The Pennsylvania Railroad

Volume 3

Railroads Past and Present

H. Roger Grant and Thomas Hoback, *editors*
Recent Titles in the *Railroads Past and Present* series

The Pennsylvania Railroad

Volume 3   The Long Decline, 1933–1968

Albert J. Churella

INDIANA UNIVERSITY PRESS

This book is a publication of

Indiana University Press
Office of Scholarly Publishing
Herman B Wells Library 350
1320 East 10th Street
Bloomington, Indiana 47405 USA

iupress.org

First Printing 2024

Manufactured in China

Library of Congress Cataloging-in-Publication Data

Names: Churella, Albert J., author.
Title: The Pennsylvania Railroad : the long decline, 1933-1968 /
    Albert J. Churella.
Description: Bloomington, Indiana : Indiana University Press,
    [2024] | Series: Railroads past and present | Includes index.
Identifiers: LCCN 2024016070 (print) | LCCN 2024016071
    (ebook) | ISBN 9780253069474 (hardback) | ISBN
    9780253069481 (ebook)
Subjects: LCSH: Pennsylvania Railroad—History. | Railroads—
    Pennsylvania—History. | BISAC: TRANSPORTATION /
    Railroads / History | TRAVEL / Food, Lodging &
    Transportation / Rail Travel
Classification: LCC HE2791.P43 C49 2024 (print) | LCC HE2791.
    P43 (ebook) | DDC 385.09748/0904—dc23/eng/20240613
LC record available at https://lccn.loc.gov/2024016070
LC ebook record available at https://lccn.loc.gov/2024016071

This history of the Pennsylvania Railroad
is dedicated to the memory of

Peter A. Hansen (1957–2020) *and* **H. Roger Grant** (1943–2023),

individuals who embodied all the virtues of scholars and gentlemen,
and to my loving and supportive wife,

Marianne Holdzkom.

CONTENTS

PREFACE

This, the third volume in a series, concludes the longest and most complex research effort that I have done, or that I am ever likely to undertake. In March 2003, when the University of Pennsylvania Press commissioned me to write a one-volume, two-hundred-thousand-word history of the Pennsylvania Railroad, I little imagined that almost precisely twenty years would pass before I put the finishing touches on a historical trilogy that encompasses nearly 1.7 million words. The time, and the length, influenced the decision of Penn Press to withdraw from the project, following publication of the first volume. The enduring appeal of the Pennsylvania Railroad and that company's significance to American history—probably more than my skills as a researcher and writer—fortuitously led to the publication of the final two volumes by Indiana University Press, as part of their *Railroads Past and Present* series.

More than any other railroad in the United States—and, I would argue, more than any other railroad in the world—the PRR's history is inextricably intertwined with a larger context that involves business, technology, geography, politics, labor, socioeconomic class, gender, race, and even elements of military and foreign policy. Weaving those disparate strands into a unifying whole has equaled the challenge associated with marshaling a vast array of primary and secondary sources and writing a seemingly endless number of words. Throughout each of the three volumes, there has been a continual trade-off between the chronological narrative that is so familiar to historians and a more analytical focus, one based on topic and theme. In some cases, the approach seemed obvious; in other instances, less so.

Volume 1, covering the years between the incorporation of the Pennsylvania Railroad in 1846 and the direct involvement of the United States in World War I in 1917, suggested a largely chronological structure. The initial chapter went further back in time, encompassing the complex and contested development of internal improvements in the Early Republic, the commercial rivalry between the great port cities that lay along the Atlantic Seaboard, and the subsequent development of Pennsylvania's Main Line of Public Works. Subsequent chapters described the PRR's incorporation, an event that owed as much to politics and to geography as to considerations of engineering and business strategy. Geography and internal politics likewise played a role in the ascendency of J. Edgar Thomson to the presidency, an event that transformed the Pennsylvania Railroad from an entity that would support the economic growth of Philadelphia to a self-governing business enterprise. The acquisition of the commonwealth's system of public works, the control over routes in the Midwest, and the critical role of the PRR and its executives during the Civil War attested to the company's relentless expansion and to the interconnectedness of business and government. Growth came at a cost, however, and initiatives by Thomson and Tom Scott—including investments in the South and West, the development of holding companies and fast freight lines, and efforts to cut labor costs during the depression of the 1870s—led to criticism from shareholders, investigations by government entities, and violence in the streets of Pittsburgh. During the years that followed, particularly under the leadership of George Brooke Roberts, executives eschewed territorial expansion in favor of an approach that blended corporate consolidation with incremental improvements to the PRR's infrastructure. By the time Roberts died in office, in January 1897, the company had established secure control over routes that connected New York and Washington and ran from Philadelphia west to Chicago and St. Louis. Block signals and the introduction of air brakes and automatic couplers made travel vastly safer, while the massive Broad Street Station constituted one of the most visible elements of the PRR's investments in transportation infrastructure. Those improvements reached their zenith after Alexander Cassatt became president in 1899. Cassatt embodied the ideal admixture of engineering skill, managerial acumen, and political savvy—which was vital as the Progressive Era transformed the 1887 Act to Regulate Commerce into a regulatory regime distinctly hostile toward the railroads. As the nation emerged from a crippling recession, Cassatt ordered construction crews to rebuild much of the railroad, creating the physical fabric that has lasted well into the twenty-first century. The process culminated in the opening of New York's Penn Station in 1910, almost four years after Cassatt's death—although it was Vice President Samuel Rea, rather than Cassatt, who oversaw that complex engineering project. Penn Station was but one component of the refashioning of the transportation infrastructure of Greater New York—a process that included the opening of the Hell Gate Bridge in April 1917, on the same day that President Woodrow Wilson urged Congress to declare war on the Central Powers.

The conflict that took place between 1914 and 1918 transformed the world, the United States, and the Pennsylvania Railroad. As noted in the opening chapter of volume 2, chronic congestion prompted the federal government to oversee the operation of the national rail network. The United States Railroad Administration at best represented little more than a modest improvement over private management, but the agency induced profound changes in the relationship between capital and labor. That transformation angered an individual who, like Thomson, Scott, Roberts, and Cassatt before him, was to have a profound effect on the PRR's history. W. W. Atterbury, the vice president in charge of operations, was instrumental to the Allied war effort, by coordinating transportation for the American Expeditionary Forces. He earned the rank of brigadier general, and his wartime service contributed to his interest in blending various forms of land, air, and water transportation. He also developed a strong desire to defend big-business capitalism from the disruptive Bolshevist influences he feared would overtake Europe and then the United States. Government meddling in the affairs of

private enterprise and the growing power of organized labor, he asserted, represented the initial stages of the collapse of American economic and political freedoms. Small wonder, then, that upon his return to the United States he sought to dismantle the labor-relations policies that the United States Railroad Administration had established. Atterbury thus contributed to the onset of the 1922 Shopmen's Strike, the most serious labor unrest to affect the railroads during the twentieth century. In cooperation with his friend, PRR advisor to publicity Ivy Ledbetter Lee, Atterbury established a company union, ostensibly to give workers a voice in corporate governance, but in reality to deny them effective workplace representation. The situation was far more complex than a simple war between management and labor, however. The third chapter of volume 2 detailed the complex development of welfare capitalism on the Pennsylvania Railroad, a process that began in earnest during the 1880s. The topical rather than chronological focus of chapter 3 also included the effects of World War I and the immediate postwar period on the African Americans and women who worked for the Pennsylvania Railroad. Chapter 4, likewise following a topical motif, discussed the complex interrelationship between the PRR and the cities it served, with particular emphasis on Chicago, Cleveland, New York, and Philadelphia. The following chapter discussed the evolution of the PRR as an integrated transportation company rather than simply a railroad—a development closely tied to Atterbury's influence. The enormous potential of intermodality nonetheless ran afoul of the Interstate Commerce Commission, in part because Atterbury and other executives intended to use buses, trucks, and cargo containers to destroy their competitors rather than improve transportation efficiency.

The rapid proliferation of automobiles and independent trucking firms created serious problems for the railroads during the 1920s, exacerbating the gap between the strong and weak railroads. As a senior executive at one of the strongest carriers, Atterbury oversaw interminable negotiations with other managers and with federal officials as he attempted to craft a plan for the consolidation of the eastern railroads—one that would be in conformity with the Transportation Act of 1920 but would also protect the PRR's strategic interests. During that period of stagnation, a series of acquisitions—as well as the formation of Pennroad, a closely affiliated investment fund—drew money and managerial talent away from more productive endeavors. The crisis of the Great Depression ended efforts at consolidation, induced additional regulatory scrutiny of the PRR's relationship with competing modes of transportation, and produced widespread opprobrium regarding

Pennroad's activities. By 1933, when volume 2 ended, Atterbury could nonetheless take comfort that his subordinate, Elisha Lee, would soon replace him as the PRR's president, while Ivy Lee would continue to offer wise counsel.

The third and final volume that you see before you continues the history of the Pennsylvania Railroad, through its 1968 merger with the New York Central. It begins with a prologue that sets the stage for an outcome that, to most readers, will not come as a surprise. The bankruptcy of the Penn Central, so soon after the merger, attested to the long decline of the railroads in the Northeast—and throughout much of the United States—during the years following World War II. That dark night had its dawn, and the subsequent formation of Conrail in 1976 and the passage of the 1980 Staggers Act were key elements in the revitalization of the national transportation infrastructure. Volume 3 seemed the most appropriate place to discuss the long and complex development of motive power on the Pennsylvania Railroad. Chapter 1 accordingly dips back into the nineteenth century, then carries the story of steam locomotion into the late 1920s—a period when the PRR's Motive Power Department seemed to have lost its way. By then, however, the company had embarked on an ambitious electrification program, one that involved new technologies and new forms of interaction between executives and government officials. That is the subject of chapter 2, along with contemporaneous, and unanticipated, changes in senior management. The third chapter examines the roles of executives and workers—including women, African Americans, and Hispanics—during the 1940s and into the 1950s. Despite the parallels with World War I, the World War II experience affected the company and its employees in substantially different ways. The motive-power story continues in chapter 4, as PRR personnel developed improved locomotives—an effort that produced a transformative struggle for power within the company and elevated a relative outsider to the presidency. The immediate postwar period involved a concerted effort

to renew the railroad's physical plant and equipment, as detailed in chapter 5. Those investments brought to completion the Philadelphia Improvements that began in the 1920s, which were described in volume 2. As noted in chapter 6, there followed a period of decline, particularly following the recession that began in 1958, from which the PRR and many other railroads never fully recovered. The following chapter, like others in this volume, breaks from a strictly chronological focus to trace the long and politically influenced development of commuter-rail services in New York and Philadelphia. The final chapter—the longest in the book, by far—traces the extraordinary complexity of the merger negotiations that involved the PRR, the New York Central, and most of the other northeastern railroads. The length in part reflects the inclusion of information regarding the PRR's diversification efforts and its involvement in a project to bring high-speed rail transportation to the United States. Those initiatives were so thoroughly interwoven with the merger process that it did not seem appropriate to banish them to another chapter in the book.

If you have read the first two volumes in this series, thank you for persevering to the end of the line. If you are beginning with this volume, I hope I have provided a coherent organizational structure for a stand-alone work. In either case, you are certainly entitled to praise or find fault with the way I have structured and written this history of the Pennsylvania Railroad and with my interpretation of events. While I have received extraordinarily valuable advice from the individuals listed in the acknowledgments, the final decisions on those matters were mine. I take full responsibility for them and for any other errors or omissions. Over the course of twenty years—nearly one-sixth of the era that the PRR was in existence—I have learned more, written more, and done more than I ever thought possible. I hope the results are worthy of the time and effort I have invested in this project and that I have done justice to the history and the legacy of the Pennsylvania Railroad.

ACKNOWLEDGMENTS

The writing and publication of the second and third volumes of this history have proceeded in tandem, spaced approximately one year apart. Many of the individuals who offered their assistance, advice, and support, and are featured in the acknowledgments for volume 2, are also listed here, and my profound apologies if I have omitted anyone. I am grateful for the assistance of Nick Fry, curator of the John W. Barriger III National Railroad Library at the St. Louis Mercantile Library and to the personnel at Railroad Museum of Pennsylvania in Strasburg and the Pennsylvania State Archives in Harrisburg—including Kurt Bell, Bradley K. Smith, Lauren Radkiewicz, Dodie L. Robbins, Michael D. Sherbon, Brett M. Reigh, Aaron McWilliams, Wesley J. Decker, and Megan Rentschler. Josué Hurtado, the coordinator of public services and outreach at the Special Collections Research Center, Temple University Libraries provided access to photographs that were vital to telling the story of the PRR's relationship to its headquarters city of Philadelphia. Many thanks to Catherine Medich and Joanne M. Nestor, at the New Jersey State Archives; Kellen Cutsforth, the digital image collection administrator at the Denver Public Library; Ethan Bowers, the collections manager at the History Center at the Allen County-Fort Wayne Historical Society; Alice Griffin, archivist, at the Center for Brooklyn History, Brooklyn Public Library; Andrea Felder at the New York Public Library; Daniel Brenner, the acting collections manager and research archivist at the New York Transit Museum; Robert Cheetham and his colleagues at Phillyhistory.org; and Andrew Williams, the digital services archivist and reference services librarian at the Historical Society of Pennsylvania. A special thanks to Mark Metz, for sharing his extensive knowledge of the Military Railway Service; to Tommy Meehan for his expertise regarding the Kaufman Act; and to Dan Cupper, who has generously provided access to a wealth of newspaper clippings from his collection. Keith Harcourt and Roy Edwards have provided valuable advice and information on the international context of railway containerization. Jim Cohen organized a special issue on high-speed rail in the *Journal of Transport History*, which brought into sharper focus my musings on the *Metroliner*. I am especially grateful to William Wister Haines Jr. for his efforts to preserve and promote the literary legacy of his father, the author of *Slim*, *High Tension*, and several short stories related to railroad electrification. The books, which are available at https://powerlineman.com/web/index.php/store/books/high-tension-detail, provide superb insights into the difficult, dangerous, and rewarding work of power linemen.

The Hagley Museum and Library in Wilmington, Delaware, has provided generous financial support for this project, in keeping with its mission to disseminate an appreciation for business history to the widest possible audience. Roger Horowitz and the indefatigable Carol Lockman have arranged housing, dealt with crises, and provided a friendly ear on my repeated visits. Jon M. Williams, the Andrew W. Mellon curator of prints and photographs at the Hagley, as well as archivist Judy Stevenson, curator Kevin Martin, and archival specialist Barbara D. Hall, have scoured the collections for book illustrations, and I have also benefited from the assistance of Terry Snyder and Lynn Catanese, a wonderful individual who left us far too soon. Reference archivist Marjorie McNinch has been superb in her role as the liaison between me and all the archival boxes that lay behind the door to the stacks. Clayton Ruminski, who has since gone on to other opportunities, and Kevin Martin were equally generous with their time and assistance. Angela Schad, the Hagley's reference archivist and digital archives specialist, was simply extraordinary. She did not flinch when I submitted a raft of requests for photographs and other illustrations, and much of the visual quality of this book I owe to her.

Most of the researchers who have worked at the Hagley Library and virtually all those who have studied the history of the Pennsylvania Railroad have benefited from the knowledge, wisdom, and counsel of assistant curator Chris Baer. I have lost count of the number of books relating to the PRR, railroad history, and business history in general that have listed his name in the acknowledgments, but they must number in the hundreds. His encyclopedic knowledge of the PRR's records is unsurpassed. He has helped to rescue a vast array of documents from destruction and, working with Craig Orr, Michael Nash, and others, has processed and cataloged the records and prepared a series of scope and content notes that encapsulate the key elements of the PRR's history. Much of that process is described in Christopher T. Baer, "Salvaging History," *Railroad History* 192 (Spring–Summer 2005): 76–87. Chris has devoted immense effort to the creation of "A General Chronology of the Pennsylvania Railroad Company, Predecessors and Successors and Its Historical Context," available at http://www.prrths.com/newprr_files/Hagley/PRR_hagley_intro.htm. His PRR Chronology is an invaluable resource for anyone studying the PRR or, indeed, any aspect of railroad history in the United States.

The publication of the second and third volumes of this history would not have been possible without the unstinting support of Indiana University Press. Tom Hoback, the founder and former president of the Indiana Rail Road, and Roger Grant, the Kathryn and Calhoun Lemon professor of history at Clemson University, have performed exemplary feats as the coeditors of the *Railroads Past and Present* series. They are committed to preserving the legacy of that form of transportation, from its origins in the early nineteenth century through the latest developments in technology, regulation, and operating practices. Roger's sudden and unexpected passing, on November 17, 2023, was a shock to me and to countless others. His coeditor, Tom Hoback, rightly indicated that "we have lost a giant" among transportation historians. I will greatly miss him.

Many thanks to IUP's associate director, David Hulsey, for expressing so much confidence in my abilities. Dan Crissman, IUP's trade acquisitions editor, with the assistance of Samantha Heffner, has shown great confidence in the viability and worth of this project. Thanks as well to Ashley Runyon, who was my first point of contact with Indiana University Press, and to Anna Francis, the current assistant acquisitions editor. Project editor Dave Miller has done a superb job of transforming my draft into publishable form. Marketing manager Stephen Williams has been indispensable in the process of bringing this project to fruition and ensuring that this book can reach the broadest possible audience. Many, many thanks to them, and to all the others at Indiana University Press, who are working so hard to turn out so many top-quality publications on transportation and on a great many other subjects. Copyeditors Jillian Bray and Carol McGillivray at Amnet Systems have provided extraordinarily thorough and insightful feedback on the manuscript, catching errors I would have otherwise missed. The value of any book, and particularly one of this length, depends greatly on the quality of the index, and I am grateful to Melissa Hyde at Ivy Indexing for ensuring that anyone looking for a person, event, or topic will be able to find it easily.

Mark H. Rose, at Florida Atlantic University, is the epitome of a scholar and a gentleman. Over a career spanning many decades, he has developed an international reputation as an expert in business history, urban history, and regulatory policy. Mark has read through at least two iterations of the manuscript, and he has spotted everything from the smallest of typographical errors to the largest of gaps in my arguments. He has been a wonderful colleague and friend throughout the entire research and writing process. It was he who first suggested that I undertake this work, as part of the American Business, Politics, and Society book series at the University of Pennsylvania Press. Richard R. John and Pamela Walker Laird, coeditors of the series, have been equally supportive of my work. Yet it was Mark, above all, who provided advice and support at every step of the process. Nor am I the only one who has benefited from Mark's wise counseling. Every time I have seen him at a conference, he is talking with graduate students and junior scholars, offering advice and providing suggestions for further research and publication. He is a role model for us all.

As a historian, it is only fitting that I acknowledge the mentorship, generously provided many years ago, by individuals who have helped me to become the scholar, and the person, I am today. I owe an enormous debt of gratitude to Mansel G. Blackford, my dissertation advisor at The Ohio State University, who transformed me from a history buff with an interest in trains to a serious scholar of transportation policy. Had it not been for him, my career and this book would not have been possible. K. Austin Kerr and William R. Childs, also on my dissertation committee, and both superbly knowledgeable regarding the political economy of the railroads, have unstintingly offered their advice and support. I learned in graduate school that Bill has an extraordinary ability to identify the key themes in a morass of verbiage—and he has continued to do so, in the sections involving coordinated rail-truck operations and executive compensation. I value his collegiality and his friendship, and I look forward to seeing him every year at the Business History Conference.

For the past two decades, I have been employed at Southern Polytechnic State University, a school that has since become a part of Kennesaw State University. I have been fortunate to be associated with colleagues who embody the virtues of collegiality and intellectual discourse. Several administrators, including department chairs Charlie Weeks, Julie Newell, Alice Pate, and Bryan McGovern and deans Alan Gabrielli, Tom Nelson, and Shawn Long, have exercised commendable patience with my pursuit of such a drawn-out project. I also acknowledge the support of SPSU and KSU, in the form of reassigned time for research, a tenured faculty enhancement grant, and reimbursement for a portion of the costs associated with the index and the photos used in this book.

I owe a special debt of gratitude to those who have shared with me their interest, enthusiasm, and passion for the history of the Pennsylvania Railroad. By disseminating their research through publications and websites and at conference presentations, they have contributed mightily to the store of knowledge pertaining to the nation's most important railroad. Many of those individuals have contacted me, offering their comments, thanks, and praise regarding the previous volumes of this series, or asking me when the next installment would be available. I am flattered and humbled by their interest in my work, and I can only hope that the final volume in this series lives up to their expectations. I cannot thank everyone who has befriended me in this manner, but I want to mention Rich Ader, Chuck Blardone, Al Buchan, Don Coulter, Al Doddroe, Walter Ernst, Walt Peters, Michael Burshtin, Dave Homer, Ken Kobus, Charlie Horan, Tommy Meehan, Frank Napoleon, Andrew Olson, Ira Silverman, Bruce Smith, Steve Staffieri, Rick Tipton, Richard Wallis, the late Robert Wayner, Ralph Weischedel, Doug White, Ron Widman, and Dan Zukowski. One of my strongest supporters will never have the opportunity to read the last two volumes of this work. Peter A. Hansen was an author, a filmmaker, a historical reenactor, and editor who possessed a deep and abiding love for all aspects of railroad history, and for his wife, Bonnie. Thanks to Bonnie's efforts, the Winter Park Library in Florida now houses the Peter Hansen Collection, preserving Pete's books and his memory.

While we value our friends and colleagues, it is our family that sustains us, and I have been fortunate to have the love and support of those who are nearest and dearest to me. Although I have no children of my own, I have doted on my fur babies, first Walnut, then Chancey and Stormy. All three are gone now, but Lindsey is here to reduce my stress and brighten our lives. My greatest blessing is the love of my life, my wife, Marianne Holdzkom. The research and writing process has been long and difficult for me, but also for her. She has listened patiently to my doubts, indecision, and even anger regarding the progress of the manuscript. My love for her is beyond description, and I could not have done this without her.

ABBREVIATIONS

AAR	Association of American Railroads		CWA	Clerical Workers' Association
ACF	American Car & Foundry		D&H	Delaware & Hudson
ACL	Atlantic Coast Line Railroad		DL&W	Delaware, Lackawanna & Western Railroad
AFL	American Federation of Labor		DT&I	Detroit, Toledo & Ironton Railroad
AFL-CIO	American Federation of Labor-Congress of Industrial Organizations		DOT	United States Department of Transportation
AGBANY	Action Group for Better Architecture in New York		EJA	Executive Jet Aviation
Alco	American Locomotive Company		EL	Erie Lackawanna Railroad (after June 1963)
AMA	American Municipal Association		E-L	Erie-Lackawanna Railroad (prior to June 1963)
ARE	Association of Railway Executives		EMC	Electro-Motive Company/Corporation
AT&T	American Telephone & Telegraph		EMD	Electro-Motive Division of General Motors
ATO	Association of Transportation Officers of the Pennsylvania Railroad		ERP	Employe Representation Plan
B&O	Baltimore & Ohio Railroad		ERPC	Eastern Railroad Presidents' Conference
BDCE	Brotherhood of Dining Car Employees		FAK	Freight-all-kinds
BLE	Brotherhood of Locomotive Engineers		FEC	Florida East Coast Railway
BLF&E	Brotherhood of Locomotive Firemen and Enginemen		FEPC	Fair Employment Practice Committee
BRT	Brooklyn Rapid Transit Company		FM	Fairbanks-Morse
BRT	Brotherhood of Railroad Trainmen		GDP	Gross domestic product
BSCP	Brotherhood of Sleeping Car Porters		GE	General Electric
CADE	Commission Against Discrimination in Employment		GM	General Motors
			HHFA	Housing and Home Finance Agency
C&NW	Chicago & North Western Railway		H&M	Hudson & Manhattan Railroad
C&O	Chesapeake & Ohio Railway		HRE	Hotel and Restaurant Employees' International Alliance and Bartenders' International League of America
CB&Q	Chicago, Burlington & Quincy Railroad		IAB	International Air Bahamas
CGW	Chicago Great Western Railway		IBM	International Business Machines Corporation
CHR	Commission on Human Relations			
CIO	Congress of Industrial Organizations		IBRC	International Brotherhood of Red Caps
CMI	Continental Mortgage Investors		ICC	Interstate Commerce Commission

IND	Independent City-Owned Subway System	PRT	Philadelphia Rapid Transit Company
IR	Ingersoll-Rand	PSC	New York Public Service Commission
LCL	Less-than-carload lot	PSC	Pennsylvania Public Service Commission
LIRR	Long Island Rail Road		(prior to March 1937)
LITA	Long Island Transit Authority	PSIC	Passenger Service Improvement
LMS	London, Midland & Scottish Railway		Corporation
LV	Lehigh Valley Railroad	PSTC	Philadelphia Suburban Transportation
MAIN	Military Authorization Identification		Company
	Number	PT&T	Pennsylvania Tunnel & Terminal Railroad
MCTA	Metropolitan Commuter Transportation		Company
	Authority	PTC	Philadelphia Transportation Company
MIDAS	Management Information Developed from	PUC	Pennsylvania Public Utility Commission
	Advanced Systems		(after March 1937)
MIT	Massachusetts Institute of Technology	PWA	Public Works Administration
MP	Missouri Pacific Railroad	PW&B	Philadelphia, Wilmington & Baltimore
MRS	Military Railway Service		Railroad
MTA	Metropolitan Transportation Authority	RCC	Railroad Credit Corporation
NAACP	National Association for the Advancement	RFC	Reconstruction Finance Corporation
	of Colored People	RLEA	Railway Labor Executives' Association
NCC	National Credit Corporation	RPO	Railway Post Office
NDMB	National Defense Mediation Board	SEPACT	Southeastern Pennsylvania Transportation
NIRA	National Industrial Recovery Act		Compact
NMB	National Mediation Board	SEPTA	Southeastern Pennsylvania Transportation
N&W	Norfolk & Western Railway		Authority
NRA	National Recovery Administration	TH&I	Terre Haute & Indianapolis Railroad
NRAB	National Railroad Adjustment Board	TOFC	Trailer-on-flatcar
NRLP	National Railway Labor Panel	TP&W	Toledo, Peoria & Western
NWLB	National War Labor Board	TWA	Trans World Airlines
NY&LB	New York & Long Branch Railroad	TWU	Transport Workers Union of America
NYC	New York Central Railroad	UMW	United Mine Workers of America
NYC&StL	New York, Chicago & St. Louis Railroad	UN	United Nations
	(aka, Nickel Plate Road)	UP	Union Pacific Railroad
NYP&N	New York, Philadelphia & Norfolk Railroad	URWA	United Railroad Workers of America
ODT	Office of Defense Transportation	USRA	United States Railroad Administration
OPA	Office of Price Administration	UTSE	United Transport Service Employees
OPDC	Old Philadelphia Development Corporation	UTTB	Urban Traffic and Transportation Board
ORC	Order of Railway Conductors	VRD	Voluntary Relief Department
OSS	Office of Strategic Services	W&LE	Wheeling & Lake Erie Railway
PB&W	Philadelphia, Baltimore & Washington	WM	Western Maryland Railway
	Railroad	WMC	War Manpower Commission
PRR	Pennsylvania Railroad	WPB	War Production Board
PRSL	Pennsylvania-Reading Seashore Lines	WSB	Wage Stabilization Board
P&LE	Pittsburgh & Lake Erie Railroad	YMCA	Young Men's Christian Association
P&WV	Pittsburgh & West Virginia Railway		

The Pennsylvania Railroad

Volume 3

Prologue

The headlines that appeared in the newspapers on the morning of June 22, 1970, were sobering but not necessarily surprising. They attested to the descent of the Pennsylvania Railroad from the world's largest corporation, during the final two decades of the nineteenth century, to a participant in the nation's biggest merger, in 1968, to a casualty of what was at that time America's most catastrophic bankruptcy. The company's terse official announcement suggested that that outcome had been unavoidable. "Because of a severe cash squeeze and having been unable to acquire from any source additional working capital," there was simply no way to pay the bills and keep the railroad running. The capital in question involved an unsuccessful effort to secure a $200 million federal loan guarantee—a lifeline that indicated the extent to which the fate of the railroad was intertwined with the policies and politics of the national government.[1]

The collapse of the Penn Central also provided an indication of the unique role railroads occupied in the transportation infrastructure and the national economy. Reorganization would take place under Section 77 of the Bankruptcy Act of 1933, which ensured that uninterrupted rail service would take precedence over the demands of creditors. New York governor Nelson Rockefeller indicated as much when he asserted that "the bankruptcy of the Pennsylvania Railroad is a most regrettable development, but I can assure commuters in the New York metropolitan area that the state's emergency program to improve the Penn Central equipment and service will continue without interruption." That statement, in which the governor conflated the names of the merged corporation and one of

its predecessors, spoke volumes about the role of the railroads in the twentieth century—indispensable to national mobility, required to maintain unprofitable services, and eligible for assistance only when they were on the brink of collapse.[2]

In Philadelphia, the headquarters city of first the Pennsylvania Railroad and then the Penn Central, reporters noted that the bankruptcy filing was "not really unexpected" and "no big surprise." John Kenneth Galbraith and Milton Friedman, the nation's preeminent economists, espoused radically different philosophies, but they agreed that the outcome had been inevitable. Neither expressed much concern about the fate of the world's largest privately owned transportation company or the welfare of its employees and investors. Instead, Galbraith suggested that the contagion might spread to other railroads, while Friedman noted that the banking system and the overall economy were insulated from the debacle. An editorial in the *Philadelphia Inquirer*—whose publisher, Walter H. Annenberg, had been a director at the Pennsylvania Railroad and, briefly, at the Penn Central—suggested that "Philadelphia has a vital public interest in efforts to resolve the financial crisis that hangs over the Penn Central. . . . It is apparent that the company has been victimized by financial mismanagement on a colossal scale but, from the public's point of view, it is not so much a financial problem as a transportation problem." Stating the obvious, the editors noted that "transportation experts, as well as financial experts, ought to have a hand in the diagnosing of the ills and the prescribing of cures." They were, perhaps unsurprisingly, ignorant of attempts by several generations of pundits and prognosticators to offer sage advice to do just that, by endeavoring to resolve problems that seemed intractable.[3]

Altoona, nestled at the base of the Allegheny Mountains, owed its existence to the Pennsylvania Railroad. In its glory years, it had been home to one of the world's largest shop facilities, capable of building the new locomotives and cars that matched the needs of the Pennsylvania Railroad. In 1970, it was a shadow of its former self, having endured a slow decline over the previous two decades. The editor of the *Altoona Mirror* waxed nostalgic, observing that in 1920, "there were 65 good trains through this city every day. They included the locals, the 'milk stop' short trains, and the long, gleaming intercity express trains of prestige and power." That observation was accompanied by a photo of a K4s Pacific, a product of the PRR's Juniata Shops, pulling one of those sixty-five passenger trains. Fifty years later, ten trains remained, a number that might fall to zero, should the Interstate Commerce Commission accede to Penn Central's request to eliminate most of the company's passenger service. "The Penn Central's operation is a matter of utmost importance to Altoona and it is of necessity to a nation which moves as much heavy freight as America," the editorial concluded. "A crisis of major proportions threatens, here in Altoona as well as in the rest of the country." That crisis, like the evolution and decline of the Pennsylvania Railroad, had been many years in the making.[4]

Catastrophe

Individuals familiar with the history of transportation often consider the Penn Central to have the same relationship to railroading as did the *Hindenburg* to aviation or the RMS *Titanic* to ocean travel. The Penn Central Transportation Company, to use its full name, came into being through the February 1968 consolidation of two railroads—the Pennsylvania and the New York Central—that were each on the verge of bankruptcy. The new paint scheme adopted for Penn Central locomotives, a stark and somber black, indicated how little money was available for aesthetic frivolities and portended the dismal future of the new firm. Rather than alleviate the troubles of its two predecessors, the Penn Central merger merely compounded them. Overwhelmed managers, often working at odds with one another, struggled to maintain even basic levels of freight and passenger service, while from the beginning, senior executives were hard pressed to raise enough cash to pay each day's bills. A mere 872 days passed between

merger and bankruptcy. When the company failed, on June 21, 1970, it was the largest bankruptcy in the history of the United States until that time, one that sent shock waves through the American economy, the ranks of labor, and the corridors of political power in Washington. When transportation journalist Dan Machalaba wrote his highly regarded article "Railroading's Biggest Blunders" for the September 2015 issue of *Trains* magazine, he had numerous mistakes from which to choose. Many people have commented on that article, often suggesting that he had been unduly pessimistic in one or more of his selections. Yet no one disagreed with his assessment that "the merger of the Pennsylvania Railroad and the New York Central in 1968 was one of the biggest railroad blunders of them all, if not the biggest," topping his list of the "13 flubs, foul-ups, and faux pas that shaped the industry."[5]

While few people took responsibility for the collapse of Penn Central, everyone was partly to blame. With the benefit of hindsight, critics in the media and in government highlighted a dysfunctional managerial culture that extended from the highest-level strategic decisions to the most mundane day-to-day operations. Alfred Perlman, formerly the president of the NYC, held the same office at Penn Central, albeit with far less authority over corporate policy than he had once enjoyed. Prior to the merger, he suspected that executives from the Pennsylvania Railroad, the larger and marginally more prosperous entity, would dominate the new company.[6]

Perlman was understandably wary of Stuart Saunders, the PRR's board chairman, who was the principal architect of the consolidation. Saunders was a lawyer and a skilled practitioner of the delicate art of politics, but he had little familiarity with—or interest in—the day-to-day operations of a railroad. His negotiating skills and willingness to make concessions to organized labor, government officials, and community leaders ensured that his lasting accomplishment would be the largest merger in American history. They were devil's bargains, however, and Saunders frittered away most of the savings the merger was supposed to achieve. A 1964 settlement with union representatives drastically limited the ability of Penn Central executives to reduce the size of the workforce. In an equally problematic arrangement, Saunders reluctantly agreed to provide a home for the bankrupt New York, New Haven & Hartford Railroad, which became part of Penn Central on New Year's Eve, 1968. In so doing, he preserved commuter and intercity passenger services that connected Greater New York with New England, but at a catastrophic cost to the Penn Central. Corporate support for the highly publicized

Metroliner program represented an expensive effort to curry favor with President Lyndon B. Johnson and other federal officials, although the *Metroliner* failed to achieve anything close to its promised 150-mph speeds between New York and Washington.[7]

The costs associated with the merger deeply concerned Pennsylvania Railroad executive David C. Bevan, who became Penn Central's chief financial officer. Since joining the PRR in 1951, he had been warning that the company's debt structure was unstainable. Bevan made considerable progress with the herculean task of reducing the PRR's bonded indebtedness, but he was less successful in his efforts to persuade operating officials to curtail capital expenditures. Like Saunders, Bevan knew little about railroad operations, but he did understand such basic concepts as capital budgets, cost accounting, and return on investment. His efforts to provide more accurate forecasting tools, through the implementation of a sophisticated computer system, alienated managers who were unfamiliar with the new technology and who objected to such close monitoring of their performance. Like his counterparts on other railroads, Bevan oversaw the PRR's diversification into nonrail subsidiaries. His logic was sound, in that he hoped that income generated by those firms would offset the PRR's chronic operating losses, giving the company time to curtail expenditures, eliminate most passenger service, abandon unprofitable routes, sell surplus urban real estate, and lay off as many employees as possible. Bevan reacted with dismay to the prospect of a merger between the Pennsylvania Railroad and the New York Central. He suspected, rightly, that Penn Central executives would demand massive capital investments, based on loosely supported assertions that such expenditures were vital to the operational integration of the predecessor companies. In a desperate attempt to absolve themselves of responsibility for catastrophic service interruptions, those managers also demanded more cars and locomotives, as well as an improved physical plant. Everything might be all right, Bevan hoped, if he could use the income generated by diversification to nurse the Penn Central through its initial stages, until the time when the promised savings generated by the merger offset the costs associated with implementing it. The hope was in vain, in part because few of the nonrail subsidiaries, originally acquired by the PRR, fulfilled their potential. One, Executive Jet Aviation, imploded into a morass of financial mismanagement, influence peddling, and morally questionable behavior by its founder, Dick Lassiter. The adverse publicity provided ample fodder for newspaper reporters and members of Congress. They ignored the relatively modest losses associated with Executive Jet Aviation and other subsidiaries, while accusing Bevan of being at best inept and at worst a perpetrator of fraud.[8]

Saunders and his subordinates spent so much time securing regulatory and judicial approval for the merger that they had not undertaken the complex and divisive process of developing a plan for staffing and operating the Penn Central. The new company adopted a "layer-cake" managerial structure, with former PRR personnel reporting to ex–NYC officials and so on up the corporate ladder. There was thus a built-in incentive to bypass the official chain of command, one that avoided cooperation and the sharing of vital information. Disputes between the "Red Team" (a legacy of the PRR) and the "Green Team" (from the old NYC) proved insurmountable. Perlman despised David E. Smucker, the vice president in charge of operations, and Henry W. Large, the vice president in charge of traffic—both former PRR executives—and the feeling was mutual.[9] Prior to the merger, Pennsylvania Railroad personnel had focused on the movement of bulk commodities such as coal and steel, while their counterparts at the New York Central had developed pricing and customer-service initiatives to capture smaller shipments of high-value traffic. The divergent business philosophies caused further impediments to operational integration. The IBM computer systems used by the two merger partners were incompatible. There were wide variations in operating and safety rules, sparking labor grievances over such seemingly minor issues as the provision of armrests in locomotive cabs. Even the most dedicated employees felt that their efforts were unappreciated, unrewarded, and incapable of saving a company destined for failure. Many competent junior executives left the Penn Central in favor of jobs on other railroads.[10]

The thousands of employees who worked for the Pennsylvania Railroad, the New York Central, and then the Penn Central were skilled and dedicated to their craft. Yet they, and the union officials who represented them, were understandably determined to secure wages, fringe benefits, and work rules that were as favorable as possible. While some executives acknowledged that the highly publicized problems associated with "featherbedding" were at least partly exaggerated, there were numerous cases where labor agreements ensured that too many people did too little work.

The severity of the railroad crisis also reflected the many layers of government oversight that had evolved since the adoption of the 1887 Act to Regulate Commerce. That legislation, followed by such enhancements as the 1903 Elkins Act, the 1906 Hepburn Act, and the 1910 Mann-Elkins Act, reflected an era when railroads held a near monopoly over long-distance land transportation. In that context, the policies adopted by the Interstate Commerce Commission and state regulatory agencies were designed to prevent destructive competition, forestall excessive returns on investment capital, and protect the interests of shippers, passengers, and local communities. Within a few years after the adoption of the Transportation Act of 1920, the railroads—especially those in the densely populated and heavily urbanized Northeast—were feeling the effects of highway competition. Yet regulatory policy remained static, even as truckers seized an ever-larger share of high-value freight and citizens spent their money on gasoline for their automobiles rather than on train tickets. Political considerations ensured the development of a fragmented regulatory state, with little opportunity for the coordination of rail, highway, water, and air transportation.[11]

Given the endemic failings of the Penn Central and the toxic environment that enveloped it, it is surprising that the company avoided bankruptcy as long as it did. Service deteriorated as years of deferred maintenance began to take their toll. Harried operating personnel cleared cars from yards and main lines by sending them elsewhere, often with scant regard for their intended destination. Given the mutual enmity between members of the Red Team and the Green Team, it was both exculpatory and satisfying to divert excess traffic to the routes that, only a few months earlier, had been operated by their rivals. Cars and even entire trains disappeared, and neither paper waybills nor the computerized data-management systems could track them down. The intense cold and heavy snowfall associated with the unusually severe winter of 1969–1970 brought operations to a near standstill. Carloads of Maine potatoes sat motionless in the former NYC yard at Selkirk, New York, and then froze, ruining most of the state's crop. Customers deserted the railroad in favor of trucks and complained loudly to reporters, regulators, and politicians that they would tolerate no more excuses.[12]

Nor was the Penn Central the only railroad in trouble. During the nineteenth century, the Reading prospered from the anthracite traffic in northeastern Pennsylvania, and that company was one of the PRR's most significant rivals. Those glory days were but a distant memory, and the Reading went bankrupt in November 1971. The closely allied Jersey Central had been in bankruptcy since 1967, and the formation of Penn Central the following year did nothing to help its prospects. The Lehigh Valley, another former anthracite carrier, had once been controlled by the

Pennsylvania Railroad—the legacy of efforts by W. W. Atterbury to shape the consolidation process initiated by the Transportation Act of 1920. It outlasted Penn Central by a month, entering bankruptcy court in July 1970. The Lehigh & Hudson River failed in April 1972. For a brief period, the Erie Lackawanna offered stiff competition against the Penn Central, particularly for lucrative piggyback traffic. Hurricane Agnes destroyed significant portions of the Erie Lackawanna, exacerbating the structural problems that afflicted all the northeastern railroads—and, in June 1972, forcing the company into receivership. Far to the west, the Rock Island endured a long, tragic, and unnecessary collapse. For a decade, the ICC delayed a proposed merger with the Union Pacific, arguing procedural niceties while the company's profits disappeared and its equipment and physical plant deteriorated. The end came in March 1975—an event that, more than any other, awakened legislators to the dysfunctional nature of the regulatory system.[13]

Resurrection

The solution to the transportation crisis in the Northeast came in stages and in a manner that upended nearly a century of regulatory policy. In the decades that followed World War II, regulators, politicians, journalists, community leaders, passengers, shippers, and the general public belatedly began to understand what railroad executives had known for quite some time. Thanks to competition from alternate forms of transportation, changing economic patterns, outdated regulatory policies, high levels of taxation, and the power of organized labor, the railroads were no longer invincible. Through the many hearings, investigations, studies, and discussions of the worsening railroad crisis, nearly everyone agreed on two, unshakable core principles. First, government subsidies to railroads were economically indefensible and politically impossible. Second, the railroads must forever remain bastions of the capitalist free-enterprise system and must never succumb to the socialistic tendencies of nationalization.

Restoring the health of the Penn Central and the other northeastern carriers depended on a growing willingness to modify those two core principles. The Penn Central operated more than a third of the nation's passenger service and generated almost two-thirds of the passenger miles east of the Mississippi River. Virtually all those routes lost money, and the situation on other railroads was scarcely better. Since the late 1960s, Stuart Saunders and other railroad executives had been exploring methods to transfer that burden to the federal government. The National Rail

Passenger Corporation, better known as Amtrak, while organizationally a private company, was—and remains—an adjunct of the national government, receiving public subsidies and yielding to political goals that are often only tangentially related to the provision of improved transportation. Amtrak began operations on April 1, 1971, too late to save the Penn Central from bankruptcy. Its creation nonetheless suggested that members of Congress had finally heeded the warnings of railroad executives that passenger operations had long imperiled profitability.[14]

By itself, the formation of Amtrak was insufficient to resolve the long-standing financial problems that had been decades in the making. Rescuing the Penn Central and other carriers from bankruptcy required an unprecedented level of federal support for the railroads. Congress responded by enacting two key pieces of legislation. The Regional Rail Reorganization (3R) Act of 1973 provided emergency funding, thus establishing a precedent for federal railroad subsidies. The 3R Act also established a government-owned corporation, the United States Railway Association, whose responsibilities included the development of a Final System Plan for the reorganization of the northeastern railway network, under the auspices of the Consolidated Rail Corporation. Three years later, the Railroad Revitalization and Regulatory Reform (4R) Act approved the Final System Plan, enabling Conrail to assume operations of the Penn Central and six other financially troubled companies. Of equal importance, the legislation gave railroad executives greater flexibility to establish rates and thus anticipated an era of widespread deregulation.[15]

During President Jimmy Carter's administration, economists and policy makers responded to stagflation—a combination of rising prices and high rates of unemployment—and the evident failures of the regulatory system—by implementing reforms in fields as diverse as commercial aviation, trucking, and banking. Those changes affected the railroads as well, thanks to legislation sponsored by Representative Harley O. Staggers (Dem., West Virginia), the chairman of the House Committee on Interstate and Foreign Commerce. The Staggers Act, which became law on October 14, 1980, gave railroad executives both wide latitude in the determination of rates and the ability to negotiate contract prices, particularly for high-volume shipments. The reforms associated with the Staggers Act spurred managerial initiative and attracted new investment capital that in turn made possible the efficient transportation of shipments that included coal, grain, and cargo containers. The successful reinvigoration of the national railroad network, despite last-ditch intransigence

from a weakened Interstate Commerce Commission, led to a final piece of regulatory reform. The ICC Termination Act of 1995 lived up to its name. The agency passed, unmourned, into oblivion, its remaining duties largely assumed by the Surface Transportation Board.[16]

Regulatory reform came too late to save the Pennsylvania Railroad from merger or the Penn Central from bankruptcy. It was nonetheless perfectly timed for the development of Conrail. When it began operations, Conrail employed a fifth of the nation's railroad workforce (nearly a hundred thousand men and women) and utilized one-tenth of the country's fleet of railroad cars and one-sixth of its locomotives to offer service across seventeen thousand route miles. Yet it was a company in deep trouble, with as much as 10 percent of its equipment broken down, its tracks in dangerously poor repair, and its employees, although highly skilled and dedicated, too often underutilized. Conrail in 1976 represented the darkest days of the American railroad industry, and its story would be a litmus test to determine whether the entire railroad industry would be part of America's transportation future or merely a rusted monument to its industrial past.

Like a phoenix rising from the ashes of a shattered transportation infrastructure, Conrail restored the railroad network in the northeastern United States. More than $3 billion in federal subsidies remedied years of deferred maintenance, with improved tracks and better service slowly pulling the company out of its "death spiral." Through a combination of skilled management and substantial public investment, Conrail repaired its tracks and rebuilt its equipment. Improved service brought new customers and enabled Conrail to participate in the innovative practices—from unit coal trains to double-stack intermodal shipments—that were making the railroads the most efficient mode of transportation in history. Paring its route structure and parting company with many of its employees, Conrail exploited a new political and regulatory climate, one that for the first time in a century decreased the level of governmental regulatory oversight.[17]

In many cases, however, Conrail's revitalization removed the physical traces of what had once been the Pennsylvania Railroad. The inclusion of the former PRR, NYC, and Erie Lackawanna routes through Ohio, Indiana, and Illinois ensured that Conrail possessed more capacity than was necessary and too many east–west main lines to keep in service. The Pittsburgh, Fort Wayne & Chicago and Pan Handle routes, once the heart of the PRR's Lines West of Pittsburgh and Erie, were casualties of rationalization, with most mileage sold to short line operators or simply abandoned. Passenger service suffered as well. In years past, the Pan Handle line to St. Louis had hosted trains such as *The St. Louisan, The "Spirit of St. Louis,"* and the all-coach *Jeffersonian,* speeding along behind streamlined K4s locomotives. There was now only the *National Limited,* whose name came from a rival service once operated by the Baltimore & Ohio. Amtrak terminated the train in October 1979, and much of the track over which it once operated is now gone. The storied *Broadway Limited* survived longer under Amtrak, but it, too, disappeared in September 1995.

The conservative revolution that followed Ronald Reagan's election to the presidency in 1980 spelled the end of government ownership of Conrail. The company's newfound profitability undermined assertions that the government was ill-equipped to meddle in the affairs of business. Initial plans to sell Conrail to the Norfolk Southern Corporation raised fears of a significant reduction in rail service as well as a financial loss to the federal government. With the backing of shippers and employees—who proudly displayed "Let Conrail be Conrail" bumper stickers on their cars—the company's management spent more than four years trying to preserve what they had created. Finally, in 1986, the Conrail Privatization Act kept the company intact, albeit under private ownership, generating the largest initial public stock offering in the history of American business. For more than a decade, Conrail flourished as a private corporation. Its success, and its access to every significant source of traffic in the Northeast, attracted the attention of two rival railroads, Norfolk Southern and the CSX Corporation.[18]

Like Conrail, NS and CSX were composed of a diverse range of predecessor companies, participants in the periodic waves of railroad mergers that had taken place during the last four decades of the twentieth century. That process began in 1959, when the Norfolk & Western merged with the Virginian. It was one of the most successful and consequential unions in the history of railroading, orchestrated by Stuart Saunders, the individual who would later oversee the consolidation of the Pennsylvania Railroad and the New York Central. After 1959, there remained only two major eastern railroads—the N&W and the Chesapeake & Ohio—that enjoyed access to the unending stream of revenues that poured from the Pocahontas coalfields.

Both economic logic and the advice of financial analysts, industry insiders, and prescient government officials suggested that one of those companies should join forces with the Pennsylvania Railroad and the other should augment the New York Central. Rather than seek salvation from the Norfolk & Western, Saunders elected to part with the PRR's substantial interest in that company, to make an alliance with Perlman—whose New York Central had once been allied with the C&O, a company that later became one of the constituent elements of CSX.

There was considerable irony, therefore, that in 1995, executives at Norfolk Southern and CSX engaged in a bidding war for Conrail, trying to gain control of a company whose predecessors they might have saved some thirty years earlier. In 1998, representatives from the two railroads agreed to partition Conrail. CSX received much of the trackage that had once belonged to the New York Central, including the famed Water Level Route that hosted trains such as the *Twentieth Century Limited.* Most of the surviving lines that had once belonged to the Pennsylvania Railroad passed to the Norfolk Southern. That, too, was an ironic outcome, as the descendent of the Norfolk & Western, a company once largely controlled by the PRR, now owned its former overseer. There followed a service meltdown, as Norfolk Southern and CSX struggled to incorporate the new routes, personnel, and equipment into their operating patterns. It was perhaps some comfort to the dwindling number of former Pennsylvania Railroad employees that the problems were most severe at CSX, along the lines once owned by the New York Central.[19]

When they split Conrail's assets between them, Norfolk Southern and CSX shop forces hurriedly stenciled new ownership markings, sufficient until they had time to repaint everything in the official corporate colors. In keeping with the historic route structure, equipment destined for CSX received temporary NYC markings. For a brief time, locomotives and cars bearing PRR lettering again crossed the commonwealth of Pennsylvania and toiled up the slopes of the Alleghenies and around the Horseshoe Curve that chief engineer J. Edgar Thomson had designed a century and a half earlier. It was a fitting tribute to the enduring legacy of the Standard Railroad of the World.

Chapter 1

Steam

On November 12, 1831, in Bordentown, New Jersey, Isaac Dripps carefully opened the throttle of the *John Bull*—carefully, because his passengers included Prince Charles Louis Napoleon Achille Murat, the nephew of Napoleon Bonaparte, and his American-born wife, Catherine, along with many other distinguished guests. Also on board was his boss, Robert L. Stevens, the president of the Camden & Amboy Rail Road & Transportation Company, who on that occasion acted as conductor. It was a short journey, less than a mile, at a pace that exceeded thirty miles an hour—faster than the passengers had ever traveled before. They reveled in the novelty of gliding along iron rails at the dawn of a new era in transportation.[1]

As its name suggested, the locomotive was a British import, built in Newcastle by Robert Stephenson & Company. Like the *John Bull*, Dripps was also an immigrant, born in Belfast in 1810. He was only an infant when his parents brought him to the United States and settled in Philadelphia. From the age of sixteen, he was an apprentice to Thomas Holloway, the city's leading builder of steamboat machinery. Holloway supplied equipment to the Union Line Stage & Steamboat Company, which offered service along the Delaware River. Its founders included Robert Stevens and his brother, the principal backers of the Camden & Amboy. The Stevens brothers assumed, correctly, that Dripps's experience with the emerging technology of steamboats meant that the twenty-one-year-old was qualified to take charge of an even more novel form of locomotion. In August 1831, when dockworkers unloaded the crates containing the disassembled locomotive, Dripps

was there to supervise the process. He then oversaw the transportation of the components to Bordentown, where he proceeded to assemble them. He had never seen a steam locomotive before, and the builder had supplied neither plans nor instructions. Dripps worked with some care, mindful of the fate of the *Best Friend of Charleston*. The first steam locomotive built in the United States, it was the property of the South Carolina Canal & Rail Road Company—like the Camden & Amboy, an enterprise whose founders hedged their bets, uncertain whether water or rail would be the dominant form of transportation in the future. The *Best Friend* was also the first American locomotive to suffer a boiler explosion, offering a clear lesson of the dangers inherent in steam power.[2]

Everything associated with the *John Bull* was the product of technology transfer from abroad, coupled with improvisation by talented—and largely self-taught—American mechanical engineers. George Stephenson, his son Robert, and others at the Newcastle manufactory based its design on the *Planet*, a locomotive built for the Liverpool & Manchester Railway. Yet the *John Bull* featured a different style of boiler, Stephenson's version of a design developed by his Liverpool rival, Edward Bury. It resembled nothing so much as an iron haystack set in front of the open platform that gave scant protection to Dripps and his fireman. The locomotive arrived without a tender to carry wood and water. Dripps made do with a whiskey barrel set atop a flatcar. He later added a large, enclosed tender, as well as a two-wheel lead truck that enabled the *John Bull* to navigate tracks that were considerably less

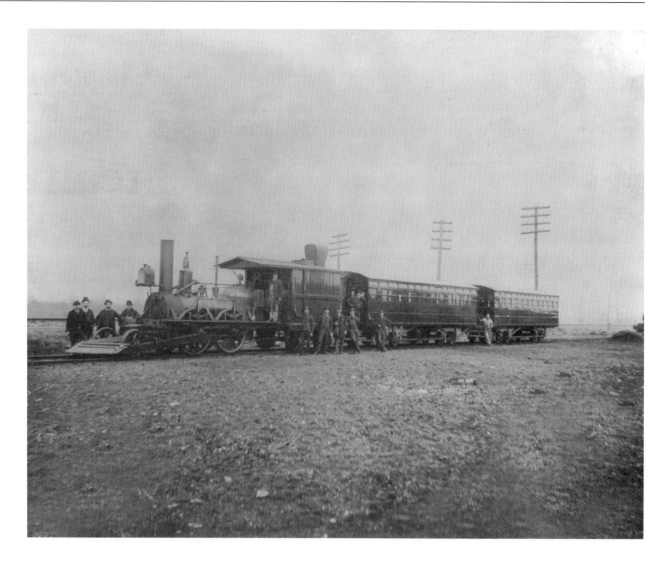

The Camden & Amboy's *John Bull*, which entered service in 1831, was the first steam locomotive to operate on any of the PRR's predecessor companies. This 1893 image shows some of the modifications undertaken by Isaac Dripps, to ensure that a British locomotive could withstand American operating conditions. It also reflects the extensive restoration necessary to make the *John Bull* presentable for the 1893 Columbian Exposition in Chicago—a city it reached under its own power. *Library of Congress, Prints & Photographs Division, LC-USZ62-71709.*

refined than anything found on British railways. A pilot, often referred to as a cowcatcher, was another concession to American lines where intrusions by livestock, vehicles, and rocks were distressingly common. The cars that carried Prince Murat and the other dignitaries were variants of the stagecoaches used on the Union Line. They rode on iron rails with a T-shaped profile, a novel design that later became standard on railroads throughout the United States and in much of the rest of the world. The stone sleepers, some of them hewn by inmates at Sing Sing prison, were far less successful and soon gave way to wood crossties.[3]

Following the public demonstrations of the power and majesty of steam locomotion, the *John Bull* sat idle for two years, awaiting the completion of the route across New Jersey. It served the Camden & Amboy faithfully for a quarter of a century, enduring numerous modifications and at last suffering the indignity of becoming a stationary steam power plant. In 1871, the Pennsylvania Railroad leased the United Canal & Railroad Companies of New Jersey, the successor company to the Camden & Amboy. The derelict *John Bull* thus became the oldest steam locomotive to operate over any route that later became a part of the PRR. Executives, proud of the company's historical antecedents, rescued the *John Bull*, arranged for its restoration by the railroad's shop forces, and placed it on display at the 1876 Centennial Exposition in Philadelphia, and in 1885, it went to the Smithsonian Institution. In 1893, the *John Bull* traveled to Chicago, under its own power, to

The E6s Atlantic that powered the 1927 Lindbergh Special was a vastly different locomotive than the one Isaac Dripps uncrated and assembled nearly a century earlier. Crew members, awaiting departure from Washington Union Station, stand beside the product of incremental improvements to traditional practices, coupled with the application of scientific principles to motive-power design. *General Negative Collection, Railroad Museum of Pennsylvania, PHMC.*

attend the World's Columbian Exposition. In 1981, under the care of Smithsonian personnel, it steamed along a short section of track, making the *John Bull* the oldest operable locomotive in the world.[4]

Nearly a century after Isaac Dripps piloted the *John Bull* down the short stretch of Camden & Amboy track and 170 miles to the southwest, James Warren waited in the cab of #460. The Pennsylvania Railroad, like other carriers, could no longer justify the assignment of names to locomotives.

In any case, that type of motive power had become so commonplace that there was no longer much value in providing a distinct identity to a piece of machinery. Many scheduled passenger trains still had names, but this one did not. On the dispatcher's train sheet, it was only Extra 460 East. The prosaic identifier belied the importance of the task ahead. Few trips would generate more renown or offer more challenges than the one that lay ahead of the #460 and its crew. Charles Lindbergh had just flown across the Atlantic, in an airplane that would soon give its name to the PRR's premier train between New York and St. Louis. He returned to the United States by water, on board the USS *Memphis*. When the cruiser arrived at the Washington Navy Yard on June 11, 1927, Lindbergh received a hero's welcome and a Distinguished Flying Cross. He would fly to New York two days later, for a ticker-tape parade the likes of which the city had never seen before. New Yorkers were not willing to wait two days to see Lindbergh, however. Newsreel crews filmed his arrival in Washington, and representatives from each company vied to be the first to place the films before Manhattan audiences. Several enterprising newscasters chartered airplanes, but officials at the International News Reel Company plotted a different strategy. Two years earlier, they had commissioned a special train to bring footage of Calvin Coolidge's inauguration from Washington to New York. A baggage car, equipped as a darkroom, enabled technicians to develop the film en route. In June 1927, however, the race to Manhattan was far more competitive, and the stakes were much higher. Success depended on the quality of the PRR's track and roadbed; the skill of its train crews; and—above all—the power, speed, and dependability of its locomotives.

The #460 was the ideal locomotive for the record-setting run. It was one of eighty-three examples of the Class E6s, whose four-wheel pilot truck, two pairs of drivers, and single-axle trailing truck were perfectly suited for fast passenger service. Its round number plate had not yet given way to the iconic keystone that would later grace the front of its smokebox, but its distinctive Belpaire firebox left no doubt that the locomotive belonged to the Pennsylvania Railroad. Built at the company's Juniata Shops in 1914, it attested to the skill with which the PRR's mechanical engineers designed locomotives that matched the railroad's traffic patterns. Shop forces had recently overhauled the #460, part of the never-ending process of keeping steam locomotives in service, ensuring that it would be ready for the most demanding assignments.

At Washington Union Station, Warren awaited the arrival of the newsreel footage from the Washington Navy Yard. He was the assistant road foreman of engines on the PRR's Baltimore Division, a rank that attested to the importance of the trip. Two additional enginemen, Harry Andrews and W. L. Anderson, were in the cab, with fireman A. Hayden ready to shovel tons of coal into the firebox. Conductor L. J. Ahern waved the highball at 12:14 p.m., and Extra 460 East accelerated away from the platform. The train reached Bowie, Maryland, 14.3 miles away, in thirteen minutes. It was soon cruising at a steady ninety-five miles per hour, three times the speed of the John Bull. A water scoop underneath the tender had long since replaced the whiskey barrel, but even modern technology was prone to failure. It malfunctioned, necessitating an unscheduled water stop in Wilmington. It took a mere seventeen minutes and thirty seconds to travel the first 23.3 miles north of that city and to the outskirts of Philadelphia. Once Extra 460 East navigated the intricate terminal trackage to the west of the Schuylkill River, the train quickly regained speed. The 66.6 miles between Holmesburg Junction and Newark went by in a mere forty-seven minutes. At 3:09 p.m., the train reached Manhattan Transfer, site of

the changeover to electric power. The #460 had covered the 216 miles from Washington in two hours and fifty-five minutes, at an average speed of seventy-four miles per hour. The airplanes chartered by rival news organizations made the trip more quickly, but ultimately lost the race to the theaters. The International News Reel's technicians developed the film during the journey, and audiences cheered Lindbergh's visage only fifteen minutes after the train arrived at Penn Station.[5]

Much more than time and distance separated the John Bull from the #460. The newer locomotive represented the same basic technology of steam power that had evolved incrementally since 1831. Some of its features, including the Belpaire firebox and its Walschaerts valve gear were—like the John Bull—influenced by developments in Europe. Yet so much had changed that Isaac Dripps would scarcely recognize the locomotive that was the descendant of the one he had uncrated and assembled. The length of the #460, including its tender, was seventy-two feet, six inches—more than four times that of the John Bull in its original configuration. The total weight of the locomotive had increased twentyfold, indicating that PRR maintenance-of-way forces had long since transcended the limitations of the primitive iron T-rail and stone sleepers. At 205 psi, the boiler pressure of the #460 would have blown the John Bull to atoms, for that locomotive's boiler was rated at only 70 psi. Metallurgy had facilitated some of that process, as steel replaced iron in the PRR's locomotives and in the rails they sped across.

Of equal importance, however, were the intellectual contributions of several generations of mechanical engineers who worked for the Pennsylvania Railroad. Beginning in the 1860s and continuing for many decades thereafter, the extraordinary success of the company's Motive Power Department depended on the skills of a few key individuals. Their ranks included several immigrants and more than a few iconoclasts. In a classic case of being in the right place at the right time, skilled practitioners such as John Laird, John Collin, Theodore Ely, Francis Casanave, James Wallis, Alfred Gibbs, William Kiesel, and Axel Vogt combined engineering expertise with artistic sensibilities, developing locomotives that were beautiful as well as functional. Time after time, they produced designs that were ideally suited to the PRR's operating conditions, always matching increased traffic demands and the threats emanating from competing railroads with motive power that met the challenge.[6]

By the early twentieth century, individuals in the PRR's Motive Power Department had applied the techniques of data-driven scientific analysis to the design and construction of steam locomotives. In the process, they gradually abandoned their reliance on improvisation, intuition, inherited knowledge, and rule-of-thumb engineering. While #460 originated from the drafting pens of talented mechanical engineers, the refinements that made the locomotive perform so spectacularly came from a laboratory. That facility—the Altoona test plant—was far removed from the world of Isaac Dripps, who had pieced together the *John Bull* without plans, without instructions, and with only a conceptual idea of how a steam locomotive was supposed to operate. In 1831, Dripps would hardly have foreseen those changes, any more than James Warren and the other crewmen in the cab of the #460 would have predicted that, less than thirty years after they sped between Washington and New York, the steam locomotive would have vanished from the Pennsylvania Railroad.

Early Locomotives on the Pennsylvania Railroad

In the autumn of 1848, with construction crews pushing their way west along the Juniata River, the PRR's directors authorized the purchase of the company's first locomotives. Matthias Baldwin, whose Philadelphia workshops soon grew into the nation's largest and most successful steam-locomotive builder, did not wait for the PRR to place its orders. Instead, he approached chief engineer J. Edgar Thomson, offering to provide "to the Company two or three locomotives" that he had originally built for the Baltimore & Ohio. Priced at $9,300 apiece, Baldwin was willing to accept as payment two hundred shares of PRR stock, plus a portion of the proceeds of a loan provided by the city of Philadelphia. Two of those locomotives were probably the *Dauphin* (delivered in December 1848) and the *Perry* (which arrived soon after).[7] The *Mifflin*, the *Indiana*, and the *Blair*, named for on-line counties, entered service in July 1849.[8] The three locomotives, designed for passenger traffic, embodied an unusual feature. Each had a single pair of drivers, with the axle linked to a set of "carrying wheels" by a "traction increaser" that, Baldwin claimed, would improve adhesion by redistributing the locomotive's weight when accelerating. Many of those earliest locomotives proved unsatisfactory. The PRR sold both the *Dauphin* and the *Perry* to the Philadelphia & Reading in October 1850. The *Westmoreland*, a similar locomotive, performed well enough that it remained in service until 1866.[9]

The small but growing collection of locomotives represented a substantial capital investment, one that required careful oversight. In the spring of 1849, Thomson—in collaboration with principal assistant engineer Herman Haupt—developed an organizational structure for managing the day-to-day operations of the Pennsylvania Railroad. Based on the one that Thomson had earlier used on the Georgia Railroad, it reflected standard practice on railroads throughout the United States. It included four categories, for "conducting transportation," "maintenance of way," "maintenance of cars," and "motive power." Haupt, who became the PRR's superintendent of transportation a few months later, oversaw the operation and repair of the company's locomotives, among his many other responsibilities. He soon delegated matters to the foreman at the Harrisburg Shops, at that time the principal service and repair facilities on the PRR. In December 1852, Enoch Lewis assumed control of the railroad's motive power, as the second assistant superintendent of motive power and shops, and a unit of the Transportation Department. Before joining the PRR, Lewis had been an employee of Eastwick & Harrison, another Philadelphia-based locomotive builder. Although far smaller than Baldwin, the firm enjoyed a reputation for technological innovation. Its founders sought a way to burn anthracite in locomotive fireboxes. Lewis shared that inventive spirit and, beginning in 1853, experimented with wood, coke, and a variety of hard and soft coals.[10]

In October 1857, Lewis assumed new responsibilities within the Transportation Department, eventually rising to the rank of general superintendent. Responsibility for locomotives and rolling stock then passed to Alexander McCausland, appointed as the master of machinery. McCausland took charge of a unit that would henceforth be known as the Motive Power Department. The new entity was now organizationally outside the Transportation Department, but McCausland and his successors reported to whichever executive oversaw the railroad's operations. For a time, McCausland continued his predecessor's investigations into locomotive fuel. Near the end of Lewis's term, mechanical engineer Alexander Lyman Holley, the editor of the *American Engineer*, provided further impetus for research. In September 1857, Holley organized a conference in New York, regarding best practices in the railroad industry, including the conversion of locomotives from wood to coal. Even though neither the PRR nor any other trunk line sent representatives to the meeting, Holley's ideas were soon in general circulation. In November 1857, Thomson hired William Jackson Palmer as his personal assistant. Palmer would soon join other PRR associates associated with the Westmoreland Coal Company and serve as that company's secretary. He was thus ideally suited to investigate coal use in PRR locomotives. Between 1859 and 1860, Palmer supervised a battery of tests

The Pennsylvania Railroad had been in existence for less than a decade when the Norris Locomotive Works supplied #85, the *Nescopeck*. It was a 4-4-0 American, the ubiquitous workhorse of the era. Shop forces at Altoona rebuilt the locomotive in 1865 as they gained experience with design and construction techniques, and it would be retired nine years later. Still in its first year of operation, the locomotive paused at Anderson's Siding, between Lewistown and McVeytown. *General Negative Collection, Railroad Museum of Pennsylvania, PHMC.*

to determine whether coal could provide sufficient heat without showering passenger cars with smoke and soot. He was particularly interested in copper fireboxes, manufactured by Gill & Company, as they seemed well suited to the combustion of coals commonly found in southwestern Pennsylvania.[11]

Later tests resulted in the development of new boiler designs and the installation of brick firebox arches, which distributed heat more evenly. Yet those hotter coal fires tended to soften and distort the iron crown sheets that separated the top of the firebox from the rearmost portion of the water-filled boiler. Shop forces were not able to rectify

that problem until early 1861, when they received the first, Baldwin-built, locomotives with steel fireboxes. After 1867, steel boilers became standard on all PRR locomotives. At the insistence of PRR motive-power officials, Baldwin began manufacturing steel boilers in 1868; in the same year, the PRR's Altoona Shops introduced steel boiler tubes. While shop forces gradually eliminated the difficulties associated with burning coal, the traffic demands associated with the Civil War accelerated the conversion process. By 1862, they had converted all freight locomotives to coal, and the remainder of the motive-power fleet followed suit by 1864.[12]

Thanks to ongoing construction and the acquisition of existing companies, Lewis, McCausland, and their successors oversaw a rapid growth in the PRR's collection of motive power. That expansion included the locomotives added in 1849, when the company began operating the Harrisburg, Portsmouth, Mountjoy & Lancaster Railroad. In January 1850, the board authorized the purchase of ten more locomotives, although Thomson elected to order only eight, again from Baldwin. That company's asking price was $7,000 cash, or $7,100 if funded by 75 percent cash and 25 percent stock. It was superior to a proposal from the Norris

Locomotive Works, another Philadelphia-based company, for $7,500 (with one-third in PRR stock, or a 1.4 percent discount for cash). Negotiations were quite informal, and Thomson "did not think it necessary to take any written contract as he thought it advisable to not do so as the plans might be changed as the business of the road developed itself." Between 1849 and 1852, Baldwin supplied sixteen locomotives, built to a design that was rapidly becoming ubiquitous on American railroads—so much so that they became known as "Americans." The dome-shaped Bury boiler developed in the 1830s was beginning to give way to a wagon-top design, so called because the rearmost portion of the boiler exhibited a distinct hump where it rested atop the firebox.[13] Steam produced in the boiler flowed through cylinders and propelled pistons that actuated Stephenson valve gear. The mechanism, developed by two employees of the British locomotive builder Robert Stephenson, was renowned for its simplicity and dependability. It produced the reciprocal motion that powered the four drivers. The locomotives also possessed a four-wheel lead truck (also referred to as a pilot truck or a pony truck) that guided the locomotive through switches and around curves. There was no corresponding trailing truck, and the firebox rested on the frame, between the drivers. Under the standard Whyte classification system, in common use after 1900, the American wheel arrangement held the designation of 4-4-0. Given the relationship between J. Edgar Thomson and Matthias Baldwin, it was entirely appropriate that Baldwin supplied the first American to operate on the Pennsylvania Railroad. It was the *Juniata*, completed in October 1849 and scrapped in March 1873.[14]

PRR executives, based in Philadelphia, relied heavily on Baldwin's factory, located in the nearby Spring Garden district. At a time of rapid transformation in the emerging locomotive industry, however, Lewis, McCausland, and other officials were also willing to experiment with the products of other builders. Perhaps the most unusual examples were eleven "camel" locomotives (so called because the cab rested atop the boiler, vaguely resembling a camel's hump) that arrived from the Baltimore manufactory of Ross Winans. The relocated cab allowed for a much wider firebox that could burn anthracite coal rather than wood. However, it also isolated the engineman from the fireman, making communication almost impossible. PRR shop forces soon rebuilt the camels into more conventional locomotives, with the cab at the rear. In that capacity, some remained in service until the early 1880s. Norris supplied a dozen fast passenger and eight freight locomotives in 1853 and 1854, all of the American type. Unfortunately, the Norris products were prone to boiler explosions, and PRR

officials quickly soured on that builder's offerings. So did their counterparts on other railroads, and Norris—once the largest locomotive builder in the United States—failed soon after the end of the Civil War.[15]

While the PRR and other railroads routinely employed 4-4-0 Americans in freight service, the grades over the Allegheny Mountains suggested the need for heavier motive power. The 2-6-0 (or Mogul) type was well suited to that purpose. Baldwin supplied a dozen of them in 1852 and 1853. Norris built two Moguls, while the Alexandria, Virginia, workshops of Smith & Perkins furnished another twelve. By 1857, the PRR had purchased 132 additional locomotives of varied wheel arrangements, more than half of them built by Baldwin. In that year, the railroad gained control over the Main Line of Public Works and thus acquired the 71 locomotives operated by the Philadelphia & Columbia Railroad, as well as the much smaller number operated by the Allegheny Portage Railroad. Some were modern and highly efficient machines, while many others represented outdated designs and were soon out of service.[16]

Altoona

The evolution of locomotive design and production methods was evident throughout the PRR system, but nowhere more so than in a community nestled in the eastern slope of the Allegheny Mountains. In 1846, when the state legislature chartered the Pennsylvania Railroad, the future location of Altoona was not far removed from the status of wilderness. The canal that constituted the Juniata Division of the Main Line of Public Works followed its namesake river to Hollidaysburg. There, it made a connection with the Allegheny Portage Railroad for the trip west to Johnstown and Pittsburgh. Thomson chose a different route for the Pennsylvania Railroad, one that passed eight miles to the north of Hollidaysburg. At that location, the moderate ascending grade west of Harrisburg met the far steeper climb to the summit at Gallitzin. The substantial change in topography, to the east and to the west of Altoona, necessitated an equally stark difference in the type of motive power used on each section. It made considerable sense, therefore, to move the PRR's shop facilities from Harrisburg to a location where employees could service and repair the widest assortment of locomotives.

Although Thomson demanded a new location for the shop facilities, he delegated the details to PRR director John Armstrong Wright. Wright's search was an easy one. He was intimately familiar with the area because, in 1838, he had conducted surveys for a proposed replacement to the Allegheny Portage Railroad. His father, Archibald Wright, was a useful intermediary, camouflaging the PRR's involvement and preventing a rapid escalation in real estate prices. In April 1849, the elder Wright purchased a farm from David Robeson (or Robinson). He immediately transferred the property to his son, who in turn sold it to the railroad. According to local lore, Wright also selected the name for the new town, based on the North Georgia Cherokee Indian word *Allatoona*, meaning "high lands of great worth." It was equally likely, however, that Thomson suggested the name, based on his familiarity with Allatoona Pass in northern Georgia. Allatoona soon became Altoona, and that was the name used upon the community's incorporation as a borough in February 1854. The owners of nearby farmlands, who were now sensitive to the increased value of their properties, began selling lots in the new districts of Greensburg and Loudensville. They remained separate communities until 1867, when they became part of the newly incorporated city of Altoona.[17]

In addition to serving as the location for shop facilities and the commencement of the westbound helper grade, Altoona also marked the junction between the main line and the short branch, completed in 1850, that provided a temporary connection to the tracks of the Allegheny Portage Railroad at Duncansville. That junction, laid out in the shape of a south-facing Y, accounted for the unusual street layout in the city. In East Altoona, 9th Avenue (also known as Branch Street) and other streets paralleled the branch that, even after the abandonment of the Allegheny Portage, led south to Hollidaysburg. To the west, however, 10th Avenue (Main Street) and its associated roadways followed the course of the main line west over the Horseshoe Curve, and all efforts to impose a more rational street plan met with failure.[18]

Construction on the PRR shops began early in 1850. Strickland Kneass, an experienced civil engineer who had earlier accompanied Charles Schlatter's surveying parties through the area, designed the initial facilities. He placed the principal buildings along the south side of the main line, west of 9th Street and paralleling 9th Avenue. The buildings included an eight-track roundhouse, with space for a paint shop and a freight car repair shop. A separate, single-story structure housed a machine shop, a car shop, and a locomotive repair facility, with an ancillary foundry—in short, all the resources necessary to maintain and repair motive power and cars in what at the time must have seemed a virtual wilderness.[19]

After Thomson became president in 1852, he transferred the headquarters of the Transportation Department from Harrisburg to Altoona. A new machine shop, built in 1852

and 1853, could handle virtually any task associated with the repair of steam locomotives, including the milling of massive side frames. Shop forces at Altoona soon undertook the rebuilding of locomotives—the first was the *Greene* in April 1853—and freight and passenger cars. In 1854, the PRR opened Engine House No. 2, referred to in later years as the Central Engine House. It contained twenty-six stalls and even at a considerable distance was readily identifiable by its ninety-foot-high cone-shaped roof. A new foundry and erecting shop also entered service. The acquisition of the Main Line of Public Works in 1857 induced a significant expansion in the shop facilities, with the construction of a sewer system, a car shop, a paint shop, and a transfer table. The PRR also increased the size of several existing buildings, at times making use of the stone sleepers that had been salvaged from the now-abandoned Portage Railroad. A new freight car shop and a paint shop entered service in 1858. Railroad officials also arranged to secure adequate coal supplies for the growing number of locomotives, installed gas lighting in some of the shop buildings, and built a water system—one that ultimately included ten reservoirs and fifty-four miles of pipeline to quench the thirst of a growing number of locomotive boilers.[20]

The town of Altoona grew rapidly, thanks to the rapid expansion of the Pennsylvania Railroad. In 1854, Altoona boasted a population of two thousand people, more than half of whom worked in the PRR shops. By 1870, Altoona's population had increased to ten thousand and to forty-two thousand by 1895. While it was never a true company town, Altoona nonetheless depended almost entirely on the jobs and the services that the Pennsylvania Railroad provided. Unlike coal-mining communities in Appalachia or such industrial centers as Pullman, Illinois, the PRR did not own houses or stores, nor was there a sustained campaign to dictate how or where employees should live.[21] Pennsylvania Railroad officials claimed that "the only moral force exercised by the Company was that the men should be what is termed 'good citizens,' and that employees trusted by their fellow-workmen with their money should be good citizens and worthy of the trust confided in them." To that end, executives sponsored a wide variety of activities that, they hoped, would keep shopworkers and other employees away from saloons, gambling dens, union halls, and other diversions that ran counter to the company's interests. In July 1853, even before the completion of the first shop facilities, the board of directors provided $500 to furnish a library. The following year, PRR officials encouraged the creation of the Altoona Mechanics' Library and Reading-Room Association, its name indicative of the highly skilled employees who would presumably make the best of citizens. While the Altoona Cricket Club catered principally to executives, its grounds hosted baseball games and other athletic activities that provided employees with wholesome recreation and camaraderie. The Logan House Hotel, built adjacent to the passenger station during 1852 and 1853, provided PRR executives and other distinguished visitors with some of the finest facilities in western Pennsylvania.[22]

A sustained expansion of the Altoona facilities took place during the Civil War and in the years that followed. The railroad and the city that it served were critical to Union military efforts and thus represented a potential target for Confederate raiding parties. The danger became acute in the summer of 1863, when General Robert E. Lee led the Army of Northern Virginia into Pennsylvania. Frantic efforts to safeguard Altoona and the PRR main line from the same type of devastation that befell the Baltimore & Ohio were prudent—but unnecessary, as Confederate soldiers never reached the western part of the state. Expansion continued throughout the war, and in 1862, construction crews doubled the size of the original Engine House No. 1 (now known as the Eastern Engine House). Repairs to locomotives and rolling stock benefited from the addition of a new brass foundry in 1863, followed by a new machine shop and a freight car shop in 1865. Engine House No. 3 (often referred to as the Western Engine House), completed in February 1867, added another forty-four locomotive stalls.[23]

Postwar growth in traffic and system mileage increased the demand for locomotives, freight cars, and passenger cars, and thus taxed the capacity of the Altoona Shops. In 1868, Alexander Cassatt, then the superintendent of motive power and machinery, recommended the construction of an entirely new, separate shop complex to augment the existing, crowded facilities. Construction began on the new Altoona Car Shops in 1869, with the work largely completed two years later. Located along Chestnut Avenue, east of 7th Street, the car shops specialized in the construction and repair of freight and passenger equipment. By the late 1870s, the car shops covered 42½ acres. The 250 employees at the freight car shop could build as many as five hundred cars per month or repair as many as two thousand. The one hundred employees at the passenger car erecting shop were able to complete thirty-four cars per month. Their efforts included a hundred austere passenger cars, lacking the ornamentation that was characteristic of the era and constructed to handle the increased traffic associated with the Centennial Exposition in Philadelphia. The cabinet shop and the upholstery shop were busy places, given the

need for the fine woodwork that graced more sumptuous equipment. Some thirty-five square yards of canvas, often elaborately decorated, covered the interior of passenger cars, expertly applied by workers in the car lining shop. Roof coverings and other components emerged from the tin shop, while the blacksmith shop, with thirty-four forges and a melting furnace, manufactured prodigious quantities of cast- and wrought-iron components. The paint store and mixing house supplied the paint shop and the varnishing shop—an important place, given that multiple coats of varnish protected the exterior of passenger cars, providing a widely used synonym for luxury express trains. Wood was the dominant component in both freight and passenger cars of that era, hence the need for a timber kiln and a massive lumberyard that contained eight million lineal feet of timber, stored on a twelve-acre site. A firehouse was an obvious necessity, as was a powerhouse that furnished the energy required to keep the complex in motion.[24]

To the south, the buildings of the original shop complex, some of which predated the Civil War, were now referred to as the Altoona Machine Shops. The size of the machine shops grew rapidly in the years following the Civil War, soon covering nearly thirty acres of land between 9th and 10th Avenues and between 11th and 16th Streets. A new erecting shop, 350 feet long and 66½ feet wide, opened in 1874, replacing the one that dated to 1854. It contained three parallel tracks, each long enough to accommodate seven locomotives, running the length of the building. The two outermost lines were dedicated to repairs, while the one in the center was set aside for the assembly of new locomotives. A separate boiler shop specialized in the construction of boilers and their related equipment, as well as the fabrication of tender tanks. A new blacksmith shop, augmenting the one that dated to 1852, contained twenty forges, two air-blast forges, and two steam hammers. The foundry, completed in stages between 1872 and 1874, contained three units. The main foundry, located in a building 250 feet long and 100 feet wide, included two small blast furnaces that could process up to thirty tons of iron per day. The more specialized brass foundry and wheel foundry ensured that the PRR could manufacture virtually any component necessary to fabricate or repair a locomotive or piece of rolling stock. Employees at the wheel shop fitted wheels to axles, and they were also responsible for items such as grade-crossing signs and signal parts. The duties of the telegraph shop were self-explanatory, while the tube shop (also known as the flue shop) and the tin shop performed similarly specialized functions. The pattern shop housed the masters, typically made of wood, that ensured

the uniformity of parts and subassemblies. Before entering revenue service, many locomotives and cars made a final stop at the paint shop, where the company maintained a consistent color scheme through the simple expedient of entrusting the mixing of pigments and binders to the care of a single individual.[25]

Other Shop Facilities

Altoona was by no means the only shop on the Pennsylvania Railroad. The Harrisburg Shops remained in operation and handled the running repairs to the motive power on the Middle Division and general repairs to a small number of locomotives. The Conemaugh Shops were located a mere thirty-six miles from Altoona. Freight trains operating between Altoona and Pittsburgh changed motive power there, and the route over the summit of the Alleghenies was so taxing that it was necessary to provide facilities for locomotives assigned to helper service or those that experienced difficulties en route. Located at the junction between Lines East and Lines West, the Pittsburgh Shops employed more than three hundred people. Fourteen miles east of Altoona, the Tyrone Shops—located at the junction of the main line and the Tyrone Division—employed a small staff that provided minor repairs to cars and locomotives. Additional shop facilities at Lewistown, Mifflin, Huntingdon, and Blairsville performed only minor repairs.[26]

The 1871 lease of the United Canal & Railroad Companies of New Jersey added both locomotives and shop facilities to the PRR system while inducing another corporate reorganization. The new system, adopted in March 1873, divided the bulk of the routes east of Pittsburgh into the Pennsylvania Railroad, United New Jersey, and Philadelphia & Erie Grand Divisions. The general superintendent on each grand division oversaw a superintendent of motive power (as well as a superintendent of transportation). Altoona functioned as the principal shop facility for the Pennsylvania Railroad Grand Division and for the entirety of the Lines East of Pittsburgh and Erie.[27]

The most significant remaining shop facilities were those located at the headquarters of the other two grand divisions. For many years, the Camden & Amboy's shops at Bordentown had accommodated the construction and rebuilding of steam locomotives, under the supervision of Isaac Dripps and his successor, Samuel B. Dougherty. Shortly after the PRR assumed control of the United Companies, however, executives closed the Bordentown shops and dismissed Dougherty. A new facility offered greater efficiency, in conformity with the standardization of design and construction practices at Altoona. Located on the United New Jersey Grand Division, the Meadows Shops were second only to Altoona in importance. Built between 1872 and 1874, they were at that time the best organized facilities on the PRR system. Workers drove nearly seven thousand piles into the marshy ground of the Hackensack Meadows and then constructed an engine house with a capacity of fifty locomotives, an erecting shop, a machine shop, a blacksmith shop, a boiler shop, a car shop, and a paint shop. The completion of the Meadows Shops downgraded the older facility at Jersey City to an insignificant status, with the principal shop building converted to a freight house. The South Amboy Shops and the Lambertville Shops were more important and served the needs of their respective divisions. The Renovo Shops, associated with the Philadelphia & Erie Grand Division offices in Williamsport, Pennsylvania, possessed the capacity to build locomotives and freight cars based on designs and standards furnished by Altoona. The Erie Shops and the Sunbury Shops could do no more than perform running repairs to cars and locomotives, with periodic maintenance and the rebuilding of damaged equipment referred to the superior facilities at Renovo.[28]

The location and responsibilities of the various shops changed regularly, according to the PRR's operating patterns, but the massive capital investments of the early twentieth century led to the establishment of new or enlarged facilities at several locations. The construction of low-grade freight lines and the integration of trackage around Harrisburg led to the installation of extensive yards and support facilities at Enola, across the Susquehanna River from the state capital. To the east, Wilmington, Delaware, housed shop facilities constructed in 1854 by the Philadelphia, Wilmington & Baltimore Railroad, long before it became a PRR subsidiary. In 1901, twenty years after acquiring the PW&B, the Pennsylvania Railroad undertook a series of improvements in Wilmington, elevating the right-of-way, adding tracks, and constructing a new passenger station. Between 1902 and 1904, construction crews dumped fill over a large plot of land located between Brandywine Creek and Shellpot Creek, two miles north of the city. A forty-four-stall engine house served the 260-odd locomotives on what was now the Philadelphia, Baltimore & Washington Railroad. The main shop building covered ninety-two-thousand square feet and included areas set aside for the erecting shop, machine shop, boiler shop, and tank shop. The complex could service as many as thirty-five locomotives and seventy-five freight cars a month. As a completely new facility, the Wilmington Shops embodied the latest technological advances, ranging from electric motors to a factory-style layout designed to speed production. At its height, during the early twentieth century, the Wilmington Shops were the largest employer in the city, with more than two thousand workers. The Great Depression induced layoffs and the possibility of closure. However, the extension of electrification between New York and Washington made the centrally located Wilmington facility an ideal setting for locomotive maintenance and repair—a function that continues under Amtrak as of this writing. The extension of catenary west to Harrisburg ensured that the shop facilities at Enola gained increased importance, eventually tending to the diverse needs of electric, steam, and diesel motive power.[29]

Lines West Shops

The Lines West of Pittsburgh and Erie also maintained an extensive network of shop facilities. The constituent carriers largely functioned as separate operating entities prior to the 1920 corporate reorganization. The Pittsburgh, Fort Wayne & Chicago Railway's route to Chicago was by far the most important. After 1890, it was at the core of the Northwest System of Lines West, a group that also included major lines such as the Cleveland & Pittsburgh Railroad and the Erie & Pittsburgh Railroad. The Grand Rapids & Indiana Railroad, while geographically connected to the Northwest System, remained a separate entity, with dedicated shop facilities and, at times, an idiosyncratic roster of steam locomotives. The corresponding Southwest System included the Pittsburgh, Cincinnati, Chicago & St. Louis Railway (often referred to as the Pan Handle Route) and other minor subsidiaries, with lines that connected each of its namesake cities. The companies west of Indianapolis, collectively known as the Vandalia Lines, like the GR&I, featured locomotives that often differed from those that operated on the larger PRR network.

The Northwest System and the Southwest System were each under the authority of a general superintendent

—subject to the policies established by the general manager of Lines West—who in turn oversaw a superintendent of motive power. Motive-power officials on the two systems thus possessed considerable discretion in the design, construction, and maintenance of steam locomotives. At times, they acquired locomotives, built at Altoona, that were either copies of Lines East designs or else had features that were unique to Lines West. In other cases, they supervised the construction of locomotives according to blueprints provided by the Motive Power Department in Altoona. Yet the Lines West shops, particularly those at Fort Wayne, were also a source of innovation during the nineteenth and well into the twentieth centuries. Lines West personnel and methods often spread to the east and exerted a profound influence over motive-power development on the entire Pennsylvania Railroad system.

The first train from the east entered Fort Wayne, Indiana, in October 1854, and work was soon underway on locomotive-servicing and shop facilities. A seven-stall brick engine house, built during the winter of 1855–1856, replaced an earlier wood structure. A few months later, in July 1856, the three companies linking Pittsburgh and Chicago—the Ohio & Pennsylvania, the Ohio & Indiana, and the Fort Wayne & Chicago—consolidated into the Pittsburgh, Fort Wayne & Chicago Railroad. The following year, that company purchased the land and buildings of the Wayne Car & Engine Works from Jones, Bass & Company. The small collection of frame buildings became the nucleus for the railroad's Fort Wayne Shops, under the direction of master mechanic Samuel Cummings. A sixteen-stall engine house, constructed in the winter of 1857–1858, was the first new building on the site.[30]

In 1859, the same year the company opened the complete route between Pittsburgh and Chicago, Isaac Dripps arrived in Fort Wayne and replaced Cummings as master mechanic. He was the same individual who had taken charge of the assembly and operation of the Camden & Amboy's *John Bull* in 1831. Dripps left the Camden & Amboy in 1853, long before it became a part of the Pennsylvania Railroad, and he assumed a partnership in the Trenton Locomotive & Machine Works. Despite Dripps's expertise, the firm could not compete effectively against Norris and Baldwin. His presence in Fort Wayne, a community of no more than seven thousand inhabitants, attested to the importance of the Fort Wayne Shops and to the role that those facilities would later play in the development of motive power on the Pennsylvania Railroad. Over the next decade, Dripps transformed the shops with new equipment and work methods. It was under his supervision

Employees at the Fort Wayne Shops repaired and built a wide variety of locomotives as well as freight and passenger cars. While conforming to the overall dictates of system policy, mechanical engineers and draftsmen enjoyed the freedom to develop designs that suited the operating conditions on Lines West. On more than one occasion, their innovations became incorporated into the products of Lines East. *History Center, Allen County–Fort Wayne Historical Society.*

that its employees built their first locomotive, in 1867. By 1870, that facility vied with Altoona as one of the premier examples of shop practice in the United States, if not the world.[31]

As at Altoona, the traffic increases brought about by the Civil War resulted in a rapid expansion of the Fort Wayne Shops. The facilities included a new engine house, car shop, boiler shop, blacksmith shop, and machine shop. In 1863, a grand ball, attended by 2,500 guests, celebrated the opening of the largest shop building. A Union army band provided music while 375 gas jets, colored lanterns, and locomotive headlights illuminated tables and a dance floor that covered an area of 80 feet by 220 feet. Four years later, workers at the facility demonstrated the physical strength and forcefulness that was a characteristic of

shop labor. Edward Ryan's saloon, located near the shops, had acquired a reputation as a watering hole and refuge for some of the least desirable individuals in Fort Wayne. One such criminal robbed a traveler at the PFW&C depot and hid in the saloon. Five hundred shopmen took the law into their own hands, surrounding the building and setting it on fire. Local newspaper editors offered a token condemnation of vigilante justice but excused the shopworkers—as well as the firefighters who declined to intervene. The year 1867 also marked the completion of the first of many locomotives built at the Fort Wayne Shops. Improvements during that time included the rebuilding of the blacksmith shop; improvements to the boiler shop were not undertaken until 1873.[32]

By 1890, the Fort Wayne Shops were, according to a correspondent for the *Railroad Gazette*, all that "might be expected on a progressive road, which acts as one of the most important feeders to the Pennsylvania." The facilities included a machine shop and an erecting shop, contained in the same building. In addition to the ongoing repair of existing motive power, the shopmen who worked there could build three new locomotives a month. Their counterparts at the truck shop could assemble twenty trucks per day to a standard PRR design developed at Altoona. Equipment in the blacksmith shop included a forge capable of stamping a wide variety of parts, as well as a crane system for conveying dies, patterns, and templates. The boiler shop was less well equipped, and a hydraulic flanger had not yet replaced hand-flanging. A reorganization of the woodworking shop ensured that all work flowed in an assembly line fashion, moving through the building without interfering with other projects or machinery. Components for as many as ten cars per day then traveled, stacked on flat cars, a mile to an erecting shop dedicated to rolling stock. Offices contained in a three-story brick building included space for the superintendent of motive power and four draftsmen, as well as a drawing room and a blueprinting room.[33]

The management of the Fort Wayne Shops included individuals who would also influence the development of motive power on Lines East. One was a French immigrant, Francis D. Casanave. He began his career in 1862 as an apprentice at the Altoona Shops. He rose rapidly through the ranks, and in 1876, he became the assistant master mechanic at Altoona. It was not uncommon for talented individuals to move between assignments on Lines East and Lines West, and Casanave conformed to that pattern. In 1881, he became the master mechanic at the Fort Wayne Shops. Six years later, he was promoted to the superintendent of motive power for the Pennsylvania Company, the PRR subsidiary that in turn controlled the Pittsburgh, Fort Wayne & Chicago. One of his most important subordinates was David F. Crawford, who in February 1892 left Altoona to become the master mechanic at the Fort Wayne Shops. By November 1899, Crawford was the superintendent of motive power for the Northwest System of Lines West. Like Casanave, he would make significant contributions to locomotive design and construction practices on the entire PRR system.[34]

While the personnel at Fort Wayne served as a source of innovative ideas in locomotive design, workers' skills and determination created a substantial amount of creative tension within the larger company. "In the design of equipment it is a matter of the greatest difficulty to reconcile two branches of the same Department," the PRRs general superintendent of motive power for Lines East noted in 1911, "as, for instance, the Motive Power Department of the lines East and West of Pittsburgh, and usually a forced decision has to be made if anything is to be done."[35]

The development of the shop facilities on the corresponding Southwest System was considerably more complicated. The initial components of what became known as the Pan Handle Route included the Steubenville & Indiana Railroad (chartered in 1848) and the Pittsburgh & Steubenville Railroad (incorporated the following year).

Steubenville, located on the western side of the Ohio River, was the junction of the two railroads and the logical site for their shop facilities. The interplay of politics and railroad development in the state of Ohio soon changed matters, however. William Dennison Jr., who enjoyed considerable success as a lawyer and banker, attained even greater stature when he married the daughter of William Neil, one of the wealthiest individuals in Columbus. Dennison served as governor of Ohio between 1860 and 1862, and his involvement in state government facilitated his various entrepreneurial activities. He assisted in the incorporation of numerous railroads, most of which were connected to the expanding PRR system. They included the Columbus, Piqua & Indiana Railroad and its successor companies, which eventually became a key component of the PRR's route between Columbus and Chicago. In 1864, he organized the Dennison Land Company, in collaboration with PRR president J. Edgar Thomson, Vice President Tom Scott, and several other investors who were closely connected with the PRR's allied lines in Ohio. The company acquired 450 acres of land situated 93 miles west of Pittsburgh and 100 miles east of Columbus. It was an ideal location for a division point and shop facilities. The distance to Pittsburgh was shorter but over undulating terrain that reduced train speeds and often required the use of helpers. It was necessary to change both crews and locomotives for the remaining route to the state capital, over relatively flat land.[36]

Work soon began on new shop facilities, although the town, named in Dennison's honor, was not established until the following year. By 1868, the PRR had merged the Pittsburgh & Steubenville and the Steubenville & Indiana into the Pittsburgh, Cincinnati & St. Louis Railway. The new company promptly built new offices in Dennison, which now served as the junction between the Pittsburgh Division and the Columbus Division of the PC&StL. While the Steubenville Shops would remain in operation for another two decades, they declined in importance. Dennison grew steadily, with the 1870 population of eight hundred more than doubling a decade later, and the adjacent city of Uhrichsville expanded at a similar rate. During the 1880s, the Pan Handle made numerous improvements in Dennison. In addition to the large roundhouse and locomotive-servicing facilities, Dennison boasted a car shop, a machine shop, a boiler shop, a carpenter shop, a tin shop, and a brass foundry. While large, the shops nonetheless ranked well behind Altoona in terms of output. In 1884, for example, the Dennison and Altoona facilities together built two passenger coaches, three baggage cars, eleven cabin cars (cabooses), twenty-four boxcars, eight stock cars, and one flatcar. Fewer than 15,000 freight cars received light repairs, with 336 receiving heavy repairs.[37]

In Dennison, as in Altoona, railroad executives encouraged wholesome and beneficial activities among the employees, without establishing a true company town. Thomas Denmead, the master mechanic at the Dennison Shops, and division superintendent W. W. Card oversaw the establishment of a Presbyterian church, often referred to by locals as the railway church. Officials supported the establishment of the Pan Handle Athletic Club. Its baseball stadium could accommodate ten thousand spectators, and during the 1920s, it hosted several systemwide athletic competitions.[38]

The Dennison Shops enjoyed their greatest importance during the first two decades of the twentieth century. At that time, more than 3,000 of the residents of Dennison and Uhrichsville worked for the Pennsylvania Railroad. Seven hundred people made running repairs to locomotives, while another 800 handled class repairs to as many as 450 locomotives. Their counterparts in the car shops tended to more than 50,000 cars per year. The 1920 census showed that 5,524 people lived in Dennison, moving the community from a village to the status of a city. The population declined swiftly during the following decade, thanks in large measure to the Shopmen's Strike of 1922. On September 8 of that year, PRR officials dispatched a group of 500 loyal employees and new hires to Dennison, part of a systemwide effort to break the strike. In the aftermath of the labor unrest, the PRR closed many of the shop facilities in Dennison, retaining only those needed to service locomotives and cars.[39]

While labor militancy influenced the managerial decision regarding the fate of the Dennison Shops and the community that surrounded it, the ongoing shift of facilities and personnel to Columbus was also of considerable importance. Columbus was an important railroad junction, the largest generator of traffic on the Pan Handle Route, and the logical location for extensive shops. The main stem of the Southwest System led due west, from Pittsburgh to Columbus. From the Ohio state capital, five routes radiated outward. They included lines that angled southwest to Cincinnati, west toward Indianapolis and St. Louis, and northeast toward Cleveland. The tracks that headed northwest, toward Chicago, carried considerable freight traffic and provided relief for the often-congested line of the Pittsburgh, Fort Wayne & Chicago. The final segment ran almost due north to Sandusky and carried large quantities of coal—often received at Columbus from the Norfolk & Western or the Chesapeake & Ohio—destined for transshipment to lake boats.[40]

The first shop facilities in Columbus dated to about 1857, with expansion at the site, near Spruce Street, continuing until the early 1870s. Constructed by the Columbus, Piqua & Indiana, they were known as the Piqua Shops. That railroad eventually became part of the Columbus, Chicago & Indiana Central Railway, created in 1868 to consolidate numerous routes in Ohio and Indiana. Many of those lines were precariously financed and badly managed, with their bloated capital structures retarding improvements to equipment and the physical plant and placing them in danger of bankruptcy. During the 1880s, PRR executives increased their oversight of those western lines, bringing them more firmly under their control. That process included the reorganization of the Columbus, Chicago & Indiana Central Railway and its 1883 inclusion in the Indiana and Illinois components of the Chicago, St. Louis & Pittsburgh Railroad. A further consolidation in September 1890 resulted in the creation of the Pittsburgh, Cincinnati, Chicago & St. Louis Railway, still referred to as the Pan Handle, and the establishment of the Southwest System of Lines West. Throughout that process, Columbus gained importance as a railroad junction that was roughly at the geographic center of the Southwest System and as a location where a substantial manufacturing base ensured a ready pool of skilled shop labor.[41]

During the 1880s, the growth of the Columbus Shops complemented the activities at Dennison and spelled the end of all but routine maintenance operations at Steubenville. In May 1883, the executive committee of the Pittsburgh, Cincinnati & St. Louis approved the construction of new shops in Columbus, and work began a month later. By the end of 1885, the general manager of the Southwest System, James McCrea, indicated that the new facilities were "about completed." Located on the east side of the city, the 20th Street Shops superseded the activities at the old Piqua Shops. Employees at the Steubenville paint shop were also transferred to Columbus on February 1, followed in July by individuals engaged in car repairs. All were under the supervision of Robert Curtis, who on August 1 became the first master mechanic at the Columbus Shops. "The entire transfer," McCrea noted, "was completed about December 15," to the undoubted consternation of merchants and civic leaders in Steubenville. In 1888, the Columbus Shops constructed 13 passenger cars, 2 baggage cars, 11 cabin cars, and 101 freight cars of various types, while all such work was suspended at Steubenville and Dennison. The output was inadequate for the needs of the companies that would soon become a part of the Southwest System, and those entities continued to receive equipment from Altoona. The manufacture of steam locomotives nonetheless suggested that employees at the Columbus Shops rivaled the abilities of their Altoona counterparts.[42]

The massive capital investments that began during the Cassatt administration stimulated the growth of the Columbus Shops, with a significant expansion occurring in 1902 and 1903. The additional facilities, built at a cost of more than half a million dollars, included a new erecting shop, engine house, and power station, as well as an expansion of the blacksmith shop, machine shop, and passenger car paint shop. Construction crews worked around the existing structures, which of necessity remained in constant use. They built the shell of the new powerhouse around the older, smaller one and were able to install a longer turntable in a mere five hours. The upgrades raised the capacity of the erecting shop from eleven locomotives to a minimum of twenty-six or a maximum of forty, depending on size. The construction of new steam locomotives continued at that facility until 1897, longer than at any other location on the system outside of Altoona. In tandem with the shops at Dennison and the smaller facilities at Indianapolis, Terre Haute (on the Vandalia Lines), and Logansport, Indiana, the Columbus Shops were well equipped to accommodate the motive-power and rolling-stock requirements of the Southwest System.[43]

The Standardization of Motive Power Design

The use of locomotives built to a standard design offered obvious efficiencies in manufacturing, maintenance, and repair. Yet the rapid expansion of the Pennsylvania Railroad, coupled with the equally precipitous evolution of steam-locomotive technology, complicated efforts to achieve standardization. Enoch Lewis, Alexander McCausland, and other motive-power officials oversaw locomotives that represented a wide assortment of builders, wheel arrangements, driving-wheel diameters, boilers, valve gears, and a host of other devices. As early as 1850, the PRR rostered fourteen different locomotive classes. Ten of those classes contained only one locomotive apiece, while two others were represented by two locomotives each. By 1856, the number of locomotives had increased to 133, divided into 43 classes. At the end of the following year, the company owned 216 locomotives, supplied by seven different builders. Many decades later, famed locomotive builder Samuel M. Vauclain recalled the difficulties that faced the company's mechanics: "My early career was with the Pennsylvania and from a small boy became very familiar with the various types of locomotives in service on that

road. And, believe me, it was difficult to find any two that were quite alike."[44]

Although PRR personnel had been using standard patterns in the car shops as early as 1858, the year 1862 marked the initial development and standardization of motive-power designs. It was the first full year of the Civil War, a time marked by disastrous reversals for Union forces and by growing traffic demands on all the railroads of the North. The war strained the railroad's facilities to the utmost and increased the number of repairs to cars and locomotives. In June 1862, to improve Altoona's performance, the board appointed John P. Laird as master of machinery—a title that changed to the superintendent of motive power and machinery the following year. Laird, born in 1826, had emigrated from his native Scotland at the age of nineteen. He was employed at both the Rogers Locomotive & Machine Works, in Paterson, New Jersey, and at the Latham Machine Shop. In the years that followed, Laird became the master mechanic of the Marietta & Cincinnati Railroad, a company that later became part of the Baltimore & Ohio.[45]

Laird typified the authority that skilled mechanics, schooled on the shop floor rather than in the classroom, could maintain over railway technology. When he arrived at Altoona, Laird confronted a bewildering array of steam locomotives, ranging from Bury-boilered 2-4-0s to ubiquitous 4-4-0 Americans to ungainly 0-8-0 Winans camels. Baldwin had built 143 of the 263 locomotives that the PRR owned in 1862, and Norris accounted for an additional 59. Twenty-seven, mostly relics from the Philadelphia & Columbia Railroad, came from another on-line producer, the Lancaster Locomotive Works. The concentration of 87 percent of the PRR's locomotive roster among the products of just three builders might indicate a high degree of standardization, but such was not the case. Most of those locomotives had been built during the 1850s, at a time when the manufacturers, along with any number of master mechanics and individual inventors, had experimented with new types of boilers, valve gears, suspensions, and wheel arrangements.[46]

Laird proceeded to rid the railroad of outdated motive power, rebuilding or scrapping a great many locomotives. He also began to standardize on a narrow range of the latest and most efficient designs. The use of parts and subassemblies that were common to different types of locomotives simplified the design and manufacturing process and made it easier for shop forces to maintain and repair the company's motive power. Of equal importance, locomotives built to the same basic design exhibited similar performance characteristics (especially speed and tractive effort, or pulling power), thus greatly simplifying the work of assembling and dispatching trains. Under Laird's direction, shop forces at Altoona rebuilt the 0-8-0 Winans camels into 2-6-0 Mogul types, gaining valuable experience in locomotive construction. Laird also designed new locomotive components, both improving efficiency and ensuring that builders would increasingly standardize on the PRR's technology rather than the disparate devices they themselves had developed.[47]

Laird left the employ of the Pennsylvania Railroad after less than four years, and his successor, Robert E. Ricker, served only fifteen months in that capacity. Alexander J. Cassatt became the superintendent of motive power and machinery in November 1867, a post he held until March 1870. Cassatt was one of three future PRR presidents to take command of the Motive Power Department. Like Frank Thomson (1873–1874) and W. W. Atterbury (1901–1903), Cassatt was a talented individual who possessed a thorough understanding of locomotive technology and operating methods. The three executives nonetheless served primarily in an administrative capacity, ensuring that the Motive Power Department conformed to the larger needs of the Pennsylvania Railroad. They honed the skills they would need as they advanced to positions of greater responsibility within the corporation but exerted comparatively little influence over locomotive design and construction.[48]

The day-to-day management of the Motive Power Department, as well as many of the technological innovations associated with it, typically came from the subordinate position of mechanical engineer. That was certainly true in the case of John B. Collin. In common with several other highly skilled locomotive designers on the PRR, Collin was an immigrant, born in Malmo, Sweden, in 1828. After immigrating to the United States, he worked for several years in various New England machine shops. Beginning in 1858, he alternated between work at Altoona and in Massachusetts. In October 1864, he returned to the PRR for the remainder of his career, initially as the general foreman of the Altoona Shops. In the spring of 1866, Collin undertook a three-month tour of various western railroads, paying close attention to matters of locomotive design, construction, and maintenance. Upon his return to Altoona, he became the PRR's mechanical engineer, a post he held until his death in 1886.[49]

Under Cassatt's direction, Collin began to establish standards for the PRR's motive power. Collin soon sought to emulate Baldwin's manufacturing capabilities as well.

With the Civil War at an end, the Pennsylvania Railroad enjoyed ample excess capacity at Altoona. Unlike Philadelphia and other northeastern cities, Altoona lacked a network of machine shops and manufactories that might provide temporary employment for skilled workers, until they could be called back to the railroad. Executives wanted to prevent their machinists, boilermakers, and foundrymen from drifting away to other locales. In that context, in-house production of locomotives offered a means to achieve that end, while reducing costs and giving the company greater control of the design and manufacturing process. A major milestone occurred in December 1866, when employees at that facility completed #142, a 4-4-0. Three other locomotives, also of the American type, followed, with #148 completed in June 1867, #127 in September, and #239 a month later. They were the first of 6,873 locomotives that would be built at Altoona over the next eighty years.[50]

For the next ten months, between October 1867 and August 1868, the personnel at the Altoona Machine Shops concentrated on the rebuilding of older locomotives—often to a common set of standards—rather than the construction of new ones. The hiatus provided Collin with the opportunity to classify and standardize the PRR's motive power. With very few exceptions, all new construction at Altoona would follow the drawings and blueprints prepared by Collin and his successors. Crucially, so would those manufactured at Baldwin and other outside suppliers, whose executives thus agreed to furnish products they had not designed. Initially, Collin employed standardization to improve the efficiency of manufacturing and repair operations rather than increase the power of locomotives. The PRR thus built or purchased as few locomotive types as possible. Collin eventually settled on eight classes that would provide the optimal flexibility for the diverse requirements of freight, passenger, and shifting (switching) service. Each design carried an alphabetic designation, assigned in chronological order rather than according to wheel arrangement. Classes A, B, and C were 4-4-0 American locomotives—the first for fast passenger service, the second as a helper in mountainous territory, and the Class C as a dual-service locomotive that could handle either freight or passenger trains. Class D and Class E locomotives were 4-6-0 "Ten-Wheelers," a type that was rapidly gaining favor on American railroads as a powerful freight locomotive. As with the Americans, one (with 56-inch drivers) was for flatland running, while the other (with 50-inch drivers) was better suited for the grades to the west of Altoona. Class F was an 0-6-0 tank locomotive (so called because it carried its water supply in a tank that lay atop and alongside the boiler), while the comparable Class H possessed the same wheel arrangement but with a more conventional tender. Lacking a pilot truck, representatives of both classes spent most of their time shifting cars in freight yards. The first standard-design locomotive to emerge from the Altoona Machine Shops, construction number 5, was a Class D 4-6-0, in August 1868. Shop forces completed the initial Class A locomotive in September, followed by the Class B (April 1869), Class E (May 1869), Class C (June 1869), Class F (November 1869), and Class G (November 1870). It would be October 1872, however, before the employees of the Altoona Machine Shops built the first Class H 0-6-0 shifter, the 146th locomotive fabricated there.[51]

As Collin was in the process of designing and bringing into production the initial eight classes of locomotives, he reported to superiors in an office that changed occupants with considerable frequency. The corporate reorganization that took place in April 1870 elevated Cassatt to the post of general superintendent of the Pennsylvania Railroad. His replacement, Isaac Dripps, was the former master mechanic at the Fort Wayne Shops. While Dripps possessed a wealth of experience, he was already sixty years old, and within a few years, the stress of the job took its toll. George Clinton Gardner replaced him in the spring of 1872, and for the next six years, Dripps remained with the PRR as an advisor and consultant, undertaking experimental projects as his health permitted.[52]

Despite Dripps's undoubted abilities, most of the innovations that occurred in the Motive Power Department during the 1870s could be attributed to the painstaking, methodological efforts of John Collin. Thanks to his ongoing standardization efforts, the various locomotive classes shared common components. They included firebox doors and frames, drivers, bearings, brake shoes and wedges, sand domes, and eccentric straps. Three types of crossheads sufficed for all classes. While the designs and their intended applications exhibited considerable variety, standardization ensured that the PRR never needed to manufacture, purchase, or carry in inventory more than four variants of any brass or iron casting. Most castings, 129 in all, were common to at least three classes, while 48 were dual-use, and none were unique to a single class of locomotive. By 1873, nearly 43 percent of the railroad's 873 locomotives conformed to one of Collin's standard designs, and that figure increased to 57 percent only three years later. Nearly 70 percent of the power that operated on the Pennsylvania Railroad Grand Division, the main line between Philadelphia and Pittsburgh, conformed to the principles of standardization. It was a remarkable achievement, given that the PRR continued to operate locomotives from so many of its subsidiaries—including the recently acquired United Canal & Railroad Companies of New Jersey. By the end of 1889, while some of its subsidiaries operated a considerable number of nonstandard locomotives, the Pennsylvania Railroad itself had achieved a phenomenal standardization rate of 99.5 percent.[53]

Collin's commitment to standardization did not come at the expense of efforts to develop new locomotive designs, as operating requirements dictated. One of the first initiatives involved a continuation of the experiments that Enoch Lewis had begun in 1853 to determine the feasibility of burning anthracite in locomotive fireboxes. The result was a variant of an existing 4-4-0 design, the Class CA, also referred to as a Canth. The Altoona Machine Shops built fifteen of them between June and November 1875, with assignments along various routes in New Jersey.[54]

By the time the anthracite-burning locomotives entered service, several important changes had taken place in the Motive Power Department. The PRR lines east of Pittsburgh expanded rapidly, thanks in large measure to the 1871 lease of the United Canal & Railroad Companies of New Jersey. J. Edgar Thomson also established firm control over the company's western affiliates, creating the Pennsylvania Company in 1871 and laying the foundation for the creation of the Northwest System and the Southwest System in 1890. In 1873, the PRR adopted a full-fledged line-and-staff organizational structure, with the system split into three grand divisions. Each grand division possessed a superintendent of motive power (as well as a superintendent of transportation), reporting directly to a general superintendent. Frank Thomson, the superintendent of motive power for the Pennsylvania Railroad Grand Division, was the first among equals, as he possessed the authority to establish standards and policies for the entire railroad. He was a skilled engineer, but his abiding interest was in the condition of the track and roadbed—to such an extent that he established prizes for the divisions with the highest-quality physical plant. Collin continued in his role as mechanical engineer, overseeing most of the details associated with the design and construction of locomotives.

Very soon, however, Collin joined forces with an individual who was equally gifted in the intricacies of steam locomotives. Theodore Newel Ely was born in Watertown, New York, in 1846. He earned a degree in civil engineering from Rensselaer Polytechnic Institute in 1866 and

Between 1874 and his retirement in 1911, Theodore N. Ely (1846–1916) was the guiding force in the development of steam locomotives on the Pennsylvania Railroad. He possessed an uncanny knack for blending power, efficiency, and beauty into his designs. *Alamy Stock Photos.*

went to work at the Fort Pitt foundry in Pittsburgh before making the transition to a mining engineer along the Monongahela Valley. Ely joined the PRR system in 1868 as a maintenance-of-way engineer on the Pittsburgh, Fort Wayne & Chicago. He became an assistant engineer on the Philadelphia & Erie Grand Division of the Pennsylvania Railroad and quickly rose to the rank of assistant general superintendent and then superintendent of motive power. In 1874, he became the superintendent of motive power for the Pennsylvania Railroad Grand Division, replacing future president Frank Thomson. Ely retained the same basic responsibilities for the next thirty-seven years, even as his title changed to general superintendent of motive power for Lines East (in 1882) and then chief of motive power for Lines East and West in 1893, a post he held until his retirement in 1911.[55]

Like John Laird before him, Ely was more than simply an administrator, assigned to that office in order to bend the activities of the Motive Power Department to the larger needs of the PRR's corporate policy. He was an

extraordinarily talented mechanical engineer who was an active member of many professional organizations, including the American Society of Civil Engineers, the American Society of Mechanical Engineers, the Franklin Institute, and the American Association for the Advancement of Science. Less typically, Ely belonged to the American Historical Association and the American Philosophical Society. He was also an honorary member of the American Institute of Architects—a testament to the aesthetic sensibilities he incorporated into the designs of Pennsylvania Railroad locomotives.[56]

Consolidations and Americans

The early years of Ely's long tenure as the head of the Motive Power Department included many significant advancements. One was associated with an improved version of a locomotive that would become the most common type on the PRR system. John Laird initiated the process when he supervised the rebuilding of numerous outdated 0-8-0 locomotives. One was the *Bedford*, delivered by Baldwin in March 1854. In 1864 or 1865, Laird added a single-axle lead truck of his own design, transforming the 0-8-0 into a 2-8-0. The locomotive did not perform well and thus offered Laird little incentive to replicate it.[57]

In 1866, however, Alexander Mitchell proved the worth of the 2-8-0 concept. Mitchell, the master mechanic of the Lehigh & Mahanoy Railroad—a company that was not a part of the PRR system—developed a freight locomotive with greater pulling power than the 4-4-0 or the 4-6-0. He relied on four sets of drivers, ensuring good adhesion and weight distribution. A single-axle lead truck was sufficient to guide the slow-moving freight locomotives through curves and switches, ensuring that most of the weight would remain on the drivers. The prototype of Mitchell's 2-8-0 entered service at the same time as the merger of the Lehigh & Mahanoy and the Lehigh Valley Railroad, hence the name Consolidation. It was the progenitor of more than thirty-three thousand locomotives built in the United States with the 2-8-0 wheel arrangement.[58]

The Pennsylvania Railroad received its first true, as-built Consolidation from Baldwin in 1868. In 1870, Baldwin supplied four Consolidations, assigned to the Philadelphia & Erie Division, followed by nine more, sent to the Northern Central Railway in 1873. All featured a wagon-top boiler, which possessed a noticeable upward slope from the front to the rear course of the boiler, over the crown sheet, and back toward the cab. The design, which by the 1850s had largely supplanted the Bury boiler, provided for greater steam capacity and could better accommodate poor-quality water. Wagon-top boilers were notoriously weak, however, and prone to explosion. The boiler's hump and the position of the steam dome, generally located just in front of the cab, also impeded forward visibility.[59]

Shortly after he arrived in Altoona, Ely oversaw the development of a new version of the Consolidation. The process in most respects reflected the work of his immediate subordinate, John Collin. By the time the Northern Central took delivery of the Baldwin Consolidations, Collin was already working on a larger and more powerful 2-8-0, with features unique to the Pennsylvania Railroad. One of the key elements of the design had a long and convoluted history, typical of the diffusion of early locomotive technology. In 1846, Robert Stevens temporarily relinquished the presidency of the Camden & Amboy, to rest and travel abroad. While visiting England, he observed a locomotive with an unusual 6-2-0 wheel arrangement, one that Thomas R. Crampton had patented four years earlier. When Stevens returned to the United States, he instructed Isaac Dripps to design a similar locomotive. Dripps feared, correctly, that the sole pair of 96-inch drivers would provide insufficient tractive effort. His design for the *John Stevens* nonetheless contained several innovative features that influenced the development of later, more successful locomotives. Rather than employ the wagon-top design, Dripps utilized a firebox with a crown sheet that sloped downward, from front to rear. A combination of crown bars (iron strips, set on edge and bolted to the crown sheet) and stay bolts (threaded rods that connected the crown sheet and the sides of the firebox to the outer walls of the boiler) held the top of the firebox in place and counteracted the outward expansive force of the steam that collected in the boiler.[60]

During the 1850s, the Philadelphia & Reading's master of machinery, James Millholland, conducted numerous experiments related to the use of anthracite coal. In the process, he appropriated elements of the firebox that Dripps had designed for the ill-fated *John Stevens*. Millholland's version also featured a firebox with a pronounced downward slope, from front to rear. He dispensed entirely with the crown bars and relied solely on stay bolts to hold the crown sheet and the top and sides of the boiler in position. Ross Winans incorporated Millholland's innovation into the numerous camel locomotives that he built for the Reading and for other customers. The PRR's roster of Winans 0-8-0 camel locomotives included the *Pluto* (built in February 1853), the *Logan* (February 1854), and the *Seneca* (April 1856). The PRR rebuilt them into conventional 2-6-0 Moguls, beginning with the *Seneca* in 1862,

followed by the *Pluto*, with the *Logan* completed in 1867—a year after Collin became the PRR's first mechanical engineer. They retained their downward sloping fireboxes and never received a wagon-top boiler. Collin may have drawn inspiration from those three locomotives. When he became the PRR's superintendent of motive power and machinery in 1870, Isaac Dripps may have reinforced Collin's willingness to replace the wagon-top boiler with a better system. Dripps doubtless remembered the sloping firebox he had designed for the *John Stevens*. He would logically have mentioned it to Collin, who was his direct subordinate.[61]

Whatever the source of the idea, the first of the new Class I Consolidations, #113, featured a firebox with a steeply sloping crown sheet. Unlike the Consolidations supplied by Baldwin between 1870 and 1873, the new Class I had a boiler barrel with a straight top from the smokebox to the front of the cab. From there, the boiler's roof sheet descended at a slightly steeper angle than that of the crown sheet. Crown bars were becoming obsolete, particularly on coal-burning locomotives, and they were in any case better suited to wagon-top boilers or straight boilers (an arrangement in which both the crown sheet and the top of the boiler barrel were horizontal). Collin thus used stay bolts exclusively. He also incorporated a large firebox, with ample grate area, that extended well into the cab of the locomotive, while making numerous other improvements. C. H. Caruthers, the superintendent of the car department of the Westmoreland Coal Company and an expert on early steam locomotives, was effusive in his praise of the work of Dripps, Collin, and their colleagues. "Pennsylvania designers added, in their various types of boilers, a superior arrangement of boiler mountings for convenient handling, and cabs affording a remarkably unobstructed view of the line and its surroundings in every direction," he noted. The arrangement was known throughout the United States as the "Altoona boiler," and it quickly became standard practice on the PRR.[62]

After completing the initial Class I Consolidation in April 1875, the Altoona Machine Shops built another seventeen in November and December. Baldwin also received an order for fourteen Consolidations. One was a star attraction at the Baldwin exhibit at the 1876 Centennial Exposition in Philadelphia. The Class I locomotive was as impressive on the railroad as it had been on static display. In September 1876, a Class I brought a freight train, consisting of 110 cars, into Harrisburg, unaided. Three months later, Consolidation #41 hauled 87 cars laden with grain and a further 13 containing oil, weighing 2,201 tons and stretching 3,127 feet. Shop forces began building one Class

By the 1880s, the Class I Consolidation had become the dominant freight locomotive on the Pennsylvania Railroad. The Altoona boiler on #811 has replaced the distinctive hump of the now-obsolete wagon-top boiler. *Pennsylvania Railroad Negative Collection, Hagley Museum & Library, acc. 1993.300.*

I after another, and during the peak output in 1883, the Altoona Machine Shops, the Fort Wayne Shops, Baldwin, the Pittsburgh Locomotive & Car Works, and the Grant Locomotive Works completed 154 of them. By the time production ended in 1886, the PRR had acquired 545 Class I locomotives.[63]

As the new Consolidations were proving their worth in revenue service, Ely began work on the first PRR locomotive class that was truly of his own design. The 4-4-0 American type handled most passenger assignments and, despite the inroads of the Class I Consolidations, was often used in freight service as well. When Alexander Cassatt, in his role as the superintendent of motive power and machinery, mandated standard locomotive designs, it was fitting that the first of those designations, Class A, was for a 4-4-0. Half of the original eight classes—the B, C, and G, as well as the A, were Americans. Prior to the reclassification that occurred in April 1897, more than half of all the PRR's locomotive types (fourteen out of twenty-five) were of the 4-4-0 wheel arrangement. The bituminous coal that was widely available along the PRR provided fuel for most of those locomotives, although some were equipped to burn anthracite. The Class C featured 62-inch

drivers, while those of the Class G were even smaller, at 56 inches—enabling them to surmount the grades of the Allegheny Mountains with relative ease and at a moderate speed. The 68-inch drivers on some locomotives, including thirteen representatives of Class A, were better suited for fast passenger service on level terrain.

Competitive pressures induced PRR executives to increase the speeds of passenger trains, requiring two things that even the Class A could not provide. One was larger drivers, so that each revolution of the wheel would cover a greater distance. The other was a larger firebox, capable of burning more fuel and thus increasing the amount of steam produced by the boiler. Conventional wisdom suggested that it would not be possible to make both modifications simultaneously. In traditional construction, the firebox rested between the main frame of the locomotive, thus restricting its width. It was certainly possible to elevate the firebox above the frame, but doing so was likely to create a top-heavy locomotive that would be dangerously unstable, particularly at high speed.

By early 1881, Ely had perfected a design that combined large drivers with the ample steaming capacity associated with a capacious firebox. His considerable talents included a willingness to learn from the larger community of motive-power experts on other railroads—chief among them the rival Philadelphia & Reading. Since the 1840s, the Reading had been hauling anthracite from northeastern Pennsylvania to tidewater. Burning the fuel in locomotive fireboxes was a trickier proposition, however. Proper combustion, especially of culm, the low-grade coal waste that was widely available in the region, required an exceptionally

During the final two decades of the nineteenth century, nothing could match the performance of the Class K Americans when it came to passenger service between Jersey City and Washington. Locomotive #10, the prototype of "Ely's Engine," was beautiful as well as functional. *Pennsylvania Railroad Negative Collection, Hagley Museum & Library, acc. 1993.300.*

wide firebox. In 1877, Reading superintendent of motive power John E. Wootten oversaw the construction of a 4-6-0 locomotive with a wide firebox, set over the rear drivers. Because it was not possible to place the cab atop or behind such a wide firebox, Wootten located it in the middle of the locomotive. He thus resurrected the camel design that had enjoyed brief popularity in the 1850s before falling out of favor.[64]

In his quest for a faster passenger locomotive, Ely borrowed some of the principles that Wootten applied to a design more commonly known as camelbacks. A retrospective in the *Railway Age Gazette*, published on the occasion of Ely's 1911 retirement, suggested that

> it was Mr. Ely that took the first step alone, against the protests of many by whom he was surrounded, that has led to the development of the large locomotives of today. While builders and engineers considered that the end had come, that the locomotive had reached the limit of its power because of the restrictions current construction put upon the size of the firebox, Mr. Ely lifted his whole boiler into the air, set his

foundation ring on top of the frames, widened his firebox and gave the machine a new lease of life. Many and dire were the predictions made as to the instability of the new design, but we all know the result. It did not upset, but ran with unexampled smoothness and with construction revolutionized the whole country followed in his wake.[65]

It was a charming story and a fitting retirement present, but one that exaggerated the extent of the opposition and derision that Ely supposedly encountered. Given contemporaneous developments on the Reading and other railroads, Ely could be reasonably certain that the PRR's newest 4-4-0 locomotive would remain stable, even at high speed. The resulting Class K was an outstanding machine, nonetheless. The firebox, set atop the main frames, was large enough to produce the heat—and the steam—necessary to power massive 78-inch drivers. The first Class K locomotive, construction number 532, left the Altoona Machine Shops in March 1881.[66] Assigned #10 as a road number, it earned its nickname of "The Monster." Total engine weight was 96,700 pounds, well above the 77,700 pounds of a Class A 4-4-0 and comparable to that of a Class I Consolidation. The boiler pressure on the Class K was 140 psi, likewise a substantial increase over the 125 psi of the earlier classes of Americans.[67]

From the beginning of its long and distinguished service on the Pennsylvania Railroad, Ely's design attracted widespread praise. The nineteen examples of Class K, built at Altoona between 1881 and 1883, offered the speed and the tractive effort necessary for the PRR's premium passenger trains.[68] Assigned to the New York Division, they experienced little difficulty moving five-car trains, weighing 130 tons, at an average speed of 48.3 miles per hour. Along the route between Jersey City and Philadelphia, sustained operating speeds over sixty miles per hour were commonplace. On one notable run, undertaken on March 10, 1890, #10 pulled a three-car special. The train, carrying the members of Albert M. Palmer's Madison Square Theatre Company, sped between Jersey City and Philadelphia in less than two hours. The following year, a train pulled by a Class K locomotive conveyed distinguished guests to the opening of a hotel in the nation's capital. It covered the distance from Jersey City to Washington in a mere four hours and eleven minutes. On a more somber occasion, Class K #958 powered the train carrying the mortally wounded president, James A. Garfield, to a seaside cottage at Elberon, New Jersey. The healthful atmosphere was not sufficient to save Garfield's life, and on September 21, 1881, the #958 returned the president's body to Washington. The legacy of the Class K locomotives proved so enduring that in 1994 the US Postal Service issued a twenty-nine-cent stamp that featured #10, the prototype of "Ely's Engine."[69]

The Belpaire Firebox

By the early 1880s, the Class I Consolidations had become the dominant freight locomotives on the Pennsylvania Railroad. Sustained traffic growth nonetheless taxed their abilities, and Ely sought a replacement that would be as successful as the latest 4-4-0 passenger locomotives. In 1885, working in collaboration with Collin, he developed the Class R Consolidation. Like the Class K Americans, the new design featured a substantial increase in boiler pressure relative to the earlier Class I 2-8-0 locomotives, from 125 to 140 psi. At 114,620 pounds, total engine weight was also substantially greater.[70]

The most significant innovation associated with the Class R involved a new firebox design, one that would soon become standard on the Pennsylvania Railroad's locomotives. Even though Collin claimed that the Altoona boiler on the Class I possessed superior steaming qualities to the straight boiler, naysayers suggested that that circumstance was more likely the result of an increase in grate size. C. H. Caruthers observed that the Altoona design appeared to draw water away from the crown sheet while the locomotive was running at full throttle, particularly while climbing moderate or steep grades. He speculated that the boiler itself was steaming properly but that the water glass was not giving an accurate indication of water levels.

Regardless of the cause, engine crews tended to run with more water over the crown sheet than was necessary. It was a sensible precaution, given the potentially catastrophic consequences associated with an exposed crown sheet—although Caruthers acknowledged that he had seen few Class I Consolidations with scorched crown sheets, and none that had suffered boiler explosions.[71]

Ely and Collin were nonetheless sensitive to the problems associated with the Altoona boiler, and they sought an alternative to the design they had developed a decade earlier. Once again, they blended their expertise with ideas imported from outside the company—and, in that instance, from outside the country as well. In 1860, Alfred Jules Belpaire was the chief of the Motive Power Department of the Belgian State Railway. Like John Wootten in the United States, he experimented with fireboxes that could efficiently burn the poor-quality coal that was abundant in Belgium. He devised a firebox that was essentially a cube, with a horizontal crown sheet that intersected the sides nearly at a right angle. As such, the crown sheet of the firebox and the roof sheet of the boiler were horizontal and parallel. Belpaire's new locomotives were successful, although—as with so many other elements of motive-power design—it was not clear whether the new firebox or other, complementary improvements were responsible for the more efficient performance. Belpaire's ideas soon appeared in other countries, and the 1862 London Exhibition featured a similar locomotive from the Northern Railway of France. Ten years later, Beyer, Peacock & Company completed the first Belpaire-equipped locomotives built in Britain, destined for the Malines & Terneuzen Railway in Belgium. The Belpaire firebox soon became common on western European railways, particularly those in Great Britain, and engineering journals gave the design extensive coverage. In 1874, the Rogers Locomotive & Machine Works installed Belpaire fireboxes on several locomotives sent to the Matanzas Railway in Cuba. Collin and Ely, therefore, were clearly aware of the concept.[72]

When the Altoona Machine Shops completed the first Class R Consolidation in October 1885, it featured the distinctive Belpaire firebox.[73] Collin, backed by Ely, suggested that the Belpaire design improved the locomotive's steaming ability by providing a slightly larger combustion chamber and thus increasing the evaporative capacity of the boiler. That assertion may have been correct, but the 12 percent increase in boiler pressure and the 34.8 percent expansion of the grate area, relative to the Class I, undoubtedly contributed to the results. The new arrangement presented certain manufacturing challenges, particularly with respect to the transition between the square firebox

The Class R Consolidation was the first to feature the Belpaire firebox, with its distinctive square shape. While uncommon in the United States, it soon became nearly universal on the Pennsylvania Railroad. The Altoona Machine Shops completed #111 in December 1890, as construction number 1568. *Pennsylvania Railroad Negative Collection, Hagley Museum & Library, acc. 1993.300.*

and the cylindrical boiler, but such matters did not tax the abilities of the craftsmen at Altoona. In compensation, the Belpaire design greatly facilitated the installation of stay bolts. A more traditional cylindrical boiler-and-firebox combination, also referred to as a radial-stay boiler, employed stay bolts of varying lengths, whose centerlines would converge at an imaginary point in the middle of the firebox—that is, set at progressively increasing or decreasing angles, relative to the vertical plane. The Belpaire, in contrast, used stay bolts that were typically of a uniform length, set at right angles to the crown sheet and the side sheets of the firebox. That feature simplified the installation of stay bolts, facilitated maintenance, and may have provided better resistance to the outward pressure of the boiler. Collin and Ely certainly believed that the Belpaire firebox would reduce the admittedly slim possibility of

burned crown sheets and catastrophic failures that were supposedly a drawback of the Altoona boiler.[74]

Lines West employed a similar, somewhat lighter locomotive, the Class S Consolidation.[75] The Fort Wayne Shops built the first examples in 1886, with a cylindrical boiler and crown bars rather than stay bolts.[76] In 1888, however, Baldwin began supplying Class S locomotives that featured Belpaire fireboxes.[77] Over the next twelve years, Baldwin and the Pittsburgh Locomotive & Car Works augmented PRR production at the Altoona Machine Shops, the Allegheny Valley Railroad shops at Verona, Pennsylvania, and the Lines West shops at Fort Wayne, Logansport, Columbus, and Dennison.[78]

Not for the first time, motive-power experts at other railroads and at the various independent builders reacted with respectful skepticism to the idiosyncratic approach of the Pennsylvania Railroad. Aside from the PRR, only the Great Northern acquired significant numbers of Belpaire-equipped locomotives. The Class R was nonetheless a triumph, and it soon became the railroad's standard freight locomotive, with more than eight hundred built between 1885 and 1892. In 1890, a Class R, #1334, hauled what may have been the heaviest train ever moved by a single locomotive, to that time. It included seventy-nine cars loaded with iron ore and six boxcars filled with pig

Motive-power officials at the Fort Wayne Shops worked in coordination with their counterparts at Altoona, but they nonetheless designed locomotives that suited the operating characteristics of Lines West. They included this rather battered Class S locomotive, once a formidable rival to the Lines East Class R but now demoted to yard service. *Pennsylvania Railroad Negative Collection, Hagley Museum & Library, acc. 1993.300.*

iron, for a total weight of twenty-four hundred tons. The Consolidation could do no better than six miles per hour on largely level track, and PRR officials concluded that the experiment could not be repeated in regular service. It was an impressive demonstration, nonetheless. A writer for the *Railroad Gazette* used it as an opportunity to illustrate the differences between operating conditions in the United States and Europe. "Some of our English readers," he noted, "do not seem to appreciate the capacity of our locomotives when hauling heavy trains." Thanks to the performance of the #1334, British railroaders whose "opinions are not based upon American experience, or conditions anything like those which obtain here," were beginning to appreciate what their counterparts in the United States were up against and what they were capable of doing.[79]

If skeptics harbored any remaining doubts about the abilities of American railroads and their locomotives, the performance of #263 must have dispelled them. In August 1892, the typical representative of Class R hauled a train, more than a thousand feet long and weighing more than two thousand tons, from Chicago to the Girard Point grain elevator in Philadelphia. Each of the forty boxcars carried thirty-three tons of wheat, some 2.64 million pounds of grain in all. The trip took four days, at an average speed of fifteen miles per hour. Although the locomotive made frequent stops to take on water and coal, it was never uncoupled from its train. The performance of #263 enabled the PRR's president, George Brooke Roberts, to announce that his company would soon be competitive against boats operating on the Great Lakes. "The question is," Roberts asked, "can the all-rail lines transport freight as cheap as the lake-and-rail lines. To determine this a struggle will ensue, but I am led to believe that the all-rail routes will be victorious." Thanks to Collin, Ely, and the Class R Consolidations, Roberts possessed a powerful advantage in his efforts to transform that prediction into reality.[80]

The Juniata Shops

Fittingly, a Class R Consolidation, #692, was the first locomotive built at the PRR's newest manufacturing facility. In 1886, with locomotive production straining the capacity of the Altoona Machine Shops, PRR officials sought a substantial increase in capacity. Construction began in September 1888, on a thirty-three-acre site to the east of the car shops. The facility would be named the Juniata Shops, a reference to the river the PRR's tracks followed for much of the distance between Harrisburg and Altoona. Workers laid the first bricks in May 1889, and the installation of machinery began early in 1891. Thereafter, the Altoona Machine Shops concentrated primarily on the repairing and rebuilding of existing motive power, although the construction of new locomotives continued until January 1904. The opening of the Juniata Shops also enabled PRR executives to accelerate the ongoing process of concentrating locomotive and rolling-stock construction at Altoona. In 1897, employees at the 20th Street Shops at Columbus, on the Southwest System of Lines West, completed their final steam locomotive. Thereafter, Lines West personnel, particularly those based at the Fort Wayne Shops, would continue to exert a substantial influence over the development of motive power. They would no longer be able to build what they had designed, however.[81]

When #692 entered service in July 1891, the Juniata Shops ranked among the most modern and efficient locomotive manufacturing facilities in the world. The nearly eight hundred craftsmen who worked there could build as many as 150 new locomotives a year. The complex featured an erecting shop that measured 70 feet by 354 feet, with components supplied by a two-story machine shop, a blacksmith shop, and a massive boiler shop. A paint shop, a paint storehouse, a two-story office building, a boiler house, and a gas house were also present. The electricity and hydraulic building attested to Ely's confidence that new power sources should be incorporated into the facility. "To give an idea of what the Pennsylvania Railroad Company thinks of the electric light," observed the editor of the *Railroad Gazette*, "I might say that its new Juniata shops at Altoona, having about 100,000 sq. ft. of floor space, are lighted entirely by the electric light; there is not a pipe for illuminating gas in any of the buildings." Electricity also powered the massive overhead cranes that could lift entire locomotives into the air. When officials at the Grant Locomotive Works announced in February 1891 that they would be building a new factory in Chicago, the *Railway Gazette*'s editor lamented that "they will not have as many special tools as are to be found in the new Juniata Shops of the Pennsylvania Railroad." While Pennsylvania Railroad officials were still willing to order locomotives from Baldwin and other independent suppliers, Ely and his colleagues possessed state-of-the-art manufacturing facilities that set the standard for others to follow. As such, they possessed considerable market power, and they were no longer beholden to outsiders.[82]

Production Costs

Locomotive production increased steadily during the early 1890s, prior to the cutbacks that accompanied the Panic of 1893. By February 1893, less than two years after #692 left the erecting shop, workers at the Juniata Shops completed their two hundredth locomotive. Master Mechanic H. D. Gorgon presided at a celebratory banquet, held at the Logan House. Ely was in attendance, as were forty other officers, clerks, and foremen—although the shopmen who had built the locomotive found sustenance elsewhere. The lavish bill of fare suggested that a three-thousand-pound trip hammer had manufactured the chicken croquettes from "selected scrap," served alongside roast turkey that was "cold sawed, with hardened steel bushings." While there was no corresponding celebration, the personnel at the car shops had just completed the world's largest freight car, a behemoth designed to transport the 124-ton Krupp gun from Baltimore to the Columbian Exposition in Chicago. By the end of 1893, the employees at the Altoona Machine Shops and the Juniata Shops had built 244 locomotives, more than in any other year of the Pennsylvania Railroad's history. The new facility employed 789 workers in the depression year of 1895—impressive, but still well below the 2,364 who worked in the car shops and the 4,051 in the machine shops.[83]

The early 1890s also featured significant changes in the management of the Altoona shop facilities. In March 1893, less than two years after the Juniata Shops began operations, the PRR adopted a new corporate structure. Ely, the general superintendent of motive power for Lines East, earned a promotion to a newly established office. As the chief of motive power, based in Philadelphia, he held jurisdiction over Lines West and Lines East. He reported directly to Charles Pugh, the third vice president, in charge of transportation, purchasing, real estate, insurance, and construction functions. Francis D. Casanave, the former superintendent of motive power on the Northwest System, replaced Ely as the general superintendent of motive power on Lines East. Holding similar responsibilities on Lines West were George L. Potter, the new superintendent of motive power on the Northwest System, and his Southwest System counterpart, Samuel Prescott Bush, grandfather of one US president and great-grandfather to another.[84]

The construction of the Juniata Shops afforded Pennsylvania Railroad executives the opportunity to introduce the newest techniques for organizing and controlling a skilled workforce. In Altoona and at countless other manufacturing facilities, there were two basic methods for the

MASTER MECHANIC & FOREMEN–ALTOONA MACHINE SHOPS
(1882)

S. Abrahims   L.A.Walton   W.H.Markland   T.M.Goodfellow   T.H.Wiggins   A.C.Davis   H.H.Stone   C.M.Pimlott   J.Gearhart   Geo.Deitrich   J.A.Lotz   D.E.Spielman

W.T.Miller   C.W.Mason   E.Mc.Lean   J.A.Beamer   H.B.Kendig   Jos.Davis   A.W.Mechen   W.Cook   P.Moore   T.J.Mc.Kiernan   W.S.Douglass

J.H.Carr   W.S.Jackson   Jos.Nixon   W.Jacobs   G.Hawksworth G.W.Stratton,M.M. T.A.Baxter A.H.Maxwell   G.W.Rosenberg   L.Kiefer   W.B.Ford   G.F.Mc.Noldy

By the time of this 1882 photo, foremen had implemented a piece rate system that increased efficiency and, they claimed, rewarded employees for their individual efforts. They reported to George W. Stratton, appropriately seated front and center in this photograph, who served as master mechanic at the Altoona Machine Shops from the Civil War era through his retirement in 1906. *Pennsylvania Railroad Negative Collection, Hagley Museum & Library, acc. 1993.300.*

assessment of wages. One reflected the number of hours that employees worked, and the other was a measure of the quantity and value of the items they produced. Most employees preferred to be awarded an hourly wage, irrespective of their level of productivity.

By the time that the Juniata Shops opened, however, many executives who were associated with manufacturing firms favored an alternate method of compensation. In the years following the Civil War, scientific analysis and engineering expertise greatly improved the efficiency of machinery. It was equally likely, argued proponents of what came to be known as scientific management, that the

same techniques could eliminate waste and inefficiency in the workforce. They asserted that piece rates, payments based on the quantity of output rather than time on the job, increased efficiency and—in theory—offered the best workers an opportunity to maximize their earnings. By the early twentieth century, the name of Frederick Winslow Taylor was virtually synonymous with the principles of scientific management. Taylor, a Philadelphia native, began his career in 1878 at the Midvale Steel Works, a significant PRR customer. His specialized techniques, including extensive reliance on time-and-motion studies, were only one facet of a much broader movement that gained momentum during the 1880s and 1890s, but they nonetheless attracted considerable publicity.[85]

On the Pennsylvania Railroad, the shops at Altoona and other locations offered the closest equivalent of the manufacturing facilities that were the focus of Taylor and other proponents of scientific management. Like their counterparts at many other companies, PRR executives adopted only those components of scientific management that best suited their needs. Moreover, while workers at shop facilities produced many standard items and often engaged in routine, repetitive tasks, there was enormous diversity in their output. As such, it was more difficult to quantify and regulate the behavior of shopworkers relative to employees of manufacturing firms such as Midvale Steel. Perhaps for that reason, Taylor's influential 1912 book, *Shop Management*, did not contain a single reference to railroads in any of its more than two hundred pages.[86]

Pennsylvania Railroad managers nonetheless enthusiastically supported one key element of scientific management, in the form of piece rates. That advocacy began well before Taylor started his career and before anyone else had articulated the principles associated with the scientific regimentation of the workforce. The company's officials introduced piece rates at Altoona as early as 1873 for workers involved in the casting of car wheels. The depression of the 1870s seriously affected the PRR's revenues and provided an economic incentive for the more widespread application of piece rates. By 1877, most shopworkers at Altoona were on the piece rate system. In the car shops, for example, it required twelve employees to complete the exterior of a freight or passenger car. Each work group selected one of its own as a foreman, who assigned specific tasks and ensured that everyone completed them. If any member of the team gave insufficient effort or performed substandard work, it was the responsibility of the foreman to notify management. Payment depended on the timely completion of the work, calculated at five or six days for a freight car, depending on complexity, and somewhat longer for a passenger car. Additional labor, beyond the allotted period, would come with a sharp rebuke for the foreman and his crew rather than additional compensation. It was a certainty that the foreman and the more productive workers would in turn pressure slackers to exert greater effort in the future.[87]

By 1880, the economic recovery and a backlog of deferred maintenance revived operations at the Altoona Machine Shops and the Altoona Car Shops. In an effort to control rising production costs, executives sought to impose piece rates on employees, many of whom were new to the shop floor. Francis Casanave was particularly adept at the implementation of piece rates in the company's shops. In 1886, he wrote a series of articles in the *Railroad Gazette* in which he articulated the core principles of the piecework system and advocated forcefully for its adoption. "To those who are willing to give the subject an impartial and careful hearing, it is proposed to show that piece, or contract work, *can* be applied to railroad work," Casanave emphasized, and "that the system is *profitable* and *fair*." He suggested that the piece rate "system is entirely free

from many of the elementary causes of discord necessarily underlying the day-rate system" and would thus enable workers to "understand and fully realize that the employers' interests are inseparable from their own and therefore identical." With piece rates in place, Casanave concluded, employees would have every incentive to work quickly (to maximize their income) and to produce quality products (the only basis for compensation, as defective components would be rejected). Shopmen "would use their brains as well as their hands," Casanave concluded, and "will give more attention to their work and become better workmen." He acknowledged that many individuals were not capable of becoming better workers and would thus earn lower compensation than their fellows. That was eminently fair, Casanave concluded. The process also enabled employers to further refine the division of labor. "Fortunately," he noted, "in every shop will be found labor adapted to men in all grades of intelligence and skill, and but little difficulty will be experienced in assigning to each one work suited to his ability." Once that division of labor had been established, the piece rate system would greatly reduce the burden on shop foremen, who would be freed from the twin responsibilities of policing slackers and overseeing quality control.[88]

Casanave devoted three of his seven articles to an effort to undermine managerial criticism of the piece rate system, a circumstance that underscored the reluctance to alter long-established shop practice. Only then did he offer suggestions regarding the implementation of piecework in railroad facilities. He devised a system of order cards, material cards, and service cards. When used in conjunction, they resolved the difficulties that arose when shop forces fabricated multiple identical parts, often to be held in inventory, and without knowing which locomotive or car would ultimately receive them. Each card listed the names of the workers assigned to a specific task, a measure of their individual output, and the corresponding earnings. The same techniques, he concluded, could just as readily be applied to car and locomotive repairs, tasks that were notoriously difficult to standardize.[89]

In addition to paying workers based on their individual output, it was also necessary to accurately allocate the costs associated with the centralized manufacture and repair of locomotives and equipment to the various divisions and grand divisions. The shops charged only the actual cost of the job, plus a percentage of overhead expense, along with interest and depreciation costs. There was considerable debate, however, concerning the way in which those overhead expenses would be calculated and allocated. Accountants at Altoona determined the facility's operating expenses only once per year. Because final adjustments were not made until the shops had completed all the projects undertaken in a particular year, that meant that the final reckoning did not take place until March or April of the following year. Beginning in 1890, in an effort to resolve some of those difficulties, Casanave devised accounting methods to assign operating expenses at Altoona to specific units of the Pennsylvania system. After 1899, the shops billed various divisions according to the amount of labor and material that each job consumed. Starting in 1910 or 1911, however, the accountants calculated the value of a job based solely on the amount of labor required. The new system therefore demanded a particularly accurate method of calculating that expense, and PRR managers concluded that piece rates constituted the most reliable mechanism of determining labor costs.[90]

Piecework thus remained an integral part of operations at Altoona during the late nineteenth century and became even more important in the years that followed. The opening of the Juniata Shops, expertly organized for the efficient production—almost on an assembly line basis—of locomotives that conformed to a small number of standard designs, offered an excellent opportunity for the implementation of piece rates. A writer for the *Railroad Gazette* observed that "the machine tools in these shops are of the most modern design, and work is done entirely by the piece."[91] Echoing one of the claims most used by proponents of scientific management, he asserted that "under this system the men are enabled to make good wages at a low cost of output to the company."[92]

Despite Casanave's claims that "the opposition to the system will not spring from the better class of workmen, but from grumblers and shirks," piece rates were highly unpopular with employees. That discontent triggered worker militancy at Altoona and other shop facilities, particularly in the years immediately following World War I. During the war years, and in keeping with the prolabor policies of President Woodrow Wilson, the United States Railroad Administration abolished piece rates in favor of an hourly wage. Postwar policies by executives on the PRR and other railroads to restore piece rates culminated in the violent Shopmen's Strike of 1922. Even before then, however, there were drawbacks to managerial efforts to impose engineering rationality, order, and system on the highly skilled craftsmen who fabricated complex pieces of machinery. During the 1890s, the general superintendent of the Pennsylvania Railroad Grand Division lamented that the new Juniata Shops lacked the "inherited knowledge" of a multigenerational workforce. "No matter how improved your appliances are," Frank L. Sheppard concluded, "if you have not the men you can not do the work."[93]

A New Classification System

Only a few years after the opening of the Juniata Shops, Theodore Ely was giving serious consideration to the development of a new classification system for Pennsylvania Railroad locomotives. The original practice, adopted by superintendent of motive power and machinery Alexander Cassatt in 1868, created eight alphabetical designations for the company's standard locomotive designs. Four classes (A, B, C, and G) were 4-4-0 Americans, principally differentiated by the diameter of their drivers. Classes D and E were reserved for 4-6-0 Ten-Wheelers, while 0-6-0 shifters were in Classes F and H. Each time the Motive Power Department developed a new locomotive, it received the next sequential letter. The first of the modern Consolidations, Class R, appeared in 1885, followed a year later by the Lines West version of that wheel arrangement, the Class S. In October 1892, the Altoona Machine Shops completed #1515, the sole representative of Class T, a 4-4-0 designed for high-speed passenger service on the New York Division. Ely and his colleagues were also working on a design for a 0-4-0 shifter, initially designated as Class U, which entered production in January 1895. The Fort Wayne Shops on Lines West were already building the Class X, another Ten-Wheeler. It would not be long, therefore, before the Pennsylvania Railroad would reach the end of the alphabet. Furthermore, the single-letter designation made it difficult to differentiate among locomotives with the same wheel arrangement and driver diameter but with modifications to the boiler, firebox, or other components.[94]

Francis Casanave, ever attentive to matters involving organization, developed a new classification system for the Pennsylvania Railroad's locomotives. In 1887, shortly after he wrote his seven-part series on the efficacy of piece rates, he became the superintendent of motive power for the Northwest System, the more complex and demanding half of Lines West. By the time he moved back east in 1893, as superintendent of motive power, Casanave possessed a thorough understanding of the principles of locomotive design and construction and a familiarity with the operating requirements of a large portion of the Pennsylvania Railroad.[95]

Casanave's new classification system became effective on April 26, 1897, replacing the chronological alphabetical sequence that had been in use since 1868. Casanave assigned a capital letter to each wheel arrangement, with numerical designations for major design revisions. Lowercase letters categorized more modest variations in a locomotive class, typically involving the type of boiler or valve gear and—in later years—the installation of superheaters. Casanave assigned the first letters of the alphabet to the PRR's shifters, including the 0-4-0 (Class A), 0-6-0 (Class B), and 0-8-0 (Class C) locomotives.[96] After 1897, the 4-4-0 locomotives in the old Class A (68-inch drivers) became the Class D1 (if burning bituminous coal) or Class D7 (if equipped to burn anthracite, and with 68-inch drivers) or Class D7a (anthracite-burners with 62-inch drivers); those in Class B became the D2 (bituminous) or D2a (anthracite); Class C became the D3 (bituminous) or D4 (anthracite, 62-inch drivers), with fifteen later converted to Class D4a (68-inch drivers); and the Class G became the Class D5 (56-inch drivers). The representatives of the original Class K—"Ely's Engine"—became Class D6 (78-inch drivers) or Class D6a (72-inch drivers).[97] The PRR did not yet own any of the 4-4-2 wheel arrangement that would soon become the railroad's dominant passenger power, but Ely set Class E aside for that purpose. Class F represented the small number of 2-6-0 Moguls that heretofore had not received an alphabetical designation. The old Class D, Class De, and Class E Ten-Wheelers joined Classes G1, G1a, and G2, while the Lines West Class X—a design that quickly passed from the scene—was awarded Class G3 or G3a. The Consolidations that were rapidly becoming the most important freight locomotive on the Pennsylvania Railroad received the designation of Class H. The obsolete Class I and Lines West Class S locomotives became the H1 and the H2, respectively, while the PRR's mainstay, the old Class R, now belonged to Class H3, H3a, or H3b. Casanave's system proved both versatile and enduring. It was in place until the end of steam operations on the Pennsylvania Railroad and provided the basis for electric-locomotive classifications that lasted even longer.[98]

Compounds and a New American

By the late nineteenth century, mechanical engineers on two continents were endeavoring to increase the efficiency of steam propulsion. One solution involved compounding. Rather than exhaust spent steam into the atmosphere, compound locomotives directed the output of the boiler into one or more high-pressure cylinders and then into one or more low-pressure cylinders. Proponents of compounding claimed that the technique made more efficient use of steam and thus lowered fuel and water consumption.

In practice, the additional complexity and the associated maintenance difficulties negated those advantages, and the concept quickly fell from favor.

Samuel Vauclain, the general superintendent at Baldwin, was the most enthusiastic American proponent of compounding. Fittingly, he was closely associated with the Pennsylvania Railroad. In 1831, his father, Andrew Constant Vauclain, found employment at the Philadelphia workshops of Matthias Baldwin. After a stint at the Reading, he moved to Altoona in 1856, the year of Samuel Vauclain's birth. A decade later Andrew Vauclain became the assistant foreman in the erecting shop and eventually earned a promotion to become the foreman of the Altoona Shops. In 1872, he secured a position for his son, as a shop apprentice. Eight years later, Samuel Vauclain went to Philadelphia, to oversee the fabrication of sixty locomotives that Baldwin was building for the PRR. His intense work ethic, domineering presence, and managerial skills attracted the attention of Baldwin executives. Vauclain began working for Baldwin in 1883 and he rose through the ranks with astonishing speed, becoming general superintendent in 1886. Thanks to his efforts, Baldwin delivered a 4-4-0 American locomotive to the Baltimore & Ohio in 1889. It was a balanced compound, with a high-pressure cylinder set atop a low-pressure cylinder, in the vertical plane, on each side of the locomotive. The B&O locomotive was successful, and it was the first of more than twenty-five hundred compounds that Baldwin completed prior to 1909.[99]

The Pennsylvania Railroad experimented with the Vauclain system and several other, less successful compounding arrangements. The first extensive tests occurred in 1892. Officials in the Motive Power Department evaluated six experimental locomotives, five of which were compounds. The oldest and most exotic contender was an English import designed by Francis William Webb, the locomotive superintendent of the London & North Western Railway, at Crewe—a community that was in many respects the British equivalent of Altoona. For many years, Webb was engaged in a friendly rivalry with his PRR counterparts. In February 1888, shop forces at Crewe completed a six-coupled goods (freight) locomotive in twenty-five hours and thirty minutes. That June, their counterparts at the Altoona Machine Shops built an anthracite-burning Class A 4-4-0 (later assigned to Class D7) in sixteen hours and fifty minutes.[100] The British would not regain the lead until December 1891, when James Holden, the locomotive superintendent of the Great Eastern Railway workshops at Stratford, exhorted his personnel to build a locomotive in just under ten hours.[101]

In August 1888, the PRR placed an order for a Webb compound locomotive. The Crewe workshops were a unit of the London & North Western, however, and did not supply the American market. As such, Beyer, Peacock & Company built the locomotive and shipped it to the United States in December 1891. The #1320 arrived in Philadelphia a month later, accompanied by a British driver (engineman) and a British mechanic. The locomotive was virtually identical to the London & North Western's *Marchioness of Stafford*, built in 1888. Its English origins were immediately apparent and included an open cab and a six-wheel tender. The PRR's enginemen and firemen demanded, and received, the protection of an enclosed cab and other safety equipment. Following a series of modifications at Altoona, test runs began in March. The Webb locomotive featured a 2-4-0 wheel arrangement, uncommon on American railroads. Webb's compound design was even more unusual, with the high-pressure cylinders propelling the rear drivers and their low-pressure counterparts doing the same for those in front. Because the two pairs of 75-inch-diameter drivers were powered independently, unconnected by side rods, the #1320 was technically a nonarticulated 2-2-2-0 locomotive. Extensive testing on Lines East and Lines West revealed that the Webb compound was an extraordinarily fast locomotive that was a worthy example of British craftsmanship. It was also underpowered and incapable of handling passenger trains on the Pennsylvania Railroad.[102]

Despite the disappointing performance of the Webb locomotive, the potential advantages of compounding were so great that Ely authorized further experiments. The #1320 soon had company, in the form of a 4-6-0 Baldwin compound, #1502, with 72-inch drivers. Baldwin also furnished #1510, a 4-4-0 with even larger 78-inch drivers. A 4-6-0 passenger locomotive, #1503, with 74-inch drivers, incorporated a rival design developed by Albert J. Pitkin, the chief draftsman of the Schenectady Locomotive Works. Schenectady also supplied #1504, a simple (i.e., noncompound) 4-4-0.[103]

The Altoona Machine Shops contributed #1515, the sole representative of Class T.[104] One of the most distinctive locomotives ever built at Altoona, it outwardly resembled the Webb compound imported from England a few years earlier. Like the #1320, it featured a six-wheel tender and low running boards with curved sections—splashers in British parlance—that covered the upper portion of the drivers. "In appearance it is the handsomest of the recent passenger engines," suggested an observer from the *Railroad Gazette*. "Great pains have been taken to get harmonious lines and to give the engine and tender what artists call 'composition.' By careful arrangement of the details the whole engine has the outward appearance of simplicity, so characteristic of English locomotive work. If it proves to be a capable and economical machine, it will doubtless establish a class."[105]

The mechanical and aesthetic qualities of the #1515 owed much to the exacting standards of its designer, an individual who was one of most talented engineers of his generation. Axel Vogt was born in Kristianstad, Sweden, in January 1849—making him an almost exact contemporary of Theodore Ely—and was educated in that city's public schools. After immigrating to the United States, Vogt began working for the Pennsylvania Railroad in 1874, as a draftsman in the office of the mechanical engineer at Altoona. He became chief draftsman two years later, followed by positions as the assistant engineer of tests in 1883 and assistant engineer in 1886. In March of the following year, he became the PRR's mechanical engineer, retaining that position until he reached the mandatory retirement age of seventy in February 1919. Thereafter, he worked as a consultant to the Baldwin Locomotive Works, the PRR's primary outside supplier of motive power, until his death in 1921. Like Ely, Vogt exhibited an extraordinary range of talents. In addition to his native Swedish, he was fluent in English, French, and German, and he regularly read technical journals in each of those languages. Along with other senior PRR executives, Vogt was a founding member of the Art Club of Philadelphia—a role that indicated both his privileged status and his ability to blend artistic beauty with engineering skill. He was idiosyncratic and rarely appeared in the office before 11:00 a.m., although he typically worked past midnight. The unusual behavior initially astonished his immediate supervisor, but Ely knew talent when he saw it and wisely left Vogt to his own devices. Vogt likewise tended to avoid the conventions of the Master Car Builders' Association and the Master Mechanics' Association—and, when he did attend, he never participated in the discussions or contributed to the published proceedings.[106]

During 1892, Vogt oversaw a comprehensive evaluation of the experimental compounds under a variety of operating conditions. The concept interested him, both because of its novelty and because he perceived a possible solution to the limitations to traditional motive power. For many decades, mechanical engineers in the United States and Europe had asserted that most locomotives possessed a firebox that was too small for the size of the boiler. Logic suggested that a firebox with a larger grate area could generate more heat and thus produce more steam in the boiler. Vogt was not convinced, however. Based on his long

The Class L, soon to become the Class D16b, represented the perfection of the American-type locomotive. Exhibiting both speed and beauty of design, #80 roars past the Waverly Yard, near Newark, early in the twentieth century. A 1903 graduate of the Juniata Shops, the locomotive was unable to cope with heavier steel cars and would be retired in 1922. *General Negative Collection, Railroad Museum of Pennsylvania, PHMC.*

experience with a variety of locomotives, he concluded that a simple increase in grate area could not continue indefinitely to keep pace with the ongoing increase in the weight and speed of trains. If engine crews could not manage a larger fire and thus generate additional steam, the only solution was to make more efficient use of the steam they were able to produce. Compounding, as Vauclain, Webb, and others asserted, was one possible way to do so.

Unfortunately, neither the #1515 nor any of the other compounds were able to meet the exacting demands of Pennsylvania Railroad passenger service, and none were ever duplicated. The 1892 tests were not a waste, however. Vogt and Ely temporarily rejected the principle of compounding, but they incorporated elements of the experimental locomotives into later designs. Much of the work was undertaken by Francis Casanave after he became the general superintendent of motive power for

Lines East in March 1893. In July of that year, workers at the Juniata Shops built six modified Class P 4-4-0 locomotives, with three assigned to the route between New York and Philadelphia and the others handling trains south to Washington.[107] The changes, based in part on the tests of the compound locomotives, included larger drivers and sandboxes relocated from a position underneath the wheel covers to one atop the boiler. The next iteration of the Class P, introduced in 1894, featured more extensive changes, which included a complete redesign of the valve gear, with the extensive use of lightweight components.[108]

In 1895, the Juniata Shops began production of a larger and more powerful American-type locomotive. Initially assigned to Class L, under the post-1897 identification system, it became a Class D16.[109] In addition to the now standard Belpaire firebox, the new design featured improved crosshead guides, developed by Vogt, and exceptionally light crossheads formed from a single piece of steel. The new running gear accordingly reduced dynamic augment—the repeated pounding of the drivers on the track—and minimized intrusions from dirt, cinders, and other debris. The locomotive featured a boiler pressure of 185 psi, ten pounds above that of the Class P. Grate area was the same, at 33.2 square feet, largely because Casanave and Vogt concluded that a larger and deeper firebox would prove difficult for the fireman to regulate.

That circumstance suggested that Vogt had been correct in his assessment that a larger firebox, in and of itself, was not sufficient to cope with heavier and faster trains. The initial batch of seventy-three Class L locomotives featured 80-inch drivers, were extraordinarily fast, and developed a respectable tractive effort of 17,500 pounds. On October 24, 1895, one of them, #1651, maintained an average speed of 57.6 miles per hour between Jersey City and Philadelphia, while hauling six passenger cars. The seventy-six locomotives with 68-inch drivers developed 20,580 pounds of tractive effort, although at the expense of speed.[110] Unfortunately, the factor of adhesion—the weight of the locomotive on its drivers divided by tractive effort—was no better than that of the earlier Class K and Class P locomotives.[111]

The new 4-4-0 locomotives had little difficulty handling the relatively light wooden passenger cars that were prevalent in the earliest years of the twentieth century. No D16 was ever able to match the speed generated by the New York Central's corresponding 4-4-0, the 1893-built #999, but that company's heavily publicized claims of a record-setting run were highly implausible. There was nonetheless little doubt that Ely, Vogt, and Casanave had designed an extraordinarily fast locomotive. One D16a covered the twelve miles between Metuchen and Rahway, New Jersey, in eight minutes, at an average speed of 102 miles per hour. In 1902, a two-car special train, pulled by D16a #804, sped Alexander Cassatt from Philadelphia to Jersey City in seventy-seven minutes, for an average speed of 70.16 miles per hour. When the PRR inaugurated the *Pennsylvania Special*, the direct antecedent of *The Broadway Limited*, D16a #1395 was the regularly assigned power, between Jersey City and West Philadelphia. The high-drivered 4-4-0 locomotives were equally suited for the run between Camden and the Jersey Shore, where competition with the Reading was intense. In August 1900, a representative of Class D16d, #5, achieved an average speed of 87 miles per hour, taking just fifty-two minutes to move a five-car train between Atlantic City and Camden.[112]

The D16 was as beautiful as it was functional. Ely and Vogt were sensitive to aesthetic considerations, and the proportions of the smokebox, firebox, boiler, and cab seemed exactly right. The tapered, flared stack; the smoothly rounded sand and steam domes; the clean lines of the valve gear and drive rods; and even the shape of the tender provided an unbeatable combination of power, grace, and beauty. As the editors of *Railway and Locomotive Engineering* observed, Ely and Vogt were each talented in their own right, and "the combination of the two gave an artistic feature to the designs of the Pennsylvania equipment that stamped it with an individuality of its own, which distinguishes it from that of any other designers in the country."[113]

The various representatives of the D16 class were both versatile and durable. After production of the 4-4-0 wheel arrangement ended in 1910, PRR shop forces rebuilt many of them with superheaters, larger cylinders, and new valve gear. The more powerful locomotives of the early twentieth century demoted many of the Class D16 to work pulling branch-line passenger trains or commuter services. One D16sb, #1223 lasted long enough to appear in *Broadway Limited*, a 1941 comedy produced by Hal Roach Studios, and it survives today at the Strasburg Railroad in Pennsylvania.[114]

The ubiquitous 4-4-0 American left an enduring legacy on the Pennsylvania Railroad. The company built or purchased more than eight hundred locomotives with that wheel arrangement. More than three hundred remained on the roster as late as 1924, long after they had vanished from most other large railroads. Well before then, however, Ely, Vogt, and Casanave had concluded that a new wheel arrangement would be necessary to bring the PRR's passenger locomotives into the twentieth century.

The Triumph of the Consolidations

The development of new passenger power did not occur in a vacuum, however, and proceeded in tandem with the search for a more modern freight locomotive. Between 1893 and 1895, Ely, Casanave, and Vogt responded to efforts by PRR managers to increase throughput by raising the speed with which trains flowed along a route of limited and increasingly strained capacity. New technological advancements, including air brakes and automatic couplers, made it possible to operate longer and faster trains. Shippers likewise demanded improved service, particularly for produce, livestock, and high-value merchandise. The depression of the 1890s created excess capacity in the railroad network, ensuring that power rested with the consumers rather than the providers of transportation. "Sharp competition and constantly falling freight rates," observed the editor of the *Railroad Gazette* in 1896, "make it more and more difficult for railroads to earn their expenses and as a result it becomes necessary to haul the heaviest freight trains at a speed that a few years ago was considered about right for passenger trains." Representatives from the PRR's Association of Transportation Officers met regularly to determine the optimal speed for freight operations. In the past, they recommended speeds of no more than a dozen miles an hour, particularly for trains carrying coal and other low-value bulk commodities. By the second half of the 1890s, however, they had little choice other than to endorse the assessment by the *Railroad Gazette* that "the conditions of traffic on some roads now require that the run be made at from 30 to 35 miles an hour."[115]

By the middle of the 1890s, however, it was not clear that the Class R (after 1897, the H3/H3a) Consolidation, with its 50-inch drivers, was the most appropriate choice for high-speed freight on the Pennsylvania Railroad. "Their well-known 'Class R' consolidation has done excellent service," the trade press observed, "but it is not sufficiently powerful, considering the needs of the future, and as soon as such an engine is run at anything like high speed, the wear and tear on the machine itself becomes great, making repairs too costly."[116]

The 2-6-0 Mogul offered a possible alternative. Employees at the Altoona Machine Shops produced the first Moguls during the 1860s by rebuilding obsolete locomotives into the new wheel arrangement. In the decades that followed, however, it was the 2-8-0 Consolidation rather than the Mogul that increasingly supplanted the 4-4-0 Americans in freight service. The general speedup of freight operations during the 1890s gave the 2-6-0 wheel arrangement a new lease on life. In 1895, Axel Vogt and Francis Casanave developed an improved version of the Mogul, with #768 completed at the Juniata Shops in December. Under the newly adopted classification system, it became the first representative of Class F1. The PRR also acquired four experimental compound Moguls, each employing a different valve-gear system and all assigned to Class F2.[117]

The 1892 experiments had not convinced Vogt of the virtues of compounding, and he remained skeptical of the new Moguls. As noted in the *Railroad Gazette*, "The Pennsylvania officers do not intend to adopt any kind of compound locomotive as standard until after exhaustive trials and experiments which may require a long time yet to complete." Between 1895 and 1897, the Altoona Machine Shops and the Juniata Shops collectively completed a total of forty-three F1 and F1a Moguls, and none were compounds. The new locomotives employed 62-inch drivers, significantly larger than the 50-inch drivers on the H3 Consolidations. The grate area in the ubiquitous Belpaire firebox was slightly smaller (29.9 vs. 31.2 square feet) but nonetheless sufficient to generate 185 psi in the boiler, well above the 140 psi on the H3. The weight on drivers increased as well, from 100,590 pounds to 127,000 pounds. The tractive effort of the F1a, at 28,400 pounds,

was 24 percent greater than that of the H3, and sustained operating speeds were much higher.[118]

Beginning in 1901, Baldwin began deliveries of the Class F3, with a boiler pressure increased from 185 psi to 205 psi. Additional variants followed, including the F3b, with a wide firebox and a radial-stay boiler, and F3c, with a Belpaire firebox. The Vandalia Lines also operated a wide assortment of Moguls, some dating to the 1870s and others built new in the early twentieth century. Regardless of their origins, the 2-6-0 design was unable to keep pace with the weight of new all-steel cars or with demands from shippers for ever-faster transit times. The powerful, plodding Consolidations were far more numerous, and the PRR's brief involvement with the Mogul held little lasting significance.[119]

Steady improvements to the 2-8-0 ensured that the Consolidation would become the company's dominant freight locomotive. The impetus for larger and more powerful Consolidations came from Lines West, but the design quickly spread to the eastern portion of the system. "We believe," observed a correspondent for the *Railroad Gazette*, "that the design in general was made at Fort Wayne, but naturally it must have had its final revision and approval at Altoona and in the office of the Chief of Motive Power" in Philadelphia. Despite the uncertainty, the comment was an accurate reflection of the genesis of the H4 and its successors. Much of the work was undertaken by George Potter, since 1893 the superintendent of motive power for the Northwest System of Lines West. In that capacity, he enjoyed the support of his predecessor, Francis Casanave, who had been promoted to general superintendent of motive power on Lines East.[120]

By December 1897, five Class H4 locomotives were in service, hauling trains between Pittsburgh and the Lake Erie ports, with five more under construction at Altoona. Lines West motive-power officials had concluded that the firebox of the H3 Consolidation was unnecessarily large, with 31.2 square feet of grate area. The grate of the H4 was slightly less capacious, at 29.7 square feet. Nothing else was smaller, however. The H4 employed drivers that were 56 inches in diameter, half a foot more than those on the H3a. Boiler diameter increased from 60 to 68 inches, and the H4 had a noticeably "fatter" appearance. There was also a substantial increase in boiler pressure, from 140 psi on the H3 (or 150 psi on the H3a) to 205 psi on the H4. Cylinder dimensions expanded from 20 by 24 inches to 22 by 28 inches, identical to the F1a. The weight of the H4 was 40 percent higher than the H3a, and weight on drivers rose by 46 percent—something that was only possible thanks

While slightly less robust than its H5 predecessor, the Class H6 was nonetheless a massive locomotive, well suited to almost every type of road freight and yard service. The #1868 is shifting cars in Long Island City in 1920. *Harris Negatives Collection, Railroad Museum of Pennsylvania, PHMC.*

to a superbly maintained right-of-way. Tractive effort increased by 67 percent, from 21,500 to 35,800 pounds. In the quest for greater power, the PRR's newest Consolidation regained the lead from Class F1a Mogul, which could generate only 28,400 pounds of tractive effort.[121]

Like Casanave, James McCrea served on the western portion of the PRR system, before moving to Lines East. Although he hailed from Philadelphia, McCrea had been a Lines West executive since 1882. When the H4 Consolidations entered service, seventeen years later, he was the first vice president of Lines West, in charge of all operations west of Pittsburgh. McCrea was thus familiar with the potential of the H4 design. He was also well positioned to recommend the locomotive to Frank Thomson, the president of the Pennsylvania Railroad. Thomson, who had served briefly as the PRR's superintendent of motive power and machinery, an earlier version of the office that Casanave now occupied, quickly appreciated the benefits of the H4 and recommended widespread use on Lines East. Frank

Sheppard, the general superintendent of the Pennsylvania Railroad Grand Division, incorrectly assigned credit for the H4 to McCrea rather than Potter or Casanave, but his assessment of Thomson's reaction to that locomotive was probably more accurate. The president of the Pennsylvania Railroad made "an inspection of McCrea's big engine," Sheppard recalled, and said, "'Let's build an engine bigger than this,'" for use on Lines East.[122]

By early 1898, work was underway on the H5, the Lines East counterpart to the H4.[123] The revisions included slightly larger cylinders and a more capacious firebox. Boiler pressure was nonetheless somewhat lower, at 185 psi. Engine weight was an astonishing 198,000 pounds, nearly 73 percent greater than the H3a. Weight on drivers increased from 100,500 pounds on the H3a to 186,000 pounds on the H5. The H5 generated a total tractive effort of 43,400 pounds, making it one of the heaviest and most powerful locomotives that had ever been built. The ponderous H5 nonetheless embodied the graceful appearance that Ely, Casanave, and mechanical engineer Axel Vogt incorporated into its design. "We think the reader will agree with us," noted the editors of the *Railroad Gazette*, "that this engine has remarkably handsome lines for such an enormous machine." When the first H5 left the erecting shop, its designers knew only its calculated rather than its actual weight, as the locomotive was too heavy for any track scale then in use.[124] It was also too long for any available turntable. It performed well in its intended role, pushing freight trains up the eastern slope of the Alleghenies, but it returned to Altoona in reverse, as there was no way to turn it.[125]

The fifteen H5 locomotives did everything that designers expected of them, and the trade press frequently mentioned them as the standard setters for large Consolidations on other railroads. One fourteen-hour trip, made in August 1898, was particularly notable. The first H5 to enter service, #872, moved 130 cars of coal from Altoona to Columbia, Pennsylvania, in a train that stretched 3,877 feet and weighed 5,212 tons. The performance attested to the power of the H5 as well as to the improved facilities that enabled crews to turn the locomotive. Motive-power officials nonetheless concluded that the behemoth was best suited for pusher duties and was not appropriate for general freight service on the Pennsylvania Railroad.[126]

Based on their experience with the H5 Consolidations, Casanave and Vogt designed a similar locomotive, one that was better suited for road service. The H6 weighed 186,500 pounds, somewhat less than its predecessor. Its Belpaire firebox had a grate area of 33.3 square feet, but the size of its cylinders was slightly smaller. Boiler pressure was notably higher, increasing from 185 psi to 205 psi. The H6 developed a maximum tractive effort of 42,170 pounds, nearly equaling the 43,400 pounds generated by the H5. That was more than double the 20,400 pounds developed by the Class H1 Consolidations introduced in 1875 and close to four times the output of an 1868-vintage D3 passenger locomotive.[127]

The performance of the first Class H6 Consolidations, delivered in early 1899, justified large-scale production. In March, Baldwin received an order for twenty-five of them, and by November another ten were under construction at the Juniata Shops. In October 1900, PRR officials announced they would soon replace all the 2-6-0 Class F Moguls on the Philadelphia Division with Consolidations. Even though the Pennsylvania Railroad would acquire Moguls as late as 1906, it was clear that in the future the 2-8-0 would be the company's dominant freight locomotive. When production ended in 1913, the PRR and its subsidiaries had acquired 1,707 examples of the Class H6, in numerous variants. It was the largest group of locomotives, built to the same basic design, on any railroad, anywhere in the world.[128]

The original version of the H6 demonstrated one serious impediment that limited its potential. Its firebox, which sat between the drivers, was long and narrow, and even the most skilled fireman found it difficult to fully utilize the ability of the capacious boiler. Casanave and Vogt soon devised a solution in the form of a firebox that sat atop

the rearmost drivers rather than between them. The first representatives of Class H6a, built by Baldwin in 1901, had a grate area of forty-nine square feet, a 47 percent increase from the H6. The modification unleashed the full potential of the design, and the PRR ultimately acquired 1,242 H6a locomotives. Capacity limitations at Altoona, combined with the urgent need for additional motive power, ensured that, by 1905, Baldwin constructed 1,017 of them. In one spectacular rush order, that company completed 160 locomotives in a six-week period, between October 10 and November 22, 1905. The total cost of each locomotive, including a 10 percent profit for Baldwin, was $17,764.32. Most of that amount—slightly over $10,000—involved materials, with barely $4,000 attributable to what Baldwin executives labeled "productive labor." Pattern work cost a mere $1.20, and the cost of drawings was zero, illustrating the advantage of building hundreds of locomotives to the same design. True manufacturing standardization was an elusive goal, however, as evidenced by nearly $60.00 worth of "errors and defects," most likely failed castings or improperly machined parts.[129]

The development of the ultimate Consolidation began in 1905, when Alco built two experimental Class H28 locomotives, one for Lines East and the other for Lines West. They resembled the Class G5 Consolidations used on the New York Central—hardly surprising, as Alco was the NYC's preferred outside supplier for motive power. They featured wide fireboxes, like the H6a, but used a radial-stay boiler rather than the PRR's standard Belpaire. The fat boiler on the H6 became even fatter on the H28, with the diameter increasing from 69½ inches to 80 inches. The 63-inch drivers were vastly larger than the 50-inch versions on the old H3, and even exceeded, by an inch, the F1a Mogul that Vogt and Casanave had once envisioned as the PRR's standard fast freight locomotive.[130]

While the PRR never duplicated the two Class H28 locomotives, the information obtained from road tests led to the development and widespread production of three classes of Consolidations: the H8, the H9, and the H10. All three used the same boiler design, 76¾ inches in diameter, with an operating pressure of 205 psi.[131] Driver diameter was also the same, at 62 inches. The PRR rushed the H8 into production so quickly that the Juniata Shops could not keep up with the demand. The company eventually acquired nearly a thousand of the Class H8 and its various subclasses, built by the PRR, Alco, Baldwin, and Lima. After the first H8 left the Juniata Shops in January 1907, it became clear that the large boiler generated more than enough steam to supply the 24-inch by 28-inch cylinders. As such, the cylinders on the H9s featured a diameter that

Class H10s #9895, built by Alco at its Pittsburgh Locomotive & Car Works facility in 1913, was the ultimate expression of the Consolidation design. While primarily employed in freight service, it was equally adept at handling mail and express trains, such as the one seen here in 1933, near Indianapolis. *Otto Perry photograph, Denver Public Library, Western History Collection, call number OP-14447.*

was one inch larger, with a comparable increase on the H10s, to 26 inches by 28 inches. With the larger cylinders and the application of superheaters to the two later classes came a corresponding gain in tractive effort, from 45,330 pounds on the H8 to 49,180 pounds for the H9s and 53,200 pounds for the H10s. The PRR's most powerful Consolidations, used principally on Lines West, carried 223,000 pounds on their drivers, more than double the 100,590 pounds of the 1880s-vintage Class H3. At 53,200 pounds, the tractive effort of the H10 was also a vast improvement over the 22,850 pounds of the H3 and the 28,400 pounds of the F1a Mogul.[132]

The success of the H8, H9s, and H10s classes ensured that the Consolidation was the most common freight locomotive on the Pennsylvania Railroad through the end of steam operations. While it is difficult to identify the precise number of locomotives provided by outside suppliers or constructed in the PRR's various shop facilities, it is probable that the Pennsylvania Railroad acquired more

than 4,000 Consolidations between 1875 and 1916. By 1923, the PRR owned 7,366 locomotives, of which more than 3,300 were H-Class 2-8-0s. By 1930, there were still 2,300 Consolidations in service. The traffic declines associated with the Great Depression ensured that about 900 of these would be retired by 1935. Most were the older, less robust Consolidations, and many others of that wheel arrangement remained in service on main lines, on branch lines, and as shifters in railroad yards.[133]

The Birth of the Limiteds

Even as they were developing the Consolidation into the PRR's dominant freight locomotive, Ely and his subordinates could not afford to neglect the design of motive power that was more appropriate for passenger service. During the last third of the nineteenth century, as the American yielded to the Consolidation in freight service, the 4-4-0 remained the mainstay of the PRR's passenger fleet. The refinement of the design continued through the introduction of the Class K in 1881 and culminated with the Class L (D16) in 1895.

The development of those locomotives coincided with the emergence of some of the most beautiful and luxurious trains to ever operate on the Pennsylvania Railroad. By the 1880s, numerous incremental technological advancements coalesced into revolutionary new designs for passenger equipment. Suppliers, most notably Pullman's Palace Car

Company, developed improved manufacturing techniques while employing skilled craftsmen who could turn the prosaic passenger car into a work of art. Pullman and other car builders incorporated air brakes and automatic couplers, increasing both safety and operating speeds. Enclosed vestibules permitted passengers to pass from one car to another. Those cars included sleepers, observation lounges, and the diners that were increasingly replacing trackside eateries. The recirculating hot-water system developed by William C. Baker was far safer than the potbelly stoves that it replaced and provided greater comfort for passengers.[134] Lighting improved as well thanks to the replacement of kerosene lamps with the Pintsch gas system. Beginning in 1882, the PRR's chief chemist, Charles Dudley, initiated experiments with electric lighting in passenger cars, although it would be many years before that technology would become widespread.[135] The rapid development of big business in the United States created a large group of entrepreneurs and senior executives, individuals who had a need to travel frequently and who possessed the means to do so. They reveled in the ostentatiousness that accompanied the Gilded Age, boasting of their ability to move faster and in greater luxury than anyone had done before. That such speeds could at times prove dangerous only added to the thrill. For those who could afford it, there was no better way to travel than onboard the deluxe, extra-fare limited.[136]

The first of the limiteds connected the heavily populated cities along the Atlantic Seaboard. In the summer of 1873, the completion of the Baltimore tunnels enabled the PRR to offer through service over what advertisements dubbed the "Pennsylvania Air Line" from Jersey City south to Philadelphia, west to Lancaster, south to York, then southeast to Baltimore and on to Washington. Later that year, the PRR replaced that roundabout route with a more direct one that relied on the Philadelphia, Wilmington & Baltimore, at that time still an independent company. Within a year, the railroad had inaugurated its first limited, extra-fare, all-Pullman train over the route— the *Washington Limited Express* southbound and the *New York Limited Express* in the opposite direction. They were the first PRR trains to offer only first-class, extra-fare service, with passengers accommodated in Pullman parlor cars. The *New York Night Express* and the *Washington Night Express*, established in 1873, offered comparable overnight service between the two cities, with through sleeping cars continuing to destinations in the South.[137]

Rivalries with the Baltimore & Ohio, particularly for traffic between New York and the South, influenced the development of the PRR's passenger service. In June 1880,

George Brooke Roberts replaced an ailing Tom Scott as president, with Alexander Cassatt promoted to first vice president. Early the following year, Cassatt negotiated the purchase of the Philadelphia, Wilmington & Baltimore, giving the PRR a direct link from Jersey City south to Washington and dealing a serious blow to the B&O. In April, Roberts and Cassatt hired James R. Wood as the general passenger agent. Recruited from outside the company, Wood had been the Michigan Central's assistant general passenger agent and later the general passenger agent of the Chicago, Burlington & Quincy. He possessed more than a decade of experience in the management of passenger service and had served as president of the Western Association of General Passenger and Ticket Agents.[138]

At the end of October 1881, Wood extended the extra-fare limited concept to the much longer route between Jersey City and Chicago. "If travelers desire speed enough to pay the extra charge for it," a writer for the trade journal *Railroad Gazette* observed, "they now have an opportunity to show it." The *New York and Chicago Limited* departed Jersey City at 7:55 a.m., reached Philadelphia two hours and twenty minutes later, and pulled into Pittsburgh at 8:00 that evening. As it entered the tracks of the Pittsburgh, Fort Wayne & Chicago, it became the *Limited Express*, crossing Ohio and Indiana in the night and arriving in Chicago at 9:40 the following morning.[139] The trip took a mere twenty-six hours and thirty-five minutes, with connecting service from Pittsburgh reaching St. Louis in thirty-six hours. The schedule provided for an average speed of 34.3 miles per hour—not lightning fast, perhaps, but still well above most trains of the day.

The introduction of the *New York and Chicago Limited*, coupled with the rivalry between the PRR and the New York Central, produced one of the greatest public-relations blunders in the history of American business. On October 8, 1882, William Henry Vanderbilt was making his way west from New York. He was the president of the New York Central and its most important subsidiaries, and he was in the process of inspecting his various properties. At Michigan City, Indiana, *Chicago Tribune* reporter John D. Sherman and freelance correspondent Clarence P. Dresser joined Vanderbilt for the two-hour trip to Chicago. Dresser was young, aggressive, and determined to provoke Vanderbilt into providing sensationalistic material. The journalist succeeded beyond his wildest expectations. "Does your limited express pay?" queried Dresser, making a reference to the NYC's efforts to match the speed of the PRR's *New York and Chicago Limited*. "No, not a bit of it," Vanderbilt replied. "We only run it because we are forced to do so by the action of the Pennsylvania Road. It doesn't pay expenses.

We would abandon it if it was not for our competitor keeping its train on." Dresser's follow-up question—"But don't you run it for the public benefit?"—allegedly caused the head of the New York Central to suggest that "the public be damned." Dresser certainly embellished the quotation and in all likelihood he modified or fabricated the context in which their conversation took place. Regardless of the circumstances, however, the quest for speed had produced a disaster. No lives were lost, but Vanderbilt's reputation never fully recovered.[140]

The *New York and Chicago Limited* survived long after Vanderbilt's debacle. Beginning in 1887, Lines West personnel preferred the shorter and more romantic name *Pennsylvania Limited*, and Lines East adopted the moniker in October 1891. By then, travel time had been reduced by nearly an hour, to an unprecedented twenty-five hours and forty minutes. The cost was likewise breathtaking, with a $3.00 extra fare applied to the customary New York-Chicago tariff of $5.00. As the PRR's flagship train, the *Pennsylvania Limited* received the most modern and luxurious equipment that Pullman's Palace Car Company could produce. In 1887, the railroad leased five cars from Pullman, including the sleepers *America*, *England*, and *France*, along with the *Esperanza*, the first lounge car built in the United States. All featured vestibules that enabled passengers to easily and safely walk between cars. The PRR soon operated four identical trains, necessary to provide daily service in both directions. Each included a baggage/smoking car complete with a bath, barbershop, and library; a diner; and three sleepers. Beginning in August 1889, the PRR assigned an end-of-train sleeper with an observation lounge, often occupied by ladies who, for the sake of propriety, dared not set foot in the smoking section at the front of the train. The upgrade induced a reporter from the *New York Times* to describe the *Pennsylvania Limited* as "the most perfectly-appointed passenger train in the world." A fourth sleeper stayed with the consist between Jersey City and Pittsburgh before following the Pan Handle route to Cincinnati. Pullman built all the sleepers to its standard designs, although with luxurious embellishments that included electric lighting, plush upholstery, and elaborately inlaid woodwork.[141] Most of the accommodations on the *Pennsylvania Limited* were nonetheless open sections, the most basic type of sleeping arrangements. Within a few years, however, wealthy patrons—and eventually almost all passengers—would demand their own private space.[142]

Additional refinements soon followed. For the tenth anniversary of the *Pennsylvania Limited*, in 1891, general advertising agent Frank N. Barksdale prepared a commemorative booklet to advertise the service. While not the first publication to promote a passenger train, it was one of the best, with rich halftone drawings by Charles Dana Gibson and other artists.[143] In 1893, in conjunction with the World's Columbian Exposition in Chicago, Pullman introduced new equipment for the train, with vestibules that spanned the width of each car. The Pullman Strike, which began in May of the following year, seriously delayed production, however. The Pennsylvania Railroad received the first of the new observation cars in January and February 1898, with additional equipment arriving through the end of the year. Each trainset included a combination baggage and library/smoking car, a diner, two sleeping cars, and a sleeper observation.[144] According to legend, PRR officials inspecting the Pullman plant took note of cars being built for Mexican president Porfirio Díaz, resplendent in red, green, and cream yellow colors that mimicked his nation's flag. They insisted on the same striking paint scheme for the new equipment that would be used on the *Pennsylvania Limited* and on the Jersey City–Washington *Congressional Limited*. Regardless of the source of the inspiration, the 1898 *Pennsylvania Limited* was indeed a stunning train, one of the most beautiful to operate on the American rail network. It soon acquired the nickname the "Yellow Kid," a reference to the Richard Felton Outcault comic strip that debuted in the *New York World* in 1896.[145]

Perfecting the Passenger Locomotive

While the Yellow Kid was the most visible example of the PRR's commitment to passenger service, hundreds of lesser trains carried travelers throughout the Northeast and the Midwest. Each of them required motive power that could provide the optimal combination of speed, power, and efficiency. The continuing rivalry with the Reading, particularly on the highly competitive run between Camden and Atlantic City, induced the development of a wheel arrangement that would for a time become the dominant type of passenger motive power on the Pennsylvania Railroad. In the spring of 1889, the Reading consolidated its southern New Jersey subsidiaries into the Atlantic City Railroad and soon offered exceptional service to the burgeoning shore resorts. The PRR followed suit in May 1896, merging several of its affiliates into the West Jersey & Seashore Railroad. Both companies poured money into tracks, roadbed, and bridges, creating a physical plant that could accommodate high-speed passenger service, with long trains pulled by heavy and powerful locomotives. "The fastest running in the world, considering distance and weight" observers noted in 1899, "has been done for some years on the two lines from Camden, opposite Philadelphia, to Atlantic City."[146]

By the last years of the nineteenth century, however, the American type was approaching the outer limits of what that wheel arrangement could accomplish in main line passenger service. As the national economy was slowly emerging from the recession that began in 1893, passenger traffic began to increase, as did the length of the average train. Travelers on the most luxurious extra-fare limiteds demanded additional amenities—such as enclosed vestibules, dining cars, and smokers—that added further weight. The axle-mounted generators that provided electricity on those trains also increased drag and taxed the ability of the locomotive fleet. PRR executives sought to maintain a competitive edge over services offered by other companies and accordingly instructed Transportation Department personnel to increase passenger-train speeds, even in mountainous territory.

As the existing 4-4-0 classes were confronting their limitations, mechanical engineers at several railroads and representatives from the locomotive builders were proposing larger and faster designs. Their cooperation, and their rivalry, led to the near-simultaneous development of the 4-4-2 Atlantic and the 4-6-2 Pacific. In both instances, the addition of a single-axle trailing truck permitted an extension of the firebox, with the larger grate area providing the heat necessary to generate additional steam power. The most obvious difference in the two designs involved the number of drivers. Those who favored the 4-4-2 asserted that the design minimized the complexity of the valve gear and other components and thus simplified construction and maintenance. Advocates for the Pacific countered that the additional pair of drivers was necessary to support a larger boiler and to distribute the locomotive's weight more evenly without creating undue stresses on the track, roadbed, and bridges.

Given the size of the PRR system, the diversity of operating conditions, and the long-standing division between Lines East and Lines West, it was perhaps not surprising that the railroad's motive-power experts recommended different strategies for the development of more powerful passenger locomotives. Ely, who since 1893 served as chief of motive power for both halves of the system, theoretically possessed the authority to oversee a single research-and-development program to design a standard locomotive for every portion of the network that linked the East Coast with Chicago and St. Louis. In practice, however, he awarded considerable discretion to individuals

such as David Crawford, the general superintendent of motive power on Lines West.

It was the ongoing rivalry between the Pennsylvania Railroad and the Reading rather than the one between Lines East and Lines West that encouraged Ely and his associates to develop the 4-4-2. In the spring of 1896, the Baldwin Locomotive Works delivered two of those locomotives to the Reading's Atlantic City Railroad, thus establishing the nomenclature that would correspond to all others of that wheel arrangement. Like the Reading's earlier 4-4-0 design, they featured wide Wootten fireboxes, which in turn necessitated the position of the cab in the middle of the locomotive, in classic camelback fashion. They were also Vauclain compounds, whose high- and low-pressure cylinders made efficient use of steam. The Reading's new locomotives were extraordinarily fast and powerful, and there was little chance that the PRR's 4-4-0 Americans could keep up.[147]

PRR executives responded quickly to the threat posed by the Reading. By June 1899, the Juniata Shops had completed the #698, the first of three representatives of the E1 class—and just in time for the booming summer resort traffic along the Jersey Shore. In many respects, the #698 and its two companions resembled the Reading locomotives that were their rivals. The most obvious similarities involved the wide Wootten firebox for the combustion of anthracite, necessitating the camelback design. With a grate area of sixty-eight square feet, the firebox may have been the largest used on any steam locomotive up to that time. Yet the E1 was correspondingly larger than the Reading Atlantics and was the first locomotive on any railroad to exceed one hundred thousand pounds on two pairs of drivers. The tender featured three axles in a rigid frame, more typical of European practice, rather than the swiveling trucks generally used in the United States. As an observer from the *Railroad Gazette* acknowledged, the Class E1 constituted a "radical departure from the recognized standard type of locomotives built by the Pennsylvania Railroad."[148]

To the gratification of Ely and his colleagues, the E1 delivered impressive results. In a test run on June 20, 1899, the #698 pulled a ten-car passenger train weighing 410 tons between Philadelphia and Jersey City. Despite two intermediate station stops and two speed reductions—necessary to scoop water from track pans—the locomotive covered the ninety miles in one hour, forty-nine minutes. "The engine arrived perfectly cool," PRR officials observed, "and the test proved that it could do considerably better than this." The PRR's three Atlantics performed equally

Among the rarest of all PRR locomotives were the three Class E1 Atlantics, built in 1899. Neither the Camelback design nor the six-wheel tender established a precedent, but the #698 and its two companions proved the value of the 4-4-2 wheel arrangement for high-speed passenger service. *Pennsylvania Railroad Negative Collection, Hagley Museum & Library, acc. 1993.300.*

well in their intended role, speeding along the fifty-eight miles between Camden and Atlantic City in record time. On July 18, an E1 and a seven-car train covered that distance in fifty-one minutes, at times reaching eighty-three miles per hour. Two days later, an E1 with eight cars made the trip in fifty-three minutes. It was the first time that the PRR had been able to pull that many passenger cars at sustained high speeds. On July 31, another eight-car train traveled between Atlantic City and Camden, against a headwind, in just over fifty minutes.[149]

Despite its many virtues, the E1 was by no means a perfect locomotive. The camelback design placed the engineman in the center of the locomotive, where he found it difficult to communicate with the fireman who was stationed at the rear, just ahead of the tender. There was thus no independent verification of signal indications and, should the engineman become incapacitated, no one would notice the emergency and take action to

stop the train. An experiment never to be repeated, they were the only camelback locomotives to wear the livery of the Pennsylvania Railroad.[150] As an alternative, Ely first experimented with a single modified E1, #269. The use of a radial-stay boiler permitted the cab to be moved to a more conventional location. Otherwise, aside from a slight increase in length, the #269 was nearly identical to its three predecessors.[151]

Even though Ely, Vogt, and Casanave rejected the camelback design, the Class E1 proved the worth of the 4-4-2 wheel arrangement for high-speed passenger service. Beginning in 1901, the PRR acquired 305 of the Class E2 Atlantics. The most visible differences from the E1 included a cab at the rear of the locomotive and a conventional eight-wheeled tender. Other changes were more subtle but equally important. A two-wheel radial truck replaced the single-axle rigid rear side frame on the E1. Improved-quality steel enabled an increase in boiler pressure from 185 psi to 205 psi—a transformation that was occurring on all the PRR's locomotive designs. The use of bituminous rather than anthracite coal permitted a reduction in the grate area from 68 to 55.5 square feet. Total locomotive weight was slightly higher on the E2, while tractive effort increased by more than 10 percent.[152]

The further development of the Atlantic depended heavily on the contributions of yet another superbly talented locomotive designer, Alfred Wolcott Gibbs. His father, Alfred Gibbs, was a career officer in the US Army,

Despite the installation of safety equipment suited to operating conditions in the United States, there was no mistaking the European ancestry of de Glehn compound Atlantic #2512. While it could not match the pulling power of the PRR's E2 Atlantics, it contained features that sparked further innovation by the Motive Power Department. *General Negative Collection, Railroad Museum of Pennsylvania, PHMC.*

who served with distinction in both the Mexican-American War and the Civil War. In the period between those two conflicts, he was assigned to the western frontier—including Fort Filmore, where his son was born in October 1856. General Gibbs died in 1868, but the fatherless youngster was able to continue his education, attending Rutgers College and in 1878 graduating from the Stevens Institute of Technology. He soon began his railroad career, advancing in quick succession from a special apprentice at the Altoona Machine Shops to the role of draftsman. He spent several years in the South with the Richmond & Danville Railroad before returning to the PRR in July 1893, as assistant mechanical engineer. In September 1902, he became the superintendent of motive power for the Philadelphia, Wilmington & Baltimore—perhaps owing to the recommendation of his cousin, George Gibbs, the electrical engineer who was instrumental to the New York Improvements. It was an extraordinary opportunity. In another two months, the PW&B would merge with the

Baltimore & Potomac Railroad to form the Philadelphia, Baltimore & Washington Railroad, in the process combining motive-power rosters and shop facilities. Gibbs did not remain with the PB&W for long, however. On January 1, 1903, President Cassatt selected W. W. Atterbury as the general manager of Lines East, to alleviate the operating bottleneck in and around Pittsburgh. Gibbs then filled Atterbury's former role as the general superintendent of motive power for Lines East, working closely with Ely and Vogt. He was subordinate to Ely, but the PRR's chief of motive power was in increasingly poor health, and he delegated much of his authority to Gibbs. Given Ely's unique talents, it was hardly surprising that when he retired in July 1911, the PRR abolished his job title. Nor was it unexpected that Gibbs thereafter filled many of his responsibilities in the newly created post of chief mechanical engineer—a role he held until his death in May 1922.[153]

The involvement of Alfred Gibbs in the design of improved Atlantic locomotives attested to the willingness of PRR officials to borrow elements from American and European railway practice and to transform locomotive development from the nineteenth-century reliance on tradition and instinct to a twentieth-century dedication to the techniques of scientific analysis. Little more than a year after becoming the PRR's general superintendent of motive power for Lines East, Gibbs was involved in a comprehensive series of experiments to determine which new technologies would be most appropriate for the PRR's needs.

During the 1890s, to make more efficient use of steam, Ely, Vogt, and Casanave had experimented with several versions of compound locomotives. None proved successful. The added complexity associated with compounding did not discourage locomotive designers, in Europe or the United States, from pursuing that technology. One of the many proponents of compounding was Alfred George de Glehn, who was associated with the Société Alsacienne de Constructions Mécaniques facility in Belfort, France. Unlike the Vauclain system, the high- and low-pressure cylinders on each side of a de Glehn locomotive drove pistons that were in opposition to one another, with one moving forward and the other in reverse. The de Glehn design ensured that the locomotive rode smoothly even at very high speeds, while keeping dynamic augment to a minimum.[154]

The PRR borrowed a de Glehn compound Atlantic in the spring of 1904 as part of the ongoing effort to develop faster and more powerful passenger locomotives. The #2512 arrived in the United States in pieces, which the employees at the Juniata Shops then assembled. The locomotive was a near duplicate of those built for the Northern Railways of France and—from the convex smokebox front to the low running boards and splashers—its European origins were unmistakable. On May 30, the de Glehn locomotive underwent trials on the West Jersey & Seashore, over the hotly contested territory between Camden and Atlantic City. The results were not encouraging. An eleven-car train left Camden twelve minutes late and failed to make up any time on the journey. Engineman Doughty confessed that the arrangement of the cab controls was so alien that he could not exploit the locomotive's full potential. The unusual features included a geared wheel that took the place of the conventional reverse quadrant (commonly referred to as a Johnson bar) that controlled the amount of steam admitted into the cylinders. Subsequent tests were no more encouraging. "The engine at no time," remarked an observer, "showed signs of being able to compete with the Pennsylvania fliers in making up lost time with bursts of speed." The ultimate assessment came from Doughty and other crewmen, who complained that "she did not touch the fliers built in the Pennsylvania Railroad shops."[155]

The setbacks on the Atlantic City run were of scant consequence, as Ely and his subordinates never intended to purchase de Glehn locomotives in quantity. Instead, they planned to incorporate elements of the de Glehn design into motive power that was more appropriate for the PRR's operating conditions. "Granting that the engine as a whole might not suit our conditions," Gibbs explained, "the value of the lessons to be learned from it would fully justify the expense of the experiment, and I am glad to say that these expectations have been fully realized."[156]

Into the Twentieth Century

Alexander Cassatt's presidency coincided with a rapid growth in traffic and, thanks to his ability to control rebates and maintain adequate rates, a corresponding rebuilding of the physical plant. In November 1899, five months after Cassatt took office, the PRR broke all previous records for the movement of eastbound freight through Altoona. A total of 160,266 loaded cars passed through the city at a rate of 5,342 cars per day. Most of the traffic, some 40 percent, was coal, 30 percent was grain, and the remainder iron and general merchandise, consigned mainly to Philadelphia and Greater New York. Regardless of the nature and the destination of the cargoes, the traffic placed an enormous strain on the PRR's motive power, and thus on the facilities in and around Altoona. By the summer of 1904, construction crews had reopened the long-abandoned New Portage Railroad and had completed the quadruple-tracking of the main line between Altoona and Pittsburgh. The construction of Penn Station, hundreds of miles to the east, also affected work at Altoona. The PRR would require hundreds of new all-steel passenger cars that could be used in the tunnels under the Hudson River. Steel would soon replace wood in many freight cars as well. The transition ensured that the Altoona Car Shops would have plenty of work, while the additional weight of steel cars meant that Theodore Ely and his colleagues would soon need to design and build a new generation of powerful steam locomotives.[157]

The yard and shop facilities at Altoona benefited from a rapid infusion of capital. In 1899, the PRR opened a new machine shop and completed a new classification yard for eastbound coal traffic the following year. In East Altoona, construction of a hump yard for westbound traffic began in 1902 and it entered service a year later. Between 1903 and 1906, PRR personnel greatly expanded the capacity of the Juniata Shops into a facility with an annual capacity of 275 engines. The improvements included expansion of the erecting shop, boiler shop, machine shop, and blacksmith shop, accompanied by the construction of a new storehouse and a second machine shop. A third erecting shop, built between 1905 and 1907, provided further manufacturing space. In 1904, the PRR opened new yards and a fifty-two-stall engine facility at East Altoona, permitting

The employees crossing the 12th Street pedestrian overpass during the afternoon shift change on August 24, 1926, constituted only a small portion of the more than fifteen thousand people who staffed the Altoona Works. The surrounding buildings were still part of the Altoona Machine Shops, even though locomotive production had long since shifted to the nearby Juniata Shops. The area became the 12th Street Car Shops in 1938. *Pennsylvania Railroad Negative Collection, Hagley Museum & Library, acc. 1993.300.*

the abandonment of the fifty-year-old Engine House No. 1. To the south, at Hollidaysburg, the PRR completed a new twenty-four-stall engine house and freight yards, further relieving the pressure on Altoona. One of the most significant expansions began in 1903, when the PRR acquired eighty-five acres of land in South Altoona. The South Altoona Foundries, opened in 1905, could cast as many as nine hundred wheels per day. Employees at the facility also mixed lubricating oils and grease and supplied them to the entire PRR system, ensuring a high degree of quality control. The South Altoona Foundries employed four hundred workers—out of some fifteen thousand in the entire Altoona Shops complex.[158]

After 1905, the operations at Altoona consisted of four specialized and interdependent components. Workers at the Altoona Car Shops were making the transition to the construction of steel-underframe and all-steel freight cars, as well as all-steel passenger cars, often using components supplied by the South Altoona Foundries. In January 1904, the craftsmen at the Altoona Machine Shops completed a Class B4a shifter, which was the last of the 2,289 steam locomotives built at that facility. Thereafter, the Altoona Machine Shops specialized in the repair and rebuilding of older locomotives, while the Juniata Shops was kept busy with the construction of new ones. Until production ended in June 1946, the Juniata Shops manufactured 4,584 locomotives, in addition to those completed at the Altoona Machine Shops prior to 1904.[159]

The Locomotive Test Plant

Amid the construction of new facilities at Altoona, one element of the Cassatt-era expansion was destined to have an outsized effect on the development of the Pennsylvania

Railroad's motive power. For much of the nineteenth century, the design and construction of steam locomotives remained more of an art than a science. Rule-of-thumb methods prevailed, often based on personal experience. Locomotive builders also relied heavily on knowledge inherited from predecessors or borrowed from a community of technological practitioners whose members readily shared information through engineering conferences and professional journals. Few mechanical engineers or corporate executives, on the PRR or elsewhere, worried that another railroad or independent supplier might appropriate proprietary information and use it solely for its own purposes. The larger danger was that excursions into unknown territory, in the form of radical design changes, the adoption of new wheel arrangements, or the installation of unproven components, might produce a locomotive that failed to match its predicted abilities. It was also unwise to make too many simultaneous alterations to existing designs, as there was no certain way to determine which adjustment was responsible for altered performance characteristics. Disappointing results at the very least represented an irretrievable loss of time, money, and intellectual energy. Those who designed the locomotive would also face the unpleasant task of defending their decisions, coupled with the knowledge that their careers could be at risk.[160]

Most mechanical engineers thus adopted a cautious, conservative approach to locomotive design. Officials in the Motive Power Department paid close attention to developments on other railroads, at Baldwin and other locomotive builders, and in Europe. They selectively incorporated a limited number of incremental improvements into new locomotives rather than making wholesale changes. The process typically relied on the construction of one or two prototypes, which would undergo rigorous in-service testing under a variety of operating conditions. As such, and with the significant exception of the Altoona boiler and then the Belpaire firebox, Pennsylvania Railroad locomotives of the late nineteenth century relied on the same fundamental principles that had been in place since the end of the Civil War. Experience, the greater availability of high-quality steel, and improvements to the right-of-way ensured that the PRR's most modern locomotives were larger, faster, and more powerful than their predecessors. Such changes nonetheless attested to gradual evolution rather than a revolution in mechanical engineering practice.

The conservative approach that had served the PRR well for much of the nineteenth century eventually reached its limits. The recovery from the severe recession of the 1890s placed unprecedented traffic demands on American railroads, necessitating massive capital investments in equipment and the physical plant. As the weight and speed of trains increased, traditional methods increasingly failed to produce new locomotives that were up to the task. "The conditions of present day railroading have made necessary the use of big engines," observed the editors of one professional journal, "but in many cases the big engine has failed in service due to defects in design. Ratios that did well for small engines have been found incorrect when applied to very heavy power."[161]

The first decade of the twentieth century witnessed a transformation of locomotive design, from methods based on intuition and tradition to those that depended on rigorous and replicable scientific analysis. That process affected all railroads and all independent builders, but it began on the Pennsylvania Railroad. It occurred principally during the presidency of Alexander Cassatt, between 1899 and 1906. Many years earlier, Cassatt had served briefly as the superintendent of motive power and machinery, and for the remainder of his career he displayed a keen interest in the design, construction, and operation of steam locomotives. From bitter experience, Cassatt was also aware that the political climate of the Progressive Era was rapidly becoming unfavorable to the railroads. Business leaders, journalists, regulators, and elected officials were increasingly blaming the carriers for high rates, inadequate service, and a worsening safety record. The PRR's critics often ignored the correlation between higher rates and the capital investments that would enable trains to operate more quickly and more safely. Instead, they argued that it was the responsibility of railroad executives to make their businesses operate with greater efficiency. Faced with the prospect of steadily increasing expenses and stagnant revenues, Cassatt and his contemporaries had little choice but to comply. The Progressive Era was also a time when public-relations pioneers like Ivy Lee were endeavoring to provide businesses with a positive image. In that context, Cassatt and his subordinate, W. W. Atterbury, valued the ability to demonstrate that the PRR was a modern and progressive corporation, committed to the use of impartial scientific analysis as a basis for safe and efficient operating practices.

The Louisiana Purchase Exposition, held in St. Louis between April and December 1904, gave nearly twenty million people an opportunity to see that commitment to science, progress, and better service. The Pennsylvania Railroad's thirty-three-thousand-square-foot exhibit illustrated the massive betterment programs that were part of the Cassatt administration. A large model of the

Philadelphia yard and terminal facilities suggested the investments that the PRR had made in its headquarters city. Even more impressive was a series of displays relating to the New York Improvements. They included a large model of Penn Station and a section of cast-iron lining for the tunnels under the Hudson River.[162]

A locomotive test plant was the unquestioned highlight of the PRR exhibit. Attendees were mesmerized at the sight of a massive steam locomotive, pouring forth steam and smoke, its drivers spinning in perpetual motion while technicians peered intently at dials, gauges, and paper charts. The test plant was no mere display, however. Instead, it was part of an evolutionary process that transformed locomotive design. With scientific data at their command, mechanical engineers now possessed the confidence to go beyond the conservative, traditional approach of their predecessors and build locomotives that could meet the motive-power needs of the twentieth century.

While the PRR's test plant was the best-known and most influential facility of its kind anywhere in the world, the company did not originate the principles associated with the scientific evaluation of motive power. During the 1880s, Alexander Borodin constructed a locomotive test plant for the tsarist railways, but few people outside Russia were aware of that development. A decade later, William F. Goss, a mechanical engineer associated with both the University of Illinois and Purdue University, independently developed a rudimentary stationary testing apparatus in West Lafayette, Indiana. The Chicago & North Western Railway constructed a similar device in 1895, with another, at Columbia University, opening in 1899. In Britain, the Great Western Railway installed a test plant at its Swindon workshops in 1904. By the time of the St. Louis World's Fair, therefore, Ely and his fellow mechanical engineers at the PRR were thoroughly familiar with the concepts associated with the stationary testing of steam locomotives.[163]

With Cassatt's support, PRR executives nonetheless envisioned the most modern—and the most publicly visible—test plant that had ever been built. Planning began in 1903, at a time of transition in the Motive Power Department. On August 1, Edward D. Nelson, the superintendent of motive power at the Philadelphia & Erie Grand Division, became the new engineer of tests. Nelson and Ely in turn delegated responsibility for the development of the test plant exhibit to Francis Casanave—the individual who, in his role of superintendent of motive power on Lines East, had been the principal architect of the PRR's 1897 locomotive classification system. In October 1901, Cassatt's community of interest enabled Casanave to become the general superintendent of motive power at the Baltimore

& Ohio. He returned to the Pennsylvania Railroad during the summer of 1903, appointed as a special agent responsible for overseeing the installation of the test plant in St. Louis.[164]

Even as Casanave sailed to Europe to solicit locomotives that could be evaluated on the test plant, PRR executives were reimagining its role at the fair. Initially, they suggested "that such a plant would serve merely as an exhibit which, after the close of the Exposition, would be given a permanent location on the company's property, and utilized in the study of locomotive design. Further development of this idea, however, led to the determination to carry on in St. Louis a series of tests and endeavor to enlist the interest of the engineering profession and railroad companies in making them as comprehensive as possible." To that end, Ely and Nelson convened an advisory panel, chaired by William Goss, the designer of the test plant at Purdue University. Representatives from the American Society of Mechanical Engineers and the American Railway Master Mechanics' Association also provided advice. "The tests shall be upon the highest scientific basis," noted an observer from the Railroad Gazette, "and the effort will be made to obtain results which will be of permanent value."[165]

PRR personnel evaluated eight locomotives over the course of the exposition. The first, a Class H6a Consolidation, was the only Pennsylvania Railroad locomotive placed on the test plant. The New York Central & Hudson River, the Lake Shore & Michigan Southern, and the Michigan Central furnished locomotives for testing—an Atlantic from the parent company and a Consolidation from each of its affiliates. The Santa Fe provided two locomotives, both compounds. Atlantic #535 was intended for passenger service, while a representative of the comparatively new 2-10-2 wheel arrangement, afterward known as the Santa Fe type, was suited for freight operations. Two imported Atlantics, each of which relied on a different system of compounding, rounded out the testing program. One was the property of the Royal Prussian Railways. The other was the #2512, the de Glehn locomotive—still the property of the Société Alsacienne de Constructions Mécaniques—that had recently completed road tests between Camden and Atlantic City.[166]

The 727-page summary of tests featured copious information, including graphs and comparison charts. PRR officials made the data freely available to anyone who might use it to design a better locomotive. The willingness to share the results of the experiments received widespread praise from the larger engineering community. The test plant exhibit received a Special Commemorative Grand

Prize from the fair's organizers, "awarded to the Pennsylvania Railroad System for its original series of scientific investigations of locomotive performance conducted at the Louisiana Purchase Exposition, the results of which are a permanent contribution to the advancement of engineering knowledge."[167]

Axel Vogt, in his capacity of mechanical engineer, designed the test plant installation, according to the suggestions of Goss and other representatives of the advisory panel. Ever sensitive to aesthetic as well as engineering considerations, Vogt won praise from his superiors "for a design of testing plant of unusual beauty and perfection of details, and of such excellence of operation that under severe conditions of service, interruptions were more frequently due to locomotive defects than to difficulties with the plant." Shop forces at Altoona fabricated most of the components, with others supplied by William Sellers & Company, the leading instrument and specialty equipment manufacturer in Philadelphia.[168]

Workers began the installation of the test plant by digging a large pit in the floor of the exposition's Transportation Building. Longitudinal cast-iron bed plates supported a series of pedestals that housed journal boxes. The axles on supporting wheels, similar to the driver pairs on a steam locomotive, fitted into the axle boxes. One set of three pairs, with seventy-two-inch wheels, permitted the testing of passenger locomotives with large drivers, while the five-pair set that utilized fifty-inch wheels was suited for freight power. Removable rails permitted locomotives to be eased into place, with each driver atop its corresponding supporting wheel. By connecting the locomotive's drawbar to a dynamometer, workers could easily calculate tractive effort. Careful measurement of the coal and water supplied to each test locomotive enabled an accurate measurement of efficiency at various speeds. A water-based hydraulic braking system enabled technicians to accurately adjust the corresponding level of resistance placed on the drivers, thus simulating varying train weights and the effects of grades. During the testing process, it was a simple matter to make minor adjustments to the locomotive's controls, thus providing an accurate statistical measurement of performance.[169]

During the St. Louis World's Fair, Nelson supervised a staff of thirty-six engineers and technicians. Ten were kept busy observing the dials and gauges that monitored each aspect of the locomotive's performance. Three held the title of "computer," a responsibility that attested to the mountain of arithmetical data generated by the test plant. One of them, Charles D. Young, would eventually succeed Nelson as engineer of tests and, in that capacity,

oversee the collection of information that contributed to the design of some of the finest locomotives ever used on any American railroad.[170]

Following the fair, the railroad stored many of the remaining exhibits in boxcars, ready to be shipped anywhere, anytime. The New York Improvements display reappeared in 1907 at the poorly attended Jamestown Ter-Centennial Exposition, then again two years later at the Alaska-Yukon-Pacific Exposition in Seattle. The section of tunnel lining found a more practical use. In storage after the exposition, it would be used two years later as the last ring in the south tunnel under the Hudson River. The test plant found a new lease on life as well. Workers dismantled the facility and in 1905 began erecting it in a purpose-built structure at the southern end of the Altoona Machine Shops. Vogt made slight alterations in the design, ensuring that the facility could accommodate any locomotive that the PRR owned or that the Motive Power Department might develop in the future. The first tests at Altoona began on December 28, 1906—coincidentally, the day of Alexander Cassatt's death. Thereafter, the test plant played a critical role in the application of scientific methods to the development of newer and more powerful locomotives, enabling designers to expand performance criteria with a high degree of certainty that their efforts would be successful.[171]

With the test plant in its permanent home, however, there was some managerial disagreement regarding the best way in which to utilize it. The debate in some sense reflected the universal tension between the boundless scientific curiosity associated with pure research and the pragmatic return-on-investment calculations that were linked to the development of new technologies. In the 1890s, before PRR officials had envisioned a testing facility, Frank Sheppard, the general superintendent of the Pennsylvania Railroad Grand Division, observed differences in opinion between the "men who are interested in the performance of the locomotive from a financial standpoint in the returns it will give to the stockholders" and "the practical locomotive builder." The latter contingent, Sheppard concluded, generally held sway over locomotive design and construction. They included "scientific fellows like Ely, who never had to consider the question of traffic in building their locomotives and were governed by certain conventional rules."[172]

The development of the test plant exacerbated the tension between finance and science. W. W. Atterbury, the general manager of Lines East, insisted that the facility's principal function should be to educate crewmen in more efficient firing techniques and should only secondarily be used to determine the scientific basis for improved locomotive performance. In contrast, Alfred Gibbs, the general superintendent of motive power for Lines East, favored extensive testing that would facilitate a data-driven approach to new locomotive designs. As an expert in his field, he had little desire to share those insights with executives who sought to influence the development of new types of locomotives. "There is a great deal of this information that has not generally been distributed" through formal channels, he complained, "although it is continually used" informally by operating officials—individuals who wanted to influence the work of the Motive Power Department and to encourage the experts at Altoona to produce locomotives that were suitable for operating characteristics on their division, although not necessarily for the railroad as a whole. Gibbs was happy to share test plant data with his counterparts at other railroads. He nonetheless balked at a proposal, issued by the Association of Transportation Officers, that asked him to provide that information to division superintendents and other mid-level managers. "If designs are to be held up while being submitted for criticism" by those outside the Motive Power Department, he warned, "it will be readily understood that the design would remain incomplete for many months." The ATO's plan to incorporate managerial prerogatives into the design process, Gibbs emphasized, would lead to endless debates over details large and small, and, he concluded, was "beautifully arranged to stop any progress."[173]

The Need for Speed

Alfred Gibbs was fully justified in his fears that unwarranted managerial interference might retard progress. By the beginning of the twentieth century, the American public had embraced a fascination with speed, and the operation of fast passenger trains called for a new generation of steam locomotives. Despite the beauty and the luxury of the 1898 Pennsylvania Limited, it would spend less than four years at the apex of the PRR's passenger service. It soon fell victim to the intense rivalry between the Pennsylvania Railroad and the New York Central. The NYC operated the Empire State Express as the primary competitor to the PRR's Pennsylvania Limited. Comparable in luxury, it also matched the PRR's rapid pace, thanks to a fleet of fast and powerful 4-4-0 American-type locomotives. In May 1893, one of those engines reportedly reached speeds in excess of one hundred miles per hour. In reality, the train barely topped eighty, but that mattered little to the journalists who touted the New York Central's locomotive #999 as

the fastest transportation in the history of the world. That summer, the NYC introduced the Exposition Flyer, a luxury train that carried the wealthy from New York to Chicago, site of the Columbian Exposition, in a mere twenty hours. That rate of speed was too expensive to sustain, however, and the end of the fair, as well as the contemporaneous effects of the Panic of 1893, also marked the end of the Exposition Flyer.[174]

Improved economic conditions as the nation emerged from the depression of the 1890s reinvigorated the competition for speed and luxury. Railroads across the United States invested heavily in new locomotives and cars and the wholesale rebuilding of the physical plant. The PRR was in the forefront of that effort, and when Cassatt became president in 1899, he authorized a host of improvements—paid for in part with the higher rates that were associated with his successful campaign to curtail rebating. While a large portion of those expenditures addressed the rapid increase in freight traffic, Cassatt was acutely aware of the public-relations value associated with improved passenger service. He was also sensitive to developments at the New York Central, the company that dominated passenger travel between New York and Chicago. On June 15, 1902, the NYC inaugurated the Twentieth Century Limited as the railroad's new flagship train, again operating on a twenty-hour schedule.

Cassatt was unwilling to offer service that was inferior to what the New York Central provided, and he had already insisted that the PRR introduce a new premier train on the same day. The Pennsylvania Special, likewise operating on a twenty-hour schedule between Jersey City and Chicago, offered virtually identical amenities. Eschewing the complex paint scheme of the "Yellow Kid," the new train earned its nickname of the "Red Ripper" as a string of Tuscan red cars streaked by crowds of suitably impressed onlookers. In the competition for affluent travelers, New York Central had the advantage of a more gently graded, although longer "Water Level Route" along the Hudson River to Albany, thence westward toward Buffalo, Cleveland, and Chicago. The PRR's Pennsylvania Special enjoyed a shorter and more direct route through Pittsburgh, saving more than fifty miles in distance, but was handicapped by the rugged Allegheny crossing and, until Penn Station opened in November 1910, required passengers to take a ferry between Manhattan and Jersey City.[175]

The reliable daily operation of such a fast train required substantial resources, something the PRR was not always able to provide. The traffic congestion that affected Pittsburgh in 1903 and 1904 gave PRR officials little choice other than to discontinue the *Pennsylvania Special*. The decline in revenue was minuscule, but the loss in prestige was immense. By May 1905, with the congestion crisis averted, PRR officials began to transform the hiatus from an embarrassing operational failure to an opportunity to launch the fastest train in the Western Hemisphere. They had learned that their counterparts on the New York Central were planning to cut the running time of the *Twentieth Century Limited* to nineteen hours—a reasonable reduction, but one that would nonetheless place an enormous strain on the railroad's track, equipment, and engine crews. Rather than simply match their competitor, Pennsylvania Railroad executives elected to cut another hour from the timetable—giving the *Pennsylvania Special* a blistering eighteen-hour timing between Jersey City and Chicago. The announcement caught NYC officials off guard, but it was a virtual certainty that they would respond in kind. One of the railroad's low-level officers promised to "go them an hour better or bust." The NYC's senior executives were not so brash as to consider a seventeen-hour schedule, but on June 6, they concluded that they had little choice other than to match the PRR's initiative. One day earlier, the PRR had operated two test trains, one between Jersey City and Pittsburgh in eight hours and fifty minutes, and the other covering the remaining distance to Chicago in seven hours and thirteen minutes, together averaging 55.9 miles per hour. Flushed with success, Lines West general manager George L. Peck brashly asserted that "at that rate we can make the run from New York to Chicago in fifteen hours." Quickly dismissing the PRR's achievement, Charles F. Daly, the NYC executive in charge of passenger traffic west of Buffalo, suggested that his company had some time previously operated a train between New York and Chicago in less than sixteen hours. He could not remember the precise details, prompting Colin Studds, the PRR's eastern passenger agent, to assert that "I have never heard about such a run." The Pennsylvania Railroad operated another test train on June 9, covering the 352.2 miles between Pittsburgh and Philadelphia in six hours and seven minutes. That was nearly twenty minutes faster than the previous record, set by President Cassatt's special train on April 29.[176]

Executives from other railroads were unanimous in their refusal to be drawn into the looming confrontation between the *Pennsylvania Special* and the *Twentieth Century Limited*. "This speed war is likely to prove an expensive experiment to both the competing lines," observed Grand Trunk executive George W. Vaux. That rivalry, he noted, "is a fight between the Central and the Pennsylvania," and

no one else. Denying the obvious, spokesmen from both railroads announced that "we are entering into no speed contest." Studds insisted that "we are not striving to bring about a rivalry in speed" and suggested that the new eighteen-hour schedule was "in deference to public demand." The *New York Times* saw the merit in both arguments, editorializing that "the rivalry, which we are asked to accept as purely incidental and not at all unfriendly . . . probably answers to a real demand of the traveling public [as] time becomes more precious with each of the inventions for saving it."[177]

Despite the willingness of newspaper editors to restate the familiar adage that time is money, only a small portion of the traveling public was willing to pay for the privilege of cutting a few minutes off their journey time. As their name suggested, luxury trains were extraordinarily comfortable, and—for those who could afford to travel in style—offered excellent accommodations, superb food, and attentive service. In all likelihood, wealthy individuals sought the bragging rights associated with travel at a record-setting pace rather than the time saved as a result. If newspapers suggested that such practices were inherently dangerous, then those titillating warnings would only embellish stories told in the gentlemen's club, at a social gala, and onboard one's yacht.

Speed could nonetheless come at a considerable cost, and innovative marketing campaigns could not exempt either the PRR or the NYC from the laws of physics. "Train acceleration is very much more a function of the mechanical department than of the General Passenger Agent's office," the *Times* concluded. If the demand for ever-faster trains "is the outgrowth of a competition in which the managements of two great systems are willing to 'take chances' which their judgment disapproves, its business wisdom is open to question." It was a warning that executives representing both railroads would have done well to heed.[178]

The inaugural run of the restored *Pennsylvania Special* departed Jersey City at 3:55 on the afternoon of June 11, 1905. There were only four cars—a combination baggage/buffet/smoker; a diner; a twelve-section, one-drawing room, one-stateroom sleeper; and a six-compartment observation lounge. Each passenger paid $35 for a ticket, which included the regular rail tariff of $20, an additional $5 for a Pullman berth, and a $10 extra fare for the privilege of traveling on the PRR's fastest train. That amount represented nearly a month's wages for the average American worker.[179] The train was nearly full, but many of those aboard were reporters or PRR officials, not paying passengers. Division superintendents assigned thousands of employees to examine the track for the most minute of defects, before and after the train had passed by—one indication of the enormous cost associated with high-speed operations. Fresh engines stood ready at Harrisburg, Altoona, Pittsburgh, Crestline, and Fort Wayne. PRR crews cut out the dining car at Altoona rather than force the motive power to drag the additional weight over the Alleghenies. A hotbox delayed the train east of Crestline, threatening the promised on-time arrival in Chicago. Equipped with a new locomotive, the *Pennsylvania Special* tore across Ohio, reaching a reported top speed of 127.1 miles per hour. The new record was as implausible as the one allegedly posted by the NYC's #999 twelve years earlier, and it was doubtful that the train ever traveled much above eighty miles per hour. The sensationalistic press coverage nonetheless left NYC officials little choice other than to proceed with their plans to emulate the PRR's eighteen-hour schedule between New York and Chicago, effective June 18.[180]

Such speeds compromised safety, with the New York Central bearing the brunt of the resulting accidents. On June 21, just three days after the new schedule went into effect, the *Twentieth Century Limited* hit an open switch at Mentor, Ohio, killing nineteen passengers and five members of the crew. New York Central president William H. Newman canceled the train, perhaps hoping that Pennsylvania Railroad officials would deescalate the competition for speed. They did not, instead announcing that they were "astonished" at Newman's action and pledging to maintain the eighteen-hour timing of the *Pennsylvania Special*. One executive from the PRR's Transportation Department laconically and unsympathetically suggested that "accidents will happen" and asserted that "there is no greater reason why an accident should befall the Pennsylvania Special than the slowest accommodation train."[181] Newman had no choice other than to yield, and the suspension of the *Century* lasted for only a single day. As speed returned to the New York Central, so did the accidents. On August 27, the NYC's premier train derailed just after 4:00 in the morning while entering the station at Syracuse, New York. Fortunately, no one was injured in what reporters referred to as the "18-hour flier accident." A year later, another open switch, near Elyria, Ohio, caused a derailment that injured several passengers.[182]

Nor was the Pennsylvania Railroad exempt from accidents that affected its most visible passenger train. Shortly after 5:00 in the morning of July 15, 1905, a month after the implementation of the faster schedule, the eastbound *Pennsylvania Special* was approaching Port Royal, Pennsylvania, near Harrisburg. A few minutes earlier, the engineman on a PRR freight train, perhaps unused to the relatively new technology of the air brake, had stopped too quickly, causing his train to buckle and nudging one of the boxcars onto the adjacent track. Engineman Calvin Miller on the *Pennsylvania Special* spotted the danger, threw his locomotive into reverse, set the air, and jumped. He alone suffered injuries, and the sleeping passengers noticed no more than a mild bump. It could have been much worse—a remarkably similar accident only a few months earlier and just a few miles away sent the *Cleveland and Cincinnati Express* crashing into a boxcar loaded with dynamite. The collision at Lochiel, Pennsylvania, created a conflagration that incinerated twenty-eight passengers. The Port Royal wreck, while mercifully far less severe, nonetheless illustrated the dangers associated with high-speed operation.[183]

The same journalists who sensationalized accidents involving fast trains on the NYC, the PRR, and other railroads periodically pressed railroad officials to defend their business practices. One executive, who preferred to remain anonymous, asserted that many stretches of track could safely accommodate trains traveling at sixty miles per hour or more—but acknowledged that any attempt to maintain average operating speeds that exceeded fifty miles per hour was inviting disaster. He noted that many railroads at first introduced short, light trains and later added cars to keep up with the additional business, with officials insisting that operating personnel keep to the originally advertised schedule. His views were sensible but distinctly in the minority. Citing the public's "speed mania," NYC senior vice president William C. Brown noted that "the railroads must listen to the demands of their passengers" rather than the preferences of "railroad men [who] would prefer a schedule which could be maintained throughout the year" and regardless of weather conditions. Conveniently ignoring the Mentor accident that had occurred eighteen months earlier, Brown insisted that "speed had nothing to do with" such calamities.[184]

One day after Brown's interview appeared in the morning newspapers, another incident demonstrated the folly of his remarks. The *Pennsylvania Special*, running fast to make up lost time, slammed into the side of a Wheeling & Lake Erie locomotive at a diamond crossing in Canton, Ohio. The W&LE engineman suffered fatal injuries, but by some miracle, the PRR train remained upright, and even the engine crew survived virtually unscathed. The following February, the *Pennsylvania Special*, ninety minutes late, was under the control of an engineman who was determined to bring his charge in on schedule. The train derailed at Mineral Point, just east of Johnstown. More than fifty passengers suffered injuries, with the casualty list including Ohio congressman Beman Gates Dawes. The cause was almost certainly a defective brake hanger on one of the tender trucks, but in a master stroke of public relations, the railroad placed the blame squarely on a batch of experimental steel ties produced by US Steel. Echoing the PRR's indifference in the aftermath of the Mentor wreck, NYC vice president Alfred H. Smith told reporters that "the question of taking off the Twentieth Century Limited train on the New York Central Lines was not considered." Smith's further comment that "the accident on the Pennsylvania might have happened on any of the slower trains" defied both common sense and the laws of physics and tarred the entirety of the PRR's passenger service with the same broad brush. PRR officials nonetheless agreed with Smith's assessment that "the public is demanding fast service [and] they insist on getting it," and they made no effort to suspend or slow the *Pennsylvania Special*.[185]

Other high-profile accidents continued to plague the PRR's premier trains. In March 1907, the *Chicago Limited*—a train only slightly less prestigious than the *Pennsylvania Special*—derailed just east of Pittsburgh. There were no fatalities, but the presence of Cleveland mayor Tom Loftin Johnson among the passengers ensured widespread, and unfavorable, media coverage.[186] Less than five years later, on February 15, 1912, the eastbound *Pennsylvania Limited* derailed at Warrior's Ridge, thirty miles east of Altoona. The train slid thirty feet down an embankment and into the last remaining set of locks on the old Main Line of Public Works, leaving three dead and more than fifty injured. PRR officials quickly traced the cause of the accident to a broken equalizing bar on the tender truck of the second locomotive. Yet reporters were quick to observe that the train had arrived in Altoona almost an hour late and that it was probably traveling more than fifty miles an hour through a series of sharp curves, as the crew struggled to make up lost time. Any luxury limited was bound to carry a host of prestigious and influential passengers. The wrecked train was no exception, and the dazed survivors included two members of the House of Representatives and the nephew of a US senator. To make matters worse, the westbound *Pennsylvania Limited* derailed near Fort Wayne two days later, leaving four dead and ten injured.[187]

In the end it was up to regulatory officials to protect affluent travelers from their "speed mania." The New York Central's Water Level Route was more susceptible to harsh winter weather than the PRR's more southerly line, occasioning a longer wintertime schedule for the *Twentieth Century Limited*. It was a wise precaution, and one that could be ignored only at the railroad's peril. The seven-car *Century* left Chicago at 3:30 on the afternoon of March 12, 1912, but by the following morning, it was running nearly two hours late. Engineman James Ryan, operating one of the most powerful locomotives on the railroad, was doing his best to make up as much time as possible. NYC officials later stressed that Ryan was going no more than forty-five or fifty miles per hour. Passengers claimed that the actual speed was closer to seventy, a reasonable estimate given the intense pressure placed on operating employees to bring their trains in on time. Between Hyde Park and Poughkeepsie, the train encountered a stretch of roadbed damaged by the late-winter cycle of thawing and refreezing. While the engine remained upright, the passenger cars tore up two thousand feet of track, then tipped sideways, slid down an embankment, and broke through the ice that covered the surface of the Hudson River. It was, fortunately, just before 9:00 in the morning, and most passengers were awake. They nonetheless recoiled in terror as frigid water began to fill the cars, several of which briefly caught fire. Architect Frank Mills Andrews told reporters that "we expected to be either drowned or roasted to death." No one was, thanks to the strength of the steel cars the NYC had recently added to the *Twentieth Century Limited*, but the injuries and the photographs of the train lying partially submerged in the Hudson prompted regulators to act.[188]

Subsequent investigations by the ICC and the New York Public Service Commission demonstrated that frost heaving had caused the wreck, not the broken rail that NYC officials had initially blamed. Nor were PSC officials willing to cast aspersions on maintenance-of-way forces, who were battling "the end of one of the most severe Winters known." They suggested that the train had been traveling at almost sixty miles an hour—a little slower than what passengers had estimated but much faster than NYC officials had acknowledged. More broadly, the PSC investigation gave the lie to long-standing assertions by PRR and NYC executives that accidents to limiteds were unrelated to the high rate of speed at which they traveled. Each railroad, claimed PSC investigators, operated trains on "schedules too fast for safety." Regulators accordingly called on the carpet the leading operating officials of both railroads, strongly suggesting that they reduce the speeds of their fastest trains, at least during the winter months. The executives agreed, with a sense of relief that the government had enabled each railroad to reduce the cost and the risk of high-speed operations without sacrificing any competitive advantage to its rival. The reductions are "sure to please the railways," observed the *New York Times*, "and ought to please the traveling public. It is from the public the demand for speed comes. No railway officer wants to operate at an excessive speed, and every engineer at times takes his throttle in hand with fear and trembling." The last assertion may have been more hyperbole than reality, but such statements marked a clear refutation of the news media's earlier celebration of "speed mania." It was certainly an exaggeration to suggest that extra-fare limiteds were "deadlier than artillery," but the sinking of the RMS *Titanic*, barely a month after the Hyde Park wreck, caused many Americans to reexamine their confident assumptions that faster was better. "Just as the slower and more comfortable steamships are growing in favor with experienced ocean travelers," speculated the editorial staff of the *Times*, "so slower and more comfortable trains might be made acceptable to railway riders disillusioned by excessive shedding of blood."[189]

Even though the *Pennsylvania Special* traveled less than a mile through the Empire State, all underground, Pennsylvania Railroad officials had ample reason to comply with the New York Public Service Commission recommendation for lower train speeds. The transition to steel cars, made necessary by the subterranean approaches to Penn Station, increased the weight of the train and taxed the ability of locomotives to pull the new equipment at such a rapid pace. Given the meager capacity of the *Pennsylvania Special* and the high cost associated with its operations, the train almost certainly operated at a loss, even during periods of high demand. George D. Dixon, the new vice president in charge of traffic, conceded that safety and operating efficiency superseded the favorable publicity associated with high-speed operation. On July 29, the day after meeting with PSC officials, Dixon announced that the Pennsylvania Railroad was prepared to increase travel time between New York and Chicago to twenty hours when the new autumn timetables took effect. The slower schedule, Dixon admitted, would practically eliminate the refunds paid to passengers on late-arriving trains, save the PRR a considerable amount of money on operating costs, and reduce pressure on conductors and enginemen to bring their trains in on time, no questions asked. He nonetheless made the change contingent on the actions of New York Central officials, ensuring that that company would be the first to withdraw from the battle for high-speed travel.[190]

Dixon and other Pennsylvania Railroad officials had one significant advantage over their rivals at the NYC. Advertising agents and others in the PRR's Passenger Department informed Dixon that travelers found it difficult to distinguish between the *Pennsylvania Special* and the original, only slightly less prestigious, but nonetheless slower *Pennsylvania Limited*. The solution would be to rebrand the PRR's flagship train, allowing the Advertising Department to promote a new name and a new service, without dwelling on the slower running time. On November 24, 1912, the PRR renamed the *Pennsylvania Special* as *The Broadway Limited*, wisely restoring the twenty-hour running time that had been in place in 1902 and 1903.[191] Grateful NYC officials simultaneously added two hours to the schedule of the *Twentieth Century Limited* but lacked the promotional opportunities associated with a newly renamed train.[192]

Perfecting the Atlantic

Even as Pennsylvania Railroad and New York Central officials declared a truce in the quest for ever-higher speeds, motive-power designers at both companies were busily developing passenger locomotives that could meet scheduled operating times. The PRR's test plant was central to that effort, enabling personnel in the Motive Power Department to apply the techniques of scientific analysis to improve speed, power, and efficiency. While in its temporary home in St. Louis, the test plant provided valuable data pertaining to improvements in the design of the 4-4-2 Atlantic that had rapidly become the mainstay of the PRR's passenger service. From September through November 1904, Motive Power Department personnel evaluated the performance of four Atlantics, including the de Glehn compound. A series of mechanical problems, particularly exceptionally hot components in the running gear of the #2512, hampered their efforts. Their work was frequently interrupted by a series of repairs and modifications undertaken at the PRR's Vandalia Lines Shops in Terre Haute, Indiana. While the technicians who operated the test plant ultimately resolved many of the glitches in the #2512, their final assessment was that "considerable difficulty was encountered in getting the locomotive to steam." That was a fatal flaw, for which there was no remedy. In November, the PRR nonetheless purchased the locomotive from its builder, and the French import was sent to Altoona. It spent most of its remaining years parked outside the office of John C. Mengel, the master mechanic. Shop personnel, finding humor in the situation, unceremoniously referred to the mothballed de Glehn compound as "Mengel's paperweight."[193]

Despite the failure of the #2512, the locomotive did offer one important feature that would soon become widespread on the PRR's locomotive fleet. Prior to 1905, most steam locomotives on the Pennsylvania Railroad, and throughout the world, employed Stephenson valve gear. Named for locomotive pioneer Robert Stephenson but developed by the employees at his company, the system enjoyed the virtues of simplicity and adaptability to various wheel arrangements, driver diameters, and operating velocities. The rapid increase in speed and pulling power of the PRR's locomotives generated new levels of complexity that taxed the adaptability of the Stephenson design. The transition from the universal 4-4-0 American to the more specialized 4-4-2 Atlantic and the 2-8-0 Consolidation proved particularly problematic. "When we departed from the simple eight-wheel type," Gibbs observed in 1906, "and introduced additional driving wheels, filling up the space between them with spring rigging, brake shoes and other appliances, the situation at once became more complicated."[194]

The solution came from Egide Walschaerts, a foreman at the Brussels-Midi terminal of the Belgian National Railways and a subordinate of Alfred Belpaire. Whereas Stephenson valve gear was typically located inside the side frames of the locomotive, the Walschaerts system was readily visible, outside the drivers. That arrangement simplified maintenance and made additional room available for the appliances that Gibbs described. The relatively unobstructed space between the frames also permitted the installation of additional cross-bracing—necessary because, as the weight of locomotives increased, cracking and even catastrophic failure of frame components was becoming a distressingly common problem. The Walschaerts motion also made it much easier for an engineman to adjust the cutoff—the length that the piston traveled down the cylinder when the closing of the inlet port prevented the further admission of steam. Proper adjustment of the cutoff improved the balance between the power needed to start a heavy train or surmount a grade and the efficient use of steam while operating at a steady speed over level terrain.[195]

Despite its many faults, the #2512 was equipped with the Walschaerts system, and evaluation on the test plant demonstrated its value. "The history of the Walschaert [sic] valve gear on the Pennsylvania Railroad," Gibbs observed, "dates from the importation of the de Glehn locomotive."[196] That may have been a slight exaggeration, as Gibbs would have been familiar with the performance of a Baltimore & Ohio locomotive, featuring Walschaerts valve gear, that entered service in 1905. Even so, Gibbs was particularly impressed with the lightness of the running

gear on the de Glehn Atlantic. He acknowledged that some of the components were "expensive to construct and, unless a high grade of workmanship is obtained, are likely to give trouble," but he was nonetheless determined to use similarly lightweight components on PRR locomotives, wherever possible. Gibbs also appreciated the advantages of the geared wheel, used to set the cutoff, that had so perplexed engineman Doughty. By the late nineteenth century, steam locomotives had become so large and powerful that enginemen found it both difficult and dangerous to change the cutoff, by moving the Johnson bar, while underway. In extreme cases, the Johnson bar could spring forward, causing severe injuries to anyone operating it. "We all know of engines which runners are afraid to handle while running, for fear of being pulled through the front of the cab," Gibbs conceded in 1906, "with the result that the reverse lever once set in its position on the quadrant remains in that position, up hill and down dale, to the next stop and start." Many enginemen declined to adjust the reverse lever while the train was moving, a prudent move that nonetheless prevented the locomotive from operating efficiently. The geared wheel, like the one installed on #2512, made the process of setting the cutoff much easier and safer, to the undoubted relief of enginemen, while reducing fuel and water consumption in a manner that was likely to please the PRR's accountants.[197]

Based on the test results obtained at the Louisiana Purchase Exposition, Gibbs ordered the installation of Walschaerts valve gear on ten Consolidations then under construction at the Baldwin Locomotive Works. He dispatched them to every grand division on the railroad for evaluation under varying conditions. Delays at Baldwin ensured that operating personnel had little more than a month to assess the new system before the PRR placed its next order, for 160 Consolidations. "The reports we received from the road people," Gibbs noted, "were so favorable that we did not hesitate to continue the application of the Walschaert [sic] motion." In addition to the installation of the Walschaerts apparatus on the Class H6 Consolidations, now designated as Class H6b, it soon appeared on the newest Class E2d and Class E3d Atlantic passenger locomotives. By November 1906, the PRR rostered more than 400 Walschaerts-equipped locomotives, 352 on Lines East and 55 on Lines West. "Contrary to our expectations," Gibbs concluded, "no protest whatever came from the road when these Walschaert [sic] gear locomotives were introduced, the road people placing without exception high value on the accessibility of the gear." With astonishing rapidity, the Walschaerts valve gear supplanted the Stephenson system that seemed little more than a relic of the nineteenth century.[198]

During the first years of the twentieth century, the PRR's newest passenger locomotives bridged the transition from radial-stay to Belpaire fireboxes and boilers and from Stephenson to Walschaerts valve gear. The Class E2 was the most numerous of the Atlantics, with more than three hundred examples in various subclasses. Some had radial-stay boilers and Stephenson valve gear, others employed a Belpaire firebox (Class E2a and E2c with slide valves and E2b with piston valves), while the final group (Class E2d) came with Belpaire fireboxes, piston valves, and the more modern Walschaerts valve gear—a system that had recently proven its worth on the Class H6b Consolidations. Nearly 200 locomotives were in the E3 class, including 8 with radial-stay boilers, 114 (Class E3a) with Belpaire fireboxes and Stephenson valve gear, and the remaining 56 (Class E3d) with Belpaire fireboxes and Walschaerts valve gear. The Vandalia Lines subsidiary acquired nineteen Atlantics in the E21, E22, and E23 classes. The Pennsylvania Railroad manufactured most of those locomotives in-house at the Juniata Shops. The demand for new power was so acute and production capacity at Baldwin so limited that PRR officials turned to Alco—a company more closely associated with the New York Central—for the E2c and some of the E2b locomotives, as well as the Atlantics destined for the Vandalia Lines.[199]

The E2 and E3 Atlantics quickly established a reputation as fast and reliable locomotives, and they soon became commonplace at the head end of the PRR's most important passenger trains. When the easing of traffic congestion through Pittsburgh permitted the reestablishment of the *Pennsylvania Special*, in June 1905, it was entirely appropriate that a Class E2, #7002, pulled the company's most prestigious train between Crestline and Fort Wayne. It was a spectacular run, made at an average speed of more than 68 miles per hour, and engineman J. W. McCarthy made up twenty-five minutes of lost time. McCarthy's skilled handling of his locomotive encouraged Pennsylvania Railroad publicists to fabricate the claim that he had achieved a new land speed record of 127.1 miles per hour. The enduring legend nonetheless highlighted the pride of corporate executives in their flagship passenger locomotive. Despite its unprecedented eighteen-hour pace between Jersey City and Chicago, the westbound *Pennsylvania Special* arrived on time 328 days in the year following June 11, 1906, and on 14 additional days, the train was less than ten minutes late. Such a consistently strong performance would not have been possible without the new Atlantics. Closer to their

namesake ocean, the Class E2 and E3 locomotives matched or beat the schedules of Reading locomotives, between Camden and Atlantic City. On the fast, level run between Jersey City and Washington, they had no rivals. Some of them remained in service, typically assigned to the Long Island Rail Road or in work trains, into the 1940s.[200]

Despite the success of the Class E2 and Class E3 Atlantics, steadily increasing traffic and rapid developments in locomotive technology induced Ely and his subordinates to make further experiments with the 4-4-2 wheel arrangement. In addition to proving the worth of Walschaerts valve gear, the de Glehn compound influenced the design of four locomotives ordered in 1905. Two (Class E28) came from Baldwin; the others (Class E29) came from Alco. All four were balanced compounds and differed only in minor details. Their performance, like that of the de Glehn locomotive, did not warrant full-scale production. The two Baldwin locomotives nonetheless featured improvements to the spring-equalization system that connected the rear driver with the two-wheel trailing truck. In keeping with the long-standing interchange of ideas between railroads and locomotive builders, it was hardly surprising that Ely incorporated the same basic design into future locomotive production at Altoona. Alco also built two Class J28 2-6-2 locomotives for the PRR. The Prairie wheel arrangement, as its name suggested, found favor with western railroads, such as the Santa Fe, that combined fast passenger service with lightly built track and bridges. Such limitations rarely existed on the PRR's principal routes, and Ely concluded that the added complexity associated with an additional set of drivers did not justify the lighter axle loadings associated with the Prairie design.[201]

Even as Ely dismissed as impracticable the balanced-compound Atlantics and the Prairie designs, he grew increasingly determined to develop a passenger locomotive that was more powerful than the Class E2 and E3 Atlantics. The rapid expansion of the subway system in New York provoked widespread—and understandable—public concern regarding the vulnerability of wooden cars to collision and fire. In 1902, shopworkers at Altoona completed a prototype all-steel subway car. The simultaneous New York Improvements ensured the PRR and the Long Island Rail Road would use only steel cars in the tunnels under the Hudson and East Rivers. In practical terms, that meant that all trains operating between New York and Washington, as well as through trains to Chicago and St. Louis, could no longer be equipped with all-wood or wood-bodied, steel-underframe cars. In 1907, Pennsylvania Railroad officials announced that the company would acquire two hundred all-steel passenger cars, and their counterparts at Pullman pledged to convert to steel as well. Ely thus faced a serious problem, in that increases in passenger traffic, coupled with the conversion to steel cars, meant that trains were becoming both heavier and longer—just as renewed competitive pressures were again encouraging PRR executives to demand faster schedules on the railroad's premier trains.[202]

The pressing need for more robust passenger locomotives stimulated one of the most productive rivalries that developed between motive-power officials on Lines East and Lines West. Even as Ely, Vogt, and Gibbs were refining the design of the 4-4-2 Atlantics, David Crawford was having some difficulties of his own. The general superintendent of motive power on Lines West was well aware that the steel passenger cars that were leaving the subterranean confines of Penn Station would continue on to his section of the vast PRR system. Crawford accordingly needed a locomotive that could cope with the undulating terrain that lay west of Pittsburgh and that was equally capable of fast running along the flatlands that spanned the remaining distance to Chicago. In collaboration with the staff of the Pittsburgh Locomotive & Car Works (since 1901 a part of the American Locomotive Company), Crawford suggested the addition of another pair of drivers, transforming the Atlantic into a 4-6-2 Pacific.[203] The result was #7067, the sole representative of the Class K28. The locomotive possessed a radial-stay boiler rather than the Belpaire configuration that had become almost universal on Lines East. It was also a massive, hulking machine, probably the largest passenger locomotive in the world at that time, and engine crews frequently referred to it as "Fat Annie." After entering service in 1907, the K28 quickly proved its worth along the route between Pittsburgh and Chicago, pulling longer and heavier trains than the E2 and E3 Atlantics could manage.[204]

In Altoona, Vogt and Gibbs were simultaneously preparing a preliminary design for another version of a Pacific, to be assigned to Class K1. The advantages of the K28 were so great, however, that they modified that design for use on Lines East, where the need for modern locomotives was most acute. Between 1910 and 1913, the railroad acquired 153 K2 and 75 K2a locomotives, built at Altoona and at Alco's facility in Schenectady, New York. They featured a Belpaire firebox—the most notable departure from the K28 design—but otherwise to a substantial degree embodied Crawford's expertise.[205]

By 1910, the comprehensive rebuilding of the physical plant, initiated during the Cassatt presidency, ensured that main line tracks and bridges could accommodate large six-coupled locomotives like the K2. Yet Ely retained his long-standing aversion to the mechanical complexity associated with a Pacific. The use of even one additional set of drivers, Ely concluded, increased construction and maintenance costs. "On the portions of our lines where passenger trains are not frequent and the trains are very heavy, we use, to some extent, three pairs of drivers," he informed the members of the International Railway Congress. "But we do not approve of this practice for general express service.... We think that every pair of drivers adds complications of machinery and friction." No statement better encapsulated Ely's small-engine philosophy. He made those remarks in July 1895, and the events of the following decade did little to change his assessment.[206]

Ely's use of the term we was accurate, at least on Lines East, as his subordinates and successors initially shared that small-engine philosophy. Even though he acknowledged the virtues of the experimental K28 and the production-model K2 that it inspired, Gibbs was wary of the 4-6-2 design. The valve gear on the K2, he observed, included exceptionally large and heavy components—a situation that increased manufacturing costs, created additional wear on the mechanism, and made dynamic augment a more serious problem. Firemen experienced difficulties as well. The firebox of the K2 consumed massive amounts of fuel, necessary to produce steam in the exceptionally large boiler, and a typical run between Manhattan Transfer and Washington consumed fifteen tons of coal in five hours. While David Crawford favored the use of automatic stokers on Lines West, Ely and Gibbs were hesitant to accept the additional complexity of the Crawford underfeed stoker on the eastern portion of the system.[207]

Rather than devote their limited time and resources to the development of an improved version of the K2 Pacific, Gibbs favored the refinement of the familiar Atlantic design. The 4-4-2 wheel arrangement afforded the simplicity, ease of maintenance, and use of lightweight components that Gibbs and Ely favored. By the end of the first decade of the twentieth century, ongoing improvements to the physical plant ensured that it was possible to place a large amount of weight on each driver—thus obviating the need for the lighter axle loadings that constituted one of the virtues of the 4-6-2 design. Moreover, and thanks to the timely arrival of the first K2 locomotives in 1910, Gibbs possessed the time and freedom he needed to develop the ideal Atlantic, without imperiling the PRR's need for passenger motive power. His starting point was the E3d, a locomotive that featured a Belpaire

Thanks to the use of superheated steam and Walschaerts valve gear, the E6s was a superb machine, proving that the Atlantic type was both fast and powerful enough to handle long consists of steel passenger cars at high speed. Even standing still, it attracted attention—witness #230 on display at Harrisburg in November 1915, little more than a year after it emerged from the Juniata Shops. Rugged and dependable, it remained in service until 1952. *Pennsylvania Railroad Negative Collection, Hagley Museum & Library, acc. 1993.300.*

firebox and modern Walschaerts valve gear. The fifty-six examples of that class, built between 1906 and 1910, were in many respects like the contemporaneous E2d. The principal difference lay in the size of the cylinders, which were considerably larger on the E3d than on the E2d. That circumstance reflected Gibbs's advocacy for larger cylinders and was in keeping with his assessment that the performance of the K2 suffered because of inadequate cylinder volume.[208]

The success of the E3d Atlantic vindicated Gibbs's design philosophy and provided him with the key elements for a more robust 4-4-2 passenger locomotive. He specified a large boiler, large cylinders, and Walschaerts valve gear, and then turned the details over to Axel Vogt and assistant mechanical engineer William F. Kiesel Jr. A decade younger than Gibbs, Kiesel was born in Scranton, Pennsylvania, in September 1866. He graduated from the mechanical engineering program at Lehigh University in 1887. He worked briefly at the Lehigh Valley, where he was involved in the testing and evaluation of that company's steam locomotives. Kiesel took that experience to the PRR the following year, as a draftsman. Over the next fourteen years, he rose to the position of assistant engineer, as Gibbs's direct subordinate. In 1902, when Gibbs became the superintendent of motive power for the Philadelphia, Wilmington & Baltimore, Kiesel replaced him as assistant mechanical engineer. He became the PRR's mechanical engineer in 1919, following Axel Vogt's retirement. He was as outgoing as Vogt was introverted, always ready to share a joke or a story. By the time Kiesel ended his forty-eight years with the PRR, in October 1936, he had secured 135 patents related to improved mechanical devices on locomotives and cars. One of the most significant, dating to

1894, was for an improved water scoop that was able to fully utilize the potential of the railroad's track pans.[209]

As they collaborated on the new Atlantic, Vogt used his drafting skills to design an extraordinarily beautiful locomotive. Its clean, flowing lines suggested a combination of size, power, grace, and speed. Kiesel oversaw the development of many of the smaller components, including the single-axle trailing truck. On many earlier locomotives, mechanical engineers struggled to properly equalize the rear driver's inside axle box, which was incorporated into the frame, with the outside journal box of a trailing truck that of necessity moved in compensation with curves and irregularities in the track. Drawing in part on the E28 experimental locomotives furnished by Baldwin in 1905, Kiesel developed and patented an innovative new design for the trailing truck. The Kiesel trailing truck, constructed from cast rather than fabricated steel components, greatly improved stability and riding quality. It appeared first on the dozen examples of the Class E5—essentially a slightly upgraded version of the E3—and it soon became standard equipment on many classes of PRR steam locomotives.[210]

In 1910, Gibbs, Vogt, and Kiesel brought together the constituent elements of what would become one of the most extraordinary locomotives in the history of railroading. As the prototype of the E6 class, the #5075 reflected Gibbs's preference for a massive boiler, one that provided a 26.3 percent increase in heating surface compared to the E3. The customary Belpaire firebox was, conversely, slightly smaller than on the earlier class of light Atlantics but provided ample heat.[211] The combination of firebox and boiler was quite similar to the one employed on the Class H8 Consolidations, reflecting the standardization across classes that contributed to lower construction and maintenance costs. Many of the smaller appliances, including the pilot, headlight, piping, and placement of controls on the backhead, were also identical to those on other classes. The cylinders resembled those on a K2 Pacific more than those on the E3, while the installation of Walschaerts valve gear attested to the proven virtues of that design. Beneath the cab, Kiesel's recently developed trailing truck, only recently applied to the E5 class, provided stability at high speed. The #5075 was an exceptionally heavy locomotive for its wheel arrangement, carrying 133,300 pounds on its two pairs of drivers. Few other railroads in the United States possessed track that could accommodate such high wheel loadings.[212]

The first representative of the Class E6 quickly proved its worth. Beginning in early 1911, the #5075 sped across the Middle Division, between Harrisburg and Altoona, usually in charge of the *Pennsylvania Special*—soon to be renamed *The Broadway Limited*. On one trip, the locomotive pulled eight steel cars along the steady uphill westbound grade, and without the helper that was often assigned to trains headed by a K2 Pacific. An eastbound special train carrying First Vice President Charles E. Pugh, under the command of the #5075, covered the Middle Division at an average speed of 69.6 miles per hour and traversed the entire distance between Altoona and Philadelphia at an average speed of 67.4 miles per hour. The results on Lines West were equally impressive, with the locomotive managing a nine-car train at an average speed of 75.3 miles per hour between Fort Wayne and Valparaiso, Indiana. The #5075 generated a drawbar pull of fourteen hundred horsepower, proving that it was the most powerful Atlantic that had ever been built by any railroad.[213]

The Science of Steam

While the E6 Atlantics were ideally suited for the level topography along the Atlantic Seaboard, the routes that lay to the west called for a different type of locomotive. Motive-power officials on railroads across the United States increasingly employed the 4-6-2 Pacific to move long, heavy passenger trains at acceptable speeds, even over hilly terrain. Theodore Ely had considered the potential of six-coupled locomotives, as shown by the two J-Class Prairies of 1905, as well as the sole K28 locomotive that followed two years later. Full-scale production of the K2 began in 1910, even before the E6 entered service. Yet Ely remained wedded to the small-engine philosophy, which suggested "that every pair of drivers adds complications of machinery and friction." He and his subordinates were also reluctant to deviate too radically from established design principles, lest they create a locomotive that performed poorly. By making too many changes at once, they also risked the possibility that they would not be able to determine whether each alteration, on its own, exerted a positive, negative, or inconsequential effect.

Two developments freed the Motive Power Department from the final constraints of nineteenth-century engineering practice, permitting the development of the finest 4-6-2 Pacific to serve on any railroad in the United States. One involved the ongoing work at the test plant, where technicians accumulated a massive amount of data relating to locomotive performance under a wide range of parameters. That information gave designers the confidence that they could build larger locomotives, while making simultaneous changes to multiple interrelated components, and achieve the expected performance criteria. They could also undertake subtle modifications to a single prototype and, using the test plant, quickly evaluate the effects of those alterations without extensive and time-consuming road testing.

A series of changes in the composition of the Motive Power Department reinforced the potential benefits associated with the test plant. The retirement of Theodore Ely on July 1, 1911, fortuitously occurred precisely when the need for improved locomotives was most urgent. No one could doubt Ely's abilities, but he was in some respects a representative of a bygone era, more comfortable with intuition and traditional practice than with modern techniques of scientific analysis. His repeated emphasis on the desirability of small locomotives, with the fewest possible drivers and a minimum of complex mechanical devices, made sense at a time when each component was prone to manufacturing defects, complications in construction, and failure in service. Yet more drivers and additional appliances were now precisely what the Pennsylvania Railroad needed, if the company was to provide efficient transportation.

With Ely's retirement, the PRR abolished the office of chief of motive power. Alfred Gibbs earned a promotion to the new office of chief mechanical engineer, in charge of locomotive development at Altoona. He was a decade younger than Ely and more receptive to newer design and production methods. Axel Vogt, continuing in his role as mechanical engineer, had engineered the test plant, and he was correspondingly in favor of basing decisions on the results that it generated. Charles Young, who had been a "computer" at the St. Louis exhibit, became the new engineer of tests on October 1. To an even greater extent than his predecessor, Edward Nelson, Young was intimately familiar with the most effective ways to use the Altoona installation of the test plant to monitor the performance of locomotives.

A timely if tragic circumstance added another talented mechanical engineer to the PRR's design team. In July 1911, Richard N. Durborow, the superintendent of motive power on the Eastern Pennsylvania Grand Division, replaced Gibbs as the general superintendent of motive power for Lines East. He died at his post barely five months later, felled by a heart attack. His replacement, James T. Wallis, became an integral member of the team that included Gibbs, Vogt, and Kiesel, and he soon became one of the most influential individuals associated with the Motive Power Department. Born in New Orleans in 1863, Wallis attended the University of Louisiana and Georgetown University before graduating from the Stevens Institute of

James T. Wallis (1868–1930) became the general superintendent of motive power on Lines East at the beginning of 1912, just as his colleagues in the Motive Power Department were initiating the development of a new class of passenger locomotives. Working in collaboration with Alfred Gibbs, Axel Vogt, and William Kiesel, he played a leading role in the development of the K4s Pacific. *Collection of the Historical Society of Pennsylvania.*

Technology in 1891. He immediately began working for the Pennsylvania Railroad and in less than a decade rose to the rank of assistant master mechanic at the Altoona Machine Shops. Between 1907 and 1911, as the Juniata Shops were building the 153 Class K2 locomotives for Lines West, Wallis was the superintendent of motive power for the Erie Grand Division and Northern Central Railway. In May 1911, he became the superintendent of the West Jersey & Seashore Railroad and the Philadelphia & Camden Ferry Company. In that capacity, he would have had daily exposure to the Class E Atlantics. Effective January 1, 1912, as both the Atlantics and the K2 were revealing their limitations in mountainous terrain, Wallis became the general superintendent of motive power on Lines East.[214]

In his new role, Wallis was instrumental in the development of what would become the Pennsylvania Railroad's iconic steam locomotive. His first task was to explain why the K2, a design that looked good on paper, was performing poorly on Lines West. A decade earlier, there would have been no way to provide a scientific explanation for the deficiency. In the absence of unassailable data, it would have been reasonable to assume that the problems associated with the K2 could be attributed to an unwise deviation from Ely's small-locomotive policy. Moreover, there would have been little guidance regarding the modifications that might make the K2 into a satisfactory locomotive—and little incentive to engage in costly and time-consuming experiments—at a time when the E6 was generating superb results.

Following the installation of the test plant at Altoona in 1906, however, Wallis, Vogt, and Gibbs possessed a growing body of analytical data that enabled them to determine why locomotives performed the way they did and how to make them better. For several years, test plant personnel conducted experiments in a granular and haphazard manner, evaluating small components in isolation from one another. Under Charles Young's leadership, however, activities at the test plant became more systematic and generated a comprehensive body of knowledge regarding the fundamental aspects of locomotive performance. A series of trials conducted between 1911 and 1913 were of particular importance. Collectively, they turned a very good locomotive—the E6—into a superb performer and transformed another—the K2—from a disappointment into a stunning success.[215]

One of the most significant tests involved a K2a locomotive, #877. In 1911, shop forces applied a superheater, a device that transformed highly saturated (or "wet") steam into drier steam that flowed to the cylinders at a far higher temperature, and thus exerted a proportionately greater force on the pistons. Mechanical engineers in Germany pioneered the principle. It soon spread to North America, with installations on Canadian Pacific locomotives between 1903 and 1905. There was yet no comprehensive data that conclusively demonstrated the superiority of superheated locomotives over their more traditional, saturated-steam counterparts. Given the contemporaneous debate regarding the advantages of compounding, even the most experienced locomotive designers found it difficult to predict which technology would produce the greatest gains in power and efficiency.[216]

The PRR's K2a Pacific, now equipped with a superheater and thus classified as a K2sa, soon underwent trials, and the data from the test plant was unambiguous. The superheater greatly improved the locomotive's performance, generating a level of efficiency far greater than that obtained from the mechanically complex and problematic compounding systems developed by Samuel Vauclain and his contemporaries. "It is seen," Young observed, "that the saturated steam locomotive used practically 15,700 pounds of water per hour more than is required for the same power when the steam is superheated, or nearly 48 per cent." Young put the results in a manner that was more appealing to operating officials who faced the need to get heavy trains across their divisions as quickly as possible. "For equal weights of water consumed," he noted, "there is an increase in horse-power by superheating of 28 per cent." The data, Young emphasized, "points out strikingly the economies which very highly superheated steam will give when furnished to a simple engine in preference to compounding." While personnel in the Motive Power Department continued to evaluate compound locomotives, on a sporadic basis, it had become clear that compounding would never become commonplace. The #877 performed so well that the PRR adopted the superheater as standard equipment on Lines East beginning in April 1912. Thereafter, the company installed superheaters on most of the existing Class K2 locomotives, transforming them into Class K2s. To the undoubted disappointment of David Crawford, the general superintendent of motive power on Lines West, subsequent tests of another K2sa, #7166, did not indicate the value of the mechanical stoker he had designed. "From the results obtained," Young observed, "the variation in engine performance makes it difficult to find a very material difference in the boiler performance when comparing locomotives with and without a stoker and with no other difference." Undeterred, Crawford demanded the installation of the Crawford underfeed stoker on the corresponding locomotive that he designed for Lines West. The result was the K3s, built in much smaller numbers (thirty in total) by Baldwin in 1913. As the classification indicated, all came from the erecting shop with superheaters as standard equipment.[217]

The greatly improved performance of the first K2sa provided compelling evidence that the installation of superheaters could make the outstanding E6 Atlantic an even better locomotive. Despite the extraordinary success of the #5075 prototype, Gibbs was the first to acknowledge that modifications to the E6 design might be warranted. Gibbs oversaw the construction of two additional Atlantics in the Juniata Shops—#89 in May 1912 and #1092 the following month. Both featured superheaters as well as minor changes in the valve gear and other details. The installation of a brick arch in the firebox produced more

While the Class E6s Atlantics were ideally suited for flatland running between New York, Washington, and Atlantic City, their older counterparts, the E2 and E3 classes, handled trains in more mountainous territory. The awe-inspiring sight of three such locomotives lifting a westbound passenger train around Horseshoe Curve and to the summit at Gallitzin did little to cheer accountants who fretted at the cost of so many crews. *General Negative Collection, Railroad Museum of Pennsylvania, PHMC.*

efficient combustion while minimizing rapid fluctuations in temperature. After the customary shakedown process in road service, #89 went to the Altoona test plant in 1913. The results vindicated Gibbs's faith in the value of a superheater. The new locomotive could produce the same power as the saturated-steam Atlantic, #5075, while reducing coal and water consumption between 23 and 46 percent. More significantly, given the necessity of pulling heavy trains at high speeds, the #89 generated a 30 percent increase in horsepower over the original E6, while using the same amount of fuel and water.[218]

Based on the performance of the #89, Gibbs authorized further modifications to the initial E6 Atlantic. The #5075 received a new number (#1067, appropriate for its

intended assignment to the New York Division) as well as a superheater, an all-metal pilot, and larger cylinders. A screw-type reversing gear replaced the earlier Johnson bar and provided a much safer alternative for enginemen. Gibbs and Vogt redesigned the valve gear, with lighter components and fewer moving parts, with a total weight of less than a thousand pounds on each side of the locomotive. The changes led to a modest 200-pound reduction in the weight carried on the drivers, but the total locomotive weight was a robust 240,000 pounds—extraordinarily heavy for an Atlantic. "This apparently excessive weight on drivers is permissible," an analyst for the *Railway Age Gazette* noted, because "these locomotive do not deliver as heavy a blow on the rail, nor do they have as bad an effect on the track so far as strain is concerned, as the majority of passenger locomotives which have a weight on drivers of from 10,000 lb. to 12,000 lb. less per axle." The tender trucks, newly designed by Kiesel, permitted great stability at high speed, while his time-tested water scoop facilitated long nonstop runs.[219]

The performance of the #1067 removed any doubt regarding the ability of a 4-4-2 to maintain fast schedules with long trains of all-steel cars. In August 1913, it easily handled the thirteen-car *Cincinnati, Indianapolis & Chicago Express* from Manhattan Transfer to Broad Street Station in Philadelphia. Pennsylvania Railroad executives had little hesitancy regarding full-scale production of the locomotive that, with a superheater, was now classified as an E6s. With astonishing speed, the personnel at the Juniata Shops built eighty of the locomotives between February and August 1914. Typically assigned to the routes east of Harrisburg, including the line from Camden to Atlantic City, they accommodated the heaviest of trains with ease. Officials at the Reading took one look at the locomotive, simmering in the Camden yards, and knew they were in trouble. They developed a design for a 4-4-4 Baltic locomotive, converted it to a more conventional 4-4-2, and finally gave up the race to Atlantic City as a lost cause.[220]

Perfecting the Pacific

The eighty-three representatives of the Class E6s were superb locomotives, but they did not solve the PRR's motive-power needs. While they easily accommodated passenger trains east of Harrisburg, the moderate westbound grades of the Middle Division presented difficulties. The steeper terrain along the Pittsburgh Division, particularly over the territory between Altoona and the summit of the Alleghenies at Gallitzin, was even more problematic. The K2 Pacifics, built at Altoona between 1910 and 1911, handled most passenger assignments. Longer trains nonetheless required the use of two or even three locomotives to maintain schedules. Given their success with the Atlantic, however, there seemed little reason why Wallis, Gibbs, Vogt, and Kiesel could not develop a better Pacific.

In perfecting the design of their new Pacific locomotives, officials in the Motive Power Department borrowed heavily from outsiders, while using the test plant to provide a scientific basis for modifications. The accumulated data provided precise measurements of the effects associated with alterations in cylinder dimensions and in the all-important valves that regulated the flow of steam in and out of the cylinders. The ongoing tests also demonstrated the value of superheaters and put an end to further discussions regarding the widespread use of compound locomotives.

Perhaps most significantly, the Altoona test plant provided the data that overcame the last resistance to Ely's small-engine policy and made possible the development of the PRR's most enduring passenger locomotives. In assessing the results of numerous tests of the K2 Pacific, Charles Young could find scant evidence to support Ely's assertion "that every pair of drivers adds complications of machinery and friction." That may have been true in the nineteenth century, but rigorous analysis showed that it was no longer the case. "While the Pacific type locomotive has been credited with greater machine friction than is found in

the Atlantic type, these tests do not serve to confirm this impression," Young concluded. "The machine friction was approximately the same as with four-coupled locomotives and there should be no hesitation on this account in using a six-coupled locomotive for high-speed work as compared with a four-coupled one." Ely had retired, and a new generation of locomotive designers was in the ascendancy. The test plant showed that Ely's small-engine philosophy was no longer the governing factor in motive-power development, while providing data that enabled his successors to transcend the limitations of traditional practice. Equipped with the most modern techniques of scientific analysis, they improved the Atlantic, but they ultimately concluded that the future belonged to the Pacific.[221]

Wallis took the lead in designing the PRR's new Pacific, in collaboration with Vogt and Gibbs. He drew much of his inspiration from a single locomotive, Class K29 Pacific #3395, which differed from traditional PRR practice in many respects. It was designed by Francis J. Cole, Alco's mechanical engineer, rather than PRR personnel, and it came from Schenectady rather than Baldwin or the Juniata Shops. By the early twentieth century, Cole had established an international reputation as a supremely talented designer who placed great reliance on the value of empirical science. He was responsible for Alco's pathbreaking Pacific, a demonstration model referred to as #50000 and later sold to the Erie. Even though the Pennsylvania Railroad also rostered many talented motive-power experts, they deferred to Cole's reputation in the design of the #3395, a locomotive like the #50000. They acquiesced to the installation of a radial-stay boiler rather than the now standard Belpaire arrangement, as well as a mechanical stoker, a superheater, and a brick arch. Alco's variant of the screw reverse gear, while similar to that employed on the E6s, was an improvement over the PRR's design.[222]

After Alco completed the locomotive in November 1911, Pennsylvania Railroad officials sent it to the Altoona test plant, without the customary evaluation in revenue service. The subsequent report may well have been the most significant of the many documents generated during the long history of that facility. "These tests are unique," Young emphasized, "in presenting a complete series of results at very high speed and power, with the largest passenger locomotive of its type, and one fully equipped with the devices which are known to add to the power of the locomotive and the convenience of its operation." In the past, when trials took place on the railroad rather than in a laboratory, it would have been impossible to accurately assess a locomotive fully equipped with a variety of devices. In the absence of controllable, quantifiable, and replicable scientific data,

M.E.796A

Built by Alco in 1911 and based on a design by Francis J. Cole, the #3395 was one of the best steam locomotives ever built. Even though the PRR owned only a single Class K29 Pacific, results from the Altoona test plant led to the construction of a massive fleet of K4s locomotives. *Pennsylvania Railroad Negative Collection, Hagley Museum & Library, acc. 1993.300.*

no one could be certain how each of those components affected a locomotive's performance, either individually or in combination. Under Young's supervision, test plant personnel could now perform as many experiments as necessary to determine which variables needed adjustment.[223]

The older Atlantics, rather than the E6s, constituted the primary basis for comparison. Young nonetheless suggested that "the worst performance of the K29 is superior to the best performance of the E2a." Of greater significance, Young concluded that "a locomotive of this size will eliminate all necessity for double-heading excepting on the

Eastern Slope of the Pittsburgh Division, Keating Summit and Kane Hill, and will give a large margin of power for making up time." His final assessment attested to the abilities of Francis Cole and the revolutionary changes that the K29 would have on the PRR's fleet of steam locomotives. "The locomotive has been in course of development for upwards of a century," Young noted in awe, "and it is a notable fact that the greatest economy and highest sustained power of which we have record have been obtained with this locomotive by the use of new and comparatively simple devices, as shown in the remarkable series of trials" at the test plant. Vogt and Gibbs shared Young's assessment that the K29, which they had not designed, was the best steam locomotive ever built.[224]

While Young lacked the authority to make policy recommendations, the data he presented to his superiors unequivocally indicated that the PRR should acquire a fleet of similar locomotives. He suggested several relatively minor modifications to Alco's design, including changes to the stack, reduced cylinder clearance, and a reduction

As a group, the Class K4s Pacifics were among the finest passenger locomotives to operate anywhere in the world. The #5379 exhibited grace and style as it moved the eleven-car *Fort Dearborn* across the Susquehanna River on August 19, 1933. The train by that name ran for only six years, but the locomotive lasted considerably longer. Built in June 1924, near the end of its career it conveyed spectators bound for Dwight D. Eisenhower's January 1953 presidential inauguration. *Otto Perry photograph, Denver Public Library, Western History Collection, call number OP-14393.*

in the weight of the valve gear. The substitution of a Belpaire firebox for Alco's radial-stay boiler was apparently taken for granted. Young acknowledged that "a stoker when applied to a boiler of this size, which is beyond the capacity of a fireman, justifies its application through the fact that the maximum power which the boiler is capable of developing can be obtained." He did not, however, include a mechanical stoker in his list of key recommendations.[225]

With the report of the Test Department in hand, Wallis moved ahead with the design of #1737, the prototype for a new class of 4-6-2 locomotives. As its designation indicated, the first representative of Class K4s was fitted with a superheater—and Walschaerts valve gear, which was likewise becoming ubiquitous on the PRR. The expectation that a skilled fireman could handle the large locomotive initially

overrode Young's concerns, and there was no automatic stoker. Alco's version of a power reverse gear permitted the cab of the K4s to be significantly shorter than that of the K2. Like its Alco progenitor, the #1737 featured large, 27 by 28-inch cylinders and drivers that were 80 inches in diameter. The cast-steel frame for the single-axle trailing truck closely resembled the Kiesel design employed on the E6s. Further refinements, in cooperation with Charles T. Westlake at the Commonwealth Steel Corporation, produced the KW trailing truck, with a three-point suspension system that ensured stability at high speeds. The #1737 was slightly heavier and more powerful than the K29, with a total locomotive weight of 304,500 pounds. The tender was smaller than what might be expected for such a large locomotive. The use of track pans and the availability of closely spaced and efficiently operated coaling facilities initially obviated the need for extensive onboard fuel and water capacity, however.[226]

The #1737 displayed impressive results. Its maximum tractive effort of 44,460 pounds was 36 percent higher than the K2 and 42 percent greater than an E6s. Data from the test plant indicated that the locomotive generated a maximum of 3,184 horsepower at the drawbar. Young concluded that #51, a representative of the most modern class of Atlantics, "shows very good economy of coal, exceeding that of the other locomotives at the higher dynamometer horse-powers, excepting the K4s." The prototype K4s could generate one horsepower for every 97 pounds of locomotive weight and 1.52 pounds of coal burned. Those results were slightly less impressive than the ones generated by the E6s. In terms of the ability to pull ten- and twelve-car trains over the Pittsburgh Division, however, the K4s proved its worth through a substantial reduction in the cost and delays associated with helper service while keeping to rigorous operating schedules.[227]

The success of the #1737 led to full-scale production of the K4s, for use on all parts of the system. There was a delay, however, given the more pressing need to build freight locomotives. The Juniata Shops produced an initial group of 41 K4s locomotives in 1917, followed by a further 111 in 1918, 15 in 1919, and 50 the following year. There was a brief hiatus, induced by the postwar recession, but shop forces were soon back at work. They built 57 K4s locomotives in 1923, 50 in 1924, 92 in 1927, and a final batch of 8 in 1928. The PRR acquired 425 copies of the versatile locomotive, making it one of the largest classes in service. Most came from Altoona, but Baldwin built 75 of them; none came from Alco's facility in Schenectady—to the undoubted chagrin of the employees who had designed the K29. The K4s soon displaced the various classes of K2 locomotives from the most important assignments on the Middle and Pittsburgh Divisions. With equal rapidity, they made inroads on Lines West, where the K3s had heretofore held sway. While they were the obvious choice for heavy passenger trains in territories with moderate or severe grades, the K4s locomotives could eventually be found in a variety of assignments, including commuter service on the New York & Long Branch Railroad and even, on rare occasions, pulling freight trains.[228]

While the overall design of the K4s remained essentially unchanged during its 1914–1928 production run, officials in the Motive Power Department often used the locomotive as a test bed to evaluate new innovations. David Crawford, the general superintendent of motive power on Lines West, had long been an advocate of automatic stokers, which—at his insistence—were standard equipment on the K3s. It was hardly surprising, therefore, that during the 1920s, shop forces began to install stokers on K4s locomotives operating west of Pittsburgh. As engineer of tests Charles Young had predicted, the appliance enabled the locomotive to unleash the full potential of its massive boiler and large cylinders. Debates regarding the abilities of shovel-wielding firemen in any case became moot after December 1937, when the Interstate Commerce Commission ordered the installation of automatic stokers on all passenger locomotives that carried more than 160,000 pounds on drivers—a category that included the K4s. Larger tenders became standard on locomotives

built in 1923 and thereafter, allowing for greater coal and water capacity while reducing the expense associated with operating track pans and coaling stations. By late 1924, the multitalented Kiesel had developed another new tender design that featured simplified construction and a one-piece cast-steel underframe. Kiesel subsequently designed a far larger "coast-to-coast" tender, applied to eleven members of the Class K4s and to many freight locomotives as well.[229] Other incremental innovations included power reverse gear, trailing-truck boosters, smoke lifters, mechanical lubricators, better injectors, cab signals, train phones, and a variety of valve gear designs. Roller bearings reduced both friction and the possibility of catastrophic mechanical failure, yet the PRR applied them to only two locomotives in that class.[230]

The streamlining craze that swept across the United States during the 1930s produced the most visible changes to the K4s, although only to a small number of locomotives. Noted industrial designer Raymond Loewy worked with the PRR's engineering staff to develop twenty-four preliminary concepts, which underwent wind-tunnel tests at New York University. In 1936, locomotive #3768 received a sheet-metal cowling that almost completely hid its running gear and other mechanical parts. It garnered favorable publicity and made an appearance at the 1939 New York World's Fair. The cost of conversion, coupled with complaints from mechanical forces who found it difficult to service and maintain the locomotive, ensured that future streamlining efforts would be less extensive. Four other locomotives (#1120, #2665, #3678, and #5338) received more modest, and less aesthetically pleasing, modifications in 1940 and 1941. Despite their enhanced appearance, the five locomotives rarely appeared on the premier *Broadway Limited*—largely because that train operated mostly at night, with limited public visibility. Accordingly, the streamlined K4s locomotives mostly found work on the all-coach *Jeffersonian* to St. Louis and on the *The South Wind*, the Chicago–Florida service operated by the PRR in conjunction with the Louisville & Nashville, the Atlantic Coast Line, and the Florida East Coast.[231]

Modern Freight Locomotives

All steam locomotives, whether engaged in passenger or freight service, embodied some combination of speed, power, and efficiency. While those were not mutually exclusive performance criteria, every mechanical engineer acknowledged that efforts to modify one variable would of necessity affect the others. Near the end of his long and distinguished career, Theodore Ely had pushed his long-standing small-engine policy to its limits. The E6, particularly when equipped with a superheater, pulled heavy passenger trains at high speeds, while making economical use of coal and water. Subsequent reliance on test plant data enabled James Wallis, Alfred Gibbs, Axel Vogt, and William Kiesel to design an equally superb Pacific, the K4s. Together, the two classes would satisfy the PRR's requirements for passenger service for many years to come.

Freight was another matter, however. In 1904, even as he was supervising the development of the H-Class Consolidations, Gibbs expressed concern regarding the type of freight locomotive that would best meet the PRR's needs. "It can scarcely be said that at the present time we have any thoroughly suitable locomotive for fast freight service," he complained to W. W. Atterbury, the general manager for Lines East, "and until we have definite information as to what such a locomotive must perform we cannot prepare a satisfactory design." He was awaiting the outcome of discussions by the representatives of the Association of Transportation Officers to determine the speed at which freight trains should move across the system. Gibbs feared that, even though the nearly new "class 'H6a' locomotives do make the schedule, they are seriously racked by so doing and the failures from breakages are entirely too numerous." He reminded Atterbury, an individual who had preceded him as the Lines East general superintendent of motive power, "that an all-around locomotive has not yet been designed" and noted "that our present designs should be gone over with the view of making a more reliable locomotive." Yet Gibbs warned that he could not proceed until Atterbury and the members of the ATO had informed him of "the first step, [which] is to know what the locomotive is expected to do."[232]

Despite such frustrations, Gibbs and his colleagues possessed several key advantages in the quest for a new generation of freight locomotives. One was the Altoona test plant, which furnished a steady stream of data regarding all aspects of locomotive performance. Another was the corresponding wealth of experience derived from simultaneous work on new passenger locomotives. This included the construction of the Lines West–inspired K28 in the spring of 1907, the development of the E6 Atlantic, and the introduction of the K2 Pacifics in 1910 and the K29 the following year. Superheaters became standard equipment on Lines East in April 1912—hence their installation on the H9s and H10s locomotives—and they soon made their appearance on production-model E6s Atlantics and on the K3s, which debuted in 1913. Given the Motive Power Department's long tradition of standardization, it was a certainty that many of the innovative designs associated

with passenger locomotives would be applied to freight locomotives as well.

Initial experiments with locomotives that could move massive quantities of freight, albeit at low speeds, proved disappointing. At the beginning of the twentieth century, motive-power officials on several railroads were showing a keen interest in articulated locomotives. They featured two, and, in rare cases, three, engines—that is, the integrated units consisting of the cylinders, valve gear, and drivers. The forward engine could pivot independently from the frame, boiler, and firebox assembly, enabling even very long locomotives to navigate curves and switches with relative ease. There were in turn two types of articulated locomotives. Simple articulateds directed steam from the boiler into both pairs of cylinders, with the spent steam then exhausted into the atmosphere. Compound articulateds relied on a set of rear, high-pressure cylinders, with the spent steam then moving to a pair of larger, low-pressure cylinders on the front engine. Baldwin's Samuel Vauclain was a longtime proponent of compounding, but it was a European contemporary who lent his name to compound articulated locomotives. Anatole Mallet, a Swiss native who worked in France, first applied the principles of compound articulation to narrow-gauge locomotives used at the Paris Exposition of 1889, and to standard-gauge locomotives soon thereafter. Alco produced the first American Mallet locomotive in 1904, a 0-6-6-0 for the Baltimore & Ohio. Ely and his subordinates would certainly have been aware of that development, both through coverage in technical journals and because Alexander Cassatt's community of interest established close ties between the PRR and the B&O.[233]

With their customary thoroughness, representatives from the PRR's Motive Power Department evaluated the potential of simple articulateds and Mallet locomotives.[234] The company eventually acquired thirteen articulated locomotives, two prior to World War I and the remainder in 1919. When #3396 arrived in October 1911, it was the first simple articulated to operate on any railroad in the United States and featured a 2-8-8-2 wheel arrangement. Built by Alco, it was in some respects the equivalent of two H-Class Consolidations operating back-to-back, hence the designation of Class HH1s.[235] The radial-stay boiler was rated at 160 psi, lower than some of its contemporaries. The #3396 generated an impressive 99,144 pounds of tractive effort, more than double the output of a Class H8 Consolidation. In 1912, Baldwin supplied #3397, a Class CC1s 0-8-8-0 that was the first Mallet to operate on the PRR.[236] Unlike its counterpart, it featured the PRR's customary Belpaire firebox. It operated at a much higher steam pressure of

The capabilities of the L1s Mikado in freight service matched those of its passenger counterpart, the K4s, and the two locomotives featured many common design elements. An eastbound train, moving at a respectable forty miles per hour through Stelton, New Jersey, on August 19, 1937, attests to its versatility—and to the persistence of steam operations in electrified territory. *Otto Perry photograph, Denver Public Library, Western History Collection, call number OP-14341.*

205 psi, necessary to ensure that sufficient steam reached the secondary, low-pressure cylinders. The locomotive's tractive effort was, at 82,716 pounds, nonetheless considerably lower than that of the #3396 simple articulated. Pennsylvania Railroad officials tested both locomotives in pusher service, and they were not impressed with the results. While undoubtedly powerful, they were often out of service, and they were expensive to maintain. The flexible steam connections between the high- and low-pressure cylinders on the #3397 were particularly troublesome, a circumstance they shared with Mallets operated by other railroads. Such problems only reinforced the aversion of Gibbs, Vogt, and others to locomotive designs that seemed unnecessarily complicated. While #3396 and #3397

remained on the roster until 1929 and 1931, respectively, neither would be duplicated. The aversion of PRR officials to articulated locomotives hardly indicated any failings in the Motive Power Department, however. Instead, it reflected the extraordinary success with which Gibbs, Vogt, Wallis, and Kiesel refined more conventional designs for freight locomotives.[237]

The Mikado and the Decapod

James Wallis, the PRR's superintendent of motive power, was an extraordinarily busy person during 1913. In addition to developing the K4s, Wallis oversaw the design of a locomotive that would go beyond the abilities of the H-Class Consolidations. The addition of a single-axle trailing truck to the 2-8-0 wheel arrangement permitted the use of a more capacious firebox and created a 2-8-2 wheel arrangement. First used on the Bismarck, Washburn & Great Falls Railway, the Mikado enjoyed widespread popularity on railroads across the United States. Wallis adopted that basic design for the PRR's L1s Mikado, but he added recognizable PRR features—most notably the Belpaire firebox. He took the decades-long commitment to standardization to new heights, employing the same boiler on the L1s and the K4s. Many other parts were likewise interchangeable,

With its massive boiler and small drivers, the L1s Decapods performed at their best while moving heavy trains at low speeds. On August 19, 1933, near Altoona, #4287 hauled forty-seven cars loaded with coal at twelve miles per hour. *Otto Perry photograph, Denver Public Library, Western History Collection, call number OP-14369.*

and, on both locomotives, Wallis reduced the weight of the running gear and other components to the greatest possible extent. Data from the test plant revealed that the L1s weighed 30 percent more than a Class H9s Consolidation while generating a 25 percent increase in tractive effort. Between 1914 and 1919, the PRR acquired 574 of the locomotives—the majority built at the Juniata Shops, with 205 built by Baldwin and another 25 by Lima.[238] Initially, most of the Mikados operated on Lines East, with the last of the Consolidations assigned to the western half of the system. Before long, however, the L1s could be found just about anywhere that there was freight to haul.[239]

According to those who operated them, the L1s Mikados were ideally suited for the undulating Pennsylvania coal lines that formed the heart of the railroad's route structure. Some enginemen even found them superior to

the more advanced Class M1 Mountains that came into service more than a decade later. The L1s locomotives would have been better, perhaps, had the Motive Power Department unlocked their full potential by increasing the boiler pressure and making other minor, incremental improvements. Crews noted that although the L1s was a powerful engine, its tender lacked sufficient coal and water capacity. Because they initially lacked mechanical stokers, many firemen could not keep pace with the locomotives' insatiable demand for coal while simultaneously managing the fire, checking water levels, regulating steam pressure, and assisting the engineer in observing signals and passing trains. Some enginemen and brakemen complained that they had to assist with firing, in order to develop the locomotive's full power. The additional duties prompted complaints from the Brotherhood of Locomotive Engineers and the Brotherhood of Locomotive Firemen and Enginemen, and union officials on the Williamsport Division threatened a strike unless shop forces retrofitted the locomotives with mechanical stokers. Instead, the PRR assigned two firemen to each locomotive, probably because the company had a surplus of available firemen and because executives did not want to establish a precedent for the installation of stokers on other locomotive classes or on other divisions.[240]

The L1s was a superb locomotive, but it did not fully satisfy the need to move heavy trains—drag freights—at low speeds over difficult terrain. The 3,068 Consolidations the PRR built or bought between 1901 and 1916 were likewise inadequate. Just as the Mikado generated 25 percent more tractive effort than a Class H9s Consolidation, Vogt and Wallis hoped they could gain a further 25 percent increase over the L1s. Beginning in the spring of 1916, they developed specifications for an even more powerful freight locomotive, which became the Class I1s Decapod. They chose a 2-10-0 configuration, a wheel arrangement that dated to the 1860s. That design had temporarily fallen out of favor, as its long wheelbase required generous curves. The concept enjoyed a resurgence during the 1890s, and many railroads employed Decapods in pusher service. While the PRR's motive-power experts did not ignore the possibility that the 2-10-0 could be used as a helper, they envisioned a locomotive powerful enough to pull trains that were beyond the capabilities of the L1s. As such, their design was on a scale far larger than any of its 2-10-0 predecessors. In typical PRR practice, Vogt and Wallis extrapolated from known techniques and designs, particularly those related to the L1s. The driver diameter, at 62 inches, was the same on both locomotives, and the Belpaire fireboxes were virtually identical. The Walschaerts valve gear was similar. However, the boiler on the I1s was massive, with an inside diameter nearly six inches larger than on the L1s. The size created a squat, ungainly appearance, ensuring that engine crews frequently referred to the Decapods as "Hippos." The other nickname, "Decs," was even more obvious. Steam pressure was correspondingly high, at 250 pounds per square inch, rather than 205 psi on the L1s. The Decapod's boiler was so large, even at its base, that it could not nestle between the drivers, as was the case on locomotives such as the L1s and the K4s. The wide boiler also precluded the installation of counterweights large enough to fully counteract dynamic augment. As such, the I1s was a rough-riding locomotive, even at low speeds, and was thus unpopular with engine crews.[241]

The large boiler provided steam to correspondingly voluminous cylinders, measuring 30.5 by 32 inches, necessary to permit one of the most significant innovations associated with the I1s. That was the locomotive's limited cutoff, set at 50 percent rather than the more traditional practice of 90 percent. Even when the engineman worked the reverse gear to its maximum forward position, admission of steam to the cylinders would cease when the piston had traveled half its length through that cylinder. The limited cutoff gave the steam in the cylinder greater opportunity to move the piston and thus power the drivers. That method maximized tractive effort at low speeds. While the locomotive could reach 50 miles per hour, optimal results were attained at 7.2 miles per hour—ensuring that the I1s would rarely get anywhere in a hurry. That was a small price to pay, however, as the I1s developed 90,000 pounds of tractive force, compared to 61,470 pounds for the L1s. The Decapod's weight was correspondingly greater, at 386,100 pounds. Significantly, it concentrated a far larger proportion of its total weight on its drivers, accounting for its exemplary pulling abilities—something that was only possible on a railroad with heavy rail, sturdy bridges, and a well-maintained right-of-way.[242] "Not only has the engine shown remarkable efficiency," observed James Partington, an estimating engineer at Alco, "but economy under wide ranges of load is especially remarkable." Those comments suggested that Vogt and Wallis were able to achieve an impressive balance between raw power and the efficient use of fuel and water.[243]

In December 1916, workers at the Juniata Shops completed #790, the prototype I1s, and the locomotive more than met expectations. Over the next few months, Charles Young evaluated its performance on the test plant before releasing it into road service in March 1917. Additional evaluations took place in February 1918. With the United States at war, there was a pressing need for additional motive power, and PRR officials soon authorized full-scale production of the I1s. The Juniata Shops completed 122 of them between September 1918 and September 1919. The postwar recession briefly reduced the need for additional locomotives, but the recovering economy soon forced PRR officials to acquire more Decapods. William Kiesel replaced Vogt as chief mechanical engineer in February 1919, and he accordingly oversaw some modifications to the design of the I1s. Kiesel rearranged the tubes and flues in the boiler, increasing the superheating surface and making more efficient use of steam. He added a Worthington feedwater heater, which necessitated the relocation of the air reservoir tanks to the deck of the pilot. The design made the I1s even more ungainly, but the presence of the twin air tanks at the front of the locomotive constituted an unmistakable identifying feature. In 1922, Baldwin received the order for 475 Decapods, at a total cost in excess of $31 million. By the time Baldwin completed the last I1s in 1923, the PRR owned 598 examples of that one class. No other railroad in the United States rostered so many locomotives that, aside from relatively minor differences in appearance and equipment, were essentially identical.

The 130 examples of the Class N2s, built at the behest of the United States Railroad Administration, lacked many of the features typically associated with PRR steam locomotives. The company subsequently added Belpaire fireboxes to many of them, including #7284, thereafter assigned to Class N2sa. For many years, they capably handled coal and iron-ore trains in the industrial belt that lay west of Pittsburgh. This view, in Cincinnati, dates to the summer of 1950. *Otto Perry photograph, Denver Public Library, Western History Collection, call number OP-14299.*

While they could be found across the system, most of those Decapods worked the Middle Division and the Pittsburgh Division as well as the territory stretching into far western Pennsylvania, the West Virginia Panhandle, and eastern Ohio. Often working two, three, or even four at a time, they muscled coal and ore trains over adverse grades. Unlike the 2-10-0 pushers adopted by other railroads in the 1890s, the PRR's Decapods initially seldom appeared at the end of a train. There were too few of them to spare, and helper duties often fell to the less capable L1s Mikados.[244]

Despite the praise that James Partington and other mechanical engineers directed at the I1s, the locomotive also had its share of critics. One engineman, disgusted with the poor riding characteristics of the I1s, questioned "why a railroad the size of the Pennsylvania, with the best engineering staff in the world, would design such a useless monstrosity," and he more pointedly referred to the locomotives as "just massive, worthless hunks of iron." Those who were more familiar with the principles of locomotive design suggested that the I1s was out of date, that the lack of a trailing truck precluded the use of a sufficiently large firebox, and that—despite the increase in pressure—the enlarged boiler was incapable of delivering enough steam to the large-capacity cylinders.[245]

Given the symbiotic rivalry between Lines East and Lines West, it was hardly surprising that some of the criticism came from the engineers and draftsmen at the Fort Wayne Shops. They favored the addition of a single-axle trailing truck, emulating the wheel arrangement first used by the Santa Fe in 1903. The additional support permitted a firebox that encompassed nearly seventy square feet, 14.3 percent larger than on the I1s. The Lines West locomotive, Class N1s, operated at a boiler pressure of 215 psi, slightly higher than the L1s but well below that of the Decapods. The total engine weight was considerably higher on the N1s than on the I1s, but, thanks to the use of the trailing truck, the weight on the drivers was about the same. The maximum tractive effort of the N1s, 84,890 pounds, was nonetheless lower than its Lines East Decapod rival. The Santa Fe type was also quite slow and could not exceed thirty-five miles per hour. That was of little consequence, however, and the N1s gave exemplary service, particularly

In June 1919, the Railway Supply Manufacturers' Association convention in Atlantic City featured a locomotive that earned its nickname of "Mr. Big." The front and rear cylinders were the same size, indicating that this was a simple articulated rather than a Mallet. The only example of Class HC1s, the #3700, was perhaps ahead of its time and too powerful to operate efficiently in freight service. *Otto Perry photograph, Denver Public Library, Western History Collection, call number OP-14271.*

with ore trains moving between Ashtabula, Ohio, and Pittsburgh, as well as with coal traffic from central Ohio to the Great Lakes. In 1918, Baldwin completed twenty-five N1s locomotives, while Alco built a further thirty-five.[246]

World War I and the oversight of the United States Railroad Administration saddled Lines West with a second, larger group of 2-10-2 locomotives. USRA officials elected to assign the idiosyncratic design to the Pennsylvania Railroad rather than force the company to utilize the articulated locomotives that—on other railroads—generated results that were comparable to the Decapod and Santa Fe types. In 1919, Alco and Baldwin delivered 130 members of the N2s class. As originally built, they bore little resemblance to PRR motive-power practice, and their radial-stay boilers were particularly notable. Much lighter than the N1s, they also produced considerably less tractive force. Beginning in 1923, shop forces rebuilt the locomotives, incorporating the PRR-standard Belpaire

firebox and other features. Subsequently listed as Class N2sa, they soldiered on in the same assignments as their Class N1s counterparts.[247]

Despite their aversion to unnecessary complexity, however, mechanical engineers on both Lines East and Lines West simultaneously developed new articulated locomotives. In 1919, Baldwin supplied ten 0-8-8-0 Mallet compound locomotives, designated as Class CC2s. They had the smallest drivers (51 inches) and the highest boiler pressure (225 psi) of any of the PRR's articulated locomotives, and they were the only class of articulateds that included more than a single locomotive. Initially assigned to Lines West, and in later years based in Columbus, Ohio, the CC2s locomotives proved effective in pusher service, in shoving long cuts of cars at hump yards, and in transfer runs between various yards. They worked through the Great Depression and World War II before succumbing to the scrapper's torch in the late 1940s.[248]

The other design, for a simple articulated, was much more ambitious but far less successful. In 1919, workers at the Juniata Shops completed a single 2-8-8-0 locomotive, the sole representative of Class HC1s. The #3700 was a gargantuan machine, one that earned its nickname of "Mr. Big." It weighed 603,500 pounds, 56 percent more than the ponderous I1s Decapods. The locomotive also generated an astonishing 147,640 pounds of tractive effort—more than triple the output of a Class H8 Consolidation. The boiler stretched nearly fifty-four feet—so long that designers had to make special provisions to ensure an adequate supply of water over all portions of the crown sheet while the locomotive was climbing or descending grades. An equally capacious firebox included a grate area of 112 square feet, 1.6 times the size of the ones on the L1s and I1s locomotives, and so large that it was necessary to install a corrugation in the throat sheet (the location where the front of the firebox met the rear of the boiler) to permit thermal expansion. Like the I1s, Mr. Big featured a maximum cutoff of 50 percent, ensuring economy in the use of fuel and water. The massive locomotive attracted considerable attention when placed on display at the Railway Supply Manufacturers' Association convention in Atlantic City in June 1919. It appeared alongside a Decapod and "Big Liz," the PRR's only Class FF1 electric locomotive. Mr. Big and Big Liz provided valuable lessons for the development of new steam and electric locomotives, but neither represented the solution to the PRR's motive-power needs. In some respects, they were victims of their own success, as they were too powerful for the freight cars that existed at that time. When pulling trains, they frequently shattered couplers that did not meet the latest standards established by the Master Car Builders' Association. Operating as pushers, they could cause the cars ahead of them to bunch up, in accordion fashion, and derail. They offered an indication of the potential of steam and electric locomotives, but they were too far ahead of their time. Mr. Big served the PRR for less than ten years, and Big Liz went to the scrapyard in 1940.[249]

Baldwin and the M1

In 1920, when the United States Railroad Administration returned the carriers to private management, the Pennsylvania Railroad rostered 7,656 locomotives. They included 4,996 assigned to freight service, 1,692 that pulled passenger trains, and 968 shifters. It was the largest collection of motive power the company would ever own—as well as the largest locomotive fleet in the United States, comprising more than 11 percent of the 68,592 steam locomotives in service at that time. The corporate reorganization that took place that year transformed the Altoona Shops into the Altoona Works, organizationally separate from the four newly created regions of the PRR system. James Wallis, the general superintendent of motive power on Lines East, became the systemwide chief of motive power, reporting to W. W. Atterbury, the vice president in charge of operations. The postwar recession soon led to layoffs, however, as well as a suspension in the construction of new locomotives

that lasted for more than two years. The 1922 Shopmen's Strike did not seriously affect the Altoona Works, although it disrupted other, smaller facilities across the PRR system. Those events, combined with changing operating patterns, contributed to the ongoing centralization of construction, maintenance, and heavy-repair activities at Altoona. In 1920, the PRR had twenty-six shops capable of handling class repairs, yet by the end of 1929, only four remained in operation.[250]

The prosperity that characterized the second half of the 1920s ensured that the Pennsylvania Railroad, the Altoona Works, and the surrounding community returned to prosperity. By 1926, the facilities covered more than fifty acres and employed more than thirteen thousand people in its four constituent units. The fifty-five hundred employees of the Altoona Machine Shops fabricated components and performed heavy repairs, rebuilding as many as four locomotives per day. More than three thousand people worked in the Altoona Car Shops, building and repairing a new generation of steel passenger cars. The Juniata Shops employed more than forty-two hundred personnel. They could match their Altoona Machine Shops counterparts in the pace of locomotive repairs, while producing twelve of the world's largest and most sophisticated steam locomotives each month. At the South Altoona Foundry, seven hundred employees turned out a wide variety of cast-iron and steel parts, including a thousand wheels a day.[251]

The rapid growth of highway traffic during the 1920s presented further challenges for the Motive Power Department. Senior executives acknowledged the danger of truck competition, particularly in the transportation of perishables and other high-value, time-sensitive freight. While such preference freight constituted a smaller portion of the PRR's business than was the case on rival carriers such as the New York Central, the company's managers could not afford to ignore the rapid changes in traffic patterns. Yet the locomotives that represented the height of motive-power development in the early decades of the twentieth century were at risk of obsolescence. The roster of motive power included more than three hundred antiquated 2-6-0 locomotives, all of which were retired by 1929. The arrival of the L1s Mikados and the I1s Decapods permitted the reassignment of many of the older classes of 2-8-0 Consolidations to yard service. The retirement of the oldest Class A, Class B, and Class C shifters nonetheless required the PRR to build more than two hundred replacements at the Juniata Shops during the 1920s. The growing fleet of I1s, L1s, N1s, and N2s locomotives could move vast quantities of coal and iron ore, but high-speed service was beyond their capabilities. The ponderous and generally unsuccessful articulateds were not a solution either. The K4s was a superb locomotive but was not suited for freight service, and longer passenger trains taxed its abilities, particularly in hilly terrain.[252]

Following World War I, executives on many railroads demanded further increases in the speed of freight trains, to capture high-value merchandise and perishables traffic while fending off highway competition. Engineers and technicians at the three main producers of steam locomotives—the Baldwin Locomotive Works, the Lima Locomotive Works, and the American Locomotive Works—rose to the challenge. Often working in collaboration with representatives from railroad motive-power departments, they developed new components, design principles, and testing methods. In 1925, Lima applied the term *Super Power* to locomotives that featured such incremental improvements as larger fireboxes (which necessitated four-wheel trailing trucks, often equipped with boosters), feedwater heaters, lightweight valve gear, and roller bearings. Alco and Baldwin quickly copied the basic elements of the Super Power concept. For the first time, railroads acquired fast and powerful locomotives that performed equally well in passenger and high-speed freight service.[253]

On the Pennsylvania Railroad, James Wallis crafted a locomotive well suited to the movement of time-sensitive freight, yet the design lacked many of the key elements of the Super Power revolution. The effort also benefited from the encouragement of Samuel Vauclain, the longtime proponent of compounding and, between 1919 and 1929, the president of the Baldwin Locomotive Works. In 1922, Vauclain and Wallis discussed the PRR's massive order for 475 I1s Decapods. During the conversation, Vauclain proposed that Baldwin and the PRR work together to develop the most powerful passenger locomotive in the world. Such a project would generate substantial orders for Vauclain's company, and it would encourage other railroads to follow the PRR's example and buy similar locomotives.

Despite Vauclain's desire for collaboration, Wallis and mechanical engineer William Kiesel were almost solely responsible for the design of the M1. The Juniata Shops completed the prototype, #4700, in October 1923.[254] With a 4-8-2 wheel arrangement, the locomotive in some respects resembled a K4s Pacific with an additional pair of drivers. The similarities notwithstanding, Wallis and Kiesel based the M1 on the I1s freight Decapods. The running gear was largely the same. So were the firebox and boiler, which in each case was rated at 250 psi. Despite its massive size, the

prototype M1 did not have a stoker—although Kiesel left space under the cab and tender deck, so that one could be added later. Kiesel favored the use of very large drivers, of as much as 80 inches, but that would have raised the boiler to such a height as to run afoul of clearance restrictions. As such, he made do with 72-inch drivers—a standard size originally employed on the Class G4 Ten-Wheelers, introduced a quarter-century earlier. The drivers on the M1 were nonetheless ten inches larger than those of the Decapod, and accordingly far better suited for its intended role in fast freight and passenger operations. With a tractive effort of 64,500 pounds, the M1 was by no means the most powerful locomotive on the Pennsylvania Railroad and only slightly exceeded the 61,470 pounds produced by the L1s. The Mountain class nonetheless filled an important niche in response to the growing demand for high-speed service.[255]

For more than two years, the #4700 remained the only M1 on the PRR roster. That status caused some individuals to suggest that President Samuel Rea and other top executives were resolutely opposed to the new design. According to that narrative, W. W. Atterbury, desperate for faster motive power, used his personal funds to pay for the construction of the prototype—to the extent that the M1 earned the nickname of the "Atterbury engine." That story, probably based on various railfan accounts, had no foundation in reality.[256] The PRR's vice president in charge of operations and heir apparent to the presidency had no need to finance the venture. As a PRR director himself, he would have experienced little difficulty in persuading Rea and his fellow directors of the value of the M1. The more logical explanation for the delay stemmed from the lingering effects of the postwar recession, coupled with the customary thoroughness of officials in the Motive Power Department. Lengthy evaluations indicated the potential of the M1, but they also suggested that certain modifications might be necessary. Chief among them, and to the undoubted relief of firemen, was the installation of a mechanical stoker.[257]

By 1926, the completion of the evaluation process and the growth of traffic induced Atterbury—who was by that time the PRR's president—to authorize the purchase of 200 M1 locomotives. As Vauclain had expected, 175 of the Class M1 locomotives came from Baldwin, at a cost of $65,612 apiece, while Lima produced the remainder. Slight design changes—including the more widespread use of cast rather than fabricated components, the installation of a Worthington feedwater heater, and the increased size of the tender—resulted in the Class M1a. In 1930, the PRR ordered a hundred of them, fifty from Baldwin and

M1 #6882, built in 1926 and shown here on August 19, 1933, experienced little difficulty powering a five-car eastbound passenger train around the Horseshoe Curve, at a steady twenty-five miles per hour. The PRR's Mountains were more commonly found in fast freight service, yet they lacked many of the refinements that characterized the Super Power locomotives built just a few years later. *Otto Perry photograph, Denver Public Library, Western History Collection, call number OP-14441.*

the remainder evenly split between Lima and the Juniata Shops.[258]

The M1 was a superb locomotive, but one that did not fully achieve its potential. It came just too soon to take advantage of the core elements of Super Power practice. The electrification of the routes to the east of Harrisburg ensured that electric locomotives, rather than the M1, would pull preference freight and heavy passenger trains. To the west, ample K4s locomotives were available, particularly after the Great Depression curtailed passenger traffic. Designed as dual-service locomotives, the representatives of the M1 class generally pulled only freight trains, usually on the Middle and Pittsburgh Divisions. While the M1 was a testament to the abilities of Kiesel, Wallis,

and their subordinates, it nonetheless constituted the only successful locomotive developed by the PRR between the two world wars. In many respects, moreover, it was the final great achievement of the Motive Power Department, and its blend of power, speed, efficiency, and dependability would never be repeated.

The Changing Demands of Passenger Service

The development of the M1 occurred at a critical point in the evolution of the Pennsylvania Railroad's passenger service. For all its fame, *The Broadway Limited* was only one of a wide array of prestigious trains that operated over the Pennsylvania Railroad. The most celebrated were part of the PRR's "Blue Ribbon Fleet," a name that mimicked the Baltimore & Ohio's fast and luxurious Royal Blue Service between Washington and Jersey City. The term, first used in advertising in 1903, became more common in the 1920s. While the precise composition of the Blue Ribbon Fleet changed over the years, the name typically referred to one or two of the most prestigious trains, such as *The Broadway Limited* and *The "Spirit of St. Louis,"* that operated along the routes between the East Coast and western destinations. The *Congressional Limited* (renamed *The Congressional* in 1931), which connected New York and Washington, was also accorded Blue Ribbon status. Such trains typically received the PRR's most modern locomotives.[259]

The 1920s witnessed a significant expansion of the PRR's intercity passenger service. Following the end of USRA oversight in 1920 and the subsequent easing of the postwar recession, executives on the PRR and other railroads anticipated a steady increase in demand for passenger travel. Ridership and revenues remained stagnant, however, in a trend that was linked to increased automobile ownership and the rapid growth of the highway network. The Pennsylvania Railroad carried 196.8 million intercity and commuter passengers in 1920, but that number fell steadily to 144.9 million in 1924 and 118.1 million in 1928. The decline in long-distance travel—from 79.3 million passengers in 1922 to 58.9 million in 1928—was not as severe but nonetheless represented a trend that executives found troubling. Total intercity passenger revenue declined from $143.4 million in 1922 to $125.9 million in 1928.[260] Wages and supply costs also rose steadily, further eroding the profitability of passenger operations.[261]

Pennsylvania Railroad officials sought to increase passenger ridership—in part by offering additional trains, but more commonly by rebranding existing ones. Ivy Lee, the PRR's advisor to publicity, suggested that evocative new names would humanize the railroad's operations and generate considerable public goodwill. Working with the J. Walter Thompson advertising agency and the PRR's Advertising Department, Lee provided whimsical—and, at times, nonsensical—names for many of the railroad's freight trains. He applied the same principles to passenger service. Nearly every train that featured sleepers or parlor cars received a name—from the *Bankers Special* and *The Cavalier* to the *Lock Haven Express* and *The Metropolitan Limited*. The *Nellie Bly* and the *Seagull* sped passengers to Atlantic City, the former from New York and the latter from Pittsburgh. Even the more prosaic trains operated by the subsidiary Long Island Rail Road were part of that process, and wealthy Manhattanites headed for resorts in the Hamptons and Montauk could enjoy such appellations as the *Greenport Express*, the *Shinnecock Express*, and the *Peconic Bay Express*.[262]

Lee's promotional flair and penchant for new names soon affected the PRR's passenger services, including those that connected New York and Chicago. Debuting on July 16, 1922, *The Gotham Limited* was the first of the postwar extra-fare trains. While slower than *The Broadway Limited*, its running time of twenty-two hours ensured that the PRR now operated four trains between New York and Chicago with schedules faster than twenty-four hours. On May 10, 1923, the PRR renamed the existing Washington

section of *The Broadway Limited* as the *Washington Broadway Limited*, running from the nation's capital north to Baltimore, then over the Northern Central Railway (rather than the Columbia & Port Deposit Railway) to Harrisburg, and then west to Chicago.[263] A week later, the Baltimore & Ohio upgraded its existing service between Washington and Chicago, as the *Capitol Limited*. The train was popular with employees of the federal government as well as travelers who appreciated the Chesapeake Bay cuisine served in the dining car, but the B&O remained a minor player in the east–west passenger market. The New York Central represented a far more serious threat, and for decades to come, that company repeatedly goaded PRR officials into upgrading their passenger service.[264]

While St. Louis attracted fewer passengers than Chicago, it was nonetheless an important gateway to the Southwest. As with the routes between the East Coast and Chicago, all three trunk lines implemented contemporaneous service improvements. That became apparent on April 26, 1925. The Baltimore & Ohio launched the *National Limited*—but, as with the *Capitol Limited*, the company was never a major competitor in the St. Louis market. The Pennsylvania Railroad was in a far stronger position, particularly when the company launched *The American*. The train, with amenities equal to those on *The Broadway Limited*, took precisely twenty-four hours to travel between New York and St. Louis, by way of Pittsburgh, Columbus, and Indianapolis. Not to be outdone, the New York Central debuted the *Southwestern Limited*, a train that was as luxurious as the *Twentieth Century Limited*. Even though the NYC's route between New York and St. Louis was considerably longer than the PRR's more mountainous line, the *Southwestern Limited* featured the same journey time as *The American*. Charles Lindbergh's May 1927 solo flight across the Atlantic Ocean prompted the PRR to rename and reequip the existing *The St. Louisan/The New Yorker* service as *The "Spirit of St. Louis."* It soon replaced *The American* as the PRR's premier train to and from St. Louis.[265]

The Pennsylvania Railroad also offered extra-fare service to intermediary cities, and none was more important than Pittsburgh. Train names changed frequently, according to the whims of employees in the Advertising Department. As with the PRR's other trains, however, operating personnel relied on numbers rather than names, and the frequent changes in nomenclature required minimal adjustments in train-handling practices. The PRR established the *Pittsburgh Express* in May 1896. Other westbound trains were variously known as the *Pittsburgh Night Express*, the *Pittsburgh Special*, and the *Iron City Express*.

The Steel City Express, established in 1915, offered comparable extra-fare service between Pittsburgh and Chicago. Eastbound, the *Pittsburgh Limited*, which began operations in November 1898, departed from its namesake city and soon thereafter made a brief stop at East Liberty, Pennsylvania, one of the most affluent of Pittsburgh's suburbs. It sped through the night, pausing briefly at Harrisburg to cut off cars destined for Washington. The train skirted Philadelphia, and passengers detrained only when they reached Jersey City and the ferry connection to Manhattan. In November 1903, the first section of the *Pittsburgh Limited* became the *New York Special*, a deluxe, extra-fare service that likewise bypassed Philadelphia. At the same time, the PRR established a train that would serve its headquarters city. The *Philadelphia Special* ran directly from Pittsburgh to Broad Street Station in Center City, but it also carried cars from Chicago, St. Louis, Cincinnati, and other western points of origin. In 1909, the *Philadelphia Special* became the *Philadelphia Night Express*, operating between Pittsburgh and Philadelphia and carrying through sleeping cars from Akron and Cleveland. The general upgrading of passenger service that occurred during the 1920s included the introduction of *The Pittsburgher*, inaugurated on January 14, 1924. Like the *Pittsburgh Limited* and the *New York Special*, the new extra-fare service did not accommodate any passengers between New York and East Liberty.[266] The train proved immensely popular with Pittsburgh industrialists, and US Steel commonly reserved sleeping-car space for any of its executives who needed to reach New York as quickly and as comfortably as possible. With a late-evening departure from New York and from Pittsburgh, the schedule enabled managers to enjoy a leisurely dinner before boarding, perhaps followed by conversation in the train's lounge. A good night's rest and an early morning arrival permitted a full day of business.[267]

While less important than Pittsburgh, numerous other cities benefited from direct PRR passenger service. Beginning on May 23, 1920, *The Cincinnati Limited* ran westbound between New York and its namesake city. Six years later, the PRR established comparable nomenclature in the other direction, by assigning the same name to the train previously referred to as the eastbound *Metropolitan Limited*.[268] *The Clevelander*, established in 1916, offered westbound-only service to its namesake city, with *The Buckeye Limited* carrying passengers the opposite direction. Like *The Broadway Limited*, the two trains fell victim to the USRA's efforts to promote coordination, and the names disappeared from the timetables between January 1918 and May 1920. Cleveland was in any case very much a New York Central town, and the PRR's service

only attracted travelers from Pittsburgh and other Pennsylvania locations rather than from Manhattan. Detroit, the last major city reached by the Pennsylvania Railroad, benefited from *The Red Arrow*, placed in service on September 27, 1925. Initially running only between the Motor City and Pittsburgh, with through sleepers to New York, by mid-December, the train operated eastbound directly to Manhattan, followed by its westbound counterpart on September 26, 1926.[269]

The final prosperous year of the Roaring Twenties witnessed the birth of several new luxury trains on the Pennsylvania Railroad. The inauguration of *The Senator* on July 14, 1929, provided extra-fare, all-Pullman late afternoon travel between Boston and Washington.[270] *The Rainbow*, introduced on April 28, 1929, operated eastbound only between Chicago and New York.[271] Its westbound counterpart, *The Red Knight*, enabled Manhattan theater attendees to make a late-night departure for Pittsburgh and Chicago.[272] The launch of *The Golden Arrow* in September 1929 created what was in effect a second section of *The Broadway Limited*. Both trains provided similar equipment and offered bath and barber facilities, along with a ladies' maid, valet, and a secretary. The most exotic and shortest-lived train in the Blue Ribbon Fleet was undoubtedly *The Airway Limited*, which beginning on July 7, 1929, ran westbound only between New York and Columbus, Ohio. As the eastern leg of the combined Pennsylvania Railroad/Transcontinental Air Transport rail-air service to Los Angeles, the train was an early casualty of the Great Depression and suspended service on February 16, 1932.[273]

The Last Pacific

As the representatives of the Passenger Traffic Department steadily improved the PRR's passenger services during the 1920s, their counterparts in the Operating (Transportation) Department continued to rely on locomotives whose design long predated World War I.[274] The New York Central was experiencing similar problems with its large fleet of Class K3 Pacifics, built between 1911 and 1923. After he became the NYC's chief mechanical engineer of motive power and rolling stock in January 1926, Paul W. Kiefer worked with Alco to develop a more powerful passenger locomotive. Kiefer and his counterparts at Alco borrowed many of the elements of Super Power technology that Lima had employed on its massive 2-8-4 Berkshire locomotives. The two-axle trailing truck permitted the installation of a larger firebox, with an attendant increase in steam-generating capacity. The employment of a comparable two-axle pony truck and the use of three rather than four sets of

Efforts to build a more powerful and efficient Pacific came to an end with the two examples of Class K5. Baldwin built the #5699 in 1929. The locomotive waited at Paoli in May 1937, the year in which shop forces replaced its problematic Caprotti valve gear with the more conventional Walschaerts system. The lingering effects of the Great Depression, coupled with electrification—soon to be extended west to Harrisburg—ensured that the #5698 and the #5699 would not be duplicated. *Harris Negatives Collection, Railroad Museum of Pennsylvania, PHMC.*

drivers ensured that the first example of the Class J1a was an ideal solution for the NYC's motive-power needs. The prototype entered service in February 1927 and quickly proved its worth. Over the next eleven years, the New York Central acquired 275 locomotives of the 4-6-4 wheel arrangement, named Hudsons in tribute to the railroad's water level route between New York City and Albany.[275]

The 4-6-4 was popular on railroads across the United States, but not on the PRR. Wallis, who had been one of the principal designers of the K4s, was worn out by his efforts on behalf of his employer. In February 1927, he became an assistant vice president in charge of operations, a position whose limited responsibilities suited his poor health. He died little more than three years later, at the age of sixty-two. His successor, Frederick Hankins, was a capable administrator but lacked Wallis's abilities as a designer. In 1928, a year after he replaced Wallis as the PRR's chief of motive power, Hankins oversaw an attempt to match the performance of the New York Central's Hudsons. Rather than emulate the 4-6-4 wheel arrangement, Hankins retained his loyalty to the basic concept of the K4s Pacific that had served the PRR so well since 1914.

When Kiesel took charge of the design process, however, he confronted the limitations of the Pacific. In the 1915 evaluation of the K4s, engineer of tests Charles Young had suggested "that the large locomotive in output of power shows no limitations attributable to its increased size." Under those circumstances, Young concluded, "We need not expect, then, as locomotives grow larger, that the power developed will become proportionately less." In theory, therefore, it would have been a simple matter to expand the K4s, with a bigger firebox and boiler. Doing so, however, would have made the resulting locomotive so large that it would have exceeded the PRR's clearance restrictions. The only remaining solution involved a rejection of the long-standing aversion, expressed by an earlier generation of experts such as Ely, Gibbs, and Vogt, to more complicated mechanical appliances.[276]

The most significant deviation from conventional practice involved the valve gear developed by an Italian mechanical engineer, Arturo Caprotti. He began his career at Florentia, a short-lived automobile manufacturer based in Florence. The company went bankrupt in 1912, and soon thereafter, Caprotti applied his knowledge of motor cars to steam locomotives. He developed a system of camshafts and poppet valves that replaced the piston valves used on traditional steam locomotives. Unlike piston valves, which mechanically interlocked the components responsible for the admission of steam into the cylinder and the expulsion of spent steam from the cylinder, the tappet (push) rods that were the basis of the poppet valve gear enabled the two events to take place separately. While Caprotti's valve gear was far more complex, and thus more difficult to maintain, the system enabled a locomotive to use steam much more efficiently. First employed in Italy in 1921, poppet valves attracted further attention following experiments undertaken between 1926 and 1928 by the London, Midland & Scottish Railway.[277]

Kiesel developed two versions of a new high-power Pacific, the Class K5, each completed in 1929. The Juniata Shops built #5698, equipped with the familiar and proven Walschaerts valve gear. Baldwin supplied #5699, outfitted with the Caprotti system.[278] Both locomotives featured additional, incremental improvements over the fifteen-year-old K4s design. Kiesel used the same basic boiler as the one he employed on the I1s Decapod freight locomotives produced between 1916 and 1923. He incorporated several changes, the most significant of which involved the use of nickel steel to reduce weight and increase tensile strength. The frame, cylinder, and smokebox saddle were incorporated into a single integrated steel casting, facilitating the final assembly of the locomotive and constituting a successful experiment that would be repeated on other classes of motive power. At 250 psi, the boiler pressure was considerably higher than the 205 psi of the K4s. The cylinder diameter also increased by two inches. Kiesel employed an improved superheater and added a feedwater heater, one of the few elements of Super Power practice that he incorporated into the K5.[279]

The Caprotti-equipped #5699 generated an impressive 54,675 pounds of tractive effort, more than 30 percent above the performance of a K4s.[280] The total weight on the drivers increased by a far smaller amount, a mere 6.8 percent. That figure attested to the skill with which Kiesel had incorporated the Caprotti valve gear and other improvements into the design of the K5. There was a perverse drawback to that situation, however. The K5 had a low factor of adhesion, making it prone to slipping of the drivers and thus impeding the locomotive's ability to translate raw power into useful work. Further development might

well have resolved that issue. The electrification of the PRR's principal routes east of Harrisburg, combined with the decline in passenger traffic that accompanied the Great Depression, made the issue largely irrelevant. The number and weight of steam-hauled passenger trains declined significantly, and there were ample K4s locomotives available to do the work. The #5698 and #5699 lasted into the 1950s, but neither was ever duplicated.[281]

The most significant legacy of the experimental K5 locomotives involved the Caprotti valve gear installed on the #5699. For more than seven years, Kiesel tolerated the intricacies of the Caprotti system in a vain effort to make it work properly. When Carl Steins became the assistant chief of motive power in 1936, shortly after Kiesel's retirement, he abandoned the project as hopeless and instructed shop forces to remove the Caprotti valve gear from the locomotive. The concept would soon reappear, however, as a key element of a new class of Pennsylvania Railroad locomotives.

Legacies

By the time William Kiesel retired in October 1936, the spirit of innovation had largely disappeared from the Motive Power Department. He was the last of the old guard who had made the transition from the nineteenth-century practices based on intuition and tradition to the twentieth-century reliance on rigorous testing and scientific expertise. Theodore Ely, Alfred Gibbs, and Axel Vogt were long gone as well. Absent the leadership of so many talented individuals, there was little chance that the Pennsylvania Railroad could match the performance of the New York Central's Hudsons or do any better than the storied K4s.

Even though he reported to the head of the Motive Power Department, the mechanical engineer typically took charge of locomotive development on the Pennsylvania Railroad. Between 1866 and 1936, three individuals had successively occupied that role. John B. Collin (1866–1886), Axel Vogt (1887–1919), and William Kiesel (1919–1936) constituted an unbroken chain of expertise that served the company well, through prosperity and depression, balancing the performance criteria associated with speed, power, and efficiency as the operating requirements associated with freight and passenger service continued to evolve. After 1936, the chain was broken, and never again would the Pennsylvania Railroad or the Altoona Works enjoy the same reputation for excellence in motive-power design and construction.

A small portion of the Pennsylvania Railroad's vast motive-power fleet steams quietly near the site of 30th Street Station, awaiting the next call to duty. The West Philadelphia Elevated, better known as the High Line, soars overhead, and the tower of city hall is visible through the smoky haze. On the ready tracks are (*left to right*) E6s Atlantic #1647, K2s Pacific #3367, K4s Pacific #612, and G5s Ten-Wheeler #5700, all assigned to passenger service. The PRR's Motive Power Department enjoyed considerable success in standardizing locomotive designs, and in the K4s they produced what might have been the finest steam passenger locomotive ever built. During the 1930s and 1940s, however, the railroad's personnel were less successful in crafting the next generation of steam locomotives and were likewise slow to adopt diesel power. *General Negative Collection, Railroad Museum of Pennsylvania, PHMC.*

Through the 1930s and 1940s, the new generation of personnel at the Motive Power Department produced some notable results, particularly in the design of electric locomotives. Even with the new technology, however, Kiesel's successors continued to rely on the design philosophies and classification systems associated with steam

locomotives. They succeeded in large measure because they relied on outside equipment suppliers and on consulting firms such as Gibbs & Hill—whose founder, George Gibbs, was a cousin of one of the PRR's talented steam-locomotive designers. The willingness of PRR personnel to cede so much authority to outsiders foreshadowed the rapid evolution of another source of power. In the years following World War II, the independent builders of diesel locomotives would sideline motive-power officials on the Pennsylvania Railroad and other carriers and gain full control over that technology. More insidiously, the successes associated with the development of electric locomotives convinced senior officials in the Motive Power Department that they could design and build equally large and powerful steam locomotives. The new behemoths would, they hoped, fend off the diesels, cement the loyalty of on-line coal producers, and not incidentally preserve their power within the corporation. It was not an unrealistic expectation, perhaps, given that their predecessors had repeatedly transcended the boundaries of what earlier generations had thought possible. Patterns were not destiny, however, and extraordinary success in the past provided no guarantee against failure in the future.

Chapter 2

Wired

Many thousands of individuals worked for the Pennsylvania Railroad, often for only a short time. Yet even a brief association with the electrification of the route between New York and Washington—one of the greatest engineering and technological achievements of his generation—provided the foundation for the literary career of William Wister Haines. Haines was born in Iowa in 1908, but he had deep and prominent roots in Philadelphia. Relatives on his mother's side included physician Caspar Wistar (who gave his name to the purple-flowered wisteria), horticulturist John Caspar Wister, and pioneering historic preservationist Frances Anne Wister.[1] Civil War general Isaac Jones Wistar served during the 1870s as the president of the Pennsylvania Canal Company, the PRR subsidiary that managed many of the water routes originally constructed by the Commonwealth of Pennsylvania. The continuing presence of the Wister neighborhood in northwest Philadelphia as well as Wister Woods Park and the Wistar Institute attest to the family's involvement in the community. They also possessed considerable literary talent. Ella Wister Haines, the mother of William Haines, was a highly respected author, and his uncle, Owen Wister, is best known for writing *The Virginian*.[2]

William Wister Haines became a writer only after he embraced the profession that animated many of his works. At age eighteen, a trip to a mining operation in Searchlight, Nevada, left him enthralled with the transmission towers and high-voltage electric lines that were increasingly important to the American economy. Over the next few years, he alternated between semesters at the University of Pennsylvania and work as a lineman. In 1930, Haines

was hired to string catenary over the Pennsylvania Railroad tracks that linked New York and Washington. He incorporated his experiences and those of his coworkers in two novels and five short stories. The novel *Slim*, published in 1934, featured an eponymous protagonist much like Haines, an individual whose fascination with line work led to a difficult, dangerous, and rewarding career on projects across the United States. Slim's tale culminated with his work on the PRR's infrastructure. "There was nothing essentially different from steel tower lines about that," Slim observed. "But when he looked at the maze of catenary wiring suspended from the underside of the crossbeams, his head swam." The book enjoyed a favorable reception from popular audiences and literary critics alike and became a best-selling novel. Warner Brothers subsequently hired Haines to write the screenplay for the identically named film, which starred Henry Fonda and Margaret Lindsay. In 1938, a year after the movie's premiere, Haines completed *High Tension*, a shorter work that focused solely on PRR linemen. Haines drew upon his wartime experience in the Eighth Air Force when he wrote *Command Decision*—initially intended as a stage play, then serialized in the *Atlantic Monthly*, and finally published in 1947. The popular and highly praised novel also became a Hollywood film, produced by Metro-Goldwyn-Mayer and starring Clark Gable.[3]

Haines's depiction of the brief and tragic career of one railroad lineman appeared in "Remarks, None," and was featured in Edward J. O'Brien's compendium of *The Best Short Stories of 1935*. Regan, Haines wrote, was a good lineman, one of the best. Haines's literary creation gained his considerable experience working on the long-distance, high-voltage transmission lines crisscrossing the landscape, transforming electricity from a scientific miracle to an everyday necessity. There was plenty of work, even during the early years of the Great Depression, but most of it was in remote areas, far from the bright lights in the big city. Regan was an easygoing sort and seemed happy anywhere, but his wife sought the delights of the metropolis, to bask in the glow of the neon tubes his work brought to life. Scarfe was Regan's friend, and he understood about wives and what men might do to make them happy. He knew that Regan was so besotted with her that he had spent three years awash in drink and gambling and that he had become so recklessly irresponsible that he had been banned from job after job. Jig was reluctant to risk hiring a man like that, but Scarfe had saved his life, extricating him from a tangle of sizzling wires, and he owed Scarfe a favor.

In his dialogue in "Remarks, None," Haines left no doubt that he was aware of the dangers of his profession. Jig took charge of Regan, explained to him that working on a wire train, around 14,000-volt catenary that could power a railway locomotive, was vastly more dangerous than the current that enabled ordinary men and women to flip a light switch or turn on a vacuum cleaner. Regan was a quick learner, and what he lacked in experience he made up for in hard work. He knew to look out for the trains that barreled past at sixty miles an hour. When the boss yelled for the crew to hit the deck, he did as he was told, without wasting a second. Like his fellow linemen, Regan kept his nerve—even though, Jig observed, "they was many a night's work in that yard with the gang just eighteen inches from a look at the Holy Ghost."[4]

But then Regan's old problem came back. His wife screamed at him, tormented him, hit him, and he was too much controlled by love to leave her or to fight back. He became distracted and careless—two qualities that threatened his life and the lives of everyone who worked with him. The situation became serious when the crew was working just ten feet beneath hot catenary. Despite Jig's warnings, Regan swung a long piece of hanger wire into the air. Everyone lay face down, waiting for the explosion of electricity and the acrid smell of burned and mutilated flesh. Scarfe was the only one who headed toward the danger, at the last instant knocking Regan to the platform. Scarfe begged Jig to give Regan another chance, certain that he had learned his lesson.

Regan, Haines wrote, was all right for a while and knew better to participate in the weekend craps game the crew had going. But one night, he came to work without his dinner and with a scratch on his face. The trouble with his wife had come back, and so had his bad habits. Jig and Scarfe talked it over. They knew they had to fire Regan and what would happen to him if they didn't. Regan behaved well during his last night on the job, but at about four in the morning, Scarfe needed someone to help him change the wiring at a signal bridge. He asked for Regan, so he could work with his friend one last time. Jig watched the two men head off into the darkness and climb the signal bridge, coils of wire in hand. Then he saw the flash, heard the explosion of the circuit breaker, and inhaled the horrible, unmistakable smell. Scarfe was alive, but the look on his face showed that he would never be the same. The flashlight illuminated Regan's face, just for an instant, but that was enough. Jig covered the corpse with his jacket, so no one else would have to see. "If he could of had a decent chancet at breaking in he would have been hard to beat," Jig concluded. "But he didn't, and he ain't likely to get it now until they electrify hell."[5]

The preceding excerpts from "Remarks, None," like the novels *Slim* and *High Tension*, showed that William Haines was an experienced practitioner of his twin crafts of writer and lineman. Though works of fiction, his books and short stories—and the characters he created—were firmly rooted in true-to-life experiences. They reflected the widespread public fascination with the most extensive railroad electrification program that had yet occurred anywhere in the world. At the end of October 1928, when President W. W. Atterbury announced that the PRR would electrify the route between New York and Wilmington, Delaware, the breathtaking scope of the project epitomized American technological prowess. Press releases and newspaper articles brimmed with superlatives—the company would spend $100 million to string wire over 1,300 miles of track, along routes totaling 325 miles. As many as three hundred new electric locomotives would be required, along with fifty-five million pounds of copper—more than the entire annual output of the nation's smelters just half a century earlier. Shares of the holding company that controlled Philadelphia Electric gained 5¾ points, while those of the Public Service Corporation of New Jersey rose by 1⅜. General Electric, Westinghouse, and American Locomotive Company also surged on Wall Street, with investors expecting that those companies would supply many of the locomotives and electrical equipment. The linemen Haines describes in *High Tension* felt it, too, as they discussed "how ten thousand men would be employed directly or indirectly; how many millions of bucks the road would spend; and how they'd pay for it with bonds and who was going to sell the bonds and what they'd do to the money market, and God knows what else."[6]

New Brunswick, New Jersey, along the route between Newark and Trenton, experienced some of the highest traffic densities on the PRR system. The urban setting suggests why the company's executives rejected the possibility of adding additional tracks or building new bypass lines. Electrification offered the most effective solution for increasing capacity—although the elevated right-of-way, heavy rail, and extensive catenary attest to the PRR's enormous investment in transportation facilities. *General Negative Collection, Railroad Museum of Pennsylvania, PHMC.*

The onset of the Great Depression, less than a year later, transformed the PRR's electrification initiative into a symbol of can-do Americanism and the steadfast determination of business executives to use the tools of private enterprise to put men back to work and save the nation from economic catastrophe. Atterbury was one of the foremost business executives in the United States. In February 1932, therefore, the Senate Finance Committee and reporters from Time magazine solicited his perspective on the railroads, the economy, and the state of corporate America. Atterbury's remarks to the Senate, and in *Time* magazine, attested to his desire to defend free enterprise and his suspicion of governmental involvement in the economy. Yet his interviewer was most concerned with the PRR's electrification program, now expanded to extend all the way south to the nation's capital.

Atterbury's multifaceted responsibilities indicated that he was wired into currents of economic and political power, as surely as Pennsylvania Railroad locomotives were beginning to draw electricity from high-voltage transmission lines. That energy—figuratively and literally—was essential to the Pennsylvania Railroad's operations, but it could also be dangerous and difficult to control. In the interregnum between presidential administrations, and with the real-life counterparts of Regan, Scarfe, Jig, and Slim spinning a web of wires over the PRR's tracks, it was tempting to believe that Atterbury and his fellow executives were in command of the capitalist system they defended. Increasingly, however, they shared power with Franklin Delano Roosevelt and other government officials, and with the unions that represented linemen, factory workers, and railroad employees. A staunch Republican, Atterbury had routinely emphasized the profound distinctions that separated the two major political parties. The Democrats were now in the ascendency, however. Of even greater importance, the actions of the dominant party reflected a broad political consensus that was beginning to reshape the political economy in a manner that Atterbury found unsettling. The transformation had less to do with political parties than with a profound change in the nature of the relationship between business and government. It was significant that a substantial portion of the money used to pay for electrification came from the Reconstruction Finance Corporation—one of Herbert Hoover's initiatives that Roosevelt retained and expanded—and then from the Public Works Administration, a cornerstone element of FDR's New Deal.

By picking and choosing among the alphabet soup of new government agencies, Atterbury was able to shift the expense associated with private initiative to the public sector. Atterbury's ability to do so nonetheless involved the executive and his railroad in debates regarding the rights of labor, the legality of holding companies, the proper level of executive compensation, and the propriety of executive interference in the political process. Even before *Time* magazine lauded Atterbury's achievements, forecast the date of his retirement, and predicted his likely successor, the seismic changes associated with the Great Depression were rewiring the national power grid. Whether the Pennsylvania Railroad would remain at the center of that system or else be consigned to the periphery remained to be seen.

Embracing Electrification

During the early years of the twentieth century, the Pennsylvania Railroad had been one of the great pioneers of electric traction in the United States. The New York Improvements, with miles of tunnels linking New Jersey, Manhattan, and Long Island, required the use of electric locomotives. Electrical engineer George Gibbs participated in a vigorous debate as to which type of electric propulsion was most suitable for the Hudson River and East River tunnels.[7] Low-voltage direct current transmitted through a third rail at ground level was a proven technology and was suitable for a relatively short route.

George Gibbs (1861–1940) was one of the world's foremost experts on railroad electrification. During the first decade of the twentieth century, his skills made possible the construction of the New York Improvements and the installation of low-voltage direct-current power along portions of the PRR and the Long Island Rail Road. Through his consulting firm, Gibbs & Hill, he played an equally important role in the development of a high-voltage alternating-current network that extended from New York south to Washington and west to Harrisburg. *Harry R. Hippler collection of Pennsylvania Railroad Negatives, Hagley Museum & Library, acc. 2015.279.*

High-voltage alternating current traveling through catenary provided far superior current transmission over long distances, but the technology was still under development. The New Haven had already committed to the high-voltage AC system between New York and New Haven, but installation was still in its preliminary stages, suffered several unexpected delays, and did not yet offer a clear indication as to performance under operating conditions. By November 1908 and following extensive tests, Gibbs acknowledged the potential of alternating current. Hedging his bets, he nonetheless recommended the use of low-voltage direct current as the more dependable option.

Any unforeseen setbacks in the development of alternating-current propulsion, he warned, risked delaying the opening of Penn Station. Acting on his advice, the PRR installed a 650-volt DC third-rail system from Manhattan Transfer in the New Jersey Meadowlands, east under Manhattan and onto Long Island, and on many of the LIRR's commuter routes. Thanks to the development of the rugged and reliable DD1 electric locomotive, the system worked flawlessly. By the time Penn Station opened in 1910, massive Class DD1 electric locomotives were ready to haul trains under the Hudson River. On the Long Island Rail Road, a fleet of MP41 and MP54 multiple-unit electric passenger cars, first delivered in 1908, transported commuters in and out of Penn Station. The success of the New York Improvements demonstrated the merits of direct current in mainline railroad service. The conditions there were nonetheless unique, in an environment where trains operated over short distances and the use of steam locomotives was clearly impossible.[8]

Main line electric operations and the concomitant banishment of steam locomotives from freight and passenger service were far more daunting propositions. To the west of Philadelphia, PRR executives nonetheless identified locations where electrification might yield handsome dividends. Foremost among them was the main line over the Alleghenies, between Altoona and Pittsburgh. Thanks to the engineering expertise of J. Edgar Thomson, the PRR's route, as far west as Altoona, featured modest grades. Most trains required helpers beyond that point, with the attendant burden of locomotive and crew costs. Severe traffic congestion, particularly between 1902 and 1904, highlighted the inefficiency of such operations. The same technology that would soon bring trains into Penn Station offered possibilities in western Pennsylvania as well. As early as 1908, PRR electrical engineers performed arithmetical calculations that pitted a theoretical electric locomotive against an H6 Consolidation steam locomotive along the relatively flat trackage between Harrisburg and Morrisville. The results indicated, at least on paper, that electrification would cost $10 million but would reduce annual operating expense by $750,000. Other calculations, for the Pittsburgh Division, doubled the expected savings. Both the national economy and the Pennsylvania Railroad were still recovering from the recession that began in October 1907, precluding implementation.

Improving economic conditions and a steady increase in traffic prompted another examination of main line electrification. The issue was particularly acute in Philadelphia, where commuter traffic was taxing the capacity of Broad Street Station. In contrast to conventional locomotive-hauled passenger trains, electrified commuter cars, like the equipment used in New York, were bidirectional and did not need to be turned at a terminal. That feature greatly simplified operations and increased efficiency. Replacing steam-hauled commuter trains would also reduce the need for an expensive and politically sensitive expansion of the tracks leading to Broad Street Station.

As they had in New York, PRR officials relied heavily on the expertise of electrical engineer George Gibbs. Following the opening of Penn Station in September 1910, Gibbs was available and ready to continue working for the Pennsylvania Railroad. In June 1911, he formed the engineering consultancy of Gibbs & Hill, in conjunction with partner E. Rowland Hill. A month later, the PRR engaged the services of Gibbs & Hill, whose offices were in Penn Station. Sensing the possibility of substantial equipment orders, representatives from both General Electric and Westinghouse soon sought to influence the decisions of Gibbs and PRR executives. In January 1912, Fourth Vice President W. W. Atterbury conferred with Westinghouse executive Edwin M. Herr. William Wilgus, the New York Central official who oversaw the electrification of Grand Central Terminal, was also present.[9] Wilgus was most familiar with low-voltage DC transmission, yet Herr—as well as his GE counterparts—emphasized that they would gladly furnish any system that Gibbs desired. The two suppliers offered to study the merits of each form of power. Samuel Rea nonetheless insisted that "we can do that at any time with our own staff to our entire satisfaction at any particular point on the Pennsylvania Railroad, just as we did for the New York Tunnel Extension after most careful consideration, and as we now have up in Philadelphia." Conceding that the type of power supply was "a grave matter to determine," he also acknowledged that circumstances had changed since the time, a decade earlier, when he had been in charge of the New York Improvements. "We now have," he informed Atterbury, "in connection with electrification in the Philadelphia area, to consider the question anew."[10]

In December 1912, Gibbs presented the PRR board of directors with his recommendations to alleviate congestion in Philadelphia. While Gibbs had grudgingly supported the use of direct current for the New York Improvements, in Philadelphia, he rejected the advice he had provided barely four years earlier. During that time, the New Haven's electrical engineers had resolved the difficulties associated with that railroad's 11,000-volt AC system, an application that more closely resembled the PRR's commuter lines than did the tunnels under the Hudson and East Rivers. Finally, Gibbs was now contemplating an extensive system of long-distance electrification. Direct current would barely be adequate for the initial installation in Philadelphia, and it certainly could not accommodate the movement of heavy, fast trains over longer distances.[11]

Gibbs's recommendations for a massive new engineering project delighted Rea, who became president only days after the report had been completed. In March 1913, the board of directors approved $5.5 million to electrify the twenty miles between Broad Street Station and Paoli, the traditional western limit of commuter operations. Because municipal officials and representatives from the Philadelphia Rapid Transit were discussing the possibility of building a rapid-transit line to Chestnut Hill, Rea recommended that the electrification of the twelve-mile line to that commuter suburb be held in abeyance. By September, however, the directors had approved an additional $1.63 million for the route to Chestnut Hill.[12]

During the spring of 1914, construction crews began erecting catenary along the Main Line. They elevated tracks and eliminated grade crossings, developed new methods for installing the overhead wire without interfering with steam operations, and pioneered the combined installation of integrated power and automatic-block, position-light signal systems. The railroad also developed new training methods for its crews, recruiting some three hundred employees to take courses offered by the Pennsylvania State College School of Electrical Engineering, in cooperation with the PRR branch of the Philadelphia YMCA. Railroad officials were particularly committed to educating members of the public about the dangers of electricity. Spokesmen visited local schools, warning children that they should not try to climb the catenary towers nor should they fly their kites near the overhead wires.[13]

The Paoli electrification, while far less complex than the comparable construction of the New York Improvements, nonetheless presented some novel engineering challenges. In New York, the PRR built and operated a power plant at Long Island City but rejected that level of vertical integration in Philadelphia. Reliance on the commercial power grid significantly reduced the railroad's initial capital investment. Because suburban traffic, and therefore demand for electricity, tended to peak in the mornings and afternoons, it made little sense for the PRR to maintain surplus generating capacity at other times of the day. PRR officials also wanted to avoid negative public opinion and possible regulatory consequences at a time when many reformers were condemning the interlocking ownership of railroads (particularly streetcar and interurban lines) and public utilities.[14] Moreover, integrated power generation might well alienate the owners of public utilities whose coal deliveries constituted a lucrative source of revenue.

There were nonetheless some technical difficulties associated with reliance on commercial power. Beginning in 1899, the Philadelphia Electric Company consolidated smaller firms in the Philadelphia area, soon replaced the older DC systems, and converted to three-phase, 60-cycle AC power. With the Paoli electrification underway, PRR and Philadelphia Electric Company engineers spent many months developing methods to convert the energy to the single-phase, 25-cycle current used by the railroad. The PRR received the power at the Arsenal Bridge substation at 13,200 volts, stepped it up to 44,000 volts, and dispatched it to substations at West Philadelphia, Bryn Mawr, and Paoli, which reduced the current to the 11,000 volts that flowed through the catenary. A fleet of ninety-three MP54 cars collected the electricity through pantographs, with onboard transformers stepping down the current that fed a pair of 225-horsepower Westinghouse traction motors. The MP54 cars were often noisy and uncomfortable, with poor acceleration and a low top speed. Yet they were rugged and dependable, the PRR ultimately rostered nearly five hundred of them (with nearly a thousand more on the LIRR), and some remained in service until the early 1980s.[15]

Electric operations between Center-City Philadelphia and Paoli began in September 1915. The total cost was $4.2 million, which PRR executives considered money well spent. Travel time decreased by as much as seven minutes, compared to the earlier locomotive-hauled commuter trains. More important, the conversion of seventy-eight daily trains to MP54 equipment greatly eased congestion at Broad Street Station and was the equivalent of adding two additional tracks to that facility. Although the onset of World War I, the period of USRA control, and shortages of labor and materials delayed the electrification of the line to Chestnut Hill, that project was completed in April 1918.[16]

Vice President Atterbury, who bore the ultimate responsibility for the movement of freight and passenger trains, hoped that the Paoli electrification might serve as a model for the replacement of steam locomotives in main line freight service. In January 1912, he asked Rea to authorize a cost-benefit analysis for the electrification of the Trenton Cutoff from Morrisville, Pennsylvania, to Glen Loch, then west along the main line to Enola Yard, across the Susquehanna River from Harrisburg. Rea also contemplated a resurrection of the 1908 studies on main line electrification farther to the west. He received further suggestions from Charles S. Churchill, the chief engineer of the Norfolk & Western—a company closely affiliated with the PRR. Churchill had overseen a study that delineated the economic benefits associated with the electrification of the N&W's line between Eckman and

Bluefield, West Virginia. The operating conditions were reasonably similar to the PRR's route west of Altoona, and Gibbs & Hill personnel gave the report careful scrutiny. By the end of 1912, Atterbury was decidedly in favor of electrifying the route between Altoona and Gallitzin and perhaps on to East Conemaugh, on the outskirts of Johnstown. On December 6, he recommended the use of low-voltage direct current, the same technology employed in New York but vastly different from the high-voltage AC that Gibbs would endorse three weeks later, in his report on Philadelphia suburban electrification. Rural western Pennsylvania did not yet possess a commercial power grid that could meet the PRR's needs for either type of power, however. In customary PRR fashion, Atterbury favored vertical integration and proposed that the company acquire coal lands and build coke ovens and generating stations.[17]

Atterbury's advocacy continued into the summer of 1913, by which time the board of directors had already authorized the Gibbs & Hill plan to use high-voltage alternating current on the suburban line to Paoli. PRR officials awarded Westinghouse the contract to supply the necessary equipment, largely because that company was one of the largest shippers on the Pennsylvania Railroad. When Atterbury met with General Electric vice president Anson Wood Burchard on May 16, he had the unenviable task of explaining that GE would not be participating in the project. "Naturally they could not appreciate our position," Atterbury recalled, "and while the meeting was perfectly harmonious, nevertheless I could detect that they were seriously perturbed." Combining his enthusiasm for electrification with an attempt to soften the blow, Atterbury informed Burchard that the PRR was also interested in electrifying the tracks west of Altoona. Given Atterbury's certainty that any definitive action would be delayed at least three years, pending the completion of the Paoli electrification, he "saw no objection to telling the General Electric people we would give them the opportunity of bidding on it."[18]

Irrespective of the sincerity of Atterbury's offer, several factors conspired to delay and then prevent the electrification of the tracks over the Alleghenies. James T. Wallis, the general superintendent of motive power, provided a cost estimate in March 1913, suggesting that the project might generate a return on investment that exceeded 32 percent. Four months later, Gibbs found fault with those figures and added $1.1 million to the initial expense, while increasing estimated annual charges by nearly $129,000. Even with those modifications, Rea looked favorably on a $10 million budget that promised a 20 percent return. He nonetheless urged Atterbury to adopt a wait-and-see approach to

electrification technology. Rea observed that neither the side-rod locomotives used at Penn Station nor the ones that the NYC employed at Grand Central Terminal would be suitable. "As to the question of electric locomotives," Rea concluded, "there is a great deal to be learned about them." General manager Simon Cameron Long had similar misgivings, and he reminded Atterbury that "both the General Electric and the Westinghouse Companies are working on schemes that are changing the situation quite rapidly and it is possible that six months from now they would recommend apparatus altogether different from that which they would recommend today." No one had yet decided whether alternating or direct current would be preferable, and there seemed little reason to rush that decision. "My thought, therefore," Rea concluded, "is that in case 1914 proves to be a prosperous year, we should organize for a thorough study and get up working plans for the work contemplated in this report."[19]

Neither Rea nor anyone else in the world fully anticipated the changes that would take place in 1914. With Europe plunged into war, traffic levels increased and congestion became intolerable—although that situation had more to do with backlogs at East Coast ports than with the PRR's inability to move trains between Pittsburgh and Altoona. In February 1915, Atterbury once again prodded Rea to take action. The Paoli electrification was nearing completion—service would begin seven months later—and that project conclusively demonstrated the superiority of high-voltage alternating current. With that question resolved, Atterbury recommended that Gibbs & Hill develop detailed cost estimates for the route between Altoona and Johnstown and suggested that the PRR's Motive Power Department should "design an electric locomotive, at least in sufficient detail to know the cost of one suitable to permit a train at present handled by four steam locomotives being handled by two electric locomotives."[20]

Rea recommended waiting for the results of the Norfolk & Western's electrification project, also supervised by Gibbs & Hill. Or, as Rea informed shareholders, "the Company prefers to obtain the benefit of the experience of other lines in the use of electric traction for heavy freight trains and to see a further expansion of its own revenues before procuring the new capital required for this important project." By the summer of 1915, Atterbury was losing patience, and he reminded Rea that the N&W system had been in operation for several months and was working well. The twenty-seven-mile section between Bluefield and Vivian employed 11,000-volt alternating current flowing through the catenary—essentially identical to the Paoli electrification—but easily accommodated much heavier trains that

Representatives from the PRR's Motive Power Department often sought to match wheel arrangements for steam and electric locomotives, to create designs with similar performance characteristics. At the top is "Big Liz," the sole representative of Class FF1, completed in 1917, paired with the equally rare HC1s, an experimental 2-8-8-0 articulated built in 1919. Big Liz went to the scrapyard in 1940, but its steam locomotive counterpart had an even shorter career of just ten years. *Pennsylvania Railroad Negative Collection, Hagley Museum & Library, acc. 1993.300.*

battled steep grades. In May, Atterbury secured a $40,000 appropriation to develop specifications for locomotives, power stations, and substations, based largely on the N&W example. The next step, he urged Rea, was to appropriate a further $150,000 to order two prototype passenger locomotives. Loyalty to on-line shippers was of paramount importance, and despite the promises Atterbury made to GE officials a few years earlier, the contract would go to Westinghouse. The result of Atterbury's persistence was a single locomotive, with construction authorized in 1917. The sole example of Class FF1, widely known as "Big Liz," was nearly eighty feet long and tipped the scales at 240 tons. It was the world's most powerful electric locomotive, rated at 4,800 horsepower and sufficient to pull long trains

over the mountainous route between Altoona and East Conemaugh. For the moment, however, it could operate only along the tracks between Philadelphia and Paoli. The more pressing imperatives associated with World War I also curtailed Atterbury's plans. In December, barely eight months after the experimental unit entered service, the United States Railroad Administration assumed control of the national network, retarding further expenditures on electrification.[21]

Little progress occurred during the war years. Atterbury was in Europe, supervising transportation matters there, and could no longer serve as an advocate for electrification. Rea was not prepared to invest additional funds in the electrification of the line over the Alleghenies, particularly given his suspicions that "instead of costing $10,000,000. it is more likely to cost $20,000,000. before we are through."[22] Those fears were not misplaced, given the shortages of labor and materials as well as the inflation associated with World War I. "The going prices were entirely out of joint," Wallis observed. In September 1918, and for the sake of simplicity, the PRR's general superintendent of motive power relied on prewar prices and suggested that the mountain electrification would cost $15 million. A more realistic estimate, he concluded, would be $30 million—triple Atterbury's initial projections and half again as much as Rea's more pessimistic calculations—and would take three or four years to complete.

"The expenditure of such a sum now is out of the question, of course," Wallis admitted.[23]

Given the cost and uncertainties associated with electric operation, PRR executives chose to rely on traditional steam power. Wallis emphasized that the PRR could acquire fifty-five Mallet helper locomotives for a mere $2,750,000, with the concomitant reduction in borrowing costs negating the economic advantages of electrification. Officials in the Motive Power Department had already considered but rejected the widespread use of articulated locomotives. By the end of the 1920s, however, the PRR had acquired a new generation of conventional steam locomotives, purchased in large quantities to accommodate the surge in wartime traffic. They included the 574 representatives of the Class L1s, constructed between 1914 and 1919, and a group of 123 Class I1s, built at Altoona from 1916 through 1919. More power arrived in the early 1920s, including 475 additional Class I1s (1922–1923) and 301 Class M1 and M1a locomotives (1923–1930).[24] The new locomotives provided sufficient power to boost longer, heavier trains over the mountain, thus reducing the number of train movements and alleviating much of the congestion. While electrification remained technologically feasible, the potential for a favorable return on investment decreased markedly.[25]

Advocacy for electrification did not disappear, however, particularly as the prosperity of the late 1920s gave executives plenty of money to spend. As the Pennsylvania Railroad recovered from the postwar recession, Rea expressed cautious support for yet another analysis of electrification. "I have been giving a good deal of thought to what we ought to do to increase our Net Earnings," he informed Atterbury in September 1921. "From the present outlook it does not appear that we will be called upon for important extensions in the near future, that is, in the form of new railroads," he conceded. Yet "the Pennsylvania Railroad Company proper has over $30,000,000. of capital money on deposit in the bank and only bringing 3% interest." Left unstated was the fear that such a surplus would attract the attention of regulatory agencies and make it more difficult for the PRR to increase or even maintain existing rates. The concomitant improvement reduction in transit times (as well as the elimination of smoke) associated with electrification would likewise suggest that PRR officials were committed to improved service and thus merited rate increases. Casting about for suitable investments, Rea suggested electrification between Altoona and Johnstown. Another possibility involved the routes radiating out of Pittsburgh, matching the growing suburban network in Philadelphia. In November 1923, a PRR press release indicated that Rea was still willing to consider the use of electric power in the Alleghenies. The following June, he announced even more ambitious long-term plans to electrify the heavily trafficked line between Pittsburgh and Philadelphia, followed by an extension north to New York and eventually from Philadelphia south to Washington. The estimated cost would be $60 million, double the amount of surplus capital that Rea was prepared to put to good use. As such, PRR officials observed that "the general railroad situation and the inadequacy of available funds make improbable the beginning of electrification work on a large scale in the near future."[26]

For the moment, Rea was only willing to provide funding for experimental motive power that would take advantage of innovations that had occurred since the completion of the FF1 in 1917. In 1924, the Juniata Shops built three Class L5 electric locomotives. The first of the series drew 11,000-volt alternating current from the catenary. It could operate on the electrified suburban territory around Philadelphia and serve as a test bed for electrification west of Altoona. The remaining locomotives collected 650-volt direct current from a third rail, restricting their use to the tunnels between New Jersey and Long Island. Yet all were capable of conversion to high-voltage alternating current, or even to dual DC/AC power, should additional electrified routes become available. Westinghouse, General Electric, and Brown Boveri each supplied electrical equipment for one of the three locomotives, enabling motive-power officials to select the most reliable technology. By 1928, an additional twenty-two Class L5 locomotives were in use. They did not meet expectations, however, and were ill-suited to long-distance operations. Even in New York, the older and more reliable DD1 locomotive lasted longer.[27]

By the time the first L5 locomotives entered service, Rea and Atterbury had shifted their focus. They were increasingly preoccupied with conditions between New York and Washington, an area that was considerably different from the route over the Alleghenies that had heretofore occupied so much of their attention. A steady parade of trains carried passengers, commuters, and freight along the Atlantic Seaboard, making the tracks between New York and Philadelphia the busiest on the PRR system. As early as 1913, three years after the opening of Penn Station, Gibbs & Hill suggested that it would cost $7.5 million to electrify the line between Manhattan Transfer and North Philadelphia, the location where many intercity passenger trains turned to the west. The estimate included $6.1 million from Manhattan Transfer to Bristol, Pennsylvania, with an additional $1.4 million for the section from Bristol to North Philadelphia—an amount included in the $10.3

million cost to electrify the suburban lines in Philadelphia. While the conversion of commuter service to electric power progressed incrementally—to Paoli in 1915 and to Chestnut Hill three years later—another decade would pass before intercity trains would begin to move under wire.[28]

During that decade, urban growth in the Northeast, coupled with changes that affected electric utilities, created conditions favorable to main line electrification. The traffic congestion that plagued the PRR during World War I was not the only threat to the nation's infrastructure. Increased industrial production taxed electrical-generating capacity, and only the armistice prevented a crisis similar to the one that had affected the railroads in 1917. At the same time, the efforts of the United States Railroad Administration to coordinate rail operations suggested the potential for an integrated approach to transportation and electric-power generation. The chief instigator was William S. Murray, a consulting engineer who had supervised the electrification of the New Haven. In December 1918, with the support of New Haven president Edward G. Buckland, Murray urged Secretary of the Interior Franklin K. Lane to fund a comprehensive survey of electric power

in a "superpower zone" that stretched from New England south to Washington. Murray took charge of the project, relying on an advisory board that included PRR vice president Elisha Lee and mining engineer Herbert Hoover, who was just beginning his second career as a public servant.[29] Murray completed his report in June 1921, following a year of effort. He predicted that by 1930, utilities in the superpower zone would require investments of $1.3 billion to generate the 31 billion kilowatt-hours that would be demanded by industries, municipalities, residences, and the railroads. Murray asserted that railroads could profitably electrify nineteen thousand of the thirty-six thousand track miles in the region, at a cost of $570 million, with a return on investment of 14.2 percent. Much of the savings could come from the more efficient allocation of railroad traffic, which would in turn require the same sort of coordination that USRA officials had advocated. "Under electric operation," Murray claimed, "the entire traffic between Philadelphia and Washington could readily be carried over the rails of the Pennsylvania system, those of the Baltimore & Ohio being left for future growth."[30] Murray accordingly highlighted the potential of the new technology to transcend competitive jealousies that might impede the efficient allocation of traffic. "Improvements in operation can be made more readily under electric service than under steam," he predicted, "for a change in the power system would bring fresh minds into the service and would consequently liberate the mental operations of the average railroad man from their conventional routine."[31]

Postwar advances in electric-power generation, generally concentrated in the industrialized Northeast, provided an additional impetus for the PRR to replace steam locomotives. By the early 1920s, rising demand for electric power, coupled with improved technologies, created impressive economies of scale that encouraged the construction of large generating stations and the formation of interconnected public-utility holding companies. Electrical engineers also developed reliable methods for transmitting power over long distances, ensuring that power plants could be located at a considerable distance from the urban areas that were the primary users of electricity. One suitable site was located along the Susquehanna River near Conowingo, Maryland, about five miles south of the Pennsylvania state line. The name was Susquehannock for "at the rapids," and it was a natural site for a dam.[32] In 1910, the Pennsylvania Water & Power Company built a dam and hydroelectric generating station just upriver, at Holtwood, Pennsylvania. The company's engineers also demonstrated the practicability of transmitting power as far as Baltimore. Within a few years, World War I greatly increased the demand for electricity, particularly in Philadelphia's booming manufacturing sector. A scarcity of skilled labor ensured that many factories could no longer maintain proprietary power plants, and they began to buy electricity from the commercial grid. Wartime coal shortages gave way to a postwar strike by the United Mine Workers, encouraging utility executives to look more favorably on hydroelectric power. Homeowners during the Roaring Twenties demanded refrigerators, radios, washers, and other electrical appliances. Finally, the PRR's newly upgraded commuter lines, coupled with the expansion of Thomas Mitten's Philadelphia Rapid Transit, ensured a steady demand for electricity.[33]

During 1922 and 1923, engineers working on behalf of the Philadelphia Electric Company conducted a series of feasibility studies at various locations near Conowingo. They concluded that a new hydroelectric facility would offer substantial cost savings, relative to aging coal-fired plants in Philadelphia. The project nonetheless confronted the same problem that bedeviled early efforts to establish canals and river improvements along the Susquehanna, in that construction in one state was bound to affect conditions in the other. The War Department's designation of the Susquehanna as a navigable river further complicated the situation. In the end, the intervention of two state utility commissions and a license from the Federal Power Commission enabled the project to go forward. Work commenced in March 1926 and proceeded with remarkable speed, with the first generators entering service almost exactly two years later.[34]

Even before it began producing electricity, the Conowingo Dam stimulated both immediate and long-term changes to the Pennsylvania Railroad. The dam's back-pool flooded a considerable portion of the Columbia & Port Deposit branch, necessitating the relocation of sixteen miles of track between Port Deposit, Maryland, and Fishing Creek, Pennsylvania. Contractors moved nearly 1.5 million cubic yards of earth and rock and dug three tunnels to raise the line to the 120-foot level, a dozen feet above the full-pool height of the reservoir. The line relocation complemented ongoing efforts to transform the Port Road from a rambling branch line to a major freight artery bypassing congestion in Philadelphia.[35]

Even as the enormous power output from the Conowingo facility increased the viability of widespread electrification, serious capacity problems remained along the route between New York and Wilmington, Delaware. By 1925, the tracks through Elizabeth and Trenton were clogged with traffic, creating serious delays. PRR officials anticipated that, by the end of the decade, an average mile of the New York Zone main line would accommodate 350 trains per day, compared to 38 on the Eastern Region, 25 for the PRR in its entirety, and 12 for the average Class I railroad. As PRR officials observed, "Experience indicates that with steam operation, the economic limit of the facilities ... has been reached on certain peak days." The problem was especially acute with high-value perishable traffic. The PRR carried 80 percent of the agricultural produce that moved from the South, through Washington, and on to the great cities of the Northeast. It was imperative that the railroad transport those shipments as expeditiously as possible, both to reduce spoilage and to beat back the growing threat of motor-carrier competition. Yet the extreme congestion made it impossible to do so without simultaneously raising the speed of the drag freights that carried low-value commodities along the route. Such a universal quickening of schedules would entail an enormous increase in operating costs and would be beyond the capabilities of the existing fleet of steam locomotives. Under the existing rate structure—in which low-value commodities cross-subsidized valuable and time-sensitive freight—there was little possibility that the PRR could recoup the investment necessary to expedite the movement of bulk shipments.[36]

Pennsylvania Railroad officials developed two plans for addressing the congestion issue between New York and Washington. One involved the construction of a freight-only relief line through New Jersey. The concept dated to the massive rebuilding agenda of Alexander Cassatt's presidency. In December 1905, the PRR chartered the Pennsylvania & Newark Railroad to build an extension of the 1892 Trenton Cutoff low-grade line that bypassed Philadelphia. The new route would stretch from Morrisville, Pennsylvania, cross the Delaware River, then parallel the existing main line, rejoining it in the vicinity of Newark.

By the time construction began in 1911, the plans had been modified and scaled back. The new route would extend from Morrisville only as far north as Colonia, New Jersey, midway between Newark and New Brunswick. From Colonia, two additional tracks would be added to the main line, to South Elizabeth. The fifth and sixth tracks entered service in 1915, about the time when work began on the Pennsylvania & Newark bridge across the Delaware River, a short distance downstream from Trenton. World War I halted that project, however, and neither the bridge nor the railroad were ever completed. The postwar plan to alleviate congestion envisioned a resurrection of the Pennsylvania & Newark, coupled with the installation of another track along the two- and three-track line from Wilmington, Delaware, to Washington. The estimated cost would be $20 million and would not require the adoption of electrification. The expansion of conventional facilities for trains hauled by steam locomotives would not reduce operating costs, however. As such, the project would fail to generate sufficient net income to offset the interest charges on the borrowed money and would thus ensure a negative return on investment.[37]

Electrification of the entire route between New York and Washington would require a much larger expenditure—$110 million—but it promised substantial reductions in operating costs. The resulting increase in net operating income would be sufficient to offset the interest charges on the borrowed funds as well as the increased taxes on the physical plant, while generating an annual surplus of $4 million. Powerful electric locomotives possessed the ability to increase the speed of drag freights from a mere fifteen miles per hour to twenty-eight or twenty-nine miles per hour—fast enough to match the operating requirements of trains carrying perishable freight. The operation of longer and heavier consists could reduce freight movements between New York and Philadelphia from one hundred to forty-four trains per day, and between Baltimore and Washington from forty-three trains to twenty-three. The operation of longer and faster trains offered a 25 percent increase in capacity, obviating the necessity of adding additional tracks. That was an important consideration, given the rising cost of real estate, particularly along the mothballed Colonia relief line. Electrification would also eliminate a major problem at one of the most important intermediate stops along the route. The necessity of changing between electric and steam power at Manhattan Transfer created an operating bottleneck that prevented many through trains from stopping at Newark. Absent full-scale electrification, that difficulty could only be solved by relocating the Newark passenger station and extending the existing DC electrification—and thus the change of motive power—from Manhattan Transfer to Newark.[38]

By 1925, the decision in favor of electrification became all but inevitable. The PRR released its latest study in January. Two months later, Vice President Elisha Lee informed reporters that the railroad was doing well financially. "We believe the general outlook is pretty good," he declared. "There is every indication that we will have an increasing business." In that context, he suggested that the entire route between New York and Washington would be electrified within fifteen or twenty years. Events moved more quickly than that. At the end of September, Rea retired as the PRR's president. Atterbury, his successor, had long supported electrification—both as a means of reducing operating costs and as an appealing cutting-edge technological innovation. In December, Gibbs & Hill signed a new contract with the PRR, "in connection with the railroad's plans to electrify certain suburban services out of Philadelphia, and possibly for certain through electrifications."[39]

The dual role of Gibbs & Hill as an advisor for both the Philadelphia Improvements and main line electrification had important implications for the development of both projects. The proposed station, at 30th and Market Streets, would cover a vast area above the tracks, as would the new post office that would be built just to the south of Market Street. The tracks and platforms serving intercity trains at 30th Street Station contained only small openings along the side facing the Schuylkill River. Unlike Union Station in Chicago—which had slots above the tracks—there was thus little possibility of eliminating smoke from steam locomotives. In January 1928, George Gibbs informed Lee, who was in overall command of the Philadelphia Improvements, of "a number of rather startling conclusions, especially regarding the great size of the proposed West Philadelphia Station building and the difficulty, if not impracticability, of operating steam locomotives under it." Gibbs observed that the station and the adjacent post office would cover more than one thousand feet of station trackage and platforms. "The conditions imposed are unprecedented," he emphasized. "The disturbing conclusion is reached that if we must use steam locomotives the station building itself should be moved to the side of the tracks and a train-shed be provided, as at Chicago, Washington and elsewhere. I assume this can hardly be even considered at West Philadelphia." To avoid asphyxiating its patrons, the PRR needed to either install large ventilation fans or position all trains so that their steam locomotives lay just beyond the edge of the station platforms. The situation at 30th Street suggested the value of continuous electrification from New York at least as far south as Philadelphia. The operating requirements associated with commuter traffic had already induced the board of directors to authorize the extension of electrification from Philadelphia south to Wilmington, Delaware, in January 1926. By process of elimination, Gibbs concluded, "electric traction under the station is indicated, either by cutting off road engines outside, or by electrification of the New York Division and electric operation to and from Wilmington and west to Paoli or Thorndale." As one PRR executive later recalled, the problems at 30th Street led to "the later determination of the Railroad Company, in conjunction with the Philadelphia Improvements, to electrify the Main Line from New York through Philadelphia to Washington."[40]

While electrification had demonstrated its potential on various segments of the PRR system, it was not clear that the railroad could successfully implement long-distance power transmission for main line freight and passenger trains. The technology was in its infancy, particularly with respect to the design of electric locomotives. Both the DD1 and the L5 classes relied on large electric motors, two per locomotive, driving the wheels through heavy jackshafts and side rods. Neither was suitable for intercity service, and the inadequacies of the L5 ensured that it would not be the universal freight and passenger locomotive that PRR officials had envisioned. In 1927, however, Westinghouse introduced a revolutionary new technology, in the form of a 600-volt, alternating-current, 650-horsepower electric motor. The design relied on brushes that made contact with a rotating commutator. Because the commutator motors were far smaller than their cousins—used to power the DD1 and L5 classes—they fit between the locomotive wheels, mounted to the axles. In addition to freeing considerable space in the body of the locomotive, the commutator motors offered reliable operation, high maximum speeds, and rapid acceleration. Thanks to the improved electrical-equipment technology, Atterbury asserted that the PRR's Motive Power Department, in concert with outside suppliers such as Westinghouse and General Electric, could soon develop new freight and passenger locomotives that would exploit the full potential of electrification. Based on that assumption, he supported electrification along the route between New York and Washington—at a cost initially estimated at not much more than $50 million.[41]

The simultaneous evolution of the commercial power grid provided another key element in Atterbury's electrification strategy. Philadelphia Electric's Conowingo hydroelectric facility could generate ample power, but there were other options as well. Thomas Mitten had for several years been engaged in protracted sparring with Philadelphia Electric, threatening to build a powerhouse for the Philadelphia Rapid Transit if he could not secure favorable rates. In February 1927, PRR officials began the same campaign of brinkmanship, announcing plans to construct a new generating plant in Trenton, New Jersey. While there was little likelihood of construction, the threat was sufficient to extract exceedingly favorable terms from Philadelphia Electric, and in July, the two companies signed a twenty-year contract. The following year, Philadelphia Electric, the Pennsylvania Power & Light Company, and the Public Service Electric & Gas Company of New Jersey connected their systems to the same commercial grid, providing reliable power supplies along the route between New York and Washington.[42]

By the spring of 1928, there was widespread speculation among industry insiders that the Pennsylvania Railroad was preparing for main line electrification between New York and Washington. At the end of March, PRR officials authorized the first issue of new stock since 1913. More than half of the $80 million would be used to finance existing debt, but observers suggested that much of the remainder would be used to string catenary south of New York. Two months later, the PRR board approved electrification of a portion of the Schuylkill Division, between Philadelphia and Phoenixville. Although that track was not part of the route between New York and Washington, it nonetheless indicated steady progress toward the replacement of steam locomotives in commuter service. By the end of September, electric commuter trains were in operation from Philadelphia south to Wilmington. The major commitment came on October 10, when Atterbury informed the board of directors of his plan to extend the catenary north to New York and south to Washington at an estimated cost of $110 million.[43]

On November 1, 1928, Atterbury made public the PRR's plans for the most extensive electrification project that any railroad had ever undertaken. He pledged to spend $100 million, at a rate of $15 million per year, to install catenary over 325 route miles encompassing more than 1,300 miles of track.[44] Between 250 and 300 new electric locomotives, costing as much as half a million dollars apiece, would also be needed. Construction would require fifty-five million pounds of copper, substantially more than the total annual copper production in the United States just half a century earlier. The first phase would cover the route from Philadelphia north to Trenton, with completion expected as early as 1930. Construction would then proceed in stages, from Newark south to New Brunswick, then closing the gap between New Brunswick and Trenton. The replacement of the 650-volt DC third rail with catenary would permit electric operation through the Hudson and East River tunnels as far as Hell Gate Bridge. The main line west in the direction of Harrisburg would be electrified as far as Atglen and a connection with the Atglen & Susquehanna low-grade freight line. Attention would then shift west to the operations between Altoona and Pittsburgh. Eventually, Atterbury predicted, every mile of the vast Pennsylvania Railroad system might feature electric power.[45]

The breathtaking scope of the electrification project offered an equally impressive list of potential benefits. Atterbury announced that electrification would allow the railroad to cut the number of freight trains in half, thus doubling the capacity of existing facilities. Double-headed steam locomotives, each with a separate crew, would no longer be necessary in passenger service, and the operation of second sections of popular trains would likewise be unnecessary. The elimination of locomotive smoke was certain to please both travelers and trackside residents. The anticipated 20–30 percent increase in the speed of trains carrying perishable freight was also an important consideration, as rapid improvements in highways and trucks were already giving motor carriers a significant edge over the railroads in the transportation of produce.[46]

The PRR's electrification plans produced a generally—although not universally—positive response. Not to be outdone by his longtime rival, Reading president Agnew T. Dice quickly announced a $20 million electrification program covering nearly fifty route miles in Philadelphia's suburbs.[47] Shares in the United Gas Improvement Company, the holding company that controlled Philadelphia Electric, rose by 5¾ points, while prices for Public Service Corporation of New Jersey stock also increased.[48] With the railroad's initial power demands estimated at 100,000 kilowatts—projected to rise to 250,000 kilowatts within a decade—the confidence was hardly misplaced. General Electric and Westinghouse also gained ground, well before the PRR began soliciting bids for new electric locomotives. Newspapers, trade publications, and financial journals, including *Railway Age*, *Electrical World*, the *Commercial & Financial Chronicle*, and the *New York Times*, all praised Atterbury's progressive management and his commitment to improved service. The only dissenting voice came, as might be expected, from a representative of the National Coal Association, who envisioned a future without steam locomotives.[49]

Traffic levels decreased substantially to the south of Philadelphia, but there were nonetheless compelling reasons to consider electrification from Wilmington all the way to Washington. Civic leaders and government officials in the nation's capital were continuing their campaign against locomotive smoke, and any promise that electrification was pending would likely end their protests. Many of the produce trains that Atterbury had mentioned originated at Potomac Yard in northern Virginia, and it made sense to use electric locomotives to pull the cars all the way north to Greater New York. The general speedup of passenger schedules would also increase the PRR's competitive edge against the Baltimore & Ohio's service, particularly between Baltimore and Washington.

Improvements in the city that hosted the B&O's headquarters also influenced the PRR's decision to extend catenary south of Wilmington. During the early years of the twentieth century, Baltimore's substandard facilities incurred the ire of the city's residents. Travelers walked across multiple tracks, dodging freight and passenger trains. Chastised, Pennsylvania Railroad officials soon solicited bids for a new station. In 1909, architect Kenneth MacKenzie Murchison Jr. submitted the winning proposal. Murchison had established a reputation as one of the nation's experts in station design and had recently completed work on the Delaware, Lackawanna & Western's Hoboken Terminal.[50] In Baltimore, he adopted the Beaux Arts style, with an exterior sheathed in pink Milford granite, creating a building that in some respects resembled a miniaturized version of Penn Station in New York. Because rail yards and postal and commissary tracks surrounded the site, Murchison had little choice other than to design a severely rectangular building, 60 feet wide and 275 feet long. The new facility opened in 1911, yet many critics considered it inadequate for Baltimore's needs.[51]

The Charm City and the Quaker City had long been rivals, and by the late 1920s, the PRR's expenditures on the Philadelphia Improvements encouraged Baltimoreans to demand similar investments. In 1928, Mayor William F. Broening encouraged Pennsylvania Railroad executives to cooperate with the B&O and to provide a true union station for the people of Baltimore. PRR personnel refused and drove the point home by changing the name of their proprietary facility from Union Station to Pennsylvania Station. They likewise resisted efforts to erect a completely new structure that would serve all the city's railroads. Curmudgeonly local journalist H. L. Mencken quickly sided with the Pennsylvania Railroad. "A vast new railroad station, such as is being planned," he observed, "is not needed in Baltimore."[52] While Atterbury and Elisha Lee refused to expand the existing building, they nonetheless pledged millions of dollars for other improvements in Baltimore. In that context, the extension of electrification and other changes provided important political as well as operational benefits.[53]

In October 1929, following more than a year of negotiations, PRR executives promised Baltimore city leaders that they would spend $22 million over the next five years. In addition to improvements at Pennsylvania Station, the railroad agreed to replace the old Northern Central station at Calvert Street and to build adjacent freight houses. The most notable change involved the excavation of new double-track tunnels, paralleling the existing Baltimore & Potomac and Union bores. Once completed, the PRR would have a four-track main line through the city, one that could accommodate larger locomotives and cars as well as wider and higher loads. Atterbury also agreed to electrify tracks through the city, both to satisfy the environmental concerns of local residents and to facilitate the operation of trains through the tunnels.[54]

The PRR's commitment to the Baltimore Improvements made electrification to Washington a foregone conclusion. On February 17, 1931, Atterbury announced that he was both expanding and quickening the pace of the electrification project. Brushing aside concerns that the Depression and the growth of highway competition had reduced the PRR's traffic and revenues, he anticipated "the inevitable restoration of business activity" and suggested that "the existing low volume of business can only be temporary." Like President Hoover, Atterbury emphasized a positive, can-do attitude as a cure for the economic malaise—"The Pennsylvania Railroad considers that now is the time to express its confidence in acts," he suggested— but the ready availability of labor and materials probably had more to do with the decision. "Now is the time to go forward with redoubled energy," Atterbury emphasized, citing "an exceptionally favorable time to push to conclusion the plans in hand." He now promised to spend $175 million, and to complete the work in two and a half years, eighteen months sooner than originally planned. The money would fund the completion of electrification from Sunnyside Yard on Long Island south to Potomac Yard in Alexandria, Virginia, as well as the remaining portions of the Philadelphia Improvements (including 30th Street Station) and the Baltimore Improvements that he had announced four months earlier. Newark, New Jersey, would receive a new passenger station, a lift bridge over the Passaic River, and other betterments. In Elizabeth,

the main line would be widened to six tracks, while a new freight bypass line and bridge over the Delaware River would speed traffic through Trenton. Three months later, and in keeping with Atterbury's twin promises of "confidence" and "redoubled energy," the board of directors authorized the expenditure of more than $25 million to complete main line electrification between New York and Washington. At the beginning of December, Atterbury estimated that the New York–Wilmington phase of electrification would be completed by the summer of 1932.[55]

The PRR's ambitious project guaranteed a demand for electricity and stimulated the construction of another dam and hydroelectric plant along the Susquehanna River. The Pennsylvania Water & Power Company and Consolidated Gas of Baltimore, each controlled by utility magnate John E. Aldred, jointly owned the Safe Harbor Water Power Corporation. In the spring of 1930, the company began construction at its namesake location, midway between Columbia, Pennsylvania, and the Maryland state line. Like the more southerly Conowingo Dam, the project required the PRR to relocate some ten miles of the Columbia & Port Deposit to higher ground. Of greater significance, in October 1931, the PRR signed a twenty-year contract with the three Aldred companies. The facility entered service in December 1931, several months ahead of schedule, and thereafter supplied most of the PRR's power needs.[56]

New methods of long-distance power transmission accompanied the increase in generating capacity. Two decades had elapsed since the New Haven had pioneered the use of high-voltage AC traction, ample time to prove the dependability of the technology. In most respects, the methods were identical to those employed in the electrification of the Philadelphia suburban lines. The PRR retained the 25-hertz frequency that had become the de facto standard for the New Haven and other railroads, but that was at variance with the 60 hertz employed by public utilities.[57] The most significant change was an increase in the transmission current from the 44,000 volts initially used at Philadelphia to 132,000 volts, necessary to prevent voltage drop over such long distances. Because utilities had not yet established an interconnected commercial power grid, those transmission lines followed the PRR right-of-way for the entire distance between New York and Washington.[58]

Proven technology notwithstanding, installation was no simple task, however. Construction crews were always mindful of the steady parade of trains and were careful to minimize disruptions to traffic. After surveyors had evaluated the right-of-way, workers used a purpose-built

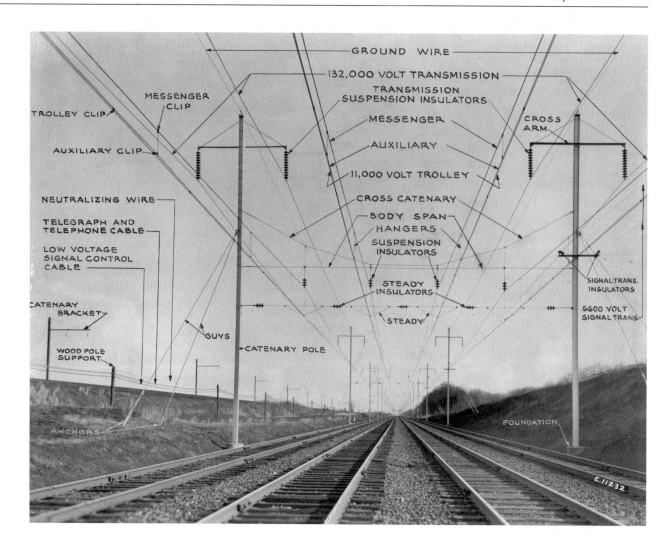

The Pennsylvania Railroad annotated this photograph, taken near Whitford, Pennsylvania, to show the extraordinary complexity of catenary construction. Notable are the 132,000-volt long-distance transmission lines leading to substations, where the power will be stepped down to 11,000 volts for the trolley lines that make contact with locomotive pantographs. *Pennsylvania Railroad Negative Collection, Hagley Museum & Library, acc. 1993.300.*

concrete train to pour footings for the catenary poles. They then erected the catenary towers, typically at 270-foot intervals, and with closer spacing on curves.[59] The towers, built from heavy H-section steel beams, varied in height from 70 feet to 110 feet. The tallest towers supported the 132,000-volt transmission lines that carried power from the generating stations to substations, located between eight and ten miles apart, that stepped the current down to 11,000 volts. A considerable portion of the fifty-five million tons of copper that the project would require went into

the fabrication of the catenary, including the span wires that crossed above the tracks, the messenger wires that carried the 11,000-volt current, and the trolley wire that made contact with the pantographs of electric locomotives. Yard and station tracks required an even more complex web of wires. The most difficult sections were the tunnels under the Hudson and East Rivers, where a hundred PRR employees removed more than twenty thousand cubic yards of ballast, to lower the rails sufficiently to permit the catenary installation. Elsewhere, crews raised bridges, eliminated grade crossings, and replaced semaphores with position-light signals and cab signaling equipment.[60]

Given the specialized nature of the electrification project, the Pennsylvania Railroad relied heavily on outside contractors. Gibbs & Hill was a natural choice, considering George Gibbs's quarter century of association with the Pennsylvania Railroad. The scope of the project necessitated reliance on many other companies, many of which possessed economic or political ties to the Pennsylvania Railroad. The Arundel Corporation of Baltimore had overseen the construction of the Conowingo Dam, and the company's chairman, Frank A. Furst, was also a director of the subsidiary Northern Central Railway. Perhaps the most controversial contracts—more than $3.5 million in the second half of 1931 alone—went to the Vare Construction Company of Philadelphia. The firm, also known as Vare Brothers, dated to the 1890s. One of its founders, George, died young, but Edwin and his younger brother William enjoyed great success, thanks in large measure to their connections to city government. The two surviving Vare brothers became ward bosses and by World War I had established a political machine that rivaled Tammany Hall in New York. Edwin's death in 1922 had left Bill Vare as the undisputed head of Philadelphia politics. Like Vare, Atterbury was both a strong opponent of Prohibition and a major force in Pennsylvania's Republican Party. They had little else in common, but Atterbury tolerated Vare for the same reason that Alexander Cassatt had worked with Tammany Hall—machine politicians may have been corrupt, but at least they could open a path through municipal bureaucracy and ensure that things got done. Under the circumstances, the electrification contracts the PRR awarded to Vare Construction represented a wise investment. In general, however, Atterbury supported the other, probusiness wing of the Republican Party, centered in Pittsburgh and represented by Treasury secretary and former PRR director Andrew W. Mellon and Joseph R. Grundy, the president of the Philadelphia Manufacturers' Association. While Mellon was a reliable ally of the Pennsylvania Railroad, Grundy was a staunch supporter of Prohibition and thus implacably opposed to Atterbury's efforts to repeal the Eighteenth Amendment. When Vare won election to the US Senate in 1926, Grundy supported efforts by outgoing governor Gifford Pinchot to withhold the certification of the results. The effort was successful, and the Senate seat remained vacant for more than two years before the new governor, John S. Fisher, appointed Grundy to an office that Vare believed was rightfully his.[61]

The events of the 1920s set the stage for a battle over power—both electrical and political—that complicated the Pennsylvania Railroad's efforts to place wires over its tracks. In the spring of 1930, just as the PRR's electrification campaign was getting underway, Gifford Pinchot announced that he was seeking another term as governor. Pinchot styled himself as a populist, suspicious of both the corporate boardroom and the ethnicity and presumed iniquity of urban life. He was always one to relish a fight, and in 1930, he had three adversaries—alcohol, utilities, and William Vare. The Philadelphia boss enjoyed undisputed

pride of place atop Pinchot's list of enemies, and his gubernatorial bid was to a considerable degree fueled by fears that Vare was rebuilding his political career. Atterbury, a probusiness wet who colluded with both Vare and with utility moguls, was only slightly less likely to draw Pinchot's ire.[62]

In the 1930 Republican gubernatorial primary, Pinchot faced the full wrath of the Vare machine and its chosen candidate, Francis Shunk Brown. Brown was the grandson of Francis Rawn Shunk, the governor who had reluctantly presided over the chartering of the Pennsylvania Railroad in April 1846. Given the close ties between Vare and the Pennsylvania Railroad, Brown also received the support of Atterbury, PRR director Richard B. Mellon, and other members of the Mellon family. Like Atterbury, Brown was opposed to Prohibition, although he refused to say so publicly. That put him at a disadvantage against a third Republican contender, Thomas Wharton Phillips Jr., an oil-industry executive and former congressman who called for the resumption of alcohol sales.[63] Pinchot campaigned openly as a dry, yet his unwillingness to vigorously enforce Prohibition during his first term in office gave him an appeal on both sides of the issue.[64]

The most disruptive influence, however, came from Joseph Grundy, the Republican who had taken Vare's Senate seat in the aftermath of the disputed 1926 election. Grundy now sought to be elected to the Senate in his own right, and he was ready to attack the Vare forces, their candidate for governor, and anyone who supported them. He accused Atterbury of using his role as a Republican Party committeeman to orchestrate a "conspiracy" by "the Philadelphia gang and the Pennsylvania Railroad" to "grab control of the State Government and the public treasury, dictate the personnel and policy of the Public Service Commission and dominate all the important relationships of this great State with the Federal Government." Grundy announced that this had happened before, when Tom Scott and other so-called robber barons had dominated Pennsylvania politics. "No railroad executive since that time," he suggested, "until W. W. Atterbury, President of the Pennsylvania Railroad, has dared even to attempt to bring the railroads of the country back into the political affairs of the States or the nation." The people had regained control of their state only after a long and bitter struggle, Grundy declared, and the maverick politician promised that he would lead a similar rescue effort. Grundy asserted that Atterbury and "the Pennsylvania Railroad-Philadelphia gang combination" were launching a three-pronged assault on the integrity of Pennsylvania politics—by supporting

Brown for governor, by backing Labor Secretary James J. Davis for the US Senate, and by acquiescing to Herbert Hoover's tariff policies.[65]

Grundy was his own worst enemy, and his histrionics constituted no more than a minor annoyance to Atterbury and the Pennsylvania Railroad. In 1911, Boies Penrose, the ward boss who had preceded the Vare machine, observed that his friend Grundy was "the best money-raiser and the worst politician since Julius Caesar." It was an apt assessment. In a stunning display of political ineptitude, Grundy managed to alienate his original backers and ensure Davis's election to the Senate. His accusations, which filled five columns in the newspaper and implicated everyone from the president of the United States to the president of the Pennsylvania Railroad, suggested more conspiracy theory than conspiracy. Asked to substantiate his allegations about Atterbury's manipulation of the political process, Grundy's insistence that "I do not have to prove that statement. Everybody knows it" constituted an exceptionally low evidentiary standard. For the moment Atterbury remained silent, but representatives from the Vare machine rushed to his defense—not to protect him so much as to hobble Grundy. Such support must have come as a relief to the PRR president, given that in 1928 he had broken with the Vare forces by opposing Hoover's bid for the Republican presidential nomination.[66]

Gifford Pinchot nonetheless perceived considerable value in a campaign of indiscriminate mudslinging. He emulated Grundy's rhetoric, suggesting that the supporters of the Vare organization "represent the very worst in politics" and "that these men would move into the Capitol at Harrisburg and raid the State as they have raided Philadelphia." He accused Atterbury of instructing PRR employees to vote for Brown in the primary and sent the railroad's president a telegram, demanding that he "cease interfering with their right as free American citizens to vote as they believe." While Grundy suggested that Atterbury was endeavoring to gain control of the state legislature and the state treasury, Pinchot accused him of dominating the judicial branch by orchestrating the appointment of justices on the Pennsylvania Supreme Court and on the US District Court for the Eastern District of Pennsylvania. Atterbury's principal goal, Pinchot alleged, was to manipulate the state's Public Service Commission, working in tandem with the Vare interests and the utility corporations. As an alternative, Pinchot pledged to abolish the PSC, replacing it with what he called a "Fair Rate Board." Those "Fair Rates" meant equal rates for all, without scale-induced reductions for large customers—something that concerned Atterbury, as he was preparing

to buy power off the commercial grid for the PRR's widespread electrification program.[67]

The May 20 Republican primary was as chaotic as the election campaign that preceded it. Partisans of the Vare machine announced that they were willing to sacrifice Davis, if that was what it took to ensure that Brown became the gubernatorial candidate. The reverse happened, with Davis trouncing Grundy and winning the Republican Senate nomination—giving credence to rumors that Atterbury would eventually resign from the PRR to undertake his own bid for a Senate seat. Thanks largely to the division of the wet vote between Brown and Phillips, Pinchot became the Republican candidate for governor, although by a much narrower margin.[68]

Atterbury showed little party loyalty in the general election, at least where Pinchot was concerned. His allies—including the Vare machine in Philadelphia and the Mellon interests in Allegheny County—ensured that state treasurer Edward Martin bested the candidate backed by Pinchot and Grundy for a seat on the Republican State Committee. The move only exacerbated Pinchot's accusations that the PRR president was attempting to gain control of the state treasury. Francis Shunk Brown, Atterbury's failed hope for governor, was still in the mix as well. At issue were some sixty thousand disputed ballots in Luzerne County, in the anthracite fields where Pinchot had long enjoyed strong support. Brown filed suit to have the ballots invalidated, and Pinchot concluded that the PRR forces were involved. "The attempt of certain public utilities and gang politicians under the leadership of Atterbury to steal the Governorship is too raw to be tolerated," he warned. "Such an assault on popular government cannot and must not win." Pinchot vowed that if Brown's court challenge succeeded, he would run as an independent, a move that would split the Republican vote and virtually ensure the election of Democratic nominee John M. Hemphill. In October, a thoroughly disgusted Atterbury resigned his chairmanship of the state's delegation to the Republican National Committee and was willing to support Hemphill, for the simple reason that Hemphill was not Pinchot. The Mellon family similarly abandoned Pinchot, as did PRR vice president Edward T. Whiter and a coalition of Pittsburgh business leaders.[69]

Pinchot, who had managed to alienate a large portion of his party, reiterated his allegations that "Atterbury has been using the employes of the Pennsylvania railroad [sic] on time paid for with money of the Pennsylvanian [sic] Railroad at the expense and to the serious cost of the stockholders of the road." No longer content to charge Atterbury and other PRR executives with voter intimidation, Pinchot listed a slew of other complaints. They included the PRR's exemption from taxation in Philadelphia, its refusal to pay $9 million in back taxes to the commonwealth, the willingness of executives to invest millions in port facilities in Greater New York while leaving Philadelphia's docks to stagnate, and the negotiation of cost-plus contracts to fund electrification and other projects with the Vare Brothers construction firm. Threading a careful path between Atterbury and the PRR's employees, whose votes might well determine the outcome of the campaign, Pinchot emphasized that "the Pennsylvania Railroad is one of the greatest economic institutions of America," a company that "has earned the respect and confidence of millions." The actions of its president, in contrast, "will result within a year either in serious loss in prestige and business for the Pennsylvania Railroad," Pinchot predicted, "or in the elimination of Atterbury as President." He was wildly inaccurate on both counts, and the PRR's directors acted quickly to defend their company and its leader. The board's official statement, released a week before the general election, mentioned neither Atterbury nor Pinchot but firmly refuted the "reckless and repeated" accusations that placed the Pennsylvania Railroad in a "false and unjust light."[70]

Pinchot's political instincts proved excellent, and on November 4, 1930, he won a second term as governor. While the attacks on Atterbury certainly helped his cause, he was more likely the beneficiary of the changing political alignments that characterized the first major election since the collapse of the stock market. Pinchot's margin of victory was small, but he felt sufficiently confident to continue his campaign against the Pennsylvania Railroad and the Public Service Commission. Within weeks of taking office in January 1931, Pinchot arranged for the state senate to launch an investigation and to issue subpoenas to Atterbury, Public Service commissioner James S. Benn, and Philadelphia mayor Harry A. Mackey. All were political adversaries of Pinchot. When Atterbury testified on February 24, he faced a barrage of questions from the governor's attorney, William A. Gray, most of which resurrected Pinchot's accusations during the previous year's campaign. Atterbury either denied the allegations or said that he had no recollection of the events in question. Pinchot characterized his adversary as "a perfect imitation of a railroad president ignorant of the essential business affairs of his own road" and predicted that the Pennsylvania House would soon launch a parallel investigation. While the Senate hearings soon stalled, Pinchot was more successful in the other legislative chamber. Urged on by the governor, House members developed a damning portrayal of links between Atterbury the railroad executive,

Atterbury the Republican committeeman, the Vare interests, the municipal government of Philadelphia, and the Public Service Commission. The assertion by the *New York Times* that the "Pennsylvania capital has gone into the investigating business" was not too far off the mark, nor was the suggestion that "Harrisburg faces a 'legislative circus.'"[71]

Atterbury scored a significant political victory—or at least benefited from exceptionally good timing—thanks to the appeal of the PRR's electrification program. On February 17, a week before he was scheduled to testify before the Pennsylvania Senate, he announced that the company would spend $175 million to push the project forward with all possible speed. There was no mention of links to Vare Brothers, whose contractors would do much of the work; to the Philadelphia political machine that bore their name; to the large utilities that would provide power; or to the members of the Public Service Commission who would exercise a measure of regulatory oversight. With thousands of jobs in the offing and with the economic situation getting worse by the day, no one much cared about Pinchot's conspiracy theories that linked together all those entities. By the end of May, much to Atterbury's relief, the state senate had rejected a House bill that would have given the governor the authority to replace members of the Public Service Commission.[72]

Pinchot's attacks on the PSC and the utilities continued, but with scant results. In the end, the governor could score no more than a symbolic victory against his political adversaries. When the Commonwealth of Pennsylvania began issuing automobile license plates in 1906, they were numbered sequentially on a first-come, first-served basis. It was indicative of Atterbury's wealth and his interest in highway transportation that he acquired both the fifth and fifty-fifth registrations. With considerable pettiness, in November 1931, Pinchot revoked the coveted one- and two-digit automobile license plates held by his foes. For whatever reason, he permitted William Vare and members of the Mellon family to retain their low numbers. Atterbury suffered more than anyone, losing tag No. 5 to highway secretary Samuel S. Lewis and tag No. 55 to Morris Gregg, a stenographer in the governor's office.[73]

The PRR and the RFC

The Great Depression presented both a crisis and an opportunity for the Pennsylvania Railroad. Nowhere was that more evident than in the project to electrify the route between New York and Washington. During his failed 1930 bid for the US Senate, Joseph Grundy stoked fears that

Atterbury and other Pennsylvania Railroad executives were controlling state government, just as Tom Scott had allegedly done half a century earlier. The political landscape had changed greatly in the intervening fifty years, however. The locus of political power shifted from Harrisburg and other state capitals to Washington, DC. Through the 1920s, Washington remained a sleepy southern town, stirring to life only when Congress was in session, and even the brief flurry of activity during World War I had done little to change its character. Behind the scenes, however, the authority of the Interstate Commerce Commission, growing reliance on national labor agreements, and the increased involvement of the president in railroad matters suggested that PRR executives would be wise to pay attention to the individuals and the institutions that inhabited the capital district. The federal government also possessed access to vast amounts of money, an important consideration at a time when the railroads found it increasingly difficult to secure badly needed investment capital.

The Depression strengthened the influence of the national government, while increasing the willingness of private companies to rely on public funds. That trend was apparent even before Franklin Delano Roosevelt launched the New Deal. His predecessor, Herbert Hoover, did more than any president before him to involve the federal government in the economy. His principal goals were, of course, to restore economic prosperity and to put Americans back to work. That agenda meshed well with Atterbury's desire to complete the PRR's vast electrification project. While he never abandoned his opposition to increased governmental involvement in the affairs of private corporations—a process he asserted would inevitably lead to Bolshevism—he was willing to take the government's money. In borrowing funds from the Reconstruction Finance Corporation, and later the Public Works Administration, Atterbury downplayed the benefits the Pennsylvania Railroad received from the public sector. Instead, he insisted—with great sincerity—that he was doing his part to help the nation recover from the Depression. While that effort dovetailed with the goals of Hoover and Roosevelt, Atterbury was never willing to accept the government as an equal partner. Atterbury also possessed a powerful lever that he could use to shape public policy to suit the PRR's interests. With unemployment levels rising and industrial production at a standstill, electrification could create thousands of jobs and help to reenergize the national economy. What followed was a protracted and intertwined negotiation between the Pennsylvania Railroad and the federal government, one that involved railroad rates, wages, working conditions, federal loans, and managerial compensation.

In June 1931, the railroads petitioned the ICC for an emergency 15 percent across-the-board increase in freight tariffs—a necessary condition, they asserted, for safeguarding the banking and financial sectors, preventing further layoffs, and maintaining the uninterrupted service vital to economic recovery.[74] Spokesmen for investment banks and insurance companies quickly endorsed the proposal. Shipper representatives, in contrast, demanded that the railroads impose all possible economies and that organized labor accept a substantial pay cut before any rate increase could be considered. Coal and oil producers also claimed that increased rates would prove disastrous for their industries and further imperil the health of the economy. Lumber dealers suggested that higher tariffs would bring the construction of new homes nearly to a standstill. While congressmen from the Northeast were generally sympathetic to the railroads' plight, their counterparts representing agricultural interests in the South and West were determined to hold the line on railroad rates. Senator Smith W. Brookhart (Rep., Iowa) accused his House colleague James M. Beck (Rep., Pennsylvania) of serving as "the Pennsylvania Railroad's own little Congressman," in that capacity attempting to "intimidate" the ICC into increasing rates. Beck retaliated by excoriating the agency for its plodding consideration of the rate application, asserting that regulators were progressively pulling the federal government toward "the philosophy of Moscow."[75]

PRR officials anxiously awaited the outcome of Ex Parte 103 (also known as the *Fifteen Percent Rate* case). As public hearings continued through the summer of 1931, ICC officials maintained secrecy and gave no indication of their inclinations. On September 23, rumors that the agency would grant a substantial increase, although perhaps not the full 15 percent, caused railroad stocks to rally in the Wall Street financial markets. They experienced the largest one-day gain in price in more than twenty years, with the aggregate value of PRR shares rising by more than $50 million. By early October, members of Congress were confident that the ICC's decision was forthcoming and that the railroads would receive about half of what they had requested. On Wall Street, railroad share prices again rose, as investors expressed their hopeful anticipation. Many observers suggested that the fate of the entire economy would depend on the actions of the Interstate Commerce Commission, in what the *New York Times* labeled "the most far-reaching and the most important decision it has ever been called on to make."[76]

The ICC's ruling, rendered on October 16 and made public four days later, was a bitter disappointment to the carriers and to Pennsylvania Railroad executives. Four months after the railroads first requested higher rates, and after collecting 11,719 pages of testimony, ICC officials concluded that a 15 percent increase was unwarranted. While acknowledging the precipitous decline in the value of railroad securities since the stock market crash, regulators asserted that a substantial rate hike would place too great a burden on commerce and on a fragile economy. As a remedy, the ICC offered a 3.5 percent change, less than a quarter of what the railroads had originally requested. PRR officials estimated that the new rates would generate $12.2 million in additional revenue between January 1932 and April 1933, when the increase was set to expire. That was far less than they had hoped to receive, and there was no guarantee that they would even be able to keep the money. The ICC required that the additional revenue be pooled among the carriers, creating an emergency relief fund to support companies that could not meet their interest payments and ensuring that the PRR and other strong railroads would subsidize their weaker competitors.[77]

Many railroad officials were furious at the ICC's terms, even to the point of advocating a rejection of the agency's offer. Two days after the commissioners released their ruling, the Association of Railway Executives held its customary autumn convention in Atlantic City. Although the ARE's Law Committee suggested that the pooling plan was probably illegal, Atterbury and the other members of a committee specially convened to discuss the matter gave their cautious assent. They nonetheless sought several alterations to the revenue-pooling program and were particularly determined to change the intercorporate transfers from outright gifts to loans. While the executives were wary of antagonizing the ICC, their principal concern lay with the operating brotherhoods. They had resolved to seek a substantial pay cut from the unions, and rejection of the ICC's offer would make that process difficult if not impossible.[78]

During the ensuing negotiations between the railroads and the ICC, President Hoover suggested that the National Credit Corporation might be able to manage the railroads' revenue pool. Introduced to the public on October 13, 1931, a week before the ICC released its ruling in Ex Parte 103, the NCC was part of Hoover's voluntarist agenda for forestalling the growing banking panic, and it enabled banks in distress to borrow from their healthier brethren. The agency proved unworkable, thanks to rules that required borrowing banks to pledge prohibitively high levels of assets as collateral for loans. Railroad executives accordingly demanded a separate corporation, which they nonetheless agreed should be managed by the banking sector. The ICC accepted both that stipulation and the

reclassification of payments from the revenue pool as loans and not gifts—paralleling the procedures of the NCC. In December, the carriers established the Railroad Credit Corporation, headed by Edward G. Buckland, the chairman of the board of the New York, New Haven & Hartford. Atterbury did his best to appear optimistic about the new revenue pool. Speaking to the Chamber of Commerce and the Traffic and Transportation Club in Birmingham, Alabama, he acknowledged that the RCC, whose coffers were expected to hold between $100 million and $125 million in revenues, would keep many carriers from the ignominy of bankruptcy.[79]

Deteriorating economic conditions soon illustrated the limits of Hoover's privately managed voluntarist approach and encouraged the president to seek more direct public intervention. A sharp downturn in the bond markets in late 1931 overtaxed the resources of both the National Credit Corporation and the Railroad Credit Corporation and persuaded Hoover to develop a more robust alternative. In January 1932, Congress approved the creation of the Reconstruction Finance Corporation. The RFC was a government agency, not a private corporation, and it possessed a war chest of $2 billion for emergency loans. Officials in the Hoover administration initially envisioned the RFC as a mechanism to reduce instability in the banking sector. Yet the agency could not achieve that goal without also assisting the railroads. During the 1920s, reductions in the quantities of US Treasury bonds in circulation had caused banks and insurance companies to increase their holdings of railroad securities.[80] With those assets in jeopardy, so too were the banks that owned them. As such, the RFC possessed the authority to make loans to railroads and to bolster the value of their securities issues, thus protecting banks from collapse. RFC officials initially envisioned that only the weakest of the carriers would apply for loans. To no one's surprise, the first significant request came from the bankrupt Wabash Railway, a company closely tied to the Pennsylvania Railroad. The PRR was as strong as the Wabash was weak, but Atterbury quickly perceived the RFC's importance to his company—not as a source of rescue but rather to secure financing at below-market interest rates. It was an important consideration, given that the PRR was experiencing difficulties in finding the money necessary to pay for main line electrification.[81]

Paying for Electrification

The PRR's electrification program, in tandem with other improvements, promised to consume a substantial amount of capital. During the ten years of Atterbury's presidency, the railroad increased its investment in physical plant and equipment by more than $300 million.[82] When coupled with the additional $193 million spent to establish control over various railroads, in response to the ICC's efforts to develop a consolidation plan, it was clear that the company's liabilities would increase sharply. That meant nearly $160 million in new stock and the sale of nearly $50 million in new bonds. The first stock offering occurred in April 1928, well before the crash, when investors had few reservations about paying $50 for shares with a market value of $70. A second issue, in December of the following year, was fortuitously timed. The full magnitude of the economic crisis was not yet apparent, and despite recent reversals, PRR stock was still selling above $80 a share. The economy showed signs of improvement during the early months of 1930, but further stock offerings were not advisable. Instead, the PRR released $60 million in forty-year bonds bearing a 4½ percent interest rate. Conditions being what they were, they were offered at 94½, a steep discount by PRR standards. Another $50 million bond issue came in March 1931, this time for 4¼ percent, fifty-year instruments, discounted at 96½. While the proceeds went to a variety of purposes, much of the money was available to fund the $175 million in betterments that Atterbury announced in February 1931.[83]

The accelerated timetable that Atterbury promised on February 17 required a similarly rapid infusion of capital. During the autumn of 1931, PRR officials met informally with representatives from the investment-banking community, and the results were not encouraging. The conversations confirmed their suspicions that the bankers lacked both the desire and the financial resources necessary to purchase another, proposed, $60 million PRR bond offering. Insurance companies and pension funds, which had traditionally acquired substantial quantities of PRR securities, were likewise too cash-strapped to buy more. The Pennsylvania Railroad possessed the authority to sell additional stock but was legally required to price the offering at par value or higher. With 1932 prices ranging from a low of 6½ to a high of 23⅜, it was unlikely that any investor would pay $50 a share for the company's stock. The PRR did own $106 million (at par value) of stock in the Wabash and the Lehigh Valley, acquired during the 1920s. That was almost precisely the estimated $110 million cost necessary to complete the electrification project.[84] That stock could not be sold for anywhere near par value, however, and it had long since stopped paying dividends into the PRR's treasury. The only remaining source of funds—short-term bank loans with high interest rates—constituted an undesirable option at best. Electrification between New York

and Washington by the summer of 1932 was no longer a realistic possibility. The new target date—sometime in 1933—was dependent on the availability of additional investment capital. By the spring of 1932, the PRR had already spent $26 million on the project, with an additional $34 million under contract. Executives could find only $13 million more. After that, all work would have to stop.[85]

With private-capital markets in disarray, the federal government offered the only remaining source of funds. On February 4, 1932, just two days after the Reconstruction Finance Corporation commenced operations, Atterbury announced that the PRR would soon submit a loan application to underwrite the cost of the electrification project. "The extent of the loan has not yet been definitely determined," Atterbury admitted, but he suggested that "a rough guess would be about $5,000,000 a month" for an indeterminate period.[86] Given that the PRR would be spending more than $100 million on the project—the maximum amount that any one company could borrow under RFC rules—that period might be quite long. Atterbury emphasized that the loans would enable the PRR to hire ten thousand workers, with independent utility companies and other ancillary suppliers boosting employment by another five or ten thousand. In addition to stressing the benefits to cities along the Atlantic Seaboard and to the national economy, Atterbury asserted that, absent RFC funds, all further electrification work would cease. In that event, he emphasized, thousands of workers would lose their jobs.[87]

It took little more than a month for PRR officials to prepare a proposal for submission to the Reconstruction Finance Corporation. On March 10, 1932, the company applied for a three-year loan of $55 million, secured by $68.3 million of stock of the Pittsburgh, Fort Wayne & Chicago and the Pittsburgh, Cincinnati, Chicago & St. Louis subsidiaries. The PRR would provide an additional $13.2 million, with the resulting $68.2 million representing the proposed expenditures for the remainder of 1932.[88] The bulk of that amount—$47 million—would go toward the New York–Washington electrification. By the time of the RFC application, the electrification of the line between New York and Wilmington was largely complete, and in practice, most of the funds would be allocated to the tracks between Wilmington and Washington. Most of the rest was slated for terminal improvements in Philadelphia ($9.8 million), Newark ($2 million), and Baltimore ($1.5 million). The remainder would be put to other uses, including the redemption of soon-to-mature security issues.[89]

Only weeks into the RFC's existence, Hoover administration officials debated the precise nature of the RFC's obligations to the railroads. Atterbury's proposal represented a significant expansion of the scope and the purpose of the Reconstruction Finance Corporation. The $55 million sought by the PRR represented nearly 3 percent of the RFC's total funding authorization. The request was more than the $47 million that the RFC had at that time approved for all the other railroads in the United States and nearly a quarter of the $235 million that the federal government had thus far spent on the program. The PRR was clearly not in danger of financial collapse, and the company's bonds, although affected by the Depression, were still widely regarded as sound investments. In that sense, the completion of the electrification effort was unlikely to provide any appreciable assistance to the nation's troubled banks. Some skeptics, such as Senator Brookhart, suggested that federal support for capital improvements would lead to the competitive overbuilding that had contributed to the railroads' current difficulties—thus making the credit crisis worse rather than better. The promised reduction in unemployment, while of obvious benefit to the country, was not initially central to the RFC's mandate. Undecided, Hoover invited representatives from the railroads, the Reconstruction Finance Corporation, the ICC, the Commerce Department, and the Railway Credit Corporation to a series of confidential conferences at the White House. The RFC's president, Charles G. Dawes, favored the maximum possible assistance to the railroads, while the agency's chairman, Eugene Meyer, demanded that banks holding railroad securities should bear at least an equal share of any loan. Meyer also suggested that Atterbury was unwilling to back his loan request with corporate funds. In volunteering to privately finance only $13.2 million of the proposed 1932 expenditure of $68.2 million, Atterbury was asking the RFC to provide more than 80 percent of the cost. That was far beyond the 50/50 split that represented the maximum that Meyer was prepared to countenance.[90]

Frustrated with the delay, on March 18, Atterbury made what he described as a brief "courtesy" call on the president. The informality of the visit was questionable, as he returned to the White House half an hour later, accompanied by senior executives from a dozen other companies—all of whom happened to be in Washington for a meeting of the Association of Railway Executives. The railroad managers were as divided as RFC officials regarding the responsibilities of the banks, but they all agreed that the availability of loans should not be jeopardized by disagreements among RFC board members. When he emerged from the White House an hour later, Atterbury was not a happy man. A reporter described his

countenance as "glum" and observed that "he shook his head, almost violently, when asked to tell what had taken place." Atterbury's demeanor was either unduly pessimistic or, far more likely, a clever theatrical performance designed to arouse fears that a parsimonious RFC might jeopardize the national economy. With that implicit threat hanging over them, RFC officials soon came to a consensus. They agreed to support the loan request, while offering a vague suggestion that banks could do more to assist the railroads—a compromise that one participant called "about two-thirds Dawes and one-third Meyer."[91]

To overcome any lingering opposition to federal support for electrification, Atterbury began an intense lobbying effort to persuade RFC officials to redirect the course of their agency. On the same evening as the meeting at the White House, PRR electrical engineer John Van Buren Duer gave reporters attending a meeting of the New York Railroad Club an update on the company's progress. As if on cue, pioneering electrical engineer Frank J. Sprague joined the conversation, asserting that "at this time of great economic depression, General W. W. Atterbury, president of the Pennsylvania Railroad, deserves the support of the entire country for his vision and courage in carrying out the electrification." Atterbury also received praise from Frederick E. Williamson, the newly installed president of the New York Central, who anticipated that RFC loans might offset some of the $118 million cost of the West Side Improvements in Manhattan. The B&O's Daniel Willard—whose railroad really was in financial trouble—was equally enthusiastic in testimony before the Senate Banking and Currency Committee.[92] The near-universal support from railroad executives, even those whose companies were in competition with the PRR, produced the desired effect. Quite quickly, the RFC broadened its goals from bank stabilization to increased employment and economic growth, portending many of the core components of Franklin Delano Roosevelt's New Deal.[93]

Not everyone was so enthusiastic about the RFC's willingness to loan money to the railroads with few questions asked. Two individuals proved to be particularly cautious. One was ICC commissioner Joseph Eastman, an individual who for some time had been suspicious of Atterbury's motives and activities. The Transportation Act of 1920 had given the Interstate Commerce Commission enormous authority over railroad finance, with the ability to approve or disallow security issues and loans—including those granted by the RFC.[94] Eastman was generally willing to vote yes, but he had deep—and legitimate—concerns that many railroads were using federal funds to refinance existing loans and bonds rather than undertaking new projects that would stimulate employment. Such financial legerdemain might have been necessary to stave off bankruptcy, Eastman acknowledged, but suggested that the RFC was subsidizing wealthy bankers rather than assisting the unemployed.[95]

The Missouri Pacific Railroad, teetering on the edge of bankruptcy, aroused Eastman's suspicions regarding the intended purpose of RFC loans. The MP was one of several railroads controlled by the Alleghany Corporation, a holding company established by the Van Sweringen brothers. The stock market crash had shattered their creatively financed real estate and railroad empire, and by early 1932, the Vans were frantically arranging stopgap measures to stay afloat. Missouri Pacific officials requested more than $23 million in RFC loans to keep the company solvent through the remainder of the year. On February 15, the Reconstruction Finance Corporation granted an emergency loan—its first ever to a railroad—for $1.5 million, barely sufficient to allow the MP to pay interest obligations that came due that month. Six weeks later, it was the ICC's responsibility to evaluate a much larger RFC loan, for $12.8 million, to the Missouri Pacific. Nearly half of that amount would go to a banking syndicate, headed by J. P. Morgan, which held a large block of MP securities. Days after the RFC received the PRR's loan application, Eastman and his fellow commissioners "with some reluctance" validated the Missouri Pacific financing. "No good reason has been shown for approving a government loan" to the MP, Eastman emphasized, but he acknowledged that Congress, in creating the RFC, had given the Interstate Commerce Commission "a responsibility which we cannot thus escape."[96]

James J. Couzens, the chairman of the Senate Committee on Interstate and Foreign Commerce, echoed Eastman's concerns, although with greater stridency and political clout. A Michigan Republican who had earned a fortune through his early association with Henry Ford, Couzens was an outspoken critic of both the banks and the railroads. He was intimately involved in debates regarding railroad labor, railroad consolidation, and holding companies, so it was perhaps inevitable that he should play a role in the issue of RFC loans as well. As early as December 1931, Couzens had supported a congressional investigation into the railroads' financial difficulties. As Congress debated the provisions of the legislation that would ultimately create the Reconstruction Finance Corporation—and to the astonishment of many of his fellow legislators—Couzens suggested that it would not be appropriate to include the railroads in the bill.[97] Without additional regulatory oversight, he suggested, the RFC would likely provide

assistance that was politically expedient but financially unwise. The inevitable result, Couzens warned, would be federal ownership and a situation in which "the government will at least find itself in possession of the least desirable and least profitable railroads."[98]

Even though he considered the PRR and the New York Central to be the only two carriers that were both desirable and profitable, Couzens was particularly vocal in his criticism of their RFC loan applications. One issue was that the PRR in particular had maintained close ties with the investment-banking community. Such connections were necessary, particularly as the company launched its massive New York–Washington electrification program, but to Couzens, they suggested that both the railroad and the purveyors of capital were profiting at the expense of the people. "We have the Pennsylvania Railroad applying for $55,000,000 from the Federal Government," Couzens observed, "in spite of the fact that bankers all through the normal years have made great profits in financing these railroads." Couzens was also displeased that the RFC had received a request for an $18.5 million loan from the bankrupt Wabash Railway, "which the Pennsylvania Railroad controls, and yet they have in no sense come forward to help their weak subsidiary."[99]

Couzens was incorrect in his assertion that the Wabash was a subsidiary of the PRR. He nonetheless tapped into widespread resentment regarding Atterbury's willingness to leave to its own devices a company he had so eagerly sought only a few years earlier. On April 1, Couzens introduced a bill that would terminate the RFC's authority over railroad loans, leaving such matters solely to the discretion of Eastman and the other ICC commissioners. Couzens emphasized that railroads should use loan funds solely to initiate new investments in the physical plant and equipment—and not to redeem security issues, to pay operating expenses, or to fund existing projects. As such, the Couzens bill would preclude public support for the PRR's New York–Washington electrification. Couzens was soon distracted by other matters, including proposals to raise the income tax, investigate bear raids on Wall Street, and empower the ICC to regulate holding companies. His bill came to naught, the RFC and the ICC retained joint control over loan applications, and that threat to the PRR's request for federal funds disappeared.[100]

Some members of the investment-banking community also expressed concerns about the PRR's loan application, although for different reasons than Meyer, Eastman, and Couzens. At the Pennsylvania Railroad's annual meeting, held on April 12, shareholders asked if the Reconstruction Finance Corporation would require the company to suspend dividends as a condition of federal aid. Atterbury replied, truthfully, that there was no such stipulation associated with the RFC application process. As a practical matter, however, the request for $55 million had already subjected the PRR's dividend policies and executive compensation to an unprecedented level of public scrutiny. A year earlier, the directors had authorized a 6½ percent dividend that drained the corporate treasury of $36.2 million, including the expenditure of $16 million in cash reserves. In the spring of 1932, however, it would have been fiscally irresponsible and politically suicidal to award such a large dividend, particularly one that was financed in part from accumulated savings rather than current earnings. On April 27, barely two weeks after Atterbury's reassurances at the annual meeting, the directors voted to suspend the PRR's quarterly dividend payment for the first time in the company's history.[101] The railroad's stock declined only one point as a result, to 12⅜, a quarter of par value. The PRR did manage to scrape together a 1 percent dividend for the year, but that was hardly sufficient to attract private investment to the railroad.[102]

Through the month of April, PRR officials placed increased pressure on the Hoover administration to support the Reconstruction Finance Corporation loan. On April 7, Vice President Albert County wrote to the RFC's Eugene Meyer, emphasizing the importance of the electrification project and the jobs that it would generate. "Unless funds from the Reconstruction Finance Corporation can be obtained," he warned the agency's chairman, "the entire improvement program will have to be halted." Nine days later, County sent a similar letter to the ICC. "The days are going by," he noted, reminding the commissioners that any further delays might force the PRR to postpone or cancel construction contracts. County suggested that "a word from you as to the next definite step would be very reassuring," but neither the letter nor a follow-up telegram, sent three days later, elicited a response.[103]

The federal government made the next move. In early May, RFC and ICC officials approached Atterbury, asking whether he might cut in half the PRR's original $55 million loan request. The board of directors discussed the issue on May 5 and again on May 11. It authorized the issuance of $27.5 million in additional bonds that would be necessary to make up the railroad's expanded share of the electrification project but left the acceptance of the RFC's terms to Atterbury's discretion. He assented and on May 12 refiled the loan application. As with the previous request, the PRR pledged the securities of the Fort Wayne and the Pan Handle as collateral and offered to provide $13.2 million in corporate funds. ICC officials indicated that they were not the least bit surprised that the PRR had been able to generate an additional $27.5 million so quickly, and they stressed that the new request represented a near-complete reversal of Atterbury's prior claims of corporate poverty. Most observers considered the PRR's capitulation to be a stunning victory for both the ICC and the RFC, in that the two agencies had held fast to their demand that private-sector bankers should equally match the government's contribution. The PRR also won a significant concession from the RFC, however, becoming only the second company (after the New York Central) to secure a loan for new construction rather than for debt relief.[104]

RFC and ICC officials suggested that they would formally approve the request, with the entire $27.5 million to be made available on October 1.[105] They nonetheless demanded that the PRR increase the security of its collateral by substituting bonds from the company's Philadelphia, Baltimore & Washington subsidiary in place of some of the Pan Handle and Fort Wayne stock.[106] One PRR executive complained that neither the RFC nor the ICC had demanded such stringent guarantees from any of the other railroads that had applied for federal assistance, but there was little that Atterbury could do but comply. With that final change, the RFC approved the $27.5 million, three-year loan carrying a 6 percent interest rate. President Hoover was delighted and contrasted the Pennsylvania Railroad project with such "non-producing" expenditures as a House bill to appropriate $132 million for highways. "The financing of 'income-producing works' by the Reconstruction Corporation," Hoover emphasized, "is an investment operation, requires no congressional appropriation, does not unbalance the budget, is not a drain upon the treasury, does not involve the direct issue of Government bonds, does not involve added burdens upon the taxpayer, either now or in the future."[107]

Investment bankers were still reluctant to lend money, however, and the PRR experienced difficulties in borrowing the matching $27.5 million. At the May 25 board meeting, Atterbury informed the directors of the problem. The following day, the PRR filed what amounted to a fourth version of a loan application, asking the RFC to provide an exemption from the private-capital requirement.[108] Owing to the capital shortage, the PRR also sought a large initial RFC payment (of $8 million) on June 1, four months earlier than previously agreed, with the entire amount made available by October 1. Atterbury also pushed back against the RFC's demand that he pledge Philadelphia, Baltimore & Washington bonds as collateral for the loan. That provision had never been popular with PRR officials, but it had now aroused concern from executives on other carriers who feared that it would set an uncomfortable precedent for their upcoming loan negotiations. In place of the PB&W securities, Atterbury proposed to substitute $11.7 million in the less valuable bonds of the New York Bay Railroad, along with $2.5 million in additional Pan Handle stock.[109]

The newest iteration of the PRR's loan application posed a significant challenge to the authority of both the Reconstruction Finance Corporation and the Interstate Commerce Commission. Atterbury had abandoned all pretense of compliance with the unwritten rule that made the federal government and Wall Street equal partners in the provision of financial relief to the railroads. PRR executives increased the stakes by again vowing to suspend work on electrification and terminal improvements in the Northeast, laying off thousands of workers in the process. Federal officials had faced that threat before, but this time there were indications that Atterbury was in earnest. Several of the individuals involved in the negotiations, speaking off the record, suggested that the earlier "enthusiasm" of PRR managers had vanished and that they had "lost interest" in the project. The reduced traffic levels associated with the Great Depression had resolved most of the capacity issues along the route between New York and Washington and had correspondingly altered the cost-benefit ratio associated with electrification. There was considerable doubt, in other words, that the PRR could earn a return on its investment that would be sufficient to service the 6 percent RFC loan.[110]

Federal officials took Atterbury's threat seriously. Herbert Hoover feared that the cancellation of the PRR's electrification project might cause at least fifteen thousand, perhaps as many as twenty-five thousand, people to be added to the unemployment rolls during a presidential election year. Both the president and Treasury Secretary Ogden L. Mills informed ICC officials that they were strongly in favor of the PRR's proposal. On May 28, the Interstate Commerce Commission gave its blessing, assenting to all the conditions the PRR had stipulated. In the process, the Reconstruction Finance Corporation moved decisively from the stabilization of the banking sector through the maintenance of securities values to the goal of reducing unemployment and stimulating industrial output.[111]

The RFC's new commitment to the maintenance of employment led to a second, far smaller loan to the Pennsylvania Railroad. During the spring of 1932, as the RFC and the ICC were considering the PRR's application for the electrification project, a group of civic officials from Rochester, New York, met with Treasury Secretary Mills. Determined to revive their city's steel output,

they recommended that the RFC issue loans to pay for repairs to more than eight thousand steam locomotives and nearly a quarter of a million freight cars that were out of service nationwide. The proposal received the enthusiastic support of the car builders. They sponsored the National Equipment Credit Corporation as a mechanism to channel federal funds, first to the carriers and ultimately to themselves. Mills turned the matter over to Robert P. Lamont, the secretary of commerce, who met with Atterbury and other railroad executives. Some managers saw no reason why their companies should take on additional debt to return unneeded cars to service as part of a government make-work program. Most, however, accepted the economic and political value of providing as many as a hundred thousand new jobs. They accordingly recommended that the RFC expand the scope of its authority by granting loans for equipment repair. President Hoover included the proposal in his nine-point plan to stimulate the economy, announced on July 29. When he emphasized the importance of "programs of increased repair and maintenance in cooperation with the agencies of the government for the purpose of expanding railway employment," Hoover was moving the RFC far beyond its original mandate to save the nation's banks. He was also using the carriers to promote a national goal that—while laudable—was not necessarily in the best interest of the Pennsylvania Railroad.[112]

In early August, the PRR became the first railroad in the United States to apply for one of the RFC's equipment loans, to build more than one thousand steel freight cars.[113] Company officials estimated that the project would provide work for seven hundred PRR shopworkers for six months or more, along with an equal number of jobs at the mills that would supply the necessary steel. The railroad had scant need for the new equipment, and it would be difficult to apply a traditional return-on-investment calculation to justify the expenditure. "The purpose of this loan," Atterbury acknowledged, "is to increase employment and stimulate business" rather than to improve the PRR's earning potential. In return for his public-spiritedness, Atterbury expected that the RFC would provide funds at 5 percent interest, a point below the rate on the $27.5 million electrification loan. Within little more than a month, both the RFC and the ICC had approved the $2 million loan, at the lower interest rate. By early November, PRR shop forces at Altoona, Pitcairn, and Enola were busy assembling the new cars.[114]

It would be the last loan the Pennsylvania Railroad would receive from the Reconstruction Finance Corporation. Shopworkers had barely finished the new boxcars and work on the electrification project was far from complete when the company began to repay the government, far ahead of schedule. Atterbury's decision to distance the PRR from the RFC had little to do with a sudden availability of private financing or with an aversion to government assistance. Instead, the PRR's about-face reflected Atterbury's unwillingness to permit federal involvement in managerial prerogatives.

Executive Pay, Revisited

The Reconstruction Finance Corporation loans to railroads and other private corporations sparked a renewed debate regarding executive salaries. Such criticisms echoed those that had accompanied the economic depression of the 1870s and the reform initiatives of the Progressive Era. At such times, labor leaders, sympathetic journalists, and some politicians questioned why a small number of executives were living well, while a far larger number of workers and ordinary Americans were struggling to get by. Wide disparities in pay were unacceptable, they argued, because blue-collar employees spent as much time on the job as did managers, often enduring working conditions that were far more difficult and dangerous. In that context, it was inconceivable that the president of the Pennsylvania Railroad, who spent ten hours a day sitting at a desk or riding in a private car, should earn many times the wages of individuals who spent the same ten hours in the cab of a steam locomotive or walking across the tops of boxcars. Executives, in contrast, adopted an entrepreneurial perspective, insisting that their pay was modest compared to the value they added to the corporation. Moreover, they suggested, their compensation reflected a justifiable recognition of their years of hard work and dedication to the company. It was also evidence that they were the best of the best, having succeeded where less worthy colleagues had failed to pass muster.

Irrespective of those two largely irreconcilable attitudes toward executive compensation, there was little the government could do to address the issue. The investigations that followed the 1877 riots had produced only scattered anecdotal information regarding compensation levels. Not until 1921 did Congress compile the first systematic list of the pay awarded to railroad executives—and, even then, the voluntary nature of the reporting ensured that the data was incomplete. There was little public pressure for the railroads to reduce salaries and, more significantly, no legal mechanism whereby Congress could force them to do so.

The Great Depression aroused the ire of millions of American voters, many of whom believed that a plutocratic elite had caused the economic debacle. Legions of workers had lost both their jobs and the optimism that had characterized much of the 1920s. They increasingly questioned the propriety of government support for some of the nation's wealthiest corporations while so many ordinary Americans had lost homes, farms, small businesses, and the savings of a lifetime. Elected officials were attuned to those sentiments and could be expected to act accordingly. In July 1932, with the November election fast approaching, Herbert Hoover voluntarily reduced his salary by 20 percent, to $60,000 per year. Whether motivated by empathy or politics, that act found favor with many Americans. The eminent historian William E. Dodd suggested that "the President's example will have a good and widespread effect" and observed that George Washington had served in the Continental army without pay and Abraham Lincoln had likewise refused to accept luxurious furnishings for the White House while the divided nation suffered through the Civil War. "But as far as I know American history contains no parallel whatsoever of President Hoover's example today," Dodd concluded. Even though Pennsylvania Railroad executives had already taken a larger salary cut (25%), Hoover's altruism caused many individuals to suggest that they should do more.[115]

For the first time in the history of business-government relations, the Reconstruction Finance Corporation gave federal officials a weapon with which they could limit executive compensation. For many RFC and ICC personnel, careful scrutiny of salaries was part of a larger concern with the spending habits of companies that received support from the federal government. While the amounts involved constituted a small portion of total expenditures, an example such as a $50,000 paycheck provided journalists, politicians, and the electorate with an easily understood indicator of all that was wrong with corporate America. Such numbers also suggested profligacy on the part of the railroads and made it more difficult for the RFC to justify loans to the railroads. Some senior RFC officials, such as board member (and later chairman) Jesse H. Jones, a Texas banker and real estate developer, were also personally invested in the issue of managerial pay. While Jones appreciated the political value of waging war against alleged plutocrats, he also saw the issue in moral terms— that it was fundamentally unfair that so few people were so well compensated while so many others were destitute.[116]

Just as the RFC and the ICC worked together to grant railroad loans, the two agencies enjoyed a symbiotic relationship in the matter of executive compensation. While the Reconstruction Finance Corporation could not require railroad companies to change the salary awarded to any

As a shrewd negotiator and a political opportunist, Texas banker and real estate developer Jesse Jones parlayed a seat on the board of Herbert Hoover's Reconstruction Finance Corporation into the leadership of one of the most important agencies in the administration of Franklin Delano Roosevelt. Seen here in July 1939, he is answering questions from the Senate Banking and Currency Committee regarding below-market interest rates for RFC loans to railroads. *Harris & Ewing Collection, Library of Congress, Prints and Photographs Division.*

executive, the agency could demand reductions as a condition for a loan. However, it was the ICC, not the RFC, that possessed the legal authority to compel the railroads to make public their salary data. Fortunately for Jesse Jones, he enjoyed an ally in ICC commissioner Joseph Eastman. For Eastman, like Jones, lavish pay seemed morally indefensible. Moreover, Eastman stressed that high salaries constituted a readily identifiable indication of waste and inefficiency that could easily be eliminated. He was not sufficiently naive to assume that plucking the low-hanging fruit associated with the salaries of a small number of top executives would restore the railroads to prosperity. Even draconian reductions would at most save the carriers no more than a few million dollars annually. Instead, Eastman indicated that situations in which executives were simultaneously well paid and asking for government assistance reflected a more pervasive problem of mismanagement and misplaced financial priorities.

In April 1932, several factors caused Eastman and his fellow commissioners to increase their oversight of executive salaries. The RFC's loan to the Missouri Pacific, which Eastman had reluctantly endorsed, suggested that investment bankers were becoming the chief beneficiaries of government support. The Pennsylvania Railroad's request for a $55 million electrification loan also disturbed Eastman—in part because of its unprecedented size, in part because it was not matched by an equal share of private investment, and in part because it was for new construction rather than for the support of existing debt. In that month, and probably at Eastman's request, the ICC required all railroads applying for RFC funds to disclose the salaries of any executive earning more than $10,000 annually between December 1929 and March 1932. With federal employees (including members of Congress) facing the prospect of a 10 percent pay cut, it was unlikely that anyone outside the business community would offer any objections to the ICC's demands.[117]

The alliance between Jones and Eastman benefited from the inclusion of a third ally. Despite his business background and his party affiliation, Michigan Republican James Couzens also viewed highly paid executives with disdain. As a senator, he was in a powerful position to translate the recommendations of the RFC and the ICC into legislative action. The contentious Missouri Pacific loan had induced Couzens to write legislation to transfer authority for railroad loans from the RFC to the ICC, and he believed that Eastman could be entrusted with that oversight. While that effort came to naught, Couzens still maintained an alliance with Eastman, and the senator wanted to see the results of the ICC's salary survey.[118]

Eastman delivered the ICC's salary report to Senator Couzens in early July, and neither individual was particularly pleased at its contents. Nor was Senator Hugo Black (Dem., Alabama), who observed that the Southern Pacific's president, Angus McDonald, had received a $135,000 salary while his company had requested an RFC loan. Most railroads, including the PRR, had reduced executive salaries by 10 percent or more since 1929, but even then, the pay struck critics as excessive. President Atterbury held a financially gratifying but politically hazardous position near the top of the list. In more prosperous times, Atterbury had received $150,000 annually, and in 1932, he was still earning a respectable $121,500. However, Atterbury's 1932 pay incurred a 56 percent federal income tax, so he kept only $53,460 of his paycheck. That afforded him a purchasing power equivalent to $40,809 in 1913—when then-president Samuel Rea's posttax earnings had been $48,500.[119] Vice President Elisha Lee earned $52,650, down from $65,000 a few years earlier. Such salaries were perhaps appropriate for the managers of the nation's largest railroad, a company that would be a key component in any effort to rebuild the national economy. The *New York Times* headline emphasizing that the "P.R.R. Leads in Size of Presidents' Pay" was nonetheless unlikely to improve the company's image.[120] With the "B. & O. and the Missouri Pacific next on [the] railway list," readers were likely to compare those two carriers—whose earlier loan applications had already garnered strong criticism from RFC and ICC officials—to the Pennsylvania Railroad. Other headlines that appeared over the next few weeks, including "Rail Heads to Seek New Union Wage Cut to Offset Losses" and "College Youths on Cruise: Sons of W. W. Atterbury and Friends Reach Bermuda on Yacht," further damaged the PRR's reputation.[121]

The tenor of the PRR's April 11, 1933, annual meeting made it clear that Atterbury could expect no more sympathy from the railroad's investors than he had received from the general public. "Salaries are entirely too high," complained Colwyn, Pennsylvania, resident John J. Welsh. "The officers are getting it all and the stockholders are getting nothing." Welsh also complained that the high unemployment levels and resulting labor surplus associated with the Great Depression had not sufficiently reduced managerial pay. He noted that Atterbury and his subordinates were not the only ones capable of running the Pennsylvania Railroad. "You can get men who will do the same work, equally well or better, for considerably less," he advised.[122]

The PRR's annual meeting occurred soon after Franklin Delano Roosevelt's inauguration, and both the president and many members of a cooperative Congress believed they had secured a national mandate to attack highly paid business executives. In keeping with his political pragmatism, Roosevelt retained many individuals who had served in the previous administration. Hoover had appointed Jesse Jones to the RFC's board of directors, but Roosevelt made his fellow Democrat chairman of the agency. Shortly after his inauguration, Roosevelt casually remarked to Jones that he saw no reason why any railroad president should earn more than $25,000 a year.[123] Jones thought that suggestion too drastic, as he believed "that most men who have been accustomed to drawing $100,000 a year salary usually lived it up, and that to cut them to $25,000 would be too severe, particularly since everybody was in debt, regardless of his bracket." He instead proposed to Roosevelt a sliding pay scale, suggesting that managers earning between $10,000 and $15,000 per year should accept a 15 percent decrease. More highly paid personnel would face progressively more severe reductions, topping out at 60 percent for those earning $100,000 per year. No executive could earn more than $60,000, which happened to be the same amount as the president's salary, following Hoover's voluntary reduction in pay. Roosevelt, who generally regarded Jones as being too conservative, nonetheless "agreed that it was a good formula, and probably severe enough."[124]

Despite Roosevelt's support, Jones lacked any legal mechanism to force railroad executives to lower their salaries. Instead, he offered to reduce the interest rate on RFC loans from 6 percent to 5 percent if executives complied with the guidelines, effectively making them an offer they could not refuse. One obvious target was the Southern Pacific, which had filed an application for a $23.2 million RFC loan. Despite a series of salary reductions, the company's three most senior executives earned considerably more than the $60,000 that Jones had suggested as the upper limit for managerial compensation. In 1929, Hale Holden, the chairman of the Southern Pacific's Executive Committee, had been tied with Atterbury for the highest salary in the industry, at $150,000 per year. By July 1932, Holden's pay had fallen to $135,000, as the dissolution of the SP's Executive Committee placed him in the less demanding role of chairman of the company's board of directors. On May 1, 1933, his salary again declined, to $109,350. President McDonald at that time earned somewhat less, $90,000 annually, with Paul Shoup, the vice chairman of the board of directors, garnering $76,500. The RFC's first test case came on May 28, 1933, when with some trepidation Jones informed the Southern Pacific officials of their new suggested salaries. To

his surprise, they were delighted, doubtless because they had put credence in earlier rumors, spread by Roosevelt and Jones, that $25,000 might be the upper limit of their compensation.[125]

Less than two weeks after the Southern Pacific's executives capitulated, Congress gave the RFC some legal authority to regulate executive salaries. With Black's sponsorship, the discussion between Jones and Roosevelt became part of an amendment to the 1932 Reconstruction Finance Corporation Act. Section 3 of the new bill, which became law on June 10, 1933, barred the RFC from issuing loans "if at the time of such subscription, purchase, or loan, any officer, director, or employee of the applicant is receiving total compensation in a sum in excess of $17,500 per annum." That section of the act contained a further stipulation that rendered the salary clause essentially meaningless—"unless at such time the applicant agrees to the satisfaction of the [Reconstruction Finance] Corporation not to increase the compensation of any of its officers, directors, or employees." The more significant restriction appeared in the following section, which enjoined the RFC from making any loan if "any officer, director, or employee of the applicant is receiving compensation at a rate in excess of what appears reasonable to the Reconstruction Finance Corporation." The June 1933 amendment to the Reconstruction Finance Corporation Act did not give Jones the legal authority to compel railroad executives to reduce their compensation. He could of course deny outright any loan application from railroads with managerial salaries that were not "reasonable," but such practices would jeopardize the fiscal stimulus and the increased employment that by that time had become the major goals of the Reconstruction Finance Corporation. As such, and despite his earlier success with the Southern Pacific, he was reluctant to fully utilize the expanded power of the RFC over managerial salaries.[126]

To a greater extent than any railroad executive in the United States, Atterbury was willing to employ economic brinkmanship to resist Jones's efforts to curtail the pay awarded to executives. During the summer of 1933, Jones made his usual offer, to reduce the interest rate (from 6% to 5%) on the PRR's $27.5 million RFC loan—the money dedicated primarily to the electrification of the route between New York and Washington. As with other railroads, the agreement included a cap on executive compensation. With the full support of the board of directors, Atterbury refused to accept salary reductions or even to disclose officers' pay levels. Instead, in what many observers suggested was a fit of pique, he ordered repayment of the entire RFC loan.[127]

Atterbury's actions were not as precipitous as his critics insinuated, however. His decision to return the RFC loan was made easier by an all-too-brief economic upturn that began not long after Roosevelt's inauguration. Revenues increased during the summer of 1933, and one PRR executive noted, perhaps a little prematurely, that advance ticket sales suggested that the Fourth of July weekend would be "like old times."[128] In that context, the Pennsylvania Railroad had little difficulty in repaying the first $5 million of the RFC loan on June 30. Four days later, the railroad returned another $4.5 million, followed by $9 million on July 14. The RFC received the final installment, a check for $6.4 million, on July 28. With that, the PRR became the first large railroad to repay all its obligations to the Reconstruction Finance Corporation. Agency officials suggested that the PRR's actions signified economic recovery and emphasized their belief that private banks would soon be able to provide financing to the railroads without government involvement. Critics, however, insisted that the early repayment indicated that wealthy corporations did not need or deserve public support.[129]

Far from signaling a return to prosperity, the PRR's repayment of the RFC loan brought progress on the electrification project nearly to a halt, throwing thousands of people out of work. The outflow of $27.5 million in less than a month strained the railroad's finances and left the company in a dangerously cash-poor position. A gradual improvement in economic conditions during the summer of 1933 softened the blow, and the PRR added eleven thousand employees between June 1 and the beginning of October. Deserted construction sites and great piles of stored material nonetheless lent credence to rumors that Atterbury no longer thought electrification south of Wilmington to be a wise investment.[130]

The decision to repay the RFC loan did not prevent the completion of electrification, nor did it signify Atterbury's unwillingness to accept government assistance. To the contrary, the company continued its relationship with the federal treasury, albeit on more favorable terms. The first hundred days following Roosevelt's March 1933 inauguration witnessed a flurry of legislative activity, as a cooperative Congress enacted virtually every measure the president proposed. One of the most significant was the National Industrial Recovery Act, which became law on June 16. In addition to creating the National Recovery Administration—a largely unsuccessful effort to control wages, prices, and output levels—the new law established the Public Works Administration. Under the leadership of Secretary of the Interior Harold L. Ickes, Congress authorized the PWA to spend $6 billion ($3.3 billion in the first year alone) on a variety of large construction projects that would increase employment and stimulate the economy.[131]

As the PWA's deputy director, Henry M. Waite was responsible for evaluating the technical merits of most of the agency's funding proposals. Trained as a civil engineer, Waite began his career on a subsidiary of the New York Central, went to several other railroads, and then served as the city manager of Cincinnati. During World War I, he was a member of the Transportation Department of the American Expeditionary Forces, under the command of General Atterbury. Between 1927 and 1933, Waite oversaw building the new Cincinnati Union Terminal, a project that also put him into close contact with PRR officials. Waite wanted to assist the nearly prostrate steel industry, and, like his counterparts in the RFC, he saw the railroads as a useful mechanism to achieve that goal. He met with representatives from the Association of Railway Executives, encouraging the railroads to borrow from the PWA to purchase up to a million tons of steel rails. The American Car & Foundry Company and other car builders—also major consumers of steel—likewise pressured Waite to encourage the railroads to order new equipment. Some executives reiterated their prior complaints that they were reluctant "to become further indebted to the government," particularly when agencies such as the RFC had "too frequently invaded the field of managerial discretion." They generally preferred to maintain their long-established contacts with the steel industry rather than permit the federal government to act as an intermediary. Moreover, the NRA's Codes of Fair Competition triggered an increase in steel prices, thus undermining efforts by Waite and other PWA administrators to encourage the carriers to purchase additional rail.[132]

Atterbury was quick to exploit the Public Works Administration for the benefit of the Pennsylvania Railroad. On June 28, Atterbury informed the board of directors that the National Industrial Recovery Act was a likely source of funding for the electrification project. Twelve days had passed since Roosevelt signed the measure into law, and in another two days the PRR repaid the first portion of the RFC loan—and Atterbury's comments undoubtedly reassured the directors that replacement funds would soon be available. It was a reasonable expectation, as Waite considered the completion of electrification between Wilmington and Washington an excellent way to benefit the steel industry, increase employment, and promote economic growth. By the end of September, two months after Atterbury had finished repaying the Reconstruction Finance Corporation, PRR and PWA officials began negotiations. Ickes and Waite suggested to President Roosevelt

On January 3, 1934, representatives from the Pennsylvania Railroad and the Public Works Administration signed a $77 million loan agreement. The bulk of the money would enable the completion of electrification between New York and Washington, but there were also provisions for new locomotives and freight cars. The railroad received funds on exceedingly favorable terms, while federal officials touted the 46 million man-hours of employment the investment would create. Standing, from left, are Vice President Albert County; Benjamin V. Cohen, the associate general counsel of the PWA; the agency's assistant counsel, Henry J. Hart; and Frank C. Wright, the director of the Division of Transportation Loans at the PWA. Seated in front is Harold L. Ickes, who served simultaneously as the secretary of the interior and as the director of the PWA. *AP Photo.*

---

that the PRR would be a suitable candidate for a massive loan, larger even than the railroad's original proposal to the RFC. On November 2, 1933, PWA officials announced that they would devote $135 million to assist the railroad industry. Of that amount, $51 million would be for the purchase of new rails, something that primarily benefited the western carriers. The remainder, $84 million, would go to the Pennsylvania Railroad, enabling the completion of electrification. Just under $16 million would be devoted to building catenary towers and stringing copper wire. Tunnel improvements in Baltimore and Washington would cost another $4.6 million, and the rest of the loan would pay for locomotives and freight cars. Waite predicted that the funds would put as many as twenty thousand people back to work on the PRR and its suppliers.[133]

Waite and Atterbury soon renegotiated the PWA loan, but it remained a superb arrangement for the Pennsylvania Railroad. A reduction in the scope of the tunnel work in Baltimore and Washington saved $7 million, but $77 million was still a very large amount of money, equivalent to nearly a quarter of the railroad's annual revenues. The loan carried a 4 percent interest rate, two-thirds that of the 1932 RFC loan, with a one-year interest moratorium.[134] There was no specified deadline for repayment, other than a general understanding that the PWA would probably recoup its investment within fifteen years—five times the period demanded by the RFC and long enough for the PRR to begin earning a return on its investment. Railroad officials agreed to pay the unskilled workers engaged on the project at least $15 per week, and, wherever possible, to buy materials from companies that subscribed to the NRA's Codes of Fair Competition. The PRR would use the money to string catenary over 646 miles of track, completing the electrification between New York and Washington. The PWA loan would also pay for 101 electric locomotives and 7,000 freight cars, constituting the largest single purchase of railroad equipment ever undertaken by any American carrier.[135]

The Interstate Commerce Commission approved the financial arrangements on January 16, 1934, and as Roosevelt, Waite, and Ickes had hoped, the PRR soon began spending the proceeds of the PWA loan. As Atterbury emphasized, the importance of governmental assistance "in putting money into the pockets of working people and helping small tradesmen, business men and farmers as well as the industries may be readily visualized." Even if most of the money went to large corporations rather than small tradesmen and farmers, the loan produced the economic multiplier effect so often associated with infrastructure projects. By the end of January, for example, the Safe Harbor Water Power Corporation and the Pennsylvania Water & Power Company placed orders for $1.25 million in equipment to supply electricity to PRR catenary south of Wilmington.[136]

Many Americans nonetheless expressed their displeasure with federal assistance to large and occasionally mismanaged corporations—what a later generation might refer to as government bailouts for companies that were too big to fail. Those feelings certainly accounted for efforts by Jesse Jones and Joseph Eastman to restrict executive salaries. A more dispassionate analysis, however, suggested that the debate over salaries was incidental to the generally positive results associated with federal assistance to the railroads. The PRR received more money from the Reconstruction Finance Corporation than all but four other carriers.[137] The $29.5 million that the Pennsylvania Railroad borrowed, however briefly, from the RFC nonetheless represented less than 5 percent of the $638 million loaned to American railroads between 1932 and 1937.[138] By 1949, all but sixteen of those companies had repaid their loans in full. The RFC did not shift the cost of running the railroads to the taxpayers, and it certainly did not lose as much as a dime on the PRR loan. The much larger and longer-lasting loan from the Public Works Administration produced even better results for the federal government. The PWA transferred the bonds used to pay for the electrification project to the RFC, consolidating all railroad finance in that agency. In January 1936, the RFC sold $30.8 million of the PRR bonds to the prominent Wall Street investment-banking house of Halsey, Stuart & Company. The bankers paid a premium of 3.55 percent, netting the federal government a profit of nearly $1.1 million.[139]

To Washington, under Wire

Despite the economic and political challenges associated with the Great Depression, the Pennsylvania Railroad completed the world's largest electrification project with astonishing speed. By the end of June 1930, the wires were energized from Wilmington as far north as Trenton.[140] Within eighteen months, catenary had superseded the third rail from Sunnyside Yard on Long Island, underneath the East River, Penn Station, and the Hudson River, as far south as Manhattan Transfer.[141] Electric multiple-unit commuter service between Exchange Place in Jersey City and New Brunswick began on December 8, 1932.[142]

The subsequent infusion of resources first from the Reconstruction Finance Corporation and then from the Public Works Administration enabled work to continue, even as economic conditions worsened. On January 16, 1933, New York's mayor, John P. O'Brien, arrived at Penn Station at 8:20 in the morning and proceeded directly to a gate that was draped with American flags. Despite his exalted office, no one recognized him—until longtime station master William H. Egan, who was accustomed to meeting celebrities, arrived on the scene. O'Brien, Egan, PRR vice president George LeBoutillier, and a gaggle of reporters descended to one of the subterranean platforms, where a train was waiting. The mayor used a pair of scissors to cut a ribbon that rather ineffectually bound the locomotive's handrail to a nearby pillar. After the obligatory photographs, the party boarded the first train to travel between New York and Philadelphia, powered solely by electricity. It was not much of a party, which was perhaps appropriate for some of the darkest days of the Great Depression. Atterbury was not present for the ceremonies. Despite all that electrification had achieved, he had presided over the layoffs of sixty-seven thousand PRR employees and, eleven months earlier, had orchestrated a 10 percent pay cut for those who remained on the job. Atterbury's deputy, chief of motive power Fred Hankins, was already denying rumors that the PRR had embraced electrification as a way to further reduce the ranks of operating employees. There was in any case so little publicity that a group of commuters

Facing, Crewmen Pierce C. Stoopes, William Farrell, and Louis Peters prepare to depart Wilmington on September 29, 1928, with the first electrified train to Philadelphia. *Courtesy of the Special Collections Research Center, Temple University Libraries, Philadelphia, PA.*

had no idea why the mayor, the flags, the photographers, and a bugler from the Sixteenth United States Infantry had gathered on an adjacent platform. Manhattan office workers had taken electric propulsion for granted, as it had been in use on the Long Island Rail Road for a quarter of a century. They nonetheless knew a celebration when they saw one and cheered gamely as the train pulled out of the station, precisely on time at 9:00. For the next hour and fifty-seven minutes, the train sped southward, underneath the Hudson River, through Newark and Trenton, and on to Philadelphia. The return trip was scheduled for a 1:00 p.m. departure, but Philadelphia mayor J. Hampton Moore arrived late—a faux pas that the *New York Times* found headline worthy. Moore enjoyed, or at least endured, a cab ride as far as North Philadelphia before returning to city hall. Over the next few weeks, the Pennsylvania Railroad incrementally replaced the steam locomotives on the forty-four daily trains that connected New York with Philadelphia. Electric power was then introduced to the smaller number of trains that continued further south, joining the commuter services that had been operating to Wilmington since 1928. Paoli, at that time the western limit of electrified territory, became the changeover point for passenger trains bound for Harrisburg and Pittsburgh. To the south of Wilmington, construction crews continued to install catenary at a rapid pace.[143]

On January 28, 1935, it was finished. Engineman C. B. Morris opened the throttle of engine #4800, the first in a new series of powerful and versatile electric locomotives. The train, carrying 128 representatives from the Pennsylvania Railroad and various state and federal agencies, accelerated out of Washington Union Station. It took just under four hours to make the 269-mile round trip to Philadelphia, at an average speed of 72 miles per hour. Returning to Washington, the train blazed through Landover, Maryland, at 102 miles per hour—proof that electrification had increased the speed, and therefore the capacity, of the trains and tracks along the Atlantic Seaboard.[144]

It was symbolic that the trip began and ended in the nation's political capital and not in the company's headquarters city of Philadelphia or in Manhattan, where Penn Station symbolized the commitment of an earlier

generation of PRR executives to improved service. Vice President Martin W. Clement represented the railroad, while Harold Ickes attended on behalf of the federal government. Predictably, each revealed his perceptions of the role of private and public enterprise in the economy. Clement offered his "appreciation to the Administration for the pleasure we have had in working with them" but heaped far more praise on "a smooth-running army of railroad employees numbering in the thousands, backed by many more in industry, [who] have again come through in the American way." Ickes, determined to highlight the accomplishments of the New Deal, thanked Clement for his help in demonstrating "what actually has been accomplished under [the] PWA when private initiative aids the Administration in carrying out its reemployment plans."[145]

Regular passenger service between New York and Washington began on February 10, 1935, but the stringing of wires continued. In January 1937, the PRR board agreed to electrify the tracks from Paoli west to Harrisburg. Several additional routes hosted mostly freight trains. They included the low-grade freight bypass from Morrisville, Pennsylvania, along the Trenton Cutoff, the Philadelphia & Thorndale Branch, and the Atglen & Susquehanna to Enola Yard on the opposite side of the Susquehanna River from the state capital. The Columbia & Port Deposit would be electrified between Perryville, Maryland (on the Philadelphia–Washington main line), and Royalton, Pennsylvania, on the east–west main line just east of Harrisburg. Additional short stretches of catenary along the west bank of the Susquehanna, at West Chester, and between Monmouth Junction and South Amboy ensured that most of the PRR's freight and passenger traffic to the east of Harrisburg would move behind electric locomotives. There would be no Reconstruction Finance Corporation or Public Works Administration loans this time. With the economy improving in the months before the "Roosevelt Recession" of 1937–1938, the PRR had little difficulty in placing an issue of $52.7 million in convertible bonds, carrying the extraordinarily low interest rate of 3¼ percent. On January 15, 1938, the westbound *Metropolitan* became the first train to enter Harrisburg under catenary, completing the largest and most expensive electrification project in American history.[146]

By the time the United States entered World War II, the Pennsylvania Railroad had developed a network of electrified lines that only a few European countries could rival. From New York south to Washington and west to Harrisburg, 673 route miles and 2,158 track miles hosted electric locomotives. That represented nearly 40 percent of the nation's electrified railway mileage and a tenth of all such track in the world. *The Congressional*, the PRR's premier train between New York and Washington, now made the trip in three hours and forty-five minutes, cutting the earlier scheduled time by half an hour. *The Pennsylvania Limited* traveled from New York to Chicago two hours faster than before, and the railroad reduced the schedule for *The Broadway Limited* from seventeen hours to sixteen hours to match the timing of the New York Central's *Twentieth Century Limited*. Even more gratifyingly, and amid the Great Depression, electrification induced some passengers to return to the rails. In the second half of 1935, passenger revenues in electrified territory increased by 5.6 percent, compared to only 2.2 percent nationwide. Electrification also reduced the travel time for freight trains between Potomac Yard and New York City by two and a half hours. As electric locomotives replaced steam engines, the PRR's motive-power costs fell by nearly $8 million a year. The biggest dividends came during World War II, when traffic along the electrified lines was 40 percent above the volume of the prosperous 1920s. Electrification enabled the railroad to handle the additional traffic with ease, avoiding a repeat of the congestion crisis—and subsequent federal operation—that had characterized the previous world war. Two political administrations—one Republican and the other Democratic—facilitated that successful outcome. The evolving partnership between the Pennsylvania Railroad and the federal government was often haphazard and poorly coordinated. Atterbury and other PRR executives, rather than elected officials and government agencies, typically dominated that process and reaped the immediate financial rewards. In the decades that followed, however, the nation and its people received the greatest long-term benefits, which continued even after the Pennsylvania Railroad disappeared from the corporate landscape.[147]

Newark

While the electrification of the PRR's eastern trackage attracted the attention of journalists and technical experts, the project involved much more than wires and catenary towers. Some of the biggest changes occurred in Newark, New Jersey. Rail service between Newark and Jersey City began in 1834 via the New Jersey Rail Road & Transportation Company. The line soon became the preferred route between New York and Philadelphia. Traffic increased steadily after the PRR acquired the property in 1871 (as part of the lease of the United Canal & Railroad Companies of New Jersey). By the end of the century, the steady parade of freight and passenger trains speeding across

city streets had made Newark one of the most dangerous locales in the country. Between 1901 and 1904, the PRR elevated tracks through the area. The company nonetheless retained its principal station, built in 1890 and located just to the south of the Passaic River at Market Street. The situation in Newark changed considerably during the second decade of the twentieth century. The 1910 opening of Penn Station in Manhattan promised to increase the number of trains operating through Newark. Manhattan Transfer, an isolated location in the Hackensack Meadows about a mile northeast of Newark, served as the changeover point between steam and third-rail electric power. Beginning in October 1911, an extension of the Hudson & Manhattan Railroad to Manhattan Transfer enabled travelers to make a convenient cross-platform connection with service through the Hudson Tubes to Lower Manhattan. Within a few months the H&M extended its line across the Passaic River to a terminus at Park Place in Newark. The Park Place facility was used primarily by commuters, as it lay an inconvenient six blocks away from the PRR's Market Street station, making a transfer at that point virtually impossible.

Newark's outdated station, the inadequacy of the Passaic River Bridge, and the separation of the Pennsylvania Railroad and the Hudson & Manhattan termini all suggested the need for a comprehensive redevelopment of the city's transportation facilities. With long-distance main line electrification in the early planning stages, the project offered the opportunity to eliminate Manhattan Transfer, facilitate the exchange of passengers with the Hudson & Manhattan, and give the city a magnificent new passenger terminal. Planning for the new station began during the summer of 1924 and involved representatives from the PRR, the Hudson & Manhattan Railroad, and the New Jersey Public Service Corporation. They envisioned an integrated transportation facility, with passengers on intercity trains able to make a convenient connection with the H&M, joining Manhattan-bound commuters. Public Service Corporation rapid-transit streetcars entering the facility below ground, via the bed of the abandoned Morris Canal, would enable the efficient distribution of traffic throughout the city. Two new bridges over the Passaic River would afford PRR and H&M trains improved access to the station site. Initial estimates suggested that the project would cost $15 million and be completed within two years.[148]

The construction of Newark's new Pennsylvania Station took far longer than initially anticipated. President Atterbury announced the PRR's plans in February 1926 at a meeting of the Bond Club of Newark, but little action was forthcoming. The project soon sparked heated debates regarding the location, design, and allocation of costs associated with the station. Residents and business owners in the southern part of Newark demanded a facility where the PRR's tracks crossed South Street, a little over a mile to the southeast of the Passaic River. They also anticipated the extension of the parallel Hudson & Manhattan line to the South Street location, to facilitate easy commutation to Lower Manhattan and Herald Square. Pennsylvania Railroad officials balked at that proposal, largely because the cooperative arrangement with the H&M, useful for moving passengers from Manhattan Transfer into Manhattan, had given way to a competition for suburban traffic. They prevailed and chose a location just to the southeast of the Passaic River crossing.[149]

There were nonetheless considerable delays in the construction of Newark Pennsylvania Station. Architects, city officials, and PRR executives could not agree on a design for the structure. There was widespread criticism of a proposal that featured trains running through the center of what looked very much like a Greek temple—or a mausoleum, as some dubbed it. Another rendering, with a semicircular head house, likewise never got off the drawing board. Nor was there any agreement on the allocation of costs between the PRR and the city. Railroad executives were willing to proceed only if an increase in passenger traffic and in overall operating efficiency could justify the massive investment in new facilities. They were also determined to make the city of Newark bear the largest possible share of the expense. Newark officials were reluctant to pay for anything beyond the relocation of nearby streets and insisted that increased tax revenues (generated by the real estate development that was certain to occur in the area) would constitute their sole financial contribution to the project. After four years of negotiations, in April 1928, PRR officials and Newark mayor Thomas L. Raymond reached an agreement on what would become the Newark Improvements. The only significant detail that had changed was the cost, which had risen to $20 million. By the time the contracts were ready the following month, the price tag was $25 million, to be divided evenly between the railroad and the city.[150] The Newark city commissioners approved the contract with the PRR in September, yet there were further delays. At the same meeting, the commissioners rejected a portion of the contract with the Public Service Commission, for the construction of rapid-transit tracks in the old Morris Canal.[151] Until that matter was resolved, Atterbury and other Pennsylvania Railroad officials were not willing

to go ahead with the project. Not until January 1929, nearly five years after the initial announcement of the new station, did representatives from the PRR, the city, and the PSC affix their signatures to the agreement.[152]

The lengthy negotiations were but a prelude to an even longer construction process, one that would take more than eight years to complete. Work on the new Passaic River crossing began in October. The new three-track lift bridge over the Passaic River spanned 230 feet and was the longest such structure in the world at that time. Pennsylvania Railroad officials did not reveal plans for the new station until May 1931, following their approval by the Newark City Commission. The railroad's executives entrusted many of their most important stations—at Washington, Philadelphia, and Chicago—to D. H. Burnham & Company or its successor, Graham, Anderson, Probst & White. New York's Penn Station had been an exception, and so, too, was the corresponding facility in Newark, with both commissions awarded to McKim, Mead & White. William Rutherford Mead, the last of the three founding partners, had died in 1928, followed three years later by William Symmes Richardson—the individual largely responsible for Penn Station in Manhattan. Their neoclassical and Beaux Arts designs were in any case increasingly out of step with the Jazz Age and the advent of Art Deco. Newark Pennsylvania Station was one of the firm's last major commissions. Along with edifices such as the Cincinnati Union Terminal and the Los Angeles Union Passenger Terminal, it was also one of the final large passenger rail stations constructed in the United States.

Lawrence Grant White, the son of Stanford White and the principal partner at McKim, Mead & White, was largely responsible for an edifice that was unmistakably Art Deco in style, strikingly at variance with earlier facilities in Manhattan and Baltimore.[153] Indiana limestone clad the exterior, while pink granite accentuated the archways over the main entrance doors. Inside, red terrazzo floors and walls of rose-yellow Montana travertine and gray marble gave way to more modern design features. Thirteen plaster medallions, set high into the walls, featured notable scenes from the history of transportation. The chandeliers featured signs of the zodiac. Fifty feet above the floor was a gently curved ceiling in blue, accentuated with gold leaf. On either side of the main waiting room, a pair of long, low walls, interrupted only by narrow horizontal slit windows, stretched from Edison Place, across Market Street, and nearly to the bank of the Passaic River. They protected travelers from inclement weather, while aesthetically hiding the trains and platforms from view. Architects had

Opened in stages between 1935 and 1937, Newark Pennsylvania
Station provided commuters and intercity travelers with access
to trains operated by the PRR and the Hudson & Manhattan
Railroad. Designed by McKim, Mead & White, the structure
reflected the growing influence of the Art Deco movement.
New Jersey State Archives, Department of State.

long since dispensed with the massive arched train sheds
originally employed at Broad Street Station and other
facilities. They were expensive to build and maintain, and
they tended to trap the smoke and soot associated with the
use of steam locomotives. While electrification promised
to eliminate much of the pollution at Newark, the location—set above street level—made a conventional train
shed doubly impracticable. Instead, the station featured
what was in effect a low canopy, interrupted by slits above
the centerline of each track. The design, also employed at
the upper level of 30th Street Station in Philadelphia, was
originally developed by Thomas Rodd, the former chief
engineer on Lines West, for Union Station in Chicago.[154]

By the end of July, the proposed facility had increased
in size, thanks to a decision to include a second entrance

for bus passengers and Hudson & Manhattan commuters.
PRR officials also agreed to clad the secondary, eastern
facade of the station with limestone rather than brick to
better match the main, western entrance. The changes,
which burdened the PRR with an additional $200,000 in
construction expense, were but the first in a series of cost
overruns. The onset of the Great Depression caused further delays and induced PRR officials to bundle elements
of the Newark Improvements with the negotiations for the
$27.5 million Reconstruction Finance Corporation elec-
trification loan that occurred during the spring of 1932.[155]

The combination of private and public support accelerated work on the Newark Improvements, even as the local
economy remained mired in the Depression. On March
24, 1935, Newark mayor Meyer C. Ellenstein presided
over the opening of the first phase of the new station. He
equated the facility with improvements to Port Newark,
the growth of the Newark Airport—at that time the busiest
in the world—and the recently completed Pulaski Skyway.
"Newark has already advanced so far on all transportation
fronts," he observed, "that Newark's dominance as a shipping and industrial distributing centre in the east should
not be a remote or extravagant prospect."[156] After arriving
at the station, the eleven-car inaugural train remained on

public display, giving spectators the opportunity to see the electric locomotive and the most modern, air-conditioned equipment the PRR and the Pullman Company could provide. Despite the festivities, the station was far from complete. The baggage room was temporarily situated in the lower-level rapid-transit lobby. Neither the dining room nor the barber shop had yet been built—although the absence of the permanent restroom facilities was probably more of an inconvenience. Only three of the planned eight tracks were in service, but the new waiting room was finished and elicited favorable reviews. Construction work would continue for another two years, and the final cost would rise to $42 million, nearly three times the initial 1924 estimate.[157]

The completion of the Pennsylvania Railroad and the Hudson & Manhattan facilities at Newark spelled the end of a place that had earned iconic status in the history of Greater New York. Between 1934 and 1937, the Hudson & Manhattan relocated its southern terminus from Park Place to Newark's Pennsylvania Station, utilizing a new lift bridge constructed just to the east of the PRR span. Manhattan Transfer remained in service following the January 1933 completion of electrification from New York south through Philadelphia, but its days were clearly numbered.[158] At 4:01 a.m. on June 20, 1937, the first Hudson & Manhattan train left Newark Pennsylvania Station, bound for Lower Manhattan. None of the railroad or political officials who had attended the opening ceremonies three years earlier were willing to make a return appearance at such an unseemly hour. Instead, the first ticket went to seventy-three-year-old Theodore D. Staats, a lifelong resident of Newark, who had been the first fare-paying passenger at the Park Place station a quarter of a century earlier. Buses and Public Service Corporation rapid-transit cars also began using the new station. Commuters and intercity travelers bound for Lower Manhattan now changed trains at Newark, and Manhattan Transfer no longer served any useful purpose. "Work of demolishing the place," the *New York Times* noted on June 21, "is already underway." PRR officials estimated that 230 million passengers had passed through Manhattan Transfer during its twenty-seven-year history. Despite its importance to the railroad's operations, the facility stood alone in the Hackensack Meadows, and it lacked both public road access and an imposing head house and waiting room. As journalist John Markland noted, "The drab, isolated, brick-and-concrete islands in the heart of the Meadows will have outlived their usefulness." For many, its platforms had been a gateway to the glittering skyline of Manhattan. "Young men and women coming to the metropolis in search of fame and fortune," Markland

recalled, "coach travelers and occupants of private compartments, political bosses from the plains States and dignified Senators from Washington, movie stars seeking their first glimpse of Broadway, schoolteachers, clergymen, convention delegates, native New Yorkers returning from the 'provinces'—these and countless others from every walk of American life have found a bit of glamor in the dilapidated station perched atop an embankment 'fill' in the Meadows just east of Newark."[159]

Perfecting the Electric Locomotive

The PRR's electrification project required a new generation of motive power that could make effective use of the high-voltage alternating current that flowed through the overhead wires. In October 1928, when President Atterbury asked the board of directors to approve electrification between New York and Washington, he reassured the directors that the Motive Power Department could develop new freight and passenger locomotives that employed the commutator motors Westinghouse had introduced the previous year. Thirteen months later, the company announced plans to spend $16 million for sixty freight locomotives and ninety passenger locomotives, each capable of greater speed and pulling power than anything that had come before them.[160]

A new generation of PRR motive-power officials struggled to match a relatively new technology with the time-tested paradigms of steam-locomotive design. During the first two decades of the twentieth century, gifted individuals such as Axel Vogt, Alfred Gibbs, and James Wallis had developed steam locomotives that were the mainstay of the PRR's operations. By the time Atterbury announced the electrification of the main line between New York and Washington, however, much of the innovative character of the Motive Power Department had disappeared. Vogt retired in 1919, Gibbs died in 1922, and Wallis was essentially invalided in place in 1927, receiving the impressive-sounding but meaningless title of assistant vice president in charge of operations. In their absence, John Van Buren Duer took charge of electric-locomotive development. As his name suggested, he was a direct descendant of President Martin Van Buren—and, before that, William Duer, a late eighteenth-century financial speculator and member of the Continental Congress. He earned a degree in mechanical engineering at the Stevens Institute of Technology in 1903 and then became an apprentice at General Electric. By 1905, he was involved in the electrification of the Long Island Rail Road and soon became that company's electrical-equipment inspector.

He joined the PRR in 1910 as a foreman of motormen, training the crews who worked on the DD1 locomotives that pulled trains underneath Manhattan. Duer earned promotion to assistant engineer for electrical work in 1913, became electrical engineer for Lines East in 1919, and accepted the same duties for the entire system the following year. He worked closely with mechanical engineer William F. Kiesel Jr. and Frederick W. Hankins, who in 1927 replaced Wallis as the chief of motive power. The three executives shared responsibility for motive-power development, yet to varying degrees. Duer possessed a comprehensive understanding of electrification, yet he stood apart from the individuals—including Kiesel, Vogt, and Gibbs—who had developed the PRR's most innovative steam locomotives. Kiesel was a supremely talented mechanical engineer, but he was nearing retirement and lacked expertise in electrical-equipment technology. Hankins was a competent administrator but not someone who was likely to produce any breakthrough motive-power designs.[161]

While Duer was intimately familiar with electric locomotives, most of his colleagues in the Motive Power Department were not. They did, however, possess considerable experience with the steam locomotives that had proven their worth in freight and passenger service. Under the circumstances, it was hardly surprising that they retained that frame of reference and endeavored to create a series of electric locomotives that would replicate the known characteristics of steam locomotives. Cousins Alfred and George Gibbs had begun that process in 1905, with the completion of locomotives #10,001 and #10,002. The presence of two pairs of axles, similar to two Class A 0-4-0 steam shifters coupled together, ensured their assignment to Class AA1. It conformed to a B+B alphanumeric designation, later introduced by the Association of American Railroads as an alternative to the Whyte system applied to steam locomotives. The units were unsuccessful, but they provided valuable lessons for the development of a more worthy successor. In an effort to reduce lateral sway, designers added a pair of eight-wheel pony trucks, creating an arrangement that resembled two Class D 4-4-0 steam locomotives coupled back-to-back—hence the designation of the Class DD1, which entered service in 1910. Under the AAR system, the DD1 was a 2-B+B-2 locomotive, with two leading axles, two pairs of powered axles in an articulated frame, and a further two unpowered trailing axles.[162]

Future electric-locomotive designs emulated the classification system applied to steam locomotives, but the similarities did not stop there. As with steam locomotives, representatives from the Motive Power Department

Frederick W. Hankins (1876–1958) began his PRR career as a machinist, in 1897. He became the chief of motive power in 1927, replacing the legendary James Wallis. While Hankins lacked his predecessor's ability, he was nonetheless receptive to emerging technologies. Hankins favored electrification of the main line over the Alleghenies, and during the 1930s, he played an important role in the development of the GG1 and other electric locomotives. *Collection of the Historical Society of Pennsylvania.*

attempted to minimize the number of axles, placing as much weight and as much horsepower as possible on each axle. Duer, Kiesel, and Hankins favored large drivers (which they believed necessary to ensure high speed) and rigid-frame construction, both typical of steam-locomotive practice. They also insisted that all the new electric locomotives should have as many interchangeable electrical and mechanical components as possible, echoing the standardization of steam-locomotive parts that their predecessors had introduced as early as the 1870s. Such standardization would allow the PRR to procure identical electrical-equipment components from either General

The Class O1, designed to mimic the performance characteristics of the Class E6s steam locomotives, proved a disappointment. Engine #7851, shown here with a passenger train in December 1930, was one of only eight built. *Pennsylvania Railroad Negative Collection, Hagley Museum & Library, acc. 1993.300.*

Electric or Westinghouse, avoiding the possibility of monopolistic practices on the part of either company.[163]

Unfortunately, Duer's attempts to mimic existing steam-locomotive designs initially proved unsuccessful. That was certainly the case with the 2,000-horsepower Class O1, the first attempt to create a locomotive that would match the demands of main line electrification. The O1 employed a 2-B-2 wheel arrangement, similar to the 4-4-2 Class E6s Atlantics that had become the mainstay of pre-electrification passenger service between Manhattan Transfer and Washington. In 1930 and 1931, the Altoona Works completed eight O1 locomotives. Two carried electrical equipment from American Brown Boveri, three from

Westinghouse, and three from General Electric to assess the relative merits of each builder's products. They were far heavier than expected, Hankins confessed, "due to an error on the part of [the] people at Altoona in not properly checking in detail the weights of the principal parts that went to make up the locomotive." Compounding the problem was the fact that only half of the locomotive's weight rested on the powered driving axles, while the rest contributed nothing to adhesion or pulling power. Representatives from both the Motive Power Department and the Transportation Department agreed that the O1 was not sufficiently powerful to accommodate heavy trains over long distances. It could pull no more than eight passenger cars at a time when the existing fleet of eighty-three Class E6s Atlantic steam locomotives routinely powered eleven-car passenger trains, at high speeds, between Manhattan Transfer and Washington.[164]

The L6 was an even greater disappointment. Like its predecessor, the L5, the locomotive employed a leading axle, four driving axles, and a trailing axle—although its rigid frame indicated an AAR classification of 1-D-1 rather than the older 1-B-B-1 wheel arrangement employed by

Motive Power Department officials intended to build sixty Class L6 locomotives, to be the mainstay of the railroad's freight service. When the GG1 displaced the P5a as the PRR's principal electric passenger locomotive, there was little need for the L6. Only three were completed, with an additional twenty-nine car bodies, fabricated at Altoona, stored until they fell victim to a World War II scrap drive. *Pennsylvania Railroad Negative Collection, Hagley Museum & Library, acc. 1993.300.*

the L5.[165] The steam-locomotive equivalent of the L6 was the 2-8-2 Mikado, Class L1s. Duer and his colleagues intended a group of sixty L6 electrics to be the equivalent mainstay of freight service on the newly electrified lines. The Altoona Works completed two prototype L6 locomotives in the autumn of 1931 and, without adequate testing, quickly ordered thirty more from the Lima Locomotive Works. Only one was completed. The remaining shells sat unfinished at the Lima plant before becoming part of a World War II scrap drive. The limitations of the L6 design influenced the decision to terminate production. So, too, did the development of an alternative, electric locomotive.[166]

The K4s Pacific was perhaps the most famous class of steam locomotive to operate on the Pennsylvania Railroad. Its electric equivalent, the P5, was less satisfactory, but it nonetheless represented a considerable improvement over

the O1 and the L6. Just as the K4s was in some respects a lengthened version of the E6s Atlantic, the P5 was ten feet longer than the O1. The extra distance permitted the use of another driving axle, creating a 4-6-2 in the case of the K4s and a 2-C-2 on the P5.[167] The P5 was certainly more powerful than the O1, developing 3,750 continuous horsepower and as much as 6,500 horsepower for brief periods. In the spring of 1931, the Altoona Works began building two P5 prototypes. Motive-power officials were so confident of their design that in May they authorized construction of another ninety units, classified as the P5a. Westinghouse provided the traction motors and related electrical equipment, assembled in a plant at Lester, Pennsylvania. Given the size of the order, and with the availability of locomotives lagging behind the progress of catenary construction, Westinghouse introduced mass-production techniques for traction-motor production for the first time in the company's history. The General Steel Castings Corporation, based in Eddystone, Pennsylvania, supplied innovative one-piece castings for the locomotive frames and then delivered them to the nearby Baldwin Locomotive Works, where carbody fabrication and final assembly took place.[168]

In August 1931, the first P5a locomotives underwent tests, and Pennsylvania Railroad officials immediately placed them into service. Depression economics nearly forced the PRR to cancel the remainder of its P5a locomotive order, however, and work resumed only after the railroad received its $27.5 million loan from the

In cooperation with General Electric and Westinghouse, the PRR's Motive Power Department developed the P5a as the electric equivalent of the K4s steam passenger locomotive. Midway through P5a production, a grade-crossing accident demonstrated the danger of placing crewmen at the front of the exposed boxcab design (rear locomotive). Subsequent units relocated the cab to a much safer location at the middle of the locomotive—as in the case of #4748, shown in the summer of 1940, leading a freight train near Washington, DC. *Otto Perry photograph, Denver Public Library, Western History Collection, call number OP-1465.*

Reconstruction Finance Corporation. On January 16, 1933, it was a P5a that had the honor of powering the first passenger train to travel under wire between New York and Philadelphia. The new locomotives were soon pulling fifteen-car trains—double what the O1 could handle—between New York and Wilmington and Paoli, at speeds of up to ninety miles per hour.[169]

The P5a soon began experiencing problems, caused in part by the decision to rush the units into production before the completion of the initial road tests. Like the smaller O1 locomotives, they tracked poorly at high speeds, producing a lateral sway that damaged rails and ties. Inspections showed that the driving axles on several locomotives had developed serious cracks. PRR officials soon imposed a seventy-mile-per-hour speed limit, ensuring that the P5

and P5a units would be no faster than the steam locomotives that they replaced. The lower speeds were far more than a blow to the PRR's prestige, as they prevented the railroad from achieving the goal of increasing capacity without adding more tracks. The boxcab design, with the operator's controls at each end of the locomotive, proved to have tragic consequences. In January 1934, a P5a pulling *The "Spirit of St. Louis"* through Deans, New Jersey, struck an apple truck at a grade crossing. The cab crumpled on impact, killing the engineman. The accident induced the Pennsylvania Railroad to redesign the P5a, placing the cab in a much safer location at the center of the locomotive.[170]

While the redesign of the P5a carbody required considerable skill, it did nothing to address the more pervasive problems affecting the performance of the locomotives. Fred Hankins worked with representatives from Baldwin, Westinghouse, and General Electric to devise solutions to what were a combination of both mechanical and electrical issues. They concluded that the high torque produced by the traction motors was causing axles to crack and break but could find no better solution than to increase the axle thickness. Even then, the locomotives remained prone to cracked axles throughout their careers, until retirement in the early 1960s. The lateral sway was an even more complex puzzle, and no one seemed entirely certain as to the cause. In April 1933, in an effort to determine the source of the problem, mechanical and electrical engineers from the Pennsylvania Railroad, Westinghouse, GE, and Gibbs

The PRR's motive-power officials initially predicted that the Class R1—built by the Baldwin Locomotive Works in 1934, utilizing Westinghouse electrical equipment—would become the company's standard electric locomotive for passenger service. Tests soon indicated that its long, rigid wheelbase made it prone to derailments. In consequence, the #number 4800, was reassigned to the prototype of the far more successful GG1. The sole member of Class R1 then became the #4999. *Pennsylvania Railroad Negative Collection, Hagley Museum & Library, acc. 1993.300.*

& Hill turned a 440-foot section of the main line, near Claymont, Delaware, into a test track. While GE and Westinghouse employed onboard sensors, PRR officials relied on the same Brinell hardness scale that they had employed in their earlier 1906-1907 tests. Based on the results of the Claymont tests, Hankins and his colleagues recommended changes to the truck design and the redistribution of weight. The modifications improved performance and reliability, but the P5a was still not an ideal locomotive. While a commendable improvement over the O1, it lacked the power to handle the longest passenger trains that the railroad operated.[171] The speed restrictions made the P5a better suited to freight service. That was the intended role for the L6, just coming into production at the Lima Locomotive Works at the time of the Claymont tests. Had both

designs been at an equal stage of development, PRR officials might well have discarded the former locomotive in favor of the latter. With numerous P5a locomotives already in service, however, it made little sense to sideline them in favor of the three L6 models then in use.[172]

Duer, Hankins, and the others enjoyed their greatest success when they began to think of electrics as a new type of technology, one with different performance characteristics than steam. They also benefited from outside expertise, provided by GE, Westinghouse, and the New Haven, whose pioneering high-voltage AC electrification had created a path for the PRR to follow. While the Claymont tests that began in April 1933 generated improvements to the P5a, they played an even more important role in the development of a locomotive that would make that design obsolete. In November, after analyzing the tracking problems associated with the P5a, PRR personnel borrowed a New Haven Class EP3a locomotive. General Electric built the unit in 1931, based on a 1929 design supplied to the Cleveland Union Terminal Company. Whereas Duer and Hankins favored a small number of axles (to maximize weight on each driver, in keeping with steam-locomotive practice), GE employed a different method with the EP3a. The New Haven electric distributed its 202 tons of weight over six powered and four unpowered axles, in a 2-C+C-2 wheel arrangement. The EP3a also possessed an articulated frame, which accommodated curving track much

The prototype GG1 excelled in tests conducted at Claymont, Delaware, and the 139 locomotives in its class easily handled passenger and freight operations in electrified territory. The first, #4800, featured a riveted car body, garnering the nickname "Old Rivets." The remaining units featured a smooth, welded skin, an idea suggested by industrial designer Raymond Loewy. *General Negative Collection, Railroad Museum of Pennsylvania, PHMC.*

more readily than the PRR's rigid-frame designs. It easily reached speeds of 120 miles per hour while generating 2,740 horsepower. That was not much more power than the P5a. The more significant difference lay in the vastly improved riding qualities and greatly reduced lateral forces. The assembled experts all concluded that the New Haven locomotive represented a vast improvement over the PRR P5a. They disagreed, however, as to the reasons. One faction insisted that certain wheel arrangements naturally tracked better than others and suggested that it would be possible to design a larger and heavier locomotive that would conform to the 2-C+C-2 configuration of the EP3a. The other group asserted that the improved tracking qualities were attributable to the reduced weight per axle, irrespective of the precise wheel arrangement. If they were correct, then a more powerful version of the EP3a would

require a larger number of axles, with an attendant increase in construction and maintenance costs.[173]

To resolve the dispute, the PRR ordered two experimental locomotives, each of which was larger than the New Haven unit. One was the Class R1, a 2-D-2 rigid-frame locomotive built by Baldwin, with electrical equipment from Westinghouse. It was basically an extended version of the P5a, in much the same manner that that locomotive was a longer variant of the O1. The R1 prototype also utilized the same heavy axle loading, reflecting the traditional PRR practice of employing as few axles as possible. It carried the number 4800, suggesting that Duer and Hankins were confident that it would be the first in a long series. The other test locomotive was the GG1, at the time numbered 4899. The mechanical components also came from Baldwin, although General Electric supplied the traction motors and related equipment. Like the New Haven test locomotive, the GG1 employed an articulated frame and a 2-C+C-2 wheel arrangement.[174] Its traction motors were smaller and individually less powerful than those on either the P5a or the R1. With six driving axles, however, the GG1 utilized twelve traction motors compared to eight on the R1 and only six on the P5a. The GG1 prototype was fifteen feet longer than the R1 but—thanks to the articulated frame—had a significantly shorter rigid wheelbase and could thus accommodate even relatively sharp curves with ease.[175]

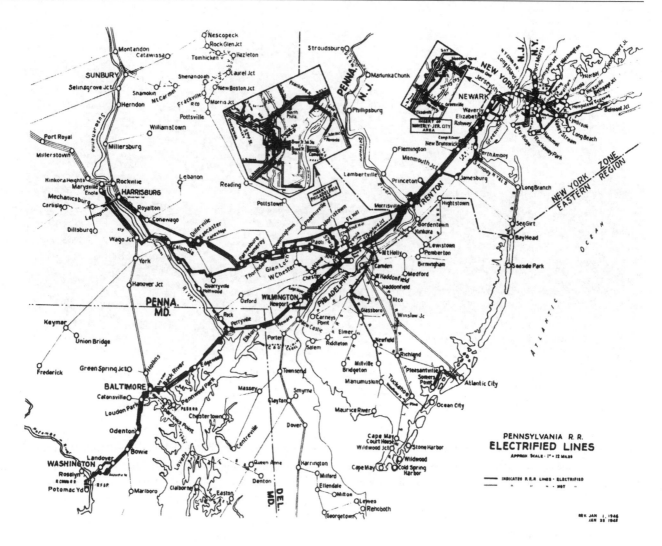

By the time German and Soviet troops invaded Poland, in September 1939, the Pennsylvania Railroad had established the most extensive network of electrified routes in the nation and was among the largest in the world. That enormous capital investment ensured that the company would have adequate capacity to cope with the unprecedented traffic demands of World War II. *Author's collection.*

Representatives from the PRR and the various equipment suppliers conducted what may well have been the most exhaustive tests the railroad had ever undertaken. The results showed that the GG1 was the overwhelming favorite. Both prototypes offered a stunning combination of high horsepower and high speed. The GG1 certainly excelled in those areas, with its twelve traction motors collectively producing 4,620 continuous horsepower and up to 8,500 horsepower in short bursts. That was sufficient to accelerate a test train from zero to 100 miles per hour in 64.5 seconds, and to reach a reported maximum speed of

129 miles per hour. Of equal importance, the GG1 exhibited far better tracking characteristics than the R1, and the reduction in lateral movement produced much lower stresses on the rail.[176]

PRR officials were elated with the success of the prototype GG1. They quickly reassigned number 4899 to the never-duplicated R1, with newly renumbered 4800 the first of what would become 139 GG1 locomotives. In November 1934, the PRR ordered the first 57 copies, from a consortium of builders.[177] With the locomotives carrying a price tag of about $250,000 apiece, the $15 million order was one of the largest in the history of American railroading, financed by a loan from the Public Works Administration. On January 28, 1935, the prototype GG1, #4800, rather than an outclassed P5a, powered the train that inaugurated service between Washington and Philadelphia. Two weeks later, on February 10, the #4800 took charge of the northbound *Congressional*, the PRR's premier train between New York and Washington.[178] The first four production-model units entered service in April 1935, and all had been delivered by 1937. The final expansion of the catenary system to Harrisburg, authorized by the board in January 1937, suggested the need for additional GG1 locomotives. The last entered service in 1943, barely in time to accommodate the surge in traffic produced by American involvement in World War II.[179]

The GG1 was both functional and beautiful, a triumphant expression of industrial design that blended the principles of Art Deco streamlining with the demanding operating conditions imposed by the Pennsylvania Railroad. Most of the credit belonged to Donald Roscoe Dohner, an Indiana native who began his career as an associate professor of design at the Carnegie Institute of Technology. He began consulting work at Westinghouse in 1926. By 1930, he had taken charge of the company's Art in Engineering Department. During the next four years, Dohner and his staff designed at least 128 products for Westinghouse. The most significant, at least in terms of the GG1, was the "visibility cab" oil-electric switch engine. By narrowing the upper sides of the locomotive, thus creating a horizontal shoulder along the midpoint of the body, extending from the cab forward, Dohner enabled crewmen at one end of the locomotive to clearly see the tracks ahead. While Westinghouse produced only fifteen visibility-cab locomotives between 1929 and 1937, Dohner remained committed to the basic concept.[180]

By early March 1934, Dohner had developed three similar designs for the PRR—one for the prototype R1, another for the prototype GG1, and the third for the center-cab version of the P5a, reconfigured in the aftermath of the January 3 wreck at Deans, New Jersey. In place of the horizontal shoulder used on the oil-electric locomotives, Dohner applied a downward slant to the lower sides, further improving visibility for enginemen who sat about twenty-five feet from the front of the locomotive. One of the conceptual models he produced—for the R1—improved the aesthetics of the large vents, located between the cab doors, by providing them with rounded corners. That feature was absent on the prototype GG1, but it is reasonable to assume that Dohner intended to incorporate the improved vents in the GG1, should PRR officials prefer that locomotive to the R1. Had Dohner remained at Westinghouse, he undoubtedly would have made further refinements to the GG1 design. In 1935, however—and just as the initial GG1 order was entering production—he left the company for a post at the Pratt Institute in Brooklyn.[181]

With Dohner no longer at Westinghouse, another individual gained the opportunity to put the finishing touches on the GG1. A French national who immigrated to the United States not long after World War I, Raymond Loewy had by 1934 established a considerable reputation as an industrial designer. He possessed little experience in railroad work, but he sensed that the PRR offered enormous potential. Loewy persuaded his friend, future US senator Stuart Symington, to write a letter of introduction, incorrectly intimating that the designer had done work for the New York Central and the Baltimore & Ohio. When he met Martin Clement and Charles D. Young in October 1934, Loewy began the conversation, chatting about their shared military service in World War I. Unlike Atterbury, neither PRR vice president had been in France, but Clement politely asked Loewy what he might like to design for the Pennsylvania Railroad. Loewy said, without hesitation, "a locomotive"—at least according to his version of events. "I recalled my whole future being decided in this moment" while Clement considered the matter, he later observed. The PRR executive offered Loewy a distinctly less glamorous assignment, redesigning the wastepaper baskets in Penn Station.[182] That task completed, Loewy returned to the executive suite, where Clement hailed him as "the great trash can specialist." After another friendly conversation, Clement called Fred Hankins, the chief of motive power, into the room. Hankins showed Loewy a photograph of the GG1 that Dohner had designed. Loewy, who rarely found it difficult to denigrate any work that was not his own, assumed that Hankins was responsible for the locomotive's appearance. Under the circumstances, he conceded that he "could hardly criticize it too harshly in front of the man who probably had developed it."[183]

Loewy had a lifelong habit of taking full credit for every design he had touched, however briefly, and the GG1 was no exception. Without ever acknowledging Dohner's contributions, Loewy made only minor changes to his predecessor's work. He enjoyed the full complicity of Clement and other executives, who could boast that the Pennsylvania Railroad, rather than Westinghouse, had styled the nation's newest and most glamorous locomotive. In November 1934, they agreed to pay Loewy $5,000 for his efforts on the GG1. That it was only the second railroad commission awarded to "the great trash can specialist" suggested how little substantive work remained to be done. Fred Hankins, who knew far more than Loewy about the locomotive's design history, vainly opposed the contract and suggested that the railroad would be "just throwing $5,000 up in the air." Given the advanced state of GG1 production, Hankins suggested that Loewy forgo the project and employ his talents elsewhere. Young, with Clement's support, instead gave the designer free rein and arranged for the construction of a full-size mockup at the PRR's Wilmington Shops. Loewy clambered over the facsimile, observing that "Hankins, who was watching me,

4800

4800

Facing, Based on his experience as an industrial designer at Westinghouse, Donald R. Dohner created the smooth, flowing lines that characterized the GG1. Raymond Loewy suggested the use of a welded rather than riveted exterior, coupled with the application of five narrow pinstripes—as indicated by this mockup, photographed in December 1934. Loewy, who was attempting to establish his reputation in the railroad industry, took full credit for the entire design, relegating Dohner to relative obscurity. *Pennsylvania Railroad Negative Collection, Hagley Museum & Library, acc. 1993.300.*

Above, By May 1935, workers at the Juniata Shops were engaged in full-scale production of the GG1. These 5 were among the first of 139 completed between 1934 and 1943—all but 15 built at the Altoona Works, with the remainder assembled by General Electric. *Pennsylvania Railroad Negative Collection, Hagley Museum & Library, acc. 1993.300.*

looked deeply interested." Loewy may well have misread Hankins's emotions, but he nonetheless prevailed on PRR officials to make subtle changes.[184]

Loewy's most significant contribution to the design of the GG1 involved the overlapping, riveted steel plates that formed the outer skin of the #4800. He suggested that welding—then a relatively new technique among suppliers of railroad equipment—would provide a more stream-lined appearance, reduce wind resistance, and decrease manufacturing costs. Loewy also made minor changes to the shape of the nose and shoulders along the side of the locomotive and replaced the boxy marker lights with an elongated teardrop shape—which in turn permitted the relocation of the number board originally mounted atop the nose. The rounded corners of the side vents were a great improvement over the squared-off version on the 4800, yet they were no different from what Dohner had intended for the R1 and probably for the production version of the

On August 19, 1937, nearly new GG1 #4828 is doing exactly what PRR and GE designers intended it to do—hauling a heavy passenger train at a steady seventy miles per hour through Stelton, New Jersey. *Otto Perry photo, Denver Public Library, Western History Collection, call number OP-14470.*

GG1 as well. Loewy recommended that the locomotives be painted in the PRR's traditional Brunswick Green—a very dark color, almost indistinguishable from black—and his only contribution was a set of gold, five-pinstripe, "cat whisker" lines running horizontally from one end to the other.[185]

After numerous false starts, the PRR's Motive Power Department had finally developed a locomotive that could fully exploit the potential associated with long-distance main line electrification. The GG1 could easily haul twenty-car passenger trains at any speed the tracks and roadbed could safely accommodate. The climb out of Penn Station toward the Bergen Hill tunnel portal—the steepest continuous grade in electrified territory—presented no problems as trains hustled south out of Manhattan. Passengers on elite services such as *The Congressional* and *The Broadway Limited* rode behind GG1 locomotives from New York south to Washington or west to Harrisburg. So did

travelers on the hourly Clocker trains that ran between New York and Philadelphia and—in later years—even commuters on the New York & Long Branch Railroad. The GG1 featured prominently in PRR promotional materials, in numerous movies, and in Lionel train sets. Once each year, a dozen or more of the locomotives, aligned in a neat row, filled the tracks adjacent to the Philadelphia Municipal Stadium, part of the fleet of equipment that brought fans to the Army-Navy football game. The GG1 moved dignitaries and spectators to Dwight D. Eisenhower's 1953 presidential inauguration, and one of them memorably overran the end bumper at Washington Union Station and crashed through the concourse floor into the baggage room. Fifteen years later, two GG1 locomotives headed the train carrying the body of Senator Robert F. Kennedy, bound for interment at Arlington National Cemetery.[186]

In addition to its ubiquity, the GG1 was both versatile and enduring. While designed as a high-speed passenger locomotive, the GG1 was equally at home pulling freight. Between 1940 and 1943, amid wartime increases in merchandise traffic, PRR shop forces regeared forty-four of the locomotives for freight service. The only thing that could stop them was the snow—not just any snow, but a fine powder that fell across the Northeast in February 1958. It blew through the air intakes, then melted and short-circuited the normally indestructible electrical equipment. It took weeks for the railroad to recover. Shop forces were soon busy relocating the intake grilles, marring the GG1's aesthetics but mostly preventing a recurrence of the problem. By 1967, with passenger traffic steadily declining and with the anticipated arrival of the new *Metroliner* train sets, the railroad had converted more than eighty of the Class GG1—including prototype #4800—to freight operations. Even the arrival of sixty-six Class E44 electric freight locomotives, intended as replacements for the P5a, in 1960 did not displace the GG1. The aging locomotives soldiered on through the 1968 Penn Central merger and subsequent bankruptcy and into the early years of Conrail. Just over three years later, in November 1979, Conrail withdrew the GG1 from freight service, followed soon after by the cessation of all electrified freight operations. The GG1 lasted even longer in passenger service. In 1973, two years after its formation, Amtrak ordered more than two dozen E60 locomotives from General Electric as replacements for the GG1 fleet. It was a poor decision, as the E60 proved unstable at high speeds. With the arrival of the AEM-7 electric locomotives late in the decade, Amtrak was finally able to remove the GG1 from passenger trains. On April 26, 1980, intercity passengers had their last opportunity to ride behind the world's most famous electric locomotive. Commuters traveling on the former New York & Long Branch, now operated by New Jersey Transit, experienced the GG1 for another three and a half years, until October 1983. Two years earlier, NJ Transit repainted GG1 #4877 into a variant of the Pennsylvania Railroad paint scheme that Raymond Loewy had designed.[187] It was a fitting tribute, and a fitting end, for a class of locomotive that had enjoyed nearly five decades of success.[188]

Executive Salaries in the New Deal

Even as journalists and officials in the Roosevelt administration celebrated the PRR's commitment to electrification, they continued to excoriate the company's executives for their compensation policies. Given the duration and the severity of the Great Depression, it was hardly surprising that opposition to the perceived excesses of managerial compensation continued through the remainder of the 1930s. W. W. Atterbury's highly publicized decision to spurn Reconstruction Finance Corporation funding rather than accept governmental interference in the affairs of a private corporation did little to harm the Pennsylvania Railroad, as the replacement Public Works Administration loan carried far better terms. The transition from one federal agency to another impeded efforts by RFC chairman Jesse

Jones to curtail executive compensation. By the summer of 1933, ICC commissioner Joseph Eastman replaced Jones as Atterbury's most vocal opponent. It was Eastman, rather than Jones, who attacked Atterbury's salary, making the issue something of a personal crusade. Atterbury, true to his combative nature, possessed an almost visceral dislike for Eastman—in large measure because Eastman had openly supported the nationalization of the railroads—and the antipathy seems to have been mutual.

In June 1933, the passage of the Emergency Railroad Transportation Act enabled Eastman to address executive compensation in both economic and moral terms. Like Jesse Jones at the RFC, Eastman asserted that market forces had failed to sufficiently reduce managerial pay. "I cannot believe that there is such a dearth of good material that it is necessary to pay the salaries which have been paid in order to get good men," he observed, "nor do I know of any reason to believe that the competency of executives can be safely judged by the salaries which they receive." Eastman also suggested that a career in railroad management possessed intrinsic rewards that transcended financial compensation and that "a railroad presidency is a job which ought to have much attraction quite apart from the money which it pays." In a similar vein, Eastman reminded managers that "money is by no means the only compensation" and that they should value the "joy of creative work well done." Such comments may have possessed a kernel of truth. However, they were strikingly at variance with the culture of managerial entrepreneurship that had emerged in American business since the end of World War I. It became increasingly common for individuals to move from company to company in search of better employment opportunities based on assertions that their unique talents could increase corporate profitability. Historically, that had not been the case on the railroads, where managers rose through the ranks of one company over many decades, with few opportunities to join a competing carrier. Stability rather than innovation characterized the railroads, and few executives wanted to accept blame for an alteration in traditional operating practices that might go badly wrong. Yet railroaders were cognizant of the larger corporate culture of the 1920s and 1930s. Even though most executives possessed an esprit de corps, a willingness to endure great hardship, and a profound loyalty to their employer, they increasingly perceived compensation as a just reward for their hard work and sacrifice.[189]

While Jones offered the incentive of RFC loans to ensure pay reductions, Eastman insisted that the Emergency Railroad Transportation Act had given him a legal mechanism to force the carriers to comply. On July 14, less than a month after he became the federal coordinator of transportation, Eastman told Atterbury and top executives from several other railroads that he expected them to voluntarily reduce their pay. "The salaries to which many executives attained were a symptom of the boom disease" of the 1920s, he asserted, and "there must be an adjustment of this matter of salaries before the railroads will stand right with the shippers, investors and labor under conditions which now exist." Eastman acknowledged that executive salaries constituted "an insignificant item" of overall corporate expense but insisted that compensation embodied "a psychological importance which much exceeds its money significance." Absent cooperation, he vowed to order pay cuts, even though it was by no means certain that the Emergency Railroad Transportation Act gave him that authority. Eastman proposed a $60,000 salary cap, a figure that was by no coincidence identical to the one that Jones and Roosevelt had agreed upon for the RFC.[190] That limit affected a mere sixteen railroad executives, of whom Atterbury was the best compensated. Whether they were intimidated by Eastman's power or merely fearful of negative publicity, most quickly fell into line. To Eastman's delight, and perhaps his surprise, fifteen of the sixteen executives agreed to reduce their salaries to the $60,000 threshold.[191]

The one exception was General Atterbury. By March 1933, his official salary had declined to $103,882, thanks to an additional round of executive pay cuts, but that was nearly double Eastman's recommended maximum and more than four times the $25,000 level that Roosevelt had informally favored. Over the next two months, PRR officials refused to indicate either their compliance with or their refusal to accept the recommendations of the transportation coordinator. For Atterbury and his colleagues, Eastman's order portended a far more serious threat than the loss of a few thousand dollars in pay. If federal officials could arbitrarily set Atterbury's salary, they reasoned, then there was nothing to prevent them from countermanding any executive decision. As such, they viewed "Mr. Eastman's 'request' for an adjustment in their salaries to be an outright invasion of managerial discretion." Representatives from the Association of Railway Executives informed Eastman that they thought it unlikely that Atterbury would yield to federal authority. Perhaps with some admiration, they emphasized that "the Pennsylvania intends to continue paying its officials in accordance with their responsibility."[192]

During the standoff, Atterbury commissioned Price, Waterhouse & Company to study trends in executive salaries and to provide evidence that would enable him

to defend the PRR's practices. In a report issued on September 11, the accounting firm concluded that $100,000 represented a fair salary for a position as important as the presidency of the Pennsylvania Railroad. Atterbury's compensation was still slightly over that mark, but company officials emphasized that his after-tax income had declined from $123,000 in 1929 to $71,500 in 1932. Of greater significance, the report observed, inflation had reduced Atterbury's posttax purchasing power from the equivalent of $75,000 in 1912, when he was a vice president, to $72,300 in 1929 and a mere $55,700 in 1933.[193]

Neither Atterbury's obstinacy nor the Price, Waterhouse report convinced Eastman to abandon his calls for austerity. On September 19, he issued an ultimatum, demanding to know whether Atterbury intended to conform to the salary guidelines. Should the answer be in the negative, the transportation coordinator intended to let the courts decide if he would become the first federal official in American history who possessed the legal authority to limit the earnings of an employee of a private corporation.[194]

The matter never went to the courts, however, as Atterbury capitulated on the following day. As he informed Eastman, by telegram, the PRR's bylaws gave the board of directors the sole authority to determine annual salaries above $6,600. In that sense, had Atterbury unilaterally cut his own pay, as executives on other railroads had done, he would have interfered with the board's prerogatives. He explained that the first scheduled board meeting following Eastman's July 14 ultimatum had not taken place until September 13, two days after the completion of the Price, Waterhouse report. It was at that meeting that Atterbury informed the directors of his willingness to limit his salary to $60,000. Given his 36 percent tax bracket, that meant that the PRR's president would now take home $38,400 for his year's work. The board agreed, denying Eastman's authority to mandate such a reduction and resolving "that having made reasonable revision of the salaries of the executives and other officers of the company it should not surrender its right to determine the compensation of its officers" to government officials or to anyone else outside the corporation.[195]

The PRR's austerity measures struck some of the company's investors as insufficient, yet they were scarcely more of a threat to executive salaries than were Jones, Eastman, or other federal officials. One elderly female shareholder at the 1934 annual meeting insisted that it was monumentally unfair that the corporation's senior executives had only lost a third of their incomes. "They can spare their fabulous salaries," she insisted, so long as "we stockholders, who put all we had into the railroad, have to be impoverished." More than two hundred attendees responded with cheers to her straightforward if monosyllabic question of "Why?" and to her proposal that managers serve without pay for the next two years. Longtime PRR director Effingham B. Morris had grown used to complaints from disgruntled investors, but the septuagenarian former president of the Girard Trust Company was taken aback. He could do no better than assert that the directors had disbursed all the dividends they could, given the PRR's meager earnings. Albert J. County, the vice president in charge of finance, quickly came to Morris's aid. A company that paid small dividends was better than one that paid no dividend at all, he observed, and pointed out that more than half of the nation's corporations were in the latter category. County also noted that eliminating the salaries of all the PRR's senior executives would increase earnings by precisely six cents per share—a response that demonstrated County's impressive command of facts and figures and also suggested that he might well have anticipated the question. The dissident shareholder nonetheless wondered why Atterbury and other senior executives "get enormous salaries—higher than the compensation of the president of the United States." Under the circumstances, County's response—that Roosevelt supplemented his income with free room and board at the White House—fell a little flat. Yet the PRR's directors and most of the shareholders saw no reason to place further restrictions on the salaries of the managers who governed their corporation.[196]

Jesse Jones at the RFC and Joseph Eastman together ultimately persuaded about two dozen railway managers to voluntarily relinquish a total of $208,000 in annual pay—an amount equivalent to 0.009 percent of all railroad operating expenses in 1932. Rather dismissively, Pennsylvania Railroad director Pierre S. du Pont claimed that Eastman's only achievement during his tenure as transportation coordinator was to force a single executive to lower his salary by $49,000.[197]

It would be tempting to regard Eastman as a grandstanding politician or anticapitalist radical. He was neither. Instead, Eastman was an extraordinarily capable public servant with decades of regulatory experience. He knew—as did Atterbury—that the Pennsylvania Railroad was a private corporation chartered to serve public needs. Everything that the railroads did affected the economic and social fabric of the United States in some manner. The federal government had long been involved in the regulation of rates, the promulgation of safety standards, and the setting of wages and working conditions. Although those developments had inevitably been politicized—they were

public-policy issues, after all—Eastman saw them as part of a logical progression toward bending private enterprise toward the public good. While salary reductions did little to reduce "wastes and preventable expense," Eastman asserted that mandatory restraint sent a powerful symbolic message to railroad executives and to the American people. Fairness, as he defined the term, demanded that all Americans acknowledge the severity of the Great Depression and shoulder equally its burdens.

What Eastman had done, perhaps, was to delay the restoration of managerial pay for railroaders by several years. Executive compensation in manufacturing industries bottomed out sometime in late 1932 or early 1933. The gradually improving economic conditions produced a corresponding rise in pay that began in the middle of 1934, nearly three years before the PRR president's salary began to recover.[198] Moreover, Eastman insisted that the trivial reduction in executive compensation had sent an important symbolic message. "A danger now exists in the fixing of salaries for executives in private business which did not once exist, and which grows out of the fact that great corporations with widely held stock are not really controlled by the owners of their properties, but rather by boards of directors who tend to become self-perpetuating," he wrote in July 1933. "It is easy for the directors to drift into the conclusion that the executives, fellow-members of these boards, are justly entitled to very large compensation for their services." That language would not have sounded out of place three-quarters of a century later, as a new generation of Americans struggled to come to terms with the relationship between corporate executives and workers reeling from the effects of the so-called Great Recession of the early twenty-first century.[199]

Significantly, federal regulators were already applying Eastman's methods to other sectors of the economy. Both the RFC and the Federal Reserve investigated banking salaries, while the Power Commission did the same for executives at utility companies. The Federal Trade Commission lacked the legal authority to compel large corporations to release salary data—but secured compliance with the simple reminder that Congress would readily legislate if the information was not provided voluntarily. The 1934 Securities Act empowered the Securities and Exchange Commission to collect data on executive compensation. Congress prevented airlines receiving federal subsidized airmail contracts from paying executives more than $17,500 per year—a fraction of Atterbury's salary, even after his "voluntary" 60 percent reduction.[200]

Ironically, the same governmental inquisitiveness that had originally sparked such outrage in the matter of railroad salaries ultimately offered PRR executives a measure of exoneration. Atterbury and his fellow railroad executives, it turned out, were so far down on the scale of executive compensation as to be almost unnoticeable. In 1937, the House Ways and Means Committee compiled a list of every corporate executive whose salary, bonuses, and other compensation totaled more than $15,000 during the 1936 tax year. More than anything else, the accounting demonstrated that new industries such as automobiles, chemicals, and entertainment offered greater profit potential than did the railroads. Nine of the sixteen individuals who earned more than $300,000 a year were General Motors executives. Their ranks included President Alfred P. Sloan Jr., who topped the list at $561,331 (equivalent to nearly $12 million in 2023, and well below the salaries of many early twenty-first century executives). In second place was his lieutenant, GM vice president William S. Knudsen, at $459,878. All told, 336 GM managers received a salary of at least $15,000. Henry Ford was parsimonious in comparison, paying his son Edsel (who held the title of president of the Ford Motor Company) only $137,564—significantly less than the compensation afforded to Vice President Peter E. Martin and mechanical engineer Charles E. Sorenson. The petroleum that fueled those cars was in demand as well, hence the $150,000 salary of the president of Standard Oil of California, and $122,500 for his counterpart at Standard of New Jersey. Six DuPont executives earned over $100,000 a year, attesting to the importance of chemicals in the modern era. Film and radio stars also did well, including Gary Cooper ($370,214), Ronald Coleman ($362,500), Claudette Colbert ($350,833), and Mae West ($323,335, three notches down from her first-place showing among entertainers the year before). Hal Roach, the president of the eponymous studio that produced many Laurel and Hardy films, declared $129,000 in income—about average for a Hollywood mogul. Noted director Fritz Lang made only $55,000. Advertising executives were well rewarded for their labors, with the head of the J. Walter Thompson Company—which had done considerable business with the PRR—making $90,020. At a mere $58,333, Bruce Barton was less successful as a partner at Barton, Durstine & Osborn—although he was perhaps more widely remembered for writing a rather bizarre book in which he compared advertising executives to Jesus and his disciples.[201]

In comparison, railroad management did not fare so well. New York Central president Frederick Williamson earned $62,495 and his B&O counterpart Daniel Willard made $60,000, while Hale Holden at the Southern Pacific likewise enjoyed a $60,000 salary. The Delaware,

Lackawanna & Western Railroad, despite its small size and the loss of much of its anthracite traffic, managed to pay President John M. Davis $63,140 a year, but the smaller Lehigh Valley could do no better than $56,413 for its president, Edward E. Loomis. Former PRR executive Leonor Loree was one of the best compensated railroaders in the United States, avoiding Eastman's $60,000 limit through the simple expedient of serving simultaneously as the president of the Delaware & Hudson Railroad ($50,260) and the Delaware & Hudson Company ($20,180).[202]

Only the Pennsylvania Railroad's president and three of the company's vice presidents earned more than $50,000 a year. The ongoing debate regarding top-tier executive compensation scarcely affected the company's other managers. In 1933, when the issue loomed large in the national press, only one individual on the PRR payroll earned a six-figure salary. The other 116,119 employees did not. In particular, the legion of midlevel bureaucrats who kept the railroad functioning on a day-to-day basis suffered the effects of the Depression as deeply as did the rank-and-file workforce. Alexander Whitney, the president of the Brotherhood of Railroad Trainmen, complained that between 1929 and 1934, layoffs, wage cuts, and underemployment had reduced the pay of railroad workers by 52 percent. During the same period, total compensation paid to executives fell by almost the same amount, 52.5 percent. By comparison, the largest manufacturing companies in the United States reduced executive salaries by an average of only 21.4 percent. Even though members of the railroad brotherhoods grudgingly accepted a 10 percent pay cut in 1933, managerial compensation on the Pennsylvania Railroad declined by a third, compared to the halcyon days of the late 1920s. After the first 10 percent salary reduction (on July 1, 1931), additional cuts came on April 1, 1932 (10%), July 1, 1932 (5%), and March 1, 1933 (10%). Not until early June 1933 did the PRR's directors authorize Atterbury to rescind the salary cuts, on a case-by-case basis. Only in the hard-hit steel industry did managerial pay decline to the same extent as on the Pennsylvania Railroad. Like their counterparts who managed the steel mills, railroaders were particularly sensitive to both the evolving nature of the economy and the financial constraints associated with the Great Depression. Salaries on the Pennsylvania Railroad reflected those external forces, but they also suggested that the vast majority of the company's executives lacked any opportunity whatsoever to take a job with another railroad, much less in a different industry.[203]

Ultimately, the Depression had more of an effect on the size rather than the compensation of the executive corps. During the 1930s, the PRR reduced the number of salaried officers by 46 percent, a more severe reduction than that faced by any class of unionized employees. As the nation emerged from the economic crisis and prepared for war, the company slowly replenished its executive ranks. Many of the desks remained unstaffed, however, as the Pennsylvania Railroad never again employed as many midlevel managers as it had during the 1920s. With salaries low and few opportunities available for employment or advancement, a career in railroad management became a far less attractive option. The Pennsylvania Railroad nonetheless continued to employ a great many competent executives, individuals who could have been successful in any sector of the economy. The excitement and the challenges associated with a railroading career offered a strong lure, as they had for previous generations of managers. To a large degree, many railroad executives agreed with Joseph Eastman's assertion that "money is by no means the only compensation" and that railroad management offered the "joy of creative work well done." Money rather than joy paid the bills, however, and if the PRR could not offer sufficiently remunerative career opportunities, it was unlikely to be—as it had been in the past—one of the best-managed corporations in the United States.

Departures

The economic crisis of the 1930s transformed many Americans into strident critics of big businesses and the individuals who managed them. Transportation Coordinator Joseph Eastman, Reconstruction Finance Corporation chairman Jesse Jones, Senator James Couzens, and Senator Burton Wheeler were in large measure responding to that groundswell of public opinion. The Pennsylvania Railroad and its executives were not their only targets, and many other corporations felt the wrath of individuals who had stood by helplessly as the prosperity of the 1920s turned into the most severe economic calamity in the nation's history. Their disdain was largely temporary, and the next major crisis—global war—redeemed the PRR and the other corporations that made possible the Allied victory. Throughout that tumultuous period in American history, Pennsylvania Railroad executives soldiered on, as their predecessors had soldiered on for nearly a century. W. W. Atterbury engaged in a war of words with Eastman, and others, who dared to challenge his salary and his authority. Yet such conflicts were largely an annoying distraction from the activity that occupied almost all his time—that of running the nation's most important railroad, and one of its largest corporations. He was the inheritor of the managerial expertise of those who had come before him and,

when his time came, he would entrust the railroad's future to the next set of capable hands.

For more than three-quarters of a century, much of the strength of the PRR's managerial system lay in the ability of presidents to identify and mentor their eventual successors while alternating between individuals who possessed differing personalities and leadership styles. Tom Scott was familiar with railroad logistics and strategy, but his principal attributes lay in his ebullient personality, his charm, and his aggressive—some would say reckless—tactics. He was a marked contrast to J. Edgar Thomson, the reticent and taciturn engineer, who selected him as vice president for precisely that reason. Yet Thomson identified other talented civil engineers and ensured their rapid advancement. While he expected Scott to succeed him, he insisted that George Brooke Roberts—a man much like himself—be the one who would replace Scott. By selecting Frank Thomson and Alexander Cassatt as his likely successors, Scott institutionalized the system of alternating managerial philosophies. With Thomson dying after little more than two years in office, Cassatt was ready to step in as a replacement. When Cassatt died in 1906, there followed two executives—James McCrea and Samuel Rea—who were much like Roberts. Rea's successor, W. W. Atterbury, was the protégé of Cassatt.

The alternating system suggested that Rea would anoint someone to follow Atterbury, but he did not do so. Despite his postpresidential advocacy for utopian projects such as a new low-grade rail line across Pennsylvania, Rea acknowledged that the era of expansion had ended. Henceforth, the Pennsylvania Railroad would have little opportunity to assess the managerial potential of individuals based on their involvement in enormous undertakings like the New York Improvements and had scant need for chief executives who were also engineers. Born in 1855, Rea did not fathom the transformative effect that internal-combustion power would have on the railroads or on competing modes of transportation. In a 1927 speech to the Engineers' Club of Philadelphia, Rea predicted that steam locomotives would, in 1977, still be powering most of the nation's freight and passenger trains.[204] Whether resigned to the extinction of his life's work or simply unable to conceive of an alternative, Rea saw little purpose in choosing a successor who shared the same training, temperament, and abilities. Atterbury represented the future, and his ability to cooperate with and battle against other railroads, labor unions, legislators, and regulators reflected the new focus of presidential responsibilities.[205]

Given Rea's hesitancy about the future, it was appropriate that Atterbury's successor would share the general's personality, managerial philosophy, and leadership style—one that Cassatt had imprinted on him. Elisha Lee was Atterbury's obvious choice. Well educated, he possessed a college degree from the Massachusetts Institute of Technology. Lee joined the PRR as a rodman, working for the division engineer at Tyrone, Pennsylvania. He became an assistant supervisor in 1899 and spent the next few years making the rounds of various divisions. Lee became a supervisor in 1901 and in 1903 became superintendent of the New York, Philadelphia & Norfolk, the Pennsylvania Railroad subsidiary that Cassatt had helped to develop during the period when he severed his formal ties to the PRR. In March 1911, Lee became the assistant to Lines East general manager Simon Cameron Long, an assignment that brought with it significantly greater responsibilities. By May 1916, when he was appointed the assistant to the general manager of Lines East, it was clear that Lee had become one of the strongest contenders for the presidency. He became more actively involved in the formulation of labor policy and, as the chairman of the Conference Committee of Managers, represented the carriers in their discussions with government officials. Long's death enabled Lee to replace him as Lines East general manager on April 1, 1917. In August, when the board of directors granted Atterbury leave to go to France with the American Expeditionary Forces, Lee became the acting vice president in charge of operations, a level of authority second only to that of President Rea. By that time, he had become involved in a variety of strategic decisions that went well beyond the scope of ordinary day-to-day operations. They included efforts to alleviate wartime congestion and to investigate the feasibility of employing women and African Americans as replacement workers. At the beginning of USRA control, Lee became the federal manager for the PRR's lines.[206]

The 1920 reorganization placed Lee as the vice president of the Eastern Region. When James A. McCrea, the son of a former president, died in October 1923, Lee took his place as the vice president of the equally important Central Region. During his time as vice president of the PRR's two most important regions, Lee was involved in labor negotiations, the development of the rail and water route along the Delmarva Peninsula and Chesapeake Bay, and efforts to shape federal legislation and regulatory policy affecting the railroads. When Atterbury became vice president on November 15, 1924, Lee became the next vice president in charge of operations. He remained in that role when Atterbury assumed the presidency on October 1, 1925, with Martin Clement, the vice president of the Central

Region, promoted to the new post of assistant vice president in charge of operations. In September 1926, the board of directors, at Atterbury's recommendation, selected Lee as the executive vice president. It was a certainty, therefore, that at some future date—likely in 1936, when Atterbury reached the mandatory retirement age of seventy—Lee would become the eleventh president of the Pennsylvania Railroad. In the interim, Lee represented the PRR at high-level conferences with political leaders, union officials, and executives on other railroads. While Atterbury retained his close personal friendship with Ivy Lee, the advisor to publicity, Elisha Lee was increasingly responsible for coordinating the PRR's public-relations efforts through the Publicity Department, organized in June 1930. He was involved in one of the few successful consolidations of the interwar period through the creation of the Pennsylvania-Reading Seashore Lines. Lee also supervised the Philadelphia Improvements, the complex project whose successful completion would provide the final confirmation that he was ready for the presidency.[207]

And then, in the summer of 1933, fate intervened. On June 24, Elisha Lee was in New York, wishing bon voyage to his wife, Angie Latimer Lee, and his youngest son, Elisha Lee Jr., who were on their way to Europe for a two-month vacation. Like her husband, Angie Latimer had been born in Chicago before her family moved to Tioga Center, New York. She shared much in common with the wives of other Pennsylvania Railroad executives, raising a family, belonging to Philadelphia social clubs, and helping those who were less fortunate through the PRR Women's Aid Society. She had been in Europe less than a week when severe abdominal pains brought her to a hospital in Neuilly-sur-Seine, on the outskirts of Paris. Doctors performed emergency surgery, and on July 4, she died on the operating table. The *Berengaria* brought home her body, escorted by her son. She was fifty-six years old.[208]

Elisha Lee was six years older than his wife, but at age sixty-two he would likely serve the Pennsylvania Railroad for another eight years. With Atterbury reaching retirement age in January 1936, at least five of those years would be as president. In the interim, Lee was entitled to spend some time away from the company to grieve for the loss of his partner in life. He spent several days in Saratoga Springs, the place where an earlier generation of PRR executives had met to create cartels that established rates and allocated the available traffic. Those days were long gone, thanks to the formation of the Interstate Commerce Commission, and rate bureaus now operated in a routinized, bureaucratic environment. Lee began the return journey to New York on August 6, in the company of three of his friends and neighbors from Philadelphia. They drove to Albany, where they boarded a New York Central train bound for Grand Central Terminal in Manhattan. A derailment blocked the tracks at 225th Street, forcing the NYC to reroute the train to the West Side Freight Line—the proprietary all-rail access to Manhattan that had complicated efforts by the Port Authority of New York to develop facilities that would be shared by all railroads. The passengers disembarked at 96th Street, where they prepared to board buses that would enable them to complete the journey. As he was crossing the tracks, Elisha Lee clutched the left side of his body and then collapsed. One of his traveling companions, Dr. Max F. Herman, could do little more than comfort Lee, felled by a stroke, as his life ebbed away. George LeBoutillier, recently appointed as the resident vice president at New York and general manager of the New York Zone, rushed to a nearby police precinct and made the necessary arrangements.[209]

Elisha Lee's body was buried in Tioga Center, next to the wife who had died little more than a month earlier. A special train left Broad Street Station at 8:15 a.m. on August 9. It swung past 30th Street Station, which had opened five months earlier. The building was the crown jewel of the Philadelphia Improvements, the great engineering project that guaranteed Lee's fitness for the presidency. With only two tracks and one platform in service, the edifice was nonetheless incomplete. Lee would never witness the sight of travelers walking through the main waiting room and concourse, which would not open until December 15, two months after his death. Not until 1952 would it finally replace Broad Street Station. A special parlor car attached to the *Erie Limited* enabled friends and colleagues from New York to bid Lee farewell as his body was laid to rest next to that of his wife. He left an estate valued at $101,042, more than half of which represented the benefit provided by his life-insurance policy.[210]

President Atterbury, speaking at the funeral, observed that "in transportation circles Mr. Lee was universally recognized as the foremost railroad executive in dealing with questions of employe relationships. He has done more than any other man that I could name to maintain those relationships upon a friendly and mutually loyal basis and to promote harmony between men and management." Atterbury must have been aware that no one would ever use those words to describe him, following his vitriolic response to the 1922 Shopmen's Strike. His further assessment, that Lee's "success in this important work was largely due to his patience, straightforward methods and

the fact that leaders among railroad labor, without exception, had complete confidence in his integrity and absolute fairness," attested to the transformation in labor-management relations that had occurred over the past eleven years. Like Baltimore & Ohio president Daniel Willard, Atterbury had come to accept that labor was a force to be reckoned with, not an enemy to be crushed. Despite Atterbury's familiarity with the person he hoped might one day succeed him, the *New York Times* did a better job of summing up a life cut short. "From the day he left college," a reporter observed, "Elisha Lee was always a railroad man. More than that, he was always a Pennsylvania Railroad man."[211]

As was customary, the *Times* provided Elisha Lee's biography. The information came, almost verbatim, from a Pennsylvania Railroad press release. Over the previous quarter century, that practice had become so common that it had long since ceased to gratify the other Lee whose fate was intertwined with that of the PRR. In October 1906, when a train derailed and plunged into the channel known as the Thorofare, just west of Atlantic City, the news media had initially blamed the Pennsylvania Railroad for a disaster that ended fifty-seven lives. Ivy Ledbetter Lee, hired earlier that year to control the damage from the ICC's investigation into the allocation of coal cars, issued a press release absolving the company of responsibility. Most papers printed the information exactly as he had written it, and the publicity consultant succeeded in shifting the blame away from his employer.

Lee, at least in his public pronouncements, never felt that he was misleading or manipulating the American people. Instead, he insisted that he was setting the record straight, providing factual information that would counter the sensationalistic propaganda fabricated by muckraking journalists, whose only goal was to increase circulation. If those facts had to be carefully selected, Lee reasoned, it was for a good cause. Labor agitation and the growth of economic and political philosophies such as socialism, communism, and anarchism, he concluded, threatened big-business capitalism and democratic freedom—the two philosophies, inextricably intertwined, that were the ineluctable foundation of the United States. Unless he could restore confidence in corporations and the men who led them, by erasing words like *monopoly* and *robber baron* from the lexicon, then America itself was at risk. He found a kindred spirit in W. W. Atterbury, with whom he shared a faith in big business, fear of organized labor, hatred of Bolshevism, and aversion to governmental interference in managerial prerogatives. Their experiences in World

War I reinforced those attitudes, with Lee sidelined by the United States Railroad Administration and Atterbury concluding that that agency had wrecked his railroad.

Their friendship notwithstanding, Lee saw the Pennsylvania Railroad as a vast laboratory for his experiments in the development of public-relations techniques. The company's size, its proximity to the centers of economic and political power, its indispensable role in the system of national transportation and mobility, its restive labor force, and even Atterbury's acerbic management style provided the publicist with ample opportunity to transform anger and suspicion into admiration and loyalty. For his part, Atterbury perceived that Lee had become an inescapable component of railroad management. It was no longer sufficient to survey new routes, design better cars and locomotives, undertake massive engineering projects, or even keep the trains running on time. Passengers, shippers, workers, legislators, and regulators demanded something that the railroads could not provide—lower rates coupled with faster trains, better service, higher wages, shorter hours, increased safety, and improved facilities. It was up to Lee to explain why the Pennsylvania Railroad and its executives could not do all those things at once.

The arrangement between Ivy Lee and W. W. Atterbury worked well during the 1920s, when it coincided with robust economic growth, the emergence of seductive new technologies, widespread antipathy toward organized labor, and the election of probusiness politicians. Lee always assumed that the critics of big-business capitalism and the managers who were associated with it were misinformed and that their counterproductive behavior could be corrected. The furor surrounding the 1914 Ludlow Massacre did not dissuade him from defending John D. Rockefeller Jr., the executive widely blamed for the deaths. The increasing severity of the Great Depression did not shake his faith in the capitalist system and the men who controlled it. In the end, Lee never seriously doubted that his clients were in the right, that they had the best interests of humanity at heart, and that they would never do anything to disgrace him.

And then he met Hitler. Beginning in 1929, during the years of the Weimar Republic, Lee had been a consultant to the giant chemical firm IG Farben. In early 1933, soon after Adolf Hitler attained power as Reich chancellor, Farben executives increased Lee's retainer and asked him to do additional work for the company. Lee declined to advise Farben on matters pertaining to labor relations, but he was interested in developing a better understanding of German attitudes. He traveled to Germany in January 1934 and attended a series of meetings that had been carefully

arranged by business and political leaders. Those individuals included propaganda minister Joseph Goebbels and, eventually, Hitler. During the conversations, Lee reiterated the same advice he had given to Pennsylvania Railroad officials—be forthright, provide accurate information, and explain policies in a clear and concise manner. If the German people, or American detractors of the Nazi regime, could not be persuaded of Hitler's good intentions, Lee insisted, then the Nazis would have to change their ways. It was a monumentally naive assessment of the situation, one that utterly failed to consider the viciousness of the Nazi regime—or the ability of Goebbels and his colleagues to manipulate an individual who prided himself on his ability to manipulate others.[212]

Lee's work with the Nazis coincided with sweeping political changes in the United States. Democrats controlled both houses of Congress, and many of them were longtime opponents of Ivy Lee, his methods, and his clients—and they had been waiting years for an opportunity to exact revenge. In May 1934, the House Un-American Activities Committee began to investigate Lee's activities on behalf of IG Farben. His health was already poor, and he was noticeably affected by the stress. Testifying in secret, Lee explained that he had warned the Nazis against distributing propaganda in the United States and that there was no way to create a positive image for their increasingly severe persecution of Jews. Lee was as charming and well-spoken as ever, and he acquitted himself well. The committee exonerated him and gave him permission to go abroad to recuperate. Lee arrived in Baden-Baden, Germany, on July 12, less than two weeks after Hitler launched a purge—commonly known as the Night of the Long Knives—that eliminated hundreds of his opponents. The members of the Un-American Activities Committee saw an opportunity to take advantage of public anger toward the Nazis while destroying Lee's reputation. On July 11, they released the transcripts of Lee's testimony. Journalists made selective use of his words, and they generated stories that portrayed Lee as an apologist for the Nazis. That outcome was richly ironic, given that Lee had devoted his career to protecting his clients from precisely that kind of treatment, and now he could not even protect himself.[213]

Lee's best client had always been the Pennsylvania Railroad and, despite the furor surrounding his relationship with the Nazis, Atterbury and other PRR executives did not abandon him. He returned to the United States on August 30. The water cure at Baden-Baden did not compensate for the debilitating effects of the adverse publicity that surrounded him, and his health was worse than ever. He nonetheless continued to meet with PRR officials—including Martin Clement and Julien Eysmans, two individuals who attested to changes in the executive ranks. Clement, until recently the vice president in charge of operations, had earned a promotion to executive vice president, replacing Elisha Lee. Eysmans had been the vice president in charge of traffic but was himself in such poor health that he was now in the honorific role of vice president, assistant to the president. They met for the last time on Monday, October 29. Lee paused during the meeting and looked at Clement and Eysmans, individuals he had known for many years. He did not recognize them, nor did he understand where he was. The Pennsylvania Railroad provided a private car to take the company's publicist from Philadelphia to Penn Station, where he was rushed to St. Luke's Hospital. A phalanx of doctors diagnosed an inoperable brain tumor, and they concluded that it had erupted four months earlier, amid the newspaper campaign that accused Lee of conspiring with the Nazis. On November 9, 1934, Lee died at the age of fifty-seven. Atterbury was in Miami, and he did not attend the funeral. The PRR's president nonetheless provided a eulogy, in which he indicated that Lee "had a brilliant mind, absolutely without prejudice. His advice was invaluable. His passing was a great loss to our country. Personally, I shall miss him sadly."[214]

Atterbury and other PRR executives would also miss Lee's ability to create a favorable public image for their company. Ivy Lee was his own best client, and the persona that he crafted for himself suggested that he alone had pioneered the field of public relations. In reality, Lee had never been solely responsible for the ideas for which he claimed credit. Early in his career, he had appropriated the innovations of his first partner, journalist George F. Parker, whom he later unceremoniously cast aside, writing Parker out of the narrative that encompassed his life's work. Parker had died in 1928 and was no longer able to contest Lee's self-aggrandizement. By August 1933, his health already failing, Lee had taken the precaution of joining forces with another partner, his onetime assistant Thomas Joseph Ross. The public-relations firm, now known as Ivy Lee & T. J. Ross, continued to serve the PRR and other clients, long after Lee's death. Its ability to sway the attitudes of journalists, politicians, regulators, and other Americans had largely disappeared, however, at least as far as the Pennsylvania Railroad was concerned.[215]

By November 1934, W. W. Atterbury had lost the executive who was his protégé and presumed successor and the publicist who was his advisor, confidant, and friend. He had also lost touch with the new political and economic realities of the United States during the Great Depression. It is a truism that the party in power will experience setbacks in the midterm elections, but the events of 1934 marked the exception to that rule. On November 6, three days before Ivy Lee's life came to an end, Americans went to the polls. The Democrats gained nine seats in the Senate, giving them better than a two-thirds majority. Nine additional House seats ensured that the majority there exceeded 75 percent. By the time the votes were counted, it was clear that only seven states would have Republican governors. Based on those results, political pundits concluded that the Republican Party was finished.

In Pennsylvania, Gifford Pinchot did not run for reelection. That was some small comfort to Atterbury, who despised Pinchot, a progressive Republican and supporter of Prohibition, who cooperated with Roosevelt's New Deal. Pinchot's replacement, Atterbury nonetheless concluded, was far worse. George Howard Earle III was born into one of the most prominent families in the United States. Raised as a Republican, like many other Americans he expressed his dismay at Herbert Hoover's ineffectual efforts to end the Great Depression. Earle campaigned on behalf of Roosevelt in the 1932 presidential elections and, in 1934, entered the gubernatorial race as a Democrat. His timing was fortuitous, as the city's Republican machine was beginning to lose its grip on municipal politics. William Vare, the last survivor of the Vare brothers, earned the enmity of Governor Pinchot, who had refused to certify his victory in the 1926 Senate race. Vare suffered a stroke in August 1928, yet slowly reestablished at least a portion of his power in Philadelphia. He died on August 7, 1934, six years to the day after his stroke and only weeks before the election. The power vacuum increased the authority of Joseph R. Grundy, the Pinchot ally who briefly occupied the Senate seat that Vare considered rightfully his. Grundy, like Pinchot, was an ardent foe of Atterbury, who had routinely cooperated with the Vare machine to get things done in the PRR's headquarters city.

Philadelphia's weakened Republican base and votes from rural counties were not enough to save state attorney general William A. Schnader, Earle's opponent in the 1934 gubernatorial race. For the first time since 1890, Pennsylvania's governor was a Democrat. After he was sworn into office on January 15, 1935, Earle launched the "Little New Deal," one that at times went beyond what even Roosevelt was able to accomplish in Washington. Earle supported the construction of the Pennsylvania Turnpike, a transportation artery that was bound to reduce patronage on the PRR's passenger trains. He courted the labor vote, increased collective-bargaining rights, and outlawed the private police forces that coal and steel company executives routinely deployed to crush strikes. Polls consistently ranked Earle as one of the most popular politicians in the United States, only slightly below the president. In 1937, he appeared on the cover of *Time* magazine, the same publication that had featured Atterbury's portrait only four years earlier.[216]

The political developments in Pennsylvania were but a local manifestation of a national transformation that Atterbury found troubling, if not terrifying. Like Earle, Atterbury had been disappointed by Hoover's actions following the stock market crash. The PRR's president was initially optimistic about Roosevelt's leadership skills and policy initiatives. Atterbury hoped that the model of business-government cooperation embodied in the National Recovery Administration—something that mirrored his own associationalist beliefs—would restore the nation to prosperity without altering the relationship between private enterprise and the public sector. An overwhelmingly Democratic Congress nonetheless pushed Roosevelt to the political Left, encouraging the president to vilify big business and court the votes of organized labor. Those policies were anathema to an executive who had spent decades battling independent unions and warning his fellow Americans about the threat of incremental Bolshevization. Section 7(a) of the National Industrial Recovery Act permitted Atterbury's Employe Representation Plan to remain the collective-bargaining agent for much of the PRR's workforce. Atterbury nonetheless became one of the chief targets of Transportation Coordinator Joseph Eastman and other federal officials, who questioned his salary and attacked his union. As the letters received by Eastman revealed, Section 7(a) persuaded many workers that Roosevelt wanted them to join independent unions and they called on their elected officials to strengthen laws protecting organized labor. The National Labor Relations Act, which Roosevelt signed into law on July 5, 1935, abolished the ERP and other company unions and, for the first time, stipulated that employers and employees would have equal power at the bargaining table. Roosevelt and the federal government had chosen sides in the battle between management and labor.

It was more than someone like General Atterbury could stand. In August 1934, wealthy and influential individuals, including Irénée du Pont and former General Motors director John Jakob Raskob, established the American Liberty League. Many of the founders had, like Atterbury, been involved in the Association Against the Prohibition Amendment. The Liberty League adopted a policy of bipartisanship, and its members defended individual

freedom and the sanctity of private property—for the affluent, at least—and resolutely opposed Roosevelt and what they considered the socialistic tendencies of the New Deal. Given his attitudes and the evolving nature of the political economy, in the years to come Atterbury would likely have played an active role in the Liberty League.[217]

He did not live that long. On July 26, 1934, Atterbury entered the Bryn Mawr Hospital, complaining of abdominal pain. Doctors diagnosed gallstones and operated the following day. It was, in all likelihood, cancer of the liver, and it was incurable.[218] Atterbury was too ill to attend the August 24 meeting of the Eastern Railroads Coordinating Committee, the group that, in collaboration with Transportation Coordinator Eastman, was supposed to restore prosperity through the elimination of waste and inefficiency.[219] Three weeks later, the board of directors temporarily relieved Atterbury of his duties, to give him time to recuperate. Martin Clement, the executive vice president, assumed Atterbury's responsibilities and became president in all but name. On October 15, a reporter for the *Philadelphia Inquirer* noted, "What appears to be a well-grounded rumor at Broad Street Station says that General W. W. Atterbury—due to a long illness—sent to the board of directors his resignation as president of the Pennsylvania Railroad." The rumor mill also suggested that "the board read the letter and answered it promptly by tearing it into shreds and by casting said sheds in the waste paper basket." Whether the story was accurate or not, on the following day, the company issued a press release stating that Atterbury would retire on January 31, 1936, when he reached the age of seventy.[220]

Atterbury left Philadelphia on October 20, the same day that the Pennsylvania Railroad announced that he would continue as president for another fourteen months. He was destined for Florida, accompanied by his wife, on board the yacht that he named in her honor. The *Arminia* arrived in

Facing, W. W. Atterbury and his wife, Arminia, enjoyed the privileges associated with his status as the PRR's president, which included spending time on the water. During the late 1920s, the two were at Montauk Point, on board the *Shadow K*, a yacht belonging to real estate developer Carl Fisher. Atterbury nonetheless preferred the vessel that he named for his spouse. The *Arminia* was docked in Miami in November 1934, when Atterbury gave one of his last interviews to reporters. He claimed to be in excellent health, but his appearance—vastly different from the demeanor shown here—shocked those who saw him. *William Wallace Atterbury Photographs, Hagley Museum & Library, acc. 1994.309.*

Miami in early November, where Atterbury was informed that Ivy Ledbetter Lee had died in a New York hospital. There was thus considerable poignancy in his comments about the loss of his friend. As for his own health, Atterbury projected optimism. Sitting in a deck chair, he told a reporter that "I haven't felt as good as I do today since last July." Thumping his chest, he announced that "I'm the livest, kick'n'est person you ever saw." The accompanying photo belied the confident assertion, showing Atterbury gaunt and ill at ease, his eyes vacant and his mouth contorted downward in a rictus of pain. Atterbury returned to Philadelphia on December 21, informing reporters that he would be back at his desk at the beginning of the new year.[221]

Atterbury never returned to his desk, and his one remaining visit to Broad Street Station was to tender his resignation, in person. He did not attend the annual stockholders' meeting on April 9. Investors voted to thank him for his service to the company and wish him a rapid recovery. One of them recommended that Atterbury receive a $15,000 bonus for his lifetime of work on behalf of the Pennsylvania Railroad. W. H. Nunamacher, a shareholder from Newark, introduced a resolution that would waive the mandatory retirement age and enable Atterbury to remain as president through 1941—long enough to see the electrification of the route between New York, Washington, and Harrisburg through to completion. The final decision on each of the shareholder motions was up to the board of directors, who would meet again on April 24.[222]

There was considerable value in maintaining investor confidence in the continuity of leadership during the economic crisis of the Great Depression, but Atterbury and his closest associates knew that the charade would have to come to an end. On April 17, Atterbury composed a letter to Percival Roberts Jr., the iconoclastic director who had resigned when the Special Committee on Organization would not accept his suggestions for reforming the 1920 corporate structure. He had since returned to the PRR and had been instrumental in the organization of Pennroad—the investment affiliate that was now drawing scrutiny from regulators and criticism from once-loyal Pennsylvania Railroad shareholders. "My continued absence since July of last year," Atterbury noted, "and the improbability that any improvement in my condition will permit me to resume active work in the near future, make it most desirable that at this next meeting my retirement be authorized and my successor elected." Eighteen months earlier, the choice of a replacement would have been obvious, in the personage of Elisha Lee. Now, everything was different. "Of course, I have but one recommendation to make as to

my successor," Atterbury informed the board, "and that is, Mr. M. W. Clement, now Vice President." Atterbury could not bring himself to make a decision of equal importance. Like Samuel Rea before him, he declined to recommend someone who would follow Clement into the presidency and who could preserve the duality of managerial philosophies that, in the past, had been critical to the PRR's success. "We have among our Vice Presidents four or five men who are of Presidential timber, but it is not necessary at this time to make a selection of Mr. Clement's possible successor," he noted. Atterbury accordingly recommended that the office of executive vice president be eliminated, leaving the company's future in the hands of Martin Withington Clement.[223]

Atterbury attended the April 24 board meeting—the first since the onset of his illness, and the last. He offered his resignation and praised the individual who would take his place, calling Clement "unquestionably the ablest railroad executive in the country." The directors accepted Atterbury's resignation, and a career that began in 1886 and stretched through the peak of the PRR's prosperity, a world war, and into the Great Depression came to an end. On September 12, 1935, Atterbury returned to the Bryn Mawr Hospital, where doctors examined him but chose not to confine him to a bed. Eight days later, he was sitting in a chair, talking with his wife. At half past three in the afternoon, and like Elisha Lee before him, the tenth president of the Pennsylvania Railroad succumbed to a stroke. As a civilian and as a soldier, Atterbury had fought innumerable battles on two continents. Now, his wars were over.[224]

More than a thousand people attended Atterbury's funeral, held at Bryn Mawr's Church of the Redeemer at 3:00 p.m. on September 23. Many arrived on an eight-car special train that ran directly from Penn Station to Bryn Mawr. The Pennsylvania Railroad's corporate offices closed at 1:00 p.m., and every train from Suburban Station, along the Main Line to Paoli, was equipped with additional coaches for those who wished to attend the service. The guests included prominent state and local politicians, investment bankers, and industrialists. Samuel Vauclain was there, representing the Baldwin Locomotive Works. So was Pierre S. du Pont, General Motors vice president Alfred H. Swayne, and the president of US Steel. There was no formal military presence, but a bounty of medals attested to the respect accorded to Atterbury by numerous fellow members of the American Expeditionary Forces. For more than a decade, Atterbury had both attacked and cooperated with executives at other railroads as he protected the PRR's interests in the various system plans that arose from the Transportation Act of 1920. Many of those allies and adversaries were there, including Patrick Crowley and Frederick Williamson from the New York Central, Edward E. Loomis at the Lehigh Valley, and the B&O's George Shriver. The Port Authority, an agency that aroused Atterbury's fierce opposition, sent three of its commissioners. At least some of the employees of the Pennsylvania Railroad forgave the Shopmen's Strike and the many other ways in which Atterbury had attempted to subordinate their interests to the welfare of the company and its management. "There were gray-haired, broad shouldered men with the heavy wrists and hands and prominent knuckles of boiler-makers and mechanics," a reporter observed, "men wearing the little buttons of the railroad brotherhoods in their lapels, the enginemen and firemen distinguished by their weather-beaten faces, marked by the innumerable crow's feet imprinted by hours of peering through fog, through rain, through the beating heat of summertime." Some of those employees were there out of sincere devotion, others because it was expected of them, and still others because they had thrown in their lot with the Employe Representation Plan rather than the independent unions that were on the verge of replacing it. Even accounting for journalistic embellishment, the description nonetheless attested to the perseverance of Atterbury's utopian vision of a shared culture of mutual respect between management and men.[225]

There was no eulogy at Atterbury's funeral, and one was not needed. All those who worked with him and fought against him, who benefited and suffered because of his actions, had their own assessment of his legacy. Even though he served only briefly in the American Expeditionary Forces, Atterbury used his military title for the remainder of his life. It was fitting that in April 1937, when the Pennsylvania Railroad introduced a new train between New York and Chicago—second only to *The Broadway Limited* in prestige—it carried the name of *The General*.[226] Executives from a multitude of companies praised his skill and his contributions to the Pennsylvania Railroad and the nation. Most workers said little, at least in public. The *Machinists' Monthly Journal*, published by the labor organization that had futilely resisted the implementation of the Employe Representation Plan, did not even mention that he had died. Perhaps the only comment that would provoke universal acknowledgment appeared in the *Philadelphia Inquirer*. "A builder and a fighter was General Atterbury," the editor suggested, "but first and last he was a railroad man of pre-eminent courage and ability."[227]

Compared to his accomplishments as a soldier and a railroader, Atterbury's financial legacy was modest. His will, probated four days after his funeral, suggested that his estate was valued at something over $257,000. The true appraisal was not filed until January 30, 1936, four days after the death of Henry Stimson Atterbury, W. W. Atterbury's brother. The full amount was $613,306.89, more than 87 percent of which represented securities—mostly of the Pennsylvania Railroad and its affiliates. It was a substantial sum, one that was certain to instill envy and anger among many Americans who continued to suffer the effects of the Great Depression. The editor of the trade journal *Railway Age* thought it necessary to defend Atterbury's affluence. "The criticism is frequently made of the organization of large corporate enterprises that managements are responsible to no one but themselves and hence are more concerned with the power, prestige and salary of their position as managers than they are with protecting the interests of the owners." That statement reflected the allegations made by Eastman during the summer of 1933 and seconded by such individuals as Couzens, Jones, and Wheeler. "Great corporations with widely held stock are not really controlled by the owners of their properties," Eastman had asserted, "but rather by boards of directors" who acceded to unnecessarily large executive compensation. Many people agreed with that assessment, but many others did not. "But when a manager of an enterprise makes stock in his company the principal basis of his estate, he identifies his interest with that of the other owners of the property," *Railway Age* declared. "There can be no better earnest of a corporate manager's sincerity and his determination to do his utmost for those to whom he is responsible than the fact that his personal fortune is linked with theirs." If Eastman, Couzens, Jones, and Wheeler found Atterbury's wealth excessive, or his estate too large, then they did not say so.[228]

After attending his predecessor's funeral, Martin Clement went back to the business of running the nation's most important railroad. Even though fate had made him president, there was little in his background to suggest that he was not up to the task. Clement, like most of his predecessors and fellow executives, had been associated with the PRR for his entire adult life. Pennsylvania Railroad freight and passenger trains were an inescapable part of Sunbury, Pennsylvania, where Clement was born in 1881. Two decades later, after graduating from Trinity College with a degree in civil engineering, he began work with his first and only employer, the Pennsylvania Railroad. He started as a rodman, assisting Samuel Rea in his early efforts to find a way underneath the Hudson River and into Manhattan. In January 1910, he earned a promotion to supervisor in the office of the general manager at Philadelphia. Clement honed his skills by making the customary tour of the system, to the Manhattan Division in June 1913 and to the Pittsburgh Division that December. He spent a little less than two years as a division engineer on the New York, Philadelphia & Norfolk, then took on similar responsibilities at the PRR proper, examining improvements in Greater New York. He moved to the New Jersey Division as principal assistant engineer and then back to the NYP&N as superintendent. In September 1918, with the Pennsylvania Railroad under USRA oversight, Clement became superintendent of freight transportation. Following the war and the 1920 reorganization, Clement became the general superintendent of the Lake Division, and by 1923, he was general manager of the Central Region. By then, Elisha Lee was being groomed for the presidency, and Clement followed one step behind—to assistant vice president in charge of operations in 1925, then to vice president in charge of operations the following year. Lee's premature death in August 1933 enabled Clement to assume the role of vice president two months later. He soon played an important role in organizing the Association of American Railroads, the trade group that enabled the carriers to present a united front against the onslaught of New Deal legislation and regulation.[229]

When Atterbury resigned abruptly on April 24, 1935, Clement was only fifty-three. He thus became the youngest chief executive since the days of J. Edgar Thomson and Tom Scott. In the past, Clement had shown evidence that he was willing to emulate the brusque and confrontational style of his predecessor, particularly in the realm of labor relations. "If a general in charge of a great army led his troops to disaster," Clement wrote in 1927, "he is in no wise responsible to the men, only to his country." There seemed little doubt, therefore, that Clement's loyalties lay with the corporation that he managed, rather than with the individuals who kept the trains running. He shared Atterbury's distaste for socialism, something that was hardly uncommon among business executives. As he told reporters two days after becoming president, "The American people are too wise to permit government ownership of the carriers," asserting that such a radical remedy for the problems created by the Depression would be nothing short of "disastrous."[230]

The PRR's newest chief executive also made it clear that he would not countenance any departure from the ventures and policies that Atterbury had left to him. "I shall certainly project into the future his plans as he laid them down," Clement emphasized. Those initiatives included the completion of electrification between New York and Washington, but little beyond that. Given the state of the economy, Clement conceded, further investments of that

Martin W. Clement (1881–1966) was a capable administrator who rose steadily through the ranks of the PRR system—yet he would not likely have ascended to the presidency had it not been for the untimely death of Elisha Lee. When he became the chief executive officer, in 1935, Clement made it clear that he would not continue Atterbury's involvement in politics, labor relations, or efforts to defend big-business capitalism against the intrusion of government. *Collection of the Historical Society of Pennsylvania.*

scale were unlikely. When a reporter asked if catenary would one day reach all the way to Pittsburgh, he replied with a question of his own. "Can you tell me when prosperity is coming back?" The rejoinder was starkly different from Atterbury's confident pronouncements early in the Depression that economic recovery was just around the corner. The divergence may have reflected personality differences between the two executives or, more likely, the sad reality that five years of economic catastrophe had left everyone exhausted and disillusioned. In any event, Clement, like Rea before him, had little difficulty asserting that steam locomotives would continue to "rule for a long time" on the Pennsylvania Railroad and other carriers. It was a prophetic comment, one that would come back to haunt Clement a decade later when the PRR waited too long to embrace dieselization.[231]

From the outset of his presidency, Clement was nonetheless determined to prove that he was no Atterbury. His realization, following the death of Elisha Lee, that he would be the next president of the Pennsylvania Railroad mellowed his tone, or at least impressed upon him the value of prudence. Clement was careful to remind workers and labor leaders that he had "no thought" of reducing wages or interfering with independent unions. He also shied away from Atterbury's attacks on Eastman and other critics who questioned the propriety of executive salaries. Following his promotion to the presidency, Clement brought home $60,470 after taxes—thanks to the willingness of the company's directors to lift the salary cap that Atterbury had grudgingly accepted.[232] Only three other PRR executives, all vice presidents, took home more than $50,000 a year—Walter Franklin at $53,033, John Deasy at $51,178, and Julien Eysmans at $50,101. That compensation nonetheless attracted the attention of Senator Burton Wheeler, still busily engaged in his investigation into railroads and holding companies. Clement reassured Wheeler that—unlike Leonor Loree at the Delaware & Hudson—his entire paycheck came directly from the Pennsylvania Railroad and not from any of its subsidiaries or affiliates. Wheeler nonetheless secured Clement's admission that his salary was "$100,000 a year gross, about $60,000 net." When the senator asked, "What becomes of the other $40,000?" Clement quickly deadpanned, "I give it to the government." The PRR executive provided a further display of his jocularity when he asked Wheeler for a copy of a photograph showing the two of them together. The politician could play the same game and promptly handed Clement a signed image, labeled "from one farm boy to another." The delicately choreographed interaction was vastly different from Atterbury's vitriolic intransigence, a persona that belonged to a different generation.[233]

Clement was also acutely aware of the criticism generated by his predecessor's dual role as a Republican national committeeman and as the nation's most prominent railroad executive. When Clement warned of the dangers associated with nationalization, something that would go far beyond the federalization of the World War I years, he averred that the issue was "awfully close to politics"—a subject that he was determined to avoid. Two years into the first Roosevelt administration, and with voters in the mood to punish business executives, Clement sought to deflect any further repercussions from perceived conflicts of interest. "The Pennsylvania Railroad is not in politics," he emphasized. "We realize that there are thirteen States in which to travel. Some are Democratic and some are Republican. As far as I am concerned the railroad is not in politics because we must deal with the powers that be in those States that we serve."[234]

Despite Clement's remarks, Pennsylvania Railroad executives would continue to be involved in politics. His comments nonetheless constituted an admission that the public policy affected the corporation to a far greater extent than the company's executives controlled the political process. The Great Depression and the New Deal had also empowered organized labor, ensuring that more employees than ever before would be able to negotiate on equal terms with their managers. Henceforth, Clement and other Pennsylvania Railroad executives would participate in a complex environment in which the corporation, the government, and the labor force were wired together in a system of mutual interdependence, and they would engage in endless negotiations for the allocation of political and economic power.

The vagaries of fate had made Clement the president of the nation's most important transportation company, an enterprise that was linked to the welfare of more than a hundred thousand employees and millions more who depended on rail service. The executive who could only ask when prosperity might return would find it difficult if not impossible to anticipate additional years of economic malaise, another global war, and the steady erosion of the railroad's freight and passenger business. Clement would go forth into that uncertain future, lacking the guidance of a political power broker, a public-relations expert, or a mentor and without any strategic vision other than to carry on as his predecessors had done before him.

Chapter 3

Adversaries

A nation at war was a nation that moved by rail. The US Army required 24,483 freight cars to provide the military ordinance of a single convoy bound for a classified destination. Seventy-five million gallons of gasoline aboard 12,500 tank cars. Four thousand freight cars bearing cases of supplies. Ten thousand trucks, 30,000 jeeps, and 500 tanks, lashed to nearly 4,500 flat cars. Twenty-five million shells, a thousand bombs, and half a billion rounds of ammunition, carefully stowed in boxcars and rigorously segregated from the rest of the cargo. Antiaircraft guns, machine guns, searchlights, airplanes, PT boats, and a hundred locomotives—the products of American industrial might—carried to the nation's bustling ports by America's preeminent carrier of freight. Almost anywhere in the United States, a young boy looking up from his favorite fishing spot, a mother anxiously shooing her children away from the railroad tracks, or a driver impatiently waiting at a grade crossing might see a steam locomotive thundering by, trailing fifty freight cars, part of that convoy of nearly twenty-five thousand. On average, seven of those cars, anywhere in America, would carry the Keystone herald of the Pennsylvania Railroad.

One of those cars was #59944, an ordinary Class X31 round-roofed fifty-foot boxcar, similar to thousands of other cars on the Pennsylvania Railroad. It left Pittsburgh on May 23, 1943, carrying machinery parts bound for Seattle. By June 12, it was being loaded with wood pulp in Everett, Washington, and four days later, it was en route to Wachusett, Massachusetts, passing through the ripening wheat fields of North Dakota on June 22. On July 2, it reached its destination, and workers quickly replaced

the wood pulp with rolls of paper. That paper, a necessary supply for the burgeoning wartime bureaucracy, arrived in the nation's capital on July 6. The car then went to Baltimore, received a load of aircraft components, then sped west to Wichita, Kansas. The parts were gone by July 19, replaced by hospital supplies, rushed west to California for shipment to troops fighting in the Pacific Theater. On August 3, the car crossed the Southern Pacific's Lucin Cutoff over the Great Salt Lake, and by August 7, it was rolling through orange groves. It carried on, along San Francisco Bay, and by August 21, it was amid the redwoods of Northern California, ready to be loaded with Feather River lumber. On September 10, workmen in Chicago pulled that lumber through the open door of PRR #59944, before sending the car again on its way.[1]

The rapid progress of boxcar #59944 was a journey of the imagination, conducted in the heads and through the pens of the Al Paul Lefton advertising agency in Philadelphia. Despite marketing claims, freight cars typically moved no more than fifty miles per day, on average. It was highly unlikely that #59944, in less than four months, covered "approximately 15,000 miles of travel, over many railroads

Facing, The 1943 travels of boxcar #59944 arose largely from the imagination of advertising executives rather than from waybills and train orders. Its journey nonetheless suggested the enormous resources that the United States could bring to bear against the Axis powers—as well as the critical role of the Pennsylvania Railroad in the war effort. *Author's collection.*

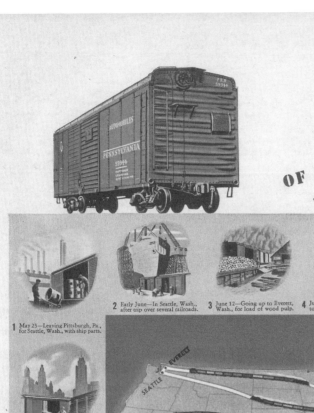

DIARY
OF A WARTIME FREIGHT CAR
— PENNSYLVANIA 59944

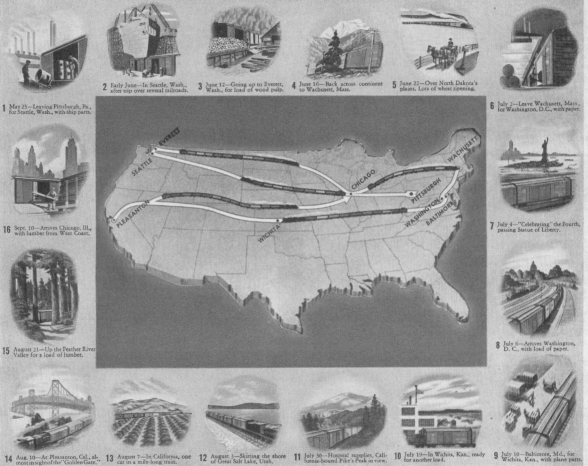

1 May 23—Leaving Pittsburgh, Pa., for Seattle, Wash., with ship parts.

2 Early June—In Seattle, Wash., after trip over several railroads.

3 June 12—Going up to Everett, Wash., for load of wood pulp.

4 June 16—Back across continent to Wachusett, Mass.

5 June 22—Over North Dakota's plains. Lots of wheat ripening.

6 July 2—Leave Wachusett, Mass., for Washington, D.C., with paper.

7 July 4—"Celebrating" the Fourth, passing Statue of Liberty.

8 July 6—Arrives Washington, D. C., with load of paper.

9 July 10—Baltimore, Md., for Wichita, Kan., with plane parts.

10 July 19—In Wichita, Kan., ready for another load.

11 July 30—Hospital supplies, California-bound. Pike's Peak in view.

12 August 3—Skirting the shore of Great Salt Lake, Utah.

13 August 7—In California, one car in a mile-long train.

14 Aug. 10—At Pleasanton, Cal., almost in sight of the "Golden Gate."

15 August 21—Up the Feather River Valley for a load of lumber.

16 Sept. 10—Arrives Chicago, Ill., with lumber from West Coast.

LET'S EXAMINE the "work sheet" of a typical freight car... Pennsylvania Railroad 59944. Let's see where it has been... what it has carried...how much work it has done.

The period covered is a short one, slightly more than three summer months of 1943. Yet note over how much territory No. 59944 has traveled, the variety of shipments it has delivered; approximately 15,000 miles of travel, over many railroads besides its "home" line ... the Pennsylvania Railroad.

An exception? Not a bit! Pennsylvania 59944 is typical of how the 1,800,000 freight cars of the American railroads are serving

the war effort. It illustrates how the railroads in a mighty and united effort have made it possible to haul more tons per trip — over longer distances — at greater speeds — than ever before in the history of railroading.

BUY UNITED STATES WAR BONDS AND STAMPS

Pennsylvania Railroad
Serving the Nation

★ 47,016 in the Armed Forces ★ 199 have given their lives for their Country

World War II placed unprecedented demands on the Pennsylvania Railroad, as raw material and manufactured goods moved toward both coasts, destined for the European and Pacific Theaters. With U-boats menacing coastal shipping, the PRR experienced a brief resurgence in oil traffic. Texas crude moved to East Coast refineries in solid trains of tank cars like this one, behind N2sa #8912, passing through Davis, Indiana. *Bud Laws photo, General Negative Collection, Railroad Museum of Pennsylvania, PHMC.*

besides its 'home' line . . . in a mighty and united effort." The assertion that the car rolled past the Statue of Liberty on the Fourth of July further strained the limits of credulity. But, as Pennsylvania Railroad officials emphasized, it was a trip that *might* have happened. They intended to reassure the American public that the traffic chaos that had characterized the previous world war would not materialize. The intrusive government control once exercised by the United States Railroad Administration was no longer necessary, they insisted, and private management could provide the transportation necessary to win a global conflict. The contributions of PRR employees, so obviously necessary to the expeditious movement of #59944, likewise took place in an environment untainted by the contentious labor

disputes of the late 1910s and early 1920s. Whatever the mistakes of the past, efficiency and harmony now characterized the Pennsylvania Railroad and the other elements of the national transportation system.[2]

While the journey of boxcar #59944 took place in advertisements rather than in reality, there was nothing imaginary about the wartime performance of the Pennsylvania Railroad. The extraordinary efforts of the railroads during World War II have often, and quite rightly, been called the industry's finest hour. During the first eight months of 1942, they handled a third more freight and half again as many passengers, compared to the same period during the pre-Depression year of 1929—despite a 25 percent reduction in the number of passenger cars and a 20 percent decrease in locomotives and freight cars. The additional traffic included millions of gallons of oil, at a time when coastal shipping was vulnerable to attacks by German U-boats.[3] By the time the war ended, on September 2, 1945, the nation's railroads carried 90 percent of the freight consigned to the army and the navy. In the forty-five months that elapsed since the attack on Pearl Harbor, more than 97 percent of all military personnel reached their destination by rail, often traveling on one of the 113,891 troop trains that carried MAIN (Military Authorization Identification Number) designations.[4]

The Pennsylvania Railroad and its employees contributed mightily to that performance, and in 1942, they handled more than 42 percent of the freight that traveled over the four eastern trunk lines. Between 1939 and 1944, the PRR's freight traffic more than doubled, while passenger volume increased four times over. Civilian travel became difficult and inconvenient, as the company gave priority to military personnel. In one representative week, between February 15 and February 21, 1942, the PRR moved 125 extra trains of military traffic—and that number would only increase as the war intensified. Travelers also included 150,000 German prisoners of war—nearly two-thirds of the number brought to the United States—who moved along the PRR for at least part of the distance to their internment camps. The Pennsylvania Railroad was also a tempting target for spies and saboteurs. The most serious attempt at espionage in wartime America occurred during the summer of 1942, when a German U-boat landed eight saboteurs on Long Island. They intended to focus their efforts on the PRR, by blowing up Hell Gate Bridge, the Horseshoe Curve, and the Newark, New Jersey, passenger station. The plot failed, thanks to poor planning and the willingness of the group's leader to defect to the United States, but it nonetheless indicated that German military planners were aware of the critical role played by the Pennsylvania Railroad in the American war effort.[5]

The Pennsylvania Railroad's greatest contribution to the war effort came from its people rather than from its locomotives, cars, and physical plant. On the home front, employees purchased more than $72 million in war bonds. They also served in all branches of the armed forces, and by late 1942 and into early 1943, they were entering military service at a rate of more than 2,000 per month. By the end of the war, 54,712—equivalent to a third of the company's 1942 workforce—had become soldiers.[6]

The extraordinary achievements of the Pennsylvania Railroad and its employees, when faced with the adversity of a global war, came at considerable cost. The greatest sacrifice came from the 1,307 PRR personnel who died in service of their country. Their memorial, *The Angel of Resurrection*, inscribed with their names, has since 1952 overlooked the concourse of 30th Street Station in Philadelphia. The consequences were no less severe for the civilian railroaders who suffered injury or death amid the surge of wartime traffic. Those who escaped unharmed nonetheless endured the relentless demands of wartime transportation, as there were never enough employees, locomotives, or cars to accommodate the trains that rolled ceaselessly across the PRR system. They likely brought home higher wages than they had ever earned before, yet they faced

pressure—often as much from the federal government as from executives—to curtail inflation by sacrificing their earnings. Native-born, White, male employees, who had long dominated the railroad workplace, increasingly labored alongside Blacks, women, and Hispanics. Both managers and federal officials substantially limited the tasks assigned to the newcomers, while asserting that they would only be employed for the duration of the war. Many White employees nonetheless suspected that even modest steps toward workplace equality would come at their expense. Far from engendering solidarity, therefore, the wartime experience at times transformed different groups of employees into adversaries.

The escalating labor costs of the war years also contributed to the PRR's disappointing financial performance, particularly in the years immediately following the Allied victory. There was nothing new about the adversarial relationship between the Pennsylvania Railroad and the Interstate Commerce Commission, and regulatory reluctance to grant rate increases was something that corporate executives no doubt expected. What was new, however, was the increasing antagonism between the PRR and the investment-banking community. Financial analysts who had waited patiently through the grim years of the Great Depression and counseled patriotic forbearance during the war expected a commensurate postwar return on investment. They did not get it, and they could now be added to the growing list of the Pennsylvania Railroad's adversaries.

Military Railroaders

Many of the Pennsylvania Railroad employees who served in the armed forces were associated with the Military Railway Service. Eighty years earlier, during the Civil War, some of their predecessors had worked for the United States Military Rail Roads, under the direction of the PRR's former chief engineer, Herman Haupt. In his simultaneous capacity as the Pennsylvania Railroad's vice president and as the assistant secretary of war, Tom Scott oversaw the movement of troops and supplies on behalf of the Union army. During World War I, W. W. Atterbury became the director general of transportation for the American Expeditionary Forces. The army acknowledged his contributions with a new training facility—Camp Atterbury—built in 1942 near Columbus, Indiana.[7]

The rapid demobilization that followed the end of World War I undermined the organizational continuity of the US Army and jeopardized national security—prompting Congress to adopt the National Defense Act of 1920. The legislation enabled the organization of thirty-two railway operating battalions and a single shop battalion, with reserve officers selected from civilian railway personnel. The 492nd Engineer Battalion (Railway), established in December 1921, was assigned to the PRR in February 1923 and headquartered in Philadelphia. American isolationism, coupled with the financial exigencies of the Great Depression, nonetheless ensured that the Military Railway Service existed largely on paper.[8]

The deteriorating political situation in Europe led to a rapid expansion in the military's transportation capabilities. In February 1939, Carl R. Gray Jr., the executive vice president of the Chicago, St. Paul, Minneapolis & Omaha Railroad, became the manager of the Military Railway Service. In one of his first acts, Gray selected Charles D. Young, the PRR's vice president in charge of real estate, purchases, and insurance, as a consultant. Young initially spent much of his time in Washington, acting as a liaison with federal officials and freeing Gray to enlist the support of railroad executives across the United States. Working in collaboration with Colonel John J. Kingman, the assistant to the army's chief of engineers, Gray and Young established the organizational structure that would enable the Military Railway Service to cope with the demands of a two-front war.[9]

By the end of the war, the Pennsylvania Railroad sponsored six Military Railway Service units, more than any other carrier. In February 1941, well before American involvement, the MRS redesignated the 492nd Engineer Battalion (Railway) as the 730th Engineer Battalion (Railway Operating), later designated as the 730th Railway Operating Battalion. It was not activated until May 1942, when PRR personnel began their training at the appropriately named Camp Thomas A. Scott, near Fort Wayne, Indiana. In January 1943, the unit arrived in Khorramshahr, Iran, assigned to the Northern Division of the Trans-Iranian Railway, between Dorud and Teheran. The PRR's soldier-railroaders spent the remainder of the war ensuring the flow of Lend-Lease supplies to the Soviet Union.[10]

In addition to the 730th, the PRR sponsored the 717th and 724th Operating Battalions, activated in December 1943.[11] The 717th also trained at Camp Scott, as did the 729th Railway Operating Battalion (New Haven) and the 745th Railway Operating Battalion (Chicago, Burlington & Quincy). Following training at Fort Sam Houston, Texas, and Camp Shelby, Mississippi, the personnel of the 724th sailed for Europe in August 1944.[12] Another Railway Operating Battalion, the 746th, sponsored by the Missouri-Kansas-Texas Railroad, included Company D, the sole unit with experience in electrified railways. As part of their training, the personnel of the 746th were assigned to a private high school in Harrisburg, Pennsylvania, close to the recently completed catenary that stretched east to Philadelphia. PRR shop forces participated in the 756th Railway Shop Battalion, which mobilized in January 1943. Their personnel arrived in England in September 1943 and soon began assembling locomotive components, sent from the United States, before moving to Marseille in November 1944. By May 1945, they had completed 10,000 freight cars in France, part of the 28,801 cars they built while stationed overseas.[13]

The PRR-sponsored 706th Railway Grand Division was one of eleven units that constituted the operational structure of the Military Railway Service.[14] Its personnel arrived in France in August 1944, and they were soon working to restore rail service to Paris. On August 24, Lieutenant D. C. Hastings, an assistant engineer of track for the 706th, became the first person to enter the newly liberated city by train, riding on a rail diesel car. The smooth functioning of the Military Railway Service in France resulted from a decision, made prior to D-Day by Allied supreme commander Dwight D. Eisenhower, to establish an Inter-Allied Railway Commission. John A. Appleton, the general manager of the PRR's New York Zone—during the war holding the rank of brigadier general—was the sole US representative on the committee. As with several of his predecessors, Appleton would use his military experience to assist the Pennsylvania Railroad in the postwar environment.[15]

Managing Wartime Transportation

The onset of war rapidly transformed the surplus of cars and locomotives, characteristic of the Great Depression, into an acute shortage. It was critically important, therefore, to more efficiently allocate the existing capacity. On December 18, 1941, President Franklin D. Roosevelt issued Executive Order 8989, creating the Office of Defense Transportation. To lead the new agency, Roosevelt selected an individual who was intimately familiar with transportation policy. Joseph B. Eastman joined the Interstate Commerce Commission in 1919 and soon established a reputation for his shrewd questioning of railroad executives on such matters as consolidation plans and investments in truck and bus operations. In 1933, Roosevelt chose Eastman as the federal coordinator of transportation in a valiant but unsuccessful effort to restore the railroads to prosperity by ensuring that they operated more efficiently. Following the passage of the Motor Carrier Act in 1935, Eastman joined the ICC's Motor Carrier Division. More than any of his regulatory contemporaries, Eastman perceived the merits of coordinated transportation entities and decried regulatory policies that segregated one mode from another.

In his newest role, Eastman noted that "there has never before been an agency like the Office of Defense Transportation." The ODT's Division of Railway Transport certainly presented a striking contrast from the United States Railroad Administration, the entity that had overseen transportation matters during World War I. It was neither necessary nor politically tenable for the federal government to renew its earlier experiment with direct government operation. Instead, Eastman acknowledged that his role was to facilitate the efforts of private management, and he followed FDR's mandate to "advise and assist" rather than to control.[16]

Unlike William Gibbs McAdoo, the wartime director of the USRA, Eastman was far less antagonistic toward railroad managers. Many of the ODT's meetings were held not in the agency's headquarters in Washington but at locations that were familiar to executives—including Penn Station in New York. Representatives from the railroads, who outnumbered their counterparts in government by a ratio of 10:1, dominated ODT meetings. Having apparently learned a few lessons from the difficulties of the earlier war, Eastman "expressed his appreciation of the cooperation of the railroads and of the opportunity to meet with their representatives to discuss these important current questions." The ODT's director likewise "stated his preference for this form of procedure to the use of orders and obligatory restrictions [and] ... asserted that he was firmly opposed to any 'hair shirt' philosophies." In matters of car supply, representatives from the War Department worked directly with individual railroads. The Military Transportation Section of the Association of American Railroads coordinated War Department requests for special equipment or troop movements. Throughout that process, the federal government acted as a purchaser of rail services rather than as the controller of the railroads.[17]

Managers—including several who were associated with the Pennsylvania Railroad—held key staff positions at the Office of Defense Transportation. The most important was Charles D. Young, the PRR's vice president in charge of real estate, purchases, and insurance. Prior to American entry into the war, he helped to revitalize the Military Railway Service. Beginning in January 1942, Young served briefly as the director of the ODT's Division of Materials and Equipment. He soon reached the military's retirement age of sixty-four, and in July, he became the assistant director of the Office of Defense Transportation, with a commission as a brigadier general. John F. Deasy, the PRR's vice president in charge of operations, was the chairman of the ODT's Eastern Operating Committee. John W. Barriger III, who began his career on the PRR in 1917 and remained associated with the company for the next decade, became the associate director of ODT's Division of Railway Transport. Herbert A. Enochs, the company's chief of personnel, was a representative of an Association of American Railroads advisory committee, whose function was to provide Eastman with recommendations regarding manpower issues.[18]

Wartime Passenger Service

Eastman's most important responsibility at the Office of Defense Transportation involved the allocation of scarce passenger service. During World War II, Americans had little choice other than to travel by train. On December 11, 1941, as Japanese forces seized control of rubber plantations in Southeast Asia, the federal government imposed restrictions on the sale of automobile tires. In January 1942, the Office of Production Management barred further production of civilian automobiles and trucks for the duration of the war. Beginning in May, gasoline rationing became a fact of life in the northeastern United States, encompassing much of the area served by the Pennsylvania Railroad, and the policy expanded nationwide on December 1. As the nation's largest passenger carrier, the PRR experienced a surge in demand, and its trains and stations were filled to overflowing. The number of intercity passengers who traveled on the Pennsylvania Railroad increased from 48.1 million in 1941 to 80.6 million the following year, 118.5 million in 1943, and 125.2 million in 1944—a record that was never exceeded, before or since. Revenue passenger miles more than tripled during the same period, from 3.9 billion to 15.5 billion. Intercity passenger revenues showed a similar upward trend, from $84.2 million in 1941 to $253.6 million in 1944.[19]

As a result of War Production Board restrictions on the manufacture of new railway equipment, PRR officials pressed every available passenger car into service. The company acquired coaches, parlor cars, and sleeper-observation cars from other railroads and from Pullman. Shop forces converted 69 coach-baggage combination cars into full coaches while adding seats to parlor cars, a business car, and even 6 track-inspection cars. In all, those measures added 175 cars and 14,000 seats to the overall capacity of the passenger fleet.[20]

To accommodate the large number of military personnel, shop forces experimented with several designs for troop cars. In February 1942, they completed a prototype for a Class P60 troop coach, based on the design of a Class X38 automobile boxcar. Given WPB limitations, it proved more expeditious to convert existing cars to military service. Most were Class X32 and Class X32a automobile cars, built between 1933 and 1936.[21] The first, in June 1942, became a Class P56 troop coach, complete with upholstered seats. Shop forces then completed fourteen Class P78 troop coaches, with slatted wooden seats.[22]

The Class P78 troop coaches were adequate for short journeys, principally between Camp Atterbury and nearby Indianapolis, but unsuitable for overnight travel. By the end of November, workers at the Altoona Car Shops completed the first of forty Class P30a troop sleepers.[23] The rebuilt cars featured porthole windows that provided a modicum of light as well as small ventilators for fresh air. They were equipped with three-tier bunks that afforded little space or comfort, and their riding qualities were not much changed from their freight-car origins. Four corresponding kitchen cars, with hard wooden bench seats, were equally basic. Another converted car was the prototype for the Class P54 recreation car. Also referred to as a command car, it could accommodate officers and other military personnel who were responsible for getting the train to its destination in secrecy and safety.[24] In December 1942, representatives from the Pennsylvania Railroad and the army tested the prototypes between Philadelphia and Fort Dix, New Jersey.[25]

The concept was sound, but the PRR had little incentive to build cars that would become useless once the war ended. Nor could a few large railroads be expected to provide equipment that would operate throughout the United States. As such, in June 1943, the Office of Defense Transportation placed an order with the Pullman-Standard Car Manufacturing Company for twelve hundred troop sleepers and four hundred kitchen cars.[26] While they featured square rather than porthole windows, they nonetheless mimicked the PRR's experimental models. To the dismay of soldiers headed for war, they were equally uncomfortable—but they were an essential component of the American military effort.[27]

Given the importance of troop movements, restrictions on civilian rail travel began early in the war. By June 1942, the Office of Defense Transportation had ordered the railroads to curtail many of their luxury services and to eliminate special trains that had once taken passengers to conventions, racetracks, and other sporting events. *The Broadway Limited* continued to operate, but the ODT required ticket agents to sell every available seat, including those in lounge cars. The ODT's General Order No. 24, which became effective on September 26, 1942, placed additional restrictions on passenger service. As with subsequent directives, however, railroad officials could request special permits from the ODT to keep certain trains in operation. The measures achieved their intended aim of concentrating available equipment on the most heavily traveled routes, often at the expense of lightly patronized branch-line services. In 1942, the PRR generated a 60 percent increase in passenger miles, while trimming passenger train miles by 22 percent, locomotive miles by 18 percent, and the number of passenger cars in service by 17 percent.[28]

By early 1945, with victory in Europe assured, the PRR and the nation's other railroads faced a new set of challenges. Military planners anticipated the need to transfer troops and equipment to the Pacific Theater, which in turn would necessitate the operation of MAIN trains from one side of the country to the other. On January 11, General Order No. 47 required the railroads "immediately to discontinue all passenger train schedules which are operated for the purpose of providing seasonal service to any resort, recreational or vacation area." The restrictions also prohibited railroads from operating any passenger service where average occupancy had not exceeded 35 percent during the month of November 1944. That stipulation, which ODT officials envisioned as a mechanism to discontinue lightly patronized branch-line passenger trains, generated little opposition from PRR officials—who, since the 1920s, had been endeavoring to curtail as much local service as possible. Resort traffic was another matter, however. J. Monroe Johnson, who became the ODT's director in April 1944 following Eastman's death, chided Martin Clement, the PRR's president, for requesting a special permit allowing weekend service to the Jersey Shore. Johnson reminded the PRR's president of the terms of General Order No. 47, emphasizing "that these orders were not written to apply to all American railroads except the Pennsylvania." The next set of ODT guidelines came on July 15, when the agency prohibited the use of sleeping cars on runs shorter than 450 miles. Pennsylvania Railroad officials accordingly canceled numerous sleeping-car lines. They also discontinued the all-Pullman *Pittsburgher*, a train that was a particular favorite of steel-company executives. *The Pittsburgher* soon reappeared as an all-coach day train but did not resume its all-Pullman status until February 1946.[29]

Labor during World War II

During World War II, the Pennsylvania Railroad faced an intense demand for labor. The steady growth of freight and passenger traffic ensured that every operating employee would be pressed into service. Maintenance-of-way and shop personnel worked around the clock to remedy the increased strain on track and equipment. At the same time, even though enginemen and other skilled workers were exempt from conscription, many of the PRR's employees were subject to the will of the draft board. In July 1942, 12,127 employees were serving their country in the military. Yet the Personnel Department calculated that 78,743 individuals between the ages of twenty and forty-four, representing nearly 50 percent of the company's workforce, were eligible for the draft. The uncertainties associated with fighting a two-front war suggested that many of those employees might leave the company on short notice.[30]

The scarcity of labor was not unique to the Pennsylvania Railroad, and federal officials developed new methods for alleviating the crisis. On April 18, 1942, Roosevelt issued an executive order that established the War Manpower Commission. The agency's commissioners oversaw efforts to expand the workforce, while allocating personnel in a manner that would most effectively meet the demands of transportation, industry, mining, and agriculture as well as the military.[31] Given the likelihood that federal officials would ask older individuals to postpone retirement or to reenter the labor force, it was appropriate that the WMC held jurisdiction over the Railroad Retirement Board. PRR chief of personnel Herbert Enochs became the sole railroad representative to the management-labor policy committee.[32]

Given the pressing need for workers, there was only so much Enochs could do to advocate for the Pennsylvania Railroad and the other carriers. James W. Oram, the PRR's assistant chief of personnel, was concerned that Enochs and the other members of the management-labor policy committee might establish the Railroad Retirement Board's Employment Service as the "exclusive public hiring agency for the railroads." Oram accordingly warned President Clement that "we certainly don't want to be under the War Manpower Commission for the recruiting of railroad labor, nor do we want to have our hiring placed entirely in the hands of the Railroad Retirement Board." Oram instead suggested that the company should be able to secure employees through any means necessary, particularly as "the railroads were very liberal in allowing men to go into the armed service; of a consequence, they ought to be equally free in their employment arrangements."[33]

In addition to the efforts to increase the size of the national labor pool, federal officials also endeavored to maintain peace between management and labor, thus preventing strikes that would hinder production. Railroad workers, many of whom remembered the temporary gains

associated with the actions of the United States Railroad Administration during World War I, hoped to achieve similar results—if for no other reason than to ensure that their wages kept pace with inflation. Union leaders shared that perspective, but they were acutely aware of the political backlash that was likely to accompany strikes or any other form of labor militancy that might interfere with the war effort. Railroad executives were often willing to grant higher wages as a mechanism to ensure an adequate labor supply, but they demanded a comparable increase in rates. The likely result would be an inflationary spiral, and Roosevelt and his advisors were determined to prevent the double-digit annual price increases that had taken place during World War I.

Wartime labor relations on the Pennsylvania Railroad thus reflected an adversarial relationship among the nation's workers, managers, and government officials, as they competed for political and economic power. As in the past, however, the railroads were a unique situation, and the leaders of the national unions were adamant in their demands for special treatment. The situation created difficulties for Roosevelt, who sought to balance the Democratic Party's labor constituency with the imperatives of national defense. As was typical of his leadership style, the president engaged in a series of experiments, creating new programs to replace those that had failed or otherwise outlived their usefulness. Roosevelt also exhibited a tendency to cultivate administrative agencies that acted in opposition to one another. A charitable assessment of that process suggested that competition among federal officials would generate a creative tension that would facilitate innovative policies. Yet it was also true that the president's methods enabled him to exercise considerable power, as the final arbiter of disputes, while giving him ample opportunity to assign blame to someone else, should things go wrong.

By the summer of 1940, as the fall of France highlighted the dangerous situation in Europe, the United States witnessed a wave of industrial strikes. To forestall additional labor militancy, Roosevelt initially relied on the informal mediating efforts of Sidney Hillman, the head of the Amalgamated Clothing Workers of America. Hillman was also a member of the advisory committee of the Council of National Defense, an agency created in 1916 and reactivated in May 1940. Although Hillman was initially successful in his efforts to dissuade workers from walking off the job, by late 1940, a new wave of strikes was affecting defense production and creating an embarrassing situation for the president. Accordingly, on March 19, 1941, Roosevelt's Executive Order 8716 established the National Defense Mediation Board. The new agency reflected the tripartite structure the Progressives had favored, with representatives from business, labor, and the public sector. Despite some early success, the NDMB was unable to placate John L. Lewis. The president of the United Mine Workers demanded the appointment of a special board, establishing a precedent that leaders of the railroad unions would later use to their advantage.[34]

Following the attack on Pearl Harbor and the American declaration of war against the Axis powers, Roosevelt orchestrated a meeting between representatives of business and labor. Executives agreed to refrain from lockouts for the duration of the war. Officials representing the American Federation of Labor and the Congress of Industrial Organizations promised that they would not countenance strikes, work slowdowns, or other forms of labor militancy. In return for their no-strike pledge, labor leaders demanded a replacement for the NDMB, one that would better represent their interests. On January 12, 1942, Roosevelt therefore reestablished the National War Labor Board, an agency Woodrow Wilson had created during World War I. The NWLB retained the tripartite structure of its Wilsonian predecessor, with the president empowered to appoint four representatives apiece from management, labor, and the public. If business executives and union officials could not resolve disputes through direct negotiation, the secretary of labor could refer the matter to the NWLB.[35]

The National War Labor Board possessed authority over transportation, mining, and industry. Like the coal miners, railroad labor was a special case, however. Any work stoppage by unionized employees would likely affect the entire transportation network—a far more serious situation than the closure of a single defense plant. By virtue of numbers alone, railroad workers possessed substantial political influence, making it more difficult for Roosevelt and other Democrats to resist their demands. Employees, particularly those who belonged to the operating brotherhoods, possessed a long history of union organization, with leaders who knew how to pull on the levers of power. Moreover, railroaders had long possessed access to federal mediation. In creating the National War Labor Board, Roosevelt had not exempted the railroads from that agency's jurisdiction. Nor did he arrange for the temporary suspension of the National Mediation Board, the entity established by the 1934 Crosser-Dill amendment to the 1926 Railway Labor Act. Representatives from railroad unions accordingly enjoyed the ability to engage in jurisdiction shopping, supporting the decisions of whichever agency or mediation body was likely to give them the highest wages and benefits. The resulting disagreements

between the National Mediation Board and the National War Labor Board at times obliged Roosevelt to create an ad hoc panel to resolve the disputes, adding yet a third potentially conflicting ruling.

Wages and Prices

The war in Europe brought the Great Depression to an end and created opportunities for railroad employees to secure higher wages and benefits. The process began in May 1940, when representatives from the fourteen nonoperating unions sought paid vacations and subsequently insisted on an additional thirty cents per hour in base pay. Those issues remained unresolved when, in May 1941, officials from the five operating brotherhoods demanded a 30 percent increase in wages as well as changes in work rules. Despite the involvement of the National Mediation Board, workers began filling out strike ballots.[36] Given the perilous foreign-policy situation and the increasing likelihood that the United States would be drawn into the war, Roosevelt was determined to avoid a national rail strike. On September 10, under the provisions of the Railway Labor Act, the president appointed an emergency board. The panel, under the direction of Wayne L. Morse, the dean of the University of Oregon Law School, acted with remarkable speed. On November 5, Morse recommended a 7.5 percent pay raise for the brotherhoods and a nine-cent increase for nonoperating employees. The gains, which would be retroactive to September 1, would—absent renegotiation—end on December 31, 1942. Railroad executives quickly accepted the recommendations, but their labor counterparts expressed dismay and renewed their strike threat. Roosevelt then took the unprecedented step of intervening personally in the dispute. The compromise settlement, announced on December 2, provided only modest increases above Morse's original proposal—a 10.5 percent gain for operating employees and ten cents per hour for their nonoperating counterparts. The changes would be permanent, however, giving union officials hope that they could retain whatever further advantages they might gain in a war that would come home to the United States only five days later.[37]

Although they succeeded in forestalling a strike, Roosevelt and other federal officials could be reasonably certain that similar disputes would erupt in the future. He first secured the cooperation of organized labor. Union officials, organized under the Railway Labor Executives' Association, seconded the no-strike pledge issued by representatives from the American Federation of Labor, the Congress of Industrial Organizations, and most other unions. On March 21, 1942, Roosevelt provided labor leaders with one of the rewards they sought by modifying the resolution procedures associated with the Railway Labor Act. Since 1926, the members of the National Mediation Board had waited until union leaders established a strike date and began circulating strike ballots to workers. Under the new policy, the NMB could intervene whenever managers or union officials stated that negotiations had reached an impasse. Roosevelt's Executive Order 9172 established a second line of defense against labor-management disputes. If the NMB could not resolve the issue, then the newly created National Railway Labor Panel could act. The president gave himself the authority to create three-person emergency boards, drawn from the members of the National Railway Labor Panel, to resolve the situation. While the rulings of the emergency board depended on voluntary cooperation by management and labor, there was little doubt that wartime conditions, coupled with the power of public opinion, would ensure compliance. The expedited process, which remained in place until 1945, minimized but did not eliminate labor unrest on the Pennsylvania Railroad and the nation's other carriers. By removing disputes involving railroad workers from the jurisdiction of the War Labor Board, Executive Order 9172 perpetuated the long-standing practice of segregating railway employees from all other workers. The National Railway Labor Panel also contributed to the increasing bureaucratization of labor-management relations, replacing strike votes and picket lines with closed-door conferences in the nation's capital.[38]

Not surprisingly, PRR officials played an important role in those discussions. Herbert Enochs, the chief of personnel, acted in his capacity as the chairman of the Eastern Carriers' Conference Committee. In June 1942, representatives from the Brotherhood of Locomotive Firemen and Enginemen presented Enochs and other management representatives with a list of demands. Some reflected the differing operating characteristics of steam locomotives, based on weight and whether they were fired by coal or by oil. Others attested to the growing prevalence of diesel locomotives, especially on the western lines, while the request for wage parity between the North, South, and West perpetuated a long-standing goal of the operating brotherhoods. On September 2, Enochs announced that the negotiations were hopelessly deadlocked and requested federal mediation.[39]

Nor were train crews alone in their quest for higher pay and more favorable work rules. On September 25, the leaders of the nonoperating unions, representing some nine hundred thousand shopworkers, clerical, and maintenance-of-way personnel, demanded a pay increase of twenty cents per hour, with a minimum wage of seventy cents. For the first time in modern memory, they also sought a closed shop, in which every newly hired employee would automatically become a union member. Managers had little difficulty in rejecting the proposal, which they claimed would add $450 million to their annual costs. As a formality, they initiated negotiations with labor leaders, but even before the first meeting had taken place, they indicated that the National Mediation Board would undoubtedly intervene to resolve the issue. Their predictions were correct, and mediation began on January 7, 1943. Nine days later, NMB representatives abandoned their efforts and turned the matter over to William M. Leiserson, the chairman of the National Railway Labor Panel.[40]

Workers' hopes for steadily rising wages soon collided with Roosevelt's determination to control wartime inflation. Those efforts began in September 1939, shortly after the German and Soviet invasion of Poland. Executive Order 8248 gave the president the authority to establish several new offices within the executive branch. They included the Office for Emergency Management, which began operations on May 25, 1940. A subsequent executive order established the Office of Price Administration and Civilian Supply on April 11, 1941 (the title was shortened to the Office of Price Administration on August 28) as a subagency within the Office for Emergency Management. The OPA became a separate agency, following passage of the Emergency Price Control Act in January 1942. When he signed the legislation, Roosevelt warned that "nothing could better serve the purposes of our enemies than that we should become the victims of inflation," an assertion that attested to the president's determinations to curtail increases in wages and prices. He conceded that rationing, limits on prices, and other measures would require "sacrifices from each of us," but he insisted that "effective price control will ensure that these sacrifices are equitably distributed."[41]

The distribution of sacrifices was as much a matter of politics as it was of national security, and issues involving railroad labor became increasingly problematic. On September 7, 1942, the president asked Congress to give him further authority to first stabilize farm prices and then wages. Legislators responded with the Stabilization Act of 1942, which became law on October 2. The following day, Roosevelt issued Executive Order 9250, with the intent of holding wages to their level of September 15. Thereafter, the National War Labor Board held broad authority to set compensation levels for most workers—with two exceptions. Farmers were exempt from NWLB guidelines, as were railroaders. Under the terms of Executive Order 9299, issued on February 4, 1943, Roosevelt stipulated that the National Railway Labor Panel would have sole jurisdiction regarding compensation for railway workers.[42]

Federal policy nonetheless required all wage adjustments involving railroad workers to comply with the rules established by the NWLB and by James F. Byrnes, the director of the Office of Economic Stabilization. The most important of those guidelines was the Little Steel formula, adopted by the War Labor Board on July 16, 1942. That policy provided a 15 percent wage increase for the period after January 1, 1941, but stipulated that no additional raises would be forthcoming until after the war. Applied initially to steelworkers at all companies other than US Steel, the formula set a pattern for other industries. Enochs was certainly pleased with the restraint embodied in Executive Order 9299, and he suggested that "today's executive order of the President sets the procedure for setting the most important wage issue which has ever been presented in this country." Making a pointed reference to the Little Steel formula, Enochs observed that "the group of nearly a million railroad employes involved in this issue has already had more than a 15 per cent increase since Jan. 1, 1941." By that measure, he concluded, no additional concessions—much less the twenty cents an hour demanded by the nonoperating employees—could be worthy of consideration.[43]

Nonoperating employees nonetheless persisted in their demands. Although union officials repeatedly emphasized their no-strike pledge, there were signs from across the Atlantic that the situation might deteriorate rapidly. On January 15, locomotive enginemen and firemen in Great Britain narrowly voted against walking off the job unless the Ministry of Labor granted significant concessions. With American railroad personnel largely isolated from the grim realities of war, it was conceivable that they might eventually follow the lead of their British counterparts. Roosevelt accordingly invoked the new dispute-resolution procedures associated with the National Railway Labor Panel. On February 20, an emergency board, chaired by University of Michigan economics professor Isaiah Leo Sharfman, began evaluating the demands of the nonoperating employees.[44]

Sharfman's emergency board was in the midst of deliberations when Roosevelt made a further attempt to rein in inflation. When he issued Executive Order 9328 on April 8, the president emphasized the necessity of blocking any additional price hikes. This was "a hold-the-line Order," he indicated. "There are to be no further increases in wage rates or salary scales beyond the Little Steel formula, except where clearly necessary to correct substandards of living."

Roosevelt's "hold-the-line" mandate brought negotiations to a halt, as Sharfman discussed the ramifications of the new policy. He ultimately declined to apply the terms of Executive Order 9328 to the nonoperating employees, on the grounds that the emergency board had begun its work before it took effect. On May 26, the emergency board thus awarded the nonoperating employees an increase of eight cents per hour, retroactive to February 1. Sharfman concluded that the increase was necessary to "correct gross inequities and aid in the prosecution of the war," but union leaders concluded that the ostensibly impartial chairman of the emergency board was yielding to a president who was determined to retain the political support of railroad workers. Irrespective of his motives, Sharfman's recommendation was less than half of what they had demanded but well beyond the limit suggested by the Little Steel formula. Enochs and other railroad executives calculated that Sharfman's ruling would cost them $204 million per year, including $85 million in back pay. They nonetheless assumed that the National Railway Labor Panel, rather than the War Labor Board or the Office of Economic Stabilization, held final authority in such matters, and they accepted Sharfman's ruling as inevitable. In that context, both managers and workers expected that approval by the Office of Economic Stabilization was a foregone conclusion.[45]

Fred M. Vinson, who had recently replaced James Byrnes as the director of the Office of Economic Stabilization, was not willing to yield so easily, however. Prior to his appointment as stabilization director, Vinson had been a federal judge with scrupulous adherence to legal procedures. He had little patience with union threats or with Roosevelt's willingness to placate labor by undermining the Little Steel formula. On June 22, he indicated that the eight-cent increase "does violence to the stabilization program and if suffered to become effective it will irretrievably break the inflation line." Vinson recommended that Sharfman reconsider the issue. Backed by William Leiserson, the chairman of the National Railway Labor Panel, Sharfman concluded that neither his emergency board nor the larger entity of the NRLP possessed the authority to do so. In that context, Roosevelt's efforts to treat railway labor as a special case led to administrative gridlock in Washington.[46]

The nonoperating employees had scant respect for efforts to hold the line on inflation, in conformity with the Little Steel formula. Nor did they have any further use for collective bargaining with management—the right they had won in a previous war and then unsuccessfully defended against W. W. Atterbury and other executives in the decade that followed. Political pressure now constituted a more effective means to advance their interests, and union officials did not hesitate to use it. On August 4, the heads of the nonoperating unions discussed the possibility of placing a strike ballot before their membership. It was unlikely that they would have taken such a drastic step, but their statements sent a clear message to the Office of Economic Stabilization, and to Roosevelt, that they were not to be trifled with. Three days later, representatives from management and labor reached a new agreement, one that was almost identical to the one that Sharfman's emergency board had recommended and Vinson had disallowed. Despite the cost, executives could afford to be sanguine, as higher wages were necessary to attract and retain workers in a tight labor market. While Roosevelt did not make any public statements on the issue and put nothing in writing, he provided backchannel assurances to union leaders that their members would receive the full eight cents per hour. On August 9, union officials released what they claimed were the terms of a settlement—one that would become binding as soon as the president gave his assent. On September 16, they discussed the matter with Roosevelt. George Harrison, the president of the Brotherhood of Railway Clerks, expressed optimism that "some basis can be developed for the culmination of our differences." The following day, however, Roosevelt's secretary informed labor leaders that the president desired to postpone further discussions involving the nonoperating employees, pending the resolution of similar matters involving the operating brotherhoods.[47]

Eleven months earlier, in January 1943, the leaders of the operating brotherhoods had demanded a 30 percent increase in pay for train-service employees, with a minimum compensation of $3.00 per day. Railroad executives denied the request, on the grounds that it was inflationary. The National Mediation Board became involved on February 18. That effort failed, as did subsequent attempts at arbitration, and on May 31, Leiserson drew on the resources of the National Railway Labor Panel and appointed an emergency board chaired by Walter P. Stacy. Sharfman was also a member, ensuring that there would be considerable continuity with the concurrent hearings involving the nonoperating employees. In their September 25 report, Stacy and Sharfman concluded that there was no evidence of substandard wages among trainmen. As such, they could not authorize any increases beyond those provided by the Little Steel formula. Since January 1, 1941, operating employees had already received a 10.5 percent raise, suggesting that only an additional 4.5 percent was permissible. That was equivalent to four cents per hour, little more than an eighth of what union officials demanded. Vinson soon

accepted the proposal, in keeping with his rigorous adherence to the Little Steel formula. His actions indicated that, even if he were to yield to the demands of the nonoperating employees, he would grant them no more than four cents per hour—precisely half of the amount specified in the agreement reached by representatives from management and labor.[48]

By the middle of October, when the American Federation of Labor held its annual convention in Boston, the leaders of the nonoperating unions were in an angry mood. Harrison indicated that his members were "desperate" as a result of Vinson's "dangerous way of dealing with wage questions and labor relations." He suggested that Vinson had assumed dictatorial powers and found it appalling that a single individual could override months of complex negotiations between labor, management, and the federal government. Harrison decried "compulsory control of labor by the Government and Government through discretionary authority." It was an intriguing statement, given that union officials had cultivated Roosevelt's discretionary authority, in the hope that he would authorize compensation for railroad workers that was at variance with national wage-stabilization policies. Ominously, Harrison acknowledged that rank-and-file employees demanded "that we put out a strike ballot," but he implausibly suggested that workers would do nothing that might impede the war effort. Maverick North Dakota senator William "Wild Bill" Langer criticized Roosevelt's "delay" in authorizing the full eight-cent increase and urged the president "to sign the findings of the railroads and the unions" as a mechanism to "prevent riots, strikes and bloodshed."[49]

Echoing the language used by the nonoperating employees, labor leaders condemned Vinson's "arbitrary" policies—which, they asserted, had "emasculated" the 1926 Railway Labor Act. Under the circumstances, they concluded, they had no choice other than to ask Congress for new legislation that would "repair the damage." Representative Hamilton Fish, a New York Democrat, obligingly introduced a bill that would force Vinson to accept the eight-cent award stipulated by Sharfman's emergency board, with comparable increases for operating personnel. Officials representing train-service employees reiterated their no-strike pledge but indicated that rank-and-file members were so angry and so determined to strike that they were beyond anyone's ability to control. Their nonoperating counterparts expressed solidarity with train crews, if for no other reason than they too wanted Roosevelt to overrule the complex dispute-resolution and wage-stabilization procedures he had established only a few months earlier. As a reporter for the *New York Times* observed, the events "further confused a situation which students of labor arbitration say is putting the railway labor arbitration machinery, long considered as 'model,' into disrepute." Union officials were equally despondent, concluding that the dispute-resolution procedures established by the Railway Labor Act were "as good as in the ash-can."[50]

Roosevelt concluded that he would need to intervene personally to settle the escalating conflicts among the government agencies he had established and the federal officials he had appointed. In doing so, he chose to act more decisively to limit inflation and to heal some of the rifts within the federal bureaucracy. By endeavoring to bring railway wage increases into line with the Little Steel formula, Roosevelt distanced himself from the informal promises, which he had made in August, to treat railroaders as a special case. Union officials glumly concluded that "all bets are off" and that they could no longer count on the president to bow to their political pressure. If they had wagered that Roosevelt would have unilaterally overruled Vinson's policies, they would have lost their bet. On October 16, two days after Harrison issued his thinly veiled strike threat, Roosevelt signed Executive Order 9388. Based on a precedent he had established less than a month earlier, in a dispute involving employees of the Pacific Electric Railway, the president constituted a new emergency board, chaired by Illinois Supreme Court justice Elwyn R. Shaw.[51]

Alexander F. Whitney, the president of the Brotherhood of Railroad Trainmen, declared that he was "on the warpath" and questioned whether either Vinson or Roosevelt had the right to interfere with the procedures established by the Railway Labor Act. "This stalling and appointing of a second emergency board has demolished the Railway Labor Act and made the processes and procedures for the settlement of a railway wage dispute a farce," he indicated. Whitney emphasized "a growing belief among the workers that labor is being betrayed by those in authority in Washington." He provided reporters with a letter from dining car steward Charles Decker, who observed that "our members now feel that the Government has deserted labor and particularly railroad labor, the best friend the Administration in Washington ever had. As far as our members are concerned, they take the position that the no-strike pledge does not exist any more." Belatedly, union officials and rank-and-file workers were beginning to realize what they probably should have understood all along. Roosevelt's promises for significantly higher wages had always been hollow, and the president was using Vinson

as a mechanism for controlling labor costs while avoiding the inevitable political backlash.[52]

Labor leaders again employed political pressure to influence the deliberations of Shaw's emergency board. They increased the virulence of their rhetoric, with Whitney asserting that "the 'no-strike' pledge is becoming more and more untenable." Endeavoring to pick and choose from among the government agencies that best suited his interests, Whitney criticized wartime government bodies that "are in a position to hog-tie the War Labor Board and the National Railway Labor Panel. Nearly all the positions in our Government," he concluded, "are now held by big business reactionaries or at best by ultra-conservatives, and the President has put them there." On October 26, and as a mechanism of applying additional political pressure, Whitney and his colleagues authorized a strike vote. Six days later, Senator Harry S. Truman (Dem., Missouri) introduced a congressional resolution that would force Vinson to accept the eight-cent increase that conformed to the August 7 settlement between management and labor. That agreement, Truman asserted, "is an appropriate and valid settlement of the dispute."[53]

The new emergency board acted with considerable speed, but to no avail. Shaw convened hearings on October 28, and his panel issued its report on November 4. It recommended a sliding scale of wage increases, from four cents per hour to as much as ten cents per hour, for the lowest-paid employees. The Shaw board's recommendation included an average wage increase of 7.2 percent (versus the 8% that union leaders demanded) and would add $184 million to the railroad's labor costs, only $20 million less than the earlier amount of $204 million. Vinson approved the proposal on November 8, and union officials just as quickly rejected it. Money was not the only issue at stake. Instead, labor leaders protested "the additional inequities," associated with a sliding scale of wage increases—something they considered to be "unworkable and impracticable of application." More broadly, they asserted that the Shaw "board was not a free agent under the order which created it and simply followed the instructions of the Director of Economic Stabilization." Simply put, labor leaders concluded that, during a time of labor shortages and acting through the established mechanism of the Railway Labor Act, they could gain greater concessions from management than the economic stabilization machinery of the federal government would otherwise allow. Railroad executives likewise called on the federal government to respect the terms of the Railway Labor Act and indicated their support for the Truman resolution. The 1926 legislation had thus succeeded in a manner that its supporters had probably never intended. It enabled representatives from management and labor to forge a harmonious bond of mutual interest—but only because they were united in opposition to the policies of the federal government.[54]

The situation involving the nonoperating unions remained unresolved as the concerns of the operating brotherhoods came to the fore. Their officials rejected as wholly inadequate the four-cent wage increase that Walter Stacy's emergency board had recommended on September 25. Despite Vinson's willingness to approve the settlement, on December 17, labor leaders announced that they would call a strike at the end of the month. Roosevelt became directly involved on December 21 and attempted to mediate the dispute at a series of conferences held at the White House. The effort failed, and the matter proceeded to arbitration, under the terms of the Railway Labor Act. On December 24, representatives from the Brotherhood of Locomotive Engineers and the Brotherhood of Railroad Trainmen called off the proposed strike. Three days later, officials from the nonoperating unions indicated that their members would also remain on the job. Despite Roosevelt's offer of additional wage increases as well as a week of paid vacation, their counterparts at the Brotherhood of Locomotive Firemen and Enginemen, the Order of Railway Conductors, and the Switchmen's Union of North America remained intransigent.[55]

Even as Roosevelt begged union leaders to call off the strike vote, as a Christmas present to the nation, he prepared to use military force to keep the trains running. On December 23, he instructed Attorney General Francis Biddle to prepare the legal documents necessary for a federal takeover.[56] The president then ordered Major General Charles P. Gross, assisted by Lieutenant Colonel Luke W. Finlay, to draw up plans for a government seizure of the entire railroad industry. Gross in turn relied on an advisory panel of railroad and union officials. President Clement was the most important executive on the panel, which also included representation from the Association of American Railroads and the American Short Line Railroad Association. Clement also served as the chief technical advisor to General Brehon B. Somervell, the chief of the Army Service Forces. Seven regional offices, akin to those employed by the United States Railroad Administration during World War I, held the authority to coordinate operations, regardless of the corporate identity of any of the individual carriers. While Gross acknowledged that he might need to employ draconian measures—including the cancellation of draft deferments for striking workers and the employment of military personnel to operate trains—there was general agreement that a symbolic takeover and an appeal to worker patriotism would be sufficient to resolve the dispute. That was just as well, as representatives from the Labor Branch of the Industrial Personnel Division pointed out, in a report highly critical of Gross's plan, that the army possessed only a small fraction of the 1.1 million workers needed to keep the railroads in service.[57]

At 7:00 on the evening of December 27 and acting under the terms of Executive Order 9412, Secretary of War Henry L. Stimson took control of the railroads on behalf of the federal government. Stimson's actions represented the only time during the war that the military had seized an entire industry. In actual practice, however, railroad operations continued as before, and the military presence was practically nonexistent. Individual railroad presidents continued to manage their respective companies, under the largely theoretical direction of the seven regional administrators. Two days later, on the eve of their threatened December 30 strike, the disaffected brotherhood officials agreed to postpone the walkout for the duration of government control. Union leaders insisted that they were still willing to resist the actions of railroad executives and even the policies of the Office of Economic Stabilization, but they acknowledged that "we will not strike against our government."[58]

Gross and his fellow officers, confident that a strike would be averted, released for other duties most of the military personnel originally assigned to operate the railroads. Despite the fears of some officials in the Labor Branch, Gross was proven correct in his assertion that railroad workers would care more about patriotism than paychecks. Alexander Whitney, the president of the Brotherhood of Railroad Trainmen, warned his members that a strike vote would be "'suicidal' not only for the brotherhood but for the whole American labor movement." The New York Times reported that an individual "in some high Government circles," widely believed to be General George C. Marshall, the army's chief of staff, suggested that the strike and military takeover of the railroads "has set back the end of the war" and "might be considered the equivalent of a military disaster which would cost added thousands of American lives." Roosevelt abandoned any pretense of impartiality and offered a stern warning to union leaders. "If any employees of the railroads now strike," the president emphasized, "they will be striking against the Government of the United States." Several members of Congress threatened to support legislation criminalizing wartime strikes, and it was abundantly clear that the American public did not have much sympathy for the unions.[59]

Two weeks later, on January 14, 1944, the remaining three brotherhoods accepted the same terms that had been granted to the BLE and the BRT on December 27. On January 17, fourteen days after Roosevelt agreed to reestablish the Shaw board, the leaders of the fifteen nonoperating unions accepted a new wage agreement. With the threat of a strike over, federal control ended on January 18, 1944. As with all compromises, all involved insisted that they had been unfairly deprived of an equitable resolution of the dispute. Workers, ignoring the changed conditions of wartime, argued that the Roosevelt administration had violated the provisions of the 1926 Railway Labor Act, had quashed their rightful demands for overtime pay, and had failed to grant the full 15 percent pay increase authorized by the Little Steel formula.[60] Some managers suggested that the government takeover had been little more than a smokescreen, designed to remove their voices from the dispute and to divert attention from Roosevelt's willingness to grant wage increases that exceeded his administration's wage-stabilization guidelines. Many business leaders and politicians were likewise disgusted at the president's tendency to ignore the recommendations of properly constituted mediation bodies, with the *New York Times* suggesting that the incident was "a perfect record of how not to handle a labor dispute."[61]

Despite such caustic assessments, the military takeover of the railroads displayed something of a theatrical quality, creating only a modest disruption to transportation and to military readiness. The same could be said for the carefully orchestrated negotiations between labor leaders, railroad executives, and government officials that had taken place over the preceding two years. What was perhaps most noticeable was the absence of Pennsylvania Railroad personnel from the headlines. In the years immediately following World War I, Vice President Atterbury had vigorously—and publicly—attacked unions whose members refused to cooperate with his vision of harmonious labor-management relations. He served as a spokesman for the railroad industry and had broadened his rhetoric to include condemnation of Bolshevism and other radical challenges to the established capitalist order. When Martin Clement replaced Atterbury as president in 1935, the PRR's newest chief executive made it clear that the onset of the New Deal and other changes in the political landscape meant that such practices were no longer tenable. "The Pennsylvania Railroad is not in politics," he told reporters just two days after taking office. It was not an idle promise. Clement refrained from making overtly political statements, or from playing an active role in party politics, as Atterbury had done. During his brief stint as civilian advisor to the US Army, he did not make any comments regarding the situation, nor did he excoriate labor leaders for imperiling military preparedness.[62]

Union officials were equally restrained in their rhetoric and correspondingly willing to engage in negotiations that were far removed from the union hall and the picket line. Even Bert M. Jewell, who remained the president of the Railway Employes' Department of the American Federation of Labor until 1946, eschewed the confrontational tactics he had employed during the 1922 Shopmen's Strike. Jewell and his colleagues at times announced, perhaps disingenuously, that they were powerless to resist rank-and-file members who were determined to break the no-strike pledge. They were not prepared to authorize a strike, however—nor could they, given the political inclinations of a wartime president. Roosevelt's support for organized labor had never matched that of Woodrow Wilson, and the defeat of the Axis powers took precedence over everything else. While it was certainly not true, as some disgruntled workers alleged, that railroad wages were frozen for the duration of the war, their pay did not increase to the extent that it had during World War I. That difference suggested that federal officials had learned a great deal in the quarter century that separated the two world wars. In addition to developing more effective methods of controlling inflation, Roosevelt and his advisors acknowledged that soft power could be more effective than outright government control. However, Roosevelt's ability to manage the competing demands of employees, executives, and consumers hinged on the overall level of worker—and public—support for the war effort. In an earlier era, Wilson had devoted considerable time and effort to selling an unpopular war to the American people, an activity that severely limited his political effectiveness. Following Pearl Harbor, Roosevelt faced no such difficulties.[63]

African American Labor in Times of Depression and War

Despite the policy differences that characterized the government's approach to World War I and World War II, each conflict created substantial opportunities for individuals who were traditionally underrepresented in the railroad workplace. Thanks to the extreme shortage of labor, Pennsylvania Railroad officials were willing to hire African Americans, women, and Mexican nationals in larger numbers than ever before. As in World War I, employment opportunities were not equally distributed, and the highest-paying jobs remained the province of native-born White men. The role of the federal government did not change much either. In both wars, public rhetoric extolling workplace equality typically yielded to a pragmatic effort to secure as much labor as possible, by any means necessary. The rapidity with which the PRR and other railroads discharged their Black, female, and Hispanic workers, following the end of the war, attested to that. The employment of individuals from diverse groups satisfied the temporary need for workers, but it also created adversarial relationships within the Pennsylvania Railroad's workforce. White workers, by virtue of both their race and their seniority, expected that they would retain their privileged status—particularly when their government had required them to doff their coveralls in favor of khaki.

Since the 1850s, the Pennsylvania Railroad had employed African American workers, yet never on the same terms as their White counterparts. While largely confined to such low-paying occupations as laborers, porters, and cleaners, a few Black workers were able to secure employment in more highly skilled occupations. Their options broadened between 1918 and 1920, with the United States Railroad Administration overseeing the operation of the railroads. William McAdoo, the director general of the USRA, was far more interested in maintaining an adequate supply of labor than in guaranteeing equal rights, and the agency's policies reflected that intent. General Order No. 27, issued on May 25, 1918, mandated equal pay for comparable work, regardless of race. In practice, it was a simple matter to assign Whites and African Americans to different job classifications, thus negating the equal-pay-for-equal-work provisions. By preventing PRR executives from offering lower wages to Black workers, moreover, the USRA eliminated any economic advantage associated with employing them. Whites—particularly those in the running trades and the shop crafts—supported the USRA's labor policies, but they could not abide the prospect of women or persons of color competing for their jobs. They and the labor leaders who represented them experienced little difficulty in convincing executives that the maintenance of a cooperative workforce depended on the exclusion of African Americans from all but the most menial of occupations. The end of governmental oversight, coupled with the severe postwar recession, led to a reduction in employment, with Black personnel often the first to be let go. Their ranks fell from nearly 13,000 in August 1923 to 9,600 in January 1924.[64]

The onset of the Great Depression created both problems and opportunities for the PRR's African American workers. Their employment on the Pennsylvania Railroad reached its lowest level since the period prior to World War I, both in absolute numbers (6,277) and as a share of the labor force (5.6%). Yet demographics were working in their favor. The great migration that began during World War I continued through the 1920s, as millions fled segregation and sought economic opportunity in the North. While nearly nine out of every ten African Americans lived in the South in 1910, by the time Franklin Delano Roosevelt took office in March 1933, more than 20 percent lived in northern cities. During the thirty years between 1910 and 1940, the African American share of the total population doubled in the Census Bureau's Northeast Region—an area that included Pennsylvania, New Jersey, and New York. The increase, from 1.9 percent to 3.8 percent, was a precursor to a new wave of internal migration during World War II that increased the Black share of the region's population to 5.1 percent by 1950. A remarkable political transformation occurred during the 1930s as well. African Americans, particularly in the North, exercised their political rights, while shifting their affiliation from the Republican Party to the Democratic Party. Roosevelt's support for civil rights was at best tepid, but his political pragmatism ensured that Black voters would become an important part of the political coalition that accompanied the presidential election of 1936.[65]

African Americans weighed their options during the 1930s and the 1940s. One choice involved their level of cooperation with the company that employed them. Pennsylvania Railroad executives—all of whom were White and male—exhibited racial attitudes that were typical for their time. Few believed in racial equality or imagined that African Americans might one day sit beside them in the corporate boardroom. More comfortable with the accommodationist philosophy of Booker T. Washington than the more radical approach of W. E. B. DuBois, they suggested that the PRR offered industrious African Americans an opportunity to engage in productive labor that would reflect well on their race.[66] In the final analysis, however, White executives employed Black workers for the simple reason that they could be paid less than their White counterparts to do the same work. When that wage differential disappeared, then the railroad's commitment to its African American employees typically vanished as well.

The PRR's Black workers faced larger impediments than the company's executives. While those managers were not racial progressives, they were for the most part not virulent racists either. They generally possessed no desire to dislodge African Americans from those occupations they considered suitable for Black labor. Moreover, and as they had demonstrated numerous times in the past, they often exhibited a genuine compassion for individual African American employees who were endeavoring to support themselves and their families. To the extent that they felt able to do so, managers intervened on behalf of Black workers, attempting to protect their careers or at least find them menial jobs that would provide some source of income.

Those executives had to tread carefully, particularly in cases where African Americans sought positions traditionally reserved for native-born Whites. In that respect, the leaders and the rank-and-file membership of the railway unions constituted the greatest impediment to racial equality on the PRR. The constitutions of the operating brotherhoods barred African Americans—as well as Hispanics, Asians, and immigrants—from membership, while the shop craft unions affiliated with the American Federation of Labor maintained similar restrictions. While the leaders of those unions had often supported the USRA's labor policies, they did not accept the equality provisions reflected in General Order No. 27. Since federal control ended in 1920, they had negotiated labor agreements that had progressively restricted the ability of managers to employ Black workers in skilled occupations. The policies of PRR executives, while discriminatory in practice, thus reflected managerial acknowledgment of segregationist policies among the railway labor unions rather than a culture of corporate racism.

Excluded from the all-White operating brotherhoods and most other national unions, African American workers faced another choice—whether to attack racism from within existing unions or to form separate all-Black labor organizations. The first approach hinged on their ability to convince White union officials that their need for additional members outweighed the intolerance of many White members. Even if they succeeded in integrating an established union, Blacks remained a minority of the whole—and it remained to be seen whether the White majority would acknowledge the concerns of African American members or accept them in leadership positions. The second approach was likewise problematic. Black unions often lacked the membership and the financial resources necessary to operate effectively. They also enabled management to adopt a divide-and-conquer strategy, pitting a White union against an African American one. On numerous occasions, officials from the former camp attacked the latter, even as they waged war against the company that employed them all.

Inspired in part by Roosevelt's political rhetoric, many of the PRR's African American employees looked hopefully toward Washington. Some federal officials did perceive that the Great Depression and World War II might provide opportunities for the government to promote the cause of racial equality. So, too, did their counterparts in diverse and cosmopolitan states such as New York. They encouraged companies such as the PRR—and, of equal importance, pressured labor unions—to provide equal opportunities for Black workers. Southern Whites and organized labor were also vital components of the new Democratic Party, however, and neither group favored additional political or economic rights for African Americans. Those divisions forced Roosevelt to engage in a delicate balancing act, as he endeavored to placate the various constituencies that formed a part of his New Deal coalition. While the federal government proved increasingly willing to defend the rights of organized labor, that protection rarely extended to Black workers or union members.[67]

During the 1930s and 1940s, the Pennsylvania Railroad provided an increasingly public arena for the battles involving workers, unions, management, government, and the civil rights movement. The company attracted attention from supporters of racial equality, many of whom excoriated the railroad for failing to safeguard the rights of Black employees. To a large extent, the PRR gained that notoriety because it was one of the largest corporations in the nation, because it employed so many African Americans, and because it served the nation's economic and political capitals, not because it was more discriminatory or more racist than any other American organization. Ultimately, managerial efforts to be conciliatory, to comply with federal policy, and to provide a modicum of protection for the rights of African Americans cost the company dearly. In assuring federal and state governments that they would protect the rights of Black employees, PRR officials alienated White workers by challenging their notions of racial superiority and by threatening to deprive them of the implicit guarantee of multigenerational employment.

The New Deal initially made conditions worse rather than better for the PRR's Black workers. Joseph Eastman, in his role as federal coordinator of transportation, was not inclined to support the demands of African American railroaders. He accepted collective bargaining through independent unions primarily as a means of improving efficiency and avoiding disruptive strikes. In that capacity he feared that efforts to protect Black workers—whose representatives often openly supported the cause of civil rights—would likely produce disharmony within the ranks of organized labor. Yet the primary culprit was the 1934 Crosser-Dill Act, legislation that amended the 1926 Railway Labor Act. The revised statute established the National Mediation Board, with the authority to oversee and certify elections to determine which unions would represent a particular craft. In most cases, Whites dominated each occupational category, and in the national certification elections, they favored established unions that denied membership to African Americans. The White leadership of the victorious unions typically insisted that railroad managers remove Black workers from the payroll or ensure that they would never be promoted to desirable jobs. Executives who were determined to prevent labor unrest saw little reason to object. African Americans were entitled to bring their grievances to the National Railroad Adjustment Board, the other body established under the auspices of the Crosser-Dill Act. They could expect little success, however, for the NRAB's labor representatives were drawn exclusively from the White unions that had prevailed in the NMB-sanctioned national certification elections.[68] Nor could Black railroaders defend their rights by forming an African American counterpart to a White union, as such efforts ran afoul of Crosser-Dill's stipulation that only one organization could represent a particular craft.[69]

Despite those structural impediments, African American workers were able to influence the course of labor relations. The most notable accomplishment came through the Brotherhood of Sleeping Car Porters, Train, Chair Car, Coach Porters and Attendants, established in 1925. Because African Americans dominated that occupation, to the exclusion of other races, the Brotherhood of Sleeping Car Porters easily prevailed in the NMB-supervised certification election. Despite resistance from the Pullman Company, the BSCP won a contract in 1937 that included union recognition. Even though the porters who staffed parlor cars and sleeping cars worked for the Pullman Company and not the Pennsylvania Railroad, their success had important ramifications for the PRR's Black employees. A. Philip Randolph, the longtime president of the BSCP, sought to expand his influence into other crafts that employed significant numbers of African American workers. Those efforts brought him into conflict with other Black organizers. The resulting jurisdictional disputes pitted Randolph and others who favored affiliation with White-dominated unions such as the American Federation of Labor against those who insisted that only separate Black unions would be receptive to the needs of Black workers. Randolph also leveraged his role as the nation's best-known African American union official to advance the cause of civil rights. His achievements in that regard, although limited by widespread labor and managerial resistance to racial equality, nonetheless enabled officials in the federal government to expand their oversight of the PRR's employment practices.[70]

The outbreak of war in Europe and the likelihood of American involvement provided Randolph with an opportunity to further his conjoined goals of improving the economic well-being of African American workers while supporting civil rights. His threatened March on Washington induced Roosevelt to ban discrimination in wartime industries. Issued on June 25, 1941, Executive Order 8802 also established the Fair Employment Practice Committee. The FEPC was nonetheless a weak agency, with scant authority to enforce its recommendations. For political reasons, Roosevelt had appointed several White southern Democrats to the committee, individuals who asserted that workplace harmony should take precedence over equal rights. Initially a part of the Office of Production Management, the FEPC's power diminished still further in July 1942, when the agency became part of the War Manpower Commission. Nor were PRR officials willing to accept the FEPC's jurisdiction in employment matters, and general counsel John Dickinson initially advised President Clement that Executive Order 8802 applied only to wartime industries and not to companies engaged in transportation.[71]

By the time the federal government established the FEPC, the number of African American employees on the Pennsylvania Railroad had more than doubled since the slack period of the Great Depression. In September 1942, the company employed 16,155 Black workers, more than any other carrier. Of those, 5,347 worked on the Eastern Region, with an additional 2,063 in the New York Zone and 548 on the Long Island Rail Road. There were a further 2,340 Black employees on the Central Region, and 2,408 on the Western Region. Only 154 were women, working in jobs as diverse as coach cleaners, matrons, marine stewardesses, elevator operators, crossing tenders, and locomotive preparers. A few of their male counterparts worked in skilled occupations—fourteen machinists, five electricians, two welders, thirty-seven marine firemen, and a dozen stationary enginemen and firemen. Yet most were relegated to tasks that required either intense physical labor or deference to White travelers. Laborers accounted for 1,184 of the total number of Black employees. Slightly more than 2,000 African American workers were freight truckers, who loaded and unloaded boxcars, while another 317 served as station baggagemen. A further 621 were station porters or porter captains. Nearly a thousand were janitors or car, locomotive, or station cleaners. The largest contingent of African American employees worked in the Dining Car Department, with 549 cooks and 2,598 waiters.[72]

The number of African American employees increased slightly as the war progressed, but their occupations hardly changed. Of the 17,469 who worked for the Pennsylvania

When assigning jobs to African American women, PRR executives paid scant attention to prevailing notions of female propriety and instead regarded them as generic Black workers, best suited for manual labor. In November 1942, six of those women—members of the PRR's first female section gang—were using ballast forks to clean debris from the gravel that stabilized the tracks at Downingtown, Pennsylvania. The photographer did not record their names but noted that they "aren't allowed to lift more than 15 pounds"—an assertion that seemed hardly credible, given the physical intensity of the work. *Courtesy of the Historical Society of Pennsylvania.*

Railroad in November 1944, nearly 4,000 were loaders and truckers, some 1,500 were coach cleaners, and 2,423 were maintenance-of-way laborers. A further 3,432 were assigned to the Dining Car Department, both on trains and at the commissaries that stored, prepared, and washed food, linens, silverware, and dishes.[73]

A quarter of the African Americans who worked for the railroad during World War II were women, and nearly 20 percent of the women who worked for the PRR during the war were African American, a far higher percentage than in the previous war. Those employees were more likely to be assigned duties based on their race rather than their gender. In October 1943, when Thelma Williams applied for a position as a file clerk in the PRR's Reservation Bureau, she observed that the application form included a category for race. Even though she received the courtesy of an interview, a supervisor informed her that the railroad did not employ African Americans in white-collar jobs. More than a thousand African American women worked as coach cleaners. Another 430 served as truckers and porters, 269 as waitresses, and nearly 200 as cooks—occupations traditionally occupied by Black men. In addition, more than 200 worked as car and locomotive oilers, an even larger number as laborers, and the PRR listed a further 366 as maintenance-of-way "Section & Extra Gang

African American men prepared and served the superlative cuisine enjoyed by White passengers onboard *The Broadway Limited*. World War II, however, disrupted the boundaries that defined the roles of Black, White, male, and female employees on board the PRR's dining cars. *Aberdon F. Sozio photo, Conrail Photographs, Hagley Museum & Library, acc. 1993.231.*

Men." Approximately 200 "colored girls" worked in dining car service. Yet 46 African American women found jobs as machinists, 30 as electricians, and 11 as turntable operators. Perhaps most remarkably, one was as a police officer and another a gang foreman of laborers.[74]

Because more African Americans worked for the Dining Car Department than in any other area of the PRR's operations, it was hardly surprising that that occupation became the focus of controversy between managers, Black workers, and White employees. Those jobs were difficult, requiring long hours, perpetual deference to White passengers and crewmen, and, for the kitchen staff, the heat and cramped conditions of a dining car kitchen. While enginemen, firemen, conductors, brakemen, and other train-service personnel worked only on their respective divisions, dining car crews worked the train for its entire journey—from New York to Chicago or St. Louis, for example. With onboard space at a premium, they could expect to spend the night sleeping on the tables in the dining car. Cooks were well paid, compared to most other African American employees, but waiters received very low wages. They might receive tips, but their pension was based on their paycheck, not their total earnings—an issue that was a source of continuing frustration for dining car crews.

Each dining car was under the supervision of a dining car steward, who directed passengers to the appropriate table, ensured that diners received prompt and courteous service, and collected payment at the end of the meal. Prior to the war, Whites invariably occupied the steward's position. African Americans, in contrast, performed all the other tasks associated with preparing and serving meals. Most were cooks or waiters. Some trains on lightly patronized routes featured a diner lounge rather than a full diner, however. Under a PRR labor agreement with the Brotherhood of Railroad Trainmen, diner lounges with no more than thirty seats employed an African American waiter-in-charge rather than a White steward. It was the most senior food-service position available to Black employees, but it paid significantly less than the wages earned by White stewards for comparable work.

Public policy and racial barriers shaped the organizational efforts of the PRR's dining car employees. The labor standards established by the United States Railroad Administration during World War I encouraged food-service workers of both races to organize and demand collective bargaining. Nationwide, more than a thousand dining car stewards (including perhaps a hundred on the PRR) belonged to the Brotherhood of Dining Car Conductors. Established in 1918, the union's membership was limited to White supervisory personnel. The far larger number of African American PRR dining car employees followed a complex path toward union representation. In 1917, some established the Dining Car Cooks and Waiters' Association, and soon attracted membership from the Baltimore & Ohio and the Delaware, Lackawanna & Western. Black workers on the New Haven were involved in a parallel organizational campaign, resulting in the 1919 incorporation of the Brotherhood of Dining Car Employees.[75] The following year BDCE grand president Rienzi B. Lemus joined forces with his PRR-based counterparts. A veteran of the Spanish American War and the Philippine Insurrection, Lemus displayed his combative stance as a union organizer. In 1919, he persuaded the USRA to establish an 8-hour day and a 240-hour month for dining car personnel. Between 1921 and 1924, Lemus testified repeatedly in front of the Railroad Labor Board in a successful effort to maintain those standards. In 1921, he secured an agreement from the PRR covering pay and work rules—an accomplishment that nonetheless stopped short of outright union recognition.[76]

Lemus's relationship with Pennsylvania Railroad management varied between cooperation and confrontation. He initially praised PRR officials, particularly after the company began transferring food-service operations at major stations from the Dining Car Department to the independent Savarin restaurant chain. Lemus credited President W. W. Atterbury for interceding with Savarin officials to preserve the jobs of African Americans at those facilities. Such consideration encouraged Lemus to suggest that "the Pennsylvania is the best and most friendly employer of the Negro railroad employee." His assertion that the PRR "contemplates no racial discrimination, doesn't permit it," while inaccurate, presumably reflected his desire to curry favor with the railroad's executives. By the spring of 1932, however, Savarin was feeling the effects of the Depression, and managers cut costs by replacing veteran African American cloakroom attendants with young White women—a change that drew protests from Lemus.[77]

Lemus's disagreements with other African American labor leaders reflected the complex interplay of racial barriers, economic goals, and the civil rights movement. Soured by the race riots of the World War I years, Lemus had little patience with suggestions by Booker T. Washington and others that African Americans might earn respectability through hard work, self-improvement, and continued deference to White authority. Nor did he accept the advice of W. E. B. DuBois and other Black intellectuals to aggressively challenge segregation and racism. At least publicly, Lemus favored the attainment of economic equality over a campaign for civil rights. He emphasized that in 1921 he had "led two successful major fights against the [PRR] dining car department . . . both of which would have been lost had we allowed any of the Negro uplift organizations in on it." Lemus was equally hostile to socialism and communism, preferring to work through established political and economic channels to secure his goals. His determination to maintain his authority within the labor movement led to disagreements with Randolph and the Brotherhood of Sleeping Car Porters and with the American Federation of Labor. Lemus was incensed that the BSCP leader—whom he referred to as "All Piffle Randolph"—refused to honor the porters' overwhelming vote in favor of a strike against the Pullman Company. Lemus was equally opposed to Randolph's eagerness to link African American unions to the American Federation of Labor. The AFL had designated the Hotel and Restaurant Employees' International Alliance as its mechanism for organizing dining car employees, and in 1926, it offered Lemus the opportunity to merge his Brotherhood of Dining Car Employees into that affiliate.[78] Lemus acknowledged the benefits of AFL membership but demanded that BDCE members become a part of the Whites-only unions that collectively formed the AFL's Railway Employees' Department rather than the hotel and restaurant workers' affiliate. That was something that neither AFL leaders nor White shopworkers were willing to accept, and the negotiations soon came to an end.

For the better part of the following decade, Lemus repeatedly warned his members to avoid subsuming their goals to the authority of any White-dominated union.[79]

By the mid-1930s, however, Lemus's power had weakened considerably. Many cooks and waiters complained that the Brotherhood of Dining Car Employees had done little to protect them from the layoffs, wage reductions, and deteriorating working conditions associated with the Great Depression. White restaurant chefs, desperate for employment, eventually filled 30 percent of the ranks of dining car cooks, displacing African American employees in the process. Filipino immigrants—the only Asians who could legally enter the United States between 1924 and 1934—likewise competed against BDCE employees for work as waiters and served as potential strikebreakers.[80] That threat became clear in February 1932, when Pullman replaced eight African American porters with sixteen Filipinos. "Rumor has it," observed a reporter for the *New York Age*, an African American newspaper, "that the shift was made upon the suggestion and responsibility of the Pennsylvania Railroad Company, which we should prefer to believe rather than to think the Pullman Company is guilty of gross ingratitude to the Negro porter who has been the largest contributory factor toward its success from the very beginning." The *Age* encouraged its readers to boycott the Pennsylvania Railroad, in favor of the Baltimore & Ohio and the New York Central—an indication that the PRR might face the economic consequences of any discriminatory actions on the part of management. Lemus also feared the ability of executives to pit one race against another. While the Brotherhood's constitution did not impose restrictions based on race, he was determined to maintain jobs for the African American members of his union. He actively campaigned against the hiring of dining car workers of other races, and few, if any, Whites or Filipinos joined his organization.[81]

The public-policy machinery that had empowered Lemus and the Brotherhood of Dining Car Employees eventually undermined both the organizer and the union he established. The 1934 Crosser-Dill amendment to the Railway Labor Act created a mechanism for federally supervised certification elections, under the auspices of the National Railroad Adjustment Board. Leaders of the AFL's affiliate, the Hotel and Restaurant Employees' International Alliance, were quick to take advantage of the changed conditions. Prior to 1936, the charter of the AFL affiliate required racial segregation. In practice, however, many locals ignored that stipulation, ensuring that the HRE was one of the few racially integrated labor organizations in the United States.[82] Yet as late as 1928, the union had no more than a thousand Black members, few of whom worked for the railroads. The following year's efforts by the HRE's White leadership to supplant Randolph's Brotherhood of Sleeping Car Porters likewise did little to suggest that the union had any commitment to racial equality. That was precisely the outcome that Lemus had feared, and he accused African Americans who joined the AFL affiliate of being "Uncle Toms."[83]

Beginning on the West Coast, dining car employees unhappy with Lemus's leadership of the BDCE nonetheless began shifting their allegiance to various HRE locals. By January 1936, the HRE's influence had reached the Pennsylvania Railroad. The most prominent HRE member was George E. Brown, an employee of the PRR's Dining Car Department. Brown (who was White rather than African American) headed Local 370, which represented workers in New York, New Jersey, and New England. Determined to exploit the certification provisions contained in the Crosser-Dill Act, Brown challenged the right of Lemus's Brotherhood of Dining Car Employees to represent PRR crewmen. Speaking to a mostly Black audience at the Harlem Labor Temple, Brown alleged that the BDCE was a "fake union," more akin to a company union than an independent labor organization. Percival A. Moore, another member of Local 370, accused Lemus of "poisoning the minds of the colored race" by spreading the "propaganda that the A. F. of L. does not cater to colored people."[84] Brown called on the National Mediation Board to oversee a secret ballot to determine which union would negotiate with Pennsylvania Railroad management. The PRR's dining car employees found his arguments persuasive and, in common with their counterparts on other railroads, rejected the BDCE in favor of the AFL's affiliate.[85]

Brown and the AFL's Hotel and Restaurant Employees' affiliate emerged victorious, displacing the Brotherhood of Dining Car Employees as the union that represented the Pennsylvania Railroad's dining car personnel. There were nonetheless indications that Lemus had been rightly suspicious of the new union's commitment to the well-being of its African American members. Brown's initial demand was that the PRR's Black waiters-in-charge should receive the same wages as White dining car stewards. Rather than defend the pay inequity in front of the National Railroad Adjustment Board, company officials complied. The equalization seemingly represented a victory for the small number of Black waiters-in-charge. In practice, however, the new policy removed any financial incentive that the railroad might have possessed to place African Americans in supervisory positions in dining cars. That was a boon to furloughed dining car stewards and White employees of the hospitality industry, who could potentially replace Black waiters-in-charge. Nor did Brown's agenda produce any benefits for the African American cooks and waiters who constituted the vast majority of the PRR's dining car employees—all of which suggested that Brown was primarily interested in advancing the economic interests of the relatively small number of White stewards who were HRE members while attempting to attract defectors from the Whites-only Brotherhood of Dining Car Conductors.[86]

Racial tensions within the HRE exacerbated the union's ineffectiveness as a bargaining agent for dining car crews. Whereas Randolph's Brotherhood of Sleeping Car Porters, also affiliated with the AFL, bargained with one employer, the HRE negotiated with the PRR and more than forty other railroads. That situation alone ensured that there was little uniformity in wages, hours, or working conditions. HRE officials were more accustomed to dealing with restaurants that did not move from place to place and with a multiplicity of small-scale local employers who lacked the economic resources that the railroads possessed. The HRE's White officials were thus poor advocates for African American railway workers. Largely ignored by AFL leadership, two Union Pacific dining car employees began to recruit disaffected HRE members. Ishmael Flory and Solon Bell were members of the American Communist Party, and it was sometimes difficult to draw a clear distinction between their political beliefs and their commitment to the economic welfare of their fellow African American workers.[87] In 1937, Flory and Bell established a Dining Car Service Branch, also known as the Dining Car Employees' Division but more properly referred to as the Joint Council of Dining Car Employees, a unit of the HRE.[88] The fifteen locals that comprised the Joint Council enrolled about 7,000 members, of whom 1,500—including Brown—were White. Between 1937 and 1939, Brown was on leave from the PRR so that he could dedicate full time to the affairs of Local 370 and the larger Joint Council. He returned to railroad work in August 1939, probably occasioned by his failure to secure a 191-hour working month for PRR cooks and waiters.[89]

George Brown's involvement with the Joint Council reflected the triangulation of race, gender, and labor-management relations. By November 1942, with wartime traffic booming, the PRR was in desperate need for people who could work in dining cars and in off-train food-service positions. For the first time in the company's history, PRR officials contemplated the employment of women in dining cars. "Our dining car people recently placed colored waitresses on one of the cars operating between New York and Philadelphia," observed Walter S. Franklin in February 1943, "to take the place of colored men entering the armed forces." The PRR's vice president in charge of traffic was careful to balance potential opposition from White employees and passengers with the opportunity to attract the goodwill of civil rights leaders and African Americans who might patronize or work for the company. "While future developments in the matter are not quite clear, and for that reason we are not promoting the girls in general publicity, I am giving pictures and data about them to a number of colored newspapers, with the thought that publicity in that quarter will be generally helpful."[90]

Ultimately, approximately two hundred Black women worked as dining car waitresses, principally on trains operating between New York and Philadelphia. A far smaller number of White women became stewardesses—the female equivalent of White male stewards, although their status was on par with that of Black waiters-in-charge. As a White man whose HRE was affiliated with the largely White American Federation of Labor, Brown grappled with the complex and adversarial intersection of race and gender. He feared that waiters-in-charge—some of whom were White, and all of whom were men—might be demoted to the status of waiters, to create additional positions for female stewardesses. He nonetheless assented, on behalf of the HRE, to accept African American men over forty-five and women as temporary employees.[91] Brown's counterparts on the Brotherhood of Railroad Trainmen, the union that represented White dining car stewards, were even more reluctant to accept White temporary stewardesses. PRR management emphasized the critical nature of the wartime labor shortage and, more pointedly, informed the BRT officials that they could choose between acquiescing to White stewardesses and accepting more African American waiters-in-charge. Rather than face that possibility, the BRT capitulated in October 1943.[92]

The Red Caps and the FEPC

By the time the PRR hired the first African American waitresses, the organizational activities of another group of predominantly Black workers encouraged George Brown and the Joint Council to advocate more forcefully for African American dining car employees. Since 1896, and perhaps earlier, red caps worked at many PRR passenger stations, assisting travelers with their luggage, conveying messages, ensuring that unaccompanied children reached their train safely, and performing a variety of other services. They did not receive pay from the rail-road or from any union-station company. Instead, they subsisted solely on tips.[93] The onset of the Great Depression induced a substantial decline in tip income. At the same time, Whites desperate for employment sought jobs as red caps.[94] Efforts to organize the red caps into a union began in 1937, at the Chicago & North Western Terminal in Chicago. The efforts soon resulted in the formation of the International Brotherhood of Red Caps.[95] The IBRC's attorney, Leon Despres, sought to exploit the provisions of the 1934 Crosser-Dill amendment to the Railway Labor Act. By October 1938, he had persuaded the Interstate Commerce Commission to acknowledge the status of red caps as railroad employees, engaged in interstate commerce. Red caps were thus eligible to receive a railroad wage—set at twenty-five cents an hour, under the terms of the June 1938 Fair Labor Standards Act. As a result, red caps anticipated that they would receive a guaranteed minimum income, supplemented by tips.[96]

The classification of red caps as employees did not end the adversarial relationship between the PRR and the IBRC. In theory, red caps were guaranteed a minimum of two dollars for an eight-hour day. That was a significant expense for the Pennsylvania Railroad, one for which the company had not previously been responsible.[97] In common with their counterparts on other lines, PRR officials adopted an "accounting and guarantee" system that classified tips as wages. Any red cap earning less than two dollars a day would receive a supplement from the railroad to make up the difference. Red caps self-reported their tip earnings, creating an incentive to understate the amount they received from passengers. The larger problem, however, was that railroad officials strongly discouraged red caps from reporting anything below the two-dollar threshold that would require the company to augment tip income. In 1939, however, the federal wages and hours administrator declared that such practices violated the terms of the Fair Labor Standards Act. In response, attorneys for the International Brotherhood of Red Caps filed suit against the PRR and four other railroads, demanding more than $2 million in back pay.[98]

Beginning at the Cincinnati Union Terminal in February 1940, and soon extended to other PRR facilities, the "dime-a-bag" plan created further difficulties for red caps. Red caps charged a flat fee of ten cents per item of luggage, without a corresponding tip. They turned over their accumulated earnings to the terminal company that operated the station at which they worked, in exchange for an hourly wage.[99] That practice probably benefited red caps at smaller stations, with comparatively light patronage. At

larger terminals—such as those in Chicago, New York, and Washington, the total pay earned by the red caps was slightly less than the amount they had collected from travelers.[100] The system also induced a flurry of protests from passengers, who insisted that paying for assistance should be discretionary rather than mandatory. They directed much of that outrage at the red caps who were standing in front of them, asking for dimes. Red caps noted that their earnings, already depressed by the accounting-and-guarantee plan, had declined still further. Industrious red caps no longer had the opportunity to earn more than the federally mandated minimum wage, in part because they could not charge for mailing letters, safeguarding children, or other ancillary services. Moreover, many red caps complained that they had sacrificed the opportunity to develop a personal relationship with their customers through the social exchange of tipping.[101]

The substantial increase in passenger traffic that accompanied the end of the Great Depression and the beginning of the war in Europe produced few benefits for the red caps or the Pennsylvania Railroad. The total number of passengers increased from 35,127,004 during the first six months of 1940 to 64,276,277 in the corresponding period of 1941. By that time, however, 95 percent of travelers chose to carry their own bags rather than pay a fee to the red caps. Edgar E. Ernest, the chief of passenger transportation, indicated that the PRR was spending $180,000 annually on wages for red caps, over and above the revenue generated by the dime-a-bag policy. Red caps expressed little sympathy for the railroad's plight and insisted that their working conditions had deteriorated—in part because they were now penalized if a passenger mislaid a baggage check tag. Their outrage was so pervasive that during the autumn of 1942, 110 red caps at Penn Station refused to permit further payroll deductions for the purchase of war bonds.[102]

The red caps sought additional recruits in their fight against what they considered an unjust compensation system. In January 1940, shortly before the dime-a-bag plan went into effect, they recast the IBRC as the United Transport Service Employees. Ernest Calloway, the secretary of the union's constitutional committee, observed that the new name would give greater "dignity" to the organization and its members, but he was also hoping that the broader title would attract other African American railway personnel. The following year, many of the members of the Brotherhood of Dining Car Employees who had not already defected to the Hotel and Restaurant Employees' International Alliance joined the recently renamed union. In 1942, UTSE became affiliated with the Congress of Industrial Organizations. As such, the CIO-linked UTSE and Brown's Joint Council of the Hotel and Restaurant Employees' International Alliance (part of the AFL) were set to compete for the loyalties of dining car personnel. While the AFL had a long history of involvement with the railroads, primarily through the Whites-only Railway Employes' Department, the upstart CIO held important advantages as well. Many of the new union's organizers possessed ties to the American Communist Party and asserted that workplace solidarity trumped racial divisions.[103] In addition, the CIO's commitment to industrial unionism precluded the assignment of Black workers to segregated crafts.[104]

Stewards and Waitresses

The issuance of Executive Order 8802 and the creation of the Fair Employment Practice Committee enabled the Joint Council and UTSE to vie for members while enlisting the federal government to gain benefits for African American dining car employees. In August 1942, Claude H. Mason, the financial secretary and treasurer of the Joint Council's Local 370, initiated a chain of events that would transform the Pennsylvania Railroad's hiring and promotion practices. A month earlier, before the implementation of wartime austerity measures, the Dining Car Department had hired additional stewards, filling those positions, as it always had, with White employees. Representing thirty-two African Americans who had applied, unsuccessfully, for the positions, Mason brought the matter to the attention of the FEPC. By December, in an attempt to forestall a full-fledged FEPC investigation, Pennsylvania Railroad executives agreed to appoint two African Americans to the newly created positions of waiter-instructor and chef-instructor. Whites nonetheless continued to occupy all the steward positions.[105]

Mason accordingly wrote to John Finnegan, the general superintendent of dining car service, regarding the "elevation of experienced waiters-in-charge to stewards in dining car service." Finnegan ignored the request, prompting Mason to contact James Regis Downes, Clement's assistant. Downes in turn sought the advice of Walter Franklin, who in July 1943 observed "that, under present conditions, it would be inappropriate for this Company to undertake to state its policy with respect to the employment of Negroes as Stewards, which hitherto has not been considered competitive service." Finnegan adopted a similar perspective. "It has been our practice to observe the traditional methods obtaining for many years in employing and assigning persons for the different types and crafts of work available to them under the regulations applicable

to each type or craft," he noted, "and that racial relations would not be helped but rather strained by any deviation from this course; that we felt we are obliged to keep the delicate balance traditionally observed in this respect." That "delicate balance," Finnegan emphasized, resulted from the unwillingness of officials from the Brotherhood of Railroad Trainmen—a union that, unlike Local 370 of the HRE's Joint Committee, represented only White stewards—to countenance the employment of African Americans in those jobs.[106]

Efforts by PRR executives to dismiss Mason's request did not resolve the situation, however. The railroad's officials soon faced other complaints before the FEPC. Petitioners maintained that the company refused to hire African American trainmen and switchmen in the Chicago Terminal Division; was biased in its hiring and promotion practices at the Wilmington, Delaware, shops; would not appoint African Americans in Columbus, Ohio, to machinists' posts; and had failed to promote Black freight handlers and stock room employees to clerical positions. In Pittsburgh, PRR officials denied Mildred Johnson a job in the company's shops—because of her race, not her gender. The railroad hired ten of the thirty White female applicants, while turning away Johnson and another African American woman. Johnson complained that the only explanation provided by PRR officials was that "they have no rest rooms for Colored women."[107]

Despite the FEPC's limited authority and the segregationist attitudes of some of its leadership, many of the agency's staff members were genuinely appalled at the extent of workplace discrimination. With few investigative resources at their disposal, they relied on data provided by civil rights organizations and other associations of African Americans. By the fall of 1942, the overwhelming evidence of discriminatory practices persuaded FEPC officials to hold public hearings on the matter. Originally scheduled to begin the following January, the investigation soon ran afoul of wartime politics. The agency was reassigned to the War Manpower Commission in July 1942, indicating that mobilization was a far more important goal than equality. The Democrats lost more than fifty House and Senate seats in the 1942 congressional elections, suggesting the waning influence of the New Deal. While Roosevelt had no desire to alienate the northern Black voters who provided a significant share of his support, he was even less willing to antagonize southern Democrats. He instructed the War Manpower Commission to suspend indefinitely the proposed FEPC hearings. Widespread protests from Randolph and other African American labor and civil rights leaders caused Roosevelt to reconsider. Executive Order

9346, issued in May 1943, made the FEPC independent of the WMC, increased the agency's budget, and permitted the investigation to go forward.[108]

The FEPC hearings that began on September 15, 1943, placed PRR executives in the uncomfortable position of supporting the exclusionary policies of the White operating unions while denying that the company maintained discriminatory employment practices. Because the FEPC lacked subpoena power, the leaders of the brotherhoods were not under any obligation to give testimony. Their absence ensured that aggrieved African Americans took center stage, posing a significant public-relations problem for the Pennsylvania Railroad. Charles E. Musser, the PRR's chief of personnel, was quick to deny allegations of racism. He insisted that the vast majority of the PRR's African American workers were content and suggested that the federal government's commitment to equality had produced more harm than good. General counsel John Dickinson reassured FEPC chairman Malcolm Ross that "there has never been any race friction of any kind in the employment relations of the Pennsylvania Railroad" and that "in many respects Negroes are favored in the treatment accorded to them as employes by this Company."[109] Musser argued that a mere handful of "Negro Intellectuals" and "Negro radicals headed by Philip Randolph of the Sleeping Car Union [sic]" had used the FEPC as a forum for their grievances—and intimated that both the Brotherhood of Sleeping Car Porters and the Joint Council maintained ties to the Communist Party while neglecting workers' welfare in favor of an aggressive civil rights agenda.[110]

Despite Musser's suggestion that by "co-operating with the Fair Employment Practice Committee, we have done a world of good for the Negro," PRR officials saw little reason to support interventionist public policies. Musser and other executives emphasized that they had no desire to practice racism and were merely acceding to the expectations of White workers and the unions that represented them. The railroad's personnel managers no longer insisted, as they had in the 1910s and 1920s, that African Americans were incapable of performing highly skilled jobs. Instead, they suggested that racial integration would undermine efficiency and morale by engendering hostility among White employees. While emphasizing that "steady progress has never been interrupted by racial issues," they suggested that FEPC involvement "would stir up racial feeling where none now exists. It would be the first step backward for the colored employes in all the years they have been advancing on the Pennsylvania Railroad." Management also accused "the so-called Committee on Fair Employment

Practice" of "stirring up strife between the races on the Pennsylvania Railroad and by trying to compel us to do things that neither of the races on the Pennsylvania Railroad would desire to have done." Managers informed the FEPC of their commitment to "the requirement that a particular employe must be able to perform his duties without friction with his fellow workers or those under his supervision or with the public and consequently without creating a situation which may cause a general disruption of the service." PRR managers thus suggested that segregation and exclusionary employment practices were necessary evils, while claiming that it was their unionized employees and not they who were racist. When asked by FEPC officials whether the railroad had "hired any bright, young colored men in the Signal Department as yet," Musser explained that the answer was no, "primarily because there has been some resistance on the part of the Signalmen's Organization against the induction of negroes [sic] in the Signal Department." Nor was such opposition confined to the Brotherhood of Railroad Signalmen. PRR officials explained to the FEPC that their "knowledge of the attitude of this Company's present [White] employes at Chicago leads to the conclusion that to employ Negroes in these occupations would make the Company incapable of continuing to carry on its operation there and . . . that that attitude would find effective expression, if not through the organizations representing these employes, then through direct action on the part of the employes themselves."[111]

No amount of rationalization, however, could overcome the overwhelming evidence of discrimination aired at the FEPC hearings. By November, the agency had released a series of findings and directives that excoriated railroad companies and unions for their discriminatory employment practices. The southern carriers were by far the worst offenders and unsurprisingly bore the brunt of the FEPC's ire. Pennsylvania Railroad executives were not exempt, however. In particular, FEPC officials had little patience with claims by Musser and others that they had no choice but to accept the racist attitudes of unionized White workers. "It is not difficult to conclude that race or color is or may be a determining factor in the employment process where, as here, the Company expands the definition of 'fitness' so as to include therein the requirement that an employe must be able to perform his duties without friction with his fellow workers or the public," the agency noted. Adopting a perhaps overly optimistic assessment of the racial tolerance of White workers and travelers, the FEPC insisted that "the Company has not correctly diagnosed the temper of its employes or the public." It concluded that a pattern of pervasive discrimination did exist, at least in the case of the Chicago switchmen and the employees of the Dining Car Department. The agency also issued a cease-and-desist order that required the PRR and twenty-two other railroads—as well as seven unions—to end discriminatory hiring and promotion practices.[112]

Most of the twenty-three railroads sanctioned by the FEPC were in the South, where executives and union officials had long conspired to banish African Americans from the ranks of firemen, brakemen, and other skilled crafts. The FEPC deemed the abuses on the PRR (as well as on the New York Central) to be less pervasive. The agency held the cease-and-desist orders in abeyance, subject to corrective action on the part of the two railroads. While the brotherhoods ignored the FEPC directives and the southern carriers issued a statement of defiance, the comparative leniency granted to the Pennsylvania Railroad created a dilemma for that company's executives. They engaged in the delicate task of placating African American workers and the FEPC while reassuring White employees that their jobs were secure. With labor in short supply, the PRR was increasingly dependent on African American employees. Unlike the southern lines, which traversed areas where White supremacists provided a powerful extralegal mechanism to force Blacks to abandon railroad careers, the PRR served cities with strong traditions of African American activism. President Clement acknowledged that "there are certain places where unrest is creeping into our colored forces—such as in New York and Chicago—and we must arrive at a determination among our own colored employes as to how we are going to best meet this issue."[113]

Musser and other PRR officials adopted a strategy that was all too familiar to African Americans, one that emphasized self-improvement and advocated forbearance. "The Fair Employment Practice Committee has done a remarkable job for the Negroes," Musser told participants attending a conference at historically Black Howard University. "If they are patient and allow the Committee to move slowly, they will obtain their legitimate place in industry. A Negro cannot be kept down if he proves that he is equal to the job." Those jobs were available on the PRR, Musser added, asserting that "the Negro is entitled to a place in our industry." Explaining that the Pennsylvania Railroad "has made more progress in the employment of Negroes than any other enterprise," Musser cited the growing number of African American employees. He observed that since December 1941, the number of Black and White PRR workers had increased by precisely the same amount, 19 percent in each case. PRR officials also suggested that, in most cases, the ratio of African American

to White PRR workers exceeded the ratio of Blacks to Whites in the general population. That was particularly apparent in New York, where African Americans made up 4.2 percent of the population but 25.6 percent of the PRR labor force.[114] Musser suggested that it was unrealistic to expect more rapid progress and that it was dangerous for African Americans to rely on the policies of the FEPC. Government-sanctioned racial equality cut both ways, he suggested, hinting that Whites might soon apply for jobs in dining cars and as red caps in New York's Penn Station. As a result, Musser claimed, "there will probably be less colored people on the railroad when the White fellows get through."[115]

Musser and his associates also orchestrated an ambitious public-relations campaign, one that suggested the PRR's willingness to provide opportunities to its African American workers. During the summer of 1942, Herbert A. Enochs, Musser's predecessor as chief of personnel, had opposed such efforts at outreach. Enochs argued that it made no more sense to hire "a Public Relations man to represent the Negro worker, than . . . to put someone on to represent any other race of workers." The FEPC's directives, coupled with Clement's desire to placate Black workers without antagonizing their White counterparts, soon produced a change in corporate policy. Gustavus E. Payne, who headed the PRR's Publicity Bureau, escorted "a local [Pittsburgh] Courier reporter and photographer over the Philadelphia Terminal Division [to take photographs] of carefully selected groups of Negro workers in various occupations."[116] Clement also favored the hiring of a consultant to keep executives "informed as to the negroes' thinking in order that Management can keep these employees satisfied." Executives made it clear that that individual would not be a labor organizer and that "he would not be located under any circumstances in a Pennsylvania [Railroad] office." Steel magnate Ernest T. Weir suggested Joseph V. Baker, a journalist who had worked for the *Philadelphia Tribune* and then became the first African American columnist at the *Philadelphia Inquirer*. Baker established a public-relations firm, specializing in the marketing of products to African American consumers, and served as the executive secretary of the National Association of Negroes in American Industry. He possessed impeccable conservative credentials—he remained a staunch Republican until his death in 1993—perhaps suggesting why Weir considered him to be "an unusually intelligent negro."[117]

In addition to their public-relations campaign, Pennsylvania Railroad executives made more substantive efforts

The labor shortages associated with World War II rearranged traditional race and gender relationships in the PRR's dining cars. On May 7, 1944, W. L. Bright discusses the menu with White passengers. Judging by his dark uniform jacket, Bright is a dining car steward rather than a waiter or a waiter-in-charge. Replacing a White steward, he is supervising an unnamed African American woman, who has taken the place of a Black male waiter. *Courtesy of the Historical Society of Pennsylvania.*

to forestall implementation of FEPC sanctions. Following the September 1943 FEPC hearings, the company hired four hundred African American mechanics and mechanics' helpers. By April 1944, executives permitted African Americans to work in ten additional job classifications, including boiler inspector, freight-car inspector, passenger-car inspector, air brake inspector, machine operator, tender repairman, sheet metal worker, and electric crane operator.[118]

The actions of the FEPC, coupled with the wartime labor shortage, reshaped race and gender roles in many of the PRR's dining cars. Further pressure came from the leadership of AFL's Joint Council of Dining Car Employees (represented on the PRR by Local 370) and the CIO's United Transport Service Employees of America (the renamed and expanded union originally known as the International Brotherhood of Red Caps). In April 1944, and under pressure from the FEPC and Black labor leaders, PRR executives declared that the railroad's forty-eight African American waiters-in-charge would be eligible for promotion to steward.[119] The complex nature of the agreements between the PRR, the Hotel and Restaurant Employees' International Alliance, and the Brotherhood of Railroad Trainmen reflected the expectations assigned to each race and to both genders. [120]

Whether they worked as stewards or in more traditional roles such as cook, waiter, or waiter-in-charge, Black men interacted with female dining car employees of both races.

White women could not serve as stewards, but a position as stewardess was the functional equivalent of a male waiter-in-charge. Their African American counterparts worked only as waitresses. John Finnegan, the head of the PRR's Dining Car Department, asserted that women had no place in the dining car and made clear "that he did not want to retain females [sic] road personnel after the war." Yet he had little choice other than to accommodate the diversity that wartime labor shortages had engendered. Finnegan and other PRR managers were quick to allay the concerns of passengers who might balk at the sight of White women working with Black men in the close confines of a dining car. Moreover, Finnegan wondered "whether the sex rather than color would control" the interactions between White female stewardesses and male African American employees. He suggested that White women "would have a rather difficult time . . . in controlling the activities . . . of the old time [African American male] cooks and waiters on the car in her charge." The most straightforward solution, Finnegan suggested, was to transfer existing racial norms from one gender to another, by placing a White stewardess in charge of a dining car staffed by Black female waitresses. The all-female crews would work on a variety of trains operating between New York and Washington, including The Representative, The Mount Vernon (second dining car), and the advance section of The Judiciary. PRR officials also contemplated assigning female dining car staff to Chicago–Detroit service on The Detroit Arrow. Black men (as stewards or as waiters-in-charge) supervised a uniformly African American staff that might include male waiters or female waitresses.[121]

The full extent and duration of the PRR's use of female dining car personnel is not clear. Still, it must have been a fascinating experience to watch as The Mount Vernon thundered through New Jersey at better than eighty miles per hour. As the train's coaches and parlor cars flashed past, trackside observers could catch a glimpse of a White male steward supervising a contingent of African American men laboring as cooks and Black women who served as waitresses while, a few cars back, a White woman was overseeing the Black women who were serving the meals prepared by African American men.

Finnegan's reluctant concessions did not end the controversy regarding employment in PRR dining cars. The leadership of the Whites-only Brotherhood of Dining Car Conductors insisted that Black waiters-in-charge would be treated as newly hired employees once they earned promotion to steward. Even though the two jobs entailed identical responsibilities, African Americans would start at the bottom of the stewards' seniority ladder. White stewards

serving in the military retained their prewar seniority and upon returning to civilian life had the right to displace their Black counterparts.[122] When George Crockett, the executive director of the United Auto Workers-CIO Fair Practices Committee asked Musser to defend the inequity, the PRR's chief of personnel claimed that "our motive was not to discriminate against Negroes." Musser emphasized that at the beginning of the war, the PRR had established separate seniority lists for all newly hired employees, irrespective of race or gender. The policy reflected management's intent to preserve the jobs and seniority rights of returning veterans while allowing the company to eliminate surplus workers once the war ended. "We have been getting the riffraff of the world because we have had a very tight labor market," Musser complained, emphasizing that the two-tier seniority system "merely gives us the right to weed out any undesirables whom we got during the war." Irrespective of Musser's rationale, few Black waiters-in-charge were willing to risk the loss of their seniority, while suffering with the hostility of White dining car employees, solely for the opportunity to become stewards for the duration of the war.[123]

National events soon outpaced the cautious efforts of PRR executives to maintain an adequate labor force while minimizing racial disharmony. In the South, the intransigence of the operating brotherhoods and railway managers shifted efforts to attain workplace equality from the executive branch to the judiciary. In January 1944, Roosevelt established a commission, named for its chairman, North Carolinian Walter P. Stacy, to resolve the dispute.[124] The members of the Stacy Commission concluded that the FEPC had probably exceeded its authority, and they elected to await the resolution of two lawsuits pending before the Supreme Court. The plaintiffs in the Steele and Tunstall cases alleged that representatives from national labor unions had conspired with executives on southern railroads to deny jobs and promotion opportunities to Black operating employees. Specifically, they argued that the maintenance of segregated seniority lists ensured that White firemen were eligible for promotion to enginemen, while their African American counterparts were not. The cases, both decided in December 1944, invalidated union rules that interfered with the seniority rights of Black firemen and precluded any opportunity for them to earn promotion to enginemen. More broadly, the court required White unions to provide fair and equal representation to African American workers. Because the PRR did not employ any African American firemen or trainmen, the company was not specifically affected by the court's decision. The rulings nonetheless indicated that executives could no longer claim that racist union officials were the sole impediment to expanded employment opportunities for African Americans.[125]

Postwar Race Relations on the Pennsylvania Railroad

As the war came to an end, seniority rights became the most significant barrier to any expansion of African American employment on the Pennsylvania Railroad. In 1940, Congress had adopted the Veterans' Reemployment Rights Act, stipulating that individuals inducted into the military would be able to reclaim their seniority when they returned to the civilian workforce.[126] Many union officials argued that seniority should not be frozen at the level attained prior to induction. Instead, they claimed that Congress had intended for seniority to continue to accrue, as if the employee had never left the civilian workforce. It would be monumentally unfair, they maintained, if someone who began working just prior to the implementation of Selective Service and was drafted soon thereafter should lose ground to a more recent hire who had accumulated several years of seniority during the war. Musser and other PRR officials supported that position, in large measure because they were reluctant to extend seniority rights to "the riffraff of the world." In common with many other companies, the PRR adopted the "escalator clause," allowing employees in military service to continue accruing seniority as if they had never left railroad employment.[127] That provision became part of a January 24, 1945, contract between the railroad and the AFL's Brotherhood of Railroad Shop Crafts of America. While the Shop Crafts did not accept African Americans as members, the contract's escalator clause nonetheless applied equally to the four hundred Black mechanics and mechanics' helpers hired since the fall of 1943. Employed on the PRR for less than two years, they could not match the seniority of a White employee hired in 1940 and drafted in 1941 who returned to civilian life in late 1945—with the escalator clause stipulating that he had accrued more than five years of seniority during that time.[128]

The number of African American employees declined after V-J Day, from a peak of 18,532 in June 1944 to 13,014 in June 1949.[129] Yet there were similar reductions among the ranks of White workers, and the share of Black employment declined only slightly, from 10.5 percent of the PRR's workforce in the former year to 10.2 percent in the latter. There was likewise little change in the types of jobs open to African American workers. A few served as boilermakers, sheet metal workers, machinists, and electrical workers. Yet most worked as section men, laborers, baggage room attendants, and dining car crewmen. While 188 women worked at the Altoona Shops in 1950, only 13 African Americans did so, suggesting that the average White male shopworker was more likely to see a woman than an African American in the workplace. More than a third of the railroad's female employees were concentrated in the system general offices, yet fewer than 15 percent of African American employees worked there, and none of them were women.[130]

During the postwar years, the presence of many southern Democrats in Congress ensured that the federal government did little to protect the rights of African American railroad employees. While southerners continued to defend discriminatory policies at the state level, at least one northern state took action, in a manner that affected the Pennsylvania Railroad. In 1945, the New York legislature passed the Ives-Quinn Act, banning racially based restrictions on employment and establishing the state Commission Against Discrimination in Employment. The commission soon took action to secure the rights of African American passengers, even though PRR executives insisted that they were not engaging in discriminatory practices. Many of the trains that departed Penn Station continued beyond Washington, to New Orleans, Miami, and other locations in the segregated South. Pennsylvania Railroad conductors considered it easier to assign African Americans to separate accommodations when they boarded the train in New York rather than ask them to relocate when they reached the nation's capital.[131] In April 1948, Lillie Belle Perez left Penn Station, bound for Florida. She was on the *Silver Meteor*—a Seaboard Air Line train hauled by the PRR as far south as Washington—and entered a car occupied by White travelers, without incident. When she reached Washington, a crewman ordered her to relocate to a car assigned to African Americans. Her experience attracted the attention of James C. Olden, a Louisville native who was serving as a visiting pastor at the Salem Methodist Church in Harlem. Olden hoped to use the situation in New York as an opening wedge to end segregated transportation throughout the South. Eliminating segregation at busy locations such as New York, Washington, Cincinnati, and St. Louis would, he asserted, ripple through the rest of the country as well. Members of the Congress of Racial Equality, established in 1942, joined Olden's demand for an investigation into the matter. PRR officials emphasized that they only recommended but did not require segregation on trains departing Penn Station, and they expressed concerns about the disruption associated with relocating—midjourney—an entire trainload of passengers and their baggage from randomly assigned to segregated accommodations. Yet railroad officials aroused the ire of Elmer Carter, an African American member of CADE, when they suggested that the only alternative was to force every passenger on the *Silver Meteor* to leave the train at Washington, where they could purchase new tickets and secure new seat assignments for points farther south. Carter threatened to initiate a public investigation into the PRR's seating policies and further pledged to bring the matter to the attention of the state attorney general. Confronted with a case that they would almost certainly lose, railroad executives relented. Beginning in October 1949, conductors at Penn Station seated passengers without regard to race.[132]

Carter and the other members of the Commission Against Discrimination in Employment were far less aggressive in their efforts to protect the PRR's African American employees. Easiest to defend were the small number who worked in skilled occupations yet were ineligible for union membership. By 1947, the commission had forced the leadership of each of the operating brotherhoods and the other Whites-only railroad unions either to repeal discriminatory membership clauses or to forgo their enforcement within New York State.[133] The concessions enabled a PRR dining car steward to become the first African American in the nation who was able to join the Brotherhood of Railroad Trainmen. By the early 1950s, all the PRR's Black stewards had been inducted into the BRT.[134]

Yet the concessions by the BRT and other unions mattered little, so long as the Pennsylvania Railroad practiced discriminatory employment policies. As Musser had suggested in 1944, the PRR had displaced African American workers—including many who resided in New York—to provide jobs for returning White veterans. Musser's willingness to maintain dual seniority lists—one for prewar workers and the other for individuals hired or promoted after the terms of the Veterans' Reemployment Rights Act took effect—ensured that the railroad and the union collaborated to relegate those Black workers to unskilled positions.

In May 1946, six Black PRR employees, demoted to the status of coach cleaners to make places available for returning White veterans, filed a complaint with the Commission Against Discrimination in Employment. That situation created a quandary for the leadership of the National Association for the Advancement of Colored People. The state of New York possessed one of the most aggressive civil rights agendas in the nation and thus served as an excellent test bed for the national battle against discrimination—even more so because the NAACP's headquarters

were conveniently located in New York City. Thurgood Marshall, who had been associated with the NAACP since 1934, nonetheless believed that any case against the PRR would be too small and localized and thus incapable of establishing any national precedents.[135] It fell to White attorney Marian Wynn Perry, assistant special counsel to the NAACP's Legal Defense Fund, to protect the seniority of the PRR's Black employees. In June 1946, she brought the matter to the attention of CADE, asserting that the PRR and the Brotherhood of Shop Crafts had conspired to keep African Americans out of skilled positions. The PRR's 1943 promotion of African Americans to mechanics and mechanics' helpers mattered little, she argued, so long as the seniority escalator clause was in effect.[136]

Carter and the other commissioners ignored Perry's advocacy, defending their inaction with the assertion that the many complex issues associated with the complaint merited careful study. Not until 1953, eight years after the end of the war, did the PRR finally provide places for all the Whites who desired to exercise their seniority rights, thus opening positions for African American workers. Yet even then African American applicants reported that they were ignored in favor of White recruits. Three of them—Charles Morris, Louis Tribble, and Leroy Hall—sought the assistance of the Railroad Employees Association Against Discrimination, a group that included workers on the PRR, the NYC, and several other railroads that served Greater New York. The subsequent investigation by CADE revealed that the PRR employed 685 passenger trainmen and 2,180 freight trainmen, all of whom were White. The 61 new trainmen hired during a three-month period in 1953 likewise did not include any African Americans. Elmer Carter, the commissioner who had earlier stonewalled Perry's efforts on behalf of the NAACP, now informed PRR officials that he expected full compliance with the 1945 Ives-Quinn Act. The company's executives agreed to notify personnel managers that they could no longer discriminate on the basis of race and pledged to forward hiring data to the commission. On October 7, 1953, Morris became the first African American brakeman hired by the Pennsylvania Railroad, and company officials promised to begin employing conductors without regard for race.[137] By May 1956, the PRR had hired 140 African American trainmen. While some subsequently left the company, the majority were still on the job in 1957, when the Commission Against Discrimination examined the 20,900 train-service jobs in New York and New Jersey.[138]

By 1958, the New York commission, acting in concert with its New Jersey counterpart, had nonetheless concluded that "Negroes have been confined to the menial jobs on the railroads—and to the non operating groups." The commissioners praised the PRR as the one railroad that had made a "striking advance" in its hiring practices. Of the company's workforce, 10.5 percent was Black, compared to 7.2 percent on the New York Central, 6.6 percent on the Baltimore & Ohio, and 8.6 percent, on average, in the United States. The Pennsylvania Railroad also kept 113 African American train-service employees on the payroll—compared to five for all other railroads combined. Yet the PRR's progressive stance was relative, and Blacks accounted for less than 1 percent of the region's operating personnel. Neither the PRR nor any of the other eighteen railroads under investigation employed African American managers, agents, clerks, police officers, or signal workers. The commissioners' joint report ascribed their exclusion from the ranks of operating employees to opposition from the major railway unions. They emphasized, "The general situation may not change rapidly unless the management of the railroads will seek to implement a program of fair employment," and called upon executives to begin "hiring competent Negroes in job categories from which up to now they have been excluded."[139]

Ninety miles to the south, efforts to reform Philadelphia's city government produced greater opportunities for African American workers on the PRR. During the years immediately following World War II, financial problems and a series of political scandals rocked the city. In April 1951, voters approved a new municipal charter (often referred to as the Home Rule Charter), which took effect the following January. The charter's many provisions included an antidiscrimination clause, reflecting the diverse membership of the reform coalition and growing local commitment to civil rights. It also made provision for the establishment of the Commission on Human Relations, the first of its kind in the nation. The new agency, which began operations in 1952, replaced the much weaker municipal Fair Employment Practices Commission that had been established in 1948. The new agency soon published *Philadelphia's Negro Population: Facts on Housing* to combat discriminatory practices. During the same year, CHR executive director George Schermer persuaded the PRR to hire its first "class A" Black clerical worker.[140]

Pressure from the federal government and from state agencies in New York and Pennsylvania caused PRR executives to gradually modify their segregationist policies. As early as 1948, James W. Oram, Musser's replacement as chief of personnel, insisted that the railroad continue to maintain detailed statistics that classified employees by race, even though there was no legal requirement to do so.[141] "In view of the present intense interest in anti-discrimination

legislation—Federal, State, and City," Oram emphasized, "it is essential that we have current information regarding colored employes." Even though those statistics indicated that Whites dominated the more desirable job classifications, Oram emphasized that PRR managers had "used the figures to good advantage at various times when we were under investigation by the F.E.P.C. and also by the New York Commission."[142]

By 1965, the company's executives had identified twenty-three African American employees that they believed suitable for managerial positions. David Smucker, the vice president in charge of operations, nonetheless remained sensitive to the intense public scrutiny that was likely to accompany such promotions. "You will recognize," he noted, "the need to be careful not to move these people too fast or into positions for which they may not qualify. The consequences of having to demote a Negro supervisor would seem to me to be quite different from the necessity to remove a white supervisor who did not adequately fill the job to which he was assigned."[143]

Despite the limited advances in New York and Pennsylvania, the anticommunist sentiment that characterized American politics during the early years of the Cold War created further problems for Black employees and the unions that represented them. In 1937, Solon Bell's opposition to Rienzi Lemus contributed to the formation of the Joint Council of Dining Car Employees, as part of the AFL's Hotel and Restaurant Employees' International Alliance affiliate. The war had done little to reduce Bell's combative nature or his loyalty to the Communist Party. Beginning in 1945, in his capacity as chairman of the Joint Council, he began to organize Committees for a Democratic Union within various dining car locals. His goal, ambitious to say the least, was to use the committees to enable the Joint Council to seize control of the larger HRE. That plan ended in April 1947, when the delegates at the HRE annual convention defeated Bell's slate of candidates, removed him from the chairmanship of the Joint Council, and adopted a resolution that prohibited communists from serving in leadership positions. Ostracized from the Joint Council and the HRE, Bell soon established the Dining Car and Railroad Food Workers Union. While the new organization enrolled members on eleven railroads, Bell concentrated his efforts on the PRR, with most of his key personnel employed by that company's Dining Car Department.[144] In 1948, he defeated the Joint Council's Local 370 in a National Mediation Board certification election, establishing the Dining Car and Railroad Food Workers Union as the sole representative of approximately two thousand PRR dining car employees.[145] Bell and his allies were soon supporting the presidential bid of Progressive Party nominee Henry A. Wallace.[146] Few of the PRR's dining car employees shared Bell's political sentiments, however, and many later testified that they felt little kinship with someone who had worked for the Union Pacific but never for their company.[147]

The prospect of a cadre of Black communists serving meals to travelers on the nation's largest passenger-carrying railroad ensured that federal scrutiny of the Dining Car and Railroad Food Workers Union was more or less inevitable. Beginning in 1951, the Senate Internal Security Subcommittee, initially under the leadership of Nevada Democrat Patrick McCarran, investigated suspected threats to national security. The McCarran Committee soon subpoenaed Bell and other members of his union. North Carolina Democrat Willis Smith oversaw most of the testimony, accused Bell of being uncooperative and hostile, and recommended that he be cited for contempt. Speaking for the McCarran Committee, Smith insisted that the leaders of the Communist Party had scripted Bell's activities, valuing dining car workers for their ability to serve as "couriers in transmitting communications, documents, and instructions in the illegal operation of the party." By controlling the activities of railway workers, Smith continued, the Communist Party could "paralyze the whole national economy" by orchestrating a general transportation strike. Bell insisted that the Dining Car and Railroad Food Workers Union was "not a corps of Communist message carriers," and concluded that "being Negro, we are not shocked by name calling even by senators of the U.S."[148]

Despite allegations of communist influence, the Dining Car and Railroad Food Workers Union remained in existence, its sole bastion the Pennsylvania Railroad. During the summer of 1955, it survived challenges from the AFL's Joint Council and John L. Lewis's United Mine Workers, winning an NMB certification election. The union continued to represent PRR dining car crews into the 1960s. In company with the Joint Council and the Brotherhood of Sleeping Car Porters, it was one of the few African American unions to continue through the civil rights era. Those unions could nonetheless do little to protect the jobs of their members. The rapid decline in passenger traffic after 1945 proved catastrophic for the PRR's dining car employees, and not even the most successful union could rectify the situation. Dining cars had always operated at a loss and existed largely as an amenity to attract travelers. As passenger deficits mounted, PRR officials sought ways to reduce the expense of onboard food service. One solution was the "Automatic Buffet-Bar Car," placed in operation along the route between New York and Washington in December 1953. Automat cars on the PRR and other railroads were never popular with patrons, but they provided basic sustenance for the dwindling number of people willing to endure increasingly Spartan and inconvenient train travel. Of greater significance to African American employees, they required only a single attendant rather than a crew of cooks and waiters. By the early 1960s, years of deferred equipment maintenance had taken their toll, and 140 of the railroad's 162 dining cars were in a poor state of repair. The recession that began in 1960 and continued into 1961 produced sharp declines in the freight revenues that had for decades subsidized passenger service. In February, the PRR eliminated dining cars on many of its trains. Those that remained served progressively fewer patrons and required smaller numbers of employees. By the summer of 1961, the PRR's Dining Car Department, which at its wartime peak had employed 3,100 African Americans, had just 650 African Americans on the payroll.[149]

The ongoing decline of the northeastern railroads affected other classes of Black PRR employees with equal severity. As business executives and affluent vacationers shifted to automobiles or airplanes, the number of Pullman porters declined from seventeen thousand to fewer than seven thousand. A reduction in rail passenger travel and the desire of executives on the PRR and other railroads to reduce expenditures in stations that were often nearly deserted ensured that red caps also lost their jobs. The number employed at Penn Station and Grand Central Terminal fell from 1,250 to 225, as patrons increasingly relied on luggage carts and their own muscles to move bags through stations. Deferred maintenance, the increased mechanization of maintenance-of-way work, and the loss of less-than-carload-lot shipments (which required considerable manual labor) likewise produced substantial reductions in the number of African Americans who worked in less skilled occupations. By 1961, a reporter for the *Pittsburgh Courier* observed, "the thinning ranks of Negro railroadmen are wondering if they are headed for complete extinction."[150]

The erosion of the color bar during the late 1950s did not signify the end of White dominance over railroad employment. Executive Order 10925, issued in March 1961, prohibited railroads carrying the United States Mail from engaging in racial discrimination, a stipulation that PRR executives quickly conveyed to union officials.[151] In the face of mounting political pressure and a judiciary willing to support racial equality, the operating brotherhoods gradually opened their membership to persons of color—the Brotherhood of Railroad Trainmen in 1960, the Brotherhood of Locomotive Firemen in 1963, and the Brotherhood of Locomotive Firemen and Enginemen the following year. The passage of the Civil Rights Act of 1964 forced the remaining unions to abandon discriminatory practices as well. Yet skilled railroad occupations remained almost entirely White and male, shaped not by the law but by a workplace culture rife with racist comments, intimidation, and occasional violence. The reduction in railroad employment during the postwar years also worked against the PRR's African American workers. As the most recent hires, they were the first to be furloughed either in the event of a downturn in traffic or simply because increased efficiency necessitated fewer people on the payroll.[152]

Pennsylvania Railroad executives engaged in a delicate racial balancing act during the 1940s and 1950s. Musser, Clement, and others attempted to convince African American employees and various government agencies that they were neither racist nor discriminatory. Discrimination, they argued, was an unfortunate circumstance created by the policies of the White brotherhoods, by the requirements of efficient railway operations, and by the seniority rules established by the federal government. At the same time, they endeavored to reassure White employees that African Americans would never replace them. As one individual explained to the general manager of the PRR's New York Zone, it was important to create a situation in which "colored employees may be given promotional opportunities without incurring the ill-will of other employees." That such opportunities were woefully inadequate by modern standards was less an indication of racist attitudes on the part of PRR managers than a reflection of the social and political attitudes at the time. Those managers, after all, were far more interested in reducing labor costs and filling gaps in the railroad's wartime workforce than they were in any notion of racial equality. Yet, in providing jobs to African Americans and in stressing greater opportunities for them, Pennsylvania Railroad executives widened the adversarial relationship between management and labor, a trend that would be exacerbated during the postwar years.[153]

Female Employment during the Interwar Period

The PRR's female workers, like their African American counterparts, experienced the vagaries of the labor market, managerial attitudes, union rules, and federal policies. They too discovered that White male workers often functioned as adversaries, rather than allies. During World War I, the United States Railroad Administration mandated equal pay, irrespective of gender, for comparable work. Yet, it was

an easy matter for executives to create separate, although similar, job categories for men and women, with disparate levels of compensation. Nor could female workers expect any support from union officials who resolutely opposed any policies that would jeopardize the employment of men. Pauline Goldmark and other members of the USRA's Women's Service Section intervened in workplace disputes, but they generally did so in a manner that protected female virtue rather than female jobs.[154]

Despite the efforts of PRR executives to eliminate nonclerical female employees after World War I, a few remained, even in highly skilled occupations. Dora Miller, hired well before the First World War and working through the Second, retired with forty-two years of service. She had the distinction of being the last female block operator on the Pittsburgh Division. Katherine Rich left a job at the Westinghouse Lamp Company in February 1918 to work as crossing watchman on the Pennsylvania Railroad. After passing the Book of Rules exam and joining the Order of Railroad Telegraphers, she served in numerous towers in the New York–New Jersey area. By 1940, she had accumulated enough seniority to secure a night shift posting at Tower F, a vital junction controlling the traffic moving from Sunnyside Yard west into Penn Station. Her career invoked the mixed symbolism that reflected the changing status of women in American society on the eve of American participation in World War II. Observers praised her masculine attributes yet emphasized her femininity. Newspaper articles reported on "the 176 [trains] that Mrs. Rich shoots along nightly into the security of the railroad station." Rich herself fondly recalled the "thrill" of climbing tall signal towers, even during inclement weather, but expressed relief that electro-pneumatic controls had eliminated the physical labor necessary to operate the older manual levers. In common with many male block operators, Rich experienced the loneliness and danger associated with her job. She watched a flood on the Delaware River inundate the first floor of her two-story tower at Belvidere, New Jersey. Equally dangerous, perhaps, was her nightly commute to work, which involved a late-night trip on "the Eighth Avenue Subway as far as Sunnyside" before she was able to "grope her way through the dark across lots and over tracks to her tower." Given the nature of her work, it was hardly surprising that she considered herself the equal of her male counterparts. "Whether it's a man or woman makes no difference," Rich asserted. "You have to have a lot of nerve and the ability to make quick decisions. I feel just as capable as any man." Overall, she found her job "interesting" and looked forward to retirement and travel on a PRR employee pass.[155]

Such women were the exception, however. Most of those who remained on the payroll after World War I served as clerks, typists, secretaries, or stenographers. More than three-quarters of the entire female workforce belonged to the Clerical Workers Association, part of the PRR's company union, the Employe Representation Plan. As longtime employees, they enjoyed the benefits of seniority, although not to the same degree as men. When employment levels contracted during the Great Depression, male clerks demanded that women, particularly married women, be the first fired. Ironically, managers—rather than union representatives—attempted to preserve their jobs. In August 1931, the president of the CWA acknowledged that female clerks had often acquired many years of seniority. The economic needs of men nonetheless took precedence, L. H. Rieffel concluded, and those male employees "should merit more consideration in retention in employment than married females who are not required to secure a livelihood through employment with the railroad." One PRR executive nonetheless asserted "that a married woman with the responsibility of a home makes a more efficient employee than an unmarried woman who is merely working to save some money to spend." Frank Fell, the PRR's comptroller, offered a different perspective. "At the close of the last War," he observed, "we found ourselves with a number of married women on our rolls, which proved to be very undesirable as it was our experience that this caused a considerable amount of lost time over and above the average employe; for instance, if the husband was sick, the wife in many instances would stay home. . . . This also had an undesirable effect upon the morale in the office." Robert Massey, the vice president in charge of personnel, offered a more sympathetic and less mercenary perspective. "There are many cases," Massey observed, "where family, financial and other conditions, including dependencies, etc., are such that employment for married women is really a necessity."[156]

As the growing economic crisis produced more layoffs, female employees offered varying perspectives on the issue. Some supported the existing seniority system, which ensured that the longest-serving individuals would be the last to lose their jobs. Marion Mixner, in contrast, agreed with Rieffel that it was unfair for the PRR to use the seniority system in a manner that deprived women of badly needed jobs. Mixner was unmarried and an orphan, and after being laid off, she had no one to support her. "Simply because we were not born a few years sooner are we to be deprived of making a living," Mixner asked, "while girls with a few more years of service to their credit, with

husbands, continue to gratify all of their selfish desires for luxuries?"[157]

Pennsylvania Railroad executives ultimately elected to target married female clerical workers for layoffs, irrespective of their level of seniority—a stipulation that they never applied to men. "During the past ten years in the interest of the National welfare," Fell recalled in August 1942, "there was considerable agitation, I might say nation-wide to weed out the married women from employment that otherwise would have been occupied by male employes." Beginning in 1932, therefore, the personnel managers required all married women to tender their resignations. For the next decade, according to PRR policy, the company hired only single women and fired them as soon as they elected to marry. "This has been very beneficial to us," Fell concluded, "and we think it is a good thing." As a result, by 1938, only twenty-five married women worked for the Pennsylvania Railroad.[158]

Despite the abrogation of long-standing seniority policies, the severity of the Great Depression ensured that few single women were able to retain their jobs either. By September 1938, the Pennsylvania Railroad employed only 240 women, out of a total workforce of nearly 96,000. Nearly a third of them worked in the Accounting Department, and most of the remainder were secretaries in the company's corporate offices.[159]

Women in the Wartime Labor Force

Even before the United States declared war on the Axis powers, the European conflict stimulated the American economy and transformed the labor surplus to a labor shortage. That situation created substantial, albeit temporary, opportunities for women on the railroads. "The railroads," as a report to President Clement noted in February 1943, "have to be free to get men wherever they can; and particularly women, if they are going to train them to replace men." On December 1, 1941, only days before Pearl Harbor, fewer than 2,500 women worked for the PRR, constituting a mere 1.7 percent of the total workforce. By mid-February 1943, female employment had increased to 14,645, representing 8.7 percent of the railroad's 167,703 employees. During the summer of 1943, nearly 18,000 women had jobs on the PRR, and the company's officials acknowledged that that was less than half of the 40,577 positions that could be filled by temporary female employees. On September 15, 1943, the PRR employed 21,825 women, more than any other railroad in the United States, and second only to the Southern Pacific in terms of the

In May 1943, twin sisters Amy and Mary Rose Lindich worked as car repairmen helpers at the PRR shops in Pitcairn, Pennsylvania. They earned seventy-two cents an hour for their contribution to the war effort. *Marjory Collins photograph, Office of War Information, Library of Congress, Prints & Photographs Division.*

percentage of female employees in the workforce. By May 1944, the number had increased to 23,000 women, some 4,500 of whom were African American. As one newspaper reporter observed, the women "do practically everything but operate the trains." The fact that so many women were engaged in so many aspects of railroad work, Clement informed the chairman of the Interstate Commerce Commission, "shows you that they really have taken over men's work."[160]

Newly hired women came from a variety of backgrounds, and their new occupations were equally diverse. Mahala Snyder, who had been a car record clerk during World War I, reentered PRR service as a car tracer in the next conflict. Love Braithwaite drove a tractor. Mary Stauffer worked loading scrap while envisioning a postwar career as a welder. Some, like Snyder, had been forced from railroad service after the end of World War I. The larger group, however, were typically unmarried, in their late teens and early twenties. Often, they had grown up in railroad towns like Altoona and were thus acculturated to the world of railroading. Several members of Sarah Price's family worked for the Pennsylvania Railroad, and two of them—her uncle and her husband—died in on-the-job accidents. She had lived in Altoona since 1932, and in February 1943, she hired on as a laborer. After spending time assisting a crane operator, she was transferred to less traditionally masculine occupations—first as a store attendant, then as a records clerk, then a data entry clerk. In the process, she acknowledged that she "had made enemies of the male clerks." Aside from the pranks and practical jokes that were often a part of the railroad workplace experience for both genders, she nonetheless recalled little in the way of overt discrimination.[161] Unlike male workers, who had their pick of YMCA facilities, bars, and clubs, women like Price socialized and ate their meals in a combination cloakroom and restroom. Price baked desserts for her fellow workers, and, in a neat intersection of traditional gender and class boundaries, she modeled clothes in a fashion show organized to help the wives of PRR managers with their Christmastime shopping—an event that was duly recorded in the company's *Mutual Magazine*.[162]

Gloria Brown had similar experiences. Also hired in 1943, she worked as a secretary, served as a stenographer, and prepared train detention reports. In doing so, she developed a thorough understanding of locomotive terminology. Following the unexpected death of the man who served as the head clerk to the master mechanic, she succeeded him in that post. Like Price, she did not recall any examples of overt sexism—perhaps because she worked in the office rather than in a railroad yard or on the shop floor and was thus largely isolated from male employees. Brown also credited a supervisor who threatened to invoke disciplinary action against any male worker who stepped out of line.[163]

As such individual stories suggested, the shortage of male labor ensured that an increasing number of women worked in occupations ordinarily practiced solely by men. At the beginning of November 1941, 84.6 percent of the women who worked for the PRR served as clerks, stenographers, or telephone switchboard operators. By September 15, 1943, female employment had surged nearly tenfold, from 2,394 to 21,825. By then, however, only 35.9 percent of those women were associated with clerical and related responsibilities. During the same time, the number of carmen helpers increased from 0 to 845, electrician helpers from 0 to 235, and machinist helpers from 1 to 643. There were no female watchmen or policemen employed in 1941, but a dozen in 1943. The four welders, four boilermakers, two pipefitters, seventy-two machinists, fourteen assistant signalmen, and three Car Shop gang foremen who worked for the PRR in 1943 were the first female individuals since World War I to have access to those jobs. As the nomenclature suggested, PRR executives typically retained the

existing masculine job classifications. There were some exceptions, however, and the lone female draftswoman who was on the payroll in November 1941 welcomed thirteen additional coworkers by September 1943.[164]

Despite their participation in skilled occupational categories, most nonclerical women did not enjoy such opportunities. In September 1943, the company employed far more women who worked as coach cleaners (2,195), common laborers (1,962), loaders and truckers (1,720), section and extra gang men (1,238), storehouse laborers (710), oilers (679), and janitors (485). African American women performed many of those responsibilities, in keeping with managerial attitudes and the racial categorization of the era. By August 1944, of the PRR's 167,800 employees, 18,222 were White women and 5,195 were African American women. In November 1942, newspapers reported that the PRR "has hired 25 negro [*sic*] women as section hands, to handle such light jobs as trimming ballast and cleaning up" along the tracks in the Philadelphia area. On the Western Region, several lower-level managers informed general manager Harry Nancarrow that White women were not well suited to the physical demands of railroad work but that Black women possessed the requisite strength and stamina. In her reports to Nancarrow, Martha Davis, the Western Region advisor for women, carefully noted the distinctions between White and African American women and generally considered the former to be more conscientious than the latter. While most White executives shared those attitudes, her painstaking recordkeeping did not reflect corporate policy. In November 1943, Clement's assistant, James Downes, asked John Deasy, the vice president in charge of operations, to "let me know how many women the Pennsylvania Railroad had in service at the outbreak of the war and the number in service now; and of this number, how many are white and how many are colored." Upon further reflection, however, Downes appended "no separation to be made as between races."[165]

Recruiting and Training Female Workers

The rapid growth of the PRR's female workforce presented managers with considerable challenges, as they sought the best way to recruit and train those new employees. As early as September 1940, Pennsylvania Railroad executives began to investigate the potential of female labor. Three months had elapsed since the fall of France revealed the seriousness of the military situation in Europe, suggested that the United States might soon be a combatant, and heightened concerns regarding a shortage of workers. Personnel in the PRR's Legal Department indicated that "we have no definite policy against the employment of women. It is our feeling," emphasized an assistant to general counsel Henry Wolf Biklé, "that the most capable person should be employed, for a particular occupation, regardless of the sex of the individual." Yet he conceded that "some of our supervisory forces raised strong objections to the employment of women to fill jobs which they considered a female was entirely unfitted to occupy." Other PRR executives suggested that women employed during World War I had not taken their responsibilities seriously. "There is to be the same discipline among women as among men," they emphasized. "The last time it was not good."[166]

Despite such localized opposition from midlevel managers, state laws affecting the hours and working conditions of women—many of them dating to the Progressive Era—constituted a more serious barrier to their employment. "These laws were possibly made to protect the female," Biklé's assistant concluded, "but it seems to me that the employer, feeling that he has more latitude in the employing of a male, prefers the latter if he is available." Some states protected traditional norms of female propriety by preventing women from serving alcohol in dining or lounge cars or from working as crew callers.[167] Others prohibited women from handling toxic substances, lifting heavy objects (typically more than fifteen pounds), or working on certain types of machinery. Some legislation, such as the Pennsylvania Female 44-Hour Week law of 1937, curtailed women's working hours, both to protect their moral and physical health and to artificially decrease the supply of entry-level labor.[168]

The constraints imposed by state law and managerial attitudes conditioned the subsequent—and cautious—development of labor policies on the Pennsylvania Railroad. Executives initially sought guidance from their counterparts in Great Britain, where the labor situation was even more critical. Some of the most useful advice came from Sir Ernest John Hutchings Lemon, vice president of the London, Midland & Scottish Railway. Lemon "considered it important to have the women interviewed in the first place by our trained Women Welfare Supervisors in order to assess suitability and physical capacity." The LMS also used those supervisors as liaisons between executives, male workers, and female employees, and in "dealing with general questions outside the actual control of work, which affect the women."[169]

President Clement also received unsolicited advice from one of the PRR's most opinionated and confrontational midlevel managers. In 1906, William Elmer, the master mechanic on the Pittsburgh Division, refused to talk with striking female car cleaners. The women then invaded the home of division superintendent Simon Cameron Long—who ordered Elmer to discuss matters with the strikers and who doubtless admonished his subordinate for the maladroit handling of the situation. More than a decade later, shortly after the end of World War I, Elmer was the acting superintendent of the Philadelphia Division. In that capacity, he attempted to dismiss as many female employees as possible, in violation of the labor policies established by the United States Railroad Administration. He was equally aggressive in his response to labor unrest by men, vowing to die rather than submit to what he considered an illegal strike, while threatening to personally expel all disloyal workers from PRR property. Those actions encouraged one USRA official to label him a "bone head," and it was clear that Elmer did not lose his obstinacy in the years that followed. By September 1941, he had long since retired and moved to Florida. Despite his questionable tactics during and immediately after the previous war, he advised Clement on the most appropriate way to utilize female labor. He forwarded a photograph of women employed at the Olean Shops during World War I, indicating that "it was a sort of a hint that maybe you ought to be getting ready for hundreds and eventually perhaps thousands of women on our tracks and in our shops." If Elmer's advice was prescient, his further recollections embodied the sexism and ethnocentrism that were widespread in the early twentieth century. "While most of them were not handsome," he suggested, "they were efficient and helped out a lot." Elmer noted that "we began hiring women for track work, as there were many strong and husky Polish to draw on." His assertion that "whereas it took 4 men with tie tongs to carry a tie, these women would up-end it alone and carry it on their heads" nonetheless suggested that his recollections were less than fully accurate.[170]

It was the federal government rather than individuals such as Elmer that provided guidance for the employment of women in wartime. Otto S. Beyer, the director of the Division of Transport Personnel at the Office of Defense Transportation, was instrumental in that process. He relied on Dorothy Sells, an expert in British labor policy, who was at that time serving as the assistant chief of the ODT's Personnel Section. She was an appropriate choice, given that she had visited England and spoken with Sir Ernest Lemon at the London, Midland & Scottish regarding the employment of women on British railways. Sells recruited Olive Dennis, the engineer of service at the Baltimore & Ohio, an individual who advocated more comfortable seats, better ventilation, and other improvements that would appeal to female travelers. The B&O had also been in the forefront of efforts to expand employment opportunities for women in railroad operations, with the first of five hundred recruits beginning work in August 1942.[171]

Beyer soon attempted to coordinate the actions and forge a consensus among representatives from railroads, urban transit operators, airlines, trucking firms, and labor unions. In March 1943, he organized a two-day "Womanpower in Transportation" conference in Washington. "Never before in the history of the nation have we so looked to women to meet such a problem," ODT officials indicated, demonstrating a remarkable ignorance of the efforts made by their USRA counterparts during World War I. E. B. Dithridge, a midlevel manager in the Personnel Department, represented the PRR, while Sells gave a presentation on British practices. Other PRR managers, who assumed that women were physically incapable of entering the masculine world of railroad transportation, had little use for such meetings, however. Their dismissive comments indicated the gender bias and their assumptions regarding female behavior. "I am opposed to these kinds of conferences," complained John Deasy, the vice president in charge of operations. "They don't produce anything except a lot of gossip."[172]

During the months following the conference, Sells and Dennis prepared a forty-two-page report on the employment of women on the railroads. Issued in January 1944, it delineated, in detail, more than 150 jobs that they considered within the capabilities of female workers. Despite William Elmer's wildly inaccurate recollections of the strength of Polish trackworkers, they concluded that physically demanding jobs, particularly in maintenance-of-way work, should remain the province of men. Sells and Dennis noted that the processing of employee records "was exactly the right kind of work for women," while managerial positions required "a background of railroad experience not usually possessed by women." It would be difficult for women to work in the field of labor relations, they noted, "because it requires dealing with labor chairmen, all of whom are men"—although they did suggest that "women of the right type make often better conciliators than men." Based on the assumption that working women were also mothers, they recommended assignments that would allow female employees to return home every evening rather than spend the night in bunkhouses or other railroad facilities. Sells and Dennis also favored the establishment of nursery schools and carpooling arrangements to alleviate the burden on working mothers.[173]

Even before the release of the ODT report, PRR executives were developing initiatives similar to the recommendations that Sells and Dennis had prepared. In late 1942, the PRR selected Jessie Wilson as a consultant, at a salary of $100 per month. Wilson was a veteran of the Women's Service Section of the United States Railroad Administration and later served as the supervisor of female employees and the administrator of the railroad's John Edgar Thomson Scholarship program. By January 1943, and probably at Wilson's suggestion, presidential assistant James Downes had selected five advisors for women—one on each of the three regions, one on the New York Zone, and one at the Altoona Works. It was of vital importance, Downes informed Clement, that "these women have been designated as 'Advisers' in every instance, so that the title will give no intimation of any supervisory capacity, since their function will be of an advisory nature, both to the employees and to the Management."[174] The five women possessed dual reporting lines and were answerable to Wilson (and thus to Herbert Enochs, the chief of personnel) and to their respective general managers and vice presidents in the Transportation Department.[175] Each of the five was the widow of a deceased PRR midlevel executive. The jobs were not sinecures, however, and Downes ensured that the women possessed ample experience—some with the PRR's Women's Aid program during the Great Depression and others at the post office or the Red Cross.[176]

Thanks to the reluctance of Deasy and others to permit the regional advisors to issue orders to men, those five women restricted their activities to matters that had little effect on corporate policy. Martha Davis, who served on the Western Region, offered one example. She had been married to William R. Davis, the master mechanic at the Harrisburg Shops, but by 1943, at age forty-six, she was a widow. She had been active in Women's Aid, and—as Downes noted—possessed "considerable practical nursing experience." Davis's advisory reports to Harry L. Nancarrow, the general manager of the Western Region, reflected her identity as an individual who was White and middle class. She spent considerable time evaluating the condition of bathroom facilities—an activity that attested to her belief in the domestic virtues of cleanliness as well as an awareness of state laws that governed female employment. Like most of the PRR's male executives, Davis suggested that African American women were best suited to tasks that required physical strength rather than intellectual ability. Davis also reported sexual misconduct in the workplace, including instances of men who harassed or had affairs with their female coworkers. During World War I, Pauline Goldmark and other representatives of the Women's Service Section embodied similar beliefs. There were important differences, however. Goldmark, a graduate of Bryn Mawr College, was far wealthier and more socially

Newly hired female employees, gathered for a safety demonstration on December 14, 1942, were among the first to take advantage of new wartime opportunities on the Pennsylvania Railroad. Over the next two and a half years, the number of women railroaders grew rapidly—and fell even more precipitously once the war ended. Aside from the protective footwear, protective glasses constitute the only other safety devices in evidence. *Pennsylvania Railroad Negative Collection, Hagley Museum & Library, acc. 1993.300.*

prominent than Davis, who attended Altoona High School before spending a year at Irving College in Mechanicsburg, Pennsylvania. Davis was also employed by the railroad rather than the federal government, and she was correspondingly less likely to challenge PRR managers or corporate policies. In her advisory capacity, moreover, she lacked the coercive authority, admittedly limited in nature, that Goldmark possessed.[177]

Wartime hiring practices also caused PRR executives to reconsider the rule, adopted in 1932, that precluded the employment of married women. In July 1942, Alice P. Koller contacted Otto Beyer at the ODT. Koller, who had worked in the PRR's Accounting Department since 1919, was among the large group of women hired during the period of USRA control of the railroads. "I am anxious to get married," she told Beyer, "which would necessitate my resigning from the Railroad." Koller noted that when female employees "get married they do not become less valuable to the Company for which they work simply because they change their status from single to married." Given her qualifications, Koller could easily find work for the federal government, as part of the Civil Service Commission, but she was reluctant to give up the pay and the seniority rights associated with railroad employment. The situation was untenable, she concluded, given the PRR's desperate need for labor.[178]

Beyer's subsequent intervention, on Koller's behalf, revealed that more than two decades after the creation of a systemwide Personnel Department, the PRR had not yet fully standardized employment practices. Downes informed comptroller Frank Fell that the Transportation Department had never based employment on marital status.[179] "In order that we may have one policy on the railroad," he informed Fell, "it would be well for you to lift the ban on the employment of married women." Herbert A. Enochs, the chief of personnel, nonetheless suggested that married women would not earn a place on the seniority list.[180]

The finite nature of the wartime labor shortage ensured that the distinction between single and married women was largely irrelevant. Pennsylvania Railroad executives, as well as union officials, insisted that all newly hired women be treated as temporary employees who would be furloughed soon after the end of hostilities. "The females are in the service for the duration only," Deasy asserted, "and they will have to devote all of their time to their immediate problems. The long-range planning will be left for post-war activity, when the ladies will have lots of time to sit, to eat and to drink tea." Deasy and his colleagues issued instructions to all supervisory personnel that they were to emphatically stress that "the new employee has no definite assurance of a railroad job when the war is terminated." PRR managers also emphasized that "extreme care must be exercised in the employment of women to guard against establishing precedents, with relation to their employment in certain occupations, that may become embarrassing in the future." The language was subtle, but it clearly suggested that women who undertook traditionally male responsibilities could not expect to do so for long.[181]

Pennsylvania Railroad executives nonetheless emphasized the equitable treatment of female labor, but for reasons of efficiency rather than equality. "Women must be utilized in filling some of the positions normally occupied by men," they emphasized. As such, "employing officers must studiously avoid any appearance of prejudice against the employment of women. On the contrary, they must recognize the necessity of encouraging and assisting these women in becoming efficient workers whose cooperation is essential in the war effort." That policy ensured that managers could justify discriminatory practices based on widely held assumptions that fundamental differences between the genders marked women as incapable of efficiently performing many types of railroad labor.[182]

The concept of gender differentiation extended to the training programs devised for newly hired female employees. Women received an on-the-job education from "trainers," as well as classroom instruction. Both training and supervision took place in a gendered fashion, based on the assumption that "some women may become nervous and sensitive to criticism and may interpret routine supervisory instruction or similar action as evidence of partiality." Personnel Department managers informed female workers that shop machinery resembled familiar household appliances and could thus be operated in much the same way—but with far greater caution and respect. Cartoons illustrated the dangers of high heels and clothing that was too loose or too tight. A PRR safety manual reassured fashion-conscious female workers that "attractive low-heeled shoes are now on the market." One drawing, entitled "Too Much!" warned women that revealing clothing might attract unwanted attention from male workers. Another set of cartoons demonstrated the dangerous conditions that women might encounter. Initial drafts of training manuals included graphic illustrations depicting a woman who lost her eyesight to a chip of flying metal, another who crushed her foot, and a third whose arm (and her entire blouse) had been pulled off by a piece of machinery—while, in the background, a lurking, sinister man offered glass eyes and false limbs. In keeping with their conception of gender norms, personnel managers concluded that women would be unduly disturbed by such images and thus deleted them from the final version of the manual. Men, they assumed, would be more likely to avoid dangerous activities if they were shown the tragic consequences of their mistakes. Women, in contrast, would become frightened, timid, and hesitant if faced with the grim realities of a dangerous workplace and thus would be more likely to commit careless accidents.[183]

Publicizing Female Employment

Most of the women who worked for the Pennsylvania Railroad performed their jobs out of public view. Whether they took dictation in offices, cleaned cars in coach yards, greased locomotives, or assisted a machinist at the Altoona Works, they were largely invisible to those outside the company. A small group of women, well-educated, usually middle rather than working class, universally White, and carefully selected and trained by management, did represent the railroad in the public arena, however. Unlike their counterparts in offices, shops, and yards, they were not typically from railroad families.

By the summer of 1942, the Pennsylvania Railroad was employing female ticket clerks on an occasional basis in New York, Pittsburgh, Fort Wayne, and Dayton. To fill those positions, executives began "to build up a staff of young college women who have the personality and temperament to deal with the public directly or over the telephone" as they provided information, planned trips, and sold tickets. Executives repeatedly emphasized that "no girls are to be employed for such work unless they have

During World War II, the PRR employed women who worked directly with the traveling public. Sergeant Leonard Blocki (*left*) and Corporal Lester Edman (*right*) were in Philadelphia's Broad Street Station in December 1943, on the way to their next deployment. PRR managers went to great lengths to ensure that the female employees such as Ruth Lofland, who staffed information desks, were college educated and dressed in suitable attire. *Courtesy of the Special Collections Research Center, Temple University Libraries, Philadelphia, PA.*

a college education"—a far more rigorous requirement
than men faced for similar jobs. Newspaper ads, used in
cities with a large PRR presence, sought "young women
between 22 and 35 years with college education or sufficient business background or other specialized training.
Character, neatness and good address essential." The last of
those stipulations—for proper diction—reflected expectations that women could make announcements in major
railroad terminals. Personnel managers soon established a
formalized training process, with schools in Philadelphia
(conducted by H. William Hawke, the organist and choir-
master of St. Mark's Episcopal Church), Harrisburg, and
New York City (under the direction of the School of Radio
Technique). Deasy informed Clement that the women's
"posture and appearance are being checked daily by supervision, and corrective action taken where required." The
employment of female announcers proved successful, and
a New York newspaper reporter noted that "the dulcet
tones of a feminine voice heard over the public address
system in the great concourse of the Pennsylvania Station
are now taking the place of the old-fashioned gibberish of
the train announcer."[184]

On both the PRR and its Long Island Rail Road subsidiary, educated, articulate, and personable White women
could advance to positions of even greater responsibility.
The running trades—enginemen, firemen, conductors,
trainmen, and brakemen—had been the exclusive domain
of men since the beginning of railroading. Those operating
employees, their union representatives, and railroad managers assumed that women lacked the physical strength,
temperament, and years of training that were vital to safe
and efficient railroad service. The severity of the wartime
labor shortage nonetheless ensured that a small number
of women were able to serve as trainmen on the PRR and
on several other carriers. John Deasy, as the head of the
Transportation Department, had at first resisted the hiring
of women for jobs in train operations. The need for skilled
workers took precedence, however, as Clement made clear
on February 4, 1943. "You are entirely too slow in getting
the girl brakemen started," he admonished Deasy. "The
first thing you know you are going to lose out."[185]

Deasy did as he was told. At 9:45 a.m. on February 6,
1943, Elizabeth B. Johns became the first woman in train
service when she left Suburban Station on the outbound
Paoli Local. Vera Ruth Demmer and Ethel P. Moore began
work later that day. Soon thereafter, the LIRR selected
fourteen women for a three-week training session. Despite
the war, plenty of men were still on the payroll and entitled
to exercise their seniority rights. As such, only six of the
women were able to secure posts as trainmen, beginning
work on April 11, 1943. By May, twenty-four were working
on passenger trains along the Philadelphia Terminal Division (in addition to fifteen in freight service), twenty on the
New York Zone (principally on commuter trains operating
between Penn Station and New Jersey), and forty-one on
the Long Island Rail Road.[186]

While classified as "female trainmen," the women
did not attain equality with their male counterparts.[187]
They worked only in commuter service in Philadelphia,
Baltimore, and Greater New York, on both the PRR and
the Long Island Rail Road. The two companies together
employed slightly more than 200 female trainmen, who
filled about a sixth of the 1,355 vacant trainmen positions.
The remainder were reserved for men. Female trainmen
possessed no authority over train operations. Instead,
they sold and collected tickets, provided information, and
announced station stops. Given their limited responsibilities, they earned about $175 per month, well below the $300
paid to men. Initially, the women also lacked union representation, as membership in the Brotherhood of Railroad
Trainmen was restricted to native-born White men. Nor,
at first, did they accrue seniority rights.[188]

While only a small percentage of the PRR's workforce was associated with train service, female trainmen
attracted a disproportionate share of media attention. The
railroad's managers, sensitive to the glare of publicity,
developed a public-relations campaign that would portray their most visible employees in the best possible light.
Those efforts included the careful selection of the uniforms
worn by female trainmen. Clement and Deasy considered
several variants and scheduled a photo shoot with models.
The two senior executives subsequently exchanged lengthy
correspondence regarding uniform style, indicating their
recommended changes by drawing on the photographs
with a grease pencil. They ultimately settled on a design,
described in the *New York Times,* that consisted of "trim
navy jackets and skirts, neatly pleated front and back, with
smart caps fashioned after Civil War Confederate hats
and mannish shirts and ties." Some of the PRR's women
trainmen complained that the skirts were impracticable,
dangerous, and clearly ill-suited to the nature of railroad

Above, While they were seldom visible to the public, women filled many jobs customarily held by men—including tending switches at Sunnyside Yard in Queens. *Aberdon F. Sozio photo, courtesy of New York Transit Museum.*

Facing, Aberdon Sozio's photograph provided the basis for the PRR's *Molly Pitcher, 1944* advertisement. The ad emphasized that—like their counterparts in the American Revolutionary War—women were temporary employees, during a time of national emergency. The visual representation of African American women, on a section gang, suggested that racial norms were less fluid than gender ones. *Author's collection.*

Molly Pitcher, 1944

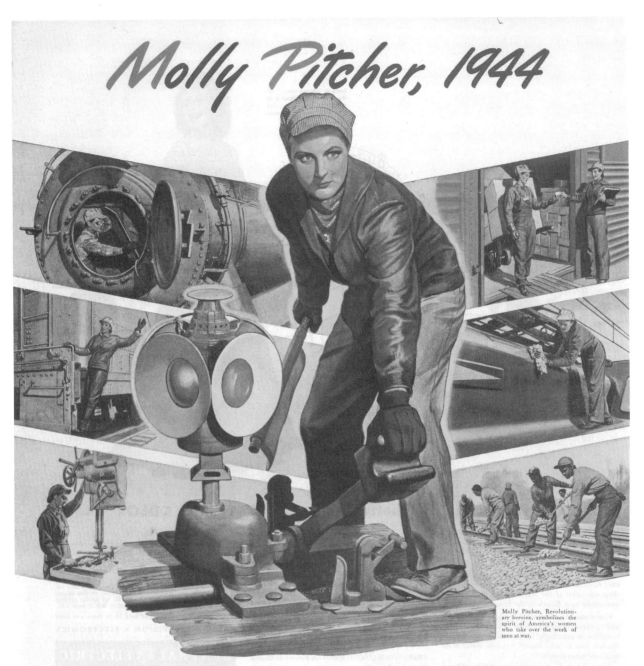

Molly Pitcher, Revolutionary heroine, symbolizes the spirit of America's women who take over the work of men at war.

Women are doing a big job on the Pennsylvania Railroad

More than 48,000 experienced Pennsylvania Railroad men have entered our armed forces. Yet, wartime's unusual needs for railroad service are being met . . . thanks in great part to more than 23,000 women who have rallied to the emergency. From colleges, high schools and homes, these women—after intensive training—are winning the wholehearted applause of the traveling public.

You see them working as trainmen, in ticket and station masters' offices and information bureaus, as platform ushers and train passenger representatives, in dining car service. Yes, even in baggage rooms, train dispatchers' offices, in shops and yards and as section hands. The Pennsylvania Railroad proudly salutes these "Molly Pitchers" who so gallantly fill the breach left by their fighting brothers-in-arms.

★ 48,128 in the Armed Forces
★ 248 have given their lives for their Country

Pennsylvania Railroad

Serving the Nation

BUY UNITED STATES
WAR BONDS AND STAMPS

work. Only after at least one woman suffered a serious injury did managers relent and permit female trainmen to wear pants.[189]

Clement and other PRR executives also developed a sophisticated advertising campaign that publicized the activities of female operating personnel. "In connection with the Pennsylvania Railroad's employment of women," emphasized publicity consultant Thomas J. Ross in December 1942, "there would seem to be a fine opportunity to get together a layout of photographs and news clippings dealing with women's activities in railroad work in a form that could be used for poster purposes around the railroad and perhaps for an advertisement." One poster, prepared in conjunction with the Al Paul Lefton Company, asked the public to "Meet MRS. Casey Jones." The associated caption indicated that women served in a variety of nontraditional occupations "where 'man-size' jobs have to be done'" and that they were "loyal, busy and able workers." The most famous advertisement, "Molly Pitcher, 1944," was based on an image, taken by freelance photographer Aberdon F. Sozio, of a woman switch tender at Sunnyside Yard. The central figure and the six surrounding vignettes depicted women performing traditionally male occupations—operating a drill press, switching cars, working inside the firebox of a steam locomotive, wiping down the exterior of a GG1 electric locomotive, and loading freight into a boxcar. In keeping with racial norms and PRR employment practices, the six African American women were depicted as working on the track, a form of manual labor that managers considered unsuitable for White women. Collectively, the women were engaged in atypical occupations, associated with "wartime's unusual needs for railroad service." The advertisement nonetheless emphasized that they had come from more traditional backgrounds in "colleges, high schools, and homes" and that their presence in the workplace was only temporary—as they "so gallantly fill the breach left by their fighting brothers-in-arms." In keeping with the general tenor of the PRR's public-relations efforts, the company also emphasized that women received "intensive training" before beginning their jobs, and that they were "winning the wholehearted applause of the traveling public."[190]

Correspondents were equally determined to publicize the personalities and actions of the small group of female trainmen. The July 18, 1943, radio broadcast by "Commando Mary" profiled the women who worked at Sunnyside Yard and included an interview with Dorothy Sells at the ODT. "Mary" was in reality Ernesto Barlow, a descendant of an influential Philadelphia Quaker family and an individual who spent several years promoting the contributions of women to the war effort. A reporter for the New York Times noted that female trainmen acted "with poise and dignity" and—like their counterparts at Penn Station—announced station stops "in strangely pleasant tones." They "collected tickets from grinning customers," who considered the altered gender roles to be both unusual and humorous. Those passengers typically remained respectful, however, and one woman trainman noted that she had experienced little difficulty with "mashers." In a memo to Deasy, Clement nonetheless suggested that it might "be a good thing to instruct or train the girl-brakemen how to defend themselves in case somebody gets fresh—possibly with the punch?"[191]

Even accounting for gender differences, the female trainmen on the PRR and the LIRR were not typical of the company's workforce. All were White, all had completed high school (and, in many cases, had attended college or had taken correspondence courses), and most were from middle-class rather than working-class backgrounds. A few hailed from railroad families. Marcell Craft, a Brooklyn native, was the daughter of an LIRR dispatcher. Her mother was the station agent at Nostrand, and her brother was an engineman. Craft's experience was unusual, however, and many of the newly hired female trainmen had been cashiers, telephone operators, bank clerks, dental assistants, or housewives. Ruth Hilger was one of the stars of Temple University's women's swimming team, but she also worked for the railroad three nights a week. Jocelyn Knowles quit her job as a receptionist at 20th Century Fox and accepted the considerably higher wage of $7.11 per day as a PRR trainman. Knowles valued more than the income, however. Having majored in literature at Columbia University, she lived in a very different world than most other PRR employees, male or female. She recalled that she "was motivated by a romantic conception of railroads acquired from movies and novels" and found that "the notion of doing 'a man's' job was in those days thrilling." Knowles judged, probably correctly, that PRR Personnel Department officials would evince little sympathy for those goals, and so she instead told them that her brother was in the military and that she wanted to contribute to the war effort to bring him home. New York resident Mary B. Robinson sought a way to support her husband, who was in the military. Bebe Thorne, in contrast, disclaimed any patriotic motivation and insisted that she was "doing it for the money." Fellow New Yorker Jocelyn Wagner had been a schoolteacher before she entered railroad service. Claire N. Frederick came from Pittsburgh and was a graduate of the prestigious Pittsburgh Academy. Gladys W. Reilly was from Kansas City, far to the west of PRR territory, but she was modeling clothes in New York City when she accepted the higher-paying job of a woman trainman.[192]

Female operating employees, fully cognizant of the high visibility that accompanied their public presence, offered a generally positive assessment of their experience on the PRR and the LIRR. They often did so in a language that emulated the masculine bravado associated with railroad men. Robinson, Wagner, Frederick, and Reilly indicated that they were "just crazy" about railroad work. Thorne, assessing the passengers on a typical commuter train, observed that "there are some pests you'd like to push their faces in, but most of them are nice." Irrespective of their reasons for taking a job with the railroad, all emphasized that their employment was solely for the duration of the war and that they would be happy to resume more traditional gender roles.[193]

The women offered varying accounts of their interactions with male employees. "On the whole," Robinson noted, "the men treat us pretty swell." Thorne, in contrast, suggested that "the situation is not so good between the men and the women." She concluded that "some of them are just old codgers who can't stand to see women doing men's work." More commonly, however, men assumed that they would have to compensate for women who were physically incapable of performing heavy railroad work. "But the *guys*—the guys have to work at everything that's called for," Thorne noted. "This makes them sore at us, because we don't have to do it." The perceived limitations of women also suggested that they were incapable of being true railroaders. Men, as one of Knowles's coworkers observed, were "proud of their hernias." When the two women struggled to throw a switch—a job normally undertaken by one man—Knowles tore away the sleeve on her jacket, while her companion lost her cap and her shoes. "We were humiliated," Knowles recalled, noting that the engineman on a passing train "was grinning as he passed us." Like Knowles, Thorne surmised that men resented the ability of PRR executives to employ low-wage labor. "But in a lot of ways they don't like us," she emphasized. "They think we're out to steal their jobs, though it doesn't seem to worry them when new men are hired."[194]

Many female trainmen concluded that membership in the Brotherhood of Railroad Trainmen would ensure higher wages and greater opportunities in the workplace. They faced a formidable obstacle, however, in the form of BRT president Alexander F. Whitney, a steadfast opponent of women in the workplace. In July 1942, Whitney noted that the employment of female trainmen offered "evidence of the aim of some carriers to obtain cheap labor so the coupon clippers might have a more bountiful harvest."[195]

More forcefully than any of his counterparts, Whitney insisted that women should only be used as a resource of last resort, hired after the railroads had exhausted the supply of men over forty-five. Above all, Whitney insisted, women should be classified as temporary personnel and thus would be ineligible for seniority. The initial agreement between the PRR and the BRT, signed in December 1942, thus emphasized that "females who are taken in the service of the Pennsylvania Railroad Company . . . during the present National Emergency and for a reasonable period thereafter . . . shall be considered temporary employees, and shall not accrue seniority" rights that overlapped those attained by men.[196]

By the summer of 1943, however, PRR executives were becoming concerned at the high rate of turnover within the ranks of female trainmen. The situation was particularly vexing, given the company's public-relations campaign, which had suggested that those women were happy in their work and grateful for the opportunity to contribute to the war effort. Of the 274 women hired as trainmen between January 6, 1943, and January 31, 1944, only 175 were still on the job—an attrition rate of 36.1 percent. The loss was the highest on the Maryland Division, where nearly half of the new hires quit the railroad, but even the best showing—on the Philadelphia Terminal Division, where 80 percent stayed on the job—was unacceptable. Charles Musser, who had replaced Herbert Enochs as the PRR's chief of personnel in July 1943, identified three principal causes for the high level of resignations. Some women objected to the irregular hours associated with railroad work, which often interfered with commitments to children or other family members. The necessity of working in all types of weather caused further problems. Other female trainmen complained that men, even those who had been hired at a later date, could bump them from the most coveted assignments. "The girls were hired for the duration of the war and not for after the war," Clement observed in December 1943. "Those who have been around for a year have commenced to be jealous of their seniority. One thing that is well known to them is that men hired since they have been hired have seniority over them right at the start. This does not seem quite equitable to the girls." Bebe Thorne complained, "They don't send us girls to Washington, Harrisburg or even Philadelphia. They only send us to jerky little [low seniority] places like Bay Head, New Brunswick and South Amboy, which pays less."[197]

To remedy the high turnover rate, Musser and other PRR executives pressured Whitney to grant seniority rights to female trainmen. In a letter to his assistant, James Oram, Musser complained that "Communists and the C.I.O."

were also asserting that female operating employees were entitled to seniority. Matters came to a head in February 1944, when Jocelyn Wagner and four other women filed a grievance with the National Railroad Adjustment Board. "We do not ask to replace the men returning from war, nor to displace the men who have been on the railroad before us," Wagner emphasized. "We believe in the principle of seniority. We merely ask for that seniority as of the date of hiring. We ask to be allowed to work the jobs we are qualified for and to be permitted to qualify for the jobs we are capable of working." On March 15, in an act of compromise, PRR and BRT officials agreed that women employed on or hired after that date would accrue seniority.[198] "Had it not been for your cooperation," Clement informed Whitney, "these young ladies would probably never have had the opportunity of taking a man's place for war." The two men had nonetheless established a separate female seniority line, ensuring that male employees with less experience could displace women at any time. That limited protection, moreover, would disappear once the war was over.[199]

Some union officials were receptive to female employees' concerns that the March 15 agreement did little to alleviate unfair employment practices. Bert Jewell, the long-standing head of the Railway Employees' Department of the American Federation of Labor, supported the creation of a single seniority list, one that would not differentiate between men and women who worked in railroad shops. Given that the PRR did not recognize the RED shopcraft unions, Jewell could do little more than offer moral support for the demands of the company's female employees. A representative from the Brotherhood of Railroad Signalmen (who, Clement noted, "doesn't agree with anybody on anything") likewise favored a single commingled seniority list. So did officials from the Brotherhood of Railway and Steamship Clerks, Freight Handlers, Express and Station Employes, a union representing occupations in which many women had worked, even prior to the wartime emergency. Some of the resulting agreements permitted women to retain their jobs after the war ended, unless displaced by a returning veteran. As a result, many women hired in those occupations during the war enjoyed long careers on the Pennsylvania Railroad.[200]

Whitney remained intransigent, however. His union was the sole operating brotherhood in a craft where women were also employed. The seniority policy endorsed by other labor leaders "was evidently news to Whitney," Clement observed, "and I don't think he is going to go along with it." In January 1944, shortly before Wagner and her colleagues filed a complaint with the National Railroad Adjustment Board, Bebe Thorne spoke with a female correspondent associated with *The Railroad Trainman*, the BRT's monthly journal. After highlighting the comparatively low wages and the discriminatory treatment she faced, compared to men, Thorne expressed satisfaction that "it's being taken up by the union." When asked to elaborate, she said, "Sure! The Brotherhood of Railroad Trainmen! Look at me, Brother Bebe! Didja hear about the four cents an hour 'raise' some jerks were trying to hand us? I guess they're afraid we haven't got enough for chewing gum or something. But Whitney says nix." The earthy language that characterized the interview reflected the intended audience of male trainmen, who used a similar vocabulary, suggesting that class solidarity took precedence over gender differences. In May, Wagner, accompanied by Mary Robinson, Claire Frederick, and Gladys Reilly, visited Whitney at the BRT's headquarters in Philadelphia. Unlike the coverage in *The Railroad Trainman*, a reporter for the *Cleveland Plain Dealer* emphasized their femininity and indicated that "they were pretty, they were glamorous." Irrespective of the difference in tone, the visiting women were likewise "impressed with the way the B.R.T. was conducting union affairs." Frederick indicated that "this business of working on the railroad has opened our eyes to a new world." It was, however, a world apart. Despite repeated challenges, Frederick and her coworkers were unable to establish a single, gender-neutral seniority list for trainmen. Nor were they able to establish seniority rights that predated March 15, 1944, or remove the provision that defined them as temporary employees. As such—and despite their enjoyment of their work and their need to earn paychecks—their only reward for their wartime service would be a furlough notice once hostilities had ended.[201]

Women in the Postwar Workplace

After World War II, female employment declined swiftly from its wartime high of more than twenty-three thousand. As the war came to an end and the company approached its 1946 centennial, PRR managers envisioned a new role for women. No longer interested in "Molly Pitcher, 1944," they planned to select a "'Miss Pennsylvania Railroad' from among [the] female employes so that the women might have a part in the celebration." Few of the PRR's female employees had anything to celebrate, however, and by the summer of 1946, half of them were off the payroll.[202] By February 1947, the company had furloughed most of its female dining car crews, satisfying the 1942 and 1943 agreements with the unions. Eight months later, most of the women who had served as shopworkers lost their jobs. Machinists, blacksmiths, electricians, and carmen represented by the Brotherhood of Railroad Shop Crafts of America were gone by August 1, 1949.[203] In 1950, only 4,997 women remained on the job, less than a quarter of those who had worked for the railroad little more than five years earlier, and only 657 of whom were African American.[204]

The speed with which the PRR released its female employees depended to a large degree on their occupation. Sarah Price spent much of the war as a clerk in the Altoona Works. That assignment saved her railroad career—for, had she remained in the more physical realm of shopwork, she would have been dismissed within six months after V-J Day. Instead, she continued to work for the Pennsylvania Railroad and then Penn Central before retiring from Conrail in 1977. Like Sarah Price, Gloria Brown held a traditionally female job as a secretary and stenographer. Her assignment to office work also preserved her job, and she worked from her date of initial hire in 1943 to her retirement from Conrail in 1987.[205]

Those stories were the exception, however. Within two years of the war's end, executives had eliminated 99.3 percent of the company's female laborers and 94.8 percent of the maintenance-of-equipment helpers. Unskilled workers fared somewhat better, as the PRR retained 39.4 percent of female crossing watchmen and 44.8 percent of coach cleaners. Overall, more than a third of the women who kept their jobs worked in the PRR system offices (nearly seven hundred in the comptroller's office alone), a clear indication that their duties were primarily clerical. In short, once the war had ended, women were universally culled from traditionally masculine occupations. Fewer than two hundred women remained at the Altoona Works, and they, too, conformed far more to the stereotype of Susie the Stenographer than Rosie the Riveter.[206]

While most women accepted their return to more traditional gender roles, a few resisted. At least one female dining car stewardess protested her dismissal. Lacking the governmental support that had existed during the USRA period and faced with the temporary nature of the wartime employment agreements, she had no recourse. The situation at the Pittsburgh freight terminal was more problematic, however. Most of the women freight handlers who remained after the war—thirty-seven out of forty-six—worked at the 11th Street facility. During the war, officials on the Pittsburgh Division had been so desperate for labor that they had hired the women without requiring them to sign special labor agreements—thus placing them in the general seniority pool, contrary to PRR hiring policies.[207]

Despite the layoffs and the overall contraction of the Pennsylvania Railroad's workforce, a few women secured jobs with the company even after the war ended. Like so many of her fellow PRR employees, Beverly Nail came from a railroad family. Her father and grandfather both worked for the company, and so did her mother. Unusually, her father only worked on the railroad for eighteen years (and was furloughed, off and on, for seven of them), yet her mother was hired in 1943 and worked for the next thirty years as a tractor operator, truck dispatcher, and clerk. It was Nail's mother who encouraged her to apply for a job in 1955, even though the railroad typically only hired single or divorced women. As a married woman, Nail credited her success to the fact that the division superintendent was on vacation when she was hired. She worked in various clerical positions, including the labor-relations section of the Personnel Department. To secure a position as the first woman head clerk in the Altoona Works, she "had to blackmail [her] boss" by refusing to train any more men to be promoted above her. Even then, her male supervisor assigned her the additional task of helping to prepare various departmental budgets.[208]

Nancy Delozier echoed Beverly Nail's frustration with managerial attitudes toward married women. She recalled being displaced while on maternity leave, with her allegedly temporary (and less capable) male replacement being kept on permanently. She spent most of her forty-one-year PRR career as a stenographer, filling out accident reports, taking dictation, and sorting through time cards. Like Sarah Price, Delozier was awestruck at the size and abundance of the rats that infested the Altoona Works. She was convinced that some of the shopmen fed them and adopted them as mascots. Price offered an alternate explanation—that the rats were fed so that they could be lured out into the open and dispatched with a piece of scrap metal. Delozier's chief complaint about railroad work nonetheless concerned the lack of suitable facilities for female workers. The nearest women's bathroom, she noted, was a quarter of a mile from her desk. Delozier probably spoke for most of the women on the PRR when she indicated that "we put up with all kinds of conditions because railroad pay was so much better than anywhere on the outside."[209]

Dawn Mangus also valued the pay associated with railroad work. Like many other PRR women, she came from a railroad family, and her father, grandfather, father-in-law, brother-in-law, and a cousin all worked for the PRR. She left the Bell Telephone Company, where it would have taken five years to reach starting railroad pay, for a stenographer's job on the PRR in 1956. She recalled more instances of sexual harassment and discrimination than did other women at Altoona. They included a supervisor who told her to use the restroom at a local gas station, another who claimed that women were not suitable employees because they might get pregnant, and a male head clerk who demanded the prerogative, reserved for her, of distributing paychecks. Mangus also pointed out that, while men and women ostensibly received equal pay for equal work, men typically filled higher-grade jobs, while women were assigned to lower-grade positions.[210]

Even after World War II, some women enjoyed long careers on the Pennsylvania Railroad, with jobs they found both financially and personally rewarding. They were nonetheless confined to a narrow occupational spectrum, unable to secure managerial positions or higher-paying jobs as skilled craftsmen or operating employees. Those changes would emerge only gradually. Today, even though railroading remains a male-dominated profession, women have made inroads into managerial ranks, railway yards, and locomotive cabs to a far greater degree than even during the years of World War II.[211] In spite of their limited participation in the PRR workforce, the contributions of women workers should not be discounted, for they paved the way for the women who later served in a wide array of railroad jobs.[212]

Hispanic Labor during World War II

As had been the case in World War I, the severe labor shortage ensured that American companies employed foreign nationals, in addition to African Americans and women. During World War II, the Pennsylvania Railroad utilized many Hispanic personnel, under *bracero* (guest worker) agreements negotiated between the US and Mexican governments. Braceros faced considerable opposition from railroad labor unions, ensuring that the program—unlike its agricultural counterpart—would end as soon as the war was over. PRR officials hoped that Anglo workers would have little reason to fear braceros, temporary employees who were not eligible for US citizenship. The influx of thousands of new workers onto PRR payrolls nonetheless exacerbated the concerns of native-born White employees, who asserted that managers were recruiting an alien group of low-wage workers who might undermine their authority in the workplace.

For several decades prior to the 1940s, Mexican nationals had worked for the PRR and other railroads in the United States. As early as the 1870s, some southwestern railroads had employed Mexican immigrants. By the turn of the century, continued migration had led some Mexicans to the Midwest and to a lesser extent the East Coast, where a few found employment with the Pennsylvania

Railroad. Beginning in 1917, despite opposition from labor unions, the PRR experienced such a shortage of wartime workers that it sent recruiting agents to El Paso to hire Mexican nationals. The United States Railroad Administration initially oversaw the program, albeit in a haphazard and inefficient fashion, and it remained in effect under private management until 1921. The political turmoil associated with the Mexican Revolution, combined with the poor oversight practices, ensured that the first incarnation of the railroad bracero program was largely a failure. Many railroads in the Midwest and Southwest continued to employ Mexican workers, however, and, in some instances, these workers comprised up to 90 percent of maintenance-of-way forces. During the prosperous years of the late 1920s, independent labor contractors supplied the PRR with some Mexican nationals. However, unlike the Italian immigrant labor of a previous generation, those Mexican workers were typically young, single men, who, once in the United States, frequently disappeared in search of more remunerative jobs. In 1928, one recruiter complained, "We ship about 500 Mexicans a month for the Pennsylvania Railroad.... Out of every 100 we bring, only about 20 stay on the job more than a few weeks." PRR personnel attempted to reduce the exodus by locking Mexican employees in railroad cars and nailing boards across the windows, but to no avail. During the 1920s, therefore, officials in the railroad's Personnel Department preferred to recruit African Americans, usually from Georgia or Florida. The relatively few workers of Mexican ancestry were generally repatriated during the depressed labor market of the 1930s.[213]

The labor shortages associated with World War II made railroad executives, including those on the PRR, enthusiastic participants in a resurrected bracero program. In September 1941, officials on the Southern Pacific requested an Immigration Service waiver to bring six hundred Mexican workers into the United States. The Immigration Service denied that request, but within a year, representatives from the railroad industry, the Office of Defense Transportation, and the War Manpower Commission were calling for the use of Mexican labor. Unions, represented by the Railway Labor Executives' Association, attempted unsuccessfully to block the importation of Mexican workers, with representatives from the United Brotherhood of Maintenance of Way Employes and Shop Laborers being particularly adamant in their opposition. Union officials attempted to recruit additional workers in the United States and pressured the railroads to increase wages for trackworkers, but the labor shortage continued.

In January 1943, State Department personnel began negotiations with representatives from the Departamento de Agricultura de México, largely because the two agencies had already worked together to establish an agricultural bracero program.[214]

By April, the two governments had established the parameters for the importation of six thousand Mexican railway workers. The agreement, signed the following month, provided substantial protections for all four of the major parties involved. The Mexican government insisted that railway braceros receive better treatment than their agricultural counterparts. The accord thus established minimum standards for wages and working conditions, transportation home at the end of each worker's contract, oversight by Mexican officials, and protection from discrimination (under the terms of Executive Order 8802). Mexican workers were also guaranteed medical care, food, and lodging equal to that of their US counterparts—a small concession, given that living and working conditions for all track workers were uniformly abysmal. While the US government posted a departure bond for agricultural braceros, guaranteeing their return to Mexico, the railroads instead shouldered that expense, at $500 per worker. Railroad executives also agreed to contribute a recruiting subsidy of $7.50 per employee. The federal government, through the Railroad Retirement Board and the War Manpower Commission, nonetheless agreed to pay for the evaluation and processing of prospective braceros before assigning them to various railroads. The unions secured a provision ensuring that bracero labor would not affect the employment, wages, or seniority of any native White worker.[215]

Thanks to the insatiable demand for labor, the bracero program grew rapidly. War Manpower Commission officials initially envisioned that the railroads would hire no more than a few thousand Mexican nationals. Eventually, however, they employed more than a hundred thousand workers, although no more than fifty thousand were on the job at any one time. Braceros served on thirty-six railroads and comprised nearly a sixth of railway maintenance-of-way forces in the United States. The WMC directed the entire initial contingent of braceros to three railroads in the West and Southwest, with the largest number assigned to the Southern Pacific, followed by the Santa Fe and the Western Pacific. By early August, however, the PRR's recently appointed chief of personnel, Charles Musser, was pressuring the War Manpower Commission for Mexican labor. In the WMC's August 1943 quota, the Pennsylvania Railroad accordingly received an allocation of a thousand braceros. Only the Southern

Pacific and the Santa Fe—the two largest carriers serving the states along the Mexican border—hosted larger contingents. PRR executives nonetheless considered that number to be insufficient. By September, they were using the Association of American Railroads to lobby the WMC for between eighteen hundred and twenty-two hundred additional workers.[216]

The PRR's maintenance-of-way executives would have to be patient, however, as the first group of one thousand braceros did not begin arriving until late December. Even though the Immigration Service and the Public Health Department assumed responsibility for screening applicants in Mexico City, PRR executives insisted that they be permitted to send two representatives there, "one to pick out the men prior to physical examination, and the other to sign all papers for each man employed." It is not clear to what extent the PRR officials were able to select the applicants whom they preferred, because prospective employees often bribed officials of the Secretaría de Trabajo y Previsión Social, who then delivered contingents of workers to the railroads. Several Pennsylvania Railroad Traffic Department representatives then accompanied the trainloads of braceros from Mexico City to El Paso and then on to St. Louis, where they reached PRR rails. While executives had initially envisioned distributing the contingent of one thousand braceros evenly throughout the system, they soon amended those plans. Instead, they assigned half to the Western Region and the remainder to the Central Region, generally in groups of twenty-five to sixty. Managers selected one individual from each group, based on his knowledge of English, to act as a combined foreman and interpreter.[217]

Pennsylvania Railroad executives continually demanded additional braceros, and both Musser and John Deasy (the railroad's vice president in charge of operations) wrote frequent letters to the War Manpower Commission and the Railroad Retirement Board. In March 1944, the WMC assigned 3,200 Mexican nationals to the PRR. During the summer, the railroad's quota had increased to 6,800, still well below the 9,360 that Deasy and Musser had requested.[218] By that time, PRR officials had assigned Mexican nationals almost equally to all three regions (Eastern, Central, and Western). The employment of more than 600 in the New York Zone (including the New York Division and the Long Island Rail Road) attested to the steady eastward spread of bracero labor. Mexican employment peaked in July 1945 at 9,592, representing 5.5 percent of the PRR's labor force at that time. Nearly half of the company's track workers as well as a fifth of its shop forces

During World War II, the PRR employed Mexican nationals as temporary workers under the federal bracero program—including ninety-three initially assigned to Philadelphia. On June 27, 1944, five of those employees were at 3210 Market Street, just west of 30th Street Station, reading a PRR safety manual that the railroad had translated into Spanish. *Courtesy of the Historical Society of Pennsylvania.*

were braceros—ratios that were well above the national average. Overall, the Pennsylvania Railroad brought 14,234 Mexicans into the United States as guest workers.[219]

Ethnic intolerance, language barriers, and the temporary status of the bracero program ensured that the Pennsylvania Railroad's White personnel had little interest in making Mexican nationals feel welcome in the United States. Mexican officials toured the PRR and spoke with many braceros, encountering numerous complaints but few examples of egregious mistreatment. The

maintenance-of-way personnel at Crestline, Ohio, were unanimous in their dislike for their foreman, Victor Plasencia, who "treated them very inhumanely," but that seemed to have been the exception rather than the rule. Living conditions were nonetheless uniformly substandard, ranging from shacks to converted boxcars. Food supplies were inadequate, with scant provision for Mexican dietary traditions. Braceros rarely enjoyed access to Mexican government officials, legal counsel, or union representation. The War Manpower Commission held back 3.25 percent of each bracero's wages, placed in a fund administered by the Railroad Retirement Board, money that workers might never collect.[220] Unlike officials on the Southern Pacific, who were widely known for their antagonistic relationship with both its braceros and the Mexican government, the PRR executives favored cooperation, and they routinely worked with Mexican consuls to resolve injury and death claims. Yet some braceros found it difficult to obtain access to medical care. In October 1945, Félix Tapia Montaña, a PRR track worker assigned to Plainsboro, New Jersey, required an emergency appendectomy. The railroad began withholding $24 of his $90 monthly paycheck in addition to the ongoing deductions for food, lodging, and retirement benefits. With his remaining earnings reduced to less than $10 per month, Tapia went on strike. With the war already over, neither the PRR nor the WMC had any further use for braceros such as Tapia. WMC officials declined to pressure the railroad to pay the striking worker's hospital bills and instead asked that he be deported.[221] Native White PRR workers were even less tolerant of their bracero counterparts, and they exhibited attitudes toward Mexicans that were typical of the time. One White female employee insinuated that they were lazy, incompetent, and unintelligible ("because they couldn't speak a word of English . . . it was gibber, gibber, gibber"); that they drank heavily; and that they were "dangerous" sexual predators, to the extent that women "had to be careful" in their presence.[222]

In anticipation of postwar repatriation, PRR officials made few efforts to mimic the Americanization programs they had offered to Italian immigrants during the 1910s and 1920s. The railroad offered little more than a smattering of instruction manuals and safety films translated into Spanish. In Philadelphia, charitable organizations, instead, assumed much of the responsibility for integrating braceros into the local community. By the early 1940s, the districts of Southwark, Spring Garden, and the Northern Liberties included substantial Spanish-speaking enclaves. Yet most residents (particularly among the cigar manufactories in Southwark) were of Spanish, Cuban, or Puerto Rican ancestry.[223] Other than a shared language, they had little in common with the more recent arrivals from Mexico. Although mutual-aid associations such as La Fraternal and La Milagrosa were involved in the assimilation process, braceros were more likely to interact with the International Institute, a non-Latino social-welfare organization. While most immigrant-welfare programs (including those that the PRR had offered during the 1910s and 1920s) emphasized Americanization, the International Institute instead encouraged both ethnic pluralism and the preservation of Indigenous cultures. In addition to English-language classes, long a staple of the Americanization movement, the institute sponsored dance and folklore groups and ethnic festivals. By 1945, Institute personnel had established the Philadelphia Regional Committee for Mexican War Workers to assist the thousand or so braceros who lived in the area. In their interactions with Mexican nationals, the committee's representatives "sensed constantly an antagonism to the railroad people." Mindful of

the tension and distrust between braceros and PRR officials, the institute's staff acted as intermediaries, working to resolve contract disputes in the absence of any sustained involvement from the WMC or Mexican government officials. Committee members also organized Sunday evening fiestas and trips to sporting events, while locating a Spanish-speaking buyer from a local department store to assist braceros with their shopping. The chairman of the committee was also concerned that many braceros returning to Mexico after the war "will, and with justification, report that they were treated as social inferiors, cheated in business transactions, and exploited by their employers." Such "ill-will ambassadorship," he lamented, would result in a postwar "setback to relations with Mexico, and the rest of Latin America"—an important consideration, as the United States and the Soviet Union were each preparing to influence the region. In September 1945, to counter such negative publicity, the Philadelphia Regional Committee began publication of *El Bracero Mexicano*, a mimeographed newsletter featuring articles and poetry written by Mexican workers. Many of the contributions were heavily scripted—or at least carefully chosen—to suggest that braceros were grateful for jobs in the United States and their opportunity to contribute to the war effort. Enrique Parra Rameríz, a PRR employee based in Philadelphia, emphasized, "I feel so very happy to have come here to work on the railway lines of North America. I am happy not only because I have come to know this Great Land of Marvels but also because I have come to meet my obligations as a good Mexican citizen and to collaborate and help attain a victory for peace." Within a few months, moreover, most braceros had been repatriated, and the committee ceased operations in March 1946. Its efforts to inculcate a positive image for the United States may or may not have worked, but in the absence of any significant social-welfare initiatives on the part of the Pennsylvania Railroad, the International Institute undoubtedly provided valuable benefits to the company's temporary Mexican workforce.[224]

The 1943 contract with the Mexican government stipulated that braceros would be confined to maintenance-of-way responsibilities. In late June, however, War Department officials emphasized that aliens could be employed in any occupation, with the exception of those involving the aviation industry and classified contracts, and that to do otherwise would render companies liable for violating Executive Order 8802. In September, the Santa Fe pushed the limits of the revised policy when it assigned Mexican nationals to work on refrigerator car icing platforms. Santa Fe executives asserted that the task was merely another form of unskilled labor, albeit one that was not explicitly covered under the terms of the contract between Mexico and the United States. Both the Mexican government and the WMC initially expressed their disapproval of such practices by threatening to bring the bracero program to a swift and premature end. The demand for labor was nonetheless such that labor reassignments became commonplace throughout the United States.[225]

Like their counterparts on the Santa Fe, PRR managers assigned bracero workers to a variety of occupations, triggering conflicts with labor unions and testing the boundaries of the company's diverse, yet rigidly compartmentalized labor force. Union officials were not initially hostile to the reassignment of Mexican workers, and by the beginning of October 1943, the Brotherhood of Maintenance of Way Employes, the AFL's Railway Employes Department, and the Brotherhood of Railway Clerks had all given their approval, provided that no native White workers were affected. The WMC accordingly created two groups of braceros, one for the PRR's Maintenance of Way Department and the other for the Maintenance of Equipment Department. When railroad executives requested an additional sixty-three hundred Mexican nationals from the WMC in early March 1944, Harry W. Jones, the chief of motive power, anticipated that more than half would be working in the New York Zone. Jones estimated that nearly eleven hundred (just over 17%) would be assigned to equipment maintenance rather than track work. By early April 1944, Vice President Deasy had requested and received permission from the WMC to employ braceros as unskilled shop laborers. Later that month, the WMC granted the railroad the authority to use Mexican nationals in some skilled occupations, including stationary firemen and oilers. PRR chief engineer John L. Gressitt nonetheless acknowledged that any commingling of bracero maintenance-of-way and maintenance-of-equipment forces would produce "serious complications."[226]

The trouble began in the Wilmington Shops, where laborers were in perennially short supply. The DuPont munitions works and Sun Oil's high-octane gasoline refinery in nearby Marcus Hook received A-1 priority for whatever workers were available. Deasy had already emphasized that he "did not want to employ any more women or riff-raff" in Wilmington or at other PRR shop facilities. And, indeed, female employees had already refused to work in the drop pits underneath the shop tracks, rigging electric-locomotive motor brushes. Shop supervisors also asserted "that the colored forces working

second and third trick do not work regularly." When shorthanded, they routinely and without authorization rousted braceros from their bunkroom and assigned them to whatever tasks were at hand.[227]

The local initiative to freely interchange workers, without regard to race, gender, or bracero classification, created two problems. By the summer of 1944, the railroad was employing fifty-four Mexican nationals at the Wilmington Shops, and seventeen of them were classified as skilled workers (eight machinists, eight electricians, and a blacksmith). It was more expedient, PRR shop managers argued, to simply promote braceros who possessed the requisite skills than to spend months or even years training novice Anglo workers to do the same tasks. Such practices were also illegal, or at the very least a violation of the bracero agreement between the governments of the United States and Mexico. When PRR officials explored the possibility of obtaining permission from the War Manpower Commission to do what they were already doing, they discovered that only the Immigration Service could grant the necessary authority. Yet, Jones admitted, a request of that nature would require a formal investigation, "to which hearing representatives of organized labor would be invited." That, in turn, would likely invoke the open hostility of labor unions, whose leaders were already suspicious that the bracero program was not so much a wartime necessity as a ploy to undermine the wages and benefits of native-born workers. "In the circumstances," Jones observed with considerable understatement, "it is not desired to open up this subject." By March 1945, the railroad had signed a contract with the Pennsylvania Federation of the Brotherhood of Maintenance of Way Employes, stipulating that "Mexican Nationals will not be upgraded or transferred . . . except upon written approval of the [union's] General Chairman [and that] available domestic employes will be afforded opportunity for upgrading or transfer."[228]

The Wilmington incident also suggested a more pervasive problem with the bracero program, one that involved overtime labor. When shop foremen had assigned Mexican nationals in lieu of native-born White or African American workers, they had also given them overtime pay, while denying that same opportunity to individuals who were US citizens. That seeming favoritism toward Mexican workers soon created a systemwide labor-relations problem. Many braceros desired to work as many hours as possible to maximize their earnings before they were required to leave the United States. Citing their own economic needs and the obvious shortage of labor, they demanded the right to collect time-and-a-half pay by routinely working ten hours a day rather than eight. In September 1944, the Mexican under-minister of labor, Padilla Nervo, informed the WMC that, unless the PRR and the New York Central permitted braceros to work overtime, then he would suspend the entire program. Overtime pay was simply not possible, Deasy countered, noting that "it would not be equitable to work Mexican nationals 10-hours per day without offering the same privilege to all domestic workers who may desire to work the same number of hours [and] . . . we are not in a position to revise our maintenance program to allow for such longer working periods." As assistant chief of personnel James Oram observed, what Deasy meant was that the increased overtime pay would cost the Pennsylvania Railroad $6 million a year in extra wages. With the Mexican government pledging to withdraw all braceros from the PRR, representatives from the War Manpower Commission warned that the railroad's "allocation would be reduced to the number that it would be if the Mexicans were to be worked on the basis of 10 hours per day." The head of the WMC's Foreign Labor Section, John D. Coates, headed for Mexico City in an effort to resolve the dispute. Coates was successful, and the problem subsided, but the overtime controversy engendered considerable ill will between PRR officials, braceros, unionized White workers, the Mexican government, and the WMC.[229]

Despite the end of the war in Europe, PRR executives lobbied for the continuation of the bracero program. In July 1945, they complained that "men released from Military Service are not returning to Railroad work and women are leaving Railroad Service" and that maintenance-of-way crews in the Eastern Region "have been employing school boys 16–17 years of age."[230] Union leaders, however, were outraged at reports that some other railroads had retained Mexican nationals while laying off native-born White workers. The concerns of PRR managers thus quickly gave way to opposition from organized labor as well as a consensus that as many jobs as possible be made available to returning veterans. In consequence, the War Manpower Commission terminated the railroad bracero program on August 28, 1945—although its agricultural counterpart remained in force until 1964. By 1949, the PRR had officially removed all Mexicans, Puerto Ricans, and Filipinos from the employment rolls, but the Immigration and Naturalization Service still held the company liable for the departure bonds of twenty-five braceros who had disappeared without returning to Mexico. The Korean War created a new round of labor shortages, but the PRR's efforts to resurrect the railway bracero program were unsuccessful. By the summer of 1951, however, the general manager of the Western Region acknowledged that he had "resorted to importing Mexicans from the state of Texas."[231] As late as 1956, officials at the Immigration and Naturalization Service alleged that fifteen Mexican nationals were still employed by the Pennsylvania Railroad.[232]

The contraction of railway employment that accompanied falling postwar traffic levels as well as the mechanization of many maintenance-of-way operations ensured that the PRR had scant need for Mexican workers. After the end of the agricultural bracero program in 1964, many farmers and agribusinesses replaced their guest workers with undocumented aliens, but such was not the case in the railroad industry and certainly not on the PRR. Native White male workers thus had little reason to fear that executives were grooming a generation of foreign workers to take their jobs. The railroad's participation in the bracero program and unsuccessful efforts to extend it indicated that Pennsylvania Railroad managers were continually exploring ways to reduce labor costs, in the process creating tensions between executives and unionized, native-born, White workers.

Casualties of War

The executives and the employees of the Pennsylvania Railroad performed magnificently during World War II, yet they hardly earned the thanks of a grateful nation. Passengers complained about trains that were crowded, late, and composed of poorly maintained equipment. They were particularly critical of the Pennsylvania Railroad, a company that faced chronic shortages of passenger cars while transporting more commuters and intercity travelers than any other carrier. Boxcars converted to emergency passenger service provided particularly dismal accommodation, and patrons paid little attention to the ingenuity of shop forces, who did the best they could with limited resources. One PRR executive acknowledged "criticisms of the Pennsylvania Railroad, not only by regular passengers, but by those in uniform" and warned that "this feeling may be carried over into the post war period, i.e., that the Pennsylvania was 'the road that made us ride in box cars.'" Many dissatisfied patrons vowed never to travel by another train again if they could possibly avoid it. They could easily make good on their threats. The postwar prosperity that followed a decade of economic calamity and five years of global war generated millions of consumer dollars for the purchase of new automobiles and other luxuries-turned-necessities. All levels of government were poised to do what the vast majority of Americans demanded, by building highways, subsidizing the home mortgages that permitted GIs to flee the cities for the suburbs, and in general facilitating a culture of automobility.[233]

Between 1940 and 1945, the PRR experienced neither the traffic congestion nor the contentious relations with the federal government that had characterized World War I. That happy outcome was related to the development of more efficient practices for transferring cargoes between railroad cars and oceangoing ships. It also reflected the substantial investments in railroad infrastructure—most notably the electrification of the lines between New York, Washington, and Harrisburg. More ominously, the increased transportation efficiency associated with World War II stemmed from the greater availability of alternate modes of transport. Victor V. Boatner, the director of the Division of Railway Transport of the Office of Defense Transportation, was probably correct when he attributed the substantial increases in productivity that had taken place in the railroad industry after 1929 to "the removal of the drudgery work primarily by the trucks." That "drudgery work" nonetheless paid the bills, particularly given a rate structure that set high tariffs for less-than-carload-lot and merchandise shipments. It remained to be seen whether the PRR and the other railroads could find off-setting sources of traffic and revenues.[234]

The federal government's efficient management of wartime transportation also worked to the detriment of the Pennsylvania Railroad. During the short-lived boom in petroleum traffic, representatives from the Office of Defense Transportation stated that "we have consistently endeavored to route symbol petroleum traffic on the Pennsylvania Railroad only in cases where it was absolutely essential from a termination requirement." Petroleum thus accounted for 6.7 percent of the PRR's gross freight revenue during the first five months of 1943, compared to 8.4 percent for the New York Central, 10.2 percent for the Baltimore & Ohio, and 10.5 percent for the Erie. Beginning in 1943, the federal government allocated supplies of iron ore to specific mills rather than permit steel-company executives to purchase their raw material on the open market. As a result, the PRR's deliveries to the Bethlehem Steel Company declined by 3.5 million tons. The Defense Plant Corporation diverted substantial freight tonnage to the Baltimore & Ohio, so that that company would have a source of revenue that would facilitate the repayment of its 1932 loan to the Reconstruction Finance Corporation. The conversion of Detroit's auto plants to aircraft production temporarily deprived the New York Central of traffic—but ensured high freight volumes once full-scale manufacturing was underway. When comparing the first eight months

of 1942 with the corresponding period in 1943, the PRR's freight revenue increased by 10.8 percent, well below the 17.1 percent on the NYC, 17.2 percent on the B&O, and 18.8 percent on the Erie. Thanks to the expense associated with managing a high volume of passenger traffic, moreover, the PRR's net railway operating income declined by 8.1 percent. Only the Erie, with an 11.7 percent decrease, did worse, while the B&O and the NYC posted gains of 26.7 percent and 27.3 percent, respectively.[235]

After 1945, efforts to provide adequate service depended on the PRR's ability to undo the deleterious effects of wartime traffic on locomotives, cars, and the physical plant. Officials in the office of the chief engineer estimated that, in 1943, the company suffered $12.1 million in deferred maintenance associated with maintenance of way and structures—an amount that increased to $19.0 million the following year. Deferred maintenance on equipment likewise expanded from $18.4 million in 1943 to $24.8 million in 1944. Managers reported shortages of 634,255 ties in 1943 and 281,000 ties in 1944. Many replacement ties were small, made from inferior wood, or not properly preserved with creosote or other materials, and they would require replacement soon after the war was over. The situation involving steel rail was even worse, with allotments falling short of requirements by 42,555 tons in 1943, 46,900 tons in 1944, and 84,700 tons in 1945. All told, the Pennsylvania Railroad received slightly less than half of the rail that it needed.[236]

As the company's assets deteriorated, PRR executives were spending more money than ever, just to keep the trains rolling. Between August 31, 1939, and October 31, 1942, they authorized $197 million in "extraordinary expenditures," over and above the amount that would have been allocated under normal operating conditions. The amount included $72.6 million in locomotives and rolling stock as well as $81.7 million in additional repairs. The added wear and tear on the physical plant consumed another $34.8 million. Overall, between 1939 and 1945, the PRR spent more than $77 million on roadway facilities, $10 million on yards, $16.5 million on port improvements, $24 million for additional main tracks and signals, and $2 million to build spurs and sidings to wartime industries—to say nothing of the millions more spent on equipment. Yet even that would not be sufficient to restore what the company had lost during the war.[237]

In the postwar world, the Pennsylvania Railroad and the other carriers were also buffeted by an attitudinal shift regarding the role of the railroads in the national economy. During much of the nineteenth century and well into the twentieth, railroads had been the defining feature of life in the United States. Operating employees were at the apex of the working class, while young boys dreamed of becoming the enginemen who guided massive steam locomotives across the country. The small-town depot and the urban railroad terminus were at the center, both literally and figuratively, of every community. Merchants, manufacturers, miners, farmers, and travelers would have accomplished little without a rail network that was indispensable to mobility. By 1945, however, the railroads had lost their novelty. Everyone was familiar with automobiles, aviation, and even the promise of space flight, and children imagined careers as pilots rather than railroaders. The generation that had come of age during a war that had introduced penicillin, radar, sonar, jet engines, and atomic energy now considered the railroads to be anachronistic. They flocked to high-paying new jobs in booming modern industries, further depriving the railroad companies of managerial talent. Many of those industries were located in the South and the West, far from PRR rails, and their activities were unrelated to the coal, iron ore, and steel that formed the traditional backbone of the Pennsylvania Railroad's freight traffic. Postwar industries also attracted the attention and capital of investors who looked with dismay at the low returns generated by railroads, particularly those in the Northeast.

Even though the national economy depended on the performance of the Pennsylvania Railroad and other carriers, the corresponding political and regulatory system did not reward that effort. The railroad rate structure, indispensable to efficient operations, modernized facilities, and adequate returns on investment, thus became a casualty of war. Franklin Delano Roosevelt and his advisors, mindful of the inflationary spiral that had taken place during World War I, were remarkably effective at holding the line on price increases. Inflation was modest in 1914 (1.3%) and 1915 (0.9%) before increasing to 7.7 percent in 1916. The following year, with the American declaration of war on the Central Powers, prices rose 17.8 percent and then a further 17.3 percent in 1918. Inflation abated only slightly following the armistice. Consumer prices increased 15.2 percent in 1919 and 15.6 percent in 1920 before a postwar recession caused a 10.9 percent decline in 1921. During World War II, however, the United States experienced only a single year of double-digit inflation—1942, when consumer prices rose 10.9 percent. In 1943, the year when Roosevelt issued the "hold the line" edict in Executive Order 9328, inflation fell to 6.0 percent, then to 1.6 percent in 1944 and 2.3 percent in 1945. Price levels for critical raw materials provided even stronger evidence of the success associated with efforts by Roosevelt and the Office of Price Administration to

control inflation. During World War I, the cost of copper increased 170.4 percent and tin 223.7 percent, while during World War II the figures were 14.3 percent and 6.6 percent, respectively. Steel prices rose 334.6 percent during the earlier conflict but did not change, even by a fraction of a percentage point, during the longer and more widespread military effort that took place between 1941 and 1945. Even dining car meals remained uniform throughout much of the war, on the Pennsylvania Railroad and across the country—eighty-five cents for breakfast, lunch for a dollar, and dinner for a dollar and a dime. Reconversion to a peacetime economy, coupled with pent-up consumer demand, caused prices to rise by 8.5 percent in 1946 and 14.4 percent in 1947—inflationary pressures more severe than anything the nation had experienced during the war. The increases came at a particularly unfortunate time for the Pennsylvania Railroad, as executives authorized the purchase of the materials necessary to rebuild the physical plant and replace equipment worn out by heavy wartime service. They also struggled to reduce the number of employees at a time when union leaders demanded compensatory adjustments in the cost of living.[238]

Despite Roosevelt's efforts to hold the line on inflation, railroad workers made significant gains in pay and benefits during the war. Thanks to the wage increases of September 1 and December 1, 1941, the labor costs of the nation's railroads increased by $389 million. Total payroll increased another $375 million by the end of September 1943. The PRR was not immune from that trend, as employee compensation increased from $226 million in 1940 to $289 million in 1941, $367 million in 1942, $437 million in 1943, and $474 million in 1944. Much of that growth was attributable to a larger labor force, which grew from 115,491 in 1940 to its wartime peak—and highest level since 1929—of 171,928 in 1944. Yet the arithmetic indicated that average annual compensation was increasing as well, from $1,959.57 in 1940 to $2,758.91 in 1944. During a period when the cost of living rose by 25.6 percent, employees enjoyed, on average, a wage increase of nearly 40.8 percent. Nor did the end of the war provide relief for the corporate treasury. Total employment declined to 168,958 in 1945, 158,687 in 1946, and 156,182 in 1947, but wages did not follow that trend. There was a slight decrease to $469 million in 1944 but then a rise to $503 million in 1946 and nearly $518 million the following year. In 1947, therefore, an average PRR employee took home $3,316.37 in pay, representing a 69.2 percent wage increase, compared to 1940.[239]

The railroads were squeezed from both sides, as there was no mechanism to offset the effects of the parsimonious rate increases that characterized the war years. Compared to the situation that accompanied World War I, railroad executives enjoyed little success in their long campaign for more remunerative tariffs. Beginning with the *Five Percent* case in 1914 and 1915 and continuing through the ICC's 40 percent rate increase in 1920, freight charges had risen 86 percent. In that context, and despite managerial complaints regarding United States Railroad Administration oversight, the carriers enjoyed significant benefits from federal control. That agency's officials, backed by the Wilson administration, had at least demanded that the ICC provide the financial resources necessary to prevent a politically embarrassing shutdown of the national transportation network.[240]

During World War II and after the return of peace, railroad executives struggled to win regulatory approval for rate increases that would match their spiraling costs. In February 1942, the Interstate Commerce Commission awarded the railroads a 9 percent increase in passenger fares. A month later, the ICC's Ex Parte 148 ruling granted a 4.7 percent rate increase, to remain in place for the duration of the war and six months thereafter. In December, however, economic stabilization director Fred Vinson petitioned the ICC to suspend the new tariff schedule, on the grounds that it contributed to inflation. The commissioners agreed to hold the higher rates in abeyance, beginning on May 15, 1943, and continuing through the end of the year—a decision that cost the PRR $30 million in lost revenue.[241] Railroad executives accepted the suspension as well as further ICC rulings that delayed the rate increase, initially until July 1, 1944, and then until January 1, 1945. In September 1944, however, representatives from several state regulatory commissions asked the ICC to rescind rather than suspend the March 1942 rate adjustments. That move prompted railroad officials to ask the ICC to restore the increases that the agency had granted more than thirty months earlier. They won only a partial victory. While federal regulators declined to withdraw the higher rates that they had provisionally granted, they held the higher tariffs in abeyance until six months after the war's end. Predictably, beginning in June 1943, the railroads' net earnings began trending downward, reversing the steady increase that had been taking place since October 1938. During 1943, the nation's carriers generated a net operating income of $1.380 billion, significantly below the 1942 figure of $1.485 billion. The PRR nonetheless managed to generate $979,733,155 in operating revenue during 1943, more than any other company in the history of American railroading.[242]

By April 1946, the war was over, but the carriers required substantial funds to rebuild the physical plant and purchase new equipment. Accordingly, executives petitioned the ICC for a 19.6 percent increase in freight rates. They also requested a continuation of the February 1942 rise in passenger fares rather than allowing their expiration six months after the end of the war. In June, the agency granted a preliminary 6 percent increase in freight rates in Ex Parte 166. With labor and material costs continuing to rise, the carriers amended their petition several times in 1946, requesting an increase of 25 percent (in July 1947), then 27 percent (in September) and 41 percent (in December). The final decision in Ex Parte 166, issued in July 1948, was at best only a partial victory for the railroads. They received a 27 percent gain, but that was not enough to offset their rising costs.[243]

Between 1940 and early 1947, the ICC had authorized a 10 percent increase in passenger fares and a 17.3 percent increase in freight rates. During the same period, hourly wages grew by 50 percent, while the cost of fuel and supplies rose by a similar amount. The PRR's costs increased by $267.6 million, yet the ICC-sanctioned rate adjustments provided the company with just $112.8 million in additional revenue. Even with the inclusion of Ex Parte 166, in 1948, rates rose by just 47 percent after 1940. President Clement, in one of his many appearances before the ICC, vented his frustration at the extent to which his company had been afflicted by the twin burdens of wartime transportation and Roosevelt's hold-the-line policies regarding inflation. "If, on the Pennsylvania Railroad, the general price of transportation had been allowed to follow up the general advance in the price level of the country," he noted, "in the 7 years 1941 to 1947 inclusive, it would have produced something over $500 more millions in profits."[244]

Higher rates did not guarantee increased revenues or profits, however. The erosion of freight and passenger traffic to the highways, underway since the early 1920s, accelerated during the years immediately following World War II. In that context, it was not clear whether the obstinance or the acquiescence of ICC commissioners portended the greatest harm for the Pennsylvania Railroad. On September 24, 1948, reporters at the *New York Times* took note of the multiple demands by railroad executives for higher rates under Ex Parte 166—the sixth such request since the end of the war. "In seeking a further increase of 8 percent in freight rates," they warned, "the nation's railroads may be playing into the hands of their competitors, in the opinion of many authorities on transportation . . . freight rates now are so high that some traffic has been diverted to trucks and waterways and the desired rise, it is argued, probably would accelerate the trend." The editors of the trade journal *Railway Age* warned executives that the "traffic diversion [was] cause for alarm" and suggested that the "Ex Parte 166 rate increases" were among the factors that were "combining to produce a substantial diversion of railroad freight traffic to highways and waterways."[245]

The nation's railroads did not reap the rewards associated with their extraordinary wartime performance, and the financial community took notice of the imbalance between revenues and expenditures. In 1943, the carriers collected a record $9.075 billion in revenues, well above the $6.280 billion generated in 1929. Expenses rose as well, and the $1.380 billion in 1943 net operating income was barely above the $1.252 billion in 1929. The nation's railroads collectively paid $215 million in dividends from their 1943 earnings, compared to the $490 million they had distributed in 1929. Investors who had endured more than a decade of low profitability during the Depression eagerly anticipated a wartime and postwar bounty. They were sadly disappointed, and they increasingly looked to industries—many of them the beneficiaries of lucrative defense contracts—that would generate a higher rate of return. For a time, the PRR's size, its consistent record of profitability, and its uninterrupted record of dividend payments insulated the company from criticism. The railroad paid respectable dividends during the war years—4 percent in 1941, and 5 percent in each of the following four years. That was certainly a better performance than in the worst of the Depression, with stockholders chafing at several years of 1 percent dividends. Share prices were nonetheless disappointing, suggesting that investors were seeking better opportunities elsewhere. From a 1941 low of $17\frac{3}{8}$, they peaked at $47\frac{1}{2}$ in early 1946 before the curtailment of government spending triggered a recession that drove prices down to 25, precisely half of par.[246]

Centennial in Crisis

Then came the centennial. One hundred years earlier, on April 13, 1846, Pennsylvania governor Francis Rawn Shunk had signed the charter that incorporated the Pennsylvania Railroad. The upstart rival to the Baltimore & Ohio and also-ran to the coal-rich Reading had since become the nation's most important railroad and the world's largest business corporation. With the war over and the Great Depression a distant memory, there seemed every reason to celebrate. Befitting such a historic event, congratulations and good wishes poured in from across the territory served by the Pennsylvania Railroad. The commissioners of Delaware County, Pennsylvania, unanimously approved a resolution praising "the great primary artery of commerce [that] serves our important industries on the

Delaware River from Darby through Eddystone, Chester and Marcus Hook" and expressing confidence that "the spirit of cooperation now existing between the Pennsylvania Railroad and Delaware County will continue on the same high plane which prevailed during the past century." Managers at Wanamaker's, the company that opened its first store in a repurposed PRR freight station, did not see fit to purchase a newspaper advertisement honoring the Pennsylvania Railroad. Strawbridge & Clothier, another iconic Philadelphia department store, hailed "the great Pennsylvania Railroad, one of the oldest in the country." Not to be outdone, their New York rival acknowledged that, when the PRR's first board meeting was taking place, "Gimbels was a little country store." Central-Penn National Bank, which for eight decades had maintained a business relationship with the PRR, honored "The Pennsylvania Railroad Company for what it has accomplished" and noted that its actions had "made possible the industrial supremacy of the great Commonwealth of Pennsylvania." The Atlantic Refining Company was ready to "congratulate the Pennsylvania Railroad Company on the vital contributions it has made to the growth and prosperity of the city, state and nation." Representatives of the Tradesmens National Bank & Trust Company, a firm only a year younger than the railroad, offered their "Heartiest Birthday Greetings" and indicated their "admiration for the prudent course of management that has distinguished its service to the nation."[247]

Newspaper articles were less overtly effusive in their praise and, more ominously, they generally focused more on the great accomplishments of the past than on the promised achievements of the future. Page 16 of the *New York Times* featured a dry, half-column recitation of key developments in the PRR's history, while the hometown *Philadelphia Inquirer* did not provide any coverage at all. The Lancaster *Sunday News* ended its story with a tally of the number of trains that ran over the PRR's tracks, without predicting what would happen next, while the *Brooklyn Daily Eagle* went no further than the electrification project that had concluded nearly a decade earlier. The *Cincinnati Enquirer* quoted President Clement's admission that "the airlines will stimulate us to do a better job, which means we've got to give passengers better food, better drinks, better accommodations and comforts than they can get elsewhere." A lengthy article, spread across two pages of the *Marion Star*, devoted only a single paragraph to "the orders to be placed for hundreds of new cars." The *Central New Jersey Home News* reminded readers that the PRR "enjoys a justly deserved reputation for stability, having returned over a billion and a quarter dollars in dividends to its owners over the years and having permitted no year since 1845 to pass without a cash return to its stockholders. . . . New Brunswick felicitates the Pennsylvania Railroad upon the completion of its first hundred years and hopes the new century which is beginning will be full of profit and progress and public service." The *Altoona Tribune*, based in a community that, more than any other, depended on the Pennsylvania Railroad, could do no better than suggest that the company "has imbedded itself after an era of pioneering, empire building, trade wars and rights-of-way competition. It has survived depressions, floods and competition."[248]

The efforts of Pennsylvania Railroad executives to celebrate their company's centennial likewise reflected a mix of nostalgia for the past and hesitancy about the future. In November 1945, Edward C. Gegenheimer, the assistant to the general manager of the Eastern Region, prepared an ambitious list of commemorative activities. As a member of the Committee on Centenary Observance, Gegenheimer recommended an expenditure of $1,713,000—equivalent to the cost of ten new steam locomotives.[249] The most expensive component, at $1,225,000, involved a greatly expanded advertising campaign in *Life*, *Time*, *Newsweek*, and the *Saturday Evening Post*, among other publications. Other planned initiatives included a series of commemorative dinners (including special meals to be served aboard *The Broadway Limited*, The "*Spirit of St. Louis*," and other premier trains); special stationery, public timetables, and dining car menus; and anniversary postcards. Gegenheimer also recommended the development of a "Railroad Educational Feature Film for exhibition in theaters, schools, clubs, chambers of commerce, etc.," with estimated production and distribution costs of $110,000. Another $45,000 would be allocated to a "Pictorial history for children and young people of the P.R.R. for wide distribution." Like his predecessor J. Elfreth Watkins, who scoured the system for historical artifacts and curiosities that could be displayed at the 1893 World's Columbian Exposition, Gegenheimer recommended the "regions to be canvassed for museum items to be displayed in conjunction with motive power exhibits and later to become part of permanent collection." Considering that those relics had little more than scrap value, the estimated $2,000 expense was eminently reasonable. The more ambitious project involved dispatching a representative sample of equipment to thirty-eight cities along the Pennsylvania Railroad. The public would thus have the opportunity to see a replica of the PRR's oldest steam locomotive (the *John Bull*) and the most unusual (the *Reuben Wells*, once assigned to the

Madison incline) alongside the most modern steam locomotives and passenger cars.[250]

Only a portion of Gegenheimer's ambitious agenda came to fruition. The scope of the advertising was much reduced, and the most elaborate commemoration came in the form of a preface to the PRR's 1945 annual report, published early in 1946. Extolling "one hundred years of transportation progress," the twenty-page color supplement traced the railroad's corporate history, interspersed with patriotic advertisements that emphasized the company's contributions to the war effort. The text also reinforced the PRR's dependence on the traditional staples of American industry, including an observation that 58 percent of freight tonnage involved the products of mines, with coal constituting more than 70 percent of that traffic.[251]

The exhibition of historical and modern locomotives and rolling stock did not take place. As late as March 1946, executives were still committed to the project, but the assistant chief of motive power observed "that this cannot be done for the expenditure of $75,000, named by the Committee."[252] Walter Franklin, the vice president in charge of traffic, cautioned that the new streamlined passenger equipment, the proposed counterpart to antiques from a prior century, would not be delivered until late 1946, after the traveling display had ended. Moreover, Franklin noted, "I doubt if it would be desirable to use this equipment for that purpose when it is delivered" rather than put it to work transporting paying customers. In the end, the delayed delivery schedule, the logistics associated with moving so much equipment around the system, and—above all—the substantial cost doomed the proposal.[253]

The "Educational Feature Film" materialized into *Clear Track Ahead!*, a twenty-seven-minute offering that the PRR released in the summer of 1946. Subtitled "A Film Story of Progress in Railroad Transportation," the narrator emphasized that "the progress of America and the progress of its railroads became one and the same thing." In the present and into the future, he asserted, "mass transportation is therefore the keystone on which the progress of America depends. In the vanguard of that progress are the railroads." Despite confident pronouncements about the future ("new cars and new trains"), the film was very much rooted in the past. The title, meant to suggest that all the company's problems were behind it, instead unintentionally foreshadowed a four-track main line that was increasingly bereft of freight and passenger traffic. The steam locomotives that played a prominent role as characters in the drama were on the verge of extinction, and the assertion that "steel is the basis of American industry" would soon ring hollow. A pioneer, bound for the West by covered wagon, delivered the most poignant line. "Dog-gone railroads, what good are they?" suggested a stubborn attachment to a preindustrial past. Yet, in 1946, it was a question asked by an increasing number of Americans who envisioned a very different future.[254]

The literary commemoration of the railroad's centennial was somewhat more complex. In January 1945, the company commissioned the engineering consulting firm Coverdale & Colpitts to prepare a four-volume work entitled *The Pennsylvania Railroad Company: The Corporate, Financial and Construction History of Lines Owned, Operated and Controlled to December 31, 1945*. Volume one covered the original corporate entity of the PRR, the second and third volumes described the development of the Lines East and the Lines West of Pittsburgh and Erie, and the final volume included affiliated and miscellaneous companies. The books featured a brief "historical sketch" of many of the hundreds of PRR subsidiaries, along with a "chronological statement" of construction milestones and extensive information on the organization, leases, mergers, and other consolidations. While providing a wealth of information for corporate attorneys and future generations of historians, *The Corporate, Financial and Construction History* was essentially unreadable. Intended for the use of a small number of senior executives, it was never meant for distribution to the news media or the general public.[255]

Based on the Coverdale & Colpitts data, however, George H. Burgess and Miles C. Kennedy prepared the 835-page *Centennial History of the Pennsylvania Railroad Company*. Published in 1949, well after the hundredth-anniversary celebrations had faded, the book was unabashedly prorailroad and promanagement. Burgess was intimately familiar with transportation matters, having begun his career in 1908 as the chief engineer of the Delaware & Hudson Company. He later served as the chairman of that firm's valuation committee, responding to the congressional mandates embodied in the Valuation Act of 1913. He joined Coverdale & Colpitts in 1925. Kennedy, many years his junior, had once been a member of the engineering corps on Lines West. He eventually attained a partnership in Coverdale & Colpitts and, as late as 1965, was undertaking studies of coal transportation in India. Burgess and Kennedy adopted an executive-driven organizational structure for the *Centennial History*, with chapters covering each presidential administration. Unsurprisingly, J. Edgar Thomson received the most coverage, totaling 280 pages. The authors betrayed their reliance on the four-volume

Corporate, Financial and Construction History, and their work contained many references to stock and bond issues, leases, mergers, and other financial transactions. They acknowledged the controversial events of the past—including the 1877 Pittsburgh riots—but the emphasis was clearly on the successes of the corporation and its managers. The contentious Shopmen's Strike of 1922 merited only two pages, mostly devoted to the PRR's compliance with the policies promulgated by the Railroad Labor Board. The one-page conclusion ("A Glance Toward the Future") echoed the long-standing claim "that the railroads were an essential factor in the economic life of the United States." In the final paragraph, Burgess and Kennedy noted that "the history of the company from its earliest day is notable for the absence of any trace of defeatism. If any prediction may safely be made, it is one soundly based on Pennsylvania tradition, to the effect that its management will face its problems, whatever they are, with unflinching courage and fortitude."[256]

In the postwar world, Martin Clement and the PRR's other executives would need all the unflinching courage and fortitude they could muster. In 1946, and for the first time in its history, the PRR lost money on its railroad operations. The deficit in January was $3.3 million, nearly doubling to $6.5 million the following month. During the first six months of the year, the company operated at a $31 million loss, and executives used accumulated cash reserves to meet the payroll and purchase equipment and supplies. The total deficit for the year was $27.6 million, fortunately offset by $19 million in federal tax credits and by dividends received from the Norfolk & Western and other investments. The overall situation was nonetheless catastrophic, with financial analysts focusing their attention on the year's net operating loss of $8.5 million. Given that the PRR had generated a net operating income of $49 million in 1945, the steep decline came as a shock to executives and investors alike.[257]

The causes of the financial disaster were easy to identify, if difficult to correct. Severe winter weather, early in the year, compounded the congestion that accompanied the return of troops and equipment from overseas. The western railroads whose finances compared so favorably with those of the Pennsylvania Railroad were desperately short of cars that could carry grain and perishables. Accordingly, in February, ICC officials ordered the PRR to send four thousand freight cars—a group that may well have included Class X31 #59944—to the West. The directive cost the railroad $2 million in lost revenue and burdened it with the $500,000 expense associated with transferring the equipment to the western lines. A succession of strikes in the coal, steel, automobile, and electrical industries deprived the PRR of badly needed traffic and revenues. Wages and other operating costs increased 50 percent, compared to the prewar period, and the ICC had not granted corresponding rate increases. Despite the steady loss of less-than-carload-lot shipments to the motor carriers, the company still maintained extensive facilities for LCL freight. As a result, the PRR lost $30 million on that category of business in 1946, exclusive of property taxes, rentals, and other fixed charges. That equated to an operating ratio of 153 percent, indicating that the company spent $1.53 to generate a dollar in LCL revenue. Perishable traffic was almost as unprofitable, with a 1946 operating ratio of 124 percent. The operating ratio for passenger traffic was 96 percent, which superficially suggested that it remained a profitable segment of the PRR's business. The inclusion of fixed charges, including those associated with expensive urban passenger terminals, nonetheless ensured that the company lost money on every commuter and intercity traveler. The PRR's overall operating ratio was 90.7 percent, the highest in the company's history and significantly worse than the 1945 figure of 83.7 percent. Even the lesser figure was well above the 70 percent operating ratio that most industry experts considered adequate, if the company was going to pay taxes, cover fixed charges on its debts, and have something left over for reinvestment and the payment of dividends.[258]

The most significant problem, however, was that the company had not reduced its workforce at the same rate that its revenues declined. The average level of employment, which was 131,000 in 1941, rose to 151,000 in 1946, even though the company generated approximately the same number of revenue ton miles.[259] High personnel levels at freight and passenger terminals were especially noticeable and were a sign of the railroad's labor-intensive LCL and passenger traffic. The number of yard employees also grew significantly, a situation that attested to traffic congestion and to the inefficiency of yard operations. The difference in employment levels equated to an additional $78 million in annual expenditures, an amount that was clearly unsustainable.[260]

Given the PRR's financial situation, prudence dictated that the company should not pay dividends in 1946. As Clement observed, in May, "after we have provided for the deficits of this year and for commitments already made, we will have to start planning on how to meet the requirements of '48 and '49 as there won't be sufficient cash to hand to meet them." Public relations and sound stewardship of the company's resources were two different

matters, however. As early as February 1946, before the full extent of the financial calamity had become apparent, Thomas J. Ross urged executives to authorize a "Centennial dividend." The individual who oversaw the consulting firm of Ivy Lee & T. J. Ross suggested that the payout "would probably result in a good deal of favorable publicity. It would afford an opportunity to emphasize again the railroad's remarkable dividend record over the years. It would no doubt be regarded as an appropriate thing to do. Completion of a century of successful operation is still very unusual and a dividend in connection with that achievement would be altogether natural." The directors concurred, and on June 26, they authorized a 1 percent dividend, payable on July 30. They acknowledged that "it has been necessary to draw in earnings of prior years to pay increased wages and increased prices for materials and supplies, and therefore its management believes that the stockholders should receive consideration through a distribution from this same source." Whatever the merits associated with that justification, the directors had little choice in the matter. In 1948 and 1949, the company would face $110 million in maturing securities. The rebuilding of the physical plant and the acquisition of new locomotives and cars would eventually consume more than $1 billion. If the directors allowed the annual dividend to expire on their watch, investors would shy away from the company, and the burden associated with financing the Pennsylvania Railroad would become even more difficult.[261]

While shareholders no doubt appreciated the modest 1946 dividend, the disbursement did little to placate members of the investment-banking community. An earlier generation of investment bankers, such as Otto Kahn at Kuhn, Loeb & Company, had established a warm and symbiotic relationship with Pennsylvania Railroad executives. The declining earnings of the railroads, the financial crisis of the Great Depression, and the intense regulatory scrutiny of the New Deal had eroded that partnership. The announcement of the PRR's 1946 operating results transformed the cooperation between railroaders and investment bankers into a far more adversarial relationship. Analysts in the Bond Department of Merrill Lynch, Pierce, Fenner & Beane were the first to sound the alarm. On February 6, 1947, they issued a report that was sharply critical of the PRR's performance. "As a result of competition from other transportation agencies, decentralization of industry and shifts of population," they warned, "there has been a general decline in the per cent of Pennsylvania system's revenues related to revenues of all Class I railroads. That this trend will be reversed in the foreseeable future is not indicated." The report suggested that the company's dependence on coal traffic was a "disturbing factor," as was the high ratio of passenger revenues to total earnings. The more serious problem, analysts noted, was that the "Pennsylvania Railroad compares unfavorably with certain other railroads in many of the operating efficiency factors." Between 1940 and 1945, the other companies that served as a basis of comparison reduced their transportation expenses, per ton mile and as a percentage of total revenues. The PRR was the exception, as both of those figures increased, while the number of gross ton miles per freight-train hour declined. The root cause was readily identifiable. "The higher than average ratio of wages," the analysts emphasized, "undoubtedly contributes to the apparently less efficient movement of traffic by Pennsylvania R.R., in comparison with other railroads."[262]

The Merrill Lynch report initiated an increasingly acrimonious exchange between Pennsylvania Railroad executives and representatives from the investment-banking community. Fairman R. Dick, an expert in railroad finance and a partner in Dick & Merle-Smith, warned Clement that "some of my rich banker friends in New York do not seem to think your railroad is doing very well." He reassured the PRR's president that "I do not quite agree with this myself" and highlighted a significant flaw in the Merrill Lynch analysis. The three comparator roads—the Great Northern, the Union Pacific, and the Santa Fe—were western transcontinentals, companies with long line hauls, low terminal costs, and relatively little passenger service. They also benefited from the war in the Pacific Theater, to a far greater extent than the PRR. Dick nonetheless asked Clement for an explanation of the company's difficulties, information that he could then use to reassure his anxious clients. "What we are trying to point out," Dick emphasized, "is that as yet there does not seem to be any real evidence that the relative credit position of the Pennsylvania cannot be maintained, given sound regulation and efficient management."[263]

Very soon, however, Dick and his fellow investment bankers concluded that both sound regulation and efficient management were in short supply. The ICC continued to forestall rate increases that would match escalating costs, and Clement and his subordinates struggled to articulate a response to growing criticism of their handling of the company. "The year 1946 should have been one of your company's most satisfactory years," he informed shareholders. "The reason your company did not have a satisfactory profit for the year was due to the lag between advancing costs and the rate increases allowed by regulatory authorities." Clement conceded that "it will take several years to get the rate structure up to where it should

be. In the meantime, there will be some deferred maintenance and curtailment of service, particularly passenger." He suggested that the transportation of passengers, perishables, and less-than-carload freight "are either going to be more profitable or they will gradually disappear so that the business which is left will be the profitable business." At no point, however, did he address the central issue—the necessity of ensuring that reductions in labor and other costs would make the company operate more efficiently. The best that Clement could do was to offer an optimistic prediction. "As I see the East developing the combination of a magnificent highway system and rail transport," he asserted, "plus the ever increasing population and the settling of business in this area, rail transportation will be a permanent factor in the economic situation." Given the decline of traditional industries, the growth of the interstate highway system, and the emerging demographic shift to the Sunbelt, his optimism was woefully misguided. Investment analyst M. P. Barrett said as much when he predicted that "if deindustrialization of industry becomes pronounced, the area served by the PRR will be one of the ones hardest hit."[264]

Fairman Dick was initially supportive of PRR management, but his tone changed after he received the PRR's dismal earning results for January 1947. "Those for your road were not encouraging," he told Clement, emphasizing that "the Pennsylvania makes a very poor showing in comparison with the other three Trunk Line roads." Significantly, he compared the PRR with the New York Central, the Baltimore & Ohio, and the Erie rather than the western lines. Dick emphasized that, between January 1940 and January 1947, the PRR's transportation ratio (transportation expenses as a percentage of revenues) had risen at a significantly faster rate than had been the case with the other three companies. Statistics also indicated that, among sixteen comparator railroads from all sections of the country, the PRR experienced the largest post-1940 increase in the operating ratio (operating expenses as a percentage of revenues). Those results inevitably affected the company's bottom line. In 1939, the Pennsylvania Railroad's gross revenues represented 10.8 percent of the national total, while its share of net operating income was 13.1 percent. By 1947, the PRR generated 10.4 percent of the nation's gross rail revenues but a mere 4.1 percent of net operating income. Confronted with such dismal results, Dick informed Clement of his "hope that you can give me some explanation of an encouraging nature," but it was clear that his patience was wearing thin.[265]

Other investment analysts were becoming increasingly critical of the Pennsylvania Railroad's performance and the company's management. They paid scant attention to Clement's excuses regarding the unwillingness of regulatory authorities to grant higher rates. A May 1947 report from Argus Research Corporation emphasized the PRR's "huge personnel" and its "heavy stake . . . in a normally unprofitable passenger business" and asserted that "the railroad has not taken drastic steps to curtail these commitments." While they acknowledged the largely unavoidable problems associated with the ICC's rate-making policies, industrial strikes, and the conversion to a peacetime economy, analysts emphasized "that the contraction in the gross profit margin comes not from traffic but rather from exorbitant costs. . . . Since the problem lies in operating expenses," they concluded, "the management sooner or later must take aggressive steps to bring a greater measure of control over its outgo." Should Clement and his subordinates prove successful in reducing costs, representatives from Argus predicted, the company could transform the $8.5 million deficit of 1946 to a positive operating income of $20 million in 1947.[266]

Despite Clement's efforts to blame everything on the Interstate Commerce Commission, his subordinates acknowledged the company's internal problems. George H. Pabst Jr., the vice president in charge of finance and corporate relations, did little more than correct a few of the statistics in the reports that the investment analysts had presented. "Generally, we think that the [Argus] Report is a pretty fair presentation of our situation," he conceded. Walter Franklin, the vice president in charge of traffic, admitted "that everything in the report has been fairly presented."[267] Franklin nonetheless informed Clement that investors were not the only ones who were dissatisfied with the president's leadership. "I think I see signs of information that could not have been obtained except through conferences with some of our officials," Franklin concluded. Even though he added a disclaimer ("I am not in any way intimating that something was said that should not have been said"), it was clear that someone, highly placed in the PRR's executive ranks, was working surreptitiously to undermine the existing power structure.[268]

The most detailed condemnation of the PRR's management came from R. W. Pressprich & Company in September 1947. Prepared by Isabel H. Benham, a veteran of the prewar Reconstruction Finance Corporation and one of the few women to work in the field of railroad finance, it provided a wealth of information regarding the railroad's difficulties.[269] "It is readily apparent," Benham concluded, "that the problems of the Pennsylvania Railroad are not due to a declining traffic level, but to progressively higher operating costs." She acknowledged the deleterious effects of passenger service but was not willing to accept that as an excuse. To the contrary, the revenue derived from unprecedented passenger volumes made the company look healthier than was the case. "In the period 1940–1945," she emphasized, "the expanding volume of passenger business and the increasing profit of this division obscured the declining efficiency and consequently the declining earnings of the freight division."[270]

The Pressprich analysis provided compelling evidence that the Pennsylvania Railroad no longer deserved its reputation for sound management and efficient operating methods. "If the 1946 performance had only equaled that of the industry as a whole," Benham concluded, "the operating expenses of the road would have been $60,122,000 less than reported, and the 1946 deficit of $8,500,000 would have been a handsome profit." She noted that costs associated with station employees rose 222 percent between 1940 and 1946, while claims for lost and damaged merchandise increased by 236 percent—figures that suggested both the unprofitability of LCL traffic and the failure of the container systems developed during the 1920s to rectify the situation. During the same 1940–1946 period, the number of people involved in the movement of trains increased by 50 percent. Coupled with periodic increases in employee compensation, the company's payroll rose by 128 percent, equivalent to $87 million. Despite the additional personnel, average freight-train speeds decreased from 14.7 to 13.8 miles per hour. That reduction ensured that more track, more yard facilities, and more cars and locomotives would be required to move the same amount of freight.[271]

The motive-power situation was particularly critical, Benham emphasized. "With the sharp increase in traffic since 1940, and the inability to acquire a large number of new and modern motive power units, Pennsylvania was forced to return to service nearly all of its old steam locomotives. It was the increasing use of these old steam locomotives which has contributed so much to higher operating costs." The PRR's difficulties were numerous, and they had one factor in common. For a decade, whether through complacency or as a result of inadequate revenues and unfavorable financial markets, executives had not invested the funds necessary to modernize their company and ensure efficient operations. "We believe that it is not lack of maintenance work, but failure to make capital expenditures for additions and betterments which has caused a decline in Pennsylvania's efficiency," Benham concluded. "No substantial capital investments have been added to the road accounts in any year since 1937."[272]

Investors and PRR officials were in general agreement on the causes of the PRR's difficulties, but reforms would be extraordinarily difficult. "Generally, the report does not touch upon anything not known to Management," one senior executive observed in October 1947, "and practically everything they bring out has been or is being actively handled." Despite the confident assertion, the company continued to struggle, incurring a loss of $4.7 million during the first eight months of 1947. The situation improved, and the company finished the year with a net income of $7.3 million. The amount was nonetheless well below the $20 million estimate that Argus Research had provided in May 1947. The favorable showing, moreover, depended on the dividends paid on the PRR's holdings in the Norfolk & Western and other affiliated lines. "Otherwise," Clement conceded, "this Company would have had a Net Deficit for the second year in succession and during a period of relatively high traffic volume."[273]

It was hardly surprising, therefore, that Smith, Barney & Company warned its clients "that money invested in Pennsylvania Railroad stock could be used to greater advantage in other issues." Roger Babson, the idiosyncratic investment advisor and financial prognosticator, who allegedly predicted the 1929 collapse of the stock market, admitted that he was insufficiently cautious regarding the brief postwar upsurge in railroad equities. "We did avoid recommending railroad common stock purchases," Babson conceded, "but unfortunately did not go so far as to include the highly regarded Pennsylvania among the many Red-Border Reports issued near the peak of the boom." The warning was well placed, for by December 1947, PRR stock was selling at $18.00 per share, little more than a third of par and 29½ points below its peak in 1946 and 1947. Bonds suffered similarly adverse effects, at a time when PRR executives were in desperate need of capital to retire older securities issues and finance betterments to the physical plant and equipment. Investment analyst M. P. Barrett noted that "top management has stated publicly that the road is run for the benefit of the shareholders and that dividends will be maintained at all cost. This attitude indicates declining security for bonds." Even if red ink no longer flowed from the pages of the Pennsylvania Railroad's annual report, red-border status and its equivalent from other investment analysts ensured that the company would find it difficult to secure the funds that were vital to greater efficiency and long-term survival.[274]

Pennsylvania Railroad executives acknowledged that massive investments would be necessary to ensure that the company remained competitive in the postwar world. Clement asserted that a more favorable rate structure, between 1941 and 1947, would have generated $500 million in additional revenue, most of which would have

gone toward badly needed improvements. Yet, the PRR's president informed regulators, "it is going to take a sum considerably greater than that to complete the evolution of the Pennsylvania Railroad from the economy of World War II to whatever economy is to come." He then provided a list of all the work that needed to be done. "With sufficient earnings to add to the cash resources of this Company," Clement informed the ICC, "we should spend at least $180,000,000 a year over the next five years." The expenditures would include $200 million to repair the wartime damage to the physical plant, $240 million for additional track and yard capacity, $30 million for signals and communication equipment, $250 million for new cars and locomotives, and a further $180 million to repair and modernize the existing fleet. "As pressing as these requirements are," Clement concluded, "we must first meet maturities amounting to $100,000,000 now before us."[275]

The problem was that no one could be certain where the money would come from. Clement observed that the Pennsylvania Railroad had spent $1 billion to rehabilitate its operations following World War I. In doing so, the company had increased its debt by $350 million between 1916 and 1929. During the years that followed, executives made steady progress in lowering the company's debt, beginning with a reduction of $8.5 million in 1938. The economic recovery and increased earnings caused further retirements, peaking at $32.9 million in 1944.[276] By the end of 1946, the PRR's debt was $892 million, well below the $1.02 billion in 1939. Clement had no desire to see the company's debt return to its former level, but that outcome seemed all but inevitable. "We should not again be forced to mortgage the future," he insisted, "because of insufficient earnings from an inadequate rate structure." His contention was that mortgaging the future was not merely unfair—it was also impossible. Investment analysts were already warning their clients to be wary of existing PRR securities, and they were hardly likely to look favorably on the issuance of new ones. Higher rates would not provide a solution, either. Even if the ICC granted the seemingly unending petitions and emendations prepared by executives, the availability of highway transportation ensured that the railroads would eventually price themselves out of the market for transportation services.[277]

Because the PRR was a common carrier, required by law to serve the public's need for mobility, Clement and others might have reasonably assumed that their company would be eligible for public subsidies that would bridge the gap between revenues and expenses. That was hardly likely, however, as the end of World War II generated a new set of adversaries and initiated a conflict that was far less destructive but also much longer lasting. The Cold War reawakened the fears of Bolshevism that W. W. Atterbury had used so effectively to attack unions and government regulation during the years that followed World War I. In that context, government subsidies represented a threat to the capitalist system and suggested that the United States was succumbing to socialism and the Soviet influence. Railroad executives lacked any rhetorical weapons in that battle, as they were ensnared in their own public-relations initiatives. For decades, they had argued that railroads were unique among all other forms of transportation because they represented pure free-market capitalism, unadulterated by government intervention, support, or control. "Our railroad systems under private ownership and management have followed a carefully charted course which thus far, in spite of inadequate earnings, has given this country in its growing needs the best and cheapest transportation system available anywhere in the world," asserted James H. Aydelott, a vice president in the operations and maintenance department of the Association of American Railroads. Subsidization was thus not merely politically intractable—it also refuted the basic tenets of American railroading.[278]

Under the circumstances, and as investment analysts had suggested, the survival of the Pennsylvania Railroad depended on the expertise of the company's managers, their willingness to adapt to new economic circumstances, and—above all—their ability to increase efficiency and reduce operating costs. Given the strength of organized labor, it would be difficult to undo wartime changes in wages, working conditions, and collective-bargaining practices, as Atterbury had done during the early 1920s. There was, as industry experts repeatedly observed, one area in which significant economies were possible. A new source of motive power, the diesel locomotive, offered lower operating costs, increased utilization, and the possibility of reducing the number of employees who worked in yards and shops, relative to steam power.

The seemingly straightforward matter of substituting one form of technology for another was anything but. Many Pennsylvania Railroad executives had spent decades progressing upward through the managerial ranks, based on their knowledge of the established way of doing things. They were determined to protect existing practices, particularly those involving motive power, and thus preserve their authority within the company. To them, the recommendations of financial analysts were misguided policies to be resisted rather than warnings to be heeded. They could point with pride to the stellar record of the Motive Power Department, an entity that had always been in the forefront of the development of steam locomotives. They could claim, with considerable justification, that such success would continue into the future. The war and immediate postwar era marked a period of relative quiescence in the long-standing adversarial relationship between management and labor. Harmony within the executive ranks would be more difficult to attain, however. The "evolution of the Pennsylvania Railroad from the economy of World War II to whatever economy is to come" would involve a struggle for power within the managerial ranks, the likes of which had not been seen since J. Edgar Thomson took control of the company in 1852.

Chapter 4

Power

Even by accounting for differences in taste and opinion, it would be impossible to choose with any degree of certainty the one time or place that would represent the railroads at their best. If limited to the United States, one might justifiably choose a Southern Pacific cab forward lifting a solid block of yellow and orange refrigerator cars over Donner Pass; a black, red, and orange Daylight sailing along the California coast; Santa Fe's "Madame Queen" assisting the warbonnet-liveried diesels powering the *Super Chief* over Cajon Pass; or a New York Central Hudson sprinting along its namesake river, propelling the *Twentieth Century Limited* toward Grand Central Terminal. As the 1940s ended, however, one of the greatest shows in railroading must surely have taken place along the Pennsylvania Railroad. Fortunate individuals could stand next to the electrified tracks that linked Washington and New York, alongside the Horseshoe Curve, or on the flatlands of Ohio and Indiana. There, they would witness an elegantly choreographed cacophony of the thousands of humming, burbling, steaming horsepower that marked the Pennsylvania Railroad at its most complex, coordinated, and best. The all-Pullman *Broadway Limited* and the other representatives of the Blue Ribbon Fleet trailed behind Art Deco streamlined, pinstriped GG1 electric locomotives, emerging from the depths of Manhattan Island, traveling south through New Jersey, transiting Philadelphia, and then heading toward Chicago. West of Harrisburg, electric power gave way to steam—a pair of K4s Pacifics, perhaps, or one of the railroad's newest locomotives, a T1 duplex. Like the GG1, the stylish and streamlined T1 was the embodiment of speed, power, and style, as it moved passenger trains across Ohio and Indiana at speeds of a hundred miles an hour.[1]

Along their way west toward Chicago, passengers could catch brief glimpses of the PRR's other motive power. It might be a brace of massive I1s Decapods—often nicknamed "Hippos" because of their wide boilers—dragging 125 cars of coal around Horseshoe Curve, with two more shoving from the rear. Also on view was the N1s and its close cousin the N2s, developed on Lines West during the closing days of World War I, and well suited for the heavy ore trains that plodded from ports on the Great Lakes to steel mills in the Monongahela Valley. Or it might have been a J1 Texas, built as an expedient in a more recent war and—as a copy of another railroad's design—unusually lacking the PRR's trademark Belpaire firebox. The Class M1 Mountain—perhaps the PRR's best all-around steam locomotive, and equally at home in fast freight and passenger service—could be seen everywhere across the system. Far less common was the Q2, designed as the modern freight counterpart to the streamlined T1. Toiling away in yards and on branch lines were hundreds of the H-Class Consolidations, the railroad's all-around workhorse for switching and light-duty freight and passenger operations.

Amid the hiss of steam and the pall of smoke produced by more than four thousand steam locomotives, a few interlopers might be visible, like tiny primitive mammals cautiously poking their heads from burrows nestled among the reptilian behemoths of the last years of the Cretaceous Period. Diesel locomotives were in widespread use on many railroads—including the Santa Fe, where they had long since taken charge of the *Super Chief*—but far less so

Until well after World War II, officials in the PRR's Motive Power Department insisted that they could develop efficient steam locomotives that would outperform diesels and placate online coal producers. Passengers demanded modern, cleaner power, forcing the railroad to purchase diesel passenger locomotives, such as the collection of General Motors, Electro-Motive Division E7 and E8 units on display at Harrisburg during the early 1950s. A nearly identical facility was located at Enola, on the opposite side of the Susquehanna River. *General Negative Collection, Railroad Museum of Pennsylvania, PHMC.*

on the PRR. Their absence attested to many factors, including the railroad's long tradition of designing and building its own motive power. Not all the steam locomotives on display along the lines of the Standard Railroad of the World had come from the Altoona Works, but since 1866, more than six thousand had done so, exerting a powerful influence on the decisions made by motive-power officials. Particularly during the years between 1875 and 1915, the Pennsylvania Railroad's engineering staff and its facilities at Altoona were the envy of railroad executives and representatives from locomotive builders throughout the world. The PRR served the bituminous mines of Pennsylvania, not the oilfields of Texas, and it seemed inappropriate that the company should replace locomotives that consumed coal with those that burned petroleum. With diesels still a relatively new technology, and with experts predicting

that the world's oil supply would soon run dry, it seemed prudent for a traditionally conservative railroad to retain a proven form of motive power.[2] Nor was there any desire on the part of PRR executives to alienate the coal producers who were among their best customers. There was also the hope that the electrification that had proven so successful in the East could be extended west of Harrisburg, obviating the need for either steam or diesel. Even if they would never operate over the Alleghenies, the performance of electric locomotives like the GG1 suggested the desirability of creating equally powerful units that could operate on other parts of the system. It was a goal that steam locomotives could at least theoretically attain, but one that was beyond the capabilities of diesels. Pennsylvania Railroad executives could thus claim ample justification for their continued loyalty to steam power. Their faith was misplaced, as was their assumption that they could apply the lessons of the past to the challenges of the future. Those who stood trackside during the late 1940s were witnessing the end of an era. Over the next decade, and with a speed that few would have predicted, steam locomotives disappeared from the Pennsylvania Railroad.

The evolution of the PRR's motive power during the 1930s, 1940s, and 1950s involved two interrelated stories. The first was the effort by personnel in the Motive Power Department to develop innovative steam locomotives—initially to replicate the impressive performance of the GG1 electric, then to fend off dieselization. It is a tale that could suggest either the rigid and blinkered conservatism of individuals who time had passed by or an innovative attempt to redefine the railroad's core capabilities under radically altered conditions. Their advocacy for increasingly unorthodox steam-locomotive designs bespoke their loyalty to an obsolete technology, as well as their desperation to save their careers. In that respect, PRR employees skilled in the design of steam locomotives were as committed to maintaining their individual power within the organization as they were to the development of motive power that could pull freight and passenger trains. Their efforts cost the railroad nearly $40 million in research-and-development costs, to say nothing of the foregone benefits that the more rapid acquisition of diesels might have produced. The second story, one that was far more praiseworthy, involved the recalibration of the PRR's motive-power strategy, personnel, and operating methods to exploit the potential of the diesel locomotive. That transformation happened within little more than three years, suggesting a company whose executives responded appropriately to an economic and political landscape that was profoundly different from the one that had existed prior to 1945. Yet it was one executive more than any other—Western Region vice president James M. Symes—who initiated that profound alteration in the PRR's strategy. His efforts, part of a larger plan to prevent a repeat of the company's 1946 operating loss, ensured that he would do more to shape the railroad's destiny than any individual since the days of W. W. Atterbury.

Railcars for Branch Lines

Symes's ability to rapidly banish steam locomotives from the Pennsylvania Railroad reflected more than two decades in the evolution of locomotive technology. During the early years of the twentieth century, branch-line passenger service provided the first opportunity for the application of internal combustion to the Pennsylvania Railroad's operations. That business had rarely been profitable, but the advent of the automobile made the situation far worse. As the largest passenger carrier in the nation, and one that served many areas that were early recipients of public highway aid, the PRR was among the first railroads to suffer acute automobile-induced losses in ridership. National rail passenger revenues fell by 25 percent during the 1920s, while the PRR's share declined by a slightly larger amount, 29.4 percent. That translated into a reduction in intercity passenger revenue from $151.2 million in 1922 to $106.1 million in 1930.[3] The number of intercity passengers reached an interwar peak of 79.6 million in 1923 and declined to

just 46.2 million in 1930. During that period, the distance traveled by the average passenger rose from 53.7 miles to 64.4 miles. The increase, although small, suggested to PRR executives that they should allocate a larger portion of passenger-service expenditures to trains that traveled longer distances while correspondingly trimming expenses on lightly traveled branch lines.[4]

Like their counterparts on many other railroads, PRR officials attempted to cut branch-line passenger-train operating costs by employing internal-combustion railcars. Compared to a conventional passenger train, which typically consisted of a steam locomotive pulling several passenger cars, a single-unit motor car provided substantial savings in crew costs, fuel, and maintenance. Most used gasoline or distillate (similar to kerosene) engines, coupled with mechanical (direct-drive) transmissions. Yet, early railcars were typically underpowered and prone to mechanical failure. Technological improvements, particularly the application of diesel engines, improved the performance and reliability of the PRR's railcars. The economic constraints associated with the Great Depression and the need to cut costs wherever possible made their use even more attractive. In the end, however, railcars did not provide a solution to the PRR's passenger-service problems. They were less expensive to operate than conventional locomotive-hauled trains, but they were just as slow and operated on similarly infrequent schedules. Internal-combustion railcars were noisy and smelly—even to the point of inducing carbon monoxide poisoning—and they drew more complaints than praise from passengers. They proved inadequate at stemming the inroads made by private automobiles, but they did nurture a technology that would eventually supplant steam power on the railroad.

A small number of experimental railcars predated the beginning of the twentieth century. The earliest were powered by steam, with the addition of a passenger-car body to a small locomotive. They rarely performed well and saw sustained use only in locations where public pressure or municipal ordinances demanded that traditional steam locomotives be disguised—typically to avoid frightening horses. These "steam dummies" rarely lasted long in intercity operations, the application that was most useful to the Pennsylvania Railroad.

During the 1860s three companies that later became part of the PRR system conducted short-lived experiments with steam cars. In 1851, Bostonians Joseph H. Moore and William P. Parrott developed one of the earliest documented examples. Moore moved west in 1856, to become the superintendent of the Pittsburgh, Fort

Wayne & Chicago. In 1860, the same year that he earned promotion to general agent at Chicago, Moore acquired a facility in Massillon, Ohio, and began the production of steam-powered railcars. Moore claimed that his design would reduce operating costs by two-thirds, compared to a conventional locomotive-hauled train. The prototype made at least one demonstration run between Pittsburgh and Chicago, attesting to its reliability. Moore produced at least two other cars to that design, but the Civil War brought a swift end to his experiments. In 1862, the War Department requisitioned the three steam cars, and they did not return from their assigned duties in the South. William Romans, the master mechanic at the Columbus, Piqua & Indiana Railroad, designed a similar car in 1861. Its name—*Economy*—reflected his effort to reduce the costs associated with the operation of passenger service between Columbus and Piqua. A second Romans car, less appropriately named the *Express*, also entered service, but neither attracted widespread attention. Another design, patented by Robert H. Long and Joseph Grice, was more successful, with sales to ten railroads. One of them was the Camden & Amboy, which purchased several cars in 1861. The disappointing results associated with early steam cars nonetheless ensured that there was little sustained development during the 1870s and 1880s.[5]

Late in the nineteenth century, four factors encouraged a renewed interest in self-propelled passenger cars. One was the severe economic depression that began in 1893, which induced railroads executives to curtail operating costs. At the same time, the rapid growth of electrified interurbans reduced patronage on branch lines. Likewise, during the late 1800s, Samuel Vauclain, the general superintendent at the Baldwin Locomotive Works, became a forceful advocate for the development of compound steam locomotives. While Vauclain envisioned compounding as a mechanism to increase the efficiency of conventional steam locomotives, he zealously attempted to apply the concept to steam cars as well. The final influence reflected the research of German engineer Rudolf Diesel. In 1893, he published *Theorie und Konstruktion eines rationellen Wärmemotors zum Ersatz der Dampfmaschine und der heute bekannten Verbrennungsmotoren* (*Theory and Construction of a Rational Heat Motor*), which established the basic principles of the engine that would bear his name. Diesel's initial experiments involved the combustion of powdered coal, rather than oil. Regardless of the fuel source, however, American mechanical engineers hoped that the new engine could be used to power railcars.[6]

Two self-propelled railcars, each built in 1899, reflected those developments. Baldwin produced a steam-powered unit for the Pittsburgh, Cincinnati, Chicago & St. Louis Railway. With a weight of fifty-eight tons, it featured a passenger section that seated forty people, as well as a small compound steam engine. Intended for use on the route between Xenia and Springfield, Ohio, it lasted barely a month before being banished to the Clearfield Coal Company in Pennsylvania. Its internal-combustion counterpart, developed by the Chicago-based Vimotum Hydrocarbon Car Company, was even less successful. Vimotum subcontracted the production of the *Eureka* to the Jewett Car Company, an Ohio firm that specialized in the manufacturing of electric streetcar and interurban equipment. The forty-one-foot car thus closely resembled its interurban counterparts, albeit powered by a three-cylinder, forty-five-horsepower Wolverine Motor Works engine rather than electricity. The unit soon underwent tests on the New York Central's Big Four affiliate and on the Indianapolis & Vincennes Railroad (a company that would soon become part of the PRR-affiliated Vandalia Railroad). One Pennsylvania Railroad official suggested that the new technology meant that the company "has no longer anything to fear from parallel electric lines." The *Eureka* moved from Columbus, Indiana, to Philadelphia, where it went on display—although, ominously, it made the trip attached to a PRR freight train, rather than under its own power. Vimotum's wildly optimistic claims suggested that the car could travel between Chicago and Pittsburgh without stopping for fuel and water, for a mere $18 in operating costs. Reporters for Indiana newspapers predicted a great future for the *Eureka* and the Vimotum Hydrocarbon Car Company. They suggested that the new technology could be applied to any PRR passenger equipment and asserted—incorrectly—that the private car of PRR president Alexander Cassatt was being converted to internal combustion. Despite the favorable publicity, both the *Eureka* and the Vimotum Hydrocarbon Car Company soon disappeared from the Pennsylvania Railroad.[7]

The Pennsylvania Railroad purchased only two motor cars from the beginning of the twentieth century until World War I. Neither was successful. In the autumn of 1909, the Sheffield plant of Fairbanks-Morse delivered a unit powered by a four-cylinder, 50-horsepower gasoline engine. It replaced a conventional passenger train on a lightly traveled branch line between Clayton and Smyrna, Delaware, part of the PRR's Philadelphia, Baltimore & Washington subsidiary. At thirty-four feet in length, the car lacked adequate seating capacity and could not accommodate the racial segregation that existed in Delaware at that time. It suffered from the limitations and defects that were common to an emerging technology, and the car lasted only three years in service. The other piece of equipment came from the McKeen Motor Car Company, a firm with close ties to the PRR's executive family. William R. McKeen Jr., the superintendent of motive power and machinery on the Union Pacific, was the son of Terre Haute & Indianapolis Railroad president—and occasional PRR nemesis—William Riley McKeen, and the brother of Benjamin McKeen, at that time the general manager of the TH&I and later a PRR vice president. Acting on instructions from Union Pacific executive committee chairman Edward Henry Harriman, McKeen developed a distinctive motor-car design, with porthole windows and a wind-splitting wedge front. While most McKeen cars went to the UP, he sold models to several dozen other railroads, including the PRR. A 200-horsepower McKeen car, #4701, arrived in the fall of 1910 and spent most of its time carrying passengers between Olean, New York, and Bradford, Pennsylvania. The crew included a McKeen technician, necessary to keep the car running and attesting to its lack of reliability. By 1918, PRR officials had removed the McKeen car from service. Over the next few years, PRR officials tested a variety of storage-battery and gasoline-powered motor cars, along with a diminutive steam car built by Baldwin for the Pittsburgh, Cincinnati, Chicago & St. Louis, but none were successful.[8]

While World War I and the period of federal control temporarily blocked additional railcar experiments, the postwar recession and steadily declining branch-line traffic levels reawakened executive interest in motor cars. The Service Motor Truck Company, based in Wabash, Indiana, prospered during World War I, before entering the railway market. Its technicians mounted a carbody, manufactured by J. G. Brill, on a truck chassis equipped with flanged wheels. Charles O. Guernsey, the chief engineer of Service's rail division, soon designed a motor car that was far better suited for railroad operations. The Model 55 featured a 68-horsepower gasoline engine, coupled to a mechanical transmission. Its forty-three-foot length was adequate for most branch-line passenger routes. The PRR took delivery of three Model 55 motor cars in early 1923 and placed an order for three more later that year. By then, Brill had transferred its expertise in the railroad equipment market to the fledgling motor-car industry, just as Service had earlier expanded from trucks into rail vehicles. In November 1923, Brill acquired the rail division of the cash-strapped Service Motor Truck Company, thus establishing the new Brill Automotive Car Division.[9]

The PRR ultimately purchased seven of the Model 55 motor cars during 1923 and 1924, and one remained in service as late as 1935. One of the cars transported railroad officials along the PRR between Philadelphia and Washington so they could attend the American Short-Line Railroad Association Convention. Even though the delegates made the trip at an average speed of only thirty-three miles per hour, they commented favorably on the utility of the railcar for branch-line service. Many PRR executives nonetheless suggested "that the field for rail motors is of a restricted character." While the Model 55 performed well on the relatively flat lines in New Jersey, Delaware, and eastern Pennsylvania, it could not surmount the steeper grades that characterized many of the routes further west. Nor could it haul a trailer—something that was essential in services that required additional passenger capacity or the fulfillment of Railway Post Office mail contracts. The railroad's operating employees may have contributed to that situation, either because they were unfamiliar with—or openly hostile to—internal-combustion technology. The PRR's chief of motive power complained that a Brill car placed in service near Altoona "was handled very poorly and it seems to be the opinion of our Inspectors that about all the operating people on the Cresson Branch desired to do was to discredit the car, instead of trying to operate it economically."[10]

Guernsey and other Brill designers responded to the limitations of the Model 55 by developing two new designs, the Model 65 and the Model 75, each of which employed a mechanical transmission. The PRR purchased only two of the Model 65 motor cars, in May 1925. The more powerful Model 75, which could tow either a conventional passenger coach or a baggage-mail car, proved only slightly more appealing, with four units placed in service in 1925 and 1926. All four were powered by a Winton Engine Company 175-horsepower gasoline engine. Guernsey also developed a variant with a gasoline engine married to a more reliable electric transmission and producing 250 horsepower. PRR officials tested one of the new Brill cars, comparing its performance with a 175-horsepower demonstrator provided by a relatively new entrant into the field, the Cleveland-based Electro-Motive Company. While both performed well, railroad officials opted for the more powerful design. Orders for five of the new Brill cars soon followed.[11]

Despite the initial setback, Electro-Motive soon supplanted Brill as the dominant supplier of railcars on the Pennsylvania Railroad and throughout the United States. Like the Service Motor Truck Company, Electro-Motive represented the transfer of highway technology to the railroads. Founded by Harold L. Hamilton, a former employee of the White Motor Company, Electro-Motive revolutionized the motor-car industry by using standardized designs and highly developed postsale customer support services.

Electro-Motive did not produce railcars. Rather, it contracted its carbody designs to outside builders, including Brill and the Pullman Car & Manufacturing Corporation (after 1934, the Pullman-Standard Car Manufacturing Company). The internal-combustion engines came from the Winton Engine Company. Winton's capabilities attracted the attention of Alfred P. Sloan and other executives at General Motors, and they acquired the firm in 1930. Upon learning that EMC was Winton's primary customer, GM officials established control over the railcar producer as well. The timing was fortuitous for EMC, as the saturation of the railcar market, the decline of branch-line passenger trains, and the onset of the Great Depression had imperiled the company's future. While EMC founders Harold L. Hamilton and Paul Turner had never been defenders of the steam locomotive, their alliance with GM reinforced their commitment to internal combustion and provided them with the capital and technological expertise necessary for expansion.[12]

The growth of the Electro-Motive Company and its affiliation with General Motors coincided with changes at the Pennsylvania Railroad. In February 1927, the PRR created a new post—chief of passenger transportation—that reflected the growing concern of senior managers regarding the loss of passenger revenue. The job went to Daniel M. Sheaffer—the son of Charles Sheaffer, who had, eleven years earlier, given W. W. Atterbury, then the vice president in charge of operations, a pessimistic assessment of the usefulness of buses as replacements for branch-line passenger trains. Sheaffer was familiar with the rapid improvements to internal-combustion technology that had occurred since then. Given the increase in automobile ownership and the spread of paved highways, Sheaffer's career prospects depended on his ability to reduce the cost associated with branch-line passenger services. Based on the data generated by the PRR's pioneering motor cars, Sheaffer recommended a series of routes where new equipment could replace conventional, locomotive-hauled trains. In December 1927, the board of directors authorized an expenditure of $635,000 to acquire thirteen railcars—the largest order to date. The first six came from Brill, as their Model 350. At seventy-three feet in length (thirteen feet longer than the previous model) and weighing sixty-five tons, the newest acquisitions in many respects resembled conventional passenger cars. Producing an impressive 350 horsepower (hence the model designation), they could easily pull one or two trailers and cope with the grades on virtually any branch line. Several months later, the PRR ordered six cars from Electro-Motive. Built by Pullman and featuring Winton engines and Westinghouse electrical

equipment, they produced only 275 horsepower—still adequate for most service. Hamilton, desiring a large order from an influential railroad, was willing to compromise his policy of standardization. He eschewed EMC's preference for General Electric electrical equipment and mounted the engine in line with the carbody rather than transversely, as was the usual practice. The thirteenth car, ordered as concession to Mack Trucks, Incorporated (although with a Brill body), was an experiment not to be repeated.[13]

With more than thirty motor cars in service, Sheaffer solicited feedback on their performance as well as recommendations that might guide future purchases. His surveys revealed that the PRR's division superintendents, who were under pressure to trim their expenditures, clamored for additional equipment. Based on their requests, Sheaffer recommended that the railroad acquire an additional sixteen cars. The board granted its approval on March 7, 1928. Thirteen came from Brill, based on their earlier Model 350 design, built by Pullman and equipped with Winton gasoline engines. Two others, also constructed by Pullman, featured Beardmore diesel engines, as an experimental measure to evaluate the new power source. They marked the beginning of vertical integration in the railcar industry, with Westinghouse building both the diesel engines (in South Philadelphia) and the electrical equipment (in East Pittsburgh). Electro-Motive provided only one motor car, fabricated at Pullman's Michigan City, Indiana, facility. All were in service by April 1929. Even while they were under construction, Sheaffer was recommending the purchase of another twenty-five cars. However, he soon discovered that division superintendents, in their eagerness to receive additional motor cars, had grossly overestimated the savings that might result.[14] A more accurate recalculation indicated that only one of the proposed assignments met the requirement, established by vice president in charge of operations Martin Clement, for a 25 percent reduction in operating costs. The PRR ultimately ordered just five of the planned twenty-five cars. All five came from Brill and featured a robust 400-horsepower engine.[15]

By the time the PRR received the final five Brill cars, in the autumn of 1930, the Great Depression further eroded passenger revenues. Brill was the most obvious casualty, and the economic calamity ended its efforts to develop and market innovative new railcar designs. Electro-Motive did far better, ultimately abandoning motor-car production in favor of diesel passenger and freight locomotives. By the end of 1930, the PRR rostered fifty motor cars—eleven of the early gasoline-mechanical cars and thirty-nine of the more reliable models with electric transmissions. The number was adequate, particularly as executives accelerated the

Internal-combustion railcars, such as the one calling at Oxford, Pennsylvania, in 1948, were capable replacements for conventional passenger trains along routes with low traffic potential. They also provided firms such as the Electro-Motive Company with an opportunity to develop organizational capabilities that would serve them well as they began to manufacture diesel locomotives. *David H. Cope Photographs, Hagley Museum & Library, acc. 2001.242.*

abandonment of passenger service. As such, many of the routes assigned to the motor cars lasted no more than two or three years. The lines where they could be used most economically, it turned out, were also the ones where nothing could be done to save rail passenger service from the effects of automobile traffic.

The Depression also encouraged Pennsylvania Railroad executives to experiment with new designs, in the hope of providing rapid, comfortable, and low-cost passenger service. That effort solidified their reliance on Electro-Motive and resurrected ties with Edward G. Budd, a design engineer who would have a similarly transformative role in the development of railway technology. Budd began his long and distinguished career at William Sellers & Company,

a firm that had enjoyed a close relationship with both the Baldwin Locomotive Works and the PRR during the nineteenth century. Budd joined another Philadelphia firm, the Hale & Kilburn Company, in 1902. Four years later, he was involved with the fabrication of stamped-metal components for the PRR's earliest steel passenger cars. The partnership with the Pennsylvania Railroad proved so lucrative that Hale & Kilburn built a new factory at 17th Street and Glenwood Avenue, close to the PRR's North Philadelphia station.[16] The aerodynamic railcars developed by William McKeen also used products supplied by Hale & Kilburn. While the McKeen design did not become popular, it encouraged Budd to think about new types of railroad equipment. In 1912, a year after J. P. Morgan acquired Hale & Kilburn, Budd founded the Edward G. Budd Manufacturing Company, initially producing truck bodies for General Motors and other companies.[17]

The onset of the Great Depression severely curtailed orders from the automotive sector. Budd sought new uses for the company's plant, located at the intersection of Stockley Street and Hunting Park Avenue since 1915. He was intrigued with the potential of stainless steel and, in cooperation with the American Aeronautical Corporation, fabricated a prototype aircraft from the strong, corrosion-resistant material. After much experimentation, Budd developed the shot welding technique, which uses electric current to join fluted stainless-steel panels into railcar bodies. Budd traded the European rights for the shot weld process to the French firm Michelin in exchange for that company's designs for applying pneumatic tires to rail wheels. That agreement led to the production of two Budd-Michelin railcars in 1932. One, the *La Fayette*, was shipped to France for testing, while the other remained in the United States. The first production model, also completed in 1932, went to the Reading, where it performed poorly. The Pennsylvania Railroad purchased two of the cars in 1933, thanks in part to Budd's friendship with Atterbury and to Atterbury's fascination with innovative transportation technologies.[18] Doubts about the viability of the new technology were nonetheless well-founded, with the two-unit railcar set frequently experiencing the novel phenomenon of a flat tire while operating on steel rails. The Cummins diesels that powered the equipment were also prone to failure. By August 1936, the Budd-Michelin cars were in the shops at Altoona for rebuilding. They emerged with new engines and without the troublesome rubber tires but still experienced numerous problems. The cars were in storage by 1940.[19] While Budd sensibly abandoned further efforts to apply tires to railroad equipment, the Edward G. Budd Manufacturing Company—like Electro-Motive—would soon enjoy considerable success in the railway equipment industry and count the PRR among its most important customers.[20]

Despite the improvements of the 1920s, railcars were still no match for the comfort and reliability of locomotive-hauled passenger trains. To the contrary, they were small, underpowered, noisy, and smelly, and they probably soured a great many travelers and railroaders alike on the very idea of internal combustion. Nor could they protect passenger safety to the same degree as conventional trains. Accidents at grade crossings were particularly dangerous, with the motorman—sitting at the very front of the unit—being most at risk. Motor cars were also far more fragile than steam locomotives, a situation that was tragically illustrated on July 31, 1940. Engineman Thomas Murtaugh, overcome by carbon monoxide fumes from the engine, allowed railcar #4648 (weight 61 tons) to drift past the location of a scheduled meet. The car collided with a freight train pulled by two I1s steam locomotives (combined weight 386 tons, plus several thousand more tons in the seventy-three cars they were hauling). The motor car's fuel tank ruptured and then exploded, incinerating forty-three passengers. Although such horrific incidents were mercifully uncommon, PRR motive-power officials had

long since concluded that railcars were not the appropriate vehicle for stemming the decline in passenger traffic.[21]

Early Diesels: Disappointment and Derision

For the first four decades of its development, the diesel engine provided little indication that it would ever displace steam locomotives from the Pennsylvania Railroad. Early diesels were large and heavy, with a low power-to-weight ratio, and thus were best suited for stationary or maritime applications. Initial efforts to use diesels to power railway locomotives produced disappointing results.

Safety concerns, shaped by public policy, nonetheless provided a small niche market where the development of diesel locomotives could proceed. On January 8, 1902, two trains collided in the smoke-filled Park Avenue Tunnel leading to the New York Central's Grand Central Depot, leaving more than a dozen people dead. The catastrophe was one of the factors that encouraged the NYC to replace the outdated station and—under the direction of electrical engineer William J. Wilgus—to electrify the route leading to the new Grand Central Terminal. The PRR's New York Improvements, then in the planning stages, also necessitated electrification between New Jersey and Long Island. Neither railroad objected to legislation, passed by the New York State Assembly in May 1903, requiring that the NYC electrify its main line south of the Harlem River by July 1, 1908.[22]

The successful operation of PRR, NYC, and New Haven trains along the electrified routes in Greater New York did not eliminate the danger or the unpleasantness associated with the steam locomotives that continued to move through the city. Although the Long Island Rail Road had electrified most of its suburban commuter lines within city limits, more than a tenth of its passengers still traveled behind steam locomotives. Other steam locomotives worked at small, isolated pier-side facilities, but the most serious problem involved the NYC's tracks along "Death Avenue" on the Lower West Side of Manhattan. In April 1923, the state legislature approved a bill, sponsored by Manhattan assemblyman Victor R. Kaufman, mandating complete railroad electrification in all five boroughs by January 1, 1926. PRR and LIRR officials, initially caught unawares by the Kaufman bill, attempted in vain to prevent Governor Alfred E. Smith from signing the measure into law. Two years later, Smith vetoed the Thayer bill, a measure that would have postponed the compliance date until January 1, 1929. Failing at the Governor's Mansion, the carriers then took the matter to federal court, with LIRR attorneys claiming that that railroad alone would have to spend as much as $30 million to satisfy the terms of the Kaufman Act. Even though LIRR officials authorized electrification on the Montauk Division between Jamaica and Babylon and along the freight line linking Bay Ridge Yard with Fresh Pond Junction, they steadfastly refused to consider any further projects. Their counterparts on the PRR, a company that operated very few steam locomotives in Greater New York, proved more conciliatory.[23] Asserting that they were making a good-faith effort to comply with the legislation, they persuaded the New York Public Service Commission to postpone the compliance date until July 1, 1927.[24] At approximately the same time, Chicago, Cleveland, and Baltimore enacted ordinances that likewise attempted to ban or severely restrict the scope of steam-locomotive operations.[25]

The Kaufman Act and its counterparts in other cities made the adoption of internal-combustion locomotives all but inevitable. Electrification was a proven technology, but it made little economic sense to electrify small urban freight terminals. PRR officials argued that any locomotive using an internal-combustion engine to create the electricity that powered the wheels was in fact an electric locomotive, at least for the purposes of the Kaufman Act.[26] In 1923 and 1924, just prior to the adoption of the Kaufman Act, the PRR had taken delivery of seven Model 55 railcars manufactured by J. G. Brill. Intended for branch-line passenger service, they were hardly suited for switching cars in Greater New York. Even in their intended role, they experienced frequent problems with their mechanical transmissions. Officials in the Motive Power Department joined forces with their colleagues at Westinghouse to develop a more reliable electric transmission, based on the system recently designed by Hermann Lemp at General Electric. John F. Deasy, the PRR's chief of freight transportation, asserted that such primitive internal-combustion units could not match the speed and power offered by steam and electric locomotives. He nonetheless acknowledged their value in areas subject to the Kaufman Act. As he told Martin Clement, then the vice president in charge of operations, in the fall of 1927, Deasy "assumed that other large cities in the future will probably impose restrictions that will force the use of engines of this type."[27]

By the time Deasy shared his opinions with Clement, several companies had developed internal-combustion locomotives. The earliest engines often burned gasoline or more readily available distillate. Both fuel sources were highly flammable and exceedingly expensive.[28] By 1924, most had shifted to the use of diesel engines as the most efficient mechanism for powering the experimental new locomotives.[29] In the face of limited demand and

high research-and-development costs, the earliest efforts arose from consortia of firms that specialized in the diesel engine, the electrical equipment that controlled the locomotive, or the chassis and superstructure. General Electric and Ingersoll Rand launched a cooperative venture in 1921, and by December 1923, they had tested a 300-horsepower locomotive. The American Locomotive Company soon became part of the consortium, and in the summer of 1925, it sold the first commercially successful diesel locomotive to the Jersey Central. The Baldwin Locomotive Works, Alco's rival, responded with a 1,000-horsepower behemoth. It used electrical equipment furnished by Westinghouse, creating a rival to the Alco-GE-IR group. During testing, the Baldwin unit became the first diesel locomotive to operate on the Pennsylvania Railroad. Its performance was unsatisfactory, and PRR officials chose not to purchase it. Instead, the first diesel-powered vehicle owned by the Pennsylvania Railroad was the *Media*—a tugboat, built in 1889, that received a 300-horsepower Southwark & Harris diesel power plant in 1917.[30]

With the outcome of the political and legal battle over the Kaufman Act still in doubt, the failure of the Baldwin-Westinghouse locomotive did not halt the gradual spread of dieselization. PRR officials evaluated locomotives of varying designs from all the major builders—a tradition that it would maintain for the next quarter century. The first tests, during July and August 1924, demonstrated that a GE gasoline-electric locomotive could perform the same functions as a Class A4 0-4-0 steam shifter.[31] By the fall of 1925, the GE-IR-Alco consortium had developed a 600-horsepower diesel locomotive, destined for the Long Island Rail Road. On December 15, it pulled a train along PRR rails, from the GE works at Erie to Harrisburg. As LIRR #401, its performance was mediocre at best and required continual maintenance and extensive modifications. The #401 was nonetheless the first diesel locomotive owned by the PRR or any of its subsidiaries. Its failings stimulated further research-and-development efforts. In January 1926, the LIRR received a 500-horsepower Brill-Westinghouse gasoline-electric locomotive (#402) but soon returned it to the builder, owing to excessive fuel consumption.[32] In May 1928, the LIRR took delivery of the first diesel locomotives produced by Baldwin-Westinghouse, a conjoined pair numbered 403A/B.[33]

While LIRR officials purchased locomotives supplied by various builders, their counterparts at the PRR experimented briefly with in-house production. While such insourcing seemed logical for a company that built more than six thousand steam locomotives, managers underestimated the technical difficulties involved. The initial

Long Island Rail Road #401 was the first diesel locomotive
to operate on the PRR or any of its subsidiaries. Generating
a mere 600 horsepower, it was no match for a steam locomotive—but it did comply with the antipollution provisions
of the Kaufman Act. *General Negative Collection, Railroad
Museum of Pennsylvania, PHMC.*

meeting of the design team occurred on April 18, 1925,
four days after Governor Smith vetoed the Thayer bill.
Designers intended to fit a 500-horsepower diesel engine
and its associated electrical equipment into the small
outline of a Class B1 electric switcher. The fabrication of
the carbodies for the three experimental units posed few
problems for the shop forces at Altoona, but the engines
were another matter.[34] While the Motive Power Department solicited bids from various manufacturers, only the
Bessemer Gas Engine Company was willing to provide a
prime mover that satisfied the railroad's size and weight
requirements. By May 1926, workers at Altoona completed
the three carbodies and waited for Bessemer to finish
research-and-development work on its new engine design.
Bessemer rebuilt their troublesome engine three times and

did not ship the first one to Altoona until the last day of
February 1928. It proved as unreliable in service as it had
been in stationary tests, and James T. Wallis, the PRR's
chief of motive power, concluded that the Bessemer engine
was "not very satisfactory." His comment was something
of an understatement, as the engine disintegrated on September 29, severely damaging the locomotive and seriously
injuring a Bessemer technician. Although the PRR had
agreed to pay Bessemer $50,000 for three engines, Besse-
mer officials spent $94,000 in a fruitless attempt to get the
first one working properly and then asked to be relieved
of the contract. Only the #3905 ever operated under the
power of its intended Bessemer engine, making it both the
first diesel locomotive on the PRR and the only one built at
Altoona. Its time as a diesel was short-lived, however, and
by early 1929, shop forces had replaced the troublesome
Bessemer engine with a Winton gasoline engine, originally designed for use in railcars. One of its counterparts
(the #3906) likewise received a Winton gasoline engine.
Assigned to Class A6, they were the first internal-combustion locomotives in regular service on the Pennsylvania
Railroad. The two locomotives performed adequately
and—in keeping with the requirements of the Kaufman
Act—spent most of their careers loading and unloading

Despite the prodigious number of steam locomotives produced at the Altoona Works, shop forces completed only a
single diesel. By the time of this scene in New York, in August
1937, the original Bessemer engine on the #3905 had been
replaced with a Winton gasoline model. *General Negative Collection, Railroad Museum of Pennsylvania, PHMC.*

car floats in Greater New York.[35] Yet they were often out
of service, owing to a shortage of trained personnel at the
LIRR shops in Morris Park, Queens, where they were sent
for maintenance.[36] The inadequate staffing highlighted the
importance—and the expense—associated with providing support facilities for a new type of locomotive.[37]

Even after more than a decade of sustained research and
development on the part of several companies, diesels were
unreliable, underpowered, and far more expensive than a
comparable steam locomotive. The reduced traffic levels
associated with the Great Depression had sidelined many
steam engines—creating a situation in which locomotive
builders, desperate for business, were prompting the railroads to acquire diesel locomotives, while railroad officials
had little interest in buying them. The glut of motive power
was particularly notable on the PRR, thanks to the electrification of the route between New York and Washington,
with the extension west to Harrisburg entering service in

January 1938. That project alone released four hundred
steam locomotives from service, and the Depression sidelined still more. Between 1930 and 1935, the PRR retired
or stored eleven hundred steam locomotives—more than
a fifth of the railroad's total motive power. The possible
extension of the catenary from Harrisburg west to Pittsburgh, the subject of sustained discussion during the 1930s,
would have rendered surplus even more steam locomotives. Although the PRR's motive-power fleet was older
than the national average by the mid-1930s, there were still
more than enough steam locomotives available to handle
the traffic without the additional capital expenditures
associated with diesel-locomotive purchases.[38]

The Necessity for Improved Passenger Service

The Great Depression and the increasing popularity of
automobile and bus travel exacerbated the troubling
ridership trends of the previous decade. Total intercity
passenger miles declined from 3.5 billion in 1929 to less
than 1.7 billion in 1933, while intercity passenger revenue
fell from $124.2 million to $48.4 million. Those statistics
suggested the need to reverse the reduction in passenger traffic associated with the Depression, by ensuring
that passengers remained loyal to rail travel. That effort
depended on the PRR's ability to offer improved service
on long-distance routes while imposing further cuts in

branch-line services and redundant long-distance trains. In the process, PRR officials elected to offer fewer but longer and better-appointed trains. Despite the introduction of lightweight streamlined equipment, the improved passenger services increasingly taxed the abilities of the K4s Pacifics that dominated operations outside electrified territory. As such, and despite the abundance of stored power, officials in the Motive Power Department faced the immediate need to develop more powerful and efficient units that would accommodate the changing demands of passenger service.[39]

By 1930, the PRR's passenger equipment was not appreciably different from the cars that had entered service two decades earlier. Innovations such as vestibules, electric lighting, and all-steel construction had become universal. Despite incremental improvements in heating and ventilating systems, however, passengers had only one sure mechanism to reduce the temperature during the hot summer months, and that involved opening a window. By doing so, they could anticipate that their clothes and possessions would be covered with soot from the locomotive and dust kicked up from along the tracks. In the process, those travelers might wonder when the air-conditioning they had experienced in buildings would also be applied to trains. In 1902, a publishing company in Brooklyn asked engineer Willis Haviland Carrier to prevent humidity-induced expansion or shrinkage of paper, particularly during the summer. Carrier solved the problem by establishing the parameters of air-conditioning, and he patented his system in 1906. The New York Stock Exchange, whose members often rode along the Pennsylvania Railroad, had been air-conditioned since 1903. In 1917, a theater in Montgomery, Alabama, became the first in the nation to install air-conditioning. Two years later, Carrier published *The Story of Manufactured Weather*, which publicized the new technology. The installation of air-conditioning in New York's Rivoli Theatre in 1925 attracted widespread attention—particularly when the system more than paid for itself, through increased ticket sales, in one summer season.[40]

During the prosperous years of the late 1920s, passengers increasingly demanded greater summertime comfort while traveling, particularly in sleeping cars and other premium accommodations. The Pullman Company conducted unsuccessful experiments with air-conditioning between 1927 and 1929, but the Baltimore & Ohio succeeded where Pullman had failed. To gain a marketing advantage over the PRR, during the summer of 1929, the B&O hired Carrier to perform a test installation. In May 1931, the B&O's *Columbian* became the first fully air-conditioned train

in the United States, on its run between Jersey City and Washington. A year later, the B&O had air-conditioned two of its overnight trains, including the Washington–Chicago *Capitol Limited*.[41]

Pennsylvania Railroad executives, hampered by cost considerations and uncertainty regarding the most effective mechanism for cooling trains, were slow to emulate the B&O's efforts. Shop forces equipped only a small number of cars, mainly diners, with air-conditioning during 1931 and 1932, as the Great Depression and the ongoing electrification project in the Northeast limited the company's ability to do more. Desperate to compete against the B&O, the PRR instead used refrigeration units at stations in New York, Philadelphia, Baltimore, Washington, Pittsburgh, Cleveland, Columbus, Cincinnati, Indianapolis, Louisville, Detroit, St. Louis, and Chicago to precool cars prior to each train's departure.[42]

Technicians at Altoona also experimented with a variety of on-board systems, ranging from ice blocks to electromechanical units to steam ejectors. Ice-block technology offered the virtue of simplicity, requiring only a pump (to move melted ice water to coils in the roof of the car) and a fan (to blow chilled air through the passenger compartment). While the use of ice was clearly impracticable in the hot and humid South, it was a reasonable alternative in the cooler northern latitudes in which the PRR operated. Each car consumed about five hundred pounds of ice per hour, however. Frequent re-icing was costly, labor-intensive, and time-consuming. Even worse, the ice water could only lower the car's temperature a maximum of fourteen degrees Fahrenheit, creating difficulties on especially hot days. Mechanical air-conditioning units eliminated those problems, but not all were suitable for use on the Pennsylvania Railroad. One system, developed by the Waukesha Motor Company, employed a self-contained, propane-fueled engine to generate power for the compressor and related equipment. While popular on many railroads, the propane tanks posed too great a fire risk in the New York tunnels. Following the earlier period of experimentation, the company generally relied on a belt-driven mechanical system supplied by Frigidaire. Although the initial installation was more expensive than ice or propane units, the Frigidaire unit lowered operating costs by 80 percent. Unfortunately, the belt-driven system could not maintain a cool temperature if the car remained stationary for any length of time. From the perspective of operating personnel, however, the more serious concern was that the axle-driven generator created additional friction, imperiling the ability of locomotives to haul long passenger trains.[43]

By the beginning of 1933, competitive pressures, coupled with a growing confidence in the new technology, prompted the widespread application of air-conditioning. In January 1933, the board of directors authorized $323,000 for the installation of equipment on trains operating between New York and Washington. Funding for passenger trains between the East Coast and Chicago and St. Louis came that September. By 1936, the PRR operated more air-conditioned equipment than any of its competitors—506, with an additional 610 Pullman sleepers and parlor cars. By the summer of 1938, the PRR had installed air-conditioning on enough cars to permit the retirement of the early precooling units. When the United States entered World War II, passengers on most regularly scheduled long-distance trains enjoyed cool air. It nonetheless took many years before the bulk of the coach fleet was air-conditioned, and most commuter equipment never received air-conditioning at all.[44]

In addition to the increased comfort provided by air-conditioning, travelers valued faster schedules that enabled them to reach their destinations more quickly. The electrification of the route between New York and Washington, and eventually west to Harrisburg, facilitated reductions in running time, at least on the PRR's premier trains. Schedule changes lowered *The Broadway Limited*'s twenty-hour trip between New York and Chicago to eighteen hours in 1932, then to 17¾ hours in 1933 and 16½ hours by September 1935, while the corresponding journey between New York and St. Louis, on *The "Spirit of St. Louis,"* went from twenty-three hours to less than twenty-one hours. Despite its status as the PRR's flagship train, *The Broadway Limited* nonetheless suffered from low ridership and routinely failed to cover its operating costs. The New York Central, which dominated the route between New York and Chicago, maintained its competitive stance by adopting matching schedules for the *Twentieth Century Limited*. The Pennsylvania Railroad was also partly to blame for declining patronage on *The Broadway*. In April 1937, the company introduced *The General*, named for its recently deceased president, W. W. Atterbury. The new service—which did not charge an extra fare—was almost as luxurious as *The Broadway* and nearly as fast.[45]

Trainsets and Lightweight Cars

By the mid-1930s, Pennsylvania Railroad executives concluded that air-conditioning and faster schedules would not be sufficient to ensure the popularity or profitability of long-distance passenger services. Success would require a new generation of passenger equipment, entailing a substantial investment that would match the commitment of competitors such as the New York Central. The redesign of the cars that would carry people across a continent coincided with the birth of the industrial-design movement. Like the PRR's efforts to retain a share of the passenger market, industrial designers were reacting to the economic calamity of the Great Depression, as manufacturers sought to reestablish the consumer culture that had generated so much prosperity during the 1920s.[46] Industrial design and transportation were two very different endeavors, however, producing tension between individuals who envisioned futuristic cars and locomotives and the railroaders assigned to build and operate them.[47]

Moreover, there was yet no clear consensus as to the best way to incorporate innovative designs into railroad service. Some individuals favored entirely new lightweight trainsets, powered by internal-combustion engines, that were incompatible with existing equipment. Others judged that more modest, incremental improvements would yield greater economy and efficiency. At the heart of the debate were two trains, the M-10000 and the *Zephyr*, that represented the marriage of new design and fabrication techniques with the latest developments in propulsion systems. Both were introduced by manufacturers who were desperate to generate additional business. Widely praised as emblematic of the American can-do spirit that was certain to overcome the Great Depression, they nonetheless embodied performance characteristics that were not appropriate for the Pennsylvania Railroad's requirements.

By the early 1930s, the companies that manufactured passenger cars were in serious financial trouble. Railroads had replaced most of their wooden passenger cars with all-steel equipment, and the Great Depression further retarded new orders. The situation was particularly severe at the Pullman Car & Manufacturing Corporation, the company that produced a large share of the passenger equipment used in the United States. During the Depression, officials at Pullman were committed to the development of new, marketable products. They worked with aircraft designer William Bushnell Stout, who had recently developed the Ford Tri-Motor aircraft employed in the PRR's short-lived transcontinental air-rail service. Stout created a hybrid of rail and aviation technology, in the form of the *Railplane*. The concept worked well enough that it attracted the attention of the executives at the Union Pacific, who were interested in operating a fast streamliner over long distances through sparsely settled territory. In February 1934, Pullman completed the Union Pacific's M-10000. A distillate engine powered the three-car articulated train, built largely of aluminum. Its sleek, low-slung

Facing, Not long after its record-breaking run from coast to coast, the Union Pacific M-10001 was on display at Broad Street Station. Its sleek exterior and bright colors contrasted with the PRR coach at the extreme right. *Courtesy of the Special Collections Research Center, Temple University Libraries, Philadelphia, PA.*

appearance offered a notable contrast with conventional heavyweight passenger cars hauled by a steam locomotive. A nationwide publicity tour, which included a stop at Chicago's Century of Progress International Exposition, generated considerable public awareness of the sleek new streamliner.[48]

A new articulated train quickly superseded the M-10000 in the national headlines and exerted an even more profound influence on the development of passenger equipment and service. While Edward Budd's Michelin-design railcars had proven a dismal failure, he saw considerable potential for the shot weld method of fabricating carbodies from stainless steel. He was also searching for additional business, and he was thus willing to offer extremely favorable terms for the construction of a trainset similar to the M-10000. He contacted his distant relative Ralph Budd, the president of the Chicago, Burlington & Quincy Railroad—a company that, like the Union Pacific, operated long passenger routes with light traffic. Much like the M-10000, the *Zephyr* included three cars, permanently coupled together. Its shiny stainless-steel exterior was a noticeable contrast from the armor-yellow and leaf-brown paint used by the Union Pacific. The power plant was different as well. In place of the distillate engine used by the UP's M-10000, the *Zephyr* featured a Model 201A diesel engine, supplied by the Winton Engine Company.[49]

Budd's Philadelphia manufacturing plant completed the *Zephyr* in early April 1934 and soon tested it on the Reading. The Pennsylvania Railroad had the honor of hosting the *Zephyr*'s public debut, however, in an event held at Broad Street Station on April 18. Fortuitously, Marguerite Cotsworth, the daughter of the Burlington's passenger manager, was a student at Swarthmore College and thus was available to break a bottle of recently legalized champagne over the nose of the train. Alfred P. Sloan Jr., the president of General Motors, was at the celebration, as were both Budds and the president of US Steel. Speaking on behalf of the PRR, Atterbury suggested that "the Burlington *Zephyr* represents modern pioneering," adding that "we are all keenly interested in the principles embodied in the Burlington *Zephyr*." The subsequent excursion, to Downingtown, paled in comparison to the

May 25 dawn-to-dusk nonstop run between Denver and Chicago. Reporters, photographers, and newsreel cameramen covered the event, while schools canceled classes so that children could join the adults who stood at trackside, waiting for the *Zephyr* to flash by. Its sunset arrival at the Century of Progress Exposition garnered national headlines and overshadowed the display of the Union Pacific's M-10000. Executives at RKO Radio Pictures sensed the public's fascination with the Art Deco streamliner. The December 1934 release of *The Silver Streak*, in which the train featured prominently, increased the *Zephyr*'s notoriety.[50]

The M-10000 and the *Zephyr* soon had company on western rails. In October 1934, Pullman delivered the M-10001 to the Union Pacific. Powered by a Winton Model 201A diesel engine, it was twice as long as its predecessor. It was also extraordinarily fast, setting a still-unbroken record pace of fifty-seven hours for a cross-country trip between Los Angeles and New York City. Soon thereafter, the M-10001 was on display at Penn Station before attracting crowds at Broad Street Station in Philadelphia. Over the next few years, Pullman (a company that became the Pullman-Standard Car Manufacturing Company in December 1934) built several additional diesel units, beginning with the M-10002. Four identical locomotive sets, numbered M-10003 through M-10006, were sufficiently powerful to pull long passenger trains, composed of conventional equipment rather than dedicated, articulated cars. The successful operation of trains such as the *City of San Francisco*, the *City of Denver*, and the *City of Los Angeles* provided strong evidence that diesels could be used interchangeably to maintain fast schedules with almost any type of passenger service.[51]

From Unit Trains to the Fleet of Modernism

The development of the *Zephyr* and the M-series trainsets inspired PRR executives to mimic the efforts of the UP and the Burlington. As early as February 1934, John F. Deasy, Walter Franklin, and other executives met to consider the future of the PRR's passenger service. Despite the depressed economic conditions, Deasy had every reason to anticipate a bright future in the company. He was born in Hamorton, Pennsylvania, west of Philadelphia and not far north of the Delaware state line. In June 1901, at age nineteen, he began his employment with the Pennsylvania Railroad as a telegraph operator. While working as a station agent on the Trenton Division, he studied law at night school, and by 1912, he had become division superintendent. Deasy became the chief of freight transportation in

1927 and the vice president of the Central Region, based in Pittsburgh, in 1931. He returned to Philadelphia in October 1933 as the vice president in charge of operations. Martin Clement's simultaneous promotion to executive vice president indicated that he would soon replace W. W. Atterbury as the head of the company, with Deasy his logical successor. If so, Deasy could only hope that Clement—less than four months his senior—would retire early and give him an opportunity to spend several years as president. Even though his ample sideburns suggested that he belonged to the era of Martin Van Buren, Deasy was attuned to modern operating methods, and he was particularly receptive to the importance of streamlined passenger equipment and powerful new steam locomotives.[52]

While Deasy could reasonably expect to become the president of the Pennsylvania Railroad following Clement's retirement, Walter Franklin likely harbored no such ambitions. Like Alexander Cassatt before him, Franklin came from a well-known, almost patrician Philadelphia family.[53] His father had been in the PRR's Engineer Corps during the 1850s, served as a colonel in the Union army during the Civil War, and in later years was the president of the Ashland Iron Company, near Baltimore. Walter Franklin was born there in 1884, attended a private school in Baltimore, and graduated from Harvard University in 1906. He soon began working for the Pennsylvania Railroad as a freight clerk at the Dock Street Freight Station in Philadelphia. His education and his family connections ensured that he would not remain a laborer for long. By July 1909, he was a freight solicitor in Baltimore and later held similar responsibilities in New Haven, Toronto, and Pittsburgh. In 1914, Franklin became one of the PRR's most important off-line freight agents, based in Atlanta and overseeing traffic solicitation in the southeastern United States. The following year, he became a division freight agent in his native Baltimore. Franklin was with General John J. Pershing's forces in Mexico as they attempted to track down Pancho Villa, and he joined Pershing again during World War I. Like General Atterbury, Franklin served in the Transportation Corps of the American Expeditionary Forces, earning the rank of lieutenant colonel. Following the armistice, he helped to coordinate the return of American troops from France. Franklin left the PRR in 1919 to serve as the president of the American Trading Company. He returned in 1928 as the railroad's general agent at Detroit. After little more than a year, President Atterbury engineered Franklin's appointment as the president of the Detroit, Toledo & Ironton, a company recently acquired by the PRR's Pennroad investment affiliate. At the beginning of 1931, Franklin became the assistant to

John F. Deasy (1882–1953) joined the PRR in 1901, as a telegrapher. He made a rapid ascent up the corporate ladder, becoming the assistant vice president in charge of operations in 1928, vice president of the Central Region in 1931, and vice president in charge of operations in 1933. Later in the decade, he explored the potential of lightweight, streamlined passenger trains. His eventual rise to the presidency seemed a foregone conclusion, but his advocacy for a new generation of fast and powerful steam locomotives proved his undoing. *Harry R. Hippler collection of Pennsylvania Railroad Negatives, Hagley Museum & Library, acc. 2015.279.*

Clement, then the vice president in charge of operations. Another reassignment occurred in October, when Franklin replaced William H. Williams, the recently deceased president of the financially troubled Wabash. Two years later, after helping to guide the Wabash into receivership, Franklin returned to the PRR as vice president in charge of traffic. It was an important job, one that involved the setting of rates as well as the solicitation of passengers and freight shipments. Franklin's duties lay well outside the two paths that had led his predecessors to the top job in the company, for he lacked expertise in either engineering or transportation.[54]

Although all railroads experienced the effects of the Great Depression, Deasy and Franklin were particularly

Walter S. Franklin (1884–1972) was from a patrician background, but he began his PRR career as a freight handler.
Franklin advanced rapidly through the corporate ranks, and in
1933, he became the vice president in charge of traffic. It was an
important post, although given Franklin's lack of experience in
matters related to operations or engineering, not one that was
likely to lead to the presidency. *Courtesy of the Historical Society
of Pennsylvania.*

determined to control costs and avoid expensive new
projects. So was the individual who, for all intents and
purposes, now ran the Pennsylvania Railroad. Just as
Atterbury embodied the ebullient spirit of the 1920s
by supporting forays into every conceivable mode of
transportation, Martin Clement was cautious and parsimonious, reluctant to spend any more money than was
necessary. That attitude became apparent by 1934, as the
PRR's vice president increasingly assumed the day-to-day
responsibilities that the ailing Atterbury was no longer
able to undertake. Given the austerity associated with the

Depression, Clement, Deasy, and Franklin conceded that
most alterations to passenger equipment would involve
nothing more elaborate than air-conditioning and minor
cosmetic upgrades.[55]

For the railroad's two premier trains, *The Broadway
Limited* and *The Congressional*, however, Deasy and his
colleagues envisioned something much more elaborate.
They took inspiration from the design philosophy of
Walter Chrysler, particularly the Chrysler Airflow automobile that was in development between 1932 and 1934. By
transferring those principles to railroad operations, they
suggested, the PRR could develop passenger trains that
featured a streamlined curvilinear profile, low wind resistance, and high speed. By January 1935, they had established
a Unit Train Committee, which included representatives
from Westinghouse, General Electric, Pullman, and Gibbs
& Hill. Raymond Loewy, who had already taken credit
for the redesign of the GG1, was also involved in the project. By March, the PRR had signed Loewy to an exclusive
contract, in which he agreed to work for no other railroad
and in which the PRR pledged to use no other industrial

Beginning in 1935, Raymond Loewy and PRR personnel developed proposals for streamlined trains, mimicking the Union Pacific M-10000 and the Burlington *Zephyr*. One version, headed by a stylish new electric locomotive, would speed passengers between New York and Washington. While they were eye-catching and modern, unit trains were ill-suited for the operating characteristics associated with the PRR's passenger service. *Pennsylvania Railroad Negative Collection, Hagley Museum & Library, acc. 1993.300.*

designer. Mimicking the basic concept of the M-10000 and the *Zephyr*, representatives of the Unit Train Committee developed plans for two articulated streamliners featuring lightweight bodies fabricated from aluminum. A fourteen-car trainset, operating as *The Congressional*, would cover the route between New York and Washington in as little as three hours, pulled by a newly designed electric locomotive. The other, thirteen-car train would provide overnight service between New York and Chicago. In January 1936, after a year of effort, the Unit Train Committee permitted a select group of Philadelphia civic leaders to see the drawings for the cars that might someday carry them to Washington or New York. As a cost-cutting measure, PRR officials had substituted a GG1 for the custom-built locomotives they had originally envisioned, but their efforts nonetheless embodied a significant departure from past practice.[56]

Despite the potential embodied in the M-10000 and the *Zephyr*, those involved in the unit-train project began to recognize the disadvantages associated with articulated trainsets. Both trains operated over long routes with few intermediate stops and little passenger traffic—operating characteristics vastly different from the busy PRR route between New York and Washington. When Clement assumed the presidency in April 1935, he suggested that the *Zephyr* and its imitators reflected the "most misunderstood situation" in the field of railroading. While appropriate for carriers with "thin service" that would "never even think of electrifying," he asserted, they were clearly inappropriate for a company with a high ratio of passenger miles to mile of line. In an August 1936 memo, Vice President Charles D. Young made a similar point. "I am afraid I did not make it clear to you two gentlemen what I was driving at insofar as the Western lines are concerned," he chided Deasy and Franklin, and he reminded them "that they are making a 'show' of running relatively few trains." Moreover, because all the cars in a unit train were permanently coupled together, even a minor defect in one car could sideline an entire train. Nor were they interchangeable with conventional passenger equipment, making it impossible to increase or decrease the length of the train to accommodate fluctuating passenger levels. The situation would be particularly problematic in the case of the New York–Chicago service, with its mix of sleeping and dining cars. Expense was also a factor. The members of the Unit Train

Committee concluded that the two train sets required for the route between New York and Washington would cost more than $1.4 million if built to the same articulated design as the M-10000 and the *Zephyr* but only half that amount if ordered as conventional equipment.[57] Finally, by 1936, the GG1 had demonstrated its ability to haul lengthy, and heavy, consists at high speeds, eliminating the need to employ aluminum in car construction.[58]

The New York Central, whose executives also sought to emulate the success of the M-10000 and the *Zephyr*, provided the PRR with an alternative to the unit-train concept. In July 1936, the NYC introduced the *Mercury* on a route between Cleveland and Detroit. The *Mercury* was sleek, modern, and stylish, and it featured largely cosmetic improvements to conventional passenger equipment rather than the unique designs employed by the Union Pacific and the Burlington. Additional *Mercury* trains followed in quick succession, one linking Detroit to Chicago and another connecting Detroit and Cincinnati. Each enhanced the NYC's dominance of the midwestern passenger market. The *Mercury* trains offered style as well as speed, thanks to the work of Henry Dreyfuss, Loewy's great rival in the field of railroad industrial design. Dreyfuss subsequently planned virtually every aspect of the new equipment, from the streamlined locomotives and the sleek and modern interiors to the souvenir tickets sold to each passenger.[59]

The popularity and favorable publicity associated with the New York Central's *Mercury* convinced PRR officials to dispense with the problematic unit-train concept. They sought instead to buy more conventional passenger cars for many of the railroad's premier trains. Clement and his subordinates were particularly concerned about articles that appeared in Chicago newspapers on August 12, 1936, announcing that the NYC had committed to upgrading the *Twentieth Century Limited*. To a far greater extent than the *Mercury*, that was a direct assault on the Pennsylvania Railroad and its flagship passenger train. "Our New York-Washington didn't bother them," Clement confided to his assistant, James R. Downes. "Their Chicago-Detroit bothers us little . . . but these are side shows." The *Century* and *The Broadway Limited* operated on identical schedules between New York and Chicago, in one of the great rivalries in the history of American railroading. The competition was largely for show, however, and the two companies coordinated many aspects of their passenger services. Preferring cooperation to confrontation, Clement conceded that "we both are going to have to step up between New York and Chicago and St. Louis" but that the "New York Central and P.R.R. should meet the situation alike. No sense in getting into a battle between New York and Chicago."[60]

In that cooperative spirit, the PRR, the NYC, and Pullman formed a joint committee to develop equipment designs for both trains. The relationship between the Pennsylvania Railroad and the New York Central was considerably more harmonious than the one between Pullman and the two railroads, however. As its name suggested, Pullman-Standard produced standard-design cars, irrespective of the railroad that hauled them. Standardization reduced construction costs and—because Pullman operated the cars under contract with various railroads—facilitated uniform national service under the Pullman brand. Although Pullman cooperated with the Union Pacific in the design of the M-10000, that trainset was distinctly unstandardized. As such, it raised the alarming possibility of an enormous variety of railroad-specific cars that would undermine efforts by Pullman executives to control production costs. The Burlington's *Zephyr* represented an even greater threat. Even though the *Zephyr* did not contain sleeping cars, Budd was nonetheless poised to challenge Pullman's monopoly of passenger-car production. Executives at both the PRR and the NYC were pleased with the newly competitive conditions, and they expressed satisfaction that they could now play one builder off against the other. "The Pullman Co. will have to play a square game with both roads," Clement informed his subordinates, "or be out."[61]

The challenge from the Budd Company came at a particularly unfortunate time for Pullman. The Great Depression reduced overall demand and convinced many penurious passengers to forgo the luxury of a berth in a sleeping car. Those who were sufficiently affluent to travel by Pullman increasingly demanded a private room rather than the open section that had been a staple of the sleeping car since the days of George Pullman and Webster Wagner. Pullman officials were slow to change their designs, in part because of the added manufacturing complexity associated with all-room cars and in part because open-section sleepers could carry half again as many fare-paying patrons. However, they could hardly argue with statistics that showed that 80 percent of sleeping-car passengers were willing to pay a premium for a lower berth rather than endure the cramped and windowless upper. The uneven demand erased any cost savings that open-section sleepers might have produced and convinced Pullman executives to offer more modern designs.[62]

The Pennsylvania Railroad and its Long Island Rail Road subsidiary also played a significant role in encouraging Pullman to replace the antiquated open-section sleepers with all-room cars. By the late 1920s, the rapid growth of suburban Long Island taxed the capacity of its namesake railroad, particularly during the morning and afternoon rush hours. The limited capacity of the platforms at Penn Station precluded the use of additional trains or longer trainsets, and the tunnels under the East River restricted the height of commuter equipment. LIRR officials looked with favor on a bi-level design developed by Albert E. Hutt in 1928. Shop forces in Altoona built a prototype car in 1932. It was only slightly taller than conventional equipment, but it seated an impressive 120 passengers and—thanks to the extensive use of aluminum components—weighed a mere thirty-six tons. The PRR built two additional cars for the LIRR, but they proved unpopular. The design required passengers to climb either up or down into small, four-person cubbyholes where they sat, face-to-face, with little legroom. The added capacity often went unused, as many female passengers in skirts refused to sit in the exposed upper level.[63]

Despite the limitations of the bi-level LIRR cars, Pullman engineers endeavored to modify Hutt's design. The result was the duplex sleeper, easily identifiable from the exterior by its two staggered rows of windows. On the inside, half of the rooms were located a few feet above the floor, permitting the end of the bed in one room to project under the corresponding berth in the adjacent compartment. Through that ingenious use of space, designers were able to replace open sections with almost the same number of individual rooms. As early as 1931, even before the LIRR cars entered service, Pullman rebuilt two sleeping cars into hybrids that featured duplex rooms at one end. The *Wanderer* and the *Voyager* spent the next year in service on the PRR and contributed to the design of two all-duplex sleepers, the *Eventide* and the *Nocturne*. All four were heavyweights, built using the same techniques that Pullman had employed since the early days of steel passenger-car construction.[64]

While Pullman was experimenting with duplex heavyweight sleepers, the company was also engaged in the development of lightweight cars. The *G. M. Pullman*—an aluminum car that weighed half as much as conventional equipment—made an appearance at the 1933 Century of Progress International Exposition in Chicago. It attracted favorable publicity, but Pullman officials were slow to implement large-scale production of lightweight cars. The M-10000, produced the following year, also made extensive use of aluminum, but it was an expensive material and in short supply. In 1933, however, US Steel developed Cor-Ten, a high-strength, rust-resistant alloy that provided

Pullman with an alternative to Budd's patented shot weld process.[65]

The trend toward private compartments coupled with the inauguration of lightweight construction offered Pullman the opportunity to fend off the challenges posed by the Budd Company. Pullman's strategy nonetheless depended on the company's ability to perpetuate its tradition of batch-produced, standard-design cars. By August 1936, the commitment of the Pennsylvania Railroad and the New York Central—the nation's two most important passenger carriers—to simultaneously reequip their prestige trains offered Pullman a superb opportunity to instill in the two competing railroads the virtues of standardization. That would not be an easy task, however, as executives from each company were determined to offer a unique experience to their patrons. PRR representatives were content with the customary Pullman practice of locating the bedrooms on the right side of the car, to minimize noise from passing trains. Their NYC counterparts, determined to maintain the marketing advantages associated with the so-called Water Level Route, insisted that the bedrooms be on the left so that passengers leaving New York could enjoy vistas over the Hudson River. Each railroad proposed different designs for lounge and observation cars. The competing artistic visions of Raymond Loewy and Henry Dreyfuss further impeded Pullman's efforts to achieve standardization. David A. Crawford, Pullman's president, insisted that the two designers be "restricted to color and fabrics and possibly other non-structural details, but under no circumstances to let Messrs. Dreyfuss and Levy [sic] get their shears to working on structural designs." Crawford had ample reason for concern, as full compliance with PRR and NYC demands could have increased production costs by as much as $20,000 per car.[66]

Nor could the two railroads agree on the types of sleeping cars they preferred. PRR personnel initially demanded a wide assortment of sleeping-car designs, including open-section and newer duplex-roomette sleepers.[67] Yet by the summer of 1937, Pullman had developed alternatives to each of those arrangements. The roomette offered greater

Facing, By the late 1930s, with short-haul passenger traffic dwindling rapidly, PRR executives increasingly focused on the needs of business and leisure travelers who were making overnight journeys. Those affluent customers demanded greater comfort and privacy, and Pullman's new all-room cars were in high demand. *Pennsylvania Railroad Negative Collection, Hagley Museum & Library, acc. 1993.300.*

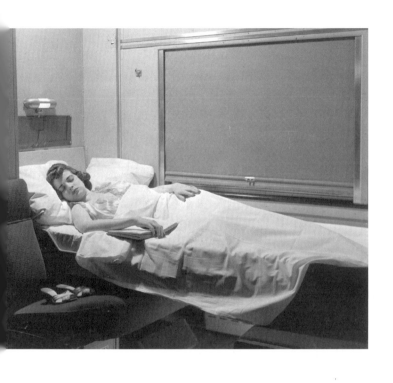

E.12960

The General, shown here passing through Gary, Indiana, in 1940, was second only to *The Broadway Limited* along the route between New York and Chicago. Both trains received modern streamlined equipment, part of the Fleet of Modernism, but at least half of the cars shown here were older, heavyweight equipment. *General Negative Collection, Railroad Museum of Pennsylvania, PHMC.*

interior space than the duplex, while avoiding the hazard and inconvenience facing passengers who had to climb up into their accommodations. Daniel Sheaffer, Deasy's assistant, offered a glowing review of the prototype roomette car and predicted that it would be a moneymaker for the railroad. With statistics showing that 82 percent of the upper berths on PRR trains were unoccupied (compared to 13 percent of the lower berths), dispensing with the open-section sleepers was not a difficult decision.[68]

The timing was propitious for the introduction of new lightweight equipment. Slowly improving economic conditions triggered an increase in the number of intercity passengers who traveled on the PRR, from 30.3 million in 1935 to 38.1 million in 1936. In 1937, 40.7 million people relied on the Pennsylvania Railroad for intercity travel, which exceeded every other year of the decade. Intercity passenger revenues likewise increased, from $55.2 million in 1935 to just under $63 million in 1936—an amount that would peak at $67.3 million the following year.[69]

On March 9, 1937, with signs of optimism abounding, the Pennsylvania Railroad and the New York Central issued a joint public announcement of their intent to buy new lightweight passenger equipment. Two weeks later, PRR and Pullman officials approved the production contract. Yet it was May before representatives from each railroad made a final determination of the quantity and the types of cars they would order. Both the PRR and the NYC requested the same number of lightweight cars—fifty-two—but their assignments would be quite different. The New York Central would have enough equipment to establish four daily sections of the *Twentieth Century Limited*, two in each direction. Clement and his staff faced a more difficult problem, however, in that many trains merited improvement. For all its prestige, *The Broadway Limited* had never enjoyed as much popularity as the *Century*. The PRR faced challenges on other fronts as well. In May 1937, the B&O assigned new diesel locomotives to its Washington–Chicago *Capitol Limited*, giving the train a faster schedule than the PRR's competing *Liberty Limited*. By using a mixture of new streamlined cars and rebuilt heavyweight equipment—styled by another designer, Otto Kuhler—the B&O introduced a modernized *Capitol* in November 1938, and the improved service further eroded the PRR's market share. The *"Spirit of St. Louis"* was holding its own against the NYC's *Southwestern Limited*, but there was nonetheless keen competition between the two railroads for passengers traveling between New York and St. Louis. The PRR's newest train, *The General*, would also benefit from improved equipment.[70]

Both the PRR's finances and limited production capacity at Pullman prevented the railroad from ordering enough lightweight equipment to fully reequip *The Broadway Limited*, *The Liberty Limited*, *The "Spirit of St. Louis,"* and *The General*. Instead, the railroad allocated its initial complement of fifty-two cars to all four trains. PRR officials collectively referred to them as the "Fleet of Modernism." The name contrasted with the NYC's "Great Steel Fleet." It also marked an effort to create a new image for the PRR's passenger service, temporarily supplanting—but never replacing—the "Blue Ribbon Fleet" designation in use since 1903. Despite the nomenclature, however, the Fleet of Modernism was not fully modern. The new consists included sixty distinctly unmodern heavyweight cars that typically received little more than a new paint scheme.[71] The mixture of equipment ensured that none of the trains presented the uniform appearance of the *Twentieth Century Limited*. As the PRR's premier train, the two sections of *The Broadway Limited* received eight eighteen-roomette sleepers (named for on-line cities); two midtrain lounge cars; two end-of-train observation cars; four four-double-bedroom, four-compartment, two-drawing-room sleepers; and two thirteen-double-bedroom sleepers. Yet the train still featured a heavyweight diner, baggage car, and Railway Post Office car—whose presence attested to the need to earn additional revenue that would offset paltry ridership figures. The other three trains made do with a few new lightweight sleepers and observation cars, heavyweight diners, and some older sleeping cars as well.[72]

By the summer of 1938, the Pennsylvania Railroad was ready to launch the Fleet of Modernism. The *City of New York*, an eighteen-roomette sleeper, was the first of the new cars to arrive from Pullman, on March 15, and the remainder of the equipment followed in quick succession. In early June, following a series of short excursion trips, the reequipped *Broadway Limited* went on display in Philadelphia, New York, and Chicago. More than forty-nine thousand curious spectators examined the train, while a further twenty-eight thousand saw *The "Spirit of St. Louis"* in Indianapolis, Dayton, and St. Louis, or *The Liberty Limited* in Washington or Baltimore. At 4:40 on the afternoon of June 15, Francis McCoy, the wife of army general Frank R. McCoy, christened *The General* at Penn Station. Less than two hours later, the granddaughter of former governor Alfred E. Smith performed the same ceremony with *The Broadway Limited*. The National Broadcasting Company carried the festivities live, including speeches by

railroad officials and performances by the New York Naval Militia Band, the PRR's Keystone Quartette, and the Singing Redcaps. Next out was *The "Spirit of St. Louis,"* sent on its way by a descendant of Stephanus Van Cortlandt, the first mayor of New York City to be born in the colonies. Farther south, at Washington Union Station, Elizabeth Farley, the wife of the postmaster general, sent *The Liberty Limited* on its way to Baltimore and Chicago. Similar ceremonies were taking place in Chicago and St. Louis, as the eastbound trains began their journeys. Celebrations were also underway at Grand Central Terminal, where the New York Central's modernized *Twentieth Century Limited* began its inaugural trip to Chicago, on the same accelerated sixteen-hour schedule as *The Broadway*.[73]

Raymond Loewy excelled in his efforts to transform the Fleet of Modernism into an Art Deco masterpiece on wheels. The insistence of Pullman executives on standardization, combined with simple engineering pragmatism, ensured that the designer could do little to alter the look of the various sleeping cars. Instead, he devoted his attention to the public areas of each train. Loewy, who wanted to avoid the tubular, tunnel-like effect so common in passenger equipment, used curved interior walls and variations in color to break each car into smaller, more intimate spaces. Modern hues, such as café au lait, two-tone burgundy, pastel blue, and lemon yellow, graced the dining cars. Everything bore Loewy's touch, from the menus to the tablecloths and silverware and even the tan jackets and burgundy pants worn by the waiters. The lounge car, also distinguished by its clean lines, boasted gray-green leather, dusty pink and copper lacquer ceilings, blue Formica tables, and gold fabric window panels. Indirect lighting and piped-in music produced a soothing ambiance. Outside, the cars were resplendent in a two-tone red paint scheme accentuated with pinstripes and simplified Futura lettering, imposing a uniformity that disguised the varied origins of each consist.[74] At the head end, on the inaugural eastbound run at least, was K4s Pacific #3768, sporting a streamlined shroud that Loewy had designed in 1936.[75]

Neither Loewy's designs nor the trains themselves were free of problems, however. Waiters on *The Broadway Limited* disliked the small tables that Loewy provided for the rebuilt dining cars, and passengers objected to the extensive windowless areas in the lounges. The side skirting on the streamlined K4s Pacific #3768 impeded PRR employees who were attempting to service or repair the locomotive. In 1940 and 1941, when shop forces streamlined four more Pacifics, #1120, #2665, #3678, and #5338, they installed smaller cowlings that detracted from Loewy's original vision but permitted access to the running gear.

A retouched publicity photo depicted *The Broadway Limited* as it existed in Raymond Loewy's vision rather than in reality. Streamlined K4s Pacific #3768 would more likely be encountered along the route to St. Louis, as the longer run ensured that the locomotive would be visible during a greater number of daylight hours. Even the prestigious *Broadway* did not initially merit a full complement of lightweight, streamlined cars in the striking Fleet of Modernism scheme, and the Railway Post Office car—necessary to augment the train's revenues—is nowhere to be seen. *Pennsylvania Railroad Negative Collection, Hagley Museum & Library, acc. 1993.300.*

Even then, the restyled locomotives rarely appeared on *The Broadway Limited*, and the train typically relied on more conventional, unstreamlined versions of the K4s.[76]

The more pervasive difficulty was that the new *Broadway Limited* failed to satisfy the traveling needs of the public or to draw sufficient passengers away from the New York Central. The PRR's premier train was by far the least successful contender in the Fleet of Modernism. In July 1939, *The General* grossed $3.87 per train mile; *The Liberty Limited*, $2.53; *The "Spirit of St. Louis," *$2.47; and *The Broadway Limited*—a mere $0.67. The new cars did not help the bottom line, as the train's gross revenue per train mile fell from $1.10 in 1936 to only $0.85 in 1939. Whereas the westbound *Twentieth Century Limited* carried an average of 71.4 passengers per trip, the westbound *Broadway* averaged only 16.3. On August 5, *The Broadway* left New York without any passengers, with the only revenue generated by two presumably well cared for, if lonely, travelers who boarded the train in North Philadelphia.[77]

The PRR's flagship train presented a clear example of the waste and needless expense that the National Transportation Committee identified in its February 1933 report to President Herbert Hoover. "The public is familiar with the spectacle of 'crack' passenger trains shuttling back and forth across the county empty or nearly so," the committee members observed, and they suggested that "empty trains should either be filled by reduced rates or taken out of service." Some PRR officials agreed with that assessment, particularly after the reequipping of *The Broadway*

Limited failed to produce satisfactory results. The train's survival depended less on profitability than on public relations and a desire to maintain parity with the New York Central. "If the Pennsylvania would discontinue the *Broadway*," emphasized Western Region vice president Horace E. Newcomet, "the Pennsylvania would immediately be recognized as being in the same class as the Erie and the B&O."[78]

The dismal financial performance of *The Broadway Limited* contrasted with the success of a new concept in train travel. In the summer of 1935, the Union Pacific introduced the *Challenger*, providing service between Chicago and the West Coast. The *Challenger* offered coach and budget sleeper accommodations, low-cost meals, and interiors designed to appeal to female passengers. Travelers enjoyed a taste of style and luxury without the expense of prestige trains such as the *City of San Francisco*, and one journalist dubbed the *Challenger* "Everybody's Limited." It was a winning combination, and the *Challenger* soon became one of the most heavily patronized trains on the Union Pacific. In November, the members of the PRR's Unit Train Committee contemplated a similar all-coach train, operating between New York and Chicago as a low-fare alternative to their proposal for an articulated *Broadway Limited*. The plan did not come to fruition, owing to the inauguration of the New York Central's *Mercury* and the subsequent efforts by both railroads to work with Pullman on the development of lightweight cars. The *Challenger* model had considerable merit, however, and it soon appeared on the PRR in a slightly different guise.[79]

In addition to paying close attention to the performance of the *Challenger*, Pennsylvania Railroad officials were familiar with other examples of low-cost travel. In February 1938, the Santa Fe matched the all-Pullman *Super Chief* with the all-coach *El Capitan*, an equally fast train between Chicago and Los Angeles. Closer to home, competition for wintertime traffic between the Northeast and Florida was almost as intense as the rivalry between the Pennsylvania Railroad and the New York Central. In December 1938, the Atlantic Coast Line inaugurated the *Vacationer*, a luxury all-coach New York–Florida train operating on PRR tracks as far south as Washington. Three months later, the Seaboard Air Line responded with the *Silver Meteor*, which featured such improvements as diesel locomotives and lightweight passenger equipment. The new trains typically catered to middle-class vacationers rather than business executives, and their popularity reflected the easing of the Great Depression and the pent-up desire for leisure travel.[80]

By the summer of 1939, both the PRR and the NYC were ready to introduce all-coach trains between New York and Chicago. The New York Central equipped its version, dubbed the *Pacemaker*, with conventional heavyweight equipment. The PRR lavished considerably more effort on its *Trail Blazer*. At Altoona, shop forces rebuilt P70 coaches with clean interior lines, individual reclining seats, sealed windows, and air-conditioning. Two of the cars became round-end observations that featured Loewy's distinctive style, albeit with more austerity than on *The Broadway Limited*. Passengers enjoyed seventy-five-cent dinners and fifty-cent breakfasts that even frugal middle-class travelers could afford. Pennsylvania Railroad officials studied the twin-unit diners employed on the *Challenger* and elected to apply a similar design to *The Trail Blazer*.[81] On July 28, 1939, *The Trail Blazer* and the NYC's *Pacemaker* staged simultaneous departures from their respective Manhattan terminals. Their identical schedules permitted passengers to reach Chicago in seventeen hours and twenty-five minutes, almost as fast as *The Broadway* and the *Century*. In addition to its modernized equipment, the PRR's luxury coach train offered eastbound passengers something the NYC could not possibly match—the opportunity to continue past Penn Station, through the East River tunnels, and on to Long Island and the site of the New York World's Fair.[82]

The Trail Blazer was both popular and profitable. The all-coach streamliner carried an average of 524 passengers each day, more than fifteen times the patronage of *The Broadway Limited*. *The Broadway*'s anemic earnings of $0.67 per train mile paled in comparison to those of *The Trail Blazer*—$2.70 per train mile during its first year of operation, and $3.28 in its second. The capital cost of the two trains was virtually identical, and *The Trail Blazer* had lower above-the-rails operating costs than *The Broadway*, as it featured fewer frills and a smaller crew. In April 1941, based on the success of *The Trail Blazer*, the PRR inaugurated the all-coach *Jeffersonian* between New York and St. Louis. It featured similar amenities, including rebuilt equipment and an end-of-train observation lounge. As an added touch of class, the typical motive power for *The Jeffersonian*, with its long daylight run, was one of the semi-streamlined K4s Pacifics that rarely made an appearance on *The Broadway Limited*, a train that operated mostly in darkness.[83]

As the 1930s came to an end, the Pennsylvania Railroad was rapidly augmenting its passenger-car fleet, replacing obsolete heavyweight equipment as fast as resources would permit. The 1937 contract with Pullman gave the PRR the option of ordering up to two hundred lightweight cars by December 31, 1941. With many other railroads vying for new equipment, it was a fortunate provision. The earliest of the 1938 Fleet of Modernism cars had caught the fancy of Pittsburgh's leading bankers and industrialists, including US Steel executives and members of the Mellon family. They had little interest in riding on *The Broadway Limited*, as the train passed through their hometown in the middle of the night. Instead, they preferred *The Pittsburgher* from New York or *The Golden Triangle* from Chicago and demanded that those trains have modern equipment as well. In April 1938, even before the Fleet of Modernism entered service, the PRR ordered fifty additional sleeping cars from Pullman. Many were soon operating in Pittsburgh service. Nor did Pennsylvania Railroad officials limit their purchases to Pullman products. As part of the initial Fleet of Modernism order, the Budd Company supplied two stainless-steel diners, which were often assigned to *The Liberty Limited*. Loewy designed the interior of the #4501, while Paul Cret, Budd's design consultant, styled the #4500. The railroad placed additional dining car orders in 1939, ultimately purchasing five cars each from Budd, Pullman, and American Car & Foundry to compare their quality and reliability.[84]

Along the East Coast, the Pennsylvania Railroad was involved in the ongoing rivalry between the Atlantic Coast Line and the Seaboard Air Line. The February 1939 launch of the *Silver Meteor* propelled the Seaboard ahead of the ACL. Ten months later, Atlantic Coast Line officials responded with *The Champion*. The two trains were the first all-coach streamliners linking New York and Florida, and each employed diesel power south of Washington. Successful operation of the trains required cooperation between the Pennsylvania Railroad and the Seaboard, but the process was not always smooth. In 1938, when Seaboard officials were developing plans for the *Silver Meteor*, they prematurely announced that the seven-car train would run as a separate consist all the way to New York, to preserve the uniform appearance of the equipment. John Deasy, the PRR's vice president in charge of operations, saw little reason to assign a GG1 to such a short train, and he demanded that the *Silver Meteor* be attached to an existing Pennsylvania Railroad schedule, north of Washington.[85] The Florida service nonetheless proved so popular that within a few years both the *Silver Meteor* and *The Champion* were long enough to provide an adequate challenge for a GG1. PRR officials accordingly agreed to contribute to the equipment pool for each train. The orders gave Budd further business, beyond the two diners assigned to *The Liberty Limited*. In 1939 and 1940, Budd completed thirty

coaches for the PRR, and many of them helped to satisfy the burgeoning wintertime demand for travel to Florida. They included three cars that matched the stainless-steel exteriors of the *Silver Meteor*, with several others assigned to *The Champion*.[86]

The market for Chicago–Florida service was much less robust, in part because the trains linking the two areas attained much lower average speeds than *The Champion* or the *Silver Meteor*.[87] In April 1940, representatives from the PRR, the New York Central, the Illinois Central, and the Chicago & Eastern Illinois—the four railroads linking Chicago to the South—discussed the development of a new streamlined all-coach train to Florida. NYC officials doubted that it would be possible to duplicate the success of *The Champion* and the *Silver Meteor*, and they declined to participate in the cooperative venture. The remaining three companies began negotiations with six southern railroads to develop three new streamliners that would follow different routes between Chicago and Florida, each operating every third day.[88] While PRR officials initially insisted on a late-afternoon departure from Chicago—to gather connecting passengers from other parts of the Midwest—they subsequently yielded to the Illinois Central's insistence that the trains leave Chicago in the morning.

In December 1940, the PRR launched *The South Wind*, in cooperation with the Louisville & Nashville, the Atlantic Coast Line, and the Florida East Coast. In contrast to the small number of cars contributed to *The Champion* and the *Silver Meteor*, the PRR owned the baggage-dormitory car, four coaches, the diner, and the buffet-lounge-observation that comprised the sole *South Wind* trainset. All the Budd-built cars were stainless steel but, in contrast to the two East Coast trains, were painted in Tuscan red Fleet of Modernism colors. Two of the streamlined K4s Pacifics, #1120 and #2665, painted in Brunswick green livery, provided the motive power. Loewy designed the interior of the train, with a soft gray background highlighted by burgundy, blue, and yellow accents. Raised plastic wall panels provided vignettes of Florida and other parts of the South. The southern practice of segregation was evident and affected Loewy's plans for the dining car. In April 1941, the US Supreme Court required railroads to afford African Americans equal access to first-class facilities and make at least a token effort to adhere to the terms of the 1896 *Plessy v. Ferguson* decision. While the ruling did not affect the PRR's operations in Illinois, representatives from the Louisville & Nashville asked that some provision be made for *The South Wind*'s African American passengers south of the Ohio River. PRR officials then instructed Loewy to design a chrome-plated rod and curtain that dining car crews (who were themselves African American) could use to screen African American patrons from White passengers.[89] *The South Wind* proved as popular as the PRR's other all-coach streamliners, generating a 78 percent increase in traffic over the previous year. While PRR officials initially planned to end wintertime service in March 1941, they continued operations into April and then announced that *The South Wind* would operate year-round. It was nonetheless difficult to determine whether the positive results stemmed from the improved equipment or from the increased economic prosperity that in turn stimulated discretionary travel.[90]

Despite the publicity surrounding the Fleet of Modernism, the vast majority of the PRR's passengers continued to travel in older and less luxurious equipment. The railroad still relied on more than a thousand of the P70 coaches that since the 1910s had formed the backbone of the company's operations. Wholesale replacement made little economic sense, but shop forces at Altoona upgraded hundreds of the cars to provide more comfortable accommodations and, in some cases, to better match the new lightweight equipment. Beginning in 1936, the PRR developed six experimental designs for rebuilding the P70, to establish the most appropriate model for a more comprehensive renovation program. Scheme 1 cars replaced the old walkover seats with those that rotated. The additional legroom and the provision of luggage racks reduced seating capacity from eighty passengers to sixty. Scheme 2 cars, while similar on the inside, featured wide picture windows. Scheme 3 cars were even more comfortable, with individually reclining seats and a total capacity of only forty-two passengers—less than half the number that some versions of the P70 had originally carried. The PRR ultimately adopted Scheme 6 as the prototype for future rebuilds. The cars were not identical, however, and they displayed considerable variance in the size and location of windows and the number of seats. Some retained their original clearstory roofs, even though the provision of air-conditioning rendered that ventilation feature unnecessary. Others received arch roofs that mimicked but did not precisely match the contours of the new lightweight equipment. The P70 rebuilds assigned to short-distance and commuter service generally conformed to the as-built pattern of two vestibules per car, while those on long-distance routes sacrificed the vestibule at one end in favor of larger bathrooms, luggage storage, and more widely spaced seats. Wartime shortages of labor and materials brought the rebuilding program to a halt in the autumn of 1942, and conversions did not resume until the spring of 1948. By then, however, the arrival of new lightweight cars and the subsequent rapid decline of intercity passenger service reduced the importance of upgrades to older equipment.[91]

Although *The Broadway Limited* offered prestige without profits, Pennsylvania Railroad officials could be reasonably satisfied with the performance of their new and upgraded passenger equipment and service. The budget streamliners such as *The Trail Blazer* and *The Jeffersonian*, as well as the Florida trains, generated impressive gains in ridership and seemed to be winning passengers back to the rails. More conventional trains such as *The General* and *The "Spirit of St. Louis"* also produced healthy earnings. The new streamlined cars, Loewy's stylistic touches, and the PRR's publicity won praise from passengers, but those factors alone were not responsible for the increase in passenger traffic. By the late 1930s, the nation was on the road to economic recovery, and Depression-weary Americans were ready to travel by any means available. Some enjoyed the comforts of the Fleet of Modernism, but most preferred the bus or the automobile. Of the estimated 740,000 people from the New York region who visited Florida in 1940, fewer than one in seven arrived on a train. From the Midwest, the situation was even worse, as more than 94 percent went by highway. Under the circumstances, even the daily addition of a few hundred passengers to Pennsylvania Railroad trains did not make much of a difference. Nor were the amenities associated with the Fleet of Modernism likely to retain passenger loyalty unless the price was right—particularly when the vast majority of the PRR's clients did not travel by streamliner but rather in the more Spartan confines of an unadorned P70 coach. In July 1938, the Interstate Commerce Commission permitted the PRR and the other eastern carriers to raise coach fares from 2 cents to 2½ cents per mile. It was an experiment, to determine whether passenger earnings would increase. They did not. Ridership sank precipitously, perhaps owing to the lingering effects of the Roosevelt Recession, and revenues promptly fell by 14 percent. The decline offered a convincing demonstration that the nation's highways provided voyagers with alternatives to rail travel and that people were willing to sacrifice comfort in order to cut costs. Nor could passenger trains compete with the freedom of the open road, as motorists could readily choose how far to travel each day, when to stop for lunch, and where to spend the night.

Some PRR executives may have interpreted the rapid increase in rail passenger traffic during World War II as a continuation of the gains that the Fleet of Modernism had achieved a few years earlier. That was not the case, and the rapid erosion of rail travel after the war demonstrated that the Fleet of Modernism had been fighting a losing battle. In the near term, however, Clement and his subordinates sought to reduce the costs associated with passenger operations. In addition to the elimination of branch-line passenger trains, that agenda called for the curtailment of duplicate services on the main line. By combining multiple trains that operated along the same route, it would be possible to accommodate the same number of passengers with fewer crews and less disruption to freight operations. Despite the addition of a small number of lightweight passenger cars, the reliance on longer consists further increased train weight, requiring the use of additional locomotives and threatening the railroad's ability to adhere to scheduled running times. Even the newest of the K4s locomotives represented technology from an earlier era, ill-suited for changed operating conditions. With electrification west of Harrisburg no longer a realistic option, Pennsylvania Railroad executives acknowledged the need for new motive power. Given the skills of the PRR's mechanical engineers and the success attained by the Motive Power Department, it seemed obvious that the next generation of locomotives should be designed and built at Altoona. By the middle years of the 1930s, however, personnel changes at the Pennsylvania Railroad, coupled with the rapid evolution of internal-combustion technology, ensured that that strategy was no longer tenable.[92]

The Need for New Motive Power

A series of events that took place between the spring of 1936 and the summer of 1937 largely dictated the development of motive power on the Pennsylvania Railroad over the following decade. For a quarter of a century, the K4s had been the reliable workhorse that powered passenger trains throughout the PRR system. It was an exemplary design, and during the 1930s, the railroad had plenty to spare. Yet the increased passenger traffic that accompanied the waning of the Great Depression taxed their abilities. Outside electrified territory, long, heavy passenger trains typically required the assignment of two locomotives, each with a separate crew. Double-heading increased operating expenses on the Western Region alone by nearly half a million dollars per year. The electrification of the main routes in the East, coupled with the success of the GG1, suggested that a single powerful locomotive could pull passenger trains at high speeds, shortening schedules and reducing crew costs. Since the 1910s, PRR executives had dreamed of extending electrified territory as far west as Pittsburgh, but the cost of eastern electrification, coupled with the severity of the Depression, put those plans on indefinite hold.

Beginning in 1936 and continuing through 1945, the PRR commissioned four electrification studies covering the territory as far west as Pittsburgh. None came to fruition, but in two ways they collectively shaped the decisions made by the personnel of the Motive Power Department. First, they assumed that the mountainous terrain between Harrisburg and Pittsburgh would eventually be converted to electric operation and that main line steam locomotives should be employed in that territory only as a stopgap measure. Second, they acknowledged that electrification on the comparatively straighter and flatter tracks that lay to the west of Pittsburgh was unlikely to occur soon, if ever. On the western lines, therefore, it was imperative to develop a new generation of steam passenger and freight locomotives that could match the performance of the GG1, maintaining fast schedules without double-heading.[93]

The PRR's program to develop powerful new passenger and freight locomotives, which began early in 1936, coincided with a shortage of talent in the Motive Power Department. To a greater extent than any other individual, Theodore N. Ely shaped the development of the PRR's locomotives during the late nineteenth and early twentieth centuries. His small-engine policy suggested that the PRR should avoid the cost and complexity associated with a large number of drivers and with new technologies such as compounding. Ely imparted that philosophy to his colleagues, at a time of remarkable continuity in the Motive Power Department. Between 1866 and 1936, three individuals successively occupied the role of mechanical engineer, taking charge of locomotive development on the Pennsylvania Railroad.[94] Each passed his skills and design philosophy to his follower, ensuring an unbroken tradition that was seldom seen on other railroads. Ely, his health broken by the stress of his job, left the PRR in 1911. Following the retirement of Axel Vogt in 1919 and the death of Alfred Gibbs three years later, chief of motive power James T. Wallis and mechanical engineer William F. Kiesel Jr. oversaw the development of new steam locomotives. They scored their greatest triumph with the 201 locomotives of the Class M1, first built in 1923, followed in 1930 by a further one hundred of the similar Class M1a. The M1 and the M1a coped admirably with the heavier and faster freight trains of the 1920s and early 1930s and even performed well in passenger service. Wallis and Kiesel lacked expertise in electrical matters, however—a circumstance that limited their role in the planning and implementation of the electrification between New York and Washington. In 1927, the ailing Wallis received a courtesy promotion to assistant vice president in charge of operations, and he died three years later at age sixty-two. Frederick Hankins became the new chief of motive power. Yet he often deferred to electrical engineer John Van Buren Duer, the matrilineal descendant of a former president, who played a critical role in the electrification project.[95] Duer became the PRR's chief electrical engineer in 1935, strengthening his alliance with John Deasy, the vice president in charge of operations since 1933.[96]

During the 1930s, Duer and his allies scored some significant triumphs of their own, most notably in the development of the GG1 electric locomotive. They hoped to apply their expertise to a massive expansion of the PRR's electric operations, but the Depression precluded that opportunity. Yet despite their eagerness to rid the Harrisburg–Pittsburgh main line of steam locomotives, they had little use for diesels either. Diesels, in their primitive state of development, could not yet match the horsepower produced by even the smallest of the PRR's main line steam locomotives—and Duer was convinced that they never would. The best alternative to electrification, he insisted, would be to develop large steam locomotives that could match or exceed the pulling power of the GG1. Duer's plans therefore represented a significant departure from the PRR's long tradition of designing and operating smaller locomotives, a policy that Ely, Vogt, and Gibbs had perfected and that Wallis and Kiesel had continued.[97]

Given Deasy's support of his protégé, few individuals were able to resist Duer's influence over motive-power development. Kiesel was set to retire in October 1936, at age seventy. The next most senior official in the Motive Power Department was Harry A. Hoke, who had joined the PRR in 1898. He earned a promotion to assistant mechanical engineer in 1919 and held several patents for improvements to steam locomotives, yet he remained primarily a draftsman who lacked conceptual design experience. In early 1936, and in anticipation of Kiesel's retirement, Warren R. Elsey joined the Motive Power Department. Since early 1929, Elsey had been the PRR's supervisor of floating equipment, overseeing maritime operations in locations such as New York Harbor and Chesapeake Bay. Those duties had little in common with the design and construction of steam locomotives, and he had much to learn. When Elsey replaced Kiesel as mechanical engineer on October 1, one of his first acts was to move the mechanical engineer's office from Altoona to Philadelphia, to be near the chief of motive power and his staff. The relocation, part of a larger effort to recentralize staff functions following the 1925 corporate reorganization, caused considerable consternation in Altoona. It also provided Elsey

and his staff with more convenient access to electrified territory and brought them close to the Baldwin Locomotive Works—whose designers possessed the expertise that the PRR's depleted ranks now lacked. The following April, the PRR appointed Carleton K. Steins as the assistant chief of motive power, reporting to Hankins rather than Elsey. Unlike Elsey, Steins possessed considerable familiarity with steam-locomotive technology, and he was responsible for ensuring that the innovations developed by the Motive Power Department could function reliably under railroad operating conditions.[98]

Inroads

Even as Deasy, Duer, and other officials in the Motive Power Department continued to emphasize their commitment to steam locomotives, personnel at Electro-Motive were equally determined to eradicate that form of motive power from the American railroad landscape. Harold Hamilton had transformed EMC into the nation's dominant producer of self-propelled railcars. The company's products soon saturated the market, particularly as railroad executives were discontinuing lightly patronized branch-line passenger trains as quickly as possible. The Great Depression brought the production of railcars almost to a standstill. Even the backing of General Motors, the company that had owned both Electro-Motive and the Winton Engine Company since 1930, could not transform the railcar business into a viable long-term endeavor.

EMC personnel marketed main line diesel passenger locomotives, often emphasizing the same attributes—faster travel times, smoke-free operation, and favorable publicity—that had accompanied the introduction of the M-10000 and the *Zephyr*. EMC's chief engineer, Richard M. Dilworth, oversaw the development of a new locomotive that could pull a dozen or more conventional passenger cars. Dilworth attempted to match the performance of the 4-6-4 Hudson steam locomotives that could generate 3,600 horsepower at speed. He accordingly placed two of the 900-horsepower Winton Model 201A engines into each of two linked carbodies, identified as #511 and #512. Hamilton and Dilworth envisioned the #511 and #512 as a test bed for the development of a better passenger locomotive rather than as a production model. To gather performance data under a variety of operating conditions, they sent the locomotives on a nationwide demonstration tour in 1935 and 1936.[99]

In March 1936, the Pennsylvania Railroad tested the #511 and #512, largely as a favor to General Motors. "We were willing to give them the tests," one anonymous official told a reporter for the *Harrisburg News*, "but they had no significance to us." The *Johnstown Democrat* published a similar story, under the heading "Old Iron Horse in No Danger, P.R.R. Says." Despite the negative press, the forty-five Pennsylvania Railroad personnel who evaluated the diesels over a five-week period provided a balanced and not entirely unfavorable assessment of the #511 and #512. Martin. L. Trumpower, the road foreman of engines on the Middle Division, acknowledged that "she handled the train nicely." Francis M. Waring, the PRR's engineer of tests, conceded that when the locomotives were operating as intended, they could match or even exceed the performance of a K4s Pacific. Given that a single K4s was not sufficiently powerful to pull long passenger trains, however, the #511 and #512 offered few benefits in terms of additional horsepower. Moreover, the diesels often did not perform reliably, and several EMC employees were continually at work fixing the recalcitrant engines. Waring and his colleagues concluded that any diesels purchased by the PRR would impose additional labor costs in the form of onboard technicians. They also disliked the placement of the engine crew at the front of the locomotive, a consideration that emerged following the 1934 grade-crossing accident that killed an engineman riding in the front of a P5a boxcab electric. PRR officials also objected to the noise of the diesel engines and the odor of diesel fumes, particularly when the train was at a station.[100]

Waring's report on the performance of the #511 and #512, released at the end of April, did little to discourage EMC executives. EMC soon sold a single, 1,800-horsepower unit to the Baltimore & Ohio and two more to the Santa Fe. The Burlington also purchased two, two-unit sets, with stainless-steel shrouding disguising their boxcab appearance. Buoyed by the potential for additional orders, GM and Electro-Motive officials planned a massive new manufacturing facility in La Grange, Illinois, one that was dedicated solely to the production of diesel locomotives. Dilworth and his colleagues also prepared a new generation of diesel passenger locomotives, based on the lessons they had learned from the #511 and #512. The first of the E-units, classed as the EA and EB, still employed the Winton Model 201A engine, but they featured a streamlined appearance and an upward-slanting, shovel nose that offered enhanced protection for train crews.[101] Already established on the Union Pacific and the Burlington, EMC extended its reach to the principal route between Chicago and Los Angeles. On May 12, two EMC locomotives, virtually identical to the #511 and #512, inaugurated service on the Santa Fe's prestige train, the *Super Chief*.[102]

A month later Fred Hankins received an audacious proposal from Paul Turner, who was serving as EMC's Eastern Region sales manager. If diesels could power the *Super Chief*, Turner emphasized, then they could certainly head the PRR's *Broadway Limited* between Paoli (then the westernmost point of electrification) and Chicago. Whether through professional curiosity or out of respect for GM's role as a shipper, Hankins provided Turner with grade profiles and other information. In late September, Turner suggested that a pair of the new EMC diesels could cut the running time for *The Broadway Limited* by as much as ninety minutes. Based on further discussions with Hankins and Duer, Turner soon expanded the offer, promising similar reductions in the travel time for *The "Spirit of St. Louis."* The proposal took full advantage of the public relations potential associated with diesels and included artist's renderings for a pair of E-units painted in a vibrant new green-and-white Pennsylvania Railroad color scheme.[103]

While PRR officials gave serious consideration to the EMC proposals, they did not consider diesels to be a viable alternative to steam power. Warren Elsey acknowledged that Turner's suggested running times for *The "Spirit of St. Louis"* were feasible but questioned those for *The Broadway Limited*. Duer doubted that the 3,600 horsepower produced by two E-series locomotives would be adequate for *The Broadway*, much less the longer trains that constituted the bulk of the PRR's long-distance passenger service. Adding a third E-unit, combined with the need to establish dedicated fueling and maintenance facilities, was certain to push the capital cost of diesels beyond that of comparable steam locomotives, he concluded.[104]

By the mid-1930s, however, an increasing number of executives on other railroads were willing to consider diesels as their motive power of choice. Diesel passenger locomotives, such as those that powered the *Super Chief* and the *City of San Francisco*, were still rare. Yet they provided the railroads that purchased them with an advertising and public-relations bonanza—particularly when combined with lightweight, streamlined passenger cars. When a railroad had purchased even a single diesel passenger locomotive, it would have to create the entire support network associated with dieselization, from fueling stations to machine shops to training programs and inspection regimens. Once established, that support system would substantially reduce the marginal cost associated with the acquisition of additional diesels. Representatives from Electro-Motive were eager to provide the necessary instruction, confident that those employees could then pass their skills on to others.

Top, Small but of enormous significance, the #3908 was the first production-model diesel locomotive acquired by the Pennsylvania Railroad. The Electro-Motive Model SW, delivered in the summer of 1937, demonstrated greater efficiency and reliability than steam shifters. Shown here at Linden, New Jersey, in 1938, it was the opening wedge in the slow dieselization of the entire railroad. *General Negative Collection, Railroad Museum of Pennsylvania, PHMC.*

Above, Baldwin's Model VO-660 and more powerful Model VO-1000 were among that company's first mass-produced diesel switchers. The PRR owned examples of each, including this VO-1000 (PRR Class BS-10), delivered in September 1943. Orders for the marginally successful Baldwin units demonstrated the willingness of PRR officials to support a longtime supplier, customer, and partner in steam-locomotive design. *Pennsylvania Railroad Negative Collection, Hagley Museum & Library, acc. 1993.300.*

Electro-Motive sales representatives such as Paul Turner also perceived a lucrative market for diesel switchers, which were ideally suited for the slow-speed movement of cars in freight yards.[105] Many companies had developed diesel- or gasoline-powered switchers in response to New York's 1923 Kaufman Act and other municipal smoke-abatement ordinances. Those locomotives—including the PRR's home-built Class A6—offered little better than mediocre performance, but they encouraged incremental improvements in switcher designs. By May 1936, when EMC's new La Grange plant began production, the company was ready with the Model SC. Equipped with a 600-horsepower Winton 201A engine, the SC and similar Model SW were well suited to yard switching, and EMC sold more than a hundred to various railroads.[106]

The PRR began the dieselization of shifting service with the purchase—albeit reluctantly—of a single Model SW. In March 1937, the PRR tested an SW in Chicago, and the vice president of the Western Region acknowledged that the locomotive offered a potential replacement for steam shifters—and not merely in those areas subject to smoke-abatement ordinances. Yet his superiors acted only when subjected to pressure from a major customer. In 1937, General Motors opened a new automobile assembly plant in Linden, New Jersey, adjacent to the New York–Philadelphia main line. GM officials barred steam locomotives from the facility, inducing the PRR to test one of their A6 locomotives as well as a borrowed Fairbanks-Morse diesel. Representatives from the automaker found fault with both units and instead recommended an SW demonstrator manufactured by their EMC subsidiary. With the Linden plant generating seventy carloads per day, there was little doubt that chief of motive power Fred Hankins would accept the advice. When it entered service on June 24, the SW demonstrated that it could handle as many cars as a steam shifter, but at significantly lower operating costs. Within a few months, optimistic EMC salesmen provided the PRR with a proposal to dieselize all the remaining steam-powered shifting operations in the New York Zone, but the railroad's management showed little interest. A similar study demonstrated that diesels could generate substantial reductions in operating costs at two freight yards in Philadelphia but likewise produced no changes in motive power.[107]

Managerial resistance to diesel switchers continued for five more years. Even those few individuals who favored the new technology needed to be cautious, lest they risk their careers by antagonizing senior executives who would not admit that a lifetime of experience with steam locomotives had become irrelevant. Further evaluation of diesel switchers largely reflected the desire of PRR executives to support the lackluster research-and-development program that was taking place at Baldwin. Those two companies maintained a long history of collaboration in steam-locomotive production, so it was hardly surprising that the Philadelphia-based builder would receive the courtesy of a trial run. The close personal and professional relationship between Charles D. Young, the PRR's vice president of purchases, stores, and insurance, and Charles E. Brinley, president of Baldwin, doubtless contributed to the decision as well. In 1940, Young offered to test a Baldwin diesel switcher, as a favor to Brinley. Hankins arranged the demonstration, but without much enthusiasm. "It should be made clear to him from the start," he told Young, "that we are not in the market for a Diesel switcher at this time." In any event, the Baldwin locomotive performed poorly and did little to encourage Hankins to consider the acquisition of additional diesels. The lack of interest stemmed in part from an abundance of steam shifters—including more than sixty mothballed H9s Consolidations in the New York Zone. EMC's Paul Turner, repeatedly frustrated in his efforts to sell diesels to the PRR, asserted that the railroad's organizational culture was hostile to the new form of motive power, irrespective of the economic issues involved. During the Philadelphia dieselization study, at least one PRR official was receptive to the new technology—and Turner observed that "this mechanical officer has not benefited from his advocacy of Diesel switchers."[108]

Resistance

As the 1930s ended, the affluent could travel from California to Chicago behind diesel locomotives, either on the Santa Fe's *Super Chief* or the Union Pacific's *City of San Francisco*. Continuing east on *The Broadway Limited*, they would have seen little evidence that anyone associated with the Pennsylvania Railroad possessed an interest in dieselization. Of the more than four thousand locomotives owned by the PRR, just four generated their power through internal combustion. Three tiny Class A6 models toiled in relative obscurity, one at a small harbor-side facility in Manhattan, a second in Brooklyn, and a third in Philadelphia. They were there only because public-policy initiatives and unusual operating conditions precluded the use of steam shifters. The PRR's sole Model SW switcher moved cars at Linden, at the behest of General Motors and its Electro-Motive subsidiary.

Pennsylvania Railroad officials had good reason to avoid diesel locomotives. In common with Pocahontas lines such as the Norfolk & Western and the Chesapeake

& Ohio, the PRR generated a significant share of its revenues from a commodity that was instrumental to the generation of steam power. The Pennsylvania Railroad transported more than eighty-five million tons of coal in 1930. A decade later, the amount had declined to seventy-six million tons, but that nonetheless represented more than 43 percent of total traffic. Petroleum products, in their myriad forms, accounted for little more than 2 percent of the railroad's business in 1940. Railroads were significant users as well as transporters of coal, and nearly a quarter of the nation's bituminous output went to fuel railroad locomotives. With so many steam locomotives in operation, the Pennsylvania Railroad burned more coal than any other company in the United States, consuming 3.5 percent of American bituminous production. In 1940, the company bought more than $19.3 million worth of coal.[109] On an average day in 1945, the railroad's steam locomotives consumed nearly sixty thousand tons of coal, enough to fill 945 hopper cars. It made sense for the PRR to burn coal. The railroad served numerous bituminous mines in western Pennsylvania, providing ready access to a commodity that was inexpensive and, according to most experts, inexhaustible.[110]

Executives from coal companies expressed concern that dieselization would create a catastrophic decline in sales to the railroads.[111] "The effect on the coal industry of a general conversion by the railways to Diesel operation would be extremely serious," PRR officials observed, while highlighting "the bitter opposition of the coal industry to the Dieselization that has already taken place." Pennsylvania Railroad executives acknowledged that the wholesale replacement of steam locomotives "would unquestionably shut down many mines on our line, and result in the loss of substantial tonnage of revenue coal traffic." The owners of those mines enjoyed close relationships with Pennsylvania Railroad traffic and operating personnel and were quick to remind them that they could ship their coal by whichever railroad showed the greatest loyalty to steam.[112]

The importance of coal traffic was nonetheless a relatively minor factor influencing the decision to develop new steam locomotives while simultaneously avoiding the purchase of diesels. In their internal correspondence, PRR executives only rarely suggested that continued reliance on steam power was necessary to secure the loyalty of on-line coal producers. The symbiotic relationship between the railroad and the collieries might nonetheless have been so deeply ingrained in the corporate culture of the PRR that it scarcely needed mentioning.[113]

Duer and his subordinates in the Motive Power Department possessed some powerful incentives to reject diesels,

motives that had little to do with the protection of the coal industry. Since 1866, the Pennsylvania Railroad had built thousands of steam locomotives at Altoona. For three-quarters of a century, PRR officials possessed almost complete control over locomotive development. In that context, diesels represented a radically different form of motive power that threatened the technical expertise of seasoned veterans in the Motive Power Department. They also challenged the organizational prerogatives of those individuals, transforming them from designers of unique steam locomotives to buyers of standardized diesels that had been developed outside the company, with minimal input from the PRR's motive-power experts. While personnel at Altoona explored the possibility of manufacturing diesels at Altoona, they quickly confronted the limits of their expertise as well as the refusal of outside suppliers to share their proprietary information.[114]

Under the circumstances, and acting in self-defense, the PRR's mechanical engineers occasionally suggested that diesels might alienate coal producers. More commonly, they adhered to their commitment to using a single locomotive to pull heavy trains—and they noted that an individual diesel could not match the power of one modern steam locomotive. They were also correct in their assertion that the initial purchase price of diesels was significantly higher than that of steam, on a dollar-per-horsepower basis. That was an argument likely to find favor with the railroad's accountants as well. At conferences and other professional meetings, PRR officials routinely encountered counterparts on other railroads who shared their misgivings about diesels. Through journals and formal proceedings, as well as through informal conversations, they shared their concerns that diesels threatened to undermine their authority within their respective companies. They were certainly aware that representatives from coal companies were equally wary of diesels, although for somewhat different reasons. In that context, PRR personnel could likely find support from both colleagues and customers as they defended steam locomotives.[115]

The Duplex Revolution

Unfortunately for Turner, Dilworth, and other Electro-Motive personnel, their plans to sell passenger diesels to the Pennsylvania Railroad coincided with a concerted effort by the Motive Power Department to develop a new generation of steam locomotives that would be capable of pulling passenger trains at high speed and with greater efficiency. Thanks to the loss of talent that culminated with William Kiesel's retirement in October 1936, PRR officials were incapable of doing so on their own. The limited expertise of the PRR's Motive Power Department personnel suggested that the railroad should turn to Baldwin, its longtime outside supplier, for advice. Yet Baldwin was also experiencing difficulties. During the 1920s, under the direction of President Samuel Vauclain, the company had expanded its manufacturing facility at Eddystone, Pennsylvania, south of Center-City Philadelphia. The project was completed in 1928. Even before the Great Depression induced a sharp decline in business, Baldwin's sales were decreasing—from 843 locomotives in 1926 to 655 in 1927, with a commensurate reduction in earnings on investment. During the summer of 1927, Charles and Frederick Fisher—whose Fisher Body Corporation was part of the General Motors empire—gained control of Baldwin in a bitterly fought battle against Vauclain and other longtime managers. In March 1929, George H. Houston, an associate of the Fisher brothers, became president of the company, with Vauclain relegated to a ceremonial role in the company he had once controlled.[116] Baldwin then invested heavily in the development of internal-combustion locomotives, in cooperation with Westinghouse. They did not sell well, reinforcing the aversion of longtime Baldwin employees to diesels. Even more disheartening was the PRR's 1934 decision to select the GG1 rather than the R1 design developed by Baldwin and Westinghouse as its preferred electric locomotive. Baldwin declared bankruptcy in February 1935, a year before PRR officials began planning a new generation of steam locomotives. For the next three and a half years, Baldwin faced a leadership crisis, with disgruntled investors demanding the removal of all senior management and insisting that the company commit to diesel-locomotive production.[117]

Embattled Baldwin executives fought back, defending their managerial prerogatives and disparaging diesel-locomotive technology. In June 1930, the same month that General Motors acquired control of the Electro-Motive Company, board chairman Samuel Vauclain provided the members of the Mechanical Division of the American Railway Association with a nostalgic retrospective on the development of the steam locomotive. He considered "this benefactor of mankind" the "greatest of all human devices," and asserted that "wherever it has gone it has promoted prosperity and carried civilization into lands at all corners of the earth." Vauclain acknowledged that the development of the diesel locomotive "is progressing well." Yet he also asserted "that we are just beginning to realize what actually can be done with the steam engine in the way of continuous performance, economical performance,

and reduction in maintenance." Those were precisely the performance characteristics where diesels excelled, and Vauclain was extraordinarily optimistic in his belief that the further development of steam locomotives could keep pace with rapid improvements in their internal-combustion counterparts. Even less credible was his prediction that the steam locomotive "can be more ably discussed in the year 1980 than it will be at this convention in 1930."[118]

Vauclain was not alone in his determination to perpetuate the reign of the steam locomotive. In April 1935, Baldwin vice president Robert S. Binkerd invoked the biblical verse "Muzzle not the Ox that Treadeth out the Corn" (1 Corinthians 9:9), asserting that railroad executives should remain loyal to the steam locomotives that had served them so well for so many years. "It was not so long ago," Binkerd informed his audience at the New York Railroad Club, "that the movie magnates thought it would be a good thing to interest the movie public in the personal lives of the movie stars. And that was all very well for a while, until finally they woke up and found this public trying to dictate what the lives of those stars should be." He suggested that the news media had similarly created a public infatuation with modern trains such as the M-10000 and the *Zephyr*. "The impressions which are being produced today are going to become the public demands of tomorrow," Binkerd warned. Injudicious experiments with diesels, he asserted, would doubtless lead to expectations that the new form of motive power could not possibly meet.[119]

One after the other, Binkerd attempted to demolish the claims made by Hamilton, Turner, and other advocates of dieselization. Ostensibly modern diesels, Binkerd demonstrated, could not match the speed developed by a 4-4-2 Atlantic steam locomotive built in 1896. "The field of probable profitable application of the Diesel locomotive is pretty generally indicated at work speeds not exceeding 10 miles an hour," he concluded. The development of Super Power technology, beginning in the second half of the 1920s, ensured that modern steam locomotives were considerably faster and more powerful than their predecessors. The price of oil was likely to increase substantially, he predicted, and steadily increasing maintenance costs would soon make diesels more expensive to operate than steam locomotives. "Whenever you set out to study the economy of installing Diesels," Binkerd concluded, "the greatest safeguard that you can have is to first set up what modern properly designed steam power will do in operation." Baldwin, a company with minimal organizational capabilities associated with diesel technology, was well prepared to supply that modern steam power, Binkerd emphasized. Many of the railroad executives in the audience were responsible for locomotive purchases, operations, and maintenance, and they listened with incredulity as Binkerd warned them that "there is danger in the ideas which are being put in the public mind today. . . . This is dangerous to the railroads because the false impressions of today will become the demands of tomorrow, coupled with a requirement of capital investment on which our railroads will not earn a return." Binkerd was in effect asserting that Baldwin's customers should absolve his company of any responsibility to produce the type of motive power that many Americans demanded—and that an increasing number of railroad executives supported. Within a few years, events proved that Binkerd had erred in every one of his predictions. At that moment, however, many railroaders thought his unflagging loyalty to steam locomotives to be misguided, and more than a few wondered if he had taken leave of his senses.[120]

Pennsylvania Railroad executives did not share Binkerd's intense and unyielding opposition to diesels, but their ongoing ties to Baldwin reinforced their suspicions regarding the new technology. They concluded that diesel locomotives could not yet—and might never—provide the power and speed they considered essential. As such, they were caught in an unfortunate moment of history, ready to replace their outdated steam locomotives with the latest developments in Super Power technology, only a few years before diesels proved their worth in all aspects of railroad operations. Their limited expertise and their willingness to abandon the small-engine philosophy that Theodore Ely had developed also made them particularly susceptible to recommendations made by Baldwin personnel.

Planning for the PRR's new generation of steam locomotives began in May 1936, when Deasy told Fred Hankins, the chief of motive power, to develop "a fast passenger steam engine of even greater capacity than now established." Hankins in turn formed a committee that included Kiesel, Duer, Elsey, and Thomas W. Demarest, the general superintendent of motive power for the Western Region. Demarest, like Kiesel, was nearing retirement, but his presence on the committee attested to the locomotive's intended use on the flat, straight track through Ohio and Indiana. Harry Glaenzer, Baldwin's vice president in charge of engineering, provided additional expertise.[121] Their first formal meeting took place on June 4, eight days before Paul Turner submitted his initial proposal to dieselize The Broadway Limited. Had Turner been able to attend that gathering of PRR and Baldwin officials, he would have

doubted his chances of selling any diesels to the Pennsylvania Railroad. Determined to match the abilities of the GG1 that had proven its worth in electrified territory, the PRR representatives on the committee developed a list of performance criteria that was both short and ambitious. To avoid undue stress on the track, the weight would be restricted to no more than sixty thousand pounds per axle. The locomotive would also have to pull a fifteen-car passenger train weighing twelve hundred tons between Harrisburg and Chicago, at speeds of up to one hundred miles per hour. EMC's new E-units were still in the preliminary design phase, but it was clear that one of those locomotives, unaided, could not match those combined speed and power requirements. PRR officials, accustomed to steam-locomotive operating practices, apparently did not consider the possibility that several E-units, coupled together and under the control of a single engineman, could fulfill the stated requirements.[122]

The committee's first task was to determine whether any established locomotive design would meet the PRR's demands. Glaenzer initially suggested a variant of the 4-8-4 Northerns that the company had built for several other railroads. While Super Power locomotives such as the 4-8-4 had already demonstrated their abilities in passenger service, the PRR officials expressed misgivings. They feared that Northerns were not sufficiently powerful to maintain high speeds with long passenger trains.[123] Moreover, sustained high-speed running by a locomotive with four drive axles threatened to tear the railroad apart. Norman Litchfield, a representative from the engineering consultants Gibbs & Hill, joined the committee to study the problem. He observed that each additional set of drivers progressively retarded the ability to convert the reciprocal motion of the pistons to high wheel revolutions per minute. The more serious problem involved dynamic augment, the rhythmic pounding of the drivers on the rails that created severe stresses on the track. Additional drivers necessitated heavier side rods and associated valve gear, with correspondingly large counterweights on the drivers—all of which substantially increased dynamic augment. The development of alloy-steel side rods, one of the elements of Super Power design, alleviated but did not eliminate the difficulty.[124]

The committee members were receptive to advice provided by Ralph P. Johnson, Baldwin's chief engineer.[125] The solution, Johnson suggested, was to employ two sets of pistons and drivers, each of which would require substantially lighter valve gear. Unlike the articulated locomotives that had never proved successful on the PRR, Johnson's

The S1 was the largest locomotive built at Altoona. It overshadowed fifty-eight of the individuals who worked on it, including one who had ignored the standard workplace admonitions regarding the use of safety glasses. *Pennsylvania Railroad Negative Collection, Hagley Museum & Library, acc. 1993.300.*

duplex locomotive featured two sets of drivers on a single, rigid frame. Thus the 4-8-4 would become a 4-4-4-4, which Kiesel agreed would be the ideal wheel arrangement to meet the PRR's needs. It was a novel but not unprecedented concept, and the members of the committee paid close attention to an experimental 4-4-4-4 locomotive, the *George H. Emerson,* completed by the Baltimore & Ohio in its Mount Clare Shops in May 1937. Despite their support of a duplex, Baldwin designers were nonetheless concerned that it might not be possible to achieve the desired drawbar horsepower without experiencing wheel slippage. It was a generally accepted principle of steam-locomotive design that smaller drive wheels and a greater number

of drivers increased adhesion—a valuable characteristic for drag freight locomotives that moved at comparatively low speeds. Larger drivers made for faster locomotives, yet also increased the likelihood that those drivers would slip, particularly on grades or where the rail was wet. The fewer the drivers, the greater the problem—which was why the PRR's Class E6 Atlantics, with just two pairs of drivers, were extraordinarily fast but also suffered from repeated wheel slipping. The proposed duplex, with two sets of two-coupled drivers, was likely to experience a similar problem. Kiesel nonetheless reassured Johnson that the limited-cutoff feature he had developed for the PRR's Class I1s freight locomotives would control wheel slip.[126]

The innovative features of the duplex did not solve the PRR's problems, however. Despite considerable effort, the committee members were unable to design a locomotive that would meet both the weight and speed requirements. The best they could accomplish was a maximum speed of ninety miles per hour and an axle loading of 67,500 pounds. PRR officials hoped that Alco and Lima might provide better results, yet they feared alienating Glaenzer

The PRR's first duplex steam locomotive dominated the Transportation Zone at the 1939 New York World's Fair and attested to Raymond Loewy's skills as an industrial designer. The "Big Engine" was too large to operate efficiently, but it served its intended role as a test bed for future motive-power designs. *Library of Congress, Prints & Photographs Division, Gottscho-Schleisner Collection, LC-G613-35557.*

and Johnson at Baldwin. Charles D. Young, the Pennsylvania Railroad's vice president in charge of purchases, stores, and insurance, organized a parallel committee that initially included representatives from Alco and Lima, but not Baldwin, as well as several of the PRR members of the Hankins committee. The secrecy and duplication of effort proved counterproductive, and by the end of 1936—and over Hankins's objections—Young had merged the two committees.[127] Now working together, representatives from the PRR and all three locomotive builders were able to reestablish a potential top speed of one hundred miles per hour. They addressed the unacceptably high axle loading by lengthening both the lead and trailing trucks to carry the extra weight and provide for a larger firebox, turning the 4-4-4-4 locomotive into a 6-4-4-6. The following March, PRR officials tested a Chicago & North Western 4-6-4 Hudson with drivers that were exceptionally large, at 84 inches in diameter. While Duer considered

the C&NW Hudson insufficiently powerful for the PRR's needs, he was relieved that the large drivers enabled high speeds without undue slipping. The 84-inch diameter then became the standard for the new design.[128]

By the spring of 1937, the committee had established the basic outlines of the new locomotive, yet there was disagreement as to its purpose. Led by Duer, many of the PRR contingent envisioned a very fast and very powerful locomotive like the GG1. The consultants at Gibbs & Hill, led by George Gibbs himself, cautioned that the condition of the track and roadbed rather than performance of the locomotive constituted the most significant impediment to high-speed operation. That perspective, shared by Baldwin's Ralph Johnson, suggested that the new locomotive would not appreciably shorten passenger-train schedules, as the GG1 had done between New York and Washington. Yet Duer rewrote Gibbs's report, consigned his warning to an appendix, and forwarded the resulting document to Deasy—who presumably supported or at least accepted the modified findings that he in turn sent to Clement. In their desire to mimic the GG1, Duer, Deasy, and their allies assigned secondary importance to the reduction of double-heading—the only significant benefit that the new locomotive was likely to produce—and instead emphasized the speed and power it would offer.[129]

The carefully structured arguments presented by Duer persuaded senior management to appropriate funds to construct a prototype locomotive. In April 1937, the board of directors approved the expenditure of $300,000 to build the PRR's first duplex, classed as the S1. Shop forces at Altoona completed the locomotive in December 1938. Assigned the number 6100, the S1 stretched 140 feet, almost as long as two standard passenger cars, and forty feet longer than the C&NW engine tested nine months earlier. Fully laden with coal and water, it weighed more than one million pounds. The locomotive was so massive that it was necessary to lengthen and strengthen the Altoona test plant to evaluate its performance.[130] The S1's tractive effort of seventy-two thousand pounds was double what that C&NW Northern could achieve. The cost of the #6100 was also substantial, at $669,780, equivalent to slightly more than $14.4 million in 2023 and more than twice what the board of directors had initially authorized. After some preliminary tests, the PRR shipped the locomotive to Long Island for display at the New York World's Fair. Visitors to the Transportation Zone saw the S1 spinning its drivers in perpetual motion, its wheels suspended on rollers.[131] They marveled at Raymond Loewy's streamlined exterior casing, including a "hemispheric" smoke box that he copied from designer Otto Kuhler. Initially emblazoned with "Pennsylvania Railroad" on its massive tender, the lettering soon changed to "American Railroads." The new moniker attested to the cooperative efforts of the World's Fair Committee of the Eastern Railroad Presidents' Conference, but it also suggested to the public that the S1 represented the future of railroading in the United States.[132]

By the time the S1 made an appearance at the New York World's Fair, PRR officials had concluded that it would not suit the railroad's needs. It steamed well, producing ample power for even the heaviest of passenger trains while easily reaching speeds exceeding one hundred miles per hour. Under normal operating conditions, however, the locomotive was simply too large and too powerful. One experienced engineman, who saw the S1 on display at the World's Fair, observed that the locomotive's size and long wheelbase precluded its use on many PRR routes. Lloyd B. Jones, the engineer of tests, complained that "nothing [had] been done to eliminate the restricted clearances on the main line both East and West of Altoona," limiting the scope of the locomotive's operations. The S1 nonetheless presented an impressive sight on the western half of the system, generally operating between Crestline and Chicago. The Crestline roundhouse could not accommodate the behemoth, requiring a thirty-foot addition to one of the stalls. Train crews had little difficulty referring to the monster as "The Big Engine" and acknowledged that it could pull

heavy passenger trains at considerable speed. Frequent malfunctions plagued the locomotive, however, and the #6100 spent a disproportionate share of its time in the shop.[133]

Even though the S1 was not practicable for regular service, officials in the Motive Power Department argued that the locomotive served as a test bed, providing information that would assist in the development of more practical duplex designs. The #6100 thus intensified the desire of Duer and others to build very large and powerful steam locomotives.[134] At no point did they give serious consideration to the use of diesels or to the incremental improvement of smaller steam locomotives that had proved their worth in revenue service. With the GG1 as their model and with Baldwin executives serving as their friends and collaborators, PRR officials saw little need to alter course. At a time when Electro-Motive was beginning to market moderately sized diesel locomotives as building blocks of motive power that could be combined, as needed, into virtually any conceivable horsepower combination, PRR officials remained focused on the development of a single-unit locomotive that could haul even the heaviest passenger and freight trains. Over the next decade the main channel of steam-locomotive development on the Pennsylvania Railroad was to flow from that premise.

New Freight Locomotives

The information gleaned from the construction and testing of the S1 contributed to parallel efforts to design duplex freight and passenger locomotives. During the fall of 1939, and acting at Clement's behest, officials in the Motive Power Department investigated methods to increase the power and efficiency of the M1/M1a.[135] Representatives from the Lima Locomotive Works offered to rebuild one of the locomotives with a four-wheel booster truck and other Super Power features, but Elsey and Hankins asserted that the modifications could not be retrofitted to the M1 design. Instead, Elsey set to work developing a variant of the recently completed S1 prototype. With a third of its motive power in storage, including forty-seven of the M1 class and nearly four hundred of the smaller L1 engines, the PRR was hardly short of locomotives. Rather, Elsey's intent was to curtail double-heading on freight trains, with its attendant crew costs.[136]

The Q1 freight locomotive that Elsey designed bore a striking similarity to the S1—including a streamlined shroud, later removed to improve access for maintenance. In an effort to reduce overall length and to increase adhesion by concentrating as much weight as possible on the drivers, Elsey chose a 4-6-4-4 wheel arrangement rather

As the sole representative of Class Q1, the #6130 facilitated the development of a duplex freight locomotive. Like the Baltimore & Ohio's *George H. Emerson*, it featured pairs of cylinders on opposite ends of the drivers—an experiment that would not be repeated. *Harris Negatives Collection, Railroad Museum of Pennsylvania, PHMC.*

than the 6-4-4-6 of the S1. Despite Clement's misgivings, the prototype of the Q1 featured drivers that were 77 inches in diameter, 5 inches larger than those on the M1.[137] While theoretically offering better performance at higher speeds, the larger drivers also increased the Q1's wheelbase. Placing both sets of cylinders ahead of their respective drivers (as on the S1) would have restricted operation through tight curves. Elsey could only overcome that problem by placing the rear set of cylinders behind the second set of drivers, tucked up against the front end of the firebox. The Q1 thus mimicked the pioneering Baltimore & Ohio duplex *George H. Emerson*, employing a concept that that railroad's motive-power experts had already dismissed as unworkable.[138] Representatives from the locomotive builders, led by Ralph Johnson at Baldwin, nonetheless predicted that Elsey's design would be successful. Based on that reassurance, in October 1940, the PRR board authorized the construction of #6130, the first and only Q1.

Completed in May 1942 at a cost of $395,322 (equivalent to nearly $7.5 million in 2023), the #6130 was eighteen feet shorter but only sixteen tons lighter than its S1 progenitor. It towered over the M1 and indeed every other class of PRR motive power. The locomotive could easily reach speeds of seventy miles per hour, yet the systemwide maximum freight-train speed was only fifty miles per hour. In that respect, the new locomotive was ill-suited for the movement of heavy trains filled with bulk commodities such as coal and iron ore. PRR officials nonetheless suggested that the Q1 would soon be able to power faster trains filled with perishables and other high-value commodities, much as the GG1 had expedited schedules in electrified territory.[139]

While more successful than the S1, the Q1 experienced its share of teething problems. Between late May and the end of July 1942, the locomotive operated in a series of shakedown runs between Harrisburg and Altoona, and subsequently west to Pittsburgh. Crews reported difficulties in maintaining adequate steam pressure and complained of excessive accumulation of cinders in the smokebox and periodic slipping of the rear drivers, among other problems. PRR shop forces gradually corrected many of those difficulties, and by October 1943, the #6130 was operating reliably. In that month, the operating personnel on the power-starved Western Region—over the objections of their Central Region counterparts—requested and received permission to operate the Q1. By June 1945, when the locomotive received its first major overhaul, it had accumulated one hundred thousand miles in service. Although that represented a monthly average that was less than a third that of a typical Super Power design used on other railroads, the low mileage was to be expected on a locomotive that was largely experimental in nature. Train crews and shopworkers who possessed limited familiarity with the #6130 also contributed to the low availability and periodic malfunctions.[140]

The Q1 succeeded reasonably well as an experimental locomotive, and its failings were by no means sufficient to discredit the plan to use duplexes in freight service. Officials in the Motive Power Department certainly intended to produce a refined design that would serve as the PRR's principal fast freight locomotive, west of Harrisburg. With sufficient time and resources, they would likely achieve their goal. Time and resources were both in short supply during the early months of World War II, however. So, too, were locomotives, as the prewar surplus of motive power gave way to an acute shortage. Although the number of locomotives owned by the PRR decreased slightly between September 1939 and April 1943—from 4,291 to 4,275—those that were serviceable jumped from 67.2 percent to 98.0 percent of the fleet, while the number of stored locomotives declined from 263 to only 7. Crews were also placing greater demands on those engines. The average PRR freight locomotive covered just 64.3 miles a day in 1937, but by September 1942, the average daily run was 104.3 miles. The corresponding increase for passenger locomotives was nearly 80 percent, from 104.3 to 187.5 miles. While the PRR did acquire additional GG1 electric locomotives, the extension of electrified territory was impossible, owing to financial constraints and shortages of both copper wire and workers.[141]

Moreover, a shakeup in the Motive Power Department had sidelined the most aggressive proponents of duplex locomotives like the S1 and the Q1 while creating a dearth of talent as severe as the one that accompanied William Kiesel's retirement in 1936. President Clement and other senior managers were hardly pleased that the S1 had cost more than twice the anticipated amount or that it performed so poorly. Nor were they willing to accept delays in the subsequent development of the T1 class, intended as the fast passenger counterpart to the Q1 freight locomotive. The result was a transfer of personnel that stopped short of outright dismissal yet nonetheless signaled that all was not well in the Motive Power Department. In February 1941, Fred Hankins lost his status as chief of motive power and became the assistant to John Deasy, the vice president

in charge of operations. More a punishment than a promotion, the reassignment reduced Hankins's direct oversight of motive-power development but nonetheless enabled him to maintain a close relationship with a vice president who supported large steam locomotives.[142] Under normal circumstances, Warren Elsey, the mechanical engineer who had participated in the joint PRR–Baldwin conferences to develop the S1, might well have replaced Hankins as chief of motive power. As events transpired, however, Elsey became the new general superintendent of motive power on the Eastern Region, with Carl Steins taking over his responsibilities. Harry W. Jones became the new chief of motive power. In that capacity, he worked closely with Lloyd Jones, the engineer of tests, and with Robert G. Bennett, newly appointed as the assistant chief of motive power. Three months later, John Duer, the chief electrical engineer, also joined Deasy's staff as an assistant to the vice president in charge of operations. The completion of electrification to Harrisburg in 1938, absent any concrete plans for an extension west to Pittsburgh, suggested that there was little need for Duer's electrical-engineering expertise. By joining Deasy's office, he nonetheless became an even more forceful advocate for large steam locomotives, including some that would be far more visionary than even the S1.[143]

By the fall of 1941, the Motive Power Department was still in some disarray, and the Q1 existed only in blueprints. There was too much at stake to bet a substantial portion of the Pennsylvania Railroad's freight traffic on an unproven design. In October, President Clement asked Charles Brinley, the president of Baldwin, for recommendations. Brinley offered some suggestions, based on existing and proposed Baldwin offerings, but without making any specific proposals. The following month Robert Bennett, the assistant chief of motive power, and mechanical engineer Carl Steins organized a special motive-power committee to develop an alternative to the M1. As had been the case with the initial development of the S1, they solicited advice from representatives at Baldwin, Lima, and Alco. Bennett and Steins considered seven designs that were in use or under construction on six railroads, assessing their potential for service on the PRR and their merits relative to the still-incomplete Q1. All but two were articulateds, a concept that had never found favor on the Pennsylvania Railroad.[144] The remaining two were rigid-frame 2-10-4 Texas locomotives that incorporated many of the Super Power developments that had emerged since the design of the M1. In February 1942, PRR officials tested one of the forty 2-10-4 locomotives that Lima had built for the

In 1942, PRR motive power officials worked with their counterparts at the Lima Locomotive Works to modify a Chesapeake & Ohio Railway design for a 2-10-4 Texas locomotive. The Class J1 lacked the Belpaire firebox and other elements of traditional PRR motive power design, and the incremental improvements that the C&O had made to its Texas fleet were also absent. The J1 was nonetheless rugged and dependable, and it lasted until the end of steam operations. Two examples, #6449 and #6421, are nearing Altoona with an eastbound train on July 15, 1953. *Otto Perry photograph, Denver Public Library, Western History Collection, call number OP-14433.*

Chesapeake & Ohio in 1930. Bennett and Steins concluded that the C&O engine could haul heavier loads than the M1, was less expensive to construct and operate, and could generate more mileage between scheduled repairs and maintenance.[145]

While PRR officials were evaluating the locomotives employed by other railroads, changes in public policy began to constrain their options. The war enabled the federal government to assume unprecedented influence over the economy, far exceeding anything that Franklin Delano Roosevelt had been able to achieve during the New Deal. In January 1942, Roosevelt signed an executive order establishing the War Production Board, initially headed by Sears executive Donald M. Nelson. In April, the agency issued General Limitation Order 97, which required railroads to obtain WPB approval before ordering any new motive power. Preference would be given to the freight locomotives that would bring raw materials to factories and expedite the movement of military supplies to ports. The order also banned the manufacture of experimental locomotives, requiring both railroads and builders to use proven designs. WPB officials insisted that the small output of diesel locomotives be directed to carriers such as the Santa Fe, where they could take advantage of existing service facilities, improve operations in an arid climate, and speed men and matériel to the Pacific Theater. There was little chance that WPB personnel would accede to any request from the coal-rich Pennsylvania Railroad for diesels—and little likelihood that the railroad's Motive Power Department would accept them.[146]

While the plans for the Q1 predated the issuance of General Limitation Order 97, WPB officials were nonetheless more inclined to approve the manufacture of locomotives that were based on those that had already proven themselves through extensive service. Pennsylvania Railroad

The twenty-six examples of the Class Q2 duplex were unde-
niably impressive machines. Yet in freight service they
performed little better than the Class J1—a locomotive,
designed by outsiders, that represented the technology of
a prior decade. The limitations of the Q2 and the need for
new freight power initiated an acrimonious debate between
supporters of steam and those who favored diesels. *General
Negative Collection, Railroad Museum of Pennsylvania, PHMC.*

officials elected to play it safe and at least temporarily forgo
the purported advantages of the Q1. In March 1942, only a
month after the PRR tested the C&O's 2-10-4 Texas locomotive, the board of directors appropriated $10.6 million
for fifty virtually identical models, assigned to Class J1.[147]
The design faithfully copied Lima's 1930 blueprints and
erection drawings, including those features that had not
been updated to reflect numerous incremental improvements in locomotive development since then. To reduce
weight, the PRR eschewed the traditional Belpaire firebox.
Other components, including a radial-stay boiler, a two-
axle trailing truck, and a trailing-truck booster, reflected
the Super Power technology of the locomotive industry
rather than customary PRR practice. The same was true
of the 69-inch drivers on the J1, considerably larger than
the 62-inch drivers that had become the PRR standard

for freight locomotives—although they were smaller than
those used on the Q1. Half of the new J1 locomotives would
be built at Altoona (at $175,000 apiece), with an equal
number assigned to Lima (at $250,000 each). Lima ulti-
mately did not produce any of those locomotives, as WPB
officials concluded that that company's facilities were more
urgently required for the manufacture of Sherman tanks
and steam locomotives for the US Army. In the first six
months of 1943, Juniata Shop forces, by dint of Herculean
effort, completed 54 J1 locomotives, which represented
nearly a third of all domestic steam-locomotive production
during that time. Ultimately, the Altoona Works completed 125 J1 and similar J1a locomotives by 1944. Although
they had a reputation for excessive coal consumption and
tended to be rough on the track, the locomotives were both
powerful and reliable. Even though the PRR adopted the
design as a temporary wartime expedient, some remained
in service until 1957—long after the more idiosyncratic
duplex locomotives designed by the Motive Power Department had been consigned to the scrapyard.[148]

The success of the J1 did not halt the PRR's efforts
to develop the ideal duplex freight locomotive, one that
would remedy the deficiencies that had become apparent
on the Q1. If anything, the tendency of the J1 to damage
track—a situation that was partly attributable to the failure
to incorporate updates to Lima's original design—reinforced the desire to employ the duplex principle to reduce

dynamic augment. In 1943, while employees at the Juniata Shops were rushing to produce as many copies of the J1 as possible, Vice President Deasy instructed the Motive Power Department to improve the Q1 design. The wheel arrangement changed from a 4-6-4-4 to a 4-4-6-4 but retained five driving axles on a rigid frame—equivalent to a 4-10-4 conventional locomotive but with a reduction in dynamic augment.[149] The more important modification involved placing both sets of cylinders ahead of their respective drivers, made possible by reducing driver diameter from 77 inches to a more practicable 69 inches. The Q2 design looked so good on paper that in October 1943 the PRR suspended production of the final batch of thirty-two of the more conventional J1 locomotives. In March of the following year, with the prototype Q2 still incomplete, the directors authorized construction of an additional twenty-five of the new design. Not until August did the initial Q2, #6131, enter service, with the remaining twenty-five locomotives completed between January and June 1945. The total cost was just under $6 million ($100 million in 2023), with additional expenditures necessary to increase the size of enginehouse stalls, lengthen track pans, and install longer turntables.[150]

At first it appeared that the PRR had received good value from its investment in the Q2. The Q2 was slightly longer and heavier than the Q1, and no more powerful nonarticulated steam locomotive has ever been built anywhere. As one PRR fireman noted, "These mammoth engines drew a lot of attention wherever we went and we felt important sitting in the cab." The locomotives nonetheless consumed unexpectedly large volumes of water. Fuel consumption was just as extreme, with nearly half of the coal fed into the massive firebox being expelled through the stack, unburned—wasting money and angering trackside residents whose homes would be covered by a blanket of soot whenever a Q2 passed by. Their innovative antislip devices, developed by the American Brake Shoe Company, did not function reliably, and the wheel slipping that was the bane of the duplex design occurred frequently. Rails wet with water, snow, or even morning dew posed particularly severe difficulties, to the extent that crews nicknamed the Q2 "the Pennsylvania Railroad's dry weather special." Enginemen also complained that the boiler was so long that they lacked a clear view of the tracks ahead while rounding curves. The more disconcerting problem was that the Q2 did not seem to perform much better than the Class J1. Officials in the Motive Power Department had not fully tested the Q2 until February 1945 and had not analyzed all the data until June, just as the last of the locomotives was emerging from the Juniata Shops. Too late,

they realized they had done little better than what their Lima counterparts designed fifteen years earlier.[151]

The Duplex in Passenger Service

Over the next two years, the limitations of the Q2 would influence the growing debate regarding whether any steam locomotive produced by the PRR could compete against modern diesels. Even as they were developing the Q1 and Q2 freight locomotives, Hankins and Elsey were applying the duplex principle to a new type of passenger locomotive. They never intended for the Class T1 to replace all the 425 K4s Pacifics that were the mainstay of the PRR's passenger service. The K4s remained a superb choice for lightly traveled branch lines, short trains, and routes with frequent stops. On the main line, they could handle up to thirteen cars at adequate speed. Longer trains, coupled with the systemwide increase in passenger-train speeds during the 1930s, overtaxed their abilities, however. Double-heading was the only solution, a step that increased operating expenses—with the Central Region alone incurring an additional $1.5 million in annual labor costs. The M1/M1a Mountain locomotives were more powerful but did not solve the problem. Despite their name (one that was in common usage on other railroads as well), the locomotive that James Wallis and William Kiesel designed was not well suited for hilly topography. It was at its best pulling fast freight trains (and some passenger trains), over level terrain. On the Western Region, they faced a speed restriction of sixty miles an hour, far below what was necessary to maintain passenger schedules—any faster and their massive side rods produced so much dynamic augment as to damage the track. Their long, rigid wheelbase also precluded operation through the sharply curving tracks that led west out of Pennsylvania Station in Pittsburgh.[152]

The new duplex would instead have one specific function—to pull long passenger trains at high speeds without double-heading, thus shortening schedules and reducing crew costs. The locomotive that PRR and Baldwin personnel created embodied the rugged beauty, the potential, and the ultimate failure associated with the final years of their efforts to develop bigger and better steam locomotives. It is likely that the T1 has received more attention from historians—and has generated more controversy—than any other class of steam, diesel, or electric locomotive that has operated in the United States. Some have regarded the T1 as a flawed concept that was doomed before it left the drawing board, an exemplar of the stubbornness and insularity of officials in the Motive Power Department as they foolishly attempted to stem the tide of dieselization.

On July 25, 1940, it required two K4s Pacifics, #5337 and #3772, to bring the fourteen cars of the westbound *Golden Arrow* into Chicago. With the development of new lightweight trainsets no longer a viable option, PRR officials were motivated to envision a single locomotive that could haul a train of this length, unaided. *Otto Perry photograph, Denver Public Library, Western History Collection, call number OP-14377.*

Others have asserted that the T1 was a rational and practicable solution to the PRR's motive-power needs and that, given just a little more attention, it would have assumed its rightful place as one of the greatest locomotive designs of all time.[153]

Buoyed by the construction of the B&O's *George H. Emerson* and the PRR's S1, by the summer of 1939, Ralph Johnson at Baldwin was proposing a range of duplex designs for service on railroads across the United States. Despite the easing of the Great Depression and the potential for war in Europe, most carriers faced a surplus of stored locomotives and showed little interest in Baldwin's efforts. Pennsylvania Railroad officials were the exception and worked with Johnson to develop both the Q1 for freight service and a smaller, faster duplex for passenger operations. In June 1940, the directors appropriated $600,000—slightly less than the final cost of the sole S1—for the cooperative development of two T1 prototypes. They placed an order with Baldwin at the end of the following month. Warren Elsey headed the Pennsylvania Railroad contingent that worked

with Johnson and his colleagues to match the performance criteria they had established for the S1, without creating a locomotive too large to be serviceable. If successful, each of the new locomotives could replace a pair of K4s Pacifics, while moving the trains of the Blue Ribbon Fleet at speeds of more than one hundred miles per hour. The resulting 4-4-4-4 wheel arrangement of the T1 copied that of the B&O's duplex, although the PRR version positioned both sets of cylinders ahead of their respective drivers. Eighteen feet shorter and significantly lighter than the S1, the T1 was designed to operate over almost any section of the railroad's main line. A massive tender permitted the locomotive to pull passenger trains between Chicago and the beginning of electrified territory at Harrisburg with only a single refueling stop at Millbrook, Ohio. By running straight through, over a distance of 713 miles, the T1 would eliminate the engine changes at Altoona and Crestline that were unavoidable with the K4s.[154]

One of the most controversial elements of the T1's design—and, in hindsight, the most unfortunate—involved the installation of poppet valves. Aside from dynamic augment, perhaps the most serious impediment to the further development of the steam locomotive involved the imprecise control of the back-and-forth motion of each piston in its cylinder. By the 1930s, most modern American steam locomotives employed piston valves, in which steam entering the cylinder propelled a piston connected to the valve gear that transferred the reciprocating motion of the pistons to the rotary motion of the drivers. Similarly,

POWER REVERSE
CONNECTING SHAFT

CONNECTING ROD (EXHAUST)

GEAR BOX

CONNECTING ROD (INTAKE)

INTERMEDIATE LEVER

As they worked to achieve optimum performance from a new duplex passenger locomotive, representatives from the PRR, Baldwin, and the Franklin Railway Supply Company paid close attention to a series of tests conducted in 1939 and 1940. The installation of poppet valves appeared to improve the performance of K4s Pacific #5399, but it was not clear whether other, simultaneous modifications had made the difference. *Pennsylvania Railroad Negative Collection, Hagley Museum & Library, acc. 1993.300.*

locomotives typically employed Walschaerts valve gear, which had proven its reliability since its development in 1844.[155] Piston valves nonetheless displayed characteristics that potentially precluded their application on the PRR's new high-speed T1 design. Locomotives powerful enough to pull a long train required correspondingly large cylinders and pistons. As the weight of the pistons increased, so too did the inertial forces created when the piston reached the end of the cylinder and was then propelled back in the opposite direction. Many locomotive

designers had concluded that, with the application of incremental Super Power improvements, they had reached the physical limitations associated with piston valves and that no further increases in speed could be expected. The other problem involved the process of controlling the flow of steam. Even though an engineman could adjust the cutoff ratio (the rate at which steam was injected into the cylinder), he often experienced considerable difficulty in regulating the exhaustion of spent steam, reducing the force exerted by the piston and consequently lowering the locomotive's efficiency. Poppet valves, an innovation that locomotive designers borrowed from the automobile industry, employed tappet rods that actuated valves that in turn regulated the amount of steam flowing in and out of each cylinder. As an alternative to piston valves, they permitted more precise control over the admission of steam into the cylinder and—of even greater importance—the exhaustion of spent steam.[156]

Despite their potential, poppet valves were a largely untested innovation. The PRR's first—and unsuccessful—experiment with poppet valves occurred in 1918, with a system developed by Austrian mechanical engineer Hugo Lentz and applied to a Class L1 Mikado, #1127.[157] In 1929, the PRR's Motive Power Department installed on one of two experimental K5 Pacifics a poppet-valve system designed by Italian mechanical engineer Arturo Caprotti. It did not perform well, in large measure because the Caprotti valve gear, like many other elements of European railway technology developed over the previous hundred years, was insufficiently robust for American railway service. Beginning in 1937, the Lima Locomotive Works and its subsidiary, the Franklin Railway Supply Company, designed the Franklin Oscillating Cam as an improvement over the Caprotti system. During the summer of 1939, the PRR loaned a K4s Pacific, #5399, to Lima for an experimental installation of the new "O. C." poppet valves. Over the next year, the locomotive ran some fifty-seven thousand miles over the fast, flat tracks between Crestline and Chicago.[158] The initial results were not encouraging, inducing Lima to suspend the tests long enough to install a new superheater and to enlarge the locomotive's steam-chest volume and exhaust passages. The #5399 ultimately demonstrated a 44 percent increase in drawbar horsepower at eighty miles per hour, compared to an unmodified K4s. In some cases, the locomotive did the work of a pair of K4s Pacifics, precisely the role that designers envisioned for the T1.[159]

While the in-service performance of the #5399 suggested the potential of poppet valves, it did not resolve the debate as to whether they should be used on the T1. By the time design work began on the T1, in 1940, Baldwin officials were not entirely convinced of the efficacy of poppet valves, perhaps because they had been designed by the subsidiary of a rival locomotive manufacturer. They warned that the use of poppet valves in conjunction with the equally novel duplex design might compound any operating problems. Franklin officials were more partisan, as they hoped that the successful application of poppet valves to the T1 would generate far larger sales associated with the retrofitting of the fleet of K4s locomotives. The members of the PRR contingent acknowledged the potential advantages of poppet valves, but they were hesitant to bet the future of the T1 on a largely untested technology.[160]

Everything now depended on the performance of a single locomotive at the Altoona test plant. During the fall of 1940, more than fifty stationary operations of the #5399 seemingly resolved the debate over poppet valves. The results showed that the installation of poppet valves and other modifications had reduced steam consumption by 18.4 percent at eighty miles per hour and an astonishing 31.7 percent at one hundred miles per hour. That was a crucial improvement, for it demonstrated one of the key

advantages of poppet valves—because they required less steam than conventional Walschaerts piston valve gear, they could reduce the size and thus the weight of the boiler and the firebox used on the T1. Equally impressive, the horsepower produced by the #5399 increased 22.9 percent at eighty miles per hour and 46.8 percent at one hundred miles per hour, compared to a conventional K4s. The test locomotive topped out at 4,267 horsepower at seventy-five miles per hour, decreasing only slightly to 4,099 horsepower at one hundred miles per hour. That was exactly the result that Hankins and Elsey hoped to achieve, and it suggested that poppet valves were ideally suited for high-speed passenger service. Unfortunately, there was no clear evidence that the poppet valves alone had caused that improvement. The many complementary modifications to a locomotive designed twenty-six years earlier may have been collectively responsible for the impressive results.[161]

The person who was untimely responsible for evaluating #5399, engineer of tests Lloyd Jones, had few misgivings about the results—or, if he did, he kept such matters to himself. In a January 1941 article in the *Railway Mechanical Engineer*, he took his profession to task, suggesting that "perhaps the greatest single handicap of the steam locomotive is the deep-rooted conservatism of American locomotive designers which has sentenced it to be a machine of two cylinders controlled by one valve apiece." He further suggested that it would be possible to avoid both the "destructive dynamic forces" and the "ineffective steam distribution" that his colleagues accepted as "necessary evils, to be tolerated rather than faced." While Jones did not specifically mention poppet valves as the resolution to those problems, the list of desirable qualities he provided exactly matched the theoretical abilities of the "experiments now under way in this country" by the PRR, Baldwin, and Franklin. His allusion to "various valve arrangements which meet this requirement more or less perfectly are extensively used in Europe" was an undoubted reference to the 335 poppet-valve-equipped locomotives that operated on French railways.[162]

Bolstered by the results of the #5399 tests, Jones suggested a solution to the design flaw that plagued the S1—that the only way to make a locomotive both fast and powerful would be to make it so big that it would be unusable. Several years earlier, when assessing the limitations of the S1, consulting engineer George Gibbs had suggested a way to reconcile the competing goals of speed, power, and weight. In a presentation to the Road Committee of the board of directors, he recommended that the PRR should replace many of its existing heavyweight passenger cars with lightweight equipment. In addition to appealing to

Class T1 duplex #6111, nicknamed "Buck Rogers," was one of two prototypes developed collaboratively by Baldwin and the PRR's Motive Power Department. Thanks to their shrouding, designed by Raymond Loewy, they presented a striking appearance. They were fast and powerful, but design problems—including the decision to use poppet valves—created ongoing operational difficulties. By the time the last of the T1 locomotives entered service, diesels had demonstrated their superiority. *Pennsylvania Railroad Negative Collection, Hagley Museum & Library, acc. 1993.300.*

the public's interest in modern streamliners, the reduction in train weight from 1,200 tons to 880 tons would enable a smaller locomotive to pull as many cars as an S1, at speeds of up to one hundred miles per hour. The process of upgrading the PRR's passenger fleet was underway, with the first lightweight Fleet of Modernism equipment arriving in 1938. Yet those 54 cars (52 from Pullman and 2 from Budd) were but a small fraction of the 4,560 passenger cars that were in service at the end of 1940.[163] Even if

replacements were limited to the most important trains on each route, it would take many years, and the investment of millions of dollars, to comply with the advice that George Gibbs had provided.[164]

Jones suggested that there was another option. Drawing on the test plant results for the #5399, he articulated the performance characteristics for an "improved locomotive"—undoubtedly a proxy for the T1. It would substantially reduce the time required to move even a heavyweight train from a stationary position to a given speed, compared to the "present locomotive" with either heavyweight or lightweight cars. He acknowledged that the "improved locomotive" would perform more efficiently with lightweight (compared to heavyweight) equipment but insisted that the differential disappeared once each hypothetical train had reached a given operating speed. As he noted, "For a given maximum speed, the saving in schedule time by the lightweight train is confined to acceleration, and if there are no stops or speed reductions, the heavy train will require only a little more time to cover a given distance than the lightweight train." Jones was

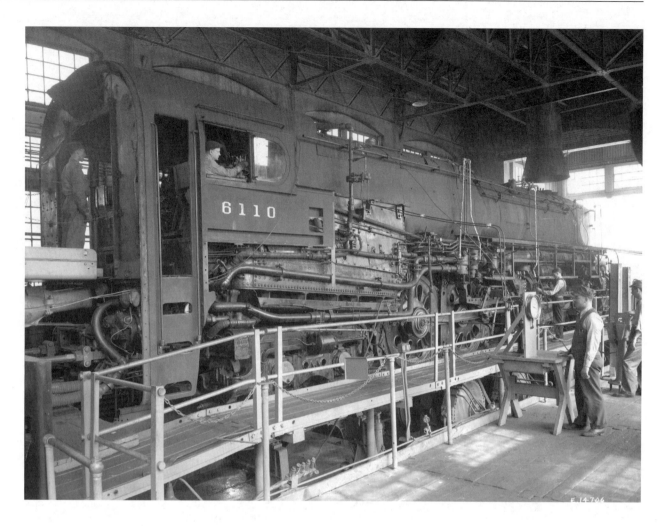

During the spring and summer of 1944, motive-power officials evaluated Class T1 #6110 at the Altoona test plant. The data they collected improved the performance of the production-model locomotives that would follow but could not eliminate all the problems associated with the T1 design. The analytical methods that had been in place for more than four decades were no longer adequate for a world in which the diesel was ascendent. *Pennsylvania Railroad Negative Collection, Hagley Museum & Library, acc. 1993.300.*

describing the ideal conditions of trains that operated at high speeds and made infrequent stops. He was also asserting that the development of the "improved locomotive" was worth the cost and the technological risk, for it potentially obviated the expense of reequipping the entire Blue Ribbon Fleet with lightweight equipment. While Jones did not explicitly state that poppet valves offered the only realistic option for the design of a single-unit locomotive that was compatible with the PRR's passenger schedules and existing equipment, he certainly suggested as much. In January 1941, Jones and his colleagues thus agreed that the

Franklin poppet valves should be included in the design of the T1. It proved to be a serious mistake, one that discredited the potential of poppet-valve technology and compromised the performance of the PRR's new passenger locomotive.[165]

During the spring of 1942, Baldwin completed the two prototype T1 locomotives, but their initial performance was disappointing to say the least. Thanks to a shroud styled by Raymond Loewy, they looked sleek and modern, and the #6110 and #6111 soon gained the nicknames "Flash Gordon" and "Buck Rogers." Loewy's sheet metal covered a Belpaire firebox, long standard on the PRR but a change from Johnson's Baldwin design. The two locomotives achieved their intended performance criteria, pulling heavy trains at speeds of a hundred miles an hour.[166] Unfortunately, metallurgical limitations contributed to the frequent failure of the Franklin poppet valves, and it was particularly difficult for maintenance forces to gain access to the gearbox for the rear set of drivers. The duplex design did reduce dynamic augment, but the trade-off was that the locomotive was prone to slipping at high speeds. One minute the locomotive would be barreling through

Indiana at ninety miles per hour, the next its drivers were spinning wildly, and it took an experienced engineman to bring it under control without coming to a complete stop.[167] The sander nozzles were misaligned and clogged frequently, while the sandbox was far too small—ensuring that it was often impossible to apply sand to the rails, thus exacerbating the slippage problem. Both locomotives steamed poorly, necessitating substantial modifications. The #6110 and #6111 generated extreme vibrations that loosened pipe joints, shattered headlight bulbs, and induced leaks in the superheater system. Engine crews endured hot cabs, air brake failures, and the pounding that ensued when the tender continually ran up against and slammed into the rear of the locomotive at high speeds. By January 1943, the PRR had temporarily abandoned efforts to use the two locomotives in regular passenger service between Harrisburg and Chicago. They instead confined them to operations in Ohio and Indiana, near the shop facilities at Crestline.[168]

Even before the United States entered World War II, the cost overruns on the S1 project and the problems associated with the design of the T1 had sidelined the careers of Fred Hankins as chief of motive power and Warren Elsey as mechanical engineer. Their replacements, Harry Jones and Carl Steins, set to work remedying the defects of the two initial T1 locomotives. Forsaking any radical changes, such as the elimination of the troublesome poppet valves, they instead undertook a series of minor adjustments that were typical of any new steam-locomotive design. In April 1944, the Altoona test plant began an evaluation of the incrementally modified #6110. The results, released in August, suggested that a single T1 produced as much horsepower as three K4s locomotives and more than a four-unit diesel locomotive at passenger-train speeds. To the consternation of officials in the Motive Power Department, however, the results attained at the test plant could not be consistently replicated in revenue service. Jones and Steins noted that many enginemen and firemen were unfamiliar with the T1 and that as they gained experience, the problems would correspondingly diminish. Vice President Deasy nonetheless acknowledged that local operating officials were routinely underreporting the prevalence of slippage, even though "the people down the line know it." Frustrated shopmen progressively stripped off bits of the Loewy-designed sheet metal streamlining in order to get access to the rear poppet-valve gearbox and other critical components. The defenders of the T1 insisted that shop forces would need more time to gain experience with the locomotives and develop new tools that would facilitate maintenance. The excuses did not produce

results, however, and in September—a month after the Test Department revealed the exemplary results of the #6110—Deasy complained that "the T1 locomotive is not performing well on the Railroad."[169]

Deasy's pessimistic assessment of the T1's abilities might well have ended the PRR's efforts to develop a duplex passenger locomotive, with the #6110 and #6111 attaining the same orphan status as the sole representatives of the S1 and Q1 classes. With the War Production Board continuing to restrict the production of passenger locomotives, while banning experimental designs, there was little possibility that the PRR could order additional T1 locomotives, much less develop a replacement. The success of the June 1944 D-Day landings altered both the course of the war and the composition of the PRR's motive-power fleet. On August 25, two days after the Test Department released its report on the T1, the Allies liberated Paris. Military planners calculated that the war in Europe would be over by the summer of 1945 at the latest. They anticipated that there would follow a massive redeployment of troops across the Atlantic to the United States, then by rail to Pacific coast ports and on to the Pacific Theater. In preparation for the expected surge in troop movements, the WPB shifted priorities to the manufacture of passenger locomotives, ensuring that the PRR would experience few impediments in the acquisition of additional copies of the T1.[170]

James Symes and the T1

With the War Production Board encouraging the construction of new passenger locomotives, the primary opposition to an expansion of the T1 fleet came from within the ranks of Pennsylvania Railroad executives. By the end of 1944, James M. Symes had become the most prominent supporter of dieselization and, correspondingly, the most forceful opponent of the T1. Born in 1897, Symes, like many others, followed his father's example of working on the Pennsylvania Railroad. His career nonetheless began in a rather atypical manner, having been recruited in 1916 as a star player for the Lines West baseball team. From his initial role as a clerk, Symes rose through the ranks. In 1934, he became the chief of freight transportation. In his later years, Symes recalled his time working for Martin Clement, the general superintendent of the Lake Division, based in Cleveland, during the early 1920s. Defying an order from a local trainmaster, Symes dispatched several locomotives in an effort to get traffic moving. His successful insubordination gained Clement's attention, and Symes became one of his protégées. Between 1935 and 1939, Symes was on loan to the Association of American Railroads, as

James M. Symes (1897–1976) began his Pennsylvania Railroad career in 1916 as a clerk—and a talented player on the Lines West baseball team. In 1934, at about the time this photo was taken, he became the chief of freight transportation. After 1939, as general manager and then as vice president of the Western Region, Symes became familiar with the diesel locomotives employed by the other railroads that served the city—and correspondingly intolerant of repeated failures by officials in the Motive Power Department to develop equally efficient steam locomotives. *Harry R. Hippler collection of Pennsylvania Railroad Negatives, Hagley Museum & Library, acc. 2015.279.*

that organization's vice president of operations and maintenance. That post removed him from the insularity of the PRR's corporate offices and introduced him to executives on many other railroads—including those who were prepared to experiment with diesel locomotives.[171]

When Symes returned to the PRR, he became the Western Region general manager. In February 1942, as the two initial T1 locomotives were nearing completion, the board promoted Symes to the vice presidency of the Western Region. Stretching from Chicago and St. Louis east to Crestline and Columbus, it was the likely home of many of the fast and powerful duplex freight and passenger

locomotives designed by the Motive Power Department, and Symes had no desire to be stuck with a lemon. Moreover, from his office in Chicago, Symes had ready access to a variety of modern steam and diesel locomotives used by other carriers, and he saw no reason why the PRR should be restricted to the products manufactured by the Altoona Works. Symes retained the obstinacy that he once demonstrated in Cleveland, and as the T1 was being tested, he made known his feelings on the matter. Unlike his counterparts in the Motive Power Department, he had little interest in the development of innovative new steam locomotives or in the graphs and charts that emanated from the test plant. His responsibility was to maximize the operating efficiency of the Western Region, and he was determined to avoid being saddled with experimental models that might fail to meet schedules or would increase maintenance costs. He was an ardent critic of the S1 and demanded that it be removed from the Western Region. He was more receptive to the Q1, but he nonetheless harbored deep suspicions regarding the viability of the duplex design.[172]

In the autumn of 1944, Symes and other PRR executives engaged in a vigorous debate regarding the locomotive that would presumably power the railroad's premier passenger trains for the next ten or twenty years. The Norfolk & Western had long been allied with the PRR and offered an alternative to the T1. The N&W Class J was outwardly like the T1, with a streamlined body that sat atop a four-wheel lead truck, four drivers, and a four-wheel trailing truck. That was the same basic arrangement as the 4-4-4-4 T1, although the N&W locomotive dispensed with the duplex drive and the associated second set of cylinders. Its designers also avoided poppet valves but insisted on the application of roller bearings on the side rods. By January 1942, three months prior to the completion of the #6110, the N&W's Roanoke Shops built the first five J-Class locomotives. They soon demonstrated exceptional performance, without any of the difficulties experienced by the T1.[173]

On October 26, Symes wrote to Deasy, insisting that the PRR test one of the N&W locomotives before committing to full-scale production of the T1. Deasy, supported by Harry Jones, asserted that the N&W locomotive was not sufficiently powerful to haul long passenger trains at high speeds. By November 3, however, the N&W's vice president in charge of operations promised Symes that he would loan one of his locomotives to the PRR for a month of testing along the routes connecting Harrisburg to Chicago and St. Louis. Officials on both railroads were concerned that the test locomotive was six inches taller and a foot wider than the T1, made possible by the N&W's generous engineering

In December 1944, at the insistence of Western Region vice president James Symes, the PRR tested a 4-8-4 locomotive borrowed from the Norfolk & Western. The #610, shown here on its home rails in Bristol, Virginia, in 1947, often exceeded the performance of the PRR's new T1 and Q2 duplex locomotives. The test results convinced Symes that the construction of additional steam locomotives at Altoona would be a waste of the railroad's resources. *General Negative Collection, Railroad Museum of Pennsylvania, PHMC.*

standards. Carl Steins and his subordinates were soon at work checking the PRR's clearance diagrams. The results were not encouraging. The tracks between Harrisburg and Pittsburgh were out of bounds, owing to numerous potential strike points. That was unfortunate, as that territory mimicked the Pocahontas grades that had established the Class J performance criteria. Clearance restrictions also eliminated the Panhandle route west to St. Louis. The only tracks over which the N&W locomotive could safely operate linked Crestline and Chicago, although even some of the terminal tracks in the Windy City were off limits. That flat, straight route was where the T1 was at its best, ensuring that the Norfolk & Western's 4-8-4 was already operating at a disadvantage.[174]

The N&W's #610 began testing in early December. Despite the unfamiliar territory, the locomotive performed

superbly. Even though its drivers were only 70 inches in diameter, 10 inches smaller than those on the T1, it reached one hundred miles per hour—although PRR officials suggested that sustained running at such high speeds would be destructive to the locomotive and the track. The road foreman of engines on the Fort Wayne Division noted that the #610 was able to maintain the PRR's schedules west of Crestline on even the heaviest of passenger trains. Lloyd Jones, the head of the Test Department, issued a report to Harry Jones that likewise acknowledged the virtues of the N&W locomotive. At the end of January 1945, Symes informed Harry Jones that all his Western Region train crews were happy with the performance of the #610 and experienced few problems with slipping drivers. The Western Region vice president emphasized the virtues of the locomotive's conventional design, familiar to the PRR's train crews and shop forces. That meant a reduction in maintenance costs, less time spent in the shop, and consequently greater availability to pull passenger trains. Symes insisted that the N&W locomotive, like its C&O 2-10-4 freight counterpart, was a viable stopgap solution for the PRR's passenger needs. The restrictions imposed by the War Production Board were still in effect, but the planned invasion of Japan was likely to bring the war to a conclusion by 1946. The return of peace would unleash a pent-up demand for diesel locomotives, and if the PRR did not act quickly, then it might face a long wait while the builders struggled to catch up. Under the circumstances, Symes argued, it made little sense to commit to the further refinement and wholesale production of the T1, a radically new class of steam locomotive that within a few years would be displaced by diesels.[175]

Symes's advocacy for the N&W locomotive was in vain. The members of the Motive Power Department had devoted the better part of a decade to the development of duplex locomotives, and it was difficult for Symes to resist the momentum of the T1 project. On December 20, while the testing of the borrowed N&W locomotive was still underway, the board of directors appropriated more than $14 million for the construction of fifty additional copies of the T1, subject to WPB approval. In March 1945, as Allied troops were crossing the Rhine and setting foot on German soil, PRR officials finalized the details of the order. The need for passenger power was so acute that the company assigned half of the locomotives to Baldwin, to expedite their construction. The Juniata Shops completed the first production T1 in November 1945, months after Japan's capitulation precluded any widespread movement of troops between the European and Pacific Theaters. In June 1946, shop forces at Altoona finished their batch of fifty locomotives, and T1 #5524 became the last of more than sixty-five hundred steam locomotives built by the Pennsylvania Railroad. The company received its final T1 from Baldwin on August 2 and would never add another steam locomotive of any type.[176]

The performance of the fifty production-model T1 locomotives suggested that the Motive Power Department had resolved some—but by no means all—of the problems that plagued the two prototypes. The poppet values nonetheless remained unreliable and contributed to the high maintenance costs and low availability of the T1.[177] By January 1947, poppet valves were cracking once a day, on average. Gearbox failures were also distressingly frequent, with most occurring in the difficult-to-access rear set of drivers. While the railroad's maintenance forces often blamed the Franklin Railway Supply Company for producing poor-quality poppet-valve assemblies, representatives of that outside supplier were equally adamant that PRR employees lacked the training, experience, and tools necessary to maintain and repair equipment that was more at home on an automobile than on a locomotive. By early 1948, however, Franklin had made modifications that significantly reduced poppet-valve failures. Given sufficient time, it is likely that that problem would cease to plague the T1.[178] The same was true of the wheel slipping that affected Flash Gordon and Buck Rogers. One solution was to reposition the sander nozzles, ensuring that sand landed on the rails in line with the drivers.[179] A more complicated remedy involved changing the springs and the equalization system, preventing the front drivers from lifting off the rails.[180]

Locomotive design involved a complex series of trade-offs, and efforts to resolve one problem produced another. Unfortunately, while the change in the locomotive's weight distribution largely eliminated the slippage problem, it exacerbated another, potentially far more serious situation. During the summer of 1945, several months before the completion of the first production-model T1 locomotives, one of the prototypes derailed on a sharp curve just west of the Pittsburgh station. In the subsequent investigation, Harry Jones and Carl Steins concluded that the mishap occurred because there was too little lateral play in the locomotive's drivers, causing them to ride up the guardrail of certain switches. On December 1, before Jones and Steins could develop a solution, one of the newly built T1 locomotives derailed under similar circumstances—this time at the 28th Street enginehouse in Pittsburgh. Several other derailments occurred in quick succession.[181] It appeared that the changes in the equalization of the front drivers, which had largely solved wheel slipping, had degraded the ability of the locomotives to stay on the rails.[182]

Under the circumstances, Ethelbert W. Smith, the vice president of the Central Region, had little choice other than to ban the operation of the T1 through Pittsburgh.[183] Deasy, the vice president in charge of operations, did not countermand the order. He did, however, demand that Jones explain why he had designed locomotives—constructed at a cost of $13 million—that were incapable of serving their intended function. Jones, who probably felt that his career would soon end, could do no better than suggest that Deasy had not been clear on precisely how the T1 was to replace the K4s. Deasy had obviously assumed that a single duplex would be able to accommodate a train from Harrisburg through to Chicago, something that had not been possible with the older Pacifics. Jones had apparently taken the concept of "replacement" somewhat more literally, asserting that three of the T1 models, operating in succession, could substitute for three pairs of K4s locomotives, retaining the long-standing practice of changing motive power at Altoona and Crestline. It was an implausible explanation, but about the best that Jones could offer under the circumstances. Plausible or not, it did not solve the problem of the Pittsburgh derailments. Jones's career did soon come to an end, although not in the manner he anticipated. The PRR's chief of motive power died on February 23, 1946, barely five weeks after his plaintive explanation for the shortcomings of the T1. He was just sixty-two years old, and the stress associated with the repeated T1 derailments may well have contributed to his death. Deasy, who had been preparing to offer Jones up as a scapegoat, must have sensed that someone else would now have to fill the void. Despite his impressive pedigree and undoubted talents as an electric engineer, John Van Buren Duer was a likely target. Yet Deasy feared that the most obvious candidate to take the blame belonged to the face that stared back at him from his mirror.[184]

Meanwhile, Steins—who was probably the PRR's most gifted mechanical engineer—was working with Baldwin officials to devise a method to prevent further derailments. The solution involved modifications that afforded more lateral play to the drivers. It was a tricky business, given that there was very little clearance between the unmodified drivers and the crossheads on the cylinders, but it worked. Unfortunately, it was too late to incorporate Steins's modifications to most of the newly built locomotives, the last of which emerged from Baldwin's Eddystone facility in August. It would take considerable time and effort to make the changes that Steins had recommended. Until then, the locomotives were largely confined to service between Harrisburg and Altoona and between Crestline and Chicago. There was, however, a further problem. The new coaling station at Millbrook, Ohio, designed to be the sole refueling stop for the T1 between Harrisburg and Chicago, was not operating efficiently. Crews reported that it could take as long as forty-two minutes to fill the tender, producing unacceptable delays. Changes, made at a cost of $95,000, reduced the dwell time to twenty minutes, but the PRR's passenger-traffic officials still complained about so much time being lost. Their counterparts in operations also expressed misgivings about operating a T1 for more than seven hundred miles without any opportunity for a thorough inspection and servicing en route. As a result, passenger trains, even with the modified T1 locomotives, required at least two engine changes between Harrisburg and Chicago, negating one of the principal advantages of the new motive power.[185]

Steam Turbines

The development of the S1, Q1, Q2, and T1 duplexes coincided with an even more radical departure from conventional steam-locomotive practice. In 1897, when British naval engineer Charles A. Parsons demonstrated the *Turbinia* at a naval review at Spithead, England, he proved the value of steam turbines in maritime applications. Motive-power officials on various railroads in Europe and the United States acknowledged the potential

for turbine locomotives. By the 1930s, steam-locomotive boilers typically achieved thermal efficiency (that is, the proportion of potential energy contained in a fuel such as coal ultimately transformed into power) approaching 70 percent. Yet by the time the steam had traveled through the cylinders, actuated the valve gear, and turned the drivers, the locomotive's thermal efficiency had fallen to somewhere between 6 and 8 percent. Turbines offered a higher potential thermal efficiency, combined with lower water consumption. Because they dispensed with traditional valve gear, they also eliminated the problem of dynamic augment—a feature particularly appealing to John Duer and other PRR officials. Yet Duer and his colleagues would face formidable challenges as they attempted to transfer maritime technology to locomotives. Trains were much smaller than ships, requiring designers to shoehorn boilers, turbine units, and associated piping into the narrow confines of a locomotive shell. Turbines operated efficiently only at high speeds, ensuring that a turbine-equipped locomotive would only be suited for fast passenger service, with few intermediate stops. Railroads were also exceedingly dirty places, and pollutants easily fouled the sensitive turbine units. Finally, the vibrations associated with sustained operating speeds were often sufficient to render the turbine inoperable.[186]

The PRR's experiments with steam turbines reflected several concurrent developments during the mid-1930s. Officials at General Electric sought additional applications for the company's generators and associated electrical equipment. They developed a range of steam-powered generator units that could produce between 1,000 and 10,000 horsepower. GE technicians completed the first boiler/turbine/generator unit in 1934. Unlike the turbines employed in naval vessels, the GE technology was small enough to fit inside a railway locomotive. As with the *Turbinia*, however, British engineers took the lead in applying turbine technology to the railroads. In 1935, William Stanier, the chief mechanical engineer at the London, Midland & Scottish Railway, developed the Turbomotive.[187] By the fall of 1936, the Turbomotive had received extensive coverage in the American railway and mechanical-engineering trade press—just as Warren Elsey, John Duer, and John Deasy were replacing the old guard represented by the retiring mechanical engineer, William Kiesel. Turbine technology meshed well with their advocacy for large locomotives, and Duer suggested that it might be a viable counterpart to the GG1 electric. Duer approached GE, which had helped to design the GG1, to determine whether that company's stationary power units could be adapted to railroad use. He also invited representatives from other railroads to participate in the research-and-development efforts, to reduce the PRR's expenditures.[188] By 1937, they were at work on a prototype, known as the Steamotive, with two units that entered service on the Union Pacific in 1938. They soon experienced many problems and went to the scrapyard in 1943.[189]

The disappointing performance of the GE Steamotive reinforced rather than discouraged efforts by Duer and other PRR officials to develop an improved steam-turbine design. The LM&S Turbomotive provided a logical starting point, and Deasy emphasized that the British locomotive was "the only one of which [the PRR had] definite knowledge to which the steam turbine idea has been applied." He acknowledged that Sir Harold Hartley, the LM&S vice president in charge of research, "was not able to furnish very much information with regard to the performance or the operating characteristics" of a design that had not yet performed consistently in revenue service. PRR vice president Charles Young nonetheless suggested that a K4s Pacific—a locomotive that employed the same 4-6-2 wheel arrangement as the Turbomotive—might be converted to turbine drive. Representatives from Baldwin and Westinghouse nonetheless cautioned that the boiler of a K4s could not accommodate the high pressures necessary to power a turbine. Duer likewise suggested that a complete rebuilding of the locomotive was not worth the cost and that the entire proposal was "undesirable."[190]

Duer and his associates continued to cooperate with Baldwin and Westinghouse on the design of a steam turbine that in many respects resembled the recently completed GE Steamotive. By the end of 1939, they had established the basic outlines for a locomotive that could haul a 1,200-ton passenger train traveling at one hundred miles per hour—the same performance criteria that they had set for the recently completed S1. The three-unit prototype would stretch 205 feet and weigh 950,000 pounds. Like the Steamotive, the design relied on a turbine to power an electric generator. The PRR-Baldwin-Westinghouse effort also relied on condensers to conserve water, even though the Union Pacific was beginning to experience significant problems with that technology. There was a significant difference from the GE design, however. The Steamotive burned Bunker C fuel oil rather than coal. That was of little consequence to GE, as a supplier of electrical equipment, but mattered a great deal to Pennsylvania Railroad executives and colliery owners. Rather than risk alienating some of the railroad's largest customers, the first iteration of the design, as well as all its successors, employed coal rather than oil as a fuel. Moreover, as they refined the steam-turbine concept, mechanical engineers at the PRR, Baldwin,

and Westinghouse moved closer to the outlines of a conventional steam locomotive. As an intermediate step, the three-unit locomotive became a single unit, 112 feet long. The problematic condensers disappeared, replaced with a 45-foot tender that would supply water. While the intermediate drawings resembled a lengthened GG1 far more than a typical steam locomotive, the concept evolved still further, to a 4-8-4 wheel arrangement. Rather than use the steam turbine to power a generator, Duer favored a direct drive, in which the steam turbine was linked to the wheels through a series of gears.[191]

By April 1941, representatives from Baldwin and Westinghouse informed their PRR counterparts that a prototype turbine locomotive could be built within a year at a cost of $340,000, with an additional $35,000 in expenditures for testing. At the recommendation of Duer and Deasy, President Clement put the matter before the board of directors on April 23. It was indeed a busy time in the Motive Power Department, with the sole S1 duplex undergoing road tests and final design work underway on the two T1 prototypes. Fred Hankins and Warren Elsey had only recently been removed from their posts as chief of motive power and as mechanical engineer, largely because they had failed to make sufficient progress with the development of duplex locomotives. Their successors, Harry Jones and Carl Steins, demanded better results, and Duer was also placing his career on the line through his support for the steam turbine and duplexes. The board approved the steam-turbine project on April 23, but there was little doubt that the directors, and the PRR's senior management, expected results.[192]

Design work on the steam turbine was incomplete when President Roosevelt established the War Production Board in January 1942. A month later, Fred Hankins (in his new role of assistant vice president in charge of operations) contacted the WPB for permission to construct what was clearly an experimental locomotive. Despite his assertion that the agreement between the PRR, Baldwin, and Westinghouse predated the war, the resulting conversation did not go well. Chief of motive power Harry Jones weighed in on the matter, but to no avail. In January 1943, Charles Young became the deputy director of the Office of Defense Transportation, a post that may have assisted the efforts of his former colleagues to gain WPB approval. Two months later, on March 9, the WPB permitted construction of the new steam-turbine locomotive. Even then, Young cautioned Motive Power Department officials "not to have too many innovations in the design of the locomotive." Of greater significance, shortages of critical materials prevented the use of nickel steel for the

As the only steam-turbine locomotive to operate on the Pennsylvania Railroad, the #6200 presented a striking profile—as here in Chicago in July 1945. The high cost of research and development efforts, coupled with the greater efficiency of diesel locomotives, ensured that this example of Class S2 would never be duplicated. *Harris Negatives Collection, Railroad Museum of Pennsylvania, PHMC.*

boiler, as originally intended. The reliance on carbon steel as an alternative increased the locomotive's weight and required an extension of the lead and trailing trucks. That change transformed the 4-8-4 into a 6-8-6, the same wheel arrangement as the S1 duplex, and accordingly assigned to Class S2 and number 6200.[193]

Unfortunately for Duer, there seemed to be no end of difficulties associated with the S2. Baldwin employees encountered repeated technical issues and material shortages. They were not able to deliver the locomotive to the PRR until October 1944. Data accumulated by the Altoona test plant disappointed Duer and other advocates of the steam turbine. The #6200 generated a peak thermal efficiency of only 7.7 percent, about equal to the performance of a conventional reciprocating steam locomotive. The decision to gear the turbine solely to the two middle sets of axles required the installation of side rods, ensuring that dynamic augment remained a problem. In service, the locomotive proved as slippery as the duplexes and achieved

a top speed of only ninety miles an hour—well below the performance of the T1. One problem followed another, and for 54 percent of the period between October 1, 1944, and June 1945, the locomotive was unavailable for duty.[194]

The sorry state of affairs threatened the reputation of the Pennsylvania Railroad as well as the careers of the individuals who supported the steam-turbine research-and-development program. Despite the ongoing problems, PRR publicists did their best to portray the #6200 as an exemplar of the railroad's progressive management. A December 1, 1945, advertisement in the *Saturday Evening Post* noted (incorrectly, given GE's brief experiments with the Steamotive) that "for the first time a way has been found to put into a locomotive the same kind of power which sends big battleships forward—turbine drive." The boasting was premature and ultimately became one of the principal reasons for the railroad's continuing investments in an unsatisfactory technology. "This locomotive," Charles Young noted in 1947, "has had such favorable and widespread publicity that every effort should be made . . . to make it an operating success regardless of the difficulties thus far experienced."[195]

PRR, Westinghouse, and Baldwin representatives blamed one another for the defects of the S2, but they were unable to develop any solutions. The turbines (one to move the locomotive forward and a smaller unit for reverse) performed well, with minimal wear on the gears and other components. The same could not be said for the boiler, however. It was of conventional construction, with riveted plates held in place by stay bolts that counteracted the outward pressure of the steam. Unlike conventional steam locomotives, which maintained ample steam reserves, the turbine could consume so much steam as to quickly lower boiler pressure—a problem that was particularly acute when the locomotive was starting from a stationary position. Even the most experienced firemen found it difficult to judge how much coal to feed into the firebox at such moments. Too little fuel, and the reduction in boiler pressure retarded speed and pulling power. Too much fuel, particularly if not precisely timed, produced clouds of soot emanating from the stack—a situation that occurred so frequently as to require the installation of smoke lifters to clear the air so that the engineman could see the tracks ahead. Moreover, the rapid fluctuations in boiler pressure placed extreme stress on the stay bolts. They failed frequently, necessitating costly repairs. During its first year, the #6200 ran only thirty-two thousand miles, and by March 1948, near the end of its service life, it had traveled only seventy-five thousand miles in three and a half years. That was well below the performance of the T1 duplexes, which averaged eighty thousand miles a year, or the newest passenger diesels, which averaged more than two hundred thousand miles annually. PRR technicians contemplated the installation of a welded, high-pressure boiler, but the possible improvement in performance was not sufficient to justify the expense.[196]

By the end of World War II, it was clear that the #6200 would not be the solution to the PRR's motive-power problems. Even if the S2 had operated as anticipated, it could not match the thermal efficiency generated by diesels. While the locomotive operated well at seventy miles an hour and above, its efficiency diminished rapidly at lower speeds. Like the T1, the S2 was thus suitable only for the longest and heaviest of intercity passenger trains. Yet that was precisely the application that best fit the performance characteristics of the diesel locomotives offered by Electro-Motive and other builders. James Symes, who had always been skeptical of the PRR's newest steam locomotives, acknowledged that the S2's "performance has been as satisfactory as could have been expected of a locomotive so radically different in design from the reciprocating steam engine." It was hardly a ringing endorsement for a locomotive that had cost more than $440,000 (more than $7.6 million in 2023 dollars) and had never performed reliably. His further observation that "there would seem to be no justification for supplanting the conventional reciprocating locomotive with the turbine type" suggested that that money had been wasted. However, Symes did not yet

have sufficient authority within the company to block the further development of steam-locomotive technology. His moment would come soon enough, as Duer and his allies suffered failure after failure in their efforts to match the performance characteristics of diesels.[197]

For the moment, the disappointing performance of the S2 did not dissuade Duer from supporting steam-turbine technology. The Southern Pacific operated numerous cab-forward reciprocating locomotives, designed to reduce engine-crew exposure to smoke in tunnels and snow sheds. Duer found the concept intriguing and hoped to design a similar cab-in-front locomotive, but one that burned coal rather than Bunker C fuel oil. By November 1941, Raymond Loewy, acting at Duer's request, had produced preliminary drawings for a cab-forward reciprocating steam locomotive. The designer chose the name Triplex, in reference to its three-unit articulated construction, with the leading cab unit carrying the coal, followed by the boiler unit, and then a tender for water. Loewy was a stylist rather than a mechanical engineer, and he sought to retain control of the Triplex name and design. Duer and other PRR officials were far more interested in establishing patent rights to the locomotive's technology, as other coal-carrying railroads such as the Chesapeake & Ohio were conducting similar experiments. At least informally, they retained the Triplex appellation—even as they made substantial alterations to the design. By early 1942, Duer and Carl Steins had sufficient confidence in the S2 development program to eliminate the conventional cylinders and reciprocating valve gear, in favor of a Westinghouse steam turbine. In November, they contemplated testing the now-discredited GE Steamotive units between Indianapolis and Louisville, partly to accumulate additional information for the design of the Triplex. They redesigned the Triplex as a two-unit locomotive, one that vaguely mimicked the preliminary designs for what eventually became the S2. The streamlined lead unit employed a 4-8-4-8 wheel arrangement—although, as it closely resembled an electric or diesel locomotive, it might more properly have been referred to as a 2D-2D.[198] It housed the coal supply, cab, and boiler, eliminating the difficulties associated with transferring fuel from one unit to another. A separate tender, as in Loewy's original design, carried 21,000 gallons of water, with a scoop to collect water from track pans. The complete locomotive, classified as a V1, would be more than 137 feet long, weigh 632,000 pounds, and generate 8,100 horsepower.[199]

During World War II, and with the T1, Q1, J1, Q2, and S2 in various stages of development, Duer and Steins were limited in the time and resources they could devote to the V1 project. It was not until the summer of 1944 that Deasy requested Clement's approval to fully develop the V1 proposal. Clement agreed, although without consulting the board of directors. There was nonetheless reason for Clement to be concerned about the PRR's latest experimental locomotive. Baldwin and Westinghouse had not yet completed work on the S2, but it was apparent that steam-turbine technology was far from perfected. Neither Duer nor Deasy were willing to state definitively whether the Triplex would be used for passenger, freight, or helper service. The turntable at Harrisburg was the only one on the system long enough to accommodate the locomotive's 122-foot, 6-inch wheelbase, and others would have to be lengthened.[200] The same was true of the track pans, to replenish the water supply in the massive tender of the V1.[201]

For a locomotive that never progressed beyond the drawing board, the V1 provoked a surprising amount of controversy among the parties involved in its design. The PRR publicized the project during the spring of 1945, and even the artist's renderings generated criticism. The president of the M. A. Hanna Company, one of the leading coal producers in the East, complained that the railroad's drawings of the V1 made the locomotive look too much like a diesel and failed to emphasize the modernity that was possible in a steam locomotive. Clement responded by noting that the Triplex ensured that "the Pennsylvania should be in a position to continue puffing smoke for years to come." Loewy insisted that the PRR had not given him sufficient credit for the exterior styling. He was quick to remind Deasy that "this conception was originated by me personally in 1941" and suggested that publicity materials "be changed to read, 'The "Triplex" was conceived by the Pennsylvania Railroad's Consulting Designer, Raymond Loewy and developed by the Railroad's Engineering Staff.'" Deasy, in turn, reminded Loewy that railroad personnel had made substantial modifications to his initial sketches, transforming a three-unit reciprocating steam locomotive into a two-unit turbine. He was nonetheless conciliatory and promised to give Loewy full credit for the styling of the V1, if it was completed. Nor was it clear who would build the prototype. PRR representatives suggested that it should be constructed in the Juniata Shops, while their Baldwin counterparts promised to do the work at a considerably lower expense. They also did their best to dissuade Duer from incorporating the superior boiler offered by Alco into the final design.[202]

Throughout the development process, Duer and Steins were concerned that officials at Baldwin and the Chesapeake & Ohio were designing a steam turbine that was extraordinarily similar to the V1. Their efforts during 1945 and 1946 principally involved protecting the PRR's patent rights rather than building a complete locomotive. When Howell Cover became the new chief of motive power in March 1946, following the death of Harry Jones, he reinforced those concerns. A native of Altoona, Cover began working for the PRR as a laborer in 1915, four years before he earned an engineering degree at Pennsylvania State College. Like W. W. Atterbury before him, Cover participated in the special apprentice program before making the customary rotation of jobs across the PRR system. He returned to Altoona in 1929 as a gang foreman at the East Altoona Shops. In 1942, he became the superintendent of freight transportation, serving only briefly in that post, prior to his assignment as the general superintendent of the Eastern Ohio General Division. In June 1946, he reminded Deasy that the courts were "inclined to very narrowly construe patents when the patentee has not reduced his invention to practice." Deasy passed the warning to Clement, who in September obtained board approval to negotiate a contract with Baldwin and Westinghouse to build the trucks, turbine drives, and other patented components of the V1. Yet amid postwar austerity and with diesel locomotives demonstrating their advantages over both reciprocating steam locomotives and steam turbines, the possibility that the PRR would spend a million dollars or more on a working V1 prototype, to retain patent rights, seemed increasingly remote.[203]

Even so, the repeated setbacks associated with the V1 did not discourage PRR executives from supporting further attempts to apply steam turbines to locomotives. Rather than bear the expense of a proprietary project and thus retain the associated patent rights, they pursued a strategy of cooperation. The project began in the spring of 1944, when Clement met with officials from other railroads that relied on coal for a significant portion of their revenues. Dieselization threatened to eliminate the more than fifty million tons of coal consumed by the eastern railroads each year, encouraging representatives from eight railroads and four large coal companies to join the consortium.[204] Acting in concert, they established the Locomotive Development Committee of Bituminous Coal Research, Incorporated, a research-and-development organization funded by coal producers. Edward L. Bachman, the PRR's general superintendent of motive power, served as vice chairman. For the next fourteen years, the committee worked to develop a gas-turbine-electric locomotive that would burn powdered coal.[205] John I. Yellott, the director of the Institute of Gas Technology at the Illinois Institute of Technology, coordinated the project. Every major company with significant experience in the design and construction of steam locomotives, turbines, and electrical equipment made contributions of varying degrees. Their efforts on behalf of the Locomotive Development Committee complemented and occasionally conflicted with their work on proprietary projects for specific customers. Alco and Baldwin designed sample locomotives, which in many respects mimicked the basic outlines of the now-halted V1. In January 1947, the PRR reminded coal-mine operators that the company was "now actively collaborating in the development of coal burning gas turbine locomotives." By the fall of 1949, Allis-Chalmers and the Elliott Company had completed prototype turbines. They burned oil, but members of the Locomotive Development Committee hoped that the technology could be adapted to the use of powdered coal as a fuel. The Standard Stoker Company and Babcock & Wilcox were working on an atomizer that could crush the coal. Combustion tests at Alco's Dunkirk, New York, facility; at the Battelle Memorial Institute in Columbus, Ohio; and at Turbodyne Corporation in Fontana, California, nonetheless revealed a disturbing problem. The burning of atomized coal produced large quantities of fly ash, an airborne particulate that corroded the turbine blades and impeded the operation of a mechanism that was far more delicate than a conventional reciprocating steam locomotive.[206]

Oblivious to the demands of coal producers, all three of the steam-locomotive producers went ahead with plans to build gas-turbine locomotives, none of which burned coal. Lima-Hamilton prepared preliminary designs for a 3,200-horsepower unit. In 1948, the PRR pledged $250,000 in funding but revoked the offer four years later after the company merged with Baldwin, and the project died on the drawing board. Baldwin subsequently produced a 4,000-horsepower demonstrator that underwent tests on the PRR during 1952. Baldwin was on the verge of exiting the locomotive business, however, and lacked the resources and the organizational commitment to make improvements. The most successful results emerged from the cooperative arrangement between General Electric and Alco. For several years, GE technicians had made a valiant effort to develop a coal-fired steam turbine, utilizing a high-pressure boiler developed by Babcock & Wilcox. The evaluation of the boiler at the Altoona test plant and at a Babcock & Wilcox facility failed to produce the desired thermal efficiency. By the spring of 1947, GE personnel had concluded that—even if they could solve the multitude of problems they encountered—the locomotive would never be competitive against the diesel. They continued with the development of a gas turbine that burned inexpensive

Bunker C fuel oil, and by November 1948, they had completed a prototype for the Union Pacific. It operated far more successfully than the prewar Steamotive, prompting UP officials to order several additional units. The success of the oil-fired turbines that GE and Alco produced for the Union Pacific did little to benefit the PRR and the other coal-carrying railroads, mine owners, or the members of the Locomotive Development Committee.[207] By 1955, PRR officials had committed at least $800,000 to the Locomotive Development Committee, but no more contributions would be forthcoming. The committee's experiments with coal-fired gas-turbine locomotive technology ended in 1958, with the test results turned over to the United States Bureau of Mines. By then, the steam locomotive had vanished from the Pennsylvania Railroad. In its place came the diesel.[208]

The Momentum Begins to Shift

Even as they were struggling to develop duplexes and steam turbines, Pennsylvania Railroad motive-power officials had lost the battle against diesels. Between 1937 and 1942, Electro-Motive transformed its formidable position in the diesel-locomotive industry into market dominance. Eugene W. Kettering, the son of famed GM engineer Charles Franklin Kettering, led a team that developed the Model 567 diesel engine as a replacement for the Model 201A. The E3 passenger locomotive, introduced in the summer of 1938, featured two Model 567 engines that together generated an impressive 2,000 horsepower. EMC's NW2 switcher also employed the new engine, with its 1,000-horsepower output nearly twice that of the PRR's lone Model SW.[209] Beginning in 1939, EMC fabricated traction motors and other electrical equipment at the La Grange plant, ending its dependence on outside suppliers such as General Electric and Westinghouse and providing tighter control over design and production methods.

Of equal significance, in 1939 EMC introduced the Model FT, a 1,350-horsepower freight locomotive. Four of them, coupled together, generated 5,400 horsepower, about as much as a Super Power steam locomotive. The FT was the first locomotive that could dieselize the freight trains that constituted most of the railroads' traffic, and EMC officials were prepared to exploit their advantage. In November, they began a nationwide demonstration tour that covered more than eighty thousand miles. The FT did not travel on the Pennsylvania Railroad, however, and representatives from the Motive Power Department declined EMC's offer to test it on their rails. John Deasy, the vice president in charge of operations, refused even to read the

The PRR's first two passenger diesels, ordered in December 1941, did not enter service until September 1945. Intended for *The South Wind*, the #5900 and the #5901 instead powered *The Red Arrow* service to Detroit. They soon proved their worth and thus doomed the efforts of the Motive Power Department to perfect a new generation of duplex and steam-turbine locomotives. *General Negative Collection, Railroad Museum of Pennsylvania, PHMC.*

data that the FT had accumulated on other railroads. With some justification, he dismissed the information as EMC propaganda and not up to the standards established by the PRR's Test Department.[210]

Yet there were signs that some PRR officials were giving greater consideration to diesel locomotives. In 1941, the PRR purchased a second diesel locomotive—an NW2, which by 1943 had replaced the original SW unit at the Linden GM plant. Many of the lower-level operating and maintenance employees who worked with those diesels commented favorably on their abilities, but their perspective rarely swayed senior executives. Charles Young, the PRR's vice president of purchases, stores, and insurance, acknowledged that the railroad had ended all purchases of steam shifters—although that decision was influenced by the large numbers of surplus steam locomotives already on the property and not by a desire to acquire diesels. Paul Turner, Electro-Motive's chief salesman, observed that

Fred Hankins had accepted the merits of diesel switchers, although he still harbored doubts about the diesel's potential for main line freight and passenger service. John Duer, the chief electrical engineer, was determined to extend electrification west of Harrisburg and had little interest in any form of diesel propulsion. He authorized numerous cost/benefit analyses relating to the acquisition of diesel switchers, but Turner was convinced that these were nothing more than a delaying tactic. By June 1941, another Electro-Motive executive suggested that the Pennsylvania Railroad "appears to be definitely forming itself into a Diesel and a [sic] anti-Diesel camp. Some of the lesser officials are becoming quite aggressive in the interests of the Diesel although there is no indication that the higher officials are anxious to make purchases in the near future." As such, Turner and his colleagues prepared study after study for the PRR and waited for the internal dynamics of the railroad to tip in their favor.[211]

The gates had begun to open in 1941, on one of the more remote corners of the Pennsylvania Railroad system. In December of the previous year, the PRR inaugurated *The South Wind* between Chicago and Miami, in cooperation with the Louisville & Nashville, the Atlantic Coast Line, and the Florida East Coast. In addition to contributing equipment to the passenger-car pool, the PRR provided a streamlined K4s Pacific like those employed on *The Jeffersonian*, the all-coach streamliner that traveled between New York and St. Louis. The L&N also employed a streamlined steam locomotive for its portion of the run, but the FEC relied on an EMC E-unit. PRR representatives to the joint project had considered a diesel as well but had initially rejected the idea. In February 1941, less than three months after the inaugural trip of *The South Wind*, Harry Jones replaced Hankins as chief of motive power, while Carl Steins succeeded Elsey as mechanical engineer. Jones and Steins proved more receptive to diesel power, particularly as the competing *City of Miami* (operated jointly by the Illinois Central, Central of Georgia, Atlantic Coast Line, and FEC) featured a single EMC E6A locomotive. Jones ordered Steins to arrange the purchase of a pair of E6A locomotives. The two units, coupled together, generated 4,000 horsepower, perhaps inadequate for the longest and heaviest passenger trains, but certainly sufficient for the seven-car consist of *The South Wind*. The board of directors authorized the purchase, based on Jones's assertions that the diesels would shorten *The South Wind*'s schedule—even if it would produce no better than a 4.5 percent return on investment. The PRR placed the order on December 9, 1941, only two days after Pearl Harbor. Restrictions imposed by the War Production Board soon encouraged the PRR to cancel the order on May 20, 1942. Even after the relaxation of WPB guidelines, the PRR had lost its place in the queue behind the many other railroads whose executives demanded diesels as quickly as possible. The locomotives, now slightly upgraded to the Model E7 (with an iconic "bulldog" nose that replaced the shovel nose on earlier versions) were not ready until September 1945.[212] The railroad's first passenger diesels entered service on *The Red Arrow* between Harrisburg and Detroit, not on *The South Wind* as originally planned. It was a pragmatic operational decision, given that K4s Pacific locomotives, commonly assigned to *The Red Arrow*, were too heavy for the access ramp leading to Detroit's Fort Street Union Depot.[213] As an added benefit, the use of Electro-Motive diesels on the route was certain to find favor at GM's corporate headquarters.[214]

By the time the PRR received the two E7 units, there had been a further transformation in the locomotive industry. The success of the Model FT and the certainty of increased military orders encouraged Alfred Sloan—the president and chairman of the board at General Motors—to establish tighter control over Winton and Electro-Motive. On January 1, 1941, EMC became a part of the new Electro-Motive Division of General Motors. Production continued on the Model FT freight locomotive, the E-series passenger locomotives, and various switchers, but the navy demanded an increasing share of EMD's output for landing craft and similar applications. The War

Production Board's 1942 controls established EMD as the sole producer of freight locomotives, with Alco and Baldwin restricted to switching and passenger units.[215]

During the war, PRR executives acknowledged that diesel switchers were superior to their steam counterparts, even in locations that were not constrained by public policy or adverse operating conditions. At the time of Pearl Harbor, the railroad operated the three gasoline-powered A6 switchers, plus two Electro-Motive diesels—the 600-horsepower Model SW and the 1,000-horsepower Model NW2. A third diesel, a Model SW1, had been on order since October but would not be delivered until August 1942.[216] It was soon at work at a GM plant in Grand Rapids, Michigan, as another concession to a valued customer. In March 1942, however, Jones recommended the acquisition of fifteen diesel switchers, three to be based in Philadelphia and the remaining dozen in the New York Zone. He noted that the only alternative involved the use of nineteen steam shifters to accommodate increased wartime traffic. Deasy supported the request and acknowledged a return on investment of nearly 14 percent. It was the first time that a senior PRR official had explicitly recommended the purchase of diesels based solely on their economic merits. All fifteen came from Baldwin, in acknowledgment of the close ties between the two companies, and of WPB restrictions that curtailed EMD switcher production. Even as the Motive Power Department was scaling up production of the Q2 and the T1, there was no further discussion of building steam shifters. Yet as late as 1947, the PRR still owned fewer than 40 diesel switchers, less than a tenth of the 591 steam shifters in service.[217]

Nor was there much interest in diesel freight power during the war. Wartime service, particularly on the Santa Fe, proved the worth of Electro-Motive's FT. In 1935, the Baltimore & Ohio had been an early adopter of Electro-Motive's first boxcab diesel design. By August 1942, the B&O had again taken the lead on the PRR, acquiring a set of FT locomotives. So did the Boston & Maine, and a *Railway Age* article regarding their performance attracted the attention of President Clement. Unlike many of his subordinates, he was at the very least curious about the potential of diesel freight service. In November 1943, three years after Deasy had declined Electro-Motive's offer to demonstrate the FT, Clement asked the vice president in charge of operations for his perspective on the locomotive. The PRR had just canceled plans to produce a final batch of J1 locomotives, based on Deasy's assurances that the Q2—still on the drawing board—was a better choice. Yet the board of directors had not yet committed the company to full-scale Q2 production. In defense of his pet project,

Deasy reassured Clement that the Q2, a locomotive that had not yet been built, would provide higher speeds and more pulling power than Electro-Motive's FT, a locomotive whose test results he had refused to evaluate.[218]

During 1943, Deasy and Duer were also involved in a revised plan to electrify the main line between Harrisburg and Pittsburgh, to cope with increased traffic. Implementation was unlikely, given the cost and the shortage of copper. EMD's Paul Turner was nothing if not persistent and suggested dieselization as an alternative. It was a bold proposal, given the WPB restrictions on EMD's output, but Turner was determined to derail the electrification study before it gained too much momentum. Despite his ties to Baldwin, Charles Young was receptive to Turner's proposal. Duer acquiesced but demanded Clement's approval before the matter went any further.[219]

The discussions between Turner and Duer proved fruitless. Duer demanded a single locomotive that could generate 6,000 horsepower, comparable to a GG1 or the proposed Q2. A four-unit set of EMD FT locomotives fell only 600 horsepower short of that goal. Yet Duer was not prepared to embrace the operational flexibility that constituted one of the most important performance characteristics associated with diesel locomotives. Like his counterparts on other railroads, Duer was legitimately concerned that the operating brotherhoods would demand separate crews for each diesel unit, thus raising labor costs to an unacceptably high level.[220] Turner resisted the demand that EMD place so much horsepower in a single unit, and he was even more adamant in his refusal to allow the PRR's Motive Power Department to buy diesel engines from EMD and install them in locomotives built at Altoona.[221] As he had done in the past, Duer was likely imposing conditions that he knew Turner would never accept so that he could truthfully inform Deasy and Clement that diesels were impracticable. Moreover, as Turner acknowledged, Duer was a passionate advocate for electrification and was prepared to dismiss diesels for that reason alone. Turner nonetheless suggested, with good reason, that Duer's attitudes "reflect some of the thinking of his superiors in connection with these matters." Having made many trips to Philadelphia, with little to show for his efforts, Turner's disgust with the PRR's Motive Power Department was evident. "If they were not such a potential market for motive power," he informed the executives at La Grange, "I would be inclined to forget them but I don't think we can afford to do this."[222]

Within three years, however, Turner's efforts had begun to pay off. By 1945, no one at the PRR was willing to oppose the use of diesel switchers, and only the cost of acquiring

new units, coupled with the surplus of steam shifters, prevented more rapid adoption. The wartime service accumulated by passenger diesels on other railroads suggested that they were a viable replacement for steam power. That was certainly true on the Santa Fe, where senior management was enthusiastically supportive of dieselization. In the East, the Baltimore & Ohio was experiencing excellent results with its growing fleet of Electro-Motive E-units, ensuring that that company's sole experiment with a duplex was never to be repeated. Of greater concern to PRR executives, their counterparts at the New York Central had also avoided duplexes—by joining the Super Power revolution and then quickly shifting allegiance to diesels. In March 1945, the NYC received the first Class S1a steam passenger locomotive. Designed by Paul W. Kiefer, the NYC's chief of motive power, and manufactured by Alco, the locomotive employed the 4-8-4 wheel arrangement that had become commonplace for fast passenger locomotives.[223] Its excellent steaming capabilities and 79-inch drivers (7 inches larger than the N&W's version of the 4-8-4, and only an inch smaller than those on the T1) generated 6,000 horsepower at high speeds. The NYC's new locomotive reflected the best traits of Super Power design, but its days were numbered. Less than a week after the first S1a arrived on the property, a New York Central passenger train left Collinwood, Ohio, twenty minutes behind schedule. A new set of EMD E7 diesels provided the power. The engineman settled into the right-hand seat, and as he notched open the throttle, the train accelerated out of the yard. "It was one of the finest runs I've ever seen," declared a NYC official. The train reached speeds of eighty miles an hour and arrived in Buffalo thirty-four minutes ahead of schedule. The railroad soon assigned diesels to the *Twentieth Century Limited*. NYC officials announced that they were also prepared to dieselize the most important passenger routes to Cincinnati and St. Louis, relegating their new, state-of-the art Super Power steam locomotives to secondary service.[224]

Clement was determined that the Pennsylvania Railroad should remain competitive in the east–west passenger market, and he was prepared to match the NYC's efforts. In September, two months before the Altoona Works completed the first of the production-model T1 locomotives, he asked Deasy whether it would be possible to dieselize *The Broadway Limited*, west of Harrisburg. At the very least, the PRR's president insisted, the company should purchase enough additional E7 locomotives to provide diesel power for every section of *The Red Arrow*, a move that was certain to please GM executives. Until the locomotives arrived, Clement suggested, the two existing E7 units could be tested on a variety of routes. Clement's request placed Deasy in an awkward position. On the same day, he had requested additional funds for the V1 steam turbine, while acknowledging massive cost overruns in its developmental phase. Its predecessor, the S2, was unquestionably a failure. So too was the original duplex, the S1, while its offspring—the Q1, the Q2, and the T1—had not demonstrated the success Deasy had promised. Under the circumstances, Deasy's response to Clement—"do not know what we want to do, but we should hurry up and find out"—demonstrated both indecisiveness and an unwillingness to accept dieselization and thereby abandon a decade of research and development on high-horsepower steam locomotives.[225]

Deasy's situation became more difficult a few days later when he received an urgent letter from James Symes, the vice president in charge of the Western Region. Symes had refused to operate the problematic S1 on his region, and he had doubts about the Q2 and the T1 as well. A year earlier, in an effort to halt the development of the T1, he had demanded tests of a Norfolk & Western locomotive, but he failed to dissuade officials in the Motive Power Department from pursuing the project. Symes did not concede defeat, and he now asked Deasy to suspend construction of as many as twenty of the unbuilt T1 locomotives in favor of purchasing passenger diesels for use on the Western Region. Deasy referred the matter to Harry Jones, who in defense of the T1 could do no better than assert that the Juniata Shops had already ordered the material for their production and that it was too late to cancel.[226]

On October 3, 1945, the day after the PRR announced that it would order ninety lightweight passenger cars for the all-coach *Jeffersonian* and *Trail Blazer*, Deasy acquiesced to the purchase of additional passenger diesels. Mimicking the motive-power assignments on the New York Central, three additional locomotive sets would enable the dieselization of a single train on the routes to Chicago, St. Louis, and Cincinnati. Deasy acknowledged that the assignments would furnish data that would permit an accurate comparison with steam locomotives. He nonetheless suggested that the new diesels were unlikely to generate much more than a 5 percent return on investment. Within a week, and probably at Clement's insistence, Deasy had expanded the proposal to seven locomotive sets, sufficient to fully dieselize *The Broadway Limited*, *The "Spirit of St. Louis,"* and *The Cincinnati Limited*. In late November, less than two weeks after the Altoona Works completed the initial production-model T1 locomotive, the PRR placed the first of several orders for the diesels that would soon replace them. Yet there was no public mention of this sea change

in the PRR's motive-power policy. The company had not yet found a buyer for the equipment-trust certificates that would underwrite the cost of each T1, and Clement concluded that such negative publicity would have jeopardized that process.[227]

The PRR's initial purchases reflected a managerial policy that favored brute horsepower, at the expense of operational flexibility. Jones "recommended that the minimum size Diesel locomotive purchased be of 6,000 H.P. capacity, which is almost identical with that of the T1 and GG1." It was the standard stipulation of the Motive Power Department and one that Deasy passed along to Clement. Pennsylvania Railroad officials explored several options for ensuring that each locomotive set generated the required 6,000 horsepower. While a group of E7 locomotives, coupled together in an A-B-A configuration, would have met the requirement, officials in the Motive Power Department held fast to their steam-era practice of placing as much weight on the (powered) drivers as possible. They objected to the six-wheel trucks used on the E7, as the middle axle was unpowered. As an alternative, they favored A-B-B-A sets of the EMD F3, the 1,500-horsepower model that had superseded the FT. Yet when they became aware of tracking problems on the F3 diesels used by the Santa Fe, they changed the order to eight E7 sets and only two sets of the Model F3.[228]

Baldwin offered a third option, in the form of the DR-12-8-1500/2. The design was more commonly known as the "Centipede," owing to its many wheels, and possessed of a distinctive front end, sometimes called a "baby face." The Centipede consisted of two permanently coupled units, each of which generated 3,000 horsepower. Both had cabs, allowing for bidirectional running, yet the two halves were not identical and could not be operated independently. The design of the Centipede thus reflected the railroads' concerns that union officials would demand multiple crews in multiple-unit locomotives.[229] It was also an extension of Baldwin's design philosophy, which even with growing diesel sales continued to emphasize the production of massive, single-unit steam engines, a practice that matched the traditions of the PRR's Motive Power Department.[230] As a new model, the Centipede had not yet demonstrated the abilities of the EMD E- and F-units, and PRR officials acknowledged that earlier Baldwin diesels had not performed well. Clement nevertheless authorized the purchase of several Centipedes, partly as a favor to Baldwin and partly to sample the products of as many builders as possible prior to committing to large orders for a single design. That strategy ensured that PRR employees would

The DR-12-8-1500/2 represented Baldwin's effort to capture a portion of the passenger diesel market. It soon gained the nickname "Centipede"—as well as an unenviable reputation for mechanical failures. Quickly banished from passenger service, the Centipedes completed their brief and unhappy careers as pushers. One set is seen rounding the Horseshoe Curve in July 1953, headed back to Altoona for another assignment. *Otto Perry photograph, Denver Public Library, Western History Collection, call number OP-14320.*

confront a great diversity of operating and maintenance conditions, given the idiosyncrasies associated with each builder's products.[231]

While the 1945 purchases represented a significant first step in the dieselization of the PRR's passenger and freight service, they did not indicate that managers had accepted the new technology. Duer, supported by Deasy, hoped for an expansion of electrified territory, with the V1 Triplex handling trains west of Pittsburgh. In July 1946, he argued that "the Pennsylvania Railroad should not build up its ownership of Diesel locomotives to such an extent as to prevent the future adoption" of the steam turbine that was still under development. Even Clement was cautious, and

he and his subordinates were careful to emphasize that the new diesels were an "experiment" that would keep traffic moving until the next generation of steam and electric locomotives could enter service. For the next year, therefore, PRR executives pursued a three-part strategy for the acquisition of motive power: buying a few diesels, continuing the production of the T1 while contemplating the manufacture of additional Q2 freight locomotives, and experimenting with the Triplex.[232]

The Triplex project never bore fruit, and the second component of that three-part strategy also proved problematic. While the T1 and Q2 locomotives at least made it off the drawing board, by the summer of 1946, it was clear that they were not performing as well as Duer and other officials in the Motive Power Department had promised. The J1 locomotives, copies of those built for the Chesapeake & Ohio fifteen years earlier, were proving themselves superior to the recently completed Q2 models that had been designed by the PRR's Motive Power Department. In July, PRR officials conducted a new round of stationary tests. While their intent was certainly to compare the Q2 against the more reliable J1, they were also determined to gather the evidence that would demonstrate that a duplex steam locomotive could generate far more power than even the best diesels that EMD could produce. Unfortunately, the data showed that the Q2 produced only slightly more horsepower than the J1 at typical operating speeds, and no one was able to determine why that was the case. Duer downplayed the Q2's high coal and water consumption rate, suggesting that further stationary testing would provide more accurate readings than data collected by Western Region operating and maintenance personnel. Those lower-level officials had observed the Q2 and the J1 at work under a variety of conditions rather than in the carefully calibrated environment of the Altoona test plant, and they were emphatic that they preferred the latter locomotive over the former. Senior management was not impressed with Duer's argument that the Q2 was performing almost as well as the locomotive it was designed to replace, and his authority within the company never recovered. Even Deasy, who had supported the Q2, eventually admitted that the Motive Power Department had brought it into production too quickly.[233]

By the time officials in the Test Department had released the data from the Q2 evaluation, Duer and Deasy had lost the ability to delay dieselization or experiment with new steam-locomotive designs. The cost of coal increased from $2.00 to $4.60 a ton between 1939 and 1949, making steam-locomotive operation increasingly uneconomical.[234] A strike by the United Mine Workers, which began on April 1, 1946, curtailed coal supplies and caused prices to double. The PRR placed 560 coal-burning steam locomotives in storage and curtailed freight and passenger operations. On May 10, the Office of Defense Transportation imposed a 25 percent reduction in the mileage of passenger trains pulled by steam locomotives, with an additional 25 percent reduction taking place less than a week later. The shortage of coal prevented the PRR from assigning more than one locomotive to many passenger trains, and the resulting decrease in the number of cars angered travelers, deprived the company of revenue, and retarded Clement's efforts to entice Americans out of their cars and onto the rails.[235]

Clement asked his staff to suggest ways to curtail coal consumption. Only one of the five responses addressed dieselization, but with steam freight and passenger locomotives consuming 80 percent of the coal used on the PRR, Clement began to give serious consideration to the wholesale replacement of the railroad's motive power. Labor costs rose 75 percent during the same period, while rates remained stagnant. As the war came to an end, freight and passenger traffic declined sharply, and net railway operating income fell from $109 million in 1944

to $87.2 million in 1945 and just $25.9 million in 1946. Under such circumstances, the operating ratio (operating expenses as a percentage of operating revenue) began to creep upward, from 72.9 in 1944 to 83.7 in 1945. The latter figure was manageable yet belied a statistic that shocked managers throughout the system—in December of that year, the operating ratio had reached the crippling level of 160.3. That could be explained by a variety of factors, including bitter winter weather, but there was no excuse for the 1946 operating ratio of 90.7. Nor could the railroad's executives deny that net revenues had declined from $45 million in 1945 to an $8 million *loss* the following year. The subsequent *New York Times* headline—"Pennsy 'In The Red'"—was unprecedented, and the statement that "the 1946 deficit occurred in spite of the fact that the road handled more traffic, both passenger and freight, than in any previous peacetime year" was equally concerning. "Never before in its 100-year history has that system, the largest in the nation, lost money," the *Times* continued. That such a situation had occurred during the PRR's centennial year only made matters that much more embarrassing. Under the circumstances, the Pennsylvania Railroad could no longer devote resources to the refinement of the freight and passenger duplexes, and there was certainly too little money available to waste on projects such as the Triplex steam turbine.[236]

Thanks to its financial worries, in its centennial year the Pennsylvania Railroad's motive-power policies changed more rapidly than at any other time in the company's history. At the beginning of 1946, all the PRR's personnel conceded that diesel switchers were superior to their steam counterparts. The crucial debate involved the freight and passenger locomotives that made up the bulk of the railroad's fleet. While some officials in the Motive Power Department were beginning to yield in the matter of passenger service, most insisted that diesels were unsuited for freight operations. In January, when Steins and Jones began to establish criteria for a new freight locomotive, they certainly reflected that philosophy. They solicited input from the regional vice presidents regarding the features that should be incorporated into a new steam-locomotive design, yet they did not offer diesels as an alternative.[237]

By the spring of 1946, however, the momentum toward dieselization had become unstoppable. Harry Jones died in February. A month later, Howell Cover became the new chief of motive power. Cover had been intimately involved in the development of the passenger and freight duplexes and, like Duer, he was trained as an electrical engineer. However, he lacked Duer's commitment to large locomotives and was more receptive to diesels. On April 1, Deasy instructed Cover to work with regional personnel to determine the optimum design for a new batch of one hundred steam locomotives. Clement's assistant, James Regis Downes, quickly suggested that diesel and electric locomotives should also be considered. Edgar E. Ernest, the chief of passenger transportation, wanted to dieselize the PRR's long-distance trains, and he echoed the concerns that Clement had expressed through Downes. Deasy and Duer mostly ignored the advice, and by August, they agreed that the PRR should build seventy-five more Q2 freight locomotives. In a concession to Ernest, Duer reluctantly recommended the acquisition of twenty-five diesel passenger locomotives, sufficient to maintain service while the Motive Power Department completed work on the steam turbine. While he downplayed the lower operating costs and increased availability of diesels, Duer nonetheless acknowledged that the railroad's existing duplexes were no longer the ideal choice for passenger service. Carl Steins was less flexible, however, and he asserted that the T1 locomotives—the last of which were nearing completion—would provide ample passenger power in the foreseeable future.[238]

As the vice president in charge of the Western Region, James Symes offered a very different perspective on the choice of motive power. The years he spent in Chicago, coupled with his service to the Association of American Railroads, had exposed him to operating practices on other carriers—and correspondingly insulated him from the corporate culture at the PRR's headquarters in Philadelphia. He was only forty-nine—fifteen years younger than Deasy—and his formative years had coincided with the emergence of the automobile as a reliable means of transportation. Unlike Deasy and many of the senior members of the Motive Power Department, Symes was comfortable with the principles of internal combustion. He had no vested interest in steam technology or in the long and expensive duplex program. He was less interested in the data produced by the Altoona test plant than he was in assessing how well steam locomotives performed in revenue service. Rather than maximize the horsepower that each locomotive could generate, Symes cared only about maximizing the railroad's return on its investment in motive power by earning as much revenue as possible while minimizing operating costs. Given the PRR's financial problems following World War II, Symes did not view diesels as a threat to steam power. Instead, he suggested that they would determine whether his century-old company would survive or perish. The return on investment

associated with the purchase of diesels, he asserted, "is so attractive that it might well be the governing factor in determining our future solvency, and I do not think we can afford to postpone it."[239]

Symes had never thought highly of the duplex, and, in the autumn of 1944, he insisted that the PRR test a Norfolk & Western locomotive before committing to wholesale production of the T1. The 1946 tests that demonstrated that the Q2 performed scarcely better than the J1 in freight service did little to improve Symes's opinion of the Motive Power Department. Symes was likewise displeased—but probably not surprised—when, in early September, two T1 locomotives loaned to the Chesapeake & Ohio performed badly in a series of tests. After reading a preliminary draft of Deasy's report, Symes thus cautioned against building any more of the Q2 freight locomotives.[240]

Duer and Deasy ignored Symes's recommendations, just as they had skirted the advice that Downes provided. Their final report, with its assertion that the PRR should invest in a further batch of seventy-five Q2 locomotives, galvanized Symes into action. On October 7, less than a month after the completion of the T1 tests on the C&O, Symes wrote a memo suggesting that further investment in the Q2—or indeed in any steam locomotives—was a waste of money. With the New York Central and the Baltimore & Ohio by now committed to the dieselization of freight trains, Symes argued, the PRR had little choice but to follow suit. Symes pointed out that diesels cost less to operate than steam locomotives, while their much greater availability ensured that they would spend more time in service, generating revenue—issues that Duer and Deasy had largely ignored. Symes emphasized that thirty-three sets of diesel freight locomotives would cost the same as the seventy-five Q2 steam locomotives but would produce at least a million additional train miles annually. Under the circumstances, Symes concluded, the PRR could no longer afford to use steam locomotives merely to avoid alienating representatives from the coal industry.[241]

Clement found the arguments persuasive, and nine days later, he appointed Symes as the deputy vice president in charge of operations. Symes was soon on his way from Chicago to the company's headquarters in Philadelphia, only feet from Clement's office and the corporate boardroom.[242] While he was Deasy's direct subordinate, by October 1946, Symes was for all intents and purposes directing the PRR's motive-power strategy. In early November, Symes ordered a comprehensive study of the PRR's future motive-power needs. His immediate goal was to accumulate the data necessary to block the acquisition of any additional steam locomotives. The larger issue, however, concerned the more than four thousand steam locomotives that were still in service. Most of the individuals in the Motive Power Department—and in all probability Clement as well—assumed that they would remain in use until they were worn out, at which point diesels would replace them. Symes, in contrast, was convinced that if the Pennsylvania Railroad were to remain competitive, dieselization should proceed as rapidly as possible, even if that meant the scrapping of the newest of the steam locomotives.[243]

While Symes did not release his final report until the end of March 1947, by early December of the preceding year, he had accumulated sufficient data to bolster his contentions. The preliminary findings reiterated the economic advantages of the diesel, in terms of greater availability and lower operating costs, while suggesting that if the PRR continued to rely on steam power, it could not remain competitive against the New York Central and the Baltimore & Ohio. He observed that at any given moment there were approximately seven thousand hopper cars full of coal, destined for locomotive use, circulating through the PRR's thirteen thousand miles of track. They occupied valuable space in yards and along the main line and consumed a significant portion of the railroad's operating capacity. Symes also attempted to quantify the previously vague assertion that dieselization would alienate mine owners, causing them to redirect their coal traffic to competing carriers. With most of the other railroads in the United States ordering diesels, Symes concluded that the coalfields would be devastated and there was not much that the PRR, alone, could do to prevent it.[244] Asserting that the market for steam-locomotive coal would soon be gone forever, Symes suggested that mine owners would soon come to appreciate the benefits of dieselization through lower freight rates and improved service. Nor was electrification a viable means to fend off dieselization or to protect the coal industry through the operation of power plants. The prewar $47 million estimate to erect catenary between Harrisburg and Pittsburgh had ballooned to $105 million, and the expected return on investment was far too low to justify such a massive expenditure.[245]

The PRR's president needed little convincing. In November, while Symes was mailing a barrage of questions to personnel in the Operating and Traffic Departments, Clement met with an official in Toledo who "made the statement that no railroad could protect its competitive situation by confining itself to steam if diesel was more productive." Thus convinced and armed with Symes's preliminary data, Clement placed the matter before the Road Committee of the board of directors. He emphasized that

it was essential that the PRR obtain new motive power as quickly as possible, but he did not insist that diesels were the only option. The members of the Road Committee nonetheless recommended, unanimously, that the board should appropriate nearly $16.4 million to purchase nineteen 6,000-horsepower passenger locomotive sets. In conjunction with the diesels already in service and on order, that would be sufficient to dieselize the railroad's highest-priority passenger trains.[246] A further six sets of EMD Model F3 diesels, each generating 7,500 horsepower, would be used to operate a single freight train between Harrisburg and Chicago and another between Harrisburg and St. Louis.[247]

The December 18, 1946, board meeting signaled that the railroad's commitment to steam locomotives was waning. The dieselization of the Blue Ribbon passenger trains rendered the T1 duplexes useless, as that was the only purpose for which they had been designed. The six freight-diesel sets seemingly posed little threat to the 1,034 large steam freight locomotives that the railroad owned—particularly when Clement acknowledged that they could only move "125 of the most important cars out of each of these towns [Chicago and St. Louis] for New York every day, [so that] the rest of the business could well follow along in the other [steam-locomotive] service."[248] Yet it was the principle rather than the numbers that mattered. The directors had validated Symes's contention—the one that had resulted in his promotion just two months and two days earlier—that neither the Q2 nor any of the PRR's other homegrown steam-locomotive designs could compete against diesels manufactured by EMD. Nor was the V1 likely to do any better. At the same December 18 board meeting that marked a new phase in the dieselization of the Pennsylvania Railroad, the directors voted to defer action on Deasy's request for $1.15 million to build a prototype of the Triplex.[249]

In January 1947, while Symes was collecting data to support his campaign for rapid dieselization, a PRR spokesman made the first public acknowledgment that steam locomotives would no longer power the principal trains of the Blue Ribbon Fleet. The diesels ordered from Electro-Motive and Baldwin had not yet arrived, and only the two E7 *Red Arrow* units, plus a collection of small switchers, mingled with the railroad's steam power. The announcement, which came five months after the completion of the final T1, suggested that the PRR was "keeping fully abreast of every modern development in all forms of motive power." Despite the admission that "diesels certainly will be more economical," railroad officials were careful to reassure coal miners, shopworkers, and potentially nervous investors that the company had not completely abandoned its commitment to steam—and cited as evidence the new Q2 and T1 locomotives.[250]

Many officials in the Motive Power Department found it difficult to accept that their skills, accumulated over a lifetime of hard work and dedication, were no longer of value. Perhaps it was just as well that Harry Jones, the chief of motive power, had died before the company's directors rejected the locomotives that had served the company well for a century. As a loyal employee of the PRR, Jones had instructed that his ashes be scattered along the Horseshoe Curve where—for a few more years at least—he would be near the last of the railroad's steam locomotives. Others were not spared the humiliation that accompanied the failure of the Motive Power Department's decade-long quest to develop the ideal steam locomotive. Chief among them was John Deasy, who became increasingly strident in his attempts to justify the duplex program. "Can't we do as well with the T1 as the General Motors Engineer and Maintenance men can do with the Diesels?" Deasy lamented. "If we give the T1's the kind of attention that General Motors give the Diesels," he argued, "we might have some hope of competing with them." Duer was even more forceful in his support for the development of new steam locomotives, particularly the V1 Triplex. In February 1947, he provided what was perhaps the most direct attempt to link the future of the steam locomotive to the PRR's chief source of traffic. "The location of the Railroad and its dependence on the transportation of coal as a commodity suggest that any long-range motive power policy be based on the use of coal-using motive power," he suggested. When referring to the Triplex, Duer admitted that it was "unlikely that this development will be completed and the engine ready for service in less than two or three years," yet he continued to oppose the widespread acquisition of diesel freight locomotives. By that point, Symes had well and truly lost patience with steam locomotives and those who advocated them. On March 14, after reading Duer's plea, Symes forwarded the missive to Clement, but not without adding his own comments, advocating dieselization and emphasizing that the PRR could not wait for the steam-turbine locomotive to be developed.[251]

Symes's final report, made available on March 29, spelled an end to any lingering hopes that Duer and his colleagues might have retained regarding the future of steam locomotives. To meet the PRR's anticipated need for freight power, the company could purchase eighty 6,000-horsepower diesel sets for $47.7 million or build another 176 Q2 steam locomotives at a cost of $52.8 million.[252] While the diesels would require an additional expenditure of nearly $7.3 million for new shop facilities (compared to $3.7 million for the Q2), only $2 million would be necessary to improve the track and roadbed—far less than the $20.8 million that would be needed to add track pans and make other changes that the steam locomotives would require. Once in service, the new diesels would save $14 million in operating costs annually, compared to the use of the Q2. It was an amount that would have more than offset the PRR's $8.5 million net operating loss in 1946. The railroad would earn a further $6.5 million if diesels, as Symes expected, produced an increase in on-time performance.[253]

The financial implications of dieselization ensured that Symes's arguments would prevail. On February 6, 1947, as Symes was completing his report, investment analysts at Merrill, Lynch, Pierce, Fenner & Beane sounded the first warnings about the PRR's dismal financial performance during 1946. Argus Research Corporation issued a similarly pessimistic assessment on May 8, followed by Smith, Barney & Company (on June 18), R. W. Pressprich & Company (in early September), and Carstairs & Company (on December 24). All indicated that the failure of management to reduce expenditures, rather than inadequate rates, constituted the primary cause of the company's difficulties. Analysts were particularly concerned about high labor costs, especially in yard operations and at stations and shop facilities.

In addition to encouraging executives to eliminate unprofitable passenger, less-than-carload-lot, and perishables traffic, investment advisors highlighted managerial unwillingness to embrace the economic efficiencies associated with dieselization. The Argus report noted that "the company experienced a number of costly engine failures in 1946, and particular disappointment appears to be manifest in the T-1 locomotives." After reading the Argus study, Symes reminded Clement that its author "suggests certain corrective action, all of which is underway and will be accelerated with the acquisition of Diesel power." Walter F. Hahn, at Smith, Barney & Company, emphasized the "inadequate dieselization of yard operations." Isabel H. Benham, at Pressprich & Company, observed that "the relatively better showing of the other carriers on yard switching fuel costs may be attributed in part to the extensive Dieselization of yard operations." Yet, she emphasized, "until 1946 there appeared to be no program for extensive use of Diesels either in the yards or on the road." Pierre R. Bretey, writing on behalf of the Railroad Department at Carstairs & Company, suggested that the "Pennsylvania's operating difficulties stem in part from an unfortunate decision to utilize all of its then steam motive power, regardless of age, following completion of electrification." Bretey was particularly critical of the Class L1s Mikados, but he concluded that even larger and more modern locomotives were no longer viable. "Had Pennsylvania continued its previous policy of maintaining technological leadership in installing all forms of power, with new emphasis on diesels, many of the operating difficulties of the past several years might well have been obviated and substantial economies effected." Yet, Bretey observed, "Pennsylvania has been very laggard in installing diesel switchers, although their profitability has been proved beyond a doubt."[254]

In a frantic effort at damage control, Clement promised reforms, but in doing so he attempted to justify the railroad's continued reliance on steam locomotives. He noted that obsolete units—particularly the L1s Mikados—"are disappearing now as we get larger and heavier freight power, both steam and diesel." Despite the Argus report's condemnation of the PRR's newest duplexes, the railroad's president emphasized the "acquisition of 52 class T1 steam locomotives, plus 40 new 6000-horsepower passenger Diesel locomotives." Clement's refusal to categorically denounce steam power reinforced the perception of investment analysts that many PRR executives were reluctant to alienate coal producers. "As the Pennsylvania carries more coal than any other system in the country," Benham suggested, "the management has been loath to follow the trend of the industry in turning to Diesel power." Analysts at Merrill Lynch came to the same conclusion and noted that "due to its heavy dependence on coal traffic, the company has been slow in acquiring Diesel locomotive [sic]." They also asserted that "because some of its best customers are coal shippers, it has dilly-dallied about using Diesels." The Argus report hinted that "the moderate conversion to diesel power [was] delayed because Pennsy has the greatest participation in coal movements to consuming areas." Investment advisors rather than PRR executives thus provided the clearest evidence of the relationship between coal traffic and a continued reliance on steam power. Whatever the nature of that relationship, and despite the unwillingness of officials in the Motive Power Department to relinquish their authority within the company, it was clear that investors were no longer willing to accept further delays in the dieselization of the Pennsylvania Railroad.[255]

Diesels and the Smoke Nuisance in Pittsburgh

Civic leaders and municipal officials provided a further incentive for the adoption of diesel power. Even as he highlighted the economic benefits associated with dieselization, Symes also observed that the new locomotives

would preclude the enforcement of existing antismoke ordinances and the enactment of new ones. It was an important consideration at a time when smoke—often seen as a sign of prosperity and industrial might during the Great Depression and World War II—became redefined as intolerable pollution. The situation was particularly acute in Pittsburgh, where municipal officials had long struggled to control the sources of pollution in both manufacturing and transportation. As early as 1868, less than two decades after the beginning of Pennsylvania Railroad service to the community, the City Council banned the use of wood or bituminous coal within city limits. Enforcement was virtually nonexistent, however. A new set of laws, adopted in the early twentieth century, sought to curtail smoke produced by locomotives, riverboats, and factories but did nothing to address the pollution emitted from thousands of homes equipped with coal-burning furnaces. The Bureau of Smoke Regulation, established in 1911, followed the typical pattern of lackluster enforcement, coupled with well-intentioned efforts to teach locomotive firemen more efficient ways to use coal. The result was continuing ill-will between railroad employees who resented being told how to do their jobs, railroad officials who wanted to maintain favorable public relations, upper-middle-class residents who complained that too little was being done to control pollution, and municipal smoke inspectors who bore the brunt of criticism from all sides. During the 1920s and 1930s, the focus shifted to the many homeowners who collectively generated a substantial proportion of the smoke, but political repercussions likewise retarded effective action.[256]

The situation began to change in the late 1930s in a city that now experienced visible smoke pollution nearly every day of the year. Smoke commissioner Raymond R. Tucker moved decisively to control the problem. In February 1941, the *Pittsburgh Press* published a series of articles highlighting the success of pollution-control efforts in St. Louis. That month, Mayor Cornelius D. Scully appointed a Commission for the Elimination of Smoke. Five months later, the City Council overwhelmingly approved a sweeping antismoke ordinance, with the section applying to railroads scheduled to take effect on October 1, 1942. Citing wartime necessity, representatives from the railroads and industries campaigned for a delay in enforcement, while attempting to prevent similar measures at the county level. In 1943, officials from the PRR and the other railroads serving the city persuaded the state legislature to weaken a law empowering Allegheny County to regulate pollution. Henceforth, all railroads in the county would be exempt from antismoke ordinances. Environmental activists

E.14590

Despite their beauty and majesty, steam locomotives fouled the air with smoke and begrimed the ground with ashes and cinders. Residents of Altoona tolerated conditions such as these, documented in November 1943—both on the grounds of wartime necessity and because the PRR was the city's leading employer. Pittsburghers were far less forgiving and, with the war over, demanded an end to pollution. *Pennsylvania Railroad Negative Collection, Hagley Museum & Library, acc. 1993.300.*

had long singled out the railroads as the most visible and objectionable sources of pollution, and the 1943 exemption focused their anger on the Pennsylvania Railroad's steam locomotives.[257]

The end of the war renewed the political battle to control smoke and to transform Pittsburgh from a gritty industrial center to a gleaming modern metropolis. Richard King Mellon, a PRR director since 1934, was the principal instigator of that Pittsburgh Renaissance. In 1945, he orchestrated a merger between the Allegheny County Conference on Community Development and the United Smoke Council, solidifying the relationship between urban renewal and pollution control. In late November 1946, Allegheny County commissioner John J. Kane demanded that the Pennsylvania Assembly reverse the 1943 act that exempted the railroads from county smoke-abatement legislation. Simultaneously, at the other end of the Commonwealth, Symes was beginning his survey of the PRR's motive-power needs. In early March 1947, three weeks before Symes released his final report that advocated rapid dieselization, the state legislature began consideration of the Fleming-Barrett bill, which would empower Allegheny County to regulate railroad smoke. Mellon's organization wrote the legislation and the well-connected banker contacted Clement, asking for his acquiescence. Pittsburgh mayor David L. Lawrence, who took office in January 1946 on an economic redevelopment and antipollution platform, threatened draconian enforcement of existing city legislation unless the railroads came to terms with the bill. Commissioner Kane and Pennsylvania governor James Duff also put pressure on the PRR, as did Benjamin

F. Fairless, the president of US Steel. Clement and other PRR officials begged for leniency, stressing the railroad's ongoing importance to the region and highlighting its 1946 deficit. By the end of March, representatives from the city's railroads had reached a compromise, dropping their opposition to the Fleming-Barrett bill in exchange for a promise of flexibility in enforcement.[258] The Allegheny County commissioners established committees that worked with the railroads and other smoke emitters, overseeing a voluntarist compliance strategy similar to that employed in cities such as Chicago during the early decades of the twentieth century.[259] There was little question, however, that community leaders expected the PRR and the other railroads serving the city to take meaningful steps to reduce pollution. The continued operation of steam locomotives, at a time when other railroads relied extensively on diesels, was certain to reignite public anger and increase calls for more forceful legislative action. Pittsburgh possessed the highest concentration of steam locomotives anywhere on the PRR system, and if they could not be used there, then they had little value anywhere—particularly if other cities followed the example provided by Allegheny County.[260]

The Changing of the Guard

In its unequivocal support for dieselization, the Symes study ended the careers of two of the champions of new steam locomotives. Harry Jones's death in February 1946 ended any possibility that John Deasy could assign blame for the failures of the Motive Power Department to his subordinate. On April 1, 1947, two days after the release of the final report, Deasy resigned as vice president in charge of operations. He remained in the ceremonial—and powerless—position of vice president, assistant to the president, until he retired in March 1948. Deasy's demotion probably had more to do with the previous year's net operating loss than with the debate over motive-power strategy. Those two issues nonetheless represented different facets of the same problem. The Pennsylvania Railroad could not continue to do business as it had in the past, and in the future the company would require a new generation of locomotives and a new generation of leadership.[261]

Without Deasy's support, John Duer's career with the Pennsylvania Railroad was over. Within a few months, he too was gone, five years shy of mandatory retirement age. During the 1930s, Duer had won universal praise as one of the heroes of the PRR's electrification project. Now, he bore the blame for the repeated failures to develop duplexes and turbines. That effort had cost the railroad nearly $40 million in research, development, and manufacturing

costs, to say nothing of the added operating and maintenance expense and the foregone revenues associated with the operation of the T1 and the Q2. Yet Duer's fall had less to do with his advocacy for large steam locomotives than with his insubordination. He had consistently exaggerated the abilities of all the railroad's steam-locomotive projects, while downplaying the performance of diesels. While suggesting that it was necessary to continue the use of steam locomotives in order to protect the coal industry, he had never attempted to quantify precisely how dieselization might affect the PRR's coal revenues. In his support of powerful locomotives, Duer chose to ignore the flexibility associated with smaller diesel units that could be coupled together to create locomotive sets of varying horsepower. He never acknowledged that the lower operating costs associated with diesels more than offset their higher initial purchase price. Nor did he admit that diesels were available for service at a far higher rate than steam locomotives—a curious omission, given that the same was true with respect to the electric locomotives he had helped to design.

Symes, who became the next vice president in charge of operations, had eliminated the last bastions of resistance to dieselization. He thus ended the tradition, stretching back nearly a hundred years, in which the Motive Power Department of the Pennsylvania Railroad internalized the customized design and manufacture of locomotives. Symes could count on the immediate and strong support of John A. Appleton, who since February 1946 had been the assistant vice president in charge of operations. Appleton, the former general manager of the New York Zone, had spent the war years as the chief of the Rail Division in the War Department, eventually rising to the rank of brigadier general. He endured nearly a year under Deasy's authority, and he found Symes's philosophy on motive power much more to his liking. Symes's other subordinates in the Motive Power Department quickly fell into line. Hal Cover, the chief of motive power, had never been a wholehearted proponent of large, experimental steam locomotives. The ostracization of Deasy and Duer had in any case made him acutely aware of the precarious state of his own career. Little more than a month after assuming his new office, Symes suggested that the Triplex project was "a waste of money" and asked Cover whether it would be worthwhile to pursue further development. Cover's answer contained no ambiguity. For the previous seven years, he conceded, the PRR had experimented with the S2 steam turbine, producing an inadequate locomotive that should never be manufactured in quantity.[262] At least another seven years of effort—and perhaps as long as a decade—would be required before the V1 would be ready for service. Even then, he acknowledged, a steam turbine would never offer the advantages of the diesel locomotives that were currently available from EMD and other builders. Cover's response, less sycophantic than realistic, probably only reinforced a decision that Symes had already made. He ordered an end to all further research-and-development work on the Triplex. Henceforth, the PRR would rely solely on outside suppliers, purchasing the same models that served on other carriers.[263]

Symes was as enthusiastic an advocate for diesels as Deasy and Duer had been for steam locomotives. During his first two months in office, he issued four separate recommendations that covered the purchase of fifty switchers and twenty-one freight-diesel sets, along with an expenditure of $4.3 million to construct service and repair facilities at Enola Yard (the western end of the Harrisburg electrification), Crestline, Columbus, and Chicago. While he reiterated his earlier emphasis regarding the high return on investment associated with dieselization, Symes also highlighted the elimination of helper districts, with their associated locomotives and crews. With Clement's support, the board of directors readily approved the expenditure of $25 million. In 1948, the board favored the construction of service and shop facilities at forty additional locations, ensuring the spread of diesels throughout the Pennsylvania Railroad system. By the end of the year, thanks to the board's approval of recommendations from Symes, the PRR had in service or on order ninety-four switchers and thirty-nine sets of freight diesels. That represented a collective investment of $115 million in new equipment, with another $16 million for support facilities.[264]

By December 1947, the investment analysts who had resoundingly criticized the PRR's continuing reliance on steam locomotives cheered Symes's increased importance within the company as well as his commitment to rapid dieselization. After detailing the PRR's financial problems, Merrill Lynch's *Investor's Reader* newsletter provided a glimmer of hope. "Into this traffic-jam last spring marched a new operations vice president. His name is James Miller Symes. A go-getter, vice-president Symes should put new zip in centenarian PA." Far from honoring the anniversary of the PRR's incorporation, the adjective *centenarian* clearly suggested that the company had become ossified and hidebound by tradition—but that Symes could implement badly needed reforms. Representatives from Merrill Lynch noted that "earlier this year, the management appointed Mr. J. M. Symes vice-president in charge of operations. A more aggressive attack on the system's operating problems is now under way." The most important

element in that attack, they concluded, involved "the substantial economies that should be derived from the new Diesels and other new equipment expected to be received during 1948." The Argus report noted approvingly that "J. M. Symes from the Chicago District, has been placed in 'Charge of Operations' and soon steps will be taken to effect major consolidations in yard personnel, reduce station employees, consolidate passenger schedules and institute savings in other categories."[265]

Echoing Symes's statements that the PRR had "turned the corner," Merrill Lynch analysts reminded investors that between 1937 and 1946 the company had generated $226 million in net earnings, in excess of dividends. Under the circumstances, they noted, "the 1946 net loss of $8.5 million pales into insignificance." Pierre Bretey and his colleagues at Carstairs & Company were "in accord with Mr. Symes' conclusions and accordingly wish to withdraw our previous bearish advices [*sic*] on all Pennsylvania securities, made at earlier higher levels." Market prognosticator Roger Babson was similarly pleased "that the management has become really active in its cost-control campaign," and he moved the PRR from his Red-Border Report to the Green-Border Report.[266]

Symes matched the investments in diesels with changes in the PRR's operating practices. Creative scheduling enabled diesels to operate on additional side trips while laying over on their regular runs—something that had not been possible with steam locomotives. While steam locomotives had generally been confined to their home divisions, the greater reliability of diesels, coupled with improved interdivisional coordination, enabled the new locomotives to run through with little more than a quick stop to change crews. In 1951, the company established the Motive Power Control Bureau to coordinate the movement of diesels that operated through multiple divisions. As motive power director Connie J. Haywood observed, the bureau employed a dedicated telephone line to "control 1400 road power units from one point."[267]

Personnel changes reinforced the new operating methods. In October 1948, the board of directors appointed Clair I. Clugh as the new manager of the Altoona Works. The first upper-level manager associated with the locomotive program to have been born in the twentieth century, Clugh was intimately familiar with diesels. During the 1920s, he had been involved in the development of the A6, the PRR's only sustained attempt to construct an internal-combustion locomotive that could comply with the Kaufman Act. Clugh and his colleagues set to work training PRR personnel in the care and maintenance of diesels. Lloyd Jones, like his late brother Harry schooled in the technology of the steam locomotive, stepped down as engineer of tests. There was in any event far less to test, now that the Pennsylvania Railroad was no longer designing and building motive power. New opportunities beckoned for those familiar with diesel power and electricity, however. In November 1950, the PRR promoted assistant electrical engineer John W. Horine Jr. to the new position of general superintendent of motive power-diesel, based in Philadelphia. Each of the three regions possessed a regional superintendent of motive power-diesel.[268]

As the 1940s came to an end, dieselization proceeded more rapidly than even Symes initially anticipated. Two factors suggested the need to accelerate the process. First, the price of the sixteen million tons of coal purchased by the PRR increased faster than the rates on the 101 million tons of coal that the railroad transported. As Symes reported to the board of directors at the end of April 1948, that situation would increase costs by $5 million a year, an expense that could only be reduced by employing diesels. There was little further point in placating mine owners through a continued reliance on steam locomotives. Coal supplies were likewise becoming undependable. In March 1948, less than two years after the resolution of the 1946 strike, members of the United Mine Workers again walked off the job. The Office of Defense Transportation had disappeared, but the Interstate Commerce Commission adopted similar policies—ordering the railroads to reduce the mileage of all coal-burning locomotives by 25 percent. A PRR spokesman acknowledged that service disruptions would be inevitable but pledged that "the road's 12 Diesel electric freight locomotives now in service (out of 51 included in the Pennsylvania's postwar re-equipment program) will be used to the maximum extent possible." Left unstated was the obvious realization that additional diesels would have prevented many of the problems facing the PRR. The final blow came on September 19, 1949, in the form of a national coal strike that increased the cost of steam-locomotive operations while illustrating the railroad's vulnerability to the suppliers that were also its customers.[269]

Second, as the first passenger and freight diesels entered service, additional data demonstrated beyond any doubt that they were vastly more efficient than any of the railroad's steam locomotives. The greater availability of diesels, coupled with improved motive-power scheduling and utilization practices, accounted for some of the difference. The E7 passenger locomotives originally assigned to *The Red Arrow* averaged more than 18,000 miles a month, compared to fewer than 8,000 miles per month with the

T1. November 1947 was a relatively poor month, with the PRR's initial passenger diesels accumulating only 13,500 miles—but that was still far better than the paltry 3,000-mile average of each freight Q2. Operating data showed that the average diesel passenger locomotive logged 228,760 miles per year, nearly triple the 79,200 miles of the T1 and greater even than the 141,240 miles of the GG1 electrics. What made such figures even more striking was that the diesel average included the Baldwin Centipedes, which had quickly established a reputation for unreliability. Had only EMD locomotives been considered, the disparity between steam and diesel would have been that much greater. Freight service demonstrated equally one-sided results. A 6,000-horsepower diesel set generated 141,480 revenue train miles per year, nearly triple the achievement of a Q2 (51,600 miles) and above the output of a GG1 (114,792 miles). The average annual operating cost per mile was $1.94 for a freight diesel and $2.37 for a Q2. While the difference of $0.43 per mile might have seemed trivial, when multiplied by the PRR's 32.5 million revenue freight-train miles, the data suggested that complete freight dieselization could save the railroad nearly $14 million per year. As more and more diesels entered service, Transportation Department personnel checked and then rechecked their data, unable to believe what they were seeing. The initial prediction of a 5 percent operating savings, derided as overly optimistic by Deasy and Duer in October 1945, turned out to be wildly inaccurate. It was far too low. The railroad's accountants calculated that additional diesel passenger and freight locomotive purchases could yield between a 20 and a 40 percent return on investment, while some diesel switchers garnered a 47.2 percent return. That data suggested that the PRR should scrap its steam locomotives as quickly as possible, regardless of their age.[270]

Symes, determined to take advantage of the high rate of return associated with rapid dieselization, steadily increased his requests for new locomotives. Clement had thoroughly renounced his May 1945 suggestion that "the Pennsylvania should be in a position to continue puffing smoke for years to come," and he accepted Symes's recommendations without question. In May 1947, not long after Symes became the vice president in charge of operations, his motive-power plan stipulated that 80 diesel freight units, 45 passenger units, and 222 diesel switchers would be in operation by January 1, 1952, permitting the retirement of 657 of the railroad's 4,372 steam locomotives.[271] By the end of 1948, Symes had recommended an increase to 82 freight diesels, 63 passenger diesels, and 449 switchers.[272] Once delivered, the new locomotives would collectively generate more than a million horsepower—sufficient to power a third of the railroad's freight ton miles and passenger-train miles, including the dieselization of the entire Blue Ribbon Fleet, while handling 40 percent of locomotive switching hours. The savings would be considerable—$18.5 million annually in fuel costs alone, with additional millions to be reaped from the elimination of double-heading and personnel reductions at the shop facilities that maintained steam locomotives.[273]

Once the new locomotives had been delivered, Symes and Clement anticipated annual orders equating to about 150,000 horsepower for each of the next ten years. It would take at least until 1958, therefore, to add 1.5 million horsepower to the million-plus horsepower that was already in service or on order. Dieselization would be a correspondingly slow process, and the schedule left open the possibility that steam locomotives might not completely disappear from the Pennsylvania Railroad. Yet the advantages of diesels were so increasingly obvious that by March 1949 the ten-year timeline had shortened to just four years. Cover soon added a year to the schedule, to better enable the railroad to finance the $120 million acquisition of another 495 diesel locomotives.[274]

The decision to aggressively embrace dieselization produced a variety of responses. Pittsburghers were delighted that locomotive smoke would soon be a thing of the past. Pennsylvania Railroad executives took every advantage of the opportunity to remind the city's residents that they were committed to advancing the public welfare. John A. Appleton, the assistant vice president in charge of operations, and a longtime supporter of dieselization, pledged that by the end of 1947 the company would banish steam shifters from downtown Pittsburgh. "This is a further effort on the part of the Pennsylvania Railroad to aid in the campaign to rid the city and county of smoke," he emphasized. The following year, Allen J. Greenough, the newly appointed general superintendent of the Eastern Pennsylvania General Division, reinforced that message. "The increased use of diesel-powered locomotives will do much to alleviate the smoke nuisance," he emphasized on his second day in office, while noting that the PRR had only "scratched the surface" when it came to the dieselization of freight operations. Irrespective of the environmental benefits associated with diesels, Greenough concluded it made little sense to waste money by sending "fuel up the stack" of inefficient steam locomotives.[275]

In Altoona and many other PRR enclaves, however, many residents anticipated the prospect of widespread

dieselization with trepidation. Residents of Tyrone listened to "Diesel Power and Its Effect on the Community," a presentation given by the district freight agent at Altoona. Joseph A. Sladen noted that the railroad still rostered fewer than a hundred diesels, compared to nearly five thousand steam locomotives. Sladen thus concluded, inaccurately, that "The use of Diesel-electric engines on the Pennsylvania railroad [sic] will have little effect on the communities which supply workers for the company." In another meeting, held in January 1949 in the Logan Room of Altoona's Penn Alto Hotel, Altoona Works manager Clair Clugh offered a more disturbing prediction. "We can't stand in the way of progress," he informed 180 foremen from the Juniata Shops. "If we do we'll get run over." Thirty months had passed since those foremen had overseen the construction of the PRR's last steam locomotive, T1 #5524. Clugh's blunt rhetoric dispelled any hope that the glory days of the Altoona Works might someday return. "We must increase our efficiency and find new ways of doing things," he emphasized. "We're going to have to go from steam to Diesel more than we anticipated." His subordinate, Juniata Shops superintendent J. E. Parker, addressed the subject that was at the center of everyone's concern. "If there is anything any of us hate it is to reduce forces, to furlough men." Following the cessation of steam-locomotive production, however, that outcome seemed inevitable. One Altoona resident had already said as much. In a letter to the editor of the Altoona Tribune, Louis Cunningham decried the locomotive "smoke nuisance" and lamented "the scenic, natural wonderland that we, through carelessness have permitted Altoona to become the filthiest city I have ever seen." Other railroads were purchasing diesel locomotives, he emphasized, and "you can take my word for it the P.R.R. is not slumbering. . . . One morning, my fellow citizens, you will wake up and that will be the day the PRR places 40 to 60 Diesels between Harrisburg, Detroit, Chicago, St. Louis. Then, it will be too late. . . . These diesels will not be built in Altoona to my best knowledge. Manpower will be lessened in the shops."[276]

Coal miners rather than railroaders expressed the greatest outrage at the rapid progress of dieselization. Unlike the personnel at the Altoona Works, they could count on the support—or at least the acquiescence—of the executives who operated the collieries. John P. Busarello, the president of United Mine Workers District 5, in Pittsburgh, complained that "every time a steam engine is driven off the railroads, two miners are out of a job." Michael Honus, the secretary-treasurer of District 4, based in Uniontown, asserted that "the 25 new diesel engines will cut coal demands 2,750 tons a day." He vowed to "fight in the state legislature . . . fight it to the last straw." John Ghizzoni, an international board member of the UMW, was more moderate in his criticism of PRR executives, indicating that "we would like to see them keep the use of coal burning locomotives as far as is possible." He disavowed any efforts to take the matter to the state legislature, but he could not block the efforts of his more radical colleagues. Montgomery F. Crowe, a Republican from East Stroudsburg and the chairman of the Mining Committee of the state senate, called for the establishment of a special legislative commission to investigate the plight of the coal industry. He nonetheless indicated that "legislation could not be passed" to prevent the PRR and other railroads that operated in the state from buying diesels, any more than a "law could make you buy one make of car instead of another."[277]

The Push to Full Dieselization

The disastrous events of 1949 accelerated the pace of dieselization and spelled the end of steam locomotives on the Pennsylvania Railroad. On March 2, the subsidiary Long Island Rail Road filed for bankruptcy. While PRR officials argued that they were not responsible for the LIRR's financial well-being or the maintenance of its commuter operations, there was a strong possibility that the parent company would ultimately bear some of the burden. The United Mine Workers staged a series of intermittent strikes during the year that did not end until early November, causing revenues to plummet and imperiling the supply of fuel for steam locomotives. Steel workers were on strike for the entire month of October and into November. While the PRR's labor relations were more harmonious, average wages continued to increase even as the overall workforce declined, given that the average hourly wage rate had more than doubled since 1940. In December 1948, a Presidential Emergency Board decreed that nonoperating employees would work a forty rather than a forty-eight-hour week, with no corresponding loss of pay. When the ruling took effect on September 1, 1949, it was the equivalent of a raise of nearly 17 percent, adding between $12 million and $15 million to the PRR's annual labor costs. As the company's officials emphasized, the new work rules "imposed on this 7-day industry a 5-day work week." Emboldened by the success of the nonoperating employees, yard trainmen and firemen also demanded a reduction in working hours that would ensure a substantial increase in overtime compensation.[278]

Nor could the Pennsylvania Railroad count on increased earnings to offset the added expenditures. In 1949, the railroad's income from freight and passenger operations was $145 million less than the year before. Partly as a result of the coal and steel strikes, between 1948 and 1949 freight traffic declined by almost 23 percent, from 58 billion to 44.9 billion ton miles, with freight revenues falling by 17.8 percent. Addressing disgruntled shareholders at the May 1950 annual meeting, PRR comptroller Elmer Hart suggested that the two strikes had cost the railroad $5 million in lost revenues and higher operating expenses. Passenger miles declined from a 1945 high of nearly 13 billion to 6 billion in 1948 and just 5 billion in 1949. The corresponding passenger revenues fell only 6.9 percent, to $202 million, thanks to management's efforts to curtail lightly patronized services and consolidate trains serving the same routes. During the first five months of 1949, the PRR culled

Facing, In November 1948, the smiling faces of the PRR's directors provided little evidence of the tensions within the company or of the personnel changes taking place. John F. Deasy, the vice president in charge of operations, had resigned from the board and the company the previous April. Still five years shy of mandatory retirement age, he took the blame for the inability of the Motive Power Department to develop a new generation of steam locomotives. His replacement, James M. Symes, standing second from right, became the de facto head of the company, although he did not yet possess sufficient experience to replace Martin Clement, who is seated third from left. Walter S. Franklin, standing at center, gained a promotion, from vice president in charge of traffic to executive vice president and heir apparent. Clement, at this stage in his career largely a figurehead, would resign the presidency in June 1949, still two and a half years short of retirement. To Franklin's left, and nearly matching his height, is C. Jared Ingersoll, the chairman of the Muskogee Company. Seated immediately in front of him is Philip C. Clarke, the president of Chicago's City National Bank & Trust Company. In 1961, at Symes's behest, Ingersoll and Clarke worked with Richard King Mellon to arrange a merger between the PRR and the New York Central. Standing directly behind Clement is George H. Pabst Jr., the vice president in charge of finance. He stepped down from that post in 1951, owing to poor health. His successor, David C. Bevan, thereafter figured prominently in the PRR's financial affairs. Isaac W. Roberts, standing between Ingersoll and Symes, was the president of the Philadelphia Saving Fund Society and the son of former PRR president George Brooke Roberts. James E. Gowen, standing next to Pabst, was the president of the Girard Trust Company. He also possessed a strong railroad pedigree, and his great-uncle was Franklin B. Gowen, president of the Reading during the 1870s and 1880s. Next in line is James R. Downes, PRR vice president and assistant to the president. *Pennsylvania Railroad Photographs, Hagley Museum & Library, acc. 1988.231.*

1.25 million passenger-train miles. By the end of the year, the cuts totaled nearly 4 million train miles, equivalent to almost 10 percent of the railroad's total passenger operations. Even that was not sufficient to stem the flood of red ink, with 1949 passenger losses reaching almost $40 million.[279] When PRR executives explored the possibility of eliminating half of all remaining train miles, however, they discovered that revenues would fall to $125 million, with losses climbing to $55 million. The PRR's operating ratio rose to 86, higher than that of either the New York Central or the Baltimore & Ohio. Net railway operating income decreased by 43.5 percent between 1948 and 1949, from $64 million to $36.1 million. The railroad's overall earnings suffered a similar decline—from $34.4 million in 1948 to $12.5 million in 1949—while the return on investment in transportation property plummeted from an already poor 2.37 percent to a paltry 1.25 percent. Clement warned that the Pennsylvania Railroad would have to become more efficient if the company was to survive. "There is no question that changed working conditions require mechanical improvement, not only in motive power but in all other activities," he told Symes in early October, "and with the very large percent of return indicated from these improvements, well spent capital should very much improve the earnings situation and eventually cut down the cost of transportation." With steam locomotives still responsible

for 43 percent of freight, 19 percent of passenger, and 42 percent of shifting duties, there was considerable room for improvement.[280]

Clement's decision to step down from the presidency in June 1949 did little to slow the pace of dieselization. He was two years shy of the mandatory retirement age of seventy, and he served out the remainder of his time as the chairman of the board of directors. It was a newly created post that, as a PRR spokesman emphasized, would "provide an executive arrangement whereby the president may share some of the newer responsibilities imposed upon the top management of a large corporation by conditions of the times." That polite language notwithstanding, Clement's new job held little power or influence.[281]

No one doubted that Symes would soon become the president of the Pennsylvania Railroad. He was only fifty-one, however. Despite his wealth of experience, he was not quite ready for the top position. Moreover, his oversight of dieselization constituted his first priority—just as, a generation earlier, Samuel Rea had been so heavily involved in the New York Improvements that he could not immediately succeed Alexander Cassatt. In the interim, Walter S. Franklin became the company's twelfth president. Demoted in 1947, Deasy retired at the end of March 1948. Franklin became the PRR's executive vice president less than three months later, a clear indication that Clement had chosen a successor. When he became president in 1949, Franklin was something of an anomaly among senior executives. For the first time in its long history, the Pennsylvania Railroad was under the control of an individual who was more familiar with the traffic side of the business than with operations. Born just three years after Clement, Franklin was already sixty-five, and he could anticipate no more than five years as chief executive. By then, however, Symes would be ready to replace him.[282]

As a caretaker president with relatively little experience in operating matters, Franklin was willing to yield to Symes on most matters of substance. That included dieselization. When he was the vice president in charge of traffic, Franklin had in any case repeatedly emphasized the value of diesels in increasing the speed and reliability of freight and passenger service. He was therefore unlikely to question Symes's advocacy for diesels, even if the railroad's finances had permitted a continued reliance on steam power. In early September, Symes recommended an acceleration in diesel-locomotive purchases. Rather than the 125,000 horsepower budgeted for 1950, he asked for nearly three times that amount—356,000 horsepower. President Franklin and the other directors readily complied, and in October 1949, the company placed orders for an additional 226 diesel locomotives. They would cost $38 million, representing a significant share of the $300 million that the railroad had spent on capital improvements since 1946. When delivered, they would augment the 594 diesels already on the property, collectively generating more than 1.4 million horsepower.[283]

While the fortunes of the Pennsylvania Railroad improved slightly during 1950, the underlying issues of increasing labor costs, rising passenger-service losses, and stagnant freight rates were largely unchanged.[284] By February, even before the PRR had taken delivery of the 226 locomotives ordered four months earlier, 90 percent of passenger service and 65 percent of freight trains were dieselized. Even so, Symes was contemplating further purchases. He suggested that another 300,000 horsepower might be appropriate. That would not be sufficient to dieselize the entire railroad west of Harrisburg, however. To do so would require the acquisition of several hundred additional units, at great expense and with a progressively diminishing return on investment. Instead, he anticipated that diesels could accommodate all passenger and shifting duties as well as between 80 and 85 percent of freight traffic. Should economic conditions further curtail the railroad's freight business, there would be no need to sideline recently purchased diesels. If traffic levels remained

the same, then steam locomotives could be concentrated in a few divisions on the Western Region, where they came closest to matching the efficiency of diesels.[285] If freight traffic surged, mothballed steam locomotives could be reconditioned and placed in service. Therefore, Symes recommended the complete dieselization of the Central Region by the end of 1952, with electrics handling the bulk of the traffic on the Eastern Region and steam remaining in place on the Western Region into the early 1960s, perhaps longer. "I do not think that the railroads will ever become one hundred percent dieselized," Symes suggested in April 1950. "Some of them perhaps yes; but most of them certainly no."[286]

By June, acting at Symes's request, the Motive Power Department had prepared yet another study of the economies of dieselization. It supported the conclusions that Symes had reached in February, noting that full dieselization would require $207 million for 877 new locomotives, with an additional $8 million for fueling stations and other servicing facilities. While such an expenditure would generate an average return on investment of 16.8 percent, that was well below the 30 or 40 percent returns associated with the initial phase of dieselization. More to the point, PRR officials were reluctant to take on so much additional debt. Instead, the report recommended the purchase of 214 diesels, producing just over half a million horsepower, with an impressive 27.7 percent return on investment. In August, the directors approved the recommendations, sufficient to give the Pennsylvania Railroad—once the champion of the steam locomotive—the most extensive roster of diesel locomotives in the United States.[287] During 1951, as the conflict in Korea boosted traffic levels, the directors approved another $72 million for 312 locomotives. In just three years, the PRR had pledged $165 million to the purchase of more than seven hundred diesel locomotives that collectively generated 1.6 million horsepower.[288] The advantages of diesel locomotives were so great, and the PRR's net operating income was in such dire circumstances, that the railroad committed to achieving what had originally been a ten-year plan in less than a third of that time.[289]

The rapid pace of dieselization encouraged PRR personnel to acquire a wide variety of locomotives from every major builder. Their experimental approach reflected a desire to determine the optimal designs for specific types of service. Motive-power officials also retained some loyalty to Baldwin, a company that continued to struggle in the diesel-locomotive industry. Finally, with other carriers placing orders with EMD, sole reliance on the dominant producer would have entailed delays of up to two years in the acquisition of new locomotives.[290] The diversified strategy, coupled with the PRR's size, nonetheless precluded the standardization of maintenance and repair methods. It also resulted in the acquisition of many unsatisfactory locomotives.

Since 1848, the Baldwin Locomotive Works had built steam locomotives for the Pennsylvania Railroad, complementing the production at the Altoona Works, and those ties ensured favorable treatment in the PRR's diesel orders. The Pennsylvania Railroad eventually owned 643 Baldwin diesels, 22 percent of that builder's total production for the domestic market. Unfortunately, Baldwin also provided some extraordinarily bad locomotives that eventually soured the PRR—and the rest of the railroads in the United States—on its designs. Baldwin's best offerings by far came in the form of switchers. The Pennsylvania Railroad eventually bought 373 of them, equivalent to nearly 44 percent of the company's total roster of diesel switchers. Although the PRR's first two switchers came from Electro-Motive, largely as a favor to General Motors, the railroad honored its traditional alliance by ordering most of its subsequent units from Baldwin. They included nine 660-horsepower switchers and six 1,000-horsepower counterparts, with one exception the only diesels added to the roster during World War II.[291] Those locomotives soon demonstrated their superiority over steam shifters, resulting in a postwar order for three more 660-horsepower and two additional 1,000-horsepower locomotives. Baldwin built them at the Eddystone plant, practically alongside the last of the T1 steam passenger locomotives. The ninety-nine units from Baldwin's Model 4-4-660, which arrived between June 1947 and November 1948, represented more than 71 percent of the total production of that design.[292] The more powerful 4-4-1000 was even better represented, with 137 examples placed in service between June 1947 and May 1950—although in that case encompassing a mere 27 percent of Baldwin's total output.[293] In May and June 1950, Baldwin completed twenty-four Model 4-4-750 switchers, providing an alternative to the 660-horsepower and 1,000-horsepower models.[294] Refinements to Baldwin's designs led to the 800-horsepower S-8, with the PRR ordering six examples in August 1950.[295] The 1,200-horsepower S-12 was more popular, with eighty-seven units delivered to the PRR between January 1951 and February 1954.[296] The Baldwin switchers performed well, and most remained in service through the mid-1960s. Many lasted into the Penn Central years, and a few even survived the creation of Conrail in 1976.[297]

The Pennsylvania Railroad's foray into Baldwin passenger locomotives proved far less successful. The Baldwin Centipede provided an impressive 6,000 horsepower in a single, two-unit locomotive and thus appealed to PRR officials during the initial 1945 discussions regarding the experimental dieselization of some passenger trains.[298] The railroad ordered the first married pair in January 1946, but it did not arrive until April 1947. The lengthy production time was a bad omen, as was a mechanical failure that delayed one of the locomotive's trial runs on The Broadway Limited. An additional eleven of the Centipedes, delivered in 1947 and early 1948, performed scarcely better. Operating officials soon banished the Centipedes to secondary passenger runs rather than tolerate repeated delays. While used briefly in freight service, by 1952 the locomotives had been reassigned as pushers, assisting westbound freight trains from Philadelphia toward Paoli and helping others over the terrain between Altoona and Johnstown. Most were out of commission by 1958, barely a decade after they were built, although the twelve units were not officially retired until 1962. Baldwin and the PRR experienced moderately better results from the eighteen A-units and nine B-units of the Model DR-6-4-2000, delivered in 1948.[299] PRR officials requested distinctive styling for the locomotives, and their counterparts at Baldwin were happy to comply—if for no other reason than to de-emphasize any connection with the "baby-face" noses of the inadequate Centipedes. The appearance of the new locomotives was indeed distinctive, with a sharply tapering, up-thrust, prowlike front end that quickly gained the appellation of "Sharknose." The similarity to Raymond Loewy's styling for the T1 steam locomotive was obvious, but it was something that the famed industrial designer could not claim as his own. It was instead a close imitation developed by the Hartford, Connecticut, design firm Hadley, Ryder & Pederson, acting as consultants to Baldwin.[300] While the passenger Sharknose was unique to the PRR, the railroad was one of several that purchased a shorter, less powerful freight version. Thirty-four A-units and a corresponding number of B-units, each generating 1,500 horsepower, entered service between February 1949 and June 1950. The period between June 1950 and April 1952 saw an influx of a 1,600-horsepower version, totaling seventy-two A-units and thirty B-units.[301] Like the passenger Sharks, they performed reasonably well but could not match the reliability of EMD locomotives. The PRR withdrew the passenger versions from service in September 1962, with the initial batch of freight locomotives retired in 1963 and 1964. The 1,600-horsepower freight units lasted a bit longer and were retired between July 1966 and January 1967.[302]

The PRR relied on Baldwin for two additional types of locomotives, road switchers and transfer units. Road

Beginning in the summer of 1948, Baldwin delivered a series of passenger locomotives that represented a significant improvement over the problematic Centipedes. The unmistakable carbody design, often mistakenly attributed to industrial designer Raymond Loewy, was the creation of stylists at Hadley, Ryder & Pederson. The #2012, delivered in February 1952 as PRR Class BF-16, was among the most modern of the Baldwin Sharknose units—but, like Baldwin's other diesels, its performance was at best mediocre. *Pennsylvania Railroad Negative Collection, Hagley Museum & Library, acc. 1993.300.*

switchers, slightly larger and more powerful than switchers, left the confines of the yard to collect and deliver freight cars along branch lines, sidings, and spurs. With many routes snaking through urban industrial zones, winding through valleys in coal country, and traversing the flatlands of Ohio, Indiana, and Illinois, the Pennsylvania Railroad required a large group of those locomotives. Some, equipped with a boiler to provide steam heat, pulled commuter trains or short passenger consists along branch

lines. The first Baldwin road switchers arrived in February 1949, in the form of two DRS 4-4-1000 locomotives.[303] Baldwin delivered four more in February 1950. Like the Centipede passenger locomotive, the DRS 4-4-1000 was not popular, and the PRR's six examples represented two-thirds of Baldwin's production for the domestic market. The Baldwin Model RS-12 was more successful, with fifty units produced—eight of which went to the PRR, beginning in April 1951.[304] Between May 1951 and February 1954, the PRR received a dozen of the six-axle, 1,600-horsepower Baldwin Model AS-616.[305] While the PRR experienced satisfactory results from its Baldwin road switchers, the curtailment of branch-line passenger and freight services as well as the availability of better models from other builders led to their gradual retirement. Baldwin also provided about half of the forty-five transfer locomotives used on the Pennsylvania Railroad. As their name implied, their principal function was to transfer long blocks of cars at low speeds between various railroad freight yards while also pulling long coal trains along branch lines and shoving cuts of cars at hump yards. They were massive machines,

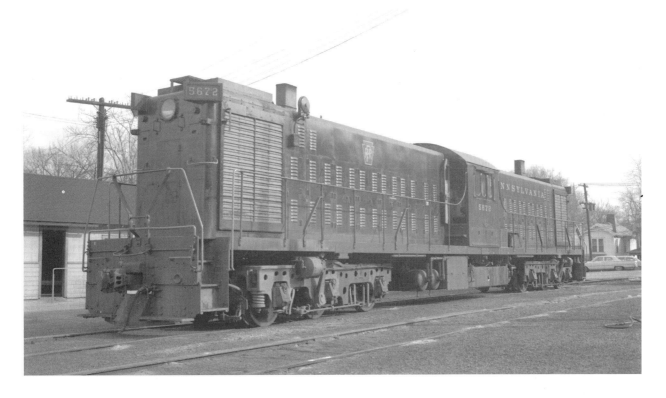

The Lima Locomotive Works was the least successful manufacturer of diesel locomotives. Its products included an ungainly transfer locomotive, PRR Class LS-25. While lacking in grace, it offered 2,500 horsepower—ideal for dragging long cuts of freight cars between yards at low speeds. Awaiting its next assignment is #5672, in Zanesville, Ohio, in March 1954. *Harris Negatives Collection, Railroad Museum of Pennsylvania, PHMC.*

heavy and slow, but extraordinarily powerful by the standards of the time. Between August 1951 and February 1954, the PRR acquired twenty-three of Baldwin's 2,400-horsepower transfer locomotives. As EMD and its competitors increased the power of their general-service freight locomotives, transfer units gradually fell out of favor. Most were sidelined by the mid-1960s, although a few survived the 1968 Penn Central merger.[306]

Lima Locomotive Works, the least successful of the diesel manufacturers, provided few locomotives to the PRR—or to any other railroad, for that matter. Lima's 1947 merger with the General Machinery Corporation gave the company—now named Lima-Hamilton—access to diesel-engine technology but did little to counteract the company's limited presence in the market. In the spring of 1950, Lima-Hamilton delivered the PRR's other twenty-two transfer units, each generating an impressive 2,500 horsepower. Within a few years, they had been concentrated

at Mingo Junction, Ohio, where they collected cars from myriad nearby coal mines. Like their Baldwin counterparts, by the mid-1960s they were obsolete, and the railroad sidelined them as they came due for repairs. By July 1966, all were out of service.[307]

Despite their relatively brief service life, both the Lima-Hamilton and the Baldwin transfer units outlasted the entity that built them. In 1951, the two weakest companies in the diesel-locomotive market merged to form Baldwin-Lima-Hamilton. The firm soon halted production at the Lima facility, which on September 11, 1951, completed its last locomotive—Pennsylvania Railroad transfer unit #5683. It was a sad end for the company that had pioneered the Super Power era and had thus indirectly contributed to the development of the duplex design on the PRR. Baldwin fared little better after the merger. The initial rush of dieselization had subsided by the early 1950s, ensuring that marginal producers would be the first to be eliminated from the industry. Any residual loyalty to the Baldwin of Samuel Vauclain and Ralph Johnson had disappeared, and only a desire to temper EMD's dominance could justify further orders from Eddystone. In 1953, the PRR placed a token order with Baldwin for an assortment of yard switchers and road switchers. With Baldwin's collapse imminent, PRR officials refused to consider further bids from that source. The company that had supplied so many steam locomotives to the Pennsylvania Railroad stopped building diesels in 1956.[308]

Fairbanks-Morse applied opposed-piston engines, developed for World War II submarines, to its range of diesel locomotives. They included switchers such as the Model FM H-10-44. This example, given the PRR classification of FS-10, is on duty at Cincinnati, Ohio, in June 1950, little more than a year after it was built. *Otto Perry photograph, Denver Public Library, Western History Collection, call number OP-14323.*

The Pennsylvania Railroad awarded several orders to Fairbanks-Morse, a longtime supplier of agricultural equipment, whose tenure as a manufacturer of diesel locomotives was almost as brief as that of Lima. Fairbanks-Morse developed an opposed-piston diesel engine that worked well in navy submarines. As World War II was coming to an end, the company entered the locomotive market to develop other applications for the OP engine. While Fairbanks-Morse was never a major player in the industry, the PRR's rush to dieselize yard operations resulted in orders for two groups of switchers—fifty-five of the Model H-10-44 and sixteen of the Model H-12-44.[309] Beginning in December 1948, the PRR received a total of thirty-eight H-20-44 road switchers, with each unit producing an impressive 2,000 horsepower.[310] A substantial number of the Fairbanks-Morse switchers and road switchers lasted until the end of PRR operations, but few saw service on the Penn Central.

The ability of a single opposed-piston engine to generate ample horsepower made Fairbanks-Morse competitive in the main line freight and passenger diesel markets.[311] Between November 1947 and March of the following year, the PRR took delivery of twenty-four "Erie-built" locomotives—so called because they were assembled at a General Electric facility in Erie, Pennsylvania, pending the expansion of the Fairbanks-Morse manufacturing plant in Beloit, Wisconsin. With two A-units flanking a cab-less B-unit, each three-locomotive set produced the 6,000 horsepower the personnel in the Transportation Department and the Motive Power Department deemed appropriate for road service. A further order of twelve units (four A-B-A sets) contained steam-heating equipment for passenger service, while twelve more locomotives (in six A-A pairs) found work as helpers.[312] All were retired by the end of 1963. With the FM plant at Beloit in full operation, the company introduced its Consolidation Line of diesel locomotives. The PRR acquired twenty-four of the 1,600-horsepower variant of the "C-Liner," in the form of sixteen A-units and eight B-units.[313] Between 1953 and 1957, Fairbanks-Morse produced 107 of the Model H-24-66. Dubbed the "Train Master," each unit could produce 2,400 horsepower, foreshadowing later developments in high-power locomotives. Only nine copies went to the PRR, delivered in August and September 1956.[314] They were the last Fairbanks-Morse locomotives that the PRR would buy.[315]

The eclectic nature of the PRR's motive-power purchases included thirty-six locomotives supplied by Fairbanks-Morse and assembled at Erie, Pennsylvania. Two-thirds of them, assigned to PRR Class FF-20, were employed in fast freight service—including this pair, rounding the Horseshoe Curve in July 1953. *Otto Perry photograph, Denver Public Library, Western History Collection, call number OP-14458.*

Although the American Locomotive Company had never matched Baldwin as a supplier of locomotives to the PRR, it was the only builder that could come close to challenging Electro-Motive. Based in Schenectady, New York, Alco was the preferred outside source of steam locomotives for the New York Central. Alco nonetheless built a substantial number of steam locomotives for the PRR—including 410 of the H-Class Consolidations, delivered between 1907 and 1917.[316] In 1925, Alco had collaborated with GE and Ingersoll Rand to build an oil-electric locomotive for the Long Island Rail Road. Alco acquired McIntosh & Seymour in 1929, thus establishing control over diesel-engine development, but remained reliant on GE electrical equipment. Even though Alco produced main line freight and passenger locomotives, the company lagged well behind Electro-Motive. Alco executives instead concentrated on the development of switchers and road switchers. The company introduced the Model RS-1 in 1941, and it remained in

production until 1960—an extraordinarily long tenure for an early locomotive design. The PRR's first Alco order was for a set of more conventional yard locomotives, with the railroad's first road switcher acquired as an afterthought. Although PRR officials generally favored Baldwin switchers, in November 1946 they ordered three Alco Model S-1 660-horsepower switchers.[317] They arrived in May and June of the following year, and they were the first Alco diesels on the railroad.[318] In June 1947, the PRR ordered eight Alco Model S-2 switchers, each capable of generating 1,000 horsepower. Within two months, however, PRR officials expressed an interest in removing steam locomotives from the Parkton Local, a commuter service that operated from Baltimore twenty-nine miles to the north along the Northern Central Railway. Chief of motive power Hal Cover was familiar with the RS-1 road switchers that Alco had delivered to the Washington Terminal Company—owned in part by the Pennsylvania Railroad—in 1944. Rather than ask the PRR board to approve an additional locomotive order, he requested that Alco substitute a single RS-1, equipped with steam-generating equipment, for one of the S-2 yard switchers.[319] The PRR's first road switcher arrived in December 1948, two months before the comparable Baldwin DRS 4-4-1000 entered service. The PRR eventually ordered an additional twenty-six of the Model RS-1, and the locomotives saw service as helpers, powering local freights, and in various passenger duties.[320]

Alco was in the forefront of the initial development of the road switcher, a versatile locomotive that was equally at home in the yard, on the main line, and on branch lines. One of the first to join the PRR's roster was #5637, an RS-1 delivered in June 1950 as the railroad's Class AS-10am. It is in Olean, New York, five years later. *General Negative Collection, Railroad Museum of Pennsylvania, PHMC.*

Alco's 1,600-horsepower road switcher, the RS-3, proved even more popular and was by far the largest class of Alco motive power that operated on the Pennsylvania Railroad. Beginning in August 1950, the PRR placed eight orders for the Model RS-3, totaling 115 locomotives, with the last units delivered in January 1956.[321] They displaced H-Class 2-8-0 Consolidations on many local services and dieselized the five commuter routes in Pittsburgh—which, aside from Chicago's Valparaiso Local, were the only PRR commuter operations west of the Alleghenies. While delivering the many RS-3 locomotives to the PRR, Alco also produced several other types of locomotives, in much smaller numbers, for specialized applications on the railroad. Six Model RSD-5 locomotives, ordered in November 1951, arrived between October 1952 and March 1953. Outwardly similar to the RS-3, and likewise developing 1,600 horsepower, the RSD-5 units employed three-axle trucks.[322] That made them well suited for lugging heavy freight trains at low speeds, for helper service, and for pushing cars

through hump yards. The five Alco Model RSD-7 locomotives ordered in September 1955 each generated 2,400 horsepower, suitable for their principal role—assisting westbound passenger trains out of Altoona and around the Horseshoe Curve to the Allegheny summit.[323]

By the time the last of the RS-3 locomotives arrived in early 1956, EMD had come to dominate the road-switcher market. To maintain its secondary position in the diesel-locomotive industry, Alco replaced its troublesome Model 244 diesel engine with the Model 251. The new prime mover gave Alco road switchers a 50-horsepower edge over their EMD competition, but that advantage was insufficient to overcome problems with the turbochargers and crankshafts that had plagued earlier Alco locomotives. By early 1956, however, PRR executives were ready to replace the last steam locomotives as quickly as possible, and they were unwilling to wait for EMD to catch up with the backlog of orders at La Grange. The PRR accordingly acquired thirty-eight of the Alco Model RS-11, an 1,800-horsepower road switcher delivered in three batches between August 1956 and December 1957.[324] The RSD-12 was a similar locomotive, also developing 1,800 horsepower, but its three-axle trucks suggested its intended role in helper service, pushing westbound freight trains upgrade out of Altoona.[325] The twenty-five RSD-12 units, delivered between December 1957 and April 1958, were the first on the PRR to replace other diesels rather than steam locomotives. The Baldwin Centipedes had been progressively

The exalted status of the engineman did not disappear with the passing of the steam locomotive. The Alco PA may have been the most visually appealing locomotive built in the United States, and this example—PRR Class AP-20, #5753—elicited awe and respect from father and son alike. *Don Wood Negatives, Railroad Museum of Pennsylvania, PHMC.*

demoted from the Blue Ribbon Fleet to secondary passenger trains and then to pusher service, and the new Alco diesels finally sidelined them once and for all. While Alco's products were far superior to those produced by Baldwin, most railroad officials had come to favor EMD's locomotives. The PRR was no exception and in 1956 ordered its last Alco road switchers—a mere six units of the 2,400-horsepower Model RSD-15.[326]

While Alco excelled in the early road-switcher market, the company was less successful in the manufacture of main line freight and passenger locomotives. In the summer of 1946, Alco began production of the Model

PA-1, and its unmistakable profile established its reputation as one of the most beautiful diesel locomotives ever designed. In January 1947, the PRR placed an order for fifteen—ten PA-1 units with cabs and five PB-1 cab-less units—that would create five 6,000-horsepower passenger sets.[327] While the Alco PA locomotives were far more reliable than the Baldwin Centipedes, they suffered from the same engine, crankshaft, and turbocharger problems that affected the company's road switchers. Delivered in late 1947, within five years they had already been reassigned to secondary passenger service.[328] Alco's freight locomotives were likewise superior to anything offered by Baldwin or Fairbanks-Morse but still a distant second to those produced by EMD. In July 1947, the PRR ordered eight copies of the Alco Model FA-1 and FB-1, a 1,500-horsepower freight locomotive that resembled a shortened version of the PA.[329] Alco delivered eight more FA/FB locomotives in March and April 1950. The PRR's 1950 locomotive-purchasing campaign included an additional eighteen of the Alco Model FA/FB. Grouped into six A-B-A sets, they reflected the changing philosophy of the Motive Power Department, whose personnel had concluded that a 4,500-horsepower package was sufficient for many freight applications. By the time production began on the 1950 order, Alco had upgraded the design to 1,600 horsepower, as the FA-2 and FB-2.[330] The PRR eventually purchased twenty-four of the FA-2 and twelve of the FB-2, yielding a dozen A-B-A sets. By the time the last of the locomotives arrived in December 1951, PRR personnel had become familiar with the limitations of the Model 244 engine.[331] The PRR kept the Alco freight units in service long enough to run out the clock on their fifteen-year equipment-trust financing and then sent them into retirement.[332]

In the years after 1945, the Electro-Motive Division of General Motors rapidly attained market dominance throughout the United States, although its superior position on the Pennsylvania Railroad took somewhat longer to achieve. Prior to the war, Electro-Motive supplied a single Model SW switcher in 1937, followed by a lone NW2 in October 1941. In January 1942, the railroad ordered one 600-horsepower Model SW1, delivered seven months later.[333] Thereafter, restrictions imposed by the War Production Board and the ingrained loyalty of PRR officials toward Baldwin virtually excluded EMD from the switcher market. Two more NW2 switchers, ordered in January 1945, and three additional SW1 locomotives requested the following month constituted the PRR's only additional wartime orders for EMD yard engines.[334] Even after the war and the dissolution of the WPB, Pennsylvania Railroad officials continued to place most switcher and road-switcher orders with either Baldwin or Alco. EMD did supply an additional twenty-nine of the Model NW2, delivered between October 1947 and December 1948, and eighty-one of the Model SW1, which arrived between June 1946 and November 1950. By the end of 1951, EMD had provided the PRR with 535 locomotives, surpassing Baldwin for the first time.[335] The largest group of EMD switchers, 119 locomotives in all, entered service between June 1950 and April 1958. All developed 1,200 horsepower and progressively represented three EMD models—first the SW7, then the SW9, and finally the SW1200. The new switchers replaced many of the H-Class Consolidations that had routinely been employed in yard service.[336]

With the PRR purchasing at least some diesel passenger locomotives from every builder save Lima, EMD did not initially dominate the PRR's passenger fleet. The convoluted process involving the first of the passenger diesels was perhaps a harbinger of things to come. After canceling and then reinstating the May 1941 order for a pair of E6 locomotives and then enduring WPB restrictions and

wartime production delays, the PRR finally took delivery of two E7 units in September 1945. The subsequent assignment to *The Red Arrow* (rather than *The South Wind*) was as much a courtesy to General Motors as it was a desire to evaluate the performance capabilities of the new type of motive power. The persistent demands of James Symes for diesels, his elevation to vice president in charge of operations, and the support of President Clement changed matters. Although PRR officials debated the relative merits of four-axle and six-axle motive power, in November 1945 they committed to a further twenty-four E7 locomotives (sixteen A-units and eight B-units).[337] The next two passenger orders, in January and in October 1946, were for the twelve Baldwin two-unit Centipede sets. Fortunately for the PRR's passengers, the railroad returned to EMD in January 1947, ordering ten E7A and six E7B locomotives.[338] Eighteen additional E7A units, delivered in March and April 1949, indicated that the PRR had begun to alter the dependence on a standard 6,000-horsepower package for passenger service. EMD's Model E8, which began production in August 1949, offered an additional 250 horsepower per unit and was well suited to the PRR's needs. By that time, the entire Blue Ribbon Fleet had been dieselized, but steam locomotives continued to power other passenger trains. The seventy-four E8A locomotives, delivered between March 1950 and November 1952, completed the dieselization of long-distance trains, just as Alco and EMD road switchers were eliminating steam from branchline and commuter operations.[339] As passenger traffic decreased, the PRR had a correspondingly reduced need for passenger locomotives, and the combined 120 E7 and E8 units proved more than sufficient. The Baldwin Centipedes were the first to be removed from passenger service, followed by the Fairbanks-Morse, the Baldwin Sharknose, and the Alco PA locomotives.[340]

Road freight units constituted the largest category of diesel locomotives in the United States, and EMD's executives were eager to cultivate the Pennsylvania Railroad as a customer. They succeeded, and EMD's four-axle F-units became the standard freight locomotive on the PRR, as they did on many other railroads. By the time the last of the 363 F-units entered service in September 1952, they represented 9.5 percent of all the locomotives (steam, diesel, and electric) that operated on the Pennsylvania Railroad and 19.6 percent of the diesel-locomotive roster. EMD's 1,500-horsepower Model F3, which entered production in the summer of 1945, was the direct descendant of the 1,350-horsepower Model FT that John Deasy had once dismissed as irrelevant to the PRR's needs. The Pennsylvania Railroad acquired its first F3 locomotives during the initial experimental phase of dieselization. In November 1945, shortly after the arrival of the first two E7A passenger locomotives, the railroad placed an order for twenty F3A and twenty F3B locomotives, geared for passenger service and sufficient to create ten 6,000-horsepower sets. John Duer and Hal Cover were concerned about the tracking characteristics of the four-axle locomotives at high speeds. A little over a year after placing the original order, they altered the specifications to eight A-B-A sets of E7 passenger locomotives and four F3A units and two F3B boosters geared for freight service, and they received authorization to purchase two additional F3B locomotives.[341] They were the first diesel freight locomotives on the Pennsylvania Railroad. The eight F-units, arranged into two A-B-B-A sets, developed the requisite 6,000 horsepower. While they constituted an insignificant share of the PRR's locomotive fleet, they symbolized the crumbling of managerial allegiance to steam. In October 1946, while the PRR's F-units were under construction at La Grange, Symes had moved to Philadelphia as the assistant vice president in charge of operations. With Clement's support, by the end of the year Symes had arranged for another EMD order. The ten F-units, in two A-B-B-B-A sets, would generate 7,500 horsepower—sufficient to pull heavy freight trains over the Alleghenies without the use of helpers.[342]

There followed a flurry of additional orders whose seemingly chaotic nature reflected the evolving policies of the Motive Power Department. As they gained experience with diesels, Cover and his associates determined that a mixture of 4,500-horsepower, 6,000-horsepower, and 7,500-horsepower packages represented the most efficient allocation of locomotives to varying freight duties. They also concluded that it was necessary to purchase A-B-A diesel sets geared for helper service, to replace steam pushers on the Allegheny summit.[343] Later, they began to question the need for a 7,500-horsepower package, as that much power was often wasted on the flatlands and insufficient to keep traffic moving through the mountains. That in turn necessitated the acquisition of additional helper sets as well as the reconfiguration of A-units and cab-less B-units into packages of varying horsepower. Regardless of their ultimate assignment, the first F3 locomotives arrived in July 1947, and by the end of the following year, 104 of them were in service. By the time that the last of the PRR's Model F3 locomotives left La Grange in February 1949, EMD had built 120 of them.[344] Less than six years earlier, EMD sales representative Paul Turner had vented his frustration with executives in the PRR's Motive Power Department, noting that "if they were not such a potential market for motive power, I would be inclined to forget

them but I don't think we can afford to do this." He had not forgotten the Pennsylvania Railroad—a company that, thanks to the 1947 managerial shakeup, was much changed from the one that had refused to allow the Model FT on the property.[345]

EMD's best-selling freight diesel, the F7, was even more widespread on the Pennsylvania Railroad. EMD's Model 567 diesel engine, in use since 1938, was far superior to the Alco Model 241 engine or any of the offerings from Baldwin, Lima-Hamilton, or Fairbanks-Morse. Yet EMD's proprietary electrical-equipment designs were less successful than the comparable technology that General Electric and Westinghouse supplied to the other builders. The F7, introduced in February 1949, generated the same horsepower as the F3 but with substantially improved traction motors and associated electrical equipment, overcoming much of the deficiency.[346] The PRR's first order, for ten F7A locomotives and an equal number of B-units, came in July 1947, with deliveries taking place in February and March 1949.[347] Additional units arrived over the following months and—like the PRR's other diesels—were assigned to replace steam locomotives in specific duties that generated the highest possible return on investment. In June 1950, however, the Motive Power Department's report to the board of directors called for a rapid increase in diesel-locomotive purchases. Stopping short of recommending complete dieselization, officials now suggested that steam locomotives should only be retained in seasonal and standby service and in a few locations where diesels would produce modest gains in efficiency. The directors were convinced, and on August 7 they approved the acquisition of 214 diesels for $85 million, by far the largest single locomotive purchase in the company's history. While EMD captured only 40 percent of the total, that portion included an order for ninety-six F7 locomotives. Even though the F7 was equally at home in passenger and freight service, the PRR's examples—classified as EF-15a—held more prosaic duties. Most hauled freight, while others labored as helpers or on heavy ore trains. When deliveries ceased in September 1952, EMD had produced 199 F7 locomotives for the Pennsylvania Railroad. Only the New York Central, the Santa Fe, and the Southern Pacific owned more. An additional group of forty Model FP7A diesels, designed for either freight or passenger service, went to the PRR as well.[348]

While the earlier F3 marked the beginning of the end for steam freight locomotives on the Pennsylvania Railroad, the arrival of the F7 units finished the job. They also marginalized Baldwin and Fairbanks-Morse and came close to doing the same for Alco. The beautifully

The EMD F7 was a stunningly successful locomotive, with 3,856 produced between 1949 and 1953. The PRR owned nearly 200 of them, geared for freight and helper operations rather than passenger service. The two A-units (led by F7A #9798) and interspersed B-unit, each generating 1,500 horsepower, are eastbound near Altoona. By the time this photo was taken, in the summer of 1953, PRR dispatchers were no longer reliant on 6,000-horsepower diesel sets. *Otto Perry photograph, Denver Public Library, Western History Collection, call number OP-14460.*

engineered Model 567 engine, combined with the vastly improved electrical equipment, made the F7 far superior to the Baldwin DR-4-4-1500 and RF-16 freight Sharks, the Fairbanks-Morse Erie-builts and C-Liners, and the Alco FA-1/FB-1 and FA-2/FB-2 freight locomotives. By the time EMD had delivered the last of the F7 locomotives, Pennsylvania Railroad officials were no longer interested in Baldwin's designs. With the exception of the tiny contingent of nine Train Masters ordered in 1956, they had no further use for Fairbanks-Morse either. Alco survived in the locomotive industry largely because of its innovative road-switcher designs. Locomotives like the RS-1 had demonstrated the utility of the squared-off configuration

that lacked an enclosed car body or an aesthetically pleasing rounded nose.[349] Alco dominated the road-switcher market in the first years after the war. Baldwin was a close second, at least on the Pennsylvania Railroad.

Alco's innovations did little to hamper EMD's success. EMD's first road switcher, the Model BL2, sold poorly, and the PRR did not buy any of them. By the autumn of 1947, however, EMD had developed the 1,500-horsepower GP7. The GP7 and its 1,750-horsepower cousin, the GP9 (which debuted in January 1954) were by far the most successful road switchers offered by any builder, with a combined total of more than seven thousand units built for the domestic and export market. The PRR acquired sixty-six of the GP7 model between January 1952 and September 1953.[350] Motive-power and operating officials were still experimenting with the assignments for various types of locomotives, and the GP7 units featured a wide variety of configurations suitable for freight or passenger service, for branch-line and main line operation, for hilly terrain and flatlands, and even for use in electrified territory. By October 1955, the initial period of experimentation had largely ended, and PRR personnel had adjusted to the operating characteristics of diesels. The 310 GP9 locomotives that arrived over the next four years were less varied—although the group included forty cab-less B-units, a feature rarely

Although Alco initially dominated the road-switcher market, it did not take long for EMD to surpass its rival. The PRR took delivery of 66 examples of the Model GP7. The slightly more powerful GP9 was even more successful, with 310 examples—including #7017, #7014, and #7028—operating on virtually every part of the sprawling PRR system. *Don Wood Negatives, Railroad Museum of Pennsylvania, PHMC.*

seen on road switchers.[351] It was a massive armada of locomotives, representing more than 12 percent of the PRR's motive power, and indicated that the company had committed to complete dieselization and had come to favor EMD as its preferred supplier. Just as the 1,200-horsepower switchers displaced the 2-8-0 Consolidations in the yards, the new EMD road switchers did the same on branch lines across the railroad.[352]

While the GP7 and GP9 locomotives were sufficiently versatile to handle almost any assignment, there remained some unusual duties that required equally specialized motive power. The 5.89 percent average grade on Madison Hill in southern Indiana was the steepest on the PRR system, and it had proven disastrous for more than one train headed down to the Ohio River. Two EMD Model SD7 locomotives, completed in November 1953, featured

dynamic brakes, instruments to control wheel slip, automatic sanders, regulators to maintain air brake pressure, and a sprayer that washed leaves and other slippery materials off the rails.[353] They replaced a group of H6 and H10s steam locomotives, also modified for service on Madison Hill, banishing steam from another small corner of the PRR system. The twenty-five examples of the EMD Model SD9, acquired in November 1957, concluded the displacement of steam locomotives, largely finishing the process that the lone Model SW switcher had started in 1937.[354] They were slightly more powerful than the SD7 and lacked the features necessary for overcoming Madison Hill. Instead, they mostly served to push cuts of cars through hump yards, eliminating the last of the I1s 2-10-0 Decapods. In addition to hump service, the new diesels handled transfer runs, culling out the final L1s Mikados and eventually rendering obsolete some of the problematic transfer units that Baldwin and Lima had provided.[355]

As the new diesels arrived, the PRR's steam power disappeared. In June 1947, the PRR owned 4,290 steam locomotives and just 45 diesels. Between 1947 and 1958, however, the PRR removed nearly 350 steam locomotives a year from service, on average. In April 1950, steam locomotives still powered 16 percent of passenger trains, 42 percent of yard switching, and two-thirds of freight traffic.

In 1948, the arrival of large numbers of diesel switchers and passenger locomotives enabled the railroad to retire 562 steam locomotives. The following year, the company removed 747 from service. By the end of 1951, the Pennsylvania Railroad had taken delivery of an additional 1,510 diesels, collectively generating slightly more than two million horsepower. By that time, only 2,155 steam locomotives were still in use. A year later, most of the motive power ordered during the rapid 1949–1951 dieselization campaign was in service, upping the horsepower total to 2.6 million. Steam locomotives remained in only 3 percent of passenger service, 9 percent of switching duties, and 18 percent of freight traffic. The 1952 diesel orders provided another 345,000 horsepower. By the beginning of January 1955, only 2,117 steam locomotives remained, and many of them were in storage. In early 1953, PRR officials announced that they had achieved "practically full utilization" of diesels, with steam locomotives commanding fewer than 20 percent of freight assignments and not even 4 percent of passenger runs.[356]

The PRR's newest steam locomotives were some of the first to be stricken from the roster. The S1 possessed little value aside from its role as a test bed for the development of the duplex concept. Symes had never thought highly of the S1 and, as vice president of the Western Region, he made clear that he would not allow it to operate over his section of the railroad. By the fall of 1945, he insisted that the locomotive be scrapped, and only pleas from Harry Jones and Carl Steins postponed its fate. Duer, desperate to preserve the legacy of his accomplishments, suggested that the S1 be donated to the Smithsonian, but to no avail. By November 1948, Jones was dead and Duer had been forced into retirement. Symes was the vice president in charge of operations, and no one was in a position to protect the S1. In that month, he signed the disposition order, and the PRR's pioneering duplex soon disappeared into scrap metal. The S2 steam turbine, by far the least successful of the experiments, had never operated satisfactorily. By the summer of 1949, the locomotive was out of service and stored at Crestline. With the cancellation of the V1 Triplex project, there was little point in keeping it, even as a prototype for other designs. The PRR dropped the locomotive from the roster in January 1952, and workers dismantled it in June. The sole Q1 freight duplex met the same fate, consigned to the dead line in 1948.[357]

The Q2 and T1 locomotives, designed to be the mainstay of the PRR's fast freight and passenger service into the 1960s, scarcely lasted longer than the prototypes that had inspired them. Most of the Q2 freight duplexes were stored serviceable at Crestline and were only occasionally sent south to Columbus to pull freight trains, when no other locomotives were available. The EMD E7 passenger diesels that arrived between September 1945 and April 1949 were ideally suited for handling the trains of the Blue Ribbon Fleet—the sole rationale for the design of the T1. Because each T1 was far more expensive to operate and maintain than one of the older, conventional Class K4s Pacifics, there was little value in assigning them to shorter, secondary passenger trains. A brief experiment with the T1 in freight service produced poor results, owing to the slipping drivers that was one of the inherent limitations of the duplex design. By early 1952, all the T1 duplexes were out of service, and a report to the board of directors suggested that the "locomotives were never a satisfactory unit for . . . operation." Within weeks, several were headed for the scrapyard, and the others followed in quick succession. In 1953, the railroad slated the remaining freight and passenger duplexes for retirement and eventual scrapping. The Juniata Shops and the Baldwin Locomotive Works had completed them less than a decade earlier. They were not fully depreciated, nor had the Pennsylvania Railroad satisfied the fifteen-year equipment-trust obligations used to pay for them. Diesels had rendered them obsolete, however, and it was cheaper to pay for their remaining cost and then turn them into scrap metal than it was to keep them in operation. All were gone by early 1956.[358]

Over the previous two decades, the PRR had spent some $38 million to develop the next generation of steam locomotives, but the last tangible results of that effort had disappeared. While the Pennsylvania Railroad preserved at least one example of most of the major classes of steam power, the duplexes proved such a disappointment that not a single one survived.[359] The short careers and ignominious ends of all the PRR's modern steam power has led to understandable assertions that key personnel in the Motive Power Department were incompetent or that at the very least they failed miserably in their effort to design viable locomotives. There can be little doubt that the S1 and the S2 were inadequate in a technical sense, and none of the steam turbine designs were likely to be successful. Those were prototypes that embodied a variety of innovative technological features, however, and not even the most confident mechanical engineer would be optimistic enough to suggest that they could be brought into full-scale production without substantial modifications. The Q2 was in many respects a satisfactory performer in fast freight service, although afflicted with the slipping wheels that were endemic to all locomotives with large drivers.

The two prototype T1 units were certainly plagued with glitches, but PRR and Baldwin officials had eliminated many of those difficulties by the time the fifty production locomotives entered service. The remaining issues—principally the malfunctioning poppet valves and the propensity for derailments at certain locations—were on their way toward resolution when the diesels began to arrive in large numbers. There was in any case little doubt that personnel in the Motive Power Department had done exactly what senior management had asked of them. They produced a locomotive that could pull long passenger trains at high speeds and eliminate the double-heading that was associated with the use of the K4s.

The Motive Power Department and the Accounting Department measured success in two very different ways, however. The purpose of the first part of the organization, as its name suggested, was to provide power that would move the railroad's trains—and the more power, the better. Individuals such as Harry Jones, Carl Steins, and Hal Cover could with justifiable pride point to results from the Altoona test plant, demonstrating that a T1 could produce as much tractive effort as three K4s locomotives. In service, some of the newer T1 locomotives averaged 9,592 miles a month, well above the 7,715 miles generated by a typical K4s. In that sense, the PRR's designers not only met but exceeded what their superiors had demanded of them. Other problems, ancillary to their principal mandate, constituted interesting (if often frustrating) technical puzzles that, given sufficient time, they could certainly have resolved. Time was not on their side, however. Even as they designed the T1 and the other duplexes, the Great Depression, World War II, and then the postwar transformation of freight and passenger-traffic patterns upset their calculations. Coal prices and labor costs escalated, and a series of strikes by the United Mine Workers ensured that supplies were unreliable. Political interests that had once accepted locomotive smoke as a necessary companion to increased mobility, well-paying employment, and economic growth now found such pollution unacceptable. By 1945, the PRR's motive-power experts had succeeded in providing locomotives that were ideally suited to conditions that existed fifteen years earlier but not those that were in place when the final T1 emerged from the erecting shop. The real tragedy, perhaps, was that if executives had delayed full-scale production of the T1 for even a year, then it is likely that Flash Gordon and Buck Rogers would have been the only locomotives of that type to have ever been built.

During precisely the same years when Pennsylvania Railroad personnel were designing and testing the duplexes, engineers at Electro-Motive transformed the diesel locomotive from a barely adequate adjunct to steam power into a reliable and economical form of transportation. In the end, that was what mattered to the PRR's accountants as well as to their counterparts on every other railroad in the United States. They stressed, correctly, that diesels cost less to operate and maintain than steam locomotives, were more reliable, and were available for revenue service for a far larger percentage of the time. Their limited horsepower, much less than that of any of the PRR's duplexes, was irrelevant, so long as individual units could operate in multiple units under the control of a single crew. The accountants' calculations told them that a set of passenger diesel locomotives cost 32 cents per mile to operate, 40 percent less than the 53.9 cents per mile associated with a T1. The T1—and indeed all the PRR's steam locomotives—were technological successes but economic failures, and that is what ultimately doomed them to extinction. The accountants won that struggle for power.[360]

The Cost of Efficiency

Many of the PRR's older and more conventional steam locomotives outlasted the duplexes. The arrival of hundreds of diesel switchers during and immediately following World War II consigned numerous Class A 0-4-0 and Class B 0-6-0 shifters as well as Class H 2-8-0 Consolidations to the scrap line. Except for the duplexes, however, the PRR did not immediately retire any major group of steam power in its entirety. As additional diesels arrived, the remaining steam locomotives would be sidelined whenever they came due for major repairs. By concentrating steam power in fewer and fewer locations, where dieselization would produce the least favorable return on investment, the PRR was able to progressively close roundhouses and shop facilities and dismantle coaling stations, water tanks, and track pans.

The greatest economies associated with dieselization came not from the elimination of coal, but from the elimination of people. That process made redundant 90 percent of the workforce associated with steam locomotives. Machinists, boilermakers, pipefitters, and other representatives of the shop crafts had always occupied a space between the operating employees and the unskilled and semiskilled workers who maintained the right of way and engaged in other menial occupations. Their demands for higher wages and union representation, strengthened by the labor policies of the United States Railroad Administration, provoked the vicious strikes of 1922. By the time of World War II, they had joined powerful unions and secured better pay and benefits. The compensation earned by shop forces represented an increasing cost to the Pennsylvania Railroad, one that diesels promised to reduce substantially. The use of standardized and interchangeable parts, manufactured by builders such as EMD rather than the railroad, reduced the need for skilled craftsmen. With few parts to machine, no pipes to fit, and no boiler to maintain, diesels enabled the PRR to cut labor costs, eliminate strictly defined job classifications, and undercut the power of the American Federation of Labor and other national unions.

During the general economic prosperity of the early 1950s, Pennsylvania Railroad officials assuaged whatever guilt they may have felt about ending so many railroad careers by insisting that those laid off could easily transition to manufacturing facilities. They noted that 85 percent of those former employees had quickly found jobs that were at least as good as those on the railroad. Even individuals in their fifties or sixties, whose age made the transition more difficult, seemed resigned to developments. "I'm not worried," an unemployed blacksmith suggested. "Something will turn up. Besides, no one can stand in the way of progress."[361]

Progress certainly affected the Altoona Works. During the 1920s, the shop facilities provided jobs for more than fifteen thousand people. The number of employees declined during the Great Depression, rebounded in the World War II years, and fell again after 1946, when locomotive production ceased at the Juniata Shops. As traffic levels fell, so, too, did the number of freight and passenger cars that rolled across the railroad and that required construction or periodic repair. The coal industry was particularly hard hit, and the number of hoppers in service declined by 27 percent. Much of the freight that remained traveled in smaller numbers of higher-capacity cars, meaning fewer sets of trucks, fewer couplers, and fewer air brake assemblies to build or repair. Between 1952 and 1956, the railroad's freight-car roster shrank by 15 percent, from 200,000 to 170,000. As the railway supply industry became more competitive after 1945, the Pennsylvania Railroad could often buy material from outside firms more cheaply than manufacturing it in-house. EMD salesmen played a particularly aggressive role in that process. One of the locomotive builder's representatives toured the Altoona facilities, and he repeatedly pointed out areas where the PRR could purchase supplies rather than manufacture them. Predictably, employees complained about the alleged inferiority of "foreign" components, but executives

who were desperate to trim operating costs could not be too choosy.[362]

Thanks to the maintenance and servicing requirements of the existing steam-locomotive fleet, employment at the Altoona Works was still a respectable 11,939 in 1949. In June 1952, as EMD and the other builders completed the massive batch of locomotives ordered over the previous three years, the PRR abolished all jobs at Altoona that did not directly support diesel maintenance or the construction and repair of freight and passenger cars. Three years later, the PRR opened the first section of the Samuel Rea Shops in Hollidaysburg, eight miles south of Altoona. The half-mile-long facility initially built new freight cars on an assembly line basis, but car repair operations were soon relocated there as well. The 12th Street Car Shops (the former Altoona Machine Shops), the Altoona Car Shops, and the South Altoona Foundries were left virtually deserted.

Beginning in June 1953, as the last steam locomotives were disappearing from the railroad, James P. Newell, the company's vice president in charge of operations, commissioned a series of studies regarding the Altoona situation. The conclusions ranged from the relatively minor emphasis on buying most nonstandard rivet sizes from an outside manufacturer to the more substantive decision to close the Grey Iron Foundry—a facility that was useless now that diesels had taken over. Newell initially hoped to find ways to put the excess capacity at Altoona to some other use. He highlighted "the production line methods that will be possible at Samuel Rea Car Shop" and suggested that the older facilities in Altoona might become competitive with outside suppliers. David Bevan, early in his time as the PRR's vice president in charge of finance, noted that the facilities and personnel at the Altoona Works could be used to manufacture and repair freight cars for other railroads. Attorney John B. Prizer observed that both the PRR's corporate charter and Pennsylvania state law prohibited such activities, and the plan never came to fruition.[363]

The recession that began in August 1957 dealt the final blow to the Altoona Works and the city that shared its name. In the immediate postwar period, some thirteen thousand people labored at the Altoona Works. By 1958, that number had declined to forty-five hundred. Even high-seniority employees could not count on steady work. Instead, they endured long furloughs, hoping to be called back for a brief interval of high-paying employment. The city's population declined as younger individuals moved away to look for jobs elsewhere. Many older residents lived in a kind of limbo, laid off from the Works but still hoping that they might be called back, unwilling to give up their seniority and too old to start over elsewhere. They subsisted on minimal incomes, and even those who retained their jobs had little confidence that they would keep them much longer.[364]

The Altoona Works had once accounted for 90 percent of the city's employment, and the cutbacks proved devastating to the local economy. The small number of people who still worked for the PRR possessed scant interest or wherewithal to invest in the community, and the city soon began to deteriorate. So many PRR employees retired and then moved to Florida that the *Altoona Mirror* published a weekly update on events in the Gulf Coast city of St. Petersburg. During the 1920s, representatives from Altoona's Chamber of Commerce had actively discouraged the establishment of new businesses that might compete with the Pennsylvania Railroad for a limited pool of local labor. Beginning as early as 1946, however, civic leaders in Altoona launched initiatives to attract new industries that would provide alternative employment. The Chamber of Commerce established Altoona Enterprises, Incorporated, an entity funded by local businesses, that would in turn provide loans and other seed money to encourage companies to locate in the city. By 1958, however, local leaders had only been able to reduce the city's rate of unemployment to 15 percent.[365]

James Symes—the executive who had done more than anyone else to banish steam locomotives from the Pennsylvania Railroad—was now the PRR's president, and he witnessed the consequences of his policies. In the spring of 1958, Pennsylvania Railroad public-relations officials visited Altoona and warned Symes of the possibility of "breadlines there within a month," something that had not been seen in that city since the dark days of the Great Depression. They informed him that any improper handling of the Altoona situation "could easily subject the Company to open criticism and community hostility in the future." As events unfolded, however, it became apparent that workers and the unions that represented them lacked the ability to make much of a difference. Politicians like Representative James E. Van Zandt—a Republican whose district included his hometown of Altoona—protested the reductions, but their voices hardly mattered.[366]

Given the dire economic circumstances, Symes authorized a public-relations campaign to diffuse the hostility of furloughed employees, the few who still had their jobs, and the townspeople who depended on the PRR's paychecks. The general theme was that intrusive regulation, excessive taxation, and competition from other modes of transportation were to blame for the Pennsylvania Railroad's, and hence Altoona's, difficulties. PRR officials assigned a "community relations man" to the staff of Clair I. Clugh, the Altoona Works manager. He was responsible for maintaining close contacts with community leaders; speaking to women's clubs, business groups, and service clubs; and generating favorable news releases for the local media. The company also contributed to the industrial development program of Altoona Enterprises, Incorporated, but PRR executives concluded that the agency's efforts were "not spectacularly successful."[367]

As conditions worsened, the crisis in Altoona attracted national attention. In March 1959, Senator Matthew N. Neely, a West Virginia Democrat, chaired a subcommittee of the Senate Committee on Labor and Public Welfare. Neely pledged to investigate the "economic disaster" in Blair County and seven other hard-hit western Pennsylvania counties. Representative Van Zandt arranged for the hearings to take place in Altoona at the Penn Alto Hotel. Neely presided, both because of his role as chairman and because he was the only subcommittee member who bothered to travel to Altoona for the hearings. The sole witness who had anything negative to say regarding the Pennsylvania Railroad was Murray Gassman, a staff representative from the Congress of Industrial Organizations. Earlier, Gassman had acquired a certain degree of local renown by pushing a series of resolutions, mostly dealing with surplus food distribution, through the Altoona City Council and the Blair County Board of Commissioners. The congressional hearings provided Gassman with a venue to launch "a bitter attack upon the Pennsylvania Railroad, its policies, and its management." According to journalists, Neely employed "all of the charm" and "political finesse" he could muster to defuse the situation. The senator recommended a change in venue, asking Gassman to present his views in Washington, a city far removed from the troubles in Altoona.[368]

Despite Gassman's vociferous attacks on the Pennsylvania Railroad, the company's public-relations campaign produced the intended results. Works manager Clugh made certain that Senator Neely was aware that the Altoona tragedy represented "the story of the decline of a once great national industry." Rather than excoriate the Pennsylvania Railroad, Neely highlighted such issues as restrictions on imported crude oil, which raised the PRR's fuel costs, and the ongoing decline of the coal industry. When Pennsylvania Railroad officials surveyed local employees and residents, they concluded that most possessed "a generally wide understanding that the Company has serious problems over which it cannot exercise adequate control."

Whether they feared alienating their former employer or were resigned to what they considered inevitable, Altoona residents acknowledged that the Pennsylvania Railroad was acting "as a matter of self-preservation."[369]

The situation in Columbus was equally dire. Once the principal repair facilities on the Southwest System of Lines West, the 20th Street Shops had at their peak employed more than 8,000 people. In early 1953, a workforce of 2,800 tended to the last of the PRR's steam locomotives. Mass layoffs began later that year, and by March 1955, only 1,364 people remained. The fit-up, boiler, tank, blacksmith, and car departments that had once provided work for more than 2,000 people were consolidated into the machine shop, which employed only 87. Every boilermaker with less than thirty years of seniority lost his job. Of the 280 blacksmiths who had worked at the 20th Street Shops, only five remained—and all had at least twenty-two years of seniority. Electricians, in contrast, were in high demand, with the youngest having been on the job for less than four years. In the main shop complex, 160,000 square feet of floor space had become vacant. The nearby Spruce Street roundhouse disappeared, as did nineteen other structures. Only 15 steam locomotives were still in use, with another 189 in storage, to be employed only in case of emergency.[370]

That emergency came only briefly, thanks to an increase in freight traffic during the mid-1950s. In May 1955, the PRR rehabilitated thirty steam locomotives at Altoona, calling skilled boilermakers and machinists back to work one last time. In some cases, however, PRR officials found it less expensive to lease steam locomotives from other railroads rather than recondition those that were in storage. They included nine Class T1 4-8-4 Northerns leased from the Reading in 1956.[371] By then, steam freight operations were confined to only a few locations that drew railfans who were prepared to document the last holdouts. On the Shamokin Branch, Class I1s Decapods battled heavy grades while moving iron ore from Erie to a connection with the Lehigh Valley, for delivery to Bethlehem Steel in its namesake town. Farther west, the Sandusky Branch hosted extensive coal traffic between Columbus and Lake Erie. The ice-free navigation season on the Great Lakes required additional motive power on a temporary basis. That meant a variety of large steam locomotives, including a dozen oil-burning 2-10-4 Texas locomotives, leased from the Santa Fe in 1956. The following year, six representatives of the PRR Class J1—the locomotives that had demonstrated their superiority to the now-scrapped Q2 duplexes—provided one of the last opportunities to see steam locomotives in action on the Pennsylvania Railroad.[372]

The brief resurgence of steam power would not last. On July 1, 1956, a nationwide steel strike involving half a million workers caused traffic levels to plummet. In response, PRR managers laid off workers and reduced the number of locomotives in operation. Sixty thousand longshoremen went on strike in November, crippling New York and other East Coast ports. In June 1957, the board of directors agreed to the purchase of two hundred additional locomotives, including RSD-12 helpers from Alco and GP9 road switchers, SW1200 switchers, and SD9 yard engines from EMD.[373] When delivered, they would be sufficient to eliminate the last pockets of steam operation on the Pennsylvania Railroad. Yet complete dieselization occurred even before all the new units entered service. A recession that began in August 1957 did not begin to abate until the following April. The remaining I1s, L1s, and J1 freight locomotives went into the dead line for the last time, never to steam again. A few K4s Pacifics remained in commuter service on the New York & Long Branch, the route that the PRR operated jointly with the Jersey Central. There had been several attempts to dieselize the service, but none of the new locomotives could match the speed, acceleration, and reliability of their older cousins. The last two steam locomotives in regular service succumbed on November 4, 1957. For a few more weeks, steam locomotives saw occasional use on commuter routes or as helpers, then they too were gone.[374]

The final displacement of steam locomotives did not end the ongoing process of dieselization. The orders placed in November 1957 ensured that ample power was available, regardless of economic conditions and traffic levels. After a five-year hiatus, however, PRR officials were again ready to buy diesels. The products of Baldwin, Lima, and Fairbanks-Morse had demonstrated their inadequacy and were ripe for replacement. Even the more reliable EMD locomotives were beginning to show their age. Both EMD and Alco—the only surviving locomotive builders—were developing new locomotive designs with turbochargers and other features that boosted horsepower. Often referred to as "second-generation" diesel locomotives, they enabled railroads to replace older models, often on a two-to-one basis. Both companies offered attractive trade-in credits on used locomotives, and by the early 1960s, the PRR was ready to cull its oldest and least efficient diesels from the roster. As they had done in the past, PRR executives spread their purchases among multiple builders, to avoid favoritism, to evaluate competing products, and to prevent one company from monopolizing the locomotive industry.[375]

The first order, placed in February 1962, went to a new entrant in the road diesel market. Since the 1920s, General

Even after full dieselization, the relics of steam operation persisted. A trio of EMD GP9 locomotives lead a train past a water crane and underneath a coal wharf—expensive facilities that could now be abandoned. Many employees, particularly those who worked in shop facilities, were similarly redundant. *Don Wood Negatives, Railroad Museum of Pennsylvania, PHMC.*

Electric had supplied generators, traction motors, and associated equipment to Alco, while the company's executives agreed to avoid the production of large diesel locomotives for the domestic market. GE personnel did develop several small switching locomotives. They included a 44-ton model that complied with a 1937 national labor agreement eliminating firemen from units weighing less than ninety thousand pounds. The PRR acquired forty-six of them, delivered between November 1947 and February 1950.[376] They were ideally suited for the tight curves of urban industrial districts but lacked the power necessary to perform their duties efficiently. In 1953, as PRR officials were trying to find a useful role for their underpowered diesel switchers, GE terminated its agreement with Alco and undertook the development of road freight locomotives. In 1959, GE began testing a 2,500-horsepower unit, later classified as the Model U25B. Demonstrations on the Pennsylvania Railroad, in February 1962, indicated the ability of the U25B to pull high-priority trains. The PRR's first order, for seven locomotives, was paid for by the federal government, as compensation for the relocation of tracks to make way for the Kinzua Dam in northwestern Pennsylvania.[377] Soon thereafter, the company ordered a further twenty-two U25B locomotives.[378] The railroad eventually owned fifty-nine, delivered between August 1962 and December 1965. By the early 1960s, operating officials were becoming disenchanted with the four-axle locomotives that since the 1940s had formed the mainstay of the PRR's freight-diesel fleet. Six axles, they concluded, were less likely to exhibit wheel slip when hauling heavy trains upgrade. Fortunately, GE offered a six-axle version of the U25B, classed as Model U25C. The PRR acquired

By the time Electro-Motive delivered these two SD40 locomotives, in March 1966, steam was long gone from the Pennsylvania Railroad. So, too, were Baldwin, Lima-Hamilton, and Fairbanks-Morse, as all three companies had ceased production. Locomotives such as the #6100 and #6101 were now replacing many of the older, inadequate models, as the PRR standardized on the products of EMD, Alco, and General Electric. The coaling tower in the background had long since outlived its usefulness, and it likely survived because of the expense associated with tearing it down. *Don Wood Negatives, Railroad Museum of Pennsylvania, PHMC.*

twenty, all delivered in 1965.[379] A further twenty of the Model U28C, a slightly more powerful six-axle locomotive, arrived between September 1966 and January 1967.[380] In 1967, the PRR placed its last locomotive order, less than a year prior to the Penn Central merger. Twenty more GE locomotives were included. With six axles and 3,300 horsepower, those Model U33C units arrived shortly after the consolidation and never featured the iconic PRR keystone.[381]

General Electric was a clear threat to Alco's secondary status in the diesel-locomotive market. Yet Alco continued to receive orders from Pennsylvania Railroad officials who acknowledged the virtues of the company's newer locomotives and who wanted to maintain competition. The PRR and other railroads had experienced numerous problems with the Model 244 engine that powered most of Alco's early diesels. The much-improved Model 251 engine went

into production in 1954—too late to be of much benefit in the initial dieselization rush but ensuring that Alco was ready to manufacture high-horsepower second-generation units. The PRR's 1962 orders removed all fifteen of the obsolete Alco PA-1 and PB-1 passenger locomotives from the roster, traded in for an equal number of the Model RS-27, a four-axle, 2,700-horsepower freight locomotive.[382] To compete against GE, its former manufacturing partner, Alco introduced the Century Series in 1962. The PRR owned a lone four-axle C-424 unit, delivered in September 1963.[383] It was soon superseded by the slightly more powerful C-425, with thirty-one examples ordered in 1964 and 1965.[384] The shift to six-axle power resulted in the delivery of fifteen Model C-628 locomotives in 1965.[385] An equal number of the Model C-630 arrived in the last months of 1966.[386] The last Alco locomotives ordered by the Pennsylvania Railroad were a group of fifteen Model C-636 units, manufactured in the spring of 1968.[387] With the Penn Central merger in place, the locomotives, like the GE Model U33C, arrived in the livery of the new company. They were the final locomotives ordered under the auspices of the Pennsylvania Railroad to enter service. They were also among the final locomotives to emerge from Alco's Schenectady manufacturing plant. It was a poor omen that the PRR's order for just fifteen units was the largest single request for the C-636. Although Alco had steadily improved its products, the company yielded secondary status to GE and ceased US production in 1969.[388]

Even though they were willing to give token orders to GE and Alco, the PRR's motive-power officials exhibited a clear preference for EMD's locomotives. Yet EMD initially lagged both of its competitors in terms of its second-generation designs. The PRR's initial 1962 purchase of second-generation power included fifteen of the Alco Model RS-27 and twenty-nine of the GE Model U25B—but not a single locomotive from La Grange. To remain competitive, EMD designers boosted the horsepower of the long-established Model 567 diesel engine, placing it in the Model GP30 locomotive. The distinctive units, with a body designed at the GM Automotive Styling Center, were but a temporary measure, until EMD could develop a more competitive product. The PRR purchased fifty-two of them, all built in the first half of 1963.[389] Between May 1964 and April 1965, the PRR took delivery of the upgraded Model GP35—119 in all, indicating the railroad's continuing reliance on EMD.[390]

Like the GP35, the SD35 developed 2,500 horsepower—low for a second-generation model. It was nonetheless in the vanguard of the transition to six-axle freight locomotives, and the PRR acquired forty of them during the first half of 1965.[391] The 1960s horsepower race nonetheless exceeded the capabilities of the Model 567 diesel engine. The new Model 645 engine debuted in 1965, perfectly timed for the second generation of locomotives. EMD's SD40 locomotives featured the new engine, atop six-wheel trucks, with each unit generating 3,000 horsepower. It was the locomotive that ensured that EMD would continue to dominate the industry, and the PRR purchased sixty-five of them in early 1966.[392] The Model SD45, introduced in 1965, generated 3,600 horsepower. That was more than double what the initial batch of F3 locomotives had been able to provide two decades earlier. Only the Alco C-636 could match that power, but its frequent mechanical problems made any comparison irrelevant. The first SD45 order, for sixty-five units, arrived incrementally between October 1966 and January 1967.[393] PRR officials were pleased with their performance. In October 1967, they ordered sixty-five more, with the last representatives arriving soon after the merger.[394]

The Limits of Dieselization

It is perhaps too much to suggest that the diesel locomotive saved the Pennsylvania Railroad, but it certainly retarded the company's long postwar decline. James Symes, who had done more than any other executive to eliminate steam, acknowledged the debt that his company owed to the new technology. As he observed in 1955, "The greatest single contribution to the economic and efficient operation of our railroads during my 40 years of association with the

industry has been the development of the Diesel locomotive." Symes was quick to add that it was not just the diesel but the Electro-Motive diesel that had revolutionized railroad operations.[395]

The increased availability, greater efficiency, and reduced maintenance expenditure associated with diesels had done much to offset rising labor costs, stagnant rates, and declining revenues. During its corporate existence, the Pennsylvania Railroad purchased just over three thousand diesel locomotives. Slightly over two thousand had been in service at any one time, as the first second-generation units arrived and before the company had disposed of many of the earlier models. It was the largest diesel-locomotive fleet in the United States but was still well below the number of steam locomotives that had been in use at any time since the 1870s. While there had been some postwar curtailments in service, particularly on passenger routes, the reduction in motive power demonstrated the extraordinary increase in efficiency that diesels generated.

Diesels could not work miracles, however, and they could not eliminate the underlying structural deficiencies that affected the Pennsylvania Railroad after 1945. World War II generated unprecedented levels of freight and passenger traffic, but shortages of labor and materials led to deferred maintenance and the erosion of the physical plant. Despite a sustained managerial commitment to rebuild the railroad's infrastructure, wartime profits did not fully compensate for the damage that wartime traffic had imposed. World War II had only temporarily masked systemic problems that affected all the railroads to varying degrees.

Despite those systemic problems, in the immediate postwar period the Pennsylvania Railroad still possessed a sterling financial reputation, competent leadership, and many thousands of talented employees. The company remained an indispensable component of the transportation network and the economic welfare of the Northeast and Midwest. The years immediately following World War II thus marked a time of renewal, as the Pennsylvania Railroad invested in new equipment and operating methods for freight and passenger service and brought to completion such long-delayed projects as the Philadelphia Improvements. Those initiatives may have been a shadow of the PRR's former glories, of a time when Alexander Cassatt and his colleagues brought trains underneath the Hudson River and into the architectural glories of Penn Station. They were nonetheless significant, and they suggested that there was cause for optimism regarding the future of the company, the communities it served, and the railroad industry it represented.

Chapter 5

Renewal

A small group of Indians moved slowly along the shore of Lake Michigan, horses and dogs dragging travois laden with their meager goods. Louis Jolliet and Jacques Marquette—Père Marquette—soon made an appearance, initiating contact between Indigenous peoples and European explorers. Wagons arrived within minutes, their wheels marking the pace of advancing civilization. Robert Stephenson's *Rocket*, fresh from its triumphant success at the 1829 Rainhill Trials, chugged across the stage. In the next half hour, Abraham Lincoln left Illinois to begin his presidency, the Transcontinental Railroad united a continent, Scandinavian farmers populated the Great Plains, and powerful diesel locomotives sped onward into a glorious future.

The occasion was the Chicago Railroad Fair of 1948 and 1949, commemorating, in Carl Sandburg's words, the city's role as "Player with Railroads and the Nation's Freight Handler." A century earlier, in October 1848, the locomotive *Pioneer* traveled along the tracks of the Galena & Chicago Union Railroad. Over the hundred years that followed, Chicago had become the second-largest city in the United States and the most important rail hub in the world. The Pennsylvania Railroad contributed mightily to that transformation, as did the other three eastern trunk lines, the midwestern granger roads, the western transcontinentals, and a host of others. Countless tons of freight had passed through the city's rail yards. Millions of people began or ended their journeys at one of Chicago's great passenger terminals, and it had recently become possible to travel directly from the Atlantic to the Pacific, transiting the metropolis without leaving the comfort of a sleeping car.[1]

The 1948–1949 Chicago Railroad Fair contained many of the familiar themes featured at past exhibitions. The Deadwood Central, a narrow-gauge railroad, skirted the perimeter of the lakeside grounds, giving fairgoers both a train ride and a taste of the Old West. Pullman offered two displays, reflecting a recent federal antitrust action that divided the company—long associated with Chicago—into two components. The manufacturing arm demonstrated the methods used to build new sleeping cars, eagerly awaited by travelers who had endured overcrowded and often decrepit equipment during the war. The other Pullman, now owned collectively by the railroads, operated those sleeping cars and exhibited their latest features. The Edward G. Budd Manufacturing Company, whose efforts to expand production sparked the antitrust battle, also displayed its wares. Several railroads maintained exhibits, although participation was far from uniform. The Chicago & Eastern Illinois offered a re-creation of Miami Beach and a replica of the Bok Singing Tower in Lake Wales, designed to encourage wintertime rail travel to Florida. The Illinois Central introduced the streamlined *City of New Orleans* in 1947 and correspondingly showed visitors the delights of the French Quarter. Western carriers were even better represented, in part because Chicago rather than St. Louis was the true gateway to the West. They were also some of the most prosperous railroads in the United States, and they could afford to put on a show. The Chicago & North Western, the company that long ago absorbed the Galena

& Chicago Union, built a replica of the city's first passenger depot. The Rock Island created Rocket Village—the name alluded to a fleet of modest if modern streamliners—complete with a western dance hall. The Santa Fe's Indian Village included an adobe pueblo and 125 Pueblo Indians. Union Pacific officials were eager to promote tourist travel, and their exhibit highlighted the scenic wonders of eleven western states. The three western lines that had once been part of James J. Hill's community of interest, prior to the *Northern Securities* case, continued to cooperate. The display jointly sponsored by the Burlington, the Northern Pacific, and the Great Northern included a dude ranch, a replica of Old Faithful, and a cohort of bears. Within a year, Denver & Rio Grande Western officials would introduce the *California Zephyr*, perhaps the most famous of the postwar streamlined trains, and their exhibit likewise stressed the scenic beauty along their tracks. According to legend, a trip along the Rio Grande's route through Glenwood Canyon inspired General Motors vice president Cyrus Osborn to invent the dome car. It was only appropriate that the locomotive and four passenger cars of GM's all-dome *Train of Tomorrow* were parked just a few yards away, with the *Star Dust*, the *Sky View*, the *Dream Cloud*, and the *Moon Glow* offering a level of comfort and style rarely seen before. Maverick railroad financier Robert R. Young, the chairman of the Chesapeake & Ohio, offered an alternative vision of the future. The ultralightweight Train X was short on comfort and style, but it was cheap to build and operate—ideal for railroads that hoped to remain competitive in the intermediate-distance passenger market.[2]

The offerings of the Pennsylvania Railroad, in contrast, were far more modest. The company carried more passengers than any other railroad, but commuters and business travelers formed a large share of the total. While luxury trains such as *The Broadway Limited* continued to offer high-class service, the PRR did not have access to Indian pueblos, Old Faithful, or playful bears, and its routes would never equal the appeal of trains like the *California Zephyr*. Even as they approved requests for expenditures on new passenger equipment, executives were already observing that the market for postwar rail travel was less robust than they had predicted. The Pennsylvania Railroad's financial difficulties, including the 1946 operating loss, in any case precluded the kind of frivolities associated with the Chicago Railroad Fair. The same held true for the other eastern railroads, and none offered an individual exhibit. Instead, the PRR and eight other carriers collaborated on a joint display. It featured a 45-foot tower fabricated from chrome-plated rails and topped with a jeweled

prism ball, a 9-foot robot that answered questions from visitors, and a dozen dioramas and photo murals. The Pennsylvania Railroad provided three of its oldest steam locomotives—a replica of the Camden & Amboy's *John Bull*, the Cumberland Valley's *Pioneer*, and the *Reuben Wells* that had spent years toiling up the steep grade of Madison Hill—and two of its newest—the sole S1 and one of the T1 duplexes that were already proving to be a poor investment. A far more successful locomotive, the GG1 electric, suggested the PRR's passenger service at its best, hauling long fast passenger trains between the densely populated cities along the Atlantic Seaboard. There were no diesels, however, even though one of the most intense struggles for corporate power in the company's history had recently resulted in a decision to replace steam locomotives as quickly as possible. A single passenger car was on display, from one of the all-coach streamliners that generated a far greater return on investment than did *The Broadway Limited*. Parked nearby was the *Robert E. Hannegan*, the only PRR Railway Post Office car to carry a name, in honor of the postmaster general. In the years to come, the mail traffic that it represented would only partly offset increasingly catastrophic losses in passenger operations. One of the four freight cars available to visitors—a boxcar equipped for merchandise traffic—would soon have little freight to haul, as many of those high-value shipments had already fallen victim to motor-carrier competition.[3]

Locomotives played a starring role at the Chicago Railroad Fair, as exhibits and as actors. Edward Hungerford, a newspaper reporter, author, and historian, recycled many of the themes he had incorporated in *Wings of a Century* (at the 1933–1934 Century of Progress Exposition in Chicago) and *Railroads on Parade* (at the 1939–1940 New York World's Fair).[4] The title of the postwar iteration, *Wheels A-Rolling*, suggested that trains were not the only—or even the dominant—mode of wheeled transportation. The script intermingled the evolution of mobility with the history of Chicago's development, embedded in an overall framework that stressed "an adventure in speed, growth, and progress." The wheel in its myriad forms, from oxcart to automobile, became the principal element in the onward march of civilization, ensuring that "today America is a nation on wheels, wheels that have rolled through wilderness and wasteland, leaving in their wake a thousand cities and ten thousand towns." As Indians, French explorers, and Chicago's early settlers passed from the scene, Stephenson's *Rocket* became the first of more than twenty locomotives that crossed the stage. The *John*

Bull that had previously appeared in Chicago was now in the Smithsonian, but a replica—constructed by PRR shop forces in 1940—followed close behind the *Rocket*. Yet the remaining equipment had little to do with the PRR, and neither the company nor any of the individuals associated with its history merited a mention in the script. The *DeWitt Clinton*, also a replica, carried the standard for New York Central predecessor Mohawk & Hudson. The Baltimore & Ohio, which maintained the preeminent collection of nineteenth-century railroad equipment in the nation, played an even more visible role. The *Lafayette* was there, as was a reference to Charles Carroll, sole surviving signer of the Declaration of Independence when he was the guest of honor at the railroad's groundbreaking in 1828. The *Tom Thumb* raced a horse, and lost, a mythical event suggesting that Joseph Pangborn's flair for promotion had outlived him. The *Atlantic* reenacted the arrival of the first B&O locomotive into the nation's capital. The setting then shifted west to the inaugural run of the Galena & Chicago Union's *Pioneer*, the California gold rush, and the breathtaking speed of a Wells Fargo stagecoach and the Pony Express. Abraham Lincoln departed Springfield in February 1861. His body returned four years later, as three newly emancipated slaves walked sorrowfully alongside a funeral train pulled by another B&O locomotive, the *William Mason*. In the aftermath of the Civil War, the completion of the Transcontinental Railroad "means indeed a union of east and west which will not be split asunder." Irish, Chinese, and Hispanic tracklayers stood side by side, watching the driving of the golden spike as "Auld Lang Syne" played in the background.

The quickening pace of progress unfolded over the remainder of the nineteenth century. Fred Harvey established his eponymous chain of trackside restaurants and dining cars, an event that was no doubt familiar to those who had seen the 1946 Judy Garland film *The Harvey Girls*. The narrator emphasized both efforts by land agents of the Burlington and the Milwaukee Road to attract Scandinavian immigrants to the Great Plains and the importance of the Northern Pacific to the development of logging. James J. Hill passed through the scene, as the "Empire Builder" who had replaced the Red River oxcart with the railway. Chicago in the Gay Nineties featured bicycles, a horsecar, a cable car, and a fashion show. The New York Central's No. 999, allegedly the fastest locomotive in the world, then dashed past the spectators.

The twentieth century did not begin until more than thirty minutes into a thirty-four-minute show, suggesting that *Wheels A-Rolling* depicted the story of the railways largely in past tense, through a nostalgic, rose-colored filter. Significantly, the modern era began with a parade of early automobiles, the technology where "American industrial genius is concentrated." It was "from these humble beginnings a new and great industry indicative of a great nation's commercial progress [was] being born." The Burlington *Zephyr* reprised its 1934 debut at the Century of Progress. When it first graced the rails, fourteen years earlier, commentators had suggested that it represented the beginning of a modern, streamlined, and prosperous future. By 1948, the internal-combustion *Zephyr* appeared as little more than a by-product of the auto industry, and "it was inevitable that the automotive vehicle would come to the road of steel." The performance ended less than a minute later, with a steam and a diesel locomotive meeting head-to-head, as the *Jupiter* and the No. 119 had done at Promontory. "For more than a century, railroads have forged our destiny in war and in peace," the narrator concluded. "They have spanned the continent and united a nation. The romance of transportation, the adventure of speed and progress, is more than the history of America, it is the lifeblood of the nation."[5]

The success of the Chicago Railroad Fair reflected the affinity of Americans for their railroads but also suggested that the nature of that relationship was changing. More than 2.5 million people attended the exhibition before it closed on October 3, 1948—still several weeks before the centenary of the *Pioneer*'s inaugural trip—and an even larger number visited the following year. Many of them traveled to Chicago by train, and the Pennsylvania Railroad and other carriers were buying new passenger equipment as fast as it could be manufactured. Those purchases were but a small part of a massive postwar campaign to eliminate years of deferred maintenance, to rebuild the railroad network, and to acquire the locomotives and rolling stock necessary to remain competitive in a rapidly evolving transportation landscape. Despite its financial difficulties, the PRR alone spent more than a billion dollars between 1948 and 1953 in the largest capital-investment program in the company's history. In the years that followed, the Pennsylvania Railroad offered travelers some of the most comfortable accommodations they had ever experienced. New intermodal services demonstrated a commitment to innovation and created a truly integrated transportation system. The completion of the long-delayed Philadelphia Improvements improved the efficiency of the railroad's operations while beginning the revitalization of the nation's third-largest city. That widespread commitment to renewal attested to managerial optimism regarding the future and confidence that the railroads would continue to play a central role in the national economy.[6]

As Americans continued their ongoing "adventure in speed, growth, and progress," however, their wheels were increasingly rolling over roads rather than rails. The war in which railroads gave such heroic service also accelerated developments in aviation. It gave rise to a group of highly trained military pilots who made the transition to civilian life by taking command of steadily improving passenger aircraft. The commitment of railroad executives to the golden age of the postwar streamliner proved to be a serious mistake, as new services lacked patronage and comfortable sleepers, coaches, and diners ran half-empty. The situation was almost as bad on the freight side of the ledger. Modern equipment and rehabilitated tracks could do little to halt the long decline of the steel industry, northeastern manufacturing firms, and other major generators of revenue. Trucks commanded an ever-larger share of the scant remaining less-than-carload-lot traffic. Intermodal shipments grew as rapidly, sparking criticism from executives who asserted that large investments in piggyback service merely shifted the railroad's business from boxcars to trailers. The redevelopment of Center-City Philadelphia initiated a fierce debate between business leaders and urban planners and indicated that activities other than railroading had become vital to the PRR's survival. All the while, rate increases lagged the growth of wages and other expenditures, maintenance and betterment programs could not keep pace with the forces of decay, and rates of return fell to levels that made the Pennsylvania Railroad unattractive to investors. The company was able to recover, although not completely, from the decline in business that occurred in the immediate aftermath of World War II and again after the end of the conflict in Korea. There would be no corresponding recovery from the far more severe recession that began in 1957 as Americans contemplated the possibility that the railroads would follow the horse-drawn travois off the national stage.

Rebuilding the Pennsylvania Railroad

In 1948, the Pennsylvania Railroad embarked on the most ambitious capital-investment program in its history. Over the next six years, the company allocated more than a billion dollars to improvements in the physical plant and in new and rebuilt equipment. The rapid dieselization program so strongly advocated by Vice President James Symes was by itself the single most expensive financial commitment that the railroad had ever made. By the end of 1950, the PRR

expended $171.6 million on diesel locomotives and their related service and repair facilities. Another $66.5 million worth of new diesels arrived the following year—part of what PRR officials estimated would be a $310.6 million commitment to new motive power. Modern streamlined passenger equipment arrived from Pullman-Standard, Budd, and American Car & Foundry, while shop forces at Altoona rebuilt and reconditioned older heavyweights. In early 1954, the company owned 3,300 passenger cars, along with 2,395 that accommodated baggage, mail, and express traffic. Freight paid the bills, however, and the investment there was even more substantial. During 1950, the Pennsylvania Railroad ordered 20,000 new freight cars and authorized the rebuilding of thousands of others, at a cost of $151.6 million. At the end of the following year, the total had grown to 31,860 new freight cars of various types, with heavy repairs scheduled for 36,000 others—and the associated expenditures rose to $258 million. New acquisitions in 1952 totaled a mere 3,438 cars—a number that nonetheless exceeded the purchases of all but a few other railroads. By the time the $1 billion capital program ended in 1953, the PRR had built or repaired more than 173,000 cars. The company then owned 67,000 boxcars, 75,000 hopper cars, 46,800 flats and gondolas, and 1,300 stock cars, with an aggregate capacity of more than eleven million tons of freight. Some 2,200 cabin cars trailed behind the trains that rumbled across the system.[7]

Expenditures on the physical plant were equally impressive. Workers cleaned ballast, replaced 11.5 million ties, and aligned rails along seventeen thousand of the PRR's twenty-five-thousand track miles. The company spent $17 million on more than six million tons of new ballast. In October 1956, track gangs began installing short stretches of continuous welded rail. It was an experiment to determine whether "ribbon rail" was more economical than conventional jointed rail, and it would soon become standard on railroads throughout the United States. Other innovations, such as an atomic switch lamp that would glow for a decade on a single charge of Krypton 85 gas, did not enjoy such widespread acceptance. Machines now performed more than half of track work, enabling the company to dispense with many of its seasonal maintenance-of-way workers. The construction, rebuilding, and ongoing repair of bridges consumed $34 million, while nearly $50 million went into yards and sidings. Efforts to increase clearance and improve freight operations led to the elimination of five tunnels along the Pan Handle route between Pittsburgh and Columbus, Ohio. Despite the steady decline in passenger service, there were new

SAMUEL REA SHOPS
Hollidaysburg, Pa.
Penna. Railroad Company
General Contractor:
Hughes-Foulkrod, Philadelphia, Pa.
Date: Photo No.

E-20705

The Samuel Rea Shops reflected the PRR's postwar reinvestment in equipment and the physical plant, incorporating the latest production methods while reducing the number of shopcraft workers. The new facility, located in Hollidaysburg, also contributed to the economic decline of nearby Altoona. *Pennsylvania Railroad Negative Collection, Hagley Museum & Library, acc. 1993.300.*

stations to serve commuters in Pennsylvania—at Paoli, Curtis Park, and Levittown—and one for intercity passengers traveling through Alliance, Ohio.[8]

Many of the improvements occurred in Pittsburgh and nearby communities. For more than a century, the board of directors had met only in Philadelphia, but on November 12, 1952, they convened in Pittsburgh, attesting to the importance of that city to the company's operations. The directors announced a $47 million campaign to improve freight service that they hoped would finally alleviate the bottlenecks that had long bedeviled the region. In the

end, they spent considerably more than that. The projects included improvements to the passenger station and the easing of the sharp curve to the west that had sealed the fate of the T1 duplex—after dieselization had made such issues irrelevant. In their quest for greater efficiency, PRR executives selected Conway Yard, twenty-two miles northwest of Pittsburgh, as the hub for eastbound and westbound freight. By the time work ended in 1958, the company spent nearly $35 million on a project that made Conway the largest and most modern classification yard in the United States. Two separate yards, one for eastbound and the other for westbound traffic, together contained 107 tracks—many of which were more than a mile in length. A bevy of technological systems, including computers, radar, cab signals, electronic scales, pneumatic tubes, and tape recorders, facilitated the tracking and sorting of freight cars. After cars moved over the hump, electropneumatic retarders slowed them to a safe speed—eliminating the rider-brakemen whose jobs had been both hazardous and expensive. The VELAC Automatic Switching System, installed by Union Switch & Signal, enabled the hump operator to select routes with the touch of a few push buttons.[9]

PRR officials planned major changes for the company's principal shops east of Pittsburgh. In the summer of 1952, with dieselization well underway, they began shutting down the portions of the Altoona Works that accommodated the building and repair of steam locomotives. The railroad also announced plans to shift much of the work associated with freight equipment to a new facility at Hollidaysburg, seven miles to the south. The first section, a small facility to reclaim components from scrapped cars, opened in 1954. Over the next two years, the PRR spent $35 million on a massive new complex for the construction and rebuilding of rolling stock. The Samuel Rea Shops—named for the PRR's ninth president, who was born in Hollidaysburg—was nearly three thousand feet long, with an interior space that covered seventeen acres. It was largely complete by the end of 1955, with the final stages finished in June of the following year. Workers produced new freight cars on an assembly line basis, far more efficiently and with much less labor than had been possible at Altoona. Entire classes of worn-out cars, scheduled for rebuilding, also passed through the Hollidaysburg facility. The Altoona Works remained in operation, with employees focusing on tasks that their counterparts at the Samuel Rea Shops could not readily accommodate. That included repairs to diesel locomotives, passenger cars, and wreck-damaged equipment. Yet both the shops and the city of Altoona were but a shadow of their former glory, shattered by dieselization, new production methods, and the overall decline of the Pennsylvania Railroad.[10]

The Pennsylvania Railroad also made significant investments at the eastern edge of the system. For many decades, the PRR transported iron ore from Great Lakes ports to steel mills in eastern Ohio and western Pennsylvania. By the early 1950s, the high-grade reserves in northeastern Minnesota's Mesabi Range were depleted, and mines had not yet made the transition to the production of taconite. Steel mills increasingly depended on ore imported from Labrador, South America, Africa, and northern Europe. In 1952, the PRR's directors authorized an expenditure of nearly $10 million to build an unloading facility at Greenwich Point in South Philadelphia. The Philadelphia Ore Pier, opened in 1954 and expanded two years later, was the largest railroad-owned facility of its type in the United States. Four unloaders could transfer six thousand tons of ore per hour from oceangoing vessels to a fleet of new freight cars. Some thirty miles north, the PRR spent another $10 million on the reconstruction of the freight yard at Morrisville, Pennsylvania. When completed in 1953, the expanded facility provided improved service to industries in the Delaware Valley—including the new US Steel plant in nearby Fairless Hills, opened in 1952.[11]

The massive prewar investment in electrification reduced but did not eliminate the railroad's operating difficulties east of Harrisburg. The most pressing problem was a shortage of electric freight locomotives. The GG1 offered the ideal combination of power, speed, and acceleration necessary to move heavy passenger trains. It quickly displaced the Class P5a, built between 1931 and 1935, relegating the smaller locomotives to freight service. The P5a proved a capable machine, but it lacked the horsepower necessary for efficient operation. Double-heading was commonplace, as was the need for helpers along the grade that led from Philadelphia west to Paoli. Locomotive shortages, particularly during periods of peak demand, necessitated the continued reliance on steam locomotives in electrified territory and imposed additional operating costs and delays.[12]

Wartime research-and-development programs at General Electric and Westinghouse resulted in numerous improvements to electrical-equipment technology. PRR motive-power officials paid close attention to those innovations, and in March 1949, they ordered prototypes from each manufacturer. If successful, each would be able to move a 150-car freight train, replacing three P5a locomotives. GE's 5,200-horsepower offering featured conventional alternating-current traction motors. Completed in the summer of 1951, it carried the PRR designation of Class E2b. Westinghouse engineers experimented with more modern technology. They used an MP54 car, #4561, as a test bed for the application of the "Ignitron" rectifier to railway service.[13] The rectifier tubes converted alternating-current catenary power to direct current, permitting the use of more efficient DC traction motors, identical to those employed on diesel locomotives. The rectifiers could also operate at either twenty-five cycles (as used on the PRR's prewar electrification) or sixty cycles (which by the 1950s had become the standard for electric utilities).[14] The results of the tests were satisfactory, and Westinghouse collaborated with Baldwin-Lima-Hamilton to produce the 6,000-horsepower Class E3b demonstrator, delivered in November 1951.[15] In both cases, the locomotive sets consisted of two mated units that—aside from their pantographs—closely resembled diesels. In 1951, in a later-day reenactment of the Claymont trials that pitted the R1 against the GG1, Pennsylvania Railroad officials evaluated the merits of their newest electric locomotives. While both the GE E2b and the Westinghouse E3b performed well during tests, they soon suffered repeated mechanical and electrical failures. By 1954, they were sidelined and placed into service only when no other electric locomotives were available.[16]

The increasing age of the GG1 and P5a locomotives, coupled with the failure to develop suitable replacements, called into question the future of electrification on the Pennsylvania Railroad. During the 1920s and 1930s, executives had repeatedly predicted that catenary would one day extend to Altoona and perhaps as far west as Pittsburgh. The Great Depression, shortages of copper during World War II, and the company's postwar financial condition made such projects unlikely. Dieselization greatly reduced the potential benefits associated with the expansion of electrified territory. Studies undertaken in November 1942 and September 1945—even before more than a small number of diesels were in service—suggested that additional installations were inadvisable. Yet a 1947 report suggested that it would be possible to operate the Middle Division, between Harrisburg and Altoona, under catenary without a substantial increase in motive power. In the spring of 1955, Symes announced what would be the last of those cost-benefit analyses, prepared by the engineering consultants Gibbs & Hill in collaboration with General Electric and Westinghouse. The timing was propitious, as prewar locomotives, catenary, and electrical equipment—as well as the venerable MP54 commuter cars—were beginning to wear out. The PRR's contract with the Philadelphia Electric Company would terminate in 1958, and arrangements with other utilities were due to expire shortly afterward. Thirty years earlier, the railroad's executives had elected to buy rather than generate electrical power. It was a sensible decision, but their successors now faced the prospect of rate increases of more than a third, potentially adding $3.5 million to the company's annual operating costs. When he briefed reporters on the study, Symes was accordingly lukewarm in his advocacy for electrification. "Should electrification be expanded," he asked, or "should it be limited to its present scope or should it be cut back? Economies may be available for any of these alternatives, and we must measure all costs to find out." In addition to assessing the development of new electric freight and passenger locomotives, Gibbs & Hill considered the electrification of the New York & Long Branch Railroad, a commuter line jointly operated by the PRR and the Jersey Central. A new generation of electric multiple-unit cars might replace the aging MP54 cars used in Philadelphia and New Jersey–New York commuter service. That technology could logically influence the development of more robust train sets that could provide high-speed travel between New York and Washington.[17]

The Gibbs & Hill study, released in October, generally affirmed the status quo. The consultants estimated that it would cost $54,000 per track mile to extend the catenary from Harrisburg west to Altoona. The need for additional locomotives, substations, and related equipment brought the estimated expenditure to $48.4 million, with an anticipated rate of return of barely 3 percent. Under the circumstances, further electrification could not be justified unless the price of diesel fuel increased or if competitive pressures mandated higher operating speeds. Gibbs & Hill could not determine whether the PRR should undertake partial electrification of the New York & Long Branch. That line briefly remained one of the last holdouts of steam locomotives on the Pennsylvania Railroad system before succumbing to dieselization in November 1957.[18]

Gibbs & Hill made only one unequivocal recommendation for further action, stressing the importance of purchasing new electric locomotives to supplement or replace the GG1. One possibility involved copying the ten Class EP-5 rectifier locomotives that General Electric built for the New Haven in 1955. Sleek and streamlined, they resembled a double-ended version of the PRR's 1951 experimental locomotives but were far more reliable. They were best suited for passenger service, however, and Pennsylvania Railroad executives had little interest in replacing the venerable GG1. The discontinuation of electric operations through the Great Northern's Cascade Tunnel offered a less expensive alternative. The timing was propitious, as the opening of the new Philadelphia Ore Pier in March 1954 ensured that there would be a steady movement of loaded ore cars west out of Philadelphia. In August 1956, therefore, the PRR acquired eight Class Y-1 electric locomotives from the Great Northern. Built by General Electric and the American Locomotive Company in 1927, they hardly embodied the latest technological innovations, were even less powerful than the P5a, and traveled at no more than thirty miles per hour. Assigned to Pennsylvania Railroad Class FF2, they nonetheless performed well in helper service, typically assisting trains up the short but steep grade between Thorndale and Paoli.[19]

By the end of the 1950s, the P5a locomotives had reached the end of their useful lives and were no longer economical to operate or maintain. While an extension of electrification was out of the question, PRR executives again debated whether to retain the system that was in place. During the 1920s, efforts to increase freight-train speeds and to move a higher volume of traffic without adding more tracks provided powerful motives for electrification. Motor carriers had since taken a large portion of preference freight, while passenger traffic east of Harrisburg had fallen by a quarter

PRR Class FF2 electric #6 is at Enola—in circumstances that recall its original assignment, laboring for the Great Northern in the snowy Cascades. They were capable locomotives but insufficient to replace the aging fleet of P5a and GG1 electrics. *Don Wood Negatives, Railroad Museum of Pennsylvania, PHMC.*

since the completion of electrification. Electrical engineer D. R. Macleod put the matter succinctly when he observed that "track capacity is no longer a problem."[20]

At that moment of executive indecision, during the summer of 1959, General Electric and the Electro-Motive Division of General Motors prepared starkly different motive-power studies for the Pennsylvania Railroad. After completing the PRR's experimental rectifier locomotives, Westinghouse abandoned further work, leaving GE as the sole remaining advocate for main line electrification. General Electric personnel recommended the wholesale replacement of the PRR's electric locomotives and commuter equipment. The acquisition of seventy-five rectifier

locomotives, similar to the New Haven EP-5, would permit the reassignment of the same number of GG1 units to freight service, eliminating the entire P5a fleet. Alternatively, a combination of modern GE freight and passenger electrics could replace the P5a while permitting the PRR to withdraw the oldest and least reliable of the Class GG1. More than two hundred multiple-unit cars could supplant the worst of the MP54 fleet, pleasing commuters who were increasingly vocal in their complaints regarding the railroad's service. Electro-Motive, in contrast, had become the dominant producer of diesel locomotives. By the end of the decade, however, steam locomotives had disappeared from American railroads and EMD officials were interested in selling diesels anywhere they could. Unsurprisingly, they suggested that diesels could economically replace much of the PRR's existing electrified operations. They observed that maintenance costs for the P5a freight locomotives were 32 percent greater than for comparable diesels, and energy costs were 78 percent higher. While the EMD study offered ten scenarios to the Pennsylvania Railroad, it broadly recommended the dieselization of all

The sixty-six Class E44 electric freight locomotives, built by General Electric between 1960 and 1963, sidelined the P5a units that were approaching their third decade of service. Their more powerful and reliable GG1 counterparts continued to soldier on, in both passenger and freight service. In March 1965, #4405 is at the beginning of a career that will last into the Conrail era. *Harris Negatives, Railroad Museum of Pennsylvania, PHMC.*

freight service and most intercity passenger operations. Commuter equipment would continue to operate under wire. Trains on the New York & Long Branch, as well as those headed for Atlantic City, would rely on something like the EMD dual-service FL9, built for the New Haven between 1956 and 1960, that could operate with either a diesel engine or electric power. Many trains entering Penn Station would, of necessity, require an engine change on the west side of the Hudson River, raising the prospect that Manhattan Transfer would rise again from the New Jersey Meadowlands. EMD predicted savings of $8.5 million annually, generating an 11 percent return on investment.[21]

Pennsylvania Railroad executives navigated a middle course between the GE and EMD proposals, declining to undertake a massive new investment while refusing to abandon much of what their predecessors had created. They showed little interest in new passenger electrics, and the introduction of modern commuter equipment proceeded slowly. In September 1959, however, the board of

directors agreed to purchase sixty-six Class E44 electric freight locomotives from GE. Delivered between 1960 and 1963, they incorporated ignitron rectifiers and DC traction motors, the same basic technology installed in the New Haven EP-5.[22] Their external appearance was closer to the twelve units of the Class EL-C that GE built for the Virginian Railway between 1955 and 1957. The E44 electrics lacked the sleek lines of the GG1 and soon earned the nickname "bricks." They were capable locomotives nonetheless and soon relegated the P5a to the scrapyard. The E44 soldiered on for several decades, for the Pennsylvania Railroad, the Penn Central, and finally Conrail. Their careers ended in 1981, when Conrail suspended electric freight operations. The PRR could never find a better passenger locomotive than the GG1, however. While Amtrak withdrew the units from the Northeast Corridor in 1980, a few of the venerable locomotives continued in New Jersey Transit commuter service until 1983. The GG1 truly was the epitome of the greatest investment in railroad electrification in the history of the United States.[23]

Philadelphia Improvements Finale

The PRR's postwar betterment program included the completion of the long-delayed Philadelphia Improvements. In 1925, the board of directors agreed to build two new railway stations in the city, one for commuters and the other for intercity passengers. The promised abandonment of

Broad Street Station and the much-detested Filbert Street Extension promised increased operating efficiency while freeing valuable land for redevelopment. Municipal officials pledged to build a new highway bridge across the Schuylkill River, at Market Street, and relocate the Market Street Elevated into a subway. In 1930, construction crews completed Suburban Station, freeing Broad Street Station from the burden of commuter traffic. By then, however, the Great Depression imperiled the city's ability to carry out its share of the improvements. Politicians such as Governor Gifford Pinchot and Mayor J. Hampton Moore condemned the 1925 agreement as an unjustifiable transfer of municipal resources to the Pennsylvania Railroad, even as corporate executives complained that they were bearing an excessive share of the project's cost. The PRR nonetheless continued to honor its commitments, opening 30th Street Station in 1933. The lower level included only two tracks and one platform, for intercity traffic between New York and Washington. Trains from New York to western points continued to stop only at North Philadelphia, while services originating or terminating in Philadelphia still relied on the facilities at Broad Street. Of necessity, the Filbert Street Extension—widely reviled as the "Chinese Wall"—remained in place, blocking the revitalization of Center-City Philadelphia. In December 1935, the agreement between the city and the Pennsylvania Railroad expired. Mayor-elect S. Davis Wilson declared the project "dead" and pressured the City Council into abandoning efforts to negotiate an extension. The city's contributions—a new Market Street Bridge and a disconnected subway tunnel under the Schuylkill River—were of little value, so long as the Market Street Elevated continued to block access to the south side of 30th Street Station. After nearly a decade of haphazard progress and a combined expenditure of $106 million—$25 million by the city and the remainder by the Pennsylvania Railroad—all progress on the Philadelphia Improvements came to a halt.[24]

World War II and the subsequent reconversion process fostered a growing public concern regarding Philadelphia's fate in a postwar world. In February 1942, *Business Week* highlighted a study by the Urban Land Institute, which suggested that the city was succumbing to urban blight. The following June, the Action Committee on City Planning, a group that included representatives from fifty civic organizations, persuaded the City Council to establish a new planning commission. Its first and most influential chairman, investment banker Edward Hopkinson Jr., was a direct descendant of one of the signers of the Declaration of Independence and was widely regarded as "the most important man in Philadelphia outside of politics."

He predicted that "the program of the City Planning Commission will touch the life and activities of every Philadelphian," and it was hardly an exaggeration. Representatives from sixty-four civic, welfare, and professional organizations soon formed a parallel entity, the Philadelphia Citizens' Council on City Planning, to maximize citizen participation and to bypass the city's notoriously corrupt Republican political machine. The group recommended an eighteen-point plan for postwar Philadelphia and suggested that at least $100 million—and perhaps as much as $200 million—would be necessary to fund all the improvements. The interest in coordinated planning took root in other areas as well. In April 1945, political and business leaders established the Committee for Economic Development to ensure that peacetime industries would be able to solicit business to replace canceled military contracts. The allocation of the PRR's intercity passenger traffic to three stations—North Philadelphia, 30th Street, and Broad Street—was unlikely to appeal to Washington bureaucrats or New York executives who were considering doing business in the Quaker City. Representatives from the Philadelphia Transportation Company did their part, offering a five-year plan to upgrade bus and streetcar service. Members of the West Philadelphia Chamber of Commerce supported the PTC initiatives. They also reminded everyone of the truncated tunnel under the Schuylkill River, walled off and largely forgotten, and they called for the completion of the long-delayed Market Street Subway.[25]

By the spring of 1946, the concerted pressure from business leaders and civic groups ensured the resurrection of the Philadelphia Improvements. The railroad, the city, and the state would each pay a share of the estimated $20 million cost, and they would reap corresponding benefits. The City Council's Public Works Committee agreed to provide $4.3 million to purchase a portion of the Filbert Street Extension. The acquisition would make possible an extension of Filbert Street, west of city hall. Initially known as Pennsylvania Boulevard and subsequently renamed John F. Kennedy Boulevard, the new route would cross the Schuylkill River on a new bridge and terminate at the eastern side of 30th Street Station. Commonwealth officials pledged $6 million to offset construction costs, while the PRR took responsibility for the remaining expense—mostly associated with the removal of the Chinese Wall. Most of the Broad Street Station headhouse would remain in place and be converted to an office building—although the northernmost portion, including the original 1881 clock tower, would have to be demolished to make way for Pennsylvania Boulevard.

Additional office buildings would replace the remainder of the land once occupied by the Filbert Street Extension. By retaining ownership of that property, PRR officials expected to profit handsomely from a real estate development initially known as "Broad Towers." The city was also slated to collect a financial windfall. So long as the area was dedicated to rail transportation—a public utility—it was exempt from municipal taxation. With the tracks gone, the land was assessed at $9.5 million—an amount that would yield $161,500 in annual tax receipts, more than sufficient to finance the city's $4.3 million investment in the project. In taking responsibility for the tax bill, Pennsylvania Railroad officials thus possessed a strong incentive to convert what would soon become an abandoned railroad facility into rentable commercial space.[26]

With the financial benefits so compelling and with Philadelphians fearing that their city was on the brink of a steady postwar decline, approval was a foregone conclusion. The City Council gave its assent on March 21 as part of a $29 million slate of municipal improvements. When voters went to the polls two months later, they had the opportunity to endorse the issuance of $78.2 million in municipal bonds—the first the city had sold since 1929. Politicians from both parties came out in support of the initiative, and it passed by an overwhelming 12–1 margin. The largest component, for $34 million, supported improvements to the sewer system, while $10 million was allocated to the city's two airports. To the delight of the members of the West Philadelphia Chamber of Commerce, the bonds provided $8 million for the completion of the Market Street Subway west to 42nd Street (later extended to 46th Street). The subsequent removal of the Market Street Elevated would eliminate one of the impediments to the completion of the facilities at 30th Street Station. The bond issue also included the $4.3 million slated for the acquisition of the portion of the Filbert Street Extension that would be occupied by Pennsylvania Boulevard.[27]

Within five months of the successful bond campaign, PRR and city officials announced the details associated with the completion of the Philadelphia Improvements. At the end of October, Richard C. Morse, the PRR's vice president in charge of real estate and taxation, led Mayor Bernard Samuel and a delegation of City Council members on a tour of the areas that would soon be affected. The railroad's surveyors marked the site of Pennsylvania Boulevard with daubs of white paint to give a better indication of the changes that were to come. The first phase, Morse explained, involved additions to facilities at 30th Street that would permit all passenger trains except the "Clockers" to New York and the nonelectrified trains to

Atlantic City to be removed from Broad Street Station. The curtailment of service to Broad Street would permit the removal of part of the Chinese Wall—something that Morse promised would occur within two years—and some of the maze of trackage that led west toward the Schuylkill River. Construction crews could then expand the capacity of Suburban Station, permitting additional reductions in service at the Broad Street facility. Finally, the railroad would abandon Broad Street Station and remove the remainder of the Filbert Street Extension, although Morse was less specific as to when that might occur. Two weeks later, the City Council approved a new agreement with the Pennsylvania Railroad, replacing the one that had expired in 1935.[28] The $8 million expenditure for the Market Street Subway, a necessary component but one that was not a part of the agreement with the railroad, also gained council approval. On December 16, the *Philadelphia Inquirer* published a full-page overview of the project, featuring before-and-after illustrations of the changes planned for Center City, 30th Street, and West Philadelphia. Realtors, who wanted to sell properties located to the north of Market Street, claimed that the land would at least double in value once the Chinese Wall was gone. The Better Philadelphia Exhibition at Gimbels department store featured a model of the city, with rotating sections that in a matter of seconds replaced the old Philadelphia with the new one.[29]

As with the initial 1920s phase of the Philadelphia Improvements, construction could not keep pace with public expectations. Pennsylvania Railroad representatives continued to express optimism that the project would soon be finished, but municipal officials were less certain. Thomas Buckley, the director of public works, warned the Budget Committee of the City Council that he could not possibly complete the ambitious postwar redevelopment program on the "depression type" budget that Mayor Bernard Samuel had proposed. His words proved prophetic, as the $20 million, three-year estimate for the completion of the Philadelphia Improvements proved extraordinarily optimistic. "One way to wish the Mayor a long life, if not a merry one," observed *Philadelphia Inquirer* political columnist John M. Cummings, "is to say to him, 'Well, Barney, I hope you'll be Mayor of this town when the Chinese Wall is removed from Market st.'" Another skeptic suggested that the elevated structure "will outlast the famous original in China." In May 1947, six months after Morse led city officials on a tour of the site, a PRR spokesman acknowledged that "at least three years of preliminary work" would be required before the Filbert Street Extension could be eliminated. By the end of the month, a year after public approval of the bond issue, Buckley's office solicited bids for the extension of the Market Street Subway between 32nd and 36th Streets. In September, construction crews resumed work that halted in 1932, but there were still no firm plans to complete the sections to the east and west.[30]

The slow pace of municipal improvements provided political opportunities for the Democratic Party and for individuals who would influence both urban development and the city's relationship with the Pennsylvania Railroad. Mayor Samuel campaigned for reelection in 1947, seemingly a formality in traditionally Republican Philadelphia. He nonetheless found it necessary to highlight the municipal progress "under leadership of the Mayor and Republican City Council" while defending his choice of projects. The city's Democrats, fighting an uphill battle, were quick to offer criticism. Michael J. Bradley, the chairman of the Philadelphia Democratic Party, emphasized that "twenty years ago Mayor Mackey in his campaign said he would do away with the Chinese Wall. . . . Nothing has been done, as is usual with this type of city planning by city government. Twenty years from now, Mayor Samuel's son will probably run for Mayor and probably make the same promises." Joseph S. Clark Jr., the vice president of the Citizens' Council on City Planning, was equally critical. "We plan to spend millions to tear down the Chinese Wall," he noted, "but apparently have no money to build homes for the thousands who do not have decent habitation." Richardson Dilworth, Clark's close friend and political ally, was an even more prominent critic of the Samuel administration. Dilworth hailed from an elite Pittsburgh family, earned a law degree from Yale, and was a veteran of two world wars. He had been involved in Philadelphia politics since the 1930s, expressing his desire to perpetuate the aims of the New Deal and to expose the city's rampant political corruption. He ran an aggressive campaign for mayor in 1947, one that tied Republican misdeeds to the slow pace of municipal improvements. Samuel won reelection, but Dilworth gained a respectable 43.8 percent of the vote. In the months that followed, his advocacy for municipal reform spawned numerous investigations that validated many of his accusations. Several prominent city officials committed suicide, others went to prison, and the Republican Party was never again able to control municipal politics. In 1949, with the city's machine politicians on the defensive, Dilworth won election as treasurer, while Clark became controller. The two Democratic mavericks were thus ideally positioned to root out illegal financial practices and to prepare for future—and successful—mayoral bids.[31]

Mayor Samuel retained control of Philadelphia's Republican machine, but attacks by Clark, Dilworth, and other Democrats suggested that he and his allies would be well advised to bring long-promised urban improvements to a speedy completion. In early November, only days after the 1947 election, the general manager for the PRR's Eastern Region addressed delegates at the Greater Philadelphia Traffic Conference. Harry L. Nancarrow promised that the entire Filbert Street Extension would be eliminated within five years. The following January, three weeks after Samuel's inauguration, the assistant to the chief engineer of the Eastern Region, Joseph M. Fox, spoke with representatives of the American Society of Civil Engineers. The removal of the six northernmost tracks at Broad Street Station would soon begin, he told them, permitting the expansion of the southern portion of Suburban Station. By the end of March, Mayor Samuel demanded that the leaders of the various city departments, boards, and commissions submit their planning recommendations by the first of June. In April, the City Planning Commission approved the design of Pennsylvania Boulevard from the Benjamin Franklin Parkway to the east side of 30th Street Station. At the same time, Mayor Samuel announced that the city would need an extra $103 million to complete all the planned improvements, an announcement that did little to mitigate the criticism from Clark, Dilworth, and other Democrats. A meeting between Samuel and Pennsylvania governor James H. Duff—also a Republican—brought a pledge of financial aid from the commonwealth and a promise that a meeting between city, state, and PRR officials would soon be arranged.[32]

The state proved to be a fickle ally. The May 1945 Urban Redevelopment Law empowered local authorities such as the City Planning Commission "to engage in the elimination of blighted areas and to plan and contract with private, corporate or governmental redevelopers for their redevelopment." That legislation did not empower the commonwealth to expend money on such projects, however. Even the promised highway funds seemed in jeopardy. Governor Duff assessed the region's transportation needs and at the end of August 1948 indicated that the Pennsylvania Boulevard project was not of the "first priority in the way of solving the city's traffic problems." Duff also observed that there was little point in the disbursement of state funds, as the Pennsylvania Railroad and the city had not yet undertaken their promised share of the improvements. Both Mayor Samuel and Buckley (the director of public works) correspondingly blamed the state government for causing further delays.[33]

The PRR's postwar financial problems, coupled with the urgent necessity of purchasing new equipment and upgrading the physical plant, ensured that the completion

The Pennsylvania Railroad

of the Philadelphia Improvements carried a low priority. Not until November did the board of directors approve the $2.9 million necessary to finish phase one of the project—the expansion of the lower level of 30th Street Station to accommodate the railroad's east–west intercity trains. On December 6, Martin Clement joined Mayor Samuel at the West Philadelphia facility for the ceremonial groundbreaking. The PRR's president briefed reporters on the scope of the changes, which he estimated would cost his company $22.5 million—well above the initial $20 million estimate for the railroad and the city combined. John Cummings, whose editorials in the *Philadelphia Inquirer* were generally critical of Democrats in both local and national government, suggested "a medal for Mart Clement, a medal bigger'n the one they're working on at the mint to mark the Truman inauguration"—but added that "this medal would be awarded to M. Clement the moment the Chinese Wall disappears from Market st."[34]

Cummings never had the opportunity to present a medal to Clement, who left the presidency well before the completion of the Philadelphia Improvements. Work ground slowly on, with representatives from the railroad, the city, and the state continuing to disagree as to who should do what and when. Not until February 1949 did the city place a $164 million bond issue with a syndicate headed by Drexel & Company, finally raising the money needed to complete the Market Street Subway and compensate the PRR for a portion of the Filbert Street Extension. A month later, the state legislature approved a five-year road-improvement bill that provided funds for Pennsylvania Boulevard. At the end of November, on the same day that Dilworth called for a state investigation into municipal corruption, Mayor Samuel announced plans for a $537 million public-works program. Nearly half of the money would be allocated to public housing—something that Dilworth ally Joseph Clark had demanded—but plenty would be available for other types of urban redevelopment.[35]

Civic leaders who had once criticized municipal inaction now turned their attention to the Pennsylvania Railroad, which they saw as the chief impediment delaying the rebirth of their city. More than a year had passed, with little accomplished. At the PRR's May 1950 annual meeting, Vice President Symes told investors that the company would need to spend an additional $15 to $18 million on its share of the project—and that the removal of the Chinese Wall might take another four years. In October, Fred Carpi, the vice president in charge of traffic, told an audience of highway planners that the structure would be gone within five years. A month later, Symes could be no

more specific than to state that "the railroad is prepared to coordinate with the city and State in going forward with its part of the program that will ultimately make possible demolition of the Chinese Wall." The news came as scant comfort to Edward Greene, better known as the "Concourse Bandit," an individual convicted of multiple counts of robbery and assault with a deadly weapon. Judge James C. Crumlish made clear that Greene would no longer be a threat to society and sentenced him to prison "for so long that the Chinese Wall will be down when he gets out." Because railroad and municipal officials had made empty promises to remove the Filbert Street Extension a quarter of a century earlier, Greene could look forward to a long period of incarceration.[36]

The Philadelphia Improvements nonetheless moved toward completion. In January 1951, Mayor Samuel presented PRR officials with a check for $1 million, the first installment of the $4.3 million set aside to compensate the company for the loss of the land needed to construct Pennsylvania Boulevard. In return, Eastern Region vice president Ethelbert W. Smith announced that the railroad had appropriated an additional $6.5 million for work on the project. Smith also provided a definitive answer regarding the fate of Broad Street Station, a question that had been the cause of much speculation among Philadelphia's citizenry. When work on the Philadelphia Improvements resumed in 1946, PRR officials had considered retaining most of the facility for conversion into office space. Well before 1951, however, they concluded that the idea was impracticable and that the station's nineteenth-century architecture was inappropriate for the modernist postwar development that would dominate the area. Smith merely acknowledged publicly what many city officials and planners had known all along—that the structure designed by Joseph M. Wilson and reimagined by Frank Furness would be destroyed.[37]

Through the summer of 1951 and into the first months of the year that followed, Philadelphians witnessed the demise of two long-standing institutions. One was Broad Street Station, as operations there began to wind down. The other was the Republican machine that had controlled urban politics since the 1880s. The anticorruption campaign waged by Clark and Dilworth, coupled with the city's financial problems, increased support for efforts to revise the municipal charter. In April 1949, the state legislature adopted the Lord Home Rule Bill, initiating the process and giving Mayor Samuel the authority to appoint members to the Charter Commission. While Samuel was initially inclined to cronyism, Democratic successes in the fall elections (in which Dilworth emerged victorious as city treasurer and Clark as controller) suggested the wisdom of integrity and bipartisanship. Influential community leaders insisted that leading citizens rather than political hacks should serve on the Charter Commission. Their most forceful representative, Robert T. McCracken, was a director of the Pennsylvania Railroad and a friend of the mayor. McCracken provided Samuel with a list of acceptable candidates and became one of the fifteen commissioners. According to Clark, the commission produced "one of the greatest municipal charters in history." The voters agreed, and in April 1951, they approved the new document. The Home Rule Charter combined many city and county offices, increased the investigatory powers of the mayor, and implemented civil-service exams as a mechanism to destroy political patronage. The City Planning Commission gained additional authority, with the mayor now required to submit the commission's recommendations and requests for funds, unaltered, to the City Council.[38]

It was fitting that Joseph Clark was so effusive in his praise for the Home Rule Charter, as he soon became the first person to benefit from its provisions. In anticipation of the 1951 elections, Clark announced his candidacy for mayor, while Dilworth sought the post of district attorney. McCracken, the PRR director, sensed the public mood and engineered the selection of Reverend Daniel E. Poling, a Baptist minister, as the Republican mayoral nominee. Poling was, by design, entirely innocent of political corruption. Poling was, sadly, largely innocent of political acumen as well, and his status as a resident of New York City ensured that he had little local support. Clark won the election with more than 58 percent of the vote, Dilworth was equally successful, and the new City Council consisted of fifteen Democrats and only two Republicans. Thereafter, PRR executives who had enjoyed close relationships with Republican municipal officials would have to forge links with key Democrats as well.[39]

When Clark took office on January 7, 1952, he was determined to make the removal of the Chinese Wall and the redevelopment of the area on the north side of Market Street signature achievements of his administration. He and his Democratic allies were determined to succeed where his Republican predecessors—who bore the brunt of his campaign against political corruption—had failed. Clark accordingly accelerated discussions with Symes and other Pennsylvania Railroad officials, pressuring them to do their part to bring the project to fruition. The mayor's timing was excellent, as his efforts coincided with the

PRR's increasing reliance on diversification and income produced by nonrail subsidiaries.[40]

Clark nonetheless faced significant challenges in his efforts to transform the Chinese Wall into a municipal showpiece. The PRR executives and the bankers and real estate moguls who were vital to the redevelopment process were generally tied to the now-discredited Republican machine, and encouraging them to change allegiance would be no easy matter. The state's 1945 Urban Redevelopment Law gave Clark the ability to influence the planning process but no funds to do so. The 1949 federal Housing Act provided plenty of money but restricted its use to the construction of public housing—a limitation that was incompatible with the commercial development that Clark and everyone else envisioned. The municipal budget was inadequate for the task, particularly given Clark's promises to fix all Philadelphia's problems at once. His efforts to increase taxes alienated many of those who had recently voted him into office and threatened the Democratic coalition that he established. Clark's integrity, although commendable in the abstract, undermined his political authority. His support for civil-service reform and his concomitant opposition to patronage politics deprived Democratic Party loyalists of their eagerly anticipated spoils following the 1951 election. Socioeconomic class and geography also impeded Clark's effort to build support for urban redevelopment. Clark came from a prosperous and long-established Philadelphia banking family and had little in common with the blue-collar workers who comprised the bulk of the city's population.[41] The same could be said for Yale Law School graduate Richardson Dilworth, the city's new district attorney and Clark's eventual successor. White, working-class residents from neighborhoods such as Kensington and South Philadelphia did not share the Clark administration's desire to entice upper-middle-class suburbanites to the city. They perceived little value in either the economic or the aesthetic value of the Broad Street Station redevelopment, and they certainly would not accept higher taxes to pay for it. That set of circumstances ensured that Clark would possess scant authority beyond moral suasion as he attempted to persuade PRR executives and real estate developers to sacrifice a measure of profitability to appease municipal planning goals.[42]

Municipal and private objectives coincided long enough to ensure the demolition of Broad Street Station and the removal of the Chinese Wall. On the evening of February 9, 1951, waiters in the dining room at Broad Street Station served the facility's last meals. The site that had hosted innumerable meetings of travelers, business executives,

Led by conductor Eugene Ormandy, members of the Philadelphia Orchestra entertain spectators as the last train pulls out of Broad Street Station on April 27, 1952. A quarter of a century had elapsed since representatives from the PRR and the city of Philadelphia agreed to remove the Filbert Street Extension and banish long-distance trains to the west side of the Schuylkill River. *George D. McDowell Philadelphia Evening Bulletin Photographs, courtesy of the Special Collections Research Center, Temple University Libraries, Philadelphia, PA.*

and politicians closed forever. The lunch counter remained open, however, as did other businesses for the passengers coming and going from the ninety daily trains that still used the facility. The following January, PRR officials informed the building's tenants to vacate by April 28, yet there was still no formal announcement regarding the termination of rail operations. Finally, on February 21, 1952, Symes addressed nearly a thousand guests attending a luncheon at the Bellevue-Stratford hotel. "Effective Sunday,

April 27 this year," he confirmed, "all passenger train service, as well as Pennsylvania Greyhound bus service, will be removed from old Broad Street Station."[43]

Symes was as good as his word and—perhaps for the first time in the long history of the Philadelphia Improvements—everything happened according to schedule. More than five thousand people crowded Broad Street Station. Many had been in line for hours, waiting for an opportunity to purchase tickets on the last train to depart. The initial group of six hundred sold out within eleven minutes, but officials ultimately sold 4,384 tickets as souvenirs. As night fell and a steady rain poured down on the building, Eugene Ormandy and the members of the Philadelphia Orchestra performed "The Star-Spangled Banner," "Finlandia," and "The Stars and Stripes Forever." Real estate developer Albert M. Greenfield, the chairman of the Greater Philadelphia Chamber of Commerce, professed sadness at the destruction of a local landmark, but he was already making plans for the site that it occupied. Greenfield acknowledged that he was "feeling a bit sentimental—I'm sure we all are—about this, but we must remember that Philadelphia and the Pennsylvania Railroad are now seeing the beginning of one of the greatest developments in the history of an American city, the beginning of a new life and new beauty." Walter Franklin, the PRR's new president, posed for photographers on the rear platform of the observation car *Queen Mary*, standing alongside a woman who had seen the first train that entered the station eighty-one years earlier. A lucky seven hundred people crowded into the cars that stood alongside the platform. They included Ormandy and his musicians, who were on the first leg of a tour to Canada and the Midwest. Just before 10:00 p.m. trumpeters, trombonists, and a drummer gathered on the rear of the *Queen Mary* and played "Auld Lang Syne" as the last train departed.[44]

Pennsylvania Railroad officials wasted no time in eliminating Broad Street Station from Philadelphia's urban landscape. On February 26, five days after Symes's announcement at the Bellevue-Stratford, Vice President James Newell informed Ethelbert Smith that the public would not tolerate further delays in the eagerly anticipated obliteration of the Filbert Street Extension. Prompt action "is very desirable not only from a psychological viewpoint," he told the vice president in charge of the Eastern Region, "but it will also show sincerity on our part in progressing the demolition work without delay." On the morning of April 28, spectators were ransacking the building for souvenirs when Mayor Clark made his way toward the top of the structure. Most of the doors leading to the roof were nailed shut, but a PRR employee found a long-disused staircase that led outside. A workman swung a sledgehammer, breaking loose a portion of the terra-cotta edging. Standing on the rain-slick roof, Clark levered a crowbar into position and dislodged a brick, the first of many that would soon be carted away. "I'm sorry to see the station go, in a way," he told reporters, "but it's in the interest of progress"—then he added, "What else can I say without sounding corny?" Thirty trucks a day were soon carrying rubble to Greenwich Point to be used as fill in the construction of the PRR's new ore import terminal. Six weeks later, workers began dismantling the Filbert Street Extension. The Philadelphia Improvements seemed destined to drag on forever, as the station's robust construction delayed demolition crews. Layoffs resulting from the depressed economy reduced the number of PRR workers assigned to the task of stripping rails and signals from atop the Chinese Wall, causing further setbacks. The Filbert Street Extension proved even more resilient than the station it had served, and the demolition company gave up on the wrecking ball and resorted to blasting it apart with

dynamite. Nearby, throngs of "sidewalk superintendents" watched the process, while workers labored underground to complete the extension of the Market Street Subway. The underground line opened to 46th Street in early November 1955, permitting the removal of the Market Street Elevated. On June 1, 1959, the opening of the Pennsylvania Boulevard Bridge across the Schuylkill River gave Center-City motorists more convenient access to 30th Street Station—and to the Schuylkill Expressway, completed the following year, which took an increasing share of the PRR's commuter traffic. The Philadelphia Improvements had begun with great fanfare more than thirty years earlier, when PRR president W. W. Atterbury and Philadelphia mayor W. Freeland Kendrick shook hands, made speeches, and predicted that everything would be done within five years at a cost of no more than $60 million. No one present at that July 28, 1927, groundbreaking of the Philadelphia Improvements could have imagined that it would take so long or that the final cost would balloon to a quarter of a billion dollars.[45]

The debate regarding the appropriate use of the land once occupied by the Filbert Street Extension was as contentious as the one regarding its removal. Buoyed by the results of the May 1946 municipal bond election, members of the City Planning Commission were determined to take charge of the redevelopment process. For inspiration, they looked north to the Rockefeller Center in New York. Undertaken with the support of the Rockefeller family, the complex reflected the best principles of coordinated planning. One of its most notable features was a sunken pedestrian esplanade, something that many Philadelphians wished to emulate. City planners also looked west to the more recent development in the "Golden Triangle" area of downtown Pittsburgh. Reform impulses that emerged during the Progressive Era culminated in 1939, when Robert Moses prepared a series of recommendations for the Pittsburgh Regional Planning Authority. Moses, already famous as an urban planner who advocated slum clearance and highway construction, proposed a $38 million slate of improvements, including a park at the junction of the Allegheny and Monongahela Rivers. "The Pennsylvania Railroad," Moses observed, "occupies a grossly disproportionate amount of land in the Triangle," and he recommended "the future removal of the Pennsylvania system west of the main freight and passenger stations at Eleventh Street."[46]

World War II delayed efforts at urban redevelopment. Civic leaders in Pittsburgh nonetheless shared the concerns of their Philadelphia counterparts regarding the looming transition to a peacetime economy. They also objected to the air pollution that made the city infamous, and their campaign for cleaner air forced the PRR to curtail the use of steam locomotives in the city. In 1946, business and political interests established the Urban Redevelopment Authority, whose responsibilities were like those of Philadelphia's City Planning Commission. The city of Pittsburgh nonetheless lacked the resources to finance widespread improvements, and the Democratic Party's control over local government raised fears regarding the confiscation of private property—with socialism presumably not far behind. Entrusting the matter to the politicians in Harrisburg alleviated some of those concerns, and in May 1946, the commonwealth ordered the acquisition of the land owned by the Pennsylvania Railroad and the adjacent Dravo Corporation. The site included the PRR's Duquesne Freight House and yards, which occupied 12.4 of the 36 acres intended for Point Park.[47] In most circumstances, railroad executives would have waged an all-out effort to save their principal freight depot in the commonwealth's second-largest city. Richard King Mellon, a PRR director, the unquestioned leader of the city's business and financial community, and an ardent advocate of urban renewal, played a critical role in bridging the divide between business and political leaders. Working with the city's Republican elite, he ensured bipartisan support for reform and diffused concerns regarding excessive government intervention in the rights of private property. Thanks to Mellon's involvement, in February 1948 the PRR transferred the necessary property to the state. The Duquesne Freight House burned in January 1951, facilitating the development of Point Park.[48] Mellon also arranged adequate funding, drawing on his personal financial resources and arranging loans from Mellon National Bank & Trust Company. His promise that both Westinghouse and the Mellon financial interests would locate their corporate offices in the proposed Gateway Center induced New York's Equitable Life Assurance Society to provide additional loans. The first three buildings of the Gateway Center opened in 1952, and work on Point Park was underway.[49]

Even as construction crews labored to finish the Gateway Center, Pittsburgh's Golden Triangle alerted Philadelphians to the possibilities of the land that lay buried under the Chinese Wall and in the largely isolated blocks that lay to the north. Members of the City Planning Commission and others increasingly referred to the "Philadelphia Triangle," expanding the twenty-two-acre site occupied by Broad Street Station and the Filbert Street Extension to include the two hundred or so acres delineated by the Benjamin Franklin Parkway, Market Street,

and the Schuylkill River. In October 1946, they hired Associated City Planners to develop proposals for the area.[50]

The resulting plan was the first of many—each of which involved a balance between profitability and an opportunity to create an architectural showpiece worthy of the Pennsylvania Railroad's headquarters city. The initial proposals envisioned integrated development encompassing all the land between Market Street and Pennsylvania Boulevard that remained under railroad ownership. In 1947, PRR officials asked industrial designer Raymond Loewy, long associated with the company, to prepare an architectural model. Loewy appropriated elements of the Associated City Planners design and added new concepts—including a complex network of underground roads, pedestrian walkways, and parking areas that knit together rail, subway, automobile, bus, and truck transportation.[51]

The railroad's postwar financial difficulties ensured that little money was available to bring Loewy's vision to reality.[52] Given the size of the twenty-two-acre parcel, it was unlikely that any one developer would risk buying the entire property. The more likely scenario involved piecemeal sales to whomever was willing to pay the highest price, effectively ending any possibility of a unified redevelopment program. In March 1949, several years prior to the demolition of Broad Street Station, President Clement made clear his willingness to sacrifice aesthetics in the interests of profitability. He informed the members of the Philadelphia Mortgage Bankers Association that the land, with its frontage along Market Street, would enable the "most attractive real estate development in the city"—but added that the "developing will have to be done by someone other than the railroad because we are going to sell the property."[53]

Clement's determination to trade the land for cash alarmed the recently appointed leader of the Philadelphia City Planning Commission. Edmund N. Bacon joined the commission in 1947 and soon collaborated with fellow architect Louis Kahn on the development of the Better Philadelphia Exhibition that debuted at Gimbels department store. Bacon became the commission's executive director two years later, a post he held until 1970. A contemporary of Robert Moses, he shared a preference for highway construction, the wholesale demolition of historic neighborhoods that he termed "blighted," and large-scale redevelopment projects. Bacon was nonetheless committed to maintaining open areas for public use rather than filling every available parcel of land with rentable office space.[54]

In May 1949, two months after Clement announced his intention to sell the land, Bacon urged the city's architects

In June 1950, architect Vincent Kling, at right, debuted his rendition of Penn Center. Edmund N. Bacon, center, the executive director of the City Planning Committee, favored Kling's aesthetically pleasing design, while Earle N. Barber, chairman of the Philadelphia Redevelopment Authority, was more focused on commercial viability. Ultimately, real estate developers, rather than planners, architects, or PRR executives, held sway over the construction of Penn Center. *George D. McDowell Philadelphia Evening Bulletin Photographs, courtesy of the Special Collections Research Center, Temple University Libraries, Philadelphia, PA.*

to develop a unified master plan for the site. Determined to preserve his vision of coordinated development, he warned that failure to take prompt and aggressive action might create "a hodgepodge and an architectural eyesore." Evoking the great public spaces of Paris and Rome, he demanded "an expression of our contemporary state of culture, a civic monument unparalleled in this country."

The *Philadelphia Inquirer* echoed Bacon's words. "Regardless of what enterprises ultimately may occupy the site," its editors observed, "it is apparent that there should be restrictions on the types of buildings that will be permitted in order that a harmonious whole will result." In June 1950, Bacon offered his vision for a "Coordinated Transportation and Commercial Center" that reflected elements of both the Associated City Planners design and Loewy's proposals. Negotiations between PRR officials and Mayor Samuel were at an impasse, however, and Bacon's recommendations carried little influence.[55]

Joseph Clark's victory in the 1951 mayoral election broke the deadlock. Following further refinements, Bacon and architect Vincent Kling debuted their design at the February 21, 1952, luncheon at the Bellevue-Stratford hotel, the event where Vice President Symes announced the closing of Broad Street Station. The architectural model of what was now called the Penn Center development was soon on display in Wanamaker's department store, giving Philadelphians an opportunity to see the changes that awaited their city. Although lacking in residential space, Bacon's design offered a creative blend of office, retail, and transportation functions. Uniform twenty-story office towers formed the heart of the complex, yet they did not dominate the site. Their slender profile and their orientation on a north–south axis enabled sunlight to flood the area. Underground walkways connected Suburban Station, a bus terminal, and the Broad Street and Market Street Subway lines. A wide pedestrian esplanade, set below street level, provided access to retail stores, while open plazas and an elevated walkway ensured ample space for pedestrians. Bacon refused to permit the Victorian opulence of city hall from interfering with his unified modernist design, and he advocated the structure's demolition.[56]

Despite its architectural merits, Bacon's vision never came to fruition. While Mayor Clark was attracted to elements of the design, he associated Bacon with the previous Republican administration and did not fully trust him. Clark also doubted that he possessed the political or legal power necessary to condemn the PRR's land, should company officials refuse to cooperate. It was a moot point, in any case, because the city was so heavily committed to a variety of public-works projects that it lacked the wherewithal to pay for the land slated for Penn Center. Urban redevelopment was by no means a new phenomenon in Philadelphia, but past projects were generally located in public spaces. While the new City Planning Commission had been in operation for a decade, its members had never confronted a massive scheme located on private property, and they questioned the limits of their authority. Other municipal officials dismissed Bacon's ideas as impracticable and out of step with economic reality. Albert Greenfield, the city's leading real estate developer, shared that view. In September 1952, he announced that he and a consortium of investors were prepared to put $50 million into the Penn Center project. In stark contrast to Bacon's integrated, open design, Greenfield proposed to cover virtually every square foot of the site with high-density office, retail, and hotel space.[57]

The controversy placed Vice President Symes in an awkward position. He supported the concept of an integrated, aesthetically pleasing development, admired Bacon's plan, and hoped to retain at least some of its elements. Symes also disliked Greenfield, perhaps because the developer vied with Pennsylvania Railroad officials for influence over municipal politics and perhaps because Greenfield's heritage as a Jewish immigrant was at odds with the native-stock Protestantism that characterized both Main Line society and the PRR's boardroom. Yet

Symes's ultimate responsibility was to the Pennsylvania Railroad and its investors—who made it clear that they expected far higher rates of return than its transportation operations were able to generate. As workers carted away the remains of Broad Street Station and the Chinese Wall, the Pennsylvania Railroad lost all income from the site. Property taxes continued, however, and until the Penn Center project got underway, the company would gain nothing from its ownership of one of the most valuable parcels of real estate in Philadelphia. Under pressure from the PRR's directors, who were principally interested in a quick return on investment, Symes grudgingly conceded the merits of Greenfield's plan.[58]

Caught between the extremes of the Greenfield and Bacon proposals—the first aesthetically horrifying and the second economically indefensible—Symes was receptive to a third option. Frank G. Binswanger, one of Philadelphia's leading commercial realtors, acknowledged that few local banks were willing to underwrite the cost of Penn Center. Binswanger sought an alliance with a New York real estate developer, Robert W. Dowling—the president of the City Investment Company and heralded for the construction of Stuyvesant Town and Peter Cooper Village on the Lower East Side of Manhattan. His work on the Gateway Center in Pittsburgh's Golden Triangle ensured that he enjoyed close ties with Pennsylvania Railroad officials. Endeavoring to move the project forward, Symes asked Dowling to prepare an alternative to the plan that Bacon and Kling had devised. Dowling's proposal, made public in January 1953, featured six office towers arranged in a manner that would block the sweeping city vistas that Bacon envisioned. The arrangement likewise preserved less open space than Bacon advocated, but it avoided the high-density construction that Greenfield favored. Bacon reluctantly accepted Dowling's proposal, particularly after he persuaded the developer to eliminate one of the buildings in favor of additional public space. Because Dowling's towers were tall and thin, all the offices would have natural light, and the corresponding rental rates—higher than what Greenfield's plan could generate—ensured that the PRR would receive adequate income. Better still, Symes would not have to work with Greenfield.[59]

Symes accordingly backed Dowling and hired him as the railroad's real estate consultant for the Penn Center project. Reporters went so far as to identify Dowling as "a spokesman for the Pennsylvania Railroad," an understandable if inaccurate characterization. Dowling hoped to obtain financing from New York's Mutual Assurance Company, the same firm that made possible the completion of

On November 24, 1953, Mayor Joseph S. Clark Jr. moved the first shovelful of earth associated with the construction of Three Penn Center. Executive Vice President James Symes (in the light suit, behind Clark's head) and President Walter S. Franklin (the tall man in the center) are interested spectators. Symes was less than pleased with the mediocre design adopted by Harold and Percy Uris, standing at right. Given the PRR's precarious financial condition, he had little choice but to acquiesce to the development agenda favored by the Uris brothers and by consultant Robert W. Dowling, at the extreme left, and Philadelphia realtor Frank G. Binswanger, who is standing between Symes and Franklin. *George D. McDowell Philadelphia Evening Bulletin Photographs, courtesy of the Special Collections Research Center, Temple University Libraries, Philadelphia, PA.*

Gateway Center. He invited potential investors to accompany him to Manhattan, traveling in a PRR office car, on what at least one participant referred to as a "junket." During the trip, Dowling suggested that financing was all but arranged. That assessment soon proved to be overly optimistic, as representatives from Mutual balked at the difficulties associated with the project. Symes, who wanted to generate backing in Philadelphia, emphasized that the plan would require the "wholehearted support of everyone in this community." Dowling was even more direct. Unless local developers were willing to provide some of the estimated $75 million cost, he emphasized, there was little chance that Penn Center would ever be built.[60]

Philadelphia real estate developers gave guarded responses to Dowling's threat, but their lack of enthusiasm was telling. Greenfield was openly contemptuous of the Dowling plan, and he worked behind the scenes to discourage Philadelphia bankers from investing in the project.

Given the Pennsylvania Railroad's continuing financial problems, there was little chance that the railroad could fund the construction of Penn Center. Symes acknowledged that his only remaining option was to permit piecemeal, uncoordinated initiatives, selling or developing smaller portions of the site as quickly as possible. In May 1953, the PRR sold the first two parcels of land, between 17th and 18th Streets, in a deal brokered by Binswanger. Walter H. Annenberg, the publisher of the *Philadelphia Inquirer*, intended to build a broadcasting center, a sports arena, and a bus terminal. While Annenberg's plans never came to fruition, his ownership of a large portion of the site ensured that coordinated development would be difficult if not impossible.[61]

The more controversial transaction involved the area between 15th and 16th Streets, opposite city hall. Binswanger again set his sights on New York and the firm of Uris Brothers. Harold and Percy Uris began their careers as residential developers. They experienced considerable success building temporary housing during World War II. By 1950, however, their dissatisfaction with the city's rent controls focused their attention on commercial real estate, particularly office buildings. The brothers were pragmatic rather than visionary, and Harold Uris recalled that "we had a policy of creating the greatest amount of space for the lowest cost." In May 1953, Dowling agreed that Uris Brothers would construct a pair of boxy, twenty-story office towers on the easternmost block of the Penn Center site. The Uris brothers' involvement destroyed any remaining chance of achieving the integrated, aesthetically pleasing development advocated first by Bacon and then by Dowling. Harold and Percy Uris proposed two plain glass boxes that were both unimaginative and uninspiring. Their construction would also preclude the creation of an underground shopping area that constituted Dowling's modification to Bacon's sunken pedestrian esplanade.[62]

The Uris proposal generated criticism from prominent architects and urban planners, and both Clark and Symes did what they could to force the brothers to alter their design. The mayor hinted that the city might condemn the property, through the power of eminent domain, if Uris Brothers did not cooperate. It was an empty threat, given the city's limited financial resources and local disinterest in an undertaking that seemed to be controlled largely from New York City. In August 1953, Clark oversaw the formation of the Citizens' Advisory Committee on Penn Center. Committee chairman Arthur C. Kaufman complained that he felt "let down" by the Uris Brothers proposal and indicated that "I'm not going to be connected with it." The committee possessed neither money nor enforcement

powers, and Kaufman's boycott was meaningless. Clark also encouraged Symes to establish an Advisory Board of Design, whose members included Bacon, Dowling, and prominent architect George Howe. Despite Symes's distaste for the Uris proposal, he was determined to generate revenue from the site as quickly as possible. Howe, Symes's ally on the advisory board, attempted to build support for building the first of the structures—yet he could do no better than to suggest that it was "not a bad building."[63]

The Uris brothers prevailed, largely because local politicians, civic leaders, business executives, developers, and bankers lacked either the will or the resources to stop them. With Pennsylvania Railroad officials determined to make money from the Penn Center site as quickly as possible, the outcome was a foregone conclusion. On November 24, 1953, Symes presided over the groundbreaking for Three Penn Center, the first of the new Uris Brothers buildings. Even as the steel girders began to rise, Bacon was desperately attempting to preserve the underground retail space that had been a key part of his coherent vision for the area. When Harold and Percy Uris refused to spend money on such a profitless proposition, Symes agreed that the Pennsylvania Railroad would manage the development and underwrite the cost of construction. He engaged Welton Becket & Associates, based in Los Angeles, to develop a sunken plaza and shops, with the potential for underground connections with the Market Street and Broad Street Subway lines. Bacon also persuaded PRR officials to install an ice-skating rink, mimicking the one at Rockefeller Center, and to purchase public sculptures by Alexander Calder.[64]

The PRR's influence over the design process was nonetheless minimal, and Penn Center's remaining components emerged in a haphazard fashion—precisely as Bacon had feared. Mathew McCloskey, the contractor who had demolished Broad Street Station, oversaw the construction of Six Penn Center, the second structure built on the site. Designed by Vincent Kling, it represented only a marginal improvement over its neighbor. In January 1957, PRR officials marked the building's completion by relocating their corporate offices from nearby Suburban Station. At the end of March, they held the first board meeting in Six Penn Center. The headquarters would remain there for the rest of the PRR's existence and through the Penn Central and Conrail years as well. Kling continued to bolster his relationship with the Pennsylvania Railroad, although not always in a manner that carried forth Bacon's vain hopes of controlling Penn Center's development. Following Howe's death in April 1955, the board of design that Symes had authorized did not meet for nearly a year. Kling eventually

For many years, James Symes took a keen interest in the buildings that would replace Broad Street Station and the Filbert Street Extension. His desire for an architectural masterpiece that would bring renown to Philadelphia and to the Pennsylvania Railroad clashed with the more mundane economic realities associated with real estate development in a city that was in decline. He is at the left in this December 1960 image, accompanied by Sylvester J. Lowery, the president of Penn Towers, Inc. *George D. McDowell Philadelphia Evening Bulletin Photographs, courtesy of the Special Collections Research Center, Temple University Libraries, Philadelphia, PA.*

replaced Howe, at Symes's request, but the board never exercised any meaningful influence.[65]

Penn Center provided significant financial benefits for the Pennsylvania Railroad yet failed to fulfill Bacon's vision for unified urban redevelopment. Symes received considerable credit for moving the project forward. He earned the 1963 Edward Powell Award, issued every four years to the individual who best promoted the commercial development of Philadelphia. When he stepped down as the PRR chairman later that year, the *Philadelphia Inquirer* noted that "Symes' career ends with Penn Center as its chief monument." That assessment slighted his many other contributions to the Pennsylvania Railroad yet attested to local satisfaction that a modern urban development had finally replaced Broad Street Station and the Chinese Wall. By 1963, the PRR had sold nearly $25 million in property and was collecting $550,000 annually in rents on the underground concourse that Harold and Percy Uris refused to build. Bacon nonetheless emphasized that one of the PRR's executives lamented that the arrangement with the Uris brothers had been a "phony deal." The second Uris building at Two Penn Center, completed in 1958, was as ghastly as the first. The skating rink, promised as the equivalent of the facility at Rockefeller Center, opened on New Year's Eve, 1958. Its popularity quickly faded, and in little more than a decade a new office tower—Eight Penn Center—emerged in its place. The fragmented nature of the construction process ensured that Bacon's unified pedestrian esplanade gave way to a series of disconnected wells between buildings. Designed to allow sunlight into the lower level of the complex, they quickly became strewn with trash, inhabited by the homeless, and avoided by almost everyone else. To the north of Pennsylvania Boulevard, atop the tracks leading to Suburban Station, the PRR and the Sheraton Corporation made plans for a one-thousand-room hotel. Opened in 1957, it was the first hotel to be built in Philadelphia in the previous three decades. That statistic suggested the paucity of interest in commercial real estate development in the center of the third-largest city in the United States. It also explained why so many Philadelphians were grateful that any kind of progress was being made, no matter how imperfectly.[66]

Nor did Penn Center succeed in breathing new life into Center-City Philadelphia. The affluent suburbanites courted by Mayor Clark and other Democratic politicians commuted to their offices in the morning and went straight home in the afternoon. There were many shopping, dining, and entertainment venues in the suburbs and little reason to linger in the city. By the late 1950s, working-class White people were increasingly concerned about crime rates and feared racially integrated neighborhoods and schools. They had little in common with municipal officials or their grand schemes for urban redevelopment. "Someday," noted a blue-collar resident from the northeastern part of the city, "I must go to Philadelphia and see what they've done." While architects and urban planners debated the merits of the structures at Penn Center, the city that the project was designed to save was in steady decline. In 1949, the City Planning Commission predicted that Philadelphia's population would increase by 23 percent over the next three decades. Between 1950 and 1980, the years that bracketed the construction of Penn Center, the city suffered an 18.5 percent population loss.[67]

Four decades after the completion of the first buildings at Penn Center, architecture critic Herbert Muschamp summed up popular disenchantment with Philadelphia's first great experiment in postwar urban redevelopment. "Louis Kahn, whose design for the area had been rejected, commented that if the plan had been submitted by a first-year architecture student, the grade would be zero," Muschamp recalled. "Later, Penn Center was reviled as a prime example of disastrous modern city planning." Bacon chafed at the limitations of Penn Center but chose not to blame the Pennsylvania Railroad for the disappointing results. Wealthy families provided political and financial support for the construction of Rockefeller Center in New York and Mellon's Gateway Center in Pittsburgh, the two principal inspirations for Penn Center. "The Pennsylvania Railroad is not a family," Bacon acknowledged. "It is a group of stockholders expecting dividends. And it certainly does not possess unlimited means."[68]

The Brief Golden Age of the Postwar Streamliner

The Pennsylvania Railroad carried more travelers than any other company in the United States, and for many decades its executives counted on passenger earnings to bolster the company's profits. Those benefits began to fade during the 1920s, as Americans increasingly took to the highways. The use of internal-combustion railcars and substitute bus service could do little to halt the decline, and patronage dwindled on branch-line and local trains. The PRR provided service to more than 79.3 million intercity passengers in 1922, but by 1929, that number had fallen to less than 56 million. The situation worsened in the following decade, as the Great Depression discouraged business and recreational travel. In 1933, fewer than 27 million people rode the PRR's intercity passenger trains. Managers employed several strategies to lure people back to the rails. The most successful involved new all-coach lightweight streamliners such as The Trail Blazer (introduced in 1939) and The Jeffersonian (which debuted two years later).[69]

Other Depression-era initiatives were less rewarding. Beginning in early 1935, the members of the PRR's Unit Train Committee—which also included Raymond Loewy, PRR mechanical engineer Warren R. Elsey, and representatives from Westinghouse, General Electric, and Pullman as well as engineering consultants Gibbs & Hill—evaluated lightweight, articulated streamliners like the Union Pacific's M-10000 and the Burlington Zephyr. They concluded that those trains were only appropriate for the light traffic loads in western states and not for the densely populated Northeast. In 1937, after two years of research, the members of the Unit Train Committee abandoned that concept. As the Depression eased and more Americans took to the rails, PRR personnel nonetheless remained interested in cutting costs and maximizing the efficiency of passenger transportation, particularly between New York and Washington. Beginning in 1940, Loewy and his staff collaborated with the Edward G. Budd Manufacturing Company to create double-deck passenger equipment.[70] By September 1940, the industrial designer developed preliminary designs for a double-deck coach, and the following year he oversaw the construction of a mockup at the PRR's Wilmington Shops. Loewy envisioned a single-level lounge area at each end of the car, over the trucks. The center section of the car could be much lower, permitting the installation of seats on two separate levels, connected by short staircases leading either up or down from the end-of-car lounge areas.[71]

Loewy also gave careful thought to the development of two-level dining cars as part of a broader effort to improve the efficiency of the railroad's dining car operations. The initial design, dating to 1937, featured a two-tier dining room located in the center of the car, between the trucks, with single-level food-preparation areas at each end. Budd revised the concept in 1940, splitting both the kitchen and dining areas into two levels inconveniently connected by dumbwaiters (for the food) and a spiral staircase (for the passengers). In 1943, Loewy proposed the only other conceivable variant of the double-deck diner, with a single-level dining area and a kitchen on two floors. Successful use of the cramped kitchen facilities depended on an idea that Loewy proposed in 1942, to centralize food preparation in commissary facilities and correspondingly reduce the role of onboard cooks. While Loewy's design provided adequate comfort for passengers, the same could not be said for crews laboring in the two-level kitchen. John W. Ebstein, who worked for Loewy between 1938 and 1963, emphasized that the cars were not suitable because "the only personnel that could work in them were midgets." That was not precisely accurate, but the maximum 6-foot headroom made the design uncomfortable and universally hated by those who used the mockup. The fatal flaw, however, was that the two-level cars were too tall to fit through the tunnels that led under the Hudson River and into Penn Station.[72]

Walter Franklin, the PRR's vice president in charge of traffic, was nonetheless sufficiently intrigued with Loewy's suggestions to establish a Dining Car Committee to translate the designer's theoretical concepts into equipment that would function in revenue service. The principal problem involved the storage of precooked food prepared in commissaries and served onboard trains. Loewy offered several solutions, none of which proved adequate. Frozen meals required an all-electric kitchen to maintain proper temperatures, but the PRR's mechanical engineers doubted the feasibility of applying the requisite generators to the railroad's dining cars. Canned foods lasted almost indefinitely, but test subjects disliked the appearance and the metallic taste. Reconstituted dehydrated meals likewise proved unappealing and drew widespread comparisons to military rations. The most innovative method involved the use of large thermos containers to transport hot and cold foods previously prepared in terminal commissaries.

Befitting Loewy's love of gourmet cuisine, menu choices included curry of chicken Bombay and shrimp Newburg—but mercifully omitted cold tongue, a particular Loewy favorite. John F. Finnegan, the PRR's manager of dining car service, nonetheless balked at the limited menu selections necessitated by the thermos-bottle system. "It is highly questionable," he warned Loewy, "that a restricted offering of prefabricated items, mostly stews and mixtures, would offer a satisfying and competitive type of service." Loewy dismissively referred to the head of the PRR's Dining Car Department as "Pan Gravy Finnegan" and paid little attention to his input.[73] A. Baker Barnhart, a Loewy partner who worked on the diner project, recalled that Finnegan "felt, for example, that if a passenger liked prunes for breakfast at home, he should be able to have them on diners." That statement was an exaggeration, but it reflected the long-standing insistence of the Dining Car Department that its cooks prepare a wide variety of traditional meals in cramped conditions while utilizing a basic pantry of ingredients. The disagreements between Loewy, Barnhart, and Finnegan notwithstanding, the problems associated with thermos containers involved more than the taste and variety of food. Full bottles dispatched from a central commissary made the return journey empty, wasting valuable space in the cramped dining car. If not sanitized properly, they could promote bacterial growth and subsequent cases of food poisoning. The thermos bottles were also difficult to obtain, as wartime military demand ensured that they carried an AA-1 priority.[74]

The problems associated with the innovative but cramped double-deck cars led Loewy and PRR officials in precisely the opposite direction, by refining traditional designs in a manner that afforded more space and luxury for each passenger. In 1943, Loewy undertook a lengthy tour of the United States, in which he rode many of the most modern passenger trains, and he took careful note of their many amenities. Because they would be "striving energetically to survive the inroads of air and highway travel" in a postwar world, Loewy emphasized that "the railroads will find it necessary to abandon some tried and tested ideologies for a different technology of transportation." Loewy insisted that "comfort, luxury, and elegance" should take precedence, with "ample space and comfort for passengers," and he warned that "overcrowding would be fatal." Ever attentive to the entire travel experience, he suggested "dust eliminators," ozone generators to mask "offensive odors," improved lighting, and movie projectors in lounge cars. Loewy did not abandon his earlier interest in "delicious prefabricated food," however, and he advocated operationally dubious schemes—so that "coaches and parlor cars may be designed so that they can be utilized as sleepers with a minimum of maintenance layover." While his recommendations for better advertising and modernized ticket counters held considerable merit, it was unlikely that PRR executives would favor the wholesale replacement of small-town stations with modular structures, the provision of connecting transportation between railway stations and airports, or the remodeling of urban terminals to include landing pads for helicopters.[75]

The demands of wartime travel strained the resources of all the carriers, even the Pennsylvania Railroad. The Office of Defense Transportation, established less than two weeks after the attack on Pearl Harbor, possessed broad authority to allocate, coordinate, and restrict virtually every form of freight and passenger travel. Using a combination of moral suasion, rationing, and sanctioning, the ODT temporarily reversed the shift from railroads to highways that had characterized the previous two decades. The railroads claimed just 9.8 percent of passenger miles in 1941, compared to 84.8 percent for private automobiles. By 1943, the railroads garnered 33.2 percent of passenger miles, while autos accounted for 54.4 percent. That trend affected the Pennsylvania Railroad, with the number of intercity passengers increasing from 39.1 million in 1940 to 48.1 million in 1941, then 80.6 million in 1942 and 118.5 million in 1943. The number of intercity passengers peaked in 1944 at 125.2 million as wartime industries boomed and as the military prepared for a massive escalation of the conflict in the European and Pacific Theaters. For the first time in its history, New York's Penn Station operated at full capacity, its grand public spaces crowded with people. The financial results were equally gratifying, as the PRR's intercity passenger revenues rose from just under $67 million in 1940 to $84.2 million in 1941, $162.4 million in 1942, and $238.1 million in 1943—peaking at $253.6 million in 1944 before falling slightly to $251.8 million the following year. The October 1942 Revenue Act eroded some of those gains, thanks to a surcharge of 10 percent on all passenger fares. In April 1944, the tax increased to 15 percent, but everyone assumed that it was a temporary wartime measure, certain to disappear when the federal government curtailed its massive military expenditures.[76]

It seemed certain that the demand for passenger travel would continue well after the end of the conflict. Policy makers, determined to avoid repeating the recession that followed World War I, laid the groundwork for a postwar economic boom that would likely produce an increase in business travel. With the reconversion process still incomplete and consumer goods in short supply, salesmen and buyers frequently faced the necessity of making multiple journeys. Attendance at conventions, sharply restricted during the war, offered further opportunities for travel. Americans buffeted by fifteen years of economic depression and world war would want to see the country that many had fought to defend. Vacation trips to Florida and California were especially popular, but equipment shortages made it difficult for anyone to get anywhere. Overwhelmed ticket agents acknowledged "that desperate reservation seekers start out by asking for a bedroom or a compartment on a streamliner but many end up by begging for any kind of space on any train." Another railroad official acknowledged that "it is really tough" and asked for patience, emphasizing that "we are trying to take care of everyone but there just aren't enough cars." By March 1946, the ODT eliminated the last of the wartime restrictions on the assignment of sleeping cars, enabling the PRR to restore Pullman service to seventeen city pairs—a group of trains that included *The Pittsburgher*. Such measures helped, but they would be insufficient to accommodate the anticipated demand. The shortage of space was only likely to increase, as passenger bookings for the first months of 1947 were 50 percent above the same period the previous year.[77]

Buoyed by record-setting demand for passenger service, PRR executives anticipated a golden age of postwar rail travel. At the very least, the company would have to repair and replace equipment worn out by wartime service. While no one suggested that the railroads could recapture branch-line and local service, managers anticipated success in two specific markets. One involved intermediate-distance routes of five hundred miles or less that linked major cities in the heavily urbanized Northeast. Passengers on such journeys had little need for amenities such as sleepers, lounges, or diners. The PRR's business strategy would accordingly depend on the availability of fast trains with lightweight equipment that cost relatively little to purchase, operate, and maintain. Executives also expressed optimism that business travelers and vacationers would continue to travel by rail. Commercial aviation was only beginning its rapid postwar growth, and a national system of multilane interstate highways did not yet exist. Trains offered the safest and most comfortable travel between cities that were more than five hundred miles apart. Passengers on those routes demanded new equipment that was luxurious, modern, and stylish. It was not difficult to see why the *New York Times* observed that the "railroads see [a] bright future" in passenger travel and why PRR executives were ready to spend lavishly on new equipment and services.[78]

Time was of the essence to fend off competition from other carriers. Despite the B&O's lackluster finances, officials from that railroad were signaling their willingness to buy new equipment and upgrade existing cars. The New York Central represented a more serious threat. In 1944, that company commissioned a study of likely postwar travel behavior, an initiative that soon caught the attention of Pennsylvania Railroad executives. The results suggested that passengers would demand larger and more comfortable accommodations—including lounge cars, all-room sleepers, and coaches with widely spaced seats. The NYC accordingly spent more than $56 million for 300 coaches and 420 sleepers. It was the largest purchase of passenger equipment in the history of American railroading and sufficient to reequip 52 trains in its Great Steel Fleet. All the NYC's new sleepers would feature enclosed rooms, a sure sign that the prewar open section had fallen out of favor with travelers who now demanded comfort and privacy rather than economy.[79]

The Pennsylvania Railroad responded with an ambitious plan to upgrade the entire Blue Ribbon Fleet. The priority for the new equipment would be *The Trail Blazer* and *The Jeffersonian*, the luxury all-coach trains between the East Coast and Chicago and St. Louis. It was a sensible choice, given that in the prewar period those two trains generated a consistently higher return on investment than more prestigious all-Pullman services such as *The Broadway Limited*. In October 1945, the board of directors approved the construction of ninety new cars, to be built at the Altoona Works. The order included seventy coaches and ten buffet-lounge cars—half with a baggage compartment to be placed at the front of the train and the remainder with an observation section for the rear. The final ten cars were diners, configured into two-unit sets like the ones added to *The Trail Blazer* when the train was inaugurated in 1939.[80] Loewy took charge of the interior styling, in collaboration with a team of PRR mechanical engineers and passenger-traffic officials. Executives optimistically predicted that the new cars would be in service by April 13, 1946, to participate in the company's centennial celebrations.[81]

The anticipated level of postwar travel, coupled with the NYC's commitment to its Great Steel Fleet, ensured that the cars for *The Trail Blazer* and *The Jeffersonian* were only the first in a series of new equipment orders. In December 1945, Pennsylvania Railroad officials announced that they would spend $21 million for 214 cars for *The Broadway Limited*, *The "Spirit of St. Louis,"* and other Blue Ribbon trains.[82] The railroad allocated the car orders to the principal builders—Budd, Pullman-Standard, and American Car & Foundry. President Clement announced another large passenger-car order in August 1948—part of a massive

$216.7 million investment that also included 566 diesel units and 4,400 freight cars. PRR officials also planned to "renovize" hundreds of older cars, mostly P70 coaches. Along with prewar lightweight equipment and unmodified heavyweight cars, the additional $51 million investment would give the PRR a vast fleet of more than two thousand pieces of long-distance passenger equipment.[83]

The much-publicized new cars were slow to arrive, owing to manufacturing delays—the inevitable result of reconversion to a peacetime economy—and competition from the other railroads that were also upgrading passenger service. Pullman-Standard in particular faced shortages of key components and was operating at less than half of its potential capacity. By May 1946, Pullman had 1,163 cars on its order books, 870 of which were ahead of the PRR's order. The Altoona Works likewise could not keep pace with the company's demand for new freight and passenger equipment. The first of the ninety coaches authorized in October 1945 would not be ready for service on *The Trail Blazer* and *The Jeffersonian* until January 6, 1947—long after the railroad's centennial—and the trains would not be fully reequipped until late the following year.[84]

The new equipment, when it finally entered service, was luxurious, complex, and expensive. In keeping with the results of Raymond Loewy's 1943 fact-finding trip and the 1944 NYC survey, PRR personnel avoided radical changes to long-established design principles. Instead, they favored incremental improvements, particularly those that would provide each passenger with more space. The coaches, assigned to Class P85BR, were five feet longer than the prewar lightweight cars assigned to *The Trail Blazer* and *The Jeffersonian*. Yet they featured only forty-four reclining seats, eight fewer than their predecessors. Capacious men's and women's lounges occupied a substantial portion of each car, further limiting the number of revenue passengers. Fourteen new features—including large windows, diffused fluorescent lights, a public-address system, and pneumatically operated doors—increased passenger comfort while contributing to the manufacturing complexity that delayed production and increased expense. Each coach cost the PRR $90,000, while the twin-unit diners carried a price tag of $130,000. Cars 7302–7305, assigned to *The Jeffersonian* in March 1948, were among the most luxurious and unusual components of the PRR's postwar passenger program. Built by American Car & Foundry, they featured a sunken buffet lounge, a game and reading room, and a tiny movie theater. A nursery and children's playroom suggested the beginnings of the baby boom. Like the new coaches, the recreation cars provided ample space per passenger, increasing operating costs without generating any additional revenue. They also reflected the PRR's evolving efforts to market the company's long-distance passenger trains. Rather than emphasizing the journey as an intrinsically enjoyable experience, it now seemed like a burden to be endured, with numerous distractions that would alleviate boredom and help time pass as quickly as possible.[85]

Pennsylvania Railroad executives had acted wisely in prioritizing the upgrading of *The Trail Blazer* and *The Jeffersonian* and in contracting so many of their passenger cars to the Altoona Works rather than to outside suppliers. The twin-unit diners that completed *The Trail Blazer* were not ready until November 1948, more than three years after PRR officials had authorized the new equipment.[86] It was nonetheless the first entirely new train on any railroad in the postwar era. The PRR and other carriers mostly pieced together whatever prewar, postwar, heavyweight, streamlined, outdated, and modernized equipment that was available to accommodate passengers, while reassuring them that better service was coming soon. Ward Allan Howe, a reporter for the *New York Times* and a lifelong rail enthusiast, reflected the public's initial optimism and subsequent rapid disillusionment. "Other fine trains are on the way," he wrote in May 1947. Barely a year later, however, he suggested that the "outlook is not bright," particularly for passengers wishing to travel in new sleeping cars. "Up to now," Howe observed, "not a single post-war car of this type has been received by any Eastern road."[87]

The situation that Howe described plagued the Pennsylvania Railroad and forced repeated postponements of the announced upgrading of the most prestigious Blue Ribbon trains. The PRR invested more than $4.6 million to reequip the 1938 version of *The Broadway Limited*, but the new cars did not enter service until March 1949. Raymond Loewy was again the designer, and he selected interiors that were considerably more austere than those he had favored in 1938. The veneers fabricated from exotic woods were gone, replaced by easier-to-maintain plastic. The equipment remained luxurious nonetheless, and the sleeper-observations *Mountain View* and *Tower View* offered some of the finest accommodations available on any railroad—including a master bedroom, complete with a shower. The most distinctive passenger cars in the PRR's fleet, they featured squared-off ends rather than the teardrop shape used on the prewar *Broadway* and on both the early and modern versions of the *Twentieth Century Limited*. The new equipment helped *The Broadway Limited* to generate passenger loads and revenues that were substantially higher than had been the case before the war, with earnings of nearly $4.00 per train mile. The *Century*

still carried far more passengers, however, and the New York Central remained the dominant carrier in the New York–Chicago market.[88]

By the summer of 1949, many of the PRR's other Blue Ribbon trains received upgrades as equipment trickled in from Pullman, Budd, and American Car & Foundry. With only two sets of equipment available for *The Broadway Limited*, the company upgraded *The General* as a companion train—in large measure to compete against the NYC, whose *Twentieth Century Limited* routinely operated in multiple sections. By July 1949, new sleepers, observation cars inherited from the prewar Fleet of Modernism, and a sixteen-hour schedule made *The General* the functional equivalent of *The Broadway Limited*. In October, the PRR announced the assignment of new equipment to *The Cincinnati Limited*, although passengers still routinely encountered prewar heavyweight cars. The train was successful nonetheless, as it was significantly faster than its closest competition, the NYC's *Ohio State Limited*. The same could not be said for *The Red Arrow*, the New York–Detroit service that had introduced passenger diesels to the Pennsylvania Railroad. The New York Central's *Detroiter* followed a more direct and speedier route and soon dominated that market. The same situation applied in Cleveland, where most travelers preferred the NYC's *Cleveland Limited* to the PRR's *Clevelander*. To the south, the Pennsylvania Railroad dominated travel between New York and Philadelphia and St. Louis, thanks to the fast schedules of The *"Spirit of St. Louis"* (which received new cars in August 1949) and *The Jeffersonian*. The *Southwestern Limited*, operated by the New York Central, was not competitive except at some intermediate points. The Baltimore & Ohio provided a more serious challenge, and its *National Limited* carried a significant share of passengers traveling between Washington and St. Louis. Even though the PRR upgraded *The Liberty Limited* in 1949, its patronage between Washington and Chicago fell well below what the B&O achieved with the *Capitol Limited* and the all-coach *Columbian*.[89] While the PRR dominated rail service between New York and Pittsburgh, the decade-old Pennsylvania Turnpike increasingly sapped passenger revenues. *The Pittsburgher*—the overnight train that had temporarily fallen victim to the ODT's restrictions on sleeping-car service—received new equipment in September 1949. It remained popular with steel-industry executives and other business travelers on expense accounts.[90]

Even as new coaches, sleepers, and diners trickled in from the builders, Pennsylvania Railroad executives concluded that passenger service faced a bleak future. Despite inroads made by highway traffic, passenger operations remained profitable through 1930 before the Great Depression generated eleven straight years of deficits. The company enjoyed substantial net passenger earnings between 1942 and 1945, but as wartime restrictions on automobile travel came to an end, the losses returned in 1946. Pennsylvania Railroad officials responded to the situation by seeking fare increases and by curtailing service. "There is no use in trying for volume in the unprofitable," President Clement observed in May 1947. He endorsed an 11.7 percent reduction in passenger-train miles between 1946 and 1947 to lower operating costs. The elimination of troop trains and the cancellation of extra sections that accommodated overflow traffic accounted for about a quarter of the decrease. In some cases, trains that once operated separately were combined for a portion of their respective routes, curtailing train mileage but increasing time-consuming switching moves at major terminals. The 1946 coal strike justified temporary reductions, but by the end of the year, it was clear that many of those changes would be permanent. In January 1947, the PRR combined the eastbound *Pennsylvania Limited* with *The St. Louisan* between Pittsburgh and New York. The same policy applied to the westbound *Akronite* and *Clevelander*, which ran as one train east of Pittsburgh. The Washington section of *The Red Arrow* disappeared, as did *The Metropolitan* between Philadelphia and Pittsburgh. The biggest casualty was *The Steel King*, the all-coach daytime train between New York and Pittsburgh. PRR officials first proposed the service in 1940 as a companion to *The Trail Blazer* and *The Jeffersonian* in an effort to win back passengers from the Pennsylvania Turnpike. It first appeared in a painting for the PRR's 1941 calendar, but World War II delayed the inauguration of the actual train until February 1946—on the same date as *The Pittsburgher* reverted to its previous all-sleeper, overnight status. Most travelers found automobiles and buses to be less expensive and more convenient, and *The Steel King* disappeared from the timetable on January 18, 1947.[91]

The initial postwar curtailments were but a prelude to an escalating series of reductions in passenger service. "There is one thing to bear in mind," President Clement informed his chief operating and traffic officers in October 1948. "Passenger service on most roads is gradually drying up." The PRR was no exception. "As to the passenger business," Clement emphasized, "we are on the horns of a dilemma. It is profitable between Washington and Boston and we do not dare sacrifice that; it bears some profit between New York and St. Louis and Chicago; but, with the exception of the primary services, there is no profit in the passenger business." Clement and other operating officials were thoroughly familiar with the conditions that accounted for the consistently poor financial performance of passenger trains. They operated at considerably higher speeds than freight traffic, and not even the PRR's four-track main line could fully accommodate that differential. Unlike freight, passengers and the trains that transported them required round-the-clock attention. Passenger service "is the first occupation of the Operating [Transportation] Dept., with 24 hours a day service everywhere," Clement complained. "It is the first occupation of the Traffic Dept., and it consumes a lot of executive time. With the tendency toward the 40-hour week it is going to be the most expensive thing on the railroad." Clement's pessimism was not exaggerated. In the autumn of 1948, products associated with the steel industry generated revenues that were double the cost of transportation—indicating an operating ratio of 50 percent. Coal traffic carried an operating ratio of 85 percent—"but it wouldn't take much to put it to 70% even though it belongs at 60%," Clement emphasized. The operating ratio for passenger service was 130 percent, indicating the PRR spent $1.30 for every dollar collected in fares.[92]

The short life of *The Steel King* was a bad omen for the PRR's postwar passenger service. Its elimination coincided with the consolidation or truncation of several secondary trains, a sure sign that business and leisure travelers were increasingly relying on automobiles and aircraft. Even as journalist Ward Howe touted the reequipping of *The Trail Blazer* and *The Jeffersonian* and the pending introduction of the *California Zephyr*, the same January 1949 issue of the *New York Times* included the article "South by Trailer." Travel writer Arthur Swift highlighted "the increase in trailer traffic all along the route and the progress made on new trailer park construction in Florida." His southbound journey proceeded at a leisurely rate—240 miles a day, on average—but the slow pace and intermediate stops were part of the fun. The cost for fuel and oil was a mere $40, equivalent to 2.9 cents per mile. That was slightly below the fare in a railroad coach and significantly cheaper than Pullman rates—and without the 15 percent wartime federal tax on rail travel. With a trailer in tow, neither Swift nor his emulators had any need for the sleeping and dining facilities provided by the passenger cars that were just entering service. Despite his love for rail travel, Howe sensed trouble for the PRR and other carriers. In May 1947, he had eagerly anticipated a new golden age of modern streamliners, and within a year he had expressed disappointment that the new equipment was so slow to materialize. By May 1949, however, he noted that the railroads "now have plenty of new equipment." What they did not have were passengers. "Beset by mounting operating costs and a disturbing decline in passenger travel," Howe emphasized, "the railroads are looking hopefully to the vacation season to start an upward trend in revenue again."[93]

When Howe suggested that the railroads had more passenger equipment than they needed, the Pennsylvania Railroad had not yet taken delivery of all the cars that it had ordered for the upgrading of the Blue Ribbon Fleet. Those cars, and the more than $50 million investment they represented, would never be utilized to anything approaching their full potential. In 1947, passenger losses were $44 million. By 1951, the Pennsylvania Railroad's passenger deficit had reached $71 million. The New York Central, a railroad where the vaunted Great Steel Fleet had generated a loss of $54 million that year, performed almost as poorly. In May of that year, Clement emphasized that "we just can't afford to continue such a big volume of business at such big losses, and the easiest way to get out is to increase rates, increase train size, and keep the number of trains that are running profitably, even though it reduces the frequency of the service." Those initiatives, while economically sound, were unlikely to increase customer satisfaction or passenger patronage. A few weeks later, in a memo to Symes, Clement offered an even more pessimistic assessment regarding the future of passenger service. "It is clearly indicated that rail passenger transportation as a general mode of transportation is passing out," he observed. "No railroad can afford to penalize its other business to try and subsidize rail passenger transportation in competition with other subsidized means of hauling people—by air or highway. I do not desire to prejudge or influence, but I have watched road after road go out of the passenger business, into the freight business, and become prosperous." Symes needed little convincing, and he agreed that passenger service should be restricted to the route between New York and Washington, with the addition of a small number of overnight trains between major cities. On the PRR, as on countless other railroads across the United States, the golden age of the postwar streamliner was ending, almost as quickly as it had begun.[94]

The PRR, Pullman, and Transcontinental Passenger Service

Clement, frustrated with the PRR's mounting passenger losses, expressed his irritation at journalists who had not yet grasped that long-distance rail travel was a relic of the past. "The western roads, even the southwestern roads, are getting high praise for their passenger service," he complained, "yet they really are not much better than two high class trains each way a day." Under that model, he concluded, the PRR might conceivably operate only *The*

Broadway Limited between New York and Chicago, and *The "Spirit of St. Louis"* to its namesake terminus. While that goal was for the moment unattainable, Clement had joined forces with the western carriers whose limited passenger service he envied.[95]

The postwar evolution of the PRR's passenger operations included an initiative that was boldly innovative and spectacularly unsuccessful. For a brief period after World War II, the Pennsylvania Railroad offered through service from the East Coast to such faraway destinations as California, Texas, and Mexico City, in collaboration with thirteen western railroads. Travelers could thus avoid the inconvenience of changing trains in gateway cities such as Chicago and St. Louis.

Initial efforts to develop transcontinental trains began prior to World War II, in response to the development of western streamliners such as the M-10000 and the *Zephyr*, and in conjunction with efforts by the PRR's Unit Train Committee to apply that technology to the routes between New York, Washington, and Chicago. The PRR's long-standing tradition of cooperative passenger service in conjunction with southern and New England carriers made officials more receptive than most to the concept of transcontinental operations. In 1934, the company's executives initiated discussions with their counterparts at the New York Central, the Santa Fe, the Union Pacific, the Chicago & North Western, the Southern Pacific, and the Baltimore & Ohio. Representatives from those railroads showed little interest, in part because they estimated that only about two hundred people per day made a transcontinental trip. Pennsylvania Railroad officials likewise acknowledged that fewer than 5 percent of all passengers traveling on *The Broadway Limited* (or on the NYC's *Twentieth Century Limited*) were heading from coast to coast. Even then, existing schedules permitted convenient connections at Chicago between eastern and western passenger trains. The Great Depression had also reduced the demand for travel while impeding the ability of the carriers to inaugurate new services.[96]

By 1937, improving economic conditions and the publicity surrounding the development of lightweight streamlined trains prompted a reconsideration of the issue. During spring and summer, the PRR and the NYC were cooperating with Pullman on the design of new lightweight equipment—including the initial Fleet of Modernism cars, delivered the following year. To the west, between 1934 and 1936 the Union Pacific took delivery of a series of streamlined trainsets, powered by internal-combustion engines. They featured low-profile, articulated equipment and as such could not accommodate the Pennsylvania

Railroad's more conventional lightweight cars. They none-theless elicited favorable media coverage, and the UP soon made plans to reequip the *City of Los Angeles* and the *City of San Francisco* with PRR-compatible cars. The Santa Fe's new, lightweight *Super Chief*, introduced in 1937, offered further opportunities for through passenger operations. It was in that context that in June 1937 PRR traffic offi-cials prepared a fifty-six-hour, forty-five-minute schedule for service from New York to Los Angeles, using either the UP or the Santa Fe as the western connection. Union Pacific board chairman W. Averell Harriman, who had been a staunch supporter of that company's streamliners, expressed some interest, but no agreement was forthcom-ing. World War II and the restrictions imposed by the Office of Defense Transportation subsequently precluded the development of experimental passenger services. It would be best to "wait until after the war and proper equip-ment became available," Clement informed the president of another potential southwestern connection, the Mis-souri–Kansas–Texas Railroad.[97]

By April 1944, however, PRR officials were ready to begin planning for the postwar passenger market. Their predictions for a high level of demand for long-distance business and leisure travel—which provided the rationale for large orders of streamlined passenger equipment—also suggested that they revive proposals for transcontinental service. By September, with the war over and travel restric-tions rapidly disappearing, Clement and other executives suggested the possibility of as many as four trains per week from the East Coast (both New York and Washington) to California (Los Angeles and San Francisco), with two more between New York and Seattle.[98]

A contentious federal antitrust prosecution soon complicated the negotiations between the PRR and its prospective transcontinental partners, while introducing a charismatic and unpredictable actor into the process. Through its two subsidiaries (the Pullman Company and the Pullman-Standard Car Manufacturing Company), Pullman, Incorporated, had for decades controlled most of the sleeping cars in the United States, building and maintaining them, staffing them, and contracting their transportation to the various railroads over which they operated. The Pullman monopoly was both practical and efficient, in that it exploited economies of scale, offered uniform service, and facilitated the movement of sleeping cars from one railroad to another. Pullman-Standard was well equipped to construct sleeping cars to the designs specified by the parent corporation. Yet the arrangement did no favors for the Edward G. Budd Manufacturing Company. Beginning with the Burlington's 1934 *Zephyr*

trainset, Budd had transitioned into the construction of full-sized stainless-steel passenger cars—including two diners delivered to the PRR in 1938. Pullman's tradition of in-house manufacturing nonetheless limited Budd's prospects in what promised to be a booming market for lightweight sleeping cars.[99]

Competition from Budd was one of several challenges facing Pullman during the 1930s. The Depression and the growth of highway and air travel halved patronage, while the growing power of A. Philip Randolph and the Brother-hood of Sleeping Car Porters threatened to increase labor costs. A more existential threat emerged from the antimo-nopoly impulses of the New Deal, as directed by Assistant Attorney General Thurman Arnold. On July 12, 1940, the Department of Justice filed suit against Pullman, alleging that that company's monopoly of both the manufacture and operation of sleeping cars had resulted in inferior ser-vice and had prevented other builders, particularly Budd, from gaining equal access to the passenger-car market. Even though Pullman's attorneys argued that the company had lowered fares and spent millions of dollars to upgrade cars and improve service, in May 1944 the Federal District Court at Philadelphia ordered the separation of the com-pany's manufacturing and operating functions. Pullman, Incorporated, executives elected to retain control of Pull-man-Standard, their manufacturing arm, while divesting the Pullman Company subsidiary that oversaw the opera-tion of a national fleet of more than six thousand sleeping and parlor cars.[100]

While the pending breakup of Pullman, Incorporated, caused few immediate changes in passenger service, it provoked a lengthy battle for control of the Pullman Com-pany and the sleeping cars that were its principal assets. In August 1944, Pullman president David A. Crawford sug-gested that the nation's railroads combine their resources to create a single operating consortium. The New York Central and its allies were inclined to follow Crawford's advice. PRR officials refused to take part, largely because they preferred individual corporate control over the own-ership and operation of equipment. Absent the cooperation of the leading passenger carrier in the United States, a national sleeping-car pool seemed an impossibility. The result was an impasse, as the deadline for divestiture grew ever closer.[101]

The railroads' inability to decide the fate of the Pullman Company provided opportunities for Robert R. Young, the charismatic and mercurial chairman of the board of the Chesapeake & Ohio. A Texas native and self-styled Prairie populist, Young repeatedly railed against the East Coast "goddambanker" elite. His rancor was to some extent

Robert R. Young (1897–1958) leveraged the wreckage of the Van Sweringen empire into an audacious effort to dominate the railroad network in the eastern United States. He is seated, second from the right, and flanked by his allies Allan Kirby (in the center of the photo) and Frank Kolbe (at far right), with attorney Walter S. Orr (at left) ready to offer advice. The year is 1937, and over the next two decades, Young will attempt to gain control of the Pullman Company, then the Chesapeake & Ohio, and finally the New York Central. *Harris & Ewing Collection, Library of Congress, Prints & Photographs Division.*

genuine and stemmed from a combination of insecurity and resentment at repeated rejections of the investment opportunities that he presented to his more cautious Wall Street colleagues. Young nonetheless mistrusted what he considered to be the dangerously socialistic tendencies of the Roosevelt administration and was probably as surprised as anyone that he attracted a loyal following of antimonopoly New Dealers. Never one to miss an opportunity for favorable publicity, Young criticized the railroads and the banks in roughly equal measure. Audacious and articulate, Young became a favorite of reporters, who could always count on him for a good story or a pithy quote. His persona increasingly involved a combination of aggressive business tactics and theatrical bombast as his myriad financial ventures rippled through the national transportation network.[102]

Young's involvement in railroading arose from the wreckage of the complex system of holding companies that Oris Paxton and Mantis James Van Sweringen had established to exploit the consolidation provisions contained in the Transportation Act of 1920. By 1935, the Vans were badly overextended. Their principal asset—the Alleghany Corporation—came under the control of George A. Ball, the youngest among the five brothers who had established an eponymous firm in Muncie, Indiana, for the manufacture of glass Mason jars.[103] The agreement provided the Van Sweringens with the opportunity to buy back their holdings, but the death of M. J. in 1935 and O.

P. the following year put an end to that arrangement. In 1937, Ball sold his shares to a consortium that included Young and two other investors, Frank F. Kolbe and Allan P. Kirby.[104] When they gained control of Alleghany, Young and his allies inherited the railway system that the Vans had created, one that included the Chesapeake & Ohio, the Nickel Plate, the Wheeling & Lake Erie, the Pere Marquette, the Missouri Pacific, and the Chicago & Eastern Illinois.[105]

With his customary bravado, Young announced that he was prepared to restore the Alleghany Corporation to solvency and consolidate its holdings into an efficient transportation network, one that would be built around the profitable Chesapeake & Ohio.[106] That was easier said than done, however. J. P. Morgan & Company refused to take part in Young's schemes, increasing the Texan's animosity toward the East Coast banking establishment. When the Depression worsened in 1937, Young experienced severe financial difficulties, followed by a nervous breakdown. In 1938, a bitterly contested proxy battle with the Guaranty Trust Company, for control of the C&O, gave Young further opportunity to rail against the Wall Street elites. He subsequently scored what he considered a major victory over both the House of Morgan and Kuhn, Loeb & Company, preventing the two major investment-banking firms from participating in the refinancing of C&O securities. Professing his dedication to the interests of small investors, he demanded competitive bidding for the new bond issue and afterward crowed that he had brought fairness and integrity to the world of railroad finance. Not until 1942, however, did Young and his allies finally oust Ball from the oversight of the C&O and achieve control over the lucrative Pocahontas coal carrier. For the next three years, Young was involved in a further round of negotiations and legal battles with the Interstate Commerce Commission and the Justice Department, primarily involving the issue of whether the Transportation Act of 1940 precluded his control of multiple railroads.[107]

To win the federal government's favor, Young cultivated the image of a progressive and visionary railroader. In the late stages of the contentious *Georgia v. Pennsylvania Railroad* case, he sided with those who contended that northern-dominated rate bureaus had suppressed economic development in the South. Young's crusade to end regional rate discrimination nonetheless concealed his efforts to negotiate a settlement between the Chesapeake & Ohio and the state of Georgia, one that would exclude companies such as the PRR. As part of that plan, he established the Federation for Railway Progress, an alternative to the Association of American Railroads.[108]

Young hoped that the "constructive elements" of management, labor, and investors could join forces "to promote free and competitive enterprise in the interest of the public" and work "to improve equipment and service, to fight for the billions in rail securities which are being unjustifiably squeezed out in reorganizations, and to preserve a fair balance between wages and rates." Once more casting himself as David battling Goliath, Young claimed that his new organization represented the interests of 90 percent of the AAR's current members, even though the managers of those companies "haven't dared do anything about it. Everybody knows that the New York Central and the Pennsylvania control the association," he concluded. Yet, perhaps as a publicity stunt, he asked the Pennsylvania Railroad to join his Federation for Railway Progress. President Clement had little difficulty in recommending that the PRR board reject the offer—in part because the inclusion of labor and investor interests weakened managerial prerogatives and in part because the federation's policy of equal representation for all railroads, regardless of size, undermined the authority that the Pennsylvania Railroad had exercised within the AAR.[109]

Young also emphasized his public-spirited commitment to improved passenger service. He demanded a centralized rail passenger reservations bureau and in 1947 issued a credit card that enabled travelers to purchase Chesapeake & Ohio tickets.[110] The Federation for Railway Progress distributed copies of its "Passenger Service Report"—a postcard enabling travelers to comment on their experience before sending it, postage free, to the federation's headquarters in Cleveland's Terminal Tower. Young announced plans to order nearly three hundred new passenger cars to replace the prewar equipment on the C&O and the Pere Marquette—and pledged to launch a new train, the *Chessie*, that would provide dome cars, a children's playroom, an aquarium, and a movie theater for passengers traveling between Washington and Cincinnati. It was a monumental miscalculation, as the C&O was primarily a coal road, with little long-distance passenger businesses.[111] Most of the new equipment never entered service, and only a single test train of the *Chessie* ever graced C&O rails.[112]

Young's efforts to improve passenger service and create an eastern railroad empire coincided with the court-ordered breakup of Pullman, Incorporated, giving the maverick financier investment and public-relations opportunities that were too good to pass up. His bid to control the Pullman Company was ultimately unsuccessful, but it complicated the disposition of the firm's assets and created a strong incentive for the Pennsylvania Railroad to become involved in transcontinental passenger service. As his support for the *Chessie* indicated, Young represented an extreme example of the confidence among railroad executives that long-distance passenger travel would remain strong after the end of gasoline rationing and other wartime restrictions that retarded the use of private automobiles. Yet the railroads would have to act quickly, Young argued, before improved highways and better aircraft could erode their share of the market. Young insisted that Pullman had failed to serve the needs of its customers and was ill-equipped to exploit the narrow window of opportunity to keep travelers loyal to the rails. In classic Young fashion, he decried a cabal of monopolists (Pullman), unimaginative dunderheads (railroad executives), and grasping plutocrats (Wall Street investment bankers), each of whom had conspired to deprive the American people of the mobility that was their natural right.[113]

The division among the railroads, between those who wanted to form a sleeping-car pool and those who sought individual ownership, goaded Young into action. The latter arrangement—favored by Clement—represented the more serious threat, in that it would have frustrated Young's grandiose national ambitions. By the end of August, Young had submitted a proposal to the US District Court in Philadelphia, offering to buy the Pullman Company in its entirety.[114] A few weeks later, he arranged a meeting with the PRR's president, who was one of the few executives willing to talk to him. Clement reiterated his insistence that Pullman's sleeping cars be allocated to the various railroads. Yet Young's relentless publicity campaign, coupled with several other proposals to acquire Pullman, encouraged Clement to reconsider his position. A month after his meeting with Young, Clement and representatives from nineteen other railroads—including the NYC—agreed to form a buying group that could counter Young's bid.[115] On October 27, the railroads matched Young's proposal, offering $75 million for Pullman and arguing that they were best equipped to maintain uninterrupted service. Pullman officials initially rejected the terms suggested by the buying group, although their preference clearly lay with the railroads rather than Young. The Justice Department, in contrast, favored the iconoclastic outsider. John Dickinson, the PRR's general counsel, took the lead in presenting the case of the railroads' buying group. The judges accepted Dickinson's argument that the railroads were more financially secure than Young and could best offer uninterrupted service for the traveling public.[116]

Young hoped that an aggressive media campaign would swing public opinion in his favor and ensure his control of Pullman. Claiming that railroad and Pullman officials had permitted service to decline to antediluvian levels, he cast himself in the role of savior. The ad campaign began in November 1945, only days after the district court began evaluating the merits of the various bids for the Pullman Company.[117] In late December, the court rejected Young's offer for Pullman. Following his initial judicial defeat and anticipating an appeal to the Supreme Court, Young accelerated his advertising campaign. Characterizing Pullman cars as "rolling tenements," Young suggested that the vast majority of the company's equipment should be sent to the scrapyard.[118] He pledged to spend half a billion dollars on new sleepers, vowing to replace passenger cars every seven years.[119] Yet Young's most outlandish criticism—as measured by the disparity between the extent of the problem and the intensity of the rhetoric that he used to attack it—involved the reluctance of Pullman and the railroads to offer transcontinental sleeping-car service. Despite the absence of passenger demand, and although the PRR had already explored the possibility of through operations to the West Coast, Young insisted that the railroads had ignored the right of travelers to pass through cities such as St. Louis and Chicago without changing trains.[120]

Although Young succeeded in gaining the support of the Justice Department—in part because his attorney, Thurman Arnold, was the former head of the Antitrust Division—the members of the Interstate Commerce Commission were less easily swayed. ICC hearings began in November 1946, on the same day that Young announced his intention to launch the *Chessie* and reequip the other C&O and Pere Marquette passenger trains with modern lightweight equipment. He continued his brazen attempt to curry public support when he testified at the hearings, reiterating his sensationalistic allegations of monopoly, Wall Street dominance, and unimaginative and incompetent Pullman and railroad executives. The public might have been impressed, but the ICC examiner was not, and in February 1947, he seconded the court's recommendation that Pullman go to the railroads. Young's last hope lay with the Justice Department, whose officials had given his antimonopoly crusade far more attention than it deserved. In March 1946, Young, representatives from the Justice Department, and two other unsuccessful bidders appealed the district court's ruling. The matter now went to the Supreme Court, with the various regulatory and judicial roadblocks extending the Pullman Company's oversight of the sleeping-car business longer than anyone had anticipated—and ironically discouraging the very modernization and innovation that Young insisted was critical to the survival of long-distance passenger rail travel.[121] At the end of March 1947, the Supreme Court affirmed the lower court's ruling, ending Young's dreams of acquiring Pullman.[122] Young had probably anticipated that outcome—which at the very least seemed to confirm his warnings regarding the conspiratorial forces arrayed against him—and the peripatetic entrepreneur had already moved on to greener pastures. Since the latter months of 1946, he had been buying New York Central stock. Within a few years, his control of that company triggered the first phase in the long evolution of its merger with the Pennsylvania Railroad.[123]

The Supreme Court and ICC rulings affirmed the transfer of Pullman's assets to the railroads, a process that had been underway since December 1945. PRR officials agreed to spend more than $8 million to purchase outright 123 heavyweight parlor cars, along with 142 lightweight sleepers that had entered service prior to World War II. At the end of June 1947, and with the removal of the last legal and regulatory impediments, the buying group—now comprising fifty-seven railroads—established a new Pullman Company.[124] The participants purchased the sleeping and parlor cars owned by the predecessor firm and then leased them back to the new corporation that in turn coordinated operations and ticket sales. The PRR was the largest single participant, with more than 16 percent of the total pool of the 6,500 cars in service. That represented an investment of $4.5 million in the new Pullman Company's stock, with millions more to buy 688 heavyweight cars assigned to its routes. A further $600,000 was allocated for the acquisition of Pullman's Wilmington, Delaware, shop facilities. All told, the demise of the original Pullman Company required the PRR to invest some $20 million, just to maintain the status quo. That constituted a major drain on capital, at a time when the railroad was struggling to dieselize and rebuild its physical plant after the deferred maintenance that stemmed from fifteen years of depression and war.[125]

Young's ad campaign ultimately failed to provide him with control of Pullman, or to dismantle the relationship between its successor company and the railroads. It nonetheless proved remarkably effective—although not precisely in the way he had hoped. In response to his invectives, both the PRR and the New York Central, as well as the Baltimore & Ohio, reconsidered the possibility of transcontinental rail service. The PRR's first formal proposal—to operate four trains a week to California and two more to Seattle, while sharing the eastern portion of the route with the New York Central—had taken shape in September 1945, the same month that Young attempted to dissuade Clement from buying the PRR's share of the Pullman equipment. Young's bravado nonetheless affected

Clement less than it did his counterparts on the NYC and the Santa Fe. In early November, as the district court at Philadelphia was hearing arguments from the various bidders for Pullman, the two railroads suggested that they would inaugurate a transcontinental sleeping car via the *Twentieth Century Limited* and the *Chief.*[126]

The joint NYC/Santa Fe announcement provoked an angry response from several other carriers. Clement demanded the opportunity to provide equivalent service by forwarding a car from *The Broadway Limited* to the *Chief.* Hedging his bets, he also contacted the Southern Pacific (which could offer service to Los Angeles via the Golden State Route, in cooperation with the Rock Island) and the Union Pacific (the critical link in the Chicago & North Western/UP/SP Overland Route to San Francisco). The irritation of Southern Pacific officials was also palpable. Like their PRR colleagues, they resented the Santa Fe's attempt to monopolize the western portion of the transcontinental market. In tandem with Rock Island managers, they also warned that any effort to establish through service would confirm the validity of Young's arguments. With the district court still in deliberations and the ICC not yet considering the issue, conformity to Young's agenda would make it more likely that he would gain control of Pullman. Following additional pressure from Pullman, whose attorneys were likewise fearful of giving Young too much ammunition, the Santa Fe and the NYC agreed to postpone an official announcement.[127]

The disagreements among the various companies portended further delays in the introduction of transcontinental service, something that provided Young with ample opportunity to lambaste the selfishness and ineptitude of railroad executives. In early 1946, he demanded, "Why Shouldn't America Have Through Sleeping Car Service from Coast to Coast?" Soon thereafter, he asked readers, "Are Chicago and St. Louis Part of America—or Not?" The ad campaign reached a stunning climax in March, when Young reminded travelers that "A Hog Can Cross the Country Without Changing Trains—But YOU Can't!" The accompanying drawing showed a self-satisfied, cigar-smoking swine, standing in the door of a stock car barreling past luggage-laden human travelers stranded alongside the tracks. Its outline suggested the porcine equivalent of the heavy-jowled investment bankers who also featured prominently in Young's publicity efforts.[128] "Last year alone," the ad suggested, "more than 560,000 people were forced to make annoying, time-wasting stopovers at the phantom China wall which splits America in half!" Young's inference that more than half a million people demanded transcontinental passenger service was a ludicrous exaggeration, but it was precisely the type of statement that made him so popular with the news media. Making the most of his initiative, Young ordered more than forty thousand offprints of the ad. Most went to the individuals listed in *Who's Who*, with some of the remainder going to every member of Congress and each cabinet secretary.[129]

While Young failed to gain control of Pullman, his intense focus on transcontinental service forced the PRR and other carriers to overcome their differences rather than face the possibility of a public-relations disaster. The resulting compromise resolved the impasse through the simple expedient of giving each of the rival railroads a piece of the action. Sleeping cars were soon crisscrossing the country on a variety of routes, providing human travelers far more options than those available to Young's cigar-smoking swine. Unfortunately, those services were competing for the same limited (and rapidly shrinking) pool of passengers, ensuring that none were likely to be successful. On March 18, 1946, two weeks after the first appearance of Young's "Hog" advertisement, the NYC and the Santa Fe released their (postponed) announcement that they would begin transcontinental sleeping-car service. The following day, the PRR followed suit, with plans for a through car from *The Broadway Limited* to be attached to the *Chief* at Chicago. The sleeping-car lines offered by the PRR, the NYC, and the Santa Fe would doubtless have been sufficient to satisfy consumer demand. Yet the competitive frenzy that followed soon led to a proliferation of service that had no rational economic basis and could only be justified as an exercise in public relations. On March 31, the first day of transcontinental operations, nine sleeping cars departed from two East Coast terminals (New York and Washington), with the same number heading east from Los Angeles and Oakland. They traveled over ten railroads, tacked onto a variety of established passenger trains.[130] The situation became more complicated in June, when an eleventh company joined the mix. The Rock Island moved a PRR sleeper from Chicago to an interchange with the Southern Pacific at Tucumcari, New Mexico, along the Golden State Route to Los Angeles.[131] PRR officials announced that passenger response to the new travel options had been "gratifying" and reported that the inaugural *Broadway Limited/Chief* car to Los Angeles had been sold out a month in advance.[132]

As the PRR's experience with Transcontinental Air Transport might have suggested, a heavily publicized and fully booked inaugural trip was not necessarily an indication of sustained demand. Initial results were nonetheless encouraging. In July, James Symes—in his final months

as vice president in charge of the Western Region—noted that more than four hundred passengers a day were taking advantage of transcontinental service.[133] With ten sleepers per day now leaving each coast, that suggested that on average each carried twenty passengers—close to a full load. Yet, Symes also noted, he was receiving an increasing number of complaints. Humans, it turned out, were far better equipped to articulate their dissatisfaction with their cross-country trip than had been the case with Robert Young's hogs. With new passenger equipment in short supply, officials on the various railroads were reluctant to commit too many cars to transcontinental service.[134] While some sleepers traveled on *The Broadway Limited*, others gave transcontinental travelers access to distinctly less glamorous PRR trains. Yet the principal objection involved the cumbersome process of switching cars between trains at Chicago. In one respect, the PRR was better positioned than its competitors, in that some of the sleepers bound for Oakland (via the Burlington, the Rio Grande, and the Western Pacific) merely needed to be shifted from one track to another at Union Station. In contrast, cars destined for the Santa Fe (at Dearborn Station), the Rock Island (at La Salle Street Station), and the Chicago & North Western (at its eponymous terminal) required lengthy (and costly) switching moves through congested urban areas. Many passengers left the train to wait in the station, have a meal in a restaurant, or even do some sightseeing. It was easier and quicker to take a taxi from the arrival station to the departure one rather than endure up to four hours in a sleeper—with neither heat nor air-conditioning—as it lurched its way through Chicago's yards.[135] Even the premier New York–Los Angeles trip required sixteen hours on *The Broadway Limited*, three hours in Chicago as the equipment was switched and serviced, and forty-eight hours on the Santa Fe—a long time to spend cocooned in the tight confines of a roomette or bedroom in a sleeping car. To solve those problems, Symes suggested the operation of entire trains, rather than individual sleeping cars, from coast to coast. The PRR's western connections, the SP in particular, were not in favor of the idea, and Clement balked at his railroad's share of the estimated $23.8 million for fourteen sets of new equipment.[136]

Rather than implement Symes's suggestion for complete transcontinental trains, Clement elected to expand through sleeping-car service to the St. Louis gateway. Since September 1945, Clement had been corresponding with Lewis W. Baldwin, the chief executive officer at the Missouri Pacific. The MP was the dominant passenger carrier to the southwest of St. Louis, but the company had been in receivership since 1933, and Baldwin showed little interest in through service to Texas. Officials with the Missouri–Kansas–Texas and the St. Louis–San Francisco sensed an opportunity, and in January 1946, they opened negotiations with the PRR, the NYC, and the B&O. Ignoring advice from his subordinates—who feared making an enemy of Baldwin—Clement agreed to begin discussions with the Katy and the Frisco. Hoping to provoke a reaction from Baldwin, he mentioned his plans to MP officials as well as representatives from that railroad's ally, the Wabash. By the beginning of April, as transcontinental sleeping cars began rolling through Chicago, the seven railroads had made little progress in their efforts to implement corresponding service in St. Louis. At first glance, the logistic considerations seemed less serious than in Chicago, as all the companies used the St. Louis Union Station. Yet the schedules operated by the eastern and western carriers provided for brief layovers in St. Louis. It was an ideal arrangement for passengers who could walk from one platform to another in a matter of minutes. Given the frequency of arrivals and departures at the station and the corresponding congestion of tracks serving the terminal, it would require two hours to switch cars from one train to another—too much time to enable a connection.[137]

Robert Young's genius for publicity soon encouraged the PRR and its six counterparts to overcome those obstacles. He had already taken credit for the partial elimination of "the phantom 'Chinese Wall' which divides this country," suggesting that "this breach at Chicago followed a series of Chesapeake & Ohio advertisements." Now it was time to bring the same benefits to another transcontinental gateway. Young demanded to know "Why Should St. Louis Be a Stepchild?" and provided a cartoon image of a sobbing infant—helpfully tagged with the name of the city—lying abandoned on a station platform. He noted that "the same old excuses are being offered!" by the railroads, but conveniently omitted any acknowledgment that those excuses were entirely valid. On April 23, following the C&O's annual meeting, Young issued a statement demanding service through St. Louis. He noted that the receivers of the MP and Frisco (which had also gone bankrupt during the Depression) were closely aligned with one another, "without specific approval of the Interstate Commerce Commission." In suggesting that the reorganization process, in common with the absence of transcontinental service, was "contemptuous of the public interest," Young was delivering a none-too-subtle message that he could enlist the assistance of the regulatory state to force offending carriers into line. He then filed a lawsuit against the MP, claiming that Baldwin's refusal to deliver through cars

to the NYC at St. Louis imperiled the competitive interests of the C&O—the railroad he hoped would forward them from Cincinnati to the East Coast as part of his planned *Chessie* streamliner.[138]

While Young's public-relations efforts, his announcement at the C&O annual meeting (with its barely concealed suggestion of blackmail), and the lawsuit primarily affected the MP, Clement was nonetheless sufficiently worried as to demand the prompt inauguration of St. Louis service. Baldwin died on May 14, silencing the individual who was most reluctant to launch a cooperative route to Texas. A month later, the PRR and the MP announced their plans—to the consternation of officials at the B&O and the other carriers who had been part of the earlier negotiations. On July 7, the inaugural run of the *Sunshine Special* eroded claims that St. Louis was a "stepchild." The new service "should be of the highest character," Clement informed his Missouri Pacific counterpart, Paul J. Neff, "and we want to make it so and expect to put in streamlined equipment and Diesel power." Clement was as good as his word, and the PRR ordered thirty new cars from Budd and ACF, as part of its contribution to a $3.3 million train. The Pennsylvania Railroad and the Missouri Pacific solved the switching problem at St. Louis by ensuring that the entire train, rather than individual sleeping cars, ran through the city. While it was not, strictly speaking, a transcontinental service—in that none of its cars reached the Pacific Ocean—it was nonetheless the first time that a regularly scheduled train operated in both the eastern and western halves of the United States. Westbound coach passengers could ride directly to San Antonio or Dallas/Fort Worth. More affluent travelers had even more options, with through sleepers to Dallas/Fort Worth, El Paso, San Antonio, and Galveston via Houston. One car went from New York to Mexico City via Laredo, a marathon four-day trip via the PRR, the MP, the International Great Northern, and the Ferrocarriles Nacionales de México. In addition to the main New York section, the Washington section carried through sleepers to several Texas destinations—even though the B&O had long dominated passenger operations between the nation's capital and points to the west. The train also featured what PRR officials referred to as a "divided coach"—a segregated "Jim Crow" car, necessary to comply with legal statutes in several southwestern states.[139]

The transcontinental operations offered through Chicago and St. Louis attracted media attention and blunted the force of Young's attacks against Pullman and the railroads. Favorable publicity did not equal profits, however, and the PRR soon began to curtail the scope of its through service. Declining patronage first became apparent in

Chicago, where the PRR and its partners had neither resolved the issues associated with shifting cars between terminals nor followed Symes's advice to operate through trains. There was an equally serious problem on the East Coast, where the PRR had never been competitive against the B&O along the route between Washington and Chicago. The PRR's direct service between the nation's capital and San Francisco lasted barely two years and ended in April 1948. By the following spring, the sleeping-car line between Washington and Los Angeles had also been discontinued. Next to go was the New York sleeper that followed the Rock Island/SP Golden State Route from Chicago west to Los Angeles, which last operated in July 1951.[140]

The corresponding through service via St. Louis fared only slightly better. The Missouri Pacific, the PRR's partner in the operation of the *Sunshine Special*, was engaged in stiff competition with the St. Louis–San Francisco and the Missouri–Kansas–Texas for both freight and passenger traffic. In October 1945, the Frisco and the Katy placed orders for diesel locomotives and lightweight passenger cars to reequip their two most important trains. Both debuted in May 1948. The Frisco's *Meteor* was an overnight train from St. Louis to Oklahoma City via Tulsa. The more serious threat to the MP came from the *Texas Special*, a joint Frisco/Katy train that operated between St. Louis and San Antonio. Ridership levels exceeded even the most optimistic projections, as passengers deserted the prewar heavyweight cars on the MP's *Sunshine Special* in favor of the *Texas Special*. The success of the *Texas Special* was a mixed blessing for the Pennsylvania Railroad, however. The PRR exploited the train's popularity by contributing two sleeping cars to the equipment pool, enabling through service between New York and San Antonio. Two additional cars ran from New York to Oklahoma City on the *Meteor*.[141] Painted in the vibrant red-and-silver scheme adopted by the Katy and the Frisco, they were among the most colorful passenger cars the PRR owned.[142] Unfortunately, the schedule of the *Texas Special* suffered from poor connections with trains arriving from the east. As a result, passengers in through sleeping cars endured long layovers in St. Louis, extending their journey time.[143]

The awkward connection with the *Texas Special* ensured the PRR's continued reliance on the *Sunshine Special*, the through train operated in conjunction with the Missouri Pacific. The MP's management, however, responded to the competition posed by the Katy and the Frisco in a manner detrimental to the interests of the Pennsylvania Railroad. New diesels and passenger cars were on order, and on August 15, 1948, the MP replaced the heavyweight *Sunshine*

Special with the streamlined, lightweight *Texas Eagle*.[144] Given the intensity of competition with the Katy and the Frisco, MP officials were understandably preparing to make the most of their investment in new equipment— even at the expense of ending through-train operations with the Pennsylvania Railroad. Several months before the *Texas Eagle* entered service, they informed the PRR that they would only permit the exchange of sleeping cars at St. Louis, beginning April 25, 1948. After just two years, the sole complete train to break through Young's "phantom 'Chinese Wall'" had run its last miles. In its place, the PRR offered eleven sleeping cars, painted in the blue-and-gray scheme that matched the MP equipment used on the *Texas Eagle*. They operated on an aptly named new train—*The Penn Texas*—between New York and St. Louis, where they were transferred to the Missouri Pacific.[145]

By the early 1950s, it was clear that the hoped-for resurgence of long-distance passenger rail travel had not materialized and that transcontinental service was no longer viable. By the early 1950s, a new generation of aircraft could fly nonstop between New York and the West Coast, turning a journey of days into one of only a few hours.[146] The Civil Aeronautics Board, whose members wanted to encourage the development of commercial aviation, authorized a one-way transcontinental fare of $80. That was roughly the same price that a passenger would spend to endure three days in a railroad coach seat and far less than the price of a berth in a through sleeping car. The speed of air travel, moreover, worked to the benefit of both passengers and the airlines. A single plane could easily make a transcontinental round trip in a single day. In contrast, the PRR and its allies needed thirty-two sleepers to maintain daily service between New York or Washington and San Francisco. The end of the economic boom associated with the Korean War caused severe financial problems for the railroads and forced many Americans to curtail their travel plans. By late 1956, occupancy rates on through cars between New York and California ranged from a respectable 58 percent to an intolerable 37 percent. Yet it was the far more severe recession beginning in 1957 that ensured that continued operation of through sleepers was no longer tenable. By the end of October, all the transcontinental routes through Chicago had been suspended. Service through St. Louis continued a little longer and was generally well patronized during the winter vacation season in the Southwest. At the beginning of the 1960s, passengers could still travel directly between New York and Houston, Dallas/Fort Worth, or San Antonio without leaving their sleeping car.[147] In June 1961, however, the PRR and the MP elected to discontinue all the remaining through cars. Despite catastrophic declines in passenger traffic, interline movements of PRR passenger trains continued east of the Mississippi River.[148] Yet after fifteen years of effort, the Pennsylvania Railroad, its partners, and its competitors had finally acknowledged that Robert Young's vision of coast-to-coast passenger operations was not meant to be.[149]

The Decline of Passenger Service

The disappointing performance of transcontinental service was only one small facet of the passenger-traffic crisis facing the Pennsylvania Railroad. The PRR carried more passengers than any other railroad—nearly a sixth of the national total—and suffered accordingly. With the war over and most veterans discharged from military service, PRR executives expected that intercity passenger-traffic patronage would decline from its 1944 peak of 125.2 million. In that respect, the decrease to 120.8 million in 1945 and 96.0 million in 1946 offered scant cause for concern. Yet the numbers continued to fall, to 73.4 million in 1947, 63.4 million in 1948, and 52.0 million in 1949—the last year in which the Pennsylvania Railroad would even come close to transporting 50 million intercity passengers. Intercity passenger revenues had peaked in 1944 at $260.9 million and in 1946 were still at a respectable $207.2 million—sufficient to generate almost $790,000 in net income. By 1949, however, passenger earnings stood at only $149.3 million, representing a loss of $49.4 million. That meant that more than 57 percent of the net income generated from still-profitable freight operations went to offset passenger losses. It was money that could not be paid to investors or used to maintain the railroad's facilities and equipment.[150]

In early 1949, after two successive years of passenger deficits, PRR officials considered several mechanisms for rectifying the situation. One alternative was to eliminate as many marginal trains as possible and concentrate passengers on those that were left in service. After the middle of January, The Clevelander and The Akronite no longer operated as second sections, east of Pittsburgh, and the same was true of The Pennsylvania Limited and The St. Louisan. The simultaneous termination of the short-lived Steel King was more troubling, for it suggested that travelers preferred automobiles and would not be returning to the rails. By May, further cuts enabled the PRR to eliminate an additional 1.25 million passenger-train miles per year, equivalent to a further 3 percent reduction since the January discontinuances. Train curtailments did not keep pace with declining demand, however. Between 1948 and 1949, for example, the number of passengers carried decreased

by 18.0 percent and passenger miles by 17.7 percent, but the PRR reduced passenger-train miles by barely half of that amount, 9.5 percent.[151]

Increased passenger fares did little to resolve the deficit problem. In November 1949, the Interstate Commerce Commission voted 6–4 to increase rates for interstate coach seats (from 3 to 3.375 cents per mile) and Pullman berths (from 4 to 4.5 cents per mile). The 12.5 percent increase was the third since the end of the war. The higher fares did not apply to commutation tickets, which accounted for 11.6 percent of the PRR's passenger miles in 1949. Nor did the ICC adjust intrastate rates, except in Illinois and Michigan—states where the Pennsylvania Railroad handled comparatively little local passenger traffic. With the inclusion of the federal tax (which meant that passengers would pay 3.887 cents per mile of coach travel), fares were now the highest that they had ever been in the history of rail travel.[152] A one-way coach ticket between New York and Chicago that had previously cost $27.30 would now be $30.71, while space in a sleeping car increased from $36.35 to $40.89. PRR officials estimated that they would receive an additional $8 million in annual passenger revenue, part of the $37.8 million gain for the eastern railroads as a group. Railroad officials discounted the possibility that the steadily rising cost of travel might encourage customers to shift to automobiles, buses, or aircraft. PRR officials acknowledged that in a worst-case scenario, they might lose as much as 5.5 percent of their passenger traffic—although they stressed that 2 percent was the more likely figure—and their counterparts on the NYC predicted that there would be no appreciable decline in business.[153]

ICC commissioner Charles D. Mahaffie, who had voted against the increase, was far more pessimistic, suggesting that the higher rates would drive so many travelers to competing modes of transportation that the carriers would suffer a net decrease in revenue. Mahaffie urged the railroads to consider reductions in ticket prices and claimed that the steep reduction in traffic since the previous rate hike, in July 1948, provided "further warning that measures other than additional increases in fares are necessary if the steady decline in passenger revenues of these roads is to be stopped." He was perhaps correct in his assertion that "vacant seats rather than inadequate fares are the prime cause of passenger deficits," yet he provided little additional advice as to how those seats might be filled. The ICC could not control the pace of highway construction, nor did it possess the authority to regulate commercial aviation. As automobile and air travel became cheaper and more convenient, however, neither Mahaffie nor any of his fellow commissioners were yet willing to accept the new reality, that long-distance rail travel had become an uncompetitive anachronism.[154]

The reluctance of ICC commissioners to authorize rate increases and the discussions among PRR executives regarding the profitability of passenger operations reflected an increasingly contentious debate over the true cost of providing that service. Some expenses were easy to calculate and were clearly associated with passenger operations. Typically referred to as out-of-pocket or above-the-rails costs, they included the maintenance of passenger cars and locomotives assigned to passenger service, crew wages, dining car supplies, and other onboard items. Other expenses were more difficult to allocate. Passenger trains obviously produced wear and tear on track and bridges, although hardly to the same extent as heavily laden coal or ore trains. Passenger trains were typically faster than their freight counterparts, however, and that speed imposed significant costs in the form of higher track-maintenance standards and signaling systems that were ill-suited to freight operations. Dispatchers struggled to route long, slow freight trains and short, fast passenger services over the same tracks, impeding overall operating efficiency and—to the frustration of Clement, Symes, and other executives—all too frequently delaying the freight shipments that paid the bills. The PRR, like the New York Central, was blessed with a four-track main line over its core territory, permitting the unimpeded movement of freight and passenger trains in each direction. Yet that blessing was also a curse, given the associated tax liability and the expense of maintaining so many tracks when, in the absence of passenger service, two or three would have been sufficient.[155]

The extent to which the elimination of a single passenger train—or even passenger service in its entirety—would affect the PRR's overall profitability was uncertain. The cancellation of a specific train (such as The Steel King) would of course eliminate the out-of-pocket costs allocated solely to that service. Assuming every passenger who had patronized The Steel King could be accommodated in empty seats on the many other trains linking New York and Pittsburgh, the savings could be considerable. If additional coaches had to be attached to those other trains, then the net gain would be reduced. Some travelers, dismayed at the reduction in service, might well choose an alternative form of transport, and the resulting decline in ticket sales would further erode the benefits associated with the train's cancellation.

Determining the precise reduction in fully allocated costs associated with the discontinuance of The Steel King was an even more difficult proposition. There would be

less wear and tear on the rails as well as fewer tasks for dispatchers and tower operators to perform—but there was no possibility of removing one main line track or of eliminating those employees. The same could be said for coach cleaners at Sunnyside Yard and ticket agents who worked at stations and reservation bureaus. Those facilities would still require staffing and maintenance to accommodate passengers traveling on other trains, and the taxes on that real estate would still have to be paid. The expensive operation of major urban terminals—which, aside from the World War II years, never operated at anything close to full capacity—constituted a significant portion of overhead costs that were allocated to each train. Perversely, discontinuing The Steel King would increase the indirect expense associated with the operation of the remaining passenger trains that shared the PRR's tracks, stations, and other passenger facilities, regardless of whether the overall level of patronage increased, decreased, or remained the same.[156]

The debate over the true extent of the PRR's passenger losses began in the summer of 1949. Charles Mahaffie, the ICC commissioner, asked President Clement to speculate on the railroad's cost savings if all passenger service were to be eliminated. Clement furnished data indicating that the company would sacrifice $216.7 million in revenue but avoid $252.4 million in expenditures—producing a $35.7 million increase in net railway operating income. Based on the railroad's 1948 financial results, a focus solely on freight transportation would translate into a 38.5 percent gain in net income, vastly increasing the amount that could be reinvested in the physical plant or paid out in dividends. There was little likelihood that regulatory authorities would permit the PRR to discontinue all intercity and commuter passenger service. The figures nonetheless indicated the danger that passenger travel posed to the overall financial health of the railroads and encouraged further discussions of the issue.[157]

In the years that followed, railroad executives and ICC officials were unable to form a consensus as to the true cost of passenger service. Six different accounting measures—each of which had proponents and detractors—provided widely varying figures. In 1950, for example, national railroad passenger revenues exceeded solely allocated, out-of-pocket costs by $136.2 million, suggesting that passenger traffic had generated a substantial profit. By that measure, the railroads had consistently generated positive returns on their passenger operations and would continue to do so until they incurred a small loss (just over $1 million) in 1953. At the other extreme, however, fully allocated costs for passenger service produced a staggering $508.5 million loss in 1950, part of a string of annual deficits that had continued unabated since 1946.[158] Railroad executives who desired to curtail passenger service naturally favored the more pessimistic assessment, while travelers and representatives from trackside communities were equally adamant in their assertion that most trains remained profitable. In 1950, nearly $645 million separated those divergent perspectives, and it initially seemed that little compromise was possible.[159]

The accounting standards mandated by the Interstate Commerce Commission, which had remained largely unchanged since the passage of the 1906 Hepburn Act, provided little guidance for the calculation of the expenses associated with passenger traffic. The ICC required all railroads to allocate their expenditures to one of four categories: those related solely to freight service; those attributed solely to passenger, express, and mail traffic; those that were common to both freight and passenger operations; and those that were associated with activities other than transportation. The first two categories—which reflected the out-of-pocket costs for either freight or passenger business—were relatively easy to calculate, and the fourth category was of little consequence. The attribution of shared expenditures to either freight or passenger trains was at the heart of the issue, and ICC commissioners were unable or unwilling to articulate a consistent policy on the matter.[160] As ICC examiner Howard Hosmer observed, "The methods of making such apportionments necessarily are more or less theoretical or arbitrary and therefore controversial."[161]

Given the vexed nature of railroad cost accounting, the easiest trains to discontinue were the ones that did not cover out-of-pocket costs. It would be difficult for even the most ardent proponents of passenger service to deny that those trains imposed a burden on the railroads, and by avoiding the issue of shared costs, it was equally difficult for the ICC to assert that curtailment would reduce overall net earnings from freight and passenger operations. Beginning as early as 1947, PRR executives adopted a policy of gradually discontinuing the relatively small number of trains that at that time failed to recoup their operating costs. Less than three months after his appointment as the vice president in charge of operations, Symes expressed his concerns regarding money-losing passenger trains that were eroding the earnings of freight service. In June 1949, as the railroad was still reequipping its Blue Ribbon Fleet, Symes suggested that drastic cuts in intercity passenger service might add more than $35 million to the bottom line each year. President Clement, supported by Franklin, nonetheless insisted that only about 15 percent of

passenger-train mileage failed to cover out-of-pocket costs, with commuter traffic representing 40 percent of that relatively small number. By that accounting, the Pennsylvania Railroad made money on 91 percent of its long-haul passenger trains. Clement reminded his subordinates of the substantial gap that separated the costs that were solely attributable to a specific passenger train and those shared expenditures that could rightfully be allocated to passenger operations. "If we take off a passenger train, we actually save about $3.00 per train mile" in above-the-rails costs, Clement emphasized, "yet that train must earn about $6.00 per train mile to pay its full cost under the I.C.C. formula," one that was based on fully allocated expense. It would not be easy to convince regulators, passengers, and politicians that a train earning more than $3 but less than $6 per mile was losing money. For the next decade, executives made little headway in their efforts to persuade the ICC and state regulatory agencies that passenger services were inexorably pulling the company toward financial ruin.[162]

By the spring of 1951, Symes had abandoned all hope that intercity passenger service might ever become profitable. The Pennsylvania Railroad was well on its way to incurring a $71.7 million passenger deficit—the highest in the company's history—and one that would consume 54.7 percent of freight earnings. Walter Franklin was now president, and Symes warned him that passenger operations had "changed from an asset part of our business, to a very serious liability part of it—so much so that it is difficult for the other principal arteries of traffic to offset the continuing and increasing losses that are occurring in its handling." Symes had lost all patience with the long-standing assumption that public convenience and necessity required the railroads to use freight revenues to subsidize passenger losses. The "excess pricing of the profitable [freight] portion of our traffic, in order to subsidize the unprofitable [passenger] portion thereof," he emphasized, "could very well lead to eventual destruction of the industry."[163]

The unsustainable nature of passenger deficits encouraged Symes to accelerate the ongoing curtailment of services. As early as March 1951, he informed Edgar E. Ernest, the chief of passenger transportation, of the need to eliminate 5,000 passenger-train miles per day—equivalent to more than 1.8 million miles a year. In June, representatives of the Transportation, Traffic, and Accounting Departments met to develop strategies for bringing the passenger-service operating ratio below the break-even point, based on the ICC formula for fully allocated costs. One of their objectives was to determine ways to generate an additional $50 million in passenger revenue based on the existing level of service. They also performed a cost/

benefit analysis on the elimination of as many as 270 inter-city trains, more than a third of those in operation. Such a wholesale reduction had the potential to lower the passenger operating ratio from 115.5 to 110.7—not enough to solve the problem but at least sufficient to curtail some of the drag on freight earnings. As Symes acknowledged, however, that figure reflected fully allocated costs. A calculation based only on the out-of-pocket expenditures assigned solely to passenger-train operation yielded a very different result and indicated that the reduction in passenger revenues would exceed any savings in above-the-rails costs by at least $2 million. Those who opposed train discontinuances, and their allies at state and federal regulatory agencies, were likely to emphasize the latter set of numbers as a reason to block the proposed cuts. As before, the safer course of action involved requests to terminate specific trains that did not cover their out-of-pocket costs. In the two years since Symes and Franklin had first discussed that subject, the number of trains in that category had increased from 9 percent to 15 percent of the total—but that was still too few to make much of a difference in the bleak overall equation.[164]

Despite the constraints imposed by regulatory practices and accounting standards, Symes and his colleagues eliminated as many underperforming passenger trains as possible. The principal targets were local trains and those serving markets—such as Baltimore, Washington, and Cleveland—where the PRR was at a disadvantage compared to other carriers. The Harrisburg–Baltimore sections of many east–west trains disappeared. So, too, did the commuter service that a PRR rail car had provided between Cleveland and Hudson, Ohio. Perhaps the most disheartening change involved the consolidation of two of the PRR's most famous trains. Since its inauguration in 1939, *The Trail Blazer* had been an early example of the all-coach streamliners that, railroad executives had hoped, would provide a taste of luxury to middle-class travelers and lure them away from the highways. Along with *The Jeffersonian*, *The Trail Blazer* was one of the first trains to benefit from the massive postwar expenditure in new passenger equipment. So had the all-Pullman *General*; by the summer of 1949, its new cars and faster schedule had made it second only to *The Broadway Limited* along the PRR's route between New York and Chicago. Passenger traffic nonetheless declined so rapidly that within a few years PRR officials had combined *The Trail Blazer* and *The General* during periods of low demand. That status became permanent in September 1951, and the railroad's premier coach streamliner and elite-status limited lost their separate identities.[165]

In some cases, however, state regulatory agencies blocked the elimination of unprofitable local service. The Pennsylvania Public Utility Commission and the New Jersey Board of Public Utility Commissioners were among the most stringent in the nation, and a substantial portion of the PRR's passenger mileage was in those two states. In January 1951, for example, the New Jersey agency denied permission to discontinue passenger service on that state's portion of the Belvidere Division between Trenton and Stroudsburg, Pennsylvania. The commissioners did not question the PRR's data, which showed substantial ongoing deficits. Rather, they gave preference to the needs of local communities, where many residents testified that they relied on the trains to reach Trenton and the PRR main line. Regulators asserted that the railroad had treated the passenger operation as "an unwanted stepchild" and had attempted to drive away business rather than attract new passengers. It was a refrain that had become increasingly familiar to PRR executives and one that would persist, in various guises, for many years to come.[166]

The Pennsylvania Public Utility Commission was likewise reluctant to permit train discontinuances, a policy that extended to intrastate portions of long-distance services. In 1948, in response to the Pennsylvania Railroad's initial postwar train reductions, the PUC asserted the right to block the cuts. The matter came to a head a decade later, when PRR officials attempted to eliminate the combined *Cincinnati Limited/Red Arrow* and the eastbound runs of *The Pennsylvania Limited* and *The Clevelander*. The Public Utility Commission required continued service between Philadelphia and Pittsburgh, the easternmost and westernmost stops on routes that had once spanned several states. They continued to operate as "ghost trains," typically consisting of a locomotive and a single coach, unlisted in public timetables and unannounced at stations. Patronage was unsurprisingly almost nonexistent, but the daily losses of $1,900 continued unabated.[167]

The cuts continued into 1952 and 1953. By February 1952, Symes—now the executive vice president—along with Edgar Ernest and James Newell, the new vice president in charge of operations, had developed a plan to shed as many passenger miles as possible. That year's goal was a reduction of fifteen thousand train miles per day, three times the target that Symes had established a year earlier. Thanks to the latest round of cuts, between August 1946 and August 1952, the PRR had trimmed its total passenger-train miles by 37 percent. *The Broadway Limited* remained popular, and in June the PRR celebrated its fiftieth anniversary, hosting veterans of the 1902 inaugural run. The full dieselization of intercity passenger trains, also achieved in

In June 1952, the eastbound *Broadway Limited* broke through a banner celebrating the train's inauguration fifty years earlier. Women in period costumes provided a suitable atmosphere, while several enginemen who were in service in 1902 enjoyed cab rides as far as Fort Wayne. Neither the festivities nor the cosmetic upgrades to *The Broadway*, undertaken a few years later, could remedy the rapid decline of postwar passenger service on the Pennsylvania Railroad. *Conrail Photographs, Hagley Museum & Library, acc. 1993.231.*

1952, lowered operating costs and eliminated passenger complaints about smoke and cinders from steam locomotives. More gratifying to Symes and other executives was the reduction in the passenger deficit to $60.5 million, more than 15 percent lower than the previous year's dismal record. Passenger losses now consumed only 44.7 percent of freight earnings, but managers hoped for better the following year. In April 1953, the all-coach *Jeffersonian* suffered the same fate as *The Trail Blazer*. Five years after

receiving all-new equipment—including the family recreation cars—*The Jeffersonian*'s coaches were added to *The "Spirit of St. Louis,"* which lost its status as an all-Pullman streamliner.[168]

While managers uniformly agreed that it was imperative to consolidate passenger services in the face of declining demand, they acknowledged that that policy alone would not be sufficient to stem the PRR's losses. In June 1954, confronting a difficult situation, Symes reminded the PRR's employees that "we have about one billion dollars invested in that phase of our operations. We can't simply afford to scrap that investment . . . you can't make money closing up the shop." The removal of individual trains, even those that operated at a loss, deprived the company of revenues. Of greater importance, regulatory agencies were unlikely to permit the abandonment of major passenger corridors or the elimination of service to large communities. As Symes had once told Franklin, "Train withdrawals or consolidations in themselves is [*sic*] not the answer" for reducing passenger deficits. Nor, he admitted, would it "be possible

By the early 1950s, PRR executives had concluded that most intercity passenger service would never become profitable. The sole exception was the route between New York and Washington, where heavy patronage justified the acquisition of new equipment for *The Congressional*, shown here behind GG1 #4909 in 1952. *Budd Negatives, Railroad Museum of Pennsylvania, PHMC.*

to make any substantial reduction in operating expenses in passenger service." Symes dismissed some suggestions for minimizing losses, such as increasing mail rates by a third or express rates by 90 percent. The ICC's most recent adjustment, in December 1950, had raised compensation for carrying the mail by nearly 50 percent, and additional benefits were unlikely.[169]

To make the best of a bad situation, Symes and other PRR executives attempted to improve service on a few select long-distance trains that remained reasonably well patronized while incrementally eliminating as many local and branch-line services as possible. Beginning in 1952, the company assigned eight supervisors of service to the premier trains of the Blue Ribbon Fleet. Their job, according to traffic vice president Fred Carpi, involved "getting acquainted with passengers on trains, obtaining suggestions for improving service, and determining whether additional refinements might be made." Each service supervisor rode a specific train, twice a week, from origin to destination, inspecting every aspect of the equipment and operations and ensuring that employees were courteous and helpful. The initiative nonetheless conflicted with an increased emphasis on cost reductions, particularly the curtailment of dining car expenditures—all of which was likely to provoke additional complaints from dissatisfied patrons.[170]

The railroad's most successful passenger operations linked New York and Washington, and executives paid particular attention to that heavily trafficked corridor. In the summer of 1948, when the PRR's passenger traffic posted an overall operating ratio of 111.7 percent, service between New York and Philadelphia generated an operating ratio of 63.4 percent. The results for the New York–Washington market—59.2 percent—were even better. By the early 1950s, executives concluded that the densely populated East Coast corridor offered the only opportunity to earn a profit in passenger service and was therefore worthy of additional investment. Accordingly, in March 1952, the PRR reequipped *The Congressional* and *The Senator* with sixty-four modern cars provided by the Budd Company. Built at a cost of $11 million, they were the first passenger cars in regular PRR service to retain their unpainted stainless-steel exteriors, save for a red letterboard. Each of the two *Congressional* sets featured eight coaches (four on each side of a coffee-shop car), a twin-unit dining car, an observation lounge, and six parlor cars. One of the parlor cars contained conference rooms, equipped with radio telephones, so that politicians and business executives could hold meetings en route. *The Senator*, which continued north to Boston, featured similar equipment but lacked the all-room parlor car and used a more conventional single-unit diner. On both trains, the interiors embodied a patriotic motif, which PRR officials suggested would evoke "the atmosphere and events in the lives of national heroes in colonial times, and historic landmarks along the route." The parlor cars employed names such as *Betsy Ross, General Lafayette,* and *Paul Revere,* while the observations, named in honor of George and Martha Washington, Ben Franklin, and Alexander Hamilton, carried the familiar keystone drumhead enclosing thirteen blue stars. Even the interior colors, such as Bunker Hill red, alluded to the American Revolution. The March 17 inauguration of the new *Senator* was important enough to draw Alban W. Barkley, the vice president of the United States, who watched his wife smash a champagne bottle across the nose of a GG1 locomotive.[171]

The combination of new equipment, smooth track, and rapid travel times between closely spaced city pairs increased ridership by 9 percent. It was a gratifying result, but not one that could be repeated elsewhere on the PRR system. The 64 cars employed on *The Congressional* and *The Senator* represented a substantial investment. Yet their numbers were small, compared to the 212 sleepers, 144 long-distance coaches, 40 diners, and 23 lounge and observation lounge cars the PRR had acquired since the end of World War II, for assignment to money-losing western routes. Even on the nation's busiest passenger rail corridor, moreover, the increase in ridership and revenues was only temporary. Patronage along the route between New York and Washington fell by half between 1952 and 1963, even as the population of those cities increased, and as early as February 1954, the PRR announced the elimination of seven passenger trains in that corridor, owing to insufficient demand.[172] When he lauded the PRR's investment in *The Congressional* and *The Senator,* journalist Ward Howe reminded travelers that thanks to the Korean War "defense restrictions on the use of metals, these are likely to be the last completely new passenger trains to appear on an American railroad for some time." It was a prophetic statement, and the shiny modern cars on the two trains represented the PRR's final significant purchase of conventional intercity passenger equipment.[173]

Curtailing Passenger Service

The efforts of PRR executives to lower costs and improve the efficiency of passenger service engendered a long and momentous relationship between the Pennsylvania Railroad and Robert Heller & Associates. Robert Heller was a management engineer and efficiency expert based in Cleveland, Ohio. His most significant project, undertaken between 1935 and 1937, involved a comprehensive reorganization of the corporate structure at US Steel. Heller also served as a consultant for the Ford Motor Company, E. I. du Pont de Nemours, the Columbia Broadcasting System, and the US Post Office. In August 1951, he completed a study, "The Future of the Pullman Company," commissioned by that firm's managers in a desperate attempt to respond to the postwar decline in passenger travel. In the aftermath of the 1944 dissolution of Pullman, Incorporated, the Pennsylvania Railroad and the New York Central were each part owners of the Pullman Company, ensuring that their executives were aware of Heller's services. "It would seem," Symes informed Franklin in September 1951, "with this transportation background, they would be well equipped to conduct an exhaustive passenger study on the Pennsylvania Railroad."[174]

By early 1952, NYC executives were even more determined than their PRR colleagues to solicit advice on ways to improve—or eliminate—passenger service. At a time when they were requesting increases of as much as 30 percent for commuter fares, NYC officials were endeavoring to defend the poor performance of their long-distance trains. The flagship *Twentieth Century Limited* was late half of the time, and only a third of the trips made by the *Empire State Express* arrived on schedule. The New York Public Service Commission responded to widespread complaints by reopening a 1942 investigation into the NYC's passenger service.[175] When hearings began on February 5, 1952, Public Service commissioner Spencer B. Eddy emphasized that he had no patience for "reasons or excuses" and suggested that he might force the NYC to reduce its passenger fares. "If there is no remedy for the problem, and we have to reconcile ourselves to second-class service," Eddy told NYC counsel Harold McLean, "then perhaps you should be prepared to show why you should not be required to accept second-class fares." McLean acknowledged that he was "gravely concerned" about the situation and that the company's executives would take prompt and decisive action. Executives announced they would cooperate with Heller & Associates in an effort to "increase passenger revenues, tailor service more closely to the public needs and wishes, and put it on a sound economic footing."[176]

Franklin had been considering Symes's endorsement of Heller since October 1951, and the New York Central's involvement made possible a coordinated endeavor that also included the Baltimore & Ohio. PRR representatives agreed to terms on January 23, 1952, and over the next two years paid Heller almost $1 million in consultancy fees—part of nearly $5 million collected from the three railroads.[177] Heller began by studying the passenger operations of the Pennsylvania Railroad and the New York Central in the Chicago, Louisville, and Cincinnati markets. He and his staff then expanded their coverage to include all the PRR's passenger and commuter services and by 1954 had begun to evaluate industrial-engineering methods for the maintenance of passenger and freight cars.[178]

Heller's report, presented to the PRR directors in June 1954, acknowledged that none of the companies would be able to regain traffic lost to automobiles and airplanes and that the railroad share of the intercity passenger market would continue to decline. Heller emphasized cost containment rather than the generation of new business. A surplus of passenger cars—many of which predated World War II—ensured that maintenance-of-equipment expenditures consumed nearly half of passenger revenues. Cavernous stations and other facilities that were far too large for the number of patrons suggested the wisdom of consolidating the three railroads' tracks and terminal facilities. Heller emphasized that the companies could also reduce both routes and train frequencies, cost-saving measures that were likely to further decrease demand for rail

travel. Of the PRR's few remaining passengers, 80 percent traveled between cities with more than one hundred thousand residents, indicating that the company should provide low-cost basic coach service in those markets, with sleeper and parlor-car operations reserved for the small number of trains that remained popular with affluent patrons.[179]

Despite the pessimistic tone of the Heller report, there were three general areas where executives might at least minimize the damage. First, it was clear that both the reduction in demand and the presence of competition dictated changes in the pricing of passenger services. It would be advisable, Heller suggested, to increase fares on some routes with high operating ratios. If there were few transportation alternatives, then the traffic would stay captive to the rails, and deficits could be reduced. In a more likely situation, where travelers possessed other options, the higher fares would drive away business that was not worth keeping, facilitating the consolidation of trains or even the outright abandonment of service. On some segments—such as the PRR between New York and Washington and the NYC between Manhattan and Albany and perhaps west to Buffalo—there was still considerable potential for high-density traffic. In such circumstances, selective fare reductions might win back travelers from other modes of transportation. There would nonetheless have to be a corresponding decrease in operating costs, something that would only be possible with the development of lightweight, high-capacity passenger cars. Mail and express traffic, which was still profitable, could be segregated from passenger operations. That practice would permit the removal of some passenger trains while increasing patronage on those that remained by expediting their schedules.[180]

Second, the study noted that for many decades each of the trunk lines had been dominant in specific passenger markets. In the context of declining demand, it made little sense for all three carriers to serve every major destination in the East and Midwest. The New York Improvements and the electrification program of the 1930s had given the PRR a strong advantage along the route linking New York and Washington, and Heller accordingly recommended that the B&O terminate the *Royal Blue* trains and other passenger services between those two cities. The Baltimore & Ohio would likewise yield Chicago to the PRR and the NYC. The *Capitol Limited* would operate no farther west than Pittsburgh—where it would terminate at the PRR's station rather than the one operated by the B&O. In return, the B&O would have a monopoly on travel between Baltimore/Washington and St. Louis. The PRR would continue to operate trains between New York/Philadelphia and both St. Louis and Chicago, as well as maintaining the Washington sections of trains serving the Windy City. The bulk of the PRR's Blue Ribbon Fleet would disappear, with only two trains—most likely *The General* and the all-Pullman *Broadway Limited*—linking New York and Chicago. The New York Central, long the preferred carrier between New York and Chicago, would retain that dominance and likewise control access to the intermediate lakeshore cities.[181]

The third and most far-reaching element of the Heller report addressed the PRR's organizational structure. It noted that both the Traffic and Transportation Departments, which shared authority over passenger service, were primarily oriented to the solicitation and movement of freight. Station operations were the responsibility of individual division superintendents, ensuring that the condition of passenger facilities varied from outstanding to deplorable. To overcome the problems caused by divided responsibilities, Heller recommended that the PRR combine control over passenger operations in one department that would be coequal with the Transportation and Traffic Departments. A new vice president of passenger services would be responsible for such diverse activities as sales, advertising, and onboard conditions as well as Pullman, dining car, and mail and express operations. Out of necessity, the Transportation Department would retain oversight of the movement of passenger trains as well as their upkeep. That would still help to reduce operating and maintenance costs, Heller suggested, because the Passenger Service Department would be charged with—and held accountable for—the expenses that it subcontracted to the Transportation Department.[182]

The Heller report was in most respects dead on arrival, owing to regulatory constraints and resistance from key PRR personnel. Fred Carpi, the vice president in charge of traffic, rejected the suggestions out of hand. He asserted that any proposals to change passenger service should be handled within the company rather than by outside consultants. Carpi insisted that earlier experiments with variable ticket prices had not improved passenger revenues and suggested that such changes would violate the long-standing requirement, imposed by the ICC and by state agencies, for a standard per-mile rate. "The regulatory bodies will never tolerate a 'hodge-podge' system [of fares] for permanent application," Carpi observed. He held a similarly dim view of Heller's suggestion for efforts to promote passenger travel. "Conceding that competitive factors have changed over the past 50 years," he suggested, "there is still no warrant in transferring our emphasis from

personal solicitation to newspaper and magazine advertising. We could not possibly afford the same advertising ratio to operating revenues as maintained by the airlines." Carpi likewise disagreed with Heller's proposal to segregate profitable mail traffic from passenger service. He labeled the idea "more theoretical than practical" and claimed that the post office would not accept the delays necessary to accumulate an entire train's worth of mail and express cars.[183]

Some managers, including operating vice president Jim Newell, supported Heller's mail-service plan, and he suggested that Carpi was being unduly pessimistic. Yet Newell was strongly critical of other aspects of the report, particularly the recommendation for faster schedules, utilizing passenger trains unencumbered by mail and express traffic. The increased speed—both in absolute terms and in comparison with slow-moving freight trains—would make life more difficult for Newell and other operating officials. Newell also reacted with alarm to Heller's suggestions for a comprehensive reorganization of train operations, one that would diminish his authority. "There is nothing to be secured from the proposal that cannot also be secured by proper personnel and proper operation of our present organization," Newell emphasized in December 1952, and he stressed that hiring and promotion of "men with initiative, vision and ingenuity" would resolve most of the problems.[184]

By early February 1953, however, Newell acknowledged that "developments in the interim" caused him to reverse his initial position. He noted that he was "now wholeheartedly in favor of progressing this organization set-up as quickly as possible" and that the Heller recommendations "should be carried forward actively and vigorously on a continuing basis." Newell acknowledged that "over the years our people have become too set in their approach and their attitude" and that "a new organization set-up . . . should bring a fresh approach to [the PRR's] problems." His change of heart probably stemmed from a realization that both of his superiors—Franklin and Symes—concluded that Heller's recommendations had merit. While relaying Newell's concerns to Franklin, Symes emphasized that the New York Central implemented its version of the Heller study, reducing passenger losses and allowing operating personnel to focus more effectively on freight service. Convinced, Newell acceded to the March 1953 reassignment of Walter W. Patchell, the vice president in charge of real estate and taxation, to the newly established office of special vice president, responsible for minimizing the passenger deficit. As his previous title suggested, Patchell was less interested in increasing passenger revenues than in providing the data necessary to demonstrate to regulatory authorities why more trains should be discontinued.[185]

Despite their commissioning of the Heller report, PRR executives were unwilling to implement its most important recommendations. Beginning in July 1953 and continuing into the autumn, PRR officials engaged in discussions with representatives from the New York Central and the Baltimore & Ohio. Long-standing competitive impulses among the railroads nonetheless made it difficult to rationalize passenger service. Some of the opposition came from Newell and other operating officials, who balked at the prospect of coordinating train movements among multiple carriers. Traffic personnel reacted instinctively against the allocation of their passenger business to competing railroads. They also insisted that the elimination of familiar services—no matter how poorly patronized—would alienate freight shippers. Representatives from the Baltimore & Ohio did not want to pay the cost of a connection with the PRR in Pittsburgh. In October 1955, they withdrew from discussions. With rail travel in steep decline, executives at the two remaining companies increasingly sensed that the wholesale abandonment of service rather than greater coordination between the carriers offered the best mechanism for reducing deficits.[186]

In the near term, because railroad executives were unwilling to abandon service to any market, even on marginal routes, each carrier retained highly unprofitable trains that reduced the average performance of each system's overall passenger operations. Accordingly, PRR managers possessed an even stronger incentive to eliminate trains and to curtail amenities on those that remained. Newell reminded Symes that it was a mistake to continue policies whereby "personnel responsible for running passenger trains may frequently be judged more by the number of complaints received than by economy of operations" and reminded him that "there will be times when every customer will not get everything that he wants." In practical terms, that meant that extra equipment would not be assigned to trains in anticipation of peak demand, even if passengers ended up standing in the aisles. Lightly patronized routes would lose Pullman and dining car services, a situation that was bound to increase customer dissatisfaction. Furthermore, in accord with Heller's recommendations, PRR officials suggested that Patchell attempt to eliminate passenger trains to communities with fewer than one hundred thousand residents while preserving both coach and Pullman options for large cities—so long as the company could "economically afford to do so." Newell emphasized that "the size of the town does not necessarily reflect the true importance of the

locality to the railroad," suggesting the need to retain some marginal passenger markets to appease major freight shippers and prevent them from complaining to politicians or regulatory officials. He nonetheless identified *The Pittsburgher*—a train popular with steel-industry executives—as one of many that should lose its Pullman sleeping cars, even if it entailed a reduction in freight revenues.[187]

Despite the willingness of Pennsylvania Railroad executives to maintain unprofitable service as a favor to valued shippers, they concluded that the long-distance passenger market had disappeared, just as branch-line traffic had evaporated during the 1920s. "Now I, for one," Symes declared in September 1955, "don't hold out much promise for long-haul rail passenger business—and by that I mean distances of over one thousand miles. Realistically, the time element is too much of a factor in favor of air service." He was more optimistic regarding "the potential mass travel available between metropolitan areas for shorter distances, with comfortable 'sit-up' trains" stripped of such expensive amenities as diners and sleeping cars. That approach, Symes emphasized, would only be successful if the PRR and the other carriers could develop new equipment "with a much lower capital investment per seat, plus the lower maintenance cost," enabling fare reductions that would generate the passenger volume necessary to earn a profit. As PRR officials acknowledged, "If the Railroad has any satisfactory place in the passenger field it would seem to be primarily as the low-cost form of transportation." That comment suggested that after a less-than-ten-year commitment to luxury streamliners, Pennsylvania Railroad executives were willing to return to the concept of the low-cost, high-density equipment that Raymond Loewy and others had advocated during the late 1930s and early 1940s.[188]

Low-Cost Streamliners

The cautious optimism of PRR executives regarding the potential for medium-distance passenger travel reflected their ongoing involvement in collaborative efforts to develop a new generation of lightweight passenger equipment. Representatives from the railroads and from manufacturers hoped to reduce production costs to no more than $1,000 per passenger seat, about a third of the expense of a standard lightweight coach. Lighter weight and low-slung profiles would also permit faster schedules, luring passengers back to the rails. That was certainly the expectation of New Haven president Patrick B. McGinnis, whose company had suffered catastrophic declines in both freight and passenger revenues. McGinnis, a securities broker with minimal railroad experience, won a bitterly contested April 1954 proxy battle for control of the New Haven. He soon announced his intention to save the railroad by attracting new business and not merely by cutting expenses. McGinnis also pledged to convince regional highway planners of the ongoing importance of railroad passenger services—a serious matter, given that work had just begun on the Connecticut Turnpike route that by 1958 would parallel much of the New Haven's right-of-way. In background and personality, McGinnis was in many respects like Robert Young, who became the New York Central's board chairman only a few weeks later. It was hardly surprising that both individuals were interested in resurrecting the TALGO system that American Car & Foundry had developed between 1946 and 1950.[189] In June 1954, the New Haven tested the train between Boston and New Haven, with McGinnis claiming that it had reached a top speed of 102.8 miles per hour—well above the 55-mile-per-hour average of the railroad's premier *Merchants Limited*. At that rate, McGinnis claimed, the TALGO could reduce New York–Boston schedules from four hours to as little as two and a half hours. He pledged to order as many as thirty TALGO trainsets, some of which would be in service within six months, at a cost as low as $500 per seat. Officials from ACF Industries, the successor to American Car & Foundry, expressed incredulity at both the price and delivery times McGinnis had promised—suggesting that the New Haven executive, like Robert Young of *Chessie* fame, was primarily engaged in a public-relations gambit.[190]

Even as he criticized other railroads for purchasing expensive and luxurious "Cadillac" passenger equipment, McGinnis sought their help in the development of a new generation of TALGO trainsets. He suggested that the sharing of expertise would facilitate the research-and-development process while generating the economies of scale necessary to reduce manufacturing costs. In June 1954, McGinnis discussed the matter with Symes and with the New York Central's new president, Alfred Perlman. They soon established the Mechanical Research Committee, which also included representatives from the Baltimore & Ohio, the Chesapeake & Ohio, and the Santa Fe. By September, McGinnis—who had adopted more realistic cost and delivery estimates than the ones he had provided a few months earlier—announced that he would postpone the New Haven's TALGO purchases for six weeks, to give the other members of the consortium time to order similar equipment.[191]

Ironically, all the participants in the consortium ultimately favored proprietary designs, rendering impossible the standardization that McGinnis had advocated. Even the three new lightweight trainsets built for the New Haven—far fewer than the twenty or thirty McGinnis had initially promised—differed from one another. Only the *John Quincy Adams* employed the TALGO system, with cars built by ACF and locomotives provided by Fairbanks-Morse.[192] The Budd Company furnished the *Roger Williams* (a set of rail diesel cars coupled together), while Pullman and Baldwin-Lima-Hamilton cooperated on the construction of the *Dan'l Webster*. The *Dan'l Webster* caught fire on its inaugural run, none of the three operated reliably, and their rough ride drove away passengers rather than attracted them. They did not last long in revenue service and were insufficient to protect the New Haven's passenger operations from worsening deficits.[193]

On the Pennsylvania Railroad, Symes favored two experimental designs, each of which owed something to the TALGO concept. The more innovative and less successful system emerged from collaborations between the Mechanical Research Committee and General Motors. As a GM vice president, Nelson Dezendorf had little stake in the railroads' passenger difficulties, and he would have been content to see passengers travel in the cars and buses that his company manufactured. As the general manager of GM's Electro-Motive Division, however, Dezendorf reacted with alarm to the disappearance of the steam locomotive. EMD had done more than any other manufacturer to facilitate rapid dieselization. With that process nearly complete, however, EMD was likely to experience a precipitous decrease in sales. Dezendorf hoped that EMD could offer "something completely new in a passenger train," a design "so inexpensive to build and operate that railroads can't afford *not* to buy it . . . by the hundreds." Neither Dezendorf nor GM president Harlow H. Curtice had any interest in gearing up for full-scale manufacture of hundreds of new passenger trains.[194] Instead, their goal was to select a variety of preexisting products, manufactured by EMD and other GM divisions, assemble them into demonstration units, and encourage railroads to buy large numbers of those basic components. The use of off-the-shelf items kept the per-seat cost at the $1,000 threshold that railroad executives had established as the basis for profitable passenger service.[195] The weight per passenger (sixty-four thousand pounds) was half that of traditional passenger equipment, with a corresponding 60 percent reduction in manufacturing costs. The train would rely on a 1,200-horsepower EMD Model 567 diesel engine, the same unit used to power the SW1200 switcher. Thanks to the styling efforts of Charles M. Jordan, the chief designer at GM's Special Projects Studio, the power car bore little resemblance to a lowly switch engine. Instead, its rakish profile, elevated sloped-back cab (akin to Jordan's 1956 Motorama Buick Centurion concept car), flattened ovoid nose (like that of the 1955 Euclid Tractor), and Cadillac-like tailfins at the end of the train bespoke the space age more than the golden age of rail travel. The ten coaches were modified 40-foot General Motors bus bodies, widened by eighteen inches, and seated forty passengers. GM's Delco Products Division supplied the generators, while the Frigidaire Division provided the air-conditioning equipment. Each unit rode on a pair of two-wheel trucks and thus lacked the single-axle TALGO design.[196] The center of gravity was three inches higher than on the TALGO but ten inches below that of a conventional passenger car. GM designers also included rubber bellows, filled with compressed air, to provide a smooth and comfortable ride for passengers. They initially referred to the project as Train Y—to convey the impression that it had longer antecedents than the Young/Pullman Train X proposals—occasionally relied on the term *Air Rider*, and finally settled on *Aerotrain*.[197]

Symes, who first discussed the *Aerotrain* concept with the PRR's directors in December 1954, was inclined to favor GM's effort to stem passenger losses. He had long been a devotee of EMD diesel engines, and he acknowledged that the commonplace General Motors bus body had "the earmarks of being a wonderful passenger transport unit." Symes was nonetheless concerned about Dezendorf's plan to simultaneously provide one unit apiece to the Pennsylvania Railroad and the New York Central, which would prevent the PRR from maximizing the public-relations value associated with the debut of the *Aerotrain*. There remained a further problem, as GM personnel complained that their PRR counterparts did not specify the type of onboard food service they preferred until very late in the design process.[198]

The *Aerotrain* attracted immediate popular interest and just as quickly fell out of favor. By September 1955, GM had completed the first of two *Aerotrain* sets, placing it on display at the Powerama exhibit in Chicago. GM then leased one *Aerotrain* apiece to the Pennsylvania Railroad and the New York Central. On January 5, 1956, the two units made simultaneous trips on the PRR (between Washington and Newark) and the NYC (from Chicago to Detroit). Six days later, the New York Central's *Aerotrain* derailed in the Park Avenue Tunnel while en route from Grand Central Terminal to Albany. Young and Perlman already favored Pullman's Train X concept, and the embarrassing accident did little to halt the development of the NYC's competing *Xplorer* design.[199]

The *Aerotrain*'s performance on the Pennsylvania Railroad was almost as disappointing. Following its inaugural run, the equipment was on public display at Penn Station, where it attracted large crowds curious about the future of rail travel. The *Aerotrain* then went on a demonstration tour in anticipation of the inauguration of regular service between New York and Pittsburgh, slated to begin on February 6. The trial runs demonstrated severe problems with noise and vibration, particularly in the rearmost cars, and passengers complained that they found it difficult to read or even walk down the aisle. Shop forces at Altoona undertook modifications that reduced but did not eliminate the problems. Regular service did not begin until February 26, when the PRR's *Pennsy Aerotrain* left Penn Station at 7:55 a.m. Despite a mechanical problem at North Philadelphia, the train arrived in Pittsburgh at 3:25 in the afternoon, slightly ahead of schedule. The seven-and-a-half-hour journey was the fastest regularly scheduled trip between those two cities, beating *The Broadway Limited* by twenty-three minutes. It was about the last favorable publicity that the *Pennsy Aerotrain* would receive. Food service initially included two options—"Buffet-Box Meals" and the "Hot Penn-Tray," served to passengers using lap boards—and the experience was hardly a substitute for the comforts of a PRR dining car. The hot meals disappeared in June, when service to New York ended and the *Aerotrain* was truncated to one round trip a day between Philadelphia and Pittsburgh.[200] The lightweight coach bodies, one of the design features stressed by PRR and GM officials, ensured that the cars were not heavy enough to track well. Despite the modifications at Altoona, passengers complained of cramped accommodations, noise, vibrations, and a rocking and bouncing motion that some likened to being on a ship at sea. According to newspaper reporters, passengers chanted the lyrics to the 1954 Charles E. Calhoun (Jesse Stone) hit "Shake, Rattle and Roll." Whether true or merely apocryphal, the stories nonetheless suggested that the PRR's efforts to market the next generation of lightweight equipment to the traveling public had failed miserably. "No one knows what is going to be the final solution for the equipment side of the railroad passenger problem," Symes acknowledged when he introduced the *Pennsy Aerotrain* in January 1956. "No one knows yet what the final answers will be either in engineering, comfort or convenience." Within less than a year, the experiment had failed on all three counts. In June 1957, the PRR withdrew the *Aerotrain* equipment from service.[201]

The second design that emerged from the efforts of the Mechanical Research Committee was more conventional and far more successful than the *Aerotrain*. It was in some

The *Aerotrain* was sleek, stylish, and modern, but that was about all that could be said in its favor. Ride quality was extraordinarily poor, and the set of articulated bus bodies would not provide a solution to the PRR's growing passenger-service losses. Don Wood captured the *Aerotrain* passing through Elizabeth, New Jersey, early in its brief career. *Don Wood Negatives, Railroad Museum of Pennsylvania, PHMC.*

respects a throwback to the "possum-belly" cars that were briefly popular during the earliest days of passenger travel in the 1830s. In February 1955, Symes announced the development of a tubular train, in collaboration with the Budd Company. As its name suggested, each car consisted of a self-supporting stainless-steel tube, a concept borrowed from aircraft manufacturers. By eliminating the traditional center sill, the cars were much lighter and considerably lower than conventional passenger equipment. The low-slung design would reduce wind resistance (and therefore fuel costs), permit faster acceleration, and facilitate high-speed operation through curves. Symes suggested that the seven-car train would "provide comfortable accommodations for nearly 600 passengers." Given the train's estimated cost, that equated to about $1,700 per seat, well above the $1,000 target and more than three times the unrealistic figure that McGinnis had promised the previous year.[202]

In June 1956, the Pennsylvania Railroad debuted the new tubular train, branded as *The Keystone*. "This is the fourth new train to be brought out in less than six months," observed Paul J. C. Friedlander, the travel editor at the *New York Times*, "and, from the passenger's point of view, it comes closest to hitting the target." That was hardly

In 1956, the PRR introduced *Keystone* service, using cars manufactured by the Edward G. Budd Company. Because the body functioned as a steel tube, Budd was able to eliminate the heavy underframe, and the resulting weight savings promised to lower operating costs. While the design was much superior to the *Aerotrain*, many passengers were nervous about riding so close to the rails and objected to the stairs at either end of the car. *Pennsylvania Railroad Negatives Collection, Hagley Museum & Library, acc. 1993.300.*

surprising, as the cars on *The Keystone* were more akin to traditional passenger equipment than any of the other designs that had arisen from the 1954 TALGO experiments. Wisely, PRR and Budd engineers avoided the articulated trainsets that were an indispensable part of the TALGO concept. *Keystone* cars rode on familiar two-axle trucks and the vestibules and couplers were at a standard height. Those design elements enabled the cars to be mated with traditional equipment and reduced the danger of telescoping in the event of an accident. The tubular construction, along with small-diameter wheels, meant that the *Keystone* cars were only eleven feet, nine inches high—twenty-one inches lower than conventional lightweight cars like those assigned to *The Congressional*. With a center of gravity that was nearly nine inches lower than normal, *The Keystone* facilitated higher speeds on curves. The cars weighed 93,000 pounds apiece, significantly less than the 130,000 pounds for more traditional designs. Each of the seven new

cars accommodated eighty-two passengers, nearly double the number housed in the P85BR coaches that Raymond Loewy had styled for *The Trail Blazer* and *The Jeffersonian*, even though their length was identical. Fifty-six people sat in the depressed-center area, between the trucks; twelve occupied seats at one end; and a lounge area at the other end accommodated fourteen. An eighth car contained a small kitchen and a diesel generator that provided electrical power for the entire train. The resulting elimination of batteries and axle-mounted generators from each car saved space and weight while reducing drag on the wheelsets. The four-wheel trucks also provided a much smoother ride than any of the single-axle designs that had been evaluated by the Mechanical Research Committee. As Friedlander observed, "One can stand and walk in the Keystone aisles at eighty without teetering and hanging on"—something not always possible on the *Aerotrain*.[203]

"Personally, I think that it is a good train," Symes told reporters during the inaugural run of *The Keystone*, "but I am not saying it is the ultimate answer to the passenger problem confronting the American railroads." It was an apt statement, for the train was neither a spectacular failure nor a revolutionary success. Many passengers objected to sitting so low to the rails, while others complained of the inconvenience and potential danger associated with the short stairways that connected the end and midcar seating areas. While the PRR could add additional, conventional cars to the *Keystone* consist, the reliance on the generator unit made it impossible to assign *Keystone* cars to other trains. The cost was also higher than Symes had originally predicted, equivalent to $2,000 per seat. That was only slightly below the inflation-adjusted purchase price of $2,300 per seat for the 1952 cars assigned to *The Congressional* and *The Senator*—although Symes expressed confidence that improvements in the manufacturing process could lower the cost of future *Keystone* cars to a more reasonable $1,500 per passenger. The train remained in service until 1968, shortly after the Penn Central merger. The PRR never replicated the design, however, and—as Symes had suggested—it was not the answer to the passenger problem.[204]

TrucTrain and the Development of Intermodal Service

On July 12, 1954, Vice President Richard Nixon addressed the governors of all forty-eight states, who were assembled in Lake George, New York. President Eisenhower had hoped to be in attendance, to ask the governors to support what would become one of the signature achievements of his administration. Tragically, his sister-in-law, Helen Eakin, had died two days earlier, at the age of forty-nine, and he wanted to be with his younger brother Milton during his time of grief. Acting in the president's stead, Nixon emphasized that "we have a transportation system which in many respects it is true is the best in the world, but far from the best that America can do for itself in an era when defensive and productive strength require the absolute best that we can have." That was why, he continued, "a Cabinet committee has just been established by the president to explore and to help formulate a comprehensive transportation policy for the Nation, taking into account the vital interests of carriers, shippers, the States and communities, the public at large. But more specifically, our highway net is inadequate locally, and obsolete as a national system." The remarks constituted an important milestone in Eisenhower's efforts over the previous year to implement a massive federal project—an expenditure of $50 billion over ten years to construct a system of interstate highways. It would be another two years before the president would sign the Federal-Aid Highway Act of 1956 into law, but it was clear that national transportation policy was bound to cause problems for the railroads. If they were to survive, they would have to improve the efficiency of their operations and find new ways to move freight from place to place.[205]

On the same day that Nixon spoke to the nation's governors, a Pennsylvania Railroad train left New York for Chicago. Its prosaic name, LCL-1, was far less romantic than anything employed by the Blue Ribbon passenger

fleet and not even a match for such earlier named freight trains as the *Greyhound* and the *Speed Witch*. Yet the inaugural trip of the LCL-1 marked the beginning of one of the most important transformations in freight transportation. It demonstrated that the PRR had taken the lead in the development of what would eventually become the single largest generator of revenue for railroads in the United States. Over the course of several decades, trailer-on-flatcar service and its close cousin, container-on-flatcar operations, have revolutionized the transportation sector and become an indispensable component of the global economy. The intermodal revolution developed gradually, however, and its benefits for the railroads came too late to save the PRR and its Penn Central successor.[206]

The PRR's involvement with intermodal transportation had begun more than a quarter century before crews loaded the first highway trailers aboard the flatcars assigned to LCL-1. Since 1924, the PRR had used trucks to augment or replace boxcars for the collection and delivery of LCL shipments. Some were engaged in "substituted service," ferrying packages from one PRR freight house to another. Other trucks provided service from the freight house or rail yard directly to the customer's door. Those store-door operations, like the simultaneous use of containers, were in part a subterfuge to undercut the rate structure that the railroads had established and that the Interstate Commerce Commission had validated. They nonetheless made the handling of LCL freight more efficient, and the ICC permitted many of those store-door routes to continue. It did not require much imagination to envision placing the entire truck, wheels and all, on board a railroad flatcar, creating something colloquially referred to as "piggyback."

The Pennsylvania Railroad was not the first carrier to place highway trailers on flatcars. As early as 1884, the Long Island Rail Road—not yet a part of the PRR system—provided a special train that carried farmers, their draft animals, and wagons filled with produce to Long Island City.[207] During the 1920s and 1930s, competition from motor carriers and worsening economic conditions encouraged officials at some railroads to experiment with piggyback operations. The Chicago, North Shore & Milwaukee established TOFC service in 1926, while a similar operation began on the Chicago, South Shore & South Bend the following year.[208] A more significant development occurred on the Chicago Great Western, one of the weakest of the midwestern granger lines. The company entered bankruptcy in February 1935, and managers considered innovative methods of addressing the railroad's financial problems. They became early advocates of dieselization and hoped to attract additional business by cooperating with independent motor carriers. Adopting the loading techniques employed by Ringling Brothers and Barnum & Bailey Circus, the CGW provided flatcars and loading ramps, while companies such as Chicago-Dubuque Motor Transportation furnished trailers and solicited business from shippers. The 1935 Motor Carrier Act had given the Interstate Commerce Commission the authority to regulate trucks as well as trains, but the new law did not adequately address shipments that blended the two modes of transportation. As a precaution, CGW officials filed a joint rail-highway tariff. Nearly two decades would elapse, however, before the ICC would clarify that aspect of the regulatory environment. The New Haven also entered bankruptcy in 1935, encouraging the company's management to emulate the CGW experiment. Highway competition affected the New Haven more than any other carrier, thanks to the proliferation of highways along a short route structure that served areas of high population density. To turn that situation to their advantage, in 1937 New Haven executives established piggyback service linking Boston, Providence, and New York.[209]

In the last few years prior to World War II, PRR executives expressed interest in the New Haven's TOFC operations. In March 1941, John F. Deasy, the vice president in charge of operations, asked the chief of motive power about the possibility of building flatcars that could accommodate as many as four truck bodies or trailers—something that not even the New Haven could achieve. Deasy and his colleagues acknowledged that, because of low motor-carrier rates, "a considerable volume of traffic has been diverted to truck service" and suggested that "the Pennsylvania Railroad should attempt to obtain the line haul by transportation of trailers on flatcars on the theory that 'half a loaf is better than none.'" In a move to undercut the average motor-carrier rate, they proposed a flat fee of $36 for each loaded trailer and half that for an empty backhaul plus $3 in terminal charges. Action was not forthcoming, and the onset of war precluded the further development of intermodal services on the PRR.[210]

Wartime public policy provided new inducements for TOFC operations. Despite repeated calls for the regulation of freight forwarders, federal law had not addressed that issue. Some forwarders nonetheless took the precaution of filing applications for certificates of convenience and necessity, under the 1935 Motor Carrier Act, and subsequently requesting joint tariffs with regulated common-carrier trucking firms. In a series of rulings between 1937 and 1939 and upheld by the Supreme Court in 1940, the ICC struck down those joint tariffs, holding that they constituted discriminatory rates. The suspension was held

in abeyance, however, given that joint rates were critical to the operation of both freight forwarders and many motor carriers. Commissioner Joseph Eastman proposed additional regulation to clarify the status of the freight forwarders, a suggestion soon seconded by the industry trade association, the Freight Forwarders Institute.[211]

The Freight Forwarders Act of 1942 transformed forwarders from shippers into carriers and placed them under ICC oversight for the first time, under Part IV of the 1887 Act to Regulate Commerce. The new law did not employ the precise term *common carrier* but for all intents and purposes instructed the ICC to treat freight forwarders as such. While Congress had prevented forwarders from controlling common carriers, legislators nonetheless allowed common carriers (Congress primarily envisioned railroads) to own or establish freight forwarders.[212]

The new law produced some unintended consequences, however. By 1950, Section 409 of the Act to Regulate Commerce allowed motor carriers—but not railroads—to give preferential rates to forwarders for distances of 450 miles or less, contributing to a situation in which forwarders under the control of trucking firms were moving even larger proportions of intercity freight. Yet the pattern of regulation—fragmented and often contradictory though it was—created several opportunities for the PRR. Railroads could act as contract haulers for independent common-carrier truckers, transporting their trailers on flatcars and allowing the motor carrier to take advantage of the Section 409 rates. They could also establish or make contracts with freight forwarders, enabling them to exploit the terminal area exemption embodied in Section 202(c) of the Act to Regulate Commerce.[213] One serious impediment remained, however, as the ICC still prohibited railroads from levying freight-all-kinds rates on merchandise carried in trailers or containers—thus ensuring their continued reliance on freight forwarders.[214]

Despite the opportunities provided by changes in regulatory policy, managers at financially stable railroads such as the PRR and the NYC were initially reluctant to emulate the examples provided by the Chicago Great Western and the New Haven. The ICC's *In the Matter of Container Service* decision occurred three years prior to the passage of the Motor Carrier Act and the beginnings of intermodal operation on the CGW. Subsequent events nonetheless suggested that regulators drew a distinction between innovative practices that could save bankrupt railroads and those that might enable prosperous companies to become even stronger. Carriers like the PRR also possessed longer line hauls than did the CGW and the New Haven, at least temporarily reducing the threat of motor-carrier competition. During the years immediately following World War II, therefore, both the PRR and the NYC avoided intermodal operations as a means of retaining LCL traffic. Managers instead focused their efforts on improvements to conventional boxcar operations. The New York Central introduced "Pacemaker" equipment in 1946, with the PRR launching "Keystone Merchandise Service" four years later. The Pennsylvania Railroad operated more than a thousand distinctively painted boxcars, with scheduled "sailings" between major points on the system. The equipment carried special placards lettered "L.C.L merchandise—this car must not be delayed." Employees received additional training, to promote the Keystone brand and speed traffic to its destination, while new accounting methods improved billing and payment processing. Keystone service was coordinated with local highway delivery, first introduced in the 1920s, and PRR officials announced that they favored the "efficient use of trucks in their proper place." Fred Carpi, the vice president in charge of traffic, praised the developments and predicted "a substantial increase" in LCL traffic.[215]

By the early 1950s, however, it was clear that faster schedules and brightly painted boxcars equipped with specialized loading racks would be insufficient to arrest the steady erosion of LCL traffic. In the fall of 1949, soon after he retired from the presidency, Clement acknowledged the seriousness of the situation. In his new position of board chairman, he observed that "the less-than-carload situation, as far as operating ratio is concerned, is worse off than the passenger situation." Clement insisted that "short haul LCL should be increased," without providing any specific suggestions as to how that might be done. In March 1951, Clement informed his subordinates that the railroad's less-than-carload-lot business "needs some drastic attention and action." Yet he could do little more than recommend "a plus charge for collection and delivery" and "a flat addition to the rates," both of which seemed tailor-made to drive even more LCL business to the truckers. A few months later, Clement asked Symes, Fred Carpi, and Eugene Hofmann (the manager of passenger transportation) to develop a thorough analysis of ways to improve the performance for both passenger and LCL traffic. "This situation is one of changing from what has long been a monopoly and suddenly has become highly competitive," Clement emphasized, insisting that managers "must develop new rates and new practices."[216]

Despite Clement's exhortations for improved performance, LCL business continued to deteriorate, both on the PRR and across the country. In 1946, the nation's railroads had originated 24.4 million tons of package freight, but by 1954 that had fallen almost 72 percent, to just 6.9 million tons. The PRR alone had originated more than 5.7 million tons of LCL in 1946, equivalent to 2.45 percent of the railroad's total traffic. In 1954, the company transported little more than 1.2 million tons, a mere 0.74 percent of the total. In the space of eight years, therefore, more than 78 percent of the PRR's less-than-carload-lot shipments had migrated to the highways.[217]

Highway competition had produced particularly severe declines in the New Haven's boxcar-based LCL traffic, encouraging that company's officials to expand the prewar experiments with piggyback service. In 1953, the struggling New England carrier secured nearly $2 million in badly needed revenue by loading more than fifty thousand trailers on flatcars. New Haven officials were ready to increase the scope of piggyback operations but were reluctant to proceed without advance advice from the ICC. They thus paid close attention to the Southern Pacific's May 1953 inauguration of piggyback service between Los Angeles and San Francisco. Unlike their counterparts at the Chicago Great Western and the New Haven, SP executives had no desire to work with independent motor carriers who functioned as both customers and competitors. Instead, the company established a subsidiary, Pacific Motor Transport, which would wholly own both the railcars and the trailers used in TOFC service, charging freight-all-kinds rates directly to shippers and dispensing with freight forwarders. The SP's arrangement was potentially in violation of the 1935 Motor Carrier Act—but as the route lay entirely within the state of California, it was exempt from ICC oversight. It was clear from the outset, however, that the SP's intrastate operation offered a valuable model for the New Haven and other railroads to emulate. In September 1953, the New Haven submitted twenty questions to the Interstate Commerce Commission, the answers to which would establish national parameters for TOFC service. PRR executives displayed a keen interest in the outcome, assigning assistant solicitor William B. Johnson to the case. Not until the summer of 1954 would the ICC conclude deliberations in *Movement of Highway Trailers by Rail*, often referred to as the *New Haven* case. Yet preliminary indications suggested that the commissioners were inclined to permit a significant expansion in the scope of intermodal services.[218]

The PRR's involvement in TOFC operations came more slowly than on other railroads, hampered by disagreements among the company's executives. The lack of consensus among Pennsylvania Railroad managers provided echoes of the previous decade's debate between supporters of steam locomotives and those who favored diesels. During

James P. Newell (1900–1982), standing at left, was willing to experiment with new operating methods, even if they ran counter to standard PRR practice. He asserted that the carriage of highway trailers on flatcars might reverse the steady decline of LCL traffic and enable the railroad to gain ground against highway competition. At right is Herman H. Pevler (1903–1978), who began his PRR career in 1927. Following the company's 1955 reorganization, Pevler became the vice president of the Northwestern Region before assuming the presidency of the PRR-affiliated Wabash Railroad in 1959. Pevler became the president of the Norfolk & Western in 1963, replacing Stuart Saunders. *Pennsylvania Railroad Photographs, Hagley Museum & Library, acc. 1988.231.*

the 1940s, James Symes had been a persistent advocate of dieselization, first as vice president in charge of the Western Region and ultimately as vice president in charge of operations. His years in Chicago had placed him near early diesels and close to the pioneering TOFC service offered by the Chicago Great Western. As the New Haven case

worked its way through the regulatory apparatus, Symes encouraged President Walter Franklin to invest heavily in piggyback. Symes's advocacy became more forceful after he became the PRR's thirteenth president on June 1, 1954.

Symes had a close ally in James P. Newell, who replaced him as the vice president in charge of operations. Newell grew up in Carthage, Missouri, and he never ventured east of Chicago until he began studying engineering at Princeton University in 1920. Following his 1924 graduation, Newell spent a year working for the Toledo Scale Company. An urge to travel motivated him to sail to Europe on an oil tanker. After ten weeks abroad, he paid for his return voyage on the SS *Leviathan* by washing dishes in the galley. His father had unwisely speculated in agricultural properties during the Florida land boom, and Newell spent time plowing fields that had lost much of their value. He joined the PRR in 1927 and rose through the engineering ranks, serving as assistant supervisor in the Maintenance of Way Department, assistant division engineer at the Altoona Works, and division engineer on the Long Island Rail Road. In 1942, Newell became the superintendent of the St. Louis Division, then general superintendent of the Southwestern General Division in 1944, followed by the corresponding office on the Eastern Pennsylvania General Division in 1946. The same year, his only child died in an automobile accident. In June 1948, Newell became the general manager of the Western Region, the post that Symes had held between 1939 and 1942. Newell thereafter followed the same path that Symes had trod before him— leading, he assumed, to the presidency of the Pennsylvania Railroad. After spending six months as the assistant vice president in charge of operations, Newell replaced Symes as the vice president in charge of operations in January 1952. Like his mentor, Newell was familiar with the methods employed by executives on other railroads, and he was not content to follow the customary PRR methods of doing things. He eagerly took charge of the development of the company's piggyback service. He believed in its potential, was eager to please Symes, and hoped that a successful effort to recapture lost LCL traffic would enable him to climb the last rung on the PRR's corporate ladder.[219]

While Symes and Newell emphasized the potential of TOFC service, other PRR executives were equally adamant in their opinion that it was a serious mistake. Chief among them was Fred Carpi, the vice president in charge of traffic. Like Walter Franklin, Carpi rose through the ranks on the traffic rather than the operations side of the company. Otherwise, however, the two men had little in common. The outgoing president was a Harvard alumnus who mingled effortlessly with the sophisticated elites who resided along the Main Line and held memberships in Philadelphia's best social clubs. Carpi possessed no education beyond high school, and his nickname—"Little Caesar"— suggested both his personality and his management style. He began his career as a clerk at the Shire Oaks Yard, outside Pittsburgh, and by 1931 had risen to the rank of traffic engineer. Three years later, he became the general freight agent at Philadelphia, where he assisted in the development of the PRR's early intermodal pickup and delivery operations. Carpi replaced Franklin as the head of the Traffic Department in June 1948. In May 1954, days before Symes became president, both Carpi and Newell were awarded seats on the PRR's Board of Directors. Carpi's relationship with Newell was prickly and his interactions with Symes not much better. As his involvement in store-door service indicated, Carpi was not resolutely antithetical to the blending of railroad and highway transportation. He nonetheless insisted that conventional boxcars—including the Keystone Merchandise Service that he had helped to implement—constituted a proven method for the movement of LCL freight. By setting piggyback rates low

Like many other PRR executives, Fred Carpi (1900–1967) rose through the ranks thanks to his grit and determination rather than a formal education. When he became the vice president in charge of traffic, in 1948, Carpi confronted the loss of once-profitable LCL service. Carpi was committed to the traditional boxcar, and he asserted that trailer-on-flatcar services were undermining his policies. He clashed repeatedly with Jim Newell, hindering the development of piggyback operations and derailing the careers of both executives. *Collection of the Historical Society of Pennsylvania.*

enough to take trucks off the roads, Carpi asserted, the PRR would cannibalize its LCL boxcar traffic, incurring additional expenses for new facilities without generating a corresponding increase in revenue.[220]

Despite Carpi's misgivings, the PRR could not afford to delay the introduction of piggyback service. The recession that had begun the previous June, following the end of the Korean War, had proved devastating. Carloadings during the first four months of 1954 decreased 19 percent from the same period the previous year, producing a net loss of more than $9.1 million. When the board met on May 26 to elect Symes to the presidency, the directors also voted to defer the payment of dividends. Precisely one month

Class F30d flatcar #475462, hastily converted to TOFC service
in April 1954, was a stopgap measure to exploit the ICC's preliminary liberalization of the conditions regulating intermodal
operations. Both the trailer and the car are owned by, and
lettered for, the Pennsylvania Railroad—a clear indication
of Plan II service. In the background is the Altoona Brewing
Company, manufacturer of Horseshoe Curve Beer. *Pennsylvania Railroad Negative Collection, Hagley Museum & Library,
acc. 1993.300.*

earlier, Newell informed Symes and Franklin that "it is
the recommendation of the Operating [Transportation]
and Traffic Departments that operation of rail-trailer service on the Pennsylvania Railroad should begin as soon
as possible." He suggested "that the railroad will furnish
the complete service, from placement of the trailer at the
shipper's door to the delivery of the loaded trailer at the
consignee's point." Newell was much less certain about
other crucial details, including "the exact volume of traffic,
the commodities to be moved, and other related matters."
He also acknowledged that "the financial results of this

venture can not be definitely determined at this time."
Franklin's public pronouncements were somewhat more
optimistic. "This new form of railroad operation promises
benefits to the commerce of our Nation," he suggested,
"and it is time to resolve with practical experience the
debate which has gone on in transportation circles during
the last two years."[221]

The novel features of piggyback operations, coupled
with the uncertain regulatory climate, ensured that the
cautious approach favored by Carpi initially prevailed.
"Service will be inaugurated between a limited number
of points," Newell emphasized, and he favored "terminal
facilities to be of an inexpensive and temporary nature."
Construction crews established TOFC loading areas at
Waldo Avenue Yard in Jersey City, Hunter Street Yard in
Newark, Kensington Yard in North Philadelphia, Island
Avenue Yard in Pittsburgh, and 12th Street Yard in Chicago. Newell recommended that the company employ 150
highway trailers, half owned by the PRR's trucking subsidiaries and the remainder leased from the Fruehauf Trailer
Company. All would be lettered for the Pennsylvania Rail-
road and would—as Newell initially recommended—be

under the control of company employees from the loading dock of the shipper to that of the consignee. Shop forces made minor modifications to 115 Class F30d flatcars. They were fifty feet long and could accommodate only a single trailer, ensuring that the railroad was unlikely to do more than break even on each shipment. Symes and Newell recognized the inefficiency associated with the single-trailer-per-car approach, and by the end of April, the PRR had pledged to purchase two hundred 75-foot cars. Even though the new, longer cars would not be ready for several months, the PRR filed tariffs with the Interstate Commerce Commission and announced that TOFC service would begin on June 16.[222]

To the consternation of PRR executives and their counterparts on five other railroads, ICC officials suggested that their earlier indications of support for intermodal operations had been premature. Truckers had been caught off guard by the railroads' actions, and they objected to total railroad control of shipments from origin to destination. Instead, they sought complete oversight (including the solicitation of traffic), simply paying the railroads to transport their trailers whenever such movements were more efficient than long-distance highway travel—what the ICC later defined as Plan I TOFC service. The prewar operations of the Chicago Great Western and the New Haven conformed to Plan I, and had the Pennsylvania Railroad embraced that model, it is likely that truckers would have had few objections. The tariffs filed by the PRR and the other five carriers, in contrast, would allow them to solicit traffic and collect and deliver shipments using railroad-owned trucks—what eventually became known as Plan II service.[223]

If approved by the ICC, the PRR's proposed Plan II operations ensured that independent truckers would be excluded entirely from the transportation of intermodal freight. Teamsters responded, belatedly, with their spokesmen charging that "wide-open" TOFC operations would produce "dangerous competition" that would adversely affect motor carriers. Two days before service was scheduled to begin, the ICC suspended the tariffs filed by the PRR; the B&O; the Erie; the Wabash; the Nickel Plate; and the Delaware, Lackawanna & Western, pending a new round of hearings on the matter. PRR executives immediately filed an appeal, asserting that the ICC's peremptory action had idled their investment of nearly $1.3 million in equipment and facilities. In a rare show of solidarity with management, the head of the Brotherhood of Locomotive Firemen and Enginemen also demanded that the commission lift the suspension. The ICC scheduled hearings to begin on July 27, and they were likely to drag on for many months. Initial indications—that the commissioners would not reach a final decision until January 1955—suggested that the financially strapped railroads would experience long delays in their attempts to generate additional business. Within a month, however, protests from railroads and their unions—as well as the dire financial condition of many of the carriers—had again persuaded the ICC to change course. On July 9, the commission permitted Plan II service to proceed on an interim basis, pending the outcome of the investigation.[224]

During the next round of ICC hearings, the railroads encountered little resistance from the trucking interests. The commissioners now permitted the carriers to introduce data on the savings—in transportation costs and loading time—associated with TOFC operations. The PRR had the best figures of any carrier, and its executives acted as representatives for the industry. Despite his continued faith in boxcars, Fred Carpi testified that the dispersal of industrial facilities away from the urban core placed the PRR under a "competitive handicap" that required the use of TOFC services. Rather than developing an unfair advantage over independent truckers, Carpi continued, "the railroads are seeking to maintain competition and thereby prevent monopoly by the motor-carrier industry in respect to a huge volume of important freight traffic—the more desirable high-rated business." On August 6, in what the New York Times correctly called "a monumental victory for the railroads," the ICC gave its final approval to Plan II service. As such, the Pennsylvania Railroad possessed full legal authority to solicit business, dispatch PRR-owned trucks to collect freight from customers, load trailers on flatcars, and deliver the shipments, by highway, to their destinations under a single bill of lading. The ruling thus clarified an issue that had been the subject of considerable debate since the passage of the 1935 Motor Carrier Act, with the ICC classifying the entire intermodal journey as a rail movement, freeing railroads of the requirement of obtaining a certificate of convenience and necessity from the ICC's Motor Carrier Division.[225]

By the time the ICC issued its ruling, the PRR's Plan II piggyback service had been in operation for nearly a month. On July 12, three days after the ICC gave its permission and hours after Richard Nixon urged the nation's governors to support a new interstate highway system, Train LCL-1 began rolling west toward Chicago as Train LCL-2 headed east.[226] The initial westbound trip involved only six trailers, carried on flatcars coupled to the boxcars that constituted the traditional method of handling LCL freight. July's total traffic amounted to a mere 29 trailers. The number rose to 62 in August and to 159 in September.

Before the year was out, Trains LCL-3 and LCL-4 were providing TOFC service to the St. Louis market, contributing to further increases in traffic, with a total of 1,354 trailers transported in 1954. The modest traffic nonetheless demonstrated strong growth potential, and PRR officials concluded that the service generated nearly twice as much revenue, per car mile, as conventional LCL boxcar service. Equipment utilization was also much improved, with each loaded trailer making five trips a month, compared to two monthly journeys for a typical LCL boxcar. There were also significant reductions in loss and damage claims from shippers.[227]

No one could quite decide what to call the new service. Newell sought an evocative name that could be trademarked. He initially favored the "Pennsy Railblazer Route," presumably a variant of the once-popular all-coach *Trail Blazer* passenger train. Vice President Walter Patchell recommended Pennsy Railtrailer as an alternative, but general counsel John Butler Prizer predicted that "the shortened phrase designation 'Railtrailer service' is little more than descriptive and might not prove registerable." The same defect befell the suggested "Pennsy Piggy Back" nomenclature. The solution came in the form of a contest, open to all employees, with the winner receiving a $500 prize. Robert A. Young, a relief agent in the Philadelphia Terminal Division, suggested "TrucTrain."[228]

TrucTrain service grew quickly, aided by the fortuitous timing of a sustained economic recovery that began in the summer of 1954. By the end of that year, after less than six months in operations, the PRR had transported 1,330 trailers, generating $251,000 in revenue. The PRR's Mechanical Engineering Department was completing work on the design for new 75-foot flatcars, based on the standards that had been adopted on July 1. The Bethlehem Steel Corporation built the first two hundred of the Class F39, which entered service in December. They were far superior to their shorter predecessors but nonetheless weighed more than was required for efficient TOFC operation—prudence dictated that they should be sufficiently robust to withstand general service, should the piggyback experiment fail. PRR shop forces were soon at work, building a further three hundred cars in the almost-identical F39a and F39b classes. By the middle of 1956, therefore, the PRR rostered five hundred modern flatcars, each capable of carrying two trailers in TrucTrain service as well as more than a hundred of the essentially obsolete single-trailer cars. The company also employed 522 trailers, assigned to TOFC operations. The trailers, painted a brighter shade of red than the Tuscan on the flatcars, bore the familiar "Pennsylvania Railroad" and "Keystone Merchandise Service" lettering that debuted on the PRR's early store-door delivery service.[229] Construction was soon underway on two new intermodal terminals, located at Meadows Yard in Kearny, New Jersey, and at the 55th Street Yard in Chicago, to replace the earlier, temporary facilities.[230]

Despite its initial success, Plan II service faced inherent limitations. The PRR was responsible for the entire cost of the trailers, flatcars, and loading facilities. It was also impossible for the railroad to transport trailers owned by independent trucking companies—something that was especially problematic given that many truckers were willing to use rail service for empty backhauls, where time and service quality was of little consequence. Moreover, ICC regulations prohibited the Pennsylvania Railroad from using its trucking subsidiaries to solicit freight from points that the company did not also serve by rail. John Prizer, the company's chief legal representative, suggested a straightforward solution to that difficulty—an amendment to the Act to Regulate Commerce that would permit the railroads to engage in over-the-road trucking. While legally sound, Prizer's suggestion did not consider the competitive pressures facing the carriers. In May 1954, two weeks before he became president, Symes reminded Prizer that "we certainly cannot obtain public support—if in one instance we attempt to get the big trucks off the highway and onto the railroads—and then turn around and advocate putting them back on the highway." If the PRR "were granted such permission," Symes concluded, "we would find ourselves in the position of advocating more lenient truck laws in the various states that could eventually destroy the railroads." It was a chance that Symes could not afford to take. Newell recognized the danger as well, and he sought to balance the evident threat of independent truckers with their role as potential customers. He also desired ways to expand the scope of the PRR's operations at minimal additional cost. To do so, the PRR would need to cooperate with independent truckers, in Plan I service, shifting the cost of the trailers to companies that in most respects were the railroad's competitors.[231]

A further, equally problematic alliance brought the Pennsylvania Railroad into a relationship with one of the foremost pioneers of intermodalism. The rapid growth of the piggyback service created both opportunities and challenges for one of the strongest proponents of intermodal operations. Eugene F. Ryan spent his early career as a transportation manager for GM's Chevrolet Truck Division before transferring to the General Motors Acceptance Corporation. In 1950, Ryan became a transportation consultant based in the railroad hub of Chicago, where he soon developed a keen interest in the TOFC operation on the Chicago Great Western. He maintained the contacts he had established with executives at GM, the railroads, and trucking firms, and he secured a retainer from Pullman, Incorporated, the parent company of the Pullman-Standard Car Manufacturing Company. In May 1952, a year before New Haven executives sent their list of twenty questions to the ICC, Ryan established the Rail-Trailer Company. Ryan functioned as a broker, acting as a liaison between the railroads and the independent, common-carrier truckers, cooperating with the former on matters related to service and with the latter on rates. He solicited loads from various independent trucking companies and offered the resulting bundle of trailers to the railroads at a uniform rate. The trucker assumed all responsibility for billing the shipper and for transporting the trailer to and from the intermodal terminals. Rail-Trailer employees took responsibility for driving the trailers on and off the flatcars at terminals and for securing the trailers to the deck of each flatcar. Cash-strapped railroads thus avoided considerable expense—an investment that would have been difficult to recoup should TOFC revenues prove disappointing. Finally, Ryan's personality—and the fact that he was not a railroader—gave him a significant mediating influence. He maintained a close relationship with Jimmy Hoffa, the vice president of the International Brotherhood of Teamsters since 1952. Ryan's persuasive skills must have been considerable, as he endeavored to persuade Hoffa that intermodal operations would enable his members to benefit at the expense of the railroads, while reassuring railroad executives that they would capture business from the motor carriers.[232]

In addition to providing terminal services, Ryan hoped to establish a nationwide pool of flatcars for use on any railroad in North America. He called on the expertise of his former colleagues, including Nelson Dezendorf (a GM vice president, the general manager of the Electro-Motive Division, and soon-to-be director of Rail-Trailer), Cyrus Osborn (a GM executive often credited with inventing the dome passenger car), and Paul Turner (EMD's vice president in charge of sales and an individual who had spent years endeavoring to sell diesel locomotives to the PRR). They launched the "Rail-Highway Coordination Program," an EMD project that developed many of the key elements of piggyback operations. The resulting concepts included a 75-foot, depressed-center flatcar that could accommodate two 35-foot trailers—the standard length at the time—while still conforming to the restricted clearances that characterized the PRR and many other eastern railroads. The EMD group also established designs for efficient intermodal terminals with sunken tracks that enabled large forklifts (developed in cooperation with the Clark Equipment Company) to easily position trailers on flatcars.[233]

Gene Ryan's success was dependent on the willingness of railroad executives to accept the design standards he had recommended and to cooperate in the formation of interline piggyback routes. Yet both endeavors would prove problematic. Many managers, including Carpi, resisted investments in specialized equipment, such as the long, depressed-center flatcars that the Rail-Highway Coordination Program had developed. Should piggyback fail, they reasoned, it would be difficult to use those cars for more conventional traffic. Even if they acknowledged the merits of Ryan's terminal layout, they cautioned that locating tracks in a trench below ground level would entail considerable initial expense—money that would be squandered should Ryan's predictions of future TOFC growth prove overly optimistic.[234] It would be more prudent, they suggested, to build the simple ramps that companies like the Chicago Great Western were using to load trailers, circus style, even if they were cumbersome to operate. Moreover, interline coordination between carriers was minimal, particularly as many traffic officials feared that piggyback services offered by one company deprived connecting railroads of their share of the total line haul.[235] Those executives who did support TOFC operations were reluctant to permit flatcars and trailers to leave their systems, for fear that directionally unbalanced demand might cause unloaded cars to accumulate in certain offline locations. Each railroad's chief mechanical engineer was responsible for the safe movement of equipment. As such, they had authority to demand changes to car length and construction as well as loading methods. Many mechanical and operating personnel, including some on the PRR, insisted that flatcars capable of carrying two trailers were too long and therefore dangerously unstable. They favored specific car designs and trailer-restraint systems, and on occasion they refused to permit equipment they considered suspect to be accepted in interchange service.

The influence of railroad mechanical officers and outside developers such as Ryan also endangered the interchangeability that was vital to the creation of a national intermodal network. The New Haven adopted a system designed by Deodat Clejan, whose Piggyback, Incorporated, competed against Ryan's Rail-Trailer Company. While in some respects superior to the equipment used by the PRR and Rail-Trailer, the Clejan cars employed an entirely different mechanism for securing the trailers to the car deck. A more serious threat emerged from the company that initially promised to be one of Ryan's best customers. In the fall of 1953, Ryan had persuaded NYC president William White to partner with Rail-Trailer and establish a TOFC operation branded as Star Service. The ink was barely dry on the contract, however, when Robert Young gained control of the company and appointed Alfred Perlman as president. Unlike Ryan, Perlman was reluctant to work with common-carrier truckers in Plan I service. He authorized the development of a proprietary system, Flexi-Van, that was wholly incompatible with the equipment used on other railroads.[236]

Following the loss of the New York Central contract, Ryan turned to his other best prospect, the Pennsylvania Railroad. His timing was fortuitous, as Newell and other PRR executives were endeavoring to expand their fledgling Plan II TOFC operations. Ryan could provide almost everything necessary to establish complementary Plan I service at minimal expense. Rail-Trailer solicited business from independent truckers—who in turn provided tractors and trailers at no cost to the railroad. Ryan's crews loaded and unloaded the trailers, and his contacts with the Teamsters ensured labor peace. Rail-Trailer's subsidiary, the Van-Car Corporation, took responsibility for billing and other clerical functions. Ryan also provided equipment, purchasing the PRR's first two hundred 75-foot flatcars (in Class F39), assigning them to Van-Car, and then leasing them back to the railroad.[237] The Pennsylvania Railroad's sole remaining responsibilities involved the maintenance and expansion of loading ramps and the operation of trains from terminal to terminal.[238]

Despite the advantages of the symbiotic relationship, the reliance on Rail-Trailer caused considerable friction among PRR executives. Ryan's advocacy of Plan I service minimized the railroad's financial exposure. Yet Carpi, as the vice president in charge of traffic, objected to Ryan's business model, which excluded his staff from the solicitation of business from customers. In Carpi's assessment, Ryan was attempting to steal organizational authority from his department, just as TOFC operations were certain to pull traffic away from the LCL boxcars that he understood so well. There were also technical problems, largely because Ryan was a promoter rather than an engineer. In his initial negotiations with the PRR, Ryan had suggested an apparently arbitrary fee of $4.00 to load each trailer onto a flatcar (aka, the "lift charge"). That was far less than Rail-Trailer's actual cost, and the disparity threatened to bankrupt Ryan's company. Rail-Trailer employee

Les Robinson—who was an engineer—devised a "kingpin grabber," later replaced by a collapsible screw hitch, that enabled the trailer to be secured to the flatcar without a time-consuming and labor-intensive system of tie-down chains. The PRR's mechanical engineer, Carl Steins, was responsible for operational safety, and he envisioned trailers breaking loose from flatcars and quite possibly causing catastrophic wrecks by fouling adjacent tracks. To protect his organizational responsibilities, Steins refused to authorize the operation of any TOFC equipment that lacked safety chains. Robinson appealed the matter to Jim Newell, who agreed to a series of endurance tests, which the new hitch passed with flying colors.[239]

With those issues resolved, the PRR initiated Plan I TrucTrain service on March 3, 1955. Dedicated TOFC trains (TT-1 and TT-2) carried trailers from trucking firms such as Cooper-Jarrett, Iowa-Nebraska Transportation, Schreiber Trucking, Eastern Motor Express, Spector Freight Systems, and Mid-States between Chicago and Kearny, New Jersey. In keeping with ICC rules governing Plan I service, the Pennsylvania Railroad charged a standard freight-all-kinds rate, as determined by the weight of the trailer and irrespective of its contents.[240] Total journey time was twenty-nine hours, quicker than any other freight train and ten hours faster than all-highway schedules. TrucTrain equipment operating between New York and Chicago was soon averaging more than three hundred revenue miles per day, more than six times the standard boxcar utilization. Within a year, the PRR was operating fourteen TrucTrain terminals, half of which offered Plan I service.[241]

Plan I TrucTrain operations ensured that PRR and Rail-Trailer personnel would become dependent on one another. That dependency increased during the summer of 1955, when Ryan proposed a plan for a national flatcar pool that offered benefits for both companies. The PRR would be relieved of the necessity of building and financing additional equipment, while Rail-Trailer could achieve the standardization and control that Ryan craved. On August 18, he presented the arrangement to Newell, who circulated the proposal to Carpi, David Bevan (the PRR's chief financial officer), and John Prizer (the general counsel). By October, representatives from the two companies had agreed to establish the Trailer Train Company, with a public announcement to that effect issued on December 21. William B. Johnson, the PRR's assistant general counsel, wrote Trailer Train's incorporation papers and created much of its organizational structure. The Pennsylvania Railroad and Rail-Trailer each received an initial allocation of 2,500 shares of stock. The Norfolk

In March 1955, the PRR expanded TrucTrain service to include the transportation of trailers owned by independent trucking companies. Newly delivered Class F39 flatcars were long enough to accommodate two trailers apiece. Drivers employed by the Rail-Trailer Company cautiously backed the trailers onto each car. It was an inefficient and time-consuming process, and the low initial cost of "circus-style" loading ramps encouraged the PRR to extend TrucTrain service to markets that ultimately proved unremunerative. Within less than a year, the PRR had joined the Trailer Train equipment pool, and a quick paint job replaced the "Pennsylvania" logo with "T.T.X." reporting marks. *General Negative Collection, Railroad Museum of Pennsylvania, PHMC.*

& Western was also a founding member, with an allocation of one thousand shares. Additional railroads invited to join the pool would each receive five hundred–share blocks of Trailer Train stock. At the insistence of Newell, Bevan, and Carpi, Ryan agreed to sell his twenty-five-hundred-share stake in Trailer Train, should a majority of the

company's directors vote to terminate the management contract. Given the close relationship between the PRR and the N&W, therefore, Newell had an initial advantage over Ryan.[242]

The incorporation of Trailer Train ensured a complex relationship among the various components of the PRR's piggyback service. Railroad personnel continued to advertise and market service under the TrucTrain brand and operated trains carrying TOFC equipment. Trailer Train maintained a pool of flatcars available to all member railroads for their use and for interline service, assessing a mileage fee and a per diem charge.[243] Ryan's Rail-Trailer Company loaded and unloaded trailers at PRR intermodal facilities and performed billing and other clerical functions. Rail-Trailer's subsidiary, Van-Car, provided managerial services to Trailer Train.[244]

Despite its status as a multicarrier freight-car pool, Trailer Train bore the unmistakable stamp of the Pennsylvania Railroad—so much so that many shippers and executives from other railroads assumed, inaccurately, that the company was a PRR subsidiary. The first group of 75-foot flatcars originally belonged to the PRR.[245] For more than a decade, those and other Trailer Train cars were painted the same Tuscan red as Pennsylvania Railroad freight equipment, and many were built in the PRR's Samuel Rea Shops. Newell served as president and as a director of Trailer Train, while retaining his position as the PRR's vice president in charge of operations. Carpi and Bevan were also on the Trailer Train board, with Stuart T. Saunders representing the interests of the N&W.[246] Trailer Train's sole initial employee, Ed Martin, had been hired from the Pennsylvania Railroad. When general manager Arthur L. Berry returned to the Pullman-Standard Car Manufacturing Company in November 1958, he was replaced by John E. Wightman Jr., until then the superintendent of transportation of the PRR's Lake Region. The PRR's Public Relations Department generated Trailer Train's press releases and other publicity material, and the railroad provided computing services for Trailer Train until that company acquired its own computer in 1961. The company initially used Pennsylvania Railroad letterhead, with the name of the railroad crossed out and replaced with "Trailer Train." Until 1966, Trailer Train's address of record was the small Main Line commuter station of Haverford, Pennsylvania—a subterfuge to avoid payment of Philadelphia taxes.[247]

The relationship between the PRR and Rail-Trailer did not initially produce the surge in piggyback traffic that Newell anticipated. In 1955, the railroad transported 32,273 trailers, about evenly split between Plan I and Plan II service, and generated $5.7 million in revenue. It was a modest amount, but it represented the only good news in an otherwise dire overall financial situation—and, as such, descriptions of intermodal service featured prominently in the PRR's annual reports and promotional materials. Railroad officials nonetheless privately conceded that "many obstacles have been encountered in soliciting TrucTrain traffic." Most shippers were satisfied with highway transportation, executives concluded, and they conceded "the ability of the Trucker to furnish dependable service, with close personal attention, has developed a relationship with industry which is difficult to break down." Independent motor carriers could also deliver partial loads to multiple en route consignees, something that could not be done with rail-bound trailers. Other potential customers feared that the PRR would eventually abandon intermodal service, and they accordingly saw considerable risk in switching temporarily to a new form of transportation. Even worse, the railroad's analysis of the initial year and a half of intermodal operations concluded that "there is no

cost advantage to industry in using TrucTrain service, and, except in bad weather, no service advantage." The tariff to ship a trailer by rail was, on average, $24 more than the corresponding all-highway trip. On short routes, moreover, TrucTrain service was slower than road transport, in part because trailers remained idle in the yards until the once-daily departure. Motor carriers thus employed piggyback primarily during periods of peak demand, when drivers and tractors were in short supply. Johnson acknowledged that "volume has fluctuated widely" and that TrucTrain did "not have anything like a full train a day each way between Chicago and New York."[248]

Within a little over a year, all but one of the independent motor carriers had deserted TrucTrain, with Spector alone remaining loyal to the Pennsylvania Railroad. Dissatisfied truckers complained that the railroad had increased charges without consulting them and that customer service was abysmal—including repeated incidents where trailers were left behind at their originating terminals, for which the truck line took the blame. Following an April 1956 meeting with motor-carrier executives, Newell acknowledged that the PRR had "given the truckers the feeling that they are at the mercy of the railroad on rates and service." The gathering, which Newell described as "a dismal failure," indicated that he had underestimated the diversity of the trucking business. He cautioned, "We cannot do business with such a large group of truckers, which includes those giving us small volume as well as those giving us large volume—the interest of these two groups of truckers are too divergent."[249]

The establishment of interline routes with other carriers offered an important mechanism to foster TrucTrain's growth. The Norfolk & Western was an obvious first choice given its close association with the Pennsylvania Railroad. In November 1955, only days after the incorporation of Trailer Train, the PRR and the N&W began moving trailers as far south as Bristol, Virginia, via an interchange at Hagerstown, Maryland. The inclusion of additional carriers was vital to the success of the Trailer Train concept, but their selection presented Newell and his colleagues with several challenges. Some railroads, such as the Baltimore & Ohio and the New York Central, were competitors, and their access to the Trailer Train equipment pool would undoubtedly erode the PRR's TrucTrain business. While Newell was willing to work with any western partner, managers on those competing lines were suspicious of one another—a situation notable at the St. Louis gateway, where the Missouri Pacific, the Katy, and the Frisco vied for traffic. Some carriers employed equipment that was not compatible with Trailer Train's standards—that group included the NYC's Flexi-Van units and the Clejan cars used by the New Haven, the Boston & Maine, and the Southern Pacific. Walter Tuohy, the president of the financially stable Chesapeake & Ohio, worried that his company might ultimately bear a large portion of the debts incurred by Trailer Train. "If the other railroads in Trailer Train went 'kaput,'" he observed, "the C&O would also probably be 'kaput' but that, at least, if they were not in Trailer Train they would still have their money in the bank." Executives at other railroads, such as the Illinois Central, labeled truckers as enemies and refused to cooperate with them. Their counterparts on the SP, who had pioneered Plan II (railroad-owned) TOFC service, wanted nothing to do with Plan I (motor-carrier-controlled) operations.[250]

Under Trailer Train's bylaws, decisions regarding which railroads to recruit for membership were the responsibility of the entire board of directors, including Ryan. In practice, however, the members of the PRR's TrucTrain Committee—Newell, Carpi, Bevan, and Prizer—oversaw identifying likely prospects. The PRR had long cooperated with the Seaboard Air Line, the Atlantic Coast Line, and the Southern, its principal partners through the Washington/Richmond gateway, and those three railroads made the initial list.[251] So, too, did the New Haven, despite its ownership of Clejan equipment and obsolete 40-foot flatcars, as that company was an important link to New England. In the west, the Santa Fe and the Burlington were clear initial favorites. To the southwest, the situation was more complicated. The Missouri Pacific was a natural choice, given its long-standing interchange of freight traffic with the PRR as well as its participation in transcontinental passenger service. The Katy was also a possibility, but its inclusion ran the risk of alienating executives at the Frisco. The St. Louis Southwestern (Cotton Belt) had considerable value as a partner, even if its parent company—Southern Pacific—was unlikely to participate.[252]

During 1956, Newell and his staff negotiated traffic agreements with the Chicago & North Western, the Missouri Pacific, the Katy, the Frisco, the Cotton Belt, and the Santa Fe, facilitating the offline movement of TOFC equipment as far west as Dallas–Fort Worth and Houston. Through service was not integrated service, as shippers could expect to receive multiple bills, one from Rail-Trailer, one from the Pennsylvania Railroad, and still more from the other participating railroads. Even worse, an initial shortage of Trailer Train cars ensured that the various railroads offering TOFC service utilized different equipment. It was thus difficult to operate through trains, and at

many interchange points, crews reloaded trailers from the cars of one railroad to those of another.[253] William Johnson, the Pennsylvania Railroad attorney who also provided legal advice to Trailer Train, emphasized that the "PRR has worked for nearly a year now to bring about a consensus of opinion among piggyback railroads . . . as to a standard form of interchange." He nonetheless observed that at "meeting after meeting . . . we have generally accepted any suggestions which are workable, reasonable and favored by others, . . . [yet] the Katy is the only railroad with which we have yet been able to get an executed trailer interchange agreement."[254]

The arrival of new Trailer Train cars would have alleviated many of the interchange issues, but it presented a new problem. Even as the PRR and Rail-Trailer were developing a 75-foot car to accommodate two 35-foot trailers, legislatures in many western states authorized the use of 40-foot trailers. They were still not legal in many of the eastern states served by the PRR, ensuring that the shorter trailers were likely to remain in service for quite some time. It nonetheless made little sense to retain flatcars that might only be able to carry a single trailer, and Newell insisted that Trailer Train should adopt 85-foot cars as the new standard. In his dual capacity as an executive with both the PRR and Trailer Train, Newell advised President Symes of the necessity for longer cars while instructing PRR mechanical engineer Harry Decker to head a development committee in tandem with his counterparts on other railroads. Newell also asked R. W. Tackbary (the manager of TrucTrain services) to serve on the committee, ensuring that the new cars would be compatible with the PRR's operational requirements. Newell's recommendations triggered a resumption of the debates associated with the development of the 75-foot flatcar and its associated tie-down mechanisms. Mechanical officers on the PRR and other member railroads—who had by that point come to accept the viability of 75-foot cars—insisted that an additional ten feet of length would be certain to cause derailments. As a compromise, Trailer Train ordered both 85-foot cars and 50-foot cars—even though, as Newell repeatedly emphasized, the shorter equipment was uneconomical to operate. In any event, the first of the new 85-foot cars would not be available until February 1959, further hampering Newell's efforts to use the Trailer Train equipment pool to facilitate the interchange of TrucTrain business with other railroads.[255]

Despite his pioneering role in piggyback operations, Ryan soon became a liability to both the Pennsylvania Railroad and Trailer Train. When something went wrong—and it often did—Rail-Trailer and PRR employees were eager to blame one another. Trailer Train had not yet become the "happy united family it should be," Newell observed. He assigned most of the blame to Ryan, whom he called a "disturbing influence." Overall, railroad personnel suggested that Ryan was primarily a salesman and promoter and that his knowledge of terminal operations was "not outstanding." They also noted that Rail-Trailer's financial situation was precarious and that Ryan was willing to sell a portion of his company's stake in Trailer Train, raising the possibility that an independent motor carrier might gain a significant degree of control over intermodal operations.[256]

The underlying problem stemmed from Rail-Trailer's dual role as both an owner of and a subcontractor for Trailer Train. Van-Car charged a hefty management fee to Trailer Train, equivalent to 20 percent of the latter company's operating expenses. Newell suggested that neither the PRR nor Trailer Train were getting their money's worth, particularly as Ryan seemed more interested in establishing better relations with independent truckers than in promoting interchange traffic among the railroads. As they gained more familiarity with intermodal operations, executives were confident that "personnel in the PRR family are better qualified . . . to do the work." In April 1957, Newell met with the railroad representatives on Trailer Train's board of directors—without informing Ryan or any other official at Rail-Trailer—to encourage them to cancel the management contract with Van-Car. Six months later Newell amended the PRR's contract with Rail-Trailer, transferring all clerical responsibilities to the railroad and limiting Ryan's company to the loading and unloading of cars at TrucTrain terminals. Ryan was further marginalized on January 10, 1958, when he relinquished his post as Trailer Train's general manager. Beginning in March 1958, the PRR transferred the management of its TOFC facilities from Rail-Trailer to a PRR subsidiary, Pennsylvania Truck Lines (also known as PennTruck), with a substantial reduction in lift charges. Rail-Trailer's participation in Trailer Train would not last much longer. In March 1959, the railroaders who now dominated the Trailer Train board of directors terminated the Rail-Trailer/Van-Car management contract, a move that forced Ryan to relinquish the twenty-five hundred shares of Trailer Train stock he had controlled since 1955.[257]

By the end of the 1950s and with Ryan's departure, Trailer Train became the successful nationwide TOFC equipment pool that Newell had intended it to be. Despite a severe economic recession that brought many of its member railroads to the verge of bankruptcy, Trailer Train experienced a 10 percent increase in business between 1957 and 1958. In the latter year, the equipment pool that Newell helped to create transported nearly half of the 276,767 trailers hauled on the nation's railroads. Trailer Train owned nearly two thousand flatcars, worth about $25 million, that generated almost $2 million per year in rental charges to the various railroads that used the service. Those earnings were reinvested in additional equipment, relieving the PRR and other cash-strapped carriers of the burden of providing rolling stock.[258]

As the piggyback business increased in volume, conventional LCL traffic all but disappeared from the Pennsylvania Railroad. The company commissioned a study, released in June 1960, that merely confirmed the obvious. The recession of the late 1950s principally affected the manufacturing and transportation sectors and left consumer goods relatively untouched. That circumstance benefited truckers, who specialized in the rapid flexible delivery of high-value items over relatively short distances, and correspondingly eroded conventional boxcar freight. Nationwide, LCL traffic fell from 10.9 million tons in 1950 to a mere 3.9 million tons in 1959—representing less than one-third of 1 percent of all freight tonnage. Revenues declined as well, from $352.9 million in 1950 to $183.9 million at the end of the decade. There was little corresponding reduction in expenditures, however, thanks to high terminal costs and the labor-intensive nature of LCL traffic. The PRR's June 1960 report provided twenty-three pages of text and exhibits, but it was not necessary to read beyond the first line: "It is recommended that we take the necessary steps to get out of the L.C.L. business." Even Fred Carpi, who recalled his efforts in 1953 and 1954 to turn things around, admitted "that we stemmed the tide so little that it was hardly noticeable. It is our firm belief," he acknowledged, "that rail l.c.l. service can never compete with the other services that have been developed to handle small package shipments." LCL operations ended in 1961, but it was unknown whether the remaining traffic would be diverted to TrucTrain or would simply follow the highways from origin to destination.[259]

Regardless of the outcome of that contest or its effects on the Pennsylvania Railroad, Newell could take considerable satisfaction from his nurturing efforts on behalf of TrucTrain, Trailer Train, and intermodal transportation in general. He spent nearly eight years in the dual role of president of Trailer Train and vice president in charge of operations at the Pennsylvania Railroad. The individual who had done so much to integrate TrucTrain service into a system of national intermodal operations left the PRR in 1963, largely because of the lingering resentments generated by his ongoing feud with Carpi, and he devoted the next six years to the full-time administration of Trailer Train.[260] In 1959, the PRR and the N&W each sold five hundred shares of stock in Trailer Train, enabling the Illinois Central and the Gulf, Mobile & Ohio to join. The following year, the PRR made available an additional fifteen hundred Trailer Train shares, facilitating the participation of other railroads. Thereafter, every member of the consortium owned an equal portion of the firm's stock. By April 1964, forty railroads and one freight forwarder were participants in the equipment pool.[261] The removal of Rail-Trailer had nonetheless enabled the PRR to continue its role as first among equals, by assuming greater responsibility for car tracing, data processing, banking, and other clerical functions at Trailer Train. By the mid-1960s, the PRR was collecting between $75,000 and $85,000 per month in management fees—a valuable addition to the railroad's bottom line.[262]

The Pennsylvania Railroad's TOFC service (still marketed as TrucTrain, despite its reliance on Trailer Train equipment) thrived during the late 1950s and early 1960s. The PRR introduced new services under the TrucTrain brand, including Plan III (in which shippers owned the trailers and delivered them to a TrucTrain terminal for loading onto Trailer Train equipment) and Plan IV (in which freight forwarders owned both the trailers and the flatcars that transported them on the rail portion of their journey). TrucTrain revenue increased from $5.7 million in 1955 (the first full year of operation) to $10.6 million in 1958. By the end of 1964, the PRR rostered nearly three thousand trailers, used in Plan II service, in addition to the thousands more owned by shippers and motor carriers that the railroad transported according to the terms of the other plans. An increasing number of dedicated TrucTrain routes carried traffic across the Pennsylvania Railroad system and onto the tracks of connecting carriers. The railroad purchased special low-slung equipment and increased tunnel clearances in Baltimore, at a cost of $300,000.[263] The modifications permitted the inauguration, in 1961, of New York–Florida service in cooperation with the Richmond, Fredericksburg & Potomac; the Atlantic Coast Line; and the Florida East Coast. The Pennsylvania Railroad added seven more terminals during the early 1960s, ranging from small towns like Terre Haute, Indiana, and York, Pennsylvania, to the larger cities of Trenton and Baltimore. A major expansion at the Kearny TrucTrain facility in 1962 and 1963 included the installation of the PRR's first overhead crane, finally eliminating circus-style unloading. Cranes soon appeared at Chicago and other large TrucTrain terminals, and economies of scale eventually led to the closure of many marginal facilities in small communities and the subsequent concentration of business in major markets.[264] In 1960, the Pennsylvania Railroad operated twenty-four TrucTrain terminals and generated more than $17 million in revenue by moving more than 93,000 trailers. By 1965, earnings had increased to $35 million on a volume of 250,000 trailers. Whether that business came at the expense of independent truckers or of the PRR's boxcars was still a matter of debate.[265]

Paying for Progress

The PRR's postwar capital needs were unprecedented, a situation that produced significant changes in the company's organizational structure and personnel. The massive betterment programs that occurred during the early years of the twentieth century ensured that the Treasury Department gained power and prestige. Even though the PRR's operating personnel were among the best in the business, they possessed scant knowledge of matters pertaining to finance. Accordingly, in May 1904 Alexander Cassatt chose an outsider, Franklin National Bank president Henry Tatnall, as the company's sixth vice president, in charge of finance. While Cassatt and Samuel Rea possessed the vision and the engineering expertise to guide the PRR's massive rebuilding program, Tatnall had found the money necessary to pay for all the projects. He retired in 1925 and passed his responsibilities to Albert J. County, initially the vice president in charge of treasury, accounting, and corporate work and later the vice president in charge of finance and corporate relations. As his portmanteau titles indicated, County spent much of his time overseeing relations with subsidiary and allied companies and developing consolidation plans for the eastern railroads. When County retired in 1938, long-term capital expenditures were virtually nil, and the railroad's accounting and treasury functions involved little more than the processing of recurring payments and the distribution of dividends and bond interest to investors. His successor, George Henry Pabst Jr., had little more to do, and the Treasury Department had scant influence within the company.[266] By April 1951, less than three years into the PRR's $1 billion improvement program, Pabst had been with the company for forty-five years, through two world wars and the Great Depression. He was still in his early sixties, but his health was failing, and he informed the board of directors that he could no longer carry out his duties. He became a vice president, assistant to the president, an office commonly set aside as a mechanism to ease faithful older employees into retirement.[267]

When asked to recommend a successor, Pabst suggested one of the rising stars of the Philadelphia financial community. Both geographically and socially, David Crumley Bevan was a product of the city's western Main Line suburbs. One distant ancestor on his father's side, Iestan ap Gwrgan, was Prince of Glamorgan, Wales, during the eleventh century. Some genealogies, perhaps overoptimistically, suggested that he was also a matrilineal descendant of King Edward III of England. Fourteen generations later, in 1683, John ap Evan left Treverigg, in Glamorganshire, South Wales, following William Penn to Philadelphia. Leading a company of settlers, he gained land in the Welsh Tract to the west of the city in the area that would later be occupied by the PRR's route through the Main Line suburbs. He later changed the commonly used appellation ap Evan (son of Evan) into Bevan. His direct descendant was Howard Sloan Bevan, David's father, who spent forty-six years in the Pennsylvania Railroad Accounting Department prior to his death in 1938.[268]

Like Henry Tatnall before him, David Bevan was an outsider who spent his formative years far away from the intense operating requirements associated with the Pennsylvania Railroad. Born in 1906, he graduated from Lower Merion High School and then attended Haverford College, an old and prestigious Main Line educational institution. The young man excelled at academics and athletics, and his fellow students noted that "perhaps the greatest thing about Dave is his ambition." After graduating in the class of 1929, Bevan went on to the Harvard Graduate School of Business Administration. He began his business career at the Provident Trust Company. During the 1940s, Bevan served on the War Production Board, then became a member of a Lend Lease mission to Australia, and finally was the deputy head of the United States Mission of Economic Affairs in London. After the war, he became the treasurer of the New York Life Insurance Company, where he enhanced his impressive knowledge of accounting and budgeting. In May 1951, at Pabst's recommendation, Bevan became the PRR's vice president in charge of finance.[269]

Bevan's appointment coincided with the rapid evolution and extraordinary consequences of the computer age. His previous employment alerted him to the potential of automation and the increased use of computers and other information-processing devices. While most Pennsylvania Railroad executives dismissed computers as irrelevant to the company's operations, Bevan had the

David C. Bevan (1906–1996), who was born in Wayne, Pennsylvania, and earned a degree from Haverford College, was very much a part of Philadelphia's Main Line. After working for the War Production Board, the Provident Trust Company, and the New York Life Insurance Company, he joined the PRR in 1951 as the vice president in charge of finance. Bevan introduced often-skeptical executives to the data-processing, accounting, and cost-control methods he had learned in the financial sector. *Philadelphia Saving Fund Society Photographs, Hagley Museum & Library, acc. 1993.302.*

support of an individual whose opinion mattered most. By the time Bevan became a PRR employee, James Symes had already demonstrated that his support for new technologies and operating methods did not end with his advocacy for diesel locomotives and TOFC service. In each case, Symes was determined to offset rising labor costs by finding other areas in which the company could economize. In December 1948, Symes—who was at that time the vice president in charge of operations—acknowledged the "recent wage increases and the 40-hour week staring us in the face." He hoped to "obtain increased production with less man-hours," and he asked his subordinates to offer suggestions for reducing expenditures. Symes also demanded a separate report "as to how mechanization can eliminate man-hours." The first computer, in the modern sense, had entered service barely a decade earlier, and it was hardly surprising that Symes did not use that term. His language nonetheless suggested that he was determined that the Pennsylvania Railroad should join the information age. He asked IBM to undertake a study "of the various departments and organizations of the railroad, with the objective of increasing efficiency and reducing the costs of office procedures to the greatest extent possible." His recommendation that the PRR establish a System Mechanization Committee attested to the centralizing effect that new technology would undoubtedly produce.[270]

Symes's interest in "mechanization" began to show results, even before Bevan joined the company. Beginning in 1949, the PRR employed Photostat machines to prepare billing documents at major terminals. An electropneumatic train performance calculator in Philadelphia determined tonnage ratings and optimal allocation schedules for the railroad's motive power. The company used punch-card tabulators, supplied by Remington Rand, in conjunction with Teletype machines, to process waybills. As John L. Webb, the manager of stations and motor service, informed Symes, "We now have the first applications of punch card-tabulating equipment to station accounting work in the United States, and from the information we are able to obtain, in the world." In 1950 and 1951, the company implemented an "Intelex" reservation system, manufactured by a subsidiary of International Telephone & Telegraph, to allocate coach and Pullman space on long-distance trains. It worked well enough to encourage the installation of "Ticketeer" machines in Pittsburgh and Philadelphia in 1953 and 1954. The system, manufactured by the Burroughs Corporation, came with a 109-page instruction manual that listed hundreds of route and fare combinations for intercity passengers and commuters, members of the clergy, and soldiers on furlough, among others.[271]

After he joined the Pennsylvania Railroad, Bevan quickly expanded the company's computing capabilities. In 1951, the company installed IBM tabulating machines to process information in the Voluntary Relief Department, replacing older Kardex equipment. The upgrade was part of a broader effort to complete an actuarial study for the PRR's benefit plan—necessary because a declining workforce was supporting a large pool of beneficiaries, threatening to overwhelm the VRD's resources. Railroad personnel quickly found new uses for the equipment, employing it to locate freight cars, perform station

accounting, and prepare payrolls. Vice President Newell—who, like Symes, welcomed the computer age—observed that "the punch card-tabulating operation is so involved and yet so productive of beneficial results, that it would appear that close coordination of all installations on our railroad is extremely desirable." In 1955, Bevan oversaw the establishment of a new Data Processing Department "to centralize machine operations to the end that the maximum machine utilization and economy may be realized." To facilitate that process, the PRR ordered one IBM Model 705 mainframe computer as well as two IBM 650 Magnetic Drum Data-Processing Machines. Both models debuted a year earlier, suggesting that the PRR was one of the earliest adopters of the new technology. The Data Processing Department worked in collaboration with the Methods and Procedures Department, established in 1955, which functioned as a centralized "electronic and mechanical data processing service" for accounting and clerical functions. The new entity was, executives noted, "created for the purpose of improving present work procedures, and planning new ones, on a systemwide basis." Computers quickly replaced the existing electropneumatic train performance calculator and helped to reduce fuel consumption, optimize tonnage ratings, and guide decisions regarding the purchase of new locomotives. The upgrades required a considerable investment—the Model 705 alone carried a rental fee of $30,000 per month—but Bevan concluded that it was money well spent. It was more difficult to calculate the intangible costs, stemming from the resistance of operating personnel to new and unfamiliar technology, the centralization of data collection and decision-making, and the growing authority of button pushers and number crunchers.[272]

Bevan's commitment to data processing reflected his larger concern that the PRR's financial-management practices were woefully out of date. He was appalled that such a large and seemingly prosperous company had failed to implement standards that had been in use elsewhere for many years. The principal difficulty stemmed from the reliance on the accounting methods that the Interstate Commerce Commission mandated under the terms of the 1906 Hepburn Act. The haphazard allocation of costs between freight and passenger operations constituted one of their many failings. A more serious problem, according to Bevan, was that ICC accounting categories were reflective in nature—that is, they provided a fair approximation of what each railroad had done in the past, but they had little value in planning for the future. The Interstate Commerce Commission thus gave the railroads scant incentive to adopt income budgets, capital budgets, or cash-flow statements that since the 1930s had represented standard operating practice at most manufacturing, financial, and telecommunications firms. Real-time statistical controls that provided managers with periodic performance updates—and thus the ability to make rapid alterations in spending—were likewise alien to the ICC system. Finally, there was little opportunity to compare expenditures with their corresponding benefits and thus hold individual managers accountable for their performance.[273]

Bevan's most immediate concern involved the rapid increase in debt associated with the PRR's postwar modernization program. From a prewar high of more than $1 billion, total system debt had gradually declined to $891.9 million in 1946. It then crept upward, again surpassing $1 billion in 1950. By the end of 1952, as Bevan completed his first full year at the Pennsylvania Railroad, total system debt exceeded $1.1 billion. The composition of that debt was also changing. In 1939, bonds accounted for 94 percent of debt, reflecting the borrowing necessary to pay for the electrification of lines to the east of Harrisburg. In the years that followed, managers shifted their focus to new equipment rather than improvements to the physical plant. There had been little major engineering work and considerable deferred maintenance during the war years, but the demand for more locomotives and cars was insatiable. Symes's campaign to make up for lost time by purchasing diesels as quickly as possible ensured further borrowing, as did managerial decisions to reequip many of the railroad's passenger trains. Bonded debt decreased by 22.7 percent between 1939 and 1952, from $990.4 million to $765.3 million. During the same period, however, borrowing for new equipment soared from $62.4 million to $350.7 million, an increase of 462.4 percent.[274]

Those securities would eventually come to maturity, providing Bevan with another set of problems. For the remainder of the decade, bonded-debt maturities would exceed $10 million in only two years (1955 and 1957), while the total maturities for all debts mostly hovered between $30 million and $40 million annually. In 1960, however, the PRR would be responsible for the redemption of more than $90 million in debt, including about $65 million in bonded indebtedness. The situation in 1965 would be far worse, with nearly $125 million in bonds and $15 million in equipment-trust obligations coming due. The total—more than $141 million—represented nearly 13 percent of the PRR's long-term debt and 5.6 percent of the company's total capitalization. In the past, Bevan's successors would have simply negotiated another round of bond sales, at a reasonable interest rate, to pay off issues that were about

to mature. Given the railroad's financial performance—to say nothing of the limited earning potential of American railroads in general—that strategy would be difficult, if not impossible. The situation involving equipment-trust certificates was even more problematic. Unlike tracks, bridges, and buildings, new locomotives and cars were movable assets that could be easily repossessed and transferred to another railroad. Historically, therefore, banks and other lenders had been willing to finance the purchase of equipment, and at low interest rates. The financial malaise that affected all the nation's railroads called into question the ability of new cars and locomotives to generate a satisfactory rate of return and suggested that repossessed equipment might not find a remunerative home anywhere in the country.[275]

The financing of equipment assumed critical proportions during the summer of 1957. In May, the PRR paid extremely high rates (4.43%) for equipment-trust certificates. Other railroads were facing the same difficulty, and the situation was indicative of a loss of investor confidence in the future of the entire railroad industry—not just individual carriers. In July, Symes told the House Commerce Committee that the PRR would be unable to raise the funds necessary to purchase an estimated $1 billion of new equipment that, he insisted, the PRR would need over the next five years. Acting on behalf of thirty-four eastern railroads, he suggested that the federal government spend up to $2.5 billion to form an equipment pool that would then lease cars and locomotives to the railroads. The plan generated opposition from southern and western lines that were in less desperate circumstances—and from opponents of an expanded government, who feared that Symes's proposal marked a preliminary step toward nationalization. After failing to secure federal assistance, Symes quietly arranged to lease 225 diesel locomotives, worth nearly $33.8 million, from EMD and Alco. Financial analysts did not learn of the arrangement until the end of December, and they cautioned that neither the leases nor the secrecy that surrounded them reflected well on the PRR's finances. Thereafter, the Pennsylvania Railroad largely abandoned equipment-trust financing in favor of equipment leasing. Lease payments on cars and locomotives constituted an operating expense, charged against earnings, rather than the servicing of debt associated with a capital investment. The practice thus lowered the PRR's total debt and appeared to increase return on investment. Leasing also reduced net income, making it more likely that the ICC would grant higher rates. The practice was perfectly legal and took place on an increasing number of railroads, but it did suggest to many investors and Wall Street analysts that new financial practices were increasingly rigging the game in favor of the Pennsylvania Railroad.[276]

Bevan's initial task, therefore, was to lower the PRR's debt and to identify additional sources of funding. He made considerable progress with the first goal, and by the end of 1959, total system debt had decreased by a fifth, to $882 million. The $49 million in consolidated mortgage bonds that constituted the largest single component of the 1960 maturities had become a more manageable $35 million, and the sale of Pennsylvania Company bonds could offset the remaining balance. There had been a similar curtailment in the $125 million in bonds that would come due in 1965 to $70 million. The debt-reduction campaign lowered the PRR's fixed charges and decreased the likelihood of default should the company experience a prolonged period of low earnings. Unfortunately, Bevan's efforts also diverted funds from the upkeep of the physical plant, exacerbating the ongoing problems associated with deferred maintenance and increasing the likelihood that he would anger operating and traffic officials.[277]

The acquisition of additional capital proved more challenging than the retirement of old debts. Given the parlous state of the Pennsylvania Railroad's finances, the issuance of additional stock was simply out of the question. The last significant offering, during the summer of 1930, had placed more than half a million shares with the PRR's employees. The Great Depression destroyed the value of their investment and that of the railroad's other shareholders. Stock prices recovered somewhat during the war years but would never come close to their precrash levels. Nor would dividends. In 1930, and perhaps unwisely, the company's directors had authorized a payout of 8 percent—the highest since 1876. Unlike many other carriers, the PRR always managed to pay a dividend during the Great Depression, which was no small accomplishment. Between 1942 and 1945, the rate had grown to 5 percent, thanks to wartime traffic. It fell to 3 percent in the first year of peace, and the operating loss incurred in 1946 caused a further decline, to the same 1 percent level seen during the worst part of the Depression. The following years were scarcely better—2 percent in 1948, 1.5 percent in 1949, and 2 percent for each of the three years that followed. During a period of general economic prosperity, therefore, the company's shareholders earned little more on their investment than they had during the worst economic crisis in American history.[278]

In common with many other companies experiencing financial difficulties, PRR officials sought creative mechanisms to increase dividend payments, maintain share prices, and reduce complaints from stockholders. Those efforts began in the autumn of 1946, five years before Bevan became the company's chief financial officer. The catalyst was a report, completed on February 1, 1946, covering all aspects of the Pennsylvania Railroad's finances. The study updated a document prepared in October 1940 and reflected the changes that had occurred during the war and the immediate postwar period. The conclusions were not encouraging, and they suggested that the PRR's practices were badly out of date. Most of the problems resulted from the development of the Lines West of Pittsburgh and Erie, largely through leases of carriers that were already in operation. The generous lease terms obligated the Pennsylvania Railroad to allocate substantial sums to the payment of interest and dividends to investors who owned securities in those subsidiaries. The Trust of 1878, established to reduce that burden, allocated a minimum of $50,000 per month to repurchasing those stocks and bonds, which then became the property of the Pennsylvania Company. Earnings from those western subsidiaries contributed to the financial strength of the Pennsylvania Company, which in turn supported the Pennsylvania Railroad.[279]

By the end of World War II, however, the Trust of 1878 had outlived its usefulness. As PRR executives explained, "So much of this stock has already been acquired through the years, and circumstances have so changed in other respects, that the fund has now outgrown its original purpose, and its continued operation without modification threatens to bring about an accumulation of moneys which might better be applied to the extinguishment of your Company's debt, and of other types of securities as to which your Company has assumed obligations." It was a convoluted way of suggesting that the modification of the Trust of 1878 could offset the PRR's rising debt burden and reduce tax liabilities. In November 1947, the directors first considered the use of the trust's assets to pay dividends, and they secured shareholder approval to do so at the May 1948 annual meeting.[280]

When Bevan began his employment with the PRR a few years later, he continued to rely on the reserves contained in the Trust of 1878, yet he cautioned restraint in the matter of dividend payments. In the ten years that followed the end of World War II, the PRR paid out 60 percent of its net income in the form of dividends. That was a departure from the tradition of "a dollar to the investors and a dollar to the property" and was also at variance with the rest of the nation's Class I railroads—where dividends averaged only 43 percent of net income. In March 1954, with the economy still enduring a post–Korean War recession and

PRR stock hovering around $16 a share, Bevan expressed his concerns to the board of directors. He reminded them that the company was paying dividends at a rate 50 percent higher than the average Class I railroad. Given that that average included relatively prosperous western carriers and Pocahontas coal roads, his conservatism was well-founded.[281]

Bevan also recommended the dissolution of the Trust of 1878. "Not only has the Trust outlived its original purpose," he emphasized, "but it now is a definite hindrance to the company's policy of corporate simplification." That goal was not new, and for decades PRR executives had been consolidating hundreds of subsidiaries into the parent company. Bevan's other motivation was more troubling. "Termination of the Trust," he noted, "would give the Company worthwhile additional advantages in the area of financial flexibility"—largely because assets held in the trust could not be used as collateral for certain types of borrowing. "Although it is not contemplated that these leased line obligations will be used," he concluded, "in the event of an emergency it would provide another medium for financing." Bevan's arguments were persuasive, and in May 1956 both the board and the stockholders complied. Whether they realized it or not, Bevan was preparing for the financial problems that repeatedly affected the Pennsylvania Railroad, as he anticipated one emergency after another.[282]

Bevan was equally concerned about other aspects of the PRR's finances. In early 1954, he commissioned Joseph R. Warner, an independent financial analyst and railroad consultant, to update the February 1946 financial report. Warner offered ample evidence that the Pennsylvania Railroad's finances were rooted in the past. The Trust of 1878, he cautioned, was only one of many indications that "the present financial set-up is largely a result of policies formulated for the most part many decades ago under vastly different economic conditions and outlook for the railroad industry now prevailing." Just as the PRR desperately needed new locomotives and cars, Warner concluded, "the financing structure of the enterprise requires overhauling and conformation to the needs of the time."[283]

Warner also took note of the unfavorable conditions associated with the Pennsylvania Railroad's equity. "The Pennsylvania, like the New York Central, with so substantial a portion of its investment in passenger facilities of uncertain future profitableness," he emphasized, "should not, and reasonably cannot, expect too much of the stock market in the way of an improvement in the price of this stock that would bring it nearer the level of years ago." Warner also emphasized that the last stock offering of any significance had occurred in 1928 and 1929, on the eve of the Great Depression, and that more than three-quarters of the outstanding shares had been issued prior to 1914. With shares currently selling for about a fifth of their book value, it was hardly surprising that no further stock issues would be forthcoming. That meant that "in comparison with any other prominent railroad, except for the New York Central, the Pennsylvania has the lowest ratio of capital stock or non-fixed charge capitalization, computed at market value, to underlying fixed charge capitalization." In short, the PRR possessed an unsustainably high debt-to-equity ratio, and the billion-dollar postwar betterment campaign was only going to make matters worse.[284]

Based on his assertion that "the financial structure of the System is not only burdensome, but unduly and seemingly unnecessarily complex," Warner recommended several reforms. While the PRR had increasingly relied on equipment-trust financing, Warner urged restraint in the future. Such obligations could not be refinanced and, he noted, the depreciation allowances on the cars and locomotives covered by equipment trusts were insufficient to pay for the cost of replacements. Warner also suggested that the PRR's stock be changed to a no-par basis, in the hope that additional shares could be issued at very low prices—perhaps in conjunction with convertible bond issues. Warner suggested replacing the general mortgage, which was secured by a lien on various subordinate companies in the Pennsylvania Railroad system, with a refunding mortgage secured by the assets of the entire corporation. Those reforms, Warner emphasized, must be undertaken in conjunction with a simplification of the PRR's organizational and financial structures. He emphasized that the division between the Pennsylvania Railroad and the Pennsylvania Company was particularly problematic.[285] "This corporate compartmental dividing line was formerly not uncommon practice in the railroad industry," he conceded, "but most roads abandoned it years ago in line with the modern concept that security holders are entitled to a comprehensive picture of the System rather than merely a corporate income account." Warner emphasized that "the non-inclusion in the published income accounts of the railroad of the income of the wholly owned Pennsylvania Company has always seemed rather inexcusable in the light of present day concepts as to what the owners of a property are entitled to know."[286]

Bevan wholeheartedly endorsed Warner's recommendations. In late March, even before the final report was ready, he briefed the board of directors on the company's financial situation. Bevan began on a positive note, highlighting the progress of efforts to retire a substantial portion of the funded debt—a policy he intended to accelerate. Like Warner, he stressed the limitations of equipment-trust financing. Bevan also suggested a new issue of $35 million in bonds, although secured by the assets of the Pennsylvania Company rather than the entire Pennsylvania Railroad system. While he did not explicitly discuss the PRR's high debt-to-equity ratio, Bevan nonetheless cautioned that dividends paid on the company's outstanding shares consumed an unsustainably large portion of net operating income. Bevan was also determined to provide greater financial transparency through the generation of consolidated reports that included all the PRR's subsidiaries, although it would require another decade—and the acquisition of companies that had nothing to do with railroading—before he could convince other senior executives of the wisdom of that policy.[287]

Armed with Warner's preliminary findings, Bevan also warned the directors about the steady decline in cash reserves. By 1954, the PRR's working capital (current assets minus current liabilities) was approximately 10.4 percent of operating revenues, about average for a railroad at that time. The corresponding average for the steel industry, also badly affected by the post–Korean War recession, was 16 percent, while the chemical industry maintained a working-capital ratio of almost 32 percent. The situation was especially dangerous in an environment where the PRR experienced large fluctuations in traffic and revenues but often lacked the ability to control wages and other operating costs. Preparing for the worst, Bevan negotiated a $50 million line of credit through a group of financial institutions headed by First National City Bank of New York. Although he had no immediate plans to use those funds, they were available in the event of a crisis. In early 1957, PRR officials nonetheless acknowledged that the level of working capital had fallen by $12.4 million during the preceding year, to $109.8 million, and was "now at a minimum required for the conduct of our business."[288]

Recession

The financial crisis that Bevan had predicted began the following year. The economic downturn that started in August 1957—often referred to as the "Eisenhower Recession"—was more severe than anything that had occurred since the Great Depression.[289] By the time the economy began to recover, the following April, the nation's industrial output had fallen by 13 percent, while gross domestic product declined by nearly 4 percent. The decrease in GDP was only slightly worse than the one that had accompanied the recession that followed the end of the Korean War, but

the causes were different. The rapid reduction in military spending disrupted the economy during 1953 and 1954 but barely affected capital spending. In 1957–1958, however, the output of producers' durable equipment was down 17.4 percent (compared to less than 5.0 percent in 1953–1954), while demand for consumer durables—essentially unchanged after the Korean War—fell by nearly 10.0 percent. The end of military operations in Korea had caused a significant decrease in rail passenger traffic but otherwise did not entail any lasting hardship for the carriers. The Eisenhower Recession, in contrast, affected demand for raw materials and manufactured goods, precisely the type of traffic that the railroads depended on for their survival. PRR suffered more severely than most other carriers, thanks to its ties to the steel industry. A series of strikes, unsustainably high wages, restrictive work rules, managerial unwillingness to invest in new technology, and the diminishment of the rich iron-ore reserves of the Mesabi Range contributed to a growth in foreign competition and the long decline of domestic steel production.[290]

A further blow was about to fall, as construction crews labored to complete the St. Lawrence Seaway. Since the 1890s, advocates of improved water navigation had repeatedly proposed a system of canals, locks, and channels that would enable oceangoing ships to reach all five of the Great Lakes. The project gained momentum during the administration of Woodrow Wilson, with supporters asserting that the railroads were monopolistic, charged unconscionably high rates, and failed to cope with wartime transportation needs. In 1932, the completion of improvements to the Weiland Canal brought part of that vision to fruition, but the Great Depression and World War II impeded further construction. During the 1950s, in addition to his support for an interstate highway network, Dwight D. Eisenhower favored the Seaway project, ensuring that the governments of the United States and Canada would coordinate the diplomatic, political, financial, and engineering aspects of the proposed waterway.[291]

Railroad executives and representatives from railway labor unions were vocal in their opposition, although their political influence was far less pervasive than earlier in the century. The Association of American Railroads took the lead in the fight against the Seaway, but Pennsylvania Railroad executives also lobbied against construction. Company officials informed shareholders that "the estimates of the traffic potential of the Seaway are questionable and the evidence presented at [Congressional] hearings indicates that the available traffic would not produce sufficient tolls to operate the Seaway and service the debt" associated with its construction, adding, "Your Company is therefore opposing the unjustifiable expenditure of Government funds to create and subsidize an unneeded transportation facility."[292]

Supporters of the St. Lawrence Seaway were quick to refute those allegations, while insisting that railroad executives were impeding the progress and prosperity of two great nations. In December 1950, journalist Freeman Lincoln suggested that a resolution by the Pennsylvania state legislature, opposing construction, "was not unaffected by the will of the Pennsylvania Railroad." In the US Senate, Vermont Republican George D. Aiken claimed that Lincoln's article "points out a fact which many supporters of the St. Lawrence development have known for a long time—that the eastern railroads and utilities have been primarily responsible for the delay and the obstruction in developing this greatest of all North American resources."[293] The following year, Representative John D. Dingell Jr., a Michigan Democrat, asserted that "the Pennsylvania Railroad, along with the Baltimore & Ohio, has managed to create seemingly unanimous opposition among business groups." He identified the PRR as one of the principal forces behind "the persistent machinations of a small but powerfully entrenched group of special interests whose chronic antipathy toward the St. Lawrence project has led them into destructive activity detrimental, in the long run, to their own, as well as the Nation's best interest." Although Dingell's claims were exaggerated, it was clear that few members of Congress evinced much sympathy for the plight of the railroads.[294] On May 13, 1954, Eisenhower signed the Wiley-Dondero Seaway Act into law, enabling construction to begin. The route opened in April 1959, and it soon affected shipments of bulk commodities by the PRR and other northeastern railroads.[295]

Even before the Seaway opened, and thanks to the recession that bore Eisenhower's name, the Pennsylvania Railroad's operating and financial results were horrific. By December 1957, freight carloadings were 22 percent below the same month in 1956, while contractually mandated cost-of-living adjustments raised wages by $28 million annually. Losses for the first two months of 1958 reached $11 million, increasing to $15 million by the end of March. The $19.6 million profit earned during the first nine months of 1957 turned into a $6.9 million loss during the same period the next year. The Pennsylvania Railroad earned a mere 2.9 percent return on investment in 1956, before the recession began, yet that figure fell to 1.4 percent in 1957. Working capital, already perilously low, plunged a further $20.6 million, to a mere $89.2 million. The board of directors reauthorized the $50 million line of credit that Bevan had negotiated in 1954 but refrained

from tapping that last remaining source of funds. They also voted to defer the first two quarterly dividends for 1958. In October, the board agreed to tap retained earnings from prior years—money that should have been used for badly needed repairs to track and equipment—to pay a twenty-five-cent per-share dividend. They did so to maintain the PRR's unbroken corporate history of annual payments to shareholders and to retain the confidence of investors. No one believed that that policy was sustainable.[296]

When the PRR's shareholders met in Philadelphia in May 1958, Symes offered little comfort. He acknowledged that revenues had declined 22 percent, compared to the previous year, and "the result," he suggested, "is that it seems extremely doubtful at this time that we will operate at a profit this year." If that prediction came true, it would be only the second loss in the railroad's history, following the disastrous events of 1946 that had set Symes on course for the presidency. Despite the deteriorating physical plant, Symes stressed that "we have reduced capital expenditures to the absolute minimum." He made "no promises" regarding the payment of dividends but suggested that "fortunately there is no imminent danger" of bankruptcy—comments that provided his audience with little reassurance regarding the value of their investments. The recitation of disasters took considerable time—so long, in fact, that it was nearly two in the afternoon before the midday meal could be served. "But if shareholders took to heart the words of James M. Symes," a reporter observed, "they didn't have much stomach for lunch."[297]

One month after the annual meeting, David Bevan addressed the New York Society of Security Analysts. He began his remarks by reminding his listeners that it was Friday the thirteenth. "We have been in the red for six consecutive months," he acknowledged, "and I fear that not only will we be in the red for the second time in our history but our deficit will attain substantial proportions." Bevan emphasized that he had been achieving success with his ongoing efforts to reduce the PRR's debt, and he admitted that that policy was necessary if he hoped to ever borrow money again from anyone. He did not mention that some of the debt reduction had occurred because the PRR had liquidated $98.8 million in assets—everything from real estate to shares in Pennsylvania Greyhound—and had realized an additional $96.5 million from the scrapping of equipment and the abandonment of branch lines. The company was running out of things to sell, however, and the economic crisis showed no signs of abating. "As far as the near-term outlook is concerned," Bevan told his audience, "the roughest period may still be ahead of us." With little likelihood of either profits or dividends in the immediate future, he conceded, "this is going to be probably the worst year" in the history of the Pennsylvania Railroad.[298]

For more than a century, railroad executives had weathered economic downturns by postponing the upkeep of equipment and the physical plant, confident in the knowledge that the future would bring prosperity and enable those deficiencies to be remedied. By the end of 1957, the railroad had accumulated $132.9 million in deferred maintenance to the right-of-way and structures, and the corresponding figure for equipment had reached $57.4 million. The Eisenhower Recession eroded many of the gains created by the $1 billion postwar modernization program and left the Pennsylvania Railroad with malfunctioning locomotives, damaged freight cars, decrepit passenger equipment, decaying structures, and tracks riddled with slow orders. The company had entered a "death spiral," a slow downward progression toward inadequate service, outraged customers, falling revenues, and possible bankruptcy.[299]

The Pennsylvania Railroad would fare worse than some and better than others in the postwar world. Some western carriers were able to weather the storm, thanks to the growing Sunbelt economy, long line hauls, modest passenger obligations, and a reliance on grain and other bulk commodities. Other companies were in far more desperate circumstances. They included the New Haven, with its obligation to provide commuter and short-haul passenger service in heavily urbanized areas that had long featured a robust highway network. Also in trouble were the lines that served the nearly deserted anthracite fields of northeastern Pennsylvania. During the 1950s and into the 1960s, the Pennsylvania Railroad was between those two extremes. There was certainly cause for optimism, given the company's sterling financial reputation, its talented employees, and the indispensable nature of its operations to the economic welfare of the Northeast and Midwest. As insiders, however, the company's executives sensed better than most that weaknesses were beginning to exceed strengths and that threats were growing faster than opportunities. The problems included a customer base affected by deindustrialization and the flight of companies to warmer and more employer-friendly regions of the country. Line hauls were shorter than the industry average, and taxes and terminal costs were higher. Many managers were ill-equipped to deal with the technological innovations, political constraints, and labor-relations conditions that characterized the postwar environment. Ambitious young men with college educations looked with disdain at the PRR's low salaries and limited opportunities for promotion, and they went elsewhere to begin their careers. The financiers who had once been eager to place the railroad's stocks and bonds with investors now shunned a company with a high operating ratio and an abysmally low rate of return. Nothing, it seemed, could prevent the Pennsylvania Railroad from entering a long period of decline.

Chapter 6

Decline

World War II was a total war, one that mobilized every element of society, all the workers on the Pennsylvania Railroad, and each member of their families. The company's executives maintained a long tradition of giving jobs to the sons of employees. When so many young men went to war, they extended that practice to wives and daughters. It was a transition that affected the Lightburn family, whose roles exemplified the railroad's pledge to "Serve the Nation" in peace and in war. James G. Lightburn was born in Lewis County, West Virginia, on March 6, 1881, and he entered PRR service in 1903 at age twenty-two. Ten years later, he earned a promotion to engineman, the most skilled and most highly respected position in the pantheon of railway labor. As one of his descendants noted, he "was a strong union man," committed to a brotherhood that linked the benefits of collective bargaining to the status of operating employees who were skilled, sober, dedicated, and industrious. During the 1930s, thanks in large measure to his service, all four of his sons found work with the Pennsylvania Railroad—James in the Freight Traffic Department, Robert in the Crestline Shops, Joseph in the Maintenance of Way Department, and Willis as a fireman. All joined the armed forces during the war and, although women did not exactly replace them, their four sisters did take railroad jobs. Sara Lightburn Snyder worked as a clerk in the Maintenance of Way Department at Crestline, Virginia Lightburn served as a clerk in the ticket office, and the remaining two Lightburn daughters worked for the Pennsylvania Railroad as well. PRR executives had ample reason to celebrate the Lightburns' contributions to victory. They did so in a 1943 advertisement that appeared in

newspapers in cities throughout the company's territory. "A Railroad Man's Family at War: The Lightburns of Crestline, Ohio" featured the entire family—the matriarch, the daughters at work, the sons in uniform, and the father, depicted most heroically of all, steadfast in the cab of his locomotive.[1]

If James G. Lightburn and his family exemplified the nobility of railroading and the PRR's commitment to its employees and their families, then a string of horrific accidents during and immediately after World War II illustrated the dangers of that profession. On March 16, 1941, *The Buckeye* derailed northwest of Pittsburgh, sending cars skidding down a snow-covered embankment and into the Ohio River. Rescuers found scores of injured passengers, five corpses, and clear evidence that someone had sabotaged the tracks. Agents from the Federal Bureau of Investigation, operating under the theory that Nazi sympathizers were at work, failed to identify the culprits. At Dunkirk, Ohio, steam pressure caused a cylinder head to

Facing, In a 1943 advertisement, the PRR highlighted the contributions of every member of the Lightburn family to the war effort. As an engineman with many years of seniority, James G. Lightburn was among the PRR's best paid and most highly skilled employees. He was also a beneficiary of the gains made by organized labor, and he expected his union to preserve his favorable wages and working conditions, even as the Pennsylvania Railroad entered a long period of postwar decline. *Pennsylvania Railroad Photographs, Hagley Museum & Library, acc. 1988.231.*

A RAILROAD MAN'S FAMILY AT WAR

The LIGHTBURNS of Crestline, Ohio

Capt. James B. Lightburn. Formerly with the Freight Traffic Department of the Pennsylvania Railroad— now in Iran with a railroad battalion.

1st Lt. Robert A. Lightburn. Previously employed in the Pennsylvania Railroad's Crestline Shops—now in the Medical Corps, San Antonio, Texas.

Lt. Joseph G. Lightburn. On furlough from the Maintenance of Way Department of the Pennsylvania Railroad—now with the Navy in the Pacific.

1st Lt. Willis Lightburn. Formerly a locomotive fireman on the Pennsylvania Railroad—now with the Air Force in North Africa.

Keeping the "Engines of War" rolling, James G. Lightburn, engineman and father of the family. He has been with the Pennsylvania Railroad 40 years.

THIS is the story of a fighting American family . . . a Pennsylvania Railroad family . . . the Lightburns of Crestline, Ohio.

On December 31, 1940 . . . a year before Pearl Harbor, the Lightburns . . . father, mother, four girls, four sons . . . held a family reunion in the pleasant home where the children were born and reared.

Today, this family group is scattered . . . all the boys officers in our Army or Navy while the girls, too, are playing vital roles.

An unusual family? Not according to "Jim" Lightburn. But a family reared in the tradition of service . . . ready when called to serve the cause of Freedom and their Country.

Pennsylvania Railroad salutes the Lightburns with pride and pleasure. A real railroad family, they are one of many railroad families who have given their sons and daughters to serve our Nation. Such families reflect the spirit and character of the manhood and womanhood which enables this and all America's railroads to meet successfully the vital transportation needs of our Country at war.

Mrs. Blanch L. Lightburn, mother of eight fine children—four boys, four girls, all serving their Country.

Mrs. Helen Lightburn Boecher is a welfare nurse.

Mrs. Sara Lightburn Snyder serves the Pennsylvania Railroad at Crestline.

Virginia Lightburn, now a clerk in the Pennsylvania Railroad ticket office at Crestline.

Jacqueline Lightburn is a member of the U. S. Cadet Nurse Corps.

★ 36,247 in the Armed Forces
∴ 65 have given their lives for their country

PENNSYLVANIA RAILROAD
Serving the Nation

BUY U. S. WAR BONDS AND STAMPS

blow out of the locomotive on a westbound freight train. It was a matter of little consequence, save that the debris landed on an adjacent track, squarely in the path of the eastbound *Pennsylvanian*. Thirteen people died in the ensuing derailment, less than a month before the attack on Pearl Harbor. Many of them were recent draftees who would never have a chance to defend their country. A passenger train traveling between Atlantic City and New York derailed near Delair, New Jersey, on May 23, 1943, owing to excessive speed, an act of carelessness that killed fourteen. Barely three months later, on September 6, the advance *Congressional* derailed at Frankford Junction near Philadelphia. The train's forward momentum drove two of the cars into a signal bridge, splitting them open and killing seventy-nine people, many of them servicemen. The Interstate Commerce Commission began an inquiry into the cause of the wreck, which investigators soon attributed to a burned-out journal bearing. A retired PRR engineman who had made hundreds of runs on *The Congressional* was more prosaic in his assessment of the tragedy. "These things happen now and then," he observed, "and sometimes no one ever knows just why or how." On June 15, 1945, with the war nearly over, a failed bearing—this time on a boxcar—sent a freight train careening into the path of the *Dominion Express*. Nineteen died in a wreck that tossed an eighty-ton steel passenger car into the air, then down again atop the cab of the locomotive, squashing it almost flat. Private First-Class Lester Calvert told reporters that the collision was "louder than anything I heard on European battlefronts." His fellow soldier, PFC Herbert E. Swan, was on his way home to Buffalo. He had endured nearly three years in a German prisoner-of-war camp, but he would not survive the last leg of his journey. Such individual tragedies were part of a troubling nationwide surge in railroad accidents that claimed the lives of some two hundred passengers during the first half of the decade—although those who considered rail travel unsafe would have been wise to reflect that nearly forty thousand Americans died in automobile crashes in 1941 alone.[2]

The accidents continued long after the war ended, as exhausted crews and worn-out equipment coped with returning veterans, recreational travelers, and the output of industries rapidly converting to peacetime production. On December 13, 1946, an eastbound freight train stopped at Coulter, Ohio, while the crew replaced a broken air hose. Another eastbound freight plowed into it and, seconds later, the westbound *Golden Triangle* hit the wreckage. Nineteen people died, including fifteen soldiers on Christmas leave. Two boys, playing along the PRR right-of-way in Walton, Indiana, wondered what would happen if they placed a coil of steel wire on the tracks. They soon found out, as a passenger train left the rails, killing six people and injuring twenty. Less than a month later, on February 18, 1947, the eastbound *Red Arrow* derailed just east of Horseshoe Curve. The cars cascaded down the side of the mountain, leaving 24 dead and 126 injured. The subsequent headline—"Most of Train Crew Die"—provided further evidence that employees rather than passengers were relatively likely to suffer the consequences of misfortune. Ten days later, at almost precisely the same location, a through sleeper on the *Sunshine Special* broke loose from its train and rolled three and a half miles down the mountain before derailing—killing a Pullman porter and injuring eleven passengers. On May 1, shortly after midnight, a westbound freight train had just passed Huntingdon when a pair of sixteen-foot-long steel plates shifted and slid sideways into the path of the overtaking *American*, en route to St. Louis. No sooner had the plates ripped open the fourth car, a sleeper, than an eastbound freight rammed the train from the opposite side, derailing the engine and fouling all four main line tracks. It was the third accident in the Alleghenies in as many months, one that left two-week-old Penelope Sims in a local hospital with a fractured leg, and her mother among the dead.[3]

Other incidents involved a far smaller loss of life but could be, in their own way, just as tragic. At 1:15 p.m. on Wednesday, October 6, 1948, Train 53, the westbound *Fort Pitt*, departed Pittsburgh on schedule. The two K4s Pacifics, #5058 and #5446, were more than adequate for the nine steel passenger cars, and within minutes the train had accelerated to sixty-five miles an hour. The four-track main line that stretched west toward Chicago was in superb condition, with newly laid 131-pound rail securely spiked to ties that lay in a deep bed of ballast. Neither the deferred maintenance of the Depression years nor the shortages of wartime impeded the progress of the train that snaked along the gentle curves that lay north of the Ohio River. At West Bellevue, less than six miles beyond Pittsburgh, the tracks followed a narrow path between the river and a sandstone bluff 120 feet high. Experienced section foremen—the Pennsylvania Railroad employed the best in the business—knew that even minor changes in geology could portend disaster. Maintenance-of-way workers periodically rappelled down the cliff face, using steel bars to pry loose any rocks that might eventually succumb to the force of gravity. Only two days earlier, a section foreman had made a careful inspection of the area. Trackwalkers patrolled the right-of-way day and night. One of them had walked by at 10:10 a.m., little more than three hours before *The Fort Pitt* passed the site, at the confluence of the Allegheny and Monongahela Rivers, that had given the train its name. Just as *The Fort Pitt* was pulling away from the platform at Pittsburgh's Union Station, an eastbound train passed safely through the area. Sometime within the next eleven minutes, a mass of rock—thirty-five feet long, twenty feet high, eight feet thick, and weighing nearly a hundred tons—calved off the face of the bluff and slid onto the tracks below. Engine crews were as vigilant as track-men for changes in the right-of-way, but they could not see around cliff-obscured curves. Four hundred and fifty feet from the rockslide, the fireman of *The Fort Pitt*'s lead-ing locomotive spotted the danger and shouted a frantic warning. His engineman threw the brakes into emergency, immediately but already much too late. For an instant, the still-spinning drivers of the second locomotive continued to propel its mate forward before its crew closed the throt-tle, and the train slid, wheels locked and sparks flying, a final few yards.

The force of the collision deflected the first locomo-tive off the rails, pitching it on its left side as the train's momentum propelled it more than four hundred feet past the point of impact. The tender came to rest at a right angle to the locomotive rather than telescoped into the cab. That was all that saved the two crewmen who, although badly injured, survived. Only the first six passenger cars derailed, with casualties there limited to nine injured passengers and an RPO clerk, who was thrown the length of his postal car, fracturing his skull. The two crewmen on the second locomotive were not so fortunate. The huge K4s Pacific flipped over, spun sideways, then jammed into the rock face. Seven thousand tons of steel passenger equipment cascaded into the disintegrating cab, which crumpled like tinfoil under the force of the impact. Silence reigned for a few moments, broken only by the low roar of steam escaping from shattered pipes. Then, from the houses on the hillside above the Ohio River, men grabbed axes, crow-bars, and whatever other tools lay near to hand and came running.[4]

Word of the accident spread quickly along the Penn-sylvania Railroad. In a long-standing tradition born of necessity, other members of the PRR family offered bereaved relatives what little comfort they could. "One great consolation," observed the engineman's widow, "is to have so many railroad men from all over the system stop in to visit with me and tell me of some little incident where his wisdom and advice was helpful." There must have been many stories, as her husband had spent forty-five years with the Pennsylvania Railroad and was less than three years shy of retirement. That interaction attested to the bond between railroad employees, but it could not make

up for what was lost. "It seems particularly lonesome here in Crestline now that I am all alone," she acknowledged. "We had planned to do so many things that, now, will never materialize."[5]

The senior executives of the Pennsylvania Railroad would generally pay little attention to any accident that claimed the lives of only 2 of more than 150,000 employees, but this was a special case. Wrecking crews required only a day to clean up the debris, rebuild the tracks, and restore service—far less time, in fact, than the week that passed before a postman delivered a letter to a modest two-story frame house at 426 West Main Street in Crestline, Ohio. The stationery was from the PRR's corporate headquar-ters, and it bore the signature of none other than President Martin W. Clement.

> My dear Mrs. Lightburn:
>
> Your husband and I knew each other for a quarter of a cen-tury. . . . To all of us on this Railroad, his death comes as a matter of great regret. It is always a sadness to me to know of the death of an employee; but it is only natural that I should feel more keenly in the case of those whom I have known well, and such was your husband. While this was a loss to all of us, yours is the great loss and I am writing to express my sympathy to you and to your sons and daughters.[6]

Labor Relations

Even in its tragedy, the story of the Lightburn family symbolized an idealized relationship between the Pennsyl-vania Railroad's managers and workers. James Lightburn lived a heroic life, sharing with his comrades the hardship and excitement associated with railroading, and he died a heroic death. He was diligent, accustomed to danger, and above all dedicated to the company that he had served for so many years. His loyalty was repaid with good wages, a lifetime of employment, and job opportunities for his sons and daughters. When tragedy struck, the support offered by his fellow workers demonstrated that the PRR was more a family than a corporation.

Labor-management relations rarely conformed to the idealized image that Pennsylvania Railroad executives had created. Most of the company's workers were not, and had never been, skilled and well-paid operating employ-ees. James Lightburn and the others who were part of that elite group had for decades prevented anyone who was not White, native-born, and Protestant from aspiring to the jobs they occupied. The comradery that the Lightburn family experienced was thus largely based on exclusion-ary policies developed by union leaders and reinforced by

PRR managers. Loyalty to the company was ultimately less important than worker solidarity, and the ties that bound employees to their employer were far more tenuous than those that connected them to their union. Time and again in the years after 1945, workers would manifest their class consciousness and union officials would demonstrate an increasingly sophisticated understanding of public relations, the law, and the political process. The result would not be harmony between workers and managers but instead a state of nearly constant warfare that would cause severe problems for the Pennsylvania Railroad.

With a few exceptions, relative peace between management and labor marked the World War II years. The principal industrial unions—the American Federation of Labor and the Congress of Industrial Organizations—honored the no-strike pledge that their leaders made in December 1941, although unauthorized "wildcat" strikes did happen occasionally. The five operating unions (the Brotherhood of Locomotive Engineers, the Brotherhood of Locomotive Firemen and Enginemen, the Order of Railway Conductors, the Brotherhood of Railroad Trainmen, and the Switchmen's Union of North America) were less cooperative. Their threat to strike in December 1943 induced Franklin Delano Roosevelt to exercise his authority as commander in chief and to seize control over the nation's railroads. Military oversight ended in less than a month, after train crews received significant wage increases. So, too, did shop workers, telegraphers, clerks, and other members of the sixteen nonoperating unions.[7]

The Allied victory over the Axis freed union officials from their pledge to avoid wartime strikes and unleashed a wave of labor unrest that rippled through the American economy. A nationwide steel strike began in January 1946, and its rapid settlement—with substantial wage increases—emboldened workers elsewhere. Beginning in October, representatives from the five operating brotherhoods began negotiating with management, seeking raises averaging 25 percent (or about $2.50 per day) and changes to work rules. In early March, less than three weeks after the resolution of the steel strike, representatives from the Brotherhood of Locomotive Engineers and the Brotherhood of Railroad Trainmen called for a nationwide walkout.[8]

Their demands posed a serious problem for President Harry S. Truman. As a Democrat and the inheritor of Roosevelt's New Deal legacy, Truman sought to retain the political support of organized labor. However, he was also sensitive to the concerns of the business community, including many who were determined to roll back the changes that had occurred during the 1930s. Depression-era austerity and wartime rationing had deprived millions of Americans of highly desired consumer goods, eroding public support for unions whose strikes and wage increases interfered with postwar spending.[9] A suspension of rail service would further impede an American economy reconverting to peacetime production while blocking the pent-up demand for business and leisure travel. On March 8, two days after the announcement of the planned BLE and BRT strike, Truman invoked the terms of the Railway Labor Act, imposing a thirty-day cooling-off period and appointing an emergency board to investigate the matter. BRT official H. F. Sites, who headed the union's PRR affiliate, insisted that he was under no legal requirement to obey the presidential directive and indicated the railroad's seventy-five hundred enginemen and trainmen would walk out as scheduled. Other union officials were more conciliatory, but they spurned the board's recommendation for a sixteen-cent hourly wage increase (equivalent to an extra $1.28 per day) and set a new strike date of May 18.[10]

On May 17, Truman seized the nation's railroads, mimicking the events that had occurred in December 1943. Despite federal control, the enginemen and trainmen rejected a final offer of 18.5 cents an hour.[11] They walked out May 23, adding to a nationwide strike wave that involved nearly a million workers. Pennsylvania Railroad officials pledged to maintain as much long-distance passenger service as possible, and the company's office personnel—still dressed in business suits—quickly donned trainmen's caps. The Senator, The Jeffersonian, and The Mount Vernon left Penn Station on time but carried only about a third of their normal complement of passengers. Managers on the PRR and the Long Island Rail Road posted notices that commuter traffic was likely to be disrupted, causing Manhattan office workers to desert their desks at 3:00 p.m., an hour before the strike deadline. A secretary, tardier than the rest, arrived just after crewmen closed the doors on one of the last trains out of Penn Station. She succeeded in climbing through a window, ensuring that her legs attracted the attention of newspaper reporters. The situation was scarcely better in Philadelphia, even though a large contingent of white-collar employees at corporate headquarters volunteered to run the trains. "We are operating at perhaps 50 per cent of normal, no better," conceded W. R. Wilson, the stationmaster at Suburban Station. Another PRR executive acknowledged that the company could accommodate "a mere trickle of traffic." Nationwide, just over 50 passenger trains operated, but more than 17,500 others did not. Of the 24,000 freight

The passengers who thronged the platform at the PRR's North Philadelphia Station on May 18, 1946, anxiously awaited any train that would convey them to their destinations. They were fortunate. The previous day the US Army had taken control of the railroads, forestalling a threatened strike by the Brotherhood of Locomotive Engineers and the Brotherhood of Railroad Trainmen. A lasting peace in the ongoing conflict between management and labor proved elusive, however. *George D. McDowell Philadelphia Evening Bulletin Photographs, courtesy of the Special Collections Research Center, Temple University Libraries, Philadelphia, PA.*

trains that crisscrossed the continent on an average day, a mere 240 were in service. Power plants, suffering from the effects of a coal miners' strike, began to run dangerously low on fuel. New York and other cities risked shortages of milk and produce. Panicked shoppers cleared store shelves of anything that was edible. In Kansas City, 500 carloads of perishables, stalled in freight yards, began to rot. California's assistant director of agriculture warned that 34,000

carloads of fruit and vegetables, ordinarily shipped eastward in June, would be lost without a speedy resolution to the strike. More ominously, any delays in the shipment of food to war-ravaged Europe might consign thousands to death by starvation. Foreign-policy experts predicted riots, the loss of American prestige around the world, and an acceleration of Soviet propaganda decrying the failure of the capitalist system. With some justification, the *New York Times* suggested that it was "the gravest transportation crisis in the history of the United States."[12]

With the railroads operating at just 1 percent of their normal capacity, military control did little to resolve the chaos. Most of the wartime railway operating battalions had been demobilized, and the two that remained were under strength. There was little likelihood that 1,000 soldier-railroaders could replace 165,000 striking enginemen and trainmen. Although the army and the navy committed all their available cargo aircraft to the movement of critical supplies, their contributions paled in comparison to what was needed. The Office of Defense Transportation was responsible for coordinating alternate plans for the movement of freight, and its officials urged motor carriers to take up the slack. Trucking executives expressed their willingness to help—and to lure business away from the railroads—but emphasized that they had not received any instructions from the ODT as to what they should do.[13]

Under the circumstances, Truman had little choice but to aggressively control the actions of the BRT and the BLE. In a radio address on the evening of May 24, he repeatedly reminded his audience that he was a "friend of labor" but emphasized that the strike "constitutes a fundamental attack upon the rights of society and upon the welfare of our country." Truman assigned blame to Alvanley Johnston and Alexander F. Whitney, the leaders of the two striking unions. "It is inconceivable," Truman asserted, "that in our democracy any two men should be placed in a position where they can completely stifle our economy and ultimately destroy our country." His comments sent a clear signal to Johnston and Whitney that the full force of the federal government would be brought to bear to end the strike as quickly as possible. The armed forces mobilized, awaiting an order from their commander in chief to move cargoes in military vehicles and, if necessary, run the railroads. On May 25, Truman proposed a series of measures to control labor—including the authority to draft strikers into the military—and the House quickly gave its assent by a vote of 301 to 13. While some enginemen and trainmen derided Truman as a "strikebreaker" and "Der Fuehrer," union officials thought it best to end the walkout as quickly as possible. They accepted a raise of 18.5 cents per hour—precisely what Truman had offered shortly before the strike began—and the increase applied to the nonoperating unions as well. At 6:42 p.m., *The Broadway Limited* departed Penn Station. It was the first intercity passenger train to operate with a regular crew since the strike began, and by late the following day, service was back to normal.[14]

Although most observers concluded that Truman scored a major victory by bringing the strike under control so quickly, his aggressive stance did not end labor militancy on the PRR or the nation's other railroads. In March 1947, nonoperating employees demanded a 20-cent increase in hourly pay. Railroad officials were quick to point out that that would entail an added expenditure of $568 million, twice their net income for the previous year. In September, an arbitration panel convened under the terms of the Railway Labor Act set the raise at 15.5 cents, increasing the PRR's operating costs by as much as $50 million annually. During negotiations, the Pennsylvania Railroad established a stockholders' committee, whose members would cooperate with executives on a lobbying campaign to influence public policy involving labor issues.

Initially, their principal role was to remind politicians—and voters—that higher wages fueled inflation and that, at the very least, the railroads should receive rate increases that would keep pace with rising labor costs.[15]

The PRR's labor-relations initiatives did little to slow the implementation of higher wages. Since the end of February 1947, the operating unions, led by Whitney, had been negotiating with executives. Whitney emphasized that he had no interest in raising pay scales but instead sought to protect forty-four work rules that governed crew size, the use of firemen on diesel locomotives, and the distance covered by operating employees as part of their normal workday. Managers were willing to continue most of the rules but demanded the elimination of twenty-five of them. The September arbitration award to the nonoperating employees emboldened Whitney and his colleagues, and at the end of October, they announced that they did in fact want higher wages—in this case, an additional 30 cents an hour. The conductors and the trainmen quickly secured half that amount—15.5 cents, worth approximately $100 million per year. Railroad executives, who had protested the earlier award to the nonoperating employees, did not even bother to submit the matter to arbitration. In compensation, they received union concessions on only four work rules, none of which involved crew size or the assignment of extra employees to freight and passenger service. The enginemen and firemen were less conciliatory; on November 19, they ended negotiations and began distributing strike ballots. The National Mediation Board intervened but by mid-January 1948 gave up efforts at resolution. In a now-familiar pattern, Truman appointed another emergency board, which investigated the situation through the end of March 1948. Its members criticized both sides for engaging in labor-management brinkmanship rather than settling matters through collective bargaining and recommended a 15.5-cent raise and some changes in work rules.[16]

The Necessity of Labor Relations

The labor unrest of the immediate postwar period induced Pennsylvania Railroad executives to embrace new methods of personnel management. Those efforts constituted another chapter in the history of a company that had long been in the forefront of efforts to control the workforce. Beginning late in the nineteenth century, an earlier generation of executives developed one of the most comprehensive systems of welfare capitalism in the United States. The Voluntary Relief Department and the Pension Department fostered the loyalty of skilled workers and co-opted similar programs offered by independent labor unions. Vice President W. W. Atterbury worked with publicist Ivy Ledbetter Lee to establish the Mutual Beneficial Association in 1913, to undercut the appeal of the operating brotherhoods. The wave of strikes that followed the end of World War I as well as the transition from federal to private oversight encouraged Atterbury to establish the Employe Representation Plan. The ERP at least superficially promised harmonious concord between management and labor, but objective observers had little difficulty in identifying it as a company union. Established in 1923, the Provident & Loan Association encouraged thrifty habits and reinforced the capitalistic ethos. The Bureau of New Ideas, implemented in 1927, solicited suggestions from employees and hinted that they could have a stake, albeit small, in the management of the company. Railroad YMCAs, reading rooms, and sports teams inculcated a family atmosphere and kept employees away from saloons and other temptations. Language courses, Americanization classes, athletic programs, and company doctors preached sobriety, industriousness, patriotism, and healthy living.

Despite the multiplicity of programs, there was relatively little centralized authority over personnel matters. Prior to 1920, Lines East and Lines West maintained separate administrative structures. The corporate reorganization that followed the end of federal control delegated responsibility for the negotiation and enforcement of labor agreements and other personnel matters to the general managers of the four regions and the Altoona Works. Each regional Labor & Wage Bureau possessed considerable autonomy, with the new systemwide Personnel Department primarily responsible for programs such as the Voluntary Relief Department and the Pension Department. Ultimate authority rested not in the president but rather with the vice president in charge of operations, whose department included nearly 95 percent of the PRR's employees.[17]

The economic catastrophe of the Great Depression, combined with the incorporation of labor into the New Deal political coalition, ensured the rapid demise of many of the PRR's welfare-capitalism initiatives. The pension system drained the company's finances, and the care of retired workers became the responsibility of the federal government. Other programs proved expensive or redundant and fell by the wayside. The Employe Representation Plan, so obviously a company union, incurred the wrath of New Dealers. Although it lingered on in the shop crafts, as a rebranded and supposedly independent union, the Employe Representation Plan would never fulfill W. W. Atterbury's determination to make it a model for labor relations on the railroads.

The war that followed transformed welfare capitalism into personnel management, both in industry and on the railroads.[18] The unprecedented output of wartime factories, as overseen by the federal government, led to the bureaucratization of labor-management relations. Railroad executives like the combative Atterbury and the more conciliatory Daniel Willard no longer served as spokesmen for various corporate factions. Executives increasingly relied on trade organizations such as the Association of American Railroads and the Eastern Railroads Presidents' Conference to ensure a measure of uniformity in wage rates and work rules and to prevent labor leaders from adopting a divide-and-conquer strategy. Union officials also acted in concert, while maintaining a close watch on the rank and file. Disagreements among labor organizations and unauthorized wildcat strikes were often far more carefully scripted than reporters suggested.

The poor relationship between managers and workers—what executives often referred to as low morale—was closely associated with an increasing number of complaints from passengers and shippers and thus a growing public-relations problem. That was one of the many issues that confronted James Symes after he became the vice president in charge of operations in 1947. "We used to be 'The Standard Railroad of the World,'" he reminded his subordinates, "and were so recognized in the 20's." That remained the case for many years, Symes noted, despite the economic privations of the 1930s and the shortages and deferred maintenance associated with the war years. "However, in the post-war period," he warned, "our service slipped badly, as did our earnings, and naturally we did not think we could, without challenge, continue to call ourselves 'The Standard Railroad of the World,' and we dropped it" as a slogan. It was not the first time the PRR had experienced such problems, but Symes emphasized that after 1945, conditions were fundamentally different. "There is a vast difference, however, in the two post-war periods," Symes emphasized. "In the post-war period of World War I we were not losing too much business as a result of inferior service, as other forms of competitive transportation were just coming into being—but this has not been the case during the post-war period of World War II when service is now an important factor, and all of us know that inferior service is now reflected in serious loss of rail traffic."[19]

The radically altered conditions of the postwar world demanded corresponding changes to the labor-relations policies of the Pennsylvania Railroad. That process began even before Symes became the vice president in charge of operations and, as had so often happened in the past,

Facing, In the spring of 1950, PRR managerial representative Jay Gilbert posted a notice in Broad Street Station informing passengers of the likelihood of a strike by the operating brotherhoods. Two of those employees, fireman R. L. Morris (*left*) and engineman G. E. Dunstan (*right*) look on. Labor disputes in the years after World War II were less confrontational and less violent than those that had occurred during the 1920s, but they had equally significant ramifications for the future of the Pennsylvania Railroad. *Philadelphia Inquirer photo, courtesy of the Special Collections Research Center, Temple University Libraries, Philadelphia, PA.*

was related to contemporaneous developments in the US military. The wartime experience illustrated the necessity of close coordination between the military and civilian defense suppliers—what would soon become known as the military-industrial complex. The Joint Board on Army and Navy Training in Industrial Mobilization played an important role in that process. It operated under the supervision of John M. Hancock—an ideal choice, given his experience as a veteran of the US navy, an investment banker, an industrial engineer, and a purchasing agent during two world wars. Hancock assigned more than three dozen officers from the Army Industrial College to year-long stints in various industrial facilities, "to increase their knowledge of the problems of production, to improve the relationship between the Armed Forces and Industry and Labor and to familiarize American Industry with the needs of military and naval procurement."[20]

Although the Pennsylvania Railroad was not an industrial corporation, Brigadier General John A. Appleton suggested that it be included in the program. Before the war, Appleton had been the general manager of the New York Zone, but he took a leave of absence to assume command of the Rail Division of the Office of the Chief of Transportation at the War Department before returning to the PRR in February 1946 as the assistant to John F. Deasy, at that time the vice president in charge of operations. Like Hancock, Appleton was well positioned to serve as a liaison between the private sector and the military. President Clement enthusiastically supported the initiative and in May 1946 suggested that the officer assigned to the Pennsylvania Railroad report directly to Deasy. Deasy's career was coming to an end, however, and he paid the price for the PRR's financial problems and for his advocacy of large steam locomotives. By the time the program was underway—and it continued at least through 1951—Symes had taken responsibility for it.[21]

Symes perceived that military officers could offer useful advice regarding the relationship between managers and employees. He asked Lieutenant Colonel Frank H. Stone of the Adjutant General's Department—the personnel management office of the US army—to evaluate the PRR's practices. Stone was familiar with the similarities between the railroad's organizational structure and that of the military. That comparison did not extend to labor relations, however. As Stone observed, personnel matters on the PRR were almost entirely decentralized at the divisional level, with such responsibilities typically "initiated and administered at the lowest echelons." Symes had only been in his new post for a few months, Stone acknowledged, and "has not yet had sufficient time to indoctrinate his subordinates with his concept of personnel management." Stone emphasized that "the tone of the organization has reflected some change. The present policy and program is, however, basically that established during the tenure of his predecessors and does not necessarily coincide with the attitude of the present incumbent." Symes's determination to break with the past was well advised, Stone concluded, given that "the present personnel program does not contain those factors which are necessary to make a satisfactorily harmonious relationship."[22]

Stone concluded that the Pennsylvania Railroad lacked even the most basic elements of proper employee relations. "The Personnel Division [*sic*]," he noted, "performs very few of the functions which would be expected in a Division so titled. In actuality it is predominantly a labor and wage bureau dealing with matters of rules, regulations, wage rates and claims, discipline and grievance appeals, and relations with the employee unions." Because the Personnel Department was focused solely on disciplinary matters and the enforcement of labor agreements, Stone warned, managers had failed to cultivate a cooperative relationship with employees. "The Company feels no responsibility toward the employe in regard to any of his activities, or lack thereof, which do not directly relate to his job performance," Stone noted. Even though "many of the employes are very loyal to the company and still retain the 'family' concept that existed throughout the organization years ago," he cautioned, "a much larger group of the employes, however, place their first allegiance to their craft unions. . . . As a result, the apparent attitude of management toward the employe group is not that of one team member to another. Rather it is an attitude of defense or self-protection against the Employe Unions."[23]

Stone's report confirmed Symes's insistence on rapid changes in the PRR's labor-relations policies. Some of those alterations were comparatively minor. They included the reorganization of the Bureau of New Ideas into the Employes' Suggestion Plan, effective on August 1, 1947—just four months after Symes became the vice president in charge of operations. Promotional campaigns increased the number of contributions from 249 in 1946 to 1,568 by the end of the following year.[24] Previously, managers had used those suggestions as an opportunity to justify corporate policies. As one executive asserted, the focus now shifted from "Tell the Worker" to "sell the worker," enabling "management to explain or sell the ideas to employes." Executives sought "to establish and maintain a situation in which communications flow freely *and in both directions*." Officials would continue to "transmit Company policy and orders, from the top down," but they would also "get the suggestions, views, reactions and cooperation of all the organization." That type of "upward communication—the hardest to get, needed the most" held the potential to "win employe confidence and trust in Company leadership." Symes's agenda quickly faltered, however, as PRR executives conceded that full implementation of the Suggestion Plan "would involve an expenditure of perhaps $200,000 to $300,000 a year to provide a director, administrative staff, necessary publicity, and adequate cash awards." It was an amount they could not afford to spend, and the suggestion boxes increasingly gathered dust. By the end of 1951, the program had been discontinued.[25]

More substantive changes occurred in November 1947, contemporaneous with the completion of Stone's report. During the 1920s, Charles E. Musser had been a loyal PRR employee, and in his role as the general chairman of the Brotherhood of Railroad Trainmen at Philadelphia, he denounced both the Outlaw Strike of 1920 and the Shopmen's Strike that erupted two years later. His promotion to chief of personnel in 1943 represented an effort to build bridges between workers and management, at a time when the employment of women, African Americans, Hispanics, and other temporary workers was engendering labor unrest. By the autumn of 1947, he was still a few years short of retirement age, but he yielded his job to an individual who was nearly thirty years his junior. James W. Oram came from a very different background, and it is doubtful that he ever threw switches or uncoupled freight cars. After graduating from Princeton University and the University of Pennsylvania School of Law, Oram joined the PRR as a law clerk in 1935. He became an assistant solicitor and an assistant general counsel, specializing in labor law and employee relations, and earned promotion to assistant chief of personnel in December 1942. Oram was not yet fifty years of age when he assumed responsibility for

the Pennsylvania Railroad's massive, restive workforce. Initially, he suffered from the same limitations on his authority that had bedeviled Musser, as regional managers retained control of most aspects of employee relations. Over the next few years, therefore, Oram and his fellow managers would find it increasingly difficult to ensure the labor harmony they desired.[26]

Continued Labor Unrest

Pennsylvania Railroad firemen were particularly willing to walk off the job in a manner they hoped would establish a national precedent. On November 14, 1947—two days before Oram became the chief of personnel—the PRR assigned five diesel switchers to yard service in Pittsburgh and in Pottstown, Pennsylvania. They were General Electric 44-ton locomotives, designed to comply with a 1937 labor agreement that permitted the elimination of firemen on diesels weighing less than ninety thousand pounds. BLF&E officials nonetheless demanded the reinstatement of firemen on the PRR's 44-ton switchers, an action that was largely in retaliation for managerial attempts to alter other work rules. "The union regards working these locomotives with one man in a cab through densely congested territories a hazardous condition," they emphasized, relying on a time-honored tactic that elevated presumed threats to safety above considerations of operating efficiency. The National Mediation Board, which had abandoned the larger dispute involving the enginemen, firemen, and switchmen, then intervened in the 44-ton switcher case. The NMB managed to postpone a threatened March 31 strike by the PRR's ten thousand firemen, but the national labor situation was again spiraling out of control. Brotherhood officials, dissatisfied with the tenor of the National Mediation Board hearings, regrouped and announced that the strike would begin on April 14. Nonoperating employees had secured hourly advances of 18.5 cents in 1946 and 15.5 cents the following year, but on April 10 their leaders demanded a reduction in the work week from forty-eight to forty hours, without any loss in pay. The same day, Truman established an emergency board to evaluate the merits of assigning firemen to five of the PRR's diesel locomotives. Given the failure of the NMB, however, that step was unlikely to do more than achieve a thirty-day postponement in the threatened BLF&E strike.[27]

National representatives from the BLF&E and the Switchmen's Union, still pursuing the thirty-cent-an-hour demand they had issued the previous October, set a new strike date of May 11. The leaders of the Brotherhood of Locomotive Engineers announced that they would probably go out as well. The National Mediation Board reconvened but, based on its past performance, was unlikely to achieve any results. Railroad executives across the United States, viewing a strike as inevitable, embargoed shipments of produce and livestock. Clement urged train crews "to consider with greatest care their obligations to their country, their families and their fellow employes and particularly their public responsibility for railroad service." He nonetheless acknowledged that "if the enginemen and firemen carry out this reckless intention to strike, it will become physically impossible to operate the railroad and, although reluctant to do so, your management may have no alternative but to shut down all departments." During the strike that had occurred two years earlier, Clement had recruited enough PRR office workers to at least keep a few trains running. This time, he was prepared to admit defeat.[28]

Truman's sole remaining option, which he exercised on May 10, was to order a resumption of federal control. Gustav Metzman, the president of the New York Central, earned a rapid promotion to colonel, as the head of the military's Eastern Region. That status reminded PRR executives of the activities of the United States Railroad Administration during World War I, when NYC executives dominated operations in the Northeast. They could nonetheless take comfort that the army placed Andrew F. McIntyre, the general manager of the New York Zone, in charge of day-to-day operational matters. In contrast to the events that had taken place in 1946, union leaders cooperated, the Pennsylvania Railroad lifted its freight embargoes, and trains continued to run. At the PRR's annual meeting, held the following day, representatives from the stockholders' committee on labor relations addressed their fellow shareholders. Hardening their stance, they recommended that the company's lobbying be expanded to include support of national legislation to block strikes.[29]

The latest round of federal oversight ended on July 9, after the leaders of the three holdout unions accepted the same 15.5 cents originally granted to the conductors and the trainmen. Even as they signed the contracts, beginning on July 30, the leaders of the operating brotherhoods demanded another 14.5 cents per hour, representing the difference between what they had received at the time of the seizure and their original call for a 30-cent raise. In October, the conductors and the trainmen accepted a compromise raise of 10 cents, and the BLE, the BLF&E, and the Switchmen assented to the same terms a month later.[30]

Nonoperating employees were correspondingly determined to secure additional gains in wages and working conditions. In early September, they reiterated their demand for a forty-hour week, overtime pay on weekends, and a twenty-five-cent raise. Less than two weeks later, they issued a strike call, and the National Mediation Board again intervened. The results were predictable— union representatives balked at the ten cents offered by the NMB (mirroring the agreements with the operating brotherhoods) and Truman appointed another emergency board. By December, the emergency board had scaled back the wage hike to seven cents, while endorsing the shorter work week. Negotiations continued until March 1949, when both sides accepted the recommendation. The shift to a forty-hour week increased the average pay for a nonoperating employee from $1.18 to $1.42 per hour, even before the addition of the seven-cent raise. All together those employees gained what amounted to an increase of nearly 30 percent—and weekend overtime promised to further fatten pay envelopes.[31]

Leaders of the railroad brotherhoods promptly asked for similar terms. The process began in March 1949, when the conductors and the trainmen demanded a forty-hour week for yard service. Truman established another emergency board to investigate the matter. The leaders of the BLF&E renewed their insistence, first made in 1939, that a second fireman be assigned to each unit of a multiple-unit diesel locomotive—even though the practice would do nothing to increase safety or operating efficiency. The union pledged walkouts on four railroads—including the PRR, west of Harrisburg—on April 26. Federal mediators managed to delay the process until May 10, but the strike by 18,000 firemen on the four carriers forced the PRR to annul *The Broadway Limited* and a host of other intercity trains while ending freight service along 90 percent of its routes. On the morning of May 12, the company furloughed 85,000 of its 120,000 employees, as there was little for them to do. Walter S. Franklin, the PRR's new president, reiterated his predecessor's warning that the company would suspend operations during the strike. Using enginemen who volunteered for firemen's duties, the railroad nonetheless managed to dispatch a few freight trains west of Harrisburg, causing union officials to set up picket lines and issue a condemnatory press release. More than fifty PRR freight trains ran on May 15, but the railroad could do no better than clear freight that had been in transit prior to the embargo.[32]

The BLF&E strike suggested that Pennsylvania Railroad officials and members of the public were growing tired of the unions' perennial calls for higher wages and benefits. Franklin suggested that the 1926 "Railway Labor Act has broken down and that the philosophy and conceptions embodied in the provisions of the Act have proved inadequate to accomplish its intended purpose." The unions, he noted, used the recommendations of impartial mediators "as only a springboard upon which to predicate additional demands." Franklin also observed that few people outside the ranks of organized labor were willing to accept the premise that firemen remained vital to railroad operations. "I know of no case," Franklin concluded, "where the public is more strongly opposed to the demands of labor than they are to this request to put additional unnecessary men on Diesel locomotives."[33]

As Franklin sensed, public opinion was beginning to turn against organized labor. Most of the coal mines in western Pennsylvania were closed, and General Motors and other large manufacturing corporations began laying off workers and suspending production. Consumers wanted to purchase new automobiles and other products that were unaffordable or unavailable during the Great Depression and World War II, and business executives were eager to satisfy that pent-up demand. Their anger at the railroad workers who interfered with their long-sought desires constituted a potent political force and gave the PRR's managers confidence that they could hold the line against wage increases.

James Oram, the PRR's new chief of personnel, assumed control of the subsequent negotiations, acting on behalf of all the eastern carriers. By May 16, he had secured an agreement that enabled both sides to claim victory. Significantly, BLF&E officials abandoned their decade-long campaign for a second fireman on diesels, accepting the verdict of two presidential emergency boards that such practices had no effect on safety. The matter of firemen on 44-ton locomotives would be left to further arbitration. A month later, the presidential emergency board recommended that trainmen and conductors be given the option to work only forty hours per week. With a corresponding hourly raise of only eighteen cents, however, those that chose the shorter week would suffer a loss in pay. The leaders of the Order of Railway Conductors and the Brotherhood of Railroad Trainmen denounced the recommendations as insufficient and on June 21 threatened to strike. By early August, ORC and BRT leaders claimed that they had lost control over rank-and-file workers and deplored the possibility of unauthorized wildcat strikes. They took the preemptive step of urging Truman to seize the railroads, for the third time since the end of the war.[34]

As the heat of August settled over Washington, the federal government's role in negotiations between labor and management was undergoing significant change. For several years, union leaders had argued that their incessant wage demands had done little more than keep pace with inflation. There was considerable truth in their assertion, given that the cost of living had risen 8.5 percent in 1946, 14.4 percent in 1947, and 7.7 percent in 1948. The following year was deflationary, however, with a 1.0 percent decrease in prices, while 1950 posted a modest 1.1 percent gain. Under those circumstances, further wage hikes became more difficult to justify. While the Interstate Commerce Commission was often willing to grant rate increases, in partial compensation for higher labor costs, the resulting gains in revenue lagged. The presence of competition from other modes of transportation also ensured that the carriers would soon reach the upper limit of what they could charge customers without driving themselves out of business. With the railroads posting disappointing financial returns during the postwar period, more and more observers suggested that the seemingly endless cycle of contentious labor negotiations, pay raises, and rate increases would eventually result in disaster. It was a "railroad carousel," editorialized the New York Times, noting that "the railroads, in seeking that illusive 'fair rate of return' once promised them in the Transportation Act of 1920, find themselves permanently in the position of the rider astride a merry-go-round horse—always chasing the horse ahead, but never catching up."[35]

By the summer of 1950, moreover, and thanks to foreign-policy considerations, strike threats and disruptions had become intolerable. On June 25, North Korean troops crossed the 38th parallel and advanced swiftly into South Korea. Truman, determined to prevent another country from following China into the communist orbit, secured a United Nations Security Council resolution permitting a multinational "police action" to repel the invaders. He committed American troops to battle, but cutbacks in military spending since the end of the previous war had left them poorly equipped. By the middle of August, they retreated to a small pocket of land on the southeastern corner of the Korean Peninsula. With American servicemen lying dead on the battlefield and coalition forces on the brink of annihilation, neither the president nor the country could afford any labor unrest that might cripple defense production, impair the movement of troops, and jeopardize national security.

When representatives from the BRT and the ORC recommended that Truman take control of the railroads, the president needed little convincing. Negotiations between labor and management broke down on August 20, despite frantic efforts by government officials to bring about a reconciliation. With a strike set for August 28, Republic Steel began shutting down its operations in Cleveland, and many of the mills along Pittsburgh's Monongahela

Valley did the same. Half a world away, UN forces were staging a last-ditch defense of the Pusan Perimeter, and there was a strong possibility that they would be overrun. When Truman seized the railroads on August 27, it came as a surprise to no one and as a relief to most. Lasting twenty-one months, it was the longest period of federal oversight since the Transportation Act of 1920 ended the involvement of the United States Railroad Administration in the operation of the carriers. Major General Frank A. Heileman, a career army officer, was in overall command. He delegated operational authority to the PRR's Andrew McIntyre, promoted to chief of freight transportation after the end of his previous military service and assigned the rank of brigadier general. One of his direct subordinates was the NYC's Colonel Metzman, again in charge of the Eastern Region. Labor leaders announced that their members would be proud to report for work as usual as part of their patriotic contribution to the war effort.[36]

The seizure was only one facet of the federal government's increased involvement in labor relations. On September 8, less than two weeks after the resumption of military control, Truman signed the Defense Production Act. Through executive order, Truman established the Economic Stabilization Agency on the following day. To control inflation, two subsidiary agencies—the Office of Price Stabilization and the Wage Stabilization Board—gave the president the authority to regulate both prices and wages.[37] More than two months passed, however, before Truman appointed the nine members of the WSB, three apiece from management, labor, and the public sector.[38]

Union leaders anticipated that the Economic Stabilization Agency would move quickly to freeze prices and wages—an action that would take place on January 26—and they were determined to lock in the highest possible raises beforehand. In October, officials from the brotherhoods asked for substantial wage increases, as did the heads of the nonoperating unions. Negotiations quickly faltered, and rank-and-file members demonstrated that they were unwilling to honor their leaders' commitment to operate trains during the national emergency. Although there was no formal strike vote, in December 1950 conductors and trainmen in Chicago began calling in sick. Despite injunctions issued by three federal courts, the sickout soon spread to other cities. The PRR was able to continue operations, thanks to the reassignment of clerical staff and other volunteers, but delays were widespread. With the Christmas season beginning, the post office announced an embargo on parcel post shipments and the movement of second-class mail. When government officials and railroad executives accused strikers of imperiling the safety

of military personnel, they responded that "we've got sons in Korea too."[39]

The wildcat strike soon ended, prompted by Truman's carrot-and-stick approach—a hardline radio address coupled with recommendations for increased wages. On December 21, the leaders of the operating brotherhoods agreed to a three-year moratorium on strikes, with a similar hiatus in their demands for higher pay and changes to work rules. In return, they accepted a raise of twenty-three cents per hour, significantly more than the presidential emergency board had recommended six months earlier. For the first time, they secured an automatic quarterly cost-of-living adjustment (often referred to as an "escalator clause"), with each 1 percent increase in the consumer price index triggering a one-cent gain in hourly pay. The resulting wage agreements—and particularly the associated escalator clause—complicated Truman's efforts to moderate inflation. They also cost the Pennsylvania Railroad dearly, with each automatic one-cent addition increasing the PRR's annual operating expenses by $3.3 million.[40]

Union leaders nonetheless continued to lobby for another of their long-standing goals—the implementation of the union shop and the deduction of union dues from paychecks. Congress assented; in January 1951, Truman signed an amendment to the Railway Labor Act, enabling those provisions.[41] By the end of the month, however, union officials indicated that they were now dissatisfied with some of the stipulations they had tentatively accepted on December 21. Another wildcat strike, led by the BRT, began on January 29. The PRR announced a "drastic curtailment" in passenger service and posted a long list of annulled trains. Automobile plants shut down, for lack of parts. Flatcars, laden with tarpaulin-covered tanks, sat idle in a Newark, New Jersey, freight yard. In Chicago and Kansas City, boxcars filled with medical supplies and military rations, destined for Korea, remained motionless.[42]

Foreign-policy considerations again prompted Truman to harden his stance against railway labor. In September 1950, amphibious landings at Inchon enabled UN forces to break out of the Pusan Perimeter and gain control over most South Korean territory. Coalition troops crossed the 38th parallel in early October and advanced rapidly northward toward the Yalu River. North Korean and Chinese forces soon counterattacked, and by the end of November American troops were in rapid retreat. On February 2, with UN forces still in disarray, Truman denounced the railway strike as a threat to national security and accused brotherhood officials of negotiating in bad faith. The president characterized BRT leaders as "a bunch of Russians" and emphasized that "interference with essential military and civilian railroad transportation" was "intolerable in an emergency." Employees trickled back to work, and on February 8 the army issued General Order No. 2, offering temporary wage increases but threatening holdouts with dismissal and the loss of their seniority.[43] Suitably chastened, BRT leaders broke ranks with their counterparts from the other operating brotherhoods and at least superficially adopted a more conciliatory stance in their negotiations with railroad executives and government officials.[44]

While the Korean War gave managers an opportunity to portray striking workers as unpatriotic, it also created economic conditions that led to a new round of labor disputes. The conflict ended an eleven-month recession that temporarily raised the purchasing power of employees who still had jobs. While consumer prices rose only 1.3 percent throughout 1950, the Korean mobilization ensured that December's inflation rate was 5.9 percent. Month by month, inflation eroded the real value of PRR wages, peaking at 9.4 percent in February and holding steady at 9.3 percent in each of the three following months. The overall inflation rate in 1951 was 7.9 percent, a figure that would not be exceeded until 1974. Determined to support their families and buy the consumer goods that everyone craved, railroad workers concluded that they would need to win substantial wage increases just to stay in the same place.[45]

Despite the inflationary pressures, both the industry and the public representatives of the Wage Stabilization Board resisted corresponding increases in pay. On February 15, the three labor representatives on the WSB claimed that that entity was biased in favor of management, and they refused to participate in any further discussions. Less than two weeks later, the National Mediation Board, still endeavoring to resolve the two-year-old dispute between management and the brotherhoods, also reached an impasse in the ongoing negotiations involving the nonoperating unions. With the WSB crippled, and in the absence of any other organizational mechanism to control wages, Truman asked his assistant, John R. Steelman, to intervene. On March 1, the nonoperating employees accepted a raise of 12.5 cents an hour, plus a cost-of-living adjustment. Under federal law, the agreement was subject to the approval of the Wage Stabilization Board, an agency that had ceased to function. As an alternative, Truman established a Temporary Emergency Railroad Wage Panel to evaluate the matter. Its members recommended acceptance, even though the cost-of-living provisions threatened to fuel inflation.[46] Not until April 21 did Truman reconstitute the Wage Stabilization Board, now with six representatives apiece from business, labor,

and the public sector.[47] Three days later, it issued Wage Adjustment Order No. 1, accepting the agreement that Steelman had negotiated and that the emergency panel had endorsed.[48] The board's acquiescence suggested that Truman was willing to award substantial concessions to labor, even if they violated his professed commitment to fight inflation.[49]

Despite the haphazard genesis of Wage Adjustment Order No. 1, it set the pattern for future negotiations with labor. Representatives from the Brotherhood of Railroad Trainmen were certainly paying close attention to the chaos at the Wage Stabilization Board. After calling off the "sickout" strike, they agreed to arbitration—the only one of the brotherhoods to do so. On May 25, they accepted an agreement that increased pay for road crews by 12.5 cents per hour, with a 27-cent raise for yard men, and both groups received a cost-of-living provision. The army remained in control of the railroads and approved the settlement—without discussing the matter with the newly reconstituted Wage Stabilization Board. Even though the provisions clearly exceeded the limits that the earlier iteration of the WSB had established (and could hardly be considered an appropriate measure to curb inflation), the federal government was under intense pressure to secure a quick resolution to the dispute. WSB approval came on June 12.[50]

The agreement with the trainmen provided a minimum basis for settlements with the other operating brotherhoods. Their leaders could afford to be patient, given that under the terms of the army's General Order No. 2, they had received wage increases ranging from 5 to 12.5 cents per hour. Union officials nonetheless expected better, and with authority divided between railroad executives, the WSB, the army, and the president, they negotiated accordingly. By the end of July, discussions involving the BLE, the BLF&E, the ORC, and the carriers had stalled. The National Mediation Board shifted responsibility to Truman, and union leaders asked for arbitration. Within a month, however, brotherhood officials accused railroad officials of adopting "a frivolous approach" to the stalemate, suggesting that efforts at arbitration were on the verge of collapse. In November, Truman established two more emergency boards—one to postpone a threatened strike by the BLF&E and the other to evaluate the demands of the nonoperating employees for a union shop. On November 27, BLF&E delegates boycotted their emergency board. Their members soon began a go-slow movement, paying extreme attention to the rulebook in order to delay train movements. Even as they did so, the leaders of the Brotherhood of Locomotive Engineers "reluctantly" asked for arbitration, but there was little likelihood that the outcome would be any better.[51]

Far from enabling PRR managers to adopt a divide-and-conquer strategy, the seemingly uncoordinated efforts of the unions worked to the detriment of the railroads. On December 14, Symes testified before the presidential emergency board investigating the complaints of the BLF&E. Attendance was sparse, as union officials had walked out of the proceedings nearly three weeks earlier. Symes suggested that leaders of each union, one by one, made unreasonable demands that management could not accept. After threatening or staging a strike, the two sides would compromise—setting a floor for equally unreasonable demands from all the other unions. As such, Symes observed, "the railroads are the victims of vicious rivalry among the unions—one trying to outdo the other in their demands on the carriers."[52]

By the autumn of 1951, therefore, Pennsylvania Railroad executives were justifiably concerned about rising labor costs and their overall effect on the company's profitability. Wages had consumed 47.9 percent of operating revenues in 1939, but that figure increased to 58.6 percent in 1951. In 1944, the year of peak wartime operations, 164,255 employees had taken home $454 million in pay. By 1949, the number of workers had fallen to 116,743, but the wage bill rose to almost $457 million. Traffic associated with the Korean War increased the PRR's workforce to 137,604 in 1951, with wages soaring to almost $502 million. Those figures indicated that each worker was becoming a more expensive commodity and suggested the importance of minimizing the number of employees while making each one as productive as possible.[53]

Education on the Silver Screen

After replacing Charles Musser as chief of personnel in November 1947, James Oram did what he could to resolve labor disputes and improve relations between managers and workers. For the first three years of his tenure, however, the PRR's Personnel Department remained decentralized, with regional and divisional managers largely free to establish and enforce labor agreements as they saw fit. The arrangement reflected long-standing assertions that locally specific operating practices, the availability of labor, and variations in the cost of living made it impossible to grant every employee the same work rules and rate of pay for comparable jobs, regardless of where they lived. While those arguments had merit, such practices generated grievances among employees who asserted that they were badly treated, compared to their counterparts on other parts of

the system. Regional variations likewise enabled union officials to argue in favor of uniform pay scales—which would naturally be based on the highest wages earned by any given class of employee. Local autonomy was also at odds with a growing emphasis by railroad executives on uniform wage rates across the nation, not merely on a single carrier. The inertia of conventional wisdom was difficult to counteract, however, and Oram initially possessed little centralized authority.

Unable at first to command, Oram sought to persuade. He resurrected the PRR's use of film as a method for educating—or indoctrinating—its workforce. The company experimented with films as early as 1915, under the supervision of the Association of Transportation Officers. Those efforts continued into the 1920s, but executives concluded that movies did not constitute an effective mechanism of teaching workers to be both safe and efficient. One of Oram's first tasks, upon assuming his new responsibilities, was to take stock of the company's existing library of safety films. They included *Stop, Look, and Live* and *Grinding Wheel Safety*, typically shown to employees at railroad YMCAs.[54]

Safety became a much more important concern by the spring of 1951, thanks in part to a series of accidents on the Pennsylvania Railroad and the Long Island Rail Road. In April, John T. Williams, the assistant manager of the Altoona Works, became the superintendent of safety for the entire PRR system. Williams presided over a thorough reorganization of the Safety Department, supervising newly appointed superintendents of safety on each region. They operated, logically, under the umbrella of Oram's Personnel Department. Like Oram before him, Williams evaluated the PRR's safety films, and he found them wanting. The company had not been as effective as other railroads and industrial corporations, Williams complained, in its efforts to emphasize "some measure of employe self-supervision" and discipline in those movies.[55]

Accordingly, Oram and Williams contracted with Unifilms, Incorporated, to produce a series of safety films. Elliott Pew, from the Sun Oil family, established Unifilms by recruiting former soldiers with wartime cinematography experience. The average age of its staff members was only twenty-six, suggesting that they were not likely to be bound by outdated traditions. Williams praised the company's methodology, noting that Pew intended to make movies "that would be motivational rather than instructional." They included *The Happy Locomotive*, a children's film produced for the Baltimore & Ohio, and *The Safe Railroader*, shown to military personnel and to the employees of some forty railroads. The breadth of the offerings suggested that Unifilms was responding to a growing sentiment among executives that the entire population—not just workers—should be encouraged to develop a favorable attitude toward the railroads. That broad reach prompted suggestions from PRR executives, each of whom thought that movies could resolve a specific problem. Williams suggested that Unifilms could "study conditions surrounding emergency operating problems." Chief engineer John L. Gressitt wanted to emphasize the proper operation of mechanized track-maintenance equipment and "dispel some of the resentment towards machines on the basis that 'machines replace men.'" Oram had a broader vision and suggested that film could serve as an effective public-relations tool, yet other executives dismissed the concept as impracticable.[56]

Unifilms accordingly produced a narrow range of safety films, beginning in 1951 with *Not by Chance*. The camera crew covered some five thousand miles of the Pennsylvania Railroad, filming hundreds of maintenance-of-way employees. Some held starring roles, portraying such characters as "an indifferent signalman," "a one-eyed trackman," and another "trackman, who thought only of saving enough oil to finish the job." The script emphasized that "the line between safety and the work breaks down—the two become interchangeable. Safety is the work—and the work is safety." The film took the audience back to a 1927 meeting of PRR executives, as they established a safety program and a book of rules for their employees. Managerial concern for employee well-being could not overcome the carelessness of workers who chose to disobey the rules, however. PRR and Unifilms officials agreed that those employees must bear full responsibility for that disobedience. "In interviews with the victims," the script noted, "each testifies to his failure to keep his wits about him." As the film emphasized, executives insisted that workers do more than simply follow the rules and unquestioningly obey managerial authority. Instead, they expected employees to internalize discipline and to make it an intrinsic part of their everyday lives. "The primary need was not to tell the men how to be safe," Unifilms personnel emphasized. "The rulebooks take care of that—but to motivate them to apply the rules, and want to apply them at all times. . . . And though the men know that the goal of no injuries is virtually impossible, the real progress that has been made is presented so dramatically that emotion destroys logic and makes the perfect goal seem within reach. The complete realism of the decreasing rate of injuries makes the thoroughly ideal goal seem plausible." The procedure for showing *Not by Chance* was as carefully scripted as the movie itself. Supervisors read a prepared set of remarks

to employees before showing them the film, mentioning the authentic Pennsylvania Railroad settings and the more than one thousand employees who took part in the production. Williams insisted that those supervisors highlight the message that "*not one man, absolutely no one, do you understand, EVER gets hurt.*"[57]

Unifilms also produced *The Breaking Point* and *Escape from Limbo*—whose dream sequence mimicked *Steve Hill's Awakening*, completed nearly forty years earlier. *Escape from Limbo* profiled a PRR employee who, rendered unconscious by a hunting accident, "dreamed he was forced after death to go back from limbo to earth to whisper encouragement to safety violators and help them to be disabled or killed." Fortunately, the employees remembered their safety training, disregarded the evil suggestions, and remained alive and unhurt. Back in limbo, the unconscious railroader reached "the conclusion that 'every man is his own keeper' and no outside suggestion can control him." In a convoluted manner, the film thus emphasized that each employee was a free agent—but that he would automatically do the right thing and avoid all temptation because he had been thoroughly conditioned into following the just rules established by his employer. *Escape from Limbo* was nonetheless sufficiently innovative to win the coveted bronze plaque (for first place) in the nontheatrical group of inspirational occupational motion pictures on safety from the National Committee on Films for Safety.[58]

By the mid-1950s, the PRR maintained a library of sixty-two films, ranging from ten to forty minutes in length, along with twenty-three sound slide films. Some, including *Survival under Atomic Attack*, were unique products of their age; others, such as the "English" and "Mexican" versions of *Men of Maintenance*, attested to the railroad's use of Hispanic labor. Most of the movies, however, emphasized that discipline was the key to safety. They encouraged employees to respect authority, obey the rules, accept responsibility for accidents, and absolve management of any blame in such matters.[59]

The Development of Public-Relations Capabilities

The development of films and new training methods coincided with substantial changes in the relationship between Pennsylvania Railroad executives, their employees, and the broader community. By the autumn of 1951, the PRR embraced two complementary efforts. One reflected a new managerial realization that the long era of public dependence on the railroads had come to an end. In an environment shaped by structural economic changes and the development of competing modes of transportation, it was clear that the PRR and the other carriers now relied on the goodwill of the public, if they were to survive. The company's ability to eliminate unprofitable passenger service, abandon obsolete facilities, reduce property taxes, and obtain higher rates depended on the acquiescence of legislatures and regulatory agencies—and the actions of those entities reflected the attitudes of the people toward the railroads. Likewise, efforts to negotiate favorable contracts with an increasingly unionized workforce, lay off unneeded workers, and obtain maximum productivity from those who remained suggested the importance of enhanced employee-relations capabilities.

Managerial initiatives coincided with the siege mentality that characterized much of the PRR's postwar decision-making. "The most primitive of impulses is self-preservation," Martin Clement informed Walter Franklin in 1951. Two years earlier, Clement had made the transition from president to chairman of the board, and he thought it appropriate to advise his successor on broad matters of corporate policy. "Self-preservation is a responsibility that rests on the management of a corporation," he reminded Franklin, acknowledging that "there isn't a county in Pennsylvania that doesn't have some railroad in it, and every county, therefore, has some anti-railroad people." When "all the 'antis' eventually accumulate into political action," Clement continued, the result was the familiar litany of higher taxation, mandates for grade-crossing elimination, the maintenance of unprofitable passenger services, full-crew laws, labor militancy, and highway competition. It was vitally important, Clement concluded, "to build back up the public contact and re-establish the Pennsylvania Railroad as a political potentiality in Pennsylvania and the other states." While he praised Franklin's commitment to improved employee relations, Clement observed that legislative relations and public relations were of equal importance and that it was the president's responsibility to ensure that "they all coordinate, and should coordinate to the greatest extent." The person in charge of those integrated initiatives, Clement insisted, must "have the same position on the Railroad that any other staff officer has—attend Board meetings and hear what the Directors have to say; definitely be the President's man."[60]

In October 1951, based largely on suggestions provided by Clement and Symes, Franklin reorganized the Publicity Department as the Public Relations Department. He hired Ralph C. Champlin for the new post of vice president in charge of public relations. As *The Commercial and Financial Chronicle* noted, Champlin's appointment represented "a new development in the Pennsylvania Railroad's public relations in establishing at the executive level a department head to carry on this function." Champlin possessed some familiarity with railroading, in that his father worked for the Central of Georgia and the Seaboard Air Line before retiring as a trainmaster on the Florida East Coast. After completing college at the University of Florida, Ralph Champlin worked in the Philadelphia branch of the William H. Rankin advertising agency. He gained further experience with Hearst International Magazines as a newsstand sales promotion manager for *Cosmopolitan* and *Good Housekeeping*. Champlin spent eight years at the advertising firm Batten, Barton, Durstine & Osborn. His work on the Ethyl gasoline account induced him to join the Ethyl Corporation in February 1937, and he became the director of public relations two years later. Champlin spent the war years as the manager of the Rubber Conservation Program for the Division of Information of the War Production Board, and then served as the chairman of both the National Conference of Business Public Relations Executives and the Public Relations Committee of the New York State Chamber of Commerce.[61]

Champlin was a staff officer who reported directly to the president, and—as two of his subordinates observed—he possessed the authority to "act in an advisory capacity to the regions and be of service to them." It was clear from the beginning, however, that Champlin sought to do more than merely advise PRR executives. During the 1920s, Stewart Mims, from the J. Walter Thompson agency, had complained that some managers were too focused on the requirements of daily operations to pay sufficient attention to customer service and public relations, while others had become personally involved in marketing campaigns despite their lack of expertise in such matters. Champlin shared those views and deplored the tendency of senior PRR managers to approve only those publicity campaigns they personally found appealing. Moreover, Champlin was critical of the tendency of executives to expand advertising budgets during prosperous times and to then suspend those efforts when their results failed to live up to expectations or when financial conditions became unfavorable.

There was some truth in Champlin's statements, yet they ignored the fundamental problem, one that had also bedeviled Mims. Broad economic and regulatory factors caused severe difficulties for the eastern railroads, and that situation could not be solved by the Pennsylvania Railroad's advertising campaigns. Champlin and his colleagues faced an environment where the PRR was increasingly at the mercy of factors outside managerial control. The growing highway network diverted freight to trucks and passengers to their automobiles. Those who still patronized the rails were increasingly vocal in their complaints regarding inad-equate service—and willing to share their unhappiness with elected officials. Efforts to adjust rates to retain or recapture traffic frequently ran afoul of a regulatory regime that dated to an era when the railroads possessed a near monopoly over transportation within the United States. The workers who demanded higher wages and increased benefits alienated many middle-class consumers, but they retained powerful political support at all levels of govern-ment. It seemed increasingly apparent that the only way to save the PRR and the other railroads was to persuade the public and the politicians alike that they should recon-ceptualize the carriers as victims rather than villains. Yet efforts to change widespread perceptions were beyond the abilities of the Pennsylvania Railroad. That broader public-relations campaign increasingly depended on the cooperation of all the carriers, coordinated by the Asso-ciation of American Railroads. Several more years would pass before that effort—which Champlin influenced but did not control—would begin to achieve success.[62]

While Champlin retained some aspects of the PRR's existing public-relations program, he also undertook sig-nificant new efforts to improve the railroad's public image. Much of that responsibility rested with Gustavus Payne, who in January 1952 became the manager of publicity. Edward C. Gegenheimer, who succeeded Edward Kaier as director of public relations in 1949, continued in that role. One of Champlin's most important new hires involved the selection of John K. Murphy as supervisor of commu-nity relations. After attending the University of Alabama, Murphy worked for the Associated Press, was on the edi-torial board of *Look*, and served as managing editor of the Picture Book Division of *Look*'s parent company, Cowles Magazines. Beginning in 1947, Murphy spent five years in the field of public relations, first with the Fred Eldean agency and then at Pendray & Company. After joining the PRR, he established a community relations program on each of the three regions.[63]

Murphy also expanded the duties of the three regional publicity representatives to include both community rela-tions and publicity. Louis Henderson, who had been the PRR's Western Region publicity representative since 1932, elected to "hire a newspaper man" to assist him in promot-ing the benefits that the PRR and its employees offered to residents. He also sought opportunities to highlight the positive contributions of Pennsylvania Railroad person-nel. In February 1953, for example, Henderson traveled to Lima, Ohio, to honor a PRR baggage handler. The previ-ous spring, Glenn McComas had raced nearly two blocks

to pull a three-year-old child out of the path of a passen-ger train, an act that had earned him a Carnegie Medal and a PRR Heroic Service Medal. Now, standing beside the editor of the *Lima News*, Henderson could congratu-late McComas upon his receipt of the Ohio State Safety Council's Nick O' Time Award and its accompanying gold watch.[64]

The strengthening of the PRR's public-relations capa-bilities led to the termination of the railroad's relationship with two of its long-standing partners. Raymond Loewy had worked with the company since 1934, when his will-ingness to design trash cans soon led to his involvement with the restyling of the GG1 electric locomotive. He sub-sequently participated in more than six hundred design projects for the Pennsylvania Railroad and was at the height of his influence during the 1940s. The railroad's increasingly strained financial circumstances and the erosion of passenger traffic reduced the need for Loewy's stylistic touches. In late 1949, after the PRR received the bulk of the new equipment used to reequip its passenger service, the company terminated most of Loewy's initia-tives and on January 1, 1950, reduced his retainer to $10,000 per year. Loewy's last project for the PRR was probably related to modifications to the station in Chester, Pennsyl-vania, which began during the summer of 1951. His contract with the railroad ended on November 1, 1952, and it was not renewed. A. Baker Barnhart, a Loewy partner who worked closely with the PRR, suggested that the rapid decline in passenger travel spelled the end of the relationship. Asked to explain the parting of ways, Loewy instead asserted that it occurred "shortly after Symes became President [*sic*] and many of my dear old friends left the railroad."[65]

Loewy's marginalization was certainly in keeping with Symes's aversion to expensive programs that did not yield reductions in cost or improvements in efficiency. After he became executive vice president at the beginning of 1952, Symes made it clear that he did not share Franklin's willing-ness to spend lavishly on advertising, public relations, and community outreach. He was most likely responsible for ending another relationship with outside consultants, one that was even older than the reliance on Loewy. Beginning in 1952, the company no longer paid a retainer to the Ivy Lee & T. J. Ross agency, as it had done since 1915. The ratio-nale for the decision is unclear, but the expanded activities associated with the new Public Relations Department may have ensured that T. J. Ross's skills were unnecessary. It is also possible that the legacy of his multifaceted wartime efforts may have come back to haunt him. In addition to consulting with the Association of American Railroads,

Ross had worked with the Eastern Railroad Presidents' Conference and had encouraged the members of that trade association to select Carl Byoir & Associates as their public-relations firm—a recommendation that PRR executives strongly endorsed. In May 1949, Ross and Byoir launched an aggressive attack on truckers, accusing them of unsafe operating practices.[66] What truckers characterized as a "vicious, corrupt and fraudulent campaign" entered a new phase in 1951, when the Pennsylvania Assembly approved a bill to substantially increase maximum truck weights. Governor John S. Fine gave credence to evidence—provided by Byoir—of the allegedly dangerous practices of the truckers, and he vetoed the measure. The Pennsylvania Motor Truck Association and several trucking firms filed a $250 million lawsuit against the ERPC, the PRR, and more than a dozen other railroads, alleging that Byoir's advertising and lobbying efforts constituted a conspiracy "to vilify and slander the trucking industry," in violation of antitrust laws. The controversy forced Byoir to end his work with the railroads and may well have poisoned Ross's reputation with the PRR as well.[67]

Champlin's activities also caused considerable friction among PRR executives, particularly by reawakening old animosities between the Transportation and Traffic Departments. He had only been on the job a few weeks before he complained to President Franklin, whose background was in traffic, that managers in the Transportation Department saw little reason to expand the PRR's public-relations functions. Operating personnel wanted to limit Champlin's role to the functions of an information bureau, preparing annual reports, answering stockholders' questions, and fielding media inquiries. In October 1952, Symes reminded Champlin that all public-relations efforts "should be channeled into the hands of operating people." Symes further suggested that the Public Relations Department "should be relatively small and should not try to undertake anything which might be done better by people in operations." Like many of his colleagues, Symes maintained a certain amount of prejudice against individuals—including Champlin—who had not risen through the PRR's ranks and who presumably spent most of their time talking rather than working. When Champlin sought to hire a staff writer from the DuPont Company, a firm that possessed far more public-relations expertise than the PRR, Symes refused the request. "I am inclined to think," he wrote, "48 years of age is a little too old for an outsider of this type to start in the railroad industry. In addition, I would take it, from reading his letter, that he is of the 'braggadocio and smart-aleck' type."[68]

Fred Carpi, the vice president in charge of traffic, shared Symes's aversion to the development of a wide-ranging public-relations agenda. Like Symes, he suggested that Champlin focus his energies within the company rather than seek to influence outsiders. "Good public relations of a lasting nature are founded on good employe relations," Carpi told Champlin. "A prerequisite of a successful program is high employe morale." Carpi intended to maintain his control over the solicitation of the railroad's freight and passenger traffic, and he resented the involvement of outside consulting, advertising, and marketing firms. "There is still no warrant in transferring our emphasis from personal solicitation to newspaper and magazine advertising," he explained, and he resented Champlin's efforts to bypass contacts cultivated over many years with impersonal community relations initiatives. Carpi acknowledged that the PRR's "street men" were more interested in selling tickets in bulk, for military and group travel, rather than to individuals, but he insisted that there was no reason to change the railroad's marketing methods. Carpi's involvement in publicity matters also strained the railroad's relationship with the Al Paul Lefton Company. He complained to Champlin of the need to "coach" the Lefton agency "and point them down the road to modern advertising practice; research, testing, planning, and writing." Champlin, whose experience in the field of advertising vastly exceeded Carpi's, pointed out that Lefton's work was far superior to that produced by J. Walter Thompson during the 1920s and that the unwillingness of PRR personnel to cooperate with Lefton constituted a more serious problem.[69]

A New Personnel Department

Even as they were enhancing the PRR's public-relations capabilities, senior executives were placing increased emphasis on employee relations. "Confidence and loyalty are seriously lacking on the part of many of our employees," Symes observed in September 1951. He concluded that that situation resulted from "the troubled labor conditions of the past decade (during which labor has been in the ascendency)" and "an organized campaign by the officers of labor unions to strengthen the loyalty of the employes to their organizations by attempting to discredit railroad management . . . to weaken employe morale and destroy employe-management relations." Unfortunately, Symes concluded, "there has been no complete and fully integrated System-wide program on our railroad to meet this problem and to secure the necessary improvement in employe morale." He also called attention to the ages of the divisional personnel assigned to labor issues—half were older than fifty, and a substantial number were in their sixties—and warned that the passage of time would soon pit their young and inexperienced replacements against seasoned union negotiators.[70]

Similar problems had bedeviled Symes's predecessors. Prior to World War I, Ivy Lee and W. W. Atterbury had developed the Mutual Beneficial Association as a mechanism to secure the loyalty of train-service personnel and to undercut the appeal of the operating brotherhoods. Although he was willing to negotiate with those skilled employees, Atterbury could not countenance efforts by shop workers, clerks, or maintenance-of-way personnel to join independent unions or otherwise interfere with managerial prerogatives. His implementation of the Employe Representation Plan and his hardline response to the 1922 Shopmen's Strike temporarily blocked gains by organized labor. Such vitriolic responses became untenable once the Great Depression and the New Deal transformed both public opinion and the political climate. Martin Clement and Walter Franklin had largely acquiesced to workers' demands, contributing to the state of labor relations that Symes found so objectionable. Symes could hardly return to the combative days of the Atterbury administration, but he concluded that a carefully orchestrated program of employee relations might achieve the same goal of managerial supremacy through the use of gentler and more politically acceptable tactics.

As had so often occurred in the past, the Pennsylvania Railroad's organizational structure changed to match corporate strategy. Symes demanded a comprehensive reorganization of the Personnel Department, one that would centralize authority at the system level. He acknowledged that "public relations and employe relations go hand in hand," but he was not willing to "await decision with respect to the final outcome of the public relations program that has been discussed from time to time." When the new organization took effect on November 1, 1951, James Oram thus focused solely on matters involving the workforce. As chief of personnel, Oram continued to work closely with his counterparts on other eastern railroads to present a united front against labor and to ensure uniformity in the application of wages, benefits, and work rules. The superintendents of labor and wages for each of the three regions and at the Altoona Works became regional superintendents of personnel, under Oram's direct authority.[71] Oram's discretion also extended to the supervisor of personnel, the division examiner, and several junior examiners on each division. Symes predicted "that the majority

of the problems will be disposed of at the Division level to avoid dissatisfaction on the part of the employes and to expedite the handling of grievances." That circumstance suggested that the divisional junior examiners should be carefully "selected in much the same manner as Junior Engineers and will be given a course of training designed to give them a well-rounded picture of the railroad to assist them in personnel work." The training program would be expensive, Symes conceded, as would the increased wages paid to the most promising examiners. The cost would be more than justified, he concluded, "in view of the money which can either be expended or saved by decisions that are made in this Department."[72]

At the headquarters level, Oram relied on the contributions of two assistants. Charles E. Alexander, the former superintendent of labor and wages for the Eastern Region, served as an assistant chief of personnel. While Oram planned a long-term labor-relations strategy, Alexander negotiated with union officials and oversaw the day-to-day application and enforcement of labor agreements. James I. Patin, Oram's other assistant, took responsibility for employee relations, an effort that was closely connected with attempts to improve customer service. "One of the main ideas of our Employe Relations Program," Patin emphasized, "is to produce a better feeling and better understanding between management and employes throughout the entire organization, so that the employes in their treatment of the public might reflect the right attitude." He faced a formidable challenge. "Things I hear about lack of cooperation among departments and divisions and regions," he conceded, "indicate that we have a long way to go internally before we can expect to get the kind of reputation we want among the public." Patin was neither an idealist nor a visionary, and he reminded his colleagues that "human relations is the art of the possible." Patin was equally dismissive of social engineering and he deplored the "crusader" who was "likely to forget the purpose of the business in his effort to carry out his theories which to him are more important than the business. We try on the Pennsylvania," Patin concluded, "to screen out the lad who comes out of the classroom with too strong a sense of mission, too deep a conviction that he can straighten out everyone by applying formulae from the textbooks."[73]

Patin, supported by Oram, insisted that managers as well as workers would need to change their behavior. To that end they worked with John E. Kennedy, the chair of the Management Training Department at Pennsylvania State College. Kennedy, who became the PRR's new manager of employee relations, worked with faculty at

Penn State, Purdue University, and ten other institutions to develop a series of training seminars. They encouraged managers to "impart information," "develop skill," and "modify attitudes" to promote safety and teamwork and create a positive approach to discipline. The overall theme—"A Satisfied Patron Is Our Security"—reflected an emphasis on cooperative labor-management efforts to rectify complaints from shippers and passengers and thus retain their business.[74]

During the spring and summer of 1953, Patin oversaw a comprehensive management-training initiative. More than five thousand PRR executives attended sessions offered at New York, Philadelphia, Washington, Harrisburg, Fort Wayne, Indianapolis, and other locations. Professors such as psychologist Charles H. Lawshe and former railroader Virgil Samms facilitated the discussions. As the author of books such as *Psychology of Industrial Relations* and *Principles of Personnel Testing*, Lawshe was more attuned to streamlining the managerial structure than he was in placating passengers and shippers. He segregated attendees by rank, encouraging them to speak freely without fear of reprimand from more senior executives. James Newell, who had replaced Symes as the vice president in charge of operations, emphasized that the entire process would be "something of a two-way street," one that would offer "an added opportunity for the men to give the management the benefit of their ideas, developed through years of experience, as to ways of improving service and facilities." The seminars initially highlighted improvements to the chain of command within the organization, and only later touched on improved customer relations.[75] Trainmasters, yardmasters, and other supervisory employees learned "how to get along with subordinates" and "the delicate, subtle game of dealing with the various types of personalities who make up any organization."[76]

Patin also enlisted the support of labor leaders, suggesting that diligent employees would create satisfied customers and ensure the profitability of the Pennsylvania Railroad—prosperity that would underwrite future increases in wages and benefits. Two training films, one scripted for depot and clerical forces and the other for train crews, emphasized the twin themes of safety and the prevention of loss and damage through the careful handling of freight. In a pamphlet titled "Insuring Your Prosperity," the leaders of the nonoperating unions stressed a similar theme, encouraging employees to be conscientious in their daily tasks. Workers and union representatives prepared a set of "Recommendations of Train Masters, Assistant Train Masters and Yard Masters to the Upper Management of the Pennsylvania Railroad," listing dysfunctional elements associated with both customer relations and interaction among employees and their supervisors. The Brotherhood of Railroad Trainmen—whose members were more likely to interact with passengers than those who belonged to other operating unions—sponsored sessions designed to "improve 'customer relations' and strengthen relations with fellow employees."[77]

A new employee magazine was an integral part of efforts to improve customer service and inculcate loyalty within the workforce. In September 1951, when he recommended the reorganization of the Personnel Department, Symes observed that "we do not have a satisfactory method of communicating with our employes . . . and their families whereby they can be kept informed" of various issues facing the company. Those issues included safety, the prevention of loss and damage claims, the development of new technology, the PRR's financial situation, and the overall problems facing the railroad industry. A monthly magazine should "humanize the officials and acquaint the employees with them," Symes suggested, "make the employees and their families proud of being a part of the Pennsylvania Railroad, and do much to counteract the vicious anti-management propaganda reaching the employes through regular Brotherhood publications such as 'Labor,' 'Trainmen's News,' etc." Symes was adamant that the monthly publication should be mailed to employees at their homes rather than be handed directly to them. Individual workers might ignore the promanagement message or simply toss the magazine in the trash, Symes suggested, but their family members could exert considerable influence on their attitudes and behavior. He also hoped that the magazine might replace the moribund Employes' Suggestion Plan, which he and other executives deemed too expensive to continue.[78]

In June 1952, the PRR's Public Relations Department released the first issue of *The Pennsy*. The title reflected ongoing efforts to identify a modern slogan for the PRR. Patin had little patience with "a title such as 'The Friendly Railroad' or 'Standard Railroad of the World,'" noting that "the difficulty of getting uniformity of behavior over so much territory and by so many employees make us vulnerable to criticism which such a slogan might actually invite." With "The Standard Railroad of the World" both outdated and cumbersome and "The Friendly Railroad" already in use by the Southern Pacific, a simpler slogan seemed in order. "The word 'Pennsy' is friendly and informal," one executive noted, "and it seems to me that we should call ourselves it more often." That was indeed the case, as the shortened version of "Pennsylvania," once absent from official correspondence, began to appear with increasing regularity.[79]

While outwardly like the *Mutual Magazine* that Atterbury had encouraged when he was the vice president in charge of operations, *The Pennsy* eschewed that publication's narrow focus on issues that might interest clerks, machinists, and other skilled employees. At Symes's insistence, *The Pennsy* excluded news items relating to specific employees, ensuring that readers would instead focus solely on managerial initiatives and concerns. In addition to the immediate audience of PRR employees and their families, Murphy intended that *The Pennsy* would also influence the broader public. The magazine stressed the railroad's ongoing investments in equipment and the physical plant; exhorted employees to provide better customer service; and condemned high taxes, regulations, and government support for competing modes of transportation.

Murphy recruited some of the best available talent for the new magazine. Ik Shuman managed *The Pennsy* and supervised a seven-person staff. In 1948, he had left his post as executive editor at *The New Yorker* to take charge of *Script*, a West Coast version of his former employer. Shuman purchased the failing company for a dollar, but publication ceased the following year and left Shuman deeply in debt—perhaps explaining his interest in Murphy's offer of employment. Shuman's art director, Alfred C. Strasser, once worked for the Art Department of the New York advertising agency Dorrance, Sullivan & Company during the 1920s and was more recently the art director for the Biow Company. In the 1930s and 1940s, Biow had been one of the top agencies in the United States, thanks to a client list that included Philip Morris. By the early 1950s, a tax scandal and the loss of several major accounts sounded the firm's death knell, and Strasser was doubtless relieved to join the staff of *The Pennsy*. When he became part of the Public Relations Department in 1953, Strasser devoted most of his time to the company magazine and to the preparation of artwork for annual reports, timetables, and displays. Over the next five years, however, he increasingly assumed the industrial-design responsibilities that had once belonged to Raymond Loewy—including concepts for passenger-car interiors, stations, and corporate offices. Associate editor Joseph Shallit was a Russian émigré and a reporter for the *Philadelphia Record*, who scored his greatest journalistic coup in 1942 when he was arrested for photographing the Liberty Bell on the Fourth of July. After military service during World War II, he wrote mystery novels and science-fiction magazine articles.[80]

Collectively, the diverse backgrounds and the undoubted talents of *The Pennsy*'s editorial staff suggested that Champlin, Murphy, and PRR executives were willing to devote considerable resources to its publication. Accordingly, they allocated $350,000 annually to the production and mailing of 180,000 copies of each issue to current and retired employees.[81]

The Pennsy moniker also lent its name to the Pennsy Family Clubs, which included both executives and blue-collar workers in a variety of social events. There was a clear business purpose as well, and Symes emphasized that the Pennsy Family Clubs would "encourage teamwork to promote sales and improve service and public relations and help create warm personal relations among PRR people." Those initiatives included the airing of a fifteen-minute film, in which Symes explained the problems facing the PRR and highlighted managerial initiatives to improve the situation. By the end of 1956, thirty Family Clubs were in operation at various points across the system. There were additional, occupation-specific clubs for station agents and yardmasters, the outgrowth of the management-training program at Penn State College. The Personnel Department provided guest speakers, who highlighted important developments affecting the railroad and offered suggestions for improved job performance and career advancement.[82]

The growing importance of health care as part of overall labor costs prompted Oram and his subordinates to increase the responsibilities of the PRR's Medical Department.[83] The formal provision of medical care to employees began in 1883, when the board of directors donated land in Altoona for a hospital that opened two years later. The railroad expanded its medical services over the next several decades, keeping pace with a larger workforce and improvements in health care practices. By 1925, the PRR employed a chief medical examiner and two assistants, one stationed in Philadelphia, the other in Cleveland. Fifty-three district examiners and ninety-seven assistant district examiners served at division points and other locations with high concentrations of employees. By 1948, the railroad was subsidizing a total of 283 hospitals, operating on a pay-as-you-go basis, at an annual expenditure of $308,000. Fifty full-time medical examiners and assistants plus 427 part-time company surgeons and medical specialists cost a further $457,000.[84]

Unless they had the misfortune to be injured, operating employees typically encountered Medical Department personnel only when they were called upon to demonstrate that they were physically able to perform their jobs. Enginemen and firemen, the two classes of employees who would most obviously incite disaster if incapacitated, received annual checks of visual acuity, color perception (vital for the correct reading of signals), and blood pressure. Employees who failed the exam would be transferred to other work or, more rarely, given disability retirement, assuming that the condition was permanent. Those who failed the medical exam could appeal their test results to the chief medical examiner in Philadelphia, but some employees had a simpler method of getting back on the job. One engineman, for example, took a local doctor's advice to drain a pint of blood before having his blood pressure tested in Philadelphia. Such tactics suggested that employees perceived the Medical Department as a mechanism for managers to control employees rather than make them well again.[85]

By the time of the 1951 Personnel Department reorganization, Oram confronted several difficulties relating to the company's health care capabilities. With the workforce shrinking steadily, he wanted to reassure employees that Medical Department personnel were not interested in weeding out high-seniority workers and ending their careers. In keeping with his emphasis on improved productivity, Oram also stressed preventive medicine and the avoidance of accidents and injuries that might retard the movement of freight and passengers, create ill-will among employees, and sully the railroad's public image. Finally, in an increasingly litigious society, Oram was acutely sensitive to the relationship between the quality of medical care and "the level of costs of personal injury settlements." It was for that reason that he considered, but ultimately rejected, organizational and administrative links between the Medical Department, which examined injured workers, and the Claim Department, which paid out any damage settlements that might result from an accident or from mishandled shipments. Oram, who was a personnel manager rather than a lawyer, was not concerned that a relationship between the two departments would result in excessive liability claims. Instead, he feared that workers might conclude that the company's medical facilities existed primarily to prevent them from suing their employer. Because the railroad was "engaged in a broad program of improving Management-Employe relations," Oram observed, "it would be a serious mistake to put the doctors under Claim Department jurisdiction, [as] such action would simply confirm the existing views of the employe representatives as to the relations between our doctors and Claim Department interests."[86]

Oram's multifaceted concerns prompted a thorough overhaul of the Medical Department during the summer of 1953. The PRR recruited its new medical director, Dr. Norbert J. Roberts, from the Standard Oil Company of New Jersey, a common move for a company that overwhelmingly promoted from within its own ranks yet relied on outsiders for new or unfamiliar areas of specialized expertise. Roberts presided over 56 full-time PRR physicians—many of them newly hired—who were stationed at locations across the system. A further 350 consultant physicians and surgeons, paid on a case-by-case basis, were available to perform physical examinations and treat the victims of on-the-job accidents. The new structure gave the medical director broad policy authority while delegating day-to-day administrative issues to four assistant medical directors—one at each of the three regions and one at the Altoona Works. Those directors could call on the expertise of what was essentially a central staff office, consisting of specialists in internal medicine and other disciplines. Medical records became confidential, ensuring that employees who sought help were unlikely to face retribution from their superiors. Blue-collar workers received varying levels of medical benefits, depending on the stipulations of union collective-bargaining contracts. Beginning in 1956, the PRR provided both a medical plan and group life insurance for officers and salaried employees who were not covered by union agreements.[87]

New Tactics by Organized Labor

The reorganization of the Personnel Department did little to halt the steady upward progression of wages or the spread of the union shop. In scarcely more than a year following the January 1951 amendments to the Railway Labor Act, executives on more than forty railroads agreed to union-shop representation for some of the sixteen nonoperating unions, covering 215,000 employees. By February 1952, the members of the presidential emergency board saw no reason why that condition should not become universal. They emphasized that they were "both puzzled and struck by the fact that the carriers appear before us bitterly opposing the union shop on basic principle and yet have themselves recently entered into such agreements with other unions on their properties." PRR executives were among those who bowed to pressure from organized labor, and on May 8, 1952, they gave the CIO's United Railroad Workers of America affiliate a union-shop contract. The agreement, covering forty-five thousand shopcraft employees, represented the first time that any of that union's maintenance-of-equipment employees gained that form of representation. By the end of August, the PRR and the other eastern carriers had signed contracts with all the nonoperating unions, providing for union-shop representation.[88]

Operating employees—particularly those enrolled in the BLE, BLF&E, and ORC—favored more contentious tactics. More than five thousand staged a strike in March 1952, affecting the New York Central. In Cleveland, federal judge Emerich B. Freed declared the walkout a threat to military operations in Korea and ordered the strikers back to work. Several hundred refused to comply, but the temporary truce spurred further negotiations. Truman's most recent seizure of the railroads, by now nearly two years old, was due to end on June 1 and could not be extended without congressional authorization. With elections less than six months away, the president was reluctant to follow that course of action, lest he alienate an important component of the Democratic Party's political constituency. On May 19, railroad executives and representatives from the three recalcitrant unions reached an agreement that promised road crews a 12.5-cent hourly increase, with 27 cents for those working in yards. Each group received a 10-cent cost-of-living adjustment, ensuring further escalations in the PRR's expenditures. In return, management gained slightly greater authority to alter work rules. The disputes that would inevitably result from the application of those work rules were still subject to the nonbinding recommendations of a chairman appointed by the National Mediation Board, suggesting that a harmonious relationship between management and labor was likely to remain elusive. Union officials indicated that they had accepted the arrangement only reluctantly, and with "some disappointment," but a more objective analysis suggested that they had met virtually all their goals.[89]

As the threat of strikes subsided, the army relinquished authority over the railroads on May 23. The NYC's Gustav Metzman and his aide, Illinois Central division engineer Wayne Smith, were all smiles as they posed for photographers and traded their uniform jackets for civilian clothes. The PRR's Andrew McIntyre and other executives returned to their respective railroads, and the fifty regular army officers assigned to railway operations assumed more traditional responsibilities. Everyone expressed relief that the process that had cost the federal government more than $45,000 a month was over. The truce would not last, but observers indicated that "the brotherhoods and the carriers seem to have learned one lesson from their experience—to stay as far from the Government as possible in future disputes." Following years of strikes, seizures, injunctions, mediation, and arbitration, neither side

wanted to expose its agenda to the uncertainties of intervention by the public sector.[90]

Despite pledges to negotiate wages and work rules outside the political process, the federal government continued to structure the PRR's labor relations. By the summer of 1952, the union shop was widespread, and the universal cost-of-living adjustments for railroad workers ensured that labor leaders could no longer claim that wages were not keeping pace with inflation. In July, they sought a new mechanism for securing higher pay for their members. In keeping with Wage Stabilization Board policies, the contracts negotiated over the preceding sixteen months permitted additional pay raises that were tied to increases in worker productivity. Railroad executives argued that it was difficult if not impossible to separate labor's role from dieselization, mechanization, and the many other complementary technological developments that led to greater efficiency. Union leaders counterattacked, claiming that cost-of-living provisions were not sufficient—and even if they were, they did not enable workers to secure higher real (inflation-adjusted) wages.[91]

At the beginning of December, Truman asked Paul N. Guthrie, an economics professor at the University of North Carolina and a former public member of the WSB, to determine whether increased productivity provided sufficient grounds to renegotiate the labor agreements. Guthrie concluded in the affirmative and called for a new set of hearings to begin on January 5, 1953. On March 18, Guthrie awarded a productivity bonus of four cents per hour, a decision that would cost the nation's railroads $120 million per year. James P. Shields, the grand chief engineer of the BLE, insisted that the increase was inadequate, as did other labor leaders. William P. Kennedy, the president of the BRT, was more positive, asserting that the award was "history making because it recognized for the first time the workers' participation in increased productivity."[92] Kennedy and his colleagues nonetheless agreed that they had established a new mechanism to secure steadily increasing wages. Executives, in contrast, feared that any improvements in operating efficiency, acquired through capital investment, would rebound solely to labor and not to shareholders. Daniel P. Loomis, the chairman of the Association of Western Railways, also joined his colleagues in pointing out just how far economic policy had drifted from President Truman's original goal of controlling inflation.[93]

By the time Guthrie issued his recommendations, inflation was no longer Truman's problem. The November 1952 elections had gone badly for the Democrats, who lost control of the House, the Senate, and the Oval Office. Dwight D. Eisenhower's sympathies lay more with management than with labor, but that did not prevent the operating brotherhoods from initiating their fourth major round of bargaining since 1946. In addition to wage increases of up to 30 percent, they demanded that the prior cost-of-living adjustments be made permanent. It was a wise precaution, given that inflation had abated to just 0.8 percent that year, and the consumer price index would even decline slightly in 1955.[94]

As PRR executives negotiated with the various brotherhoods, the nonoperating unions presented a more complex problem. In January 1954, the railroad granted its thirty-six thousand shop workers a five-cent hourly wage increase. Representatives from the shopcraft unions were also able to solidify their earlier cost-of-living gains. They nonetheless abandoned any further reliance on the escalator clause—a provision that held little value in an economy where inflation was virtually nonexistent. Instead, they secured additional vacation time and other fringe benefits for high-seniority employees. Union officials made similar claims on the nation's other railroads, and on January 16—less than a week after the PRR's concessions—it was Eisenhower's turn to appoint an emergency board to investigate the matter. The panel rejected three-quarters of the unions' demands but nonetheless recommended additional vacation time, holiday pay, and medical benefits. The carriers accepted on August 21, averting a strike and adding $140 million per year in operating costs. A similar agreement, signed in December of the following year, further expanded health care coverage and provided a 14.5 cent hourly wage—in that instance, increasing personnel expenditures by $300 million annually.[95]

Of the many disputes associated with the nonoperating employees, the most contentious involved those who belonged to the Transport Workers Union. Since the late 1930s, three unions had waged a concerted campaign to secure the allegiance of the PRR's shop workers. One was the Brotherhood of Railroad Shop Crafts of America, the rump end of the old Employe Representation Plan. Another was the Railway Employees' Department of the American Federation of Labor. The most successful, at least on the PRR, was the United Railroad Workers of America, part of the Congress of Industrial Organizations. Two rounds of National Mediation Board certification elections, one in March 1947 and the other in November 1951, empowered the URWA to serve as the bargaining agent for all the PRR's shopcraft employees, save the blacksmiths and the machinists.[96]

Despite the CIO's support, the URWA failed to achieve a national scope, and most of its forty-two thousand members worked for the Pennsylvania Railroad. In October 1954, they voted to merge with the Transport Workers Union of America. Michael J. Quill had founded the TWU in New York City twenty years earlier. As a former courier for the Irish Republican Army and a supporter of the American Communist Party, Quill aggressively pursued the organization of the city's transit workers. He was nothing if not adaptable, however, and after World War II, his commitment to expanding his union quickly supplanted his political principles. The Communist Party treated New York's nickel subway fare as sacrosanct, but Quill perceived fare increases as a mechanism for raising the wages of TWU members. The anticommunist provisions associated with the 1947 Taft-Hartley Act also influenced his behavior, but the following year's presidential election made the break complete. The Communist Party underwrote the disastrous Progressive Party campaign of Henry Wallace, causing Quill to side with the CIO and mainstream political liberalism. CIO leaders rewarded his loyalty, and by the early 1950s, Quill had built the TWU into an organization with about 150,000 members. They included flight attendants, baggage handlers, and other aviation workers, but the union's strength still lay along the subway, streetcar, and bus routes in New York and Philadelphia.[97]

By the end of 1954, two issues shaped Quill's reaction to the Pennsylvania Railroad's management. The first involved merger negotiations between Quill's CIO and the American Federation of Labor. The two unions had been bitter rivals for the better part of two decades and had a long history of jurisdictional disputes—including repeated battles over the allegiance of shopcraft workers. Quill was opposed to the consolidation—but, if it were to occur, he expected to gain a high-profile position within the new organization. His repeated attacks on the New York City Transit Authority and the Philadelphia Transportation Company were his primary vehicle for self-promotion, but the PRR was also a highly visible target. Of more concern to TWU members, however, dieselization and the steady decline of passenger service thinned the ranks of shop personnel, and Quill was as determined to preserve jobs as he was to secure higher wages and fringe benefits. He was particularly incensed by curtailments at the PRR's Wilmington Shops and the transfer of some of that work to Altoona. TWU members organized a picket line at Penn Station, providing homeward-bound commuters with leaflets accusing the company of "gambling with the safety of passengers by reducing its inspection and maintenance force to a dangerously low level." In March 1955, again in September, Quill threatened strikes against the PRR, and just as quickly called them off. The National Mediation Board intervened in each case, although with little practical effect. Quill's demands—including a twenty-five-cent hourly raise and a thirty-hour workweek—struck many as unreasonable. PRR officials insisted that their equipment was in excellent condition. Moreover, by 1955 the company had a surplus of passenger cars, suggesting that a prolonged walkout by TWU maintenance forces would not interrupt operations. Finally, Quill had made more than a few enemies within the labor movement, and both CIO leaders and the heads of the other shopcraft unions declined to support a TWU walkout. Another threatened strike, set to take place a few days before Christmas, likewise failed to materialize. In each case, Quill excused his inaction by reminding TWU members that the thirty-day cooling-off period mandated by the Railway Labor Act precluded any immediate efforts to make good on his threats.[98]

Even as he waged war against the Pennsylvania Railroad, Quill pledged that neither he nor TWU members would interfere with operations on the Long Island Rail Road. He need not have bothered, as the Brotherhood of Railroad Trainmen was using many of his tactics against the PRR's subsidiary. In August 1955, BRT leaders postponed a walkout against the Long Island Rail Road, pending the outcome of federal mediation. The eleven hundred union members who worked for the LIRR—98 percent of whom had voted in favor of a strike—were reportedly "so mad" that they were prepared to put down their tools and head home. The commuter carrier could ill afford the $1.5 million in additional labor costs associated with the BRT's proposal, and there was little political will to raise fares in compensation. LIRR shop workers remained on the job for another month, while mediation ran its course. That effort failed, and in early September employees began calling in sick. On September 12, a coordinated go-slow campaign threw the morning rush hour into chaos, delaying ninety thousand commuters by more than an hour. The two sides soon reached an accord, one that cost the LIRR little more than a tenth of what its negotiators originally estimated. There was no corresponding fare increase, however, ensuring that the company's financial problems would continue to worsen.[99]

By early 1956, with Quill seemingly in the position of the little boy who cried wolf, the labor leader reverted to his earlier efforts to turn public opinion against the PRR. TWU members entertained commuters with another picket line at Penn Station. On February 24, *The Embassy*

derailed near Odenton, Maryland, killing three passengers and two PRR employees. Quill blamed the accident on layoffs of maintenance personnel and warned of "additional railroad tragedies" in the future. A month later, another strike threat led to federal mediation. In September, Quill denounced as unwise a walkout threatened by the Motormen's Benevolent Association, a rival union, against New York's Transit Authority—and promptly announced that the TWU would strike against the Pennsylvania Railroad. He abandoned the plan a few hours later, acceding to arbitration. The PRR's shop workers accepted the cancellation of the latest proposed walkout, but some twenty-five hundred gathered, on company time, to discuss their concerns. The meeting lasted twenty-four hours, drawing a swift restraining order from district judge Sylvester J. Ryan. "This high-handed and last minute gag of the workers' protest against the Pennsylvania's criminal neglect of their just grievances and complaints," Quill emphasized, "has caused a new and extremely explosive situation among Pennsylvania workers, which is now spreading beyond the New York area into the entire Pennsylvania system." The situation was not new, nor was it particularly explosive, but it did result in a new contract between the PRR and the TWU in December, one that provided substantial wage increases to some thirty-five thousand shop workers.[100]

The gains achieved by the Transport Workers Union were not sufficient to silence Mike Quill. In October 1957, he criticized PRR management for the "persistent violation" of its contract with the union, particularly with respect to the furloughing of shop workers. James Oram, by now promoted to the railroad's vice president in charge of personnel, had a somewhat different perspective. "We think Mr. Quill is moved in this instance," Oram commented, "by the fact that a convention of his union opened in New York on Monday and that it would be politically expedient for him to appear before the convention with this 'call for strike' on the record." Regardless of Quill's motivation, his actions, like all those that preceded, fizzled out into nothing more than rhetoric. Oram and other PRR executives would have been in error, however, if they assumed that the feisty Irishman was all talk and no action. Time and time again Quill engaged in collective-bargaining brinkmanship, threatening and calling strikes in an effort to preserve jobs and wages. At the end of the 1950s and as the PRR's financial problems worsened, Quill was prepared to translate his words into action. As the next decade began, he accomplished what the Civil War, two world wars, the Great Depression, a score of blizzards, and the labor unrest of 1877, 1920, and 1922 failed to achieve.

In 1960, Mike Quill would orchestrate a strike that, for the first time in history, shut down the Pennsylvania Railroad.[101]

Postwar Reorganization

The changes involving the Personnel Department were but a prelude to a far more widespread corporate reorganization, the most significant to have occurred since 1920. Throughout its history, the Pennsylvania Railroad's senior executives charted a course between the extremes of centralization and decentralization, attempting to identify the proper relationship between a single, all-powerful headquarters and autonomy at the local level. Prior to World War I, the PRR's organization reflected the company's policy—dating to the 1860s and 1870s—of expanding into Ohio, Indiana, and Illinois by leasing or acquiring the securities of existing railroads rather than by constructing new lines. For nearly half a century Pittsburgh was the dividing line between Lines East and Lines West, and in terms of day-to-day management, the two halves of the system functioned in relative isolation from each other. The World War I years illustrated the difficulty in moving traffic through Pittsburgh and correspondingly demonstrated the value of increased coordination between Lines East and Lines West. In 1920, contemporaneous with the end of federal oversight, the Pennsylvania Railroad became a truly integrated company for the first time. The board of directors achieved greater centralization by combining the two halves of the system while simultaneously decentralizing authority among four new regions. The arrangement freed senior executives in Philadelphia from involvement in routine operating matters and gave them more opportunity to focus on overall corporate policy and business strategy. The four regional vice presidents possessed considerable autonomy and in turn were expected to maximize efficiency and increase the level of traffic in their assigned regions.[102]

Changing operating conditions, the retirement of key personnel, and the preferences of individual executives incrementally altered that structure over the ensuing decades. The four regions, while covering geographic areas that were roughly equal in size, did not generate an equivalent level of traffic, nor did they place comparable demands on operating employees. There was also considerable duplication of effort among staff officers on the various regions, negating many of the efficiencies associated with the 1920 reorganization. During the first half of the 1920s, the PRR stripped the regions of many of their staff functions, leaving only the Transportation Department on a decentralized basis. In 1925, the company combined the Northwestern and Southwestern Regions—the least productive, in terms of traffic and revenues—into the Western Region, headquartered in Chicago. To the east, however, the high level of traffic and intensity of operations in Greater New York provoked the opposite response. In 1928, the operational responsibilities for the Long Island Rail Road and the New Jersey General Division became part of the New York Zone—which in many respects represented a new regional entity.

Throughout the system, division superintendents remained in charge of the day-to-day movement of trains as well as routine maintenance of equipment and the physical plant. The regional vice presidents functioned principally to transmit instructions from the system offices in Philadelphia to their subordinate divisions, to establish coordination among division superintendents, and to ensure the timely flow of information upward to corporate headquarters. For the next thirty years, the PRR remained a three-region organization, even as faster schedules, the increased prevalence of through trains, changes in union agreements, and service reductions progressively reduced the forty divisions that existed in 1920 to just nineteen divisions in 1955. During that time, the challenges associated with motor-carrier competition, the Great Depression, World War II, dieselization, and declining passenger traffic occupied the attention of PRR executives, and those managers demonstrated little enthusiasm for wholesale changes to the corporate structure. President Clement, who had been the general superintendent of the Lake General Division at the time of the 1920 reorganization, acknowledged that regions were competing against one another to persuade businesses to select industrial sites in one location or another—but, aside from calling for greater coordination, he did not offer any solutions.[103]

Demands for change emanated not from Philadelphia, but from the opposite end of the system. When he was the vice president in charge of the Western Region, James Symes was eager to apply lessons he had learned from other railroads to improve the efficiency of the PRR's operations. He encountered stiff resistance from his superiors, particularly with respect to his advocacy for dieselization, and he was almost as critical of constraints on his authority as he was of the railroad's duplex steam locomotives and steam turbines. Symes was concerned that the incremental organizational changes that had occurred since 1920 were depriving the railroad of the benefit of innovations emerging from the regions and divisions, outside the closed circle of system headquarters. When informed of plans to consolidate the Indianapolis Terminal Division into the St. Louis Division, he warned Clement that the change would reduce the level of contact between local employees and their new staff officers. The brief response that Clement added in the margins of Symes's letter—"too bad"—suggested the president's lack of interest in the opinions of regional or divisional personnel.[104]

Symes's 1947 promotion to system headquarters, as the vice president in charge of operations, vindicated his views on diesels while affording him the opportunity to give regional managers the autonomy he thought was their due. His responsibilities were still limited to the Transportation Department, yet his supervision of 94 percent of the railroad's employees gave him considerable scope to implement changes that would undo the creeping recentralization that had occurred since 1920. He supported a 1949 internal review of the corporate structure, which indicated that "centralization of authority became very noticeable during Government operation during the First World War, and was accelerated materially with the consolidation of the Lines East and Lines West and the formation of the Regions in March, 1920." That statement alone suggested that other PRR officials had forgotten that one of the principal goals of the 1920 organization had been to increase regional autonomy. The report stressed that "this [centralization] continued until Mr. Symes assumed the position of Operating Vice President some years ago, when, so far as the Operating [Transportation] Department was concerned, it was decided to return more authority to the Regions and to the Divisions." A key step in that process took place in the summer of 1951, when Symes asserted the need "to return the responsibility for operating the railroad back down the line and make the Superintendent, in effect, the General Manager of his Division, with complete charge and authority over practically all of the activities on his Division."[105]

Walter Franklin, serving as president since the summer of 1949, was more receptive than Clement had been to Symes's calls for organizational reform. Probably at Symes's suggestion, Franklin discussed the PRR's organization with at least two of the company's directors. Leonard T. Beale, the president of the Pennsylvania Salt Manufacturing Company, seconded Franklin's acknowledgment that the PRR organization was "a bit antiquated" and gave his support to efforts to reorganize the company.[106] Banker Richard King Mellon was familiar with Cresap, McCormick & Paget, management consultants to US Steel, and he suggested that that firm should conduct a study of the railroad's bylaws and organization charts.

Franklin ignored the recommendation, but he solicited advice from Roger M. Blough, the steelmaker's general solicitor. Blough observed that his company, like the Pennsylvania Railroad, was affected by increased competition, a rapidly shrinking workforce, and declining profits. He was confident that a change in corporate structure might improve the situation, and he was accordingly one of the principal architects of a comprehensive reorganization at US Steel, completed in 1951. He shared the preliminary outlines of his new organization chart with Franklin but swore the PRR president to secrecy. Franklin responded with tentative reorganization sketches, based in part on the steel company's corporate structure.[107]

At the beginning of 1952, Symes became the PRR's executive vice president, second in command and the clear successor to Franklin. After barely five months in his new role, Symes could boast that "we have practically revamped the organizational setup of the Operating [Transportation] Department." He had set his sights on a much larger challenge, addressing the corporate structure of the entire railroad. On April 30, he was in Pittsburgh, meeting with representatives from the Transportation and Traffic Departments. Highlighting the problems that faced the Pennsylvania Railroad, he emphasized that solutions would require "proper industrial relations, proper public relations, and to some extent labor relations" as well as "better contacts with state regulatory authorities." Despite the creation of the Public Relations Department the previous October, Symes suggested that the railroad lacked integrated policies in each of those areas. With Franklin and other senior executives seated beside him, Symes listened to suggestions and complaints from the managers who were in attendance. The responses reinforced his conclusion that there was a pronounced absence of coordination within the Transportation Department and between that department and other units of the company. While few in the audience realized the ramifications of that meeting, Symes left Pittsburgh determined to implement a thorough reorganization of the PRR's corporate structure.[108]

Symes was particularly concerned that the existing organization chart impeded the development of managerial initiative and made it more difficult for senior executives to identify and promote promising junior officers to positions of greater responsibility. The problem stemmed in part from the ongoing contraction in the number of divisions and the concomitant reduction in managerial employment. Divisional consolidation ensured that there were fewer opportunities to train and evaluate midlevel managers. Paradoxically, many of those executives were younger, less experienced, and less well equipped to manage the increasing size and complexity of a declining number of divisions.

The absence of more experienced managers in turn owed much to the austerity programs of the 1930s and to military service requirements during World War II, each of which created a bimodal distribution of executives in the 1950s. Those in the older group were nearing retirement and had little enthusiasm for change, while their more junior counterparts were reluctant to risk their careers by challenging the long-established status quo. Top management had always relied heavily on input from local operating officials, those closest to the action. Unfortunately, just as the railroad needed that wisdom the most, the supply of initiative and the innovative ideas that accompanied it seemed to be drying up. That situation led to an erosion of élan, divisional prestige, and morale. Even though senior management "experienced no difficulty in having [their] orders transmitted down the line, and in most cases having them acted upon," Symes and Franklin observed, they were "not getting the benefit of the comments and suggestions of those down the line." Local divisional and regional personnel complained that all real estate acquisitions and sales had to pass through the system vice president in charge of real estate, purchases, and insurance, and that it was impossible to scrap an obsolete freight car—even one that had been virtually destroyed in an accident—without the approval of the vice president in charge of operations. Some managers asserted that they "could do so much more if Regional authority permitted."[109]

Jim Newell, who replaced Symes as the vice president in charge of operations, and who was one of his key allies, suggested that the problem had been years in the making. "As a result of the depression and war years, coupled with the union activities during that time," Newell emphasized, "many [executives] on the railroad lost the desire to assume their responsibility. They were merely content to do a passable job and carry out orders—sometimes half-heartedly—to avoid wherever possible any real mental activity, any use of foresight, or any planning." Samuel R. Hursh, the PRR's chief engineer, made much the same point when he told Newell that "a great portion of [the centralization of authority] was caused by the war and the many restrictions that were placed not only on the railroads but on other industries by the many and various control boards instituted by the Federal Government, which were continued after the war and to a great extent during the Korean conflict."[110]

Symes was particularly concerned that his efforts to streamline the Transportation Department had created a severe mismatch with the railroad's Traffic Department. Operating personnel typically restricted their activities to specific divisions and were often headquartered in communities where there were extensive railroad facilities but relatively few shippers. Traffic officials were more likely to extend their oversight across multiple divisions while soliciting business in large cities and off-line locations as far away as Europe. The two departments also maintained a long-standing history of incompatible organizational cultures, with Transportation Department personnel valuing their no-nonsense practicality and their willingness to accept physically demanding and dangerous labor—while denigrating the glib salesmanship of their counterparts in the Traffic Department.[111]

Under the 1920 organization, the Transportation and Traffic Departments had been given similar territories, and the railroad subsequently assigned a division or district freight agent to the headquarters of each superintendent. By 1952, however, the railroad had incrementally eliminated one region, one zone, thirteen general superintendents' territories, and twenty-five superintendents' divisions—yet the organization of the Traffic Department remained almost unchanged. That situation produced some unusual problems of coordination. The division superintendent at Indianapolis worked with five Traffic Department division or district freight agents—in St. Louis, Terre Haute, Peoria, Indianapolis, and Louisville. In Detroit, the staff of the Traffic Department was under the supervision of Western Region headquarters in Chicago, while Transportation Department employees housed in the same building reported to Central Region headquarters in Pittsburgh. Transportation Department and Traffic Department personnel in the key city of New York answered to two different sets of managers in Philadelphia—the former to Eastern Region headquarters and the latter to the corporate offices. Throughout the system, traffic agents solicited business without contacting the transportation personnel who were to move it from one place to another, Transportation Department superintendents allocated freight cars among multiple freight agents, and managers found it difficult to coordinate advertising and marketing campaigns. System officers routinely negotiated agreements with shippers, consolidators, and freight forwarders with little input from divisional personnel.[112]

Based on his assessment of the April 30 meeting in Pittsburgh, Symes initially favored a consolidation of the Traffic Department's structure, one that would align each traffic manager's territory to match the existing operating divisions that were under Newell's authority. Fred Carpi, the vice president in charge of traffic, did not share Newell's loyalty toward Symes and insisted that the solicitation of business and the carrying of freight were fundamentally different functions that did not conform to the same geographic constraints. "After giving a great deal of thought to the possibility of making the jurisdiction of the Traffic Department office coextensive with those of the Operating [Transportation] Department," Carpi told Franklin, "I have reached the conclusion that the idea is wholly impracticable."[113]

After the board of directors elevated Symes to the presidency on June 1, 1954, reorganization discussions began in earnest. Symes envisioned a new corporate structure modeled on successful manufacturing firms outside the transportation field. He acknowledged that his vision was "somewhat revolutionary in the railroad industry but is similar in many ways to the new line and staff plans of organization which some of our leading manufacturing companies have adopted in recent years." Symes assigned his right-hand man, Jim Newell, to plan and implement the changes. Not surprisingly, Newell also supported "the decentralization of authority as a means of accelerating action, encouraging initiative and acceptance of responsibility, and increasing efficiency."[114]

One of Newell's first tasks was to explore the PRR's organizational history. He hoped to determine the motivations for the 1920 reorganization and to explain how the company had changed in the intervening thirty-four years. Chief engineer Hursh, who had been on the payroll since 1916, offered his perspective on the situation. "The Regions were formed in 1920 for the sole purpose of decentralizing power," Hursh recalled, "basically putting the Vice President and General Manager in charge of what could be considered a separate railroad, and they only refer matters to the system office that pertain to policy and money." While that structure may have been adequate at a time when a relatively small amount of traffic crossed divisional boundaries, Newell was concerned that it was no longer appropriate for circumstances in which diesel locomotives and through freight trains often ran from one end of the system to the other. Despite Hursh's contention that the system office exercised full control over policy and money, Newell concluded that the current structure provided division superintendents little incentive to undertake the personnel reduction and other cost-cutting measures that were vital to the company's survival. The railroad, in its "present financial situation could not afford to allot the money so saved [in one Division] to that particular Division exclusively," Newell observed, because "there might be projects of much more importance on other Divisions."[115]

At Symes's request, Newell began soliciting opinions from senior executives regarding the proposed changes to the corporate structure. Not everyone agreed with Symes that decentralization was an urgent necessity, and some suggested that railroads were inherently ill-suited to that type of organization. James Oram, in charge of personnel, emphasized the importance of systemwide labor agreements—and insisted that neither their negotiation nor their enforcement could be entrusted to local officials. The railroad suffered from "a problem of education rather than any important changes in the organizational setup," Oram concluded. Operating officials also expressed their misgivings. Harry L. Nancarrow (the assistant vice president in charge of operations, in Newell's former job), Andrew F. McIntyre (the chief of freight transportation), and Edgar E. Ernest (the chief of operating practices) suggested that decentralization could produce regional variations in train-handling methods—something that might impair safety. At the very least, they insisted, the railroad should establish a mechanism to coordinate passenger and freight schedules, train consists, and operating rules among various divisions—similar, perhaps, to the long-vanished Association of Transportation Officers. Any deviation from system practices, Nancarrow reminded Newell, "can only lead to trouble."[116]

Other executives seconded Nancarrow's resistance to change. They asserted that divisional personnel were claiming that the existing corporate structure was flawed, to excuse their failure of leadership at the local level. T. Clarence Stiegler, who supervised many of the PRR's budgetary functions, insisted that "authority is [already] decentralized to a great extent on the Pennsylvania Railroad and our problem is to encourage the exercise of the decentralized authority now existing." He insisted "that complaints concerning lack of authority are alibis." Stiegler concluded that local officials were reluctant to do anything that might get them into trouble, and he suggested that the "authority which Superintendents and minor officials now have is not exercised through fear." Howell T. Cover, who served as the chief of motive power, responded "that in many cases some embarrassing problem is settled by the excuse that Regional or System authority controls do not permit handling at Divisional level; in other words, claim of restriction by high level authority is often used as an excuse for inaction." Overall, as Newell informed Symes, "the prevailing opinion among the staff is that, so far as formal organization or action is concerned, decentralization of authority has already gone as far as practicable or necessary."[117]

Despite those objections, Symes pushed ahead with his decentralization planning, his efforts heavily influenced by the consultancy firm of Robert Heller & Associates. Between October of 1951 and January 1954, the railroad paid Heller nearly a million dollars to study methods for reducing passenger-train losses. Heller took on additional responsibilities in October 1953, as the company's consultants began to evaluate the PRR's accounting practices. In addition to implementing modern budgeting methods, Heller personnel also sought to apply consistent standards to all regions. In July 1954, less than two months after succeeding Franklin as president, Symes announced that Heller would evaluate the PRR's organizational structure. As they had done in their passenger studies, Heller personnel interviewed hundreds of PRR employees, ranging from top-level managers to trainmasters and station agents. Newell's earlier conversations with senior executives left little doubt that Symes supported reorganization, a circumstance that probably influenced the responses that Heller collected.[118]

Although some PRR officials complained that the railroad's much-publicized billion-dollar postwar betterment program had not even come close to modernizing the physical plant and equipment, that opinion was scarcely relevant—neither revenues nor borrowing could generate the funds necessary to make things right. As such, the Heller study concluded that investment was more than adequate and that it merely had to be utilized more effectively. Some respondents expressed concern about the youth and inexperience of many of the railroad's managers, but Heller's findings applauded "a lot of foresight in recruitment and development over the years," such that the railroad was "fortunate to have good people to do the job." Just as they had dismissed concerns regarding the corrosive effects of deferred maintenance, Heller staffers saw no need for additional investments in the PRR's personnel. "The main problem is to fully utilize . . . manpower resources with the right plan of organization and up-to-date organization policies," they concluded. According to the Heller report, improvements in communication, equipment, technology, and operation had combined to render the 1920 organization obsolete, and that excessive centralization retarded individual initiative—precisely as Symes had maintained all along.[119]

In June 1955, Symes presented the final reorganization plan to the board of directors. He suggested that the new corporate structure would improve coordination, while providing a concomitant increase in the ability of local managers to attract additional business and use scarce

resources more effectively. Sensitive to widespread complaints from shippers, Symes emphasized that the new organization would permit "close supervision of service typical of a smaller railroad" while enabling the company to "capitalize on the advantages of larger size." The changes recommended by Heller & Associates would open channels of communication between the line and staff officers, he asserted, "thus avoiding the 'ivory tower' approach" and allowing for "the constant infusion of 'fresh blood.'" In addition to nurturing budding managerial talent, Symes expected that the reorganization would generate substantial cost savings by eliminating an entire stratum of supervision, at the old regional level, and allow "key men on the firing line [to work] directly with their counterparts at System headquarters instead of going through another level of authority."[120]

The new organization took effect on November 1, 1955, transforming the railroad's three regions and eighteen of its nineteen divisions into a new nine-region system.[121] Each of the nine regional managers possessed virtually unlimited control over operations, repairs to equipment, and maintenance of the physical plant. "He and his staff will not only produce transportation but sell it and promote it," Symes observed, suggesting that he would be "Mr. PRR" in his territory. In addition to building budgets and generating proposals for capital expenditures, the regional managers oversaw sales, marketing, and public-relations functions, and controlled the use and disposition of real estate. They reported to Newell but yielded authority to the central office only in matters of scheduling and other elements of system coordination. The elimination of the divisional structure ensured direct contact between the nine regional managers while offering the potential to save costs by increasing coordination, reducing duplication and other forms of inefficiency, and eliminating some midlevel executives.[122]

The regional managers and their assistants supervised the full complement of line and staff officers necessary to carry out the four basic functions of a railroad—the movement of trains (through the regional superintendent of transportation and his staff), the maintenance of locomotives and rolling stock (the superintendent of equipment), the upkeep of the physical plant (the regional engineer), and the solicitation of business (the freight traffic manager and the passenger traffic manager). The passenger and freight traffic managers were responsible for maximizing revenues at stations throughout their respective regions, which they were to treat as retail sales outlets. The nine regional supervisors of transportation engineering oversaw the physical plant. They worked in tandem with the supervisors of cost control in maintenance of way, officials whose titles attested to the importance of reducing wasteful expenditures.[123] Despite James Oram's support for the centralization of employment matters, each region employed a superintendent of personnel. Likewise, the nine regional managers of public relations exercised considerable autonomy while also coordinating their activities with the system Public Relations Department.[124]

At the system level, Symes exercised authority over his principal line executive—Vice President Newell—and the staff officers who oversaw what railroad officials generally referred to as "service departments." Those personnel included the secretary, the comptroller, and the director of real estate—who yielded many of his responsibilities to the nine regional real estate managers and their counterparts, the managers of industrial development. The new Financial Department was under the authority of David Bevan, the vice president in charge of finance, subsuming the old Treasury, Accounting, Tax, Insurance, Pension, and Voluntary Relief Departments. That aggregation gave Bevan nearly complete authority to procure outside investment capital as well as the oversight of the financial assets of the Pennsylvania Railroad and subsidiaries such as the Pennsylvania Company. John B. Prizer served as vice president and general counsel, in charge of the Legal Department. For the first time in the railroad's history, the Transportation Department lost control over systemwide personnel functions, and the Personnel Department (headed by Oram) now reported directly to Symes.[125] That divorcement freed transportation officers to concentrate on train operations while giving Oram the authority to address labor policy—including negotiations with union representatives and government officials over matters such as wages, work rules, full-crew laws, and attrition. He would have his work cut out for him. Oram's subordinate, Charles E. Alexander, observed that the railroad was "still heavily loaded with an accumulation of sins of the past," and he hoped that Oram's department could "dig out of that situation" as rapidly as possible.[126]

Ralph Champlin also had a lot of digging to do. As part of the corporate reorganization, he became the vice president in charge of public relations, supervising the manager of publicity, the manager of community relations, the manager of advertising, and the art director. Champlin and his staff took charge of systemwide advertising campaigns and the preparation of timetables and other literature while giving regional officials the opportunity to build goodwill in their local communities.

Champlin and his staff experienced little success in their efforts to improve the public's attitude toward the Pennsylvania Railroad. Despite the favorable publicity surrounding the new streamlined cars that arrived during the late 1940s, most of the railroad's passenger equipment was outdated. By 1952, the average Pennsylvania Railroad passenger car was thirty years old and in poor condition—about average for an American railroad. Given the decline in patronage, it made little sense to repair or replace aging rolling stock.[127] Travelers who endured dirty and malfunctioning cars often faced the additional burden of discourteous or surly crew members. The problem was particularly acute during World War II, when PRR managers noted that "employee attitude toward the public is deteriorating," and they placed "the proper education of employees" at the top of their postwar list of priorities. Passenger-train crews received instruction in courtesy and other aspects of customer relations. Those efforts, plus the arrival of new equipment, seem to have satisfied many customers. By the early 1950s, however, the level of criticism was again on the rise. The most troubling complaints came from business executives, whose patronage was critical to the viability of the PRR's intercity passenger operations. One corporate president, Harry G. Kitchin, noted that his traveling salesmen "got the fastest ride on the PRR but the roughest personal treatment" and suggested that "for a great many years we all dreaded a ride on the Pennsylvania Railroad due to the unfriendly and inconsiderate attitude of the company's employees." Herbert W. Hoover Jr., the assistant vice president of the Canton, Ohio, company famed for the manufacture of vacuum cleaners, was similarly critical of the PRR's passenger service. He complained that PRR train crews demonstrated "utter disregard of their responsibility to the public." The situation was so bad, Hoover informed a reporter from *Time* magazine that his executives refused to ride on the company's passenger trains. Even in the busy New York–Washington market, travelers complained of rough track, dirty trains, and inedible food. Many claimed they would be willing to devote an additional hour to the journey and patronize the Baltimore & Ohio instead.[128]

Pennsylvania Railroad executives relied on consultants to evaluate and correct the torrent of passenger grievances. The Dining Car Department was a particular area of interest, as executives wanted to improve service while reducing a deficit that averaged eighty cents per meal. Beginning in 1948, two firms collected data from passengers. The first was Cresap, McCormick & Paget, established by individuals associated with the pioneering management-consulting firm Booz Allen Hamilton. One of them, Willard F. McCormick, had done work with US Steel and with Westinghouse, bringing him to the attention of PRR executives. The Cresap, McCormick & Paget data suggested that the PRR's dining car operations were "acceptable but not impressive."[129]

The more influential firm was the Opinion Research Corporation, whose initial dining car surveys soon expanded into a series of studies regarding public perceptions of the Pennsylvania Railroad. Cofounded in 1938 by statistician and pollster George Gallup, the company pioneered many of the techniques of political polling and in 1943 began publishing the *Public Opinion Index*, a monthly compendium of attitudes toward business. Pennsylvania Railroad executives placed increasing reliance on the Opinion Research Corporation, perhaps because that firm had recently worked with the Association of American Railroads, sampling overall public perceptions toward the carriers. In 1953, Opinion Research personnel conducted 2,750 interviews with shippers, passengers, and residents in ten cities across the PRR system.[130] In addition to questions related to the customers' experiences, they inquired about public attitudes toward the railroads, particularly in matters relating to taxation and subsidies for competing modes of travel.[131]

The Opinion Research Corporation survey, released during the summer of 1954, suggested that the activities of the Public Relations Department had not produced the hoped-for results. The consultants emphasized that the PRR enjoyed a generally favorable reputation. Half of those interviewed believed that the company was "quick to adopt new ideas," 47 percent thought that it was a "top railroad," and 61 percent concluded that its managers and employees were "running its business efficiently." The more frequently they rode passenger trains, however, the less likely respondents were to have a "general good feeling" toward the Pennsylvania Railroad. Moreover, fewer than 10 percent of those surveyed agreed with the perspective of PRR executives regarding earnings, taxes, and regulation. On the crucial matter of regulatory reform, 59 percent favored keeping "things as they are now," and the proportion who saw no need for tax relief (44%) or rate increases (49%) was almost as high.[132]

It mattered little that people thought highly of the Pennsylvania Railroad if they did not also support the public policies that were crucial to the company's survival. Jim Newell, the vice president in charge of operations, reminded Champlin that "the attitude of the public toward our railroad can be: (1) one of resentment, antipathy, or opposition; (2), passive acceptance—more or less neutral; (3) hearty enthusiasm and active support." Unfortunately, Newell explained, "in the past year or two, we may have accomplished much towards moving from (1) to (2). However, there is no question in my mind but that we have a long ways to go to reach the attitude expressed in (3)."[133]

The Opinion Research Corporation study, released at the beginning of June 1954, suggested Champlin's inability to cultivate good relationships with passengers and shippers. Symes, who became president on the same day, was not happy with its findings, and that dissatisfaction constituted one of the most significant motivations for the November 1955 reorganization. Symes expected results, and Champlin hoped that organizational decentralization would enable him to bolster the PRR's public image and save his job. "The new Regional set-up has gone a long way toward re-establishing the proper relationships with our customers and with the residents of the communities in which our customers operate," he told Symes in March 1956. "Our officers have been able to meet and deal with many more state and community leaders on a person-to-person basis." As a result, Champlin continued, "because Regional Managers and members of their staffs have been able to assess more of these local situations accurately, and because they have the authority to deal with them, in many cases we have been able to resolve them before they developed into problems."[134]

Champlin was being overly optimistic, with respect to the future of his department and to the viability of his career. The crippling recession of 1957–1958 made it necessary to eliminate every possible expense, and publicity was an easy target. The advertising budget declined from nearly $2.3 million in 1951 to a mere $481,804 in 1958. During the 1950s, the Osborne Company charged the railroad more than $110,000 per year for developing and printing three hundred thousand wall calendars, mainly given to shippers. There was little evidence that those calendars ensured customer loyalty, and the expense was increasingly difficult to justify. The Grif Teller painting of Conway Yard that adorned the 1958 calendar was the last of its breed. The following year the company simply reused a photo from the 1957 annual report, with lighted windows in the Six Penn Center office building spelling out the letters "PRR." Teller earned the commissions for the 1960 and 1961 calendars, but the illustrations were much smaller than their predecessors. Thereafter, the company published calendars in *The Pennsy*. With its editorial staff largely gone, that magazine declined significantly in quality. It was published only bimonthly and was handed to employees rather than mailed to their homes. On April 1, 1960, Symes dismissed Champlin and dissolved the Public Relations Department. He assigned its surviving functions to the Personnel Department, under the authority of James Oram, in his expanded title of vice president of public and employee relations. As part of the retrenchment, the company eliminated the post of manager of community relations in favor of the narrower duties of the manager of public relations, under the guidance of John Murphy. Within a few years, the PRR would again rebuild its public-relations capabilities, but it would take the arrival of a new chief executive and the need to establish public and political support for a merger with the New York Central to make that happen.[135]

The reorganization of the Traffic Department promised to bring its structure into conformity with that of the Transportation Department while giving its executives direct control over rates, service, and marketing.[136] Prior to 1955, Fred Carpi had been the vice president in charge of traffic, with authority over the solicitation of both freight and passenger business. In common with his counterparts on other railroads, Carpi understandably focused on the freight traffic that generated the bulk of the PRR's business, and he was correspondingly less committed to passenger service. Following the reorganization, Carpi retained his most important responsibilities, as the vice president in charge of freight sales and services. J. Benton Jones became the vice president in charge of passenger sales and services, part of a fruitless effort to stem the decline in rail travel. Along with the NYC and the Southern Pacific, the PRR was thus one of only three railroads in the United States with a vice president who was solely responsible for catering to the needs of people rather than freight. While Jones bore the ultimate responsibility for the PRR's passenger service, there was nonetheless little to suggest that he possessed either the experience or the authority to achieve satisfactory results. Unlike Carpi, Jones rose through the ranks of the Transportation Department, and he had little experience with traffic functions.[137] He was also unlikely to prevail in any requests for new equipment or improved schedules, if they interfered with Carpi's insistence on moving freight as efficiently as possible. Like Ernest C. Nickerson, his counterpart on the NYC, Jones was primarily responsible for eliminating severely unprofitable passenger trains and routes rather than engaging in a quixotic effort to return travelers to the rails.[138]

Both Carpi and Jones were mindful of the potential associated with new transportation technologies. They had high hopes for intermodal service and for the passenger-equipment innovations that had emerged in the

aftermath of the New Haven's 1954 TALGO trials. Walter Patchell, the vice president in charge of the newly established Research and Development Department, reporting to the president, took charge of those efforts. Assisted by a business analyst, a manager of research and development, and a team of project engineers, Patchell sought to develop equipment suitable for TrucTrain service as well as a new generation of passenger cars that would reduce operating and maintenance costs. The Research and Development Department's activities were not strictly technical in nature, and the business analyst was responsible for long-range forecasting and planning. Those efforts were in part an attempt to accumulate the data necessary to demonstrate the PRR's need for higher rates, lower taxes, reduced interference from unions, and the discontinuance of passenger trains. Patchell, in cooperation with the Legal Department, also oversaw public-policy and regulatory issues, including those related to commuter transportation and urban regional planning.[139]

Three additional vice presidents represented the most important cities served by the Pennsylvania Railroad. The vice president at New York (James L. Cranwell) and the vice president at Pittsburgh (John A. Appleton) oversaw communities that generated considerable traffic and required correspondingly complex operating methods.[140] Aside from its role as a gateway to the southern railroads, Washington offered relatively few business opportunities. It was, however, the political center of the United States. Regulatory and legislative issues thus occupied the time of Frank J. McCarthy, the vice president at Washington. Unusual for a PRR employee, McCarthy started his career on the New York Central, first in the Indianapolis Shops of its Big Four subsidiary and then as a passenger representative for the parent company. In 1942, he became the chairman of the Associated Railways of Indiana, an industry trade group, and that post brought him to the attention of Pennsylvania Railroad officials. McCarthy joined the PRR in 1945, as a special assistant in the Legal Department, based in Washington. After 1951, he was the railroad's assistant vice president at Washington, still under the authority of the Legal Department, and responsible for monitoring federal legislation and regulatory initiatives. As they were finalizing the details of the 1955 reorganization, Symes and Newell reaffirmed McCarthy's duties of "keeping the President and his staff informed regarding all national and state legislative matters of interest to the Company." At that time, however, the PRR and the railroads in general were suffering from the negative publicity associated with the antitruck lobbying activities of Carl Byoir & Associates.

Executives did not want to perpetuate accusations that McCarthy would be collecting a substantial salary while using corporate resources to manipulate the political process. They accordingly acknowledged that there was "grave doubt in the minds of some of [the railroad's] officers as to the advisability of spelling out in detail the anticipated functions of this department." McCarthy's new post nonetheless signaled that PRR officials had abandoned the less formal lobbying mechanisms associated with the stockholders' committee established in 1947. The members of that group were never successful in their efforts to work with managers and with public officials to influence regulatory, rate, and labor policies. They abandoned their work in March 1955, little more than seven months before the new organizational structure took effect.[141]

The most significant change at the headquarters level involved the reallocation of the responsibilities formerly assigned to the vice president in charge of operations. To coordinate the solicitation of business and the movement of freight, Symes recommended eliminating the separate offices of vice president in charge of operations and vice president in charge of traffic. Both functions came under Newell's jurisdiction, in his capacity as vice president. Newell also served as the mediator between the nine regional organizations and the staff offices. Or, as PRR officials described the arrangement, "in the organization of 1955, there was created what might loosely be termed an hourglass form of System-Regional contact, with the Vice President at the junction of the upper and lower segments of the glass." His role as an intermediary made Newell—the individual who was responsible for developing and implementing the new corporate structure—an indispensable part of the company's operations, more so perhaps than even the president. It was a crushing workload but—particularly as he could count on Symes's ongoing support—Newell had every reason to believe that he would one day take charge of the Pennsylvania Railroad.[142]

Newell held direct supervisory authority over the nine regional managers as well as three senior executives. Clarence Stiegler served as budget manager, while Charles Alexander became the manager of labor relations. Newell's most significant subordinate, however, was Allen J. Greenough, the former Eastern Region vice president. As the new vice president of transportation and maintenance, Greenough's function was in many respects equivalent to the former post of vice president in charge of operations. He did not have control of the Personnel Department, but he retained oversight of systemwide responsibilities involving transportation, maintenance of equipment, and upkeep of the physical plant, as well as authority over the PRR's police force. Howell Cover became the assistant vice president and chief mechanical officer, responsible for the Altoona Works and other system shops. Samuel Hursh, who had previously given Newell a historical overview of the evolution of the PRR's managerial system, retained his post as chief engineer, his duties largely unchanged. Greenough's most important subordinate—entrusted with the safe and efficient movement of trains—was John D. Morris, the general manager of transportation. Morris in turn oversaw seven system personnel, including the manager of freight train operations. Another new position—manager of TrucTrain service, under Howard C. Kohout—attested to the rapidly increasing potential of intermodal operations. The solicitation of that business was the responsibility of Collins S. Van Gunten, the manager of TrucTrain sales, who reported to Newell's adversary, Fred Carpi, the vice president in charge of freight sales and services. Edgar Ernest, who had earlier warned Newell against delegating train-handling practices to the regions, became the manager of operating rules, ensuring conformity across the system.[143]

The 1955 restructuring was at least as disruptive as the one that had occurred in 1920, and Pennsylvania Railroad personnel struggled to adapt to the new way of doing business. The Research and Development Department was quickly overwhelmed with a slate of projects that included new passenger cars, analyses of the rapidly evolving merger landscape, and plans to improve suburban commuter service. Walter Patchell, the vice president of research and development, was soon demanding a substantial expansion in funding and personnel. The decentralization of authority ensured that each of the nine regional managers oversaw local research-and-development functions—ideally but not always in collaboration with the head office. Patchell acknowledged that those efforts were often "poorly coordinated," impairing standardization and creating needless duplication of effort. He questioned whether his department should "function as a Service Department for all other Departments and the Regions (as is the case with General Electric)" and asked whether the "work that is now being carried on independently in little niches and crannies elsewhere throughout the system can be assigned here, . . . similar to the action taken by U. S. Steel." He noted that many projects required the temporary assignment of R&D staff from the various regions to corporate headquarters in Philadelphia. The cost of those relocations often exceeded the expense of permanent transfers and created a constant pressure to finish projects quickly, so that personnel could return to their regions and to their families.[144]

The reorganization plan centralized the Comptroller's Department, assigning to it the work previously performed by the three Regional Accounting Offices. Those additional responsibilities, combined with the creation of three Methods and Cost Control groups (as the Heller report had recommended), tripled the workload of the Comptroller's Department, while their personnel decreased. The Communications and Signals Department suffered the opposite problem, as the assignment of many of their activities to the nine regional engineers ensured that they had substantially more personnel at the central office than they required. The new organization also continued one long-standing practice, as Comptroller Hugh J. Ward complained, that "traditionally, and for no clear reason, the Insurance Department has for years been under the jurisdiction of the Vice President, Purchases, Stores & Insurance," where it did not properly belong. Responsibilities concerning taxation were not so much decentralized as trifurcated, split between the Real Estate Department, the Accounting Department, and the Legal Department.[145]

Despite Newell's role as an intermediary, the reorganization also proved less than successful at improving communication between the central office and the regions. Newell reminded Fred Carpi that senior executives should make more frequent visits to each of the regions and that "it would help the Regional organizations if they are kept currently informed of detailed policy decisions" made in Philadelphia. Because 80 percent of the railroad's freight traffic traveled across more than one region and many large shippers maintained facilities in multiple locations, Newell and Carpi considered it "essential that a strong centralized System contact be maintained with these industries"— something that regional freight traffic managers could not accomplish. Newell also complained that Carpi's staff requested the same information that each of the regions provided to Allen Greenough, the vice president in charge of transportation and maintenance—to the annoyance of regional managers who resented the needless duplication of effort.[146]

There was also evidence to suggest that regional personnel were more interested in their local territories than in the well-being of the entire company. Some executives feared that "policies adopted in one Region looking to its own individual good, could conceivably not work for the full benefit of the other Regions or the System as a whole." Newell noted "a great variance in the content and approach" employed by the nine regional managers

as they appraised their 1956 performance and developed a set of objectives for the following year. The Philadelphia Region focused on "transportation efficiency and monetary savings," the Northern Region submitted a detailed outline of staff responsibilities, while the Buckeye Region merely suggested ways that the system officers could better serve the regions. With a single exception, Newell complained, the regional managers had failed to adequately address "one extremely important item . . . the delegation of greater responsibility and authority to the Regional and supervisory forces," which was ostensibly the entire reason for the reorganization in the first place. Even as late as 1959, regional personnel still had not fulfilled their original charge to develop master plans for their regions. It also became increasingly difficult to coordinate interregional engineering, communications, and signaling work, and Newell soon gave several of the more important regions authority over their smaller counterparts in those matters.[147]

Symes and Newell anticipated that the reorganization would reduce the thick layers of middle management, along with the associated expense, yet they failed to achieve that objective. Executives whose departments received new responsibilities were quick to demand a corresponding increase in personnel, while those whose duties shrunk rarely acknowledged that they could make do with less. By the end of February 1957, sixteen months after the changes took effect, Newell "recognized that possibly more positions were being created than were necessary but that this would be desirable in order to ensure the successful operation of the new organization." The situation soon got out of hand, however. Supervisory personnel on the individual regions requested additional staff as well as increases in pay for those already on the job.[148] Many of the intended corresponding reductions in personnel were never carried out. That often occurred because the railroad created sinecure posts for managers who were no more than eighteen months away from retirement, trusting that attrition would eventually thin the executive ranks. When those individuals retired, however, regional administrators often neglected to abolish the positions, instead hiring or promoting new personnel to take their place. Newell worried that the railroad was "beginning to be 'top heavy' on executives" and contemplated a blanket prohibition on further managerial promotions and hiring at that level. By that time, even though the Heller study had anticipated that the 1955 reorganization would save $900,000 per year in personnel costs, the actual result was a $2.7 million annual *increase*. Within another year, the number of system staff officers reporting to the president increased to fourteen, confirming the "fear in the minds of some of our Directors and officers that the group reporting to the President was too large for effective administration."[149]

The upheavals in the managerial ranks increased the importance of identifying and promoting the most promising talent—and conversely sidelining individuals who could not meet expectations. The PRR implemented a supervisory appraisal program in March 1957 to improve communications and identify the potential for advancement. The performance reviews extended as far down as midlevel managers such as engine house foremen, track supervisors, and train masters. There was also a strong possibility that the PRR might lose some of its most senior executives, lured away by better offers on smaller but more prosperous carriers. That concern had prompted the implementation of a Contingent Compensation Plan in 1952. Five years later, the board of directors and the shareholders approved a stock-option plan for senior executives, with Symes eligible for thirty thousand shares, followed by vice presidents Newell, Carpi, Bevan, and Patchell, entitled to as many as twenty thousand shares each. In later years, the ownership and disposition of that stock would raise many questions regarding the potential for conflicts of interest.[150]

The Passenger Crisis

The economic downturn that began in August 1957 and continued into April 1958—often referred to as the Eisenhower Recession—marked the turning point in the PRR's commitment to passenger service. Decreased travel demand and competition from highways and airlines caused ticket sales to plummet. Since the record $72 million passenger operating deficit in 1951, the Pennsylvania Railroad had made steady progress in stemming the tide of red ink, to $44 million in 1954.[151] The shortfall increased slightly the following year, to $50 million, but that amount represented only 42 percent of freight earnings—the lowest figure since 1948. Increased fares in 1955 and 1956 produced $4 million in additional passenger revenue, while continual reductions in train mileage trimmed operating costs by $5 million. Wages, supplies, and taxes increased by $14 million during that time, however, and the passenger situation became even more drastic. In 1956, the deficit was nearly $55 million, consuming 44.9 percent of the net income generated by freight service. The following year, passenger losses were $57 million.[152]

The expanding Interstate Highway System only made the situation worse. In 1947, Americans traveled 47 million miles by train, representing 13.4 percent of all intercity mileage. By 1956, passenger miles had fallen to 28.5 million, just 4 percent of the total. The primary culprit was the automobile rather than the airplane, as car travel increased from 273 million miles in 1947 (77.6% of the total) to 617.7 million miles in 1956 (88%).[153] Sometime during the second half of 1948, the number of cars driving along the Pennsylvania Turnpike exceeded the number of passengers traveling on the PRR's Middle Division, and the gap continued to widen in the years that followed. By December 1951, eastward and westward extensions of the turnpike created a four-lane highway virtually the entire distance from Philadelphia to the Ohio state line. In 1954, construction crews completed the road to the west bank of the Delaware River, where a bridge—opened two years later—afforded access to the Garden State. On January 15, 1952, Governor Alfred E. Driscoll dedicated the final section of the New Jersey Turnpike. In conjunction with the Lincoln Tunnel and the Holland Tunnel, cars and buses could easily reach the heart of Manhattan. To the west, the Ohio Turnpike had been in the planning stages since 1947, and by 1955 a limited-access route extended to the state's western border—where the Indiana Toll Road, built between 1954 and 1956, was waiting to take traffic to the outskirts of Chicago. A modern highway system now paralleled the PRR's main line for the entire distance between New York, Philadelphia, Pittsburgh, and Chicago. The Pennsylvania Railroad faced the same situation as the New York Central, whose investment in the Great Steel Fleet had been rendered meaningless by the construction of the New York Thruway. Even before Dwight D. Eisenhower affixed his signature to the Federal-Aid Highway Act of 1956, therefore, the core territory of both companies had been penetrated by multilane expressways. Even if the PRR had been able to continue W. W. Atterbury's pioneering investments in coordinated rail, air, and bus service, such efforts would have been fruitless in competition with the family automobile.[154]

The rapid growth of air travel gave PRR executives additional cause for concern. After World War II, various government entities invested more than $645 million in the seven airports (three in Greater New York, two in Washington, and one each in Baltimore and Philadelphia) that served the railroad's greatest potential passenger market. Millions in additional government subsidies offset annual operating losses at those airports. Airline capacity doubled between 1949 and 1954, driving most business travelers away from the railroads. In 1946, air travel accounted for 1.7 percent of intercity passenger miles. By 1956, that figure was 3.6 percent—still small, but most of that growth had come at the expense of intercity trains.

The following year, for the first time, aviation passenger miles exceeded rail passenger miles—hardly surprising, as commercial airlines offered an unbeatable combination of speed and value. The PRR charged $65.92 for a roomette between New York and Chicago, while a first-class airfare was only $47.95. Thirty nonstop flights connected New York and Pittsburgh in one hour and forty-five minutes, far shorter than the seven and a half hours posted by the record-setting pace of the once-daily *Aerotrain*. There were twenty-three direct flights from Washington to Chicago, imperiling both the PRR's *Liberty Limited* and the B&O's *Capitol Limited*. In the summer of 1951, American Airlines inaugurated "commuter service" between New York and Chicago. Every hour on the hour between 8:00 a.m. and 5:00 p.m., a DC-6 departed from each city on a nonstop flight that lasted a little less than three hours. The planes flew past each other somewhere over the Alleghenies, not far from where *The Broadway Limited* was making its sixteen-hour trek between the nation's two largest cities. No reservations were necessary, and missing a flight meant a wait of no more than an hour before the next plane was ready to depart. It was doubtful that many New Yorkers or Chicagoans commuted between the two cities—but with American alone offering twenty-five nonstop flights in each direction, every day, people had their pick of travel options. Trans World Airlines provided only thirteen roundtrips per day—but reported average load factors of more than 87 percent. Like United and Capital, which also served the route, American and TWA employed propeller-driven planes. The previous year, however, an Avro Canada C102 Jetliner made a test flight between New York and Chicago in just under two hours. The pilot informed reporters that he avoided any effort to set a record time for the journey and had not bothered to fly at maximum speed.[155]

The only short-term response to the overwhelming superiority of highway and airline competition was to discontinue as many trains as possible. The year 1956 alone saw the elimination of *The American* and *The Gotham Limited*. *The Pennsylvania Limited*, *The Admiral*, *The Red Arrow*, *The Cincinnati Limited*, and *The Liberty Limited* were downgraded, combined with other trains, or stripped of the observation cars and the other amenities that had historically made trains more enjoyable than cars, buses, or aircraft. The severity of the Eisenhower Recession encouraged further cuts. *The Liberty Limited*, a casualty of more competitive Baltimore & Ohio service, ended service in October 1957. *The Akronite* and the westbound *Admiral* went in 1958, followed by the westbound *St. Louisan* in 1959. After July 1959, *The Red Arrow* no longer served Detroit and

became a plodding local linking Crestline and Toledo. The trains that survived were a shadow of their former glory. Mail and express traffic predominated, causing lengthy delays during loading and unloading operations. The practice was less deliberate than on the New York Central, where executives issued orders to lengthen trains and decrease average speeds in order to reduce patronage and facilitate petitions for discontinuance. The head-end traffic nonetheless helped to trim the PRR's passenger deficits, and officials were willing to put schedules in jeopardy and irritate an ever-dwindling number of passengers to retain that all-important business.[156]

By the late 1950s, the golden age of postwar rail travel had come to an end, on the Pennsylvania Railroad and on countless other carriers. In 1954, 80.7 percent of the trains in the premier Blue Ribbon Fleet reached their destinations on time. By 1958, that figure had fallen to 67.5 percent, suggesting that a third of all passengers would, in the future, have ample reason to choose other modes of transportation. As service deteriorated, travelers increasingly complained of dirty, outdated, and poorly maintained equipment as well as "frequent discourteous treatment" from train crews demoralized by the state of the Pennsylvania Railroad's passenger operations. Under pressure from the Pennsylvania Public Utility Commission, PRR officials admitted that a quarter of the 675 cars used in the commonwealth needed interior maintenance, while another quarter were not being adequately cleaned. Arguing that they lacked the $9.5 million necessary to amend the situation, they nonetheless agreed to spend a much smaller amount—some $175,000—to improve service. By the early 1960s, as part of an ongoing attempt to increase passenger-crew morale, the company's officials released a training film, *The Irate Customer*, to encourage employee courtesy. Judging by the number of complaints that the railroad received, there were plenty of irate customers to work with.[157]

As train after train disappeared from the timetable, *The Broadway Limited* remained one of the last examples of the golden age of rail travel. In 1957, the New York Central added coaches to the *Twentieth Century Limited*, ensuring that the Pennsylvania Railroad operated the only all-Pullman train in the New York–Chicago market, and one of the few in the nation. Vice President Newell sensed an opportunity to gain additional patronage at the NYC's expense and called for "an advertising campaign . . . proper cleaning of the train, . . . paint touch-up, [and] necessary repairs to the hardware" on *The Broadway Limited*. With so few trains running, the PRR concentrated its best equipment and its best crews on *The Broadway*. Track improvements and, more troublingly, declines in freight traffic allowed the streamliner to travel on the fastest schedule in its history. Managers told employees to "Brag about the Broadway," insisted that the train reach its destination on time, and cited its performance as an indication that their railroad still cared about passenger service. *The Broadway Limited* briefly experienced a 14 percent increase in ridership and regularly drew more travelers than the *Twentieth Century Limited*. Yet by August 1958, a year after the NYC downgraded its passenger service, the increased patronage on *The Broadway* amounted to only fourteen additional passengers per day. That represented a revenue gain of $200,000 per year—sufficient reason to maintain high-quality service on that one train but hardly enough to offset chronic passenger deficits. The positive results were not destined to last, and by 1966, only fifty-four people rode *The Broadway Limited* on an average trip.[158]

While there was considerable value in the PRR's incremental approach to a reduction in the passenger deficit, a long-term solution would depend on changes to the legal and regulatory environment. Since the late 1940s, railroad executives, government officials, and members of the public displayed fundamental disagreements regarding the determination of costs associated with passenger service. There was little consensus as to whether solely assigned or fully allocated costs—or some intermediate measure between those two extremes—best represented the financial results. As late as 1952, community leaders and other individuals who opposed train discontinuances could argue that the nation's railroads earned a $49.7 million passenger surplus. They were correct, to the degree that during that year ticket sales, combined with mail and express revenues, exceeded out-of-pocket costs by that amount. Passengers and their advocates were correspondingly skeptical of railroad executives who argued that they had suffered a $642.4 million loss based on fully allocated expenditures. In 1953, however, and for the first time in their history, the railroads could not even cover the solely allocated costs of passenger service. The difference was small—only a little over $1 million—but it grew to $38.3 million in 1954, $45.7 million in 1955, and $81.6 million in 1956. In 1957, out-of-pocket expenses consumed $114.0 million above earnings, and no one could convincingly deny that passenger operations were bleeding the railroads white.[159]

By the mid-1950s, a variety of economists and policy makers were beginning to articulate suggestions for mitigating passenger deficits and alleviating the overall financial problems facing the PRR and the nation's other railroads. While their perspectives varied, they challenged four core elements of federal and state regulatory policy. First, they rejected the long-standing assumption that railroads could monopolize the transportation sector of the economy. Second, they were critical of rates set according to the value of service, and instead favored cost-of-service rate making. The third, related recommendation was that the Interstate Commerce Commission permit changes in rates, irrespective of possibly deleterious effects on other modes of transportation. Finally, analysts shared the view that the financial well-being of the railroads overrode any public necessity associated with the provision of barely used passenger services and that the process for train discontinuances should be simplified.[160]

One of the first policy recommendations emerged in April 1955, when Commerce Secretary Sinclair Weeks released the report of the Presidential Advisory Committee on Transport Policy and Organization. Weeks emphasized that the railroads' problems could only be solved by reducing rather than increasing regulation. It was a watershed moment, although it would take another quarter century of intense political debate before that philosophy was fully incorporated into federal law. The Weeks report also recommended providing the Interstate Commerce Commission with greater authority to discontinue passenger trains—correspondingly reducing the power of state regulators who often insisted on a continuation of service.[161]

The Weeks report challenged the regulatory status quo and encouraged ICC officials to reexamine their accounting and rate-making policies, particularly with respect to passenger service. In April 1957, the commission initiated the *Separation of Operating Expenses between Freight and Passenger Services* investigation to determine whether the traditional formula for the allocation of shared costs was still appropriate. That inquiry, which ended the following January, concluded that changes were unnecessary. One piece of testimony, however, gave railroad executives cause for concern. Representatives of the National Association of Railroad and Utilities Commissioners insisted that "the present separation rules have no purpose other than the development of statistical data." They thus argued that the ICC's accounting categories did not accurately measure the avoidable costs associated with passenger service— that is, those that could be eliminated if the carriers were responsible only for freight operations. Nor were they willing to accept assertions from railroad executives that the ICC data grossly underestimated avoidable costs. Instead, officials from the state regulatory agencies supported "a change in the rules to reflect the out-of-pocket costs of the passenger service. The City of Philadelphia takes a similar position." That standard suggested that the elimination of passenger trains would curtail only those costs that were solely allocated to passenger operations, ignoring the burden placed on the physical plant and the employees who maintained it. Under the proposed guidelines, most trains at least broke even. It would have been impossible, therefore, for the PRR and other carriers to discontinue more than a small fraction of their passenger service, suggesting why executives were determined to follow Weeks's recommendation that state commissions be stripped of their power to interfere with efforts to curtail passenger operations.[162]

The other ICC investigation began earlier, yet it lasted longer and held far greater significance. In March 1956, the commissioners appointed examiner Howard Hosmer to conduct a wide-reaching investigation of the causes of passenger-train deficits. Hearings began in June 1957 and continued for just over a year—an indication of Hosmer's determination to consult every interest group involved. Those who testified included passengers and the shippers of the freight that subsidized the cost of their transportation. Spokesmen from the National Coal Association were particularly committed to supporting the carriers, given that their mines were captive to the railroads and as such were likely to endure higher rates that would be necessary to offset passenger losses. Representatives from three state regulatory agencies, all of which were outside the PRR's territory, also gave testimony. Their ranks included Alan S. Boyd, chairman of the Florida Railroad and Public Utilities Commission, who was in his midthirties and getting his first exposure to the national regulatory landscape.[163]

Harvard economist John R. Meyer provided some of the most controversial testimony. He headed a team acting on behalf of the Aeronautical Research Foundation—which, despite its name, was funded by the Association of American Railroads. Meyer and his colleagues were careful to assert that "the services of these researchers were arranged by the AAR, but their findings were completely their own." That impartiality was debatable, and even the trade journal Railway Age mistakenly listed Meyer as a witness for the railroads rather than the Aeronautical Research Foundation. Meyer's principal goal was to provide yet another measure of avoidable costs, diametrically opposed to the one suggested by state regulators in the Separation of Operating Expenses investigation. "Simply because fully distributed costs are a poor measure of avoidable costs does not mean that solely-related costs are necessarily a better measure," he emphasized. Meyer concluded that proper cost-accounting techniques indicated that the total expense associated with the provision

of passenger service, nationwide, equaled $1.975 billion in 1955, significantly higher than the $1.743 billion calculated by the ICC. He set the corresponding passenger deficit at $708 million, far more than the $476 million suggested by the ICC's mechanism for determining fully allocated costs. While Meyer was undoubtedly correct in his assertion that reliance on solely attributed costs was far too simplistic a mechanism to avoid the difficult questions regarding the allocation of shared costs, economists employed by the General Services Administration correspondingly insisted that his "ARF study flounders in a mire of unfortunate and distinctly avoidable errors."[164]

Given the wide variations in estimates of passenger-service costs and deficits, it was hardly surprising that examiner Hosmer was unable to suggest a path forward. He outlined the all-too-familiar causes of the passenger crisis, including competition from other modes of transportation, expensive commuter services, declining mail and express traffic, escalating operating costs, heavy tax burdens, and high wages and arcane work rules for train-service employees. Hosmer also observed that discount pricing, family-plan tickets, the provision of modern equipment, and experiments with lightweight streamliners such as the Aerotrain had failed to stem the loss of passenger traffic. He found credible the views of the AAR's president, who noted "when every other resource has failed, the railroads have reduced passenger train operations to avoid further loss. Unfortunately, the latter course is more and more proving the only remedy." Given the rapid changes in transportation patterns that occurred during the previous decade, Hosmer acknowledged that rail passenger service might be unsalvageable. "At the present time the inescapable fact—and certainly to many people an unpleasant one," he suggested, "seems to be that in a decade or so this time-honored vehicle may take its place in the transportation museum along with the stage coach, the sidewheeler, and the steam locomotive."[165]

Many observers reacted with incredulity, unable to believe that the luxurious streamliners that had debuted barely a decade earlier were already obsolete. Given the rapidity with which travelers were taking to the highways and the air, and the pace of train discontinuances, Hosmer predicted that all parlor and sleeping-car travel would disappear by 1965 and that the last intercity coach trains would stop running by 1970.[166] With so few options available, Hosmer could do little more than urge state regulators "to adhere vigorously to the principle that where the service cannot be made compensatory, abandonment should be permitted, having due regard for public convenience and necessity." He also sounded a warning to public officials, reminding them that the passenger crisis was part of a larger set of problems facing the railroads. "In fact there is here a disturbing overtone due to an implication that the passenger deficit may be a symptom of more deep-seated infirmities for which some remedy must be found if the railroads are to survive."[167]

Hosmer's pessimism was not misplaced. The Eisenhower Recession ended in April 1958, as far as the nation was concerned, but the same could not be said for the railroads, particularly those in the Northeast. The recession, the passenger deficits, and the declining financial health of the carriers increased pressure to remake a national regulatory apparatus that had experienced extraordinary growth in size and power since the adoption of the 1887 Act to Regulate Commerce. Much of the impetus came from railroad executives and their supporters, who blanketed the country with books, articles, pamphlets, speeches, and interviews, all focused on the seriousness of the railroad crisis. *Railway Age* devoted almost the entirety of the October 7, 1957, issue to a special report—entitled simply "Outrage"—that delineated the problems facing the carriers. Six months earlier, on March 29, a federal judge ordered the liquidation of the New York, Ontario & Western Railway. The struggling regional carrier had been in bankruptcy—a situation that many other railroads had experienced—since 1948. It was, however, the first Class I railroad to be abandoned, an event that underscored the seriousness of the transportation crisis. President Symes and his counterparts on other railroads emphasized that the collapse of the railroads would cripple American industry and put at risk the military's ability to defend the nation. John Meyer, who led the thinly disguised Association of American Railroads effort to maximize the tally of avoidable costs associated with passenger service, continued his research and his advocacy. He coauthored *The Economics of Competition in the Transportation Industries*, in which he acknowledged the complacency of many railroad executives. Meyer and his colleagues nonetheless laid most of the blame at the door of the ICC, an agency whose rate-making policies "failed miserably as an allocator of transportation resources." James Nelson, acting on behalf of the Brookings Institution, wrote *Railroad Transportation and Public Policy*, called for rate liberalization, and demanded an end to the umbrella rate making that attempted to protect all modes of transport. Meyer, Nelson, and others, disagreed on specific reforms, but all suggested that the regulatory apparatus should be curtailed rather than enhanced.[168]

The Economics of Competition and *Railroad Transportation and Public Policy* did not appear in print until 1959, but the research of Meyer, Nelson, and their colleagues, as well

as the evidence that Hosmer collected, contributed to the first major change in railroad regulation since 1940. George A. Smathers (Dem., Florida), chairman of the Surface Transportation Subcommittee of the Senate Committee on Interstate and Foreign Commerce, initiated hearings on the crisis facing the railroads.[169] "A mighty industry has come upon sick and precarious times," he told reporters. "Our railroads are in a very serious condition." Daniel Loomis, recently appointed president of the Association of American Railroads, emphasized that the recession caused the national economy to contract by 3.7 percent but that railroad earnings had declined by 10 percent, while net income fell by 17 percent. Symes was the second person to testify, and the remarks of the PRR's president set the tone for the rest of the hearings. "I have never seen the outlook for the industry so alarming as it is now," he warned, referring to a career that began in 1916. Between 1948 and 1957, Symes asserted, the PRR lost $523.8 million on its passenger operations, cancelling out nearly half of the company's $1.1 billion in net operating income from freight service. "On the Pennsylvania we have had to defer all heavy maintenance," Symes emphasized. "We are operating with equipment averaging 31 years old for our passenger fleet, and 27 years for freight cars, with 26,000 freight cars now in bad order and not useable." The president of the New York Central appeared before the Smathers Subcommittee on the following day, and he told much the same story. Even as they were attacking the outmoded regulatory system, railroad executives and ICC officials continued to rely on their traditional method of negotiating rate increases that might keep pace with rising operating costs. Totaling 22 percent between December 1956 and February 1958, they contributed to the problem by increasing the attractiveness of competing modes of transportation.[170]

Like Loomis and numerous other railroad executives, Symes stressed that the problems facing the carriers were far more severe than most policy makers acknowledged. He advocated a variety of remedies—not all of which found favor with executives at other companies. His suggestion that the federal government purchase rolling stock and lease it to the railroads, something he initially proposed the previous June, struck opponents as the first step toward the nationalization of the railroad network.[171] Other recommendations were less controversial, at least among railroad executives, and their familiarity was indicative of the political impasse that for years had deferred substantive reforms. They included the repeal of the excise tax on passenger fares, subsidies for the commuter operations that cost the PRR alone $7 million per year, permission to diversify into other modes of transportation, and greater freedom to negotiate rates. Even as he criticized Washington's regulatory policies, Symes favored the granting of additional power to the federal government. He echoed the voices of Weeks, Hosmer, Nelson, Meyer, and others in their insistence that Congress provide the ICC with greater authority over train discontinuances, at the expense of state regulatory agencies. Symes also called for a new cabinet-level agency, a department of transportation, that could formulate a balanced national transportation policy.[172]

The recommendations of the Smathers Subcommittee, released at the end of April, largely reflected the perspectives of railroad executives. "It was obvious from the testimony that the railroads no longer are a monopoly in the transportation field," Smathers acknowledged. That statement as well as the assertion that the primary "reason for the decline of railroads is overregulation" reinforced the ideas that Meyer and Nelson were incorporating into the books that they would publish the following year. Smathers's further comment "that the railroads' financial position results, in a large measure, from the general passenger deficit" offered hope that the ICC and state regulatory agencies would ease restrictions on train discontinuances. In acknowledgment of the railroads' inability to borrow money for improvements, the report recommended that the federal government provide a $700 million loan fund. It highlighted the losses associated with commuter service, asked states to evaluate their tax policies, and called on unions to ease work rules. Smathers reserved some of his harshest criticism for the Interstate Commerce Commission, an agency that had established "habits of belaboring relatively unimportant details involving form rather than substance, while procrastinating on coming to grips with important policy matters that involve serious matters of public interest." The statements that followed mirrored the earlier comments by railroad executives who were asking for speedier adjudication of rates, greater clarification of distinctions between various modes of transportation, and a tariff structure that would enable them to attract new business. Of greatest immediate consequence, the Smathers report suggested specific changes to the Act to Regulate Commerce and called on Congress to pass appropriate legislation.[173]

The congressional response, in the form of the Transportation Act of 1958, stopped short of what Smathers recommended and what Symes and other railroad executives sought to achieve. Legislators acted with remarkable speed yet in their haste pieced together a variety of short-term remedies without establishing a sustainable national transportation policy. They eliminated the excise tax on

freight traffic but—nearly thirteen years after the end of World War II—the 15 percent surcharge on passenger tickets remained in place. The new law enabled the federal government to issue up to $500 million in loan guarantees but did not exempt the railroads from reliance on market interest rates. Congress instructed the ICC to alter certain elements of the commodity rate structure, and by permitting rate liberalization asserted that the commission should not consider the effects of those tariffs on other modes of transportation. Mindful of the policies of state regulatory agencies, legislators also gave the ICC more authority over intrastate rates and the right to intervene in decisions involving intrastate passenger trains. Commuter services were particularly burdensome on the PRR's finances, and the company benefited from the mandate that local communities would be required to pay a significant share of their cost.[174]

While Symes and other railroad officials foresaw benefits from the Transportation Act of 1958, the new law was not the panacea they hoped for. Ten weeks after Congress acted, the PRR's president was sufficiently confident in the improving economic conditions to restore the 10 percent reductions in executive salaries that had been in place since April. The move did little to reinforce the claims of corporate poverty he had made during the Smathers investigation. Members of the Pennsylvania Public Utility Commission reluctantly acquiesced to the ICC's enhanced authority and permitted the discontinuance of many of the "ghost trains," omitted from public timetables, that made their lonely way from one part of Pennsylvania to another. The reductions in service, however insignificant, gave community leaders further cause to criticize the PRR's lack of public spirit. The directive that the ICC permit rates that might prove destructive to other modes of transportation, which was one of the most important provisions of 1958 legislation, was the victim of a political compromise that made it ineffective. The stipulation that the commission was responsible for "giving due consideration to the objectives of the national transportation policy" ensured that the railroads were hamstrung in their efforts to lower rates on commodities where they possessed an inherent competitive advantage over motor carriers and barge lines. The only way forward, it seemed, were across-the-board rate increases that would further price the railroads out of the transportation marketplace.[175]

In the absence of meaningful changes in federal regulatory policy, Symes and other executives could do little more than focus on the "Help by the Industry" section of the Smathers report to Congress. Smathers echoed Meyer's allegations of managerial complacency—"there has been a failure to recognize changing conditions, times, and tastes"—but the senator offered few concrete suggestions for the revitalization of executive expertise. Instead, Smathers adopted the same rhetoric once manifested in Louis Brandeis's comments in the 1910 rate hearings, the policies of the United States Railroad Administration, the consolidation provisions associated with the Transportation Act of 1920, and Joseph Eastman's role as federal coordinator of transportation. Greater cooperation and the implementation of more efficient operating practices would save the railroads from ruin, Smathers suggested, without necessitating meaningful sacrifices from shippers, passengers, workers, or residents of local communities. In the latest revival of that utopian vision, Smathers asserted that "the railroad industry has not, in the subcommittee's opinion, been sufficiently interested in self-help in such matters as consolidations and mergers of railroads [and] joint use of facilities in order to eliminate waste."[176]

Given the ICC's lack of leadership in transportation planning, it was perhaps unfair to lay the blame for that situation exclusively on the shoulders of railroad executives. Nor was it certain that the consolidations and mergers that Smathers recommended would save any single railroad, restore the railroads as a group to prosperity, or bring into being a sound and balanced national transportation system. In the absence of all other alternatives, however, merger seemed the only way forward. As the president of the Pennsylvania Railroad, Symes embodied that philosophy. Even as the Smathers hearings were underway, he was a participant in what promised to be one of the most significant mergers in American history.

Antecedents to a Merger

The consolidation impulse was not new. For fifteen years following the passage of the Transportation Act of 1920, railway executives, ICC officials, and transportation economists endeavored to allocate the nation's railroads into systems with comparable earning potential. They failed, in part because W. W. Atterbury and other PRR executives refused to relinquish their investments in affiliated lines. The ICC's lack of leadership, coupled with the financial crisis of the Great Depression, halted the development of system plans, and the Transportation Act of 1940 ended the consolidation provisions Congress had mandated twenty years earlier.

Yet the incentive to merge never disappeared, even though the intense operating pressures of the World War II years left little time for such considerations. A 1944 case involving the trucking industry facilitated postwar efforts to rationalize the railroad network. In *McLean Trucking Co. v. United States*, the Supreme Court upheld the combination of several small motor carriers, instructing the ICC to permit consolidations where the benefits of increased efficiency offset the disadvantages of reduced competition. Having failed to prevent his competitors from working against him, Malcom McLean soon found another route to success and helped launch the intermodal revolution that would transform the railroads. The more immediate effect, however, lay in the reduced burden of proof necessary to win regulatory approval of rail mergers. Advances in operating methods and improvements in communications systems facilitated the movement of trains over longer distances, permitting the establishment of ever-larger railroad systems. By the early 1950s, declining traffic and the more efficient use of the physical plant ensured that eastern railroads in particular suffered from excess capacity. To the extent that mergers enabled workforce reductions, route abandonments, and the elimination of duplicate facilities, they might restore the railroads to prosperity.[177]

Entrepreneurs who looked with dismay at the low earning potential of the railroads also perceived considerable opportunity for financial gain. Once they acquired large blocks of securities, a merger—or even the announcement of one—would likely produce a notable increase in value. Such financial legerdemain, many investors concluded, was the only way to make money from a railroad. They rarely acknowledged their motives, however, since politicians, regulators, and the news media were sensitive to any suggestion that such manipulation might conflict with the public interest. Instead, speculators in railroad securities predicted that mergers would increase the efficiency of the transportation network and prevent disruptions in service, or else claimed that they intended to remedy the ills of transportation companies addled by managerial ineptitude.

Robert Young was one of the first to take advantage of the changed environment regarding mergers. During the 1930s, he pulled the Alleghany Corporation from the dying grip of the Van Sweringen brothers. With it came the Chesapeake & Ohio, a prosperous coal road. Young's chairmanship of that carrier provided the financier with endless opportunities for self-promotion while perpetuating his mistaken assumption that he possessed the skills necessary to successfully manage any railroad in the United States. In 1945, Young attempted to orchestrate a four-way merger between the C&O, the Pere Marquette, and the Nickel Plate Road (each of which he influenced through the Alleghany Corporation), and the Wheeling & Lake Erie (which he did not). If successful, Young would gain control of a significant portion of the Alphabet Route, an affiliation of carriers that provided service between Chicago and the Atlantic Seaboard.[178] That was a possibility that aroused the concerns of PRR executives, including some who had battled the Van Sweringens' earlier efforts to do much the same thing. In 1929, they had established the Pennroad Corporation, ostensibly as an investment opportunity for loyal PRR shareholders but more accurately as a mechanism to influence the development of a national consolidation plan. Pennroad again joined the fray in June 1945, purchasing $4.4 million of W&LE stock from the Pittsburgh & West Virginia, another participant in the Alphabet Route.[179] It was a sensible precaution but an unnecessary one, as Young's efforts came to naught. The directors of the C&O, the Pere Marquette, and the Nickel Plate dutifully approved the merger (although their shareholders refused to do so), but no one at the W&LE wanted anything to do with the arrangement. Like George Gould and the Van Sweringens before him, Young failed in his efforts to create a fifth trunk line. He merged the Pere Marquette into the C&O in May 1947, but it was small consolation for an ambitious entrepreneur.[180]

With the remnants of the old Van Sweringen empire falling to pieces around him, Young soon set his sights on bigger game. The New York Central was precisely the kind of railroad that excited him—prestigious, newsworthy, and home to the storied *Twentieth Century Limited* and other glamorous passenger trains. In the fall of 1946, Young began purchasing NYC stock. His timing was propitious, given that the company, like the PRR, performed badly in the immediate postwar period. In 1946, the New York Central lost more than $10 million. There was no possibility of paying dividends, and as common stock fell from $35 to $13 a share, Young made his move. He was astute enough to realize that the ICC would never permit him to take charge of the New York Central so long as his Alleghany Corporation portfolio included the parallel line of the Nickel Plate. At the beginning of February 1947, and even as he denied that he was attempting to establish control over the NYC, Young pledged his willingness to divest his holdings in the Nickel Plate, should that become necessary. He soon offered Alleghany's Nickel Plate holdings to the PRR. Nearly twenty years earlier, Atterbury might have jumped at the offer—if in fact Young meant to be taken at his word—but Martin Clement lacked both the resources and the inclination to acquire the superbly engineered line along the south shore of Lake Erie.[181]

In March 1947, NYC president Gustav Metzman reluctantly provided Young and ally Robert J. Bowman with

seats on the board of directors, subject to ICC approval. By August, Young had lost his highly publicized bid to control the Pullman Company, and he became more determined than ever to dominate the New York Central. He told reporters that he was willing to relinquish his control of the Alleghany Corporation to avoid Clayton Act prohibitions on interlocking directorates. Young also pledged to distribute to Chesapeake & Ohio shareholders that company's holdings in the Nickel Plate.[182] He then proposed that there be three great powers in the East—a combination of the C&O and the NYC, the Baltimore & Ohio, and the Pennsylvania Railroad.[183]

Young predicted great benefits from an alliance between the Chesapeake & Ohio and the New York Central over a consolidated system that would move vast quantities of coal from the Pocahontas mines to the cities of the Northeast. That prospect terrified executives at the Virginian, long the NYC's preferred interchange partner, who feared isolation from their traditional markets. At the ICC hearings that began in September, representatives from the Virginian delivered blistering attacks on Young, characterizing him as an irresponsible speculator whose impracticable schemes would disrupt the entire eastern railroad network. ICC examiner Charles E. Boles needed little convincing, and in December he concluded that "the stock of the New York Central was not purchased as an investment but for the specific purpose of injecting applicant Young's influence and policies into the affairs of the New York Central," a situation that would "substantially lessen competition" between the C&O and the NYC. It was precisely the outcome that Metzman had hoped for and possibly the one that Young expected as well. If nothing else, it provided Young with ample opportunity to excoriate the ICC (with its "two-faced justice" by a "Government bureaucrat"), Wall Street insiders, and career railroad executives. The net result of Young's second attempt to dominate the eastern railroad network was that he forced the C&O to relinquish a controlling interest in the Nickel Plate—one of the premier railroad properties in the East—in a failed effort to control a company that was on the verge of financial ruin.[184]

Robert R. Young was nothing if not persistent, and he and his allies continued to acquire New York Central stock. By the fall of 1951, Young suggested that he would terminate his connections with the C&O, make himself chairman of the board at the NYC, and install longtime ally Allan Kirby as that company's president—and then just as quickly denied that he would do any of it. Reporters puzzled over his motives (and misspelled Kirby's name), but they delighted in the stories that Young's antics provided. The headlines practically wrote themselves, with the *New York Times* labeling him a "'rebel' of the railroad industry" and making much of the fact that his "R. R." initials were an appropriate shorthand for "railroad." Young accused Metzman and other NYC executives of ineptitude and blamed them for the company's poor performance. As the chairman of a prosperous coal-hauling railroad with minimal passenger service and low terminal costs, Young did not bother to mention the underlying structural factors that hobbled the NYC. To the contrary, he pledged that if he gained control of that company, he would revitalize tired freight operations and develop a new generation of passenger trains that would win travelers back from the highways and airports. They were absurd statements, but they caused the NYC's directors to coax Metzman into retirement and replace him with William White, formerly the president of the Delaware, Lackawanna & Western. Not long before Symes commissioned Heller & Associates to review the PRR's management structure, White did something similar at the NYC, relying on the services of Cresap, McCormick & Paget. White authorized improvements to the physical plant, finally undoing much of the damage inflicted by wartime traffic. Senior executives were optimistic that, in time and under White's leadership, the NYC would soon reclaim its status as a profitable and efficient company.[185]

White might have succeeded had not the recession that followed the end of the Korean War affected the NYC's revenues. That situation gave Young ample opportunity to expand his control over the company and further humiliate its management. The struggle unfolded during the first six months of 1954, just as White was working with Gene Ryan at Rail-Trailer to implement the piggyback service that might have proved the NYC's salvation. In January, Young announced that he had substantially increased his holdings of NYC stock. He also resigned his post as board chairman at the C&O and arranged for the Alleghany Corporation to sell all its holdings in that company. Young had now severed his ties with one of the most profitable railroads in the United States, removing the last legal and regulatory impediments to his effort to dominate the New York Central. There followed a long and grueling proxy battle, with Young skillfully exploiting his connections with the media to appeal to NYC shareholders. The fight culminated on May 26 during a bizarre train ride from New York to Albany. Young and White were both on board, making last-minute appeals for support—although they refused to speak to each other. By the time the tallying

of the proxies concluded on June 2, Young had fulfilled his ambition and gained control of the New York Central.[186]

Young's victory lent credence to the adage that it is best to be careful about achieving one's desires. In March, two months before the NYC's hotly contested annual meeting, Young told reporters that he had selected Alfred E. Perlman to be the president of the company he intended to control. The announcement came as a surprise to many people, including Perlman, who insisted that "I've never met Mr. Young, and I've never considered holding the position of Central president." When they met in person, however, Perlman found Young to be knowledgeable and charming, and the two men shared a deep-seated distaste for lawyers and Wall Street insiders. When Young walked triumphantly into the New York Central's Park Avenue headquarters on June 14, Perlman displaced White as president, with Young serving as chairman of the board at a salary of $1 per year. Perlman had been the executive vice president of the Denver & Rio Grande Western and helped pull that company out of bankruptcy through dieselization, the mechanization of track work, and the creation of a research-and-development laboratory—precisely the sort of cutting-edge initiatives that Young insisted would revitalize moribund carriers like the NYC. Perlman was unquestionably a capable executive, yet he had presided over a small company that enjoyed relatively long line hauls, faced minimal highway competition, and operated only one passenger train of any significance, the still-profitable *California Zephyr*. He was doubtless honored to take command of such a storied road as the New York Central, but his first inspection trip shattered the mystique associated with the route of the Vanderbilts.[187] The physical plant was in deplorable condition, passenger facilities were woefully underutilized, and the only shippers who were not complaining about the poor quality of freight service were the ones who had diverted their business to trucks. A cursory review of the books showed that the NYC was practically bankrupt.[188]

Perlman fortuitously benefited from the lingering effects of the reforms White had implemented, before Young deposed him, and from an economic upturn that coincided with the beginning of his presidency. Young took full credit for the subsequent increase in NYC earnings and share prices, claiming that those happy developments vindicated his methods. He and Perlman evicted Gene Ryan and Rail-Trailer from the property, in favor of the innovative Flexivan system that was at best marginally successful. Despite Perlman's warnings that passenger service would never be profitable, Young eagerly

New York Central president Alfred Perlman, at left, and James M. Symes, the Pennsylvania Railroad's board chairman, maintained an uneasy alliance born of necessity. Their November 1957 merger announcement followed behind-the-scenes efforts by Symes to prevent the NYC from joining forces with any other company. The acrimonious relationship between the two executives contributed to the suspension of merger talks. The declining financial conditions facing the two railroads nonetheless prompted another effort at consolidation. Here, Perlman and Symes strike a pensive pose as they prepare to testify in the merger hearings held in Pittsburgh on January 14, 1963, almost exactly a year after they signed a formal merger agreement. The process is far closer to its beginning than to its end, and more than five years will elapse before the consolidation will take place. *AP Photo/Dozier Mobley.*

pursued a pet project that had fascinated him since 1946. Train X, based on the Spanish TALGO design, would be modern, fast, cheap to build, and popular with travelers. During Young's tenure at the C&O, he devoted considerable resources to the development of Train X, and in 1956 it came to fruition on the New York Central. The NYC's *Xplorer* was cramped, rough-riding, noisy, and distinctly

unpopular with travelers—and provided conclusive evidence that Young's advocacy for improved passenger service was nothing more than a mixture of naivete and self-promotion.

The Eisenhower Recession—far more severe than the one that made William White vulnerable to Young's attacks—caused serious problems for both the NYC and the PRR. Despite a 7 percent increase in rates, the Pennsylvania Railroad's net earnings fell from $31.3 million during the first nine months of 1956 to $19.6 million for the comparable period the following year. The New York Central was in far worse condition. In August 1957, the company operated at a loss for the first time since Young gained control. That October, Perlman attempted to reassure a group of New York security analysts, one of whom asked whether the NYC "is going to go busted?" Perlman acknowledged that he had "never seen a pattern of carloadings as scrambled up as has taken place in the last two months." Freight revenues, he noted, were "down when they ought to go up and going up when they ought to go down" and conceded that "I'm just as confused as everybody in the United States as to where the economy is going." Perlman projected optimism, emphasizing that the NYC had plenty of cash on hand and indicating that he was including that company's bonds in his children's investment portfolios—but he chose not to provide specific financial data. When the company did release that information a few days later, the numbers were shocking. The New York Central's net earnings declined from $28.2 million during the first nine months of 1956 to just $8.7 million in the initial three quarters of 1957. The company managed to pay its final dividend of the year only by tapping its holdings in the Reading and distributing that company's shares to investors.[189]

For the first time, executives at the two companies began to seriously consider the possibility of a merger. In late September, Symes went to Young's Manhattan apartment to discuss the situation. Later, after everything had fallen apart, Perlman insisted that the PRR's president had initiated the meeting. That may well have been true, although it was equally likely that the whole thing had been Young's idea—and, as only one of the two participants was still alive, it was difficult to determine the precise chain of events. Like Young, Perlman supported consolidation as a mechanism to eliminate duplication and increase efficiency.

Perlman nonetheless harbored grave doubts regarding the wisdom of a merger with the Pennsylvania Railroad. During the 1920s, he studied transportation economics at the Harvard Business School under William Z. Ripley, the chief architect of the ICC's never-implemented final system plan. Based on that experience, Perlman concluded that the Pennsylvania Railroad would be a poor partner for the New York Central. He considered the PRR to be a much more regimented organization, its personnel focused on the technical aspects of maintaining a complex physical plant and operating trains carrying bulk commodities. The NYC, he asserted, was a company whose executives favored flexibility, innovation, and marketing initiatives—the same qualities that he brought to the Rio Grande. Perlman also doubted that the ICC would approve a consolidation of the two largest railroads in the United States, particularly as they served similar territories. The New York Central was the smaller and financially weaker railroad, and Perlman reasoned that in the event of a merger, he and his associates would likely be displaced by Symes and the PRR management team. As an alternative, Perlman hoped that the NYC might merge with the Baltimore & Ohio, given that the two companies shared complementary route structures and organizational cultures. The PRR, he suggested, could logically assume outright control of the Norfolk & Western, a company it had dominated for decades.[190]

Despite his misgivings, Perlman acknowledged the NYC's perilous financial condition, and he soon bowed to Young's entreaties. On November 1, 1957, the two presidents made separate announcements regarding the proposed merger, Symes in Philadelphia and Perlman in New York. The identically worded statements suggested that their "railroads are faced with other difficulties beyond their own control," and in the absence of any mechanism to increase revenues, cost containment offered the only opportunity for survival.[191] It was, a reporter for the New York Times observed, "one of the best-kept secrets in investment circles in recent years." If approved, the merger would create the eleventh-largest corporation in the United States, with assets of more than $5.5 billion and revenues exceeding $1.5 billion a year. Transportation writer Robert Bedingfield saw the announcement as an indication that the "signal turns red" for the entire railroad industry, and he had little doubt that the rationale for the merger was the adage that "two can live as cheaply as one."[192]

Wall Street analysts expressed surprise at the proposal, pointed to the numerous regulatory obstacles associated with combining the two dominant eastern carriers, and doubted that it would ever come to pass. Some, mindful of Young's genius for promotion, suggested that it was an elaborate publicity stunt intended to convey the seriousness of the railroad crisis. "At first glance, however, I would say that it just won't ever happen," suggested Gerald M. Loeb, an analyst at E. F. Hutton, "and it strikes me as a bold move being made in an effort to gain legislation that will afford them some relief." Oscar Lasdon, a former member of the New York Stock Exchange and an expert in the valuation of railway securities, put the matter more succinctly when he asserted that "these guys have something else up their sleeve. Undoubtedly they have taken this approach in the hope of getting something else in return." Wall Street's ever-pessimistic bears suggested that the PRR/NYC proposal was "the switch—long expected in some quarters—onto a steep downgrade with a dead end at the bottom." Smith Barney's Walter Hahn concluded that "all they are planning to do is merge weakness with weakness." It was a view shared by many investors and share prices for both companies barely budged. Neither Symes nor Perlman was willing to speak with reporters—a PRR spokesman suggested that both presidents "have a lot of other things to handle at the moment"—and their absence gave experts in transportation and finance little confidence that the merger negotiations would succeed. Perhaps the most prescient comment regarding the proposal came from Joseph Small, at Paine, Weber, Jackson & Curtis. "It looks very much like something of a trial balloon," he suggested. "Undoubtedly they will carry their planned studies out. But those studies will go on for a long, long time."[193]

Executives from other railroads were generally supportive of the proposal. The leaders of the Santa Fe, the Illinois Central, the Erie, the Boston & Maine, and the PRR-affiliated Wabash suggested that mergers were inevitable and that the proposed consolidation held considerable merit. Many of them were contemplating merger proposals of their own and hoped that prompt ICC approval for the largest railroad merger in American history would establish a favorable precedent. They predicted that the East would logically be dominated by four, three, or perhaps even two large systems. Baltimore & Ohio president Howard E. Simpson was more reticent and issued a terse "no comment" as he considered his options. James A. Hood, the president of the Short Line Association, echoed the comments of many investment analysts, suggesting that the merger announcement was "a pretty emphatic way of bringing to the attention of the general public the fact that the railroad industry, as we know it in the populous east, is up against a stone wall." He was less optimistic about the possibility that Symes, Perlman, and Young could achieve the anticipated reduction in expenditures, and he did not "have too much confidence in the ability of so large an organization to render effective service." Most railroaders nonetheless agreed with the comments of T. C. Burwell, the outgoing president of the National Shippers Board. The merger was a "step in the right direction," he asserted, acknowledging that the railroads "have to do something."[194]

Officials at the Interstate Commerce Commission and the Justice Department were also taken aback by the proposed merger. ICC chairman Owen Clarke asserted that the agency would "handle it like any other case if they ever file an application." It was an audaciously optimistic prediction, in advance of the largest and most complex case that would ever appear before the commission. The initial statement from the attorney general's office—"no comment—it's an ICC matter"—would prove even more inaccurate. Senior officials in the Eisenhower administration, who preferred not to be named, suggested that the White House might look favorably on any consolidation that could reduce operating costs and rates, improve service, and avoid the necessity of federal aid to the carriers. Senator Estes Kefauver (Dem., Tennessee) was far less sanguine. As the chairman of the Subcommittee on Antitrust and Monopoly of the Senate Judiciary Committee, Kefauver vowed to oppose the merger and emphasized that the PRR and the NYC could provide "better competition when they operate independently." Labor leaders likewise voiced their disapproval, none more forcefully than Mike Quill of the Transport Workers Union. "If the

financial jugglers who control the New York Central and Pennsylvania Railroads are permitted to merge these two railroad empires," he said in letters to Kefauver and Attorney General William P. Rogers, "we might as well scrap our anti-trust and anti-monopoly laws."[195]

As a financier rather than a railroader, Young had always been the primary supporter of consolidation. The process would keep his name in the headlines and provide an opportunity to distance himself from the uncomfortable reality that none of his visionary experiments at the New York Central had produced any positive outcome. As 1957 came to an end, and as Wall Street was abuzz with rumors regarding the merger, it became clear that Young and Perlman had not been able to overcome the effects of that year's recession. The NYC's 1956 earnings of $39.1 million fell to just $8.4 million the following year. The company's rate of return on investment was below 1 percent, about the same as that of the Pennsylvania Railroad. Meanwhile, the Chesapeake & Ohio and the Nickel Plate Road—the companies that Young had relinquished, to control the New York Central—remained two of the most prosperous railroads in the United States.[196]

In January 1958, the NYC's directors traveled to Palm Beach, where Young kept a winter home, to discuss the desperate financial situation. Young was despondent, virtually silent as the board agreed to eliminate the company's quarterly dividend. His supporters insisted that he felt remorse for exposing both his friends and a legion of small investors to the financial consequences of his actions. Others less charitably suggested that he was unable to cope with repeated failures to transform his inflammatory rhetoric into results. In some respects, Young resembled Reading president Franklin B. Gowen, the talented but emotionally troubled individual who bedeviled PRR executives between 1870 and his suicide in 1889. On January 25, 1958, Young ended his life in much the same way, locked in the billiard room of his Palm Beach mansion, holding a shotgun.[197]

Young's death did little to reduce the disruptive influences he had initiated. Planning for the merger continued, although without much support from Perlman and his fellow New York Central executives. On the PRR, Symes and his associates were more invested in the process, in a manner that increased their workload and prompted a partial reversal of the organizational changes implemented in 1955. The burden on Newell was particularly heavy. As vice president, he served as the sole conduit for information moving between the central office and each of the nine regions, and he was also responsible for coordinating regional activities. Newell made few friends and many enemies, as he was often the person who imposed constraints on regional operating officials. "It is obvious that the money available for maintenance and capital expenditures during the next ten years will not come up to the expenditures desired by the Regions," he warned the nine regional managers in February 1957. As the vice president in charge of transportation and maintenance, Allen Greenough also supported efforts to more accurately allocate scarce resources. He agreed with Newell's suggestion for "some type of a master plan—to avoid applying money on a 'hit or miss' basis during the next ten years." Yet Greenough argued that regional officials should not be required to provide forecasts of track-maintenance expenditures or requirements for additional yard locomotives—and without those critical figures, accurate forecasting and budgeting would be impossible. President Symes was more sympathetic to Newell's objectives but assigned to his subordinate the thankless responsibility "to coordinate these plans as between Regions—and that will be a System job." Newell's task would be that much more difficult, given Symes's insistence that "I do not want to hand the Regions their program—I want them to hand one to us." Moreover, Newell's position in the narrowest part of the "hourglass" that separated system and regional functions resulted in a crushing workload. As the PRR's executives acknowledged, that role "has at times created bottlenecks, by throwing an almost impossible burden on one man."[198]

Symes was also overworked, although for reasons that had little to do with the management of the Pennsylvania Railroad as a stand-alone entity. Instead, his efforts were directed outward, focusing on merger negotiations with the New York Central, political affairs in Washington, and the activities of executives on other carriers. Symes acknowledged that by the beginning of 1958, he was spending a third of his time focusing on "the common interests of all railroads, in order to endeavor to bring about new concepts of regulation and avoid further impairment of the position of the railroads in the field of competitive transportation." In the context of the worst economic downturn since the Great Depression, with passenger traffic dwindling and freight revenues plummeting, and with labor leaders steadfastly refusing to permit workforce reductions or changes in operating practices, Symes would need to employ all his persuasive abilities to shape public policy.[199]

The changing roles of senior executives prompted an overhaul of the corporate structure. The PRR's new organization, implemented on March 1, 1958, preserved the nine regions but reversed many of the other changes that had characterized the railroad's headquarters since 1955.

The most obvious alteration involved the creation of three "major" (Transportation, Sales, and Financial) and five "lesser" staff departments. Newell's burden eased somewhat, thanks to the reestablishment of the position of vice president in charge of operations, which again became his title. He remained a liaison between the regions and the Sales and Financial Departments but yielded much of his authority over traffic functions. Newell's Transportation Department gained control of the Safety Department, indicating that such matters were closely linked to the movement and repair of trains. In addition to relinquishing safety matters, the Personnel Department lost its authority over labor negotiations and employee grievances. The director of labor relations, whose staff now reported directly to Newell, likewise reflected the long-standing situation in which nearly all employees were part of the Transportation Department. The necessity of fielding a coordinated marketing strategy, particularly with respect to large industries, mandated the reimplementation of a centralized sales force, essentially the same as the old Traffic Department. That return to traditional practices induced the combination of the Freight Sales and Services and the Passenger Sales and Services Departments into the Service Department, now increasingly isolated from operations.[200] Fred Carpi, in his new role as vice president in charge of sales, regained full control over traffic functions, increasing his authority relative to that of his rival, Newell.[201]

The 1958 reorganization also strengthened David Bevan's status within the company. The consolidation of the Financial Department and the old Accounting Department (sometimes simply referred to as the Comptroller's Office) enabled Bevan to oversee all matters relating to taxation and insurance as well as employee benefits. Bayard Roberts, the PRR's secretary and the grandson of former president George Brooke Roberts, had traditionally handled the heretofore largely routine and bureaucratic function of shareholder relations. At a time when investors were becoming increasingly vocal regarding the railroad's poor financial performance, Bevan also took charge of those activities, as part of his Financial Department. Of greater significance, the changes improved Bevan's ability to monitor financial data and to develop cash-flow predictions, an income budget, and plans for capital expenditures.[202]

Shortly after the 1958 reorganization, Bevan used his enhanced status to ensure that his office would be an integral part of day-to-day operations on the Pennsylvania Railroad. In early 1954, and thanks to Bevan's efforts, the Accounting Department began the development of a system of responsibility accounting. Work progressed slowly, and by the autumn of 1958, Bevan had not yet achieved the project's objectives. The initiative was also backward-looking, in the sense that it represented an attempt to determine costs and allocate them to the departments and divisions responsible for incurring the expense. In addition to antagonizing many operating officials whose financial management—or mismanagement—had heretofore been concealed, responsibility accounting was of limited value in the shaping of future operating methods.

Bevan intended to correct that deficiency, and in early October 1958, he held a series of meetings with representatives of Peat, Marwick, Mitchell & Company. The Philadelphia-based accounting firm had worked with several railroads, including the New York Central, the Baltimore & Ohio, the Chesapeake & Ohio, and the Southern Pacific. One of the firm's partners, Thomas H. Carroll, recommended a thorough survey of the PRR's accounting practices, to be undertaken by the Transportation Department and the Management Controls Department. "Our experience has shown," Carroll informed Bevan, "that the accounting and reporting systems of most railroads fail almost completely in one very important aspect—they fail to meet the test of what should be the primary objective of all accounting—to serve as a real and effective tool of operating management." He emphasized "that an operating budget should be an integral part of a cost control system."[203]

The Peat, Marwick, Mitchell report, completed in March 1959, found considerable fault with the PRR's practices. The consultants indicated that the company's cost-accounting methods were "antiquated and clumsy." The poor oversight of purchases and stores was noteworthy, with "paperwork archaic and unnecessary" and "control over inventories weak." Peat, Marwick, Mitchell also identified pervasive deficiencies with personnel, with "many 40 year veterans and not always receptive to change" and other individuals who "sometimes appear to be unqualified." The study also highlighted the "prevalence of defensive attitude on PRR," with a "'keep my boss out of trouble'" approach that "seems to be more a question of protection or ascribing blame than on positive or constructive action. Even senior executives reflect this attitude." No names were mentioned, but outside observers clearly identified a systemic failure at the top levels of PRR management.[204]

The most senior of those executives, James Symes, listened politely to the consultants' briefing while doodling on the eighteen-page synopsis they provided. Whatever his feelings, he nonetheless permitted Bevan to engage the

services of Peat, Marwick, Mitchell as the first outside auditors in the Pennsylvania Railroad's history. Lower-level managers were far less supportive. They had risen through the ranks of the Transportation Department, based largely on their experience with the pragmatic matters of day-to-day railroad operations, and they could not have been happy at the prospect of consultants from the "Management Controls Department" telling them how to do their jobs. They likely bristled at Thomas Carroll's promise that the PRR's operating budget could be transformed "into an effective tool for controlling and measuring operations." Carroll acknowledged "the need to 'sell' the program to operating personnel," but those executives would likely blame Bevan for attempts to subvert their hard-won authority within the company.[205]

One further alteration to the 1958 corporate structure reflected the profound changes that had taken place on the Pennsylvania Railroad since the end of World War II. Not much more than a decade earlier, the Motive Power Department had spent millions of dollars developing a new generation of duplex steam locomotives, unique to the company. It was the culmination of a long-standing tradition, where new designs flowed from the drafting pens of Theodore Ely, Alfred Gibbs, Axel Vogt, and William Kiesel to skilled craftsmen at the Juniata Shops who translated their drawings into steel. Even after dieselization shifted locomotive design and production from Philadelphia and Altoona to La Grange and Schenectady, PRR executives hoped they could continue to tailor specific technologies to suit their railroad. The staff of the Research and Development Department, established in 1955, would have little scope to work on such elaborate projects as the K4s or the T1. They could nonetheless exploit the potential of low-cost, lightweight passenger cars and develop intermodal equipment for TrucTrain service. By 1958, those days were over. The *Aerotrain* traveled its last miles between Philadelphia and Pittsburgh in June 1957, before being banished to the Union Pacific and then the Rock Island. Its failure, like that of Young's *Xplorer*, indicated that there was little value in expending additional resources in a vain effort to capture a dwindling passenger market. Trailer Train's nationwide flatcar pool satisfied the PRR's demands for TrucTrain service, and there was no longer any need to create specialized equipment that could not be used on other railroads. Walter Patchell's Research and Development Department lost its identity in the 1958 reorganization, with the few remaining R&D responsibilities assigned to various staff offices. The Department of Tests remained in existence, but there was little left to test. Most research-and-development activities as well as the evaluation of finished products were now the responsibility of manufacturers, engineering societies, trade associations such as the AAR, or the federal government. "While the conception of the position seemed to be sound, and outside industry successfully uses this instrument," PRR officials suggested, "we have found that it does not adapt itself to our form of operation." It was a graceful way of saying that the Pennsylvania Railroad had once and for all abandoned nearly a century of efforts to control the technology it utilized.[206]

The surviving functions of the Research and Development Department had little to do with the development of new technologies or operating practices. Instead, they principally related to merger planning and to efforts to discontinue or to find public support for commuter operations. Those functions became the responsibility of the Department of Special Services, under Patchell's direction. The name was sufficiently innocuous to allay suspicions that Patchell was attempting to shape public policy, yet that was precisely his role. His office would focus solely on the financial, legal, and regulatory issues affecting "the important subject of the consolidation of railroads," thus removing much of that responsibility from Symes and Newell. Initially, Patchell and his staff were responsible for developing a merger plan for the PRR and the New York Central, and that activity consumed much of their time.[207]

Planning for the merger had begun in November 1957. The effort was under the direction of John D. Morris, Patchell's subordinate in what was at that time still the Research and Development Department. Prior to his reassignment, Morris had been the general manager of transportation. He started his PRR career in 1926 as a rodman and later held the offices of division engineer, division superintendent, assistant general manager of the Eastern Region, and general manager of the Western Region. He spent time on reassignment to the Accounting Department, which gave him some of the skills he would need in his new role. His fellow PRR representatives on the Operating Committee for Merger Planning included a methods engineer, a transportation engineer, an assistant train master, a superintendent of equipment, and a boat master familiar with New York Harbor operations. Their NYC counterparts, led by general manager John C. Kenefick, featured two industrial engineers, a transportation inspector, and the general superintendent of shops.[208] Another committee, which included two PRR and three NYC officials, evaluated the potential effects of the merger on passenger and mail traffic. Given their close association with the PRR, three other

carriers—the Wabash, the Lehigh Valley, and the Detroit, Toledo & Ironton—each furnished a representative. None of the nineteen individuals involved in the merger study were familiar with legal or financial matters, and only one possessed experience with traffic and the marketing of service. The exchange ratio between PRR and NYC stock, irrelevant from an operating perspective but critical for shareholder approval, was left to a separate committee.[209]

The task of Morris, Kenefick, and the others was not so much to fit the two railroads together as to persuade politicians and regulators that the benefits of the merger would outweigh the loss of competition—in keeping with the standard established by the 1944 McLean case.[210] That lesson was not lost on Kenefick. In December 1957, he spoke with Ernest C. Poole, the retired manager of the Bureau of Transportation Research at the Southern Pacific. Poole was at that point a transportation consultant working for the Pittsburgh & Lake Erie. He was an expert in rates and cost accounting, and in 1962 he would publish Costs: A Tool for Railroad Management, widely used at carriers across the United States. Poole reported to P&LE president John W. Barriger III, an executive with a reputation as a progressive railroader and an individual who enjoyed a good relationship with regulators and politicians. Fortunately for Kenefick, the P&LE was a New York Central subsidiary, and thus Poole and Barriger were ready and willing to give advice. "I understand Mr. Poole's statistical approach has been accepted by the Interstate Commerce Commission in rate cases in the past," Kenefick informed NYC vice president John Francis Nash, "and I assume that it would be a useful basis for presenting a case for a merger to the Commission now."[211]

Irrespective of their standing with the Interstate Commerce Commission, Poole and his team created what was at best a haphazard estimate of the potential cost savings associated with the merger. They divided the study into three phases, only one of which would be directly relevant to the merger application before the ICC. The first, Poole noted, "should be prepared as soon as possible. It should be sufficiently accurate to prove the case and indicate the areas where substantial economies could be effected immediately when and if such consolidation should be approved." The next component, principally concerning the structure of freight rates and reductions in passenger service, "can be progressed while awaiting decision after submitting study 1" to the ICC, Poole suggested. The final phase, he concluded, "should be a much more complete and accurate study than made in stages 1 and 2"—something that should be undertaken "if and when consolidation is approved." In other words, representatives from the two companies would determine whether the merger was economically viable only after the consolidation of the Pennsylvania Railroad and the New York Central had become irreversible.[212]

The desire of PRR and NYC officials to act as quickly as possible and to generate data that proved the economic efficiencies associated with the merger led to some questionable methods and assumptions. To determine the optimal routing of freight traffic—the largest potential area for cost reductions—Poole and his associates relied on a fifteen-waybill sample, in turn divided into approximately one hundred subsamples. All were from 1956, an unusually prosperous year for the northeastern railroads. Poole also overestimated the salvage value of facilities made redundant by the consolidation. His assumption that "the abandoned freight houses can often be rented to advantage" was highly unlikely—as was the assertion that "what is true of the freight house and the trackage serving them will often be true but to a greater degree for passenger stations and the trackage serving them." Given the rapid decline in passenger service coupled with the population shift from the urban core to the suburbs, it was doubtful that anyone would want to purchase and maintain a decaying passenger terminal. Barriger sensed as much. When he subsequently conveyed Poole's "rough estimate" to Perlman, he acknowledged that the figures were "somewhat arbitrary." Poole's study nonetheless claimed that the merger would likely save the combined companies $146.2 million per year, an amount well above what PRR and NYC officials were suggesting publicly.[213] Despite the uncertainties associated with that prediction, Perlman received the reassurance that "unquestionably the savings will be very substantial." It was a simple matter to round up, and "this estimate shows $150,000,000 a year as the expected savings and is more likely to be the lower limit rather than the upper limit when all factors are considered."[214]

Despite the favorable predictions, cooperation among Pennsylvania Railroad and New York Central executives was by no means assured. In the NYC camp, the November 1957 merger announcement prompted neither a corporate reorganization nor any apparent urgency to accelerate the planning process. Perlman regarded the merger as Young's project, not his, and feared that he would lose much of his authority in the consolidation. While Symes highlighted Morris's involvement in the merger study and promised reporters that he would provide them with periodic updates, Perlman refused to release a list of the NYC officials who were working on the consolidation. John

Nash, the New York Central's vice president in charge of operations, also expressed frustration with his PRR counterpart. "We still do not agree with their thinking," he informed Barriger, following a late-December meeting with Newell and his staff. "We are firmly convinced that a statistical study is the only way to approach this problem to get an idea of the estimated savings." That methodology, coordinated by Poole, clashed with the PRR's reliance on estimates generated by staff officers and the nine regional managers. The disparity reflected the differences between the NYC's centralized corporate structure and the decentralized approach favored by the PRR and embodied in the 1955 reorganization. Barriger, who enjoyed an insider's view of the negotiations, later reminded Perlman that "the brief period of the proposed NYC-PRR alliance . . . represented a strange interlude in NYC policy—and that of PRR, too. It is explained only by the distressing financial pressures that were generated by the business recession beginning during the third quarter of 1957 and lasting for about a year." The resulting courtship, based largely on economic necessity, was unlikely to produce a happy marriage—particularly when Perlman was reluctant to escort the New York Central down the aisle.[215]

By February 1958, the members of the Operating Committee were able to set aside their differences and generate the first iteration of a merger report. They released a revised draft in March and the final version on April 21. There were minor revisions, but none changed the basic presumptions regarding the operation of a merged railroad. While Perlman was probably correct in his expectation that PRR executives would dominate the new company, he could take comfort that the lines of the former New York Central would see increased use. "In general," noted members of the planning committee, "we felt that every advantage should be taken of the virtually gradeless Central main line to New York, and business should be moved over the Pennsylvania line over the Allegheny Mountains only when excessive mileage would be involved in the first route." The Pennsylvania Railroad would be banished from freight operations in Greater New York, with the NYC alone serving the area as far south as Metuchen, New Jersey. The four-track PRR main line across the Commonwealth of Pennsylvania would be restricted largely to traffic moving between Pittsburgh and Philadelphia.[216] Shipments from the Chicago area destined for East Coast points south of Metuchen would travel along the NYC to Cleveland and then south along the PRR to Pittsburgh. The Pennsylvania Railroad lines to the west of the Pittsburgh-Youngstown-Cleveland corridor would see the most drastic reductions. The Pittsburgh, Fort Wayne &

Chicago, once the heart of Lines West, would be downgraded to little more than a branch line. The same was true of the old Southwest System. The PRR's route provided ready access to the center of large cities such as Indianapolis—an important consideration for passenger operations that were rapidly nearing extinction but an impediment to efficient freight service. There would be little use for the line between Chicago and Columbus, Ohio, by way of Logansport, Indiana. Much of the track to the west of Columbus would likewise be downgraded or abandoned. Traffic from the St. Louis gateway would follow the former New York Central as far east as Union City, Ohio, en route to Columbus. With most freight between Chicago and the East Coast sent through Buffalo, even the original Pittsburgh, Cincinnati, Chicago & St. Louis (Pan Handle) link between Columbus and Pittsburgh would see a substantial reduction in use. The merger plan suggested that traffic on the PRR lines would decrease by more than thirty-eight billion gross ton miles per year, while that on the NYC would grow by a corresponding amount. The imbalance might increase, the report concluded, if the railroads succeeded in their ongoing efforts to repeal full-crew laws in the state of New York.[217]

The final report of the Operating Committee suggested the problematic nature of the merger proposal. The Pennsylvania Railroad would bear the brunt of the efficiencies and economies associated with the consolidation. That situation was of scant concern to investors, assuming that representatives from the two companies could negotiate a satisfactory exchange ratio for their securities. PRR workers and their union representatives were another matter, however. They began mobilizing to save their jobs or, at the very least, prevent mass reassignments to other work locations. Elected officials in Pennsylvania were particularly sensitive to those concerns. They also feared that the reduction in service would further undermine manufacturing firms that were feeling the effects of deindustrialization and the steady migration of economic output to the Sunbelt.

The Operating Committee report also cast doubt on the $146.2 million in annual savings that Poole identified. The total was now less than $94.2 million—still substantial, but no one could explain the wide variation in the two estimates.[218] The reduced amount included $15.5 million associated with the consolidation or elimination of passenger service. That was substantially less than the $31.1 million that Poole had calculated, but both figures contained an obvious bias.[219] The PRR and the NYC were each moving aggressively to curtail passenger operations and would continue to do so as independent companies. The

additional reduction in passenger expenditures, attributable solely to the merger, was likely to be far smaller.[220]

Faced with two conflicting estimates of the benefits associated with the merger, Symes split the difference. At the end of March 1958, nearly a month before the release of the Operating Committee's final report, Symes presented preliminary results to the PRR's board of directors. Consolidation, he predicted, would within a few years save the combined company as much as $100 million annually. The number had little basis in fact, and it did not even represent an accurate portrayal of the imperfect calculations of the PRR and NYC officials who were planning the merger. It sounded impressive, however, particularly to individuals who saw consolidation as the only mechanism to prevent the nationalization of the railroads or the collapse of the northeastern transportation network.[221]

Perlman was less interested in the potential for long-term cost savings than in a frantic effort to save his railroad. The New York Central had eliminated 30 percent of its workforce since 1954, yet the company was still not earning a profit. At the 1958 Smathers hearings, Perlman testified that the NYC had suffered half a billion dollars in passenger losses in the previous eight years and acknowledged that capital expenditures for that year would be zero. "Unless you take steps now," he told members of the subcommittee, "don't expect to wave a magic wand when an emergency or catastrophe is upon the country and expect to have up-to-date, modern and efficient railroads to do your bidding. Then it will be too late." The New York Central incurred a $3.1 million loss in April, with gross revenues down more than 20 percent compared to the same month in 1957. On May 21, as shareholders prepared for the next day's annual meeting, the NYC announced a $19.6 million loss for the first four months of 1958 and predicted that the deficit would reach $50 million by the end of the year. A consortium of New York and Chicago banks declined to authorize a $50 million line of credit, like the one that Bevan had negotiated for the PRR, judging the proposition too risky. Perlman told investors that he saw no signs that industrial output in the Northeast—or the NYC's carloadings—would increase any time soon. When asked by a shareholder if he thought the company was heading for bankruptcy, Perlman could only answer "I do not want to say. I have no crystal ball." Through the first half of 1958, the NYC suffered a loss of more than $25 million. At the beginning of July, Perlman threatened to eliminate the NYC's Manhattan commuter services and abandon Grand Central Terminal unless the company received municipal subsidies. In October, the company leased its Park Avenue headquarters—the same building that had seen the triumphant arrival of Young and Perlman in 1954—to a local real estate entrepreneur. The following month, newspapers announced that since 1955, Perlman had sold more than three-quarters of his New York Central stock.[222]

As 1958 came to an end, Wall Street had little reason to be optimistic about the future of either the Pennsylvania Railroad or the New York Central. At first glance, the PRR's 1958 gross revenues of $844.2 million and net earnings of $3.5 million seemed reasonable, even commendable, given the severity of the recession. It was nonetheless a steep decline from the $19.1 million the company earned in 1957 while grossing $987.3 million. Simple arithmetic indicated that revenues had fallen by just under 14.5 percent, while net earnings plummeted by a far steeper amount—almost 81.7 percent. Those results, disappointing as they were, would have been little short of disastrous had not the PRR's accountants used a $3.2 million tax credit and an arrearage of $13 million in payments from the post office to offset catastrophically poor operating results.[223] Absent those one-time benefits, the Pennsylvania Railroad would have been awash in a sea of red ink. Perlman faced a situation that was no less serious. The New York Central's operating revenues fell from $741.6 million to $659 million, while net earnings were more than cut in half, from $8.4 million to $4.1 million. It was the worst showing since the $10.5 million loss incurred in 1946. The retroactive increase in mail rates of $18.7 million and tax credits of $1.7 million had likewise saved the company from an overall deficit.[224]

Merger Mania

The Eisenhower Recession affected the nation's railroads to varying degrees, while increasing the resolve of executives who were determined to protect themselves from the proposed PRR/NYC colossus. The first response occurred in January 1958, when Baltimore & Ohio president Howard Simpson suggested to his Chesapeake & Ohio counterpart, Walter Tuohy, that the two companies should explore an alliance. The B&O and the C&O were in many respects competitors, but Simpson and Tuohy were ready to save each other in order to save themselves. They hoped that the Nickel Plate would join the group, but representatives from that company feared that they would retain little power once swallowed by the two larger systems. The Nickel Plate's accountants also took a close look at the finances of the B&O, by far the weakest of the three lines, and that was enough to end the discussions.[225]

The announcement of the PRR/NYC merger produced equally disruptive effects on other eastern railroads. After

his dismissal from the New York Central, William White became president of the Delaware & Hudson, and he had good reason to fear his former employer. By September 1956, he had opened negotiations with the Erie and the Delaware, Lackawanna & Western regarding a possible consolidation to better compete against the largely parallel routes of the New York Central. Two years later, in November 1958, White organized representatives from seven northeastern railroads, exploring the possibility of a defensive alliance against the looming PRR/NYC juggernaut. The B&O, the C&O, and the Nickel Plate sent delegates, as did the Erie, the Lackawanna, and the Reading. "The purpose of the meeting," White told reporters, "was to consider means of competitive survival in the event the Pennsylvania and New York Central Railroad systems carried out their projected consolidation." White emphasized that the attendees' cooperative spirit was based on a shared desire to fight against Symes and Perlman rather than a collaborative effort to attract new business or improve operating efficiency. "What are we going to do, each of us," he mused, "if a Pennsylvania-Central merger proposal should reach the Interstate Commerce Commission?"[226]

White's question set the tone not only for the November meeting but for all the merger negotiations that unfolded, nationwide, over the following decade. Few people possessed the perspicacity or simple common sense to ask whether railroad consolidations would improve service or restore the carriers to financial health. Instead, all involved were determined to make the best deal they could, protecting the interests of their respective companies while blocking initiatives proposed by rivals. Five of the seven railroads represented in Cleveland (although, ironically, not White's Delaware & Hudson) would lose their corporate identity through merger. They were not the only ones caught up in a series of realignments triggered by the proposed PRR/NYC combination.

The first of those mergers involved two companies that were not represented in Cleveland, one of which was closely allied to the Pennsylvania Railroad. Since Robert Young first attempted to gain control of the New York Central in 1947, officials at the Virginian had been carefully considering their company's competitive position. The consolidation battles that occurred during the interwar period induced the Virginian to build a connection with the NYC, at Deepwater, West Virginia. The link enabled traffic from the Midwest to reach Hampton Roads and transformed the Virginian from a coal carrier to a company that also handled significant amounts of carload freight. Since then, the New York Central was closely affiliated with the Virginian, although it lacked the securities ownership that bound the Norfolk & Western to the Pennsylvania Railroad. "The Virginian," Perlman emphasized, "was regarded in early consolidation plans as a natural partner of the New York Central," and he clearly expected that association to continue. In addition to its ties to the NYC, the Virginian was also associated with the Chesapeake & Ohio and recruited many of its executives from that larger company. The NYC/C&O alliance that Young proposed in 1947 would nonetheless have drastically reduced the interchange traffic that flowed between the New York Central and the Virginian, across Deepwater Bridge. Regulatory constraints on Young's activities ended that threat. A merger between the New York Central and the Pennsylvania Railroad would be just as bad. The combined company would undoubtedly rely on the Norfolk & Western's access to the Pocahontas coalfields, to the exclusion of the Virginian, and would have little incentive to route traffic along the Deepwater connection.[227]

Even as Virginian managers contemplated their future, changes were taking place on the Norfolk & Western. Stuart T. Saunders spent his youth in Bedford, Virginia, before graduating from Harvard Law School in 1934. He went to work for the N&W in 1939 as assistant general solicitor. After World War II, he clashed repeatedly with Robert H. Smith, the N&W's president. Smith rose through the operating ranks, and he had little use for lawyers. He was also enamored of steam power, in part because he hoped to retain the loyalty of on-line coal producers. Smith authorized the construction of new steam locomotives at the Roanoke Shops as late as 1950, long after the PRR and other railroads committed to dieselization, and he supported the development of the *Jawn Henry*, the N&W's experimental steam turbine. Much like John Duer and his colleagues in the PRR's Motive Power Department, Smith stressed the horsepower that the *Jawn Henry* and other steam locomotives could provide while ignoring the cost considerations associated with their servicing and repair. Saunders provided unassailable data that demonstrated the efficiency of diesels, infuriating Smith but ending the N&W's status as one of the last railroads to operate steam locomotives.[228]

Smith retired at the end of March 1958, and Saunders replaced him as president. While the move was not unprecedented, it was nonetheless rare for a lawyer, unschooled in operating matters, to assume command of one of the leading railroad systems in the United States. The PRR/NYC merger announcement occurred five months earlier, and executives on dozens of railroads were pondering their place in the new competitive landscape. Saunders had long coveted the Virginian, a company with access to

massive coal reserves. The Virginian, completed decades after the N&W, also provided easier grades for eastbound coal trains headed for tidewater. Because the two systems essentially paralleled each other, there was considerable scope for directional running, to take advantage of the N&W's superior westbound grades. The exploratory committee that Saunders organized predicted that a merger would produce savings of more than $12 million per year. That amount was far less than the projected benefits associated with the merger between the Pennsylvania Railroad and the New York Central. The disparity reflected the smaller size of the Norfolk & Western and the Virginian, as well as a far more realistic assessment of the merger's likely outcome.[229]

After evaluating the merger study, Saunders and his staff took care to discuss the proposal with all the parties that would be affected. Virginian officials were sufficiently frightened of the PRR/NYC combination to set aside their historic antipathy toward the Norfolk & Western. They also hoped that an alliance with the N&W would provide the funds for new motive power while increasing merchandise traffic that could balance cyclical coal revenues. Saunders placated his counterparts on the Chesapeake & Ohio by offering them trackage rights. Mine operators and representatives from the United Mine Workers were supportive, as they saw an opportunity for increased coal production. Labor leaders were initially opposed to Saunders's plans—until he reassured them that all personnel reductions would take place through attrition, without any reduction in pay. Saunders could afford to be generous to his employees in large part because the coal business was booming, and he needed the workers. That was at variance with conditions in the rapidly deindustrializing Northeast, but the N&W's attrition agreement established a baseline for the labor negotiations associated with all future mergers. The widespread support that Saunders cultivated ensured that the merger proposal generated little opposition. The situation was very different from the experiences of PRR and NYC officials, whose plans generated a torrent of complaints from shippers, unions, and local communities. In contrast with the PRR, much of the coal transported by both the N&W and the Virginian was destined for export. The ICC had historically permitted higher rates than those that applied to purely domestic shipments, and overseas customers lacked the political influence necessary to oppose the consolidation. With all the stars aligned in Saunders's favor, on December 1, 1959, the Norfolk & Western absorbed the Virginian. While executives from other companies had talked extensively of their merger plans, and politicians, regulators, and financial analysts had weighed in on the issue, the N&W/ Virginian combination was the first significant railroad consolidation of the postwar era, and it was one of the most successful. Stuart Saunders achieved a considerable victory and established a reputation as a man who could make mergers happen.[230]

Perlman, it seemed, was the only person who was not favorably disposed toward the merger of the two Pocahontas coal lines. For the remainder of his life, Saunders never wavered from his assertion that the consolidation was solely his idea, carried out in collaboration with N&W general counsel John P. "Jack" Fishwick. While Saunders was first and foremost acting in the interest of the Norfolk & Western and its investors, those stakeholders included the Pennsylvania Railroad. The timing of his decision to pursue the Virginian struck Perlman as suspicious, not because it so closely followed Saunders's elevation to the N&W's presidency but because it occurred so soon after the PRR and the NYC agreed to merge.

Perlman felt betrayed. "While we were engaged in this study with the Pennsylvania," he complained, "we did not, of course, offer to institute contemporaneous merger studies with any other railroad. I felt it would not be fair to the Pennsylvania to engage in any other negotiations while making a joint study with them. However, during the very same time we were making this study with the Pennsylvania, its subsidiary Norfolk & Western was actively negotiating a merger agreement with the Virginian Railway, which had always been one of Central's friendly connections." Perlman assumed that Symes—who was a director of both the Pennsylvania Railroad and the Norfolk & Western—had coached Saunders into pulling the Virginian out of the New York Central's sphere of influence and into the PRR's orbit. By depriving the NYC of access to the Virginian's traffic, Symes was now in a much stronger position to dictate merger terms to Perlman. Moreover, if the merger talks failed—Perlman certainly entertained that possibility—then the PRR would have superb access to the Pocahontas coalfields, and his company would suffer accordingly.[231]

The announcement of the pending consolidation of the N&W and the Virginian dampened whatever enthusiasm Perlman may have felt for a merger between his company and the Pennsylvania Railroad. By November 1958, knowledgeable insiders suggested that Perlman had "cooled" on the idea and was raising the possibility that the "timing" was not propitious. Representatives from the two companies failed to establish the all-important ratio for the conversion of stock into shares of the new company, even though PRR sources insisted that negotiations were

ongoing. In December, David Bevan suggested that the financing plan—the last stage of the merger proposal— was nearing completion. At the next NYC board meeting, however, the company's directors voted to abandon the project. Following the decision, announced on January 9, Perlman suggested that the Eastern Railroad Presidents' Conference could take responsibility for developing a comprehensive consolidation plan that would "bring about in the East three or four systems of nearly balanced economic strength." It was a naive suggestion, given that the initial merger announcement, thirteen months earlier, produced the same every-man-for-himself mentality that doomed the planning process during the 1920s and 1930s.[232]

Perlman excused his change of heart by saying that his earlier statements regarding the progress of the merger negotiations had been made "in the past tense." He nonetheless indicated that he was "very pleased" with the results of the consolidation study. Perlman also hoped that he could continue to cooperate with the PRR, short of merger, to increase efficiency and benefit both companies.[233] Yet he seemed unconcerned that the union that was supposed to save both companies was not going to happen. "He was understood to have said privately," the New York Times suggested, "that he would not be unduly distressed if obstacles to a merger of the Pennsylvania and Central were found to be insurmountable." Given Perlman's exclusion from the September 1957 meeting between Young and Symes, it suggested to some that the whole business had been an elaborate publicity stunt on the part of the now-deceased financier, one that had been designed to draw attention to the problems facing the railroads. Perlman's final comment on the matter indicated that he had never been in love with the Pennsylvania Railroad or with the idea that the two companies should be combined. "Before we marry the girl," he told reporters, "we want to make sure that no other heiress is around that might fall into our lap."[234]

Symes professed surprise at the collapse of the merger negotiations. "None of the reasons for the New York Central's decision to withdraw, so far published by the newspapers, were given to us until they read us their public announcement just moments before its release." He also offered a blunt reaction to the apparent nonchalance of Perlman and the NYC's directors. "I, too, am pleased with the results of the study," he emphasized, "but amazed as to the lack of definite action taken by them in connection therewith. It is well recognized throughout the industry that coordination of facilities is not a substitute for corporate mergers—if it were, the question of mergers would not now be considered." Symes likewise had little patience for Perlman's assertions regarding poor timing, or his pronouncement that negotiations might resume at some future date. "As a practical matter," Symes noted, "consideration of corporate mergers must move forward or stop. They cannot, in good faith, be held in abeyance and revived at the will of any one participant." The language in the PRR's annual report, released a few weeks later, echoed Symes's contention that Perlman had been responsible for the debacle. "It is self-evident that a productive corporate merger can be accomplished only when all parties are enthusiastic about it," the company informed its shareholders. "The proposed merger with the New York Central therefore cannot be accomplished—at least not until there is a change of attitude on their part."[235]

Symes had good reason to be angry at Perlman, given the economic and competitive conditions that faced the Pennsylvania Railroad. Even as he spoke to reporters, maintenance crews were struggling to repair facilities affected by flooding along the Ohio River and its tributaries. The damage, which was particularly severe in the Youngstown steel-producing region, saddled the PRR with $2 million in repair costs and forgone revenues and contributed to a $6 million loss during the first quarter of 1959. The company incurred a $44 million passenger deficit in 1958, and the following year was unlikely to show much of an improvement. Corporate realignments spawned by the fruitless merger announcement promised to inflict further harm on the Pennsylvania Railroad. Along the PRR's southern flank—and even without the cooperation of the Nickel Plate—officials from the Baltimore & Ohio and the Chesapeake & Ohio were discussing a defensive alliance. To the north, William White proposed a three-way consolidation of the Delaware & Hudson, the Lackawanna, and the Erie. The recession caused D&H officials to sour on the arrangement, but the executives at the other two companies vowed to proceed, nonetheless. Since the September 1957 meeting with Young, Symes had inadvertently helped to strengthen his rivals without producing any appreciable benefit for his company. Alluding to the nearly complete but now abandoned merger studies between the PRR and the NYC, Symes again told reporters that the consolidation would have saved the combined company at least $100 million a year—but now it was not to be.[236]

Destiny

By the end of October 1959, most of the autumn leaves had fallen from Philadelphia's trees, and the pleasant fall weather was becoming cold and harsh. Although the Eisenhower Recession had ended, the Pennsylvania Railroad had not recovered, and would never fully recover, from its effects. September's operating loss of nearly $2.3 million ensured an overall deficit during the first nine months of the year. A steel strike, the fifth since the end of World War II, had been underway since July and showed no signs of abating. It cost the PRR $65 million in lost revenue and caused layoffs of 11,600 railroad workers. The walkout would last nearly four months, and historians would later identify it as the beginning of the end of an American steel industry that for so many decades had been a principal source of the PRR's revenues. Railway labor was restless as well, and government mediators were doing their best to prevent a nationwide strike. Union officials demanded more of the same wage increases that had contributed to the Pennsylvania Railroad's deficits while managers—for the first time since the Great Depression—were seeking to reduce employee pay. Passenger service continued to hemorrhage money, and many Pennsylvania Railroad executives fervently hoped for the accuracy of Howard Hosmer's prediction that it would disappear by 1970, if not sooner.[237]

Yet despite the PRR's multifaceted problems, the trains continued to run. Although James Symes served as the company's president, as he had since the spring of 1954, Allen J. Greenough bore the ultimate responsibility for the safe and efficient operation of the railroad. Greenough was born in San Francisco but soon became an easterner, attending Princeton Preparatory School and graduating from Union College in Schenectady, New York. Intending to be a sanitary engineer, he was attracted to the Pennsylvania Railroad by the promise of a salary of $155 per month. He started with the company in 1928 as an assistant electrical engineer based in Jersey City. By 1933, he was a track supervisor. In 1945, he became superintendent of the Wilkes-Barre Division, then general superintendent of the Eastern Pennsylvania General Division, and finally general superintendent of transportation for the Eastern Region in 1950. He served as general manager of the Central Region and then headed back east as the vice president of the Eastern Region in 1953. The 1955 reorganization elevated Greenough to the post of vice president in charge of transportation and maintenance, in charge of keeping traffic moving and ensuring that the physical plant remained in acceptable condition. By the autumn of 1959, he was fifty-four years of age and secure in his career, seemingly destined for another sixteen years of labor followed by a comfortable retirement.[238]

On the morning of October 28, President Symes presided over a meeting of the board of directors and shared with them the continued disappointment of the railroad's financial results. Three of those directors—Jim Newell,

David Bevan, and Fred Carpi—held dual roles as board members and corporate vice presidents. Symes informed each of them that he would need to make drastic changes if the Pennsylvania Railroad were to survive. First and foremost, he would resign the office of president. Far from leaving the PRR, however, Symes planned to increase his control over the company. He intended to serve as chairman of the board—an office created when Martin Clement left the presidency in 1949 but abandoned upon his retirement two years later.[239] Symes would retain the status of chief executive officer, in charge of corporate strategy. The new president, Symes's replacement, would be reduced to the role of chief administrative officer, managing day-to-day operating matters.[240]

Just after noon and without warning, Symes summoned Greenough into his office. It was a private conversation, no one took notes, and no reporters were present. The *Philadelphia Bulletin* later reconstructed a reasonable facsimile of the brief meeting between the two executives. Symes began by offering his congratulations to Greenough, causing his subordinate to ask, "What have I done now?" Given the PRR's difficulties, Greenough could be forgiven if he imagined that Symes's remark carried a measure of sarcasm coupled with a sinister undertone. He need not have worried, however, as Symes announced the board's decision to appoint him as president. Greenough's response—"President of what?"—was not unreasonable. Despite the ongoing process of corporate simplification, the PRR still controlled nearly one hundred subsidiary companies, many of which required ceremonial chief executive officers. The response—"president of the Pennsylvania Railroad"—was both straightforward and entirely unanticipated.[241]

Everyone, including Greenough, was taken completely by surprise. His responsibilities had been such that no one had previously thought it necessary to appoint him to the railroad's board of directors—a situation that was soon remedied. The three executives who were on the board made no public comment, but their private feelings were not difficult to predict. As the vice president in charge of sales, Fred Carpi would have been an unlikely choice for president. His selection would not have been unprecedented, however, given Walter Franklin's presidency and the emphasis that the 1955 reorganization had placed on the traffic side of the company. It was more traditional to promote the vice president in charge of operations to the top of the executive ranks, and Jim Newell accordingly considered himself to be Symes's rightful successor. He had, after all, taken charge of the development of Truc-Train and the subsequent formation of Trailer Train, with

intermodal operations serving as one of the few bright spots in an otherwise dismal freight business. Newell's support for intermodal transportation nonetheless sparked a feud with Carpi, who for far too long remained loyal to traditional, boxcar-based, less-than-carload-lot traffic. That resentment intensified during the last few years of Symes's presidency, as both executives jockeyed for position. By the time of the board meeting in October 1959, relations between the two men had become toxic, and they were increasingly unwilling to work with each other for the good of the company. Greenough had no intention of putting up with such infighting and considered Carpi the more valuable asset to the company. In one of his first actions as president, he invited Newell to resign. The vice president in charge of operations appealed the matter to Symes, who promptly ended Greenough's initiative. Symes had protected Newell in the past and would do so again in the future, securing a place for him in the Trailer Train organization. Newell's career had reached a dead end, however, and his bitterness against Greenough and Carpi—two of the five top executives in the company—increased in the months that followed.

David Bevan had only been with the Pennsylvania Railroad for eighteen years, not long by the standards of the company's upper echelons, but he too aspired to a higher office. The 1958 alterations to the organizational structure gave him almost complete control over the railroad's finances. He knew, better than anyone else associated with the PRR, just how precarious that financial situation was. Largely isolated from senior operating and traffic officials, Bevan charted his own course through the corporate hierarchy, doing his best to curtail expenses, pay down the company's debt, diversify into more profitable areas of business, and borrow money wherever and however he could. He was nonetheless an outsider, the sole senior executive who focused on accounting, budgeting, and the control of costs rather than on the business of transportation. Bevan's continual advocacy for financial restraint, coupled with his willingness to accentuate the negative aspects of the PRR's performance, made him the target of criticism by individuals in the Transportation and Traffic Departments. They rarely admitted that Bevan was correct, and they quickly blamed him for the company's financial difficulties. "The Board likewise looks to me primarily to safeguard the correctness and soundness of our figures," he complained to Greenough. "If anything goes wrong I am the one who will be held primarily responsible." While he did not share Carpi's visceral hatred of Newell, Bevan nonetheless clashed with the head of operations over the cost of improvements and service initiatives. Like Carpi, he saw Newell as a rival for power within the organization.[242]

It was unclear whether Bevan wanted the presidency or was qualified for that office, but Symes made a point of reassuring him. Now that he had taken on the strategic functions associated with the board chairmanship, Symes emphasized, the presidency required an expert in railroad operations and nothing more. Bevan nonetheless insisted that Greenough, despite his rank, was not the best candidate available. He thought more highly of Herman H. Pevler, who until four months earlier had been the general manager of the Northwestern Region. Pevler left the PRR to become the president of the Wabash as part of Symes's attempt to influence the rapidly shifting merger landscape. He could easily have been summoned back to the Pennsylvania Railroad, but Symes lacked confidence in his abilities as a manager. Bevan may have shared that view and believed that he could dominate a weak and indecisive Pevler.[243] While he refused to accept Bevan's advice, Symes dangled a carrot in front of the railroad's chief financial officer. As chairman of the board, Symes explained, he could assist Greenough and provide the leadership that his chief administrative officer lacked. Bevan might one day do the same, Symes hinted, replacing him as the PRR's chief executive. At age fifty-three, Bevan could afford to be patient and wait for the stars to align in his favor.[244]

In assessing Greenough's promotion, reporters pondered the board's "dramatic and unexpected action" and concluded that the directors had "apparently decided yesterday that the time had come to stress the maintenance and the day-to-day train performance throughout the system's 9,000 miles of line." Transportation analysts suggested that the Pennsylvania Railroad was preparing to rectify years of decay on the physical plant and embark on an aggressive marketing program designed to attract additional freight traffic. They were at least partly correct, in that the promotion denied Greenough any meaningful contribution to the development of long-term corporate strategy. As the PRR's new chief administrative officer, his responsibilities extended to the practical matters of railroad operations and no further.[245]

Largely, however, observers and prognosticators badly misinterpreted the managerial realignments on the Pennsylvania Railroad. Greenough earned his promotion not because the PRR was focusing on its core competencies but because his marginalization freed Symes to pursue a loftier and more ambitious agenda. In his dual role as chief executive officer and chairman of the board, Symes intended to supervise Greenough's performance while focusing on the implementation of the PRR's long-term

strategic goals. As *Trains* editor David Morgan observed, "The shift will allow him to ease Greenough over the first hurdles of his job as well as permit the chairman to assume an elder statesman role, free of the distractions of running the road itself." Symes's most important task as elder statesman would be a merger with the New York Central. Circumstances that included Robert Young's suicide, Alfred Perlman's obstinacy, deteriorating economic conditions, and the defensive merger of the N&W and the Virginian thwarted an earlier attempt at consolidation. Symes intended to retire in three years' time, at sixty-five; before he did so, he wanted to try again, and this time succeed. The merger with the New York Central would save his company, but it would also be his legacy. Over the next few years, Symes would use all his skill and influence to convince politicians, regulators, financial analysts, and labor leaders that a merger would promote the public interest as the only remaining opportunity to preserve the northeastern railroad network. He would also try to win over a reluctant Alfred Perlman, who had been led down the garden path of consolidation by a flamboyant and publicity-seeking financier who was now dead. Until those merger plans could come to fruition, Symes had a railroad to run and to protect from bankruptcy. He presided over a company whose president held a job that he had not sought and did not want, a chief financial officer increasingly at odds with the men who kept the trains moving, and leaders of the Transportation and Traffic Departments who loathed each other. If Greenough faced many hurdles, then so, too, did Symes.[246]

In the annals of business history, many factors have encouraged corporate mergers—a desire to achieve economies of scale, to safeguard patents, to generate a quick speculative profit, to increase shareholder value, and even to achieve personal renown. For the Pennsylvania Railroad, however, merger would mean nothing less than a chance at survival. Merger was to be the unalterable destiny of the Pennsylvania Railroad as well as the crowning achievement of the individual who had relinquished its presidency in order to gain greater power over the company. Symes was an outsider, who built his career at the far western edge of the PRR system. He was also an iconoclast, gaining renown for challenging traditional managerial practices. By relentlessly advocating for the purchase of diesel locomotives and the abandonment of steam, he had pulled the Pennsylvania Railroad back from the brink of financial ruin. Now, he hoped to do so again. So did David Bevan, who insisted that his financial abilities offered the one remaining opportunity to rescue the company from its latest crisis. Among all the senior executives, the chief financial officer expressed the deepest doubts regarding the wisdom of a merger with the New York Central. The costs associated with combining the facilities and operations of the PRR and the NYC, he reminded Symes and anyone else who would listen, would derail his efforts to control expenditures and thus prove disastrous to both companies.

A union of the two greatest railroads in the United States would also be the legacy of Alfred Perlman. He was a reluctant merger partner and—as the first Jew to become president of a major railroad—an outsider among the resolutely Protestant executives who worked with him and fought against him. At the Norfolk & Western, Stuart Saunders was also an outsider, trained in the law rather than in railroad operations—yet he shared with Symes a willingness to speak truths that flew in the face of tradition. Saunders was also destined to play a pivotal role, both politically and organizationally, in the implementation of the merger between the Pennsylvania Railroad and the New York Central. Alan Boyd, the Florida regulator, was just beginning a long association with the federal government, one that would reach its apex during the administration of Lyndon B. Johnson. His participation in the passenger-train hearings overseen by ICC examiner Howard Hosmer served as a prelude to his involvement in national regulatory politics. The complex interaction between Symes, Bevan, Perlman, Saunders, Johnson, Boyd, and a host of others ensured that the merger would take far longer to achieve than Symes—or anyone else—had anticipated. Nearly a decade elapsed before the Pennsylvania Railroad and the New York Central became one company. The hard-fought effort to achieve that goal became one of the greatest accomplishments of those executives and public servants. It was also one of the greatest disasters in the history of American business.

Chapter 7

Commutation

"The most significant thing that ever happened in Philly," Kitty Foyle observed, "was when it quit being the terminus of the Pennsy Railroad and grand old Broad Street Station became just a turn-around for the suburban trains."[1] Although Kitty lived only on the pages of Christopher Morley's eponymous novel, few characters—and few books—have more effectively captured the mystique of Philadelphia during the middle decades of the twentieth century. Working-class and Scots-Irish, Kitty grew up in urban Frankford—"a long way from the Main Line," she emphasized, "if you know what that means in Philly." Everyone in Philadelphia did know, as did many people who had never been to Philadelphia and who had little knowledge of the city's geography. Morley was certainly familiar with the distinction between the industrial city and its wealthy, elitist suburbs. "He knows Philadelphia," suggested *New York Times* literary critic Margaret Wallace, "and pokes fun at it constantly, with a sharpness born of long and affectionate intimacy." Morley spent much of his adult life in suburban Long Island, but he grew up in the Main Line community of Haverford. He graduated from Haverford College, where his father taught mathematics, not far from the Cheswold estate once occupied by Pennsylvania Railroad president Alexander J. Cassatt.[2]

The doomed romance that is at the heart of *Kitty Foyle* was both improbable and symbolic of the deep divisions within Philadelphia society. Kitty occupied her childhood by making paper dolls and naming them after Main Line socialites. At some future day, Kitty dreamed, she might be included in their society. Kitty was not so much from the wrong side of the tracks as from the urban side of a small

stream, in tandem with the intersecting City Line Avenue, which marked the boundary between Philadelphia and its suburbs. The Pennsylvania Railroad's main line to Pittsburgh began in West Philadelphia, but the Main Line started at Overbrook. "All those vintage Main Liners pride themselves to be just lovely with the lower classes," was Kitty's sarcastic assessment of the situation, "as long as they don't go beyond their proper station, which would probably be Overbrook." Kitty transcended both the geographic boundaries and the restrictions on social class that Morley so deftly conjoined in one sentence. Wynnewood "Wyn" Strafford VI, the love of Kitty's life, embodied the geography of the Main Line and reflected Morley's subtle mockery of the region's social institutions. His first and last names each represented stops along the PRR's commuter line to Paoli. The route had been electrified since 1915—causing Kitty to muse, inaccurately, that "there's no steam engines at Broad Street Station."[3] The daily migration of Philadelphia's self-conscious and insular Main Line aristocracy took the city's elites from their homes to their important occupations in Center City, and rarely anywhere else. "Like all Main Line people," mused Kitty, "Wyn figured a train ought to go to Broad Street Station, or it might as well stay home on a siding." The people of Frankford, in contrast, rode the subway and elevated line that stretched from Center City, past the PRR's 30th Street Station to a terminus at 69th Street in West Philadelphia. Save for its last few hundred yards, the Market–Frankford Line remained within city limits and was of little value to Main Liners and other affluent suburbanites. "In Philly, Wyn and his crowd hardly even knew there *was* a subway,"

Kitty noted. "They rode the snobway instead; the suburban trains." Even today, time spent on Philadelphia's impressive network of commuter rail lines and on its inadequate subway system will quickly reveal the class divide between city and suburb.[4]

Kitty Foyle's Main Line was only one of many commuter routes along the Pennsylvania Railroad and was in truth one of the least significant of any such service in the Northeast. It paled in comparison to the network of lines operated by the subsidiary Long Island Rail Road that fanned out to the east of Penn Station.[5] To the west of the Hudson River, half a dozen carriers brought commuters to the ferries that would take them the final mile to Manhattan. The New York, New Haven & Hartford extended north through Westchester County and into Connecticut, through a constellation of communities far larger and wealthier than anything that could be found along the Main Line. Commuters in New York, and increasingly in Chicago as well, routinely traveled long distances to and from work—thirty or even fifty miles, in some cases. Main Line executives and office workers had far less time to read the morning newspaper or play a game of cards on their journey home, as their trips rarely exceeded ten miles in either direction. Those Philadelphians seldom enjoyed access to the bar cars and parlor cars that made the daily sojourn to and from Manhattan somewhat more bearable, at least for those who could afford such luxuries. And there were many in New York with the means to partake of those amenities, as the city's suburbs housed some of the richest individuals in the United States. Wealthy Americans resided in Philadelphia, too, but theirs was an old-money aristocracy, and they often depended on legacies accumulated in the nineteenth century, and perhaps even in the one before that. Nor was the Main Line initially the most fashionable of Philadelphia's suburban enclaves. That honor fell to Chestnut Hill, home to the oldest of the old money, and a community that was served by PRR and Reading branch lines.[6]

Popular culture—rather than statistics involving personal wealth, commuting times, or passenger volumes—ensured that the Main Line attained renown in a manner that other suburban enclaves never did. Christopher Morley's 1939 novel, and the film that followed a year later, were only a couple of the artistic and cultural references to the Main Line. A similar book-and-movie pairing—Richard P. Powell's The Philadelphian and Paul Newman's featured role in The Young Philadelphians—gave 1950s audiences a taste of the area's tortured social relationships. George Cukor's 1940 film, The Philadelphia Story, nonetheless epitomized the virtues and the vices of Main Line society.

Simultaneously lauding and belittling individuals who survived the Great Depression financially unscathed, the actors poke fun at elites with too much time and money and too little sense. The occasional use of thee and thou acknowledged the lingering influence of the Quakers, who had long since ceased to dominate the city's economic and political life. It was entirely fitting that Katherine Hepburn portrayed the female protagonist, given that in 1928 she graduated from Bryn Mawr College—an elite educational institution located at the apex of the Main Line, on land once owned by the Pennsylvania Railroad.

During the 1830s, when construction crews completed the Philadelphia & Columbia Railroad, Bryn Mawr did not yet exist. The principal transportation artery, built in the 1790s by the Philadelphia & Lancaster Turnpike Road Company, linked the Quaker City with the Susquehanna River. It later became Lancaster Avenue, the principal commercial street along the Main Line, running parallel and a short distance to the south of the tracks. On the other side of the Main Line lay Montgomery Avenue, traversing a sparsely settled area and connecting large farms that often had been in the same family since the arrival of the Quakers in the 1680s. The Commonwealth's Main Line of Public Works gave the region both its name and a transportation route that came under the control of the Pennsylvania Railroad in 1857. President J. Edgar Thomson oversaw the rebuilding of the line that became the PRR's Philadelphia Division. In 1860, the railroad added a small station and telegraph office at Whitehall, currently the intersection of Bryn Mawr Avenue and County Line Road. Four years later, in May 1864, the PRR began local service as far west as Paoli, initiating the storied tradition of the Paoli Local.[7]

Following the Civil War, PRR engineers began to straighten the route through the area, to eliminate a long southerly bend through Whitehall. In 1868, chief engineer of construction William Hasell Wilson began purchasing the necessary land in nearby Humphreysville, acquiring entire farms rather than a narrow strip for the right-of-way. Humphreysville was part of the old Welsh Tract, dating to the days of William Penn. One of Penn's followers, Rowland Ellis, was born in 1650 at the farmstead of Bryn Mawr, near the Welsh village of Dolgellau in the district of Meirionnydd. Ellis employed the same name for his new home in America, both as a tribute to his Welsh heritage and as a literal description of the beautiful hill at the site. Wilson resurrected Bryn Mawr, a more romantic and evocative name than Humphreysville, and one that he hoped would entice affluent Philadelphians to buy lots and build luxurious summer homes. The railroad stipulated that no residence could cost less than $5,000—far more than an unskilled laborer could hope to earn in a decade. Those along Montgomery Avenue carried a value of at least $8,000. Factories, saloons, and other offensive and unsavory structures were prohibited. "It is proposed," a Philadelphia newspaper noted, "to make this locality one of the most desirable of the numerous out-of-town but near-the-city places of residence now to be found around Philadelphia in every direction." In April 1871, the railroad provided three Pullman Palace drawing-room cars for an inspection trip to entice prospective buyers—unnecessarily luxurious for the nine-mile trip out from the city, but indicative of the clientele that Wilson favored. In 1874, he took charge of the railroad's new Real Estate Department, which continued to promote the community until 1886.[8]

Under the watchful supervision of Pennsylvania Railroad executives, Bryn Mawr slowly evolved from a summer resort destination to an affluent commuter suburb. In 1872, the company opened the first portion of the Bryn Mawr Hotel. Despite the catastrophic depression that began soon afterward, prosperous Philadelphians were eager to partake of modern comforts that included bathtubs, gas lighting, and an elevator. The hotel, which could accommodate 250 guests, was by no means the only lodging available to those wishing to escape the heat and the filth of summertime Philadelphia. By 1874, more than fifty hotels and boarding houses between Overbrook and Downingtown provided beds for 1,330 lodgers. At a time when many people perceived a direct correlation between altitude, pure air, and good health, Bryn Mawr drew business away from Chestnut Hill, thanks to its higher elevation. The difference, admittedly, was a mere four inches, but the claim was valid nonetheless. Despite Bryn Mawr's popularity, the economic crisis discouraged the sale of lots and the construction of homes, although in a manner that gave birth to Katherine Hepburn's alma mater. In April 1878, the Pennsylvania Railroad sold land to Quaker physician John W. Taylor for $1,500, well below the normal asking price. The arrangement reflected the reduction in demand, as well as Taylor's assurance that he would build a seminary for the instruction of young society women. Bryn Mawr College opened in 1885, a few miles from another Quaker institution, Haverford College.[9]

The Bryn Mawr Hotel became less popular during the 1880s, as neither the PRR nor the concessionaire who operated the facility were willing to make improvements. The building burned in 1887, but by 1890, a far more elaborate replacement was welcoming visitors. Designed by the Philadelphia architectural firm of Furness, Evans & Company, the four-story granite structure offered comfortable although hardly luxurious accommodation. Its residents included PRR vice president Joseph N. Du Barry; the parents of another vice president (Alexander J. Cassatt); and his sister, the artist Mary Cassatt. Many other affluent Philadelphia families settled in for the summer, with mothers and children escaping the oppressive conditions in Center City and fathers commuting to their offices. By the end of the nineteenth century, however, the growing popularity of resorts along the Atlantic Ocean, in the Catskills, and in even more distant locations gave Philadelphians far more enticing options than the Bryn Mawr Hotel.[10]

As the Main Line became less attractive as a resort destination, it became more popular with commuters who made the daily trek to and from the city. The transition was gradual, and it did not please everyone. Through the time of the Civil War, gentlemen farmers dominated the area, overseeing estates that had been passed down from generation to generation, and they had little use for hotel guests, summer visitors, or daily commuters. One of the area's longtime residents, John W. Townsend, recalled nostalgically that "the Pennsylvania Railroad did not cater much to commuters in the Sixties. There were only six trains a day each way. If the 6 P. M. was missed there was nothing till 'the Emigrant' at midnight.... It was unpleasantly odiferous. There was naturally no going to the city for theatres, evening entertainments or club attractions." Commuters disembarked at the PRR's terminus in West Philadelphia, Townsend emphasized, necessitating a long walk or a horsecar ride to Center City. He noted that "'Haverford College Station,' like most other stations on the Line, was then only a dirty frame box, about six feet square and ten feet high." The characterization was not accurate, nor was it sufficient to discourage ever-increasing numbers of Philadelphians from intruding on Townsend's idyllic rural retreat.[11]

Whatever the accuracy of Townsend's statements, conditions gradually improved as an increasing number of permanent residents moved to the area. In 1876, as Wilson's new Real Estate Department was continuing to promote Bryn Mawr, there were a dozen trains a day into the city.[12] As part of the Whitehall line relocation, the PRR built new stations at Elm (renamed Narberth in 1892), Wynnewood, Haverford, and Bryn Mawr. The opening of Broad Street Station in December 1881 brought commuters directly into Center City, opposite city hall, and eliminated the streetcar transfer at West Philadelphia. In April 1882, the PRR established a new station, at 21st Street, along the Filbert Street Extension, that served "local accommodation trains" to a variety of destinations favored by commuters.[13] By that time, twenty-one trains offered service to Bryn Mawr each weekday, with eighteen of them continuing

Merion, six miles west of Center-City Philadelphia, was near the eastern edge of commuter territory. While a fashionable community, it lacked the renown of more distant locales such as Bryn Mawr. The station, built in 1914, the parklike setting, and the well-groomed right-of-way attested to the quality of commuter service along the Main Line. *City Parks Association Photographs, courtesy of the Special Collections Research Center, Temple University Libraries, Philadelphia PA.*

to Paoli. They departed Broad Street Station every half hour through 6:45 p.m., providing adequate service for outbound commuters, while trains at 10:15 and 11:30 p.m. ensured that theatergoers would have ample opportunity to reach their suburban homes. Within a decade, commuters had access to trains that left Broad Street Station for Bryn Mawr every half hour between 6:15 a.m. and 10:45 p.m. In increasing numbers, they clutched multiple-ride commutation tickets, purchased at discounted ("commuted") prices that saved them money and gave a name to the activity that became one of the defining characteristics

of their lives. Such tickets, PRR publicists emphasized in 1894, were "sold at a rate that places them within the purse-power of every class of people. The commutation rates, considering the quality of the service, have been reduced to the lowest figure at which passengers can be carried with any percentage of profit."[14]

The first generation of Main Line residents scarcely needed to worry about limits on their purse power, as their large estates attested to their wealth and social standing. Their ranks included numerous Pennsylvania Railroad executives who were now favoring the area over the older community of Chestnut Hill. Frank Thomson resided in Merion, while Vice President Charles E. Pugh preferred Overbrook. Yet nothing could match Cheswold, Alexander Cassatt's estate along Montgomery Avenue in Haverford. Designed by Henry Augustus Sims, civil engineer turned architect, construction began in 1872 on a project that eventually cost $50,000. Cassatt's passion for horses motivated his support for carriage roads through the area and induced him to purchase Chesterbrook Farm in Berwyn, farther west along the Main Line. Cassatt's protégé, Samuel Rea, occupied a less grandiose home that stood half a block from the station at Bryn Mawr.[15]

Many representatives from the upper-middle class were joining the wealthy along the Main Line. In 1880, financier Anthony J. Drexel and George W. Childs, the editor of *The Public Ledger*, purchased a large tract of land near Louella. They chose a more glamorous name for the community, in honor of Revolutionary War hero "Mad" Anthony Wayne. In response to criticism that Wayne was too far from Philadelphia, Childs responded that it would give commuters on the Pennsylvania Railroad sufficient time to read the *Ledger* before their train arrived in Center City. Rapid growth occurred in other communities, many of which adopted fashionable Welsh-sounding names. Eagle, midway between Strafford and Devon, fell by the wayside. Morgan's Corners gained status as Radnor, and Athensville became Ardmore, just as Whitehall was transformed into Bryn Mawr. The renamed communities joined Wayne, Rosemont, Wynnewood, Narberth, Merion, Overbrook, and the long-established town of Haverford as suburban enclaves. In 1915, the Pennsylvania Railroad completed the electrification of the Main Line, as far west as Paoli. For many decades, that community would be the customary outer limit of the commuter territory that began at Overbrook, where the tracks left city limits and crossed into Montgomery County. The PRR operated five other commuter routes in Philadelphia and a great many more that served other cities, but none could match the aura of the one along the Main Line. "Nothing," wrote Christopher Morley in 1952, "was so holy as the Local to Paoli."[16]

Few others described the Pennsylvania Railroad's commuter services in such lyrical or affectionate terms. Longtime Main Liner John Townsend, who expressed himself in a manner that was both nostalgic and acerbic, was as critical of the PRR's passenger operations in the 1920s as he had been in the 1860s. Broad Street Station had long since replaced the inadequate facilities in West Philadelphia, but at least in the old days "there was no herding behind iron bars, like animals in a Zoo, and no gate slammed in one's face when the time to go has come, whether the train goes or not." Generations of commuters empathized with that experience, as they followed the well-established channels that led from home to train to work and back again. Like Townsend, they both cursed and depended on the railroad that conveyed them between suburb and city, bemoaning late trains, crowded cars, inadequate heat, and air-conditioning that depended entirely on their ability to force open a window. Pennsylvania Railroad executives may have bragged about inexpensive "commutation rates, considering the quality of the service," but many commuters

judged the cost to be far too high and the level of amenities far too low.[17]

Townsend's self-described "meanderings of an old man's memories" identified the Pennsylvania Railroad's role in fostering a complex and not entirely symbiotic relationship between the cities and their suburbs. "Unfortunately for the city," he concluded, "this western movement has taken many prominent and helpful citizens out of civic life. . . . These Philadelphia emigrants pay no taxes to the city where they earn their living, but when they travel they register from 'Philadelphia.'" In Philadelphia, New York, and elsewhere, the tracks of the Pennsylvania Railroad passed through many political jurisdictions. The lines on a map, invisible to commuters reading their newspapers or staring listlessly out the window, represented bastions and fortress walls in an unending battle to determine who would pay for the services that connected the suburbs and the city. When it came to matters of funding, the commuter operations that were vital to everyone were always someone else's problem.[18]

For the company that operated commuter trains, the interrelationship between revenues and expenses was, in the final analysis, the Pennsylvania Railroad's problem. The 1894 assertion that ticket prices "have been reduced to the lowest figure at which passengers can be carried with any percentage of profit" was accurate and left precious little allowance for deleterious changes in business conditions. On the Main Line, on Long Island, and elsewhere, low commutation rates fostered suburban development. Commuters came to expect low rates as their due, for a routine yet vital journey that they made for reasons of necessity rather than pleasure. Rising wages, higher taxes, and more expensive supplies increased the cost of the PRR's operations, yet suburbanites saw little reason why those factors should affect ticket prices. The twice-daily surge of short-haul passenger traffic in and out of the city represented a poor model for the utilization of crews, equipment, and the physical plant, but office workers demanded fares that were lower than those on intercity trips with balanced demand patterns. The construction of expressways and feeder roads, the proliferation of automobiles, and the eventual transition to a five-day workweek reduced patronage, but not the insistence of passengers, politicians, and regulatory agencies that high-quality commuter rail service should remain widely available.[19]

The suburban exodus greatly increased the number of people who traveled to and from the city center each day, but with scant benefit for the commuter railroads. As early as the 1920s, Pennsylvania Railroad executives identified disturbing trends in commuter traffic. The general prosperity of the decade, coupled with a pervasive belief that the railroads were both monopolistic and invulnerable, ensured that regulators and other public officials were largely insensitive to the problem. The economic crisis of the 1930s was so pervasive that it masked many of the structural issues associated with commuter rail. Tire and gasoline rationing during World War II produced a surge in traffic and revenues but left commuters with unpleasant memories of crowded trains and substandard equipment. After 1945, however, no one who truly understood either railroads or cities could deny the scope of the problem. The voters who flocked to the suburbs called on elected officials to finance the construction of new highways, confident that those transportation arteries would eliminate traffic congestion. The assumption was mistaken, as new roads generated an increased demand for travel, which in turn bred delays and gridlock. Frustrated motorists demanded more highways but balked at tax increases to pay for them. Few suburbanites wished to live near railroad tracks, and they were generally unwilling to walk long distances to the nearest station. They could drive to a park-and-ride lot, but once in their cars, most preferred to continue all the way to the city center. Suburban shopping malls lured housewives who in days past might have taken a commuter train into the city, while the popularity of television kept the evening theater crowd off the rails. By the 1950s, commuter rail ridership was increasingly concentrated into the morning and afternoon rush hours, with little demand during the remainder of the day. As such, the PRR and other carriers found themselves in the perverse position of having inadequate equipment and facilities to serve peak demand, even as overall patronage declined precipitously.

By the late 1950s, Pennsylvania Railroad executives, joined by their counterparts on other carriers, were pleading for relief. The statistics that they provided to the federal government attested to the commutation crisis. The PRR's commuter traffic peaked in 1923, at nearly 72.4 million revenue passengers, representing 48.9 percent of total passenger traffic. In 1956, commuters still accounted for 37.9 percent of the railroad's passenger business, but only 11.2 percent of passenger miles and 8.7 percent of passenger revenue—a clear indication of the short-haul and low-fare nature of the traffic. Despite the decline in business, in 1956 nearly 23.7 million people a year rode to and from their jobs along the tracks of the PRR. The statistics indicated two incompatible realities. Commuter service was vital to the cities the Pennsylvania Railroad served and could not be eliminated, yet it would have to be scaled back or abandoned, if the company were to survive. For PRR executives, "commuted" traffic suggested an alternate meaning,

one that had little to do with discounted multiride tickets. Required by law to accept the punishing effects of commuter traffic, they sought to reduce or curtail that sentence as much as possible. To do so, they would have to enlist government officials as allies, pledging to increase mobility in the metropolis while threatening to abandon urban residents to an overcrowded highway network.[20]

The awareness of the extent of the commuter problem began first at the municipal level, in cities such as New York and Philadelphia, and quickly spread to the nation's capital. Politicians and urban planners concluded that commuter railroads offered the only alternative to exponential increases in highway funding. Federal regulators also perceived that staggering losses incurred in commuter services threatened the overall financial health and even the survival of the Pennsylvania Railroad and many other carriers in the Northeast. That realization influenced Florida Democrat George A. Smathers, who chaired a Senate subcommittee investigating the railroad crisis.[21] "Because of the burden that these losing intrastate services are imposing on interstate commerce," Smathers observed in April 1958, "the Federal Government can no longer stand aside to the extent it has in the past."[22]

The dawning realization of the scope of the postwar commuter crisis was not accompanied by any clear or immediate solutions. In the past, the ICC or state regulatory agencies could raise rates to a level sufficient to guarantee a fair return on investment. That strategy would do little to alleviate the burden of commuter traffic, however, as it would only entice more people to leave the railroads and take to the highways, while incurring fierce opposition from urban and suburban politicians. "It is evident that fares which would theoretically return a profit for the railroads," Smathers acknowledged, "would generally result in charges substantially greater than commuters are accustomed to paying and, in some instances, prohibitive charges." Despite his assertion that the federal government could no longer sidestep the issue, the senator maintained that "the commuter service problem is a local one having both social and economic implications." Under those circumstances, he thought "it desirable to leave to the local government agencies involved the job of seeking specifically tailored solutions to their particular problem." It was a realistic assessment of the situation, given the initial reluctance of federal officials to intervene in state and municipal affairs. Smathers's advice nonetheless characterized local government as a monolithic entity, whose representatives would work in harmony to resolve a crisis that threatened them all. It was an inaccurate perception that ignored deep divisions between cities and their suburbs. By the time of the Smathers Committee hearings, officials at all levels of government had concluded that something must be done to save the commuter services operated by the Pennsylvania Railroad and other carriers. Yet no one could agree on precisely what they should do. For more than a decade, representatives from urban, suburban, state, and national governments alternately cooperated with and battled against one another, even as the Pennsylvania Railroad and its counterparts moved closer to financial collapse.[23]

Commuting in Greater New York

Greater New York was the largest city in the United States and home to one of the most extensive commuter rail systems in the world. The Pennsylvania Railroad operated three principal commuter services in the region. One followed the heavily trafficked route between New York and Philadelphia. Commuter trains operated as far south as Trenton, although most people who worked in Manhattan did not venture that far afield.[24] Princeton, linked by a short branch to the main line at Princeton Junction, was the most prestigious source of commuter traffic. A substantial number of New Jersey commuters worked in Newark, which through the 1950s provided employment for many middle and lower managers in banks, department stores, and corporate headquarters. The opening of Penn Station in 1910 greatly facilitated commuting to Midtown but was of little practical benefit to the larger number of New Jersey residents headed for Lower Manhattan. Many detrained at Newark, taking the Hudson & Manhattan Railroad to the Hudson Terminal at the intersection of Church and Cortlandt Streets. The Hudson Tubes also served Exchange Place, the PRR's rail terminal in Jersey City. Until January 1950, commuters had the option of taking a Pennsylvania Railroad ferry from Exchange Place to the foot of Cortlandt Street in Manhattan.[25] They joined thousands of others who utilized the ferries that called at the Communipaw Terminal of the Central Railroad of New Jersey; the Erie's Pavonia Terminal; the Hoboken facility of the Delaware, Lackawanna & Western; and the Weehawken Terminal of the New York Central's West Shore Railroad subsidiary.[26]

A less conventional service connected Penn Station and Exchange Place with the once-fashionable New Jersey shore community of Long Branch. During the 1870s, the New York & Long Branch Railroad, a subsidiary of the Jersey Central, built a new line from Perth Amboy, southeasterly toward Long Branch, and eventually as far south as Bay Head. The PRR also constructed a line to Bay Head

in 1881—although the tracks approached from the south via Camden and Pemberton. Pennsylvania Railroad executives contemplated a northern extension yet ultimately elected to compromise with the Jersey Central. The 1882 agreement that gave the Pennsylvania Railroad trackage rights over the NY&LB initially facilitated travel from Philadelphia to resorts along the Jersey Shore. The depression of the 1890s, coupled with moralistic crusades against drinking, gambling, and horse racing ended the allure of Long Branch, and it became a working-class resort. Outlying areas—including Asbury Park and Bay Head to the south and Sea Bright through Rumson to Red Bank in the north—provided summer homes for wealthy New Yorkers. They could afford to pay for a long commute, and they demanded the amenities that befitted their status and that typically exceeded anything available along Philadelphia's Main Line. The PRR named the principal commuter trains on the New York & Long Branch—something that was also seen on the Long Island Rail Road and other lines that served Greater New York. The best known, largely because of its longevity, was *The Broker*, but there were many others.[27] Prior to the Great Depression, many trains carried parlor cars and bar cars. When economic conditions forced the PRR to retrench, private commuter clubs paid the railroad to operate deluxe equipment solely for their members.[28]

Middle-class and even working-class commuters eventually joined their wealthier counterparts on the New York & Long Branch. Workers from communities such as Elizabeth, Newark, and Jersey City found it more convenient to use the NY&LB rather than the Pennsylvania Railroad's more westerly route between Philadelphia and New York. In 1912, seven daily NY&LB trains operated into Penn Station, diverting from the Jersey Central's tracks at Woodbridge Junction, just north of Perth Amboy. A further five went to the Exchange Place terminal. The PRR also offered direct New York & Long Branch service into Midtown, a route that appealed to outbound beach goers as well as inbound commuters. By terminating other NY&LB trains at Jersey City, the PRR preserved track capacity at Penn Station and avoided the need to change from steam to electric power. As such, neither the Pennsylvania Railroad nor the Jersey Central could justify the cost of electrifying the route, and PRR steam locomotives remained in service on the New York & Long Branch until 1957.[29]

The Pennsylvania Railroad's commuter traffic in New Jersey was substantial but paled in comparison to the business conducted by its subsidiary in New York. The Long Island Rail Road carried more people than any

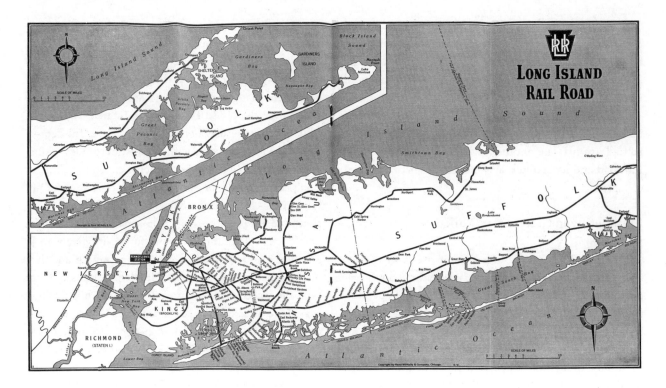

Originally part of a short-lived rail-and-water route between New York and Boston, by the 1880s the Long Island Rail Road served farmers, vacationers, and a growing number of commuters. The Pennsylvania Railroad gained control of the LIRR in 1900, electrified the busiest portions, and beginning in 1910 brought commuters directly to Midtown Manhattan. Decade by decade suburbia expanded outward, from the boroughs of Brooklyn and Queens east into Nassau County and eventually into Suffolk County. Rising costs and competition from an expanding subway and highway network drove the PRR subsidiary into bankruptcy in 1948, a year after this map appeared in timetables. *Author's collection.*

other company in the United States, and it was the only Class I carrier to earn more than half of its revenues from passenger traffic. The LIRR, which operated fewer than four hundred route miles, carried more than 72.7 million passengers in 1920—nearly 40 percent of the number that traveled on the entire Pennsylvania Railroad system. Yet the LIRR's aggregate passenger mileage was less than 17 percent of the nearly 6.3 billion miles generated by its corporate parent, a reflection of the short but frequent trips undertaken by most commuters. That circumstance contributed to an operating deficit of $1.3 million in 1920. Each time the wheels of an LIRR passenger train rolled across a mile of track, the company lost another 21.5 cents. The situation was the same in most years, as even large passenger volumes could not compensate for wages, taxes, and real

estate costs that were among the highest in the country. As an independent company, the problems—and possibly their solutions—would have been readily apparent. As a subsidiary of the Pennsylvania Railroad, however, the situation was far more complicated.[30]

The Long Island Rail Road, chartered in 1834, was originally part of a rail and water link between New York and Boston, through the ferry terminal at Greenport. The completion of the New Haven's all-rail route in December 1848 caused LIRR managers to solicit local traffic. As early as 1854, promoters organized parallel, competing railroads that drew traffic from the LIRR. During the 1870s, the LIRR absorbed those rival lines, creating what amounted to a transportation monopoly on Long Island. The company nonetheless entered bankruptcy in 1877, largely as result of the severe economic depression that began in 1873. New York investment banker Austin Corbin acquired a controlling interest in the railroad, and beginning in December 1880, he served as its receiver. Corbin reorganized the LIRR, became its president in October 1881, and oversaw improvements in service and the construction of new lines. By the late 1800s, an increasing number of commuters traveled on the LIRR to Long Island City before boarding ferries that would take them across the East River to Manhattan. The LIRR's other western terminus, at Flatbush Avenue, was far less convenient. Travelers there faced a transfer to a streetcar or elevated railway to reach a ferry or, after 1883, the Brooklyn Bridge. The lines to Long Island City and to Flatbush Avenue converged at Jamaica, the most important junction on the Long Island Rail Road. From there a network of branches fanned out—south to Far Rockaway and Long Beach, north to Port Washington and affluent Oyster Bay, and east as far as Greenport and Montauk. Whether they hailed from blue-collar suburbs, worked in middle-class professions, or enjoyed the elite prerogatives of a drink and a card game in a parlor car, most of the LIRR's commuters became familiar with the oft-repeated instruction to "change at Jamaica."[31]

After assuming the presidency of the Pennsylvania Railroad in June 1899, Alexander J. Cassatt pushed forward plans to take the PRR into Manhattan. He also favored a connection with the New Haven, via Long Island and a new bridge over the East River. Thus, in 1900, the board of directors voted to purchase substantially all the outstanding stock and bonds of the Long Island Rail Road. Following the completion of the New York Improvements, PRR trains traveled through the East River tunnels from Manhattan to the Sunnyside Yard on Long Island via the tracks owned by the Pennsylvania Tunnel & Terminal Railroad Company, another PRR subsidiary. Some continued north over the New York Connecting Railroad (since 1902, jointly owned by the PRR and the New Haven) and across the Hell Gate Bridge and access to New England.

The close financial and administrative relationship between the Pennsylvania Railroad and the Long Island Rail Road continued long after Cassatt's death. The LIRR's corporate offices were located at Pennsylvania Station in New York, and PRR executives ensured that the two companies maintained a close strategic relationship. The Long Island Rail Road rented locomotives and rolling stock from its parent company and paid fees for the use of PRR facilities, particularly those associated with Penn Station. The PRR underwrote the cost of extensive improvements that benefited the LIRR far more than the parent company. They included the installation of third-rail electrification along heavily traveled routes in Brooklyn and Queens, as well as the purchase of all-steel, multiple-unit cars for commuter service. Between 1903 and 1905, workers completed the Atlantic Avenue Improvements. The massive grade separation project used a succession of tunnels and elevated structures to carry the busy main line from the LIRR's Flatbush Avenue terminal in Brooklyn to the East New York station. The remainder of the route, east to Jamaica and a junction with the line originating at Penn Station, remained largely at street level, suggesting that further construction would soon be necessary.

The relationship between the PRR and its subsidiary created problems for managers at both companies. First, it was difficult to accurately divide the cost of shared facilities between each carrier. Should PRR executives set the rental fees at Penn Station at a level that was too low, they would be depriving their company of the moneys rightfully due from the LIRR. High rental rates, however, left PRR managers open to charges that they were exploiting their LIRR subsidiary and gouging captive commuters on Long Island. Second, the LIRR was an intrastate railroad, yet it was closely affiliated with an interstate carrier. Its assets were in the New York City boroughs of Brooklyn and Queens, it offered service to Manhattan, and it operated in Nassau and Suffolk Counties, outside city limits. As such, it was not clear whether the Interstate Commerce Commission or state and local regulatory agencies held jurisdiction over fares and conditions of service. At various times, PRR and LIRR executives, representatives for commuter groups, local and state officials, and Interstate Commerce Commission regulators asserted that the LIRR was or was not an interstate carrier, as they thought best suited their interests—and, on more than one occasion, they changed their position on that issue, to exploit conflicts between different levels of government.

Jurisdictional disagreements began early in the twentieth century. In 1907, New York governor Charles Evans Hughes gave his support to the Page-Merritt Public Utilities Act. The new law created two regulatory commissions, each possessing considerable authority over rates and services for railroad, mass-transit, gas, and electric companies. Effective July 1, 1907, the Public Service Commission for the First District replaced the Board of Rapid Transit Railroad Commissioners as the regulatory agency overseeing rail service in the five boroughs. The agency's responsibilities included oversight of the Dual Contracts, a 1913 agreement by the city, the Interborough Rapid Transit Company, and the Brooklyn Rapid Transit Company to expand the subway system. The corresponding state agency, the Public Service Commission for the Second District, oversaw railroad and utilities regulation outside New York City—an area that included Nassau and Suffolk Counties on the eastern end of Long Island.[32]

While the Long Island Rail Road operated solely within the state of New York, the Interstate Commerce Commission also governed its operations. In 1914, the US Supreme Court expanded the ICC's control over intrastate rates, particularly where freight charges between points within a state placed comparable interstate traffic at a competitive disadvantage.[33] The Transportation Act of 1920 further strengthened the agency, now empowered to establish tariffs that would guarantee a uniform rate of return among all carriers. The first test of the ICC's authority occurred later that year. Railroad executives across the United States petitioned the commission for sweeping rate adjustments, in compensation for wartime inflation and rapidly escalating labor costs. In August, the ICC granted a 20 percent increase in passenger fares. The ruling was of great potential benefit to the LIRR, a company with little freight traffic, and executives raised ticket prices accordingly. The Public Service Commission for the Second District exercised its jurisdictional authority and blocked increases in intrastate passenger fares throughout the state. In November, ICC officials overruled the state PSC, based on the precedent established in 1914 and on the enhanced authority afforded by the Transportation Act of 1920. Allowing state regulatory commissions to mandate per-mile intrastate rates that were lower than comparable interstate fares, the commissioners argued, constituted discrimination and imperiled the ability of carriers to generate a uniform and equitable return on investment. Justice Russell Benedict, representing the Second Department Appellate Division of the New York Supreme Court, sharply criticized the ICC's intervention into matters involving intrastate commerce, and he enjoined the Long Island Rail Road from complying with the ICC directive to increase rates. The court voided the injunction in January 1921, on the grounds that state courts lacked the authority to block the actions of federal agencies. LIRR officials immediately announced a 20 percent fare increase, but the company received less benefit than did any of the sixty-two other railroads that provided intrastate passenger service in New York. The changes did not apply to commuters or schoolchildren, as that traffic was clearly intrastate in nature and lacked a corresponding interstate basis for comparison. As a result, ticket prices on the traffic that accounted for two-thirds of the LIRR's revenues remained unchanged through the Roaring Twenties, the Great Depression, and World War II.[34]

John Francis Hylan, mayor of New York between 1918 and 1925, caused further damage to the Long Island Rail Road. A self-styled populist with ties to Tammany Hall, Hylan made low-cost mobility a central tenant of his administration. He exploited widespread public sentiment asserting that the 1913 Dual Contracts represented a cozy duopoly that retarded the expansion of the vitally important subway system. By the time Hylan took office, the existing network was overburdened by wartime traffic, with inflation precluding sorely needed improvements and pay raises. Like many of his constituents, Hylan nonetheless held the five-cent subway fare as sacrosanct, blocking any increases that could provide additional revenue. Even though he had once worked as a motorman on the Brooklyn Union Elevated Railroad, a constituent company of the BRT, Hylan was unconcerned that the nickel fare also

John Francis Hylan (1868–1936) was the grandstanding, populist mayor of New York City between 1918 and 1925. He held the nickel subway fare to be sacrosanct, and he supported the construction of a municipally owned transit network, as a mechanism to exert control over the Interborough Rapid Transit Company and the Brooklyn–Manhattan Transit Corporation. Hylan also attacked the alliance between the PRR and the Long Island Rail Road—which, he claimed, was responsible for imposing unconscionably high fares on commuters from the boroughs of Brooklyn and Queens. *George Grantham Bain Collection, Library of Congress, Prints & Photographs Division.*

undermined efforts by rapid-transit employees to secure higher pay. Inadequate wages contributed to a November 1918 strike by BRT employees. The situation soon became horrific, when an ill-prepared replacement motorman caused an accident at Malbone Street, killing more than ninety passengers. Outraged New Yorkers demanded manslaughter charges against the BRT as well as a complete overhaul of the subway system, and Hylan enthusiastically supported both requests.[35]

While BRT personnel escaped manslaughter convictions, Hylan's efforts to transform the subway system eventually proved more successful. In 1919, Hylan appointed fellow Tammany stalwart John H. Delaney to the new post of transit construction commissioner.

Delaney commissioned transportation engineer Daniel Lawrence Turner to prepare an ambitious plan, completed in September 1920, for a massive expansion in the subway, elevated, and streetcar systems. Turner envisioned a $350 million program that would add 830 miles of track, substantially greater than the existing Dual Contract lines. Hylan and Delaney counted on the support of Governor Alfred E. Smith, given that all three individuals were connected with the Tammany Hall political machine. The victory of reformer Nathan L. Miller in the 1920 gubernatorial elections derailed those plans and prompted the new governor to establish tighter control over transit operation in New York City. Despite Hylan's vitriolic protests against the loss of local political autonomy, in March 1921 the state legislature replaced the First District and Second District commissions with a single, statewide Public Service Commission. The redesigned PSC regulated all energy and telecommunications within the state of New York and possessed authority over railroad operations outside the city of New York. Its remit included LIRR operations in Nassau and Suffolk Counties. A new state agency, the Transit Commission, oversaw rail service within the five boroughs, including that offered by the Long Island Rail Road. Hylan refused to acknowledge the authority of the Transit Commission and celebrated Smith's return to the governor's office in January 1923. In February 1924, following prolonged negotiations between Smith and the state's Republican political leaders, the legislature limited the responsibilities of the Transit Commission to the LIRR and other privately owned rail lines within the city of New York. A new agency, the New York City Board of Transportation, fulfilled a part of Hylan's ambition, giving Tammany loyalists control over the completion of the Dual Contracts and the construction and operation of a new subway network. The arrangement also precluded the development of an integrated transportation system in Greater New York, with authority divided between rival city and state agencies.[36]

Work soon began on the Independent City-Owned Subway System, rivaling the privately funded Interborough Rapid Transit Company and Brooklyn-Manhattan Transit Corporation, the 1923 successor to the Brooklyn Rapid Transit Company. The success of the IND's expansion program depended heavily on the ability of its new rapid-transit lines to attract commuters in Brooklyn and Queens, boroughs that accounted for a substantial portion of the LIRR's traffic. Political pressure ensured that fares on all the city's subway, elevated, and surface lines remained at five cents, a situation that did not change until 1948. That nickel fare created an upper limit on the LIRR's

rates and ensured that, as rapid transit expanded, the railroad retreated into Nassau and Suffolk Counties. The 1924 legislation that created the Board of Transportation also stipulated that a municipally owned transit system would eventually have to become self-supporting. Hylan and Delaney (who became the first chairman of the new agency) thus possessed two powerful incentives to attack the Long Island Rail Road. In addition to the competition between the LIRR and the IND, Hylan was eager to please his many constituents who complained about high fares and poor service on the PRR's subsidiary.[37]

Coinciding with Hylan's tenure as mayor, the growing population of Long Island and the increasing popularity of the automobile created additional problems for the LIRR. Urban and suburban development increased land values, producing a 650 percent rise in the company's property taxes between 1903 and 1922. The latter amount—nearly $1.8 million—consumed 23.3 percent of the net revenue generated by railway operations. Company officials claimed that nearly $94,000 of the tax bill went to pay for the construction of highways that drew riders away from the railroad. The increase in auto traffic contributed to a spate of accidents at grade crossings and accelerated political pressure to minimize such tragedies. World War I and the postwar recession postponed those efforts, but by July 1922, LIRR officials had conceded the necessity for improvements. Following a meeting with the Transit Commission, they agreed to eliminate four grade crossings near Jamaica, as part of an effort to increase the main line to four tracks through the area. Representatives from municipal and state governments funded a third of the $1.5 million cost, but the LIRR was responsible for the remainder. Railroad personnel reminded regulators that the project was likely to spur calls for other, equally expensive changes to the physical plant.[38]

The warning proved prophetic. In January 1923, the Transit Commission ordered the LIRR to eliminate all highway crossings along its main line between Jamaica and the eastern border of the city. The following month Acting Mayor George Murray Hulbert called for the removal of all grade crossings within city limits. During 1922, Hulbert emphasized, collisions between automobiles and LIRR trains had killed three people and injured twenty others. He asked the state legislature to support "humanitarian legislation" to remedy the problem, while cautioning that "past experience has demonstrated that in the matter of elimination of grade crossings valuable time is consumed through obstacles of delay, usually indulged in by the Long Island Railroad." Hulbert's demand helped to reawaken public opposition to the LIRR's operations along Atlantic

Avenue in Brooklyn. The Atlantic Avenue Improvements, completed two decades earlier, left portions of the route between East New York and Jamaica at ground level. Maurice E. Connolly, the president of Queens Borough, dubbed the LIRR tracks along Atlantic Avenue as "the greatest railroad menace to the world." His further comment that LIRR officials were "stubborn and unreasonable" likewise echoed Hulbert's claims of obstructionism. In the summer of 1925, the Transit Commission proposed a ten-year program along the lines that Hulbert had suggested. That fall, Smith announced his support for an amendment to that state constitution, permitting the legislature to appropriate $300 million to pay a quarter of the cost associated with the elimination of highway crossings. Local communities contributed an equal share, with railroads responsible for the remaining half of the expense. The Public Service Commission counted 455 crossings along the LIRR and estimated that $55.7 million would be required to remedy the problem.[39] Even though the railroad was responsible for only half of that amount, it nonetheless represented a substantial drain on the corporate treasury. New Yorkers who feared for their lives at grade crossings also objected to the pollution produced by the relatively small number of steam locomotives that served the city. The 1923 Kaufman Act mandated the operation of electric locomotives within city limits after January 1, 1926. Long Island Rail Road officials estimated that compliance would cost between $25 million and $40 million, asked for an extension in the deadline, and did their best to respond to accusations that such delays represented a deliberate effort to obstruct the will of the people.[40]

In his dual role as a PRR and LIRR executive, George LeBoutillier (1876–1952) bore the brunt of Hylan's attacks. His efforts to coordinate the operations of the two companies and to use the Pennsylvania Railroad's resources to help its subsidiary ensured that Long Islanders had access to inexpensive, reliable transportation. Many commuters nonetheless asserted that LeBoutillier was enriching the PRR at their expense. *Collection of the Historical Society of Pennsylvania.*

Rates and Rentals at Penn Station

George LeBoutillier, the vice president of the LIRR, bore the brunt of attacks from Mayor Hylan, disgruntled commuters, and fractious residents of local communities. Like many other senior managers, LeBoutillier began his career as a rodman, in his case in 1895 on the PRR's Lines West of Pittsburgh and Erie. He earned promotion to division engineer in 1903 and division superintendent eleven years later. With the end of federal oversight in March 1920, LeBoutillier became the general superintendent of the Eastern Pennsylvania Grand Division. By January 1923, LIRR president Ralph Peters was in poor health and requested that LeBoutillier serve as his vice president, assistant, and eventual successor. Peters died less than eleven months later, giving LeBoutillier an opportunity to restore the company's financial health and public image. Educated at

the University of Cincinnati, he was probably more articulate and personable than many other railroad executives. LeBoutillier won praise for his decision to commute to work by train rather than automobile, to gain firsthand experience of the LIRR's service. "With precisely the spirit which the late Count Tolstoy displayed in eating and dressing like a moujik and working as hard as anybody in his own fields," the *Brooklyn Daily Eagle* editorialized, "his devotion and self-sacrifice cannot be too highly commended." Yet LeBoutillier was trained as an engineer and had honed his craft as an expert in operating matters. He possessed limited experience with the complex task of navigating through a landscape of politicians, journalists, and concerned citizens. LeBoutillier had been on the job

Harried Long Island Rail Road commuters rarely saw the grand interior spaces of Penn Station. Instead, they scuttled in and out of the building through separate entrances, segregated from intercity passengers. Their fares nonetheless paid for the upkeep of the entire building, leading many to wonder if they were being exploited and forced to subsidize the Pennsylvania Railroad. *Courtesy of the New York Transit Museum.*

for less than six months when federal Prohibition agents raided his private car, confiscated twenty-two cases of wine, whiskey, and gin, and arrested Charles Jones, the steward who was unlucky enough to be on board. Despite Jones's rather implausible assertion that the alcohol was his personal property, the agents seized the car as contraband. Mayor Hylan and most of his constituents were at best lackluster supporters of Prohibition, and the incident probably elicited more amusement than outrage. The media coverage nonetheless suggested that both LeBoutillier and

the Long Island Rail Road were very much in the public eye.[41]

LeBoutillier's honeymoon was regrettably brief, as his arrival coincided with efforts by PRR officials to reallocate the costs associated with the operation of Penn Station. Since 1910, LIRR trains bound for Manhattan had traveled through the East River tunnels and into their Manhattan terminus, over the tracks of the Pennsylvania Tunnel & Terminal Railroad Company. For the privilege of using the station, the tunnels, and a portion of Sunnyside Yard in Queens, the LIRR paid an annual rental to the PT&T— although as both companies were Pennsylvania Railroad subsidiaries, there was little internal disagreement regarding the terms of the lease.

At the beginning of the twentieth century, President Cassatt envisioned a monumental gateway that would welcome intercity passengers to New York, and he badly underestimated the population growth that would occur on Long Island in the following decades. During the 1910s, Manhattan's population decreased slightly, while the number of residents in Brooklyn and Queens increased by 30 percent. Commuters soon overwhelmed the inadequate waiting room and concourse set aside for their use. By the end of 1916, Penn Station had been in operation less than a decade, but construction crews had completed three major expansions of the Long Island Rail Road facilities. In that year, more than 13.2 million people boarded or disembarked from LIRR trains in Manhattan. They accounted for 73 percent of the passenger volume at Penn Station, nearly three times the level of PRR patronage. The situation was the reverse of what Cassatt had envisioned little more than a decade earlier. In 1919, the first full year of peace and the last full year of federal oversight, the LIRR transported more than 19.8 million commuters in and out of Penn Station. Over the years that followed, rising real estate prices and worsening congestion pushed suburbanites further east, beyond city limits and into Nassau County, increasing the Long Island Rail Road's dependence on Penn Station.[42]

The unexpected imbalance between commuter and intercity traffic rendered untenable the June 1912 agreement that governed the shared use of Penn Station. The LIRR paid the Pennsylvania Tunnel & Terminal (and thus the PRR) $156,000 annual rental for trackage rights west of Sunnyside Yard. By 1922, the fee had increased to $300,000, but that was still far below the LIRR's share of the cost associated with maintaining tracks, platforms, signals, and other infrastructure—to say nothing of the provision of electricity that powered multiple-unit commuter equipment.[43] Even though the LIRR accounted for more than 70 percent of the traffic at Penn Station, the company paid only 35 percent of the facility's operating costs. In one respect, the subsidization was irrelevant, as the artificially low rental improved the LIRR's financial performance, and any resulting profits could—in theory—simply be transferred to its corporate parent. In practice, however, the LIRR routinely operated at a deficit, and the losses would only increase if the company paid a fair share for its use of Penn Station. Commuters, politicians, and regulators took the existing arrangements for granted. They saw little need to accept higher ticket prices, particularly as Long Island commuters rarely used the grand public spaces in Penn Station. Fares thus remained low, and in 1919, the LIRR earned only 1.526 cents per passenger mile, while the New York Central and the New Haven—the other two companies that provided commuters with direct rail access to Manhattan—generated 2.527 and 2.212 cents per passenger mile, respectively.[44]

In September 1923, however, Pennsylvania Railroad officials sought permission from the Transit Commission to raise the LIRR's annual rental for tracks and facilities at Penn Station. For the railroads' executives, it was a straightforward matter of bringing the financial relationship between the two companies into alignment with their operating and traffic patterns. After all, they argued, since the station had opened in 1910, the number of LIRR passengers at Penn Station had tripled, while the company's rental fees at that facility had only doubled. It was appropriate, argued Pennsylvania Railroad vice president Albert County, that his company should earn a modest 4 percent return—equivalent to slightly more than $3.3 million—on the money that it had devoted to the New York Improvements. That would only be possible, he continued, if the LIRR paid its proportionate share, amounting to approximately $1.8 million. The possibility of a sixfold increase in the LIRR's rental payments, however reasonable, generated widespread condemnation from Long Islanders and their elected officials. More than two-thirds of the LIRR's passengers did not use Penn Station or the East River tunnels, and they saw little reason why they should have to pay for those facilities. With the company operating at a loss, many suspected—correctly—that a request for higher ticket prices would soon follow.[45]

Unhappily for George LeBoutillier, the beginning of his tenure as the LIRR's vice president coincided with the reassessment of rental payments, a rapid increase in the company's operating costs, growing complaints regarding service, and Mayor Hylan's campaign to defend local political and regulatory autonomy. In July 1923, a committee of one hundred prominent Long Island residents presented LeBoutillier and PRR president Samuel Rea with a list of suggestions for improvement. They included faster and more frequent trains, in effect transforming the LIRR into a rapid-transit line, at least within city limits. The committee members also recommended schedules that would preclude the need for passengers to transfer at Jamaica, where the routes to Penn Station and to Flatbush Avenue converged—an activity that had long been the bane of commuters. While they did not explicitly state that the Pennsylvania Railroad should pay for those changes, they nonetheless asserted that the larger company should assume direct operation of its smaller subsidiary. LeBoutillier emphasized the engineering and financial difficulties associated with the committee's recommendations, which he predicted would cost a quarter of a billion dollars. He attempted to co-opt their recommendations by pledging a ten-year, $84 million improvement program—which, he emphasized, could only be funded by the earnings of the Long Island Rail Road and not its corporate parent. "I presume everybody is now 'watching me,' as they did Ralph Peters, to see how many more millions the beneficent Pennsylvania Railroad will contribute toward carrying out this tentative program," LeBoutillier warned, "but I'm afraid the Pennsylvania cow has already been milked dry, and the money will have to come from other sources." Given the heavily urbanized character of Greater New York, the bovine metaphor occurred with surprising frequency—usually employed by commuters who asserted that the money they paid for tickets flowed directly to the PRR's corporate headquarters in Philadelphia.[46]

Residents of Brooklyn and Queens turned to their elected officials for support, first at the federal level. Representative Emanuel Celler, a Democrat whose district included portions of both boroughs, was just beginning a fifty-year career in Congress. He found the LIRR a popular target, and in early 1924, he warned his constituents that the company was preparing to increase fares by 20 to 40 percent. On March 31, LeBoutillier confirmed those rumors and acknowledged that members of his staff were preparing applications for a joint hearing by the Transit Commission and the Public Service Commission. The additional revenue, LeBoutillier emphasized, would be used to pay the increased rental fees at Penn Station, eliminate grade crossings, comply with the Kaufman Act, acquire new equipment, and make other improvements in service. The members of the Transit Commission, who had approved the 1922 increase in rental payments, were likely to be receptive to those arguments. Celler therefore took his grievances to the PSC, claiming that the Transit Commission was as responsible as the Long Island Rail Road for the unacceptable conditions in his district. He also demanded an Interstate Commerce Commission investigation into the "most miserable" conditions along Atlantic Avenue and at the Flatbush Avenue terminal. ICC chairman Mark W. Potter suggested "that the company is dealing very well with a very difficult and trying situation" and refused to act. Some labor leaders detected a suspicious coincidence in the recent arrest of steward Charles Jones, and they suggested that LeBoutillier had intended to use the alcohol stored in his private car to bribe the freshman congressman into turning his attention elsewhere.[47]

Frustrated by the inaction of the ICC, the Transit Commission, and the Public Service Commission, commuters demanded to know why state and federal agencies had failed to protect them. They concluded that the local government would have to step into the breach. On April 16, LeBoutillier attended a meeting at Flushing High School. More than fifteen hundred people were gathered to protest curtailments in service on the Whitestone Branch,

a line that generated little traffic and substantial losses. Barely two weeks had passed since the announcement of the fare increase, and the attendees were in a combative mood. Wisely, LeBoutillier remained mute during the proceedings, but his silence provided Mayor Hylan with ample opportunity to air his grievances against both the LIRR and the Transit Commission. The grandstanding politician who said he had "come to listen" managed to do a considerable amount of talking as well. "The Vice President of the Long Island," Hylan asserted, "came here a few months ago from Chicago, and he's going to get away with jobs like this if the people will let him."[48] Driving home his characterization of LeBoutillier as an outsider, Hylan pointed a figure at the LIRR executive, exclaiming, "I don't know, sir, whether I've pronounced your name right, but if it's war you want, we are ready to start whenever you are!" The events of the evening suggested that neither the mayor nor the citizenry were likely to be supportive of LeBoutillier's request for higher fares.[49]

Long Island residents might not have shared Hylan's bombastic fervor, but they were equally determined to prevent the Long Island Rail Road from raising fares or decreasing service. They soon formed the Association of Long Island Commuters. Each of the organization's seventy-five vice presidents represented a different civic association, taxpayers' association, or chamber of commerce in communities scattered throughout Long Island. Together, they could mobilize some seventy-five thousand daily commuters and a quarter of a million residents. Thanks to Hylan's influence, the executive board enjoyed free use of the Jamaica town hall as a headquarters. The association's general counsel, Maurice Hotchner, took charge of negotiations with both the Transit Commission and the Public Service Commission, securing a postponement of the rate hearings and giving the coalition additional time to build political support. Hotchner also resurrected the long-standing Progressive Era allegation that LIRR stock was watered, presumably explaining the company's low dividends. While Hotchner worked behind the scenes, executive vice president Hobart Carson Fash rallied Long Islanders to the cause. His ancestors had settled the area when it was still a Dutch colony, and in more recent times, one of them served as an aide to George Washington. Fash edited the financial sections of the *New York Tribune* and the *New York Herald*, and he was both articulate and familiar with corporate spreadsheets.[50]

In the face of such well-organized opposition, LIRR officials soon abandoned their efforts to obtain fare increases as high as 40 percent. On June 24, they announced that 20 percent would now constitute the upper limit. Even then, their appearance at a joint session of the Transit Commission and the PSC did not go well. Hylan attended the first day's hearings, accompanied by corporation counsel George C. Nicholson. The mayor announced that he was merely a spectator who had no desire to influence the outcome of the proceedings, and he graciously if disingenuously asked the commissioners to ignore his presence. Regulatory officials showed little interest in LIRR data that demonstrated substantial increases in operating costs over the previous few years. Instead, they relied on the ICC's 1916 tentative valuation of the railroad's assets as a basis for determining a fair rate of return. Hobart Fash, speaking on behalf of the Association of Long Island Commuters, attacked anyone who believed that higher ticket prices were necessary. "A few sincere, though misguided, residents of Long Island," Fash declared, "have taken the position that perhaps it might be well to concede to the Long Island an increase in rates so that it may the better afford a greater efficiency of service, improved equipment and a general improvement in the facilities of the system." He instead insisted that the proposed fare increase would generate just enough money to pay for the added rental fees at Penn Station, with nothing left over for betterments. In that context, Fash insisted, higher ticket prices served solely as a mechanism to transfer money from the pockets of Long Island commuters to the corporate coffers of the Pennsylvania Railroad.[51]

Over the next few years, the Association of Long Island Commuters continued to do battle against the threat of higher ticket prices, although without the assistance of their chief spokesman. Hobart Fash, hailed as the "Paul Revere of Long Island," died of throat cancer in February 1925—the result, his supporters claimed, of having delivered so many speeches against the fare increase. "My doctors tell me that I have brought my present condition on myself by the campaign," Fash whispered from his deathbed, "but Long Islanders have shown that they can pull together and fight for a cause when once aroused." Newspapers labeled him a "martyr," and his followers did indeed continue their struggle without him. So did Mayor Hylan, as he entered his final months in office. Citing a "vehement expression of popular disapproval," he ordered corporation counsel Nicholson to "carry on the legal battle on behalf of the Long Island Railroad commuters" and block the company's "proposed extortion" of the city's voters. Not until July 4, 1925, did the Transit Commission reach an agreement regarding the LIRR's rental payments at Penn Station. Commissioner LeRoy T. Harkness emphasized "that nothing has developed in these hearings to question the good faith of the officials of the Pennsylvania and Long

Island companies in negotiating this agreement. Any loose talk of the Pennsylvania 'milking' the Long Island company is unsupported by a scintilla of evidence."[52]

Residents of Queens and Brooklyn, particularly those who lived along the dangerously congested Atlantic Avenue corridor, took little solace in the comments of Commissioner Harkness. They demanded that the remaining tracks along Atlantic Avenue, between East New York and Jamaica, be placed underground or on an elevated structure—something that could easily be done, they alleged, if Pennsylvania Railroad executives ceased shirking their responsibilities to the company that they owned and controlled. LeBoutillier informed the Transit Commissioners that "the Long Island is ready and willing at any time to discuss the situation with the city in an effort to solve the grade crossing problem," but he balked at the expense of relocating more of the line along Atlantic Avenue into a trench below street level. "I'll be perfectly frank with you," he informed the commissioners, "the Long Island is in no position to meet the expense of this track depression." Instead, he threatened to end service between Jamaica and Flatbush Avenue, asserting that "the Long Island wants to get out of Brooklyn."[53]

It was not the only potential curtailment of service. Rather than eliminate thirteen grade crossings on the chronically unprofitable Whitestone Branch, LeBoutillier announced that he was prepared to sell the line to the city. "This branch as a cold business proposition is losing money for the Long Island Railroad," he asserted. "I feel that the moral obligation of providing transit service for the communities on this branch rests more heavily upon the city than the Long Island Railroad. The entire line is within the boundaries of New York City and I feel that the city should take it over."[54] Queens Borough president Maurice Connolly had little patience with such threats. "The Long Island is continually crying poverty," he asserted. "It may not have the money in its own bank, but the Pennsylvania has it, and should pledge its credit as it has done before."[55]

Representatives from the city government and the Association of Long Island Commuters were thus convinced that the PRR could easily fund improvements to the Long Island Rail Road. They continued to resist the 20 percent fare increase that was still pending before the Transit Commission and the Public Service Commission. LeBoutillier attempted to persuade them of the LIRR's poor financial condition, but to no avail. Over the next five years, he testified, the carrier would need to spend $57 million on improvements—a sum that included a new $5 million terminal at Long Island City and $37.5 million to eliminate grade crossings. While PRR executives marshaled an impressive body of data to support their position, they nonetheless made comments that offered ample fodder for their critics. Hobart Rawson, an electrical engineer at the LIRR, testified that he hoped that Nassau and Suffolk Counties would stop gaining population, to reduce the burden on the railroad's facilities—a sentiment that LeBoutillier quickly refuted. Albert County, in his capacity as both an LIRR and PRR vice president, complained that commuters "still go on like Tennyson's brook, causing the railroad company to lose money."[56] When reminded that commuters comprised the bulk of the railroad's customers, County replied, "Yes, that is what keeps us poor." LeBoutillier emphasized that the LIRR had not paid dividends since 1896, four years before the Pennsylvania Railroad acquired control of the company. He could hardly deny that the PRR owned virtually all the railroad's stock and more than 10 percent of its bonds but insisted that "the Long Island runs its affairs with a free hand, and its officials control all its activities, even to purchasing."[57] Without a rate increase, LeBoutillier warned, the LIRR could not offer adequate service, cope with the rapidly growing population of Long Island, or avoid serious financial repercussions. "The Long Island is just one jump ahead of the Sheriff," he insisted. "If the Pennsylvania support was taken from us, we would be in bankruptcy so quickly it would make your head swim."[58]

Attorneys for the city and the Association of Long Island Commuters continued to favor the opposite perspective—that far from benefiting from the PRR's assistance, the LIRR was subsidizing its parent company. They asserted that the LIRR's commuter operations were "highly profitable," that the company had exaggerated pending expenditures and understated future revenues, and that rates were higher than those charged by the New Jersey railroads that accommodated commuter traffic. Association representatives also argued that LIRR officials had deliberately overvalued the property (and thus understated return on investment) by fraudulently listing many of the company's assets in the area, outside city limits, that lay under the jurisdiction of the PSC. The Flushing United Association adopted an even more sophisticated strategy, based on the uniform-rate provisions established by the Transportation Act of 1920. As a wholly owned subsidiary of the Pennsylvania Railroad, they suggested, the LIRR was for all intents and purposes an interstate carrier, and thus subject to the jurisdiction of the ICC, not the PSC. Regulators gave little credence to that creative effort at jurisdiction shifting, and likewise found fault with some of the data and the conclusions that the protestants had generated. They were equally condemnatory of the case

that railroad officials had prepared. "The burden of proof to justify the reasonableness of the proposed tariffs was upon the Railroad Company," PSC officials observed, ruling that "the failure to supply additional or more persuasive cost figures" negated any possibility of a fare increase.[59]

During the last years of the 1920s, LIRR personnel struggled to maintain service in the face of growing traffic, increased costs, and stagnant rates. In December 1925, LeBoutillier admitted that the company would be unable to comply with the electrification requirements by the January 1, 1926, deadline stipulated in the Kaufman Act. He suggested that the LIRR would need to spend at least another $12.6 million and that steam locomotives might remain in freight service until 1929. In May 1926, LeBoutillier again offered to sell the chronically deficit-plagued Whitestone Branch to the city, rather than pay for grade-crossing remediation and other improvements. It was part of an ongoing effort by LIRR officials to abandon service within Brooklyn and Queens, areas better suited to the expanding subway and rapid-transit system. In the autumn of 1927, the *New York Evening Post* published a series of articles lambasting the LIRR for frequent delays. Company officials acknowledged "that service was unsatisfactory and that congestion was the principal cause." They continued to plead poverty and emphasized that a rate increase would be necessary to fund improvements.[60]

Like LeBoutillier, W. W. Atterbury emphasized the "continued reliance" of the LIRR "on the Pennsylvania Railroad Company for advances to carry out its improvement work and to meet its maturing obligations." Atterbury, who was president of both companies, suggested offering commuters the option to purchase LIRR preferred stock—an opportunity to raise capital while turning the company's critics into its investors. Even then, he warned, improvements "must be seriously delayed, if not curtailed, and the overcrowding of trains and facilities cannot be prevented." Atterbury hoped that the Transit Commission and the Public Service Commission would reconsider the 20 percent fare increase, and he hoped that "a change in public opinion will ultimately bring about a change in conditions that will make it possible to earn a fair return on the value of the property and facilities provided for the public, and bring to the company the financial strength and ability to undertake the forward program which it realizes the public requires, but which cannot be provided promptly because of longstanding disabilities." It was a powerful if long-winded message, but one that suffered from excruciatingly poor timing. Less than three weeks earlier the directors of the LIRR—whose ranks included Atterbury and LeBoutillier—voted to pay a 4 percent dividend on the company's common stock. It was the first dividend in nearly thirty years of PRR ownership and it transferred almost $1.4 million to the corporate treasury of the Pennsylvania Railroad. Under the circumstances, it was difficult for LIRR officials to suggest that the company was on the verge of bankruptcy, to demand a fare increase, or to deny assertions that the PRR was milking the Long Island Rail Road for all it was worth.[61]

Operational considerations reinforced public perceptions that the Pennsylvania Railroad and the LIRR constituted a single unified company. In November 1927, a systemwide surge in freight and passenger traffic induced the PRR to appoint a resident vice president at New York, to coordinate operations throughout the region. The job went to George LeBoutillier, who retained his role as vice president of the Long Island Rail Road. Long Island commuters were abuzz with rumors that Atterbury, as president of the PRR, was "dissatisfied" with the LIRR's performance and had demanded a "shake-up" of management. LeBoutillier emphasized that such reports were "absolutely without foundation," but no one doubted that every important decision regarding the company emanated from Philadelphia rather than Manhattan. The following June, the Interstate Commerce Commission issued a ruling in the *Hell Gate Bridge* case, crippling efforts by the Port of New York Authority to manage all the region's railroads as part of a unified transportation system. Significantly, the decision affirmed the status of the Long Island Rail Road as a component of the PRR system rather than a truly independent carrier. In October 1928, as part of the ongoing consolidation of operations in the area, the Pennsylvania Railroad established the New York Zone by combining the PRR's New Jersey General Division with the LIRR. LeBoutillier, promoted to the vice presidency of what was in most respects a PRR region, now held full authority over the activities of both railroads in Greater New York. Jesse F. Patterson, the former LIRR general manager, became the general manager of the New York Zone and LeBoutillier's direct subordinate. C. D. Baker, who had been the general superintendent on the Long Island Rail Road, went to Philadelphia as a PRR employee. LeBoutillier emphasized that the coordination of operations and personnel would eliminate duplication, cut costs, improve service, and benefit consumers. To journalists, however, it was clear that "from an operating standpoint the Long Island Railroad thus becomes an integral part of the Pennsylvania Railroad . . . and its activities are extended beyond the Hudson River for a considerable distance beyond the territory already served." When the ICC issued its Final System Plan in December 1929, the commissioners

disallowed efforts by PRR executives to expand the railroad's influence through control of other carriers, with but one exception. The Pennsylvania Railroad would remain as it was, but no one entertained any serious thoughts of ending the long-standing relationship between that company and the LIRR.[62]

A Union between Two Railroads

The 1930s provided a repeat of the controversies surrounding the LIRR's rates and its relationship with the Pennsylvania Railroad, set against the backdrop of the Great Depression. In 1930, when commuters complained of overcrowded trains, a company official declared that "the idea of a seat for every passenger during rush hours is an absurdity" and certainly not something that was possible on the city's subway lines. The statement prompted a member of the Transit Commission to insist that commuters "have a right to expect railroad convenience and railroad convenience certainly implies a seat for every passenger"—particularly when they were paying as much as eight times subway fare. Municipal officials and regulators sought to alleviate overcrowding by increasing the length of LIRR trains to fifteen cars—an accommodation that would require a $13 million expenditure to lengthen platforms at Penn Station. LeBoutillier informed the PSC and the Transit Commission that he would gladly accept a reduction in the number of LIRR passengers rather than spend the extra money. His statement was in keeping with a long-standing effort to shift traffic within the boroughs to the subway and rapid-transit system, but it did little to improve the company's public image.[63]

LeBoutillier soon saw his wish fulfilled, thanks to the deteriorating economic situation. In 1929, and for the first time in its history, the Long Island Rail Road carried more passengers than the entire Pennsylvania Railroad system. Thanks to the preponderance of short trips, coupled with the reluctance of regulators to grant fare increases, passenger revenue on the LIRR was barely 20 percent of that earned by its corporate parent.[64] Patronage soon began to decline, however. In 1930, the reduction was a barely perceptible one-half of 1 percent—a mere 608,277 riders out of a pool of more than 118 million. The situation became more ominous during 1932, when only 91.7 million passengers utilized the LIRR. During that year, the company borrowed $1.6 million from the state of New York, for the elimination of grade crossings, and received an infusion of $2.5 million from the PRR. During 1934, as the nation began to experience some of the worst months of the Depression, the LIRR carried fewer than eighty million passengers, a decrease of nearly a third from the peak year of 1929. As a result, the LIRR lost $1.25 million on its commuter services and earned only a slight profit on noncommutation traffic. The Long Island Rail Road nonetheless paid $18 million in dividends to the Pennsylvania Railroad between 1927 and 1933—the last dividends the company would ever generate. Those funds more than offset the financial support received from the parent corporation and fueled accusations that Long Island commuters were subsidizing a company headquartered in Philadelphia.[65]

To the consternation of Pennsylvania Railroad officials, the declining patronage encouraged efforts to solidify the company's corporate relationship with the Long Island Rail Road. In June 1933, President Franklin Delano Roosevelt appointed ICC commissioner Joseph B. Eastman as the federal coordinator of transportation. Eastman took seriously his mandate to increase the efficiency of the national railway network, and he sought to eliminate waste and the unnecessary duplication of effort. Ernie Adamson, an attorney specializing in transportation law, drew Eastman's attention to the possibility of consolidating the PRR and the LIRR. Eastman found the argument persuasive and forwarded Adamson's letter to W. W. Atterbury. The PRR's president predicted "that ultimately this consolidation will take place" but suggested that "the management of this company has not regarded the time as ripe for this action, and has thought, before it is consummated, that further development of the relations between the two companies is desirable." Adamson dismissed the response as "evasive," but Eastman acknowledged that he was "without power to enter an order with respect to any matter"—an absence of coercive authority that plagued the coordinator's office throughout its short existence. For his part, Atterbury had no desire to saddle the Pennsylvania Railroad with a commuter operation that was unlikely to ever demonstrate sustained profitability.[66]

Displaying little sympathy for patrons affected by the Great Depression, on August 30, 1935, LIRR officials applied for a 15 percent fare increase within New York City and 20 percent in Nassau and Suffolk Counties. Commuter representatives quickly seized on the discrepancy, particularly as LIRR managers had employed the same cost figures to justify different rates. The request reawakened the old allegations that the LIRR paid too much for the use of Penn Station and that Long Island commuters were responsible for subsidizing the company's exploitation by the Pennsylvania Railroad. It was certainly familiar ground for Maurice Hotchner, the counsel for the Association of Long Island Commuters, who had spent the

previous decade honing strategies to counter fare increases and reductions in service.[67]

LIRR managers did themselves few favors when they accumulated the statistics they used to justify the rate increase. To determine ridership levels, LIRR conductors counted the number of passengers on board each car, while performing their other duties. "No other help was employed. The instructions were meager," observed a representative of the Public Service Commission. "Apparently the count was not even supervised by men with a competent knowledge of how the results were to be used." Railroad accountants relied on cost figures for a single week in 1934 as a proxy for the entire year, adding to suspicions that the data could not be trusted. Regulators also calculated that, based on the cost data the railroad had provided, the requested rate increase would not be sufficient to eliminate the operating deficit "or to bring the total net earnings up to a fair rate of return. This fact," PSC officials asserted, "necessarily raised a doubt as to the accuracy of the railroad's figures."[68]

During his testimony before the combined Transit Commission and Public Service Commission rate hearing, George LeBoutillier again bore the brunt of the attacks on the Long Island Rail Road. He warned that, even with efforts to reduce operating costs, the steady decline in commuter traffic portended a $1 million deficit in 1935, with even larger losses the following year. LeBoutillier admitted that his duties as a PRR vice president consumed 70 percent of his time, with little left over for the concerns of the smaller company. He defended a 40 percent reduction in maintenance expenditures between 1931 and 1933 by suggesting that it was "good management" to economize in that area, even as the company paid dividends to the PRR. LeBoutillier's remarks were perhaps ill-advised and certainly badly timed. On one of the mornings that he testified in the rate hearings, an LIRR train struck a school bus at Holbrook, New York. Three children died and several more suffered serious injuries in an accident that made the front page of local newspapers. The Holbrook crossing lay well outside city limits and was not a part of the ongoing program of grade separations. Hotchner nonetheless insisted that the decision of LIRR executives to allocate dividends to the PRR rather than invest them in safety measures had contributed to the tragedy. LeBoutillier further alienated New Yorkers when he recalled that he had made the decision to ask for higher fares after discussing the matter with a Pennsylvania Railroad executive—but without consulting the LIRR's board of directors. City attorneys suggested that that admission alone was enough to warrant dismissal of the petition. The sole moment of levity during the hearings occurred when LeBoutillier confessed that he did not know whether he was a director of the Pennsylvania Tunnel & Terminal Railroad, the PRR subsidiary that owned the tracks leading into Penn Station. He was, as an aide subsequently determined, but at a time when many Americans vilified the murky structure of holding companies as a cause of the Great Depression, LeBoutillier's confusion did not sit well with regulators.[69]

Efforts by Pennsylvania Railroad executives to keep the LIRR at a distance took on increased importance as the Great Depression exerted a downward pressure on national rail passenger rates. In February 1936, to increase demand for travel, the ICC commissioners narrowly approved a reduction in coach and Pullman fares. Baltimore & Ohio president Daniel Willard lobbied for the change, but his PRR counterpart was far less enthusiastic. Martin Clement, president for less than a year, declared that the decision was a "big surprise," one that would "have a serious effect on our revenues." The reduction in coach fares from 3.6 cents to 2.0 cents per passenger mile reduced the cost of a ticket between New York and Pittsburgh from $15.82 to $8.78, cheering travelers but giving Clement ample cause for concern. Commuters on the Long Island Rail Road had reason to rejoice as well. The new schedule of rates suggested that a trip from Penn Station to Montauk, at the eastern extremity of Long Island, should decrease in price from $4.24 to $2.26. At those rates, railroad officials warned, patronage on the LIRR would have to increase by 66.34 percent for the company to maintain revenue neutrality.[70] Such a massive gain in ridership was unlikely, and in many cases the Long Island Rail Road lacked the capacity to accommodate the additional commuters.[71]

To the undoubted relief of both Clement and LeBoutillier, the LIRR operated solely within the state of New York and was thus exempt from ICC-sanctioned rates. With intercity passenger fares set to decline by nearly 40 percent, it nonetheless became increasingly difficult for LeBoutillier to explain to the Transit Commission and the Public Service Commission why the LIRR merited a 15 or 20 percent increase in ticket prices. "It is clear that the decision makes the Long Island's attempt at a fare boost look mighty ridiculous," observed Hotchner. Jacob Abelson, a textile salesman from Queens, drew cheers from his fellow commuters when he graciously offered to pay 25 cents for the 11.3-mile trip from Jamaica to Penn Station—worth 22.6 cents under the new ICC rules—but refused to give the conductor the posted 34-cent fare. Representatives from the Transit Commission highlighted Section 57a of the state's Railroad Law, which prohibited intrastate carriers from charging higher rates than the interstate

companies that owned them. LIRR officials continued their plea for a fare increase, although without much expectation of success, but their immediate concern was to avoid compliance with the reductions in interstate rates. The eastern carriers, save the B&O, offered to compromise at 2.5 cents per mile, and the matter deadlocked the ICC. Joseph Eastman favored the greater efficiencies that he suggested would accompany lower rates and increased volume. In his capacity as transportation coordinator, he lacked the authority to compel obedience from the railroads, but his ongoing status as an ICC commissioner was another matter. In April 1936, he cast the deciding vote, rejecting the railroads' appeal.[72]

While the PRR and the other interstate carriers headed for the courts, LIRR officials filed a further petition. They demanded special consideration for the company's status as an intrastate commuter route and suggested that rates be set at three cents per mile. On May 20, the ICC likewise rejected that argument, mandating two-cent fares on the Long Island Rail Road. Emulating the actions of their corporate parent, LIRR officials sought judicial relief, but to no avail.[73] State supreme court justice Francis Bergan gave little credence to arguments regarding the unique characteristics associated with commuter operations and ruled that the LIRR provided service that was "identical in every respect" to intercity rail transportation. LIRR officials, claiming that the company would suffer losses of more than $1.7 million annually, vowed to appeal the matter to the US Supreme Court.[74]

The Long Island Rail Road soon suffered another defeat, when the Transit Commission and the Public Service Commission denied the rate petitions that had been under consideration for the previous year. The hearings revealed a profound disconnect between the railroad executives who perceived the LIRR in strictly financial terms and commuters who viewed the company as a public utility. Even before the railroad came under PRR control, managers had promoted residential development on Long Island to generate additional traffic. Representatives from numerous community groups now argued that the Long Island Rail Road had trapped commuters on an island, utterly dependent on rail service. That explanation ignored the presence of the subway and elevated transit network in Brooklyn and Queens as well as the rapidly expanding parkway system that connected suburban motorists to the city. Regulators nonetheless found the argument persuasive. Public Service commissioner George R. Lunn wrote the decision, with no dissenting votes. He concluded that LIRR officials had implicitly promised low rates and other inducements to commuters and could not rescind that obligation. "The [LIRR's] cost study method," he noted, "gives no recognition to the basic fact that commuter fares were established on a cost level distinctly below what the present apportionment methods would call for, and the entire development of residential suburbs is bound up with the fares so fixed. Now to abandon this system would work great hardship on established communities, especially to homeowners who are wholly dependent on commutation service in retaining both their homes and their means of livelihood." Under that set of circumstances, the scale of the railroad's losses was irrelevant. PSC chairman Milo R. Maltbie authored a concurring opinion that was blistering in its condemnation of the LIRR, its management, and its ties to the Pennsylvania Railroad.[75] "The Long Island Railroad went to rather unusual lengths in attempting to persuade people to build on Long Island," Maltbie emphasized. "It induced thousands to build homes all over the territory," he concluded, and that "so far as rail transportation upon Long Island is concerned, the Long Island Railroad has induced a virtual monopoly outside of the city of New York." As such, he continued, "the residents of Long Island are apt to think that the railroad company considers that it has them securely hooked and that as they cannot escape, it is somewhat indifferent to their protests." It was a common allegation, in New York, in Philadelphia, and elsewhere, and one that placed the parsimony of commuters ahead of the economic well-being of the PRR and its subsidiaries.[76]

Regulators reiterated their earlier assertions that the PRR was exploiting the LIRR, to the detriment of the area's commuters. "The Pennsylvania Railroad has insisted upon receiving a larger percentage of the income of the Long Island Railroad that [sic] it formerly received," Maltbie declared, "and the Long Island Railroad now desires to recoup a large part of the alleged losses from its former income through increased commutation rates." By siphoning away the LIRR's revenues, regulators asserted, the PRR had given commuters a choice between an unjustified fare increase and inadequate service. "The Long Island Railroad has not had the confidence and support of the traveling public," Maltbie emphasized. "It seems to me," Transit commissioner Leon G. Godley reflected, "that the Long Island might well devote its efforts first to the improvement of its service. . . . Other railroads have met a decrease in passenger revenue much greater in proportion than the Long Island's by improving service with much faster trains and installing better equipment, such as air conditioned coaches."[77]

Maltbie, Godley, and other regulators declined to explain how the LIRR would pay for those improvements,

however. The series of dividend payments to the PRR had ended in 1933 and would never resume. The expenditures for the elimination of grade crossings continued unabated and were likely to increase in tandem with the growth of competing highway traffic. Between 1899 and 1938, the LIRR eliminated 389 grade crossings, at a cost of $37.5 million, and managers estimated that an additional 697 high-risk crossings remained. The largest single project involved the long-standing demand for the removal of tracks along the Atlantic Avenue corridor, between East New York and Jamaica. Work began in October 1939, as contractors laid a temporary line that allowed trains to bypass the construction site. Over the next three years, they built a 4.6-mile-long tunnel, at a cost of $23 million, while eliminating more than twenty street crossings.[78] Aside from a slight reduction in travel time between Jamaica and the Flatbush Avenue terminal, the improvements offered few corresponding benefits for the Long Island Rail Road. Except for the passenger platforms at Woodhaven Station, where the new line crossed the Rockaway Branch, all the stops between East New York and Jamaica were abolished. The LIRR thus lost all the local business along the route, although by 1942, most commuters in the area were more accustomed to travel by bus or by subway.[79]

Beginning in 1933, various federal New Deal agencies (principally the Public Works Administration and the Works Progress Administration) funded a national effort to remove grade crossings, but too little money was available to make much of a difference. In 1938, the New York Assembly adopted new legislation that assigned the entire cost of crossing-mitigation projects to the state. Under the terms of the 1938 law, however, the state was entitled to recover the cost of all improvements that were unnecessary to ensure the safe movement of highway traffic, including those that provided a net operating benefit to the LIRR. A highway overpass, for example, would improve public safety, but it also might allow LIRR trains to travel more rapidly. The value of that higher speed could thus be charged to the railroad, up to 15 percent of the total cost of the project. Likewise, any related improvements that did not produce a direct public benefit (using the overpass as an opportunity to improve the railroad's alignment, for example) required the LIRR to contribute its own resources. What concerned LIRR officials even more, however, was that the railroad bore the increased property tax liability associated with the entire value of the improvement, since the 1938 law made no provision for tax relief.[80]

The Long Island Rail Road was caught between stagnant rates, rising costs, higher taxes, and increased competition from the highway network, and it seemed unlikely that it could survive as an independent company. Total operating revenues fell from $41.3 million in 1929 to $23.8 million by 1935, while return on investment declined from a healthy 6.63 percent to a paltry 0.39 percent. Net income decreased from $3 million in 1929 to $329,452 in 1934, followed by a loss of more than $1 million in 1935. The deficits grew to $1.2 million in 1940 and $1.3 million the following year. Pennsylvania Railroad officials emphasized that they charged the LIRR only one-third of the customary rate for locomotive rentals, and that they had loaned their subsidiary $10.5 million in 1938 and an additional $11.5 million in 1939. They insisted that commuter service had improved substantially since 1900 and stressed that the LIRR "made this progress only by means of the financial backing of the Pennsylvania Railroad."[81]

Even the 1939–1940 New York World's Fair failed to generate badly needed revenues. The Eastern Railroad Presidents' Conference sponsored the *Railroads at Work* display and the *Railroads on Parade* pageant, each of which featured contributions from the Pennsylvania Railroad. Long Island Rail Road officials, in contrast, were more concerned with plans to transport millions of visitors to and from the exhibition grounds. As early as the autumn of 1936, various LIRR subcommittees began planning for the event. Based on estimates that the fair would generate as many as six million passengers per year, executives agreed to build a World's Fair station along the Port Washington Branch and to spend nearly $3 million on new passenger equipment. The Interborough Rapid Transit Company and the Brooklyn-Manhattan Transit Corporation also served the fair, while the Independent Subway System built a new route (the World's Fair Line) solely for the exposition. The resulting competition, coupled with lower-than-expected attendance, cut deeply into the LIRR's revenues. The General Motors *Futurama* exhibit, far more popular than the railroad displays, foreshadowed the postwar boom in freeway construction—a development that was certain to imperil the Long Island Rail Road and other commuter services.[82]

Gaining Public Support

Under the circumstances, some commuters and political leaders began to support public ownership and operation of the Long Island Rail Road. In September 1935, former state senator John A. Hastings, a resident of Great Neck, suggested the creation of a new state agency, the Long Island Rapid Transit Authority. Senator Thomas F. Burchill, a Manhattan Democrat who chaired the Committee on Public Service, thought it was a splendid idea. He soon

introduced legislation that would enable the state to issue bonds to underwrite the purchase and improvement of the LIRR and perhaps other commuter lines as well. Frank A. McNamee, a spokesman for the railroad, called the plan "impractical" and suggested that "a reading of the obligations and requirements in the form of taxes and maximum fares . . . should persuade even the most gullible that the scheme is doomed to failure at the outset." His comments illustrated the difficulty of securing private investment for any company that would never earn a profit. The bill failed, providing commuter advocates such as Maurice Hotchner with an additional reason to despise the PRR. "The public should know that the onus for this rests squarely on the Pennsylvania Railroad," stated the attorney who had for the previous decade represented the Association of Long Island Commuters. "It was they, and they alone, who spurned the way out offered them through purchase of the Long Island Railroad by the Long Island Rapid Transit Authority." The solution that Hastings, Burchill, and Hotchner recommended—public ownership and management—would indeed resolve many of the problems facing the Long Island Rail Road, but it was a plan that would require another quarter century to implement.[83]

To stem the mounting losses, PRR and LIRR officials sought ways to improve the railroad's public image, thus increasing the possibility that the PSC and the Transit Commission would approve future requests for higher fares. In June 1941, the PRR directors authorized a consulting firm, the J. G. White Engineering Corporation, to prepare a report on the Long Island Rail Road situation. The consultants developed questionnaires and conducted interviews with LIRR employees, business leaders, local government officials, and commuters. They reviewed PSC complaint files, to ascertain why the LIRR suffered from so much negative publicity and launched "a special investigation by a woman inspector trained in the observation of railroad operations and customer relations." Those efforts, the consultants suggested, would help the LIRR to improve its tarnished image by "offering an impressively superior form of railroad service." Despite the focus on improved customer relations, White's initial instructions were to provide PRR and LIRR executives with data they could use to persuade local governments to reduce property taxes. "Through the contemplated educational campaign, White's consultants suggested, "there might be created a more sympathetic and cooperative attitude on the part of the public and the taxing authorities in the communities affected." However, by the time the consultants released *The Long Island Rail Road—Its Problems and Future*, a year later, their recommendations had broadened considerably. They now included a general indictment of governmental interference in the LIRR's affairs. White suggested that public support for highway construction, coupled with commuter rates that had not increased since 1918, prevented the LIRR from earning adequate revenues and improving service. The report recommended $30 million in betterments but stressed that they could only be justified if accompanied by increased fares.[84]

The LIRR continued to feel the effects of highway construction, increased automobile use, and the opening of new subway lines. Between 1930 and 1940, the company's commuter traffic declined by nearly 43 percent, from 83.3 million to 47.7 million patrons. In 1931, 42.8 percent of the commuters who used the LIRR lived within fifteen miles of Pennsylvania Station. Portions of five Independent City-Owned Subway System lines (6th Avenue, 8th Avenue, Crosstown, Fulton Street, and Queens Boulevard) opened during the 1930s, providing residents of Brooklyn and Queens more frequent train service, lower fares, and—for those headed to Lower Manhattan—the opportunity to ride to their destination without changing trains. As a result, by 1941 only 11.4 percent of the Long Island Rail Road's commuter traffic originated from within a fifteen-mile radius of Penn Station. Yet, aside from eliminating the Whitestone Branch, LIRR officials had little choice other than to maintain facilities and service in that area. Nearly 70 percent of the railroad's commuter traffic originated in the next territorial belt, from fifteen to twenty-five miles distant from Manhattan, but the likely spread of expressways, bus lines, and even subway routes threatened the future of that business as well. The expense side of the ledger offered an equally dismal picture. In the preceding twenty years, taxes increased nearly threefold, from $1.5 million to $4.1 million. By 1941, the cost of grade-crossing eliminations totaled nearly $40 million, and there was little chance that the company could keep pace with the expanding highway network. Between 1934 and 1941, the Pennsylvania Railroad provided $9.3 million in additional funding, to compensate for the ongoing deficits in passenger operations, but that assistance could not continue indefinitely.[85]

World War II proved a mixed blessing for the Long Island Rail Road. Soldiers, Manhattan-bound commuters, and workers traveling to new defense plants on Long Island boosted the company's traffic but did not resolve its financial difficulties. "There is now enjoyed by the railroads a revival in patronage which could never have been dreamed of last Winter," insisted the chief counsel of New York's Public Service Commission. "One is not required to be a soothsayer to predict that passenger traffic will probably reach a level never known in American history." Walter S. Franklin, the vice president in charge of traffic for both the Pennsylvania Railroad and the Long Island Rail Road, highlighted the fallacy in that argument. "Some people apparently draw the inference that because the Long Island Railroad is carrying a great many people, it must be making money. Of course that does not follow. If business is done at a loss, the fact that a large amount of it is being done is no proof of prosperity."[86]

The possibility of additional revenue offered hope for LIRR executives, but ultimately succumbed to conflicts between state and federal agencies. In December 1941, the Class I carriers filed for a 10 percent increase in passenger fares in Eastern Territory, and the ICC assented in January 1942. Representatives from the Public Service Commission and the Transit Commission blocked implementation in New York City, however, arguing that the ICC had no authority over intrastate commuter rates. The New York Central then filed a petition with the ICC, arguing that the state's regulatory action was unfairly prejudicial to intrastate commerce. The ICC began hearings on April 13, 1942, first in Washington and later in the St. George Hotel in Brooklyn.[87]

Despite careful preparation, representatives from the Long Island Rail Road failed to present an effective argument in favor of the fare increase. President Clement insisted that Franklin should emphasize "the philosophy of the situation," including an assertion "that at the present time the railroad is being supported by the Pennsylvania Railroad." Rather than allow Franklin's key points to be lost in a morass of facts and figures, Clement suggested that "it is much better that somebody else should stand examination on all statements and exhibits, so that there cannot be any confusion brought into Mr. Franklin's testimony by a long and detailed cross-examination on exhibits." That strategy may have been a mistake. The attorney for the PSC objected to every part of Franklin's carefully prepared testimony, usually by invoking the phrase "irrelevant and immaterial." The LIRR representative who did present the statements and exhibits bungled the job. After insisting that the railroad's equipment and service were equal to that provided by other commuter lines, the PSC counsel reminded him of the J. G. White report that the railroad commissioned a year earlier—which suggested precisely the opposite.[88]

The poor outcome of the ICC hearings in Brooklyn distressed advertising executive T. J. Ross, hired by the railroad to bolster the LIRR's public image. He observed at least some of the testimony and quickly spotted the source of the problem. "So far as public support is concerned," Ross told Clement's executive assistant, "I still do not think that you are going to arouse any enthusiasm among the people of Long Island for higher rates until something more visible and substantial is done by the Railroad to meet demands for action to improve existing conditions." Until commuters saw firsthand the benefits associated with new equipment and more frequent service, Ross concluded, "it seems to me futile to expect people to enthuse about paying higher fares, even though they thoroughly understood that in this particular situation the Long Island Railroad is being discriminated against as compared with other railroads benefited by the ICC rate increase." Clement followed the advice, but not precisely in the way that Ross had intended. James Regis Downes, speaking on Clement's behalf, authorized an advertising campaign that would begin the following summer. "The theme of this advertising," Downes asserted, "should be that the Railroad is prepared to make improvements to service, facilities, etc., when the returns from operations are in the black, which is not the case at the present time." Ross and Downes were speaking a similar language but were largely talking past each other. The advertising executive asserted, correctly, that regulators, politicians, and the citizenry would not support a fare increase until they enjoyed a slate of expensive improvements. With equal conviction, the president's assistant emphasized that it would be both foolish and irresponsible to build new facilities and purchase additional equipment—with money that would ultimately have to come from the Pennsylvania Railroad—unless regulatory agencies granted a rate increase to pay for it. The situation was not new, but it was a catch-22 from which there would be no escape.[89]

Postwar Crisis on the Long Island Rail Road

By the end of the war, commuters had lost patience with the Long Island Rail Road. They demanded immediate improvements, although without displaying any desire to raise ticket prices to pay for better service. In April 1946, the Public Service Commission initiated an investigation into the company's operations and finances. The study revealed that the most pressing demand was for new equipment that would alleviate the crowded conditions that forced many passengers to stand during their journey. LIRR officials attempted to generate favorable publicity by purchasing modern cars, yet their efforts fell far short of commuters' expectations. On March 6, 1947, the LIRR introduced the first of ten bi-level commuter cars, representing a collective expenditure of more than $1 million. They each seated 134 people, tightly packed in

seats that faced one another—conditions that prompted a new round of complaints to the PSC. In any event, ten cars would do little to remedy chronic overcrowding. George A. Arkwright, the commissioner who for the previous eleven months had presided over the investigation into the LIRR, estimated that the company would need to purchase at least 160 new cars. For the moment, there was no way to use that equipment effectively, given the length of the platforms and the insufficient number of tracks available at Penn Station. Arkwright thus limited his recommendations to 59 additional units, the most that the existing facilities could accommodate. There was a larger problem, moreover, in that frequent train movements were overtaxing the aging third-rail electric system, resulting in severe voltage drops during peak travel times, and additional cars would only exacerbate the problem. Even if LIRR managers had possessed the resources necessary to upgrade the electrical system, to run additional trains, the tunnels under the East River were nearing capacity, and there was no feasible solution to that problem.[90]

On March 7, the day after placing the first of the new double-deck cars on public display, LIRR officials petitioned the Public Service Commission for a 25 percent increase in commuter fares—which had not changed since 1918. The higher rates, they emphasized, would pay for $17.6 million in improvements to the physical plant and equipment. Regulators were quick to emphasize that they would not consider the matter until LIRR managers pledged major improvements in service. On March 11, the PSC commissioners demanded that the company develop a plan for better equipment utilization. Arkwright highlighted the limitations at Penn Station, the heavy traffic through the East River tunnels, and the congestion at the busy junction of Jamaica. He demanded an expanded investigation into the LIRR's management as well as the company's ties to the Pennsylvania Railroad—a process he thought might take two or three years. Yet "the need for a solution to the Long Island Rail Road problem is urgent," he emphasized, "and the work should be started as soon as possible." That language suggested that the PSC would demand improvements immediately yet delay indefinitely a rate increase to fund the expenditures. LIRR superintendent of operations and maintenance Eugene L. Hofmann estimated that betterments to the physical plant would require at least $25 million, irrespective of the cost of new equipment, and it was money the company did not possess.[91]

The PSC rate hearings continued through the spring of 1947. Executives noted that "a number of persons" testified in favor of a fare increase, apparently persuaded that the added expense was preferable to the poor-quality service that the LIRR was providing. PRR officials observed that "one person, stating that he represented 580 Communists on Long Island, appeared and read into the record the salaries of Pennsylvania Railroad officers." Other witnesses reiterated the long-standing assertion that the PRR was profiting at the expense of Long Island commuters. That argument carried far less force than it had during the 1920s and 1930s, since PRR managers had recently announced that their company had lost money in 1946, for the first time in its history. On July 9, 1947, the PSC awarded the LIRR a temporary 20 percent fare increase in commuter fares, set to expire on June 30, 1948. Executives would have to be content with an additional $4 million in annual revenue—$1 million less than they had sought—and the satisfaction of winning the first increase in commuter fares in nearly three decades.[92]

PRR and LIRR officials reasoned that the temporary higher fares would accomplish little, unless they could reduce costs and persuade the public of the necessity of additional, permanent rate adjustments. The J. G. White Engineering Corporation played an important role in both efforts. Prior to World War II, PRR executives had touted electrification as a mechanism for alleviating congestion in Philadelphia, New York, and along the main line that connected Manhattan to Washington. By war's end, however, rising costs had rendered that technological solution impracticable. In a June 1947 supplement to their initial 1942 report, White personnel asserted that the electrification of the more remote lines on Long Island would be prohibitively expensive. Instead, they suggested the replacement of steam-hauled commuter trains with diesels. Little more than a month later, LIRR officials ordered five new diesel locomotives, at a cost of $402,909, and curried favor with residents by emphasizing the resulting improvements in air quality. Privately, however, they were more impressed with the estimated 22.1 percent annual return on investment associated with dieselization and made plans to acquire an additional thirty-eight units, to retire fifty-four steam locomotives.[93]

Diesels alone would not save the Long Island Rail Road. The situation prompted two Republicans in the state legislature, Senator Seymour Halpern and Assemblyman Fred W. Preller, to resurrect the prewar Long Island Rapid Transit Authority bill. The two legislators from Queens suggested that "this authority would convert a deficient operating enterprise that gives unspeakably poor service, totally inadequate facilities, ancient equipment, and a destructive fare structure into a modern system with up to date equipment, better service and low postalized fares." Halpern and Preller were not the first individuals to

suggest that commuter tickets should be priced according to travel zones rather than on a per-mile basis. That policy eventually became commonplace throughout the United States.[94] Less plausible was their insistence that a $50,000 legislative appropriation would be adequate to fund preliminary studies and establish the administrative structure for the new agency.[95]

As legislators took steps, however tentative, toward public ownership of the Long Island Rail Road, there were growing indications that PRR officials were getting ready to sell. A new generation of LIRR managers carried the conviction that the status quo was untenable and that only a substantial rate increase could forestall bankruptcy and the collapse of commuter service. Pennsylvania Railroad executives accordingly worked with White's consultants to sever their ties with a subsidiary that could never break even, much less earn a profit. The situation was no longer of any concern to George LeBoutillier, who retired in February 1946, transferring to John C. White his responsibilities as vice president of the LIRR and of the PRR at New York. Effective March 1, 1948, the PRR Board of Directors selected David E. Smucker as the new general manager and Henry A. Weiss as the new traffic manager of the Long Island Rail Road.[96]

White, Smucker, and Weiss were nonetheless Pennsylvania Railroad veterans and very much a part of that company's organizational structure.[97] Their principal instructions were to develop a coordinated public-relations campaign for the railroad. They considered hiring former AT&T vice president Arthur W. Page as a consultant. Page declined, although he would later do considerable work for the PRR. Instead, the LIRR employed Verne Burnett on a one-year, $25,000 contract. Burnett was the former vice president in charge of public relations for the General Foods Corporation and in 1947 had published *You and Your Public: A Guidebook to the New Career—Public Relations*. He acknowledged that fascist propaganda had enabled the rise of totalitarian regimes but optimistically predicted that, in the postwar world, the same techniques could engender industrial harmony. Burnett's duties with the LIRR were somewhat more prosaic, and he emphasized that "we have a rate problem which must be solved satisfactorily if the property is to bring any return to its owners and give a satisfactory service to the public."[98]

On November 9, 1949, PRR officials attempted to resolve the rate problem by petitioning the Public Service Commission for permanent increases ranging from 20.97 to 34.41 percent. Smucker noted that the LIRR suffered a loss of nearly $4 million in 1947 and, absent additional revenue, projected a $5.6 million deficit in 1948.[99] Even in the unlikely event that the PSC granted the entire rate adjustment, the additional revenue would offset less than 60 percent of the company's losses. Walter S. Franklin, the executive vice president of both companies, informed the PSC that he was willing to support a three-year, $18 million betterment program, even though the LIRR's existing "financial needs, in themselves, fully justified the increases in fares." The improvements would include the acquisition of fifty bi-level cars, the rehabilitation of existing equipment, the construction of new electrical substations, and the provision of new and renovated station facilities. Residents were not willing to accept Franklin's deal. Emulating the efforts of their prewar counterparts, a new generation of commuter advocates mobilized their forces. The Suffolk County Commuters Association, organized the previous month, swung into action. Irving T. Bergman, the chairman of the Nassau–Suffolk Commuters' Committee, called the proposed rates "unjustified" and insisted that "the basis upon which the railroad is seeking a rate increase is a fictitious one." Bergman and his allies thought little of managerial promises for reform, particularly after Smucker admitted that even fifty new cars would not eliminate the standee problem.[100]

Given the LIRR's financial difficulties, bankruptcy seemed increasingly likely. On March 9, 1948, even as Burnett was expounding on the link between public relations and fare increases, PRR executives had provided a further assignment for the J. G. White Engineering Corporation. They asked its consultants to examine nine questions pertaining to the LIRR situation. The most important of those was whether the PRR should retain ownership of its subsidiary. By November 20, 1948, White's preliminary report was in the hands of senior PRR executives. James M. Symes, the vice president in charge of operations, revealed the worst to President Clement. "White concludes the [Long Island] Railroad has no earning power for the Pennsylvania," Symes emphasized, and that the consulting firm recommended a forced receivership, followed by sale. Symes pointed out that a $39.9 million LIRR bond issue would come due on March 1, 1949. The PRR board was certainly positioned to forgive that debt, since it held title to the bonds. The directors might also guarantee a new bond issue (in the amount of $46 million), as they had done several times previously. This time, Symes emphasized, the PRR should provide no such coverage. PRR officials spoke privately with representatives from the leading financial institutions, who confirmed that they would not purchase LIRR securities without a guarantee from the parent company. "Obviously without a Pennsylvania guarantee there would be no market," Symes observed. "The Pennsylvania

should promptly demand payment of the note, and upon failure to receive the money, throw the Long Island into Receivership. This is considered," Symes concluded, "the only way to impress the interested Commissions and users of the Long Island of the seriousness of the Road's financial plight."[101]

Symes was not exaggerating the gravity of the situation. LIRR accountants calculated that that carrier had incurred a deficit of more than $6 million during 1948, the greatest loss in the company's history. It was $55 million in debt, the treasury contained less than $60,000 in cash, and managers could barely cover current expenses. In addition to the looming bond maturity, the Long Island Rail Road owed its parent $12 million in loans and car-service balances, and an additional $2 million to other railroads. Since the war, in their efforts to placate commuters and regulators, LIRR officials had spent $12.5 million on equipment, stations, and other improvements. They nonetheless estimated that an additional $5 million to $7 million would be required over each of the next five years—money that was simply unavailable. From 1940 through 1948, expenses had risen by $23 million, while freight and passenger revenues had increased by only $16 million. In the brief period between July 1947 and November 1948, the PSC's temporary rate increases generated an additional $5 million in revenue, yet costs grew by $7 million. Expenditures on fuel and supplies had risen 80.9 percent between 1940 and 1948, at a time when commutation fares had increased by 25 percent, freight rates by 45 percent, and basic passenger fares by 50 percent. The mediation boards established by the 1926 Railway Labor Act awarded large raises during 1941, 1943, and 1946. A federal emergency board, which President Harry S. Truman established on March 8, 1946, recommended that LIRR operating employees receive a further seven-cent hourly pay raise and a forty-hour work week. As a result, by the autumn of 1948, wages were 81.6 percent above their 1940 level. Franklin, who chaired a committee on the LIRR situation, noted that the resulting increase in labor costs "is the final blow." The situation was so severe,

Facing, After World War II, commuters demanded better equipment, lower fares, and more frequent service. Instead, as the Long Island Rail Road entered bankruptcy, they received largely superficial improvements. In August 1949, Grace Schaefer of Richmond Hill demonstrated the new ticket vending machines installed in Penn Station. Conditions on board the LIRR's trains were distinctly less modern. *Brooklyn Daily Eagle Photographs, Brooklyn Public Library, Center for Brooklyn History.*

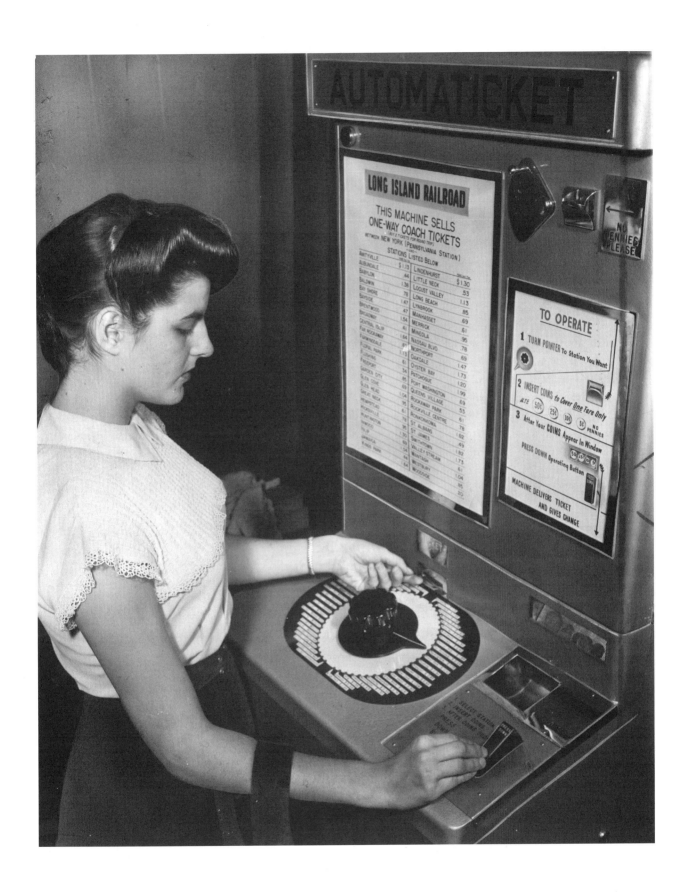

Franklin asserted, that higher fares alone would do little to save the LIRR. "There is apparently no hope of working out a plan which would enable the Company to operate at a profit in the foreseeable future, even if the approval of the New York Public Service Commission could be obtained," he emphasized.[102]

On December 22, the PRR's board established a committee to determine the future course of the Long Island Rail Road. The directors' task was not to decide whether the LIRR should go bankrupt but instead how they would implement that unavoidable decision. At their January 12 meeting, the board members concluded that the LIRR would never become profitable and that any further subsidies would constitute an irretrievable waste of the PRR's resources. On January 26, the directors of the Pennsylvania Railroad authorized the American Contract & Trust Company to purchase the LIRR's bonds and demand payment in full. "The Pennsylvania Railroad Company will no longer support The Long Island Rail Road Company by making advances to cover its deficits," the company informed shareholders, "and the Long Island—not being self-supporting—may have no recourse but to apply for legal relief in the courts." Franklin was brusquer in his comments, informing commuters that he expected the Long Island Rail Road to "stand on its own feet for everything from now on."[103]

Franklin's announcement that the LIRR would soon have to fend for itself belatedly awakened regulatory officials to the seriousness of the situation. Representatives from the Public Service Commission reevaluated the LIRR's accounts and conceded "the somber fact that the company is face to face with the gravest financial emergency in its history. . . . The stark issue and the only present choice seems to be: Is there going to be railroad transportation on Long Island continued and improved," they emphasized, "or is there likely to be disintegration of service, confusion, and receivership?" On March 1, the PSC approved a temporary 25 percent increase in commuter fares. It was a last-ditch—and futile—effort to save the company. The Long Island defaulted on its obligations the following day and filed for Chapter 77 bankruptcy, listing $11 million in assets and $55 million in debts.[104]

To the area's commuters, the company's financial collapse, so soon after receiving a substantial rate increase, constituted a final act of betrayal. Irving Bergman, the chairman of the Nassau–Suffolk Commuters' Committee, emphasized that "the commission has not provided enough money by new rates to take the road out of bankruptcy. It has merely forced the commuters to throw good money after bad." One longtime patron summed up the

matter more succinctly, observing "that's just like the Long Island, always late—even getting into bankruptcy court."[105]

The reorganization of the LIRR did not proceed smoothly. On March 14, federal judge Harold M. Kennedy, representing the US District Court for the Eastern District of New York, named three trustees who would be responsible for managing the company's operations and protecting its creditors. One—David Smucker—had earned the enmity of commuters in his role as the LIRR's general manager. The others, Hunter L. Delatour and James D. Saver, were legal associates and friends of the judge who appointed them. A month later, the Interstate Commerce Commission ratified the appointment of Smucker and Delatour but concluded that a third trustee represented an unjustifiable expense.[106]

The *New York Times* announced that "the Long Island Rail Road officially became an orphan" on April 27. With Smucker and Delatour in charge of the company, Pennsylvania Railroad officials abolished the New York Zone. They transferred all PRR operations in the area to the Eastern Region, while segregating the LIRR for the first time since 1928. By the end of 1949, shop crews were busy repainting the company's locomotives and passenger equipment. The traditional Tuscan red paint scheme, in use for half a century, gave way to a palette of dark green and light slate gray, developed by industrial designer Lester Tichy. The company's old herald—intertwined LIRR initials, surrounded by a keystone—likewise disappeared. In its place was a simple LI, set inside a circle. Once the new livery became widespread, the casual observer would find little evidence of a connection between the Long Island Rail Road and the PRR, the company that still owned it—and that was precisely the point.[107]

The bankruptcy removed the Pennsylvania Railroad from the management and operation of the Long Island Rail Road but did little to placate commuters. While the reorganization proceedings sheltered the company from creditors, the cessation of PRR support meant that its financial situation worsened rather than improved. Within days of taking charge of the LIRR, Smucker and Delatour announced that they were canceling most improvements to the physical plant and equipment. Additional train frequencies were also unlikely, Smucker acknowledged, despite the rapid postwar growth of Long Island suburbs. By the end of May, a month after the ICC endorsed their appointment as trustees, Smucker and Delatour petitioned the Public Service Commission for a rate increase on one-way, noncommutation tickets. If granted, the higher fares would take effect just as summertime crowds were preparing to travel to shore resorts and other holiday destinations.[108]

Catastrophe

With the LIRR in bankruptcy and relations with commuters at an all-time low, the railroad plunged repeatedly into disaster. Six months after defaulting on its financial obligations, and at the height of the evening rush hour, two Long Island Rail Road trains collided near Sunnyside Yard. Mercifully, both were empty of passengers, but the accident killed two crew members, injured six others, and delayed the homeward journeys of twenty-five thousand commuters. The situation was much worse on February 17, 1950. Eastbound Train 192 and westbound Train 175 were scheduled to meet near Rockville Centre. The line was double tracked, but the railroad and the state of New York had jointly funded the building of an overpass at a highway crossing where nine people had died and a further twenty-four had been injured over the previous twelve years. While construction was underway, the two tracks had been reduced to one. Sometime after 10:00 p.m., motorman Jacob Kiefer overran a stop signal and allowed Train 192 to enter the short section of single track, directly into the path of the westbound train. After the collision, rescue workers labored into the night to extricate the wounded and the dead from the wreckage, while doctors amputated the limbs of survivors to free them. Radio stations broadcast calls for welders, the only people who possessed the skills and the equipment needed to cut through the shattered cars that encased the victims. One man, impaled by a steel beam, begged for someone to kill him. Another commuter sat perfectly upright in his seat, as if traveling home from a routine day at the office, save that he was missing the top of his head. Thousands of people lined the parallel Sunrise Highway, asking for news about loved ones, and watching as police officers and firefighters carried more than thirty bodies to a temporary morgue at the nearby Negro Second Baptist Church.[109] The dead included Harold W. Worzel, one of the leaders of the Suffolk County Democratic Party, and John M. Weeks, a contributing editor at *Time* magazine—ensuring that the Long Island Rail Road would receive special attention from both politicians and journalists. The Public Service Commission soon launched an investigation, but few doubted where to place blame for the tragedy. Motorman Kiefer, who somehow survived, was subsequently charged with manslaughter but was ultimately acquitted. The real villain, a reporter for *Time* magazine asserted, was "the slipshod Long Island," and echoed calls from commuters to "investigate the whole

operation of the Long Island, [and to] rescue it from what passengers were sure was its undisputed status as the worst Class I railroad in the U.S."[110]

Month after month, the horrors continued. On August 5, an LIRR passenger train collided with a freight train at Huntington, injuring forty-six. During the evening rush hour on November 22, two eastbound commuter trains, carrying a total of some twenty-two hundred people, departed Penn Station. At Richmond Hill, a mile west of Jamaica, the brakes seized on Train 780, the Hempstead Local.[111] Within minutes, Train 174, bound for Babylon and traveling at an estimated sixty miles per hour, smashed into Train 780. Richmond Hill, like Rockville Centre, was a heavily populated area, and this time five thousand horrified spectators watched the rescue personnel who worked through the night and into the following morning, Thanksgiving Day. The accident killed seventy-nine people and injured more than three hundred. Thirteen of the dead were residents of Rockville Centre, the community devastated by the collision that had occurred there nine months earlier. Benjamin J. Pokorny, the motorman on Train 174, was directly responsible for the catastrophe, but, once again, the public blamed the management of the Long Island Rail Road. The "city's Thanksgiving is quiet owing to war and disaster," the *New York Times* noted, equating the Richmond Hill wreck with the tenuous military situation in Korea. "The shocking Thanksgiving-eve tragedy on the Long Island Rail Road leaves the public with a sense of mingled sympathy for the bereaved families and angry indignation at the railroad," the paper editorialized. The response by LIRR officials satisfied no one. David Smucker, the railroad's trustee and chief operating officer, refused to speak with reporters. Joseph N. Kanzler, Smucker's assistant, rejected calls to install automatic speed-control equipment, similar to the technology employed on the city's subway lines. "We feel we have every safety device we need," Kanzler indicated.[112]

When coupled with the earlier disaster at Rockville Centre, the Richmond Hill wreck suggested that the LIRR's trustees were no longer capable of managing the company. At 1:00 a.m. on the night of the accident, while rescuers were still cutting victims from the wreckage, Acting Mayor Joseph T. Sharkey told reporters that "something must be done to stop this carnage. If public ownership is the answer, that's it." Mayor-elect Vincent Impellitteri cut short a vacation in Cuba and rushed back to New York. On November 23, immediately following his return to the city, Impellitteri created the Long Island Railroad Commission (also known as the Patterson Commission) to investigate the LIRR's operations. Chaired by

Following the Rockville Centre disaster, Major General William H. Draper Jr. (1894–1974) became the sole trustee for the bankrupt Long Island Rail Road. He soon demonstrated his commitment to the safety of the railroad's passengers. In February 1951, Draper was in Chicago, standing third from the left, as Santa Fe signal engineer George K. Thomas explained the operation of that railroad's automatic train stop system. Santa Fe train control engineer Roy Lister and LIRR signal engineer Samuel B. Higginbottom observed the proceedings. *Brooklyn Daily Eagle Photographs, Brooklyn Public Library, Center for Brooklyn History.*

former Secretary of War Robert P. Patterson, its members also included Parks Commissioner Robert Moses and former New York State Supreme Court justice Charles C. Lockwood. Given that the cause of the tragedy was heartbreakingly obvious, the members of the Patterson Commission initially devoted their attention to the selection of a more useful scapegoat than motorman Pokorny. "The mob demanded scalps," *Railway Age* editorialized,

"and, as always, the politicians obliged."[113] Subsequent events bore out the assertion that "*The management of a poverty-stricken public service corporation is vulnerable and will be crucified, without regard to justice, whenever a plausible excuse can be found.*" Governor Thomas A. Dewey, acting on the committee's recommendation, demanded the resignations of Smucker and Delatour "on the short grounds that they have lost public confidence." He called for a "complete housecleaning of management and the installation of a new, widely experienced and highly competent direction" and threatened legal action if necessary. On November 29, Smucker and Delatour announced that they would resign as trustees, effective December 22. Their replacement, Major General William H. Draper Jr., was an investment banker and a partner at Dillon, Read & Company. Draper took his responsibilities seriously, selling his house in Tarrytown and buying one in Garden City, so that he could commute to work on the LIRR. "He always traveled in either the front car or the rear car," his son recalled, "in order to dissuade others from fearing them." The new trustee, the *New York Times* acknowledged, "will have to be a man of great gifts and courage, for he will probably be expected to achieve miracles without long delay." The words proved prophetic, as the public's tolerance for mistakes was growing thin. On December 14, even before Draper could assume his new duties, a switchman mistakenly routed a group of empty cars into the path of a train that had stopped at the Valley Stream station. Terrified passengers stampeded to the rear of the first car as the opposing train bore down on them. It stopped seventy-five feet—one car length—short of a head-on collision.[114]

The series of disasters and near catastrophes reawakened allegations that the Pennsylvania Railroad had drained the LIRR of resources, to the detriment of New York commuters. It mattered little that during the previous twenty-two years of PRR oversight, prior to the bankruptcy, not a single passenger fatality had occurred on the Long Island Rail Road. At a time when no one knew who would be responsible for the LIRR's management, or who would pay for improvements to equipment and the physical plant, the PRR became a political target. New Yorkers asserted that the Pennsylvania Railroad bore ultimate responsibility for the carnage and that that company had a financial, legal—or, at the very least, moral—obligation to remedy the situation. Mayor Impellitteri derided the LIRR as "this disgraceful common carrier" but added that the company was "the stepchild of a callous, indifferent and arrogant landlord operating by remote control from another state." Orrin G. Judd, special counsel for Nassau County, asserted that "the Long Island has been under the shadow of the Pennsylvania for many years. No one has ever been sure how much the Pennsylvania was taking out of the Long Island, and one of the tasks of the new trustee is to straighten out this question."[115]

Both the Interstate Commerce Commission and the New York Public Service Commission conducted sweeping investigations of the Long Island Rail Road, and their preliminary recommendations were equally comprehensive. Human error and "disobedience of orders" provided a ready explanation for each of the incidents, yet state regulators also observed systemic managerial inadequacies. The company's record was "replete with failures in operating practices," the PSC emphasized, coupled with a "serious breakdown in safety practices and a deterioration in the morale of many employees. . . . The primary cause of that breakdown in morale has been the pressure of operating an antiquated road under modern, high speed, and congested conditions presently existing on the Long Island." Rather than attribute those antiquated conditions to the unremunerative rates that they had endorsed, PSC officials assigned blame to the Pennsylvania Railroad. "The

withdrawal of Pennsylvania Railroad support after the bankruptcy brought the improvement program to a dead stop," they emphasized. PSC officials noted, "We are convinced that absentee management coupled with absentee ownership is inconsistent with satisfactory service under safe-operating conditions."[116]

Pennsylvania Railroad and LIRR officials soon went on the offensive, attributing the accidents to the refusal of regulatory officials to authorize an increase in commuter rates between 1918 and 1947. Walter Franklin, president of the company that still owned the LIRR, issued a lengthy statement refuting PSC allegations that absentee management had contributed to the disaster. "This criticism is entirely unjustified and disproven by the facts," Franklin emphasized. "If any blame can be placed for the alleged unsatisfactory conditions on the Long Island Rail Road and for the alleged low state of morale on the Long Island, it must rest squarely on the New York Public Service Commission for its starvation policy. . . . Nothing tends to destroy the morale of an organization more rapidly than being forced to operate continually at a loss with constant criticism and ridicule." Objectively, Franklin's connection between low rates and poor performance had merit. In the aftermath of three major accidents that killed more than a hundred people, few New Yorkers cultivated much sympathy for the slim wallets and bruised egos of LIRR officers and employees.[117]

The ICC and PSC investigations brought sweeping changes to the Long Island Rail Road. Safety was understandably the top priority. The Interstate Commerce Commission, the Long Island Railroad Commission, and the Public Service Commission recommended a host of improvements, with the ICC mandating the installation of automatic train stop technology on the company's busiest routes. The changes would cost an estimated $6 million, an amount that was far beyond the LIRR's resources. "The only reason that I was asked to go in," Draper recalled, "was with that problem in mind, and so almost to the exclusion of all other problems I devoted my attention to that important problem." Draper established a companywide Safety Department, the first in the LIRR's history. Judge Kennedy, who possessed ultimate authority over the railroad's finances, soon authorized Draper to spend $265,000 for the installation of red warning lights on each train. It would be more difficult to pay for the $6 million worth of safety improvements demanded by the PSC and the Patterson Commission, however. The company did not possess more than a small portion of the necessary funds, and PRR executives were unwilling to make good the shortfall. After failing to secure a loan from the Reconstruction

478

Finance Corporation, Draper cajoled his fellow investment bankers into acting for the public good. He exploited his contacts at the First National Bank, where he had started his career before moving to Dillon, Read, and they in turn secured the participation of four other Manhattan lenders and twenty-four banks on Long Island. The bankers—"very properly . . . in view of the conditions," Draper acknowledged—demanded that their loan constitute a first lien on the LIRR's assets, giving them precedence over all other creditors. The condition was both unusual and illegal, and it forced Draper and his allies to press Congress for modifications to federal bankruptcy law. Draper also spoke with representatives from nearly every political jurisdiction served by the LIRR, asking them to yield their claims to back taxes to the bankers' insistence on priority for repayment. It was an odd manifestation of Daniel Defoe's reference to "Things as certain as Death and Taxes," for Draper was asking local politicians to choose between those two alternatives. Only by relinquishing the tax revenues that they needed to fund municipal services, he suggested, could they halt the string of accidents that had claimed the lives of so many members of their communities.[118]

Draper prevailed at both the local and at the federal levels. Community leaders grudgingly assented to tax deferments, and on October 24, President Truman signed HB 4693, amending Section 77 of the Bankruptcy Act to permit safety-related trustees' certificates to take precedence over all other liens. Additional relief came from another source. In May 1950, a fire destroyed a portion of an LIRR trestle over Jamaica Bay, severing the company's Rockaway Beach Branch. With service suspended, LIRR officials proposed to abandon the line. The misfortune coincided with efforts by the New York City Board of Transportation, in the planning stages since 1929, to extend a municipally owned rapid-transit line to the area. In September 1951, the city offered $7 million in

cash for the route, plus $1.5 million in credits relating to depreciation and grade-crossing abatement. Long Island Rail Road officials also combed the property for scrap metal and surplus electrical equipment, offered for sale at inflated Korean War prices. The additional resources funded a modest improvement program but were insufficient to fully rehabilitate the railroad, much less restore it to profitability. Changes in bankruptcy law facilitated investments in safety equipment but not comprehensive programs to improve service. The sale of scrap metal and the shedding of components such as the Rockaway Beach Branch could not continue indefinitely. Political leaders in New York City and other lineside communities were not willing to support an unending exemption for the railroad's property taxes.[119]

Draper's creativity enabled the Long Island Rail Road to undertake a $14 million improvement program. The single largest expenditure, $6 million, attested to demands for increased safety. In May 1951, the company completed the installation of automatic train stop equipment on the route linking Brooklyn and Jamaica. A further section, between Long Island City and Port Washington, entered service in September. The system relied extensively on the technology pioneered on the Pennsylvania Railroad during the 1920s. Cab signals replicated the fixed signals located along the track. Should the motorman fail to respond to the signal indication, a whistle would sound in the cab. Absent corrective action, the brakes would engage.[120] "A robot engineer that forced compliance with signal rules rode alongside a veteran engineer," one reporter observed, and he praised "the railroad's apparently successful demonstration of a new safety device that will erase the possibility of human failure to heed signals." In the aftermath of the tragedies at Rockville Centre and Richmond Hill, the confidence in supposedly fail-safe technology was understandable. The remaining funds were sufficient to purchase new equipment. A dozen Fairbanks-Morse diesels permitted the retirement of seventeen steam locomotives. The first four 2,400-horsepower C-Liners entered service in October 1951, increasing operating efficiency and eliminating the smoke nuisance that had generated complaints from passengers and lineside residents. In April 1952, the company ordered twenty new passenger cars from Pullman-Standard, for use in electrified territory.[121]

Finding a Home for the Long Island Rail Road

The intractable financial situation suggested the difficulty of identifying a permanent entity to own and operate the Long Island Rail Road. Governor Dewey acknowledged that the LIRR situation was unprecedented. He nonetheless indicated that neither he nor other members of the Republican Party favored the establishment of a state transit authority, if any means existed to keep the company under private ownership. Despite Dewey's misgivings, public control seemed likely. On January 21, the Long Island Railroad Commission recommended the creation of a state transit authority to operate the company.[122] "Under any presently foreseeable circumstances," Patterson, Moses, and Lockwood conceded, "the Long Island Rail Road under private ownership offers little hope as a sound private investment." They dismissed as impracticable long-standing if unrealistic suggestions that a growth in LIRR freight revenues could restore the company to profitability. Nor could the company survive without additional passenger revenue. "There is no use shouting 'no increase'" in fares, they noted, in a manner that was certain to disappoint and alienate commuters. Financial recovery, they emphasized, would occur only when the railroad could be relieved of local property taxes as well as PSC oversight. The members of the Patterson Commission called on the legislature to authorize the new agency to issue up to $100 million in bonds—although they doubted that the rehabilitation of the LIRR would cost more than two-thirds of that amount. They also made clear that the exercise of public control would not necessitate the expenditure of public funds. "The suggestions that either the Federal or State governments hand out money from their treasuries to rehabilitate and improve the Long Island Rail Road under the guise of extreme necessity, war mobilization, civilian defense, analogy with the E.C.A. [Economic Cooperation Administration, the federal agency responsible for disbursing aid under the Marshall Plan] or depression spending are so manifestly indefensible that we refrain from further characterization," they emphasized. It was a striking statement, one that seemed monumentally naive when judged against the transformation in public assistance for urban mass transit that would take place over the following decades. Rather than ask the national government for support, the Patterson Commission advocated two changes in federal policy—the termination of all ICC control over the Long Island Rail Road and revisions in bankruptcy law that would expedite the company's reorganization.[123]

While PRR officials endorsed most of the committee's report, they disagreed vehemently with its guarded analysis of the relationship between the LIRR and the Pennsylvania Railroad. "No plan which contemplates further absentee ownership and operation of the Long Island Rail Road by the Pennsylvania would have the slightest chance of

general acceptance," warned Patterson and his colleagues. "We find that the overwhelming weight of opinion among commuters, Long Island taxpayers and others is that the first consideration, after restoration of safety and morale, is the complete and permanent separation of the Long Island from the control of the Pennsylvania Railroad." The members of the Long Island Railroad Commission avoided any discussion as to how that permanent separation might take place, or what, if anything, the Pennsylvania Railroad might recoup from its $144 million investment in the Long Island Rail Road.[124] "We make no estimate as to the remaining equities of the Pennsylvania," they noted, "except to indicate that they have been drastically reduced." The three commissioners nonetheless refuted "uninformed guesses and random charges of sympathy for the Pennsylvania" and emphasized that "we did not and do not advocate, as was suggested by a few critics, overpaying the Pennsylvania as owner of the Long Island."[125]

Given the tenor of those remarks, PRR executives perceived an immediate danger of seizure without adequate compensation, coupled with a long-term threat that government entities might selectively demand control over additional portions of their railroad. Invoking pervasive fears of spreading communism, President Franklin warned the PRR's shareholders that they faced "a major threat to the security of private property in this country." The proposed transit authority represented "a direct and undisguised confiscation of private property for the purpose of advancing the policy of public ownership by unjust means," he insisted. "For government to destroy the earning power of private property by oppressive regulation and taxation, and then attempt to expropriate the property at a depressed price brought about by the government's own acts," Franklin concluded, "would be the essence of state socialism at its worst."[126]

Dewey shared Franklin's aversion to public ownership of the Long Island Rail Road and did his best to blunt legislative efforts to implement the plan the Patterson Commission had endorsed. Rather than purchase and operate the LIRR, the governor insisted, the transit authority's responsibilities should be limited to the preparation of a reorganization plan to resolve the bankruptcy and restore the company to profitability. "If the new authority, with the powers that I have proposed, should still fail to achieve a reorganization of the railroad and to induce the investment of the necessary new capital," Dewey emphasized, "then, as a last resort, it should have the power to acquire the railroad and operate it." William Draper, the company's trustee, likewise favored the retention of private control but announced that "the authority would be a solution and I would cooperate with it in the absence of any other." He was defending a proposal, pending before the Public Service Commission, for a 20 percent fare increase. The added funds, he conceded, would not end the LIRR's losses but would merely be sufficient "to get a railroad worth riding on."[127]

Commuters were quick to condemn the policies of both the governor and the trustee. Howard Meyer, representing the Unity Club of Nassau, charged that Draper sought the fare increase to make the company more attractive to private investors, thus "burying the authority alive." Irving Bergman, the longtime chairman of the Nassau–Suffolk Commuters' Committee, used a different metaphor when he accused the governor of "putting the cart before the horse." He emphasized that Dewey's proposal did not specify a deadline for efforts to restore the LIRR to its status as a self-sustaining private corporation. If the initial plan failed, Bergman asserted, it was unlikely that supporters of public ownership could regain the momentum they currently possessed. County executive J. Russell Sprague, a loyal Republican, observed that "the people of Nassau County are for private enterprise, but their primary concerns are safety, improved service and reasonable rates. These three essentials they will demand from any operation."[128]

Even as Sprague reiterated the usual trinity of commuter demands, the newspapers informed New Yorkers that none of them were likely to come to fruition any time soon. The PSC ultimately granted the 20 percent fare increase that Draper had recommended, suggesting that the LIRR—as an independent line or as a stepchild of the PRR, in bankruptcy or out, controlled by the public or by the capitalists—was inevitably going to pick the pockets of its passengers. A sickout by the Brotherhood of Railroad Trainmen halted commuter operations throughout Greater New York, throwing the highways into chaos and emphasizing the importance of lines such as the LIRR. Safety continued to suffer as well. On February 6, *The Broker*—a commuter train operated by the PRR rather than the LIRR—derailed near Woodbridge, New Jersey. Eighty-five people died when the train plunged off an embankment adjacent to a temporary bridge over the New Jersey Turnpike, in an accident reminiscent of the Rockville Centre tragedy on Long Island.[129]

Despite clear signals that privately owned commuter services were increasingly unable to provide economical, reliable, or safe operations, the governor and his Republican allies retained their aversion toward the concepts of public ownership and management. On March 31, 1951, Dewey signed legislation creating the Long Island Transit Authority, embodying at best a tentative step toward government control. In addition to its small paid staff—four full-time employees—LITA depended on the services of three unsalaried commissioners. LITA had the authority to hire consultants, conduct studies, and formulate a plan to rehabilitate the Long Island Rail Road, but the agency could not directly operate the line. Only if the LITA commissioners failed to restore the company to profitability could they contemplate more aggressive governmental intervention. For the next year, and under LITA administration, the railroad would be able to set rates without approval from the Public Service Commission. State and local governments agreed to forgive some $20 million in debts attributed to the cost of grade-crossing elimination and unpaid franchise fees and property taxes. The railroad would also benefit from the deferment of future franchise obligations and a 60 percent reduction in its $3.7 million annual real estate tax liability. That exemption would cease when the railroad emerged from bankruptcy court and the back taxes came due—suggesting an imperative for a speedy reorganization, before the arrearage assumed staggering proportions.[130]

On the last day of June, Dewey appointed Draper, investment banker George Emlen Roosevelt (one of the nation's leading experts on railroad reorganizations), and former undersecretary of the army Tracy S. Voorhees to administer LITA.[131] Voorhees spoke for all three when he asserted that private enterprise is "the natural way of doing things in America," yet he also conceded that "it might be harder to finance now than it would have been six months ago. We can't keep moving rates to adjust to every change in the inflationary cycle." He was doubtless referring to the 20 percent increase in commuter rates, granted by the PSC on April 11, promising an additional $4.6 million in annual revenue. That was almost precisely the LIRR's deficit for 1950, and rapidly increasing labor and supply costs would soon erode whatever financial progress the company had made. The commissioners urged the public to absolve the PRR from responsibility for the situation. "It has been popular to blame the Long Island's plight on its affiliation with the Pennsylvania Railroad," they declared, but highlighted the larger company's inability to secure any return on the more than $100 million it had invested in the commuter carrier. Draper, Roosevelt, and Voorhees also cautioned commuters against the expectation of any quick or easy remedies. There were "formidable legal obstacles," they indicated, and "many financial problems" and "a number of important items of expense and income are still unsettled."[132]

The overriding task of the three commissioners was to extricate the Long Island Rail Road from receivership. "It is obvious," Voorhees observed, "that the railroad ought not to be left hanging in bankruptcy court indefinitely." Within two months Voorhees, Roosevelt, and Draper issued a preliminary report, acknowledging that "a very difficult problem exists" and that "no financial miracle can be expected, and none will be attempted." The resuscitation of the LIRR presented issues of unprecedented complexity, they cautioned, yet they reiterated their confidence in private ownership and operation and hoped "that before the end of this year most of these questions will have been sufficiently clarified to permit definite decisions concerning the type of reorganization."[133]

By the second anniversary of the Richmond Hill wreck, Dewey's commitment to the private ownership and operation of the Long Island Rail Road had begun to evaporate. On November 19, 1951, Walter Franklin and David Bevan filed an LIRR reorganization plan with the Interstate Commerce Commission and with Judge Kennedy of the US District Court for the Eastern District of New York. Franklin was acting in his capacity as president of both companies, while Bevan—six months into his tenure as the PRR's vice president in charge of finance—was providing an early demonstration of his desire to reduce drains on the corporate treasury.[134] Their assertion "that it is clearly possible to reorganize the debtor as a private enterprise" was in concord with Dewey's sympathies, but in all other respects, the PRR's reorganization proposal fell flat. Franklin and Bevan asked the ICC to set a target rate of return for the Long Island Rail Road, allowing the company full authority to raise fares as necessary to achieve that goal. Officials in the reorganized LIRR would also have the power to reduce unremunerative operations or abandon marginal lines, as they saw fit. Such a course would of necessity permanently bar the New York Public Service Commission from setting rates or terms of service. The PRR plan demanded adequate compensation for the company's investments in the Long Island Rail Road—although it emphasized that the true investors were the PRR's 186,000 small shareholders, many of whom resided in New York, rather than a corporate colossus based in Philadelphia. Making good on those obligations would require a new LIRR bond issue and the reduction or elimination of virtually all state and local taxes, an amount that would exceed $5 million annually. In effect, the PRR plan placed the sanctity of private property and with it the

preservation of free enterprise as "the paramount issue over and above all other issues," including the demands of commuters, state regulatory agencies, and on-line communities.[135]

The members of the Long Island Transit Authority soon demonstrated their opposition to the PRR's suggestions. Draper still served as LITA's chairman, but he was no longer the trustee of the Long Island Rail Road. He had resigned that post two months earlier, at the insistence of PRR executives—who insisted, Draper noted, "that they should not negotiate concerning a possible reorganization with the members of the authority so long as I was also trustee." In accepting the resignation, Judge Kennedy praised Draper's efforts and suggested that the situation "was precipitated by the refusal of the Pennsylvania Railroad" to cooperate.[136]

The ongoing disputes between LIRR, PRR, and LITA representatives characterized the agency's recommendations to Dewey as well. On the last day of 1951, they submitted an "Informal Report to the Governor," acknowledging the necessity of rapid reorganization. While "recent attempts to increase earnings and effect economies" had stabilized the LIRR's financial situation, they acknowledged that "the road if operated in a way to give safe and adequate transportation is not, and gives no good prospect of, earning enough to pay present taxes"—much less the arrearage that had accumulated. Draper, Roosevelt, and Voorhees nonetheless emphasized that "the Pennsylvania's plan of reorganization is illegal" since "it calls for virtually complete exemption of a private company from State control of rates and service; also for relief from all State and local taxes except those on real estate." Draper and his colleagues pointed to a fundamental difference between their approach to reorganization and that favored by railroad managers. "In the past, taxes have come ahead of interest," the report emphasized. "In the Pennsylvania's plan, a return on its investment would be put ahead of taxes. Realistically we cannot expect the road to be able to pay both." The document suggested that the bankruptcy "plan shows that the Pennsylvania is unwilling to sponsor a reorganization under existing state laws and taxes."[137]

The three LITA representatives thus presented Dewey with a stark choice. He could preserve the profits that were essential to ongoing private ownership and operation. If he did so, however, he would need to relinquish both the taxes that were an important component of local revenues and the PSC regulation that had for decades protected the public interest. "Does the value of continuing private enterprise in the operation of this railroad justify further relief from taxes as a fixed charge and in a way bring about a closer alignment of the interest of the public with that of the private owner and operator?" the LITA commissioners asked the governor. "Or is it desired that we proceed with a plan for state ownership and authority supervision if—as seems probable—we cannot secure an acceptable reorganization by private enterprise under existing law?" LITA representatives proceeded cautiously and refused to recommend a specific solution. "It seems to us," they emphasized, "that a question is presented which is not for us but for the state to decide." Draper, Roosevelt, and Voorhees nonetheless took a dim view of the PRR's insistence on a reduction in both taxes and regulation. They likewise acknowledged that if Dewey and the state legislature refused to alter state law in a manner that would facilitate the PRR's proposal, no other private owner was likely to step forward. The LITA report cautioned against direct governmental operation of the Long Island Rail Road, in large part because employees refused to submit to civil-service examinations. Their recommendation for an intermediate measure—public ownership under LITA, with day-to-day operations contracted to a private firm—nonetheless represented a vastly different arrangement than the one Dewey had proposed a few months earlier.[138]

However tentative its recommendations, the LITA report coalesced growing opposition to the PRR's ongoing operation of the Long Island Rail Road. Faced with the potential loss of tax revenues, representatives from suburban communities rapidly shed their formerly steadfast commitment to the sanctity of private property. J. Russell Sprague, Nassau County's executive, insisted that in any attempt to "preserve Pennsylvania ownership of the Long Island there must be some strict control over management to be sure that the railroad is operated for the interests of the people and not the Pennsylvania." Sprague's condition was antithetical to the terms of the PRR's reorganization proposal and fundamentally incompatible with the principles of private ownership. Irving Bergman, representing the Nassau–Suffolk Commuters' Committee, asserted that continued PRR control would be "undesirable" and emphasized that those he represented "have had plenty of experience with its selfish principles."[139]

In Albany, Governor Dewey hosted a marathon four-hour meeting with Republican lawmakers, hoping to save the LIRR without expanding the authority of the state government. Draper had resigned as the LIRR's trustee, and he was reaching the limits of his endurance with respect to his role as the head of the Long Island Transit Authority. In early February, President Truman selected Draper as ambassador at large. As Draper left office, he acknowledged that the railroad's deficit for the first three quarters of 1951 was $1.8 million more than it had been during the same period of the previous year. The transition nonetheless enabled Dewey to elevate investment banker George Roosevelt—an unassailable champion of corporate capitalism—to the chairmanship of the Long Island Transit Authority.[140]

Roosevelt worked with Dewey to craft a carefully worded addendum to LITA's December 31 report. At the end of February, Roosevelt and Voorhees—the sole remaining members of LITA, following Draper's resignation—reminded the governor that "we are handicapped in our negotiations for a private enterprise reorganization because we have neither title to the road to offer, nor any basis to determine the price which a purchaser might have to pay for it." The best solution, they concluded, would be for LITA to file a new plan of reorganization, contesting the one the PRR had generated the previous November. If LITA failed to sell the Long Island Rail Road to a private company—an outcome that appeared increasingly likely, they acknowledged—then the new reorganization plan would enable the agency "to stand ready to take the property and control its operation." That would be done, Roosevelt emphasized, "without filing a certificate that private enterprise reorganization is impossible."[141]

Dewey used similarly convoluted language when he presented the recommendations to the legislature on March 5. The governor praised the "tentative plan to enable the authority to seek reorganization on a private enterprise self-supporting basis" and only grudgingly acknowledged that "if such a private reorganization is not attainable, operation of the road by the authority through a controlled corporation would be possible until such time as a transfer to private operation becomes feasible." Dewey's proposal met some resistance—primarily from legislators who wanted clarification regarding the amount of money the state might have to pay to acquire the LIRR—but the measure became law on April 2. It increased the likelihood of a state takeover of the company, but only after all other options had been exhausted. "The best argument for private enterprise," Dewey asserted, "lies in the notoriously unsuccessful results of government operation of transportation in this country and elsewhere." It was a pointed reference to the financial problems associated with the New York City Board of Transportation, whose municipal rail and bus operations were well on their way to posting a 1952 deficit of nearly $25 million. He could have added that private enterprise was not faring much better. The Hudson

& Manhattan Railroad was staggering under losses that would soon lead to bankruptcy, while commuter services were sapping the financial strength of the PRR, the New York Central, the New Haven, and several carriers that terminated on the New Jersey side of the Hudson River.[142]

Dewey's criticism reflected long-standing tensions between the metropolis and the remainder of the state, but his aversion to government ownership was more a matter of political rhetoric than economic reality. Increased state support seemed inevitable, but it was better to face that than the economic and political consequences associated with the collapse of public transportation in Greater New York. On March 26, 1952, the New Jersey Legislature established a state rapid-transit commission, and Governor Dewey signed corresponding New York legislation a few days later. Unlike the powerful Port of New York Authority, the two five-member commissions operated separately, although with a mandate to develop a coordinated solution for the region's transportation problems. Less than a year later, Dewey signed a bill establishing the New York City Transit Authority, a public corporation responsible for owning and operating the subway, elevated, streetcar, and bus lines in the five boroughs. It would take considerably longer to achieve a similar solution for the Long Island Rail Road, but the result would be the same.[143]

During the summer of 1952, Roosevelt and Voorhees prepared the agency's bankruptcy plan. Submitted to Judge Kennedy on August 18, it suggested public ownership and operation, as a temporary expedient pending the selection of a private corporation to assume those responsibilities. Under LITA control, the tax deferments—equivalent to approximately $4 million annually—would continue, but they would ultimately become the responsibility of the new owner. Roosevelt and Voorhees promised a "speedy, fair and equitable reorganization," one that included "a substantial provision for the Pennsylvania." Yet they emphasized that "the state and its political subdivisions have no intentions of making these sacrifices . . . for the purpose of increasing profits and thereby enhancing the equity of . . . the Pennsylvania." They suggested a purchase price of $20 million, adding that it "is all we can afford to give the Pennsylvania."[144] The amount was less than half of the $55 million in LIRR bonds owned by the Pennsylvania Railroad. It also failed to consider another $55 million in loans and unpaid charges, which the Long Island Rail Road owed to its corporate parent. Those outstanding debts, Roosevelt and Voorhees suggested, were "at best worth only a fraction of their face value."[145]

Pennsylvania Railroad officials, predictably, were opposed to the LITA proposal. This is "not a plan for reorganization," they complained, "but a plan for confiscation." Judge Kennedy thus faced two wholly incompatible reorganization plans—one submitted by the PRR and labeled "illegal" by LITA personnel, and the other provided by the agency and condemned as "confiscation" by railroad executives. Denis M. Hurley, the corporation counsel for the city of New York, asserted that both plans were "defective and should be opposed by the city" and suggested that "what is needed now is an impartial re-examination of the entire problem by the I.C.C."[146]

The Interstate Commerce Commission held the ultimate authority to decide who would control the Long Island Rail Road. ICC hearings began on December 1, 1952, and proceeded in fits and starts for the next fifteen months. In his opening statement, PRR counsel John B. Prizer insisted that Section 77 of the Bankruptcy Act "is not a device for compelling public ownership," a comment that encapsulated the attitude of railroad officials toward the proposal submitted by the Long Island Transit Authority. President Franklin highlighted the $13.5 million the PRR had loaned the LIRR between 1935 and 1949, and he attributed the carrier's problems to excessive taxation and the unwillingness of the Public Service Commission to grant adequate fare increases. The rectification of those situations, Franklin suggested, would be sufficient to restore the line to safe and efficient operation under private control. LITA chairman George Roosevelt warned the ICC examiner that the railroad's tax arrearage had reached $18 million and was now increasing at the rate of $5.5 million a year. If Pennsylvania Railroad officials did not act "promptly," Roosevelt warned, the agency would withdraw its $20 million purchase offer. He conceded that $20 million was far less than the PRR had invested in the property but reiterated his earlier assessment that LITA could not afford anything more.[147]

Near the end of April, both sides requested an adjournment, hoping to reconcile the reorganization plans in a less public forum than an ICC hearing room. During the interregnum, PRR officials sweetened their proposal, pledging to invest an additional $30 million in the Long Island Rail Road. Franklin's insistence that "reasonable fare increases, in addition to partial tax relief, undoubtedly will be required to make this plan succeed," ensured that Roosevelt and Voorhees were unlikely to accept the offer. After the ICC hearings resumed in November, Roosevelt reminded regulators "that increases in fares of the kind contemplated by the Pennsylvania plan could not be absorbed by the Long Island community." He was equally contemptuous of Franklin's assertion that the PRR should be exempt from PSC oversight. "The Pennsylvania's plan,"

Roosevelt continued, "is not a plan for private ownership, as we understand private ownership. It is really a device by which profits can be guaranteed, in part by public subsidy, without any real public supervision." Governor Dewey was even more blunt, condemning "an effort by the Pennsylvania Railroad either to gain control of the Long Island free of state regulation or, in the alternative, to force the State of New York to socialize the railroad and pay them (the P.R.R) $60,000,000 in condemnation of the property."[148]

As the ICC hearings ground on, commuter opposition to the Long Island Rail Road showed no signs of abating. In August 1951, two months prior to his resignation as trustee, William Draper engaged William Wyer & Company to prepare a series of operating and reorganization plans for the company. Wyer, a consulting engineer, proposed the elimination of service on three marginal lines—including those serving Greenport and Montauk, at the eastern end of Long Island. The routes clearly operated at a substantial loss, but representatives from Nassau and Suffolk Counties refused to accept the cessation of rail service. The LIRR's unpaid taxes proved a particularly contentious issue. Wyer persuaded the city of New York to accept $8.8 million, in settlement for a $13 million tax arrearage. The resolution of the outstanding tax liabilities enabled the LIRR to generate a small positive net income, but Roosevelt and Voorhees had planned to use that money to pay for upgrades to the railroad and demanded that the city return the $5.5 million paid. They announced that—absent a refund—they would have no choice other than to curtail LITA's $28 million program of improvements.[149] The two commissioners also alerted the ICC that his tax settlement might scuttle their reorganization plan. When Draper resigned as the LIRR's trustee, moreover, William Wyer replaced him. Wyer's appointment generated concerns regarding a conflict of interest, and his relationship with residents and with the Long Island Transit Authority was at times contentious. In addition to his trustee's salary of $30,000, Wyer's firm billed the LIRR $75,000 annually for comprehensive operating studies. LITA representatives soon accused Wyer of conspiring with the PRR to prolong the bankruptcy as long as possible, to maximize his consulting fees. Despite Wyer's assurance that he did not profit personally from the arrangement, Kennedy's court blocked his efforts to gain the additional business for his company.[150]

First as a consultant and then as a trustee, Wyer concluded that the LIRR could not survive without a substantial increase in fares. His perspective heightened allegations that he was in league with Pennsylvania Railroad executives. The state's Public Service Commission acknowledged that "this commission was engaged in an unrelenting effort to block the increase," giving Wyer little choice other than to take the matter to the federal level. His April 1953 application to the ICC aroused the ire of Lawrence E. Walsh, the legal counsel for the PSC. "We have memoranda from the Pennsylvania's files," Walsh asserted, "which show that it is a proceeding either worked out jointly by the two railroads or worked out with silent approval or acquiescence of the Long Island." In addition to accusations of "sinister collusion" between the Pennsylvania Railroad and the Long Island Rail Road, PSC personnel asserted that their control over rates superseded the authority of the Interstate Commerce Commission. Nassau County executive A. Holly Patterson was equally determined to retain low rates and local control, and he hoped to "forbid I.C.C. interference with passenger fares on railroads of purely local character such as the Long Island." When an ICC examiner granted a 25 percent fare increase in November—while noting that it would eliminate less than two-thirds of the company's operating deficit—Public Service Commission officials made clear their disapproval. PSC chairman Benjamin F. Feinberg accused Wyer of "an inherent disregard by the trustee of the normal regulatory procedure and the hope of obtaining thereby an unconscionable advantage to the detriment of the people who must look to the Long Island for transportation." Feinberg and his fellow commissioners "took the position that the passenger service of the Long Island, being entirely of an intrastate character, its fares are subject to State regulation and asked the Federal agency to dismiss the Pennsylvania's application," while ensuring that they "opposed the Pennsylvania at every turn."[151]

The disagreements between William Wyer and the Public Service Commission paralleled an increasingly dysfunctional relationship between the LIRR's trustee and the members of the Long Island Transit Authority. The twenty new Pullman-Standard passenger cars, often referred to as "Wyer cars," were not scheduled to enter service until October 1953. Even then, they would be rare examples of modernity in a fleet of nearly twelve hundred cars, many of which dated to the 1920s. In an effort to eliminate overcrowding and alleviate the problems associated with older equipment, Long Island Rail Road officials surveyed commuters on the optimal design for new rolling stock. The company hired Howard Ketcham, a color and design engineer, to craft a more modern interior, with improved lighting. "The result of Mr. Ketcham's efforts will be better lighted, more cheerful cars, with an integrated color scheme and new types of upholstery," Wyer emphasized. Ketcham indicated that he was also committed to the provision of coat hooks and "windows that can really be opened"—a statement that indicated the decrepit nature of much of the LIRR fleet. Company officials polled commuters on the optimal design for new cars. Patrons evaluated three samples, placed on display at nine stations. A clear majority favored a color palette that included a cream ceiling, blue-green walls, rust-red floor tile, and blue spruce upholstery. Despite Ketcham's interest in aluminum coat hooks, most commuters rejected that feature. On the more important question of seating arrangements, the largest number of votes went to a design that squeezed 148 people in each car. The efficient use of seats nonetheless required passengers to sit fully upright, in what company officials labeled "good posture" seats—something that few commuters were willing to accept. The compromise choice was for more comfortable seating in a car that accommodated 128 people. Based in part on the results of the passenger survey, the LIRR ordered more than a hundred new cars, for use in electrified and nonelectrified territory.[152]

Wyer also authorized the rebuilding of older equipment, largely as a stopgap measure until the new cars could arrive. In January 1953, he announced that shop crews would begin refurbishing cars at a rate of seventeen per month. George Roosevelt, who chaired the Long Island Transit Authority, had little patience for such halfhearted measures. "The announced class repair of 17 cars per month, or 204 cars per year," he observed, "differs little from the average annual rate of 210 cars during the period from 1929 until the time Mr. Wyer took over as trustee." It was a stinging rebuke, given the extended period of deferred maintenance during the Great Depression. "Over the years Long Island passenger cars have been allowed to deteriorate shamefully," Roosevelt concluded. "What is really needed is a major car purchase and rehabilitation program." Relations between Roosevelt and Wyer, which were never good to begin with, sank even lower when LITA officials accused the LIRR's trustee of impeding the agency's rehabilitation program. The subsequent Public Service Commission inspection underscored Roosevelt's critical remarks. Following an evaluation of 1,314 cars, PSC officials indicated that 242 required major rehabilitation, 945 exhibited less-serious defects, and 455 were dirty.[153] On some crowded rush-hour trains, nearly 30 percent of commuters stood in aisles or vestibules.[154]

In the face of mounting criticism from LITA, the PSC, and Long Island commuters, Wyer ordered Long Island Rail Road personnel to find a solution to the equipment problem. Their initial report, delivered to Wyer in February 1953, recommended the expenditure of $28.8 million for the purchase of 112 new cars and the rehabilitation of 558 others, all for use in electrified territory. A parallel study favored a similar approach for rolling stock on the nonelectrified lines. The hybrid policy, Wyer emphasized, would cost far less than the replacement of the LIRR fleet with new equipment, or the complete rehabilitation of all the existing cars. Even the more economical solution, however, would cost far more money than the Long Island Rail Road possessed.[155]

Emerging from Bankruptcy

As 1953 ended, the combatants in the Long Island Rail Road reorganization battle faced two critical, unresolved issues. One was the long-standing tension between the "illegal" plan proposed by the PRR and the "confiscation" model favored by the Long Island Transit Authority. The first was politically untenable, and the second, economically indefensible. The other struggle pitted local authority—in the form of LITA and the PSC—against the Interstate Commerce Commission and the federal regulatory apparatus. On December 10, Roosevelt and Voorhees reminded Governor Dewey that the LIRR would soon enter its fifth year in receivership, suggested that the prolonged ICC hearings constituted a "roadblock" to reorganization, and asserted that the overlapping jurisdictions of state and federal agencies "are causing an indefinite prolongation of the bankruptcy and complexities in the reorganization to a degree making impossible an early solution of the Long Island's problems." On the following day, Dewey spent more than forty-five minutes with President Dwight D. Eisenhower, complaining about the ICC's "usurpation" of state authority and "unprecedented interference" in the LIRR's affairs. Dewey also hinted that the president possessed the authority to dictate policy to the Interstate Commerce Commission. "Conceivably," the governor told reporters after the meeting, "the I.C.C. could find it doesn't have jurisdiction over the Long Island Rail Road." A month later, the New York Assembly unanimously approved a petition asking Congress to give the Public Service Commission sole authority over the Long Island Rail Road. Legislators could not pass up the opportunity to simultaneously heap additional criticism on the embattled William Wyer, asserting that his proposal to end service on the easternmost portions of the railroad was "gravely detrimental to the public interest."[156]

Despite Dewey's misgivings regarding increased governmental control over the Long Island Rail Road, two developments pushed him in precisely that direction. One, on March 4, was the release of the report prepared by the New York and New Jersey rapid-transit commissions. "Transit and traffic in the metropolitan area have now exceeded the point of full saturation," the commissioners warned. "Self-strangulation is becoming increasingly acute." They suggested closer cooperation and further studies, noting that "a full-scale economic investigation is in order, since one of the most serious aspects of the whole picture is the continuing state of financial crisis which constantly faces most of mass transit facilities." *New York Times* reporter Leonard Ingalls responded with a series of articles highlighting the difficulties faced by the Long Island Rail Road and other commuter carriers. "After thirty years of concern over its mass transportation problems," Ingalls reminded his readers, "the New York metropolitan region faces a basic decision. It must resolve the rivalry between rail and rubber." His insistence on "giving rail travel the attention and priority it deserves in the public interest" suggested his clear preferences in the matter. By June, the New York and New Jersey legislatures had transformed the two parallel transit agencies into the bistate Metropolitan Rapid Transit Commission. The new agency hired business and public-relations consultant Arthur Page as project director, in charge of a series of transportation studies. Page had a long history of collaboration with the Pennsylvania Railroad—as did William Wyer and the consulting firm of Coverdale & Colpitts, two of the many subcontractors on the project. The studies would not be completed until 1958, but preliminary research suggested that rail transit could not survive long without a massive increase in public-sector involvement.[157]

The second factor that pushed Dewey toward public ownership and operation involved the ongoing jurisdictional dispute between the Public Service Commission and the Interstate Commerce Commission. On March 5, 1954, the day after the New York and New Jersey transit commissions issued their joint report, the ICC dismissed Wyer's request for a 25 percent increase in fares. It was hardly a victory for local political autonomy, however. Interstate Commerce Commission officials emphasized that the additional revenue sought would be insufficient to cover the LIRR's losses. They also gave the PSC sixty days—soon amended to "a reasonable time"—to consider the matter. The implication was clear. Unless the members of the Public Service Commission abandoned their implacable opposition to a rate increase, the ICC would grant one on rehearing. "An increase of 25 per cent in commutation fares was inevitable," PSC officials concluded, "without any binding commitment of improvement in the service."[158]

Predictably, Dewey thought the ICC's actions "inappropriate," while his insistence that "both effective management and new capital are absolutely essential"

suggested that he was equally critical of Wyer's actions as trustee and the unwillingness of PRR officials to invest additional funds in their subsidiary. He ordered LITA to prepare a plan for the rehabilitation of the Long Island Rail Road, one that would remove the company from bankruptcy, rebuild its physical plant and equipment, and exempt the carrier from ICC jurisdiction. Dewey suggested that at least $50 million in capital improvements would be necessary, although he left Roosevelt and Voorhees with the unenviable task of determining where that money would come from. Above all, the governor emphasized, any fare increase would have to be well below the 25 percent threshold that the ICC was prepared to authorize.[159]

Acting with considerable speed, Roosevelt and Voorhees submitted a proposal to the governor on May 26. They recommended legislative amendments to the 1951 Railroad Redevelopment Act that would terminate the bankruptcy proceedings while extinguishing LITA. In its place would be a new railroad redevelopment corporation, empowered to spend nearly $59 million on improvements over the next twelve years. For the first nine of those years, the LIRR would pay a maximum of $1.8 million annually in taxes. Roosevelt and Voorhees complied—albeit barely—with Dewey's stipulation regarding rates, limiting the initial fare increase to 20 percent. "So far as we can now foresee," they suggested, "this 20 per cent increase in fares should be adequate to carry forward the rehabilitation program. This is based, of course, on the assumption that no substantial increases in operating costs or further declines in business should occur." Given that those circumstances had continually afflicted the LIRR since the end of World War II, Roosevelt and Voorhees were making an assumption that was unlikely to prove correct. Their accompanying stipulation that rising costs would trigger a corresponding increase in rates, without approval of the Public Service Commission, thus constituted more of a warning than a reassurance. In other respects, however, the proposal preserved PSC control over rates and service, enjoining railroad officials from appealing such matters to the Interstate Commerce Commission.[160] Roosevelt and Voorhees pledged to devote any gains in revenues to improvements in equipment and service, with nothing to be paid to the Pennsylvania Railroad. In addition to foregoing any return on their investment in the LIRR, PRR officials pledged to lend the new redevelopment corporation $5.5 million— money that could be used as a down payment on new passenger cars, in the expectation that higher fares could be used to pay the balance of the cost. The Pennsylvania Railroad would continue to own and operate the company, but with all management based locally rather than in Philadelphia. It was an arrangement that suited Walter Franklin, soon to reach the PRR's mandatory retirement age. He resigned the company's presidency, and thereafter served solely as president of the Long Island Rail Road, assisting in the reorganization.[161]

The parties most directly connected with the operations of the Long Island Rail Road were enthusiastic in their support of the proposal developed by Roosevelt and Voorhees. William Draper, the former LITA chairman and LIRR trustee, wrote from Mexico City, suggesting that it was "a modern miracle of successful railroad finance." Governor Dewey boasted that the arrangement ended the bankruptcy proceedings, preserved the principle of private ownership, ensured the supremacy of state regulation over that of the federal government, and diffused the threat of a massive fare increase. He called the plan "a truly remarkable achievement," while emphasizing the cooperation of Franklin and other PRR executives. Pennsylvania Railroad officials made modest concessions to the state, but they received considerable benefits in return. They included the potential for unlimited fare increases, as necessary to keep pace with rising costs—something they had been demanding for decades. Roosevelt and Voorhees also acknowledged the PRR's "existing investment in the railroad of over $100 million." It was a significant concession, and one that increased more than fivefold the $20 million LITA had offered to pay for the Long Island Rail Road. Pragmatism rather than generosity prompted that statement, however. "It must, therefore, be recognized by everyone," Roosevelt and Voorhees admitted, "that without agreement with the Pennsylvania Railroad, as virtually the sole creditor and owner, it is impossible either to bring about a prompt termination of the bankruptcy or to provide the new capital so badly needed to launch a rehabilitation of the Long Island."[162]

Despite the newfound harmony between PRR officials, LITA representatives, and the governor's office, the May 1954 agreement engendered controversy in the areas served by the Long Island Rail Road. The New York City corporation counsel calculated that the tax concessions would cost the city more than $16 million over the nine-year abatement period. Newly elected Mayor Robert F. Wagner Jr. labeled the proposal "unsound and discriminatory" and vowed to take the battle to the state legislature and the courts. Democratic state chairman Richard H. Balch insisted that "the people of Long Island will resent this arrogant move by the Governor. They know it means that the Governor is mandating a 20 per cent fare increase upon them and in return they will receive nothing but a

lot of pie-in-the-sky promises." Long Beach Democratic assemblyman Joseph F. Carlino likewise emphasized that his constituents would not look favorably on "cheap political stunts." The Democratic leader of Nassau County, Lawrence W. McKeown, reiterated the long-standing assertion that "there cannot be any satisfactory operation of the Long Island under Pennsylvania domination." Democrats were in the minority in the state legislature, however. After Dewey called a special session on June 7, they failed to alter the bill the governor favored. On June 15, he signed an amendment to the Railroad Redevelopment Act, placing into law the suggestions that Roosevelt and Voorhees had made a few months earlier.[163]

Thomas Goodfellow, characterized by the *New York Times* as "an earnest, conscientious man who realizes the seriousness of his responsibility," resigned the superintendency of the PRR's Pittsburgh Division to become the general manager of the LIRR. James A. Schultz, a veteran of both the Pennsylvania Railroad and Pan American World Airways, became the new director of public relations. On August 12, the PRR regained control over the Long Island Rail Road, bankruptcy proceedings ended, commuters braced themselves for the 20 percent fare increase that would take effect at one minute past midnight, and the controversial trustee William Wyer was in search of a new job. In his place, the fifteen-member LIRR Board of Directors included some familiar Pennsylvania Railroad faces, including Franklin, James Symes (the new president), James Newell (the vice president in charge of operations), and David Bevan (the vice president in charge of finance). Governor Dewey appointed five public directors, including Roosevelt and Voorhees.[164]

Despite the political controversy, even justifiably cynical Long Island commuters were impressed with improvements in service that the new legislation engendered. "The ugly duckling," a reporter for *Time* magazine suggested, "is sprouting a few swanlike pinfeathers." Goodfellow pledged that LIRR shopworkers would upgrade a further 696 pieces of equipment, providing sixteen thousand additional seats. In May 1955, Goodfellow announced that the LIRR was adding sixty more trains to its midday and evening commuter service. A month later, he promised that diesels would soon replace the last of the railroad's steam locomotives. Railroad personnel addressed deferred maintenance along dozens of miles of tracks and at more than fifty stations. Goodfellow improved the LIRR's image, supporting an employee course in public relations, demanding that passengers be kept informed of the reasons for any delays, and creating an "engineer for a day" program. During the last quarter of 1954 and the first three quarters of 1955, the LIRR even turned a profit of just over $1 million—money that was off limits to the PRR and could thus be reinvested in the property.[165]

The honeymoon was short-lived. Thanks in large measure to aggressive wage demands by the Brotherhood of Railroad Trainmen, the 20 percent fare increase proved inadequate to pay for the railroad's operation and rehabilitation. In November 1955, Goodfellow announced higher ticket prices—the LIRR's seventh increase in eight years. Under the terms of the amended Railroad Redevelopment Act, representatives from the Public Service Commission could not refuse the request, so long as the money would be allocated solely to improvements. Less than a year after the PSC acquiesced, Goodfellow announced that rates would rise for the eighth time, adding fifty cents to the cost of weekly commutation tickets. "We know people aren't going to be happy about the fare increase," he conceded, and he thought it necessary to remind customers that "nobody pockets a penny, either in dividends or in interest or principal payments, on more than $60,000,000 of old indebtedness" held by the Pennsylvania Railroad. "The hardest part of my job," Goodfellow lamented, "is dealing with those people who think I take a bag of gold down to Philadelphia every Friday afternoon."[166]

Despite Goodfellow's reassurances, commuters and elected officials criticized the LIRR's steadily increasing fares. Nathan M. Klein, the president of the North Shore Commuters Association, accused the railroad of treating its passengers with "utter contempt" and asked Governor W. Averell Harriman to investigate the matter. Harriman, a Democrat who was more critical of business corporations than his predecessor, suggested that the state legislature investigate the management of the Long Island Rail Road. Albany Republicans deflected the effort, securing instead the promise of a Public Service Commission inquiry into the railroad's affairs. As Democrats feared, the PSC accomplished little, but the ongoing rate increases fueled the anger of the governor and state legislators. On March 27, 1958, Harriman signed a bill reestablishing full PSC control over rates on the Long Island Rail Road. Goodfellow warned that "retrogression to the old system of protracted hearings on fare adjustments would plunge us hopelessly into the hole." Symes, the PRR's president, condemned the "baldfaced breach of faith by the State of New York" and asserted that the "ill-advised tampering with the Redevelopment Law reverses the Long Island's steady improvement and sends it skidding downhill again." Harriman acknowledged that the new measure might constitute grounds for the dissolution of the May

1954 agreement between the state, the PRR, and the Long Island Rail Road, but he reassured legislators that he could develop a new mechanism for resolving the situation and continuing the improvement program.[167]

With commuters again given the opportunity to choose between unending fare increases and a deteriorating railroad, some began to support a third option. In April 1958, the chairmen of the Liberal Party in Queens, Nassau, and Suffolk Counties suggested that the Railroad Redevelopment Act was "ineffective in stopping the decline of the road or in building it into an adequate public service." They urged public ownership, a concept that politicians from both mainstream parties had resisted for decades. Like their Liberal Party counterparts, Long Island Republicans and Democrats now had access to the studies produced by the Metropolitan Rapid Transit Commission—which suggested improvements that were clearly beyond the reach of the PRR-controlled Long Island Rail Road. Meeting the suggestion that the LIRR should provide nine thousand additional rush-hour seats was sufficiently problematic, but the assertion that "a new East River rail crossing is essential to Long Island transit improvements" was entirely beyond the railroad's abilities. Transit Commission personnel, echoing the prewar recommendations from the Committee of One Hundred, suggested that "the Long Island Rail Road should be assigned the function of serving only Nassau and Suffolk commuters," with those living in Brooklyn and Queens relying on the routes operated by the municipally controlled New York City Transit Authority. Such coordination would only be possible through public ownership of all passenger rail operations in the area.[168]

Thomas Goodfellow, the president of the Long Island, was not yet ready to relinquish his company to the state. By early 1959, however, he and his colleagues had abandoned all hope that private enterprise could resolve the situation. "Scores of studies over the past decade have agreed on at least one point," he conceded. "A profitable commuter operation, under present-day conditions, is completely impossible. Railroads in the New York metropolitan area have long realized this. With no profit motive, incentive disappears." While Goodfellow did not go so far as to suggest government ownership, he acknowledged that "at best, our present rehabilitation program is only a stop-gap measure." He suggested that at least $70 million in capital investments would be required over the next few years, yet he acknowledged that the LIRR could not reasonably ask for any additional fare increases. Instead, he encouraged the city's mayor and the governors of New York, New Jersey, and Connecticut to create a new government agency that would purchase passenger equipment and lease it to the region's commuter railroads at a nominal cost. The inclusion of states that the LIRR did not serve embodied Goodfellow's recognition that the commuter rail crisis affected every railroad that served Greater New York. It also reflected changes in federal law that were causing that crisis to become far more severe.[169]

Weehawken Ferry

When Republican Nelson Rockefeller replaced Averell Harriman as governor, on January 1, 1959, the possibility that the state might purchase the Long Island Rail Road seemed even more remote. Yet Rockefeller was a moderate and as a candidate had undermined Harriman's support in Greater New York by offering improvements in the region's transportation infrastructure. He had good reason to make such promises. By the spring of 1959, Manhattan office workers could look a mile or so to the west, across the Hudson River, for a glimpse of the dark future that likely awaited the city's commuter rail services. Among its many provisions, the Transportation Act of 1958 restricted the ability of state regulatory commissions to block the discontinuance of unprofitable passenger trains. Members of Congress probably envisioned the elimination of myriad branch-line trains that trundled from one small town to another, bereft of passengers. Executives from many of the railroads serving the New Jersey side of the Hudson River nonetheless perceived an opportunity to reduce the financial drain associated with commuter routes that did carry a great many passengers—some eighty thousand a day. Since 1957, officials representing the New York Central had been fighting to discontinue the company's interstate ferry service between Manhattan and Weehawken, New Jersey. Their goal was to end commuter traffic on the NYC's West Shore Line, which would be effectively useless without a ferry connection to Manhattan. On March 2, 1959, two months after Nelson Rockefeller became governor of New York, and based on the provisions of the 1958 legislation, the US Supreme Court upheld the NYC's petition. When the ferries stopped running on March 26, more than five thousand commuters switched to automobiles or buses, and passenger traffic on the West Shore Line fell by 85 percent. The New York Central's initiative inspired other railroad executives to make similar reductions. The Delaware, Lackawanna & Western sought to discontinue its entire commuter operation. Representatives from the Erie announced that they had no plans to abandon the region's commuters—but that, without subsidies, cutbacks were inevitable.[170]

The closing of the Weehawken ferry awakened the area's residents and politicians to the seriousness of the crisis. Austin J. Tobin, the executive director of the Port Authority, was more worried than most, although his concerns had little to do with the plight of commuters. By the time he joined the agency in 1927, Port Authority officials had grown frustrated with the intractability of the railroad problem in Greater New York, and they directed their effort to the construction of bridges and tunnels for highway traffic. They also recognized the inherent unprofitability of rapid-transit and commuter rail operations and assiduously avoided involvement with those modes of transportation. By 1958, however, the Port Authority was in danger of becoming the victim of its success. The agency possessed a reserve fund of more than $64 million, largely accumulated through automobile and truck tolls. As the surplus grew, so did political pressure from both states to spend the money on commuter rail service. To deplete the Port Authority's reserves, Tobin advocated two new development projects—an airport in New Jersey and an international trade center in Lower Manhattan—that would theoretically offer benefits for both states. Acknowledging that the Port Authority's remaining funds would be too tempting for politicians to resist, he also sought legal restrictions on the amount of money the agency could allocate to commuter subsidies. Finally, Tobin worked behind the scenes, encouraging politicians in New York and New Jersey to establish another bistate compact, one that would use tax revenues rather than Port Authority funds to subsidize the LIRR, the PRR, and other commuter operations.[171]

Tobin enjoyed more success in New York than he did in New Jersey. On March 15, 1959, Robert W. Purcell, the director of the New York Office of Transportation, briefed the newly inaugurated governor on the state of commuter services operated by the LIRR, the New York Central, and the New Haven. Purcell recommended an unprecedented level of government support, including a reduction of $15 million per year in the railroads' state and local taxes. He cautioned against public ownership but advocated the creation of a bistate transit commission, managed by five representatives apiece from New York and New Jersey. Residents of the seventeen New York and New Jersey counties within the district would accept higher taxes, in exchange for improved commuter service. Purcell suggested that the Port Authority purchase $20 million in new passenger equipment, to be leased to the three railroads, with loan guarantees that would enable the carriers to borrow an additional $80 million. The suggested figure of $20 million was more than Tobin wanted to spend, but a finite equipment obligation that would deplete less than a third of the Port Authority's reserves was far preferable to the unending subsidization of commuter rail deficits that were approaching $140 million per year. Representatives from the NYC and the New Haven praised the Purcell plan, but officials at the LIRR suggested that it was "a moot question at this point," since the company could not afford to lease equipment from the Port Authority or anyone else. Democratic Party state chairman Michael H. Prendergast criticized the proposal as a "multi-million give-away to the railroads at the expense of commuters and taxpayers," and every Democrat in both houses of the state legislature voted against it. So did some Republicans, but on March 26—at the close of the legislative session—it secured approval by extremely narrow margins.[172]

Tobin's strategy failed miserably on the other side of the Hudson River. New Jersey residents were generally suspicious of the Port Authority, suggesting that the agency was promoting the economic growth of New York City at their expense. Governor Robert B. Meyner and legislators in Trenton nonetheless reacted with alarm to the plight of the commuter railroads, including the PRR. In Washington, New Jersey senator Harrison A. Williams Jr. sponsored a bill to prohibit the elimination of commuter service. The following day, Jersey City Democrat Dominick V. Daniels introduced parallel legislation in the House of Representatives. In Trenton, Meyner pledged to protect commuters, although he also vowed that he would not increase taxes to do so. It was a rash promise, given that New Jersey was at that moment facing its worst fiscal crisis since the Civil War. Excessive reliance on excise taxes, coupled with opposition to further increases in real estate assessments that were already the highest in the country, ensured that little money would be available to assist the railroads. Despite the revenue shortfall, on April 13 the New Jersey Assembly approved membership in the bistate transportation compact. The state senate passed the measure on May 4, and Meyner immediately signed the bill into law. The $100 million in potential funding for commuter equipment benefited only the Long Island Rail Road, the New York Central, and the New Haven, and thus provided scant immediate benefit for hard-pressed New Jersey commuters. By expanding the responsibilities of the two states represented in the Port Authority, the agreement nonetheless established a precedent for further negotiations.[173]

Interstate cooperation took time, however, leaving Meyner to fend for himself. In June, he introduced a plan to use surplus funds accumulated by the New Jersey Turnpike Authority to support commuter operations. He was careful to avoid the use of the word *subsidy* and instead

asserted that the money would enable the state to purchase commuter service on behalf of its residents. The plan drew harsh criticism, particularly from downstate legislators whose constituents rarely traveled to Manhattan. The funding arrangements for the New Jersey Turnpike stipulated that tolls would end when the Turnpike Authority redeemed the bonds used to finance construction. Diversion of surplus toll revenues to commuter railroads would delay the advent of free travel. Truckers likewise saw little reason why their operating costs should increase, to assist railroad commuters.[174]

Despite such opposition, the legislature approved the measure on August 31. Meyner's relief plan would not take effect, however, unless voters gave their approval at the November elections. The governor staked his political reputation on the outcome of the referendum, and he received bipartisan support from many civic leaders. The strongest opposition came from Hudson County, which would lose $11 million in revenue if proposed tax abatements for the railroads' waterfront properties took effect. On Election Day, Hudson County residents voted four-to-one against the measure, contributing to a crushing statewide defeat. Putting a brave face on the disaster, Meyner promised to do everything he could to forestall reductions in commuter service. Two days after the election, the Associated Railroads of New Jersey, the trade group representing the PRR and the state's other carriers, held a meeting in Penn Station to discuss strategy. A subsequent conference, at the headquarters of the Delaware, Lackawanna & Western, included government officials who could offer exhortations but not assistance. In the absence of public funding, on December 30, PRR officials requested Interstate Commerce Commission approval of a 28 percent increase in fares for the railroad's ten thousand daily New Jersey commuters.[175]

Left to their own devices, executives from the Pennsylvania Railroad and the Central Railroad of New Jersey sought ways to reduce costs through shared trackage and the abandonment of duplicate facilities. Worn down by short hauls, high terminal costs, and a decline in coal traffic, and heavily dependent on commuter service, the Jersey Central was in serious trouble. The company possessed extensive—and heavily taxed—pier-side facilities in Hudson County, a mile-long combination of bridges and trestles over Newark Bay that constituted a maintenance nightmare, and an expensive ferry service between Jersey City and Liberty Street in Lower Manhattan. In 1958, the company incurred a passenger deficit of nearly $7.8 million—principally attributable to commuter service—and an overall loss of more than $1.9 million. The

PRR's problems in the area were not so severe, but the company's New York & Long Branch service was losing more than $1.5 million annually. The completion of the parallel Garden State Parkway in 1957 halved the number of railroad passengers headed for the Jersey Shore. Creeping suburbanization created double-digit increases in commuter patronage, but, as on Long Island, short hauls, low rates and high taxes rendered that traffic profitless. "Under present conditions," PRR executives concluded, the "financial results of these services will not improve."[176]

The situation made PRR officials receptive to Meyner's efforts to save commuter service in New Jersey. State Highway commissioner Dwight R. G. Palmer, a supporter of the ill-fated effort to use turnpike funds to support the railroads, also asked PRR executives to assist in the seemingly hopeless task of alleviating the Jersey Central's commuter problems. On July 15, 1959, the PRR released the results of a study overseen by James W. Diffenderfer, the railroad's director of special services. A month had passed since Governor Meyner proposed tapping the highway surplus, and voters had not yet rejected the proposal. During the interregnum, however, Diffenderfer prepared for the worst. At Aldene, a few miles west of Elizabeth, the Lehigh Valley crossed over the Jersey Central route that led to the Communipaw ferry terminal. The construction of a short connecting track between the two lines would enable eastbound Jersey Central commuter trains to follow the Lehigh Valley to a junction with the Pennsylvania Railroad main line, just south of Newark. At Newark, commuters possessed several options, including the Hudson & Manhattan Railroad and the PRR route leading to Penn Station in Midtown. With the Aldene connection in place, the Jersey Central could abandon the Communipaw Terminal. The Pennsylvania Railroad might also assist the Jersey Central by assuming sole control over passenger traffic on the New York & Long Branch. The economies resulting from the elimination of redundant facilities might be sufficient to save the Jersey Central from bankruptcy and preserve the company's remaining commuter operations—without obligating the New Jersey state government to spend any money to fix the problem.[177]

Diffenderfer's willingness to come to the rescue of both the Jersey Central and the state of New Jersey came with certain conditions, however. Chief among them was that the PRR should be permitted to discontinue all service to its ferry terminal at Jersey City. Diffenderfer also demanded the right to eliminate some trains and to close stations. He insisted that the state should grant tax relief on facilities and equipment used in passenger service as well as assume sole responsibility for grade-crossing

improvements—a policy that would be in keeping with the governor's willingness to use highway funds to support commuter railroads. Finally, Diffenderfer made clear that the Aldene plan was no more than a temporary solution to a much larger problem. In the long term, he expected that a public-transit authority—yet nonexistent—would pay for new equipment, upgrade station facilities, and electrify the New York & Long Branch.[178]

In the aftermath of the November 1959 defeat of Meyner's Turnpike proposal, Diffenderfer's cooperative spirit and his dire warnings encouraged the governor to develop another strategy for funding commuter railroads. In April 1960, Highway commissioner Palmer presented a comprehensive set of recommendations to Meyner and the New Jersey legislature. Palmer suggested annual payments of $6 million to the railroads. The PRR would receive the largest share, nearly $1.7 million.[179] It was barely more than a token gesture, given that the ten companies operating in New Jersey collectively lost more than $27 million on their passenger services during 1959. Palmer also appropriated the principal elements of Diffenderfer's proposal, including the construction of the Aldene connection. The new rail link, Palmer emphasized, would enable seven thousand Jersey Central commuters to have an all-rail ride directly to Lower Manhattan or to Penn Station in Midtown, albeit with a change of trains at Newark.[180] The project's viability ultimately depended on the ability of the Hudson Tubes to accommodate the commuters who would no longer be able to utilize the Jersey Central's ferry service. Unfortunately, the Hudson & Manhattan Railroad had been in bankruptcy since November 1954, and its financial prospects were even worse than those of the Jersey Central. Palmer accordingly called for legislation, in both New York and New Jersey, that would require the Port Authority to buy ninety new passenger cars and lease them to the H&M.[181]

Pennsylvania Railroad officials paid close attention to the legislative debates relating to the Palmer plan. The outcome would determine whether the PRR would divert Jersey Central trains to Newark and establish a new operating pattern for the New York & Long Branch—and whether the Jersey Central would abandon its Jersey City terminal and its associated ferry service. Most New Jersey residents supported the proposal, but budget director Abram H. Vermeulen reminded legislators that the state's financial situation was "too tight" to pay for it. Meyner suggested imposing an income tax on the 150,000 New Jersey residents who worked in Manhattan, irrespective of how they reached the city, and equal to what they paid to New York State. Because they could deduct the new levy from their New York taxes, New Jersey residents would come out even. The state of New York would not, however, and stood to lose as much as $40 million in annual revenue. It was not the sort of policy that would foster the bistate cooperation necessary to solve the crisis on the Hudson & Manhattan. Secure in the knowledge that New York would pay for the rehabilitation of New Jersey's commuter railroads, however, the legislature overwhelmingly approved the subsidy bill. Meyner signed the measure into law on June 22, but he astutely avoided a vote on the income-tax proposal. Three months later, the Highway Department's Division of Railroad Transportation signed a contract with the Pennsylvania Railroad for an initial nine-month subsidy of just over $1.4 million. A recently concluded strike by the company's nonoperating employees generated systemwide losses of $40 million, suggesting that the state funds would not be sufficient to rescue commuter services or save the company that operated them.[182]

New Jersey's commuter tax district did not guarantee the survival of the Hudson & Manhattan or the fulfillment of the goals James Diffenderfer recommended. One portion of Palmer's recommendations—Port Authority assistance for the Hudson & Manhattan—required the support of the same New Yorkers who were outraged by the income tax on New Jersey commuters. Even as Meyner signed the rail subsidy bill, he possessed sufficient political acumen to allow the clock to run out on the 1960 legislative session without acting on the tax measure. The year's delay gave Governor Rockefeller the opportunity to encourage the Port Authority to assist the Hudson & Manhattan. Rockefeller was not particularly happy with Meyner's innovative plan for funding commuter rail subsidies. Nor was Austin Tobin, the Port Authority's executive director, eager to oversee the operation of the Hudson Tubes. However, both favored the development of a World Trade Center in Lower Manhattan. The proposed location, adjacent to the East River, was convenient to Long Island, but difficult to reach from New Jersey. Meyner accordingly emphasized that New Jersey's approval of the Port Authority's involvement in the World Trade Center project was contingent on two factors—assistance for the Hudson & Manhattan and shifting the site to the west side of Manhattan, atop the H&M terminus at the corner of Church and Cortlandt Streets. The pressure proved effective. In September 1960, Tobin ended a Port Authority policy eschewing involvement in commuter rail, one that had been in place for forty years. He offered $20.5 million in Port Authority funds for the purchase of the Hudson & Manhattan, with an additional $49.5 million set aside for new passenger equipment and for real estate development.[183] Tobin made clear that the offer depended on the construction of the Aldene

connection and the termination of the Jersey Central's ferry service to Jersey City—thus funneling additional passengers into the Hudson Tubes.[184] He also demanded legislation in both states, preventing the Port Authority from being saddled with any other commuter rail service in either New York or New Jersey.[185]

The Port Authority's involvement nonetheless depended on New Jersey's approval, giving Meyner a valuable bargaining chip in his efforts to save the Hudson & Manhattan and to bolster his state's commuter rail service. In New York, legislators approved a single bill that combined the World Trade Center development and the Port Authority rescue of the Hudson & Manhattan. Rockefeller signed the legislation on April 8 and appealed to Meyner to support both proposals. In Trenton, Meyner and state legislators demonstrated New Jersey's long-standing suspicion that the Port Authority's activities favored New York. They demanded separate votes on each measure, giving them the opportunity to saddle the Port Authority with the H&M without affording the agency the corresponding benefits associated with the redevelopment project in Lower Manhattan. In November, Richard J. Hughes won New Jersey's gubernatorial election, and even before he took office, he indicated that he was prepared to demand a high price for the state's cooperation with the World Trade Center. Meyner's commuter income tax was now in place but facing a constitutional challenge in federal court. Preparing for any eventuality, Hughes demanded that the Port Authority assume the $6 million in annual commuter rail subsidies being funded by the diversion of income taxes from New York to New Jersey. While he did not gain Port Authority assistance for New Jersey's commuter lines, Hughes did win a significant concession—the relocation of the World Trade Center site to the west side of Manhattan, significantly closer to his state. The final agreement came in January 1962, only days after Hughes took the oath of office in Trenton.[186]

The certainty that the Hudson & Manhattan would survive enabled the Pennsylvania Railroad to implement one of the recommendations associated with the company's July 1959 commuter rail study. On November 17, 1961, the last passenger trains called at the Exchange Place terminal in Jersey City, ending 127 years of rail service at that location. Thereafter, commuters would most likely change at Newark, riding to Manhattan through the Hudson Tubes. By the end of 1963, construction crews demolished the terminal head house and most of the ancillary facilities. The connection between the Jersey Central and the Lehigh Valley, the key to the Aldene plan, remained unbuilt. It would take several more years to complete that project and to secure additional funding for the PRR's commuter operations in New Jersey.[187]

Buying the Long Island Rail Road

By 1964, the state redevelopment corporation had been managing the Long Island Rail Road for more than ten years, and the twelve-year life span provided by the 1954 Railroad Redevelopment Act was about to end. In August 1966, the LIRR would relinquish the tax deferments that had collectively saved the company $65 million. PRR officials, who were now facing serious financial problems on their own railroad, would be legally entitled to demand compensation for the Long Island Rail Road securities that had been effectively frozen for more than a decade. The LIRR's operating costs continued to increase, and both regulators and commuters had begun to lose patience with continual requests for higher rates.[188] The company relied on assistance from Nassau County and the city of New York to keep stations in even a basic state of repair. Despite pressure from Governor Rockefeller, Suffolk County officials refused to cooperate, prompting LIRR executives to seek higher fares that would apply solely to residents of that county. Members of the Public Service Commission were unsympathetic; in July 1962, they blocked the increase. When the Long Island Rail Road filed another application for higher rates in September 1964, the PSC delayed the matter pending further investigation. The PSC relented in November, but the company was well on its way to incurring a 1964 deficit of more than $2.1 million, its worst showing in a decade.[189]

In addition to providing modest assistance for the Long Island Rail Road, Nassau County furnished a template for efforts by the state government to rescue the faltering carrier. The Nassau County Planning Commission sponsored a 1963 study that recommended a six-year, $103 million slate of improvements.[190] "The basic economic and physical configuration of Long Island," the report noted, "is such that *capital expenditures for railroad service expansion can be justified.*" Projects included the electrification of the route between Mineola and Bethpage, to ensure faster transit times and to reduce the need to change trains at Jamaica. Widespread elimination of grade crossings, the installation of additional tracks, and the rehabilitation of service between Roosevelt Field and Bethpage rounded out the changes within Nassau County. The agenda for New York City was even more ambitious, with a new double-track tunnel under the East River and a connection to Grand Central Terminal.[191] The report implausibly suggested that

increased ridership would generate additional revenue that would be more than adequate to fund the improvements. Representatives from the Planning Commission nonetheless indicated that increased financial support for the LIRR would generate numerous ancillary benefits for the region. Improved transportation, they noted, would facilitate access to jobs, increase opportunities for economic growth and upward social mobility, afford transportation to those too young to drive, and boost property values. Perhaps most compellingly, the study emphasized that a robust commuter rail system would "assist in relieving present and future traffic congestion arising from the growing number of automobiles." The alternative "*cost of accommodating more traffic* through the construction of new arterial highways *is extremely high.*" While the report did not recommend either public subsidies or government ownership, the rationale for increased expenditures on commuter service expanded far beyond the borders in Nassau County. The association of social benefits—particularly the avoidance of expensive and politically divisive highway construction—with commuter rail increasingly affected policy debates in New York, and eventually in the nation's capital.[192]

In September 1964, Rockefeller established a five-person committee, headed by William J. Ronan, to devise a plan for the future operation of the Long Island Rail Road. While Ronan was officially Rockefeller's secretary, he was also the governor's principal advisor on transportation matters as well as one of his closest political associates. Beginning in August 1961, Ronan led the Tri-State Transportation Committee, established to coordinate policies in New York, New Jersey, and Connecticut. In February 1965, acting on Ronan's recommendations, Rockefeller urged the legislature to buy the LIRR at a "reasonable price." Rockefeller recommended a $200 million investment in the Long Island Rail Road—a tenth of the amount that would be necessary to build the twenty-six lanes of freeways necessary to replace the commuter carrier. At his urging, the legislature passed the Metropolitan Commuter Transportation Act in June 1965. The law established a new state agency, the Metropolitan Commuter Transportation Authority, headed by Ronan and empowered to acquire and operate the Long Island Rail Road. Rockefeller insisted that he had no intention of succumbing to "creeping socialism," and he characterized the MCTA as a measure of last resort. "I've been trying to avoid this for six years," he told reporters, emphasizing that his actions were "definitely not a prelude to taking over any other railroad." State senator Earl W. Brydges seconded that assessment, suggesting that "we've got to do almost anything within reason to keep the Long Island operating. And it begins to look as though this is the only thing we can do."[193]

Given the long and contentious debate regarding control of the Long Island Rail Road, the establishment of a "reasonable price" occurred quickly and quietly. Rockefeller refused to name a precise figure, although he reminded his constituents of the $20 million offer made by the Long Island Transit Authority in 1952. Ronan quickly added that the Pennsylvania Railroad held LIRR debts of $61 million as well as capital stock carried at a book value of $78 million. Senate majority leader Joseph Zaretski, a Democrat, suggested a price of $25 million, while Suffolk County executive H. Lee Dennison recommended $115 million, a mere $4 million less than the amount proposed by PRR executives. The Interstate Commerce Commission provided several valuation estimates, ranging from $120 million to $230 million. New York City councilman Paul O'Dwyer suggested that bankruptcy destroyed whatever value had once existed in the LIRR and asserted that "the railroad should now be taken for no more than a token price of $1."[194]

Fortunately for Pennsylvania Railroad executives, O'Dwyer played no role in the negotiations. Board chairman Stuart Saunders initially represented the PRR, but once he discovered that Rockefeller was not involved in the discussions, he quickly lost interest. David Bevan, the PRR's chief financial officer, thus worked with Ronan and his staff to set a purchase price. They relied on a report prepared by the engineering consultants Stone & Webster, which suggested that it would cost $400 million to replace the railroad and that it was worth $94.8 million as scrap. By the end of May 1965, Bevan and Ronan had agreed on a price of $65 million, which reporters erroneously reported as the LIRR's scrap value. The amount was little more than half of what PRR executives claimed the company was worth, but—even adjusting for inflation—it was a far better result than LITA's 1952 offer of $20 million. Ronan made additional concessions that increased the value of the transfer to about $120 million, suggesting that Bevan had been spectacularly successful in his negotiations. The PRR retained its still-profitable Bay Ridge freight line as well as the air rights over the Long Island City freight yards and at Sunnyside Yard in Queens. As a state agency, the LIRR would continue to pay the PRR $500,000 a year in rental fees for the use of the East River tunnels and facilities at Penn Station. Saunders, who had initially doubted that Bevan could obtain such favorable terms, quickly took sole credit for the successful negotiations.

On January 20, 1966, the Pennsylvania Railroad accepted the final installment ($55 million) of the $65 million purchase price and relinquished control over the Long Island Rail Road to the Metropolitan Commuter Transportation Authority.[195]

Seven months later, Ronan announced an aggressive three-year program to rehabilitate the Long Island Rail Road. The proposed improvements included five hundred new cars, worth $90 million, as well as the installation of high-level platforms and the extension of electrified territory. Governor Rockefeller suggested that the LIRR would thus become "the finest commuting facility, not only in the United States, but anywhere in the world." Ronan announced that, with the cooperation of labor and reliance on federal funds, the upgrades would probably not require an increase in rates. "We hope all these radiant expectations will not be derailed after Election Day," the *New York Times* editorialized, "but the L.I.R.R. commuter is entitled to a dream or two while waiting for the millennium."[196]

MCTA ownership did not solve all the Long Island Rail Road's problems. Thomas Goodfellow remained in charge of the company's operations. James Schultz, who had become the LIRR's vice president in charge of public relations, reassured commuters that "absolutely nothing has changed." For many passengers, that was precisely the problem, as the company coped with severe winter weather, equipment shortages, and degraded facilities. Rockefeller's assurances that "creeping socialism" would not affect other railroads proved misplaced. The near collapse of commuter operations throughout Greater New York, coupled with state and local initiatives to obtain a share of federal transportation funds, soon enlarged the MCTA's purview. In May 1967, the governor signed the Transit Unification Bill, giving the agency jurisdiction over the New York City subway and bus services, the Staten Island Rapid Transit, and the commuter services operated by the New York Central and the New Haven. The measure took effect on March 1 of the following year, at which time MCTA became the Metropolitan Transportation Authority, with Ronan serving as its chairman. The last act of the old agency was to release *Metropolitan Transportation: A Program for Action*, a $2.9 billion plan to upgrade the region's transportation facilities. The subway system would be the primary beneficiary, but the LIRR would receive some improvements as well. Despite the availability of state bond funding, the ongoing operation of the LIRR remained expensive, and one of the first tasks of the successor agency was to request a substantial increase in rates. "Nobody is more unhappy about that fare hike," Ronan asserted in a television interview, than "the management of the Long Island Railroad or the Metropolitan Transportation Authority Board." Many Long Islanders begged to differ, indicating that they possessed a significantly higher degree of unhappiness. The old LIRR "was running better than you're running it," an exasperated commuter told Ronan. "It's worse now." Another was more specific, lamenting that "for $42.50 a month, you have to stand." In response to protests from Nassau County commuters, state supreme court justice William J. Sullivan ordered MTA officials to demonstrate that the higher ticket prices were not "arbitrary, capricious and an abuse of discretion." Such language would have sounded strikingly familiar to Hobart Fash, the 1920s Paul Revere of Long Island—to say nothing of commuters who battled the Long Island Rail Road in the decades that followed.[197]

For much of the twentieth century, the Long Island Rail Road proved a financial and a public-relations embarrassment for PRR executives. With considerable justification, they blamed regulatory officials for the plight of the LIRR, emphasizing that in the three decades following the end of World War I, costs had risen considerably, while commuter fares remained the same. Just as the Interstate Commerce Commission was not a monolithic national entity, neither was there a unified state or local regulatory conspiracy against the railroad. Rather, agencies such as the New York Transit Commission and the Public Service Commission were the products of the complex interplay of local and state politics. As such, their policies often depended on events unconnected with the LIRR's operations. During the 1920s and 1930s, PRR and LIRR executives nonetheless regarded higher rates as their due and thus adopted an astonishingly cavalier attitude toward the collection of operating cost data. In presenting such incomplete information to regulatory officials, they undermined the strength of their position.

Ultimately, however, the nature of the relationship between the Long Island Rail Road and the Pennsylvania Railroad did far more damage to the two companies than did the actions of managers or public-sector officials. Because the LIRR was both a part of and separate from the PRR, it was never precisely clear whether one company was taking advantage of the other or whether a railroad that carried commuters between Long Island and Manhattan was engaged in intrastate or interstate commerce. Jurisdictional disputes complicated the efforts of railroad executives, regulatory officials, and politicians, all of whom wanted to ensure that commuters had access to safe and efficient transportation. Despite the creation of quasi-public agencies in the 1920s and afterward, civic leaders in

Greater New York never succeeded in developing a comprehensive transportation plan that would integrate the commuter rail lines, subways, bridges, tunnels, ferries, and highways into a seamless network. In the absence of planning, forceful individuals such as Mayor John F. Hylan and Parks commissioner Robert Moses implemented subway and highway projects that suited their own interests, without considering the ramifications for existing Long Island Rail Road service. As those new transportation arteries drew business away from the LIRR, and with commuter fares stagnant, the railroad's managers could not afford to increase capacity, improve service, or even keep the public safe from accidents. By the early 1950s, an increasing number of New Yorkers set aside their fears of "creeping socialism," at least to the degree that it suited their personal welfare. They supported some form of governmental operation of the LIRR—but it was not until 1958, when voters elected Nelson Rockefeller as their governor, that a resolution to the commuter crisis was possible. The creation of the Metropolitan Commuter Transportation Authority was a blessing for the PRR, in that it allowed the company's managers to recover an unexpectedly large portion of their investment in the Long Island Rail Road. It was an even greater victory for New York residents, however, for it embodied a widespread realization that public transit offered social benefits that private corporations could not be expected to provide.

Commuters and Urban Politics in Philadelphia

The fate of commuter service in Philadelphia proved even more problematic than it had been on Long Island. While New York was the nation's largest city, with the greatest number of commuters, they made their way to and from work on a wide variety of railroads—including the New York Central, the New Haven, and several New Jersey carriers. By the 1960s, about forty thousand Greater New York commuters utilized the PRR each day, as a company separate from the Long Island Rail Road. That was little

Facing, Philadelphia possessed a superb network of commuter rail lines, operated by the Pennsylvania Railroad and the Reading. Municipal efforts to subsidize commuter operations gained enthusiastic support from officials in Bucks and Montgomery Counties. Their counterparts in Delaware County, home to affluent communities along the Main Line, were opposed the use of local tax revenues to support the initiatives of politicians in Center-City Philadelphia. *Courtesy of the Special Collections Research Center, Temple University Libraries, Philadelphia, PA.*

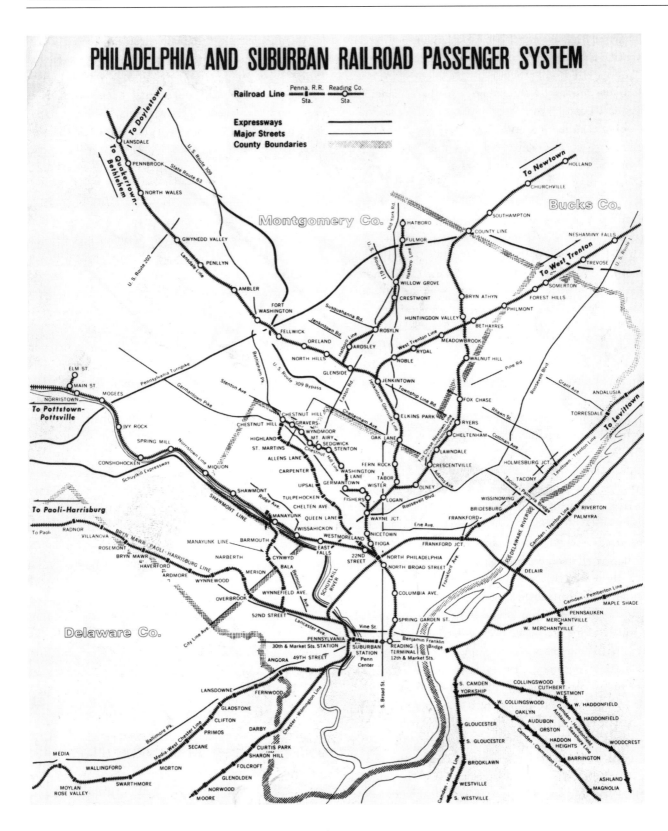

PHILADELPHIA AND SUBURBAN RAILROAD PASSENGER SYSTEM

more than half of the seventy thousand who traveled the PRR's six commuter routes in Philadelphia. Two of those lines—from Center City north to Trenton and south to Wilmington—represented local service along the busy link between New York and Washington. The Media–West Chester Local, part of the old West Chester & Philadelphia Railroad, traversed prosperous communities in the vicinity of Swarthmore before petering out into a sparsely populated area that generated few passengers. The Norristown Local ran along the industrialized valley of the

Schuylkill River as far as its namesake city, through largely working-class neighborhoods. North of Center City, the Chestnut Hill Local provided service to one of the more desirable residential communities in the Philadelphia region. The most prestigious addresses lay along the Main Line. It was the PRR route to the west, hosting luxury trains such as *The Broadway Limited* as well as the storied Paoli Local commuter service. The lines converged on the upper level of 30th Street Station before heading a mile east to terminate at Suburban Station in Center City. The Reading operated another six commuter lines, extending northward and westward from Reading Terminal. One paralleled the route of the PRR's Norristown Local, while another terminated in Chestnut Hill, only a few hundred feet from the PRR station. The remaining four Reading commuter lines served Doylestown, Warminster, Fox Chase, and West Trenton. There was, however, no connection between the PRR and Reading facilities in Center City, although the possibility that one might be created animated urban planners for the better part of half a century.[198]

Population growth and the transition from the Great Depression to a wartime economy increased the strain on the PRR's commuter operations in Philadelphia. In January 1942, John Deasy and Walter Franklin, the PRR's vice presidents in charge of operations and traffic, reported that the number of people living in the Main Line suburbs had tripled since 1900. About 20 percent of that growth occurred during the previous decade, yet commuter traffic decreased steadily between 1930 and 1937—suggesting that those who still had jobs preferred to reach them by automobile. While there had been a slight gain in the last years of the 1930s, thanks to the improving economic situation, an even greater surge in demand occurred during the first few months of 1942. The cause was easy to identify. Officials at the Office of Price Administration feared that the rubber plantations in Southeast Asia would soon fall under Japanese control. They began restricting tire sales on December 11, 1941, just four days after the attack on Pearl Harbor. The following January, the newly established War Production Board announced that the manufacture of new civilian automobiles would be suspended for the duration of the war. In May, the OPA imposed gasoline rationing along the East Coast—largely as a mechanism to conserve tires rather than fuel—and the restriction applied nationwide in December. The wartime regulations ensured that the rapidly growing Philadelphia workforce would be dependent on the commuter services provided by the Pennsylvania Railroad and the Reading.[199]

Martin Clement, the PRR's president, correctly predicted that "conservation of private automobiles is going to throw a lot of commuters on our railroad," while acknowledging that the company did not have enough equipment to accommodate them. In early January, he observed that some trains were standing room only, a situation that was likely to become more serious. Supply shortages precluded the construction of new equipment for commuter traffic. Moreover, as Clement emphasized, the increase in business was a "temporary necessity; and, after the emergency is over, it will be back to where it was." He suggested that it might be possible to assign seats to commuters who had patronized the railroad for years, allowing those with less seniority to stand—but admitted that such a system would be difficult to implement and likely to produce many complaints. Eventually, shop crews added windows, doors, and seats in fifty box cars, transforming them into Class P78b cars that resembled the P78a coaches used on troop trains. The equipment was nonetheless uncomfortable, rode poorly, and was clearly nothing more than a stopgap measure. Mindful of the inadequate accommodations, Clement was quick to remind his subordinates that they "must be prepared to answer in an intelligent way the complaints that we are going to receive."[200]

The discontent that Clement predicted continued after the end of the war. Philadelphia's suburbs expanded rapidly, encouraged by provisions in the 1944 Servicemen's Readjustment Act—better known as the GI Bill—that provided returning veterans with access to low-cost mortgages. Real estate developers were quick to respond to the exodus from the city and into its northern and western suburbs. In 1951, as he was completing his iconic Long Island community, William J. Levitt turned his attention to Philadelphia, building a second Levittown in Bucks County. Governmental support for highway construction played a role as well, enabling suburbanites easy access to the jobs and amenities located downtown. City officials

Facing, Commuters traveling between the suburbs and Center-City Philadelphia were always relieved to see an approaching train, but perhaps never more so than on this bitterly cold morning at Claymont, Delaware, in February 1961. Peak loads during the morning and afternoon rush hours—occasionally augmented by motorists unwilling to brave icy highways—produced such a small return on investment that the PRR could not justify replacing equipment such as these aging MP54 multiple-unit cars. *Courtesy of the Special Collections Research Center, Temple University Libraries, Philadelphia, PA.*

began planning the Schuylkill Expressway in 1947, and construction commenced two years later. As a result, while the population of the city of Philadelphia declined by 6 percent between 1950 and 1970, the suburbs grew by 30 percent.[201]

Not all those suburban pioneers lived near PRR and Reading commuter lines, but those who did were quick to demand improved service. A 1948 editorial in Ardmore's *Main Line Times* noted that "progress and gracious living on the Main Line are tied closely with the Pennsylvania Railroad and its Paoli Local." Such complimentary language notwithstanding, commuters frequently found fault with those suburban trains. A November 1947 resolution adopted by the Lower Merion Chamber of Commerce was typical in its demands for more frequent service, additional equipment, the installation of air-conditioning, and improvements to Suburban Station in Center-City Philadelphia. "The type of commuter who is moving into Overbrook and Merion is one who is not interested in that consideration which the service requires," Clement complained—meaning that they were not accustomed to long waits, crowded trains, or the other inconveniences associated with public transportation. Moreover, he asserted, suburbanites were happy to drive to work in good weather but demanded a comfortable seat on a commuter train whenever summer rains or winter snows made the highways difficult to navigate. As another PRR executive explained to an irate commuter, "The public has abandoned the railroad before the railroad has been forced, as a result, to curtail or abandon service."[202]

Despite his aversion to commuter operations, Clement was willing to address the complaints that flooded his office—primarily to avoid the political fallout associated with unhappy patrons. He nonetheless framed the situation as a public-relations problem rather than as a business opportunity. The Pennsylvania Railroad was losing money on commuter traffic, and Clement possessed scant financial incentive to authorize improvements in equipment or services. He made that attitude clear, as early as January 1948, when he discovered that some of his subordinates, perhaps out of habit, were preparing to block the expansion of competing bus services. "I see by the papers that we are opposing the granting of bus licenses to the center of Philadelphia," Clement admonished his staff. "Why oppose bus lines from Delaware and Montgomery counties? We should make an appearance at the hearing and make our position clear; that we are anxious to get out of the commuter business; that we want to close the stations nearer to town; that we want to increase our rates, and in granting those [bus] permits, which we favor as a natural means of

travel." Clement's recommendations—rate increases and the eventual withdrawal from commuter operations—would characterize the PRR's agenda in Philadelphia for many years to come.[203]

Absent any possibility that the Pennsylvania Public Utility Commission would authorize the abandonment of service, PRR officials hoped that a show of good faith would placate commuters and alleviate the worst of their complaints. Clement encouraged the PRR's "officers, particularly the traffic men, living in the suburban territory," to "become active members in the various civic and other influential organizations in their territory," as a mechanism to build better relationships with suburban commuters. In 1952, executives engaged Robert Heller & Associates—the same consulting firm that was concurrently evaluating the PRR's intercity passenger operations—to study commuter operations in the Philadelphia area. Heller's staff recommended more frequent service as well as park-and-ride facilities at stations along major commuter routes. They evaluated the Media–West Chester Local and concluded that there was insufficient patronage to warrant a continuation of service between Media and West Chester.[204] The consultants also observed that "suburban business is of sufficient financial importance to the Railroad, and its operation is so different from other passenger business, that it requires specialized management of sales and service policies." Left unstated was the certainty that such specialized oversight would also entail close contact with government officials. At no point, however, did Heller recommend that commuter operations be handed over to local governments. Heller instead favored a concentration of authority in the hands of "a full-time Traffic Officer assigned exclusively to the Eastern commuter service." Acting on that suggestion in May 1953, the PRR appointed Thomas J. Costello as the manager of suburban services so that he rather than senior executives would coordinate news releases, interviews, and other public-relations matters.[205]

Costello experimented with off-peak fares, to reduce the imbalance of demand—mostly inbound in the early morning, outbound in the late afternoon, and virtually nonexistent during the remainder of the day—that was the bane of all commuter operations. Working with Ralph C. Champlin, the vice president in charge of public relations, Costello blanketed the suburbs with newspaper advertisements, brochures, direct mailings, and flyers placed on car seats. Much of the advertising encouraged suburban housewives—labeled "General Managers in Charge of Family Purchases"—to use "Thrift Tickets" to travel into the city at off-peak hours to do their shopping. Service

In 1958, the Pennsylvania Railroad acquired six Pioneer III multiple-unit cars from the Budd Company. They experienced numerous mechanical problems, but they did suggest to commuters and municipal officials that better service was possible. *Courtesy of the Special Collections Research Center, Temple University Libraries, Philadelphia, PA.*

reductions on lightly patronized routes permitted a corresponding increase in schedules serving Paoli, Bryn Mawr, and other communities that generated more traffic. Park-and-ride lots provided a solution to another problem that commonly bedeviled commuter operations—sprawling suburbs where few people lived within walking distance of a rail line.[206]

Public response to the PRR's promotional efforts could at best be described as mixed. Jim Newell, the vice president in charge of operations, complained that the cartoon illustration on one brochure was so poorly done that "the front of the MU train car has every appearance of a 'Chic Sale'"—a reference to long-deceased vaudevillian Charles Partlow Sale, but more commonly a euphemism for an outhouse. John K. Murphy, the PRR's supervisor of community relations, rode a commuter train to Swarthmore and observed "that only one person was reading the pamphlet" that Champlin and Costello had developed, "while the rest were sitting on them or had pushed them off on the floor." The only commuters who seemed to know anything about the alterations in the PRR's schedules were those who were irate about the reductions on lightly traveled lines. Members of the Levittown Commuters Club, furious at the complete absence of commuter service between 10:00 a.m. and 4:00 p.m., organized a mass meeting, a carpool, and a boycott of the Pennsylvania Railroad. Other commuters demonstrated little sympathy for managerial claims that investments in profitable freight operations took precedence over deficit-ridden services that moved people to and from their jobs. One disgusted suburbanite informed the *Welsh Valley Herald* that he would likely enjoy

When the Budd Company completed the first of the six Pioneer III cars sold to the PRR, President Symes took the opportunity to play the role of motorman. Edward G. Budd Jr., Budd Company's president, looks on with interest—no doubt hoping that commuter equipment will prove the company's salvation, after the market for intercity passenger equipment had disappeared. PRR executives were unwilling to pay for additional equipment to replace the vast MP54 fleet, and they expected government agencies to provide the necessary funds. *Budd Negatives Collection, Railroad Museum of Pennsylvania, PHMC.*

better conditions if he could be nailed into a packing crate and shipped to Center-City Philadelphia by boxcar.[207]

Even those commuters who benefited from more frequent service complained about the condition of the MP54 cars, the first of which had entered service in 1915. Beginning in 1950, the company rehabilitated a hundred of them, installing roller-bearing trucks and aluminum window frames and improving ventilation. Some received air-conditioning, but executives judged the conversion too expensive for widespread application. The Heller commuter study noted that the equipment was expensive to maintain and increasingly prone to mechanical failure.

"In view of the amount of service the Company will be required to provide for many years," the report emphasized, "it would be unsound financial policy further to defer a broad program of fleet improvement." Newell agreed, highlighting "the urgent need for new equipment which would produce a much more favorable maintenance rate, and possibly attract more traffic and have a good employe and public relations effect."[208]

The Budd Company provided the Pennsylvania Railroad with an alternative to the aging MP54 fleet. By the mid-1950s, orders for new intercity passenger equipment had dwindled to practically nothing, and Budd's self-propelled Rail Diesel Car proved less successful than the company's executives had anticipated. By the summer of 1956, Budd developed the Pioneer III, an ultralight, stainless-steel coach.[209] Along with the TALGO, the *Aerotrain*, and the *Keystone* tubular train, it was one of many efforts to revitalize intermediate-distance passenger service. Budd suggested a price of $95,000 per car on orders of fifty or more, substantially less than the $125,000 cost of a conventional passenger car. Spartan in every respect, the all-plastic interior was minimalist, sterile, and uncomfortable. Twenty feet longer than the MP54, the Pioneer III accommodated 125 passengers, a 74 percent increase, in a cramped 3–2 seating arrangement.[210]

Like its counterparts, the Pioneer III coach attracted little sustained interest. Given Heller's warning regarding the maintenance expense associated with the MP54 equipment, James Symes—the PRR's president since 1954—nonetheless saw possibilities in the new design. Standing alongside Edward Budd, he inspected a prototype exhibited at—or, more precisely, underneath—the Waldorf-Astoria Hotel in Manhattan. Symes encouraged Budd to redesign the Pioneer III into an electrically powered, multiple-unit configuration intended for suburban service. After testing the car along the route between New York and Washington, the PRR ordered six production models, with an option for an additional forty-four. The PRR's vice president in charge of research and development, Walter W. Patchell, hinted that the Pioneer III might eventually replace the five hundred plus MP54 cars that served commuters in Philadelphia, New York, Baltimore, and Washington. The six new cars entered service in June 1958. The addition of pantographs, rectifiers, traction motors, and other electrical equipment increased the cost of each car to $250,000, well above the price that Budd had originally quoted for the locomotive-hauled coach. Should the PRR order the full fifty cars, the expense would drop to $180,000 each, but that was still a significant investment in a service that was generating losses rather than profits. As

an experimental design, the Pioneer III cars were prone to mechanical failure. Symes was accordingly more circumspect than Patchell had been, announcing that it would take "some little time" before the Pennsylvania Railroad purchased the remaining forty-four cars. Even that commitment would fall far short of the hundreds that would be necessary to eliminate the MP54 fleet, something he estimated would cost $36 million.[211]

Given the Pennsylvania Railroad's deteriorating financial situation, the company possessed little incentive to invest in additional Pioneer III cars, or any other new equipment. In 1957, the PRR carried 14.3 million riders on its Philadelphia commuter routes, but that figure represented a decline of almost a third, compared to the 21 million who used the services in 1946. PRR officials calculated that they were subsidizing each regular commuter in the amount of $200 annually. After raising fares in 1952 and again in 1955, within two years the PRR was petitioning the Public Utility Commission for another increase. Representatives from the city of Philadelphia bitterly opposed the request, as did suburbanites who complained that 10 percent or more of those who rode the commuter trains were deadheading PRR employees who traveled for free. Offering the Pioneer III as a tantalizing example of what might be possible, Symes made clear that he would go no further without some form of subsidy. He was nonetheless mindful of the political opposition that would likely accompany any request that the government provide money to a private corporation. As such, he favored the same policy that was being discussed in Greater New York—that the public sector would purchase additional transportation on behalf of passengers. "Arrangements should be worked out with local governments whereby the railroads will operate commuter service as their agent, he declared." That suggestion, simple in principle, would nonetheless take another two decades to implement.[212]

Traffic Jam

By the time Budd delivered the six Pioneer III cars, Symes had reason to be optimistic regarding local support for Philadelphia's commuter operations. In April 1951, voters approved a new city charter, a document that would prove instrumental in the city's efforts to stabilize the commuter rail services offered by the PRR and the Reading. The Home Rule Charter crippled the Republican machine by stripping power from the City Council, transferring it to the mayor's office. The mayor had nearly unlimited authority to select municipal personnel, and the city solicitor, who served in the mayor's cabinet, was the only staff member whose appointment required approval by the City Council. The 1951 charter also made provisions for the merging of city and county government offices, an arrangement solidified by the August 1953 Philadelphia City–County Consolidation Act.[213]

The November 1951 mayoral elections gave Democrats virtually unfettered access to the levers of municipal power. They won fifteen seats on the City Council, rendering the two Republicans councilmen virtually irrelevant. Voters by a substantial majority endorsed Democrat Joseph S. Clark Jr. for mayor, and his close friend and ally, Richardson Dilworth, became the city's district attorney. Neither had much in common with their working-class constituents, however. Clark was a member of one of Philadelphia's leading banking families, while Dilworth held a degree from the Yale School of Law. In pledging to eliminate municipal corruption, they alienated both Republicans and Democrats accustomed to the benefits of political patronage. Clark and Dilworth further distanced themselves by courting affluent suburbanites, whom they hoped to lure back to the city for work, shopping, and recreation.[214]

The rapid changes in Philadelphia politics came as a relief to the influential private citizens who had long supported the involvement of responsible government in the process of urban redevelopment. In 1943, they pressured the City Council to establish a new Planning Commission. Having achieved their principal goal, the members of the coalition shifted their priorities to oversee the integrity of the planning process—a wise decision, given the notorious political corruption that characterized municipal government. They established the Philadelphia Citizens' Council on City Planning, which served thereafter as a watchdog organization, particularly with respect to transportation, zoning, and land-use issues. Since 1948, the members of the Citizens' Council had been marshaling community support for the Schuylkill Expressway and attempted to influence its route.[215]

In 1954, the same year that Citizens' Council established a Committee on Comprehensive Planning, the opening of a new section of the Schuylkill Expressway offered an object lesson in the limits of automobility. Transportation planners had devoted most of their attention to battles over the location and financing of the new superhighway, but they had given little thought to the subsequent movement of automobiles through the city's notoriously narrow surface streets. At its temporary eastern terminus, the freeway disgorged traffic onto City Line Avenue, creating what the *Philadelphia Inquirer* described as a "grand-slam traffic jam" and a "monumental snafu." Characterizing the

The 1951 municipal elections in Philadelphia ended nearly seven decades of uninterrupted Republican control of city government and facilitated public support for the PRR's commuter operations. Joseph S. Clark Jr. (1901–1990), at left, won the mayor's race, while Richardson Dilworth (1898–1974) became the new district attorney. *Courtesy of the Historical Society of Pennsylvania.*

gridlock as a "warning," the *Inquirer* observed that "unless immediate steps are taken, the Expressway may be completed all the way to central Philadelphia without anything having been done to diffuse incoming traffic, as much as possible, and handle the rest when it pours into town."[216]

The chaos on City Line Avenue encouraged Mayor Clark to make commuter rail an important component of his political strategy. Transportation planning was central to his efforts to slow the suburban exodus and bring the middle class back to the city. That process required Clark to forge political connections between the newly Democratic city government and the staunchly Republican constituencies of outlying counties. "It was the understanding of Joe Clark, particularly," one of his deputies recalled, "that Philadelphia was a part of a region and that it couldn't make decisions alone—that it had to build bridges to the suburbs." On December 17, 1953, the City Council authorized Mayor Clark to establish the Urban Traffic and Transportation Board, to study the development of an integrated regional transportation system. The following September, less than a month after the ill-fated opening of the newest portion of the Schuylkill Expressway, Mayor Clark announced plans to form a multicounty, bistate regional development board initially known as the Delaware Valley Authority. It would have an extensive remit, but transportation was among its top priorities.[217]

Clark reassured suburbanites that the city of Philadelphia had no plans to annex or otherwise take control over their communities. It was an important caveat, and one that was coded in the language of race relations. Less than five months earlier, the Supreme Court's ruling in the *Brown v. Board* school desegregation case accelerated the exodus out of Philadelphia and other cities, and few Whites wanted integration to follow them into the suburbs. "We must win Philadelphia's suburban towns over to our side," Clark emphasized. "We must persuade them that we have a common interest. We must sell regionalism—my term for government cooperation or metropolitan operation with a local government, self-government base. Nothing must disturb local autonomy. And we must assure everyone that no one could get hurt by cooperation of this sort." Clark's remarks set the tone for the complex relationship between the city of Philadelphia, its suburbs, and the Pennsylvania Railroad. Improved commuter rail services, funded by the city, would help to "win Philadelphia's suburban towns over to our side," while Clark's reluctance to "disturb local autonomy" greatly complicated his efforts, and those of his successors, to develop an integrated transit plan.[218]

Sitting in the audience, and listening intently to Clark's carefully worded comments, was John Weeks Bodine, the president of the Citizens' Council on City Planning. A Rhodes scholar and prominent attorney, Bodine was a resident of the affluent suburban community of Wyndmoor, just northwest of Philadelphia's city limits and adjacent to the termini of the PRR and Reading Chestnut Hill commuter lines. Like many of his neighbors, Bodine was concerned that the development of new suburban shopping malls had eroded the vitality of Germantown Avenue, the core of the Chestnut Hill community. One of those neighbors, Lloyd Wells, established a businessmen's organization known as the Development Group, and he asked Bodine to serve on its Publication Board. Bodine and his fellow board members created a new community newspaper, the *Chestnut Hill Cymbal*, first published in December 1955. Within three years, the name had changed to the *Chestnut Hill Local*, an obvious reference to the commuter service that connected the area to Center-City Philadelphia. Wells observed that the paper's mission was to "create public interest in the problems facing our community

today"—of which transportation was one of the most important. Bodine was equally active in civic affairs in the city of Philadelphia, and in 1964 he would become the president of the Academy of Natural Sciences. He was also a longtime proponent of coordinated development, assisting in the creation of the City Planning Commission during the 1940s, and in 1959 he became the president and executive director of Penjerdel, a regional planning entity sponsored by the Ford Foundation. Members of the Citizens' Council had tried, unsuccessfully, to divert the Schuylkill Expressway away from Fairmount Park, and Bodine deplored "the rape of the park" that resulted. He may well have reacted to the debacle on City Line Avenue with a sense of grim satisfaction, given his insistence that "the expressway was obsolete before it was ever opened; it couldn't handle the traffic that it was hoped would use it."[219]

Bodine's dislike for the Schuylkill Expressway and his affinity for rail transit soon influenced the Urban Traffic and Transportation Board study that had been underway since December 1953. During the deliberations involving the enabling legislation that created the UTTB, a member of the City Council added an amendment that a representative of a citizen's group be appointed to that body. Mayor Clark was surprised by the change, but he had little difficulty in persuading Bodine to serve in that capacity. Bodine recalled that the UTTB

> was formed for two reasons, one of which was made public and one of which was sort of the secret agenda. The purpose, as I recall, as set forth in the ordinance, was to study traffic conditions in the city and see what could be done about them ... they being, admittedly, in chaos. The secret agenda was to prove the proposition ... that it would be far cheaper for the city to subsidize the commuting railroads, than it would be to allow them to go into bankruptcy and be discontinued, and be forced to build sufficient numbers of lanes of expressways on which the people who would have normally commuted on railroads, would go back and forth commuting by car.[220]

Bodine later insisted that "the board succeeded triumphantly in demonstrating this proposition" regarding the superiority of commuter rail over highway construction. The UTTB study, entitled "Plan and Program 1955," issued in December of that year, recommended a "complete evaluation of existing transportation facilities and services in the entire region and the reappraisal of current policies financially challenging and confronting the Philadelphia region." Construction on the Schuylkill Expressway would continue (it would be completed in 1960) but the members of the UTTB did not envision additional highway projects on that scale. They feared that the new freeway would become congested during rush hour, balked at the expense of additional lanes for periods of peak use, and stressed that the railroads should accommodate the majority of rush-hour commuting journeys. Most of the members of the Urban Traffic and Transportation Board lived in the suburbs, not the city, and their proposals reflected their suburban bias. That bias created further impediments to the already haphazard program of subway construction within city limits but ensured a more favorable reception to Symes's request for assistance relating to commuter service.[221]

The "Plan and Program 1955" study eventually landed on the desk of Richardson Dilworth, who in January 1956 succeeded Clark as mayor. Dilworth and the new city solicitor, David C. Berger, soon played important roles in preserving Philadelphia's commuter rail network. If Dilworth was a consummate politician, well suited for the mayor's office, then Berger was likewise ideally placed for his municipal post. After graduating first in his class from the University of Pennsylvania Law School in 1936, he clerked in both the Pennsylvania Supreme Court and the US Court of Appeals for the Third Circuit. Berger served in the navy during World War II, survived the 1942 sinking of the USS *Hornet*, and later met Marine Captain Dilworth in New Guinea. The two men vowed that if they made it home alive, they would reform Philadelphia's notoriously corrupt Republican political machine. Berger became a trial lawyer, joined the city's law department, and became city solicitor in 1956—a post he held until 1963.[222] The 1953 Philadelphia City–County Consolidation Act made the city treasurer an appointed rather than an elected office, ensuring that Philadelphia voters would find it difficult to punish Berger for his efforts to use municipal funds to subsidize services that primarily benefited residents of suburban communities. Berger's new status did not shield him from the influence of John Bodine and other suburbanites who could not even vote in Philadelphia city and county elections. Recalling his unsuccessful efforts to protect Fairmount Park from the Schuylkill Expressway as part of the Citizens' Council on City Planning, Bodine acknowledged that "we did not make much impact on whoever it was that was doling out the money." When it came to matters involving commuter rail, neither Bodine nor the Citizens' Council would make the same mistake again.[223]

In 1956, the Citizens' Council Subcommittee on Transportation began a review of the UTTB "Plan and Program 1955" report. Given the problems that had occurred on City Line Avenue, the members of the subcommittee were concerned that too much expressway traffic would be funneled onto residential streets. The group was so "dismayed by what it saw of the Arterial Street Plan that it [advocated] . . . some modification of the plan." While Citizens' Council representatives supported the UTTB's emphasis on the value of public transportation, they questioned the underlying assumption "that motorists would return to using mass transit facilities if those facilities were attractive and reasonably priced." Those civic leaders noted that that was an untested hypothesis and suggested "an experimental six-month program to make an actual test of whether motorists can be attracted back to mass transit." Ignoring the report that Cleveland-based Heller & Associates had completed for the PRR in 1953, the Citizens' Council hired a local consulting firm—yet rejected its findings on the grounds "that the actual conditions of the experiment differ so greatly from the assumptions made by the market research consultants that the levels of success outlined in their report are probably impossible of attainment." The members of the Citizens' Council instead supported an expansion of existing Philadelphia Transit Company bus service in the inner-city area, accompanied by park-and-ride facilities at suburban stations, thus creating a "distribution network" and a "collector network."[224]

Representatives from the Citizens' Council were not the only ones who were criticizing the activities of the Urban Traffic and Transportation Board. Mayor Dilworth balked at the UTTB's "Plan and Program 1955" recommendation for expenditures of $1.6 billion over the next twenty-five years—a sum that would place considerable strain on the city's limited resources. The report also emphasized the importance of coordinated regional planning. Yet establishing harmony between the city and county of Philadelphia, eight suburban counties, and the governors and legislatures of Pennsylvania and New Jersey presented a daunting prospect, to say the least. Dilworth accordingly streamlined the Urban Traffic and Transportation Board, reducing its membership from twenty-three to nine. He also insisted that the reconstituted board restrict its focus to the solution of specific current transportation problems. Long-term planning became the responsibility of a second agency, born out of a June 1957 meeting of Pennsylvania, New Jersey, and federal highway officials, as well as representatives from various county governments. Carrying forth Mayor Clark's September 1954 proposal to create a Delaware Valley Authority, they established the Penn-Jersey Transportation Study, an entity that in 1965 would become the Delaware Valley Regional Planning Commission. Their initial task was to exploit the provisions of the 1956 Federal-Aid Highway Act, a mandate that made them less inclined than their counterparts at the UTTB to favor commuter rail.[225] Thereafter, representatives of the UTTB and Penn-Jersey pursued their respective transportation agendas in separate offices located almost five miles apart.[226]

While representatives from the UTTB, Penn-Jersey, the Planning Commission, and the Citizens' Council were contesting one another's authority over the planning process, officials from the Pennsylvania Railroad and the Reading were experiencing a similar set of problems. During the summer of 1957, Symes complained to Dilworth that the PRR was suffering "staggering losses," more than $4 million a year, on its Philadelphia commuter operations. The mayor was nonetheless more sympathetic to the concerns of Philadelphia voters than to the financial interests of the Pennsylvania Railroad. Thanks in large measure to opposition from the city government, the two companies failed to win the higher commutation fares that they requested. On April 7, 1958, the state's Public Utility Commission asserted "that the arguments advanced by the railroads to substantiate the increase was [sic] one of the most deficient in point or quality of proof ever made before the commission."[227]

The stinging rebuke from the PUC encouraged both companies to work more closely with municipal leaders. Dilworth hoped that a combination of lower fares, more frequent service, and improved facilities would increase ridership and alleviate pressure on the highway network.[228] He also suggested that growing passenger volume would enable the railroads to at least break even on their commuter operations, eliminating the need for long-term public subsidies. Symes and other PRR and Reading officials were willing to accept financial support from the city as an alternative to a politically contentious rate increase, and they promised to do their part by improving the condition of stations and boarding platforms and investigating the purchase of new equipment.[229]

The new spirit of cooperation between the city and the railroads made possible the small-scale demonstration projects recommended by the Citizens' Council. Municipal officials initially favored the PRR service from Suburban Station northwest to Manayunk—the outermost stop on the route to Norristown that was still within the city and county of Philadelphia.[230] That line, which traversed a largely industrial district, enjoyed much lighter patronage than the more direct Reading service to Norristown. It nonetheless appealed to commuters in the Wynnefield section of northwestern Philadelphia.

Some affluent and politically well-connected residents of Bala-Cynwyd, just across the Montgomery County line, also found it more convenient than the PRR's Main Line service to Paoli. The corresponding Reading route would be the lightly patronized line to Fox Chase, northeast of Center City. Joined by their counterparts at the Reading, PRR officials encouraged city representatives to consider alternatives that would offer a better measure of the economic effects associated with municipal support. They recommended the parallel PRR and Reading routes that led from Center City to Chestnut Hill, entirely within city limits.[231] The prosperous Chestnut Hill area was home to Citizens' Council president John Bodine and other influential Philadelphians, ensuring a strong level of political support. City solicitor David Berger asked members of the City Council to appropriate funds for expanded service, asserting that they would "for the first time be stemming the tide of attrition" in commuter rail service.[232]

The experiment, branded as Operation Northwest, began on October 26, 1958. The City Council approved a subsidy of $160,000—with $113,000 allocated to the PRR and the remainder to the Reading—for a six-month trial. As Berger emphasized, the money was not a gift to the railroads, but "more a subsidy to commuters." The additional funds enabled the two companies to reduce the maximum single-ride fare between Center City and Chestnut Hill from fifty-three cents to thirty cents, while weekly and monthly commutation tickets declined from forty-four cents to twenty-nine cents per ride. Thanks to an agreement with the Philadelphia Transportation Company, passengers could buy a connecting bus ticket for an additional dime. Municipal officials emphasized that the arrangement would serve as a model for stricken commuter services in other locales, with elected officials from many cities "in the Nation anxiously looking to Philadelphia for an answer to one of the most pressing of all metropolitan area problems."[233]

The new fare structure saved regular daily commuters about $75 per year and proved modestly successful at improving patronage. The two companies added 218 trains a week, with the PRR offering service every fifteen minutes during rush hour and hourly during off-peak periods. During the first month of the experiment, 132,492 people traveled the Pennsylvania Railroad's Chestnut Hill line, representing a gain of only 400 riders. As PRR officials were quick to emphasize, however, patronage during the month prior had declined by 10 percent from the same period the previous year, and merely halting that erosion of traffic represented a notable success. Walter Patchell,

Operation Northwest, which began in October 1958, suggested the potential for integrated rail-bus mass transit, and the concept soon expanded to other routes. This ribbon-cutting occurred at Swarthmore, on the PRR's line to West Chester. *Courtesy of the Special Collections Research Center, Temple University Libraries, Philadelphia, PA.*

the railroad's vice president for special services, was "very encouraged with the results so far and hopeful that the steadily increasing trend will continue." Berger suggested that municipal assistance had generated benefits that were "far beyond what we had expected. Mayor Dilworth and I are very much encouraged by the rise." The city solicitor also noted, although without precise traffic counts to support his estimates, that Operation Northwest had removed six hundred cars a day from downtown streets.[234]

After three months, Berger boasted that the experiment had increased Chestnut Hill commuter traffic by 14.9 percent (compared to a 6 percent decline on other lines), giving the PRR and the Reading four thousand additional riders each week. He declared that he was "immensely pleased that the program is achieving the primary goal of reducing downtown traffic congestion"—one of the principal objectives of the Urban Traffic and Transportation Board. Berger asserted that expanded service eliminated three thousand automobile trips a week, reducing the expense associated with police and street maintenance by $3,000 per day. "Undoubtedly," he concluded, "extension of the plan to other communities would benefit them also." Berger was as good as his word, and he and Mayor Dilworth persuaded the City Council to fund a six-month extension of Operation Northwest. In September 1959, the city launched Operation Northeast along the Reading's Fox Chase commuter line.[235]

Even as they were praising the achievements associated with Operation Northwest, city officials were developing much more elaborate plans. Dilworth suggested that the city should take control of all twelve commuter routes operated by the PRR and the Reading, assuming responsibility for the maintenance of equipment, tracks, and stations, as well as all personnel matters. He planned to pay the two railroads precisely nothing for their facilities, asserting that the opportunity to escape chronic deficits was benefit enough. "To ask us to donate our property is silly," the PRR's Walter Patchell noted, perhaps tempering his language. He emphasized that his company could not legally give away assets that were encumbered by bonded indebtedness—to say nothing of the problems that would occur if the railroad relinquished control over several routes that were vital to freight operations.[236]

Along with his counterparts at the Reading, Patchell was further distressed by the perverse results associated with Operation Northwest and Operation Northeast, characterized by one observer as "traffic up, deficits up." Following the initial six-month trial of Operation Northwest, PRR officials announced that the lower fares had produced a 15 percent increase in ridership while generating a 28 percent reduction in the revenue generated by ticket sales. As they informed the company's investors, the city's assistance "emphasized rather than solved the problem." Although "the operation succeeded in diverting many people from the congested streets and highways," the annual report noted, "the increased patronage was not sufficient to overcome revenue losses from reduced fares." In economic terms, the operations had not shifted the positive externalities associated with commuter rail services to the balance sheets of the railroads that generated them. "We contend that we need at least a 30 percent increase in passengers on the lines to make it worth our while," a railroad spokesman emphasized, adding, "Some day the city will be called upon to decide whether it is worth the cost to keep the riders in mass transit." To Dilworth's dismay, PRR executives announced that they were prepared to request a 30 percent rate increase, should municipal support continue to prove inadequate.[237]

Objecting to both the parsimonious subsidies and to Dilworth's plan to confiscate their property, representatives from the two railroads proposed an alternate solution—they would provide whatever level of service Dilworth requested and send the bill to the city of Philadelphia or to a nonprofit municipal development corporation. Under that scenario, the City Council would be responsible for annual deficits totaling $7.5 million, plus as much as $45 million to purchase new equipment—amounts that would make the initial $160,000 appropriation for Operation Northwest seem utterly insignificant.[238] John A. Bailey, the executive director of the Urban Traffic and Transportation Board, doubted that the railroads' losses were as high as their executives claimed and asked the City Council for a $15,000 appropriation to study the matter. Until the two sides could come to some agreement about the actual cost of service, little progress seemed possible. Moreover, as Patchell observed, the city of Philadelphia lacked the authority to own facilities, operate services, or assign new equipment to portions of routes located in the suburbs. The prospect of commuters changing trains at the Philadelphia county line was both absurd and unthinkable, and Patchell doubted that suburban politicians would participate in Dilworth's plan once they became aware of the costs that would be involved. Berger's comment that communities located outside of city limits would be "on their own with the railroads" was not likely to foster the regional cooperation Mayor Clark had promised in 1954.[239]

Money from Washington

By the autumn of 1959, the debates regarding the funding of commuter rail services in Philadelphia had become intertwined with a national political dialogue regarding urban mass transit. The Interstate Commerce Commission's *Passenger Train Deficit* investigation that began in 1956 offered Pennsylvania Railroad officials the opportunity to highlight the growing losses associated with commuter operations. Walter Patchell was a key witness, and he devoted a considerable portion of his testimony to an explanation of the problems in Philadelphia. In January 1958, the US Supreme Court upheld a ruling by the Illinois Commerce Commission that forced the Milwaukee Road to continue a deficit-plagued commuter service in Chicago, on the grounds that the company's operations in Illinois earned an overall profit. That ruling, focused narrowly on a single railroad's commuter business in one state, led directly to the comprehensive Smathers Committee investigation into the nearly endless array of problems facing the industry. Perhaps because of the scope of the

Smathers hearings, the committee's twenty-five-page summary report devoted barely a page to the deleterious effects of commuter operations. Although it was a direct outgrowth of the Milwaukee Road case, the Transportation Act of 1958 likewise offered few concrete solutions to the commuter crisis. The new law enabled carriers to borrow from a $500 million fund—which in principle might have been used to upgrade commuter operations—but few railroads were willing to shoulder the high interest rates that accompanied the loans. Of greater significance, the act also eased regulatory barriers to the discontinuance of intrastate trains. Beginning with the New York Central's petition to discontinue the Weehawken ferry, several carriers serving Greater New York quickly announced their intent to eliminate many of their commuter services. With PRR and Reading officials arguing that the Philadelphia's meager financial support was insufficient to cover their $7.5 million annual losses, even a politician with far less perspicacity than Richardson Dilworth could easily guess what was likely to happen next.[240]

Determined to preserve Philadelphia's commuter rail network, Dilworth pursued two parallel, complementary strategies, one in Washington and the other in his hometown. As early as 1956, he had been pressuring federal officials to divert highway funds to public transit. He also encouraged Representative William J. Green Jr. (Dem., Pennsylvania) to sponsor legislation that would establish a $500 million fund within the Department of Commerce, to be dedicated to urban transit projects. Those efforts proved fruitless, defeated by the Eisenhower administration's commitment to highway construction and by opposition from members of Congress who represented rural districts. Dilworth then enlisted the support of railroad executives and the mayors of other large cities. By the end of 1959, that coalition, under the aegis of the American Municipal Association, had released *The Collapse of Commuter Service*. Dilworth and Symes also cooperatively revised the bill Representative Green had introduced in 1958. Their alliance was not unprecedented, but it was unusual. Philadelphia's mayor was more supportive of rail-based transit than his counterparts in other cities, and the Pennsylvania Railroad's president was one of the few executives willing to accept government assistance as a mechanism to preserve rather than end commuter operations.[241] Representatives from the AMA—rather than Dilworth and Symes—orchestrated support for the legislation, to avoid any suggestions that federal funds might be used to benefit one city or one of the largest corporations in the United States. In March 1960, freshman senator Harrison

A. Williams (Dem., New Jersey) introduced the bill that Dilworth and Symes had helped to write. In the face of stiff resistance from Congress and the Department of Commerce, Williams reoriented the commuter rail crisis as an urban problem rather than a transportation problem. He trimmed the loan fund to $100 million and proposed that it be placed under the authority of the Housing and Home Finance Agency. The Senate approved the measure in June, but the bill stalled in the House.[242]

Even as Dilworth and Symes were lobbying for federal funds to support Philadelphia's commuter services, they were collaborating on local funding arrangements. Direct municipal payments to the PRR and the Reading raised a host of uncomfortable political and legal questions that Dilworth was trying to avoid. In October 1958, the city's powerful Committee of Seventy claimed that the Operation Northwest experiment violated the state constitution, which prohibited the diversion of public funds to a private corporation. David Berger, the city solicitor, suggested that the arrangement was not "foreign to the material interests and general prosperity of the municipality," language carefully chosen to echo a precedent established more than sixty years earlier.[243] Berger's reassurance was hardly the same as a ruling from the Pennsylvania Supreme Court, however, and as the level of payments increased, legal challenges seemed inevitable. Moreover, the congressional debates regarding the bills sponsored by Representative Green and Senator Williams suggested that whatever moneys might be forthcoming from the federal government would be awarded only to a municipal corporation rather than to the city directly.[244]

Planning for a new municipal transit corporation began in July 1959. Dilworth and Berger oversaw the process, coordinating their efforts with Symes and Patchell at the PRR and with Reading president Joseph A. Fisher. Given his multiple duties as mayor, Dilworth delegated responsibility to his former law firm, Dilworth, Paxson, Kalish, and Levy, with most of the work assigned to William T. Coleman Jr.[245] Edson L. Tennyson, hired as the city's transit engineer in 1956, also played an important role in the planning process. Tennyson was well suited to the task, as he began his career at Pittsburgh Railways and remained a lifelong advocate of rail-based transit.[246]

On January 20, 1960, Dilworth, Symes, and Fisher announced the formation of the Passenger Service Improvement Corporation, with Berger applying for a charter the following day. While it was for all intents and purposes a municipal agency, PSIC's corporate status enabled it to accept federal funds. The members of the City

Council lacked direct control over PSIC, although they could threaten to withhold local funding. The mayor suggested that PSIC was the first entity of its kind, yet it bore a strong similarity to the municipally owned Philadelphia Industrial Development Corporation that he and Berger created in 1958. In the process of establishing PSIC, Pennsylvania Railroad and Reading officials pledged that they would maintain existing service for the next two years. They also promised that they would not raise fares within city limits—but on March 1 petitioned the state Public Utility Commission for a 25 percent increase for all suburban destinations. By maintaining the status quo within the city and county of Philadelphia, Berger emphasized, the PSIC would be "providing a 'breathing space' during which a permanent solution for the commuter line crisis may be worked out."[247]

The Passenger Service Improvement Corporation both reflected and reinforced long-standing notions regarding the relationship between the city of Philadelphia and its suburbs, as well as predictions for future regional growth. In May 1960, four months after the formation of PSIC, the City Planning Commission released *Comprehensive Plan: The Physical Development Plan for the City of Philadelphia*. The document, updated three years later, embodied fears—well-founded, as events transpired—that suburban growth would drain the population and economic vitality of Center City. The members of the Planning Commission emphasized that "the well-being of Center City Philadelphia is basic to the well-being of the entire Delaware Valley region," that "Center City must always remain the principal place for doing business," and that "Center City serves as the springboard from which waves of revitalization spread outward as suburban families are re-attracted to urban living." Planners suggested that the city's population would grow from 2,002,512 in 1960 to 2,521,000 in 1970 (in fact, it declined to 1,949,996) and to as many as 2,755,000 inhabitants in 1980 (the actual result was a further decline to 1,688,210). They suggested that rail transportation would play a critical role in Philadelphia's urban renaissance yet demonstrated little interest in the needs of working-class city dwellers. As such, the plan called for only a modest ten-mile increase in the subway network, and even smaller investments in surface streetcar and bus routes. The study's authors were far more solicitous of the transportation needs of affluent suburbanites, who they saw as critical to the city's demographic and economic revitalization. They also assumed, incorrectly, that the suburbs would continue to function largely as bedroom communities, and that most office jobs, shopping, and recreational activities

would remain in the urban core.[248] As such, they recommended "a completely connected commuter rail rapid transit system to deliver peak loads to Center City from outlying suburban areas."[249]

PSIC representatives were fully in accord with the role that commuter railroads would play in the fulfillment of the hub-and-spoke vision embodied in the 1960 City Plan. The eleven directors of the municipal corporation, appointed by the mayor, were more attuned to the transportation needs of affluent White suburbanites than to those of the urban working class who would more likely ride the subway, bus, or streetcar lines. Casimir A. Sienkiewicz, the board chairman, was the president of Central-Penn National Bank of Philadelphia, yet he lived in Doylestown, in suburban Bucks County. Henry M. Chance II, the president of United Engineers & Constructors, resided in Kennett Square. As the president of Food Fair Stores, Louis Stein was kept busy opening a string of new suburban supermarkets. The family of Clifford E. Frishmuth, the vice president of the Sealtest Foods Division of the National Dairy Products Corporation, hailed from Merion. Patchell and Reading vice president and general counsel H. Merle Mulloy protected the interests of their respective railroads, and the president of the Brotherhood of Railroad Trainmen and the secretary of the Railway Labor Executives' Association did the same for unionized workers. Two city councilmen, the city's managing director, and the director of finance promoted Dilworth's views.[250]

John A. Bailey, PSIC's executive director, was principally responsible for the agency's day-to-day operations. He possessed a wealth of planning experience and, like Edson Tennyson, he was a passionate advocate for rail transportation. Bailey worked in the Pittsburgh area before moving to Philadelphia in 1953, as the chief of refuse disposal in the Streets Department. Three years later, he was the city's deputy managing director as well as the executive director of the Urban Traffic and Transportation Board. Bailey professed his determination "to smooth over political problems rather than create them if new directions indicated something had been done that was incorrect," yet his steadfast determination to do what he thought proper gained him many enemies. He clashed repeatedly with Streets Department personnel and was openly critical of David Smallwood, Dilworth's choice as street commissioner. Smallwood, Bailey suggested, did not comprehend regional or intermodal transportation needs, "had no real interest in research," and displayed "very little interest in analysis of traffic systems."[251]

While waiting for Congress to fund a "permanent solution for the commuter line crisis," Dilworth and Bailey began to expand the scope of PSIC's operations. They were careful to emphasize that they were buying additional service rather than subsidizing the PRR and the Reading. Under that arrangement, PSIC guaranteed at least $1.4 million to offset operating costs on the two railroads, while the new agency received all the revenues collected in the service it sponsored.[252] After assuming oversight of Operation Northwest and Operation Northeast on July 28, 1960, PSIC personnel developed similar arrangements on three other commuter routes. One (Operation Shawmont) affected only the Reading, but the remaining two operated along the Pennsylvania Railroad. The eight miles of Operation Manayunk resurrected the original 1957 proposal for service along the Schuylkill Valley, as far as the last stop within city limits. Operation Torresdale covered 15.8 miles from Suburban Station toward Trenton. At Torresdale, the northernmost station inside the city and county of Philadelphia, PSIC officials proposed a balloon track that could be used to turn equipment, lest it stray into an adjacent political jurisdiction. The PSIC implemented the combination of increased service and reduced fares on October 30, 1960, giving the municipal government responsibility for six of the twelve commuter lines that served Philadelphia.[253]

Silverliners, Subsidies, and SEPACT

The following month, Philadelphia voters approved $6 million in loans for PSIC-supported service. The measure—part of a $47 million loan package that both political parties had endorsed—permitted a short extension of the Reading's electrified territory, the construction of park-and-ride lots, and the acquisition of twenty-six new commuter rail cars. Edson Tennyson, the city's transit engineer, took charge of the design process. His starting point was the group of six Pioneer III cars that the Pennsylvania Railroad purchased in 1958. Working with PRR and Budd engineers, Tennyson remedied many of the problems that plagued the Pioneer III equipment. He received less cooperation from Pennsylvania Railroad personnel in the matter of seating inside the cars. Anticipating an increase in commuter traffic, railroad officials sought to accommodate as many passengers as possible by giving them a mere seventeen inches of seat width—slightly less than what was available on the older MP54 equipment. Backed by Bailey, Tennyson insisted that passengers be allotted nineteen inches of seat width, to make the ride more comfortable. Rather than accept a 17.6 percent reduction in

capacity (from 125 passengers to 103), PRR personnel narrowed the aisles from thirty-six inches to a mere twenty inches. By doing so, they could incorporate two seats on one side of the aisle and three on the other, restoring the higher capacity they had favored.[254]

Like the PRR and Reading executives who preceded them, PSIC personnel confronted the unpleasant economic realities associated with commuter traffic. The increased service frequencies and reduced ticket prices induced a 44 percent gain in ridership during the first six months of 1961. Casimir Sienkiewicz, PSIC's chairman, suggested that such results "indicated a public response probably without precedent in modern railroading." Increased patronage produced larger deficits—hardly a surprising outcome, given that the price of each ticket was substantially below fully allocated operating costs. Given the number of passengers carried on the six subsidized lines (just over 3 million on the PRR and slightly more than 3.2 million on the Reading), the city was providing a subsidy of $0.25 per passenger, per trip—equivalent to about $2.57 in 2023 funds. In 1961, the first full year of all five "Operations," the city allocated $1.57 million to the PSIC, nearly ten times the $160,000 subsidy for the initial six-month Operation Northwest experiment. The revenue situation showed few signs of improvement, and city officials estimated that the PSIC would spend nearly $1.8 million in 1962. That was money that could not be directed toward housing, street repair, police and fire protection, subway construction, or the city's other pressing needs. Under those circumstances, PSIC support increased traffic—but added to the railroads' losses while imposing a steadily rising financial obligation on the city, one that could not be sustained indefinitely. Further expansion—and even the survival of the existing experiments—would depend on the involvement of other political jurisdictions in the process of transportation planning. "The problem goes beyond the city line," David Berger emphasized. "It is more than a local problem; it is a regional one, or even a federal one."[255]

Any expansion of regional support for PRR and Reading commuter rail operations depended on the cooperation of the affluent suburbs that PSIC could not yet legally serve. Many suburbanites, however, suspected that the cordial relations between the city, the PSIC, and the railroads had come at their expense, and they were reluctant to commit financial resources to rail operations. Residents of outlying counties desired improved commuter service, one city official observed, but "they backed away from it when it appeared that it was going to cost them money." Neither the PUC nor the ICC objected to the rate increase that the

PRR and the Reading had requested, for service outside the city, and it took effect on April 1. The new fares increased costs for regular suburban commuters by as much as $100 per year. That compared unfavorably to the $75 annual savings for those living inside the city, who were able to take advantage of PSIC subsidies. PRR and Reading executives indicated the rate increase would produce just over $1 million in increased revenue each year. Even with steadily increasing PSIC support, that was far short of their $7.5 million annual losses. Absent federal assistance, it was reasonable to assume that suburban governments—should they join forces with the city of Philadelphia—would be responsible for much of the funding gap that remained. Suburbanites who kept a tight grip on their pocketbooks were also determined to protect their local political autonomy from the steadily increasing authority of city government. "We are not interested in absorption, annexation or the political situation of any area beyond the city limits of Philadelphia," Berger assured suburban audiences, echoing the rhetoric that Mayor Clark had used six years earlier. "We want to see a good commuter line, with reasonable fares and good service, for the people who are required to come into Philadelphia." Despite such promises, Republican suburban politicians remained reluctant to cede tax revenue and political authority to a Democratic administration in the city.[256]

While the situation in Philadelphia looked increasingly dire, in Washington there were signs that efforts to secure federal funding for mass-transit projects were finally beginning to bear fruit. *Federal Transportation Policy and Program*, issued by the Commerce Department in March 1960, reinforced the Eisenhower administration's aversion to federal aid for local mass-transit projects, but the report also offered hope for the future. Ernest W. Williams Jr., the study's director, and deputy director David W. Bluestone authored an appendix that deviated from the conclusions the president and the Commerce Department had endorsed. They asserted that "mass transportation is clearly much less expensive per passenger mile than total costs of the private automobile." Moreover, Williams and Bluestone suggested that "Federal or State loans to municipalities or metropolitan authorities may need to be considered especially where localities may acquire commuter rail facilities and equipment and lease them to the carriers." They made specific reference to Philadelphia, at that time the only city where commuter operations received substantial public support. While Williams and Bluestone acknowledged that "the net revenue of the [PRR and Reading] railroads was not materially changed because the benefit from increased traffic was offset by the

reduced rates which went into effect at the same time," they emphasized that "the area as a whole derived real benefits by the diversion of traffic from the highways to mass transit vehicles"—precisely the argument that Dilworth and his successors had used. For the first time, officials at both the local and federal levels of government were stressing the social benefits (or positive externalities) associated with commuter rail service as a justification for federal assistance. Williams and Bluestone were also committed to a transportation agenda in which the "essential purpose is to move people rather than vehicles," maintaining sensitivity to the deleterious effects of freeway construction on urban neighborhoods. Finally, they were deeply concerned that the cessation of commuter operations would necessitate a massive compensatory increase in federal highway expenditures—in effect transferring to the public sector the losses that the railroads had carried since the end of World War II.[257]

The November 1960 elections enabled Republicans to make slight gains in Congress but gave Democrats control of the White House. John F. Kennedy demonstrated his support for urban, Democratic mayors while addressing the multitude of issues facing American cities. May 1961 hearings before a subcommittee of the House Banking and Currency Committee promised further support for urban mass transit. At issue was legislation, sponsored by New York Democrat Abraham J. Multer, that attempted to revive the $100 million aid package that Harrison Williams had sponsored the year before. Testifying in support of the bill, Dilworth highlighted the success of the PSIC experiment. He nonetheless acknowledged that "it is obvious that a city budget can never carry investments of this scale without a drastic change in the taxing system which would earmark substantial amounts of the gasoline tax for city purposes" and suggested that "a Federal program can help bridge the gap between the poor city and the suburb." The PRR's Symes also asked Congress to provide federal funds, but he was less optimistic about the benefits associated with PSIC. He read a lengthy prepared statement in which he highlighted the company's $13 million annual loss in systemwide commuter operations and noted that "from the railroad's viewpoint these innovations have been a financial failure, but from the standpoint of the city they have been a huge success because they have increased rail ridership." It was a set of circumstances that exemplified the uneasy alliance between Symes and Dilworth. "My job then as president of the Pennsylvania Railroad," Symes emphasized, "was to eliminate losses from the various services." That was a strikingly different goal than the one favored by municipal officials, who sought to move as many people as possible in and out of the city without placing more strain on the overburdened highway network. The testimony was effective nonetheless, and less than six months after taking office, Kennedy signed the Housing Act of 1961. The measure authorized the Housing and Home Finance Agency to provide low-interest loans that municipalities could use to purchase new equipment and improve transit facilities. Congress also appropriated $25 million for urban mass-transit demonstration projects, based on a two-for-one match with local funds.[258]

Ultimately, the prospect of two federal dollars for every one raised locally proved too tempting for elected officials in most suburban counties to resist. Twenty percent of area highways were over capacity, and demographic studies predicted that the Philadelphia metropolitan area (which included Bucks, Chester, Delaware, and Montgomery Counties) would grow from 3.6 million to almost 4.5 million people between 1960 and 1975—placing further strain on the region's roads. Transportation planners noted that the construction of freeways into the suburbs was falling behind schedule and that railroads were indispensable for regional transportation. In June 1961, the local CBS affiliate aired a special program, "Dead End: 1975?," suggesting a dystopian future of endless traffic jams and hellish commutes. Through the process of elimination, host John Facenda suggested that commuter rail service offered the only possible solution to the dilemma. Walter Patchell, the PRR's vice president for special services, was Facenda's most prominent guest. He explained the economic conditions that made it impossible for the railroad to make money on commuter operations and suggested that government assistance offered the only alternative to a series of fare increases.[259]

Montgomery County officials were the first to demonstrate a serious interest in rail transit, offering $100,000 for a six-month trial. Other counties soon emulated that example. In September 1961, Bucks, Chester, and Montgomery Counties joined the city of Philadelphia to create the Southeastern Pennsylvania Transportation Compact. The new agency was closely linked to the Passenger Service Improvement Corporation. Casimir Sienkiewicz, PSIC's chairman, represented the city at SEPACT board meetings. Bailey, the executive director of PSIC, was initially SEPACT's secretary, although that title slighted his considerable influence over both urban and suburban transportation policies. Unlike PSIC, a municipal corporation that channeled city funds to the railroads, SEPACT was solely a planning body whose function was to coordinate various local governments and to pursue negotiations with the PRR and the Reading. The new agency's "greatest

significance," as its staff members informed the Department of Transportation, "lay in its pioneering development of regional cooperation between a large metropolitan city and its surrounding suburbs." SEPACT representatives intended to reduce highway congestion, increase rail ridership in low-density suburban areas where cars remained an attractive option, and foster cooperation that would facilitate the eventual creation of a regional transportation authority similar to PSIC. Suburbanites preserved local control by insisting that each county (including the city and county of Philadelphia) possess equal representation on the SEPACT board.[260]

Suburban cooperation and federal assistance—in the form of SEPACT and the HHFA, respectively—came in the nick of time for the cash-strapped city of Philadelphia. Dilworth resigned the mayor's office in February 1962, to run for governor. His successor and fellow Democrat, former City Council president James H. J. Tate, did not share Dilworth's enthusiasm for public-transit projects, particularly those that required municipal support. Bailey was likewise pessimistic, having discovered that the suburban counties that joined SEPACT, in anticipation of federal funds that had not yet materialized, were unwilling to offer much in the way of local support. In March 1962, he warned that the city's financial commitment to commuter rail would fall at least $35,000 short of the amount needed to keep the "Operations" running during the last four months of 1962. "By this time next year," he complained to Tate in September 1962, "the city will have gone about as far as it can on its own. . . . We have agreed to bear all that I feel [the city of] Philadelphia can support vis-à-vis the suburbs."[261]

Bailey hoped that the HHFA would come to Philadelphia's rescue. "We are attempting to save money by shifting two-thirds of present PSIC costs of Operation Torresdale to the United States Government," he reassured the mayor. SEPACT was one of the first entities to take advantage of the mass-transit provisions of the 1961 Housing Act. On May 4, Bailey filed an application for $2.9 million in federal matching grants.[262] A substantial portion would fund the purchase of new equipment for the Reading, with money left over for park-and-ride lots and other station improvements.[263] City solicitor David Berger informed federal officials of plans for improved facilities, lower fares, and additional trains on several PRR and Reading routes. Two-thirds of the estimated $4,339,000 cost would come from the HHFA, with seed money furnished by the city of Philadelphia, via PSIC ($864,000), Bucks County ($165,000), and Montgomery County ($417,000). The plan represented an unprecedented use of federal funds, and

While outwardly similar to the Pioneer III equipment, Budd's Silverliner cars were much improved and a welcome change from the aging MP54 equipment. Municipal funds, funneled through the Passenger Service Improvement Corporation, nonetheless paid for only thirty-eight PRR Silverliners—far too few to address the needs of commuters. *Pennsylvania Railroad Negative Collection, Hagley Museum & Library, acc. 1993.300.*

neither Berger nor Bailey could be certain that an agency focused primarily on housing matters would be agreeable to the proposal. "We got no formal commitment" from the HHFA, Bailey indicated, "but I am heartened by the reception that our application received." In October, however, Bailey complained that federal officials were delaying consideration of the city's request for assistance but nonetheless hoped that the HHFA would "agree reluctantly" to provide the requested funds. Bailey also informed Mayor Tate that "PSIC staff must be increased"—ultimately at the city's expense—to cope with the vast quantities of data demanded by the HHFA.[264] Despite the difficulties, in November 1962, the HHFA awarded $3.1 million in funding, slightly more than Bailey originally requested, for a three-year trial period.[265] The local share had likewise

increased, with $930,400 contributed by the city of Philadelphia, $178,000 from Bucks County, and $449,000 from Montgomery County.[266]

Federal money was not entirely free, and the Philadelphia City Council appropriated nearly a million dollars to PSIC, as its share of SEPACT's costs. That amount represented nearly a sixfold increase in municipal subsidies in only two years. Further city funding for the PRR and the Reading now depended on the outcome of a November 6, 1962, ballot initiative. The Citizens' Loan Improvement Committee, which counted Mayor Tate as its honorary chairman, urged voters to approve nearly $37.5 million in three categories of municipal bonds. Of that amount, $16.2 million would fund general infrastructure improvements (including upgrades to the subway and elevated transit lines), with $16.5 million allocated to the municipal waterworks and $4.8 million to commuter rail service. Committee members asked the public for "a vote to turn back the creeping paralysis that menaces the economic and social health of many of America's metropolitan centers." The election, held only days after the Cuban missile crisis pushed the world to the brink of nuclear war, affected the fates of commuter rail and of the politician who had been one of its chief proponents. Voters approved all three loans by wide margins, with more than 71 percent supporting increased municipal assistance for the PRR and the

The formation of SEPACT for the first time permitted munici-pally owned Silverliner cars to leave Philadelphia's city limits. The December 3, 1962, celebration of the inauguration of Oper-ation Levittown service, held on the platform of Suburban Station, featured dignitaries and beauty queens—but also one of the aging MP54 units rather than the modern equipment that constituted the city's contribution to the new regional transportation agency. *Photo courtesy of PhillyHistory.org, a project of the Philadelphia Department of Records.*

Reading. Richardson Dilworth did not fare so well. The gubernatorial campaign was one of the most vicious and bitterly contested races in Pennsylvania's history, and the former mayor lost badly to Republican business executive William W. Scranton. Following the setback, Dilworth returned to his law firm, Dilworth Paxson, working on transportation matters in Philadelphia and in Washing-ton.[267]

The success of the ballot measure enabled PSIC offi-cials to authorize parking lots and improvements at

several stations and to begin replacing antiquated PRR and Reading equipment. They placed an order with the Budd Company for fifty-five modern cars, more than double the number authorized by the $6 million bond issue voters had approved two years earlier. Based on Tennyson's design, thirty-eight would be allocated to the Pennsylvania Rail-road and the remainder to the Reading. The PRR assigned them to Class MP85B, but thanks to their unpainted stainless-steel exteriors, they quickly became known as Sil-verliners. The city purchased and owned the cars, through PSIC, and leased them to the railroads for twenty-five years, with an option to purchase them at that time, for a dollar apiece. While they were municipal property, the Silverliners could legally operate along PRR and Reading routes in each suburban county that had joined SEPACT, as part of the city's contribution to that agency.[268]

HHFA grants, the municipal bond issue, and the for-mation of SEPACT gave Bailey an opportunity to extend subsidized service into the suburbs. Pennsylvania Railroad officials cooperated enthusiastically. They understood the city had reached the limit of its financial abilities but were hopeful that the federal government could provide a bottomless pool of money to offset the massive losses associated with commuter operations. One of the routes caused little controversy. On December 3, 1962, SEPACT officials rebranded the PRR's Operation Torresdale as Operation Levittown, extending service to that suburban community, twenty-seven miles from Center City. The inaugural celebrations included Mayor Tate, a group of Bucks County commissioners, and two beauty queens, Miss Philadelphia and Miss Bucks County. Their smiles suggested the harmony between city and county governments, made easier by the willingness of HHFA to pay a substantial portion of the costs.[269]

Delaware County

The situation along the PRR's Main Line could not have been more different. The formation of SEPACT, coupled with steady increases in PSIC subsidies, outraged officials from Philadelphia's two remaining privately owned transit systems. Banker and real estate developer Albert M. Greenfield organized the Philadelphia Transportation Company in 1940, as a successor to Thomas Mitten's Philadelphia Rapid Transit. PTC controlled the city's bus and streetcar lines and operated the subway system under a fifty-year contract that expired in 1957. PRT and its successor shared a heritage of bitterly antagonistic labor-management relations, and both companies incurred the enmity of Philadelphia commuters. Greenfield's interactions with James Symes were not much better, and the two men clashed over the most appropriate use for the land once occupied by Broad Street Station and the Filbert Street Extension. As chairman of PTC's executive committee, Greenfield relied on his close ties to the city's Republican political machine for protection. When the Democratic Clark-Dilworth administration gained power, its efforts to please both the public and organized labor made the PTC a tempting target. In 1953, it initiated the first of a series of confrontations with Greenfield in an unsuccessful effort to block a fare increase. After Dilworth became mayor in January 1956, he announced that the city would purchase the PTC's assets, although it took more than a decade to bring that plan to fruition. Dilworth privately described Greenfield as a "ruthless" businessman who "was only interested in making money" and characterized him as "the most selfish son of a bitch who ever lived." Matters of political expediency mellowed the relationship in the years that followed, transforming it into something approaching genuine friendship. Dilworth and Greenfield cooperated on the Penn Center project along the site of Broad Street

Station and the Filbert Street Extension, as well as in the Society Hill district to the south of Independence Hall.[270]

By the time of SEPACT's formation in September 1962, Greenfield was well into his seventies and winding down his business affairs. He had resigned from PTC's board of directors in January of that year, but he was still heavily invested in the company and was solicitous of its welfare. Greenfield was appalled at municipal support for the Pennsylvania Railroad and the Reading, and equally critical of the laudatory coverage that the Philadelphia Inquirer awarded to PSIC and SEPACT. The paper's January 1962 editorial, criticizing "an endless succession of fare rises" by the Philadelphia Transportation Company drew a quick response from Greenfield. He noted that the PSIC subsidy of twenty-six cents per passenger was higher than the total PTC fare, even after the latest increase.[271] "PTC could carry its passengers absolutely free—and throw in a morning cup of coffee—if it received the same per-passenger subsidy as do PSIC railroads," Greenfield complained. While he acknowledged that "the objectives and accomplishments of PSIC are commendable," he suggested that "those who would use that agency as a yardstick to measure PTC's performance should take account of its diminutive dimensions in the overall transportation picture, the limited areas of the city in which it operates, and its extremely high per-passenger cost to taxpayers." It was a valid point, given that the PTC—functioning without a municipal subsidy—carried nearly fifty times as many Philadelphians as did the six "Operation" routes supported by the city. Greenfield also had just cause to criticize the use of municipal funds to draw business away from his company. PSIC officials calculated that the payments to the PRR and the Reading had enabled those two companies to poach 30 percent of PTC's riders, costing Greenfield's company as much as $200,000 in lost revenue per year.[272]

Merritt Taylor Jr. was even more steadfast in his opposition to PSIC, particularly to the possibility that SEPACT might extend subsidized transportation to the suburbs. His grandfather, A. Merritt Taylor, was the city's first transit director, beginning in 1912, and played an instrumental role in the development of streetcars, elevated railways, subways, and interurban lines. Son and grandson followed a similar path, managing the family's diverse transportation empire. By the time of SEPACT's formation, Merritt Taylor Jr. operated the Philadelphia Suburban Transportation Company, popularly referred to as the Red Arrow Lines. Its principal rail route linked Norristown—a community also served by PRR and Reading commuter trains—with the 69th Street terminus of the Market Street subway and elevated line. The Red Arrow Lines remained profitable during the late 1950s, thanks in part to Taylor's austerity campaign that focused on efficient, if basic, transportation rather than passenger amenities. That profitability made Taylor reluctant to cooperate with municipal officials or join forces with the PRR and Reading services that were hemorrhaging money. Taylor was also a staunch political conservative, with an aversion to any form of governmental involvement in business. He used his influence in Delaware County to prevent that jurisdiction, located to the south and west of Center City, from joining SEPACT. It was an unfortunate omission, given that the county was home to several commuter lines, including a substantial portion of the all-important PRR route to Paoli. Taylor also refused to coordinate PSTC streetcar and bus routes and schedules with the commuter rail network, thus compromising the process of regional transportation planning.[273]

By the summer of 1962, Taylor had a specific reason to resist the activities of the city of Philadelphia, PSIC, and SEPACT. Civic planners had always assigned an important role to buses, as feeders to the Pennsylvania Railroad and Reading commuter rail lines, and the earliest Operation Northwest and Operation Northeast experiments included a joint one-fare arrangement with the PTC for precisely that type of service. By the spring of 1962, however, PTC and Red Arrow had developed a cooperative express-bus operation from Center City to Ardmore that had proven extraordinarily successful. A considerable portion of that ridership came at the expense of the Paoli Local. Taylor planned a new route between King of Prussia and Center City, and he suggested that the increased capacity of Red Arrow buses could create "a phantom fourth lane" on the Schuylkill Expressway, "without any city subsidy" or other obligations to taxpayers. "There has got to be an integrated system," Taylor acknowledged, but "of course, not all rail lines make sense." The proposed bus service offered the two companies an opportunity to recapture much of the commuter traffic that the PSIC-supported PRR and Reading had taken away from them, but it also threatened to undermine the impressive ridership gains the "Operation" lines had achieved. PSIC officials—who had pledged to take pressure off the overburdened Schuylkill Expressway while making it easier for commuters to reach Center City—now found themselves in the odd position of blocking an initiative that promised to achieve those goals. The city of Philadelphia accordingly opposed the PTC/PSTC application when it came before the state Public Utility Commission.[274] Ultimately, efforts by the PRR, the Reading, PTC, and Red Arrow to capture a limited number of nonhighway commuters indicated a

troubling situation. Lower fares and improved rail service were not proving effective at pulling people out of their cars and easing the pressure on the Schuylkill Expressway and surface streets. Instead, those initiatives were simply encouraging commuters to move from one form of mass transit to another.[275]

Taylor's opposition to public support for commuter rail reached a fever pitch in May 1962. Bailey was ready to implement service improvements along the PRR's Main Line to Paoli. He began pressuring the Delaware County commissioners to join SEPACT and contribute the seed money necessary to secure HHFA funds. Geography played against him, however. Once the PRR's route to Paoli left city limits, just past the Overbrook station, it ran through Montgomery County. The bulk of the $449,000 that Montgomery County had contributed to SEPACT went to Operation North Penn–Hatboro, for improvements on two Reading lines that lay north of Center City.[276] The remainder was allocated to Operation Bryn Mawr, along the Main Line. The name reflected the contentious nature of suburban politics, as the PRR's stop at Bryn Mawr was the westernmost location in Montgomery County but well short of the end of commuter territory at Paoli. The Bryn Mawr station was situated perhaps a thousand feet northeast of County Line Road. Just beyond lay the tracks of Merritt Taylor's Red Arrow Lines, with approximately two-thirds of its route to Norristown located within Delaware County. Past Bryn Mawr, the PRR line cut through the northernmost corner of that county, crossed over the Red Arrow tracks and—shortly before Strafford—entered Chester County (which was also a participant in SEPACT) for the remaining distance to Paoli. While there was one further station in Montgomery County, at Rosemont, Bryn Mawr was as far as westbound Silverliners could go before crossing over to the eastbound tracks for their return trip to Center-City Philadelphia.[277]

Both PSIC and PRR officials were prepared to extend Operation Bryn Mawr the full distance to Paoli, but they could not receive federal funds without the cooperation of the Delaware County commissioners. Bailey requested a $190,000 contribution, as part of the buy-in to the HHFA grant. Taylor was determined to prevent the county commissioners from authorizing the use of local and federal funds to subsidize a competitor. At Taylor's urging, the *Main Line Chronicle* ran a front-page headline asserting that a "$180,000 Rail Subsidy Got Pennsy Only 4 New Riders—Chicanery Exposed by Red Arrow." The associated article referred to the "Propagandists for the Pennsylvania Railroad, the Reading Company, and the city of Philadelphia [who] have been seeking to convince the suburbs that their counties should hand out subsidies to the railroads through additional real estate taxation." The accompanying editorial cartoon showed the city's "Billy (Green) Penn" shoving the nose of a "Pennsy/Reading" camel into the tent of suburban tax revenues.[278]

Taylor was well connected with Delaware County's Republican establishment, and he had a powerful ally in G. Robert Watkins, the chairman of the county commissioners. Watkins's opposition was hardly surprising, as SEPACT represented everything he despised. He was a conservative Republican and a loyal member of the notoriously corrupt county political machine controlled by former state senator John J. McClure. Both politicians recoiled with horror at the loss of Philadelphia's municipal government to the Clark, Dilworth, and Tate administrations, and both worked to ruin Dilworth's chances in the 1962 gubernatorial contest. Watkins and McClure had established successful business careers and had little use for government intervention in any form—and they certainly could not abide by public subsidies. McClure was a paving contractor who prospered from the expansion of the highway network, although he conveniently ignored the role of government in financing those improvements. Watkins organized the Blue Line Transfer Company in 1932, and he was a member of the Pennsylvania Trucking Association and the American Trucking Association. In their respective capacities, therefore, neither Watkins nor McClure were sympathetic to the problems experienced by the Pennsylvania Railroad. Watkins asserted that Operation Bryn Mawr represented "an attempt by the railroad to pressure the county communities into accepting the SEPACT program." He claimed that as many as eight thousand PRR employees rode the line each day for free, to get to and from their jobs. By comparison, he insisted, no more than twelve thousand Delaware County residents used the service as paying passengers, adding that it was "unfair to tax the real estate of all property owners in order to reduce the fares paid by a relatively small minority of commuters." Instead, Watkins suggested, it would be better to use federal funds to improve the Red Arrow service operated by his friend and political ally Merritt Taylor.[279]

PRR and SEPACT officials did their best to win over the Delaware County commissioners, but to no avail. Railroad personnel distributed sample petitions to twenty civic organizations, asking their members to sign and forward them to the commissioners. James W. Diffenderfer, Walter Patchell's assistant, exploited his status as a resident of Delaware County to promote the program to his neighbors. At a speech before the Main Line Kiwanis Club, Diffenderfer emphasized the ridership gains on other "Operation"

lines and the inadequacy of the highway network. He stressed that PRR officials "are convinced that it is in the best interest of residents and taxpayers in suburban communities to join SEPACT in its rail service expansion program." Patchell was active as well, telling an audience at the Bellevue-Stratford Hotel that he fervently hoped that Delaware County would join SEPACT and contribute to the support of the PRR's commuter operations. "Such a contract does not subsidize the railroads," Patchell reassured his audience, "but only pays the carrier for rendering a public service in much the same way that municipalities contract for street lighting and other essential services." He also noted that "tax funds appropriated for contracting rail services are 'peanuts' by comparison with the millions of dollars spent to build highways, bridges and parking lots to transport these additional people to and from the suburbs." Patchell was arguing against both perception and reality, however. The amount requested from Delaware County was indeed small, but statistics clearly demonstrated that the funds contributed by the city of Philadelphia, and by Bucks and Montgomery Counties, exceeded initial estimates—and many of Delaware County's residents did not want to suffer the same fate. Moreover, as Bailey acknowledged a month earlier, there were significant conditions associated with the HHFA grants. They included "the requirement that our programs be shifted from revenue-supported to tax-supported" and ensured that "the Federal agency will have to get deeply into the decisions on the value of each project and even into City/PTC negotiations." Those stipulations made it far more difficult for Bailey and Patchell to argue that the SEPACT "Operations" represented anything other than a taxpayer-funded subsidy, stoked suburbanites' fears of a more intrusive federal presence in their communities, and gave Greenfield, Taylor, and their associates further reasons to mistrust the Democratic administrations that held power in both Philadelphia and Washington.[280]

The May 17 meeting of the county commissioners did little to clarify the situation. Municipal officials made the trek to Delaware County in hopes of influencing the outcome, although without much success. David Berger, a Democratic Jewish lawyer from Center City, probably did not expect a friendly welcome from Protestant, Republican suburbanites, and he did not receive one. An attorney representing Taylor's Red Arrow Lines declared that SEPACT was illegal and "an atrociously un-American scheme" developed by the "selfish interests" of the Pennsylvania Railroad. Taylor predicted that subsidies would "skyrocket," while enabling SEPACT to "rob" his company of passengers. A representative from the West End Civic

Association insisted that the arrangement would impose "an unconscionable tax burden" on area residents, a sentiment endorsed by Commissioner Watkins. "I never like to pay your taxes," he told Berger, and "I hate to contribute one penny to the city of Philadelphia when we need it so badly out here." Patchell reminded the commissioners of the railroad's continuing losses, raised the frightening specter of as many as four new freeways slicing through the county, and asserted that the PRR and the city "will not be destroyed" by the cost of commuter service. When the three commissioners cast their votes, Watkins was emphatic in his opposition to SEPACT. William A. Welsh, the sole Democrat on the county commission, was equally enthusiastic in his support for the agency. The third commissioner, Albert H. Swing—who controlled a vote that matched his name—announced that he was "on the fence" and that he would need at least an additional month of study before he could make up his mind. Welsh had hinted that the fracas was "entirely political," a statement so blindingly obvious that it need not have been said. Bailey reassured Mayor Tate that the situation constituted "more of a side show than a serious attempt to obtain facts on a program of importance to the county," but until Swing made up his mind, neither SEPACT nor the Pennsylvania Railroad could move forward with plans to resolve the commuter crisis.[281]

It took Swing until October to reach a decision, but he did so with a vengeance. Within a week after the May 17 commissioners' meeting, Swing received more than four hundred letters from his constituents. Three-quarters of them supported Delaware County's participation in SEPACT. Welsh, the Democratic commissioner, negotiated several conditions with Berger, further alleviating Swing's concerns.[282] Watkins remained steadfast in his opposition, and his obstinacy prompted Swing to join forces with his Democratic counterpart. Welsh and Swing together removed Watkins from the chairmanship of the Delaware County commissioners, on account of his "obstructionist tactics." An infuriated Watkins reminded reporters that "the people of Delaware County elected two Republicans to run their government. Mr. Swing, with his marriage to the Democrat county commissioner, is defeating the will of the people demonstrated at the polls." He had harsher words for Welsh, "whose philosophy for spending transcends even that of Mr. Swing." Although he yielded the chairmanship to Swing, Watkins was still a county commissioner, and one whose opposition to the SEPACT program had only increased. Despite his role in Watkins's ouster, Swing refused to state his position regarding the county's involvement in the project. As the

ultimate decider of the fate of commuter rail operations along the Main Line, Swing was in a powerful position, and he used that authority to demand additional concessions from Bailey.[283]

Informal negotiations dragged on for months, and formal talks between Delaware County officials and SEPACT representatives did not begin until March 10, 1963. They occurred as Philadelphia commuters were beginning to recover from strikes that successively affected the Philadelphia Transportation Company and the Red Arrow Lines.[284] Bailey recalled that because of the crisis "Jim Tate decided that it was time to have a regional solution," one that would prevent further transportation paralysis. The mayor convened a task force and instructed its members to evaluate regional transportation authorities in other cities. He also put pressure on Merritt Taylor and his Delaware County allies, while offering them a share of the money that was beginning to flow from the nation's capital. Taylor spoke at a meeting of the American Transit Association in Washington, advocating federal legislation that would provide private companies—including his Red Arrow system—with the same federal funds that were available to SEPACT. Commissioner Welsh, who was no friend of Taylor, suggested that the Red Arrow strike could be resolved if that company became part of SEPACT, with ample resources to satisfy the unionized workers who were an important part of his constituency. Residents of Delaware County, with Taylor's backing, nonetheless announced that they were prepared to file a lawsuit on behalf of taxpayers, to prevent the county from contributing money to commuter rail. McClure, the county's power broker, decided that both Watkins and Swing had become toxic, and arranged for them to be left off the slate of nominations in the May 1963 Republican primary. Meanwhile, officials in Chester County—home to the westernmost stations along the route to Paoli—announced that they were ready to provide financial support to SEPACT, as soon as their Delaware County counterparts agreed to join. The *Philadelphia Inquirer*, which had long advocated improved commuter rail service, editorialized that "Delaware county has continued to be the missing link in the transportation improvement program for the Philadelphia area." That statement was a clear reference to the region's geography and the location of the PRR's Main Line, but observers could not help but wonder whether the farcical behavior of Delaware County's politicians represented a missing link of a different sort.[285]

As the county commissioners debated and attacked one another, SEPACT officials periodically released data showing impressive ridership gains on the other

"Operation" lines, while stressing the continuing improvements in equipment, facilities, and service. On October 28, SEPACT launched the long-delayed Operation Bryn Mawr, disingenuously rebranded as Operation Main Line. The reduced fares and additional trips—often made with new, air-conditioned Silverliner equipment—stopped just short of the Delaware County line. Another service—Operation Southwest—also began that day, along the PRR route toward Media and West Chester. Like its Main Line counterpart, it extended only as far as Angora, without entering the county whose commissioners had not yet offered financial support for SEPACT. Delaware County commuters began sending letters to the commissioners and to the newspapers, asking why they should not receive similar benefits. One letter to the editor prompted a response from a Levittown resident, apparently highly pleased with the PRR's service in Bucks County. "The answer is very simple," he noted. "About a year ago the Delaware County Commissioners refused to join SEPACT." In November 1963, Stuart Saunders, the PRR's chairman, pledged a "new look" for commuter facilities along the entire Main Line. It was part of a systemwide initiative known as "Operation Beaver" and represented only cosmetic improvements to a rapidly decaying physical plant. At the encouragement of PRR officials, the *Philadelphia Inquirer* and other newspapers nonetheless portrayed the announcement as an indication that the Pennsylvania Railroad was prepared to grant a significant boon to Delaware County residents who did not deserve it.[286]

From SEPACT to SEPTA

The resolution to SEPACT's difficulties emerged slowly, through an understanding that everyone would get a share of federal resources. Just as municipal officials established the Passenger Service Improvement Corporation as a repository for the money they hoped would accompany the Housing Act of 1961, regional transportation planners envisioned a new agency that would complement another federal mass-transit initiative. Despite Kennedy's earlier disinterest in transportation matters, by early 1962 he was increasingly receptive to the concerns of urban Democrats who constituted an important segment of his political constituency. On April 5, 1962, the president sent a message to Congress on "The Transportation System of our Nation." Basing his remarks on a report prepared by Secretary of Commerce Luther H. Hodges and Housing and Home Finance administrator Robert C. Weaver, Kennedy recommended comprehensive planning on matters relating to urban transportation—an approach that would necessitate

increased federal support for mass transit. John Bailey attended a Democratic Party State Finance Committee dinner in Harrisburg on September 20, and he noted that the president twice mentioned the issue. New Jersey senator Harrison Williams introduced the latest iteration of his bill in August, but like its predecessors, it stalled in Congress. Bailey lamented, "The transit bill has apparently been lost for this session," and he insisted that "Philadelphia should utilize all its available energy to accomplish its passage in the next Congress."[287]

In January 1963, Williams reintroduced his transit bill, and the Senate approved the legislation in April. Progress was much slower in the House, owing to opposition from southern Democrats and to Kennedy's assassination that November. The new president, Lyndon Johnson, was a strong advocate for the measure, and he secured bipartisan support for its passage. Like Richardson Dilworth before him, Mayor Tate lobbied heavily for the legislation, testified before Congress regarding the urgent necessity for federal assistance, and took credit for the bill's success. The Urban Mass Transportation Act of 1964, which the president signed on July 9, provided $375 million in federal funds over the next three years, including $10 million for demonstration grants to be awarded in 1965 and twice that the following year. While the amount was modest, compared to the funds spent on highway construction, the 1964 Transportation Act provided urban mayors with some hope that they could resurrect commuter rail and other mass-transit systems. As subsequent events would demonstrate, the legislation also facilitated more visionary schemes, including the potential for high-speed rail service connecting cities along the Atlantic Seaboard. Tate and other municipal officials predicted that Philadelphia would receive nearly a tenth of that amount—$36 million—and they announced their first application on July 8, 1964, one day before Johnson signed the bill into law. Of more immediate concern to Pennsylvania Railroad executives, federal funds provided the opportunity to escape the deficits associated with commuter operations. George C. Vaughan, the manager of the PRR's Philadelphia Region, observed "that the general concept of public participation in paying the costs of suburban service has been established" and that it was now time to seek additional compensation from government agencies.[288]

As urban, suburban, and state officials tracked the bill's progress through Congress, they established a new agency that—like PSIC at the municipal level—could legally accept the predicted infusion of federal funds. They based their newfound spirit of cooperation on the premise that Washington would provide the bulk of the

Given the long and acrimonious debates among officials in suburban counties, the finger-pointing that accompanied the first meeting of SEPTA's commissioners, on February 6, 1964, was probably appropriate—the smiles, perhaps less so. In the back row are, left to right, Chester County commissioner Leo D. McDermott, Walter B. Gibbons (Governor Scranton's representative), and Delaware County commissioner Harry S. McNichol. At the front are A. Russell Parkhouse, the president of the Montgomery County Commission; Philadelphia mayor James H. J. Tate; and John J. Bradley, the president of the Bucks County Commission. *Courtesy of the Special Collections Research Center, Temple University Libraries, Philadelphia, PA.*

money necessary to subsidize mass transit in southeastern Pennsylvania. In August 1963, the Pennsylvania Assembly adopted the Metropolitan Transportation Authorities Act, permitting counties to establish regional transit agencies. The legislation also created the Southeastern Pennsylvania

Transportation Authority. Initially, SEPTA existed solely to solicit federal grants and channel them to the companies that provided transportation services. It gained the necessary political support, according to vice chairman James McConnon, because no one at the city, county, or state level "was going to have to put any money in" to the agency. That proved an unrealistic expectation. Limitations on federal funding, the high costs of commuter rail operations, and the desire of SEPTA personnel to acquire the Philadelphia Transportation Company and the Red Arrow Lines ensured that representatives from both the state and county governments became liable for costs they had not anticipated.[289]

Even though they boycotted SEPACT, the promise of state and federal support prompted the Delaware County commissioners to join SEPTA in December. Each of the five metropolitan counties would have equal membership on SEPTA's board of directors, alongside one representative appointed by the governor. John Bailey eventually relinquished his duties as executive director of PSIC and as the secretary of SEPACT, becoming the deputy general manager of the new agency. Robert Watkins, the lame-duck commissioner, managed to set aside his earlier opposition to SEPACT long enough to indicate that "we will stand with the rest of you that are honored to be in this authority."[290]

SEPTA began operations in February 1964, but considerable time elapsed before the agency relieved the Pennsylvania Railroad of the cost of its commuter operations. The *Philadelphia Inquirer* predicted "a year of treading water" as the new agency recruited staff and began negotiations to purchase PTC and the Red Arrow Lines. In the interim, SEPACT continued to coordinate commuter service in the region. By May, some Silverliner cars were running beyond Bryn Mawr, giving Chester County commuters access to the benefits associated with a transportation compact they had joined in 1961. Twenty additional Silverliners, ordered from the St. Louis Car Company, augmented the thirty-eight Budd cars that PSIC had leased to the Pennsylvania Railroad. Even though those cars were city property, by the summer of 1964, the PRR was using them in weekend and off-peak service between Philadelphia and New York. They covered the eighty-six miles between Penn Station and North Philadelphia in seventy-five minutes, offering a demonstration of the potential for modern high-speed rail service connecting the major cities of the Northeast.[291]

"Treading water" was perhaps too charitable a description of the chaos that ensued over the next few years. Not until September 1965 did SEPTA assume the managerial and coordinating functions formerly undertaken by PSIC and SEPACT. SEPTA management of the PRR and Reading "Operations" did not begin until February 1966. In the meantime, suburban politicians discovered that they would not receive as much federal funding as they had anticipated—and that they would bear a far larger share of SEPTA's operating costs than they had expected. Representatives from the four suburban counties initially pledged $5,000 apiece for SEPTA's operations, to be matched by the city of Philadelphia, but they soon volunteered to triple that amount. City and SEPTA officials pressured the counties for a further increase, to $40,000, but Lawrence G. Williams, one of the two SEPTA board members representing Delaware County, insisted that the agency could make do with less. John Cramp, the other SEPTA commissioner from Delaware County, was more conciliatory and suggested that "Delaware county will pay up if SEPTA shows that the money was needed." The City Council, which had earlier pledged to allocate $60,000

to SEPTA, refused to release the funds until Delaware County paid its share. Not until April 1965 did the various entities reach a resolution, enabling Philadelphia's City Council to disburse the promised contribution. Coupled with $115,000 offered by the Commonwealth, it provided SEPTA with an annual operating budget of $435,000—barely sufficient to begin the process of coordinated transit planning. The amount was certainly minuscule, compared with the $2.4 million that the city of Philadelphia had allocated for the various commuter rail operations under PSIC and SEPACT. Moreover, there were indications that both the mayor and the City Council had reached the limit of their endurance.[292] Requests to increase the 1965 subsidies to almost $2.9 million collided with Mayor Tate's "hold-the-line" restrictions on spending, implemented after the city shouldered $4.2 million in unexpected costs associated with a race riot that ripped through North Philadelphia during August.[293] Even the addition of county funds and federal HHFA grants would prove inadequate to address the scope of the region's transportation problems.[294]

The limited nature of public support became clear on July 29, when Reading vice president and general counsel H. Merle Mulloy threatened to eliminate the company's commuter service, a move that would affect nineteen thousand Philadelphians a day. The Reading received $1.8 million in PSIC and SEPACT assistance during 1963, falling far short of eliminating the railroad's $5.1 million deficit from commuter operations. No one was happy about the situation, least of all Stuart Saunders, the PRR's chairman. While the Pennsylvania Railroad was not yet in such desperate financial straits as the Reading, Saunders nonetheless complained that his company carried half again as many commuters, lost more money on those operations, and was accordingly more deserving of public support. He also noted that 82 percent of Reading commuters benefited from the various "Operations," compared to only 31 percent on the PRR. "Of the $16 million lost by the Pennsylvania on suburban services throughout its system," Saunders emphasized, "the deficit on Philadelphia area lines totaled $6.3 million. Only $1.6 million of this was covered by public contract payments." Before he was prepared to support additional funding for the Reading, Saunders demanded a corresponding share of assistance for the Pennsylvania Railroad. "The conclusion is inescapable," he reminded Philadelphians, "that what is needed is extension and expansion of contract payments on all our suburban lines."[295]

Political battles at the state and local levels complicated efforts to implement coordinated transit planning that would replace what Saunders decried as a "fragmented" system. "It was clear that the Governor's representative had his ideas," for SEPTA, Bailey complained, "that Larry Williams from Delaware County had a slightly different set; and the rest of the people were together." In Harrisburg, Governor Scranton was pressuring the assembly to support a statewide transit bill, like those adopted in New Jersey, New York, Connecticut, and Massachusetts. Joseph Sharfsin, the chairman of the Public Utility Commission, instead proposed that the PRR assume the operation of the Reading's commuter services, with state funding made available to offset the deficits. None of the Reading's routes served Delaware County, inducing SEPTA board member Lawrence Williams to withhold his support and threaten legal action. He emphasized that the Reading contracts had been negotiated by PSIC and SEPACT rather than SEPTA and that the new agency had no role to play in the crisis. Yet it was equally clear that he had little interest in the fate of commuters in Montgomery County, where most of the Reading's tracks were situated. In retaliation, Montgomery County officials refused to continue subsidies for the Operation Main Line trains that had entered service the previous October—arguing that the initiative primarily benefited Delaware County, which had accepted membership in SEPTA but had never joined SEPACT. On October 25, slightly less than a year after the long-awaited launch of Operation Main Line, the PRR discontinued the initiative. At the same time, Mayor Tate's "hold-the-line" budget austerity threatened even the original service within city limits. On October 16, Edward A. Harvey, Bailey's replacement as PSIC's executive director, announced that the thirty-cent fares to Overbrook would return to their earlier level of forty-four cents, and that a reduction in train frequencies was also likely. "It's merely a question," Harvey observed, "of whether the city or SEPTA can raise funds to make up the deficit or obtain Federal experimental program funds for the line." With the survival of Reading's commuter service very much in doubt, SEPACT officials announced that it was "too early to tell" whether public support could preserve the city's commuter rail lines. Nearly two-thirds of the way through the demonstration period financed by the HHFA, it seemed clear that "payments made by SEPACT have reduced the burdens on the railroads, but it remains to be seen whether . . . commuter rail service can be saved from discontinuance."[296]

The fate of the PRR and Reading commuter operations again depended on the actions of the federal government. In March 1965, SEPACT filed another application with the HHFA, for more than $2.9 million. When matched with state and local funds, it would provide $4.7 million

in aid to the beleaguered Reading. Mayor Tate and representatives from Bucks and Montgomery Counties were delighted. Officials from Chester County expressed misgivings regarding their continued contributions to SEPACT without any corresponding benefits, following the discontinuance of Operation Main Line. Their counterparts in Delaware County reiterated their unwillingness to join SEPACT or assist in any way with the agreements that that agency had negotiated, and they refused to pay the $40,000 assessment owed to SEPTA for its 1965 operations. "The problem in Delaware county is unique and different from the other four counties that are members of SEPTA," observed board member Lawrence Williams. He announced that the county commissioners were not willing to subsidize "just the railroads" and demanded that PTC and Red Arrow receive a corresponding share of SEPTA funding. His obstinacy ensured that the three PRR commuter routes serving the county—to Paoli, to West Chester, and to Wilmington—were the only ones in the metropolitan area that did not receive the benefits of reduced fares and enhanced service. Merritt Taylor continued to rail against the "un-American" subsidies awarded to the railroads that were draining traffic and revenues from the Red Arrow Lines, while simultaneously demanding that he receive his fair share of government support. His allies in Delaware County suggested that the public should perhaps control Red Arrow, but as part of local transit authority. Albert Greenfield and other investors in the Philadelphia Transportation Company announced that they were willing to sell and named two different prices—one for the city and the other for SEPTA. Both were wildly inflated and unlikely to win political support. SEPACT was so short on staff that it took six months to prepare the application for HHFA funds—so long that Reading managers withheld the printing of passenger and employee timetables, for fear that federal aid would fail to materialize and that commuter operations would have to be curtailed.[297]

SEPTA made slow progress, although without offsetting the Pennsylvania Railroad's deficits associated with commuter service. In August 1965, the Delaware County commissioners agreed to honor the $40,000 payment to SEPTA, while promising to cooperate with the agency. On September 1, SEPTA assumed oversight for the PSIC and SEPACT programs. Both predecessor entities remained in existence as advisory groups, and PSIC retained title to the Silverliner cars that operated on the PRR and the Reading. City Controller Edward G. Bauer Jr. announced that he would safeguard PSIC's authority to "look out for Philadelphia interests," potentially undermining the regional unity that Bailey was determined to preserve. By the end of October, SEPTA officials had negotiated a contract with the PRR to continue subsidized service to Levittown, funded by contributions from the city of Philadelphia, Bucks County, the Commonwealth, and the federal government. The obstinacy of the Delaware County commissioners ended in December, when they agreed to provide $150,000 in SEPTA funding for 1966—but only on the condition that some of the money would be allocated to the Red Arrow Lines. The long-awaited improvements to the Paoli Local and the other two commuter routes serving Delaware County began on February 20, 1966. SEPTA's $6.5 million program included nearly $4.2 million allocated to the PRR—still inadequate to cover the railroad's losses. The funds permitted the addition of thirty-one weekday trains, many of them equipped with city-owned Silverliner equipment. Unlike the earlier PSIC "Operations," however, there would be no reductions in fares. John K. Tabor, the Pennsylvania secretary of commerce, suggested that the new service represented "government at its very best." Given the long and complex struggle to achieve harmony between city, county, state, and federal jurisdictions, it was a statement that was difficult to take seriously.[298]

In September 1966, SEPTA officials—who had by then gained oversight of all twelve of the region's commuter lines—announced an ambitious $457.7 million, ten-year capital-improvement program. The $168.9 million budgeted for commuter rail was more than a thousand times the city's initial $160,000 appropriation for the Passenger Service Improvement Corporation, suggesting that efforts to avoid costly highway construction had fostered equally expensive mass-transit initiatives. Even though it carried only a third of the region's rail commuters, the Reading would be the primary beneficiary, thanks to thirty-one new cars, the extension of the company's electrified territory, and the rebuilding of the viaduct that carried tracks out of Reading Terminal. Pennsylvania Railroad officials would have to be content with fifty cars and the construction of a new maintenance facility—although long-term plans called for the replacement of the PRR's aging MP54 equipment. The shift from local funding to state and federal support—which had been unavailable when PSIC began—was also notable. The city would provide only $10 million for the capital improvements, with the remaining $136.5 million coming from Harrisburg and from Washington.[299] The most visionary—or foolhardy—aspect of the plan involved funding for a tunnel linking Suburban Station with Reading Terminal. Officials from both railroads had little interest in the project, which SEPTA officials

initially estimated would cost $47 million. The tunnel may have facilitated regional transit planning and offered some convenience for commuters, but it would do nothing to offset either railroad's financial losses.[300]

The accomplishments of SEPTA officials fell far short of their ambitions. The steadily rising cost of the conflict in Southeast Asia, without a corresponding tax increase, restricted federal support for urban areas. Officials in cities across the United States, inspired in part by Philadelphia's example, competed for whatever funds were available. The impressive results associated with the initial HHFA grants also worked against the city's transit planners. "But now, at least as far as SEPTA is concerned," noted a senior government official who preferred to remain anonymous, "these demonstration grants have dried up because there is nothing left to demonstrate." SEPTA's efforts to acquire the Philadelphia Transportation Company and the Red Arrow Lines proved more complicated and more expensive than its staff members had anticipated. Bailey resigned abruptly as SEPTA's deputy general manager, ostensibly to pursue a more lucrative career as a university professor and transportation consultant. Insiders suggested that simultaneous investigations by City Controller Alexander Hemphill and the governor's office had prompted the hasty departure. A series of scandals rocked the agency, prompting Hemphill to withhold the PSIC's $950,000 contribution. The precipitous action threatened more than $4 million in federal subsidies, money that PRR and Reading executives were counting on to reduce their operating deficits. The continued flow of money from Harrisburg proved equally problematic. The executive director of the state's House Appropriations Committee suggested that SEPTA officials had failed to justify their request for funds. With the Commonwealth facing a budget crisis of its own, he recommended massive cuts in SEPTA's appropriation. Chairman Casimir Sienkiewicz complained that SEPTA's transit program would be "seriously impeded" and withheld nearly $800,000 owed to the Pennsylvania Railroad for commuter operations during the second quarter of 1967. Stuart Saunders, desperate to prevent the PRR from bearing the full weight of expanded commuter operations, reminded Philadelphia residents "that unjustified criticism of SEPTA can jeopardize receipt of monies from Federal and other government agencies on which the whole program depends."[301]

The new equipment SEPTA officials had promised likewise failed to placate commuters. A prolonged strike at the St. Louis Car Company and shortages associated with the Vietnam War ensured that the new batch of twenty Silverliners did not begin to arrive until August 1967, a year behind schedule. They joined the thirty-eight-car Budd Silverliner fleet, giving the PRR enough modern equipment to provide only a basic level of service.[302] Rush-hour commuters were more likely to encounter one of the 175 MP54 cars that remained in use. The situation stemmed in part from the success of the "Operations," as increased ridership had produced crowded trains and required the PRR to rely on even the oldest and most badly maintained equipment. Matters became worse in January 1968 when a broken wheel derailed a PRR train near Chestnut Hill. Soon traced to a design flaw that caused the brakes to overheat, the accident temporarily sidelined all twenty of the Silverliners manufactured by the St. Louis Car Company.[303]

PSIC officials and their successors had been promising better service for the previous decade, but with so few Silverliners running along the PRR, commuters grew tired of waiting. SEPTA officials acknowledged that "additional equipment will have to be provided if the railroads are to maintain effective service." Edson Tennyson, the city transit engineer who had helped to design the Silverliners, observed that "SEPTA is struggling valiantly for a large number of new cars," but no one was quite certain who would pay for them. Tennyson acknowledged that trains were frequently late, with the aisles packed with standees. "Some passengers were not able to board the train and return to their homes and travel to town by automobile," Tennyson admitted. He remained a loyal patron of the PRR's services but conceded that his train had arrived on time "only once." Commuters who lacked Tennyson's affinity for rail transit exhibited less sympathy for SEPTA's problems. "For the past two years there has been a shortage of seats and comfort and safety," one complained. His criticism of the PRR's "cattle car treatment" of its passengers suggested that not much had changed since 1954, when a counterpart considered the possibility of riding into Center City in a packing crate. SEPTA chairman Casimir Sienkiewicz grilled PRR and Reading officials, demanding an explanation for the poor quality of service. Representatives from Bucks County, one of the earliest and most dedicated supporters of SEPACT, were likewise

disappointed that their investment had not produced better results. "The runs by the Reading and Pennsylvania railroad are nothing but milk runs," complained the chairman of the Lower Bucks County Regional Cooperation Commission. "We're members of SEPTA," he observed, "but in name only." A decade of public support for commuter operations provided little relief from either deficits or complaints from disgruntled passengers. The public-private partnership gained the Pennsylvania Railroad few friends and a whole new set of enemies.[304]

Beginning with the city's Passenger Service Improvement Corporation "Operations," and continuing through SEPACT and SEPTA, transportation planners generated increased ridership for both the PRR and Reading commuter lines—although whether those gains resulted from taking cars off the highways or from taking passengers away from PTC and the Red Arrow Lines remained unclear. What the planners had not done, however, was to stem the losses that were draining millions of dollars each year from the PRR's treasury. By 1967, local, state, and federal officials had a reasonably good idea of the cost that was involved—and they did not want to pay it. The subsidies they could not legally call subsidies were inadequate, and the new Silverliner cars were too few to make more than an occasional appearance among a vast fleet of aging and decrepit MP54 units—some of which had carried Doughboys to their homes, following the armistice. Regardless of the availability of equipment, the track and roadbed were in such poor condition that they could not support high-speed operation. The Pennsylvania Railroad certainly could not afford to make repairs, and no government agency was willing to commit the necessary funds. Instead, all eyes were on another high-speed demonstration project, one that grew out of Philadelphia's pioneering experiments. Unsurprisingly, efforts to create a high-speed rail corridor linking the cities along the Atlantic Seaboard involved the same mixture of personalities and politics that had characterized local transportation planning since that late-summer day in 1954 when the opening of the Schuylkill Expressway generated a grand-slam traffic jam along City Line Avenue.[305]

The City of Philadelphia's Passenger Service Improvement
Corporation owned the Silverliner cars, the Southeastern
Pennsylvania Transportation Compact managed their use,
the Pennsylvania Railroad operated them, and a combination
of city, county, and federal funds paid for the service they
provided. Passengers at Paoli—the traditional outer limit of
commuter service on the Main Line—probably knew little
about the political battles that made it possible for that equipment to operate through Chester, Delaware, and Montgomery
Counties and into Center City. That process culminated in
the formation of a new agency, the Southeastern Pennsylvania
Transportation Authority. SEPTA assumed control of PSIC
and SEPACT operations in the fall of 1965, about the time
this photograph was taken. *Philadelphia Railroad Stations,
Red Arrow Lines, Trolley, Truck, and Bus Photographs, Hagley
Museum & Library, acc. 1995.238.*

Chapter 8

Merger

Barely forty years after its creation, Penn Station began to die. When it opened in 1910, the grandest of the nation's passenger terminals was but one component of a construction project that was exceeded in scope only by the completion of the Panama Canal. Neither Charles Follen McKim, the architect who claimed credit for its construction, nor Alexander Johnston Cassatt, the Pennsylvania Railroad president who authorized the New York Improvements, lived long enough to see the culmination of a vision translated into steel and stone. From the date it opened, however, their Beaux Arts masterpiece was declining into obsolescence. Humble commuters from Long Island and New Jersey rapidly supplanted the wealthy intercity travelers for whom Cassatt and McKim had planned a grand gateway to Manhattan. The rise of the automobile and the onset of the Great Depression induced an erosion in long-distance travel from which there was but one brief respite. More than one hundred million people passed through the station in 1945, a record the facility would never again equal. Soon after World War II ended, the Pennsylvania Railroad's intercity passenger service was in irreversible decline, while the company's financial problems were becoming far more severe. Penn Station was a colossal white elephant, expensive to maintain, and ill-suited for the travel patterns of the mid-twentieth century. The pollution from automobiles that clogged Manhattan streets blackened the exterior of pink Milford granite, while years of deferred maintenance ensured that the interior spaces were equally dismal.

Penn Station, moreover, stood on some of the most valuable real estate in the world, due in large measure to the convenient transportation connections established by the PRR and the Long Island Rail Road. There seemed little reason to preserve a structure solely for aesthetic or sentimental reasons. As early as 1950, Pennsylvania Railroad officials considered building a parking garage above the station's south courtyard. Two years later, the president of the Governor Clinton Hotel offered to pay $29.5 million for the facility, which would be replaced by a mixed-use development. The 1954 Heller passenger-service study reinforced the willingness of the railroad's executives to find a more profitable use for Penn Station. Asserting that "other than for cleanliness, lighting, and the ease of boarding and leaving trains, the average passenger is probably little concerned with the appearance and arrangement of stations," Heller recommended leasing space to concessionaires, as a means of generating additional income. The report also suggested that the railroad "actively pursue efforts to dispose of the passenger station building in New York, retaining ground rights and station space in new structures."[1]

Even as Robert Heller was preparing his recommendations, New York City's leading real estate developer was in negotiations with PRR officials. Through his company, Webb & Knapp, William Zeckendorf agreed to pay $4 million for the air rights associated with the open space between 9th and 10th Avenues, west of the General Post Office Building. Soon, however, Zeckendorf turned his attention to Penn Station itself. "If the studies are favorable," Zeckendorf announced, "the passenger station will be thoroughly modernized below the street level and a new building will be built above it, with adequate street level entrances and exits for the passenger station." The precise function of the new building remained nebulous, and Zeckendorf suggested possibilities ranging from an office tower to a trade center. During the summer of 1955, Zeckendorf sat beside the PRR's president, James Symes, in the office car *Pennsylvania*, pen in hand. The developer agreed to pay the railroad $30 million as part of a $100 million project to build a "Palace of Progress" atop the site. It would be the world's largest and most expensive structure, with seven million square feet of space in a tower that stretched five hundred feet into the Manhattan skyline. An office building and heliport would be constructed on the site that originally attracted Zeckendorf's attention, bookending the post office. The passenger station would pale into insignificance, although Symes promised to allocate $13 million of the money he received from Zeckendorf to build a new underground facility. A writer for the *New York Times* described the proposal as "a dream that can only be described in superlatives and punctuated with exclamation points." The paper's editors mentioned potential problems involving subway congestion, automobile traffic, and parking but said nothing about the incipient destruction of one of the city's greatest architectural monuments. Little more than six months later, Zeckendorf announced that he was abandoning the Palace of Progress. In its place was an even more ambitious development scheme that would cover the area between 9th and 12th Avenues and 30th and 38th Streets.[2]

While Zeckendorf was planning the future of Manhattan, PRR officials were marring the architectural integrity of Penn Station with kiosks and advertising signs. The worst insult came in February 1957, with the opening of a new ticket counter in the main concourse. Designed by architect Lester Tichy, it resembled nothing so much as a giant plastic clamshell incongruously placed in the middle of a Roman bath. It was a symbol, the *New York Times* observed, that "the Age of Elegance bowed to the Age of Plastic." Like Zeckendorf, Tichy was interested in demolishing Penn Station and developing the air rights over the tracks. "Every function of the station, except the glory, occurs below street level," he noted. It was a perspective that could have come straight from the Heller report, and one that was utterly dismissive of Charles Follen McKim and the other architects who won lavish praise for their work half a century earlier.[3]

Despite the various proposals, Penn Station remained much as it was, its Milford pink granite slowly disappearing under a layer of urban soot. In early 1960, PRR officials calculated that the company was losing $1.5 million a year on the facility's operation, to say nothing of the forgone

revenues from new real estate development. Symes, now the PRR's chairman, indicated that the railroad would save a considerable amount of money by bulldozing the station and turning the site into a parking lot while awaiting a new use for the land. His statement coincided with a new round of expensive investments in the PRR's freight operations, all of which required a massive infusion of capital. David Bevan, the railroad's vice president in charge of finance, experienced increasing pressure to raise the necessary funds, and the sale of real estate assets was one way to achieve that goal. Even as Symes and Bevan planned the station's destruction, the facility celebrated its fiftieth birthday on November 27. The PRR made no announcement of the event, there was no celebration, and a reporter who mentioned the significance of the date to a station employee received in response the sarcastic and apathetic query, "Is that so?"[4]

While Pennsylvania Railroad executives were deciding what to do with a station they no longer wanted, entrepreneur Irving M. Felt was moving forward with plans of his own. During the early 1950s, Felt gained control of Graham-Paige, a failing automobile manufacturer, and transformed the company into a real estate development firm. In 1959, Felt arranged for Graham-Paige to purchase Madison Square Garden, built in 1925 at 8th Avenue and 50th Street. The following November, Felt announced plans for a new Madison Square Garden. He did not indicate where it would be located, other than to suggest that "it won't be far" from the original site. He was true to his word and was soon negotiating with PRR officials for the air rights at the Penn Station site, fifteen blocks to the south.[5]

In contrast with previous development proposals, Felt's plans for a new Madison Square Garden moved quickly toward fruition. By the following summer, J. Benton Jones, the PRR's vice president in charge of purchases and real estate, briefed the board of directors on two possible uses for the site. One, from Lester Tichy, proposed an office, tower, a hotel, and an exhibition space tied to the city's nearby Garment District. Jones and the directors agreed that Tichy was unlikely to secure the cooperation of the notoriously fragmented clothing manufacturers and that his concept was not likely to succeed. Felt's vision was far more realistic. On June 28, the directors signed Penn Station's death warrant, approving $21.5 million for the demolition of the building and preliminary design work on the replacement terminal. The story broke on July 24, when PRR officials acknowledged that the new Madison Square Garden would be built atop Penn Station. There was considerable ambiguity, and newspapers initially reported that "the main waiting room of Pennsylvania Station will be left as is." The formal announcement came on July 26, when Symes and Felt highlighted a $75 million project to build a twenty-five-thousand-seat arena; a smaller, four-thousand-seat facility; a twenty-eight-story hotel; a thirty-four-story office building; and a parking garage accommodating three thousand cars. Construction would be overseen by the Madison Square Garden Corporation, with Graham-Paige controlling 75 percent of the stock and the PRR the remaining quarter. Felt promised that the sparkling new facility would be completed before the opening of the 1964 New York World's Fair. Clarifying rumors, the *New York Times* reported that "the present station structure will be razed to the street level." The matter-of-fact notice suggested that the newspaper's editors had little interest in interfering with the march of progress. "A new Madison Square Garden," they emphasized, "makes a constructive contribution to New York City above and beyond its obvious attraction for sports and entertainment."[6]

Despite the laconic response to the impending destruction of Penn Station, an effort to save the facility was underway. The acerbic architectural critic Lewis Mumford was the first to sound the alarm. Generally regarded as modernist, he suggested that "Pennsylvania Station turned out to be the dying note of the classic revival that had begun in 1893 with the Chicago World's Fair."[7] In his criticism of the Beaux Arts style, Mumford was thus not dogmatically opposed to the construction of new buildings to replace old ones. Yet he deplored what he perceived to be the soulless and corrupting influence of capitalism, which crassly elevated the profit motive above aesthetics and everything else that gave meaning to life. Mumford criticized the grime, the tattiness, the vending machines, and the advertising displays that cluttered Penn Station, and he insisted that the building was in its death throes long before Irving Felt announced the construction of the new Madison Square Garden. "One suspects," he informed readers of *The New Yorker* magazine in 1958, "that the subversion of McKim's masterly plan was due simply to the desire to make the whole design an immense advertising display." Tichy's clamshell ticket counter was the last straw, and a despairing Mumford suggested that "no one now entering Pennsylvania Station for the first time could, without clairvoyance, imagine how good it used to be, in comparison to the almost indescribable botch that has been made of it." The building had lost its soul, if not yet its physical existence, and Mumford concluded that "nothing further that could be done to the station could damage it."[8]

When it became clear that the building would be destroyed, others blended Mumford's lament for glories lost with a determination to preserve whatever remained of its original grandeur. "Although the interior has been almost entirely ruined, its great space and nobility are still visible," observed architecture critic Aline Saarinen, the widow of architect Eero Saarinen. "I would do everything possible to urge its restoration and imaginative re-thinking in order to make it again functional," she observed. The news editor of *Progressive Architecture* lamented that "New Yorkers will lose one of their finest buildings, one of the few remaining from the 'golden age' at the turn of the century, for one reason and one reason only: that a comparatively small group of men wants to make money." The battle between aesthetics and commerce would become the defining feature of the efforts to save Penn Station, and of the historic-preservation movement in general.[9]

Penn Station gained powerful supporters, including many who were outside the architectural community. In September 1961, the Municipal Art Society and the National Trust for Historic Preservation both denounced the Madison Square Garden Project. So did the *New York Times*, whose editorial policy quickly changed to reflect support for the preservationists. Editors expressed disgust that matters of sordid finance were taking precedence over art and beauty. "The ultimate tragedy," they observed, "is that such architectural nobility has become economically obsolete, so that we must destroy it for shoddier buildings and lesser values."[10]

Norval White, assistant professor of architectural design at The Cooper Union, spearheaded what soon emerged as the most vocal organization in support of Penn Station's preservation. In May 1962, White wrote a letter to the *New York Times* in which he characterized the building as "a strong part of our urban landscape." The station was indeed a glorious architectural creation, White emphasized, "but even more importantly, it is a sequence of glorious entrance spaces to our city." The Port of New York Authority owned or oversaw the other grand entrances to New York as well as many of the city's iconic structures. Therefore, White asserted, Penn Station should be added to that list. While representatives from the Port Authority wanted nothing to do with the building, White had more success in his efforts to build a grassroots coalition of architects, artists, writers, and other concerned citizens. His organization, the Action Group for Better Architecture in New York, published a call to arms in the August 2 issue of the *New York Times*. The announcement listed more than 175 prominent supporters, and reiterated White's Port Authority proposal. AGBANY members nonetheless conceded that "it may be too late to save Penn Station; next month the workers will move in for the kill.

But it is not too late to save New York." The group called for a demonstration at the station's 7th Avenue entrance that evening. Some two hundred picketers carried signs bearing such inscriptions as "Save Our Heritage," "Be a Penn Pal," and "Don't Demolish It! Polish It!" That evening, AGBANY leaders met Mayor Robert F. Wagner Jr. at the airport as he was returning from a European vacation, and they handed him a letter asking for his support.[11]

Wagner was sympathetic, but there was not much he could do. "In a city changing as rapidly and being rebuilt as rapidly as New York," he observed, "there is a constant danger that structures of historic interest or high esthetic value may be overwhelmed by the rebuilding rush." Two months before the AGBANY demonstration, Wagner established the Committee for the Preservation of Structures of Historic and Esthetic Importance. Headed by architect Geoffrey Platt, the advisory group worked with the Municipal Art Society and the Fine Arts Federation and recommended the creation of a permanent Landmarks Preservation Commission. Those developments coincided with 1961 alterations to the city's 1916 zoning law, meant to provide New Yorkers with more light, better public spaces, and improved parking. On April 21, 1962, Wagner appointed Platt to head the newly constituted Landmarks Preservation Commission. On the same day, the New York chapter of the American Institute of Architects condemned the loss of "a great architectural monument" that was Penn Station. "Like ancient Rome," they noted, "New York seems bent on tearing down its finest buildings." Echoing a familiar theme, they stressed that "the generation that conceived the station accepted the dictum: 'Well building hath three conditions: commodity, firmness and delight,' and the greatest of these was delight." Sadly, they concluded, "no opinion based on the artistic worth of a building is worth two straws when huge sums and huge enterprises are at stake."[12]

Pennsylvania Railroad executives had little patience with activists' efforts to elevate aesthetics over finance. In an August 1962 letter to the *New York Times*, President Allen Greenough asked the city's residents, "Does it make any sense to attempt to preserve a building merely as a 'monument' when it no longer serves the utilitarian needs for which it was erected? It was built by private enterprise, by the way, and not primarily as a monument at all but as a railroad station." Greenough emphasized that "the railroads that use the station have a grave responsibility to the public, their stockholders and their employees to operate as efficiently as possible. No private enterprise," he reminded New Yorkers, "can operate at a continuing loss." Irving Felt shared that perspective. "What's the

alternative?" he asked reporters. "Who pays for the large expenditures we already have made? Who subsidizes the Pennsylvania Railroad?"[13]

Greenough's perspective dictated Penn Station's fate and—for the moment at least—the shape of the built environment. The PRR selected Charles Luckman Associates as the architects for the project and contracted with the Turner Construction Company to demolish the historic structure and build the foundations for Madison Square Garden. In September, the board of directors approved the arrangements. Greenough pledged to spend $10 million on "a newly designed, efficient terminal that recognizes both the convenience and the requirements of the day" and would feature such improvements as escalators and air-conditioning. While Greenough was promising a new and improved Penn Station, those who opposed the destruction of the old one were powerless to stop it. A group of architects and civic leaders presented their concerns to Mayor Wagner, as did the Fine Arts Federation of New York. The newly constituted Landmarks Preservation Commission lacked the authority to interfere in the demolition of a privately owned structure, and the City Planning Commission could only withhold a building permit for the new Madison Square Garden if it failed to meet municipal ordinances. For the final time, Port Authority representatives stressed that they could not lawfully take control of Penn Station and that they had no desire to do so.[14]

The controversy—which accelerated the momentum of the historic-preservation movement and led to the passage of the 1965 New York City Landmarks Law—came too late to save Penn Station. On October 28, 1963, workers removed the four granite eagles from the 33rd Street facade of the station. The PRR's J. Benton Jones, accompanied by Irving Felt and Thomas M. Goodfellow from the Long Island Rail Road, watched as the first of Adolph Weinman's sculptures came down from its aerie. Later in the day, AGBANY protestors donned black armbands and picketed the site, their cries of "shame" drowned out by the roar of jackhammers attacking the station's Doric columns. "This is a sad day for us," commented architect Norman Jaffe, who called the building "an index to an era of America that was great and noble." John Rezin, the foreman of the demolition crew, was less evocative. He noted that the destruction of the Pennsylvania Railroad's iconic architectural achievement was "just another job." Two days later, the *New York Times* published one of the most memorable editorials in the paper's history. "Until the first blow fell no one was convinced that Penn Station really would be demolished or that New York would permit this monumental act of vandalism against one of the largest

Once considered one of the nation's greatest architectural achievements, by the 1950s Penn Station had lost its commercial value. As they withdrew from unprofitable passenger operations and struggled to raise money wherever they could, Pennsylvania Railroad executives sold the air rights to the four-block site and condemned the station to destruction. Workers incrementally dismantled the Beaux Arts edifice while erecting the framework for Madison Square Garden in its shell. This was the situation on June 9, 1966. *AP Photo.*

and finest landmarks of its age of Roman elegance," the paper conceded. "Any city gets what it admires, will pay for, and, ultimately, deserves. Even when we had Penn Station, we couldn't afford to keep it clean. We want and deserve tin-can architecture in a tin-horn culture. And we will probably be judged not by the monuments we build but by those we have destroyed."[15]

The demolition of Penn Station continued for another three years. By September 1964, the remains of the Doric columns lay shattered in the New Jersey Meadowlands, where they could be seen by passengers speeding by on board the Pennsylvania Railroad's trains. The unceremonious dumping marked the final blow to preservationists who suggested that it might at least be possible to save parts of the facade, to display them in a park. It was "a matter of economics," emphasized Morris Lipsett, who headed the demolition contractors. "If anybody seriously considered it art, they would have put up some money to save it." One of his competitors, Harry Avirom, was even more enthusiastic in his assessment of the reconstitution of Greater New York. "We are entering a great new era of demolition," observed the president of the Wrecking Corporation of America. "All of the little garbage has been torn down, so now we are sinking our teeth in the big stuff." All across the city, so much was disappearing so fast that the market for used bricks had collapsed, and it was difficult to find demolition cranes at any price.[16]

While the city they had once known disappeared around them, more than two hundred thousand passengers a day continued to use Penn Station. Like wayward children daubing finger paint over the *Mona Lisa*, construction workers built the new station even as they were dismantling the old one. Commuters and intercity travelers navigated a maze of scaffolding and colossal piles of rubble. Passengers and red caps yelled at one another, the only way they could communicate above the din. The station master rearranged the wiring for the public-address system, so that patrons might be able to understand the announcements for arriving and departing trains. People passing through the station soon reported hearing intermittent bursts of music echoing faintly through what remained of the cavernous structure. Electronics experts speculated that steel beams, stripped of their ornamental covering and crisscrossed with temporary wires, acted as a giant radio receiver. A security guard making his lonely nighttime rounds indicated that it was easy to "get to wondering if it isn't the voice of the station, moaning 'Please help me! Please help me!'" Correspondents for *The New Yorker* "were convinced that we'd been looking for an explanation of the music in the wrong world altogether." It was, they speculated, "a ghost sound in the ghost of a building, in a city that doesn't believe in ghosts." For those who looked to the future, anticipating the fulfillment of a murdered president's vow to land a man on the moon and return him safely to Earth, the sounds may have resembled the final garbled transmissions of an out-of-control spacecraft careening toward the most distant reaches of the galaxy. Those who favored the past could imagine the end of the age of the dinosaurs and the last breaths of a dying behemoth that lay astride a dying railroad.[17]

The Merger Landscape

As New Yorkers were deciding the fate of Penn Station, the entire eastern railroad network was moving toward collapse. The problems were familiar to anyone who paid attention to the basic elements of transportation economics—highway and airline competition, rapidly decreasing passenger traffic, stagnant freight revenues, increased labor costs, high taxes, expensive terminals, decaying branch lines, and chronically unprofitable commuter operations. Executives universally assumed they suffered from overcapacity and that there were simply too many miles of track and too many companies for any of them

to be profitable. The most likely outcomes seemed to be either the bankruptcy of the weakest railroads, with the attendant disruptions to local communities, or else nationalization. With considerable faith and a growing sense of urgency, railroad officials concluded that mergers offered the only realistic mechanism for restoring financial health. Joined by a growing number of politicians and shippers, they predicted that the consolidation of firms, the rationalization of facilities, and the elimination of excess capacity would enable the railroads to compete against the highways and inland waterways. While there were many players in the escalating merger movement that began in the late 1950s, one individual would prove more influential than any other. When the Pennsylvania Railroad announced that Penn Station would give way to Madison Square Garden, he was nearly five hundred miles away, in the comparative quietude of the Blue Ridge Mountains. He had distinguished himself as an expert in mergers, and he was rapidly gaining a reputation as the man who would save the railroads.

Stuart Saunders did very well during his first twenty months as the president of the Norfolk & Western Railway. On November 1, 1957, five months before Saunders took office, James Symes and Alfred Perlman announced their intention to merge the Pennsylvania Railroad and the New York Central. Their plans threatened to upend the entire eastern railway network. The Pocahontas region was a small but unusually prosperous portion of that network, and Saunders's Norfolk & Western was about as successful as any railroad could be during the late 1950s. The PRR owned 45 percent of the N&W and used dividends from the coal carrier to bolster its increasingly dismal net income. Symes sat on the Norfolk & Western's board of directors, and Saunders could be reasonably confident that his company would be well treated in a merger between the PRR and the NYC. The same could not be said for the Virginian, a company that rivaled the N&W in its ability to move coal efficiently and profitably to tidewater and to overseas markets. For many years, the Virginian also delivered coal to the NYC at Deepwater, West Virginia, bound for cities and industries in the Northeast and the Midwest. Yet the relationship between those two companies lacked the close financial ties that bound the Norfolk & Western and the Pennsylvania Railroad. Should the PRR-NYC merger take place, the Norfolk & Western was bound to prosper, and the Virginian would assuredly be cast aside. When Saunders became the N&W's president on March 31, 1958, he found Virginian executives receptive to any merger that would assure the company's survival. Saunders, an affable and charismatic attorney with excellent political connections, masterfully orchestrated a consolidation with the Virginian, winning approval by the Interstate Commerce Commission, placating on-line shippers and communities, and promising workers that jobs would be sacrificed solely through attrition.

The December 1, 1959, consolidation of the Norfolk & Western and the Virginian was the first of many mergers that would take place over the following decades. At less than three thousand route miles, the newly expanded N&W was small by PRR standards, yet the company and the merger that Saunders had engineered proved enormously consequential. He emerged as one of the leading railroad executives in the United States, with a reputation for savvy negotiating skills and the skillful manipulation of the regulatory process. Saunders always claimed that the absorption of the Virginian was solely his idea, without any coaxing on the part of Symes or other PRR officials. Perlman nonetheless felt blindsided and betrayed. On January 8, 1959, he announced that he was suspending negotiations between the New York Central and the Pennsylvania Railroad.

For all his reluctance to join forces with the Pennsylvania Railroad, Perlman was the first to respond aggressively, both to acquire partners that could bolster the NYC's low earnings and to protect his company from the other eastern trunk lines. His most immediate concern involved his predecessor. After William White became president of the New York Central in August 1952, he made steady progress in his efforts to rebuild the physical plant, improve service, and increase earnings. His tenure lasted less than two years before financier Robert Young gained control of the company and installed Perlman as president. White quickly found a job as head of the Delaware & Hudson, where he began to forge alliances with other regional carriers whose executives felt threatened by Young, Perlman, and the New York Central. Two of those companies—the Erie and the Delaware, Lackawanna & Western—would be devastated by the proposed merger between the New York Central and the Pennsylvania Railroad.

The same 1954 recession that enabled Young to discredit White's leadership of the NYC also encouraged officials from the Erie and the DL&W to explore cooperative efforts to ameliorate their shared economic misery. They included joint use of the Lackawanna's Hoboken Terminal and the consolidated operation of parallel tracks along seventy route miles through south-central New York. White, who had been the Lackawanna's president before joining the New York Central, was eager to develop a more formal relationship between the two railroads—both to protect

his interests and to extract a measure of revenge against the management team that had displaced him. Using the strategically located Delaware & Hudson as a base, in September 1956 he sought a three-way merger with the Erie and the DL&W. The proposed consolidation of the PRR and the NYC, announced little more than a year later, portended the creation of a railroad colossus that could destroy both the Lackawanna and the Erie and made officials from both companies disposed to cooperate. White prudently sought the advice of financial consultants, and in April 1959, they cautioned him to stay well clear of the two larger railroads. Executives at the Erie and the Lackawanna carried on without him. The immediate threat of the PRR-NYC merger had ended, but the financial situation of the two companies was still dire. With remarkable speed, representatives from the Erie and the Lackawanna agreed to merge and sought ICC approval on July 1, 1959.[18]

The Erie-Lackawanna consolidation created a serious problem for Symes, who considered the merger negotiations with the New York Central to be paused rather than terminated. A strengthened system on the PRR's northern flank, even one composed of two weak carriers, was bound to do his company no good, and would certainly harm the NYC as well. However, he could hardly oppose the merger of two parallel east–west trunk lines—on the grounds that it would reduce competition and injure competing railroads—without acknowledging that an even larger and stronger PRR-NYC consolidation would do precisely the same thing. Publicly, Symes's course of action was clear. To the surprise of many Erie and DL&W executives, the PRR's chairman suggested that the merger would solve the difficulties that faced both railroads. His further comment that "this should be a good example to encourage other railroads to do the same thing" was a none-too-subtle reference to his plans for the New York Central.[19]

Privately, however, Symes did what he could to hobble the merger application. He suggested that, although he supported the creation of an Erie-Lackawanna system in principle, he felt duty bound to remind ICC officials that it would do serious harm to both the Wabash and the Lehigh Valley, two companies in which the PRR maintained a controlling interest. Symes was only half-right. ICC examiner Hyman J. Blond conceded that the Wabash might lose $1 million of revenue annually, should the Erie-Lackawanna merger win approval. No one, however, could envision a scenario in which the Lehigh Valley might be negatively affected. Symes asked Wabash president and former PRR executive Herman H. Pevler—whose company had the better case—to oppose the consolidation of the two railroads. It was unlikely that Symes's behind-the-scenes machinations could have thwarted a merger that almost everyone said was a sound idea. Instead, Symes hoped that Pevler could extract significant concessions. They included trackage rights that would provide the Wabash with better access to Buffalo and enable the PRR to create what amounted to a new trunk line between New York and the Midwest, via the Lehigh Valley and the Wabash. Representatives from the Erie and the Lackawanna complained that their capital investments would be used for the benefit of their competitors, but to no avail. In April 1960, Pevler negotiated an agreement that provided him and Symes most of what they wanted. Five months later, the ICC gave its assent to the creation of the Erie-Lackawanna Railroad.[20]

The Erie-Lackawanna merger talks, in large measure the product of the failed discussions between the PRR and the NYC, in turn rippled outward in two directions. One involved Stuart Saunders and the Norfolk & Western—which meant that it unavoidably touched on the interests of the Pennsylvania Railroad as well. Even as he relished the acquisition of the Virginian, Saunders sought other opportunities for his company. The newly expanded N&W was well equipped to carry large volumes of coal to the Virginia coast but did not reach the large urban markets of the Northeast and the Midwest. Saunders was also concerned about the N&W's reliance on a single commodity that could be disproportionately affected by economic downturns. The New York, Chicago & St. Louis Railroad solved both of those problems. The company, better known simply as the Nickel Plate Road, offered service to Buffalo, Cleveland, Toledo, St. Louis, and Chicago—ready markets for Pocahontas coal. The Nickel Plate specialized in high-speed merchandise traffic, complementing the N&W's bulk-commodity base. It was also a very prosperous company—and if Saunders learned one thing from his negotiations involving the Virginian, it was that it was much easier to merge two successful firms than two failing ones.[21]

While the Nickel Plate prospered as an independent carrier, its managers had reason to be worried as the 1950s came to an end. The 1957 recession adversely affected the company, more so than many of its competitors. Declining iron-ore production in the Mesabi Range reduced shipments to steel mills located along the Nickel Plate. Perlman's efforts to improve service along the New York Central also hurt the company's revenues, while the Erie-Lackawanna merger portended additional problems. The Nickel Plate's president, Felix Hales, was initially receptive to a union with the Chesapeake & Ohio, one that would re-create a significant portion of the old Van

Sweringen system. The Baltimore & Ohio would also be a participant, however, and a cursory examination of the B&O's books was sufficient to cause Nickel Plate officials to look elsewhere. Saunders welcomed them enthusiastically, for a union of the two prosperous railroads would create one of the most profitable transportation enterprises in the United States. In November 1959, Saunders and Hales began discussing the possibility of a merger.[22]

Alfred Perlman and other New York Central officials reacted with alarm to the rapid restructuring of the eastern railroad network. A merger between the Erie and the Lackawanna was bound to affect the NYC's east–west trunk-line traffic, but the Norfolk & Western proposal was far worse. The Nickel Plate Road, which had once been a part of the New York Central, possessed a superbly engineered route between Buffalo and Chicago, as well as a network of lines that penetrated deep into NYC territory. A union with the N&W would make it an even more formidable competitor, while excluding the NYC from the lucrative traffic that flowed between the Pocahontas coalfields and the Great Lakes. To worsen matters, the PRR joined forces with the Santa Fe, gaining control of the Toledo, Peoria & Western Railway. On December 14, a few days after Saunders and Hales began merger discussions, the United States Supreme Court resolved a legal battle—underway since the summer of 1955—for control of the short but strategic line that extended the PRR's reach farther into the West while offering a freight bypass around the congested city of Chicago.[23]

Perlman blamed the Pennsylvania Railroad for instigating the consolidation of the Norfolk & Western and the Virginian, and it was hardly surprising that he perceived the same forces at work in the latest developments. Shortly after receiving word of the negotiations between Saunders and Hales, he asked John W. Barriger III to study the matter. Barriger, the president of the Pittsburgh & Lake Erie, a New York Central subsidiary, was an expert in such matters. He had recently offered his opinion on the now-abandoned merger discussions with the PRR, and he was thoroughly familiar with the eastern railroad situation. His report, delivered on December 16, 1959, confirmed Perlman's worst suspicions. "There are clear signs that the Pennsylvania now intends to expand its territorial and mileage sphere of influence," Barriger warned. "The Pennsylvania's sixty-year development of its 'community of interest' policy has brought about control of the Norfolk & Western (and now the Virginian) together with the Wabash, the Lehigh Valley, Detroit, Toledo & Ironton Railway and (a half interest in the) Toledo, Peoria & Western. Even this impressive group of satellites does not represent the probable ultimate limit of the Pennsylvania's rail empire."[24]

The creation of empires bespoke acts of violence, and Barriger relied heavily on militaristic language. "The Pennsylvania's location may be regarded as similar to that of the 'Central Powers' in World War I," he told Perlman, "with the New York Central on one flank, the Baltimore & Ohio on another, and the Van Sweringen lines in between, competing with both the PRR and the Norfolk & Western." Barriger credited the PRR's success to the "short interior lines that pass through the greatest freight traffic producing and consuming areas of the nation" as well as to "a fairly consistent policy dating back to the Cassatt administration." The latest battle, Barriger concluded, demonstrated that "one of the Pennsylvania's historic ambitions is a route along the south shore of Lake Erie. Acquisition of the Nickel Plate would provide such a line." It made little difference that it was the Norfolk & Western rather than the Pennsylvania Railroad that was poised to capture a lakeshore route. As far as Barriger and Perlman were concerned, the two companies were one and the same.[25]

While no one could know with certainty whether the Erie-Lackawanna or the Norfolk & Western merger proposals would prove successful, Perlman thought it best to be prepared for any eventuality. Barriger was ready with suitable advice, and he noted that "the NYC, B&O and C&O are so complementary and supplementary to one another that they should promptly enter into emergency consolidation conversations in order to develop in detail the advantages that would follow from the unification of their physical and corporate structures." He acknowledged that the lingering effects of the 1958 Eisenhower Recession still affected the PRR but concluded that "only a system the size of a NYC-B&O-C&O combination will enable the non-Pennsylvania railroads to maintain permanent traffic parity with the Pennsylvania not alone for the present but during a period in the future when the Pennsylvania will again become dynamic and successful." The limiting factor, Barriger emphasized, was that the merger between the Norfolk & Western and the Virginian ensured that only two large Pocahontas coal carriers remained. Given the steady decline of the northeastern railroads, he concluded, it was unlikely that any large company could survive without the mine-to-tidewater traffic that the N&W and the Chesapeake & Ohio could generate. "A two-party consolidation of eastern railroads appears inevitable," Barriger insisted, "because no possible combination of lines could make a third system that would be geographically complete and competitively well balanced." Perlman accepted that

reasoning, and later informed the ICC that "the merger of the Virginian into the Pennsylvania system reduced the number of Pocahontas lines to two, the Norfolk and Western and the Chesapeake and Ohio. This militates against, if it does not actually prohibit, the evolution of more than two systems in official territory."[26]

Perlman and Barriger thus anticipated the development of two great eastern railroad networks. One would be based on the Pennsylvania Railroad, with the assumption that that company would forever control the Norfolk & Western (and with it the Nickel Plate and the Wabash), the Lehigh Valley, the DT&I, and the TP&W. The other would continue the historic alliance between the New York Central and the Baltimore & Ohio (as well as the Reading and the Jersey Central), with the Chesapeake & Ohio providing all-important access to revenues from the Pocahontas coalfields. The remaining unaligned carriers would, of necessity, gravitate to one or the other of the two giant systems.[27] Barriger suggested that a union of the NYC, the C&O, and the B&O could increase their combined net railway operating income by $150 million per year—well above the purported economies associated with a merger between the New York Central and the Pennsylvania Railroad. His logic was impeccable, and subsequent events demonstrated that his predictions were uncannily accurate. It would, however, take nearly forty years to translate Barriger's visions into reality.[28]

In the near term, predictions of a two-system East quickly succumbed to a cascading series of merger proposals that ultimately favored the development of three eastern networks. Symes and other PRR executives played an important role in most of those initiatives, although often behind the scenes. Those developments contained their own inexorable logic, and they led back to the outcome that both Barriger and Perlman wanted to avoid—the resurrection of a consolidation between the New York Central and the Pennsylvania Railroad.

Restructuring the Eastern Railroads

As 1959 gave way to 1960, Perlman received frequent confirmation of the accuracy of Barriger's warnings. Stuart Saunders's efforts to join forces with the Nickel Plate depended almost entirely on the attitude of Symes and other Pennsylvania Railroad officials. Many outside observers suggested that the Norfolk & Western was for all intents and purposes a subsidiary of the Pennsylvania Railroad and ready to do Symes's bidding to restructure the eastern railroad network. "If the Nickel Plate and the

Norfolk and Western were to merge," *New York Times* transportation reporter Robert E. Bedingfield observed, "the Central, the B. & O. and the C. & O. would find themselves surrounded by the Pennsylvania Railroad system and its controlled lines." Despite such assertions, Symes had good reason to oppose an expanded Norfolk & Western. For many decades, the N&W funneled coal to the Pennsylvania Railroad at interchange points such as Cincinnati and Columbus, Ohio, and Hagerstown, Maryland. A Norfolk & Western-Nickel Plate alliance would deprive the PRR of a significant share of that traffic. Moreover, a stronger Nickel Plate, one that could efficiently move freight between the East Coast and the Midwest, was bound to cut into the PRR's trunk-line business. The negative effects would be far greater for the New York Central, the railroad whose tracks paralleled the Nickel Plate for much of its length—save that a weakened NYC would be of little value to Symes, who still favored a merger with that company.[29]

Symes possessed considerable power over the Norfolk & Western's merger proposal. The Virginian merger reduced the PRR's control of the N&W from 45 percent to 34 percent. That was still a significant investment, as a one-third vote of N&W shares was sufficient to block mergers and other strategic decisions. There was also the matter of geography. A consolidation of the Norfolk & Western and the Nickel Plate made superb financial sense. The movement of traffic was another matter however, as the two railroads lacked a physical connection. There were only two options, and each depended on the cooperation of the Pennsylvania Railroad. One involved the Detroit, Toledo & Ironton Railroad, linking its eponymous cities, and originally part of Henry Ford's vertically integrated automobile-manufacturing empire. In 1929, during the final heady stages of the consolidation battles that characterized that decade, the Pennroad investment trust bought the railroad from Henry Ford, on behalf of the PRR, and at a wildly inflated price. The Pennsylvania Railroad operated the line as an independent subsidiary and acquired outright control from Pennroad in 1951. Despite Ford's claims that he had built one of the most efficient railroads in the United States, the southern end of the DT&I was a ramshackle line, not well suited to the movement of N&W coal trains from Ironton to a junction with the Nickel Plate, near Toledo.

Saunders could nonetheless take advantage of one significant characteristic associated with the DT&I, in that Symes had few qualms about getting rid of the company. The same could be said for two other marginal properties,

like the DT&I acquired during the irrationally exuberant 1920s, and investments that had long since lost their luster. One was the Lehigh Valley, hobbled by poor management and by the long-term decline of anthracite traffic. Its connection with the Nickel Plate, at Buffalo, could offer the expanded Norfolk & Western access to Greater New York, but not much else. The other was the Wabash, a perennially struggling carrier that the PRR both controlled and competed against. When Saunders announced the merger negotiations with the Nickel Plate on March 18, 1960, Symes immediately perceived an opportunity to offload all three of the marginal companies on the N&W. At a board meeting held five days later, Symes informed the PRR's directors of the negotiations, emphasizing that only their company could fill the gap between the N&W and Nickel Plate lines. He then suggested that the Norfolk & Western could lease the DT&I, the Lehigh Valley, and the Wabash from the Pennsylvania Railroad.[30]

Symes was ultimately able to find a home at the Norfolk & Western for only one of the PRR's three foundlings. Saunders wanted no part of the DT&I's connection with the Nickel Plate. There was a far better option—the PRR's Sandusky Branch, which connected with the N&W at Columbus, Ohio, offered direct access to Lake Erie, and crossed the Nickel Plate at Bellevue, Ohio. Symes, however, was reluctant to part with the 110-mile line, a link that was far more valuable to the PRR than was the case with the DT&I. He drove a hard bargain. So did David Bevan, the PRR's vice president in charge of finance, who was improving the railroad's liquidity by raising cash anywhere he could. The PRR eventually received $27 million for the Sandusky Branch—an amount that N&W executives thought excessive, particularly as they soon had to spend millions more rebuilding it. They could at least console themselves on avoiding a forced lease of the DT&I, and that company remained a part of the PRR system. The same was true of the Lehigh Valley. The Wabash was a different matter, however. Bevan and Symes demanded that the Norfolk & Western lease the Wabash, as a condition tied to the sale of the Sandusky Branch, and under terms that were highly favorable to the Pennsylvania Railroad. Significantly, the agreement included a provision that would enable the PRR to exchange its Wabash stock, receiving in exchange the much more valuable shares of the N&W. Saunders was willing to accept the arrangement, in part because he needed the Sandusky Branch so badly. He also conceded that the Wabash would provide access to Kansas City, Omaha, and Detroit, valuable markets for coal and merchandise traffic, and that the Wabash line to

St. Louis was far superior to the one maintained by the Nickel Plate. The resulting reductions in transit times and improvements in service played a major role in Saunders's efforts to convince the ICC that the N&W–Nickel Plate–Wabash merger served the public interest.[31]

Symes's efforts to resolve the Lehigh Valley situation did not go as smoothly. By the autumn of 1960, two things were abundantly clear about the struggling anthracite carrier. It would not be included in the N&W merger, and it was on the verge of bankruptcy. The latter situation would have caused Symes little anxiety, save that the Pennsylvania Railroad—either directly through the Pennsylvania Company or indirectly through the Wabash—owned 44 percent of the Lehigh Valley, representing an investment of $64 million. Earlier that year, Pevler at the Wabash and Cedric A. Major, president of the Lehigh Valley, negotiated preferential access to Buffalo from the participants in the Erie-Delaware, Lackawanna & Western merger negotiations. Those concessions were far too little to save Major's company or the PRR's investment in it. In mid-September, Major inquired about a merger between the Lehigh Valley and the Pennsylvania Railroad. That was farther than Symes was prepared to go, but in October he recommended to the board of directors that the PRR buy the Lehigh Valley's remaining stock. To bolster his position, Symes cited a report—prepared by vice presidents Walter Patchell and Fred Carpi—predicting annual savings exceeding $6 million, largely through the elimination of duplicate facilities and personnel. Control over the Lehigh Valley would also give the Pennsylvania Railroad access to the Bethlehem Steel facilities in its namesake town. Symes's offer of one PRR share for every 2⅜ shares of Lehigh Valley stock was far from generous, but the company's other investors had little choice but to accept. On February 3, 1961, the same day that the Lehigh Valley ended its passenger service, the Pennsylvania Railroad petitioned the ICC for full control of the company. To save the Lehigh Valley, Symes told regulators, he would need permission to remove the stock, owned by the Wabash and the Pennsylvania Company, from the voting trust where it had resided since 1941. His predecessors implemented the agreement, now nearly two decades old, to overcome the objections of New York Central officials who would not tolerate PRR management of the Lehigh Valley. Its proposed dissolution signaled to Perlman that, as with the N&W–Virginian merger, Symes was waging war against his company.[32]

Direct Pennsylvania Railroad control of the Lehigh Valley required the approval of the Interstate Commerce Commission, and hearings began in March 1961. Symes's timing was fortuitous. Both the 1957 recession and the subsequent congressional hearings that led to the Transportation Act of 1958 highlighted the problems facing the eastern carriers. Under the circumstances, Symes's promise to use the PRR's resources to save the Lehigh Valley held considerable appeal. "Let me make it clear that we have only one objective," he testified, "and that is to prevent the financial collapse of the Lehigh Valley and thereby save our large investment in its stock." Symes tied that immediate goal to the long-standing efforts of Pennsylvania Railroad executives to dictate the structure of the eastern railroad network. In December 1960, just four days after the Lehigh Valley's board of directors assented to the purchase agreement, Symes told reporters of his enthusiastic support for mergers that would transform thirty-five carriers into two or at most three large systems. While he declined to explain precisely which railroads would be allocated to which groups, it went without saying that the Pennsylvania Railroad would be at the core of one of them—and that it would have two competitors, at most. Rapid consolidation, Symes emphasized, constituted the only viable alternative to multiple railroad bankruptcies and perhaps the nationalization of the entire railroad network. He had no patience for those who counseled restraint. "The sooner more mergers are started the better," Symes concluded. He was nonetheless careful to dismiss concerns that the PRR might become an even larger and more dominant system. "I can assure you that there are no definite plans to go any further" in the merger process, he declared, although he averred that "eventually all of these properties might become involved in mergers not now contemplated."[33]

Symes's testimony at the Lehigh Valley control hearings suggested that his magnanimous plan to merge the eastern railroads into prosperity was largely a facade, obscuring his desire to make the Pennsylvania Railroad more powerful than ever. He casually and—according to PRR attorneys—inadvertently mentioned that he planned to install centralized traffic control along the Lehigh Valley. Such an investment would make sense only if the Pennsylvania Railroad planned a massive increase in traffic along that company's line between the East Coast and Buffalo. It could be inferred that many of those freight cars would continue west along the Wabash, via the improved connection negotiated as part of the Erie-Lackawanna merger agreement. A cursory analysis of traffic patterns indicated that the PRR possessed ample excess capacity along the routes linking the Atlantic Seaboard with Chicago and St. Louis, and thus could hardly justify expensive upgrades to the Lehigh Valley. Symes's statement nonetheless suggested to the ICC that the Lehigh Valley's financial stability and increased operating efficiency, funded by the PRR, took precedence over any potential reduction in competition. His allusion to the creation of what amounted to a new trunk line was also a thinly veiled threat to the New York Central, and Perlman took it as such.[34]

Journalists, Wall Street insiders, and executives at many railroads put the various pieces together. They concluded that Symes was assembling a Pennsylvania Railroad system that included two of the most prosperous railroads in the country (the Norfolk & Western and the Nickel Plate), a second trunk line via the Lehigh Valley and the Wabash, and a north–south route along the Detroit, Toledo & Ironton and the Ann Arbor Railroad, a subsidiary of the Wabash. Such a corporate colossus would have catastrophic consequences for both the New York Central and the newly created Erie-Lackawanna. Panic-stricken Erie-Lackawanna officials insisted that they be permitted to merge into the Pennsylvania Railroad if the PRR gained full control of the Lehigh Valley. In March 1961, Symes indicated that he was "not interested at this time" in making any arrangement with the Erie-Lackawanna, a company that was likely headed for financial collapse.[35]

The PRR's increased control over the Lehigh Valley and Saunders's efforts to merge the Norfolk & Western with the Nickel Plate were not the only realignments that created problems for Perlman and his fellow New York Central executives. Equally troubling were the activities of Walter J. Tuohy, president of the Chesapeake & Ohio. The initial impetus for Tuohy's actions came from Robert Young, the financier who selected Perlman for the presidency of the New York Central. During the early 1950s, Young attempted to merge the NYC with the C&O. In some respects, it would have been an ideal match, a more formal version of the relationship between the Pennsylvania Railroad and the Norfolk & Western. In each case, a declining although still powerful trunk line could rely on the revenues of a Pocahontas coal carrier. Yet it was not to be. Young badly mishandled negotiations with the C&O, alienating both investors and regulators. He turned instead to the Pennsylvania Railroad, and the November 1957 announcement of merger talks frightened Tuohy. If the New York Central joined the PRR, he reasoned, the consolidated entity could rely on the Norfolk & Western for access to the Pocahontas coalfields, and Perlman would have scant reason to continue the NYC's long-term alliance with the Chesapeake & Ohio. In 1958, that realization encouraged Tuohy to discuss matters with Baltimore

& Ohio president Howard Simpson and representatives from the Nickel Plate. The B&O's poor financial condition ensured that Nickel Plate officials soon lost interest, and they turned instead to the Norfolk & Western as a merger partner.

Two years later, Tuohy and Simpson were ready to try again. The evolving N&W–Nickel Plate merger talks, and the near certainty that the ICC would approve the consolidation, encouraged them to consider a defensive maneuver involving the C&O and the B&O. The two sets of negotiations occurred at almost the same time, and each affected the other. Perlman, who concurred with journalistic assessments that Symes was creating a vast Pennsylvania Railroad empire that would surround and destroy the New York Central, was keenly interested in the discussions between Tuohy and Simpson. Formal negotiations began in February 1960, shortly after Stuart Saunders made his opening gambit for the Nickel Plate Road but before he announced his plans to the public on March 18. Little more than a month later, Herman Pevler negotiated the Buffalo concessions that strengthened both the Wabash and the Lehigh Valley and made possible the Erie-Lackawanna merger—all of which portended serious harm to the NYC. The Chesapeake & Ohio annual meeting took place on April 28, as the company's investors assembled in Williamsburg, Virginia. Tuohy suggested that the C&O would join forces with the B&O and that the New York Central might also be a participant. Robert Bedingfield, the *New York Times* transportation reporter, suggested that the latest consolidation proposal was the inevitable response to the PRR's efforts to reshape the eastern railroad network. "If the three roads should merge," he suggested, "the Pennsylvania Railroad in effect could be identified as the catalytic agent."[36]

When Tuohy spoke with reporters at the annual meeting, he indicated that "the C. & O. has been and is looking at a couple of possibilities that have merit." It was a guarded statement, and an accurate one. The range of potential merger options reflected the differing goals of Tuohy, Simpson, and Perlman. In the chaos that followed, none of them were able to get precisely what they wanted. Simpson, aware of his company's financial difficulties, sought a merger with the prosperous C&O, one that would forever bind the destinies of the two railroads. Tuohy was more cautious and preferred to control the B&O through stock ownership. Acquisition of at least 80 percent of the outstanding shares would permit the two companies to post a consolidated balance sheet, enabling the C&O to reap substantial tax benefits resulting from the B&O's losses.

Simpson glumly concluded that that arrangement would permit Tuohy to cut the Baltimore & Ohio adrift should its financial performance deteriorate further.[37]

Simpson's disappointment at the B&O's subordinate role in the proposed system was a minor matter, compared to Perlman's frantic effort to win inclusion for the New York Central. Shortly after the collapse of the PRR-NYC merger negotiations, Perlman spoke with Simpson and suggested "that we proceed jointly to consider what advantages might be gained by a merger of the Baltimore and Ohio and Central." Simpson was receptive and recalled a statement made years earlier by then-president Daniel Willard that the two companies were "natural allies." Over the next few months, as the two executives began to consider the full ramifications of the N&W–Virginian merger, they agreed that the Chesapeake & Ohio was a necessary addition to the group. John Barriger endorsed that view in December 1959, five months before the C&O shareholders' meeting, when he recommended a two-system East. While a merger between the NYC and the B&O would have some merit, Barriger concluded, only by including the Chesapeake & Ohio could Perlman hope to compete against the Pennsylvania Railroad. Perlman recalled that "Mr. Simpson expressed some doubt that the Chesapeake & Ohio would be interested in any merger" but suggested he discuss the matter with Tuohy.[38]

Simpson's pessimism was well-founded. During a series of meetings that began in January 1960, Perlman did his best to convince Tuohy and C&O board chairman Cyrus Eaton of the advantages associated with a three-way merger. "I expressed my concern that the Chesapeake and Ohio, the Baltimore and Ohio and the New York Central were about to be surrounded by the expanding Pennsylvania system," Perlman insisted, "and my belief that if we did not get together, we would find it impossible to compete against the Pennsylvania system as independent railroads." Perlman reminded the C&O executives of the historic ties between the two companies and spoke of the need to "maintain competitive balance" between two systems, each one tied to a Pocahontas coal carrier. He also "pointed out to Mr. Eaton"—presumably with a straight face—"that the long-range future of coal, the one commodity on which the Chesapeake and Ohio was highly dependent, was uncertain." It was an extraordinarily weak argument, made by the president of a railroad that was on the verge of bankruptcy to the chairman of a company that was, thanks to coal, one of the most profitable transportation enterprises in the United States.[39]

Perlman's entreaties were in vain. In meeting after meeting, Tuohy and Eaton acknowledged that a three-way merger was worthy of serious consideration, but they declined to make any specific promises. The three executives had dinner in New York City on May 18, and Perlman was "shocked to learn, at the meeting, that the control of the Baltimore and Ohio by the Chesapeake and Ohio had been agreed to by the Boards of both railroads." It was a fait accompli, the news media had been informed, and no one at either company had thought it necessary to consult Perlman on the matter.[40]

For Perlman, a merger of the Chesapeake & Ohio and the Baltimore & Ohio, without the inclusion of the New York Central, was the worst possible outcome. It would strengthen another east–west trunk line while simultaneously depriving his company of much of the coal traffic it had traditionally received from the Chesapeake & Ohio. His assertion, at the NYC's annual meeting, that Tuohy and Simpson were not bargaining in good faith did little to calm the railroad's investors. The New York Central's directors were equally nervous, and they authorized Perlman to buy as much Baltimore & Ohio stock as possible. It was unlikely that the NYC could acquire a majority interest, but even 20 percent was enough. If Perlman could block Tuohy's goal of 80 percent control, he would have the leverage he needed to extract significant concessions from the C&O and the B&O and might even win inclusion in the merger.[41]

Through the summer and into the autumn of 1960, Perlman continued his desperate bid for inclusion in any arrangement that involved the Baltimore & Ohio. For a time, Simpson wavered. He knew Tuohy could guarantee his company's salvation, but he also saw advantages in Perlman's eagerness to join forces. On July 20, he told both Perlman and Tuohy that a three-way consolidation would benefit each of the constituent companies and that it was clearly in the public interest. The president of the Chesapeake & Ohio remained aloof. A month later, Perlman offered to merge solely with the Baltimore & Ohio, to the exclusion of the C&O. Studies began on September 26 and continued—"with encouraging prospects," Perlman noted—for several months. Simpson announced that "in the pursuit of these Central and B. & O. studies the C. & O. would, of course, be a welcome addition at any time." Perlman said much the same thing. He reiterated those assertions the following month while on board the *Empire State Express*, heading for a special shareholders' meeting in Albany. One of the other items on the agenda that day was an admission that the NYC was omitting its fourth-quarter dividend, an indication of the increasingly dire financial circumstances that motivated Perlman to find a merger partner as soon as possible.[42]

Tuohy had expressed his desire to steer well clear of the New York Central, and he was equally determined to prevent an agreement between the NYC and the B&O. He reassured Simpson that the B&O's problems were temporary, stemming in large measure from the recession of 1957, but emphasized that the NYC's difficulties were systemic and perhaps impossible to remedy. Tuohy also threatened to withdraw the lifeline he had offered to the B&O, informing reporters that "if we can't sell the idea that the C. & O. is the best offer for the B. & O., we'll withdraw gracefully." His further statements that "we can bow out of the deal" and that the "C. & O. will pick up its marbles" were sufficient to persuade Simpson that an alliance with Perlman would be fatal to the B&O's prospects. Through the remainder of 1960—and to the delight of Baltimore & Ohio shareholders—Tuohy and Perlman fought each other for control of the company. Simpson initially encouraged those efforts, in part because the bidding war was raising the price of B&O stock. By the time the proxy battle ended in February 1961, Perlman spent $13 million to acquire 369,775 B&O shares. Tuohy invested $29 million, for 489,720 shares. That was well short of 80 percent, but unquestionably sufficient to enable a merger between the Chesapeake & Ohio and the Baltimore & Ohio, subject to ICC approval. Tuohy then improved his offer to the B&O, and at the same time informed that company's directors that they must abandon merger talks with Perlman. A year earlier, Tuohy had encouraged the New York Central's president to hope for inclusion in the merger studies with the Baltimore & Ohio and the Chesapeake & Ohio. "Now I learn," Perlman complained to the NYC's shareholders, "that this friendly effort has been used to minimize our opposition before the I. C. C. of C. & O. control of B. & O."[43]

In the Manhattan offices of the New York Central, Alfred Perlman was rapidly running out of options. The Erie-Lackawanna merger strengthened a carrier that served much of the same territory. As an ancillary outcome, the Pennsylvania Railroad tightened its control over the Lehigh Valley. The consolidation of the Norfolk & Western, the Nickel Plate, and the Wabash, made possible through the PRR's cooperation, did indeed appear to surround the New York Central with adversaries. Perlman's failed bid for the Baltimore & Ohio ensured that he would not be a part of a merger with that company, or with the Chesapeake & Ohio—and that the C&O's coal traffic was likely to disappear from his railroad. On April 28, three days after the New York Central announced that it suffered a $4.26 million deficit in the previous month, general solicitor Robert D. Brooks offered a grim vision

of the company's future. At a press conference, Brooks asserted that the NYC "would become bankrupt" unless it could win inclusion in one of the impending mergers. Only the Norfolk & Western and the Chesapeake & Ohio offered access to the Pocahontas coalfields, he observed, and, he reiterated, "it is vital that Central be joined with one or the other network." Echoing Perlman's sentiments, Brooks indicated that the C&O–B&O system would be the best fit for his company, but his comments left no doubt that beggars could not be choosers.[44]

Two strategies now suggested themselves, and both depended in large measure on the actions of the Interstate Commerce Commission. Perlman could ask the ICC to disallow both the N&W–Nickel Plate and the C&O–B&O merger applications. As an alternative, he could assert that the public interest, and the rights of NYC investors, demanded that he be included in the merger negotiations—whether Saunders, Tuohy, Simpson, or anyone else wanted him to participate or not.

Perlman's reliance on the Interstate Commerce Commission began in June 1960 when he asked the agency to establish "ground rules" for consolidations and to consider all merger applications collectively rather than individually. The ICC's refusal to plan comprehensively, Perlman argued, was certain to "result in a chaotic situation based on survival of the fittest." His remarks echoed the consolidation recommendations of the 1920s, although he acknowledged that "changes in competition, technology, corporate structures and traffic patterns have made the planning of the past obsolete." What he did not admit, at least not publicly, was that studies conducted during the 1920s delayed indefinitely the rationalization of the eastern railroad network. There was no reason to believe that the outcome during the 1960s would be any different. Transportation reporter Robert Bedingfield had little difficulty discerning Perlman's motives. "To force the Interstate Commerce Commission to hold broad hearings on railroad consolidation," he observed, constituted "a move that in the past has always been sure death to all merger efforts within the industry." Some Wall Street analysts praised Perlman's delaying tactics, suggesting that they would give him more time to show consistently strong earnings from the managerial changes and capital-improvement programs he had authorized since assuming the presidency six years earlier. Executives on other railroads, who possessed a more realistic perspective on the New York Central's prospects, concluded that Perlman ineptly managed negotiations with the C&O and the B&O and that he was now trying to destroy a merger in which he could not participate. Symes, the only senior manager willing to share his opinions on the record, sardonically observed that if Perlman had been more cooperative a few years earlier, the New York Central would already be in the sheltering embrace of the Pennsylvania Railroad.[45]

Symes characterized Perlman as an obstructionist who was so determined to protect the New York Central that he would permit the nation's railroads to succumb to bankruptcy or nationalization. At the PRR's annual shareholders' meeting, he suggested that Perlman was "attempting to throw a roadblock" in the path of mergers that would restore the eastern carriers to financial solvency. The New York Central executives who were once so reluctant to accept a consolidation with the Pennsylvania Railroad, Symes observed, were now "very anxious" to merge with the Chesapeake & Ohio, the Norfolk & Western, or any other company that would accept Perlman's overtures. "And if they can't," Symes concluded, "then they will do everything in their power to block or delay them." Norfolk & Western president Stuart Saunders, who attended the meeting in his capacity as a PRR director, echoed Symes's perspective. Perlman's demand to be included in the N&W–Nickel Plate merger was not sincere, Saunders asserted, but was instead "just another delaying tactic."[46]

Symes crafted the image of an avuncular elder statesman, one who was understandably committed to protecting the legitimate interests of PRR shareholders, yet sagacious enough to act in the best interests of the railroads as a group. When he anointed himself the savior of the eastern carriers, however, he had not yet decided how he would achieve that goal. During the spring and summer of 1961, he contemplated two grand strategies for gathering the most important eastern railroads into competitive and self-sustaining systems. One variant preserved long-standing relationships among the carriers and created a logical competitive balance. The inclusion of the New York Central in the C&O–B&O merger might displease Tuohy, but it would give Perlman access to a steady income stream from the Pocahontas coalfields. Symes could achieve the same end by consolidating the Pennsylvania Railroad with the Norfolk & Western and the Nickel Plate, with the Wabash and the Lehigh Valley and perhaps the Erie-Lackawanna included as well. As an alternative to a two-system East, Symes considered a three-system variant. In that model, the N&W–Nickel Plate merger would eventually expand to include the Erie-Lackawanna, providing an essential northeastern tidewater outlet for a system that was strong in the Midwest and the Pocahontas region. The New York Central would be left out of the C&O–B&O merger, as

Tuohy demanded, but would find a home with the Pennsylvania Railroad.[47]

With a C&O–B&O–NYC merger increasingly unlikely, Symes was rapidly losing interest in a two-system East. The alternative, three-system model required Perlman to do several things he desperately wanted to avoid—tolerate unrestricted PRR control over the Lehigh Valley, accept exclusion from both the C&O–B&O and the N&W–Nickel Plate merger negotiations, and, most distasteful of all, join forces with the Pennsylvania Railroad. Perlman did not go down without a fight, however. He lost his first battle on June 15, when the Interstate Commerce Commission declined to consider the eastern mergers as a group or to develop a comprehensive plan for the region's rail network. Perlman's next campaign began four days later, when the ICC initiated hearings on the control of the Baltimore & Ohio by the Chesapeake & Ohio. Perlman depicted the consolidation as an existential threat to the New York Central, strengthening his competitors and depriving his company of access to the Pocahontas coalfields. Tuohy reprised his familiar role as the savior of the Baltimore & Ohio, a company that had suffered a $15 million loss during the first four months of the year. It was doubtful, Tuohy asserted, that the company could survive for long, absent support from the C&O. Howard Simpson, recently replaced as the B&O's president by Jervis Langdon, followed a similar script. Any discussion of the NYC's inclusion would likely take years, Simpson emphasized, and noted that the B&O "cannot wait that long. Its need is for help as soon as possible, and only the Chesapeake and Ohio can provide this." Tuohy and Simpson acknowledged that the B&O had fallen on hard times, but they insisted that the company's problems were temporary and that consolidation with the C&O, more aggressive management, and renewed investment in the physical plant would quickly turn things around. Neither executive had any desire to add the New York Central, and they characterized its deficiencies as permanent and irredeemable. They refused to accept the NYC's $1 billion in debt, arguing that forced inclusion would destroy the credit rating of the consolidated firm and preclude improvements in service.[48] As if to underscore their remarks, a week later the NYC announced losses of nearly $25.3 million during the first five months of 1961—the worst performance in the company's history. Tuohy and Simpson were in effect offering the ICC commissioners a stark choice. If forced to accept Perlman as a merger partner, they would all go down together. As an alternative, the ICC could permit the Chesapeake & Ohio to save the

Baltimore & Ohio, while abandoning the New York Central to its fate.[49]

When he testified before the ICC in July, an increasingly desperate Perlman floated as many proposals as he could, each of them designed to prevent the New York Central from being left aside in the great merger battle. Perhaps, he suggested, a "cooling-off" period in the C&O–B&O merger would be possible. Or, if the ICC would not force those two companies to include Perlman in their merger, the NYC and the C&O might arrange joint ownership of the Baltimore & Ohio. Chesapeake & Ohio attorney Edward K. Wheeler disputed Perlman's claims that the consolidation of his company with the Baltimore & Ohio would drive the New York Central into bankruptcy. Wheeler reminded the commissioners of the late-1950s talks between PRR and NYC officials and observed that Perlman would always have "some place else to go." The obvious inference was that the New York Central would merge with the Pennsylvania Railroad.[50]

Perlman fared no better in his efforts to block Stuart Saunders at the Norfolk & Western. On March 17, 1961, the N&W asked the ICC for permission to merge with the Nickel Plate, lease the Wabash, and purchase the Sandusky Branch.[51] Saunders asserted that the consolidation, which would expand the Norfolk & Western to 7,400 route miles, would generate savings of $25 million annually. Each of those transactions depended to some degree on the cooperation of the Pennsylvania Railroad, and N&W attorneys were careful to stress their freedom from PRR influence. Yet the statement that the "Pennsylvania does not control or have the power to control Norfolk" did little to put the matter to rest. Only a week after the filing of the N&W merger petition, Symes gave a speech in Cincinnati, one of the gateway cities that linked the two roads together. "The Norfolk & Western is more than a friend" of the Pennsylvania Railroad, he observed. With the ICC hearings into PRR control over the Lehigh Valley beginning at precisely the same time, it was hardly surprising that the New York Central's recently released 1960 annual report referred to the "Pennsylvania Railroad's ever growing rail empire."[52]

Perlman was not the only one who feared the PRR's expansionist potential. The Erie-Lackawanna was less than six months old, but there were indications that the benefits associated with that merger were slow to materialize. The combined companies suffered an operating loss of nearly $20 million in 1960, and the results for the following year were not likely to be much better. Erie-Lackawanna executives reacted with alarm to the PRR's long-standing ties to the Norfolk & Western, now coupled with the bid to

gain control over the Lehigh Valley. While an independent Lehigh Valley was not much of a threat, a PRR–N&W–LV colossus was a different matter entirely. They concluded that their best strategy for survival involved inclusion in a larger and more prosperous system, and they set as their first target the company they claimed was trying to destroy them. On March 7, 1961, Erie-Lackawanna executives suggested that a "program of unification" with the Pennsylvania Railroad would be in the public interest. Less altruistically, they vowed to block PRR control of the Lehigh Valley, unless they got what they wanted. The E-L had little bargaining power, however, as ICC officials were showing signs that they were willing to accept Symes's dominance of the Lehigh Valley, as the only viable mechanism for saving that company. Symes had little patience with such threats and announced that he was "not interested at this time" in any association with the Erie-Lackawanna.[53]

Symes's rebuff had far-reaching consequences for the Pennsylvania Railroad. A month later, Erie-Lackawanna officials, desperate for sanctuary, petitioned for inclusion in the Norfolk & Western-Nickel Plate merger. Here they were on much firmer ground, as that system projected as much power as the Lehigh Valley embodied weakness. Regulators were accordingly receptive to the E-L's protective inclusion in the N&W system. Stuart Saunders and other N&W executives were alert to the danger, and they soon announced they had no intention of taking on the failing company. "We have no plans for any additional mergers," they emphasized, "and Erie-Lackawanna's attempt to link these applications with the merger plans of any other railroads, including those of the Pennsylvania Railroad, is based on fancy rather than fact." For nearly another seven years, however, the efforts of Erie-Lackawanna executives to hitch their wagon to the N&W's star would postpone the only merger that James Symes really cared about—the one between his company and the New York Central.[54]

The Erie-Lackawanna was not the only company that intruded, unbidden, into the Norfolk & Western-Nickel Plate merger case. After the Chesapeake & Ohio and the Baltimore & Ohio rejected his advances, Perlman sought refuge with the N&W. On April 28, the New York Central filed a petition with the ICC, requesting inclusion. Perlman was becoming accustomed to rejection, first from Tuohy at the C&O, then Simpson at the B&O, and now Stuart Saunders at the Norfolk & Western. Near the end of May, the N&W's president announced that he was not willing to provide a "second-choice" haven for the New

York Central and that Perlman's maneuvers would produce "only unnecessary and fruitless delay" in the merger he was arranging with the Nickel Plate. Saunders suggested that Perlman's initiative represented "another step in the Central's efforts to delay or destroy any mergers in the East which do not embrace that railroad." Like their C&O counterparts, N&W officials also denigrated Perlman's suggestion that the ICC develop a comprehensive plan for the eastern railroad network. "The New York Central is trying to turn the clock back almost half a century to the Transportation Act of 1920," they asserted, noting that "consequent abandonment of the compulsory approach reflects congressional recognition that realistic, voluntary mergers are the only kind that can be achieved in a free enterprise system." The statement highlighted two themes that would characterize the eastern merger movement for the remainder of the decade: that private enterprise was far better equipped than regulatory agencies to rationalize and revitalize the railroads and that any merger deemed economically viable, however imperfect, was vastly preferable to a utopian restructuring that could never be implemented. Tuohy reminded the ICC that consolidation would need to be a "voluntary process," and that any attempt to force the New York Central into an expanded C&O system "will surely kill it for all time." Saunders held the same views, with respect to his efforts to extend the scope of the Norfolk & Western.[55]

That free-enterprise system was hardly free of public-sector involvement, however. Representatives from New York State shared Perlman's fear that the N&W–Nickel Plate and C&O–B&O consolidations would cause great harm to the New York Central and thus to the state for which it was named. They supported Perlman's call for comprehensive merger planning and for the NYC's inclusion in one or the other of those networks. Even with the backing of state officials, however, Perlman's likelihood of success was extremely low. The ICC commissioners were indeed reluctant "to turn the clock back almost half a century to the Transportation Act of 1920," and they had little desire to consider all the mergers as a group or to engage in a comprehensive restructuring of the eastern railroad network.

Perlman's sole glimmer of hope came from the Justice Department. Robert Kennedy, the new attorney general, had little interest in comprehensive transportation planning. He nonetheless shared the concerns of his brother, recently inaugurated as president, regarding the potentially monopolistic practices associated with big business. Everywhere he looked, Robert Kennedy saw evidence that Symes was manipulating the consolidation process

to ensure preferential treatment for the Pennsylvania Railroad. He mistrusted the ICC and suggested that the commissioners were too willing to accept mergers to protect the financial health of the railroads, irrespective of the deleterious effects on competition. Even as regulators and railroaders alike insisted that consolidation and rationalization should proceed as quickly as possible, before the companies deteriorated even further, the attorney general sought to delay consolidations that, once implemented, would be irreversible. During the summer of 1961, Perlman could not yet know that the economic criteria adopted by the Interstate Commerce Commission would collide headlong with the Justice Department's legalistic defense of competition. What he did know—or at least had reason to suspect—was that the leaders of the other great eastern railroad systems were making plans that did not include the New York Central. If he could not become part of the C&O–B&O merger or the expanded Norfolk & Western system, then he could save his railroad only by submitting to the authority of the company, and the executive, he had so recently spurned.[56]

The Last Heiress

In January 1959, when he announced the suspension of merger talks with the Pennsylvania Railroad, Perlman flippantly remarked that "before we marry the girl, we want to make sure that no other heiress is around that might fall into our lap." By the summer of 1961, it was clear that Perlman was unable to find any suitable partners, heiresses or otherwise. The Erie-Lackawanna merger was not showing the promised savings, but even in its feeble state, the company was offering stiff competition for the New York Central. Although B&O officials were cautiously receptive to Perlman's overtures, Walter Tuohy at the C&O was adamant that the NYC be kept at a distance. Stuart Saunders and his allies at the Nickel Plate felt the same way, and even if they did not, Pennsylvania Railroad executives would never yield the Sandusky Branch to a system that would include the New York Central. In his testimony before the ICC, Symes's assertion that he wanted to rescue the Lehigh Valley was disingenuous but plausible. While the LV would never offer a serious challenge to the New York Central, Perlman viewed the situation as another PRR victory in a campaign to encircle his railroad. When Perlman testified before the ICC in July 1961, he acknowledged "that he had talked with practically every Eastern railroad president about merger." None were interested. There was no heiress, and no one left to marry.[57]

Perlman's desperation gave considerable agency to the Pennsylvania Railroad. Even as Perlman battled for inclusion in some merger, any merger, the future of the New York Central was being settled, through an arranged marriage. During the summer of 1961, three Pennsylvania Railroad executives traveled to the Greenbrier Hotel in White Sulphur Springs, West Virginia. Their ranks included Symes; David Bevan, the vice president in charge of finance; and Fred Carpi, the vice president in charge of traffic. Walter Tuohy was familiar with the Greenbrier's location along the Chesapeake & Ohio's main line, as his company owned the hotel. He was in attendance, as was his chief financial officer, John Kusik. While Symes and Bevan were also directors of the Norfolk & Western, that company's president, Stuart Saunders, did not receive an invitation. Neither did Perlman or any other New York Central executive, even though the discussions would seal the fate of their company.[58]

The five executives who gathered at the Greenbrier acknowledged that the C&O–B&O and N&W–Nickel Plate–Wabash consolidations would transform competitive patterns throughout the eastern United States, to the detriment of the New York Central. Both Symes and Tuohy recognized that the Interstate Commerce Commission would not likely tolerate the bankruptcy of the NYC, as collateral damage associated with the merger between the Chesapeake & Ohio and the Baltimore & Ohio. Symes accordingly perceived an opportunity to restructure the region's entire rail network, a responsibility that the ICC had just declined to undertake. In his role as kingmaker, Symes was particularly committed to a three-system East, a policy that would ensure his long-desired merger with the New York Central. Tuohy was, predictably, opposed to a PRR-NYC merger, one that would create a strong rival to the C&O–B&O system that was still awaiting ICC approval. He and Kusik also shared Perlman's suspicions that Symes dictated the policies of the Norfolk & Western and was therefore responsible for the equally threatening consolidation between the N&W, the Nickel Plate, and the Wabash. Symes nonetheless made his most persuasive case. He argued that the PRR did not control the Norfolk & Western (an assertion that was barely plausible), that without the immediate rationalization of the eastern railroad network the most vulnerable carriers would soon be in bankruptcy (an outcome that was highly likely), and that he could exert considerable influence to block the C&O–B&O merger application before the ICC (an obstructionist tactic he would almost certainly exercise). It would be far easier, Symes suggested, if everyone present

at the Greenbrier agreed to cooperate. He would accept Chesapeake & Ohio control of the Baltimore & Ohio, provided that Tuohy and Kusik waived their right to object to ICC approval of the N&W–Nickel Plate merger. The two C&O executives would also accede to a union between the Pennsylvania Railroad and the New York Central, should one be arranged. The resulting three-system East would encompass what would be by far the largest railroad in the United States—PRR-NYC—and two smaller but more profitable ones—C&O–B&O and N&W–Nickel Plate–Wabash.[59]

After resisting Symes's entreaties for most of the morning, Kusik advised Tuohy to accept a merger between the Pennsylvania Railroad and the New York Central. In return, Symes pledged that neither he nor Stuart Saunders at the Norfolk & Western would object to the consolidation of the Chesapeake & Ohio and the Baltimore & Ohio. Tuohy demanded another concession, one that stemmed from the long-standing community of interest that linked Philadelphia and the N&W's headquarters at Roanoke. The Pennsylvania Railroad would sell its investments in the Norfolk & Western, and Symes, Bevan, and the two other PRR executives who served on the N&W's board of directors would resign. That was the only way, Tuohy and Kusik insisted, to maintain competitive balance in the East.[60]

In the aftermath of the meeting at the Greenbrier Hotel, the actions of the Interstate Commerce Commission were largely formalities. On September 20, Symes testified before the ICC, announcing that he supported the Chesapeake & Ohio's application to control the Baltimore & Ohio. Symes's unexpected testimony aroused suspicions that he had made a deal with Walter Tuohy—an accusation he vigorously denied, even though it was true. Perlman, however, was still resolutely opposed to any arrangement between the C&O and the B&O that did not include the New York Central. As everyone had agreed at the Greenbrier, Symes's next task was to destroy Perlman's efforts to win inclusion in the C&O–B&O combination. Perlman's dire predictions regarding the future of the NYC were groundless, Symes testified, and he promised that the New York Central could obtain salvation through a merger with the Pennsylvania Railroad. Symes reminded regulators that merger negotiations between the two companies began in 1957 and offered a baseless explanation as to why Perlman had abandoned them. The NYC's president allegedly feared that the combination was not in the public interest, that it would destabilize the eastern railroad network, and that it would not win ICC approval.

Perlman declined to engage in a debate regarding matters that had occurred nearly five years earlier. He nonetheless reiterated his long-standing position that Symes's encouragement of the merger between the Norfolk & Western and the Virginian represented a show of bad faith that ended any possibility of an agreement between the PRR and the NYC.[61]

The bickering between Symes and Perlman at the C&O–B&O hearings belied their growing cooperation. Regardless of how much Perlman knew about the meeting at the Greenbrier Hotel, Symes's testimony made it clear that some deal was in the works and that the New York Central would never win inclusion in either the C&O–B&O or the N&W–Nickel Plate systems. For the protection of his company, therefore, Perlman authorized a resumption in merger negotiations with the Pennsylvania Railroad. The discussions initially involved only the heads of the two companies, held on neutral ground in Washington during breaks between ICC hearings. Despite the secrecy, experts in railroads and in finance sensed that something was about to happen. Preliminary hearings on the Chesapeake & Ohio application to control the Baltimore & Ohio ended on October 9, three weeks after Symes promised a safe haven for the New York Central. It was too soon for Perlman to publicly disavow his antipathy toward the Pennsylvania Railroad, but in the weeks that followed, he was oddly reticent to share his grievances with reporters.[62]

When the Norfolk & Western-Nickel Plate case opened on October 10, Perlman was ready to reiterate his charges that the PRR controlled the N&W and that Symes was complicitous in efforts to destroy the New York Central. Stuart Saunders denied those allegations in his prepared testimony, and by the beginning of November, the Norfolk & Western president was prepared to endure a scathing cross-examination by NYC attorneys. The attack did not come, and Perlman dropped his objections to a merger he had bitterly opposed less than a month earlier. Erie-Lackawanna officials were also conciliatory, based on Saunders's vague and never-fulfilled promise to form an affiliation between that company and the Norfolk & Western. The New York Central withdrew opposition to PRR control of the Lehigh Valley on January 16, 1962, and to the C&O's control of the B&O on January 29. Perlman, who had been fighting simultaneous battles in all three Interstate Commerce Commission hearings, now surrendered on all fronts. He also abandoned his insistence that the ICC engage in comprehensive merger planning and instead focused his efforts solely on obtaining approval for the union between the Pennsylvania Railroad and the New York Central.[63]

Second Effort

On November 8, the public announcement of a merger between the Pennsylvania Railroad and the New York Central confirmed rumors that had been swirling for weeks. Symes emphasized that the consolidation would "conservatively" yield savings of $100 million per year, the same figure he offered during the 1957–1959 negotiations. If true, the reduction in expenditures would come as a welcome relief to two companies that were in serious financial trouble. The joint press release offered a terse rationale for the resumption of a process that had disintegrated nearly three years earlier. The problems facing the eastern carriers "have worsened appreciably," the two railroads emphasized. "Time to assure maintenance of rail transportation as a private enterprise is running out, and we have no choice but to try every means at hand to help our companies better their ability to compete more effectively in the transportation field and avoid Government ownership." Left unsaid was Symes's determination to block "every means at hand," save the one he wanted.[64]

Still, few could argue with the grim statistics. A rapid decline in the PRR's net income, from $41.5 million in 1956 to $19.1 million in 1957, first induced Symes to support consolidation with the New York Central. By November 1961, however, even the 1957 results seemed a long-vanished echo of a glorious past. Profits in 1960 declined to zero. During the first nine months of 1961, the PRR suffered an operating loss of nearly $12.8 million, and only the dividends received from the Norfolk & Western enabled the company to eke out a profit. The situation for the New York Central was even worse. Net income fell from $42.8 million in 1956 to $12.2 million in 1957. By 1960, that figure was down to $4.6 million. The loss during the first nine months of 1961 was $24.8 million, nearly double the PRR's total—and Perlman lacked a Pocahontas coal carrier whose dividends could come to his rescue. In January 1959, when Perlman ended the first round of merger negotiations, a share of New York Central stock sold for 29⅜. When discussion resumed in the autumn of 1961, each NYC share was worth 18⅜. In only one area did the Pennsylvania Railroad exhibit the more severe problem. Its 1960 passenger losses were $30.9 million, compared to $17.8 million for the New York Central. The combined total approached $49 million, nearly half of the promised $100 million in annual savings associated with the merger.[65]

The directors of the two companies held simultaneous but separate meetings on November 8. Each board approved the merger in principle and established a negotiating committee. Banker Richard King Mellon, Philadelphia civic leader C. Jared Ingersoll, and Philip R. Clarke, an investment banker at Lehman Brothers, were on the PRR committee, with Symes as an ex officio member. Their New York Central counterparts were Isaac B. Grainger, the former president of Chemical Bank; retired surgeon and Baltimore city comptroller R. Walter Graham Jr.; Seymour H. Knox, the chairman of the board of the Marine Midland Trust Company; and Perlman. Everyone involved in the merger negotiations was committed to the maintenance of adequate freight transportation, yet each thought that his respective railroad was best equipped to handle the bulk of the traffic. Most of them were bankers and financiers, suggesting that they and their allies believed that it would be far easier to make money by raising the prices of PRR and NYC securities rather than by moving trains across a consolidated system.[66]

The eight committee members faced a formidable task. They would engineer the largest corporate merger in the history of American business, creating a twenty-thousand-mile rail network with assets of more than $5.5 billion and debts that exceeded $2 billion. The combined PRR-NYC system would operate 10 percent of the rail mileage in the United States, employ 12 percent of the railroad workforce, and generate 15 percent of freight revenues and 30 percent of passenger receipts. And they would carry out their work with extraordinary speed. Symes promised that the two companies would place a merger proposal before the Interstate Commerce Commission within eight weeks of the November 8 announcement and that hearings would begin in early 1962. The deteriorating financial condition of the two companies accounted for the haste, but only in part. The ICC had not yet issued a ruling in either the B&O–C&O or the N&W–Nickel Plate cases, and Perlman wanted the opportunity to reintroduce his demand for inclusion, should talks with the Pennsylvania Railroad prove fruitless.[67]

The merger negotiations proceeded so rapidly that there was little time to discuss how the operations of the two companies would be integrated or what specific changes might produce the tantalizing and oft-cited figure of $100 million in annual savings. Such contentious matters, everyone assumed, could safely be left until later and would be more deftly handled by operating executives rather than corporate directors. The committee members instead focused on two basic issues. One was the all-important

ratio of exchange between the shares of the Pennsylvania Railroad and the New York Central. Despite Perlman's insistence that the 1957–1959 merger negotiations ran counter to the public interest, the inability to agree on an exchange rate had been a far more significant issue. The second round of negotiations proceeded far more smoothly. Each railroad selected an investment bank to assess relative share values. First Boston Corporation was an obvious choice for the PRR, given its connection to Richard King Mellon. Morgan, Stanley & Company continued its long-standing ties to the New York Central.[68] The two banks in turn chose Glore, Forgan & Company as a kind of arbiter. Whether by accident or by design, all the bankers came to the same conclusion. The new company would issue 1.3 shares of stock in exchange for each NYC share, with an equal exchange for holders of PRR securities.[69]

The selection of the officers and directors became, and remained, a far thornier problem. The difficulties stemmed in part from the incompatible managerial cultures on the two railroads. The PRR had long specialized in the transportation of coal, iron ore, and other bulk commodities that were largely captive to the rails. Division superintendents and other midlevel managers possessed considerable autonomy, yet they were careful to avoid initiatives that might result in ignominious disaster. Promotion upward through the ranks depended on hard work, common sense, dogged determination, and a willingness to stick close to the herd. Traffic Department personnel were equally averse to experimentation. They routinely sought across-the-board increases in rates, while accepting as inevitable the steady loss of business to trucks, competing railroads, and the inland waterways. The New York Central, in contrast, had long endured competition from the Great Lakes and the Erie Canal, which exerted a downward pressure on bulk-commodity rates. Traffic managers aggressively sought additional business through improvements in service and by tailoring rate reductions to target specific, high-value commodities. Even before he came to the NYC, Perlman was enamored with technology and its potential to vastly increase the efficiency of railroad operations. He talked repeatedly about cybernetics, a vague and untested proposition that computers could impose order and routine on disorderly operating practices. Perlman favored aggressive young college-educated managers who possessed drive and initiative. The New York Central's management structure, in contrast to the PRR, was hierarchical and headquarters driven, and local officials possessed scant discretionary authority.[70]

The financial difficulties that plagued both the PRR and the NYC, coupled with the inevitable jostling for position within the new company, exacerbated the deeply ingrained differences in managerial philosophy. Symes and Perlman openly disparaged each other's oversight of their respective railroads, each blaming the other for poor performance. Backed by their respective management teams, they asserted that it would be the height of foolishness to entrust their opposite numbers with leadership in the new corporation. The issue came to a head on December 27, 1961, when Symes, Perlman, and Grainger met to select the top management. The PRR's chairman announced that he intended to continue in that role following the merger. When he retired, he would promote Allen Greenough to succeed him. The date when the transition might take place was unclear. Symes had announced his decision to step down at age sixty-five, in August 1962—but he also indicated that he was under considerable pressure to remain at his post for a while longer. Either way, Symes and Greenough would control the merged company, effectively making the NYC an appendage of the Pennsylvania Railroad. Perlman warned that the New York Central's directors would not accept that arrangement. He was five years younger than Symes and insisted that he should become the new chief operating officer—someone who could impose the NYC's methods on the Pennsylvania Railroad. That was something that the Pennsylvania Railroad board of directors could not accept, Symes insisted. While no one discussed the issue openly, it was also clear that the PRR's directors would never tolerate a Jew as the head of the new corporation. After lengthy and acrimonious debate, Perlman and Symes agreed to serve as inactive vice chairmen of the board following the merger. The Pennsylvania Railroad would select the new chief executive officer, while the NYC would name the president.[71]

Remarkably, the negotiating committee fulfilled the two-month timetable that Symes had promised in November 1961. On January 12 of the following year, the directors of the two companies, again meeting separately and simultaneously, approved the creation of the Pennsylvania New York Central Transportation Company.[72] The new firm, chartered in Pennsylvania, would be the eleventh-largest corporation in the United States. Under the agreed-upon exchange ratio, PRR shareholders would receive 60.8 percent of the 21,646,144 shares in the new company, while the NYC's investors would control the remaining 39.2 percent. That ratio entitled fourteen of the PRR's directors and eleven from the New York Central to serve on the new board. Under the terms of the December agreement, the PRR's directors possessed the authority to select the

new chief executive officer, while their New York Central counterparts would do the same for the president. The dispute between the senior officials at the two companies was now out in the open, with reporters informing investors, bankers, politicians, and regulators "that the Pennsylvania's directors have been bitterly opposed to Mr. Perlman's serving either as chairman or as president of the consolidated company, and that they have made their views clear to him."[73]

The early demonstration of managerial infighting portended difficulties for the merger. The arrangements had proceeded so quickly that no one was able to explain how the Pennsylvania New York Central Transportation Company would fulfill Symes's promise of a $100 million reduction in annual expenditures. Neither Symes nor Perlman would commit to a specific level of savings, and they were willing to say only that "present indications are, however, that they will be substantial." Some New York Central directors indicated that they had been promised economies of as much as $125 million per year. By the time shareholders from both companies voted on the proposal, on May 8, Perlman lowered the estimate to $75 million annually, after five years. Given the financial problems afflicting the two companies, the precise amount was largely irrelevant. Of the PRR shares voted on May 8, 98.57 percent were in favor of the merger, while the corresponding figure on the New York Central was 99 percent.[74]

Wall Street was less enthusiastic. Eschewing the cumbersome Pennsylvania New York Central Transportation Company designation, financial analysts combined letters from the *Pennsylvania And New York Central* railroads into an acronym for the PANYC Line. Pronounced "panic," the name did little to inspire confidence in the merger. The less pejorative monikers of Pennsy-Central or simply Penn Central soon found favor, but financial-sector apathy continued. While stocks in both companies rallied briefly following the January 12 merger announcement, on January 15 they began to decline, and finished the day at a loss. Although financial analysts remained confident that the efficiencies associated with consolidation would generate profitability, they now suspected that the path to merger would be long and difficult.[75]

Naysayers had good reason to be pessimistic. The economic and political environment was substantially different in 1962 than it had been in January 1959, when Perlman withdrew from the first round of merger talks. For a brief period during the late 1950s and early 1960s, many economists, politicians, and regulators viewed consolidation as a panacea, one that would restore the financial health of the railroads, improve the quality of service, and prevent nationalization. It was in some respects a revisitation of the old Progressive Era assertion of Louis Brandeis, that the elimination of waste and inefficiency would ensure ample benefits for investors, workers, and shippers. By the late 1950s, however, the railroad crisis was so severe that regulators largely abandoned any Brandeisian aversion to monopoly. Moreover, paved highways had long since reached every corner of the country, giving passengers and shippers a multitude of transportation options. "So long as the public has a choice of transport," observed economist Charles Phillips, analyzing the implications of the 1959 merger between the Norfolk & Western and the Virginian, "the elimination of inter-railroad rivalry cannot be equated with the elimination of competition." The success of that merger bolstered Stuart Saunders's reputation and offered compelling evidence that consolidation guaranteed financial health. Saunders nonetheless possessed significant advantages that his successors did not. The N&W and the Virginian were small regional railroads, lines that were not integral to the eastern rail network. Both were highly profitable, with low terminal costs, minimal passenger service, and the prospect of steadily increasing coal traffic that was secure from motor-carrier competition.[76]

By the beginning of 1962, however, the earlier consensus in favor of mergers had largely disappeared. The situation in the Northeast was far more complex than the one in the Pocahontas region, with much less scope for success. Except for a few sound companies, such as the Nickel Plate, all the carriers endured high terminal costs, short hauls, extensive passenger losses, competition from other modes of transportation, and substantial real estate taxes. Stagnant or declining traffic levels ensured excess capacity, an unnecessarily large workforce, and low labor productivity. Despite optimistic pronouncements by Symes, Perlman, and other proponents of mergers, it was increasingly obvious that the surest way to increase efficiency involved layoffs and the abandonment of duplicate lines. Reductions in capacity suggested that some communities might experience a curtailment or even the elimination of rail service.[77]

The consolidation of lines serving the same territory reawakened deeply rooted fears of monopoly, which lingered long after the railroads ceased to monopolize the transportation sector of the economy. The July 1960 announcement that the Great Northern, the Northern Pacific, and the Chicago, Burlington & Quincy intended to merge contained echoes of the Northern Securities Company that the Supreme Court declared illegal in 1904. A decade passed before the Burlington Northern merger won regulatory approval, attesting to widespread opposition

from a region that would be served by a single major carrier. The proposed N&W–Nickel Plate and C&O–B&O mergers promised to divert traffic away from large and politically powerful cities like New York and Philadelphia, and toward Virginia. Such concerns became more evident after January 1961, when Democrats took control of the White House and became increasingly solicitous of voters in the urban Northeast. During the Kennedy and Johnson administrations, successive attorneys general began to look more closely at antitrust issues than their Eisenhower-era predecessors had done. The contentious battles for inclusion—particularly Perlman's unsuccessful proxy battle for the B&O and Symes's behind-the-scenes manipulation of the consolidation process—provided reporters with ample opportunity to portray railroad executives as robber barons and unscrupulous financial manipulators. There were also growing indications that the consolidation of two or more struggling railroads would make their problems worse rather than better. Transportation economist Kent Healy asserted that companies that grew too large through merger became difficult to manage effectively. The 120,000-strong combined labor force of the Penn Central lay well beyond Healy's threshold of 19,000 employees, the point at which diseconomies of scale set in. The recently consummated Erie-Lackawanna merger seemed to prove Healy's point, as the company struggled to maintain service and generate profits.[78]

Labor leaders sensed that their members would bear the brunt of the economies associated with the merger of the Pennsylvania Railroad and the New York Central. Given the events of the preceding few years, they had considerable justification for their cynicism. The economic recession of the late 1950s caused severe problems for the nation's railroads, and executives sought to cut labor costs as much as possible. Between October 1953 and July 1959, the PRR's total workforce declined by 33.8 percent, to 84,034. The executive ranks survived largely intact, with a loss of 11.6 percent. Employment in train service fell by almost a quarter, thanks in part to a steady reduction in the number of passenger trains. The most widespread layoffs occurred among maintenance-of-way forces (52.3%) and maintenance-of-equipment employees (41.3%). The mechanization of track work, a decrease in the passenger-car fleet, and the transfer of many locomotive manufacturing and rebuilding functions to outside suppliers such as Electro-Motive accounted for much of the attrition. Of greater concern to managers, shippers, and investors, a steadily increasing burden of deferred maintenance attested to the PRR's poor financial condition. In early 1959, Symes acknowledged that nearly a quarter of the company's freight equipment was in storage and in need of repairs. The forty thousand cars sitting idle represented an investment of a third of a billion dollars. "More than a year at best," Symes acknowledged, would be required to get that rolling stock in a "reasonable state of repair." Absent an increase in business, however, there was no money to fix the cars, and no freight for them to haul, even if they were in working order. It was probably just as well that there was so little freight and passenger traffic, as the railroad was riddled with slow orders, decrepit structures, aging bridges, and malfunctioning signal systems. The remaining maintenance employees, who struggled to patch together the remains of a once-proud railroad, reflected on the grim statistic that in less than three years nearly half of their colleagues had disappeared from the railroad. Given the shambles that surrounded them, they bristled at managerial assertions that there were still too many workers on the payroll and that those who had survived attrition were not pulling their weight.[79]

The Labor Issue

Even as the late-1950s recession thinned the ranks of railroad employees, executives launched a concerted attack on those who were left. During the spring of 1959, the carriers initiated a widespread advertising and public-relations campaign, coordinated by the Association of American Railroads, to draw attention to practices that managers characterized as "featherbedding." The pejorative term referred to a wide range of work rules, codified into law or written into collective-bargaining agreements, that restricted managers' ability to allocate workers as they saw fit.[80] Full-crew laws, many of which dated to the Progressive Era, ostensibly improved safety but generally ensured that trains operated with more employees than would otherwise have been necessary. The definition of daily trip lengths of approximately one hundred miles was reasonable in an era when freight trains traveled at no more than a dozen miles an hour but ensured that postwar crews could often earn a full day's pay after only a few hours of work. Rules prohibiting train crews from running through multiple operating divisions were increasingly out of step with the rapid, long-distance movement of trailers on flatcars and other high-priority freight. Complex seniority and job-classification provisions made it difficult for supervisory personnel to reassign employees from yard crews to road crews on an as-needed basis. The continuing requirement to provide firemen for freight trains hauled by diesel locomotives constituted another expense that railway executives asserted was unnecessary.[81]

Altogether, AAR officials claimed, such policies imposed unnecessary costs of $500 million a year, including $46.5 million for the Pennsylvania Railroad alone. Some PRR executives nonetheless expressed misgivings about the true cost of featherbedding. James Oram, who oversaw the Personnel Department, acknowledged that "there is no doubt a certain amount of featherbedding on the railroads—but I still think that we have caused the public to feel that there is a great deal more than there actually is, and that fostering that idea does more harm to the railroads than good." David Bevan, the company's chief financial officer, had little firsthand knowledge of employment practices. He nonetheless "discussed the matter with our Operating Officers who are much more familiar with the subject, and they express the view that the problem is not nearly as great as the general public may believe." Delaware & Hudson attorney Daniel P. Loomis, the AAR's president, was a strong opponent of organized labor, and he paid little attention to the perspectives of individuals such as Oram and Bevan. Loomis declared "war on featherbedding" and generally received the backing of reporters—including transportation journalist Robert Bedingfield—who asserted that the practice consumed as much as a quarter of railroad payrolls.[82]

The issue of work rules came to a head in the summer of 1959, after President Dwight D. Eisenhower declined the request of railroad executives to establish a commission to study the matter. He voiced an "earnest hope" that labor and management would resolve their differences in the next round of collective bargaining, scheduled to begin on November 1. Well before that date, however, the leader of the most combative labor organization on the Pennsylvania Railroad announced that he had little interest in negotiations. Headed by Michael J. Quill, who delighted in personal attacks on PRR executives, the Transport Workers Union of America represented more than twenty thousand of the company's shop forces. Talks relating to work rules had been underway for twenty months, Quill observed, and neither he nor his subordinates saw any hope of results. Most of the operating brotherhoods were more accommodating, and by the summer of 1960, their tactics diverged from those practiced by the TWU. On July 6, representatives of the brotherhoods requested a presidential commission to study the work-rules dispute. It was a complete reversal of their earlier position, and one that might impose lengthy delays, but that was precisely the point. There would be a presidential election in a few months, and brotherhood leaders were hopeful that a new, Democratic, president would be more receptive to their concerns than Eisenhower had been.[83]

Quill's Transport Workers Union followed a different path. Its members pledged to strike the PRR on June 6, an outcome averted when Eisenhower established an emergency fact-finding board. After investigators released their recommendations on June 25, Quill complained that "we got nothing from the fact-finders—apparently all they found was that the railroad runs from east to west and west to east." On July 7, the day after the brotherhoods demonstrated their willingness to negotiate, Quill set a new strike date of July 25 "or some days thereafter." Discussions with management continued, and the PRR made substantial concessions. Quill nonetheless demanded the retention of existing work-rule classifications in shop facilities, something executives were not willing to accept. He also refused to permit outside suppliers to maintain and repair equipment—a practice that was becoming increasingly common, as diesel-locomotive manufacturers provided parts and subcomponents.[84]

The Transport Workers Union strike hit the Pennsylvania Railroad just after midnight on September 1, 1960. For the first time in its 114-year history, the company suspended all operations, halting the daily movement of 870 trains that carried 136,000 commuters and intercity passengers and 118 million ton miles of freight. The nation was about to enter the Labor Day weekend, making the effects of the walkout that much more severe. Six governors and eleven mayors sent telegrams to each side, calling for a speedy resolution to the dispute, but to no avail. "Mr. Quill seems to feel that, in effect, he can seize a major railroad with impunity," Symes complained, and suggested that TWU officials "did it to further their own personal ambitions." Regardless of his motives, Quill was unwilling to compromise. He suggested that "it has taken 114 years to close down this system and it may take 114 years to open it up again." Symes conceded that "if Quill is in that mood, it might last that long." The warring parties settled the strike in only twelve days, rather than 114 years, but the effects on both sides were nonetheless catastrophic. The PRR's employees sacrificed $14 million in lost wages, with most of the suffering borne by the fifty thousand workers, not part of the strike, who were furloughed when the railroad suspended operations. Symes estimated that the company lost $40 million in revenue, to say nothing of the public-relations disaster associated with the cessation of service.[85]

Quill's chaotic and expensive shutdown of the Pennsylvania Railroad reinforced the determination of the leaders of the operating brotherhoods to work within the political process. On September 7, midway through the TWU strike, Secretary of Labor James P. Mitchell presided over a meeting between executives and union officials. Five

weeks later, they agreed to the formation of a presidential Railroad Commission. "We wholeheartedly welcome this presidential study commission as a major contribution to the public welfare," explained Guy W. Knight, the PRR's director of labor relations, "and will help in every way to make its work a success." Knight and his fellow managers accepted one of the brotherhoods' principal demands—that the commission's recommendations would not be binding—as they were increasingly confident that the railroads' antifeatherbedding campaign was turning the tide of public opinion in their direction.[86]

To the dismay of labor leaders, the presidential Railroad Commission offered railroad executives almost everything they wanted. In late December, as he entered his final month in office, Eisenhower appointed the fifteen members of the work-rules commission. Five individuals apiece represented the public sector, labor, and management—including the PRR's Guy Knight. Predictions of a long and complex process proved correct, and the investigation continued through John F. Kennedy's first year as president. On the last day of February 1962, the new secretary of labor, Arthur J. Goldberg, delivered the commission's final report. Goldberg was not easily swayed by the arguments of railroad executives, and he encouraged management to "tone down its featherbedding propaganda and talk about the real problems of the railroad industry." He nonetheless recommended the elimination of at least thirty thousand and perhaps as many as forty-five thousand workers—equivalent to about a fifth of the overall membership of the five operating brotherhoods. Most would be firemen in freight or yard service. Employees with more than ten years' seniority would retain their jobs until retirement age, and their younger colleagues would receive severance pay. Many of those who continued to work for the railroads would earn better wages, but the highest-paid employees would see a reduction. Executives would possess increased authority to implement mechanization and other labor-saving practices, along with greater flexibility in assigning workers. Managers could not, however, fully commingle road and yard crews or override the provisions set by the states' full-crew laws. "We are disappointed in some of the provisions," the Association of American Railroads acknowledged, "but we realize that no subject as complex as this can be settled to the complete satisfaction of everyone." Labor leaders were far less sanguine and expressed their "shock and disappointment" at the outcome. The five union representatives dissented from the findings, and the assistant grand chief engineer of the Brotherhood of Locomotive Engineers refused to sign the letter of transmittal to the president. Quill was not represented on the panel, but he offered his opinion that the report elevated "profits before people" and reflected "Stone Age thinking." Regardless of the thought process involved, the willingness of all five of the commission's public members to agree with most of the arguments offered by management suggested which side was likely to win the public-relations battle regarding featherbedding.[87]

The presidential Railroad Commission completed its work at almost the same moment that Symes and Perlman announced their plans to combine the Pennsylvania Railroad and the New York Central. Union leaders, preparing to resist the implementation of the commission's recommendations, were equally determined to block a new threat to their livelihoods. On January 12, 1962, the same day that Symes and Perlman announced the merger agreement, the Railway Labor Executives' Association asserted that "the giant railroads now proposing mergers are already too large for competent management, and further enlargement will only weaken their own position in the industry and create greater inefficiency in their operation." While they did not mention Penn Central by name, union officials nonetheless decried "the most catastrophic proposal in its potential effects upon the future welfare of the nation and the railroad industry itself which has ever been placed before the public." Mike Quill, the bombastic head of the Transport Workers Union, was even more blunt in his criticism of the merger proposal. He threatened to lead a walkout by the twenty-five thousand Pennsylvania Railroad and New York Central employees who were TWU members unless he received a guarantee that the combined company would not reduce employment or retirement benefits. Both the PRR and the NYC swiftly obtained injunctions blocking the strike, but Symes and his colleagues had not heard the last of Mike Quill. Echoing growing suspicions that a small number of investors intended to profit from the merger, the combative labor leader demanded that attorney general Robert Kennedy "launch an immediate investigation of this $4,400,000,000 stock manipulation."[88]

Even before Quill spoke to reporters, both the president and his brother were growing increasingly concerned about the eastern merger situation. After the ICC rejected Perlman's demand for a comprehensive study of railroad mergers in June 1961, Robert Kennedy and his staff at the Justice Department assumed the mantle of national transportation planners. The attorney general accordingly began monitoring both the antitrust implications of the three plans that would realign the eastern railroad network and the Northern Lines merger proposal to bring together the Great Northern, the Northern Pacific, and the CB&Q. He feared that executives from the largest and

strongest railroads were uniting to save themselves while leaving their weaker counterparts to possible bankruptcy, abandonment, or nationalization. The willingness of ICC officials to give pro forma approval to merger applications, coupled with their refusal to develop a comprehensive plan for the East, suggested that it would be the attorney general's responsibility to ensure competitive balance. In that respect, it would be difficult to imagine any action more disruptive than the consolidation of the two largest railroads in the United States. PRR and NYC officials were aware of the danger, and on December 14, 1961—three weeks before the official merger announcement—they discussed their plans with the attorney general. They did not win Robert Kennedy's blessing, however. On January 13, the day after the directors of the two companies approved the creation of the Penn Central, Justice Department officials announced that they would take a "hard look" at the proposal. The statement dampened investor confidence in the Penn Central merger, and the two constituent companies soon suffered declines in share prices. At that time, Robert Kennedy asserted that antitrust issues and the deleterious effect on organized labor overrode any potential economic benefits associated with the Penn Central. It was the same argument he used in opposition to the Northern Lines merger proposal. There was a profound difference between the two outwardly similar consolidation plans, however, and it involved a bankrupt railroad linking New York and Boston.[89]

New Haven

Even as they were vowing to take a hard look at the Penn Central merger proposal, officials in the Kennedy administration were struggling to resolve one of the most serious crises in the northeastern transportation network. The financial problems that afflicted the New York, New Haven & Hartford Railroad seemed far removed from the potentially anticompetitive effects associated with the combination of the Pennsylvania Railroad and the New York Central. Thanks in large part to Attorney General Kennedy, however, the two issues became inextricably intertwined, ensuring that the New Haven's woes would add appreciably to the complexity of the Penn Central merger.

Since the late 1800s, the New Haven served as a logical northern extension for the Pennsylvania Railroad, providing access to Boston and other locations in New England. The symbiotic relationship became more important when Alexander Cassatt authorized the New York Improvements. Those betterments included the jointly owned

New York Connecting Railroad that carried freight and passenger trains over the Hell Gate Bridge, from Long Island to the New Haven's tracks in the Bronx. During the Progressive Era, the close cooperation exacerbated fears that financier J. P. Morgan and New Haven officials were establishing a transportation monopoly in New England. In 1914, those concerns produced both an ICC investigation and a Justice Department antitrust suit that curtailed the New Haven's plan to acquire competing interurban, bus, and truck lines. During the 1920s, the New Haven enjoyed a last, brief surge of prosperity but was even then suffering from high terminal costs, short hauls, and highway competition.

The consolidation impetus that unfolded during the 1920s failed to produce a resolution to the problems that faced the New Haven and other New England carriers. Transportation economist William Z. Ripley ambitiously began his efforts at planning by studying the New England situation, but he soon abandoned those efforts in favor of less taxing issues. Pennsylvania Railroad officials supported the independence of the New England lines rather than risk being burdened with any of them. The ICC's final system plan proposed the creation of two stand-alone regional carriers (one based on the New Haven, the other on the Boston & Maine), yet it was not clear that either of them would be financially stable. President W. W. Atterbury was reluctant to assume the New Haven's problems, but he nonetheless wanted to protect the PRR's interests in the region. The subsequent Pennroad purchase of New Haven and Boston & Maine stock convinced many New Englanders that Atterbury intended to monopolize rail transportation, to the detriment of their region.

During the 1930s, fears of monopoly control gave way to concerns about the New Haven's survival. The company declared bankruptcy in October 1935, rendering Pennroad's investments nearly worthless. The New Haven emerged from receivership in 1947, but its problems were hardly over. Patrick B. McGinnis gained control of the company in 1954, following a bitter proxy fight—one that bore similarities to Robert Young's battle for the New York Central at almost precisely the same time. Like Young, McGinnis was a financier with little practical railroad experience. The chairman of the NYC and the president of the New Haven each predicted a resurgence in passenger-rail travel and spoke optimistically of a new generation of lightweight, high-speed trains. Those efforts proved disappointing, as did the administrations of the two executives. Young died by his own hand in 1958, while McGinnis lost control over the New Haven two years earlier. He went to the Boston & Maine, where his financial dealings led to a brief stint in

federal prison. McGinnis's management of the New Haven had been suspect as well, thanks to his decision to defer maintenance in order to demonstrate artificially inflated earnings. The policy left the company ill-equipped to respond to two serious problems that emerged in 1958. One was the opening of the Connecticut Turnpike, paralleling the New Haven and depriving the company of a substantial portion of its freight and passenger revenue. The second was the short-lived but severe economic downturn of the Eisenhower Recession.

During the final eighteen months of the Eisenhower administration, it was clear that the New Haven was in serious trouble. In the summer of 1959, the company sharply curtailed intercity and commuter passenger operations, yet by year's end still suffered a passenger-service deficit of $12.6 million, of which nearly half was attributable to commuter traffic. The New Haven announced that it lost $10.8 million in 1959 and expected to lose $14.3 million in 1960 and applied for a federally guaranteed loan under the terms of the Transportation Act of 1958. Three months into the new year, the Interstate Commerce Commission began an investigation into the situation. The ICC's report, issued in November, lambasted the "follies" of the New Haven's prior management—a clear reference to the now-departed McGinnis. The current president, George Alpert, did not fare much better, and ICC investigators criticized his "indulgence in loud complaint and self pity." Yet the commission also objected "to excessive state and local taxation, to the discriminatory promotional policies of government agencies and to the short-sightedness manifested at times by patrons and by employes of the carrier." The ICC predicted that the New Haven would need a $35 million increase in annual revenues, merely to enable the company to rehabilitate its physical plant and break even. The agency endorsed fare increases of between 20 and 30 percent in commuter rates—something that would likely cause catastrophic declines in ridership—but emphasized that such measures would be ineffective unless accompanied by a reduction in taxes and a corresponding increase in local public-sector financial support. "The commuter problem is essentially, but not exclusively, a state and local problem," ICC commissioner Charles A. Webb observed in a comment that seemed to absolve the agency of any further responsibility in the matter.[90]

Webb's language accurately reflected federal policy, and it was clear that neither he nor anyone in the Eisenhower administration wanted to involve the national government in the New Haven's problems. In late October, the ICC refused to approve a $6 million emergency loan for the New Haven, pending the development of a rescue plan by local and state governments. New York governor Nelson Rockefeller and his Connecticut counterpart, Abraham A. Ribicoff, accordingly began discussing ways to resolve the crisis. The conversations resulted in the creation of an Interstate Staff Committee on the Rail Problem. Headed by William J. Ronan, one of Governor Rockefeller's key aides, the committee was an extension of Ronan's efforts to preserve commuter rail operations in Greater New York. Representatives from the four states served by the New Haven developed a plan to cut the company's expenses by $14 million per year. The proposal depended on the willingness of labor to make concessions, local communities to accept lower property taxes, and Congress to repeal the 15 percent tax on rail passenger fares. Alpert, acutely aware that his company's survival depended on state support, dutifully traveled to Albany to meet with Rockefeller. The governor, a loyal Republican, was busy promoting Richard Nixon's campaign for the presidency and kept Alpert waiting. The resulting photograph of the New Haven president sitting patiently in an anteroom appeared in the *New York Times*, with the caption "hat in hand." The sartorial reference was literally correct, but the symbolism spoke volumes about the New Haven's desperate financial situation and its utter dependence on local, state, and national governments.[91]

By the time John F. Kennedy won the 1960 presidential election—despite Rockefeller's support for Nixon—the New Haven was on the verge of collapse. None of the stakeholders associated with the railroad proved cooperative, and the $14 million in annual savings recommended by the Interstate Staff Committee on the Rail Problem proved elusive. State and local officials asked the president to support an emergency $5.5 million loan, under the auspices of the Defense Production Act. Southern Democrats had little interest in rescuing the New Haven, and one of them—Virginia senator A. Willis Robertson—chaired the Joint Committee on Defense. Robertson considered the loan to be illegal, and his opinion made Kennedy reluctant to act. Myer Feldman, Kennedy's deputy special counsel and one of the president's most important aides, was likewise opposed to federal support. On July 6, 1961, the Office of Civil and Defense Mobilization denied the loan, and the New Haven declared bankruptcy the following day. Reporters quickly sought the advice of Howard S. Palmer, the retired president who guided the New Haven through its previous receivership—a situation that attested to the company's chronic financial problems. "I don't know the answer," Palmer conceded, in a remark that was as apt in 1961 as it had been in 1935. The problem was that no one else knew the answer either.[92]

The Penn Central merger threatened to destroy the New Haven once and for all. The New Haven depended on the PRR and NYC family of companies for nearly 44 percent of its freight traffic in interchange service.[93] Because the New York Central possessed good access to New England, through its Boston & Albany subsidiary, the Penn Central would have little need to route freight via the New Haven. Transportation economists, hired by the trustees of the bankrupt railroad, predicted that annual freight revenues would decrease by $9.5 million.[94] Given the depth of passenger losses, any further reductions in freight earnings would be catastrophic. On January 16, four days after the announcement of the Penn Central consolidation, New Haven officials warned that they could only guarantee continued operation "through the end of summer." The governors of the four states served by the railroad echoed Perlman's earlier insistence, which he had since abandoned, on comprehensive transportation planning and the inclusion of foundering carriers in merger arrangements. "We have a deep concern," the four governors noted, "that consolidation, merger and control proceedings now under way or projected may not provide for the inclusion and continuance of essential roads like the New Haven unless there is a federal transportation policy to provide a framework within which such combinations can be encouraged and achieved." Given the depth and the intractable nature of the New Haven's problems, it was clear that its survival also depended on an alliance with a larger and stronger carrier. Richard Joyce Smith, one of the trustees for the bankrupt company, insisted that "no plan for the New Haven will be successful unless the service of the road is merged into a trunk line operation."[95]

Smith did not mention a specific trunk line, but there could be little doubt that he was referring to the Penn Central. A month earlier, he discussed the New Haven situation with Allen Greenough at the PRR and Alfred Perlman at the New York Central. Neither executive had any interest in the New Haven, a company with little local freight business and massively unprofitable commuter and intercity passenger services. "The impression I received" from the meeting, Smith suggested, "was that it was hopeless for us to even start talking with them till our own house was in order." Unable to secure an invitation to join the Penn Central, in June Smith requested that the ICC mandate inclusion in the merger. "It would appear that a successful reorganization of the New Haven system would be impossible to achieve," absent affiliation with the Penn Central, Smith and his associates warned the commissioners, "and the system would have to terminate operations." PRR and NYC officials instead suggested that the New England lines, including the Boston & Albany, should be consolidated into a single regional carrier, with equal access for all—something that Atterbury had proposed more than three decades earlier. That they were willing to relinquish the Boston & Albany suggested their determination to avoid being lumbered with the New Haven as well as their assessment that the New England railroads constituted more of a liability than an asset.[96]

Even as PRR and NYC executives were doing their best to distance themselves from the New Haven, the president of the United States was setting in motion a chain of events that would drive the companies together. John F. Kennedy faced two conflicting realities during the summer of 1962. It would be difficult if not impossible to muster the federal resources necessary to save the New Haven, and it would be politically inexpedient to allow the company to die. The governors of the four states served by the railroad dispatched a telegram to the White House, asking for federal assistance. They hoped Congress would repeal the 15 percent federal tax on passenger tickets without a corresponding reduction in fares—a step that would add $3 million to the New Haven's annual revenues. They also asked Kennedy to appoint a federal representative to the Interstate Staff Committee on the Rail Problem. The president did not deign to respond, and it was up to Feldman to tell the governors that federal support would not be forthcoming. Feldman threw the matter back to the states, demanded evidence of the governors' "specific plans" for the New Haven's rehabilitation, and emphasized his desire to "encourage" local communities to develop innovative solutions. While he welcomed the opportunity to engage in informal discussions with New Englanders, Feldman also emphasized that there would be no federal representative to the Interstate Staff Committee.[97]

Railroad Mergers and National Transportation Policy

Although Kennedy was not willing to involve the federal government in local efforts to save the New Haven, he nonetheless began to take executive action through initiatives he could control. On March 6, Under Secretary of Commerce for Transportation Clarence D. Martin Jr. met with local, state, and federal officials. Two weeks later, Commerce Secretary Luther H. Hodges—acting on Martin's recommendations—selected nine railroad experts for a "professional survey group" that would address the New Haven situation. Headed by Fredric B. Whitman, the president of the Western Pacific, all nine represented midwestern or western carriers, far removed from the merger

battles raging in the East. Yet Whitman and his colleagues soon concluded that the fate of the New Haven was but one of many troubling developments in the transportation sector. Further railroad bankruptcies seemed inevitable, they warned, and would be accompanied by increased calls for federal funding or nationalization. The three big merger proposals in the East, coupled with the Northern Lines petition in the west, raised the disturbing specter of monopoly. Nor were such antitrust concerns limited to the railroads. On March 23, two days after he announced the formation of Whitman's professional survey group, Kennedy received a report from the House Committee on the Judiciary. Headed by New York Democrat Emanuel Celler, who launched his political career with a series of attacks on PRR and Long Island Rail Road officials, the committee warned that a proposed merger between Eastern Air Lines and American Airlines would be contrary to the public interest.[98]

The prospect of repeated railroad bankruptcies, coupled with monopolies both on the land and in the sky, prompted the president to move in the direction of a national transportation policy. In his April 5 message to Congress, Kennedy emphasized the need to save the carriers, without public ownership or government subsidy. He recommended rate liberalization, the removal of restrictions on intermodal service, and the implementation of user charges for private companies that took advantage of inland waterways, air-traffic control centers, and other federal investments in the transportation infrastructure. Symes and other railroad executives were lobbying for precisely those reforms, yet they could not expect the president to endorse their additional recommendation to increase efficiency through mergers. Regulatory approval, Kennedy insisted, should depend upon "the realization of genuine economies"—something that PRR and NYC officials had not yet clearly demonstrated. Kennedy was also concerned about the ICC's seeming willingness to disregard the competitive effects associated with railroad consolidations, with scant input from the Justice Department or any other federal agency. As an alternative, he endorsed the creation of an Interagency Committee on Transport Mergers. "This group will examine each pending merger in transportation," the president emphasized, to ensure protection for workers and "effective competition . . . between competing firms in the same mode of transportation."[99]

The Interagency Committee on Transport Mergers represented an effort to give key federal agencies the opportunity to reach consensus on transportation policy, without direct and periodic involvement from the White

House. Chaired by Clarence Martin, the under secretary of commerce for transportation, the group also included Assistant Attorney General William H. Orrick Jr., Assistant Secretary of Labor James J. Reynolds, and John P. Lewis, representing the Council of Economic Advisers. Charles L. Schultze, the assistant director of the Bureau of the Budget, served in an advisory capacity. So did Washington attorney E. Barrett Prettyman Jr.[100] Although Prettyman was sympathetic to Robert Kennedy's concerns regarding the anticompetitive effects associated with the railroad mergers, he instead focused on the lack of coordination between the various federal agencies involved in transportation planning. The attorney general "had this problem at the Justice Department," Prettyman recalled, "where the people in his Antitrust Division who were supposed to be dealing with railroads and other transportation problems were not even speaking to the people at the ICC and other agencies who were supposed to be handling the same problems, so everything had come to a standstill." Prettyman noted that he "simply got everybody in a room [and] brought in heads of railroads, brought in the chief people at the Antitrust Division, brought in experts in the field . . . sat down with them, had a series of meetings, found out what the problem was, and wrote the Attorney General a memo with recommendations."[101]

It was one thing for the Kennedy brothers to promise a coordinated national transportation policy, but fulfilling that pledge was another matter altogether. The president feared that railroad officials placed individual concerns ahead of national interests and that they would not accept his public-spirited leadership. The ICC's willingness to give the PRR complete control over the Lehigh Valley, announced the day before Kennedy's message to Congress, offered ample evidence that railroad representatives, like the ICC commissioners who were supposed to be regulating them, were pursuing monopolistic practices and flaunting presidential initiatives. Such managerial intransigence was not limited to the railroads. In early April, as he was asking Congress for a clear national transportation policy, Kennedy pressured the United Steelworkers of America to accept modest wage increases, as an act of self-sacrifice that would stop an inflationary spiral. On April 10, US Steel's board of directors nonetheless voted to increase prices, prompting the president to famously recall that "my father always told me that all businessmen were sons of bitches."[102] The president's acerbic comment did not signify a declaration of war against corporate executives. It did, however, suggest that Kennedy would be less tolerant than Eisenhower of the actions of railroad officials

and the acquiescence of the Interstate Commerce Commission.[103]

Some members of Congress were receptive to Kennedy's argument that railroad mergers portended monopoly. Chief among them was Tennessee Democrat Estes Kefauver. He joined the House of Representatives in 1939, near the tail end of congressional investigations into abusive business practices. The urgency of World War II temporarily blunted such concerns, but after 1945, Kefauver resumed his crusade against economic concentration. He became a senator in 1949 and seven years later chaired the Senate Subcommittee on Antitrust and Monopoly. Kefauver expressed growing unease regarding the tide of railroad merger proposals, with the arrangement between the PRR and the NYC at the top of his list. Their efforts to combine, he told President Kennedy, "would only result in a snowballing of other large consolidations as a matter of economic survival." Kefauver sought to delay all further mergers until the end of 1963 so the federal government could develop a comprehensive national transportation plan. The suggestion was reminiscent of Perlman's June 1960 request that the ICC evaluate all merger proposals in unison.[104] Times had changed since then, however. Now that the New York Central had finally found a home, both Perlman and Symes were determined to block Kefauver's proposal.[105]

During June and July 1962, a familiar parade of railroad executives, economists, and regulators gave testimony at the Kefauver hearings. As the head of the nation's largest railroad and the self-appointed coordinator of the eastern merger movement, Symes was a star witness. He reiterated the familiar story of government operation during World War I, the rise of motor-carrier competition, the traumatic effects of the Great Depression, the heroic service of the railroads during World War II, government subsidies for competing modes of transportation, and the carriers' inexorable postwar decline. Symes refuted allegations that widespread managerial incompetence led the railroads to their current sorry state and emphasized that consolidation constituted the sole available remedy. "A prompt regrouping of the railroad industry in the Northeastern section of the United States," he testified, "is an absolutely indispensable step for rescuing those railroads from the inevitable results of a steadily deteriorating situation." Sensitive to Kefauver's campaign against economic concentration, Symes turned the argument on its head. "I think that there is at present only one danger of monopoly in railroad transportation," the PRR's chairman observed. "Many railroads cannot long survive present conditions as private enterprise. Today in the East we are actually looking down the road to nationalization of our railroad system. To my mind that is the most dangerous monopoly of all, a subsidized nationalized railroad system. . . . The public is likely to see the very ultimate in monopoly in transportation; namely, Government ownership and operation." In response to a barrage of questions from members of the Subcommittee on Antitrust and Monopoly, Symes carefully explained why the Penn Central merger would produce a massive reduction in operating costs without adversely affecting freight and passenger service. He also deflected demands that the large and healthy railroads should extend the charity of inclusion to those, such as the New Haven, that were small and weak. While the Kefauver hearings attracted considerable media attention, they accomplished little. Never reported out of committee, the Kefauver bill disappeared at the end of the legislative session and would not return. The congressional testimony nevertheless increased the likelihood that the Justice Department would in the future look more closely at the various proposals for railroad consolidation.[106]

Third in Line

Representatives from the Interstate Commerce Commission were also busy during the summer of 1962, simultaneously evaluating the three major eastern merger applications. The Penn Central case was the last in line and the only one that did not include a Pocahontas coal carrier, yet it was the largest and undoubtedly the most important. The Pennsylvania Railroad and the New York Central filed their application with the ICC on March 9, 1962, and hearings began on August 20. That placed the case about a year behind the Chesapeake & Ohio's petition to control the Baltimore & Ohio (where hearings began in June 1961) and the Norfolk & Western bid for the Nickel Plate and the Wabash (with the first testimony taking place that October). Even though they would undoubtedly suffer from the competitive effects of the Penn Central, the executives representing the other two proposed systems refrained from criticism. Symes had eliminated their opposition, tying Saunders's acquiescence to the sale of the PRR's Sandusky Branch and securing Tuohy's cooperation during the meeting at the Greenbrier Hotel. Saunders and Tuohy could say little in any event, given that their plans to expand the Norfolk & Western and the Chesapeake & Ohio bore a strong similarity to Symes's agenda for the Pennsylvania Railroad. The Penn Central application was in fact useful to Saunders and Tuohy. They could convincingly argue

that their merger proposals, still under consideration by the ICC, represented a form of preemptive self-defense against the pending Penn Central colossus. Symes was equally tolerant of the other two eastern merger applications, as their success would make the Penn Central case that much stronger. He acknowledged as much at the Kefauver hearings, when he noted that "if the C. & O.—B. & O. is approved, that is going to help the Nickel Plate case and if that is approved, it is going to help our case, going to go right around the circle."[107]

With each of the eastern merger applications affecting the others, it was hardly surprising that those left out of the consolidation scramble demanded protection. They hoped that the ICC would reconsider its refusal to develop a comprehensive plan for the region's railroads. The initial impetus came not from Perlman at the New York Central but from William White, the company's previous president. White feared that "a merger of the Pennsylvania Railroad and the New York Central System could do great harm to the Delaware & Hudson." He hoped that consolidated hearings would provide the best opportunity to emphasize the plight of the smaller carriers and to persuade the ICC to include the D&H in the Norfolk & Western merger. White could count on the support of Robert Kennedy and other Justice Department officials who likewise feared that the members of the Interstate Commerce Commission would approve each application, one after the other, with scant concern for the integrity of the eastern rail network.[108]

Despite White's protests, the ICC demonstrated a willingness to approve each merger in turn, as a mechanism for preserving the constituent railroads. The consolidation of the Chesapeake & Ohio and the Baltimore & Ohio presented few difficulties. The meeting at the Greenbrier Hotel a year earlier ensured Symes's support, while the January 1962 agreement between the PRR and the NYC removed Perlman's objections. On May 1, ICC examiner John L. Bradford concluded that the two companies were ideal partners and that C&O control of the B&O was clearly in the public interest. Walter Tuohy was delighted. So was Symes, for the examiner's report conformed precisely to his vision of a three-system East. The recommendation, he declared, "was another step in bringing about mergers in eastern territory that are so necessary to the future well-being of the industry." Perlman, who spent the better part of two years endeavoring to either block or win inclusion in the arrangement between the C&O and the B&O was equally—and almost identically—effusive in his praise. "We look on this," he noted, "as the first step in establishing three balanced competitive systems in the East." Oral arguments before the full commission began on October 23, the day after President Kennedy announced the presence of Soviet missiles in Cuba. With Americans anticipating war, B&O president Jervis Langdon explained that without assistance from the Chesapeake & Ohio, his company would soon be unable to provide the transportation that was vital to national defense. It was a compelling argument, and on December 17, the commission approved the consolidation.[109]

The Norfolk & Western's application to merge with the Nickel Plate and lease the Wabash was next in line. Approval seemed assured, given the outcome of the C&O–B&O hearings, but two critical differences threatened the proceedings. One involved the fate of the Erie-Lackawanna. During the spring of 1961, that company's executives petitioned for inclusion, first in the Penn Central and then in the Norfolk & Western. They received a frosty reception from officials at both companies, none of whom were interested in a marginally profitable company with a massive debt. As the N&W–Nickel Plate merger hearings were progressing, Delaware & Hudson president William White was engaged in negotiations with his Norfolk & Western counterpart, Stuart Saunders. They failed to reach agreement, and at the last possible instant, White asked the ICC to mandate the inclusion of his railroad in the expanded N&W. Patrick McGinnis, who had abandoned the New Haven to take charge of the Boston & Maine, had similar preferences. On June 13, less than a month before the N&W merger hearings ended, fate—in the form of a federal investigation into allegations of criminal wrongdoing—forced McGinnis to resign. His replacement, Daniel A. Benson, was receptive to membership in the New England regional system advocated by Symes and Perlman. As such, he abruptly reversed course and announced that the Boston & Maine did not want to become an appendage to the Norfolk & Western.[110]

Aside from the inclusion question, the other principal problem involved the PRR's close relationship with the companies involved in the Norfolk & Western merger proposal. The Pennsylvania Railroad owned virtually all the Wabash and a third of the N&W, suggesting to Justice Department officials that the three balanced systems proposed by Symes were in reality two unbalanced ones. Within weeks of the January 1962 Penn Central merger announcement, the Justice Department became involved in the N&W hearings, asserting that that company was under the control of the Pennsylvania Railroad. Symes had long since accepted that he would need to relinquish control over the N&W, as part of the Penn Central merger. He

acknowledged as much when he met with Walter Tuohy and John Kusik at the Greenbrier Hotel. The arrangement with the two C&O executives was not entirely secret, but it was informal and unenforceable. It was up to the Interstate Commerce Commission to add legal sanction to that arrangement.

When he testified at the Kefauver hearings in July 1962, Symes conceded that "we have agreed that we would divest ourselves of our holdings in N. & W. over a reasonable period of time." He was more reticent about the length of that period of time, as well as when it would begin. His clarifying statement "that if our merger is approved, the Pennsylvania-Central, we will dispose of it" suggested that stock sales would begin only after the ICC and the Justice Department acquiesced to the consolidation of the Pennsylvania Railroad and the New York Central. Symes was nonetheless hoping to avoid a worst-case scenario, in which the PRR would relinquish the N&W stock and the $12 million in dividends it generated each year, with no assurance that the ICC would allow him the opportunity to reap the savings associated with the Penn Central merger. Should the consolidation fail to win approval, Symes emphasized, "I do not know what our board of directors would do. But, I would recommend they not dispose of it because we have it as an investment." Ever solicitous of the welfare of the eastern railroads, Symes suggested that he might change his mind, should the ICC ratify the N&W–Nickel Plate merger, "for the good of the cause here, knowing that we could not have three competitive systems and we have that big ownership in N. & W." Symes's rather convoluted statement, when decoded, promised a three-part deal with regulators: Interstate Commerce Commission approval of the Norfolk & Western merger, followed by the PRR's sale of that company's stock, which the ICC would in turn reward with validation of the Penn Central. During that summer, the PRR sold a small block of Norfolk & Western shares, in what *Trains* magazine called a "sign of good faith." It was much more than that. The decrease from 33.72 percent to 32.09 percent was sufficient to deprive the Pennsylvania Railroad of the one-third ownership stake necessary to exercise veto powers over the Norfolk & Western's strategic decisions. The transaction clearly suggested that Symes was willing to give up his influence over the N&W, to facilitate the creation of a three-system East.[111]

By October 1962, other PRR officials were willing to strengthen Symes's previously vague promises. David Bevan, the PRR's vice president in charge of finance, testified that he would sell the railroad's $300 million worth of N&W stock, should the ICC approve the Penn Central merger. He asked only that he be allowed to do so gradually, to prevent a collapse in share prices. In the interim, he hoped to place the securities in a trust—one that would continue the flow of N&W dividends while he sought a replacement for the $12 million in annual income that, just barely, ensured the PRR's profitability. Regardless of the precise financial arrangements, Bevan and Symes clearly expected that full divestment would occur only after they were certain of the outcome of the Penn Central merger hearings.[112]

Regulators soon made it clear that continued Pennsylvania Railroad influence over the Norfolk & Western would prevent that company's merger with the Nickel Plate. On April 17, 1963, ICC examiner Lester R. Conley recommended the approval of the N&W–Nickel Plate consolidation, coupled with the new company's lease of the Wabash. There was one major condition, however. Conley concluded that Pennsylvania Railroad ownership of N&W and Wabash securities, in whatever form, would be inconsistent with the public interest. During the months that followed, the full ICC came under considerable pressure to approve Conley's stipulation. Norfolk & Western executives, fearing that the fate of their merger hung in the balance, pressured the PRR to divest and to remove its officers from the N&W's board of directors. John P. "Jack" Fishwick, the N&W's vice president in charge of legal affairs, had little patience with Symes's conditional promise, made nearly two years earlier. Complaining that the PRR could not "have its cake and eat it too," Fishwick demanded a formal divestiture agreement. If the PRR was not willing to provide one, he suggested that the commissioners should make it clear that neither the N&W–Nickel Plate nor the Penn Central merger would be approved. Because the merger agreement endorsed by Norfolk & Western and Nickel Plate shareholders mandated implementation no later than March 1, 1966, Fishwick was not willing to wait for ICC approval of Penn Central. There were accordingly two clear threats contained in his statement that "if our unification plan fails, it will bring, in all probability, a halt for years of any further substantial realignment of the eastern railroads." The first, directed at the ICC, suggested that any impediments to his merger would prevent the consolidations that seemed to be the only way to preserve rail service in the Northeast. The second, made for Symes's benefit, indicated that the PRR's failure to cooperate would destroy the arrangements between the N&W and the Nickel Plate—but that outcome would in turn preclude the formation of Penn Central. Justice Department attorney Jack Pearce was far less oblique in his comments. The attorney general would acquiesce to

the N&W–Nickel Plate merger, Pearce indicated, "if and only if" the PRR undertook "complete prompt, and full" withdrawal from the Norfolk & Western.[113]

When the ICC commissioners assented to the N&W–Nickel Plate merger on June 24, 1964, they imposed more stringent conditions than those associated with the C&O–B&O decision. They fully supported examiner Conley's divestment recommendations and gave the Pennsylvania Railroad ninety days to prepare a plan for relinquishing its interest in the N&W and its 99.5 percent share of the Wabash. Sales could proceed gradually over the next ten years, but in the interim, the Norfolk & Western could preferentially solicit interchange traffic from the PRR's competitors. During that time, the Norfolk & Western stock would be in a voting trust, although direct PRR control of the Wabash stock could continue. The other major stipulation reflected the concerns of New York State and the Port of New York Authority, whose representatives wanted to protect the Erie-Lackawanna and to prevent the further migration of traffic southward to Virginia. Backed by the Justice Department, they demanded that the merger agreement formalize the vague promises that N&W officials had offered, regarding cooperation with the E-L. As such, Appendix O of the ICC decision gave the Erie-Lackawanna, as well as the Delaware & Hudson and the indecisive managers of the Boston & Maine, an opportunity to petition for inclusion in the Norfolk & Western-Nickel Plate consolidation at any time within the next five years.[114]

The provisions associated with ICC approval of the N&W–Nickel Plate merger ensured that Pennsylvania Railroad executives would need to make one of the most important decisions in the company's history. Official consummation occurred on August 20, giving PRR officials thirty days—until September 18—to decide whether they would accept the divestment provisions, and a further sixty days to develop a plan for doing so. They could refuse and thus scuttle the N&W's merger with the Nickel Plate. In that scenario, the PRR would retain both the Sandusky Branch and the Wabash as well as the all-important stream of N&W dividends. Maintenance of the status quo, however, would ensure the enmity of Norfolk & Western executives and render ICC approval of the Penn Central merger highly unlikely.

Yet acquiescence to the divestment provisions did not guarantee the success of the Penn Central application. The only certain outcome was that the PRR would forever relinquish at least $12 million in annual dividend income, funds that made the difference between the parent company's profit and loss. Gone, too, would be the $5 million or

$6 million in annual revenue from the line to Sandusky. In a worst-case scenario, without regulatory approval of the Penn Central, the situation might push the Pennsylvania Railroad to the brink of insolvency. "You are going to crucify the Central and the Pennsylvania," Symes warned the ICC commissioners, if they approved the first merger but not the second. That outcome was unlikely. Although the commissioners could not legally promise endorsement of the Penn Central application, they strongly hinted that they would do so—provided that the PRR cooperated with the Norfolk & Western. That cooperation, moreover, was essential to the development of a three-system East and to the rationalization of the region's railroad network. "It should be borne in mind that there are very strong factors of self-interest impelling all of the parties to work in good faith to keep alive the opportunity leading toward ultimate consummation," the commissioners emphasized in the N&W–Nickel Plate decision. "For them to plan and negotiate a new eastern railroad restructuring of comparable magnitude would be extremely difficult, costly, and time consuming." They also reminded everyone involved that Justice Department officials were determined to sever all ties between the Pennsylvania Railroad and the Norfolk & Western, even though they harbored misgivings regarding the ICC's oversight of railroad mergers. "The Pennsylvania, having perhaps more to gain in the status quo than any of the others," the commissioners observed, "would have also to evaluate the likelihood of Government-enforced divestiture of its N&W control regardless of the merger situation."[115]

The principal issue that faced Pennsylvania Railroad executives, therefore, was in the nature of a bet. They gambled that the removal of all regulatory and legal impediments to the Penn Central merger would occur before the loss of the N&W dividends and the continuing erosion of the eastern railroad network produced irreversible harm to the merger partners. If so, the anticipated savings associated with the consolidation would overcome those problems and ensure sustained profitability. If not, then there was a very real possibility that the steady decline of the PRR and the NYC would make it difficult to raise the capital that would be necessary to integrate the operations of the two companies. In that respect, the Penn Central merger proposal was not merely a decision to be made by the regulatory state. It was a race against time.

Forty Thousand Pages

On August 20, 1962, the Interstate Commerce Commission began consideration of the largest, longest, and most complex case in the agency's history. The process unfolded at an exceptionally busy time, while the agency was moving toward a decision in the C&O–B&O and the Norfolk & Western–Nickel Plate cases. Along with eleven other merger proposals that portended massive changes in the national railroad network, the events were enough to overwhelm both the commission and the reporters who covered its activities. The *New York Times* heralded the opening day of the Penn Central hearings with barely two column inches on page 33, labeling it "the next clinic on the ills of American railroads." Seven months had elapsed since the directors of the Pennsylvania Railroad and the New York Central approved the consolidation. The progress of the Penn Central application was somewhat slower than Symes initially predicted, but he remained confident that the process would move expeditiously toward approval. Individuals knowledgeable in regulatory matters seconded that assessment and suggested that the proceedings would last three weeks, possibly a little longer.[116]

Symes's optimism was misplaced, and by the time the hearings concluded, two and a half years later, he was no longer the PRR's chairman. During that time, eighteen cities hosted a parade of 461 witnesses and 337 attorneys. The 129 days of testimony generated forty thousand pages of transcripts. None of the staff members at the ICC were able to keep pace with the number of spoken words, and the agency hired an outsider to transcribe the oration. Craig W. Wallace took only one break from the case, giving him the opportunity to win his third consecutive world stenography championship. The volume of material damaged the eyesight of Jerome K. Lyle, the ICC's chief hearing examiner, so badly that he had to purchase new glasses midway through the proceedings. His much-younger colleague, Henry C. Darmstadter Jr., spent the final months of the hearings holding the voluminous transcripts in one hand while feeding his newborn twins with the other.[117]

It was entirely appropriate that Symes was the first witness to take the stand. His testimony occupied the better part of a day, and the subsequent cross-examination lasted more than a week. His supposed equal in the merger, NYC president Alfred Perlman, said not a word during that time. Symes began by reading a prepared statement—all fifty-six pages of it—and highlighted a further forty-six pages of exhibits. It was nonetheless a mercifully short dossier, given the multitude of tasks he intended to accomplish. Symes was careful to refute two potential objections to the merger. One was that financiers had instigated the consolidation, in search of speculative profits. Citing his "close contact with many investment firms," Symes asserted that "there has never been an attempt on the part of any of them to persuade me that railroad mergers should be undertaken for the reasons mentioned." The other allegation was that the Penn Central would be excessively large, to the point where it would exert an overwhelming dominance in the East. Symes acknowledged the primacy of the proposed company, with respect to assets and miles of track. "However, from the standpoints of net earnings and return on investments, which are more significant than other factors," he emphasized, "the two railroads are pretty far down on the list, and it is these reasons, rather than size, that motivated the merger." Lest anyone think that Symes was solely interested in profits for PRR and NYC investors, however, he tied the outcome of the merger to the fate of the eastern railroad network. The current situation "cannot continue without a number of bankruptcies in the East that could eventually cause nationalization of the industry," he cautioned.[118]

Symes also devoted a considerable portion of his testimony to his self-appointed role as master planner for the railroads. He highlighted his vision for a three-system East, assigned virtually every railroad in the area to one of those combinations, and emphasized the desirability of an independent regional network in New England—an arrangement that ensured that the most problematic carriers in the nation would become someone else's problem. Making no mention of the arrangements at the Greenbrier Hotel, Symes explained that prompt approval of the C&O–B&O and N&W–Nickel Plate petitions constituted an essential element of his plan to save the railroads by grouping them into three systems. "They must be expedited to the fullest degree, and not delayed one for the other," he warned, "which would lead to the failure of all." The Penn Central was a natural—almost inevitable—component of that three-system East, he continued. Ignoring the massive organizational differences between the PRR and the NYC, he suggested that the two companies were like "two peas in a pod." It would be a simple matter to integrate their operations and reap the economic benefits associated with increased efficiency, Symes noted, because they served virtually identical territories. That assertion in and of itself suggested just how much things had changed since the Progressive Era and indicated the new willingness of regulators to countenance a substantial decrease in competition in a desperate attempt to save the eastern railroads. Symes's statement also amounted to a declaration of war against the Antitrust Division of the Justice Department, whose representatives were among the 250 people packed into the hearing room.[119]

Despite the provocation, Justice Department attorney Joseph Gallagher refrained from attacking Symes or the

merger. More than seven months had elapsed since the attorney general's office promised to take a "hard look" at the Penn Central proposal. During that time, officials in the Kennedy administration were struggling to find a balance between competition, efficiency, economic growth, and the bolstering of the national transportation network. As that process unfolded, Gallagher awaited further instructions. He could also expect that other interested parties would make his case for him. On the fourth day of the hearings and following a short cross-examination, Gallagher announced that he needed more time to develop his brief. Examiners Lyle and Darmstadter granted a deferment, but Symes and his colleagues had not heard the last of Gallagher or the Justice Department.[120]

The witnesses who testified over the following two and a half years were mostly drawn from four groups: other eastern railroads, shippers, local and state governments, and organized labor. Representatives from the two other nascent systems in the East offered no objections to the merger that would create their most formidable competitor.[121] With the C&O–B&O and the N&W–Nickel Plate cases still awaiting approval by the ICC, they could hardly do otherwise. Symes had laid the groundwork for their cooperation, and all were participants in a tripartite relationship of mutual assured destruction. If any one of them opposed either of the other two mergers, then all three consolidations were unlikely to surmount the regulatory hurdles. Six railroads and Seatrain Lines indicated they would support the consolidation if the ICC endorsed arrangements they had negotiated with the PRR or the NYC—principally regarding the interchange of traffic. Ten other carriers made reference to minor matters, easily resolved.[122]

The remaining six railroads, however, sought protection through inclusion in the Penn Central system. Executives at each of those six companies expressed legitimate concerns that the three-system East would drive them out of business. Given the amount of excess capacity in the region, there seemed little reason why any of the big networks—least of all the Penn Central—would have any incentive to route freight over their lines. Representatives from the New York, Susquehanna & Western Railroad and the eleven-mile-long Brooklyn Eastern District Terminal particularly feared the catastrophic diversion of traffic and sought protective inclusion in Penn Central. There was nonetheless an element of crassness in their demands, for investors had long since concluded that the smaller eastern carriers were unlikely to ever demonstrate sustained profitability. The negotiation of a favorable purchase price with one of the major systems seemed the only way to increase shareholder value, and their demands for inclusion thus smacked of extortion.[123]

The inclusion problem was most acute on the New Haven. Richard Joyce Smith and his fellow trustees concluded that consolidation with the Penn Central offered the best hope for maintaining service, while bondholders sought the chance to recoup as much of their investment as possible. They petitioned for inclusion in June 1962, two months before the merger hearings began, and they were not willing to accept Perlman's plan for an independent New England regional system. Joseph Auerbach, the New Haven's legal counsel, alleged that that proposal was a chimera, intended merely to prevent his employer's inclusion in Penn Central. Perlman rather implausibly denied the assertion and blamed the entire region for the New Haven's problems. "New England sits on its chair and watches the rest of the world go by," he suggested. Perlman was even more dismissive of New Haven managers who had repeatedly "fouled the ball" by failing to meet motor-carrier competition. "They ought to clean up their own house before they run to pop," he concluded. Replacing his paternalistic scolding with a more avuncular tone, Perlman suggested that the unification of the New England carriers would assuage fears that the Penn Central might monopolize rail transportation in the Northeast. Regional consolidation would give the Norfolk & Western and the C&O–B&O systems equal access to the area, he argued. To allow the Penn Central to control both the New Haven and the Boston & Albany would exclude competition from the region, Perlman concluded, a step that "would kill the public interest."[124]

The fate of the New Haven remained a hotly contested issue into the early months of 1963. Several noted transportation economists insisted that the company could only survive through inclusion in the Penn Central merger. Smith testified that the loss of income stemming from a merger between the PRR and the NYC would prevent reorganization and "require its liquidation and possibly its nationalization." Smith was also hoping to reduce opposition from Symes and Perlman, and to make the New Haven a more attractive partner. The company's passenger-service deficit must be eliminated through the use of public operating subsidies, he conceded, as "a prerequisite for inclusion in the merger." PRR attorney Windsor F. Cousins responded that it was more likely that proposed tax reductions and any potential for public support of passenger service would disappear as soon as the New Haven became part of a larger and more prosperous company. It was a reasonable assumption. For decades, New Yorkers resisted similar support for the Long Island Rail Road, on the grounds that the PRR had ample funds to cover its losses. Cousins also observed that the New Haven's stock was effectively valueless and that it would be difficult to set a fair price for purchasing the company. Regardless of the terms and conditions, Pennsylvania Railroad and New York Central officials wanted nothing to do with the New Haven, whose inclusion would complicate their merger application. In a joint statement, they indicated that any attempt to delay the formation of Penn Central until "a solution had been found for the ailing New England Lines might effectively nullify the benefits of the merger to the public, shippers, employes, communities and the national defense."[125]

Equally problematic inclusion petitions came from three railroads whose officials were entirely familiar with the process. Both the Erie-Lackawanna and the Delaware & Hudson requested inclusion in the Norfolk & Western-Nickel Plate merger. So had the Boston & Maine, only to withdraw its request in favor of participation in the New England regional system advocated by Symes and Perlman. Negotiations were ongoing, and there was no guarantee that the B&M would receive conditions that its managers found acceptable. It would be another two years, moreover, before the ICC gave its final approval to the Norfolk & Western merger and its associated Appendix O inclusion provisions—and in 1962, that outcome was by no means guaranteed.

As a fallback option, in January and February 1963 representatives from all three carriers demanded the right of inclusion in the Penn Central. Erie-Lackawanna executives were particularly adamant, claiming that their company would likely lose a quarter of its freight traffic to the new system. "Because of the unavoidable existing uncertainty as to whether Erie-Lackawanna will accomplish an affiliation with the Norfolk & Western and because of the fatal damage and impairment that the Pennsylvania-New York Central merger would cause," they stressed, "we herein filed our petition requesting that Erie-Lackawanna be included in the pending transaction upon equitable terms in the event that Erie-Lackawanna is unable to accomplish affiliation with the Norfolk & Western and that otherwise the authority for the Penn-Central merger be denied." In somewhat less convoluted language, the other two carriers adopted essentially identical positions.[126]

Symes and Perlman considered the Erie-Lackawanna, the Boston & Maine, and the Delaware & Hudson to be almost as unappealing as the New Haven. Whether they remained independent, joined the Norfolk & Western, or became part of a New England system was largely irrelevant, so long as they did not become a burden to the Penn

Central. Yet each of those carriers had intervened in the merger proceedings, and there was not much Symes or Perlman could do about it. "The Pennsylvania and the New York Central Railroads found themselves last week in the position of a hostess at a private party suddenly confronted with unwanted guests demanding access," observed *New York Times* business reporter John M. Lee. "The social graces in such a situation were strained further by the equivocations of some of the would-be gatecrashers who, while sticking a foot in the Pennsy-Central door, made it clear that their first choice was the party across the street." Lee made those remarks in February 1963, five years before the last of the gatecrashers found a party where they would be included, although not welcomed. In the meantime, executives at the E-L, the B&M, and the D&H were trying to delay the creation of Penn Central as long as possible, while awaiting the outcome of negotiations for inclusion in the Norfolk & Western.[127]

The criticism from shippers and trade associations was less vociferous. Of the 220 or so representatives who testified, 121 stated their enthusiastic and unqualified endorsement of the merger, four offered conditional support, and eight had no opinion one way or another. Only twelve indicated their opposition, and a majority merely asked the ICC to impose conditions that would mollify their concerns. Fifteen chambers of commerce supported the creation of Penn Central, and only three did not. Most shared the optimism of PRR and NYC officials and predicted that the savings associated with the merger would guarantee vastly improved service. The remaining witnesses discussed the likely effects of Penn Central on its competitors and expressed their fear that the Erie-Lackawanna and the other eastern railroads would collapse, depriving them of competitive freight service. Those accounts, however, were based largely on lurid headlines in local newspapers, predicting rusted rails and economic catastrophe. "In very few instances," Lyle and Darmstadter observed, "were these witnesses qualified to testify as to the actual effects of the proposed merger upon applicants' financial or other conditions nor upon the overall service improvements to be provided by the merged company." Qualified or not, many shipper representatives demanded inclusion or some other form of protection for the railroads that were likely to be affected by the Penn Central merger.[128]

Officials from state and local governments were decidedly less tolerant of the merger arrangements. Their respective positions depended in large measure on what was perhaps the most important document associated with the proceedings. During the first half of 1962, Pennsylvania Railroad and New York Central personnel worked frantically to prepare a preliminary operating plan that would integrate the facilities and services of two very different companies. Two managers, one from each railroad, headed a joint committee consisting of ten PRR and eleven NYC personnel. Nine zone committees, each of which included officials from both railroads, examined operating issues in specific territories. In developing their recommendations for the distribution of freight traffic, the delegates relied on waybill data for only two months—October 1960 in the case of the NYC and August 1961 for the PRR. Each of the ten committees specialized in transportation matters, to the exclusion of the traffic departments of the two railroads.[129]

There was, at first, no one specifically assigned to coordinate the activities of those ten committees. Before long, however, Symes selected Walter W. Patchell, the PRR's vice president in charge of special services, to take charge of the herculean task. Patchell never met with either the joint committee or any of the zone committees and discussed matters only with the two executives who coordinated the joint committee. He encountered varying levels of cooperation, tempered with suspicion that the merger would retard or destroy the careers of managers at each company. Financial matters were the most contentious, and David Bevan, the PRR's chief financial officer, found little common ground with his New York Central counterparts. Transportation officials were somewhat more cooperative, although most advocated for the continuance of the operating methods employed on their respective railroads, while identifying a long list of capital improvements that would be necessary to make the two companies work as one.[130]

The postmerger operating routines associated with the Patchell plan were largely irrelevant, however. The report's principal function was to provide unimpeachable evidence that the cost savings associated with the consolidation would be more than adequate to rehabilitate the two railroads, improve service, and generate a rate of return sufficient to attract additional investment capital. "The Patchell report which was presented to the ICC was not a plan for the merger nor was it intended to be," representatives from the Securities and Exchange Commission later observed. "It had not attempted to set out savings or costs that would result from the actual operations of the merged railroad." Long after the Interstate Commerce Commission approved the Penn Central merger and oversaw the company's subsequent bankruptcy, that agency offered a similar assessment. "We realize that conditions change; however, there appears so little correlation between the claims and the realities as to seriously question whether a realistic merger plan ever existed."[131]

Patchell's goal was quite simply to generate a plausible document that would offer a compelling economic rationale for the Penn Central merger. Working backward from that objective, his staff concluded that, following an eight-year consolidation process, the merger would produce annual savings of $81.2 million. The purported efficiencies included reductions in freight-terminal operating costs ($42.1 million) and road freight service ($14.5 million), as well as benefits associated with shared use of passenger facilities ($6.8 million) and equipment maintenance ($6.4 million). General traffic and expenses, a catch-all category, would yield another $11.7 million in savings per year. The increased costs associated with the joint use of facilities would raise annual operating expenses by a mere $300,000, practically a rounding error amid the extraordinary benefits stemming from the merger. Patchell acknowledged that operational coordination would require substantial capital investments, principally in the form of new or upgraded freight yards and physical connections between PRR and NYC tracks at forty-four locations. Those changes would necessitate an up-front cost of $75 million. Happily, Patchell concluded, the Penn Central could offset all but $30 million of that amount through the sale of real estate and equipment made redundant by the merger. Nearly eight thousand members of the combined workforce of 120,000 would also be made redundant—although with furloughs averaging 11,000 a year over the previous decade, the additional hardship was likely to be negligible.[132]

The traffic patterns and operating routines elucidated in the Patchell report would not have come as a surprise to anyone with a basic working knowledge of geography and transportation economics. Both Symes and Perlman wanted out of the passenger business, but political considerations dictated their promise that there would be no significant reductions in service. *The Broadway Limited* and the *Twentieth Century Limited* would continue their simultaneous runs, despite steadily declining patronage. They would share terminal facilities, as the former New York Central would shift its intercity trains to Penn Station in New York and Union Station in Chicago. The more significant modifications involved freight service along two parallel trunk lines that served 142 points in common. Despite the extraordinary engineering achievement associated with the Horseshoe Curve, the New York Central's Water Level Route offered far easier grades. All through freight between the Atlantic Seaboard and the Midwest would flow through Albany, Buffalo, and

Cleveland, bypassing the commonwealth of Pennsylvania. The altered operating patterns in turn dictated the single largest investment associated with the merger—a $19.7 million classification yard at Selkirk, New York, near Albany. The PRR's main line would be restricted to freight traffic from the coal and steel territory, east of Youngstown and Columbus, Ohio, that had historically generated most of the company's revenues. Shipments routed between Chicago and Pittsburgh would avoid the Pennsylvania Railroad entirely, moving east along the New York Central to Cleveland and then south along the NYC's Pittsburgh & Lake Erie subsidiary. The Pittsburgh, Fort Wayne & Chicago, once the heart of the Pennsylvania Railroad's Lines West, would become little more than a branch line, reduced to a single track. The PRR's old Vandalia Line would correspondingly thrive under the new arrangements, carrying traffic from St. Louis as far east as Terre Haute. East of there, the New York Central route would take precedence. Altoona would be the home of the principal shop facilities of the combined system, to the detriment of the NYC's operations at Collinwood, near Cleveland. Penn Central would have little need for the outdated Pitcairn Yard, east of Pittsburgh, but would make extensive use of the larger and more modern Conway Yard, west of the city. Representatives of the two railroads were not willing to indicate whether the Penn Central's headquarters would be located in Philadelphia or in Manhattan, nor were examiners Lyle and Darmstadter prepared to choose between those two alternatives. Despite the proposed changes, PRR and NYC officials emphasized that they could achieve the promised savings without any line abandonments or reductions in service. It was an implausible assertion—but a necessary one, given the potential opposition to the changes produced by the merger.[133]

The Pennsylvania Railroad and the New York Central released the Patchell report on July 17, 1962, in a three-hour press conference at Penn Station.[134] Officials from the two companies immediately began contacting interested parties in more than thirty cities, from Boston as far south as Norfolk and as far west as Chicago and St. Louis, reassuring them that only good things would come from the merger. Despite those claims, representatives from state and local governments immediately began their own assessment of the merger's probable effects on local employment, tax revenues, and access to transportation services. The state of Illinois reacted against the consolidation, as did many local governments. The city of Peoria expressed concern over the effects on the Toledo, Peoria & Western, which offered a connection between the PRR and the Santa Fe. The proposed downgrading of the Fort Wayne line ensured opposition from many communities in Indiana and Ohio. The city of Cleveland protested a loss of competition, principally with respect to coal shipments. The Maryland Port Authority predicted that the merger would reduce traffic at Baltimore but was willing to accept that outcome if the ICC mandated steps to protect the Western Maryland.[135] The state of New Jersey, the New Jersey Public Utilities Commission, the city of Newark, and various other Garden State communities indicated strong opposition to the formation of Penn Central. Their principal complaint was that the new system would destroy the Erie-Lackawanna, eliminating competition and jeopardizing much of the region's commuter service. New Jersey officials nonetheless acknowledged that they might modify their position, if the ICC guaranteed the Erie-Lackawanna's inclusion in the Norfolk & Western—or, barring that, the Penn Central.[136]

The situation involving the two states that lent their name to their respective railroads was, to say the least, complicated. Some of the jurisdictions along the New York Central's route between Albany and Buffalo supported the merger, predicting that the new traffic patterns would result in improved service. The promised construction of Selkirk Yard, conveniently located near the state capital in Albany, promised both jobs and economic growth. Yet residents of Buffalo and some other upstate communities deplored the rationalization and relocation of facilities and personnel. Farther south, along the route of the Erie-Lackawanna, opposition was fierce and based on the familiar charge that the Penn Central would drive the railroad lifeline into bankruptcy. New York State, New York City, and the Port of New York Authority—some of the most formidable intervenors in the case—announced they would support the merger only on one condition: the Erie-Lackawanna must have an opportunity for inclusion in the Norfolk & Western system, lest the Penn Central obtain a near monopoly of rail operations in the state.[137]

It was in Pennsylvania, however, that the merger aroused its most vocal opposition. The state's chamber of commerce, as well as its offshoots in Philadelphia and in Pittsburgh, offered enthusiastic support—on the grounds that a more efficient transportation network was certain to benefit the regional economy. Governmental bodies courted a much broader constituency and consequently adopted a starkly different assessment of the merger. They were dismayed that the Patchell plan, like its 1958 predecessor, routed the preponderance of east–west freight traffic through New York. Like the managers of the Pennsylvania

Railroad and the New York Central, they were also caught up in the politics of postwar industrial decline. By some measures, the state's coal and steel industries reached maturity around 1910, well before the previous world war. They had nonetheless done well during the 1920s, survived the Great Depression, and boomed as a result of the temporary surge in orders during World War II. The briefer Korean War expansion likewise disguised some of Pennsylvania's underlying economic problems, but the situation rapidly deteriorated during the remainder of the 1950s. Union agreements designed to maintain labor harmony produced unsustainably high levels of wages and fringe benefits—inducing many companies to relocate to the South or the West and to replace workers with machines. In the early 1950s, John L. Lewis agreed that the United Mine Workers of America would no longer oppose the mechanization of the coal industry. The arrangements preserved wage rates and curtailed strikes, but they portended devastating long-term consequences for miners. Nor could the UMW halt the steady decline of coal production in Pennsylvania. A lack of entrepreneurial vision and constrained access to capital prevented steelmakers from investing in new technologies. US Steel and Bethlehem Steel did not adopt the basic oxygen process until 1964, twelve years after its first commercial use in Austria. A series of strikes roiled the steel industry, with the 1959 walkout giving Japanese and other foreign competitors a chance to penetrate the market. By 1960, Japan accounted for 6 percent of global production, a figure that increased to 16 percent in 1983. During the same period, American steel output fell from a quarter to a tenth of the global total. Much of the steel production that remained was increasingly concentrated in locations such as Chicago, and even as far west as the Los Angeles basin, rather than in the Mon Valley. Nor were other industries immune. New Kensington, twenty miles up the Allegheny River from Pittsburgh, had once produced more aluminum than any other city in the world. By the time of the 1958 recession, there were clear indications that the Alcoa plant there was in trouble. Union officials accepted a new contract in 1966, giving significant concessions to management. Their willingness to sacrifice wages and benefits merely postponed the day of reckoning, and in 1970 Alcoa announced that the New Kensington facility would close. The Pennsylvania Railroad was the victim rather than the cause of those problems. That distinction was lost on many of the blue-collar Pennsylvanians whose jobs—and often their entire way of life—seemed to be under siege. In that context, the merger with the New York Central suggested that the nation's financial and political elites were enriching themselves, while furthering the decline of industrial America.[138]

The divergent attitudes toward the merger placed Governor David L. Lawrence in a difficult position. He had once been the mayor of Pittsburgh and had worked with Richard King Mellon, Symes, and others associated with the PRR as part of that city's urban renaissance. He was also a Democrat and accordingly sensitive to the concerns of organized labor—particularly when representatives from the Brotherhood of Railroad Trainmen and the Pennsylvania AFL-CIO demanded that he oppose the merger. "One of the things that I am concerned about," Lawrence indicated, "is, here you have the leaders of labor in the State opposing it and you have the Chambers of Commerce supporting it." Unsure of the correct course of action, Lawrence appointed David H. Kurtzman, the secretary of administration, to head an investigative committee. Kurtzman could not make up his mind, either, but he thought it prudent to study the matter further and see what transpired in the ICC hearings. Patchell's suggestions, and particularly the proposed diversion of through traffic to the New York Central, caused Kurtzman to recommend that the governor take action to protect the commonwealth's interests. In September 1962, two months after the release of the Patchell study, Governor Lawrence announced that he had asked the ICC for the right to intervene in the Penn Central case. He stressed that he had not taken a specific position but indicated he would soon do so.[139]

On January 3, 1963, eleven days before ICC hearings were to commence in his home city of Pittsburgh, Lawrence ordered state attorney general David Stahl to oppose the Penn Central merger. The policy, based on recommendations from Kurtzman's committee, pleased representatives of organized labor. The members of the Pennsylvania Chamber of Commerce announced their "surprise and disappointment" at the decision. James Oram, the PRR's vice president in charge of public and employee relations, reiterated the official position that the merger would cause no harm to Pennsylvania and rather dismissively suggested that the committee's recommendation was attributable "perhaps to a lack of comprehension of the evidence."[140]

Lawrence was a lame-duck governor, and his term would expire on January 15. It remained to be seen whether his successor, Republican William W. Scranton, would continue to fight the merger. Before he left office, Lawrence authorized a $50,000 study, aided by a computer at the University of Pittsburgh, to quantify the effects that the consolidation would produce. Stahl, the outgoing attorney general, convinced Scranton and incoming attorney

general Walter E. Alessandroni to see the study through to its conclusion. Researchers fed eight million bits of information into the computer, which promptly crashed and then spit out a forty-page summary that AFL-CIO attorney Albert Brandon labeled "unintelligible." Advocates of pen and paper expressed glee at the breakdown, and the ICC permitted commonwealth officials to postpone their testimony while they reprogrammed the computer. The results were ready at the end of June 1963 and offered little if any clarity. They suggested that Patchell had *underestimated* the savings associated with the merger—but that the Penn Central's gains would be temporary, as the company met increasingly stiff competition from truckers, pipelines, and inland waterways. Pennsylvania would probably suffer as a result of the diversion of traffic but, the report concluded, "the damage is not likely to be very large." In contrast, the study suggested that "the impact on railroad labor in Pennsylvania would probably be greater than estimated by the applicants" and that the ripple effects associated with "secondary employment may be a serious problem." Labor leaders considered themselves vindicated. So did representatives from the city and county of Philadelphia, who had also announced their opposition to the merger. The computer suggested that the city and its port would suffer serious economic harm. Patchell, ready to defend his version of the situation, suggested that the competing study "indicates no real opposition to the merger itself, but rather a desire to develop the best method of operating the merged company." That was the situation in August 1963 as Scranton weighed his options.[141]

The concerns of many Pennsylvania residents provided a political cause célèbre for one of the most implacable and outspoken opponents of the Penn Central merger. Milton J. Shapiro grew up in Cleveland and earned a degree in electrical engineering, graduating during the worst year of the Great Depression. He moved to Pennsylvania, began selling electronic components, and changed his last name to Shapp, to disguise his Jewish heritage. He founded the Jerrold Electronics Corporation in 1948, took advantage of the postwar boom in telecommunications, and was soon doing $25 million a year in business. Even before Shapp sold the company in 1966, he possessed both the wealth and the time to become involved in politics. A staunch Democrat, he associated with John F. Kennedy and contributed suggestions that led to the establishment of the Peace Corps. Shapp also enjoyed close ties to Philadelphia's Democratic mayors. Given his professional background, as well as his religion, Shapp was far removed from the concerns of coal, steel, and Pennsylvania's other traditional economic mainstays. Even as he deplored the commonwealth's sagging industrial base, he advocated education and retraining programs that would prepare the workforce for the new electronic economy.[142]

The Penn Central merger proposal afforded Shapp a superb opportunity to highlight Pennsylvania's declining economic fortunes—and to assign blame to the Pennsylvania Railroad. His opening salvo appeared in the *Philadelphia Inquirer* on October 15, 1962, in the form of a nearly full-page ad attacking the consolidation.[143] The massive typeface proclaiming that "the proposed merger of the Pennsylvania and the New York Central Railroads could spell economic catastrophe for our State" was certainly adequate to attract the attention of his intended audience—all business executives and chambers of commerce across the breadth of the commonwealth. Shapp concluded that Symes's testimony before the ICC "reveals vividly how the merger, as presently conceived, will reduce rail service in all areas of Pennsylvania, cripple future industrial growth for many hard-hit communities, and make it virtually impossible to attract new industries and to create new employment opportunities in our State." Selectively employing statistics from the Patchell report, Shapp asserted that Philadelphia would lose nearly a quarter of its daily freight service, and Johnstown nearly a third, with the Oil City-Titusville area suffering a decline of 73 percent. Turning the logic of the merger on its head, he suggested that the Penn Central proposal represented managerial ineptitude rather than an opportunity for executives to implement greater efficiencies. "It is time for the PRR—one of the wealthiest companies in the nation," Shapp contended—"to stop pleading poverty and government interference and to start offering better service to the public as a means of revitalizing its declining business."[144]

After dismissing managerial claims of government meddling as irrelevant, Shapp proceeded to ask the government to intervene on his behalf. The ICC hearings were in Philadelphia on January 16, 1963, and Shapp took full advantage of the opportunity to air his views. Speaking in his capacity as the vice chairman of the National Public Advisory Committee on Area Redevelopment, he recommended the creation of a state agency that would coordinate and regulate all modes of transportation. He reiterated his criticism of PRR and NYC executives and decried "featherbedding in the top levels of railroad management." It was another attempt to turn the tables on his opponents and to suggest it was they, rather than regulators and unionized workers, who were responsible for the ills of the railroads.[145]

If anyone could exceed Shapp's apocalyptic predictions regarding the merger, it was Mike Quill. Even before the

hearings began, the president of the Transport Workers Union claimed that the consolidation would produce "a loss of 40,000 to 50,000 jobs." That was a vastly higher number than the Patchell report predicted, and Quill did not explain how the Penn Central could function after furloughing more than a third of its workforce. Despite the scant accuracy of his statements and the limited efficacy of his tactics, Quill nonetheless represented only the most vocal component of fierce labor opposition that began as soon as the two companies announced their merger plans in January 1962. Between December 1955 and December 1962, the PRR's workforce plummeted from 113,213 to 64,041, and the proposed consolidation with the New York Central suggested that further declines were inevitable. Like Quill, representatives from the Railway Labor Executives' Association denounced the merger as little more than a stock swindle, one that would have disastrous repercussions for workers, shippers, passengers, and the overall economy. The Brotherhood of Railroad Trainmen paid for a full-page ad in the June 10, 1962, Sunday edition of the *New York Times*, slightly larger than the one Shapp had placed in the *Philadelphia Inquirer*. "A wholesale consolidation of railroad properties should *never* be permitted on a showing of financial manipulators," asserted BRT president William Parker Kennedy. "To allow these two giant railroads to merge will cause great harm to the eastern half of the United States," he suggested, and "will threaten the very survival of our business enterprises." In language certain to appeal to the Antitrust Division of the Justice Department, he warned that "approval of this merger would establish the pattern of government sanction not only for monopoly in railroads but, as already is evident in the proposal to merge American and Eastern Airlines, in all other transportation." Albert Brandon, representing the Pennsylvania Federation of Labor, AFL-CIO, adopted a scattershot approach during his cross-examination of Symes and Perlman, peppering them with random accusations in the hopes of catching them off guard. He emphasized that the boards of directors of the PRR and the NYC included "some of the largest banking houses, the largest industrial corporations, and the largest originators and receivers of shipments" in the country, suggesting a clear conflict of interest.[146]

The problem facing the unions was that the old Progressive Era arguments against banker dominance, the trusts, and the heartless attitudes of robber-baron railroad executives no longer worked as well as they had in the past. By 1962, no one could seriously argue that the railroads monopolized the transportation sector of the economy. The railroads' antifeatherbedding campaign was proving remarkably successful in the court of public opinion, if not in every state legislature. Railroading was a far less dangerous occupation in the 1960s than it had been at the turn of the century, and unions found it increasingly difficult to assert that full-crew laws were vital to safety. Fewer and fewer people worked for the railroads, knew someone who worked for the railroads, or traveled by train. Under the circumstances, unionized railway workers were at worst a nuisance and at best irrelevant. The demise of the Vermont-based Rutland Railway, which abandoned operations in 1963 following a prolonged strike, offered an object lesson in corporate suicide at the hands of organized labor. That transformation was not lost on politicians, particularly Republicans, who increasingly favored business profits, economic growth, and the creation of jobs in the abstract—rather than the protection of specific workers in specific industries. Even Democrats had to wonder whether full-fledged support for unions remained sound amid rapidly shifting economic and political ideologies.

As an alternate tactic, labor leaders adopted an approach that was precisely opposite the rationale that Symes and Perlman provided for the merger—yet one that was increasingly in alignment with federal policy. The Railway Labor Executives' Association commissioned a report by economist Leon Keyserling, who chaired the Council of Economic Advisers during the Truman administration. His initial findings, released in February 1962, subsequently became the basis for *The Move toward Railroad Mergers: A Great National Problem*, published later that year. Keyserling called for a halt to all such consolidations, pending the development of a national transportation policy—recommendations identical to those that Estes Kefauver was airing in the Senate, at practically the same time. RLEA officials were keenly aware of the similarity and organized a rally of fifteen hundred cheering PRR and NYC employees—giving the senator another opportunity to demand that the Kennedy administration establish a coherent policy on mergers. Not surprisingly, given the RLEA sponsorship, Keyserling concluded that railroad mergers jeopardized jobs, economic development, and national security. He asserted that the railroads were far more prosperous than their propaganda indicated—"I can't imagine any subject on which the public has been more brainwashed," he suggested—but somewhat contradictorily alleged that mergers among healthy companies might threaten the survival of their weaker competitors. His strongest argument, however, was that Symes, Perlman, and others were woefully misguided in their claims that the railroads suffered from excess capacity. More

effective management, Keyserling suggested, would fill the rails with traffic, ensure universal prosperity without the need for mergers, stimulate economic growth, and—most significantly—increase rather than decrease the demand for workers. Keyserling's prediction that railroading was a growth industry seemed bizarre beyond belief to anyone who actually worked for a northeastern railroad. His timing was nonetheless excellent, as the publication of his recommendations coincided with the recovery from the 1958 recession. The eastern railroads enjoyed a last, brief period of prosperity, and Keyserling was not the only one who thought that such gains would continue indefinitely. Officials from the Justice Department, who still had not offered formal testimony at the ICC merger hearings, incorporated Keyserling's growth model as they refined their response to the Penn Central application.[147]

PRR and NYC officials attempted to blunt labor opposition, with varying degrees of success. Walter Patchell, the PRR vice president whose operating plan produced so much outrage from union leaders, warned commissioners Lyle and Darmstadter that job guarantees and other concessions to labor would cause significant delays in the realization of the cost savings associated with the merger. Symes held up well under cross-examination from union attorneys and scored points when he insisted that the consolidation might "very well increase employment" as the Penn Central captured a larger share of the nation's freight traffic. Perlman did less well, particularly when Brandon bored into him. The NYC president accused the AFL-CIO attorney of attempting "to trap me" into saying that truck competition was the sole cause of the railroad's problems. The two men ended their exchange by shouting at each other—precisely the sort of incident that labor leaders calculated would capture the public interest.[148]

Despite the drama in the ICC hearing room, PRR and NYC officials were prepared to yield ground to organized labor. They knew as well as their union adversaries that any delays to the merger would be costly, and a strike even more so. It was simply a matter of balancing the value of concessions against the political and economic losses associated with disruptions in service. Even as Symes and Perlman endured cross-examination from Brandon and other labor representatives, they were attempting to resolve the featherbedding issue. During the spring and summer of 1962, in the months before the hearings began, the National Mediation Board failed to end the work-rules dispute between the operating unions and the carriers. Executives subsequently accepted arbitration, but labor leaders did not, and the unions then filed suit to prevent implementation of the recommendations issued by Kennedy's presidential Railroad Commission in February. In retaliation, railroad officials announced that they were no longer willing to accept the commission's criteria but would instead adopt the more draconian cuts they had proposed in 1959. They also demanded the creation of a presidential emergency board as a mechanism to avoid lengthy litigation and a possible nationwide strike. The Supreme Court weighed in on the matter the following March and in a unanimous decision held that the carriers were legally entitled to implement work-rule changes. The Pennsylvania Railroad immediately announced plans to furlough thirty-one hundred firemen in freight service, and other railroads prepared to do the same.[149]

The featherbedding issue was by no means resolved, and the judicial ruling provoked a combative response on the part of the operating unions. Negotiations between management and labor quickly broke down, and executives pledged to eliminate forty thousand firemen on April 8, with another twenty-five thousand to follow. Union officials responded with a nationwide strike call. Everyone involved was paying close attention to the Florida East Coast Railway, where a walkout was rapidly evolving into one of the longest and most violent labor disputes in the history of twentieth-century railroading.[150]

Kennedy, who sought to prevent the problem from spreading, established yet another emergency board. Railroad officials accepted a new set of work rules, prepared by Secretary of Labor W. Willard Wirtz, and set implementation for July 11, 1963. The brotherhoods, predictably, rejected the Wirtz recommendations and called for a nationwide walkout at midnight on July 9. Hours before the strike deadline, Kennedy called both sides to the White House and proposed that Supreme Court justice Arthur J. Goldberg arbitrate the dispute. It was an unusual choice for what Kennedy called an "extraordinary situation," but critics condemned the commingling of two supposedly independent branches of the federal government. Despite Goldberg's credentials as the former general counsel for the United Steelworkers of America and former secretary of labor, union officials refused to submit to compulsory arbitration—although they agreed to delay the strike until the end of the month. That would give sufficient time for Kennedy's Advisory Committee on Labor-Management Policy to act. The president appointed a six-person subcommittee to investigate the issue. Wirtz and Secretary of Commerce Luther Hodges constituted the federal government's contingent, AFL-CIO president George Meany and Brotherhood of Railway Clerks grand president George

M. Harrison advocated for the unions, and Inland Steel chairman Joseph L. Block represented industry. Norfolk & Western president Stuart Saunders was the sole railroad executive on the subcommittee.[151]

As the work-rules dispute passed its fourth anniversary, the featherbedding issue slowly moved toward an uneasy resolution. The carriers agreed to postpone implementation until the end of August, giving Wirtz an opportunity to persuade union officials to accept the principle of arbitration. Labor leaders were not willing to specify precisely what matters would be subject to arbitration, although they indicated that they were willing to discuss crew size and the severance arrangements for firemen and other furloughed employees. The brotherhoods had good reason to be cautious, as every previous government recommendation had been more favorable to management than to labor. They had little choice in the matter, however, as both the House and the Senate were considering bills that would bar a strike and force the unions to submit to arbitration. Confident of political support from Congress as well as the Kennedy administration, on August 24 the carriers posted new work rules that eliminated the jobs of thirty-two thousand firemen. The proposal, scheduled to go into effect on August 29, prompted the brotherhoods to issue another strike call. On August 28, less than six hours before the beginning of a walkout that would paralyze the national economy, Kennedy signed legislation blocking the strike. The bill passed the House by a vote of 286 to 66 and prevailed in the Senate by a margin of 90 to 2, suggesting the degree to which political support for organized labor had atrophied. In addition to barring strikes for 180 days, the measure mandated arbitration for issues related to crew size and the elimination of firemen. It was the first use of compulsory arbitration in peacetime, and some observers questioned whether "the free institution of collective bargaining" was headed for extinction. Collective bargaining was far from dead, however, as it remained the mechanism of choice for addressing all the other disputes—and there were many—between management and labor. Nor did the national legislation terminate the battles in state legislatures, regarding the repeal of full-crew laws. Like the eastern railroads themselves, the leaders of the railway unions were fighting an existential battle for survival. They faced enemies on many fronts, and the ongoing Penn Central merger hearings suggested that much of the increased efficiency ballyhooed by executives was going to come at their expense.[152]

Union leaders were not the only ones surrounded by enemies. James Symes had enjoyed a remarkably varied

Pennsylvania Railroad career, as a ringer on a company baseball team, an operating official exiled to the far western end of the system, a relentless advocate for dieselization, a chief executive officer, and an indefatigable supporter of the Penn Central merger. He had climbed to the very top of the corporate ladder by way of the Transportation Department, a unit of the company not generally known for fostering tact and diplomacy. Yet he had acquitted himself well at the ICC hearings, controlling his temper, refusing to be baited, and displaying an impressive command of the voluminous data associated with the case. Symes worked assiduously to overcome opposition to the merger while trusting President Allen Greenough to keep the railroad running. Yet the hearings dragged on, day after day, month after month, and the hostility from government entities, local communities, labor leaders, and competing railroads showed little sign of abating. If Symes mollified one complainant each week, he could perhaps eliminate all the absolute and conditional objections to the merger in something like two years. The Pennsylvania Railroad did not have that much time, and neither did Symes. For the merger to succeed, he would need to yield authority to a younger man, someone with the combination of legal training, political connections, and personality necessary to make friends in high places and to guide the Penn Central merger through the regulatory process. To do so, Symes looked to the South, to an executive he knew very well.

The Gentleman from Roanoke

On July 8, 1962, five days after he testified at the Kefauver hearings, James Symes celebrated his sixty-fifth birthday. He had arranged to remain as the PRR's chairman, during a critical stage in the merger negotiations. By early 1963, however, it was becoming clear that Symes would not become the first chairman of the Penn Central. The merger was taking longer than he expected, and he could not postpone his retirement indefinitely. By training and temperament, he was likewise ill-suited to the organizational, legal, and regulatory challenges associated with joining two companies with very different corporate cultures.

The most serious impediment to Symes's continued oversight of the Pennsylvania Railroad, however, was that he did not get along with Alfred Perlman. At all. Both executives rose through the ranks, and they possessed a wealth of practical experience in railroad operations. Yet Perlman, and many of his subordinates, considered the PRR to be overly bureaucratic, rigidly traditional, and out of touch

with the basics of modern railroading. They were particularly dismissive of Fred Carpi's Traffic Department and its continual demands for ICC approval of higher tariffs, refusal to authorize selective rate reductions, and willingness to make so many concessions to shippers that traffic often moved at a loss. Symes and his staff, in contrast, denigrated the NYC as a company obsessed with unproven technology and run by marketing experts who knew little about making the trains run.

Symes's efforts to restructure the eastern railroad network exacerbated those underlying tensions. During the first iteration of the proposed PRR-NYC merger, it was Robert Young who persuaded Symes to participate, while Perlman was never more than grudgingly cooperative. Perlman was convinced that Symes orchestrated the merger between the Norfolk & Western and the Virginian, with its attendant harm to the NYC, and that perceived betrayal was sufficient to end the first round of negotiations. When Symes met with Chesapeake & Ohio executives at the Greenbrier Hotel, to create the three-system East, he never bothered to invite his future merger partner. Symes subsequently undermined Perlman's efforts to win inclusion in the C&O–B&O and the N&W–Nickel Plate consolidations, ensuring that the NYC's president would have to choose between the Penn Central merger and probable bankruptcy. Once Perlman agreed to unite the two companies, he abandoned his efforts to create a two-system East and with it any opportunity to head one of those networks. It was a bitter pill to swallow. Perlman, like Young, thought of the New York Central as the classiest railroad in the United States, regardless of its relative size or financial position.

Given that the PRR was the nation's biggest railroad, and the NYC second, it was clear which leadership team would dominate the Penn Central. The contentious December 1961 negotiations over the structure of the new company reflected Symes's determination that PRR executives would remain in charge and that their operating and managerial methods would predominate. Perlman was superbly equipped to serve as the Penn Central's chief operating officer, and NYC directors demanded that he do so. PRR president Allen Greenough was capable but not exemplary in that regard, yet he would be in charge of the Penn Central's day-to-day affairs. The agreement that both Symes and Perlman would serve as cochairmen of the Penn Central's board of directors hardly resolved the situation. Given the similarity of their backgrounds, coupled with their profoundly different operating philosophies, Symes and Perlman were likely to come into conflict time and time again. Symes excluded Perlman from merger-planning meetings through the simple expedient of neglecting to tell him when and where they were to take place. Perlman's demand that he become an officer likewise met resistance, coupled with vague explanations. While Symes never acknowledged the presence of antisemitism in the executive ranks, he indicated that some of the PRR's directors considered Perlman to be "socially unacceptable."[153]

By the end of 1962, even as the ICC was overseeing the Penn Central merger hearings, the hostility between Symes and Perlman threatened the agreement between the Pennsylvania Railroad and the New York Central. PRR director Howard Butcher III pushed for a resolution, in the process becoming one of the company's most influential board members. After graduating from the University of Pennsylvania in 1923, Butcher went to work at his father's brokerage firm, and he became a partner in July 1929. The collapse of the stock market, only a few months later, influenced his investment strategy, which generally involved the purchase of shares he believed to be undervalued. Butcher's emphasis on what he called "special situations" led to the acquisition of securities in railroads and public utilities. By the 1950s, the family firm had become a boutique brokerage house, discreetly undertaking transactions on behalf of a small number of wealthy clients. The offices of Butcher & Sherrerd were located in Philadelphia, and Butcher lived along the Main Line, yet he consistently encouraged his investors to sell whatever Pennsylvania Railroad shares they owned. The recommendation would doubtless have come as a disappointment to his great-grandfather, Washington Butcher, who served as a PRR director between 1849 and 1873. Howard Butcher's attitude changed in early 1959, when he acknowledged that he "really studied" the PRR's 1958 annual report. The data convinced him that the railroad's stock was undervalued and that the company was selling assets at extremely low prices. The problem, he thought, was that investors denigrated the railroads in general and characterized the PRR as one of the least exciting carriers in the United States. "In my thirty-nine years at this desk," he emphasized, "I have never seen a stock with so much promise selling so low in relation to its assets with the market selling so high." He began buying shares "a little bit early," he acknowledged, as he lost money at first. Then, during the early 1960s the railroads experienced a brief resurgence, seemingly vindicating Butcher's investment philosophy. In less than three years, he acquired 1.4 million PRR shares—150,000 for himself and the remainder for his family, friends, and clients. When Norfolk & Western president Stuart Saunders

resigned from the PRR board on January 12, 1962, as part of the gradual separation of the two companies, Butcher was a logical successor.[154]

It was entirely appropriate that the change in the board's composition occurred on the same day that the PRR directors signed the consolidation agreement with their NYC counterparts, as Butcher became one of the merger's most enthusiastic proponents. He expected the union to increase the prestige and profitability of the system and predicted that he would at least triple his initial $25 million initial investment.[155] The failure of the merger negotiations would be correspondingly disastrous, and as Butcher took his seat on the PRR board, he feared the rift between Symes and Perlman was leading in precisely that direction. He encouraged Symes to step down as chairman and to find a suitable replacement.[156]

The search for the Pennsylvania Railroad's new chairman and CEO reawakened some of the ill will that emerged in the autumn of 1959, when Symes selected Allen Greenough as the PRR's president. Greenough was the vice president in charge of transportation and maintenance, not the customary choice for promotion. The most traditional contender was James Newell, the vice president in charge of operations—but Newell was engaged in a toxic feud with Fred Carpi, the head of the Traffic Department. Bevan preferred Herman Pevler—someone, he hoped, who lacked strategic vision and would thus offer no impediment to his goal of succeeding Symes as chairman. As he sought his replacement during the spring and summer of 1963, Symes quickly dismissed Greenough, Newell, Pevler, and Bevan from consideration. The PRR's president was doing a competent job, but the limited horizons associated with his attention to day-to-day operating matters made him ill-suited to the chairman's position. Newell had more enemies than friends in the executive suite and survived only because he enjoyed Symes's protection. After Symes passed him over for promotion in 1959, Pevler went to the Wabash, where he greatly improved the performance of that PRR subsidiary. He could be recalled, but Bevan's assessment of Pevler's limited strategic vision was largely correct. Bevan himself was increasingly valuable to the Pennsylvania Railroad, as its financial condition worsened. He possessed no experience in railroad operations, however, and his elevation to the chairmanship would have provided ample evidence that the consolidation with the New York Central was nothing more than an elaborate exercise in financial manipulation. Of equal significance, Bevan expressed serious misgivings regarding the wisdom of that merger. He possessed a thorough understanding of the PRR's operating statistics, and he had a pretty fair knowledge of those on the New York Central as well. He doubted that the merger would produce anything like $100 million a year in economies. He also knew, from experience, that operating officials on the new Penn Central were likely to demand massive capital investments—far more than either Symes or Perlman predicted—to integrate the operations of the two predecessor companies. As the most vocal naysayer among the executive ranks, he was hardly the appropriate person to guide the Pennsylvania Railroad through its merger with the New York Central.

Because Butcher's investment strategy depended entirely on the success of the Penn Central merger, he sought an expert in railroad consolidations rather than railroad operations. No one had a better reputation in that regard than the Roanoke lawyer who headed the Norfolk & Western. By June 1963, Symes and Butcher concluded that Saunders would be the next chairman of the board. In some respects, the president of the Norfolk & Western was an unlikely choice to head the nation's largest railroad. "Saunders was no railroader," recalled Basil Cole, the PRR's assistant general counsel. "He didn't know anything about railroads, any more than I did." With little knowledge of railroad operations, Saunders often set arbitrary performance goals and became enraged when his subordinates could not achieve them.[157]

In his social life, however, Saunders was the epitome of the charming and gracious southern gentleman. He had little interest in golf or any other form of physical activity, but he was a passionate bridge player who enjoyed French cuisine and vintage wines. His attire was impeccable, with a neatly pressed three-piece suit accentuated by a gold watch chain. Such elegance was hardly the norm for a career railroader, but it represented a carefully cultivated persona. Soon after he joined the Norfolk & Western, Saunders recruited public-relations expert William A. Lashley from the Ford Motor Company. Lashley became his personal assistant, responsible for remaking Saunders into an individual who epitomized the public's perception of a skilled railroad executive. Journalist and transportation consultant Rush Loving Jr. suggested that Lashley "made Stuart Saunders his personal project, by molding him in the image of a transportation innovator and a king of industry." Joseph Califano Jr., a key aide in the Kennedy and Johnson administrations, characterized Saunders as "a businessman whose impeccable attire and cherubic countenance provided cover for his tenacity and political street smarts."[158]

From his youth, Saunders was something of an outsider. A childhood acquaintance from Bedford County, Virginia,

described Saunders as "the fat little boy we used to chase home from school." Those experiences may have increased Saunders's sensitivity to issues of discrimination and marginalization. The 1954 *Brown v. Board* decision produced a White-supremacist backlash known as Massive Resistance and led to the 1957 election of staunch segregationist J. Lindsay Almond as governor of Virginia. Late the following year, Saunders organized a delegation of business executives who shared his concern that Massive Resistance was harming the Virginia economy and making it more difficult to entice northern industries to locate in the state. Under Saunders's guidance, the Virginia Industrialization Group pressured Almond to abandon his support for Massive Resistance and permit the integration of public schools.[159] Despite that controversial stance on race relations, Symes suggested that Saunders and his "charming and capable wife" would likely "fit into the Philadelphia picture quite well." Saunders, however, did not share such barely concealed antisemitism. He broke ranks with his fellow WASPs and socialized with Jews. He was the guest of honor at a 1965 dinner of the National Conference of Christians and Jews, principally on account of his efforts to improve labor-management relations. Such public actions suggested that he would be more willing than Symes and other PRR executives to work with Perlman. Yet those who knew Saunders suggested that his commitment to social justice was both mercenary and insincere and always designed to achieve some goal related to his business interests.[160]

Saunders's elevation of self-interest to an art form also colored his political affiliations. He was a Democrat, typical for any White man who established his career in Virginia during the first half of the twentieth century, yet a rare commodity among the ranks of senior railroad executives. Califano described Saunders as "a heavy Democratic money man," willing to spend lavishly to gain political influence. Saunders enjoyed a close relationship with members of the Kennedy family—including the president and the attorney general who possessed considerable authority over the Penn Central merger proposal. John F. Kennedy's assessment that Saunders was "a smart fellow" suggested that the two got along well. In May 1963, Saunders and Henry Ford II served as cochairmen of the Business Committee for Tax Reduction. Kennedy encouraged the initiative—which he called "the most important domestic economic measure to come before Congress in 15 years"— that culminated in the Revenue Act of 1964. In his efforts to avert a nationwide railroad strike during the summer of 1963, the president asked Saunders to serve as the carriers' representative on the work-rules subcommittee of the Advisory Committee on Labor-Management Policy. In later years, Saunders was one of the original trustees of the John F. Kennedy Library.[161]

For Symes and Butcher, Saunders's most important credential involved his reputation as the nation's leading expert on railroad mergers. That status alone suggested that the Penn Central was destined for success, if he was at the helm. When he brought together the Norfolk & Western and the Virginian, Saunders initiated a consolidation movement whose momentum continued through the remainder of the twentieth century. The announcement of the N&W–Nickel Plate–Wabash proposal brought further renown to the executive the *New York Times* dubbed the "master of mergers" and "the man who kicked off the modern merger movement and supplied much of its relentless power." Symes concurred with that assessment, suggesting to board member C. Jared Ingersoll that Saunders "has done a wonderful job in merging the Norfolk & Western with the Virginian. He worked out a plan to merge the Norfolk and Western with the Nickel Plate and lease the Wabash." Saunders, presidential aide Joseph Califano observed, "was determined to consummate the biggest railroad merger in American history" and "was obsessed with doing the biggest ever, Penn-Central."[162]

While Jared Ingersoll chaired the committee of PRR directors responsible for hiring the next chairman, there was little question that Symes and Butcher had the final say in the matter. On June 26, 1963, the board chose Saunders. His new salary would be $130,000 a year, not that much higher than what he earned as president of the N&W, but generous stock options made the offer more attractive. Saunders assumed his new duties on October 1, the day after Symes retired. While the change in leadership was not entirely unexpected, many observers questioned Saunders's decision to leave the most prosperous railroad in the United States so that he could take command of one of the weakest ones. One analogy, that he was forsaking the leadership of the New York Yankees to coach the Mets, did not suggest that Saunders was a man of sound judgment. Butcher, whose economic fortunes depended on the success of the Penn Central merger negotiations, adopted a different sporting reference. "Saunders is like a football player who finally gets the ball on the four-yard line," he suggested, noting that those final four yards were the most difficult ones on the field. Saunders defended his decision by suggesting that the implementation of the nation's largest corporate merger marked the logical progression of his career trajectory. "I took this job because I think I can make the greatest contribution of which I am capable," he emphasized, "to the eastern railroads."[163]

On October 1, 1963, James Symes, at right, yielded his post as chairman of the board to Stuart Saunders, the former president of the Norfolk & Western. The transition of power, from a highly skilled railroader to an attorney with impeccable political connections, attested to the importance—and the difficulty—of guiding the Penn Central merger application through the regulatory process. *AP Photo/Warren M. Winterbottom.*

The training, personality, and political street smarts that Califano described gave Saunders the skills he needed to orchestrate the perfect merger. His legal background and political connections were essential for steering the merger through the Interstate Commerce Commission and the Justice Department. Symes thought that Saunders "is an excellent witness"—an invaluable quality during the interminable hearings that accompanied the Penn Central application. Saunders also held the respect of other railroad presidents, representatives from the coal industry and other shippers, investors, and bankers, Symes concluded. Saunders's willingness to eschew any fixed ideology also made him extraordinarily adept at achieving compromise and consensus. "He was a problem-solver," recalled attorney Basil Cole. "In my opinion, he was a terrible manager, but the world's greatest problem solver." William Lashley, the public-relations expert, suggested that "Saunders was a deal maker, and Saunders also argued for compromise" and was someone who "would work every angle that he could to get his job done." In his single-minded commitment to merge the Pennsylvania Railroad with the New York Central, there was nonetheless a very real possibility that Saunders might destroy the company he was attempting to save. The extent to which Saunders was willing to compromise, to get the job done, was itself a compromise. If he yielded too little to those who opposed the merger, he risked the possibility that the ICC or the courts would bar the consolidation. If he gave away too much, he might erode the savings the merger was supposed to achieve.[164]

When he moved to Philadelphia, Saunders was not altogether in unfamiliar territory. Several of his PRR colleagues, including Bevan, had served with him on the board of the Norfolk & Western. Saunders's new office at the Pennsylvania Railroad headquarters at Six Penn Center was just down the hall from the one that he had at his disposal, when he was the N&W's president. He asked Lashley, who had done so much to shape his image as a traditional-yet-progressive railroad executive, to accompany him to Philadelphia, as the PRR's assistant vice president in charge of public relations and advertising. A. Paul Funkhouser, the N&W's assistant general counsel, also accepted a new position with the PRR, as an assistant vice president.[165]

The transition of power rippled through the executive ranks. Herman Pevler, who spent many years working for the PRR before taking charge of the Wabash, replaced Saunders as the president of the Norfolk & Western. David E. Smucker, the president of the Detroit, Toledo & Ironton, became the PRR's vice president in charge of operations. The reshuffling of personnel among the firms in the Pennsylvania Railroad's orbit did little to silence critics in the Justice Department and elsewhere, who feared that the company's senior managers were poised to monopolize the rail network in the Northeast. David Bevan, promoted to the PRR's chief financial officer and chairman of the Finance Committee, possessed marginally greater authority after Saunders took charge of the PRR. He hoped that Saunders would be more receptive to his repeated calls for fiscal discipline than Symes had been. To the extent that Bevan ever believed that he might serve as Symes's replacement, he was nonetheless disappointed in the turn of events. He felt increasingly ostracized by his fellow executives, and as a diversion began to explore private

investment opportunities. Jim Newell suffered the most. As the vice president in charge of operations, he clashed with Traffic Department head Fred Carpi and incurred so much enmity that he survived only because Symes protected his job. That shield included an opportunity for escape, and Newell became increasingly involved in the intermodal operations at Trailer Train. With his guardian headed for retirement, Newell wisely became the president of Trailer Train, with Smucker replacing him at the Pennsylvania Railroad.

The personnel changes that followed Saunders's arrival were but a prelude to more sweeping modifications to the corporate structure and traffic patterns. In 1955, Symes decentralized the railroad, transforming three regions and their associated divisions into a system consisting of nine decentralized regions. Relying on advice from the consulting firm Robert Heller & Associates, Symes suggested that regional executives would be able to adapt quickly to unique local conditions, without submitting routine operating matters to corporate headquarters for approval. Problems soon emerged, however, as it became clear that the new system could not adequately accommodate interregional traffic. TrucTrain service accelerated soon after the development of the nine-region system. In March 1955, the PRR handled 1,010 trailers, equivalent to about 250 per week. By the summer of 1963, the company was routinely transporting more than four thousand trailers each week. It was one of the few bright spots in an otherwise dismal freight-traffic picture, yet those vital long-distance movements crossed numerous regional boundaries.[166]

The PRR was also one of the first carriers to adopt the concept of unit trains, consisting of dedicated sets of cars that moved directly from mines to power plants without expensive and time-consuming yard switching. Railroad executives had always taken coal traffic for granted, as it was ill-suited to long-distance truck transportation, and most mines did not have direct access to inland waterways. By the mid-1950s, however, two threats emerged to the Pennsylvania Railroad's coal traffic. One came from coal-slurry pipelines, which transported pulverized coal mixed with water. In 1951, the Pittsburgh Consolidation Coal Company completed a 17,000-foot-long demonstration pipeline at Cadiz, Ohio. Company president George H. Love, who had long complained of high railroad rates, declared the project a success and worth the half-million dollars spent to develop it. In 1954, the Cleveland Electric Illuminating Company pledged to invest more than $2 million in a full-scale commercial slurry pipeline stretching across 110 miles of Pennsylvania Railroad territory. The company's director of purchasing anticipated savings of $1.25 per ton, compared to rail rates. "It may be that the high cost of transporting coal by rail," observers noted, "will lead to a vast change in the method of handling coal." If that assessment were correct, it was a change that would destroy the Pennsylvania Railroad and a great many others. Another threat stemmed from a proposed coal conveyor belt, linking Lake Erie and the Ohio River. Its principal backers were the rubber and steel companies located in Akron and Youngstown, a region of northeastern Ohio that generated a substantial portion of the PRR's traffic and revenues. Although proposals dated to 1949, it was not until the spring of 1955 that the Ohio General Assembly began to discuss the prospect of granting Riverlake Belt Conveyor Lines the power of eminent domain. During the decades that followed, railroad opposition, financing issues, environmental concerns, and resistance from landowners doomed both the coal-slurry pipelines and the conveyor belts. As the PRR struggled to survive the recessionary economy of the late 1950s, however, executives could not take chances with the railroad's most important commodity.[167]

The first unit-train experiments took place in 1962, ferrying gravel from a quarry in Cable, Ohio, forty miles to a processing plant in Columbus. The PRR soon signed a contract with Pennsylvania Power & Light to move coal from mines located in Indiana County, Pennsylvania, to a generating station along the Delaware River. The increased operating efficiency associated with unit trains permitted significant rate reductions. So did changes in ICC tariff policies, which now permitted rate reductions even in areas not subject to water-carrier competition. The ICC also abandoned its earlier instance that trainload rather than carload rates constituted unlawful discrimination against smaller shippers. Traffic increased rapidly, as the PRR, the Baltimore & Ohio, and the Norfolk & Western repeatedly undercut one another's rates. By the summer of 1964, the Pennsylvania Railroad was operating more than three hundred unit trains per month. As with TrucTrain service, they moved long distances, usually without changing motive power, and they were similarly ill-suited to the decentralized nine-region organizational structure.[168]

The ninefold duplication of various staff functions also created unnecessary expense and a top-heavy management structure. The 43 percent decrease in the workforce that occurred between December 1955 and December 1962 was not matched by a corresponding reduction in the number of managers. "Each of these . . . individuals," complained Allen Greenough in January 1963, "have, in the interim since the jobs were created, justified their existence," regardless of whether their services were vital to

the company. A few months later, Greenough and Symes addressed some of those deficiencies by placing engineering, equipment, and maintenance-of-way personnel on an interregional basis.[169]

As the Pennsylvania Railroad's new chairman, Saunders soon dispensed with the dysfunctional nine-region structure. The new organization, which became effective on March 1, 1964, established three new regions—Eastern, Central, and Western—each with four divisions. The three regional managers retained control over transportation, sales, maintenance, accounting, transportation engineering, and labor relations. Activities pertaining to public relations, industrial development, industrial engineering, accounting, real estate, storekeeping, medical care, claims, and coal and ore sales were stripped from the regions and assigned to the central office. Despite Saunders's claim that the 1964 reorganization created "a complete, closely-knit operating team," executive morale continued to decline. The anxiety was most severe among nonoperating personnel, as nine contingents of managers competed for the three sets of jobs at the regional level. In the end, the PRR found alternate posts for nearly everyone affected by the reorganization. The changes were nonetheless disruptive, as executives fretted about the possibility of relocation or reassignment to less desirable positions. The ongoing merger situation only exacerbated those concerns.[170]

Taking Charge of Transportation Policy

There were indications that Saunders arrived in Philadelphia just in time to save the Penn Central merger. Symes's efforts to locate a successor coincided with the early stages of a decade-long struggle between the Interstate Commerce Commission and the Justice Department, regarding the formulation of national transportation policy. That conflict long predated the 1960s, and it was the attorney general's office rather than the ICC that was responsible for the 1904 *Northern Securities* case that prevented the reordering of the railroad network in the Northwest. Congress subsequently made the situation more complicated. The Transportation Act of 1920, designed to address the weak road–strong road problem, gave the Interstate Commerce Commission the authority to develop consolidation plans. While the ICC could not mandate consolidation, the law suggested that any mergers approved by the agency, in line with national transportation policy, would be exempt from antitrust prosecution. The Transportation Act of 1940, legislated at the end of an economic crisis that attested to the carriers' vulnerability, reinforced those antitrust provisions.

Given the failure of consolidation initiatives over the previous two decades, it was hardly surprising that the new law relieved the ICC of proactive responsibility for transportation planning. The agency would now apply a four-part test to evaluate the effects of merger proposals on employees, competing carriers, the financial well-being of the merger partners, and the public's right of access to adequate transportation services.[171] With national consolidation plans no longer an option, the ICC after 1940 increasingly acquiesced to merger proposals that promised to increase transportation efficiency. The commissioners relied on their newly granted power to mandate inclusion

in a merger application, to protect the weaker railroads. It was that authority that enabled the commissioners to insert Appendix O into the conditions associated with the consolidation of the Norfolk & Western with the Nickel Plate and the Wabash. Any resulting decrease in competition was outside the scope of the Justice Department. If the ICC judged merger proposals to be consistent with the public interest, then the carriers involved "shall be and they are hereby relieved from the operation of the antitrust laws and of all other restraints." Two subsequent Supreme Court decisions reinforced the ICC's authority to grant railroads broad exemptions from antitrust prosecution.[172]

Facing, Three federal officials, none of whom worked for the Interstate Commerce Commission, exerted an outsized influence over the Penn Central merger negotiations. One was Attorney General Robert F. Kennedy, at right, who pledged that the Justice Department would not override the ICC's ruling. By the time of this photo, February 8, 1965, he was a senator representing New York. In that capacity, he demanded that the PRR and the New York Central come to the rescue of the bankrupt New Haven. Nicholas Katzenbach, at center, feared that the Penn Central might monopolize rail transportation in the Northeast. The date is February 8, 1965, during the Senate confirmation hearings that followed President Lyndon Johnson's announcement that he would appoint Katzenbach as Kennedy's successor and Ramsey Clark, at left, as deputy attorney general. *AP Photo.*

For most of the following two decades there were few railroad mergers of any consequence, and the Eisenhower administration showed little interest in antitrust concerns. The 1959 N&W–Virginian merger—which indicated the ICC's willingness to countenance a loss of competition to improve the health of the railroads—likewise attracted little attention from the Justice Department. The subsequent Northern Lines, N&W–Nickel Plate, C&O–B&O, and Penn Central consolidation initiatives gave the ICC commissioners ample opportunity to create a more efficient and profitable transportation network, as Congress had instructed, while largely ignoring the issue of economic concentration.[173]

The spate of merger proposals during the early 1960s nonetheless raised alarm among the senior staff at the Justice Department, now under the command of Robert Kennedy. Antitrust matters were ultimately his responsibility, but issues ranging from the civil rights movement to the Cuban missile crisis occupied much of the attorney general's attention. He delegated matters involving transportation and economic policy to the deputy attorney general, Nicholas deBelleville Katzenbach, who in turn relied on Lee Loevinger, the assistant attorney general in charge of the Antitrust Division. Katzenbach considered Loevinger to be "a terrible administrator" who "could not run his division." Other critics complained of a "scattershot" approach to antitrust actions, and journalists noted "a widespread complaint that the antitrust division has had no policy in the last few years, that it has flailed in various directions without knowing why." Loevinger nonetheless enjoyed the support of Senator Hubert Humphrey and Secretary of Agriculture Orville Freeman, and it took the attorney general some time to arrange a suitably important

alternate post. The situation began to change in June 1963, when the Senate confirmed Loevinger as a member of the Federal Communications Commission.[174]

Loevinger's replacement, State Department official William H. Orrick Jr., lacked prior experience in antitrust prosecutions but accepted the responsibility—"like a good soldier," Katzenbach recalled, "albeit reluctantly." The new head of the Antitrust Division established a Policy Planning Group—what reporters described as "a bright-young-man operation close to Mr. Orrick." He reduced the number of cases under investigation, husbanding the limited resources of the Justice Department by focusing instead on a smaller number of big targets. One, in process since April 1961, included allegations that General Motors monopolized the manufacture of diesel-electric railway locomotives, through its Electro-Motive Division. Orrick was concerned that the railroad consolidation proposals—some of the largest and potentially most destructive mergers in history—lay outside the purview of the Justice Department. Deputy Attorney General Katzenbach did not share that perspective, and he was content to allow the ICC to have the final say in the matter. In the autumn of 1963—shortly before Saunders replaced Symes as the PRR's chairman—Orrick asked Robert Kennedy for support. The attorney general's willingness to "tell Nick to get off his lazy behind and get his work done" suggested that the Justice Department was preparing to intercede where the ICC feared to tread.[175]

Orrick served as the Justice Department's representative to the Interagency Committee on Transport Mergers, the group President Kennedy established to coordinate transportation planning. His antitrust concerns prevented that body from developing a consensus regarding the structure of the eastern railroad network. As the undersecretary of commerce for transportation, Clarence Daniel Martin Jr. chaired the committee. He concluded that mergers provided the best hope of rehabilitating the northeastern railroad network and thus promoting the economic prosperity that was central to his area of responsibility. He supported the Penn Central proposal as well as the Norfolk & Western–Nickel Plate and C&O–B&O applications that were pending before the ICC. Orrick was equally steadfast in his opposition to all three mergers. More forcefully than any other senior official in the Justice Department, he stressed the catastrophic decline in competition—something that could never be reversed—and its resulting deleterious effect on businesses and communities throughout the eastern United States. His caustic attitude toward his Commerce Department counterpart reflected that difference of opinion. "Dan Martin is a good friend of mine,"

Orrick recalled, "but he is hopeless; he didn't understand it, he's just not very bright, but he certainly came to the meetings." Robert Kennedy shared Orrick's critical assessment of Martin's leadership of the Interagency Committee. "Now, Dan Martin from the Department of Commerce, since Barrett Prettyman has left, is heading that up," he told Lyndon Johnson in the spring of 1964, "and between ourselves, that's not very satisfactory."[176]

With the attorney general's support, Orrick soon displaced Martin from decision-making authority, and in the process the Justice Department superseded the Commerce Department as the agency that effectively controlled the Interagency Committee on Transport Mergers. Ultimately, Orrick and other Justice Department officials simply marginalized those who disagreed with them. Somewhat ironically, given President Kennedy's intent to coordinate the activities of various federal departments, they pursued an antitrust agenda, irrespective of the recommendations made by the Interagency Committee on Transport Mergers. "They haven't liked the Committee's advice," observed economist Gardner Ackley, who chaired the Council of Economic Advisers. Ackley complained that Justice Department officials "have been operating independently without even keeping the members of the Committee informed." Orrick's assertion that "we moved the Department of Commerce" was likewise a clear indication that the Interagency Committee would ultimately frame its recommendations in antitrust language rather than the jargon of economic efficiency.[177]

Orrick was at a severe disadvantage in his efforts to move the Department of Commerce, however. While he could muster powerful legal arguments against consolidation, any calculation of the economic merits of the various merger proposals fell under the purview of the statisticians and researchers at the Commerce Department. They were under the supervision of Edward Grosvenor Plowman, the deputy under secretary of commerce for transportation, who was an unabashed proponent of mergers. Plowman had established a reputation in the private sector as an expert in logistics, as a traffic manager for the Colorado Fuel & Iron Company, and as vice president in charge of traffic at US Steel. During the Korean War, he served as the director of the Defense Department's Military Traffic Service. Like Pittsburgh & Lake Erie president John Barriger III before him, Plowman's assessment reflected the presence of the two remaining Pocahontas coal carriers. Plowman concluded that the preservation of the northeastern railroad network depended on the assignment of the region's lines to one or the other of two massive systems. One preserved the historic relationship between the

PRR and the Norfolk & Western, with the N&W's prospective merger partners also included. The other mimicked Alfred Perlman's desire to couple the New York Central with the Chesapeake & Ohio and the Baltimore & Ohio. Drawing on his experience as a US Steel executive, he also questioned the wisdom of permitting the Penn Central to implement a near monopoly of rail transportation in the Pittsburgh region. The Baltimore & Ohio did serve the city, but its influence could hardly equal that of the PRR or the Pittsburgh & Lake Erie, an NYC subsidiary. Of greater importance, there would be no independent route between Pittsburgh and the Great Lakes. More broadly, Plowman asserted that any union between the PRR and the NYC would make it impossible to preserve balanced competitive transportation patterns in the Northeast.[178]

Few people supported Plowman's recommendations, but some found them useful. His subordinates at the Commerce Department, who had undertaken most of the research on the northeastern merger situation, instead favored a three-system option—one that entailed ICC approval of all three merger proposals. They concluded that the creation of two systems would produce complacency rather than competition. Because each group could count on a steady stream of coal revenues—from either the N&W or the C&O—managers would find it much easier to subsidize the other, less profitable eastern lines rather than make the innovative and dynamic reforms that were so obviously necessary. Many Commerce Department staffers acknowledged that the Penn Central would be larger than either the N&W–Nickel Plate–Wabash or C&O–B&O systems. Yet it would also be financially weaker. That was a blessing rather than a curse, they suggested, as it would force the managers at Penn Central to put their affairs in order, and quickly. It was the position of the Commerce Department that "a three-system plan represents a more dynamic competitive position than any balanced two-system plan, because the two smaller systems—Norfolk and Western and Chesapeake and Ohio—have sufficient capital resources to improve their services while the high-cost position of Penn-Central would limit their competitive efficiency in the earlier post-merger period"—thus blunting concerns that Penn Central could overwhelm its competitors. In the long run, however, Penn Central executives "would be encouraged in the face of the well financed competition of the two smaller lines to improve their costs." Many officials at the Department of Commerce stressed that it would be unwise to impede the momentum of the three merger applications, just when railroad executives were prepared to collectively remedy the defects of the northeastern railroad situation. "The energy with which the railroad industry was promoting merger was constructive," emphasized Lowell K. Bridwell, Martin's assistant, "and should not be obstructed by government opposition." With an eye toward the rapidly deteriorating situation in New England, Bridwell hinted "that Penn-Central, as a condition for merger, could be maneuvered into solving the New Haven Railroad problem and other vexing problems troubling the government."[179]

Plowman's two-system plan was also anathema to Orrick, for reasons that had little to do with the promotion of economic growth, the momentum of the merger movement, or the rescue of the New Haven. The allocation of every northeastern carrier to one or the other of two equally balanced groups reflected a massive reduction in competition, he asserted, only one step short of a regional transportation monopoly. Nor could Orrick support the competing three-system plan favored by most other Commerce Department officials. To do so would require the Justice Department to reverse course and withdraw its opposition to each of the three merger proposals pending before the ICC. Any such admission that economic necessity superseded an aversion to monopoly power held disturbing implications for the attorney general's involvement in nearly every aspect of the business landscape. Instead, Orrick recommended the creation of four balanced systems. One would be based on the N&W and its affiliates and a second on the combined C&O–B&O. The PRR and the NYC would remain separate, and most of the remaining unaligned carriers would be allocated to one or the other of them. The four-system plan achieved Orrick's principal goal, in that it precluded the creation of Penn Central, yet his approach held several pitfalls. As a matter of transportation economics, it was highly doubtful that the Pennsylvania Railroad and the New York Central, each burdened with a constellation of failing carriers, could survive as independent companies. As a legal matter, Orrick's strategy necessitated that the Justice Department acquiesce to two of the three eastern consolidation proposals under consideration by the ICC, while resolutely battling against a third.

In an effort to blunt opposition from the Department of Commerce, Orrick proposed a fallback option. Some restructuring of the eastern railroad network was necessary, he conceded, and his four-system plan would allow two of the three mergers to proceed. The two consolidations would provide a clear test of whether the economic benefits claimed by merger supporters would come to fruition and whether there would be a significant reduction in competition. Continued opposition to the Penn Central would prevent the further, irreversible contraction of the eastern railroad network. The four-system plan would also demonstrate that competition could stimulate the progressive thinking and innovative business practices that could rescue the railroads—without further mergers, subsidies, or public ownership. His plan would work, Orrick assured the other representatives on the Interagency Committee on Transport Mergers. But if it did not, then and only then would he be prepared to countenance an additional round of mergers, along the lines Plowman had suggested, to couple the Pennsylvania Railroad to the N&W and the New York Central to the C&O and the B&O. Whatever the outcome, the Penn Central merger would never occur. As Bridwell summarized the situation, "the Justice Department, wishing to oppose all the Eastern mergers, accepted the mechanics of the Plowman approach, because it enabled them to oppose the Penn-Central merger, without committing themselves to Plowman's two-system concept."[180]

While the Interagency Committee's nineteen-page analysis of the merger situation in the Northeast relied on data compiled by the Commerce Department, its recommendations provided a clear demonstration of Orrick's strategizing. The committee analyzed six basic plans as well as numerous variants of each. Only two conformed to the three-system plan that included the creation of Penn Central. One left the unaligned railroads to fend for themselves, while the other placed those smaller carriers in the sheltering embrace of the Penn Central, the Norfolk & Western-Nickel Plate, or the Chesapeake & Ohio-Baltimore & Ohio. Neither version was acceptable, and the report emphasized "that no combination which included a Penn-Central merger was in the public interest." Furthermore, the grouping of the strongest carriers into three systems would preclude future restructuring of the northeastern railroads. There was also no clear mechanism to force the Penn Central, N&W, and C&O–B&O groups to accept every unaligned carrier that was in imminent danger of failure.

The study, completed shortly before Symes yielded the PRR's chairmanship to Saunders, disputed managerial assertions regarding the savings associated with the merger, and the members of the Interagency Committee on Transport Mergers were "not in agreement as to whether this sum has been overstated or understated." That perspective, one that was shared by executives from the two railroads, exemplified the nebulous nature of the data used to justify the merger. Despite the presence of Under Secretary of Labor James J. Reynolds on the Interagency Committee, the report showed scant concern for organized labor. It suggested that "the possible adverse effect on employees, and indirectly upon communities, is not in itself a sufficient ground for opposing this merger."[181]

Despite Clarence Martin's advocacy for each of the three mergers on economic grounds, the report reflected Orrick's refusal to accept the creation of Penn Central. "The core of the problem of the Penn-Central merger," the study concluded, "lies in its adverse effect on competition." Orrick insisted that "the railroads are in the process of stabilizing their competitive position vis-à-vis other modes"—a perspective reflected in the collective statement that "neither the PRR nor NYC is in imminent danger of failure." The more likely outcome was that the Penn Central would dominate the northeastern railroad network, monopolize service to many communities and industries, and drive the region's small carriers into bankruptcy. The committee acknowledged that the company would be "weak in some respects," principally its high ratio of employees to mileage and revenues and its dependence on connecting lines for a large portion of its coal traffic. Those would be more than offset by the Penn Central's dominance in the Pittsburgh region, its control over the best routes between the East Coast and the Midwest, and its influence over freight rate bureaus.[182]

The outright rejection of either of the three-system options led the committee to consider multiple variations of a four-system plan, an arrangement strongly favored by the Justice Department. Of those, the one supported by Orrick and "tentatively" endorsed by the committee, "attempts to take into account proposals already pending before the ICC and achieve a balance in as many ways as possible between each system, improved service, optimum competition between key cities, and other factors." The committee, with Orrick's blessing, acknowledged that "the control of the B&O by the C&O would appear to be in the public interest." That system would also include the three carriers that were historically tied to those companies—the Reading, the Jersey Central, and the Western Maryland. The arrangement also accepted as inevitable ICC approval of the consolidation of the Norfolk & Western, the Nickel Plate, and the Wabash.[183] The Erie-Lackawanna and the New Haven would be included in the N&W system, partly to provide access to New York and New England but principally to give those companies a refuge from impending collapse. The New York Central would retain control of the Boston & Albany, the Peoria & Eastern, and the Pittsburgh & Lake Erie while gaining the Boston & Maine, the Lehigh Valley, the Monon, and the Chicago & Eastern Illinois. The Pennsylvania Railroad would change the least, with the inclusion of the Detroit, Toledo & Ironton and the Ann Arbor. The report suggested that the PRR should also "be offered the D&H, which might prove attractive because of its earning record and its access to Albany, Montreal and Northern New England."[184]

The Interagency Committee's four-system plan, developed at Orrick's behest, contained some attractive features for the Pennsylvania Railroad. Significantly, it enabled the company to escape the distribution of the weakest unaligned carriers—particularly the New Haven—all of which went to the other systems. From the perspective of Symes and Saunders, however, it contained a fatal defect, in that it forever precluded the consolidation of the PRR and the NYC. The same was true of the committee's fallback option, in the event that the four-system plan failed to adequately rationalize the northeastern railroad network. The members of the Interagency Committee considered three variations of Plowman's two-system plan, even if it did "not seem feasible at this time for the Government to recommend such a drastic step." Two of the variants joined the PRR with the Norfolk & Western, while the third offered the C&O–B&O as a substitute. Even in a stripped-down two-system Northeast, however, the Pennsylvania Railroad and the New York Central would never be permitted to combine.[185]

Orrick had good reason to be pleased with the recommendations of the Interagency Committee, as they reflected the position the Justice Department had developed and would continue to support over the next four years. The creation of three eastern systems—Symes's cherished goal, the one endorsed by many in the Commerce Department—was absolutely out of bounds. A four-system East was the only viable alternative, with a further reduction to two systems an unlikely worst-case scenario. The N&W–Nickel Plate–Wabash and the C&O–B&O mergers were acceptable, while the Penn Central was not. Merger applications called for a cautious, prudent, and conservative approach, while the consolidation of the PRR and the NYC would be both radical and irreversible. Thus, the committee concluded, "it would not seem wise for the Government to take any irrevocable position that did not leave room for consideration" of new information and changing circumstances. As Orrick demanded, the maintenance of competition and the prohibition of transportation monopolies took precedence over the economic well-being of the Pennsylvania Railroad and the New York Central.[186]

The assignment of the New Haven to the Norfolk & Western was an important element of Orrick's strategy, "assuming that studies already under way in the

Department of Commerce . . . indicate that this is the appropriate course." Plowman also supported the allocation of the New Haven to the N&W, although for different reasons. The deputy under secretary of commerce for transportation defined the issue in terms of economic balance, judging that the strongest of the big systems would have the best chance of rehabilitating the weakest of the New England lines. Orrick conceded the point, but he principally sought to remove any possible incentives that favored the combination of the Pennsylvania Railroad and the New York Central. By decoupling the New Haven from the Penn Central merger application, Orrick removed one of the most compelling arguments in favor of the consolidation and made ICC approval that much less likely. Commerce Department staffers were inclined to agree. They "considered whether the solution of the problem of the New Haven by inclusion of that carrier in the proposed Penn-Central system would outweigh the adverse effects of the merger. The conclusion was in the negative." Something had to be done with the struggling New England railroad, however. Norfolk & Western executives were distancing themselves from their earlier, and remarkably vague, promises to assume control over the Erie-Lackawanna. It was highly unlikely that they would accept the New Haven as well.[187]

The members of the Interagency Committee acknowledged only two potential difficulties with the plan to rearrange the northeastern railroad network and prevent a looming transportation crisis. "The conclusions must necessarily be tentative in terms of precisely which of the smaller carriers should go with each system," they admitted. The larger problem, they conceded, was that "there is no simple way to force the carriers to accept the lines which the Committee has assigned to them." Based on experience, they knew full well that "the ICC, of course, has limited authority to impose conditions on its approval of any merger." The realistic assessment of the limits to the ICC's power, coupled with the use of the word *force*, suggested that the federal courts would play an important role in delineating the merger landscape. While Clarence Martin and his staff at the Commerce Department evaluated the economic effects of the various merger proposals and the assignment of weak carriers to larger systems, their influence over that process steadily decreased. A more legalistic strategy indicated the primacy of William Orrick and the Justice Department. The Interagency Committee on Transport Mergers would soon be paralyzed by disagreements among representatives from the agencies that comprised it. Far from enabling PRR executives to

implement their merger agenda, with minimal federal interference, that paralysis would delay and complicate those efforts.[188]

At their September 1963 meeting, the members of the Interagency Committee distilled their nineteen-page report to a two-page set of conclusions. The brief document even more clearly reflected Orrick's willingness to accept two mergers, to prevent a third. The committee emphasized that "the Government does not oppose rationalization per se of the Eastern District, and in fact feels that some rationalization in this area is inevitable." That restructuring included the N&W and the C&O–B&O applications, which "would appear to be in the public interest if the N&W system were willing to assume control of the E-L and the NH." However, "the Penn-Central merger as presently proposed would not be in the public interest because of its substantial adverse effect on competition and the ability of other carriers to survive, and the fact that it forecloses other more balanced restructuring both now and in the future."[189]

The conclusions of the Interagency Committee were not unanimous, however. Orrick, backed by Assistant Secretary of Labor Reynolds and Council of Economic Advisors representative John Lewis, voted in favor of the four-system strategy and in opposition to the Penn Central merger. Martin opposed the recommendations, on behalf of the Commerce Department, yet he did not endorse the two-system plan his deputy, E. Grosvenor Plowman, had recommended. With the urging of other Commerce Department officials, Martin concluded that "merger is essential in the eastern district." He also accepted that "a three-system plan evolved by the railroads is a workable system having the support of industry," and that "any severe opposition to the industry's own policy would curb initiative and destroy the benefits of merger." In particular, Martin suggested, "a Penn-Central merger would solve certain severe problems in the east; notably, it would take over the New Haven Railroad with its debt to the Government." Within a short time, the salvation of the New Haven as a condition of the Penn Central merger would become increasingly popular within the Interagency Committee, the ICC, and the White House. In September 1963, however, Martin was outvoted three to one. Orrick possessed a clear majority in his efforts to block the Penn Central, but one that stopped well short of an absolute mandate. He accordingly discussed the matter with Attorney General Robert Kennedy, who in turn spoke with the president. The position of the Justice Department prevailed. Orrick received permission to appear before the Interstate

Commerce Commission to present his perspective on the Penn Central merger and not that of Clarence Martin.[190]

On October 1, bolstered by the Interagency Committee's majority recommendation and confident of Robert Kennedy's support, Orrick publicly attacked the Penn Central merger proposal. His timing was impeccable. Stuart Saunders became the PRR's new chairman that morning, and the ICC hearings that had been underway for fourteenth months were scheduled to end the following day. At such a late date in the proceedings, none of the interested parties would be able to present evidence challenging the position of the Justice Department. Moreover, and because he was not officially a party to the case, Orrick could not be recalled as a witness or subjected to cross-examination. In reading a prepared statement, Orrick reiterated the familiar admission that the Northeast "would benefit by some rationalization of the existing railroad facilities." That concession justified Orrick's abandonment of the Justice Department's opposition to the "ultimate integration of the Chesapeake & Ohio and the Baltimore & Ohio, with proper conditions which may be imposed by the Commission." He was less certain about the N&W–Nickel Plate–Wabash application, which "as currently filed does not in our opinion adequately protect the public interest." While not implacably opposed to the consolidation, Orrick insisted that the Justice Department would demand several concessions. They included PRR divestiture of Norfolk & Western stock and the inclusion in the N&W system of the Erie-Lackawanna and—pending further study—the New Haven. The proposed allocation of the New Haven was diametrically opposed to Clarence Martin's recommendation that it go to the Penn Central and reflected Orrick's determination to prevent the PRR and the NYC from using the bankrupt New England carrier as a bargaining chip.[191]

In contrast to his willingness to countenance a restructuring of the eastern railroad network, Orrick emphasized "the Government's conclusion is that a Pennsylvania-New York Central merger is not in the public interest." He asserted that "the combination of these two large railroads would eliminate a vast amount of beneficial rail competition" and "would also endanger the service capabilities, the prospects, and even the continued existence of several smaller railroads." Orrick also cautioned the ICC to await the outcome of the N&W and C&O proposals before committing irretrievably to a course of action that would give the Penn Central dominance over transportation in the Northeast. "Finally, and of very great importance in our view," he emphasized, "the proposed merger of these two systems would preclude more balanced restructuring of

the Eastern district railroads both now and in the future." His views were a direct challenge to Symes's plan for a three-system East and a rebuke to the ICC commissioners who seemed poised to support it. It mattered little that, as those commissioners later noted, "the [Justice] Department submitted no evidence in support of its four-system plan, but only an opinion that it is preferable to the consolidated rail systems that have emerged in the East." Orrick was nonetheless determined to oversee transportation planning, a strategy that required him to disparage the ICC's capabilities in those areas.[192]

Stuart Saunders, confronting the first of many crises he would face as the PRR's new chairman, made no immediate comment to Orrick's statement. The company's general solicitor, Windsor Cousins, nonetheless indicated that Saunders was "very sorry" and suggested that Orrick demonstrated "poor taste by coming to our party and approving everybody's merger but ours." On October 11, Saunders broke his silence. He called the criteria established by the Interagency Committee on Transport Mergers "impractical and unrealistic" and insisted that the policies of the Kennedy administration "would have tragic consequences, including bankruptcy, for a number of railroads." When "the committee undertook to suggest a complete realignment of railroads in the East," he asserted, they demonstrated a shocking ignorance of the conditions that faced the PRR and the other railroads that served the area. What might have made sense in the 1920s no longer did, Saunders insisted, and, he emphasized, "the plain fact is that there just is not enough railroad business to support four systems." Above all, Saunders condemned the intervention of the Justice Department—and the federal government as a whole—in a matter that he considered to be the prerogative of private enterprise. "If all of these proposals could be consummated fairly promptly," he said in reference to the various merger applications before the ICC, "the Eastern segment of the industry could get down to reshaping itself."[193]

Procedurally, the Justice Department possessed no more influence than any of the railroad executives, shippers, labor leaders, or community representatives who testified at the regulatory hearings. Orrick's opinion nonetheless carried disproportionate weight. His acceptance of the Chesapeake & Ohio's control of the Baltimore & Ohio removed the last significant obstacle to that consolidation, and the Supreme Court gave its assent on December 9. The N&W–Nickel Plate merger proposal would take longer, but there now seemed little reason to doubt the outcome. Penn Central was another matter, however. Orrick's opposition carried with it the implied threat that the Kennedy administration could create endless political and legal barriers. Saunders's most important task, therefore, was to neutralize Justice Department opposition to the merger. He used his political influence to ensure that private enterprise shaped public goals rather than the other way around. On October 25, Saunders and Perlman were at the White House, in conversation with Orrick, the other members of the Interagency Committee on Transport Mergers, and the president's aide, Myer Feldman. Orrick observed that the two railroad executives "took sharp issue with the administration statement of policy made to the ICC three weeks ago" and pleaded for more sympathetic treatment. Saunders was apparently pleased with the outcome of the meeting. "They listened very sympathetically," he told reporters. "They gave good attention to what we had to say." Saunders's optimism was not misguided, as the federal official whose opinion mattered the most was indeed paying attention. When Orrick briefed Robert Kennedy on the outcome of the meeting, the attorney general asked only one, rhetorical question regarding Saunders's entreaties—"I would like to cooperate, wouldn't I?"[194]

The president's death, a month later, scarcely affected Saunders's campaign to win the support of the White House, the Justice Department, and the Interagency Committee on Transport Mergers. "If you ever knew Stuart Saunders," Orrick recalled, "he wasn't stopping at any committee like that. He was in to President Johnson; he was in with Bob" Kennedy, who remained as attorney general following his brother's assassination. Johnson is "a good friend of mine," Saunders boasted to reporters. "I had a good relationship with the White House, yes. A lot of these people are good friends of mine.... That was no problem." In typical Saunders fashion, his political affiliations were nonetheless selective, conditional, and grounded in an ulterior motive. "He was a friend of the President's," Joseph Califano recalled, "and he was, I think, [a] financial supporter of the Democratic Party, or at least the Lyndon Johnson Democratic Party." Between June 1964 and December 1968, Saunders visited the White House at least eighteen times, for a variety of reasons.[195] Regardless of the stated purpose, each encounter afforded Saunders an opportunity to advocate for the merger. Saunders was a member of Johnson's Advisory Committee on Labor-Management Policy and the Balance of Payments Advisory Committee. He continued to support the corporate tax-cut proposal that began in the Kennedy administration, and after the measure became law in February 1964, he noted that "all of the good things that were predicted—and none of the bad ones—have happened." Saunders joined a Business Advisory Committee to help administer nearly

a billion dollars in federal funds, part of Johnson's War on Poverty. Johnson considered Saunders for the secretary of the treasury, before settling on Henry H. Fowler for that post. Following the 1964 presidential election, the *New York Times* described Saunders as "one of the businessmen who lined up support for President Johnson." Fowler was more effusive in his praise, suggesting that "Stuart Saunder's [*sic*] career is a kind of parable, an epitome, of what the full function of the businessman ought to be in today's world. For he has excelled in the three primary roles which that world demands of a business leader—the role of leader in his company and his industry; the role of leader in his home community, his city and his state; and the role of leader in national affairs."[196]

Concessions

In his role as a leader and in his bid to win support for the Penn Central merger, Saunders would have to overcome considerable opposition from state and local governments, organized labor, and—most ominously of all—the US Department of Justice. To do so, he was prepared to make substantial concessions, each of which was likely to be expensive. Saunders nonetheless operated with the assurance, contained in the Patchell report, that the consolidation would generate more than $81 million in annual savings, once the merger was fully implemented. Many investment bankers and railroad experts openly asserted that the benefits were likely to be much larger than that, perhaps more than $100 million a year. That gave Saunders a considerable budget for compromise, as he balanced the estimated cost of the concessions against the predicted gains resulting from the creation of Penn Central. There were only two potential pitfalls, neither of which seemed to concern Saunders. The first was that, in an exuberant flurry of nonstop dealmaking, he might grant favor after favor, each individually inconsequential but collectively burdening the new company with massive obligations. The second was that he might be overestimating the savings associated with the merger while underestimating the cost of the arrangements he made to achieve it. Either outcome would be problematic, and both together would be disastrous.

Saunders acknowledged that the merger faced widespread opposition from state governments and local communities. Many of those constituencies demanded minor concessions or asked the ICC to include the Erie-Lackawanna in the Norfolk & Western—outcomes Saunders was perfectly willing to accept. The situation in his home state of Pennsylvania was far more complex and correspondingly difficult to untangle. When David Lawrence left the governor's mansion in January 1963, a committee he appointed was still working on a computer-assisted study to determine how Penn Central might affect the commonwealth. His successor, Republican William Scranton, permitted the research to continue, but he did not indicate whether he would reverse his predecessor's opposition to the merger. Scranton asked the Governor's Council of Business and Industry to study the matter, and on September 5, they recommended approval, "provided that suitable assurances are received that all communities needing it will continue to receive adequate rail transportation." Saunders became the PRR's chairman less than a month later, and his negotiations with the governor continued through the final months of 1963. On January 18, 1964, Scranton suggested that he might grant "conditional approval" to the merger. A few days later, one of Scranton's close confidants indicated that the governor "is leaning in that direction" but opaquely emphasized that "it is kind of obvious that this is not a 'yes' or 'no' matter in any case."[197]

Scranton did not make up his mind until February 8. He agreed to support the merger but extracted a heavy price for doing so. Scranton asked the ICC to impose eight conditions, each of which was certain to prove financially or politically costly to the Penn Central. Several of those related to freight service, including the retention of existing through trains between Philadelphia and the West, a year's advance notice for reductions that affected local communities, and a requirement that the Penn Central obtain ICC authority prior to the discontinuance of trains. Residents from Erie reacted with panic to the section of the Patchell plan that recommended the closing of the city's coal-handling facilities, and Scranton insisted that the Penn Central would also have to maintain its routes to that city. The company would have to provide—and pay for—retraining programs for displaced employees. For eight years following the consummation of the merger, the Penn Central would not be able to curtail interchange traffic with feeder railroads, principally the anthracite carriers in the northeastern portion of the state. Saunders also agreed to invest in improved facilities and service at Philadelphia's Delaware River waterfront. Finally, in a manner that was certain to inflame the long-standing rivalry between Pennsylvania and New York, Scranton insisted that the Penn Central headquarters should be located in Philadelphia. None of those conditions would become effective until they were mandated by the ICC. Saunders nonetheless indicated that he would not object to the commonwealth's conditional acceptance of the merger, and

there was thus every likelihood that Scranton would get what he wanted.[198]

The situation in Philadelphia mirrored the complexity of developments at the state level. Scranton's conditions were insufficient to mollify municipal residents, but they did help to reduce the intensity of local opposition. Despite Saunders's promises, however, the location of the Penn Central's headquarters was by no means settled. Examiners Lyle and Darmstadter knew a political minefield when they saw one, and they diplomatically suggested that it would not be appropriate for the ICC to choose between New York and Philadelphia.[199] The local chamber of commerce favored the merger from the beginning, but the municipal government did not—in part because officials feared that the Penn Central would destroy the Reading and thus preclude efforts to improve commuter service on its suburban routes. As late as June 1964, municipal officials asserted that "no city, no State, and certainly no shipper, can stand before this Leviathan"—a position that accorded well with the stance of the Antitrust Division of the Justice Department. Representatives from the Delaware River Port Authority feared that reductions in freight service would divert shipments to New York Harbor, Baltimore, and Hampton Roads.[200]

Under Saunders's relentless pressure, municipal opposition began to dissipate. The PRR had for some time employed former mayor Richardson Dilworth as a consultant and a lobbyist, principally to secure federal funding for passenger-rail services. The *Philadelphia Inquirer* noted that Dilworth was ideally placed to encourage Philadelphians to support the merger. So was Walter Annenberg, the paper's owner, whom Saunders courted assiduously. Despite his wealth and influence, Annenberg's Jewish faith kept him outside the orbit of Main Line Protestant society. Saunders perceived an opportunity, and soon after he became the PRR's chairman, he made a point of befriending the publisher. He sponsored Annenberg for membership at Philadelphia's Gulph Mills Golf Club, perhaps out of friendship, but more likely as a calculated political move. The precise motivations made little difference, however, as the membership committee immediately blackballed Annenberg's application—an outcome that did not bode well for Alfred Perlman, should the Penn Central's headquarters be located in Philadelphia. Howard Butcher, one of the railroad's most influential investors, also kept company with Annenberg, as did fellow director John Dorrance, the chairman of Campbell's Soup. Friendships aside, Annenberg was a sincere and enthusiastic supporter of the Pennsylvania Railroad and concluded that the welfare of that company, and its successor, would rebound to the benefit of Philadelphia. Happily for Saunders, he was also a determined foe of Milton Shapp, whom he battled relentlessly in the pages of the *Philadelphia Inquirer* and elsewhere.[201]

By the summer of 1964, the resistance of city officials appeared to be softening. On August 19, Mayor James H. J. Tate, Dilworth's successor, attended a meeting with Saunders and representatives of various labor unions. Saunders promised that the Penn Central would expedite shipments to the city's docks, emphasizing that "the service we give has a definite relation to our financial capacity." Despite his promises to Scranton, some six months earlier, Saunders informed Tate that he could not yet guarantee that the Penn Central would be based in Philadelphia. That was a problem, and Tate explained that Saunders was "a very persuasive person who has presented a very positive program, but the location of the headquarters is very much at the heart of the city's position." Yet Saunders could offer one further reassurance, one he had not been able to promise Governor Scranton. In the presence of union officials, he noted that labor and management had reached an accord on personnel matters and that job losses would be minimal. It was not enough to guarantee municipal support for the merger, but it was sufficient for Tate to acknowledge that the matter was now "very much under consideration."[202]

The labor agreement that Saunders highlighted on August 19 became one of the most important, expensive, and controversial concessions associated with the Penn Central merger. Like many of Saunders's other initiatives, it represented his determination to overcome all obstacles to the merger, regardless of their cost, coupled with an inability to predict how long the approval process would take. By the spring of 1964, the state of labor relations on the Pennsylvania Railroad, the New York Central, and the other railroads in the United States was turbulent and uncertain. Legislation enacted by Congress in August 1963 prevented a nationwide strike, but it did not end the controversy over crew size or the assignment of firemen to freight trains. On November 26, four days after Kennedy's assassination, the presidential arbitrators that he appointed concluded that the railroads could eliminate 90 percent of freight-service firemen. The ruling affected more than forty thousand employees, the vast majority of whom would keep their jobs until they resigned, retired, were dismissed for cause, or died. No one would follow in their footsteps, however, or fill their places in union membership rolls, and labor leaders soon filed lawsuits challenging the decision. Furthermore, so long as state

full-crew laws remained in effect, there was little the railroads could do to eliminate redundant employees. With strong support from the PRR and the NYC, Governor Nelson Rockefeller sponsored a bill in the New York Assembly to repeal full-crew legislation enacted in 1913. In March 1964, it went down to defeat. Farther west, a wildcat strike on the Illinois Central threatened to mushroom into a nationwide walkout. President Johnson secured a fifteen-day cooling-off period, but not every worker got the message. Picketers delayed commuter trains in New York City, the PRR canceled several long-distance passenger trains, and trainmen in Columbus, Ohio, stayed home. A separate dispute, involving 160,000 shopworkers, had been underway since May 1963. Another presidential emergency board, established a year later, failed to achieve results, and the president extended its tenure until June. In Vermont, the managers of the Rutland Railway ceased operations rather than yield to organized labor. To the south, strikers along the line of the Florida East Coast Railway were shooting at locomotives operated by replacement crews, dynamiting tracks, and wrecking trains.[203]

Finally, on the evening of April 22, 1964, Johnson announced that federal mediators had resolved the work-rules dispute that began in February 1959. The president pressured railroad executives to implement pay raises for one hundred thousand employees, a concession that would cost $64 million annually. Union leaders accepted changes to work assignments and permitted the removal of firemen from freight trains, with an attendant saving of $317 million a year. Johnson and his advisors nonetheless acknowledged that confrontations were likely to continue. The lawsuit filed by the operating brotherhoods was still in process, and it would be several more days before the Supreme Court declined to hear the case. Nor did the settlement eliminate state full-crew laws, which were certain to produce lengthy political and legal battles. A representative from the Brotherhood of Locomotive Firemen and Enginemen complained of the railroads' arbitrary application of the new rules and indicated that "our people are being incited to riot." Wildcat strikes soon erupted, including one at the PRR's Conway Yard.[204]

Johnson was determined to avoid any further situations that might antagonize the railroad unions. The Penn Central merger, with the attendant possibility of substantial job losses, was a case in point. Representatives from the Pennsylvania Railroad and the New York Central were scheduled to present their case to the members of the Interagency Committee on Transport Mergers on April 23, the day following Johnson's labor-relations triumph. While

William Orrick and his staff at the Antitrust Division of the Justice Department were not particularly concerned with the merger's effect on organized labor, Johnson was. In anticipation of the meeting, and even as he prepared to announce that he had prevented a national strike, the president asked Attorney General Robert Kennedy for advice. Kennedy explained that the Justice Department initially opposed the Chesapeake & Ohio's application to control the Baltimore & Ohio as well as a never-consummated proposal to merge the Santa Fe and the Western Pacific. The attorney general acknowledged that his office had since reversed its position in both cases but continued to block the formation of the Penn Central. Johnson's reply—"Can you give me any suggestion what I ought to do?"—indicated that Saunders's ties to the Democratic Party had not yet influenced White House policy. Kennedy cautioned the president that "you have to take some care in saying, you wouldn't want to take it on yourself, but that the people in government have the responsibility to look at it, you'd make sure that they'd looked at it and considered all points of view, obviously you haven't had a chance to examine it yourself so you couldn't say but you'd make sure that everybody got a fair shake and that's what we want too." The advice was noncommittal and stopped well short of an endorsement for the merger. Mindful of the disaster he had narrowly averted and sensing the likelihood of future conflicts between management and labor, Johnson observed that "if the Pennsylvania and the New York Central merge, it would probably throw people out of work." Kennedy admitted that the C&O–B&O consolidation had produced precisely that outcome—although not to the extent that the unions had feared. "That's why the unions would be opposed to it," he advised Johnson, "so that's why I don't think you could probably go further." When the members of the Interagency Committee discussed the matter with PRR and NYC officials on the following day, it was evident that labor opposition would be an insurmountable obstacle to a successful outcome for the merger hearings.[205]

In addition to Johnson's concerns, the ICC would not have permitted wholesale job losses to accompany the Penn Central merger. The issue had come up many times before on various carriers, thanks to mechanization and the overall contraction of the railroads. In May 1936, the Washington Agreement provided displaced employees with severance pay equivalent to 60 percent of their wages for six months to five years, depending on seniority. It was the outcome of a collective-bargaining agreement and did not necessarily set a precedent for the future. While most union officials were willing to accept that arrangement,

Brotherhood of Railroad Trainmen president Alexander F. Whitney demanded more generous benefits. At his urging, Representative Vincent Harrington (Dem., Iowa) sponsored a bill that instructed the ICC to provide explicit guarantees to displaced workers. Under the 1944 *Oklahoma* conditions, managers possessed the authority to reassign employees, so long as they guaranteed at least the same level of pay for the next four years. The stipulations initially applied to railroads that had abandoned operations or sold routes to another carrier—something that would not be the case with Penn Central—but they soon became commonplace whenever there was a contraction in employment. In 1948, the ICC made significant modifications to that doctrine when it articulated the *New Orleans* conditions. Because the job losses associated with the completion of a new passenger terminal in New Orleans would not take place for another four years—precisely when the *Oklahoma* conditions would expire—the ICC developed a hybrid of the Washington and *Oklahoma* models. Employees would enjoy *Oklahoma* protections for those four years, eliminating the incentive for the affected railroads to proactively cull the labor rolls before the new station opened. After four years, when large-scale layoffs were likely, displaced workers would enjoy legally guaranteed severance benefits equivalent to those established under the Washington Agreement.[206]

The *New Orleans* conditions severely constrained Saunders's ability to achieve immediate savings from the merger, through the rapid displacement of redundant employees. The apparent resolution of the nationwide work-rules dispute and the agreement regarding the elimination of firemen was not likely to help much, either, given the need to offer severance pay. Still, prompt approval of the merger would set the clock running on the *New Orleans* conditions and eventually ensure a reduction in the labor force. Much had changed since 1948, however, and labor leaders saw clear evidence that the decline of the eastern railroads, coupled with the concessions regarding firemen, were causing steep reductions in union membership. Rather than fight for higher wages, shorter hours, and improved working conditions, as they had in the past, labor organizers sought to preserve the status quo, enabling their members to remain employed until retirement. It was an understandable strategy, given the difficulty that displaced workers in their fifties and sixties were likely to encounter as they made the transition to a new career—even with a few years of severance pay in their pockets.

During the spring of 1964, the unions were ideally positioned to implement their goals in the context of the Penn Central merger. Mike Quill's Transport Workers

Union had shut down the Pennsylvania Railroad, and the combative labor leader was vowing to create even more disruptions. Johnson had just finished resolving a drawn-out dispute between management and labor, and he did not want to face another one during an election year—particularly at a time when confrontations over the issue of civil rights were increasingly occupying the attention of the president and the attorney general. At the state and local level, politicians were advocating vigorously for job protection, retraining programs, and other expensive guarantees to safeguard the economic and political interests of their working-class constituents.

On May 20, Saunders and Perlman reached an accord with most of the labor organizations that would be affected by the merger. The Luna-Saunders agreement reflected the participation of Charles Luna, the president of the Brotherhood of Railroad Trainmen and one of the more aggressive defenders of worker rights, and Stuart Saunders, the PRR chairman who could not allow labor opposition to delay the merger. Slightly less than a month had passed since Robert Kennedy cautioned the president that he could not support the merger until the unions were willing to accept it. George Leighty, the chairman of the Railway Labor Executives' Association, acknowledged that the settlement "provides what the labor organizations themselves agree is adequate protection, and therefore removes this objection to the merger." The pact initially covered seventeen unions, but twenty-three would ultimately participate in the Luna-Saunders agreement.[207] The compromise affected seventy-seven thousand Pennsylvania Railroad and New York Central employees, 75 percent of their combined labor force, and virtually all their unionized workers.[208]

Saunders gained the acquiescence of organized labor, but at a steep price. The Luna-Saunders agreement stipulated that layoffs could occur only in cases where the new company suffered a reduction in traffic and revenues of at least 5 percent, over a thirty-day period. Otherwise, employees at the two predecessor companies could continue to work for Penn Central as long as they desired, and they could only be removed through voluntary resignation, retirement, death, or dismissal for cause. Their paychecks would also continue, without any reduction in wages or fringe benefits, even if there was no work for them to do. With attrition rates averaging 5 percent annually, it seemed reasonable to assume that few redundant workers would be employed for any length of time. The Luna-Saunders agreement contained a further stipulation, however, preventing managers from transferring employees from one craft to another, and likewise restricted their ability to move workers across seniority lines. Union representatives

calculated that PRR and NYC officials possessed a strong incentive to decrease the workforce as much as possible, in anticipation of the reduced staffing needs associated with the consummation of the merger. Accordingly, they received Saunders's guarantee that the provisions would be retroactive to January 1, 1964. Crucially, the reductions in force would begin on the date the merger became effective, rather than on May 20, 1964, when Saunders and Luna reached a settlement. If, as he expected, Saunders could overcome the objections of the Justice Department and other opponents and win quick approval of the merger, then that stipulation was of scant consequence. Any significant delays, however, would require the PRR and the NYC—and ultimately the Penn Central—to maintain thousands of unnecessary workers, year after year, based on 1964 employment levels.[209]

The Luna-Saunders agreement caused further divisions among the four members of the Interagency Committee on Transport Mergers. The previous September, and by a 3–1 vote, they had opposed the Penn Central merger. Only the Commerce Department dissented, based on Under Secretary Clarence Martin's assertion that the Pennsylvania Railroad and the New York Central could only provide adequate transportation by joining forces. With railroad executives willing to restructure the eastern railroad network, he concluded, it would be the height of folly for the federal government to stand in their way. Martin also suggested that the Penn Central could rescue the New Haven. That idea was rapidly gaining popularity, as the condition of the New England carrier worsened and as managers at the Norfolk & Western were making it clear that they wanted nothing to do with the company.

Martin reiterated those arguments in the May 15, 1964, meeting of the Interagency Committee. Orrick had heard Martin's spirited defense of economic efficiency many times before, but he remained opposed to the merger. On May 20, the date of the Luna-Saunders agreement, he wrote a lengthy memo to Myer Feldman, the gatekeeper to the president of the United States, again raising the specter of monopoly. The assistant attorney general was rapidly losing his influence over the Interagency Committee on Transport Mergers, however. Only two people signed the document—John Lewis, the representative from the Council of Economic Advisers, and Charles Schultze, the assistant director of the Bureau of the Budget, who acted in a nonvoting advisory capacity to the committee. The Interagency Committee was now deadlocked on the question of the Penn Central merger. When he organized that body, President Kennedy envisioned a mechanism to bring together the federal officials who were most closely connected to the national transportation system so they could reach consensus and present unified policy recommendations to the White House. Myer Feldman, and by extension President Johnson, now faced a flurry of memos, as dissenting members of the committee attempted to make their own arrangements with the next president.

Two of those missives came from Clarence Martin at the Commerce Department. He suggested that the railroad network—including the PRR—was on the verge of collapse and that desperate times called for prompt and aggressive measures. "Merger is an absolute necessity for the survival of private enterprise railroads in the Eastern District of the United States," read the opening line of one of his memos. His emphasis on "earning power" ignored the possibility of reduced competition, which had long been Orrick's principal focus. To the contrary, Martin insisted that the Penn Central would be far weaker than either the N&W or the C&O–B&O system and thus hardly capable of dominating the eastern railroad network. Martin observed that "eight small Class I railroads in this Northeast area have lost much of their viability during the decade 1953–62," and he predicted a succession of bankruptcies, as the New Haven, the Boston & Maine, the Erie-Lackawanna, and then the New York Central fell like a row of dominoes. Rejection of the Penn Central merger proposal, Martin insisted, would not save the unaligned carriers—it would destroy them. "The railroad situation in the East is such that we can no longer afford to wait five years or more for another comprehensive attack on its problems."[210]

Martin informed Feldman that the situation required "drastic surgery" to ensure the "further reduction of unneeded and underutilized railroad transportation capacity in the Northeast." That surgery included the assignment of the Erie-Lackawanna, the Delaware & Hudson, and the Boston & Maine to the Norfolk & Western, and the New Haven to the Penn Central, as conditions for ICC approval of the respective merger applications. He asserted that "whether what is left of our former regulated rail service and network can be helped to survive by means of Federal actions, ICC approval of the Penn-Central and N&W mergers would constitute substantial help." Martin was less than enthusiastic about the circumstances, and he conceded that "Penn-Central is not ideal, but it is practicable." Even if it possessed no other virtues, he insisted, "the advantage of this plan is that it can be implemented quickly once accepted by the carriers without destroying the momentum gained by the present merger procedures." Martin's comment that "the Penn-Central plan should be accepted as a logical outcome of events" gave considerable

primacy to railroad executives and intimated that neither the Interstate Commerce Commission nor the Justice Department should interfere with those prerogatives. After seventy-five years of ICC oversight and multiple attempts to establish a coordinated transportation policy, it was becoming increasingly difficult to argue that federal regulation had benefited the railroads, or the country. Martin concluded, "The Penn-Central merger thus has become not only an opportunity but a necessity."[211]

Following the Luna-Saunders agreement, James Reynolds reversed his earlier position and indicated that "the Department of Labor is not opposed to the merger of the Pennsylvania and the New York Central." He noted that "we have recently been informed by both the Penn-Central interests and representatives of the railroad employees that the parties have concluded to their satisfaction an arrangement to protect employees adversely affected by the merger." Like Orrick, Reynolds connected the merger to the issue of competition, but he did so in a very different manner. Ignoring the possibility that the Penn Central would destroy its smaller competitors and monopolize rail traffic, the assistant secretary of labor asserted that the new company would enable the railroads to compete against other modes of transportation, preserving thousands of jobs in the process. Reynolds also echoed Martin's willingness to accept the consolidation as an inevitable, if imperfect, mechanism to save the eastern railroad network. "While a Penn-Central merger may not be the most desirable vehicle to attain this goal," Lewis conceded, "it may be the most feasible under present circumstances."[212]

The earlier 3–1 vote against the merger had thus evolved into an even split. The Justice Department strongly opposed the merger, with the Council of Economic Advisers offering a slightly less negative assessment. Martin's Commerce Department was equally adamant in its support of the consolidation, while the Department of Labor provided a more tepid endorsement. For the next year, the members of the Interagency Committee on Transport Mergers were in a state of organizational paralysis, and they simply stopped discussing the largest and most consequential merger in American history.

The disagreements among the members of the Interagency Committee coincided with Johnson's efforts to shift the oversight of transportation policy from the Commerce Department to a new federal agency. The initiative continued the policies advocated by John F. Kennedy in his April 1962 Special Message to Congress on Transportation, but they bore the unmistakable imprint of Johnson's political style. During the summer of 1964, he established a task force on transportation policy, one of fourteen such bodies that would guide the administration's 1965 legislative agenda. The committee offered a veneer of apolitical expertise, yet it met in secret, attesting to Johnson's determination to control the process. Chaired by historian and transportation economist George W. Hilton, its members included economist John R. Meyer. Each of those individuals had previously encouraged the Interstate Commerce Commission to ease the regulatory burden on the railroads. They delivered their report on November 16, days after Johnson won a sweeping electoral victory, with a strongly Democratic Congress. Hilton suggested greater rate flexibility for the railroads and other measures that promised to increase the efficiency of the transportation network. The task force also recommended the creation of a federal transportation department, one that would assume many of the responsibilities of the Department of Commerce.[213]

Johnson's preliminary efforts to increase presidential control over transportation policy occurred during a hiatus in the ICC hearings on the Penn Central merger. When testimony resumed September 16, solely to consider the labor provisions, Saunders was the only witness. He informed examiners Lyle and Darmstadter that the labor issue had been resolved to everyone's satisfaction. The PRR's chairman indicated that acceptance of the *New Orleans* conditions would have imposed costs of nearly $83 million over the first eight years of Penn Central's operation. The Luna-Saunders agreement, he boasted, would cost the Penn Central only $78.2 million, almost all of which would be spent during that eight-year period. It was still an expensive proposition, but—if Saunders's calculations were correct—the amount would be less than a single year of savings associated with the merger, following the completion of the eight-year transition period. The figures Saunders provided proved to be inaccurate, however. The examiners observed that he had calculated the attrition rate without fully acknowledging restrictions on the transfer of workers from one job classification to another.[214] More seriously, Saunders based his predictions on his assumption that the merger would win speedy approval, with implementation taking place by the end of 1965 at the latest. That did not happen, and the company that emerged on February 1, 1968, did so with the obligation to maintain as many employees on the payroll as had been in place more than four years earlier.[215]

The arrangements that Saunders brokered with labor leaders and state and local officials in Pennsylvania were only the most significant portions of a wide-ranging agenda of concession and compromise. Negotiation by negotiation, his targets reconsidered their initial opposition to

the merger. One was William Gural, New Jersey's deputy attorney general, who in February 1964 wrote a letter to the ICC, informing the examiners of what local newspapers characterized as a "slightly changed position toward the consolidation." The slight change amounted to a complete reversal of policy, as Gural now acquiesced to the merger that the state had until recently opposed. In return, he asked the ICC to safeguard the interests of organized labor, maintain existing levels of freight and passenger service, and protect the Erie-Lackawanna—conditions that Saunders readily accepted.[216]

The negotiation of so many concessions did not guarantee acceptance of the Penn Central merger, however. ICC approval looked increasingly likely, as intervenor after intervenor accepted the formation of Penn Central. The Interagency Committee on Transport Mergers was gridlocked into insignificance. Johnson's tentative proposal to establish a federal transportation department had not yet faced what was certain to be a long and contentious period of legislative scrutiny. In the resulting power vacuum, only one agency within the federal government possessed the organizational coherence necessary to mount an effective campaign against the consolidation of the Pennsylvania Railroad and the New York Central. Despite his many successes, Stuart Saunders still faced one particularly daunting obstacle. Unless he could convince the US Department of Justice to fall into line, there was little chance that the merger could take place.

The 482-Word Memo

As Saunders silenced critics of the merger, one by one, officials at the Justice Department remained implacably opposed to his plans. On June 1, 1964, William Orrick and his staff filed a 269-page brief with the ICC. A more detailed version of the objections that he raised the previous October, the document reflected Orrick's view that "the expanding economy of the nation in the years to come" would assure the prosperity of the PRR and the NYC as separate companies. As such, Orrick insisted, "the public interest in the long term would be better served by alignments in which the Pennsylvania and the Central would remain independent of each other." He noted that the merger would reduce or eliminate competition at 149 locations currently served by both carriers. The Penn Central would also control the bulk of the rail traffic in the East, as well as east–west trunk-line service, a circumstance that portended serious consequences for other railroads. While the Penn Central merger would undoubtedly harm all the New England carriers, the New Haven would be particularly affected, thanks to the diversion of traffic to the Penn Central. Until the Pennsylvania Railroad and the New York Central could guarantee some form of protection for the New Haven, Orrick emphasized, their merger application would face relentless opposition from the Justice Department.[217]

The ICC received a second brief on June 1. Issued jointly by the Pennsylvania Railroad and the New York Central, and, at 179 pages, only moderately shorter than the one generated by the Justice Department, it attempted to remove the New Haven situation as an impediment to the merger. PRR and NYC officials suggested that even negative consequences for the New Haven might be consistent with the public interest—in effect asserting that the benefits associated with the Penn Central merger would far outweigh any problems that might affect a company in bankruptcy. As an economic argument, it possessed some validity, and perhaps even conformed to the narrow dictates of regulatory law. It was a politically indefensible position, however, and unlikely to find favor with an attorney general whose family had strong ties to New England.

As an alternative, the PRR and the NYC offered three plans to assist the New Haven and the other struggling New England carriers. One resurrected earlier proposals for a unified regional system, coupled with vague promises that the Penn Central would be "willing to promote" interchange traffic with those carriers. The Penn Central might instead allow the New Haven and the Boston & Maine to lease the NYC's Boston & Albany subsidiary, again as part of a regional system. As an alternative, Pennsylvania Railroad and New York Central representatives promised to operate freight service on the New Haven for a period of ten years. Boston & Maine president Daniel Benson was receptive to the possibilities of regional consolidation, but he sensibly demanded greater clarity than PRR and NYC executives were willing to provide regarding their willingness to promote interchange traffic. Richard Joyce Smith, the New Haven's principal trustee, had repeatedly rejected the creation of an independent New England system and labeled the proposals "unrealistic and unacceptable." Smith likewise balked at any arrangement that would deprive his company of the profits associated with freight service while forcing him to continue the New Haven's money losing passenger operations.[218]

The dueling briefs forced Saunders to confront the role of the New Haven in the Penn Central merger. A week after he declared the joint PRR-NYC proposals unrealistic and unacceptable, Smith petitioned the ICC to reopen the merger hearings, to ensure adequate protection for the New Haven. Further testimony would, at a minimum,

delay approval of the merger. Given the inclusion criteria associated with the Transportation Act of 1940, the ICC might require the Penn Central to absorb the New Haven—including its commuter and intercity passenger service. The Appendix O inclusion provisions associated with the commission's preliminary approval of the Norfolk & Western-Nickel Plate merger certainly suggested that possibility.[219]

The initial discussions regarding the purchase of the New Haven coincided with the Interstate Commerce Commission's final approval of the Norfolk & Western-Nickel Plate merger, issued on August 20. That action triggered the thirty-day period allotted to the company that owned nearly a third of the N&W's stock. By September 18, Saunders would need to decide whether the Pennsylvania Railroad would dispose of those shares. If he refused to do so, he would cripple the N&W's merger plans, and doubtless those of the Penn Central as well. Acceptance of the terms would eliminate the dividends that shored up the PRR's earnings, with no guarantee that he would win the Penn Central merger and its anticipated savings. With the Justice Department still opposed to the consolidation of the PRR and the NYC, Saunders prudently sought a guarantee that his cooperation would be rewarded. While Robert Kennedy held only a passing interest in the relationship between the Pennsylvania Railroad and the Norfolk & Western, the financial health of the New Haven was something he took seriously. Any successful resolution of the New Haven situation thus gave Kennedy, and the Justice Department, a powerful incentive to mitigate the opposition to the Penn Central merger.

On August 21, 1964, the day after the ICC ruling in the N&W–Nickel Plate case, six men gathered at the Department of Justice to settle the fate of the New Haven and determine the outcome of the Penn Central merger hearings. Saunders and Perlman represented their respective railroads. The presence of George Leighty, the chairman of the Railway Labor Executives' Association, indicated that the Luna-Saunders agreement had transformed the unions from fierce opponents to staunch supporters of the consolidation. The other three individuals were from the Justice Department. They included Robert Kennedy and Deputy Attorney General Nicholas Katzenbach. As the head of the Antitrust Division, William Orrick was the sole representative of the Interagency Committee on Transport Mergers, a body that had long since ceased to reflect any interagency cooperation whatsoever.[220]

Saunders first discussed the terms of the N&W–Nickel Plate merger. He did not consider the Appendix O inclusion provisions for the Erie-Lackawanna, the Boston &

Maine, and the Delaware & Hudson to be of any great significance, and the attorney general did not make a policy statement on that issue. The disposition of the PRR's investment in the Norfolk & Western assumed far more importance. Saunders, according to Kennedy, "requested to be informed whether the Government intended to continue to oppose the Penn-Central merger under all conceivable circumstances. He indicated that the Government's attitude would have an influence on the Pennsy's decision as to divestiture."[221]

The conversation then turned to the preservation of the New Haven, an issue directly related to Robert Kennedy's political ambitions. On the following day, August 22, Kennedy would announce his bid for a US Senate seat in New York. Despite his experience and family connections, Democratic Party officials were unenthusiastic about his candidacy. Republican incumbent Kenneth Keating had ample opportunity to characterize his opponent as an opportunistic outsider whose ties to New York were tenuous at best. "There is nothing illegal about the possible nomination of Robert F. Kennedy of Massachusetts as Senator from New York, but there is plenty that is cynical about it," the New York Times observed. "If he became a candidate, he would merely be choosing New York as a convenient launching-pad for the political ambitions of himself and others." Kennedy's campaign would benefit immeasurably if he could announce that he had secured a promise to protect the New Haven, without burdening the taxpayers. Saunders, the "heavy Democratic money man," was also in a position to direct both financial and political support to Kennedy's campaign. As such, the senatorial candidate who supported the merger for political reasons embodied a very different perspective from the attorney general who opposed it for legal ones. He listened intently as Saunders and Perlman briefed him on negotiations to protect the New Haven. As Kennedy recalled the conversation, "They reasserted their previously expressed willingness to cooperate with the Department [of Justice] or the ICC in assuring that transportation services will continue to be rendered by the New Haven Railroad and that such services will not be impaired by the Penn-Central merger."[222]

Despite Kennedy's cooperative mood, he planned to resign from the attorney general's office on September 3, and he thus told Saunders and Perlman that it would be impossible to commit his successor to any specific policy regarding the merger. "I informed Mr. Saunders that since we had only recently reviewed our position of opposition to the merger, had concluded on the merits that we should continue to oppose it, had publicly reasserted that

opposition, and the case is now under submission to the [ICC] hearing examiners," Kennedy explained, "it would be inappropriate to take any action to the contrary at this time." Kennedy instead offered to write a memorandum of understanding to his successor, who was seated beside him, to be kept on file at the Justice Department. Assuming that Saunders and Perlman honored their promises, the 482-word document yielded authority over the Penn Central merger to the Interstate Commerce Commission, with the Justice Department refraining from any further interference in the case. "If the hearing examiners' recommended decision should be contrary to the Government's position and favorable to the merger and the merger applicants have by that time formulated terms for inclusion of the New Haven in the proposed Penn-Central system which are satisfactory to the New Haven's trustee [sic], and to the District Court," Kennedy promised, "and unless circumstances have materially changed, it would be my recommendation that the Department of Justice not continue opposition to the merger beyond that point." There was a certain amount of ambiguity in the document, particularly regarding Saunders's role, as the attorney general noted, "in assuring that transportation services will continue to be rendered by the New Haven Railroad and that such services will not be impaired by the Penn-Central merger." Both the precise nature of those services and the way in which the New Haven would be protected remained undetermined. Moreover, and given the rapidly evolving nature of the eastern railroad network, the stipulation that the Justice Department would abandon opposition "unless circumstances have materially changed" preserved considerable flexibility for Kennedy's successors. When he received a copy of the Kennedy memo on September 4, however, Saunders had little reason to be concerned about the possibility that the agreement might be renegotiated. Katzenbach, who was now the acting attorney general and Kennedy's obvious successor, added a brief note in which he indicated that "I am in agreement with its conclusions."[223]

The understanding between Saunders and Kennedy—which stopped well short of a binding commitment by either party—ensured that the Pennsylvania Railroad would soon lose control of its most valuable asset. On September 14, four days before the deadline imposed by the ICC, Saunders announced the largest securities transaction in the history of the Pennsylvania Railroad. Within ten years, he indicated, the PRR would sell $425 million in N&W and Wabash stock. In the interim, the shares would remain in trust. Saunders, Bevan, and Symes promised to resign from the N&W board, their places assumed by three neutral directors approved by the ICC.[224] "We would not take this crucial step," Saunders emphasized, "without complete confidence that our Pennsylvania-New York Central merger will be authorized in due course." He called the divestment agreement "an act of faith," without acknowledging that he kept in his office a document—bearing Robert Kennedy's signature—that suggested he was not exactly leaping into the abyss. Herman Pevler, the former PRR and Wabash executive who was now the N&W's president, expressed his relief that the decision "removes the last major obstacle" to the consolidation plan engineered by his predecessor. On October 9, the Interstate Commerce Commission gave final approval to the merger of the Norfolk & Western and the Nickel Plate, and the subsequent lease of the Wabash.[225] At 12:01 a.m. on Friday, October 16, a Norfolk & Western train left Columbus, Ohio, and headed north on tracks that a few minutes earlier had belonged to the Pennsylvania Railroad. The relinquishment of N&W stock would take considerably longer, but Saunders's pledge to do so was unalterable.[226]

Diversification

Well before Saunders promised Robert Kennedy that the Pennsylvania Railroad would abandon its holdings in the Norfolk & Western and the Wabash, the company's chief financial officer had been preparing for just such an eventuality. On May 21, 1963, five weeks after ICC examiner Lester Conley ruled that the Pennsylvania Railroad controlled the Norfolk & Western, David Bevan addressed the members of the PRR's Finance Committee. Symes, who served as committee chairman, reminded his fellow board members that the consolidation of the Norfolk & Western and the Nickel Plate—and as a subsidiary outcome the merger of the Pennsylvania Railroad and the New York Central—now depended on the disposition of nearly 2.3 million shares of N&W stock, worth almost $290 million. Bevan then reassured the directors that the PRR was financially sound but warned them that "the next seven years will be the most difficult from a financial standpoint of any period of the history of the Company." Net earnings for the previous five years amounted to a paltry $695,000, and the railroad had been able to maintain service only by burning through its cash reserves at an alarming rate—$110 million between 1952 and 1962. Bevan estimated that the cash loss for 1963 would exceed $20 million. Even if the company did not borrow any funds for new capital expenditures, he would be responsible for refinancing $565 million in bonds, loans, and other debt that would mature between 1963 and 1970. Yet the pending merger with the New York Central

would require massive capital investments, on the order of $75 million over five years. Bevan estimated that $45 million of that amount could be recouped through the sale of surplus equipment and real estate, but that still left a net investment of $30 million before any appreciable savings associated with the consolidation would become apparent. Bevan also knew that the NYC was in equally poor shape and could not be expected to fund its full share of the merger-related capital investments.[227]

While the Pennsylvania Railroad was experiencing chronic financial difficulties, Bevan nonetheless emphasized that its subsidiary, the Pennsylvania Company, was doing quite well. Its annual net income more than doubled between 1946 and 1962, from $11 million to $24 million. The Pennsylvania Company's investments in companies such as the N&W; the Detroit, Toledo & Ironton; and the Toledo, Peoria & Western generated $209 million in the decade preceding the meeting of the Finance Committee. Most of that amount—$198 million—went to the parent company, and the money was crucial to the PRR's ability to maintain operations. "These earnings," Bevan insisted, "must be maintained."[228]

The ICC divestment requirement, coupled with Bevan's dire predictions regarding the PRR's financial future, sparked considerable debate among the company's directors. William L. Day, the chairman of the First Pennsylvania Banking & Trust Company of Philadelphia, proposed allocating most of the proceeds from the sale of the N&W stock to pay down the PRR's debt. Some would be used to rebuild the physical plant and buy new equipment, with the remainder paid out to PRR shareholders as a special dividend. Howard Butcher likewise favored improvements to the railroad, coupled with a steady stream of increased dividends. Butcher also advocated a $20 million investment in new passenger equipment, in a vain attempt to attract travelers back to the rails.[229]

For Bevan, such suggestions were anathema. Given his projections of future cash losses exceeding $20 million a year, it would not take long to dissipate $280 million worth of Norfolk & Western securities. No amount of money would ever redeem the PRR's passenger service, and additional dividends would fritter away the company's windfall without generating any corresponding benefit. It would be the height of foolishness, he suggested, to reallocate the proceeds from the sale of the N&W stock to capital expenditures that would generate a minuscule return on investment, probably no more than 1 or 2 percent. Bevan cautioned against converting the investments into new locomotives and freight cars, rails, bridges, and other improvements. In 1959, he emphasized, Symes authorized

$260 million to buy new equipment and upgrade the physical plant, yet by 1962 that investment had not generated a corresponding increase in net earnings. Bevan also knew that the railroad's operating officials were always willing to blame inadequate service on deficiencies in tracks and equipment and ready to propose a new capital expenditure that would surely fix the problem. Such pressure was difficult for the board of directors to resist. As Bevan noted, once the proceeds from the sale of Norfolk & Western stock went into the physical plant, the money was gone forever and could no longer be used as collateral for the borrowing that he needed to keep the Pennsylvania Railroad operating. If those funds were "invested in fixed assets with the Pennsylvania Railroad," he observed, "we will have destroyed our liquidity and also seriously injured our credit position." Such a strategy might also generate lawsuits from the debtors of the Pennsylvania Company—the PRR subsidiary that was the registered owner of the N&W stock—based on assertions that Bevan was engaged in asset stripping.[230]

If there was any fear that kept Bevan awake at night, it was that he would not be able to borrow the massive sums that were necessary to maintain the solvency of the Pennsylvania Railroad. Given the nature of the tax code, Bevan emphasized, as well as the PRR's bleak earnings picture, the use of the N&W proceeds to retire debt carried at 6 percent interest would be the equivalent of securing a 2.88 percent return in other, nonrailroad investments. By allocating the entire proceeds from the sale of the N&W's investments to the redemption of maturing debt obligations, he would still be left with a shortfall of $285 million in unfunded debt. Bevan would need to borrow that money from somewhere. Despite his excellent connections with the New York banking community, those bankers were reluctant to invest in a railroad with such low rates of return, absent the security guaranteed by the Pennsylvania Company's assets.[231]

The only way forward, insisted Bevan, was to trade the bulk of the Norfolk & Western holdings for corresponding investments in nonrailroad subsidiaries. He recommended that the PRR reduce its stake to no more than 15 percent of the N&W, with sales to occur gradually so as not to depress market values. The divestment would initially generate about $98 million, while the 1965 sale of the Long Island Rail Road to the state of New York—under extremely favorable terms that Bevan negotiated—would provide an additional $65 million. Rather than squander the proceeds on the Pennsylvania Railroad, Bevan recommended the acquisition of at least 80 percent of firms unaffected by the vagaries of railroad operations. The 80 percent threshold

reflected provisions in tax law that permitted the PRR and its new subsidiaries to file consolidated income-tax returns. That stipulation would in turn enable Bevan to use the tax credits stemming from the railroad's losses to offset what he hoped would be high net earnings generated by the subsidiaries. Profits from the subsidiaries would replace the earnings from the N&W holdings, generating a profit for the company as a whole and enabling the board of directors to continue the uninterrupted stream of dividends that would maintain investor confidence. The highly rated securities of the new subsidiaries could preserve the PRR's liquidity, provide an emergency reserve to guard against inevitable downturns in the railroad industry, and furnish the collateral Bevan needed to refinance the company's debt. That process could continue indefinitely, Bevan suggested, provided that the PRR and ultimately the Penn Central could control expenditures and prevent the further erosion of revenues.[232]

Over time, the efficiencies associated with the merger, coupled with the possibility of regulatory reform and reductions in passenger service, might allow rail operations to become robustly profitable in their own right. During the early 1960s, as Bevan was charting the railroad's financial future, stasis or even a slight improvement seemed a realistic possibility. Since the passage of the Transportation Act of 1958, executives were making slow headway in their efforts to curtail passenger operations and obtain operating subsidies for commuter services. A nationwide campaign coordinated by the Association of American Railroads was aggressively pushing for the repeal of state full-crew laws, while orchestrating public-relations efforts that highlighted the deleterious effects of government support for competing modes of transportation. If Bevan's strategy could keep the Pennsylvania Railroad afloat for another decade, then perhaps the company could again enjoy a healthy rate of return.

The PRR's chairman and the other directors acquiesced to Bevan's plan, although Symes soon relinquished his authority over the company's financial affairs. He remained on the board but yielded the post of chairman and CEO to Saunders on October 1, little more than four months after the pivotal May 21 meeting of the Finance Committee. Saunders, busily cultivating support for the merger with the New York Central, initially showed little interest in financial matters yet—according to Bevan—was a strong supporter of the diversification program.[233]

Bevan's diversification efforts relied heavily on the advice of Charles J. Hodge, a broker at Glore, Forgan & Company. The relationship between the PRR's vice president in charge of finance and a mediocre agent at a lackluster brokerage firm exemplified the railroad's declining status in the postwar financial world. It was certainly a humbling transition from the early twentieth century, when Pennsylvania Railroad executives forged a close and mutually beneficial alliance with individuals such as Jacob Schiff and Otto Kahn at Kuhn, Loeb & Company.[234] Both Hodge and the firm he represented had a long and complex history, which included multiple points of intersection with the Pennsylvania Railroad. The brokerage began operations in March 1920, as the partnership of Glore, Ward & Company, and by the end of the year had become Marshall Field, Glore, Ward & Company. Just twenty-six years old, Marshall Field III was the grandson of the famous Chicago department store magnate, and his wealth and name recognition proved invaluable to the partnership. The firm went through several name changes, as well as incorporation in the state of Delaware, before Field left the concern in 1935. The founder and now head of the firm, Charles F. Glore, was well acquainted with the railroads that served Chicago, and he served as a director of the Chicago, Burlington & Quincy. Cofounder J. Russell Forgan spent the war years as a senior official in the Office of Strategic Services and eventually was in command of the agency's operations in Europe. After 1945 he kept in close contact with his fellow OSS veterans, organizing periodic reunions.[235]

When Charles Glore died in 1950, control of the firm passed to his two sons, the son of Russell Forgan, and several new partners. Their ranks included Charles Hodge, who had been with the firm since the end of World War II. Hodge made a noteworthy contribution to the Allied victory in that conflict as the commanding officer of the 117th Mechanized Cavalry Reconnaissance Squadron. The unit saw service in Tunisia and Sicily before taking part in Operation Dragoon, the amphibious landings in southern France. Despite fierce German resistance near Savasse, along the Rhône River, he delivered what some observers "regarded as one of the finest performances of any cavalry reconnaissance unit." Hodge accepted the surrender of Lieutenant General Ferdinand Neuling, the commander of the German LXII Corps, and thereafter kept Neuling's sidearm as a prized souvenir of his wartime service. Brigadier General Hodge also returned home with a Bronze Star and the Croix de Guerre, and in civilian life continued to use his military title. He also relied on Forgan's connections with former OSS operatives, individuals who could be counted on to perform tasks with efficiency and discretion.[236] Hodge's personality differed markedly from Bevan's cautious and conservative approach to the PRR's finances. Hodge was charismatic and assertive,

continually optimistic about the stock market, and always envisioning a bright future for American financial capitalism. While the railroad's chief financial officer relied on Hodge's advice—and was perhaps too easily won over by the broker's ebullience—the relationship between the two men was based primarily on business necessity rather than friendship.[237]

Bevan's interest in diversification began sometime in 1957, well before the May 1963 meeting that committed the PRR to that policy. He asked Hodge for advice regarding pipeline companies, a mode of transportation barely affected by swings in the economic cycle. Hodge dismissed several possibilities but in July 1960 enthusiastically recommended the Buckeye Pipe Line Company. Buckeye began operations in 1886 as a unit of the Standard Oil Trust. The Supreme Court's 1911 antitrust decree established Buckeye as an independent company. Prior to 1960, the firm operated two disconnected systems, one in Ohio, Indiana, and Michigan and the other in Pennsylvania, New York, and New Jersey. Its lines were, as Hodge observed, "within the area covered by the Pennsylvania Railroad and its subsidiaries and/or area covered by any future consolidations." The second part of the sentence was a clear reference to the New York Central, whose territory overlapped that of Buckeye as precisely as did the region served by the PRR. When Hodge wrote to Bevan, Buckeye executives were negotiating for the purchase of the Tuscarora Pipe Line, a link that would connect the eastern and western units of Buckeye into an integrated 7,500-mile system. Buckeye thus needed capital, which the Pennsylvania Railroad could provide. There were, as Hodge emphasized, substantial advantages associated with PRR control of Buckeye. The railroad's losses could be used to offset Buckeye's federal income-tax liability. The pipeline could also deliver fuel to diesel locomotives at most points on the system—and, as Bevan noted, "every railroad operating in the Buckeye area is a source of potential traffic." Finally, as Hodge suggested, Buckeye's management "is believed to fall in the category of very satisfactory, not excellent." That comment suggested that careful oversight by PRR executives would produce synergistic benefits.[238]

Despite Hodge's recommendation, the Pennsylvania Railroad did not begin purchasing Buckeye stock until January 1963. Under the terms of its corporate charter, the PRR could not directly own any company unrelated to its core rail operations. Bevan therefore relied on the American Contract & Trust Company, a holding company incorporated in 1886. It lay dormant for several decades, but during the 1920s, it housed the firms associated with W. W. Atterbury's ventures in intermodal transportation.

The PRR had disposed of most of those companies by the early 1960s, when Bevan reincorporated the entity in Delaware, as the American Contract Company. He also established the Delbay Corporation—the former Harborside Warehouse Corporation—as a subsidiary of the American Contract Company. By the end of July 1963, Delbay acquired 203,300 Buckeye shares, representing about 10 percent of the company. Hodge brokered all the transactions, through Glore, Forgan, and billed the PRR for $200,000 in fees. The purchases accelerated after October 1, 1963, when Stuart Saunders became the new chairman and chief executive officer. Within a month, the PRR owned 29 percent of Buckeye, financed through the sale of N&W stock and from the retained earnings of the Pennsylvania Company. Pipeline consultant Herbert E. Fisher addressed the PRR's Finance Committee, encouraging the directors to add to the company's holdings. Fisher provided the same advice that Hodge had given to Bevan more than three years earlier. Of the eighty-seven pipeline companies in the United States, Fisher emphasized, only three were available for purchase, adding "that Buckeye Pipe Line is the only one which serves the same general area as the lines of The Pennsylvania Railroad Company . . . and finally that in his opinion it would be an ideal arrangement if it were to be owned and operated by the Pennsylvania."[239]

Based on Fisher's recommendation, Saunders and the other members of the Finance Committee endorsed further purchases, to ensure ownership of at least 80 percent of Buckeye's stock. To finance the acquisition, Bevan proposed that the Pennsylvania Company issue at least $42.5 million in nonvoting preferred stock, to be traded for Buckeye shares. The new securities would be attractive to Buckeye's existing shareholders, both because they promised a guaranteed dividend and because they were convertible to Norfolk & Western common stock. It was a risky strategy, in that it obligated the Pennsylvania Company to make good the dividends from its earnings, including those that flowed from Buckeye. However, Bevan assured the members of the Finance Committee that the tax advantages associated with PRR ownership of Buckeye would increase the subsidiary's earnings from $1.75 per share to $3.50 per share. Based on that forecast, the Pennsylvania Company would generate an additional $1.3 million per year from Buckeye, even after paying dividends to the owners of its preferred stock. By the summer of 1964, the PRR, through the Pennsylvania Company, owned more than 2.7 million shares of Buckeye Pipe Line common stock, acquired at a cost of just over $100 million.[240] The transaction required the Pennsylvania Company to issue

more than $70 million worth of preferred stock, a significantly higher amount than the Finance Committee endorsed in December 1963.[241]

While Buckeye Pipe Line meshed with the PRR's territory and operating practices, the railroad's other forays into diversification took Bevan and Hodge further afield. Beginning with the creation of the Real Estate Department in 1874, the Pennsylvania Railroad and its subsidiaries acquired land for stations and other facilities, promoted the growth of suburban communities such as Bryn Mawr, and encouraged industrial development along the right-of-way. During the 1960s, however, Bevan favored real estate projects that had nothing to do with railroad transportation. They were located principally in the booming Sunbelt, far from the PRR's territory.

The first of those acquisitions brought Bevan and other Pennsylvania Railroad executives into contact with a maverick Texan, Angus G. Wynne Jr. In 1956, Wynne and his uncle, Toddie Lee Wynne, established the Great Southwest Corporation, a real estate development firm. With additional financing provided by David Rockefeller and the Rockefeller Center, Incorporated, Wynne transformed the Waggoner Ranch, midway between Dallas and Fort Worth, into an industrial park. After visiting Disneyland, Wynne decided to construct a similar facility—Six Flags Over Texas—on a portion of one of his industrial sites. To finance the venture, Great Southwest issued 418,223 shares of stock, brokered by Glore, Forgan & Company. Most of those shares sold quickly, but in February 1962, Hodge persuaded Bevan to allocate a modest contribution of PRR funds—$21,900—toward the acquisition of twelve hundred leftover shares of Great Southwest.[242]

Even though Great Southwest completed the Six Flags park in 1961, Wynne soon experienced serious financial problems. At the 1964 New York World's Fair, he oversaw the development of the Texas Pavilion, a 2,560-seat music hall that featured the lavish—and horrifically expensive—"From Broadway with Love" musical revue. He raised the necessary funds by pledging ninety thousand shares of Great Southwest stock as collateral for the loan. The fair generated attendance and revenues that were well below expectations, and Wynne suffered more than most. "We had everything but the paying customers," he conceded, and admitted that he was losing more than $100,000 a week. The Music Hall closed in July and its parent company, Wynne-Compass Fair, Incorporated, declared bankruptcy. The debacle widened an existing rift between Wynne and his uncle, who from the beginning opposed involvement in the fair. Like Toddie Lee Wynne, the Rockefeller interests were also ready to part ways with

Great Southwest, and an open-market sale of its stock would remove Angus Wynne from control of the company he founded.[243]

Angus Wynne's financial difficulties presented both a problem and an opportunity to Charles Hodge, the broker who arranged much of the real estate developer's financing through Glore, Forgan. The timing was propitious, in that the firm's underwriters were negotiating a merger with William R. Staats & Company. Glore, Forgan's principal activities were in Chicago and New York, although the company also maintained offices in Boston, Los Angeles, and San Francisco. Staats, in contrast, operated nineteen offices in Arizona and Southern California. The merger, announced in December 1964, gave Glore Forgan, William R. Staats, Incorporated, a strong presence in the Southwest, precisely the area where Wynne operated.[244]

Hodge approached Bevan to see if the PRR might invest in Wynne's Great Southwest Corporation. In June 1964, Saunders—acting in his capacity as the president of the Pennsylvania Company—recommended spending $12 million to acquire 49 percent ownership in Great Southwest. Purchases from the Wynne family and from the Rockefeller interests began the following month and continued through October 1966. By that time, the Pennsylvania Company allocated $51.2 million to Great Southwest, with a far smaller amount—$738,150—contributed directly by the Pennsylvania Railroad. As with Buckeye Pipe Line, Glore Forgan, Staats brokered many of the transactions. The purchases gave Saunders, Bevan, and PRR treasurer William R. Gerstnecker seats on the board of Great Southwest. Wynne nonetheless received a guarantee that he would remain as president, limiting the degree of control that Bevan and other Pennsylvania Railroad executives would have over the company.[245]

PRR and Pennsylvania Company purchases gave Wynne the capital he needed to develop real estate in the same area of Southern California where Glore Forgan, Staats maintained many of its offices. Bevan was impressed with the region's potential, and he encouraged Wynne's plans to establish a California subsidiary, Great Southwest Pacific. Hodge and other representatives at Glore Forgan, Staats offered an alternative and volunteered to broker a merger with the Macco Corporation. Macco specialized in the construction of single-family homes, a business model that differed considerably from Wynne's expertise in shopping centers, industrial sites, and amusement parks. Wynne nonetheless insisted that Macco was an exceptionally well-managed company and would complement the activities of Great Southwest. During 1965, and acting on Wynne's advice, Saunders and Bevan approved the use of

$39 million in Pennsylvania Company funds to purchase Macco's stock.[246]

The next real estate acquisition took place at the other end of the Sunbelt. Arthur Vining Davis, president and board chairman at Alcoa, began acquiring Florida real estate in 1947, particularly in the area around Boca Raton. In 1958, he established the Arvida Corporation, a portmanteau of the first two letters in each of his names, to develop the land. Arvida was soon involved in numerous projects on both the Atlantic and Gulf coasts, as well as in the Florida Keys. During the summer of 1965, and acting on Bevan's recommendation, first the PRR and then the Pennsylvania Company spent $18.3 million to acquire slightly over half of Arvida from the estate of Arthur Vining Davis.[247] Even though the Pennsylvania Railroad owned a controlling interest in the company, it appointed only three of Arvida's twelve directors—Saunders, Bevan, and Charles Hodge at Glore Forgan, Staats.[248]

Penphil

The close association between Bevan and Hodge created a set of investment opportunities that were parallel to but separate from the activities of the Pennsylvania Railroad and the Pennsylvania Company. Both men were familiar with the investment opportunities available to the Pennsylvania Railroad, and they chose to exploit that information to earn personal profits. While neither the broker nor the PRR executive were wealthy, they earned healthy incomes, did not live beyond their means, and thus scarcely needed the additional money. For Bevan in particular, those side investments had more to do with recreation than remuneration. They were a hobby and a diversion for a talented manager who could climb no higher on the corporate ladder. Since arriving at the PRR in 1951, Bevan repeatedly chastised the operating officials who dominated the railroad's senior ranks, demanding that they curtail capital expenditures, improve data-management practices, and seek additional sources of funding so he could put the railroad's financial house in order. The pending retirement of James Symes, as chairman and chief executive officer, offered Bevan a superb opportunity to take charge of the company and impose fiscal discipline. Symes remained on the job for another year, while he looked for a successor who would clearly be someone other than Bevan. His decision to select Saunders—a lawyer with minimal experience in traffic, operations, or finance—was a bitter blow to Bevan's ambitions. He began his personal investments a month after Symes reached retirement age. When Saunders replaced Symes, in June 1963, Bevan's disenchantment—and his outside interests—increased accordingly. Not surprisingly, given that Bevan had always felt ostracized by other PRR executives, he declined to tell Saunders or the board of directors of his private investment activities.[249]

In July 1962, Bevan and Hodge incorporated the Penphil Company, as an investment club. While there was some superficial resemblance to the Pennroad Corporation, they were two entirely different entities. The PRR created Pennroad in 1929 as a mechanism to gain control over other railroads, during the articulation of the various consolidation plans, without running afoul of the Interstate Commerce Commission. Pennsylvania Railroad shareholders were eligible to invest in Pennroad, and more than forty thousand did so. While Pennroad was a legally separate entity from the railroad that sponsored it, its small administrative staff came largely from the ranks of former PRR managers. Atterbury and other PRR executives served as Pennroad trustees and they, rather than investors, controlled the firm's activities.

Penphil, in contrast, began with a mere sixteen investors, with ten more joining in the years that followed. Membership was by invitation only and was restricted to individuals associated with the Pennsylvania Railroad, its subsidiaries, the banks and brokerage firms with which the company did business, and a few others. Many of the initial investors were members of "The Silverfish," a fishing club that Bevan established. David Bevan and his brother, Thomas R. Bevan, a partner in the law firm of Duane, Morris & Heckscher, each owned thirty-three hundred shares of Penphil. So did Hodge, although he registered the securities in his wife's name. The same was true with respect to Dorothy Warner, the wife of Theodore K. Warner Jr., the chief tax counsel in the PRR's Legal Department. Treasurer William Gerstnecker, assistant treasurer and director of investments Robert Haslett, and Paul D. Fox, the assistant vice president in charge of finance, were also members—although Gerstnecker later claimed that he "was never consulted prior to any of Penphil's investments."[250]

From the beginning, Penphil participants benefited from David Bevan's association with the Pennsylvania Railroad. Each invested the modest sum of $16,500, far too little for the projects that Bevan and Hodge contemplated. In August 1962, they negotiated the first in a series of loans—totaling $1.8 million over the next seven years—from New York's Chemical Bank. The Pennsylvania Railroad had done business with Chemical Bank since 1898 and by the end of 1961 maintained a balance of approximately $5 million, with more than $22 million in loans outstanding. The bank's officials offered extraordinarily favorable terms, based in part on the reputation of Bevan and his associates and in part as a favor to an individual who was able to steer the PRR's financial transactions toward any bank he preferred. The Penphil loan was at prime rate, contained no specific repayment terms or repayment deadline, and relied on the value of Penphil's investments as collateral. "Frankly the rate on the proposed loan is too low," conceded one of Chemical Bank's executives, "but in view of the size of the deal and the fact that it has such good friends connected with it, WSR [William S. Renchard, the bank's chairman] felt it was preferable not to quibble with Mr. Bevan over the rate."[251]

Given Bevan's dual role as an investment advisor to both Penphil and the Pennsylvania Railroad, it was perhaps inevitable that the two portfolios displayed some notable similarities. In some cases, the PRR's initial investment in a particular company preceded Penphil purchases and at times it was the other way around, but generally the activities of the railroad and the investment club proceeded simultaneously. Penphil's first significant purchase, funded by the loan from Chemical Bank, was a case in point. Interest in the Kaneb Pipe Line Company arose from the ongoing discussions between Bevan and Hodge that triggered the investment in the Buckeye Pipe Line Company. Unlike Buckeye, Kaneb's operations were far removed from the railroad's territory and—as the name suggested—included lines located in Kansas and Nebraska. In addition to serving as president of Kaneb, Herbert Fisher was the president of Pipe Line Technologists, a consulting firm that since the late 1950s had advised Bevan on the development and expansion of the railroad's pipeline subsidiaries. Glore, Forgan served as Kaneb's investment banker, and Hodge held one of the three seats on the company's executive committee. Despite weak 1961 net income of $38,547, Hodge urged Bevan to purchase Kaneb stock, on behalf of both the PRR and Penphil. Between February and June 1962, the PRR acquired 25,434 shares of the pipeline company, with Hodge brokering the transactions through Glore, Forgan. A month after the PRR purchases ended, Bevan committed Penphil to 22,633 shares, again arranged through Hodge and Glore, Forgan. Hodge remained busy during much of 1963, processing a series of Kaneb purchases by the Pennsylvania Railroad, Penphil, and individual Penphil members on their own account. By the end of the year, all those associated with the transactions collectively owned about a quarter of Kaneb.[252] Amid those sales, Fisher indicated that he would like to participate in Penphil, and he became a member on July 1, 1963.[253]

The Tropical Gas Company, based in Coral Gables, Florida, was also in the energy business, distributing liquefied petroleum gas throughout South Florida, the Caribbean, and Central America. Hodge was the company's vice president. He was also a member of Tropical's executive committee, along with President Frederick H. Billups and Glore, Forgan vice president Hobart Ramsey. At some point prior to May 1962, Bevan directed the Pennsylvania Railroad to purchase twenty-three hundred Tropical shares. Over the next year, the railroad acquired another twenty-nine thousand shares, with the transactions consummated by Glore, Forgan and Hemphill, Noyes & Company—whose managing partner, Lawrence M. Stevens, was a founding member of Penphil, albeit with shares registered in his wife's name. In June 1963, not long after Bevan completed the PRR's purchases of Tropical stock, Hodge invited Billups and Ramsey to join Penphil.[254] Over the next month, Penphil bought ten thousand shares of Tropical. In November 1964, Bevan became a Tropical director while also serving as the PRR's chief financial officer, chair of the finance committee, PRR-board member, and a participant in Penphil. It was in those conjoined capacities that he authorized the acquisition of a further fifty-six thousand shares of Tropical stock between June 1965 and October 1968.[255]

The Great Southwest Corporation also suggested just how thoroughly Hodge and Bevan intertwined the activities of Penphil and the Pennsylvania Railroad. The company's president, Angus Wynne, received an invitation to join Penphil in September 1962, well before his financial problems at the New York World's Fair and almost two years before the PRR's initial investment in his company. In July 1963, Penphil purchased ten thousand shares of Great Southwest. The cost was a modest $165,000. A year later, after the PRR acquired control of Great Southwest, two of the three directors associated with the railroad—Bevan and Gerstnecker—were also members of Penphil, with Stuart Saunders the only individual who was not simultaneously linked to the investment club, the railroad, and its real estate subsidiary. Within a year, Great Southwest's executive committee consisted of Bevan, Hodge, Wynne, and Saunders, three of whom were also members of Penphil. It was not until December 1965, however, that Bevan acknowledged a conflict of interest in the matter. He arranged for Penphil to sell its Great Southwest stock, while observing that "all members of Penphil made a sacrifice in this connection." Bevan and his fellow investors could nonetheless take comfort in a 130 percent return on their investment, over the span of less than twenty-nine months. The buyer of Penphil's Great Southwest shares

was the Pennsylvania Railroad. Hodge brokered the transaction through Glore Forgan, Staats and collected a $4,300 commission for his efforts.[256]

While Penphil did not invest in Arvida, the company established by Arthur Vining Davis, the investment consortium was closely linked to the development of Florida real estate. By the end of 1965, Bevan, Hodge, Gerstnecker, and Wynne served as Arvida directors as well as Penphil members. Acting on the advice of Arvida chairman Comer J. Kimball, they invested more than $400,000 in the First Bank & Trust Company of Boca Raton and the University National Bank of Boca Raton.[257] An interest in real estate financing also contributed to involvement with Continental Mortgage Investors. The impetus came from Lawrence Stevens, the managing partner at Hemphill, Noyes & Company and a member of Penphil's investments committee—one of the rare cases where Hodge did not play a leading role. Stevens suggested that CMI shares were undervalued and Francis A. Cannon, a fellow Penphil member, purchased a block of 500 in April 1964. Penphil bought 10,000 shares the following month, with Hemphill, Noyes handling the transaction. At the same time Bevan used money from the PRR's pension fund to acquire a separate block of 10,000 CMI shares, as well as $1 million of CMI notes. Thanks to additional purchases, by December 1967 the Pennsylvania Railroad owned 37,500 shares of CMI stock and more than $2 million of the company's debt.[258]

Executive Jet Aviation

While Bevan's dual involvement with the Pennsylvania Railroad and Penphil raised obvious conflict-of-interest issues, none of his investment decisions generated more controversy or criticism than the ones involving Executive Jet Aviation. The company and its checkered history were inextricably linked with another retired general, one who was far more flamboyant and attention seeking than Charlie Hodge. Olbert F. "Dick" Lassiter displayed a lifelong passion for aviation, making his first solo flight in 1935, at the age of fifteen. During World War II, Lassiter flew sixty-five combat missions in P-38, B-25, and B-29 aircraft. After the war, he was a stunt pilot for several Hollywood movies, including two starring Jimmy Stewart. In 1947, Lassiter flew a modified B-29 that set the world speed and distance record. On a later flight, he traveled more than nine thousand miles in a propeller-driven aircraft, without refueling—a record that has never been broken. Lassiter was the test pilot and project officer for a nonstop, round-the-world flight in a B-50 bomber, and he also served as one of the principal test pilots on the B-47 Stratojet. He was the first head of the Strategic Air Command at Thule Air Force Base in Greenland, commanded the 801st Air Division at Lockbourne Air Force Base in Ohio, and headed the 99th Bombardment Wing at Westover Air Force Base in Massachusetts. During the final years of his Air Force career, Lassiter oversaw a fleet of small planes used to transport officers between bases. By the time he retired from the Air Force at the end of 1964, Lassiter had flown more than three hundred different aircraft types and was undoubtedly one of the most accomplished pilots in the world. He was also a risk-taker and an extraordinarily charismatic individual with a passion for parties, nightclubs, alcohol, and attractive young women.[259]

Prior to his retirement, Lassiter began planning his career as a civilian. He sensed that an air-taxi service like the one he had organized for the military would be highly profitable. Corporate executives could charter planes at short notice and enjoy convenience and luxury without the need to invest in a company aircraft. Lassiter incorporated Executive Jet Aviation in 1964 and relied on the support of prominent backers from both the Air Force and the entertainment industry. They included General Curtis LeMay, the former Air Force Chief of Staff; retired Air Force general Perry M. Hoisington; and James Hopkins Smith, the former assistant secretary of the navy. Another investor was retired general Fred Billups, the president of Tropical Gas Company. Jimmy Stewart and the entertainer Arthur Godfrey also served on EJA's board of directors. To gain the capital he needed for the venture, Lassiter contacted Bruce G. Sundlun, an officer in the Air Force Reserve and a Washington attorney specializing in aviation law. Sundlun traveled to New York and presented the proposal to Sam Hartwell, a partner at Glore, Forgan, who turned the matter over to Hodge. When Hodge broached the subject with Bevan, in the autumn of 1964, the PRR's chief financial officer took a keen interest. So did board member Richard King Mellon, whose responsibilities as a financier and as a major general in the Army Reserve gave him frequent opportunities to travel in executive aircraft.[260]

Like Atterbury during the 1920s, both Bevan and Saunders were interested in expanding the company's activities into other modes of transportation—including the services offered by Buckeye Pipe Line and Kaneb Pipe Line. They were also concerned about developments in commercial aviation that threatened to erode a substantial portion of the PRR's freight business. In May 1964, a few months before Lassiter retired from the Air Force, the major airframe and jet-engine manufacturers submitted proposals to build a military cargo plane with greater capabilities

than the C-141 Starlifter. The CX-Heavy Logistics System project ultimately led to the development of the Lockheed C-5 Galaxy, which first flew in January 1968. The Air Force initiative to design a heavy-lift cargo plane encouraged the three largest airframe manufacturers to develop the first of a new generation of wide-bodied commercial jets. They included the Boeing 747, which debuted in February 1969, and the Lockheed L-1011 TriStar and the McDonnell Douglas DC-10, each of which underwent test flights in 1970. All three were in the preliminary design stage when Hodge offered to play matchmaker between Lassiter and Bevan, but PRR executives did not have to see them fly to sense what they might do to the company's rail traffic. If Bevan harbored any lingering doubts, they disappeared after he discussed the latest trends in aviation with one of the board members at Executive Jet Aviation. "I talked with General LeMay," Bevan recalled, "and he said that with the big planes coming out what is going to happen to railroad freight business will be beyond belief by 1975."[261] Henry Large, the PRR's vice president in charge of traffic, offered a more optimistic prediction of future developments. Large observed that "air freight and express volume" was "exploding," and he wanted "to see whether EJA might fit into a plan for PRR-NYC Transportation Company entry into this field." While a handful of executive jets would provide little immediate benefit for the Pennsylvania Railroad's freight operations, Lassiter possessed the nucleus of an airline, coupled with valuable military contacts—all of which suggested that he offered Bevan an opportunity to bootstrap the PRR into commercial aviation.[262]

There was a substantial regulatory impediment to Pennsylvania Railroad ownership of Executive Jet Aviation, however. The Federal Aviation Act of 1958 prohibited railroads and other surface carriers from acquiring an airline without the approval of the Civil Aeronautics Board, based on a ruling that such a consolidation was consistent with the public interest. On March 31, 1965, Hugh Cox, an attorney at the prestigious Washington law firm of Covington & Burling, advised Bevan that Executive Jet Aviation was an "air carrier" under the terms of the 1958 law and that PRR control would be illegal. Aviation lawyer Bruce Sundlun was now EJA's general counsel, and he provided a very different interpretation of the Federal Aviation Act of 1958. The Civil Aeronautics Board could not classify Executive Jet Aviation as an "air carrier," Sundlun insisted, because the company operated chartered rather than scheduled service, and because its planes weighed less than the 12,500-pound threshold specified in the legislation. Sundlun also emphasized that the law governed only the initial acquisition of an air carrier by a surface carrier and not the airline's subsequent operations. His inference, therefore, was that EJA, once under Pennsylvania Railroad control, could expand its business activities without obtaining a certificate of convenience and necessity from the CAB. As one of the railroad's executives later conceded, "rail carriers, under the law, cannot become involved in the operation of air freight services. The whole project was undertaken, however, in the hope that Executive Jet would expand into the freight area and at some future date laws might be changed," giving the railroad the opportunity to maintain an intermodal transportation system. David Wilson, the PRR's assistant general counsel, was more cautious. He suggested that the railroad should avoid any investment that would furnish managerial control over EJA. "Instead of our acquiring immediately a majority equity position," Wilson warned, "we might prefer to begin with a creditor relationship . . . which would permit us to obtain the majority equity position at our discretion in the future." Wilson also recommended that Bevan proceed with as little publicity as possible. "For reasons of policy," Wilson suggested, "we would prefer that none of these questions be taken up either formally or informally at this particular time with the [CAB] agency or any of its staff people if our identity would have to be disclosed."[263]

In keeping with Wilson's advice, Bevan and his associates worked indirectly and quietly to gain control over Executive Jet Aviation. In November 1964, Lassiter received an initial cash advance of $275,000—which he promised to repay, although neither Bevan nor PRR treasurer William Gerstnecker established an interest rate for the loan. Over the next seven months, Bevan and Gerstnecker directed $4.7 million to EJA through the PRR's American Contract Company subsidiary. Only then did Bevan secure a written agreement with Lassiter and announce the project to the Pennsylvania Railroad's board of directors. Some of the money—about $328,000—funded the acquisition of 655,960 shares of class B Executive Jet Aviation stock. The rest was simply a loan, to be repaid incrementally beginning in 1970, with the interest rate dependent on EJA's earnings. The funds enabled Lassiter to buy Lear jets, which initially served as the collateral for the loan. Lassiter's capital needs were insatiable, however, and by the end of August 1966, the PRR provided him with more than $13 million. Furthermore, between 1965 and 1968 Bevan persuaded the National Newark & Essex Bank, the Philadelphia National Bank, and the First National City Bank of New York to loan EJA more than $17.8 million. Bevan's pledge of support for EJA, coupled with the value of the Pennsylvania Railroad's business, encouraged officials at the three banks to dismiss concerns regarding Lassiter's

creditworthiness. Bank managers nonetheless insisted that Lassiter pledge the fleet of Lear jets as collateral for the loans, and Bevan agreed to yield the PRR's prior claim to the aircraft.[264]

Bevan's indirect strategy provided the Pennsylvania Railroad with a substantial stake in Executive Jet Aviation, although without the ability to control that firm's activities. The class B stock did not have voting rights, leaving Lassiter in sole control of the company he established. The audacity and recklessness that made Lassiter such an accomplished pilot also made him an incompetent business executive. He saw little distinction between corporate and personal expenditures and spent company funds lavishly on travel, entertainment, and a house in Beverly Hills for one of his many girlfriends. All the while Executive Jet Aviation continued to generate a cascade of red ink. During the fiscal year that ended on August 31, 1966, EJA earned $2.8 million in revenues, but still managed to lose $1.8 million. Two of the company's best customers were Lassiter, who made more than half of EJA's administrative flights, and the Pennsylvania Railroad. Over a five-year period, the PRR's Manor Real Estate subsidiary spent nearly $400,000 for 348 trips—60 percent of which were for Bevan, Gerstnecker, or Hodge. Many were short hops, including a jaunt from Newark to Philadelphia, two cities connected by frequent Pennsylvania Railroad passenger service. There were rumors that some of those flights took longer than necessary, to facilitate sexual liaisons in the cabin.[265]

While Lassiter's lifestyle was a public-relations embarrassment, his desire to expand the scope of EJA's business caused more serious difficulties. In August 1966, he purchased an 80 percent interest in Johnson Flying Service. The company, based in Missoula, Montana, operated a fleet of air tankers, used to fight wildfires under a contract with the US Forest Service. Crucially, it possessed Civil Aeronautics Board certification as a supplemental air carrier. It was one of only about a dozen such companies in the United States and the least expensive to purchase, at a cost of $1.75 million. Lassiter obtained an option to buy Johnson Flying Services without informing Bevan, and he may have completed the purchase before telling the PRR's chief financial officer what he had done. "I know the recent acquisition of the Johnson group must have seemed like a Chinese fire drill to you," he told Bevan, "and in some respects it did seem like that to us, also." Despite Lassiter's customarily insouciant attitude, the acquisition of Johnson Flying Service was very much in keeping with the strategy developed by Bevan and Saunders, to give the PRR some influence over the operation of heavy-lift cargo aircraft.

The transaction thus offered the possibility of substantial benefits for both Lassiter and his principal backer. The general envisioned the creation of a commercial passenger carrier. Charter flights would give him prestige and pleasure, as he accompanied tour groups jetting off to the Bahamas and other exotic locales, on planes staffed with beautiful flight attendants. Bevan hoped that EJA's operations would prove enormously profitable, bolstering the earnings of the Pennsylvania Railroad while enabling the company to increase the transportation options offered to customers.[266]

Threading Johnson Flying Service through the regulatory needle would be a formidable task, however. CAB officials were likely to take a dim view of Bevan's efforts to include commercial aviation in the Pennsylvania Railroad's investment portfolio. The owners of independent air carriers were also quick to point out that the PRR's financial support for the company impaired their ability to compete and was thus in violation of the Federal Aviation Act of 1958. Hugh Cox, the attorney at Covington & Burling, had warned Bevan that Pennsylvania Railroad investments in EJA might be illegal. Cox was even more concerned about the further expansion into supplemental aviation, given that Johnson was without doubt an "air carrier," as defined by federal law. "If the CAB were to find that EJA was controlled by the Pennsylvania," he noted, "it would undoubtedly not approve the acquisition of the supplemental air carrier." The independent counsel therefore suggested that either the PRR could control Executive Jet Aviation or EJA could acquire Johnson Flying Service— but not both. PRR attorney David Wilson echoed that assessment, suggesting that the CAB would undertake "a much more formal and fuller investigation" than had been the case with the railroad's initial investments in EJA and that "there would be a distinct possibility that the question of PRR relationship would come up."[267]

Despite warnings from Cox and Wilson, Lassiter forged ahead with his ambitious expansion plans. In September, he spent $26.2 million on two Boeing 707 and two Boeing 727 aircraft—planes far larger than the Lear jets EJA used to transport executives from one city to another. Lassiter's decision to buy four massive passenger airliners apparently caught Bevan by surprise. "The EJA board made the decision to go ahead and order the four planes," he insisted. "This was their judgment." Without CAB approval of the company's acquisition of Johnson, however, the new planes could not leave the tarmac. Despite that impediment, Lassiter signed a letter of intent with Lockheed to buy six L-500 aircraft for $136.5 million—far more money than EJA possessed, and a sum that would strain even

the PRR's generosity. Lassiter's buying spree revealed his intent to operate a full-service commercial airline. That much was clear to CAB examiner Milton H. Shapiro. On April 11, 1967, Shapiro insisted that the acquisition of Johnson Flying Service depended on the PRR's divestment of its holdings in Executive Jet Aviation.[268] Bevan prepared a partial divestiture plan, presented to the CAB in October, that nonetheless retained the PRR's status as the largest stockholder and the largest creditor of Executive Jet Aviation. It took little time for the CAB to reject the proposal and to insist on the complete liquidation of the PRR's aviation investments.[269]

Lassiter's headlong plunge into the world of commercial aviation alarmed Bevan. Because the PRR's investments were in the form of nonvoting stock and cash advances, there was not much he could do about it, other than threaten to withhold additional funds from EJA. Yet even that approach was ineffective, as the curtailment of new investment jeopardized the PRR's existing holdings. In early 1967, Lassiter reluctantly agreed to a review of the company's structure, finances, and operations. Bevan commissioned William W. Abendroth, executive officer at the Wharton School's Management Science Center, who gave his report to Lassiter on May 31. Abendroth provided six specific recommendations, all contained in a two-page summary at the beginning of the document. He politely emphasized Lassiter's lack of managerial skills and suggested that he be removed from the presidency of EJA, placed in a ceremonial planning role, and excluded from all day-to-day operating decisions. Lassiter gave copies of Abendroth's report to EJA executives, but only after excising the first two pages and any mention of his inadequacies. He rejected all but two of Abendroth's recommendations and ignored guidelines contained in a supplemental report that the consultant completed in November. The president of a Boston-based consulting firm, Colonial Management Associates, offered similar advice a month later, when he recommended the hiring of a new president and chief executive officer with significant business experience. It is not clear whether Bevan received any of those reports. He was nonetheless aware of Lassiter's failings yet could do little about them without confronting regulatory policies that prevented more direct PRR control over Executive Jet Aviation.[270]

Rather than liquidate the PRR's holdings in Executive Jet Aviation, as the CAB demanded, Bevan reoriented the investments. In October 1967, the American Contract Company repaid $16.2 million that it had borrowed from the Pennsylvania Railroad, funds Bevan had advanced to Lassiter. At the same time, American Contract borrowed

$16.3 million from the Pennsylvania Company. Subsequent congressional investigations placed great emphasis on one significant difference between the bylaws of the two subsidiaries—those for American Contract required the reporting of cash advances, while those of the Pennsylvania Company did not. Federal officials accordingly assumed that Bevan was attempting to maintain, and perhaps increase, the PRR's control over Executive Jet Aviation, in defiance of federal law and CAB directives. Bevan offered a much simpler explanation, suggesting that he was unwilling to abandon Executive Jet Aviation to bankruptcy while there was still a chance of preserving the PRR's investments in the company. "We actually put money in under the CAB trusteeship," he noted. "We didn't want them to go under."[271]

Lassiter's empire was indeed about to go under, and his efforts to attract additional financial support and to find a use for the four Boeing jets created further problems for the Pennsylvania Railroad. Bevan acknowledged that the cost of the aircraft "ate their heads off," and he pressured Lassiter to lease them to an airline that could legally operate them. That process, which began just as the PRR and the New York Central were merging into the Penn Central, proved extraordinarily complex, financially disastrous, and possibly illegal. In February 1968, Carl Hirschmann, the vice chairman of EJA's European affiliate, bought a 90 percent interest in Transavia, a small European airline. EJA then leased one of the 707 aircraft to Transavia, without CAB approval. A month later, Hirschmann acquired 70 percent of International Air Bahamas, a carrier whose principal asset consisted of landing rights in the Bahamas and in Luxembourg. The IAB connection soon became highly controversial—particularly because it involved the acquisition by the Penphil investment trust of a small travel agency based in Tampa. Its owner, Irene Bowen, feared that retail agencies such as hers—which sold airline tickets and booked tours for individual customers—were no longer economically viable. She wanted to relocate to Miami and specialize in package holidays, but she lacked the money necessary to make the transition. Bowen mentioned the situation to Tampa attorney Julian Lifsey, who in turn brought it to the attention of his friend, Dick Lassiter. In early January 1968, Lassiter joined Penphil, persuading his fellow investors to spend $25,000 on a 51 percent share of Bowen's agency. Penphil also provided the agency—renamed Holiday International Tours—with a $200,000 line of credit. Bevan and the three Penphil members who were also directors of EJA—Lassiter, Hodge, and Tropical Gas's Fred Billups—mediated the resulting arrangement. Executive Jet Aviation leased the other

707 to International Air Bahamas and provided crews to fly the plane. All three firms would thus enjoy a symbiotic relationship, with Holiday International arranging group tours that included charter flights on International Air Bahamas, using aircraft leased from Executive Jet Aviation.[272]

Lassiter was neither a businessman nor a lawyer, and his desperate efforts to find a use for the Boeing aircraft produced even more problems for EJA and its investors. He made suggestions that others took as binding agreements, and generally gave indications that he was prepared to turn Executive Jet Aviation into a major international airline. Given the limitations on both his financing and his organizational abilities, it is unlikely that Lassiter could have accomplished such a feat. His reckless tactics nonetheless alarmed officials from the CAB, Icelandic Airlines, and—most seriously of all—Pan American Airlines. On January 24, 1968, days before the Penn Central merger, Examiner Shapiro encouraged all the parties to quietly resolve the dispute, without additional formal hearings. A month later, Bevan informed Saunders that "the position taken by the examiner and the Bureau of Enforcement for the CAB was not favorable." The only recourse involved a total divestment of holdings in Executive Jet Aviation. That would be a difficult task, as Lassiter's ineptitude ensured that EJA was hemorrhaging money, with 1969 deficits reaching $12.5 million. Efforts to sell the company to the United States Steel Corporation and to Burlington Industries proved unsuccessful. As Saunders and Bevan searched for another buyer, they had little choice other than to advance additional money to Executive Jet Aviation, to prevent the company from going into liquidation. Not until March 1972 were they able to sell EJA to Bruce Sundlun, the aviation-attorney-turned-executive, who had won a vicious battle with Lassiter for control of the company. The purchase price was $1.25 million. The remainder of the PRR's $21 million investment in Executive Jet Aviation simply disappeared.[273]

The Benefits and Costs of Diversification

Following the collapse of the Penn Central, the EJA saga attracted an inordinate share of attention from House and Senate subcommittees, the Securities and Exchange Commission, and the Interstate Commerce Commission. Politicians, federal investigators, and newspaper reporters seeking salacious headlines profiled Dick Lassiter's outrageous behavior and reckless management of the company. Even though Bevan and other PRR executives could not exercise direct control over EJA or curtail Lassiter's actions, they suffered guilt by association. More broadly, the many critics of Bevan's diversification program asserted that the $163.5 million obtained from the disposition of the Norfolk & Western stock and the sale of the Long Island Rail Road could have been put to better use. In 1970, Wright Patman, the chairman of the House Committee on Banking and Currency, observed that the PRR invested a somewhat smaller amount—$144 million—in its four principal non-railroad subsidiaries: Buckeye, Great Southwest, Arvida, and Macco. "The decision to diversify," congressional staffers calculated, "meant that the Railroad was deprived of the potential use of $144 million in cash at a time when it was heavily in debt." Patman also highlighted the $115.5 million that the PRR and the Pennsylvania Company borrowed to add to their portfolio of subsidiaries. Only Buckeye, Patman insisted, produced substantial returns, and the four companies together generated just $19.9 million that could be used to offset the railroad's operating losses. "Accordingly," Patman concluded, "it is clear that the diversification program, in effect, represented a very substantial cash drain on the Railroad." While Patman's committee concluded that diversification squandered $175 million, its Senate counterpart placed the outflow at $41.8 million—a much lower figure, but nonetheless a damning indictment of Bevan's policies.[274]

While it was clear to Patman and his colleagues that the PRR's diversification program was an unmitigated disaster, a more objective analysis suggests that Bevan accomplished most of his goals. Patman's insistence that Bevan should have allocated the funds to railroad operations mirrored the advice he received at the May 1963 meeting of the Finance Committee, but that perspective made as little sense in 1970 as it had seven years earlier. Executive Jet Aviation was a clear failure, but one that consumed little more than 7.5 percent of the $279 million that the PRR committed to diversification. EJA was also an unfortunate outlier amid a group of largely successful companies. Buckeye Pipe Line was the most lucrative, generating an average annual rate of return of 9.5 percent from 1964 through 1968. While Macco Realty's net earnings were lower, its rate of return on investment was an astonishing 24.5 percent between 1965 and 1968. Great Southwest also did well, with returns reaching 16.9 percent in 1967 and 35 percent the following year. By the middle of 1969, the company had a market value over $1 billion.[275] Arvida was something of a disappointment, with an average rate of return of little better than 2 percent—but the boom in Florida real estate would eventually create much more favorable conditions. The overall return on the diversification investments was approximately 5.5 percent, well above what the company

could earn on its railroad operations. Bevan was not seeking explosive short-term market gains. He instead favored slow, steady growth, in the expectation that the nonrail subsidiaries would be able to offset the railroad's operating losses for many years to come. Neither he nor anyone else associated with the PRR or the NYC anticipated that Penn Central would hemorrhage funds as rapidly as it did, or reach bankruptcy so quickly.[276]

In contrast to Patman and others who argued that Bevan starved the railroad of capital, the diversification program he advocated and managed did little to curtail investments in the physical plant and equipment. In 1963, the year Bevan persuaded the members of the Finance Committee to follow his advice, the cash investment in nonrail subsidiaries represented only 13.8 percent of the money reinvested in the railroad. That figure declined to 7.3 percent in 1964, rose to 15.3 percent in 1965, and fell thereafter to 5.8 percent in 1966 and 6 percent in 1967. During the diversification period, therefore, the Pennsylvania Railroad invested more than nine times as much in locomotives, cars, rails, bridges, and other facilities as it did in the companies that Bevan recommended.[277]

In the final analysis, however, the financial results associated with diversification mattered little to politicians, regulators, reporters, and the public. They did not take kindly to Bevan's association with Charlie Hodge, Dick Lassiter and other individuals who were never employees of the Pennsylvania Railroad, yet who seemed to possess an inordinate degree of control over the company's finances. The role of the Pennsylvania Company and the American Contract Company in the diversification program—necessary to comply with federal law, regulatory policies, and the terms of the PRR's corporate charter—awakened long-standing fears of insider trading and interlocking directorates. Patman, who had been railing against the trusts since the 1930s, emphasized that it was the Pennsylvania Company, rather than the Pennsylvania Railroad, that received most of the profits from Bevan's investments. Little of that money reached the PRR's core rail operations, he suggested. Even as the Penn Central plunged into bankruptcy and as Saunders, Bevan, and other executives begged for assistance from the federal government, the Pennsylvania Company remained profitable. In Bevan's opinion, that circumstance validated his assertion that diversification could have saved the Pennsylvania Railroad, if operating officials had only taken to heart his continual insistence to keep costs under control. They did not, and that, he reflected, was not his fault. To those outside the firm, however, Bevan's diversification strategy represented an effort to treat the Pennsylvania

Company as a lifeboat, filling it to overflowing with lucrative assets, while leaving the workers, shippers, investors, and communities who depended on the Pennsylvania Railroad to go down with the ship.[278]

Saving the New Haven

While David Bevan was busily diversifying the Pennsylvania Railroad, the New Haven was slowly dying. The growing fear that the New Haven was on the verge of collapse offered Saunders a mechanism to build political support for the merger. There was considerable risk in doing so, however, as the company's chronic passenger deficit would erode a substantial portion of the $81 million in the annual savings that Saunders expected to achieve in the merger. Rescuing the New Haven made sense only if Saunders was able to limit Penn Central's responsibilities to the New Haven's marginally profitable freight service. Saunders hoped that most intercity passenger service between New York and Boston could be abandoned, while essential commuter operations would receive state or federal subsidies. By the summer of 1964, there were indications that public support might materialize. On July 9, President Johnson signed the Urban Mass Transportation Act, providing $375 million in federal funds for urban transit systems. In September, the state of Connecticut agreed to provide the New Haven with a $450,000 annual subsidy for the next two years. Given that the company lost $8.6 million on passenger service the previous year, the grant was both inadequate and temporary. It did, however, indicate that public agencies would cushion at least a part of the blow associated with the New Haven's inclusion in the Penn Central.[279]

Preliminary negotiations between PRR, NYC, and New Haven officials began in June 1964 and proceeded under the assumption that the public agencies would either eliminate or support passenger and commuter operations along the route between New York and Boston. The warning that PRR attorney Windsor Cousins provided at the ICC hearings proved prophetic, and it was difficult if not impossible to establish a fair value for a bankrupt carrier with minimal earning potential. Perlman considered the New Haven's commuter service to be "beyond rescue by private enterprise." He likewise had no use for the inclusion of marginal New Haven branch lines in Penn Central—"that would be suicide," he observed. Walter Grant, the NYC's vice president in charge of finance, suggested that he did not "want the New Haven for $1, or at any price." Grant's estimate was unlikely to win the support of the New Haven's trustees or its bondholders, and he conceded that the company might

be worth as much as $41 million. Richard Joyce Smith and the other trustees considered that amount to be wholly inadequate, demanded that they receive at least $128 million (which they calculated as the New Haven's liquidation value), and balked at a counteroffer of $80 million.[280]

The negotiations dragged on until February 1965 and, when they concluded, Smith and his colleagues had every reason to be pleased with the outcome. Following the consummation of the merger, the Penn Central would spend $140 million to acquire the New Haven. That amount included 950,000 shares of Penn Central stock, with an estimated value of just over $44 million, as well as $23 million in Penn Central bonds and $8 million in cash. The agreement also saddled the Penn Central with $25 million in pension obligations for New Haven employees and $29 million in equipment-trust obligations, accompanied with a promise to make good the company's freight losses in 1965, 1966, and 1967. It was a steep price for a bankrupt company unlikely to ever demonstrate a profit—but a necessary expense, Saunders concluded, if the Penn Central merger were to secure the approval of the Interstate Commerce Commission and the Justice Department. Saunders set one inviolable condition, to which Smith and the other New Haven trustees readily assented. The Penn Central would never be responsible for the company's catastrophically unprofitable passenger service.[281]

As the negotiations reached their conclusion, however, elected officials in New York and New England upended Saunders's assumption that the Penn Central would be exempt from the burden of the New Haven's passenger operations. The August 21, 1964, meeting at the Justice Department provided an informal agreement on the relationship between Penn Central and the New Haven, one that was subject to interpretation. The memorandum of understanding, signed by Attorney General Robert Kennedy, was sufficient to induce Saunders to part with the PRR's investments in the Norfolk & Western and the Wabash, clearing the way for the merger agreement that also involved the Nickel Plate Road. The concession encouraged Kennedy, now battling for a Senate seat in New York, to downplay his earlier opposition to the Penn Central merger. "Conditions have dramatically changed," he announced in October, justifying his abrupt policy reversal. The catalyst was the worsening commuter crisis in New York, Massachusetts, and other states where Kennedy, Johnson, and other Democrats were hoping to secure substantial margins in the 1964 elections. Criticizing a Republican opponent who favored "studies and surveys and discussions—but no action," Kennedy proposed a consolidation of the PRR, the NYC, and the New Haven, with the Long Island Rail Road thrown in for good measure. "The new system," Kennedy noted, "would be in an excellent competitive position to attract the lucrative traffic of the northeastern United States, with profitable freight and through passenger routes." Kennedy's proposal was politically useful, even though it possessed no economic merit whatsoever. It mattered little that Saunders was pushing to divorce the LIRR from the Pennsylvania Railroad or that he wanted nothing to do with the New Haven. Kennedy expected the Penn Central, rather than the federal government, to bear the brunt of the New Haven's commuter service. "It is now clear," he concluded, "that merger with a strong New York State system is the best if not the only hope for the New Haven's survival."[282]

Despite Kennedy's confidence, the situation in Philadelphia and in Washington was far less clear. On September 4, the day after Kennedy's resignation from the Justice Department, Acting Attorney General Nicholas Katzenbach sent a copy of the August 21 memo to Saunders. As the accompanying cover letter made clear, the two individuals held differing interpretations of the agreement. Saunders discussed the matter with Katzenbach by telephone on September 8 and dispatched a letter to the Justice Department the following day. "It was agreed, as I recall," Saunders noted, "that we would diligently seek to find a fair and reasonable basis to include the New Haven in the proposed system." The PRR's chairman nonetheless indicated his assumption that inclusion "was not to be an absolute condition and such action did not necessarily have to be taken prior to the date that the [ICC] Examiners filed their report." Moreover, Saunders reiterated his understanding that "if the Trustees of the New Haven were unreasonable or if terms could not be found that were mutually fair to the security holders of both companies," then the Penn Central would not have to accept the bankrupt New England carrier. Katzenbach had a different recollection of the August 21 meeting. Summarized by Saunders, he suggested "that terms for inclusion of the New Haven in the proposed system must be satisfactory to the New Haven Trustees and to the District Court [overseeing the bankruptcy proceedings] and that they must be formulated by the time of the Examiners' recommended decision."[283]

The acrimonious exchange set the tone for future negotiations between PRR and NYC executives, Justice Department officials, and the New Haven's trustees. On January 8, 1965, Saunders and Perlman again traveled to Washington to discuss the issue with Katzenbach and William Orrick, the head of the Antitrust Division. Both sides held firm to their earlier assertions, although Saunders suggested that Katzenbach and Orrick were not "adhering to

the position" that Kennedy had promised the previous August. In truth, they were continually reassessing one another. Katzenbach and Orrick were probing to see how many concessions Saunders and Perlman were willing to yield to merge their respective railroads, while the two executives were assessing how badly the federal government wanted to rescue the New Haven.[284]

Farther to the north, the New Haven's trustees and local political leaders were trying to obtain as much support from the Penn Central as possible, without demanding such unreasonable terms as to make Saunders and Perlman call off the merger. The sorry state of the New Haven's commuter and intercity passenger service had always been the principal impediment to cooperation with the PRR and the NYC, and the New Haven's supporters were attempting to make that burden as light as possible. On January 6, two days before the latest meeting at the Justice Department, New York senator Jacob K. Javits and Representative Ogden Reid, both Republicans, endorsed the creation of a four-state transit agency that would fund the New Haven's passenger operations. The following day, Senator Claiborne Pell, a Rhode Island Democrat, hosted a meeting with the governors of the four states served by the New Haven. ICC chairman Charles A. Webb and Commissioner William H. Tucker were also present, ensuring that the federal regulatory agency with the power to decide the fate of the Penn Central merger was well represented.[285]

The trustees also endeavored to secure greater public assistance and make their company more attractive to Saunders and Perlman. On January 8, they announced plans to curtail commuter operations, affecting about seventy-five hundred daily commuters, and to gradually eliminate all intercity passenger service. Panicked mayors called the plan "disastrous" and scrambled to find any source of funds that would keep the trains running. Governor Rockefeller of New York insisted that "the Federal Government should have a role." With the support of Connecticut governor John N. Dempsey, he sought a grant from the Housing and Home Finance Agency of the Department of Commerce. Rockefeller conceded that $3 million from Washington would only offset a small portion of the New Haven's losses, and he could only hope that local communities would generate the necessary matching funds. The two governors also vowed to provide as much as $20 million to the New Haven, principally for new and refurbished passenger cars. A former New Haven executive suggested that the Port of New York Authority should take over the company, but that agency wanted nothing to do with public transit. In Washington, Senator Javits and Representative Reid proposed that New York and

Connecticut would provide funds to offset two-thirds of the New Haven's operating deficit, with the federal government furnishing the remainder. Rhode Island's Claiborne Pell favored a similar plan, expanded to include Rhode Island and Massachusetts. Connecticut senator Thomas J. Dodd introduced a bill to provide $75 million in federal support.[286]

When the legislative session opened on March 2, the Dodd legislation was the most generous of four bills that awaited members of Congress. The resulting hearings indicated that railroad officials and members of Congress held starkly different opinions regarding the relationship between Penn Central and the New Haven. Trustee Richard Joyce Smith, desperate to save his railroad, reiterated his assertion that Penn Central should not have to accept any of the New Haven's passenger operations. "We believe, if the Pennsylvania-Central merger is approved by the Interstate Commerce Commission," Smith insisted, "that a satisfactory basis for inclusion in the merged system of the New Haven's principal freight operations will have been achieved." His further comment that "we have not been able to negotiate for a continuation of our freight service on any basis that would involve the taking over of the passenger service by the Penn-Central group" suggested that Saunders and Perlman—if pushed too far—might simply abandon their merger plans and allow the New Haven to die an agonizing death.[287]

Members of Congress possessed a very different agenda, however. The financial well-being of the New Haven's investors was a minor matter, compared to the welfare of the millions of voters who depended on the company's service. Their statements reiterated a consistent theme. They acknowledged that some federal assistance was essential but insisted that the ICC should require the Penn Central to bear the burden of the New Haven's passenger service, as a condition associated with the merger. Robert Kennedy, successful in his 1964 Senate race, showed the most restraint. "We must be aware at all times that we are dealing with two kinds of passenger traffic—commuter and intercity or long haul," he observed. "The first line of approach for the future of the long haul operation is to require the Pennsylvania and New York Central Railroads to run it, should their merger be approved and should they take the New Haven's freight operations into their system." Kennedy highlighted his August 1964 memorandum of understanding with Saunders and Perlman yet committed the two executives to more than they had expected. "Prior to the time I left as Attorney General, I wrote a letter to my successor and left it in the files that it was my recommendation that opposition to the Pennsylvania and New

York Central merger should be withdrawn if the merger was approved by the ICC with the proviso that the New York Central and the Pennsylvania Railroad should take over the New Haven Railroad. And that was not to take over the New Haven freight service, but take over the New Haven freight and passenger service." When asked if the additional burden would cause the PRR and the NYC to withdraw their merger application, Kennedy predicted that the savings associated with the consolidation—which he predicted would reach $100 million per year—would preclude such a drastic outcome. "This merger is so attractive to them," he emphasized, "there is every reason to believe that the new combination could operate the New Haven's long haul passenger service without undue burden."[288]

Other elected officials volunteered to further expand the Penn Central's obligations. Jacob Javits, the other New York senator, also highlighted $100 million in economies, an amount $19 million above what Saunders had officially promised. "When they do merge and they are going to have to use a little of that money," Javits noted, to employ "a little of what they are saving by the merger in order to serve the public interest which allows them to continue as monopolies. And part of that public interest is going to be some continuance of some kind of passenger service." While Javits acknowledged the necessity of federal support for commuter rail services, he did not absolve the Penn Central of the ultimate responsibility of operating them. Nor did Connecticut senator Abraham Ribicoff. "For a long time there has been talk about the merger of the New York Central and the Pennsylvania," he observed. "It is my understanding that these railroads are more than willing to take over the freight part of the New Haven road. They are not interested in taking on the commuter and passenger service because they feel that this is too great a loss for them to carry. For them, it is a business proposition. Yet if a merger is to take place, it would seem to me that the tail should go with the rest of the animal." Ribicoff insisted that "we ought to use persuasion and encouragement and inducement more than compulsion," and he urged railroad executives and state and federal officials to "sit down and talk this over." Yet there was little doubt that elected representatives were increasingly willing to use the financial resources of the Pennsylvania Railroad and the New York Central to solve a difficult political problem.[289]

Rhode Island governor John H. Chafee was the only one who urged restraint. Forcing the PRR and the NYC to accept passenger service "appears to be a very risky step," he cautioned, "and I think should be approached warily because of the danger that the Penn-Central, who has been entering the marriage with the New Haven freight operations as a somewhat reluctant bridegroom, could well balk at this requirement and back out of the whole arrangement." Collapse of the merger agreement, Chafee concluded, would destroy the New Haven, "leaving Rhode Island without any class I railroad. While an organization might come in and pick up the pieces or some of them, the possibilities are so doubtful that I would hope great caution would be used before jeopardizing acquisition by the Penn-Central of New Haven's freight operations."[290]

Recommendation

Congressional testimony regarding the New Haven's future had barely concluded when the Interstate Commerce Commission decided the fate of the Penn Central merger application. On March 29, 1965, examiners Jerome Lyle and Henry Darmstadter suggested that the full commission should support the creation of the Pennsylvania-New York Central Transportation Company. Their exhaustive report, 446 pages long with appendixes that added a further 145 pages, devoted considerable attention to the underlying economic situation facing the eastern carriers. Lyle and Darmstadter noted that six of the seven railroads that were party to the proceedings were experiencing severe financial difficulties. The New Haven was bankrupt and on the verge of collapse and the Erie-Lackawanna and the Boston & Maine were posting chronic deficits. The modest profits earned by the PRR and the NYC over the preceding twelve years were attributable solely to income from investments in nonrail subsidiaries. Only the Delaware & Hudson generated respectable returns, and those were likely to disappear in the event of further deterioration in the eastern rail network. The examiners dismissed any notion that rapid growth in the American economy would restore the carriers to profitability. "We can see in the record no reason for optimism on the applicants' traffic level," they asserted, in a direct rebuke to the arguments made by the Justice Department. Lyle and Darmstadter also countered any lingering assertions—which reached their height decades earlier, during the Progressive Era—that the railroads continued to dominate the transportation sector of the economy or used monopoly power to extract exorbitant rates from passengers and shippers. "These roads, large as they may be, are engaged in a struggle for basic survival," they emphasized. Nor was the danger of ruin limited to the Pennsylvania Railroad and the New York Central. "We are dealing here essentially with a 'failing' industry," they suggested, "and not simply with an isolated instance of corporate collapse or impotency."[291]

Lyle and Darmstadter acknowledged that "the proposed merger clearly does not provide a panacea for the ills attending the applicants or the rail industry in the East." They nonetheless suggested that Saunders, Perlman, and other PRR and NYC executives had done everything that could reasonably be done with the resources available to them. Demolishing another Progressive Era shibboleth, they noted that "management has performed remarkably well in cutting costs, in achieving greater efficiency, and in reducing overall price, no mean feat in an inflationary economy." The ICC examiners presumed that the Penn Central merger would enhance those positive trends, enabling managers to improve service and generate a respectable rate of return on investment. They noted that all the opposition to the application came from adversely affected railroads, from state and local governments, and from the Justice Department—and none from shippers. The customers who used the Pennsylvania Railroad and the New York Central, Lyle and Darmstadter noted, accepted pledges, made by executives, that things could only get better once the merger took place. Their overview of the merger's effects on labor occupied no more than a dozen pages and noted that the May 1964 Luna-Saunders agreement ensured that the number of displaced workers would be zero.[292]

Given the limited and focused nature of the opposition, Lyle and Darmstadter were principally concerned with protecting other railroads that would likely suffer as a result of the merger. Chief among them was the New Haven. They acknowledged that the company had been in serious trouble since the late 1950s and "that without some radical change in existing conditions, even if this merger were denied, N. H. would face almost hopeless odds in extricating itself from bankruptcy." The examiners nonetheless had little patience with politicians in New York and New England who suggested that the Penn Central would be sufficiently powerful to underwrite the cost of rail transportation in the area. "While undoubtedly the public has a right to demand that private enterprise, employed in providing an essential service, meet its obligations to the public, this right does not embody the requirement that they commit fiscal or corporate suicide in providing an overall service for which no reasonable opportunity to attain an adequate return exists." For the ICC to mandate such a policy, they suggested, "would simply delay for a short time the complete abandonment of rail service into New England." Even worse, the inclusion of all New Haven services might drag the Penn Central into disaster. Such an arrangement "would require the merged company and shippers throughout the area served by the former literally to subsidize rail transportation in New England and the basic struggle for the survival of the railroad industry in the East is too closely drawn to impose such a burden."[293]

By the spring of 1965, however, the salvation of the New Haven had become a potent political force, and Lyle and Darmstadter could hardly ignore the issue. In an effort to balance the survival of that company against the financial welfare of the Penn Central, they concluded that the ICC should "provide for inclusion of N. H. but only to the extent necessary to protect it from the adverse affects [sic] flowing from the merger." In practical terms, the ICC would require the Penn Central to operate the New Haven's freight service—the only part of the company that was even modestly profitable and the only portion that was likely to suffer because of the merger of the Pennsylvania Railroad and the New York Central. Rather than saddle the Penn Central with the "staggering passenger burden" of the New Haven, Lyle and Darmstadter expected government agencies to come to the rescue. They observed that New England possessed a robust highway and airline network and that the abandonment of the New Haven's passenger service would cause little inconvenience—something that was not true with respect to freight operations. It was up to elected representatives to decide whether commuter and intercity passenger trains were worth saving. Any effort to force the Penn Central to provide passenger-service subsidies, the examiners concluded, was guaranteed to absolve political leaders of responsibility in that regard and to ensure that little public funding would be made available. A long-term solution to the passenger problem lay beyond the examiners' remit, and they cautioned that the matter remained unresolved. "This is not to say that any level of government is obligated to underwrite passenger service provided by any railroad," they concluded, "for in the final analysis, such action is a matter between the governing body and its citizens."[294]

When Lyle and Darmstadter proposed shifting the New Haven's passenger service to the public sector, it seemed initially that federal and state governments were willing to accept that responsibility. In truth, they had little choice. On March 30, the railroad's trustees made public the details associated with the $140 million PRR-NYC agreement to buy the company and incorporate its freight operations into the Penn Central. Trustee Richard Joyce Smith conceded that the New Haven "will proceed for elimination of all passenger service." He nonetheless placated commuters and intercity travelers with assurances that the PRR and the NYC "have expressed a willingness to continue operations on the New Haven's passenger service if suitable arrangements with public authorities can be made."

Public authorities heeded their side of the bargain on April 20. New York and Connecticut agreed to contribute $1.5 million in commuter subsidies as the local match for a $3 million federal demonstration grant funded by the Urban Mass Transportation Act. The money would only last for eighteen months, but everyone expressed confidence that it would allow ample opportunity to work out a permanent source of funding. Nelson Rockefeller was in Venezuela, but Acting Governor Malcolm Wilson reassured commuters that the agreement "will remove the sword of Damocles that has been hanging over them for a considerable time." The New Haven's future seemed assured, and few seemed concerned that Wilson tempered his confident predictions with the word hopefully.[295]

While the examiners imposed many additional conditions related to the merger's potential effects on other railroads, only one possessed any significance. The original 1957 PRR-NYC merger proposal frightened executives at the Erie and the Delaware, Lackawanna & Western into a consolidation. The Erie-Lackawanna struggled from its inception in 1960, and the 1964 union of the Norfolk & Western, the Nickel Plate, and the Wabash heralded further difficulties. For that reason, the ICC mandated the Appendix O provisions in their approval of the N&W merger. If the E-L, the Boston & Maine, or the Delaware & Hudson could demonstrate a loss of traffic and revenue, they had until 1969 to petition for inclusion in the Norfolk & Western system. Any hesitancy that E-L officials might have felt about becoming part of the N&W disappeared once it became apparent they would be surrounded by the Penn Central colossus. Erie-Lackawanna executives were abundantly clear in their preference to join the N&W but indicated that they expected the right of inclusion in the Penn Central, should their first preference prove unattainable. Persuading the ICC to implement the Appendix O provisions would not be an easy task, however. The Erie-Lackawanna's precarious financial position prevented the company from filing a petition for retroactive inclusion in the N&W merger. Nor would they find a warm welcome in their preferred home. Herman Pevler and his associates at the Norfolk & Western were prepared to move heaven and earth to distance themselves from the E-L, a company burdened with nearly a third of a billion dollars in debt.[296]

The situation placed Lyle and Darmstadter in an awkward position, one that reflected the difficulties associated with the ICC's unwillingness to evaluate the eastern mergers as a group. If they recommended approval of the Penn Central merger, they would likely be signing the Erie-Lackawanna's death warrant—unless that company could become part of the Norfolk & Western.[297] However, they lacked the authority to revisit the ICC's 1964 approval of the N&W merger or to force the commissioners to exercise the inclusion provisions associated with Appendix O. Nor could they mandate the addition of the Erie-Lackawanna to the Penn Central, so long as the E-L's relationship to the N&W remained unresolved.[298]

To protect the Erie-Lackawanna, the Norfolk & Western, and the Penn Central, Lyle and Darmstadter recommended a new set of inclusion provisions. Erie-Lackawanna executives would have a full decade to produce evidence of harm arising from the Penn Central merger. Barring their preferred option, inclusion in the expanded Norfolk & Western, they could then petition for consolidation into the Penn Central system. The Boston & Maine and the Delaware & Hudson enjoyed similar provisions, yet their relative financial strength suggested that the resolution of their Appendix O claims would be correspondingly less complicated. More significantly, neither the B&M nor the D&H demanded a delay in the Penn Central merger proceedings. The Erie-Lackawanna did, forcing Lyle and Darmstadter to exercise extreme care in the wording of their recommendations. "Considering all of these diverse factors," they emphasized, "inclusion of E-L into this merger cannot be provided for until some decision as to its proposed entry into the N&W System is made. On the other hand, to delay consummation of the instant [Penn Central] merger pending a change in the E-L's financial condition, so that terms and conditions for its inclusion into N&W can be drafted, may be too long in coming and too expensive, not only to the many carriers whose economic life is largely dependent on the outcome of the instant merger proceeding, but to the numerous shippers and communities which are dependent upon them."[299]

The examiners' Solomonic efforts to protect the Erie-Lackawanna without delaying the Penn Central merger fell rather short of the mark. Lyle and Darmstadter acknowledged that powerful political forces—including the states of New York and New Jersey, as well as the Port of New York Authority—were determined to protect the E-L through inclusion in a larger system. "It may well be that the governmental bodies which have so strongly advocated inclusion of E-L and demand that the latter continue to operate deficit-ridden passenger services may be in a position to provide an answer," Lyle and Darmstadter observed. "We cannot do so, and must make a choice designed to maximize the opportunities to achieve a sound and efficient transportation system." With that goal in mind, the examiners concluded that "an indefinite delay in consummation here [in the Penn Central

case] would have a broader and more direct affect upon applicants, those carriers dependent upon this merger and shippers and communities served by it. In other words, the major injury caused by delay clearly outweighs the smaller caused by consummation as soon as possible." Simply put, they were willing to sacrifice the Erie-Lackawanna to attain the greater benefits promised by the Penn Central. Yet they undermined that argument in a single, critical sentence—one that would present enormous difficulties for Saunders and Perlman. "Our assessment of competitive balance," Lyle and Darmstadter emphasized, "requires that the petition of E-L be first tested in the N&W proceeding before it is permitted inclusion in the instant merger."[300]

With the best of intentions, Lyle and Darmstadter suggested that the Penn Central merger should go forward, in the expectation that the Erie-Lackawanna could join at some point within the subsequent decade—ample time to sort out that railroad's possible inclusion in the Norfolk & Western. Erie-Lackawanna executives adopted a very different interpretation of that language, however. They argued that the Pennsylvania Railroad and the New York Central could not consummate their merger *until* the ICC decided whether the Erie-Lackawanna would be added to the Norfolk & Western. That perspective also appealed to William Orrick and other officials in the Antitrust Division of the Justice Department. The seemingly satisfactory resolution of the New Haven crisis greatly weakened their ability to block the formation of Penn Central. As one door closed, another opened, and Orrick discovered an alternate—and even more compelling—argument against the merger. Lyle and Darmstadter even pointed the way, when they acknowledged that "no consideration has been given to the effect of the proposed inclusion here of the D&H, B&M and/or E-L upon competition, and no effort has been made to assess or accommodate the antitrust laws in light of such action." As they well knew, the monopolistic issues associated with the various merger proposals were the responsibility of the ICC rather than the Justice Department. Orrick knew that too, but such subtleties hardly mattered. By styling the attorney general's office as the protector of the Erie-Lackawanna, the Boston & Maine, and the Delaware & Hudson, he found new hope that he might prevent the largest merger in American history.

Preparing a Company for Consolidation

The examiners' recommendation for approval of the Penn Central merger came as welcome—but not unexpected—news to Pennsylvania Railroad and New York

Central officials. Since arriving in Philadelphia eighteen months earlier, Stuart Saunders had done an outstanding job of undermining opposition to the consolidation, causing petitioner after petitioner to inform the ICC that their initial protests had been misguided. PRR and NYC share prices declined following the March 29 announcement, suggesting that the Wall Street analysts who praised the latest development in railroad finance had anticipated a favorable outcome. Investors also acknowledged that Lyle and Darmstadter had issued only preliminary recommendations, and that every policy they advocated was subject to modification by the full body of ICC commissioners. With the thorny problem of the New Haven seemingly resolved, however, there seemed little reason to doubt that the commission would quickly endorse the examiners' report. In a joint statement, Saunders and Perlman noted "that the conditions do not impose any insurmountable obstacles to consummation of the merger." Two weeks later, representatives from the two railroads held a planning session in New York and agreed that final ICC approval would likely occur by February 1966.[301]

In the aftermath of the positive examiners' report, Pennsylvania Railroad and New York Central executives began to make sincere efforts to integrate the personnel, organizational structure, and facilities of the two companies. The first alteration involved the senior leadership that would guide Penn Central. In December 1961, two weeks prior to the initial merger announcement and long before Saunders arrived on the scene, Symes, Perlman, and their respective allies reached an uneasy truce. The PRR board, whose members were hostile to Perlman, would select the Penn Central's chief executive officer. Their New York Central counterparts possessed the authority to appoint the president, who would act as the chief administrative officer. Symes and Perlman would occupy advisory roles as inactive cochairmen on the board. It was an unworkable arrangement, given the obvious friction between the two executives, and the October 1963 appointment of Saunders as the PRR's chairman did not solve the problem. Saunders was an attorney, and he delegated operating matters at the Norfolk & Western to his subordinates. He continued that practice on the Pennsylvania Railroad and intended to do so at Penn Central. Perlman, in contrast, possessed decades of experience in the practicalities of day-to-day railroading, but he was correspondingly less comfortable with the political and regulatory maneuvering at which Saunders excelled. In March 1965, shortly before Lyle and Darmstadter recommended approval of the merger, NYC director Isaac Grainger recommended a solution. Grainger had been a member of the committee that devised the initial

leadership team in 1961, and he saw firsthand the acrimony that accompanied that process. Now, he suggested that Saunders become the Penn Central's board chairman and CEO, in charge of corporate strategy, with Perlman serving as president and the chief administrative officer who would run the railroad's day-to-day operations. The two companies announced the decision on April 29, precisely one month after the release of the examiners' report. It was perhaps the only logical arrangement available, but it placed Perlman—who commanded the fierce loyalty of many of the NYC's executives—under the authority of a lawyer who was not a career railroader.[302]

The development of an operating plan for Penn Central was far more complex, and the process would not be completed until November 1967. Beginning in early 1962, PRR and NYC executives began working on the problem, under the direction of Walter Patchell, the vice president in charge of special services.[303] The Patchell report fulfilled its intended purpose. It helped to convince Lyle and Darmstadter—as well as many of those who were skeptical of the merger proposal—that the Penn Central would generate more than $81 million in annual savings while improving service and causing minimal disruption to shippers, workers, and local communities. The document could hardly be considered an effective operating plan, however, particularly as it often changed to accommodate local political considerations.[304]

Not long after the release of the examiners' report, Saunders and Perlman appointed themselves as the heads of a new merger steering committee and informed senior executives that the Patchell plan would be replaced by an entirely new document. "The necessity for these decisions," wrote one executive, "has arisen from an inability of the representatives of the two companies to agree or make compromise agreements during much of the pre-Merger planning period." Each railroad appointed a merger coordinator—PRR assistant general counsel Basil Cole and his NYC counterpart, Ferdinand L. Kattau—and established several intercompany committees. The effort, which involved more than seventy executives, represented a concerted effort to blend the best practices at each of the two companies. "The aim is not to fit one organization into the mold of the other," Saunders told the PRR's board of directors, "but to take what is best of each or formulate something new so that the merged company will be superior to either of its components. To this end, the focus has been on the essential functions performed by each department. Once it is decided just what is to be done, the organizational structure best suited to the job will be adopted."[305]

It was an ideal strategy, but one that quickly fell to pieces. The two companies exhibited such profound differences in transportation and traffic matters, as well as organizational cultures, that a truly hybrid system became impossible. Instead, it was soon apparent that one company's system must supersede the other, ensuring that one set of managers would overpower their rivals in the corresponding department on the other railroad. Under those circumstances, most of the executives associated with the intercompany committees fiercely defended their organizational prerogatives and gave scant support for alternate methodologies. Operating officials at the New York Central were directly answerable to corporate headquarters. They were accustomed to the speedy movement of high-value merchandise and were generally willing to emulate Perlman's fondness for cutting-edge equipment and methods. Their counterparts at the PRR, despite the mitigating effects of the 1964 reorganization, functioned on a far more decentralized basis. Their goal was generally to move bulk cargoes at low speeds. To do so, they relied on proven techniques that stood the test of time—and that NYC officials frequently dismissed as outdated. The Pennsylvania Railroad operated only 6.8 percent more track miles than the New York Central, yet in 1957 it generated 32 percent more ton miles. That statistic reflected the slow, heavy trains operated by the PRR. Those shipments correspondingly caused considerable damage to the track, which was in worse shape than that on the NYC. Despite that disparity, the New York Central invested more heavily in the repair of the physical plant. In 1955, for example, the company allocated 12.15 percent of earnings to maintenance of way and structures, compared to 10.87 percent on the Pennsylvania Railroad. The NYC also relied more heavily on mechanization, while the PRR continued to employ more traditional, labor-intensive practices.[306]

Marketing issues were similarly incompatible. NYC traffic personnel moved aggressively to solicit new business and to prevent shipments from being lost to the nearby New York Thruway and the St. Lawrence Seaway. They favored selective rate cuts and tailored services—practices that ICC regulators were just beginning to accept. Like their colleagues in transportation, they regarded the PRR as hopelessly old-fashioned. They complained that traffic personnel such as Fred Carpi and his successor, Henry W. Large, demanded across-the-board rate increases without generating any statistics regarding the actual cost of movement associated with each shipment. Prospective investors were well aware of the disparity between the two companies. "It is our impression that the Central is taking positive steps to revise its rate structure for the purpose of regaining traffic from nonrail competitors but with a due regard for operating costs," securities analyst Henry Lyne Jr. informed the Finance Committee of the Penn Mutual Life Insurance Company. "On the other hand, we have gained the impression that the Pennsylvania has shown a less positive interest in competitive rate revisions, outside of their 'piggyback' operations. Also, we are unaware of any major PRR property improvement program either in progress or projected except for the building of freight cars." Lyne was equally critical of the PRR's poor operating practices. "In the course of our conversations with large railroads in the west, south and southwest," he informed Treasurer William Gerstnecker, "we have quite frequently been told that effective competition with non-rail carriers for long haul traffic interchanged with the Pennsylvania was made more difficult for them because of the unreliability of your service."[307]

The profound differences in corporate cultures and operating practices perversely ensured that PRR and NYC officials agreed on one crucial matter. On merger day, it would not be possible to begin integrated operations of the two companies as a single entity. Cole and Kattau emphasized "the formidable array of operating problems which must be dealt with during the early weeks and months of the merged company." The initial structure of the combined firm envisioned a vice president in charge of operations—an individual who had not yet been chosen—with oversight over two chief operating officers. One would oversee the "Southern Lines," that had formerly been part of the PRR and the other the "Northern Lines" of the NYC. Each half of the Penn Central would include three regions that in turn controlled twenty-three divisions, three fewer than the combined total prior to the merger. Cole and Kattau nonetheless warned that "the Operating officers of both companies feel that it would not be practicable to go to the presently planned twenty-three divisions and six regions on M-Day." They also cautioned that "it will be some months before a uniform accounting system can be installed and implemented in the new company." The leaders of the planning process acknowledged warnings provided by managers at both companies, who were "particularly concerned that a minimum of 90 days lead time is mandatory to effect the changes in the Freight Car Movement Reporting system"—something that was vital to ensure the proper routing of shipments over the Penn Central. The absence of work-rules agreements with the unions likewise indicated the necessity of "operating as two distinct railroad properties (though merged)." Cole and Kattau thus suggested "that, on M-Day, the officers and personnel . . . will have the same relationship to the

Penn-Central as they now have individually with either the Pennsylvania or the Central." Even though that incremental strategy would leave "a myriad of management and personnel type problems to be resolved," they concluded, "it is felt that this course of action, although giving the appearance of moving more slowly toward integration of the new company, will actually result in a more orderly transition."[308]

Despite the differing corporate cultures, at least the PRR and NYC operating and traffic personnel cooperated, to varying degrees, with the intercompany merger committees. Those associated with financial matters did not. After joining the Pennsylvania Railroad in May 1951, Bevan grew increasingly concerned at the company's deteriorating financial position. He attempted to restrain capital expenditures advocated by operating personnel, cautioned against excessive dividends, and sought new methods of generating money. The 1957–1958 recession produced catastrophic consequences for the PRR and gave Bevan both a determination to implement financial reforms and an opportunity to exploit the crisis mentality among senior executives. In February 1958, Vice President Newell warned the nine regional managers of "the very unsatisfactory financial outlook for the year 1958, necessitating drastic reductions in our forces, without affecting the efficiency of our operations." As part of that initiative, Newell asked regional personnel to prepare detailed lists of their overhead expenditures. It was up to Bevan to make sense of that data, and he recommended a multifaceted approach for doing so. "We believe that in certain respects we can probably strengthen our budgetary and cost controls and establish a cost accounting system," he informed the regional managers in December. "It is also our desire to be able to render income statements by Region that will be accepted by all of you as being sound and accurate."[309]

In his effort "to end up with the best accounting and budgetary setup in the railroad industry," Bevan demanded an ambitious program that "as now envisioned will probably take from two to three years." As a preliminary step, he secured the appointment of the accounting firm Peat, Marwick, Mitchell & Company "to make an overall study of our accounting, budgeting and cost control operations." He used the results of the study to bolster his long-standing advocacy for computing and centralized data-management systems. In March 1962, Bevan's Financial Department established an Electronic Data Processing Division, with a new IBM computer system. A few months later, Bevan persuaded William S. Cook to leave General Electric and become the PRR's deputy comptroller, in charge of the modernization of the railroad's accounting methods.

Other initiatives followed, including the installation of car-control and inventory-control computer systems in 1963. Working in collaboration with Peat, Marwick, Mitchell, Bevan used computers in conjunction with new accounting techniques that could generate accurate and up-to-date income and capital budgets. The more precise budgetary forecasts, in turn, were vital to Bevan's efforts to control costs, generate additional investment capital, and pay down a portion of the PRR's massive debt. He had little use for the ICC's accounting methods, which dated to the Progressive Era and assigned revenues and costs to largely arbitrary categories. Based on his experience with banking and industry, Bevan favored responsibility accounting, which could accurately allocate expenditures to specific departments and divisions. The new system offered a mechanism to compare the performance of one manager against another—a competitive standard that won Bevan few friends among operating personnel. In September 1964, the PRR began using commercial telephone lines during off-peak hours to transmit payroll data stored on magnetic tape between Computer Data Centers in Philadelphia, Pittsburgh, and Chicago. By the following summer, technicians were implementing the MIDAS (Management Information Developed from Advanced Systems) initiative, which collected information from 181 locations across the company. Within five hours, MIDAS could process data and transmit reports to supervisors throughout PRR territory. Further progress occurred after Bevan hired Carl G. Sempier in the spring of 1966. Sempier had been IBM's marketing manager for transportation at Philadelphia and thus possessed a wealth of knowledge regarding both computers and railroad operations. He soon developed an integrated system that could keep track of car loadings, car movements, waybills, and revenues.[310]

Bevan's methods, which began to show results in 1963, had little appeal to executives at the New York Central. He despised his counterpart, NYC vice president in charge of finance Walter R. Grant, and the feeling was mutual. Grant's accountants continued to employ ICC methods, with their attendant limitations. Perlman relied heavily on

Facing, David Bevan recruited Carl Sempier from IBM and instructed him to integrate computers into the PRR's operating, accounting, and budgeting functions. Sempier nonetheless encountered resistance from many longtime executives, individuals who were familiar with railroad operations but who possessed little knowledge of an alien technology. *Pennsylvania Railroad Photographs, Hagley Museum & Library, acc. 1988.231.*

capital budgets, generally developed in lengthy meetings that enabled senior managers to advocate for their favorite projects. Unlike Bevan, however, he was not familiar with income budgets, and therefore possessed scant ability to accurately allocate costs to specific units or to evaluate one official against another. Despite Perlman's belief in centralized control, the NYC's computer system was poorly integrated, and Sempier complained that that company's data-management resources were "spread throughout the organization. For instance, data origination and terminal management are within operations; data communications and network are within communications and signals; computer operations are within the financial department; and operations research is within the operating department." That dispersal ensured that the New York Central could not match the functionality Bevan had achieved at the PRR, nor could it use computers to effectively coordinate operations, car-tracking, costs, and budgeting. Moreover, the NYC system generated an error rate of 10 percent, twenty times that on the PRR, suggesting that much of the accumulated data was either inaccurate or simply useless. In 1965, during the merger-planning process, Bevan suggested that Grant adopt the PRR system, with Sempier to oversee implementation. It was a generous offer, but one that would ensure that Bevan rather than Grant would have pride of place in the Penn Central. Grant refused and promised that the New York Central would have a Univac 418 system in service within a year. It was not, and on the eve of the merger, Sempier dismissed the NYC technology as only "partially operational."[311]

Saunders was not particularly interested in computers and data-management systems, but he wanted to prepare the Pennsylvania Railroad's equipment and facilities for the merger. His efforts benefited immensely from the PRR's modest prosperity during the early 1960s, which increased both revenues and the demands from operating officials for an increasing number of improvements to the physical plant. In October 1964, months before Lyle and Darmstadter released their report, Saunders pledged to increase that year's $120 million in capital spending to $150 million in 1965. The following January, he again raised the amount, to $166 million. The budget included $34 million for 150 new freight locomotives, part of an effort to replace the initial contingent of diesels with more modern and efficient second-generation motive power. The railroad would also buy sixty-one hundred new freight cars and rehabilitate eighty-two hundred others. It was one of the largest such investments in the PRR's history, one that would accommodate what Saunders hoped would be steadily increasing freight traffic. One of the less expensive

components of the betterment program involved the conversion of ninety sleeping cars into maintenance-of-way equipment—a sure sign that passenger traffic had left the railroad and would not return.[312]

While the PRR's operating officials eagerly anticipated the new equipment and improvements to the physical plant, Bevan became increasingly concerned at the rapidly mounting cost of the betterment program. He had seen this before, and he knew from experience that Symes's lavish expenditures had done little to improve the PRR's rate of return on investment. Bevan's new accounting and budgeting systems enabled him to calculate some troubling trends. Between 1956 and 1965, the PRR's capital budget averaged $87.5 million annually. For the three years 1964 through 1966, however, the $480 million in capital expenditures equated to $160 million a year. Unfortunately, as he informed Saunders in December 1965, the PRR's earnings had not kept pace with those expenditures. While operating personnel projected profits of $50 million in both 1964 and 1965, the actual results were $29 million the first year and $28 million the second. Large projects, many of them not directly related to transportation, were incurring lengthy delays and cost overruns. They included the demolition of Penn Station and the development of Madison Square Garden, which in 1965 exceeded its budget by more than $800,000. Bevan, who was ultimately responsible for borrowing the money needed to finance the various improvements, also warned that interest charges and the need to establish larger depreciation allowances were imperiling the railroad's working capital and undermining his efforts—underway since he joined the company in 1951—to reduce debt burdens.[313]

As Bevan informed Saunders, the New York Central was also enjoying reasonable profits, without matching the PRR's level of capital spending. Between 1962 and 1966, the NYC invested $73 million per year in the physical plant and equipment, compared to $137.6 million on the Pennsylvania Railroad. In the more recent period, 1964–1966, the disparity was even greater—$95 million for the NYC and $180.1 million for the PRR in an average year. Bevan's data indicated that the Pennsylvania Railroad, a company that was a quarter larger than the New York Central, was spending nearly twice as much on capital improvements. Much of the variance, Bevan suggested, was attributable to the vastly different budgetary procedures at each company. The PRR's division superintendents and other operating personnel frequently made vague and unsubstantiated assertions regarding the payoff associated with a particular project. Perlman, in contrast, demanded that New York Central executives demonstrate at least a 20 percent return on investment, with a 30 percent threshold for initiatives that involved only labor costs. As he progressively implemented improved accounting methods—which in turn permitted the generation of accurate income budgets and capital budgets—Bevan warned that the PRR's spending policies were woefully out of date and out of step with the methods employed by its merger partner.[314]

Readjustment

Despite the desire of PRR and NYC officials to move forward with merger planning, final ICC approval of the consolidation was by no means assured. Following the favorable recommendation by examiners Lyle and Darmstadter, on March 29, 1965, protesting parties had until July 14 to file exceptions to their report, and twenty-six did so. Eleven were railroads.[315] None of those eleven carriers objected outright to the consolidation of the Pennsylvania Railroad and the New York Central, nor did they deny that the merger was in the public interest. Instead, they each sought some measure of protection against the harm that the Penn Central was likely to do to them. In compensation, they demanded trackage rights, guaranteed interchange of traffic, and preferential routings. Fifteen objections came from government agencies and associated parties in seven states. Most related to the precise terms associated with the New Haven's inclusion in Penn Central, and several others were from Pennsylvania jurisdictions concerned about reductions in jobs and service. The twenty-odd replies to the examiners' report followed a similar pattern.[316] Such concessions were to be expected, were unlikely to cause the commissioners to make significant alterations to the recommendations made by Lyle and Darmstadter, and would not likely delay final approval of the merger.[317]

The most serious difficulty involved the future of the New Haven's intercity and commuter passenger service. Lyle and Darmstadter feared that the addition of those services to Penn Central's formidable responsibilities might imperil the financial stability of the newly merged company. If regulators or railroad executives believed that the examiners' report excused the Penn Central from accepting the "staggering passenger burden" of the New Haven, however, then they were badly mistaken. The editors of the *New York Times* lamented that "the much-jolted commuters of the bankrupt New Haven Railroad have now had official confirmation that they will be orphans in the projected absorption of the New Haven into a merged Pennsylvania-New York Central system." Elected officials quickly volunteered to protect their orphaned constituents,

although they were more reticent about the possibility of public funding for the orphanage. Two Connecticut politicians—Senator Thomas Dodd and Representative Donald J. Irwin—complained that Lyle and Darmstadter had done too little to protect passenger service in their state. The state's governor, John Dempsey, was even more direct in his recommendations. "I am disappointed that the examiners did not recommend inclusion of the passenger service provided by the New Haven," he told reporters. "Savings resulting from the merger should be used by the [Penn Central] system to offset any passenger deficit. I will ask the Interstate Commerce Commission to reconsider the examiners' report."[318]

The modest proposals to provide government subsidies for commuter service were at any rate inadequate, temporary, and subject to the vagaries of the political process. In an announcement that inadvertently coincided with the examiners' report, the Housing and Home Finance Agency dealt a serious blow to the commuter-assistance plan developed by Dempsey and his New York counterpart, Nelson Rockefeller. Federal officials noted that they would "probably" approve the $3 million demonstration grant—but the money would last only for eighteen months and was restricted to the routes between New York City and Westchester and Fairfield Counties in Connecticut. A larger HHFA award for new equipment was unlikely unless the agency received "assurances that the commuter services were going to continue in operation for a long period." What would happen next was anyone's guess, and the agreement provided no assistance whatsoever for the New Haven's remaining commuter operations, or for its equally problematic intercity passenger service. The most politically expedient choice involved assigning the problem to the Penn Central. Elected officials could not help but notice that the PRR's consolidated net earnings grew steadily during the early 1960s, from $8.6 million at the beginning of the decade to more than $60 million in 1964. The largest annual increase occurred in the year that preceded the ICC examiners' report, and politicians eagerly echoed Saunders's public predictions that such growth would continue indefinitely. If so, there seemed little reason why some portion of those profits could not be redirected to the preservation of the New Haven's commuter and intercity passenger service.[319]

The political situation in Pennsylvania remained complex, and remarkably fluid. Representatives from the state government again reversed course, and they now vowed to oppose the merger. State attorney general Walter E. Alessandroni highlighted the damage the Penn Central would do to the Erie-Lackawanna and the anthracite carriers in northeastern Pennsylvania. At the very least, he informed the ICC, the E-L should be protected through inclusion in the Norfolk & Western. Alessandroni also demanded a guarantee that the Penn Central would ignore key elements of the Patchell report and maintain the existing level of freight service along the PRR's main line.[320]

Municipal officials in Pittsburgh became more conciliatory, thanks in part to Saunders's support for urban redevelopment. In the immediate aftermath of World War II, PRR officials cooperated with board member Richard King Mellon and other advocates of the Pittsburgh Renaissance. By 1952, work was well underway on the Gateway Center and Point Park, much of which was situated on land formerly occupied by the PRR's Duquesne Freight House. Saunders, Mellon, and former governor David Lawrence backed the even more ambitious Penn Park development. PRR facilities occupied 80 percent of the 148-acre site, and construction would require the removal of Union Station, a large portion of its associated coach yard, a produce yard, and the Fort Wayne bridge over the Allegheny River. Planning began in 1966, when David Bevan and his assistant, William Gerstnecker, toured the site. They subsequently solicited the advice of Vincent Kling, one of the architects associated with the development of Penn Center in Philadelphia. On May 5, 1966, Saunders highlighted the project to a group of business executives and government officials gathered at the Duquesne Club, causing Mellon to remark that "this is the biggest thing that has ever happened in Pittsburgh." In his determination to gain favorable publicity, Saunders made the announcement without informing the PRR's other directors and—more problematically—before the railroad had acquired all the necessary land. Real estate prices increased by $5 million, and the added cost of the project, coupled with protests from residents who would be displaced by the redevelopment, ensured that Penn Park never came to fruition. It was a disappointing fiasco, although one that saved a large urban passenger terminal from destruction. Regardless of the outcome, the redevelopment initiative significantly assuaged local fears that Pittsburgh would be almost wholly dependent on the Penn Central for rail service.[321]

Following the release of the examiners' report, Milton Shapp intensified his opposition to the merger. He continued to highlight the loss of freight traffic as well as the willingness of PRR executives to modify operating routines to suit political considerations. Shapp remained vigilant for any mistake on the part of Pennsylvania Railroad executives, to help make his case. On December 16,

1965, Saunders addressed the mayor and the city council in New Castle, Pennsylvania, some fifty miles northwest of Pittsburgh. The elected officials were strongly opposed to the merger—and had said as much to the ICC—thanks to the proposed downgrading of the Fort Wayne line and the rerouting of traffic over the Pittsburgh & Lake Erie. For the PRR's chairman, it was simply another episode in a seemingly endless effort to pick off the merger's opponents, one by one. In this instance, he indicated that Patchell might have been somewhat hasty in his conclusion that a substantial portion of the Penn Central's freight traffic should bypass the city. To prove his point, Saunders offered two books of modified operating plans, suggesting that New Castle would thrive under the new regime. Suitably reassured, the city council reversed course and voted to support the merger. Shapp did not attend the council meeting, but he soon heard the results, and he obtained a tape recording and a transcript of the proceedings. The new proposals, Shapp insisted, offered no guarantees that Penn Central would maintain traffic levels in Pennsylvania, and merely proved that Saunders would say whatever was convenient at the moment, in order to disorient his opponents. On January 3, 1966, Shapp demanded that the ICC reopen the record, so he could use the New Castle incident as an argument against the merger. As a private citizen, Shapp lacked legal standing in the case—a situation he remedied through the simple expedient of buying a few shares of PRR stock. Saunders dismissed this latest annoyance, insisting that the New Castle documents "were not new plans for merged operations as Mr. Shapp asserted, but actually were progress reports on planning for implementing phases of merger operations." ICC officials were equally dismissive of Shapp's arguments, noting that he submitted as evidence only those small portions of the transcript that supported his opinion. "We find no serious impediment in this respect," they declared, "and can see no basis for this exception."[322]

Political leaders representing the city and county of Philadelphia feared a reduction in both jobs and freight service, but a new round of concessions from Saunders quickly overcame their objections. On July 12, 1965, two days after Alessandroni filed objections on behalf of the commonwealth, Mayor James Tate announced that he now supported the merger. Tate's about-face reflected the ongoing rivalry between eastern port cities. In December 1963, the Supreme Court upheld the ICC directive for the Chesapeake & Ohio's control of the Baltimore & Ohio. The following spring, the combined C&O–B&O system sought to include the Western Maryland. Those realignments were bound to strengthen Baltimore and its port, to the detriment of Philadelphia. The consolidation of the Norfolk & Western, the Nickel Plate, and the Wabash would similarly shift traffic south to Hampton Roads, at the mouth of Chesapeake Bay. The PRR's chairman saw the threat and with it the corresponding opportunity to win Tate's support. He reiterated promises to improve port facilities along the Delaware River waterfront and pledged to maintain an adequate level of freight service to Philadelphia. "Mr. Saunders is well aware of Philadelphia's growth potential and has expressed his eagerness in helping us promote it," the mayor emphasized. "The Pennsylvania is participating actively and constructively in many port projects for improving Philadelphia." Tate also praised the PRR's efforts, which never proceeded beyond the planning stage, to build a sports complex over the tracks at the northern end of 30th Street Station.[323] He further emphasized that he had received assurances from Saunders that "not only will there be no loss of total employment in Philadelphia, but the city actually stands to gain several thousand new jobs by virtue of the consolidation." While neither Tate nor Saunders said so publicly, the agreement was in effect an admission that the Penn Central's headquarters would be located in Philadelphia rather than in New York.[324]

Saunders's final concession meshed with Tate's interest in using local, state, and federal funds to improve the city's suburban commuter rail operations. The logical next step would be a larger program to revitalize passenger service from New York to Washington, by way of Philadelphia. "Situated as we are between the Nation's political and financial capitals," the mayor emphasized, "this service would be a great asset to Philadelphia." Such projects were expensive, however, and public funding was rarely easy to obtain. Tate hinted that the Penn Central would undoubtedly have the resources to pay for the development of a high-speed rail corridor. If that merger included the New Haven, then so much the better, as single-line service could be extended north to Boston. "Also of great importance to Philadelphia," Tate concluded, "would be the increased capacity of the merged railroads to develop high-speed passenger service between Washington, New York and Boston."[325]

By the time Tate withdrew Philadelphia's objections to the Penn Central merger, Saunders had committed the Pennsylvania Railroad to the development of a modern passenger-rail corridor linking the great metropolitan areas of the Northeast. The project was bound to be expensive and fraught with technological difficulties, but

it also offered some compelling benefits. The least significant was the opportunity to increase patronage on the only PRR passenger service that still generated a profit. As Mayor Tate's comments indicated, the political benefits could be even more substantial. It was indeed fortuitous for Saunders that investments in high-speed rail helped to win Tate's loyalty, but the City of Philadelphia was not his principal target. Two presidents—first Kennedy and later Johnson—saw the project as a way to revitalize urban areas, keep pace with technological developments in other countries, gain federal control over transportation policy, win votes in the Northeast, and ensure the loyalty of Democrats in Congress. With the Justice Department still firmly opposed to the Penn Central merger, improved passenger service gave Saunders a powerful bargaining chip, one that he could use to gain support from the White House. The PRR's chairman had made concession after concession, in his bid to overcome opposition to the merger, and he was willing to make one more. A unique combination of political circumstances provided Saunders with a vehicle to secure approval of the merger, one that moved at 150 miles an hour.

Metroliner

During the late 1950s and early 1960s, two developments stimulated interest in high-speed rail travel along the Eastern Seaboard. Japan's rapid recovery from World War II overtaxed the capacity of the country's narrow-gauge railway network. The 1956 electrification of the nation's most important rail route, between Tokyo and Osaka, failed to keep pace with demand. Despite widespread perceptions that auto and air travel would soon render railways irrelevant, Shinji Sogō, the president of Japanese National Railways, was a forceful advocate of a completely new, standard-gauge line between the two cities. He succeeded in part because Japanese business and government leaders wanted to demonstrate the country's economic and technological prowess, and to offer a transportation showpiece to coincide with the 1964 Tokyo Olympic Games. In December 1958, the Japanese government accepted the proposal. Construction expenses ballooned to double the original estimates, ending the careers of both Shinji Sogō and his engineering deputy, Hideo Shima. Observers in the United States paid little attention to the cost overruns, however. Nor did they appreciate that the goal of Japanese transportation planners was to create a high-capacity, rather than a high-speed, railway—in that context, velocity was merely a necessary, albeit inspiring, means

The *Metroliner* project represented the PRR's last-ditch effort to save passenger service between New York and Washington while dampening opposition to the proposed merger with the New York Central. Transportation planners and federal officials perceived an opportunity to emulate Japanese successes in high-speed rail travel, solve the transportation problems in the Northeast, and win support for the Democratic Party. Those goals did not align well, and the smiles on the faces of board chairman Stuart Saunders (*left*) and Transportation Secretary Alan Boyd (*right*) disguised serious conflicts between the railroad and the federal government. *Courtesy of the Special Collections Research Center, Temple University Libraries, Philadelphia, PA.*

to shove as many vehicles as possible down a fixed guideway. Instead, Americans marveled at the sleek and modern *Shinkansen* "bullet trains" that zipped between Tokyo and Osaka at speeds of 130 miles per hour.[326]

The second, contemporaneous development arose from the scholarship of French geographer Jean Gottmann. Fleeing the Nazi onslaught, Gottmann immigrated to the United States, where he taught initially at Johns Hopkins University and later at Princeton's Institute for Advanced Study. Gottmann was thus intimately familiar with the urban geography of the Northeast, a subject that animated his research for the remainder of his career. In 1957, he published a seminal article, "Megalopolis, or the Urbanization of the Northeastern Seaboard," followed four years later by an eight-hundred-page book, *Megalopolis: The Urbanized Northeastern Seaboard of the United States.* At a time when many people regarded urban sprawl as "a menace or a cancer," Gottmann perceived instead "the cradle of a new order in the organization of inhabited space." This "pioneer area" stretched six hundred miles between southern New Hampshire and northern Virginia and was home to thirty-seven million people. With a "personality all its own," Gottmann asserted, the megalopolis demanded integrated regional planning that transcended the activities of local and state governments. The editor of the *New York Times* supported Gottmann's recommendations, reminding readers that "whether we like this urbanization drift or not, we have to accept it and we have the opportunity and the obligation to make it as livable as possible."[327]

Significantly, when the editor of the *Times* acknowledged that the megalopolis "scares some of us, whether we look at it on a map or from the air or try to steer a motor car through it," one mode of transportation was notable by its omission. That perspective was understandable, given the rapid growth of commercial aviation and highway travel in the Northeast. In April 1961, Eastern Air Lines introduced the Air-Shuttle, offering hourly flights between New York and Washington. Reservations were not necessary, and the cost was $12.75. That was only slightly more expensive than the $10.65 ticket price for the PRR's slower and less frequent rail service. Business travelers increasingly headed to the airport rather than to the train station, and the decision of PRR managers to reduce train frequencies, defer equipment maintenance, and sideline dining cars did little to bring them back. Those who preferred to drive could take advantage of the federal government's $2 billion investment in the region's road network. On November 14, 1963, President John F. Kennedy presided over the opening of the last major segment of Interstate 95, placing in service a superhighway linking Boston and Washington.[328]

Despite travelers' preferences for air and highway travel, some politicians were beginning to emphasize the value of an improved rail network that would serve the millions of voters who lived in the megalopolis. While Japanese engineers and construction crews were building the *Shinkansen* and Jean Gottmann was describing "a new order in the organization of inhabited space," a profound transformation was taking place within the Democratic Party. John F. Kennedy prevailed in the 1960 presidential election by the closest popular-vote margin in American history, a situation created in part by the exodus of White southerners toward the Republicans. If the president were to have any hope of reelection, he would need to build support in the cities and suburbs of the megalopolis. His prospects looked brightest in Philadelphia, where first Joseph Clark and then Richardson Dilworth displaced a series of mayors who depended on the support of both the Republican political machine and the Pennsylvania Railroad. Each possessed a reputation for integrity and good government. By the time Kennedy was in the White House, Clark was at the other end of Pennsylvania Avenue, as a reliable ally in the Senate.

The situation in New York was less promising. Both of the state's senators were Republicans, as was Governor Nelson Rockefeller. Robert F. Wagner Jr. was the latest in a string of Democratic mayors in a reliably Democratic city. Yet that was part of the problem, as Wagner was also part of a long tradition of politicians linked to Tammany Hall. As Kennedy well knew, middle-class suburbanites living in the megalopolis had little stomach for urban political corruption. That was something that might drive them away from the Democratic Party, just as his support for civil rights had alienated southerners. Journalist James Reston sensed the tension as he covered the president's visit to New York in November 1961, shortly before the mayoral election. Kennedy's "usual statement of support" for Wagner, Reston observed, "was dutiful and dry, like kissing your sister."[329] Kennedy, he suggested, was also "identified with the Democratic politics of Boston, which are about as bad as politics come." Channeling Gottmann's imagery of a megalopolis, Reston emphasized something that Kennedy clearly knew—"in this sprawling conglomeration, which can easily hold the balance of national political power, there is probably more bad government than in any other urban complex in America, most of it identified with the Democratic party."[330]

Kennedy's efforts to change the party's image in time for the 1964 election would depend on both his success in reorienting political power from the cities to Washington and his ability to recruit unimpeachable allies in Congress. One of his best prospects was a recently elected senator from Rhode Island—a state that occupied an important position in the megalopolis, midway between Boston and New York. Claiborne Pell was an iconoclastic politician, considered by his colleagues as "the ultimate outsider" and initially dismissed by Kennedy as the "least electable man in America."[331] An unpretentious individual, Pell often rode city buses and wore threadbare clothes that he washed himself at a laundromat. He knew the Kennedys well, and once dated JFK's sister Kathleen. Pell ran without the endorsement of the state's Democratic Party leadership, and therefore avoided many of the accompanying political obligations. Like Kennedy, he skillfully exploited the new medium of television. In January 1961, five days after Pell took the oath of office, a CBS News correspondent dubbed him a "beardless Lincoln," largely because of his height rather than his limited catalog of legislative achievements. That August, Pell urged restraint in the Berlin Crisis, in a speech that drew national attention. During his freshman year in the Senate, Pell supported the president's efforts for expanded unemployment compensation, a higher minimum wage, economic aid to depressed areas, assistance for education and housing, and an extended tenure for the federal Civil Rights Commission. He earned a 100 percent rating from Americans for Democratic Action, a liberal political organization that counted among its members many of the individuals associated with the Kennedy administration.[332]

Pell's mannerisms and political style held important implications for the development of high-speed rail travel in the Northeast and for the PRR's role in that process. Pell preferred to travel to and from Washington by train, and he saw firsthand the steady deterioration of the New Haven and the Pennsylvania Railroad. At some point, perhaps on one of those trips, he read Gottmann's *Megalopolis*. Pell found the geographer's work informative and inspirational, and in 1966 he published a personal perspective on the subject, *Megalopolis Unbound: The Supercity and the Transportation of Tomorrow*. In May 1962, Pell issued a statement that pulled together his commitment to governing for the public good, his concern for the failing health of the railroads, and his fascination with an integrated northeastern urban environment. "The number of passengers riding the Pennsylvania is about 61 per cent of what it was ten years ago," he emphasized, noting that "this trend was also reflected in a decline in passenger cars." Using information that came directly from Gottmann's research, Pell stressed the importance of rail transportation to "our Eastern 'Megalopolis.'" He highlighted the potential of Philadelphia's recently established Passenger Service Improvement Corporation—an ideal model, given that it arose from a rare example of a city whose Democratic government was more closely associated with reform than with corruption. Pell called for a similar public agency, spanning eight northeastern states and the District of Columbia, with authority to issue $500 million in bonds.[333] The funding, he predicted, would ensure that "the railroad passenger traffic should soon be back to what it was in 1950. Perhaps even to what it was in 1910. And in a few more years we would find this strip of railroad track the economic link binding this whole area together, bringing decent, clean transportation to people throughout the Northeastern Seaboard states at a fair price."[334]

It was a compelling vision, yet one that suggested Pell knew little about either railway economics or transportation technology. "The inherent problem with Pell's proposal," one PRR executive observed, "was that the authority would not make grants to the railroads for the development of this service, but loans which would have to be repaid." Given the steady postwar decline in passenger service, it would be a foolhardy executive indeed who

would borrow such sums in the hope that improved service could lure travelers back to the rails. Pell's suggestion that trains might one day rely on monorails or rocket propulsion reflected the technological enthusiasm of the era rather than the realities of railroad transportation. Boston & Maine president Patrick McGinnis labeled the plan "pie in the sky." A Wall Street analyst employed the words *nonsense* and *naive*, while asking "if Senator Pell assumed that it can be done by government, why can't it be done by industry?"[335]

Despite the criticism, Pell's vision captured the imagination of journalists, urban planners, and politicians. The *New York Times* editorialized that it was one of the only "new, fresh, imaginative and workable ideas" to emerge from "President Kennedy's generation" and expressed relief that "it neither adds to Federal costs nor Federal power." Two months after Pell unveiled his proposal, the New York Regional Plan Association—like Pell, inspired by Gottmann's work—issued a report addressing the most serious issues facing that corner of the megalopolis.[336] Planners suggested that a "modern high-speed rail system from Boston to Washington might possibly save precious air and airport space by diverting short-haul air passengers to railroads"—to the consternation of Eastern Air Lines officials, who insisted that their Air-Shuttle was not overtaxing the region's transportation capacity. While they did not explicitly endorse Pell's visionary rocket-propelled trains, the members of the Regional Plan Association called for top operating speeds of two hundred miles per hour—something that had never been achieved or even remotely approached by any rail system.[337]

Such audacious claims were in keeping with the optimism of the space age and the insecurities of the Cold War. On February 20, 1962, less than four months prior to the publication of the editorial in the *New York Times*, John Glenn became the first American to orbit Earth. His achievement suggested that the United States was catching up to—and might soon surpass—the Soviet Union. In September, Kennedy told Americans, "We choose to go to the Moon in this decade." A massive financial commitment from the federal government ensured success in that endeavor. Under the circumstances, there could be little doubt that efforts to develop high-speed rail in the Northeast, a project that evolved at almost precisely the same time as the Apollo program, would experience anything other than a comparable level of success.[338]

Pell's controversial proposal, as well as the more impractical schemes that accompanied it, garnered support from the one individual whose opinion mattered most. On October 3, Pell wrote to President Kennedy, calling attention to the increasing congestion of highway and air travel as well as to the issue of airline safety. Pell, entranced by the possibilities of the Japanese *Shinkansen*, was convinced "that with no radical change in design, passenger railroads can give better than 100 mile per hour service, including stops!" It was a modest and potentially attainable goal, but it fell far short of the 200-mph mark set by the New York Regional Plan Association. Kennedy appreciated the value of the high-speed transportation to the metropolitan corridor that could well decide his fate in the 1964 election, and he sought to maintain Pell's role as an energetic young Democrat. "I share your concern," he reassured Pell. On October 9, 1962, Kennedy asked his deputy special counsel, Myer Feldman, to create a task force, composed of representatives from the Department of Commerce, the Housing and Home Finance Agency, the Council of Economic Advisers, and the Bureau of the Budget. The Cuban missile crisis began exactly a week later, temporarily diverting everyone's attention to foreign policy issues. By December 1962, Feldman's task force concluded that a larger study would be necessary to properly evaluate the region's transportation needs. Based on that recommendation, Kennedy instructed Commerce Secretary Luther Hodges to coordinate the effort. Hodges had little experience with railroads. But he feared that Kennedy, if reelected in 1964, might not renew his cabinet appointment. As such, he unhesitatingly supported the president's transportation initiative.[339]

Competing Visions for Modern Passenger Transportation

Pell's enthusiasm spawned two parallel initiatives, one by the Pennsylvania Railroad and the other on behalf of the Department of Commerce. PRR officials quickly spotted one of the benefits of Pell's proposal—not to increase mobility for residents of the megalopolis but rather to attract federal subsidies for the company's passenger service. In early November 1962, Allen Greenough established a committee to evaluate all aspects of the passenger operations between New York and Washington. The group included Jacob D. Fuchs, the PRR's manager of passenger transportation, who served as chairman, and John J. Clutz, the railroad's director of research. They sought to determine how much money—if any—the PRR should invest in roadbed and equipment to improve service and attract additional patronage. Fuchs retired in February 1963, and James W. Diffenderfer took charge of the study. As the director of special services, Diffenderfer made numerous appearances before regulatory bodies and public forums, defending the railroad's attempts to raise fares or reduce

the number of passenger trains. He was also skilled at persuading municipal officials to subsidize commuter rail operations, most notably in the case of Philadelphia's 1960 Passenger Service Improvement Corporation and 1961 Southeastern Pennsylvania Transportation Compact. Richardson Dilworth had been instrumental in the development of both agencies, and he was well acquainted with both PRR executives and Washington insiders. He was also available for hire, given that he lost the November 1962 governor's race and returned to his law firm Dilworth, Paxson, Kalish, Kohn & Dilks. In January 1963, the PRR employed Dilworth as outside counsel, and he was tasked with securing Housing and Home Finance Agency grants for the railroad's commuter operations. In that capacity, he was also well positioned to influence intercity transportation planning along the metropolitan corridor. Dilworth was closely associated with fellow Philadelphia attorney and Kennedy aide Myer Feldman, as was David Berger, who served as city solicitor and was responsible for legal matters associated with the city's commuter rail operations.[340]

The second proposal developed under the auspices of the Department of Commerce. It was an agency that Dilworth knew well, as it oversaw the HHFA grants for urban commuter rail systems like the one in Philadelphia. Feldman encouraged Commerce Secretary Hodges to name Dilworth as the public chairman of the Northeast Transportation Study Committee, also referred to as the Boston-Washington Corridor Study. The same Commerce Department personnel involved in the high-speed rail initiative were also accumulating data regarding the economic effects of the Penn Central merger application—to the extent, they acknowledged, that "the reports of most of the research contractors were of value to both areas of inquiry." Congress initially provided a modest $625,000 in funding for the conjoined investigations, released in late May 1963. Work began the following month, bolstered by a $2 million appropriation for the 1964 fiscal year. Most of the money went to fourteen outside contractors—four of whom were involved solely in the merger study, four in the high-speed transportation initiative, and six in both.[341]

Clarence Martin, the under secretary of commerce for transportation, had invited representatives from engineering universities, the Port of New York Authority, and the Canadian National Railway to take part in a conference to "cover all aspects of transportation by all modes, both freight and passenger, between these major cities and intermediate points [and] consider land use patterns, population factors and user preferences in the light of alternatives ranging from existing technology to development of improved technology offering greater safety, higher speed and lower unit cost." It was an extraordinarily broad mandate, one that included improvements to highways and even research involving V/STOL aircraft and attested to the willingness of senior Commerce Department officials to support radical new technologies. Neither the Pennsylvania Railroad nor the New Haven received an invitation to send representatives. Their influence would have been circumscribed, in any event, as Commerce Secretary Hodges preferred "no preconceived notion as to what is the best kind of transportation, or the best combination of the different modes of transportation needed to meet the future development of the megalopolitan area in [the] northeastern United States."[342]

Hodges's willingness to dispense with any "preconceived notion" was at variance with efforts by PRR officials to focus federal attention on modest improvements to conventional passenger service between New York and Washington. Dilworth soon clashed with Hodges regarding the nature of the transportation program. The former Philadelphia mayor suggested that in his "opinion no study needs to be made beyond one necessary to implement Senator Pell's proposal." Hodges, however, insisted that narrowing the focus of the study solely to rail passenger transport "could have an adverse impact upon the Administration's transportation program." He acknowledged that "any study of transportation facilities in the Washington-Boston corridor necessarily must give consideration to the operations and to the future of the Pennsylvania Railroad as well as the New Haven Railroad." Yet Hodges was suspicious of Dilworth's motives, reiterating that the former mayor "has in the recent past, if not now, been retained by the Pennsylvania Railroad as a legal and political consultant." On May 1, 1963, therefore, Dilworth resigned as legal counsel for the PRR.[343] He nonetheless retained his informal ties to Pennsylvania Railroad executives as well as his sympathy for their motives. So did Berger, whom Dilworth invited to join him on the advisory panel for the Boston-Washington Corridor Study.[344]

While Dilworth was the public—and political—face of the Boston-Washington Corridor Study, the more pragmatic technical details fell to Robert A. Nelson, a transportation economist at the University of Washington. In June 1963, Hodges selected Nelson as the director of the Commerce Department's Office of High Speed Ground Transportation. Nelson reported directly to Clarence Martin, the under secretary of commerce for transportation. He nonetheless worked most closely with Edward Grosvenor Plowman, the deputy under secretary for transportation policy and the individual preparing the

eastern railroad consolidation studies for the Interagency Committee on Transport Mergers. Nelson acknowledged that he "wasn't very much interested in passenger transportation at that time" and that he was "no train buff." His research was more closely aligned with inland waterways, and he possessed little practical experience regarding railroad operations. Nelson was enamored with high-tech transportation solutions, including automated highways—characteristics that made him a poor fit with PRR executives who favored modest improvements in conventional rail operations. He gained his federal post largely because his fellow Washingtonian, Warren Magnuson, chaired the Senate Commerce Committee. Nelson tended to elicit strong and highly polarized opinions and made few friends among Pennsylvania Railroad employees. "He was abrasive, difficult, and terribly obstinate," a fellow federal official recalled. "At times we felt he was either a bloody ass or a genius." James Diffenderfer, the PRR's manager of special services, suggested that "the main problem with Bob Nelson was that he hated incompetence. He hated guys who didn't know what they were talking about. He'd see right through them and call their bluff." During the years that followed, Nelson grew increasingly frustrated with what he perceived as the failure of the Pennsylvania Railroad and its equipment suppliers to implement high-speed transportation in a timely manner. Some of those criticisms were justified. More commonly, however, Nelson greatly underestimated the difficulties associated with translating theoretical concepts of modern high-speed travel to the practical realities of a railroad that had been in operation for well over a century. Nor did he acknowledge that the Apollo program, the military-industrial complex associated with the Cold War defense buildup, and the escalating conflict in Vietnam consumed the talents of engineers and technicians who might otherwise have assisted in the development of passenger-rail travel.[345]

Dilworth's Boston-Washington Corridor Study completed its preliminary report in November 1963, days before Kennedy's assassination. Not until February 1964 did Pell, Dilworth, Feldman, and other senior federal officials resolve to develop a proposal for a high-speed rail route between New York and Washington. By March, they were ready to commission studies that would calculate the cost and the likely ridership levels associated with the improved service. Lyndon Johnson nonetheless initially demonstrated little interest in the project. Pell grew increasingly frustrated with the delays, and in late March 1964, he wrote a five-page letter to the new president. "I invite your attention to a domestic matter which I believe to be of real political consequence in this election year: the problem of inter-city transportation in our highly urbanized Northeast," Pell emphasized. "It is a problem which I believe you can solve with dramatic success." Yet "with the assassination of President Kennedy and in the absence of your personal involvement in this project," he complained, "the objective of an early action program seemed to diminish." Pell highlighted the principal elements of his proposal, including the creation of an eight-state transportation authority and average operating speeds of one hundred miles per hour—and offered the *Shinkansen* as evidence "that this idea is practicable." Also practicable, as Pell emphasized, was that federal investments in modern transportation would give Johnson additional political support in the Northeast. Presidential advisor Lee White noted that "Senator Pell was extremely anxious that this be included in the president's 'night reading material.'" It was, and White received the assurance that "he read this." Through the remaining months of 1964, presidential involvement ensured that the Commerce Department's high-speed rail initiative gained increased political visibility and funding.[346]

Before Johnson became fully invested in the project, its low profile worked to the advantage of Pennsylvania Railroad officials. The limited resources focused attention on the most critical area—the PRR route between New York and Washington—and temporarily precluded consideration of larger transportation issues. In early December, with the nation still in mourning, the Commerce Department provided nearly $1 million for a study evaluating the costs associated with various types of high-speed rail systems. Nelson engaged the engineering consultants Louis T. Klauder & Associates, who performed extensive calculations. They hoped to answer one of the most basic questions arising from Pell's proposal—whether it would be more cost-effective to upgrade the existing PRR and New Haven tracks or to replace them with a completely new route, as the Japanese were doing. Klauder also offered the first analysis of potential ridership, to test the implicit but unproven hypothesis that faster travel times would attract additional patronage. By February 1964, the members of the Boston-Washington Corridor Study concluded "that satisfactory, high-speed rail service, from New York to Boston, cannot be self-liquidating." Without public funding, moreover, even the existing "Corridor from New York to Boston could conceivably lose all rail service, including commuter rail service, in the near future unless a workable plan is forthcoming." South of New York, along the Pennsylvania Railroad, Commerce Department officials suggested that high-speed service could be profitable. In late March 1964, they concluded that a modest

improvement, to permit a 100-mph maximum speed, "need not be further considered because it is insufficient from the standpoint of time-in-transit reduction." They suggested that 125 miles per hour constituted "the correct goal," with an increase to 150 miles per hour a "highly desirable future goal." At that velocity, travelers could zip between New York and Washington in two hours and fifteen minutes or less.[347]

The Commerce Department's Boston-Washington Corridor Study proceeded simultaneously, although independently, with the committee Allen Greenough had established in November 1962. Diffenderfer and his staff concluded that the railroad's passenger service between New York and Washington was no longer competitive with highway and air travel. The federal government had spent $2 billion to complete Interstate 95 between Boston and Washington, as well as a roughly equal amount to improve commercial aviation in the Northeast. The PRR, in contrast, could offer barely a hundred modern, stainless-steel coaches. All featured vestibules on only one end of the car, delaying loading and unloading at intermediate stops. About 60 percent of the equipment used between New York and Philadelphia consisted of prewar heavyweight cars, with an even higher ratio on weekends and during peak travel periods. All relied on steam heat and axle-driven electrical generators, systems prone to malfunction. The GG1 locomotives were continuing to offer good service, but they were approaching the point of obsolescence. Under union rules, they also required a fireman, with the attendant labor costs. "Thus," Diffenderfer concluded, "a 'turning point' had been reached. Something had to be done to check this downward trend if the railroad was to avoid getting into a heavy deficit situation as had occurred with passenger services in other, less densely settled, portions of its system." Diffenderfer predicted that—absent at least minimal upgrades to equipment and service—by 1970 the railroad would incur a $7.4 million annual deficit in its New York–Washington passenger services. While PRR executives agreed that the future appeared grim, there was little consensus regarding the appropriate response. "We had to decide whether we were going to stay in this service or get out of it," Diffenderfer observed. "There were arguments in favor of both positions."[348]

Although Diffenderfer's committee did not release its report until June 16, by March PRR executives decided to compete for additional passenger business between New York and Washington. Diffenderfer proposed that the railroad acquire at least 94 new self-propelled, electrified passenger cars—assuming patronage remained the same—and as many as 178 units, should ridership double. They would feature vestibules at both ends, cutting loading time in half. The bidirectional cars could facilitate terminal operations, sideline many of the aging GG1 locomotives, and—if the operating unions could be placated—dispense with firemen. Lower labor costs, reduced maintenance, and increased patronage, Diffenderfer concluded, might generate a profit of $7.8 million annually.[349]

Like Nelson and other Commerce Department officials, Diffenderfer and his colleagues emphasized the importance of high-speed travel and reduced journey times. Their recommendations nonetheless embodied a very different conception of speed and the money it would require achieving it. In 1963, several members of the Diffenderfer committee toured the New Tōkaidō route, still under construction, as part of an eleven-member American delegation sponsored by the United Nations Economic Commission on Asia and the Far East. The visit convinced them that the Japanese project represented an unprecedented level of business-government cooperation, one that the Pennsylvania Railroad could not duplicate. It would cost at least $500 million to emulate the Japanese system between New York and Washington, they concluded. Even if the Pennsylvania Railroad possessed that much money, it made little sense to challenge the federal government's $4 billion investment in highway and air travel. "Building a completely new line in the competitive environment of this route was out of the question," Diffenderfer asserted. He also rejected out of hand the possibility of top operating speeds of 150 miles per hour, or of two-hour, fifteen-minute travel times between the two cities. He informed Greenough that "the large initial investments required for a high-speed rail passenger service to permit the often-mentioned 2½-hour New York-Washington schedules are too great to warrant the risk of private capital." Diffenderfer reiterated that "private financing of the costs to provide a modernized 100 mph operation is even a risk" and that "operation at speeds above 125 mph is not presently contemplated for revenue service." There was, moreover, little point in investing massive amounts of irreplaceable capital in a high-speed rail service, if it would not generate a corresponding rate of return. Diffenderfer accordingly recommended a cautious, incremental approach, "to measure public reaction to improved, more frequent service, faster schedules, smoother and more comfortable rides, various levels of fares and other amenities." It was a policy that placed as much emphasis on marketing and customer relations as on speed. The goal was to give travelers an enjoyable experience rather than to simply move railroad cars between New York and Washington as rapidly

as possible. Diffenderfer insisted that only if, "as a result of this demonstration, it was found that a shift could be made toward using a public carrier on the surface, projections could be made to determine the effect of even higher speeds and other improvements for design of future transport needed in that corridor area."[350]

Given the PRR's poor financial condition, the interest of federal officials in high-speed rail transportation provided the company with an extraordinary opportunity. "At the same time we faced these 'turning points,'" Diffenderfer observed, "the government had some problems of its own. Increasing expenditure of public funds for air and highway facilities seemed to result only in ever-increasing congestion."[351] Proposals, such as the one offered by Pell, indicated that the federal government might pay for a significant portion of the incremental upgrading program that Diffenderfer supported. In keeping with his recommendations, the Pennsylvania Railroad budgeted $17.5 million, to be spent over two years, for improvements to the tracks between New York and Washington. That amount was just 3.5 percent of Pell's unrealistically low estimate of the cost associated with rebuilding the megalopolitan rail system. The expenditure nonetheless demonstrated that PRR executives were engaged in a good-faith effort to cooperate with the federal government, for the shared goal of improved transportation in the Northeast. Officials from the Engineering, Operating, and Legal Departments informed Commerce Department personnel that additional improvements would require federal funding. Diffenderfer "suggested that a construction subsidy may well be in order for railroad cars, similar to the ship-building subsidy for ship building, since the high speed train could well be purchased in Japan [and] all P.R.R. personnel present concurred that this was a good idea." Two weeks later, Dilworth and his colleagues made much the same point, stressing "that the entire risk of investment loss should be borne by appropriate government agencies in some manner."[352]

Diffenderfer's support for the Commerce Department's efforts to bring high-speed transportation to the megalopolis was an approach fraught with peril. By accepting federal funding, Pennsylvania Railroad executives acquiesced to a set of goals vastly different from their own. Diffenderfer sensibly set 125 miles per hour as the upper limit for speed on a railroad alignment that was well over a century old. At the insistence of Commerce Department officials, he nonetheless pledged "to extend tests beyond 125 mph to a possible maximum of 150 mph to develop information relative to the margin of safety beyond 125 mph, and for future consideration in case such higher speeds are contemplated for future operations." Diffenderfer emphasized that speeds matching the *Shinkansen* would only be possible if the "Government should underwrite a research and development program, covering prototype equipment, catenary and road facilities, and involving automatic operation at speeds up to at least 150 mph." Nelson and other Commerce Department personnel agreed that it was a laudable suggestion, but they declined to offer a binding commitment to fund those expenditures. In common with his PRR colleagues, Diffenderfer also recommended a cautious and incremental effort to attain higher speeds, but members of the Johnson administration demanded quick results, ideally in time for the 1966 congressional elections. While Diffenderfer held a degree in civil engineering from Bucknell, his role as director of special services reflected his desire to use railway technology to suit the larger ends of customer service, community relations, and ultimately the financial well-being of the Pennsylvania Railroad. Federal officials, in contrast, became fixated on the talismanic goal of 150-mph operation and the equipment needed to reach that speed.[353]

The radically different criteria favored by PRR and Commerce Department personnel placed Louis Klauder in a difficult position. As an engineering consultant hired by the Commerce Department, he was predisposed to favor high-speed transportation technology. Yet he was also pragmatic, and while he did not explicitly endorse Diffenderfer's caution he nonetheless warned against some of the federal government's more ambitious goals. In June 1964, Klauder delivered a preliminary report to the Commerce Department. He concluded that "it would be less expensive to operate trains over the present Pennsylvania Railroad route at speeds which would shorten the trip to 2 hours, than to build an entirely new railroad from the center of New York City through the centers of Newark, Trenton, Philadelphia, Wilmington, and Baltimore to Union Station in Washington in order to accomplish the same result." In keeping with the modest—and attainable—goals favored by PRR officials, Klauder evaluated a top operating speed of 125 miles per hour along the route between New York and Washington. Klauder estimated that the associated improvements to the physical plant between New York and Washington would cost $200 million, more than ten times the PRR's initial $17.5 million commitment.[354]

At first blush, Klauder's estimate was not out of line with the $500 million that Pell judged sufficient to upgrade the entire route between Washington and Boston. However, the phrase "which has not been included in the $200,000,000 estimate of railroad improvements"

appeared with depressing frequency. Aside from two test cars, the budget did not include the cost associated with a fleet of "new high-speed multiple-unit, self-propelled electric passenger cars," priced at $375,000 apiece. Options for additional betterments included the elimination of all grade crossings ($23 million), parking lots and other improvements to stations ($32 million), a replacement bridge across the Hackensack River ($15 million), and new tunnels under Baltimore ($200 million). Klauder's base estimate included an astonishing $66 million in contingencies, engineering fees, and administrative overhead—necessary, Louis Klauder admitted, "because we have not prepared preliminary designs for each of these improvements."[355]

Only by conducting additional, detailed evaluations could the consulting engineers determine how much time, effort, and money would be necessary to transform a 120-year-old railway alignment into something resembling the *Shinkansen*. The last comprehensive study of railway braking characteristics had taken place in 1937, and no one on Klauder's staff was willing to predict how high-speed operations would affect equipment design, deceleration characteristics, or stopping distances. Those conditions in turn dictated signal spacing, and it was anyone's guess as to whether the PRR's existing system would be adequate. There was a possibility that the distance between tracks would have to be increased to prevent the partial vacuum created by two trains passing at speed from canting one set of cars into the other. The optimal degree of superelevation was also unknown, and raising the height of one rail too far above the other on curves would be expensive and could negatively affect the operation of conventional trains. Unlike the system used on the *Shinkansen*, the PRR's catenary was not under constant tension, and it tended to contract during the winter and sag during the summer. Catenary height varied by as much as eight feet, with pantographs reaching skyward along portions of the route and nearly pressed against the tops of cars and locomotives transiting the Baltimore and Hudson River tunnels. The corresponding vertical play on the New Tōkaidō line was less than twelve inches. Nor was the Pennsylvania Railroad's catenary indexed as that in Japan, where the contact wire moved gradually from side to side, in the horizontal plane, to prevent grooves from forming in the pantograph. Making the best of a bad situation, Klauder observed that the PRR's tracks were so badly out of alignment that the yawing of cars at even moderate speeds produced the same effect as indexing and prevented damage to the pantographs. His pragmatism did little to camouflage concerns regarding the amount of work required to upgrade an electrical system that had not been state-of-the-art since his father had founded Klauder & Associates in 1921.[356]

Officials at the Commerce Department, far from expressing dismay at the many unknown factors and unpredictable costs associated with Klauder's preliminary findings, instead pushed the consultants to expand the scope of their work. Deputy Under Secretary Plowman instructed Louis Klauder to examine the feasibility of two-hour travel between New York and Washington, something that would only be possible with top speeds approaching 150 miles per hour. Plowman "extended our assignment to include a quick look at an entirely new railroad between New York and Washington," Klauder informed Dilworth. "In addition, he would like us to make a preliminary investigation of the railroad between New York and Boston." In his revised report, Klauder offered options ranging from a top speed of 125 miles per hour, for a two-and-a-half-hour trip, to a two-hour journey at speeds of up to 150 miles per hour. "American railroads have sufficient experience with speeds up to 125 mph so that this speed should not pose any serious problem to the Pennsylvania Railroad," Klauder observed. Despite his warning that "this is about as high as American railroads have ever gone," he referred to the New Tōkaidō line, and could "see no reason why 150 mph should not be easily attainable in this country."[357]

Privately, however, Klauder was far less sanguine regarding the possibility of duplicating the *Shinkansen* in the United States. "Unfortunately," he confided to the chief construction engineer at the Japanese National Railways, "our government is not at the moment inclined to spend the money to put in a completely new high speed railroad as you have done and is limiting us to the present right-of-way with modest changes in some of the more restricted areas. Even so, we will probably end up with an investment of $500 million, in order to reduce the running time from 3 hrs.-50 min. to 2 hrs.-40 minutes for our 225 mile run" between New York and Washington. Klauder's 160-minute timing was ten minutes longer than even the slowest estimate that he had offered to the Commerce Department and served as an early indication that promises for high-speed operation would not live up to expectations.[358]

Klauder's revised study provided four estimates for equipment and track upgrades between New York and Washington. They ranged from $329 million to $764 million, depending on speed and travel time. Even the least expensive option was well above the $500 million that Pell had suggested, given that it did not cover the extension of high-speed service from New York north to Boston. The resulting revenue projections were even more sobering. If the four levels of investment failed to produce an increase in ridership, then each would incur a substantial operating loss—of as much as $33 million annually, in the case of 150-mph, two-hour service. Only two scenarios could potentially generate an operating profit, and both depended on the project's ability to double ridership in the corridor. The most attractive option was also the slowest, with the $329 million investment generating $9 million in net profit. That represented a 2.7 percent rate of return, far too low to attract the private capital that Pell had predicted would be readily available. Klauder noted that a slightly less expensive option was available, one that would generate a modest improvement in profitability. It depended on a reduction in crew size, and the labor unions that constituted a vital part of the Democratic political coalition were already mobilizing to preclude that possibility.[359]

The expanded scope of the project, particularly the potential for upgrades along the New Haven route to Boston, was certain to please Senator Pell. The same could not be said for Dilworth, who learned about Plowman's revised instructions to Klauder—after the fact—from his consulting engineer. Pennsylvania Railroad executives were equally dismayed with the changes. High-speed service north of Manhattan was of little value to the PRR. Given the New Haven's ongoing bankruptcy and deplorable physical condition, moreover, that carrier was likely to soak up most of the available federal dollars. A new alignment between New York and Washington would preclude federal funding for the upgrading of the PRR's existing tracks between those two cities, which the company still needed for freight and commuter service. Yet even improvements to the existing right-of-way to permit 150-mph operation threatened to impose substantial costs on their company, even with federal support. As Klauder admitted to Dilworth, "Jim Symes had been less than eager to have the Pell Plan proceed because he was convinced that it was going to cost the Pennsylvania $500 million in capital improvements, which he was not willing to recommend to the Board of Directors." Chester J. Henry, the PRR's chief engineer, warned Klauder of the dangers associated with operating high-speed passenger trains adjacent to tracks used in freight service—something the designers of the New Tōkaidō line had avoided from the beginning. While he did not dismiss the possibility of 150-mph operation, Henry's "memorandum leaves the implication that 125 mph is possible but that 150 is scarcely practical." Nor was Henry being unduly pessimistic. "I note your concerns about 150 mph speed," Klauder acknowledged, "and we, obviously, have the same concern." Ultimately, Klauder acknowledged, "the Pennsylvania Railroad will not be willing to sign a contract to operate a high-speed service until after it has had an opportunity to see what practical and/or technical problems are raised by such high-speed operation." That stipulation ensured that further development would not occur unless the Commerce Department allocated substantial funds for a demonstration project, one that could resolve the many unanswered questions associated with high-speed operation in the American context.[360]

While Klauder's preliminary and amended reports did not explicitly suggest that high-speed rail service would require substantial subsidies from the federal government, the implication was obvious. He shared that sentiment in a letter to a Commerce Department official, in which he suggested that Pell's enthusiasm had not taken root with his congressional colleagues or among the electorate. "The public, and particularly the Congress, have never seen or probably never even heard of the Japanese developments and therefore have no idea of how attractive or how different from conventional railroading the service we are providing actually is. If they could see what is involved in a modern high-speed railroad," Klauder emphasized, "they would be disabused of the idea that this is something which the railroads really should pay for out of their own capital." Like PRR officials, Klauder emphasized that the Commerce Department should fund a demonstration project—both to give the public a tantalizing glimpse of the potential for high-speed travel and, he emphasized, "so that all of our various reports do not end up in the storage vaults."[361]

Diffenderfer's PRR study and the Commerce Department's Klauder reports each suggested that massive investments in high-speed rail made little economic sense. Politics was another matter, however, and both the president of the United States and the president of the Pennsylvania Railroad had ample reason to favor the project. Johnson, mindful of the damage the Dixiecrats had done to Harry Truman's 1948 campaign, suspected that his commitment to civil rights legislation might produce a corresponding erosion of support in the South. Like Kennedy, he hoped that the great urban conglomeration of the Northeast would generate offsetting votes. His July 9 signature on the Urban Mass Transportation Act provided funding for the Southeastern Pennsylvania Transportation Authority and other transit agencies and attested to his desire to cultivate the region's voters. As Diffenderfer observed, Johnson also hoped to "find a solution to many of its corridor transportation problems by upgrading, at relatively minimal cost, the existing, high-capacity rail facilities, rather than pouring additional billions of dollars exclusively into highways and airways." It was the same logic that induced Richardson Dilworth and other politicians to support commuter rail, alleviating congestion in suburban Philadelphia while courting affluent suburban voters who might be persuaded to switch allegiance from the Republicans to the Democrats. For Johnson, a highly publicized initiative to provide high-speed intercity transportation, particularly one that could be announced prior to the 1964 election, would be a great asset.[362]

The high-speed-rail project, and its potential value to the Johnson administration, provided Pennsylvania Railroad executives with benefits that had nothing to do with ridership and revenue. Howard Butcher III, a Philadelphia investment banker, reflected that symbiotic relationship. Beginning in the spring of 1959, Butcher acquired more than 1.4 million shares of PRR stock. In April 1964, when Louis Klauder was studying the corridor's technical and financial aspects, he sat down to lunch with the financier. Butcher, he noted, "seemed very enthusiastic about how much the New York–Washington high-speed railroad service would help the Pennsylvania Railroad. He was particularly interested in its effect on the public image of the Pennsylvania. Perhaps," Klauder concluded, "his ownership of a million and a half shares of their stock may influence his thinking in this regard." Butcher also anticipated the benefits of a merger with the New York Central, another company in which he held substantial investments. By assisting Johnson's efforts to court northeastern voters with high-speed transportation, Butcher expected that Johnson would encourage the Justice Department to moderate its opposition to the consolidation. Butcher "seemed to feel that he might be helpful in suggesting ways in which the Railroad and the Government could work together," Klauder observed. "His suggestion was that if he and we could find some program that sounded good to him, he would be glad to help us sell Stuart Saunders."[363]

In reality, Saunders needed little convincing. His predecessor, James Symes, was schooled in railroad operations and recognized that passenger service drained the PRR's resources while interfering with freight traffic. Symes perceived little value in high-speed travel. Saunders, in contrast, was a lawyer, an accomplished networker, and someone who valued high-level political connections. As a Democrat who socialized with both John F. Kennedy and Lyndon Johnson, he was well equipped to solicit their support for the merger. While acknowledging Symes's reluctance to devote substantial sums to the development of high-speed rail, Butcher reassured Klauder "that Mr. Saunders has a much broader view and that he felt there was a whole new and more enthusiastic management now than under the Symes regime." Diffenderfer shared that perception. "If Stuart Saunders hadn't been on the scene," he observed, the "project wouldn't have gotten started."[364]

The Politics of High-Speed Rail Transportation

On August 11, and with the 1964 election fast approaching, the Commerce Department provided President Johnson with a summary report based on the Klauder data. The phrase "Northeast Corridor" replaced the cumbersome Boston-Washington Corridor Study designation and would thereafter be the default name for the project and the region. The initial emphasis on 125-mph operation disappeared. In its place, Commerce Department officials suggested that "the cost of capital improvements, depending upon various levels of service, ranges up to a probable maximum of $1 billion for speeds on the order of 150 miles per hour." That was twice the projected expense Pell had offered two years earlier.[365] Only in that respect would the Northeast Corridor project ever resemble the New Tōkaidō line—with the route between Tokyo and Osaka completed two months later, at double the initial cost estimates. As if to divert attention from the massive investment associated with the Northeast Corridor rail line, the Commerce Department highlighted the estimated $700 million to $1 billion that would be required to expand the region's airports. Given that short flights within the corridor accounted for two-thirds of all air traffic, offsetting investments in rail service seemed appropriate.[366]

In accordance with Klauder's recommendations and the demands of PRR executives, the Commerce Department recommended a series of engineering surveys and research projects. With luck, they would resolve many of the unknown technical issues associated with high-speed rail travel. President Johnson concluded that "the promise of efficient, low cost, fast rail service along the Corridor is sufficient to warrant proceeding with detailed investigation and evaluation, including research, design, testing, and demonstration." He also "expressed his conviction that private industry would cooperate with the Department of Commerce in this effort." The president instructed the Commerce Department to provide a progress report by October 15, effectively committing the federal government and the Pennsylvania Railroad to participation in the Northeast Corridor high-speed rail initiative. Pell praised the president's "determination to continue to work until we get the answers" but warned that the Commerce Department must "soon change research reports into action recommendations," to prevent "our railroads from going the way of the horse and buggy or the dodo."[367]

To the consternation of PRR officials, Nelson and his associates at the Commerce Department had concluded that conventional rail passenger transportation had gone the way of the dodo. They instead favored revolutionary new schemes, ones that promised scant benefit for the Pennsylvania Railroad. Nelson had little use for the *Shinkansen*, a system that represented the outer limits of traditional wheel-on-rail technology. He cautioned that the cost of building an American version of the New Tōkaidō line would require "some careful thinking as an area of expenditure by the Federal Government" and that it would be obsolete by the time it was completed. It made little sense to spend more than $2 billion to duplicate the Japanese system between Washington and Boston, Nelson argued, when the United States could leapfrog beyond what that country accomplished. "There hasn't been any significant research and improvement in rail transportation in more than 20 years," Nelson complained, "so it is a question for us of starting almost from scratch, of getting free of old concepts of locomotion and suspension and roadbeds and safe speeds."[368]

Nelson's suggestions characterized an era of technological exuberance that reached its zenith with the Apollo program. His recommendations moved more or less in tandem with the president's Advisory Committee on Supersonic Transport, established in April 1964. Commerce Secretary Hodges noted that a surface-transportation study similar to the one undertaken for the SST "should mean greater thoroughness and should inspire greater confidence than we now have." Donald F. Hornig, the presidential science advisor and head of the Office of Science and Technology, considered the two projects to be "of the same order of magnitude" and therefore required similar economic feasibility studies. Like Nelson, Hornig demonstrated little interest in "a replication of the Japanese system." In August 1964, he had argued that experiments to incrementally improve the PRR's existing facilities were "premature" and "would reveal little." Hornig aired those views at a September 2, 1964, meeting, convened by Hodges, with the attendees agreeing that the development of futuristic transportation technologies should be coupled with efforts to rehabilitate the PRR's existing service between New York and Washington.[369]

Lyndon Johnson saw little value in innovative transportation projects that would not be completed until long after his political career had ended. Nelson's proposals—visionary schemes that critics dubbed the "blue sky" approach—included high-velocity monorails, pneumatic tubes, magnetic levitation, and a twenty-four-foot-wide

"RRollway Train" that carried automobiles at a right angle to the tracks—enabling passengers to drive themselves off the cars and onto feeder roads. Doing it right, Nelson now conceded, could cost as much as $4 billion, and some railroad officials thought a more realistic estimate would be more than $5 billion in construction costs alone—to say nothing of the difficulty and expense associated with the acquisition of real estate through eminent domain. Myer Feldman, who was as close to Johnson as he had been to Kennedy, informed Martin that "the White House would never O.K. such a proposal."[370]

Even as Nelson was highlighting his blue-sky proposals, the president and his aides were seeking more practical and tangible results. As an unelected president, Johnson was seeking victory in November 1964. Through the summer of that year, Johnson was also exploring the creation of a new federal agency that would remove transportation matters from the Department of Commerce. Even though Johnson was at the height of his political power, getting the measure through Congress would be extraordinarily difficult. A request for $5 billion for a single project, benefiting only the Northeast, would not make that task any easier. Johnson's unwillingness to ask Congress for billions of dollars in railroad transportation funding ensured the restraint that PRR executives also favored.

On October 15, two weeks after the highly publicized opening of the New Tōkaidō route and three weeks before the presidential election, Louis Klauder presented Johnson with a proposal for a $15 million demonstration project. In addition to upgrades to twenty miles of track and catenary, Klauder proposed to acquire a pair of cars from each of the three major builders—Budd, Pullman-Standard, and American Car & Foundry—to serve as test beds. General Electric and Westinghouse would supply the traction motors and related power-control systems. Testing would take place along the route between Trenton and New Brunswick, New Jersey. The "Raceway," as it would become known, boasted the best track and the fastest running times on the entire PRR system and was hardly representative of the entire distance between New York and Washington.[371]

The initial component of the two-phase project, Klauder noted, "would establish the basic facts concerning the problems of high-speed operation as they relate to track, aerodynamics, and trolley wire system"—a research agenda that would take two years and nine months. Only then would engineers move on to "the second phase, or developmental section, [that] would test the ability of the equipment to perform satisfactorily and would include the allowance of time and money for making a number of changes to the prototype equipment and tests of the changes." That process would require an additional two years and nine months. Further time would be required to fabricate the equipment necessary to begin regular service. Assuming there were no unexpected delays, Klauder emphasized, "cars could be delivered for the start of high-speed passenger service in 7 years from the authorization of the first preliminary test program." Based on his engineering expertise, Klauder thus warned that—even in the unlikely event that the Commerce Department immediately released the necessary funds—full-scale operations along the Northeast Corridor could not begin until August 1971 at the earliest.[372]

Johnson moved quickly to secure congressional support for the high-speed-rail demonstration project. Elected in a landslide, and with both houses of Congress firmly under Democratic control, he felt sufficiently confident to emphasize a program that was broader than the one Louis Klauder recommended. "I will ask for funds to study high-speed rail transportation between urban centers," the president announced in his January 4, 1965, State of the Union address. "We will begin with test projects between Washington and Boston. On high-speed trains, passengers could travel this distance in less than four hours."[373] Luther Hodges's fear that the president would not renew his appointment as secretary of commerce proved accurate. Two weeks after the State of the Union message, Johnson selected John T. Connor, a supporter of high-speed rail, for that post—another signal that the president was willing to make a substantial commitment to rail transportation in the Northeast. In his January 25, 1965, budget message to Congress, Johnson announced that he would "propose legislation to authorize a comprehensive program of research and development on high-speed intercity surface transport." It was a vague statement that left open the possibility of the blue-sky proposals that Nelson favored. In the meantime, the president pledged to "begin demonstrations of possible improvements in existing rail passenger services in the Northeast Corridor in the Nation" and asked Congress for $20 million in preliminary funding. Newspaper reporters suggested, inaccurately, that four-hour travel along the corridor was something that "most experts consider attainable within two or three years," and emphasized Nelson's even more outlandish predictions that "within a decade or so, advanced systems may make possible surface transportation at approximately the speed of sound."[374]

On March 4, Johnson encouraged congressional approval of the $20 million appropriation he had promised earlier in the year. His comment that "evolutionary improvement in the existing railroad system must be compared to much more radical and longer term developments" indicated that transportation planners had still not decided between attainably pragmatic and impossibly visionary goals. The amount of money that the president offered was insignificant, and in effect represented a placeholder until Commerce Department officials decided the level of funding that would be required. They suggested three amounts—$15 million, $50 million, and $99 million—for studies along the entire route between Boston and Washington. PRR executives labeled the least expensive version the "Mediocre Commerce Proposal," an editorial comment for which Saunders later apologized. On May 25, Commerce Secretary Connor requested a $90 million appropriation, to be assigned to the Office of High Speed Ground Transportation. Even that amount represented no more than a token effort to resolve the transportation issues in the megalopolis. "No one in the field knows where the money will come from," suggested Cabell Phillips, the Washington correspondent for the *New York Times*, "but everyone knows that there is only one source for the bulk of the money—the Federal Government."[375]

It was up to Congress to decide the extent of federal funding for high-speed ground transportation in the Northeast. While everyone acknowledged that the requested appropriation of $90 million would only fund preliminary research and development, there was considerable disagreement regarding the ultimate direction of those exploratory efforts. In anticipation of the congressional hearings that began on May 19, 1965, Nelson and other "blue-sky" advocates were ready to make their case for a radically new transportation infrastructure. He relied on a Commerce Department study, authorized in September 1964, that he hoped would reveal the next generation of transportation technology. Known as Project Transport, the research was under the direction of William Seifert, the assistant dean of engineering at the Massachusetts Institute of Technology. Like Robert Nelson, Seifert was keenly interested in futuristic transportation systems, thus making him particularly susceptible to the blandishments of lobbyists from the defense and aerospace industries. Seifert and a colleague from MIT visited Japan in March and April 1965, spent time with Japanese transportation officials, and rode on the *Shinkansen*. They announced that they "were very favorably impressed with the job JNR and its contractors did in bringing the New Tokaido Line into operation." Within a few months of returning to the United States, however, Seifert had moved well beyond what the Japanese had been able to accomplish. Summarizing the

ongoing MIT study, he emphasized "that a new high-speed ground transport (HSGT) system could be achieved technologically, but it would differ radically from passenger trains and railways as we know them today. It would be, in fact, a new mode of transport." Seifert predicted "that main-line speeds in excess of 200 miles per hour or even 300 miles per hour would be required to provide the character of service needed in the era of the 1980's and beyond." He emphasized "effective coupling between intercity and urban transport systems." Many transport planners favored the integration of local and long-distance transportation, something that Seifert had seen to good effect in Japan. He took the word "coupling" literally, however, and noted that the MIT researchers were "examining means for accelerating vehicles from a local station to main line speed and connecting them with the main line vehicle, at speed." Lest critics scoff at the impracticability of coupling cars together at speeds approaching three hundred miles per hour, Seifert observed that engineers at the National Aeronautics and Space Administration were attempting to do the same thing, by docking spacecraft together while orbiting Earth. Given the highly speculative nature of Seifert's proposals, however, few could argue with his comment that "this approach will necessarily take several years."[376]

Seifert made his remarks during the congressional hearings on the $90 million appropriation for the Commerce Department's Office of High Speed Ground Transportation. It was hardly surprising that Claiborne Pell was the first to speak. Much of the testimony came from equipment suppliers, including the consortium represented by the Railway Progress Institute, as they were the ones that stood to gain the most from massive federal expenditures on new transportation systems. Robert Nelson was there as well, promising the same type of revolutionary technological change that Seifert advocated. He supported "newer concepts which could have a tremendous impact on the Nation's transportation systems," although he admitted that "not a great deal of work has been done on the speeds which we contemplate here, 150 to 250 miles per hour." John Connor, the secretary of commerce, was slightly more cautious. While he admitted that visionary technologies might someday replace conventional railroad service between Boston and Washington, he advocated the incremental approach. "In view of the experimental nature of the demonstration project," he conceded, "present equipment on the corridor routes will not be replaced in its entirety."[377]

Connor's comments provided some reassurance to Stuart Saunders, who also testified in support of the legislation. He chose his words with great care, hoping that Congress would provide adequate funding for the Pennsylvania Railroad, but not enough to enable visionary blue-sky proposals that would do the company no good whatsoever. Saunders had little use for pneumatic tubes, RRollway Trains, or other utopian projects that threatened to squander precious time and financial resources. Instead, he recited the familiar litany of facts and figures—growing population, overcrowded highways and airports, and the PRR's ongoing investments in passenger travel between New York and Washington. "As one of the Nation's great transportation arteries," he reminded legislators, "our Washington-New York line is a readymade base on which fast, high-volume passenger service can be developed quickly and economically." He predicted that it would cost nearly $1.5 billion to replicate the New Tōkaidō line between those two cities and offered as a cautionary tale the enormous expense associated with San Francisco's new rapid-transit line. In cooperation with the Commerce Department, however, Saunders promised additional improvements to the physical plant and new equipment "capable of accelerating to 125 miles per hour in 150 seconds, and operating in the future at speeds up to at least 150 miles per hour." The statement did not commit the PRR to sustained 125-mph service, did not specify when 150-mph operation might begin, and provided no suggestion that speeds of 200 mph or greater might be possible. Saunders further clarified his position a month later, when he asked Representative Oren Harris, the bill's sponsor, to place a $90 million cap on appropriations. "This would have a strong tendency to keep the research projects within practical and realistic fields," Saunders emphasized.[378]

Despite Saunders's determination to keep the attention of the Commerce Department firmly focused on the Pennsylvania Railroad, the forty faculty and twenty-five graduate students associated with the MIT study had other ideas. Delivered to the Commerce Department in June 1965, the report replicated, almost word-for-word, the earlier comments of project director William Seifert. High-speed ground transportation was "feasible," the study concluded, but "would differ radically from passenger trains and railways as we know them today." Also present was Seifert's earlier assertion that transportation conditions in the 1980s would require travel speeds of between two hundred and three hundred miles per hour. "Traditional modal orientation must be avoided if new ideas are to be generated," MIT personnel emphasized. "Rather, the purpose of HSGT research is to explore new approaches to high-speed ground transportation offering minimum door-to-door transit time." The report outlined twenty-two areas for future research, most of which had nothing to do with the Pennsylvania Railroad or with conventional railway technology. There were more than one hundred charts and tables. Only a few covered issues such as the wear produced by steel wheels on steel rails, something that had long concerned PRR maintenance-of-way engineers. Most provided data on subjects such as "human tolerance to periodic vertical accelerations" and "modified steady subsurface guideway enclosure temperature rise per ton of vehicle versus vehicle speed." Seifert and his MIT colleagues could easily devote the remainder of their careers to the exploration of such complex and intrinsically fascinating topics. Saunders and the others connected with the Pennsylvania Railroad did not have that long to wait.[379]

Transforming a Vision into Reality

Through the spring and summer of 1965, and as they awaited the congressional verdict on the $90 million appropriation, Commerce Department personnel used existing funds to begin the demonstration project. They worked with Pennsylvania Railroad officials and representatives from equipment suppliers, hoping to produce tangible results that would generate additional federal funding. "If Congress will approve the project's first step," Connor promised, "the Commerce Department, working with the Pennsylvania Railroad, will have 50 high-speed, electric-powered cars operating between Washington and New York by late 1966." It was an impossibly ambitious timetable, and one that was far shorter than the seven years Louis Klauder had suggested. Klauder was an engineer rather than a politician, and political considerations in the Johnson administration ensured that his preliminary timetable quickly fell apart. Connor's deadline of "late 1966" in reality meant November 8, 1966, the date of the midterm elections. Connor and Johnson agreed that by any means necessary East Coast newspapers would be able to publish photographs of modern high-speed trains zipping along the PRR's right-of-way before voters went to the polls.[380]

Despite reassurances that most of the necessary funds would come from the federal government, Commerce Secretary Connor demanded that the PRR contribute substantial resources as well. By the summer of 1965— and following the recommendations of the committee that President Greenough had established in 1962—the company had invested $17.5 million in passenger operations between New York and Washington. In March, Commerce Department officials announced that they expected the railroad to spend at least another $8 million on new equipment. The news came as a surprise to Stuart Saunders, yet he refrained from criticism. At the annual shareholders meeting on May 10, he reminded investors that the company had lost $34.9 million on its systemwide passenger operations during 1964. He emphasized that the route between New York and Washington was the only one that could possibly generate a profit from passenger service, conceded the necessity of the $8 million expenditure, and announced that high-speed trains "may" be operating by late 1966. A month later, Alan S. Boyd, Clarence Martin's successor as the under secretary of commerce for transportation, rejected "any so-called exotic modes of transportation." He nonetheless promised that the project could produce trains that ran at a top speed of 150 miles per hour. Three days later, Saunders pledged to match federal support, dollar for dollar, an amount he anticipated would total $10 million. "This is not money we would spend in any event," he informed members of Congress, "but funds specifically required to support the Federal program." Saunders emphasized that the PRR would provide "the finest passenger equipment in the world," and he endorsed Boyd's promise of 150-mph operation.[381]

The passenger equipment that Saunders praised so highly was under development, but it would fall far short of setting the standard as the finest in the world. Representatives from the Budd Company were eager to exploit their expertise in the manufacture of commuter rail equipment and replace at least a portion of the now-vanished demand for intercity streamliners. Their High Speed Passenger Equipment Study, completed in July 1963, reflected the parallel research efforts undertaken by the PRR and the Commerce Department. By the following May, Budd engineers had developed initial specifications for test trains capable of 150-mph operation. In August 1964, Edward G. Budd Jr. suggested that trains capable of 125-mph operation were "feasible and desirable." Albert Dean, the chief engineer of Budd's Railway Division, echoed those sentiments. Philip W. Scott, who had recently replaced Budd as the company's president, suggested that the experimental train could reach speeds of 160 miles per hour and that it could be in service within eighteen months. Yet Budd executives cautioned that they had not yet built a prototype, and they could offer the newspapers nothing more than an artist's rendering of the proposed design. The Budd Company had allocated $750,000 to research and development efforts, Scott reminded reporters, and would spend no more "unless someone backs it up with a development program."[382]

Further progress depended on a substantial infusion of federal funds. Not until the autumn of 1965 did Congress appropriate the money necessary to pay for the Northeast Corridor demonstration project. On September 30, Johnson signed the High Speed Ground Transportation Act. He congratulated "Senator Pell, who harassed me week after week until he got me to take some action," and thanked "the hard working, intelligent Members of what is, in my opinion, one of the best Congresses in the history of this country." The law allocated $90 million over three years, an amount that paled in comparison to that year's $275 million for aviation research—to say nothing of the federal dollars spent on highways. Johnson expressed his confidence that the demonstration project would produce tangible results by the autumn of 1966, yet Congress earmarked less than a third of the $90 million for the implementation of actual high-speed service. Some $60 million would fund research into the conceptual designs favored by Robert Nelson and his colleagues. "The same science and technology which gave us our airplanes and our space probes," Johnson remarked at the signing ceremony, "could also give us better and faster and more economical transportation on the ground. And a lot of us need it more on the ground than we need it orbiting the earth." It was an idea that refused to die. A month later, New York Times correspondent Lawrence Galton headlined developments that would permit "commuting at 1,000 M.P.H." Paying scant attention to the demonstration project that "would be almost immediately" implemented along the Pennsylvania Railroad, Galton described at great length such familiar proposals as the RRollway Train, "torpedo trains," and the five-hundred-mile-per-hour "Levatrain."[383]

Despite the allure of visionary proposals, the High Speed Ground Transportation Act involved three focused areas of research and development, two of which had little bearing on the Pennsylvania Railroad. Because there was no realistic possibility of extending catenary north of New Haven, Commerce Department officials worked with the United Aircraft Corporation to develop the gas-turbine TurboTrain, for service to Boston. The design represented improvements to Robert R. Young's 1950s "Train X" concept and paralleled research by the Société Nationale des Chemins de fer Français. In January 1966, Claiborne Pell announced that the Commerce Department would purchase two TurboTrains for operation along the New Haven tracks that ran through his home state. The first units entered revenue service in April 1969. They suffered a series of mechanical problems, however, and could not overcome the deteriorating condition of the route. The second involved efforts to blend rail and highway transportation. While the RRollway Train never materialized, in 1971 the concept evolved into the Auto-Train, using conventional equipment to transport passengers and their automobiles between northern Virginia and central Florida.[384]

The third component of the High Speed Ground Transportation Act provided about $12 million in federal funds for the PRR's demonstration project between New Brunswick and Trenton. Most of the money would be used to purchase experimental cars, which would be owned by the Commerce Department, and production models that would be the property of the Pennsylvania Railroad. On December 10, the Commerce Department signed a $952,000 contract with the Budd Company to construct four cars for testing purposes. They were little more than stripped-down Silverliners, with more robust traction motors, trucks, and brakes, and they would never be suitable for revenue service. Had Nelson adhered to Klauder's recommendations, both the modified Silverliners and the TurboTrain would undergo thorough evaluations prior to the ordering of any additional equipment. "The Department of Commerce is expected to order 50 cars of one type," a reporter suggested, but only "after both super-trains have been tested." The compressed timetable made that procedure impossible, however, and ensured that the testing and production phases would occur simultaneously. "Although the railroad endeavored to convince the Department of Commerce people that the four laboratory test cars could not be evaluated as prototype cars," PRR engineers lamented, "Dr. Nelson was not interested in building another prototype train, but rather wanted to put several trains into the demonstration program." Yet the conflation of the research and production phases ensured that the inevitable modifications resulting from experimental testing—something that might otherwise be corrected with a few strokes of a pen to blueprints on a drafting table—would need to be retrofitted into cars while they were under construction or even in revenue service.[385]

By the end of December—even though Budd had not yet completed, much less tested, the four modified Silverliners—the PRR and the Commerce Department received bids for the fifty high-speed multiple-unit cars, intended for revenue service. The St. Louis Car Company warned "that the time allowed to produce these cars leaves no cushion for significant delays from suppliers" and demanded indemnification for any penalties that might result from their inability to meet the autumn 1966 deadline. United Aircraft proposed two test trains, to be completed within ten months, and a further eight revenue-service train sets that would follow five months later. Despite the clear preference of PRR engineers for the Silverliner concept, the United Aircraft design closely resembled a TurboTrain

with a pantograph and a keystone herald on the nose. Its principal advantage, the company's representatives stressed, was a tilting suspension system that reduced the need to ease sharp curves or increase superelevation to the point where it interfered with slow-speed freight service. There was little doubt about the outcome of the bidding process, however. Given the Budd Company's experience with the Silverliners, its reputation for timely delivery, and the contract for the four test cars, PRR and Commerce Department personnel agreed that Budd would build the equipment at its Red Lion facility, near Philadelphia.[386]

The Contract

Passage of the High Speed Ground Transportation Act, with its assurance of a modicum of federal support, persuaded PRR officials to allocate corporate funds to the implementation of improved rail service between New York and Washington. On April 15, 1966, Pennsylvania Railroad and Commerce Department representatives signed the contract for the high-speed demonstration project. Sixty pages long and subsequently amended at least eight times, it was the first agreement between any railroad and the federal government for the operation of a specific passenger service. In addition to paying for the four demonstration cars, which would remain the property of the Commerce Department, the agency would provide $9.6 million to buy fifty cars for revenue service. The Commerce Department's other expenditures were far more modest. They included assistance in the development of specifications, the evaluation of proposals from suppliers, the formulation of advertising and marketing programs, and the distribution of passenger surveys. During a two-year demonstration period, the PRR would operate at least six of a planned eleven daily passenger services between New York and Washington, employing modern high-speed equipment. Initially, federal officials demanded that the demonstration period begin in April 1967. PRR executives asserted that it would be impossible to implement the new technology so quickly and negotiated an extension until October. Even so, it was a far shorter period than the seven years that Louis Klauder thought to be a realistic timetable for the implementation of high-speed service.[387]

Saunders acknowledged that the Pennsylvania Railroad would spend "at least as much money and probably more" than the federal government. The contract certainly reflected that concession, even though a host of transportation economists had cautioned against reliance on private capital for the resurrection of passenger-rail service in the megalopolis. Nelson pledged that the federal government would exert substantial control over the redevelopment of the Northeast Corridor, without bearing a corresponding share of the costs. "We are not specifying that the Pennsylvania Railroad spend any given amount of money," he informed the members of a House Appropriations subcommittee. "What we are doing is establishing track standards, roadbed standards, which we expect to check very carefully." That level of oversight ensured that the Pennsylvania Railroad would pay for the improvements he and his colleagues demanded. The company's initial obligation involved $1.5 million in improvements to the No. 3 track between Trenton and New Brunswick, where testing would take place. Yet Pennsylvania Railroad officials had signed what was essentially an open-ended commitment to rebuild the entire route between New York and Washington, which would ultimately cost nearly forty times that amount. The railroad's responsibilities also included the remaining $10.4 million of the $20 million cost of the cars. The contract provisions—which one Pennsylvania Railroad representative summarized as "may include but not limited to"—required the railroad to renew ties and ballast, lay continuous welded rail, upgrade the catenary, improve signaling, rebuild bridges, eliminate grade crossings, and build high-level boarding platforms in three cities—Wilmington, Baltimore, and Washington. Nelson suggested that the PRR would spend between $20 million and $36 million to upgrade the right-of-way, far more than the amount the federal government was contributing to the project. Even that was an underestimate. Should the demonstration grant produce increased profits from the Northeast Corridor service, then that money would be used to repay the federal government. It was an uneven arrangement, what one executive labeled "the worst contract ever negotiated in the 120-year history of the Pennsylvania Railroad."[388]

It is unlikely that Stuart Saunders, the PRR's chairman, expected that the company's expenditures on high-speed rail travel would generate a favorable return on investment. He nevertheless anticipated corresponding political benefits associated with the proposed merger with the New York Central. On April 27, twelve days after the signing of the contract between the Pennsylvania Railroad and the Commerce Department, the Interstate Commerce Commission endorsed the consolidation. Officials at the Justice Department continued to oppose the merger, however, as did labor leaders. Many observers suggested that Saunders's display of good corporate citizenship—and his willingness to pay for a substantial portion of a transportation project that would increase the Democratic Party's popularity in the Northeast—reflected his desire to see the merger consummated at any cost. "I have no doubt,"

Robert Nelson asserted, "that Saunders' softness in negotiating the contract with the government can be directly related to his feeling that this was one of the things he had to do to get the Penn Central merger approved."[389]

From the beginning, Nelson was determined to control every aspect of the demonstration project, to ensure that it met the goals of the Commerce Department rather than those of the Pennsylvania Railroad. "I had far more decision-making power than anyone over at the Pennsylvania Railroad except for Stuart Saunders," he boasted. He demanded a top speed of at least 150 miles per hour, even though PRR representatives on the design committee strongly favored 125 miles per hour. The contract contained a domestic-content provision, limiting the ability of the PRR to take advantage of recent advances in high-speed rail technology in Japan and Europe. Federal officials also mandated the development of additional stations in suburban locations, hoping to attract affluent passengers with free parking and easy access to the freeway network—but the resulting dwell times necessitated a higher top speed to maintain favorable end-to-end journey times.[390]

The fifty high-speed cars, which the Commerce Department ordered from Budd on May 6, provoked further disagreements between Nelson and Saunders. Nelson initially insisted that Budd would manufacture only coaches, perhaps because he saw no reason why the federal government should subsidize luxury travel. Under pressure from PRR personnel, Nelson agreed to expand and reorient the order to include cars with minimal food-preparation facilities. Saunders, attentive to potential travel demand along the Northeast Corridor, insisted that parlor cars should constitute a fifth of the order. Nelson refused. Fearing "that this might be the only opportunity to re-equip the New York–Washington service," Saunders agreed to pay for ten parlor cars. That concession increased the PRR's expenditures on equipment from $20 million to $21.6 million, without any corresponding increase in federal funding. Along with twenty coaches and a further twenty snack-bar coaches, the parlor cars constituted the initial roster of high-speed equipment. Those fifty cars were hardly sufficient to replace the equipment utilized in New York–Washington service. For the moment, however, they were all that Commerce Department officials were willing to sanction.[391]

Political rather than engineering considerations ensured that the development of the Budd cars proceeded at a rapid, and perhaps reckless, pace. Pennsylvania Railroad officials and Budd technicians, as well as Louis Klauder and his staff, acknowledged the wisdom of completing and fully evaluating the Commerce Department test cars, before Budd began constructing the fifty coaches, snack-bar coaches, and parlor cars. It was nonetheless clear that Robert Nelson, the Commerce Department consultant who lacked any significant experience in railway engineering, would have a substantial influence over the design process. He was under intense pressure from more senior government officials to ensure that the test cars demonstrated clear results—and generated favorable publicity—prior to the November 1966 elections. Nelson expected that revenue service between New York and Washington would commence by October of the following year. The May 6 contract between the Commerce Department and the Budd Company certainly reflected that goal. It required the carbuilder to complete the fifty-car order within fifteen months. That was a slight concession from Nelson, who originally demanded that the cars be completed by the beginning of May 1967. Even with the modest extension, it was an impossibly short timetable—especially considering that almost everything associated with the cars was new and untested.[392]

The Demonstration Project

Philadelphia's Silverliner commuter equipment, which entered service in the summer of 1963, constituted an obvious starting point for the development of the test cars. The design owed much to city transit engineer Edson Tennyson and his desire to provide a replacement for the obsolete MP54 cars.[393] PRR officials acknowledged that the Silverliners earned "the dubious distinction of endeavoring to avoid the pitfalls of the rather calamitous six Pioneer III prototypes" that debuted in 1958. Despite the improvements, the Silverliners were so new that PRR and Budd officials had scant opportunity to evaluate their performance.[394] They were suitable only for commuter service, with a top speed of 85 miles per hour. Budd officials promised that "special gearing and partial streamlining will enable this equipment to determine the necessary test data." As early as July 1964, however, they warned the Commerce Department that "the propulsion apparatus will not withstand continuous 150 mph service." It was hardly an ideal approach, but it conformed to demands from Commerce Department and White House officials to deliver visible results as quickly as possible. Budd's vice president for sales acknowledged the need "to minimize the time required for engineering and production and to hold all costs down wherever possible," stipulations that necessitated reliance on the Silverliner design. It was a fateful decision, one that made the mandated performance characteristics almost impossible to achieve.[395]

In July, Budd's Red Lion plant completed the four modified Silverliner test cars, numbered T-1 through T-4. One car measured the interaction of the pantographs and the catenary, the second evaluated track geometry, the third contained equipment (provided by AT&T and Bell Labs) that would enable passengers to make telephone calls in transit, and the fourth evaluated the trucks and overall ride quality. Melpar, Incorporated, a research consultancy based in Falls Church, Virginia, provided most of the instrumentation and the technicians who monitored it.[396] While each car could function independently, Commerce Department specifications required all four to operate in unison, on at least four trial runs at a sustained speed of 150 miles per hour for a minimum of six miles. Only then would the federal government pay the Budd Company for the test cars. Budd briefly evaluated the four cars on the Reading's electrified line at Jenkintown, where a pantograph snagged the contact wire and destroyed a section of the catenary. Despite the inauspicious debut, Budd dispatched the cars to the PRR's yard at Morrisville, Pennsylvania. Located just beyond the New Brunswick–Trenton test zone, Morrisville became the home base for the test cars and then the production models during the lengthy evaluation process. By early August, PRR crews had finished the installation of welded rail along the line between Trenton and New Brunswick, and they were upgrading the catenary with heavier wire. Progress was slow, however, threatening to delay the beginning of high-speed test runs.[397]

During the summer of 1966, PRR engineers worked frantically to ensure that the railroad and the Commerce Department would have something to demonstrate by election day. On September 21, the company assigned oversight of the high-speed rail project to Robert B. Watson, as the coordinator of the Northeast Corridor Demonstration Project.[398] Watson was a second-generation Pennsylvania Railroad employee, born in Altoona, and the son of a man who spent most of his career in the Test Department. Beginning in 1951, he worked as a probationary junior engineer. Two years later, he graduated from Pennsylvania State College with a degree in mechanical engineering. Watson served with the 765th Railway Shop Battalion and the 724th Railway Operating Battalion in Korea, returned to the PRR in 1955, and in 1958 earned a degree in railway operations and economics from Yale University. By the spring of 1966, he was the PRR's master mechanic at Philadelphia, prior to taking on his new responsibilities. For the next six years he would be the principal liaison between Pennsylvania Railroad executives, government officials, and representatives from Budd, GE, Westinghouse, and the other equipment suppliers.[399]

Nelson and other Commerce Department officials, determined to demonstrate results prior to the November election, demanded a "profile run" with two of the four test cars on October 17. It was to be followed by a ceremony at Washington Union Station with Barbara Castle, the British minister of transport, as the guest of honor. On October 10, however, GE engineers acknowledged that the traction-motor mounts were subject to forces more than nine times Earth's gravitational pull. A week later, on the day scheduled for the profile run, Watson issued the first in a long series of coordinator's reports, each one a litany of problems and concerns regarding the performance of the high-speed equipment. In summarizing the results of a seminar held on October 13 and 14, Watson listed twenty "items in which more than a passing interest was expressed"—by which he meant issues that no one knew how to solve. GE technicians reassured Watson that the cars could be moved safely to Washington, "if normal timetable limits were not exceeded." It was neither a ringing endorsement nor a promising start for high-speed operation.[400]

Two of the test cars made their public debut at Washington Union Station on October 20, less than three weeks prior to election day. The advance publicity for the event went exactly according to plan but unfortunately nothing else did. Based on optimistic pronouncements from the Commerce Department, journalists anticipated something akin to the *Shinkansen*. They were badly disappointed. "The press reaction was generally poor," Watson noted, "mainly because of the confused arrangements, and the inability of those conducting the briefing to convey the true purpose of the cars and the test program." The previous day, on the trip south from Morrisville, cracked sensor brackets disabled a significant portion of Melpar's instrumentation. Shortly after the train arrived in Washington, Commerce Department personnel announced that members of Congress would be unable to attend the next day's demonstration. They therefore canceled the planned trip to Odenton, Maryland. Everyone received word of the change—except reporters, who began arriving at 6:30 the following morning. They berated Commerce Department officials, who unilaterally announced that the excursion was on again. By the time PRR personnel assembled a crew, the train left an hour after its scheduled departure time. There were seventy-nine people, including thirty-eight reporters, in the two cars—each of which was crowded with instrumentation but contained no seats. "The train was late," complained a reporter from the *Philadelphia Inquirer*. "Most of the passengers had to stand. The top speed achieved was a measly 85 miles an hour"—well

below the promised benchmark of 110. The headline that appeared in the *Philadelphia Bulletin*—"Pennsy Unveils Its Speedy Train—Standing Still"—was even less forgiving. The equipment remained parked at Union Station the following day, and if the Right Honorable Baroness Castle of Blackburn harbored any criticism of American high-speed equipment that contained no seats and did not move very fast, then she was much too polite to say so. "In order to preclude any future coverage of this kind," Watson concluded, "the Department of Commerce has asked to call a meeting of all the public relations groups and their respective operating people to set up some ground rules for future PR functions." Belatedly, those involved in the demonstration project were beginning to appreciate that selling the value of high-speed rail operations to the American people was as important as the technology that made that service possible.[401]

From Commerce to Transportation

The first, halting steps coincided with Lyndon Johnson's efforts, underway since the summer of 1964, to create a new cabinet-level agency that would coordinate national transportation policy. In the November 1964 report of the presidential task force on transportation policy, economists George Hilton and John Meyer recommended just such an entity, as well as rate-making flexibility and the integration of multiple modes of transport. Not until July 1965, however, did the president ask his key assistant, Joseph Califano, to coordinate an agency with a $6 billion budget and a hundred thousand employees. Alan S. Boyd, recently appointed as Clarence Martin's successor as the under secretary of commerce for transportation, headed an advisory panel that would work out the details. Boyd's report, delivered to Califano on September 2, echoed many of the initiatives recommended by Hilton and Meyer. Boyd also endorsed a proposal that would enable the president to appoint the chairman of the Interstate Commerce Commission—an initiative that would increase Johnson's control over transportation policy. The president received Boyd's report on September 22, and he was delighted with its provisions.[402]

Despite the potential benefits associated with transportation coordination, Johnson was facing what Califano later described as "the toughest legislative fight of the 89th Congress." Ignoring the president's focus on the collective efficiency associated with the new policies, representatives from all modes of transportation sought what was best for their respective companies. They included Stuart Saunders, who emphasized that he favored "an integrated transportation system." In a resurrection of policies advocated by W. W. Atterbury in the 1920s, Saunders made it clear that the PRR—and ultimately the Penn Central—should be able to own air carriers and trucking firms associated with its trailer-on-flat-car services. The proposal drew condemnation from competitors who feared that the Penn Central would monopolize all transportation in the Northeast, not just the railroads. Officials from existing federal agencies—most notably the Federal Highway Administration, the Federal Aviation Administration, the Army Corps of Engineers, and the Maritime Administration—sought to maintain their existing institutional prerogatives. The subsequent political maneuvering eliminated several of the features Johnson supported. There was now little emphasis on deregulation or the type of transportation coordination that Saunders, as well as Hilton and Meyer, favored. Nor would the president be able to appoint the chairman of the Interstate Commerce Commission. Johnson nonetheless claimed victory and signed the enabling legislation on October 15, 1966. He selected Boyd as the first secretary of transportation, the individual who would inherit from the Commerce Department the oversight of the high-speed rail project. The Department of Transportation would also have control over the urban transit programs funded by the Housing and Home Finance Agency (after September 1965, part of the Department of Housing and Urban Development). The transition suggested that federal officials now perceived mobility issues within American cities as a transportation problem rather than an urban problem. The transfer also offered a measure of protection against growing conservative opposition to social-welfare projects that principally benefited an urban, Democratic constituency. The same perceptions threatened the high-speed demonstration project, and it was just as well that the Commerce Department reassigned the effort to the Department of Transportation.[403]

It was fortunate that Johnson signed the transportation bill into law when he did. Less than three weeks later, the Democrats fared badly in the 1966 elections, losing three seats in the Senate and forty-seven in the House. The situation had little to do with the politics of high-speed rail and instead reflected opposition to Johnson's social-welfare programs and his advocacy of civil rights. The Republican gains, coupled with the escalation of the war in Vietnam, nonetheless sharply curtailed the president's Great Society. Had Claiborne Pell waited a few more years before proposing modern railroads as a solution for the transportation crisis in the megalopolis, it is doubtful that Johnson would have given such strong support to that policy agenda.

The Department of Transportation began operations on April 1, 1967. Both Nelson and the Office of High Speed Ground Transportation became part of the DOT's Federal Railroad Administration, under the command of A. Scheffer Lang. Unlike Nelson, Lang had significant experience with railroad operations, working at the Denver & Rio Grande Western and at the US Army Transportation School at Fort Eustis, Virginia. Between 1961 and 1965, he was the director of operating data systems at the New York Central, overseeing the application of computers to railroad operations. As the deputy under secretary for transportation research at the Commerce Department, he was familiar with both Nelson and the Northeast Corridor project. He was also supportive of high-speed rail transit, while restraining some of Nelson's more visionary tendencies. "My most important contribution," Lang recalled, "was to keep the bureaucrats and the power-grabbers away from Nelson so he could get his work done in peace." In his role as coordinator of the demonstration project, Watson was nonetheless more likely to interact with T. F. Murray, the DOT's test director—an individual who, the PRR engineer observed, "is well versed in instrumentation and test programs, but has no railroad experience."[404]

Watson and his colleagues made slow progress during the remaining months of 1967 and into the year that followed. Less than a week after the badly managed debut at Washington, the test cars exceeded 130 miles per hour for the first time. Prudently, Watson favored incremental increases in speed with each test run, to identify and correct any new problems that might develop and to give PRR maintenance-of-way crews sufficient time to complete upgrades to the track. Budd Company officials were less patient, as the Commerce Department would not release payment until there had been four test runs at speeds exceeding 150 miles per hour. "We are experiencing considerable pressure from them for unrestricted speeds on the entire test track," Watson complained, reiterating his philosophy that "the higher speeds must be approached gradually rather than a one-shot 150 M.P.H. run which Budd seems to want." Given the limitations inherent in the repurposed Silverliners, he observed, "there is considerable doubt that the cars as they presently stand will achieve 150 M.P.H." Watson was being unduly pessimistic. On November 18, and on their twenty-seventh trip, the cars held a sustained speed of 152 miles per hour for three miles. The success was possible only because shop crews had removed the pantographs from two of the four cars, to reduce the arcing produced by catenary that displayed abrupt changes in height. Watson also ordered an increase in catenary voltage, admitting that the procedure "created a highly undesirable condition for the Philadelphia Electric Company which will not be duplicated." The high speeds threw chunks of ballast in every direction, with some pieces landing on the roofs of the cars and others disabling underfloor instrumentation. Watson dampened the celebrations of Budd Company officials, noting that the three-mile high-speed run was only half of the minimum distance specified in the Commerce Department contract. Another two months would pass before the test cars would again operate at 150 miles per hour. Despite the initial, tantalizing burst of speed, much work remained to be done before the technology worked as intended.[405]

Month after month, Watson and his fellow engineers identified and corrected problems. General Electric refused to make any further modifications to the traction motors, and their engineers recommended operation at no more than 130 miles per hour. They also advised long intervals between test runs, to allow the overheated traction motors to cool. GE technicians rejected recommendations to install cooling fans and suggested that an additional six months of research would be needed to resolve the problem. Watson sought permission from federal officials to apply a shroud around the leading edge of the pantographs and to add a streamlined cowling to the front end—a change that would make it difficult to install signal lights and couplers on the production-model cars. One day's operation created a groove one-sixteenth of an inch deep into the pantograph wear strips, suggesting that improvements to the track had succeeded in keeping the cars in line, but at the expense of exacerbating the problems associated with the absence of indexing in the catenary. By the middle of January, Watson observed, "Budd was at this time confident that the 150-mph acceptance speed could be attained, but was doubtful that it could be held for the required 6 miles." When representatives from the car builder requested modifications to the acceptance criteria, Nelson suspended all testing until the parties could work out an agreement. The Office of High Speed Ground Transportation canceled a press run, scheduled for February 8, because there was no progress to demonstrate.[406]

As they struggled to overcome the problems associated with the development of high-speed rail technology, personnel from the PRR, Budd, and the other suppliers and contractors did their best to accommodate the diverse transportation agenda favored by federal officials. Technicians from Bell Laboratories and AT&T spent considerable time testing a telephone system that would permit passengers to make calls while en route—a highly publicized amenity that possessed no operational value whatsoever. In January 1967, shop forces cut a massive hole in one of

the test cars. After being loaded with two automobiles (a Ford Mustang and a Chevrolet Chevelle), the Commerce Department dispatched it to Florida to test the auto-train concept. Given the stipulations of the Commerce Department contract, acceptance could not take place until the wayward auto carrier returned from Florida and all four cars could operate as a complete set. All the while, Watson and his team were inundated with visitors—including delegations from Japan, France, India, and Canada, congressional staffers, and the engineering personnel of various American railroads. "We must severely limit the number of persons having unrestricted access to the cars if we are to expect timely and economical completion of our research program," complained Edward Ward, the deputy director of the Office of High Speed Ground Transportation. "We cannot tolerate any distractions to the personnel operating the cars and instrumentation."[407]

Watson prepared for another series of test runs, designed to prove that the Budd Company had achieved the performance criteria stipulated in the contract with the Commerce Department. "Budd is under severe pressure from the Department of Commerce," he observed, "and now has the added threat of unfavorable publicity from the New York Times." The qualifying runs took place in early morning on Sunday, April 2—a time chosen because little other traffic would draw current from the catenary. Pennsylvania Railroad substations sent fourteen thousand volts surging through the overhead wires, something that never would have been sustainable under normal operating conditions. The first trip remained steady at 100 miles per hour, to ensure the track was in acceptable condition. On the second test, the train accelerated to a maximum speed of 155.5 miles per hour, as a hail of dislodged ballast hit the underside of the cars. It took eight attempts, but the cars fulfilled their contractual requirements.[408]

While Watson and his staff pushed the test cars to their limits, marketing personnel sought ways to tailor high-speed rail service to suit potential demand. Traditionally, PRR conductors tallied both the number of passengers who boarded at each large station and overall patronage. That methodology ensured that yard crews added the correct number of cars to each train but did not measure the origin or the destination of each traveler. Commerce Department representatives introduced small prepunched tickets, which they based on their experience with sales and inventory-control procedures employed in retail stores. When fed into a computer, the data provided the first accurate information regarding passenger volumes and demand patterns for each origin-destination pair. Computer simulations also indicated optimal speeds and running times for each section of the route, assisting in the development of schedules and the issuance of public timetables. Surveys, mock-ups, and other techniques established consumer preferences for food service, seating, and related amenities. The PRR's longtime marketing consultant, the Al Paul Lefton Company, developed a new brand image for the service. Lefton created a logo that resembled two teardrops sliding past each other, evocative of both speed and direction. Lefton's staff considered many possible names for the high-speed operation, including *Speedliner* and *Railblazer*. Ultimately, they acknowledged the urban character of the megalopolis that stretched from New York to Washington and selected the name *Metroliner*.[409]

Capitaliners to Harrisburg

Efforts to implement high-speed service between New York and Washington inspired a similar proposal along the 104 miles of Pennsylvania Railroad track linking Philadelphia and Harrisburg. Depending on one's perspective, the result was either a commendable effort to provide better transportation in southeastern Pennsylvania or an unconstitutional and anticompetitive demonstration of administrative overreach. The initiative was an outgrowth of efforts by the Philadelphia municipal government to preserve PRR and Reading commuter service in the region—first through the Passenger Service Improvement Corporation, then through the Southeastern Pennsylvania Transportation Compact, and finally with the Southeastern Pennsylvania Transportation Authority. It became clear, early in that process, that neither the city and suburban governments nor the two railroads possessed the financial resources necessary to subsidize commuter operations. Even though PSIC, SEPACT, and SEPTA performed different functions, all three agencies demonstrated increasing reliance on federal subsidies. The money came first from the Housing and Home Finance Agency and later through the Department of Housing and Urban Development. In each case, the justification for federal support depended on the assertion that improved rail service was a means to achieve the desired end of urban improvement. When the Department of Transportation replaced the Commerce Department as the agency responsible for supporting rail service, the focus on the urban environment largely disappeared. Moreover, an increasing number of municipalities competed with Philadelphia for a limited supply of federal dollars. Even with federal subsidies, support for passenger-rail service still required local matching funds. The Pennsylvania Assembly only grudgingly assented to the creation of SEPTA in 1963.

Legislators from rural districts possessed little incentive to favor a transit system that served only five of the state's counties. The extension of high-speed rail operations from Philadelphia west to Pittsburgh—ideally paid for by the federal government and the Pennsylvania Railroad—would ensure a much broader base of political support. Improved passenger service would also offset the loss of through freight traffic following the proposed Penn Central merger.

People from across the commonwealth shared the widespread public fascination with technology and high-speed travel, giving Governor William Scranton an opportunity to mobilize geographically diverse constituencies. In January 1965, he announced Operation Alert, a three-part plan to "attract space age industries to Pennsylvania." The program called for the establishment of a Materials Advisory Board, a three-year study to increase the utilization of computers, and a proposal to implement high-speed rail service between Philadelphia and Pittsburgh. Scranton also sought a full-time science advisor, mimicking Donald Hornig's role in the Johnson administration. The advocacy group 100,000 Pennsylvanians for the Promotion of Economic Growth would pay the scientist's salary, suggesting that Scranton was primarily concerned with minimizing the costs associated with Operation Alert. The same budget-conscious philosophy conditioned his support for rebuilding and reequipping the PRR route to Pittsburgh.[410]

The Commerce Department's advocacy for high-speed rail service in the Northeast Corridor suggested to politicians in both Philadelphia and Harrisburg that a further source of federal assistance might be available. In November 1965, less than six weeks after President Johnson signed the High Speed Ground Transportation Act, the Pennsylvania Department of Commerce hired Louis T. Klauder & Associates to evaluate the possibility of a Keystone Corridor to match the Northeast Corridor.[411] State commerce secretary John Tabor announced a "dramatic and significant" initiative to emulate the proposed high-speed service between New York and Boston, and hinted that further extensions west toward Chicago lay in the future. Newspapers from Allentown and York to Oil City and Pittsburgh covered the story, suggesting that politicians from across the commonwealth might be favorably disposed toward the project. The *Philadelphia Inquirer*, located in the city that had the most to gain from both Northeast Corridor and Keystone Corridor service, gushed praise in an editorial that reiterated many of the unrealistic promises offered to travelers living between Boston and Washington. "It is self-evident that the economic results of such a 'Keystone

Corridor' would be to widen the dimensions of the Eastern Seaboard megalopolis that is steadily taking shape," editor Walter Annenberg insisted. Operation at 150 miles per hour would cut in half the two-hour trip from Philadelphia to Harrisburg, he suggested, with trains operating on hourly frequencies. The question was not if but "how soon such a project would be self-supporting." Other newspapers, inspired by the pervasive allure of high-speed travel, predicted "possible routes for 150 mph and 300 mph services across the State." It was as if the boosters who during the 1820s promoted the Main Line of Public Works had come to life again, promising that people in all corners of Pennsylvania would see improved transportation reaching their very doorsteps.[412]

Thanks to their work on the Northeast Corridor, staff members at Klauder & Associates were becoming intimately familiar with the potential and the limitations of high-speed rail service. They did not deliver the final report to the state Commerce Department until April 1967, but the incomplete nature of the study did not restrain Scranton's enthusiasm for the project. "If we don't do this kind of thing," he emphasized, "we won't be on the main line." On August 30, 1966, Scranton announced a proposal to spend nearly $22 million on the Keystone Corridor. Like many such initiatives, it offered less than it promised, while minimizing the amount of money that the state government would contribute. The state's share was a mere $6.75 million, ostensibly for a high-speed demonstration project along the Keystone Corridor. The bulk of the funding, $12.8 million, would come from the federal government. Because neither the state nor the federal government could legally give money or equipment to the Pennsylvania Railroad, Scranton had little choice other than to rely on SEPTA as an intermediary. Most of the federal and state funds would be put to far more prosaic uses than the development of high-speed rail service, however. It would enable SEPTA to acquire fifty-five Silverliners, for conventional commuter service in suburban Philadelphia. The remainder of the $19.6 million equipment budget was sufficient for only eleven high-speed cars, clones of the *Metroliner* design. [413] Those, too, would be owned by SEPTA and assigned to the Pennsylvania Railroad under a fifteen-year lease. Often referred to as *Capitaliners*, both their name and their reliance on the PRR's catenary suggested that—at least for the moment—the Keystone Corridor would extend no farther west than Harrisburg.[414] Smaller pools of state money could be used to eliminate grade crossings between Philadelphia and Harrisburg ($1.6 million), fund an engineering and research program ($250,000), and support a $400,000 marketing campaign. The Pennsylvania Railroad would

contribute $2.3 million, principally for improvements to tracks, catenary, and station facilities. It was a small price to pay for the cooperation of state officials in the matter that most concerned Stuart Saunders and other PRR and NYC executives. On December 29, four months after Scranton announced that the Pennsylvania Railroad would begin high-speed service along the Keystone Corridor, Pennsylvania's attorney general informed the US Supreme Court that he no longer opposed the railroad's merger with the New York Central. The timing suggested that there was a link between the two developments, much as the PRR's commitment to improved service between New York and Washington helped overcome opposition at the federal level.[415]

Governor Scranton declared that the four-year demonstration project would "put Pennsylvania on the main line of America," but service along the Keystone Corridor represented, in microcosm, many of the inflated expectations and unfulfilled promises associated with the development of high-speed rail travel in the United States. Until the PRR completed improvements to the right-of-way, Scranton acknowledged, the new high-speed cars would be limited to no more than 90 miles per hour. Before long, he indicated, 150-mph service would be in place, at least as far west as the state capital. Subsequent announcements indicated that the eleven cars would be equipped for operation at speeds of up to 110 miles per hour—significantly slower than the 150-mph standard that Tabor had mentioned the previous autumn.[416]

Just as Lyndon Johnson demanded a successful test run in the Northeast Corridor prior to the November 1966 elections, Scranton was also in a hurry. Under Pennsylvania law, he could not run for reelection. Scranton's term would end in January 1967, and he wanted to achieve measurable results before he left office. On November 3, representatives from the Pennsylvania Railroad, the state government, SEPTA, and the Budd Company agreed to the terms for improvements to the Keystone Corridor. A demonstration trip, for the benefit of the news media, took place on November 29. Regular service began on December 5, a month before Scranton left office. Neither the *Capitaliner* cars nor the improved roadbed were available, and the Keystone Corridor instead hosted conventional Silverliner equipment, owned by PSIC, managed by SEPTA, and assigned to and operated by the Pennsylvania Railroad. Even as an interim measure, the cars were easily able to reach speeds of 80 miles per hour, trimming fifteen minutes from the two-hour schedule. Frequencies increased from three to eight round trips per day. "Pennsylvania now becomes the first State in the Nation to sponsor and develop high-speed ground transportation," bragged Scranton. "It is a partnership—it is new, it is unique, it puts Pennsylvania out front." John Tabor, the state commerce secretary, echoed the governor's promises of faster trains. Allen Greenough, the PRR's president, was more reticent. "Our goal on the Pennsylvania," he emphasized, "is to produce faster, more convenient and more comfortable passenger service"—but only, he added, "where there is sufficient demand." Greenough was familiar with the condition of the tracks between Philadelphia and Harrisburg, and he declined to endorse statements by government officials that the cars could routinely reach speeds of 110 miles per hour.[417]

Philadelphia city officials were even more reticent and feared that the Keystone Corridor would divert equipment and funds from the regional commuter rail system they had created. They observed that SEPTA was a regional transportation agency, one whose authority extended only as far as the western border of Chester County. Despite Scranton's claims, it was not certain that SEPTA possessed jurisdiction over PRR operations that continued west to Lancaster and Harrisburg.[418] Philadelphians expressed dismay that the state planned to pay for the new high-speed Capitaliner cars by diverting money from SEPTA's budget appropriation, in the anticipation that offsetting federal funds would eventually materialize. Even the stop-gap Silverliner operation depended on cars that the city purchased through the Passenger Service Improvement Corporation, with the intention that they would be used solely along suburban commuter routes. Edson Tennyson, the city transit engineer, emphasized that "this experimental service was instituted until high-speed trains are put into use by the railroad," but his claims of temporary expediency reassured no one. Merritt Taylor, the president of the Red Arrow Lines and a longtime critic of government transportation subsidies—particularly those that drew traffic away from his company—asserted that the Harrisburg service represented another "sop to the classes at the expense of the masses, particularly those in Philadelphia." He demanded that the state Public Utility Commission rather than SEPTA manage the region's transportation services. Staff members of the Delaware Valley Regional Planning Commission also refused to endorse the Capitaliner plan, declaring that they were willing to accept the fifty-five commuter cars but not the eleven that would be dedicated to high-speed operation.[419] Politicians also spoke out against the arrangement. When he was city controller, Alexander Hemphill had been sharply critical of SEPTA's management. He resigned that post in January 1967, but in his new role as mayoral candidate, he was more determined than ever to safeguard Philadelphia's financial interests. He complained that the city "is spending millions to provide modern cars for local commuters, but SEPTA has been parceling them out to the Pennsylvania Railroad for Philadelphia-to-Harrisburg service." Hemphill's outrage increased after a rockslide demolished a $250,000 Silverliner near Elizabethtown, ninety miles west of the municipality that owned it.[420]

Scranton's advocacy for the Keystone Corridor also concerned the regulatory officials who served on the state's Public Utility Commission. While they were not averse to economic development or increased mobility, they possessed a responsibility to maintain a competitive balance among various modes of transportation. The owners of rival bus lines took little comfort in the assertion by James Diffenderfer, the PRR's director of special services, that there was "a role for everyone" and that "it is not our desire to hurt or undercut anyone." Representatives from the Red Arrow Lines, Greyhound, Capitol Trailways, and twenty-one other bus companies appealed their case to the PUC. They argued that the Capitaliner project provided a subsidy, in violation of both the federal and state constitutions, while conferring an unfair advantage on the PRR. The commission launched an investigation, asserting that the new service "could result in injury to competitors" of the Pennsylvania Railroad. Regulators questioned SEPTA's authority to organize and provide funding for areas that lay well beyond the Philadelphia metropolitan area and suggested that "SEPTA has not made a full and complete disclosure of the facts in light of the far-reaching effects this proposed agreement would have on the transportation system of the Commonwealth." Governor Scranton soon faced a PUC subpoena and was in the odd position of defending an agency that was the legacy of his bitter political rival, Richardson Dilworth.[421]

Pennsylvania Railroad officials quickly concluded that the potential legal, political, and financial liabilities associated with the Harrisburg service far outweighed whatever modest increase in ridership the railroad might gain. Pennsylvania Railroad attorney Charles E. Mechem insisted that the company had no desire to exempt the Philadelphia–Harrisburg route from the PUC's oversight. Following the precedent established by the PRR and Reading commuter operations in Philadelphia, Mechem explained that government funding constituted the purchase of additional service rather than an outright subsidy. While technically correct, the assertions largely fell on deaf ears. With the outcome of the PRR-NYC merger still in doubt, it was a poor time to alienate the members of Pennsylvania's Public Utility Commission. In early

February 1967, barely two months after Silverliners began running to Harrisburg, Mechem announced "revisions" to the railroad's agreement with SEPTA. "I am not in a position at this time to say just what the revisions will consist of," Mechem stated. "The new contract will be the same as the old one in many respects. But there will be one or two changes." Mechem's reference to "changes" was something of an understatement, and on February 20, the PUC approved the railroad's request to withdraw from the contract that its representatives signed on November 3.[422]

The Pennsylvania Railroad's abdication did little to discourage advocacy for the Keystone Corridor. When he took office in January 1967, Governor Raymond P. Shafer demonstrated the same enthusiasm for high-speed rail as his predecessor—and faced the same level of criticism. "We do not have to conduct this program or demonstration," acknowledged state commerce secretary Clifford Jones. "But if we don't, it will be done south of us in Maryland or north of us in New York State. If that happens, the Keystone State will be bypassed entirely from a transportation point of view and from future economic growth." Governor Shafer declared that Pennsylvania had to act quickly, lest "the rapidly increasing demand for high-speed transportation may result in an alternative route or system located outside Pennsylvania which hurts, rather than helps, Pennsylvania's economy." It was a poignant comment, given that PRR and NYC officials were planning to eliminate most through freight service between Philadelphia and Pittsburgh once the Penn Central merger took place. Citing the recently completed Klauder report, Shafer indicated that "those who made the study conclude that it would be economic suicide for Pennsylvania not to develop such a high-speed corridor." It was an argument that echoed political advocacy for the Main Line of Public Works during the 1820s and 1830s, stoked by fears that the Erie Canal and other rival transportation arteries would capture the trade of the West and transform the state into an economic backwater.[423]

In a reprise of the political debates that took place well over a century earlier, elected officials from all parts of the commonwealth heaped scorn on the proposal. "The Scranton and now the Shafer administrations are changing Pennsycare from a program to help sick people to one that helps healthy railroads," argued Milton Shapp, making reference to the recent enactment of Medicare, one of the signature achievements of the Johnson administration. Shapp, a staunch critic of both the PRR and its proposed merger with the New York Central, insisted that "the sole benefactor of this entire project will be the Pennsylvania Railroad." He suggested that the *Capitaliner* cars will "wind

up being paid for by Pennsylvania taxpayers and used by the PRR between Washington and New York." Erie's Democratic senator, William G. Sesler—who represented a district that included the General Electric plant that manufactured equipment for the *Metroliners*—asserted that it was foolhardy to order the eleven *Capitaliner* cars before the improved roadbed was ready to receive them. "We're giving away $7 million," complained Representative Jules Filo, a fellow Democrat, "and I don't like to give away $7 million." Even though the Pennsylvania Railroad served his native city of Pittsburgh, Filo charged that the proposal represented an illegal state subsidy to the company.[424]

During the 1820s and 1830s, political battles over funding for the commonwealth's system of internal improvements involved contentious debates between the "Mainliners" and the "Branch Men"—a situation resolved only after legislators agreed to extend canals into every corner of Pennsylvania. When he released the full Klauder report to the General Assembly on May 11, Shafer was channeling a similar strategy. The proposal recommended a high-speed route along the existing PRR right-of-way from Philadelphia to Harrisburg. West of the capital, a new alignment along the Pennsylvania Turnpike would bring trains to Carlisle, the junction for possible high-speed lines to Chicago and St. Louis. Spurs would provide fast service to Reading, Allentown, Bethlehem, Wilkes-Barre, Scranton, and Erie. With so many routes crisscrossing the state, it would be difficult to find a community of any significant size that would be denied the benefits of modern rail travel or any politicians who could not deliver some spoils to their constituents. Klauder suggested that a new two-track main line from Philadelphia to Pittsburgh could be in service by 1975, with passenger trains operating at the visionary default speed of 150 miles per hour. By 1990, two additional tracks could host freight service at 90 miles an hour, but thirty or forty years might elapse before hovertrains or similar technologies permitted passenger speeds that exceeded 300 miles per hour.[425]

The breathtaking magnitude of the project, far from uniting legislators behind the creation of a comprehensive high-speed rail network, led to its undoing. Shafer asked the assembly to provide $24 million to acquire the land needed to construct the main route across Pennsylvania. It was a manageable sum, although one that represented about half of the state Commerce Department's annual budget. Yet an expenditure of that magnitude was tantamount to a binding commitment to see the plan through to completion. At a time when the federal government allocated no more than $12 million in public funds to the *Metroliner* project along the Northeast Corridor, the Klauder study estimated the cost of the initial Philadelphia–Pittsburgh passenger line at $1.178 billion. With that, the vision for a statewide high-speed rail corridor passed into the realm of fantasy, a land from which it never returned.[426]

High Speed Comes to the Northeast Corridor, at Last

Even as Pennsylvanians struggled to create a local high-speed network, federal officials forged ahead with the demonstration project along the Northeast Corridor. Ever mindful of the importance of public relations, they scheduled a daytime demonstration run for the benefit of the news media. PRR officials were careful to inform reporters that "this is the four-car electric test train recently delivered to the Department of Transportation by the Budd Company. It is not the high-speed electric train being constructed for the Pennsylvania Railroad by the Budd Company for [the] regular schedule of high-speed transportation between New York and Washington this October." On May 24, 1967, the test equipment—now the property of the Department of Transportation rather than the Commerce Department—zipped through Princeton Junction at 156 miles per hour. During the second run, a piece of dislodged ballast struck a wheel-slip sensor and disabled the traction motors on one of the cars. It was a frequent occurrence, yet it did little to dim the enthusiasm of the two hundred spectators. The reporters and photographers who stood on the station platform offered enthusiastic assessments of the high-speed project. So did the guests fortunate enough to go along for the ride, despite having to stand in cars packed with equipment and concrete blocks that provided ballast. Correspondents received membership cards in the "150 Club" and in return granted the project favorable publicity. They noted that the brief journey was both smooth and surprisingly quiet, thanks in large measure to the recent installation of continuously welded rail along the route. Road foreman of engines Elton B. Selover, nattily attired in a bright red sport coat, white shirt, and black tie, offered the eminently quotable opinion that "this means the end of the cinder goggles, the bibb overalls and the high button shoes; this is the beginning of a new era."[427]

Even as Selover was predicting a new era of high-speed rail transportation, the project was falling apart. PRR officials had gone to great lengths to remind reporters that the four instrument-filled and seatless test cars were not representative of the modern and luxurious equipment that the Budd Company was constructing at its Red Lion plant. They offered assurances that at least some of the new cars

would be available when regular service began on October 29. Budd president Philip W. Scott announced that equipment would "positively" be ready by autumn and capable of reaching speeds of up to 160 miles per hour. Scott's estimate proved wildly optimistic. Had the PRR and its equipment suppliers undertaken—and completed—a slow and incremental evaluation of the four test cars, Bob Watson and his team could have eventually resolved many of the problems they encountered. Instead, technicians struggled to remedy defects in as-delivered cars that were scheduled to enter revenue service.[428]

While numerous difficulties plagued the Budd cars, the most serious involved their all-important traction motors and associated electrical equipment. If the selection of a car builder represented an easy decision on the part of Pennsylvania Railroad officials, then the choice of electrical components was not. Budd possessed considerable expertise in the fabrication of the stainless-steel car bodies, but the traction motors and control systems could only come from General Electric or Westinghouse. While both companies boasted a long tradition of manufacturing components for electric and diesel-electric locomotives, neither had much experience with the rigorous conditions that accompanied high-speed operation. As such, there was scant precedent to guide PRR executives in their selection of electrical equipment. The decision fell to David Smucker, the vice president in charge of operations, who was reluctant to commit to either manufacturer. "Rather than face the possibility of being 100% wrong in the choice of a single propulsion supplier," Watson observed, "the railroad could be assured of at least being 50% correct by splitting the propulsion order" between GE and Westinghouse. The split was not quite 50/50, as the twenty coaches would employ Westinghouse technology, with the twenty snack-bar coaches and ten parlor cars using equipment provided by GE. Had this exercise in technological coin-flipping been limited to the four test cars, then mistakes on the part of either supplier would have been of little consequence. With Budd gearing up for full-scale production, however, problems with either company's products could sideline a significant portion of the fifty-car fleet.[429]

Pressure from the Johnson administration, the Commerce Department, and later the Department of Transportation forced the PRR and Budd to begin building production-model equipment well before the completion of the testing program. Three PRR officials—assistant electrical engineer J. W. Irvin, mechanical engineer George R. Weaver, and assistant mechanical engineer R. W. Reed—were responsible for evaluating and approving Budd's proposals and engineering drawings. Yet

By late May 1967, four modified Silverliner cars, owned by the recently created Department of Transportation, provided a successful public demonstration of high-speed operation. The project was nonetheless well behind schedule, and the technicians who were involved expressed little confidence that trains would be operating in revenue service between New York and Washington in time for the 1968 elections. *Pennsylvania Railroad Photographs, Hagley Museum & Library, acc. 1988.231.*

they were simultaneously responsible for the construction of twenty new Silverliners, built by the St. Louis Car Company for the Passenger Service Improvement Corporation, and thirty-five Jersey Arrow cars, owned by the New Jersey Department of Transportation. Along with the fifty Budd high-speed units, they would all operate along the PRR. Each design was nonetheless different from the others, and the three engineers had a difficult time keeping abreast of the crushing workload. Neither PRR nor

Budd employees could execute any changes without first securing approval from the Office of High Speed Ground Transportation. It was "almost impossible to achieve the adequate review and evaluation of the car builder's proposals," Watson complained, "especially since so many of the plans were being submitted in an 'as-built' form rather than for approval prior to construction." David Smucker shared Watson's concerns and chafed at the delays that occurred as Budd employees corrected problems on the production line rather than on the drawing board. "Some day within a reasonable length of time, Budd should have at least two cars de-bugged to an extent which will warrant presenting them to us for acceptance testing," he complained at the end of October 1967. "Then, for the first time, we will be free to begin to evaluate the performance of the cars that have been built for this service—not for commuter service, not for fruitless running up and down pretending to be testing something more than my waning patience." Smucker looked forward to the day when "we will not be obliged to pay any attention to anyone but the seller and he

The interior of the repurposed Silverliner cars, although filled with instrumentation provided by Melpar and other contractors, lacked seats and other amenities. The reporters packed inside could only speculate about the luxurious, airplane-like accommodations that, as PRR officials promised, would be incorporated into *Metroliner* equipment. *Pennsylvania Railroad Photographs, Hagley Museum & Library, acc. 1988.231.*

and his electrical suppliers, to us as the buyer"—an indication of his loathing for DOT officials and his desire to dispense with their oversight. Yet Smucker expressed optimism that the amount of money at stake would encourage Budd and the other equipment suppliers to get their house in order. Given the PRR's "$21.6 million hold on these people," he concluded, "I am sure that no engineering or scientific stone will be left unturned."[430]

The vice president in charge of operations placed far too much confidence in the coercive value of the $21.6 million that the Pennsylvania Railroad promised to pay Budd for the fifty new cars. David Bevan, the PRR's chief financial officer, was desperately trying to find sufficient cash to keep the railroad operating, and he had long cautioned restraint in matters of capital expenditures. To Bevan, the Northeast Corridor project represented an unsustainable drain on the corporate treasury rather than an opportunity to showcase the allure of high-speed passenger travel. Even though the DOT's two-year demonstration period could not begin until at least some of the new Budd cars were in service, Bevan did his best to avoid spending money on them. As early as December 1966, Watson became aware that "one of the reasons for the slow delivery schedule of the new cars is that Mr. Bevan does not want to pay for them until 1968. . . . It would seem," Watson concluded in a masterpiece of understatement, "that the inception of the demonstration train in October, 1967 is not compatible with the desire to delay payment for the cars until 1968." To postpone the expenditure as long as possible, Bevan encouraged Budd to give priority to the eleven commonwealth-owned *Capitaliner* cars intended for service between Philadelphia and Harrisburg. Several months passed before Robert Nelson, the director of the Office of High Speed Ground Transportation, learned of the subterfuge. When he did, he recalled, "I literally raised hell. For the next three weeks I was sitting on Budd's doorstep. I forced them to put on another production line." Nelson's obstinacy moved the project forward but in the process

gave the company's engineers and technicians less time to correct the many problems they were observing.[431]

Bevan's delaying tactics were in some respects the least serious impediment to the completion of the fifty new *Metroliner* cars. In July, three months before the scheduled initiation of service, reporters toured the Red Lion plant and inspected the first completed car, a seventy-six-seat coach. Budd representatives assured them that forty cars would be available by October 29 but that they would initially travel no faster than 110 miles per hour. By early September, however, it was evident that few if any of the cars would be ready in time. Budd executives absolved themselves of all responsibility for the delays and instead shifted the blame to the component suppliers. Even though the Red Lion plant was in operation six days a week, they emphasized, Budd employees were struggling to modify GE and Westinghouse electrical and braking equipment to the PRR's specifications. General Electric declined to comment on the problems, while a Westinghouse representative insisted that "the charge is debatable," without offering any further explanation.[432]

Even as Budd was slowly completing the *Metroliner* cars, Watson and his fellow engineers were attempting to resolve problems that threatened to preclude high-speed operation along the Northeast Corridor. The comprehensive test plan for the pantographs and the catenary would not be ready until August, but there were ample indications that those components constituted the Achilles heel of the entire project. "The alarming results already found with the test cars above 100 mph," Watson noted in September, "indicate that pantograph performance is the major problem facing us." Watson's statement was more of a confirmation than a discovery. As early as March 1966 consultants at Gibbs & Hill—who knew the PRR's catenary better than anyone—"came to Melpar to convince them of the complexity of the wire behavior vs pantograph behavior problem on MU trains at speeds above 100 MPH and to see if they could get in the act. They said the Pennsy system would not work above 100 MPH and that there was no successful analytical approach to the problem. They said there might be as many as 150 variables involved." The installation of heavier contact wire did not remedy the severe arcing that occurred with catenary that was neither indexed nor properly tensioned and that rose and fell at a steep gradient whenever the tracks went through tunnels or underneath highways. Ward, the deputy director of the Office of High Speed Ground Transportation, privately confided to Watson that the PRR would probably have to bear the additional expense of altering the catenary profile at those locations. Test pantographs provided by Stemmann-Technik GmbH, adequate for European electrified railways, proved too weak for the PRR's application. Those supplied by its French competitor, Faiveley, performed better but were still inadequate at speeds above one hundred miles an hour. Despite their early offer to "get in the act," the staff at Gibbs & Hill did not receive instructions to work with the equipment suppliers until October 20. Less than three weeks later, with the problems still unresolved, DOT personnel "stated that the test cars were needed for other work and could see no benefit from further pantograph runs." With the experimental equipment on its way north, for a track survey on the New Haven, there was little Watson could do to improve the key link between the high-speed trains and the wires that powered them.[433]

The autumn of 1967 marked the nadir of the high-speed rail project in the Northeast Corridor. On September 14,

PRR executives traveled to Washington to inform DOT officials that regular operations could not possibly commence at the end of October. Even though Nelson insisted that it was "extremely desirable for a number of reasons to get this service started," the absence of suitable equipment and unresolved problems with the catenary and pantographs made delays unavoidable. "We need a full complement of cars in order to give the public the new vastly improved service which it has been given reason to expect from this project," he conceded. Six days later, a spokesman for the Department of Transportation announced that the first passenger runs would not take place until the beginning of the new year. The terse announcement appeared on page 94 of the *New York Times*, indicating just how far the story had fallen from the headlines. In an adjacent article, the senior vice president and general manager of Eastern Air Lines predicted steadily increasing costs for airport construction, coupled with lengthening delays for those traveling by plane. "Even more disturbing," Arthur D. Lewis observed, "there are no technological improvements in the foreseeable future which will reverse these unfavorable trends"—suggesting that the dire warnings regarding impaired mobility in the megalopolis were beginning to come true. Unable to launch the new *Metroliner* service, PRR officials instead raised the speed limit for the *Afternoon Congressional*—a conventional passenger train powered by GG1 locomotives—to one hundred miles per hour. The new three-hour, twenty-minute schedule lasted just six months, before reverting to a three-hour, thirty-five-minute travel time. The short-lived experiment suggested both the difficulty in maintaining sustained high-speed operation and the embarrassment that was likely to result when the new *Metroliner* cars could do no better than trim twenty-one minutes off a journey undertaken with equipment more than a decade old. It remained to be seen whether that insignificant reduction in travel time would be worth the massive investment required to achieve it.[434]

Reporters, primed to offer glowing reviews of the inauguration of high-speed rail travel, instead filled column inches with vituperative criticism. On October 27, two days before the now-postponed inauguration of 110-mph service, Ward announced that the Pennsylvania Railroad had failed in its efforts to upgrade the catenary. The *New York Times* provided a description of the test cars passing by with "a section of new and heavier overhead trolley line flapping behind like a loose clothesline." It was a memorable image but hardly the one that PRR officials wanted to portray. Cecil Muldoon, the railroad's manager of public relations, initially denied that there were any problems with the catenary and pantographs but within hours had acknowledged that "we are not completely satisfied with their over-all performance." The negative media coverage and Muldoon's poor response to the situation finally caught the attention of Chairman Stuart Saunders. "It is only recently that I learned the current collection problem is going to present any serious problem to us," he told David Smucker. Saunders nonetheless insisted that recommendations for a reduction in maximum speed were "absolutely unthinkable" and that "we will be subject, and rightly so, to public criticism and even ridicule if we do not make much better speeds than some of our people have been talking about."[435]

Smucker had taken the precaution of assigning blame to most of the parties involved, save the Pennsylvania Railroad. He complained that Melpar's technicians "have never progressed beyond their original jim-crackery featuring a closed circuit television observation system on just one pantograph. . . . They frankly stated that they had no idea how to go about designing instruments or methods to measure displacement of the over-head system, stresses induced therein, or in the pantograph structure or, in short, any causative factors leading to excessive arcing which can be observed by a child standing along the track." Smucker was even more disgusted with the multiple initiatives undertaken by federal officials, suggesting that "it was necessary to go over the head of Dr. Nelson's entire group to win grudging allocation of test time." Above all, he concluded, "we would be further down the road if the Office of High Speed Ground Transportation were staffed with men who could either project their mind and imagination, or pay some attention to others by whom this problem is regarded as one to be surmounted and not to the contrary." Saunders cautioned his subordinate that "all of our officers should refrain from making public statements which tend to create discord between the Department of Transportation and the Pennsylvania," but it was rather a case of closing the barn door after the horse had bolted. The conflicting messages and indiscriminate mudslinging were symptomatic of the poor coordination between railroad and government officials as well as the growing friction between the participants in the *Metroliner* debacle.[436]

Even as they were defending the delays in the *Metroliner* project, PRR executives complained of obstacles established at all levels of government. The initial Department of Commerce contract required the railroad to add intermediate suburban stops for high-speed trains operating between New York and Washington—a stipulation that would undermine efforts to maintain competitive end-point travel times. "Right now the cheapest way to take out a few minutes" from the timetable, insisted Smucker, "is to tell the people who want the trains to stop twice at their double-houses that these are high-speed service trains which are scheduled to be run as limited service trains, and not as street-cars." PRR officials also highlighted the presence of more than twenty grade crossings along the route between Philadelphia and Washington. At the insistence of residents, county governments in Maryland refused to close even rarely used crossings or pay for grade separation. One such crossing served only the village landfill, a location that was accessible by other routes—and the prospect of a train traveling at more than a hundred miles an hour striking a fully laden garbage truck was too horrific to contemplate. Yet neither the DOT nor any other federal agency possessed the authority to mandate the elimination of those hazards.[437]

Richard A. Rice, the project director for transportation science studies at Princeton University, suggested that the quest for high speed had been doomed from the start. It was a poor imitation of Japanese and European railroad technology that was a decade more advanced than that in the United States, he asserted. Rice condemned the buy-American provisions in the Commerce Department contract that prevented the Pennsylvania Railroad from taking full advantage of technological advancements in those countries. He suggested that the initiative was "hastily conceived, terribly restricted in its technological concept, and unrealistic in its fare plan." Rice was quick to identify the cause as "pressure by and on the administration in Washington for something concrete the public can see." The eagerness of the Johnson administration to get results as quickly as possible, he suggested, produced an unrealistic development schedule. "It should take from three to four years from the time you contract such a project to the time trains are running," Rice emphasized, "and they've tried to do it in two years." He agreed with the assessment of PRR executives that "political pressure will apparently require four to five intermediate stops, which cancels all possibility that the service can match its European and Japanese counterparts." Rice predicted that shorter travel times would increase ridership by 30 percent at most, far less than the 70 percent gain necessary to earn a positive rate of return on the additional investment in infrastructure and equipment. He doubted that the PRR would ever be able to operate at sustained speeds over 110 miles per hour, making the new trains too slow to compete with air travel. His assessment comported almost precisely with the recommendations that Louis Klauder had furnished in 1965 and likewise would have come as no surprise to Bob Watson and the others involved in the test program.[438]

Given the adverse publicity, federal officials demanded meaningful results. On November 9, Transportation Secretary Alan Boyd visited the Red Lion facility. Budd had completed only sixteen of the *Metroliner* cars and had delivered none of them to the Pennsylvania Railroad. Boyd nonetheless declared that he was "very satisfied" with the equipment, while minimizing concerns about the chronic delays. "I would be much more worried if the project were moving ahead without a hitch," Boyd insisted. "That would mean that everyone involved was doing something easy and familiar. We are supposed to be developing a new service, offering something as new as the jet is from the DC-3." It was an apt comparison, save that in the late 1950s the Boeing Company spent nearly $200 million on the development of the 707, the first commercially successful passenger jet—to say nothing of the billions of private and public dollars allocated to aviation research and development, aeronautical engineering programs, and airport construction.[439] By that measure, the *Metroliner* was very much done on the cheap.[440]

Robert Nelson set a new deadline, promising that service would begin on February 1, 1968, "if no more bugs developed." In September, Budd delivered the first two *Metroliner* coaches, 800 and 802, and tested them on the Reading line at Jenkintown. The initial evaluation exposed serious problems with the Westinghouse electrical equipment, particularly the control circuits on the thyristors. On November 15, Budd nonetheless sent the cars to the PRR's Morrisville Yard, with two more units arriving in December. During their shakedown runs, it soon became evident that Nelson's qualifier had been well-founded, and Watson uncovered more bugs than anyone had anticipated. "There was no favorite failure," he recalled. "Everything had problems and everyone was in trouble." Watson's engineers and technicians identified sixteen "major problem areas which persist with little or no improvement" as well as more than 130 less serious inadequacies. "In addition to the chronic major problem areas," Watson complained, "minor spasmodic defects are continually being encountered and corrected only to be replaced by others." Along with the now-familiar difficulties associated with the pantographs, Watson's technicians experienced many problems that "have cropped up only to disappear before they can be conclusively located." Unintended brake applications slowed the trains and ground flat spots into the wheels. The air leaked from the brake system. The automatic doors operated sporadically. Watson observed that "Car 802 has been dead in forward motion on several occasions with no cause found." Snow driven into the air intakes melted and dripped onto the seats. "There is no doubt that these deficiencies will be overcome," Watson asserted, "but the radically new designs and involved circuitry are making the solution very difficult."[441]

The situation was little better when the first of the GE-equipped *Metroliners* arrived the following March. David Smucker's reluctance to "face the possibility of being 100% wrong in the choice of a single propulsion supplier" dictated the involvement of both GE and Westinghouse in the design and manufacturing process. Unfortunately, his plan to "be assured of at least being 50% correct by splitting the propulsion order" proved overly optimistic. The two systems proved incompatible, delaying the introduction of complete consists with the proper mix of equipment. Federal antitrust laws prevented GE and Westinghouse engineers from discussing their proprietary technologies unless the meeting included a representative from the Department of Transportation and attorneys from both companies. Watson cataloged more deficiencies in the Budd-GE parlor cars and snack-bar coaches than in the earlier Westinghouse cars. Most were relatively minor, however, and sustained evaluation and testing identified the problems and enabled Watson's team to eliminate them one by one. The Westinghouse inadequacies, while fewer in number, were more systemic and not so easily corrected. In early March, railroad officials placed the Westinghouse cars in storage. They sat motionless while railroad, Budd, DOT, and Westinghouse officials argued over who would bear the financial responsibility for fixing them. Not until January 1969, nearly a year after the Pennsylvania Railroad disappeared from the corporate landscape, did the first *Metroliner* begin revenue service. With Lyndon Johnson preparing to leave the White House only a few days later, neither the president nor anyone else bothered to mention that the United States had failed to emulate the *Shinkansen*.[442]

Betrayal

Stuart Saunders cared little for high-speed passenger-rail travel, other than as a means of generating favorable publicity and overcoming opposition to the formation of Penn Central. The *Metroliner* was but a small element in his grand plan to orchestrate the perfect merger, and with it take command of the restructuring of the eastern railroad network. He shared with his predecessor, James Symes, a desire to create a three-system East, with the Penn Central ranking as first among equals. During the summer of 1961, Symes had placed that plan into motion. His meeting with

Chesapeake & Ohio executives at the Greenbrier Hotel ended Alfred Perlman's hopes of a merger between the C&O and the New York Central, and thus made a union between the NYC and the Pennsylvania Railroad all but inevitable. Perlman accused Walter Tuohy and other C&O executives of betrayal, and his opinion of Symes was scarcely better. It was hardly the ideal start to the second iteration of a marriage proposal between the Pennsylvania Railroad and the New York Central.

The Penn Central merger application was only the last of three major consolidation proposals placed before the Interstate Commerce Commission during the early 1960s. ICC officials nonetheless lacked the authority, or the inclination, to consider the three proposals as a group, and as a mechanism to plan the future of the northeastern railroad network. Instead, the agency's officials considered separately Tuohy's effort to enable the C&O to control the Baltimore & Ohio, Saunders's desire that the N&W should merge with the Nickel Plate Road and lease the Wabash, and Symes's effort to create Penn Central. The realignments produced significant changes in the relationship between the Pennsylvania Railroad and the Norfolk & Western, including stock divestiture, the sale of the Sandusky Branch, and—most significantly—the appointment of Stuart Saunders as the PRR's board chairman and new chief architect of the Penn Central merger.

In March 1965, ICC examiners Jerome Lyle and Henry Darmstadter recommended approval of the Penn Central merger proposal. They inserted few conditions. The most onerous involved the assumption of the New Haven's freight service. Both Lyle and Darmstadter agreed with Saunders, Perlman, and the New Haven's trustees that the New Haven's commuter and intercity passenger operations were so catastrophically unprofitable that they would reduce the economic benefits associated with the merger and perhaps even imperil Penn Central. Officials in the Commerce Department likewise favored the merger, and they agreed with Saunders that the purported $81 million in annual savings would rescue the eastern railroad network without resorting to federal subsidies or government ownership. Their counterparts in the Justice Department—led by Assistant Attorney General William Orrick—focused instead on the potentially anticompetitive effects associated with the Penn Central merger. The disagreement drove a wedge through the president's Interagency Committee on Transport Mergers, paralyzing into inaction the only body engaged in any form of national transportation planning. Robert Kennedy's decision to enter the 1964 New York senate race deprived Orrick of much of his leverage. In a carefully worded memo, the

attorney general agreed to drop opposition to the Penn Central merger, pending certain conditions—including, as Saunders would later discover, support for the New Haven's passenger operations. To Orrick's dismay, even that burden was insufficient to cool Saunders's ardor for the consolidation, and the head of the Antitrust Division sought another mechanism to hobble the PRR's chairman. His best opportunity lay in the terms of the Norfolk & Western merger, a union he had once opposed but later grudgingly accepted. Appendix O alerted Orrick to the problems facing the Erie-Lackawanna, the Boston & Maine, and the Delaware & Hudson while offering another potential avenue to block the Penn Central merger.

There matters stood in the spring of 1965, as Walter Tuohyof the C&O and the N&W's Herman Pevler and Jack Fishwick gathered at the Greenbrier Hotel. Nearly four years had passed since Tuohy and Symes agreed on the outlines of a three-system East. Symes was still on the board of directors of the Pennsylvania Railroad, although no longer as chairman, but neither he nor any other PRR executive was present at the meeting. In their place were representatives from the Norfolk & Western—a situation that indicated how quickly industry leadership was changing and the extent to which access to Pocahontas coal separated the weak from the powerful. The attendees included N&W president Herman H. Pevler, who was a former PRR executive, and Vice President John P. Fishwick, who served as the company's chief strategist. Despite their strength, the leaders of the C&O and the N&W were concerned about a much more recent event—the March 29 announcement that examiners Lyle and Darmstadter had recommended approval of the Penn Central merger. As so often happened, action produced reaction, and one consolidation proposal begat another. Assuming a posture of self-defense, C&O and N&W officials concluded that a three-system East was no longer viable—at least, not for them. Their concord shattered the plans that first Symes and then Saunders had so carefully laid. By the summer of 1965, the machinations of both Symes and Saunders were about to come full circle, in ways that they should probably have expected—but apparently did not. Like Perlman before him, Saunders would soon suffer the sting of betrayal. What made the situation that much worse was that the newest threat to the Penn Central merger came from Jack Fishwick, Saunders's protégé and one-time ally at the Norfolk & Western.

From the beginning, the entire rationale for the Penn Central merger depended on one key point. It was the vision, first articulated by Symes and later echoed by Saunders, that there would be three great rail systems in the

East. It was that philosophy that underpinned the pivotal meeting at the Greenbrier Hotel during the summer of 1961, when Symes orchestrated his grand design for the eastern carriers. That entente cordiale also explained the lack of PRR and NYC opposition to the Norfolk & Western-Nickel Plate-Wabash and the Chesapeake & Ohio-Baltimore & Ohio consolidation proposals. When the regulatory process finally came to an end, there was no question that the Penn Central would be first among equals, easily able to fend off the competitive threats posed by the other two combinations. Saunders had little interest in the remaining, unaligned eastern carriers. He was aware that the Erie-Lackawanna, the Boston & Maine, and the Delaware & Hudson each possessed the right to petition for inclusion in the Norfolk & Western system—a stipulation mandated by the Interstate Commerce Commission in Appendix O, when regulators approved the N&W's consolidation proposal. If the ICC forced his former employer to shoulder the burden of three ailing railroads, then so much the better.

In the months that followed the release of the examiners' report, there was just one thing that might seriously threaten the financial performance of the company that Lyle and Darmstadter endorsed. The Norfolk & Western and the Chesapeake & Ohio were two of the most profitable railroads in the United States. Even with the inclusion of weaker lines such as the Wabash and the Baltimore & Ohio, each system possessed financial strength that rivaled what the Penn Central would be able to generate. A union of those two systems would, from Saunders's perspective, be little short of disastrous. The 1961 Greenbrier Hotel meeting and its aftermath—including regulatory approval of the N&W–Nickel Plate–Wabash and C&O–B&O consolidations—was based on the unshakable premise that those two systems would always be competitors rather than partners. It was certainly true that Saunders, then the head of the Norfolk & Western, had not attended the meeting at the Greenbrier. Given his subsequent move to the PRR, he had little doubt that his former colleagues would remain cooperative. As the near certainty of the Penn Central merger reshaped the railroad landscape in the East, that assumption proved woefully misguided.

At the Norfolk & Western, Jack Fishwick had a new set of problems to occupy his attention. The company's vice president for legal affairs was largely responsible for corporate strategy, in cooperation with Herman Pevler, the former PRR and Wabash executive who was now the N&W's president. The N&W–Nickel Plate–Wabash consolidation that Saunders engineered was by all accounts a success, but Fishwick and Pevler feared the actions of

the C&O. During the community-of-interest period, early in the twentieth century, the Baltimore & Ohio acquired a controlling interest in the Western Maryland. The tracks of those two railroads paralleled each other for a considerable distance, and the two companies were obvious competitors. Both the Clayton Act and ICC scrutiny ensured that an outright merger was impossible and that the stock remained in trust. During the early 1960s, Walter Tuohy began buying Western Maryland stock, on behalf of the Chesapeake & Ohio. By the time the ICC granted Tuohy the authority to control the Baltimore & Ohio, he was positioned to integrate the Western Maryland's operations into the C&O–B&O system. Tuohy also possessed a measure of influence over two other companies, likewise the inheritors of the community-of-interest system. Half a century earlier, the Baltimore & Ohio had acquired 39 percent of the Reading Company, which in turn controlled the Jersey Central. The New York Central maintained a slightly smaller share of the Reading—about 29 percent of the company's preferred stock—and the arrangement provided the two trunk lines with good access to most of the territory between New York and Washington. The NYC began selling its Reading stock in 1957, but Perlman retained substantial holdings as a precautionary measure, as he awaited the outcome of the eastern merger battles. His commitment to join Penn Central ended the Reading's usefulness in that regard, and in March 1965, the NYC sold the last of its investment in that company. The stock went to speculators, who hoped to secure favorable terms through inclusion in a larger and more prosperous system—and either the C&O–B&O or the Norfolk & Western would do. Tuohy was interested. Despite their precarious financial position, the Reading and the Jersey Central could give his expanded Chesapeake & Ohio system improved access to Greater New York.[443]

Norfolk & Western officials expressed both surprise and anger at Tuohy's plans. The Western Maryland, with access to tidewater at Baltimore, was a valuable eastern connection for the expanded N&W system. That link was likely to increase in importance once the Penn Central began poaching the N&W's traffic. Pevler and Fishwick were also concerned that C&O control of the Reading and the Jersey Central would exclude the Norfolk & Western from access to the great cities of the Northeast. Tuohy, Pevler, and Fishwick shared a common enemy, however. As the financial performance of the PRR and the NYC improved steadily, year by year, during the first half of the 1960s, the three executives sensed that the Penn Central might be a far stronger competitor than they had anticipated. The obvious countermeasure required them to overcome their mutual enmity and join forces. During the spring of 1965, the three executives elected to discuss the issue at the Greenbrier Hotel, in the manner that most such issues moved toward resolution. After giving the matter considerable thought, Fishwick proposed a merger between the Norfolk & Western and the Chesapeake & Ohio, one that would also include the Baltimore & Ohio and the Western Maryland. Overcoming his initial surprise, Tuohy began to appreciate the merits of the proposal, and secret negotiations took place over the following months.[444]

The need for secrecy was related, in part, to the Appendix O inclusion provisions associated with the October 1964 merger between the Norfolk & Western and the Nickel Plate. Despite considerable pressure from such entities as New York State and the Port of New York Authority, N&W executives continued to block the addition of the Erie-Lackawanna to their company. Fishwick's proposed N&W–C&O system was certain to destroy the E-L as well as the Boston & Maine and the Delaware & Hudson. Representatives from those three companies would accordingly demand that the ICC reopen the N&W–Nickel Plate merger proceedings and add them to that consolidation, as a prerequisite for approval of the N&W–C&O merger.

The fate of the Erie-Lackawanna was particularly significant. Even as E-L executives debated their strategy for inclusion in the Norfolk & Western system, new management was beginning to improve the company's prospects. After Robert Young forced him out of the New York Central in 1954, William White served as president of the Delaware & Hudson, and in June 1963, he became the chairman of the board and CEO at the Erie-Lackawanna. In a symbolic gesture, White rehabilitated the *Phoebe Snow*, the railroad's premier passenger train. More substantively, he aggressively solicited intermodal traffic, purchased new equipment, paid off the company's back taxes, and reduced the burden of commuter operations. The new Erie Lackawanna (White preferred to avoid the hyphen) became a respectable competitor against the New York Central, a situation that portended difficulties for the Penn Central. Fishwick took notice of the improvements on the Erie Lackawanna. He was now willing to make that company a part of the Norfolk & Western but not on the terms White advocated. An outright merger between the two companies would saddle the N&W with the Erie Lackawanna's $350 million debt, something White had been unable to eliminate.[445]

Fishwick also considered the status of the other two railroads affected by the ICC's Appendix O inclusion order. While the Delaware & Hudson was in reasonable shape, the heavy debt burdens of the Boston & Maine made it an unattractive merger partner. The same was true of the Reading and the Jersey Central. Neither railroad had been promised inclusion in the earlier merger between the N&W and the Nickel Plate. Given their precarious financial circumstances, however, it was likely that they would demand protection in any subsequent consolidation of the N&W and the C&O. To a substantial degree, moreover, both companies were a part of that proposed system, in that the C&O and the B&O together owned 48.97 percent of the voting stock of the Reading—and that company, in turn, controlled the Jersey Central. As such, it made sense to resolve the fate of all five railroads, as a group. By adopting a preemptive strategy, Fishwick hoped to gain control over those companies on his terms rather than those dictated by the Interstate Commerce Commission.[446]

The solution came in the form of a holding company, Dereco, Incorporated, whose name reflected the initials of most of the impoverished carriers that would be added to the system.[447] The investment bankers at R. W. Pressprich & Company placed Fishwick's idea into a financially viable format. They were determined to protect the N&W and the C&O–B&O from the massive debts associated with the weaker railroads while exploiting the tax-loss carry forwards associated with their chronic deficits. Bringing the project to fruition would depend on the successful resolution of a great many issues. They included the cooperation of the weaker companies, changes in federal tax law, further reductions in commuter service, and the approval of the Interstate Commerce Commission.[448]

By August 1965, a year had passed since the ICC's approval of the N&W–Nickel Plate–Wabash consolidation, and neither Pevler nor Fishwick had made any public effort to protect the Erie Lackawanna from the effects of the pending Penn Central merger. An ICC examiner concluded that "serious question arises whether that carrier is actively conducting good-faith negotiations toward affiliation with the Erie-Lackawanna." Based on those findings, on August 19, 1965, New York State, New York City, and the Port of New York Authority petitioned the ICC to reopen the N&W–Nickel Plate case, to ensure the addition of the Erie Lackawanna. Norfolk & Western executives had irrevocably assented to the inclusion clause, which would not expire until July 1969, and it seemed likely that the ICC would soon force the Erie Lackawanna on them, under conditions they considered extremely unfavorable. In response, representatives from the Norfolk & Western and the Chesapeake & Ohio announced their merger plans on August 31. They highlighted the formation of Dereco—which, they claimed, resolved the inclusion issues associated with the Erie Lackawanna and the other small railroads. Newspapers touted the "sweeping merger of 7 eastern carriers" and highlighted a route structure that resembled a net entrapping the territories that would be served by the Penn Central. Pevler, Fishwick, and Tuohy proposed a railroad colossus with 26,460 route miles, assets of $5.9 billion, and gross revenues of $1.8 billion a year—slightly larger than the Penn Central and considerably more profitable.[449]

The merger proposal shattered the three-system East arranged by Symes and Saunders and led to a final break between the Pennsylvania Railroad and the Norfolk & Western. "We are committed to fighting the N. & W.-C. & O.'s merger plan," Saunders warned, and he asserted that the arrangement was "not in the public interest." The PRR's chairman insisted that "it wouldn't produce a balanced system. They would have a monopoly of coal." Making the best of a bad situation, Saunders suggested that the N&W–C&O announcement increased the likelihood that the ICC commissioners would speedily grant final approval to Penn Central. "This new proposal," he emphasized in a joint statement with Perlman, "makes it absolutely necessary that the Pennsylvania-New York Central merger be approved at an early date. The existing independent C. & O. and N. & W. systems already have shown their competitive force against the Pennsylvania and New York Central railroads and the proposal emphasizes their determination to press these advantages even more vigorously in the future."[450]

The Pennsylvania Railroad's efforts to facilitate the N&W–Nickel Plate merger made the matter even more galling. "The Pennsylvania, looking toward a balanced three-system plan in the East, made the competing system possible," a Pennsylvania Railroad attorney later informed the Interstate Commerce Commission. Norfolk & Western executives had been entirely responsible for the efforts to control the Nickel Plate and the Wabash, he emphasized, without any encouragement or interference from the Pennsylvania Railroad. To the contrary, the PRR had acquiesced to the consolidation, had generously parted with the Sandusky Branch, and had agreed to relinquish its $350 million investment in N&W stock. No one at the PRR bothered to inform regulators that that behavior was in keeping with the secret—and private—1961 arrangement between Symes and Tuohy, to dictate the future of the eastern railroad network.[451]

Fishwick fought back, asserting that since the early 1900s the Pennsylvania Railroad had dominated the Norfolk & Western, something he had not thought to say earlier. "The Pennsylvania always had a thumb" capable of applying pressure, Fishwick told the ICC, "and I think

anybody on the N&W knew that thumb would be exercised if we did anything they really didn't want us to." Following the resignation of PRR executives from the N&W's board of directors—a condition specified by the April 1963 examiner's report in the N&W–Nickel Plate–Wabash case—Fishwick suggested that he was now able to speak freely. Like every other aspect of his carefully scripted testimony, the accusation was designed to convince the ICC of the necessity of the N&W–C&O merger. Now that he and Pevler were finally able to govern without interference, they demanded protection from the company that had once controlled them. That perspective helped to explain why the same Norfolk & Western officials who supported the Penn Central merger in 1963 were now implacably opposed to it. When confronted with that inconsistency, Fishwick also suggested that both the PRR and the NYC had "shifted from two sick railroads to two that were growing stronger, and this growth had been slow, but it was accelerating."[452]

Representatives from the US Department of Commerce viewed the developments with concern. Two years earlier, Deputy Under Secretary of Commerce for Transportation E. Grosvenor Plowman had recommended a two-system East—but not *this* two-system East. Acting on behalf of the Interagency Committee on Transport Mergers, Plowman suggested that the Pennsylvania Railroad and the New York Central should each be allied with one of the only two available Pocahontas coal carriers—the first with the Norfolk & Western and the second with the Chesapeake & Ohio. The union of the N&W and the C&O, against the proposed Penn Central, was an outcome Plowman had not seriously contemplated and would never have endorsed. It fell to his replacement, Alan Boyd, to determine what to do next. On September 1, the day after the announcement of the Dereco arrangement, Boyd briefed Commerce Secretary John T. Connor on its provisions. Approval of the Penn Central merger had now become inevitable, Boyd suggested, as "appearance of this fundamental merger proposal undermines the last argument against consolidation of all the Eastern railroad merger cases in a consolidated proceeding before the ICC." Boyd acknowledged the possibility that one or the other of the two giant companies might monopolize rail transportation in many areas of the Northeast, but he noted that there was little possibility that the Penn Central would be sufficiently powerful to destroy its sole remaining competitor. "While the two systems would have the appearance of equal size and financial strength," Boyd observed, "the N&W-C&O system would be much stronger in terms of cash resources." He was not ready to concede to Saunders's demands for immediate approval of the Penn Central merger proposal, however. Boyd suggested two possible responses. The first involved a petition to the Interstate Commerce Commission, to defer a decision in the Penn Central case until the unaligned carriers could be adequately protected. As an alternative, the ICC could impose a moratorium on both merger proposals until the agency could complete a comprehensive investigation of the railroad situation in the Northeast. Either option entailed substantial delay, something Saunders could ill afford.[453]

As events transpired, Boyd did not need White House intervention or an ICC investigation to impose further impediments to the Penn Central merger. In the aftermath of the Dereco announcement and in the absence of any consistent federal transportation policy, the managers of the privately owned railroads proved themselves more than capable of imposing one delay after another. It soon became clear that the fate of each merger proposal depended on the outcome of the other. It also went without saying that Saunders wanted the ICC to approve the creation of the Penn Central before the commissioners ruled on the N&W–C&O application, while Pevler, Fishwick, and Tuohy wanted the order to be reversed.

Given that the Penn Central case had been under consideration by the ICC since March 1962, Saunders was in the enviable position of being in the regulatory pipeline ahead of Tuohy, Pevler, and Fishwick. There was only one aspect of the N&W–C&O proposal that might possibly interfere with Saunders's plans. If the weakest railroads in the East accepted membership in Dereco, then they would satisfy the Appendix O inclusion provisions in the 1964 N&W–Nickel Plate merger and remove the most significant obstacle to the consolidation of the N&W and the C&O. By sweeping up most of the unaffiliated carriers in the East, Dereco also eliminated regulatory concerns that the Penn Central might destroy those companies. Dereco would thus reduce the threat to the Erie Lackawanna, the Boston & Maine, and the Delaware & Hudson, undercutting the Justice Department's sole remaining legal argument against the Penn Central. The biggest problem was that the weak railroads might refuse membership in the Dereco holding company and instead demand a more traditional merger with the Norfolk & Western. Pevler and Fishwick would almost certainly resist that outcome, inducing lengthy regulatory and legal battles over the terms of inclusion.

For Saunders, that nightmare scenario seemed to be coming true. Fishwick apparently believed that officials on the Erie Lackawanna and the other small railroads would be relieved, if not overjoyed, at the generous offer

for participation in Dereco. They were not, and their representatives considered the holding company a poor substitute for full-fledged inclusion in the Norfolk & Western. Several Reading directors, seeking speculative profits that had not yet materialized, issued a statement characterizing Dereco as "an unconscionable attempt to shamelessly abuse the investment public." The president of the Boston & Maine insisted "that the financial terms suggested for the acquisition of the B. & M. are completely unacceptable." In his dual role as president of the D&H and chairman of the EL, William White asserted that Dereco "does not adequately protect the interest of the Delaware & Hudson in the restructuring of the railroad systems in the east, through mergers or otherwise, nor are the financial terms satisfactory." Robert G. Fuller, the chairman of the EL's Finance Committee, was more succinct in his assertion that the company's board of directors "couldn't recommend it," and he demanded that the N&W "live up to its obligations" as dictated by the terms of Appendix O. In September 1965, the Erie Lackawanna filed a petition with the ICC, demanding a more conventional merger with the N&W, one that would obligate that company to assume the Erie Lackawanna's debt.[454]

When the N&W and the C&O submitted their merger application on October 11, representatives from all three aggrieved carriers demanded inclusion—on their terms rather than the ones Jack Fishwick had devised. Pevler dismissed the EL's proposal as "perfectly ridiculous," while another N&W executive emphasized that any arrangement that required his company to assume the Erie Lackawanna's debt "would be unthinkable." If the situation was not complicated enough, each side demanded diametrically opposing methods of resolving their differences. Pevler, Fishwick, and Tuohy wanted the ICC to consolidate the Appendix O inclusion hearings in the reopened N&W–Nickel Plate case with the new merger application filed by the Norfolk & Western and the Chesapeake & Ohio. Their all-or-nothing approach would enable them to back away from their consolidation arrangement, should the ICC's Appendix O ruling prove too onerous. William White and his fellow executives at the Erie Lackawanna, the Boston & Maine, and the Delaware & Hudson demanded that the ICC resolve the Appendix O matter before assenting to the N&W–C&O application. That strategy raised the possibility that the commissioners would force the N&W to accept the three companies, on terms that Pevler and Fishwick found unacceptable, while disallowing the union with the Chesapeake & Ohio that had triggered the controversy in the first place. Nor was the matter likely to be resolved any time soon. Erie Lackawanna officials wanted to prolong the hearings, as they awaited action on their efforts to discontinue commuter operations in New Jersey. They got their wish, and the ICC did not rule on the matter until February 1966, nearly a year after examiners Lyle and Darmstadter recommended approval of the Penn Central merger.[455]

To the dismay of Norfolk & Western executives, regulators agreed with White's demand for separate hearings. First in line would be the reopening of the N&W–Nickel Plate merger, to resolve the Appendix O inclusion provisions. Testimony was not scheduled to begin until April and was likely to take considerable time. Only when the ICC and the courts resolved that matter could they begin to consider the consolidation of the Norfolk & Western and the Chesapeake & Ohio. Of greater concern to Saunders, however, was that Tuohy, Pevler, and Fishwick were not willing to commit to the N&W–C&O merger until they received the ICC's guarantee that they could accept the weak eastern carriers through Dereco rather than through a straight merger. The issue was critical, for two reasons. First, representatives from the ICC and the Justice Department were unlikely to endorse the Penn Central merger until they could be assured that the Erie Lackawanna, the Boston & Maine, and the Delaware & Hudson would be protected. Second, should the N&W–C&O proposal fall apart, they would have that much less reason to support the creation of an eastern system that would be far larger than either of those two railroads on its own. In both respects, therefore, the Dereco proposal dictated the outcome of the Penn Central merger.

Even though Saunders remained optimistic that the ICC would permit the formation of Penn Central, he found the situation intolerable. The PRR's chairman was in the process of granting concessions to organized labor and to state and local governments. At the very least, those agreements were eroding the $81 million in savings that, he claimed, would result from the merger. Saunders knew, better than anyone, that the merger must happen quickly, before the added costs associated with the concessions and the consolidation process bankrupted the two corporate partners. Like Symes before him, he had made careful arrangements with the other eastern carriers, to ensure that nothing would go amiss. Thanks to the N&W–C&O merger proposal, something had gone badly wrong, in a spectacularly convoluted way that portended further delays. To make matters worse, the crisis had originated from his former employer and from an executive he had once considered a friend. Stuart Saunders and Jack Fishwick were among the few senior executives who rose to prominence because of their legal training rather than their experience in railroad

operations. In his early days at the Norfolk & Western, shortly after World War II, Saunders hired Fishwick and mentored the younger man as both managers rose through the ranks. Their friendship ended in August 1965, with the public announcement of the negotiations between the Norfolk & Western and the Chesapeake & Ohio. At the subsequent merger hearings, the two met, by accident, in the cavernous halls of the Interstate Commerce Commission building on Constitution Avenue. Stung by what he perceived as a personal and professional betrayal, Saunders told his former protégé, "You're going to regret your action." In his relentless efforts to bring about the Penn Central merger, Saunders had relinquished the Pennsylvania Railroad's most valuable asset, its Norfolk & Western stock. Now, thanks to his opposition to the merger of the Norfolk & Western and the Chesapeake & Ohio, Saunders also abandoned his relationship with one of the N&W's most capable executives.[456]

Breaking a Promise

The events of 1965 may well have dampened Saunders's characteristically ebullient personality and taxed his faith in humankind. No sooner had he suffered Fishwick's betrayal than he received a similar blow from another lawyer, someone he believed he could trust. The political consequences were substantial, given that that individual was once the attorney general and was now a United States senator. When Jerome Lyle and Henry Darmstadter released the examiners' report in the Penn Central merger case, Stuart Saunders and Alfred Perlman had little reason to fear that the Justice Department would offer any significant impediments to the consolidation of their railroads. Both executives were present in Robert Kennedy's office the preceding August when the outgoing attorney general promised to withdraw opposition if the examiners agreed that the merger was consistent with the public interest. Nicholas Katzenbach, who was also in the room, supplied Saunders with Kennedy's memo on the subject and agreed with its recommendations. There were only three specific sections of the document that left open any potential for ambiguity or that offered the Justice Department an excuse for breaking the implied promise that Kennedy granted to Saunders and Perlman. First, Kennedy emphasized that his recommendation would not bind his successors or dictate their policies—something that everyone accepted. The possibility that the Justice Department might again oppose the merger if "circumstances have materially changed" likewise constituted an uncontroversial acknowledgment that Kennedy could not predict the future. Finally, Kennedy's rapid transition from attorney general to senatorial candidate was responsible for the agreement "assuring that transportation services will continue to be rendered by the New Haven Railroad and that such services will not be impaired by the Penn-Central merger." That stipulation, Saunders and Perlman assumed, applied only to the New Haven's freight operations.[457]

Within days after the examiners' report, however, it became evident that the Justice Department was willing to interpret all three of those ambiguous statements in a manner that would create significant impediments to the Penn Central merger. The situation might have been different if Katzenbach had taken a keen interest in the matter. He did not, and his autobiography made no mention of Saunders, Perlman, the Penn Central, or the Kennedy memo. As Kennedy's successor, Katzenbach had many other responsibilities, including numerous civil rights cases, and he left antitrust issues to the discretion of Assistant Attorney General William Orrick. On April 23, barely three weeks after the release of the examiners' report, Saunders was in Richmond, Virginia, demanding the formation of a presidential commission to address what he called antiquated and economically damaging restrictions on business consolidations. "Mergers must continue," Saunders emphasized, "not only in banking and railroading but in industry generally, for they are vital to the growth of our economy." On the same day and a hundred miles to the north, Orrick was offering a very different view of the situation. He was testifying before the Senate Subcommittee on Antitrust and Monopoly, still grinding on more than eighteen months after the death of chairman Estes Kefauver. "Congress's dedication to antitrust goals," Orrick emphasized, "has always rested on its recognition that concentration of industrial power may lead to the police state." Hyperbole aside, the ICC examiners' favorable assessment of the Penn Central represented a humiliating defeat for Orrick—and one that, in light of the Kennedy memo, suggested that he could no longer object to the merger. The head of the Antitrust Division was not willing to yield so easily, however. It was perhaps appropriate that Saunders was speaking in the former capital of the Confederacy and his opponent in the seat of the federal government. The nation's foremost supporter of mergers and the Justice Department's most ardent foe of monopoly were about to collide head-on, in a very uncivil war.[458]

In his determination to block the Penn Central merger, Orrick was willing to selectively interpret at least two of the three of the ambiguous clauses in the Kennedy memo. Kennedy refused to bind his successors because there was no legal way he could do so—but he, along with Saunders

and Perlman, agreed that the Justice Department would honor that commitment. Orrick, in contrast, viewed the statement as an indication of the integrity and autonomy of the attorney general's office, and an assertion that Antitrust Division personnel retained full authority to prosecute cases as they saw fit. As such, Orrick responded to the examiners' report by beginning work on a brief opposing the merger. It explicitly demanded that the full ICC disallow the Penn Central merger—in direct contravention of the spirit and intent of the Kennedy memo.

Orrick also took a close look at the section "assuring that transportation services will continue to be rendered by the New Haven Railroad." During the August 1964 meeting, Saunders, Perlman, and Kennedy each assumed that commuter and passenger operations would be subsidized by government agencies, curtailed, or abandoned. The ICC examiners came to a similar conclusion, stipulating that the Penn Central should operate the New Haven's freight trains and nothing more. Yet even as Lyle and Darmstadter made their recommendations, it was looking less and less likely that adequate subsidies would become available. Every politician between Manhattan and Boston was nonetheless demanding the continuation of the New Haven's intercity passenger and commuter trains. Given the PRR's increasingly respectable financial performance during the early 1960s, Orrick was not the only one who believed that "transportation services" meant both freight and passenger operations. That view became clear on April 19, three weeks after the release of the examiners' report. Saunders met Attorney General Katzenbach in Washington to discuss terms for the New Haven's inclusion in the Penn Central system. If the PRR's chairman thought the issue was settled, he was badly mistaken. Orrick was also in the room, and his views guided the Justice Department's position on the New Haven. Kennedy's agreement with Saunders "assuring that transportation services will continue to be rendered by the New Haven Railroad" became, in Orrick's words, "an agreement to take the New Haven" and all its passenger operations. It was a bitter pill to swallow, and Orrick recalled that "Saunders went out of there crying." Orrick may have exaggerated Saunders's reaction, but Pennsylvania Railroad and New York Central officials were uniformly dismayed by the changing terms. Walter Grant, the NYC's vice president for finance, later admitted that he had been "horrified" to learn that the Penn Central would be required to operate the New Haven's passenger service.[459]

It was some consolation to Saunders that William Orrick would soon cease to bedevil him, even if that circumstance did not alter the Justice Department's position on the merger. In June 1965, Orrick resigned as the head of the Antitrust Division. Lyndon Johnson had little interest in the details of antitrust policy. He was nonetheless sensitive to the concerns of business executives, who suggested that Orrick was too aggressive in his attacks on large corporations. As a replacement, Katzenbach suggested Donald F. Turner. Johnson was skeptical, as Turner's Harvard pedigree suggested uncomfortable parallels with the Kennedy brothers. Katzenbach nonetheless emphasized Turner's strong academic credentials, noting that he would forgo a Populist trust-busting ideology in favor of a rational and economically based evaluation of monopolistic practices. Deputy Attorney General Ramsey Clark seconded the endorsement, as did Johnson confidant Clark Clifford. Senate confirmation hearings produced some heated exchanges between antimonopoly New Dealers and an alliance of Republicans and probusiness Democrats, but Turner won confirmation on June 24.[460]

Turner soon disappointed Johnson, demonstrating that he was not as resolutely probusiness as Saunders and other executives had expected. While he lacked Orrick's tenacious commitment to the preservation of competition, Nelson's more scientific approach created equally severe obstacles to the creation of Penn Central. "We should not attack a merger," he noted shortly after taking office, "simply because the companies are large in the absolute sense, and we should not attack aggressive but fair competitive conduct simply on the basis that some competitors are hurt." Yet the new head of the Antitrust Division placed great store in economic data, which he characterized as an accurate measure of monopoly power. Rather than resisting market concentration per se, Turner favored a balance of competition, innovation, and efficiency. Based on his knowledge of the economic literature, Turner concluded that there was no appreciable increase in economies of scale once a company exceeded $5 million in assets—roughly one-one-thousandth the size of the proposed Penn Central. He concluded that very large firms were neither efficient nor innovative and that the consolidation of two or more giant firms simply made the problem worse. "The best economic information and thinking available to us indicates that a strong anti-merger policy, at least insofar as horizontal type mergers are concerned, is almost certainly right," he observed. In short, Turner held that the deleterious effects associated with consolidations grew exponentially as the size of the firm increased—something that did not bode well for Saunders, as he attempted to orchestrate the largest merger in American history.[461]

Inasmuch as regulators suggested that the increased efficiency associated with the Penn Central merger provided adequate compensation for the associated decrease in competition, the goals of the ICC and the Justice Department were in alignment. Turner nonetheless asserted that neither the courts nor regulatory agencies possessed the ability to assess a merger's effects on interfirm competition. To an even greater extent than his predecessor, therefore, Turner had little patience with the actions of the Interstate Commerce Commission. On July 14, less than three weeks after his Senate confirmation, he demonstrated his distaste for administrative regulation and his unwillingness to abide by the terms of the Kennedy memo. Turner's twenty-page brief, filed with the ICC, did not specifically mention the antitrust implications of the merger or its likely effects on other railroads. In a separate statement, however, the attorney general's office indicated that those concerns were still valid and should be considered part of the document by inference. Turner and his staff were "aware that other factors may nevertheless persuade the [Interstate Commerce] commission to conclude that the merger is in the public interest." They nonetheless cautioned regulators that sacrificing competition to achieve the dubious benefits of economic efficiency constituted a poor bargain. Turner deplored the commissioners' willingness to permit a series of reactive mergers, and he suggested that their eagerness to prevent the further decline of the eastern railroad network blinded them to the broader economic consequences of their policies. The ICC commissioners got the message, and they conceded that "although modifying its earlier position of outright opposition to one recognizing that conditional approval may be justified, the [Justice] Department expresses alarm at the dominance which the Transportation Company will acquire in the Eastern District as a result of the merger."[462]

Although Turner did not explicitly demand that the ICC block the merger, he recommended three conditions. He insisted that the New York Central relinquish control over the Pittsburgh & Lake Erie, in order to preserve competition in the Pittsburgh area—even though ICC officials had concluded that the P&LE probably could not survive as an independent carrier. The Justice Department also called for an eighteen-month postponement in the merger proceedings, to give the Erie Lackawanna, the Boston & Maine, and the Delaware & Hudson time to seek inclusion in the Norfolk & Western system. Turner was yet unaware of the Dereco plan, announced two weeks later, or the controversies it would generate. His concerns nonetheless suggested something that had not been a part of the 1964 Kennedy memo—a growing awareness that the Penn Central might destroy the three smaller railroads, an outcome potentially more disastrous than the collapse of the New

Haven. The third condition in the Justice Department brief was by far the most burdensome and reinforced Orrick's demand that had allegedly reduced Saunders to tears. Like Orrick, Turner asserted that the "transportation services" provision in the Kennedy memo reflected a pledge by Saunders and Perlman to meet the needs of commuters and intercity passengers. "Failure to include the New Haven's passenger operations in the proposed system may well lead to an immediate abandonment of passenger services," Turner emphasized, inducing "a great loss to the public in the geographic area concerned, and an alteration of conditions which may make eventual restoration of service extremely costly if not impossible."[463]

Despite his supposed breakdown in front of William Orrick, Saunders was still unwilling to assume the New Haven's passenger operations. He mounted an offensive to refute Turner's assertions, calm the fears of commuters, and persuade the ICC commissioners that Lyle and Darmstadter had been right all along. Saunders scheduled meetings with the four governors who represented the New Haven's territory, pressuring them to find public funds to keep commuter operations running. His first target was Governor Dempsey of Connecticut. "I am quite hopeful we can work out a mutually satisfactory agreement," Saunders told reporters after a closed-door meeting, and he emphasized that "we're not trying to discontinue service here." In August, the PRR and the NYC provided the Interstate Commerce Commission with a joint response to the Justice Department brief, reminding the commissioners that it would be unwise to force Penn Central's shippers "literally to subsidize rail transportation in New England." They warned the ICC that efforts to placate the Justice Department would work to the detriment of the New Haven and all its services. "If the merger is delayed," they emphasized, "the New Haven will not survive long enough to be included."[464]

Saunders possessed unlikely allies in the New Haven's trustees, who hoped to gain his cooperation and maximize the amount that the Penn Central would pay to acquire their bankrupt company. To do so, they divided passenger service into two categories. Like Saunders, they demanded adequate public subsidies for the maintenance of commuter operations. On October 11, 1965, the trustees revealed the second part of their strategy. They filed an application to discontinue all 274 of the New Haven's intercity services. It was the largest passenger-train discontinuance petition the ICC had ever received. The request was unlikely to be successful, given the efforts by Claiborne Pell and the Johnson administration to establish high-speed rail service between Boston and Washington.

It was nonetheless a useful ploy to increase the likelihood of government funding. The trustees also hoped to coax the ICC commissioners into accepting the examiners' recommendation, that the Penn Central's role be limited to freight operations. Regulators would need time to study the matter, however, and Saunders could anticipate still more delays in the resolution of the Penn Central merger application. On October 15, the agency ordered the New Haven's intercity passenger service to continue until at least July 1, 1966. Given the urgency of the situation, the ICC dispensed with the customary examiner's investigation and proceeded with hearings overseen by commissioner William H. Tucker.[465]

Eleven Commissioners

On October 20, 1965, the eleven members of the Interstate Commerce Commission began hearing oral arguments in the Penn Central merger case. Only nine days had elapsed since the New Haven's trustees petitioned to end all intercity passenger service. The ICC evaluated the two cases separately but concurrently, as each clearly affected the other. Attorneys representing the Pennsylvania Railroad and the New York Central announced that they were willing to accept the "most burdensome" condition—the assumption of New Haven freight operations—as well as all the other requirements recommended by the two examiners, Lyle and Darmstadter. The New Haven's trustees struck a similar tone and indicated that they would "unequivocally urge" prompt approval of the merger, likewise without the inclusion of passenger operations. "There is reason to think that New Haven passenger service will be preserved," noted PRR general solicitor Windsor F. Cousins, but his use of passive voice suggested that the railroads would not be the ones who would bear the cost. He indicated that the Penn Central might retain some through passenger trains between Boston and Washington, a gesture that would be critical to the implementation of high-speed rail service, but he made no further promises.[466]

The hope that the railroads might distance themselves from the New Haven's passenger operations quickly faded, thanks to the refusal of regional governments to accept that responsibility. The attitude of Roy C. Papalia, the chairman of the Massachusetts Department of Public Utilities, was representative. The maintenance of commuter and intercity passenger trains, he explained, "can be resolved on a basis which will be fair to the states and will not constitute an unreasonable burden on the New Haven or any acquiring carrier." In case the commissioners missed the point,

Papalia demanded approval of the Penn Central merger "only on the basis of inclusion of both freight and passenger service." Papalia enjoyed the support of numerous allies, including the Port of New York Authority and the City of New York, the Connecticut Public Utilities Commission, the Brotherhood of Locomotive Engineers, the International Association of Machinists, and the Railway Labor Executives' Association.[467]

Crucially, the Justice Department also tied the Penn Central merger to maintenance of New Haven passenger operations—as well as the welfare of the Erie Lackawanna, the Boston & Maine, and the Delaware & Hudson. When he testified before the ICC, federal attorney Joseph J. Saunders made no mention of Robert Kennedy's 1964 memorandum. Instead, he reiterated the conditions Donald Turner had announced earlier that year. "The public interest would be better served if the Pennsylvania and the New York Central became components of competing systems," Joseph Saunders emphasized, making reference to the Justice Department's preferred four-system plan for the East. If the ICC were to approve the consolidation, he insisted, then the New York Central must relinquish the Pittsburgh & Lake Erie and the Penn Central should be required to operate the New Haven's passenger service. The merger might also be delayed by eighteen months, he suggested, to give the Erie Lackawanna, the Boston & Maine, and the Delaware & Hudson the opportunity to petition for inclusion in the Norfolk & Western.[468]

It mattered little that, by the summer of 1965, almost everyone else supported the Penn Central merger. Even though it was the responsibility of the ICC rather than the Justice Department to evaluate the competitive implications associated with the Penn Central, it was also clear that Turner and his staff at the Antitrust Division were eager to maintain their authority over transportation planning. According to Lowell Bridwell, the deputy under secretary of commerce for transportation, that stance was based largely on Turner's desire to maintain "consistency with past Government policy before the Commission." Bridwell noted that "the Government now stands practically alone in opposition. Major affected States and areas have accepted or have muted their previous opposition. Labor, once violently opposed, now acquiesces." By "Government," Bridwell meant Turner and the Justice Department. The secretary of commerce had supported the merger from the beginning, and the Luna-Saunders labor-protection agreement secured the cooperation of the secretary of labor. Like William Orrick before him, Turner endeavored to be first among equals, with a disproportionate share of influence over the Interagency Committee on Transport

Mergers. At the committee's June 28, 1965, meeting, Turner reiterated his opposition to the merger. Orrick's obstinacy had frozen that entity into a paralysis of indecision. The committee met again in September 1965, a month before the ICC hearings began, and it never again discussed the Penn Central merger. That circumstance offered fairly convincing evidence that the agenda established by the Justice Department was now the only one that mattered.[469]

As the eleven ICC commissioners began their deliberations, their decision would indicate both the terms of the Penn Central merger and their willingness to cede influence over national transportation planning to the Justice Department. By the end of the year, there were credible rumors, published in the *Wall Street Journal*, suggesting that the ICC had approved the merger and would issue a formal order in mid-January 1966. The New Haven passenger-service discontinuance case, which began in December 1965, plodded along. At the beginning of February, regulators announced that, by working nights and weekends, they were "hopeful" that they might reach a decision sometime in early March. The hearings related to the N&W's Appendix O inclusion provisions affecting the Erie Lackawanna, the Boston & Maine, and the Delaware & Hudson were not scheduled to begin until April. Representatives from the three inclusion railroads insisted that the commissioners should not rule on the Penn Central consolidation until they had exhausted every regulatory and legal possibility for merging with the Norfolk & Western. Should that effort fail, they asserted their right to be included in Penn Central. Their determination suggested that the Justice Department's call for an eighteen-month delay would seem mercifully short by comparison. The Norfolk & Western and the Chesapeake & Ohio had not filed their merger application with the ICC until October 11, nine days before the full commission began hearing oral arguments in the Penn Central case, and their stockholders had not yet voted on the matter. Even though there was little doubt that they would support the initiative—with the proviso that Dereco be a part of the arrangement—formal ICC hearings would not begin until April 1967. Such regulatory complexity attested to the rapidly shifting dynamic of competitive patterns in the railroad industry and highlighted the failure of the ICC to take seriously calls by Perlman and others to develop a comprehensive plan for the East. Given the interrelated nature of those cases, moreover, nothing could be decided until everything was decided.[470]

The middle of January came and went, and in the absence of a set of definitive regulatory conditions associated with the consolidation, many of the interested parties began reinforcing their positions. Some of the highest-profile figures appeared at the New Haven passenger-service discontinuance hearings, which had been underway for nearly two months. Senator Kennedy eliminated some of the ambiguity present in his 1964 memo, when he demanded that the Penn Central continue to operate "essential" passenger services along the New Haven. If Saunders, Perlman, and the New Haven trustees could not resolve the issue, Kennedy concluded, the ICC should "define the terms for them." His Republican counterpart, Jacob Javits, and New York City mayor John Lindsay enthusiastically supported the recommendation. Governor Nelson Rockefeller testified on January 24, offering a tepid promise that the government would subsidize commuter operations. "New York and Connecticut will continue to operate commuter service just as we have taken over the Long Island Rail Road," he stressed. Yet Rockefeller's pledge of support made no mention of intercity passenger trains, and he was unsure who would pay the commuter subsidies once the federal demonstration grant expired on July 1. Rockefeller was in a difficult position, however. While he was not entirely oblivious to political pressure from affluent Westchester County commuters, he was far more committed to the Penn Central's role in promoting the economic welfare of the entire state of New York. "When the merger takes place," the governor emphasized, in a distinct break with the other three New York politicians, "they will take over the freight lines." He concluded that "it's too late" to expect the ICC to assign the New Haven's passenger service to Penn Central. The editors of the *New York Times* seconded Rockefeller's assessment, noting that "what this really represents is a concentration of political force on the I.C.C. to make a political rather than an economic or a transportation decision on the terms under which it will permit the Pennsylvania and the New York Central to consolidate."[471]

Decision

The unanimous decision by the Interstate Commerce Commission came on April 6, 1966. It was four years and one month after the PRR and the NYC filed their petition to merge, and one year and one week had elapsed since examiners Lyle and Darmstadter recommended approval. The outcome remained a closely guarded secret until the official announcement came on April 27, although increases in share prices for both companies suggested that Wall Street representatives knew what was about to happen. By acquiescing to the merger, the commissioners acknowledged that the consolidation was in the public interest and

that the creation of a more efficient transportation system overrode any danger of monopolistic practices and the resulting loss of competition. They disagreed with almost every underlying contention made by the Justice Department, dismissing the antitrust concerns that first Orrick and then Turner had raised. "The very fact that Congress has seen fit to enter into the comprehensive regulation of transportation contradicts the notion that competition is favored without qualification," emphasized commissioner Kenneth H. Tuggle. He further marginalized the Justice Department with the assertion that "today competition is but one of several important factors to be considered in determining the public interest and applying the national transportation policy." The commissioners acknowledged that "the merger proposed herein will, without a doubt, lessen railroad intramodal competition to some degree." It was more significant, they argued, that Penn Central would reduce costs, improve service, and generate healthy profits that would sustain the company for the indefinite future. "There is no question," the commissioners emphasized, "but that the transaction will permit more economical and efficient use of the applicants' transportation facilities."[472]

The decision reiterated many of the statistics the two railroads provided to the ICC—a 27 percent reduction in freight transit times between Boston and Cincinnati, 36 percent between Buffalo and East St. Louis, 11 percent between New York and Chicago, and 26 percent between Jersey City and Detroit. The combined company would spend $75 million on nearly a hundred projects to integrate the physical plant, the commissioners emphasized. It would be possible to eliminate six million train miles a year without sacrificing the quality of service. Regulators accepted, without dispute, managerial assertions that the merger would generate at least $81 million in annual savings. "We do not mean to imply that merger is a magic touchstone of success," the commissioners acknowledged, noting that "too many other elements are essential: research, progressive technology, salesmanship, alert management willing to face today's problems on a realistic basis, etc." They did not provide any guidance on how the Pennsylvania Railroad and the New York Central would incorporate those vital elements, but they were content with assurances by executives at both companies that that process would happen.[473]

The commissioners also refuted the Justice Department's assertion that robust economic growth would ensure sufficient traffic to support a four-system East. "Notwithstanding the relatively high levels of business activity in 1964 and 1965, and applicants' improvement

On April 27, 1966, Alfred Perlman, president of the New York Central Railroad, at left, and Stuart Saunders, board chairman of the Pennsylvania Railroad, celebrated the news that the full Interstate Commerce Commission had approved the largest merger in American history. Nearly two more years would pass before the combined system, depicted on the map behind them, would become a reality. *AP Photo/John Lindsay*.

in revenue and net income," they emphasized, "the fact remains that even in this economic climate PRR had a rate of return on net investment in transportation property of only 1.77 percent in 1964 and 1.91 percent in 1965; and NYC's return rose to only slightly above 2 percent in 1964 and to 3.01 percent in 1965." That was, they noted, well below the average of almost all seventy-three industry groups and vastly inferior to the 4.5 percent yield on

Treasury bonds. While conceding that the financial results of both companies had improved since the filing of the merger application, ICC officials still acceded to Saunders's insistence that the PRR and the NYC could only become profitable through the elimination of duplicative and unneeded facilities. "In approving the PRR-NYC merger," the commissioners noted, "it is our purpose to open the way for the development of a modernized railroad system trimmed of unnecessary plant, unencumbered by service obligations no longer responsive to the public needs, and free and able to grow as and where the Nation's transportation requirements dictate. Mergers are not for shrinkage any more than the pruning of a fruit tree is for reducing the yield of fruit."[474]

Vice chairman William H. Tucker stood alone in his assertion that the merger was a necessary evil, whose outcome attested to the ICC's inability to develop a comprehensive transportation plan for the eastern railroads.

"On the day that the Commission approved the C&O-B&O unification," he noted,

> the success of this merger application became practically inevitable. When, in a separate decision a year and a half later, the Commission approved the unification of the N&W, Nickel Plate, and Wabash Railroads, any remaining doubt as to the outcome of the instant proceeding was removed. By its disposition of those two separate cases, the Commission effectively signified its complete acceptance of the principle of a predetermined three-system rail structure for the East. But it did this on a case by case basis, without having before it a picture of that three-system structure in its entirety. But in fact, a "panic button" response was sought—and achieved—when the C&O-B&O case was advanced before the Commission on the principal basis that B&O was on the verge of "collapse," and could only be saved by C&O's immediate assumption of its control. Once again that useful button was employed when N&W said it would lose its merger chance if the Commission failed to observe an approaching "deadline" on the parties' private agreements and stockholder authorization.[475]

The willingness of the ICC to openly countenance a substantial reduction in competition, in the face of sustained protests from the Justice Department, stood in stark contrast to the other great merger decision announced on April 27. The Northern Lines application to unite the Great Northern, the Northern Pacific, and the Chicago, Burlington & Quincy had been under consideration since 1960. While those three railroads benefited from longer hauls, lower terminal costs, and minimal passenger service, they still felt many of the same pressures that afflicted the PRR and the NYC. Like Penn Central, the Northern Lines proposal would merge essentially parallel systems, thus reducing competition—offset, executives claimed, by the elimination of duplicate facilities and ensuing cost reductions that would underwrite improvements in service. The ICC disagreed and denied the application. Even the most casual observer of the two parallel cases would find it easy to spot the key difference between the two. The Penn Central conditions included the preservation of the New Haven, but the Northern Lines had no bankrupt carrier to rescue.[476]

Observers noted that the decision in the Penn Central case cast doubt on the apolitical nature of the regulatory process. While the full ICC generally followed the guidelines suggested by examiners Lyle and Darmstadter, there were significant differences. Each seemed to confirm the suspicions of the *New York Times* editorial staff that the eleven commissioners made "a political rather than an economic or a transportation decision." One was a requirement

that the Penn Central indemnify the Erie Lackawanna, the Boston & Maine, and the Delaware & Hudson, if the merger caused their revenues to fall below what they had earned in 1964. The amounts involved were small—less than a million dollars a year, well within the Penn Central's budget. The ultimate fate of those three companies was more problematic. "It is doubtful that, without inclusion in a major system, these three carriers could withstand the competition" from the Penn Central, the commissioners noted. While retaining the Appendix O provisions associated with the 1964 Norfolk & Western-Nickel Plate merger, the three railroads now received "as an alternative to their first preference" a ten-year window for consolidation with the Penn Central. The commissioners expressed their hope that the inclusion matter would be settled promptly and harmoniously, through Dereco, and they emphasized the importance of "active cooperation in the implementation of conditions imposed by us." With representatives from the three companies and those from the N&W and the C&O holding diametrically opposing views about the nature of the consolidation process, it was unclear how that harmony would be accomplished or how long it would take. That, at least, was something Saunders would not have to worry about, as the ICC specified that the Penn Central merger could take place first, with the inclusion provisions to be determined later.[477]

The second striking difference between the examiners' report and the commissioners' ruling was even more overtly political and reflected the only area where the ICC and the Justice Department were in complete agreement. The ICC required the Penn Central to assume the New Haven in its entirety, including its passenger service. To do otherwise, the commissioners asserted, would be inconsistent with the public interest. To soften the blow, they made a simultaneous announcement in the New Haven passenger-service discontinuance case, permitting the elimination of about half of that company's intercity trains. The commissioners also emphasized that "the inclusion of New Haven's passenger service shall in no way be applied or construed to mean that New Haven passenger deficit operations, if undue, must be borne by the savings resulting from this merger." Likewise, they noted, "it should be made clear that, merely because it may be viewed as the embodiment of new efficiency and enterprise in railroad transportation, the [Penn Central] Transportation Company is not to become the repository for all the ailing railroads in the East nor the sop for their financial and operating problems." By inference, government agencies would assume much of the burden associated with the New Haven's passenger operations, but that was something the

Interstate Commerce Commission could not guarantee. As was the case with the inclusion provisions affecting the EL, the B&M, and the D&H, the commissioners emphasized that the resolution of the New Haven's problems should not delay the formation of the Penn Central and the realization of the associated economic benefits. Following the consummation of the merger, the Penn Central would have six months to prepare a plan for purchasing the New Haven and assuming its freight and passenger operations. That proposal would be subject to ICC approval—but, again, that could come later. The arrangement amounted to a promise that PRR and NYC personnel would safeguard the New Haven's rail service and employees, but it offered neither details nor guarantees regarding the protection of that company's investors.[478]

Reactions

Stuart Saunders had long anticipated the outcome of the hearings as well as the new conditions that the commissioners added to the examiners' report. In his determination to consolidate the Pennsylvania Railroad and the New York Central, he had made numerous concessions, and a few more would hardly destroy his plans. The Interstate Commerce Commission approved the merger, and that was what mattered. At a press conference, held in New York, Saunders and Perlman issued a joint statement emphasizing that they "don't anticipate any problems" with the implementation of the merger or the inclusion of the New Haven, "provided we get cooperation from the several states served by that system." Perlman conceded that his earlier—and emphatic—refusal to have anything to do with the New Haven's passenger service was a mistake, now that he was aware of "the cooperative attitude of the various New England states." Investment analysts dismissed any notion that the New Haven, with $15 million in annual losses, would impose "too great a burden" on the PRR and the NYC, whose combined earnings totaled $123 million.[479]

The reactions from those who were endeavoring to preserve the New Haven's passenger service ranged from jubilation to cautious optimism to a resigned and cynical pessimism. Governor Rockefeller, who saw in the ICC's terms benefits for both Manhattan commuters and upstate shippers, trumpeted "a great victory for New York," one that "fully substantiates New York State's position that the merger was in the public interest and that the merged system should include the New Haven in its entirety." Senator Javits applauded "a very fine understanding of the public interest," given the ICC's "move to continue the

commuter service." Robert Kennedy was slightly more restrained, merely acknowledging "a great breakthrough, with major implications for the entire region." Connecticut senator Thomas Dodd was "pleased that as a condition of merger, these two rail giants must include the New Haven Railroad and its freight and passenger operations." The New Haven commuters who read newspapers on their way to and from Grand Central Terminal discovered that the *New York Times* was somewhat more cautious. Acknowledging that the company "has operated for years on little more than rails and a prayer," the principal comment on the Penn Central merger was that "final approval came yesterday, and none too soon." Nor did the paper's editors view the consolidation as the panacea that so many others envisioned. "The outlook for commuters on the bankrupt New Haven Railroad has been greatly improved by the Interstate Commerce Commission's approval of the Pennsylvania-New York Central merger," they suggested, "but they should not mistake the green light for a permanent guarantee of operation."[480]

Given the generous terms of the Luna-Saunders agreement, unionized workers had little cause to fear unemployment. The merger nonetheless exacerbated concerns about the changing nature of railroading and the slow but steady decline of the workforce. PRR operating employees at Pitcairn, Pennsylvania, recalled that a facility that provided jobs for nearly four thousand people during the early 1950s now rostered no more than four hundred. The 1956 opening of Conway Yard, on the other side of Pittsburgh, was principally responsible for that decline, and the proposed operational changes would likely cause further curtailments. They could keep their jobs, but might lose their seniority, and would doubtless have to move away from their homes, their friends, and their communities. The situation was so bad that many had accepted lower wages at nearby manufacturing facilities. To the northeast, in Williamsport, PRR and NYC crews nevertheless dutifully posed beside their locomotives, smiling and shaking hands. It was an acknowledgment that when the merger took effect on June 1, they would be coworkers rather than competitors. Yet the sight of the two engines facing each other on the same stretch of track evoked disturbing images of the prelude to a train wreck.[481]

And then it all began to go horribly wrong. Like most such rulings, the terms of the ICC decision granted thirty days for appeals, although legal challenges in the courts might continue indefinitely. Saunders had done his best to anticipate and minimize those delays, yet his arrangements for doing so had not anticipated the other great merger battle in the East. Herman Pevler and Jack Fishwick at the

Rivals no longer, the crew of the Pennsylvania Railroad locomotive, at left, shake hands with their New York Central counterparts at Newberry Junction, near Williamsport, Pennsylvania. Executives struggling to mesh two incompatible organizational cultures were being far less cooperative. *AP Photo/Paul Vathis.*

Norfolk & Western and Walter Tuohy at the Chesapeake & Ohio acknowledged that the Penn Central decision facilitated ICC approval of their merger plans. Until those arrangements could come to fruition, they feared the competitive strength of the Penn Central. They were also disheartened at the ICC's denial of the Burlington Northern merger—which, like their proposal, represented an effort to combine prosperous rather than declining carriers. "Tuohy and Pevler have a real job on their hands now," one investment analyst suggested, emphasizing that they could not make the same claim of poverty and excess capacity that served Saunders and Perlman so well in the Penn Central merger hearings.[482]

Even as he celebrated victory in the Penn Central merger case, Saunders could not resist further meddling in the strategic relationships of the eastern railroads. He desired to block the union of the Norfolk & Western and the Chesapeake & Ohio, and now felt that he had little reason to fear reprisals from the likes of Pevler, Fishwick, and Tuohy. As such, his pent-up disgust at the actions of his rivals soon erupted into open warfare. His initial weapon involved the PRR's portfolio of Norfolk & Western stock, which was now under the control of three trustees. If two of them voted their shares against the N&W–C&O merger, then the plan would likely fail. Saunders telephoned each of the trustees, emphasizing that the combined N&W–C&O system would cause great harm to the Pennsylvania Railroad and asking them to make the "right" decision. The calls were not illegal, but they were provocative and generated an immediate response. In his last act on Earth, Walter Tuohy attacked Saunders and the Penn Central merger. He suffered a fatal heart attack on May 12, as he was putting the finishing touches on a speech exhorting C&O shareholders to approve the union with the N&W. His remarks, delivered posthumously, echoed the sentiment of the Justice Department while mocking the pruning that the Penn Central was prepared to undertake. "The N.&W.-C.&O. merger plan is for growth and not for diminution," he wrote. "Our merger does not rest on cutbacks in service, but upon the creation of a system to meet the expanding American economy that lies ahead." Tuohy's death only slightly dampened the euphoria of shareholders in Cleveland and Roanoke, who overwhelmingly approved the merger proposal—in part as a retaliation against Saunders's precipitous action. Further punishment came shortly thereafter, as both the N&W and the C&O filed petitions to delay the Penn Central merger. The assertion, unsurprisingly, was that Saunders's efforts to influence the trustees proved that the Pennsylvania still influenced the Norfolk & Western, in contravention to the ICC's ruling in the Nickel Plate merger case.[483]

Despite the actions of N&W and C&O officials, the first official delay came from the commissioners who had only recently, and unanimously, approved the merger. On May 17, the ICC postponed the consummation of the merger until the end of July, to give the Erie Lackawanna, the Boston & Maine, and the Delaware & Hudson more time to prepare a response to the ruling. While representatives from the B&M were soon in negotiations with PRR and NYC officials, their counterparts at the EL and the D&H proved more obstinate. William White was the chairman of both companies, and he enthusiastically embraced the opportunity to attack Saunders and Perlman, the man who had cost him his job as president of the New York Central. White demanded that the ICC's indemnification and inclusion provisions "be considerably changed so that those protective conditions could be made equitable and workable." In plain English, White sought to delay both the Penn Central merger and the N&W–C&O consolidation as long as possible, so that he could negotiate favorable inclusion terms in one of those systems. He vastly preferred a straight merger with the Norfolk & Western, but he was willing to accept a place in the Penn Central

rather than see his companies consigned to the N&W's Dereco subsidiary. The ICC facilitated White's strategy and further postponed the effective date of the Penn Central merger until at least August 12. On the Fourth of July, the Reading joined the fray, its lawyers charging that the "novel" indemnification provisions encouraged the EL, the B&M, and the D&H to poach its traffic. Unlike those three carriers, the Reading did not have any opportunity for inclusion in the N&W–Nickel Plate merger. "Since the proposed N.&W.-C.&O. is the only transaction which involves inclusion of the Reading," the company's lawyers complained, "any ability on the part of the Pennsylvania to influence N.&W. stockholders would seriously jeopardize the Reading's opportunity to become part of a major system"—another instance where Saunders's telephone calls came back to haunt him.[484]

Given the volume and complexity of the petitions, the ICC waived the thirty-day filing deadline, extending the time limit until July 11. The complaints from the Norfolk & Western, the Chesapeake & Ohio, the Erie Lackawanna, the Delaware & Hudson, and the Reading were only at the top of a very large pile. Negotiations between PRR-NYC officials and the Boston & Maine broke down, and that company's executives demanded modifications to the indemnification provisions. The Chicago & Eastern Illinois also sought concessions—as did the Norwich & Worcester, a tiny affiliate of the New Haven. The investment banking firm of Oscar Gruss & Son was determined to protect $10.5 million in New Haven first mortgage bonds under its stewardship. The firm had not been a party to the merger hearings and its agents were appalled that the ICC was willing to allow the Penn Central to begin operations without securing guarantees for the New Haven's investors. The Gruss interests now demanded that Saunders and Perlman make good those securities, as a condition for final approval of the merger. The financiers indicated that, absent such reassurances, they would demand the New Haven's liquidation—the only certain way to recoup some of their investment. The always combative Milton Shapp submitted what was simultaneously the longest (at ninety-four pages) and the least relevant petition. No friend of Robert Kennedy, he denounced "the junior Senator from New York" and his "attempt to saddle Pennsylvania with the ills of bad management on the New Haven." Shapp was referring to the commonwealth rather than the railroad and charged that it was "essential for the economy of Pennsylvania that this merger be disapproved." His further allegation that Penn Central "would be the greatest disaster facing the Commonwealth of Pennsylvania since the opening of the Erie Canal in 1825" reawaked the economic rivalries that led, well over a hundred years earlier, to the development of the Main Line of Public Works and then to the chartering of the Pennsylvania Railroad.[485]

While the ICC had long since dismissed Shapp as a self-absorbed blowhard with minimal legal standing, the other petitions posed a significant threat to the timely consummation of the Penn Central merger. Given the number of objections, the ICC postponed the final decision until September 30. It was the third delay countenanced by the commissioners since they approved the merger on April 27. The latest setback did not discourage investors or cause share prices to fall. One securities broker called the ruling "good news" and speculated that the ICC "is determined to have a bullet-proof record in the event one of the opposing parties to the merger decides to appeal to the courts."[486]

When the Pennsylvania Railroad and the New York Central held simultaneous shareholder meetings the following day, in Philadelphia and in New York, executives from both companies insisted that combined operations would surely begin on October 1, or soon thereafter. They highlighted impressive improvements in earnings—causing one NYC investor to somewhat spoil the party by asking, in light of such prosperity, why a merger was necessary. Perlman, unable to control his temper, leaped from his chair and asserted "an $81 million savings looks good to me yet." That was the figure that the two companies provided to the ICC, but Perlman was now saying publicly that the merger would surely generate economies of $100 million annually. Far from curtailing his optimism, some Wall Street insiders suggested that the benefits were likely to be even higher. Ninety miles south, Saunders emphasized that the ICC's "delaying tactics" caused him little concern, although he thought that each week's postponement would impose unnecessary costs of at least $1.5 million. Even worse, he suggested, "would be to deprive our nation's economic and industrial heartland of the modern railroads which are so desperately needed." Ten days after the dual shareholder meetings, the two companies filed a petition of their own, emphasizing that they were willing to accept without protest all the ICC's conditions in return for prompt consummation of the merger.[487]

While Saunders and Perlman remained nonchalant, important political figures were growing restive at the series of postponements. The most prominent were all eight senators—including two Kennedy brothers—from the four states served by the New Haven. On July 23, they informed ICC chairman John W. Bush that "they were greatly disturbed that even though the Penn-Central merger has been approved, attempts are being made to delay indefinitely its effective date." While they were

mindful of the concerns of the Erie Lackawanna and the other petitioners, their primary aim was to save the New Haven by foisting it onto the Penn Central before it was too late. "The I.C.C. should not allow delaying tactics to be invoked in the face of the great crisis which faces the New Haven," they emphasized. New Haven trustee Richard Joyce Smith shared those concerns. Speaking before the Rotary Club of Greenwich, Connecticut, he warned that his company "has been living off of steadily declining capital for many years and we are now at a point where, in my opinion, we cannot continue to function very much longer as an independent enterprise." At the end of July, Smith and his cotrustees filed a petition with the ICC, seeking to expedite rather than delay the merger. Further postponement, they asserted, could result in the New Haven's liquidation, and under such circumstances, the likelihood that freight and passenger service could ever be resurrected "must be deemed remote." If there was any further delay in the consummation of the merger and the inclusion of the New Haven in the Penn Central, they indicated, there would be no New Haven left to save.[488]

The political pressure made little difference. The disaster came on August 8, when the Justice Department demanded a further postponement of the Penn Central merger. Less than two years had passed since Attorney General Robert Kennedy issued a 482-word memo, promising Stuart Saunders that his office would honor the examiners' recommendations, but it might as well have been a century. Even allowing for the ambiguity in the memo, Kennedy secured what he desired most—an opportunity to promise voters in the 1964 New York senate race that he had saved the New Haven and its passenger service. Saunders clearly did not get what he wanted, and the Justice Department had consistently opposed the merger, even after Lyle and Darmstadter issued their favorable report. Saunders yielded in the matter of the New Haven's passenger service, even though that provision was not clearly stated in the Kennedy memo. Nor did that document make any mention of the welfare of the Erie Lackawanna, the Boston & Maine, or the Delaware & Hudson.

The contents of the Kennedy memo were irrelevant to Donald Turner and his staff at the Antitrust Division. In clause after clause of their April 27 decision, the eleven commissioners refuted nearly every argument raised by the Justice Department—from the assumption that rail traffic would grow, to the demand for a four-system East, to the assertion that the prevention of monopoly overrode any economic benefits that might accrue from the merger. Turner was not willing to be written out of the largest and most complex merger case in American history, and he was determined to throw whatever impediments he could in the path of the Penn Central. "It now appears that critical facets of the transaction may not have been fully explored before the commission," noted attorneys for the Justice Department—another way of saying that they had lost and wanted another bite at the apple.[489]

The Justice Department's August 8 brief cited three principal reasons for delay. Turner found suspicious the willingness of PRR and NYC executives to accept all the conditions mandated by the ICC, in exchange for a speedy consummation of the merger. "Whether such reversal of normal procedure is sound in policy or in law is open to considerable doubt," he noted. Saunders's phone calls to the trustees overseeing the Norfolk & Western stock gave Turner an opportunity to emphasize the PRR's ongoing influence at that company. Turner also expressed concern about the harm the Penn Central might inflict on the Chesapeake & Ohio and the Norfolk & Western, and he deplored that those two railroads intended to merge in response. The N&W–C&O combination would decisively end any plans to establish a four-system East, claimed Turner, while producing another massive and undoubtedly monopolistic corporation. The most significant objection, however, concerned the welfare of the three inclusion roads. Emphasizing the "novel" nature of the ICC's indemnity provisions, the Justice Department asserted that "the conditions are inadequate as protection and allow Penn-Central permanently to strip the E.-L., D.&H. and B.&M. of their traffic." By the time they could win inclusion in the N&W–Nickel Plate merger, therefore, the Norfolk & Western would inherit three companies, "the competitive capabilities of which have been destroyed." With New Englanders favoring the Penn Central merger in order to save the New Haven, and Saunders and Perlman reluctantly willing to accept that company's passenger service, Turner and his colleagues at the Justice Department saw little opportunity to block the Penn Central merger on that score. Instead, Turner styled the Justice Department as the savior of the Erie Lackawanna, the Boston & Maine, and the Delaware & Hudson. That issue, something that Robert Kennedy never addressed in his August 1964 memo, now became the chief legal argument against the consolidation of the Pennsylvania Railroad and the New York Central.[490]

The Norfolk & Western Appendix O inclusion hearings resumed on August 3, with executives from the three smaller railroads still demanding a conventional merger, and Pevler insisting on their membership in Dereco. Eight days later, the Erie Lackawanna sought another postponement in the Penn Central case, to give the company

sufficient time to pursue their negotiations with the N&W. Two weeks after that, and for the first time, the ICC refused to countenance any further delays. After four months of listening to complaints, the commissioners finally abandoned efforts to create "a bullet-proof record in the event one of the opposing parties to the merger decides to appeal to the courts."[491]

Amid the chaos, it was only a matter of time before the aggrieved parties turned to the courts. On September 8, the Erie Lackawanna filed suit in the US District Court for the Southern District of New York, calling for "permanently enjoining, annulling or setting aside" the ICC's April 27 order. The company's lawyers insisted that the ICC's protective conditions are "plainly and grossly unjust to the Erie." They sought to undermine political support for the merger by suggesting that it was "uncertain whether the New Haven will ever be included in a Penn-Central system." In an obvious ploy to attract the attention of the Justice Department, the EL's brief asserted that the ICC "had erred in failing to require the development of an adequate record as to the anticompetitive, or monopolistic, effects of the merger." It was not at all clear whether the company's lawyers could convince the three-judge panel as to the merits of their case, but they did not have to. They merely needed to stall the formation of Penn Central long enough to resolve the terms of inclusion in the Norfolk & Western. With observers suggesting that it could take two years, possibly longer, for the case to work its way through the judicial process, they would have plenty of time.[492]

The Erie Lackawanna's lawsuit opened the floodgates for aggrieved parties who abandoned the regulatory apparatus in favor of the courts. The Delaware & Hudson, also under White's supervision, became a party to the suit on the following day. On September 12, the Norfolk & Western, the Chesapeake & Ohio, the Baltimore & Ohio, and the Chicago & Eastern Illinois joined the proceedings, as did the Reading, the Jersey Central, and the Western Maryland. A week later, with the situation rapidly spiraling out of control, the ICC dismissed all the regulatory appeals filed since April and announced that the merger would take place on September 30. The commissioners' sole concession to the firestorm of opposition was an acknowledgment that they might be willing to consider slight modifications to the indemnity provisions. That process, ICC attorney Robert W. Gennane conceded, might take "three months, six months and possibly a full year." With a total of ten railroads now demanding judicial abrogation of the merger, it may have been the least relevant announcement in the history of the Interstate Commerce Commission. On September 21, the district court issued a temporary restraining order, preventing the consummation of the merger until the case had worked its way through the judicial process.[493]

None of the plaintiffs objected to the Penn Central merger in principle or denied that it was in the public interest, but each developed alternate forms of protest designed to delay or destroy it. Attorneys for the Erie Lackawanna reiterated their claim that the consolidation "would have inevitable and irreversible consequences" and "may ultimately mean a very significant monopoly for the merged company." Postponement was imperative, they insisted, until they could persuade the ICC to adopt adequate inclusion terms in the Norfolk & Western. A lawyer representing the N&W, the C&O, and the B&O emphasized the role of "political pressure" when he testified that "the thing putting the pressure on is the New Haven Railroad." The ICC "hasn't done its job" to ensure the inclusion of that company in the Penn Central, he noted. Until the New Haven had a guarantee of protection, he concluded, the merger should not go forward. Gennane, the ICC attorney, insisted that it would take at least a year for the Penn Central to become efficient and prosperous enough to cause harm to anyone. During that time, he suggested, there was a "large likelihood that the I.C.C. can come up with a system of protection for the smaller roads"—in effect asserting that everyone should trust the agency to do the right thing. Gennane nonetheless acknowledged the importance of saving the New Haven, something that could only be done through inclusion in the Penn Central. "The commission isn't going to take a chance on an indefinite postponement of that merger," he reiterated.[494]

The New York District Court's ruling, issued on October 4, failed to settle the matter. Judge Henry J. Friendly was unwilling to issue an injunction blocking the Penn Central merger, as attorneys for the Erie Lackawanna and the other nine plaintiffs had demanded. Yet he extended the restraining order to permit an appeal to the US Supreme Court—a likely outcome, and one that would impose additional delay. Friendly, who wrote the majority opinion in the 2–1 decision, sensed that the protesting carriers were seeking to delay the merger solely as a means to bolster their respective bargaining positions. That conclusion, in turn, reflected his assertion that the ICC, rather than the courts, should be responsible for shaping transportation policy. "The Commission surely can appraise far better than we what effect a year's delay of consummation would have on the jockeying of these roads and of the three plaintiffs in the C&O, B&O, and N&W actions for price and position in respect of other mergers which,

despite all the words, is what we suspect these actions to be mostly about," Friendly suggested. "We would be assuming powers not confided to us if, once we have acquitted ourselves of our limited task, we were to pit our necessarily ill-informed judgment on these imponderables and their procedural entailments against the unanimous conclusion of the agency to which Congress has given authority for decision and on which it has placed responsibility for achievement." Friendly also supported the ICC's contention that prompt consummation of the Penn Central merger represented the only possible mechanism to rescue the New Haven. He dismissed as unrealistic an $80 million plan, announced a week earlier by Governors Rockefeller and Dempsey, to acquire that railroad's commuter operations. The proposal depended on a massive infusion of federal funds that Congress had not yet allocated—and, given the rising cost of the conflict in Vietnam, was not likely to provide. The lone dissenter, District Judge Edward Weinfeld, adopted precisely opposite interpretations of the two principal issues under consideration—insisting that the inclusion roads were desperately in need of protection and that rumors of the New Haven's demise were greatly exaggerated.[495]

The disaffected carriers' decision to take the matter to the Supreme Court was one of the few aspects of the Penn Central merger that proceeded with alacrity. We "are in a state of shock," an attorney for one of the smaller railroads conceded. "We certainly thought it was in the bag for us." Within days, nine of the ten railroads filed appeals with the Supreme Court.[496] Only the Boston & Maine refrained from further legal action, while its executives attempted to negotiate a separate peace with the PRR and the NYC—reinforcing Judge Friendly's suspicions regarding "jockeying" for position. Sensing an opportunity for further concessions, representatives from the city of Scranton and seven other communities in Pennsylvania and New Jersey also submitted briefs.[497]

Milton Shapp joined the appeal to the Supreme Court, as an opportunity to bolster his political career. Earlier in the year, Shapp faced state senator Robert P. Casey in the Democratic primary. Casey enjoyed the support of party insiders, including former governor David Lawrence, but Shapp dipped into his personal wealth to finance a statewide media campaign and win the contest. Party loyalty only went so far, however, and fellow Democrats soon found fault with Shapp's opposition to the merger. Not long after the primary, Commerce Secretary John Connor was in Philadelphia and publicly criticized Shapp's stance on the issue. So did Saunders ally Walter Annenberg, and his *Philadelphia Inquirer* undermined Shapp's chances in the general election. Shapp struck back, calling Saunders a "robber baron." Saunders talked with Shapp in early July, asking him to moderate his opposition to the merger. Shapp refused and, predictably, each individual offered radically different accounts of the meeting. Saunders recalled that he had merely emphasized the benefits associated with the merger, while Shapp alleged that the PRR's chairman offered financial support for his campaign—tantamount to a bribe—if he reversed his position. Regardless of the details, Shapp was more convinced than ever that Saunders, Annenberg, the leadership of the Democratic Party, and key officials in the Johnson Administration were conspiring against him. On October 7, he became a party to the appeal.[498]

Saunders and Perlman initially predicted that the Supreme Court would refuse to consider the appeals from the New York District Court. Had it done so, Judge Friendly's restraining order would have become void, and the merger could go forward as early as November 1. Instead, on October 18, the justices agreed to hear the case, referred to as *Baltimore & Ohio v. United States*, and they scheduled arguments to begin on January 9, 1967. One Washington attorney noted that such speed "is almost unprecedented," but given that the merger battle was about to enter its fifth year, it seemed the least that the court could do. Observers also attached great significance to the justices' insistence that the ICC should proceed with its rehearing of the protection and indemnification conditions, scheduled to begin on October 31. A rapid resolution of that issue, they hoped, might placate the protesting railroads and render a judicial decision unnecessary. Regardless of the circumstances, however, it was clear that neither the formation of the Penn Central nor the rescue of the New Haven could take place until the new year.[499]

The heads of the Pennsylvania Railroad and the New York Central tried to make the best of a bad situation. Saunders suggested that the consummation of the merger "is relatively near at hand," while Perlman asserted that he would deplore "the necessity for further delay of the merger but remain confident of its approval." Yet the two executives now faced a legion of enemies, on two battlefields. While the contest in front of the Supreme Court would not begin until January, the reopened Interstate Commerce Commission indemnification hearings presented a more immediate problem. Managers and lawyers from a dozen railroads filled the ICC's largest hearing room. Regulatory officials acknowledged that it would take six weeks or more merely to hear all the testimony, while a New Haven

attorney predicted "months and months of hearings." The two ICC examiners, Robert Murphy and Henry J. Whitehouse, suggested that the process might last more than a year.[500]

Their caution was well advised, as the agency faced a new issue associated with the Erie Lackawanna, the Boston & Maine, and the Delaware & Hudson. The ICC had required the Penn Central to indemnify the three railroads for any revenue losses they might suffer because of the merger, until they could be included in the Norfolk & Western system. Saunders quickly accepted that condition, judging that payments of less than a million dollars a year would barely make a dent in the savings related to the merger. Representatives from the three beleaguered carriers now demanded that the PRR and the NYC indemnify them for the loss of shareholder value, until they could find refuge with the N&W. The amount involved could be substantial, ranging from $65.5 million to as much as $142.4 million. New York Central general counsel James B. Gray, who also represented the PRR's interests in the matter, insisted that such a capital-indemnification plan was unprecedented, and probably illegal. It would in any event be extraordinarily difficult to determine whether the steady erosion of shareholder equity stemmed from the Penn Central consolidation or—more likely—the general decline of the northeastern railroads. Gray had strong support from the Norfolk & Western's lawyers—"understandable," he noted, as "they are trying to keep the price down." Norfolk & Western senior vice president Jack Fishwick was indeed appalled at the proposal, which would vastly increase the price his company might have to pay to acquire the three railroads. Fishwick labeled the payments "death benefits," language that was hardly likely to appeal to the leaders of the three railroads he hoped to include in Dereco.[501]

While Fishwick was as eager as Saunders to block the capital-indemnification plan, he was still resolutely opposed to the terms of the Penn Central merger. Ominously, the Justice Department supported the N&W's position, strongly suggesting the possibility that it would intervene when the merger case came before the Supreme Court in January. Saunders hoped to avoid appearing at the ICC hearings, but he agreed to testify after the Norfolk & Western threatened him with a subpoena. In his testimony, Saunders described the Penn Central as a "pitiful giant" and a "physical giant with few or no teeth that couldn't fight anyone." The highly publicized remarks were unlikely to inspire much confidence among PRR and NYC investors. When confronted with the improved financial performance of the two merger partners during the early 1960s, Saunders acknowledged that "there is a lot of talk in this record about the spectacular and miraculous improvement of the Pennsylvania and New York Central in recent years." Discounting earnings from nonrail subsidiaries, he emphasized that the rosy financial picture "is sheer propaganda. It is completely misleading, and the facts do not justify it." The Norfolk & Western, he emphasized, was by comparison truly and unnecessarily prosperous. "I wish I had a railroad like that to run," he noted longingly—causing more than one observer to recall that, until just a few years earlier, he had. Saunders repeated his long-standing contention that the Norfolk & Western, once coupled with the Chesapeake & Ohio, would claim most of the Penn Central's coal traffic. Above all, the PRR's chairman excoriated that company for wrecking his plans for a three-system East. "With the N.&W. it is a matter of rule or ruin," he complained. "They have a two-fold plan either to destroy the Eastern railroad merger movement or dictate how to restructure" the area's railroad network. Saunders told the examiners that he had lost patience with the Norfolk & Western for "trying to wreck the entire Eastern railroad movement by their delaying tactics and constant obstructionism." It was an audacious statement from an executive who practiced much the same tactics.[502]

Saunders had made those allegations before, although perhaps never so vehemently. His testimony contained a new threat, however, one that was at striking variance with his earlier optimism in the face of repeated delays. He noted that at one time more than seventy executives were planning the integration of the PRR and the NYC but that considering the ongoing impediments, "only a handful of people" were still doing so. The two railroads were "decelerating" their merger planning, Saunders emphasized, and they would not complete any additional studies until they knew with certainty "when this merger is going to take effect." Now Saunders speculated that the merger might never happen. The ICC, he emphasized, had clearly established that the consolidation of the Pennsylvania Railroad and the New York Central would rescue the New Haven, advance the public interest, preserve the northeastern rail network, and prevent the massive infusion of public funds or the government ownership that might be necessary to save it from destruction. None of that would occur if the ICC and the courts failed to act promptly, Saunders warned. If there were any further delays, he noted, the largest merger in American history "is going to collapse."[503]

The one bit of good news came from Pennsylvania, where Milton Shapp had spent more than $3.4 million of his substantial fortune in an effort to capture a job that paid $45,000 a year. On November 8, he suffered a bruising defeat at the hands of Republican Raymond P. Shafer, part of a nationwide movement toward the political right. Shapp garnered a smaller-than-expected plurality in Philadelphia and Pittsburgh, and his crusade to save the commonwealth of Pennsylvania from the Penn Central was insufficient to offset steep losses in rural areas. In the Philadelphia Inquirer, Walter Annenberg expressed his gratitude that "Pennsylvania voters have done a thorough-going job in averting the calamity of Milton Shapp in the Governor's office." Annenberg soon received appropriate compensation for his unwavering support of the Penn Central merger. Saunders was unable to reward his ally with a membership in the Gulph Mills Golf Club, but he proved more successful with the PRR's board. In March 1967, he recommended Annenberg, who on May 8 became the first Jewish director of the Pennsylvania Railroad.[504]

As Americans prepared to celebrate the Thanksgiving holiday, Stuart Saunders had little reason to be thankful. The Interstate Commerce Commission hearings on the indemnity provisions was likely to continue indefinitely, and there was no guarantee that the examiners' findings and the commissioners' rulings would be free of additional legal challenges. Representatives from the Erie Lackawanna and the Delaware & Hudson were still demanding inclusion in the Norfolk & Western, refusing to accept participation in Dereco, and insisting that the Penn Central merger be postponed until the matter could be resolved. Their counterparts at the Norfolk & Western and the Chesapeake & Ohio would not consider taking in those marginal carriers through any mechanism other than Dereco. Until the ICC resolved that issue, the Erie Lackawanna, the Boston & Maine, and the Delaware & Hudson would maintain their right of inclusion in the Penn Central, and the N&W and the C&O would not drop their opposition to that merger. Hearings in the N&W–C&O case would not begin until April 1967, would be prolonged, and were certain to face legal challenges. A short distance away, at the Supreme Court, the justices would not begin to hear the legal challenges to the Penn Central merger until January, and the Baltimore & Ohio v. United States case could drag on for many months. The Justice Department had not intervened in the New York District Court but had supported the N&W's demand that Saunders testify before the ICC. With the largest merger case in the nation's history about to go to trial before the Supreme Court, it was inconceivable that the head of the Antitrust Division should abrogate his responsibility to uphold federal law.

Donald Turner was at that moment working with Solicitor General Thurgood Marshall to craft a brief opposing the Penn Central merger conditions, thus undermining the ICC's prerogatives as a determiner of national transportation policy. While he could not block the merger solely on antitrust grounds, Turner could at the very least impose additional delays. To do so, he asked the court to order the ICC to reinvestigate the indemnification and inclusion provisions applying to the Erie Lackawanna, the Boston & Maine, and the Delaware & Hudson. Until that investigation ended, and the ICC implemented protections that the Justice Department found acceptable, the merger could not go forward.

What made the situation all the more frustrating was that, more than two years earlier, Saunders had negotiated a noninterference agreement with the Justice Department. He met the principal stipulation—a favorable examiners' report—in March 1965. He also accepted, albeit reluctantly, the further demands that the Penn Central assume the New Haven's passenger service and protect the smaller railroads that were also its competitors. Despite those concessions, the Justice Department repeatedly blocked the merger, time and time again clashing with the government agency whose responsibility it was to oversee the regulation of the railroad network. Saunders had in his possession a document, endorsed by the attorney general of the United States, and pledging to sweep away all obstacles before him, yet it did not seem to be worth more than the paper on which it was written. Until November 1966, Saunders had shown considerable restraint in the face of such adversity. With his efforts to consummate the perfect merger on the verge of being irretrievably lost, however, Stuart Saunders did what any virtuous citizen would do when confronted with the perceived inequities of the political system. He reached for the telephone.

Thanksgiving Week

In 1966, Lyndon Johnson spent the week of Thanksgiving at his Texas ranch, and he was not in the best of spirits. The president was recovering from throat surgery, the conflict in Vietnam continued to escalate, and the cost of that war was jeopardizing his Great Society programs. The 1965 Voting Rights Act, one of Johnson's signature achievements, greatly increased African American voter turnout in the midterm elections that took place a few weeks earlier. The president's support for civil rights nonetheless alienated many southern Democrats and cost the party dearly. Republicans failed to take control of Congress, but they

gained three Senate seats, forty-seven seats in the House, and displaced seven Democratic governors. Johnson acknowledged that many of his Democratic allies would not return to office, and he concluded that "most of them are not because of this damn fool Turner." While the actions of the head of the Antitrust Division probably had little to do with the Democratic losses, the comment reflected Johnson's growing frustration with Donald Turner and with the Justice Department. That summer, Turner suspended an antitrust action against Anheuser-Busch. Weeks later, he accompanied Vice President Hubert Humphrey to the All-Star Game in St. Louis, as a guest of the brewery and in a company aircraft. The trip represented poor judgment rather than corruption, but it proved politically embarrassing for both Johnson and Humphrey.[505] The Justice Department, citing antitrust concerns, also interfered with a bank merger in Houston, one that Johnson strongly supported. "Well I have no confidence whatever in Turner," the president told Ramsey Clark, the individual who had recommended Turner for the post of assistant attorney general. Clark was now the acting attorney general, after Nicholas Katzenbach resigned on October 2 to become the under secretary of state. Robert Kennedy was in the Senate, and William Orrick, the former head of the Antitrust Division, was in private practice in San Francisco. As such, all three of the government representatives who participated in the August 1964 meeting with Saunders and Perlman had severed their ties with the Justice Department.[506]

As Solicitor General Thurgood Marshall prepared the Justice Department's brief opposing the Penn Central merger, Saunders called in as many political favors as he could. He first contacted Joseph A. Califano Jr., the special assistant to the president and Johnson's most important domestic-policy aide.[507] The PRR chairman asserted that both Robert Kennedy and Lyndon Johnson had agreed to honor the examiners' findings, despite the preferences of the members of the Antitrust Division. "Saunders was a little fuzzy about the time, place, and specifics of the president's commitment," Califano recalled, and he discounted the claim as uncreditable. Saunders was on much firmer ground with matters pertaining to the former attorney general, however, and he sent Califano a copy of the 1964 memorandum. On the Monday of Thanksgiving Week, Califano informed Johnson of the matter, sent him Robert Kennedy's memo, and conveyed his dubious appraisal of the pledge that the president had allegedly made to Saunders. "You told him if he ran into any problems delaying the merger, to get in touch with you and you would 'move things along,'" he suggested to Johnson. "In the absence of any indication from the White House," Califano continued, "Ramsey would file before the Supreme Court recommending that the case be remanded to the ICC for further hearings" regarding the inclusion and indemnification provisions. "This, in effect, would delay the merger and would be interpreted by Saunders as a violation of an agreement he feels he has with the Administration and with you personally." The controversy caught the president by surprise—an example, he later complained, of a situation where "I get it after the fact instead of before." Johnson had never read the Kennedy memorandum, nor was he even aware that it existed.[508]

The conversation between the president and the acting attorney general did not take place until Wednesday evening, November 23, the day before Thanksgiving. There was little time to resolve the matter. In two days, Clark would reveal his position on the Penn Central merger to the Supreme Court and the news media.[509] The flurry of telephone calls began when presidential aide Jake Jacobsen informed Califano that he had talked with Johnson, who disavowed all knowledge of any agreement with Saunders. But Kennedy's memo "sure sounds like it does commit," Jacobsen conceded, and he questioned whether there was any need for Solicitor General Marshall to file a brief before the Supreme Court. Jacobsen emphasized that he was giving a personal assessment of the situation, but Califano recognized that it represented Johnson's feelings on the matter.[510]

In Washington, Califano hurriedly arranged a meeting with Katzenbach and Clark. Katzenbach had just begun his duties as under secretary of state, and he was no longer invested in the affairs of the Justice Department. He seconded the position of Jacobsen—and, by extension, Johnson—that the Kennedy memo constituted a firm promise to Saunders. Clark emphatically disagreed and announced that he had no intention of being bound by an informal document negotiated by his predecessor's predecessor. He reminded Califano that the Justice Department had consistently opposed the consolidation and could not abruptly reverse course for no apparent reason. Reiterating the position taken by the solicitor general in *Baltimore & Ohio v. United States*, Clark balked at a "no-brief" option. "When the largest merger in the history of the United States is before the Supreme Court and the United States is a statutory party," he declared, "the United States is obligated to give the Court its views of the case."[511]

With the former and the acting attorneys general firmly committed to precisely opposite interpretations of the

Kennedy memo, Califano had little choice but to involve the president. Late that evening, Clark and Johnson discussed the matter in a testy telephone conversation that lasted nearly forty minutes. Califano recalled that Clark "was a strong-willed attorney general with strong views," and subsequent events supported that assessment. Clark defended his decision, reminding Johnson of Kennedy's unwillingness to "bind my successor in office as to views on the proposed merger." The acting attorney general also emphasized that the Justice Department would honor the memo's nonbinding commitment "unless circumstances have materially changed." In his conversation with the president, Clark noted that "they have materially changed." He pointed to the economic growth that occurred during the early 1960s, benefiting the Pennsylvania Railroad and the New York Central. "The railroad's been making money for three years now, big money," Clark emphasized. Clark thus had little sympathy for Saunders's insistence that the merger must be consummated as quickly as possible. It seemed more likely, Clark suggested, that the Penn Central would become the dominant railroad in the East. As such, it would constitute a far more severe threat to the Erie Lackawanna, the Boston & Maine, and the Delaware & Hudson than either Kennedy or Katzenbach had predicted. "But I think the overriding thing is that this is the biggest merger in the history of the United States and it affects transportation in a vital part of the United States," Clark told the president, "and we're in a time where we can see it is probably a growth industry and the two members of the merger are making money and have been for the first time in some time and have made more money each year for three consecutive years, so that the conditions up there have changed, but the merger has not provided for these three little railroads, and if anything happens to them as a result of this merger, it's gonna fall right on us."[512]

Clark relied heavily, and unsurprisingly, on legalistic arguments to justify his position. When referring to "these three little railroads," he emphasized that "the three of them combined are a much greater problem than the New Haven." Under those circumstances, he argued, the Justice Department possessed a legal obligation to protect the public interest, and any failure to do so would represent a shocking abrogation of his constitutional duties. "It would just be an incredible thing if we failed to do it," he told Johnson. Clark's resolute stance clearly reflected pressure from Turner, the head of the Antitrust Division. "The assistant general's office says that that just hasn't happened and is really almost inconceivable to them. So, our responsibility is to represent the public interest in the courts."

Moreover, Clark concluded, "any intelligent treatment of the problem requires you to be sure before you permit a merger that can't be undone."[513]

Johnson, in contrast, never wavered from his position that the Kennedy memo constituted a good-faith promise, one that the federal government had yet failed to honor. "I'm not a lawyer," he reminded Clark, "but I do have some sense of justice." The president had long since lost patience with the Antitrust Division and suggested that he—rather than legalistic principles—should govern the actions of the Justice Department. Nor was he sympathetic to Clark's desire to adopt policies that differed from those practiced by his predecessors. "Of course the new attorney general has a right to change it," Johnson acknowledged, "but they haven't got a new president, and it seems to me I have some obligation to try to stabilize what we say and make our word good." Coupling the Penn Central case with the incidents in St. Louis and Houston, Johnson suggested that the Antitrust Division was out of step with presidential politics. Disgusted, he indicated that "I'm just beginning to think that we ought to call y'all when we want you to file something, otherwise tell you to sit at your goddamn desk 'til you're employed to do it."[514]

Johnson's assertion that "it seems to me like the government has really adjudicated the thing and merged it" left little room for disputes between the Interstate Commerce Commission and the attorney general's office. Since the formation of the Interagency Committee on Transport Mergers, the Justice Department imposed a legal rather than a regulatory framework on what was supposed to be a coordinated planning process. In his conversation with Clark, however, Johnson decisively shifted the balance of power back to the ICC. "It seems to me," the president observed, "like the Interstate Commerce Commission is charged with the law to determine whether it's in the public interest to merge or not and they determined that it was, and we agreed beforehand by memorandum by the Attorney General Kennedy that we would abide by that decision. And, it went against us, so we're not really complying with what we agreed in the memorandum, both Kennedy and Katzenbach, that's the way it looks to me."[515]

Johnson's support for the ICC also revealed his frustration with Donald Turner and with Ivy League experts in general. "I just wonder," he commented, "why it's not in the public interest to assume that the Interstate Commerce Commission knows as much about the effect of the merger and the wisdom of the merger and the economics of the merger as some damn Harvard professor." Even as he defended the ICC's prerogatives, the president also

asserted his right to shape national transportation policy. "I don't like to superimpose the judgment of some jerk lawyer over there for people who deal in these things every day. I don't want that lawyer's legal judgment to be superior to the president of the United States. . . . Who the hell is Turner? What special qualifications equip him to be mister God in these things? . . . Who the hell is this little jerk from Boston to come down and say, 'to hell with all of you?'"[516]

Johnson framed his support for the merger as the obligation to honor a commitment rather than a duty to uphold the principles of antitrust law. "I know all these people are going to think that I'm the guy that doubled 'em, and that's the way the ball always bounces," he complained. The Kennedy memo, he told Clark,

> had a good deal of appeal to me because first I thought, probably thought that way, and second I don't know how many government agencies a fella has to get cleaned up with before he finally gets out where he can operate. And I felt it was a pretty strong implication not only that Attorney General Kennedy feels that if the decision was reached that they could merge but that Katzenbach reaffirmed it and said that is his view too. They all knew it was mine. Now, the ball did bounce their way, and now for us to go back in and keep on fighting it, it looks like to me it was not just quite cricket.

Johnson acknowledged that he had never promised Saunders that the Justice Department would accept the merger but insisted that he was duty bound to honor the terms of Robert Kennedy's memo. "Two attorney generals [sic] told him that but it didn't amount to a goddamn thing. It's just like a Mexican certified check—bank draft—letter of credit," the president continued. "Every one of these people that had the assurance and thought that they had the thing worked out, and we had told they did have it worked out; they're going to say, well, you double-crossing son-of-a-bitch, and they have a right to. I feel I am myself. If Bobby Kennedy's letter and Nick Katzenbach's letter, and my general attitude, if a man had treat [sic] me that way I think I'd have a right to expect something out of it."[517]

Late that evening, Johnson called Califano and told him to arrange a meeting at 9:00 a.m. on Thanksgiving Day, one that included every senior federal official with any possible connection to the merger. The participants included Clark, from the Justice Department; Gardner Ackley, the chairman of the Council of Economic Advisers; fellow council member Arthur Okun; W. Willard Wirtz, the secretary of labor; Commerce Secretary John T. Connor; and Alan Boyd, soon to become the first secretary of transportation. Califano reviewed the latest draft of Marshall's brief, which, he recalled, "raised all sorts of questions about the merger and asked that the case be sent back to the ICC for a whole new round of proceedings." Most of the people in the room were quick to comment on the provisions. Ackley, Okun, and Connor defined the issue in terms of business efficiency and thus favored the rapid consolidation of the PRR and the NYC into the Penn Central. Wirtz indicated that employees would retain their jobs and that the potential for a stronger railroad network would undoubtedly produce benefits for workers in many other industries. Clark upheld the authority of the Justice Department, insisting that legal issues took precedence in all discussions of the merger. Boyd asserted that the formation of Penn Central was first and foremost a matter of transportation policy, which naturally fell under his purview. He demanded that Marshall file a brief indicating that the Justice Department was favorably disposed to the merger—an option that Johnson was willing to accept as a second-best alternative to his preference for no brief at all.[518]

Later that morning, Califano told Johnson that the discussions were hopelessly deadlocked. The president made another phone call, contacting someone he identified initially as "the best lawyer I know." Nearly two decades earlier, the legal acumen of Abraham Fortas enabled Johnson to win the somewhat irregular Texas senate race of 1948, preserving a political career that led to the post of senate majority leader and, eventually, the White House. Thereafter, Johnson relied on the legal counsel provided by Fortas, whom he nominated to the Supreme Court in 1965.[519]

On the afternoon of Thanksgiving Day, Fortas received the first of two phone calls from the ranch. The president of the United States asked the associate justice for advice, regarding the most effective way to undermine the authority of an attorney general and a solicitor general who were preparing arguments in a case pending before the Supreme Court. Califano considered the request to be "extraordinary," and even Johnson knew enough about the potential legal implications to order the tape recordings of those conversations to be destroyed. Over the course of two discussions with Johnson, Fortas shared his opinion that the Justice Department was usurping the authority of agencies and individuals—particularly Boyd—whose task it was to determine transportation policy. Fortas was not willing to endorse the president's no-brief recommendation, presumably because he thought it would be difficult for Clark, Marshall, and Turner to offer a convincing explanation for the abrupt reversal of course. Instead, Fortas insisted that the solicitor general should prepare a brief

that reflected Boyd's assessment of the merger. Fortas then called Califano, who was shocked to discover that "the best lawyer I know" was in fact an associate justice of the Supreme Court.[520] "I knew the President felt free to talk to Fortas about almost anything that troubled him," Califano recalled, "including constitutional issues that might someday come before the Court, but this was different. Johnson was talking to Fortas about what to put in a brief about to be filed with the Supreme Court in a pending case."[521]

Califano, who confided to Fortas that "my Thanksgiving had been ruined by the President," was now about to ruin someone else's Thanksgiving.[522] Thurgood Marshall was in Atlantic City when Califano called. Califano told the solicitor general that Johnson very much wanted the Justice Department to modify its brief in *Baltimore & Ohio v. United States*—although, sensibly, he did not mention that the advice had come from Fortas. "Marshall balked at what he considered an intrusion on his turf," Califano recalled. "He felt there was no way he could refrain from presenting his views to the Supreme Court in a case of this magnitude."[523]

At the president's request, Califano arranged two meetings on Saturday, November 26. At one, Ackley and Okun put pressure on Marshall. The representatives from the Council of Economic Advisers emphasized the president's desire to drop the proceedings. Before they concluded the hour-long discussion, they reminded the solicitor general about the need to act quickly to protect the PRR, the NYC, and especially the New Haven. They insisted that the merger was in the public interest, downplayed concerns regarding monopoly power, and suggested that the terms of the consolidation offered adequate protection for the smaller northeastern railroads. Marshall, Ackley recalled, reiterated his position that it was "inconceivable that the Solicitor General could fail to take a position before the Supreme Court." Ackley informed Califano that "Marshall is obviously unhappy with the situation in which he finds himself, and would like to find a way out. But he is being pressed very hard in the other direction by his staff." At the other meeting, Larry Levinson, the president's deputy special counsel, attempted to influence Donald Turner—although he declined to inform Turner of the near-simultaneous conference in which Ackley and Okun were doing the same thing to Marshall. Levinson found Turner to be flexible and pragmatic in his personal views regarding the situation. The assistant attorney general nonetheless insisted that the Justice Department had ample grounds for opposition to the merger. At some point during that day, Turner's immediate superior, Ramsey Clark, received a phone call from Peter Edelman, Robert

Kennedy's legislative assistant. Edelman emphasized that the senator "still favors the merger and feels that any delay will be harmful to the public interest," and he pointed out that both Kennedy and Katzenbach strongly recommended compliance with the August 1964 memo.[524]

While Marshall adamantly refused to withdraw all Justice Department opposition to the case, he was willing to submit a new brief that reflected the views of Alan Boyd rather than those of Ramsey Clark. Crucially, the solicitor general now conceded that the merger was consistent with the public interest, effectively abandoning all opposition on antitrust grounds and acknowledging the ICC's primacy in matters of transportation regulation. "We emphasize that, in questioning the Commission's procedure, we do not quarrel with the merits of the Penn-Central merger proposal itself," Marshall stated. "Indeed, the agencies of the Executive Branch that have substantive responsibilities for the formulation of economic and transportation policy believe that the merger is in the public interest and that its consummation should be promptly effected." The revised brief did not amount to Marshall's complete acquiescence to the merger, however. Most of the people who met with Califano on Thanksgiving morning agreed with Ramsey Clark's contention that it would be unwise to let the Erie Lackawanna, the Boston & Maine, and the Delaware & Hudson fend for themselves. Therefore, Marshall insisted, "the commission and the Court should not have allowed consummation of the Penn-Central merger until the fate of the smaller roads affected had been resolved." That language endorsed the conditions that the ICC stipulated on April 27, when the agency approved the examiners' recommendation in favor of the merger. Yet the Interstate Commerce Commission had not yet specified the precise nature of those protective conditions, nor had the commissioners determined whether the three companies would remain independent, become part of the Norfolk & Western system, or join the Penn Central. Until they resolved that issue, Marshall insisted, the Supreme Court should withhold for "a reasonable time" any ruling regarding the case, giving the ICC commissioners an opportunity to correct their error.[525]

Stuart Saunders had every reason to be delighted with the conversations that took place over Thanksgiving Week. He spent the holiday ensconced in the Hay-Adams Hotel in Washington, preparing for the ICC hearings that were set to resume on November 28. Saunders called Califano on that Monday morning and received assurances that the president had handled the situation. From that point forward, Califano promised, the Supreme Court "could retain jurisdiction over the case and simply have the ICC quickly correct certain procedural technicalities to permit the merger to proceed." Once the regulatory apparatus specified the fate of the three small railroads, the court could permit the October 4 ruling by the US District Court for the Southern District of New York to stand. Judge Friendly's temporary restraining order would be moot, and there could be no further legal challenges to the consolidation of the Pennsylvania Railroad and the New York Central.[526]

Califano promised more than the president could deliver, however, and Saunders's optimism did not adequately account for the complexity of the regulatory process. On November 28, the Interstate Commerce Commission concluded hearings on the indemnification arrangements for the Erie Lackawanna, the Delaware & Hudson, and the Boston & Maine. New York Central general counsel James Gray presented the strongest opposition, asserting that the ICC lacked the legal authority to indemnify the smaller lines against any loss of shareholder value that might be associated with the Penn Central merger. Representatives from the Norfolk & Western and the Chesapeake & Ohio were equally hostile toward the proposal. Their attorneys reiterated their contention that indemnification would at the very least raise the cost of acquiring any of the smaller lines and might eventually produce a cascading series of reparation payments tied to any future rail merger in the United States. The indemnification controversy, like others before it, seemed beyond the power of the ICC to resolve. The impasse suggested that the Supreme Court would after all be the ultimate arbiter of the Penn Central merger.[527]

As the fifth year of the merger battle drew to a close, there was little indication that the Interstate Commerce Commission would articulate a speedy resolution to the crisis involving the weak carriers in the Northeast. On December 5, the latest round of hearings began before the ICC examiners. Agency chairman John W. Bush told reporters that he was confident that the commission would resolve the indemnification issue, determine the inclusion of the smaller roads in a larger system, and settle the outcome of the N&W–C&O merger proposal—all before the end of the year. If he were correct, the Supreme Court would no longer have any reason to continue the *Baltimore & Ohio v. United States* case or to block the Penn Central merger. Bush's optimism was remarkable, given the glacial pace of the various regulatory and legal proceedings up to that point. Yet Bush acknowledged that the PRR and the NYC were beginning to experience serious financial difficulties and that the New Haven was sinking fast. Under those circumstances, he admitted, speed was of the essence. "I just don't believe that the Pennsylvania and the

Central, under any practical circumstance, would be able to hold off the consummation of their merger as long as it would take to decide the merger request of the Norfolk & Western and Chesapeake & Ohio railways," he observed, echoing language Saunders had used in ICC testimony a month earlier. "That's elementary to anybody."[528]

The Feud

Conditions inside the PRR's executive suite mirrored the regulatory chaos that enveloped the Penn Central case. Operating officials sought an infusion of capital funds to rebuild the physical plant and prepare for the service integration with the New York Central. The repeated delays in the approval process convinced many executives that those expenditures should begin as soon as possible, so that they would be ready for merger day. The anticipatory strategy ensured that the Pennsylvania Railroad would shoulder the costs associated with the merger, well before any of the corresponding savings could be realized. David Bevan, the PRR's chief financial officer, initially accepted the railroad's increased investments in equipment and facilities—provided that they could be conservatively financed through a combination of retained earnings, depreciation reserves, and judicious external borrowing. Beginning in 1964, however, Saunders's limited knowledge of railroad operations enabled division superintendents to advocate for massive increases in capital spending, without demonstrating a corresponding rate of return. By the summer of 1966, the problem had become so severe that Bevan was no longer willing to acquiesce to the seemingly unending demands for locomotives, cars, and betterments to the right-of-way.

In late August, Bevan received the proposed capital budget for 1967, and he was shocked to discover that operating personnel demanded a $232 million investment, including $175 million for cars and locomotives. Even though Saunders knew relatively little about operating or financial matters, he conceded that the amount was far too high and promised to reduce equipment purchases to $140 million. The concessions were insufficient to satisfy Bevan, who reiterated his long-standing assertions that massive capital expenditures were consistently failing to produce an adequate rate of return. He argued that the PRR could afford to spend no more than $85 million on equipment. Substantially greater amounts, Bevan emphasized, would imperil his ability to borrow the necessary funds. He was having trouble in that regard, as the days when the Pennsylvania Railroad could simply issue additional stocks or bonds had long since passed. The company

became increasingly reliant on commercial paper, high-interest loans that constituted financing of last resort. Bevan negotiated the initial arrangement with New York's First National City Bank in 1954—the first time any railroad had used that source of funds. The money, he emphasized, should be used solely in an emergency, and he was able to adhere to that policy for more than a decade. In the spring of 1965, he worked with First National for a similar, $30 million unsecured line of credit. Less than a year later, the amount increased to $50 million, coupled with an additional $50 million bridge loan that would become available in March 1968. Bevan warned that ongoing capital expenditures, coupled with that type of financing, might result in a downgrading of the railroad's credit rating.[529]

The battle over capital spending in turn shaped another disagreement between Saunders and Bevan. The PRR, and indeed all the eastern carriers, posted abysmally low rates of return during the postwar period. That situation discouraged investment, led to widespread assumptions that the railroads were dying, and made it more difficult to finance the betterments that would be necessary to integrate the operations of the Pennsylvania Railroad and the New York Central—and thereby generate the higher rates of return that investors demanded. Beginning in 1964, and not long after he became chairman, Saunders encouraged substantial increases in dividends. The move was justified, given the PRR's impressive gains in earnings over the preceding few years, but Saunders also thought it necessary to demonstrate that his leadership and support for the merger had produced financial benefits that would continue indefinitely. Saunders combined those two motives when he provided the investment analysts who were the PRR's most important creditors with an update on the state of the nation's railroads. "He assured the forum," transportation journalist Robert Bedingfield noted, "that the pay-off from new rate-making policies and the expenditure of billions of dollars of new equipment was just beginning."[530]

Saunders coupled those assurances with money. For each year between 1958 and 1962, the PRR paid dividends of just $0.25 per share. The rate doubled in 1963. The following September, and for the first time since 1957, the directors authorized the payment of a third-quarter dividend—a decision that cost the company $3.4 million. By year's end, investors received $1.25 per share. The largesse continued into 1965, when the PRR paid another third-quarter dividend, plus a special year-end dividend of $0.85. The year's total, $2.00 per share, gave shareholders the highest return they had experienced since the booming war years of 1942–1945. Few people expressed misgivings that the PRR's corporate earnings totaled just $2.45 per share. With nearly 82 percent of those earnings distributed to shareholders, however, the railroad was far from the historic—and prudent—standard of a dollar reinvested in the property to match each dollar awarded to investors. On July 27, 1966, the directors increased the quarterly dividend from $0.40 to $0.60 a share. Saunders justified the decision to reporters, highlighting the railroad's continued prosperity—even as he acknowledged that the company would need to make further increases in capital spending to provide the public with adequate service. Two days earlier, the Dow Jones railroad average set a new low for the year and heralded the beginning of a bear market. The Pennsylvania Railroad nonetheless continued to pay its investors well. In late November, it offered a supplemental dividend of $0.30 a share. The bonus raised the annual dividends to $2.30 per share, a 15 percent increase over the previous year. Observers marveled that the PRR, despite the financial setbacks of the railroads, had paid dividends every year since 1848, a longer tenure than any other company on the New York Stock Exchange.[531]

By the end of 1966, however, the PRR's dividend policies concerned Bevan almost as much as did the company's expenditures on equipment and infrastructure. He knew, as did the company's investors, that corporate earnings per share offered a reasonable indication of an appropriate level of dividends. The Pennsylvania Railroad was not one company, however. Instead, it was more than a hundred incorporated entities operating under one administrative framework. While the Pennsylvania Company and many other subsidiaries were refreshingly profitable, the Pennsylvania Railroad was not so fortunate. As such, Saunders favored the preparation of consolidated income statements that would disguise the poor performance associated with the company's rail service. The process began in early 1964, when Saunders boasted of a consolidated profit of $24 million, most of which came from nonrail subsidiaries. Bevan initially supported the issuance of consolidated income statements, as that practice was in keeping with the accounting methods at the conglomerates that were assuming increased importance in the American business landscape. As the economy began to decline through 1966 and into 1967, however, Bevan increasingly suspected that the consolidated financial statements were part of Saunders's broader strategy to manipulate the company's financial results in a manner that would justify large dividends and capital expenditures. He noted that the PRR, in comparison to the New York Central, distributed only a slightly larger percentage of its net earnings in the form of dividends. Based solely on the earnings of the core transportation operations, however, the NYC's dividends averaged between 40 and 48 percent of net earnings—an appropriate standard—while the rate on the PRR varied from 70 to 75 percent.[532]

Bevan's opposition to the restatement of earnings produced an irreparable break with Saunders and other key executives. In April 1967, the PRR reported a 5 percent reduction in freight volume during the first quarter of the year, accompanied by an even more substantial decline in net income. It was an ominous sign of things to come and suggested the necessity for immediate reductions in dividends and capital expenditures. Instead, they continued unabated—necessary, Saunders insisted, to maintain investor confidence and ensure that the railroad's facilities were prepared for the merger. By the end of 1967, and to Bevan's dismay, the PRR would disburse dividends that totaled 232 percent of the railroad's net income. That September, Bevan's staff calculated that the company's working capital was $57 million less than it had been a year earlier. The situation would be even worse—an $88 million decrease—if the company followed proper accounting protocols. Bevan warned Saunders that by the end of 1967 the railroad's cash balance would decline to $6 million—far below the $40 million that constituted the minimum necessary to pay bills and maintain bank balances. The finances of the Pennsylvania Company remained solid and could be used as the basis for the issuance of up to $75 million in bonds. Bevan could not do so, however, without exceeding the debt ceiling specified in the merger agreement with the New York Central. It would be possible to renegotiate the matter with NYC officials, but at the cost of negative publicity and the attendant disapprobation from the investment community. Increasingly, Bevan joined Saunders in the hope that the merger would be completed as quickly as possible, believing that the blending of the two railroads' finances would solve a multitude of problems.[533]

The chronic shortage of working capital added to Bevan's concern that Pennsylvania Railroad executives were routinely overestimating earnings and underestimating expenditures. His accounting techniques disclosed that division superintendents, whose careers in large measure depended on their ability to generate solid net earnings, drew down inventories without entering a corresponding expense. Operating officials, who were critical of Bevan's reluctance to countenance capital expenditures and his willingness to divert money into the diversification program, now became even more resolutely opposed to the railroad's chief financial officer. In late August, Bevan began compiling a dossier of letters, memoranda, and other materials, cataloging his interactions with Saunders and other executives. He kept his activities a secret, and he intended to use what he called his diary as evidence to protect himself, should circumstances require.[534]

Matters came to a head in November 1967 as executives anxiously awaited final approval of the merger. By late August, it was evident that the prosperity of the preceding years had disappeared. Saunders accordingly informed one of Bevan's subordinates that it would be necessary to generate an additional $5 million in third-quarter revenues, to maintain a facade of financial stability. Bevan dismissed the incident, apparently believing that Saunders wanted to create additional business rather than manipulate the corporate accounts. A few days later, Bevan informed Saunders of the propensity of division managers to understate inventory consumption and indicated that a correction would add $4 million to the PRR's third-quarter expenditures. Saunders balked and, to buy time, promised that the vice president in charge of operations, David Smucker, would investigate the matter. Even though Saunders avoided the inclusion of the inventory charges, the publicly announced third-quarter financial results were still dismal. Operating revenues decreased by nearly 10 percent, and profits were 41 percent below the corresponding period in 1966. Corporate earnings fell from $4.94 to $2.93 a share. The results would have been far worse had it not been for the reliance on consolidated financial statements, as the profits on the PRR's rail operations declined by almost 78 percent. If there was any consolation, it was that the New York Central posted results that were far worse, with a $3.9 million third-quarter loss. Saunders blamed the problems on strikes on the railroads and in the automobile industry and claimed that the declines were only temporary. The final three months of the year, he promised, "will be much better, which should be very helpful in our over-all results for 1967."[535]

Once Saunders promised excellent returns for the final quarter of 1967, he was determined to achieve them. The matter of the understated inventory levels had not yet been resolved, and Bevan indicated that a $3 million charge would be necessary in the fourth quarter. Saunders again demanded postponement. He considered the amount to be trivial and suggested that the discrepancy would be unnoticeable, following the integration of NYC and PRR accounts. Bevan considered that request to be tantamount to fraud and threatened to bring the matter to the attention of the Interstate Commerce Commission. Saunders and his assistant, Basil Cole, encouraged Bevan to step into line. Failing there, Cole pressured William Cook, the comptroller, to undermine Bevan's authority and accept the postponement. Bevan, incensed at the latest challenge

to his authority, threatened to resign. His defection, on the eve of the merger, would be little short of catastrophic, and Saunders promised that he would no longer interfere with matters of accounting and finance. Whether he would honor his promise remained to be seen. The growing feud between the two executives, visible only to those who were in the executive suite, was an inauspicious portent for the future. It also undermined the organizational capabilities of the Pennsylvania Railroad, as the company entered the final stretch of the interminable merger process.[536]

The Last Full Year

Pennsylvania Railroad executives and attorneys were fully occupied during January 1967 as they fought regulatory and judicial battles to save the Penn Central merger. The ICC hearings on the inclusion of the New Haven—along with the railroad's passenger service—began on January 16. Trustee Richard Joyce Smith testified that the Penn Central offered the only conceivable option for ending the receivership and preventing the company from suspending operations. Representatives of the New Haven's bondholders were less committed to the maintenance of operations. Faced with the ongoing delays in the resolution of the company's fate, they concluded that liquidation would be a surer way to recoup a portion of their investment. Smith acknowledged that abandonment was "not in the best interests of the railroad or the public," but he suggested that the scrap value of the New Haven might be as much as $160 million. The sum was slightly greater than the $140 million purchase price negotiated with the PRR and the NYC. That discrepancy caused lawyers representing New Haven bondholders to demand that the railroad be dismantled and sold off piecemeal. That arrangement would wreck efforts by politicians in New York and New England to preserve commuter and intercity passenger service. Such draconian tactics were also likely to provoke multiple lawsuits that would delay the resolution of the New Haven's finances—and thus the consummation of the Penn Central merger—by many years. Walter Grant, the New York Central's vice president for finance, repeated his assertions that the Penn Central would be doing everyone a favor by accepting the New Haven at any price. "The Central and the Pennsylvania considered and continue to consider the New Haven as a loss operation incapable of being transformed into a profitable concern," he emphasized. As if to underscore his remarks, the New Haven posted an $11.5 million deficit for 1966—a figure that represented no more than a modest improvement over the $15.1 million shortfall incurred during the preceding year.

In 1964, when he first began negotiations with the trustees, Grant insisted that the company was not even worth a dollar, then recommended a fair purchase price of $41 million, and grudgingly accepted a negotiated settlement of $140 million. By February 1967, however, Grant suggested that the need to assume the New Haven's outstanding obligations would raise the cost to the Penn Central to $238.8 million. It was an amount that, even under the most optimistic projections, would not be recouped until at least eight years into the merger.[537]

Then, on March 27, the Supreme Court issued its ruling in *Baltimore & Ohio v. United States*. The outcome reflected Johnson's efforts to undermine the authority of the Justice Department but was nonetheless not as favorable as either the president or Saunders had hoped. Procedurally, the justices overturned the October 4, 1966, decision by the US District Court for the Southern District of New York that blocked further legal challenges to the merger. The 5–4 verdict reflected Thurgood Marshall's concession that the formation of the Penn Central was consistent with the public interest and thus an acknowledgment that the Interstate Commerce Commission held jurisdiction. "At the outset," Justice Tom C. Clark emphasized, "we make it clear that we do not pass on the validity of the merger." Clark, writing for the majority, nonetheless declined to endorse the ICC's handling of transportation planning. He agreed with Marshall's contention that the agency failed to make adequate provision for the Erie Lackawanna, the Delaware & Hudson, and the Boston & Maine, either in the existing Norfolk & Western system or in the proposed Penn Central. "We hold only that, under the uncontradicted findings of the Commission," Clark wrote, "it was necessary for it to conclude the inclusion proceedings, as to the protected railroads, prior to permitting consummation of the merger" between the Pennsylvania Railroad and the New York Central.[538]

A slim majority of the justices, therefore, were unwilling to accept the assurances of the ICC commissioners that adequate protective conditions could be developed and put into action, following the implementation of the Penn Central merger. Instead, they demanded that the ICC articulate those provisions prior to the consolidation of the PRR and the NYC—afterward would be too late. Echoing the warning that Ramsey Clark issued to President Johnson the previous November, Justice Clark emphasized that "our experience with other mergers, and common sense as well, indicate that the 'scrambling' goes fast, but the unscrambling is interminable, and seldom effectively accomplished." Happily, Justice Clark concluded, the ICC's reconsideration of the inclusion provisions should

"entail only a very short delay before the Commission"—a small price to pay, he suggested, to avoid a catastrophic and irreversible restructuring of the eastern railroad network. Iconoclastic justice William O. Douglas went much further, issuing a concurring opinion in which he decried the absence of a coordinated national transportation policy, called for an investigation into the debilitating influence of "predatory finance," and suggested that the nationalization of the railroads might be appropriate. "In the context of these modern mergers," he warned, "there is the terrible specter that the Federal Government may be creating new Frankensteins who will be running the country in a way that people can ill afford."[539]

Abe Fortas was less than pleased at the results of his behind-the-scenes efforts to undermine the Justice Department's opposition to the merger. Astonishingly, he did not recuse himself from the case—perhaps because an honest account of his reasons for doing so might result in impeachment proceedings against himself and quite possibly the president. To the amazement of Joseph Califano, Fortas volunteered to write a blistering dissent, in which he asserted that the majority ruling represented "a reversion to the days of judicial negation of governmental action in the economic sphere." Fortas downplayed the role of the Justice Department and emphasized that only the agencies associated with transportation matters—the ICC and Alan Boyd's Department of Transportation, which was set to begin operations four days later—could properly evaluate the Penn Central merger. "Indeed," he noted, "the Solicitor General has represented to the Court that 'the agencies of the Executive Branch that have substantive responsibilities for the formulation of economic and transportation policy believe that the merger is in the public interest, and that its consummation should be promptly effected.'" That language had an interesting pedigree, as it reflected a statement that Fortas made to Johnson, conveyed in turn to Califano, who persuaded Marshall to place it in his brief, so that the associate justice who suggested the idea in the first place was able to quote the words in his dissenting opinion before the court. The process did not, perhaps, reflect the epitome of judicial integrity or the ideal functioning of the administrative state.[540]

Fortas also echoed the president's contention that the judiciary should avoid interference in a matter that had been settled by a regulatory agency. "A vast realignment of the sort involved here always has elements of the unique," he concluded, "and only a doctrinaire approach, separated by the miles that lie between the quiet of theoretical condemnation in this Court and the pressures of realistic problems in the administrative agency, can explain this Court's readiness to insist that an unknown and unknowable solution be prescribed in advance." Yet Fortas exhibited little praise for the Interstate Commerce Commission, and he observed that "the history of ICC proceedings is a source book for dilatory tactics and a monument to the successful burial of good projects by over-elaborate procedures manipulated by experts in the art. Meanwhile, national policy continues unfulfilled; urgent national needs for improved long-haul and local rail service are impeded; the desperate erosion of the New Haven continues at a rapid pace, and the public and communities urgently in need of improved rail service continue to suffer."[541]

Fortas's harsh language reflected the momentous nature of the disaster associated with *Baltimore & Ohio v. United States*, for the Pennsylvania Railroad, the New York Central, and especially the New Haven. The decision meant that the Penn Central merger could not proceed until the ICC decided what to do with the Erie Lackawanna, the Boston & Maine, and the Delaware & Hudson. That process could take years, particularly as the Supreme Court had greenlighted the legal challenges that were certain to follow any regulatory outcome. It also meant that the Justice Department would continue its involvement in the merger case—ostensibly to protect the three smaller carriers, but also as a backdoor mechanism to address antitrust issues and curtail the ICC's restructuring of the railroad network.

Executives from the three railroads that were to become part of the Penn Central offered varying reactions to the setback. Saunders indicated that he was "not disheartened by the decision, since it appears that only a brief delay will be involved." Wall Street was less optimistic, and the announcement of the judicial ruling triggered nearly a 1 percent drop in the Dow Jones rail average. The executive vice president of the New York Central lamented that the court's decision "will have adverse effects on the health of the entire Eastern railroad picture." The trustees of the New Haven hoped the ruling "would not prove fatal" yet acknowledged that further delay would produce "serious additional questions concerning continued operations." Underscoring the severity of the crisis, the trustees asked the federal judge supervising the reorganization whether the New Haven "can and should be continued in operation." With public support for passenger operations woefully inadequate, time was running out to save the company.[542]

Representatives from the two systems that were to form the other great eastern railroad network likewise exhibited little support for the decision in *Baltimore & Ohio v. United States*. Executives at the Norfolk & Western faced the possibility that the ICC, now operating under clear instructions from the Supreme Court, might force the inclusion of the Erie Lackawanna, the Boston & Maine, and the Delaware & Hudson in the 1964 Nickel Plate merger—but without making a commitment regarding the fate of their proposal to consolidate with the Chesapeake & Ohio. The forced inclusion of the three railroads, moreover, would clear the way for the Penn Central merger, long before there was any realistic chance that the ICC might approve the N&W–C&O combination. Gregory S. DeVine, the president of the combined C&O–B&O system, was even more critical of the court's decision, which set an uncomfortable precedent for judicial interference in the ICC's oversight of mergers. If the Penn Central "gets caught in the switches and dissolves," DeVine did not "think there is any chance" that he could secure approval for consolidation with the Norfolk & Western. His N&W counterpart, Herman Pevler, testified before the ICC that he would continue to pursue negotiations with the C&O and the B&O, with scant concern for the fate of the Penn Central—but he declined to explain how the courts might delay one merger but not the other.[543]

In an unfortunate case of bad timing, the Supreme Court's decision in *Baltimore & Ohio v. United States* coincided with the initial stages of the collapse of the eastern railroad network. Economic growth slowed during the second half of 1966 and into the beginning of 1967. The cost of the Vietnam War, without a corresponding tax increase, caused a steady gain in the rate of inflation. By the end of the year, the post office terminated most Railway Post Office routes, ending a source of income that subsidized many passenger trains. The combination of declining revenues and rising costs ensured that the Pennsylvania Railroad and the New York Central were no longer making "big money," as Ramsey Clark asserted to President Johnson. The PRR's net earnings fell from $90.3 million in 1966 to $60.3 million in 1967. The combined return on investment for the two companies that would form the core of the Penn Central declined from 2.7 percent in 1966 to 0.8 percent in 1967.[544]

The entire structure of the eastern railroad network now depended on the disposition of the three companies championed by the Justice Department (the Erie Lackawanna, the Boston & Maine, and the Delaware & Hudson) and the two other lines (the Reading and the Jersey Central) that were to form a part of Dereco. Yet even before the end of the year, it was apparent that efforts to merge the northeastern carriers into prosperity were doomed to failure. On March 22, the Jersey Central declared bankruptcy for the fourth and final time. Pevler emphasized that the collapse of the Jersey Central "does not kill the Dereco plan," but his reassurances were lost in a rising tide of problems affecting one railroad after another. At the Boston & Maine, a committee of dissident shareholders attempted to seize control of the company and depose the railroad's management. On April 6, William White, the board chairman and CEO who guided the Erie Lackawanna toward a modicum of prosperity, died of a heart attack in the office of the company physician. He lived just long enough to complete a message to the shareholders, and President Gregory W. Maxwell shouldered the unenviable task of reading it at the annual meeting. The profits of 1966 had disappeared, replaced by a deficit for the first quarter of the new year. Maxwell informed holders of income bonds and common and preferred stock that they would probably not see any interest or dividend payments in the foreseeable future. The company was $13.6 million in arrears on its obligations to investors, and more than $50 million in debt would mature between 1969 and 1973. Shareholders demanded a complete overhaul of the board of directors—not to restore the company to profitable, independent operation but instead to find a merger partner that would save it. Norfolk & Western executives, who wanted to avoid the Erie Lackawanna's third of a billion dollars of indebtedness, became even more determined to block inclusion in the merger agreement with the Nickel Plate. Their alternative, Dereco, was equally unpalatable to Erie Lackawanna officials, and Maxwell informed shareholders that the Dereco plan "is dead."[545]

The continuing problems on the railroads forced Lyndon Johnson to intervene more aggressively, to secure approval of the Penn Central merger. On May 16, the front page of the *New York Times* carried an above-the-fold photograph of the president, walking toward a meeting in Windsor Locks, Connecticut. Trooping along behind him were the governors of all six New England states. Attorney General Ramsey Clark, Secretary of Transportation Alan Boyd, and ICC chairman William Tucker were also in attendance. During the two-hour session, Johnson promised improved communication "between the White House and the State House." Much of the conversation involved the New Haven, as representatives from Massachusetts, Rhode Island, Connecticut, and New York shared their concern that the railroad would suspend operations unless the creation of the Penn Central happened quickly. The president promised to issue a "directive that immediate action be planned" to rescue the New Haven. He suggested that the governors travel to Washington the following week, for further discussions. Governor Dempsey of Connecticut spoke for his colleagues when he announced that

he was "delighted" with Johnson's "grasp" of the New Haven matter. Clark seemed to be the only person in the room who was not delighted, perhaps because he received the designation of scapegoat. The governors "yelled at me for opposing the merger before the ICC," he recalled, "citing the argument that the New Haven had to be saved." The yelling continued on board Air Force One, during the hour-long flight back to Andrews Air Force Base. This time it was the president who made it clear that the Justice Department had created what appeared to be an insurmountable crisis.[546]

Johnson's determination to rescue the New Haven soon prodded the ICC into action. Within days of the Windsor Locks conference, ICC chairman Tucker promised presidential aide Marvin Watson that the commission would do whatever it could to facilitate the Penn Central merger. Watson informed the president that "this is a result of your recent meeting with the New England Governors" and called the governors in question to reassure them of the ICC's cooperation. On June 9, little more than three weeks after Johnson's trip to Connecticut, the commission satisfied the requirements of the March Supreme Court ruling in *Baltimore & Ohio v. United States*. The decision, authored by Chairman Tucker and announced on June 12, ordered the Norfolk & Western to assume control of the Erie Lackawanna, the Boston & Maine, and the Delaware & Hudson, effective July 18, even before the Penn Central initiated operations.[547] "The commission directed that three of railroading's unwanted children," transportation journalist Robert Bedingfield observed, would "be adopted by the wealthy Norfolk & Western Railway." The ruling came as a relief to executives from the three beleaguered railroads, who had finally found a place of refuge.[548] New Yorkers were also satisfied, as the inclusion of the Erie Lackawanna in the N&W prevented the Penn Central from establishing a near monopoly of rail transportation in the area. No one, however, was more pleased than Stuart Saunders and his fellow PRR and NYC officials. With the survival of the three weak railroads assured, the Penn Central merger could take place as early as August 1.[549]

The only people who were not happy, it seemed, were representatives from the Norfolk & Western. Chairman Tucker suggested that the company would benefit from the Erie Lackawanna's access to New York, but Herman Pevler was more reticent. To his dismay, the ICC required the N&W to accept the three foundering railroads prior to regulatory approval of the company's merger with the Chesapeake & Ohio. Moreover, while Dereco protected the N&W from the EL's massive debt, stock ownership was another matter entirely. Tucker endorsed the ratio proposed by EL executives, in exchange for stock in the N&W. The cost of including the Erie Lackawanna in Dereco was far more than what the company's securities were worth.[550] Pevler labeled the exchange rate "ridiculous," which was not a good sign. The N&W's protest with the ICC a month later added further adjectives, including "outrageous," "unconscionable," and "unlawful." The words bespoke further interminable delays in the inclusion of the three smaller carriers—and, as the Supreme Court decreed, until that matter was resolved, there would be no Penn Central merger.[551]

Pevler could take some comfort that the ICC's inclusion order gave him another opportunity to delay the Penn Central merger until he completed his proposed consolidation of the N&W with the C&O–B&O system. On the day following the announcement from the Interstate Commerce Commission, Norfolk & Western attorneys asked the US District Court in Roanoke, Virginia, to set aside the directive. By the end of the week, they were in New York, where the September 1966 suit in the US District Court was still in process. They asked Judge Friendly to delay the Penn Central merger until the ICC's order could be adjudicated. Legal representatives from the Erie Lackawanna were equally busy in Roanoke and in New York, supporting an ICC decision that was exceedingly favorable to their company. The opposing briefs contained only one element in common—that the Penn Central merger should be postponed indefinitely, until the judiciary resolved the terms of the Erie Lackawanna's inclusion in the Norfolk & Western. No one knew how long that process might take. As Judge Friendly met in chambers with lawyers from nearly a dozen railroads, it was reasonable to assume that the delays would be extensive.[552]

By the end of June, moreover, it was evident that Johnson had not yet succeeded in bringing the Department of Justice under control. Stuart Saunders was in San Francisco on June 23, telling reporters that he remained "committed to fighting the N.&W.-C.&O.'s merger plan," yet he expressed confidence that he could overcome the legal obstacles that those companies were using to block the Penn Central consolidation. "I am still very hopeful that our merger won't be enjoined by Judge Friendly's court," he announced. On the same day, three thousand miles to the east, federal attorneys in New York were asking Friendly to prevent the union of the Pennsylvania Railroad and the New York Central. It was the third time the ICC and the Justice Department were in opposition regarding a merger that both sides now agreed was in the public interest. In the latest—and final—iteration of the dispute, the ICC commissioners argued that they had provided a

mechanism to protect the Erie Lackawanna, the Boston & Maine, and the Delaware & Hudson, precisely as the Supreme Court demanded. They acknowledged that legal appeals were inevitable but that they must not be allowed to delay the process. "It is difficult to believe that a majority of the [Supreme] court could have intended an automatic and continuing stay of consummation of the merger merely because somebody filed a suit, on some ground, in some court, challenging some aspect" of their decree, the ICC's lawyers argued. Representatives from the attorney general's office, in contrast, insisted on the resolution of all possible legal challenges to the ICC's directive for the inclusion of the three railroads in the Norfolk & Western. "The plain intendment of the Supreme Court's decision," they insisted, "is that final determination of their fate comprehends both a decision by the commission for their inclusion in a major Eastern railway system and final affirmation by the courts if timely judicial proceedings are instituted to challenge the commission's order." Given the multitude of lawsuits in opposition to the ICC's directive, that process would take many months, if not years.[553]

Saunders's penchant for dealmaking soon added further impediments to the Penn Central merger. The Reading and the Jersey Central did not join the September 1966 lawsuit seeking to block the consolidation, although they did demand the same degree of indemnification that the ICC was willing to grant to the Erie Lackawanna, the Boston & Maine, and the Delaware & Hudson. As such, they were the only two of the five presumptive Dereco roads that lay beyond the judicial umbrella provided by the Justice Department and the Supreme Court. Since then, however, the Jersey Central plunged into bankruptcy, and its trustees were seeking salvation anywhere they could. They approached Saunders and inquired whether their company might be included in the Penn Central. From an operational and financial perspective, the Jersey Central had little to offer. Until it could find a home, however, the consolidation of the PRR and the NYC could not proceed. The same was true of the Reading, which controlled the Jersey Central prior to the March 1967 bankruptcy filing. The chaos that followed the June 12 announcement of the ICC's disposition of the EL, the B&M, and the D&H made that issue more pressing and increased the likelihood of further lawsuits. At the end of June, Saunders made a preemptive arrangement with Reading president Charles E. Bertrand. Neither the PRR nor the NYC would oppose the inclusion of the Reading and the Jersey Central in the Chesapeake & Ohio-Baltimore & Ohio system, which meant that the two foundering companies would likely become a part of the merger with the Norfolk & Western as well. In return, neither the Reading nor the Jersey Central would join the latest round of lawsuits seeking to block the Penn Central merger. If for some reason the C&O–B&O would not accept the two companies, then the Penn Central would give them safe harbor.[554]

The problem was that neither the Reading nor the Jersey Central were truly independent companies. The Chesapeake & Ohio owned more than 90 percent of the Baltimore & Ohio, while that company owned 38 percent of the Reading, which in turn oversaw the Jersey Central. Gregory DeVine, the president of both the C&O and the B&O, was extremely solicitous of the two carriers, even though one was bankrupt and the other was on the verge of collapse. If nothing else, they offered the proposed N&W–C&O–B&O system access to New Jersey and eastern Pennsylvania. Like Herman Pevler at the N&W, DeVine was willing to accept the Reading and the Jersey Central as a part of Dereco, which would prevent their financial problems from infecting their more prosperous parents. DeVine was less interested in an outright merger with the Reading and the Jersey Central, as the investors in those companies preferred. More than that, however, he could not countenance the addition of the two companies to the Penn Central. DeVine put pressure on Bertrand to end discussions with Saunders, a move that caused a schism within the Reading's board of directors. Bertrand put down the revolt and yielded to DeVine's entreaties. The Reading soon joined the list of companies seeking an injunction against the Penn Central merger. At the end of August, the three dissident Reading directors filed suit against their colleagues, alleging that DeVine's influence had prevented the board from acting in the best interest of the company's investors. The internal dissension among the Reading's directors, who acted like drunken sailors brawling on the deck of a sinking ship, did the company no favors. From Saunders's perspective, moreover, his meddling in the affairs of the Jersey Central had only made a bad situation even worse.[555]

The terms for the inclusion of the New Haven in Penn Central continued to bedevil judges and regulators alike. The most aggrieved party was Oscar Gruss & Son, representatives of the New Haven's bondholders, who objected to the two-phase inclusion plan proposed by the trustees. "If the merger is consummated first," Gruss complained, "there can be no assurance that the New Haven will ever be included. If inclusion of the New Haven is frustrated for any reason, the damage to the first mortgage bondholders will be utterly irredeemable." The Supreme Court declined to intervene, indicating that Gruss should await the outcome of the ICC's hearings.[556] Those proceedings ended

four days later, on May 12, when examiner Arthur S. Present brought to an end seventeen weeks of testimony. Final arguments before the full commission would not begin until June 15, and complainants could file briefs as late as July 17. Gruss was unwilling to wait—and believed that the ICC was prepared to ignore the bondholders' rights in the interest of maintaining service on the New Haven. Joined by Chase Manhattan Bank and a bondholders' committee, Gruss took the matter to the US Circuit Court of Appeals. On May 29, the court ruled that the New Haven trustees could not transfer the company to the Penn Central until they had resolved the claims of the bondholders. In a worst-case scenario, the conflict between the trustees and the creditors would require reorganization and thus the approval of both the ICC and the New Haven bankruptcy court—a process that could take years. Even if the appeals court authorized liquidation, the piecemeal disposition of the New Haven's assets could not take place until and unless the ICC authorized abandonment. Like the still-disputed inclusion terms associated with the Erie Lackawanna, the Boston & Maine, and the Delaware & Hudson, the latest judicial ruling provided yet another impediment to the Penn Central merger and the ultimate salvation of the New Haven. It was hardly surprising that Robert Kennedy expressed frustration on behalf of his New York constituents, and Americans in general. The regulatory process was "not as fair, equitable and expeditious" as it should be, Kennedy complained, and he made a particular reference to the stalled Penn Central merger as "an example of the administrative process gone awry."[557]

Gruss and his fellow bondholders were fully justified in their suspicions that the political pressure to maintain the New Haven's passenger service took precedence over the legal rights of the bondholders and other creditors. An attorney representing the state of Connecticut asked the Interstate Commerce Commission to order temporary inclusion. That step would enable the PRR and the NYC to operate the line—and thus consummate their merger—prior to the sale of the New Haven and the resolution of that company's bankruptcy. In early August, the ICC took note of the New Haven's "worsening financial condition" and ordered the Penn Central to begin operating the New Haven on merger day. If the courts still interfered with the purchase agreement that Saunders and Perlman had negotiated, then a leasing arrangement must "be ready as an alternative immediately available upon consummation of the Penn-Central merger."[558]

A resolution of the New Haven's financial arrangements was of little consequence if the company collapsed prior to inclusion in the Penn Central. In August, New York senator

Jacob Javits arranged a meeting at the White House, one that included representatives from the Department of Defense, the US Post Office, and the Department of Transportation, to plead for as much as $10 million in emergency federal assistance. His Connecticut colleague, Abraham Ribicoff, suggested that Transportation Secretary Boyd had done virtually nothing to help the struggling company, and reminded his fellow senators that "the end of the New Haven's cash resources is only a few months away." Ribicoff suggested that either money from the Office of High Speed Ground Transportation or a Department of Housing and Urban Development demonstration grant could rescue the company. With the line's cash reserves well below $5 million and falling rapidly, there was nonetheless too little time to wait on the vagaries of the federal appropriations process. At the end of August, PRR and NYC officials agreed to create a $25 million loan fund, to be made available to the New Haven as soon as the Penn Central merger took place.[559] They expected that the additional cash would keep the company solvent for at least three years, long enough to resolve the issues associated with the bondholders and other creditors. While that money did not exactly constitute a bribe, it was obvious that it would only be made available if the ICC ignored the concerns of the New Haven bondholders and gave prompt approval to the Penn Central merger.[560]

Mollified by the $25 million pledge of support from Penn Central, the ICC speedily resolved the New Haven's fate. The initial merger would involve only the Pennsylvania Railroad and the New York Central. The New Haven inclusion terms would be decided later—perhaps much later—with the final purchase price likewise yet to be determined. For the moment, however, the ICC concluded that the New Haven's liquidation value was $125 million, significantly lower than the $230.3 million claimed by the company's trustees.[561] The more meaningful number was $159 million, the amount that the Penn Central would spend to acquire the bankrupt New Haven—a company no one wanted—and continue its freight, passenger, and commuter service. In recognition of the New Haven's chronic deficits, the ICC ordered the Penn Central to assume that company's entire operating loss, prior to the date of inclusion. Mercifully, the amount was capped at $5 million in any one year.[562]

When they released their decision on November 21, the commissioners showed little sympathy for complaints by PRR and NYC officials that they would have to spend an exorbitant amount of money for the New Haven. "Calling upon Penn-Central to pay more than the NH is worth as a going concern is not unreasonable," they observed. "For

the scope of our inquiry as to fair and equitable terms may reasonably go beyond the mere valuation of the carrier to be acquired. The Penn-Central merger (which will bring substantial dollar savings to the merger applicants) was approved with the thought that some of the merger savings would be available specifically to ward off a liquidation and shutdown of the NH so that adequate transportation service would remain available to the public which now relies on the NH." That statement was starkly at variance with the initial recommendations of examiners Lyle and Darmstadter. Yet it constituted only the latest of many indications that the rescue of the New Haven constituted the principal justification for regulatory approval of the Penn Central merger.[563]

Even as they burdened the Penn Central with the overpriced wreckage of the New Haven, the commissioners had little patience with the efforts of Gruss and other bondholders to postpone the merger until their claims were adjudicated. "Delaying such a decision, as advocated by the Committee and Gruss, until NH's reorganization is completed would most assuredly preclude a timely rescue of the NH as an operational common carrier," they emphasized,

> for there could be no hope that Penn-Central would be authorized in time to assume operation of NH before the latter exhausts its funds and shuts down. The choice is clear: either the public at large is forced to stand in the wings awaiting progress in transportation while the NH creditors haggle on stage over the wasting corpus of the NH estate, or, on the other hand, the overall objectives of the law are served, with the broad public interest brought into the scene in the form of improved service through a consummated Penn-Central merger including an operational NH, while the NH creditors are freed to litigate at will the distribution of their estate.

It was soon apparent that litigation was unlikely to be successful. Within a week, the Justice Department indicated that it, too, placed a far higher value on the preservation of the New Haven than on the rights of the bondholders or the fate of the Erie Lackawanna, the Boston & Maine, and the Delaware & Hudson. Prompt approval of the Penn Central merger was vital, the department's brief indicated, "if the New Haven is to survive as a railroad."[564]

For trustee Richard Joyce Smith, it was an encouraging sign, but one that might have come too late. On December 15, Lyndon Johnson expressed confidence that the Penn Central merger would soon win judicial approval—but "in the meantime," he noted, "the New Haven is close to financial disaster. Within months it will not be able to meet its payroll. It needs help now." That assistance came in the form of a $28.4 million grant from the Department of Housing and Urban Development, to purchase new commuter equipment and rebuild the New Haven's catenary and signaling systems. The federal government would also expedite payment of a $500,000 award from the Office of High Speed Ground Transportation and forgive $1.7 million loaned to the company. "These actions are not the final answers for the New Haven," Johnson acknowledged, but "they do help avert an immediate crisis." The assistance came barely in time. The New Haven's operating deficit for the first eight months of the year reached $15 million, well above the $8.2 million during the corresponding period in 1966. The company's trustees estimated that by the end of February 1968, they would have no more than $850,000 in the bank. Federal aid notwithstanding, without prompt implementation of the Penn Central merger, the New Haven had only weeks to live.[565]

As the ICC and the president were prioritizing the rescue of the New Haven, changes at the Department of Justice also worked in the Penn Central's favor. Ramsey Clark spent nearly four months as acting attorney general, before formally taking office on March 10, 1967. The delay was in part the result of a potential conflict of interest, as his father was a justice on the Supreme Court. Tom C. Clark retired from the court on June 12, enabling Johnson to nominate a replacement the following day. His choice was Thurgood Marshall, the solicitor general who insisted that it would be inconceivable for the attorney general's office to stand aside in the largest merger case in American history. Marshall's nomination was an important civil rights milestone, one that Johnson acknowledged when he emphasized that "it is the right thing to do, the right time to do it, the right man and the right place." It was also the right thing to do and the right time to do it for Stuart Saunders and other supporters of the Penn Central merger. As his nomination worked its way through the Senate Committee on the Judiciary, Marshall left ongoing prosecutorial efforts to Erwin Griswold, slated to be the new solicitor general. Griswold, who would not officially assume his new responsibilities until October 23, was sympathetic to the "no brief" strategy that Johnson preferred. On July 20, and under Griswold's direction, the Justice Department asked the US District Court in New York to prohibit the filing of additional lawsuits related to the merger—a move designed to halt the proliferation of legal actions that emerged after the ICC announced the protection provisions for the Erie Lackawanna, the Boston & Maine, and the Delaware & Hudson. For the first time, the Justice Department was acting to expedite rather than delay the creation of Penn Central. The request, seconded

by the Interstate Commerce Commission, also represented the end of the long-standing dispute between the two agencies.[566]

While legal actions were still pending in Pennsylvania and Virginia, only two courts now mattered. One was the District Court in New York, where the lawsuits to block the merger had first begun in September 1966. The other was the US Supreme Court, which had demanded adequate protection for the three smaller railroads, without disputing that the merger was in the public interest. The justices in Washington possessed the authority to dismiss all legal challenges to the union of the Pennsylvania Railroad and the New York Central—and would likely do so, if they believed that the ICC adequately implemented the protective conditions stipulated in *Baltimore & Ohio v. United States.*

The legal battles in New York resumed in September. On September 5, lawyers from virtually every railroad in the eastern United States filed briefs asking the district court for an indefinite postponement of the merger. They included representatives from the Norfolk & Western, the C&O–B&O system, the Western Maryland, the Reading, the Erie Lackawanna, and the Boston & Maine, all of whom wanted the three judges to annul the inclusion and indemnification provisions in the ICC's June 12 order. Delaware & Hudson attorneys continued their request for delay, even though Frederic C. Dumaine—who took charge of the company only six weeks earlier—announced that he no longer supported that policy. "The sooner they get on with the job, the better off we'll be," Dumaine asserted, leading observers to question whether the D&H had a consistent policy on the matter. Dumaine boasted that his company was highly profitable and could readily form the nucleus of an independent system that included the Boston & Maine. That was an outcome Saunders still favored, causing Norfolk & Western attorneys to charge that the PRR's chairman had made yet another backroom deal to expedite the union with the New York Central. When hearings began on September 18, Judge Friendly spent considerable time attempting to determine the Delaware & Hudson's position on the merger. The issue created further delays, as the company's lawyers were now requesting the court to enforce rather than block the ICC inclusion order. That suit would not be heard until September 28, ten days after what Friendly had earlier promised would be the final legal action relating to the Penn Central merger that would take place in his courtroom.[567]

Not until October 19 did the merger clear its penultimate legal barrier. Judge Friendly's district court in New York upheld the terms of the ICC's June 12 inclusion order. In addition to blocking suits by the N&W and other eastern railroads, the court dismissed with prejudice the legal action undertaken by Milton Shapp and by the city of Scranton. The same was true of efforts by Oscar Gruss & Son to protect the New Haven bondholders. "We are elated," observed ICC attorney Fritz R. Kahn. "We couldn't be happier" at a decision that "went way beyond our expectations." Kahn clearly viewed the outcome as a vindication of his agency's regulatory principles, when in truth it had far more to do with political pressure from the Johnson administration.[568]

Following the ruling, Saunders and Perlman issued a joint statement, declaring that the merger would be consummated "at an early date," perhaps as soon as December 1. Regulators, bankers, and politicians were equally optimistic. The PRR's stock rose $0.75 a share, while the NYC's went up by $1.62. New Haven bonds rose by $20, to $320, as speculators took chances on a bankrupt railroad's securities that carried a principal amount of $1,000. Rhode Island senator Claiborne Pell echoed the familiar "save the New Haven" mantra that caused the president to push the Penn Central merger through the regulatory and judicial arenas. The court's ruling "is notable for its promptness," Pell declared, "and also for its clear acknowledgement of the relationship between the merger and the very survival of rail service to the New England area." Fellow Democrat Abraham Ribicoff agreed that the court had approved "the most satisfactory long-range answer to the crisis on the New Haven," one that affected his Connecticut constituents. "The court's decision is very welcome to those of us seeking to insure [sic] continued rail service in New England," emphasized New York Republican Jacob Javits, demonstrating that the desire for privately funded public transportation transcended party lines.[569]

The only cause for concern was the fifteen-day stay granted by the district court. "If anyone is unhappy with the decision," commented transportation reporter Robert Bedingfield, "the court gave him 15 days to appeal to the United States Supreme Court." Thomas M. Goodfellow, the president of the Association of American Railroads, provoked laughter when he told a Washington audience that he was "delighted to hear that it's finally boiled down to a matter of 15 days." The latest timetable was, as usual, overly optimistic. The appeals to the Supreme Court began on November 1. Milton Shapp continued his war against the merger as the sole remaining combatant arguing that the arrangement failed to promote the public interest. More substantive objections came from the major players in the other big eastern merger battle—the Norfolk & Western, the Chesapeake & Ohio, the Baltimore & Ohio,

and the Western Maryland. Attorneys for those railroads filed a brief with Justice John M. Harlan, objecting to both the Penn Central merger and the inclusion terms for the three smaller railroads. The Supreme Court now had the opportunity to evaluate both issues at the same time, something the Interstate Commerce Commission had been unable to do.[570]

The *Penn-Central Merger and Norfolk & Western Inclusion Cases* demonstrated the newfound unity of purpose between the Interstate Commerce Commission and the Justice Department. On November 6, the two agencies issued a joint petition to the Supreme Court, noting that the matter had been under adjudication since April 1966 and that there were no remaining substantive issues to be resolved. Solicitor General Griswold informed the court that he would not object to a full judicial review of the case, but he emphasized that "substantial further delay" would not be in the public interest. Griswold noted that the ICC's June 12 inclusion order had satisfied the concerns that his predecessor, Thurgood Marshall, had raised earlier in *Baltimore & Ohio v. United States*. "Times have changed," Griswold emphasized. "In our view nothing of substance remains." When hearings began on December 4, Griswold informed the justices that the ICC had acted "intelligently and fairly" in its efforts to protect the Erie Lackawanna, the Boston & Maine, and the Delaware & Hudson.[571]

On December 18, nearly three weeks after the date Saunders and Perlman had predicted would mark the beginning of the Penn Central's operations, the Supreme Court declined to take any action on the appeal. With the court in recess until January 15, 1968, the consolidation could not possibly take place before February 1. Pennsylvania Railroad and New York Central officials expressed surprise and disappointment at the lack of decisive action. The trustees of the New Haven were less disappointed than terrified. Even though they were expecting their first installment of federal funds, Richard Joyce Smith acknowledged that there was barely enough money available to continue operations through the end of January. "A major snowstorm or other cash-draining event would, of course, reduce this period considerably," he acknowledged. Absent a $25 million emergency loan from the Penn Central—a company that did not yet exist—the New Haven was on the verge of shutting down.[572]

Resolution

And then it was done. On January 15, 1968, with Stuart Saunders in attendance, the Supreme Court issued its ruling in the *Penn-Central Merger and Norfolk & Western*

Inclusion Cases. In a 7–1 verdict, the justices removed the last obstacle to the merger.[573] In addition to permitting the formation of the Penn Central, prior to the addition of the New Haven, the justices concluded that the bankrupt carrier had a value that did not exceed $90 million. The stipulations indicated that the court was satisfied that the ICC had resolved the mandate contained in *Baltimore & Ohio v. United States.* Solicitor General Thurgood Marshall was now an associate justice and, given the nature of his involvement in the earlier case, he had little choice other than to recuse himself from this one. Abe Fortas showed no such restraint. He had written a dissent in *Baltimore & Ohio v. United States,* and now he authored the majority opinion in the case that followed. That role afforded him the opportunity to highlight his conception—one that Johnson shared—of the relationship between monopoly power and the determination of a national transportation policy. "Competition," Fortas emphasized, "is only one of many considerations in determining the public interest in the merger."[574]

Fortas's opinion did much more than suggest the death knell of postwar antitrust concerns. It also indicated that the court was willing to go to extraordinary lengths to save the New Haven's passenger service while minimizing the amount that government agencies would have to spend on that problem. "Continuation of the operations of the NH, which the [Interstate Commerce] Commission has found to be essential," Fortas declared, "can be assured only upon and after effectuation of the merger of the Penn-Central." Saunders and Perlman reinforced that perspective in a joint statement to the media, promising that the merger "will make it possible to extend early financial aid" to the New Haven.[575]

Richard Joyce Smith and William J. Kirk, cotrustees of the bankrupt line, agreed that the creation of the Penn Central "is the necessary condition for saving the New Haven." They anticipated a speedy resolution "in the succeeding months on the matters to be resolved pending the New Haven's full inclusion in the Penn-Central System." Local officials were equally enthusiastic. "It's wonderful and I am delighted," announced Edwin G. Michaelian, the top political official in Westchester County. Alvin R. Ruskin, the mayor of New Rochelle, simply indicated that the court's approval of the merger was "wonderful" and let it go at that. They did not bother to state that their constituents, who resided in some of the wealthiest communities in the United States, would be able to transfer the New Haven's commuter deficit to the Penn Central. Nor did they mention that the Supreme Court had not resolved the issue of when the Penn Central would buy the New Haven

or how much it would cost. New Haven bondholders were less pleased. Led by Oscar Gruss, they had waged a long campaign, demanding that the company be included in the Penn Central at the time of the merger or that it be sold off for scrap value. Both the ICC and the Supreme Court prevented those outcomes, as inconsistent with the public interest and regardless of the financial consequences to the New Haven's investors.[576]

The Supreme Court's ruling affected nearly every other eastern railroad, with some treated more favorably than others. The verdict reaffirmed the ICC terms for including the Erie Lackawanna, the Boston & Maine, and the Delaware & Hudson in the 1964 merger of the Norfolk & Western and the Nickel Plate. Erie Lackawanna executives announced that they were "gratified"—as well they should have been, given that their company was on the verge of bankruptcy. The corresponding figure for the B&M was far less favorable, and that company's president announced that he would continue "to assert its rejection of these terms." No one was quite certain what to make of the Delaware & Hudson, whose directors were content to accept inclusion in the N&W and whose president told the court that "he is in a position to recommend an alternative which in his judgment is in the better interests of the stockholders." As for the other two railroads that were supposed to become part of Dereco, the court permitted the Reading to petition the ICC for inclusion, and the bankrupt Jersey Central was not a party to the case.[577] Even though the Reading had long been the PRR's principal competitor in eastern Pennsylvania, President Charles Bertrand welcomed the creation of Penn Central. He noted that the court's decision "is in line with the position heretofore taken by the Reading that mergers are necessary to preserve the health of the industry." It was a gracious and public-spirited announcement, but one that only barely concealed his determination to increase the value of Reading securities through whatever merger he could arrange.[578]

The resolution of the Penn Central merger was exactly what the president of the Norfolk & Western expected. Herman Pevler, in Roanoke, emphasized that "the decision of the Supreme Court makes it more imperative than ever that the Norfolk & Western-Chesapeake & Ohio merger be approved by the I.C.C. promptly."[579] The statement would not have escaped the attention of James Symes, who was still a PRR director, and the chairman of the company's executive committee. "If the C.&O-B.&O. is approved, that is going to help the Nickel Plate case and if that is approved, it is going to help our case, going to go right around the circle," he had told the Kefauver

Committee during the summer of 1962. Now, nearly six years later, the endless merger merry-go-round continued to spin and seemed destined to create what neither Symes nor Saunders wanted—a second massive railroad system in the East.[580]

Reckoning

No further obstacles remained. The Penn Central would begin operations on the earliest possible date, at 12:01 a.m. on February 1, 1968. On merger day, the new company would become the nation's largest transportation enterprise, with assets of $6.3 billion. It would be second only to the Soviet railway system as the biggest rail carrier in the world. The Penn Central would belong to 121,262 investors who owned twenty-two million shares of stock. More than four thousand locomotives and nearly two hundred thousand freight cars would travel along 19,286 miles of routes linking communities in fourteen states, the District of Columbia, and two Canadian provinces.[581] The PRR, the NYC, and the New Haven were, respectively, the first, second, and third largest privately owned passenger carriers in the United States, and the Penn Central would possess some five thousand cars to transport commuters and intercity travelers. Saunders and other executives were eager to eliminate as much of that service as possible or else to shift the responsibility to public agencies, but that was a problem that could wait for another day. Thanks to the 1964 Luna-Saunders agreement, the Penn Central's 95,883 employees possessed an extraordinary measure of job security. The total workforce was nonetheless well below half of what the Pennsylvania Railroad alone had maintained five decades earlier, and it was clear that in the years to come, railroading would present fewer and fewer career opportunities.[582]

The only thing the Penn Central did not possess was a plan for integrating the managerial, transportation, and traffic capabilities of the Pennsylvania Railroad and the New York Central, or for operating the combined company. The planning process began in early 1962, shortly after the two railroads announced their intent to merge, but the sole function of the resulting Patchell report was to ensure that the Penn Central application passed through the regulatory minefield. During the spring of 1965, not long after examiners Lyle and Darmstadter recommended approval of the merger, Saunders and Perlman informed senior executives at the two railroads that a completely new document would supersede the Patchell study. The replacement plan consumed two and a half years of intense effort, while the political, legal, and regulatory battles associated

with the merger continued unabated. The six-volume report was not ready until November 1967—just in time, it seemed, as the Supreme Court's approval of the merger was only weeks away. The document recommended that the two companies continue as separate operating entities under a unified management, with the integration of transportation and traffic functions to proceed slowly and incrementally. By the beginning of 1968, however, both the PRR and the NYC were in serious financial trouble. Saunders and Perlman demanded cost reductions as rapidly as possible—if for no other reason than to prove to investors that they could generate the enormous gains in efficiency they had promised. They mandated an accelerated timetable for the integration of operations and insisted that most of the associated construction projects should be completed within two or at most three years. Come merger day, Penn Central managers and workers would be simultaneously mixing two distinct leadership styles, implementing uniform operating and sales networks, and undertaking expensive betterments to the physical plant. It was an implausible scenario and at odds with the recommendations given to Saunders and Perlman. On November 28, two months prior to the implementation of the merger, Perlman insisted that all copies of the study be marked as "Preliminary." They went into a filing cabinet in his office and were never used again.[583]

Nor was there any consensus on the leadership team that would bring the Penn Central into being. Perlman still resented the Pennsylvania Railroad and its senior management. He had not forgotten Symes's role in the Norfolk & Western-Virginian merger or the subsequent efforts to prevent the New York Central from combining with the Chesapeake & Ohio and the Baltimore & Ohio. Perlman's relationship with Saunders was somewhat better, but throughout the merger hearings, he played a distinct second to the PRR's new chairman. He still regarded the merger as a Pennsylvania Railroad takeover of the New York Central. Perlman resented his assigned role as the president and chief administrative officer of the new company, lacking the authority held by Saunders as chairman and chief executive officer. Allen Greenough, the PRR's president, was still three years shy of retirement, but no one explained what role, if any, he would play at Penn Central. Saunders despised David Bevan, largely because the PRR's chief financial officer resisted his frequent requests for capital expenditures and his efforts to massage the railroad's earnings. Bevan increased his unpopularity when he warned Saunders, in December 1967, that the two companies had not yet made arrangements to integrate their accounting, data-processing, waybill, and car-tracking functions. Without basic efforts in that direction, Bevan noted, efforts to dispatch cars along the entirety of the Penn Central system were likely to result in chaos. Bevan continued to disparage the NYC's accounting personnel and methods, particularly the company's reliance on ICC protocols that were distinctly out of step with prevailing financial practices in other industries. For his pains, Bevan received word in late December that his seat on the PRR's board would not convert to a corresponding post on the Penn Central. While he would retain the chairmanship of the Finance Committee, Bevan would lose authority over accounting, budgeting, taxes, insurance, and banking. Those would become the responsibility of Walter Grant, a New York Central executive whom Bevan regarded with contempt. Bevan would report directly to Saunders rather than the Penn Central's board of directors, while Grant would be Perlman's subordinate, further imperiling cooperation. Carl Sempier, the computer expert whom Bevan recruited from IBM, would be under the supervision of Robert G. Flannery, a New York Central executive. In the end, Bevan would only retain control over the pension fund, diversification initiatives, and the critical task of generating the additional investment capital necessary to support the betterment program—and, increasingly, simply to keep the Penn Central running. The demotion was so severe that Bevan was again ready to offer his resignation. He reconsidered only when PRR director Richard King Mellon begged him to stay, told him that his skills were critical to the survival of the Penn Central, and promised to protect him from Saunders. Similar feuds were emerging in department after department, as executives on both the PRR and the NYC attempted to determine who would be in charge and who would be subordinate. There was little clarity on the matter, as Saunders feared that a precise delineation of personnel assignments would erode morale and cause so much jockeying for position as to imperil the Penn Central's operations. On merger day, therefore, only two individuals—Saunders and Perlman—possessed specific titles and job descriptions in the Penn Central's corporate hierarchy. "We were," one disgruntled executive observed, "in the same situation as if we had planned the invasion of Europe without having General Eisenhower named until D-Day."[584]

In the immediate aftermath of the Supreme Court's decision, however, the problems that would afflict the Penn Central seemed far, far away. The future of the nation's railroads, their workers, and the people and communities they served paled in comparison to relief that the merger that had been in the making for eleven years was finally going to happen. Wall Street was not so much enthusiastic

as cautiously optimistic. On the day that the Supreme Court cleared the way for the consolidation, Pennsylvania Railroad shares finished down a quarter, while the New York Central was unchanged. Analysts emphasized that the blasé performance was attributable to repeated predictions of a favorable outcome, and they anticipated "the longer-term benefits of the merger and the inherent strength of the new road."[585]

Stuart Saunders gloried in his success. The Virginia lawyer who knew almost nothing about railroad operations had created the world's largest privately owned railroad. He came from Roanoke to Philadelphia to orchestrate the greatest merger in American history and—after many trials and tribulations—had done it. The saga began in 1957, when Robert Young first discussed the matter with James Symes. In the years that followed, Symes pressured Alfred Perlman into taking part, then expressed anger and dismay when the New York Central balked. He restarted negotiations, acknowledged his personality conflict with Perlman, and worked with Howard Butcher to recruit Saunders, an executive who had just completed what may have been the most successful merger in the history of railroading. With a staff of seventy to undertake the grueling process associated with fitting together two astonishingly different companies, Saunders was free to use his charm and influence to transform widespread opposition into overwhelming support. To do so he made concession after concession, in the end bargaining away all the benefits that the merger was supposed to achieve. He also ignored the growing friction between PRR and NYC executives, as well as clear indications that, come merger day, neither group would cooperate with the other. That Saunders was oblivious to such concerns reflected his priorities. In the final analysis, his goal had been to create the perfect merger rather than the perfect company.

Along the way Saunders took advantage of the carnage that characterized the northeastern railroad network during the 1960s. He claimed that the Pennsylvania Railroad and the New York Central were too weak to survive attacks by other carriers but that the combined Penn Central would not be so strong as to inflict the same sort of damage on others. He asserted that his way, the way of consolidation, represented the only alternative to the nationalization of the railroads or the collapse of the transportation network. His insistence on a three-system East clashed with the antitrust impulses of the Justice Department and defied the basic logic of railway economics. Saunders had many allies in his crusade, from members of the ICC who had run out of options, to executives at rival railroads who possessed merger agendas of their own,

Paintbrush in hand, car repairman Robert Whalen poses for photographers. The date is February 1, 1968, and the nation's newest railroad is in business. *Courtesy of the Special Collections Research Center, Temple University Libraries, Philadelphia, PA.*

to politicians who wanted to preserve commuter services without asking their constituents to pay for that privilege. Saunders had the backing of an attorney general, the president of the United States, and an associate justice of the Supreme Court, all of whom were willing to set aside procedural niceties in the interest of what they saw as the greater good. Rather than continue the traditional enmity between management and labor, he gave union officials whatever they demanded, to ensure their acquiescence. Saunders imposed his will on many other railroaders, including the president of his merger partner. He fought an internal feud with his chief financial officer, who never supported the consolidation and balked at the accounting and budgeting methods associated with it. Each of those institutions and actors, and many more, shaped the creation of the Penn Central. Yet when the January 26, 1968, issue of *Time* magazine appeared on the newsstands, it was Saunders, and Saunders alone, whose picture was on the cover.

Milton Shapp may have been the only person ungracious enough to publicly criticize the Penn Central while carrying on a battle that was already lost. The merger "could represent a serious economic blow to the economic future of many communities within Pennsylvania," he complained. It was an attack he had made many times before and would make again in 1970, when he renewed his quest for the governorship. Walter Annenberg, the Pennsylvania Railroad director who would soon join the board of the Penn Central, once more used the pages of his newspaper to portray Shapp as an obstructionist, a malcontent, and a sore loser, someone who failed to appreciate the extraordinary benefits that the Penn Central would produce for the commonwealth. "Consummation of the merger of the Pennsylvania and the New York Central Railroads," Annenberg editorialized in the *Philadelphia Inquirer*, "will open the door to a new era of opportunity for improved transportation services in States where the combined rail system . . . will operate." He praised an event that "marks the birth of a new era in railroading for Philadelphia, the Penn Central headquarters city, and for scores of communities in the East and Midwest that stand to share in the benefits of improved rail service." The delays associated with the merger, as well as the problems that faced the participating railroads, were well and truly in the past, Annenberg predicted. "Now, at last, the light is green and the Penn Central is rolling."[586]

Finale

Wednesday, January 31, was a delightful day in Manhattan, sunny and with temperatures that just touched fifty degrees. In the late afternoon, perhaps an hour before sunset, the usual crowds thronged Penn Station. Most were destined for the cars of the Long Island Rail Road, once a Pennsylvania Railroad subsidiary and now a ward of the state. The facilities they used, twice each weekday, had never been adequate for their needs or for the unexpected growth in commuter traffic that had occurred over the preceding half century. During its life span of less than six decades, urban soot begrimed the exterior of Charles Follen McKim's architectural masterpiece. Advertising displays and Lester Tichy's absurdly inappropriate clamshell ticket booth marred the grand spaces that lay inside. "No one entering Pennsylvania Station for the first time,"

architect Lewis Mumford observed in 1958, "could, without clairvoyance, imagine how good it used to be, in comparison to the almost indescribable botch that has been made of it." The subsequent destruction and replacement of Penn Station with a maze of subterranean conduits that seemed designed to engender claustrophobia went far beyond even the most expansive definition of the word *botch*. The imposition of Madison Square Garden atop what remained of the terminus had done little to improve matters. The new entertainment complex would open in less than two weeks, in a ceremony featuring one of America's most popular comedians. "There's a crazy set of trains in the basement," Bob Hope would tell his audience, relegating what remained of the Pennsylvania Railroad's greatest engineering achievement to the status of an amusing but ultimately irrelevant toy.[587]

Intercity travelers constituted a much smaller contingent of the people scuttling through Penn Station's underground passageways. They were heading for one of the Pennsylvania Railroad trains bound for Washington, along a route that the chairman of the railroad and the president of the country had promised would soon become a high-speed ground transportation corridor the equal of any in the world. Very few set their sights on the best—indeed, practically the only—passenger train to operate between New York and Chicago. At one time *The Broadway Limited* and the New York Central's *Twentieth Century Limited* had been among the finest trains in the world. They operated on identical sixteen-hour schedules between the nation's two largest cities, pacing each other on parallel tracks through suburban Chicago and thundering across a third of the continent. The *Century* disappeared nearly two months earlier, removed as a part of Alfred Perlman's determined campaign to eliminate the New York Central's long-distance passenger service. For a mere ten days *The Broadway* was the last remaining all-Pullman luxury limited in the United States. On December 13, 1967, the PRR combined the train with *The General* and its coach traffic. It was still called *The Broadway*, but it was not the same train nor was anything about the Pennsylvania Railroad's passenger operations the same as it once was. The observation-lounge cars *Tower View* and *Mountain View* disappeared, and the dining car lost much of its panache. It was the most visible portent of even greater declines that would come in the near future, accompanied by the nationalization of rail passenger service. Stuart Saunders and Alfred Perlman acknowledged that most travelers preferred to fly for journeys of more than three hundred miles. Even as they promised that the merger would improve freight operations, they pledged steep cuts in the Penn Central's passenger routes. "People simply aren't interested in riding the trains long distance any longer," Saunders emphasized. After noting that it took as many as seventy-eight employees to operate a service that carried only sixty or seventy passengers per trip, Saunders conceded defeat. "We can't compete" with the airlines, he observed, "and we are fooling ourselves if we think we can." Judging by the number of aircraft that would fly above the half-full *Broadway Limited* that night, making as many as three round trips in the time it took for the train to travel one way, Saunders was correct in his assessment of the public's evolving demand for mobility.[588]

At five minutes past five o'clock, sixty feet below the blasted stump of Alexander Cassatt's monumental Beaux Arts gateway to Manhattan, *The Broadway Limited* lurched into motion. It passed beneath the post office building that initially represented the sole profitable development of air rights associated with the station—a disappointing outcome, given the New York Central's experience with the contemporaneous Grand Central Terminal. *The Broadway* was soon in one of the mile-long tunnels underneath the Hudson River. Completed sixty years earlier, they epitomized the greatest civil engineering work of the age, and one of the last significant railway improvements undertaken anywhere in Greater New York. As the train exited the Bergen Hill portal and curved to the south, the fading sunlight revealed an aging and battle-scarred GG1 locomotive, its Raymond Loewy pinstripes long since replaced by a more utilitarian and economical paint scheme. Crossing the New Jersey Meadowlands, only the most knowledgeable traveler could identify the long-abandoned location of Manhattan Transfer. Prior to the massive electrification projects of the 1920s and 1930s, side-rod electrics had gone that far and no farther before yielding to steam locomotives. Passengers who rode through the Hudson Tubes, from New York's Financial District, long ago had boarded Pennsylvania Railroad trains at Manhattan Transfer. More than four decades had passed since the isolated interchange inspired the title of John Dos Passos's first commercially successful novel, and it would be another year before it gave its name to a jazz vocal group.

Within minutes the train crossed a massive lift bridge and pulled into Newark Pennsylvania Station. Hudson & Manhattan trains entered the city on a parallel right-of-way. Like the Long Island, the bankrupt H&M had passed from private to public ownership, and it now operated as Port Authority Trans-Hudson. Invisible from within the sheltering cocoon of *The Broadway Limited*, large areas of Newark lay in ashes—the aftermath of riots, less than a year earlier, that occurred because police officers beat into

unconsciousness an unarmed and unresisting Black man. The destruction in Newark was tragically characteristic of the long, hot summer of 1967, when protests erupted in 159 cities across the United States. They would reemerge barely two months later, following the assassination of the iconic leader of the civil rights movement. Lyndon Johnson worked closely with Martin Luther King Jr., hoping that liberation theology and social-gospel Christianity would temper the growing strength of Black power and Black nationalism. In October, when Tommie Smith and John Carlos stood on the podium at the Mexico City Olympics and raised their fists in the air, it was nonetheless clear that the civil rights movement had changed profoundly during the 1960s. Such concerns were far removed from passengers on *The Broadway*, as they made their way to the dining car. The train's December 1967 downgrading spelled an end to such sumptuous dishes as oxtail soup and breast of Cornish hen à la Kiev, but the menu was still far superior to anything available on an airplane. In a continuation of a long-standing tradition, the meal was prepared by African American cooks, served by African American waiters, and overseen by a White steward. Afterward, travelers returned to their compartments, where a Black Pullman porter attended to their every need. The evolving nature of race relations in the United States, it seemed, was neither uniform nor all-encompassing.[589]

The less fortunate passengers on *The Broadway* bedded down for the night on their coach seats—a poor substitute for a Pullman berth but still far more luxurious than air travel. A few months before, those coaches had been carried by *The General*, one of many trains that once made the nightly parade west toward Pittsburgh and Chicago. During the 1922 Shopmen's Strike, that train's namesake, Brigadier General W. W. Atterbury, established an unyielding and unenviable reputation as a supporter of company unions and a foe of organized labor. Such intransigence put him at odds with more progressive executives, such as Daniel Willard at the Baltimore & Ohio, who determined that cooperation with government and with labor could produce more effective results than resistance against both. Regardless of method, labor peace proved elusive, as workers fought for better wages and working conditions and then battled to preserve their jobs as an entire system of transportation collapsed all around them. Atterbury also oversaw the electrification of the main line between New York and Washington, at a time when the United States led the world in cutting-edge electric railway technology. By 1968, the decline of the eastern railroads had long since precluded projects that could compete with the Japanese *Shinkansen*. That much was evident, as *The*

Broadway left Trenton and crossed the Delaware River into Pennsylvania. A short distance to the west lay the yards at Morrisville, where Bob Watson and his colleagues were frantically debugging the *Metroliners*, endeavoring to somehow fulfill the promise of space-age rail travel along a corridor that predated the Civil War.

Whether in coaches or sleepers, many passengers whiled away the evening hours with that day's newspaper, keeping abreast of a planet that even in the first month of 1968 seemed to be spinning rapidly out of control. That morning's headlines told of events half a world away, as the Tet offensive exploded across South Vietnam, and Viet Cong operatives attempted to seize control of the American embassy in Saigon. The Pentagon released word that a navy crewman, Duane Hodges, died from injuries sustained a week earlier, when North Korean forces captured the USS *Pueblo*. Reassurances that the remaining sailors were being "properly treated" proved sadly inaccurate. As they suffered in captivity, it would be up to Under Secretary of State Nick Katzenbach, one of the witnesses to the Kennedy memo, to devise a strategy for bringing them home. Domestically, an Advisory Commission on Intergovernmental Relations provided an analysis of the 1967 riots, declaring that the "threatened anarchy" in the nation's cities portended "the greatest crisis since the Civil War." The chancellor of New York's state university system barred all drug use on campus and denied "sanctuary for those who violate state and Federal narcotics laws." It was part of a nationwide pushback against the counterculture movement, one that would soon enable Richard Nixon to make a second, successful bid for the White House. The headlines that seemed so troubling on that last day in January would only become more so as the year unfolded. To the extent that optimism arises from an inability to predict the future, it was probably just as well that no one knew what the remainder of 1968 would bring. Those events would include the assassination of Martin Luther King, a renewal of race riots, antiwar protests, an escalating military conflict that ended Lyndon Johnson's chances for reelection, and the attorney general who made possible the Penn Central merger dying in the kitchen of the Ambassador Hotel, cradled in the arms of a Mexican immigrant.[590]

At half past six, *The Broadway Limited* reached Philadelphia. Had the train continued south, toward Baltimore and Washington, it would soon have skirted the eastern edge of Woodlands Cemetery. In the unlikely event that someone was there to visit the graves of J. Edgar Thomson or Tom Scott, they could easily have seen the railroad that those executives created, with a continual parade of trains passing only a few hundred feet away. Anyone paying homage to the company's founding fathers would not have seen *The Broadway*, however, as that train skirted a city that was the birthplace and the headquarters of the Pennsylvania Railroad. For more than a century, Philadelphia had been the scene of regular cooperation and frequent conflict between railroad executives and local politicians. Broad Street Station and the Chinese Wall, long a source of contention, had disappeared, replaced by the gleaming and featureless boxes of Penn Center. The opening of the replacement station, at 30th Street, was delayed repeatedly by economic depression, global war, and the unwillingness of municipal officials to pay for the expense of urban improvement. It was a magnificent edifice, but one that *The Broadway*'s passengers would not see. The Philadelphia Improvements were incomplete and did not allow southbound trains to enter the station and then proceed toward Harrisburg. The small number of passengers who boarded the train did so at the aging North Philadelphia station, an unprepossessing gateway to a declining city.

One hundred and twenty years earlier, as the Pennsylvania Railroad was in its infancy, Philadelphia's Quakers had expressed dismay at American involvement in another war, one far removed from the fighting in Southeast Asia. The conflict with Mexico divided the United States, with supporters vowing to bring progress and freedom to a benighted and primitive people, and detractors condemning the unprovoked, imperialistic aggression of a world power against a far weaker rival. During the 1840s, the Quaker merchants who demanded a rail link to the west never imagined that Philadelphia would regain its prominence over New York. That contest for commercial supremacy was well and truly lost. Their rival was Baltimore, a city ideally positioned to capture cargoes transported along the Susquehanna River and funnel them through Chesapeake Bay and to the South. In that contest they succeeded, and Philadelphians in 1968 could take some comfort in the sure and certain knowledge that whatever problems their city was experiencing, those facing Baltimore were far worse. The city's long-ago failure to capture the western grain trade nonetheless illustrated the perils of tying a private corporation to the public good of urban prosperity and improved mobility. It was a lesson that politicians and regulators ignored when they expected the Penn Central to underwrite the preservation of the northeastern manufacturing economy, rescue the New Haven, and fund the cost of high-speed passenger service.

The original Pennsylvania Railroad began at Philadelphia, along a route pioneered by the Main Line of Public Works. The name persisted, long after the publicly financed internal improvements disappeared, and gave identity to the city's most iconic commuter suburbs. In the decades following World War II, the route to Paoli witnessed the opening of the Schuylkill Expressway, the decline of rail service, and efforts by municipal officials to avoid the cost of highway construction by putting commuters on trains. A complex mix of local, state, and federal politics rescued the network of commuter lines that radiated outward from Center City. Public support remained inadequate, however, and through the windows of *The Broadway Limited*, aging MP54 cars were more likely to be seen than modern Silverliners. Such problems were foreign to Stuart Saunders, who resided along the Main Line, at Ardmore. A limousine took him to and from the PRR's headquarters at Six Penn Center each day—unlike Perlman, he refused to travel by commuter rail.

A short distance to the west, the burial ground of Bryn Mawr's Church of the Redeemer provided a house of worship and a final resting place for a score of Pennsylvania Railroad executives—including some whose service to the company had imperiled their health and shortened their lives. W. W. Atterbury's funeral took place there, in a service attended by shopworkers, executives, financiers, and army officers.[591] During the 1920s and into the 1930s, Atterbury had blocked numerous plans for the restructuring of the eastern railroads. Decades later, his manipulations on behalf of the Pennsylvania Railroad found an echo in the dealmaking orchestrated by James Symes and Stuart Saunders. Alexander Cassatt was buried in the churchyard, a short distance from his estate at Cheswold. So was his protégé Samuel Rea, who had once lived nearby. Many members of the Thayer family were as near to Cassatt and Rea in death as they had been during their careers. Conspicuously absent was Second Vice President John Borland Thayer Jr., a passenger on the *Titanic* and lost forever in the frigid waters of the North Atlantic. The others lay close enough to the tracks that one might almost imagine that they could still hear *The Broadway Limited* passing by.

Beyond Paoli, homes became sparser while farms and barns became more evident. *The Broadway* followed the original route of the Philadelphia & Columbia Rail Road, which briefly gave Thomson experience as a surveyor. Those responsible for the Main Line of Public Works preferred a canal, and they accepted a railway to the Susquehanna River only after geographic constraints made their first choice impossible. That circumstance suggested the evolving nature of transportation technology and ensured that the hybrid rail-water system of the Main Line would never be able to compete with the Erie Canal. Just to the west of Lancaster, *The Broadway* briefly left the alignment of the state works, heading north and west along a stretch of track that became an early and integral component of the Pennsylvania Railroad. The Harrisburg, Portsmouth, Mt. Joy & Lancaster bypassed the westernmost portion of the commonwealth's railroad as well as the section of the Eastern Division Canal that followed the Susquehanna River north to Harrisburg. It succeeded because Pennsylvanians sought the fastest and most direct route to their intended destination. They demonstrated little loyalty to the outdated and often mismanaged system that was supposed to ensure their state's economic prosperity.

When *The Broadway* reached the Pennsylvania capital, shortly after 8:00 p.m., it paused only blocks away from the statehouse. In 1846, that building's predecessor was the scene of acrimonious conflicts over the future of Pennsylvania's western hinterland. Philadelphians sought to preserve their city, while their Pittsburgh rivals eagerly followed the progress of the Baltimore & Ohio. Political maneuverings, including those that blocked the B&O, reflected a consistent theme in the Pennsylvania Railroad's history. The citizens of Philadelphia and Pittsburgh paid a significant share of the initial construction cost of the Pennsylvania Railroad, under terms that ensured that they relinquished control to corporate executives. Public policy nonetheless gave birth to, and forever after shaped the actions of what would eventually become the largest private corporation in the world.

For the dwindling number of Pennsylvania Railroad employees who worked at Harrisburg in 1968, those events in the remote past carried little importance. Stationed at the end of electrified territory, their most immediate task involved removing *The Broadway*'s GG1 and replacing it with diesels. Not much more than a decade had passed since the last steam locomotives disappeared from the Pennsylvania Railroad, an outcome that earlier executives, including John Van Buren Duer, John Deasy, and Martin Clement, would have found unthinkable. Long after other railroads committed to dieselization, they poured resources into the development of duplexes and steam turbines, in a futile effort to match the new technology, preserve the company's vaunted tradition of locomotive construction, and placate on-line coal shippers. It had taken James Symes, a relative outsider from the western edge of the PRR system, to set matters to rights and propel himself into the leadership of the Pennsylvania Railroad.

Soon after leaving Harrisburg, *The Broadway* crossed the massive Rockville Bridge that spanned the Susquehanna River. The structure was part of a nationwide railroad revitalization, following the crippling depression of the 1890s. Its stone arches represented the contributions of Italian immigrants, who formed only a small part of the extraordinarily diverse yet ethnically and racially segregated workforce that built, maintained, and operated the Pennsylvania Railroad. Despite its size and complexity, the Rockville Bridge was only one of the many betterments approved by Cassatt, whose presidency fortuitously coincided with the prosperity that marked the dawn of the twentieth century. Those systemwide improvements, far more than the construction of Penn Station in New York, ensured that the Pennsylvania Railroad would always have ample capacity for the coal, iron ore, steel, and other bulk commodities that formed the core of the company's business. That traffic flowed across a landscape shaped by public policy, and Cassatt proved adept at manipulating the political process and the regulatory apparatus to suit the PRR's needs. His influence over the 1903 Elkins Act caused later generations to decry the ability of firms to capture the agencies that were supposed to be controlling them. Cassatt's life ended before the reformist impulses of the Progressive Era turned decisively against the railroads. The 1906 Hepburn Act, followed by the economic recession of 1907, ensured that the Pennsylvania Railroad could never again undertake the capital-improvement programs that produced Penn Station and the Rockville Bridge. The governmental support that had stimulated the construction of canals and railroads now turned its attention to highways and airports. The secular decline of America's industrial heartland hollowed out the PRR's traffic base. It was an economic transformation that gubernatorial candidate Milton Shapp never acknowledged, as he characterized the company as the villain rather than the victim in the unfolding of the Rust Belt. The problem of excess capacity—something Cassatt and his contemporaries had not anticipated—plagued all the eastern railroads and was the instigating agent in the merger movement of the 1960s. Only the Pocahontas coal carriers remained strong, and they alone could provide a financial lifeline to their weaker brethren. Yet there were only two of them in the early 1960s, and transportation economists recognized that that circumstance should dictate the structure of the eastern railroad network. As the vice president in charge of operations, James Symes mandated rapid dieselization and thus saved the Pennsylvania Railroad. As chairman of the board, he was so determined to merge with the New York Central and create a three-system East that he severed ties with the Norfolk & Western and set the Pennsylvania Railroad on a path to destruction.

Once off the Rockville Bridge, *The Broadway Limited* sped west along the valley of the Juniata River. This, too, had once been the route of the Main Line of Public Works, although the last vestiges of the Juniata Division Canal

had all but disappeared. Despite the loss of traffic and the concomitant decline in revenues, freight trains were still very much in evidence. They flowed along a transportation artery that retained the four tracks that had been in place since the completion of Cassatt's ambitious betterment programs. How many trains and how many tracks would remain, after Penn Central began operations, was a matter of much concern to Pennsylvania residents. As *The Broadway* continued west, town after town flew by in the darkness—Marysville, Duncannon, Port Royal, Mifflin, Lewistown, Mount Union, Huntingdon, and Tyrone. Along the way, the Pennsylvania Railroad parted company with the remaining traces of its antediluvian predecessor, whose remains were in the process of being converted into a National Historic Site. The inclined planes of the Allegheny Portage Railroad that stretched west from Hollidaysburg toward Johnstown were an engineering marvel but an operational nightmare that doomed the Main Line of Public Works. The state legislature approved the construction of a replacement line in 1850. The New Portage Railroad came too late, and like the rest of the Main Line, it became an appendage to the vast Pennsylvania Railroad empire. The outcome was emblematic of the commonwealth's inability to blend patronage politics and transportation economics. It likewise attested to the transfer of public works to the private sector, a process that was largely complete even before the Civil War began.

The Pennsylvania Railroad's four-track main line along the Juniata carried the commerce of a nation. *The Broadway Limited* pulled past westbound freights ascending the gentle grade toward the foothills of the Alleghenies, while eastbounds roared past with blaring horns and a whump of compressed air. Some carried coal and steel, the traditional mainstays of a railroad dedicated to the low-cost transportation of the bulk commodities that underpinned the American industrial economy. There were nonetheless clear indications that the Penn Central could no longer count on that traffic. Steel manufacturing had entered a period of inexorable decline, and municipalities such as New York were moving to restrict the use of high-sulfur eastern coal. Earlier that day, the city's Air Pollution Control commissioner announced that he had persuaded Consolidated Edison to convert its power plants to oil. Other utilities soon followed suit. Vast quantities of export coal nonetheless continued to flow to tidewater along the rails of the Norfolk & Western, the company that the PRR had relinquished in order to make possible the merger with the New York Central. Decades later, low-sulfur coal from Wyoming's Powder River Basin kept generating stations compliant with environmental regulations. The resulting traffic—moving in unit trains that the PRR had pioneered—helped to revitalize the railroads but would come too late to assist the Penn Central. The same could be said for the intermodal shipments that flashed by *The Broadway Limited*. The rapid growth of TrucTrain service and the Trailer Train equipment pool suggested that the NYC's focus on fast merchandise trains had superseded the PRR's reliance on heavy freight. The piggyback revolution would also prove vital to the rebirth of the railroads. Like the unit trains, the new methods developed by Pennsylvania Railroad personnel would not pay dividends for many more years.[592]

Shortly after 11:00 p.m., *The Broadway Limited* reached Altoona. If any of the train's passengers were awake at that late hour, they could hardly miss seeing the station. Five years earlier, the cosmetic improvements associated with Operation Beaver produced nothing more substantive than a coat of white paint, to cover bricks begrimed by decades of locomotive soot. The few travelers who boarded at Altoona bemoaned the loss of the train shed, demolished in 1960. The station itself would suffer the same fate in 1971, and its destruction was symbolic of the fate that awaited the surrounding community. For more than a century, every aspect of life in Altoona was intertwined with the fortunes of the Pennsylvania Railroad. The company's shops built and repaired thousands of locomotives and cars. Mechanical engineers such as Theodore Ely, Axel Vogt, Alfred Gibbs, James Wallis, and William Kiesel designed new steam locomotives that were ideally suited for the PRR's needs. Railroad officials from across the United States and around the world flocked to the Altoona Works, to witness and learn from the extraordinarily sophisticated operations of a fully integrated transportation company. The Test Department enshrined the PRR's reputation as the Standard Railroad of the World. Those days were in the past. The E6s Atlantics and K4s Pacifics of the early twentieth century proved ill-suited for the longer, heavier, and faster trains that were necessary to meet highway competition. During the 1930s and 1940s, the PRR's motive-power officials failed miserably in their efforts to compete against diesels. After World War II, the cessation of locomotive construction and the opening of the Samuel Rea Shops in Hollidaysburg turned large sections of the Altoona Works into something resembling a ghost town.

The Broadway Limited pulled away from the stricken community and headed for the summit of the Allegheny Mountains. It soon encountered the Horseshoe Curve, J. Edgar Thomson's engineering masterpiece. Like most PRR passenger trains, *The Broadway* passed through the area during the night, when the national civil engineering landmark was hidden from view. In the apex of the curve, nearly invisible in the darkness, reposed a K4s Pacific, immobilized on a section of track barely long enough to contain its wheels. The locomotive that had once reflected the genius contained in the Motive Power Department had been superseded by a new form of technology. Vogt, Gibbs, and Wallis, the creators of the K4s, were long gone. So was Harry Jones, the chief of motive power and one of the individuals who had attempted in vain to develop a steam locomotive that could keep the diesels at bay. He never left the railroad that he loved, and his ashes, scattered along Horseshoe Curve, had become part of the ground over which trains passed, day and night.

Next came the summit tunnels at Gallitzin, followed by the descent into the valley of the Little Conemaugh. To the west of the summit lay South Fork, an isolated location that in 1889 became indelibly etched on the American consciousness. The flood that ravaged Johnstown, erasing miles of track and devouring entire trains, could not destroy the underlying economic advantages of the railroads or the vitality of the PRR. Within weeks, an army of workers had restored the line to service, and only an empty reservoir and a cemetery filled with headstones attested to the dangers of human error. By 1968, however, both the power of the railroads and the strength of this particular railroad had disappeared—and nothing, not even the greatest merger in American business history, could restore them.

For most of the passengers on *The Broadway Limited*, the crisis affecting the railroads and the problems of the world paled in comparison to their individual concerns. Matters involving jobs, relationships, families, or illness either lulled them to sleep or plagued them like demons in the night. The train would soon arrive in Pittsburgh, the city of coal, iron, and steel. Beyond lay the fertile farmlands of Ohio and Indiana. It had been nearly half a century since the tracks that crisscrossed that region had been part of the Lines West of Pittsburgh and Erie. That designation was a legacy of efforts by Thomson and Scott to secure control over the PRR's western connections, with a minimum of investment and new construction, and without running afoul of restrictions in the company's charter. The separation of Lines East and Lines West also attested to the difficulty of coordinating the operations of a massive railway empire. Despite their optimistic pronouncements of the extraordinary efficiencies associated with the merger, poor coordination was something that Penn Central executives were about to experience full force. By the following morning, just after breakfast in the diner, *The Broadway* would be in Chicago, a city built by the railroads, and one that had long since replaced Pittsburgh as the true gateway to the West.

Descending the western slope of the Alleghenies, *The Broadway Limited*'s engineman stared through the darkness and the swirls of snow churned up by the passage of the finest passenger train in the eastern United States. By virtue of his seniority, he was one of the most experienced and best paid of all railway employees and the leading edge of a confraternity that included thousands of trainmen, switchmen, tower operators, signal maintainers, shopworkers, and car cleaners. The actions of each required the contributions of all the others, just as every freight and passenger train on the sprawling Pennsylvania Railroad moved in an integrated and harmonious system of mutual interdependency. The links stretched back through time and connected everyone on *The Broadway Limited* to the long-dead generations of promoters, boosters, entrepreneurs, engineers, workers, strikers, passengers, shippers, lawyers, regulators, and politicians who shaped the history of the Pennsylvania Railroad. The towers and position-light signals that guided *The Broadway Limited* through the night attested to that coordination and interdependence and to the continued reliance on the legacy handed down from the past. Signal after signal, mile after mile, and hour after hour, the train rolled on as trains had moved across Pennsylvania for more than a century. Somewhere along the valley of the Little Conemaugh River, as the inevitability of planetary motion plunged that part of the earth into its deepest darkness, midnight marked the transition to a new month as well as the promise of impending dawn. No one could predict what the new day would bring, any more than they could foresee the future of the Penn Central. The only things that could be known with certainty were that the passage of time could never be turned back and that what the architects of the merger had done could never be undone. The clock ticked forward one more minute, and after nearly 122 years of corporate existence, the life of the Pennsylvania Railroad came to its end.

NOTES

Prologue

1. "Penn Central's Announcement," *New York Times*, June 22, 1970 ("squeeze").

2. Linda Charlton, "Penn Central Is Granted Authority to Reorganize Under Bankruptcy Laws," *New York Times*, June 22, 1970 ("regrettable").

3. Hoag Levins, "Penn Central History Shows Court Action 'Not Really Unexpected,'" *Philadelphia Inquirer*, June 22, 1970 ("unexpected," "surprise"); Michael J. Clark, "Court Move May Affect Nation's Railways," *Philadelphia Inquirer*, June 22, 1970; "Penn Central Distress," *Philadelphia Inquirer*, June 22, 1970 ("vital," "experts").

4. "The Rails' Thunder Fades," *Altoona Mirror*, June 23, 1970 ("good," "operation," "crisis").

5. Dan Machalaba, "Railroading's Biggest Blunders," *Trains* 75, no. 9 (September 2015): 46–57 ("flubs").

6. Robert Sobel, *Fallen Colossus: The Great Crash of the Penn Central* (Washington, DC: Beard Books, 1977), 212–20; Joseph R. Daughen and Peter Binzen, *The Wreck of the Penn Central* (Boston: Little, Brown, 1971; Washington, DC: Beard, 1999), 54–55, 111–13; Stephen Salsbury, *No Way to Run a Railroad: The Untold Story of the Penn Central Crisis* (New York: McGraw-Hill, 1982), 78–82, 135–36.

7. Daughen and Binzen, *Wreck of the Penn Central*, 92–98, 220–21; Salsbury, *No Way to Run a Railroad*, 90–95.

8. Richard Saunders Jr., *Merging Lines: American Railroads, 1900–1970* (DeKalb: Northern Illinois University Press, 2001), 404–5; Rush Loving Jr., *The Men Who Loved Trains: The Story of Men Who Battled Greed to Save an Ailing Industry* (Bloomington: Indiana University Press, 2006), 40–47; Sobel, *Fallen Colossus*, 258–70; Daughen and Binzen, *Wreck of the Penn Central*, 103–5, 177–205; Salsbury, *No Way to Run a Railroad*, 57–74, 172–74.

9. The most memorable interaction occurred when Perlman accused Smucker of operating "a wooden-wheeled railroad," a pointed reference to the allegedly outdated methods used on the PRR. Smucker and some of his former PRR associates responded with private comments that were often unprofessional and at times deeply antisemitic. Daughen and Binzen, *Wreck of the Penn Central*, 90–116, "wooden" at 116.

10. Sobel, *Fallen Colossus*, 269–77; Robert E. Gallamore and John R. Meyer, *American Railroads: Decline and Renaissance in the Twentieth Century* (Cambridge, MA: Harvard University Press, 2014), 149–58; H. Roger Grant, *Visionary Railroader: Jervis Langdon Jr. and the Transportation Revolution* (Bloomington: Indiana University Press, 2008), 170–71.

11. For an overview of the fragmented nature of transportation regulation, see Mark H. Rose, Bruce E. Seely, and Paul F. Barrett, *The Best Transportation System in the World: Railroads, Trucks, Airlines, and American Public Policy in the Twentieth Century* (Columbus: Ohio State University Press, 2006).

12. Saunders, *Merging Lines*, 378–87; Daughen and Binzen, *Wreck of the Penn Central*, 252–55.

13. Saunders, *Merging Lines*, 416–17; H. Roger Grant, *Erie Lackawanna: The Death of an American Railroad, 1938–1992* (Stanford, CA: Stanford University Press,

1994); Gregory L. Schneider, *Rock Island Requiem: The Collapse of a Mighty Fine Line* (Lawrence: University Press of Kansas, 2013); H. Roger Grant, *A Mighty Fine Road: A History of the Chicago, Rock Island & Pacific Railroad Company* (Bloomington: Indiana University Press, 2020).

14. Geoffrey H. Doughty, Jeffrey T. Darbee, and Eugene E. Harmon, *Amtrak: America's Railroad: Transportation's Orphan and Its Struggle for Survival* (Bloomington: Indiana University Press, 2021), esp. 3–11, 52–89.

15. Richard Saunders Jr., *Main Lines: Rebirth of the North American Railroads, 1970–2022* (DeKalb: Northern Illinois University Press, 2003), 94–122; Gallamore and Meyer, *American Railroads*, 159–90.

16. Rose, Seely, and Barrett, *Best Transportation System*, 170–76, 207–8; Gallamore and Meyer, *American Railroads*, 218–56.

17. Saunders, *Main Lines*, 200–206; Grant, *Visionary Railroader*, 176–85, 208–13; Gallamore and Meyer, *American Railroads*, 191–217; Loving, *Men Who Loved Trains*, 227–37.

18. Saunders, *Main Lines*, 233–40; Gallamore and Meyer, *American Railroads*, 191–218.

19. Saunders, *Main Lines*, 322–28, 340–42; Gallamore and Meyer, *American Railroads*, 297–301; Loving, *Men Who Loved Trains*, 286–340.

1. Steam

1. John H. White Jr., *The John Bull: 150 Years a Locomotive* (Washington, DC: Smithsonian Institution, 1981), 23–24.

2. Jan Onofrio, *Pennsylvania Biographical Dictionary, Third Edition, Volume 1: A–K* (St. Clair Shores, MI: Somerset, 1999), 328–29; White, *John Bull*, 22–23.

3. John H. White Jr., *American Locomotives: An Engineering History, 1830–1880, Revised and Expanded Edition* (Baltimore, MD: Johns Hopkins University Press, 1968, 1997), 248–68; White, *John Bull*, 12–24; Charles E. Fisher, "The Steam Locomotives of the Pennsylvania Railroad System," *Railway and Locomotive Historical Society Bulletin* 89 (November 1953): 139–58, at 140.

4. White, *American Locomotives*, 251–52; White, *John Bull*, 32–49.

5. Frederick Westing, *Apex of the Atlantics* (Milwaukee, WI: Kalmbach, 1963), 123–35.

6. As one historian has noted,

The Motive Power Department of the PRR was unique in American railroading. From 1866–1936, seventy years,

only three men sat in the Mechanical Engineer's chair at Altoona, if you discount the one-year term of John W. Cloud: John B. Collin 1866–1886, Axel Vogt 1887–1919, and William F. Kiesel Jr. 1919–1936. For thirty-seven of those years Theodore N. Ely was either General Superintendent of Motive Power, Lines East (1874–1893) or Chief of Motive Power (1893–1911). For the most part the pedigrees of these men read: Apprentice, Altoona Machine Shop. They were trained in America's school of practical railroading. The PRR Motive Power Department was a place where tradition could develop, where design principles could be carried out and passed from generation to generation, to teacher, to pupil.

Richard D. Adams, with John M. Prophet and Roger L. Keyser, "The I-1s," *Keystone* 10, no. 1 (March 1977): 2–11 ("unique").

7. At their November 22, 1848, meeting, the board of directors authorized an expenditure of $19,200, payable to Baldwin. That was presumably a payment for two locomotives, although the amount was $600 more than the stated $9,300 per-locomotive cost. The third locomotive might have been a 0-6-0 that the PRR never purchased and that Thomson encouraged Baldwin to sell to the B&O.

8. There has been considerable debate regarding the identity of the first locomotive to operate on the Pennsylvania Railroad. Following an extensive analysis of PRR and Baldwin records, the late Richard Adams has provided convincing evidence that the honor goes to the *Dauphin*. Furthermore, Adams has noted, the PRR named locomotives for counties that lay along the route between Harrisburg and Pittsburgh. They were, from east to west, Dauphin, Perry, Juniata, Mifflin, Huntingdon, Blair, Cambria, Indiana, Westmoreland, and Allegheny—suggesting that locomotives were delivered and placed in service in that order. Much of the confusion, Adams has observed, has occurred because the *Dauphin* and the *Perry* arrived before the railroad was open for revenue service. The *Mifflin* was probably the first locomotive delivered after the PRR opened the line between Harrisburg to Lewistown, on September 1, 1849, and thus was the first new motive power received by the railroad as an operating entity.

9. PRR BOD Minutes, September 27, 1848, 118–19; October 11, 1848, 12; Richard D. Adams, "PRR's First Locomotive," *Keystone* 55, no. 3 (Autumn 2022): 68–77; Fisher, "Steam Locomotives of the Pennsylvania Railroad System," 146; Paul T. Warner, *Motive Power Development on the Pennsylvania Railroad System, 1831–1924*, reprinted from *Baldwin Locomotives* (Philadelphia: Pennsylvania Railroad Company, 1924), 11–12.

10. Joseph Harrison Jr., *The Locomotive and Philadelphia's Share in Its Early Improvements* (Philadelphia: George Gebbie, 1872); White, *American Locomotives,* 288–89; William Bender Wilson, *History of the Pennsylvania Railroad, with Plan of Organization, Portraits of Officials and Biographical Sketches,* vol. 1 (Philadelphia: Henry T. Coates, 1899), 58–59, 91; Test Department and Motive Power Department Organization from 1849 until June 13, 1939, Pennsylvania Railroad Company Records, Accession 1807/1810, Manuscripts and Archives Department, Hagley Museum and Library, Wilmington, DE (hereafter, HML), Box 3; James A. Ward, "Power and Accountability on the Pennsylvania Railroad, 1846–1878," *Business History Review* 49, no. 1 (Spring 1975): 37–59, at 44–45.

11. Paul T. Warner, "Boiler Development on the Pennsy," *Mutual Magazine,* February 1936, 7–12.

12. Warner, "Boiler Development on the Pennsy"; Warner, *Motive Power Development,* 19–21, 24; White, *American Locomotives,* 98.

13. Englishman Edward Bury developed the boiler that bore his name in 1830. Owing to its dome shape, it is often referred to as a haystack boiler.

14. PRR BOD Minutes, January 30, 1850, 246; February 20, 1850, 256; April 30, 1852, 431 ("necessary"); Adams, "PRR's First Locomotive," 69, 72–73; George H. Burgess and Miles C. Kennedy, *Centennial History of the Pennsylvania Railroad Company, 1846–1946* (Philadelphia: Pennsylvania Railroad Company, 1949), 53–54, 84–85; White, *American Locomotives,* 94–95, 194–98.

15. By the early 1860s, the PRR rostered some three hundred locomotives, including seventy-three manufactured by Norris. Those seventy-three locomotives were collectively responsible for 60 percent of the boiler explosions that occurred between 1857 and 1864. Warner, *Motive Power Development,* 11–12, 14–15; Andrew Dawson, *Lives of the Philadelphia Engineers: Capital, Class and Revolution, 1830–1890* (Aldershot: Ashgate, 2004), 28.

16. Warner, *Motive Power Development,* 11–14.

17. J. Simpson Africa, *History of Huntingdon and Blair Counties, Pennsylvania* (Philadelphia: Louis H. Everts, 1883), 135; James J. D. Lynch Jr., "Overview of the History and Development of the Pennsylvania Railroad's Altoona Shops," *Keystone* (Autumn 1996): 18–61, at 18–20; A. Howry Espenshade, *Pennsylvania Place Names* (Harrisburg, PA: Evangelical, 1925), 176. Information regarding the history of Altoona and of the PRR facilities in the city is also in Richard E. Beeler, *Altoona Centennial Booklet: Noteworthy Personages and Historical Events: Official Souvenir Program, Altoona's Centennial Celebration, August*

6th to 14th, 1949 (Altoona, PA: Altoona Centennial, 1949); William Hasell Wilson, *The Columbia-Philadelphia Railroad and Its Successor* (1896, republished by Morris M. Green Jr., ed. [York, PA: American Canal & Transportation Center, 1985]), 58–59; and the Pennsylvania Railroad Company, "Altoona Works, 1941," Penn Central Railroad Collection, M. G. 286, Pennsylvania Historical and Museum Commission, Pennsylvania State Archives, Harrisburg (hereafter, PHMC), Box 161 (262–66).

18. William B. Sipes, *The Pennsylvania Railroad: Its Origin, Construction, Condition, and Connections; Embracing Historical, Descriptive, and Statistical Notices of Cities, Towns, Villages, Stations, Industries, and Objects of Interest on Its Various Lines in Pennsylvania and New Jersey* (Philadelphia: Pennsylvania Railroad Passenger Department, 1875), 138–39; William Mason Cornell, *The History of Pennsylvania from the Earliest Discovery to the Present Time: Including an Account of the First Settlements by the Dutch, Swedes, and English, and of the Colony of William Penn, His Treaty and Pacific Measures with the Indians; and the Gradual Advancement of the State to Its Present Aspect of Opulence, Culture, and Refinement* (Philadelphia: John Sully, 1876), 325–26.

19. William Bender Wilson, *History of the Pennsylvania Railroad: With Plan of Organization, Portraits of Officials and Biographical Sketches,* vol. 2 (Philadelphia: Henry T. Coates, 1899), 208; Lynch, "Overview," 21–22.

20. John C. Paige, *A Special History Study: Pennsylvania Railroad Shops and Works, Altoona, Pennsylvania* (Washington, DC: US Department of the Interior, National Park Service, 1989), 6–9, 10–11, 26–29, 41–42.

21. The similarities to Pullman were nonetheless strong enough that, following the 1894 Pullman Strike, PRR officials immediately undertook a comparative analysis of the two facilities. The railroad's managers concluded that "when the town of Altoona was established the line of policy adopted was directly opposite to that afterwards adopted by the Pullman people."

22. Comments of Frank L. Sheppard, interview by J. Elfreth Watkins, April 25, 1898, J. Elfreth Watkins Collection, Smithsonian Institution National Museum of American History, Behring Center, Archives Center, Box 2, folder 2 ("moral," "opposite"); PRR BOD Minutes, July 9, 1853; Africa, *History of Huntingdon and Blair Counties,* 163; Paige, *Special History Study,* 4–7.

23. Wilson, *History of the Pennsylvania Railroad,* vol. 1, 411–14.

24. Burgess and Kennedy, *Centennial History,* 85, 291; Paige, *Special History Study,* 6–7, 13, 20; Lynch, "Overview," 23, 44–53; James Dredge, *The Pennsylvania*

Railroad: Its Organization, Construction, and Management (New York: John Wiley and Sons, 1879), 90–95.

25. Dredge, *Pennsylvania Railroad*, 76–90; Lynch, "Overview," 23–37.

26. Dredge, *Pennsylvania Railroad*, 97–103.

27. Albert J. Churella, *The Pennsylvania Railroad, Volume I: Building an Empire, 1846–1917* (Philadelphia: University of Pennsylvania Press, 2013), 388–92.

28. *Railroad Gazette*, November 2, 1872, 477; Dredge, *Pennsylvania Railroad*, 97–103.

29. *Railway Age* 37, no. 15 (April 8, 1904): 752–64; Bruce Seely, "Wilmington and Its Railroads: A Lasting Connection," *Delaware History* 19 (Spring–Summer 1980): 1–19; White, *John Bull*, 77–80.

30. Merle D. Rice, ed., *The History of the Pennsylvania Railroad's Fort Wayne Shops* (Fort Wayne, IN: Fort Wayne Public Library, 1966), 2–8; John H. White, "Railroad Car Builders of the United States," *Railroad History* 138 (Spring 1978): 5–29, at 28; Bert Joseph Griswold, *The Pictorial History of Fort Wayne, Indiana: A Review of Two Centuries of Occupation of the Region about the Head of the Maumee River, Volume 1* (Chicago: Robert O. Law, 1917), 411, 446–47, 488.

31. American Railway Master Mechanics' Association, *Report of the Proceedings of the Twenty-Fifth Annual Convention* (New York: De Leeuw, Oppenheimer & Company, 1892), 226–27.

32. Rice, *History of the Pennsylvania Railroad's Fort Wayne Shops*, 8–12; Griswold, *Pictorial History of Fort Wayne*, vol. 1, 313, 480.

33. *Railroad Gazette*, April 11, 1890, 244–45 ("progressive").

34. *New York Times*, September 28, 1901; *Railroad Gazette*, December 16, 1881, 719; November 4, 1887, 724; February 12, 1892, 128; 31, no. 44 (November 3, 1899): 768; *Railway and Locomotive Engineering* 16, no. 7 (July 1903): 328; Frederick Westing, "An American Beauty," *Trains* 14, no. 10 (August 1954): 22–26, at 22.

35. A. W. Gibbs to A. Feldpauche, March 7, 1911 ("design"), HML, Box 419, folder 564–567.

36. Dover, OH, *Daily Reporter*, May 18, 1965.

37. J. H. Newton, J. G. Nichols, and A. G. Sprankle, *History of the Pan-Handle: Being Historical Collections of the Counties of Ohio, Brooke, Marshall and Hancock, West Virginia* (Wheeling, WV: J. A. Caldwell, 1879), xi–xiii; *The History of Tuscarawas County, Ohio* (Chicago: Warner, Beers & Company, 1884), 594–97; *Seventeenth Annual Report of the Board of Directors of the Pittsburgh, Cincinnati & St. Louis Railway Company to the Stockholders, for the Year ending December 31, 1884* (Philadelphia: Review Printing House, 1885), 64.

38. *History of Tuscarawas County*, 594–97; Dover, OH, *Daily Reporter*, May 18, 1965.

39. Colin J. Davis, "Strategy for Success: The Pennsylvania Railroad and the 1922 National Railroad Shopmen's Strike," *Business and Economic History* 19 (1990): 271–78, at 277; Dover, OH, *Daily Reporter*, May 18, 1965.

40. Rick Tipton, *The Pennsylvania Railroad in Columbus, Ohio* (Kutztown, PA: Kutztown, 2011), 9.

41. Tipton, *Pennsylvania Railroad in Columbus*, 90.

42. "Abstracts from the General Manager's Report," *Eighteenth Annual Report of the Board of Directors of the Pittsburgh, Cincinnati & St. Louis Railway Company to the Stockholders, for the Year ending December 31, 1885* (Philadelphia: Review Printing House, 1886), 66 ("completed," "transfer"); *Twenty-First Annual Report of the Board of Directors of the Pittsburgh, Cincinnati & St. Louis Railway Company to the Stockholders, for the Year ending December 31, 1888* (Philadelphia: Review Printing House, 1889), 72; Charles E. Fisher, "The Steam Locomotives of the Pennsylvania Railroad System: Part II," *Railway and Locomotive Historical Society Bulletin* 90 (May 1954): 133–46, at 140; *Railroad Gazette*, August 28, 1885, 556–57.

43. Further expansion took place during World War I, at which time employment peaked at eight thousand workers. The PRR built additional facilities in 1919, including a transverse erecting shop, manufacturing machine shop, wheel shop, flue shop, boiler shop, and tank shop, as well as an enlarged powerhouse. The workforce fell to thirty-seven hundred during the difficult years of the Great Depression before rebounding during World War II and declining rapidly thereafter. The shop facilities at Jeffersonville, Indiana, handled repairs but did not build new cars. Tipton, *Pennsylvania Railroad in Columbus, Ohio*, 90–92; *Railroad Gazette* 25, no. 16 (April 17, 1903): 278–80; Mardo Williams, "Pennsy Shops Lose Their Steam," *Columbus Dispatch*, March 13, 1955; "The Columbus Shops," *Mutual Magazine*, December 1936, 7–10.

44. Burgess and Kennedy, *Centennial History*, 711–12; "Address by S. M. Vauclain to the American Railroad Association," *Railway Age* 88, no. 25D (June 25, 1930), 1548D141 ("alike").

45. White, *American Locomotives*, 542; Paul T. Warner, "Standardized Locomotives on the Pennsylvania," *Mutual Magazine*, November 1935, 2–5, at 2; Paige, *Special History Study*, 43.

46. Warner, *Motive Power Development*, 22; Steven W. Usselman, *Regulating Railroad Innovation: Business,*

Technology, and Politics in America, 1840–1920 (Cambridge, MA: Cambridge University Press, 2002), 68–73.

47. Warner, "Standardized Locomotives on the Pennsylvania," 2–7; White, *American Locomotives,* 187.

48. Warner, *Motive Power Development,* 26.

49. *Altoona Tribune,* March 25, 1886.

50. In his study of the PRR shops, John Paige indicated that the first locomotive built by the Altoona Machine Shops was #86, completed in May 1862, renumbered as #73 in 1869, and scrapped in 1885. That assertion is in turn based on a memo from J. A. Lockard to Hal T. Cover, dated January 31, 1949, in Box 1, Chief of Motive Power File, HML. Joseph Lovell, a PRR employee at Altoona who meticulously cataloged the output of the Altoona Machine Shops and the Juniata Shops, listed the #142 of December 1866 as construction number 1. It is possible that #86 of 1862 was a rebuilt locomotive rather than new construction. In any case, Lovell listed a locomotive #86, construction number 50, as being built at the Altoona Machine Shops in December 1869—the same year that Paige provided as the date when the original #86 became #73. Joseph D. Lovell, *Pennsylvania Railroad Altoona Machine Shops: Construction Number List, 1866–1904* (Philadelphia: National Library of American Transportation, 1984), 1.

51. Warner, "Standardized Locomotives," 3–4; Warner, *Motive Power Development,* 27–30; Lovell, *Pennsylvania Railroad Altoona Machine Shops,* 1–5.

52. American Railway Master Mechanics' Association, *Report of the Proceedings,* 226–27.

53. Warner, *Motive Power Development,* 29–30, 50–51.

54. Warner, *Motive Power Development,* 29; Lovell, *Pennsylvania Railroad Altoona Machine Shops,* 8–9.

55. *Railway Age Gazette* 61, no. 18 (November 3, 1916): 822.

56. *Railway Age Gazette* 61, no. 18 (November 3, 1916): 822; *New York Times,* October 30, 1916.

57. According to the historian John H. White Jr. (*American Locomotives,* 65 ["hybrid"], 407–8), "In all, the *Bedford* was something of a hybrid and had little direct influence on the subsequent development of the 2-8-0. It is mentioned here because of its priority, not its excellence."

58. Lovell, *Pennsylvania Railroad Altoona Machine Shops,* 8; William L. Withuhn, *American Steam Locomotives: Design and Development, 1880–1960* (Bloomington: Indiana University Press, 2019), 43–44.

59. Warner, *Motive Power Development,* 33; White, *American Locomotives,* 95–96; Paul T. Warner, "Old Pennsylvania 'Jacks,'" *Mutual Magazine,* May 1941, 13–17,

at 13–14; Paul T. Warner, "Boiler Development on the Pennsy: Past and Present Designs of Special Interest," *Mutual Magazine,* February 1936, 7–12.

60. White, *American Locomotives,* 102–3; White, *John Bull,* 62–74.

61. John H. White, "James Millholland and Early Railroad Engineering," *Contributions from the Museum of History and Technology* 252 (1968): 3–36; White, *American Locomotives,* 105; Fisher, "Steam Locomotives of the Pennsylvania Railroad System," 150–51; C. H. Caruthers, "Sloping Fireboxes on Locomotives," *Railroad Age Gazette* 45, no. 14 (September 4, 1908): 861–64.

62. Richard D. Adams, "The Altoona Boiler," *Keystone* 4, no. 1 (March 1971): 3–5; Caruthers, "Sloping Fireboxes on Locomotives," 861 ("designers"); Paul Carleton, *Pennsy Steam: A Second Look* (Dunnellon, FL: D. Carleton Railbooks, 1991), 40; Warner, "Boiler Development," 9–11.

63. *Exhibit of Locomotives by Burnham Parry Williams & Co., Baldwin Locomotive Works, Philadelphia, Pa.* (Philadelphia: J. B. Lippincott, 1876), 14–16; Fisher, "Steam Locomotives of the Pennsylvania Railroad System, Part II," 136; Warner, "Jacks," 16–17; Norman J. Perrin, *P.R.R. Classification Series, Number 2: Pennsylvania Railroad Consolidation Classes, Part I: 2-8-0 Built 1907 (H6b, H8, H8a)* (Baltimore, MD: Norman J. Perrin, 1943), 1.

64. James L. Holton, "Wootten and the Reading Shops," *Railroad History* 141 (Autumn 1979): 61–76.

65. *Railway Age Gazette* 51, no. 1 (July 7, 1911): 62 ("alone," "revolutionized").

66. After 1897, it was reassigned to Class D6.

67. *Railroad Gazette,* November 11, 1881, 625–29; Warner, *Motive Power Development,* 29, 34–36.

68. After 1897, the PRR reclassified the Class K as the Class D6 (78-inch drivers), with seven later rebuilt to Class D6a (72-inch drivers).

69. Westing, "American Beauty," 22–26; Warner, *Motive Power Development,* 36; Fred Westing, *Pennsy Steam and Semaphores* (Seattle: Superior, 1974), 9–10.

70. Warner, *Motive Power Development,* 39–40.

71. *Railroad Gazette,* November 11, 1881, 862–63.

72. Richard D. Adams, "The Introduction of the Belpaire Firebox on the PRR," *Keystone* 18, no. 4 (Winter 1985): 54–58; Warner, "Boiler Development on the Pennsy," 10; Withuhn, *American Steam Locomotives,* 50–51; White, *American Locomotives,* 102, 539; *Locomotives and Locomotive Building: Being a Brief Sketch of the Growth of the Railroad System and of the Various Improvements in Locomotive Building in America, together with a History of the Origin and Growth of the Rogers Locomotive*

& Machine Works (New York: William S. Gottsberger, 1886), 26.

73. After 1897, the Class R locomotives were assigned to Class H3, Class H3a, or Class H3b.

74. Withuhn, *American Steam Locomotives*, 50–51; Warner, *Motive Power Development*, 39–40.

75. The Class R weighed 100,600 pounds and featured a grate area of thirty-one square feet, while the Class S weighed 94,200 pounds and featured a grate area of twenty-three square feet. A correspondent for *Railroad Gazette* observed that "the 'class S' can just haul 22 cars over the hill between Allegheny and Alliance when she is worked to a maximum, whereas the 'class R' will do the same work readily and easily at a good speed."

76. After 1897, Class H2a.

77. After 1897, Class H2.

78. Fisher, "Steam Locomotives of the Pennsylvania Railroad System: Part II," 140; *Railroad Gazette*, January 10, 1890, 30; February 21, 1890, 131; April 11, 1890, 252 ("maximum"); Perrin, *Pennsylvania Railroad Consolidation Classes*, 1–2.

79. *Railroad Gazette*, April 11, 1890, 252 ("appreciate," "opinions").

80. *Railroad Gazette*, April 29, 1892, 314 ("question"); May 27, 1892, 397; August 19, 1892, 620.

81. Wilson, *History of the Pennsylvania Railroad*, vol. 1, 208–9; Fisher, "Steam Locomotives of the Pennsylvania Railroad System: Part II," 141; Tipton, *Pennsylvania Railroad in Columbus, Ohio*, 90.

82. *Railroad Gazette*, August 16, 1889, 544–55; February 13, 1891, 118 ("special"); February 27, 1891, 143 ("idea"); December 2, 1892, 893–94; Charles B. Clark, *History of Blair County Pennsylvania, from Its Earliest Settlement, and More Particularly from Its Organization, in 1846 to June 1896* (Altoona, PA: C. B. Clark, 1896), 94; William D. Edson, *Keystone Steam & Electric: A Record of Steam and Electric Locomotives Built for the Pennsylvania Railroad since 1906* (New York: Wayner, 1974), 131; Warner, *Motive Power Development*, 43; *Railway Age* 79, no. 21 (November 21, 1925): 935–39.

83. *Railroad Gazette*, March 3, 1893, 176 ("scrap," "bushings"); April 21, 1893.

84. J. Elfreth Watkins, *Pennsylvania Railroad Company, 1846–1896, in Its Relation to the Pennsylvania State Canals and Railroads and the Consolidated System East and West of Pittsburgh* (unpublished ms., 1896, original at the Smithsonian Institution, with microfilm copies at HML and PHMC, with an additional microfilm copy in the author's possession), vol. 2, "Organization and Departments," 15–19.

85. For a general overview of the principles of scientific management, see Daniel Nelson, *Frederick W. Taylor and the Rise of Scientific Management* (Madison: University of Wisconsin Press, 1980); Samuel Haber, *Efficiency and Uplift: Scientific Management in the Progressive Era, 1890–1920* (Chicago: University of Chicago Press, 1964, 1973); and Judith A. Merkle, *Management and Ideology: The Legacy of the International Scientific Management Movement* (Berkeley: University of California Press, 1980). For information on Taylor, see Frank Barkley Copley, *Frederick W. Taylor, Father of Scientific Management* (New York: Harper and Brothers, 1923); Hugh G. J. Aitken, *Scientific Management in Action: Taylorism at Watertown Arsenal, 1908–1915* (Cambridge, MA: Harvard University Press, 1960, Princeton, NJ: Princeton University Press, 1985); and Robert Kanigel, *The One Best Way: Frederick Winslow Taylor and the Enigma of Efficiency* (New York: Viking, 1997).

86. Frederick Winslow Taylor, *Shop Management* (New York: Harper and Brothers, 1912).

87. Robert L. Emerson, *Allegheny Passage: An Illustrated History of Blair County* (Woodley, CA: Windsor, 1984), 47.

88. *Railroad Gazette*, July 2, 1886, 459 ("willing," emphasis in the original); July 9, 1886, 471–72 ("discord," "understand," "brains"); July 16, 1886, 487 ("fortunately").

89. *Railroad Gazette*, August 6, 1886, 542–43; August 13, 1886, 555–56; August 20, 1886, 572–73.

90. By 1913, James Wallis, the general superintendent of motive power, could boast that "these [Altoona] plants are operated exactly like any other manufacturing plant throughout the country, except that no percentage is added to cover wages, etc., of general officers of this Company, and no profit is charged on the output." Wallis to W. Heyward Myers, August 10, 1910, HML, Box 467, folder 2.

91. *Railroad Gazette*, December 2, 1892, 893 ("modern").

92. *Railroad Gazette*, December 2, 1892, 893 ("enabled").

93. *Railroad Gazette*, August 20, 1886, 572–73 ("opposition"); Comments of Frank L. Sheppard, Watkins Collection ("inherited," "men").

94. Fisher, "Steam Locomotives of the Pennsylvania Railroad System: Part II," 140–44.

95. *New York Times*, September 28, 1901; *Railway and Locomotive Engineering* 16, no. 7 (July 1903): 328; Westing, "American Beauty," 22.

96. The old Class Q became the Class A1 (44-inch drivers), Class A2 (50-inch drivers, with tender), or Class A2a (50-inch drivers, with side tanks). The few surviving members of Class F became Class B1, followed by Class B2 (old Class H) and Classes B3, B4, and B4a (old Class M). In 1897, the PRR did not own any standardized 0-8-0 locomotives, although there were a few nonstandard examples on Lines West—including #634, constructed in 1896 for use on the steep grade of Madison Hill in southern Indiana. Casanave nonetheless reserved Class C for future acquisitions. The only significant subcategory was Class C1, a group of ninety built by the Juniata Shops between 1925 and 1927 (with three identical units supplied to the Washington Terminal Company). The PRR's motive-power officials typically used obsolete road locomotives, particularly the older Class H Consolidations, as shifters, hence the lack of interest in the 0-8-0 wheel arrangement.

97. The newer 4-4-0 Americans were assigned to Class D8 (old Class N); Classes D8a, D9, D9a, D10, and D10a (old Class O, depending on driver diameter and boiler diameter); D11, D11a, D12, D12a, D13, D13a, D13b, D13c, D14, and D14a (old Class P); D15 (old Class T); and D16 and D16a (old Class L).

98. *Railroad Gazette*, September 11, 1896, 651; 29, no. 50 (December 10, 1897): 864; 30, no. 19 (May 30, 1898): 339 ("issued"); 33, no. 5 (February 1, 1901): 74–75; Paul Carleton, *Pennsy Steam: A to T* (Dunnellon, FL: D. Carleton Railbooks, 1989), 22–23.

99. *New York Times*, February 5, 1940; Withuhn, *American Steam Locomotives*, 99–110. For additional information on Andrew and Samuel Vauclain, see G. A. Crimmins, *Vauclain: A History of the Vauclain Family in France and America, ca. 950 to the Year 2010* (Orland Park, IL: Rutledge, 2011).

100. "The time," observed the *Railroad Gazette*, "is believed to be the quickest time in which anything of this kind was ever done, the best previous record being about 24 hours," yet cautioned that "an inspection of our engravings shows, however, that the different parts of the engine were not only completed, but to a certain extent assembled together before erection commenced."

101. *Railroad Gazette*, August 31, 1888, 572 ("time," "inspection"); September 28, 1888, 634–35; *Railway Age and Northwestern Railroader*, January 8, 1892, 33–34.

102. *Railroad Gazette*, July 20, 1888, 468; February 1, 1889, 80; Fisher, "Steam Locomotives of the Pennsylvania Railroad System: Part II," 141.

103. *Railroad Gazette*, June 17, 1892, 445; October 14, 1892, 775; Paul T. Warner, "Eight-Wheelers between New York and Philadelphia 1870–1900," *Railway and Locomotive Historical Society Bulletin* 96 (May 1957): 44–62, at 51; Arthur Tannatt Woods and David Leonard Barnes, *Compound Locomotives*, 2nd ed. (Chicago: Railway Age and Northwestern Railroader, 1893), 262: Paul T. Warner, "Increasing Locomotive Efficiency," *Mutual Magazine*, February 1939, 12–18, at 14–15.

104. After 1897, known as Class D15, and not to be confused with the later Class T1 4-4-4-4 duplex.

105. *Railroad Gazette*, November 25, 1892, 888 ("handsomest," "capable"); Woods and Barnes, *Compound Locomotives*, 130; Westing, *Pennsy Steam and Semaphores*, 10–11.

106. *Railway and Locomotive Engineering* 34, no. 12 (December 1921): 323; A. W. Gibbs, "Obituary: Axel S. Vogt," Proceedings of the Session of the Association of American Railroads, Mechanical Division, Atlantic City, New Jersey, June 14–21, 1922 (New York: Association, 1923), 490.

107. After 1897, Class D14. They were preceded in 1892 by another variant of the original Class P, with less extensive modifications, reclassified as Class D13a.

108. After 1897, the D14a. Warner, *Motive Power Development*, 44–46; Warner, "Eight-Wheelers," 51–52; Fisher, "Steam Locomotives of the Pennsylvania Railroad System: Part II," 141–43.

109. According to PRR motive-power experts Norman Perrin and Frederick Westing, the design briefly carried the designation of Class P and then became Class L in January 1896, apparently reusing the letter earlier assigned to "Jumbo," the PRR's sole 2-4-6T locomotive (which had been scrapped in early 1894) before being reclassified as Class D16 in 1897.

110. After 1897, Class D16a and D16, respectively.

111. Warner, *Motive Power Development*, 45–47; Warner, "Eight-Wheelers," 52–53; Fisher, "Steam Locomotives of the Pennsylvania Railroad System: Part II," 143–44.

112. Fisher, "Steam Locomotives of the Pennsylvania Railroad System: Part II," 143–44.

113. *Railway and Locomotive Engineering* 34, no. 12 (December 1921): 323 ("artistic").

114. Westing, "American Beauty," 24–26.

115. *Railroad Gazette*, September 18, 1896, 651 ("competition," "conditions").

116. *Railroad Gazette*, September 18, 1896, 651 ("sufficiently").

117. Warner, *Motive Power Development*, 22, 48, 5.

118. Warner, "Increasing Locomotive Efficiency," 15–16; Fisher, "Steam Locomotives of the Pennsylvania

Railroad System: Part II," 144; *Railroad Gazette*, December 20, 1895, 835; September 18, 1896, 651 ("intend").

119. Charles E. Fisher, "The Steam Locomotives of the Pennsylvania Railroad System: Part III," *Railway and Locomotive Historical Society Bulletin* 91 (October 1954): 130–52, at 133, 148, 150; Lovell, *Pennsylvania Railroad Altoona Machine Shops*, 54–55.

120. *Railroad Gazette* 29, no. 50 (December 10, 1897): 864 ("believe").

121. *Railroad Gazette* 29, no. 50 (December 10, 1897): 864; 30, no. 9 (March 4, 1898): 165–66; 30, no. 24 (June 17, 1898): 436; Warner, *Motive Power Development*, 40, 50; Perrin, *Pennsylvania Railroad Consolidation Classes*, 2.

122. Sheppard also suggested, inaccurately, that the H5 was "Mr. Thomson's locomotive, not Ely's, not Casanave's, Vogt's or anybody else's." Comments of Frank L. Sheppard, Watkins Collection.

123. The PRR acquired 111 Class H4 and 15 Class H5 locomotives between 1897 and 1907.

124. Motive-power officials originally estimated that the H5 weighed 208,000 pounds. When they finally devised a scale that could weigh the locomotive, they discovered it was 10,000 pounds lighter than they had anticipated.

125. *Railroad Gazette* 30, no. 22 (June 10, 1898): 401; 30, no. 27 (July 8, 1898): 491; 30, no. 30 (July 29, 1898): 547 ("agree"); Perrin, *Pennsylvania Railroad Consolidation Classes*, 2.

126. *Railroad Gazette* 30, no. 32 (August 12, 1898): 584.

127. *Railroad Gazette* 31, no. 28 (July 14, 1899): 502–3; Warner, *Motive Power Development*, 50–51.

128. *Railroad Gazette* 31, no. 9 (March 8, 1899): 158; 31, no. 45 (November 10, 1899): 784; 32, no. 42 (October 12, 1900): 677; Perrin, *Pennsylvania Railroad Consolidation Classes*, 2–3.

129. Office [of] Chief [of] Motive Power Clerk, "Manner of Billing for New Locomotives Built by Baldwin Locomotive Works Under Sliding Scale Contract," March 20, 1913, HML, Box 467, folder 2; Warner, *Motive Power Development*, 57–58.

130. Fisher, "Steam Locomotives of the Pennsylvania Railroad System: Part III," 133–34.

131. The larger boiler on the modern Consolidations proved so successful that Gibbs's successors (principally, mechanical engineer William F. Kiesel Jr.) used a nearly identical design on the G5s Ten-Wheeler. The class, built at the Juniata Shops, included ninety locomotives for the PRR (built in 1922 and 1923) and thirty-one for the Long Island Rail Road (built between 1924 and 1929). Designed for the unique operating conditions of commuter service (particularly the need to accelerate rapidly after making many closely spaced stops), the G5s was an exceptionally powerful locomotive, generating more tractive effort than any other locomotive with a 4-6-0 wheel arrangement.

132. Warner, *Motive Power Development*, 62–63; Perrin, *Pennsylvania Railroad Consolidation Classes*, 3–4.

133. Carleton, *Pennsy Steam: A Second Look*, 81–87, 111; Westing, *Apex of the Atlantics*, 34; Edson, *Keystone Steam & Electric*, 9; Eric Hirsimaki, *Black Gold, Black Diamonds: The Pennsylvania Railroad and Dieselization*, vol. 1 (North Olmstead, OH: Mileposts, 1997), 11, 13; Perrin, *Pennsylvania Railroad Consolidation Classes*, 4.

134. As early as 1879, the PRR experimented, unsuccessfully, with a hot-water heating system in individual cars before settling on the industry-standard Baker system. Steam heat, supplied by the locomotive, began to replace individual car stoves in 1885. By 1893, the PRR had converted 41 percent of the passenger equipment on Lines East and 56 percent on Lines West to steam heat.

135. PRR officials initially favored a different technology, the more luminous—and more expensive—Frost "dry carburetor." The Frost system, which relied on the controlled combustion of pressurized gasoline vapor, was apparently not as dangerous as one might imagine, and by 1892, the PRR used it on nearly a quarter of its passenger car fleet. Publicly announced plans to convert the remainder of the fleet to the Frost system never came to fruition, however. The pending opening of the tunnels under the Hudson and East Rivers prompted the PRR to ban Pintsch lamps and other open flames. Beginning in 1902, with the Class PL coaches, the company began incorporating axle-mounted generators into all newly constructed passenger equipment. In 1904, shop crews began retrofitting the older Class PK cars with generators, and all the new steel cars came so equipped.

136. *Philadelphia North American*, September 20, 1882, reprinted in *Railroad Gazette*, September 22, 1882, 587; *Railroad Gazette*, May 31, 1889, 355–56; *Railroad Gazette*, June 10, 1892, 427; *Railway Age Gazette* 57, no. 23 (December 4, 1914): 1067; *Western Electrician* 16, no. 4 (January 26, 1895): 44; *Electrical Journal* 1, no. 10 (October 15, 1895): 201; "The Passing of the Wooden Passenger Car from This Railroad," July 1928, HML, Box 1414, folder 34; John H. White Jr., *The American Railroad Passenger Car* (Baltimore, MD: Johns Hopkins University Press, 1985), 389, 418–26; Burgess and Kennedy, *Centennial History*, 757–58.

137. PRR Passenger Traffic Department, *History [of] Passenger Train and Through Car Service [on the]*

Pennsylvania Railroad, 1849–1947, ed. Douglas Wornom (Philadelphia: Pennsylvania Railroad, 1947), 2, 4–7; "Original Schedule of the New York and Chicago Limited, November 27, 1881," Watkins Collection, Box 2, folder 2; Christopher T. Baer, "Named Trains of the PRR including Through Services," September 8, 2009, http://www.prrths.com/newprr_files/Hagley/PRR%20NAMED%20TRAINS.pdf, 43, 47–48, 78.

138. *Railroad Gazette*, February 18, 1881, 102; April 1, 1881, 187; April 22, 1881, 223.

139. In late December, and to attract more patronage during the slack winter travel season, the PRR changed the train's New York departure time from 8:00 a.m. to a more convenient 9:00 a.m., with the arrival in Chicago also pushed back by one hour.

140. According to historian John Steele Gordon and others, Dresser initially attempted to sell his story to the *Chicago Daily News*. In that version, the journalist interrupted Vanderbilt's dinner, refused to wait for him to finish, and complained, "But it is late, and I will not reach the office in time. The public—," whereupon Vanderbilt uttered his famous retort. The editor was not interested in that account, prompting Dresser to fabricate an alternate narrative. Some accounts suggest that Sherman, rather than Dresser, asked Vanderbilt the question that provoked the infamous response. Vanderbilt's nephew, Samuel Barton, was also present, and he provided yet another perspective, one that was unsurprisingly favorable to his uncle. *New York Times*, October 9, 1882 ("pay," "forced," "benefit," "damned"); Elmo Scott Watson, "The Truth about That 'Public Be Damned' Interview," *Cambridge Sentinel* 31, no. 45 (November 7, 1936): 2; John Steele Gordon, "The Public Be Damned," *American Heritage* 40, no. 6 (September/October 1989).

141. Each train set (with the Cincinnati car included) offered thirty-six sections, three drawing rooms, and eight staterooms, for a maximum capacity of ninety-seven passengers.

142. Al Westerfield, "The New 'Pennsylvania Limited,'" *Keystone* 34, no. 1 (Spring 2001): 18–45; *New York Times*, August 14, 1889 ("perfectly"); Arthur D. Dubin, *Some Classic Trains* (Milwaukee, WI: Kalmbach, 1964), 76–77 ("triumph"); Joe Welsh, *Pennsylvania Railroad's Broadway Limited* (Minneapolis, MN: Voyageur, 2006), 31–32; White, *American Railroad Passenger Car*, 300.

143. Barksdale joined the PRR in 1883 as a clerk and became the general advertising agent in 1890. He wrote the text for the *Pennsylvania Limited* booklet but was uncredited. The first commemorative passenger booklet used in the United States was for the 1888–1889 *Golden Gate Special*. Michael E. Zega, "PRR's Colonel Frank N. Barksdale, Inventor of the Limited Booklet," *Railroad Heritage* 1, no. 1 (Spring 2000): 12–13.

144. As with the previous (narrow-vestibule) *Pennsylvania Limited*, most passengers rode in open sections.

145. Prior to 1898, the equipment that Pullman assigned to the PRR was probably painted a standard Pullman color—perhaps a dark green or a chocolate brown. As early as May 1902, and certainly by November of that year, President Alexander Cassatt instructed Pullman to paint or repaint all equipment assigned to the PRR (including the cars assigned to the *Pennsylvania Limited* and the *Congressional Limited*) with Tuscan red. Arthur D. Dubin, "The Broadway Limited," *Trains* 22, no. 4 (February 1962): 16–33; Welsh, *Broadway Limited*, 35–37; Joel Rosenbaum and Tom Gallo, *The Broadway Limited* (Piscataway, NJ: Railpace, 1988), 17; Westerfield, "New 'Pennsylvania Limited,'" 19–27.

146. *Railroad Gazette* 31, no. 40 (October 6, 1899): 687 ("fastest").

147. *Railroad Gazette* 28 (June 19, 1896): 429–31.

148. *Railroad Gazette* 31, no. 27 (July 7, 1899): 487 ("departure"); Westing, *Apex of the Atlantics*, 13–19.

149. *Railroad Gazette* 31, no. 27 (July 7, 1899): 487 ("arrived"); 31, no. 32 (August 11, 1899): 563; Norman J. Perrin, *PRR Classification Series Number 4: Pennsylvania Railroad Light Atlantics: Classes E1-5, E7* (Baltimore, MD: Norman J. Perrin, 1944), 15–16.

150. The PRR later reassigned those camelbacks to the Long Island Rail Road.

151. The PRR later reclassified #269 as a Class E1a. Westing, *Apex of the Atlantics*, 19; Perrin, *Pennsylvania Railroad Light Atlantics*, 16–17.

152. Warner, *Motive Power Development*, 54; Westing, *Pennsy Steam and Semaphores*, 31; Perrin, *Pennsylvania Railroad Light Atlantics*, 17–18.

153. *Bulletin of the American Railway Engineering Association* 24, no. 248 (August 1922): 33–36.

154. Withuhn, *American Steam Locomotives*, 108–10.

155. *The Pennsylvania Railroad System at the Louisiana Purchase Exposition* (Philadelphia: Pennsylvania Railroad Company, 1905), 392; *New York Times*, May 31, 1904 ("bursts," "touched").

156. *American Engineer and Railroad Journal*, November 1906, 431–32, at 432 ("granting").

157. *Railway World*, December 16, 1899, 1397.

158. Paige, *Altoona Shops and Works*, 22–24.

159. Burgess and Kennedy, *Centennial History*, 85, 291; White, *American Locomotives*, 19; Paige, *Special History Study*, 6–7, 13, 20; *Eighth Annual Report of the Directors*

of the Pennsylvania Railroad Company to the Stockholders, February 5, 1855 (Philadelphia: Crissy and Markley, 1855), 51; Lovell, *Pennsylvania Railroad Altoona Machine Shops*, 61.

160. Withuhn, *American Steam Locomotives*, 175–76.

161. *Railroad Gazette* 35, no. 33 (August 14, 1903): 589 ("failed").

162. Pennsylvania Railroad, *The Pennsylvania Railroad to the World's Fair, St. Louis, Mo.* (Philadelphia: Allen, Lane & Scott, 1904), 13.

163. Ron Goldfeder, "'The Cleverest Thing in the World': A Comprehensive Look at U.S. Steam-Locomotive Test Plants," *Railroad History*, 228 (Spring-Summer 2023): 14–36; Ron Goldfeder, "Test Plants Abroad: A Global Survey of Locomotive Analysis," *Railroad History* 228 (Spring-Summer 2023): 37–45; Usselman, *Regulating Railroad Innovation*, 210; Paige, *Special History Study*, 68.

164. *Railroad Gazette* 35, no. 21 (May 22, 1903): 366; 35, no. 33 (August 14, 1903): 589.

165. *Railroad Gazette* 35, no. 27 (July 3, 1903): 486 ("scientific"); *Pennsylvania Railroad System at the Louisiana Purchase Exposition*, i ("merely").

166. *Pennsylvania Railroad System at the Louisiana Purchase Exposition*, 124–86.

167. *Pennsylvania Railroad System at the Louisiana Purchase Exposition*, 2–3 ("awarded").

168. *Pennsylvania Railroad System at the Louisiana Purchase Exposition*, i–v ("beauty"), 24, 62–65.

169. *Pennsylvania Railroad System at the Louisiana Purchase Exposition*, 24–61; Withuhn, *American Steam Locomotives*, 177–79.

170. *Pennsylvania Railroad System at the Louisiana Purchase Exposition*, 66–67.

171. PRR, Third Vice President's Office, "Jamestown Exposition," July 2, 1907; "Pennsylvania Railroad System's Exhibit at the Alaska–Yukon–Pacific Exposition," 1909; PRR press release, December 15, 1909; all in HML, Box 609, folder 30; Withuhn, *American Steam Locomotives*, 179.

172. Comments of Frank L. Sheppard, Watkins Collection.

173. Usselman, *Regulating Railroad Innovation*, 355–58; A. W. Gibbs to A. Feldpauche, March 7, 1911 ("information," "criticism," "understood," "progress"), HML, Box 419, folder 564–67.

174. Welsh, *Broadway Limited*, 35–37; Karl R. Zimmerman, *20th Century Limited* (St. Paul, MN: MBI, 2002); Dubin, *Some Classic Trains*, 58–63.

175. When the *New York Times* highlighted the 1889 upgrading of the *Pennsylvania Limited*, a reporter emphasized that "the Limited leaves New-York, foot of Cortlandt and Desbrosses streets, every day at 9 A. M. for Chicago and Cincinnati," but there was no need to mention that that location was a ferry rather than a rail terminal. *New York Times*, August 14, 1889 ("leaves"); Rosenbaum and Gallo, *Broadway Limited*, 6, 19, 24, 28; Welsh, *Broadway Limited*, 39–42.

176. *New York Times*, June 3, 1905 ("bust"); June 4, 1903; June 6, 1905 ("fifteen"); June 9, 1905; June 7, 1905 ("heard"); June 10, 1905.

177. *New York Times*, June 7, 1905 ("expensive," "contest," "deference"); June 8, 1905 ("war," "fight," "incidental").

178. *New York Times*, June 6, 1905 ("acceleration," "outgrowth").

179. US Department of Commerce and Labor, Bureau of the Census, *Bulletin 93: Census of Manufacturers: 1905: Earnings of Wage-Earners* (Washington, DC: United States Government Printing Office, 1908), 11, lists $10.06 as the average weekly earnings for all classes of wage-earners in 1905.

180. *New York Times*, June 7, 1905; June 12, 1905; June 14, 1905; June 18, 1905; *Railroad Gazette* 38, no. 25 (June 23, 1905): 718; 38, no. 26 (June 30, 1905): 751; Mark Wegnmman, *American Passenger Trains and Locomotives Illustrated* (Minneapolis, MN: Voyageur, 2008), 19–20.

181. He may have been tempting fate, for three months later, on September 25, the PRR's *New York Limited* slammed into an accommodation train halted at Paoli, killing five and injuring twenty. *New York Times*, September 26, 1905.

182. *Railroad Gazette* 38, no. 25 (June 23, 1905): 715; *New York Times*, June 19, 1905; June 22, 1905; June 23, 1905 ("astonished," "happen," "befall"); August 28, 1905; August 19, 1906.

183. *New York Times*, July 16, 1905.

184. *New York Times*, December 15, 1906 ("mania," "prefer," "nothing").

185. *New York Times*, December 17, 1906; February 23, 1907; February 24, 1907 ("question," "slower," "demanding"); Welsh, *Broadway Limited*, 42–44; *Printer's Ink*, January 23, 1913, 169.

186. The accident resulted from sabotage (through the removal of bolts and fishplates and the turning of one rail on its side, while leaving intact the bond wires that carried low-voltage signal current) rather than excessive speed, but reporters often linked all such occurrences, regardless of the causes.

187. *New York Times*, March 23, 1907; February 16, 1912.

188. *New York Times*, March 14, 1912 ("drowned").

189. *New York Times*, April 4, 1912; July 29, 1912 ("severe"); July 30, 1912 ("schedules," "please," "slower," "artillery").

190. *New York Times*, July 30, 1912; Welsh, *Broadway Limited*, 42–44; *Printer's Ink*, January 23, 1913, 169.

191. From the beginning, it was evident that the name "Broadway" was a reference to the corresponding street in Manhattan. In January 1913, Frank Barksdale, the head of the PRR's Advertising Department, emphasized that "the nearest railroad station to Broadway is the leaving and arriving point of this train." Therefore, as he informed the advertising journal *Printer's Ink*, "the embodying of Broadway in its title seems to identify it with the life and activities of the great thoroughfare." When the United States Railroad Administration permitted the PRR to reestablish *The Broadway Limited* in May 1919 (following a suspension in service that began in December 1917), it was clear that the train was not competitive against the *Twentieth Century Limited* along the route between New York and Chicago. With the train increasingly reliant on Philadelphia passengers, there would have been a certain logic in appealing to their parochialism, but there was scant attempt to do so. In 1923, the PRR introduced a slogan that suggested that the railroad was "The Broad Way to and from the West," "The Broad Way of Scenic Beauty," "The Broad Way of a Nation's commerce," and "The Broad Way of a Nation's passenger traffic." The 1926 advertising campaign developed by advisor to publicity Ivy Lee and the J. Walter Thompson agency likewise emphasized the PRR as "The Broad Way of Commerce." In addition to highlighting the company's four-track main line between Philadelphia and Pittsburgh, the slogan suggested that PRR management was progressive, broad-minded, and open to new ideas. One 1926 guidebook to Philadelphia's port facilities noted that "the Pennsylvania Railroad well serves the Nation as 'The Broad Way of Commerce,' whether in the matter of freight traffic or passenger traffic." Yet the same page also featured a timetable for the "BROADWAY LIMITED: *The Aristocrat of the Rails.*" The use of the single word *Broadway* in that context suggests that the PRR's advertising campaign (which ended with the Great Depression) did not attempt to persuade gullible Philadelphians into believing that the train's name was based on anything other than the New York street.

192. *Printer's Ink*, January 23, 1913, 169 ("nearest"); *Long Island Railroad Information Bulletin* 3, no. 2 (April 24, 1924): 54 ("West," "Beauty," "commerce," "traffic"); City of Philadelphia, Department of Wharves, Docks and Ferries, *Port of Philadelphia: Its History, Advantages and Facilities* (Philadelphia: n.p., 1926), 14 ("serves," Aristocrat," emphasis in the original); Zega, "Colonel Frank N. Barksdale," 13; Dubin, "Broadway Limited," 22, 26.

193. *Pennsylvania Railroad System at the Louisiana Purchase Exposition*, 39 ("difficulty"); Fisher, "Steam Locomotives of the Pennsylvania Railroad System: Part III," 132 ("paperweight").

194. *American Engineer and Railroad Journal*, November 1906, 431–32, at 431 ("departed").

195. Withuhn, *American Steam Locomotives*, 69–73.

196. Gibbs was technically correct in leaving the *s* off Walschaerts's name. Belpaire would not permit Walschaerts to patent the valve gear under his own name, so a colleague did so on his behalf—but, in the process, misspelled the name on the patent application.

197. *American Engineer and Railroad Journal*, November 1906, 431–32, at 432 ("history," "expensive," "afraid").

198. *American Engineer and Railroad Journal*, November 1906, 431–32, at 432 ("reports," "expectations").

199. Westing, *Apex of the Atlantics*, 19–20, 161–62; Perrin, *Pennsylvania Railroad Light Atlantics*, 17–26.

200. The PRR rebuilt both classes from Class E2 locomotives between 1916 and 1920. Both classes featured superheaters (hence the "s" designation). The E2s (ninety units) featured a Belpaire firebox, while the E2sa (fourteen units) used a radial-stay boiler. All featured piston valves (replacing the slide valves on the original locomotives) and Stephenson valve gear. One of those locomotives (Altoona-built E2a, rebuilt to an E7s) survives and is currently displayed at the Railroad Museum of Pennsylvania. PRR officials selected the locomotive, originally #8063, for preservation and display at the 1939 New York World's Fair and renumbered it as #7002. *New York Times*, June 7, 1905; June 12, 1905; June 14, 1905; June 18, 1905; *Railroad Gazette* 38, no. 25 (June 23, 1905): 718; 38, no. 26 (June 30, 1905): 751; Perrin, *Pennsylvania Railroad Light Atlantics*, 17, 21.

201. Warner, "Standardized Locomotives," 7; Warner, *Motive Power Development*, 41, 55–56; Charles Lake, "Compound Locomotives at Home and Abroad," *Railway Engineer* 26 (July 1905): 193–98; Westing, *Apex of the Atlantics*, 19; Carleton, *Pennsy Steam: A to T*, 109.

202. Westing, *Apex of the Atlantics*, 19.

203. Crawford did not pioneer the 4-6-2 wheel arrangement, which was in use in New Zealand as early as the 1880s and first appeared in the United States with locomotives delivered to the Missouri Pacific in 1902—which was in all likelihood the origin of the name "Pacific."

204. Carleton, *Pennsy Steam: A Second Look*, 78–79; Carleton, *Pennsy Steam, A to T*, 111; Westing, *Apex of the*

Atlantics, 23–24; Frederick Westing, "'Fat Annie'—Pioneer 'Pennsy' Pacific," *Railway and Locomotive Historical Society Bulletin*, 100 (April 1959): 44–51.

205. Carleton, *Pennsy Steam: A Second Look*, 78–79; Carleton, *Pennsy Steam, A to T*, 111; Westing, *Apex of the Atlantics*, 23–24; Westing, *Pennsy Steam and Semaphores*, 97.

206. *Bulletin of the International Railway Congress, Volume X* (Brussels: P. Weissenbruch, 1896), 836 ("portions," "approve").

207. Westing, *Apex of the Atlantics*, 24–28.

208. Westing, *Apex of the Atlantics*, 32–33.

209. Kiesel's grandson, William F. Kiesel IV, was equally talented and worked at Grumman Aerospace as a fluid power engineer, associated with the Apollo space program. *Railway Age* 101, no. 15 (October 10, 1936): 538–39; James Alexander Jr., "Scooping Water in the Age of Steam," *Trains* 53, no. 5 (May 1993): 62–67; David Hugh Onkst, "The Triumph and Decline of the 'Squares': Grumman Aerospace Engineers and Production Workers in the Apollo Era, 1957–1973" (PhD diss., American University, 2011), 477.

210. Westing, *Apex of the Atlantics*, 44.

211. Experience with the E3d suggested that that locomotive's firebox was considerably larger than was necessary for efficient combustion.

212. Westing, *Apex of the Atlantics*, 39–45; Carleton, *Pennsy Steam: A Second Look*, 92–93.

213. Westing, *Apex of the Atlantics*, 47–51; Carleton, *Pennsy Steam: A Second Look*, 92–93.

214. *Railway Age Gazette* 51, no. 2 (July 14, 1911): 103; 51, no. 24 (December 15, 1911): 1255; *Altoona Tribune*, November 8, 1930; *Philadelphia Inquirer*, November 8, 1930.

215. Withuhn, *American Steam Locomotives*, 180.

216. Withuhn, *American Steam Locomotives*, 180.

217. Pennsylvania Railroad Company, *Locomotive Testing Plant at Altoona, Penna., Bulletin No. 18: Tests of a Class K2sa Locomotive* (Altoona, PA: Pennsylvania Railroad Company, 1914), 3–5, 89 ("seen," "equal"), 109 ("stoker"), 116 ("strikingly").

218. Westing, *Apex of the Atlantics*, 59–69.

219. *Railway Age Gazette* 5, no. 8 (February 20, 1914): 356–59, at 356 ("apparently"); Westing, *Apex of the Atlantics*, 71–77.

220. Westing, *Apex of the Atlantics*, 79–90.

221. *Bulletin No. 18: Tests of a Class K2sa Locomotive*, 130–31 ("credited").

222. Carleton, *Pennsy Steam: A Second Look*, 95; Withuhn, *American Steam Locomotives*, 133–41, 181.

223. As Young observed, "Road tests of similar locomotives, almost as large, have been made, but these results were obtained under Test Plant conditions, where complete and accurate measurements are possible and conditions are uniform for a considerable length of time." Pennsylvania Railroad Company, *Locomotive Testing Plant at Altoona, Penna., Bulletin No. 19: Tests of a Class K29 Locomotive, 1912* (Altoona, PA: Pennsylvania Railroad Company, 1913), 3 ("unique," "uniform").

224. *Bulletin No. 19: Tests of a Class K29 Locomotive, 1912*, 4 ("development"), 136 ("performance"), 143 ("eliminate").

225. *Bulletin No. 19: Tests of a Class K29 Locomotive, 1912*, 143 ("applied").

226. Frederick Westing, "K4s," *Trains* 16, no. 10 (August 1956): 45–58, at 46–48; Carleton, *Pennsy Steam: A Second Look*, 97.

227. Pennsylvania Railroad Company, *Locomotive Testing Plant at Altoona, Penna., Bulletin No. 22: Comparison of Passenger Locomotives* (Altoona, PA: Pennsylvania Railroad Company, 1915), 35 ("exceeding"); Westing, "K4s," 48; Carleton, *Pennsy Steam: A Second Look*, 97.

228. Westing, "K4s," 48; Withuhn, *American Steam Locomotives*, 185.

229. The name was an exaggeration, as locomotives so equipped seldom ran through more than three divisions (one or two was more typical) and regular trips never exceeded five hundred miles. Part of the problem had to do with the inherent mechanical limitations of the steam locomotive, with its need for frequent lubrication and maintenance. Moreover, the "coast-to-coast" tender weighed so much that adding one meant removing a revenue-generating passenger car from the train.

230. Westing, "K4s," 49–51.

231. From the beginning, the Florida East Coast assigned an Electro-Motive E3 diesel—streamlined and painted in vibrant colors—to its portion of *The South Wind*. The Louisville & Nashville also acquired several sets of passenger diesels. PRR officials vacillated on whether to buy diesels for the train, at first electing to use streamlined K4s locomotives. They eventually agreed to order a pair of Electro-Motive diesels for the train, ran afoul of wartime production restrictions and a backlog in production at Electro-Motive, and eventually assigned the PRR's first two passenger diesels to the New York–Detroit *Red Arrow*. For a detailed overview of the design and subsequent operation of streamlined K4s Pacific #3768, see Chris Baer, "Chronology for the Streamlining and Painting of K4s 3768," *Keystone* 55, no. 4 (Winter 2022): 10–20. *Railway Age* 100, no. 10 (March 7, 1936):

391–92; "The New Engine," *Mutual Magazine*, April 1936, 5–6; Westing, "K4s," 51.

232. Alfred Gibbs to W. W. Atterbury, September 21, 1904 ("scarcely," "racked," "all-around," "step"), HML, Box 415, folder 307–310.

233. Withuhn, *American Steam Locomotives*, 101–2.

234. While every Mallet was an articulated locomotive, only a compound articulated could be properly called a Mallet.

235. The sole Class HH1s, #3396, should not be confused with the six examples of Class HH1, acquired from the Norfolk & Western in 1943, to cope with wartime traffic. They were built in 1919, as N&W Class Y3, and, like the #3396, utilized a 2-8-8-2 wheel arrangement.

236. The class designation reflected the assignment of 0-8-0 shifters to Class C.

237. Paul T. Warner, "Giants of the Pennsy," *Mutual Magazine*, January 1936, 8–9.

238. During World War I, the PRR acquired thirty-eight Class L2s Mikados, assigned to the PRR and to its Grand Rapids & Indiana subsidiary. They conformed to a design developed by the United States Railroad Administration, but that effort to create industrywide locomotive designs did not match the PRR's own notion of standardization (particularly in their lack of Belpaire fireboxes). In 1923, the PRR sold most of those locomotives to other carriers, retaining only five on the GR&I.

239. Withuhn, *American Steam Locomotives*, 64–65; Carleton, *Pennsy Steam: A to T*, 149–59; Carleton, *Pennsy Steam: A Second Look*, 99; Hirsimaki, *Black Gold, Black Diamonds*, vol. 1, 9, 13.

240. John W. Orr, *Set Up Running: The Life of a Pennsylvania Railroad Engineman, 1904–1949* (University Park: Penn State University Press, 2001), 71–76, 139–42, 239–40.

241. Bert Pennypacker, "Dinosaurs of the Alleghenies," in Carleton, *Pennsy Steam: A to T*, 63–94, at 64–67.

242. The total weight of the L1s was 320,700 pounds. The I1s carried 352,500 pounds on its drivers (91.3 percent of total locomotive weight) versus 240,200 pounds for the L1s (74.9 percent of total locomotive weight).

243. *Railway Age Gazette* 6, no. 11 (March 17, 1916): 524; 62, no. 24 (June 15, 1917): 1241–43; *Railway Mechanical Engineer* 95, no. 11 (November 1921): 673–77, at 676 ("efficiency"); Withuhn, *American Steam Locomotives*, 48, 289; Carleton, *Pennsy Steam: A Second Look*, 99; Adams, "I-1's"; Hirsimaki, *Black Gold, Black Diamonds*, vol. 1, 13–16, 19, 23; Pennypacker, "Dinosaurs," 64–67.

244. Pennypacker, "Dinosaurs," 66–71.

245. Orr, *Set Up Running*, 77–82, 87, 91–92 ("useless," "massive").

246. Richard D. Adams, "PRR Class N1s Locomotives," *Keystone* 8, no. 3 (September 1975): 2–8; Fisher, "Steam Locomotives of the Pennsylvania Railroad System: Part III," 141; Carleton, *Pennsy Steam: A to T*, 177; Carleton, *Pennsy Steam: A Second Look*, 106–7.

247. Fisher, "Steam Locomotives of the Pennsylvania Railroad System: Part III," 141–42; Carleton, *Pennsy Steam: A to T*, 181; Carleton, *Pennsy Steam: A Second Look*, 107–8; Eugene L. Huddleston, *Uncle Sam's Locomotives: The USRA and the Nation's Railroads* (Bloomington: Indiana University Press, 2002), 70.

248. Warner, "Giants of the Pennsy"; Fisher, "Steam Locomotives of the Pennsylvania Railroad System: Part III," 142.

249. *Railway Age* 66, no. 24b (January 19, 1919): 1493; *Railway and Locomotive Engineering* 32 (July 1919): 193–94; Carleton, *Pennsy Steam: A Second Look*, 109–10; Fisher, "Steam Locomotives of the Pennsylvania Railroad System: Part III," 142; Warner, "Giants of the Pennsy."

250. Hirsimaki, *Black Gold, Black Diamonds*, vol. 1, 17, 32; Burgess and Kennedy, *Centennial History*, 596–97.

251. In 1938, the PRR suspended all locomotive repair work at the Altoona Machine Shops. The facility, renamed the 12th Street Car Shops, focused on the construction of freight and passenger cars. Howard W. Schotter, *The Growth and Development of the Pennsylvania Railroad Company* (Philadelphia: Allen, Lane & Scott, 1927), 432–36.

252. Hirsimaki, *Black Gold, Black Diamonds*, vol. 1, 7–10.

253. Withuhn, *American Steam Locomotives*, 213–21; David Weitzman, *Superpower: The Making of a Steam Locomotive* (Boston: David R. Godine, 1987); Tom Morrison, *The American Steam Locomotive in the Twentieth Century* (Jefferson, NC: McFarland & Company, 2018), 346–93.

254. The #4700 featured a superheater, but in 1923, the PRR suspended the use of the "s" portion of the class designation.

255. Carleton, *Pennsy Steam: A Second Look*, 113–14; Carleton, *Pennsy Steam: A to T*, 161; Bert Pennypacker, "Atterbury's Engines," *Trains* 39, no. 12 (October 1979): 22–32.

256. In her unpublished biography of Atterbury, Patricia Talbot Davis suggested that "the company in 1922 had just spent $31,500,000 for 475 new engines so Atterbury's design seemed destined never to leave the drawing board. Yet he felt this M-1 was so important he

paid $68,317 of his own funds to Baldwin Locomotive Works to have it built, and then leased it to the Pennsylvania, recovering his investment." The story also appears in Pennypacker, "Atterbury's Engines," 26.

257. Fred Westing, "The Mighty M1's," *Keystone* 12, no. 2 (June 1979): 4–10; Walter P. Keely Jr., "The 4700 and W. W. Atterbury: Development of the First M1," *Keystone* 29, no. 2 (Summer 1996): 45–48; *Railway Age* 81, no. 21 (November 20, 1926): 989–92; Patricia Talbot Davis, "The Railroad General: William Wallace Atterbury," unpublished manuscript, revision 1.31, June 5, 1990, 116, Atterbury Family Papers, Accession 2053, Hagley Museum & Library, Wilmington, DE, Box 10, folder 2 ("destined").

258. Carleton, *Pennsy Steam: A Second Look*, 113–14.

259. Welsh, *Broadway Limited*, 116–17; Baer, "Named Trains of the PRR," 14, 39, 55, 68.

260. Separate figures for intercity and commuter traffic are not available prior to 1922.

261. Interstate Commerce Commission Docket No. 31954: Passenger Train Deficit, Item 7, Exhibit Accompanying Testimony of Walter W. Patchell, Vice President, Research and Development, The Pennsylvania Railroad Company, 1957, 10–13.

262. Roland Marchand, *Creating the Corporate Soul: The Rise of Public Relations and Corporate Imagery in American Big Business* (Berkeley: University of California Press, 1998), 120–21; Baer, "Named Trains of the PRR"; Christopher T. Baer, "Named Trains of the Long Island Rail Road," September 8, 2009, http://www.prrths.com/newprr_files/Hagley/LIRR%20NAMED%20TRAINS.pdf.

263. In September 1925, the PRR renamed the *Washington Broadway Limited* as *The Liberty Limited*; under that name, the train continued to operate until October 1957.

264. Welsh, *Broadway Limited*, 28, 59–61, 121–22, 144–45. For additional information on the *Capitol Limited*, see Dubin, *Some Classic Trains*, 96–107; Harry Stegmaier, *Baltimore & Ohio Passenger Service, 1945–1971—Volume 2: The Route of the* Capitol Limited (Lynchburg, VA: TLC, 1997); and Joe Welsh, *Baltimore & Ohio's* Capitol Limited *and* National Limited (Saint Paul, MN: Voyageur, 2007).

265. Baer, "Named Trains of the PRR," 65, 72, 75, 80; Welsh, *Broadway Limited*, 130–32. For additional information on the *National Limited*, see Harry Stegmaier, *Baltimore & Ohio Passenger Service, 1945–1971—Volume 1: The Route of the* National Limited (Lynchburg, VA: TLC, 1996); and Welsh, *Baltimore & Ohio's* Capitol Limited *and* National Limited.

266. The two New York stops were at Manhattan Transfer (for passengers destined to and from Lower Manhattan) and Penn Station (for Midtown and connecting trains).

267. Baer, "Named Trains of the PRR," 35, 48, 57–91, 61, 66.

268. The *Metropolitan Limited* was the former *Metropolitan Express* (the name change occurred on May 26, 1925), which had in turn been the *Chicago Special / New York Special* prior to 1913.

269. Baer, "Named Trains of the PRR," 3, 9, 16, 18, 62–63; Welsh, *Broadway Limited*, 136–37.

270. The *Judiciary*, established in 1932 and offering daytime service between New York and Washington, honored another branch of the federal government. By that time, *The Senator* had lost its extra-fare status and added coaches to the previously all-Pullman consist—common changes as PRR executives struggled to cut costs during the early years of the Great Depression.

271. The train took its name from the army's 42nd Infantry Division, organized at the beginning of World War I by combining National Guard units from twenty-six states and the District of Columbia. Then-major Douglas MacArthur suggested that the division would "stretch over the whole country like a rainbow." The name was thus a reference to the division's geographic rather than racial or ethnic diversity, and the US military would remain segregated until 1948. Despite MacArthur's comment, the desire of the Wilson administration to spread the inevitable initial casualties over the entire country rather than concentrate them in a specific geographic area offered the more likely explanation. Martin Gilbert, *The First World War: A Complete History* (New York: Henry Holt, 1994), 400.

272. In April 1930, the PRR renamed *The Red Knight* as the westbound *Rainbow*, ensuring that the latter name applied to the train in both directions.

273. The *Airway Limited* actually operated as the advance section of the westbound *American*, while the eastbound *American* accommodated the small number of passengers arriving from Los Angeles and intermediate points. Baer, "Named Trains of the PRR," 2, 35, 58, 66, 68; Welsh, *Broadway Limited*, 122–26, 139.

274. During the nineteenth century and into the early twentieth century, the PRR generally employed the term *Transportation Department* to describe the core functions associated with moving trains. By the 1920s, the term *Operating Department* was more common and was employed almost exclusively in the years following World War II.

275. Withuhn, *American Steam Locomotives*, 241–57.
276. *Bulletin No. 22: Comparison of Passenger Locomotives*, 46 ("limitations," "larger"); Frederick Westing, "Pennsy's Pluperfect Pacific," *Trains* 17, no. 11 (September 1957): 52–55.
277. Westing, "Pennsy's Pluperfect Pacifics," 53; J. Parker Lamb, *Perfecting the American Steam Locomotive* (Bloomington: Indiana University Press, 2003), 21–22, 153–54.
278. The Italian origins of the Caprotti mechanism earned the locomotive the nickname of "Mussolini." The #5698, despite its equally un-American Walschaerts valve gear, became the "General Butler." The name was a reference to Smedley Butler, who had recently become the youngest major general in the history of the Marine Corps. Many Philadelphians knew him better for his role earlier in the decade as the city's director of public safety. In that capacity, Butler forcefully suppressed the city's illicit liquor traffic—typical behavior, perhaps, for an individual who during the 1930s developed some fascist tendencies of his own.
279. Westing, "Pennsy's Pluperfect Pacifics," 54–55.
280. The comparable figure for the #5698 was slightly lower, at 54,675 pounds.
281. Carleton, *Pennsy Steam: A to T*, 147; Carleton, *Pennsy Steam: A Second Look*, 97; Westing, "Pennsy's Pluperfect Pacifics," 55.

2. Wired

1. Different branches of the family employed the spellings Wistar and Wister.
2. Isaac J. Wistar, *Autobiography of Isaac Jones Wistar, 1827–1905, Volume II* (Philadelphia: Wistar Institute of Anatomy and Biology, 1914), 119–24, 132–33.
3. William Wister Haines, *Slim* (Boston: Little, Brown, 1934; 6th ed. 2016), 344 ("essentially"); Haines, *High Tension* (Boston: Little, Brown, 1938, reprinted San Jose, CA: Dehart's Media Services, 2016). In addition to "Remarks, None," the other four short stories associated with railroad line work are "Just Plain Nuts," *Atlantic*, July 1934, 35–49; "Hot Behind Me," *Atlantic*, June 1935, 683–95; "Night Off," *Saturday Evening Post*, January 20, 1962; and "Killer on High," *Saturday Evening Post*, May 26, 1962; all republished in Haines, *High Tension*, 185–271. Biographical information for William Wister Haines is available in *Slim*, 425–77, and *High Tension*, 164–84. The author extends his deep appreciation to William Wister Haines Jr. for arranging for these works to be republished and widely distributed and for his efforts to

increase awareness of the livelihood that the Bureau of Labor Statistics has consistently ranked as among the ten most dangerous vocations, undertaken by individuals who are most appreciated when they get the poles back up and the lights back on after storms. For a further perspective on Haines's contributions to the literature of railroading, see Frank P. Donovan Jr., *The Railroad in Literature: A Brief Survey of Railroad Fiction, Poetry, Songs, Biography, Essays, Travel and Drama in the English Language, Particularly Emphasizing Its Place in American Literature* (Boston: Railway and Locomotive Historical Society, 1940), 11, and Frank P. Donovan Jr. and Robert Selph Henry, eds., *Headlights and Markers: An Anthology of Railroad Stories* (New York: Creative Age, 1946), 280; Bureau of Labor Statistics, "Workplace Hazards Facing Line Installers and Repairers," *Monthly Labor Review*, February 2018, 1–12. Both books, *Slim* and *High Tension* (which contains five short stories of line work, including "Remarks, None"), have been republished and can be purchased through either the website Powerlineman.com or slimthelineman.com.
4. William Wister Haines, "Remarks, None," *Atlantic Monthly* 154 (August 1934): 143–55, reprinted in Edward J. O'Brien, *The Best Short Stories 1935* (London: Jonathan Cape, 1935): 387–409, at 393 ("yard").
5. "Remarks, None," 387 ("hell").
6. *New York Times*, November 1, 1928; November 2, 1928; November 5, 1928; Haines, *High Tension*, 3 ("employed").
7. Born in 1861, Gibbs graduated from the Stevens Institute of Technology, served as the chief of the Department of Tests for the Chicago, Milwaukee & St. Paul Railroad, and later worked closely with both George Westinghouse and Samuel Vauclain (of the Baldwin Locomotive Works). Ernest Rowland Hill became his chief assistant in 1906, while work on the New York Improvements was underway. The two men became partners in 1911 and incorporated the firm of Gibbs & Hill in 1923. Gibbs died in 1940. David B. Sloan, *Pioneers in Railroad Electrification* (New York: Newcomen Society in North America, 1957).
8. "Minutes of the Board of Engineers on Philadelphia Terminal Improvements," January 3, 1911; January 9, 1911; Pennsylvania Railroad Company Records, Accession 1807/1810, Manuscripts and Archives Department, Hagley Museum and Library, Wilmington, DE (hereafter, HML), Box 1550, folder 20; William D. Middleton, *When the Steam Railroads Electrified*, rev. 2nd ed. (Bloomington: Indiana University Press, 1974, 2001), 112–31; William D. Middleton, *The Pennsylvania Railroad*

Under Wire (Milwaukee, WI: Kalmbach, 2007), 10–29; Henry T. Raudenbush, "LIRR MU Car Fleet: History and Development Prior to M-1 Cars," *Keystone* 51, no. 2 (Summer 2018): 11–62, at 16–30.

9. Wilgus was no longer associated with the NYC at that time, and he was working as an independent consultant.

10. Samuel Rea to W. W. Atterbury, January 17, 1912, HML, Box 145, folder 23 ("satisfaction," "grave," "anew").

11. *Railway Age* 64 (May 10, 1918): 1177–81; Michael Bezilla, *Electric Traction on the Pennsylvania Railroad, 1895–1968* (University Park: Pennsylvania State University Press, 1980), 56, 60–61; Middleton, *When the Steam Railroads Electrified*, 314.

12. PRR BOD Minutes.

13. Bezilla, *Electric Traction*, 62–68.

14. The Philadelphia Rapid Transit Company also relied on power supplied by the Philadelphia Electric Company, under the terms of a 1911 contract.

15. Bezilla, *Electric Traction*, 62–68; Middleton, *When the Steam Railroads Electrified*, 314–15.

16. In 1924, crews added catenary to a six-mile branch off the Chestnut Hill route to Whitemarsh, Pennsylvania. Middleton, *When the Steam Railroads Electrified*, 315.

17. Rea to Atterbury, January 17, 1912; HML, Box 145, folder 23; Rea to Atterbury, December 3, 1912, HML, Box 137, folder 19.

18. Atterbury to Rea, December 6, 1912, HML, Box 137, folder 19; Atterbury to Rea, June 30, 1913, Penn Central Railroad Collection, M. G. 286, Pennsylvania Historical and Museum Commission, Pennsylvania State Archives, Harrisburg (hereafter, PHMC), Box 64 (12–1894), folder 93/12 ("naturally," "objection").

19. S. C. Long to Atterbury, July 23, 1913 ("changing"); Rea to Atterbury, July 31, 1913 ("question," "prosperous"); Atterbury to Rea, May 11, 1915; all in PHMC, Box 64 (12–1894), folder 93/12.

20. Atterbury to Rea, May 11, 1915 ("design"), in PHMC, Box 64 (12–1894), folder 93/12.

21. The subsequent abandonment of PRR's electrification plans, west of Altoona, ensured that "Big Liz" spent the remainder of its career (nearly a quarter century) operating in pusher service under the catenary between Overbrook and Paoli. Atterbury to Rea, June 2, 1915; J. T. Wallis to Rea, August 24, 1917; both in PHMC, Box 64 (12–1894), folder 93/12; Middleton, *When the Steam Railroads Electrified*, 180–95; Middleton, *Pennsylvania Railroad Under Wire*, 110–11; Bezilla, *Electric Traction*, 82–87 (includes Pennsylvania Railroad, *Sixty-ninth*

Annual Report, 1916, 9 ["experience"]); *Railway Age* 66, no. 25b (June 21, 1919): 1648.

22. Rea instead favored the construction of a low-grade freight relief line from Sheridan to Conemaugh, part of a series of projects that would ultimately give the PRR six tracks between New York and Pittsburgh. In addition to avoiding the cost and uncertainty associated with electric operation, the new routes would give the railroad additional options for diverting freight and passenger trains whenever a catastrophic wreck blocked the existing four-track main line.

23. Rea to Atterbury, October 18, 1916 ("costing"); Wallis to R. L. O'Donnel, September 21, 1918 ("joint," "expenditure"); both in PHMC, Box 64 (12–1894), folder 93/12; PRR, Mountain Electrification Study, September 12, 1917; HML, Box 467, folder 10.

24. The PRR also acquired 60 Class N1s and 130 Class N2s locomotives in 1918 and 1919, although they were primarily used on Lines West, moving heavy ore trains from the Great Lakes ports to Pittsburgh.

25. Wallis to O'Donnel, September 21, 1918, PHMC, Box 64 (12–1894), folder 93/12; Paul Carleton, *Pennsy Steam: A to T* (Dunnellon, FL: D. Carleton Railbooks, 1989), 73–77; Bezilla, *Electric Traction*, 84–89, 91–93, 97–101.

26. Rea to Atterbury, November 12, 1921 ("thought," "outlook," capital"); Rea to Atterbury, May 2, 1922; Rea to Atterbury, June 12, 1922; all in PHMC, Box 64 (12–1894), folder 93/12; *New York Times*, June 18, 1924 ("inadequacy").

27. Bezilla, *Electric Traction*, 91–93, 97–101; Middleton, *Pennsylvania Railroad Under Wire*, 111–13.

28. E. R. Hill to A. J. County, October 29, 1913, HML, Box 137.

29. George and Alfred Gibbs also contributed their expertise to the study, as did chief of motive power James T. Wallis.

30. Murray was not far off in his predictions, as the former PRR (now Amtrak) electrified line between Philadelphia and Washington carries all intercity passenger traffic, while the former B&O (now CSX) line handles only freight and commuter service.

31. William Spencer Murray et al., *A Superpower System for the Region between Boston and Washington*, United States Geological Survey Department of the Interior (Washington, DC: United States Government Printing Office, 1921), 9–12, 27, 30, 50 ("improvements," "entire"); Bezilla, *Electric Traction*, 95–96.

32. The Susquehanna Water Power & Paper Company built the first dam at the site in 1884 to provide power for a paper mill.

33. Leonard Palmer, History, "Electrical Installations and Power Uses of Conowingo Project," 1928, Records of Phi Mu, Special Collections, University of Maryland Libraries; Robert E. Geasey, "Conowingo: The Source of Our Electric Power," Tredyffrin Easttown Historical Society, *History Quarterly* 33, no. 4 (October 1995): 131–46.

34. Geasey, "Conowingo."

35. *Railway Age* 84, no. 21 (May 26, 1928): 1193–96.

36. Reconstruction Finance Corporation, Railroad Division, "Application of the Pennsylvania Railroad Company for a Loan of $27,500,000," May 14, 1932, 25 ("experience"), Records of the Reconstruction Finance Corporation (RG 234), National Archives and Records Administration, College Park, MD (hereafter RFC Records), Box 677; *Railway Age* 76, no. 4 (January 26, 1924): 295–96; Middleton, *Pennsylvania Railroad Under Wire*, 32–33.

37. Reconstruction Finance Corporation, "Application of Pennsylvania Railroad Company for a Loan of $27,500,000: Preliminary Report," May 14, 1932, 25–26; John W. Barriger III Papers, St. Louis Mercantile Library, St. Louis, Missouri (hereafter, Barriger Papers), Series 262, Box 158, folder 2–18, and Box 167, folder 9–48.

38. RFC, "Preliminary Report," 26–28.

39. *New York Times*, March 6, 1925 ("outlook," "indication"); George Gibbs and E. R. Hill, contract with Elisha Lee, December 7, 1925, HML, Box 1571, folder 7.

40. Gibbs & Hill to the Advisory Board, Philadelphia Improvements, January 3, 1928, 4–5, HML, Box 1487, folder 26 ("unprecedented," "indicated"); Gibbs to Lee, January 6, 1928, HML, Box 1550, folder 17 ("conclusions"); F. C. Sweeton memorandum, December 30, 1931, HML, Box 758, folder 17 ("determination").

41. William D. Edson, *Keystone Steam & Electric: A Record of Steam and Electric Locomotives Built for the Pennsylvania Railroad since 1906* (New York: Wayner, 1974), 13.

42. Bezilla, *Electric Traction*, 102–6, 110.

43. *New York Times*, March 29, 1928; PRR BOD Minutes.

44. The PRR's capital-improvements budget was at that time approximately $70 million per year, suggesting that a $15 million annual expenditure on electrification would not unduly strain the company's resources.

45. *New York Times*, November 1, 1928; November 3, 1928; Bezilla, *Electric Traction*, 104, 106–17, 111–12.

46. *New York Times*, November 1, 1928; J. V. B. Duer, "The Pennsylvania Railroad Electrification," *Transactions of the American Institute of Electrical Engineers* 50, no. 1 (March 1931): 101–5.

47. While Dice's announcement followed Atterbury's by less than two weeks, the Reading's electrification plans had been long in development and reflected the same crush of commuter traffic at Reading Terminal that had affected the PRR at Broad Street Station. Like Atterbury, Dice predicted that his entire railroad would one day operate solely under electric power.

48. The Public Service Corporation of New Jersey was the parent company of the Public Service Electric & Gas Company and Public Service Coordinated Transport.

49. Bezilla, *Electric Traction*, 112–15; *New York Times*, November 2, 1928; November 12, 1928.

50. Murchison was responsible for numerous other facilities, including two terminals in Buffalo, New York—one for the DL&W and the other for the Lehigh Valley. He died while emerging from a railway station in 1938—Grand Central Terminal, which he did not design.

51. John A. Droege, *Passenger Terminals and Trains* (New York: McGraw-Hill, 1916), 96–97; Frank A. Wrabel, "Terminals, Tunnels and Turmoil," *Keystone* 28 (Spring 1995); *Railway Age* 98, no. 18 (May 4, 1935): 686–90; *New York Times*, December 16, 1938.

52. Mencken's acerbic assessment was probably on the mark. The Great Depression ended any further talk of a new facility. Although World War II temporarily taxed the station's capacity, the decline in passenger service during the postwar years ensured that there were ample empty benches in the waiting room. While passenger traffic between New York and Washington remained robust (compared to the PRR's other long-distance services), Baltimore's population peaked during the early 1950s and decreased thereafter. Unlike Penn Station in New York, declining property values and the inconvenient location of the Baltimore station ultimately ensured its salvation. Surrounded by rail yards in an area well north of the city center, the land that it occupied held little commercial value. Placed on the National Register of Historical Places in 1975, the station benefited from a thorough, multimillion-dollar restoration during the early 1980s. It continues to serve Amtrak and MARC commuter trains as well as a light rail system. Wrabel, "Terminals, Tunnels and Turmoil," 58–61.

53. Wrabel, "Terminals, Tunnels and Turmoil," 51–52; *Baltimore Sun*, March 5, 1928, quoted in S. T. Joshi, *H. L. Mencken: An Annotated Bibliography* (Lanham, MD:

Scarecrow, 2009), 196 ("vast"); *New York Times*, February 24, 1928.

54. *New York Times*, October 22, 1929; PRR BOD Minutes; *Engineering News-Record*, April 11, 1935, 509–15; *Railway Age* 98, no. 15 (April 13, 1935): 572–77; *Mutual Magazine*, June 1935, 31–32.

55. *New York Times*, February 18, 1931 ("restoration," "confidence," "redoubled," "favorable"); December 5, 1931; PRR BOD Minutes.

56. *New York Times*, October 7, 1931; December 8, 1931; *Railway Age* 91, no. 16 (October 17, 1931): 610; PRR BOD Minutes.

57. The PRR's electric locomotives employed commutator (rather than induction) motors that accommodated DC and low-frequency AC but were ill-suited to higher-frequency AC. In deference to its largest customer, the Safe Harbor hydroelectric plant included one (later two) generators that produced 25-hertz current, with the remainder dedicated to 60-hertz power for the commercial grid.

58. Duer, "Pennsylvania Railroad Electrification"; Charles Herbert Ludwig, "The History and Methods of Electrification of the Pennsylvania Railroad between Baltimore and Washington, D.C.," 1934, Records of Phi Mu, Special Collections, University of Maryland Libraries.

59. Electrical engineers demanded a uniform tower spacing, both to ensure that the catenary spans on each side of each tower would be of equal weight and to facilitate the mass fabrication of the catenary spans. When adjustments were necessary, they occurred in fifteen-foot modular intervals.

60. Ludwig, "History and Methods"; Middleton, *Pennsylvania Railroad Under Wire*, 34–35; "Application of the Pennsylvania Railroad Company for a Loan of $27,500,000"; Duer, "Pennsylvania Railroad Electrification"; H. C. Griffith, "Single-Phase Electrification on the Pennsylvania Railroad," *Journal of the Institution of Electrical Engineers* 81, no. 487 (July 1937): 91–103; Bezilla, *Electric Traction*, 116–19.

61. *Railway Age* 91, no. 3 (July 18, 1931): 112–13; 91, no. 22 (November 28, 1931): 846; Arthur P. Dedden, "The City Embraces 'Normalcy,' 1919–1929," in *Philadelphia: A 300-Year History*, ed. Russell F. Weigley (New York: W. W. Norton, 1982), 566–600, at 581–87; Richard C. Keller, "Pennsylvania's Little New Deal," *Pennsylvania History* 29, no. 4 (October 1962): 391–406; Paul B. Beers, *Pennsylvania Politics Today and Yesterday: The Tolerable Accommodation* (University Park: Pennsylvania State University Press, 1980), 61–66.

62. John Morrison McLarnon III, *Ruling Suburbia: John J. McClure and the Republican Machine in Delaware County, Pennsylvania* (Newark: University of Delaware Press, 2003), 101–3.

63. Phillips was effectively a front man for the Association Against the Prohibition Amendment, an organization that received heavy financial support from the du Pont family. Its members also included Raymond Pitcairn—whose father, John Pitcairn Jr., had worked for the Pennsylvania Railroad before founding the Pittsburgh Plate Glass Company and whose uncle, Robert Pitcairn, served as one of the PRR's most important executives. Atterbury was an active member of the Association Against the Prohibition Amendment. He used Robert Kelso Cassatt (son of a previous PRR president) as an intermediary to pressure Phillips into withdrawing from the race. That effort was unsuccessful, as was Atterbury's attempt to induce Raymond Pitcairn to back Brown. Phillips and Brown thus split the wet vote, ensuring that neither would win the election.

64. *New York Times*, March 16, 1930; March 27, 1930; March 30, 1930; March 31, 1930; April 8, 1930; May 18, 1930; Beers, *Pennsylvania Politics*, 92–93; Samuel John Astorino, "The Decline of the Republican Dynasty in Pennsylvania, 1929–1934" (PhD diss., University of Pittsburgh, 1962), 20–120.

65. *New York Times*, March 31, 1930 ("conspiracy," "gang," "grab," "executive," "combination").

66. Beers, *Pennsylvania Politics*, 112 ("best"); *New York Times*, March 31, 1930 ("everybody"); April 1, 1930.

67. *New York Times*, March 31, 1930 ("worst," "raided"); April 6, 1930; May 14, 1930 ("cease"); Astorino, "Decline of the Republican Dynasty," 134.

68. *New York Times*, May 19, 1930; May 20, 1930; May 21, 1930; Beers, *Pennsylvania Politics*, 93.

69. *New York Times*, June 8, 1930; July 11, 1930 ("attempt," "assault"); July 12, 1930; July 25, 1930; August 21, 1930; October 10, 1930; October 19, 1930; Beers, *Pennsylvania Politics*, 93.

70. *New York Times*, October 10, 1930 ("using"); October 28, 1920 ("reckless," "false"); October 30, 1930; November 1, 1930 ("greatest," "prestige"); PRR BOD Minutes.

71. *New York Times*, November 5, 1930; February 19, 1931; February 25, 1931 ("ignorant"); March 1, 1931 ("investigating," "circus"); Astorino, "Decline of the Republican Dynasty," 134–37.

72. Not until 1934 would Pinchot have the authority to appoint additional commissioners, but by then he was a spent political force. He left office in January 1935, waited

out the next four years, and suffered a resounding defeat in the Republican gubernatorial primary. *New York Times*, February 18, 1931; May 27, 1931.

73. *New York Times*, November 7, 1931; July 24, 1932; Astorino, "Decline of the Republican Dynasty," 137.

74. "Emergency" was not a generic indication of the seriousness of the crisis; rather, it indicated that the ICC would allow the rates to become effective immediately rather than suspend them during the customary period of investigation and testimony associated with a rate application. Railroad officials did not seek an increase in passenger rates (set at 3.6 cents per mile), as such a move would guarantee the further loss of passengers to buses and automobiles.

75. A decade earlier, while serving as US solicitor general, Beck had fought against the PRR's efforts to block the wage recommendations issued by the Railroad Labor Board. Subsequently, as an attorney in private practice, Beck defended fellow Republican William Vare. The connections between the Vare brothers, the Vare political machine, the Pennsylvania Railroad, and Philadelphia city politics contributed to the assertion that Beck was a puppet of the PRR. *Chicago Tribune*, December 11, 1921; *New York Times*, June 18, 1931; August 19, 1931; August 20, 1931; September 4, 1931; September 24, 1931 ("little"); September 29, 1931 ("Moscow"); Samuel J. Astorino, "The Contested Senate Election of William Scott Vare," *Pennsylvania History* 28, no. 2 (April 1961): 187–201.

76. *New York Times*, September 24, 1931; October 10, 1931; October 12, 1931; October 21, 1931 ("far-reaching").

77. The idea of a revenue pool had come not from the ICC but from Luther M. Walter, legal counsel for the National Industrial Traffic League. When ICC officials in turn proposed the idea to railroad executives, they universally—with the sole exception of those representing the Seaboard Air Line—rejected it as unworkable. It was a policy that offered no benefit whatsoever to strong railroads such as the PRR—other than the opportunity to subsidize their weaker competitors. *New York Times*, October 21, 1931; October 22, 1931.

78. *New York Times*, October 23, 1931; October 29, 1931; November 13, 1931; November 14, 1931.

79. *New York Times*, October 18, 1931; November 13, 1931; November 19, 1931; November 20, 1931; December 7, 1931; December 8, 1931; December 9, 1931; December 12, 1931; December 15, 1931; December 17, 1931; December 20, 1931; January 4, 1932; January 16, 1932; March 11, 1932; James S. Olson, "The End of Voluntarism: Herbert Hoover and the National Credit Corporation," *Annals of Iowa* 41, no. 6 (Fall 1972): 1104–13; Joseph R. Mason,

"Reconstruction Finance Corporation Assistance to Financial Intermediaries and Commercial and Industrial Enterprises in the United States, 1932–37," in *Resolution of Financial Distress: An International Perspective on the Design of Bankruptcy Laws*, eds. Stijn Claessens, Simeon Djankov, Ashoka Mody (Washington, DC: World Bank, 2001): 167–204, at 168–69; Kincaid A. Herr, *The Louisville and Nashville Railroad, 1850–1963* (Lexington: University Press of Kentucky, 2000), 253.

80. In 1933, railroad securities made up 16 percent of bank assets and 24 percent of insurance-company assets and constituted 20 percent of the bond market. Daniel A. Schiffman, "Shattered Rails, Ruined Credit: Financial Fragility and Railroad Operations in the Great Depression," *Journal of Economic History* 63, no. 3 (September 2003): 802–25, at 806.

81. Mason, "Reconstruction Finance Corporation," 178; James Butkiewicz, "Reconstruction Finance Corporation," EH.net, https://eh.net/encyclopedia /reconstruction-finance-corporation/, accessed June 24, 2015; *New York Times*, February 5, 1932.

82. This amount included $261,233,000 in road and equipment on the PRR proper, with a further $39,190,000 on leased property. The period was December 31, 1925– December 31, 1934, almost but not precisely the term of Atterbury's presidency.

83. George H. Burgess and Miles C. Kennedy, *Centennial History of the Pennsylvania Railroad Company, 1846–1946* (Philadelphia: Pennsylvania Railroad Company, 1949), 626–28.

84. The PRR's cost estimates exhibited considerable variation over the course of the electrification project—in part because the Depression reduced the price of labor and materials, in part because some projections included terminal improvements and others did not, and in part because executives made adjustments in order to make the proposal more attractive to RFC officials. In early 1932, PRR officials suggested that they would need $110 million to complete the project. It was perhaps not coincidental that that was precisely double the $55 million the PRR requested from the RFC on March 10—at a time when there was an emerging consensus among government officials that the federal government and private financiers should provide financial assistance in a 50/50 ratio. When the RFC approved the PRR's revised loan application (for $27.5 million) on May 19, company officials suggested that the final cost of the project, including terminal improvements at Newark, Philadelphia, and Baltimore, would be approximately $264.7 million, of which about 40 percent had already been spent. That

would leave $158.8 million worth of incomplete work, $48.8 million higher than some earlier estimates.

85. Burgess and Kennedy, *Centennial History*, 804; *New York Times*, February 5, 1932; March 11, 1932; A. J. County to the Reconstruction Finance Corporation, May 25, 1932, RFC records, Box 676; "Application of the Pennsylvania Railroad Company for a Loan of $27,500,000"; *New York Times*, January 16, 1932; Bezilla, *Electric Traction*, 128.

86. Atterbury's vagueness was understandable, as the RFC did not release the application procedures until February 8. They were complex, to say the least, taking up nearly half a page in the *New York Times*.

87. *New York Times*, February 3, 1932; February 5, 1932 ("extent," "guess").

88. If approved, the RFC was to release the money in monthly installments on May 1 ($7 million), June 1 ($1 million), July 1 ($5 million), August 1 ($6.5 million), October 1 ($3 million), November 1 ($16 million), and December 1 ($16.5 million).

89. Within days, the Baltimore & Ohio also filed an application for a $55 million loan. While the intended uses of the B&O loan were much more varied than was the case with the PRR's application, the bottom line was that the B&O needed the RFC loan in order to solve a cash-flow crisis and stave off bankruptcy. The value of RFC loans that were under consideration, authorized, and disbursed changed on an almost daily basis. The figures here are from the *New York Times* of March 26, 1932. It should be noted that $50 million of the $235 million authorization was allocated to the Department of Agriculture, and it was in turn up to that agency to determine its ultimate disposition. *New York Times*, March 11, 1932; March 17, 1932; March 23, 1932; PRR BOD Minutes; J. G. Watson, certification of actions of a meeting of the PRR board of directors, May 25, 1932; RFC Preliminary Report; all in Barriger Papers, Series 262, Box 167, folder 9–47.

90. *New York Times*, February 5, 1932; February 7, 1932.

91. *New York Times*, March 19, 1932 ("glum," "shook"); March 20, 1932 ("about").

92. It also helped that the chief examiner of the RFC's Railroad Division was Miles Coverdale Kennedy, once a member of the engineering corps on Lines West, who would later become one of the authors of the PRR's officially sanctioned corporate history.

93. Finance professor Joseph R. Mason has suggested that "after 1933 the railroad loan program shifted its objective, becoming a means of stabilizing general business activity and maintaining employment." The level of

support for the PRR loan request and other similar loans suggests that the shift began much sooner, probably not long after the RFC's February 1932 inception. Mason, "Reconstruction Finance Corporation," 178; *New York Times*, February 5, 1932; February 7, 1932; March 19, 1932 ("deserves").

94. Section 20 (a) of the 1887 Act to Regulate Commerce (as amended by the Transportation Act of 1920) specified, "It shall be unlawful for any carrier . . . to assume any obligation or liability . . . unless and until, and then only to the extent that . . . the Commission by order authorizes such issue or assumption."

95. Congress did not specifically address the issue of corporate failure in the RFC's enabling legislation. By March 1932, however, there was a growing consensus in government and financial circles that the Hoover administration would not permit any large corporation to go bankrupt, so long as the federal government possessed the legal and financial resources to prevent that occurrence.

96. Despite the RFC loans, the Missouri Pacific went bankrupt in 1933. *New York Times*, February 5, 1932; February 6, 1932; February 16, 1932; March 26, 1932 ("reluctance," "reason," "escape"); March 31, 1932.

97. Couzens instead recommended the resurrection of the $300 million fund established under the terms of the recapture clause of the Transportation Act of 1920.

98. *New York Times*, December 6, 1931; December 11, 1931; December 22, 1931; March 31, 1932 ("desirable").

99. *New York Times*, March 31, 1932 ("applying," "bankers," "controls").

100. *New York Times*, April 2, 1932.

101. During several prior instances, the board had voted to pay quarterly dividends in scrip, to be redeemed later for cash, after economic conditions and the company's finances had improved.

102. *New York Times*, April 13, 1932; April 28, 1932; May 13, 1932.

103. *New York Times*, April 8, 1932 ("unless"); May 13, 1932 ("days," "reassuring").

104. The arrangement with the PRR, along with the grudging approval of the Missouri Pacific loan (on March 23) and the ICC's decision in May to sharply reduce the B&O's proposed $55 million loan (on May 16), effectively locked into place the 50/50 rule supported by Meyer, Eastman, and Couzens. Because the PRR had pledged to spend $68.2 million on electrification and related improvements (including the original $13.2 million corporate contribution, the new $27.5 million bond issue, and the RFC's $27.5 million loan), the RFC's

contribution was actually only 40.1 percent of the project's cost. PRR BOD Minutes; *New York Times*, May 13, 1932.

105. The PRR was in something of a legal catch-22, in that the two agencies would only approve the loan if the PRR could demonstrate that it could raise the remaining amount from the private sector, while investment bankers demanded assurances that the RFC loan would be forthcoming, prior to committing to an additional PRR bond issue. The provisional assurance, while not legally binding, nevertheless sent a clear signal to the investment-banking community.

106. The PRR's application for the $27.5 million loan initially pledged 175,000 shares of Fort Wayne stock and 237,000 shares of Pan Handle stock. With a par value of $100 in each case, the stock was theoretically worth $41.2 million. The prevailing market value would have been considerably less and was in any case difficult to determine accurately, as the PRR owned virtually all the shares of the two subsidiaries. The revised proposal (the one approved by the ICC and the RFC) substituted 185,000 shares of Fort Wayne stock, 52,800 shares of the Pan Handle, and $11.7 million in PB&W bonds. The stated value had fallen to $35.2 million, but that amount was probably much closer to market price. The agencies also demanded that the PRR could not use any of the Fort Wayne's assets as security for any new bond issue until the RFC loan had been repaid.

107. *New York Times*, May 20, 1932; May 22, 1932; *Railway Age* 92, no. 22 (May 28, 1932): 920, 927 ("non-producing," "financing").

108. PRR executives made a rather lackluster commitment to authorize "the sale of securities through banking and investment channels before the end of the year, if business and financial conditions make it possible to do so, upon reasonable terms."

109. PRR BOD Minutes; *New York Times*, May 26, 1932.

110. *New York Times*, May 26, 1932 ("enthusiasm," "interest").

111. Atterbury apparently believed he was the one doing the federal government a favor by accepting an RFC loan that would enable his company to contribute to economic recovery. "In view of the reduction of unemployment, increase of purchasing power brought about by this work, and the lack of return under present volume of traffic," he informed Gerard Swope, the president of General Electric, "it would seem that the Government should provide this money without interest during construction." Atterbury to Swope, July 26, 1933, RFC records, Box 681 ("view"); *New York Times*, May 29, 1932.

112. Hoover's most significant proposal, as part of the nine-point plan, was to use RFC loans to pay for highways and other public-works projects—many of which would make the railroads more vulnerable to competition from motor carriers. A. J. County to Atterbury, August 3, 1932; County to Elisha Lee, September 21, 1932; both in HML, Box 326, folder 18; *New York Times*, July 30, 1932 ("programs"); July 31, 1932; August 3, 1932.

113. The original proposal was for 1,500 X-29 boxcars, subsequently changed to 925 boxcars and 360 automobile cars.

114. PRR BOD Minutes; *New York Times*, August 13, 1932 ("purpose"); September 20, 1932; October 12, 1932; November 5, 1932.

115. Dodd, a professor of American history at the University of Chicago, was referring to historical precedent for voluntary sacrifice rather than his personal political convictions. A staunch Democrat, he was Roosevelt's eventual choice for ambassador to Germany. He served between 1933 and 1937, a period of steadily worsening relations between the two countries. *New York Times*, July 16, 1932 ("widespread," "parallel").

116. Mason, "Reconstruction Finance Corporation," 179, 184.

117. Kevin J. Murphy, "The Politics of Pay: A Legislative History of Executive Compensation," in *Research Handbook on Executive Pay*, eds. Randall S. Thomas and Jennifer G. Hill (Northampton, MA: Edward Elgar, 2014), 11–18, at 12; *New York Times*, April 27, 1932; April 28, 1932.

118. Louis Brandeis perceived the broader implications of the ICC's salary report. He wrote to Felix Frankfurter (at that time a professor of law at Harvard University), suggesting that the release of salary information for public utilities, banking, and manufacturing executives would be "far more important" than the data pertaining to the railroad industry. Brandeis to Frankfurter, July 12, 1932, quoted in Harwell Wells, "'No Man Can Be Worth $1,000,000 a Year': The Fight over Executive Compensation in 1930s America," *University of Richmond Law Review* 44 (January 2010): 689–768, at 738–39, 752.

119. Adjusted for inflation, Atterbury's 1929 salary would be worth $2,693,210 in 2023, while his much-reduced 1932 compensation would be the equivalent of $2,742,916—with the slight increase in purchasing power attributable to the deflationary pressures of the Great Depression. By the standards of early twenty-first-century corporate America, neither amount seemed excessive. Tax rates calculated from Historical US Federal Individual Income Tax Rates & Brackets, 1862–2021,

https://taxfoundation.org/historical-income-tax-rates
-brackets/; cost-of living adjustments calculated from
United States Bureau of Labor Statistics, "CPI Inflation
Calculator," https://www.bls.gov/data/inflation
_calculator.htm, both accessed September 22, 2023.

120. The newspaper was technically correct but was
misleading in its assertion that Atterbury was the most
highly paid railroad *president*. Hale Holden, the chairman of the Southern Pacific's executive committee,
earned $135,000 in 1932.

121. The yacht in question was the *Arminia*, owned
by the PRR president, and was the same vessel that
revenue agents had boarded in 1931 to seize Atterbury's
stock of liquor. *New York Times*, July 10, 1932 ("Leads");
July 15, 1932; August 7, 1932 ("Youths"); August 10, 1932
("Offset").

122. Shareholders were also concerned that RFC regulations required that borrowers repay loans before paying
dividends to shareholders. That provision, necessary to
protect the federal government's investments in railroad
corporations, was clearly appropriate for companies
teetering on the edge of insolvency. For stronger carriers
such as the PRR, however, the no-dividend requirement
served to discourage private investment. That was particularly true in states, such as New York, that prohibited
banks and trust companies from owing railroad stocks
that did not pay annual dividends of at least a quarter of
fixed costs. The New York minimum-dividend requirement changed in 1932, in response to the Great Depression. *New York Times*, April 12, 1933 ("salaries," "work");
Mason, "Reconstruction Finance Corporation," 184;
Schiffman, "Shattered Rails," 805.

123. Jones had a similar conversation with Senator
Couzens, who suggested that insurance companies
receiving RFC aid should not pay their executives more
than $25,000 a year. The identical salary caps for two
different industries indicated a remarkable coincidence, a
convergence of thinking on the issue, or—more likely—
that Couzens had had a similar "informal" meeting with
Roosevelt. Jones provoked the senator by reminding him
that they each earned only $10,000 per year. The two
men then agreed to split the difference and recommend
that insurance company executives earn a maximum of
$17,500 annually. In keeping with his political acumen,
Roosevelt's suggestion of a $25,000 maximum annual
salary for railroad executives was probably not an offhand
remark. Even though it was unlikely that the president
could have justified such a low level of compensation,
Jones and others could nonetheless spread rumors that

Roosevelt might implement starvation pay, if railroad
executives did not voluntarily reduce their salaries.

124. Jesse H. Jones, *Fifty Billion Dollars: My Thirteen
Years with the RFC (1932–1945)* (New York: Macmillan,
1951), 110–11 ("accustomed," "formula").

125. Jones, *Fifty Billion Dollars*, 111; *New York Times*,
April 20, 1933; May 29, 1933; June 2, 1933; September 24,
1940.

126. Section 4 contained a similar clause as the previous section ("the applicant agrees to the satisfaction
of the Corporation not to increase the compensation of
any of its officers, directors, or employees"), but it was an
"and" statement rather than an "unless" statement. Act
of June 10, 1933, chap. 55, § 4; 48 Stat. 120 (1934), codified
at 15 USC § 605h (1934), ("subscription," "satisfaction,"
"reasonable"); Wells, "No Man," 752–53.

127. *New York Times*, July 15, 1933; July 21, 1933; July 29,
1933.

128. *New York Times*, July 1, 1933.

129. *New York Times*, July 15, 1933; July 21, 1933; July 29,
1933; Bezilla, *Electric Traction*, 147–48.

130. Michael Bezilla, "The Development of Electric
Traction on the Pennsylvania Railroad, 1895–1968," *Penn-
sylvania History* 46, no. 3 (July 1979): 195–211, at 206; *New
York Times*, October 11, 1933.

131. For the genesis and operations of the PWA, see
William D. Reeves, "PWA and Competition Adminis-
tration in the New Deal," *Journal of American History* 60,
no. 2 (September 1973): 357–72; Harold L. Ickes: *Back to
Work: The Story of the PWA* (New York: Macmillan, 1935);
and Jason Scott Smith, *Building New Deal Liberalism: The
Political Economy of Public Works, 1933–1956* (Cambridge,
MA: Cambridge University Press, 2009).

132. Transportation Coordinator Eastman resolved the
dispute over rail prices, negotiating a compromise rate of
$36.375 per ton—exactly midway between the carriers'
preferred price of $35.00 per ton and the (NRA-sanc-
tioned) steel-company price of $37.75. *New York Times*,
September 27, 1933 ("indebted," "invaded"); October
21, 1933; November 3, 1933; September 2, 1944; James
Guthrie Harbord memoirs, included in "General William
Wallace Atterbury," Indiana Military History, http://
www.indianamilitary.org/GENERALATTERBURY
/Bio.htm, accessed July 2, 2015; R. W. Harbeson, "The
Emergency Railroad Transportation Act of 1933," *Journal
of Political Economy* 42 (February 1934): 106–26, at 125.

133. PRR BOD Minutes; *New York Times*, November 3,
1933; *Railway Age* 95, no. 20 (November 11, 1933): 695–97;
Bezilla, *Electric Traction*, 148–50.

134. The railroad pledged as security $45.8 million in collateral, including $11.7 million in New York Bay Railroad bonds, $6.5 million in Pan Handle bonds, $12 million in Western New York & Pennsylvania stock, $10 million in Pan Handle stock, and $5.6 million in Fort Wayne stock. The remaining $32 million of the PWA loan (for the electric locomotives and freight cars) was secured by equipment-trust certificates.

135. PRR press release, January 30, 1934, Barriger Papers, Series 262, Box 161, folder 6–13; *New York Times*, November 3, 1933; December 27, 1933; December 30, 1933; January 7, 1934; January 17, 1934; *Railway Age* 95, no. 29 (November 11, 1933): 695–97; 96, no. 1 (January 6, 1934): 15–17; Bezilla, *Electric Traction*, 148–50; Burgess and Kennedy, *Centennial History*, 614.

136. *New York Times*, January 31, 1934 ("pockets"); February 1, 1934.

137. The four leading borrowers were the Great Northern ($105.4 million), the Baltimore & Ohio ($82.1 million), the Chicago & North Western ($46.6 million), and the Illinois Central ($39.3 million).

138. Mason, "Reconstruction Finance Corporation," 179–80.

139. *New York Times*, January 10, 1936; January 11, 1936; Jones, *Fifty Billion Dollars*, 105.

140. Commuter service to Norristown, on the Schuylkill Division, began a few weeks later, although the Depression prevented the planned extension of catenary to Phoenixville.

141. Third-rail DC remained in place as far west as the west (Bergen Hill) portal in New Jersey, making it possible to operate work trains while the catenary was deenergized.

142. The PRR operated a test train between Jersey City and Millstone Junction, near New Brunswick, on December 1. *New York Times*, December 2, 1932; December 8, 1932.

143. For a comprehensive overview of the construction process, see *Railway Age* 94, no. 8 (February 25, 1933): 270–96; General Electric, "The Pennsylvania Railroad Electrification," Barriger Papers, Series 262, Box 161, folder 6–13; and *Mutual Magazine*, March 7, 1935, 15–19, 38. For extensive coverage of the design and installation of the PRR's catenary, see Mike Nesladek, "Overhead Catenary of the PRR," *Keystone* 29, no. 4 (Winter 1996): 15–40. *New York Times*, January 17, 1933; January 23, 1933; January 30, 1933; Bezilla, *Electric Traction*, 127, 133–34; Roland Marchand, *Creating the Corporate Soul: The Rise of Public Relations and Corporate Imagery in American Business* (Berkeley: University of California Press, 1998), 128.

144. *New York Times*, January 26, 1935; January 29, 1935; *Railway Age* 98, no. 5 (February 2, 1935): 196–97.

145. Bezilla, *Electric Traction*, 15; *Railway Age* 98, no. 2 (February 1935): 106 ("appreciation," "accomplished"); *New York Times*, February 9, 1935.

146. "Harrisburg—Enola Electrification," December 18, 1936; John F. Deasy to Clement, January 5, 1937; PRR press release, October 11, 1937; April 14, 1938; all in HML, Box 233, folder 12; *Mutual Magazine*, November 1938, 50–54; *Railway Age* 102, no. 5 (January 30, 1937): 234; *New York Times*, February 9, 1935; PRR BOD Minutes; Burgess and Kennedy, *Centennial History*, 614, 647–50, 679; Middleton, *Pennsylvania Railroad Under Wire*, 36–37.

147. Bezilla, *Electric Traction*, 154–58, 161–65; Middleton, *Pennsylvania Railroad Under Wire*, 37–38.

148. PRR BOD Minutes; *New York Times*, October 9, 1924.

149. As a concession, they permitted an extension of the Hudson & Manhattan tracks, almost to South Street, but no station was ever built at that site. Today, Port Authority Trans-Hudson, H&M's successor, uses those tracks to store cars, outside of rush hour.

150. The agreement stipulated that the PRR would build two new lift bridges over the Passaic River, extend the H&M tracks a mile south as far as Parkhurst Street (approximately half a mile south of the station site), and pay for the intercity, H&M, and bus facilities at the station. The city would pay for street relocation, the underground rapid-transit facilities (including a boulevard atop the Morris Canal bed and transit line), and a plaza fronting the station.

151. Specifically, the commissioners refused to exempt the Public Service Commission from a 5 percent franchise tax on the gross receipts generated by the rapid-transit line.

152. *New York Times*, February 17, 1926; April 13, 1928; May 9, 1928; May 10, 1928; September 15, 1928; January 10, 1929; *Railway Age* 90, no. 23 (June 6, 1931): 1103–6.

153. Kenneth MacKenzie Murchison, the principal architect of Baltimore Pennsylvania Station, was an accomplished designer of railroad facilities, but rarely for the PRR.

154. *Railway Age* 98, no. 13 (March 30, 1935): 485–92; John A. Droege, *Passenger Terminals and Trains* (New York: McGraw-Hill, 1916), 38–40.

155. *New York Times*, May 14, 1931; July 30, 1931; August 1, 1931; March 10, 1932; May 12, 1932; May 19, 1932.

156. The mayor did not mention the contentious hearings before the ICC, concluded only a few weeks earlier, in which representatives from the Newark Chamber of Commerce accused the Pennsylvania Railroad of employing a discriminatory rate structure that drove freight traffic away from the city. In April 1934, the Chamber of Commerce claimed that the PRR was discriminating against Port Newark by requiring shippers to pay loading and unloading expenses, while absorbing similar charges at Philadelphia and Baltimore. On March 5, 1935, the ICC dismissed the complaint.

157. *New York Times*, April 7, 1934; March 6, 1935; March 23, 1935; March 24, 1935 ("advanced").

158. In April 1933, the PRR began changing motive power on its principal east–west trains at Paoli. Some New York & Long Branch trains continued to change motive power at Manhattan Transfer until the summer of 1936. The altered operating practices sparked a minor rebellion among NY&LB commuters riding between their homes along the New Jersey Shore and their offices in Lower Manhattan. They were accustomed to detraining at Manhattan Transfer and then boarding the connecting Hudson & Manhattan service. For a brief time, until the Hudson & Manhattan began service to the new Newark station in June 1937, commuters who had not taken a train to the ferry terminal at Exchange Place had little choice other than to ride all the way to Penn Station—paying a supplemental charge of fifteen cents for the privilege—and then make their way south by subway. Within three months, more than a hundred commuters refused to pay the additional fare.

159. John Markland, "A Landmark Faces Doom," *New York Times*, June 13, 1937 ("drab," "glamor"); *New York Times*, April 10, 1933; July 8, 1936; June 20, 1937; June 21, 1937 ("demolishing"); *Railway Age* 102, no. 26 (June 26, 1937): 1044–50.

160. *New York Times*, November 21, 1929.

161. *Railway Age* 123, no. 1 (July 5, 1947): 72.

162. According to the Whyte classification system for steam locomotives, a DD1 would be a 4-4-0+0-4-4, but simplified as a 4-4-4-4, the same wheel arrangement later employed by the Class T1 duplex steam locomotive.

163. F. W. Hankins to Martin Clement, May 9, 1931; HML, Box 334, folder 15; *Keystone*, 12, no. 1 (March 1979): 4–9; Middleton, *Pennsylvania Railroad Under Wire*, 95; Eric Hirsimaki, *Black Gold–Black Diamonds: The Pennsylvania Railroad and Dieselization, Volume 2* (North Olmsted, OH: Mileposts, 1997), 59–65; Bezilla, *Electric Traction*, 119–23, 144; Frederick Westing, "Development of the P5 Electric," in Frederick Westing, Mike Bezilla,

and Roger L. Keyser, *The Pennsy's P5 Electrics* (Altoona, PA: Pennsylvania Railroad Technical & Historical Society, 2002): 4–47, at 4–5.

164. *Railway Age* 92, no. 21 (May 21, 1932): 869–73; Hankins to Clement, June 16, 1930 ("error"), HML, Box 334, folder 15; Bezilla, *Electric Traction*, 123, 137; Westing, "Development," 5.

165. The L5 locomotives, built between 1924 and 1928, employed a 1-B-B-1 wheel arrangement (one unpowered axle, two pairs of non-articulated powered axles, and one unpowered axle), equivalent to two 2-4-0 locomotives coupled back-to-back. The 2-4-0 steam locomotive was rare in the United States, however, and the PRR owned none. Therefore, the PRR used the same classification as the L1s Mikado steam locomotives, which employed a 2-8-2 wheel arrangement.

166. *Railway Age* 94, no. 8 (February 25, 1933): 273–76; Middleton, *Pennsylvania Railroad Under Wire*, 92; Bezilla, *Electric Traction*, 124; Westing, "Development," 7.

167. Just as the 2-B-2 Class O1 was not a precise mimic of the 4-4-2 E6s, the P5 was the equivalent of a 4-6-4 rather than a 4-6-2 Pacific. That was a bit of an embarrassment, perhaps, as the 4-6-4 was also known as a "Hudson," in recognition of its role as the premier steam passenger locomotive for the rival New York Central.

168. As in previous locomotive orders, General Electric also provided electrical equipment, building about a third of the locomotives. The PRR built the last batch of P5a locomotives in Altoona, using a combination of Westinghouse and GE electrical equipment. *New York Times*, May 28, 1931; September 6, 1931; Westing, "Development," 10–20; Ludwig, "History and Methods," 24–31.

169. Michael Bezilla, "The Pennsylvania's P5/P5a Electric Locomotives," *Keystone* 12 (March 1979): 4–15; Westing, "Development," 21–23.

170. While all the P5a locomotives were internally identical, about a third were of the modified, center-cab design. Westing, "Development," 24–34.

171. The limitations of the P5a were in keeping with those of its steam-locomotive counterpart, the K4s, which also often required double-heading in order to pull long passenger trains.

172. Bezilla, "Pennsylvania's P5/P5a Electric Locomotives"; Middleton, *Pennsylvania Railroad Under Wire*, 92–99; Bezilla, *Electric Traction*, 138–40; Westing, "Development," 7, 25–26.

173. Bezilla, *Electric Traction*, 138–39, 142–43; Karl R. Zimmerman, *The Remarkable GG1* (New York: Quadrant, 1977), 15.

174. The 2-C+C-2 wheel arrangement of the GG1 corresponded to a 4-6-0+0-6-4 wheel arrangement under the Whyte classification system—the equivalent of two 4-6-0 Ten-Wheeler steam locomotives coupled back-to-back. The PRR assigned Class G to those steam locomotives, hence the "GG" designation for the electric locomotive.

175. The R1 was 64 feet, 8 inches long, with a total wheelbase of 54 feet and a rigid wheelbase of 23 feet, while the GG1 was 79 feet, 6 inches long, with a total wheelbase of 69 feet and a rigid wheelbase of just 13 feet, 8 inches.

176. *Railway Age* 101, no. 11 (September 12, 1936): 374–80; 101, no. 12 (September 19, 1936): 412–18; Bezilla, *Electric Traction*, 144; Hirsimaki, *Black Gold–Black Diamonds*, 59–65.

177. General Electric built fourteen at its plant in Erie, Pennsylvania, and supplied electrical equipment for nine others. The remaining electrical components came from the Baldwin facility in East Pittsburgh. Baldwin provided the chassis for twenty-five locomotives (in addition to the fourteen built by GE in Erie), with PRR employees installing the electrical equipment at Altoona. Altoona shop forces built the final eighteen locomotives, in their entirety.

178. Because the PRR owned only one GG1 at that time, the southbound *Congressional* relied on a center-cab P5a, #4780.

179. *New York Times*, November 11, 1934, Zimmerman, *Remarkable GG1*, 15, 17–20; *Mutual Magazine*, March 1936, 7–9; May 1936, 9–12.

180. Carroll Gantz, *Founders of American Industrial Design* (Jefferson, NC: McFarland & Company, 2014), 34–35; Hampton C. Wayt, "Donald Dohner: The Man Who Designed 'RIVETS,'" *Classic Trains* 10, no. 2 (Summer 2009): 30–35; Albert J. Churella, *From Steam to Diesel: Managerial Customs and Organizational Capabilities in the Twentieth-Century Locomotive Industry* (Princeton, NJ: Princeton University Press, 1998), 30.

181. Hampton C. Wayt, "Update on the GG1's Genesis," *Classic Trains* 11, no. 3 (Fall 2010): 86–87.

182. Loewy claimed that he spent three days observing passenger behavior at Penn Station before preparing his trash-can design, likely one of his many exaggerations.

183. Raymond Loewy, *Never Leave Well Enough Alone, with a New Introduction by Glenn Porter* (Baltimore, MD: Johns Hopkins University Press, 1951, 2002), 135–40 ("locomotive," "future," "specialist," "criticize"); Jeffrey L. Meikle, *Twentieth Century Limited: Industrial Design in America, 1925–1939*, 2nd ed. (Philadelphia: Temple University Press, 1979, 2001), 60–67, 89.

184. Fred W. Hankins to Deasy and C. D. Young, November 1, 1934 ("throwing"), HML, Box 334, folder 17; Loewy, *Never Leave*, 140–41 ("watching").

185. The Loewy pinstripes were a variant of an earlier design that appeared on Dohner's wooden conceptual models as well as on the initial GG1 prototype. There is evidence to suggest that an employee at General Electric suggested the pinstripe design and that Dohner in turn incorporated that concept into his work. The PRR officially referred to the carbody color as "dark green locomotive enamel." Deasy to Raymond Loewy, November 2, 1934; Loewy to Deasy, November 3, 1934; John F. Hankins to Deasy, November 7, 1934; Deasy to Loewy, December 18, 1934; all in HML, Box 334, folder 17; Middleton, *Pennsylvania Railroad Under Wire*, 94–96; Wayt, "Donald Dohner," 34; Bezilla, *Electric Traction*, 154–56, 161–65; Hirsimaki, *Black Gold–Black Diamonds*, 59–65; Zimmerman, *Remarkable GG1*, 16–17.

186. Zimmerman, *Remarkable GG1*, 17–19, 27–58.

187. The #4877 sported five pinstripes, but the carbody was Tuscan Red rather than Brunswick Green—a scheme the PRR adopted for a small number of GG1 locomotives (a group that did not include the #4877) for use on trains such as *The Congressional*, *The Senator*, and *The Keystone*, which featured unpainted stainless-steel equipment.

188. Zimmerman, *Remarkable GG1*, 17–19, 27–58; Dan Cupper, "Remarks from the National Railway Historical Society, Harrisburg Chapter, GG1 Dedication," Harrisburg Transportation Center, Harrisburg, Pennsylvania, November 15, 1986, chrome-extension://efaidnbmnnnibpcajpcglclefindmkaj/https://static1.squarespace.com/static/60d4047b4ab96c060b0672f5/t/60e753a593885d09ce557a0b/1625772965813/GG1Cupper.pdf, accessed September 21, 2023; Middleton, *When the Steam Railroads Electrified*, 413.

189. *New York Times*, July 15, 1933 ("dearth," "competency," "compensation"); Joseph Eastman, press release, August 25, 1933, quoted in Earl Latham, *The Politics of Railroad Coordination, 1933–1936* (Cambridge, MA: Harvard University Press, 1959), 124 ("attraction," "joy").

190. Other than the suggested $60,000 maximum, Eastman did not provide a formula for pay cuts or salary levels. Railroads might by inference follow the sliding scale that Jesse Jones had developed for the RFC.

191. *New York Times*, July 15, 1933 ("symptom," "adjustment," "insignificant," "psychological").

192. President's Salary, n.d., but ca. 1947; PHMC, Box 30 (9-1626); *Chicago Daily Tribune*, September 20, 1933 ("invasion," "accordance"); *New York Times*, September 20, 1933.

193. The report's calculation of inflation rates seems at odds with the CPI Inflation Calculator maintained by the Bureau of Labor Statistics. A salary of $75,000 in 1913 (as far back as the data series extends) would be equivalent to $129,545 (not $72,300) in 1929 and $98,485 (not $55,700) in 1933. Presumably, the lower figures reflect earnings after taxes.

194. *New York Times*, September 20, 1933.

195. *Railway Age* 95, no. 13 (September 23, 1933): 447 ("reasonable").

196. *New York Times*, April 11, 1934 ("spare," "higher").

197. While his comments were understandable, du Pont ignored Eastman's substantial achievements during his three years as transportation coordinator. They included increased efficiencies in rail and water operations in Greater New York (which saved as much as $3 million annually), the shaping of truck pickup and delivery operations on the PRR and other carriers, and the establishment of a Science Advisory Board (of which Atterbury was a member). Eastman's views on coordinated transportation contributed mightily to the passage of the Motor Carrier Act of 1935. *New York Times*, September 20, 1933; September 21, 1933 ("revision"); Harbeson, "Emergency Railroad Transportation Act," 125–26; Ari Hoogenboom and Olive Hoogenboom, *A History of the ICC: From Panacea to Palliative* (New York: W. W. Norton, 1976), 129–30.

198. John C. Baker, "Executive Compensation Payments by Large and Small Industrial Companies," *Quarterly Journal of Economics* 53, no. 3 (May 1939): 404–34, at 410–11.

199. *New York Times*, July 15, 1933 ("danger," "easy").

200. The $17,500 figure was the same one that Jones and Couzens had earlier decided would be appropriate for executives in the insurance industry, representing the average of their own salaries and the $25,000 amount that Roosevelt had suggested. Baker, "Executive Compensation Payments," 405; Harwell Wells, "U.S. Executive Compensation in Historical Perspective," in *Research Handbook on Executive Pay*, eds. Thomas and Hill, 41–57.

201. *New York Times*, January 9, 1938; Bruce F. Barton, *The Man Nobody Knows* (New York: Bobbs-Merrill, 1925).

202. *New York Times*, January 9, 1938.

203. *New York Times*, March 16, 1933; September 20, 1933; PRR BOD Minutes; John C. Baker, "Fluctuation of Executive Compensation of Selected Companies, 1928–36," *Review of Economics and Statistics* 20, no. 2 (May 1938): 65–75, at 66; Baker, "Executive Compensation Payments," 429.

204. Rea was not alone in such inaccurate predictions. In 1935, when diesel locomotive technology was considerably more advanced than it had been in 1927, Baldwin Locomotive Works vice president Robert S. Binkerd invoked the biblical verse "Muzzle not the Ox that Treadeth out the Corn" (1 Corinthians 9:9), asserting that railroad executives should not abandon the steam locomotives that had served them so well for so many years.

205. *Railway Age* 84, no. 3 (January 21, 1928): 205; 98, no. 16 (April 20, 1935): 618–19; Samuel Rea, *Future in Engineering, 1977* (Philadelphia: Pennsylvania System, 1927).

206. *Railway Age* 95, no. 7 (August 12, 1933): 249–50.

207. *New York Times*, August 7, 1933.

208. *New York Times*, July 5, 1933.

209. *New York Times*, August 7, 1933.

210. *New York Times*, August 8, 1933; November 5, 1933.

211. *New York Times*, August 7, 1933 ("college"); August 8, 1933 ("relationships").

212. Eldon Hiebert, *Courtier to the Crowd: The Story of Ivy Lee and the Development of Public Relations* (Ames: Iowa State University Press, 1966), 284–90.

213. *New York Times*, July 11, 1934; July 12, 1934; July 14, 1934; Hiebert, *Courtier to the Crowd*, 308–10.

214. *Philadelphia Inquirer*, November 11, 1934 ("brilliant"); *New York Times*, August 31, 1934; November 10, 1934; Hiebert, *Courtier to the Crowd*, 310–11.

215. Hiebert, *Courtier to the Crowd*, 155, 309.

216. Edwin B. Bronner, "The New Deal Comes to Pennsylvania: The Gubernatorial Election of 1934," *Pennsylvania History* 27, no. 1 (January 1960): 44–68; Richard C. Keller, *Pennsylvania's Little New Deal* (New York: Garland, 1982).

217. Frederick Rudolph, "The American Liberty League, 1934–1940," *American Historical Review* 56 (October 1950): 19–33; George Wolfskill, *The Revolt of the Conservatives: A History of the American Liberty League, 1934–1940* (Boston: Houghton Mifflin, 1962).

218. The exact nature of Atterbury's illness cannot be verified. When Atterbury's adopted son donated his father's papers to the Hagley Museum & Library, as accession #2052, he indicated that his father suffered from liver cancer. Atterbury's death certificate lists the primary cause of death as "apoplexy," with "arteriosclerosis" as the contributing cause. An autopsy was performed, but the section on the death certificate marked "What test confirmed diagnosis?" was left blank.

219. Atterbury resigned from the committee on October 18 and was succeeded by Martin Clement, the executive vice president.

220. *Philadelphia Inquirer*, July 28, 1934; August 24, 1934; October 15, 1934 ("rumor"); October 18, 1934; October 19, 1934; October 20, 1934; PRR BOD Minutes.

221. *Philadelphia Inquirer*, November 9, 1934; November 18, 1934; December 22, 1934; *New York Times*, November 8, 1934 ("felt," "livest"); *Railway Age* 98, no. 17 (April 27, 1935): 651–52.

222. *Philadelphia Inquirer*, April 10, 1935; *New York Times*, April 10, 1935.

223. Atterbury to Roberts, April 17, 1935, in United States Congress, Senate, Committee on Interstate Commerce, Investigations of Railroads, Holding Companies, and Affiliated Companies. Additional Report of the Committee on Interstate Commerce Pursuant to S. Res. 71 (74th Congress): A Resolution Authorizing an Investigation of Interstate Railroads and Affiliates with Respect to Financing, Reorganizations, Mergers, and Certain Other Matters. Railroad Combination in the Eastern Region, Part 18: The Pennsylvania Railroad System, Corporate Structure (Washington, DC: United States Government Printing Office, 1939), 7962 ("absence," "recommendation," "timber").

224. *Philadelphia Inquirer*, April 25, 1935 ("ablest"); September 21, 1935; *Railway Age* 99, no. 13 (September 28, 1935): 393–94.

225. *Philadelphia Inquirer*, September 24, 1935 ("shouldered").

226. Camp Atterbury, established in 1941 near Columbus, Indiana, also attested to Atterbury's military legacy.

227. *Philadelphia Inquirer*, September 21, 1935 ("builder"); *New Albany Tribune*, August 7, 1942.

228. *New York Times*, September 28, 1935; January 26, 1936; January 31, 1936; *Railway Age* 100, no. 7 (February 15, 1936): 271 ("criticism," "principal," "linked").

229. *Philadelphia Inquirer*, April 25, 1935; *Railway Age* 98, no. 17 (April 27, 1935): 652; Burgess and Kennedy, *Centennial History*, 645–47.

230. Clement to Ivy Lee, January 21, 1927, Ivy Ledbetter Lee Papers, Public Policy Papers, Department of Special Collections, Princeton University Library, quoted in Hiebert, *Courtier to the Crowd*, 85 ("disaster"); *New York Times*, April 27, 1935 ("wise," "disastrous").

231. Clement suggested that diesels were suited only for carriers with "thin service." He was referring to experiments such as the Union Pacific's M-10000 and the Chicago, Burlington & Quincy's *Zephyr*, self-propelled streamlined passenger trains that were incompatible with existing passenger equipment. His contention, reasonable given the state of diesel-locomotive technology in 1935, was that those locomotives were insufficiently powerful to pull the heavy passenger and freight trains that were commonplace on the PRR. *New York Times*, April 27, 1935 ("future," "prosperity," "rule," "thin").

232. Effective January 1, 1937, the board raised Clement's salary to $100,000, ensuring that, like his predecessor, he was the best-rewarded railway executive in the United States. Clement's post-1937 compensation was hardly lavish, however, nor did it reverse the periodic reductions that had occurred earlier in the decade. In terms of purchasing power, it was certainly lower than the $49,000 that Atterbury had sacrificed to appease Eastman and far below the president's $150,000 salary in 1929. Thanks to the deflation that accompanied the Great Depression, $100,000 went further in 1937 than it had in 1929. Still, Clement's 1937 salary would have to have been set at $118,750 to match Atterbury's 1929 level of compensation. *New York Times*, April 29, 1938; October 6, 1938.

233. *New York Times*, December 16, 1937 ("gross," "becomes," "give"); *Railway Age* 103, no. 26 (December 25, 1937): 13 ("farm").

234. *New York Times*, April 27, 1935 ("thought," "close," "thirteen").

3. Adversaries

1. Ian Fischer, "The Wagontops," *Keystone*, March 1981; Gregory P. Ames, "Diary of a Wartime Boxcar," *Railroad Heritage* 3 (Spring 2001): 18–19.

2. PRR advertisement in author's collection ("travel").

3. Nationwide, shipments of oil by rail peaked at 856,710 barrels during the week that ended September 19, 1942. Secretary of the Interior Harold L. Ickes, who served as petroleum coordinator, acknowledged that the railroads could not sustain such performance indefinitely. By the end of 1942, however, improved sea and air defenses ensured that coastal shipping was relatively safe from attack. The construction of the "Big Inch" and "Little Big Inch" pipelines from East Texas to the Northeast further alleviated the pressure on the railroads. With the completion of Big Inch to Norris City, Illinois, on February 13, 1943, the PRR and the other eastern trunk lines were kept busy relaying crude oil to East Coast refineries. Following the completion of the line to Philadelphia and Linden, New Jersey, on August 14, 1943, oil shipments by rail declined precipitously. Jerrell Dean Palmer and John G. Johnson, "Big Inch and Little Big

Inch," Texas State Historical Association, https://www.tshaonline.org/handbook/entries/big-inch-and-little-big-inch, accessed November 10, 2022; *Railway Age* 113, no. 14 (October 3, 1942): 546; 113, no. 17 (October 24, 1942): 668.

4. Association of American Railroads, *A Chronology of American Railroads* (Washington, DC, AAR, 1957), 6; F. J. Fell Jr. to Martin Clement, March 5, 1942, Penn Central Railroad Collection, M. G. 286, Pennsylvania Historical and Museum Commission, Pennsylvania State Archives, Harrisburg (hereafter, PHMC), Box 82 (9-1678). A somewhat dated but nonetheless valuable summary of the railroads' wartime activities can be found in S. Kip Farrington Jr., *Railroads at War* (New York: Coward-McCann, 1944).

5. ODT meeting minutes, Penn Station, New York, October 9, 1942; ODT meeting minutes, Washington DC, October 29, 1942; C. H. Buford to Joseph Eastman and V. V. Boatner, November 5, 1942; all in Office of Defense Transportation records (R.G. 219), National Archives and Records Administration, College Park, Maryland (hereafter, ODT records), Box 274; "Synopsis of Meeting of Operating and Traffic Officers at Pittsburgh, September 29, 1943," Pennsylvania Railroad Company Records, Accession 1807/1810, Manuscripts and Archives Department, Hagley Museum and Library, Wilmington, Delaware (hereafter, HML), Box 306, folder 5; Roger D. Thorne, "When German Prisoners of War Passed through Paoli," *Tredyffrin Easttown History Quarterly* 48, no. 1 (March 2011): 4–31, at 7; *New York Times*, June 28, 1942; Dennis P. McIlnay, *The Horseshoe Curve: Sabotage and Subversion in the Railroad City* (Hollidaysburg, PA: Seven Oaks, 2007).

6. "The Railroad's War Record," HML, Box 808, folder 9; George H. Burgess and Miles C. Kennedy, *Centennial History of the Pennsylvania Railroad Company, 1846–1946* (Philadelphia: Pennsylvania Railroad Company, 1949), 683–88; Carl Landeck and Roger Thorne, "The Pennsylvania Railroad during World War II," https://www.tehistory.org/hqda/html/v42/v42n2p035.html#MTT, accessed November 11, 2022.

7. Carl R. Gray Jr., *Railroading in Eighteen Countries: The Story of American Railroad Men Serving in the Military Railway Service, 1862 to 1953* (New York: Charles Scribner's Sons, 1955), 1–16; Don DeNevi and Bob Hall, *United States Military Railway Service: America's Soldier-Railroaders in WW II* (Toronto: Stoddart, 1992), 9–14; Dorothy Riker, ed., *The Hoosier Training Ground: A History of Army and Navy Training Centers, Forts, Depots, and Other Military Installations within the State Boundaries during World War II: Indiana in World War II, Volume III* (Bloomington: Indiana War History Commission, 1952), 8–21.

8. DeNevi and Hall, *Military Railway Service*, 14–17.

9. Gray, *Railroading in Eighteen Countries*, 17–20.

10. The 730th was deactivated in October 1945, reactivated as a reserve unit in April 1948, and deactivated in May 1959. Gray, *Railroading in Eighteen Countries*, 29, 36, 256–68; Mark Metz, correspondence with author, November 4, 2013; DeNevi and Hall, *Military Railway Service*, 17–18.

11. The 742nd Operating Battalion existed on paper but was never activated.

12. The 724th had a long association with the military. It was deactivated in January 1946, then reactivated as a reserve unit in March 1948, and transferred to active status in August 1950. Following deployment to Korea, between June 1951 and May 1955, the unit was deactivated in September 1955.

13. Mark Metz, correspondence with author, November 21, 2013; Gray, *Railroading in Eighteen Countries*, 25–27, 37–39, 167, 185, 200, 218, 228–30, 312; James M. Symes to F. R. Gerard and P. E. Feucht, June 11, 1941; Jno. C. Rill to Lewis T. Ross, July 17, 1941; Rill, "Selection of Commissioned Officer Personnel," October 13, 1941; all in HML, Box 435, folder 15; "Railway Battalions Sponsored by the Pennsylvania Railroad," October 10, 1944, HML, Box 389, folder 7; Rill, "Subject: Training of 746th Railway Operating Battalion," September 22, 1944, HML, Box 389, folder 8; Rill, "Subject: Formation of the 706th Headquarters and Headquarters Company," May 8, 1943, HML, Box 389, folder 9; Dawes E. Brisbine to Clement, October 26, 1943, HML, Box 389, folder 18; "Manpower Situation on the Pennsylvania Railroad as of March 5, 1945," HML, Box 306, folder 2; "'Pennsy's' 724th Tells Its Story," *Mutual Magazine* 30, no. 12 (June 1945): 9–12.

14. Under the original organizational structure of the Military Railway Service, each Railway Grand Division included two or more Railway Operating Battalions and a Railway Shop Battalion, although during World War II, many Grand Divisions lacked Shop Battalions. The 706th Railway Grand Division included the 716th (Southern Pacific), 718th (Big Four), 732nd (Great Northern), and 759th (Missouri Pacific) Railway Operating Battalions.

15. Gray, *Railroading in Eighteen Countries*, 25, 28, 37, 143, 171–73, 177, 179, 181–83, 197, 237, 271–72, 283.

16. Joseph B. Eastman, "The Office of Defense Transportation," *Annals of the American Academy of Political and Social Science* 230 (November 1943): 1–4 ("never");

Franklin D. Roosevelt, "Executive Order 8989, Establishing the Office of Defense Transportation," December 18, 1941, American Presidency Project, https://www.presidency.ucsb.edu/documents/executive-order-8989-establishing-the-office-defense-transportation, accessed November 9, 2022; Franklin D. Roosevelt, "Executive Order 9294, Further Defining the Functions and Duties of the Office of Defense Transportation," January 4, 1943, American Presidency Project, https://www.presidency.ucsb.edu/documents/executive-order-9294-further-defining-the-functions-and-duties-the-office-defense, accessed November 9, 2022 ("advise").

17. ODT meeting minutes, October 29, 1942 ("expressed," "preference"); ODT records, Box 274; Army Industrial College, Department of Research, *Study of Experience in Industrial Mobilization in World War II* (Washington, DC: Army Industrial College, 1945), chap. 8, 8–9.

18. *New York Times*, June 30, 1942; *Railway Age* 114, no. 3 (January 16, 1943): 215; *Victory* 3, no. 6 (February 10, 1942): 22; *Victory* 3, no. 24 (June 16, 1942): 21.

19. Geoffrey Perrett, *Days of Sadness, Years of Triumph: The American People, 1939–1945* (Madison: University of Wisconsin Press, 1985); *Interstate Commerce Commission Docket No. 31954: Passenger Train Deficit, Item 7, Exhibit Accompanying Testimony of Walter W. Patchell, Vice President, Research and Development, The Pennsylvania Railroad Company*, 1957, 10–11, 13.

20. Additional information is in Chuck Blardone, "PRR War-Emergency Coaches," *Keystone* 34, no. 2 (Summer 2001): 17–46; Ian S. Fischer, "The War-Emergency Box Car Conversions," *Keystone* (Autumn 1998): 21–38, at 21–22. Fischer indicates that the PRR added 14,198 seats, while Blardone sets the figure at 13,879 in intercity civilian passenger equipment, plus 6,776 seats in commuter equipment and troop cars converted from boxcars, for a total of 20,655 seats added.

21. The sole exception was a single X29 boxcar, briefly converted into a kitchen car and subsequently returned to freight service.

22. The war caused an increase in commuter traffic, with many existing cars (such as P70 coaches) assigned to long-distance service. Beginning in May 1943, shopworkers at Altoona converted six Class X32a boxcars to P78a coaches. Assigned to commuter service in Pittsburgh, they were outwardly similar to the P56 troop coaches. Later that year, the PRR rebuilt fifty X32a boxcars into essentially identical Class P78b commuter coaches. Fischer, "War-Emergency Box Car Conversions," 22–26, 36–37.

23. The prototype car, #6898, was briefly classified as a P30 but soon joined the remaining thirty-nine cars of Class P30a, built between May and November 1943.

24. PRR and military officials originally planned to operate the troop cars in twenty-four-car sets, subdivided into three eight-car blocks (with a kitchen and a recreation car at the center of each set, bracketed by three troop sleepers on each end). The command car was the sole representative of its class, and in March 1943, shopworkers converted it to a P78a coach for Pittsburgh commuter service.

25. Fischer, "War-Emergency Box Car Conversions," 26–38.

26. The cars were the property of the Defense Plant Corporation, a subsidiary of the Reconstruction Finance Corporation.

27. *Railway Age* 115, no. 12 (September 18, 1943): 449–51.

28. Specifically, as indicated in *Railway Age*, General Order No. 24 "prohibits railroads, with certain exceptions, from running special trains, adding new trains to existing schedules, or running extra sections to regular trains unless such extra sections have been run at least 20 per cent of the time during the past 90 days to handle the flow of traffic." *Railway Age* 113, no. 4 (October 3, 1942): 545 ("prohibits"); ODT meeting minutes, Penn Station, New York, October 9, 1942; ODT meeting minutes, Washington, DC, October 29, 1942; C. H. Buford to Joseph Eastman and V. V. Boatner, November 5, 1942; all in ODT records, Box 274.

29. J. M. Johnson to Clement, July 2, 1945 ("written"), Office of Defense Transportation records, Box 277; *Railway Age* 118, no. 3 (January 20, 1945): 198 ("discontinue"); Joe Welsh, *Pennsy Streamliners: The Blue Ribbon Fleet* (Waukesha, WI: Kalmbach, 1999), 48.

30. "Number of Positions Filled by Employes Subject to Call for Service in U.S. Armed Forces. As of July, 1942," HML, Box 863, folder 11.

31. The commissioners included the federal security administrator, who served as chairman, and representatives from the Department of War, the Department of the Navy, the Department of Agriculture, the Department of Labor, the War Production Board, the Labor Production Division of the War Production Board, the Selective Service System, and the United States Civil Service Commission.

32. Franklin D. Roosevelt, "Executive Order 9139, Establishing the War Manpower Commission," April 18, 1942, American Presidency Project, https://www.presidency.ucsb.edu/documents/executive-order-9139

-establishing-the-war-manpower-commission, accessed November 9, 2022; *Victory* 3, no. 24 (June 16, 1942): 22.

33. J. W. Oram to John F. Deasy, March 2, 1943 ("exclusive"); PRR memorandum for the president, February 25, 1943 ("certainly"); Clement to J. J. Pelley (President AAR), March 19, 1943; United States Railroad Retirement Board, "Personnel Needs and Surpluses in the Railroad Industry," May 1, 1943; all in PHMC, Clement papers, Box 23 (9-1619), folder 011.

34. Lewis's principal demand was that the closed shop, already in place in independent mines, be extended to "captive" mines owned by US Steel and other steel producers. Andrew A. Workman, "Creating the National War Labor Board: Franklin Roosevelt and the Politics of State Building in the Early 1940s," *Journal of Policy History* 12, no. 2 (2000): 233–64, at 237–50; James B. Atleson, *Labor and the Wartime State: Labor Relations and Law during World War II* (Urbana: University of Illinois Press, 1998), 20–37.

35. Franklin D. Roosevelt, "Executive Order 9017, Establishing the National War Labor Board," January 12, 1942, American Presidency Project, https://www .presidency.ucsb.edu/documents/executive-order-9017 -establishing-the-national-war-labor-board, accessed November 9, 2022; Workman, "Creating the National War Labor Board," 251–53.

36. The nonoperating unions announced plans to strike on September 11, 1941, with the brotherhoods to begin the strike incrementally from September 15 through September 17.

37. *Report to the President by the Emergency Board Appointed September 10, 1941, Under Section 10 of the Railway labor Act, to Investigate the Facts as to the Disputes Between Certain Common Carriers by Rail and Certain of their Employees Respecting Vacations with Pay, Rules of Service, and Wage Increases, and to Report Thereon* (Chicago: Fred J. Ringley, 1941); James W. Bennett Jr., "The Railway Labor Act of 1926" (PhD diss., University of Florida, 1955), 164–82; Herbert R. Northrup, "The Railway Labor Act and Railway Labor Disputes in Wartime," *American Economic Review* 36, no. 3 (June 1946): 324–43, at 326–27.

38. Bennett, "Railway Labor Act of 1926," 182–84; Northrup, "Railway Labor Act," 328–29.

39. *New York Times*, June 27, 1942; July 15, 1942; August 6, 1942.

40. *New York Times*, September 26, 1942; January 17, 1943.

41. Franklin D. Roosevelt, "Executive Order 8734, Establishing the Office of Price Administration and Civilian Supply," April 11, 1941, American Presidency

Project, https://www.presidency.ucsb.edu/documents /executive-order-8734-establishing-the-office-price -administration-and-civilian-supply; "Executive Order 8875, Establishing the Supply Priorities and Allocations Board," August 28, 1941, American Presidency Project, https://www.presidency.ucsb.edu/documents /executive-order-8875-establishing-the-supply-priorities -and-allocations-board, accessed November 20, 2022; Franklin D. Roosevelt, "Statement by the President on Signing the Emergency Price Control Act, January 30, 1942," in *The Public Papers and Addresses of Franklin D. Roosevelt, 1942 Volume*, ed. Samuel I. Rosenman (New York: Harper & Brothers, 1950), 67 ("victims"), 68 ("sacrifices").

42. Franklin D. Roosevelt, "Executive Order 9250, Establishing the Office of Economic Stabilization," October 3, 1942, American Presidency Project, https://www .presidency.ucsb.edu/documents/executive-order-9250 -establishing-the-office-economic-stabilization, accessed January 28, 2023.

43. *New York Times*, February 6, 1943 ("procedure," "group"); "Decisions of the National War Labor Board, August and September 1942," *Monthly Labor Review* 56, no. 1 (January 1943): 59–67, at 59; United States Department of Labor, Bureau of Labor Statistics, *Problems and Policies of Dispute Settlement and Wage Stabilization during World War II* (Washington, DC: United States Government Printing Office, 1950), 133–36, 162; Northrup, "Railway Labor Act," 328–29.

44. *New York Times*, January 16, 1943; Bennett, "Railway Labor Act of 1926," 216–17; Northrup, "Railway Labor Act," 329–30.

45. *New York Times*, June 24, 1943 ("inequities"); August 7, 1943; "White House Statement and Executive Order to 'Hold the Line' on Prices and Wages. Executive Order No. 9328. April 8, 1943," in *Public Papers of the Presidents of the United States, 1943 Volume* (New York: Harper & Brothers, 1950): 148–57, at 148 ("hold"), 149 ("increases").

46. *New York Times*, June 24, 1943 ("violence").

47. *New York Times*, August 5, 1943; September 17, 1943 ("basis"); October 2, 1943; October 19, 1943; October 27, 1943.

48. Bennett, "Railway Labor Act of 1926," 221–26.

49. *New York Times*, October 15, 1943 ("desperate," "dangerous," "compulsory," "strike"); October 19, 1943 ("delay," "sign," "riots").

50. *New York Times*, October 17, 1943 ("confused"); October 19, 1943 ("arbitrary," "emasculated," "repair," "good"); October 20, 1943.

51. *New York Times*, October 19, 1943 ("bets");
Northrup, "Railway Labor Act," 333–35.

52. *New York Times*, October 20, 1943 ("warpath,"
"betrayed," "deserted"); October 21, 1943 ("stalling");
Northrup, "Railway Labor Act," 333–35.

53. *New York Times*, October 23, 1943 ("untenable,"
"positions"); October 27, 1943; November 2, 1943;
November 8, 1943; November 9, 1943 ("appropriate").

54. *New York Times*, November 9, 1943 ("inequities,"
"unworkable," "agent"); November 10, 1943; Bennett,
"Railway Labor Act of 1926," 220–21.

55. *New York Times*, December 20, 1943; December 21,
1943; December 22, 1943; December 23, 1943; December
24, 1943; Bennett, "Railway Labor Act of 1926," 226–28.

56. Section 9 of the 1940 Selective Training and
Service Act permitted the military to seize vital industries in cases where strikes or other labor disputes
threatened production of military necessities. That law,
however, made no provision for intervention in cases
where management either refused to negotiate with
employees or declined to abide by NWLB recommendations. In response to several problems in the aviation
and coal industries, on June 25, 1943, Congress passed
the Smith-Connally Act (also known as the War Labor
Disputes Act), over Roosevelt's veto. The legislation
increased the ability of the NWLB to impose settlements
and afforded the US Army broad authority to seize and
operate railroads, factories, mines, and other facilities
critical to the war effort. Atleson, *Labor and the Wartime
State*, 121–22; John H. Ohly, *Industrialists in Olive Drab:
The Emergency Operation of Private Industries during
World War II*, ed. Clayton D. Laurie (Washington, DC:
Center of Military History, United States Army, 1999),
59–64, 93–111.

57. During the war, the federal government did seize
and actively manage several railroads. They included the
Fairport, Painesville & Eastern Railroad; the Toledo,
Peoria & Western Railroad; the American Railroad
Company of Puerto Rico; and the Bingham & Garfield
Railway. Those were each modest operations, however—
only a small fraction of the size of the Pennsylvania Railroad. *New York Times*, December 21, 1943; December 24,
1943; Ohly, *Industrialists in Olive Drab*, 2–7, 87–92, 133–37.

58. *New York Times*, December 30, 1943 ("strike");
January 2, 1944; January 9, 1944.

59. Henry L. Stimson, "Subject: War Department
Operations of Railroads," December 27, 1943; Luke W.
Finlay to C. H. Buford, December 31, 1943; both in HML,
Box 306, folder 1; Franklin D. Roosevelt, "Executive
Order 9412, Seizure and Operation of the Railroads,"
September 27, 1943, American Presidency Project,
https://www.presidency.ucsb.edu/documents/executive
-order-9412-seizure-and-operation-the-railroads,
accessed November 9, 2022 ("any"); *New York Times*,
January 1, 1944 ("circles"); January 2, 1944 ("suicidal");
Ohly, *Industrialists in Olive Drab*, 137–39.

60. Railroad workers received nine cents per hour in
increased wages, and their six days of annual paid vacation was the equivalent of an additional two cents per
hour. Union officials thus had some cause to argue that
the eleven-cent effective raise fell well short of the Little
Steel maximum.

61. *New York Times*, January 2, 1944; January 9, 1944
("perfect"); January 15, 1944; January 16, 1944; January
20, 1944; Bennett, "Railway Labor Act of 1926," 227–30.

62. *New York Times*, April 27, 1935 ("politics").

63. *Kansas City Star*, December 4, 1968.

64. Wintertime reductions in maintenance-of-way
forces accounted for a large portion of that decline, but
the abundance of White labor ensured that few Black
track workers could expect to be rehired come spring.
"Comparison of Number of Negro Employes in Service
as of August 16, 1923 and January 16, 1924," HML, Box
760, folder 5.

65. "Memorandum Listing Numbers of Negro and
Mexican Employees, June 30, 1949," HML, Box 309,
folder 14 (file 011.11); Campbell Gibson and Kay Jung,
*Historical Census Statistics on Population Totals by Race,
1790 to 1990, and by Hispanic Origin, 1970 to 1990, for the
United States, Regions, Divisions, and States* (Washington,
DC: United States Census Bureau, 2002), 19–23. For
information on the shifting political alliances of Afri-
can Americans during the 1930s, see Nancy Joan Weiss,
*Farewell to the Party of Lincoln: Black Politics in the Age of
F.D.R.* (Princeton, NJ: Princeton University Press, 1983).

66. For one of many studies of the differences between
philosophies of Washington and DuBois, see Jacqueline
M. Moore, *Booker T. Washington, W.E.B. Du Bois, and the
Struggle for Racial Uplift* (New York: Rowman & Little-
field, 2003).

67. For information relating to Roosevelt's relation-
ship with African Americans, see *The Black Cabinet:
The Untold Story of African Americans and Politics during
the Age of Roosevelt* (New York: Grove Atlantic, 2020);
Lauren Rebecca Sklaroff, *Black Culture and the New Deal:
The Quest for Civil Rights in the Roosevelt Era* (Chapel
Hill: University of North Carolina Press, 2009); and
Patricia Sullivan, *Days of Hope: Race and Democracy in
the New Deal Era* (Chapel Hill: University of North Car-
olina Press, 2014).

68. White operating employees in the South were particularly aggressive in using the terms of the Crosser-Dill Act to arrange for African American firemen and brakemen to be fired or demoted. By 1942, under intense pressure from the Brotherhood of Railroad Trainmen, the NRAB had finally resolved the "colored trainmen" issue, mandating that the railroads replace African American porter-brakemen with White brakemen who were members of the BRT. Such exclusionary practices had little effect on the PRR, for the simple reason that management had long since dismissed all the company's Black porter-brakemen and had never authorized the employment of Black firemen.

69. Bernstein, "Racism, Railroad Unions, and Labor Regulation," 242–42; Eric Arnesen, *Brotherhoods of Color: Black Railroad Workers and the Struggle for Equality* (Cambridge, MA: Harvard University Press, 2001), 86–87, 94, 126–27, 136, 187.

70. Arnesen, *Brotherhoods of Color*, 82, 94–95.

71. The War Manpower Commission worked closely with the Office of Defense Transportation, headed by Joseph Eastman, to recruit and allocate railroad labor. Eastman, who had earlier asserted that his role as transportation coordinator reflected a mandate to ensure transportation efficiency rather than civil rights, correspondingly held that the ODT's function was limited to war mobilization—even if African Americans suffered discrimination in the process. John Dickinson to Martin Clement, November 23, 1943, PHMC, Box 23 (9-1619), folder 010.4; Arnesen, *Brotherhoods of Color*, 106–7, 186–87, 190–92.

72. "Occupational Status of Negro Railroad Employees," *Monthly Labor Review* 56, no. 3 (March 1943): 484–85.

73. "Number of Negro Employes in All Departments on the Pennsylvania Railroad System as of October 15, 1944," HML, Box 817, folder 21.

74. Herman D. Bloch, "The Employment Status of the New York Negro in Retrospect," *Phylon Quarterly* 20, no. 4 (Autumn 1959): 327–44, at 329; "Number of Female Negro Employes in All Departments on the Pennsylvania Railroad System as of December 15, 1944," HML, Box 817, folder 21 ("Section," "girls").

75. A similarly named organization, the National Brotherhood of Dining Car Employees, was generally only a force in the Midwest and West, although it did represent some PRR employees based in Chicago.

76. Estelle M. Stewart, *Handbook of American Trade-Unions*, 1936 Edition, Department of Labor Bulletin No. 618 (Washington, DC: United States Government Printing Office, 1936), 246–47, 252, 256–58; *Who's Who in Colored America: A Biographical Dictionary of Notable Living Persons of African Descent in America*, 6th ed. (New York: Thomas Yenser, 1944), 323; *New York Times*, January 17, 1934.

77. [Baltimore] *Afro-American*, March 7, 1931 ("friendly," "permit"); *New York Age*, April 9, 1932.

78. In 1920, the organization, established in 1890 as the Waiters and Bartenders' National Union of the United States, received authority from the AFL to recruit dining car employees.

79. [Baltimore] *Afro-American*, March 7, 1931 ("successful"); Lemus ("Piffle") quoted in Larry Tye, *Rising from the Rails: Pullman Porters and the Making of the Black Middle Class* (New York: Henry Holt, 2004), 150; Arnesen, *Brotherhoods of Color*, 96–97.

80. The 1882 Chinese Exclusion Act sharply reduced Asian immigration to the United States, as did the 1907–1908 "Gentlemen's Agreement" with Japan. The Immigration Act of 1924 (also known as the Johnson-Reed Act) imposed additional restrictions. Only residents of the Philippines, under the control of the United States since 1898, were exempt. Soon after the Spanish-American War, the US Navy began recruiting Filipinos, and many arrived in the United States because of their military service. The navy restricted all Filipinos—regardless of their education or skill level—to work as stewards or mess attendants. That training doubtless explained why many sought jobs as Pullman porters or dining car waiters following their release from military service. Pullman began hiring Filipinos in 1925, soon after Randolph organized the Brotherhood of Sleeping Car Porters—and the threat that they might be employed as strikebreakers was unmistakable. In addition to implementing a procedure for Philippine independence, the 1934 Tydings-McDuffie Act limited Philippine immigration to the United States to only fifty people per year. Yen Espiritu, "The Paradox of Assimilation: Children of Filipino Immigrants in San Diego," in *Ethnicities: Children of Immigrants in America*, ed. Ruben Rumbaut and Alejandro Portes (Berkeley and New York: University of California Press and Russell Sage Foundation, 2001): 156–86.

81. Like Randolph at the BSCP, Lemus (unsuccessfully) favored an addition to the Crosser-Dill bill that would have restricted railroad employment to US citizens (ostensibly as a mechanism for protecting the jobs of "true" Americans) that would at least have eliminated the threat posed by Filipino workers. *New York Age*, February 27, 1932 ("Rumor"); Barbara M. Posadas, "The Hierarchy of Color and Psychological Adjustment in an Industrial

Environment: Filipinos, the Pullman Company, and the Brotherhood of Sleeping Car Porters," *Labor History* 23, no. 3 (Summer 1982): 349–73; Lorenzo J. Greene and Carter G. Woodson, *The Negro Wage Earner* (Washington, DC: Association for the Study of Negro Life and History [ca. 1930]), 232–33.

82. Prior to 1936, the HRE constitution stipulated that any African American who moved to a city that lacked a "colored local" could meet with White members but would officially remain a member of the local in his city of origin. That provision represented an effort by the HRE's White leadership to attract African American members without alienating the Whites who formed the bulk of the membership.

83. Stewart, *Handbook of American Trade-Unions*, 11–12, 325–27; Howard W. Risher Jr., *The Negro in the Railroad Industry* (Philadelphia: University of Pennsylvania Press, 1971), 54; Luke Mielke, "Racial Uplift in a Jim Crow Local: Black Union Organizing in Minneapolis Hotels 1930–1940," *American Studies Honors Projects*, Paper 15, 2016, 91–92; Herbert R. Northrup, "Organized Labor and Negro Workers," *Journal of Political Economy* 51, no. 3 (June 1943): 206–21, at 209; Posadas, "Hierarchy of Color," 364.

84. As was often the case, there was a personal backstory in the interunion dispute. Moore had been the treasurer of the BDCE before he defected to become one of the organizers of the HRE's Local 370. Lemus accused his former ally of being a "crook" and a "thief" after Moore refused to relinquish the BDCE's account books and funds. Moore proved victorious in the ensuing court case, after proving that he was still a member of the BDCE while simultaneously working on behalf of the AFL affiliate. By December 1934, Moore had countersued Lemus, alleging defamation of character. *Pittsburgh Courier*, December 22, 1934 ("crook," "thief").

85. [New York] *Afro-American*, January 25, 1936 ("fake,"); Arnesen, *Brotherhoods of Color*, 97–99, includes Moore quote ("poisoning"), at 98.

86. *San Antonio Register*, August 25, 1939; Risher, *Negro in the Railroad Industry*, 54.

87. Flory was the more politically active of the two, and his long career included running twice in the Illinois gubernatorial race (in 1972 and 1976) as a Communist Party candidate as well as two bids for the US Senate (in 1974 and 1984).

88. Randolph, whose BSCP had gained recognition from Pullman in 1937, was involved in the establishment of the Joint Council. The Joint Council was often at odds with AFL leadership, in part because of its commitment to civil rights (including support for an antilynching bill) and thanks to the Communist Party membership of two of its principal organizers.

89. Arnesen, *Brotherhoods of Color*, 98–99; Andrew E. Kersten, "Joint Council of Dining Car Employees," in *Encyclopedia of U.S. Labor and Working-Class History, Volume 1*, ed. Eric Arnesen (New York: Routledge, 2007), 723–25; Charles H. Wesley, "Organized Labor and the Negro," *Journal of Negro Education: The Present and Future Position of the Negro in the American Social Order* 8, no. 3 (July 1939): 449–61, at 456; *San Antonio Register*, August 25, 1939; Risher, *Negro in the Railroad Industry*, 54–55.

90. Walter S. Franklin to James R. Downes, February 16, 1943 ("placed," "developments"), PHMC, Box 32 (9-1628).

91. According to the agreement between the PRR and the HRE, African American waiters-in-charge demoted to the rank of waiter (to make room for White female stewardesses) would continue to receive their former pay and would be guaranteed a return to their former rank once the war ended.

92. "Extract from Memorandum of Discussion Had by the General Superintendent Dining Car Service with Representatives of the Dining Car Employees' Union, Local 370," September 2, 1942; Agreement between the Pennsylvania Railroad and the Hotel and Restaurant Employees' International Alliance, Dining Car Employees' Union, Local No. 370; R. G. Robinson to George E. Brown, December 19, 1942; Agreement between the Pennsylvania Railroad and the Employes in the Dining Car Department Represented by the Brotherhood of Railroad Trainmen, October 5, 1943; Agreement between the Pennsylvania Railroad and the Employes in the Dining Car Department Represented by the Brotherhood of Railroad Trainmen, December 10, 1943; all in HML, Box 863, folder 13.

93. While the red caps were technically trespassing on railroad property, officials on the PRR and other carriers were happy to permit the practice, as it saved them the expense of hiring railroad employees to assist travelers. In addition, stationmasters frequently insisted that red caps spend a portion of their (unpaid) time cleaning floors, operating elevators, or running messages in order to gain permission to assist passengers for tips—again saving the railroad money that would otherwise have gone to wages.

94. In contrast to African American red caps, many of whom held college degrees, their White counterparts tended to possess little education—a disparity that

impeded efforts by the red caps to attain solidarity and establish a union.

95. The full name was the International Brotherhood of Railroad Depot, Bus Terminal, Airport, and Dock Red Caps, Attendants, and Porters.

96. *New York Times*, October 9, 1938; Arnesen, *Brotherhoods of Color*, 153–70; Daniel Levinson Wilk, "The Red Cap's Gift: How Tipping Tempers the Rational Power of Money," *Enterprise & Society* 16, no. 1 (March 2015): 5–50, at 33–34; Patricia Romero, "The Early Organization of Red Caps, 1937–1938," *Negro History Bulletin* 29, no. 5 (February 1966): 101–2, 114.

97. PRR executives estimated the annual expense would be $495,087 during the first year that the ruling was in place, increasing to $800,616 annually after the seventh year.

98. *New York Times*, October 14, 1939; November 10, 1939.

99. In March 1942, the Supreme Court ruled that tips could be counted in lieu of wages, under the terms of the Fair Labor Standards Act.

100. The disparity prompted another lawsuit, filed in February 1940, seeking $790,000 in back pay from the PRR and the Pennsylvania-Reading Seashore Lines.

101. Association of American Railroads, Weekly Information Letter No. 384, November 23, 1940; No. 458, April 25, 1942; Clement to Deasy and Franklin, October 15, 1941; Deasy to Clement, October 14, 1938; all in PHMC, Box 32 (9-1628); *New York Times*, January 31, 1940; March 21, 1940; August 5, 1941; March 2, 1942; Arnesen, *Brotherhoods of Color*, 170–80; Levinson Wilk, "Red Cap's Gift," 35–42.

102. *New York Times*, August 14, 1941; Clement to Deasy, September 14, 1942, PHMC, Box 32 (9-1628).

103. The links between UTSE/CIO organizers and the Communist Party caused President Clement to wonder "whether the activity is an unfortunate 'pro'-racial activity, with 'anti' consequences, or whether it is plain ordinary subversiveness, or just the result of competitive union activities"—the latter comment presumably a reference to the rivalry between the AFL's Joint Council and the CIO's UTSE. Clement to Deasy, October 20, 1942 ("activity"), PHMC, Box 23 (9-1619), folder 011.

104. *New York Times*, January 14, 1940 ("dignity"); Arnesen, *Brotherhoods of Color*, 151–80.

105. Memo, RE: "Communication from Lawrence W. Cramer," January 23, 1943, HML, Box 309, folder 13.

106. Franklin to Downes, June 19, 1943; Downes to Mason, June 19, 1943; Downes to Franklin, July 8, 1943 ("elevation"); Downes to Franklin, July 12, 1943; Franklin to Downes, July 15, 1943 ("conditions"); Downes to Mason, July 21, 1943; Franklin to Downes, August 20, 1943 ("traditional"); all in PHMC, Box 32 (9-1628).

107. "Comparative Statement Showing the Total and Negro Employes of this Company to the Total and Negro Population, by States and the District of Columbia, in which the Pennsylvania Railroad Operates," August 19, 1943, HML, Box 817, folder 21; Milded Johnson to George M. Johnson, November 16, 1942, quoted in Arnesen, *Brotherhoods of Color*, 186 ("rest rooms").

108. Arnesen, *Brotherhoods of Color*, 192–95.

109. Dickinson was a direct descendant of founding father John Dickinson, whose accomplishments included writing most of the initial draft of the Articles of Confederation. He served as assistant attorney general until 1936, when the leftward drift of the Roosevelt administration induced him to pursue private practice.

110. John Dickinson to Malcolm Ross, November 23, 1943 ("friction," "favored"), PHMC, Clement papers, Box 23 (9-1619), folder 010.4; C. E. Musser to Deasy, September 20, 1943, HML, Box 309, folder 13 ("Intellectuals," "radicals").

111. "Statement to the President's Committee on Fair Employment Practice," November 29, 1943, PHMC, Clement papers, Box 23 (9-1619), folder 010.4; "Notice to the Colored Employes of the Pennsylvania Railroad," November 26, 1943 ("so-called," "stirring"), HML, Box 309, folder 13; "Post-War Industrial Outlook," 115 ("co-operating"). George L. Haskins, "John Dickinson, 1894–1952," *University of Pennsylvania Law Review* 101, no. 1 (October 1952): 1–25; Musser memorandum, October 7, 1943 ("bright," "resistance"), HML, Box 309, folder 13; "Answer to Summary of Complaints against the Pennsylvania Railroad Company before the President's Committee on Fair Employment Practice," September 13, 1943 ("requirement," "knowledge"), HML, Box 817, folder 22; Lawrence W. Cramer to Clement, December 31, 1942, PHMC, Box 23 (9-1619), folder 011.

112. Unattributed memorandum, November 26, 1943, HML, Box 309, folder 13; "Summary of Report of President's Committee on Fair Employment Practice in the Case of the Pennsylvania Railroad, Issued November 18, 1943," Office of War Information, President's Committee on Fair Employment Practice, press release, December 1, 1943; both in PHMC, Box 23 (9-1619), folder 010.4. An overview of these events is also available in Malcolm Ross, *All Manner of Men* (New York: Reynal & Hitchcock, 1948), 118–41.

113. Clement to Deasy, October 20, 1942 ("unrest"), PHMC, Box 23 (9-1619), folder 011.

114. The large number of passenger car cleaners and dining car personnel who were based at Sunnyside Yard on Long Island contributed to the high ratio, but such statistics did not address either wage inequality or exclusionary hiring and promotion practices. Equally unconvincing was the assertion that the PRR officials had endeavored to preserve positions as dining car cooks and waiters for African Americans rather than open those jobs to White workers.

115. "Memorandum of discussion with C. E. Musser, chief of personnel," November 24, 1943, PHMC, Box 23 (9-1619), folder 010.4 ("fellows"); Musser, remarks at "The Howard University Studies in the Social Sciences: The Post-War Industrial Outlook for Negroes: Papers and Proceedings of the Eighth Annual Conference of the Division of the Social Sciences," October 18–20, 1944 (1945), 91, 115 ("remarkable," "patient," "entitled," "progress"), https://dh.howard.edu/gs_pub/5, accessed January 31, 2023; Arnesen, *Brotherhoods of Color*, 181, 195–98.

116. The *Pittsburgh Courier* was the largest African American newspaper in the world, with a circulation of some two hundred thousand.

117. Despite Weir's recommendation, Clement elected not to use Baker's services. H. A. Enochs to Deasy, July 21, 1942 ("represent"); "Adviser-Colored Employes," January 20, 1943 ("informed," "located"); Musser to Deasy, September 20, 1943; Ernest T. Weir to Deasy, December 7, 1943 ("intelligent"); all in HML, Box 309, folder 13; Gustavus E. Payne to Downes, November 20, 1942 ("reporter"), PHMC, Box 23 (9-1619), folder 011; Biographical Note, Joseph Vaudrey Baker papers, 1935–1974, Emory University, Stuart A. Rose Manuscript, Archives, and Rare Book Library, https://archives.libraries.emory.edu/repositories/7/resources/2335, accessed October 8, 2023.

118. FEPC press release, April 5, 1944, HML, Box 309, folder 14; Association of American Railroads Weekly Information Letter No. 560, April 8, 1944; A. J. Muste to Clement, April 20, 1944; both in PHMC, Box 23 (9-1619), folder 010.4.

119. The Chicago & North Western and the Milwaukee Road made similar concessions. While PRR records indicate that the company employed forty-eight waiters-in-charge, the *New York Times* set the number at fifty-eight, likely a misprint.

120. Female employees apparently worked only as far south as Philadelphia. J. F. Finnegan memorandum, July 18, 1944 ("retain"), HML, Box 863, folder 13; *Lancaster* [Pennsylvania] *New Era*, April 5, 1944.

121. Finnegan to C. H. Musser, September 23, 1943 ("sex," "difficult"); memorandum of telephone conversation, Musser and Whitney, October 1, 1943; both in HML, Box 863, folder 13.

122. The Milwaukee Road maintained a similar dual-seniority system, while the Chicago & North Western permitted Black waiters-in-charge to carry over their seniority to steward positions. Resetting the clock on seniority was common in the running trades, and White firemen who earned promotion began at the bottom of the enginemen's seniority ladder. There were two important differences, however. First, the job of engineman carried substantially higher responsibilities (and correspondingly greater pay) than the classification of fireman. Second, if a surplus of enginemen occasioned a reduction in forces, a newly minted engineman could exercise his fireman's seniority rights and return to his old job by pushing progressively younger employees down the firemen's seniority ladder.

123. The postwar decline in passenger service perversely worked in favor of African American waiters-in-charge. To cut costs, the PRR replaced many diners with diner-lounge cars that contained fewer than thirty seats. Under the railroad's agreement with the BRT, a waiter-in-charge (who would likely be African American) would thus replace a steward, almost all of whom were White. Rather than accept a furlough (which, given the irreversible decline in passenger service, was likely to be permanent), dining car stewards could bid on waiter-in-charge positions—but they would start at the bottom of that seniority ladder, well behind the Black employees who (because of the BRT's discriminatory policies) had been confined to those jobs for many years. In 1957, three of those White stewards complained to the National Railway Adjustment Board, noting that the number of (White) dining car stewards had declined from two hundred to one hundred since 1946. Remarkably, they accused PRR managers of racism for *not* appointing Whites to waiter-in-charge positions. "Summary of Report of President's Committee on Fair Employment Practice in the Case of the Pennsylvania Railroad, Issued November 18, 1943," HML, Box 309, folder 13; E. J. V. to J. W. Oram, December 13, 1943, HML, Box 817, folder 21; FEPC press release, April 5, 1944, HML, Box 309, folder 14; *New York Times*, April 6, 1944; November 26, 1957; Willard Townsend, remarks at "Howard University Studies" conference, 98; Musser, remarks at "Howard University Studies" conference, 116 ("discriminate," "riffraff," "undesirables"); George F. McCray, "The Labor Movement 1944–1945," in *The Negro Handbook, 1946–1947*, ed.

Florence Murray (New York: Current, 1947), 109–28, at 110; Arnesen, *Brotherhoods of Color*, 107.

124. In addition to Stacy, the commission included Judge William H. Holly, representing the US District Court in Chicago, and Cleveland mayor Frank J. Lausche.

125. *Steele v. Louisville & Nashville Railway Company*, 323 US 192 (1944); *Tunstall v. Brotherhood of Locomotive Firemen and Enginemen*, 323 US 210 (1944); Arnesen, *Brotherhoods of Color*, 200–201, 205–10; Bernstein, "Racism, Railroad Unions, and Labor Regulations," 243–45; H. E. S. to Dickinson, January 3, 1944, PHMC, Box 23 (9-1619), folder 010.4.

126. The provision originally applied only to draftees (as part of the Selective Training and Service Act of 1940), but Congress extended its provisions to volunteers in 1941.

127. The validity of the escalator clause was uncertain until the Supreme Court upheld the practice in May 1946.

128. *Federal Register* 70, no. 242 (December 19, 2005): 75246, 75270, 75291; *Fishgold v. Sullivan Drydock and Repair Corporation* 328 US 275 (1946); Samuel F. Wright, "What Is the Escalator Principle?" *Law Review* 15102, November 2015, https://cdn.ymaws.com/www.roa.org /resource/resmgr/LawReviews/2015/15102-LR.pdf, accessed October 7, 2018; Herman D. Bloch, "The Employment Status of the New York Negro in Retrospect," *Phylon Quarterly* 20, no. 4 (Autumn 1959): 327–44, at 333.

129. The number of African American employees declined to 10,208 on October 15, 1949, largely because of the seasonal reduction in maintenance-of-way activity.

130. The PRR began laying off workers, both White and African American, well before the end of the war. On July 15, 1945, African American employment had declined to 17,207, or 9.9 percent of the workforce at that time. "Memorandum Listing Numbers of Negro and Mexican Employees, June 30, 1949," HML, Box 309, folder 14; "Number of Female and Negro Employes as of October 15, 1950," December 19, 1950; "SE-322—Statement Showing Number of White Female Employes and Colored Employes (Divided Between Male and Female)," Central Region, December 15, 1954; both in HML, Box 817, folder 22; "Number of Female and Negro Employes as of October 15, 1949," HML, Box 863, folder 19.

131. Maryland was the only segregated state along the route between New York and Washington, and the PRR apparently enforced racial segregation on intrastate trains but not on through services. In 1904, the Maryland legislature mandated separate accommodations for passengers on steam railroads and ships (although not those traveling on urban horsecar or streetcar lines) operating within the state. The law remained in effect until 1951, when the state legislature voted in favor of repeal. David S. Bogen, "Precursors of Rosa Parks: Maryland Transportation Cases between the Civil War and the Beginning of World War I," *Maryland Law Review* 63, no. 4 (2004): 721–51, at 743–44, 750–51.

132. Risa L. Goluboff, *The Lost Promise of Civil Rights* (Cambridge, MA: Harvard University Press, 2007), 195–96; Martha Biondi, *To Stand and Fight: The Struggle for Civil Rights in Postwar New York City* (Cambridge, MA: Harvard University Press, 2003), 86; Catherine A. Barnes, *Journey from Jim Crow: The Desegregation of Southern Transit* (New York: Columbia University Press, 1983) 60; *New York Times*, March 15, 1949 ("inequality"); October 20, 1949; June 6, 1950; January 30, 1951; November 26, 1955; *Atlanta Constitution*, October 11, 1950.

133. The unions in question were the Brotherhood of Locomotive Engineers; the Brotherhood of Locomotive Firemen and Enginemen; the Order of Railroad Telegraphers; the Brotherhood of Railroad Trainmen; the Brotherhood of Railway Carmen; the Order of Railway Conductors; the United Brotherhood of Maintenance of Way Employes and Shop Laborers; the Brotherhood of Railway and Steamship Clerks, Freight Handlers, Express and Station Employees; and the Switchmen's Union of North America.

134. Goluboff, *Lost Promise*, 195–96; Biondi, *To Stand and Fight*, 101–2.

135. Marshall's mentor, Charles Hamilton Houston, held a different opinion and suggested that precedents established on the railroads might ultimately apply to every other public utility. Houston also asserted that a defense of working-class Black railroaders would broaden the base of the civil rights movement, which in the 1940s and into the early 1950s typically focused on cases involving higher education and the jobs of middle-class professionals.

136. Bloch, "Employment Status of the New York Negro," 332–33.

137. Personnel managers on the subsidiary Long Island Rail Road was more obstinate, and until January 1955, they refused to provide application forms to African American job seekers.

138. *New York Times*, October 21, 1953; "Summary of Joint Report of New York and New Jersey State Commissions against Discrimination on Subject of Railroad Employment," May 1958, HML, Box 351, folder 25.

139. Ralph C. Champlin to Richard K. Mellon, November 19, 1952, HML, Box 309, folder 14; "Summary of Joint Report" ("confined," "advance," "situation," "hiring"); J. W. Oram to James M. Symes et al., May 23, 1958; both in HML, Box 351, folder 25; Arnesen, *Brotherhoods of Color*, 232–34, 315n12; Risa Lauren Goluboff, "'Let Economic Equality Take Care of Itself': The NAACP, Labor Litigation, and the Making of Civil Rights in the 1940s," *UCLA Law Review* 52, no. 1393 (June 2005): 1393–1486, at 1416–17, 1454, 1472; Goluboff, *Lost Promise*, 195–96; Biondi, *To Stand and Fight*, 101–2; "Penn. R.R. Hires First Negro Brakeman," *Jet* 4, no. 26 (November 5, 1953): 27.

140. Matthew J. Countryman, *Up South: Civil Rights and Black Power in Philadelphia* (Philadelphia: University of Pennsylvania Press, 2006), 58–60; The Committee of Seventy, *The Charter: A History* (Philadelphia: Committee of Seventy, 1980); Philadelphia Commission on Human Relations, "History of the Commission," https://www.phila.gov/departments/philadelphia-commission-on-human-relations/about/our-history/, accessed October 9, 2023.

141. In contrast, the Interstate Commerce Commission required railroads to report the number of male and female employees.

142. James W. Oram to John A. Appleton, March 1, 1948 ("view"); Oram to Nancarrow, March 13, 1950 ("advantage"); both in HML, Box 863, folder 19.

143. David E. Smucker memo, June 8, 1965 ("careful"), HML, Box 885, folder 11.

144. Bell intended to use dues collected from PRR employees to launch an organizing campaign on the NYC, and presumably from there to other railroads.

145. Various statements give the number of PRR employees who were members of the Dining Car and Railroad Food Workers Union as one thousand, two thousand, and twenty-two hundred, with slightly over two thousand the most probable number.

146. Once Roosevelt's vice president, Wallace had come under the influence of the Communist Party; in the 1948 campaign, he called for the nationalization of the railroads.

147. United States Congress, Senate, Committee on the Judiciary, Subcommittee to Investigate the Administration of the Internal Security Act and Other Internal Security Laws, *Subversive Influence in the Dining Car and Railroad Food Workers Union: Hearings before the Subcommittee to Investigate the Administration of the Internal Security Act and Other Internal Security Laws of the Committee on the Judiciary*, United States Senate, 82nd Cong., 1st sess. (Washington, DC: United States Government Printing Office, 1951); Arnesen, *Brotherhoods of Color*, 113; Ervin James III, "Unity, Justice and Protection: The Colored Trainmen of America's Struggle to End Jim Crow in the American Railroad Industry [and Elsewhere]" (PhD diss., Texas A&M University, 2012), 2–4.

148. *Subversive Influence*, VI ("couriers," "paralyze"); *Jet* 1, no. 7 (December 13, 1951): 19 ("corps," "shocked").

149. *New York Times*, July 25, 1955; *Locomotive Engineers Journal* 88 (1954): 236; Kersten, "Joint Council of Dining Car Employees," 724–25; Enoc P. Waters, "Negro Railmen Nearly Extinct," *Pittsburgh Courier*, July 1, 1961; Gregory L. Thompson, "How Cost Ignorance Derailed the Pennsylvania Railroad's Efforts to Save Its Passenger Service, 1929–61," *Journal of Transport History* 16, no. 2 (September 1995): 134–58, at 150.

150. Waters, "Negro Railmen," 7 ("thinning").

151. The executive order applied to all government contracts, including the transportation of troops and military equipment, not just the US mail.

152. PRR, "Notice to Labor Unions or Other Organizations of Workers," November 30, 1961; J. P. Newell to Morton S. Smith et al.; both in HML, Box 351, folder 25; John H. White Jr., "Oh to Be a Locomotive Engineer, Part 2," *Railroad History* 190 (Spring-Summer 2004): 56–77; Ray Marshall, "The Negro and Organized Labor," *Journal of Negro Education* 32, no. 4 (Autumn 1963): 375–89, at 375–76; Arnesen, *Brotherhoods of Color*, 231–35.

153. Joseph E. Dyer to Herman T. Frushour, n.d. but ca. 1944, HML, Box 309, folder 13 ("opportunities").

154. Albert J. Churella, *The Pennsylvania Railroad, Volume 2: The Age of Limits, 1917–1933* (Bloomington: Indiana University Press, 2023), 234–46.

155. [Harrisburg] *Evening News*, February 9, 1940; *Trenton News*, September 6, 1940 ("shoots," "thrill," "grope," "nerve," "interesting").

156. L. H. Riffel to W. C. Higgenbottom, August 24, 1931, HML, Box 987, quoted in Michael Nash, "Women and the Pennsylvania Railroad: The World War II Years," *Labor History* 30, no. 4 (Fall 1989): 619 ("merit"); H. L. Peeks to Horace E. Newcomet, July 9, 1928, HML, Box 987, quoted in Nash, "Women and the Pennsylvania Railroad," 620 ("efficient"); Fell to Downes, August 17, 1942 ("undesirable"), PHMC, Box 32 (9-1628); Massey to J. F. Patterson, August 30, 1928; Massey to C. S. Krick et al., May 5, 1930 ("dependencies"); both in HML, Box 863, folder 18.

157. Marion Mixner to Massey, August 6, 1931, HML, quoted in Sharon Hartman Strom, *Beyond the Typewriter: Gender, Class, and the Origins of Modern American Office*

Work, 1900–1930 (Champaign: University of Illinois Press, 1992), 397 ("deprived").

158. F. J. Fell Jr. to J. R. Downes, August 17, 1942 ("welfare," "beneficial"), PHMC, Box 32 (9-1628); Nash "Women and the Pennsylvania Railroad," 620.

159. Nash "Women and the Pennsylvania Railroad," 620.

160. PRR memorandum to the president, February 25, 1943 ("free"), PHMC, Box 23 (9-1619), folder 011; "Number of Female Employes on the Pennsylvania Railroad System in 1938"; E. J. Vogel memo, February 20, 1943; both in HML, Box 863, folder 9; "Training of Women Workers on the Pennsylvania Railroad," February 15, 1943, HML, Box 863, folder 16; "Statement of Number of Women That Could Be Employed and Number Employed in All Departments of the Pennsylvania Railroad System and Percent of Actual Force as of April 15, 1945," HML, Box 863, folder 17; C. E. Musser to G. LeBoutillier et al., August 30, 1943; PRR draft press release, November 1942; both in HML, Box 394, folder 5; Otto S. Beyer to Clement, April 30, 1943; Clement to J. Haden Alldredge, November 4, 1943 ("shows"); both in PHMC, Box 9–1628; *Wellsboro* [Pennsylvania] *Gazette*, March 4, 1943 ("practically"); Washington *Times-Herald*, October 4, 1942.

161. The most serious example occurred when she was asked to fill in for a vacationing janitor. The male clerks who regarded her with considerable contempt made certain that she cleaned their spittoons—which she did, with creosote.

162. Sarah Price interview, in Betty Wagner Loeb, *Voices of the Pennsylvania Railroad* (Altoona, PA: Altoona Mirror, 2001), 32–35.

163. Gloria Brown interview, in Loeb, *Voices of the Pennsylvania Railroad*, 58–61. Like Price, Brown saw evidence of the dangers of a railroad career—a close friend of hers died while clearing a wrecked train from the tracks.

164. "Statement Showing Number of Female Employes on the Pennsylvania Railroad System in Various Occupations on November 1, 1941, Compared with September 15, 1943," PHMC, Box 32 (9-1628); "Number of Female Employees on the Pennsylvania Railroad System as of February 15, 1943," HML, Box 863, folder 16; "Number of Female Employes in All Departments of the Pennsylvania Railroad System as of October 15, 1944," HML, Box 309, folder 13.

165. "Statement Showing Number of Female Employes on the Pennsylvania Railroad System in Various Occupations on November 1, 1941, Compared with September 15, 1943"; Downes to Deasy, November 1, 1943 ("separation");

both in PHMC, Box 32 (9-1628); [Zanesville, Ohio] *Signal*, November 25, 1942 ("hired"); Patricia Cooper and Ruth Oldenziel, "Cherished Classifications: Bathrooms and the Construction of Gender/Race on the Pennsylvania Railroad during World War II," *Feminist Studies* 25 (Spring 1999): 7–41, at 9–10, 22–23, 29–31.

166. PRR Legal Department to Samuel H. Cady, September 13, 1940 ("definite," "supervisory," "laws"), HML, Box 863, folder 9; "Memo for staff meeting," November 25, 1942 ("discipline"), PHMC, Box 32 (9-1628).

167. Crew callers needed to awaken train crews at any hour, day or night; they had to enter boarding houses and might see men who were naked, inebriated, or in the company of prostitutes—and those factors mitigated against the use of women for that occupation.

168. Enochs to Rill, September 2, 1937; Enochs to Franklin et al., November 13, 1942; Enochs to R. C. Morse et al., December 19, 1942; all in HML, Box 394, folder 5; Deasy to Enochs, January 19, 1943, HML, Box 863, folder 8; Morse to Enochs, March 17, 1943, HML, Box 863, folder 8; Legal Department to Cady ("laws"); Office of Defense Transportation, Division of Transport Personnel, "State Legislation Affecting Women Workers in Transportation," March 1943; both in PHMC, Box 32 (9-1628).

169. London & North Eastern Railway, "Recruitment and Training of Women Porters," "Syllabus for Training of Women: Traffic Department," "Details of Work at Present Being Done by Fully Qualified Fitters Which Could Be Delegated," December 28, 1940; Sir Ernest Lemon to F. W. Hankins, November 24, 1942 ("considered," "dealing"); all in PHMC, Box 32 (9-1628).

170. Churella, *Pennsylvania Railroad*, 107, 235, 243; William Elmer to Clement, September 2, 1941 ("handsome," "husky," "heads"); Elmer to Clement, February 16, 1942 ("hint"); both in PHMC, Box 32 (9-1628).

171. Lemon to Hankins, November 24, 1942; Hankins to Downes, December 16, 1942; both in PHMC, Box 32 (9-1628); *Baltimore Sun*, August 28, 1942.

172. Office of War Information, press release, March 9, 1943; March 16, 1943; March 18, 1943 ("Never"); Deasy to Downes, May 29, 1943 ("opposed," "gossip"); all in PHMC, Box 32 (9-1628).

173. *Railway Age* 116, no. 6 (February 5, 1944): 323; *New York Times*, January 27, 1944 ("exactly," "background," "requires," "conciliators").

174. The new terminology was a deliberate change from the title "Supervisor—Women Employees" used during World War I.

175. The exception was Helen L. Shull, widow of the former master mechanic at the Juniata Shops, who reported to Harry W. Jones, the chief of motive power.

176. Downes to Clement, November 24, 1942 ("intimation"); Downes to Deasy, January 2, 1943 ("over-all"); Downes to Clement, January 4, 1943; "Administrative Personnel for Women Employees"; all in PHMC, Box 32 (9-1628); Cooper and Oldenziel, "Cherished Classifications," 10.

177. While the USRA's Women's Service Section had long since disappeared, the US Women's Bureau, established in 1920 as a branch of the Department of Labor, performed some of the same functions. The bureau published numerous studies of wages and working conditions in wartime industries but did not focus solely on matters of railroad labor. Its inspectors, including May Bagwell, who was active in Chicago, were likewise committed to the implementation of proper restroom facilities for women. Downes to Clement, January 4, 1943 ("considerable"), PHMC, Box 32 (9-1928); Cooper and Oldenziel, "Cherished Classifications," 7, 12–14, 20–32; Jordynn Jack, "Acts of Institution: Embodying Feminist Rhetorical Methodologies in Space and Time," *Rhetoric Review* 28, no. 3 (2009): 285–303, at 293; United States Department of Labor, Women's Bureau, *Office Work in Philadelphia, 1940, Bulletin of the Women's Bureau, No. 188-5* (Washington, DC: United States Government Printing Office, 1942).

178. Alice P. Koller to Beyer ("anxious," "valuable"): Koller to Clement, August 4, 1942; both in PHMC, Box 32 (9-1628).

179. Downes also discovered that, among the eastern railroads, only the Erie and the Boston & Maine had ever discriminated based on marital status, and that both companies had suspended that policy for the duration of the war.

180. Downes to Fell, August 25, 1942 ("order"): Enochs to Downes, August 25, 1942; Fell to Downes, September 17, 1942; Downes to Clement, December 15, 1942; Oram to Clement, December 7, 1942; all in PHMC, Box 32 (9-1628).

181. Deasy to Downes, May 29, 1943 ("duration"), PHMC, Box 32 (9-1628), "Instructions Governing Employment of Women for Railroad Service," ca. 1943, 8 ("assurance"), HML, Box 1416, folder 11; "Women Employes" memo, January 25, 1943 ("care"), HML, Box 863, folder 16; Nash, "Women and the Pennsylvania Railroad," 616–17.

182. "Instructions Governing Employment of Women," 1 ("utilized"), 11 ("studiously").

183. "Instructions Governing Employment of Women," 11 ("nervous"), 12–13. "Health and Safety for Women Workers—Maintenance of Equipment, Maintenance of Way, and Station Departments," ca. 1943 ("Much"), HML, Box 1416, folder 11; Enochs to LeBoutillier et al., January 22, 1943, HML, Box 863, folder 11.

184. [Harrisburg] *Sunday Courier*, September 13, 1942 ("personality"); [Harrisburg] *Telegraph*, September 14, 1942; [Clearfield, PA] *Progress*, January 4, 1943 ("young"); [Charleroi, PA] *Mail*, March 10, 1944 ("gibberish"); PRR press release, September 13, 1942; E. E. Ernest memo, June 4, 1942 ("employed"); both in HML, Box 394, folder 5; Deasy to Clement, March 16, 1944 ("posture"), PHMC, Box 32 (9-1628).

185. Clement to Deasy, February 2, 1943, PHMC, Box 32 (9-1628) ("slow").

186. "Memorandum for File: Female Trainmen in Service as of June 15, 1943," HML, Box 394, folder 6; Enochs to Deasy, August 26, 1942; PRR press release, September 13, 1942; both in HML, Box 863, folder 11; "Women Trainmen Employed," November 31, 1943; PRR press release, February 6, 1943; both in PHMC, Box 32 (9-1628).

187. PRR executives solicited suggestions regarding the title that would be assigned to those female train-service employees. They ranged from the unimaginative but eminently logical (Trainettes, Railettes, Pennsy-ettes, and Ticketresses) to the demeaning (Trainmaids, Trainmisses, Girl Guards, Tabbies, Tixies, Carmolls, Railbirds, Servettes and Public's Assistants for Train Travel [PATTs]) to the truly bizarre (Brake-coeds, Warriorettes, Cruets, Spartans, Corpees, Brakema'ams, Pennies, and Punchettes). Executives initially seemed to prefer the appellation "Rails" but ultimately settled for the rather contradictory "women trainmen." "Suggested Names for P.R.R. Trainwomen and Brakewomen," January 22, 1943, HML, Box 394, folder 6.

188. Nash, "Women and the Pennsylvania Railroad," 611, 615.

189. *Philadelphia Inquirer*, April 18, 1943; *New York Times*, April 12, 1943 ("trim"); Clement to Deasy, May 26, 1943; Clement to Deasy, June 1, 1943; both in HML, Box 394, folder 6; Jocelyn W. Knowles, "The Lady Brakeman," *American Heritage* 46 (July–August 1995): 62–74.

190. T. J. Ross to George H. Pabst Jr., December 8, 1942, PHMC, Box 32 (3-1628); posters in author's collection.

191. Clement's comment about "the punch" was presumably a reference to the use of the conductor's ticket punch as a weapon and not a suggestion that female employees resort to fisticuffs. Martin Grams Jr., "The Story of Commando Mary," http://martingrams

.blogspot.com/2012/11/the-story-of-commando-mary
.html; Grams, "Commando Mary, Part Two," http://
martingrams.blogspot.com/2012/11/commando-mary
-part-two.html; both accessed December 26, 2022; *PM's
Daily Picture Magazine*, May 19, 1943 ("lot," "mashers");
New York Times, July 15, 1942; April 12, 1943 ("poise,"
"strangely," "grinning"); Clement to Deasy, February 4,
1943 ("instruct"), PHMC, Box 32 (9-1628).

192. [Lancaster] *Sunday News*, April 30, 1944; Knowles,
"Lady Brakeman"; *PM's Daily Picture Magazine*, May 19,
1943; J. A. Wadovick, "Lady Brakemen Give Railroad
Glamor—and Plenty of Work," *Cleveland Plain Dealer*,
May 11, 1944; Edith M. Feich, "An Interview with a Lady
Trainman," *Railroad Trainmen*, January 1944, 21, 27, at 21
("money").

193. Wadovick, "Lady Brakemen" ("crazy"); Feich,
"Interview," 21 ("pests").

194. Wadovick, "Lady Brakemen" ("swell"); Feich,
"Interview," 21 ("situation"), 27 ("codgers," "sore," emphasis in the original, "steal"); Knowles, "Lady Brakeman"
("proud," "humiliated").

195. Whitney was apparently referring to the coupons
attached to corporate bonds.

196. Nash, "Women and the Pennsylvania Railroad,"
614 ("clippers"); "Labor Agreement between the Pennsylvania Railroad and the Baltimore & Eastern Railroad," December 22, 1942 ("taken"), PHMC, Box 32
(9-1628).

197. Clement to Deasy, December 15, 1943 ("hired");
Personnel Department, "Labor Turnover among Women
Employed as Passenger Trainmen," February 7, 1944;
Musser to Downes, February 5, 1944; all in PHMC, Box
32 (9-1628); Feich, "Interview," 27 ("jerky").

198. The provisions were not retroactive, ensuring that
women hired prior to March 15 would not have any additional seniority rights.

199. Musser to Oram, May 18, 1943, HML, Box 864,
folder 3, quoted in Nash, "Women and the Pennsylvania
Railroad," 616 ("Communists"); "Five Women Trainmen
Allegedly Improperly Furloughed," HML, Box 864,
folder 4, quoted in Nash, "Women and the Pennsylvania
Railroad," 616–17 ("replace"); Clement to Alexander F.
Whitney, May 16, 1944 ("cooperation"), PHMC, Box 32
(9-1628).

200. Dawn Mangus interview, *Voices of the Pennsylvania
Railroad*, 18; Clement to Deasy and Enochs, May 27, 1943
("agree"), PHMC, Box 32 (9-1628).

201. Clement to Deasy and Enochs, May 27, 1943
("news"), PHMC, Box 32 (9-1628); Feich, "Interview,"

27 ("union"); Wadovick, "Lady Brakemen" ("pretty,"
"impressed," "business").

202. That number remained relatively stable in the
years that followed, and in 1955, the PRR employed 4,940
women, of whom 553 were African American. Still, the
number of African American female employees had
declined precipitously (by more than 85%) since peak
employment of nearly 4,200 in 1944. "Number of Female
Negro Employes in All Departments on the Pennsylvania Railroad System as of December 15, 1944," January
15, 1945, HML, Box 817, folder 21; "Number of Female
Employes in All Departments of the Pennsylvania Railroad System as of June 15, 1946," HML, Box 863, folder 19;
"Number of Female and Negro Employes as of October
15, 1950," December 19, 1950; "Female Employes—September 15, 1955"; both in HML, Box 817, folder 22.

203. The same provisions applied to men who were past
the age of forty-five at the time of initial hire.

204. Finnegan to Joseph Quinn, January 23, 1947; U. D.
Hartman to Finnegan, February 12, 1947; Finnegan to
Hartman, February 19, 1947; "Temporary Workers—M.
E. Department," October 19, 1946; H. L. Nancarrow et al.
to P. D. Reese, July 1, 1949; all in HML, Box 863, folder 13;
"SE-322—Statement Showing Number of White Female
Employes and Colored Employes (Divided between
Male and Female)," Central Region, December 15, 1954,
HML, Box 817, folder 22; George H. Patchell to Downes,
November 26, 1945 ("select"), PHMC, Box 45 (9-1641),
folder 110.01; Nash, "Women and the Pennsylvania Rail-
road," 620.

205. Sarah Price interview, Loeb, *Voices of the Pennsylvania Railroad*, 32–35; Gloria Brown interview, Loeb, *Voices
of the Pennsylvania Railroad*, 58–61.

206. "Number of Female Employes in Certain Occupations . . . as of November 15, 1947," HML, Box 863, folder 19.

207. Musser to Finnegan, April 30, 1947; Musser to
Vera V. Kyle, April 30, 1947; "Memorandum of Meeting,"
February 7, 1947; all in HML, Box 863, folder 13; Oram
memo, August 27, 1948, HML, Box 863, folder 19.

208. Beverly Nail interview, Loeb, *Voices of the Pennsylvania Railroad*, 82–84 ("blackmail"). Nail retired in
1972. Nail's daughter, Theresa Wilt, hired on to the Penn
Central in 1975, making three generations of women to
work for the PRR or its successors.

209. Delozier recalled one worker who came to her,
early in the shift, after having hit himself in the finger
with a hammer. After lunch, he accidentally hit himself in
the head with a hammer. The foreman apparently ignored
Delozier's eminently sensible advice that "they should
have taken the hammer away from him," and the worker

returned a third time with another, unspecified injury. Nancy Delozier interview, Loeb, *Voices of the Pennsylvania Railroad*, 72–74 ("conditions").

210. Dawn Mangus interview, Loeb, *Voices of the Pennsylvania Railroad*, 18–21.

211. According to John H. White Jr. ("Oh, to Be a Locomotive Engineer," Part 2, 74), female engineers were not regularly employed in the United States until the early 1970s. That statement echoes the comments of veteran PRR engineman William P. Haxel (in Loeb, *Voices of the Pennsylvania Railroad*, 6), who recalled working with two women who graduated from the training school, established in 1974 by Penn Central at Conway Yard.

212. One of the best perspectives on women in the modern railroad landscape can be found in Linda Niemann, "Railroad Women," *Railroad History* 187 (Fall-Winter 2002): 50–59; Linda Niemann, "The Hospital Yard," *Trains* 63, no. 1 (January 2003): 43–49; Linda Grant Niemann, "The Lord of the Night," *Trains* 66, no. 9 (September 2006): 42–47; Linda Grant Niemann, "Why I Quit the Railroad," *Trains* 66, no. 10 (October 2006): 52–57; and Linda Niemann, *Boomer: Railroad Memories* (Berkeley: University of California Press, 1990).

213. Paul S. Taylor interview of Mr. Soots, 1928, Field Notes 44–216, Paul S. Taylor Papers, Bancroft Library, University of California, Berkeley, MSS-74/187c, quoted in Gunther Peck, "Reinventing Free Labor: Immigrant Padrones and Contract Laborers in North America, 1885–1925," *Journal of American History* 83 (December 1996): 848–871, quotation at 859; Barbara A. Driscoll, *The Tracks North: The Railroad Bracero Program of World War II* (Austin: Center for Mexican American Studies, the University of Texas at Austin, 1999), 19, 29–31, 41–48.

214. Driscoll, *Tracks North*, 61–66.

215. "Agreement for the Temporary Migration of Mexican Workers to the United States for Nonagricultural Employment," April 29, 1943, HML, Box 492, folder 16; Albert A. Nickerson to Paul V. McNutt, July 1, 1943, HML, Box 809, folder 1; Driscoll, *Tracks North*, 67–74, 90–91, 99, 134–37; Erasmo Gamboa, *Bracero Railroaders: The Forgotten World War II Story of Mexican Workers in the U.S. West* (Seattle: University of Washington Press, 2018), 48–50. For additional information on the Mexican railroad workers and the railroad bracero program, see Thomas A. Guiler and Lee M. Penyak, "Braceros and Bureaucracy: Mexican Guest Workers on the Delaware, Lackawanna and Western Railroad during the 1940s," *Pennsylvania History: A Journal of Mid-Atlantic Studies* 76, no. 4 (Autumn 2009): 422–69; and Daniel Morales, "The Making of Mexican America: Transnational Networks

in the Rise of Mass Migration, 1900–1940" (PhD diss., Columbia University, 2016), esp. 228–95.

216. Joseph L. Burke to Musser, August 12, 1943; "Status of Relief to Labor Supply, as of October 14, 1943"; Deasy to Franklin, December 15, 1943; all in HML, Box 809, folder 1.

217. "Pertinent Details as Developed at Meeting with War Manpower Commission and Railroad Retirement Board, 12-13-43," ("pick"); "Distribution of Mexican Laborers," December 15, 1943; both in HML, Box 809, folder 1; "Distribution of Mexican Laborers," December 16, 1943; HML, Box 492, folder 16; Driscoll, *Tracks North*, 83.

218. As of May 31, 1944, the State Department had authorized 53,279 Mexican nationals to enter the United States for railroad work, with 4,121 assigned to the PRR. Of that number, 47,519 had been cleared to proceed to their new employers (3,634 in the case of the PRR). *Railway Age* 116, no. 24 (June 10, 1944): 1112–16.

219. "Memorandum Listing Numbers of Negro and Mexican Employees, June 30, 1949," HML, Box 309, folder 14; "Employment Report," June 30, 1949; PHMC, Box 23 (9-1619), folder 011; C. H. Buford to Deasy, January 29, 1944, HML, Box 809, folder 2; Musser to R. R. McCurry, February 28, 1944, HML, Box 492, folder 16; John D. Coates to Deasy, July 24, 1944, HML, Box 492, folder 17; Office of the Chief Engineer, "Distribution of Mexican Labor," October 1944, HML, Box 492, folder 18; Driscoll, *Tracks North*, 117, 134–46.

220. A combination of language issues, poor record-keeping, and corruption by Mexican banking and government officials ensured that few repatriated braceros were able to collect those retirement benefits.

221. Neil Foley (*Mexicans in the Making of America* [Cambridge, MA: Belknap Press of Harvard University Press, 2014], 132 and 288n34) provides a different account of what is undoubtedly the same event. "In one camp in New Jersey," Foley writes, "two braceros for the Pennsylvania Railroad went on a hunger strike to protest the fact that they were required to pay for emergency appendectomies that would have cost them their total wages for the length of their contracts, leaving nothing for themselves or their families." The expanded scope of the incident (two appendectomies rather than one, a hunger strike rather than a refusal to work, and the loss of all wages rather than a garnishment of $24 per month) suggests that disaffected workers may well have exaggerated the account that Gamboa relates on pages 136–37 and 212n29 of *Bracero Railroaders*. It is perhaps significant that the less severe incident, mentioned in Gamboa,

is drawn from an archive in the United States (General Records of the Department of Labor, RG 174, National Archives and Records Administration), while the more objectionable scenario, listed in Foley, comes from El Archivo de la Embajada de México en los Estados Unidos de América, in El Archivo Histórico de Secretario de Relaciones Exteriores, in Mexico City.

222. Ricardo B. Perez to Enochs, May 25, 1944, HML, Box 492, folder 17 ("treated"); Gloria Brown interview, Loeb, *Voices of the Pennsylvania Railroad*, 59 ("gibber," "dangerous," "careful"); Gamboa, *Bracero Railroaders*, 76–94, 136–37, 172–77; Driscoll, *Tracks North*, 117.

223. The War Manpower Commission initially refused to hire Puerto Ricans, largely because neither that agency nor the Office of Defense Transportation possessed the funds necessary to transport an estimated three thousand experienced track workers from that island to the United States mainland. By the end of 1943, however, the labor shortage was so acute that the federal government was studying the idea more carefully. The railroad hired some Puerto Ricans and Filipinos but did not have a formal employment program for those two groups. They served in a variety of occupations other than track work, and one Black Pullman porter recalled that the PRR employed Filipino lounge-car attendants because "not all our colored boys were" available. "Status of Relief to Labor Supply, as of October 14, 1943," HML, Box 809, folder 1; "Use of Mexican and War Prison Labor for Railroad Maintenance," November 16, 1943, HML, Box 492, folder 16; Interview with John Tibbs, conducted with Peter V. Tilp, September 1980, in Welsh, 54–59 ("colored").

224. Enrique Parra Rameríz, *El Bracero Mexicano* 4 (November 30, 1945) ("happy"), quoted in Maria Möller, "Philadelphia's Mexican War Workers," *Pennsylvania Legacies* 3, no. 2 (November 2003): 16; Víctor Vázquez, "Tobacco, Trains, and Textiles: Philadelphia's Early Spanish-Speaking Enclaves, 1920–1936," *Pennsylvania Legacies* 3, no. 2 (November 2003): 12–15; Víctor Vázquez, "The Development of Pan-Latino Philadelphia, 1892–1945," *Pennsylvania Magazine of History and Biography* 128, no. 4 (October 2004): 367–84; Maria Möller, "Philadelphia's Mexican War Workers" (includes quotations "antagonism," "justification," "ambassadorship," "setback") from Records of the Nationalities Services Center, Temple University Libraries, Urban Archives (box and file numbers not listed).

225. "Joint Statement by the Secretary of War, the Attorney General, the Secretary of the Navy, and the Chairman of the Maritime Commission on the Employment of Aliens," June 7, 1943, HML, Box 492, folder 15; Driscoll, *Tracks North*, 142–43.

226. Thomas G. Finucane, "Board of Immigration Affairs, In re: The Importation of 6,000 Unskilled Mexican Laborers," October 2, 1943, HML, Box 809, folder 1; Deasy to Robert L. Clark, December 11, 1943, HML, Box 492, folder 16; PRR Office of Chief of Motive Power, "Request of System for Additional Mexicans," March 4, 1944, HML, Box 492, folder 16; Deasy to Clark, April 8, 1944, HML, Box 492, folder 17; Earl G. Harrison to Clark, June 15, 1944, HML, Box 492, folder 18; John L. Gressitt to H. W. Jones, July 18, 1944, HML, Box 492, folder 17 ("complications").

227. Chief of motive power memo, August 9, 1944 ("employ"); Chief of motive power memo, September 23, 1944; P. S. Mock to G. S. West, August 21, 1944 ("forces"); all in HML, Box 492, folder 18.

228. "Application for Upgrading Mexican Nationals to Higher Skilled Positions—Wilmington Shop, Del.," August 1, 1944; H. W. Jones to W. C. H., September 23, 1944 ("hearing," "desired"); both in HML, Box 492, folder 18; "Agreement between the PRR and LIRR and the Pennsylvania Federation of the Brotherhood of Maintenance of Way Employes," March 14, 1945, HML, Box 809, folder 17.

229. J. W. Oram, "Memorandum for File," March 22, 1945, HML, Box 492, folder 20 ("equitable," "allocation").

230. "Meeting with the Works Manager and General Sup'ts Motive Power—Phila., Pa., July 18, 1945," HML, Box 492, folder 21 ("released," "employing").

231. In all likelihood, those individuals were either undocumented aliens or else agricultural braceros illegally recruited into railroad service. The employment of Puerto Ricans seems to have been more common, however, at least on the eastern portion of the system.

232. J. B. Jones to Oram, June 20, 1951, HML, Box 1024, folder 9 ("resorted"); Coates to Deasy, January 3, 1945; J. J. Pelley, "To Executives of Member Roads," February 9, 1945; both in HML, Box 492, folder 19; James P. Newell to J. L. G., January 2, 1953, HML, Box 309, folder 22; Driscoll, *Tracks North*, x–xi, 134–35, 146, 152.

233. "Criticisms" quote is from Ian S. Fischer, "The War-Emergency Box Car Conversions," *Keystone* 31, no. 3 (Autumn 1998): 21–38, at 38, original source not listed.

234. ODT meeting minutes, Penn Station, New York, October 9, 1942, ODT records, Box 274.

235. Franklin to Clement, October 13, 1943 ("endeavored"), PHMC, Box 82 (9-1678).

236. Office of Chief Engineer, "Pennsylvania Railroad Regional System: Estimated Deferred

Maintenance—Years, 1943 and 1944," March 6, 1945; Office of Chief Engineer, "Material Situation (Maintenance of Way)," March 6, 1945; both in HML, Box 306, folder 2.

237. *New York Times*, December 18, 1942 ("extraordinary"); *Mutual Magazine* 35, no. 7 (1949): 25.

238. Federal Reserve Bank of Minneapolis, "Consumer Price Index (Estimate), 1800-," https://www.minneapolisfed.org/about-us/monetary-policy/inflation-calculator/consumer-price-index-1800-, accessed November 18, 2022; "Facts You Should Know," Statement No. 2, Office of Price Administration, November 1943; "Price Stabilization for Meals on Trains," Fact Sheet #19, Office of Price Administration, circa 1943; both in Defense Council Records, Folder 8, box 35, information presented in Shemia Fagan, Oregon Secretary of State, "Life on the Home Front: Oregon Responds to World War II: Holding the Line on Inflation: Price Controls Fight the Rise," https://sos.oregon.gov/archives/exhibits/ww2/Pages/services-price.aspx, accessed November 18, 2022.

239. "Testimony by Mr. Clement" at ICC rate hearing, October 28, 1948, 8–9, PHMC, Box 82 (9-1678), 9; Burgess and Kennedy, *Centennial History*, 808.

240. "Testimony by Mr. Clement," 3–4.

241. The ruling also set aside rate increases on interstate commuter traffic, such as that between Manhattan and points in New Jersey. The increased passenger fares remained in effect.

242. *New York Times*, December 13, 1942; "Testimony by Mr. Clement," 8, 9; Burgess and Kennedy, *Centennial History*, 690.

243. *Railway Age* 122, no. 20 (May 17, 1947): 989; 132, no. 5 (August 2, 1947): 56 (210); 123, no. 23 (December 6, 1947): 66–67 (994–95); 125, no. 14 (October 2, 1948): 62 (648); 125, no. 15 (October 9, 1948): 72 (688).

244. "Testimony by Mr. Clement," 3–4, 14 ("allowed"); Argus Research Corporation, "Pennsylvania Railroad," May 8, 1947, 1–2, PHMC, Box 55 (9-1651).

245. *New York Times*, September 24, 1948; September 27, 1948 ("seeking"); *Railway Age* 125, no. 17 (October 23, 1948): 27 ("alarm"), 50–52 (772–74).

246. *Railway Age* 116, no. 1 (January 1944): 1–4; Burgess and Kennedy, *Centennial History*, 783, 804.

247. *Delaware County Daily Times*, April 13, 1946 ("artery," "cooperation"); *Philadelphia Inquirer*, April 12, 1946 ("accomplished," "supremacy," "vital," "Birthday," "prudent"); April 14, 1946 ("great"); *Pittsburgh Press*, April 12, 1946 ("store").

248. *New York Times*, April 13, 1946; [Lancaster, PA] *Sunday News*, April 14, 1946; *Brooklyn Daily Eagle*, April 13, 1946; *Cincinnati Enquirer*, April 13, 1946 ("airlines"); *Marion Star*, April 13, 1946 ("orders"); *Central New Jersey Home News*, April 13, 1946 ("reputation," "felicitates"); *Altoona Tribune*, April 13, 1946 ("imbedded").

249. The basis of comparison is the twenty-five Class J1 locomotives built at Altoona during World War II, at $175,000 apiece. The postwar cost would probably have been somewhat higher (the same was true for the remaining twenty-five examples of the J1 class, built by Baldwin for $250,000 apiece).

250. The *John Bull* in question would undoubtedly have been the reproduction locomotive, built by PRR shop forces in 1940, for operation at the New York World's Fair, as the original was at the Smithsonian. The *Reuben Wells*, constructed in 1868, spent its career hauling cars up and down the steeply graded tracks leading to the Ohio River at Madison, Indiana. *Altoona Tribune*, April 26, 1945; E. C. Gegenheimer to Downes, November 15, 1945; Deasy to Downes, March 6, 1946; "Centennial Exhibition: Display Points for the Following Equipment," March 5, 1946; all in HML, Box 325, folder 2 ("Educational," "children," "canvassed").

251. The Pennsylvania Railroad Company, *Ninety-Ninth Annual Report, for the Year Ended December 31, 1945* (Philadelphia: n.p., 1946).

252. The Committee on Centenary Observance proposed a budget of $75,000 for the traveling display of locomotives and a further $20,000 for historic and modern passenger cars.

253. R. G. Bennett to Deasy, March 7, 1946 ("cannot"); Franklin to Downes, December 4, 1945 ("desirable"); both in HML, Box 325, folder 2.

254. Oram, "Memorandum for File," December 31, 1947; Oram, "Report of Activities January 9th to February 25th—Safety," February 25, 1948; both in HML, Box 859, folder 16; Audio Productions, Incorporated, *Clear Track Ahead!*, 1946, archived at https://www.youtube.com/watch?v=VxwaWt43Sz4, accessed January 31, 2013 ("doggone" at 1:40, "progress" at 6:15, "steel" at 14:15, "new" at 18:05, "keystone" at 26:22); *Railway Age* 125, no. 1 (July 3, 1948): 33.

255. Coverdale & Colpitts, *The Pennsylvania Railroad Company: The Corporate, Financial and Construction History of Lines Owned, Operated and Controlled to December 31, 1945, Volume I: The Pennsylvania Railroad Proper* (Philadelphia: Allen, Lane & Scott, 1946); Coverdale & Colpitts, *The Pennsylvania Railroad Company: The Corporate, Financial and Construction History of Lines Owned,*

Operated and Controlled to December 31, 1945, Volume II: Lines East of Pittsburgh (Philadelphia: Allen, Lane & Scott, 1946); Coverdale & Colpitts, *The Pennsylvania Railroad Company: The Corporate, Financial and Construction History of Lines Owned, Operated and Controlled to December 31, 1945, Volume III: Lines West of Pittsburgh* (Philadelphia: Allen, Lane & Scott, 1946); Coverdale & Colpitts, *The Pennsylvania Railroad Company: The Corporate, Financial and Construction History of Lines Owned, Operated and Controlled to December 31, 1945, Volume IV: Affiliated Lines, Miscellaneous Companies, and General Index* (Philadelphia: Allen, Lane & Scott, 1946).

256. *Engineering Journal* 11, no. 2 (February 1928): 147; N. E. Carlson to Hans Adler, March 12, 1965, The World Bank Group Archives, Records of the South Asia Regional Vice Presidency, India-Coal Transport Study-Correspondence-Volume 2, folder 1846464, https://thedocs.worldbank.org/en/doc/3884716159 82820224-0240021965/original/WorldBankGroup ArchivesFolder1846464.pdf, accessed January 30, 2013; Burgess and Kennedy, *Centennial History*, 365–73, 571–72, 705 ("Glance," essential," "defeatism").

257. *Railway Age* 124, no. 7 (February 14, 1948): 75 (361).

258. Argus, "Pennsylvania Railroad," 1, 3.

259. Several reports by investment analysts incorrectly indicated the average 1946 employment level as 159,000.

260. Argus, "Pennsylvania Railroad," 1, 3; James M. Symes to Clement, June 5, 1947, PHMC, Box 55 (9-1651).

261. Clement to Pabst, January 24, 1945; T. J. Ross to Deasy, February 20, 1946 ("Centennial," "publicity"); Clement to Franklin, May 16, 1946 ("provided"); PRR, "For the Information of the Public," June 26, 1946 ("necessary"); July 29, 1946; all in PHMC, Box 55 (9-1651).

262. Merrill Lynch, Pierce, Fenner & Beane, "Suggested Bond Exchanges, No. 94: Pennsylvania Railroad Company," February 6, 1947 ("competition," "disturbing," "compares," "higher"), PHMC, Box 55 (9-1651).

263. Fairman Dick to Clement, February 24, 1947 ("rich," "agree"); Fairman R. Dick, "Pennsylvania Railroad Company," February 24, 1947 ("trying"); both in PHMC, Box 55 (9-1651).

264. *Railway Age* 124, no. 7 (February 14, 1948): 75 (361) ("satisfactory"); Clement to Dick, February 26, 1947 ("years," "profitable," "developing"); "Review: Penna. R. R. Co.," 7 ("deindustrialization"); both in PHMC, Box 55 (9-1651).

265. M. P. Barrett, "Review: Penna R. R. Co.," February 15, 1949, 7; Dick to Clement, March 10, 1947 ("road," "hope"), PHMC, Box 55 (9-1651); Argus, "Pennsylvania Railroad," 2.

266. Argus, "Pennsylvania Railroad," 2 ("huge," "stake," "drastic"), 3 ("exorbitant," "aggressive"), 6.

267. Clement, doubtless influenced by the assessment of Pabst and Franklin, likewise informed James E. Gowen, the president of Philadelphia's Girard Trust Company and a PRR director, that "the report is a very fair analysis of the situation."

268. Pabst to Clement, June 9, 1947 ("Generally"); Franklin to Clement, June 10, 1947 ("fairly," "signs," "intimating"); Clement to Gowen, July 18, 1947 ("situation"); all in PHMC, Box 55 (9-1651).

269. Benham, born in Buffalo, New York, in 1909, earned a degree in Economics from Bryn Mawr College in 1931. In 1932, shortly after the inception of the Reconstruction Finance Corporation, she began working for the new agency. She later joined Pressprich & Company, becoming the head of the Transportation Research Department in 1940. Benham, who became the first female partner at any Wall Street bond firm, was an anomaly, both in railroads and in the realm of finance—to the extent that PRR executives who had never met her wrote letters with the salutation "Dear Mr. Benham." On a personal note, when the author was a second-semester freshman at Haverford College (a partner institution of Bryn Mawr) in early 1983, he had the privilege of taking a course in railroad finance, taught by Benham. He earned an A.

270. R. W. Pressprich & Company, "The Pennsylvania Railroad Company: An Analysis of Operating Expenses," September 1947, PHMC, Box 55 (9-1651), 1 ("apparent"), 3 ("equaled"), 13 ("period"); Douglas John Bowen, "Obituary: Isabel H. Benham, 103," *Railway Age*, June 14, 2013, https://www.railwayage.com/regulatory /obituary-isabel-h-benham-103/, accessed November 19, 2022.

271. Pressprich, "Pennsylvania Railroad Company," 2–6 ("equaled" at 3).

272. Pressprich, "Pennsylvania Railroad Company," 10 ("locomotives"), 16 ("failure," "substantial").

273. E. Hart to Deasy, October 14, 1947 ("Generally"); "Testimony by Mr. Clement," 22 ("Otherwise"); both in PHMC, Box 55 (9-1651).

274. Dow Jones, "Pennsylvania R. R.," September 30, 1948; Smith, Barney, "Pennsylvania Railroad Company Stock," 3 ("advantage"); "Review: Penna. R. R. Co.," 7 ("stated"); Richard D. Wood to Downes, November 25, 1947 (includes Babson "unfortunately" quote); Carstairs & Company, "Pennsylvania Railroad," 4; all in PHMC, Box 55 (9-1651); *Railway Age* 124, no. 7 (February 14, 1948): 75 (361).

275. "Testimony by Mr. Clement," 14 ("sum"), 24 ("pressing," sufficient").

276. Federal tax legislation stipulated that, beginning in 1941, excess profits carried a 90 percent tax rate, but that 10 percent of that tax liability could be applied to debt reduction—thus creating a powerful incentive to reduce system debt.

277. "Testimony by Mr. Clement," 21–22 ("mortgage"); Burgess and Kennedy, *Centennial History*, 698–700; Pennsylvania Railroad, *One Hundredth Annual Report, for the Year Ended December 31, 1946* (Philadelphia: n.p., 1947).

278. *Railway Age* 123, no. 16 (October 18, 1947): 76 (672) ("private").

4. Power

1. Industrial designer Raymond Loewy took credit for both the design of the T1 steam locomotive and the GG1 electric. While the first claim is legitimate, the distinctive styling of the GG1 was the product of Donald R. Dohner at Westinghouse.

2. Geologist Marion King Hubbert is generally credited with developing the theory of peak oil, which he delineated in a 1956 paper presented at a meeting of the American Petroleum Institute. Well before then, however, prognosticators predicted that demand for oil would soon outstrip supply. Those assertions generally coincided with periods of exceptionally high demand (such as World War I and World War II) or the depletion of highly developed oilfields and did not take into account the opening of new fields or the development of more efficient extraction techniques. As early as 1914, Secretary of State William Jennings Bryan warned President Woodrow Wilson that domestic oil reserves would soon be depleted and that a military occupation of Veracruz, Mexico, was necessary to ensure adequate fuel supplies for American warships. Edward Hurley, the director of the United States Shipping Board during World War I, likewise feared the consequences of dwindling reserves. The Great Depression sharply reduced the profitability of the petroleum business and restricted the development of new oilfields. In December 1941, only days before the attack on Pearl Harbor drew the United States into World War II, Secretary of the Interior Harold Ickes informed President Roosevelt that domestic oil supplies would likely last no more than fifteen years. Subsequent Japanese control over the oil-producing regions of Southeast Asia reinforced those concerns. During the late 1940s, and prior to the rapid increase in Mideast oil production, PRR executives would likely have been aware of predictions that, over the coming decades, diesel fuel would become scarcer and much more expensive. M. King Hubbert, "Nuclear Energy and the Fossil Fuels," paper presented at the spring meeting of the Southern District, Division of Production, American Petroleum Institute, San Antonio, Texas, March 7–9, 1956, https://web.archive.org/web/20080527233843/http://www.hubbert-peak.com/hubbert/1956/1956.pdf, accessed October 20, 2023; Roger Stern, "Oil Scarcity Ideology in US National Security Policy, 1909–1980," working paper, Oil, Energy, and the Middle East Program, March 14, 2012, https://oeme.princeton.edu/sites/g/files/toruqf1156/files/roger_stern_oil_scarcity_ideology_in_us_national_security_policy.pdf, accessed October 20, 2023.

3. With the inclusion of commuter traffic, total passenger revenues fell from $163.5 million in 1921 (and $155.4 million in 1922) to $115.4 million in 1930. Separate figures for intercity and commuter passenger revenues are not available for years prior to 1922. PRR annual reports provide slightly different figures, indicating a reduction in combined intercity and commuter passenger revenues from $155.1 million in 1921 (and $147.4 million in 1922) to $113.8 million in 1930.

4. Average trip length is based on total intercity passenger miles in 1923 (4,277,642,000) and 1930 (2,976,495,000). *Interstate Commerce Commission Docket No. 31954: Passenger Train Deficit, Item 7, Exhibit Accompanying Testimony of Walter W. Patchell, Vice President, Research and Development, The Pennsylvania Railroad Company, 1957*, 10–13; Pennsylvania Railroad Company, *Ninety-Ninth Annual Report, for the Year 1945* (Philadelphia: n.p., 1946), 31.

5. John H. White Jr., *The American Railroad Passenger Car* (Baltimore, MD: Johns Hopkins University Press, 1985), 581–83.

6. Rudolf Diesel, *Theory and Construction of a Rational Heat Motor*, translated by Bryan Donkin (New York: Spon and Chamberlain, 1894). For additional information on the career of Rudolf Diesel, see Donald E. Thomas, *Diesel: Technology and Society in Industrial Germany* (Tuscaloosa: University of Alabama Press, 1987). For additional information on Samuel Vauclain and his advocacy for compounding, see chapter 1 in this volume.

7. *Logansport* [Indiana] *Pharos-Tribune*, May 21, 1899; *Cincinnati Enquirer*, December 26, 1899; *Fort Wayne Sentinel*, December 26, 1899; *Pittsburgh Press*, December 29, 1899; *Atlanta Journal*, December 30, 1899 ("fear");

Columbus [Indiana] *Republican*, April 5, 1900; White, *American Railroad Passenger Car*, 585–86, 593.

8. Debra Brill, *History of the J. G. Brill Company* (Bloomington: Indiana University Press, 2001), 3–5, 30, 152, 157; Mike Schafer and Brian Solomon, *Pennsylvania Railroad* (Minneapolis, MN: Voyageur, 2009), 60; Edmund Kielty, *Interurbans without Wires* (Glendale, CA: Interurban, 1979), 55–57; Eric Hirsimaki, "Help From Above," *Keystone* 31, no. 4 (Winter 1998): 36–40; Brian Solomon, *Streamliners: Locomotives and Trains in the Age of Speed and Style* (Minneapolis, MN: Voyageur, 2015), 17–24; Richard T. Wallis, with Lin Bongaardt, "The Maltese Cross: Rail Motor Cars on the Pennsylvania Railroad," *Keystone* 50, no. 3 (Autumn 2017): 11–80, at 14–16: White, *American Railroad Passenger Car*, 593–97.

9. Brill, *History of the J. G. Brill Company*, 3–5; *Dunn's International Review* 30 (August 1918): 54; Wallis, "Maltese Cross," 16–18; W. L. Bean, "The Gasoline Railroad-Car for Branch Lines," *SAE Transactions* 19, no. 2 (1924): 448–69.

10. "Proposed Memorandum from E. L. [Elisha Lee] and J. L. E. [Julien L. Eysmans] to President Atterbury," December 18, 1925, Pennsylvania Railroad Company Records, Accession 1807/1810, Manuscripts and Archives Department, Hagley Museum and Library, Wilmington, Delaware (hereafter, HML), Box 1144, folder 12 ("restricted"); *Railway Age* 72, no. 19 (May 13, 1922): 1125–26; *Power Wagon* 28 (June 1922): 20; "discredit" quote is from Brill, *History of the J. G. Brill Company*, 158, original source not identified.

11. Brill informally referred to the five cars as Model 25 (based on their ability to develop 250 horsepower), but PRR Motive Power Department officials designated them as Model 80. Wallis, "Maltese Cross," 18–22.

12. Franklin M. Reck, *On Time: The History of Electro-Motive Division of General Motors Corporation* (General Motors Corporation, Electro-Motive Division, 1948), 36–62; Franklin M. Reck, *The Dilworth Story* (New York: McGraw-Hill, 1954), 10–45; Albert J. Churella, *From Steam to Diesel: Managerial Customs and Organizational Capabilities in the Twentieth-Century American Locomotive Industry* (Princeton, NJ: Princeton University Press, 1998), 31–36.

13. Wallis, "Maltese Cross," 22–24.

14. For example, divisional personnel often used large and therefore expensive-to-operate steam locomotives as a basis for comparison rather than smaller locomotives that would eliminate most of the cost savings associated with railcars.

15. Wallis, "Maltese Cross," 24–33; Westinghouse Electric & Manufacturing Company, *Oil Electric Locomotives and Rail Cars* (East Pittsburgh, PA: Westinghouse, 1930), 43.

16. The location was also adjacent to the PRR's crossing of the Reading line, and access to the two competing railroads that served Philadelphia made the site particularly attractive.

17. Mark Reutter, "The Life of Edward Budd, Part 1: Pulleys, McKeen Cars, and the Origins of the Zephyr," *Railroad History* 173 (Spring 1995): 5–34, at 5–26; Karl Zimmermann, *Burlington's Zephyrs* (St. Paul, MN: MBI, 2004), 17–18; Robert Masciantonio, "The Budd Company: An Industrial Icon That Broke the Mold," *Hidden City: Exploring Philadelphia's Urban Landscape*, https://hiddencityphila.org/2018/08/budd-company-an-industrial-icon-that-broke-the-mold/, accessed November 11, 2021.

18. Budd produced a sixth car, for the Texas & Pacific. It also performed poorly.

19. The PRR sold the cars to the Washington & Old Dominion Railroad, where they operated for a short time before being scrapped in 1948.

20. Reutter, "Life of Edward Budd, Part 1," 26–30; Mark Reutter, "The Life of Edward Budd, Part 2: Frustration and Acclaim," *Railroad History* 173 (Autumn 1995): 58–101, at 58–69; *Railway Age* 95, no. 1 (July 1, 1933): 23–25; 95, no. 20 (November 11, 1933): 692–94; White, *American Railroad Passenger Car*, 623; Zimmermann, *Burlington's Zephyrs*, 18–20; Harold M. Cobb, *The History of Stainless Steel* (Materials Park, OH: ASM International, 2010), 136–38, 166–67, 286; PRR BOD Minutes; Wallis, "Maltese Cross," 31–37.

21. John Bruce, "'It Was the Most Horrible Sight . . .': Collision and Fire at Cuyahoga Falls, Ohio, July 31, 1940," *Keystone* 18, no. 3 (Autumn 1985), reprinted in *Keystone* 39, no. 1 (Spring 2006): 47–55.

22. John F. Kirkland, *Dawn of the Diesel Age* (Glendale, CA: Interurban, 1983), 75–76. For a thorough discussion of the various projects associated with the construction of Grand Central Terminal, see Kurt C. Schlichting, *Grand Central Terminal: Railroads, Engineering, and Architecture in New York City* (Baltimore, MD: Johns Hopkins University Press, 2001).

23. Much of Sunnyside Yard had already been electrified as part of the New York Improvements, and it was a relatively simple matter to extend third-rail electrification (later augmented with catenary during the New York-to-Washington electrification project) and acquire a few more electric switchers. In addition,

the PRR operated two float bridges and associated yards with steam shifters—one at the North 4th Street Freight Station in Brooklyn and the other at West 37th Street in Manhattan.

24. The railroads proved successful in court, gaining a permanent injunction against the 1923 Kaufman Act—but the legislature soon passed an amended version, with July 1, 1931, set as the date when steam locomotives would be banished from the five boroughs.

25. The author is grateful for the assistance of Tommy Meehan, who shared his expertise regarding the Kaufman Act. *New York Times*, June 2, 1923; April 4, 1924; April 15, 1925; March 27, 1926; July 7, 1926; *Brooklyn Daily Eagle*, September 10, 1926; Joseph B. Raskin, *The Routes Not Taken: A Trip through New York City's Unbuilt Subway System* (New York: Fordham University Press, 2014), 1–11; Philip M. Goldstein, Paul F. Strubeck, Joseph S. Roborecky, and Thomas R. Flagg, "Industrial, Offline Terminal Railroads & Rail-Marine Operations in Brooklyn, Queens, Staten Island, Bronx & Manhattan," http://www.trainweb.org/bedt/IndustrialLocos.html #Kaufman, accessed November 21, 2018; "North 4th/Fourth Street Freight Station," http://members.trainweb.com/bedt/indloco/prrn4.html, accessed December 30, 2018; "West 37th Street Freight Station—Pier 77 & 78," http://members.trainweb.com/bedt/indloco/prr37.html, accessed December 30, 2018; Kenneth L. Douglas and Peter C. Weiglin, *Pennsy Diesels, 1924–1968: A-6 to EF-36* (Mukilteo, WA: Hundman, 2002), 44.

26. Clarence Heiserman, the railroad's chief legal counsel, suggested that internal-combustion locomotives with electric transmissions would probably conform to the requirements of the Kaufman Act. He cautioned that it would nonetheless be prudent to receive a waiver from the New York Public Service Commission.

27. John F. Deasy to Martin Clement, October 29, 1927 ("assumed"), HML, Box 334, folder 15; William D. Middleton, *When the Steam Railroads Electrified*, rev., 2nd ed., (Bloomington: Indiana University Press, 1974, 2001), 38; Eric Hirsimaki, *Black Gold, Black Diamonds: The Pennsylvania Railroad and Dieselization, Volume I* (North Olmsted, OH: Mileposts, 1997), 37; Douglas and Weiglin, *Pennsy Diesels*, 13.

28. In 1929, gasoline cost fifteen times as much as diesel fuel. Distillate, while less expensive, was still three times the cost of diesel.

29. In this book (and in most other works on the subject), the diesel *engine* refers solely to the power plant, while a diesel *locomotive* includes the diesel engine, the chassis and superstructure, and (except where noted)

the generators and other electrical equipment needed to transfer the output of the engine to the traction motors that enable propulsion. In that sense, most diesel locomotives should more properly be referred to as diesel-electric locomotives, but that terminology will not be used here, except to differentiate them from the much smaller number of diesel-mechanical or diesel-hydraulic locomotives.

30. The conversion of the *Media* to diesel power was not successful, and the vessel was later converted back to steam power. Upon completion in 1924, the *No. 16*, subsequently named the *Detroit*, was the first PRR tugboat built with a diesel engine. Hirsimaki, *Black Gold, Black Diamonds, Volume I*, 38–40.

31. The PRR often employed the term *shifter* for locomotives that spotted cars and assembled trains. I have elected to retain that term for steam locomotives but use the widely accepted term *switcher* for diesel and electric locomotives that performed that function.

32. After withdrawing the Brill unit from service, the LIRR acquired another GE-IR-Alco locomotive, which inherited the number 402.

33. Hirsimaki, *Black Gold, Black Diamonds, Volume I*, 40–44; Douglas and Weiglin, *Pennsy Diesels*, 44.

34. The float yards in Brooklyn and Manhattan were each to receive one of the new locomotives, with the third held in reserve in the event of malfunctions.

35. In 1930, the railroad installed a Brill gasoline engine in the #3907. Owing to minor design changes, the #3907 was assigned to Class A6b. Originally intended as the relief engine in New York, it was instead assigned to the terminal tracks at 30th Street Station in Philadelphia.

36. The Morris Park facility also maintained the two LIRR switchers as well as a gasoline-electric railcar.

37. In January 1928, the PRR's directors appropriated funds for a fourth locomotive, to be powered by a newly developed Cummins engine. While the Cummins engine performed better than the Winton (and far better than the Bessemer) engines, in May 1930 the railroad canceled the project as a Depression-induced economy measure and never completed the fourth locomotive. PRR BOD Minutes, J. T. Wallis to William F. Kiesel, September 14, 1927; Wallis to Clement, October 15, 1927; F. W. Hankins to Wallis, November 29, 1927; Wallis to Clement, December 12, 1927 ("satisfactory"); Elisha Lee to W. W. Atterbury, January 9, 1928; Hankins to Lee, January 14, 1928; Clement to George Hannauer, February 2, 1928; Lee to Atterbury, November 8, 1929; Hankins to Deasy, May 7, 1930; Clement to Atterbury, May 8, 1930; all in HML, Box 334, folder 15; Hirsimaki, *Black Gold, Black Diamonds,*

Volume I, 44–47; Mark G. Mapes, "Losing Steam: The Decision-Making Process in the Dieselization of the Pennsylvania Railroad" (PhD diss., University of Delaware, 2000), 184–89; Douglas and Weiglin, *Pennsy Diesels*, 13, 44–49.

38. Hirsimaki, *Black Gold, Black Diamonds, Volume I*, 57, 74; Paul Carleton, *Pennsy Steam: A Second Look* (Dunnellon, FL: D. Carleton Railbooks, 1991), 129.

39. Patchell Testimony, 10–13.

40. Roger Chang, "The Golden Age of Cooling: Historic Theaters and Their Impact on Air Conditioning Today," *ASHRE Journal* 61, no. 12 (December 2019): 44–53.

41. White, *American Railroad Passenger Car*, 408–9.

42. "This was," as PRR historian Chuck Blardone has suggested, "a pathetic, stop-gap program."

43. Chuck Blardone, "D78, The Lines West Diner," *Keystone* 36 (Spring 2003): 9–62, at 29 ("pathetic"); John K. Tuthill, *Transit Engineering: Principles and Practice*, 1st ed. (Urbana, IL: n.p., 1935), 186; White, *American Railroad Passenger Car*, 405–6, 410–12; George H. Burgess and Miles C. Kennedy, *Centennial History of the Pennsylvania Railroad Company, 1846–1946* (Philadelphia: Pennsylvania Railroad Company, 1949), 761–63.

44. Joe Welsh, *Pennsy Streamliners: The Blue Ribbon Fleet* (Waukesha, WI: Kalmbach, 1999), 15.

45. Welsh, *Pennsy Streamliners*, 16–17; Joe Welsh, *Pennsylvania Railroad's Broadway Limited*, (Minneapolis, MN: Voyageur, 2006), 77–78.

46. As historian Jeffrey L. Meikle has observed, "Industrial designers have always considered their profession a 'depression baby.' Even though advertising agents and department store executives took product styling seriously two years before the crash, it did not concern most manufacturers until after full economic collapse. They turned to radical solutions because they had nothing to lose; to the optimistic or the desperate it seemed a panacea."

47. Jeffrey L. Meikle, *Twentieth Century Limited: Industrial Design in America 1925–1939* (Philadelphia: Temple University Press, 2001), 68 ("considered").

48. Carl R. Byron, *The Pioneer Zephyr: America's First Diesel-Electric Stainless Steel Streamliner* (Forest Park, IL: Heimberger House, 2005); Solomon, *Streamliners*, 32–37; Zimmermann, *Burlington's Zephyrs*, 23–24; Julian Leggett, "The Iron Horse Goes Modern," *Popular Mechanics* 60, no. 3 (September 1933): 330–33.

49. Since 1930, Winton had been a subsidiary of the General Motors Corporation. GM had also acquired Electro-Motive, given that it was Winton's largest customer. Under GM stewardship, Winton and Electro-Motive continued to market railcars but soon experienced much greater success in the production of diesel locomotives. Zimmermann, *Burlington's Zephyrs*, 23–30; Churella, *From Steam to Diesel*, 42–45.

50. Reutter, "Life of Edward Budd, Part 2," 70–82; *Philadelphia Inquirer*, April 19, 1934; Atterbury remarks at Broad Street Station, April 18, 1934, are quoted in Welsh, *Pennsy Streamliners*, 11; Joe Welsh, *Pennsylvania Railroad's Broadway Limited* (St. Paul, MN: MBI, 2006), 69; Meikle, *Twentieth Century Limited*, 155–62; Reck, *On Time*, 63–87.

51. Harold E. Ranks and William W. Kratville, *The Union Pacific Streamliners* (Omaha, NE: Kratville, 1974); Don DeNevi, *Tragic Train: The City of San Francisco: The Development and Historic Wreck of a Streamliner* (Seattle: Superior, 1977).

52. *Railway Age* 122, no. 15 (April 12, 1947): 770–71.

53. His brother, Philip Albright Small Franklin, became president of the International Mercantile Marine Company in 1916, in large part because of his public-relations efforts following the sinking of the RMS *Titanic* four years earlier.

54. George R. Prowell, *History of York County Pennsylvania, Volume 1* (Chicago: J. H. Beers, 1907), 390–91; PRR Press Release, May 11, 1954, HML, Box 271, folder 11; *Philadelphia Inquirer*, June 7, 1949.

55. Welsh, *Pennsy Streamliners*, 12; Meikle, *Twentieth Century Limited*, 68 ("considered").

56. Welsh, *Broadway Limited*, 69–70; Welsh, *Pennsy Streamliners*, 12–14.

57. Cost considerations likewise precluded the conversion of P70 coaches, sidelined by the Depression, into short trainsets that could provide fast service between New York and Washington. A similar proposal, to use modified P70 coaches on a deluxe all-coach train between New York and Chicago, also went nowhere.

58. *New York Times*, April 27, 1935 ("misunderstood," "thin," "think"); Charles D. Young to Deasy and Franklin, August 17, 1936, HML, Box 577, quoted in Gregory L. Thompson, "How Cost Ignorance Derailed the Pennsylvania Railroad's Efforts to Save Its Passenger Service, 1929–61," *Journal of Transport History* 16, no. 2 (September 1995): 134–58, at 143; Mike Schafer and Joe Welsh, *Classic American Streamliners* (Osceola, WI: MBI, 1997), 33; Welsh, *Pennsy Streamliners*, 13–14; Welsh, *Broadway Limited*, 72.

59. Richard J. Cook Sr., *New York Central's Mercury: The Train of Tomorrow* (Lynchburg, VA: TLC, 1991). For additional information on the later career of the *Mercury* as well as other aspects of the NYC's post–World War II

passenger service, see Geoffrey H. Doughty, *New York Central's Great Steel Fleet: 1948–1967* (Lynchburg, VA: TLC, 1995).

60. Welsh, *Broadway Limited*, 74; James R. Downes to John F. Deasy and Walter S. Franklin, August 24, 1936, quoted in Welsh, *Pennsy Streamliners*, 16 ("bothers," "alike"), 17.

61. Downes to Deasy and Franklin, August 24, 1936, quoted in Welsh, *Pennsy Streamliners*, 16 ("square"); Reutter, "Life of Edward Budd, Part 2," 89–92.

62. White, *American Railroad Passenger Car*, 277–79.

63. Between 1947 and 1949, the PRR built sixty bi-level cars (Class MP70) for the LIRR, to a somewhat different design. They were more successful, and some remained in service until 1972. *Railway Age* 93, no. 7 (August 13, 1932): 221–22; White, *American Railroad Passenger Car*, 193–94; Henry T. Raudenbush, "LIRR MU Car Fleet: History and Development Prior to M-1 Cars," *Keystone* 51, no. 2 (Summer 2018): 11–62, at 30–34.

64. White, *American Railroad Passenger Car*, 279–80.

65. White, *American Railroad Passenger Car*, 178–79, 280–82.

66. D. A. Crawford to Hale Holden, May 7, 1937, Pullman Archives, quoted in Welsh, *Pennsy Streamliners*, 18–19 ("restricted"), 21.

67. The PRR's initial preference was for a fourteen-section sleeper; an eight-section, two-compartment, two–double bedroom sleeper; a three–drawing room, six-compartment sleeper; a seventeen-room duplex sleeper; and a sleeper-observation as well as a diner, a lounge-bar car, and a baggage-postal car.

68. Welsh, *Pennsy Streamliners*, 18–20.

69. Patchell Testimony, 10–13.

70. Welsh, *Pennsy Streamliners*, 16–17; Welsh, *Broadway Limited*, 77–78.

71. Pullman repainted twenty-nine heavyweight sleepers, while PRR shop forces upgraded thirty-one heavyweight diners, coaches, combines, and RPO cars. Heavyweight diners #4420 and #4423 received the most extensive upgrades and were subsequently assigned to *The Broadway Limited*.

72. Anita A. Pins, "The Pennsylvania Railroad Streamlined by Raymond Loewy," *Keystone* 24 (Spring 1991): 46; Welsh, *Pennsy Streamliners*, 21–23, 25; Welsh, *Broadway Limited*, 78; Joel Rosenbaum and Tom Gallo, *The Broadway Limited* (Piscataway, NJ: Railpace, 1988), 40; Pennsylvania Railroad, "A Fleet of Modernism Led by a Newer and Finer *Broadway Limited*," 1938, reprinted in Rosenbaum and Gallo, *Broadway Limited*, 10.

73. "Pennsylvania Railroad 'Broadway Limited' pre-view run New York to Philadelphia, Pa., and return, Wednesday, June 8, 1938," John W. Barriger III Papers, St. Louis Mercantile Library, St. Louis, Missouri (hereafter, Barriger Papers), Series 262, Box 158, folder 2–1; *Mutual Magazine*, July 1938, 9–16; Welsh, *Pennsy Streamliners*, 23–26; Welsh, *Broadway Limited*, 79.

74. The exterior reflected the paint scheme that Loewy had chosen for the GG1, although—like many of the other distinctive features associated with that locomotive—it may have been the work of Donald Dohner or perhaps an unknown individual at General Electric.

75. Rosenbaum and Gallo, *Broadway Limited*, 32–36, 39; Welsh, *Pennsy Streamliners*, 27–28.

76. Welsh, *Broadway Limited*, 76; Jan B. Young, *Fashion in Steel: Streamlined Steam Locomotives in North America* (lulu.com, 2017), 134–39.

77. Rosenbaum and Gallo, *Broadway Limited*, 31; E. Lewis Pardee, "*Broadway Limited* Heavyweight Lounge Cars, 1922–1938," in Rosenbaum and Gallo, *Broadway Limited*, 24.

78. Welsh, *Pennsy Streamliners*, 36–38, includes H. E. Newcomet to Deasy, September 29, 1941 ("discontinue"); *New York Times*, March 18, 1933 ("familiar").

79. Charles F. A. Mann, "Everybody's Limited," *Colliers* 98, no. 5 (August 1, 1936): 22–23 ("Everybody's"); Patrick C. Dorin, *Union Pacific's Challenger: An Unusual Passenger Train, 1935–1971* (Lynchburg, VA: TLC, 2001); Robert Wayner, *Car Names, Numbers, and Consists* (New York: Wayner, 1972), 148.

80. Joseph M. Welsh, *By Streamliner New York to Florida* (Andover, NJ: Andover Junction, 1994), 16–30.

81. Each twin-unit diner saved $32,000 a year in operating costs compared to the use of two separate cars, and the PRR subsequently ordered more for assignment to other trains.

82. *Mutual Magazine*, September 1939, 7–8; Welsh, *Pennsy Streamliners*, 31–35; PRR Passenger Traffic Department, *History* [of] *Passenger Train and Through Car Service* [on the] *Pennsylvania Railroad, 1849–1947*, ed. Douglas Wornom (Philadelphia: Pennsylvania Railroad, 1947), 21.

83. Like *The Trail Blazer*, *The Jeffersonian* generated impressive patronage and earnings. July 1941 passenger revenues along the route were $100,000 higher than in July of the prior year (before the train's introduction), although the general economic recovery that accompanied the war in Europe undoubtedly contributed to some of that growth. Welsh, *Pennsy Streamliners*, 38–40.

84. In 1945, technicians at the PRR's Test Department concluded that the ACF cars had fared the best, the Budd cars the worst. Welsh, *Pennsy Streamliners*, 23–24, 42.

85. The southbound *Silver Meteor* was typically attached to *The Constitution*, while its northbound counterpart left Washington behind *The Statesman*. The ACL's *Champion* was also combined with PRR trains between the two cities.

86. Welsh, *By Streamliner New York to Florida*, 16–60, 142–43; Welsh, *Pennsy Streamliners*, 25, 65–66.

87. In 1940, passenger rail travel between Chicago and Florida was a fifth that of the New York–Florida corridor. Prior to the introduction of *The South Wind*, Chicagoans could reach Miami more quickly by bus than by train.

88. The Illinois Central was in charge of the *City of Miami* from Chicago to Birmingham, Alabama. From there, the train relied on the Central of Georgia, the Atlantic Coast Line, and the Florida East Coast. The *Dixie Flagler* followed the most complicated route, along the Chicago & Eastern Illinois: the Louisville & Nashville; the Nashville, Chattanooga & St. Louis; the Atlanta, Birmingham & Coast; the ACL; and the FEC.

89. The PRR made a similar provision on *The Jeffersonian*. Because segregation was in force only for the short distance between St. Louis Union Station and the Mississippi River, it is unlikely that the curtain received much use.

90. *Mutual Magazine*, January 1941, 5–7; Chuck Blardone, with Myron Bilas, Larry Goolsby, Lyle Key, and Theodore Kornweibel Jr., *From the Midwest to Florida by Rail, 1875–1979, Vol. 1: C&EI, IC, PRR, L&N, NC&StL, Monon, M&O* (Kutztown, PA: Kutztown, 2014), 405–14.

91. Robert A. Liljestrand and David R. Sweetland, *Passenger Equipment of the Pennsylvania Railroad, Volume 1: Coaches* (Hanover, PA: Railroad, 2001), 3–6.

92. *New York Times*, September 26, 1938; Blardone et al., *From the Midwest to Florida by Rail, Vol. 1*, 405.

93. Neil Burnell, "A Reassessment of T1 #6110 and #6111: Comparing the Two T1 Prototypes, 1942 to 1945," *Keystone* 37, no. 1 (Spring 2004): 18–39, at 18; David R. Stephenson, "PRR T1 Tests on C&O and N&W," *Keystone* 42, no. 2 (Summer 209): 35–66, at 35; Michael Bezilla, *Electric Traction on the Pennsylvania Railroad, 1895–1968* (University Park: Pennsylvania State University Press, 1980), 168–70.

94. They were John B. Collin (1866–1886), Axel Vogt (1887–1919), and William F. Kiesel Jr. (1919–1936). John W. Cloud was also the PRR's mechanical engineer during that period, but he was in office for barely six months, in

1886 and 1887. Cloud later worked for the Westinghouse Air Brake Company, primarily with its British subsidiary.

95. Duer's mother, Sarah Anna Vanderpoel Van Buren, was the granddaughter of Martin Van Buren. His father's side of the family was almost equally prestigious. His third great grandfather was William Duer (1743–1799), born in England, who signed the Articles of Confederation, served in the New York legislature, and was assistant secretary of the Treasury during the Washington administration, subordinate to Alexander Hamilton. At least partly responsible for a failed investment scheme tied to the creation of the first Bank of the United States that in turn precipitated a financial panic in 1792, William Duer paid a stiff price for his manipulation, as he became bankrupt and was sentenced to debtors' prison. J. V. B. Duer's uncle, James Gore King Duer, was a director of the Long Island Rail Road between 1882 and 1897, prior to its acquisition by the PRR. That family connection probably helped Duer begin his railroad career on the New York Improvements, first as an employee of Gibbs & Hill, then working for the LIRR before joining the PRR in 1910. Author's correspondence with Christopher Baer, March 22, 2019 and April 8, 2019. For additional information regarding William Duer's career, see Robert Francis Jones, *The King of the Alley: William Duer, Politician, Entrepreneur, and Speculator, 1768–1799* (Philadelphia: American Philosophical Society, 1992), and David J. Cowan, "William Duer and America's First Financial Scandal," *Financial History* 97 (Spring 2009): 20–35.

96. PRR BOD Minutes; *Altoona Mirror*, November 8, 1930; Richard D. Adams, with John M. Prophet and Roger L. Keyser, "The I1s," *Keystone* 10, no. 1 (March 1977): 2–11.

97. Officials on competing railroads such as the Baltimore & Ohio chose not to emulate that strategy. Lacking the PRR's resources, unconstrained by the influence of a successful main line electrification program, and without ideologues such as Duer, they proved more receptive to the use of diesels as a replacement for steam locomotives and as an alternative to electrics. Paul T. Warner, *Motive Power Development on the Pennsylvania Railroad System, 1831–1924*, reprinted from *Baldwin Locomotives* (Philadelphia: Pennsylvania Railroad Company, 1924), 71.

98. *Railway Mechanical Engineer* 115, no. 3 (March 1941): 122–23.

99. Reck, *On Time*, 97–104; Reck, *Dilworth Story*, 54–61.

100. *Altoona Tribune*, March 4, 1936 ("handled"); *Harrisburg News*, March 5, 1936; "willing" quoted in Mark Reutter, "The Great (Motive) Power Struggle: The Pennsylvania Railroad v. General Motors, 1935–1949,"

Railroad History 170 (1994): 15–33, at 20; Hirsimaki, *Black Gold, Black Diamonds, Volume I*, 78–79; Mapes, "Losing Steam," 218–20, includes "Danger" quotation from *Johnstown Democrat*, March 6, 1936.

101. The "E" was a reference to the 1,800 horsepower developed by the two Winton Model 201A engines in each locomotive. The series that began with the EA/EB continued through the E1 and E2, all employing the Model 201A. The subsequent E3 (introduced in 1938) through E9 models, the last of which remained in production until 1964, used variants of the improved Model 567 diesel engine and developed as much as 2,400 horsepower.

102. Unlike the M-10000 and the *Zephyr*, the Santa Fe's new train employed standard passenger equipment. It only operated once a week, however, with a six-car consist—hardly equivalent to the dozens of PRR long-distance trains, each carrying as many as fourteen cars, that connected all the major destinations on the system. Nor could PRR officials have been impressed that one of the Santa Fe units caught fire on a November 1935 test run, delaying the introduction of the *Super Chief.*

103. Most of the proposed reduction in running times on the two trains was based on the removal of speed restrictions, made possible by the short rigid wheelbase of the diesel locomotives. Michael W. Flick, "The Super Chief: Part One, 1936–1947," *Warbonnet* 24, no. 4 (Fourth Quarter, 2018): 6–31, at 8–9; Mapes, "Losing Steam," 220–21.

104. Reutter, "Struggle," 21–22; Hirsimaki, *Black Gold, Black Diamonds, Volume I*, 80–81; Welsh, *Pennsy Streamliners*, 66; Mapes, "Losing Steam, 221–22.

105. Unlike steam locomotives, which develop progressively higher horsepower as speeds increase, diesels exhibit constant horsepower at all speeds. Their high tractive effort at low speeds enabled diesels to move, albeit slowly, long cuts of cars that would pose difficulties for steam shifters. Because diesel switchers could operate almost continuously, crews could avoid unproductive trips to engine houses or maintenance facilities. Diesels also benefited from light axle loadings, enabling them to traverse lightly built or poorly maintained industrial and branch-line tracks.

106. Jerry A. Pinkepank, *The Second Diesel Spotter's Guide* (Milwaukee, WI: Kalmbach, 1973), 29–30.

107. David R. Sweetland, "PRR's EMD SW1 and NW2 Switchers," *Keystone* 43, no. 2 (Summer 2010): 73–80; Mapes, "Losing Steam," 194–98; Douglas and Weiglin, *Pennsy Diesels*, 159–60; Hirsimaki, *Black Gold, Black Diamonds, Volume I*, 81–84.

108. Hankins to Young, December 16, 1939, HML, Box 597, file 7 ("clear"), quoted in Mapes, "Losing Steam," 198–99; Hirsimaki, *Black Gold, Black Diamonds, Volume I*, 83–84, includes "advocacy" quotation, original source not listed, 95–96.

109. The figure (from the 1940 *Annual Report*) includes the categories for "yard switching fuel" ($3,458,543) and "locomotive fuel" ($15,892,194). The cost of electricity in electrified territory was included in the separate categories of "train power produced," "train power purchased," "yard switching power produced," and "yard switching power purchased."

110. *Railway Age* 85, no. 5 (August 4, 1928): 232–33; The Pennsylvania Railroad Company, *Eighty-Fourth Annual Report, for the Year Ended December 31, 1930* (Philadelphia: n.p., 1931), 28; The Pennsylvania Railroad Company, *Ninety-Fourth Annual Report, for the Year Ended December 31, 1940* (Philadelphia: n.p., 1941), 29, 32–33; Pennsylvania Railroad Company, "Bituminous Coal Situation for Locomotive Use, February 10, 1945," HML, Box 500—and the author thanks Chris Baer for locating this information in the Chief of Motive Power Records; Mapes, "Losing Steam," 214, 256, 283; Hirsimaki, *Black Gold, Black Diamonds, Volume I*, 74–75.

111. The proposed electrification from Harrisburg west to Pittsburgh caused little anxiety among coal-company officials. While the existing electrified routes depended heavily on hydroelectric power, the lack of suitable water sources precluded that option in western Pennsylvania. The electricity would instead have to come from coal-burning power plants, negating any loss in business associated with the replacement of steam locomotives.

112. "Effect if railroads, generally, go into Diesel Engine Operation," December 12, 1946 ("effect," "bitter," "unquestionably"), HML, Box 326, folder 39, also quoted in Reutter, "Struggle," 16.

113. In "Losing Steam" (pp. 284–85), Mark Mapes uncovers only two instances, one in 1935 and the other in 1937, when a PRR executive discussed the importance of coal as a reason to avoid dieselization. Duer was the author in each case, and he emphasized that coal was a more economical fuel source than petroleum. Yet he did not explicitly state that steam locomotives were necessary to retain the loyalty of coal-mine owners, regardless of the economic merits of each source of power. As Mapes observed on pages 273–74, much of the evidence regarding coal's effect on the selection of motive power comes from secondary sources such as Don Ball Jr., *The Pennsylvania Railroad: 1940s–1950s* (Chester, VT: Elm Tree, 1986), and Alvin Staufer, William Edson, and E.

Thomas Harley, *Pennsy Power II, 1847–1968* (Medina, OH: Alvin Staufer, 1993), and may be based on hearsay and legend.

114. In 1947, once the PRR had committed to rapid dieselization, some of the railroad's motive-power experts were attempting to copy the designs, tooling, and manufacturing methods that Electro-Motive employed at its La Grange, Illinois, plant. It is highly unlikely that PRR officials ever planned to build complete diesel locomotives. It is more probable that they intended to purchase diesel engines from Electro-Motive (as they were by far the best available) and electrical equipment from Westinghouse or General Electric (which through the 1950s was generally superior to what Electro-Motive could provide) while building the running gear and superstructure at Altoona. Electro-Motive officials were adamant in their refusal to sell engines or nonreplacement components to the PRR, and their counterparts at Westinghouse and GE were equally reticent. Hirsimaki, *Black Gold, Black Diamonds, Volume I*, 166–67; Mapes, "Losing Steam," 286–87.

115. Mapes, "Losing Steam," 273–74, 286–87.

116. The Fisher brothers were interested in the sheet-metal stamping presses developed by the Southwark Company, a Baldwin subsidiary. They also perceived the potential for the redevelopment of the land in Spring Garden (near Center-City Philadelphia) vacated when Baldwin's operations relocated to Eddystone. For additional information on the takeover, see *New York Times*, July 6, 1927; July 30, 1927; August 26, 1927; August 27, 1927; August 31, 1927; September 9, 1927; September 30, 1927; November 11, 1927; March 29, 1929; Churella, *From Steam to Diesel*, 178–79n45.

117. *New York Times*, December 31, 1927; February 10, 1928; John K. Brown, *The Baldwin Locomotive Works, 1831–1915: A Study in American Industrial Practice* (Baltimore, MD: Johns Hopkins University Press, 1995), 216; Thomas G. Marx, "Technological Change and the Theory of the Firm: The American Locomotive Industry, 1920–1955," *Business History Review* 50, no. 1 (Spring 1976): 1–24.

118. "Address by S. M. Vauclain to the American Railroad Association," *Railway Age* 88, no. 25D (June 25, 1930), 1548D143 ("benefactor," civilization"), 1548D144 ("greatest," "progressing," "beginning," "discussed").

119. Railroad clubs, common in the first half of the twentieth century, included midlevel managers (typically those associated with mechanical, electrical, or civil engineering matters, or traffic functions) from multiple railroads. They enabled officials to exchange industrywide information and were not for railfans or amateur enthusiasts. Robert S. Binkerd, "Muzzle Not the Ox That Treadeth Out the Corn," address delivered at the New York Railroad Club, April 25, 1935, *Baldwin Locomotives Magazine* (1936): 11–20, at 11 ("long," "impressions").

120. Binkerd, "Muzzle Not the Ox," 15 ("profitable"), 17 ("study"), 19 ("danger").

121. When Kiesel retired, Harry Hoke joined the committee.

122. Mapes, "Losing Steam," 162–64, 220, includes Deasy to Hankins, May 22, 1936, HML, Box 561, folder 16 ("established"), at 162.

123. Since the summer of 1936, Deasy and Young had been exploring the development of lightweight passenger cars for the Pennsylvania Railroad, and Gibbs & Hill had been considering the issue as well. While PRR officials generally dismissed as impracticable the compact articulated cars employed on the M-10000 and the *Zephyr*, the availability of lighter equipment suggested that the Hankins committee had set the 1,200-ton performance threshold unnecessarily high.

124. Neil Burnell, "In Defense of the 5500's: Dispelling the Myths," *Keystone* 41, no. 1 (Spring 2008): 15–55, at 18.

125. Kiesel and Johnson had been largely responsible for developing the accepted methodology for calculating steam-locomotive drawbar horsepower. See Ralph P. Johnson, *The Steam Locomotive: Its Theory, Operation and Economics* (New York: Simmons-Boardman, 1942).

126. Neil Burnell, who is probably the leading expert on the PRR's duplex locomotives, has quoted Charlie Meyer's assessment that Baldwin officials were unaware of the limited-cutoff concept and believed that the wheel slippage "problem was insurmountable." Baldwin's ignorance seems unlikely, given that PRR and Baldwin officials had cooperated on the design and construction of the I1s and given that the limited cutoff was an element of Super Power technology. Deasy to Clement, December 13, 1944, HML, Box 326, folder 34; Reutter, "Struggle," 22–23; Hirsimaki, *Black Gold, Black Diamonds, Volume I*, 84–85; Tom Morrison, *The American Steam Locomotive in the Twentieth Century* (Jefferson, NC: McFarland, 2018), 385; Burnell, "In Defense," 19 ("problem").

127. Glaenzer, from Baldwin, chaired the committee, whose other members included William E. Woodward from Lima and Joseph B. Ennis from Alco.

128. Mapes, "Losing Steam," 164–66, 168; Hirsimaki, *Black Gold, Black Diamonds, Volume I*, 85–86.

129. Mapes, "Losing Steam," 167–68.

130. As Duer observed, it would be necessary to "fix up the plant for the use of one engine, having in mind that we will get the use of the one at the New York World's Fair eventually." Duer to Hankins, June 14, 1939, HML, Box 609, folder 4.

131. The rollers were returned to Altoona and added to the locomotive test plant. Duer to Carl Breer et al., April 9, 1942; Breer to Duer, April 27, 1942; both in HML, Box 609, folder 6.

132. PRR employees often referred to the #6100, both obviously and unimaginatively, as "The Big Engine." More lascivious-minded fairgoers, fascinated by the protruding smokebox front, promptly dubbed the locomotive "Mae West"—perhaps not the precise form that Loewy was attempting to convey. PRR BOD Minutes; Paul Carleton, *Pennsy Steam: A to T* (Dunnellon, FL: D. Carlton Railbooks, 1989), 191.

133. L. B. Jones to Hankins, June 22, 1939; HML, Box 609, folder 4 ("nothing"); John W. Orr, *Set Up Running: The Life of a Pennsylvania Railroad Engineman, 1904–1949* (University Park: Pennsylvania State University Press, 2001), 291–92, 308–9; David W. Messer, *Conquest II: Crestline to Fort Wayne, Grand Rapids and Indiana Branch, Toledo, Sandusky and Akron Branches* (Marceline, MO: Walsworth, 2021), 32.

134. The development of the S1 thus reflected what historian Mark Reutter has labeled "the psychology of bigness" in the Motive Power Department. Reutter, "Struggle," 27.

135. The specific goal was a 10,000-pound increase in tractive effort, relative to the M1a.

136. Hirsimaki, *Black Gold, Black Diamonds, Volume I*, 108; Neil Burnell, "The Q1: An Alternate View," *Keystone* 39, no. 2 (Summer 2006): 13–17, at 8.

137. Deasy observed that the Q1's designers had initially favored 78-inch drivers but reduced the diameter by 1 inch, to limit the locomotive's rigid wheelbase. PRR and Baldwin officials asserted that in addition to producing a higher maximum speed, the larger drivers increased the locomotive's efficiency, reduced dynamic augment, and eased wear and tear on the track.

138. The arrangement limited the size of both the Q1's firebox and the adjacent rear cylinders while exposing those cylinders to excessive heat and debris from the firebox.

139. PRR BOD Minutes; Hirsimaki, *Black Gold, Volume I*, 108–11; Carleton, *Pennsy Steam: A to T*, 183–84; Burnell, "Q1," 13–17.

140. Hirsimaki, *Black Gold, Black Diamonds, Volume I*, 108–19; Eric Hirsimaki, *Black Gold, Black Diamonds: The Pennsylvania Railroad and Dieselization, Volume II* (North Olmsted, OH: Mileposts, 2000), 59–60, 62; E. Thomas Harley, *Pennsy Q Class: Classic Power 5* (Hicksville, NJ: N. J. International, 1982), 6–7.

141. Hirsimaki, *Black Gold, Black Diamonds, Volume I*, 119.

142. The following year, the board further marginalized Hankins by naming him the assistant to the vice president in charge of real estate, purchases, and stores. He retired in 1944 and Elsey replaced him in that post.

143. PRR BOD Minutes; Burnell, "Q1," 10.

144. One of those, a 2-6-6-4 from the Norfolk & Western, had already been evaluated by PRR personnel and found wanting.

145. Hirsimaki, *Black Gold, Black Diamonds, Volume I*, 111–18.

146. For information on the WPB, see United States, Civilian Production Administration, *Industrial Mobilization for War: History of the War Production Board and Predecessor Agencies, 1940–1945, Volume 1: Program and Administration* (Washington, DC: United States Government Printing Office, 1947), and Donald M. Nelson, *Arsenal of Democracy: The Story of American War Production* (New York: Harcourt, Brace and Company, 1946).

147. The PRR locomotives were somewhat heavier than their C&O predecessors and maintained a slightly higher boiler pressure.

148. Hirsimaki, *Black Gold, Black Diamonds, Volume I*, 111–19; Reutter, "Struggle," 24; Carleton, *Pennsy Steam, A to T*, 100–107.

149. The 4-10-4 wheel arrangement was uncommon and lacked an equivalent Whyte designation. A four-wheel lead truck was generally unnecessary on freight locomotives—hence the far more popular 2-10-4 Texas type, of which the PRR's wartime Class J1 was an outstanding example.

150. PRR BOD Minutes; Harley, *Pennsy Q Class*, 3, 69; Hirsimaki, *Black Gold, Black Diamonds, Volume I*, 126; Carleton, *Pennsy Steam: A to T*, 185–89.

151. Paul C. Dietz, *Firing on the Pennsy: A Fireman on the Pennsylvania Railroad Describes the Last Hurrah of the Steam Engine, 1943–1947* (Baltimore, MD: Gateway, 2001), 9 ("mammoth"), 20 ("dry"); Harley, *Pennsy Q Class*, 24–27, 56, 62; Hirsimaki, *Black Gold, Black Diamonds, Volume I*, 118, 128–30, 152–53.

152. Charlie Meyer, "What Derailed the T1?" *Milepost* 7, no. 2 (Spring 1989): 15–17; Charlie Meyer, "Just How Slippery Was the T1?" *Milepost*, July 1991, 19–21.

153. PRR officials never intended to replace all the K4s locomotives with the T1. The K4s remained the clear

choice for local trains, short consists, and situations where stops were frequent. Like the GG1, the T1 was at its best hauling passenger trains over long distances at high speeds with few intermediate stops. Burnell, "Reassessment," 18; Stephenson, "PRR T1 Tests," 35. Neil Burnell and David R. Stephenson, both strong supporters of the T1 design, provide a brief discussion of the controversy in Burnell, "In Defense," at 15, and Stephenson, "PRR T1 Tests," at 35.

154. PRR BOD Minutes; Brian Solomon, *Baldwin Locomotives* (Minneapolis, MN: Voyageur, 2010), 113–15; Hirsimaki, *Black Gold, Black Diamonds, Volume I*, 103, 107; Charlie Meyer, "Tracking the Pittsburgh T1 Derailments," *Milepost*, Winter/Spring 1990, 12–15.

155. Most early steam locomotives employed slide valves. Developed in the late 1800s and named for Belgian mechanical engineer Egide Walschaerts, the Walschaerts system rapidly gained popularity in the early twentieth century. There were five other valve-gear designs, of which the Baker was the most popular.

156. J. Parker Lamb, *Perfecting the American Steam Locomotive* (Bloomington: Indiana University Press, 2003), 21–22, 153–54.

157. Lentz first used poppet valves in 1905; over the next decade or so, mechanical engineers in most European nations experimented with that system. The biggest success came in the Grand Duchy of Oldenburg State Railways, with forty-eight locomotives built between 1909 and 1921. When the Deutsche Reichsbahn took control of the line in 1922, it quickly removed the locomotives from service, in part because they impeded a rigid policy of motive-power standardization. William T. Hoecker, "Thirty-Five Years of Poppet-Valve Experience," *Railway Mechanical Engineer* 115, no. 5 (May 1941): 192.

158. In addition to offering ideal operating conditions for fast and heavy passenger trains, the route between Crestline and Chicago provided ready access to the Lima Locomotive Works facilities, situated approximately midway between Crestline and Fort Wayne.

159. *Railway Mechanical Engineer* 115, no. 4 (April 1941): 125–30; Hirsimaki, *Black Gold, Black Diamonds, Volume I*, 88–92.

160. In July 1940, Lima officials recommended a second application, to a Class M1 locomotive, but the staff at the Motive Power Department suggested that there was little advantage in applying the technology to a locomotive used principally in freight service. In December 1945, Lima tested an improved version of the poppet value, but by that time the T1 was already in production. Lamb, *Perfecting the American Steam Locomotive*, 154–55, 159;

Bill Withuhn, "Excerpts from *The Railroad Enthusiasts Bulletin*, New York Division," *Keystone* 47, no. 3 (Autumn 2014): 47–61; Hirsimaki, *Black Gold, Black Diamonds, Volume I*, 92.

161. The PRR built #5399 in the Juniata Shops in 1924, but that locomotive embodied only marginal changes from the initial K4s produced in 1914. In a May 1941 article describing the tests, *Railway Mechanical Engineer* observed that "while this improvement is largely due to the poppet valves, it should be stated that, in addition to the improved superheater, the No. 5399 was equipped with a larger dry pipe, front-end throttle, and larger steam pipes and exhaust passages, all of which contributed to the better performance." An editorial in the same issue was less restrained, suggesting that "the results of these tests open an era in which poppet valves and adequate cross-sectional area through the entire chain of passages from boiler to exhaust nozzle provide the means for developing great locomotive capacity within conservative limits of size and weight." *Railway Mechanical Engineer* 115, no. 5 (May 1941): 169–75, at 169 ("largely"), 189 ("era").

162. In a subsequent letter to the editor of *Railway Mechanical Engineer*, William T. Hoecker refuted Jones's charge that deep-rooted conservatism accounted for the limited application of poppet valves on American railroads. Hoecker observed that most of the European railway systems that had experimented with either Lentz or Caprotti poppet valves had replaced them with conventional piston valves, or else had removed the locomotives from service. Even in France, with the world's largest contingent of poppet-valve-equipped locomotives, plans were underway to build a new fleet of conventional piston locomotives—a policy that was interrupted only by the outbreak of war and subsequent German invasion. "The piston valve also retains its place because nothing better is at present available," Hoecker concluded. Yet his acknowledgment that "much experimental work in the past has been desultory and half-hearted" may well have been sufficient to reassure Jones that he might succeed where others had failed. L. B. Jones, "Train Acceleration," *Railway Mechanical Engineer* 115, no. 1 (January 1941): 15–17, 20–21, at 17 ("handicap," "dynamic," "ineffective," "evils"), 21 ("experiments," "Europe"); Charlie Meyer, "Poppets on the PRR T1, Part 1 of 2," *Milepost*, November 1990, 21–23; Hoecker, "Thirty-Five Years" ("retains," "experimental").

163. The total number of passenger cars in service did not include the sleeping cars owned and operated by Pullman, virtually all of which were heavyweights.

164. Burnell, "Q1," 11; Pennsylvania Railroad Company, *Ninety-Fourth Annual Report*, 21.

165. Jones, "Train Acceleration," 17 ("improved," "present"); Hirsimaki, *Black Gold, Black Diamonds, Volume I*, 108.

166. There have been persistent rumors that the T1 could reach speeds as high as 140 miles per hour, but such stories have little concrete evidence to support them. The PRR did not have speed recorders installed in the T1 locomotives. The company did retrofit some of them with speedometers but did not require enginemen to record train speeds. An employee of the Franklin Railway Supply Company, riding in the cab, used a stopwatch and a visual observation of mileposts to estimate that the T1 locomotives "were frequently exceeding 140 mph for sustained periods." It should be noted that railroad mileposts were rarely spaced precisely 5,280 feet apart, which would affect the estimated times. Moreover, the Franklin employee was ready to assign blame for failures to the poppet valves (which his company had guaranteed for 100 mph continuous operation, with short bursts of up to 125 mph) on the PRR's operating practices rather than on Franklin's poor workmanship. In any event, Franklin's logbooks no longer exist, and their purported contents survive only as thirdhand accounts. For an additional discussion of the top speed of the T1, see Neil Burnell, "90 mph and Beyond: An Introduction to Poppet Valves and Fast Steam Speeds in the 1930s and 1940s," *Keystone* 47, no. 3 (Autumn 2014): 44–79; and Withuhn, "Excerpts," 59 ("frequently").

167. The T1 did not have any antislip devices, even though the PRR had installed them on the Q2.

168. Burnell, "Reassessment," 24; Hirsimaki, *Black Gold, Black Diamonds, Volume I*, 103–8.

169. Deasy to Jones, November 20, 1944 ("people"); Deasy to Cover, July 31, 1946; Deasy to Cover, October 26, 1946; "Finance Docket—Board Meeting, March 12, 1952"; all in HML, Box 326, folder 35; David R. Stephenson, "Pennsy Tests the Norfolk & Western Class J," *Keystone* 41, no. 4 (Winter 2008): 9–21, at 10–11 ("performing").

170. Burnell, "Reassessment," 24–39; Burnell, "In Defense," 17–18.

171. PRR Press Release, May 11, 1954, HML, Box 271, folder 11; *New York Times*, August 5, 1976; Michael Bezilla, "Symes, James Miller (1897–1976)," in *Encyclopedia of North American Railroads*, ed. William D. Middleton, George M. Smerk, and Roberta L. Diehl (Bloomington: Indiana University Press, 2007), 1038–39.

172. PRR BOD Minutes, Douglas and Weiglin, *Pennsy Diesels*, 16; Reutter, "Struggle," 27.

173. Stephenson, "Pennsy Tests," 9–10.

174. Stephenson, "Pennsy Tests," 12–15.

175. Stephenson, "Pennsy Tests," 12–21; David R. Stephenson, "PRR Tests the N&W Class J, Part II," *Keystone* 42, no. 2 (Summer 2009): 67–70; Deasy to Clement, December 13, 1944, HML, Box 326, folder 34; Hirsimaki, *Black Gold, Black Diamonds, Volume I*, 136–37.

176. PRR BOD Minutes; Hirsimaki, *Black Gold, Black Diamonds, Volume I*, 137, 150.

177. By the end of 1945, just as the T1 was entering production, Franklin introduced an improved poppet valve (the Type B). The PRR installed one of the Type B valve assemblies on a K4s Pacific; the T1 locomotives relied on the Type A.

178. Franklin officials considered the Type B easier to maintain than the Type A. However, they also suggested that the Type B was generally reliable only when the locomotive was traveling forward and that it was better suited for freight service. In 1948 and 1949, the PRR modified two T1 locomotives, the #5500 and the #5547—the first with a rotary-cam valve system and the second with the Walschaerts valve gear that Baldwin designers had originally advocated. The extensive valve-gear modification to the #5547 caused the locomotive to be assigned as the sole member of the PRR's Class T1a. The rebuilding efforts alleviated some of the problems associated with the locomotives, but by that time it was clear that their days were numbered.

179. PRR officials apparently intended that the capacity of the sandboxes on the fifty production T1 locomotives would be 70 cubic feet (more than double the 33-cubic-foot capacity on the two prototypes), to prevent the locomotives from running out of sand before they completed their runs. Through some oversight, neither Baldwin nor the Altoona Works incorporated that change, and the larger sandboxes were not added until the locomotives came due for class repairs.

180. Charlie Meyer, "Poppets on the PRR T1, Part 2 of 2," *Milepost*, April 1991, 22–23; Meyer, "Just How Slippery Was the T1?"; Withuhn, "Excerpts," 58–60; Jon C. Branch, "Pennsylvania Railroad T1 and T1a Duplex," https://revivaler.com/pennsylvania-railroad-t1-t1a-duplex/, accessed February 18, 2019; Neil Burnell, with David Slee, "The Case for the T1a #5547: A Quiet Achiever," *Keystone* 39, no. 3 (Autumn 2006): 40–52.

181. The initial derailment occurred at US Tower along a sharply curved section of track connecting the Pittsburgh station to the Fort Wayne line over the Allegheny

River and west toward Chicago. It was the same curve that had prevented the use of the M1/M1a locomotives on westbound passenger trains. The problem was not the curve itself but rather a #8 frog slip switch laid with rail weighing 130 pounds per yard. Similar #8 slip switches with 131-pound rail had a slightly smoother curve and could generally be traversed by a T1, moving at speeds of no more than five miles an hour, without incident.

182. Meyer, "What Derailed the T1?"; Meyer, "Tracking the Pittsburgh T1 Derailments."

183. Charlie Meyer, who has done extensive research on the derailment problem (as well as other aspects of the performance of the T1), was the stepson of Ethelbert Smith and thus had a certain amount of insider knowledge about the situation.

184. Meyer, "Tracking the Pittsburgh T1 Derailments."

185. Meyer, "Tracking the Pittsburgh T1 Derailments."

186. Neil Burnell, "The Trials and Tribulations of #6200," *Keystone* 45, no. 3 (Autumn 2012): 36–67, at 36; Adrian Osler, *Turbinia* (Newcastle: Tyne and Wear County Council Museums, 1981), https://www.asme.org /wwwasmeorg/media/resourcefiles/aboutasme/who %20we%20are/engineering%20history/landmarks /73-turbinia-1897.pdf, accessed October 29, 2023; Walter Simpson, *Turbine Power* (Waukesha, WI: Kalmbach, 2020), 12–15.

187. LM&S officials apparently referred to the locomotive only by its road number, 6202, with railway enthusiasts coining the unofficial name of *Turbomotive*.

188. The Chesapeake & Ohio, the Virginian, the Reading, the Illinois Central, and the Louisville & Nashville supported the project to varying degrees, in large measure because coal was an important source of revenue for each carrier. The PRR's share of the estimated $1.5 million R&D cost would be $400,000, with an equal amount contributed by GE. The other railroads pledged between $5,000 and $165,000 each. The New York Central, the Atlantic Coast Line, and the Baltimore & Ohio demonstrated initial interest but dropped out of the effort. Officials at the Erie elected not to participate.

189. Chuck Blardone, "6202 Background," *Keystone* 46, no. 1 (Spring 2013): 38–39; Bill Horsfall, *London, Midland & Scottish: Britain's Greatest Railway* (Bloomington, IN: AuthorHouse UK, 2014), 224; William L. Withuhn, *American Steam Locomotives: Design and Development, 1880–1960* (Bloomington: Indiana University Press, 2019), 403–8; Michael C. Duffy, *Electric Railways: 1880–1990* (London: Institution of Engineering and Technology, 2003), 236–39; "Steamotive: A New Compact Power Unit," *Log* 28, no. 4 (January 1937): 13–15; Hirsimaki, *Black Gold, Black Diamonds, Volume I*, 76–77.

190. J. F. Deasy, "Historical Sketch in Connection with Steam Turbine Locomotive and Tender to Be Built by the Baldwin Locomotive Works for Experimental Purposes," April 19, 1941 ("knowledge," "furnish"); Duer to Deasy, October 25, 1940 ("undesirable"); both in HML, Box 326, folder 32; Burnell, "Trials and Tribulations," 36–37.

191. The 4-8-4 design featured the same wheel arrangement as the R1, the solitary Baldwin-Westinghouse locomotive that had come up short in the 1934 comparison with the GG1. Had it been built according to its original design, it would have carried PRR Class R2. Steam-turbine locomotives lacked cylinders and thus did not conform exactly to the Whyte system. The R2 locomotive (and its S2 successor) relied on gearing between the second and third drivers, with the second driver connected to the first driver and the third driver connected to the fourth driver through a series of siderods. As such, the R2 design could just as easily have been classified as a "T2," with the same 4-4-4-4 wheel arrangement as the T1 duplex. Hirsimaki, *Black Gold, Black Diamonds, Volume I*, 76–78, 130.

192. Burnell, "Trials and Tribulations," 41–42; and "Abstract of Proposed Agreement Covering Patents in Connection with the Design and Construction of 6500 h.p. Coal-Burning Steam-Turbine Geared Locomotive," March 15, 1943, HML, Box 326, folder 32 for details. PRR BOD Minutes; Hirsimaki, *Black Gold, Black Diamonds, Volume I*, 130; Duer to Deasy, December 11, 1940; Deasy to Clement, April 11, 1941; Deasy to Duer, April 16, 1941; Deasy to Jones, April 24, 1941; all in HML, Box 326, folder 32.

193. Deasy to Downes, February 23, 1943; Young to Clement, March 13, 1943 ("innovations"); both in HML, Box 326, folder 32; Hirsimaki, *Black Gold, Black Diamonds, Volume I*, 130; Burnell, "Trials and Tribulations," 42–47; Charles Kerr Jr., "The Steam Turbine: Coal's New Hope," *Trains* 7, no. 8 (June 1947): 14–18; Simpson, *Turbine Power*, 22.

194. Mapes, "Losing Steam," 177; Simpson, *Turbine Power*, 22–27.

195. *Saturday Evening Post* advertisement reprinted in David Jackson, "Turbine Power," *Keystone* 28, no. 2 (Summer 1995): 23 ("battleships"); Young to Clement, March 13, 1947 ("favorable"), HML, Box 326, folder 33; Simpson, *Turbine Power*, 25.

196. David Evans, "Thoughts on Neil Burnell's S2 Article," *Keystone* 46, no. 1 (Spring 2013): 32–33; David E. Slee, "Problems with the Operation of the S2," *Keystone*

46, no. 1 (Spring 2013): 33–41; Burnell, "Trials and Tribulations," 51–67; Hirsimaki, *Black Gold, Black Diamonds, Volume I*, 130–32; Hirsimaki, *Black Gold, Black Diamonds, Volume II*, 18.

197. The #6200 did not operate after the summer of 1949 and was scrapped in June 1952. Jackson, "Turbine Power"; Burnell, "Trials and Tribulations," 67, includes Symes to George H. Pabst, March 30, 1948, HML, Box 562, folder 11 ("performance"); Mapes, "Losing Steam," 277, includes Symes to Pabst, March 30, 1948 ("justification"); Hirsimaki, *Black Gold, Black Diamonds, Volume I*, 132; Withuhn, *American Steam Locomotives*, 409–10.

198. In the standard diesel classification system employed by the Association of American Railroads, each truck carried an alphanumeric designation, with letters referring to the number of powered axles and numerals signifying unpowered idler axles that helped to distribute the locomotive's weight.

199. Hirsimaki, *Black Gold, Black Diamonds, Volume I*, 125, 132–33.

200. In April 1945, Warren Elsey explored the possibility of transforming the V1 from a direct-drive locomotive to an electrical drive. In addition to increasing the cost, the change would have made the locomotive even longer—far too long to be serviceable.

201. Hirsimaki, *Black Gold, Black Diamonds, Volume I*, 133–34.

202. Clement to George M. Humphrey, May 7, 1945, HML ("puffing"), quoted in Reutter, "Struggle," 26; Raymond Loewy to Deasy, March 20, 1945 ("conception," "changed"); Deasy to Loewy, March 26, 1945, HML; both in HML, Box 326, folder 36; Hirsimaki, *Black Gold, Black Diamonds, Volume I*, 134.

203. *Altoona Tribune*, March 15, 1946; Deasy to Loewy, March 26, 1945, HML; Cover to Deasy, June 13, 1946 ("construe"), HML, Box 326, folder 36.

204. In addition to the PRR, the other railroad participants were the Baltimore & Ohio, the Chesapeake & Ohio, the Illinois Central, the Louisville & Nashville, the New York Central, the Norfolk & Western, and the Virginian, who joined forces with the M. A. Hanna Company, the Island Creek Coal Company, the Pocahontas Fuel Company, and the Sinclair Coal Company. The New York, Chicago & St. Louis (Nickel Plate) and the Union Pacific later joined the consortium. Duer disagreed with Clement's decision to enlist coal producers in the development of a steam turbine (he suggested that they did not understand the requirements of locomotive design) and argued that the project should be restricted to the PRR, Baldwin, Westinghouse, and Gibbs & Hill.

205. The gas turbine bore a closer resemblance to a jet aircraft engine than the steam turbines used on the S2 and proposed for the V1. An atomizer crushed coal to a powder, which was then ignited, with the hot exhaust gases expanding through a conically shaped turbine. As the gas progressed through the stages of the turbine, each a larger diameter than the one that preceded it, it expanded and thus turned the turbine blades that generated electricity that powered the wheels. The thermal efficiency of a gas turbine was between two and three times that of a conventional steam locomotive but could only achieve about two-thirds of the thermal efficiency of a diesel locomotive. Because coal was relatively less expensive than diesel fuel, however, proponents of the gas turbine predicted lower operating costs (as well as lower maintenance costs, given the relative simplicity of the turbine design compared to that of a diesel engine). They also emphasized—incorrectly, as events transpired—that oil production would peak in the next twenty or thirty years and suggested that it would be prudent to continue research and development efforts on some form of coal-fired locomotive.

206. PRR BOD Minutes; PRR press release, January 22, 1947, HML, Box 233, folder 10 ("collaborating"); *Railway Age* 124, no. 21 (May 22, 1948): 37–39 (1025–27); 126, no. 26 (June 25, 1949): 118–20 (1277–78); 127, no. 2 (July 9, 1949): 59–61 (103–105); S. G. Liddle, B. B. Bonzo, and G. P. Purohit, *The Coal-Fired Gas Turbine Locomotive: A New Look* (New York: American Society of Mechanical Engineers, 1983); M. E. Lackey, *Summary of the Research and Development Effort on Open-Cycle Coal-Fired Gas Turbines* (Oak Ridge, TN: Oak Ridge National Laboratory, 1979), 5–6; Widen Tabakoff, *Erosion Study in Turbomachinery Affected by Coal and Ash Particles, Phase 1* (Cincinnati, OH: University of Cincinnati, 1978), 25; Morrison, *American Steam Locomotive*, 550; Hirsimaki, *Black Gold, Black Diamonds, Volume I*, 154–58.

207. The completion of three steam-turbine-electrics for the Chesapeake & Ohio and one for the Norfolk & Western likewise provided little benefit for mine owners or coal-carrying railroads. In 1947 and 1948, Baldwin and Westinghouse built three massive units for the Chesapeake & Ohio, one of the nation's preeminent coal-hauling railroads. With the gas turbine still under development, the C&O Class M-1 locomotives in many respects resembled the PRR's V1 design. PRR officials had nonetheless abandoned their commitment to the V1 and with it any interest in protecting the patent rights for key elements of steam-turbine technology. It mattered little in any event, as the C&O turbines were unreliable

and expensive to operate. Their unofficial nickname ("Sacred Cow") attested to unrealistic managerial demands that they perform efficiently and fend off dieselization. All three were out of service by 1950. The Norfolk & Western's *Jawn Henry*, built by Baldwin-Lima-Hamilton and Westinghouse in 1954, provided a more satisfactory performance. The locomotive was nonetheless too long for any of the N&W's turntables, afforded limited visibility to train crews, and was difficult for inexperienced enginemen to operate. N&W president Robert H. Smith, a lifelong supporter of steam locomotives, favored the purchase of additional steam turbines. Stuart T. Saunders, the N&W's vice president and general counsel, observed that the cost/benefit analysis—prepared by the Operations Department in a manner that supported Smith's views—failed to take depreciation and other expenses into account. Saunders angered Smith but dissuaded him from ordering additional turbines—a momentous decision for a railroad that supported steam power longer than most. Lamb, *Perfecting the American Steam Locomotive*, 160–64; E. F. Pat Striplin, *The Norfolk & Western: A History*, rev. ed. (Forest, VA: Norfolk & Western Historical Society, 1997), 115–17.

208. PRR BOD Minutes; Thomas Lee, *Turbines Westward* (Manhattan, KS: T. Lee, 1975); Tabakoff, *Erosion Study*, 25; Reutter, "Struggle," 24.

209. The NW2, which remained in production until 1949, was popular with the railroads, with 1,143 units sold in the United States and Canada.

210. Deasy may have been correct in his suspicions regarding the data provided by EMC. According to an unfinished manuscript by the late railroad historian and photographer Wallace Abbey, EMC inflated the number of railroads that tested the FT demonstrator while downplaying the many problems that the locomotives experienced. Reck, *On Time*, 131–42; Churella, *From Steam to Diesel*, 48–50; Pinkepank, *Second Diesel Spotter's Guide*, 36–37, 90. Hirsimaki, *Black Gold, Black Diamonds, Volume I*, 94–98; Jeffrey W. Schramm, *Out of Steam: Dieselization and American Railroads, 1920–1960* (Bethlehem, PA: Lehigh University Press, 2010), 73–74; Bill Metzger, "When and Where Did the 'Diesel That Did It' Actually Do it?," *Observation Tower*, October 6, 2014, archived at http://cs.trains.com/trn/b/observation-tower/archive/2014/10/06/when-and-where-did-the-diesel-that-did-it-actually-do-it.aspx, accessed December 30, 2018; Diesel Era, *The Revolutionary Diesel: EMC's FT* (Halifax, PA: Withers, 1994).

211. Hirsimaki, *Black Gold, Black Diamonds, Volume I*, 97–98, includes EMC memo, June 13, 1941 ("appears"); Douglas and Weiglin, *Pennsy Diesels*, 161.

212. Unlike most other railroads, the PRR did not employ the model designations developed by EMD or the other builders. When the E7 locomotives arrived, the PRR assigned them to Class 3(A1A-A1A)20E, representing three units coupled together (initially two, with a third to be added later), two sets of three-axle trucks, with the middle axle unpowered, the horsepower in hundreds, and the first initial of the builder. By 1947, that designation had been simplified to EP-3, for **E**MD, **P**assenger, **3** units. A further change occurred in 1951, when Class EP-20 referred to **E**MD, **P**assenger, **2,0**00 horsepower. A thorough discussion of the PRR locomotive classification system is provided in Douglas and Weiglin, *Pennsy Diesels*, 23–29. For the sake of clarity, this book employs the model numbers used by EMD and other builders rather than the PRR system, with the corresponding PRR 1951 classifications listed in the notes.

213. The PRR used shifters to move trains the short distance to and from the depot, imposing delays and added operating expense.

214. The L&N had acquired passenger diesels in 1942, yet the company's executives objected to paying the prorated cost associated with a lease of the PRR's new E6A locomotives. The New York Central dominated the passenger market between Detroit and the East Coast, and PRR officials no doubt hoped that the use of Electro-Motive diesels would encourage GM executives to instead travel on *The Red Arrow*. The PRR established three fueling stations (at Harrisburg; Mansfield, Ohio; and Detroit) along the 562-mile route. Mapes, "Losing Steam," 225–29; Douglas and Weiglin, *Pennsy Diesels*, 51; Hirsimaki, *Black Gold, Black Diamonds, Volume I*, 141–42.

215. Churella, *From Steam to Diesel*, 76–79.

216. The SW1, introduced in December 1938, was an upgraded version of the Model SW, with EMC's new Model 567 engine replacing the earlier Winton Model 201A.

217. Mapes, "Losing Steam," 201–2; Douglas and Weiglin, *Pennsy Diesels*, 14.

218. Mapes, "Losing Steam," 233–35.

219. Hirsimaki, *Black Gold, Black Diamonds, Volume I*, 121–33.

220. Electro-Motive officials addressed the issue of labor costs by designing the FT as a two-unit locomotive. The A-unit, which contained a cab, was attached to the corresponding cab-less B-unit with a permanent drawbar. Many purchasers of diesels (including the Santa Fe

and the PRR) took the further precaution of assigning the same number to each locomotive set (with suffixes such as L ["locomotive"], A, and B) rather than numbering the locomotives individually.

221. Duer also suggested that the PRR might be interested in diesels if EMD could convert them to burn coal—something that Rudolf Diesel had initially envisioned, although the use of coal-fired diesels soon proved impracticable.

222. Hirsimaki, *Black Gold, Black Diamonds, Volume I*, 121–23 (includes "reflect," "potential," original source not listed).

223. In acknowledgement of the railroad's location, NYC officials referred to the 4-8-4 wheel arrangement as a Niagara rather than a Northern.

224. Kiefer was determined to defend the locomotive he had designed, and in late 1946, he oversaw a series of trials between the steam and diesel locomotives. While he considered the performance of each locomotive to be roughly equivalent, he could not deny that diesels required far less maintenance and consequently offered much greater availability. *New York Times*, March 11, 1945; March 16, 1945 ("finest"); Paul W. Kiefer, *A Practical Evaluation of Railroad Motive Power* (New York: Steam Locomotive Research Institute, 1947).

225. Schramm, *Out of Steam*, 161–62; Welsh, *Pennsy Streamliners*, 67–69; Charlie Meyer, "So Quickly Gone—What *Really* Happened to the T1?" *Milepost*, November 1991, 20–23; Mapes, "Losing Steam," 229–30; Hirsimaki, *Black Gold, Black Diamonds, Volume I*, 142 ("know," original source not listed).

226. Hirsimaki, *Black Gold, Black Diamonds, Volume I*, 142–43.

227. PRR BOD Minutes; Mapes, "Losing Steam," 230; Hirsimaki, *Black Gold, Black Diamonds, Volume I*, 143; Meyer, "What Derailed the T1?" 16.

228. Jones to Deasy, October 2, 1945 ("recommended"), HML, Box 326, folder 40; Paul Withers, *Pennsylvania Railroad Diesel Locomotive Pictorial, Volume 7: EMD and Alco Passenger Cab Units* (Halifax, PA: Withers, 2002), 471; Jack Consoli, "A Guide to PRR F-Units and Their Evolution, Part 1," *Keystone* 37, no. 3 (Autumn 2004): 3–78, at 8–10.

229. The asymmetrical design of the Centipede reduced the likelihood that the unions representing operating employees could claim that it was two separate locomotives. Clement nonetheless asked Deasy to inquire whether Baldwin could combine the two units into one, "built so the cab would be a continuous cab over the entire length of the engine, articulated of course, but

with a set of bellows, so it would have the appearance of one cab." That was not merely for aesthetic reasons but might help convince the operating brotherhoods that, as a single locomotive, it would require but one crew. Clement to Deasy, April 5, 1946, HML, Box 326, folder 37.

230. Unlike their counterparts at Baldwin, engineers at Electro-Motive elected to build smaller locomotives that could be operated in multiple, with one crew, to produce a variety of horsepower combinations. Richard Dilworth's biographer observed that "the competitor set about to build a 6,000-horsepower locomotive, all in one piece, while Electro-Motive continued to put out its four units of 1,350." Dilworth, the biographer continued, "was aware that a certain railroad was hoping to duplicate in a Diesel one of its most powerful electric locomotives, a monster that required 156-pound track to support it. He knew that this didn't make sense. He wanted to sell locomotives not only to this line but to others that couldn't afford to rebuild their tracks to support mammoths." The reference to the PRR and the GG1 is obvious and suggests why salesmen like Paul Turner found it difficult to interest the railroad's officials in diesels. Reck, *Dilworth Story*, 84 ("competitor").

231. Douglas and Weiglin, *Pennsy Diesels*, 55–57.

232. Duer to Downes, July 31, 1946 ("ownership,"), HML, Box 327, folder 8; Hirsimaki, *Black Gold, Black Diamonds, Volume II*, 5.

233. Officials in the Motive Power Department were considering the use of welded rather than riveted boilers in the proposed new batch of Q2 locomotives. Because neither the Altoona Works nor Baldwin's Eddystone facility possessed a furnace large enough to anneal the boilers (to relieve the stresses caused by welding), they proposed to buy boilers from Alco and to complete the remainder of each locomotive at Altoona. Discussions with Alco personnel continued through November 1946. "Program for 100 New Engines," August 26, 1946; Deasy to Clement, August 26, 1946; both in HML, Box 327, folder 8; Hirsimaki, *Black Gold, Black Diamonds, Volume I*, 126–30, 153, 159; Harley, *Pennsy Q Class*, 3, 17–20, 24–27, 30–34, 69.

234. Increased wartime demand for coal and the growing power of the United Mine Workers contributed to the escalation in coal prices, but public-policy initiatives during the New Deal produced the most significant increase. In 1933, the federal government negotiated a Code of Fair Competition for bituminous producers in an attempt to regulate price and output levels under the terms of the National Industrial Recovery Act. In the 1935 *Schechter* case, the Supreme Court invalidated the

NIRA. In August 1935, Congress passed the Bituminous Coal Act, which reestablished many of the provisions of the National Recovery Administration codes that affected the coalfields. The Supreme Court also declared that law unconstitutional, leading Congress to adopt the Bituminous Coal Act of 1937. The law reestablished the National Bituminous Coal Commission, which had been a feature of the 1935 act (the NRA relied on the National Bituminous Coal Industrial Board for the establishment of industrywide standards) with the power to set minimum prices for coal. Its establishment of a price floor for locomotive fuel, effective in December 1937, added $20 million annually to the operating costs of American railroads. Waldo E. Fisher and Charles M. James, *Minimum Price Fixing in the Bituminous Coal Industry* (Princeton, NJ: Princeton University Press, 1955), 20–64; *Railway Age* 103, no. 23 (December 4, 1937): 812.

235. J. J. Pelley to Executives of Member Roads, May 3, 1946; PRR Press Release, May 6, 1946; Clement to Pelley, May 6, 1946; PRR Press Release, November 21, 1946; all in Penn Central Railroad Collection, M. G. 286, Pennsylvania Historical and Museum Commission, Pennsylvania State Archives, Harrisburg (hereafter, PHMC), Clement papers, Box 32 (9-1628).

236. James M. Symes, "Motive Power Progress," *Mutual Magazine*, May 1949, 4–5; Pennsylvania Railroad Company, *One Hundred and First Annual Report, for the Year Ended December 31, 1947* (Philadelphia: Pennsylvania Railroad, 1948), 4; Hirsimaki, *Black Gold, Volume I*, 144; Reutter, "Struggle," 26; Mapes, "Losing Steam," 238–40; *New York Times*, February 20, 1947 ("red," "occurred," "never").

237. Mapes, "Losing Steam," 237–42.

238. PRR BOD Minutes; Mapes, "Losing Steam," 237–42.

239. Hirsimaki, *Black Gold, Black Diamonds, Volume I*, 148–49; Symes to Clement, September 6, 1949 ("attractive"), quoted in Hirsimaki, *Black Gold, Black Diamonds, Volume II*, 107, original source not listed.

240. The Norfolk & Western conducted similar tests in 1948. As with so many other aspects of the T1, the interpretation of the tests on the C&O and the N&W remains controversial. Historians such as Neil Burnell and David Stephenson have suggested that C&O personnel did not adequately prepare the locomotives for the tests and that both C&O and PRR officials misinterpreted the results generated by the C&O's dynamometer car. Regardless of the validity of such assertions, Symes and a growing number of PRR executives asserted that the T1 had performed poorly and used the test results to bolster their

contention that the locomotives should be replaced with diesels as soon as possible. Hirsimaki, *Black Gold, Black Diamonds, Volume I*, 154; Stephenson, "PRR T1 Tests," 36–52; Mapes, "Losing Steam," 243.

241. Mapes, "Losing Steam," 243–47.

242. Symes's promotion coincided with the demotion of Vice President Richard C. Morse, whose Eastern Region had demonstrated particularly poor financial results. Morse became the vice president in charge of real estate and taxation, while Ethelbert Smith—who had first sounded the alarm about the T1 derailments at Pittsburgh—became the new vice president of the Eastern Region.

243. PRR BOD Minutes.

244. One of the questions in Symes's survey—and apparently something that no one had ever asked before—concerned the ability of the PRR and the Pocahontas coal carriers (including the Norfolk & Western and the Chesapeake & Ohio) to protect the coal industry if all the other railroads in the United States dieselized.

245. "The Pennsylvania Railroad Company, Bituminous Coal for Locomotive Use—Situation as of 12:01 A.M., 11-2-45 and 11-9-45," HML, Box 500, and the author extends his thanks to Chris Baer for locating this information in the Chief of Motive Power Records; Mapes, "Losing Steam," 246–49.

246. The order also included a single EMD E7B unit, to be used with the two E7A diesels initially intended for *The South Wind* but ultimately assigned to *The Red Arrow*.

247. Martin Clement to Walter Franklin, November 11, 1946 ("statement"), HML, Box 326, folder 40; PRR BOD Minutes; Hirsimaki, *Black Gold, Black Diamonds, Volume I*, 158–60; Mapes, "Losing Steam," 249–51, 303.

248. The number of large road freight locomotives is taken from data provided by Hirsimaki, *Black Gold, Black Diamonds, Volume I*, 138–39, and includes all subclasses of the I1s, J1, L1s, M1, N1, Q1, and Q2.

249. PRR BOD Minutes; Clement to Franklin, November 11, 1946 ("important"), HML, Box 326, folder 40; Reutter, "Struggle," 28.

250. *New York Times*, January 23, 1947 ("abreast," "economical").

251. Deasy to Cover, October 26, 1946 ("well"), HML, Box 326, folder 35; Duer to Downes, Deasy, and Franklin, February 12, 1947; Duer to Young, February 12, 1947 ("location," "unlikely"); Symes to Clement, March 14, 1947; all in HML, Box 327, folder 8.

252. Even though each diesel set was more expensive than a comparable steam locomotive, design and manufacturing improvements at EMD and the other builders

had reduced that disparity. The cost of a single steam locomotive had nearly doubled since 1939, while (thanks to rapid improvements in technology and manufacturing practices) the price of diesels increased by less than 10 percent during the same period.

253. Hirsimaki, *Black Gold, Black Diamonds, Volume I*, 158–60; Mapes, "Losing Steam," 252–56.

254. Argus Research Corporation, "Pennsylvania Railroad," May 8, 1947, 4 ("experienced"); Symes to Clement, June 5, 1947 ("underway"); Smith, Barney & Company, "Pennsylvania Railroad Company Stock," June 18, 1947 ("inadequate"); R. W. Pressprich & Company, "The Pennsylvania Railroad Company," September 1947, 2 ("appeared"), 10 ("relatively"); Carstairs & Company, "Pennsylvania Railroad Company," December 24, 1947 ("unfortunate," "continued," laggard"); all in PHMC, Box 55 (9-1651).

255. Clement to Leonard Beale, October 14, 1947 ("disappearing"); "Comment in connection with the Pressprich Report covering the Pennsylvania Railroad Company," October 14, 1947, 1 ("acquisition"); Pressprich, "Pennsylvania Railroad Company," 10 ("loath"); Merrill Lynch, Pierce, Fenner & Beane, "Review No. 155: Pennsylvania Railroad," December 22, 1947 ("dependence"); Merrill Lynch, Pierce, Fenner & Beane, *Investor's Reader* 9, no. 12 (December 10, 1947): 23–24, at 24 ("dilly-dallied"); Argus, "Pennsylvania Railroad," 5 ("participation"); all in PHMC, Box 55 (9-1651).

256. Joel Tarr, "The Metabolism of the Industrial City: The Case of Pittsburgh," *Journal of Urban History* 28, no. 5 (July 2002): 511–45, at 523–55.

257. Tarr, "Metabolism of the Industrial City," 525–57; Sherie R. Mershon and Joel A. Tarr, "Strategies for Clean Air: The Pittsburgh and Allegheny County Smoke Control Movements, 1940–1960," in *Devastation and Renewal: An Environmental History of Pittsburgh and Its Region*, ed. Joel A. Tarr (Pittsburgh, PA: University of Pittsburgh Press): 145–73, at 145–64; Joel A. Tarr and Karen Clay, "Pittsburgh as an Energy Capital: Perspectives on Coal and Natural Gas Transitions and the Environment," in *Energy Capitals: Local Impacts, Global Influence*, ed. Joseph A. Pratt, Martin V. Melosi, and Kathleen A. Brosnan (Pittsburgh, PA: University of Pittsburgh Press, 2014), 5–29.

258. The bill became law on May 9, 1947.

259. In October 1948, poisonous smog emitted from US Steel's Donora Zinc Works blanketed Donora, a mill town along the Monongahela River south of Pittsburgh, killing twenty people and making additional antipollution legislation all but inevitable. The result was a new

Allegheny County smoke-control ordinance that took effect on June 1, 1949. The new legislation also relied on a voluntarist approach.

260. St. Louis had adopted an antismoke ordinance in 1940 following a severe smog incident the year before, and that legislation served as a model for Pittsburgh. Compliance came quickly, and by January 1953, steam locomotives accounted for only 21 percent of the motive power operated by the PRR and other railroads in Allegheny County. Complete dieselization had been achieved by 1958. Mershon and Tarr, "Strategies for Clean Air," 164–69; Allen Dieterich-Ward, *Beyond Rust: Metropolitan Pittsburgh and the Fate of Industrial America* (Philadelphia: University of Pennsylvania Press, 2016), 75–79.

261. PRR BOD Minutes; Hirsimaki, *Black Gold, Black Diamonds, Volume I*, 149; Hirsimaki, *Black Gold, Black Diamonds, Volume II*, 62–63.

262. As Cover admitted to Symes in 1947, "We started the development of the S-2 turbine locomotive back in 1940, and in seven years have not progressed it to the point where we would feel safe in moving off in quantities of a locomotive of this kind." Cover to Symes, May 14, 1947 ("started"), quoted in Reutter, "Struggle," 28; Symes to Clement, November 17, 1948; Symes to Clement, December 3, 1948; both in HML, Box 326, folder 33.

263. Symes to Cover, May 8, 1947 ("waste"), quoted in Reutter, "Struggle," 28; Cover to Symes, May 14, 1947, HML, Box 326, folder 36; Hirsimaki, *Black Gold, Black Diamonds, Volume II*, 62–67.

264. PRR BOD Minutes; Mapes, "Losing Steam," 259–61.

265. Merrill Lynch, *Investor's Reader*, 24 ("zip"); Merrill Lynch, "Review No. 155" ("appointed," "substantial"); Carstairs & Company, "Pennsylvania Railroad," 5 ("steps"); all in PHMC, Box 55 (9-1651).

266. Merrill Lynch, "Review No. 155" ("corner," "pales"); Carstairs & Company, "Pennsylvania Railroad," 1 ("bearish"); Argus, Richard D. Wood to Downes, November 23, 1947 (includes Babson "active" quote); all in PHMC, Box 55 (9-1651).

267. *Lehigh Alumni Bulletin* 38, no. 4 (December–January 1950–1951): 37; *Railway Signaling and Communications* 49, no. 11 (November 1956): 51 ("control").

268. PRR BOD Minutes; Mapes, "Losing Steam," 262–63; Hirsimaki, *Black Gold, Black Diamonds, Volume II*, 17, 63.

269. PRR BOD Minutes; *New York Times*, September 19, 1949; *Railway Age* 128, no. 17 (April 29, 1950): 62 (840); PRR Press Release, March 26, 1938, PHMC, Clement papers, Box 32 (9-1628) ("maximum").

270. Hirsimaki, *Black Gold, Black Diamonds, Volume I*, 142–43; Hirsimaki, *Black Gold, Black Diamonds, Volume II*, 17, 32; Mapes, "Losing Steam," 263.

271. Slated for retirement were 468 freight locomotives (a category that included numerous Class H Consolidations employed in shifting service), 128 passenger locomotives, and 61 steam shifters.

272. For freight and passenger service, the reference is to multiple-unit locomotive sets.

273. In August 1948, the PRR announced plans to order 566 diesels, part of a massive $216.7 million capital program that also included 395 new lightweight passenger cars, 273 rebuilt passenger cars, 4,400 new freight cars, and 8,149 rebuilt freight cars. Clement to Humphrey, May 7, 1945 ("puffing"), quoted in Reutter, "Struggle," 26; *Modern Railroads* 3, no. 10 (October 1948): 8; *Altoona Mirror*, August 26, 1948; Hirsimaki, *Black Gold, Black Diamonds, Volume II*, 13; Mapes, "Losing Steam," 260–64.

274. PRR BOD Minutes; Mapes, "Losing Steam," 264–66.

275. [Williamsport, PA] *Gazette and Bulletin*, May 29, 1947 ("effort"); [Harrisburg] *Evening News*, June 2, 1948 ("increased," "scratched," "stack").

276. [Tyrone] *Daily Herald*, March 19, 1948 ("effect"); *Altoona Tribune*, February 14, 1946 ("carelessness," "slumbering"); January 31, 1949 ("progress," "efficiency," "furlough").

277. Crowe's primary concern involved the possible conversion of the Big Inch and Little Big Inch pipelines to carry natural gas—which, he estimated, could eliminate the jobs of 50,000 Pennsylvanians. [Indiana, PA] *Evening Gazette*, January 23, 1947 ("driven," "cut," "fight"); January 24, 1947; [Connellsville, PA] *Daily Courier*, January 29, 1947 ("legislation").

278. Pennsylvania Railroad Company, *One Hundred and Third Annual Report, for the Year Ended December 31, 1949* (Philadelphia: Pennsylvania Railroad, 1950), 11 ("imposed"), 12; Hirsimaki, *Black Gold, Black Diamonds, Volume II*, 106–7, 138–39.

279. With the route between New York and Washington demonstrating a clear profit, and well-patronized long-distance trains still breaking even, much of that deficit was attributable to commuter services and the transportation of mail and express.

280. Clement to Symes, October 4, 1949 ("question"), PHMC, Franklin papers, Box 59 (9-2091), folder 230; *One Hundred and Third Annual Report*, 29, 31, 34; PRR BOD Minutes; *New York Times*, May 10, 1950; Hirsimaki, *Black Gold, Black Diamonds, Volume II*, 117.

281. *Philadelphia Inquirer*, June 9, 1949 ("provide").

282. PRR Press Release, May 11, 1954, HML, Box 271, folder 11; *Philadelphia Inquirer*, June 7, 1949.

283. Existing diesels generated 1,062,300 horsepower, with the 226 new locomotives producing 370,800 horsepower—slightly more than what Symes had recommended a month earlier when he advocated an acceleration in purchases. *New York Times*, November 10, 1949; Hirsimaki, *Black Gold, Black Diamonds, Volume II*, 108.

284. The 1950 operating ratio declined to 84.3 (compared to 86 in 1949), with return on investment climbing from 1.25 percent to a still-abysmal 1.92 percent.

285. Symes recommended the continued use of steam locomotives on the St. Louis, Fort Wayne, Columbus, Cincinnati, Indianapolis, and Toledo Divisions.

286. PRR BOD Minutes; "Statement of J. M. Symes, Vice President—Operation, The Pennsylvania Railroad, before a Presidential Fact-Finding Board," Chicago, Illinois, April 4–6, 1950, 124, ("think"), Barriger Papers, Series 262, Box 167, folder 9–33; Hirsimaki, *Black Gold, Black Diamonds, Volume II*, 117–18.

287. The board instructed that the order, like its predecessors, would be allocated among all the producers of diesel locomotives, with approximately 40 percent to EMD, 30 percent to Baldwin, 15 percent to Alco, 10 percent to Fairbanks-Morse, and 5 percent to Lima-Hamilton. The 214 locomotives represented 335 individual units, as many of the road freight and road passenger models were arranged in cab-booster configurations. That meant 128 units for EMD (38.2%), 108 units for Baldwin (32.2%), 62 units for Alco (18.5%), 26 units for Fairbanks-Morse (7.8%), and 11 units for Lima-Hamilton (3.3%).

288. Mapes provides figures of 787 locomotives (rather than a total of 752) and a cost of $166 million, probably because of changes in the various proposals and orders.

289. PRR BOD Minutes; Hirsimaki, *Black Gold, Black Diamonds, Volume II*, 117–21. Mapes, "Losing Steam," 264–66.

290. As of January 1, 1947, there were 3,946 diesels on US railroads; by February 28, 1947, EMD had an order backlog of 1,037 locomotives, of which 85 were destined for the PRR. Hirsimaki, *Black Gold, Black Diamonds, Volume I*, 165.

291. The PRR classifications were the BS-6 and BS-10 (**B**aldwin **S**witcher, **6**00 horsepower and **1,0**00 horsepower, respectively).

292. PRR Class BS-6a.

293. BS-10a and BS-19am, with the *m* indicating locomotives that were equipped with multiple-unit controls

that enabled one engineman to operate several locomotives in tandem.

294. PRR Class BS-7 and BS-7m.

295. The PRR also assigned those locomotives to Class BS-7 or BS-7m.

296. PRR Class BS-12 and BS-12m.

297. Paul K. Withers and Dan Cupper, "Baldwin and the Pennsylvania Railroad," in John D. Hahn Jr., *Pennsylvania Railroad Diesel Locomotive Pictorial, Volume 2: Baldwin Switchers and Road Switchers* (Halifax, PA: Withers, 1995): 61–62; Gary W. Dolzall and Stephen F. Dolzall, *Diesels from Eddystone: The Story of Baldwin Diesel Locomotives* (Milwaukee, WI: Kalmbach, 1984), 13–22, 26–51; Douglas and Weiglin, *Pennsy Diesels*, 163–64, 167–68, 173–77, 183–84, 188–91; David R. Sweetland, "PRR BS7 Switchers," *Keystone* 45, no. 3 (Autumn 2012): 68–73; Hirsimaki, *Black Gold, Black Diamonds, Volume II*, 49–50, 88–89, 129.

298. PRR Class BP-60a.

299. The use of two A-units, mated with one B-unit, would produce the standard 6,000-horsepower package that PRR officials deemed appropriate for passenger service. On the PRR, they were classified as the BP-20, later changed to BF-16z after the PRR reassigned the locomotives to freight service (with the suffix *z* denoting a major modification to an existing locomotive).

300. Before they established the firm in 1946, Donald L. Hadley had been a design consultant for Westinghouse, the company that supplied Baldwin with electrical equipment, while the other two principals had been associated with General Electric, Alco's electrical-equipment supplier.

301. The PRR listed the 1,500-horsepower version as the BF-15 (**B**aldwin **F**reight, 1,**5**00 horsepower) and the 1,600-horsepower version as the BF-16.

302. In December 1959, Alco upgraded three of the units with an 1,800-horsepower diesel engine. Despite the resulting improvement in power and reliability, the return on investment was too small to justify any additional conversions. John D. Hahn Jr., *Pennsylvania Railroad Diesel Locomotive Pictorial, Volume 4: Baldwin Cab and Transfer Units* (Halifax, PA: Withers, 1998), 205–61; Douglas and Weiglin, *Pennsy Diesels*, 55–61, 80–81, 85–86, 95, 117, 120–23, 136–39, 197–99; Hirsimaki, *Black Gold, Black Diamonds, Volume II*, 50–51, 90–91; *Machinery* 52, no. 12 (August 1946): 238; Dolzall and Dolzall, *Diesels from Eddystone*, 52–67, 118–29.

303. Class BS-10as on the PRR. The *s* reflected the locomotive's ability to generate steam heat, thus making it suitable for passenger service.

304. They were variously classed as BS-12as, BS-12ams, and BS-12am, depending on their equipment and intended use.

305. Assigned to PRR Class BS-16m or BS-16ms, depending on whether they featured boilers to generate steam heat. One of the twelve locomotives was owned by the Pittsburgh & West Virginia and leased by the PRR (which purchased the unit in 1963). The Pennsylvania-Reading Seashore Lines (owned jointly by the PRR and the Reading) acquired sixteen Baldwin AS-16 locomotives (the four-axle version of the AS-616). The Reading's ownership of forty-three AS-16 locomotives probably influenced the decision by PRSL management to buy those units.

306. Hahn Jr., *Pennsylvania Railroad Diesel Locomotive Pictorial, Volume 4*, 262–71; Dolzall and Dolzall, *Diesels from Eddystone*, 72–117; Douglas and Weiglin, *Pennsy Diesels*, 117, 120–23, 136–39; Hirsimaki, *Black Gold, Black Diamonds, Volume II*, 156–58, 161.

307. Douglas and Weiglin, *Pennsy Diesels*, 195–96; Hirsimaki, *Black Gold, Black Diamonds, Volume II*, 89, 133–34, 161.

308. John F. Kirkland, *The Diesel Builders, Volume 1: Fairbanks-Morse and Lima-Hamilton* (Glendale, CA: Interurban, 1985), 69–95; Withers and Cupper, "Baldwin and the Pennsylvania Railroad," 62.

309. PRR Class FS-10 (**F**airbanks-Morse **S**witcher, 1,**0**00 horsepower) and FS-12/FS-12m, respectively. The PRR owned more H-10-44 (FS-10) switchers than any other railroad, representing more than a quarter of total Fairbanks-Morse production of that model.

310. PRR Class FS-20 and FS-20m. The order represented more than a third of total production of that model.

311. In July 1948, Westinghouse gained control over the floundering Baldwin Locomotive Works, largely to safeguard continued demand for Westinghouse electrical equipment. The new management promptly canceled work on Baldwin's Model 2000 diesel engine, under development since 1944. By November, the PRR had received the first batch of Fairbanks-Morse "Erie-builts," and the railroad's officials were initially impressed with the performance of the opposed-piston engine that powered the locomotives. They in turn pressured Baldwin and Westinghouse executives to develop an opposed-piston engine to supersede the terminated Model 2000 project. Baldwin's engineering staff objected to the opposed-piston concept and resented the abandonment of four years of research and development work, but they began improving a design originally developed by

the German aircraft manufacturer Junkers in 1911. The same impediments that had rendered the Junkers engine unfit for aviation use also plagued the R&D efforts on the Baldwin Model 547 opposed-piston engine, and the company abandoned the project in 1951. By that time, PRR officials had soured on the opposed-piston engine as well and within five years had ceased all further orders of Fairbanks-Morse locomotives. The wasted effort on the Baldwin Model 547 opposed-piston engine further retarded the company's success in the diesel locomotive market and represented one of the final collaborations in its century-long relationship with the Pennsylvania Railroad. Kirkland, *Dawn of the Diesel Age*, 50–51.

312. PRR Class FF-20 and FP-20.

313. PRR Class FF-16. By April 1965, all had been stricken from the roster.

314. PRR Class FS-24m.

315. They outlasted their Erie-built and Beloit counterparts, with Penn Central keeping them in service until late in 1970. Kirkland, *Diesel Builders, Volume 1*, 11–67; Paul K. Withers, *Pennsylvania Railroad Diesel Locomotive Pictorial, Volume 5: Fairbanks-Morse Locomotives* (Halifax, PA: Withers, 2000), 276–344; Douglas and Weiglin, *Pennsy Diesels*, 72–75, 84, 124–25, 151–52, 178–79, 192; Hirsimaki, *Black Gold, Black Diamonds, Volume II*, 25–28, 95–97, 122–25; David Sweetland, "Class FS-24m Diesels," *Keystone* 40, no. 3 (Autumn 2007): 13–22.

316. Alco, the product of a 1901 consolidation of eight companies, built the PRR Consolidations in Schenectady and at Dunkirk, New York (in the former Brooks Locomotive Works). Alco also built the PRR's sole Class K28 locomotive, #7067, and the sole Class K29, #3395, which served as test beds for the development of the K4s Pacific.

317. Not to be confused with the PRR's original duplex, the S1.

318. The PRR placed three additional orders for the Alco Model S-1: in October 1947 (four units, delivered between February and March 1949), in February 1948 (ten units, delivered between March and May 1949), and in November 1949 (ten units, delivered between May and June 1950). The LIRR acquired an additional fourteen of the Model S-1. In August 1950, the PRR ordered thirteen copies of the Model S-3, an upgraded version of the S-1 that also developed 660 horsepower. They were delivered between November 1950 and March 1951. The PRR assigned both the S-1 and the S-3 to Class AS-6 (**A**merican **L**ocomotive Company **S**witcher, **6**00 horsepower).

319. Additional S-2 orders followed, including five in October 1947 (delivered in February 1949), ten in February 1948 (delivered between February and March 1949), and twenty in November 1949 (delivered between March and April 1950). The PRR also acquired thirty-four copies of the similar Model S-4, with sixteen ordered in August 1950 (delivered between November 1950 and June 1951), thirteen ordered in November 1951 (delivered in May and June 1952), and five ordered in June 1953 (delivered in January and February 1954). The PRR assigned both the S-2 and the S-4 to Class AS-10 or AS-10m (if they were capable of multiple-unit operation). In August 1957, the PRR ordered six Alco Model T-6, 1,000-horsepower switchers. Delivered in March 1958, they became PRR Class AS-10a, with the *a* denoting a significant difference between the T-6 and the S-2/S-4 locomotives assigned to the same AS-10 builder/category/horsepower classification.

320. The largest order, for twenty-two units, was in November 1949 (delivered between June and August 1950), with two units ordered in August 1950 (delivered in March and April 1951) and a final two in November 1951 (delivered in May 1952). The PRR assigned the locomotives to Class AS-10s, AS-10am, AS-10as, or AS-10ms. The *a* represented the clear difference between the RS-1 road switcher and the AS-10 designation applied to the 1,000-horsepower Alco Model S-2 yard switchers.

321. PRR Classes AS-16, AS-16m, and AS-16ms. In 1955, the PRR leased six additional Alco road switchers from the Delaware & Hudson and purchased them three years later. Alco built the units in 1950, as the company was making the transition from the 1,500-horsepower RS-2 to the 1,600-horsepower RS-3. Alco rated the six locomotives at 1,600-horsepower, but their exact model designation is subject to dispute. The PRR assigned them to Class AS-15m, indicating that the railroad's motive power department rated them at only 1,500 horsepower.

322. PRR Class AS-16a, later assigned to Class AS-16am, following the installation of multiple-unit controls.

323. PRR Class APS-24ms, representing **A**lco, **P**assenger, **S**witcher, **2,4**00 horsepower, **m**ultiple-unit connections, **s**team heat. The locomotives were not successful in that service, as the limiting factor was the output of the traction motors rather than that of the diesel engine. PRR officials contemplated using the RSD-7 to dieselize commuter operations on the New York & Long Branch but discovered that the two-year-old diesels could not match the speed and acceleration of the K4s Pacifics, some of which had been built more than forty years earlier. Kirkland, *Dawn of the Diesel Age*, 88–89; David Sweetland, "PRR Alco Switchers," *Keystone* 42,

no. 1 (Spring 2009): 79–82; Hirsimaki, *Black Gold, Black Diamonds, Volume II*, 57–58, 169; Douglas and Weiglin, *Pennsy Diesels*, 25, 117–20, 131–35, 141–42, 145, 147–50, 169–70, 180–82, 193; John D. Hahn Jr., *Pennsylvania Railroad Diesel Locomotive Pictorial, Volume 1: ALCo RS Series* (Halifax, PA: Withers, 1995, 2002), 7–36, 47–48; Paul K. Withers and Dan Cupper, "ALCo and the Pennsylvania Railroad," in Hahn, *Pennsylvania Railroad Diesel Locomotive Pictorial, Volume 1*, 5–6; Paul K. Withers, *Pennsylvania Railroad Diesel Locomotive Pictorial, Volume 9: Alco and GE Switchers* (Halifax, PA: Withers, 2005), 669–722.

324. PRR Class AS-18m.

325. PRR Class AS-18am, in keeping with the three-axle trucks that distinguished them from the RSD-11.

326. PRR Class AS-24m. The PRR intended to use them as yard engines and in hump service in Philadelphia, but as with other Alco high-horsepower, six-axle units, the traction motors rather than the diesel engine limited their performance. Douglas and Weiglin, *Pennsy Diesels*, 153–54, 156–57; Hahn, *Pennsylvania Railroad Diesel Locomotive Pictorial, Volume 1*, 37–43, 49–55.

327. PRR Class AP-20, later AFP-20, when regeared and reassigned to freight service. The PRR's massive January 1947 order for passenger power included the ten Alco PA and five Alco PB locomotives, twenty-seven Baldwin DR-6-4-2000 "Sharknose" locomotives (eighteen A-units and nine B-units), and sixteen EMD E7 locomotives (ten A-units and six B-units, including an extra B-unit to be added to the initial *South Wind/Red Arrow* E7A units).

328. By the late 1950s, many of the PA/PB locomotives were pulling freight cars in the Philadelphia area, and in 1960, eight of them suffered the indignity of hauling coal trains from the Monongahela Valley through Pittsburgh to Altoona.

329. PRR Class AF-15. The initial order, delivered in July and August 1948, included four A-units and four B-units, indicating that the locomotives were to be used in an A-B-B-A configuration to produce 6,000 horsepower. The PRR's July 1947 order for road freight locomotives also included twenty-two of EMD's Model F3. Prior to that order, the first eight F3 locomotives had been completed by EMD, and forty-eight more were in the manufacturing process.

330. PRR Class AF-16.

331. By the time Alco's improved Model 251 engine was ready, in 1954, the company had ceased production of all freight and passenger cab units, including the PA/PB and the FA/FB series.

332. Paul K. Withers, *Pennsylvania Railroad Diesel Locomotive Pictorial, Volume 6: EMD and Alco Freight Cab Units* (Halifax, PA: Withers, 2001), 449–63; Douglas and Weiglin, *Pennsy Diesels*, 62–63, 69, 79, 89–90.

333. PRR Class ES-6 (**E**lectro-Motive, **S**witcher, **6**00 horsepower).

334. EMD completed one of the NW2 locomotives in November 1945, the other in April 1946, with the SW1 locomotives delivered in June.

335. While EMD had won barely a third of the PRR's diesel locomotive orders through 1951, by 1968 the division had produced more than half of the diesels in service on the PRR, triple the number supplied by Alco and more than double the number supplied by Baldwin. Hirsimaki, *Black Gold, Black Diamonds, Volume II*, 168.

336. Regardless of their EMD model designation, the PRR assigned all the locomotives to Class ES-12 or ES-12m. Mapes, "Losing Steam," 203; Douglas and Weiglin, *Pennsy Diesels*, 159–62, 165–66, 185–87; Paul K. Withers, *Pennsylvania Railroad Diesel Locomotive Pictorial, Volume 10: EMD Switchers* (Halifax, PA: Withers, 2006), 740–816; Sweetland, "PRR's EMD SW1 and NW2 Switchers."

337. For the most part, the PRR rejected four-axle diesel locomotives in passenger service. The principal exception involved the forty-two EMD FP7A locomotives (PRR Class EFP-15), delivered between April and August 1952. As their model designation suggested, they were suited for either freight or passenger service (and could generate steam heat) but with a top speed that was limited to seventy-seven miles per hour.

338. The January 1947 order enabled the PRR to create five A-B-A sets that generated the requisite 6,000 horsepower, with the remaining B-unit augmenting the two initial E7A order that was delivered in September 1945 and assigned to *The Red Arrow*. That extra B-unit arrived quickly (in April 1947), but EMD did not complete the remainder of the order until February 1948.

339. The PRR assigned the E8 locomotives to Class EP-22.

340. By the early 1960s, there was even a surplus of EMD passenger units. While PRR officials experimented with their use in fast freight service, they were not well suited to that role. Surviving E7 locomotives were often demoted to commuter service on the New York & Long Branch and increasingly cannibalized for parts that could be used on the newer E8 models. The creation of Amtrak in 1971 offered the Penn Central a golden opportunity to unload forty-eight of the increasingly decrepit E8 locomotives. Another eighteen went to the Metropolitan

Boston Transportation Authority and New Jersey Transit. Douglas and Weiglin, *Pennsy Diesels*, 51–55, 64–66, 87–88.

341. PRR Class EF-15.

342. Consoli, "Guide to PRR F-Units, Part 1," 3–13; Douglas and Weiglin, *Pennsy Diesels*, 69–71, 76–78; Withers, *Pennsylvania Railroad Diesel Locomotive Pictorial, Volume 6*, 349–51.

343. PRR Class EH-15.

344. Twenty-five of the locomotives, produced after October 1948, carried the EMD model designation of F5, essentially an F3 upgraded with more robust electrical equipment but without an increase in horsepower. The PRR assigned those locomotives to Class EF-15a. In March 1952, the PRR purchased four F3B units from the Bangor & Aroostook, yielding a total of 124 F3 locomotives in service, of which 80 were A-units and the remainder were B-units. Of those 124 locomotives, 39 were classified as helper units, arranged in 13 A-B-A sets.

345. Consoli, "Guide to PRR F-Units, Part 1," 3–37; Douglas and Weiglin, *Pennsy Diesels*, 69–71, 76–78; Withers, *Pennsylvania Railroad Diesel Locomotive Pictorial, Volume 6*, 349–82.

346. The Model F5, as noted above, was an incremental step in the transition from the F3 to the F7 but more closely resembled the earlier design than the later one.

347. PRR Class EF-15a, the same class assigned to the twenty-five EMD Model F5 locomotives, with the *a* reflecting the improved electrical equipment.

348. Although many railroads—most notably the Santa Fe—used the F7 and other F-unit locomotives in passenger service, the PRR did not. Douglas and Weiglin, *Pennsy Diesels*, 76–78, 81–83; Withers, *Pennsylvania Railroad Diesel Locomotive Pictorial, Volume 6*, 383–448; Consoli, "Guide to PRR F-Units," 24–78; Jack Consoli, "A Guide to PRR F-Units and Their Evolution, Part 2," *Keystone* 38, no. 1 (Spring 2005): 3–62.

349. Although EMD continued to produce the F9 (a 1,750-horsepower version of the F7) through 1960, railroads increasingly preferred the newer and more functional designs. The PRR did not purchase any EMD Model F9 locomotives.

350. PRR Class ES-15m and ES-15ms.

351. All were classed as EFS-17m.

352. Douglas and Weiglin, *Pennsy Diesels*, 117, 126–31, 142–45, 155; Paul K. Withers, *Pennsylvania Railroad Diesel Locomotive Pictorial, Volume 8: Early EMD Road Switchers* (Halifax, PA: Withers, 2003), 564–652.

353. PRR Class ES-15a.

354. PRR Class ES-17m.

355. Withers, *Pennsylvania Railroad Diesel Locomotive Pictorial, Volume 8*, 653–64.

356. PRR press release, December 12, 1952, HML, Box 233, folder 10; "Anticipated Use of Diesel and Electric Power as of April 1, 1953" ("practically"), PHMC, Franklin Papers, Box 17 (9-2047), folder 010.1; Hirsimaki, *Black Gold, Black Diamonds, Volume I*, 168–69; Hirsimaki, *Black Gold, Black Diamonds, Volume II*, 59, 82, 117, 140, 148, 164–65, 167; Mapes, "Losing Steam," 269–71.

357. Mapes, "Losing Steam," 269–70.

358. Reutter, "Struggle," 23–24; Hirsimaki, *Black Gold, Black Diamonds, Volume I*, 133; Burnell, "Trials and Tribulations," 67; Carleton, *Pennsy Steam: A to T*, 185–86, 199; "Finance Docket—Board Meeting, March 12, 1952," HML, Box 326, folder 35 ("satisfactory").

359. The members of the T1 Trust, founded in 2013, are currently building a new T1 duplex, #5550 (the next in the T1 numbering sequence, had production continued past the initial fifty-two units). In addition to rectifying the PRR's failure to preserve a T1, the trust intends to further refine the duplex design and, if possible, set a new steam locomotive world speed record. The estimated cost of the project is $10 million, with completion scheduled for 2030. "Announcing the Creation of the Pennsylvania Railroad T1 5550 Steam Locomotive Trust," *Keystone* 47, no. 1 (Spring 2014): 3–4; "The T1 Trust," https://prrt1 steamlocomotivetrust.org/, accessed February 1, 2019.

360. It is worth noting that the same economic factors that sidelined the PRR T1 also doomed the NYC's S1a/S1b Niagara. As a 4-8-4, the Niagara represented the epitome of Super Power design; generated high horsepower at speed; and did not suffer from excessive wheel slip, derailments, or any of the other issues associated with the T1. The first of the new locomotives were only a few months old when the NYC downgraded them to secondary passenger trains. The economics of diesel passenger power proved so compelling that all the Niagaras were out of service by the summer of 1956. None have been preserved. Meyer, "So Quickly Gone."

361. Not even the employees who possessed skills appropriate for dieselization could escape change. In February 1964, PRR officials announced plans to shift shop work from Columbus to Conway and Altoona, affecting between two hundred and three hundred workers. Mardo Williams, "Pennsy Shops Lose Their Steam," *Columbus Dispatch*, March 13, 1955, archived at Columbus Railroads, http://www.columbusrailroads.com/new/?menu=05Steam_Railroads&submenu=15Pennsylvania_Railroad&submenu4=401955%2020th%20Street%20

Shops, accessed February 2, 2019 ("worried"); Clearfield, Pennsylvania, *Progress*, February 8, 1964.

362. J. P. Newell to David C. Bevan, August 2, 1956, HML, Box 335, folder 6; U. F. Carter to Symes, March 6, 1958; Symes to Carter, March 24, 1958; all in HML, Box 335, folder 6; Symes to Rep. James E. Van Zandt, July 23, 1958; Cover to W. W. Patchell, September 25, 1956; both in HML, Box 358, folder 7, *Altoona Mirror*, March 30, 1955.

363. The only solution would have been for the PRR to establish a separate manufacturing subsidiary, as the New York Central had done. Newell to Bevan, June 26, 1956 ("methods"), HML, Box 335, folder 6; John B. Prizer to Bevan, October 3, 1957, HML, Box 358, folder 7.

364. Ralph C. Champlin and J. W. Oram to Symes, April 25, 1958, HML, Box 358, folder 7.

365. Representatives from Altoona Enterprises later claimed that, by 1965, they had created 12,200 new jobs in Altoona, nearly double the total employment of 6,500 that the PRR had provided in 1961. If true, it would have brought the employment base back to roughly the same level as the number of employees who worked for the Pennsylvania Railroad in the immediate postwar period. It is not clear that all those new jobs existed at the same time, however. Moreover, in a microcosm of the Rustbelt economy, most of those jobs required little skill and came with low pay and few fringe benefits. Kim Wallace, *Railroad City: Four Historic Neighborhoods in Altoona, Pennsylvania* (Washington, DC: Historic American Buildings Survey/Historic American Engineering Record, National Park Service, United States Department of the Interior, 1990), 39–40; "Altoona: One-Company Town in Search of Industry," *Business Week* (May 10, 1952): 76–82; Reutter, "Struggle," 30; Newell to Symes, May 16, 1958, HML, Box 335, folder 6.

366. Champlin and Oram to Symes, March 17, 1958 ("breadlines"); Champlin and Oram to Symes, April 25, 1958 ("hostility"); both in HML, Box 335, folder 6.

367. Champlin and Oram to Symes ("relations," "successful"), April 25, 1958, HML, Box 335, folder 6; *Altoona Mirror*, March 30, 1955.

368. *Pittsburgh Post-Gazette*, March 31, 1955 ("disaster," "bitter," "charm," "finesse").

369. "Statement to be Presented by Mr. C. I. Clugh at the Hearing Before the Sub-Committee of the Senate Labor Committee, March 29, 1955" ("decline"); Champlin and Oram to Symes, April 25, 1958 ("understanding," "preservation"); both in HML, Box 335, folder 6.

370. Eric Hirsimaki, "Buying Time," *Keystone* 32, no. 3 (Autumn 1999); Williams, "Pennsy Shops."

371. The Reading T1 was built to a very different design than the PRR's T1 duplex, and the use of the same classification was only coincidental.

372. Columbus Railroads, "Sandusky Branch," http://www.columbusrailroads.com/new/?menu=05Steam_Railroads&submenu=15Pennsylvania_Railroad; "Santa Fe 2-10-4 Locomotives on the Sandusky Branch," http://www.columbusrailroads.com/new/?menu=05Steam_Railroads&submenu=15Pennsylvania_Railroad&submenu4=20Santa%20Fe%20Class%205011; both accessed February 1, 2019; Gus Welty, "Dedieselization," *Trains* 15, no. 11 (September 1955): 42–45.

373. The PRR did not place the orders until November. Douglas and Weiglin, *Pennsy Diesels*, 91, 155–56, 186.

374. In June 1955, officials from the Long Island Rail Road indicated that they would retire the last twelve steam locomotives by the autumn of that year. On October 8, the LIRR staged a retirement ceremony for two of the locomotives at the station in Hicksville, New York. On October 16, the Branford Electric Railway Association commissioned a 160-mile farewell-to-steam excursion over the LIRR. The LIRR donated the locomotive that powered the final steam operation, Class G5s #35, to Nassau County, under the stewardship of the Oyster Bay Railroad Museum. It is currently undergoing restoration. It is unclear when the last steam locomotive operated over the PRR. The last use of steam locomotives in revenue service probably took place in late November 1957. The PRR kept about 135 locomotives stored serviceable, and they were incrementally stricken from the roster when their ICC boiler certification expired. It is possible that a steam locomotive operated as late as 1959, crossing the Delair Bridge from New Jersey to the 44th Street Engine House in West Philadelphia. See comments by G. W. Laepple and Jim Boylan on "Railway Preservation News," June 19, 2008, http://rypn.org/forums/viewtopic.php?f=1&t=25465, accessed February 6, 2019, and Reutter, "Struggle," 33n86. National Bureau of Economic Research, "US Business Cycle Expansions and Contractions," https://www.nber.org/cycles.html, accessed February 2, 2019; United States Department of Labor, Bureau of Labor Statistics, *Analysis of Work Stoppages, 1956*, Bulletin No. 1218 (Washington, DC: United States Government Printing Office, 1957), 21–22; Don Wood, Joel Rosenbaum, and Tom Gallo, *The Unique New York & Long Branch* (Earlton, NY: Audio Visual Designs, 1985), 128–32; *New York Times*, June 15, 1955; October 9, 1955.

375. EMD in particular offered to remanufacture older diesel locomotives to newer designs. The locomotive that

emerged from the rebuilding process bore little resemblance to the original (and in many cases reused only the trucks), but the tax issues associated with depreciation as well as the nature of equipment-trust financing ensured that many locomotives were "rebuilt" rather than merely replaced.

376. PRR Class GS-4 (**G**eneral Electric, **S**witcher, **4**00 horsepower) and GS-4m. The installation of multiple-unit controls on such a small locomotive indicated how little power each unit produced.

377. PRR officials claimed that the construction of the dam would require a longer routing for some freight trains, hence the need for additional locomotives.

378. PRR Class GF-25.

379. PRR Class GF-25a.

380. PRR Class GF-28a. While manufacturing the PRR's order, GE increased the horsepower of the design, and the last five units were delivered as Model U30C, PRR Class GF-30a.

381. PRR Class GF-33a. Tim Garner, "The Little Engine That Couldn't: PRR's GS4—The GE 44-Tonner," *Keystone* 45, no. 3 (Autumn 1012): 14–20; Douglas and Weiglin, *Pennsy Diesels*, 97–99, 108, 110–12, 170–72; Withers, *Pennsylvania Railroad Diesel Locomotive Pictorial, Volume 9*, 723–34; Paul K. Withers, *Pennsylvania Railroad Diesel Locomotive Pictorial, Volume 11: Alco and GE Road Switchers* (Halifax, PA: Withers, 2008), 865–910.

382. PRR Class AF-24.

383. PRR Class AF-24a.

384. PRR Class AF-25.

385. PRR Class AF-27.

386. PRR Class AF-30.

387. PRR Class AF-36.

388. The Montreal Locomotive Works continued to manufacture locomotives designed by Alco. Douglas and Weiglin, *Pennsy Diesels*, 100–103, 106–7, 112; Withers, *Pennsylvania Railroad Diesel Locomotive Pictorial, Volume 11*, 821–64.

389. PRR Class EF-22.

390. PRR Class EF-25.

391. PRR Class EF-25a.

392. PRR Class EF-30a. The purchase of the sixty-five SD40 locomotives was part of a series of orders that also included fifteen GE Model U28C and the same number of Alco Model C-630. It was the first time the PRR had ordered only six-axle motive power and indicated the clear preference for EMD products.

393. PRR Class EF-36.

394. Douglas and Weiglin, *Pennsy Diesels*, 101, 104–5, 108–9, 113–15; John D. Hahn Jr., *Pennsylvania Railroad Diesel Locomotive Pictorial, Volume 3: Second-Generation EMD Road Switchers* (Halifax, PA: Withers, 1996), 133–98.

395. United States Congress, Senate, Committee on the Judiciary, Subcommittee on Antitrust and Monopoly, *The Industrial Reorganization Act, Hearings before the Subcommittee on Antitrust and Monopoly of the Committee on the Judiciary, United States Senate, Ninety-Third Congress, Second Session, Part 4: Ground Transportation Industries* (Washington, DC: United States Government Printing Office, 1974), 2561 ("contribution,"); also in James M. Symes, "Railroad Needs of the Nation Ten Years Hence," address delivered at the General Motors Powerama, Chicago, Illinois, September 7, 1955, 1; Reutter, "Struggle," 30.

5. Renewal

1. Carl Sandburg, "Chicago," *Poetry: A Magazine of Verse* 3, no. 6 (March 1914): 191–92 ("player").

2. Descriptions of the stationary exhibits are from *Chicago Railroad Fair Official Guide Book and Program for the Pageant 'Wheels A-Rolling,'* at http://livinghistoryofillinois.com/pdf_files/1948%20Chicago%20Railroad%20Fair%20Official%20Guide%20Book%20Wheels%20a-Rolling.pdf, accessed August 10, 2019, and *Railway Age* 125, no. 4 (July 24, 1948): 187–94.

3. When the fair reopened for the 1949 season, PRR officials made one further addition. In 1905, Class E2 Atlantic #7002 hauled the *Pennsylvania Special* at an alleged (and highly improbable) speed of 127.1 miles per hour. Despite its fame, the PRR scrapped the #7002 in 1935. In its place, the company reconditioned a Class E6 Atlantic, #8063, and provided the stand-in with the number 7002. The locomotive is currently at the Railroad Museum of Pennsylvania, still bearing its subterfuge number.

4. Hungerford attained national renown in 1927 when he planned the Baltimore & Ohio's centennial commemoration, the Fair of the Iron Horse.

5. Descriptions of the Wheels A-Rolling Pageant and all associate quotations are from John Ott Pictures, "Wheels A-Rolling: 100 Years of Railroad Progress," https://archive.org/details/6241_Wheels_A-Rolling_100_Years_of_Railroad_Progress_01_01_12_22, accessed August 10, 2019.

6. *New York Times*, October 4, 1948; October 4, 1949.

7. Pennsylvania Railroad Company, *One Hundred and Fourth Annual Report, for the Year Ended December 31, 1950* (Philadelphia: n.p., 1951), 4; Pennsylvania Railroad Company, *One Hundred and Fifth Annual Report, for the*

Year Ended December 31, 1951 (Philadelphia: n.p., 1952), 5; Pennsylvania Railroad Company, *One Hundred and Sixth Annual Report, for the Year Ended December 31, 1952* (Philadelphia: n.p., 1953), 12; Pennsylvania Railroad Company, *One Hundred and Seventh Annual Report, for the Year Ended December 31, 1953* (Philadelphia: n.p., 1954), 17; Pennsylvania Railroad Company, *One Hundred and Thirteenth Annual Report, for the Year Ended December 31, 1959* (Philadelphia: n.p., 1960), 14–15.

8. Pennsylvania Railroad, *One Hundred and Seventh Annual Report*, 12–15; *Railway Age* 127, no. 5 (July 30, 1949): 34–38; 141, no. 18 (October 22, 1956): 11; 145, no. 18 (November 3, 1958): 7.

9. Pennsylvania Railroad, *One Hundred and Sixth Annual Report*, 16–17; Pennsylvania Railroad, *One Hundred and Seventh Annual Report*, 12–13; Pennsylvania Railroad Company, *One Hundred and Tenth Annual Report, for the Year Ended December 31, 1956* (Philadelphia: n.p., 1957), 16; Pennsylvania Railroad Company, *One Hundred and Eleventh Annual Report, for the Year Ended December 31, 1957* (Philadelphia: n.p., 1958), 14; Eastern Division, Pennsylvania Railroad, "Information Concerning the New Eastward Classification Yard, Conway, Pa.," n.d., but ca. 1958; "Conway Yard on the Pennsylvania Railroad," n.d., but ca. 1958; Pennsylvania Railroad and Union Switch & Signal, "Conway Yard: Ultra-Modern Freight Classification Yard," n.d., but ca. 1958; documents digitized by Rob Schoenberg, at http://prr.railfan.net/documents/, accessed August 7, 2019.

10. John C. Page, *A Special History Study: Pennsylvania Railroad Shops and Works, Altoona, Pennsylvania* (United States Department of the Interior, National Park Service, 1989), 36–39; *Railway Age* 139, no. 18 (October 31, 1955): 29–33.

11. Pennsylvania Railroad Company, *One Hundred and Sixth Annual Report*, 16; Pennsylvania Railroad Company, *One Hundred and Tenth Annual Report*, 16–17.

12. Michael Bezilla, "The Pennsylvania's Pioneer Rectifiers," *Railroad History* 137 (Autumn 1977): 64–79, at 64–66.

13. "Ignitron" was the trade name of a patented mechanism developed by Westinghouse and used by GE under license that produced an arc when a high-resistivity rod came into contact with mercury.

14. An extension of electrified territory west to Altoona or Pittsburgh would almost certainly rely on sixty-cycle power, suggesting that a rectifier locomotive could be used throughout the system. Moreover, PRR executives were contemplating the conversion of the existing electrified lines from twenty-five cycles to

standard sixty-cycle commercial power—a change that might reduce the electric bill as much as 20 percent, in part because utilities could use the PRR's long-distance transmission lines as "tie lines" to interconnect their power grids. Conversion to sixty-cycle power would necessitate either the scrapping of the existing fleet of electric locomotives or such extensive conversions as to make the project uneconomical. If the acquisition of new rectifier locomotives coincided with the renegotiation of commercial-power contracts and a transition to sixty-cycle power, then the economic benefits associated with the replacement of the GG1 and the P5a fleet might be considerable, even if electrification did not proceed west of Harrisburg.

15. Westinghouse delivered a second locomotive pair in 1952. It was essentially identical to the first set but had three axles per truck rather than two (as on the Class E3b) and was accordingly assigned to Class E3c.

16. The PRR removed the experimental rectifier locomotives from the roster in 1964 and scrapped them the following year. PRR BOD Minutes; *Railway Age* 128, no. 12 (March 25, 1950): 35–37; 132, no. 4 (January 28, 1952): 35–40; 132, no. 10 (March 10, 1952): 68–69; 132, no. 26 (June 30, 1952): 66–69; 136, no. 10 (March 8, 1954): 67–68; Bezilla, "Pioneer Rectifiers," 66–78; William D. Middleton, *When the Steam Railroads Electrified*, rev. 2nd ed. (Bloomington: Indiana University Press, 1974, 2001), 416–19; Eric Hirsimaki, *Black Gold–Black Diamonds: The Pennsylvania Railroad and Dieselization, Volume II* (Montoursville, PA: Paulhamus Litho, 2000), 143–46.

17. *Railway Age* 138, no. 20 (May 16, 1955): 12; Gibbs & Hill, "Pennsylvania Railroad Commercial-Frequency Electrification Harrisburg to Pittsburgh," September 26, 1957; A. J. Greenough to J. P. Newell, February 24, 1958; "Memorandum for the File: Future Motive Power Requirements in Electrified Territory," April 9, 1958; Gibbs & Hill, "Memorandum: P.R.R.—P.E. Power Contract," April 29, 1958; D. R. MacLeod, "Pennsylvania Railroad Electrification," June 26, 1958; PRR to Paul R. Turner, August 13, 1958; Greenough to Newell, February 24, 1958; all in Pennsylvania Railroad Company Records, Accession 1807/1810, Manuscripts and Archives Department, Hagley Museum and Library, Wilmington, Delaware (hereafter, HML), Box 357, folder 18; *Philadelphia Inquirer*, May 9, 1955 ("should").

18. Gibbs & Hill, "Pennsylvania Railroad Commercial-Frequency Electrification Harrisburg to Pittsburgh."

19. The Class Y1 locomotives became available after diesel locomotives and an improved ventilation system in the Cascade Tunnel allowed the Great Northern to

discontinue electric operation. The Great Northern had streamlined one of the eight locomotives (for passenger service), and the PRR cannibalized it to keep the other seven in operation. Frederick Westing, "What's New Under Pennsy Pantographs," *Trains* 18, no. 8 (June 1958): 45–49.

20. D. R. MacLeod, "Pennsylvania Railroad Electrification," June 26, 1958, HML, Box 357, folder 18 ("capacity").

21. General Electric Company, Locomotive & Car Equipment Department, "Pennsylvania Railroad Electric and Multiple-Unit Car Replacement"; General Motors, Electro-Motive Division, "Analysis of Future Motive Power Requirements, Electrified Territory, Pennsylvania Railroad," September 1959; both in HML, Box 357, folder 18.

22. GE built most of the locomotives with Ignitron rectifiers but equipped the final six with silicon diode rectifiers. GE later upgraded some of the older locomotives with silicone diode rectifiers and improved traction motors, with a resulting increase from 4,400 horsepower to 5,000 horsepower. They became Class E44a. The modifications ended as a result of the Penn Central bankruptcy. Thanks to the Penn Central merger, all three types of modern electric locomotives—the PRR E44, the New Haven EP-5, and the Virginian EL-C (later sold to the New Haven and assigned Class EF-4)—served together.

23. PRR BOD Minutes; Bezilla, "Pioneer Rectifiers," 77; Middleton, *When the Steam Railroads Electrified*, 419.

24. *Philadelphia Inquirer*, December 24, 1935 ("dead"); November 8, 1946.

25. *Philadelphia Inquirer*, April 29, 1944; September 17, 1944; *New York Times*, April 8, 1966; Margaret B. Tinkcom, "Depression and War, 1929–1946," Russell F. Weigley, ed., *Philadelphia: A 300-Year History* (New York: W. W. Norton, 1982): 601–48, at 646–67.

26. *Philadelphia Inquirer*, February 7, 1946; February 8, 1946; March 12, 1946; March 15, 1946; May 20, 1946.

27. A small portion of the $4.3 million would be used for the relocation of water and sewer lines. *Philadelphia Inquirer*, March 22, 1946; May 22, 1946.

28. City Council's Public Works Committee approved the agreement on November 7, with full council approval occurring on November 14. A hearing before the state Public Utility Commission—a formality that took less than an hour—occurred on December 27, with PUC approval occurring on January 9, 1947.

29. *Philadelphia Inquirer*, November 1, 1946; November 4, 1946; November 8, 1946; December 16, 1946; December 28, 1946; January 6, 1947; August 19, 1947; August 31, 1947.

30. *Philadelphia Inquirer*, November 15, 1946 ("depression"); May 5, 1947 ("least"); May 25, 1947; June 2, 1947; July 5, 1947 ("way"); September 7, 1947; February 7, 1948 ("outlast").

31. *Philadelphia Inquirer*, October 16, 1947 ("twenty"); October 22, 1947 ("leadership"); October 23, 1947 ("plan"); Joseph S. Clark Jr. and Dennis J. Clark, "Rally and Relapse, 1946–1968," in *Philadelphia: A 300-Year History*, ed. Russell F. Weigley (New York: W. W. Norton, 1982): 699–703, at 650–53.

32. *Philadelphia Inquirer*, November 11, 1947; January 28, 1948; March 23, 1947; April 18, 1948; April 19, 1948; May 20, 1948.

33. Urban Redevelopment Law, Act of May 24, 1945, Public Law 991, No. 385 ("engage"), http://www.fcadc.com/pdf/Urban%20Redevelopment%20Law.pdf, accessed January 13, 2023; *Philadelphia Inquirer*, August 31, 1948; September 1, 1948; September 5, 1948 ("priority"); Guian A. McKee, "Blue Sky Boys, Professional Citizens, and Knights-in-Shining-Money: Philadelphia's Penn Center Project and the Constraints of Private Development," *Journal of Planning History* 6, no. 1 (February 2007): 48–80, at 56.

34. PRR BOD Minutes; *Philadelphia Inquirer*, December 5, 1948; December 8, 1948; December 27, 1948 ("medal").

35. *Philadelphia Inquirer*, March 10, 1949; April 13, 1949; April 26, 1949.

36. Greene's sentence was eighteen to thirty-six years. *Philadelphia Inquirer*, November 27, 1949; May 10, 1950; May 27, 1950 ("long"); October 6, 1950; November 5, 1950 ("prepared").

37. *Philadelphia Inquirer*, January 14, 1951.

38. In September 1951, the City Planning Commission submitted to Mayor Samuel its first budget under the new charter. It called for $558.5 million in projects, of which the removal of the Filbert Street Extension was but a small part. Committee of Seventy, *The Charter: A History* (Philadelphia: Committee of Seventy, 1980), 8–12, 42–44, 60–61, 70–71, includes Joseph S. Clark Jr., "A Reformer Tells His Story: Clark, Dilworth Start to Crack GOP Hold," *Philadelphia Bulletin*, September 20, 1971 ("greatest" quote at 12); *Philadelphia Inquirer*, September 9, 1951.

39. Clark and Clark, "Rally and Relapse," 654–57.

40. Those efforts accelerated when David Bevan became the company's vice president in charge of finance in May 1951, eight months before Clark became mayor. McKee, "Blue Sky Boys," 51.

41. In 1837, Enoch White Clark established E. W. Clark & Company, with Jay Cooke serving as a partner between 1842 and 1858. In the decades following the Civil War, the firm specialized in railroad, public-utilities, and streetcar and interurban railway securities. Joseph Sill Clark Sr. (Mayor Clark's father) and his brother, Percy Clark, operated a law firm that worked in conjunction with the banking operations. In 1904, Percy Clark married Elizabeth Williams Roberts, the daughter of PRR president George Brooke Roberts. Their daughter, Mary Todhunter Clark, was the first wife of New York governor Nelson Rockefeller.

42. *New York Times*, April 22, 1999; James Grant Wilson and John Fiske, eds., *Appletons' Cyclopædia of American Biography, Volume 1* (New York: D. Appleton and Company, 1888), 718; "The Residents: Percy Clark's Willoughby," *The First 300: The Amazing and Rich History of Lower Merion*, Lower Merion Historical Society, http://lowermerionhistory.org/texts/first300/part28.html, accessed October 1, 2020; McKee, "Blue Sky Boys," 56, 68–69; Timothy Lombardo, *Blue-Collar Conservatism: Frank Rizzo's Philadelphia and Populist Politics* (Philadelphia: University of Pennsylvania Press, 2018), 26–27, 40–42.

43. *Philadelphia Inquirer*, February 11, 1951; January 4, 1952; February 22, 1952; April 29, 1952; James Symes, "Statement on Penn Center Plan," address made at the luncheon of the Citizens' Council on City Planning, February 21, 1952, Philadelphia City Planning Commission Papers, A-2193, quoted in Gregory L. Heller, *Ed Bacon: Planning, Politics, and the Building of Modern Philadelphia* (Philadelphia: University of Pennsylvania Press), 98 ("effective").

44. *Philadelphia Inquirer*, April 27, 1952; April 28, 1952 ("sentimental").

45. In September 1953, the city released the final portion of the $4.3 million set aside to buy the land that would be occupied by Pennsylvania Boulevard. PRR press release, April 17, 1952, HML, Box 259, folder 18; Newell to Smith, February 26, 1952, HML, Box 1486, folder 23 ("desirable," "sincerity"); *Philadelphia Bulletin*, July 6, 1952; *Modern Railroads*, August 1952, 61–65; *Philadelphia Inquirer*, April 28, 1952; April 29, 1952 ("sorry"); June 13, 1952; July 7, 1952; July 15, 1952; September 21, 1952; September 27, 1953; October 16, 1955; October 27, 1955; October 28, 1955; October 29, 1955; December 10, 1955; June 1, 1959; *Philadelphia Bulletin*, May 31, 1959.

46. Stefan Lorant, "Between Two Wars," in *Pittsburgh: Story of an American City*, 5th ed., ed. Stefan Lorant (Pittsburgh, PA: Esselmont, 1999): 321–72, at 368–72;

Robert Moses, *Arterial Plan for Pittsburgh* (Pittsburgh, PA: Pittsburgh Regional Planning Association, 1939), 7 ("removal"), 8 ("grossly").

47. The city already owned all but 16.7 acres of the land required for Point Park.

48. The train shed of the Wabash Terminal also succumbed to fire, in March 1946, fortuitously removing another obstacle to the redevelopment of Pittsburgh's Golden Triangle.

49. PRR BOD Minutes; *Pittsburgh Post-Gazette*, May 2, 1946; *New York Times*, January 4, 1951; David L. Lawrence, "Rebirth," in *Pittsburgh: Story of an American City*, 5th ed., ed. Stefan Lorant (Pittsburgh, PA: Esselmont, 1999): 373–448, at 378–86, 417–37; Tracy Neumann, *Remaking the Rust Belt: The Postindustrial Transformation of North America* (Philadelphia: University of Pennsylvania Press, 2016), 26–28; Allen Dieterich-Ward, *Beyond Rust: Metropolitan Pittsburgh and the Fate of Industrial America* (Philadelphia: University of Pennsylvania Press, 2016), 73–75, 81–84; McKee, "Blue Sky Boys," 67–78.

50. McKee, "Blue Sky Boys," 50.

51. Heller, *Ed Bacon*, 93.

52. PRR executives suggested that city officials had made it impossible to pursue Loewy's plans, which "were tidily dismissed because of the erupting ideas of the newly formed city planning commission." "Penn Center: Let's Face the Facts," *Delaware Valley Announcer*, June 1959, 18–22, HML, Box 259, folder 24 (the story was essentially a "plant" by PRR publicists—see memo to Symes et al., June 1, 1959, HML, Box 259, folder 24).

53. *Philadelphia Inquirer*, March 15, 1949 ("attractive," "sell"); July 28, 1952.

54. Heller, *Ed Bacon*, 93–94; McKee, "Blue Sky Boys," 53–54.

55. *Philadelphia Inquirer*, May 26, 1949 ("hodgepodge," "expression"); May 27, 1949 ("Regardless"); June 10, 1950 ("Coordinated").

56. *Philadelphia Inquirer*, February 24, 1952; Heller, *Ed Bacon*, 93–94; McKee, "Blue Sky Boys," 53–54.

57. McKee, "Blue Sky Boys," 55–57; Heller, *Ed Bacon*, 92–93.

58. McKee, "Blue Sky Boys," 57.

59. McKee, "Blue Sky Boys," 58–60.

60. *Philadelphia Inquirer*, January 30, 1953; January 31, 1953; March 7, 1953 ("wholehearted"); September 19, 1953 ("spokesman"); Heller, *Ed Bacon*, 95–103.

61. PRR BOD Minutes; *New York Times*, May 24, 1953; *Philadelphia Inquirer*, May 19, 1953; McKee, "Blue Sky Boys," 71–73.

62. *New York Times*, March 29, 1982 ("policy"); McKee, "Blue Sky Boys," 61.

63. *Philadelphia Inquirer*, June 5, 1953; October 10, 1953 ("down," "connected," "bad"); Heller, *Ed Bacon*, 103–6; McKee, "Blue Sky Boys," 61–65.

64. "Penn Center: Let's Face the Facts," 18–22; PRR press release, June 4, 1953, HML, Box 259, folder 2; C. P. Schants, "Penn Center—Progress Report," November 1, 1954, HML, Box 1549, folder 28; "Memorandum: Opening of Penn Center Ice Skating Rink," December 9, 1958, HML, Box 1549, folder 29; *Philadelphia Inquirer*, November 22, 1953; November 25, 1953; McKee, "Blue Sky Boys," 63.

65. By May 1956, Kling was in any case involved in another PRR project, a seventy-five-thousand-seat, $15 million stadium over the northern approach to 30th Street Station, to be built with municipal funds. City officials rejected that proposal; three years later, the PRR officials floated an equally unsuccessful plan for a sixty-thousand-seat stadium that would be built without public support. PRR BOD Minutes; Heller, *Ed Bacon*, 107–9; *Philadelphia Inquirer*, January 11, 1956; September 20, 1959; PRR press release, October 22, 1958, HML, Box 259, folder 25.

66. *Pittsburgh Press*, March 15, 1963; *Philadelphia Inquirer*, October 1, 1963; Heller, *Ed Bacon*, 108–15, includes Edmund N. Bacon, Mayor Reports, May 28, 1959 ("phony"), at 110; *Philadelphia Inquirer*, October 25, 1953; *New York Times*, June 25, 1953; Pennsylvania Railroad Company, *One Hundred and Eighteenth Annual Report, for the Year Ended December 31, 1964* (Philadelphia: n.p., 1965), 19; McKee, "Blue Sky Boys," 70.

67. Adolph Katz, "The Northeast: A Boom Town Is Growing Up," *Philadelphia Evening Bulletin*, March 9, 1961, quoted in Lombardo, *Blue-Collar Conservatism*, 40 ("Someday"); Committee of Seventy, *Charter*, 38.

68. Heller, *Ed Bacon*, 108–15; "Dream of Penn Center Being Realized, Planner Feels," *Philadelphia Bulletin*, August 25, 1959 ("family," "means"), at 110; June 17, 1998 ("rejected," "reviled").

69. Interstate Commerce Commission Docket No. 31954: Passenger Train Deficit, Item 7, Exhibit Accompanying Testimony of Walter W. Patchell, Vice President, Research and Development, The Pennsylvania Railroad Company, 1957, 10 (hereafter, Patchell Testimony); Joe Welsh, *Pennsy Streamliners: The Blue Ribbon Fleet* (Milwaukee, WI: Kalmbach, 1999), 31–40.

70. The two-level design embodied some of the concepts associated with Pullman's 1931 *Eventide* and *Nocturne* duplex sleepers, the PRR's subsequent *Brook*-series sleepers for the 1938 Fleet of Modernism, and the experimental gallery car built for the Long Island Rail Road in 1932. None of those earlier examples were true bi-level cars, however, in that they relied on a single central aisle that provided access to compartments or seats on varying levels.

71. Anita A. Pins, "The Pennsylvania Railroad: Streamlined by Raymond Loewy," *Keystone* 24, no. 1 (Spring 1991): 9–50, at 37–44; John H. White Jr., *The American Railroad Passenger Car* (Baltimore, MD: Johns Hopkins University Press, 1978), 193–94, 278–79.

72. Beginning in 1954, the Santa Fe acquired true double-deck cars for its all-coach *El Capitan* streamliner. That equipment, designed without any reliance on Loewy's efforts, was too tall to have been used on eastern lines. Pins, "Streamlined by Raymond Loewy," 37–44; Chuck Blardone, "Interviews with John W. Ebstein," *Keystone* 26 (Autumn 1993): 23–33 ("high"); White, *American Railroad Passenger Car*, 195–96.

73. The stylish and sophisticated Loewy recalled that Finnegan lacked "epicurean finesse," although he acknowledged that the head of the Dining Car Department "did a good job anyway, especially steaks." Given Loewy's French heritage, his most stinging rebuke of Finnegan may have been that "he was not so good at sauces."

74. Pins, "Streamlined by Raymond Loewy," 37–44 (includes Finnegan to Loewy, June 15, 1943 ["questionable"]; Barnhart to Pins, February 13, 1978 ["prunes"]; and Loewy to Pins, April 15, 1978 ["finesse," steaks," "sauces," "gravy"]).

75. Raymond Loewy Associates, "An Industrial Designer Looks at Postwar Travel," December 8, 1943, Penn Central Railroad Collection, M. G. 286, Pennsylvania Historical and Museum Commission, Pennsylvania State Archives, Harrisburg (hereafter, PHMC), Box 66 (9-1662) ("striving," "abandon," "comfort," "ample," "dust," "odors," "delicious," "utilized").

76. Bradley J. Flamm, "Putting the Brakes on 'Non-Essential' Travel: 1940s Wartime Mobility, Prosperity, and the US Office of Defense," *Journal of Transport History* 27, no. 1 (March 2006): 71–92; Patchell Testimony, 10, 13.

77. *New York Times*, October 28, 1945; February 3, 1946 ("desperate," "tough"); March 4, 1947; Welsh, *Pennsy Streamliners*, 84.

78. *New York Times*, October 28, 1945 ("future").

79. *New York Times*, December 13, 1945; Welsh, *Pennsy Streamliners*, 64.

80. A further twenty-two cars were under construction and destined for trains operating between New York and the South.

81. Welsh, *Pennsy Streamliners*, 62; *New York Times*, October 2, 1945; February 3, 1946.

82. The PRR order included 129 full sleepers in various configurations, 21 sleeper-lounges, 9 sleeper-observations, 11 twin-unit diners (22 cars total), 6 single-unit diners, 21 coaches, 2 coach-lounges, and 4 baggage-dorms.

83. The new equipment did not include dome cars, such as the ones employed on the *Train of Tomorrow*. Built as a collaborative venture between General Motors and Pullman-Standard, the E7 diesel locomotive and four dome cars made a series of demonstration tours, in addition to their appearance at the Chicago Railroad Fair. During its East Coast tour in the autumn of 1947, the train was open for public viewing in cities such as New York, Philadelphia, and Baltimore. PRR officials examined the train but refused to publicize it; they permitted it to travel over their railroad only when no other option was readily available. Owing to restrictive clearances along much of the East Coast (including the tunnels under the Hudson River), the PRR could not use dome cars in revenue service. There was thus little value in promoting a technological innovation that could only be used by rivals—including the Baltimore & Ohio, which did use dome cars on several passenger trains. "Steam Passenger Car Equipment Ownership and Percent, Air Conditioned," November 28, 1945; John F. Deasy to Martin W. Clement, December 17, 1945; "New Passenger Car Program—Production Schedule, Cost and Probable Retirement Program," December 27, 1945; "Post-War Passenger Car Program," December 27, 1945; all in HML, Box 327, folder 7; *New York Times*, January 6, 1946; Welsh, *Pennsy Streamliners*, 64–66; Ric Morgan, *The Train of Tomorrow* (Bloomington: Indiana University Press, 2007).

84. *New York Times*, December 24, 1946; November 10, 1948; Welsh, *Pennsy Streamliners*, 70–72.

85. *New York Times*, December 24, 1946; January 5, 1947; May 4, 1947; May 2, 1948; Welsh, *Pennsy Streamliners*, 73–76; Pins, "Streamlined by Raymond Loewy," 42–46.

86. The diners for *The Jeffersonian* entered service in December.

87. *New York Times*, May 4, 1947 ("fine"); May 2, 1948 ("outlook," "now"); November 28, 1948; April 19, 1977.

88. Equipment assigned to the 1949 *Broadway Limited* included three 21-roomette sleepers; seven 10-roomette, 6-double-bedroom sleepers; four 4-compartment, 4-double-bedroom, 2-drawing-room sleepers; two 12-duplex roomette, 4-double-bedroom sleepers; two 2-double-bedroom/lounge cars; and 2 end-of-train observation cars—but the PRR added equipment as necessary. Joel Rosenbaum and Tom Gallo, *The Broadway Limited* (Piscataway, NJ: Railpace, 1988), 47, 60; Welsh, *Pennsy Streamliners*, 73, 76, 78; Arthur D. Dubin, *Some Classic Trains* (Milwaukee, WI: Kalmbach, 1964), 92–93.

89. In 1941, the B&O introduced the *Columbian* in response to the success of the PRR's *Jeffersonian*. The *Columbian* received new equipment in May 1949 (including dome coaches, which could not operate on the PRR, owing to restricted clearances). Although the B&O also acquired many new passenger cars in the early postwar era, it did not spend as lavishly as the PRR or the NYC—partly because the B&O operated fewer passenger routes and partly because executives in the chronically under-funded company relied on refurbished and secondhand equipment. That decision, which did not appreciably harm the B&O's competitive position in markets where geography gave the company an advantage, facilitated investments in freight service with money that might otherwise have been squandered on passenger cars.

90. Welsh, *Pennsy Streamliners*, 76–89; Dan Cupper, "Tycoon's Train," *Trains* 60, no. 11 (November 2000): 54–59; Dan Cupper, *Crossroads of Commerce: The Pennsylvania Railroad Calendar Art of Grif Teller* (Mechanicsburg, PA: Stackpole, 1992, 2003), 110–11.

91. Deasy and Franklin to Clement, January 31, 1947; Clement to Franklin, May 19, 1947 ("volume"); "Pennsylvania Railroad Company—Passenger and Allied Services," 1947; all in PHMC, Box 55 (9-1651); "Trains Discontinued Account Coal Strike That Will Not Be Restored," December 9, 1946, PHMC, Box 82 (9-1678).

92. Clement to Symes and Carpi, October 27, 1948 ("drying"); Clement, memo to staff, November 5, 1948 ("dilemma," "occupation," "wouldn't"); both in PHMC Box 73 (9-1669), folder 520.1.

93. *New York Times*, January 30, 1949 ("increase"); May 8, 1949 ("equipment," "beset").

94. Clement to Franklin, May 8, 1951, PHMC, Box 82 (9-1678), folder 600.11 ("afford"); Clement to Symes, May 21, 1951, HML, quoted in Gregory L. Thompson, "How Cost Ignorance Derailed the Pennsylvania Railroad's Efforts to Save Its Passenger Service, 1929–61," *Journal of Transport History* 16, no. 2 (September 1995): 134–58, at 147 ("afford"); Welsh, *Pennsy Streamliners*, 125–26.

95. Clement to Franklin, May 8, 1951, PHMC, Box 82 (9-1678), folder 600.11 ("praise").

96. Douglas Wornom, *History: Passenger Train and Through Car Service, Pennsylvania Railroad, 1849–1947* (Chicago: D. Wornom; distributed by O. Davies, 1974), 10; Wornom, "History of Coast-to-Coast Through Train and Car Service," in *Passenger Train and Through Car Service*, 54/1; Welsh, *Pennsy Streamliners*, 91–92.

97. Wornom, "History of Coast-to-Coast Through Train and Car Service," 55/2; Welsh, *Pennsy Streamliners*, 91–92; Clement to Donald V. Fraser, January 16, 1946 ("wait"), PHMC, Box 74 (9-1670).

98. Wornom, "History of Coast-to-Coast Through Train and Car Service," 55/2–56/3; Welsh, *Pennsy Streamliners*, 92.

99. Mark Reutter, "The Life of Edward Budd, Part 2: Frustration and Acclaim," *Railroad History* 173 (Autumn 1995): 58–101, at 89–92.

100. Joseph Borkin, *Robert R. Young: The Populist of Wall Street* (New York: Harper & Row, 1969), 71–74.

101. Borkin, *Robert R. Young*, 76–78.

102. Borkin, *Robert R. Young*, 1–11, includes "goddam-banker" at 3.

103. In September 1935, Ball and the Van Sweringens formed the Midamerica Corporation, a holding company that would receive the assets Ball would shortly acquire from the two brothers.

104. Young began working for General Motors in 1922, and he became an assistant treasurer in 1928. He resigned from GM and joined forces with Kolbe, another former GM assistant treasurer, to form the investment firm Young, Kolbe & Company. They soon began purchasing stock in the Alleghany Corporation, the centerpiece of the Van Sweringen financial empire, on behalf of Alfred P. Sloan and other General Motors executives. By 1937, when Sloan and his GM associates were preparing to add the Ball holdings to their investment portfolio, they received a warning from Senator Burton K. Wheeler that his Senate Interstate Commerce Committee would oppose any GM participation in the railroad business. The GM contingent withdrew from the consortium, and most of the capital subsequently came from Kirby, the son of one of the founders of the F. W. Woolworth Company.

105. Borkin, *Robert R. Young*, 24–41, provides an overview of those financial transactions. A more extensive account is available in United States Congress, Senate, Committee on Interstate Commerce, *Investigations of Railroads, Holding Companies, and Affiliated Companies. Additional Report of the Committee on Interstate Commerce Pursuant to S. Res. 71 (74th Congress): A Resolution Authorizing an Investigation of Interstate Railroads and Affiliates with Respect to Financing, Reorganizations, Mergers, and Certain Other Matters. Railroad Combination in the Eastern Region, Part 7: Young, Kolby, Kirby Syndicate, Acquisition of Control of Alleghany System* (Washington, DC: United States Government Printing Office, 1938).

106. Young wisely promised to divest the Missouri Pacific—both because it was in bankruptcy and because its acquisition by the Van Swerigens violated the traditional separation between eastern and western lines, and angered westerners who feared the domination of eastern investment bankers.

107. Even though the ICC and the Justice Department permitted Young to retain control of the railroads in the Alleghany group, in 1945 he failed in his efforts to combine the C&O with the Nickel Plate. In 1947, the Pere Marquette merged into the C&O, but Alleghany sold its holdings in the Nickel Plate and the Wheeling & Lake Erie that year. Borkin, *Robert R. Young*, 43–69.

108. The *Georgia v. Pennsylvania Railroad* case was extraordinarily complex but ultimately inconsequential. In 1944, Georgia governor Ellis G. Arnall filed suit, on behalf of the state's citizens, against the PRR and nineteen other eastern and southern railroads. The Association of American Railroads was not named as a defendant, but the trade association was clearly central to the collaborative ratemaking process. In brief, Arnall alleged that the railroads' rate bureaus had conspired to set rates in a matter that favored northern manufacturing interests, thus impeding Georgia's ability to industrialize, and thereby crippling the state's economy. The case went to the Supreme Court in January 1945, where PRR chief legal counsel John Dickinson argued on behalf of the railroads. In March 1946, the court appointed a special master, Lloyd K. Garrison, to evaluate the merits of Georgia's argument. Garrison, the great-grandson of abolitionist William Lloyd Garrison, was a partner in the law firm of Weiss and Wharton, and the future dean of the University of Wisconsin law school. While Garrison was considering the matter, Congress passed the June 1948 Reed-Bulwinkle Act, which exempted rate bureaus from antitrust prosecution, further complicating the issue. Garrison did not accept Young's argument that, because the C&O and the Nickel Plate had withdrawn from the Association of American Railroads on January 15, 1947, the charges against those companies should therefore be dismissed. Garrison nonetheless concluded that the Georgia case lacked merit. He found little evidence of discriminatory rates, and he noted that railroads had almost always granted requests by Georgia shippers for rate relief. With Arnall no longer in office, there seemed

little point in continuing a lawsuit that had dragged on for more than five years. In November 1950, the Supreme Court dismissed the suit, at the request of both sides. *Georgia v. Pennsylvania Railroad Company*, 324 US 439 (1945); *Georgia v. Pennsylvania Railroad Company*, 331 US 788 (1947); *Georgia v. Pennsylvania Railroad Company*, 340 US 889 (1950); *Railway Age* 118, no. 13 (March 31, 1945): 584–86; 119, no. 7 (August 18, 1945): 310; 119, no. 14 (October 6, 1945): 576; 120, no. 12 (March 23, 1946): 651; 128, no. 24 (June 17, 1950): 73–76; *New York Times*, November 28, 1950; William T. Coleman and Donald T. Bliss, *Counsel for the Situation: Shaping the Law to Realize America's Promise* (Washington, DC: Brookings Institution, 2010), 101.

109. *New York Times*, October 16, 1946 ("constructive," "promote," "improved," "dared"); *Tracks* 38, no. 6 (June 1953): 22–24; PRR BOD Minutes.

110. The Nickel Plate and the Pere Marquette, the two other railroads under Young's control, were also a part of his "pay-as-you-go" plan. Effective April 1, 1947, the New York Central and more than forty other railroads—although not the PRR—offered a competing system under the auspices of the Rail Travel Credit Agency. Several years later, James Newell, the PRR vice president in charge of operations, was willing to "recognize that the whole tendency of modern times is for people to purchase on credit," and he supported the use of "identification cards" to facilitate the practice. *New York Times*, January 26, 1947; March 30, 1947; Newell to J. W. Leonard, August 18, 1954 ("recognize"), HML, Box 341, folder 2.

111. The aquarium installed in each of the tavern-lounge cars reflected, in miniature, Young's inability to reconcile his grandiose visions with the practical realities of rail travel. Each aquarium contained goldfish (whose colors matched the bright yellow letterboard on the exterior of each car), but the constant sloshing of the water in the tank caused them to die of trainsickness. The three Class M-1 steam-turbines that Baldwin and Westinghouse built for the C&O (in 1947 and 1948) were to be used on the *Chessie*. Like the passenger train, the locomotives—designed to provide modern, streamlined motive power that would ensure the loyalty of coal producers—never lived up to expectations.

112. Dubin, *More Classic Trains*, 478–81.

113. Borkin, *Robert R. Young*, 80; Herbert H. Harwood, writing as Geoffrey H. George, "This Was the Train That Was (But Never Was)," *Trains* 28, no. 9 (July 1968): 38–47; Thomas W. Dixon Jr., *Chesapeake & Ohio's Pere*

Marquettes: America's First Postwar Streamliners 1946–1971 (Lynchburg, VA: TLC, 2004).

114. Officially, Young's bid for Pullman came from Otis & Company (the Cleveland investment bank he had enlisted to block the Morgan and Kuhn, Loeb interests by agreeing to competitive bidding for the securities issued to refinance the C&O), although everyone acknowledged that Young was the driving force behind the entire operation. The Standard Steel Spring Company and the Chicago firm of Glore, Forgan & Company also submitted bids in October 1945, making in all four sets of potential buyers.

115. The principal organizer of the buyers' group was Willard F. Place, the NYC's vice president in charge of finance. On September 9, a week after Clement's meeting with Young, Place sent letters to various railroads (the PRR must have been his principal target) warning that the threat posed by Young required a united response that would override whatever merits might be associated with a policy of individual ownership.

116. *New York Times*, August 17, 1945; August 28, 1945; September 28, 1945; October 6, 1945; October 14, 1945; October 28, 1945; October 30, 1945; November 5, 1945; November 6, 1945; November 7, 1945; November 14, 1945; November 17, 1945; November 18, 1945; December 2, 1945; December 7, 1945; December 8, 1945; December 12, 1945; PRR BOD Minutes; Borkin, *Robert R. Young*, 55–57, 77–82.

117. As Young planned his advertising campaign, his lawyers advised him that Justice Department and ICC officials might look with disfavor at Young's dual role as the C&O's chairman of the board (and as an investor in the Alleghany Corporation) and as an individual attempting to purchase Pullman. As such, the ads clearly suggested Pullman's failings and the benefits that the C&O might provide but avoided any direct mention of Young's plans to acquire Pullman.

118. Young directed some of his strongest objections at the open-section sleeping car. Pullman officials had come to the same conclusion, particularly after demand for upper berths declined sharply during the 1930s. After some unsuccessful experiments with enclosed rooms in 1931, Pullman completed its first all-roomette car in 1937 and supplied all-room cars as part of the initial Fleet of Modernism order. Between 1935 and 1941, Pullman rebuilt more than three hundred open-section heavyweight cars into room cars. Had not the war intervened, Pullman would doubtless have accelerated plans to convert more heavyweights while building more all-room lightweight cars. Postwar orders for new equipment were

overwhelmingly for cars that featured enclosed rooms, with perhaps a few open sections. Even as Young was delineating the horrors of "rolling tenements," Pullman officials assumed that open sections would rapidly disappear from the national railroad network. The last new all-open-section cars were a set of six built by Budd in 1948 for the *California Zephyr*. Open sections remained valuable, although perhaps not popular, for federal government employees, who were required to use the lowest-cost sleeping-car space available. For that reason, in 1955, the New Haven purchased several sleepers that contained some open sections, and PRR/New Haven overnight trains between Washington and Boston continued to offer open-section accommodation until 1968. Young was thus emphasizing a problem that was well on its way toward a solution. Moreover, Young—the self-styled Populist—ignored the fact that room accommodations were significantly more expensive than open sections and that the abolition of "rolling tenements" would exclude the least affluent travelers from the opportunity to enjoy a comfortable night's sleep. On a personal note, the author has traveled many thousands of miles in various types of sleeping-car accommodations and has concluded that the lower berth in an open section offers a far better night's rest than any of its alternatives. White, *American Railroad Passenger Car*, 277–85.

119. Young's assertion that all passenger cars (not just sleepers) should be replaced on a seven-year cycle made little sense given the longevity of modern stainless-steel equipment. Some cars built in the late 1940s and early 1950s remained in service—as part of Amtrak's Heritage Fleet—until early 2018. As with many other aspects of Young's supposed commitment to the welfare of the traveling public, such artificial limitations on service life would have unnecessarily raised ticket prices.

120. Borkin, *Robert R. Young*, 83–93, includes "tenements" at 93; *New York Times*, December 19, 1945.

121. Pullman's profits declined from $13.9 million in 1945 to barely $2 million in 1947, even though the company generated a record number of passenger miles. *New York Times*, March 24, 1947.

122. The issue was not resolved until May 1947, when the ICC approved the sale to the railroads.

123. *New York Times*, March 5, 1946; August 1, 1946; November 15, 1946; November 16, 1946; November 18, 1946; November 19, 1946; November 28, 1946 ("misled"); January 1, 1947; February 1, 1947; March 4, 1947; April 1, 1947; April 29, 1947; May 15, 1947; June 27, 1947; Borkin, *Robert R. Young*, 83–93.

124. Two more railroads later joined the buying group. At the time of the 1968 PRR-NYC merger, Penn Central owned 31.57 percent of the Pullman Company's stock—and Pullman's massive deficits were only adding to the railroad's financial difficulties. On July 1, 1968, Penn Central began direct operation of all Pullman parlor and sleeping cars on its lines, with Pullman retaining oversight of interline service. The loss of its largest client forced the Pullman Company to cede oversight of sleeping and parlor car operations and staffing to the remaining member railroads, effective January 1, 1969, although the company continued to maintain equipment. There were then approximately 1,000 sleeping cars in operation in the United States—a tiny remnant of the 9,860 cars operated in 1930. The Pullman-Standard Car Manufacturing Company continued to build freight cars and commuter and rapid-transit equipment but did not construct a new sleeping car after 1956. Following the 1944 antitrust proceedings, it remained a subsidiary of Pullman, Incorporated, which became a highly diversified enterprise. When Amtrak began operations in 1971, it acquired many of the former Pullman sleepers and later acquired new Viewliner and Superliner sleeping cars. Amtrak currently owns less than two hundred sleeping cars. *New York Times*, November 23, 1968; December 31, 1968; Arthur D. Dubin, *More Classic Trains* (Milwaukee, WI: Kalmbach, 1974), 93.

125. Deasy and Franklin to Martin Clement, June 6, 1944; "Pullman Situation," November 24, 1945; "Proposed Pennsylvania Acquisition and Operation of Sleeping and Parlor Cars,"; all in HML, Box 264, folder 8; *New York Times*, May 15, 1947; June 12, 1947; June 27, 1947; July 1, 1947; Welsh, *Pennsy Streamliners*, 75; White, *American Railroad Passenger Car*, 264–65.

126. Wornom, "History of Coast-to-Coast Through Train and Car Service," 56/3; Welsh, *Pennsy Streamliners*, 92.

127. Welsh, *Pennsy Streamliners*, 92–93.

128. Young was factually incorrect in his assertion that a hog could travel across the country without changing trains. Regulations dating to 1873 and further defined in the 1906 Twenty-Eight Hour Law (34 Stat. 607) required all livestock to be unloaded, rested, fed, and watered after no more than twenty-eight hours in a stock car.

129. It is unclear where Young obtained the "more than 560,000 people" figure. In all probability, it referred to the total number of travelers who changed trains in gateway cities such as Chicago, St. Louis, and New Orleans, regardless of origin, destination, or length of trip—if indeed that statistic had any factual basis whatsoever. Borkin, *Robert R. Young*, 83–93, includes "Shouldn't"

and "Part" (87), "Hog" (89), and "China" (88); *New York Times*, January 5, 1946; November 28, 1946.

130. The ten railroads included three in the East—the PRR, the NYC, and the B&O—and seven in the West—the Santa Fe (Chicago to Los Angeles); the Chicago & North Western and the Union Pacific (Chicago to Los Angeles, with the Southern Pacific handling the Oakland cars west of Ogden); and the Burlington, the Denver & Rio Grande Western, and Western Pacific (Chicago to Oakland on the *Exposition Flyer* via Denver, the same route that would later be used by the *California Zephyr*). The car interchanged with the *Exposition Flyer* offered daily service to New York, alternating between the PRR's *General* and the NYC's *Commodore Vanderbilt*. In March 1949, the through car shifted to the new *California Zephyr*, with the PRR providing one lightweight sleeping car to that train's equipment pool. While the PRR/Santa Fe car from New York to Los Angeles traveled on *The Broadway Limited* and the *Chief*, the car delivered to the C&NW in Chicago (for Los Angeles, via the *Los Angeles Limited*) initially operated on *The Golden Arrow* (westbound) and *The Manhattan Limited* (eastbound). The PRR's Washington–Los Angeles car initially went west on *The Admiral* and returned on *The Rainbow*. Perhaps ironically, given Robert Young's condemnation of "rolling tenements" coupled with his demand for transcontinental service, the Washington car was usually a twelve–open section, one–drawing room prewar heavyweight sleeper—precisely the type of equipment Young had railed against. The New York–Oakland car (destined for the C&NW/Union Pacific/Southern Pacific *Overland Limited*) was attached to *The Golden Arrow* (westbound) and *The Manhattan Limited* (eastbound). The corresponding car from the nation's capital to Oakland employed the Washington section of each of those trains as far as Harrisburg and combined there with the New York section. The Oakland cars were also prewar heavyweights with open sections.

131. The sleeper initially used *The Golden Arrow* or *The Pennsylvanian* (westbound) and *The Admiral* (eastbound). West of Chicago, it traveled on the *Golden State Limited* (soon renamed the *Golden State*).

132. *New York Times*, April 1, 1946 ("gratifying"); Wornom, "History of Coast-to-Coast Through Train and Car Service," 23–24, 56/3–57/4; Welsh, *Pennsy Streamliners*, 93–96.

133. That equated to a respectable 146,000 through passengers per year—although that figure was substantially below the "560,000 victims" Robert Young had claimed in his "Hog" ad.

134. Journalist and railroad enthusiast Ward Allan Howe observed that transcontinental service "is popular but is considered by some as hardly more than a token service because of the difficulty in obtaining accommodations. There are not enough sleeping cars to make the plan really effective." *New York Times*, May 4, 1947 ("token").

135. Such practices largely defeated the purpose of through service, and there was correspondingly little value in relieving passengers of the need to transfer their luggage from one station to another. The Parmelee Transportation Company held a long-standing monopoly on the movement of passengers and luggage between Chicago's railway terminals, and by the time transcontinental rail service was inaugurated, the company was developing bus service between downtown Chicago and Midway Airport. Most through rail tickets included a free voucher for Parmelee's transfer services from one station to another. See George M. Smerk, "Parmelee Transfer Service," in *Encyclopedia of North American Railroads*, ed. William D. Middleton, George M. Smerk, and Roberta L. Diehl (Bloomington: Indiana University Press, 2007), 818–19; Robert D. Parmelee, *Chicago's Railroads and Parmelee's Transfer Company: A Century of Travel* (New York: Golden Hill, 2003).

136. Welsh, *Pennsy Streamliners*, 96–99; Rosenbaum and Gallo, *Broadway Limited*, 47.

137. Welsh, *Pennsy Streamliners*, 100–101; *New York Times*, April 24, 1946; Baldwin to Clement, November 8, 1945, PHMC, Box 74 (9-1670), folder 521.3.

138. Borkin, *Robert R. Young*, 87 ("phantom," "breach," "Stepchild"); *New York Times*, April 24, 1946 ("without," "contemptuous"); Welsh, *Pennsy Streamliners*, 100–101.

139. On July 7, the PRR also launched through sleeper service between New York and San Antonio in cooperation with the Frisco and the Katy. This was only a single car (rather than a complete train) traveling on *The American* east of St. Louis and on the *Texas Special* to the west. *The American* also carried a through car to Oklahoma City and transferred to the Frisco *Meteor* in St. Louis. Gustavus E. Payne to James R. Downes, July 8, 1946; Norman B. Pitcairn to Clement, June 8, 1946; Clement to Paul J. Neff, July 27, 1946 ("highest"); PRR press release, January 13, 1947; Clement to Neff, April 3, 1947; all in PHMC, Box 74 (9-1670), folder 521.3; *New York Times*, May 15, 1946; November 28, 1948; Wornom, "History of Coast-to-Coast Through Train and Car Service," 57/4; Welsh, *Pennsy Streamliners*, 102–8; Dubin, *More Classic Trains*, 463–68.

140. Welsh, *Pennsy Streamliners*, 99–100.

141. Through service to Oklahoma City was cut back to Tulsa within a few months after its July 1946 inauguration, and that route ended in 1949.

142. The Katy and the Frisco together contributed two cars to the transcontinental pool for the *Texas Special*, while the Frisco provided two cars for the *Meteor* (connecting with the PRR's *American* at St. Louis) to run through to New York. The four PRR cars (*Cascade Brim* and *Cascade Ravine* on the *Meteor* and *Cascade Range* and *Cascade Meadow* on the *Texas Special*) had smooth sides, as was typical of PRR equipment, while the *Texas Special* featured fluted-side cars. As such, Pullman applied shadowlining, a time-consuming and expensive process that used paint to create a trompe l'oeil effect, mimicking fluting.

143. Welsh, *Pennsy Streamliners*, 108–11; Dubin, *More Classic Trains*, 258–63.

144. The original *Eagle* (later renamed the *Missouri River Eagle*) entered service in March 1940. World War II delayed the MP's plans to upgrade other trains and make them part of the *Eagle* brand. Not all those trains materialized, however. The initial MP plan was for the *Sunshine Special* to become the *Sunshine Eagle*, operating as two trains (one from St. Louis to Dallas–Fort Worth and El Paso and the other from St. Louis to Palestine, Texas, splitting there into sections for Houston/Galveston and San Antonio [and continuing to Mexico City]). Ferrocarriles Nacionales de México chose not to bear the cost of new streamlined equipment, prompting the MP to rename the train as the *Texas Eagle* and truncate the route in San Antonio. Neither the *Sunshine Special* nor its *Texas Eagle* replacement should be confused with the *Texas Special*, the joint Frisco/Katy train that also carried PRR through cars.

145. For a few months after the MP changed the name of its half of the *Sunshine Special* to the *Texas Eagle*, the PRR operated a train with the same name between New York and St. Louis before renaming it *The Penn Texas*. Through sleepers continued to operate to a variety of Texas destinations, as far west as El Paso, but the car line to Mexico City was discontinued. In 1949, the PRR reassigned the cars destined for the Katy/Frisco from *The American* to *The Penn Texas* (which by that time was second only to *The "Spirit of St. Louis"* as the best train operating between New York and St. Louis). Peter Forbes, "PRR Through Service to the Southwest," *Keystone* 12, no. 3 (September 1979): 16–18; Welsh, *Pennsy Streamliners*, 103–10; Dubin, *More Classic Trains*, 463–68.

146. Beginning in 1933, the Boeing 247 enabled transcontinental air service without a change in planes—but with a range of only 745 miles, multiple intermediate refueling stops were necessary. By 1946, the Lockheed Constellation and the Douglas DC-6 possessed sufficient range to enable one-stop transcontinental service. The introduction of the Lockheed L-1049 Super Constellation in 1951 caused TWA to offer nonstop eastbound scheduled transcontinental service between Los Angeles and New York beginning in October 1953, with a travel time of eight hours (the corresponding westbound service stopped in Chicago to refuel, owing to the effects of headwinds). TWA Museum, "TWA History," https://twamuseum.org/history, accessed November 2, 2023; Welsh, *Pennsy Streamliners*, 91.

147. Through service from Dallas–Fort Worth to El Paso ended in January 1958.

148. The primary through train routes were Chicago to Florida, New York/Washington to Florida and Atlanta and New Orleans, and Washington to Boston.

149. *New York Times*, May 4, 1947; Welsh, *Pennsy Streamliners*, 100, 106–8; *Railway Age*, 143, no. 12 (September 16, 1957): 11.

150. Patchell Testimony, 1, 10–11, 14.

151. PRR BOD Minutes; Pennsylvania Railroad Company, *One Hundred and Third Annual Report, for the Year Ended December 31, 1949* (Philadelphia: n.p., 1950), 25; Welsh, *Pennsy Streamliners*, 128.

152. The ICC granted a 10 percent fare increase during the war, another 10 percent increase in 1947, and a 17 percent increase in 1948. After the 1949 fare adjustment, therefore, passenger rates were approximately 44 percent higher than they had been prior to June 30, 1946, and about 50 percent above prewar levels. The previous highest coach fare, in 1921, had been 3.6 cents per mile, but without the wartime federal tax.

153. Patchell Testimony, 11; *New York Times*, November 15, 1949; Pennsylvania Railroad Company, *One Hundred and Third Annual Report*, 5.

154. "Increased Fares, Eastern Railroads, 1949," ICC Docket No. 30256, *Interstate Commerce Commission Reports: Decisions of the Interstate Commerce Commission of the United States, Volume 276, August 1949–January 1950* (Washington, DC: United States Government Printing Office, 1950), 433–449, at 446 ("warning").

155. The NYC experienced even greater difficulties in paying for the upkeep of a four-track main line. By the time Alfred Perlman became NYC president in 1954, the two passenger mains were maintained and signaled for 80-mph operation—even though passenger revenues were steadily declining—while the two freight mains were riddled with slow orders and barely capable of

30-mph speeds—too slow to permit the fast and efficient freight service that Perlman thought essential to the company's survival.

156. For an additional perspective on that issue, see Thompson, "Cost Ignorance," 149–51.

157. Clement to Franklin, July 8, 1949, John W. Barriger III Papers, St. Louis Mercantile Library, St. Louis, Missouri (hereafter, Barriger Papers), Series 262, Box 158.

158. The six methodologies for the calculation of net passenger revenues included the following: (1) solely attributed expense ($136.3 million surplus in 1950); (2) solely attributed expense and tax accruals ($102.3 million surplus); (3) solely attributed expense, tax accruals, and net rents ($72.8 million surplus); (4) fully allocated expense ($398.0 million deficit); (5) fully allocated expense and tax accruals ($506.6 million deficit); and (6) fully allocated expense, tax accruals, and net rents ($508.5 million deficit).

159. Those debates were by no means new to the postwar era of declining passenger patronage. As early as 1897, representatives from the Association of Transportation Officers considered "the arbitrary division of expenses not exclusively passenger or freight" and relied on a simplistic formula based on engine mileage. The ATO identified at least one instance where a misallocation of expenses had transformed ostensibly profitable passenger service into a money-losing proposition. On the Columbia & Port Deposit, they noted, a correct attribution of expenses would have changed a $13,000 passenger loss for 1896 into a profit of $2,000. ATO, "Report of the Committee on Conducting Transportation on the Question of 'The Division of Expenses Now in Practice as Applying to Passenger and Freight Service,'" October 18, 1897, HML, Box 407, folder 8; James C. Nelson, *Railroad Transportation and Public Policy* (Washington, DC: Brookings Institution, 1959), 295.

160. Numerous historians have emphasized the declining competency of the ICC in the postwar period. Ari and Olive Hoogenboom, for example, have suggested that "two factors contributed to the commission's debilitation in the postwar years: the proportion of nonregulated interstate traffic increased as rail service declined, and weak appointments left the commission bereft of leadership and dependent upon an entrenched staff following established procedures." The assessment is apt, and the second characteristic contributed to the ICC's inability to decisively address the cost of passenger service. Ari and Olive Hoogenboom, *A History of the ICC: From Panacea to Palliative* (New York: W. W. Norton, 1976), 145 ("factors").

161. Nelson, *Railroad Transportation and Public Policy*, 294; Interstate Commerce Commission, Docket No. 31954, "Railroad Passenger Train Deficit: Report of Howard Hosmer, Hearing Examiner" (Washington, DC: Interstate Commerce Commission, 1958), 3 (hereafter, Hosmer Report), 4 ("methods").

162. Symes to Clement, June 30, 1949; Clement to Franklin, September 6, 1949 ("save"); both in PHMC, Franklin papers, Box 59 (9-2091), folder 230.

163. Symes to Franklin, July 11, 1951, HML, Box 339, folder 22 ("asset," "pricing"); Patchell Testimony, 14.

164. Symes to E. E. Ernest, March 21, 1951; Symes to Franklin, September 18, 1951; both in HML, Box 339, folder 22.

165. At peak travel times, particularly during the Christmas season, the two trains operated separately but shared a common timetable designation. Craig Sanders, *Akron Railroads* (Charleston, SC: Arcadia, 2007), 59; Welsh, *Pennsy Streamliners*, 127–28.

166. *New York Times*, January 13, 1951 ("stepchild").

167. PRR attorneys took the matter to the state's superior court, which ruled in favor of the railroad. The PUC, joined by the cities of Philadelphia and Pittsburgh, filed an appeal with the state supreme court, which overturned the lower court's ruling and restored the PUC's authority over the intrastate portions of interstate trains. There matters stood until 1959 when, under the terms of the Transportation Act of 1958, the PUC relented and permitted the trains' discontinuance. *Philadelphia Inquirer*, May 26, 1959.

168. Ernst to Newell, October 14, 1952; Newell to E. W. S. et al., November 3, 1952; both in HML, Box 339, folder 23; *New York Times*, February 20, 1953; Welsh, *Pennsy Streamliners*, 128–30.

169. Symes to Franklin, July 11, 1951, HML, Box 339, folder 22 ("withdrawals," "substantial"); Symes, speech to employees, June 10, 1954, quoted in Welsh, *Pennsy Streamliners*, 132 ("invested").

170. *Railway Age* 133, no. 15 (October 13, 1952): 16 ("acquainted"); 134, no. 5 (February 2, 1953): 46-47.

171. "Gleaming $11,000,000 Streamliners Placed in Service by the Pennsylvania Railroad," *Mutual Magazine*, April 1952, 11–20; *Railway Age* 132, no. 11 (March 17, 1952): 76–89.

172. When testifying before the ICC in 1958, two PRR vice presidents provided diametrically opposing views of the profitability of passenger service between New York and Washington. One emphasized that it "is about 40 percent of our total and it does meet its full costs," while another asserted that traffic had fallen from more than

sixty thousand passengers per day in 1947 to fewer than thirty thousand daily passengers in 1957 and that "on the total cost basis" the service incurred a deficit. Hosmer Report, 70 ("percent," "basis").

173. Symes to Clement, February 6, 1948; E. Hart to Clement, November 20, 1948; both in PHMC, Box 55 (9-1651); *New York Times*, March 16, 1952 ("restrictions"); February 20, 1954; *Lancaster Dispatcher* 48, no. 3 (March 2017): 8; PRR, *New York Philadelphia Washington Passenger Service*, 1964 Report (Philadelphia: PRR, 1964), exhibit 1, exhibit 2A; Fred W. Frailey, *Twilight of the Great Trains* (Waukesha, WI: Kalmbach, 1998), 178.

174. Christopher D. McKenna, *The World's Newest Profession: Management Consulting in the Twentieth Century* (Cambridge, MA: Cambridge University Press, 2006), 90–96; Francis L. Elmendorf, *Robert Heller of Cleveland: His Life and Work* (New York: Newcomen Society in North America, 1955); *New York Times*, January 24, 1973; Symes to Franklin, September 18, 1951, HML, Box 339, folder 22 ("background").

175. In the initial hearing, the PSC required the NYC to either change its schedules or revise its operating practices if more than 20 percent of passenger trains were late. Given the level of wartime traffic, the PSC elected not to enforce the order. Periodic assessments of the NYC's performance resumed after the war, but through 1949 PSC officials concluded that the NYC was making a good-faith effort to improve service and operate trains on time.

176. *New York Times*, January 17, 1952; February 6, 1952 ("reasons," "remedy," "concerned"); February 10, 1952 ("increase").

177. The PRR initially paid Heller between $27,000 and $32,000 per month, an amount that soon increased to $40,000 per month. By December 1952, the PRR had paid $357,000 to Heller, and the total reached $955,243 by January 1, 1954.

178. Contract, Robert Heller & Associates and the Pennsylvania Railroad Company, January 11, 1952; "The Pennsylvania Railroad Company Passenger Operations—Draft of Report, July 26, 1954"; Franklin to Symes and Carpi, October 9, 1951; Laurence T. Mayher to Symes, April 4, 1952; Symes to Franklin, December 12, 1952; "Extension of Contract with Heller Associates, Board meeting 12-17-52"; Walter W. Patchell to Franklin, May 29, 1953; Patchell to Franklin, January 18, 1954; all in PHMC, Box 76 (9-2124), folder 521.3; Peter Lyon, *To Hell in a Day Coach: An Exasperated Look at American Railroads* (New York: Lippincott, 1968), 240.

179. Ira Silverman, "Cutting and Pasting," *Railroad History* 223 (Fall–Winter 2020): 54–61.

180. "The Pennsylvania Railroad Company Passenger Operations—Draft of Report, July 26, 1954," PHMC, Box 76 (9-2124), folder 521.3.

181. "Draft of Report, July 26, 1954"; Silverman, "Cutting and Pasting," 59–60.

182. "Draft of Report, July 26, 1954"; Mayher to Symes, September 26, 1952; both in PHMC, Box 76 (9-2124), folder 521.3.

183. "Draft of Report, July 26, 1954" ("tolerate"); Newell, Carpi, and Patchell to Symes, in response to Heller report, July 1954; both in HML, Box 341, folder 2 ("conceding," "theoretical").

184. Newell to Symes, December 10, 1952 ("secured," "initiative"); both in PHMC, Box 76 (9-2124), folder 521.3; Silverman, "Cutting and Pasting," 57.

185. Symes to Franklin, December 18, 1952; Newell to Symes, February 4, 1953 ("developments," "wholeheartedly," "people," "fresh"); both in PHMC, Box 76 (9-2124), folder 521.3.

186. Harry L. Nancarrow to Newell, July 17, 1953, PHMC, Box 76 (9-2124), folder 521.3; "Robert Heller Associates—Coordination of Services," minutes of meetings, October 1, 1953, October 7–8, 1953, October 14–15, 1953, October 22–23, 1953, HML, Box 341, folder 2; PRR memorandum, June 3, 1953, PHMC, Box 76 (9-2124), folder 521.3; Silverman, "Cutting and Pasting," 59–61.

187. Newell to Symes, September 28, 1954, HML, Box 341, folder 2 ("responsible," "wants," "economically," "necessarily"); "Memorandum to Mr. W. W. Patchell Regarding Steps and Progress in Eliminating Passenger Deficit," PHMC, Box 76 (9-2124), folder 521.3.

188. James M. Symes, "Railroad Needs of the Nation Ten Years Hence," address delivered at the General Motors Powerama, Chicago, Illinois, September 7, 1955, 17 ("promise," "potential," "lower"); "Draft of Report, July 26, 1954" ("satisfactory"), PHMC, Box 76 (9-2124), folder 521.3.

189. Development work on the TALGO began in Spain in 1942, and the name was an acronym for Tren Articulado Ligero Goicoechea Oriol (articulated lightweight train of Alejandro Goicoechea and José Luis Oriol). Goicoechea designed the system, with financing provided by Oriol. ACF delivered TALGO trainsets to Spain in 1950. They operated successfully along a mountainous line linking Madrid with the French border, but observers noted the extremely poor riding quality. Spain had not fully recovered from the brutal civil war of the 1930s, remained under the autocratic rule of Francisco

Franco, and was one of the least economically developed nations in Europe. The TALGO units were thus adequate for a country where there were fewer air and highway travel options than in the United States. ACF did not receive the contract to build additional TALGO sets for the Spanish market. In 1953, the company built a demonstrator in hopes of winning domestic orders. Later TALGO equipment demonstrated a vast improvement in quality and is currently in use in Spain, the United States, and several other countries.

190. *New York Times*, April 22, 1954; May 6, 1954; June 30, 1954; White, *American Railroad Passenger Car*, 627–28; Talgo North America, "History," http://web.talgoamerica.com/history, accessed June 22, 2019.

191. *New York Times*, June 30, 1954 ("Cadillac"); July 4, 1954; September 20, 1954; February 24, 1955; March 6, 1955.

192. The Boston & Maine (controlled by the New Haven) operated the *Speed Merchant*, a close copy of the *John Quincy Adams*.

193. The New York Central more closely followed the Train X concept that Young had brought with him from the Chesapeake & Ohio. The result was the NYC's *Xplorer*, which entered service in 1956 and was withdrawn in 1957. Santa Fe officials went in a radically different direction. Taking advantage of their railroad's generous clearances, they worked with Budd to develop bi-level passenger cars that were larger than traditional equipment. The Santa Fe ordered two experimental bi-level cars in 1954. The results of the lightweight train research consortium convinced Santa Fe officials of the superiority of their design, and they ordered an additional forty-seven cars in 1956. Used on the *El Capitan* luxury coach streamliner, the cars were the culmination of the designs that Raymond Loewy had advocated a decade earlier. They were also the only successful result of the discussions that McGinnis had initiated in 1954. *New York Times*, March 6, 1955; January 9, 1957; January 10, 1957; February 13, 1957; John F. Kirkland, *The Diesel Builders, Volume 1: Fairbanks-Morse and Lima-Hamilton* (Glendale, CA: Interurban, 1985), 62–65; Sy Reich, "Twilight of the New Haven Electrics," *Railroad Magazine* 70, no. 4 (June 1959): 48–51; White, *American Railroad Passenger Car*, 195–96.

194. Curtice emphasized that GM "has no intention of going into the railroad-passenger-car building business. It is primarily interested in the promotion of the use of its diesel motive power and presents the new cars as a service to its customers."

195. Each trainset cost $1.2 million, but that included the power unit.

196. In addition to the two *Aerotrain* power units and associated coaches, in 1956 GM also provided an identical power unit for The Rock Island's *Jet Rocket*, operating between Chicago and Peoria, Illinois. ACF built the coaches to the TALGO design, and it was the first train of its type to enter regular revenue service in the United States.

197. Clifford B. Hicks, "Ten Buses Grow into a Train," *Popular Mechanics* 104, no. 3 (September 1955): 81–86 ("completely" at 82, "intention" at 83); *Railway Age* 139, no. 10 (September 5, 1955): 38–39; December 26, 1955, 30–31; Robert Tate, "Remembering Chuck Jordan, a Great Designer," *Motor Cities*, May 22, 2019, https://www.motorcities.org/story-of-the-week/2019/remembering-chuck-jordan-a-great-designer, accessed June 22, 2019.

198. Symes to Nelson C. Dezendorf, January 24, 1955 ("earmarks"); C. K. Steins to H. T. Cover, March 4, 1955; Dezendorf to Symes, March 17, 1955; "Memorandum of Meeting Held at LaGrange, Illinois," March 31, 1955; "Birth of a New Train," n.d., ca. 1955; W. W. Patchell to Symes, September 1, 1955; all in HML, Box 341, folder 3; *New York Times*, January 8, 1956; February 5, 1956; White, *American Railroad Passenger Car*, 629.

199. *New York Times*, December 20, 1955; January 6, 1956; January 12, 1956; *Railway Age* 140, no. 3 (January 16, 1956): 6–7.

200. Service between New York and Philadelphia proved problematic, for two reasons. First, with diesel power banned in the Hudson River tunnels, an electric locomotive was required to move the train in and out of Penn Station. Second, high-level platforms made it difficult for passengers to enter and exit the train.

201. The New York Central's experience with its *Aerotrain* was even shorter and was equally poor. Regular operations between Chicago and Detroit began on April 29, 1956. Less than a month later, the train stalled near Battle Creek, Michigan, forcing the transfer of passengers to another train. The same complaints regarding poor riding qualities led the NYC to discontinue the service on October 27. GM transferred the train to the Union Pacific for evaluation on the route between Los Angeles and Las Vegas. The UP also subsequently used the ex-PRR *Aerotrain* along that line. In addition to the usual issues involving noise and swaying, the 1,200-horsepower engines in each unit were not sufficiently powerful to climb the grades of Cajon Pass without a helper. The UP withdrew both *Aerotrains* from service, and the trains

finished their brief careers hauling commuters on the Rock Island. *New York Times*, January 6, 1956 ("knows"); January 8, 1956; January 18, 1956; February 22, 1956; February 26, 1956; February 28, 1956; April 19, 1956; June 24, 1956; June 26, 1956; October 9, 1956; September 13, 1958; *New York Daily News*, March 9, 1956.

202. *New York Times*, February 24, 1955 ("accommodation"); March 6, 1955; White, *American Railroad Passenger Car*, 196–97.

203. *Railway Age* 138, no. 13 (March 25, 1955): 6; 140, no. 25 (June 18, 1956): 36–40; *New York Times*, June 17, 1956 ("target," "teetering"); June 23, 1990.

204. Between 1958 and 1961, PRR officials studied twelve other possibilities for improved New York–Washington service. They included the Curtiss-Wright "Propeller Train" and the "Minneapolis-Honeywell Jet-Capsule Tube"—which, for an estimated investment of $1 billion, would have used turbo-prop engines to propel passenger pods through a 10-foot-diameter low-pressure pipeline at speeds of three hundred miles per hour. *Plainfield* [New Jersey] *Courier-News*, June 14, 1956 ("personally"); *New York Times*, June 17, 1956; White, *American Railroad Passenger Car*, 196–97.

205. Address of Vice President Richard Nixon to the Governors' Conference, Lake George, New York July 12, 1954, https://www.fhwa.dot.gov/infrastructure/rw96m .cfm, accessed May 7, 2019 ("transportation," "Cabinet").

206. James D. Panza, Richard W. Dawson, and Ronald P. Sellberg, *The TTX Story, Volume 1* (Kutztown, PA: Pennsylvania Railroad Technical and Historical Society, 2018), 9; Chuck Blardone; *Pennsylvania Railroad Advertising Art, Featuring the Ed Lied Collection* (Bryn Mawr, PA: Pennsylvania Railroad Technical and Historical Society, 2013), 110.

207. The Long Island Rail Road built some specialized cars for this purpose in 1886, but the service declined in popularity and was abandoned after about a decade.

208. Initially, the North Shore owned both the flatcars and highway trailers used in TOFC service. In 1932, the company offered to transport the equipment of shippers and independent motor carriers, causing a surge in business. The following year, the Wisconsin Public Service Commission concluded that the operation enabled truckers to avoid highway taxes and banned the practice. The agency reversed the order in 1936, and traffic again grew substantially, but it ended in 1947. The South Shore service ended in the mid-1930s. Both companies were interurban lines; as such, their TOFC equipment could not be interchanged with the PRR or other main line railroads.

209. The Denver & Rio Grande Western, the Rock Island, and the Burlington also experimented with piggyback during the 1930s. "Brief History of Piggyback," n.d., HML, Box 1417, folder 21; David J. DeBoer, *Piggyback and Containers: A History of Rail Intermodal on America's Steel Highway* (San Marino, CA: Golden West, 1992), 17–25; Panza, Dawson, and Sellberg, *TTX Story, Volume 1*, 10–15; Brian Solomon, *Intermodal Railroading* (St. Paul, MN: Voyageur, 2007), 26–31; H. Roger Grant, *The Corn Belt Route: A History of the Chicago Great Western Railroad Company* (DeKalb: Northern Illinois University Press, 1984); 119–21.

210. J. F. Deasy to H. W. Jones, March 26, 1941; "Transportation on Flat Cars of Trailers of Motor Truck Carriers Operating over the Highway," July 16, 1941 ("volume," "attempt"); both in HML, Box 334, folder 7.

211. Giles Morrow and G. Lloyd Wilson, "Some Problems of Freight Forwarders," *Annals of the American Academy of Political and Social Science* 230 (November 1943): 110–15, at 111–12; Hoogenboom, *History of the ICC*, 130–31; Mark H. Rose, Bruce E. Seely, and Paul F. Barrett, *The Best Transportation System in the World: Railroads, Trucks, Airlines, and American Public Policy in the Twentieth Century* (Columbus: Ohio State University Press, 2006), 115.

212. Regardless of who controlled them, forwarders could employ trucks or other vehicles for local pickup or delivery operations but were not permitted to own or operate their own equipment in intercity service. Morrow and Wilson, "Some Problems of Freight Forwarders," 111–12; Jeffrey S. Wood, "Intermodal Transportation and the Freight Forwarder," *Yale Law Journal* 76 (1967): 1360–96, at 1369, 1391–92.

213. Under the terminal area exemption, motor carriers could transport freight within a municipal zone free from ICC regulation, even if the movement crossed state lines—a situation that applied in areas such as New York, Philadelphia, and St. Louis.

214. As had long been the case with boxcar and container service, LCL shipments by rail were based on the class-rate structure. Once a freight forwarder collected and bundled a diverse collection of packages into a single lot suitable for transportation by boxcar, container, or truck trailer, it was able to present a single shipment to the railroad, one that traveled under a weight-based freight-all-kinds (all-commodity) rate. William E. Thoms, "Rollin' On . . . to a Free Market: Motor Carrier Regulation, 1935–1980," *Transportation Law Journal* 13, no. 1 (1983): 44–86, at 66–67; "Intermodal Transportation and the Freight Forwarder," 1369, 1382.

215. *Railway Age* 128, no. 5 (February 4, 1950): 56; 128, no. 8 (February 25, 1950): 33–37 ("delayed," "efficient"); 138, no. 15 (April 11, 1955): 12 ("substantial").

216. Clement to Franklin, September 6, 1949 ("worse," "increased"); Clement to Franklin, July 31, 1950; Clement to Franklin, March 23, 1951 ("drastic," "charge," "addition"); all in PHMC, Franklin papers, Box 59 (9-2091), folder 230; Clement to Symes, Carpi, et al., June 6, 1951 ("competitive," develop"); all in PHMC, Box 59 (9-2091), folder 230.

217. Panza, Dawson, and Sellberg, *TTX Story, Volume 1*, 9–10; Pennsylvania Railroad Company, *One Hundredth Annual Report, for the Year Ended December 31, 1946* (Philadelphia: n.p., 1947), 27; Pennsylvania Railroad Company, *One Hundred and Ninth Annual Report, for the Year Ended December 31, 1955* (Philadelphia: n.p., 1946), 60.

218. *Railway Age* 136, no. 3 (January 18, 1954): 8–9; 136, no. 18 (May 3, 1954): 9–10; 137, no. 23 (December 6, 1954): 36–39; December 13, 1954, 51–61; *Movement of Highway Trailers by Rail*, 293 ICC 93 (1954); Panza, Dawson, and Sellberg, *TTX Story, Volume 1*, 15–16; Solomon, *Intermodal Railroading*, 32; John H. Mahoney, *Intermodal Freight Transportation* (Westport, CT: Eno Foundation for Transportation, 1985), 9, 44–45; DeBoer, *Piggyback and Containers*, 35–41; Richard Saunders Jr., *Merging Lines: American Railroads, 1900–1970* (DeKalb: Northern Illinois University Press, 2001), 127.

219. "Pennsylvania Railroad: Management Organization, Effective November 1, 1955," HML, Box 1646, folder 1; Robert E. Bedingfield, "Personality: Ex-Rail Official Now on Siding," *New York Times*, March 13, 1966; Panza, Dawson, and Sellberg, *TTX Story, Volume 1*, 39; DeBoer, *Piggyback and Containers*, 34–35.

220. Carpi was not alone in his fears, as officials on many railroads moved cautiously into TOFC service for that very reason. David DeBoer—whose career with both the NYC and the Federal Railroad Administration enabled him to become one of the key architects of rail-based intermodalism—has observed that piggyback rates "had to be put low enough to attract the trucker, but high enough (under value of service pricing) to cover the most expensive freight in the trailer so that as a result of this charge other similar high-value freight would not be drawn out of boxcars." *Wall Street Journal*, January 12, 1956; DeBoer, *Piggyback and Containers*, 21–25, 35 ("attract").

221. *New York Times*, April 30, 1954; May 27, 1954; Newell to Franklin and Symes, April 26, 1954 ("recommendation," "furnish," "volume," "financial"); PRR press release, April 30, 1954 ("benefits"); both in PHMC, Box 85 (9-2236).

222. Newell to Franklin and Symes, April 26, 1954 ("inaugurated," "facilities"); Newell to David C. Bevan, May 12, 1954; Bevan to Newell, May 13, 1954; Bevan to Franklin, May 19, 1954; all in PHMC, Box 85 (9-2236); *Railway Age* 136, no. 18 (May 3, 1954): 8; 136, no. 21 (May 24, 1954): 6; Mike Nesladek, "Pennsy's TrucTrain Service," *Keystone* 25, no. 3 (Autumn 1992): 17–48, at 19–20.

223. *Railway Age* 136, no. 25 (June 21, 1954): 7–8; Josephine Ayre, "History and Regulation of Trailer-on-Flatcar Movement," *Highway Research Record* 153 (1967): 1–30, at 4–7; Eugene D. Anderson and Dickson R. Loos, "Piggyback Plans," *Boston College Industrial and Commercial Law Review* 3, no. 3 (Spring 1962): 335–54, at 338–39.

224. *New York Times*, June 16, 1954; June 18, 1954; June 23, 1954; June 30, 1954 ("wide," "dangerous"); July 30, 1954.

225. For an overview of the complex legal and regulatory issues associated with TOFC service, see Irving Kovarsky, "State Piggyback Statutes and Federalism," *Industrial and Labor Relations Review* 18, no. 1 (October 1964): 45–59; and "'Piggyback' Service under the Interstate Commerce Act," *Columbia Law Review* 66, no. 2 (February 1966): 318–37. *New York Times*, July 10, 1954; July 30, 1954 ("maintain," "competitive"); August 7, 1954 ("monumental"); *Railway Age* 137, no. 24 (December 13, 1954): 52; *Railway Age* 137, no. 23 (December 6, 1954): 36–39; Panza, Dawson, and Sellberg, *TTX Story, Volume 1*, 15–16; Solomon, *Intermodal Railroading*, 32; Mahoney, *Intermodal Freight Transportation*, 9, 44–45; DeBoer, *Piggyback and Containers*, 35–41; Saunders, *Merging Lines*, 127.

226. The Wabash, Erie, Lackawanna, and Nickel Plate also began Plan II service on July 12.

227. "Questions That Are Most Likely to Be in the Minds of Stockholders," 1955, 14–15; PHMC, Box 35 (9-2186), folder 111.01; "Back-Up Data: TrucTrain Report," Appendix B, Exhibit 1, Sheet 2; PHMC, Box 85 (9-2236), folder 620.05; *New York Times*, July 13, 1954; March 4, 1955; *Pittsburgh Post-Gazette*, January 3, 1955; *Railway Age* 137, no. 16 (October 18, 1954): 8; 137, no. 24 (December 13, 1954): 52; Pennsylvania Railroad Company, *One Hundred and Eighth Annual Report, for the Year Ended December 31, 1954* (Philadelphia: n.p., 1955), 12–13; Nesladek, "Pennsy's TrucTrain Service," 19–21; Panza, Dawson, and Sellberg, *TTX Story, Volume 1*, 18–21.

228. Walter Patchell to Newell, May 6, 1954; J. B. Prizer to Newell, May 7, 1954 ("registrable"); Newell to Prizer, May 10, 1954; Prizer to Newell and Carpi, May 18, 1954;

all in PHMC, Box 85 (9-2236); *Railway Age* 136, no. 24 (June 14, 1954): 7.

229. By the time the PRR began TOFC service, the company had consolidated its trucking subsidiaries into three groups that corresponded with the Eastern Region (Scott Brothers and Merchants' Trucking, based in Philadelphia), the Central Region (Pennsylvania Truck Lines and Buffalo Storage & Carting, based in Pittsburgh), and the Western Region (the PennTruck Company, based in Chicago). In 1953, PennTruck established the PennTruck Leasing Company, which in turn leased intermodal trailers to the PRR.

230. *Railway Age* 138, no. 21 (May 23, 1955): 31–32; Nesladek, "Pennsy's TrucTrain Service," 26–36; Panza, Dawson, and Sellberg, *TTX Story, Volume 1*, 22–24.

231. Newell to Symes, May 13, 1954; Symes to Newell, May 14, 1954 ("support," advocating"); Newell to Prizer, May 19, 1954; all in PHMC, Box 85 (9-2236).

232. Even as vice president, Hoffa had considerable influence over the operation of the union and the negotiation of labor agreements. He became president of the Teamsters in 1957. In an effort to gain Hoffa's support, Ryan agreed that Teamsters would perform all draying operations for Rail-Trailer, including those at PRR facilities. That agreement gave Hoffa considerable leverage in his efforts to make the Teamsters the bargaining agent for all railroad employees who worked at freight houses, based on the logic that freight-house operations inevitably involved truck transportation. *Railway Age* 137, no. 14 (October 4, 1954): 7; DeBoer, *Piggyback and Containers*, 27–28, 45; Solomon, *Intermodal Railroading*, 40; Saunders, *Merging Lines*, 126.

233. DeBoer, *Piggyback and Containers*, 27–31; Solomon, *Intermodal Railroading*, 40; *Railway Age* 137, no. 23 (December 6, 1954): 44; Panza, Dawson, and Sellberg, *TTX Story, Volume 1*, 25, 116.

234. The desire to avoid the expensive facilities that Ryan and his EMD team had recommended in turn doomed the depressed-center flatcar they had designed. Because it was lower in the center than at the ends, the car required the use of a side-access forklift and could not be loaded and unloaded, circus style, at the inexpensive piggyback ramps that railroad executives typically favored.

235. For example, boxcar LCL freight moving between Providence and Baltimore would logically travel over the PRR south of New York. The New Haven's TOFC service, however, might encourage truckers to offload trailers in New York and drive them south to Baltimore, thus depriving the PRR of any share of the revenue.

236. Karl A. Borntrager, *Keeping the Railroads Running: Fifty Years on the New York Central* (New York: Hastings House, 1974), 189–90; New York Central System, *Headlight*, February 1954, 1; Panza, Dawson, and Sellberg, *TTX Story, Volume 1*, 14–15, 114–19; DeBoer, *Piggyback and Containers*, 29–31, 34, 51–54, 63–65, 83.

237. The subsequent group of PRR-built F39a and F39b cars as well as the shorter F30d cars remained PRR property.

238. *Railway Age* 138, no. 10 (March 7, 1955): 7–8; DeBoer, *Piggyback and Containers*, 40–44.

239. Even after the development of the American Car & Foundry Model A retractable kingpin hitch in 1956, many railroads refused to accept loaded cars in interchange unless the trailers were also secured with tie-down chains. Nesladek, "Pennsy's TrucTrain Service," 39–40; DeBoer, *Piggyback and Containers*, 45–48; Curtis D. Buford, *Trailer Train Company: A Unique Force in the Railroad Industry* (New York: Newcomen Society in North America, 1982), 15–16.

240. The ICC required that the PRR employ a "mixing rule" in its Plan II (railroad-owned) service, such that each trailer must contain at least two commodities (each of which traveled at a separate rate) and no one commodity could account for more than 60 percent of the shipment.

241. PRR press release, June 21, 1956, HML, Box 278, folder 6; Nesladek, "Pennsy's TrucTrain Service," 30; DeBoer, *Piggyback and Containers*, 39; Buford, *Trailer Train Company*, 12–13; *Popular Science* 166, no. 5 (May 1955): 102–3.

242. The membership date of record for the PRR, the N&W, and Rail-Trailer was March 17, 1956. The key to Trailer Train's success was not the relatively small amount of equity that each member railroad contributed when it acquired a block of the company's stock. Rather, it lay in the commitment of each member railroad to guarantee a proportion of Trailer Train's debt, thus enabling the company to secure the financing that its operations required. Newell and other Trailer Train officials initially avoided reliance on equipment-trust financing (in which banks or other creditors would accept a lien on the equipment as security for the loan), as that would have necessitated a 20 percent down payment and would have required Trailer Train to register with the Securities and Exchange Commission. Instead, Trailer Train employed conditional sales agreements, in which member railroads agreed to fulfill payment obligations should Trailer Train default. Trailer Train Company, press release, December 21, 1955; Howard C. Kohout to

Allen J. Greenough, April 8, 1956; "Trailer Train Company (TTX): Report by James P. Newell to the Board of Directors of the Pennsylvania Railroad Company," June 25, 1958; Newell "Trailer Train Company," September 23, 1958; all in PHMC, Box 211 (9-2380); Panza, Dawson, and Sellberg, *TTX Story, Volume 1*, 25–34, 77–78, 86; DeBoer, *Piggyback and Containers*, 59, 67–69, 74, 105–7; Buford, *Trailer Train Company*, 13–14, 21.

243. Trailer Train acquired the PRR's flatcars along with the two hundred owned by Rail-Trailer's subsidiary, Van-Car, that had been leased to the PRR.

244. DeBoer, *Piggyback and Containers*, 67–69, 74, 105–7; Buford, *Trailer Train Company*, 13–14, 21.

245. They included the two hundred Class F39 cars (built by Bethlehem Steel) from Van-Trailer as well as the three hundred Class F39a and F39b cars built by the PRR. Subsequent Trailer Train purchases also conformed to PRR designs.

246. PRR officials occupied most of Trailer Train's executive positions as well. They included secretary Bayard H. Roberts (who was also the PRR's secretary), comptroller Hugh J. Ward (also the PRR's comptroller), vice president Paul D. Fox, treasurer William R. Gerstnecker, and assistant treasurers John H. Shaffer and D. M. Cull (the PRR's assistant vice president in charge of finance, treasurer, assistant treasurer, and assistant to the treasurer, respectively). Gene Ryan, Trailer Train's vice president and general manager, was the only Rail-Trailer representative among the ranks of senior executives.

247. While all official correspondence bore the Haverford address, beginning in October 1959, Trailer Train's corporate offices were located at Six Penn Center in Philadelphia, a building that was part of the PRR's redevelopment of the Broad Street Station site. Trailer Train's operational headquarters was in Chicago, at the PRR's Polk Street Freight House—for which the company paid the PRR a monthly rental of $30. Both locations reinforced perceptions that the PRR controlled Trailer Train. Newell and other PRR executives insisted that the Polk Street office be kept separate from the headquarters of Rail-Trailer, on North La Salle Street, to avoid giving the impression that Rail-Trailer dictated policy to Trailer Train. David Bevan to P. N. Cristal, February 23, 1956, HML, Box 278, folder 4; Newell to Symes, November 26, 1958; Trailer Train Company press release, December 23, 1958; W. A. Lashley to Stuart Saunders, July 24, 1964; all in PHMC, Box 211 (9-2380); Panza, Dawson, and Sellberg, *TTX Story, Volume 1*, 25–34, 86–88.

248. William B. Johnson to John B. Prizer, March 23, 1956 ("fluctuated," "anything"), HML, Box 278, folder 5;

"Back-Up Data: TrucTrain Report," Appendix B, Exhibit 1, Sheets 3–4 ("obstacles," "ability," "advantage"), PHMC, Box 85 (9-2236), folder 620.05.

249. "Appendix B—Growth of Trailer-on-Flatcar Service," HML, Box 125, folder 8; J. P. Newell, minutes of April 20th meeting with PRR and trucking industry representatives, April 24, 1956, HML, Box 278, folder 6 ("feeling," "dismal," "divergent"); DeBoer, *Piggyback and Containers*, 48–49.

250. Newell, "Memorandum Covering Meeting of TTX and PRR Officials with Officers of the Chesapeake & Ohio Railroad," September 25, 1959 ("kaput"), PHMC, Box 211 (9-2380); Nesladek, "Pennsy's TrucTrain Service," 36–37.

251. While SAL, ACL, and Southern officials were generally supportive of TOFC service and inclusion in the Trailer Train equipment pool, there was nonetheless considerable discussion regarding the avoidance of the PRR's restricted-clearance tunnels in Baltimore and Washington.

252. Panza, Dawson, and Sellberg, *TTX Story, Volume 1*, 53–62.

253. The transfer of trailers from one railroad car to another at interchange points was anathema to Newell, but it benefited Ryan—if Rail Trail held the contract to perform terminal services.

254. The Frisco joined Trailer Train on May 4, 1956, followed by the MP and the Katy (on May 14), then the Boston & Maine and the Burlington (on November 26). The Chicago & North Western joined in 1957. The B&O's 1958 membership was an important milestone in the history of Trailer Train, as it was the first direct competitor of the PRR to join the consortium. The Atlantic Coast Line and the Seaboard Air Line became members in 1959 (along with the Illinois Central; the Gulf, Mobile & Ohio; the Louisville & Nashville; the Nickel Plate; the Cotton Belt; and the Western Pacific). The Santa Fe and the Southern did not join until 1960. The New York Central was one of the last carriers to gain membership in Trailer Train, effective March 1, 1964. William B. Johnson to R. W. Tackbary, August 3, 1956 ("worked"); Johnson to C. R. Tucker (draft), August 1956; PRR press release, June 12, 1956; PRR press release, September 7, 1956; J. P. Newell memo, April 11, 1956; "TrucTrain Service for Motor Common Carriers to and from New England," April 4, 1956; all in HML, Box 278, folder 6; "TrucTrain Expansion," November 15, 1955, HML, Box 278, folder 1; *New York Times*, September 7, 1956.

255. Wisely, Trailer Train officials made the specifications of the Class F85 flatcar available to railroads that

were not members of Trailer Train—ensuring compati-
bility and making their integration into the Trailer Train
fleet an easy matter should those carriers later join the
equipment pool. Nesladek, "Pennsy's TrucTrain Service,"
40; DeBoer, *Piggyback and Containers*, 68–70; Panza,
Dawson, and Sellberg, *TTX Story, Volume 1*, 136–39.

256. "PRR Relationship to Rail-Trailer—Effect on
Interchange Arrangements for Common Carrier Traffic,"
April 1956 ("outstanding"), HML, Box 278, folder 6; J. P.
Newell to E. F. Ryan, January 30, 1956, HML, Box 278,
folder 3; Panza, Dawson, and Sellberg, *TTX Story, Volume
1*, 43–45 ("happy," "disturbing"), 51.

257. "PRR Relationship to Rail-Trailer" ("qualified").

258. *Wall Street Journal*, April 9, 1959.

259. "L. C. L. Study, June 1960" ("recommended");
"Less Car Load Traffic—Class I Railroads," January 12,
1961; "Gross Freight Revenue from LCL and Forwarder
Traffic," January 31, 1961; Carpi to Patchell, November
9, 1960 ("stemmed," "compete"); Newell to Patchell,
November 11, 1960; Carpi to Greenough, February 14,
1961; Newell to Patchell, February 15, 1961; all in PHMC,
Box 85 (9-2236).

260. Newell's career change was not entirely voluntary.
Based on his post as vice president in charge of operations and augmented by the success of the TrucTrain
service he had supported, Newell could reasonably have
expected to succeed Symes as the PRR's president. Newell's ongoing disagreements with Fred Carpi had become
increasingly divisive, however, ensuring that neither
executive could be promoted to that post. On November
1, 1959, Allen J. Greenough (the vice president in charge
of transportation and maintenance) became the surprise
choice (even to him) for the presidency. Symes remained
in power as chief executive officer in the reestablished
office of chairman of the board. Newell survived Greenough's subsequent attempts to force him out of the
company only because he could rely on the protection
of his patron, Symes. During the summer of 1963, in
anticipation of his retirement, Symes recruited Stuart
Saunders—the Norfolk & Western's original representative on the Trailer Train board—to succeed him as board
chairman and CEO. With Symes's departure at the end
of September, Newell's days at the PRR were numbered.
Symes assisted his old ally one last time, arranging for
Newell to become Trailer Train's full-time president and
CEO on November 1.

261. Each of the forty-one members owned 500 shares
apiece, requiring the periodic issuance of additional
stock—reaching a maximum of 20,500 shares, compared
to the initial 1955 issue of 6,000 shares.

262. Panza, Dawson, and Sellberg, *TTX Story, Volume 1*,
39, 64–65, 84–85.

263. Fred Carpi, who remained skeptical of the benefits
of intermodal service, considered the modifications to
the Baltimore tunnels to be a waste of money. Symes,
who tended to back Newell in such matters, suggested
"that it is highly desirable that we round out our pig-
gy-back service between our Eastern seaboard points
and the South. A $300,000 expenditure is negligible as
compared with the overall benefits." "Memorandum:
Baltimore, Maryland—B&P Tunnel—TrucTrain
Clearance," May 26, 1959; Newell to Carpi, May 29, 1959;
Symes to Newell, June 3, 1959 ("desirable"); all in PHMC,
Box 211 (9-2380).

264. In 1966, two years before its merger with the
New York Central, the Pennsylvania Railroad operated
thirty-two TrucTrain terminals. The introduction of a
variety of straddle cranes, culminating with Pacific Coast
Engineering's Paceco TransTrainer, required a significant capital outlay (PRR officials estimated between
$40,000 and $75,000 per facility), and there was little
economic justification for their installation at low-vol-
ume terminals.

265. TrucTrain service continued after the Penn Central merger but was soon consolidated with the NYC's
Flexi-Van operations under the trade name TrailVan.
"Questions That Are Most Likely to Be in the Minds of
Stockholders," 1956, 14; "Questions That Are Most Likely
to Be in the Minds of Stockholders," 1959, 15; both in
PHMC, Box 35 (9-2186), folder 111.01; *Pennsy*, December
21, 1964, 7; September 1, 1965, October 1, 1965, 7; October
15, 1965, 7; September 15, 1967, 7; Nesladek, "Pennsy's
TrucTrain Service," 40–48; Ayre, "History and Regu-
lation," 5–8; DeBoer, *Piggyback and Containers*, 85–86;
Panza, Dawson, and Sellberg, *TTX Story, Volume 1*, 16–18;
Solomon, *Intermodal Railroading*, 34–35; Peter E. Lynch,
Penn Central Railroad (St. Paul, MN: MBI, 2004), 19;
Anderson and Loos, "Piggyback Plans," 339–40.

266. Pabst had been with the company since 1906, when
he was a clerk in the Accounting Department. He later
became an assistant to Samuel Rea. When Henry H. Lee
resigned the treasurer's office in 1929 to assume the presidency of the Pennroad investment trust, Pabst replaced
him. Eleven years later, Pabst became the vice president
in charge of finance and corporate relations.

267. PRR BOD Minutes.

268. Many years later, David Bevan recalled that Martin
Clement attended the funeral and put his arm around the
shoulders of a grieving son. John Woolf Jordan, *Colonial
and Revolutionary Families of Pennsylvania: Genealogical*

and Personal Memoirs (New York: Lewis, 1911), 136–41; James J. Levick, "The Early Welsh Quakers and Their Emigration to Pennsylvania," *Pennsylvania Magazine of History and Biography* 17, no. 4 (1893): 385–413.

269. Stephen Salsbury, *No Way to Run a Railroad: The Untold Story of the Penn Central Crisis* (New York: McGraw-Hill, 1982), 33–34, 40–54; *Haverford College, The Record—1929*, 30 ("ambition"); *Altoona Tribune*, April 26, 1951; *Philadelphia Inquirer*, October 24, 1938; Andy Wallace, "David C. Bevan, 89, of Gladwyne, Penn Central Railroad Executive," *Philadelphia Inquirer*, April 11, 1996.

270. Symes to Herman Pevler et al., December 30, 1948 ("recent," "obtain," "mechanization"); Study of Possibilities of Use of Mechanical Devices on the Pennsylvania Railroad to Reduce Cost of Assembling, Compiling and Using Records Essential for Efficient Operation, January 12, 1949; Symes to Carpi et al., February 10, 1949 ("objective"); all in HML, Box 315, folder 8.

271. John L. Webb to Symes, September 19, 1951, HML, Box 315, folder 8 ("first"); *Railway Age* 127, no. 12 (September 17, 1949): 90–91; 128, no. 24 (June 17, 1950): 80; 129, no. 2 (July 8, 1950): 36–37; 130, no. 12 (March 26, 1951): 32–33; 130, no. 18 (May 7, 1951): 42–44; 139, no. 5 (January 31, 1955): 33; 140, no. 12 (March 19, 1956): 13; 141, no. 12 (September 17, 1956): 24–25; Ticketeer Circular #1, July 30, 1954, https://www.multimodalways.org/docs /railroads/companies/PRR/PRR%20Ticketeer%20 Circular%20%231%207-30-1954.pdf; Ticket Sales and Service Matrices for Ticketeers July 26, 1954, https://www .multimodalways.org/docs/railroads/companies/PRR /PRR%20Ticket%20Sales%20Matrices%207-26-1954 .pdf; accessed November 3, 2023.

272. Pennsylvania Railroad Voluntary Relief Department Actuarial Report, July 6, 1963, HML, Box 853, folder 1; "Memorandum in Connection with Installation of I.B.M. Machines in the Relief Department," HML, Box 853, folder 3 ("desirable"); "Memorandum of Items for Stockholders' Meeting, April 6, 1956," HML, Box 326 folder 8 ("centralize," "electronic," "improving"); *Railway Age* 138, no. 12 (March 21, 1955): 7; 144, no. 7 (February 17, 1958): 22.

273. Salsbury, *No Way to Run a Railroad*, 50–54.

274. Pennsylvania Railroad, *One Hundred and Sixth Annual Report*, 65.

275. Pennsylvania Railroad, *One Hundred and Sixth Annual Report*, 9.

276. *New York Times*, July 25, 1957; December 31, 1957; *Railway Age* 143, no. 5 (July 29, 1957): 11–12; 143, no. 6 (August 5, 1957): 13–14; 143, no. 15 (October 7, 1957): 9–11; 143, no. 16 (October 14, 1957): 9–10; 143, no. 19

(November 4, 1957): 30–33; "Limitations on the Scope of the After-Acquired Property Clause," *Columbia Law Review* 53, no. 3 (March 1953): 392–406; Frank J. Fabozzi, *Fixed Income Securities*, 2nd ed. (New York: John Wiley Sons, 2002), 153–56.

277. Pennsylvania Railroad, *One Hundred and Thirteenth Annual Report*, 10.

278. Pennsylvania Railroad, *One Hundred and Sixth Annual Report*, 37.

279. Joseph R. Warner, "Pennsylvania Railroad Financing, Part VIII," May 1, 1954, HML, Box 288, folder 14.

280. PRR BOD Minutes; Pennsylvania Railroad, *One Hundred and First Annual Report*, 11–12 ("already"); Pennsylvania Railroad Company, *One Hundred and Second Annual Report, for the Year Ended December 31, 1948* (Philadelphia: n.p., 1949), 14.

281. The directors apparently heeded that advice, at least in part, and in June they agreed to suspend the quarterly dividend, for the first time since 1949.

282. Bevan, Memorandum regarding proposed termination of the "Trust of 1878," HML, Box 326, folder 15 ("outlived," "flexibility," "contemplated").

283. Warner, "Pennsylvania Railroad Financing, Part VIII," 3 ("formulated," "overhauling"); [Hagerstown, MD] *Daily Mail*, May 12, 1953; *Railway Age* 109, no. 17 (October 26, 1940): 586–89.

284. Warner, "Pennsylvania Railroad Financing, Part VIII," 5 ("comparison"), 6 ("passenger").

285. "When we deal with the capitalizations of the Pennsylvania and the New York Central System, we have a factor that does not appear in like degree in any other major system. This is the existence of a large number of leaseholds, involving fixed charge rentals to cover interest on bonds and guaranteed dividends on stocks of lessor companies whose outstanding securities do not appear in the balance sheet or what is generally considered as embraced within the capital structure of the lessee . . . The Pennsylvania picture has been further complicated by its past practice of reporting gross rentals paid and including with other income the proportion of such rentals that flow back to the Pennsylvania Railroad Company as the owner of some of the leasehold companies' securities, but not those that came back to the System through the medium of the Pennsylvania Company. The latter were only taken over as and when the Pennsylvania Company paid over its earnings, in the form of dividends, to the Pennsylvania Railroad."

286. Warner, "Pennsylvania Railroad Financing, Part VIII," 4 ("complex"), includes "Capital Structure of Pennsylvania RR System and trend thereof over last

quarter century," 1 ("complicated," "compartmental"), 5 ("inexcusable").

287. PRR BOD Minutes; Thomas H. Carroll to Bevan, October 17, 1958 ("experience," "integral"), PHMC, Box 103 (9-2254), folder 110.01.

288. Pennsylvania Railroad, *One Hundred and Eighth Annual Report*, 9, 11; Pennsylvania Railroad, *One Hundred and Tenth Annual Report*, 23 ("minimum"), 32–33; PRR BOD Minutes; *New York Times*, June 24, 1954; Salsbury, *No Way to Run a Railroad*, 46–47.

289. Steep declines in new car sales and housing construction rather than Eisenhower's policies triggered the recession. The president nonetheless drew criticism for his aversion to fiscal policy remedies—a decision rooted in Republican economic conservatism and a fear of inflation. Richard W. Gable, "The Politics and Economics of the 1957–1958 Recession," *Western Political Quarterly* 12, no. 2 (June 1959): 557–59.

290. Domestic raw steel production decreased from 112.7 million tons in 1957 to 85.3 million tons in 1958. Output increased to 93.4 million tons in 1959, but a lengthy strike that year gave foreign producers an excellent opportunity to penetrate the American market, shifting the United States from a net exporter to a net importer of steel. Stephen K. McNees, "The 1990–91 Recession in Historical Perspective," *New England Economic Review* (January/February 1992): 3–22; Richard M. Duke, Richard L. Johnson, Hans Mueller, P. David Qualls, Calvin T. Roush Jr., and David G. Tarr, United States, Federal Trade Commission, Bureau of Economics, *The United States Steel Industry and Its International Rivals: Trends and Factors Determining International Competitiveness* (Washington, DC: United States Government Printing Office, 1977), 69–71.

291. For information on the development of the St. Lawrence Seaway, see William R. Willoughby, *The St. Lawrence Waterway: A Study in Politics and Diplomacy* (Madison: University of Wisconsin Press, 1961) and Daniel Macfarlane, *Negotiating a River: Canada, the US, and the Creation of the St. Lawrence Seaway* (Vancouver, UBC Press, 2014).

292. Pennsylvania Railroad Company, *One Hundred and Fifth Annual Report*, 16 ("estimates," "unjustifiable").

293. Electric utilities opposed the construction of the St. Lawrence Seaway because the project included the generation of competing hydroelectric power.

294. Dingell's claim that PRR executives instructed their counterparts at the Norfolk & Western to oppose the St. Lawrence Seaway was plausible. Less so were his assertions that PRR officials dictated policy to the

Richmond, Fredericksburg & Potomac Railroad, and "that the Pennsylvania Railroad's influence extends into Kansas and the southwestern territory through [the] Kansas, Oklahoma & Gulf Railroad, all of the directors of which are from Philadelphia and some holding interlocking directorates with the Pennsylvania Railroad."

295. Despite their opposition to the Seaway, PRR officials anticipated some benefits from the project. In 1957, for example, and in anticipation of increased traffic on Lake Michigan, the company spent $1.3 million to purchase Calumet Harbor Terminals, which maintained dock facilities along Lake Calumet, near Chicago. George D. Aiken, "The St. Lawrence Seaway," *Congressional Record*, 81st Cong., 2nd sess., 96, part 12 (December 11, 1950), 16405 ("fact"); "Extension of Remarks of Hon. John D. Dingell of Michigan in the House of Representatives, *Congressional Record*, 82nd Cong., 1st sess., 97, part 15 (October 11, 1951), A6319-20 ("opposition," "machinations," influence"); Freeman Lincoln, "Battle of the St. Lawrence," *Fortune*, December 1950, 84–90, 184–89, at 86 ("unaffected"); *New York Times*, April 25, 1959; *Railway Age* 143, no. 2 (July 8, 1957): 24–27; Willoughby, *St. Lawrence Waterway*, 210, 230–31, 256–58.

296. Exhibit Accompanying Testimony of James M. Symes, President, The Pennsylvania Railroad Company, Before the Surface Transportation Subcommittee, Senate Committee on Interstate and Foreign Commerce, Hearings on the Railroad Situation, January 1958, 11–13 (hereafter, Symes Testimony), 9–10; *New York Times*, October 23, 1958; Pennsylvania Railroad, *One Hundred and Eleventh Annual Report*, 12, 28–29.

297. *New York Times*, May 14, 1958 ("doubtful," "reduced," "promises," "fortunately"); *Pittsburgh Post-Gazette*, May 19, 1958 ("stomach"); Pennsylvania Railroad Company, *One Hundred and Twelfth Annual Report, for the Year Ended December 31, 1958* (Philadelphia: n.p., 1959), 16–17.

298. "Remarks by David C. Bevan, Vice President, Finance, the Pennsylvania Railroad Company, Before the New York Society of Security Analysts, June 13, 1958" ("red"); *New York Times*, June 14, 1958 ("outlook," "worst").

299. Symes Testimony, 9–10; "Remarks by David C. Bevan."

6. Decline

1. "A Railroad Man's Family at War: The Lightburns of Crestline, Ohio," n.d., but ca. 1943; Edgar E. Ernest to Martin Clement et al., October 6, 1948; Chief of

Passenger Transportation memo, October 8, 1948; all in Penn Central Railroad Collection, M. G. 286, Pennsylvania Historical and Museum Commission, Pennsylvania State Archives, Harrisburg (hereafter, PHMC), Box 21 (9-1617), folder 010.031; *Robert C. Lightburn, Benjamin Lightbourne/Lightburn of Westmoreland County, Pennsylvania and His Descendants* (Bloomington, IN: iUniverse, 2019).

2. *New York Times*, November 10, 1941; May 23, 1943; May 24, 1943; May 25, 1943; September 7, 1943 ("happen"); September 8, 1943; June 16, 1945 ("louder"); *Pittsburgh Post-Gazette*, March 17, 1941; Leon Barcousky, "Eyewitness: 1941: Saboteurs Never Found in Deadly Train Disaster," *Pittsburgh Post-Gazette*, April 3, 2011; National Highway Traffic Safety Administration, Fatalities and Fatality Rates (1899–2021), https://cdan.dot.gov /tsftables/Fatalities%20and%20Fatality%20Rates.pdf, accessed November 20, 2023.

3. *New York Times*, January 28, 1947; January 30, 1947; February 19, 1947 ("Most"); March 1, 1947; May 2, 1947; Bill Godby, "The Wreck of the Golden Triangle," *Keystone* 41 (Summer 2008): 55–60; Bill Godby, "The Wreck of the Red Arrow," *Keystone* 41 (Summer 2008): 60–65.

4. *Interstate Commerce Commission, Investigation No. 3206, the Pennsylvania Railroad Company, Report in re: Accident at West Bellevue, Pa., on October 6, 1948*, United States Department of Transportation, Office of the Assistant Secretary for Research and Technology, National Transportation Library, Investigations of Railroad Accidents, 1911–1993, https://planeandtrainwrecks.com /Document?db=DOT-RAILROAD&query=(select +0+(byhits+(general+(phrase+West+Bellevue)))), accessed November 20, 2023.

5. Mrs. James G. Lightburn to Clement, February 13, 1949 ("consolation," "lonesome," "planned"), PHMC, Box 21 (9-1617), folder 010.031.

6. Clement to Mrs. James G. Lightburn, October 11, 1948, PHMC, Box 21 (9-1617), folder 010.031 ("husband").

7. The sixteen nonoperating unions included the International Association of Machinists; the International Brotherhood of Boilermakers, Iron Shipbuilders, and Helpers of America; the International Brotherhood of Blacksmiths, Drop Forgers, and Helpers; the Sheet Metal Workers' International Association; the International Brotherhood of Electrical Workers; the Brotherhood of Railway Carmen of America; the International Brotherhood of Firemen, Oilers, Helpers, Roundhouse, and Railway Shop Laborers; the Brotherhood of Railway and Steamship Clerks, Freight Handlers, Express, and Station Employees; the Brotherhood of Maintenance of Way Employees; the Order of Railroad Telegraphers; the Railroad Yardmasters of America; the Brotherhood of Railroad Signalmen of America; the National Organization of Masters, Mates, and Pilots; the National Marine Engineers' Beneficial Association; the International Longshoremen's Association; and the Hotel and Restaurant Employees' International Alliance.

8. BRT and BLE officials submitted to arbitration in an attempt to resolve disputes relating to wages and work rules, while the other three brotherhoods (the Brotherhood of Locomotive Firemen and Enginemen, the Order of Railway Conductors, and the Switchmen's Union of North America) were only interested in the wage issue.

9. For additional information on the complex relationship between the consumer society and organized labor, see Lizabeth Cohen, *A Consumers' Republic: The Politics of Mass Consumption in Postwar America* (New York: Vintage, 2003); Lawrence B. Glickman, *A Living Wage: American Workers and the Making of Consumer Society* (Ithaca, NY: Cornell University Press, 1997); and Glickman, *Buying Power: A History of Consumer Activism in America* (Chicago: University of Chicago Press, 2009).

10. *New York Times*, March 6, 1946; March 7, 1946; March 8, 1946; March 9, 1946; April 26, 1946; May 1, 1946; May 3, 1946; May 4, 1946.

11. At that rate, the pay raise would have been $1.44 to $1.98 per day, depending on job classification.

12. *New York Times*, May 17, 1946; May 18, 1946; May 24, 1946 ("operating," "gravest"); May 25, 1946; *Philadelphia Inquirer*, May 25, 1946 ("trickle").

13. *New York Times*, May 24, 1946.

14. *New York Times*, May 25, 1946 ("fundamental," "inconceivable"); May 26 ("strikebreaker," "Fuehrer").

15. *New York Times*, March 26, 1947; September 3, 1947; PRR BOD Minutes.

16. *New York Times*, February 28, 1947; June 21, 1947; September 3, 1947; November 15, 1947; November 20, 1947; November 21, 1947; January 17, 1948; March 28, 1948.

17. "Organization and Functions of the Labor Relations Department," May 26, 1964, PHMC, Box 168 (9-2237), folder 110.1.

18. The terminology associated with labor-management relations has varied considerably over the twentieth century. During the 1920s, the use of the term *industrial relations* became common, embracing the subsidiary concept of personnel management. As economist Bruce E. Kaufman has observed, "Personnel management approaches the study of work and employment from the employer's perspective. It focuses on the goals of

employers, the practices employers use to attract, retain, motivate, and develop the labor input of workers." Bruce E. Kaufman, "Human Resources and Industrial Relations: Commonalities and Differences," *Human Resource Management Review* 11, no. 4 (Winter 2001): 339–74, at 341 ("approaches").

19. "Remarks of J. M. Symes, Vice President-Operation, at Joint Meeting with Representatives of Labor and Management on Employe Relations at Pittsburgh, Pa., November 29th–30th, 1951," Pennsylvania Railroad Company Records, Accession 1807/1810, Manuscripts and Archives Department, Hagley Museum and Library, Wilmington, Delaware (hereafter, HML), Box 1494, folder 3 ("recognized," "slipped," "difference").

20. Donald Armstrong to Clement, May 21, 1946 ("knowledge"); Clement to Armstrong, May 23, 1946; both in HML, Box 305, folder 16.

21. John R. Noyes to J. C. Rill, April 23, 1947; Paul F. Yount to Clement, June 5, 1947; G. C. Bunting to Symes, February 24, 1950; R. P. Alexander to Walter S. Franklin, April 28, 1951; all in HML, Box 305, folder 16; Carl R. Gray Jr., *Railroading in Eighteen Countries: The Story of American Railroad Men Serving in the Military Railway Service 1862 to 1953* (New York: Charles Scribner's Sons, 1955), 271–72, 283.

22. Frank H. Stone, "A Report on the Personnel Program, The Pennsylvania Railroad," November–December 1947, HML, Box 808, folder 8 ("initiated," "indoctrinate," "established," "contain").

23. Stone, "Report on the Personnel Program" ("performs," "responsibility," "loyal").

24. Of these, 65 contributors received awards in 1946, 143 in 1947. The average award increased from $7.38 (an amount that might explain the lackluster employee participation in 1946) to $13.60, with the highest award being $100.

25. James R. Downes to Clement, July 14, 1947; "The President Outlines the Employes' Suggestion Plan Which Becomes Effective August 1, 1947," "Operations of Employes' Suggestion Plan," January 19, 1948; both in PHMC, Box 21 (9-1617), folder 010.04; "Employe Relations Program, Item 6—Employe's Suggestion Plan," HML, Box 258, folder 23; J. P. Newell, memo to staff, February 24, 1960, HML, Box 351, folder 12 ("sell"); Personnel Department, Pennsylvania Railroad, "A Program to Improve Communication" and "Philosophy and Objectives of the Company," January 28, 1958, HML, Box 1494, folder 2 ("establish," emphasis in the original, "transmit," "trust"); C. E. Musser to Franklin et al., July 12, 1947; J. W. Oram to Franklin et al., March 8, 1948; Oram to

Symes, May 16, 1956 ("involve"); all in HML, Box 233, folder 18.

26. *Mutual Magazine* 33, no. 6 (December 1947): 19–20.

27. *New York Times*, March 25, 1948 ("hazardous"); March 27, 1948; March 28, 1948; April 11, 1948.

28. *New York Times*, April 29, 1948; May 7, 1948 ("consider," "reckless").

29. *New York Times*, May 10, 1948; May 11, 1948; May 12, 1948; PRR BOD Minutes.

30. *New York Times*, July 10, 1948; July 31, 1948; October 6, 1948; October 7, 1948.

31. *New York Times*, September 9, 1948; September 18, 1948; September 21, 1948; November 13, 1948; December 18, 1948; December 21, 1948.

32. *New York Times*, December 21, 1949; March 21, 1950; April 20, 1950; May 10, 1950; May 12, 1950.

33. Testimony of Walter S. Franklin, RE: Labor Relations, May 23, 1950, John W. Barriger III Papers, St. Louis Mercantile Library, St. Louis, Missouri (hereafter Barriger Papers), Series 262, Box 167, folder 9–32, 2 ("broken"), 4 ("springboard"), 7 ("opposed").

34. *New York Times*, May 16, 1950; May 17, 1950; June 16, 1950; June 22, 1950; August 10, 1950; August 12, 1950.

35. *New York Times*, July 10, 1948 ("carousel," "illusive"). Information on the inflation rate is from the Federal Reserve Bank of Minneapolis, "Consumer Price Index, 1913-," https://www.minneapolisfed.org/community/financial-and-economic-education/cpi-calculator-information/consumer-price-index-and-inflation-rates-1913, accessed January 21, 2023.

36. *New York Times*, August 20, 1950; August 24, 1950; August 26, 1950; August 27, 1950; Francis A. O'Neill Jr. et al., *Administrative History: Railroad and Airline Wage Board, September 1951 to March 1953* (Washington, DC: Economic Stabilization Agency: Railroad and Airline Wage Board, 1953), 47.

37. The Wage Stabilization Board, in existence from 1950 to 1953, should not be confused with the National Wage Stabilization Board, established in 1946 and disbanded the following year. Beginning in May 1951, there was considerable discussion regarding the specific needs of transportation employees. Those conversations led to the formation of a Temporary Emergency Railroad Wage Panel and, on September 27, the Railroad and Airline Wage Board. For the sake of convenience, the WSB terminology will be used throughout.

38. B. C. Roberts, "Wage Stabilization in the United States," *Oxford Economic Papers*, New Series 4, no. 2 (July 1952): 149–62, at 199–51; O'Neill, *Administrative History*, 5, 13.

39. *New York Times*, October 10, 1950; October 11, 1950; October 21, 1950; October 21, 1950; October 26, 1950; December 14, 1950; December 15, 1950 ("sons"); December 16, 1950.

40. *New York Times*, December 22, 1950; Pennsylvania Railroad Company, *One Hundred and Fifth Annual Report, for the Year Ended December 31, 1951* (Philadelphia: n.p., 1952), 12.

41. The new legislation overturned a portion of the 1934 Crosser-Dill Act, which had barred compulsory union membership—largely to ban company unions such as the PRR's Employe Representation Plan.

42. *New York Times*, January 11, 1951; January 31, 1951; February 1, 1951; February 2, 1951 ("drastic"); February 3, 1951; February 4, 1951; February 5, 1951; February 6, 1951.

43. The wage increases amount to 12.5 cents per hour for yard crews and 5 cents for those in road service. That was approximately half of what Truman had offered the previous December.

44. *New York Times*, February 3, 1951; February 9, 1951 ("Russians," "interference," "intolerable"); February 20, 1951; February 25, 1951; February 26, 1951; O'Neill, *Administrative History*, 47–48.

45. "Historical Inflation Rates: 1914–2020," https://www.usinflationcalculator.com/inflation/historical-inflation-rates/, accessed October 15, 2020.

46. On February 27, two days before the agreement between the railroads and the nonoperating unions, the remaining industry and government members of the WSB issued General Wage Regulation No. 6, recommending that wage increases be limited to no more than 10 percent. While the 12.5-cent increase fell below that threshold, the inevitable cost-of-living adjustments would exceed it.

47. As an intermediate step, Truman convened a National Advisory Board on Mobilization Policy, in which business and labor enjoyed equal representation. That body, in turn, advised the president to reestablish the WPB.

48. The agreement was retroactive to February 1, 1951.

49. O'Neill, *Administrative History*, 5–7; Roberts, "Wage Stabilization," 151–55; *New York Times*, February 26, 1951; February 27, 1951; March 2, 1951.

50. O'Neill, *Administrative History*, 9–11, 48–49; *New York Times*, March 31, 1951; May 26, 1951.

51. O'Neill, *Administrative History*, 9–11, 48–49; July 25, 1951; July 26, 1951; August 23, 1951 ("frivolous"); November 7, 1951; November 16, 1951; November 28, 1951; November 30, 1951 ("reluctantly"); Pennsylvania Railroad, *One Hundred and Fifth Annual Report*, 8–10.

52. *New York Times*, December 15, 1951 ("victims").

53. Pennsylvania Railroad, *One Hundred and Fifth Annual Report*, 9.

54. Oram, "Memorandum for File," December 31, 1947; Oram, "Report of Activities January 9th to February 25th—Safety," February 25, 1948; both in HML, Box 859, folder 16; *Railway Age* 125, no. 1 (July 3, 1948): 33.

55. John T. Williams to Oram, June 1, 1951, HML, Box 859, folder 16 ("measure"); *Altoona Tribune*, April 24, 1951.

56. Williams to J. I. Patin, June 2, 1951; Williams to Oram, September 6, 1951; J. L. Gressitt to Oram, August 2, 1951 ("dispel"); Oram to E. W. Smith, J. A. Appleton, and Herman H. Pevler, July 17, 1951; all in HML, Box 859, folder 16; Williams to Oram, September 3, 1952 ("conditions"); Oram to Smith, Appleton, and Pevler, November 7, 1952; both in HML, Box 859, folder 17.

57. E. C. Gegenheimer to Oram, July 30, 1951 ("interchangeable"); Prospectus for Narrative Drama "Not by Chance," produced by Unifilms, New York, 1951 ("primary," "rulebooks," "impossible"); both in HML, Box 859, folder 16; Film Summary: "Not by Chance" ("interviews"); Williams, "Suggestions in Connection with the Showing of 'Not by Chance,'" December 1951 ("hurt," emphasis in the original); both in HML, Box 859, folder 17.

58. PRR press releases, April 20, 1953 ("dreamed"); February 11, 1954; William Englander to Williams, April 6, 1954; HML, Box 859, folder 17.

59. In later years, films served many of the public-relations functions that Oram envisioned. In 1956, the PRR used a "classroom on wheels" as a theater to show commuters and elected officials that the company's financial difficulties necessitated the elimination of some services. In 1965, as executives sought to build support for the merger between the PRR and the New York Central, they considered proposals for films to be shown to employees. *United We Stand* stressed the positive elements of the merger. The film opened with PRR chairman Stuart Saunders explaining that "united, the Penn-Central *can* make even greater strides in the future." He called the merger "a natural, an inevitable step forward," based on his assertion that the entire history of American railroading involved a joining of forces. Alfred Perlman, the president of the NYC, emphasized that a merger would produce the best of both systems. "Five . . . ten years from now," he predicted, "every one of us will look back to the date of the merger as a beginning . . . a start of a great advance in railroading." Personnel executives stressed that no one would be laid off and only a few people would be transferred because of the merger. The ordinary

employee, so evident in earlier films, was nowhere to be found, except in the audience. *The Ballad of the Steel Wheel* also accentuated the positive, letting employees know that they would, at worst, suffer a few minor inconveniences but that the merger "will contribute to . . . security and to future opportunities"—with greater efficiency and economic strength but not at the expense of employees. *Railway Age* 141, no. 27 (December 24, 1956): 15 ("classroom"); Creative Department, Close and Patenaude, "Outline and Cost Estimate of 35mm Color-Sound Filmstrip on Penn-Central Merger," March 16, 1965 ("united," "natural," "years," "contribute"); Andrew D. Genron to J. S. Stewart, March 23, 1965; both in HML, Box 885, folder 7.

60. Clement, memorandum for Franklin, October 24, 1951, PHMC, Box 47 (9-2079), folder 110.01 ("primitive," "responsibility," "county," "accumulate," "build," "coordinate," "position").

61. PRR press release, September 28, 1951, HML, Box 231, folder 10; *Commercial and Financial Chronicle* 174, no. 5053 (October 8, 1951): 8 ("development").

62. Champlin to Carpi, February 3, 1953; Carpi to Champlin, February 25, 1953; J. K. Murphy and James A. Schultz to Champlin, February 12, 1954 ("advisory"); all in PHMC, Box 85 (9-2133), folder 602; *Princeton Alumni Weekly*, June 14, 1929, 1099.

63. Champlin to Allen J. Greenough et al., March 9, 1954, PHMC, Box 47 (9-2079), folder 110.01; *Altoona Tribune*, January 14, 1952.

64. Champlin to Newell, October 22, 1953 ("newspaper"), PHMC, Box 47 (9-2079), folder 110.01; *Lima News*, February 15, 1953.

65. Loewy was presumably referring to Symes's appointment as executive vice president, on January 1, 1952, as his promotion to the presidency occurred after the designer ceased his association with the PRR. Symes to Franklin, September 16, 1949; Franklin to Symes, September 17, 1949; Newell to Raymond Loewy Associates, September 24, 1952; all in PHMC, Box 47 (9-2079), folder 110.1; Chuck Blardone, "Raymond Loewy PRR Project Listing," *Keystone* 24, no. 1 (Spring 1991): 54–58; Anita A. Pins, "Thesis Questionnaire," *Keystone* 24, no. 1 (Spring 1991): 51–53 (Loewy's "friends" quote at 51).

66. The eastern railroads allegedly paid Byoir & Associates $425,000 annually, with the PRR hoping to retain $5 million in annual revenue that might otherwise be lost to trucks. In return, Byoir recruited expert witnesses who testified about the dangers of trucks and organized grassroots citizens groups to oppose legislation that favored motor carriers. Such tactics proved particularly

effective in Pennsylvania and in Ohio, where Governor Frank J. Lausche made opposition to the trucking interests a major element of his 1952 reelection campaign.

67. The matter was seemingly resolved in April 1955, when the trucking interests agreed to drop the suit, provided that the ERPC and other eastern carriers end their opposition to the bill increasing truck weights. A less-well-publicized element of the peace accord involved Byoir's withdrawal from railroad work. News of a settlement was premature, thanks to the testimony of Sonya Saroyan, a secretary who had either resigned or been fired from Byoir & Associates. She claimed that she had leaked details of the Byoir campaign to the Pennsylvania Motor Truck Association in return for a payment of $25,000 (which she claimed she never received). The titillating details guaranteed widespread media coverage. Saroyan's revelations also caused the ERPC and the railroads to countersue the Pennsylvania Motor Truck Association for $140 million. In October 1957, Judge Thomas J. Clary of the US District Court for the Eastern District of Pennsylvania ruled in favor of the truckers and ordered a small but symbolically significant award of $852,000 in damages—20 percent paid by Byoir & Associates and the remainder by the PRR and other eastern railroads. In 1961, the Supreme Court overturned the award, finding that the advertising campaign orchestrated by Byoir and the railroads was constitutionally protected free speech. That ruling also resolved a separate suit, brought by the trucking firm Riss & Company, which alleged that Byoir, the PRR, and eighty-four other railroads had conspired to deny them the opportunity to transport explosives on the grounds that their operations were unsafe. *New York Times*, April 7, 1955 ("vilify"); November 6, 1960; *Eastern Railroad Presidents' Conference, et al. v. Noerr Motor Freight Incorporated, et al.*, 365 US 127 (1961) ("vicious"); *Association of Western Railways, et al. v. Riss & Company, Incorporated*, 99 F.2d 133 (1962); Joseph R. Daughen and Peter Binzen, *The Wreck of the Penn Central* (Boston: Little, Brown, 1971; Washington, DC: Beard, 1999), 49–52; Scott M. Cutlip, *The Unseen Power: Public Relations: A History* (Hillsdale, NJ: Lawrence Erlbaum, 1994), 129–30, 574–81.

68. Champlin to Franklin, January 8, 1952; Champlin to Symes, October 3, 1952; Symes to Champlin, October 6, 1952 ("channeled," "inclined," "think"); all in PHMC, Box 47 (9-2079), folder 110.01.

69. Newell to Symes, September 28, 1954, HML, Box 341, folder 2 ("warrant," "possibly," "street"); Carpi to Champlin, April 27, 1953 ("lasting," "prerequisite"), PHMC, Box 47 (9-2079), folder 110.01; Champlin to

Carpi, February 3, 1953; Carpi to Champlin, February 25, 1953 ("coach," "road"); both in PHMC, Box 85 (9-2133), folder 602.

70. Symes to Franklin, September 20, 1951 ("lacking," "troubled," "campaign," "integrated"); "Employe Relations Program," n.d., but ca. September 1951; both in PHMC, Box 18 (9-2048), folder 011.

71. James M. McFarland, formerly based in Chicago, became the superintendent for the Eastern Region, replacing Alexander. His direct subordinate was John J. Maher, likewise based in Philadelphia. B. O. Wilson was responsible for personnel matters at Pittsburgh, the headquarters of the Central Region, along with his assistant, T. V. Murphy. Herman Kendall, who had previously been Alexander's subordinate at Philadelphia, moved to Chicago to take charge of the Western Region, assisted by A. E. Myles. A seventh manager, W. Lamont Goetz, became superintendent of personnel at the Altoona Works—an organizationally separate entity from the three regions and a location with many union employees. There was no assistant superintendent of personnel at Altoona.

72. Symes to Franklin, September 20, 1951 ("public," "decision"); "Employe Relations Program" ("majority," "selected," "money").

73. Patin emphasized that several ironclad rules dictated the proper attributes for a personnel manager, but chief among them was his exhortation to never "hire a man with a mission." The other rules were to avoid individuals who liked working with people (because personnel management was a bureaucratic staff position), anyone who was a "personality boy" (because popularity did not necessarily equate with ability), people who had not functioned well in other areas of the company (because personnel management was too important a function to entrust to individuals who received a sinecure), and former union officials (because they could not be trusted by management and were regarded as traitors by labor). *Indiana* [Pennsylvania] *Evening Gazette*, November 1, 1951; PRR press release, October 30, 1951; "The Pennsylvania Railroad Employe Relations Program," September 16, 1952; both in HML, Box 258, folder 23; Charles E. Alexander to Oram, October 22, 1952; Patin to James P. Newell, November 2, 1953 ("ideas," "hear," "title," "vulnerable"); Newell to Patin, October 23, 1953; "Memorandum for use of vice president-operation at staff meeting 11-24-53"; J. L. Webb to Newell, January 28, 1954; all in HML, Box 859, folder 20; James I. Patin, "Self Development of Personnel Men," *Michigan Business Review* 13, no. 1 (January 1961): 2–5 ("possible,"

"crusader," "forget," "screen," "mission"); *Railway Age* 131, no. 20 (November 12, 1951): 72.

74. *Modern Railroads*, March 1953 ("impart," "develop," "modify"); *Railway Age* 135, no. 16 (October 19, 1953): 73–75.

75. PRR officials emphasized that "public opinion about the railroad . . . depends, first, upon the impression the railroad has made upon its own employees, and, secondly, how well the railroad has shown its employees the importance of the impression they make upon the public."

76. *Indianapolis Star*, June 7, 1953 ("depends," "subordinates," "subtle"); "Employe Relations Program, Item 3—Supervisory Training," September 16, 1952; Oram to Fred Carpi et al., January 10, 1952; both in HML, Box 258, folder 23; Newell to J. W. Corbett, May 4, 1953, HML, Box 309, folder 10 ("street," "opportunity").

77. Newell to Corbett, May 4, 1953, HML, Box 309, folder 10 ("Satisfied," "Recommendations"); *New York Times*, April 3, 1953 ("improve"); Pennsylvania Railroad Company, *One Hundred and Seventh Annual Report, for the Year Ended December 31, 1953* (Philadelphia: n.p., 1954), 18–19.

78. "Employe Relations Program," n.d., but ca. September 1951 ("satisfactory," "humanize," "proud"), PHMC, Box 18 (9-2048), folder 011.

79. Patin to Newell, November 2, 1953 ("vulnerable"), in HML, Box 859, folder 20; Norbert J. Roberts to Newell, December 19, 1953 ("informal"), PHMC, Box 18 (9-2048), folder 011.

80. The incident in Philadelphia occurred because Shallit objected to restrictions that precluded visitors from photographing the Liberty Bell, forcing them to pay the commercial photographers who were selling the photographs of that symbol of American freedom, particularly at a time of global war. "Education of a Martian," published in 1952, reflected Shallit's disapproval of school segregation in the South, two years before the Supreme Court addressed that issue in *Brown v. Board of Education*.

81. Champlin to Thomas W. Phelps, August 31, 1953, PHMC, Box 18 (9-2048), folder 011; *Railway Age* 132, no. 25 (June 23, 1952): 86; 144, no, 18 (May 5, 1958): 17–21; *New York Times*, May 3, 1948; Burton Lindheim, "Milton Biow Dies," *New York Times*, February 3, 1976; *Time*, March 21, 1949; *Printer's Ink* 123, no. 5 (May 3, 1923): 153; State University of New York, Long Island Agricultural and Technical Institute at Farmingdale, *Catalogue and Announcement* 27 (September 1, 1955): 19; *Ad Age*, September 15, 2003; University of Waterloo, "About Joseph

Shallit," https://cs.uwaterloo.ca/~shallit/joseph.html, accessed May 26, 2019; *Philadelphia Record*, July 4, 1942.

82. "Questions that are most likely to be in the minds of stockholders," 1955, 23–24; "Questions that are most likely to be in the minds of stockholders," 1957, 31; both in PHMC, Box 35 (9-2186), folder 111.01.

83. During the World War II years, unionized workers in the mining and manufacturing sectors gained an increasing level of fringe benefits, in large measure to avoid the inflationary characteristics associated with wage increases. That trend accelerated after 1945, and in 1952, American businesses allocated more than $8 billion to a variety of fringe benefits. The most important involved paid vacations and medical care, each representing about a quarter of the total. *New York Times*, August 2, 1953.

84. The care was free only within the first twenty-four hours of an accident. In 1916, the PRR kept seventy-two doctors in private practice on retainer, to be employed on an as-needed basis. PRR BOD Minutes, June 15, 1859, 429; Richard E. Beeler, ed., *Altoona's Centennial Booklet: Noteworthy Personages and Events, Altoona History, 1849–1949* (Altoona, PA: Altoona Centennial, 1949), 23, in PHMC, Box 44 (9-1640), folder 110.01; "Memo for Board," February 11, 1949, PHMC, Box 26 (9-1622), folder 011.3; "Outline of Report to the President Respecting the Relief Department," 1935, HML, Box 310, folder 34; E. B. Hunt to G. W. Creighton, June 30, 1916; HML, Box 467, folder 2; A. J. County, "Improving Human Relations in the Transportation Industry," transcript of paper presented at the Ninth Annual Conference on "Human Relations in Industry," Lake George, NY, October 1926, HML, Box 855, folder 6.

85. John W. Orr, *Set Up Running: The Life of a Pennsylvania Railroad Engineman, 1904–1949* (University Park: Pennsylvania State University Press, 2001), 165–67, 199–201.

86. Likewise, PRR officials chose not to link the Medical Department to the Voluntary Relief Department, which paid death and disability benefits for injured workers. Oram to Newell, September 28, 1951 ("costs," "engaged"), HML, Box 854, folder 14.

87. Oram to Newell, September 28, 1951, HML, Box 854, folder 14; PRR press release, July 30, 1953, HML, Box 854, folder 16; Pennsylvania Railroad, *One Hundred and Seventh Annual Report*, 18; *New York Times*, July 30, 1953; *Railway Age* 135, no. 8 (August 24, 1953): 89–90; "Questions that are most likely to be in the minds of stockholders," 1959, 36, PHMC, Box 35 (9-2186), folder 111.01.

88. The August 1952 union-shop agreement required all newly hired employees to join their respective union within sixty days but did not provide for automatic dues deductions from paychecks. Executives on western and southern railroads refused to accept the union shop. O'Neill, *Administrative History*, 27; *New York Times*, February 15, 1952 ("puzzled"); February 16, 1952; May 9, 1952; August 30, 1952; October 4, 1952.

89. *New York Times*, May 24, 1952; O'Neill, *Administrative History*, 59–60.

90. *New York Times*, March 12, 1952; May 20, 1952; May 22, 1952 ("disappointment"); May 23, 1952 ("lesson").

91. O'Neill, *Administrative History*, 32–33; Roberts, "Wage Stabilization," 160–61.

92. Guthrie was quick to point out that that statement was not accurate, since earlier adjustments reflected gains in efficiency.

93. *New York Times*, January 1, 1953; January 13, 1953; March 19, 1953 ("history"); March 21, 1953; O'Neill, *Administrative History*, 33–35.

94. *New York Times*, September 11, 1953; October 1, 1953.

95. *New York Times*, January 13, 1954; January 17, 1954; May 16, 1954; August 22, 1954; December 22, 1955.

96. *New York Times*, March 7, 1947; March 18, 1947; July 4, 1947; November 11, 1949.

97. John C. Paige, *A Special History Study: Pennsylvania Railroad Shops and Works, Altoona, Pennsylvania* (Washington, DC: United States National Park Service, 1989), 83; Transport Workers Union Local 2001, "History," http://local2001.twu.org/history/, accessed July 8, 2015; *New York Times*, July 16, 1954; October 2, 1954. For more information regarding Quill's early career, see Shirley Quill, *Mike Quill, Himself: A Memoir* (Greenwich, CT: Devin-Adair, 1985); L. H. Whittemore, *The Man Who Ran the Subways: The Story of Mike Quill* (New York: Holt, Rinehart & Winston, 1968); and Joshua B. Freeman, *In Transit: The Transport Workers Union in New York City, 1933–1966* (New York: Oxford University Press, 1989).

98. *New York Times*, December 24, 1954; February 16, 1955 ("gambling"); September 1, 1955; September 3, 1955; October 28, 1955; December 16, 1955; December 23, 1955.

99. *New York Times*, August 3, 1955 ("mad"); August 4, 1955; August 5, 1955; August 6, 1955; August 7, 1955; August 8, 1955; August 9, 1955; September 7, 1955; September 8, 1955; September 13, 1955; September 14, 1955; September 16, 1955; September 23, 1955.

100. *New York Times*, January 26, 1956; February 25, 1956 ("tragedies"); March 23, 1956; March 28, 1956; March 29, 1956; September 14, 1956; September 15, 1956; September 22, 1956 ("gag"); December 5, 1956.

101. *New York Times*, October 20, 1957 ("persistent," "moved"); November 9, 1957.

102. For an overview of the 1920s reorganization, see Albert J. Churella, *The Pennsylvania Railroad, Volume 2: The Age of Limits, 1914–1933* (Bloomington: Indiana University Press, 2023), 65–81.

103. Clement to Deasy and Franklin, October 6, 1944, PHMC, Box 44 (9-1640), folder 100.01.

104. Symes to Clement, January 21, 1946 ("bad"), PHMC, Box 44 (9-1640), folder 100.01.

105. For example, on November 1, 1949, the Central Pennsylvania General Division merged into the Eastern Pennsylvania General Division, headquartered in Harrisburg, under General Superintendent Allen J. Greenough. The Lake General Division became part of the Eastern Ohio General Division, headquartered in Pittsburgh. The railroad combined the Williamsport Division with the Wilkes Barre Division (except for the area around Norristown) to form the Susquehanna Division. The Cleveland Division and the Erie and Ashtabula Division were consolidated into the Lake Division, headquartered in Cleveland. The Monongahela Division became part of the Pittsburgh Division, with headquarters in its namesake city. The railroad also abolished the Logansport Division, splitting the remaining trackage between the Columbus Division and the Chicago Terminal Division (which was then renamed the Chicago Division). Patchell, "Notice," October 31, 1949; PRR, "Notice," April 30, 1949; H. L. Nancarrow, "Notice," October 31, 1949; PRR press release, April 27, 1949; Symes to Clement, April 18, 1949; Clement to Symes, April 22, 1949; all in PHMC, Box 44 (9-1640), folder 100.01; "Memorandum for use of Vice President—Operation at Staff, 11-24-53," HML, Box 309, folder 5; Ernest to Newell, June 21, 1954; "Memo for Road Committee, April 13, 1949" ("centralization," "continued"); "Memorandum for Staff Meeting, November 25, 1952" ("return"); all in HML, Box 309, file 011.0. That memorandum indicated that decentralization planning had been underway "for over a year."

106. Beale agreed with Franklin that "as you say, the chart you sent me is a bit antiquated and I am sure that the one on which you are working will be a vast improvement." Franklin to Leonard T. Beale, November 7, 1950; Beale to Franklin, November 8, 1950 ("antiquated"); both in HML, Box 309, file 011.0.

107. Mark W. Cresap Jr. letter, January 19, 1951; Richard M. Paget to Franklin, March 7, 1951; Franklin memorandum, May 9, 1951; Richard King Mellon to Franklin, December 14, 1951; Franklin to Robert M. Blough,

November 30, 1950; all in PHMC, Box 47 (9-2079), folder 110.01; *New York Times*, January 1, 1964.

108. Symes to Franklin, June 3, 1952 ("revamped"), PHMC, Box 47 (9-2079), folder 110.01; "Remarks of J. M. Symes, Executive Vice President, at Joint Meeting of Operating and Traffic Officers, Pittsburgh, Pa., April 30, 1952," HML, Box 1494, folder 3 ("proper," "contacts").

109. "Memorandum for Staff Meeting, November 25, 1952," HML, Box 309, file 011.0 ("experienced"); "Pennsylvania Railroad: Summary of Staff Views with Regard to Decentralization of Authority in Operating Department," August 18, 1954, HML, Box 309, file 011.0; Unattributed comment made at the June 10, 1954, labor-management meeting, quoted in Newell to Greenough et al., June 14, 1954, HML Box 1494, folder 1 ("more").

110. "Remarks of J. P. Newell, Vice President—Operation, at Joint Meeting of Operating and Traffic Officers, Pittsburgh, Pa., April 30, 1952," HML, Box 1494, folder 3 ("result"); S. R. Hursh to Newell, June 24, 1954, HML, Box 1494, folder 1 ("portion").

111. Carpi to Franklin, June 27, 1952, Box 47 (9-2079), folder 110.01.

112. Symes to Franklin, June 3, 1952, PHMC, Box 47 (9-2079), folder 110.01.

113. Carpi to Franklin, June 27, 1952 ("thought"), Box 47 (9-2079), folder 110.01.

114. Symes quoted in PRR press release, September 29, 1955 ("revolutionary"), HML, Box 1418, folder 5; Newell to Greenough et al., June 14, 1954 ("accelerating"), HML Box 1494, folder 1.

115. Hursh to Newell, June 24, 1954, HML, Box 1494, folder 1 ("formed"); Newell to Greenough, June 28, 1954; Newell to Greenough et al., August 19, 1954 ("situation"); both in HML, Box 309, file 011.0; *Pittsburgh Post-Gazette*, September 29, 1934.

116. Oram to Newell, June 19, 1954 ("education"); Ernest to Newell, June 21, 1954; Nancarrow to Newell, June 24, 1954 ("trouble"); Oram to Newell, June 19, 1954; Andrew F. McIntyre to Newell, June 17, 1954; all in HML, Box 309, file 011.1.

117. T. Clarence Stiegler to Newell, June 23, 1954 ("complaints"); Howell T. Cover to Newell, June 23, 1954 ("embarrassing"); Stiegler to Newell, June 23, 1954 ("encourage"); "Pennsylvania Railroad, Summary of Staff Views with Regard to Decentralization of Authority in Operating Department," August 1954 ("prevailing"); all in HML, Box 309, file 011.0.

118. Laurence T. Mayher to Symes, October 27, 1953, PHMC, Box 76 (9-2124), folder 521.3.

119. PRR press release, July 19, 1954; Heller report quoted in "Announcing the New Organization of the Pennsylvania Railroad," November 1955; both in HML, Box 1418, folder 5 ("foresight," "fortunate," "utilize").

120. "Memorandum Covering Developments of, Recommended Changes in, and Additions to the Research and Development Organization," September 17, 1956, PHMC, Box 125 (9-2276), folder 110.01 ("avoiding," "infusion"); "Announcing the New Organization of the Pennsylvania Railroad" ("key"); *Railway Age* 139, no. 15 (October 10, 1955): 46–52 ("supervision," "capitalize" at 46).

121. Most of the Atlantic Division was not included in the reorganization, as it continued to operate as part of the Pennsylvania-Reading Seashore Lines. The nine regions were New York, Philadelphia, Chesapeake, Northern, Pittsburgh, Lake, Buckeye, Northwestern (later, Chicago), and Southwestern. Not all nine regions shared equal authority. The managers of the Chicago and Pittsburgh Regions held vice presidential status, while at New York, Pittsburgh, and Washington, resident vice presidents represented the central office.

122. David Bevan, the vice president in charge of finance, suggested that the regional managers should have control only over operating and traffic issues, not real estate, industrial relations, public relations, or maintenance. He was overruled, however. *Railway Age* 139:15 (October 10, 1955): 46–52 ("produce," "Mr." at 46).

123. The organizational changes coincided with extensive tests, conducted on the Fort Wayne Division during the summer of 1955, that evaluated a wide range of machinery associated with track maintenance—something that promised to generate further increases in efficiency, coupled with a reduction in employment. By the summer work season of 1956, both the new equipment and the refined organization were ready for implementation.

124. PRR press release, October 10, 1955, HML, Box 1418, folder 5; "Announcing the New Organization of the Pennsylvania Railroad"; Herbert A. Archdeacon, "The Mechanization of Track Work, Part 1: Track Surfacing and Lining," *Keystone* 41, no. 3 (Autumn 2008): 80–81; Archdeacon, "The Mechanization of Track Work, Part 2: The Renewal of Crossties," *Keystone* 54, no. 2 (Summer 2021): 76–77.

125. *The Pennsy* was an employee magazine; it (along with its editor, Ik Shuman) was under Oram's supervision, as part of the Personnel Department.

126. PRR press release, October 10, 1955; "Announcing the New Organization"; Oram to Newell, January 2, 1957; both in PHMC, Box 126 (9-2277), folder 110.01; Alexander to Newell, January 21, 1957 ("loaded," "dig"), HML, Box 1874, folder 22.

127. During 1952 and 1953, the railroad culled its passenger fleet, eliminating more than six hundred coaches, diners, sleepers, and head-end cars. Some were transferred to maintenance-of-way service, a few were sold to other carriers (including the Long Island Rail Road), and many went to the scrapyard.

128. "Memorandum to Mr. W. W. Patchell Regarding Steps and Progress in Eliminating Passenger Deficit"; "The Pennsylvania Railroad Company Passenger Operations—Draft of Report, July 26, 1954"; both in PHMC, Box 76 (9-2124), folder 521.3; "Synopsis of Meeting of Operating and Traffic Officers at Pittsburgh, September 29, 1943" ("attitude," "proper"), HML, Box 306, folder 5; H. G. Kitchin to James I. Patin, January 4, 1954 ("roughest," "dreaded"); Oram to Newell, January 6, 1954; both in HML, Box 309, folder 10; *Time*, July 2, 1951, 84 ("disregard"); Joe Welsh, *Pennsy Streamliners: The Blue Ribbon Fleet* (Milwaukee, WI: Kalmbach, 1999), 66.

129. Joseph C. Bevis to Franklin, May 18, 1948 ("acceptable"); Franklin to Arthur W. Page, May 12, 1948; T. J. Ross memo to Clement et al., July 28, 1948; Dilman M. K. Smith to Champlin, January 8, 1953; Franklin to Champlin, March 9, 1954; all in PHMC, Box 85 (9-2133), folder 602; Alfonso A. Narvaez, "Willard F. McCormick, 85, Dies; Led Management Consulting Firm," *New York Times*, April 11, 1989.

130. The locations were Trenton, New Jersey; Lancaster and Williamsport, Pennsylvania; and Salisbury, Maryland (Eastern Region); Pittsburgh; Alliance and Canton, Ohio (Central Region); and Columbus, Ohio; Fort Wayne, Indiana; and Effingham, Illinois (Western Region).

131. Opinion Research Corporation, *What People Think about the Pennsylvania Railroad*, 1954, digitized at Multimodalways, https://www.multimodalways.org/docs/railroads/companies/PRR/PRR%20Survey%201954.pdf, accessed November 21, 2023; Champlin to County, Appleton, and Patchell, November 24, 1953, HML, Box 305, folder 1.

132. *What People Think about the Pennsylvania Railroad*, 6 ("adopt," "top," "efficiently"), 12 ("things"); W. J. Gaskill to Ross, April 1954 ("feeling"); PHMC, Box 85 (9-2133), folder 602.

133. Newell to Champlin, December 29, 1954 ("attitude," "accomplished"), HML, Box 305, folder 1.

134. Champlin to Symes, March 26, 1956 ("re-establishing," "meet," "assess"), PHMC, Box 35 (9-2186).

135. "Questions that are most likely to be in the minds of stockholders," 1959, 58, PHMC, Box 35 (9-2186), folder 111.01; Greenough to Newell et al., March 25, 1960, PHMC, Box 126 (9-2277), folder 110.01; Dan Cupper, *Crossroads of Commerce: The Pennsylvania Railroad Calendar Art of Grif Teller* (Mechanicsburg, PA: Stackpole, 1992, 2003), 49, 73, 146–47; *Pennsy* 13, no. 2 (March–April 1964).

136. In practical terms, the actual business of moving trains over the railroad took place at the regional level; that process, as always, was dominated by the Transportation Department, not the Traffic Department.

137. Jones served as general manager of the New York Zone beginning in 1948; in 1953, he became the vice president in charge of real estate and taxation—replacing Walter Patchell, who had been reassigned to head a committee charged with reducing passenger-service losses.

138. In his seminal article, "Who Shot the Passenger Train?" *Trains* editor David P. Morgan noted that the "passenger traffic manager . . . is still a salesman rather than a true executive. . . . In no instance is the passenger man granted *both* responsibility and authority." David P. Morgan, "Who Shot the Passenger Train?" *Trains* 19, no. 6 (April 1959): 14–51, quote at 25, emphasis in the original; *New York Age*, February 22, 1958; Michael Conant, "The Railroad Passenger Deficit: A Comment," *Land Economics* 33, no. 4 (November 1957): 363–65.

139. Patchell called for a division of responsibilities that "would separate what GE calls their service functions from their manufacturing functions" and suggested that the new Research and Development Department could "produce the results comparable with those being produced on the C&O, Southern Pacific and Canadian National." *Business Week*, October 8, 1955, 80; PRR press release, September 29, 1955, HML Box 1418, folder 5; "Memorandum for the File: Mr. Symes Talk to Stockholders on May 8," March 28, 1956, HML, Box 326, folder 8; "Memorandum Covering Developments of, Recommended Changes in, and Additions to the Research and Development Organization," September 17, 1956; Patchell to Newell, October 5, 1957; both in PHMC, Box 125 (9-2276), folder 110.01; "Announcing the New Organization."

140. During World War II, Appleton served as the head of the Military Railway Service in the China-Burma-India Theater. He later helped to coordinate the operation of French railways following D-Day and earned promotion to brigadier general. The Pittsburgh vice presidency may have been a sinecure for Appleton, who lost his post as assistant vice president in charge of operations because

of the 1955 reorganization. In June 1956, seven months after the reorganization took effect, he resigned as vice president at Pittsburgh (in anticipation of his retirement the following year), and the office was then abolished. Following the 1920 reorganization, the company made similar arrangements for longtime senior executives who were nearing retirement.

141. *Indianapolis Star*, October 2, 1955; "Draft No. 4, Organization for Conducting the Business of the Pennsylvania Railroad Company, Effective November 1, 1955," HML, Box 233, folder 22 ("informed," "doubt"); PRR BOD Minutes; Joseph Bykofsky and Harold Larson, *United States Army in World War II: The Technical Services, the Transportation Corps: Operations Overseas* (Washington, DC: Office of the Chief of Military History, Department of the Army, 1957), 572–74; Charles F. Romanus and Riley Sunderland, *United States Army in World War II: China-Burma-India Theatre: Stilwell's Command Problems* (Washington, DC: Center of Military History, United States Army, 1987), 265–73.

142. "Proposed Change in Organization of the Pennsylvania Railroad Company," February 21, 1958 ("hourglass"), PHMC, Box 126 (9-2277), folder 110.01.

143. "Announcing the New Organization."

144. Patchell to Newell, January 15, 1957 ("poorly"); "Memorandum Covering Developments of, Recommended Changes in, and Additions to the Research and Development Organization," September 17, 1956; Patchell to Newell, January 15, 1957 ("function," "niches"); all in PHMC, Box 126 (9-2277), folder 110.01.

145. H. J. Ward to Newell, January 16, 1957; "Proposed Change in Organization of the Pennsylvania Railroad Company," February 21, 1958 ("traditionally"); both in PHMC, Box 126 (9-2277), folder 110.01.

146. Newell to Carpi et al., February 11, 1957 ("help"), HML, Box 1874, folder 22; "Proposed Change in Organization of the Pennsylvania Railroad Company," February 21, 1958 ("policies"), PHMC, Box 126 (9-2277), folder 110.01.

147. The one executive in question was not named. Newell to Herman H. Pevler et al., February 14, 1957 ("variance," "delegation"), HML, Box 1874, folder 22; Symes, memorandum, October 8, 1959, HML, Box 818, folder 5; Newell to Symes, October 10, 1958, PHMC, Box 126 (9-2277), folder 110.01.

148. For example, Oram to Newell, March 12, 1957, regarding a request from the Buckeye Region that a senior claim agent be promoted to a district claim agent, with a corresponding salary increase from $612.90 to $661.50 per month. Oram did not see "any exceedingly

strong arguments in favor of the change" and was "loath to favor the creation of this additional position of fairly high rank." In Newell to G. C. Vaughan, March 25, 1957, "It would appear that supervision on first trick is entirely too heavy." Also, Newell to Greenough, March 4, 1957; Newell to J. B. Prizer, March 1, 1957; Oram to Newell, March 12, 1957; Oram to Newell, March 11, 1957; all in HML, Box 1874, folder 22.

149. Newell to Pevler et al., December 21, 1956; Newell to Pevler et al., February 28, 1957 ("recognized"); Newell to M. S. S., February 27, 1957 ("heavy"); all in HML, Box 1874, folder 22; "Proposed Change in Organization of the Pennsylvania Railroad Company," February 21, 1958, PHMC, Box 126 (9-2277), folder 110.01 ("fear").

150. "Questions that are most likely to be in the minds of stockholders," 1957, 3, 5; "Questions that are most likely to be in the minds of stockholders," 1958, 2, 29; both in PHMC, Box 35 (9-2186), folder 111.01; PRR BOD Minutes.

151. The PRR's $43.7 million passenger loss in 1954 was more than that of the NYC ($38.8 million) or the B&O ($31.8 million) but well below the massive losses incurred by several western lines—including the Union Pacific ($53.0 million), the Southern Pacific ($51.1 million), and the Santa Fe ($46.3 million). The PRR's 1954 passenger-service operating ratio was 114, equal to that of the NYC and considerably better than the 173 on the B&O.

152. Interstate Commerce Commission, *Docket No. 31954: Passenger Train Deficit, Item 7, Exhibit Accompanying Testimony of Walter W. Patchell, Vice President, Research and Development, the Pennsylvania Railroad Company, 1957*, 1, 14 (hereafter, "Patchell Testimony"); Welsh, *Pennsy Streamliners*, 135–36; *New York Times*, September 4, 1955.

153. Bus travel, which enjoyed rapid growth prior to 1945, fell out of favor as an increasing number of Americans obtained access to automobiles—although bus patronage rose from 24 million passenger miles in 1947 (6.8 percent of the total) to 25.5 million in 1956, the latter figure represented 3.6 percent of total passenger miles in that year.

154. Patchell Testimony, 9; *New York Times*, January 16, 1952; *Cleveland Plain Dealer*, September 24, 2015; Interstate Commerce Commission, *Docket No. 31954, Railroad Passenger Train Deficit: Report of Howard Hosmer, Hearing Examiner* (Washington, DC: Interstate Commerce Commission, 1958), 12 (hereafter, "Hosmer Report").

155. Welsh, *Pennsy Streamliners*, 132; *New York Times*, July 29, 1951 ("commuter"); Hosmer Report, 12, 24, 39–44.

156. Between April 1958 and March 1959, *The Red Arrow*'s earnings exceeded out-of-pocket costs by $42,000. In August 1958, however, the PRR ended all other passenger service to Detroit. As the sole remaining train serving the city, *The Red Arrow* bore the entirety of terminal expenses, and the resulting calculation based on fully allocated costs indicated that the service incurred a $161,000 loss. By terminating *The Red Arrow* in Toledo, traffic manager Earle R. Comer hoped that the elimination of Detroit terminal expenditures would be more than sufficient to offset the loss of revenue on the truncated service. In July 1959, the former *Red Arrow* became a two-car coach service between Crestline and Toledo, with a connecting sleeper carried on *The General*. The need to set out a sleeper in Crestline slowed *The General*'s schedule, which was bound to reduce patronage on that train. During heavy travel times, the through sleeper between the East Coast and Toledo (which carried few passengers) prevented the addition of an extra coach to *The General*, depriving that train of $30,000 in revenue and making that train a more likely candidate for elimination. By January 1960, PRR officials predicted that the Crestline–Toledo service would incur $60,000 in fully allocated losses. On that basis, the Ohio Public Utilities Commission permitted discontinuance, effective August 15, 1960. Welsh, *Pennsy Streamliners*, 138–40, 143–47.

157. "Questions that are most likely to be in the minds of stockholders," 1955, 12; "Questions that are most likely to be in the minds of stockholders," 1959, 18; both in PHMC, Box 35 (9-2186), folder 111.01 "Pennsy Agrees to Polish Trains, Manners," *Philadelphia Inquirer*, April 17, 1959 ("discourteous"); Welsh, *Pennsy Streamliners*, 147.

158. Newell to Greenough et al., April 28, 1958 ("advertising"), HML, Box 358, folder 17; Carpi to Symes, August 25, 1958, PHMC, Box 35 (9-2186); Welsh, *Pennsy Streamliners*, 141–42 ("Brag").

159. The fully allocated deficit increased at a slower rate, from $704.5 million in 1953 to $723.7 million in 1957 (and was below $700 million in each of the intervening years). That situation was largely the result of the declining number of passenger trains, which accordingly consumed a smaller percentage of funds expended on the upkeep of the right-of-way. James C. Nelson, *Railroad Transportation and Public Policy* (Washington, DC: Brookings Institution, 1959), 295.

160. Ari Hoogenboom and Olive Hoogenboom, *A History of the ICC: From Panacea to Palliative* (New York: W. W. Norton, 1976), 151–54.

161. Presidential Advisory Committee on Transport Policy and Organization, *Revision of Federal*

Transportation Policy: A Report to the President (Washington, DC: United States Government Printing Office, 1955).

162. Hosmer Report, 4–5 ("rules").

163. The other state commissioners were Harold K. Davison of New Hampshire and Ewald W. Lund of Minnesota. Hosmer Report, 2, 9–10.

164. *Railway Age* 143, no. 14 (September 30, 1957): 10; 143, no. 15 (October 7, 1957): 14; 143, no. 16 (October 14, 1957): 54 ("services"); Hosmer Report, 7–9 ("flounders").

165. Hosmer Report, 11–17, 71 ("resource"); 69–70 ("inescapable").

166. "It is of course possible that some development may stop the decline and stabilize the traffic at some level lower than that of the present time," Hosmer observed, "but no such development is now in sight." Hosmer was remarkably accurate in his predictions, and most privately operated passenger service in the United States ended with the formation of Amtrak in 1971 (one year after the date he had suggested).

167. Hosmer Report, 20 ("adhere"), 22–62, 69–70 ("development"), 72 ("overtone"); David P. Morgan, "No Passenger Trains by 1970?," *Trains* 19, no. 2 (December 1958): 42–44.

168. *Railway Age* 142, no. 14 (April 8, 1957): 12; 143, no. 15 (October 7, 1957): 20–100; John R. Meyer et al., *The Economics of Competition in the Transportation Industries* (Cambridge, MA: Harvard University Press, 1959), 243 ("failed"); Hoogenboom and Hoogenboom, *History of the ICC*, 152–53; Mark H. Rose, Bruce E. Seely, and Paul F. Barrett, *The Best Transportation System in the World: Railroads, Trucks, Airlines, and American Public Policy in the Twentieth Century* (Columbus: Ohio State University Press, 2006), 138.

169. Alan Boyd backed Smathers's political campaigns, and Smathers returned the favor by supporting Boyd's successful 1954 bid for election to the Florida Railroad and Public Utilities Commission. In 1958, Smathers introduced Boyd to Lyndon Johnson, who was contemplating a bid for the 1960 Democratic presidential nomination. Smathers told Johnson that Boyd could orchestrate his victory in the Florida primary—thus beginning a relationship that would lead Johnson to appoint Boyd as undersecretary of commerce and in 1966 as the first secretary of transportation. Alan S. Boyd, *A Great Honor: My Life Shaping 20th Century Transportation* (Portland, ME: Artisan Island, 2016), 108–11, 147–54; Jeff Davis, "A Conversation with Alan Boyd, the First Secretary of Transportation," *Eno Transportation Weekly*, February 1, 2016, https://www.enotrans.org/article/conversation-alan-boyd-first-secretary-transportation/, accessed June 30, 2019.

170. United States Congress, Senate, Committee on Interstate and Foreign Commerce, *Problems of the Railroads: Report of the Subcommittee on Surface Transportation* (Washington, DC: United States Government Printing Office, 1958), 3, (hereafter, "Smathers Report"); "Statement of James M. Symes, President, The Pennsylvania Railroad Co.," May 23, 1958, *Railroad Problems: Hearings Before a Subcommittee of the Committee on Interstate and Foreign Commerce*, 85th Cong., 2nd. Sess. (Washington DC: United States Government Printing Office, 1958), 297-310 ("defer" at 298); *Time*, January 27, 1958 ("sick"); *New York Times*, January 6, 1958; January 12, 1958; January 14, 1958 ("alarming"); January 15, 1958; Robert B. Carson, *Main Line to Oblivion: The Disintegration of the New York Railroads in the Twentieth Century* (Port Washington, NY: Kennikat, 1971), 177–84.

171. *New York Times*, July 25, 1957; December 31, 1957; *Railway Age* 143, no. 5 (July 29, 1957): 11–12; 143, no. 6 (August 5, 1957): 13–14; 143, no. 15 (October 7, 1957): 9–11; 143, no. 16 (October 14, 1957): 9–10; 143, no. 19 (November 4, 1957): 30–33.

172. *New York Times*, January 14, 1958.

173. Smathers Report, 2 ("obvious"), 3 ("measure"), 4 ("overregulation"), 6 ("belaboring").

174. Hoogenboom and Hoogenboom, *History of the ICC*, 155–59; Carson, *Main Line to Oblivion*, 188–90; Daniel P. Loomis, "The Transportation Act of 1958," *Analysts Journal* 14, no. 5 (November 1958): 57–61.

175. Hoogenboom and Hoogenboom, *History of the ICC*, 155–59 ("consideration"); Carson, *Main Line to Oblivion*, 188.

176. Smathers Report, 4 ("recognize"), 5 ("Help," "interested").

177. *McLean Trucking Co. v. United States*, 321 US 67 (1944); Richard Saunders Jr., *Merging Lines: American Railroads, 1900–1970* (DeKalb: Northern Illinois University Press, 2001), 78.

178. The carriers were the New York, Chicago & St. Louis (Nickel Plate Road), the Wheeling & Lake Erie, the Pittsburgh & West Virginia, and the Western Maryland—the NYC&StL/W&LE/P&WV/WM initials made the Alphabet Route nickname an obvious choice. The inclusion of the Reading, the Jersey Central, and the New Haven enabled shipments to follow the Alphabet Route traffic to New York and Boston. Thanks to aggressive marketing and traffic-solicitation campaigns, as well as expedited service, the managers of the allied companies created what amounted to a fifth trunk line, offering

stiff competition for through traffic against the PRR, the New York Central, the Baltimore & Ohio, and the Erie.

179. Pennroad was the only bidder for the block of 59,400 shares—hardly surprising, as Pennroad controlled the Pittsburgh & West Virginia, a legacy of the investment trust's dealings with the Taplin brothers during the 1930s.

180. To save face, Young blamed Nickel Plate executives and investors for the fiasco. He would do no further favors for that company, and it no longer had any place in his strategic vision. In May 1947, Young announced that he intended to sell Alleghany's holdings in the W&LE, which were of little value if a connection with the Nickel Plate could not be achieved. That proposal left the Nickel Plate in a difficult position. If Pennroad acquired the W&LE stock and added it to the block previously purchased from the P&WV, it would give the PRR control over a significant portion of the Alphabet Route. Despite the drain on its corporate treasury, the Nickel Plate bought the W&LE shares that Young controlled and by 1949 had received permission from the ICC to lease the Wheeling & Lake Erie. *New York Times*, June 14, 1945; August 22, 1945; December 5, 1945; January 17, 1946; July 20, 1946; March 15, 1947; April 16, 1947; Saunders, *Merging Lines*, 84–89.

181. *New York Times*, February 5, 1947; February 27, 1947.

182. The distribution of Nickel Plate stock to C&O shareholders (as a special dividend) took place in November. The largest single C&O stockholder was the Alleghany Corporation—but the ICC had already ruled that Alleghany would have to place that Nickel Plate stock in trust, removing it from Young's influence.

183. Saunders, *Merging Lines*, 91–97; Joseph Borkin, *Robert R. Young: The Populist of Wall Street* (New York: Harper & Row, 1969), 94–111.

184. Boles also insisted that the four hundred thousand shares of NYC stock that Young had purchased remain in trust, supervised by Chase National Bank—in keeping with conditions that the ICC imposed in 1945, when the Alleghany Corporation acquired securities in the C&O, the Pere Marquette, and the Nickel Plate. As such, Young could not vote those NYC shares. The ICC's refusal to permit Young to influence the NYC, coupled with the Nickel Plate's purchase of the W&LE (ensuring that those companies were protected from Young's strategizing) rendered Pennroad's investment in the W&LE redundant. In August 1949, the investment trust earned a tidy $2.4 million profit when it disposed of the stock it had purchased four years earlier. *New York Times*, December 11, 1947 ("injecting," "lessen," "justice,"

"bureaucrat"); January 3, 1948; July 22, 1948; March 19, 1949; August 30, 1949; Saunders, *Merging Lines*, 91–97; Borkin, *Robert R. Young*, 111–31.

185. *New York Times*, November 27, 1951; November 28, 1951 ("rebel"); Borkin, *Robert R. Young*, 136–39; Karl A. Borntrager, *Keeping the Railroads Running: Fifty Years on the New York Central* (New York: Hastings House, 1974), 156–63, 173–82.

186. *New York Times*, January 20, 1954, January 21, 1954; January 24, 1954; Borkin, *Robert R. Young*, 140–210.

187. Journalist and transportation consultant Rush Loving Jr., who had numerous interactions with Perlman, suggested that "he did let his ego overrule his good judgment on occasion"; acquiescing to Young's entreaties may have been a case in point.

188. *New York Times*, March 30, 1954; March 31, 1954 ("never"); Borkin, *Robert R. Young*, 66, 209–19; Rush Loving Jr., *The Well-Dressed Hobo: The Many Wondrous Adventures of a Man Who Loves Trains* (Bloomington: Indiana University Press, 2016), 64–68 ("ego" at 64).

189. *New York Times*, October 19, 1957 ("pattern," "down," "confused"); October 22, 1957; November 1, 1957; November 2, 1957.

190. Borkin, *Robert R. Young*, 217–18, 222; Loving, *Well-Dressed Hobo*, 65–66, 71; Rush Loving Jr., *The Men Who Loved Trains: The Story of Men Who Battled Greed to Save an Ailing Industry* (Bloomington: Indiana University Press, 2006), 20, 25–26; *New York Times*, November 2, 1957.

191. The list included such familiar problems as inadequate rate increases, high taxes, and the unwillingness of regulatory authorities to permit the discontinuance of passenger trains.

192. *Railway Age* 143, no. 20 (November 11, 1957): 9–13; *New York Times*, November 2, 1957 ("faced," "secrets," "signal," "cheaply").

193. *Railway Age* 143, no. 20 (November 11, 1957): 10; *New York Times*, November 3, 1957 ("switch"); November 5, 1957 ("glance," "sleeve," "weakness," "handle," "balloon"); Saunders, *Merging Lines*, 142–43.

194. *Railway Age* 143, no. 20 (November 11, 1957): 13–14 ("comment," "emphatic," "confidence," "direction," "something").

195. *Railway Age*, 143, no. 20 (November 11, 1957): 13 ("matter"); *New York Times*, November 2, 1957; November 3, 1957; November 20, 1957 ("jugglers").

196. In 1959, the C&O's rate of return on invested capital was 7.4 percent (higher than any other large railroad except the Norfolk & Western and the Seaboard Air Line, and equal to that of the Denver & Rio Grande

Western, Perlman's former employer), while the Nickel Plate was earning 5.5 percent.

197. Borkin, *Robert R. Young*, 223–24; Saunders, *Merging Lines*, 122–23.

198. Symes to Newell, February 5, 1957 ("coordinate," "hand"); Greenough to Newell, February 8, 1957; Newell to Regional Managers, February 26, 1957 ("obvious," "master"); all in HML, Box 327, folder 21; "Proposed Change in Organization of the Pennsylvania Railroad Company," February 21, 1958 ("bottlenecks"), PHMC, Box 126 (9-2277), folder 110.01.

199. "Proposed Change in Organization of the Pennsylvania Railroad Company," February 21, 1958 ("common"), PHMC, Box 126 (9-2277), folder 110.01.

200. J. Benton Jones, the former vice president in charge of passenger sales and services, became the vice president in charge of purchases and real estate, replacing Warren Elsey—who had occupied essentially the same role since 1944, after being blamed for problems with the T1 duplex, and who was now preparing for retirement.

201. "Proposed Change in Organization" ("major," "lesser").

202. *One Hundred and Twelfth Annual Report of the Pennsylvania Railroad Company, for the Year Ended December 31, 1958* (Philadelphia: n.p., 1959), 18; Stephen Salsbury, *No Way to Run a Railroad: The Untold Story of the Penn Central Crisis* (New York: McGraw-Hill, 1982), 50–54, 102.

203. Carroll to Bevan, October 17, 1958 ("experience," "integral"), PHMC, Box 103 (9-2254), folder 110.01.

204. Peat, Marwick, Mitchell & Co., Management Controls Department, "Survey of Accounting Activities (Oral Presentation), The Pennsylvania Railroad Company, March 1959," 3 ("trouble," "protection"), 7 ("antiquated," "unqualified"), 17 ("archaic," "weak," "receptive"), PHMC, Box 103 (9-2254), folder 110.01.

205. Carroll to Bevan, October 17, 1958 ("effective," "sell").

206. "Proposed Change in Organization" ("conception").

207. Symes to Newell et al., February 26, 1958, PHMC, Box 126 (9-2277), folder 110.01; "Proposed Change in Organization" ("important").

208. John Kenefick began his career by working briefly for the NYC, before taking a job at the Union Pacific. He went to the Rio Grande in 1952, at a time when Perlman was that company's executive vice president. Both individuals went to the NYC in 1954. When the merger studies began, Kenefick was the general manager of the New York District, but in 1958 he was promoted to systemwide general manager of transportation. In 1966, Kenefick became the NYC's vice president in charge of operations, a role he retained until the 1968 Penn Central merger, when he became the vice president in charge of transportation. On May 1, 1968, he left a dysfunctional company that would soon be bankrupt, becoming the vice president in charge of operations on the Union Pacific. Kenefick became the UP's president in 1971. During the next fifteen years, he oversaw the UP's expansion into the coalfields of the Powder River Basin; its response to the provisions of the 1980 Staggers Act; and the company's merger negotiations with the Missouri Pacific, the Western Pacific, and the Chicago & North Western. He retired in 1983 as the UP's chairman and chief executive officer, with a legacy as one of the most influential executives in the modern railroad industry.

209. *New York Times*, November 27, 1957; October 1, 1971; Tara Siegel Bernard, "John C. Kenefick, Former Rail Executive, Dies at 89," *New York Times*, July 20, 2011; *Headlight* 20, no. 5 (May 1959): 12; *Clearfield* [Pennsylvania] *Progress*, October 4, 1963; [Baltimore] *Evening Sun*, December 23, 1966.

210. The effort to find sufficient cost savings to ensure ICC approval of the merger continued for almost another decade, even after Patchell retired in 1963, with Morris serving as his replacement. Assisted by James W. Diffenderfer, Morris would also spend an increasing portion of his time seeking government subsidies for those passenger services that the PRR could not abandon. They included commuter operations in Philadelphia but by the mid-1960s would involve one project in particular—the development of high-speed trains between New York and Washington, an effort that would be instrumental in the cultivation of political support for the PRR/NYC merger.

211. E. C. Poole, "The Carriers' Use of Costs," *I.C.C. Practitioners' Journal* 23, no. 10 (September 1956): 1106–69; Ernest C. Poole, *Costs—A Tool for Railroad Management* (New York: Simmons-Boardman, 1962); "Force Assigned Merger Study," n.d., but ca. December 1957; J. C. Kenefick to J. F. Nash, December 15, 1957; both in Barriger Papers, Series 259, Box 155, folder 3–2 ("statistical").

212. Poole study, memo to Barriger, December 2, 1957 ("prepared," "progressed," "complete," "approved"), Barriger Papers, Series 259, Box 155, folder 3–2.

213. The anticipated reductions included decreases in freight train miles and car miles ($33.5 million), passenger train and car miles ($29.6 million), transportation overheads ($23.1 million), maintenance-of-equipment expenditures ($14.0 million), maintenance-of-way

expenditures ($10.0 million), costs associated with traffic functions ($13.3 million), general expenses ($6.7 million), passenger switching ($1.5 million), and miscellaneous operations ($1.5 million).

214. Poole study, memo to Barriger, 7 ("abandoned," "passenger"); Barriger to Perlman, n.d., but ca. December 1957 ("rough," "arbitrary," "unquestionably," "limit"); both in Barriger Papers, Series 259, Box 155, folder 3–2.

215. Barriger to Perlman, December 16, 1959, 2 ("alliance"); Barriger Papers, Series 259, Box 155, folder 3–5; Nash to Barriger, December 23, 1957 ("thinking"), Barriger Papers, Series 259, Box 155, folder 3–2.

216. The initial report of the Operating Committee thus coincidentally mirrored the policies of the United States Railroad Administration during World War I. The USRA, whose Eastern Region was dominated by New York Central managers, favored the routing of through freight over the NYC, with the PRR's Lines East (as part of the Alleghany Region) restricted largely to shipments between eastern Ohio and western Pennsylvania and the East Coast.

217. "N.Y.C.—P.R.R. Operating Committee Report No. 1," February 3, 1958, 2 ("advantage"); "N.Y.C.—P.R.R. Operating Committee Report No. 2," March 17, 1958; "N.Y.C.—P.R.R. Operating Committee Report No. 3: Final," April 21, 1958; all in Barriger Papers, Series 259, Box 155, folder 3–4.

218. The April 1958 final report of the Operating Committee suggested annual savings in freight operations ($24.6 million), freight terminal operations ($20.8 million), passenger operations ($15.5 million), maintenance-of-way ($11.1 million), New York Harbor operations ($10.1 million), general and traffic expense ($10.0 million), back shop ($1.2 million), and freight stations ($0.9 million).

219. The $31.1 million amount included Poole's estimates for passenger train and car miles ($29.6 million) and passenger switching ($1.5 million).

220. "N.Y.C.—P.R.R. Operating Committee Report No. 3: Final."

221. PRR BOD Minutes.

222. New York Times, January 15, 1958 ("unless"); May 21, 1958; May 22, 1958; May 23, 1958 ("say"); July 3, 1958; October 16, 1958; November 13, 1958; January 27, 1959; Borkin, Robert R. Young, 223.

223. In June 1958, the ICC authorized a substantial increase in mail rates, retroactive to June 1956.

224. New York Times, January 9, 1959; January 27, 1959.

225. Saunders, Merging Lines, 122–23, 143–44.

226. New York Times, November 20, 1958 ("purpose," "proposal,"); Saunders, Merging Lines, 144, 168–69; PRR BOD Minutes.

227. Statement of Testimony of Alfred E. Perlman Before the Interstate Commerce Commission, Finance Docket Nos. 21160, 21161, 21237, 21238, June 2, 1961 (revised July 7, 1961), 6 ("regarded"), Barriger Papers, Series 259, Box 155, folder 3–9; Saunders, Merging Lines, 63, 93–97, 145–46; E. F. Pat Striplin, The Norfolk & Western: A History (Roanoke, VA: Norfolk & Western, 1981), 240–41; Joseph A. Strapac, "'The Richest Little Railroad in the World': A Brief History of the Virginian Railway," Railroad History 223 (Fall–Winter 2020): 14–43.

228. Striplin, Norfolk & Western, 174–75; 205–8.

229. Striplin, Norfolk & Western, 221.

230. Striplin, Norfolk & Western, 219–24, 240–41; Saunders, Merging Lines, 145–46.

231. Statement of Testimony of Alfred E. Perlman, 8–9 ("engaged"); Striplin, Norfolk & Western, 221; Saunders, Merging Lines, 145–46.

232. In February, the representatives of the Eastern Railroad Presidents' Conference agreed that their organization was not equipped to formulate a plan for consolidating thirty-seven large eastern railroads into the three or four systems that Perlman recommended. That decision ended the cooperative efforts that White attempted in Chicago. With both the ERPC and the ICC unwilling to exercise leadership, it was more apparent than ever that representatives from every carrier—the PRR included—should try to make the best arrangements they could. Equally puzzling was the statement from the NYC's directors, who were apparently surprised that the seven-railroad meeting that White organized in Chicago a few weeks earlier signaled "a new climate among Eastern railroads in regard to merger." NYC personnel must have sensed that even the possibility of a merger with the PRR would cause corporate realignments throughout the Northeast. New York Times, November 20, 1958 ("cooled"); January 9, 1959 ("balanced," "climate"); January 29, 1959 ("timing").

233. One proposal for coordination, which took effect on January 1, 1958, allowed passengers to purchase a PRR or NYC round-trip ticket and use either carrier for the return journey. The plan extended to only nine cities in the Midwest and came at a time when Perlman in particular was determined to eliminate passenger service as rapidly as possible. Perlman also suggested coordinated passenger service to St. Louis as well as joint use of passenger facilities in Detroit, and he predicted an annual expenditure reduction of $14 million. Symes dismissed

such projects as a poor alternative to the merger, insisting that "the possible alternative savings that might be made through coordination of facilities or services would be relatively small by comparison." *Railway Age* 143, no. 25 (December 16, 1957): 7; 146, no. 3 (January 19, 1959): 9–10; PRR press release, January 28, 1959, HML, Box 271, folder 13 ("possible").

234. *New York Times*, January 9, 1959 ("past," "pleased," "understood"); January 13, 1959 ("marry").

235. *New York Times*, January 29, 1959 ("amazed," "practical"); February 20, 1959; *One Hundred and Twelfth Annual Report*, 5 ("enthusiastic"); PRR press release, January 28, 1959, HML, Box 271, folder 13 ("reasons").

236. *New York Times*, January 29, 1959; *Railway Age* 146, no. 5 (February 2, 1959): 32; Saunders, *Merging Lines*, 169.

237. Pennsylvania Railroad Company, *One Hundred and Thirteenth Annual Report of the Pennsylvania Railroad Company, for the Year Ended December 31, 1959* (Philadelphia: n.p., 1960), 5–8.

238. *New York Times*, October 29, 1959; Wolfgang Saxon, "A. J. Greenough, Last Pennsy Head," *New York Times*, September 23, 1974; PRR BOD Minutes.

239. Clement's role as board chairman ensured continuity of leadership and enabled him to influence the actions of his successor, Walter Franklin. The board chairmanship was also a politically expedient way to ease Clement out of power, following the PRR's disastrous postwar financial performance. Clement remained on the board of directors until April 1957.

240. *Trains* 20, no. 3 (January 1960): 8; Salsbury, *No Way to Run a Railroad*, 89.

241. *Trains* 20, no. 3 (January 1960): 8 ("done," "what," "Railroad").

242. Bevan to Greenough, December 6, 1960 ("safeguard"), PHMC, Box 125 (9-2276), folder 110.01.

243. Pevler left the Wabash in 1963 to serve as president of the Norfolk & Western, a post he retained until 1970. He clashed with the N&W's general counsel, Jack Fishwick, who considered Pevler to be a poor administrator. Pevler later sent Fishwick to Cleveland to oversee efforts to incorporate the Erie Lackawanna into the N&W family—a move that Fishwick's supporters interpreted as banishment, so that Fishwick would not outshine Pevler. By 1970, there were growing concerns among N&W insiders that Pevler was using creative accounting techniques to inflate the railroad's earnings. When Pevler attempted to select an executive at the rival Chessie System as his successor, Fishwick engineered a coup that gained him control of the N&W. Loving, *Men Who Loved Trains*, 99–101.

244. The most comprehensive coverage of the infighting involving Newell, Carpi, and Bevan is in Salsbury, *No Way to Run a Railroad*, esp. 89–91.

245. *New York Times*, October 29, 1959 ("dramatic," "decided").

246. *Trains* 20, no. 3 (January 1960): 8 ("shift").

7. Commutation

1. The lament was not entirely accurate. For many years prior to 1939 PRR passenger trains between New York and western destinations had bypassed Broad Street Station, in favor of the North Philadelphia Station. The opening of 30th Street Station in March 1933 ensured that trains operating between New York and Washington used the new facility, located in West Philadelphia. Many long-distance trains that originated or terminated in Philadelphia, including the hourly Clocker service to New York, continued to use Broad Street Station and would do so for more than a decade after the publication of *Kitty Foyle*.

2. Christopher Morley, *Kitty Foyle* (New York: Grosset & Dunlap, 1939), 15–16 ("way"), 41 ("significant"); Margaret Wallace, "Mr. Morley's Sparkling 'Kitty Foyle,'" *New York Times*, October 29, 1939; *New York Times*, "Christopher Morley, Author, 66, Is Dead," March 29, 1957.

3. Steam locomotives continued to operate into Broad Street Station until that facility closed in 1952—most were bound for the Delair Bridge and then to Atlantic City, over a route that had never been electrified.

4. Morley, *Kitty Foyle*, 20 ("steam"), 51 ("snobway," emphasis in the original), 253 ("ought").

5. The PRR's commuter operations were not limited to Philadelphia and Greater New York. At Baltimore, the PRR offered service to Washington (which continues to operate as Maryland Area Regional Commuter) and to Parkton along the Northern Central Railway toward Harrisburg (which ended in 1959). To the west, many Harrisburg commuters relied on PRR trains that ran toward Lancaster, as well as those operating over the Northern Central and the Cumberland Valley Railroad. At Pittsburgh, the PRR served commuters along the Pittsburgh Division main line east to Greensburg (with some continuing to Derry); on the Eastern Division to Sharon; on the Monongahela Division to Brownsville; on the Allegheny Division to Kiskiminetas Junction (with some service continuing along the Conemaugh Division to Torrance); on the Chartiers Branch to Washington; and over the Panhandle Division to Burgettstown. The

PRR also operated modest commuter services between Buffalo and East Aurora, New York; between Cleveland and Youngstown (ended in 1965); and between Cincinnati and Loveland (ended in 1923) and Cincinnati and Morrow (ended in 1934). In Chicago, there was a short-lived commuter service along the Pan Handle route, which quickly succumbed to competition from elevated railways. There was a Chicago–Hegewisch–Hammond–East Chicago loop service in the Calumet District, which ended in 1919. The most successful service linked Chicago with Valparaiso, Indiana—it continued through the formation of Penn Central, then Contrail, eventually becoming an Amtrak train, the *Calumet*, and ended in 1991. The author extends his thanks to Chris Baer for compiling a list of the PRR's varied commuter operations.

6. Christopher T. Baer and William D. Middleton, with additional contributions from Norman Carlson and Arthur L. Lloyd, "Commuter Railroads," in *Encyclopedia of North American Railroads*, William D. Middleton, George M. Smerk, and Roberta L. Diehl (Bloomington: Indiana University Press, 2007): 308–24, at 314–15. For information on the development of Chestnut Hill, see David R. Contosta, *Suburb in the City: Chestnut Hill, Philadelphia, 1850–1990* (Columbus: Ohio State University Press, 1992), esp. 36–117.

7. John W. Townsend, *The Old "Main Line"* (Philadelphia: n.p., 1922), 51–52; Lawrence Grow, *On the 8:02: An Informal History of Commuting by Rail in America* (New York: Mayflower, 1979), 126–27.

8. PRR BOD Minutes; Thomas Allen Glenn, *Merion in the Welsh Tract, with Sketches of the Townships of Haverford and Radnor: Historical and Genealogical Collection Concerning the Welsh Barony in the Province of Pennsylvania, Settled by the Cymric Quakers in 1682* (Norristown, PA: Herald, 1896), 205–34; *Evening Telegraph*, April 22, 1871 ("proposed"); *Philadelphia Inquirer*, April 22, 1871; Alison Janet Reed, "The Bryn Mawr Hotel: The Relationship between the Main Line of the Pennsylvania Railroad and the Nineteenth-Century Railroad Resort Hotel" (master's thesis, University of Pennsylvania, 1989), 95–118; Lower Merion Historical Society, "Bryn Mawr," *First 300: The Amazing and Rich History of Lower Merion*, http://www.lowermerionhistory.org/texts/first300/part14.html#122, accessed February 23, 2020; Lower Merion Historical Society, "The Pennsylvania Railroad and the Development of the Main Line," *First 300*, http://www.lowermerionhistory.org/texts/first300/part08.html#72, accessed February 23, 2020; William Hasell Wilson, *The Columbia-Philadelphia Railroad and*

Its Successor (York, PA: American Canal & Transportation Center, 1985, repr. 1992), 61–65.

9. Townsend, *Old "Main Line,"* 52–57; Reed, "Bryn Mawr Hotel," 120–50; Lower Merion Historical Society, "The Bryn Mawr Hotel," *First 300*, http://www.lowermerionhistory.org/texts/first300/part09.html#80, accessed February 22, 2020; Lower Merion Historical Society, "Bryn Mawr College," *First 300*, http://www.lowermerionhistory.org/texts/first300/part18.html#162, accessed February 22, 2020.

10. The facility remained in business until 1922, when it became part of the Baldwin School. Reed, "Bryn Mawr Hotel," 170–211.

11. The Pennsylvania Railroad did not complete its line to Chestnut Hill (as the Philadelphia, Germantown & Chestnut Hill Railroad) until 1884. Townsend, *Old "Main Line,"* 21 ("cater"), 27–28 ("dirty").

12. Chestnut Hill residents, in contrast, could choose from thirty daily round trips on the Reading.

13. During the 1880s and 1890s, the PRR operated "Park Trains" that made frequent stops along the short route that connected Broad Street Station and the 21st Street Station to a station at the intersection of 52nd Street and Elm Avenue (now Parkside Avenue), at the entrance to Fairmount Park and near the site of the 1876 Centennial Exposition. It could not compete with the more frequent service offered by streetcars, and service ended around 1900.

14. The PRR offered a range of ticket options, typical of most commuter lines. Monthly tickets (60 trips) and quarterly tickets (180 trips) appealed to businessmen on a six-day workweek. School tickets (46 trips) attested to the large numbers of children who took the train, long before local governments provided bus transportation. Family tickets (50 trips at any time during a one-year period) enabled housewives to shop or socialize in the city and could also be distributed to one's domestic servants. Firm tickets followed the same pattern and were given to employees. A variety of excursion tickets provided recreational opportunities for suburbanites as well as additional patronage for the railroad during off-peak periods. *York Dispatch*, April 3, 1882 ("accommodation"); *Philadelphia Inquirer*, April 7, 1882; Wilson, *Columbia-Philadelphia Railroad*, 63–64; Pennsylvania Railroad Company, *Suburban Homes on the Lines of the Pennsylvania Railroad within a Radius of Thirty Miles around Philadelphia, with Useful Information for Summer-Home Seekers* (Philadelphia: Allen, Lane & Scott, 1894), 3, 6–7 ("purse-power"); John Henry Hepp IV, *The Middle-Class City: Transforming Space and Time in Philadelphia, 1876–1926*

(Philadelphia: University of Pennsylvania Press, 2003), 30, 197; Baer and Middleton, "Commuter Railroads," 308.

15. After he became president in 1913, Rea moved to a one-hundred-acre estate in still-rural Waverly Heights, midway between the Main Line and the Schuylkill River. Townsend, *Old "Main Line,"* 78–79; Lower Merion Historical Society, "Alexander J. Cassatt's Cheswold," *First 300,* http://www.lowermerionhistory.org/texts/first300/part26.html, accessed February 20, 2020.

16. The phrase appeared in Morley's "Elegy in a Railroad Station," a tribute to the soon-to-be-demolished Broad Street Station. The poem, as well as the syncopation of the text, is a clear reference to a steam locomotive beginning to move a train—something that had not taken place on the actual Paoli Local in nearly forty years. "Elegy in a Railroad Station (Broad Street, Philadelphia, obit, 1952)"; Christopher Morley, *Christopher Morley's Philadelphia,* ed. Ken Kalfus (New York: Fordham University Press, 1990), 133–34; Henry Graham Ashmead, *History of Delaware County, Pennsylvania* (Philadelphia: L. H. Everts, 1884), 682–84; E. Digby Baltzell, *Philadelphia Gentlemen: The Making of a National Upper Class* (Glencoe, IL: Free Press, 1958), 203–4; Grow, *On the 8:02,* 126–28.

17. Townsend, *Old "Main Line,"* 21 ("herding").

18. Townsend, *Old "Main Line,"* 5 ("meanderings"), 8 ("unfortunately").

19. George W. Hilton, "The Decline of Railroad Commutation," *Business History Review* 36, no. 2 (Summer 1962): 171–87, at 173–74.

20. *Interstate Commerce Commission Docket No. 31954: Passenger Train Deficit, Item 7, Exhibit Accompanying Testimony of Walter W. Patchell, Vice President, Research and Development, Pennsylvania Railroad Company,* 1957, 10–14.

21. Officially, the Surface Transportation Subcommittee of the Senate Committee on Interstate and Foreign Commerce.

22. United States Congress, Senate Committee on Interstate and Foreign Commerce, *Problems of the Railroads: Report of the Subcommittee on Surface Transportation of the Committee on Interstate and Foreign Commerce,* April 30, 1958 (Washington, DC: United States Government Printing Office, 1958) (hereafter, Smathers Committee Report), 4–5 ("burden").

23. Smathers Committee Report, 4 ("implications"), 5 ("evident," "desirable").

24. In the mid-1930s, for example, the PRR operated ten local trains from Jersey City to New Brunswick and a further five from Penn Station to New Brunswick. Of those, eight continued to Trenton (one from Jersey City and seven from Penn Station). Eastbound, there were eight local trains originating at Trenton (three to Jersey City and five to Penn Station). An additional twelve trains originated at New Brunswick, of which seven terminated at Jersey City and five at Penn Station. John W. Barriger III Papers, St. Louis Mercantile Library, St. Louis, Missouri (hereafter, Barriger Papers), Series 262, Box 158, folder 2–18.

25. Longtime Jersey City mayor and political boss Frank Hague coerced the PRR into continuing trans-Hudson ferry service long after the opening of the Hudson Tubes made the operation unnecessary. Hague, threatened with prosecution for his numerous misdeeds, resigned as mayor in 1947, but he remained influential for two additional years. His fall from power in 1949 enabled PRR officials to curtail ferry service, and the last boat ran on January 6, 1950.

26. Grow, *On the 8:02,* 43–46, 58–60, 83–116.

27. As a named train, *The Broker* appeared in the PRR's public timetables between 1931 and 1941 and remained listed as such in employee timetables until 1967. PRR trains bound for Penn Station changed from steam or diesel power to electric locomotives at South Amboy, followed the Jersey Central tracks a short distance north to Woodbridge Junction, then proceeded along a PRR subsidiary (the Perth Amboy & Woodbridge Railroad) eight miles northwest to the main line at Rahway. *The Broker* and other trains bound for Exchange Place in Jersey City followed the same route, but as they did not enter the tunnels under the Hudson River, they did not change power at South Amboy.

28. Histories of the New Jersey shore resorts are available in Christopher T. Baer, William J. Coxey, and Paul W. Schopp, *Trail of the Blue Comet: A History of the Jersey Central's New Jersey Southern Division* (Palmyra: New Jersey Chapter of the National Railway Historical Society, 1994). Don Wood, Joel Rosenbaum, and Tom Gallo, *The Unique New York & Long Branch* (Earlton, NY: Audio-Visual Designs, 1985), 13–65, 164–67; Rosenbaum, "A History of *The Broker,*" *Keystone* 38, no. 3 (Autumn 2005): 45; George H. Burgess and Miles C. Kennedy, *Centennial History of the Pennsylvania Railroad Company, 1846–1946* (Philadelphia: Pennsylvania Railroad, 1949), 416–17.

29. Baer and Middleton, "Commuter Railroads," 312; Grow, *On the 8:02,* 97–102.

30. The Long Island Rail Road Company, *Thirty-Ninth Annual Report, For the Year Ended December 31, 1920* (New York: Hosford, 1921), 16–17, 25.

31. Burgess and Kennedy, *Centennial History,* 472–81.

32. *New York Times*, March 10, 1907; April 7, 1907; Clifton Hood, *722 Miles: The Building of the Subways and How They Transformed New York* (Baltimore, MD: Johns Hopkins University Press, 1993), 131–32.

33. *Houston, East & West Texas Railway Company, et al. v. United States*, 234 US 342 (1914), aka, the *Shreveport Rate* cases.

34. *New York Times*, July 6, 1920; November 19, 1920; November 20, 1920; January 29, 1921.

35. *New York Times*, November 2, 1918; November 8, 1918; November 26, 1918; December 13, 1918; November 1, 2018; John Francis Hylan, *Autobiography of John Francis Hylan, Mayor of New York* (New York: Rotary, 1922), 17–18; Brian Cudahy, *The Malbone Street Wreck* (New York: Fordham University Press, 1999); Robert A. Slayton, *Empire Statesman: The Rise and Redemption of Al Smith* (New York: Free Press, 2001), 115–16, 221–24.

36. Daniel L. Turner, *A Report by the Chief Engineer Submitting for Consideration a Comprehensive Rapid Transit Plan Covering All Boroughs of the City of New York* (New York: Office of Transit Construction Commissioner, 1920); *New York Times*, October 3, 1920; January 18, 1921; State of New York, *First Annual Report of the Public Service Commission, for the Year Ended December 31, 1921, Volume I* (Albany, NY: Commission, 1922), 7–8; Arthur W. Macmahon, "The New York City Transit System: Public Ownership, Civil Service, and Collective Bargaining," *Political Science Quarterly* 56, no. 2 (June 1941): 161–98.

37. *New York Times*, February 7, 1924; Joseph B. Raskin, *The Routes Not Taken: A Trip through New York City's Unbuilt Subway System* (New York: Fordham University Press, 2014), 1–11; Andrew J. Sparberg, *From a Nickel to a Token: The Journey from Board of Transportation to MTA* (New York: Fordham University Press, 2015), 59–66.

38. *New York Times*, July 28, 1922.

39. The PRR maintained precisely the same number of grade crossings in New York. The New York Central was the undisputed leader, with 2,680 crossings, and only the Erie (921); the Delaware & Hudson (677); the Lehigh Valley (662); and the Delaware, Lackawanna & Western (554) featured more grade crossings than the LIRR and its corporate parent. Because the LIRR operated relatively few track miles, while serving a densely populated urban area, the number of crossings per route mile was higher than was the case for most other railroads—and the financial consequences correspondingly greater.

40. *New York Times*, January 18, 1923; February 12, 1923 ("humanitarian," "experience"); November 23, 1923;

December 12, 1923; December 5, 1925 ("menace," "stubborn"); February 4, 1926; *Railway Age* 86, no. 6 (February 9, 1929): 349–52; State of New York, *Fifth Annual Report of the Public Service Commission, for the Year 1925, Volume I* (Albany, NY: Commission, 1926), 23–27.

41. *New York Times*, January 19, 1923; April 18, 1924; *Harrisburg Telegraph*, January 18, 1923; *Brooklyn Daily Eagle*, January 21, 1923 ("spirit"); *Railway Engineering and Maintenance* 19, no. 11 (November 1923): 468.

42. The rapid increase in commuter traffic at Penn Station came largely at the expense of the LIRR's Long Island City rail and ferry terminal, which lay directly atop the eastern end of the East River tunnels. Passenger counts at Long Island City decreased from 6.3 million in 1910 (when Penn Station was only in service for the last three and a half months of the year) to fewer than 1.2 million in 1916. The LIRR's Flatbush Avenue terminal in Brooklyn remained heavily patronized, as it possessed a direct connection to the Interborough Rapid Transit subway line to the Financial District in Lower Manhattan. Nearly 13.5 million commuters passed through Flatbush Avenue in 1910, and the number grew to nearly 19.7 million in 1916 and 27.5 million in 1919—in each case exceeding the number of Long Islanders who used the facilities at Long Island City. *Brooklyn Daily Eagle*, November 5, 1917; C. Francis Harding, "Handling Suburban Traffic at Congested Centers," *Transit Journal* 56, no. 14 (October 2, 1920): 663–74, at 663–66; Chamber of Commerce of the Borough of Queens, *Queens Borough, New York City, 1910–1920: The Borough of Homes and Industry* (New York: L. I. Star, 1920), 58.

43. In 1920, shortly after the end of USRA control, the PRR raised the rental fee to $240,000 annually. Two years later, the Transit Commission approved a further increase, to $300,000, but that figure still represented a substantial subsidy from the larger company to its subsidiary.

44. *New York Times*, June 2, 1922; Case No. 2511, 160–66; *Reports of Decisions of the Transit Commission of the State of New York, Volume II, January 1, 1922, to December 31, 1922* (New York: Commission, 1922); Harding, "Handling Suburban Traffic," 664.

45. Case No. 2511, 165; *New York Times*, September 6, 1923.

46. *New York Times*, July 15, 1923; July 17, 1923; October 14, 1923; *Brooklyn Daily Eagle*, July 16, 1923; *Wall Street Journal*, July 17, 1923 ("watching").

47. "Far be it from us to insinuate that there was any connection between the two incidents," observed representatives from the International Brotherhood of

Electrical Workers—which, of course, was exactly what they were insinuating. *Journal of Electrical Workers and Operators* 23, no. 6 (May 1924): 397 ("insinuate"); *New York Times*, April 1, 1924; April 6, 1924 ("miserable," "dealing"); June 25, 1924.

48. LeBoutillier had recently moved from Harrisburg, not Chicago, but Hylan's lack of geographic accuracy probably did not concern members of the audience.

49. *New York Times*, April 17, 1924 ("listen," "jobs," "war").

50. *New York Times*, July 6, 1924; *Brooklyn Daily Eagle*, February 20, 1925.

51. *New York Times*, June 25, 1924; June 26, 1924; August 6, 1924; August 10, 1924 ("sincere").

52. *Brooklyn Daily Eagle*, January 27, 1925 ("Revere," "doctors," "martyr"); February 20, 1925; *New York Times*, July 8, 1925 ("vehement," "battle," "extortion"); *New York Times*, March 26, 1925; July 5, 1925 ("faith"); November 26, 1925; March 28, 1930; December 27, 1930; *Railway Age* 87, no. 16 (October 19, 1929): 944.

53. The sale or abandonment of LIRR tracks along Atlantic Avenue, between Jamaica and the Flatbush Avenue terminal, would not have affected the LIRR routes to Long Island City (which was in Queens rather than Brooklyn) or to Penn Station. Several years earlier, the Committee of One Hundred suggested modifications that would transform the LIRR into something akin to a rapid-transit line within city limits. LeBoutillier turned that argument on its head, suggesting that the municipally owned subway system that Hylan had proposed should purchase and operate the route along Atlantic Avenue. *New York Times*, December 5, 1925 ("ready," "frank," "expense," "out").

54. LeBoutillier also offered to sell the Manhattan Beach and Rockaway Beach branches to the city. The LIRR subsequently ended passenger service on the Whitestone Branch in 1932.

55. *New York Times*, March 9, 1926 ("branch," "moral").

56. "For men may come and men may go/But I go on for ever." Alfred Tennyson, *Song of the Brook* (Boston: Joseph Knight, 1893).

57. The PRR owned 99.92 percent of the $34.1 million in LIRR common stock.

58. *New York Times*, February 11, 1927; February 12, 1927 ("affairs," "jump," "bankruptcy"); March 2, 1927 ("brook," "poor"); April 25, 1928; *Railway Age* 84, no. 2 (February 4, 1928): 321–23.

59. *In the Matter of the Fare Increases*, Case No. 2042, decided February 28, 1928, State of New York, Department of Public Service, *Annual Report of the Public Service Commission for the Year 1928* (Albany: J. B. Lyon, 1929), 139 ("profitable"), 158 ("reasonableness," "burden").

60. *New York Times*, December 22, 1925; May 6, 1926; October 25, 1927 ("unsatisfactory").

61. *New York Times*, April 25, 1928 ("reliance," "curtailed," "opinion"); May 2, 1928; January 5, 1929; January 23, 1929.

62. *New York Times*, November 24, 1927; January 21, 1928 ("dissatisfaction," "shake-up," "foundation"); October 25, 1928 ("integral").

63. *New York Times*, March 1, 1930; May 8, 1930 ("absurdity," "implies").

64. In 1929, the LIRR carried 118,888,797 passengers, at 1.471 cents per passenger mile, for a total revenue of $27.8 million, at an average revenue per passenger of 23.4 cents. The PRR carried 113,713,128 passengers, at 3.173 cents per passenger mile, for a total revenue of $27.8 million, equivalent to an average revenue per passenger of $1.18.

65. *New York Times*, April 10, 1930; May 2, 1931; April 29, 1933; April 24, 1934; October 25, 1935; June 17, 1936.

66. *New York Times*, September 6, 1933; October 3, 1933 ("ultimately," "ripe," "evasive," "power"); October 4, 1933.

67. State of New York, Transit Commission, *In the Matter of the Passenger Tariff Schedule of the Long Island Railroad Company*, Case No. 3232, decided July 21, 1936, Penn Central Transportation Company Records, 1796–1986, Manuscript Collection 2372, New York Public Library, Humanities and Social Sciences Library, Manuscripts and Archives Division (hereafter, NYPL), Box 295.

68. New York Public Service Commission, *In the Matter of the Proposed Increased Commutation Fares of the Long Island Railroad Company*, Case No. 8626, July 15, 1936, July 20, 1936, NYPL, Box 295 ("meager," "doubt").

69. *New York Times*, October 25, 1935; December 19, 1935 ("management"); December 20, 1935; December 21, 1935; January 9, 1936.

70. The corresponding figure on the PRR was 87.24 percent.

71. *New York Times*, February 29, 1936 ("surprise," "effect"); April 19, 1936.

72. *New York Times*, February 29, 1936 ("ridiculous"); April 19, 1936; May 21, 1936.

73. On July 8, the New York Court of Appeals barred the LIRR from charging fares higher than two cents per mile within New York City. Five days later, the New York State Supreme Court issued a similar ruling affecting the remainder of the LIRR system, in Nassau and Suffolk Counties. The outcome of the latter case was a foregone

conclusion, because in the New York judicial system, the court of appeals outranks the state's supreme court.

74. *New York Times*, May 21, 1936; May 26, 1936; May 29, 1936; June 2, 1936; June 4, 1936; June 5, 1936; June 6, 1936; June 10, 1936; June 16, 1936; June 23, 1936; June 30, 1936; July 1, 1936; July 4, 1936; July 10, 1936; July 14, 1936 ("identical"); July 15, 1936; July 22, 1936.

75. In 1929, at the request of Philadelphia mayor Harry A. Mackey, Maltbie conducted a thorough audit of the Philadelphia Rapid Transit Company and its associated holding company, Mitten Management, Incorporated. The audit revealed widespread irregularities and may have contributed to Thomas E. Mitten's mysterious drowning later that year—events that affected the PRR's involvement in the Philadelphia Improvements. Jan Onofrio, *Pennsylvania Biographical Dictionary*, 3rd ed., vol. 2 (St. Clair Shores, MI: Somerset, 1999), 164–65.

76. New York PSC, Case No. 8626, July 15, 1936, 577 ("recognition"), 583 ("induced," "virtual"), 585 ("unusual," "hooked"); *New York Times*, July 22, 1936.

77. New York PSC Case No. 8626, 584 ("confidence"), 578 ("opinion"); New York Transit Commission, Case No. 3232, decided July 21, 1936, NYPL, Box 295 ("seems").

78. The eastern end of the tunnel was at the LIRR's Morris Park engine facility in Richmond Hill, a short distance to the west of Jamaica Station.

79. J. G. White, *The Long Island Rail Road—Its Problems and Future*, September 1942, 10; US District Court, Eastern District of New York, *In the Matter of the Long Island Rail Road Company*, Case No. 47970, August 14, 1952; both in NYPL, Box 295; *New York Times*, December 26, 1942; December 28, 1942; *Leader-Observer*, December 31, 1942.

80. Mark Aldrich, *Death Rode the Rails: American Railroad Accidents and Safety, 1828–1965* (Baltimore, MD: Johns Hopkins University Press, 2006), 127–28, 214; D. P. White to James Deasy, June 25, 1943, "RE: Reduction of Property Taxes on the Long Island Railroad," NYPL, Box 295.

81. White, *Long Island Rail Road*, 23 ("progress"), 46; Long Island Rail Road, *Sixty-Sixth Annual Report* (1947), 16; Long Island Rail Road, Operating Results, Barriger Papers, Series 179, Box 97, folder 2–7.

82. "New York World's Fair—1939, Summary of Expenditures," Pennsylvania Railroad Company Records, Accession 1807, Manuscripts and Archives Department, Hagley Museum and Library, Wilmington, Delaware (hereafter, HML), Box 1525, folder 20; LeBoutillier to John F. Deasy, May 8, 1937; LeBoutillier to Grover A. Whalen, July 13, 1937; both in HML, Box 1525, folder 18; "Division of Cost of Capital Expenditures incurred by the Long Island Railroad," May 4, 1939, HML, Box 1525, folder 20; LIRR press release, May 1, 1939; HML, Box 1525, folder 21; *Railway Age* 94, no. 21 (May 27, 1933): 754–59.

83. *Mid-Island Mail*, September 11, 1935; *New York Times*, March 19, 1936 ("gullible"); July 23, 1936 ("onus"); *New York Times*, April 24, 1936; *Railway Age* 99, no. 11 (September 14, 1935): 343.

84. White, *Long Island Rail Road*, 27 ("investigation"), 30 ("impressively"); White to John Deasy, June 25, 1943 ("Reduction of Property Taxes on the Long Island Railroad"), NYPL, Box 295 ("sympathetic").

85. The Long Island Rail Road Company, transcript of testimony of Walter S. Franklin before Commissioner J. Haden Alldredge, Interstate Commerce Commission, July 20, 1942, 5 ("apparently"), Penn Central Railroad Collection, M. G. 286, Pennsylvania Historical and Museum Commission, Pennsylvania State Archives, Harrisburg (hereafter, PHMC), Clement Papers, Box 82 (9-1678), folder 601.11.

86. Franklin Testimony, 6–7, 9–11; *Brooklyn Daily Eagle*, July 20, 1942 ("revival," "soothsayer").

87. *Increased Railway Rates, Fares, and Charges*, 248 ICC 545 (1942), 255 ICC 357 (1943); "Memo to Mr. Franklin—Subject: I.C.C. 28815—New York Intrastate Commutation Fares," November 23, 1945, NYPL, Box 295; Louis J. Carruthers to LeBoutillier, June 8, 1942; Carruthers to LeBoutillier, June 12, 1942; Carruthers to LeBoutillier, July 3, 1942; *New York Times*, July 21, 1942; October 15, 1943; *Brooklyn Eagle*, July 20, 1942; Testimony of Walter S. Franklin before Commissioner Alldredge; all in PHMC, Clement Papers, Box 82 (9-1678), folder 601.11; *New York Herald-Tribune*, January 30, 1942; Samuel P. Huntington, "The Marasmus of the ICC," *Yale Law Journal* 61 (April 1952): 467–509; "Carriers: Power of the Interstate Commerce Commission to Regulate Intrastate Rates," *Virginia Law Review* 31 (September 1945): 939–43.

88. The situation became more complicated in August 1942 when Leon Henderson, the head of the Office of Price Administration, asked the ICC to dismiss all petitions for an increase in commuter fares, arguing that higher rates constituted war profiteering and interfered with his ability to prevent inflation. In October 1943, the New York Court of Appeals ruled that the ICC maintained jurisdiction in the matter; it ordered the PRR, the New York Central, and the Staten Island Rapid Transit to increase their rates. The ruling had scant effect on the LIRR, however, given the relatively small amount of

noncommutation traffic. Martin W. Clement to James R. Downes, July 2, 1942 ("philosophy," "supported," "examination"); T. J. Ross to Downes, July 21, 1942; Frank Kivlan to Ross, July 25, 1942; Long Island Rail Road press release, August 11, 1942; Downes to Franklin, August 4, 1942; all in PHMC, Clement Papers, Box 82 (9-1678), folder 601.11.

89. Ross to Downes, April 29, 1942 ("enthusiasm"); Downes to Ross, May 1, 1942 ("theme"); both in PHMC, Clement Papers, Box 82 (9-1678), folder 601.11.

90. *Petition of the Long Island Railroad Company before the Public Service Commission of New York*, Case No. 12989, November 11, 1948, NYPL, Box 295; *New York Times*, March 11, 1947.

91. *New York Times*, March 11, 1947 ("solution").

92. Pennsylvania Railroad Company, April 9, 1947, NYPL, Box 295 ("number," "represented"); *Sixty-Sixth Annual Report of the Long Island Rail Road Company* (1947), 3.

93. *New York Times*, July 28, 1947; H. T. Cover to James M. Symes, April 22, 1949; Symes to Clement, June 6, 1947; both in NYPL, Box 80; J. G. White Report, October 15, 1948, NYPL, Box 295.

94. In 1939, for example, former New York state senator John A. Hastings suggested dividing the United States into ten travel zones, with ticket prices set accordingly. Hastings tied his proposal to efforts to reduce travel costs for those contemplating a visit to the New York World's Fair, an event that attracted far fewer visitors than its organizers had anticipated.

95. *New York Daily News*, February 25, 1948 ("deficient"); *Railway Age* 106, no. 11 (March 18, 1939): 504.

96. PRR BOD Minutes.

97. White had been general manager of the Central Region since 1939. Smucker graduated from The Ohio State University in 1929 and soon thereafter began working for the Pennsylvania Railroad. He became the company's vice president in charge of operations in 1963. Weiss joined the PRR in 1930 as a clerk in the office of the general passenger agent at Penn Station. He became the assistant general passenger agent of the LIRR in 1941.

98. Verne Burnett to Walter S. Franklin, March 5, 1948 ("problem"), Franklin to Burnett, March 8, 1948; J. G. White Report, October 15, 1948; all in NYPL, Box 295; Noel L. Griese, *Arthur W. Page: Publisher, Public Relations Pioneer, Patriot* (Atlanta: Anvil, 2001), 220; Joseph R. Daughen and Peter Binzen, *The Wreck of the Penn Central* (Boston: Little, Brown, 1971), 113–15; *New York Times*, December 5, 1964; *Palm Beach Post*, May 19, 1996.

99. The actual 1948 deficit exceeded $6 million.

100. New York Public Service Commission, Case No. 12989, Decided November 11, 1948 ("although"); *New York Times*, November 10, 1948 ("unjustified," "fictitious"); November 11, 1948; November 15, 1948.

101. Symes to Clement, November 20, 1948, NYPL, Box 295 ("obviously," "concludes," "demand").

102. The Pennsylvania Railroad Company, *One Hundred and Second Annual Report, For the Year Ended December 31, 1948* (Philadelphia, 1949); President Harry S. Truman, Executive Order 9702, March 8, 1946; "Petition of The Long Island Railroad Company before the Public Service Commission of New York, Case No. 12989," November 11, 1948; "L.I.R.R. Co. Board," February 28, 1949; Pennsylvania Railroad Company, January 12, 1949 ("final," "hope"); all in NYPL, Box 295; "The Pennsylvania Railroad and the Long Island Rail Road: An Analysis of Their Relations—Supplement to the Statement of February 8, 1951, to the Stockholders of the Pennsylvania Railroad by Walter S. Franklin, President, Barriger Papers, Series 179, Box 97, folder 3–4; *New York Times*, March 2, 1949.

103. PRR BOD Minutes; "The Pennsylvania Railroad Company, January 12, 1949," NYPL, Box 295; PRR, 1948 Annual Report, 6 ("support"); *New York Times*, March 1, 1949 ("stand").

104. *New York Times*, March 2, 1949 ("somber," "stark").

105. *New York Times*, March 4, 1949 ("provided"); *Trains* 9, no. 7 (May 1949): 4 ("late").

106. *New York Times*, March 15, 1949; April 8, 1949.

107. *New York Times*, April 28, 1949 ("orphan"); *Trains* 10, no. 5 (March 1950): 5; 11, no. 2 (December 1950): 37.

108. *New York Times*, May 6, 1949; May 28, 1949.

109. The disaster ultimately claimed thirty-two lives, with the final victim dying on March 9, three weeks after the collision.

110. "Disaster: Late Train Home," *Time*, February 27, 1950 ("slipshod"); *New York Times*, December 23, 1949; February 18, 1950; February 19, 1950; February 21, 1950; March 1, 1950; March 3, 1950; March 10, 1950.

111. The Richmond Hill wreck is often referred to as the Kew Gardens accident, as the two Queens Borough communities are adjacent.

112. *New York Times*, August 6, 1950; November 24, 1950 ("quiet," "shocking," "device"); November 25, 1950.

113. *Trains* 12, no. 1 (November 1951): 6, provided a slight variation on the *Railway Age* editorial: "The mob demanded scalps and, as usual, the politicians supplied them."

114. The Rockville Centre and Richmond Hill wrecks cost the LIRR more than $14.4 million, including $11.4

million in claims (of which insurance covered $2 million) and another $5 million in safety improvements. Most railroads used corporate funds to satisfy the legal costs of accidents, but the combination of the bankruptcy and the Rockville Centre and Richmond Hill wrecks forced LIRR officials to contact Lloyds of London, regarding external insurance coverage. US District Court, Eastern District of New York, *In the Matter of the Long Island Rail Road Company*, Case No. 47970, August 14, 1952; *New York Times*, November 23, 1950 ("carnage"); November 24, 1950; November 25, 1950 ("grounds," "housecleaning"); November 29, 1950; December 1, 1950 ("miracles"); December 2, 1950; December 15, 1950; *Business Week*, December 2, 1950, 93–96; *Time*, December 4, 1950, 20–21; "Statement of Brig. Gen. William H. Draper Jr., Retired, Trustee of the Long Island Railroad Co., and Chairman of the Long Island Transit Authority," United States Congress, House, *Railroad Reorganization: Hearings before Subcommittee No. 4 of the Committee on the Judiciary, House of Representatives*, 82nd Cong., 1st sess. (Washington, DC: United States Government Printing Office, 1951), 3–4; *Railway Age* 130, no. 4 (January 29, 1951): 14 ("scalps," "vulnerable," emphasis in the original); William H. Draper III, "Early Bay Area Venture Capitalists: Shaping the Economic and Business Landscape," Interview Conducted by Sally Smith Hughes, April 7, 2008, Regional Oral History Office, The Bancroft Library, University of California, Berkeley, 3 (01–00:15:23) ("traveled"); Edgar A. Haine, *Railroad Wrecks* (New York: Cornwall, 1993), 126–27; Aldrich, *Death Rode the Rails*, 293–94.

115. *New York Times*, November 25, 1925 ("disgraceful," "callous"); December 15, 1925 ("shadow"); *Trains* 12, no. 1 (November 1951): 6.

116. United States Congress, House, *Long Island Railroad: Hearing before a Subcommittee of the Committee on Interstate and Foreign Commerce, House of Representatives, Accident Near Jamaica, N.Y., on November 22, 1950*, 81st Cong., 2nd sess. (Washington, DC: United States Government Printing Office, 1951), 47–48 ("disobedience," "replete," "breakdown," "withdrawal," "absentee"); *New York Times*, January 5, 1951.

117. *Trains* 11, no. 5 (March 1951): 7–8 ("unjustified," "ridicule"); *New York Times*, January 7, 1951.

118. "Statement of Brig. Gen. William H. Draper, 4 ("reason"), 5 ("properly"); Draper, "Early Bay Area Venture Capitalists"; *New York Times*, January 25, 1951; February 20, 1951; Daniel Defoe, *The History of the Devil* (London: T. Warner, 1727), 269 ("taxes").

119. *Brooklyn Daily Eagle*, May 31, 1950; *New York Times*, September 3, 1951; September 4, 1951; September 6, 1951; *I.C.C. Practitioners' Journal* 19, no. 2 (November 1951); Raskin, *Routes Not Taken*, 223, 14–16, 145, 235–37; John J. Scala, *Diesels of the Sunrise Trail* (Mineola, NY: Weekend Chief, 1984), 27.

120. The automatic train stop system also prevented a train from entering an occupied block at speeds of greater than 12 miles per hour.

121. In October 1950, prior to Draper's September 1951 announcement of the betterment program, the LIRR received permission from the US District Court for the Eastern District of New York to purchase the first four FM diesels. The remaining eight locomotives, also manufactured by Fairbanks-Morse, were of 1,600 horsepower. *New York Times*, May 25, 1951; September 13, 1951 ("robot"); September 21, 1951; October 15, 1951; *Railway Age* 129, no. 16 (October 14, 1950): 57; 129, no. 19 (November 4, 1950): 93.

122. The Patterson Commission issued its final report (which did not differ appreciably from the preliminary version) on February 4.

123. *New York Times*, January 21, 1951 ("circumstances"); January 22, 1951; February 5, 1951 ("shouting," "suggestions").

124. At the March 23, 1949, PRR board meeting, Symes reported the PRR's investment in the LIRR at $143.8 million. In his February 1951 response to the report of the Long Island Railroad Commission, President Franklin set the value of the investment at a lower amount, $110 million.

125. PRR BOD Minutes; *New York Times*, January 21, 1951 ("contemplates," "overwhelming," "equities," "sympathy," "overpaying").

126. "The Pennsylvania Railroad and The Long Island Railroad: A Review of Their Relations and the Present Situation, A Statement to the Stockholders of The Pennsylvania Railroad by Walter S. Franklin, President," February 8, 1951, 19–20 ("confiscation," "security," "socialism"); *New York Daily News*, February 19, 1951; "Battle for the Long Island," *Time*, March 5, 1951.

127. *New York Times*, March 7, 1951 ("solution," "worth"); March 8, 1951 ("powers").

128. *New York Times*, March 7, 1951 ("burying"); March 8, 1951 ("cart," "concerns").

129. *New York Times*, February 6, 1951; February 7, 1951; April 13, 1951.

130. *New York Times*, April 13, 1951.

131. George Emlen Roosevelt was one of the leading members of the Oyster Bay branch of the Roosevelt

family (which doubtless accounted for his involvement with the LIRR), and his grandfather was Theodore Roosevelt's uncle. He was also a first cousin once removed of Franklin Delano Roosevelt.

132. US District Court, Case No. 47970, August 14, 1952 ("responsibility," "tangle"); *New York Times*, July 1, 1951 ("natural," "finance"); September 30, 1953; William H. Draper Jr., George E. Roosevelt, and Tracy S. Voorhees, "An Initial Message from the Long Island Transit Authority," Barriger Papers, Series 179, Box 97, folder 3–5 ("popular" at 4, "legal," "financial" at 5, "unsettled" at 6); Robert Gerwig, "Public Authorities in the United States," *Law and Contemporary Problems* 26 (Autumn 1961): 591–618.

133. *New York Times*, July 1, 1951 ("hanging"); August 30, 1951 ("difficult," "miracle," "clarified").

134. Officially, Bevan was acting in his simultaneous capacity as vice president of the American Contract & Trust Company, the holder of LIRR securities.

135. "Plan of Reorganization Presented by the Long Island Rail Road Company, Debtor, The Pennsylvania Railroad Company, Creditor and Stockholder, and American Contract and Trust Company, Creditor," US District Court for the Eastern District of New York, No. 47970, In the Matter of Long Island Rail Road Company, Debtor, November 19, 1951, Barriger Papers, Series 179, Box 97, folder 3–3; *New York Times*, November 20, 1951 ("clearly"); David P. Morgan, "Long Island: What Plan d'ya Read?" *Trains* 13, no. 2 (December 1952): 26–30, at 29 ("paramount").

136. *New York Times*, October 30, 1951 ("negotiate"); October 31, 1951 ("refusal").

137. Draper, Roosevelt, and Voorhees, "An Informal Report to the Governor by the Long Island Transit Authority," December 31, 1951, Barriger Papers, Series 179, Box 97, folder 3–5 ("attempts," "operated," "illegal," "virtually"); *New York Times*, January 2, 1952 ("taxes," "realistically," "sponsor").

138. *New York Times*, January 2, 1952 ("continuing," "seems").

139. *New York Times*, January 3, 1952 ("strict," "undesirable," "selfish").

140. *New York Times*, November 16, 1951; February 8, 1952.

141. Roosevelt and Voorhees, "Second Report to the Governor by the Long Island Transit Authority," February 29, 1952, Barriger Papers, Series 179, Box 97, folder 3–5 ("handicapped," "ready"); *New York Times*, March 6, 1952 ("without").

142. *New York Times*, March 6, 1952 ("tentative," "attainable"); March 7, 1952; April 3, 1952 ("argument").

143. *New York Times*, March 27, 1952; April 5, 1952; May 25, 1953; Metropolitan Rapid Transit Commission, *Rapid Transit for the New York-New Jersey Metropolitan Area: Report to His Excellency, Governor Averell Harriman, and the Members of the New York Legislature [and] His Excellency, Governor Robert B. Meyner, and the Members of the New Jersey Legislature* (New York: Commission, 1958), 11–13.

144. The $20 million in new bonds would be secured by a mortgage on the Bay Ridge freight line, effectively the only profitable portion of the LIRR.

145. Roosevelt and Voorhees, "The Long Island Transit Authority's Plan for the Long Island Rail Road," August 14, 1952, Barriger Papers, Series 179, Box 97, folder 3–5; *New York Times*, August 18, 1952 ("speedy," "provision"); Morgan, "Long Island," 30 ("fraction," "intention").

146. *New York Times*, August 19, 1952 ("confiscation"); Denis M. Hurley to Hon. Vincent Impellitteri, November 20, 1952, NYPL, Box 295 ("defective").

147. *New York Times*, November 29, 1952 ("promptly"); December 2, 1952 ("compelling"); January 9, 1953; April 22, 1953.

148. *New York Times*, April 29, 1953; September 24, 1953 ("reasonable"); November 6, 1953; November 25, 1953 ("absorbed," "understand"); December 12, 1953 ("effort").

149. The bankruptcy court reduced the settlement to little more than $2 million. Although the LITA commissioners wanted the LIRR to issue long-term bonds to cover the expense, Wyer elected to sell off part of the railroad, trading the Rockaway Branch to the city in exchange for tax forgiveness. Wyer's resolution of the tax dispute between the LIRR and the city of New York prompted the PRR's September 23 offer to invest $30 million in the carrier, provided it could receive similarly favorable treatment with respect to taxes outside the city.

150. *New York Times*, August 15, 1951; May 23, 1952; May 27, 1952; October 3, 1952; October 6, 1952; October 30, 1952; October 31, 1952; November 7, 1952; November 29, 1952; May 23, 1953; May 24, 1953; May 26, 1953; June 11, 1953; June 13, 1953; July 3, 1953; July 10, 1953; July 17, 1953; July 21, 1953; February 23, 1977; Hurley to Impellitteri, November 20, 1952; Chauncey H. Hand to C. E. Boles, August 15, 1952; both in NYPL, Box 295.

151. *New York Times*, April 24, 1953 ("memoranda," "sinister"); November 28, 1953 ("forbid"); December 12, 1953 ("disregard"); State of New York, *Annual Report of the Public Service Commission, Department of Public Service, for the Year 1954* (Albany, NY: Commission, 1955), 63 ("unrelenting," "position," "turn").

152. *New York Times*, February 12, 1952 ("results," "windows"); September 3, 1952 ("posture"); October 8, 1953.

153. Many cars exhibited multiple deficiencies.

154. *New York Times*, January 30, 1953 ("announced," "deteriorate," "needed"); June 3, 1953.

155. *New York Times*, February 9, 1953.

156. The two Republican sponsors of the bill, Senator S. Wentworth Horton (from Greenport) and Assemblyman Elisha T. Barrett (from Brightwaters) represented districts in Suffolk County, from an area threatened with the loss of LIRR passenger service. *New York Times*, December 11, 1953 ("roadblock," "indefinite"); December 12, 1953 ("usurpation," "unprecedented," "conceivably"); January 19, 1954 ("gravely").

157. *New York Times*, March 5, 1954 ("saturation," "strangulation," "investigation"); March 13, 1954; March 23, 1954; March 24, 1954 ("concern," "rivalry," "attention"); *Rapid Transit for the New York–New Jersey Metropolitan Area*, 11–13; Metropolitan Rapid Transit Commission, *Rapid Transit Needs of the New York–New Jersey Metropolitan Area: Staff Report to the Members of the Commission* (New York: Commission, 1957), 17–21; Metropolitan Rapid Transit Survey, Metropolitan Rapid Transit Commission, *Report of the Project Director to the Metropolitan Rapid Transit Commission* (New York: Commission, 1957).

158. *Annual Report of the Public Service Commission, for the Year 1954*, 64 ("reasonable," "inevitable").

159. *New York Times*, May 14, 1954 ("inappropriate," "essential").

160. The New York State legislature could not supersede federal law or block the ICC's role as a regulatory agency. However, any petition to the ICC regarding increased rates would automatically terminate the agreed-upon 20 percent fare increase, as well as the tax-abatement provisions, thus constituting an effective deterrent.

161. *New York Times*, May 26, 1954 ("foresee"); June 21, 1954; *Annual Report of the Public Service Commission, for the Year 1954*, 64–66.

162. *New York Times*, May 26, 1954 ("existing"); June 3, 1954 ("miracle"); June 8, 1954 ("remarkable"); *Annual Report of the Public Service Commission, for the Year 1954*, 66 ("recognized").

163. Opponents of the legislation filed three lawsuits, with the city government abandoning the effort in April 1955. *New York Times*, May 28, 1954; June 8, 1954 ("arrogant"); June 10, 1954 ("unsound," "cheap," "satisfactory"); June 11, 1954; June 16, 1954; June 18, 1954; June 26, 1954; August 13, 1954; December 28, 1954; February 24, 1955; April 19, 1955; *Annual Report of the Public Service Commission, for the Year 1954*, 67–68.

164. *New York Times*, August 14, 1954 ("earnest"); August 16, 1954; August 19, 1954; *Annual Report of the Public Service Commission, for the Year 1954*, 67.

165. The rebuilding program and the acquisition of new cars from Pullman-Standard cost $24 million. In addition to the $5.5 million provided by the PRR, the LIRR contributed $500,000, with the remaining $18 million coming from conditional sales agreements on the new cars. Typical improvements to the interior of each rebuilt car included a new tile floor, the replacement of 2-2 seating with 3-2 seating (and thus narrower aisles), new seat coverings, luggage racks, ceiling fans (but not air conditioning), and replacement windows. LIRR shop crews offered a visible demonstration of their progress by painting a "modernization number" (red numerals inside a yellow circle with a red border) adjacent to the right-side vestibule of each car. The modernization numbers were assigned sequentially, as cars emerged from the shop facilities, and bore no relationship to the car number. The modernization program ended in the early 1960s, by which time the LIRR had improved, at most, 522 cars—about 45 percent of the fleet, and well short of the 696 cars initially promised. The program added about twelve thousand seats, rather than the sixteen thousand originally specified. Despite its limitations, the modernization program ensured that cars built in the 1920s remained in service for a few more years, placating commuters and government officials pending the arrival of new equipment. "New Deal on the Long Island," *Time*, August 1, 1955 ("duckling"); William D. Middleton, "The Long Island Comes Back: The Story of the Nation's Busiest Passenger Railroad," *Trains* 18, no. 2 (December 1957): 14–32; *New York Times*, June 25, 1954; August 14, 1954; May 4, 1955; June 15, 1955; December 9, 1955; Mike Boland, "Upgrading the Fleet: LIRR's Passenger Car Modernization Program of 1954," *Keystone* 56, no. 3 (Autumn 2023): 22–39; Mike Boland, "Upgrading the Fleet: LIRR's Passenger Car Modernization Program of 1954, Part 2 of 2," *Keystone* 56, no. 4 (Winter 2023): 24–41.

166. *New York Times*, November 23, 1955 ("penny"); December 16, 1955; December 20, 1955; December 15, 1956 ("happy"); Middleton, "Long Island Comes Back," 32 ("gold"); State of New York, *Annual Report of the Public Service Commission, Department of Public Service, for the Year 1956* (Albany, NY: Commission, 1957), 14–15.

167. *New York Times*, January 10, 1957; January 23, 1957 ("contempt"); February 13, 1957; March 26, 1958 ("retrogression," "baldfaced," "tampering"); March 28, 1958;

State of New York, *Annual Report of the Public Service Commission, Department of Public Service, for the Year 1957* (Albany, NY: Commission, 1958), 28–29.

168. *New York Times*, April 6, 1958 ("ineffective"); *Rapid Transit Needs of the New York–New Jersey Metropolitan Area*, 18 ("crossing"), 19 ("function").

169. Thomas M. Goodfellow, "Suggestions for Solving the Commuter Problem: A Resume Presented to Governors Rockefeller, Meyner and Ribicoff and Mayor Wagner, February 10, 1959," HML, Box 231, folder 12 ("scores," "impossible," "best").

170. *New York Times*, March 3, 1959; March 26, 1959; April 5, 1959; Ari and Olive Hoogenboom, *A History of the ICC: From Panacea to Palliative* (New York: W. W. Norton, 1976), 155–59; Robert B. Carson, *Main Line to Oblivion: The Disintegration of the New York Railroads in the Twentieth Century* (Port Washington, NY: Kennikat, 1971), 188–90; Daniel P. Loomis, "The Transportation Act of 1958," *Analysts Journal* 14, no. 5 (November 1958): 57–61.

171. Jameson W. Doig, *Empire on the Hudson: Entrepreneurial Vision and Political Power at the Port of New York Authority* (New York: Columbia University Press, 2001), 379–82.

172. In November 1961, New York voters approved a constitutional amendment committing the state to guarantee the Port Authority's $100 million bond issue for that purpose. Even before Rockefeller signed the amendment the following April, LIRR officials ordered thirty new cars, and they were negotiating for the purchase of another thirty. The first ten arrived in August 1963, well in advance of the anticipated increase in traffic that would accompany the 1964 New York World's Fair. *New York Times*, March 16, 1959; March 17, 1959 ("moot"); March 21, 1959; March 26, 1959 ("give-away"); April 7, 1962; August 10, 1962; August 28, 1963; Joseph F. Zimmerman, "Public Transportation," *Proceedings of the Academy of Political Science* 31 (May 1974): 214–24; Doig, *Empire on the Hudson*, 380–81.

173. *New York Times*, March 21, 1959; April 5, 1959; April 14, 1959; April 26, 1959; May 5, 1959.

174. *New York Times*, June 17, 1959; June 18, 1959.

175. *New York Times*, September 1, 1959; September 2, 1959; September 3, 1959; September 18, 1959; September 23, 1959; September 30, 1959; October 8, 1959; October 9, 1959; October 16, 1959; November 4, 1959; November 5, 1959; November 6, 1959; November 13, 1959; December 31, 1959.

176. Pennsylvania Railroad, New York Region, "A Study of the Physical Feasibility and Economics of Handling Jersey Central Passenger Trains via the Pennsylvania Railroad," July 15, 1959, archived at Multimodalways, http://www.multimodalways.org/docs/railroads/companies/PRR/PRR%20CNJ%20Passenger%20Study%207-15-1959.pdf, accessed February 19, 2020, 1–7 ("conditions" at 2).

177. "Physical Feasibility and Economics," 7–15, 51–57.

178. "Physical Feasibility and Economics," 51–57.

179. Palmer also recommended assistance for the Delaware, Lackawanna & Western; the Jersey Central; the Lehigh Valley; the New York, Susquehanna & Western; the New Jersey & New York (a subsidiary of the Erie); and the Pennsylvania-Reading Seashore Lines (in which the PRR maintained half ownership).

180. Although railroad and civic officials claimed that that the route between Aldene and Jersey City traversed an industrial wasteland, communities such as Bayonne, Elizabeth, and Roselle generated substantial commuter traffic. The opening of the Aldene Connection and the termination of Communipaw ferry service forced residents to make a roundabout trip to Lower Manhattan, via Newark, utilizing stub service between Bayonne and Cranford that ended in 1978. The longer commutation times hastened the residential exodus from the area.

181. *New York Times*, April 5, 1960.

182. *New York Times*, April 6, 1960 ("tight"); April 14, 1960; April 29, 1960; May 2, 1960; May 4, 1960; May 21, 1960; June 7, 1960; June 23, 1960; September 27, 1960; Hilton, "Decline of Railroad Commutation," 180.

183. When the Port Authority submitted a formal offer to purchase the H&M in January 1961, the promised funding for new equipment and site redevelopment increased to $63 million.

184. Beginning in October 1956, the Delaware, Lackawanna & Western's ferry terminal in Hoboken also accommodated the Erie's commuter and intercity passenger trains, as a prelude to the October 1960 merger of those two companies. Tobin, who was determined to give the Port Authority sole control over all traffic between New York and New Jersey, insisted on the closure of that facility.

185. *New York Times*, September 28, 1960; January 28, 1961; March 12, 1961; May 29, 1961; May 30, 1961; May 31, 1961; Doig, *Empire on the Hudson*, 382–84; Richard Saunders Jr., *Merging Lines: American Railroads, 1900–1970* (DeKalb: Northern Illinois University Press, 2001), 165–66.

186. Later that year, the Port Authority established a subsidiary, Port Authority Trans-Hudson, to operate the Hudson & Manhattan Railroad. The World Trade

Center opened in 1973. Tobin's other initiative to deplete the Port Authority's reserve fund—a new airport in New Jersey—generated widespread opposition. It was never built, and the proposal constituted one of Tobin's few defeats during his many years with the Port Authority. *New York Times*, March 21, 1961; March 24, 1961; March 26, 1961; April 9, 1961; May 24, 1961; December 21, 1961; December 23, 1961; December 28, 1961; December 29, 1961; January 23, 1962; Doig, *Empire on the Hudson*, 383–90.

187. *New York Times*, November 18,1961; *Trains* 24, no. 4 (February 1964): 54.

188. Between 1946 and 1963 the consumer price index increased 40 percent, while the LIRR's fares tripled.

189. *New York Times*, July 18, 1962; July 20, 1962; September 29, 1964; February 17, 1965.

190. The amount did not include the cost of 370 new cars, necessary to replace obsolete equipment.

191. The connection to Grand Central came to fruition in early 2023, at a cost that exceeded $11 billion.

192. Nassau County Planning Commission, *Better Rail Service for Nassau County* (Mineola, New York: The Commission, 1963), iv ("configuration," "cost," emphasis in the original), vii ("congestion").

193. *New York Times*, September 29, 1964; February 26, 1965 ("reasonable," "creeping," "avoid," "prelude"); February 27, 1965 ("anything"); "A New Long Island Rail Road: A Report to Nelson A. Rockefeller, Governor of New York, from The Special Committee of the Long Island Rail Road," February 1965; reprinted as Exhibit 8, *Metropolitan Transportation Authority vs. County of Nassau*, New York Supreme Court, Appellate Division, 35 AD 2nd 739 (1970).

194. *New York Times*, February 26, 1965; February 27, 1965; June 3, 1965; June 7, 1965 ("token").

195. *New York Times*, June 7, 1965; June 11, 1965; September 3, 1965; December 27, 1965; January 21, 1966; "Memorandum of Understanding Concerning the Sale of the Long Island Rail Road," June 9, 1965, Exhibit 9; William J. Ronan and William A. Shea, "A Report to the Governor and the Legislative Leaders on a Reasonable Price for the Purchase of the Long Island Rail Road by the State of New York from the Pennsylvania Railroad, June 1965, Exhibit 10; "Agreement between Pennsylvania Railroad Company and Metropolitan Commuter Transportation Authority Concerning Purchase of Stock of the Long Island Rail Road Company," December 22, 1965, Exhibit 11; all exhibits in *Metropolitan Transportation Authority vs. County of Nassau*; Stephen Salsbury, *No Way to Run a Railroad: The Untold Story of the Penn Central Crisis* (New York: McGraw-Hill, 1982), 60–62.

196. Parsons Brinckerhoff Gibbs & Hill, Consulting Engineers, "Long Island Rail Road Modernization Program," August 1966; Barriger Papers, Series 179, Box 97, folder 2–13; *New York Times*, August 31, 1966 ("finest," "radiant").

197. *New York Times*, May 3, 1967; February 10, 1968; February 29, 1968; March 6, 1968; March 22, 1968 ("arbitrary"); January 27, 1969 ("worse," "stand"); March 18, 1969; *Wall Street Journal*, October 6, 1969; New York Metropolitan Commuter Transportation Authority, *Metropolitan Transportation: A Program for Action, Report to Nelson A. Rockefeller, Governor of New York* (New York: MCTA, 1968); "Transcript: The WINS News Conference," March 10, 1968, Exhibit 14, *Metropolitan Transportation Authority vs. County of Nassau* ("unhappy"); Zimmerman, "Public Transportation," 217–21.

198. In addition to the various commuter districts that extend to the north, south, and west of Philadelphia, the PRR offered extensive service on the New Jersey side of the Delaware River. In addition to the Camden-Trenton link, they included Camden-Pemberton on the PRR proper, as well as Camden-Glassboro-Millville and Camden-Hammonton and Camden-Haddonfield along the Pennsylvania-Reading Seashore Lines, (which also carried summertime commuters from Atlantic City). *Philadelphia Inquirer*, July 25, 1965.

199. Deasy and Franklin to Clement, January 29, 1942, PHMC, Clement Papers, Box 74 (9-1670), folder 521.3.

200. Clement to Deasy, Franklin, and Downes, PHMC, Clement Papers, Box 74 (9-1670), folder 521.3 ("conservation," "temporary," "complaints").

201. Joseph S. Clark Jr. and Dennis J. Clark, "Rally and Relapse, 1946–1968," in *Philadelphia: A 300-Year History*, ed. Russell F. Weigley (New York: W. W. Norton, 1982): 699–703, at 668; Dianne Harris, ed., *Second Suburb: Levittown, Pennsylvania* (Pittsburgh, PA: University of Pittsburgh Press, 2010).

202. [Ardmore, PA] *Main Line Times*, October 21, 1948 ("progress"); Maxwell Smith to Clement, February 15, 1949; "Minutes of a Joint Committee Meeting of Lower Merion Civic Associations," November 6, 1947; Clement to Symes, February 13, 1948 ("consideration"); Richard R. Champion to Clement, February 25, 1948; Charles W. Patterson to Clement, March 28, 1949; all in PHMC, Clement Papers, Box 76 (9-1672), folder 521.34; Walter W. Patchell to David H. W. Dohan, June 18, 1953, HML, Box 340, folder 22 ("abandoned"); *Wall Street Journal*, December 9, 1958.

203. Clement, "Memo to Staff," January 2, 1948, PHMC, Clement Papers, Box 76 (9-1672), folder 521.34 ("opposing," appearance").

204. There was generally strong demand for commuter services between Media and Center-City Philadelphia, thanks to intermediate stops at prosperous communities such as Swarthmore. In 1986, SEPTA truncated service on the R3 line at Media. Rapid suburbanization prompted the rehabilitation of tracks to Wawa, with the extension entering service in 2022.

205. Symes to Newell, February 3, 1953; Robert Heller & Associates, "The Pennsylvania Railroad Company, Suburban Service, December 31, 1953" ("sufficient"); "The Pennsylvania Railroad Company Passenger Operations—Draft of Report, July 26, 1954" ("assigned"); "Extension of Contract with Heller Associates, Board meeting 12-17-52"; all in PHMC, Franklin Papers, Box 76 (9-2124), folder 521.3.

206. Clement to Symes and Franklin, March 8, 1948, PHMC, Clement Papers, Box 76 (9-1672), folder 521.34 ("officers"); James P. Newell to Gustavus E. Payne, June 9, 1953, HML, Box 340, folder 21; Patchell to Dohan, June 18, 1953, HML, Box 340, folder 22; Ralph C. Champlin to James P. Newell, August 27, 1953, HML, Box 340, folder 23 ("Purchases"); Railway Age 134, no. 26 (June 29, 1953): 13–14; Baer and Middleton, "Commuter Railroads," 315.

207. Newell to Champlin, August 6, 1953 ("appearance"); Murphy to Champlin, September 11, 1953 ("reading"); both in HML, Box 340, folder 23; Saturday Evening Post 226, no. 30 (January 23, 1954): 12; [Ardmore, PA] Main Line Times, November 20, 1956; Philadelphia Daily News, July 1, 1955.

208. Heller & Associates, "Suburban Service" ("unsound"); Newell to Symes, September 28, 1954, HML, Box 341, folder 2 ("urgent"); John H. White Jr., The American Railroad Passenger Car (Baltimore, MD: Johns Hopkins University Press, 1978), 632, 636–38.

209. The Pioneer III name paid tribute to Budd's initial efforts with a stainless steel airplane ("Pioneer I") and to the Burlington Zephyr ("Pioneer II"). The eighty-five-foot length, unusual for commuter equipment, conformed to Budd's practices for the construction of intercity cars and minimized the number of vestibules (which added both weight and manufacturing expense) per train.

210. White, American Railroad Passenger Car, 639.

211. New York Times, February 15, 1952; Philadelphia Bulletin, August 15, 1957; May 16, 1957; Philadelphia Inquirer, August 16, 1957; Railway Age 141 (July 23, 1956): 38–42; 144 (June 30, 1958): 18–19, 22 ("some"); New York Times, July 17, 1956.

212. Railway Age 144 (June 23, 1958): 9 ("Arrangements").

213. Philadelphia City–County Consolidation Act of August 26, 1953, P.L. 1476, No. 433; Clark and Clark, "Rally and Relapse," 649–703, at 650–57; The Committee of Seventy, The Charter: A History (Philadelphia: Committee of Seventy, 1980), 5–13.

214. Clark and Clark, "Rally and Relapse," 654–57; Timothy J. Lombardo, Blue-Collar Conservatism: Frank Rizzo's Philadelphia and Populist Politics (Philadelphia: University of Pennsylvania Press, 2018), 26–27, 30–31, 40–42.

215. Aaron Levine, "Citizen Participation," Journal of the American Institute of Planners 26, no. 3 (August 1960): 195–200.

216. "Pressures in the Process of Administrative Decision: A Study of Highway Location," University of Pennsylvania Law Review 108, no. 4 (February 1960): 534–86; Philadelphia Inquirer, September 2, 1954; September 3, 1954 ("jam," "snafu," "immediate").

217. "John A. Bailey Oral History, June 23, 1976," Walter Massey Phillips Oral Histories, Temple University Libraries, 11 ("understanding").

218. Philadelphia Inquirer, September 3, 1954 ("win," "persuade").

219. Chestnut Hill Local, April 4, 2019, 12 ("create"); Philadelphia Inquirer, January 23, 1991; July 14, 2017; New York Times, January 11, 1964; "John W. Bodine Oral History, October 20, 1977," Walter Massey Phillips Oral Histories, Temple University Libraries, 7 ("rape," "obsolete"); Contosta, Suburb in the City, 218–54.

220. Bodine Oral History, 5, 8–9 ("reasons").

221. Bodine Oral History, 9 ("triumphantly"); "Plan and Program 1955," quoted in "Condition of Philadelphia with Respect to a Regional Transportation Plan," James Tate Papers, Philadelphia City Archives, Box 12, A-6335 ("evaluation"). For an overview of the city-suburban bias, see Jacob Kobrick, "'Let the People Have a Victory': The Politics of Transportation in Philadelphia, 1946–1984 (PhD diss., University of Maryland, 2010).

222. In later years, Berger pioneered the development of class-action lawsuits, including one on behalf of the shareholders of the Penn Central.

223. New York Times, February 24, 2007; Philadelphia Inquirer, February 24, 2007; Bodine Oral History, 7 ("impact"); "Interview with David Berger 6/11/79," Walter Massey Phillips Oral Histories, Temple University Libraries, 2–5.

224. Citizens' Council on City Planning to the Philadelphia City Planning Commission, October 14, 1959 (PRR—VP Finance, "Operation Northeast") ("dismayed"); Citizens' Council on City Planning, Statement Presented to the City Council on the Urban Traffic and Transportation Board Proposal for the Chestnut Hill Commuter Lines, September 22, 1958 ("motorists," "experimental"); "Draft Statement on 'Operation Northwest,'" n.d. ("conditions," "distribution," "collector"); all in Temple University Urban Archives (hereafter, TUUA), Box 16.

225. In January 1962, the participants in Penn-Jersey released a plan that offered five options to address the region's future transportation requirements. One contemplated the gradual elimination of all commuter rail transit by 1985. At the other extreme, the study suggested better coordination and increased funding for commuter rail, with a new connection to be built through Center City to link the termini of the PRR and the Reading.

226. Alexander Hemphill, "Passenger Service Improvement Corporation of Philadelphia, 1961," Report of the Controller's Office, 6–8; David N. Phillips to Albert M. Greenfield, January 15, 1962; both in Tate Papers, Box 12, A-6335.

227. PRR and Reading officials demanded a rehearing, at which they presented additional evidence of their rapidly increasing passenger losses; in June 1958, the PUC granted a fare increase. *Philadelphia Inquirer*, April 4, 1957; *Philadelphia Bulletin*, May 7, 1958 ("substantiate"); Patchell to Symes, May 9, 1957, HML, Box 252, folder 13; Symes to Dilworth, June 3, 1957, City of Philadelphia, Department of Records, City Archives, RG 60–2.4, Administration of Richardson Dilworth; quoted in Kobrick, "Let the People Have a Victory," 108 ("staggering").

228. City officials also opened negotiations with the privately owned Philadelphia Transportation Company to establish a uniform fare structure for the various forms of mass transit.

229. Kobrick, "Let the People Have a Victory," 109–11.

230. The route to Norristown, built under the auspices of the Pennsylvania Schuylkill Valley Railroad Company, opened in 1884. It was part of a larger project to parallel the Reading's vastly superior route along the Schuylkill Valley, as part of the PRR's largely unsuccessful effort to capture a share of northeastern Pennsylvania's anthracite traffic and as a bargaining chip in the ongoing competitive system building that pitted the PRR against the Reading and the Baltimore & Ohio.

231. The PRR route from Suburban Station was 12 miles in length, and the somewhat more direct Reading route was 10.8 miles.

232. Patchell to Symes, May 9, 1957; T. A. V. Jr. to Robert W. Large, May 21, 1957; both in HML, Box 252, folder 13; *Philadelphia Inquirer*, April 4, 1957; *Railway Age* 145 (September 29, 1958): 14 ("tide"); "Passenger Service Improvement Corporation," 9–11.

233. "Passenger Service Improvement Corporation," 13–14; *Railway Age* 145 (October 27, 1958): 82; (March 2, 1959): 13 ("subsidy"); "Draft Statement on 'Operation Northwest,'" n.d., TUUA, Box 16 ("looking").

234. "Passenger Service Improvement Corporation," 13–14; *Philadelphia Inquirer*, April 4, 1957; *Wall Street Journal*, October 17, 1958; December 9, 1958 ("hopeful," "beyond").

235. Dilworth also proposed to include the lines owned by the Philadelphia Transportation Company in the arrangement. *Railway Age* 145 (October 27, 1958): 82; (March 2, 1959): 13 ("pleased," "undoubtedly"); *Philadelphia Inquirer*, March 13, 1959; "Passenger Service Improvement Corporation," 10–11; *Trains* 20, no. 1 (November 1959): 6.

236. *Trains* 20, no. 1 (November 1959): 6 ("donate"); *Philadelphia Bulletin*, July 9, 1959.

237. In pursuing a 30 percent fare increase, PRR officials attempted to isolate that request from a smaller, although contemporaneous, petition for higher rates on its northern New Jersey commuter operations. Reading officials publicly stated that they would refrain from asking for a rate increase, to avoid antagonizing city officials and jeopardizing ongoing negotiations regarding the level of financial support they received from the city. They nonetheless confided to their counterparts on the PRR that—should negotiations break down—they were prepared to request a 60 to 70 percent increase in fares to price the Reading out of the commuter rail market. The Pennsylvania PUC granted a temporary 25 percent commuter fare increase to both railroads, effective April 1, 1960. The Pennsylvania Railroad Company, *113th Annual Report for the Year Ended December 31, 1959*, 16 ("emphasized," "diverting"); *Philadelphia Inquirer*, March 13, 1959 ("contend"); October 20, 1959; February 17, 1960; March 22, 1960; *Wall Street Journal*, March 23, 1960; Fred Carpi to William P. Roan, February 18, 1960; Carpi to Roan, February 29, 1960; both in TUUA, Box 11 (Legal Department); *Trains* 20, no. 1 (November 1959): 6 ("up").

238. By the autumn of 1959, the city's payments to the PRR and the Reading (for both Operation Northwest and Operation Northeast) had reached $525,000.

239. *Philadelphia Inquirer*, March 13, 1959 ("contend");
October 20, 1959; *Philadelphia Bulletin*, July 9, 1959
("own").

240. Patchell testimony, 10–13; Interstate Commerce
Commission, *Railroad Passenger Train Deficit*, Docket
No. 31954 (Washington, DC: Interstate Commerce
Commission, 1958); *Chicago, Milwaukee, St. Paul & Pacific
Railroad Company v. Illinois*, 355 US 300 (1958); *Interstate
Commerce Commission Reports: Decisions of the Interstate
Commerce Commission of the United States, Volume 306,
February 1959–June 1959* (Washington, DC: United States
Government Printing Office, 1960), 464–65; George W.
Hilton, "The Hosmer Report: A Decennial Evaluation,"
ICC Practitioners Journal 36 (March 1969): 1470–86;
Hilton, "Decline of Railroad Commutation," 175; George
M. Smerk, *The Federal Role in Urban Mass Transportation*
(Bloomington: Indiana University Press, 1991), 60–61.

241. Other mayors typically favored highway construction. Their ranks included New York's Robert F. Wagner
Jr.—backed by City Planning commissioner Robert
Moses, who was openly contemptuous of commuter rail.
Many railroad executives feared that federal support for
commuter services could lead to a governmental takeover of commuter operations, possibly an opening wedge
to the nationalization of financially troubled railroads or
indeed the entire railroad network. Executives representing many carriers, particularly in the western states,
worried that public subsidies would impede the efforts to
discontinue all passenger service.

242. Smerk, *Federal Role in Urban Mass Transportation*,
56–57, 67–71; Richard F. Weingroff, *Busting the Trust:
Unraveling the Highway Trust Fund, 1968–1978* (Washington, DC: Federal Highway Administration, 2013), 20–21.

243. *Commonwealth v. Pittsburg*, 183 Pa. 202, 38 Atl.
628 (1897) held that it was permissible for a municipal
government to award funds to private individuals who
were investigating the feasibility of a canal connecting
Pittsburgh and Lake Erie.

244. Dilworth also supported the creation of a municipal transportation corporation in anticipation of the
city's purchase of the assets of the Philadelphia Transportation Company. The city's negotiations with PTC
were long, convoluted, and contentious, and they did not
conclude until 1968. *Wall Street Journal*, October 17, 1958
("foreign").

245. Several years earlier, Dilworth recruited Coleman,
the first African American attorney at the firm. Coleman
became secretary of transportation in 1975—another
individual associated with Dilworth who shaped national
transportation policy.

246. *Philadelphia Inquirer*, October 12, 1956; March 13,
1959; January 21, 1960; February 12, 1960; April 19, 2009;
Todd C. Peppers, "William Thaddeus Coleman Jr.:
Breaking the Color Barrier at the U.S. Supreme Court,"
Journal of Supreme Court History 33, no. 3 (November
2008): 353–70; William T. Coleman Jr., with Donald
Bliss, *Counsel for the Situation* (Washington, DC: Brookings Institution, 2010), 137–41; "Remembering Edson L.
Tennyson, Icon of Rail Public Transport Advocacy and
Development," *Light Rail Now*, July 20, 2014, https://
lightrailnow.wordpress.com/2014/07/20/remembering
-edson-l-tennyson-icon-of-rail-public-transport
-advocacy-and-development/, accessed October 17, 2019.

247. *Philadelphia Inquirer*, April 1, 1960; *Railway Age* 160
(January 25, 1960): 9; *Philadelphia Citizen*, April 27, 2017;
"Statement by City Solicitor David Berger," March 2,
1960 ("breathing"), TUUA, Box 11 (Legal Department);
"Minutes, Passenger Service Improvement Corpora-
tion of Philadelphia, May 9, 1960"; Passenger Service
Improvement Corporation of Philadelphia, "Meeting of
Board of Directors, June 15, 1960"; both in Tate Papers,
Box 12, A-6335; Bailey Oral History, 16–17; Kobrick, "Let
the People Have a Victory," 141–42.

248. The conclusion that traffic congestion was responsible for the decline of the central business district was
also inaccurate. Clogged highways had been characteristic of Center-City Philadelphia for decades, and the abandonment of the urban core had more to do with a fear of
crime and a desire to move to more spacious and more
racially homogenous suburban communities.

249. Philadelphia City Planning Commission, *Compre-
hensive Plan: The Physical Development Plan for the City of
Philadelphia* (Philadelphia: City Planning Commission,
1960), 92 ("connected"); Philadelphia City Planning
Commission, *The Plan for Center City Philadelphia* (Phil-
adelphia: City Planning Commission, 1963), 7 ("basic,"
"remain," "serves"); "The View from Mid-Century:
Philadelphia's Comprehensive City Plan of 1960," *Greater
Philadelphia Regional Review* (Fall 2003): 8–13; Kobrick,
"Let the People Have a Victory," 115, 138–39; Hilton,
"Decline of Railroad Commutation," 182–83.

250. Many of the board members knew one another
through their involvement in earlier municipal-planning
issues. Frishmuth was chairman of the Urban Traffic
and Transportation Board, and he served with Dilworth,
Berger, Symes, and Reading president Joseph A. Fisher
on the Old Philadelphia Development Corporation,
established in 1956. Edward T. Moynahan was equally
involved in urban affairs, as both a member of the OPDC
and the PSIC board. "Passenger Service Improvement

Corporation," 3–5; "Minutes, Passenger Service Improvement Corporation of Philadelphia, May 9, 1960" ("eminence"); *Asbury Park Press*, May 12, 1954; *Philadelphia Inquirer*, January 13, 1954; August 9, 1955; *Remaking Center City: A History of the Central Philadelphia Development Corporation* (Philadelphia: Central Philadelphia Development Corporation, 2006), 69.

251. *Philadelphia Inquirer*, October 12, 1956; March 13, 1959; January 21, 1960; February 12, 1960; April 19, 2009; Bailey Oral History, 8 ("interest," "smooth"); Peppers, "Coleman"; Coleman and Bliss, *Counsel for the Situation*, 137–41; "Remembering Edson L. Tennyson."

252. PSIC officials estimated that the City Council's 1960 appropriation (representing the payments used to offset the railroads' operating expenses, less fare revenues) would be $425,000. The city's payments compensated the PRR and the Reading for the out-of-pocket (variable) costs associated with the provision of additional service. In that respect, they did not reduce the significant losses that the two companies were incurring on their existing commuter operations. Given the notorious complexity associated with the allocation of variable costs, and because the provision of off-peak service required only a slight increase in marginal cost (because equipment and crews laying over during the middle of the day were otherwise unutilized), it is likely that the payments were something of an accounting fiction—that is, each railroad collected more than the true variable cost associated with the expanded service and could then use the surplus to offset losses on services that PSIC had not commissioned. Walter Patchell, the PRR's head of special services, observed that the company received $227,400 in city subsidies during 1959 "and just about broke even"—that is, the city's payments were sufficient to offset the cost of added service and the revenue lost to reduced fares, while leaving the overall passenger deficit associated with commuter operations unchanged. "In 1961," Patchell predicted, "we will probably receive $950,000 which will put $600,000 cash in our pocket"— suggesting that nearly two-thirds of the 1961 subsidy would reduce the PRR's recurring losses, with little more than a third representing the amount that the city paid to support new service. Patchell to Symes and Greenough, November 9, 1960, HML, Box 252, folder 16 ("even," "pocket").

253. *Philadelphia Daily News*, March 2, 1960; *Philadelphia Inquirer*, May 13, 1960; July 29, 1960; "Passenger Service Improvement Corporation," 13.

254. *Philadelphia Inquirer*, August 12, 1960; November 9, 1960; February 1, 1961; April 5, 1961.

255. Hemphill, "Passenger Service Improvement Corporation of Philadelphia, 1961"; David N. Phillips to Albert M. Greenfield, January 15, 1962; both in Tate Papers, Box 12, A-6335; Kobrick, "Let the People Have a Victory," 142, includes *Philadelphia Evening Bulletin*, September 1, 1960 ("indicated"); *Philadelphia Inquirer*, March 9, 1960 ("beyond").

256. R. R. B. to J. B. P., March 8, 1960 ("backed"), in Tate Papers, Box 12, A-6335; *Philadelphia Inquirer*, March 9, 1960 ("more," "interested"); April 1, 1960; Kobrick, "Let the People Have a Victory," 146–47.

257. US Department of Commerce, *Federal Transportation Policy and Program* (Washington, DC: United States Government Printing Office, 1960); Ernest W. Williams Jr. and David W. Bluestone, *Rationale of Federal Transportation Policy: Appendix to Federal Transportation Policy and Program* (Washington, DC: United States Government Printing Office, 1960), 52–54 ("expensive," "loans," "materially," "benefits," "essential"); Smerk, *Federal Role in Urban Mass Transportation*, 62–63.

258. Statement of James M. Symes, *Hearings before Subcommittee No. 1 of the Committee on Banking and Currency, House of Representatives, 87th Cong., 1st sess., May 10, 1961* (Washington, DC: United States Government Printing Office, 1961), 47 ("viewpoint"), 59 ("job"); Testimony of Richardson Dilworth, *Hearings before Subcommittee No. 3 of the Committee on Banking and Currency, House of Representatives, 87th Cong., 1st sess., June 27 and 28, 1961* (Washington, DC: United States Government Printing Office, 1961): 164–67, at 165 ("obvious," "gap"); PRR press release, June 27, 1961, HML, Box 252, folder 16; Smerk, *Federal Role in Urban Mass Transportation*, 62–63.

259. Kobrick, "Let the People Have a Victory," 139–41.

260. "Passenger Service Improvement Corporation," 16–17; Southeastern Pennsylvania Transportation Authority, *Commuter Railroad Improvements for a Metropolitan Area (SEPACT I): Final Report to the U.S. Department of Transportation (DOT) on Mass Transportation Demonstration Project—No. PA-MTD-1, October 28, 1962–October 30, 1965*, April 1, 1969, 5 ("significance"); *Philadelphia Inquirer*, May 13, 1960; January 12, 1962; R. R. B. to J. B. P., May 3, 1960; W. G. S. S. Jr. to R. H. C., May 9, 1960; R. H. C. to R. R. B., December 11, 1961; all in TUUA, Box 11 (Legal Department).

261. Bailey to Tate, September 26, 1962 ("time"), Tate Papers, Box 12, A-6335.

262. The first HHFA grant, for $270,000, went to Detroit, for additional service on bus routes in that city.

263. Twelve new Budd Rail Diesel Cars would serve the Reading's nonelectrified commuter lines between

Pottsville, Bethlehem, and Newtown, and along the route to Newark and Jersey City. The PSIC would own the cars and lease them to the Reading, with the lease payments eventually liquidating the loan and giving the Reading ownership. The interest rate would be between 2.5 and 3.75 percent, far below what the financially strapped company could expect to pay in private capital markets. Reading officials agreed to repay the loan but, should they fail to do so, the terms of the HHFA loan protected the city from any financial liability.

264. "I have a strong belief," John Bailey reminisced, "that no regional planning agency can ever do what the Feds had asked them to do." Bailey Oral History, 8 ("belief").

265. The additional amount was apparently related to an HHFA grant, in the amount of $291,667, for "a series of integrated analytical studies" to determine the effectiveness of the SEPACT experiment.

266. *Philadelphia Inquirer*, April 14, 1962; April 20, 1962 ("heartened"); May 3, 1962; May 5, 1962; November 5, 1952; Southeastern Pennsylvania Transportation Authority, *Commuter Railroad Improvements for a Metropolitan Area (SEPACT I)*, 6, 12–15; Bailey to Tate, March 23, 1962 ("shifting"); Bailey to Tate, April 5, 1962; Louis A. Johanson to Tate, May 4, 1962; Bailey to Tate, September 26, 1962; Bailey to Tate, October 17, 1962 ("reluctantly"); November 7, 1962 ("increased"); all in Tate Papers, Box 12, A-6335; Robert C. Weaver to Bailey, June 20, 1963 ("integrated"), Tate Papers, Box 11, A-6362.

267. Citizens' Loan Improvement Committee, "Vote 'Yes' Nov. 6 on question 3 for commuter rail improvements" ("creeping"), Tate Papers, Box 12, A-6335; *Philadelphia Inquirer*, November 6, 1962; November 7, 1962; Peter Binzen, with Jonathan Binzen, *Richardson Dilworth: Last of the Bare-Knuckled Aristocrats* (Philadelphia: Camino, 2014), 177–84.

268. Bert Pennypacker, "PRR vs. Car, Plane, Bus," *Trains* 28, no. 1 (November 1967): 18–28, at 23.

269. *Pennsy* 12, no. 1 (January–February 1963): 4–5; *Philadelphia Inquirer*, November 5, 1952; *Levittown Times*, December 3, 1962.

270. Dan Rottenberg, *The Outsider: Albert M. Greenfield and the Fall of the Protestant Establishment* (Philadelphia: Temple University Press, 2014), 141–42, 238–51; Binzen and Binzen, *Richardson Dilworth*, 132 ("ruthless," "money," "selfish"), 152–54; Guian A. McKee, "Blue Sky Boys, Professional Citizens, and Knights-in-Shining-Money: Philadelphia's Penn Center Project and the Constraints of Private Development," *Journal of Planning History* 6, no. 1 (February 2007): 48–80, at 55–57.

271. Greenfield's anger would have increased had he seen the data, calculated by PSIC staff six months later, indicating that the per-passenger subsidy on PRR "Operation" lines was 32 cents, above the 26 cents he cited and greater than the 30.9-cent average fare paid by each passenger.

272. PSIC personnel relied on passenger surveys to determine which commuters had left their cars at home to use PRR/Reading services and which had abandoned the PTC. They concluded that many passengers had falsely placed themselves in the first category, as an indication that they were sufficiently affluent to own a car and thus were not captive to some form of public transit. George Hilton has observed that commuter fares account for approximately 1.5 percent of household expenditures, compared to 9.7 percent for automobile use. Subsidized commuter fares, therefore, would not likely persuade motorists to give up their cars but might persuade them to abandon other forms of public transport, in favor of PRR or Reading commuter trains. Rottenberg, *Outsider*, 251; Albert M. Greenfield to Editor, *Philadelphia Inquirer*, January 15, 1962 ("coffee," "objectives"); "PSIC Subsidy Data—1961," June 12, 1961; "PSIC Program: Diversion of PTC Passengers to Subsidized Railroads," May 25, 1962; all in Tate Papers, Box 12, A-6335 *Philadelphia Inquirer*, January 10, 1962 ("endless"); January 17, 1962; February 16, 1962; *Sunday Bulletin*, September 29, 1968; Hilton, "Decline of Railroad Commutation," 184–85.

273. *New York Times*, June 8, 1937; Fallon Samuels Aidoo, "Red Arrow Lines," *Encyclopedia of Greater Philadelphia*, https://philadelphiaencyclopedia.org/archive/red-arrow-lines/, accessed September 26, 2019.

274. PSIC personnel also found it necessary to answer criticism from Penn-Jersey, the regional planning entity that Mayor Dilworth had split off the Urban Traffic and Transportation Board eight years earlier. Penn-Jersey officials favored services that were flexible, required little in the way of public investment, and could be implemented quickly—criteria that clearly favored buses over commuter rail. The conflict between the municipally based and the regionally based planning bodies in part arose from disagreements regarding the construction of a rapid-transit line across the Delaware River to New Jersey. More broadly, however, the dispute between PSIC and Penn-Jersey reflected differing transportation philosophies. It also suggested that whatever federal funds might become available would be limited in scope and that interagency competition for those resources would be a zero-sum game.

275. *Philadelphia Bulletin*, May 20, 1962 ("phantom," "subsidy,"); June 11, 1962 ("integrated," "sense").

276. The Operation North Penn-Hatboro service went into effect on October 28, 1962, and was the first of the extensions outside city limits to receive HHFA grants. *Philadelphia Inquirer*, October 23, 1962; October 28, 1962.

277. Unlike Bryn Mawr, Rosemont lacked crossovers or any other mechanism that would permit commuter trains to cross from No. 4 Track (the outermost westbound track that handled most commuter trains) to the corresponding No. 1 Track that was the outermost eastbound line. The author extends his appreciation to Richard Allman for noting that even though Rosemont was the final station in Montgomery County, before tracks entered Delaware County, it was effectively off-limits to SEPACT.

278. *Main Line Chronicle*, May 17, 1962 ("Chicanery," "Propagandists").

279. *Philadelphia Inquirer*, April 18, 1962 ("pressure"); May 11, 1962 ("unfair"); *New York Times*, August 9, 1970; John Morrison McLarnon, *Ruling Suburbia: John J. McClure and the Republican Machine in Delaware County, Pennsylvania* (Newark: University of Delaware Press, 2003), 189.

280. *Philadelphia Inquirer*, May 2, 1962 ("contract," "peanuts"); Bailey to Tate, April 5, 1962 ("requirement," "deeply"); April 18, 1962 ("convinced"); May 5, 1962; Tate Papers, Box 12, A-6335.

281. *Philadelphia Inquirer*, May 11, 1962 ("political"); May 18, 1962 ("atrociously," "selfish," "skyrocket," "rob," "unconscionable," "like," "destroyed," "fence"); Bailey to Tate, May 23, 1962, Tate Papers, Box 12, A-6335 ("show").

282. The conditions included Berger's pledge that SEPACT would give equal consideration to commuter rail, bus, and streetcar lines and that station improvements (rather than payments to the PRR) would constitute the initial form of SEPACT support.

283. *Philadelphia Inquirer*, May 25, 1962; June 14, 1962; October 9, 1962 ("obstructionist," "people," "philosophy").

284. The PTC strike began on January 15, 1963, and lasted for nineteen days. The Red Arrow strike began on February 8, 1963, and ended on March 13.

285. *Philadelphia Inquirer*, June 17, 1962 ("link"); October 21, 1962; October 23, 1962; December 9, 1962; December 5, 1962; March 10, 1963; March 13, 1963; March 14, 1963; March 17, 1963; June 19, 1963; Bailey Oral History, 20 ("decided"); Kobrick, "Let the People Have a Victory," 152–53.

286. *Philadelphia Inquirer*, July 26, 1963 ("simple"); November 13, 1963 ("look"); February 9, 1964.

287. John F. Kennedy, "Remarks in Harrisburg at a Democratic State Finance Committee Dinner," September 20, 1962, American Presidency Project, https://www.presidency.ucsb.edu/documents/remarks-harrisburg-democratic-state-finance-committee-dinner, accessed December 7, 2023; Bailey to Tate, September 26, 1962 ("lost"), Tate Papers, Box 12, A-6335; Smerk, *Federal Role in Urban Mass Transportation*, 86–87.

288. G. C. Vaughan to J. P. Newell, April 18, 1963 ("concept"), HML, Box 357, folder 1; George M. Smerk, "The Urban Mass Transportation Act of 1964: New Hope for American Cities," *Transportation Journal* 5, no. 2 (Winter 1965): 35–40; Smerk, *Federal Role in Urban Mass Transportation*, 88–94; Weingroff, *Busting the Trust*, 28–43; Kobrick, "Let the People Have a Victory," 229–30.

289. Kobrick, "Let the People Have a Victory," 153–54 (includes Kobrick interview with McConnon, March 4, 2009 ["money"]).

290. *Philadelphia Inquirer*, December 2, 1963 ("honored"); February 2, 1964; February 13, 1964; June 14, 1964; September 16, 1964; October 1, 1964; Kobrick, "Let the People Have a Victory," 152–54.

291. *Philadelphia Inquirer*, February 2, 1964 ("water"); February 28, 1964; *Trains* 24, no. 11 (September 1964): 8; 25, no. 3 (January 1965): 10.

292. Philadelphia's 1964 budget included $2,009,000 for the original PSIC service (within city limits) and a further $341,000 for its share of the four-county SEPACT operations.

293. The approved city subsidy for 1965 was $2.35 million, including SEPACT contributions of $1.03 million for the PRR (a slight decrease from the $1.11 million in 1964) and $1.13 million for the Reading (up from $1.06 million the year before). The remainder went to SEPTA and—even when matched with contributions from the outlying counties—was hardly sufficient to do more than hire a few office personnel and study methods to achieve an integrated transit system.

294. *Philadelphia Inquirer*, May 7, 1964; September 16, 1964; January 17, 1965; February 26, 1965; April 15, 1965 ("needed"); Kobrick, "Let the People Have a Victory," 232–33.

295. *Philadelphia Inquirer*, July 30, 1964; August 6, 1964; August 10, 1964 ("system," "conclusion").

296. Bailey Oral History, 20 ("clear"); *Philadelphia Inquirer*, August 10, 1964 ("fragmented"); September 29, 1964 ("early," "payments"); October 10, 1964; October 16, 1964; October 17, 1964 ("merely"); October 27, 1964;

"Interview with Joseph Sharfsin," November 29, 1977, Walter Massey Phillips Oral Histories, Temple University Libraries, 1–3.

297. *Philadelphia Inquirer*, January 16, 1965; February 11, 1965; February 14, 1965; March 16, 1965; April 23, 1965; July 28, 1965 ("problem," "just").

298. *Philadelphia Inquirer*, August 15, 1965; September 22, 1965; February 20, 1966 ("look"); October 28, 1965; December 25, 1965; February 12, 1966 ("government").

299. Much of the remaining amount would be funded by $22.4 million in earnings from the "Operation" services.

300. *Philadelphia Inquirer*, September 17, 1966; May 6, 1967; December 10, 1967; Kobrick, "Let the People Have a Victory," 234–35, 241–50.

301. In March 1966, SEPTA officials denied rumors that they were prepared to offer Albert G. Lyons, the president of PTC, the job of general manager (at a $75,000 salary), to secure his cooperation for the inclusion of PTC in SEPTA. Hemphill's refusal to release city funds, in August, occurred in response to his belief that Bailey had withheld a report that characterized his agency as a "hodgepodge" organization and its employees as incompetent. Hemphill also asserted that SEPTA board chairman Casimir A. Sienkiewicz had failed to honor his promise to provide the controller's office with access to SEPTA's financial records. *Philadelphia Inquirer*, March 9, 1966; August 24, 1966 ("hodgepodge"); December 11, 1966; December 12, 1966 ("unjustified"); December 20, 1966; February 19, 1967 ("demonstration"); June 10, 1967; July 7, 1967 ("impeded"); August 3, 1967.

302. SEPTA classified the twenty St. Louis Car Company units as Silverliner III, referring to the fifty-five original Budd cars (delivered in 1963) as Silverliner II. The six 1958 Pioneer III cars (which were not compatible with the newer equipment) became Silverliner I.

303. *Philadelphia Inquirer*, January 17, 1968.

304. *Philadelphia Inquirer*, March 9, 1966; March 26, 1967 ("return," "once"); June 25, 1967 ("equipment," "shortage," "cattle"); September 2, 1967 ("struggling"); September 17, 1967 ("runs," "name").

305. *Philadelphia Inquirer*, November 24, 1966.

8. Merger

1. "The Pennsylvania Railroad Company Passenger Operations–Draft of Report, July 26, 1954" ("appearance," "dispose"), Penn Central Railroad Collection, M.G. 286, Pennsylvania Historical and Museum Commission, Pennsylvania State Archives, Harrisburg (hereafter, PHMC), Franklin Papers, Box 76 (9-2124), folder 521.3; Hilary Ballon, *New York's Pennsylvania Stations* (New York: W. W. Norton, 2002), 95–96.

2. *New York Times*, November 30, 1954 ("modernized"); January 15, 1955; June 8, 1955; June 9, 1955 ("superlatives"); January 6, 1956; PRR BOD Minutes; Peter Moore, Barbara Moore, Eric Peter Nash, and Lorraine B. Diehl, *The Destruction of Penn Station: Photographs by Peter Moore* (New York: Distributed Art, 2000), 14–17, 25; Ballon, *Pennsylvania Stations*, 95–98.

3. *New York Times*, September 29, 1962 ("plastic"); "Old Setting, New Gleam," *Architectural Forum*, August 1957 ("function"); Eric J. Plosky, "The Fall and Rise of Pennsylvania Station: Changing Attitudes toward Historic Preservation in New York City" (MCP thesis, Massachusetts Institute of Technology, Department of Urban Studies and Planning, 2000), 20–21.

4. *New York Times*, May 11, 1960; November 28, 1960 ("so"); Ballon, *Pennsylvania Stations*, 98–99.

5. PRR BOD Minutes; *New York Times*, November 4, 1960 ("far"); Plosky, "Fall and Rise," 22; Ballon, *Pennsylvania Stations*, 98–100.

6. PRR BOD Minutes; J. B. Jones to Allen J. Greenough, June 26, 1961; James W. Oram to James M. Symes et al., July 25, 1961; both in Pennsylvania Railroad Company Records, Accession 1807/1810, Manuscripts and Archives Department, Hagley Museum and Library, Wilmington, Delaware (hereafter, HML), Box 339, folder 6; *New York Times*, July 25, 1961; July 26, 1961 ("left"); July 27, 1961 ("razed"); November 5, 1960 ("contribution"); *New York Herald Tribune*, July 25, 1961; Plosky, "Fall and Rise," 23–24.

7. Like many Modernists, Mumford favored the Concourse, with its glass and exposed steel beams. That portion of the station was also the least functional, as the roof leaked and drafts of cold air regularly blew out of the tunnels and into areas occupied by passengers.

8. *New York Times*, December 30, 2015; Lewis Mumford, "The Disappearance of Pennsylvania Station," *New Yorker*, June 7, 1958 ("dying," "suspects," "clairvoyance," "further").

9. "Penn Station to Give Way to Madison Square Garden; Great Space in Peril; RR to Go Underground," *Progressive Architecture*, September 1962, quoted in Plosky, "Fall and Rise," 33–34 ("ruined," "lose").

10. *New York Times*, March 21, 1962 ("tragedy"); Plosky, "Fall and Rise," 34–39.

11. *New York Times*, May 17, 1962 ("landscape," "sequence"); August 3, 1962 ("save"); Plosky, "Fall and Rise," 41–44; Ballon, *Pennsylvania Stations*, 101–2.

12. *New York Times*, July 12, 1961 ("changing"); December 3, 1961; April 22, 1962 ("Rome," "dictum"); July 15, 1985; July 25, 2016.

13. *New York Times*, August 23, 1962 ("sense," "responsibility"); September 23, 1962 ("who"); Ballon, *Pennsylvania Stations*, 102.

14. *New York Times*, June 29, 1962; September 11, 1962; September 18, 1962; September 23, 1962; September 28, 1962 ("efficient"); PRR BOD Minutes; Ballon, *Pennsylvania Stations*, 105–7.

15. *New York Times*, October 29, 1963 ("shame," "index," job"); October 30, 1963 ("destroyed").

16. *New York Times*, October 9, 1964 ("economics"); December 27, 1964 ("era").

17. *New York Times*, October 30, 1964; October 20, 1965; July 14, 1966; September 13, 1966; *New Yorker*, September 18, 1965, 42–44 ("voice," "world," "ghost"); Plosky, "Fall and Rise," 49; Ballon, *Pennsylvania Stations*, 103–5.

18. Richard Saunders Jr., *Merging Lines: American Railroads, 1900–1970* (DeKalb: Northern Illinois University Press, 2001), 165–70.

19. H. Roger Grant, *Erie Lackawanna: Death of an American Railroad, 1938–1992* (Stanford, CA: Stanford University Press, 1994), 94, includes press release, October 7, 1959 ("example"); *Trains* 20, no. 2 (December 1959): 5; Saunders, *Merging Lines*, 176–77.

20. Grant, *Erie Lackawanna*, 94–100; *New York Times*, September 16, 1960.

21. E. F. Pat Striplin, *The Norfolk & Western: A History* (Roanoke, VA: Norfolk & Western Railway, 1981), 245–47.

22. Striplin, *Norfolk & Western*, 245–46, 248–49, 299.

23. *New York Times*, December 15, 1959.

24. J. W. Barriger to Alfred Perlman, December 16, 1959, 1 ("development"), 5 ("signs"), John W. Barriger III Papers, St. Louis Mercantile Library, St. Louis, Missouri (hereafter, Barriger Papers), Series 259, Box 155, folder 3–5.

25. Barriger to Perlman, December 16, 1959, 1 ("policy"), 2 ("location," "interior"), 5 ("historic").

26. "In order to maintain competitive balance," Perlman continued, "it is essential that each system have single-line access to the coal origin territory of the Pocahontas region and to the Tidewater ports." Barriger to Perlman, December 16, 1959, 6 ("lesser"), 7 ("balanced"), 7–8 ("complementary," "size"); Statement of Testimony of Alfred E. Perlman Before the Interstate Commerce Commission, Finance Docket Nos. 21160, 21161, 21237, 21238, June 2, 1961 (revised July 7, 1961), 13

("reduced," "maintain"), Barriger Papers, Series 259, Box 155, folder 3–9.

27. In a January 1961 memo to Perlman, Barriger suggested that the Erie-Lackawanna should be allocated to the PRR system. Barriger, "Memorandum for Mr. A. E. Perlman," January 18, 1961, Barriger Papers, Series 259, Box 155, folder 3–6.

28. The 1998 breakup of Conrail allocated most former PRR routes to the Norfolk Southern Corporation (the inheritor of the N&W, the Nickel Plate, and the Wabash) and most former NYC lines to the CSX Corporation (the successor to the C&O and the B&O)—thus creating, in broad outlines, the two-system East that Barriger envisioned in December 1959.

29. *New York Times*, April 29, 1960 ("surrounded"); Saunders, *Merging Lines*, 191.

30. *New York Times*, March 19, 1960; PRR BOD Minutes; Saunders, *Merging Lines*, 191.

31. PRR BOD Minutes; *New York Times*, December 1, 1960; Striplin, *Norfolk & Western*, 246–47, 250–53; Saunders, *Merging Lines*, 200–207.

32. PRR BOD Minutes; *New York Times*, December 17, 1960; February 4, 1961; March 24, 1961; Saunders, *Merging Lines*, 191–94.

33. *New York Times*, December 22, 1960 ("sooner"); March 24, 1961 ("objective"); May 10, 1961 ("assure," "eventually"); *Pennsylvania Railroad Company–Control–Lehigh Valley Railroad Company*, 317 ICC 1139 (1962).

34. *New York Times*, December 17, 1960 ("absorb"); Saunders, *Merging Lines*, 191–95.

35. *New York Times*, March 8, 1961 ("interested").

36. *New York Times*, April 29, 1960 ("identified"); Saunders, *Merging Lines*, 186–87.

37. *New York Times*, April 29, 1960 ("merit"); Saunders, *Merging Lines*, 186–88.

38. Statement of Testimony of Alfred E. Perlman, 10 ("proceed," "allies," "expressed").

39. Statement of Testimony of Alfred E. Perlman, 11 ("concern"), 11 ("uncertain"), 13 ("balance").

40. Statement of Testimony of Alfred E. Perlman, 14 ("shocked"); Saunders, *Merging Lines*, 195–99.

41. Saunders, *Merging Lines*, 187–88.

42. Statement of Testimony of Alfred E. Perlman, 16 ("encouraging"); *New York Times*, September 22, 1960 ("pursuit"); September 27, 1960; October 5, 1960.

43. *New York Times*, August 9, 1960 ("withdraw," "deal," "marbles"); May 22, 1961 ("choice, "unnecessary"); May 26, 1961 ("learn"); Saunders, *Merging Lines*, 188–90.

44. A few weeks earlier, on April 3, the Erie-Lackawanna filed a similar petition with the ICC, demanding to

be a party to the N&W–Nickel Plate merger. *New York Times*, April 4, 1961; April 29, 1961 ("bankrupt," "vital").

45. *New York Times*, June 14, 1960 ("rules," "chaotic," "obsolete"); June 15, 1960 ("force"); Saunders, *Merging Lines*, 187.

46. *New York Times*, May 10, 1961 ("anxious," "power," "tactic").

47. Symes presented the two variants to the PRR's directors at the October 25, 1961, board meeting, but he had been contemplating the relative merits of the two-system East and the three-system East for some time.

48. Tuohy conceded that C&O and NYC personnel had sporadically discussed a merger as early as 1954, when Robert Young had first broached the idea. It was still a possibility, Tuohy suggested, and "given reasonable time, it is entirely possible that a system including the B. & O., the C. & O., and the N. Y. C. could evolve in the East." It was a vague prediction that stopped well short of a promise.

49. *New York Times*, June 16, 1961; June 20, 1961 ("reasonable"); June 21, 1961 ("wait"); June 27, 1961; June 30, 1961.

50. *New York Times*, July 11, 1961 ("else," "cooling-off").

51. The application indicated that the N&W would lease the Wabash for fifty years, with the right to acquire outright control (through stock ownership) at any time, once the lease had been in effect for six years.

52. *New York Times*, March 18, 1961; *Trains* 21, no. 8 (June 1961): 4 ("empire"), 6 ("control," "friend"); *Railway Age* 150, no. 13 (March 27, 1961): 9–10.

53. *New York Times*, March 8, 1961 ("unification," "interested"); Grant, *Erie Lackawanna*, 106–7.

54. *New York Times*, April 4, 1961; April 12, 1961; April 25, 1961 ("fancy").

55. *New York Times*, May 18, 1961 ("step"); May 22, 1961 ("fruitless"); *Poughkeepsie Journal*, May 18, 1961 ("clock"); June 20, 1961 ("voluntary," "kill").

56. *New York Times*, June 16, 1961; Saunders, *Merging Lines*, 207–8.

57. *New York Times*, July 11, 1961 ("gargantuan," "talked").

58. Stephen Salsbury, *No Way to Run a Railroad: The Untold Story of the Penn Central Crisis* (New York: McGraw-Hill, 1982), 85.

59. Salsbury, *No Way to Run a Railroad*, 85; Charles W. Turner, Thomas W. Dixon Jr., and Eugene L. Huddleston, *Chessie's Road*, 2nd ed. (Alderson, WV: Chesapeake & Ohio Historical Society, 1986), 193.

60. Salsbury, *No Way to Run a Railroad*, 85.

61. *New York Times*, September 21, 1961.

62. Saunders, *Merging Lines*, 200.

63. *New York Times*, November 7, 1961; November 9, 1961.

64. *New York Times*, November 8, 1961 ("conservatively"); November 9, 1961 ("worsened," "assure").

65. *New York Times*, November 9, 1961; January 13, 1962.

66. PRR BOD Minutes; United States Congress, House Committee on Banking and Currency, Wright Patman, Chairman, *The Penn Central Failure and the Role of Financial Institutions* (Washington, DC: United States Government Printing Office, 1972; hereafter, Patman Report), 11; *New York Times*, February 3, 1961; November 9, 1961; July 9, 1988; *Chicago Tribune*, March 23, 2007.

67. *New York Times*, November 8, 1961; November 9, 1961; United States Securities and Exchange Commission, Hon. Harley O. Staggers, Chairman, *The Financial Collapse of the Penn Central Company: Staff Report of the Securities and Exchange Commission to the Special Subcommittee on Investigations* (Washington, DC: United States Government Printing Office, 1972; hereafter, SEC Report), 154.

68. The 1933 Glass-Steagall Act separated investment and commercial banking, with First Boston Corporation established as the investment-banking counterpart to the First National Bank of Boston, and Mellon Securities Corporation enjoying a similar relationship with Mellon Bank. Mellon Securities and First Boston merged in 1946, retaining the latter corporate name. J. P. Morgan was closely associated with the NYC, as an investment banker and a securities holder. J. P. Morgan & Company became a commercial bank, with Morgan Stanley as the corresponding investment bank.

69. PRR BOD Minutes; SEC Report, 154; Salsbury, *No Way to Run a Railroad*, 86.

70. United States Congress, Senate Committee on Commerce, Warren G. Magnuson, Chairman, Special Staff for the Penn Central Enquiry, *The Penn Central and Other Railroads: A Report to the Senate Committee on Commerce* (Washington, DC: United States Government Printing Office, 1973; hereafter, Magnuson Report), 89–91; Saunders, *Merging Lines*, 251–60.

71. SEC Report, 154; *New York Times*, January 13, 1962.

72. Reporters quickly shortened the cumbersome name to Pennsy-Central or simply Penn-Central, but that phrase did not become a part of the company's official title until after the merger. On merger day, February 1, 1968, the consolidated firm was the Pennsylvania New York Central Transportation Company. It became

the Penn Central Company on May 8, 1968, and was renamed the Penn Central Transportation Company on October 2, 1969.

73. *New York Times*, January 13, 1962 ("bitterly").

74. *New York Times*, January 13, 1962 ("substantial"); May 9, 1962; Interstate Commerce Commission, Finance Docket No. 21989, *Pennsylvania Railroad Company–Merger–New York Central Railroad Company*, and Finance Docket 21990, *Pennsylvania Railroad Company–Stock Issuance*, also reported in Pennsylvania *Railroad Company–Merger–New York Central Railroad* 327 ICC 475 (1966), at 566–1072.

75. *New York Times*, January 16, 1962.

76. Charles F. Phillips Jr., "Railroad Mergers: Competition, Monopoly and Antitrust," *Washington and Lee Law Review* 19, no. 1 (Spring 1962): 1–22, at 17 ("equated").

77. As early as March 1961, *Railway Age* indicated the decreased tolerance for mergers, in an article entitled "Cooler Merger Climate Seen." *Railway Age* 150, no. 13 (March 27, 1961): 65 ("Cooler").

78. Saunders, *Merging Lines*, 216–39.

79. PRR, Number of Active Employes, July 15, 1959, HML, Box 351, folder 3; *Railway Age* 146, no. 8 (February 23, 1959): 53 ("year").

80. For information on the legal context of featherbedding, see William Gomberg, "Featherbedding: An Assertion of Property Rights," *Annals of the American Academy of Political and Social Science* 333 (January 1961): 119–29.

81. J. A. Lipowski, "Featherbedding on the Railroads by Law and by Agreement," *Transportation Law Journal* 8 (1976): 141–65, at 141–46.

82. PRR Personnel Department, "Featherbedding," April 28, 1959; James Oram to Roy C. Champlin, October 1, 1957 ("doubt"); James Newell to L. A. Gossage, April 9, 1952; David Bevan to Gossage, March 5, 1952 ("problem"); all in HML, Box 233, folder 22; *Chicago Daily News*, February 5, 1959 ("war").

83. *New York Times*, August 21, 1959; August 27, 1959; September 12, 1959 ("hope"); September 29, 1959; November 1, 1959; November 2, 1959; June 16, 1960; July 7, 1960.

84. *New York Times*, June 25, 1960; July 8, 1960 ("nothing," "days"); September 1, 1960.

85. *New York Times*, September 1, 1960 ("impunity," "ambitions"); September 2, 1960 ("taken," "might"); September 3, 1960; September 4, 1960; September 6, 1960; September 7, 1960; September 8, 1960; September 10, 1960; September 11, 1960; September 12, 1960; September 13, 1960.

86. *New York Times*, September 7, 1960; September 8, 1960; October 19, 1960 ("welcome").

87. *New York Times*, December 23, 1960; March 1, 1962 ("provisions," "shock," "thinking"); *Railway Age* 150, no. 13 (March 27, 1961): 64 ("tone").

88. *New York Times*, January 13, 1962 ("giant," "catastrophic"); January 16, 1962 ("manipulation"); January 21, 1962; January 24, 1962; January 31, 1962; February 1, 1962; May 9, 1962.

89. Saunders, *Merging Lines*, 207–8; Ralph W. Hidy, Muriel E. Hidy, Roy V. Scott, and Don L. Hofsommer, *The Great Northern Railway: A History* (Minneapolis: University of Minnesota Press, 1988, 2004), 298; *New York Times*, January 14, 1962 ("look").

90. *New York Times*, July 1, 1959; September 17, 1959; November 22, 1960 ("follies," "indulgence," "excessive," "essentially").

91. *New York Times*, October 26, 1960 ("hat"); July 7, 1961.

92. *New York Times*, July 3, 1961; July 5, 1961; July 6, 1961; July 7, 1961; July 8, 1961 ("answer").

93. The figure of 43.9 percent is based on the level of the New Haven's interchange traffic in 1961 (690,222 loaded cars), factored against the number of cars interchanged with the PRR (145,952 cars), the LIRR (13,694), the Lehigh Valley (34,431), and the New York Central (79,715). The 29,529 cars operating over the New Haven in bridge service between the Boston & Maine and the PRR would also likely be lost in the event of the Penn Central merger.

94. The New Haven's freight revenues—the only service that made money—had fallen by nearly 31 percent between 1957 and 1963, from $91.5 million to $63.5 million.

95. *New York Times*, January 17, 1962 ("summer," "concern," "successful"); February 13, 1963; Finance Docket 21989, 329–30.

96. *New York Times*, January 27, 1962 ("talking"); June 9, 1962 ("appear"); June 20, 1962.

97. *New York Times*, January 17, 1962; January 28, 1962 ("specific," "encourage"); March 22, 1962.

98. New York Times, March 22, 1962 ("professional"); United States Congress, House, Committee on the Judiciary, Proposed Merger of Eastern Air Lines and American Airlines: A Staff Report to Subcommittee No. 5 of the Committee on the Judiciary (Washington, DC: United States Government Printing Office, 1962).

99. John F. Kennedy, "Special Message to Congress on Transportation, April 5, 1962," *Public Papers of the Presidents of the United States: John F. Kennedy, January*

1 to December 31, 1962 (Washington, DC: United States Government Printing Office, 1963) 292–306 ("examine," "effective," "economies" at 298); Magnuson Report, 166–67; Saunders, *Merging Lines*, 229–31.

100. In his role as special assistant to the US attorney general, Prettyman possessed little experience with railroads or any other mode of transportation. He speculated that the appointment arose from his role in planning the return to the United States, by aircraft, of some eleven hundred Cuban exiles captured in the Bay of Pigs invasion—an accomplishment that brought him to the attention of the Kennedy brothers.

101. "Statement of Assistant Attorney General William H. Orrick Jr., in the Pennsylvania–New York Central Merger Case, before the Interstate Commerce Commission," October 1, 1963, General Records of the United States Department of Transportation, Record Group 398, National Archives and Records Administration, College Park, Maryland (hereafter, DOT Records), Box 43; Historical Society of the District of Columbia Circuit, E. Barrett Prettyman Jr., Esq., Oral History Text & Documentation, Text of Interview (October 3, 1996); https://dcchs.org/sb_pdf/interview-5-e-barrett-prettyman/, accessed May 23, 2020, 140–41 ("problem," "everybody").

102. There are many variants of the quotation, including "SOBs" rather than "sons of bitches," as well as additional comments ranging from "and now I know what he meant" to "but I never believed it until now" to "but I never knew how right he was until now."

103. Saunders, *Merging Lines*, 229–31.

104. Kefauver's proposal did not apply to mergers involving less than $200 million in assets or to companies in bankruptcy.

105. *New York Times*, February 19, 1962 ("snowballing"); Saunders, *Merging Lines*, 231–32.

106. "Statement of James M. Symes," July 3, 1962, United States Congress, Senate, Committee on the Judiciary, *Rail Merger Legislation*, 87th Cong., 2nd sess. (Washington, DC: United States Government Printing Office, 1962), 367 ("prompt"), 371 ("monopoly"); Saunders, *Merging Lines*, 231–39.

107. Symes Testimony, *Rail Merger Legislation*, 397 ("approved"); *New York Times*, June 20, 1961; October 11, 1961; October 25, 1962; Saunders, *Merging Lines*, 195.

108. White comments are from the Delaware & Hudson annual report, reprinted in *Rail Merger Legislation*, 1575 ("harm").

109. A month later, when it was too late to block the consolidation, the Interagency Committee on Transport Mergers issued a preliminary set of criteria to govern

such decisions. A supplemental report, released on March 3, provided a list of ten stipulations to govern railroad and aviation mergers. Phrased as questions, they recommended the protection of competition, service levels, employees, creditors, and the public interest. In seeking a more efficient use of resources, the criteria also included speculation regarding "alternatives [to mergers] more easily revocable which promise to be of comparative effect in accomplishing the improvement in over-all efficiency." *New York Times*, May 2, 1962 ("necessary," "balanced"); March 7, 1963; "Criteria to Implement the Merger Provisions of the President's Transportation Message—Report of the Interagency Committee on Transport Mergers Provided in the President's Transportation Message of April 5, 1962," *Congressional Record*, 88th Cong., 1st sess., Volume 109, Part 3, February 22, 1963 to March 14, 1963 (Washington, DC: United States Government Printing Office, 1963), 3671–73 ("alternatives"); Magnuson Report, 166–67; Saunders, *Merging Lines*, 239–41.

110. *New York Times*, July 11, 1962.

111. Symes Testimony, *Rail Merger Legislation*, 396 ("divest," "approved," "cause"); *Trains* 22, no. 10 (August 1962): 6 ("sign"); Saunders, *Merging Lines*, 241–43.

112. The carefully worded arrangements offered by Symes and Bevan posed a problem for the ICC commissioners who evaluated the Norfolk & Western and Penn Central mergers as separate cases. They could approve the first of those applications, thus giving Symes some measure of control over perhaps two-thirds of the eastern railroad network, and then hope that they could impose divestment from the N&W as a condition of the Penn Central merger. If, in contrast, the commissioners required that separation as part of the N&W–Nickel Plate docket, then they risked the possibility that Symes might withdraw the Penn Central application. In that eventuality, it would then be their responsibility to find a home for the foundering New York Central—a near impossibility, following the creation of the C&O–B&O and N&W–Nickel Plate systems. *New York Times*, October 31, 1962.

113. *New York Times*, April 13, 1963; April 23, 1964 ("cake," "fails," "prompt").

114. Norfolk & Western Railway–Merger–New York, Chicago & St. Louis Railroad, 324 ICC 1 (1964), at 29–32; *New York Times*, April 23, 1964; Saunders, *Merging Lines*, 243–44.

115. Norfolk & Western Railway–Merger–New York, Chicago & St. Louis Railroad, 57 ("impelling); *New York Times*, May 29, 1964 ("crucify"); August 21, 1964.

116. *New York Times*, August 20, 1962 ("clinic"); August 21, 1962.

117. Two sources (*Trains* and the *New York Times*) mention forty thousand pages of testimony, while the PRR's 1963 annual report lists twenty thousand pages of testimony. The *New York Times* and the annual report indicate 128 days of testimony, while the 129-day figure in *Trains* reflects a single day of additional testimony on September 16, 1964. *New York Times*, August 21, 1962; March 30, 1965; *Trains* 25, no. 8 (June 1965): 3; Pennsylvania Railroad Company, *117th Annual Report for the Year Ended December 31, 1963* (Philadelphia: n.p., 1964), 14.

118. *New York Times*, August 21, 1962 ("contact," "attempts," "standpoints," "list," "continue"); August 25, 1962.

119. *New York Times*, August 21, 1962 ("expedited," "peas").

120. *New York Times*, August 25, 1962.

121. Both the C&O and the B&O were intervenors in the proceedings, but they were among six such railroads that did not offer evidence.

122. Finance Docket 21989, 12–13.

123. *New York Times*, August 25, 1962.

124. *New York Times*, August 28, 1962 ("chair"); August 29, 1962 ("fouled," "house," "kill"); Joseph R. Daughen and Peter Binzen, *The Wreck of the Penn Central* (Boston: Little, Brown, 1961, Washington, DC: Beard, 1999), 60–61.

125. *New York Times*, February 12, 1963 ("require," "prerequisite," "solution"); February 13, 1963; February 19, 1963; February 20, 1963.

126. *Pennsylvania Railroad Company–Merger–New York Central Railroad Company*, 327 ICC 475 (1966), 480; *New York Times*, March 26, 1963 ("unavoidable").

127. *New York Times*, February 18, 1963 ("hostess").

128. Finance Docket 21989, 13, 212–29 ("instances" at 213).

129. Finance Docket 21989, 110–12.

130. Finance Docket 21989, 110–12; *New York Times*, November 7, 1962.

131. SEC Report, 17–18 ("correlation"), 155 ("presented").

132. Finance Docket 21989, 131–43; *New York Times*, July 18, 1962; January 16, 1968.

133. Finance Docket 21989, 100, 120–31; *New York Times*, July 18, 1962; *Rails Northeast* 43 (February 1978): 13–21; 44 (March 1978): 12–21.

134. The July 17 version of the Patchell study predicted an annual savings of $75 million, but the figure subsequently presented to the ICC was $81.2 million. Another iteration of the study set the projected savings at $85.8 million.

135. Specifically, the termination of direct NYC control over the Pittsburgh & Lake Erie and the placement of P&LE stock in trust.

136. *New York Times*, July 18, 1962; Finance Docket 21989, 229–42, 254–56.

137. Finance Docket 21989, 242–54.

138. Glenn McLaughlin, *The Growth of American Manufacturing Areas: A Comparative Analysis with Special Emphasis on Trends in the Pittsburgh District* (Pittsburgh: University of Pittsburgh Press, 1938); John N. Hoffman, "Pennsylvania's Bituminous Coal Industry: An Industrial Review," *Pennsylvania History: A Journal of Mid-Atlantic Studies* 45, no. 4 (October 1978): 351–63; Marvin B. Lieberman and Douglas R. Johnson, "Comparative Productivity of Japanese and U.S. Steel Producers, 1958–1993," *Japan and the World Economy* 11 (1999): 1–27; Irwin M. Marcus, "The Deindustrialization of America: Homestead, A Case Study, 1959–1984," *Pennsylvania History: A Journal of Mid-Atlantic Studies* 52, no. 3 (July 1985): 162–82; Dale A. Hathaway, *Can Workers Have A Voice? The Politics of Deindustrialization in Pittsburgh* (State College: Pennsylvania State University Press, 1993); John Hoerr, *And the Wolf Finally Came: The Decline of the American Steel Industry* (Pittsburgh: University of Pittsburgh Press, 1988); Barry Bluestone and Bennett Harrison, *The Deindustrialization of America: Plant Closings, Community Abandonment, and the Dismantling of Basic Industry* (New York: Basic, 1982); "Deindustrialization: A Panel Discussion," *Pennsylvania History* 58 (1991): 181–211.

139. *Philadelphia Inquirer*, September 22, 1962 ("concerned").

140. *New York Times*, January 4, 1963; *Philadelphia Inquirer*, January 4, 1963 ("surprised," "disappointment").

141. *Philadelphia Inquirer*, June 9, 1963 ("unintelligible"); June 22, 1963 ("damage," "impact," "secondary"); August 7, 1963 ("indicates").

142. *Philadelphia Inquirer*, February 11, 1961; June 29, 1961; *New York Times*, November 26, 1994; Daughen and Binzen, *Wreck of the Penn Central*, 71–72.

143. The ICC merger hearings recessed on August 31, following the testimony and cross-examination of Symes and Perlman. Shapp timed the ad to coincide with the reopening of the hearings on October 15.

144. *Philadelphia Inquirer*, October 15, 1962 ("vividly," "wealthiest").

145. *New York Times*, January 17, 1963 ("featherbedding"); *Philadelphia Inquirer*, January 17, 1963; Daughen and Binzen, *Wreck of the Penn Central*, 73.

146. Allen Greenough to Symes, January 16, 1963 ("individuals"), PHMC, Symes / Saunders papers, Box 125 (9-2276), folder 110.01; *New York Times*, January 13, 1962; January 16, 1962; May 9, 1962; June 10, 1962 ("wholesale," emphasis in the original, "harm," "pattern"); July 18, 1962 ("loss"); August 25, 1962 ("largest"); Saunders, *Merging Lines*, 267–68.

147. *New York Times*, February 11, 1962 ("imagine"); September 20, 1962; Leon H. Keyserling, *The Move toward Railroad Mergers: A Great National Problem* (Washington, DC: Railway Labor Executives' Association, 1962, Westport, CT: Greenwood, 1978); Saunders, *Merging Lines*, 238, 267.

148. *New York Times*, August 23, 1962 ("increase"); August 31, 1962 ("trap"); November 7, 1962.

149. *New York Times*, April 19, 1962; May 18, 1962; May 19, 1962; May 22, 1962; June 2, 1962; June 6, 1962; June 23, 1962; June 28, 1962; June 30, 1962; July 7, 1962; August 7, 1962; March 5, 1963.

150. *New York Times*, March 5, 1963; March 14, 1963; March 16, 1963; April 3, 1963; April 4, 1963.

151. *New York Times*, April 4, 1963; July 3, 1963; July 4, 1963; July 5, 1963; July 6, 1963; July 7, 1963; July 8, 1963; July 9, 1963; July 10, 1963 ("extraordinary"); July 11, 1963; Lipowski, "Featherbedding on the Railroads," 155–56.

152. *New York Times*, July 25, 1963; August 16, 1963; August 17, 1963; August 24, 1963; August 25, 1963; August 27, 1963; August 28, 1963; September 1, 1963 ("institution"); Lipowski, "Featherbedding on the Railroads," 156–59.

153. Rush Loving Jr., *The Men Who Loved Trains: The Story of Men Who Battled Greed to Save an Ailing Industry* (Bloomington: Indiana University Press, 2006), 35 ("unacceptable").

154. *New York Times*, January 13, 1962; January 28, 1962 ("situations," promise," "early"); *Lancaster New Era*, January 13, 1962.

155. Butcher and his associates began buying PRR stock in the range of $15 to $16 per share, and went as high as $18 to $19 apiece, before the stock fell to about $11, while they continued to make additional purchases. Assuming an average share price of $16, their 1.4 million shares represented an investment of about $22.4 million, and perhaps as high as $26.6 million, in the unlikely event that Butcher acquired all shares at the highest possible ($19) price. At the exchange ratio established by the PRR and NYC directors, on January 12, 1962, those PRR shares would become 1,820,000 Penn Central shares. Financial analysts suggested that following the merger, Penn Central shares would be worth about $50,

indicating that the Butcher holdings would be valued in the range of $91 million—representing a quadrupling of his initial investment.

156. *Boston Globe*, April 8, 1965; Loving, *Men Who Loved Trains*, 35–36.

157. Loving, *Men Who Loved Trains*, 36–37.

158. *New York Times*, April 28, 1965; Rush Loving Jr., "The Penn Central Bankruptcy Express," *Fortune* 82 (August 1970): 104–9, 164–71 ("project"); Joseph A. Califano, *The Triumph & Tragedy of Lyndon Johnson: The White House Years* (New York: Simon & Schuster, 1991), 154 ("impeccable").

159. Saunders incurred the enmity of the powerful political organization headed by Senator Harry F. Byrd Sr. He was sufficiently proud of his role in the process that in 1980, as a retirement project, he chronicled his achievements in "The Unpublished Role of Virginia Business and Professional Leaders in Establishment of the Virginia Division of Industrial Development and in Opposition to Massive Resistance."

160. Symes to Jared Ingersoll, n.d., but ca. June 1963, reprinted in Daughen and Binzen, *Wreck of the Penn Central*, 64–65 ("charming," "fit"); Richard A. Hodges, "Massive Resistance and the Origins of the Virginia Technical College System," *Inquiry: Journal of the Virginia Community Colleges* 22, no. 2 (2019): Article 6; George M. Cochran, "Virginia Facing Reality: The 1959 Perrow Commission," *Augusta Historical Bulletin* 42 (2006): 1–13; Alexander Stewart Leidholdt, "The 'Virginian-Pilot' Newspaper's Role in Moderating Norfolk, Virginia's 1958 School Desegregation Crisis" (PhD diss., Old Dominion University, 1991), 203–7; James J. Hershman Jr., "Massive Resistance Meets Its Match: The Emergence of a Pro-Public School Majority," in Matthew D. Lassiter, Andrew B. Lewis, and Michael D. Lassiter, eds., *The Moderates' Dilemma: Massive Resistance to School Desegregation in Virginia* (Charlottesville: University Press of Virginia, 1998): 104–33, at 112–13; Rush Loving Jr., *The Well-Dressed Hobo: The Many Wondrous Adventures of a Man Who Loves Trains* (Bloomington: Indiana University Press, 2016), 55–56; Loving, *Men Who Loved Trains*, 36–37 ("chase"), 41; "Remarks by the Honorable Henry H. Fowler, Secretary of the Treasury, at the Dinner of the National Conference of Christians and Jews, in Honor of Stuart T. Saunders," New York, June 16, 1965.

161. *New York Times*, May 4, 1963; John F. Kennedy, "Radio and Television Announcement Following Action to Postpone the Nationwide Rail Strike," July 10, 1963, *Public Papers of the Presidents of the United States: John F. Kennedy: Containing the Public Messages, Speeches, and*

Statements of the President, January 1 to November 22, 1963 (Washington, DC: United States Government Printing Office, 1964), 561; John F. Kennedy, Transcript of Off-the-Record Meeting with Wilbur Mills, Lawrence O'Brien, and C. Douglas Dillon, July 29, 1963, *Papers of John F. Kennedy: Presidential Papers: President's Office Files, Presidential Recordings, Transcripts, Tax Cut Proposals, Volume II* (Boston: John F. Kennedy Library, n.d.), 40 ("fellow"); John F. Kennedy, "Remarks at National Conference of the Business Committee for Tax Reduction," September 10, 1963; John F. Kennedy Presidential Library, Papers of John F. Kennedy: Presidential Papers, President's Office Files, Speech Files, JFKPOF-046-033-p0002 ("important"); "1964 Corporation Trustees," John F. Kennedy Presidential Library, https://www.jfklibrary.org/about-us/about-the-jfk-library/history/1964-corporation-trustees, accessed April 26, 2020; Califano, *Triumph & Tragedy*, 156 ("heavy").

162. Symes to Ingersoll, in Daughen and Binzen, *Wreck of the Penn Central*, 64–65 ("wonderful"); Califano, *Triumph & Tragedy*, 154 ("determined," "obsessed"); *New York Times*, April 28, 1965 ("master," "kicked").

163. Daughen and Binzen, *Wreck of the Penn Central*, 65; *Patterson* [New Jersey] *News*, April 21, 1964 ("football," "contribution").

164. Symes to Ingersoll, in Daughen and Binzen, *Wreck of the Penn Central*, 64–65 ("excellent"); Loving, *Men Who Loved Trains*, 37 ("opinion," "deal," "angle").

165. PRR BOD Minutes; *New York Times*, May 13, 1965; SEC Report, 257; Saunders, *Merging Lines*, 242–43.

166. "Questions that are most likely to be in the minds of stockholders," 1955, 14; "Questions that are most likely to be in the minds of stockholders," 1956, 14, both in PHMC, Box 35 (9-2186), folder 111.01; *Philadelphia Letter on Current Railroad Developments* 7, no. 1 (August 1, 1964): 2, HML, Box 885, folder 1.

167. *New York Times*, April 4, 1951 ("change"); March 19, 1953; April 21, 1954; "Questions that are most likely to be in the minds of stockholders," 1955, 26, PHMC, Box 35 (9-2186), folder 111.01.

168. *New York Times*, August 23, 1964; Albert E. Brinkley, "Pennsy Initiates Unit Coal Train Service," *Modern Railroads* 19, no. 8 (August 1964): 48–51; John T. Starr Jr., *The Evolution of the Unit Train, 1960–1969* (Chicago: University of Chicago Department of Geography, 1976), 47–62; *Philadelphia Letter*, August 1, 1964, 1.

169. Greenough to Symes, January 16, 1963 ("individuals"), PHMC, Symes/Saunders papers, Box 125 (9-2276), folder 110.01; *Pennsylvania Railroad Management Letter* 12 (February 1964), 3; HML, Box 1418, folder 7.

170. *Pennsylvania Railroad Management Letter*, 2–3 ("team"); Greenough to Symes, January 16, 1963; "PRR Moves Forward with Revised Organization," *Pennsy*, March–April 1964, 9–13.

171. "(1) the effect of the proposed transaction upon adequate transportation service of the public; (2) the effect upon the public interest of the inclusion, or failure to include, other railroads in the territory involved in the proposed transaction; (3) the total fixed charges resulting from the proposed transactions; and (4) the interest of the carrier employees affected." 54 Stat. 906 (1940), 49 USC sec. 5 par. 2(c) (1958).

172. *McLean Trucking Company v. United States*, 321 US 67 (1944); *Minneapolis & St. Louis Railway v. United States*, 361 US 173 (1959); 54 Stat. 906 (1940), 49 USC sec. 5 par. 11 (1958) ("restraints").

173. Phillips, "Railroad Mergers," 9, 16–22.

174. *New York Times*, June 11, 1963; June 20, 1963; October 27, 1963; January 6, 1964 ("scattershot," "widespread," "bright"); December 29, 1964; Nicholas deB. Katzenbach, *Some of It Was Fun: Working with RFK and LBJ* (New York: W. W. Norton, 2008), 64 ("terrible," "run").

175. *New York Times*, January 6, 1964 ("bright"); William H. Orrick Jr., recorded interview by Larry J. Hackman, April 14, 1970, Robert F. Kennedy Oral History Program of the John F. Kennedy Library, 112 ("lazy"); Katzenbach, *Some of It Was Fun*, 65 ("soldier").

176. Orrick Oral History, 113 ("friend"); Conversation with Robert Kennedy, April 22, 1964, https://millercenter.org/the-presidency/secret-white-house-tapes/conversation-robert-kennedy-april-22-1964-0 ("satisfactory").

177. Orrick Oral History, 33 ("moved"); Memo, Gardner Ackley to Joseph Califano, November 28, 1966, Lyndon Baines Johnson Library, quoted in David M. Welborn, *Regulation in the White House: The Johnson Presidency* (Austin: University of Texas Press, 1993), 191 ("liked," "independently").

178. *Indiana* [Pennsylvania] *Gazette*, September 21, 1950; *Railway Age* 133, no. 19 (November 10, 1952): 12; 135, no. 4 (July 27, 1953): 15; E. G. Plowman, "Survey of Transportation Research," *Transportation Journal* 3, no. 3 (Spring 1964): 17–20; Lowell K. Bridwell to Alan S. Boyd, June 17, 1965, DOT Records, Box 44.

179. Boyd to John T. Connor, June 20, 1966 ("dynamic," "encouraged"), DOT Records, Box 43; Bridwell to Boyd, June 17, 1965 ("energy," "condition"), DOT Records, Box 44. Both documents were written after the Interagency Committee's initial discussions of the Penn Central merger proposal but represent a transfer of

administrative knowledge to a new generation of Commerce Department officials.

180. Bridwell to Boyd, June 17, 1965 ("wishing"), DOT Records, Box 44.

181. "Outline of Tentative Conclusions and Recommendations of the Interagency Committee on Transport Mergers in Regard to the Penn-Central and Related Railroad Mergers," n.d., but ca. September 1963, 1 ("agreement"), 4 ("employees"), 6, 8–10 ("combination" at 10), 16, DOT Records, Box 43.

182. "Outline of Tentative Conclusions and Recommendations," 2 ("stabilizing"), 3 ("failure," "core"), 9 ("weak"), 10.

183. The Akron, Canton & Youngstown and the Pittsburgh & West Virginia were included in that arrangement.

184. "Outline of Tentative Conclusions and Recommendations," 6–16 ("tentatively," "pending" at 12, "offered" at 13, "control" at 16).

185. "Outline of Tentative Conclusions and Recommendations," 10–11 ("feasible").

186. "Outline of Tentative Conclusions and Recommendations," 15 ("wise"), 16 ("studies").

187. "Memorandum for Myer Feldman," May 20, 1964, 3 ("considered"), DOT Records, Box 43; "Outline of Tentative Conclusions and Recommendations," 16 ("studies").

188. "Outline of Tentative Conclusions and Recommendations," 15 ("conclusions," "force").

189. "Text of Conclusions of Report on Pennsylvania-New York Central Merger, September 1963, by Interagency Committee on Transport Mergers," ("appear," emphasis in the original, "presently"), DOT Records, Box 43.

190. Boyd to Connor, June 20, 1966 ("essential," "workable," "solve"), DOT Records, Box 43.

191. "Statement of Assistant Attorney General William H. Orrick Jr. in the Pennsylvania–New York Central Merger Case, before the Interstate Commerce Commission," October 1, 1963 ("benefit," "filed"), DOT Records, Box 43.

192. "Statement of Assistant Attorney General William H. Orrick" ("conclusion," "combination," "endanger," "importance," "preclude"); New York Times, October 2, 1963; Pennsylvania Railroad Company–Merger–New York Central Railroad Company (1966), 502 ("submitted"); Magnuson Report, 167; Saunders, The Railroad Mergers and the Coming of Conrail (Westport, CT: Greenwood, 1978), 196; Daughen and Binzen, Wreck of the Penn Central, 66.

193. New York Times, October 2, 1963 ("sorry," "taste"); October 12 ("impractical," "tragic," "undertook," "plain," "consummated").

194. Orrick Oral History, 112 ("sharp," "cooperate"); New York Times, November 7, 1963 ("listened," "attention").

195. Some of Saunders's White House visits were largely ceremonial, including his attendance at the signing ceremonies for the Demonstration Cities and Metropolitan Development Act on November 3, 1966. Saunders was a frequent guest at luncheons or dinners, typically in the company of other prominent business executives. Meetings of the president's Advisory Committee on Labor-Management Policy (on June 29, 1964; May 3 and May 4, 1966; May 2, 1967; and December 6, 1968), indicated Saunders's willingness to represent the entire railroad industry. Some visits, such as a July 10, 1964, meeting that included Johnson, Perlman, George E. Leighty (the chairman of the Railway Labor Executives' Association) and key presidential aide Myer Feldman, were clearly related to the merger. The number and purpose of meetings is based on listings in the President's Daily Diary Collection, LBJ Presidential Library, https://www.discoverlbj.org/solr-search?q=Saunders+&page=1, accessed January 27, 2024.

196. Orrick Oral History, 112 ("stopping"); Conversation with Wilbur Mills, March 18, 1965, Miller Center, University of Virginia, https://millercenter.org/the-presidency/secret-white-house-tapes/conversation-wilbur-mills-march-18-1965, accessed May 23, 2020; New York Times, August 11, 1964; October 18, 1964 ("predicted"); March 23, 1965; April 23, 1965 ("support"); Daughen and Binzen, Wreck of the Penn Central, 75 ("friend," "relationship"); "Remarks by the Honorable Henry H. Fowler," June 16, 1965 ("parable"); Oral history transcript, Joseph A. Califano, interview 38 (XXXVIII), November 15, 1988, by Michael L. Gillette, LBJ Library Oral Histories, LBJ Presidential Library, https://www.discoverlbj.org/item/oh-califanoj-19881115-38-11-92, accessed January 27, 2024 ("friend").

197. Philadelphia Inquirer, January 19, 1964 ("provided," "conditional"); January 21, 1964 ("leaning," "obvious").

198. Philadelphia Inquirer, February 9, 1964; Finance Docket 21989, 256–69, 100–101; Daughen and Binzen, Wreck of the Penn Central, 66.

199. "In light of the need for some degree of flexibility in attaining the broad objectives of the merger, we believe the imposition of such a condition would be inconsistent with the logical achievement of such goals and an unwarranted excursion into the arena of legitimate managerial discretion necessary to carry them out."

200. *Philadelphia Inquirer,* June 2, 1964; Finance Docket 21989, 100–101 ("flexibility"), 256–69; Daughen and Binzen, *Wreck of the Penn Central,* 67.

201. *Philadelphia Inquirer,* January 29, 1963; Loving, *Men Who Loved Trains,* 41; Christopher Ogden, *Legacy: A Biography of Moses and Walter Annenberg* (Boston: Little, Brown, 1999), 383; Daughen and Binzen, *Wreck of the Penn Central,* 67, 78–81.

202. *Philadelphia Inquirer,* August 20, 1964 ("capacity," "persuasive," "consideration").

203. *New York Times,* December 27, 1963; January 3, 1964; January 6, 1964; January 9, 1964; January 10, 1964; February 16, 1964; March 26, 1964; April 8, 1964; April 9, 1964; April 10, 1964; April 11, 1964; April 18, 1964; April 22, 1964.

204. *New York Times,* April 22, 1964; April 23, 1964; May 6, 1964 ("riot"); May 8, 1964.

205. Lyndon Johnson, Conversation with Robert Kennedy, April 22, 1964, https://millercenter.org/the-presidency/secret-white-house-tapes/conversation-robert-kennedy-april-22-1964-0, accessed July 28, 2020 ("suggestion," "care," "throw," "further").

206. *Oklahoma Railway Company Trustees Abandonment of Operation,* 257 ICC 177 (1944); *New Orleans Union Passenger Terminal Case,* 282 ICC 271 (1952); Lipowski, "Featherbedding on the Railroads," 147–48; Saunders, *Merging Lines,* 134–36.

207. Two of the more combative unions—the Brotherhood of Railroad Trainmen and the Transport Workers Union—stood apart, but they soon fell into line, as did several other labor organizations.

208. *New York Times,* May 21, 1964 ("provides"); Finance Docket 21989, 143–44; *Pennsylvania Railroad Company–Merger–New York Central Railroad Company* (1966), 543–46.

209. Lipowski, "Featherbedding on the Railroads," 148–49; Saunders, *Merging Lines,* 269–70.

210. Martin, Memorandum for Myer Feldman, May 21, 1964, 1 ("necessity"), 2 ("attack," emphasis in the original), DOT Records, Box 43; Martin to Feldman, May 20, 1964, 1 ("viability"), 3 ("earning").

211. Martin to Feldman, May 20, 1964, 1 ("whether," emphasis in the original, "surgery"), 3 ("logical," emphasis in the original, "necessity," emphasis in the original), 6 ("advantage," emphasis in the original); Martin, Memorandum for Feldman, May 21, 1964, 3 ("ideal").

212. "Position of the Department of Labor with Respect to the Proposed Pennsylvania-New York Central Merger," attached to memorandum, Reynolds to Martin, May 18, 1964, 1 ("informed"), 3 ("opposed," "desirable"), DOT Records, Box 43.

213. Mark H. Rose, Bruce E. Seely, and Paul F. Barrett, *The Best Transportation System in the World: Railroads, Trucks, Airlines, and American Public Policy in the Twentieth Century* (Columbus: Ohio State University Press, 2006), 134–39.

214. "In this respect, applicants' studies fail to indicate one instance where it would be necessary to maintain the earnings of an employee affected by merger if all the vacancies created by attrition within the same union group could be filled by members whose jobs have been abolished due to merger."

215. Finance Docket 21989, 149 ("respect"); Saunders, *Merging Lines,* 269–70.

216. [Camden, NJ] *Courier-Post,* February 18, 1964 ("position"); Daughen and Binzen, *Wreck of the Penn Central,* 66–67.

217. *New York Times,* June 2, 1964 ("expanding," "alignments").

218. *New York Times,* June 2, 1964 ("promote," "unrealistic").

219. *New York Times,* June 9, 1964.

220. Magnuson Report, 328–29.

221. Kennedy to Katzenbach, September 9, 1964, DOT Records, Box 43, and reprinted in Magnuson Report, 714–15 ("requested").

222. *New York Times,* May 16, 1964 ("cynical"); August 2, 1964; Kennedy to Katzenbach, September 9, 1964 ("reasserted"); Califano, *Triumph & Tragedy,* 156 ("heavy").

223. Robert Kennedy, "Penn-Central Merger," September 3, 1964 ("informed," "circumstances," "assuring"); Katzenbach to Saunders, September 4, 1964 ("agreement"); Kennedy to Katzenbach, September 9, 1964; all in DOT Records, Box 43.

224. Pending the gradual sale of N&W and Wabash stock, the First National Bank of Atlanta, the Riggs National Bank of Washington, DC, and the United States Trust Company of New York served as trustees. In December, the ICC barred the three banks from direct representation on the N&W board of directors.

225. The decision also permitted the N&W to lease the Pittsburgh & West Virginia Railway and to purchase the Akron, Canton & Youngstown Railroad.

226. *New York Times,* September 15, 1964 ("confidence," "obstacle"); October 10, 1964; October 16, 1964 ("faith"); December 9, 1964; Striplin, *Norfolk & Western,* 266.

227. Minutes of the Meeting of the Finance Committee of the Board of Directors of the Pennsylvania Railroad,

May 21, 1963, reprinted in Magnuson Report, 730–31 ("standpoint").

228. Finance Committee Minutes, May 21, 1963 ("maintained").

229. Salsbury, *No Way to Run a Railroad*, 65–66.

230. Salsbury, *No Way to Run a Railroad*, 64–67 ("invested" at 67).

231. Finance Committee Minutes, May 21, 1963.

232. Finance Committee Minutes, May 21, 1963; Salsbury, *No Way to Run a Railroad*, 66–71.

233. Salsbury, *No Way to Run a Railroad*, 68.

234. Coincidentally, Kuhn, Loeb, like the PRR, declined rapidly in the years following World War II, as more aggressive and risk-tolerant investment bankers attained dominance. The firm merged with Lehman Brothers in 1977, a year after Penn Central became part of Conrail.

235. During the summer of 1934, the PRR's president, W. W. Atterbury, and Vice President Albert County investigated the refinancing of $16 million in the bonds of the Chicago Union Station Company—in which the railroad was both tenant and part owner. In earlier years, the Chicago Union Station Company would have relied on the services of J. P. Morgan & Company. However, the recently adopted Banking Act of 1933 (often referred to as the Glass-Steagall Act) forced Morgan to abandon investment banking in favor of commercial banking, and Glore, Forgan stepped into the breach. Glore encouraged Burlington president Ralph Budd to recommend him for the job and later told Budd that he "secured a position very largely, if not entirely through your help." There does not, at that point, appear to have been any direct connection to Atterbury, County, or any other PRR official. The author extends his thanks to Chris Baer for clarifying the firm's involvement in the project. In 1945, Glore, Forgan made an unsuccessful bid for control of the Pullman Company, following the antitrust consent decree mandating the separation of equipment manufacturing from the operation of sleeping cars—the development that brought so much public notoriety to maverick entrepreneur Robert R. Young. US District Court for the Southern District of New York, *Opinion of Harold R. Medina, United States Circuit Judge: In United States v. Henry S. Morgan, Harold Stanley, et al., October 14, 1953* (New York: Record, 1953), 74–75, 235, 320; United States Congress, Temporary National Economic Committee, *Investigation of Concentration of Economic Power: Hearings before the Temporary National Economic Committee, Congress of the United States, Seventy-Sixth Congress, Second Session, Pursuant to Public Resolution no. 113 (Seventy-Fifth Congress) Authorizing and Directing a Select Committee to Make a Full and Complete Study and Investigation with Respect to the Concentration of Economic Power in, and Financial Control Over, Production of Goods and Services, Part 22–23: Investment Banking* (Washington, DC, United States Government Printing Office, 1940), 11442–8, 11621–43, includes Glore to Ralph Budd, January 25, 1936 ("secured" at 11643), 11802–15; *New York Times*, February 1, 1974.

236. Their ranks included Joseph H. Rosenbaum, a former colonel in the OSS, and his brother Francis Newman Rosenbaum. They later played an important role in arranging financing for Executive Jet Aviation, the least successful and most controversial aspect of Bevan's diversification program. In 1970, Francis Rosenbaum drew a lengthy prison sentence for unrelated activities, involving a scheme to defraud the federal government in the sale of missile launchers. He was also convicted, in 1977, of defrauding the Penn Central. *New York Times*, February 11, 1970; March 31, 1977.

237. The author extends his thanks to Chris Baer for his insights regarding Hodge and his connections to Forgan and other former OSS officers. *Bridgewater Courier-News*, May 9, 1940; July 17, 1946 ("finest"); *Philadelphia Inquirer*, August 1, 1950; Museum of American Finance, "Francis I. duPont & Co. Genealogy: Part X," posted April 3, 2019, https://wherearetheynowblog.blogspot.com/2019/04/francis-i-dupont-co-genealogy-part-x.html, accessed March 3, 2020; Jeffrey J. Clarke and Robert Ross Smith, *Riviera to the Rhine: United States Army in World War II, European Theater of Operations* (Washington, DC: Center of Military History, United States Army, 1993), 178–80, 313, 338; Frank Carlone, "History of the Essex Troop," *Newark Military*, https://oldnewark.com/military/essextroop/historycarlone.php, accessed January 28, 2024; Daughen and Binzen, *Wreck of the Penn Central*, 154–55; Salsbury, *No Way to Run a Railroad*, 218–19.

238. Magnuson Report, 493–99, 531, includes Hodge to Bevan, July 28, 1960 ("within" at 493, "category" at 494); and PRR Finance Department Memorandum, May 10, 1963 ("potential" at 496).

239. Patman Report, 37–41, includes Minutes of PRR Finance Committee Meeting, November 1, 1963 ("serves" at 40); Magnuson Report, 531.

240. To secure the tax advantages, it became necessary to transform Buckeye into a holding company (which then spun off its assets to a subsidiary company) that in turn merged with the Pennsylvania Company.

241. Patman Report, 39–42: *New York Times*, July 25, 1964; July 27, 1964.

242. Patman Report, 47; SEC Report, 121.

243. *New York Times*, May 12, 1960; July 10, 1964; July 17, 1964; July 21, 1964; July 27, 1964; July 31, 1964; March 14, 1979; Patman Report, 49; SEC Report, 122; Salsbury, *No Way to Run a Railroad*, 226.

244. *New York Times*, December 15, 1964.

245. Magnuson Report, 533–35; Patman Report, 28, 44–48; SEC Report, 122; *New York Times*, July 17, 1964.

246. The PRR owned 80 percent of Macco, with Great Southwest and Forgan, Staats owning 10 percent apiece. Macco merged into Great Southwest in early 1969. SEC Report, 122; Patman Report, 49–54.

247. The PRR purchased the bulk of the Arvida stock on July 28, 1968, and transferred those securities to the Pennsylvania Company on September 30. The Pennsylvania Company made further, small purchases as late as December 28, 1966, increasing the railroad's ownership to 58 percent of Arvida, at a cost of $22 million.

248. *New York Times*, July 27, 1965; May 18, 1984; J. L. Delahunty, Charles Roberts, and Gilliam Breary, "Arvida and the Planned Sprawl of West Boca," *Florida Geographer* 40 (2009): 101–18; SEC Report, 320; Patman Report, 42–44; *New York Times*, August 14, 1965.

249. Journalists Joseph R. Daughen and Peter Binzen, who were overtly critical of Bevan's role in the financial difficulties of both the PRR and the Penn Central, suggested that "at the age of fifty-five [which occurred during the same year that Symes reached retirement age], Bevan began to develop other interests, interests that the chairman of the railroad would not have been expected to consider." Daughen and Binzen, *Wreck of the Penn Central*, 154–55 ("develop").

250. The remaining nine initial members of Penphil were Warren H. Bodman, a partner in Yarnall, Biddle & Company; C. Carroll Seward, also at Yarnall, Biddle; John K. Acuff, from Brooke, Sheridan, Bogan & Company; Francis A. Cannon, the administrative vice president of First Boston Corporation; Frederick B. Holmes, the vice president of the Gladfelter Paper Company; Leslie M. Cassidy, chairman of the Johns-Manville Corporation; Benjamin F. Sawin, the chairman of the board at Provident International Corporation; Edward D. Meanor (a private investor and one of David Bevan's neighbors); and Dorothy B. Stevens, the wife of Lawrence M. Stevens, a partner at Hornblower & Weeks-Hemphill, Noyes. Patman Report, 189–96, 208 ("consulted"); SEC Report, 303–6, 329–30; Daughen and Binzen, *Wreck of the Penn Central*, 156–57; Salsbury, *No Way to Run a Railroad*, 216–17.

251. Patman Report, 190, 198–204, includes memo from C. A. McLeod to William S. Renchard and M. A. Chamberlain, 1962, at 198; SEC Report, 307–9; Daughen and Binzen, *Wreck of the Penn Central*, 157–59.

252. As of December 31, 1963, the PRR owned 56,974 shares, Penphil owned 29,462 shares, and various Penphil members owned 158,597 shares in their personal accounts.

253. SEC Report, 309–12; Daughen and Binzen, *Wreck of the Penn Central*, 165–66; Salsbury, *No Way to Run a Railroad*, 222–23.

254. The PRR purchased another 2,900 Tropical shares in July 1963.

255. SEC Report, 316–17; Patman Report, 220–29; Daughen and Binzen, *Wreck of the Penn Central*, 166–69; Salsbury, *No Way to Run a Railroad*, 223–24.

256. Patman Report, 195–99, 215–19 ("sacrifice" at 218); Salsbury, *No Way to Run a Railroad*, 225–27.

257. The impetus for Penphil's banking investments came from Benjamin F. Sawin, chairman of Provident International and a founding member of the investment club. Sawin's friend and neighbor was Thomas Fleming, the chairman of both First Bank & Trust and University National. Fleming was interested in selling to Arvida a large tract of land, more than three thousand acres, that he co-owned with his wife.

258. SEC Report, 317–23; Patman Report, 230–44; Daughen and Binzen, *Wreck of the Penn Central*, 169–71; Salsbury, *No Way to Run a Railroad*, 229–30.

259. "Brigadier General Olbert F. Lassiter," United States Air Force Biographies, https://www.af.mil/About-Us/Biographies/Display/Article/106466/brigadier-general-olbert-f-lassiter/, accessed March 8, 2020; Daughen and Binzen, *Wreck of the Penn Central*, 176–78; Salsbury, *No Way to Run a Railroad*, 243.

260. Patman Report, 57–58; Daughen and Binzen, *Wreck of the Penn Central*, 178; Salsbury, *No Way to Run a Railroad*, 243–44.

261. Saunders seconded that assessment and predicted in February 1969 that airfreight, carried in wide-bodied jets, "could be the last straw" for the railroads' business in all freight traffic other than coal, grain, and similar bulk commodities. *New York Times*, February 21, 1969 ("straw").

262. Daughen and Binzen, *Wreck of the Penn Central*, 183 ("talked"); Salsbury, *No Way to Run a Railroad*, 244, 249, includes Large to Bevan, June 24, 1966, and July 1, 1966 ("volume," "exploding," "plan"); Ben Kocivar, "Giant Tri-Jets Are Coming," *Popular Science* 197, no. 6 (December 1970): 50–52; Bill Norton, *Lockheed Martin C-5*

Galaxy (North Branch, MN: Specialty, 2003), 8–13; Clive Irving, *Wide Body: The Triumph of the 747* (New York: W. Morrow, 1993); Guy Norris and Mark Wagner; *Boeing 747: Design and Development since 1969* (St. Paul, MN: MBI, 1997); Walter J. Boyne, *Beyond the Horizons: The Lockheed Story* (New York: St. Martin's, 1998); Günter Endres, *McDonnell Douglas DC-10* (St. Paul, MN: MBI, 1998).

263. Patman Report, 59–60 ("undertaken," "Instead," "policy"); Daughen and Binzen, *Wreck of the Penn Central*, 182–84; Salsbury, *No Way to Run a Railroad*, 246–47.

264. Patman Report, 58–59, 61–62, 75–77; Daughen and Binzen, *Wreck of the Penn Central*, 181–82; Salsbury, *No Way to Run a Railroad*, 247.

265. The trip from Newark to Philadelphia probably began in Manhattan, also a city with good rail connections to Philadelphia. Subsequent congressional investigations were sharply critical of PRR reliance on EJA's air services. It is possible, however, that Bevan and other senior PRR executives—whose time was quite valuable—made use of EJA aircraft that would have otherwise been sitting idle. Patman Report, 90–91; Daughen and Binzen, *Wreck of the Penn Central*, 184, 196–205.

266. Patman Report, 62–63, includes Lassiter to Bevan, August 19, 1966 ("drill"); SEC Report, 71; Daughen and Binzen, *Wreck of the Penn Central*, 184–85; Salsbury, *No Way to Run a Railroad*, 249–50.

267. Patman Report, 63, includes Cox memorandum, August 4, 1966 ("undoubtedly"); Wilson to Bevan, July 27, 1966, quoted in Salsbury, *No Way to Run a Railroad*, 249–50 ("formal," "possibility").

268. The CAB confirmed the examiner's decision on June 30, 1967.

269. Patman Report, 64–66; Daughen and Binzen, *Wreck of the Penn Central*, 184–87 ("decision" at 187); Salsbury, *No Way to Run a Railroad*, 250–55, 259–60.

270. Patman Report, 87–90, 104.

271. Patman Report, 66–67; Daughen and Binzen, *Wreck of the Penn Central*, 186–87 ("actually").

272. Patman Report, 79–87, 146–47; Daughen and Binzen, *Wreck of the Penn Central*, 185–86 ("ate"), 187–88, 194–96; Salsbury, *No Way to Run a Railroad*, 267–75.

273. Patman Report, 55, 67–71, 78–79, 148; Daughen and Binzen, *Wreck of the Penn Central*, 187–91, 196; Salsbury, *No Way to Run a Railroad*, 264–67, 270–71, 275–88, includes Bevan to Saunders, February 15, 1968 ("position" at 265).

274. Patman Report, 27 ("accordingly"), 28 ("diversify"); Magnuson Report, 15; Salsbury, *No Way to Run a Railroad*, 70.

275. Great Southwest stock reached an all-time high of $40.25 per share, shortly before the inflation-control policies imposed by President Richard M. Nixon tightened access to credit and caused the company's share prices to plummet.

276. Magnuson Report, 15, 410–11; Salsbury, *No Way to Run a Railroad*, 69, 125, 176–77, 227.

277. Magnuson Report, 410–11.

278. Patman Report, 28–30; Salsbury, *No Way to Run a Railroad*, 177.

279. *New York Times*, July 1, 1964; July 10, 1964; September 11, 1964; Finance Docket 21989, 328.

280. *New York Times*, February 3, 1965 ("rescue," "suicide"); February 15, 1967 ("price").

281. *New York Times*, April 1, 1965.

282. *New York Times*, October 25, 1964 ("conditions," "studies," "competitive," "clear").

283. Saunders to Katzenbach, September 9, 1964, reprinted in Magnuson Report, 715 ("agreed," "diligently," "absolute," "unreasonable," "terms").

284. Saunders to Katzenbach, January 14, 1965 ("adhering"); Saunders to Orrick, January 14, 1965; both reprinted in Magnuson Report, 715–16.

285. *New York Times*, January 7, 1965; January 8, 1965.

286. *New York Times*, January 9, 1965 ("disastrous"); January 13, 1965; January 14, 1965; January 19, 1965; January 20, 1965 ("role").

287. *New York Times*, January 22, 1965; January 28, 1965; February 5, 1965; February 15, 1965; February 20, 1965; February 24, 1965; February 25, 1965; February 26, 1965; March 3, 1965; March 25, 1965; April 15, 1965; Statement of Richard Joyce Smith, March 3, 1965, United States Congress, Senate, *The Crisis in Passenger Train Service* (Washington, DC: United States Government Printing Office, 1965), 119 ("believe"), 124 ("negotiate").

288. Statement of Robert F. Kennedy, March 2, 1965, *Crisis in Passenger Train Service*, 99 ("aware"), 100 ("prior," "attractive").

289. Statement of Hon. Abraham Ribicoff, March 2, 1965, *Crisis in Passenger Train Service*, 46 ("understanding"), 48 ("persuasion," "talk"); Statement of Hon. Jacob Javits, March 2, 1965, 88 ("monopoly").

290. Statement of John H. Chaffee, March 4, 1965, *Crisis in Passenger Train Service*, 216 ("risky," "doubtful").

291. Finance Docket 21989, 195–211 ("optimism" at 207), 400–405 ("dealing" at 401, "struggle" at 403); *New York Times*, March 30, 1965.

292. Representatives from the commonwealth of Pennsylvania were the only ones who raised any objections on labor grounds, and that was only because they feared that

the Penn Central's proposed operating patterns would cause a contraction of industry and employment in their state. Finance Docket 21989, 143–55, 402 ("performed"), 405 ("panacea").

293. Finance Docket 21989, 403 ("suicide"), 411 ("hopeless"), 412 ("delay," "subsidize"); *New York Times*, March 30, 1965.

294. Finance Docket 21989, 412 ("paradox," "provide," emphasis in the original), 413 ("staggering," "obligated"); *New York Times*, March 30, 1965.

295. *New York Times*, April 1, 1965 ("elimination," "willingness"); April 21, 1965 ("remove," "hopefully").

296. Lyle and Darmstadter observed that the Erie-Lackawanna "is restricted by implication against filing of a petition for inclusion in the N&W System because of its existing financial condition, particularly its heavy debt structure." Finance Docket 21989, 417 ("restricted").

297. "We believe," Lyle and Darmstadter warned, "the conclusion is warranted that E-L would have little, if any, chance of survival in face of the proposed merger were it to remain independent and reliant solely on its own resources to compete with the merged system."

298. "Furthermore, inclusion of E-L into the P.R.R./N.Y.C. at this time is no more possible than in the N&W System for the framing of terms and conditions of such inclusion would demand the Commission to require either E-L be subjected to some form of reorganization as a condition for it to be absorbed into P.R.R./N.Y.C. or require the latter to assume the entire debt structure of the E-L, a result which would defeat the very principle upon which the instant merger is justified." Finance Docket 21989, 374 ("survival"), 417 ("furthermore").

299. Finance Docket 21989, 415–46, 417 ("considering"); *New York Times*, March 30, 1965.

300. Finance Docket 21989, 418 ("governmental," "indefinite").

301. *New York Times*, March 30, 1965 ("insurmountable").

302. SEC Report, 154; *New York Times*, April 29, 1965.

303. Patchell retired in the autumn of 1963, and John D. Morris assumed his responsibilities.

304. PRR BOD Minutes; SEC Report, 18–19.

305. SEC Report, 18–19 ("aim"); Agenda for Meeting with PRR Merger Coordinator, April 27, 1966 ("necessity"), PHMC, Box 21 (9-3375), folder 21–13; *New York Times*, May 10, 1966.

306. Memorandum in Connection with Comparison of PRR–NYC M.W. Forces, June 23, 1958, HML, Box 351, folder 1; SEC Report, 19.

307. Henry Lyne Jr. to William R. Gerstnecker, August 28, 1959, HML, Box 327, folder 21 ("impression," "conversations"); SEC Report, 19.

308. Agenda for Meeting with PRR Merger Coordinator; "Memorandum regarding Merger Meeting April 29, 1966," May 3, 1966, 2 ("distinct"), 4 ("concerned"); Basil Cole and F. L. Kattau, "Memorandum," May 31, 1966 ("formidable," "practicable," "uniform," "relationship," "myriad," "appearance"); all in HML, Box 21 (9-3375), folder 21–13.

309. Newell to Regional Managers, February 4, 1958 ("unsatisfactory"); Bevan to Regional Managers, December 15, 1958 ("believe," "desire"); both in HML, Box 356, folder 23.

310. PRR BOD Minutes; Pennsylvania Railroad Company, *117th Annual Report*, 1, 5; SEC Report, 19; *Philadelphia Letter on Current Railroad Developments* 7, no. 3 (October 1, 1964): 4; 7, no. 12 (July 1, 1965): 3; both in HML, Box 885, folder 1; Salsbury, *No Way to Run a Railroad*, 50–55, 100–101, 120–21, 188–89.

311. Salsbury, *No Way to Run a Railroad*, 119–22, 153, includes Sempier to Cook, December 5, 1967 ("spread"), at 119; Sempier to R. G. Flannery, F. J. Lesh, R. E. Mann, R. C. Karvwatt, and J. McCrain, December 1, 1967 ("partially" at 121).

312. *New York Times*, October 27, 1964; [Hanover, PA] *Evening Sun*, January 18, 1965.

313. Salsbury, *No Way to Run a Railroad*, 102–3, 106.

314. Salsbury, *No Way to Run a Railroad*, 103–4, 107–8, 342.

315. In addition to the E-L, the B&M, the D&H, the Reading, and the Jersey Central, the railroads included the Brooklyn Eastern District Terminal, the Boston & Providence Railroad, the Chicago & Eastern Illinois, the Monon, the Peoria & Eastern Railway, and the Western Maryland.

316. The Boroughs of East Rochester, Freedom, Ambridge, Baden, and Conway, Pennsylvania; the Chamber of Commerce of Greater Pittsburgh; Allegheny County; the Cities of Allentown and Pittsburgh; B&M; D&H; E-L; the Greater Hazleton Chamber of Commerce; interested parties from Baltimore; New York City, State, and Port Authority; and the trustees of the New Haven. A reply was a less serious matter than an exception, as it did not allege that the examiners had erred on procedural grounds.

317. *Pennsylvania Railroad Company–Merger–New York Central Railroad Company* (1966) 478–80.

318. *New York Times*, March 30, 1965 ("orphans"); March 31, 1965 ("disappointed").

319. *New York Times*, March 30, 1965 ("probably," "continue"); August 17, 1965; Pennsylvania Railroad System, *119th Annual Report for the Year 1965*, 6, 16.

320. *Philadelphia Inquirer*, July 11, 1965.

321. *New York Times*, May 6, 1966 ("biggest"); Salisbury, *No Way to Run a Railroad*, 62–64.

322. *Pennsylvania Railroad Company–Merger–New York Central Railroad Company* (1966), 482 ("impediment"), 483–84, 491; *New York Times*, January 4, 1966 ("implementing").

323. In 1956, the PRR hired Penn Center architect Vincent Kling to design a sports arena, north of 30th Street Station, to be built with city funds. The station, unlike its counterpart in New York, would remain yet be overshadowed by a seventy-five-thousand-seat, $15 million stadium over the station approach tracks. Municipal officials rejected that proposal, and three years later, the railroad floated an equally unsuccessful plan for a sixty-thousand-seat stadium that would be built without public funds. The Pennsylvania Railroad resurrected the stadium proposal in the early 1960s. In the summer of 1961, PRR executives planned to create the Philadelphia Stadium Corporation, jointly owned by the railroad (25%), the city (50%), and the four major professional sports franchises (25%, divided among the Phillies, Eagles, Warriors, and Ramblers). The corporation would build the stadium, leasing air rights from the railroad at $840,000 a year. In response to its enormous liquidity problems, the railroad soon replaced the annual air-rights rental with an offer to the city for a one-time sale price of $3 million. The city could then resell the air rights to a redevelopment authority for $1 million, with that agency contracting with a stadium corporation (owned jointly by the railroad and the construction contractors) to build the facility. The railroad then applied, unsuccessfully, to the Urban Renewal Administration to have the area surrounding 30th Street Station designated as a "blighted area" and thus eligible for federal funds. The city would have used those funds to purchase the air rights from the railroad, with the cost now increased to $4 million. The project aroused considerable opposition from residents from West Philadelphia and conflicted with alternate proposals, never enacted, to build a science center in the area. The stadium complex was ultimately located in South Philadelphia. *Philadelphia Inquirer*, January 11, 1956; September 20, 1959; June 6, 1964; June 17, 1964; June 28, 1964; *Philadelphia Bulletin*, June 21, 1964; June 28, 1964; June 30, 1964; *Philadelphia Daily News*, May 25, 1964; *Philadelphia Evening Bulletin*, April 14, 1964; June 3, 1964; PRR press release, October 22, 1958, HML, Box 259,

folder 25; Memo, "Subject: Philadelphia, Pa.–30th and Arch Sts.–Proposed lease of 'air rights' as site for all-purpose, all weather, domed stadium," June 15, 1961; undated memo, "Stadium," 01182–19; Bevan to Greenough, November 12, 1962; all in HML, Box 259, folder 26.

324. *Philadelphia Inquirer*, July 13, 1965 ("aware," "employment").

325. *Philadelphia Inquirer*, July 13, 1965 ("situated," "importance").

326. Roderick A. Smith, "The Japanese Shinkansen: Catalyst for the Renaissance of Rail," *Journal of Transport History* 24, no. 2 (2003): 222–36, at 225–27; Hideo Shima, "The Birth of the Shinkansen—A Memoir," *Japan Railway & Transport Review* 3 (1994): 45–48. For a broader overview of the development of high-speed rail in Japan, see Christopher Hood, *Shinkansen: From Bullet Train to Symbol of Modern Japan* (London: Routledge, 2006).

327. Jean Gottmann, "Megalopolis or the Urbanization of the Northeastern Seaboard," *Economic Geography* 33, no. 3 (July 1957): 189–200, at 190 ("pioneer"); Gottmann, *Megalopolis: The Urbanized Northeastern Seaboard of the United States* (New York: Twentieth Century Fund, 1961), 9 ("cradle"); *New York Times*, November 17, 1961 ("menace"); November 27, 1961 ("personality"); December 4, 1961 ("urbanization"); March 2, 1994.

328. Several segments of the route remained unfinished, as residents of the upscale Society Hill neighborhood in Philadelphia fought the project. Most construction work was complete by 1979, but a short segment near the Philadelphia International Airport did not open until 1985. *New York Times*, December 4, 1961 ("scares"); Bruce Goldberg and David C. Warner, *The Metroliners: Trains That Changed the Course of American Rail Travel* (Bucklin, MO: White River, 2016), 7.

329. During his visit, Kennedy persuaded Wagner to part company with Tammany power broker Carmine G. DeSapio and was gratified that the mayor won reelection anyway.

330. *New York Times*, November 3, 1961 ("statement," "dutiful," "Boston," "conglomeration"); March 12, 1997; Richard M. Flanagan, *Robert Wagner and the Rise of New York City's Plebiscitary Mayoralty: The Tamer of the Tammany Tiger* (New York: Palgrave Macmillan, 2015), 47–75. For additional information on the political context of the northeastern cities, see Peter Siskin, "Growth and Its Discontents: Localism, Protest and the Politics of Development on the Postwar Northeast Corridor" (PhD diss., University of Pennsylvania, 2002).

331. The "least electable" comment may be apocryphal, but it appears in several guises, including Joseph Biden's

eulogy at Pell's 2009 funeral and in tributes from Rhode Island senators Sheldon Whitehouse and Jack Reed.

332. G. Wayne Miller, *An Uncommon Man: The Life & Times of Senator Claiborne Pell* (Hanover, NH: University Press of New England, 2011), 5 (Biden, "electable"), 101–11; United States, Congress, *Congressional Record: Proceedings and Debates of the 111th Congress, First Session, Volume 155–Part 1, January 6, 2009 to January 16, 2009* (Washington, DC: United States Government Printing Office, 2009), 58–61 (Reed "electable" at 60); Floor Statement of Sheldon Whitehouse, "A Tribute to U.S. Senator Claiborne Pell, January 6, 2009" (Whitehouse "electable"); Scott Mackay, "The Life and Times of an Uncommon Man: Sen. Claiborne Pell," *On Politics*, Rhode Island National Public Radio, October 20, 2011.

333. On June 1, Pell introduced Senate Resolution 194, calling on Congress to pass the legislation necessary to create a national transit agency similar to PSIC.

334. *New York Times*, May 21, 1962 ("number," "trend," "Eastern," "decent"); Miller, *Uncommon Man*, 113.

335. Robert B. Watson, "Memorandum, Subject: Northeast Corridor Project," n.d., but ca. Autumn 1969, 1 ("inherent"), Robert B. Watson Professional Papers, Accession 2577, Manuscripts and Archives Department, Hagley Museum and Library, Wilmington, Delaware (hereafter, Watson Collection), Box 2, folder 5; *New York Times*, May 22, 1962 ("pie," "nonsense," "naïve," "industry").

336. The Twentieth Century Fund—the entity responsible for the publication of Gottmann's *Megalopolis*—also funded the Regional Plan Association study, which included planners from the entire length of the metropolitan corridor.

337. *New York Times*, June 3, 1962 ("fresh," "generation," "adds"); July 30, 1962 ("precious," "modern").

338. As David Reinecke has noted, "The federal government engaged in an Apollo-style moonshot to innovate high-speed rail services in the Northeast United States." Likewise, James K. Cohen emphasized that "the Zeitgeist of that era" (including jet propulsion, the space race, and the development of atomic weapons) stimulated interest in high-speed rail, especially in the form of nonconventional systems. David Reinecke, "Moonshots to Nowhere? The Metroliner and Failed High-Speed Rail in the United States, 1962–1977," *Journal of Transport History* 43, no. 1 (2022): 33–53, at 34 ("engaged"); James K. Cohen, "Development of a Futuristic Technology Programme: How the Aerospace Industry (Almost) Transformed Ground Transportation in the United States (1960–1972)," *Journal of Transport History* 43, no.

1 (2022): 82–106, at 89 ("Zeitgeist"); John F. Kennedy, Address at Rice University, Houston, Texas, September 12, 1962, 3, John F. Kennedy Presidential Library and Museum, Papers of John F. Kennedy: Presidential Papers, President's Office Files, Speech Files, JFKPOF-040-001-p0001, https://www.jfklibrary.org/asset-viewer/archives/JFKPOF/040/JFKPOF-040-001, accessed January 7, 2023 ("choose"); John W. Jordan, "Kennedy's Romantic Moon and Its Rhetorical Legacy for Space Exploration," *Rhetoric and Public Affairs* 6, no. 2 (Summer 2003): 209–31.

339. Claiborne Pell to John F. Kennedy, October 3, 1962 ("radical"); Kennedy to Pell, October 9, 1962 ("share"); Myer Feldman, memorandum for Clarence D. Martin, October 17, 1962; all in DOT Records, Box 45; "U.S. Department of Commerce, Summary Progress Report, Northeast Corridor Transportation Project," July 21, 1964, 1–2, Louis T. Klauder and Associates, Office of High Speed Ground Transportation Job Files, Accession 2609, Manuscripts and Archives Department, Hagley Museum and Library, Wilmington, Delaware (hereafter, Klauder Collection), Box 4, folder 7; Walter Shapiro, "The Seven Secrets of the Metroliner's Success," *Washington Monthly*, March 1973, 7–15, at 13.

340. Berger and Feldman both attended the University of Pennsylvania Law School during the 1930s, graduating two years apart. Watson Memorandum, 2–3; *Penn Law Journal* 42, no. 1 (Spring 2007): 77–79; Cohen, "Futuristic Technology Programme," 90–91.

341. "Statement Containing Information Concerning Northeast Merger and Corridor Studies," n.d., but ca. July 1964, 2 ("possible"), DOT Records, Box 45; *New York Times*, May 26, 1963.

342. As Cohen has observed, "The targeted lobbying and public relations activities of the powerful and influential aerospace industry" shaped federal policies associated with experiments in nontraditional high-speed transportation technologies. Clarence D. Martin and J. Herbert Hollomon to L. M. Boelter et al., December 14, 1962 ("aspects"); Luther Hodges to Myer Feldman, March 6, 1963 ("preconceived"); "Summary: Northeast Corridor Transportation Study," August 1964; all in DOT Records, Box 45; Cohen, "Futuristic Technology Programme," 87–90, 100, "targeted" at 90.

343. Although the initial draft of Dilworth's press release indicated that he was severing his ties with the PRR, the Commerce Department insisted that this statement be left out of the final version, as it "only serves to call attention to the fact that he has been associated

with at least one railroad that is integrally involved in the corridor study."

344. Hodges to Feldman, March 6, 1963 ("opinion," "impact," "necessarily"); "Proposed Press Release on Dilworth Appointment," "Statement Dilworth Proposes to Make"; Hodges to Richardson Dilworth, April 16, 1963; Lowell K. Bridwell to Hodges, May 24, 1963 ("serves"); Department of Commerce Press Release, September 13, 1963; all in DOT Records, Box 45.

345. The most favorable assessments of Nelson's—and the federal government's—role in the project come from Walter Shapiro's article in the *Washington Monthly*. The magazine's founder, Charles Peters, was a New Deal Democrat predisposed to favor large federal public-works projects. Shapiro, "Seven Secrets," 12 ("wasn't," "buff," "abrasive," "problem"); Watson Memorandum, 3–4; Cohen, "Futuristic Technology Programme," 93–94.

346. Cohen, "Futuristic Technology Programme," 92; Claiborne Pell to Lyndon Johnson, March 23, 1964, 1 ("attention"), 2 ("practicable"), 3 ("assassination"); Lee White to Bill Moyers, April 9, 1964 ("anxious"); Moyers to White, n.d. ("read"); all in the John F. Kennedy Library, Boston, MA, Myer Feldman Personal Papers (R.G. #363), Box 90, folder 3. The author extends his appreciation to Jim Cohen for making these sources available.

347. Martin to Hodges, RE: "Comments on Richardson Dilworth Communications of March 16, March 6, and February 19, 1964" ("satisfactory," "Corridor"); Minutes of the Second Meeting of the Public Committee of the Washington-Boston Study, held March 24, 1964, at the Department of Commerce ("standpoint," "correct," "desirable"); both in DOT Records, Box 45.

348. Watson Memorandum, 3; James W. Diffenderfer, "High Speed Passenger Transportation in the Northeast Corridor of the United States of America, Utilizing Existing Facilities," Address at the International Railway Congress Association, International Union of Railways, Vienna, Austria, June 17–22, 1968, 6 ("reached," decide"), Klauder Collection, Box 13, folder 18.

349. Diffenderfer, "High Speed Passenger Transportation," 6.

350. Pennsylvania Railroad, *New York Philadelphia Washington Passenger Service*, 1964 Report (Philadelphia: PRR, 1964), Exhibit 16 ("presently"), Exhibit 18 ("financing"); Diffenderfer et al. to Greenough, June 16, 1964; both in DOT Records, Box 45; Diffenderfer, "High Speed Passenger Transportation," 6 ("investments"), 9 ("measure," "result"), 14–15, 43.

351. The phenomenon that Diffenderfer described is now well understood by economists and transportation planners. In the 1960s, however, most engineers and policy experts asserted that the provision of additional transportation options would reduce congestion. Instead, investments in highways and airports supplied additional mobility and thus lowered the monetary and nonmonetary costs of that mobility, in turn increasing the demand for mobility—i.e., when travel became more convenient, people traveled more, ceteris paribus, thus clogging the highways and the airports. The most effective method of reducing congestion involved making travel more difficult and more expensive—although few politicians have the desire to implement such draconian public policies.

352. "New York-Washington Passenger Service: High-Speed Operation, Program for Government," March 11, 1964; *New York Philadelphia Washington Passenger Service*, Exhibit 16 ("contemplated"); Peter Engelmann to Nelson, March 12, 1964; Minutes of the Second Meeting of the Public Committee of the Washington-Boston Study, held March 24, 1964, at the Department of Commerce ("borne"); all in DOT Records, Box 45; *Congressional Record: Proceedings and Debates of the 89th Congress, First Session, Volume 11, Part 14, July 28, 1965, to August 9, 1965* (Washington, DC: United States Government Printing Office, 1965) 15839–40; Diffenderfer, "High Speed Passenger Transportation," 8 ("problems").

353. *New York Philadelphia Washington Passenger Service*, Exhibit 16 ("extend"), Exhibit 18 ("underwrite").

354. Louis T. Klauder and Associates, "Preliminary Engineering Report on Possible Improvements to Railroad Passenger Service between New York and Washington, Prepared for the United States Department of Commerce in Connection with Its Washington-Boston Corridor Research Project," June 1, 1964; Louis T. Klauder to E. Grosvenor Plowman, June 1, 1964 ("expensive"); both in Watson Collection, Box 9, folder 6; *New York Times*, December 20, 1964.

355. Klauder, "Preliminary Engineering Report" ("prepared," "included," "new").

356. Klauder to Kenshiro Kunimatsu, March 26, 1964; Klauder to Engelmann, June 1, 1964; Klauder to Charles Code, August 11, 1964; all in Klauder Collection, Box 1, folder 14; James W. Diffenderfer, "Metroliner Experiences: An Engineering and Economic Review of Developments After a Year's Token Operation," transcript of paper presented at the American Railway Engineering Association Sixty-Ninth Annual Convention, Chicago, Illinois, March 18, 1970, 832–39, at 837.

357. Klauder to Dilworth, August 20, 1964 ("extended," "preliminary"); Louis T. Klauder and Associates, "Supplemental Engineering Report on Possible Improvements to Railroad Passenger Service between New York and Washington," June 12, 1964 ("experience," "high," "reason"); both in Klauder Collection, Box 1, folder 14.

358. Klauder to Masao Nagahama, January 23, 1964, Klauder Collection, Box 1, folder 14 ("inclined"); *New York Times*, December 31, 1963.

359. Klauder, "Supplemental Engineering Report."

360. Klauder to Dilworth, April 14, 1964 ("eager"); Klauder to Engelmann, June 1, 1964 ("willing"); Klauder to C. J. Henry, August 17, 1964 ("memorandum," "concerns"); all in Klauder Collection, Box 1, folder 14.

361. Klauder to Engelmann, June 1, 1964 ("attractive," "vaults"); Klauder Collection, Box 1, folder 14.

362. Diffenderfer, "High Speed Passenger Transportation," 13 ("solution").

363. Klauder to Dilworth, April 14, 1964 ("enthusiastic," "ownership," "helpful," "suggestion"); Klauder Collection, Box 1, folder 14; *New York Times*, January 28, 1962.

364. Klauder to Dilworth, April 14, 1964 ("broader"); Klauder Collection, Box 1, folder 14; Shapiro, "Seven Secrets," 10–11 ("scene").

365. The figure was nonetheless in keeping with an estimate offered by Paul E. McBride, the director of research for the Massachusetts Port Authority. McBride emphasized the cost of improvements to a century-old right-of-way as well as the expense associated with extending electrification from New Haven north to Boston. *New York Times*, September 25, 1964.

366. The report noted that "highway needs in the Corridor region are essentially independent of impact from service improvements from rail and air facilities"—undercutting an initial argument that suggested that improved rail service could unclog highways and preclude federal investments in road construction. "U.S. Department of Commerce, Summary Progress Report," 4 ("cost"), 6 ("independent").

367. Office of the White House Press Secretary, Press Release, August 11, 1964 ("promise," "conviction"), Klauder Collection, Box 4, folder 7; *New York Times*, August 12, 1964 ("determination," "change," "dodo").

368. *New York Times*, December 20, 1964 ("careful"); March 5, 1965 ("scratch").

369. Donald F. Hornig to Luther H. Hodges, August 19, 1964 ("magnitude," "replication"); L. K. Bridwell to Hodges, August 13, 1964 ("rapid"); Hornig to Hodges, August 28, 1964 ("premature," "little"); Hodges to Martin, September 1, 1964 ("inspire"); Hodges to Martin

and Bridwell, September 9, 1964; all in DOT Records, Box 45: Cohen, "Futuristic Technology Programme," 94–95.

370. *New York Times*, December 20, 1964 ("sky"); March 5, 1965 ("hasn't"); Dilworth to Plowman, June 16, 1964 ("never"), DOT Records, Box 45.

371. Louis T. Klauder & Associates, "New York-Washington High-Speed Service Suggested Test and Development Program," August 17, 1964; United States Department of Commerce, "Northeast Corridor Study–Phase II, Sub-Project B-3: Design of Demonstration Project for High-Speed Railroad Technology"; both in Klauder Collection, Box 4, folder 5.

372. Klauder to Plowman, August 17, 1964 ("establish," "developmental"), Klauder Collection, Box 1, folder 14; "New York-Washington High-Speed Service Suggested Test and Development Program" ("delivered" at 5).

373. The comment reflected Johnson's enthusiasm and his lack of familiarity with the project he was supporting. None of the engineers who studied the constraints of the Northeast Corridor believed it would be possible to cover the 457 miles separating Boston and Washington in so short a time. Instead, they favored a four-hour schedule between Boston and New York, with at least an additional two and a half hours necessary to reach Washington.

374. Lyndon B. Johnson, "Annual Message to the Congress on the State of the Union," January 4, 1965, *Public Papers of the Presidents of the United States: Lyndon B. Johnson, 1965, Volume I*, entry 2 (Washington, DC: United States Government Printing Office, 1966): 1–9 ("ask," "begin," at 6); Johnson, "Annual Budget Message to the Congress, for Fiscal Year 1966," January 25, 1965, *Public Papers of the Presidents, Volume I*, entry 32, 82–99 ("legislation," "demonstrations" at 93); *New York Times*, January 26, 1965 ("experts," "decade").

375. "Letter to the President of the Senate and the Speaker of the House on High-Speed Interurban Ground Transportation," March 4, 1965, *Public Papers of the Presidents, Volume I*, entry 97, 248–50 ("evolutionary" at 249); "Meeting March 23, 1965, between Representatives of the Department of Commerce and Representatives of the Pennsylvania Railroad" ("Mediocre"), DOT Records, Box 40; *New York Times*, March 5, 1965 ("field"); May 26, 1965.

376. Massachusetts Institute of Technology, "Survey of Technology for High Speed Ground Transport: Prepared for the United States Department of Commerce, Washington, DC, Under Contract C-85-65," June 15, 1965, B-18 ("impressed"); Statement of William W. Seifert,

Assistant Dean of Engineering, Massachusetts Institute of Technology, June 29, 1965, *Commerce Department Transportation Research: Hearings before the Subcommittee on Transportation and Aeronautics of the Committee on Interstate and Foreign Commerce, House of Representatives, on H.R. 5863, a Bill to Authorize the Secretary of Commerce to Undertake Research and Development in High-Speed Ground Transportation and for Other Purposes*, United States Congress, House, 89th Cong., 1st sess. (Washington, DC: United States Government Printing Office, 1965), 123 ("achieved," "excess,"), 124 ("coupling," "accelerating," "approach"); Cohen, "Futuristic Technology Programme," 93.

377.   Statement of Robert A. Nelson, Director for Transportation Research, Office of Under Secretary for Transportation and Manager, Northeast Corridor Transportation Project, US Department of Commerce, May 25, 1965, *Commerce Department Transportation Research*, 86 ("concepts"), 87 ("work"); Statement of Hon. John T. Connor, Secretary, US Department of Commerce, *Commerce Department Transportation Research*, May 25, 1965, 43 ("experimental").

378.   Statement of Stuart T. Saunders, Chairman of the Board, Pennsylvania Railroad Company, June 30, 1965, *Commerce Department Transportation Research*, 141 ("arteries"), 142 ("accelerating"); Saunders to Oren Harris, July 20, 1965, in *Commerce Department Transportation Research*, 162 ("realistic").

379.   "Survey of Technology for High Speed Ground Transport," vii ("modified"), viii ("human"), I-1 ("feasible," "radically"), II-6 ("traditional," "approaches," emphasis in the original).

380.   *New York Times*, May 26, 1965 ("approve"); June 15, 1965.

381.   *New York Times*, March 19, 1965; May 11, 1965 ("may"); June 14, 1965; June 17, 1965 ("money," "finest").

382.   Jonathan Michael Feldman, "High-Speed Rail and Barriers to Innovation: The Budd Company and the Limits of US Indirect Industrial Policy in the 1960s and 1970s," *Journal of Transport History* 43, no. 1 (2022): 54–81; "A High-Speed Bid for Business," *Business Week*, February 4, 1967, 126–28; Samuel W. Madeira to Klauder, January 22, 1964, Klauder Collection, Box 1, folder 14; Budd Company, "Preliminary Specifications for High Speed Passenger Test Trains for Operation between New York and Washington on the Pennsylvania Railroad," May 27, 1964, revised July 20, 1964, Klauder Collection, Box 1, folder 19; *New York Times*, August 12, 1964 ("feasible"); August 17, 1964; June 30, 1965 ("unless"); [Philadelphia] *Sunday Bulletin*, August 16, 1964.

383.   The Levatrain (a successor to the Levacar) was a project of the Ford Motor Company. The Levatrain was technically a railroad vehicle, in that it followed a fixed metal guideway, with "Levapads" providing jets of air that elevated the superstructure a fraction of an inch above a fixed guideway. Designers suggested that the Levatrain could travel ninety miles in thirty-eight minutes. That was, perhaps not coincidentally, the distance between New York and Philadelphia, although the initial Levatrain route would connect New York and Atlantic City. Ford designers proposed a demonstration model, with a propeller, driven by a gas-turbine engine, affixed to a stripped-down DC-3 fuselage. "But when the hard-nosed boys in the accounting department began adding thing up," observed *Baltimore Sun* reporter Ralph Stein in February 1963, "they found the experimental model would cost $5 million. So Ford's Levatrain is back on the old drawing board." Eighteen months later, a massive infusion of federal funds portended a possible resurrection of the Levatrain. United States Congress, House, 89th Cong., 1st sess., Public Law 89–220, 79 Stat. 893, A Bill to Authorize the Secretary of Commerce to Undertake Research and Development in High-Speed Ground Transportation and for Other Purposes, September 30, 1965 (Washington, DC: United States Government Printing Office, 1965); Lyndon B. Johnson, "Remarks at the Signing of the High Speed Ground Transportation Act," September 30, 1965, Public Papers of the Presidents of the United States: Lyndon B. Johnson, 1965, Volume II, entry 536 (Washington, DC: United States Government Printing Office, 1966): 1024–26 ("harassed," "intelligent," "science," "better"); *New York Times*, September 30, 1965; October 1, 1965; October 24, 1965 ("Commuting," "immediately"); Miller, *Uncommon Man*, 134; Ralph Stein, "Tomorrow's Railroads in the Sky," *Baltimore Sun*, February 3, 1963, 8–10, at 10 ("hard-nosed").

384.   Secretary of Commerce, "First Report on the High Speed Ground Transportation Act of 1965," September 1966, Klauder Collection, Box 13, folder 8; *New York Times*, January 22, 1966; *Penn Central Post*, May 1970, 5; Doug Riddell, *Auto-Train: The Planning, Formation, Demise, and Ultimate Resurrection of the Auto-Train Concept* (Fredericksburg, VA: RF&P Historical Society, 2016).

385.   Watson Memorandum, 5–7 ("convince," "interested"); *New York Times*, December 11, 1965 ("supertrains"); September 25, 1966.

386.   The Pennsylvania Railroad, "Specifications for Electric Multiple Unit Railroad Passenger Cars for Use in the Demonstration Project between New York and

Washington in Cooperation with the Northeast Corridor Transportation Project of the United States Department of Commerce," n.d., but received by Louis T. Klauder & Associates, October 29, 1965, Klauder Collection, Box 4, folder 1; Budd Company, "Presentation 3054–016: The Pennsylvania Railroad Price Inquiry No. 4899 for Fifty High-Speed Electric Multiple Unit Railroad Passenger Cars," December 29, 1965, Klauder Collection, Box 2, folder 7; Edward D. Meissner Jr. to J. S. Fair, December 27, 1965 ("cushion"), Klauder Collection, Box 1, folder 22; United Aircraft Corporate Systems Center, "Proposal for High Speed Electric Multiple Unit Railroad Passenger Cars, Submitted to Pennsylvania Railroad Company," December 29, 1965, Klauder Collection, Box 3, folder 13.

387. Martin to Saunders, April 15, 1965; "Memorandum of Understanding between the Pennsylvania Railroad and the Department of Commerce"; Bridwell to Saunders, June 11, 1965; all in DOT Records, Box 40; PRR BOD Minutes; Watson to G. C. Vaughan, December 13, 1966, Klauder Collection, Box 13, folder 6.

388. Watson, "Memo: Summary of Major Commitment" ("may," emphasis in the original); New York Times, May 5, 1966; September 25, 1966 ("specifying"); Rockland County Journal-News, May 5, 1966 ("spend"); Shapiro, "Seven Secrets," 11 ("worst").

389. Shapiro, "Seven Secrets," 11 ("doubt"); Goldberg and Warner, Metroliners, 10.

390. Watson, "Memo: Summary of Major Commitment of N.E.C. Demonstration Train Contract," Watson Collection, Box 4, folder 3; New York Times, May 5, 1966; Shapiro, "Seven Secrets," 13 ("power").

391. Watson, "Memorandum," 5–6 ("opportunity").

392. When they submitted their bid in December 1965, Budd officials reluctantly agreed to deliver the first two cars within 360 days of the initial order. To their good fortune, however, PRR maintenance-of-way personnel indicated that they would need two summer seasons to complete upgrades to the track, and the contract instead specified a fifteen-month delivery window.

393. The Passenger Service Improvement Corporation purchased the Silverliners and leased them to the PRR, where they were assigned to Class MP85B.

394. Even with little more than a year's experience, Pennsylvania Railroad personnel had uncovered one flaw in the Silverliner design—the innovative air-cushion suspension system, designed to provide a smoother ride, was prone to malfunction. The decision to revert to conventional cast-steel trucks and steel-coil springs provoked little dispute among the PRR's engineering staff. The same could not be said for Nelson and other members of

the Commerce Department. "Long after the cars were ordered," PRR officials complained, "the government people still wanted to have air springs."

395. Madeira to Plowman, July 31, 1964 ("gearing," "propulsion," "minimize"), Klauder Collection, Box 1, folder 19; Watson, "Memorandum," 8 ("pitfalls," "after," "springs").

396. Established in 1945, Melpar experienced rapid growth because of defense contracts; in 1951, it became a subsidiary of the Westinghouse Air Brake Company. By the mid-1960s, however, the company was beginning to falter, in part as the result of reductions in the government's military and space programs and in part the result of a vending-machine scandal surrounding Bobby Baker, the secretary for the majority Democratic caucus in the US Senate, which tangentially involved Melpar.

397. New York Times, August 11, 1966; Goldberg and Warner, Metroliners, 13–14.

398. Watson's appointment became effective on September 21. John Clutz, the PRR's director of research, died in July, at age sixty-two, following heart surgery. The company would later appoint James L. Forrester as his replacement, but Forrester, like Clutz before him, possessed systemwide responsibilities.

399. New York Times, July 22, 1966; "The Pennsylvania Railroad Biographies: R. B. Watson, Coordinator of the High Speed Demonstration Project, Philadelphia, Pa.," Watson Collection, Box 3, folder 9; "Coordinator High Speed Demonstration Project," November 2, 1966, Klauder Collection, Box 16, folder 3.

400. Pennsylvania Railroad, US Department of Commerce, "High-Speed Test Cars: Tentative Operation Outlined by Department of Commerce 10/4/66," Klauder Collection, Box 13, folder 1; "Northeast Coordinator Demonstration Project, Coordinator's Report No. 1," October 17, 1966 ("items," "normal"), Klauder Collection, Box 12, folder 18.

401. "Northeast Coordinator Demonstration Project, Coordinator's Report No. 2," October 24, 1966 ("reaction," "preclude"), Klauder Collection, Box 12, folder 18; Philadelphia Inquirer, October 21, 1966 ("late"); Philadelphia Bulletin, October 21, 1966 ("Unveils").

402. Rose, Seely, and Barrett, Best Transportation System, 139–41.

403. Rose, Seely, and Barrett, Best Transportation System, 141–50, includes "toughest" quotation from Joseph A. Califano, A Presidential Nation (New York: W. W. Norton, 1975), 51, reprinted at 149 and "integrated" quotation from Lee C. White, Memorandum for the Files, December 14, 1965, reprinted at 142; George M.

Smerk, *The Federal Role in Urban Mass Transportation* (Bloomington: Indiana University Press, 1991), 103–6.

404. United States Congress, House Appropriations Committee, Department of Transportation Appropriations for 1968, Hearings before a Subcommittee of the Committee on Appropriations, House of Representatives, 90th Cong., 1st sess. (Washington, DC: United States Government Printing Office, 1967), 759; *MIT News*, January 29, 2003; Shapiro, "Seven Secrets," 13–14 ("contribution"); "Northeast Coordinator Demonstration Project, Coordinator's Report No. 21," April 17, 1967 ("versed"); Bert Pennypacker, "PRR vs. Car, Plane, Bus," *Trains* 28, no. 1 (November 1967): 18–28, at 21.

405. "Northeast Coordinator Demonstration Project, Coordinator's Report No. 3," November 3, 1966 ("pressure," "gradually," "doubt"); "Northeast Coordinator Demonstration Project, Coordinator's Report No. 4," November 21, 1966 ("undesirable"); both in Klauder Collection, Box 12, folder 18; *New York Times*, December 1, 1966.

406. "Northeast Coordinator Demonstration Project, Coordinator's Report No. 6," December 5, 1966; "Northeast Coordinator Demonstration Project, Coordinator's Report No. 8," December 19, 1966; "Northeast Coordinator Demonstration Project, Coordinator's Report No. 9," December 27, 1966; "Northeast Coordinator Demonstration Project, Coordinator's Report No. 11," January 23, 1967 ("doubtful"); "Northeast Coordinator Demonstration Project, Coordinator's Report No. 12," January 30, 1967; all in Klauder Collection, Box 12, folder 18.

407. "Northeast Coordinator Demonstration Project, Coordinator's Report No. 5," November 28, 1966; "Northeast Coordinator Demonstration Project, Coordinator's Report No. 6," December 5, 1966; "Northeast Coordinator Demonstration Project, Coordinator's Report No. 9," December 27, 1966; "Northeast Coordinator Demonstration Project, Coordinator's Report No. 10," January 9, 1967; "Northeast Coordinator Demonstration Project, Coordinator's Report No. 12," January 30, 1967; "Northeast Coordinator Demonstration Project, Coordinator's Report No. 11," January 23, 1967; "Northeast Coordinator Demonstration Project, Coordinator's Report No. 13," February 6, 1967; "Northeast Coordinator Demonstration Project, Coordinator's Report No. 14," February 13, 1967; "Northeast Coordinator Demonstration Project, Coordinator's Report No. 16," February 27, 1967; all in Klauder Collection, Box 12, folder 18; Edward J. Ward to Watson, March 8, 1967, Klauder

Collection, Box 16, folder 21; Ward to "All Test Car Personnel," April 3, 1967 ("limit"), Klauder Collection, Box 16, folder 3.

408. Watson originally listed the maximum speed as 157.0 mph but noted that subsequent instrument recalibrations lowered the actual speed to 155.5 mph. "Northeast Coordinator Demonstration Project, Coordinator's Report No. 20," April 3, 1967 ("pressure"); "Northeast Coordinator Demonstration Project, Coordinator's Report No. 22," May 1, 1967; both in Klauder Collection, Box 12, folder 18; *Philadelphia Evening Bulletin*, April 25, 1967.

409. Diffenderfer, "High Speed Passenger Transportation," 17–22; *Lancaster Dispatcher* 45, no. 6 (June 2014): 6; Goldberg and Warner, *Metroliners*, 31.

410. *Evening Standard*, January 25, 1965 ("attract").

411. Klauder & Associates initially held a three-month contract, which the commonwealth extended by fourteen months in January 1966.

412. *Philadelphia Inquirer*, November 12, 1965 ("dramatic"); November 13, 1965 ("self-evident," "soon"); *Pittsburgh Press*, April 21, 1966 ("routes").

413. Commonwealth officials estimated the cost of the eleven high-speed cars to be $4.5 million, with the federal government providing $3 million and the commonwealth and the PRR sharing the remaining expense.

414. The terms *Capitaliners* and *Capitoliners* have been used almost interchangeably, but the former seems more appropriate, given that the Keystone Corridor served the entire city of Harrisburg and not merely the building where the assembly convened.

415. *Philadelphia Inquirer*, August 31, 1966; [Lancaster, PA] *Intelligencer Journal*, August 31, 1966; *Scranton Times*, September 20, 1966 ("don't").

416. *Philadelphia Inquirer*, August 31, 1966 ("line").

417. *Philadelphia Inquirer*, August 31, 1966 ("first," "partnership," "goal"); November 24, 1966.

418. SEPTA paid the PRR $198,000 a year to operate the service as far as the western border of Chester County. The railroad bore the expense for the remaining distance to Harrisburg, using the Silverliner cars that the company leased from SEPTA.

419. Planning commissioners voted to overrule the report, asserting that the request was a "package" that could not be subdivided.

420. *Philadelphia Inquirer*, August 31, 1966 ("sop"); November 24, 1966 ("package"); February 1, 1967; February 24, 1967 ("experimental," "spending").

421. *Philadelphia Inquirer*, November 12, 1965 ("role," "undercut"); November 13, 1965; January 12, 1966;

December 20, 1966 ("injury," "disclosure"); January 11, 1967; January 19, 1967; February 3, 1967.

422. *New York Times*, December 30, 1966; *Philadelphia Inquirer*, February 11, 1967 ("revisions," "changes"); February 21, 1967.

423. *Intelligencer Journal*, April 18, 1967; *Wilkes-Barre Times Leader*, April 18, 1967 ("demand," "suicide"); *Lancaster New Era*, April 26, 1967 ("conduct," "bypassed").

424. [Hazelton] *Standard-Speaker*, April 28, 1967 ("giving"); [Scranton] *Tribune*, May 26, 1967 ("changing," "benefactor," "taxpayers").

425. *Indiana Gazette*, May 1, 1967; *Pittsburgh Press*, May 11, 1967; August 28, 1967; October 31, 1967.

426. In 1980, high-speed rail advocates in Ohio initiated an Interstate High Speed Intercity Rail Passenger Network Compact, which also included Pennsylvania, Illinois, Indiana, Kentucky, Michigan, Missouri, New York, Tennessee, and West Virginia. In 1981, the Pennsylvania Assembly established the Pennsylvania High Speed Intercity Rail Passenger Commission. The body issued a report in 1985, but there has been no sustained effort to develop a high-speed corridor across the state. Parsons Brinckerhoff/Gannett Fleming, *Pennsylvania High Speed Rail Feasibility Study: Preliminary Report, Phase I* (n.p.: Pennsylvania High Speed Intercity Rail Passenger Commission, 1985), 1.2–1.3; Shishir Mathur, "High-Speed Rail Projects in the United States: Identifying the Elements of Success, Part 2," San Jose State University, *Faculty Publications, Urban and Regional Planning* (2007), 56–59.

427. "Northeast Coordinator Demonstration Project, Coordinator's Report No. 23," May 15, 1967; "Northeast Coordinator Demonstration Project, Coordinator's Report No. 24," May 29, 1967; both in Klauder Collection, Box 12, folder 18; Watson to Cecil Muldoon, July 18, 1967; "Memorandum to Correspondents," n.d. ("delivered," emphasis in the original); "News from the Pennsylvania Railroad News Bureau," May 19, 1967; Muldoon to H. P. Morgan, May 17, 1967; all in Klauder Collection, Box 16, folder 14; *Philadelphia Daily News*, May 25, 1967; *Baltimore Sun*, May 25, 1967; *Newark Star-Ledger*, May 25, 1967; *Trenton Times*, May 25, 1967; *Philadelphia Inquirer*, May 25, 1967; *Washington Post*, May 25, 1967; *New York Times*, May 25, 1967 ("goggles").

428. *New York Times*, May 10, 1967 ("positively").

429. Watson Memorandum, 8–9 ("possibility"); Robert H. Shatz to Fair, December 29, 1965, Klauder Collection, Box 3, folder 13; *New York Times*, May 7, 1966.

430. Watson Memorandum, 9–10 ("impossible"); David Smucker to Saunders, October 30, 1967 ("reasonable,"

"evaluate," emphasis in the original, "obliged," "hold"), Klauder Collection, Box 15, folder 18.

431. Watson to G. C. Vaughan, December 13, 1966 ("understand," "compatible"), Klauder Collection, Box 13, folder 6; Shapiro, "Seven Secrets," 12 ("literally").

432. *New York Times*, July 20, 1967; September 15, 1967 ("debatable").

433. "Northeast Coordinator Demonstration Project, Coordinator's Report No. 25," June 14, 1967; "Northeast Coordinator Demonstration Project, Coordinator's Report No. 26," July 7, 1967; "Northeast Coordinator Demonstration Project, Coordinator's Report No. 24," May 29, 1967; "Northeast Coordinator Demonstration Project, Coordinator's Report No. 27," July 17, 1967; "Northeast Coordinator Demonstration Project, Coordinator's Report No. 29," August 14, 1967; "Northeast Coordinator Demonstration Project, Coordinator's Report No. 31," September 1, 1967; "Northeast Coordinator Demonstration Project, Coordinator's Report No. 33," October 2, 1967; "Northeast Coordinator Demonstration Project, Coordinator's Report No. 35," October 30, 1967; Northeast Coordinator Demonstration Project, Coordinator's Report No. 36," November 13, 1967 ("benefit"); all in Klauder Collection, Box 12, folder 18; D.W. A. Memo, "Subject: Catenary Wire Dynamics Discussion of Mar. 24, 1966 with Melpar and Gibbs & Hill," March 25, 1966, Klauder Collection, Box 4, folder 7; W. E. Lehr to J. A. Miller, October 6, 1967; Klauder Collection, Box 15, folder 17; Watson to C. H. Gaut, June 8, 1967; Watson to Gaut, July 6, 1967; Watson to Gaut, July 14, 1967; "Memorandum: Pantograph Tests," July 6, 1967; "Test Results Related to Pantograph and Catenary System," July 14, 1967; "Memorandum: Reasons for requesting immediate Testing Program for pantographs used in NEC project," September 1, 1967; Watson to T. F. Murray, September 14, 1967 ("alarming"); Watson to Vaughan, September 27, 1967; all in Klauder Collection, Box 15, folder 18.

434. *New York Times*, September 15, 1967 ("desirable," "complement"); September 21, 1967 ("disturbing"); Goldberg and Warner, *Metroliners*, 22.

435. *New York Times*, October 28, 1967 ("clothesline," "satisfied"); Saunders to David Smucker, November 6, 1967 ("recently," "unthinkable," "subject"), Watson Collection, Box 2, folder 5.

436. Smucker to Saunders, October 30, 1967 ("progressed," "necessary," "staffed"), Klauder Collection, Box 15, folder 18; Saunders to Smucker, November 6, 1967 ("refrain"), Watson Collection, Box 2, folder 5.

437. Smucker to Vaughn, October 19, 1967, Klauder Collection, Box 15, folder 10 ("street-cars"); Diffenderfer, "Metroliner Experiences," 834.

438. *New York Times*, November 19, 1967 ("should"); [Philadelphia] *Sunday Bulletin*, November 19, 1967 ("hastily," "concrete," "cancels").

439. The R&D cost for the 707, which debuted in 1958, was $1.3 billion in 2004 dollars. After adjusting for inflationary increases in the Consumer Price Index between 1958 and 2004, that would suggest an expense of more than $197.4 million, in 1958 dollars. "The Geography of Transport Systems, Development Costs for Selected Aircraft," adapted from J. Bowen, *The Economic Geography of Air Transportation: Space, Time, and the Freedom of the Sky* (London: Routledge, 2010), https://transportgeography.org/?page_id=2487, accessed January 31, 2020.

440. *New York Times*, November 10, 1967 ("satisfied," "worried").

441. Feldman, "High-Speed Rail," 66; "Northeast Coordinator Demonstration Project, Coordinator's Report No. 37," December 2, 1967 ("cropped," "dead," "doubt"); "Northeast Coordinator Demonstration Project, Coordinator's Report No. 38," December 16, 1967; "Northeast Coordinator Demonstration Project, Coordinator's Report No. 40," January 15, 1968 ("spasmodic," "major," emphasis in the original); "Northeast Coordinator Demonstration Project, Coordinator's Report No. 41," January 29, 1968; all in Klauder Collection, Box 12, folder 18; *New York Times*, November 10, 1967 ("bugs"); Goldberg and Warner, *Metroliners*, 21 ("favorite," "Everything").

442. A combination of political pressure and dogged determination on the part of engineers and technicians eventually produced results. On January 15, 1969, a ceremonial inaugural run carried VIPs from Washington to New York. Alan Boyd was on board, as was John A. Volpe, the Nixon appointee who would soon replace him as secretary of transportation. At 8:30 a.m. the following day, the first regular *Metroliner* departed Penn Station. With four days to spare, Lyndon Johnson had fulfilled his promise to implement high-speed rail transportation during his presidency. A second daily round trip began on February 10. That was far less than the hourly frequency PRR officials had promised several years earlier and was insufficient to fulfill the terms of the Commerce Department contract. Not until October 26, 1970, was there enough functioning equipment available to expand service to six round trips per day. That milestone marked the long-delayed beginning of the two-year

demonstration period specified in the April 1966 contract between the Pennsylvania Railroad and the Commerce Department. It was almost precisely three years after the October 29, 1967, target that Robert Nelson and other Commerce Department personnel had stipulated. The seven-year estimate that Louis Klauder provided in August 1964 came closer to the mark. That Watson and his colleagues were able to implement regular service ten months earlier than what Klauder considered possible was a testament to their determination to overcome more obstacles than they could have possibly foreseen.

Even if the equipment functioned properly, however, it was often impossible to maintain the two-hour, fifty-nine-minute schedule between New York and Washington. The timing was only twenty-one minutes faster than what the *Afternoon Congressional* achieved between October 1967 and April 1968 with GG1 locomotives and conventional passenger cars. The modest increase in speed came at a considerable cost. By the spring of 1970, the Pennsylvania Railroad and the Penn Central invested $65 million in the *Metroliner* project. That was more than five times the $12.9 million in funding provided by the federal government. The expense was a small but nonetheless significant factor in the Penn Central's bankruptcy.

New York Times, June 14, 1967; January 17, 1969; February 6, 1969; February 9, 1969; March 2, 1969; March 16, 1969; March 19, 1969; March 28, 1969; April 4, 1969; *Penn Central Post*, March 1969, 1–2; Nelson to Boyd, "Summary of Estimated Total Funding for Northeast Corridor Rail Demonstration," July 18, 1969, DOT Records, Box 310; Diffenderfer, "Metroliner Experiences"; Dan Cupper, "The Demotion of a Faded Speedster," *Passenger Train Journal*, January 1982, 9–11, at 11; Goldberg and Warner, *Metroliners*, 20–25, 29–30, 33–34, 104–5; Donald M. Steffee, "Tomorrow's Trains Today on Yesterday's Tracks," *Trains* 30, no. 11 (September 1970): 36–47. For a comprehensive analysis of the contested development of high-speed rail in the Northeast Corridor after the PRR era, see Jonathan English, "Getting off Track: The Northeast Corridor Project in an International Context," *Journal of Transport History* 43, no. 1 (2022): 107–30.

443. Saunders, *Merging Lines*, 359–61; *New York Times*, March 17, 1965.

444. Saunders, *Merging Lines*, 364–65; Striplin, *Norfolk & Western*, 327–29.

445. Grant, *Erie Lackawanna*, 126–49.

446. *New York Times*, August 31, 1967.

447. D for Delaware & Hudson, E for Erie Lackawanna, and Re for Reading, with no corresponding letter for the Boston & Maine. The first iteration of the name—Derjco—paid tribute to the Jersey Central but suffered from the substantial disadvantage that it was unpronounceable.

448. Saunders, *Merging Lines*, 366–67; Striplin, *Norfolk & Western*, 330–31; Grant, *Erie Lackawanna*, 151–52.

449. *New York Times*, August 20, 1965; September 1, 1965; September 2, 1965 ("sweeping"); October 12, 1965; Striplin, *Norfolk & Western*, 329–31.

450. *New York Times*, September 2, 1965 ("necessary"); June 24, 1967 ("committed," "monopoly"); Striplin, *Norfolk & Western*, 331 ("interest").

451. *Trains* 26, no. 3 (January 1966): 16 ("possible").

452. Saunders, *Merging Lines*, 367–72; Rebuttal of John Fishwick, December 14, 1967, Finance Docket 21510, *Norfolk & Western Railway–Merger–New York, Chicago & St. Louis Railroad*, supplemental report, 330 ICC 780 (1967), quoted in Saunders, *Merging Lines*, 371 ("stronger"); Saunders, *Merging Lines*, 367; Finance Docket 23832, *Norfolk & Western Railway Company–Merger–Chesapeake & Ohio Railroad Company*, 262, quoted in Saunders, *Merging Lines*, 364 ("thumb").

453. Boyd to Connor, September 1, 1965 ("fundamental," "equal," "stronger"), DOT Records, Box 44.

454. *New York Times*, September 2, 1965 ("unconscionable," "unacceptable"); September 29, 1965 ("adequately," "recommend," "obligations"); October 14, 1965; February 15, 1966 ("ridiculous"); Grant, *Erie Lackawanna*, 152–53.

455. *New York Times*, February 15, 1966 ("unthinkable").

456. *New York Times*, March 17, 1968 ("regret"); Saunders, *Railroad Mergers*, 254.

457. Kennedy to Katzenbach, September 9, 1964 ("circumstances," "assuring").

458. *New York Times*, April 23, 1965 ("continue," "dedication").

459. Orrick Oral History, April 14, 1970, 112 ("agreement," "crying"); *New York Times*, February 15, 1967 ("horrified").

460. Welborn, *Regulation in the White House*, 170–71; Mark J. Niefer, "Donald F. Turner at the Antitrust Division: A Reconsideration of Merger Policy in the 1960s," *Antitrust* 29, no. 3 (Summer 2015): 53–59.

461. Donald F. Turner, Address before the National Industrial Conference Board, March 3, 1966 ("horizontal"); Turner, Address before the Antitrust Section of the American Bar Association, August 10, 1965 ("attack"); quotations reprinted in Niefer, "Donald F. Turner," 54–55.

462. *New York Times*, July 15, 1965 ("factors"); *Pennsylvania Railroad Company–Merger–New York Central Railroad Company* (1966), 502–3 ("modifying").

463. *New York Times*, July 15, 1965 ("failure").

464. *New York Times*, July 21, 1965 ("satisfactory," "discontinue"); August 17, 1965 ("delayed").

465. *New York Times*, October 11, 1965; October 20, 1965; *New York, New Haven & Hartford Trustees Discontinuance of All Interstate Passenger Trains*, 327 ICC 151 (1966), at 152–53; *Trains* 26, no. 3 (January 1966): 6.

466. *New York Times*, October 21, 1965 ("burdensome," "urge," "preserved").

467. *New York Times*, October 21, 1965 ("resolved," "basis"); *Pennsylvania Railroad Company–Merger–New York Central Railroad Company* (1966), 479.

468. *New York Times*, October 22, 1965 ("served").

469. Bridwell to Boyd, June 17, 1965, 3 ("consistency," "alone"), DOT Records, Box 44.

470. *Trains* 26, no. 5 (March 1966): 16–17; *New York Times*, February 2, 1966 ("hopeful").

471. *New York Times*, January 25, 1966 ("essential," "define," "freight," "late"); January 26, 1966 ("represents").

472. *Pennsylvania Railroad Company–Merger–New York Central Railroad Company* (1966), 490, 491 ("transaction"), 501, 505 ("contradicts," "factors"), 512 ("lessen"); *New York Times*, April 26, 1966; April 28, 1966.

473. *Pennsylvania Railroad Company–Merger–New York Central Railroad Company* (1966), 519 ("touchstone").

474. *Pennsylvania Railroad Company–Merger–New York Central Railroad Company* (1966), 496 ("trimmed"), 499–500 ("notwithstanding").

475. *Pennsylvania Railroad Company–Merger–New York Central Railroad Company* (1966), 549–50 ("inevitable").

476. *New York Times*, April 28, 1966; May 1, 1966; Saunders, *Merging Lines*, 142, 273–74.

477. *Pennsylvania Railroad Company–Merger–New York Central Railroad Company* (1966), 532–34 ("doubtful," "alternative," "cooperation"), 546–48; *New York Times*, April 28, 1966.

478. *Pennsylvania Railroad Company–Merger–New York Central Railroad Company* (1966), 524 ("embodiment"), 526 ("construed"); *New York, New Haven & Hartford Trustees Discontinuance of All Interstate Passenger Trains*, 201–18; *New York Times*, April 28, 1966.

479. *New York Times*, April 28, 1966 ("provided," "attitude"); May 1, 1966 ("burden").

480. *New York Times*, April 28, 1966 ("victory," "substantiates," "understanding," "breakthrough," "pleased," "prayer," "soon"); April 30, 1966 ("outlook").

481. *New York Times*, April 28, 1966.

482. *New York Times*, May 1, 1966 ("job").

483. *New York Times*, May 4, 1966 ("right"); May 13, 1966 ("growth"); June 21, 1966; July 5, 1966 ("transaction").

484. *New York Times*, May 18, 1966; June 22, 1966 ("considerably"); July 9, 1966.

485. *New York Times*, July 12, 1966 ("junior," "saddle," "essential," "disaster").

486. *New York Times*, July 21, 1966 ("bullet-proof").

487. *New York Times*, July 22 ("looks," "delaying," "provide"); August 2, 1966.

488. *New York Times*, July 21, 1966 ("declining"); July 23, 1966 ("disturbed," "invoked"); August 1, 1966; August 2, 1966 ("remote").

489. *New York Times*, August 2, 1966; August 9, 1966 ("facets").

490. *New York Times*, August 9, 1966 ("reversal," "novel," "inadequate," "capabilities").

491. *New York Times*, August 3, 1966.

492. *New York Times*, August 13, 1966; August 27, 1966; September 9, 1966 ("unjust," "uncertain," "erred"); *Erie-Lackawanna Railroad Company v. United States*, 259 F. Supp. 964 (S.D.N.Y. 1966).

493. *New York Times*, September 10, 1966; September 13, 1966; September 20, 1966; September 22, 1966 ("months"); October 1, 1966.

494. *New York Times*, September 22, 1966 ("pressure," "chance"); September 28, 1966 ("inevitable," "monopoly").

495. *Erie-Lackawanna Railroad Company v. United States*, 973, 981 ("assuming"); *New York Times*, September 28, 1966; October 5, 1966.

496. Initially, the appellants filed with Justice John M. Harlan, whose purview included the New York District Court. Harlan subsequently referred the matter to the full Supreme Court.

497. *New York Times*, October 5, 1966 ("shock"); October 7, 1966; October 8, 1966; October 12, 1966.

498. *New York Times*, October 8, 1966; Daughen and Binzen, *No Way to Run a Railroad*, 77–89.

499. *New York Times*, October 19, 166 ("unprecedented").

500. *New York Times*, October 20, 1966 ("relatively," "necessity"); November 1, 1966 ("months"); November 19, 1966.

501. *New York Times*, November 1, 1966; November 2, 1966 ("benefits"); November 29, 1966 ("understandable").

502. *New York Times*, November 11, 1966; November 17, 1966 ("pitiful," "fight," "spectacular," "propaganda," "wish," "rule," "destroy," "wreck").

503. *New York Times*, November 17, 1966 ("handful," "effect," "collapse").

504. *New York Times*, November 9, 1966; March 24, 1967; *Philadelphia Inquirer*, November 10, 1966 ("calamity").

505. Turner insisted that he only discovered at the last minute that the plane belonged to Anheuser-Busch and that it was too late to make alternate travel arrangements. The trip nonetheless attracted unflattering media attention—including an article in the *Wall Street Journal*, rather predictably titled "Take Me Out to the Ball Game."

506. *Wall Street Journal*, July 16, 1966; Telephone conversation #11053, sound recording, LBJ and Ramsey Clak, November 23, 1966, 6:45 p.m., Recordings and Transcripts of Telephone Conversations and Meetings, LBJ Presidential Library, https://www.discoverlbj.org/item/tel-11053, accessed February 05, 2024 ("fool," "confidence," "tour"); Mark H. Rose, *Market Rules: Bankers, Presidents, and the Origins of the Great Recession* (Philadelphia: University of Pennsylvania Press, 2019), 27–29.

507. In a November 1988 interview, Califano recalled that he received Saunders's telephone call on November 3, 1966. Oral history transcript, Joseph A. Califano, interview 37 (XXXVII), November 15, 1988, by Michael L. Gillette, LBJ Library Oral Histories, LBJ Presidential Library, https://www.discoverlbj.org/item/oh-califanoj-19881114-37-11-91, accessed February 4, 2024, 8.

508. As Johnson told Ramsey Clark on the afternoon of November 23, "No other human being has talked to me about this, that I even remember, since this memo was written. As a matter of fact, I didn't know the memo was written 'til they read it to me today." It should be noted that Robert Kennedy explicitly mentioned the memo in his March 2, 1965, testimony before Congress, so it is not clear whether Johnson was sincere in his profession of ignorance. Califano memo to Johnson, November 21, 1966, LBJ Library, reprinted in Califano, *Triumph & Tragedy*, 156 ("indication"); Welborn, *Regulation in the White House*, 195–96 (includes memo, Califano to Johnson, November 21, 1966, LBJ Library ["delaying"]); Telephone conversation # 11051, sound recording, LBJ and Ramsey Clark, November 23, 1966, 6:45 p.m., Recordings and Transcripts of Telephone Conversations and Meetings, LBJ Presidential Library, https://www.discoverlbj.org/item/tel-11051, accessed February 05, 2024, ("after").

509. The next day, in his telephone call to the president, Clark informed Johnson that "Friday's our deadline" for filing the Justice Department's brief with the court "and we have the galley proof back from the printer with our brief all printed out, the press is ready to roll

Friday morning." Johnson, his voice rising in frustration, noted, "Well, that's a mighty poor reason, though, for doing something you oughtn't be doing. The question is, 'should it be done?'" Johnson then indicated that "if I think something's right, I want to be able to do what I think's right without some fella forcing me because it's the last night to do something that I think is wrong. Now I think this is wrong." Telephone conversation #11052, sound recording, LBJ and Ramsey Clark, November 23, 1966, 6:45 p.m., Recordings and Transcripts of Telephone Conversations and Meetings, LBJ Presidential Library, https://www.discoverlbj.org/item/tel-11052 accessed February 05, 2024 ("deadline," "poor," "right").

510. Califano, *Triumph & Tragedy*, 156 ("commit").

511. Clark memo to Califano, November 21, 1966, LBJ Library, quoted in Califano, *Triumph & Tragedy*, 156 ("obligated").

512. Joseph A. Califano, interview 37, 3 ("strong-willed"); Telephone conversation #11051 ("materially," "money," "overriding,").

513. Telephone conversation, #11051 ("combined," "incredible," "inconceivable," "intelligent").

514. Telephone conversation #11052 ("lawyer," "change," "desk").

515. Telephone conversation #11051 ("adjudicated," "charged").

516. Telephone conversation #11051 ("professor"); #11052 ("superimpose," "jerk").

517. At no point in the conversation did Johnson mention Saunders's importance as a contributor to the Democratic Party or the PRR executive's connections to the Kennedy and Johnson administrations. Of course, Johnson possessed sufficient political experience to suspect that any request for special treatment on Saunders's behalf was likely to make Clark even more determined to protect the independence and the integrity of the attorney general's office. Telephone conversation #11051 ("appeal"); Telephone conversation #11053 ("doubled," "amount," "assurance"); Welborn, *Regulation in the White House*, 196.

518. "The meeting in my office," Califano recalled, "was not a twenty-minute meeting." I believe we met for two or three hours with people bitching about not getting home for Thanksgiving dinner." Joseph A. Califano, interview 37, 11 ("meeting"); Califano, *Triumph & Tragedy*, 157–58 ("raised"); Welborn, *Regulation in the White House*, 195–96.

519. Califano, *Triumph & Tragedy*, 157–58 ("best").

520. Following his first conversation with Fortas, Johnson told Califano that he had discussed the matter with "the best lawyer I know." Califano initially believed that the president was referring to either Donald Thomas or A. W. Moursund, Texas attorneys who were friends of Johnson. Johnson called Fortas a second time, later that afternoon—presumably after the associate justice had had an opportunity to think about the matter, then called Califano again, and either deliberately or unintentionally acknowledged that Fortas was "the best lawyer."

521. "Nothing was being done here for venal reasons," Califano concluded. "What was being done was being done because the President thought it was right. And once having decided that, you just went and did it. I don't think he ever felt any inhibitions on how we'd get there." Califano, *Triumph & Tragedy*, 157–58 ("extraordinary," "different"); Joseph A. Califano, interview 38, 6–9, 14 ("venal").

522. Fortas responded by telling Califano that "years ago, after I started working for this man, I began celebrating Thanksgiving on the day before. He ruins every Thanksgiving Day."

523. Califano, *Triumph & Tragedy*, 158 ("ruined").

524. Califano, *Triumph & Tragedy*, 155 ("favors"), 158–59 ("balked," "felt," "started"), includes Ackley memo to Califano, November 26, 1966, LBJ Library ("inconceivable," "unhappy"); Welborn, *Regulation in the White House*, 196.

525. *New York Times*, December 1, 1966 ("allowed," "reasonable"); January 18, 1967; *Baltimore & Ohio Railroad Company v. United States*, 386 US 372 (1967), at 384 ("quarrel"); Califano, *Triumph & Tragedy*, 158–59 (includes expanded version of the "quarrel" quotation); Welborn, *Regulation in the White House*, 196–97.

526. Califano, *Triumph & Tragedy*, 158 ("retain").

527. *New York Times*, November 29, 1966.

528. *New York Times*, December 6, 1966; December 14, 1966 ("circumstance," "elementary").

529. Salsbury, *No Way to Run a Railroad*, 104–5; Patman Report, 18.

530. *New York Times*, January 6, 1964 ("assured").

531. *New York Times*, April 22, 1964; September 10, 1964; April 20, 1965; November 30, 1965; July 27, 1966; July 28, 1966; November 24, 1966; Patman Report, 180–83.

532. *New York Times*, January 21, 1964; Patman Report, 174.

533. *New York Times*, April 25, 1967; Salsbury, *No Way to Run a Railroad*, 104–5; 109–11; Patman Report, 172; SEC Report, 36–40, 91–92.

534. Salsbury, *No Way to Run a Railroad*, 104–7, 110; SEC Report, 36, 77.

535. *New York Times*, October 26, 1967 ("better"); October 27, 1967; Salsbury, *No Way to Run a Railroad*, 110–111; SEC Report, 36–40.

536. Salsbury, *No Way to Run a Railroad*, 112–14.

537. *New York Times*, January 18, 1967; January 19, 1967; January 21, 1967; February 15, 1967 ("considered").

538. *Baltimore & Ohio v. United States*, 378 ("validity," "findings").

539. *Baltimore & Ohio v. United States*, 392 ("unscrambling," "delay"); 454 ("predatory"), 455 ("context"); *New York Times*, March 28, 1967.

540. *Baltimore & Ohio v. United States*, 463 ("represented"), 478 ("reversion"); Califano, *Triumph & Tragedy*, 158–59.

541. *Baltimore & Ohio v. United States*, 469 ("realignment"), 471–72 ("dilatory").

542. *New York Times*, March 28, 1967 ("disheartened," "adverse," "fatal," "questions"); April 7, 1966 ("continued").

543. *New York Times*, April 1, 1967 ("caught"); April 19, 1967.

544. *New York Times*, May 9, 1967; January 25, 1968; June 14, 1985.

545. *New York Times*, March 30, 1967; April 12, 1967 ("dead"); April 14, 1967; April 18, 1967 ("kill"); April 19, 1967; Grant, *Erie Lackawanna*, 153–54.

546. *New York Times*, May 16, 1967 ("between"); Welborn, *Regulation in the White House*, 197–98; "Press Briefing with the Governors Following the New England Governors' Conference," May 15, 1967, LBJ Public Papers, 53–54, quoted in Welborn, 197 ("directive," "delighted," "grasp"); Mark J. Green, with Beverly C. Moore Jr. and Bruce Wasserstein, *The Closed Enterprise System: Ralph Nader's Study Group Report on Antitrust Enforcement* (New York: Grossman, 1972), 43 ("yelled").

547. A second decision, announced at the same time, required the PRR and the NYC to pay indemnities (for lost revenue rather than the loss of capital) to the three small railroads, if the Penn Central merger occurred before the EL, the B&M, and the D&H could be included in the N&W. PRR and NYC officials had agreed to those indemnification conditions, and the provision was both expected and uncontroversial.

548. In the unlikely event that the EL, the B&M, or the D&H declined inclusion in the Norfolk & Western, they would forgo the opportunity to merge with the Penn Central.

549. Welborn, *Regulation in the White House*, 197–98; Memo, Watson to Johnson, June 6, 1967, LBJ Presidential Papers, quoted in Welborn, 198 ("result"); *New York Times*, June 10, 1967; June 13, 1967 ("unwanted").

550. The terms for the Boston & Maine were far less generous, with one share of N&W stock set as the equivalent of ten shares of nearly worthless B&M stock—a situation that was likely to lead to legal action by B&M investors.

551. *New York Times*, June 13, 1967 ("ridiculous"); July 15, 1967 ("outrageous," "unconscionable," "unlawful").

552. *New York Times*, June 14, 1967; June 17, 1967; June 21, 1967.

553. *New York Times*, June 24, 1967 ("committed," "hopeful," "intendment"); June 28 ("difficult").

554. *New York Times*, July 12, 1967; *Trains* 27, no. 11 (September 1967): 6, 16.

555. *New York Times*, July 12, 1967; August 31, 1967; *Trains* 27, no. 11 (September 1967): 6, 16; 28, no. 2 (December 1967): 49–50.

556. The justices acknowledged that the process of incorporating the New Haven into the Penn Central would be "a fairly long one in view of the reorganization problems" and saw no reason to delay the merger on that account. Should Gruss object to the regulatory outcome, they noted, his firm could appeal to a lower court.

557. *New York Times*, May 9, 1967 ("frustrated," "long"); May 13, 1967; May 29, 1967 ("fair," "awry"); May 30, 1967.

558. On September 1, the New Haven's trustees provided the ICC with a reorganization plan. They intended to create a new investment company that would oversee the proceeds from the sale to the Penn Central (950,000 shares of Penn Central stock, $23 million in Penn Central bonds, and $8 million in cash) and allocate them to the bondholders and other creditors, in the form of shares in the investment company. Representatives from the bondholders objected to that arrangement, suggesting that the Penn Central stock that would underwrite a significant portion of the investment company's bonds was "a highly speculative and volatile commodity." *New York Times*, June 16, 1967; July 18, 1967; August 4, 1967 ("worsening," "alternative"); September 2, 1967; November 30, 1967 ("speculative").

559. The loans in effect constituted an advance against the future purchase price of the New Haven and would be deducted from the amount that the Penn Central would eventually pay to acquire that company.

560. The New Haven trustees expressed their gratitude at the generosity of their future merger partners yet simultaneously demanded indemnification against any traffic losses attributable to the Penn Central until the inclusion matter could be resolved. *New York Times*,

August 17, 1967; August 23, 1967 ("end"); September 1, 1967; September 26, 1967; September 27, 1967.

561. The trustees' insistence that the New Haven was worth $230.3 million in liquidation was strikingly higher than the $160 million scrap value that trustee Richard Joyce Smith placed on the company in January 1967.

562. *New York Times*, November 22, 1967; August 13, 1968.

563. *Pennsylvania Railroad Company–Merger–New York Central Railroad Company*, 331 ICC 643 (1967), at 687–88 ("calling," "scope").

564. *Pennsylvania Railroad Company–Merger–New York Central Railroad Company* (1967), at 653–54 ("haggle"); *New York Times*, September 27, 1967; November 22, 1967; November 28, 1967 ("survive").

565. *New York Times*, September 26, 1967; December 16, 1967 ("meantime," "actions").

566. *New York Times*, June 14, 1967 ("right"); July 21, 1967.

567. *New York Times*, September 6, 1967 ("sooner"); September 19, 1967; September 29, 1967.

568. *New York Times*, October 21, 1967 ("elated").

569. *New York Times*, October 20, 1967 ("early"); October 21, 1967 ("notable," "satisfactory," "welcome").

570. The ICC hearings into the N&W–C&O–B&O–Western Maryland consolidation were scheduled to resume on November 27. *New York Times*, October 19, 1967; October 20, 1967 ("unhappy"); October 21, 1967 ("delighted"); November 1, 1967; November 2, 1967.

571. *Philadelphia Inquirer*, November 7, 1967 ("delay"); November 28, 1967 ("substance"); December 5, 1967 ("intelligently"); January 16, 1968 ("times").

572. *New York Times*, November 7, 1967; December 19, 1967 ("snowstorm").

573. Consequently, and as a formality, on January 30 Judge Friendly's New York court removed the stay that had blocked the merger, while simultaneously denying efforts by New Haven bondholders to prevent the New Haven from borrowing $25 million from the Penn Central.

574. *Penn-Central Merger and Norfolk & Western Inclusion Cases*, 389 US 486 (1968), at 487 ("competition"); *New York Times*, January 31, 1968.

575. *Penn-Central Merger and Norfolk & Western Inclusion Cases*, 510–11 ("continuation").

576. "While the rights of the bondholders are entitled to respect," Fortas insisted, "they do not command Procrustean measures. They certainly do not dictate that rail operations vital to the Nation be jettisoned despite the availability of a feasible alternative. The public interest is not merely a pawn to be sacrificed for the strategic purposes or protection of a class of security holders whose interests may or may not be served by the destructive move." *Penn-Central Merger and Norfolk & Western Inclusion Cases*, 510–11 ("rights"); *New York Times*, January 16, 1968 ("extend," "necessary," "resolved," "delighted," "wonderful").

577. The Supreme Court upheld the circuit court ruling denying the Reading the right to appeal the ICC's determination that the Reading was unlikely to suffer a loss of traffic and revenues because of the Penn Central merger. However, the Supreme Court's decision was without prejudice, indicating that the Reading possessed the right to re-petition the ICC, in the event it could prove harm arising from the formation of the Penn Central. The Jersey Central was not a party to the circuit court case (*Erie-Lackawanna Railroad Company v. United States*, 259 F. Supp. 964) and was therefore not included in *Baltimore & Ohio v. United States* or the *Penn-Central Merger and Norfolk & Western Inclusion Cases*.

578. *New York Times*, December 4, 1967 ("alternative"); January 16, 1968 ("gratified," "assert"); *Philadelphia Inquirer*, January 16, 1968 ("necessary").

579. The N&W incorporated Dereco on March 1, 1968. A month later, the Erie Lackawanna Railroad became the Erie Lackawanna Railway, its assets a part of Dereco. The Delaware & Hudson became part of Dereco in July. The Boston & Maine was not included in Dereco—largely because its parent company, Boston & Maine Industries, concluded that the inclusion provisions were insufficient. On March 20, 1969, an ICC examiner recommended the approval of the merger between the Norfolk & Western and the Chesapeake & Ohio, provided that the Reading and the bankrupt Jersey Central would become part of Dereco. The Erie Lackawanna declared bankruptcy on June 26, 1972, demonstrating the wisdom of N&W executives who favored the creation of Dereco, rather than a straight merger arrangement. The N&W nonetheless wrote off $55.8 million in Dereco equity because of the Erie Lackawanna's collapse. The catastrophic performance of the Penn Central, combined with declining earnings on the Chesapeake & Ohio, ensured that the N&W–C&O merger never took place. Striplin, *Norfolk & Western*, 335–47; Richard Saunders Jr., *Main Lines: Rebirth of the American Railroads, 1970–2002* (DeKalb: Northern Illinois University Press, 2003), 70–74.

580. Symes Testimony, *Rail Merger Legislation*, 397 ("approved"); *New York Times*, January 16, 1968 ("imperative").

581. Penn Central did not initially include the New Haven, and the company's woes continued. Five litigants demanded further concessions in the inclusion proceedings. They included representatives of the bondholders and officials from the Erie Lackawanna—whose executives demanded guarantees for traffic exchanged at the Maybrook, New York, gateway. A special three-judge federal court concluded that the New Haven's liquidation value, established by the ICC, was "significantly too low"—but that the cost to Penn Central, under the ICC's November 1967 ruling, was "significantly too high." Appeals Judge Henry Friendly, who by that point was thoroughly familiar with the New Haven's condition, "with some regret" ordered the ICC to conduct a new assessment of the New Haven's value.

It was also increasingly clear that both ICC and Penn Central officials had woefully underestimated the New Haven's losses. In November 1967, Penn Central executives agreed to make good all the New Haven's deficits for the first year of operation—but that that amount was not to exceed $5 million. During the first six months of 1968, however, the New Haven lost $11 million.

Circuit Court Judge Robert P. Anderson, who had overseen reorganization proceedings since the New Haven's 1961 bankruptcy filing, nonetheless exhibited little patience for the Penn Central's delaying tactics. "The right to merge was granted," he reminded Saunders and his colleagues, "the merger has taken place, and the price should be paid." On August 12, Anderson's federal bankruptcy court ordered the Penn Central "to physically take over and commence operating" the New Haven prior to January 1, 1969. After that date, he could no longer countenance additional borrowing by the New Haven, and the railroad would therefore suspend operations. Saunders indicated that the deadline was "impossible" and insisted that "we have done nothing to prevent its inclusion or to delay it."

The subsequent ICC ruling, released on December 2, set the liquidation value of the New Haven at $162.7 million, substantially above the $125 million figure established the previous November, but well below the $230.3 million demanded by the trustees. The agency ordered the Penn Central to pay $140.6 million for the New Haven, while assuming $5 million in 1968 operating losses. Additional expenses relating to labor-protection agreements, pension obligations, and equipment-trust payments raised the total cost to $178 million. The ICC also ordered the Penn Central to begin operating the New Haven by January 1, 1969, validating Judge Anderson's ruling. On December 23, Penn Central attorneys asked Judge Friendly to issue a restraining order, blocking implementation of Anderson's ruling. Acting with remarkable speed, a special three-judge statutory court, headed by Friendly, convened on December 27. Following two hours of oral arguments, they dismissed the request for a restraining order, removing the last impediment to the inclusion of the New Haven in the Penn Central.

Penn Central officials surrendered on December 30. On the afternoon of December 31, hours before Anderson's deadline, representatives from the two railroads signed more than two thousand legal documents, making the New Haven a part of the Penn Central system. "Neither Penn Central nor any other acquiring carrier can magically solve the New Haven's problems—problems that really began many, many years ago," concluded William H. Tucker, a former ICC commissioner who was now a Penn Central vice president in charge of the New Haven. It was an apt assessment of a carrier whose problems would contribute significantly to the Penn Central's bankruptcy. *New York Times*, July 11, 1968 ("significantly," "regret"); July 27, 1968; August 13, 1968 ("granted"); September 6, 1968 ("impossible," "prevent"); December 3, 1968; December 24, 1968; December 26, 1968; December 28, 1968; December 31, 1968; January 1, 1969 ("magically").

582. *Philadelphia Inquirer*, January 16, 1968.

583. SEC Report, 19–20; Salsbury, *No Way to Run a Railroad*, 119.

584. SEC Report 20 ("situation"); Salsbury, *No Way to Run a Railroad*, 122–27.

585. *New York Times*, January 16, 1968 ("benefits").

586. *Philadelphia Inquirer*, January 16, 1968 ("represent"); January 17, 1968 ("consummation"); February 1, 1968 ("birth," "green").

587. Mumford, "Disappearance of Pennsylvania Station" ("botch"); *Penn Central Post*, April 1, 1968 ("crazy").

588. *New York Times*, May 10, 1966 ("interested," "compete").

589. Joel Rosenbaum and Tom Gallo, *The Broadway Limited* (Piscataway, NJ: Railpace, 1989), 63. The menu selections are from November 1967, shortly before the consolidation of *The General* and *The Broadway Limited*.

590. *New York Times*, January 31, 1968 ("treated," "anarchy," "crisis," "sanctuary").

591. Following the funeral service, Atterbury was buried in the nearby cemetery of St. David's Episcopal Church in Radnor.

592. *New York Times*, February 1, 1968.

INDEX

PRR refers to the Pennsylvania Railroad.
PC refers to Penn Central.
Page numbers in *italics* indicate illustrations and captions.

Binswanger, Frank G., 330, *331*, 332

Binzen, Peter, 830n249

Bismarck, Washburn & Great Falls Railway, 72

Bituminous Coal Act, 758n234

Black, Hugo, 113–14

Blair, 11

Blardone, Chuck, 727n20, 746n42

Block, Joseph L., 569

Blocki, Leonard, *191*

Blond, Hyman J., 534

Blough, Roger M., 414

Blue Line Transfer Company, 519

Blue Ribbon Fleet: dieselization of, 282, 289, 299–300, 304; duplex locomotives for, 260, 264; electrification and, 217; poor conditions of, 424; postwar upgrades, 337–38, 340, 351, 771n80; premier passenger trains, 79–81; service improvement, 354, 424; suspension of, 357

Bluestone, David W., 513

Board of Rapid Transit Railroad Commissioners, 455

Boatner, Victor V., 206

Bodine, John Weeks, 505–7

Bodman, Warren H., 830n250

Boecher, Helen Lightburn, 387

Boeing Company: Boeing 247, 776n146; Boeing 707, 601–2, 649, 841n439; Boeing 727, 601; Boeing 747, 599; Executive Jet Aviation and, 601–2

boiler designs: Altoona boilers, 26–27, 27, 29–30, 51; barrels, 26; Belpaire firebox, 29–30, 30, 40, 42, 60–61, 63, 69, 71–72, 74, 75, 76, 217, 709n200; brick firebox arches, 12; Bury, 13, 22; "camel" locomotives, 13, 22, 23, 26; camelback locomotives, 46–47, 707n150; cylindrical, 30; diameter increases, 40, 42, 61–63, 706n131; high-pressure, 272, 274; psi ratings, 12, 38, 40–42, 47, 75–76, 83; radial-stay, 30, 42, 47, 60–61, 67, 69, 71, 76, 709n200; smokeboxes, 10, 26, 39, 49, 83, 254–55, 751n132; steel, 12; thermal efficiency, 269, 271–72, 274, 755n205; throat sheet, 77; wagon-top boiler, 25–26, 27; Worthington feedwater heaters, 74

Boles, Charles E., 430, 798n184

Bonaparte, Napoleon, 7

Booz Allen Hamilton, 419

Bordentown Shops, 17

Borodin, Alexander, 52

Boston & Albany Railroad, 554–55, 562, 590

Boston & Maine Industries, 846n579

Boston & Maine Railroad: capital-indemnification plan, 669; Dereco holding company and, 654, 667, 680–81, 845n550; financial difficulties and, 652; FT locomotives, 276; ICC protection for, 679–80, 682, 685; impact

of PRR-NYC merger, 654, 657–59, 665, 679; N&W–C&O merger, 652, 845n548; operating losses, 607; Penn Central indemnification, 662, 665, 667, 669–71, 675, 682, 685, 687, 832n315, 845n547; petition for merger inclusion, 559, 562–63, 608, 651–52, 659; PRR-NYC merger appeal, 685; regional rail system, 553, 558, 590; shareholder criticism of, 681; *Speed Merchant*, 779n192; Trailer Train Company and, 375, 783n254; women employees and, 737n179

Boston & Providence Railroad, 832n315

Boston–Washington Corridor Study, 621–28. *See also* high-speed rail

Bowen, Irene, 602

Bowman, Robert J., 430

Boyd, Alan S.: Florida Railroad and Public Utilities Commission, 797n169; high-speed rail, 632, 637, 649, 841n442; *Metroliner* project, *618*; on N&W–C&O merger, 653–54; New Haven crisis and, 684; passenger-train hearings, 426, 446; PRR-NYC merger, 653–54, 675, 681; Thanksgiving meeting on merger, 673–74; transportation policy and, 636, 674, 679

bracero program. *See* Hispanic workers

Bradford, John L., 557

Bradley, John J., 522

Bradley, Michael J., 323

Braithwaite, Love, 185

Brandeis, Louis, 429, 549, 719n118

Brandon, Albert, 566–68

Branford Electric Railway Association, 765n374

Bretey, Pierre R., 283–84, 287

Bridwell, Lowell K., 579, 659

Bright, W. L., *177*

Brill Automotive Car Division, 221–22

Brinley, Charles E., 248, 256

Broad Street Station (Philadelphia): arched train sheds, 122; closure of, 325–26, *326*, 327; commuter traffic in, 89, 321, 447, 449–51, 801n1; demolition of, 324–27, 330, 332; electrification projects, 89–90; intercity passenger trains and, 89–90, 321; Park Trains, 802n13; planned conversion of, 321–22, 324; PRR redevelopment of area, 328–33, *333*; steam locomotives and, 801n3; strikes and, 394–95; Union Pacific M-10001, 230, 231, *231*

Broad Street Subway, 330, 332

The Broadway Limited: 50th anniversary, *353*; all-Pullman, 217, 337, 357; combination with *The General*, 691–92, 796n156; dieselization of, 246, 251, 277; gross revenue, 240, 243; limited public visibility of, 70, 241–42; low ridership on, 229, 238, 240–41, 564, 692; New York–Chicago service, 229, 235, 340, 352, 357, 424; New York–Washington service, 120; postwar upgrades, 338,

Burlington Northern, 549; C&O–B&O, 540–46, 549,
557–58, 561; Eastern railroads, 533–44; Erie-Lackawanna, 534–36, 539, 541–44, 820n27; federal consolidation provisions, 3, 429; four-system plan, 579–82,
659–60, 666–67; ICC and, 4, 106, 429, 433–34, 438,
536, 538, 541–44, 546, 552, 556–57, 575–77, 581, 799n210;
impact on labor force, 549–50, 586; impact on NYC,
534–43; Justice Department and, 552, 557–60, 576–82;
labor negotiations, 441; monopolies and, 544, 549,
553, 555–56; N&W–Nickel Plate, 541–43, 545–46, 549,
557–61, 573, 823n112; N&W–Virginian, 441–42, 534–36,
546, 549, 573; national transportation policy and,
554–56, 568, 823n109; Northern Lines, 549, 552, 555, 577,
662, 664; organized labor, 411; potential cost savings,
437–39, 441; PRR expansion and, 535–39, 543; public
opposition to, 549, 822n77; railroads and, 432–35,
437–42, 445–46, 533–34, 799n208; three-system plan,
542, 545, 557–58, 560–61, 570, 578–82, 649–51, 653, 662,
670, 689, 695, 821n47; transportation efficiency goals,
576–77; trucking industry, 429; two-system plan, 536,
540, 542, 570, 578–81, 653–54, 687–88, 820n28, 821n47;
Young attempts, 429–31. *See also* Penn Central Railroad; Pennsylvania Railroad-NYC merger
Merrill Lynch, 283–84, 287
Meteor, 348, 775n139, 776n142
Metroliners: cost of developing, 649; electrification projects, 135; high-speed rail service, 639–40, 642; inaugural run, 841n442; luxurious design, 645; problems
with, 3, 649, 693; production delays, 646, 646, 647,
647, 648–49; PRR and Penn Central investment in,
841n442; PRR passenger service, *618*
Metropolitan Commuter Transportation Authority,
495–96
Metropolitan Express, 712n268
The Metropolitan Limited, 80–81, 119, 339, 712n268
Metropolitan Rapid Transit Commission, 487, 489
Metropolitan Transportation Authorities Act (1963), 522
Metropolitan Transportation Authority, 495–96
Metzman, Gustav, 397, 399, 410, 430–31
Meyer, Charlie, 750n126, 754n183
Meyer, Eugene, 107–8, 718n104
Meyer, Howard, 481
Meyer, John R., 426–28, 636–37
Meyner, Robert B., 491–93
Michaelian, Edwin G., 687
Michigan Central Railroad, 44, 52
Midamerica Corporation, 772n103
MIDAS (Management Information Developed from
Advanced Systems), 612

Middle Division (PRR): Decapods, 75; diesel locomotives, 246; electrification projects, 318; freight cars, 79;
passenger service, 63, 67, 423; running repairs, 17; steep
gradients and, 67, 70
Mid-States Express, Inc., 372
Midvale Steel Works, 33–34
Mifflin, 11, 700n8
military: freight movement by, 150, 152–53; German
prisoner of war transport, 153; industry seizure during
labor disputes, 163, 729n56; operation of the railroads,
163–64, 729n57; PRR employees in, 153–54, 157; PRR
service to, 150, 152–53; railway battalions, 153–54,
726n10, 726n14; seniority rights and, 179, 734n126;
transfer of troops and equipment to Pacific Theater,
156; troop cars, 152–53, 155–56, 727n20, 727n22, 727n24;
wartime passenger service, 155, 727n20, 727n22. *See also*
World War I; World War II
Military Railway Service, 153–55, 726n14, 796n140
Miller, Calvin, 56
Miller, Dora, 183
Miller, Nathan L., 457
Millholland, James, 26
Mills, Ogden L., 110
Milwaukee Road, 314, 509–10, 713n7, 733n119, 733n122
Mims, Stewart, 403
Minneapolis-Honeywell Jet-Capsule Tube, 780n204
Missouri–Kansas–Texas Railroad (Katy), 154, 341, 348,
374–75, 775n139, 776n142, 783n254
Missouri Pacific Railroad: Alleghany Corporation and,
343; bankruptcy and, 718n96, 772n106; *Eagle* brand,
776n144, 776n145; mergers and, 799n208; RFC financ-
ing for, 108, 113, 718n96, 718n104; St. Louis gateway, 374;
Trailer Train Company and, 375, 783n254; transcon-
tinental service, 346–48, 776n144, 776n145; wheel
arrangements, 709n203
Missouri River Eagle, 776n144
Mitchell, Alexander, 25
Mitchell, James P., 551
Mitten, Thomas E., 95, 97, 517, 806n75
Mitten Management, Incorporated, 806n75
Mixner, Marion, 184
Mohawk & Hudson Railroad, 314
Monongahela Division (PRR), 793n105
Monon Railroad, 832n315
Montauk Division (PRR), 225
Montgomery County Commission, 522
Montreal Locomotive Works, 766n388
Moon Glow, 313
Moore, Ethel P., 193

New York, NY: City Planning Commission, 531; commuter traffic in, 448, 801n5; electrification projects, 89, 93, 224–25; freight service to, 49; historic preservation efforts, 530–31, 819n7; Landmarks Preservation Commission, 531; passenger service, 2–3, 28, 54–56, 58, 79–81, 85, 93, 95–96, 224; Peter Cooper Village, 330; Rockefeller Center, 327, 332–34; smoke-abatement ordinances, 248; Stuyvesant Town, 330; subway system in, 60, 411, 454, 455–57; Tammany Hall, 456–57; World Trade Center, 493, 811n186. *See also* Greater New York

New York, Ontario & Western Railroad, 427

New York, Philadelphia & Norfolk Railroad (NYP&N), 140

New York, Susquehanna & Western Railroad, 561

New York & Long Branch Railroad, 70, 134–35, 308, 318, 320, 453, 492, 722n158

New York and Chicago Limited, 44–45

New York Central Railroad (NYC): *Aerotrain*, 779n201; African American employees, 181; attempts to discontinue Weehawken Ferry, 490, 510; B&O and, 536, 540–41; bulk commodities and, 547; C&O merger planning, 6, 441, 539–40, 821n48; capital investment and, 614–15; centralized corporate structure, 438, 614; Class S1a, 271, 764n360; Class S1b Niagara, 764n360; coal freight and, 533, 535, 540–42; commuter services, 460, 495–96; computing technologies and, 612, 614; dieselization of, 277, 281–82, 764n3600; dividend payments, 433–34; Eisenhower Recession effects, 432–33; electrification projects, 224; elimination of passenger trains, 424, 691; financial improvement, 661, 669–70, 672; Flexi-Van system, 372, 375, 431, 784n265; four-track main line, 350, 776n155; freight revenue, 206; grade crossings and, 804n39; Great Steel Fleet, 239, 337, 340, 423; Heller recommendations and, 357–58; impact of mergers on, 534–39; Kenefick and, 437, 799n208; locomotive test plant, 52; maintenance and repair, 611; mechanization and, 611; *Mercury*, 235, 241, 746n59; operating losses, 430–34, 439–40, 541–42, 678, 688; passenger cars, 235, 746n59; passenger credit cards, 773n110; passenger losses, 439; passenger service, 355–56, 756n214, 778n175, 796n151; passenger train speed, 39, 54–58; Pittsburgh & Lake Erie Railroad, 824n135; postwar capital investment, 337–38; postwar revenue, 213, 340, 614; PRR merger, 2–3, 6; RFC financing for, 107; rivalry with PRR, 44–45, 54–58, 80; strikes and, 410; TALGO system and, 359; trailer-on-flat-car service, 372, 431; Trailer Train Company and, 783n253, 783n254; Train X concept, 360, 432, 779n193; transcontinental service, 340, 345–47, 775n130; Virginian and, 440–42; Water Level Route, 6, 54, 57, 82, 236,

564; workforce reductions and, 439; Young and, 342, 345, 430, 432, 798n184. *See also* Penn Central Railroad; Pennsylvania Railroad–NYC merger

New York City Board of Transportation, 457, 479, 483

New York City Landmarks Law (1965), 531

New York City Transit Authority, 411–12, 484, 489

New York Connecting Railroad, 553

New York Division (PRR), 29, 35, 66, 97, 201

New York Improvements, 48, 88, 88, 89–90, 356, 455, 528, 552, 744n23

New York Limited Express, 44, 708n181

New York Night Express, 44

New York Office of Transportation, 490

New York Railroad Club, 107, 250

New York Regional Plan Association, 621

New York Society of Security Analysts, 384

New York Special, 81, 712n268

New York Thruway, 423, 611

New York Tunnel Extension, 89

New York World's Fair (1939), 70, 241, 253, 254, 313, 468, 807n94, 811n172

New York World's Fair (1964), 530, 595, 598

New York Zone, 413, 464, 471, 474

Nichol, J. M., 479

Nicholson, George C., 462

Nickel Plate Road (New York, Chicago & St. Louis Railroad): Alphabet Route and, 797n178; C&O shareholders and, 798n182; merger planning, 429, 440, 772n107; pay-as-you-go plan, 773n110; Pocahontas-region coal trade and, 535; profitability of, 434, 535; trailer-on-flat-car service, 369, 781n226, 783n254; W&LE investment, 798n184; Young and, 343, 429–30, 798n180. *See also* Norfolk & Western–Nickel Plate–Wabash merger

Nickerson, Ernest C., 420

Nixon, Richard, 363, 369, 554, 693, 831n276

NMB. *See* National Mediation Board (NMB)

Nocturne, 770n70

nonoperating unions: employee safety films, 407; postwar wage increases, 392, 396–97; threat of strikes, 397, 399, 411–12, 728n36; union shop and dues, 410; wage negotiations and, 399–400, 411–12, 789n43, 789n46; wartime wage adjustments, 159–64. *See also* organized labor

Norfolk & Western Railway (N&W): Akron, Canton & Youngstown purchase, 828n225; C&O merger proposal, 652–53; Class HH1s locomotives, 711n235; Class J locomotives, 266–67, 267, 268; coal traffic and, 21, 248–49, 535, 537, 575; control of B&M, 681, 845n550; control of D&H, 681; control of Erie Lackawanna, 681–82; disinterest in Erie Lackawanna, 608–9, 652;

and, 166, 175–76, 178, 180–81; status of, 207, 299, 386; threat of strikes, 399; union shop and dues, 410; wage negotiations and, 392, 397, 399–400, 411; wartime wage adjustments, 161–64. *See also* labor/workforce; organized labor

Opinion Research Corporation, 419

Oram, James W.: on centralization of personnel, 418; employee medical care and, 408–9; employee safety films, 401–2, 789n59; on featherbedding, 550; on female seniority rights, 197–98; films as public relations, 402, 789n59; labor relations and, 396, 398, 401, 412, 416; on overtime pay, 205; Personnel Department, 157, 181, 401, 406–7; public relations and, 420; racial classification of employees, 181

Order of Railroad Telegraphers (ORT), 183, 734n133, 787n7

Order of Railway Conductors (ORC), 163, 390, 398, 400, 410, 734n133, 787n8

organized labor: African American unions, 166–67, 170–73, 182; closed shop demands, 159, 728n34; collective-bargaining rights and, 144; cost-of-living adjustments, 410–11; elimination of freight-service firemen, 550, 569, 585; featherbedding and, 3, 550, 567–69, 822n80; fringe benefits, 411, 792n83; full-crew laws, 403, 418, 439, 550–51, 568–69, 585, 593; industrial strikes, 157–58; interunion disputes, 171, 731n84; Little Steel formula, 160–62, 164, 729n60; Luna-Saunders agreement, 587, 590, 607, 663, 688, 828n207; national strikes, 390–92, 443, 585; no-strike pledge and, 158, 160, 162, 164, 390; occupational representation, 166–67; opposition to bracero program, 200; opposition to PRR-NYC merger, 565–69, 583, 585–86; pay cuts and, 104–5, 117, 138; political power and, 158, 404; postwar unrest, 390–93, 395–401; public opinion and, 398; racial discrimination and, 165–67, 170–72, 175, 178–79, 183; relocation of companies, 565; union shop and dues, 399, 409–10, 789n41, 792n88; wartime wage adjustments, 158–64, 729n60; wildcat strikes, 390, 393, 398–400; women employees and, 172; work-rules dispute, 550–51, 568–69, 585. *See also* labor/workforce; nonoperating unions

Oriol, José Luis, 778n189

Ormandy, Eugene, 326, 326, 327

Orr, Walter S., 342

Orrick, William H., Jr.: anticompetitive effects of merger, 588–89, 650; antitrust laws and, 656, 660; Erie Lackawanna merger with N&W, 609; four-system plan, 579–80; Interagency Committee and, 556, 577–83, 586–88, 590; merger opposition, 577, 579–80; New Haven acquisition, 605, 656; opposition

to PRR-NYC merger, 581–83, 587–90, 656, 658; resignation of, 657

Osborn, Cyrus, 313, 371

Osborne Company, 419

Oscar Gruss & Son, 665, 683, 686

Otis & Company, 773n114

Outcault, Richard Felton, 45

Outlaw Strike of 1920, 396

Overland Limited, 775n130

Oyster Bay Railroad Museum, 765n374

Pabst, George H., Jr., 214, 290–91, 377–78, 742n267, 784n266

Pacemaker, 241

Pacific Coast Engineering, 784n264

Pacific Electric Railway, 162

Pacific Motor Transport, 365

Padilla Nervo, Luis, 205

Page, Arthur W., 471, 487

Page-Merritt Public Utilities Act, 455

Paige, John, 703n50

Palmer, Albert M., 29

Palmer, Dwight R. G., 492, 811n179

Palmer, Howard S., 554

Palmer, William Jackson, 11

Pan American Airlines, 602

Pangborn, Joseph, 314

Pan Handle (Pittsburgh, Cincinnati, Chicago & St. Louis Railway): commuter service and, 802n5; consolidation and, 21; elimination of tunnels, 315; passenger service and, 5–6; PRR-NYC merger and, 439; PRR shares in, 719n106, 721n134; rationalization and, 5; shop facilities, 20–22; Southwest System and, 18, 21–22; steam cars, 220–21

Pan Handle Athletic Club, 21

Panic of 1873, 32

Papalia, Roy C., 658–59

Parker, J. E., 289

Parkhouse, A. Russell, 522

Parmelee Transportation Company, 775n134

Parra Rameríz, Enrique, 203

Parrott, William P., 219

Partington, James, 74–75

passenger cars: air-conditioning in, 228–29, 360; all-coach, 241–42, 773n118; aluminum use, 229, 234–36; aquariums in, 343, 773n111; Art Deco designs, 131, 217, 239; bi-level cars, 236, 470, 779n193; branch line, 219–24; *Brook*-series, 770n70; *Capitaliners*, 640–42, 645, 839n414; Class P78a, 498; Class P78b, 498; dome cars, 313, 771n83; double-deck, 236, 334–35, 470, 747n63,

postwar reorganization, 436, 795n137, 795n139; PRR-NYC merger cost savings, 563–66, 568, 824n134; on purchase of Lehigh Valley, 538; Research and Development Department, 420, 436–37; retirement of, 832n303; stock-option plan for, 423

Patin, James I., 406–7, 791n73

Patman, Wright, 603

Patterson, A. Holly, 485

Patterson, Jesse F., 464

Patterson, Robert P., 476, 480

Paul Revere, 355

Pavonia Terminal, 453

Payne, Gustavus E., 176, 404

Pearce, Jack, 559

Peat, Marwick, Mitchell & Company, 436, 612

Peck, George L., 55

Peconic Bay Express, 80

Pell, Claiborne: call for national transit agency, 834n333; high-speed rail proposal, 620–26, 628, 630, 658; as "least electable," 619, 833n331; New Haven Railroad and, 605–6, 686; TurboTrain and, 632

Penn, William, 448

Penn Center (Philadelphia), 329, 329, 330, 331, 332–34

Penn Central Company, 822n72

Penn-Central Merger and Norfolk & Western Inclusion Cases, 686–87

Penn Central Railroad: bankruptcy of, 1–5, 135, 603, 768n22, 841n442, 847n581; coal traffic and, 670; Conrail and, 5, 829n234; diesel locomotives, 763n340; electric locomotives, 320; failures of, 846n579; federal subsidies and, 5; financial difficulties and, 2–3, 578, 612, 680, 688, 830n249; freight operations, 568, 584–85, 616, 642, 660, 691–92; headquarters in Philadelphia, 584–85, 617; high-speed rail, 841n442; incompatibilities and, 3, 570–71, 611–12, 614, 664, 688–89; indemnification of independent railroads, 662, 665, 667–71, 675, 682, 845n547; integration plan, 610–12, 688–89; labor impacts, 831n292; leadership of, 570, 610, 688; Luna-Saunders agreement, 688; merger approval for, 2–3, 548, 552, 607–10, 660–61, 661, 662–64, 664, 686–88; NH acquisition, 604–8, 617, 665–68, 671, 678–81, 683–87, 845n556, 845n558, 845n560, 847n581; NH freight service and, 608; NH loan fund, 684, 845n559, 846n573; passenger service, 2, 4, 687, 692; Perlman as president, 610; public and political support for, 420, 660, 666–67; Pullman Company and, 774n124; Supreme Court resolution of, 686–90, 690; transportation coordination, 637; TrucTrain service, 784n265; value of shares, 825n155; workforce reductions and, 549–50. *See also* Pennsylvania Railroad–NYC merger

Penn Central Transportation Company, 662, 822n72. *See also* Penn Central Railroad

Penn-Jersey Transportation Study, 506–7, 814n225, 817n274

Penn Mutual Life Insurance Company, 611

Pennroad Corporation, 146, 537, 553, 597, 798n178, 798n180, 798n184

Penn Station (NY): air rights, 528–29, 532; commuter traffic and, 453, 459, 460, 469–70, 528, 803n27, 804n42; construction of, 49; decline of, 528; demolition and redevelopment of, 528–33, 614, 691; electrification projects, 89; improvements to, 472, 473; intercity passenger trains, 459, 460, 691; Madison Square Garden project, 529–32, 532, 533, 691; passenger service and, 120; preservation efforts, 530–32, 819n7; PT&T rental rates, 455, 459, 459, 460–61, 466, 495, 804n43; rates and rental fees, 460; red caps at, 182

The Pennsy (magazine), 407–8, 419, 794n125

Pennsy Aerotrain, 360

Pennsy Family Clubs, 408

Pennsylvania & Newark Railroad, 95–96

Pennsylvania Canal Company, 85

Pennsylvania Chamber of Commerce, 566

Pennsylvania Company: Arvida stock, 596; bond repurchasing, 381; Buckeye Pipeline stock, 595, 597, 829n240; establishment of, 24; financial structures and, 382–83; Great Southwest stock, 596, 598; Lehigh Valley stock and, 538; Macco stock, 596; motive power and, 20; non-railroad diversification, 603; profitability of, 677; PRR dividends, 592–93, 785n285; Tropical Gas Company shares, 598, 830n254

Pennsylvania Federation of Labor, AFL-CIO, 567

Pennsylvania Greyhound, 384

Pennsylvania High Speed Intercity Rail Passenger Commission, 840n426

The Pennsylvania Limited: combined with *The Clevelander*, 352; combined with *The St. Louisan*, 339, 349; derailment of, 57; discontinuation of, 424; luxurious design, 45, 54; open section seating, 707n144; repainted Tuscan red, 707n145; travel speed, 58, 120; upgrades and, 708n175

Pennsylvania Motor Truck Association, 405, 790n67

The Pennsylvanian, 388, 529, 775n131

Pennsylvania–New York Central Transportation Company, 548, 607, 821n72. *See also* Penn Central Railroad

Pennsylvanians for the Promotion of Economic Growth, 639

Pennsylvania Power & Light Company, 97

Pennsylvania Railroad (PRR): accounting practices, 377, 379, 417, 436–38; adversarial relations with the ICC,

Stoopes, Pierce C., *118–19*

Stout, William Bushnell, 229

Strasburg Railroad, 39

Strasser, Alfred C., 408

Stratton, George W., *33*

streamliners: *Aerotrain*, 360, *361*, 779n200; articulated, 234, 334; Chicago–Florida service, 242; Class K4s, 239–40, *240*, 241–42; curvilinear profiles, 233; diesel locomotives, 246; discontinuance of, 426; double-deck cars, 334–35, 770n70, 770n72; electric locomotives, 234, *234*; freight locomotives, 254, 263; lightweight, 334, 340; Loewy design for, 70, 133, 334–35, 779n193; low-cost, 358; M-10000, 229, 231, 234, *234*, 235–36, 245, 250, 334, 340, 725n231, 749n102, 750n123; New York-Florida service, 242; shrouding design, 239, 246, 254, 265; *Zephyr*, 229, 231, 234–35, 245, 250, 314, 334, 340

strikes: BLE and, 390–92; Brooklyn Rapid Transit Company, 456; BRT and, 390–92; coal workers, 288, 290; Hispanic workers, 203, 739n221; longshoremen, 308; lost revenue from, 290; military seizure of railroads, 163, 729n56; moratorium on, 399; no-strike pledge and, 158, 160, 162; operating employees, 410; private police actions against, 143–44; PTC and, 520, 818n284; Red Arrow Lines, 520, 818n284; shopworkers, 585; steel workers, 290, 308, 443, 565; Transport Workers Union, 551; United Mine Workers, 95, 305; as unpatriotic, 399–400; wartime labor militancy, 157–58; wartime wage increases, 158–63; wildcat, 390, 393, 398–400; 585; work-rules dispute, 569. *See also* Shopmen's Strike of 1922

Studds, Colin, 55

Suburban Station (Philadelphia): commuter services and, 498, 507, 512, 814n231; completion of, 321; expansion of, 322–23; female trainmen, *192, 193, 193*; improvements to, 500; Operation Levittown service, *516*; Penn Center planning and, 330, 332, 334; strikes and, 390; tunnel to Reading Terminal, 525

subway systems: expansion of New York, 60, 454, 455–57; five-cent fares in New York, 411, 456, *456*; in Philadelphia, 321–24, 327–28, 330, 332, 447–48

Suffolk County Commuters Association, 472

Sullivan, William J., 496

Sunbury Shops, 17

Sundlun, Bruce G., 599, 602

Sunnyside Yard, 99, 196, 350, 455, 475, 495, 733n114, 744n23

Sunshine Eagle, 776n144

Sunshine Special, 347–48, 388, 776n144

Super Chief, 217, 241, 246, 248, 341, 749n102

Surface Transportation Board, 5

Susquehanna & Western Railroad, 811n179

Susquehanna Division (PRR), 793n105

Susquehanna Water Power & Paper Company, 715n32

Swan, Herbert E., 388

Swayne, Alfred H., 146

Swift, Arthur, 339

Swing, Albert H., 520

Switchmen's Union of North America (SUNA), 163, 390, 396–97, 734n133, 787n8

Swope, Gerard, 719n111

Symes, James M., *291*; advancement of, 265–66, *266*, 367; *Aerotrain* concept, 360; as board chairman, 444–45; Broad Street Station land and, 517; changes in operating practices, 287; on closure of Broad Street Station, 326–27; commuter services and, 502, 503, 506, 510; computing technologies and, 378–79; control of Lehigh Valley, 538–39; cost-benefit analyses, 318; cost-cutting and, 378–79; criticism of new steam locomotives, 266–67, *267*, 268; decentralization planning, 413, 416–17, 419, 421, 574–75; as defacto president, 290, 291–92; dieselization advocacy, 265–66, *266*, 281–83, 285–89, 292, 300, 311, 315, 366, 413–14, 695, 758n244; dissolving of Public Relations Department, 420; divestment of N&W stock, 559–60, 823n112; employee relations and, 405–8; equipment-trust certificates and, 380; federal funding request, 513; on freight service, 549–50; Heller recommendations and, 357; hostility between Perlman and, 432, 541–42, 570–71, 610; Kefauver hearings, 556–58, 570; on *Keystone* concept, 362; labor relations and, 401, 405–6; on lack of experienced managers, 415; Lehigh Valley and, 537–38, 544; on limited steam operations, 292, 760n285; LIRR and, 472, 488–89; managerial philosophy, 548; merger planning, 429, 432, 433–35, 438–39, 442–43, 445, 533, 536–37, 543–48, 552, 556–57, 580, 687, 695; military liaisons and, 395; N&W locomotives, 266–67, *267*, 268; N&W stock divestment, 592; Newell and, 415–16, 418, 444, 784n260, 784n263; opposition to Erie-Lackawanna merger, 534–35; outside consultant cancellations, 404, 790n65; passenger service cuts, 340, 351–54, 358; Pell Plan and, 626; Penn Center planning and, 330, *331*, 332–33, *333*; Penn Central advisory role, 610; Penn Station development, 529–30; personnel management and, 395–96; on Philadelphia Improvements, 324; piggyback operations and, 366; postwar reorganization, 413–21; as president of PRR, 307, 416, 419; promotion of, 281, 758n242; on PRR investment in LIRR, 808n124; PRR-NYC merger hearings, 560–61, 567–70, 824n143; public relations and, 393, 405; rate of return with diesels, 281–83, 287–89, 292; on regulatory policies, 427–28; resignation of, 444; on revenue

ALBERT J. CHURELLA is Professor of History in the History and Philosophy Department at Kennesaw State University. He is author of *From Steam to Diesel: Managerial Customs and Organizational Capabilities in the Twentieth-Century American Locomotive Industry*, *The Pennsylvania Railroad, Volume I: Building an Empire, 1846–1917*, and *The Pennsylvania Railroad, Volume II: The Age of Limits, 1917–1933*. Churella is also president of the Lexington Group, Inc., an organization dedicated to transportation history and practice.

For Indiana University Press

Tony Brewer *Artist and Book Designer*

Dan Crissman *Trade and Regional Acquisitions Editor*

Anna Garnai *Editorial Assistant*

Brenna Hosman *Production Coordinator*

Katie Huggins *Production Manager*

David Miller *Lead Project Manager/Editor*

Dan Pyle *Online Publishing Manager*

Pamela Rude *Senior Artist and Book Designer*

Stephen Williams *Marketing and Publicity Manager*